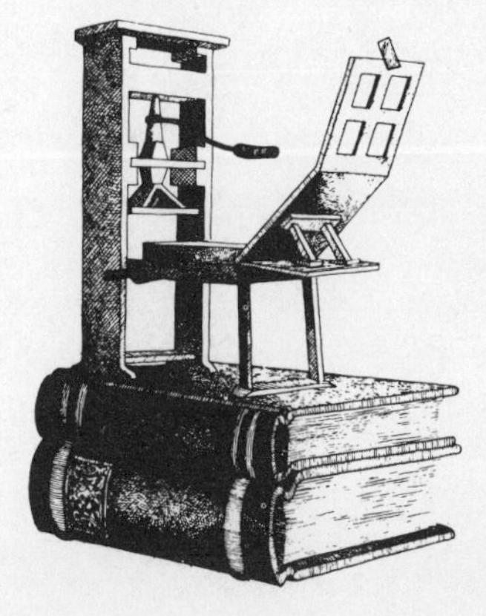

# THE PENGUIN COMPANION TO EUROPEAN LITERATURE

*Edited by*
*ANTHONY THORLBY*

McGraw-Hill Book Company
NEW YORK • ST. LOUIS • SAN FRANCISCO • TORONTO

Library of Congress Catalog Card Number: 74-158063

07 049279 4

Printed in Great Britain

# CONTENTS

# EDITORIAL FOREWORD

The English have never been as insular in their reading habits as occasional critics have supposed. Today, more English readers than ever, on both sides of the Atlantic, have some contact with the literature of the European continent. There is a wide public for the increasingly abundant translations of European classics, and many people follow the work of contemporary authors as soon as it is translated, often within weeks of its original publication abroad.

Apart from those who enjoy reading at leisure whatever they find attractive, there are others who pursue courses of more systematic reading, usually in a foreign language, and for some academic purpose. And in schools and universities there are also many students, besides those concerned directly with literary history and criticism, who need sometimes to look up basic information about an author or a text. The growing interest in Europe as a supranational community may find in literature the most accessible aspect of a common cultural heritage; the more frequent the occasions when it is discussed, the more frequent the questions and references to which such discussion gives rise. This book is meant to provide basic answers to the more obvious questions about European literature since the fifth century A.D.

Which are the more important European authors? Which are their main works? What, briefly, are these about? What editions and translations are available? What critical commentaries are to be recommended?

These are the questions which the contributors to this volume have had in mind. They have only included a few details about each author's life, in order to place him and to throw light on his work. Minor works have often not been mentioned and consequently some authors have received very brief notices. Nevertheless, prolific authors have inevitably tended to claim the most space, and it should be said that the *length* of an article should not be understood as any exact indication of a writer's excellence. In the case of some philosophers, the biggest part of their works has not been described at all, but only an aspect of it which happened to be important for literary reasons. The same is true of several historians, a class of writers not generally included, except where tradition has granted them some degree of literary standing. But it is to be admitted that the convention which acknowledges Michelet and Taine, but not Ranke or Burckhardt, is somewhat arbitrary. Indeed, all the borderline decisions to include or omit an author have seemed arbitrary. Does Ortega's writing really have more connexions with literature than Gentile's, or Keyserling's more than Berdyayev's? Any comparison tends to look odious when it results in the exclusion of an author, the more so when judgement has to be made on purely literary grounds – grounds which are notoriously liable to the most impure subjective error. This liability has been particularly great where there has been such fierce international competition for the available space.

*

*Editorial Foreword*

It would be almost an impertinence for an editor to express his thanks to 135 contributors for their help, when it is they, after all, who have written this book. Rather, an editorial apology is due to them for the way their articles have been cut, largely because the original estimates of space proved to be wrong.

However, besides the articles they contributed, several colleagues have given invaluable advice at difficult moments, and it is a pleasure to record this. Professor R. Auty, Mr C. Chaffin, Professor J. Cruickshank, Mr S. B. John, Mr R. Milner-Gulland, and Professor A. Terry have made admirable suggestions; if they have not been perfectly implemented, the fault is mine.

I am particularly grateful also to Mrs Fiona Harrington and Mrs Erika Poole, who have managed the files and the correspondence with untiring efficiency: without their secretarial assistance this book could not have been produced.

ANTHONY THORLBY

*University of Sussex*

# PUBLISHER'S NOTE

*Bibliographies*

The bibliographies in small type which generally follow an entry are arranged as follows. The first paragraph lists editions of texts and of translations of texts not already given in the entry itself. The second paragraph lists critical works concerning the subject of the entry. In cases where only one paragraph is given, it will be clear from the titles of the works listed whether they are texts or criticism.

The list of critical works is deliberately selective – further bibliographical information can usually be found in the listed works themselves.

Places of publication are not generally given for texts published in the author's own country or for critical works and translations published in the British Isles.

Abbreviated titles are explained in the List of Abbreviations on pages 17–27.

Bibliographies have been compiled by the contributors of the relevant articles – their initials are placed before the bibliographies only for convenience.

*Cross-references*

Cross-references (⇨ = see, ⇨⇨ = see also) from one article to another are made in the following cases: (a) when relevant information can be found in the articles cross-referred to; (b) when the writer cross-referred to is comparatively minor and the reader may wish to know who he is, even though he has not much relevance to the article in which cross-reference occurs.

# CONTRIBUTORS

AIW A. I. Watson, Senior Lecturer in Spanish, Birkbeck College, University of London

AJP A. J. Pryor, Gravesend, Kent; formerly Lecturer in Department of Hispanic Studies, University of Cardiff

AK A. Kinnunen, Assistant Professor of Aesthetics and Comparative Literature, University of Helsinki

AKT A. K. Thorlby, Professor of Comparative Literature, University of Sussex

AL Annette Lavers, Lecturer in French, Westfield College, University of London

AN-N A. Nyka-Niliūnas, author, Baltimore, U.S.A.

AP Avril Pyman, Moscow

ARM A. R. Milburn, Fellow of University College and University Lecturer in Portuguese and Spanish, University of Cambridge

ARP A. R. Pugh, Lecturer in French, Queen's University of Belfast; Visiting Professor, University of New Brunswick

AS A. D. Stokes, Fellow of University College and University Lecturer in Russian, University of Oxford

AT A. Terry, Professor of Spanish, Queen's University of Belfast

BJ B. Juden, Lecturer in French, University of Sheffield

BLN B. L. Nicholas, Lecturer in French, University of Sussex

BR J. Batista i Roca, formerly University Lecturer in Spanish, University of Cambridge

CAB C. A. Burns, Professor of French Studies, University of Strathclyde, Glasgow

CAHR C. A. H. Russ, Lecturer in German, University of Kent at Canterbury

CAM C. A. Mayer, Professor of French, University of Liverpool

CC C. Chadwick, Reader in Modern French Literature, University of Manchester

CCS C. C. Smith, Fellow of St Catharine's College and University Lecturer in Spanish, University of Cambridge

CEC C. E. Chaffin, Lecturer in Classical and Medieval Studies, University of Sussex

CF C. Fahy, Reader in Italian, Birkbeck College, University of London

CJ C. Jenkins, Senior Lecturer in French, University of Sussex

CLC C. L. Campos, Lecturer in French, University of Sussex

CRB C. R. Boxer, Emeritus Professor of Portuguese, University of London; Visiting Research Professor, Indiana University

DGR D. G. Rees, Lecturer in Italian, University of Birmingham

DLS D. L. Shaw, Lecturer in Hispanic Studies, University of Edinburgh

DO D. Obolensky, Professor of Russian and Balkan History, University of Oxford

DP D. Parmée, Fellow of Queen's College and University Lecturer in French, University of Cambridge

DR D. de W. Rogers, Lecturer in Spanish, University of Durham

EB E. Beaumont, Reader in French, University of Southampton.

ECR E. C. Riley, Professor of Spanish, Trinity College, University of Dublin

EDG E. D. Goy, Lecturer in Slavonic Studies, University of Cambridge

EDT E. D. Tappe, Reader in Rumanian Studies, School of Slavonic and East European Studies, University of London

EE Elizabeth E. Eppler, Senior Research Officer, Institute of Jewish Affairs, London

EJF E. Jane Freeland (*née* Woodcock), Southampton; research student; formerly Lecturer in Spanish, University of Durham

ELB E. L. Bredsdorff, Reader in Scandinavian Studies, University of Cambridge

FB F. Brittain, Fellow of Jesus College, University of Cambridge

FP-BN F. Pérez-Barreiro Nolla, journalist and broadcaster, London

FWAG F. W. A. George, Senior Lecturer in French, University College of Swansea

FWL F. W. Leakey, Reader in French, University of Glasgow

GBG-M G. B. Gybbon-Monypenny, Senior Lecturer in Spanish, University of Manchester

GC G. Connell, Lecturer in Hispanic Studies, University of Glasgow

GD G. Dego, Lecturer in Italian, Bedford College, University of London

GJ Gillian Jondorf, Lecturer, Department of Romance Languages, Howard University, Washington, D.C.

GMC G. M. Carsaniga, Lecturer in Italian, University of Sussex

HG H. J. G. Godin, Reader in French, Queen's University of Belfast

HMW H. M. Waidson, Professor of German, University College of Swansea

HTM H. T. Mason, Professor in European Literature, University of East Anglia

IHW I. H. Walker, Lecturer in French, University of Edinburgh

IL S. I. J. Lockerbie, Senior Lecturer in French, University of Stirling

IM I. Michael, Lecturer in Spanish, University of Manchester

IR Irma Irene Rantavaara, Professor of Aesthetics and Comparative Literature, University of Helsinki

ISM I. Mészáros, Lecturer in Philosophy, University of Sussex

IWA I. W. Alexander, Professor of French and Romance Studies, University of North Wales, Bangor

JA J. Atherton, Associate Professor of French, New York University

JC J. Cruickshank, Professor of French, University of Sussex

JF J. F. Falvey, Lecturer in French, University of Southampton

JFR J. F. Ray, London

JG J. Gibbs, Lecturer in Spanish, University of Birmingham

JGC J. G. Clark, Professor of Modern Languages, The New University of Ulster, Coleraine; Professor of French, Magee University College, Londonderry

JLC J. L. Cano, Editor, *Insula*; Professor, Middlebury College, Madrid, Spain
JLIF J. L. I. Fennell, Professor of Russian, University of Oxford
JMA J. M. Aguirre, Reader in Spanish, University College of South Wales and Monmouthshire, Cardiff
JMC J. M. Cohen, writer and translator, Reading
JNJP J. N. J. Palmer, Lecturer in General Studies, Sir John Cass College, London
JP J. Peterkiewicz, Reader in Polish Language and Literature, School of Slavonic and East European Studies, University of London
JPS J. P. Stern, Fellow of St John's College and University Lecturer in German, University of Cambridge
JRFP J. R. F. Piette, Lecturer in Breton and Cornish, University College of Wales, Aberystwyth
KB K. Brusak, Visiting Lecturer in Czech Literature and History, University of Cambridge
KF K. Fehr, Titular-Professor, University of Zürich
KG K. Garrad, Professor of Spanish, Flinders University, South Australia
LL L. Löb, Lecturer in German, University of Sussex
LM L. Michelina, Professor of Indo-European Linguistics, Universidad Literaria de Salamanca
LPH L. P. Harvey, Professor of Spanish, Queen Mary College, University of London
LSR L. de S. Rebelo, Lecturer in Portuguese Literature, King's College, University of London
LTT L. T. Topsfield, Fellow of St Catharine's College and University Lecturer in Provençal and French, University of Cambridge
LV L. Viljanen, Professor Emeritus of Finnish Literature, University of Helsinki
MAS M. A. Screech, Professor of French, University College, University of London
MB M. A. Bond, London; lately research student, Hans Bredow Institute, Hamburg
MG Militsa Greene, Senior Lecturer in Russian, University of Edinburgh
MI M. H. Impey, Assistant Professor of Spanish, University of Kentucky
MK M. Kusseff, Head of Religious Knowledge Department, Archway School, London
MM M. Moran, Lecturer in Philosophy, University of Sussex
MMC Margaret M. Callander, Lecturer, Department of French, University of Birmingham
MRM M. Ruth Morgan, Lecturer in French Medieval Literature, Queen Mary College, University of London
MW Margaret Wilson (Mrs Borland), Lecturer in Spanish, University of Hull
NG Nadejda Gorodetzky, formerly Professor of Russian, University of Liverpool
ONVG O. N. V. Glendinning, Professor of Spanish, University of Southampton
PB P. Bridgwater, Lecturer in Modern German Literature, University of Leicester

PC P. C. Cogman, Lecturer, Department of French, University of Southampton
PGF P. G. Foote, Professor of Old Scandinavian, University College, University of London
PH P. Henry, Senior Lecturer, Department of Russian Studies, University of Hull
PHN P. H. Nurse, Reader in French, University of Kent at Canterbury; Visiting Professor, University of California
PK P. K. King, University Lecturer in Dutch, University of Cambridge
PMJ The late P. Mansell Jones, Professor of Modern French Literature in the University of Manchester, 1951–6
PO P. A. Ouston, Senior Lecturer in French, University of St Andrews
RA R. Auty, Professor of Comparative Slavonic Philology, University of Oxford
RB R. E. Batchelor, Lecturer in French, University of Nottingham
RCL R. C. Lane, Lecturer in Russian, University of Durham
RCW R. C. Willis, Lecturer in Portuguese, University of Manchester
RDBT R. D. B. Thomson, Lecturer in Russian Language and Literature, School of Slavonic and East European Studies, University of London
RF R. H. Freeborn, Professor of Russian Literature, School of Slavonic and East European Studies, University of London
RG R. D. D. Gibson, Professor of French, University of Kent at Canterbury
RGP R. G. Popperwell, Fellow of Clare Hall and University Lecturer in Norwegian, University of Cambridge
RGV R. G. Veasey, Assistant Lecturer in French, University of Sussex
RHC R. H. Cosford, Education Officer, School Broadcasting Council (North West Division)
RJN R. J. North, Professor of French, University of Birmingham
RM-G R. R. Milner-Gulland, Lecturer in Russian, University of Sussex
RPH R. Peter Heller, journalist, Stanmore, Middlesex
RRB R. R. Bezzola, Professor of Romance Literature, University of Zürich
RS Ruth Spiers, translator, London
RSS R. S. Short, Lecturer, School of European Studies, University of East Anglia
RT R. J. Taylor, Professor of German, University of Sussex
RTC R. T. Cardinal, Lecturer in French, University of Kent at Canterbury
RV R. Velling, Helsinki
SAB S. A. Bergmann, Gottenberg; formerly Lecturer in Swedish, University College, University of London
SBJ S. Beynon John, Reader in French, University of Sussex
SEM S. E. Mann, Reader in Czech and Albanian Language and Literature, School of Slavonic and East European Studies, University of London
SH S. Hackel, Lecturer in Russian, University of Sussex
SJP S. J. Papastavrou, Fellow of Peterhouse and Lewis-Gibson Lecturer in Modern and Medieval Greek, University of Cambridge
SMD Sheila M. Bell (*née* Dingwall), Lecturer in French, University of Kent at Canterbury

SSP S. S. Prawer, Professor of German, Westfield College, University of London
TA T. Anhava, poet and critic, Helsinki
TJB T. Binyon, Lecturer in Russian, University of Oxford
TR The late T. Rogers, Lecturer in German at the University of Durham, 1965–6
VK V. Kaukonen, Assistant Professor of Finnish Literature, University of Helsinki
VKS V. Suomi, Assistant Professor of Finnish Literature, University of Helsinki
VP V. Pinto, Lecturer in Bulgarian Language and Literature, School of Slavonic and East European Studies, University of London
VS V. Swoboda, Lecturer in Russian and Ukrainian, School of Slavonic and East European Studies, University of London
WA W. Anderson, Head of Publications, Nuffield Science Teaching Project, Chelsea College of Science and Technology, University of London
WAC W. A. Coupe, Reader in German, University of Reading
WEY W. E. Yates, Lecturer in German, University of Durham
WGM W. G. Moore, Fellow of St John's College, University of Oxford
WHB W. H. Barber, Professor of French, Birkbeck College, University of London
WNI W. N. Ince, Senior Lecturer in French, University of Leicester
WPH W. P. Hanson, formerly Lecturer in Modern Languages, University of Manchester

# ABBREVIATIONS OF TITLES

Adam, *HLF*. A. Adam, *Histoire de la littérature française au XVIII^e siècle* (5 vols., Paris, 1949–56).

*AGR*. *American German Review* (Philadelphia, 1934–).

Alberto, *SP*. Asor-Rosa Alberto, *Scrittori e popolo*, vol. ii (Rome, 1966).

Alborg, *HANE*. J. L. Alborg, *Hora actual de la novela española* (Madrid, 1958).

Allwood, *TCSP*. M. S. Allwood, *Twentieth Century Scandinavian Poetry* (Helsingfors/Oslo, 1950).

Alonso, *EEG*. D. Alonso, *Estudios y ensayos gongorinos* (Madrid, 1955).

Alonso, *ESP*. D. Alonso, *Ensayos sobre poesía española* (Buenos Aires, 1944).

Alonso, *PE*. D. Alonso, *Poesía española* (Madrid, 1950).

Alonso, *PEC*. D. Alonso, *Poetas españoles contemporáneos* (Madrid, 1952).

Andrusyshen and Kirkconnell, *UP*. C. H. Andrusyshen and W. Kirkconnell, *The Ukrainian Poets 1189–1962* (Toronto, 1963) (translation).

*An. Hym*. *Analecta Hymnica Medii Aevi*, ed. G. M. Dreves, C. Blume, H. M. Bannister (55 vols., Leipzig, 1886–1922).

Antoine, *STL*. A. Antoine, *Mes souvenirs sur le Théâtre Libre* (Paris, 1922).

Antonielli, *AFN*. S. Antonielli, *Aspetti e figure del Novecento* (Parma, 1955).

Arnaldi, *PLQ*. F. Arnaldi *et al.*, *Poeti latini del Quattrocento* (Milan/Naples, 1964).

*ASR*. *American Scandinavian Review* (New York, 1915–).

*AUAU*. *Annals of the Ukrainian Academy of Arts and Sciences in the U.S.*

Auerbach, *M*. E. Auerbach, *Mimesis* (Princeton, 1953).

Austin, *SMFL*. L. J. Austin, ed., *Studies in Modern French Literature*, with Garnet Rees, Eugène Vinaver (1961).

*BA*. *Books Abroad* (Oklahoma, 1927–).

BAE. Biblioteca de Autores Españoles (Madrid).

Baer, *HJCS*. Y. Baer, *A History of the Jews in Christian Spain* (Philadelphia, 1961).

Barac, *HYL*. A. Barac, *A History of Yugoslav Literature* (Belgrade, 1955).

Bàrberi Squarotti, *AR*. G. Bàrberi Squarotti, *Astrazione e realtà* (Milan, 1960).

Bàrberi Squarotti, *NID*. G. Bàrberi Squarotti, *La narrativa italiana del dopoguerra* (Bologna, 1965).

Barnouw, *CA*. A. J. Barnouw, *Coming After. An Anthology of Poetry from the Low Countries* (1948).

Barquissau, *PC*. R. Barquissau, *Poètes créoles du XVIII^e siècle* (Paris, 1949).

Bataillon, *EE*. N. Bataillon, *Érasme et l'Espagne* (Paris, 1932).

BC. Biblioteca Contemporánea (Buenos Aires).

Beigbeder, *TFL*. M. Beigbeder, *Le théâtre en France depuis la Libération* (Paris, 1959).

Benedetto, *RDSN*. L. D. Benedetto, ed., *Rimatori del dolce stil novo* (Bari, 1939).

Bennett, *HGN*. E. K. Bennett, *A History of the German Novelle*, revised E. M. Waidson (London, 1961).

Beyer, *NL.* C. H. Beyer, *Norsk Litteraturhistorie* (Oslo, 1933).
*BH. Bulletin hispanique* (Bordeaux, 1899–).
*BHS. Bulletin of Hispanic Studies* (Liverpool, 1923–).
*BIE. Boletín del Instituto Español* (London).
Bigongiari, *PIN.* P. Bigongiari, *Poesia italiana del Novecento* (Milan, 1960).
Binni, *CI.* W. Binni, ed., *I classici italiani nella storia della critica* (Turin, 1954–5).
Biondolillo, *C.* F. Biondolillo, *I contemporanei* (Padua, 1948).
Blecua, *FLE.* J. M. Blecua, ed., *Floresta lírica española* (Madrid, 1957).
BLVS. Bibliothek des literarischen Vereins (Stuttgart).
Bo, *LC.* C. Bo, ed., *Lirici del Cinquecento* (Milan, 1941).
Boguslavskiy, *KIRSD.* A. O. Boguslavskiy, V. A. Diyev, A. C. Karpo, *Kratkaya istoriya russkoy sovetskoy dramaturgii* (Moscow, 1966).
Boisdeffre, *HVLA.* P. de Boisdeffre, *Une histoire vivante de la littérature d'aujourd'hui: 1939–1960* (Paris, 1964).
Borland, *NI.* H. Borland, *Nietzsche's Influence in Swedish Literature* (Göteborg, 1956).
Bowra, *BRV.* C. M. Bowra, *A Book of Russian Verse* (1943).
Bowra, *CE.* C. M. Bowra, *The Creative Experiment* (1949).
Bowra, *SBRV.* C. M. Bowra, *A Second Book of Russian Verse* (1948).
Brandes, *MCNL.* G. Brandes, *Main Currents in Nineteenth-Century Literature* (6 vols., 1901–5).
Braune, *AL.* W. Braune, *Althochdeutsches Lesebuch* (7th edn, Halle, 1942).
Bredsdorff, *DLET.* E. Bredsdorff, *Danish Literature in English Translation* (Copenhagen, 1950).
Brenan, *LSP.* G. Brenan, *The Literature of the Spanish People* (1951).
Bridgwater, *TCGV.* P. Bridgwater, ed., *The Penguin Book of Twentieth-Century German Verse* (1963).
*BSS. Bulletin of Spanish Studies* (1923–).
*C. Commentary* (New York, 1945–).
CA. Colección Austral (Madrid/Buenos Aires).
Calcaterra, *BA.* C. Calcaterra, ed., *Il barocco in Arcadia, e altri scritti sul Settecento* (Bologna, 1950).
Calcaterra, *LSA.* C. Calcaterra, ed., *I lirici del Seicento e dell'Arcadia* (Bologna, 1936).
Cano, *PESV.* J. L. Cano, *Poesía española del siglo XX* (Madrid, 1960).
Carr, *RE.* E. H. Carr, *The Romantic Exiles* (1933).
Cassirer, *PE.* E. Cassirer, *The Philosophy of the Enlightenment* (Princeton, 1951).
CC. Clásicos Castellanos (Madrid/Buenos Aires).
Cernuda, *EPC.* L. Cernuda, *Estudios sobre poesía española contemporánea* (Madrid, 1957).
Cernuda, *PL.* L. Cernuda, *Poesía y literatura* (Barcelona, 1960).
Chizhevsky, *HRL.* D. Chizhevsky, *History of Russian Literature from the 11th Century to the End cf the Baroque* (The Hague, 1960); or as D. Čiževskij.
Closs, *GGL.* A. Closs, *The Genius of the German Lyric* (2nd edn, 1962).
Cohen, *PA.* J. M. Cohen, *Poetry of this Age* (1959).
Cohen, *PBSV.* J. M. Cohen, ed., *The Penguin Book of Spanish Verse* (1960).
*Contemporanei. I contemporanei. Orientamenti culturali: letteratura italiana* (2 vols., Milan, 1963).

Contini, *PD*. G. Contini, ed., *Poeti del Duecento* (2 vols., Milan/Naples, 1960).

Corvin, *TNF*. M. Corvin, *Le théâtre nouveau en France* (Paris, 1963).

Cossío, *CAPE*. J. M. de Cossío, *Cincuenta años de poesía española* (*1850–1900*) (2 vols., Madrid, 1960).

CP. Clássicos Portugueses (2 vols., Madrid, 1960).

Crawford, *SDLV*. J. P. W. Crawford, *Spanish Drama before Lope de Vega* (Philadelphia, 1922).

Crawford, *SPD*. J. P. W. Crawford, *The Spanish Pastoral Drama* (2nd edn, 1938).

Croce, *LM*. B. Croce, ed., *Lirici marinisti* (Bari, 1910).

Croce, *LNI*. B. Croce, *La letteratura della nuova Italia* (6 vols., Bari, 1939–43).

Croce, *PES*. B. Croce, *Poeti e scrittori del pieno e del tardo rinascimento* (Bari, 1952).

Croce, *PPP*. B. Croce, *Poesia popolare e poesia d'arte* (Bari, 1946).

Croce, *SSL*. B. Croce, *Saggi sulla letteratura italiana del Seicento* (Bari, 1948).

CSC. Clássicos Sá da Costa.

D'Ancona, *SLI*. A. d'Ancona, *Del seicentismo nella poesia cortigiana nel secole XV*, in *Studi sulla letteratura italiana dei primi secoli* (Ancona, 1884).

Descotes, *PT*. M. Descotes, *Le public de théâtre et son histoire* (Paris, 1964).

Dietze, *JD*. W. Dietze, *Junges Deutschland und deutsche Klassik* (Berlin, 1957).

Di Francia, *N*. L. di Francia, 'Novellistica', in *Storia dei generi letterari italiani* (Milan, 1924).

Dill, *RSG*. S. Dill, *Roman Society in Gaul in the Merovingian Age* (1926).

Dilthey, *ED*. W. Dilthey, *Das Erlebnis und die Dichtung* (Berlin, 1906).

Dionisotti, *OBIV*. C. Dionisotti-Casalone, ed., *The Oxford Book of Italian Verse* (revised edn, 1952).

DLD. Deutsche Literaturdenkmale des 18. und 19. Jahrhunderts (Heilbronn, 1881 ff.).

DLE. Deutsche Literatur (Sammlung literarischer Kunst- und Kulturdenkmäler) in Entwicklungsreihen, ed. H. Kindermann (Leipzig, 1932ff.).

DNL. Deutsche National-Literatur, ed. J. Kürschner (Berlin/Stuttgart, 1882–9).

Doumic, *SI*. R. Doumic, *De Scribe à Ibsen* (Paris, 1893).

Downs, *MNL*. B. W. Downs, *Modern Norwegian Literature, 1860–1918* (1966).

*DR*. *Deutsche Rundschau* (Berlin, Baden-Baden, Stuttgart, 1934–65).

*DU*. *Der Deutschunterricht* (Stuttgart, 1955–).

Duckett, *CP*. E. S. Duckett, *Carolingian Portraits* (Michigan, 1962).

Duckett, *GMA*. E. S. Duckett, *The Gateway to the Middle Ages* (New York, 1938).

Duckett, *LW*. E. S. Duckett, *Latin Writers of the Fifth Century* (New York, 1930).

Duckett, *WS*. E. S. Duckett, *The Wandering Saints of the Middle Ages* (New York, 1959).

Ehrismann, *GDL*. G. Ehrismann, *Geschichte der deutschen Literatur bis zum Ausgang des Mittelalters* (2 vols., Munich, 1932–54).

Einarsson, *HIL*. S. Einarsson, *A History of Icelandic Literature* (1957).

Emrich, *PV*. W. Emrich, *Protest und Verheissung* (Frankfurt a.M., 1960).

Eoff, *MSN*. S. H. Eoff, *The Modern Spanish Novel* (1962).

*ER*. *Evergreen Review* (New York, 1957–).

Esslin, *TA*. M. Esslin, *The Theatre of the Absurd* (London, 1962).

Ewach, *USL*. H. Ewach, *Ukrainian Songs and Lyrics. A Short Anthology of Ukrainian Poetry* (Winnipeg, 1933) (with translations).

Faber, *RSS. Russian Short Stories* (1943).
Falqui, *PNNI.* E. Falqui, *Prosatori e narratori del Novecento italiano* (Turin, 1950).
Fechter, *ED.* P. Fechter, *Das Europäische Drama* (2 vols., Mannheim, 1957).
Fergusson, *IT.* F. Fergusson, *The Idea of a Theater* (Princeton, 1949).
Fernandez, *RI.* D. Fernandez, *Il romanzo italiano e la crisi della coscienza moderna* (with a bibliography by G. Bartolucci) (Milan, 1960).
Ferrero, *MM.* G. G. Ferrero, *Marino e i Marinisti* (Milan, 1954).
Ferretti, *LI.* Giancarlo Ferretti, *Letteratura e ideologia* (Rome, 1964).
Figurelli, *DSN.* F. Figurelli, *Il dolce stil novo* (Naples, 1933).
Filon, *DR.* A. Filon, *De Dumas à Rostand* (Paris, 1898).
Flora, *SIC.* F. Flora, *Scrittori italiani contemporanei* (Pisa, 1952).
*FMLS. Forum for Modern Language Studies* (St Andrews, 1965–).
Forster, *GP.* L. W. Forster, *German Poetry 1944–1948* (1949).
Fortini, *M.* F. Fortini, *Manabo 2* (Turin, 1960).
*FR. French Review* (New York/Baltimore, 1927–).
Frank, *MFD.* G. Frank, *The Medieval French Drama* (1954).
Frattaro, *IBLI.* R. Frattaro, *Introduzione bibliografica alla letteratura italiana* (Rome, 1963).
Friedmann and Mann, *DLZJ.* H. Friedmann and O. Mann, ed., *Deutsche Literatur im 20en Jahrhundert* (Heidelberg, 1954).
*FS. French Studies* (Oxford, 1947– ).
Gargiulo, *LIN.* A. Gargiulo, *Letteratura italiana del Novecento* (Florence, 1940).
Garin, *PLQ.* E. Garin, ed., *Prosatori latini del Quattrocento* (Milan/Naples, 1952).
Garland, *SS.* H. B. Garland, *Storm and Stress* (1952).
Garten, *MGD.* H. F. Garten, *Modern German Drama* (1959).
Getto, *MM.* G. Getto, *Opere scelte di G. B. Marino e dei Marinisti* (2 vols., Turin, 1954).
Gilman, *IPF.* M. Gilman, *The Idea of Poetry in France from Houdar de la Motte to Baudelaire* (Cambridge, Mass., 1958).
Gilson, *PMA.* É. Gilson, *La philosophie du Moyen Âge* (Paris, 1947).
*GLL. German Life and Letters* (1936–).
Golino, *CIP.* C. Golino, ed., *Contemporary Italian Poetry* (California, 1962).
Gosse, *SLNE.* E. Gosse, *Studies in the Literature of Northern Europe* (1960).
*GQ. The German Quarterly* (Lancaster, Pennsylvania, 1928–).
*GR. The Germanic Review* (New York, 1926–).
Greshoff, *HL.* J. Greshoff, ed., *Harvest of the Lowlands* (1945).
Grierson, *F.* G. J. C. Grierson, *The Flute. With Other Translations from Latin, Dutch and French* (1949).
Grossvogel, *FP.* D. I. Grossvogel, *Four Playwrights and a Postscript* (Ithaca, 1962).
Grossvogel, *TCFD.* D. I. Grossvogel, *20th Century French Drama* (New York, 1961).
Guerney, *NRS.* B. G. Guerney, *New Russian Stories* (1953).
Guerney, *TRL.* B. G. Guerney, ed., *A Treasury of Russian Literature* (1948).
Guicharnaud, *MFT.* J. Guicharnaud, *Modern French Theatre* (Yale, 1961).
*Guida*, 1959. *Guida alla lettura di . . .* (Rome, 1959) (a series of monographs published anonymously by the Istituto Poligrafico dello Stato).

Guizot, *CHF.* Guizot, *Collection des historiens de France* (Paris, 1823–4).

Gulland, *SRV.* R. M. Gulland, *Soviet Russian Verse* (1961).

Gundolf, *R.* F. Gundolf, *Romantiker* (Berlin, 1930).

Gustafson, *SSN.* A. Gustafson, *Six Scandinavian Novelists* (Princeton, 1940).

Hackett, *AMFP.* C. A. Hackett, *Anthology of Modern French Poetry* (1952).

Hamburger, *PE.* M. Hamburger, *From Prophecy to Exorcism* (1965).

Hamburger, *RE.* M. Hamburger, *Reason and Energy* (1957).

Hamburger and Middleton, *MGP.* M. Hamburger and C. Middleton, ed., *Modern German Poetry, 1910–1960* (1962).

Hare, *PRST.* R. Hare, *Pioneers of Russian Social Thought* (1951).

Havu, *FL.* I. Havu, *Finland's Literature* (Stockholm, 1958).

Hayward and Labedz, *LRSR.* M. Hayward and L. Labedz, ed., *Literature and Revolution in Soviet Russia, 1917–1963* (1962).

Heitner, *GTE.* R. H. Heitner, *German Tragedy in the Age of Enlightenment* (California, 1963).

Heller, *DM.* E. Heller, *The Disinherited Mind* (1952).

Hill and Bergin, *APT.* R. T. Hill and T. G. Bergin, ed., *Anthology of the Provençal Troubadours* (1941).

Hohoff, *GU.* C. Hohoff, *Geist und Ursprung* (Munich, 1954).

Holthusen, *JN.* H. E. Holthusen, *Ja und Nein* (Munich, 1954).

Holthusen, *KV.* H. E. Holthusen, *Kritisches Verstehen* (Munich, 1961).

Holthusen, *SW.* H. E. Holthusen, *Das Schöne und das Wahre* (Munich, 1958).

Holthusen, *UM.* H. E. Holthusen, *Der Unbehauste Mensch* (Munich, 1951).

*HR. Hispanic Review* (Philadelphia, 1933–).

Husik, *HMJP.* I. Husik, *A History of Medieval Jewish Philosophy* (1960).

Ibrovac, *APY.* M. Ibrovac, *Anthologie de la poésie yougoslave* (Paris, 1935) (French translations).

Jeanroy, *PLT.* A. Jeanroy, *La poésie lyrique des Troubadours* (2 vols., Toulouse/Paris, 1934).

*JEGP. Journal of English and Germanic Philology* (Urbana, 1871).

Jens, *DLG.* W. Jens, *Deutsche Literatur der Gegenwart* (Munich, 1961).

Kadić, *CCL.* A. Kadić, *Contemporary Croatian Literature* (The Hague/London/Paris, 1960).

Kadić, *CSL.* A. Kadić, *Contemporary Serbian Literature* (The Hague/London/Paris, 1964).

Kay, *PBIV.* G. R. Kay, *The Penguin Book of Italian Verse* (1958).

Keith-Smith, *ECGL.* B. Keith-Smith, ed., *Essays on Contemporary German Literature* (1966).

Killy, *DLTZ.* W. Killy, ed., *Die Deutsche Literatur, Texte und Zeugnisse* (Munich, 1963ff.).

Klaniczay, *HHL.* T. Klaniczay, J. Szavder and M. Szabolcsi, *History of Hungarian Literature* (1964).

Klausner, *HHHH.* J. Klausner, *Historia shel Ha-Sifrut HaIvrit Hachadashah* (6 vols., Jerusalem, 1930–50).

Klausner, *HMHL.* J. Klausner, *History of Modern Hebrew Literature, 1785–1930* (1932).

Koch, *IW.* F. Koch, *Idee und Wirklichkeit* (Düsseldorf, 1958).

Kraus, *DL.* C. Kraus, ed., *Deutsche Liederdichter des 13en Jahrhunderts* (Tübingen, 1952–8).

Kraus, *MF.* C. Kraus, *Des Minnesangs Frühling* (Leipzig, 1961).

Krzyżanowski, *PRL.* J. Krzyżanowski, *Polish Romantic Literature* (1930).

Kuncewicz, *MPM.* M. Kuncewicz, ed., *The Modern Polish Mind* (1963).

Kunisch, *HDG.* H. Kunisch, ed., *Handbuch der deutschen Gegenwartsliteratur* (Munich, 1965).

Laistner, *TLWE.* M. L. W. Laistner, *Thought and Letters in Western Europe A.D. 500–900* (1957).

Lalou, *TF.* R. Lalou, *Le théâtre en France depuis 1900* (Paris, 1961).

Lamm, *MD.* M. Lamm, *Modern Drama* (1952).

Lancaster, *FTLV.* H. C. Lancaster, *French Tragedy in the Time of Louis XV and Voltaire* (1950).

Lancaster, *HFDL.* H. C. Lancaster, *A History of French Dramatic Literature in the Seventeenth Century* (Baltimore, 1929–42).

Lavaud and Nelli, *T.* R. Lavaud and R. Nelli, *Les Troubadours* (2 vols., Paris, 1966).

Lavrin, *AMYP.* J. Lavrin, *An Anthology of Modern Yugoslav Poetry* (1963).

Levasti, *MDT.* A. Levasti, ed., *Mistici del Duecento e del Trecento* (Milan, 1935).

Levin, *GH.* H. Levin, *The Gates of Horn* (New York, 1963).

Lewis, *AL.* C. S. Lewis, *The Allegory of Love* (1938).

Liachover, *THHH.* I. Liachover, *Toldot ha-Sifrut ha-Ivrit Hachadashas* (3 vols., 1927–9).

Lind, *LPIR.* L. R. Lind, *Lyric Poetry of the Italian Renaissance* (Yale, 1954) (translations).

Lindsay, *MLP.* J. Lindsay, *Medieval Latin Poets* (1934) (with translations).

*LN. Lingua Nostra.*

*LSS. Liverpool Studies in Spanish* (University of Liverpool, 1940–).

Luckyj, *LPSU.* G. S. N. Luckyj, *Literary Politics in the Soviet Ukraine 1917–34* (New York, 1956).

Lugovskoy, *ARSP.* V. Lugovskoy, ed., *Antologiya russkoy Sovetskoy poezii (1917–1957)* (2 vols., Moscow, 1957).

Lukács, *HN.* G. Lukács, *The Historical Novel*, tr. H. and S. Mitchell (1962).

Lukács, *SER.* G. Lukács, *Studies in European Realism* (1950).

Luts'ky, *LD.* Y. Luts'ky, ed., *Lekhosynya dal'. Vaplityans'ky zbirnyk* (New York, 1963).

*M. Merkur Deutsche Zeitschrift für europäisches Denken* (Munich, 1947–).

Macri, *ESPC.* O. Macri, *Esemplari del sentimento poetico contemporaneo* (Florence, 1941).

*MAe. Medium Aevum* (Oxford, 1932– ).

*Maggiori. I maggiori. Orientamenti culturali: letteratura italiana* (2 vols., Milan, 1956).

Manitius, *GLLM.* M. Manitius, *Geschichte der lateinischen Literatur des Mittelalters* (3 vols., Berlin, 1911–31).

Mann, *ETD.* T. Mann, *Essays of Three Decades* (1947).

Manning, *UL.* C. A. Manning, *Ukrainian Literature, Studies of the Leading Authors* (Jersey City, 1944).

Manning and Smal-Stocki, *HMBL.* C. Manning and R. Smal-Stocki, *The History of Modern Bulgarian Literature* (New York, 1960).

Mariani, *GNI.* G. Mariani, *La giovane narrativa italiana tra documento e poesia* (Florence, 1962).

Markov, *MRP.* V. Markov and M. Sparks, ed., *Modern Russian Poetry* (1966) (with translations).

Markov, *PG.* V. Markov, *Priglushonnyye golosa* (New York, 1952).

Martino, *LF.* P. Martino, *Le naturalisme français* (Paris, 1923).

Mathewson, *PHRL.* R. W. Mathewson, *The Positive Hero in Russian Literature* (1958).

Matthews, *FDNC.* B. Matthews, *French Dramatists of the Nineteenth Century* (New York, 1901).

McClelland, *ORMS.* I. L. McClelland, *The Origins of the Romantic Movement in Spain* (1937).

McFarlane, *TNL.* J. W. McFarlane, *Ibsen and the Temper of Norwegian Literature* (1960).

*MDF. Mercure de France* (Paris, 1889–1965).

Meillet, *ALU.* M. A. Meillet, *Anthologie de la littérature ukrainienne* (Paris/Geneva/Prague, 1921).

Menéndez y Pelayo, *HIE.* M. Menéndez y Pelayo, *Historia de las ideas estéticas en España* (Madrid/Santander, 1946–7).

Menéndez y Pelayo, *PLC.* M. Menéndez y Pelayo, *Antología de poetas líricos castellanos* (Madrid/Santander, 1944).

Menéndez y Pelayo, *PLE.* M. Menéndez y Pelayo, *Antología de poetas líricos españoles* (Madrid/Santander, 1944–5).

Mervyn Jones, *FHW.* D. Mervyn Jones, *Five Hungarian Writers. Zrínyi, Mikes, Vörösmarty, Eötvös, Petőfi* (1966).

MGH. Monumenta Germaniae Historica, ed. G. H. Pertz *et al.* (1887).

Middleton, *GWT.* C. Middleton, ed., *German Writing Today* (1967).

Migne, *PL.* J. P. Migne, *Patrologia Latina* (221 vols., Paris, 1844–55; 2nd edn, Paris, 1878ff.).

Mijakovs'kyj and Shevelov, *TS.* V. Mijakovs'kyj and G. Y. Shevelov, ed., *Taras Sevcemko 1814–1861. A Symposium* (The Hague, 1962).

*Minori. I minori. Orientamenti culturali: letteratura italiana* (4 vols., Milan, 1961).

Mirsky, *HRL.* D. J. Mirsky, *A History of Russian Literature*, ed. F. J. Whitfield (New York, 1960).

*ML. Modern Languages* (London, 1919–).

*MLN. Modern Language Notes* (Baltimore, 1886 ff.).

*MLQ. Modern Languages Quarterly* (1940–).

*MLR. Modern Language Review* (London, 1905–).

Mongrédien, *PP.* G. Mongrédien, *Les précieux et les précieuses* (Paris, 1939).

Mornet, *SNF.* D. Mornet, *Les sciences de la nature en France au XVIII^e^ siècle* (Paris, 1911).

Motherwell, *DPP.* R. Motherwell, ed., *The Dada Painters and Poets* (1948).

Mourgue, *DDL*. G. Mourgue, *Dieu dans la littérature d'aujourd'hui* (Paris, 1961).
Mourgues, *MBPP*. O. de Mourgues, *Metaphysical, Baroque and Précieux Poetry* (1953).
Muchnic, *GP*. H. Muchnic, *From Gor'ky to Pasternak* (1963).
Muschg, *ZDL*. W. Muschg, *Die Zerstörung der deutschen Literatur* (Bern, 1956).
Natan, *GML*. A. Natan, ed., *German Men of Letters* (3 vols., 1961–3).
NBAE. Nueva Biblioteca de Autores Españoles.
Newnham, *GSS*. R. Newnham, *German Short Stories* (1964).
Newnham, *SSS*. R. Newnham, *Soviet Short Stories* (Russian and English Texts) (1963).
*NM. Neuphilologische Mitteilungen* (Helsinki, 1899–).
NDL. Neudrucke deutscher Literaturwerke des XVI. und XVII. Jahrhunderts (Halle).
Nonnenmann, *SG*. K. Nonnenmann, ed., *Schriftsteller der Gegenwart* (Olten, 1963).
Nora, *NEC*. E. de Nora, *La novela española contemporánea* (Madrid, 1962).
*NRFH. Nueva Revista de Filología Hispánica.*
Obolensky, *PBRV*. D. Obolensky, *The Penguin Book of Russian Verse* (1962).
Ollilainen, *SF*. K. V. Ollilainen, *Singing Finland* (Lahti, 1956).
Ordon, *TCPS*. E. Ordon, ed., *Ten Contemporary Polish Stories* (Detroit, 1958).
Pacifici, *CIN*. S. Pacifici, *A Guide to Contemporary Italian Narrative* (New York, 1962).
Pancrazi, *SO*. P. Pancrazi, *Scrittori d'oggi* (Bari, 1953).
Panvini, *RSS*. B. Panvini, *Le rime della scuola siciliana* (Florence, 1962–4).
Pascal, *GN*. R. Pascal, *The German Novel* (1956).
Pascal, *GSD*. R. Pascal, *The German Sturm und Drang* (1953).
Pasolini, *PI*. P. P. Pasolini, *Passione e ideologia* (Milan, 1960).
Pauphilet, *HCMA*. A. Pauphilet, ed., *Historiens et chroniqueurs du Moyen Âge* (Paris, 1952).
Peers, *SGA*. E. A. Peers, *Spanish Golden Age Drama and Poetry* (1946).
PEGS. Publications of the English Goethe Society (London, 1886–1912; new series London, 1924).
Perry, *HASP*. J. H. Perry, ed., *The Harrap Anthology of Spanish Poetry* (1953).
Peterkiewicz and Singer, *FCPP*. J. Peterkiewicz and B. Singer, ed., *Five Centuries of Polish Poetry* (1960).
Petrucciani, *PPPE*. M. Petrucciani, *Poesia pura e poesia esistenziale* (Turin, 1957).
Peyre, *LS*. H. Peyre, *Literature and Sincerity* (Yale, 1963).
Pierce, *HP*. F. Pierce, *The Heroic Poem of the Spanish Golden Age* (1947).
Pietrkiewicz, *PPV*. J. Pietrkiewicz, *Polish Prose and Verse* (1956).
Piñeyro, *RS*. E. J. N. Piñeyro, *The Romantics of Spain*, tr. E. Allison Peers (1934).
Pinto, *BPV*. V. Pinto, *Bulgarian Prose and Verse* (1957).
PLAC. Poetae Latini Aevi Carolini.
PMEP. Penguin Modern European Poets.
PMLA. Publications of the Modern Language Association of America (Baltimore, 1889–).
Poggioli, *PR*. R. Poggioli, *The Poets of Russia, 1880–1930* (1960).
Poggioli, *PS*. R. Poggioli, *The Phoenix and the Spider* (1957).

Popović, *JS*. P. Popović, *Jugoslav Stories* (New York, 1921).

*PQ*. *Philological Quarterly* (Iowa City, 1922–).

*PR*. *Partisan Review* (New York, 1947–).

*PoR*. *The Polish Review* (New York, 1956–).

Prawer, *PBGL*. S. S. Prawer, *Penguin Book of German Lieder* (1964).

Pritchard, *GE*. F. H. Pritchard, ed., *Great Essays of All Nations* (1929).

Pullini, *NIN*. S. Pullini, *Narratori italiani del Novecento* (Padua, 1959).

Pullini, *RID*. S. Pullini, *Il romanzo italiano del dopoguerra* (Milan, 1960).

*R*. *Romania* (Paris, 1872–).

Raby, *CLP*. F. J. E. Raby, *Christian Latin Poetry* (2nd edn, 1953).

Raby, *SLP*. F. J. E. Raby, *Secular Latin Poetry* (2nd edn, 1957).

RAE. Real Academia Española.

RAH. Real Academia de la Historia, Madrid.

Raymond, *DBS*. M. Raymond, *De Baudelaire au Surréalisme* (new edn, Paris, 1952).

Reavey and Slonim, *SA*. G. Reavey and M. Slonim, ed., *Soviet Literature: An Anthology* (1933).

Reich-Ranicki, *DLWO*. M. Reich-Ranicki, *Deutsche Literatur in West und Ost* (Munich, 1962).

Reményi, *HWL*. J. Reményi, *Hungarian Writers and Literature* (New Jersey, 1964).

*RFE*. *Revista de filología española* (Madrid, 1914–).

*RH*. *Revue hispanique* (New York/Paris, 1894–1930, 1933).

*RHC*. *Recueil des historiens des croisades*, Académie des Inscriptions et Belles Lettres (Paris, 1841–1906).

*RLV*. *Revue des langues vivantes* (Brussels, 1935–).

*RMS*. *Renaissance and Modern Studies* (Nottingham, 1957–61).

Roback, *SYL*. A. Roback, *The Story of Yiddish Literature* (1940).

Robertis, *SN*. G. de Robertis, *Scrittori del Novecento* (Florence, 1946).

*RoR*. *Romanic Review* (New York, 1910–).

Roscoe, *IN*. T. Roscoe, *The Italian Novelists* (1880).

Rose, *MGLV*. W. Rose, ed., *A Book of Modern German Lyric Verse, 1890–1955* (1960).

Rossetti, *DC*. D. G. Rossetti, *Dante and His Circle* (1861) (translations).

*RPh*. *Romance Philology* (Berkeley/Los Angeles, 1947–).

*RR*. *Russian Review* (Penguin Books, 1945–7).

Rychner, *A*. M. Rychner, *Arachne* (Zürich, 1957).

Rychner, *CG*. J. Rychner, *La chanson de geste. Essai sur l'art épique des jongleurs* (Geneva/Lille, 1955).

Sainte-Beuve, *CL*. C.-A. Sainte-Beuve, *Causeries du lundi* (Paris, 1851–7).

Salinari, *PLD*. O. Salinari, ed., *La poesia lirica del Duecento* (Turin, 1951).

Sanchez, *PSEO*. A. Sanchez, ed., *Poesía sevillana en la Edad de Oro* (Madrid, 1948).

Scherer-Virski, *MPSS*. O. Scherer-Virski, *The Modern Polish Short Story* (The Hague, 1955).

Schmidt, *PSS*. A. M. Schmidt, ed., *Poètes du seizième siècle* (Paris, 1953).

Schneider, *DDA*. K. L. Schneider, *Die deutsche Dichtung der Aufklärungszeit* (Stuttgart, 1948).

*SD*. *Sturm und Drang. Dramatische Schriften*, ed. E. Loewenthal and L. Schneider (Heidelberg, 1963).

Sée, *TFC*. E. Sée, *Le théâtre français contemporain* (Paris, 1950).
*SEER*. *Slavonic and East European Review* (1923ff.).
Serreau, *HNT*. G. Serreau, *Histoire du 'nouveau théâtre'* (Paris, 1966).
SG. Schriftsteller der Gegenwart (E. Berlin).
Shattuck, *BY*. R. Shattuck, *The Banquet Years: the Arts in France, 1885–1918* (1960).
Silz, *RR*. W. Silz, *Realism and Reality* (Chapel Hill, 1954).
Simmons, *RFSI*. E. J. Simmons, *Russian Fiction and Soviet Ideology* (1958).
*SL*. *Soviet Literature* (Moscow, 1942–).
Slavutych, *MP*. Y. Slavutych, *The Muse in Prison* (Jersey City, 1956).
Slonim, *MRL*. M. Slonim, *Modern Russian Literature* (1953).
Snell, *FFG*. A. L. Snell, *Flowers from a Foreign Garden. Selections from the Works of Modern Dutch Poets* (1902) (translations).
Snow and Hansford Johnson, *WT*. C. P. Snow and P. Hansford Johnson, ed., *Winter's Tales* (1961).
Soergel, *DDZ*. A. Soergel, *Dichtung und Denker der Zeit* (new edn, Düsseldorf, 1951).
Sokel, *WE*. W. Sokel, *The Writer in Extremis* (Stanford, 1959).
*SP*. *Studies in Philology* (Chapel Hill, North Carolina, 1906– ).
Sparrow, *LVHR*. J. Sparrow, 'Latin Verse of the High Renaissance', in *Italian Renaissance Studies* (1960).
Spender, *GGSS*. S. Spender, ed., *Great German Short Stories* (1960).
SRG. Scriptores Rerum Germanicarum in usum Scholarum ex Monumentis Germaniae historicis recudi fecit G. H. Pertz (64 vols., Hanover, 1839–1921).
*SS*. *Soviet Survey*.
Staiger, *MDS*. E. Staiger, *Meisterwerke deutscher Sprache* (Zürich, 1945).
Staiger, *ZE*. E. Staiger, *Die Zeit als Einbildungskraft des Dichters* (Zürich, 1953).
Steinhauer, *GS*. H. Steinhauer, ed., *German Stories* (1961).
Stern, *R*. J. P. Stern, *Re-interpretations* (1964).
Strakhovsky, *CW*. L. I. Strakhovsky, *Craftsmen of the Word* (Cambridge, Mass., 1949).
Strich, *DKR*. F. Strich, *Deutsche Klassik und Romantik* (Munich, 1924).
Struve, *RLI*. G. Struve, *Russkaya literatura v izgnanii* (New York, 1956).
Struve, *SRL*. G. Struve, *Soviet Russian Literature* (1951).
Surer, *TFC*. P. Surer, *Le théâtre français contemporain* (Paris, 1964).
Swayze, *PCL*. H. Swayze, *Political Control of Literature in the U.S.S.R., 1946–1959* (Harvard, 1962).
Taylor, *MM*. H. O. Taylor, *The Medieval Mind* (4th edn, 2 vols., 1925).
Terry, *ASP*. A. Terry, *An Anthology of Spanish Poetry, 1500–1700*, Part I (Oxford, 1965).
TFM. Textes Français Modernes.
TL. Textos Literarios.
*TLS*. *The Times Literary Supplement*.
Tompuri, *VF*. E. Tompuri, *Voice from Finland* (Helsinki, 1947) (translations).
Torrente Ballester, *TEC*. G. Torrente Ballester, *Teatro español contemporáneo* (Madrid, 1957).
Trahard, *MSF*. P. Trahard, *Les maîtres de la sensibilité française de la XVIII$^{e}$ siècle* (4 vols., Paris, 1931–3).

Trend, *OBSV*. J. B. Trend, ed., *The Oxford Book of Spanish Verse* (1940).
Tymms, *GRL*. R. Tymms, *German Romantic Literature* (1955).
*UCE*. *Ukraine. A Concise Encyclopaedia*, vol. i (Toronto, 1963).
*UQ*. *Ukrainian Quarterly* (New York, 1944–).
*UR*. *Ukrainian Review* (London, 1954–).
Valbuena Prat, *NPE*. A. Valbuena Prat, *La novela picaresca española* (1956).
Varese, *CLC*. C. Varese, ed., *Cultura letteraria contemporanea* (Pisa, 1951).
Varese, *PVQ*. C. Varese, ed., *Prosatori volgari del Quattrocento* (Milan/Naples, 1955).
Vivanco, *PEC*. L. F. Vivanco, *Introducción a la poesía española contemporánea* (Madrid, 1957).
Volz, *C*. P. Volz, *La comédie* (Paris, 1964).
Waddell, *MLL*. H. Waddell, *Medieval Latin Lyrics* (1948).
Waidson, *GSS*. H. M. Waidson, ed., *German Short Stories* (2 vols., 1957–9).
Waidson, *MGS*. H. M. Waidson, ed., *Modern German Short Stories* (1961).
Wardropper, *HPL*. B. W. Wardropper, *Historia de la poesía lírica a lo divino* (Madrid, 1958).
Waxman, *HJL*. M. Waxman, *A History of Jewish Literature* (revised and enlarged edn, 5 vols., 1960).
Weevers, *PNEC*. T. Weevers, *The Poetry of the Netherlands in its European Context, 1170–1930* (1960).
Weinberg, *HLC*. B. Weinberg, *A History of Literary Criticism in the Italian Renaissance* (1961).
Weinstein, *MDJ*. L. Weinstein, *The Metamorphoses of Don Juan* (Stanford, 1959).
Weiss, *TM*. J.-J. Weiss, *Le théâtre et les mœurs* (Paris, 1889).
Wellek, *HMC*. R. Wellek, *A History of Modern Criticism* (4 vols., 1955–).
Wellwarth, *TPP*. G. E. Wellwarth, *The Theatre of Protest and Paradox* (New York, 1964).
Wiese, *DDM*. B. von Wiese, ed., *Deutsche Dichter der Moderne* (Berlin, 1965).
Wiese, *DT*. B. von Wiese, *Die deutsche Tragödie von Lessing bis Hebbel* (Hamburg, 1948).
Wilson, *AC*. E. Wilson, *Axel's Castle* (1931).
Woledge, *PBFV*. B. Woledge, ed., *The Penguin Book of French Verse*, 1 (1961).
Yarmolinsky, *SSS*. A. Yarmolinsky, ed., *Soviet Short Stories* (New York, 1960)
Zardoya, *PEC*. C. Zardoya, *Poesía española contemporánea* (Madrid, 1961).
*Zfd A*. *Zeitschrift für deutsches Altertum* (Leipzig, 1841–53; Berlin, 1856–).
*ZRP*. *Zeitschrift für romanische Philologie* (Halle, 1877–).

# A

**Aakjær, Jeppe** (Aakjær 1866–Jenle 1930). Danish poet. The son of a smallholder, his novels of social-protest about peasant life in Jutland are now largely forgotten, but his lyrical poetry has a popularity unequalled by any of his contemporaries. Instead of protesting about them he praises the simple conditions, the patriarchal piety, the people and scenery of Jutland. He resembles Burns, whom he admired and translated. [E L B]

*Songs of the Heath*, tr. J. Glyn Davies (1962) (selection).
*ASR*, XII, 1924.

**Aarestrup, Emil** (Copenhagen 1800–Odense 1856). Danish poet. By profession a physician, he published only one volume of poems (*Digte*, 1837). ⇨ Winther produced a complete edition from posthumous manuscripts (1863) and G. ⇨ Brandes wrote the introduction for his collected poems (*Samlede Skrifter*, 1877), since when appreciation of him has steadily grown and he is now generally recognized as a highly sophisticated love poet, a daring immoralist and aesthete whose worship of the beauty of the female body is expressed with a mastery of poetic technique (see his many *ritournelles*). [E L B]

H. Brix, *E.A.* (2 vols., Copenhagen, 1952).

**Aasen, Ivar** (Ørsta, Sunnmøre 1813–Kristiana 1896). Norwegian philologist and poet. The son of a small farmer. Inspired by the current National Romanticism, he investigated the rural dialects of Norway and on the basis of some of them formulated *Landsmaal*, thus laying the foundations of *Nynorsk*, now the second official language form of Norway; his principal works in this field are *Det norske Folkesprogs Grammatik* (1848) and *Ordbog over det norske Folkesprog* (1850). His collection of poems, *Symra* (1863), which he wrote to demonstrate the literary possibilities of his new language (Danish was then the literary language of Norway), are mainly on themes from peasant life. [R G P]

*Skrifter i Samling* (3 vols., 1912); *Dikting* (1946).
I. Handagard, *I.A.* (Oslo, 1956); Beyer, *NL*.

**Abelard, Peter** (Pallet, Nantes 1079–S. Marcel, Châlons 1142). French scholastic philosopher. He studied at Paris, where his intellectual brilliance led to his appointment to a chair. His lectures became famous and attracted pupils from many countries, nearly twenty of them afterwards becoming cardinals and two of them popes (one was Celestine II). His tragic love affair with his pupil Heloisa made him withdraw for a time to the Abbey of St Denis, but clamours for his lectures soon brought about his return. The unorthodoxy of his teaching and his uncompromising character led to his expulsion in turn from the Abbey, from his oratory of the Paraclete near Troyes, from the Abbey of St Gildas in his native Brittany, and to his condemnation by church councils at Soissons and later at Sens. His last years were spent under the protection of Peter the Venerable, Abbot of Cluny, and he died in a Cluniac priory.

It was Abelard's manner rather than his conclusions that caused such violent hostility. The modern reader finds less interest in his theology and philosophy than in his *Historia calamitatum*. In this he tells the story of his love affair very frankly in the polished Latin which also characterizes his letters to Heloisa. His verse includes over a hundred hymns, written for Heloisa after she had become a nun. They show characteristic originality being in a great variety of metres, many never used before or since. Perhaps the most beautiful is 'O quanta qualia sunt illa sabbata', with its tragic undertone. [F B]

Migne, *PL*, 178; ed. V. Cousin (Paris, 1848–59); *Hymns*, ed. G. M. Dreves (Paris, 1891); *Historia calamitatum*, ed. J. Manfrin (Paris, 1959), tr. H. A. Bellows (St Paul, Minn., 1922); *Ethics*, tr. J. R. McCallum (1935); *Letters*, tr. C. K. S. Moncrieff (1925).
C. de Rémusat, *A.* (2 vols., Paris, 1845); J. G. Sikes, *P.A.* (1932); É. Gilson, *Héloïse et Abélard* (Paris, 1938); Raby, *CLP*; Taylor, *MM*.

**Abell, Kjeld** (Ribe 1901–Copenhagen 1961). Danish playwright. He reacted strongly against his respectable middle-class background, becoming an artist in Paris after graduating in economics from Copenhagen and later a stage painter in London and Copenhagen. Apart from a ballet (1934), his first play, *Melodien, der blev væk* (1935; tr. F. Sinclair and R. Adam, *The Melody that Got Lost*, 1939), produced in Copenhagen and widely abroad (London 1936), was a witty attack on the conformism and dullness of the white-collar proletariat. Another elegant and witty play, *Eva aftjener sin barnepligt* (1936), has the biblical Eve reborn into a respectable middle-class family. His most important pre-war play, *Anna Sophie Hedvig* (1939; *Scandinavian Plays of the 20th Century*, Princeton, 1945), reflects the problems of democracy *v.* Nazi tyranny in the fate of a Danish schoolmistress. Both *Judith* (1940) and *Dronning gaar igen* (1943; tr. J. F. S. Pearce, *The Queen on Tour*, in *Contemporary Danish Plays*, 1955) are clearly influenced by the German Occupation, and in 1944 Abell was forced to go underground where he worked in the Resistance. *Silkeborg* (1946) is set in occupied Denmark, and *Dage paa en sky* (1947; tr. A. I. Roughton, *Days on a Cloud*, in *The Genius of the Scandinavian Theatre*, N.Y., 1964) is concerned with the problems of the intellectuals after Hiroshima. Among his most important plays of the 1950s are *Den blå pekingeser* (1954), *Kameliadamen* (1959, inspired by Dumas's novel), and *Skriget*, produced posthumously in 1961. He was always a rebel, at first against the stuffiness of the 'Victorian', then against more recent social failings. *Synskhedens gave* (1962) contains essays and poems; a visit to China inspired the novel *De tre fra Minikoi* (1957; tr. A. I. Roughton, *Three from Minikoi*, 1960). [ELB]

Ed. S. Møller Kristensen, *En bog om K.A.* (Copenhagen, 1961); *TLS*, 18 January 1963; E. L. Bredsdorff, *K.A.* (in *The Genius of the Scandinavian Theatre*, N.Y., 1964).

**Aboab, Isaac** (*c.* 1300). Hebrew writer in Spain. Author of the most popular medieval ethical work, *Menorat ha-Maor* (1514). Its German translation (S. Bamberger, 1923) remained until recent times a household work. [EE]

Waxman, *HJL*.

**About, Edmond** (Dieuze 1828–Paris 1885). French journalist and novelist. A frequent contributor to *Figaro*, *Revue des Deux Mondes*, etc., and founder of *Le XIX siècle*. A brilliant journalist, wittily sceptical, radically democratic, his articles on social and religious questions were published in *Causeries* (1865, 1866). His stylized, colourful but moralizing stories and novels include *Les mariages de Paris* (1856), *Le roi des montagnes* (1857), *L'homme à l'oreille cassée* (1862), *Le nez d'un notaire* (1862), *Les mariages de province* (1868) and *Le roman d'un brave homme* (1880). Elected to the Académie Française, 1884. [WA]

M. Thiébaut, *E.A.* (Paris, 1936); Sainte-Beuve, *CL*.

**Abraham à Sancta Clara,** pseud. of Ulrich Megerle (Kreenheinstetten, Baden 1644–Vienna 1709). German writer. The son of a peasant-serf, educated in Jesuit and Benedictine schools, he was ordained in 1666 and became Court Preacher in Vienna in 1677, where his sermons exerted an immediate popular appeal. The plague year of 1679 brought the preacher leisure to write and he began with a series of tracts exhorting his readers to repentance, the most famous of which, the *Auf, auf, ihr Christen* of 1683, achieved immortality by Schiller's adaptation of it as the celebrated Capuchin's sermon of *Wallensteins Lager*. The characteristic qualities of these tracts, a distinctly satirical turn of mind and a gift for keen observation, a love of the rather scurrilous anecdote and a predilection for allegory and metaphor, coupled with the piling up of adjectives, nouns and verbs to achieve burlesque stylistic effects, gain their fullest expression in the 4-volume life of Judas Iscariot, *Judas der Ertzschelm* (1686–95), where Judas appears as an Oedipus figure who follows Christ out of repentance for his crimes. The thread of the narrative is frequently lost, however, because of the interpolation of long moralizing or satirical passages which in fact constitute little sermons. [WAC]

*Werke*, ed. K. Bertsche (3 vols., Vienna, 1943ff.); *Auswahl*, ed. W. Höllerer (1959).
K. Bertsche, *A. à S.C.* (Vienna, 1922).

**Abravanel (Abarbanel), Isaac** (Lisbon 1437–Venice 1508). Hebrew philosophic writer. One of the most influential Jews in Spain before the expulsion. He was Treasurer to the Kings of Portugal, Spain and Naples and in 1492 offered the Catholic Kings 30,000 ducats to prevent the expulsion of the Jews. Well versed in Latin as well as Jewish literature, he wrote a commentary to the Bible, which was in parts translated into Latin and used by Christian scholars. He was of the philosophical school of ⇨ Maimonides. [E E]

A. Heschel, *Don I.A.* (1937); B. Netanyahu, *Don I.A.* (1952).

**Abravanel (Abarbanel), Judah (Leone Ebreus, Leo Judeus)** (Lisbon *c.* 1460–Naples before 1535). Hebrew philosophic writer. Son of Don Isaac ⇨ Abravanel, he left Spain in 1492 and lived as a physician in Genoa and Naples. Influenced by Pico de la Mirandola the elder, he became a neo-Platonist and wrote his *Dialoghi dell'amore* (in Spanish or Hebrew) (tr. F. Friedeberg-Seeley and J. Barnes, *The Philosophy of Love*, 1937) in which he expounded the view that love was the governing force of the world. His son was forcibly converted; on this theme he wrote the elegy *Telunah al ha-Zeman* (1503). [E E]

B. Zimmels, *Leo Hebraeus* (Breslau, 1886).

**Abulafia, Todros** (Toledo 1247–Toledo *c.* 1303). Hebrew poet. His 800 poems of rather mediocre style and quality form an important source for the study of the period. He and his family were influential in medieval Spain. [E E]

*Gan ha-Meshalim ve-ha-Chidoth*, ed. D. Yellin (2 vols., 1932–4).
Baer, *HJCS*.

**Achard, Marcel** (Sainte Foy-lès-Lyon 1899– ). French playwright. Author of many charming diversions touched with poetry, sentiment and fancy and very consciously exploiting the characters, pantomime, improvisation associated with the *commedia dell'arte*. His fey creatures caught in insubstantial love affairs cloy in the long run. Notable successes were: *Voulez-vous jouer avec moâ* (1924), *Marlborough s'en va-t-en guerre!* (1924), *Jean de la lune* (1929), *Domino* (1931), *Le corsaire* (1938), *Auprès de ma blonde* (1947; tr./adapt. S. H. Behrman, *I Know My Love*, 1952), *Patate* (1957; tr. F. Douglas, *Rollo*, 1960) and *L'idiote* (1960; tr. H. Kurnitz, *A Shot in the Dark*, 1962). [S B J]

*Histoires d'amour* (1959) (4 plays); *L'amour ne paie pas* (1962) (4 plays).
Surer, *TFC*; Lalou, *TF*.

**Achillini, Claudio** (Bologna 1574–Bologna 1640). Italian poet. One of the most celebrated followers of ⇨ Marino, his *Rime* were published many times in the 17th century. He has left also some occasionally lively letters. He taught law at the universities of Ferrara, Parma and Bologna, and served as secretary to various prelates, among them Alessandro Ludovisi, later Pope Gregory XV. His verse is characterized by the typical features of Marinismo – hyperbole, curious images, plays on words, bizarre metaphors – but he rarely achieves the flashes of imaginative power which some of his contemporaries are capable of. One of his sonnets, 'Sudate, o fochi, a preparar metalli', quoted by ⇨ Manzoni in the *Promessi sposi*, achieved notoriety as an example of 17th-century bombastic rhetoric. [D G R]

Croce, *LM*; Getto, *MM*; Ferrero, *MM*.

**Achterberg, Gerrit** (Langbroek 1905–Amersfoort 1962). Dutch poet. Probably the most important of his generation, highly original in his central theme and his formulation of it. The death of the beloved is the point of contact with the absolute, which can literally be materialized by the magical force of words. This alchemical faith in the transmutation of poetry makes his work powerful and striking, and gave to the experimentalists around him a clearer insight into the creative function of words. [P K]

*Verzamelde Gedichten* (1963); Barnouw, *CA*; *Delta* (Summer, 1958).
*Commentaar op G.A.* (Den Haag, 1948); 'G.A.', in *Maatstaf*, 10/11, 1964.

**Acmeism.** A movement in Russian poetry of the 1910s and 1920s. Following the poet M. Kuzmin's (1875–1936) manifesto, *Concerning Beautiful Clarity* (1910), ⇨ Gumilyov and S. Gorodetsky (1884– ) established the Poet's Guild (Tsekh Poetov) in 1911; they were ironically dubbed 'Acmeists'. They reacted strongly against the imprecision and mysticism of the declining ⇨ Symbolist movement in favour of concrete imagery, conciseness and 'this-worldliness'. Two of the century's finest poets, ⇨ Mandel'shtam and ⇨ Akhmatova, belonged to the movement; many subsequent poets (e.g. ⇨ Antokol'sky, ⇨ Tikhonov, ⇨ Akhmadulina) show its influence, which is not yet exhausted. The great Acmeists conceal at times transcendental, even apocalyptic overtones behind their concrete clarity; and though basically apolitical, they were far from insensitive to the events of their time. [RM-G]

Gulland, *SRV*; Markov, *MRP, PG*; Obolensky, *PBRV*.
Strakhovsky, *CW*; Poggioli, *PR*.

**Activism.** ⇨ Hiller, Kurt.

**Acuña, Hernando de** (Valladolid 1518–Granada 1580?). Spanish poet and soldier. Famous for his sonnet in praise of Charles V and his Christian mission. [JMC]

*Varias poesías*, ed. E. Catena de Vindel (1954); ed. A. Vilanova (Barcelona, 1954); Trend, *OBSV*; Perry, *HASP*; Cohen, *PBSV*; Terry, *ASP*.
N. A. Cortés, *Don H. de A.* (Valladolid, 1913).

**'Adam, Mystère d''** or **'Jeu d'Adam'.** Medieval play in Anglo-Norman (probably 1150–70). Historically important for its partly liturgical character and detailed directions in Latin for its staging, performance and costume. The first section or 'act', about the Fall, is especially successful; Eve is a sympathetic, human figure, caring for posterity, Adam dull, harsh and concerned with his own fate. The Devil appears in the guise of a courtly seducer. The second 'act' shows the immediate consequences of the Fall, Cain's hatred for Abel, and the final section consists of a Procession of Prophets foretelling the redemption. The surviving manuscript is unfinished.

The versification in octosyllabic couplets is lively, and the dialogue is varied skilfully to convey Eve's tragic sense of wrongdoing, Adam's self-righteousness and several vivid moments of lighter humour. Decasyllables are used at solemn moments. This delightful play was performed in a 'simultaneous' setting of raised platforms, probably on the *parvis* outside the west door of a church or cathedral. (⇨ *Mystères.*) [LTT]

*Le Mystère d'Adam*, ed. P. Studer (1918); ed. P. Aebischer (Geneva, 1963); *Le Jeu d'Adam et d'Ève*, modernized ed. G. Cohen (Paris, 1936). *Neophilologus*, XLVI, 1962; Frank, *MFD*.

**Adam de la Halle** or **le Bossu** (Arras *c.* 1240–?Naples *c.* 1288). French poet. He was a leading poet and musician at the ⇨ Puy of Arras (1260–75). He accompanied his patron Robert of Anjou to Italy (before 1283), and won fame at the court of Charles of Anjou, king of Naples and Sicily.

He composed in a variety of genres: 20 debates or *jeux partis*, 30 love songs (2 to the Virgin), conventional but metrically ingenious, motets, excellent *rondeaux*, a *Dit d'amours* and *La chanson du Roi de Sicile*, a fragmentary epic in honour of Charles of Anjou. When leaving his wife and friends at Arras, probably in order to study in Paris, he wrote a *congé* (*c.* 1262) (ed. P. Ruelle, Paris, 1965), elegant but without the deep feeling of the poems by the lepers ⇨ Jean Bodel (*c.* 1205) and Baude Fastoul (*c.* 1270). The *Jeu de la Feuillée* (*c.* 1262; ed E. Langlois, 1923), closely related to life at Arras, is a complex sequence of scenes with sung refrains in which realism and satire merge with burlesque and supernatural elements, including fairies. The *Jeu de Robin et Marion* (ed. E. Langlois, 1924; K. Varty, 1962), a gaily dramatized version of the ⇨ *pastourelle*, describes with gentle irony the attempted seduction of Marion by a knight and rustic pastimes, with interludes for popular songs of the day.

Adam was a leading musician of his century, his *rondeaux* showing remarkable originality; he points ahead to the *Ars nova* of the 14th century. [LTT]

*Œuvres complètes*, ed. E. de Coussemaker (1872).
H. Guy, *Essai sur la vie et les œuvres littéraires du trouvère A. de la H.* (Paris, 1898); J. Chailley, *Histoire musicale du moyen âge* (Paris, 1950).

**Adam of St Victor** (*c.* 1110–*c.* 1180). The most prolific of all writers of Latin ⇨ sequences. Probably a Breton; canon of the Abbey of St Victor, near Paris, about 1130. His compositions are remarkable for their perfect technique, smooth rhythm, masterly rhyme (including double rhyme), elaborate typology, and closely packed content. In them 'medieval rhythmical verse reached its greatest formal perfection', yet they are practically unknown today except 'Supernae matris gaudia', of which a translation by Robert Bridges ('Joy and triumph everlasting') is in fairly common use. [FB]

*Œuvres poétiques*, ed. L. Gautier (2 vols., 1858–9; 3rd edn, 1 vol., 1894); *Les proses, texte et musique*, ed. E. Misset and P. Aubry (1900); *The Liturgical Poetry*, ed. and verse tr. D. S. Wrangham (3 vols., 1881); *Proses*, ed. M. Legrain (Bruges, 1899); *An. Hym.* 54.
Raby, *CLP*; Taylor, *MM*.

**Adamov, Arthur** (Kislovodsk 1908–1970), French dramatist. Of Russian origin, Adamov first came to the attention of the Parisian public during the theatrical season 1950–51. His abrasive plays owe something to German expressionism, though his early drama is metaphysically, rather than socially, centred, embodying the clichés of the current *avant-garde*: the helplessness and isolation of man. *Le sens de la marche* (1953) and *Les retrouvailles* (1955) both spring from an exacerbated awareness of the tyranny of parental love. In the first, the son's revolt takes the form of the murder of his grotesque father's companion and *alter ego*; in the second, the mother successfully crushes the son, a fact symbolized by the burlesque violence of the final scene in which she wheels him away in a perambulator. The force and cruelty of social conventions and pressures are graphically depicted in *L'invasion* (1950), where a scholar is dehumanized and finally distracted to the point of suicide by his hollow academic labours and the impositions of his family; in the ferocious allegory of *La grande et la petite manœuvre* (1950), when the eternal victim, the 'Mutilated One', is caught between rival factions which reduce him to a mere trunk in a wheel-chair; and in *La parodie* (1952), a parable on the failure of human communication. Perhaps the most savage of these images of social cruelty is Adamov's barely transposed version of the persecution of the Jews in *Tous contre tous* (1953), with the war against the people who limp conducted by antagonists hardly distinguishable from them. A similar kind of arbitrary humiliation is inflicted on the scholar in *Le Professeur Taranne* (1953; tr. P. Meyer, in *Two Plays*, 1962), who is accused of obscene conduct. With *Le Ping-Pong* (1955; tr. D. Prouse, in *Two Plays*, 1962), Adamov effects a transition from the world of pain and human helplessness to a more purely social world, that of the capitalist system as symbolized by the pin-table in the amusement arcade. Men are degraded by the machine but they are free not to use it or even to destroy it, just as, in *Paolo Paoli* (1957; tr. G. Brereton, 1960), the French people before the First World War are free to shake off their blind euphoria and complicity with a corrupt way of life, epitomized by Paoli who destroys beauty for gain (he trades in dead butterflies) and his vacillating and adulterous wife. The completeness of this transition to a didactic art, in which the socialistic ideas are conveyed by an expressionistic technique, may be judged by the anti-Gaullist sketches in which Adamov collaborated with G. Demoy and M. Regnant, *Théâtre de société* (1958), and by his play about the Paris Commune, *Le printemps 71* (1960). Adamov also adapted Gogol's *Dead Souls* for the Paris stage (1959). His theories on the drama are found in *Ici et maintenant* (1964).

*Théâtre* (3 vols., 1953–66).

Carlos Lynes, Jnr, 'A. and "le sens littéral" in the Theatre', *Yale French Studies*, 14 (1954–5); Esslin, *TA*; Wellwarth, *TPP*; Serreau, *HNT*.

**Ady, Endre** (Érmindszent 1877–Budapest 1919). Hungarian poet. The most significant figure of early 20th-century Hungarian literature, and leader of the modern school. Son of an impoverished country gentry family, he absorbed Protestant principles and education, studied law at Debrecen and became a journalist. A turning-point in his career came in 1899, when he went to Nagyvárad (Transylvania), then a city of bustling intellectual life, where he met his muse 'Léda', a rich, cultured bourgeois woman. With her help, Ady went to Paris (1904, 1906–7), whose cultural life strengthened his already radical views; he was especially influenced by Baudelaire, Verlaine, and the symbolists. After 1905, he became an increasingly central personality of Hungarian literary circles as the leader of the ⇨ *Nyugat* periodical and literary movement. As a notable extreme radical participant in public and political life at a time of right-wing government and conservative cultural conceptions, his ideas provoked much controversy and opposition. His poems concerning money brought a new theme into Hungarian poetry; he realistically recognized its benefits in several poems, and yet had a distaste for it and condemned the wealthy. The love reflected in his writings is egocentric (after several other affairs he married the 'Csinszka' of his poems). Ady protested unreservedly against the First World War in numerous poems (cf. *Ember az embertelenségben*, 'Man among Inhumanity', 1916). An innovator in style, epithets, metaphors and word combinations, he used mythological, Biblical and historical symbolisms to create modern myths and a radically new and personal poetry. Feeling a responsibility for the fate of his race, but at the same time egocentric and selfish, he gives expression to the deepest conflicts and problems of modern humanity. Owing to his great struggles and riotous life, he became increasingly ill. [JFR]

*Új Versek* (1906); *Vér és Arany* (1907); *Az Illés Szekerén* (1908); *Szeretném ha Szeretnének*

(1909); *A Minden Titkok Verseiből* (1910); *A Menekülő Élet* (1912); *A Magunk Szerelme* (1913); *Ki Látott Engem* (1914); *Halottak Élén* (posth.); *Az Utolsó Hajók* (posth.); trs.: *Threescore Poems of Endre Ady*, tr. A. Nyerges (Washington, 1946); *E. Ady; Poems*, tr. Vajna and Bokor (Budapest, 1941); selection tr. W. Kirkconnell, *SEER*, XXII, 58 (1944).

Reményi, *HWL*; Klaniczay, *HHL*.

**Aeneas Silvius (Enea Silvio de' Piccolomini)** (Pienza, nr Siena 1405–Ancona 1464). Latin verse and prose writer. Pope (Pius II) from 1458, though he had refused ordination until 40, being unwilling to abandon his dissolute life. Previously an advocate of the Conciliar Theory, he condemned it when he became Pope, with the famous words, 'Aeneam rejicite, Pium suscipite'. A great humanist and a prolific writer of Latin verse and prose, he is particularly famous for his frank memoirs (*Commentarii*). His other works include numerous valuable letters, a comedy (*Chrysis*) modelled on Terence, a novel (*De duobus amantibus*) and orations. [F B]

Ed. M. Hopper (Basle, 1551 and 1571); *Commentarii* (1584 and 1614), tr. F. A. Gragg (Northampton, Mass., 1937); *Epistolae*, ed. R. Wolkan (*Fontes rerum austriacarum*, Vienna, 1909–18); *De duobus amantibus*, ed. J. I. Dévay (Budapest, 1904), tr. F. Grierson, *The Tale of the Two Lovers* (1929); *Chrysis*, ed. A. Boutemy (Brussels, 1939), ed. I. Sanesi (Florence, 1941).

G. Voigt, *E.S. als Papst Pius der Zweite* (3 vols., Berlin, 1856–63); A. Weiss, *A.S.* (Graz, 1897); W. Boulting, *A.S.* (1908); C. M. Ady, *Pius II, the Humanist Pope* (1913); G. Paparelli, *E.S.* (Bari, 1950).

**Afinogenov, Aleksandr N.** (Skopin, Ryazanskaya Guberniya 1904–Moscow 1941). Russian dramatist. A member of the Communist Party since 1922, his first play, *Robert Tim*, was written for The First Working Man's Theatre of Proletarian Culture in Moscow, 1923. Like many *Proletcult* writers, he began with tub-thumping melodramas about villains and heroes of revolutionary virtue. Early work included an adaptation from Jack London, *Po tu storonu shcheli* (1926), and a number of short-lived *agit*-plays. However, as the son of a schoolmaster who was also a writer and as an educated product of the Moscow Institute of Journalism (1924ff.), he soon developed subtler dramatic sense and was among the first *Proletcult* writers to evolve from the high flights of revolutionary romanticism to a more convincing complexity. His *Chudak* (1929) is a landmark in the return of the Soviet theatre to psychological realism. *Strakh* (1931) shows the influence of Gor'ky in its bitterly sceptical approach to the doubts and torments of the liberal intelligentsia, who are depicted as arrogant, spiteful and miserly guardians of the treasures of the spirit, unfit to manage their own affairs.

In the thirties he became secretary to the dramatic sector of RAPP. His ideas of this period are set out in the pamphlet *Tvorcheskiy metod teatra. Dialektika tvorcheskogo protsessa* (1931) and embodied in the plays *Lozh'* (1933) and *Portret* (1934). In *Dalekoye* (1935, staged in London by 'Unity' in 1939) he attempted philosophical drama, but his great success – still a repertory favourite in the Soviet Union and many East European countries – is *Mashen'ka* (1940), a drama which treats the interplay of public issues and individual lives with considerable psychological insight; it was staged in the U.S.A. during the Second World War. He was killed in an air raid. [A P]

*P'yesy* (1956); *Stat'i. Dnevniki. Pis'ma. Vospominaniya* (1957); *Dnevniki i zapisnye knizhki* (1960); *Avtobiografiya* in *Sovetskiye Pisateli* 3 (Moscow, 1966).

A. Karaganov, *A.A., Kritiko-biograficheskiy ocherk* (Moscow, 1957); *Zhizn' dramatuzga* (Moscow, 1964).

**Agnon, Shmuel Yosef** (formerly **Tschatsky**) (Poland 1888–1970). Hebrew novelist and short-story writer. He settled in Palestine in 1908 and became the doyen of Hebrew literature. He chose as his subject the life of the East European Jewish diaspora. His *Hachnasat Kallah* (1922; tr. I. M. Lask, *The Bridal Canopy*, Garden City, N.Y., 1937), a long short-story, is a series of stories woven together from tales, parables, fables, proverbs and other folkloristic material. He wrote many short stories and a novel, *'Tmol Shilshom* (2nd edn 1947), describing life in Jaffa and Jerusalem before the First World War. His *Oreach Nata Lalun* (1945) is his final summing up of his life. Awarded Nobel Prize for literature in 1966.

*Collected Works* (6 vols., Tel-Aviv, 1935); *In the Heart of the Seas*, tr. I. M. Lask (N.Y., 1948); *Days of Awe*, tr. I. M. Lask (N.Y., 1948); *Two Tales*, tr. W. Lever (1966).

Waxman, *HJL*; Klausner, *HMHL*; Liachover, *THHH*.

**Agricola, Johannes,** latinized name of J. Schnitter (Eisleben *c.* 1494–Berlin 1566).

German theologian and writer. He studied theology at Wittenberg and became a devoted disciple of Luther, whom he accompanied to the Leipzig Disputation in 1519. Subsequently he quarrelled with the Wittenbergers, maintaining as the spokesman of the antinomians that true penance springs from faith, not from the Law. His real achievement lies in his 3 collections of German proverbs (1529, 1534, 1548) which, apart from their intrinsic significance for the history of the German language, cast interesting light on contemporary social and political conditions. In 1538 he published a *Tragedia Johannis Hus*, which was severely censured by Luther. [WAC]

*Sibenhundert und funfftzig Deutsche Sprichwörter*, ed. F. Bobertag (DNL 25, 1887).
G. Kawerau, *J. A. von Eisleben* (Berlin, 1881).

**Aguilar, Gaspar de** (Valencia 1561–Valencia 1623). Spanish dramatist. A member of the Valencia group, with Guillén de ⇨ Castro. His *El mercader amante* (1614) was praised by Cervantes; he wrote sacred dramas and picturesque comedies. His *Rimas* contain a few well-turned love-sonnets. [JMC]

*Comedias* (BAE 43); *Poesías*, ed. E. Mele (*BH* iii, 1901); *Fiestas nupciales . . . de Felipe III*, ed. F. Martí-Grajales (Valencia, 1910); Blecua, *FLE*.

**Aguirre, Domingo.** ⇨ Basque Literature.

**Ahad Ha-am,** pseud. of Asher Ginzberg (Skwira 1856–Tel Aviv 1927). Hebrew philosopher and essayist. He transformed Zionism, hitherto a purely political movement, into a spiritual one. He was influenced by English and French positivist thinkers and sociological and psychological theories of the time. He followed John Stuart Mill and Renan in asserting that nations, like individuals, have a distinct ego. He saw Palestine as a spiritual centre which would extend its influence upon world Jewry. He founded the famous monthly *Hashiloach* (1897–1926) which has become a most important source of modern Jewish knowledge. [EE]

*Al Parashat Derachim* (4 vols., Odessa, 1895–1913; 2nd edn, 4 vols., Berlin, 1920, with new introduction); *Igrot Ahad Haam* (6 vols., Berlin, Jerusalem, 1923–6); *Selected Essays*, tr. L. Simon (Philadelphia, 1912); *Essays, Letters, Memoirs*, ed. and tr. L. Simon (1916).
N. Bentwich, *A.H. and His Philosophy* (1927); L. Simon, *A.H. A Biography* (1960).

**Ahlgren, Ernst,** pseud. of Victoria Benedictsson (Fru-Alstad 1850–Copenhagen 1888). Swedish novelist and story-writer. After Strindberg, the greatest talent in the 'Young Sweden' group of realistic writers. Her province was Skåne (S. Sweden). She knowingly and humorously portrayed simple country people in *Från Skåne* (1884) and *Folkliv och småberättelser* (1887). Involved in contemporary issues, especially the position of women and the institution of marriage, in *Pengar* (1885) she gives a penetrating (but not altogether detached) description of an unhappy marriage. Her masterpiece, *Fru Marianne* (1887), is a study of the maturing of a young pretentious woman who, overcoming her inclination for another man, discovers her happiness in the active sharing of her husband's life on their farm. Her diaries and letters (*V.B.: dagboksblad och brev*, ed. A. Lundegård, 1928) reveal a highly complex personality, torn by inner conflicts and prone to states of depression. One may therefore assume that it was this hidden morbidity rather than external difficulties (her unsuccessful marriage to a man twice her age, and, more particularly, her unrequited love for Georg ⇨ Brandes) that drove her to suicide. [SAB]

S. Linder, *E.A. i hennes romaner* (Stockholm, 1930); F. Böök, *V.B. och Georg Brandes* (Stockholm, 1949), and *V.B.* (Stockholm, 1950); L. Maury, *L'amour et la mort d'E.A.* (Paris, 1945).

**Ahlin, Lars** (Sundsvall 1915– ). Swedish novelist and story-writer. One of the most important contemporary writers, he belongs to the number of largely self-taught authors of lower-middle or working-class background. He experienced the hardship of unemployment during the thirties and his way to literature was long and arduous. Unlike most writers of this category, e.g. ⇨ Fridegård and ⇨ Lo-Johansson, he is not concerned with the shaping of autobiographical material, however much he draws on early experiences in his native town. The hero of his first novel, *Tåbb med manifestet* (1943), is however a young unemployed worker, who after finding the Marxist gospel inadequate turns to a free interpretation of the Lutheran doctrine of Grace. The book is in essentials a prototype of its many successors: it shows the author's inclination for intellectual argument coupled with a refusal to 'bully' his characters into obedience. In several articles stating his literary programme,

Ahlin has denounced 'the novel of illusion' and spoken of himself as 'identifier' or 'mediator' and of his activity as 'intercession'. His massive second novel, *Min död är min* (1945), is Dostoyevskian in character both through its untidy, rhetorical style and loose composition and through its span and terrifying moments of emotional identification.

On the strength of these novels and two volumes of short stories, *Inga ögon väntar mig* (1944) and *Fångnas glädje* (1947), he came to be regarded as a leading name in his generation, but as yet he had no great following. The most 'theological' of his novels, *Fromma mord* (1952), did not, in spite of its ambitious character, appreciably alter this situation. Only on the publication of *Kanelbiten* (1953) did he achieve something like popular success, which he followed up with *Stora glömskan* (1954). In both of these the world is seen through the eyes of young persons. In the former, a story with tragic outcome, a hypersensitive girl is standing on the brink of womanhood and discovers that the world is not for her; in the latter, Zacharias, a boy of 13, takes a few steps towards maturity by discovering the reality of other people. Technically the books are arresting: they present kaleidoscopic sequences of events which are often bizarre but never indifferent; the result, whether intended or not, is an illusion of spaciousness and great human variety. Zacharias returns in *Natt i marknadstältet* (1957), but the book is ultimately Paulina's, his aunt's. The theme is tragic: the inability of a man to lay himself open to the reality of love on the pretext that he has to earn it. Paulina, his wife, represents Pauline charity, is an incarnation of it; this makes the reader doubtful of the book's status: is it an allegory or a straight tale? The book, however, has many facets and is remarkable not least for its style: it carries its events and its people along on a warm current of speech. Ahlin's latest novel on a large scale, the polemical *Bark och löv* (1961), is again of a more inaccessible kind. It explores the conditions in present-day society for a full artistic life and makes great demands on the reader's ability to follow a speculative line of thought. Two earlier novels, *Kvinna, kvinna* (1955) and *Gilla gång* (1958), take up the theme of married relatedness on a less overwhelming scale and against a background of everyday existence; they still reflect Ahlin's belief in a continuous creation of values and can be read as revelations of human dignity where few writers would care to look for it. [SAB]

*Ord och bild*, 4 (1958); *Bonniers Litterära Magasin*, 6 (1960); K. E. Lagerlöf, 'L.A. och maskerna', in *Samtal med 60-talister* (Stockholm, 1965); G. Palm, 'L.A. and the New Swedish Novel', in *Sweden Writes* (Stockholm, 1965).

**Aho, Juhani** (Lapinlahti 1861–Helsinki 1921). Finnish prose writer. His original surname was Brofeldt. A son of the manse, he grew up in the province of Savo (E. Finland); the rich local dialect helped form his prose style. As a university student in Helsinki he joined the literary circle which developed into the 'Young Finland' group. Aiming at the liberation of Finnish culture from foreign influences, this group was active throughout the 1880s propagating liberal views, owing something to Ibsen. In Paris in 1889 he discovered Naturalism and Impressionism. When Russian political pressure on Finland was intensified at the turn of the century, he came to be regarded as a writer with a heartening national message; later he stood aside from politics.

Despite his progressive opinions, his deepest interest was in the idyllic aspects of country life. He was at once a Finn and a European, a cosmopolitan and a son of the countryside. His attitude to simple country people is well brought out by the delicate humour of his short novel *Rautatie* (1884). The psychological novel *Papin tytär* (1885) and its sequel *Papin rouva* (1893) deal with women's emancipation, a favourite theme with the 'realistic' writers of that time; while *Panu* (1897), a historical novel, is full of the romantic nationalism inspired by the ⇨ *Kalevala*. Aho's most important work, the novel *Juha* (1911), is a colourful, neo-romantic study of the Finnish character. His later writing may have been influenced to some extent by ⇨ Lagerlöf, whom he hailed as a 'liberator'.

It is in the shorter forms that Aho produced his most characteristic writing. He published a large number of miniature pieces which he called *Lastuja* ('shavings'), and these show his stylistic qualities at their best – an impressionism with a strong leaning towards the lyrical, and a rich and elegant Finnish which served as a model for some of his younger contemporaries, notably ⇨ Sillanpää. [LV]

*Kootut teokset* (10 vols., 1918–26); *Squire Hellman and Other Stories*, tr. R. Nisbet Bain (1893).

**Aichinger, Ilse** (Vienna 1921– ). Austrian short-story writer. She began medical studies, became a publisher's reader, helped found the Institute for Adult Education, Ulm, and has lived in Upper Bavaria since she married Günter ⇨ Eich in 1953. She has written a prizewinning novel *Die grössere Hoffnung* (1948), the short stories (*Rede unter den Galgen*, 1952; new edn, *Der Gefesselte*, 1953; tr. E. Mosbacher, *The Bound Man*, 1955), imaginary dialogues, *Zu keiner Stunde* (1957), and a radio-play and drama, *Knöpfe* (1953–7). An outstanding short-story writer, Ilse Aichinger has learned from Kafka; her stories, written in a subtle, poetic style, frequently come close to surrealism. They are parables dealing ostensibly with real-life situations, but probing beneath the unreal surface in search of a symbolical dream-reality. Her latest collection is *Eliza, Eliza* (1965). [PB]

*Selected Stories and Dialogues*, ed. J. C. Alldridge (1966); Spender, *GGSS*; Steinhauer, *GS*; Waidson, *MGS*; Newnham, *GSS*; *GQ*, XXXVIII, 1, 1965.

**Akhmadulina, Bella** (1937– ). Russian poetess. Of mixed Tatar-Italian descent, she was married at 18 to ⇨ Yevtushenko, and subsequently to the short-story writer ⇨ Nagibin. Her slow-moving, rich quatrains are superficially traditional in form. But their surprising imagery and subject-matter set them apart from any other contemporary Russian verse. She can elevate such banalities as catching a cold or buying a fizzy drink into minor cosmic events; she can bring a streak of humour to play on solemn themes. Her more personal poetry is complex; mystical and fantastic strains run through it. She owes much to ⇨ Tsvetaeva and ⇨ Akhmatova, and also to ⇨Pasternak and possibly to ⇨ Zabolotsky in his elevated, half-parodying vein, but her voice is already unmistakably her own. [RM-G]

*Struna* (1962); Gulland, *SRV*; Obolensky, *PBRV*.

**Akhmatova, Anna,** pseud. of Anna Gorenko (nr Odessa 1889–Moscow 1967). Russian poetess. She grew up at Tsarskoe Selo (now Pushkin), studied in Kiev, and lived mostly in Leningrad. Her poetic gifts developed early; her verses were printed from 1907, and her first book *Vecher* ('Evening') appeared in 1912. She married ⇨ Gumilyov – already an established poet – in 1910; like him she reacted against the vagueness of Symbolist poetry, and is considered a founder of ⇨ Acmeism. Much of her early poetry deals lucidly and directly with love; typically her lyrics are brief, simply phrased, with an unanalysable intimacy (easily vulgarized by her imitators). She shows a concise brilliance in her physical settings, often of Russian countryside.

Her style was perfected early and changed little, except that since the Revolution she attempted public as well as personal themes (but still lyrically until the larger-scale work of her later years). Frequently criticized, she published no more original verse after *Anno Domini MCMXI* (1921) until her volume *Iz shesti knig* (1940). Her marriage to the ill-fated Gumilyov ended in 1918, and subsequently she married the Assyriologist Shileyko. During the war she began her long *Poema bez geroya*, and was evacuated from besieged Leningrad. In 1946 she was notoriously attacked (with ⇨ Zoshchenko) by Zhdanov, but she published occasional poems after Stalin's death, and before her death achieved a measure of due recognition at home and abroad. Her poignant cycle commemorating Stalin's victims *Requiem* has not yet been published in the U.S.S.R. Several Soviet poetesses show the influence of her fastidious, passionate-simple quatrains: among them ⇨ Berggol'ts and ⇨ Akhmadulina.

*Beg vremeni* (1966), T. J. Binyon (ed.), *A Soviet Verse Reader* (1964); Markov, *MRP*, *PG*; Obolensky, *PBRV*; *Selected Poems*, tr. R. McKane (1969).

L. I. Strakhovsky, *Craftsmen of the Word* (Cambridge, Mass., 1949).

**Aksakov, Sergey Timofeyevich** (Ufa 1791–Moscow 1859). Russian author of fictionalized reminiscences. A government official in Moscow and Petersburg; a friend and admirer of Gogol, who encouraged him to write. His *Semeynaya Khronika* (1856; tr. J. D. Duff, *A Russian Gentleman*, 1917) and *Detskiye gody Bagrova-vnuka* (1858; tr. J. D. Duff, *Years of Childhood*, 1916) paint detailed, sensitive, serene panoramas of patriarchal life in remote steppe countryside. The picture of a serf-owning society is remarkable.

His sons, Konstantin (1817–60) and Ivan (1823–86), were well-known publicists and leaders of the Slavophil movement (⇨ Khomyakov).

*Sobraniye sochineniy* (4 vols., 1955–6).

S. Mashinsky, *S.T.A.* (Moscow, 1961).

**Aksyonov, Vasily Pavlovich** (Kazan 1932– ). Soviet prose writer. Educated at the Medical Institute of Leningrad, he worked as a doctor in the port of Leningrad, then in the provinces, and from 1954 in one of the Moscow Tuberculosis Clinics. In *Yunost'* he published his first story (1959), a short novel *Kollegi* (1960; tr. A. Brown, *Colleagues*, 1962) and *Zvyozdnyy Bilet* (1962; tr. A. Brown, *A Starry Ticket*, 1962). With subsequent stories, *Na polputi k lune* and *Papa, skazhi!* (in *Novy Mir*, 1962), *Apel'siny iz Morokko* (in *Yunost'*, 1963) and *Pora, moy drug, pora* (in *Molodaya Gvardiya*, 1964), *Pobeda* (in *Yunost'*, 6, 1965) and *Na ploshchadi i za rekoy* (in *Yunost'*, 5, 1966), he became recognized as one of the most individual modern talents. He has an ear for the slangy, racy Russian of students, sailors and especially young people. His short stories abound in passages of real beauty, urban landscapes and episodic, often nocturnal sketches of scenes on the street or the road. The road plays a large part in all his stories – the romance of travel, the search for self, the refusal to settle down, whether spiritually or physically. Clearly of the same generation as Kerouac, Aksyonov is influenced by ⇨ Böll and Hemingway. His first two stories have been filmed, the second as *Mladshiy Brat*, and he is the author of a film scenario *Kogda razvodyat mosty*. The stage adaptation of *Kollegi* (1961) led to an original play *Vsegda v prodazhe* (staged 1967). [AP]

*Na polputi k lune* (1966).

**Alain**, pseud. of Émile Chartier (Mortagne-sur-Perche 1868–Le Vésinet 1951). French essayist and philosopher. Influential as a teacher of philosophy, his fame rests largely on his short articles. In 1903 he began publishing in newspapers his *propos*, short articles dealing in a highly individual manner, fraught with new insights and paradoxical affirmations, with every kind of issue of human interest. A thoroughgoing humanist and Republican idealist, suspicious of established authority in all domains, valuing above all men's freedom and the nurture of the mind, he was concerned to combat fanaticism, to show up false appearances and to maintain the lucid outlook of a Stendhal, a lucidity which banishes mystery and perhaps dispenses sometimes with depth. His writing is arrestingly fresh, at times epigrammatic, determinedly untraditional. [EB]

*Propos*, ed. M. Savin (Pléiade, 1956); *Les arts et les dieux*, ed. G. Bénézé (Pléiade, 1958); *Les passions et la sagesse*, ed. G. Bénézé (1960); *Esquisses* (1963ff.); *Cahiers de Lorient* (1963ff.); *Mars; or the Truth about War*, tr. D. Mudie and E. Hill (1930).

*Hommage à A.* (Paris, 1952); H. Mondor, *A.* (Paris, 1953); G. Pascal, *La pensée d'A.* (Paris, 1957); J. Robinson, *A. lecteur de Balzac et de Stendhal* (Paris, 1958); G. Bénézé, *Généreux A.* (Paris, 1962); B. Halda, *A.* (Paris, 1965).

**Alain-Fournier**, pseud. of Henri-Alban Fournier (La Chapelle d'Angillon 1886–Les Éparges 1914). French novelist. Son of a country schoolmaster, he was educated in Paris where, after national service in the infantry (1907–9), he became a literary columnist. His one completed novel, *Le Grand Meaulnes* (1913; tr. F. Davison, *The Lost Domain*, 1959), expresses inconsolable yearning for lost wonderment – the dominant mood in the author's own short life (he was killed in action), affecting his attitude to both religion and love. The setting, a remote part of central France in the 1890s, is the cherished countryside of his childhood; the elusive heroine is modelled on a girl he met for a few moments in 1905, worshipped for years afterwards and saw again only after the novel was finished. His other writings, all characterized by the same wistfulness, include a number of prose-poems and short stories (*Miracles*, 1924), an unfinished second novel, *Colombe Blanchet*, and the extremely revealing *Correspondance avec Jacques Rivière* (2 vols., 1948). [RG]

R. Gibson, *The Quest of A.-F.* (1953); I. Rivière, *Vie et passion d'A.-F.* (Monaco, 1963).

**Alamanni, Luigi** (Florence 1495–Amboise 1556). Italian poet. A republican opponent of the Medici, he was forced to live in exile, and found favour in Paris at the court of Francis I at a time when the prestige of Italian culture was at its height in France. He held various diplomatic posts in French service. Like ⇨ Trissino he was an extremely 'literary' poet, intent on reproducing classical forms in Italian. He cultivated the Pindaric ode, the epigram and satire (*Opere toscane*, Lyons, 1532–3), comedy (*Flora*), tragedy (*Antigone*), the mythological poem, etc. His best-known work is the didactic poem on rustic life, *La coltivazione* (Paris, 1546), which, despite its dependence on Virgil, preserves a certain freshness. In the latter part of his life he turned to the heroic poem in *Girone il cortese* (Paris, 1548) and *L'Avarchide* (a poor imitation of *The Iliad*). [DGR]

*Versi e prose*, ed. P. Raffaelli (1859); Lind, *LPIR*.

H. Hauvette, *Un exilé florentin ... L.A. sa vie et son œuvre* (Paris, 1903).

**Alan of Lille (Alanus de Insulis)** (Lille 1128?–1203). Early French humanist and Platonist. He was known in his time as Doctor Universalis, lectured at Paris, and during his later years was a monk at Cîteaux. His chief work is a long allegorical poem, *Anticlaudianus* (ed. R. Bossuat, Paris, 1955), in hexameters, dealing with the creation of the soul by God out of nothing. His *De planctu naturae* (tr. D. M. Moffat, *The Complaint of Nature*, 1908), written in alternate passages of prose and verse, deals with unnatural vice. [FB]

Ed. T. Wright, *Anglo-Latin Satirical Poets*, ii (Rolls Series, 1872).

G. R. de Lage, *A. de L.* (Paris, 1951); Raby, *CLP*, *SLP*; Taylor, *MM*.

**Alarcón, Pedro Antonio de** (Guadix 1833–Valdemoro 1891). Spanish novelist. First popular for his eyewitness account of the Moroccan campaign of 1859, *Diario de un testigo de la guerra de África* (1859), then for his delicately impressionistic journal of a visit to Italy. His romantic short stories, *Novelas cortas* (collected 1881–2), vigorous and colourful, deal with episodes in the Napoleonic wars, the Carlist campaigns, etc. His best-known work, *El sombrero de tres picos* (1874; CA; tr. J. S. Fassett, *The Three Cornered Hat*, 1918), is a fast-moving, witty, often malicious story, based on a ballad; the composer Manuel de Falla made it into one of the most famous modern ballets. *El capitán Veneno* (1881; CA) is an exciting adventure story; the more realistic *El escándalo* (1875; CA) marks his conversion from hot-headed anti-clericalism to naïve credulity, while *El niño de la bola* (1880; tr. Robert Graves, *The Infant with the Globe*, 1955) is a heroic piece in an Andalusian setting. [JMC]

L. Martínez Kleiser, *Don P.A. de A.* (Madrid, 1943); J. F. Montesinos, *P.A. de A.* (Saragossa, 1955).

**Alas, Leopoldo** (Zamora 1852–Oviedo 1901). Spanish critic and novelist. The son of a Civil Governor, Alas was trained in law, becoming professor in Saragossa (1882) and Oviedo (from 1883); his first book was a legal one, *El derecho y la moralidad* (1878). He went to Madrid in the 1870s and joined a number of the leading political and literary groups which had sprung up in the post-revolutionary atmosphere of the period. Some of the views on tolerance, the undogmatic religious idealism and morality propounded by Spanish followers of the German philosopher Krause also undoubtedly impressed him at this time, although he satirized the mystical fringes of the 'krausista' movement in his short story 'Zurita' (1886). He wrote numerous articles (collected in *Solos de Clarín*, 1881, and *Palique*, 1893) under the pseudonym 'Clarín' (bugle) and short stories in which moral and social points are expressed ironically. He was sympathetic to ⇨ Pérez Galdós and others, who were trying to re-establish the novel as a socially serious genre, and he was one of the few Spaniards to express wholehearted approval of the naturalist theories of Zola in the eighties. Alas's own first novel, *La Regenta* (1884–5), is not unlike Flaubert's *Madame Bovary* in its heroine and in its detailed description of the influence of the social ambience of Vetusta (a city modelled on Oviedo). It is a masterly study of the interplay of human passions in a complex society, whose false values are exposed to penetrating irony. The pretentiousness of people and their self-delusion are constantly revealed by a variety of methods. In his second novel, *Su único hijo* (1890), the background complexity of *La Regenta* largely disappears, and in many of his short stories, particularly the *Cuentos morales*, he contrasts rich and poor, good and evil in crude colours. Although the technique of gradually revealing his characters is employed to good effect in a number of these stories (*Dr Glauben*, for instance), the lack of moral complexity makes many of them seem sentimental or simple to the modern reader (Galdós compared him to Dickens). After a moral crisis in 1892 Alas turned from naturalism to an attitude of religious idealism, writing such tolerantly humorous stories as *¡Adiós cordera!* etc. (1892). He tried his hand at a social drama, *Teresa* (1895), and left many literary projects unfulfilled. [ONVG]

*Obras selectas*, intr. J. A. Cabezas (1947).

A. Brent, *L.A. and La Regenta* (1951); Eoff, *MSN*; *HR*, XVI (1948); *PMLA*, LVII (1949); *HR*, XXXI (1963); *BHS*, XLI (1964); *BHS*, XLIII (1966).

**Albanian Literature.** The subjugation and dispersal of Albania's population after the Turkish victory over Skanderbeg in 1468 all but eclipsed Albanian writing for many centuries.

The Roman Catholic literary tradition was kept alive in northern Albania by Buzuk's *Liturgy* (1555), three religious works by Pjetër Budi (1566–1623), a *Latin-Albanian Dictionary* by F. Bardhi, or Blancus (1606–43), and a bilingual encyclopedia of religious and secular knowledge entitled *Cuneus prophetarum* (1685) by Pjetër Bogdani. Descendants of the exiles who had fought under Skanderbeg maintained a literary tradition in Sicily and Calabria. The Sicilian-Albanian Luke Matranga (1560–1619) was the author of a *Christian Doctrine* (1592); N. Brancato (1675–1741) and D. N. Figlia, both of Sicily, wrote religious verse, and the Calabrian Gjul Variboba was the author of a versified life of the Virgin Mary (*Gjella e Shën Mëris Virgjër*) (1762). Fragments of heroic poetry, echoing the dimly remembered exploits of Skanderbeg's men, gradually took the place of religious writing, and the Bala Cycle, recording the deeds of one of Skanderbeg's henchmen, is represented in the collected folk-songs of G. Dara, Senior (1765–1832), woven together by his grandson G. Dara, Junior, into the epic, *Kënga e sprasme e Balës* (1887, 1906).

Jeronim de Rada (1813–1903), a Calabrian, initiated a period of feverish search for other fragments of Albanian epics fossilized in traditional folksongs. Norman Douglas, in *Old Calabria*, tells the sad story of this unpractical idealist. At long intervals De Rada published a number of loosely connected semi-historical 'rhapsodies' interspersed with poems, which, though often unrelated to the epic story, have a lyrical quality of their own. These are mostly in the octosyllabic trochaic rhythm of Longfellow's *Hiawatha*. Between 1883 and 1887 De Rada produced a journal, *Fjamuri i Arbënit*, to rally Albanian patriots abroad.

A return to religious themes by the Calabrian poet and playwright A. Santori (1819–94) was not maintained by other writers, and the patriotic motive, with its emphasis on language and folklore, returned with the *Saggio di grammatologia comparata sulla lingua albanese* (1864–6) by Dh. Camarda of Piana in Sicily (1821–82). To this must be added the lyrical collections of the Calabrian Z. Serembe (1843–91), and the folksong collections of Z. Schirò (1865–1927), author of two long idylls *Mili and Hajdhia* (1891), and *Te dheu i huaj* (1901). In the work of the lyricist A. Rëbeku (1867–1928) Skanderbeg themes mingle with anacreontic motifs.

In Albania proper literature languished under Turkish rule. The survival of Albanian as a literary language throughout the 18th and 19th centuries is due mainly to the efforts of two evangelists of Elbasan. Master Theodore, 18th-century author of a version of St John Chrysostom's *Liturgy* and translator of the Scriptures, was succeeded in the following century by K. Kristoforidhi (1827–95), a one-time student of London University, whose Bible translations, done at the request of the British and Foreign Bible Society between 1872 and 1879, are equalled in importance by his great Albanian-Greek Dictionary (1904, revised in modern spelling 1961). The last work was inspired largely by von Hahn, the Austrian linguist and ethnographer whom Kristoforidhi met at Yanina.

The year 1878 was the year of the national literary revival. The central figures of the movement were the brothers Abdyl, Naim and Sami Frashëri. Abdyl devoted his energies to organizing the cause of Albanian autonomy, Naim wrote several collections of lyrics on the theme of the homeland and put into verse the ideals of the Bektashi movement to which his family belonged, and Sami invented and propagated a short-lived Albanian alphabet on phonetic principles, publishing in the new spelling a pamphlet on the prerequisites for an autonomous Albania. Sami even found time to edit a Turkish encyclopedia. Tolerated for a while in Istanbul, though not in Albania for fear of sedition, these three men were joined by Kristoforidhi and J. Vreto, but after a bare five years of printing and publicity in the Ottoman capital they were forced to flee to Bucharest, where they continued to print poems and textbooks.

At about this time Vreto went on a tour of the Albanian colonies in Egypt to gain support for the reviving literary movement. As a result of his visit Th. Mitko (1820–90) and Spiro Dine (1846–1922) each brought out an anthology of folk-poetry and folktales. Somewhat apart from the movement was Anton Çako ('Çajupi') (1866–1930), who practised as a lawyer in Cairo. He became famous as a lyricist and playwright.

At the turn of the present century the

spark of the revival was kept alive by Mid'hat Frashëri ('Lumo Skendo') (1880–1949), a nephew of Abdyl, and K. Luarasi, co-founders of *Kalendari Kombiar* (1897–1927). Mid'hat Frashëri, a man of many interests, wrote and translated several educational books, and his short stories, *Hi dhe Shpuzë*, have independent literary merit. A bibliophile and bookseller, minister of state and right-wing activist in turn, he died in exile in the U.S.A.

Between the wars the Albanian colony in Bucharest continued the work of the Istanbul exiles. Best remembered is the Tosk lyricist A. S. Drenova ('Asdren') (1872–1947), author of two collections, *Rreze dielli* (1904) and *Endërra e lot*. To this colony belonged Gj. Bubani, a poet in the Greek tradition, and L. Poradeci, a symbolist poet and an admirer of ⇨ Eminescu. Poradeci now lives in Tirana. A younger poet, writing in similar vein, is Dhimitër Pasko ('Mitrush Kuteli'), born in 1907.

Albanian literature is still suffering from the divisions imposed by conflicting political regimes. The Scutari Catholic School of writers, once represented by A. M. Xanoni, linguist, lyricist and didactic poet, N. Mjedja, H. Mosi and V. Prennushi, the lyrical poets, and above all by Gj. Fishta, a fiery satirical writer and editor of *Hylli i Dritës*, chief organ of these northern writers, survives in exile under the leadership of E. Koliqi in Rome. Gj. Fishta (1871–1940) is best remembered for his epic trilogy *Lahuta e Malcís*, commemorating in racy folk-rhythms the vicissitudes of Albanian political warfare with the Serbs and Montenegrins between 1878 and 1912. Of high lyrical quality are the nostalgic poems of F. Shiroka (1859–1935), who was forced into exile in Egypt. Of a different calibre is E. Koliqi (b. 1903), whose pro-Italian sympathies often conflicted with his undoubted sincerity in wishing to raise educational standards in Albania. An admirer of Dante and Petrarch, Koliqi has evolved a rich diction in his poems, and especially in his short stories of life in the northern highlands.

With the advent of the Tosk Communists of southern Albania, now the prevailing force in Albanian literature, great changes have come about. New textbooks in great number have been produced on the basis of mainly Russian originals, and there is a great interest in the English classics, especially Shakespeare, many of whose plays were translated by the communist sympathizer Bishop Fan Noli, a southerner and founder of the Albanian newspaper *Dielli* at Boston, Mass., where he was active from 1911. Inside Albania the favoured foreign authors, apart from Shakespeare, are the Russian novelists, and Byron, Dickens and Thackeray. From the south, too, came the patriot novelists of the 1912 liberation period: Mihal Grameno (1872–1931) and F. Postoli, whose novel *Lulja e kujtimit* (1924) has recently been made into an opera. Faik Konitsa (1875–1943), for many years Albanian ambassador to Washington, was active as a political writer in the early years of the present century, and K. Floqi, another southerner, is remembered for his many satirical plays and sketches, which are for the moment out of favour in Albania.

The present literary activity is wedded to the communist theme, and is represented by the poets Sh. Musaraj, A. Çaçi, M. Ndoja, A. Varfni, K. Papajani, the anthologist Dh. Shuteriqi, the short-story writers D. Shapllo, Z. Sako, S. Spasse, M. Myftiu, the novelist F. Gjata, the playwright K. Jakova and many more. Both language and style have been enriched by the impact of translations from the major languages of Europe. The new activity is matched on a smaller scale in the autonomous Albanian Republic of Kosovo-Metohija ('Kosmet') in Yugoslavia. This community of some 750,000 souls has its political and cultural centre at Prishtinë. Its theatre shows plays by Xh. Doda of Prizrend, K. Berisha of Peja, and selected works from Albania proper. K. Kallushi, R. Kelmendi and S. Imami are successful writers of short stories, and a large poetic output is reflected in the pages of the journal *Jeta e Re* (begun in 1948), edited by Esad Mekuli. [SEM]

S. E. Mann, *Albanian Literature. An Outline of Prose, Poetry and Drama* (1955); Norman Douglas, *Old Calabria* (1923).

**Albert of Aix** (fl. *c.*1121). Medieval chronicler A canon of Aix-la-Chapelle, he did not himself go on crusade; but his *Historia hierosolymitanae expeditionis*, a history of the First Crusade and of events in Frankish Outremer 1095–1121, seems to be based on first-class documents, probably including letters from friends settled in the East. Some clearly fictitious and legendary additions put the value of this work in doubt at one time, but it is now recognized as a source of prime importance. ⇨ William of Tyre used the first six books of it as the principal source for the first eight books of his own chronicle. [MRM]

*RHC*, Hist. occ., iv; Migne, *PL*, 166; tr. Guizot, *CHF*, XX, XXI.

**Alberti, Leon Battista** (Genoa 1404–Rome 1472). Italian writer, humanist, architect, theorizer on art, student of science and mathematics (and perhaps painter). The illegitimate son of an exiled Florentine merchant. In a period when most of the leading intellectual figures preferred Latin as a means of serious communication, he upheld the potentialities of the vernacular, and wrote a substantial proportion of his many works in Italian.

His major Italian work is the dialogue *Della famiglia*. Begun in Rome before 1434, it was revised and completed in Florence between 1434 and 1443. Books I–III consist of discussions between members of the Alberti family on the maintenance and upbringing of a family and the running of a household; IV deals with friendship. The language is enriched with borrowings from Latin syntax and vocabulary, the form is a classical device beloved by the humanists, and the advice offered in the book represents the quintessence of ancient wisdom, allied with hardheaded Florentine commonsense. The *Della famiglia* lacks the grace of later Italian Renaissance dialogues, but indicates the road which Renaissance literature was to take in adopting and adapting classical models.

His other Italian works include several further dialogues – e.g. *Deifira*, *Ecatonfilea* (both written before the *Della famiglia*, and both on amorous subjects), *Della tranquillità dell'animo* (1441–2), and *De Iciarchia* (1470) – and a few poems. His major Latin work is the architectural treatise *De re aedificatoria* (completed by 1452). [CF]

*Opere volgari*, ed. C. Grayson (Bari, 1960 – in progress).

G. Mancini, *Vita di L.B.A.* (Florence, 1911); *Italian Studies*, XI, 1956; XII, 1957.

**Alberti, Rafael** (Puerto de Santa María 1902– ). Spanish poet. He belonged to the 'Generation of the Dictatorship'. His upbringing in the poorest branch of a once-rich family and his charity education in the fashionable Jesuit college of El Puerto left resentments which were to provide the basic themes of his finest poetry. Finding his adolescent talent for painting insufficiently expressive, he turned to verse. *Marinero en tierra*, inspired by the *Cancioneros* and reflecting the *purismo* and *folklorismo* of the mid-twenties, won the Premio Nacional de Literatura of 1924. In *La amante* (1925) and *El alba del alhelí* (1925–6) a similar formula is used far less successfully. The 'crisis' poems begin with *Cal y canto* (1926–7), where the brilliant technical virtuosity obscures his vain attempts to replace his lost childhood values with the 'values' of the 20th century. The hollowness of the latter is shown in his masterpiece, *Sobre los ángeles* (1927–8), sombre, violent, self-probing, splenetic, a book springing from an unhappy love-affair but which was to mark the turning-point of a whole Generation. His conversion to communism (1931) provided financial security and the means to travel in exchange for the abandonment of the subjectivity which had made his 'crisis' poems great. Only with exile did the authentic voice return sporadically. *Retornos de lo vivo lejano* (1948–56) is his finest work since 1930, and *A la pintura* (1945–52) once again demonstrates his versatility and invention; yet he still writes unoriginal political poetry (*Coplas de Juan Panadero*, 1949–53). His autobiographical *La arboleda perdida* (Buenos Aires, 1959) is an essential key to the understanding of his work. [GC]

*Poesías completas* (Buenos Aires, 1961); *Teatro* (2nd edn, Buenos Aires, 1956); *Imagen primera de . . .* (Buenos Aires, 1945); *Concerning the Angels*, tr. Geoffrey Connell (1967).

L. F. Vivanco, *Introducción a la poesía española contemporánea* (Madrid, 1961); Bowra, *CE*; C. B. Morris, *R.A.'s Sobre los ángeles: Four Major Themes* (1966); *Renaissance and Modern Studies*, III, 1959; *BHS*, XXXVI, 3, 1959; XXXVII, 4, 1960; XL, 3, 1963; *HR*, July 1965.

**Albertinus, Ägidius** (*c.*1560–1620). German writer. Born in Holland, Albertinus moved to Bavaria in his early thirties, subsequently becoming Court Secretary and librarian to Elector Maximilian I. His main achievement lies in his lengthy adaptation of Alemán's *Guzman*, by which he introduced the picaresque novel into Germany and so prepared the way for ⇨ Grimmelshausen. His voluminous output consists largely of translations and adaptations of foreign authors (Vincent de Beauvais, Guevara, Zamora, etc.) written in a style characterized by an excessive love of metaphor and simile. A devout Catholic, he is the principal literary spokesman of the Counter-Reformation in southern Germany. [WAC]

*Lucifers Königreich und Seelengejaid*, ed. R. v. Liliencron (DNL 26, 1885).
*Zeitschrift für Deutschkunde*, 44, 1930.

**Albertus Magnus** (Lauingen 1206–Cologne 1280). Dominican teacher; educated at Padua, he taught at Paris, where ⇨ Aquinas was one of his pupils, and at Cologne, and was Bishop of Ratisbon (1260–2). Especially learned in the works of Aristotle and of the Jewish and Arabic scientists and philosophers of his own time, he aimed at disseminating this knowledge throughout the West. Dante includes him in *Paradiso*, x. [FB]

Ed. A. Borgnet (38 vols., Paris, 1890–9); crit. edn, B. Geyer (Münster, 1955– ).
M. de Wulf, *History of Mediaeval Philosophy*, ii (1938); Gilson, *PMA*; Taylor, *MM*.

**Albo, Joseph** (*c.*1380–Monreal 1444). Jewish philosopher. The last in the long line of great medieval Jewish philosophers in Spain. Tried a formulation of Judaism on three basic principles by which he sought to popularize his master Chasdai Crescas. [EE]

*Sefer ha-Ikkarim*, ed. and tr. I. Husik (5 vols., Philadelphia, 1930).
Husik, *HMJP*.

**Albrecht von Halberstadt** (fl. early 13th cent.). German epic poet. Known solely from his verse translation of Ovid's *Metamorphoses*, he belongs with Hendrik van ⇨ Veldeke and Herbort von Fritzlar (*Lied von Troja*) to the group of Thuringian poets who treated subjects from Classical antiquity in the spirit of courtly chivalry. His attitudes are conventional and his style undistinguished. [RT]

Ed. K. Bartsch, *A. von H. und Ovid im Mittelalter* (Quedlinburg, 1861).
Ehrismann, *GDL*, ii.

**Albrecht von Scharfenberg** (fl. *c.*1270). German poet. Probable author of an epic poem known as the *Jüngerer Titurel* (written *c.*1272; ed. W. Wolf, 1955), a continuation and expansion of the material contained in the Titurel fragments of ⇨ Wolfram von Eschenbach. It enjoyed great popularity right down to the 15th century and preserved many of the most characteristic values of Wolfram's own art and philosophy of life. [RT]

**Alcázar, Baltasar del** (Seville 1530–Seville 1606). Spanish poet. A student, then a soldier in the fleet, he is remembered chiefly for his *redondillas* entitled *Cena jocosa*, which celebrate the pleasures of the table. He also wrote conventional love-poems and epigrams. [JMC]

*Poesías*, ed. F. Rodríguez Marín (1910); Trend, *OBSV*; Perry, *HASP*; Cohen, *PBSV*; Terry, *ASP*.

**Alcover, Joan.** ⇨ Catalan Literature.

**Alcuin** (York *c.*735–Tours 804). Medieval Latin writer. A celebrated ecclesiastic and educational adviser to the Emperor Charlemagne, who made him Abbot of St Martin at Tours. He wrote both Latin verse and prose. His verse is mostly light and occasional, including epigrams, letters in verse and inscriptions for the various rooms in a house. He also wrote a history of the see of York, in nearly 2,000 hexameters. Nearly 300 letters survive, many of considerable historical value. He was at his greatest as a teacher. [FB]

Migne, *PL*, 100, 101; *Monumenta Alcuiniana*, ed. P. Jaffé (Berlin, 1873) (letters); MGH, PLAC, i (poems).
C. J. B. Gaskoin, *A., His Life and Work* (1904); E. M. Wilmot-Buxton, *A.* (1922); E. S. Duckett, *A., Friend of Charlemagne* (N.Y.,1951); Laistner, *TLWE*; Raby, *SLP*; Taylor *MM*.

**Aldana, Francisco de** (?Naples 1537–Alcazarquivir 1578). Spanish poet and soldier. Born in Italy of distinguished Extremaduran family, he spent his early life there, soldiered in the Low Countries, and while a military adviser at the Portuguese court was killed in King Sebastião's ill-fated Moroccan expedition. Much of his verse is lost and some poems survive in a fragmentary state only. His work is uneven, at times exalted and learned, at others flat and unpolished; he uses the conventional Italianate forms, including blank verse. His themes include mystical introspection ('Carta para Arias Montano sobre la contemplación de Dios'), mythology and love poetry, some of which is Platonic and some warmly sensual. After centuries of neglect, the high value of Aldana's work has been acknowledged only in very recent years. [CCS]

*Epistolario poético completo*, ed. A. Rodríguez-Moñino (1946); *Obras completas*, ed. M. Moragón Maestre (2 vols., 1953); *Poesías*, ed. E. L. Rivers (1957); Trend, *OBSV*; Cohen, *PBSV*.
Cernuda, *PL*.

**Aldanov, Mark Aleksandrovich,** pseud. of M. A. Landau (Kiev 1886–Nice 1957). Russian novelist. He emigrated to France (1919) and the U.S.A. (1941). He is remembered chiefly for his novel series *Myslitel'* (Berlin, 1921–7; tr. A. E. Chamot, *The Ninth Thermidor*, 1926; *The Devil's Bridge*, 1928; *Saint Helena*, 1924), which depicts, with some free fabrication, the period of the French Revolution and Napoleon in a way much influenced by the author's view of the Russian revolution. *Nachelo kontsa* (1936; tr. N. Wreden, *The Fifth Seal*) is an anti-soviet satire; *Istoki* (1947; tr. C. Routsky, *Before the Deluge*, 1948) depicts European life in the late 19th century.

*Nightmare and Dawn*, tr. J. Carmichael (N.Y. 1957).

**Aleardi, Aleardo** (Verona 1812–Verona 1878). Italian romantic poet, patriot, politician and later senator. Pictured himself in the tradition of ⇨ Foscolo, dedicated to the two great loves of Woman and Italy. Like Foscolo he suffered political persecution, but his poetry, typifying the consumptive effeminate brand of late romanticism (cf. the idyll *Raffaello e la Fornarina*, 1855) against which ⇨ Carducci reacted so strongly, only rarely echoed the nobility and virility of Foscolo's (e.g. the short epic, *Le città italiane marinare e commercianti*, 1856). His poetry, the best of which he published in *I Canti* (Florence, 1864), possessed, however, a pleasing elegance of form. [RHC]

*Canti scelti*, ed. L. Grilli (1944); Dionisotti, *OBIV*.
*Minori*, iv.

**Alecsandri, Vasile** (Bacău 1821–Mircesti 1890). Rumanian poet and dramatist. He studied in Paris 1834–9, and so was among the first generation of Rumanians with Western training. Returning to Moldavia, he was chosen by the ruling Prince to be one of the three directors of the theatre at Jassy. As there were hardly any plays in Rumanian, Alecsandri was induced to contribute to the repertory and started with an adaptation of a farce. His work as a playwright extended over the next forty years, passing from farces to comedies, of which *Boieri si Ciocoi* (1874) is one of the best, and to historical dramas such as *Fîntîna Blanduziei* ('The Fountain of Bandusia', 1883). In the 1840s he became more and more interested in Rumanian folk-song, and in 1852 and 1853 he published 2 volumes of folk-ballads 'collected and corrected' by himself. The influence of these ballads on his own poetry was most beneficial; no longer was it mere imitation of French romanticism. His best poems are the volume *Pasteluri* (1875). Besides these delightful landscapes, he produced *Legende* and patriotic poems which won great popularity. As a prose-writer he excelled in reminiscences of travel, such as those of his trip to Morocco in 1853. (⇨ Rumanian Literature.) [EDT]

*Opere complete* (9 vols., 1875–80).

**Aleixandre, Vicente** (Seville 1898–    ). Spanish poet. The master of a *vers-libre* line of great power and originality, whose influence has been predominant over the young writers of Spain since the Civil War. Emerging with ⇨ Salinas and ⇨ Guillén, his early poems have affinities with theirs. In *La destrucción o el amor* (1935) he evolved his own style, already adumbrated in a few poems of *Espadas como labios* (1932). His vision of love as a chthonic force is coloured by imagery that is close to ⇨ Surrealism. Nature and man are one, love and destruction twin expressions of the same force.

He sympathized with the Republic in the Civil War, and his work was later banned. *Sombra del paraíso* (Buenos Aires, 1944) no longer identifies man with nature, but shows him rather as an exile on earth, mourning a lost state of primal bliss, often glimpsed in the paradise of childhood; his evocation of the warmth and scenery of Málaga adds a new musical quality to his verse. *Historia del corazón* (1954) returns to the theme of love, but love for his fellow-men; human solidarity, and the difficulty of communication, are recurring themes in *En un vasto dominio* (1962). *Los encuentros* (1958), a rare work in prose, contains tender sketches of his fellow poets and writers; most, though not all, of the items in his latest book of poems, *Retratos con nombre* (1965), also describe writers, past and present. [JMC]

*Poesías completas* (Madrid, 1960); Blecua, *FLE*; Cohen, *PBSV*; Trend, *OBSV*.

C. Bousoño, *La poesía de V.A.* (Madrid, 1950); Alonso, *PEC*; Vivanco, *PEC*; Zardoya, *PEC*; Cano, *PESV*.

**Alemán, Mateo** (Seville 1547–Mexico 1614?). Spanish novelist. Educated at Seville, Salamanca and Alcalá. Always poor and occasionally imprisoned for debt, he led a disordered life, eventually emigrating to Mexico at 60. His long picaresque novel *Guzmán de Alfarache* (1599–1604; repr. 5 vols. CC, 1926–36) is the account of the downfall and subsequent repentance of a young man who runs away from his home and is forced into the life of a rogue. He ends by being condemned to the galleys, where he finally realizes his hopeless state and changes his way of living. The book is a pessimistic commentary on the state of Spain and on the sinful nature of Man, with interpolated analyses of Guzmán's sins and a number of digressive stories and moralizations. The style is clear and vivid with a copious vocabulary. The work was very popular, being translated into French, Italian, English (J. Mabbe, 1621), German (⇨Albertinus), Dutch, Portuguese and Latin. Alemán also wrote a life of St Anthony of Padua, a short pamphlet on Fray García Guerra (Archbishop of Mexico), another called *Ortografía castellana*, and a translation of two odes of Horace. [JG]

E. Moreno Báez, *Lección y sentido de G. de A.* (Madrid, 1948).

**Alembert, Jean Le Rond,** known as d'Alembert (Paris 1717–Paris 1783). French scientist and man of letters. The illegitimate son of a distinguished literary hostess, Madame de Tencin, he showed early promise as a mathematician (*Traité de dynamique*, 1743) and achieved European eminence. ⇨ Diderot shared the editing of the *Encyclopédie* with him until 1759, and he is the author of its *Discours préliminaire* (1751; ed. F. Picavet, Paris, 1912), an influential essay surveying the history of human knowledge and charting its extent according to principles derived from Francis Bacon. As an exponent, in articles in the ⇨ *Encyclopédie* and elsewhere, of liberal and rationalist ideals d'Alembert was one of the most influential of the *philosophes*, enjoying wide respect, even among his opponents, as a man of moderation and integrity. [WHB]

*Œuvres philosophiques, historiques et littéraires*, ed. J. F. Bastien (18 vols., Paris, 1805–8).
R. Grimsley, *D'A.* (1963).

**Alexander de Villa Dei,** or Alexandre de Ville-Dieu (Avranches *c.*1160–after 1203). French grammarian and encyclopedist. Trained at Paris, he wrote a versified Latin grammar, the *Doctrinale* (ed. D. Reichling, Berlin, 1893), criticizing the paganizing tendency of the school of Orleans and eschewing classical authors. The work ousted Priscian and was mocked by ⇨ Erasmus (*Epist. obsc. vir.*) [CEC]

L. V. Delisle, 'A. de V.-D.', in *Bibliothèque de l'école des chartes*, 55 (1894); Manitius, *GLLM*.

**'Alexandre, Libro de.'** Spanish narrative poem of the first half of the 13th century. The work relates the life of Alexander the Great in the ⇨ *cuaderna vía* form, and consists of 10,700 lines. The main sources are Gautier de Châtillon's *Alexandreis*, the *Historia de Proeliis* and the French *Roman d'⇨Alexandre*. The author exhibits a very deep knowledge of these sources and of other Classical and medieval works. One of the most interesting aspects of the Spanish poem is the evident duality in the author's treatment of his protagonist: now great admiration for his achievements, now condemnation of his worldly pride; this duality stems from the varied character of the sources, but it is more marked in this work than in other medieval lives of Alexander. Digressions are frequent, the longest being the story of Troy, which occupies 448 stanzas. Others concern the Seven Deadly Sins and the inmates of Hell. There are some fine descriptions: Alexander's tent (which is clearly the source of Juan ⇨ Ruíz's description of the tent of Don Amor), Darius's tomb, and a pleasant May poem. The poet skilfully interlaces the digressive material with the linear narrative, producing a complex but coherent structure. The authorship is uncertain, the work having been variously attributed to, among others, ⇨ Berceo and a certain Juan Lorenzo de Astorga, mentioned in one of the two extant manuscripts. The original dialect is also not satisfactorily established, although R. Menéndez Pidal is strongly of the opinion that it was Leonese. The author appears to have been highly educated, perhaps a *clérigo d'escuela* or teacher at a *studium generale*. It is possible that the work was intended as a *speculum principis*, as R. S. Willis has suggested. The poem is the most erudite member of a learned *genre* and there is evidence of its great popularity, no doubt on account of the attraction of the theme and the enigmatic dynamism of the protagonist. [IM]

Ed. F. Janer (BAE, 57, 1864); ed. A. Morel-Fatio (Dresden, 1906); ed. R. S. Willis (Princeton, 1934).
R. S. Willis, *The Relationship of the Spanish 'Libro de Alexandre' to the 'Alexandreis' of*

*Gautier de Châtillon* (Princeton, 1934); R. S. Willis, *The Debt of the Spanish 'Libro de Alexandre' to the French 'Roman d'Alexandre'* (Princeton, 1935); M. R. Lida de Malkiel, *La idea de la fama en la Edad Media castellana* (Mexico-Buenos Aires, 1952); G. Cary, *The Medieval Alexander* (1956); *RPh*, x, 1957–8; *BHS*, XXXVII, 1960; *Anuario de Estudios Medievales*, II (Barcelona, 1965).

**'Alexandre, Roman d'.'** A medieval French cyclical romance which gave the name alexandrine to the 12-syllable verse. The various poems on this subject were put together by an unknown compiler before 1177.

The earliest surviving poem in French is a Franco-Provençal fragment of 105 octosyllabic lines describing Alexander's boyhood education. It was composed by Alberich of Pisançon, whose name occurs in a Middle High German adaptation written before 1130 by the priest ⇨ Lamprecht. The length of the German version, 7,302 lines, gives some indication of the importance of Alberich's poem, of which the main source was probably the *Res gestae Alexandri Macedonis*, a Latin translation by Julius Valerius of the 2nd-century Greek romance about Alexander made by the pseudo-Callisthenes. A further version of Alberich's work, this time by a Poitevin, was made in 10-syllable *laisses* before 1150, and this decasyllabic adaptation was continued by a poet Lambert le Tort in 12-syllable verse, in which he told of Alexander's expeditions into India, his trip in an airship, his capture of Babylon, and victory over the Amazons.

The composite *Roman d'Alexandre* consisted of: (a) a 12-syllable version of the 10-syllable Poitevin adaptation, covering Alexander's early years up to the war with Darius; (b) a poem *Fuerre de Gadres* by Eustache de Kent; (c) the long work by Lambert le Tort, mentioned above; (d) a conclusion written by the compiler himself. In this task he may have been helped by Pierre de Saint-Cloud, who is probably the author of the early ⇨ *Renart* stories.

The compiler and *remanieur* of this composite *Roman d'Alexandre* was Alexandre de Paris (or de Bernai) and this is the poem we now have, a work of sumptuous and exotic oriental descriptions and amusing and exciting adventures. Alexander is portrayed as a model ruler, generous and knightly, a man driven by intellectual curiosity.

Two *Vengeance Alexandre* were written, one by Jean le Nevelon before 1181, and the other by Guy de Cambrai about 1190. These two poems are independent of each other, and of the main work. Either Thomas or Eustache de Kent wrote another long Alexander romance in England in the late 12th century. The main source of this *Roman de toute chevalerie* was Julius Valerius. Several 14th-century romances, of which the *Vœux du paon* (1310–16) by Jacques de Longuyon is the first and most important, were composed about the Alexander legend. The *Vœux du paon* was also used later in the 14th century as the starting point of a vast prose narrative, *Perceforest*, intended to link the Alexander heroes with the legend of the Holy Grail. [LTT]

*The Medieval French 'Roman d'Alexandre'*, ed. E. C. Armstrong *et al.* (7 vols., Princeton, 1937–55).

G. Cary, *The Medieval Alexander* (1956).

**Alfasi, Isaac Ben Jacob,** known as **Rif** (nr Fez 1013–Lucena 1103). Hebrew poet and religious writer. He was a Rabbi in Fez until he had to escape to Spain in 1088. Although his poetry is lost, his *responsa* and *chalachot* (compendium to the Babylonian Talmud) form a most important part of Jewish traditional literature. [EE]

Waxman, *HJL*.

**Alfieri, Vittorio** (Asti 1749–Florence 1803). Italian poet and dramatist. He abandoned his military career to travel widely throughout Europe. The influence of French writers, his own high ideals, strong will, hatred of oppression, profound melancholy and his sense of emptiness and loneliness combined to make him Italy's leading pre-romantic and perhaps even her most essentially romantic writer. His personality is illustrated well in his memoirs – the *Vita* (first part written in Paris, 1790; second part written in Florence, 1803) – and it emerges very clearly also in the more controlled subjectivity of his *Rime*, many modelled on Petrarch, in his 17 *Satire* attacking social and political institutions (1786–97), in the anti-French outbursts of *Il Misogallo* (1793–9), and especially in the 19 tragedies (written between 1776 and 1786 and published collectively in Paris, 1789), dominated by the theme of tyranny, treated theoretically in *Della tirannide* (1777) and *Del principe e delle lettere*

(1785–6). In the best tragedies, *Saul* and *Mirra*, the element of political satire is more subdued, though in their romantic insistence on heroic willpower, whether directed towards good or evil, Alfieri's own personality still dominates the action, as much in the figure of the tyrant as in his opponents. [RHC]

*Opere*, ed. F. Maggini (2 vols., 1940); ed. L. Fassò (5 vols., 1951ff.); *Tragedie*, ed. U. Brilli (1961); *Tragedies*, tr. E. A. Bowring (2 vols., 1876); *Memoirs*, anon. tr. of 1810, revised by E. R. Vincent (1961); *Of Tyranny*, tr. J. A. Molinaro and B. Corrigan (Toronto, 1961).

W. Binni, *Vita interiore dell'A.* (Bologna, 1942); C. Jannaco, *Studi sulle tragedie di A.* (Messina, 1953); V. Branca, 'Per la storia delle *Satire* A.', in *Miscellanea E. Santini* (Palermo, 1956); M. Fubini, *Ritratto dell'A. e altri studi A.* (Florence, 1963); R. Scrivano, *La natura teatrale dell'ispirazione A. e altri scritti A.* (Milan, Messina, 1963); *Guida*, 1959; Binni, *CI*, ii; *Maggiori*, i.

**Alfonso X, El Sabio** (1221–84). Spanish patron and writer. King of Castile and León. When his father, Ferdinand III (the Saint), died in 1252, Alfonso the Wise became sovereign of a kingdom that was uncertainly united and still not completely freed from Moorish occupation. He was heavily involved in wars with the remaining Moslem rulers in Andalusia and in putting down the revolts of his own vassals. Yet he found time to establish a school of Christian, Moslem and Hebrew scholars and embarked on a plan to compose in Castilian works on every aspect of medieval culture. The choice of Castilian instead of Latin as the medium appears to have been a deliberate plan to enable works of learning to reach as many of his subjects as possible. In addition to this broad educative intention, the choice may also have been consciously coloured by the desire to achieve political unity through linguistic unity, making Castilian the national language. This desire for unity permeates the legal works of his court, all of which represent attempts to impose a unified and humane code on the existing chaos of separate municipal *fueros* or codes, many of them illogical and barbaric. These attempts culminated in the *Siete Partidas* (RAH, 1807; tr. S. P. Scott, Chicago, 1931), which go beyond the mere establishment of a national code of law and deal with every aspect of medieval Spanish society. The two great historical works, the *General Estoria* (ed. A. G. Solalinde, L. A. Kasten and V. R. B. Oelschläger, Madrid, 1930, 1957, 1961) and the *Primera Crónica General* (ed. R. Menéndez Pidal, Madrid, 1955), concern the history of the world and the history of Spain respectively. Both rely heavily on Classical works, the Bible, the Fathers of the Church and earlier Peninsular and European writings, and to a lesser extent on Moslem and Hebrew works; the latter work also made use of vernacular epic poems. The scientific and pseudo-scientific works were translated and adapted from Arabic versions of Greek and Oriental works: astronomy, astrology, the medical properties of precious stones, chess, dice, are all represented. Some of these works achieved great prestige in the rest of Europe. As well as the translations of Oriental books of fables attributed to his court, much poetry, in the fashionable poetic dialect, Galician-Portuguese, was produced; most of this is contained in the *Cantigas de Santa María* (RAE, 1889), which consist of some fine lyric and narrative poems dedicated to the Virgin Mary and relating the various miracles for which she was responsible. Alfonso's literary importance lies in the fact that he established Castilian as the normal vehicle for prose writing and brought into being a body of accessible works of learning that both widened and consolidated the culture of the period. His straightforward and unaffected prose set a stylistic pattern, soon to be taken up by his nephew, Don ⇨ Juan Manuel, that continued almost unaltered up to the 15th century. [IM]

*Antología*, ed. A. G. Solalinde (CA).

J. B. Trend, *A. the Sage and Other Essays* (1926); E.S. Procter, *A. X of Castile* 1951); D. Catalán Menéndez Pidal, *De A. X al conde de Barcelos* (Madrid, 1962); A. Ballesteros y Beretta, *A. X el Sabio* (Barcelona, 1963).

**Algarotti, Francesco** (Venice 1712–Pisa 1764). Italian popular scientist and essayist. He travelled widely throughout Europe and, in Paris, met leading scholars and artists, earning an international reputation for the agreeably clear and elegant exposition of his *Newtonianismo per le dame* (1735; tr. 1742). After a stay in London, where he met Pope, he went to Petersburg, and the record of his journey – *Viaggi di Russia* (1739) – he considered his best work. From Russia he went to Poland and Prussia, and was honoured by Frederick the Great. He was a proficient artist and enjoyed a wide reputation as a connoisseur, in 1742 being commissioned to purchase Italian paintings for the Royal Gallery at Dresden (see also the *Saggio sopra la pittura*, 1763, tr. 1764; and *Saggio sopra l'opera in musica*, 1762, tr. 1767). His writings embraced all subjects – literature, art, music, politics and sciences – the sheer universality and geniality of his work compensating for the lack of depth. Though no innovator himself, he represented the best of his age in being alive to all new currents of thought. [RHC]

*Opere complete*, ed. F. Aglietti (17 vols., 1791–4); *Viaggi di Russia*, ed. P. P. Trompeo (1961); *Saggi*, ed. G. Da Pozzo (1963).

B. Rosselli del Turco Crespi, *F.A.* (Florence, 1943); M. Fubini, 'Dall'Arcadia all'Illuminismo : F.A.', in *La cultura illuministica in Italia* (Turin, 1957); *Minori*, iii.

**Al-Harizi (Alcharisi), Judah Ben Shlomoh** (*c.*1165–1235). Hebrew poet in pre-expulsion Spain. He spent some time in Provence and even further north, where he earned a living as translator of scholarly works. His masterpiece is a translation into Hebrew of the Arabic poet al-Hariri's *Maqamas* under the title *Machberoth Ithiel*. These were Arabic short stories in rhymed prose and the translation faithfully reproduces the original style. His *Tachkemoni* is a similar book in Hebrew consisting of 50 stories, containing some humorous, some serious thoughts on Hebrew literature. His liturgical poems survive. [EE]

Waxman, *HJL*.

**Aliger, Margarita** (Odessa 1915– ). Russian poetess. She was educated in Moscow where her work was first published in 1933, and where she studied at the Gor'ky Literary Institute. During the war (in which her husband was killed) she worked as a journalist, part of the time in besieged Leningrad. She is still best known for her war-poetry, describing the sufferings of the civilian population, and for her narrative poem *Zoya* (1942), inspired by the martyrdom of a girl partisan. Some of her best work, however, has been love-poetry: e.g. the cycle *Cheloveku v puti* (1939); and after Stalin's death she took a leading part in bringing the ⇨ 'Thaw' to literature. Her poetry of the fifties shows great moral sensitivity allied with a delicate, small-scale, sometimes sombre lyricism. [RM-G]

*Stikhotvoreniya i poemy* (1953); *Iz zapisnoy knizhki 1946–1956* (1957); Gulland, *SRV*; Obolensky, *PBRV*.

**Alighieri, Dante.** ⇨ Dante Alighieri.

**Aljamiado Literature.** The literature of the Spanish Muslims written in Arabic characters but in the Spanish language (with a large admixture of Arabic and frequently with Aragonese dialectal traits). *Aljamia* (Arabic *al-'ajamiyya*) was applied in Spain to Romance: the Arabic sense is 'non-Arab', hence barbarous. The earliest text, which recounts somewhat baldly the story of Joseph (*Poema de Yúçuf*), is usually ascribed, largely on linguistic and metrical grounds, to the 14th century. Of all datable *aljamiado* manuscripts, the overwhelming majority are of the 16th century, with some from the 15th and none earlier. *Aljamiado* literature is a cultural hybrid arising in the very last period of Muslim presence in the Peninsula, beginning before the conquest of Granada (1492) and lasting until the expulsion (1609–12); during most of this period Islam was persecuted and Muslim writings could only circulate clandestinely.

Probably the first vernacular prose author was Ice de Gebir, *mufti* of Segovia, whose *Kitab Segobiano* (1462), a manual of the Muslim faith, was widely disseminated. Besides such purely theological works we have versions of Muslim legends and a doggerel account of the pilgrimage to Mecca by an Aragonese from Puey Monzón, but, not surprisingly, there is virtually nothing of a purely secular nature: the *Recontamiento del rey Alixandre* tells of the Islamic Alexander, the fairy-tale of *La doncella Carcayona* serves as a frame to a gloss on the phrase 'there is no god but Allah', even stories relating to the Muslim past (*el baño de Ziryab*) are rare. Most texts are anonymous; perhaps the only author whose personality intrudes into his writings is the Mancebo de Arévalo. In the mid 15th century he tramped Spain gathering the traditions of his faith into a series of compilations: *Sumario de la relación y exercicio espiritual*, the *Tafsira* and the *Breve compendio de nuestra santa ley*, the latter far from brief and written in collaboration with an Aragonese *faqih* Baray de Reminjo. The devotional material is interspersed with personal reminiscences which represent the chief interest of these writings today. [LPH]

*Leyendas moriscas*, ed. F. Guillén Robles (1885–6); *Las coplas del peregrino de Puey Monçón*, ed. M. de Pano y Ruata (1897); *Poema de Yúçuf*, ed. R. Menéndez Pidal (1952).

J. Ribera and M. Asín, *Manuscritos árabes y aljamiados de la Biblioteca de la Junta* (Madrid, 1912); *Memorias de la Real Academia Española*, vol. VI (1889); *R H*, 81 (1933).

**Almquist, Carl Jonas Love** (Stockholm 1793–Bremen 1866). Swedish poet, novelist, dramatist, journalist and pamphleteer. He studied at Uppsala and afterwards became a civil servant in the capital. Having been initiated into pietism by his grandfather, he later developed an independent interest in Swedenborg, and even an individual, mystical religion. The main literary achievement of his youth, *Amorina* (1822), was withdrawn from the press through the intervention of an uncle (and not published until 1839). It is the work of a feverish romantic imagination. As 'a poetic fugue' it presents a curious mixture of genres, both also of the realistic and the fantastic. The action purports to explain how the heroine, universally regarded as mad and dangerous, can at heart remain a saint. After resigning his post in the Civil Service, he married an uneducated country-girl, removed to the province of Värmland, and – to make the return to Nature complete – settled as an 'idealized farmer'. This short-lived agricultural experiment proved disastrous in all respects but the literary. During these years he conceived his vast opus *Törnrosens bok* ('The Book of the Wild Rose'), which appeared as a sequence of romantic, often exotic stories and plays from 1832 onwards becoming progressively more realistic. His many-sidedness extends beyond literature. In the 1830s he became headmaster of a progressive school and author of many textbooks. He also took orders (in 1837), which did not stop him from launching a serious attack on the institution of marriage; finally he became a full-time journalist, joining the most radical wing of the Liberal press.

Among his numerous works special attention is due to *Jaktslottet* (1832), a short novel introducing Richard Furumo, a mysterious storyteller, and his circle of admiring listeners; and *Drottningens juvelsmycke* (1834), a semi-historical novel spun round the assassination of King Gustav III, which has as its romantic heroine the mystifying androgyn Tintomara. This fantasy-figure can be seen as a symbol of Almquist's dream of emotional detachment. Greater stir was caused by the outstanding, realistically presented story *Det går an* (1839; tr. A. B. Benson, *Sara Videbeck*, N.Y., 1919) on account of its open plea for free love. In other long short stories he had already developed his talent for vivid description, e.g. *Kapellet* (1838; *The Chapel*, in the volume quoted), and on the strength of this achievement he is often considered a pioneer of realistic prose in Swedish literature. His pamphlet *Svenska fattigdomens betydelse* ('The Importance of Swedish Poverty', 1838) remains a classic of national self-characterization. Following a period of both literary and social decline, his reputation was overtaken by disaster in 1851. He suddenly fled the country, evidently to avoid a charge of attempted murder by poisoning. His later years, spent in the U.S.A., remain on the whole obscure, and although he went on filling reams of paper in exile, his notebooks have not in the main been considered worthy of publication. [SAB]

*Samlade skrifter*, ed. F. Böök (21 vols., 1921–38). H. Olsson, *Törnrosdiktaren* (Stockholm, 1956); M. Lamm, 'Studier i Almqvists ungdomsdiktning', in *Samlaren 1915* (Uppsala, 1916); A. Hemming-Sjöberg, *A Poet's Tragedy: The Trial of C.J.L.A.* (1932).

**Alonso, Dámaso** (Madrid 1898–    ). Spanish critic and scholar. He is professor of Romance Philology in the University of Madrid. His edition with prose translation of the *Soledades* of ⇨ Góngora (1927) inaugurated a reinterpretation of 17th-century poetry which has profoundly influenced Spanish taste. Influenced by the critical methods of I. A. Richards and Empson, he has studied ambiguities in the language of ⇨ Góngora and his contemporaries in *La lengua poética de G.* (1935), *Estudios y ensayos gongorinos* (1955); latterly he has done research on Góngora's biography (*Documentos gongorinos*, 1963). His interpretations of Spanish poetry range from the early Mozarabic lyrics and the *Poema del Cid* to St John of the Cross (*La poesía de San Juan de la Cruz*, 1942) and the work of his contemporaries (*Poetas españoles contemporáneos*, 1952). *Poesía española* (1950), which characterizes stylistically the chief poets of the Golden Age, is a landmark in modern Spanish criticism. His three books of poetry (principally *Hijos de la ira*, 1944) gained a rather excessive reputation at a time when Spanish poetry was at a low ebb. His rhetorical *vers-libre* resembles ⇨ Aleixandre's but is less sensitive; his prevailing theme is neurotically religious introspection. [JMC]

*Antología* (1: *Creación*, 2: *Crítica*), ed. V. Gaos (CA, 1956); Blecua, *FLE*.
Vivanco, *PEC*; Zardoya, *PEC*; Cano, *PESV*.

**Altolaguirre, Manuel** (Málaga 1905–nr Burgos 1959). Spanish poet. He echoes traditional folk-poetry, conventional in his Romantic attitudes and derivative in his fashionable neo-Gongorist devices; his principal theme is love. After the Civil War he worked in London as a printer (his original trade), and reprinted forgotten translations of Spanish poets. Later in Mexico he wrote more poetry, careful in language but even less individual than his pre-war work, collected as *Las islas invitadas* (2nd edn, Mexico, 1936). He also translated Shelley's *Adonais* and two short verse-plays by Pushkin. He was killed in a motor accident on his first visit to Spain since the war. [JMC]

*Poesías completas 1926–1959* (Mexico, 1960); Blecua, *FLE*; Cohen, *PBSV*; Trend, *OBSV*.

**Álvarez de Toledo, Gabriel** (Seville 1662–Madrid 1714). Spanish poet and historian. He was librarian and secretary to Philip V, and co-founder of the Spanish Academy. Living like a hermit in the midst of state affairs, he wrote mystical and philosophical poetry, of which the sonnet 'La muerte es la vida' is generally known, together with the mystico-philosophical poem 'A mi pensamiento' and the burlesque *Burromaquia*. His *Obras póstumas poéticas* were edited by ⇨ Torres Villaroel in 1744. [JMC]

*Poesías* (BAE 61).

**Álvarez Quintero, Serafín** (Utrera 1871–Madrid 1938) and **Joaquín** (Utrera 1873–Madrid 1944). Spanish playwright brothers who wrote in collaboration. Their plays make no claim to greatness, aiming to entertain rather than to pose emotional or moral problems, and are thus generally dismissed scornfully by the critics. Their treatment of certain themes, notably that of the *soltera* (*El amor que pasa*), foreshadows the thematic basis of the great dramas of ⇨ Lorca. They excel in the portrayal of notable eccentrics and quick-witted servants (*Doña Clarines*), the setting being generally that of their native Andalusia. Their plays remain popular. [GC]

*Obras completas* (7 vols., 1947–52); CA (selection); *Four Comedies*, tr. H. and H. Granville Barker (1932).

J. Losada de la Torre, *Perfil de los hermanos A.Q.* (Madrid, 1945); R. Pérez de Ayala, *Las máscaras*, ii (Buenos Aires, 4, 1944); Valbuena Prat, *NPE*.

**Alvaro, Corrado** (S. Luca di Calabria 1895–Rome 1956). Italian novelist. From 1917, while he was in the army, until his death he worked for some of the most important Italian dailies in various capacities, as special correspondent, theatre and cinema critic, and general editor. In his novels he tried to express the contrast, which he deeply felt in himself, between the two worlds of country and town, the former ruled by memories, traditions and customs, the latter by expediency and fashion. His 'Rinaldo Diacono' cycle (*L'età breve*, 1946; *Mastrangelina*, 1960; *Tutto è accaduto*, 1961), describing the life of the protagonist from the beginning of the century in Calabria to the end of the Second World War in Naples, is in many ways a spiritual autobiography in which he tried to clarify to himself all the problems facing an educated and urbanized Southerner, torn between the yearning for intellectual and sexual freedom and emancipation, and the longing for his native land, transfigured, once it has been safely left behind, into an image of original beauty and purity, too poetic to be realistic (*Gente in Aspromonte*, 1930). A similar unresolved dualism can be found in Alvaro's treatment of his women characters, described puritanically as corrupt social pushers, or affectionately as mythical mother goddesses and sacred prostitutes from which man takes the double gift of life, at birth and in the act of love. Some of his most beautiful stories have been collected in *Settantacinque racconti* (1955). He also wrote two interesting diaries, *Quasi una vita, giornale di uno scrittore* (1950) and *Ultimo diario* (1961). [GMC]

*Contemporanei*, ii; Pullini, *RID*; Falqui, *PNNI*.

**'Amadís de Gaula.'** Romance of chivalry of Peninsular origin. It owes much to the spirit of the *matière de Bretagne*. The hero Amadis is presented as an amorous swain in the 'service' of his lady, the princess Oriana, on whose behalf he undertakes a long series of chivalrous adventures against giants, monsters and the like. On to this basic medieval theme is grafted a new element of sensuality, normally ignored or suppressed by the courtly troubadours. Much controversy surrounds the question of the authorship, date and language of the original composition. The only known early texts, both of them extant and in Spanish, are a recently discovered (and fragmentary) 15th-century manuscript and Montalvo's printed edition (Saragossa, 1508), although references to the work were made by Castilian authors as early as the second half of the 14th century. Extensive efforts have been made to establish that the work was originally composed in Portuguese, in the 14th century, and by either Vasco de Lobeira or his forebear João. The trail of evidence is rich in clues and the Portuguese case is highly probable though not conclusively demonstrable. It is a reasonable hypothesis, however, that the fourth book of the *Amadís* is Montalvo's own composition and that he inserted new material in the first three books as well. [RCW]

M. Menéndez y Pelayo, *Orígenes de la novela*, vol. I (Madrid, 1943); G. S. Williams, *The Amadis Question*, in *Revue Hispanique*, XXI (New York-Paris, 1909); H. Thomas, *Spanish and Portuguese Romances of Chivalry* (1920); W. J. Entwistle, *The Arthurian Legend in the Literatures of the Spanish Peninsula* (1925); M. Rodrigues Lapa, *Lições de Literatura Portuguesa* (Coimbra, 1955); F. Costa Marques, *A. de G.* (Coimbra, 1960).

**Ambrus, Zoltán** (1861–1932). Hungarian writer. His whole life and career was influenced by experiences gained from literary courses at the Sorbonne. At a time when there was little contact between French and Hungarian literature, it was due to his work that French culture became the province of many Hungarian writers, as well as readers. He wrote novels (*King Midas*), short stories, worked on the editorial boards of ⇨ *Nyugat* and *Hét*, was editor of *Új Magyar Szemle*, and director of the Hungarian National Theatre (1916–22). He lacked popularity, however, mainly because he was too intimately tied to a foreign culture. [JFR]

**Amiel, Denys** (Carcassonne 1884– ). French playwright. The articulateness of his characters is simply a stratagem for concealing their profoundest feelings; dialogue is not open communication but a flurry of signs pointing elsewhere, to secret hopes and fears. He exploits this central insight, sometimes rather obviously, in a variety of plays distinguished by explorations of feminine psychology: *Le voyageur* (1912); *La souriante Madame Beudet* (1922, in collaboration with ⇨ Obey), in which the predicament of a latter-day Madame Bovary is scrupulously observed; *Le couple* (1923); *Monsieur et Madame Un Tel* (1925), etc. This scrutiny of private feelings often hinges about a topical social problem, e.g. the clash of the generations in *La femme en fleur* (1935); the freedom of the 'modern miss' in *Ma liberté* (1936). [SBJ]

Surer, *TFC*.

**Amiel, Henri-Frédéric** (Geneva 1821–Geneva 1881). Swiss writer. Of French Protestant descent, he became a professor of aesthetics, then of philosophy at Geneva. Famous for his remarkable diary, *Fragments d'un journal intime* (publ. posth. 1884). It reveals a delicate introspective nature of great critical and literary sensibility but paralysed by a feeling of mental impotence. 'I am not free because I do not possess the strength to carry out my will,' he says and he stated that he watched his life flow by as a wounded man watches the blood flow from his veins. [WA]

*Fragments*, ed. B. Bouvier (1923, 1927); *Philine* (*fragments inédits*), ed. B. Bouvier (1927); *Essais critiques* (1931); *Lettres* (1935); *Journal*, tr. Mrs Humphrey Ward (1885).

A. Thibaudet, *A.* (Paris, 1929), *Intérieurs, Beaudelaire, Fromentin, A.* (Paris, 1924).

**Amyot, Jacques** (Melun 1513–Auxerre 1593). French translator. He taught Greek at the University of Bourges (1536–*c.* 1546), where he translated Heliodorus's *Aethiopica*, the romance of Theagenes and Chariclea, for which François I gave him the abbacy of Bellozane (Normandy). He visited Italy (1547–52) to study the text of the Greek authors he proposed to translate into French. Back in France, he was appointed tutor to the sons of Henri II (the future Charles IX and Henri III); Charles IX made him Grand Almoner (1560) and Bishop of Auxerre (1570). His later years at Auxerre were troubled by the Ligueurs.

His translations helped spread a taste for heroic antiquity and moral writings; his supple, vigorous language raised the quality of French prose. His *Histoire éthiopique*, with its mixture of adventure and sentimental analysis, served as a model for a whole romanesque literature, even the device of starting the story in the middle being widely copied. It inspired Alexandre Hardy's tragedy, *Théagènes et Chariclée*, and an episode in Tasso's *Gerusalemme liberata*. He also translated seven books of the historian Diodorus Siculus (1554), the *Daphnis and Chloe* of Longus (1559), as well as his most important work, Plutarch's *Lives* (*Vie des hommes illustres*, 1559, the result of 17 years' work) and his *Moralia* (1572). Montaigne admits his generation's debt to Amyot's *Vie* ('it is our breviary') and Sir Thomas North translated it into English, furnishing Shakespeare with the plots of his Roman plays. The *Œuvres morales*, which enjoyed equally great contemporary favour, are now almost forgotten. [FWAG]

A. de Blignières, *Essai sur A. et les traducteurs du XVIe siècle* (Paris, 1851); R. Sturel, *J.A., Traducteur des Vies parallèles* (Paris, 1908); A. Ciorănescu, *Vie de J.A.* (Paris, 1941).

**Andersch, Alfred** (Munich 1914– ). German novelist and short-story writer. After six months in Dachau concentration camp in 1933 as a Communist Party member, he worked in a factory, served unwillingly in the German army, and deserted in 1944 (prisoner-of-war in the U.S.A.). Active in *avant-garde* literary circles, editor of *Texte und Zeichen* (1955–7), and on the radio; his autobiographical *Die Kirschen der Freiheit* (1952) became one of the most controversial post-war works. His prize-winning first novel, *Sansibar oder der letzte Grund* (1957; tr. M. Bullock, *Flight to Afar*, 1958), treats the conflict between totalitarianism and the individual conscience, and is remarkable for its poetic and evocative style, as is *Die Rote* (1960; tr. M. Bullock, *The Redhead*, 1961), which is again concerned with truth and individual integrity. He has also written stories: *Piazza San Gaetano* (1957) and the collections *Geister und Leute* (1958) and *Ein Liebhaber des Halbschattens* (1963), and a considerable number of radio-plays, including *Aktion ohne Fahnen* (1958). [PB]

*Bericht, Roman, Erzählungen* (1965); *The Night of the Giraffe and Other Stories*, tr. C. Armstrong (1965).

Nonnenmann, *SG*.

**Andersen, Hans Christian** (Odense 1805–Copenhagen 1875). Danish writer of fairy tales, whose father was a shoemaker and mother superstitious and almost illiterate. He came to Copenhagen in 1819 hoping to 'become famous', possibly as an actor or a singer. Working for a time as a supernumerary at the Royal Theatre, Copenhagen, he survived these years only through the help of kind benefactors. His first literary efforts, partly crude imitation of Sir Walter Scott, were published in 1822. At this time Jonas Collin, a director of the Royal Theatre, took an interest in the ambitious but almost illiterate boy and got a grant for him to attend the grammar school at Slagelse and finally Copenhagen University in 1828.

Andersen's world-wide fame is based almost entirely on his fairy tales and stories, of which he wrote altogether 168 between 1835 and 1872. The first slender volume, published in 1835, contained *Fyrtøjet* ('The Tinderbox'), *Prinsessen paa Ærten* ('The Princess on the Pea'), *Lille Claus og store Claus* ('Little Claus and Big Claus') and *Den lille Idas Blomster* ('Little Ida's Flowers'), all of which very soon became children's classics in many countries – together with *Kejserens nye Klæder* ('The Emperor's New Clothes'), *Snedronningen* ('The Snow Queen'), etc. In Andersen's lifetime a polyglot edition was published of one tale in 15 languages; today the number of languages into which his tales have been translated exceeds a hundred. Some tales are based on history, or on Danish folk-tales which he heard as a child, others on foreign sources; but the majority are his own invention, often springing from some personal event, great or small, happy or unhappy. Andersen himself, his friends and enemies, appear in the tales in a thousand different guises. Some of the tales have a childlike simplicity, others are so subtle and sophisticated that they are only properly appreciated by adults.

Andersen also wrote 6 novels, many travel books, several autobiographies, besides poems and plays. His first and most successful novel, *Improvisatoren* (1835; tr. M. Howitt, 1845), paved the way for his general recognition, both in Denmark and abroad. Like all his other novels it was a poorly disguised autobiography, on this occasion in an Italian setting. For friends in Denmark he wrote a draft autobiography in 1832 (first published in Denmark as *Levnedsbogen*, 1926), then for publication in Germany in 1847 – *Das Märchen meines Lebens ohne Dichtung* (tr. M. Howitt, *The True Story of My Life*, 1847), and finally in 1855 *Mit Livs Eventyr* (tr. W. Glyn Jones, *The Fairy Tale of My Life*, 1954).

Andersen travelled extensively in almost

every country in Europe. He considered Italy his second fatherland, but culturally his ties with Germany were much closer. He visited England and Scotland in 1847, and in 1857 he spent five weeks as the guest of Charles Dickens at Gad's Hill.

Among the innumerable English translations of Andersen's *Fairy Tales and Stories* since 1846 (first by Mary Howitt, Charles Boner, Caroline Peachey and Lady Duff Gordon), those which best recapture the spirit and the humour of the originals are by Paul Leyssac (1937), R. P. Keigwin (4 vols., 1950–60), and R. Spink (1960). [ELB]

*H.C.A.'s Correspondence*, ed. F. Crawford (1891); *The Andersen-Scudder Letters*, ed. J. Hersholt and W. Westergaard (Berkeley, 1949).

E. L. Bredsdorff, 'H.C.A. A Bibliographical Guide to his Works', in *Scandinavica*, VI, 1 (1967), *H.C.A. and Charles Dickens* (1956); R. Nisbet Bain, *H.C.A.: A Biography* (1895); E. Reumert, *H.A. the Man* (1927); S. Toksvig, *The Life of H.C.A.* (1933); C. B. Burnett, *The Shoemaker's Son* (1943); Rumer Godden, *H.C.A.: A Great Life in Brief* (1955); F. Böök, *H.C.A.: A Biography* (1962); Monica Stirling, *The Wild Swan: The Life and Times of H.C.A.* (1965).

**Andersen Nexø, Martin.** ⇨ Nexø, Martin Andersen.

**Andersson, Dan** (Grangärde 1888–Stockholm 1920). Swedish poet, novelist and story-writer. His work gained wide and lasting popularity after his early accidental death and (with that of ⇨ Koch and ⇨ Hedenvind-Eriksson) helped to inaugurate the important 'proletarian' branch of Swedish literature. Born in the province of Dalarna in a region of forest inhabited by poor, isolated communities of Finnish origin that preserved some of their own temperament and traditions (including a vein of the supernatural), he knew from his own experience the harsh, arduous, lonely life of the charcoal-burners, described in his first stories and poems – *Kolarhistorier* ('Charcoal-Burners' Tales', 1914) and *Kolvaktarens visor* (1915; tr. C. Schleef, *Charcoal-Burner's Ballad and Other Poems*, N.Y., 1943). Subsequently he published two partly autobiographical novels influenced by Dostoyevsky; artistically imperfect, they are nevertheless movingly intense. More important are the poems in *Svarta ballader* ('Black Ballads', 1917), where his concern with suffering is linked with poignant self-examination and religious search and pointed by the strange forest background.

*Samlade skrifter* (5 vols., 1930).

E. Uhlin, *D.A. före Svarta ballader* (Stockholm, (1950); *ASR*, XLII, 1954; W. Bernhard, *En bok om D.A.* (Stockholm, 1966).

**Andrada, Andrés Fernández de** (early 17th cent.). Spanish poet. Little is known of him, but he was almost certainly the author of the magnificent 'Epístola moral a Fabio', generally printed as anonymous. In admonishing his friend to put aside the ambitions of court, live a life of moderation and direct his thoughts to eternity, Andrada stands midway between the stoical acceptance of ⇨ Manrique and the world-weary sense of unreality voiced in Segismundo's monologues in Calderón's *La vida es sueño.* [JMC]

Blecua, *FLE*; Cohen, *PBSV*; Trend, *OBSV*.

D. Alonso and S. Reckert, *Vida y obra de Medrano* (Madrid, 1948–58), vol. ii, appx iv; Cernuda, *PL*.

**Andreas Capellanus** (fl. 1175–80). French author of *De amore*. Chaplain to Louis VII of France and afterwards to Marie of Champagne, granddaughter of William IX of Aquitaine. He wrote his Latin treatise, *De amore* (or *De arte honeste amandi*), for Marie. Based on Ovid's *Ars amatoria* and *Remedia amoris*, it summarizes the theory of courtly love: an extra-marital relationship in open defiance of feudal custom and ecclesiastical precept. The book was much used by later medieval writers, and from a misunderstanding of it the legend of the fabulous 'Courts of Love' was drawn. [FB]

*De amore*, ed. E. Trojel (Copenhagen, 1892); ed. A. Pagès (Castelló de la Plana, 1929; repr. with Catalan tr., 1930); ed. S. Battaglia, with Italian tr. (Rome, 1947); *The Art of Courtly Love*, tr. J. J. Parry (N.Y., 1959).

S. Painter, *French Chivalry* (Baltimore, 1940); A. J. Denomy, *The Heresy of Courtly Love* (N.Y., 1947); Lewis, *AL*.

**Andres, Stefan** (Dhrönchen/Mosel 1906– ). German novelist and dramatist. The ninth child of a miller, he began training for the priesthood, but turned to German, philosophy and art-history at Cologne, Jena and Berlin; he travelled in Italy, Greece, Egypt, lived in Positano (1937–49) and recently at Unkel am Rhein. His autobiographical first novel, *Bruder Luzifer* (1932), contains the characteristic theme of conflict between the moral law and the senses. His best-known work, the novella *Wir sind Utopia* (1942; tr. C. Brooks, *We Are Utopia*, 1954), described by Graham Greene as 'amongst the most shattering of modern literature', is the story of a monk who leaves his monastery to try to put his political idealism into practice. Andres's recent concern with social and political criticism is seen in the novels *Die Hochzeit der Feinde* (1947), *Ritter der Gerechtigkeit* (1948), and above all in the trilogy *Die Sintflut* (1949–59), an ambitious fantasy about an imaginary Hitler-type dictator, which lacks the vitality and vision to match its theme. His latest novel is *Der Taubenturm* (1966). Gifted primarily as a storyteller (his collected *Novellen und Erzählungen* appeared in 1962–4, in 2 vols.), he has attempted drama, radio-plays, and poetry (*Requiem für ein Kind*, 1948; *Der Granatapfel*, 1950). [PB]

*S.A.: Eine Einführung in sein Werk* (Munich, 1962); *S.A.: Ein biographisch-bibliographischer Abriss* (Munich, 1962); *DR*, LXXXV, 1 (1959).

**Andreyev, Leonid Nikolayevich** (Oryol 1871–Kuokkala, Finland 1919). Russian novelist and dramatist. Andreyev was born of middle-class parents and trained as a lawyer. His first stories were published in 1895, and he became a bestseller with the story *Zhili-byli* (1901). His fame and talent declined after 1908. Although he sympathized with the 1905 Revolution he rejected that of 1917 as a threat to civilization and died in exile.

Andreyev was despised by the intellectuals of his time, though he did much to popularize their themes and techniques. His morbid interest in pathological states – insanity (*Mysl'*, 1902; tr. J. West, *Thought*, 1916), sexual obsession (*Bezdna*, 1902; tr. J. Cournos, *The Abyss*, 1929) and suicide (*V tumane*, 1902) – represented one aspect of Russian thought and feeling at the beginning of the century. His fascination with psychological and religious paradoxes (*Iuda Iskariot*, 1907; tr. W. Morison, 1947) reflects the influence of Dostoyevsky, while his constant obsession with the inevitability of death and the consequent meaninglessness of life (*Zhizn' Vasiliya Fiveyskogo*, 1902) links him with L. Tolstoy. Much of Andreyev's work is spoilt by his rhetorical style and the hysterical tone of his writing; but in his best story, *Gubernator* (1906; tr. Schimanskaya and Gow, *The Governor*, 1947), an account of the last hours in the life of an official awaiting assassination, he reveals genuine power and unusual self-control.

His plays suffer from the same faults as his stories and are written in a pretentious allegorical style. *Zhizn' cheloveka* (1906; tr. C. J. Hogarth, *The Life of Man*, 1915) is the best of them. [RDBT]

*Sobraniye sochineniy* (17 vols., 1910–16).
*Kniga o L.A.* (Berlin, 1924); A. S. Kaun, *L.A.: A Critical Study* (1924).

**Andrézel, Pierre.** ⇨ Blixen, Karen.

**Andrić, Ivo** (Travnik, Bosnia 1892– ). Serbian short-story writer and novelist. Educated in Zagreb, Graz and Vienna, he was interned during the First World War by the Austrian government as a Yugoslav nationalist. After the war he entered the diplomatic service, finally serving as Yugoslav ambassador to Berlin (1940). He spent the Second World War in occupied Belgrade. He published his first important works, collections of lyrical prose, *Nemiri* and *Ex Ponto*, in 1918. These were followed by several collections of short stories and, after the Second World War, the novels *Travnička hronika* (tr. K. Johnstone, *Bosnian Story*, London/Belgrade, 1958), *Na Drini ćuprija* (tr. L. Edwards, *The Bridge on the Drina*, 1959) and *Gospodjica* (*The Woman from Sarajevo*, tr. J. Hitrec, 1966). In 1961 he was awarded the Nobel prize.

Andrić's works are dominated by a sense of human isolation, perhaps owing something to his imprisonment in youth, but in fact the basis of his philosophic view of existence. For him the main condition of man's existence is fear, the fear both of external disaster and the inner awareness of insecurity in a universe where everything is ephemeral and where the human psyche longs for constancy. Beginning with a subjective, lyrical approach to this problem, he develops in his stories and novels an almost complete impersonality, expressing himself through a rich gallery of human characters. He uses Bosnia, especially the old Turkish Bosnia with its violence, despotism and terror, as both a symbol and a canvas on which to portray man's tragic struggle against the oncoming darkness of change and death. The bridge in *Na Drini ćuprija* links the past to the present, just as it does the east to the west. Man's possible achievement, according to Andrić, is to create works of lasting beauty that bridge the gulf of change and give light and reassurance to mankind. [EDG]

*Djerzelez at the Inn*, tr. N. B. Jopson in *SEER*, XIV, 40 (1935); Lavrin, *AMYP*.
Barac, *HYL*; Kadič, *CSL*.

**Andrzejewski, Jerzy** (Warsaw 1909– ). Polish novelist. His pre-war works emulated the subjects and manner of Mauriac; e.g. *Ład serca* (1938). He tried to recapture the complex mood of his country at the end of the war in *Popiół i diament* (1948; abridged tr. D. J. Welsh, *Ashes and Diamonds*, 1962), but it was the film, based on the novel, which ten years later clarified its political ambivalence. He resorts to allegorical devices, as in *Bramy raju* (1960; tr. J. Kirkup, *The Gates of Paradise*, 1963), which is also a bold experiment in what amounts to one continuous sentence. [JP]

*Idzie skaczac po górach* (1963; tr. C. Wieniewska, *He Cometh Leaping upon the Mountains*, 1965).
Kuncewicz, *MPM*.

**Angelus Silesius,** pseud. of Johann Scheffler (Breslau 1624–Breslau 1677). German poet. Of a sternly Protestant Silesian family, he came, while a medical student at Leyden, under the influence of the Silesian mystic Abraham von Franckenberg, whose passionate adoration of Christ awakened an echo in him and who introduced him to the works of the great German mystics: Tauler, Eckhart, Weigel and Böhme. After completing his studies at Padua, he returned to Silesia as the personal physician of the Lutheran Duke Sylvius Nimrod von Öls, and thus remained close to Franckenberg. Partly because of the latter's death, partly in response to promptings of longer date, he resigned his post and returned to Breslau, where he was received into the Roman Church on 12 June 1653, taking the name Angelus Silesius. His best work was written in the years immediately following, both the *Heilige Seelenlust* and the *Geistreiche Sinn- und Schlußreime* (from the 6th edn in 1674 entitled *Der cherubinische Wandersmann*) being published in 1657. Both exemplify the mystical approach to God. The *Heilige Seelenlust* includes in its 205 poems many which are still popular with both Protestants and Catholics (*Mir nach, spricht Christus, unser Held*), but is chiefly remarkable as an example of bride-mysticism, the conventional love poetry of the age being adapted, often almost literally, to express the mystic love of the soul for Christ. The 5 books of *Der cherubinische Wandersmann* embody the more contemplative approach and express in the form of short epigrams – a form he borrowed from the Silesian mystic Daniel von Czepko – almost the whole range of mystic thought from didactic exhortations to his readers to purify their hearts to examinations of the nature and consequences of the *unio mystica*. His real achievement lies not in the power or originality of his thought, but in his consummate skill in expressing the traditional concepts of mysticism in concise poetic form. [WAC]

*Werke*, ed. G. Ellinger (2 vols., 1924); ed. H. L. Held (1949) (in progress); *A.S. A Selection*, tr. J. E. C. Flitch (1932).
G. Ellinger, *A.S.* (Breslau, 1927).

**Angilbert,** Abbot of St Riquier, Centula (*c*.814). Medieval poet and man of affairs. Of noble birth and high position in state service, he also figured as 'Homer' in Charlemagne's literary circle (⇨ Alcuin), writing elegiac verse; and after a colourful career retired to a monastery. The epic fragment *Karolus Magnus & Leo Papa* (in the style of ⇨ Fortunatus) is not by him; he is also distinct from the author of the poem *de belle quae fuit acta Fontaneto* (MGH, PLAC, ii). [CEC]

Ed. E. Dümmler (MGH, PLAC); tr. H. Althof, *Angilberts Leben und Dichtungen* (Münden, 1888).
D. Tardi, *Fortunat* (Paris, 1927); Manit us, *GLLM*; Raby, *SLP*.

**Anhava, Tuomas** (Helsinki 1927– ). Finnish poet, critic and essayist. A modernist, influenced by T. S. Eliot, he has published several collections of poems. [IR]

**Anker Larsen, Johannes** (Henninge 1874–Copenhagen 1957). Danish novelist. His works are often concerned with mystical experiences. The following novels have appeared in English: *De vises Sten* (1923; tr. A. G. Chater, *The Philosopher's Stone*, 1924); *Martha og Maria* (1925; tr. A. G. Chater, *Martha and Mary*, 1926); *Sognet som vokser ind i Himmelen* (1928; tr. R. C. Jordan, *A Stranger in Paradise*, 1930); *For aaben Dør* (1926; tr. E. and P. von Gaisberg, *With the Door Open*, 1931). [ELB]

**Annensky, Innokenty Fyodorovich** (Omsk 1856–Petersburg 1909). Russian poet, dramatist and critic. Almost unknown during his lifetime, he has since been recognized as one of the most original and talented poets of the early 20th century. His work as director of the lycée at Tsarskoe Selo, and later as inspector of schools for the St Petersburg district, left him little time for poetry, and he published only 2 collections of verse: *Tikhiye pesni*, which appeared in 1904 under the pseudonym Nik. T-o (i.e. Nobody), and *Kiparisovyy larets* (1910).

Although a contemporary of the ⇨ Symbolists, his work has little in common with theirs; he disliked the religious and mystical overtones of the Symbolist aesthetic, and his poems are more intimate and personal. Their main theme is the weariness and futility of life. He was much closer to the younger group of ⇨ Acmeists – he helped to found their journal *Apollon,* and the influence of his verse can be seen in the work of ⇨ Gumilyov and especially of ⇨ Akhmatova.

A noted Greek scholar, he translated the complete plays of Euripides, and also wrote 4 tragedies, based on Greek myths, but treated in a modern, rather than a classical manner: *Melanippa-filosof* (1901), *Tsar Iksion* (1902), *Laodamiya* (1907) and *Famira-kifared* (*Thamyras Cytharede*) (1913). His literary criticism, which deals with both Russian and foreign writers, is collected in the 2 volumes *Kniga otrazheniy* (1907) and *Vtoraya kniga otrazheniy* (1909). [TJB]

*Stikhotvoreniya i tragedii* (1959).
Vs. Setchkarev, *Studies in the Life and Works of I.A.* (The Hague, 1963).

**'Annolied.'** Medieval German narrative poem written by an unknown author, probably in the Moselle region, some time between 1075 and 1110. The hero of the poem is Bishop Anno of Cologne (d. 1075), whose life, told partly in historical, partly in legendary terms, is presented as a central event in the history of the world. The poem is interesting as an early example of idealized history and biography; it is known through an edition (1639) by M. ⇨ Opitz. [RT]

Ed. M. Rödiger in MGH (*Script. vern. lingua*, I, 2, Hanover, 1895); ed. K. Meisen (1946).

**Añón.** ⇨ Galician Literature.

**Anouilh, Jean** (Bordeaux 1910– ). French playwright. Perhaps the most superlatively gifted theatrical craftsman of his generation, his command of the Parisian boulevard theatre remains assured over thirty years after his first staged play, *L'hermine* (1932; tr. M. John, *The Ermine*, 1955). His popularity, versatility and technical deftness recall ⇨ Scribe, though he transcends Scribe's mechanical stereotypes and creates a more moving and fully human theatre. His drama constantly moves away from a minimal naturalism towards a self-consciously stylized theatre, in which the elements of artifice and play, of make-believe and pretence are pronounced, and in which the 'play' and 'pretence' infect the real. For Anouilh drama is a lie that conveys truths, and his truths are communicated through theatrical conventions of the most threadbare and obvious kind: caricature, coincidence, plays within plays. At the heart of his deliberate theatricality lies an obsession with purity which animates almost all his plays, and which is at its most absolute in his early productions. In these, his characteristic heroes and heroines reject society and live a marginal existence, e.g. Thérèse of *La sauvage* (1938) plays in a shabby and precarious café orchestra; Orphée, the hero of *Eurydice* (1942; tr. K. Black, *Point of Departure*, 1951), is an itinerant musician; Gaston, the amnesic ex-soldier of *Le voyageur sans bagage* (1937; tr. J. Whiting, *Traveller without Luggage*, 1959), inhabits a social vacuum. They are contrasted with those made callous or frivolous or corrupt by society, money or sexual appetite; with Lady Hurf in *Le bal des voleurs* (1938; tr. L. Hill, *Thieves' Carnival*, 1952), or Messerchmann, the lamentable millionaire of *L'invitation au château* (1947; tr. C. Fry, *Ring Round the Moon*, 1950); or the savagely observed gallery of middle-aged lechers and vulgarians from Thérèse's bibulous father in *La sauvage* to the promiscuous 'star' of the theatre, Madame Alexandra, in *Colombe* (1951; tr./adapt. D. Cannan, 1951). In this clash between the exigent purity of his young idealists and the craven submission of the middle-aged, Anouilh appears to identify and inflate the mood of adolescence. His early plays reveal him as a Rousseau of the boulevards, pressing to the limit the distinction between his heroes and the debased society which contains them; between moral man and immoral society. The passion for purity moves in a kind of doomed ritual towards its defeat. The 'ill-starred lovers' (the cliché is appropriate) are subjected to a series of confrontations with the standards of the 'normal' world, and the world wins. Revolt cedes to resignation; happiness cannot be reconciled with the suffering of others; sincerity is defeated by lies and social shams; fidelity and pure emotion cannot survive vulgar promiscuity. Thérèse, 'the wild one', gives up Florent and the unflawed happiness he seems to hold out; Eurydice cannot transcend her sordid past; Marc, in *Jézabel* (1932), rejects the devotion of Jacqueline and prefers to stay with his appalling mother; the heroine of *Antigone* (1944; tr. L. Galantière, 1946) prefers death to the compromises of the world, just as it is only in death that the lovers of *Roméo et Jeannette* (1946; tr./adapt. D. MacDonagh, *Fading Mansion*, 1949) find the consummation of a true love. Indeed, in many of the earlier plays, the climate of love is death; happiness survives only in fantasy. Thus, an abandoned Medea, atrocious in her grief, invokes a spectacular end upon herself (*Médée*, 1953; but written 1946; tr. L. Small, *Medea*, 1957), and poor spinster aunt Ardèle and her hunchback lover commit suicide out of desperate love in *Ardèle* (1948; tr. L. Hill, 1951). Only in *Léocadia* (1940; tr. P. Moyes, *Time Remembered*, 1954) or *Le voyageur sans bagage* or *L'invitation au château* is this fierce logic deflected. In the first, a simple shop-girl coaxes the distraught prince back to happiness; in the second, the dilemma of the amnesic soldier is resolved by the purest piece of escapism, accompanied by gay music; in the last, love survives imposture and humiliation in a fairy-tale ending. With *Ardèle*, Anouilh leaves the obsessional world of many of his early plays: the degrading poverty of *La sauvage*; the murderous sacrificial rite of *L'hermine*; the gross moral corruption of *Jézabel*; nature's obscene caricature of sex which mocks the purity of the lovers in *Ardèle* itself. Thereafter, the elements of play and pure theatricalism become stronger: the plays breathe a more urbane disenchantment. Both feeling and effects are coarsened and there is a tendency, especially noticeable in the treatment of larger subjects, to exploit a conscious vulgarity. In spite of brilliant incidentals, this is true of Anouilh's equivocal treatment of Archbishop Becket in *Becket ou l'honneur de Dieu* (1959; tr. L. Hill, *Becket or the Honour of God*, 1961), as it is of his savage assault on ideological fanaticism in *Pauvre Bitos ou le dîner de têtes* (1956; tr. L. Hill, *Poor Bitos*, 1964), a play full of cheap though striking effects. A wounded idealism still lurks below the surface of burlesque in *La valse des toréadors* (1952; tr. L. Hill, *The Waltz of the Toreadors*, 1956), where the lecherous General Saint-Pé strives to escape from loneliness and the sense of mortality amid a welter of farcical coincidence. But here, as in the clash of cynicism and innocence in *La répétition ou l'amour puni* (1950; tr. P. Hansford-Johnson and K. Black, *The Rehearsal*, 1960) or the slapstick treatment of a Don Juan in *Ornifle ou le courant d'air* (1955) or the melodramatic farrago about a class-conscious mother anxious to make her bastard son a priest in *La grotte* (1961), his talent is too self-indulgent, reflecting mere facility. *L'alouette* (1953; tr. C. Fry, *The Lark*, 1955), a tender and often lyrical treatment of the story of Joan of Arc, with some finely controlled ironies, stands out in his production since 1947. But in his self-conscious handling of all theatrical conventions, his inventiveness, sure command of racy and poetic dialogue, gay sense of fantasy and inexhaustible comic verve, he remains a supreme entertainer. He has written dialogue and scenarios for a number of films, notably *Monsieur Vincent* (1947) and *Deux sous de violettes* (1951). He has also translated and adapted Oscar Wilde's *The Importance of Being Earnest* and three comedies of Shakespeare: *As You Like It*, *The Winter's Tale* and *Twelfth Night* (1952). [SBJ]

*Pièces noires* (1945); *Nouvelles pièces noires* (1947); *Pièces brillantes* (1951); *Pièces grinçantes* (1956); *Pièces costumées* (1960); *Pièces roses* (1961).

R. de Luppé, *J.A.* (Paris, 1959); L. C. Pronko, *The World of J.A.* (1961); J. Harvey, *A. A Study in Theatrics* (1964); C. Borgal, *A. la peine de vivre* (Paris, 1966); Guicharnaud, *MFT*; Grossvogel, *TCFD*.

**An-ski,** originally Solomon Samuel Rappaport (Vitebsk 1863–Warsaw 1920). Yiddish author and dramatist. As a social revolutionary became a member of the *Bund*, the Jewish Socialist movement in Poland, and wrote its hymn ('The Oath'). He lived in France and Switzerland, but returned to Russia in 1905. He is best remembered for his play *The Dybbuk* (Odessa, 1916; tr. H. G. Alsberg and W. Katzin, 1917), first performed by the Habima Theatre in Russia in 1920. [EE]

*Gesamelte Shriften* (15 vols., Warsaw, 1925); *Ashmodai* (1904) (poems).
Waxman, *HJL*; Roback, *SYL*.

**Antokol'sky, Pavel** (St Petersburg 1896– ). Russian poet. The son of a lawyer, he went to grammar-school and university in pre-Revolutionary Moscow. His interest in the theatre (reflected in much of his later poetry) led him to join the Vakhtangov company as an actor and (after the Revolution) as producer. His work began to be printed in 1918; in the twenties he travelled abroad with his company, and in 1934 he left the theatre to devote himself to writing. His work shows a deep feeling for the classics of Russian literature (as in his poems on Pushkin and Gogol') and a strong sense of community with the Western European cultural heritage; he has made translations from French poets. The loss of his son in the war inspired a long poem of lament, his most famous single work, *Syn* (1946). As an editor and critic he has encouraged and inspired the new generation of poets.

His verse has links with ⇨ Acmeism; it is notable for its verbal precision, emotional restraint and powerfully analytical thought-content. [RM-G]

*Izbrannyye proizvedeniya* (2 vols., 1961); Gulland, *SRV*; Obolensky, *PBRV*.

**Anzengruber, Ludwig** (Vienna 1839–Vienna 1889). Austrian dramatist and novelist. Though he wrote numerous short stories and two novels (including *Der Sternsteinhof*, 1884, a character study of a peasant girl who, driven on by ambition, rises to be a rich farmer's wife), his reputation is founded principally on his dramatic works. After some years as an actor in the 1860s, he began to write for the popular Viennese stage, and, following the example of Friedrich Kaiser, a contemporary of ⇨ Nestroy, his aim as a dramatist was an educative one: in his plays, from *Der Pfarrer von Kirchfeld* (1870) onwards, he sought to communicate his ideals of tolerance and liberal 'humanity'. In an attempt to counteract the frivolity of the Vienna of his time, he set his dialect comedies such as *Die Kreuzelschreiber* (1872) and tragedies such as *Der Meineidbauer* (1871) in simple country circles, but he wrote also of Vienna, most notably in *Das vierte Gebot* (1877), a tragedy which was warmly greeted by the Naturalists in Berlin. As a playwright in the popular tradition, Anzengruber was not an innovator, though he alluded boldly to topical issues; and in competition with the operettas of Johann Strauss his plays enjoyed only limited success in the theatre and failed to effect a renascence of popular drama in Vienna. [WEY]

*Sämtliche Werke*, ed. R. Latzke, intr. O. Rommel (1920–2).
A. H. J. Knight in *German Studies Presented to W. H. Bruford* (1962).

**Apollinaire, Guillaume** (Wilhelm de Kostrowitzky) (Rome 1880–Paris 1918). French prose writer, art critic and poet. One of the most influential poets of the early 20th century. Although by instinct he was an elegiac poet, he had also a more forceful side to his personality which simple lyricism left unsatisfied. *Alcools* (1913) shows how he steadily widened his range from the near-Symbolist poems of 1899 to the modernist exercises of 1912. His modernism attempts to embrace all the dynamic forces of the new century: the urgent rhythms of modern transport and communications, the irony and iconoclasm of innovators like ⇨ Jarry, and the experiments in structure of the Cubist painters. The resulting poetry is 'modern' in combining a more complex personality with a more elliptical fragmented form. Abrupt juxtaposition, constant switches in tone and imagery, allow him to swing between his conflicting impulses with striking poignancy and immediacy.

By 1913 he was the impressario of the *avant-garde*. His enthusiastic campaign for Cubism and many other activities gave him wide notoriety. Confidently he plunged into more dubious typographical experiment with his *calligrammes* or word-pictures. During the war, at the front, he carried on experiment side by side with more traditional, and very vigorous, war and love poems, many of them included in *Calligrammes* (1918). He was badly wounded in the head in 1916. During his convalescence he produced his 'surrealist' play *Les mamelles de Tirésias*, and followed this with the manifesto of modernism, *L'esprit nouveau et les poètes*. He died in a flu epidemic in 1918, but his work opened up innumerable avenues for succeeding poets. Today, if some of his more hectic experiments have lost their interest the haunting sadness of many short poems and the exalted lyricism of two or three ambitious long poems have survived undiminished. [IL]

*Œuvres poétiques*, ed. M. Adéma and M. Décaudin (Pléiade, 1956); *Œuvres complètes*, ed. M. Décaudin (4 vols., 1966); *Selected Poems*, tr. O. Barnard (PMEP, 1965); Hackett, *AMFP*.
M. Davies, *A.* (1964); M.-J. Durry, *G.A.*, *Alcools* (3 vols., Paris, 1956–65); S. Bates, *G.A.* (1967); Raymond, *DBS*; Shattuck, *BY*.

**'Apolonio, Libro de.'** Mid-13th-century Spanish poem on the story of Apollonius (cf. Shakespeare's *Pericles*). The language contains many Aragonese features, though these may derive from copyists. The anonymous author appears to have based himself on a prose Latin version of this popular story, or on a French or Provençal version now lost. [JMC]

Ed. C. C. Marden (Baltimore, 1917–22); BAE 57; tr. Pablo Cabañas (Valencia, 1955).

**Áprily, Lajos** (Budapest 1887–1967). Hungarian poet. Principal of a girls' secondary school. His main inspiration was the natural beauty of his native Transylvania (*Nostalgia* and *Hegytetőn* (*On the Summit*); tr. W. Kirkconnell in *The Magyar Muse*, Winnipeg, 1933). He translated numerous works into Hungarian, most outstanding being his version of Pushkin's *Eugene Onegin*. [JFR]

**Aquinas, St Thomas** (Castle Roccasecca, Aquino *c.*1225–Fossa Nuova 1274). The greatest medieval philosopher. Of a noble Ghibelline family, he was educated at Monte Cassino, at the University of Naples, where he was attracted to the Dominicans, at Cologne (under ⇨ Albertus Magnus) and at Paris; he lectured in Paris, Rome, Bologna, Naples. He died on his way to the Council of Lyons (poisoned, according to Dante, *Purgatorio*, xx). The 'Angelic Doctor' was canonized in 1323.

His *Summa theologica* reconciles the truths of reason and of faith, i.e. of Aristotelian philosophy and Christian theology. The same dogmatic inspiration appears in his verse and other prose works. His five poems on the one theme of the Eucharist are of the highest rank, both as concise theology and majestic poetry. Four were commissioned by Pope Urban IV for use at the feast of Corpus Christi, which he instituted in 1264. The longest, the ⇨ sequence 'Lauda Sion', sets out the doctrine of transubstantiation in exact terms. 'Pange lingua' is a Vesper hymn. 'Verbum supernum' a hymn for Lauds almost Franciscan in spirit. [FB]

Ed. S. E. Fretté (34 vols., Paris, 1871–80); 'Leonine' edn (Rome, 1882–1903); *Summa Theologica*, tr. English Dominicans (20 vols., 1911–25); *Selected Writings*, ed. M. C. D'Arcy (Everyman, 1939, etc.); *The English Hymnal* (1906; 2nd edn, 1933) (4 hymns).
M. C. D'Arcy, *T.A.* (1930); F. C. Copleston, *A.* (1955); É. Gilson, *The Christian Philosophy of St T.A.* (1956); Raby, *CLP*; Taylor, *MM*.

**Aquino, Rinaldo d'** (13th cent.). Italian poet. One of the group of poets described as the Sicilian school whose ideal centre was the court of the Emperor Frederick II. Only a few poems are attributed to him and none of the attempts made to identify him is conclusive. Writing in the general courtly love tradition derived from Provence, he shows freshness and vigour, particularly in the famous lament of the lady whose lover is departing on a Crusade. [DGR]

Salinari, *PLD*; Contini, *PD*; Panvini, *RSS*; C. Guerrieri-Crocetti, *La Magna Curia* (Milan, 1947); Rossetti, *DC*; Kay, *PBIV*; Lind, *LPIR*.

**Aragon, Louis** (Paris 1897– ). French poet, novelist and journalist. He founded with ⇨ Breton the review *Littérature* (1919) which launched the surrealistic idea of 'automatic writing' and 'the passionate and unruly use of stupifying images' which was soon illustrated in his first poetry: *Feu de joie* (1920), *Le mouvement perpétuel* (1925) and *La grande gaîté* (1929). An early novel, *Le paysan de Paris* (1926), carried this poetic revolt into prose, suggesting through daring fantasy the everyday marvels of the city. The essays in *Le traité du style* (1928) explain the iconoclastic frame of mind of the young post-war generation. In 1930 he visited Russia and was bowled over by what he saw of reconstruction under the Soviet government – thereafter he abandoned his literary dilettantism for a life devoted to social realism and journalism. He directed the communist daily *Ce Soir* (1935–9), helping to disseminate Russian literature in France; was active in the literary circles of Madrid during the Spanish war; and fought until 1939 for the 'popular front'. He became one of the organizers of the literary resistance to Vichy, and had a hand in several clandestine news-sheets. Since the war he has edited the left-wing *Les lettres françaises*.

His poetry after 1930 returned to traditional lyrical patterns, grouped around three themes: communism (*Hourra l'Oural*, 1934), patriotism, especially during the war (*Le crève-cœur*, 1941, *La Diane française*, 1945), and his love for his lifelong companion, the writer Elsa Triolet (*Les yeux d'Elsa*, 1942; *Elsa*, 1959). He has also written a poetic autobiography, *Le roman inachevé* (1956), and *Les poètes* (1961), a pseudo-dramatic fantasy on the position and inspiration of the poet. A series of serious novels, under the general title *Le monde réel*, describes the demands of the proletariat and the slow inner erosion of the European bourgeoisie: *Les cloches de Bâle* (1933; tr. H. Chevalier, *The Bells of Basel*, 1937), *Les beaux quartiers* (1936), *Les voyageurs de l'impériale* (1942; tr. H. Chevalier, *Passengers of Destiny*, 1961), which includes the story of his youth, *Aurélien* (1945; tr. E. Wilkins, 1946) and *Les communistes* (6 vols., 1949–51). His most successful novel, *La semaine sainte* (1958), attempts to depict the world of 1815 through marxist eyes. His collection of essays and articles is important: *La lumière de Stendhal* (1954) views several classical authors through social realism, and *Littératures soviétiques* (1955) is an enthusiastic account of his discovery of ⇨ Gor'ky, ⇨ Mayakovsky and the contemporary trends in Russia. It is probably his own powers of lyrical expression rather than pseudo-automatic writing that gilded his surrealistic period: he destroyed 'style' through a style of his own. But these qualities disappear after his 'conversion': the later poetry, though powerful, occasionally rousing and full of genuine feeling, is solid rather than great – his 'realism', whether in epic or elegiac poetry, is not altogether free from bad taste. His novels blend personal experience and political inclination more convincingly, through classical qualities of narration and a gift for revealing details. Recurrent characters and a wide horizon give his books significance as documents on modern Europe. [CLC]

*Poésies* (1960) (anthology); *A Poet of Resurgent France*, ed. H. Josephson and M. Cowley (1946) (translated selection).

A. Gavillet, *A. surréaliste* (Neuchâtel, 1958); R. Garaudy, *L'itinéraire d'A.* (Paris, 1961).

**Arany, János** (Nagyszlonta 1817–Budapest 1882). Hungarian poet. Born into a poor Calvinist peasant family, he was educated in Debrecen and became a teacher, later a notary in his native town. After serving in the War of Independence (1848–9), he became Hungarian and Classics master at a Calvinist secondary school and was later appointed permanent secretary of the Hungarian Academy of Sciences. As a poet, he was an outstanding master of the Hungarian language, his work being praised by ⇨ Petőfi in 'To János Arany'. The focal-point of his art is Hungarianism; he was the most characteristically Hungarian poet. His poetic genius is perhaps best represented by his epics, though his fretting, melancholy temperament also enabled him to create powerful ballads in which he achieves an effect of mysteriousness with an impressionistic and suggestive style. His first major epic, *Az elveszett alkotmány* (1845), is an ironic satire of the political dealings of the aristocracy. His competition-winning epic masterpiece, *Toldi* (1846), is a narrative of the heroic adventures of a peasant lad at the 14th-century royal court at Buda; it is concerned with the problem of the progress of the peasantry. He later wrote two continuations of *Toldi*, the humorous *Toldi estéje* (1848; tr. W. N. Loew, *Toldi's Eve*, N.Y., 1914) and the romantic epic *Toldi szerelme*. Toldi's basic characteristic, a sudden temper which repeatedly results in murder, is symbolic of the tragedy of Magyardom. This theme reappears in his narrative *Buda halála* (1863; tr. W. Kirkconnell, *The Death of King Buda*, Cleveland, Ohio, 1936), an analytical verse-novel in which the feud of Attila and his brother Buda turns the conquering might of the Huns to internal strife. His best-known ballads are *A welszi bárdok* (tr. W. Kirkconnell, *The Bards of Wales*, in *Hungarian Poetry*, Sydney, 1955), the story of Edward I's visit to conquered Wales, which is allegorical of 19th-century Hungary under Hapsburg rule; *László V*; *Ágnes Asszony*; *Tengeri Hántás*; *Hídavatás*. Humorous narrative poems are *Családi kör* and *Bolond Istók*, which is autobiographical. His lyric poems describe bitter memories and reflections; *Autumn Bouquet* is considered to be one of the finest collections of Hungarian lyric poems; it includes 'Letészem a Lantot' and 'Epilógus'. Arany was also significant as a translator of Shakespeare, Goethe and Gogol', and as editor of the periodicals *Szépirodalmi Figyelő* and *Koszorú*. [JFR]

Reményi, *HWL*; Klaniczay, *HHL*.

**Arator** (fl. 540). Roman poet and a lawyer. He wrote an epic on the Acts of the Apostles, making St Peter and St Paul his twin heroes. He gave public readings of his epic at Rome, where it achieved great popularity. One reading was interrupted so many times by applause and by encores that it occupied four days. [FB]

Migne, *PL*, 64.
G. L. Perugi, *A.* (Venice, 1909).

**Arbuzov, Aleksey Nikolayevich** (Moscow 1908– ). Russian playwright. Experienced as actor and producer, he was first successful with *Tanya* (1938). Most of his 16 plays are lyrical in tone, easy in tempo, and often cover the fortunes of hero or heroine over a period of years to show formation of character. His bold handling of technically awkward forms such as the choir and the flashback is seen at its most professional in *Irkutskaya Istoriya* (1959; ed. S. Roberts, 1963). The charm of his work lies in his shrewd but affectionate attitude to his fellow-man; he sees through human foibles to the basic desire to lead a good and useful life, and creates plausible, even likeable, 'positive' characters. Popular in Poland, Czechoslovakia and Bulgaria, his works have been staged in W. Europe, Asia and S. America, and widely translated. [AP]

*Teatr* (1961); *Moy bednyy Marat*, in *Teatr*, 1, 1965 (tr. A. Nicolaeff, *The Promise*, Oxford, 1966); *Three Soviet Plays* (Moscow, 1962).
E. N. Zhilina, *A.N.A.*, *Ukazatel' Literatury*, ed. N. Ya. Morachevsky (Leningrad, 1958); V. A. Mamontov, *Dramaturgiya A.N.A.* (Moscow, 1965).

**Archpoet, The** (*c.* 1130–*c.* 1165). German secular Latin poet. His real name is unknown. He attached himself to Rainald of Dassel, Archbishop of Cologne and Archchancellor to the Emperor Frederick Barbarossa. His themes are simple – women, wine, a lighthearted 'confession', homage to Barbarossa, and begging for alms – but his technical skill is amazing. His 'Aestuans intrinsecus via vehementi' is probably the most famous of all secular poems in medieval Latin and certainly one of the most brilliant. Its metre – 4 trochaic lines of 7 plus 6 syllables each, in monorhyme – is commonly called the Goliardic quatrain, though there is no evidence that the disreputable clerics called Goliards wrote any verse at all. [FB]

*Die Gedichte*, ed. K. Manitius (Munich, 1913); ed. H. Watenphul, H. Krefeld (Heidelberg, 1958); K. Langosch, *Hymen und Vagantenlieder* (Basel, 1954) (texts with German tr.).
Raby, *SLP*.

**Arcipreste de Hita.** ⇨ Ruíz, Juan.

**Arcipreste de Talavera.** ⇨ Martínez de Toledo.

**Aretino, Leonardo.** ⇨ Bruni, Leonardo.

**Aretino, Pietro** (Arezzo 1492–Venice 1556). Italian writer. A prolific literary swashbuckler, his impudence and wit won him rapid favour in the Rome of Leo X. He fled on the election of Adrian VI and attached himself to Giovanni dalle Bande Nere, the famous condottiero. In the latter part of his life he established himself in security at Venice, dispensing flattery or execration as the need arose, and numbering among his friends and acquaintances many of the best-known figures of his time. His venomous and venal pen was commissioned or propitiated by many. 'Scourge of princes' and 'secretary of the world' were two of the titles he affected.

His *Letters* were published in 6 books between 1537 and 1557. Their range extends from rare moving expressions of private grief to the most portentous of public utterances, and they are a valuable commentary on the 16th-century scene. The bawdy and scurrilous *Ragionamenti* (1534–6) anatomize the life of the courtesan and plunge zestfully into the murkier depths of society. He displays the same raciness in his 5 earthy comedies, *La cortigiana* (1534), *Il marescalco* (1533), *La talanta* (1542), *L'ipocrito* (1542), *Il filosofo* (1546), which, although lacking real artistic coherence, are enlivened by an acute power of observation and an uninhibitedly spicy use of language. His tragedy *Orazia* (1546) is less successful, as are his various religious writings.

Lacking the integrity and seriousness of the dedicated artist, he nevertheless infuses a compelling vigour into his prose and is the most formidable representative of the 'anti-literary' elements in the *cinquecento*. [DGR]

*Le lettere*, ed. F. Nicolini (2 bks, 1913–16); ed. F. Flora (1960); *Ragionamenti*, ed. A. Foschini

(1960); *Teatro*, ed. N. Macarrone (1914); *Prose sacre*, ed. E. Allodoli (1914); *Scritti scelti di P.A. e di A.F. Doni*, ed. G. G. Ferrero (1951); *Lettere sull'arte*, ed. E. Camesasca (3 vols., 1957–60); *Poesie*, ed. G. Sborselli (2 vols., 1930–34); *The Works of A.*, tr. S. Putnam (N.Y., 1933) (selection); Lind, *LPIR*.
E. Hutton, *P.A. The Scourge of Princes* (1922); G. Petrocchi, *P.A.* (Milan, 1948); A. Del Vita, *L'A.* (Arezzo, 1954); *Minori*, ii.

**Argensola, Bartolomé Leonardo de** (Barbastro 1561–Saragossa 1631). Spanish poet and historian. Chaplain to the Empress María; accompanied the Count of Lemos to Naples; succeeded his brother Lupercio ⇨ Argensola as chronicler royal of Aragon in 1615. His poetry is Classical and he was acclaimed as an ally by ⇨ Góngora's enemies, but took little part in the controversies. His religious odes (deriving from those of Luis de ⇨ León) have a Miltonic flavour, e.g. battles in heaven in 'A San Miguel'. He also commands a light, satirical style as when he warns his brother against palmistry, or a pleasing realism as in the description of a country banquet; but in his religious sonnets, he reveals an existentialist malaise. Less consistently Horatian than his brother, he is a better poet. [JMC]

*Rimas*, ed. J. M. Blecua (Saragossa, 1950–1); Blecua, *FLE*; Cohen, *PBSV*; Trend, *OBSV*.

**Argensola, Lupercio Leonardo de** (Barbastro 1559–Naples 1613). Spanish poet and historian. Secretary to the Empress María and to the Count of Lemos, whom he accompanied to Naples, and chronicler royal of Aragon from 1599. He took part in the campaign against ⇨ Góngora, and wrote a memorial to Philip II, advocating the suppression of the popular theatre on moral grounds. He had himself written 3 Senecan plays. He translated and imitated Horace, and modelled his austere style on that of Luis de ⇨ León. His poem on the martyrdom of St Lawrence has some of the fervour of Crashaw, but he is better at lighter themes, e.g. the fountains in the gardens of Aranjuez. He and his brother (. . . 'come to reform the Castilian tongue', said ⇨ Lope) stand for a Malherbe-like sobriety, soon swept aside by ⇨ *culteranismo*. [JMC]

*Rimas*, ed. J. M. Blecua (Saragossa, 1950–1); Blecua, *FLE*; Cohen, *PBSV*; Trend, *OBSV*.
O. H. Green, *The Life and Works of L.L. de A.* (Philadelphia, 1927).

**Arghezi, Tudor** (Bucharest 1880–Bucharest 1967). Rumanian poet and prose-writer. He made his literary début in 1896, with verses submitted to *Liga Ortodoxă*, signed 'Ion Theo', a contracted form of his real name Ion N. Theodorescu. ⇨ Macedonski, the father of Rumanian symbolism, hailed him for his audacity in breaking with the banal imagery and conventional versification of his time. Thereafter his career followed a tortuous path. In 1899 he became a monk, re-entering the literary scene in 1904 by collaborating with his friend V. Demetrius on a new review *Linia Dreaptă*. Towards the end of 1904 he left the country to journey around Switzerland and France as a commercial traveller. On his return in 1910 he contributed to the socialist review *Viața Socială*. His violent diatribes and the pacifist opinions he consistently maintained in his own review *Cronica* earned him many enemies. After the war he was imprisoned for collaborating on the pro-German occupation newspaper *Gazeta Bucurestilor*. On his release he continued his dual career of journalist and poet, his polemics – of a rare verve and pungency – gradually giving way to a more intensive poetic output. But it was not until the appearance of his first volume of collected poems *Cuvinte Potrivite* (1927) that his name came to the notice of the Rumanian literary public at large. Arghezi, who till then had been largely disregarded by serious critics, found himself the centre of controversy, his verbal immoderacy and ruthless materialization of imagery bringing charges of facility and obscurity. Concise, sensorial, richly metaphorical, Arghezi's poetry reflects vigorously, often dramatically, sometimes with surprising suavity, a strong sense of ancestral continuity and identification with the peasant and the soil, the torment of a soul in search of the absolute, apocalyptic visions of a putrescent world.

In 1930 Arghezi published the novels *Icoane de lemn* and *Poarta neagră*, based respectively on reminiscences of his monastic and prison experiences. The volume of poems *Flori de mucegai* (1930) was also the product of his imprisonment. In this work he broke entirely fresh ground in Rumanian literature, depicting with rare sympathy the depraved elements of the prison underworld. This lyrical approach to the seamier side of life, which together with his pamphlets *Bilete de Papagal* brought grave charges of obscenity, has been compared to similar currents found in the work of

Salvatore di Giacomo and García Lorca. *Tablete din Ţara de Kuty* (1933), a satirical novel of Swiftian dimensions, was followed by other novels: *Ochii Maicii Domnului* (1934), *Cimitirul Buna-Vestire* (1936) and *Lina* (1942), as well as by further collections of poetry: *Cărticică de seară* (1935) and *Hore* (1939). He reveals here yet another direction to his poetry by affirming the value of family life and reflecting the vision of a Pantheist in his childlike obsession with the wonders of creation. It is a microscopic world, where his touch is that of a miniaturist.

Immediately after the war he continued to publish, winning the National Poetry Prize for the first time in 1947; but his period of silence (1947–54) bears witness to his uncertainty and misgivings, which were resolved with the publication of two cycles of poetry, *1907* (1955) and *Cîntare omului* (1956). Since then he has published extensively, and his position as national poet, second only to ⇨ Eminescu, is at present unchallenged. Through an excellent series of translations his poetry has won wide recognition throughout Western Europe. He has been translated into French by André Marcel, into German by Alfred M. Sperber, into Italian by Salvatore Quasimodo, into Spanish by Rafael Alberti. [MI]

**Arguijo, Juan de** (Seville 1567–Seville 1623). Spanish poet and patron. He planned 100 and wrote 61 sonnets on classical themes. His use of mythology and of stereotyped images is akin to that of ⇨ Góngora, but basically he continues the manner of ⇨ Herrera. Many sonnets are formally beautiful, but contain little feeling. His collection of anecdotes is occasionally amusing. [JMC]

BAE 32; Blecua, *FLE*; *Cruz y Raya*, 36 (Madrid, 1936); Trend, *OBSV*; Cohen, *PBSV*.

**Ariosto, Ludovico** (Reggio Emilia 1474–Ferrara 1533). Italian poet. Son of an official of the Ferrarese court, he first studied law, but later acquired a sound humanistic education. His adult life was spent in the service of the Ferrarese ducal family, particularly Cardinal Ippolito d'Este (1503–17) and his brother, Duke Alfonso (1518–33); he was governor of an outlying Ferrarese possession, the Garfagnana, 1522–5. Essentially a writer, his lifetime's service as a courtier was a burden imposed on him by economic difficulties.

His fame rests on one lengthy work, *Orlando furioso* (tr. A. Gilbert, 1954), a poem in *ottava rima*, and one of the greatest works of the Italian Renaissance. The main characters, Orlando (= Roland), Charlemagne, etc., come from the French *chansons de geste*, but the epic, heroic theme is, in Ariosto, largely subordinate to the twin themes of love and adventure – themes which are more reminiscent of the Arthurian than of the Carolingian legends. In using this material, he was not only following the taste of the time, but also the specific literary example of ⇨ Boiardo, whose *Orlando innamorato* had attempted to give this popular material the dignity of literary form. Indeed, Ariosto's poem actually continues the *Orlando innamorato*, broken off in 1494 by the French invasion of Italy and Boiardo's death.

In the *Orlando furioso* there are three main stories: the love of Orlando for Angelica; the war between the Franks and the Saracens, culminating in an assault on Paris; and the love of Ruggiero, a Saracen, for Bradamante, a Christian. These stories are interwoven with a host of minor episodes, concerned in the main with love, but also with other emotions proper to chivalry, such as friendship, devotion to one's master, heroism in battle. This kaleidoscope of scenes and emotions, of fact and fantasy, is unified by the personality of the author, serene but humorous, emotional but balanced. The episodes of magic and fantasy fill the reader with lighthearted amusement, the adventures of the knights and lovers with admiration or pathos; while the endless variety of the poem's pattern, together with the continual presence of the author, remind the reader of the finite nature of humanity, and the wisdom of moderation. Despite its fairytale elements, the *Furioso* is a work of elegant sophistication, and a fitting monument to the court society of the Italian Renaissance, which gave it birth.

The poem was probably begun about 1503. It was first published in 1516. A second, emended edition appeared in 1521, and a third, definitive edition, with substantial additions, in 1532.

The most important of Ariosto's minor works are 5 comedies, written for production in the Ferrarese court. He also wrote 7 *Satire*, in Italian, and other poems in

Italian and Latin. But in none of these works did he achieve the same standard as the *Furioso*. [CF]

E. G. Gardner, *The King of Court Poets* (1906); A. Momigliano, *Saggio su l'"Orlando Furioso'* (4th edn, Bari, 1952).

**Arjona y de Cubas, Manuel María de** (Osuna 1771–Madrid 1820). Spanish poet and canon of Seville cathedral. Once famous for a neo-Classical poem on the ruins of Rome (1808), and still remembered for the lyric 'La diosa del bosque', his ode 'A la memoria', two translations of Horace, the ⇨ *romance* 'Al pensamiento del hombre', and (unjustifiably) as a forerunner of Romanticism. [JMC]

BAE 63.

**Arland, Marcel** (Varennes 1899– ). French writer and critic. His early career was as a teacher. His prose fiction includes *Antarès* (1932), *La vigie* (1935) and *L'ordre* (1929), a study of timidity and pride (Prix Goncourt). Influenced by Gide and Mauriac, he is a fastidious and allusive writer who explores the inner life. An experienced editor, he shares, with J. ⇨ Paulhan, the direction of *La Nouvelle Revue Française*. He has published collections of critical articles and essays (*Essais critiques*, 1931; *Nouvelles lettres de France*, 1954; *La grâce d'écrire*, 1955), as well as the extended study *Marivaux* (1950), etc. His breadth of interest emerges in his *Anthologie de la poésie française* (1941), and the *Chronique de la peinture moderne* (1949). [CAHR]

J. Duvignaud, *A.* (Paris, 1962); A. Eustis, *M. A., Benjamin Crémieux, Ramon Fernandez. Trois critiques de la Nouvelle Revue Française* (Paris, 1962); *Critique*, XVII, 167, 1961.

**Arnaut Daniel** (b. Ribérac; fl. *c.*1200). Provençal ⇨ troubadour. Of noble birth, he was renowned for his skilled and elegant love songs, written between 1180 and 1210; he reputedly sang at the court of Richard Cœur de Lion and was a friend of ⇨ Bertran de Born. There survive 18 poems, including the famous sestina, 'Lo ferm voler qu'el cor m'intra', and an obscene jest 'Puois en Raimons'. In his love songs he accepts the submissive role of loyal lover to his unattainable lady; his bare and finely chiselled style was unequalled by any other troubadour. In 'En cest sonet coind' e leri' he describes how he composes on a gracious air and planes and pares his words. He is a master of the *trobar ric* with rich, unusual rhymes, complex versification and words chosen adroitly for sound and meaning.

Dante (*De vulgari eloquentia*, II: 2 and 6) praises the construction of his poems and quotes him as the model of those who have sung of love in the vernacular. In the same work (II: 10 and 13) Dante admits that he imitated Arnaut when he wrote the sestina 'Al poco giorno'. In *Purgatorio*, xxvi, the shade of ⇨ Guinizelli calls him 'miglior fabbro del parlar materno' and Arnaut's spirit replies in eight lines of Provençal poetry composed by Dante, with an allusion in the third line to one of Arnaut's own poems. Petrarch was also indebted to Arnaut and describes him in the *Trionfi* as the first among the poets of love who wrote in foreign tongues:

> Fra tutti il primo Arnaldo Daniello
> Gran maestro d'Amor. ...

Dante states (*Purgatorio*, xxvi) that Arnaut wrote prose romances. Luigi Pulci (1432–84) claims (*Morgante maggiore*, xxv, 115, 168–9; xxvii, 79–80) that an Arnaut wrote the story of Renaud's adventures in Egypt and at Roncesvalles. Tasso (*Discorsi sul poema eroico*, chap. 46, *Commentarii*, Crescimbeni, II, i, p. 25) names him as the author of a *Lancelot* in prose. [LTT]

Ed. G. Toja (Florence, 1960); ed. and Fr. tr. R. Lavaud (Toulouse, 1910).
*Speculum*, XXVII, 1952; *Filologia romanza*, VI, 1959.

**Arnér, Sivar** (Arby 1909– ). Swedish novelist, story-writer and dramatist. He belongs to the radical generation of the Swedish forties and originally shared its pessimistic outlook. Although he has talent for realistic description, it is almost invariably checked by a metaphysical concern, which makes him seek a place for the individual self in relation to other selves and to society at large, and which at times gives to his stories a quality of mystical impersonality. Complex (often inflexible) psychological constellations have always held a particular fascination for him. The majority of his novels, stories and plays are studies of marital relations, e.g. *Egil* (1948), which describes one day in the life of a schoolmaster, outwardly uneventful but filled with introspective life and retrospective episodes, prompted by the nagging question: why did my marriage fail?

*Han – hon – ingen* (1951) movingly exhibits the incompatibility of self-regarding individualism with the exigencies of mature love: only after the woman is dead does full affirmation of love become possible for the surviving partner. *Säkert till sommaren* (1954) is a collection of stories that shows his analytical mastery in a more limited form.

Since the early fifties he has taken a keen interest in political and social questions; like ⇨ Vennberg he supported a policy of non-commitment in the East–West struggle and challenged the nuclear thinking of the Great Powers. He also endeavoured to frame these convictions in allegorical form in *Fyra som var bröder* (1955), which reads like a corrective to his earlier individualism. Arnér's works for broadcasting, e.g. *Fem hörspel* (1959) and *Dag och natt* (1960), has invigorated the whole genre of radio drama in Sweden. Here his analytical acumen combines with imaginative handling of the medium: at its best it serves to convey an atmosphere of both introspection and intense relatedness. His return to the novel in recent years has been accompanied by a more relaxed manner and a more positive outlook, also by an increased interest in contemporary society and the problems of adaptation that it entails. This widening of scope has not resulted in any appreciable loss of psychological penetration, as witness *Nätet* (1962) and *Tvärbalk* (1963), yet another study of a personal relationship elaborating the theme of salvation through loving submission even at the cost of opting out of the security offered by social conformism. Of his most recent work, *ett ett ett* (1964), further documents Arnér's social orientation, while *Verkligen* (1965) is a return to the earlier intensely analytical method. Together these four novels give remarkable insights into a modern welfare society and its (not too well adjusted) members. [SAB]

*Bonniers Litterära Magasin*, 9, 1961; 5, 1959.

**Arnim, Bettina von** (Frankfurt/M. 1785–Berlin 1859). German letter-writer and essayist. The sister of ⇨ Brentano, she married Ludwig Achim von ⇨ Arnim in 1811; her lively fantasy, charm, and feeling for nature and poetry made her a centre of attraction in Romantic literary circles. Her claim to immortality rests on *Briefwechsel Goethes mit einem Kinde* (1835), built on a few meetings with Goethe and a handful of letters that she had exchanged with him, in which she portrayed her hero as the Romantics had first seen him and as he himself, in the years of his maturity, wished to be seen – as a liberator of the poetic spirit. The intensity – some might say eccentricity – of feeling which she lavished on Goethe's words she also brought to bear on the letters of a childhood friend who had become a nun (*Die Günderode*, 1840) and of those of her brother (*Clemens Brentanos Frühlingskranz*, 1844). Every word concealed an experience, every object a universal meaning. She was at one with nature in a rare serenity and harmony of spirit.

Her daughter Gisela married the essayist and short-story writer Hermann Grimm (1828–1901), son of the philologist and folklorist Wilhelm ⇨ Grimm. [RT]

G. Brandes, *Rahel, Bettina und Charlotte Stieglitz* (Berlin and Leipzig, 1896); I. Seidel, *B.* (Stuttgart, 1944); Wellek, *HMC*.

**Arnim, Ludwig (Jo-)Achim von** (Berlin 1781–Wiepersdorf 1831). German poet, dramatist and novelist. A founder of the so-called Heidelberg Romantic school. His fame, like that of his brother-in-law ⇨ Brentano, rests less on his original works than on the enthusiasms which he aroused in German Romantic writers in the early 19th century, chiefly for folk-song. The most famous collection of German folk-poetry, *Des Knaben Wunderhorn*, was published by Brentano and Arnim in 1805–8.

Arnim himself, Prussian, aristocratic, Christian, used his strain of Romantic irrationality for an openly declared moral purpose. His grandest conception was the unfinished novel *Die Kronenwächter* (1817), which, like the dramatic 'Studentenspiel' *Halle und Jerusalem* (1811; a contemporary formulation of Gryphius's *Cardenio und Celinde*) and the 2-volume novel *Armut, Reichtum, Schuld und Busse der Gräfin Dolores* (1810), exhibits a Baroque blend of flamboyant exuberance and anxious moralizing. [RT]

*Des Knaben Wunderhorn*, ed. W. A. Koch (1957). H. R. Liedke, *Literary Criticism and Romantic Theory in the Work of A. v. A.* (N.Y., 1937); Gundolf, *R*; Tymms, *GRL*.

**Arnulf of Louvain** (fl. 1240–8). A Cistercian, Abbot of Villers in Brabant, and reputed author of a long Latin poem, *De passione Domini*, a prayer addressed to various parts of the body of Christ. The last section of the poem, addressed to the face, was translated into German by P. ⇨ Gerhardt as the hymn 'O Haupt voll Blut und Wunden' (tr. Robert Bridges, 'O sacred head, sore wounded'). [FB]

Ed. G. M. Dreves and C. Blume, *Ein Jahrtausend lateinischer Hymnendichtung* (2 vols., Leipzig, 1909).
É. de Moreau, *L'abbaye de Villers en Brabant aux 12me et 13me siècles* (Brussels, 1909).

**Arolas, Juan** (Barcelona 1805–Valencia 1849). Spanish poet and priest. Of remarkable facility, he was said to scribble poems to order for lovers or blind beggars. His best poetry is amorous, and his favourite themes Moorish, in the manner of Hugo's *Orientales*; other poems treat the border wars. His religious poetry, much indebted to Lamartine, is poor. The inner contradiction led to his madness and death after long confinement in his cell. [JMC]

*Poesías*, ed. Jose R. Lomba y Pedroja (CC, 1928); Blecua, *FLE*.
J. H. Mundy, in *LSS*, I, 1940.

**Arp, Hans (Jean)** (Strasbourg 1887–Meudon 1966). German poet and sculptor. Living in Paris from 1926, he wrote poetry and stories in French and German. Closely connected with the Munich artists' circle 'Der blaue Reiter' (Marc, Kandinsky, Klee), he helped found ⇨ Dada. Though famous as the inventor of modern ageometric sculpture, his reputation and influence as a poet have been great, especially in the last decade. His poetry is contained in several selections – *wortträume und schwarze sterne* (1953), *auf einem bein* (1955), *Worte mit und ohne Anker* (1957) – and in the more recent collections *Mondsand* (1959), *Zweiklang* (1960), and *Sinnende Flammen* (1961). His collected poems (*Gesammelte Gedichte*) appeared in 1963–4. If Dada was essentially an experimental, abstract, anti-bourgeois form of art, Arp's own poetry is remarkable for its radical abstraction, its grotesque but brilliant verbal dexterity. It may be 'absurd' or 'nonsense' poetry; yet it is also – especially in his last poems – strikingly beautiful in its own eccentric way. [PB]

*Jours effeuillés* (Paris, 1967) (collected French writings); *Dreams and Projects* (New York, 1952); Bridgwater, *TCGV*; Hamburger and Middleton, *MGP*; Motherwell, *DPP*.
R. Döhl, *Das literarische Werk H.A.s, 1903–30* (1967); F. Usinger, *Die dichterische Welt H.A.s* (Mainz, 1965); *GQ*, XXXVI, 1963; *AGR*, XVI, 4, 1949/50.

**Arrabal, Fernando** (Melilla, Spain 1932– ). Novelist and playwright in French. Arrabal's is a theatre of graphic horror, rather like that of early ⇨ Adamov, but dominated by characters with the mentality of children. It is at once a personal statement and a symbolic image of much that has characterized European civilization in the past forty years. It springs from his own experience of civil war and dictatorship in Spain, with their accompaniment of terror, coercion, torture and betrayal, and revives and reorders that experience for us within the framework of a fantasy owing something to Goya and Kafka. The horror of his drama is that it conjures up a world peopled exclusively by victims and executioners, a world taken over by the sinister games of perverse children, where spontaneous tenderness gives way to gross brutality, as when Fando kills Lis in *Fando et Lis* (tr. B. Wright in *Four Plays*, 1962), or where betrayal leads to death, as when Bruno, forsaken by his fellow-prisoner Étienne, hangs himself with a lavatory chain in *Le labyrinthe* (1956). The fantasy – the squalid and prurient children's jokes, the Chaplinesque tramps – is a necessary mediation between ourselves and the brute facts: otherwise, they would be intolerable. In spite of their primitive violence, these plays are not artless. The juxtaposition of a military operation and the banalities of family life in *Pique-nique en campagne* (1959) or the use of two snivelling old men to damage the myth of the glorious dead in *Guernica* (1961) or the parody of the Passion and miracles of Christ in *Le cimetière des voitures* (tr. B. Wright, *The Car Cemetery*, in *Four Plays*, 1962) – all suggest a conscious derision of life. Ritual and erotic fantasy also mark *Le grand cérémonial* (1966). Arrabal has also written novels in a similar vein: *Baal Babylone* (1959); *L'enterrement de la sardine* (1961).

*Théâtre* (3 vols., 1958–65).
*Yale French Studies*, 29 (Spring-Summer 1962); Corvin, *TNF*; Serreau, *HNT*.

**Arrebo, Anders** (Ærøskøbing 1587–Vordingborg 1637). Danish poet. Court Chaplain, then Bishop of Trondhjem, he was defrocked for immoral behaviour, but later given a living at Vordingborg. He translated the Psalms into Danish, but his main work is *Hexaëmeron* (1630–7), a didactic poem in rhymed hexameters and alexandrines about the Creation, the most characteristic example of Danish Renaissance art poetry, though mainly an adaptation of ⇨ Du Bartas's poem *La semaine*. [ELB]

**Arriaza, Juan Bautista** (Madrid 1770–Madrid 1837). Spanish poet and diplomat (in London). An absolutist and a personal enemy of ⇨ Quintana. He translated (1807) Boileau's *Art poétique* (but was by no means a rigid neo-classicist) and published *Poesías patrióticas* (1810). Satirical, sentimental or sensual, but always facile, he achieved a certain popularity. The metrically skilful 'Terpsícore o las gracias del baile' is one of his best works.

BAE 67; Blecua, *FLE*.

**Artaud, Antonin** (Marseilles 1896–Paris 1948). French actor, producer and theorist of the stage. An important theoretician of *avant-garde* drama in a series of texts, notably *Le théâtre et son double* (1938; tr. M. C. Richards, *The Theatre and Its Double*, 1958). Artaud argued for a return to drama as a primitive rite concerned with elemental human needs and emotions; it must protest against the artificial values imposed by a rationalistic culture and throw into relief the implacable nature of the forces, internal and external, which confront man in life. Such a drama will repudiate the established conventions and forms of the modern theatre (with its reliance on texts, speech, plot, psychological analysis, and proscenium arch) in favour of 'purely irrational assemblages of sounds', 'unperverted pantomime' in which gestures symbolize ideas and effigies and bizarre objects signify cosmic forces hostile to man. The stage must surround the audience, implicating them in the action; hypnotizing them with sounds, lights, colours, rhythmic movement; submitting them to the maximum of theatricality and spectacle in order to undermine their assurance and revive a sense of the ineluctable and eternal forces latent in themselves and ranged outside them. Some of these views have had a powerful impact on the aesthetics of contemporary drama. [SBJ]

*Œuvres complètes* (7 vols., 1956ff.) (in progress); *A. Anthology* (in English), ed. J. Hirschman (San Francisco, 1965).

A. Bonneton, *Le naufrage prophétique d'A.A.* (Paris, 1961); *TLS*, 13 March 1965; J. Hort, *A.A.* (Geneva, 1960); Wellwarth, *TPP*.

**'Arte de Furtar.'** Portuguese political and moral satire in prose, published anonymously in Lisbon in 1652. For many years the authorship of this book, which has been attributed successively to many eminent Portuguese writers, has defied the most learned literary criticism. But in 1946, the Brazilian critic Afonso Pena Júnior produced massive evidence to show that António de Sousa de Macedo is the author of the *Arte de Furtar*. Macedo, who was appointed Portuguese Ambassador in London at the Court of Charles I, took an active part in shaping his country's foreign policy, after the end of the Spanish occupation (1580–1640). He was therefore in an ideal position to judge the foibles of men and the corruption of the Portuguese society of his day. The *Arte de Furtar*, written in a racy style, exposes the greed for riches and honours that took possession of the Portuguese in all walks of life, making them real experts in the art of cheating and defrauding their fellow-men. The satire is particularly virulent against the officials who were in charge of the arms supplies to the Portuguese forces during the war with Spain. To them huge profits at the expense of the national treasury were far more important than the outcome of the war. [LSR]

Afonso Pena Júnior, *A Arte de Furtar e o seu autor* (2 vols., Rio de Janeiro, 1946).

**Aseyev, Nikolay** (L'gov, nr Kursk 1889–Moscow 1963). Russian poet. Born into a middle-class family, he attended the Moscow Institute of Commerce and Moscow University. His earliest verses date from 1913, and he published his first volume (*Nochnaya fleita*) the next year. He was an organizer of LEF (Left Arts Front), and a close friend of ⇨ Mayakovsky. He did not fall out of favour after the disbandment of the ⇨ Futurist movement, to which he adhered, and in 1941 was awarded a Stalin Prize. Though an influential literary figure until his death, he never produced a real masterpiece. His earliest verse shows folklore interests reminiscent of ⇨ Khlebnikov, but he soon emulates Mayakovsky's exciting verbal and rhymic effects. His narrative poems are his best-known work: notably *Sinie Gusari*, a lament for the unsuccessful 'Decembrist' revolutionaries of 1825, and the long tribute, *Mayakovskiy nachinaetsya*. In recent years he earned the gratitude of a new generation of poets by his encouragement and defence of them. [RM-G]

*Sobraniye sochineniy* (5 vols.,1963–4); Lugovskoy, *ARSP*; Obolensky, *PBRV*.

**Ash, Sholem** (Kutno 1880–London 1957). Yiddish writer. The most prolific of the last generation of Yiddish writers of short stories and novels; he also tried his hand at drama. He had a wide experience of Jewish life in Eastern and Western Europe and America and treated the past and present with equal skill and understanding. He wrote in Hebrew and Yiddish simultaneously and portrayed life in the small Jewish communities with sympathy. He caused a great stir in Jewish literary circles by his 'Christian' novels of Jesus and Mary, but he treated them as a series of Biblical novels. Most of his work has been published in English. [EE]

*Mother* (1957); *Sabbatai Zevi*, tr. T. Whyte and F. R. Woyes (1920); *In the Beginning*, tr. C. Cunningham (1935); *Motke the Thief*, tr. W. and E. Muir (1935); *Salvation*, tr. W. and E. Muir (1951); *Three Cities*, tr. W. and E. Muir (1913); *The War Goes On*, tr. W. and E. Muir (1936) (also under the title *Calf of the Paper*); *Children of Abraham* (1942); *My Personal Faith*, tr. M. Samuel (1942); *The Nazarene*, tr. M. Samuel (1929); *Song of the Valley* (1939); *Three Novels: Uncle Moses, Claim Lederer's Return, Judge Not*, tr. E. Crouch (1938); *What I Believe*, tr. M. Samuel (1941); *The Apostle*, tr. M. Samuel (1943); *East River*, tr. A. H. Gross (1946); *One Destiny, An Epistle to the Christians* (1948); *Tales of my People*, tr. M. Levin (1948); *Mary*, tr. M. Samuel (1949); *Moses*, tr. M. Samuel (1951); *The Prophet*, tr. A. S. Caper (1956); *A Passage in the Night*, tr. M. Samuel (1952); *From Many Countries: Collected Short Stories*, tr. M. Samuel and M. Levin (1958).
Waxman, *HJL*.

**Asnyk, Adam** (Kalisz 1838–Cracow 1897). Polish poet. He was well educated in Germany, took part in revolutionary politics as a member of the secret government in 1863, and after the unsuccessful insurrection had to live in the Austrian part of Poland. In an age dominated by positivist thought and the novel, he tried hard to reconcile his sentimental lyric poetry with dispassionate philosophic arguments, as in the cycle of sonnets *Nad głębiami* (1894). But he was more at ease in travesties of popular themes after the fashion of Heine, some of whose poetry he translated. [JP]

Peterkiewicz and Singer, *FCPP*.

**'Athenaeum.'** German literary and aesthetic periodical, published 1798–1800 in Berlin. Founded by the ⇨ Schlegel brothers as the public manifesto of the new Romantic movement, it contained many of the critical statements on which the outlook of the German Romantics was based (e.g. F. Schlegel's 'Romantic poetry is a progressive universal poetry'). The *Athenaeum* survived only two years. Although it contained contributions by ⇨ Novalis and others, it was largely the work of the Schlegels themselves. The complete text of the journal was republished in a single volume by the Cotta Verlag (Stuttgart) in 1960. [RT]

**Atterbom, Per Daniel Amadeus** (Åsbo 1790–Uppsala 1855). Swedish poet. As the leader of the so-called 'Phosphorister', the Uppsala school of Romantics, he spent his early career in bitter and often unduly aggressive polemics, and as a result never received full appreciation for his considerable poetic achievement. He was particularly attracted by Schelling's philosophy and the German Romantics ⇨ Schlegel, ⇨ Tieck and ⇨ Novalis. He published a literary magazine, *Phosphoros*, and wrote a prologue for it (1810), which celebrates the advent of Romantic poetry. There followed a spate of lyrical poems whose common feature is their ethereal verse-music and metaphysical subject-matter, e.g. *Erotikon*, on the theme of Platonic love, and *Allegro och Adagio*, a dialogue between two states of mind with both of which he was familiar. A sequence of allegorical poems, *Blommorna* (1812), proved more accessible for a wider public in spite of their metaphysical inspiration. An unfinished fairy-play, *Fågel Blå* (1814), contains a fascinating study of the Romantic poet through the medium of dramatic monologue. Of a sensitive nature, he lacked the robustness required for true leadership: his polemical tracts are often obscure and diffuse.

A prolonged journey to Germany and Italy (1817–19) did much to restore him to health and vigour and provided much of the inspiration for his greatest work, *Lycksalighetens ö* (1824–7). This is another fairy-play or dramatic poem, but too long for production and too subtle ever to make popular reading. The fable of the play, however, is a folk-tale about a journey outside time to a beautiful island above the earth, but in Atterbom's handling it yields a vast, metaphysical perspective. It follows the progress of Poesy and exhibits the tragedy of the imagination: poetry, unless subjected to the purposes of religion, will remain an instrument of seduction. Acting on this insight, King Astolf returns to earth (and his death), while his beloved Felicia, the genius of poetry, returns to the higher spheres of the Empyrean. The lyrical variety of the work is impressive, and its many songs have a permanent place in Swedish anthologies, but the underlying idea of *Lycksalighetens ö* still seems remote to many readers, as it did to Atterbom's contemporaries. Its cold reception made the poet withdraw from his public. From 1841 onwards, however, Atterbom, now holding the chair in Aesthetics at the University of Uppsala, published a fine series of studies of Swedish poets and men of letters, *Svenska siare och skalder 1–6* (1841–55), and just before his death, completed a revised version of his great poetic drama. [SAB]

*Valda skrifter*, ed. F. Böök (6 vols., 1927–9).

E. Tykesson, *A. en levnadsteckning* (Stockholm, 1954); C. Santesson, *A.s ungdomsdiktning* (Uppsala, 1920), and *Mot lycksalighetens ö* (Stockholm, 1956); H. Frykenstedt, *A.s sagospel L. ö* (Stockholm, 1951).

**Aubanel, Théodore** (Avignon 1829–Avignon 1886). French poet. The outstanding Provençal lyric poet of the ⇨ Félibrige. Born of an old family of Avignon printers who enjoyed the title of printers to the Pope, he received an austere and severely Catholic upbringing. A founder member of the Félibrige, friend of ⇨ Mistral and early contributor to the *Armana Provençau*, he won fame with *La miougrano entre-duberto* ('La grenade entr'ouverte', 1860) youthful love lyrics of desire and despair which were proscribed by the Roman Catholic Church. He rejected ⇨ Roumanille's ideas of a 'localized' Provençal poetry and was well received in literary and artistic circles in Paris. He was a friend of Mallarmé and Daudet. In 1886 he published *Li fiho d'Avignoun* ('Les filles d'Avignon'), poems which abruptly declare the poet's conflict between his spiritual longings and physical passions. He was ordered by the Roman Catholic Church to withdraw this book. He died shortly afterwards. Other lyric poems, *Lou rèire-souléu* ('Le soleil d'outre-tombe') were published posthumously. He also wrote 3 plays, of which *Lou pan dóu pecat* (1882) was performed as *Le pain du péché* in Paul Arène's translation. Aubanel has a Provençal painter's eye for dazzling light and lowering shadows, for beauty transcending ugliness. He defended vigorously the victims of hypocrisy, tyranny and poverty. [LTT]

Ed. and Fr. tr. (Avignon, 1935–60); *Œuvres complètes* (Avignon, 1960– ); *Œuvres choisies*, ed. C. Liprandi (Avignon, new edn 1961) (without tr.).

L. Legré, *Le poète T.A.* (Paris, 1900); J. Vincent, *T.A.* (Avignon, 1936); G. Machicot, *T.A. poète de l'amour et de la mort* (Avignon, 1947); J. Salvat, *'La Grenade entr'ouverte' d'Aubanel* . . . (Avignon, 1960).

**Aube.** Medieval French song in which lovers regret the coming dawn. They may receive warning of this or of the approach of a jealous husband from a watchman who acts like the sentinel in medieval Latin poems alerting the sleeping camp at daylight. The genre, of popular origin, was practised by courtly ⇨ *trouvères* and especially by ⇨ troubadours in the South of France (*alba*), and was used with Christian symbolism in the 13th century. Excellent examples (*tageliet*) survive in Middle High German, especially in the poems of ⇨ Wolfram von Eschenbach. [LTT]

Jeanroy, *PLT*; Hill and Bergin, *APT*.

*Eos*, ed. A. T. Hatto (The Hague, 1965); A. Jeanroy, *Les origines de la poésie lyrique en France* (Paris, 3rd edn 1925).

**Aubignac, François Hédelin, Abbé d'** (Paris 1604–Nemours 1676). French critic. He worked for Richelieu in his efforts to raise the reputation of the theatre. He is known to have written 3 plays, which had no success, 2 essays in controversy with Ménage and a study of dramatic technique, *La pratique du théâtre* (1657; ed. P. Martino, 1927), which seems to have been discussed by those who were working out the theory and practice of a new type of play. To us it supplies evidence that the centre of discussion was not so much the unities as rules to be imposed, but the effect they were intended to achieve: concentration and continuity of dramatic illusion. This illusion would be broken by change of scene; it is intensified if the subject be taken near to its crisis and if nothing irrelevant be introduced. D'Aubignac is both a student of ancient drama and an admirer of Corneille. After the debates of 1660 (the occasion of Corneille's *Discours*) d'Aubignac, offended, turned against him and crossed out in a copy still extant all favourable references. [WGM]

R. Bray, *La tragédie cornélienne devant la critique classique* (Paris, 1927); Adam, *HLF*, ii.

**'Aucassin et Nicolette.'** A romance in the form of a *chante-fable* written about 1200 in the dialect of Picardy. The unusual form, in which prose narrative alternates with verse, has prompted the suggestion that the work was intended for dramatic recitation by two ⇨ *jongleurs*.

The story is set in the South of France, at Carthage and in the fabulous castle of Torelore. Aucassin is the young son of the lord of Beaucaire and Nicolette a girl who has been bought from the Saracens but who is the daughter of the King of Carthage. The two lovers overcome all obstacles, and after many trials and separations are happily reunited. The story is told with tenderness and realism; a delicate irony parodies the heavier genres of the heroic romance and the ⇨ *chanson de geste* and suggests the vanity of knightly prowess in comparison with true human happiness. The story is similar to that of *Floire et Blancheflor*, but the author was well-versed in the literature of his day and drew on many sources including the romances of ⇨ Chrétien de Troyes and, possibly, Arabic models. [LTT]

Ed. F. W. Bourdillon (1919); ed. M. Roques (3rd edn, 1955); tr. A. Lang (1905), M. S. Heffry (1905), H. Child (1911); Fr. tr. M. Coulon (1933), G. Cohen (1954); *R*, LXXVI, 1955.

**Audiberti, Jacques** (Antibes 1899–Paris 1965). French poet, dramatist, novelist. A journalist, he began serious writing quite late, in order to reintroduce form and rhetoric into poetry after the scourge of surrealism. *Race des hommes* (1937), *Des tonnes de semence* (1941), *La nouvelle origine* (1942) – this includes an essay on his theory of poetry – *Toujours* (1944) and *Rempart* (1953) consist of intricate, conceited and stern verse, symbolic, hermetic and didactic in turn, with here and there a truly brilliant poem. Underneath runs a playful but savage humour and an often sensuous lyricism. His little-read novels are written in poetic prose in an erudite mixture of styles rampaging from the epic to the surrealist through all the forms of realism: *Abraxas* (1938), *Cent jours* (1947), *Le maître de Milan* (1950), *Les jardins et les fleuves* (1954). His favourite themes – the war of the sexes, the resurgences of paganism, the birth of legends – are more approachable through the sensitive, creative dialogue and the complex techniques of his plays, which are regularly successful on the Parisian stage.

Audiberti's plays are characterized by an amalgam of farce and horrific melodrama fused together under the pressure of a fantasticated and burlesque poetry. There is a persistent tension between paganism and Christianity, between the surface contingency of life (as mirrored in the wildly complicated plots) and hidden, primitive forces, often representing primordial evil. Hence, in *Quoat-Quoat* (1946), the French ship bound for Mexico is a microcosm of organized society which is at the mercy of atavistic forces symbolized by the stone of the ancient god, Quoat-Quoat. Similarly, in *Opéra parlé* (1956), Christianity in the shape of Baron Massacre wins a temporary victory through marriage to the young goddess who is identified with the paganism of the dark forest, but paganism reasserts itself in violence. The presence of evil is central to Audiberti's vision: it envelopes the innocent princess of *Le mal court* (1947) who is deceived by a corrupt world; it manifests itself in the destructive sexual fury of Félicien in *La fête noire* (1948) or in the metamorphosis of men into beasts in *Les naturels de Bordelais* (1953) or in the Circe figure of *La logeuse* (1954) who enslaves her male lodgers. *Pucelle* (1950), *L'effet Glapion* (1959), *La fourmi dans le corps* (1962), *La guillotine* (1964), all reflect his belief in the continuing regenerative power of ideals, even if clothed in fantasy and myth. [CLC/SBJ]

*Théâtre* (5 vols., 1948–62); *Entretiens avec Georges Charbonnier* (1965).

Guicharnaud, *MFT*; Wellwarth, *TPP*.

**Augier, Émile** (Valence 1820–Paris 1889). French dramatist. He reacted against the extravagances of Romanticism and the facile superficiality of ⇨ Scribe with a number of insipid verse-plays: *La cigüe* (1844), *L'aventurière* (1848; tr. T. W. Robertson, *Home*, 1893), *Gabrielle* (1849). He struck his distinctive vein with dramas of social life – well observed, solidly constructed and rooted in the conventional morality of the comfortable middle classes from which he sprang. *Le gendre de Monsieur Poirier* (1854; tr. B. H. Clark, *Monsieur Poirier's Son-in-Law*, in *Four Plays*, 1915), an amiable satire on the conflict between nobility and bourgeoisie, was followed by *Le mariage d'Olympe* (1855), a realistic study of the submerged world of the *demi-monde*, and *Les lionnes pauvres* (1858; tr./adapt. A. Matthison, *A False Step*, 1879) which deals with adultery. *Les effrontés* (1861) satirized with verve the Second Empire mania for financial speculation, while *Le fils de Giboyer* (1862) attacks the politics of religion. A later play, *Les Fourchambault* (1878; tr. B. H. Clark, *The House of Fourchambault*, 1915), returns to the period theme of illegitimacy. Though his technique was not so inventive nor his effects so brilliantly manipulated as Scribe's or ⇨ Sardou's, Augier was less vulgar and meretricious and his grasp of the realities of social and economic conflict was firmer than that of ⇨ Dumas *fils* and much freer of crude didacticism. [SBJ]

*Théâtre complet* (7 vols., 1890).

P. Morillot, *E.A.* (Grenoble, 1901); L. Lacour, *Trois théâtres: E.A., A Dumas fils, V. Sardou* (Paris, 1880); Weiss, *TM*.

**Aukrust, Olav** (Lom, Oppland 1883–Lom 1929). Norwegian poet. He was brought up in a Grundtvigian milieu, trained as a teacher, and was for a time headmaster of a Folk High School. He became one of the most important of the *Nynorsk* poets, finding inspiration in a deeply rooted attachment to Norwegian nature, peasant life and its traditions. His poetry also contains a strong mystical-religious element, especially the visionary *Himmelvarden* (1916) and *Solrenning* (1930). In *Hamar i Hellom* (1926), which was intended as the first part of a trilogy, similar perspectives are combined with a passionate feeling for the traditional values of Norwegian peasant life. [RGP]

*Dikt i samling* (2 vols., 1942).

I. Krokann, *O.A.* (Oslo, 1933); H. Groth, *O.A.* (Oslo, 1948); Beyer, *NL*.

**'Auto de los Reyes Magos'** (anon., late 12th cent.). Fragment of an *auto* or liturgical play in verse, in four short scenes: the three Magi appear separately, each pondering on the meaning of the Star of Bethlehem; they then meet and agree to travel to Bethlehem to discover whether it truly heralds the Messiah; they reveal their intentions to Herod, and after their departure he summons his advisers to discuss the meaning of the Star. There the fragment ends. The contrast in attitude between the Magi, who begin in doubt but wish to believe, and Herod, who is selfishly determined not to believe that a rival King is born, is clearly brought out, and soliloquy and dialogue are both exploited in rudimentary but clearly dramatic form. The fragment is vital evidence for the existence of liturgical drama early in medieval Spain. [GBG-M]

Ed. R. Menéndez Pidal, in *Revista de Archivos, Bibliotecas y Museos* IV (1900); modern Spanish tr., F. Lázaro Carreter, in *Teatro medieval: textos íntegros* (1958).

R. B. Donovan, *The Liturgical Drama in Medieval Spain* (Toronto, 1958); *MLN*, LXX, 1955.

**Avitus** (*c.*450–*c.*525). Christian Latin poet. Bishop of Vienne in Provence in succession to his father, he was one of the best writers of Christian Latin epics. He chose scenes from Genesis as his subject, beginning with the creation of the world and ending with the crossing of the Red Sea. His style is modelled closely on Virgil. There are striking resemblances to Milton's *Paradise Lost*. [FB]

Migne, *PL*, 59; ed. R. Peiper (MGH, AA, VI, 1883); ed. V. Chevalier (Lyons, 1890).

P. Parizel, *Saint Avite* (Louvain, 1859); Duckett, *LW*.

**Avvakum, Archpriest.** ⇨ Russian Literature of the 17th Century.

**Aymé, Marcel** (Joigny, Yonne 1902–Paris 1967). French novelist, playwright and short-story writer. He worked as a journalist, then devoted himself entirely to writing after the huge success of his first novel, *La jument verte* (1933; tr. N. Denny, *The Green Mare*, 1955). A richly comic account of the complicated religious, political, social and sexual activities of a small provincial community, it contains the main ingredients of subsequent work: an extravagant but carefully handled plot and robust peasant humour, skilfully combined to convey uncanny understanding of the obscurer motives of human behaviour and sharp insight into the workings of society. As his work developed his canvas broadened and his humour acquired a more bitter and satirical edge.

Although always ready to satirize the muddle and corruption he found in present-day life – and not least in political life –

Aymé never identified himself with any political viewpoint. In *Travelingue* (1941; tr. E. Sutton, *The Miraculous Barber*, 1949) the Right bears the brunt of his satire, as he mocked the ineffectual attempts of the bourgeoisie to meet the challenge of the People's Front, whilst *Uranus* (1948; tr. N. Denny, *Fanfare in Blémont*, 1950) deals scathingly with the excesses of the dominant Left after the Liberation.

Truculent farce, Rabelaisian raciness complicated by a strain of cruelty, wild fantasy conducted with implacable logic, also mark his plays. In *Lucienne et le boucher* (1948, but written 1932), the eponymous heroine, having incited her lover, the local slaughter-house man, to kill off her inoffensive husband, charges him with murder and claims compensation for loss of her breadwinner. This epitomizes Aymé's manner. Other plays illustrate it variously: *Vogue la galère* (1936); *Clérambard* (1950; tr. N. Denny, 1952), a fantasy involving a vision of Saint Francis of Assisi; *Le tête des autres* (1952), a savage attack on the corruption of the judicial system; *Les quatre vérités* (1954), and *Les oiseaux de lune* (1955), which features a school administrator able to change inquisitive representatives of the law into birds. Incoherence of structure and a tendency to gross and vulgar caricature lend many of the plays an air of strain and contrivance. This also applies to the most recent: *La mouche bleue* (1957); *Louisiane* (1961); *Les maxibules* (1962; tr. K. Black, 1964) and *Le minotaure* (1963), but they display vitality and satirical force. [SBJ/IHW]

Pol Vandromme, *A.* (Paris, 1960); *FR*, XXXV, 5, 1962.

**Ayrer, Jakob** (Nürnberg *c.*1543– Nürnberg 1605). German playwright. After Shrovetide plays in the manner of ⇨ Sachs, he sought to quicken this native drama by importing the stage effects, the love of violence and the more sophisticated stage of the English strolling players. In his *Singspiele*, or musical plays, he similarly experimented with the introduction of music and songs into the traditional Shrovetide play. [WAC]

*Dramen*, ed. A. v. Keller (BLVS, 76–80, 1865); two plays tr. in A. Cohn, *Shakespeare in Germany* (1885).

W. Wodick, *J. A.s Dramen in ihrem Verhältnis zur einheimischen Literatur und zum Schauspiel der englischen Komödianten* (Halle, 1912).

**Azeglio, Massimo d'** (Turin 1798–Turin 1866). Italian painter, novelist and politician. A Piedmontese nobleman. An intense patriotism permeates his works, tempered, however, by the strong moral sense that, in politics, always led him away from extremism. A successful painter, specializing in classical landscapes and historical subjects, he turned in 1828 to the novel (influenced perhaps by his future father-in-law, Manzoni) enlarging upon his own canvas of the famous *Disfida di Barletta* of 1503 in the historical novel, *Ettore Fieramosca* (1833; ed. L. G. Tenconi, 1958; tr. 1880). The patriotic fervour of this and the subsequent novels, *Niccolò de' Lapi* (1841; ed. M. De Rubris, 1941; tr. 1860) on the siege of Florence in 1530, and the unfinished *Lega Lombarda* (ed. M. De Rubris, 1919) on the battle of Legnano in 1176, was intended to 'put some fire into Italians'. Vivid in the portrayal of historical incidents and in remarkable character-sketches, the novels are nevertheless spoiled by the sentimentality surrounding the languishing heroines. His literary work was interrupted by the political events of 1845–60 in which he played a leading part, supporting Piedmontese leadership of the Risorgimento, writing controversial pamphlets (e.g. *Gli ultimi casi di Romagna*, 1846), and as President of the Council of Piedmont in 1849. His unfinished memoirs, *I miei ricordi*, were published posthumously in 1867 (ed. A. Pompeati, 1958; tr. 1966). [RHC]

A. Pompeati, *D'A.* (Milan, 1946); *Guida*, 1959; *Minori*, iii.

**Azevedo, Guilherme de** (Santarém 1839–Paris 1882). Portuguese poet. Of an ailing constitution and a journalist by profession, Azevedo is essentially a minor figure in terms of his own literary output, but is of importance as a catalysing influence in that he opened new paths for Portuguese verse. His first collection, *Aparições* (1867), was nothing remarkable, composed as it was of Romantic love poetry in the manner of Lamartine. But under the influence of his study of Victor Hugo's social verse and responding to the postulates of Antero de Quental, in *Radiações da Noite* (1871) he became deeply *engagé*, ventilating many social questions in his verse. The trend of social poetry became intensified in his third and final collection, *Alma Nova* (1874), composed under the influence of *Les fleurs du* *mal*, though without any of Baudelaire's metaphysical attitudes. Poetry of the city, this collection underlined the contrasts between rich and poor and introduced a pronounced macabre and satanic element. With Antero de ➪ Quental, Azevedo was an important forerunner of the Escola Nova of Guerra ➪ Junqueiro, Cesário ➪ Verde and Gomes ➪ Leal. [RCW]

M. Dionísio, 'Guilherme de Azevedo', in *Perspectiva da Literature Portuguesa do Século XIX*, i (Lisbon, 1947).

**Azorín,** pseud. of José Martinéz Ruíz (Monóvar 1894–Madrid 1967). Spanish essayist, novelist and critic. With ➪ Baroja and ➪ Unamuno a central figure of the Generation of 1898. His novel *La voluntad* (1902) shows the intellectualized pessimism of the Generation and describes the spiritual prostration common to his age-group. He is chiefly famous for the limpid delicate style of his essays, evolved deliberately as a reaction against the florid late-19th-century Spanish prose. Many of his most famous essays, especially in *Los pueblos* (1905) and *La ruta de Don Quijote* (1905), evoke the poetic suggestiveness of the Spanish countryside, its people and traditional way of life. In later years his desire for national regeneration gave way to a more detached, aesthetic, delight in the Spanish landscape and its literary associations. His critical essays are very unequal; impressionistic rather than analytic they reveal less insight into modern literature, except the writings of his friends and contemporaries, than into that of the 16th and 17th centuries. He excels in re-creating the literary atmosphere of the Golden Age, as in *Al margen de los clásicos* (1914), and the flavour of its daily life (*Una hora de España*, 1924). His ventures into the theatre around 1930 were signally unsuccessful. His early preoccupation with the theme of time mellowed gradually into a semi-philosophic cyclic view of life in which all things are subject to a law of inevitable return. [DLS]

*Obras completas* (1959–63).

E. I. Fox, *A. as a Literary Critic* (N.Y., 1962); L. S. Granjel, *Retrato de A.* (Madrid, 1958); A. Krause, *A., the Little Philosopher* (University of California, 1948).

# B

**Babel', Isaak Emmanuilovich** (Odessa 1894–? 1941). Russian short-story writer and dramatist. Son of a Jewish tradesman he published his first stories in 1916. During the First World War he fought with the Tsarist army and in 1917 went over to the Bolsheviks. He served with the *Cheka* and later with Budyonny's cavalry in Poland. He disappeared in the purges of the 1930s and was rehabilitated in 1957.

His output is small and belongs almost entirely to the twenties. His fame rests primarily on *Konarmiya* (1926), impressions of his service in Poland. This series of brief but intense sketches combines his gifts of anarchic romanticism and a finely controlled objectivity. His protagonists are uninhibited primitives or else weak and sensitive intellectuals. The narrator is both a horrified participant and a detached observer of events. Appalling cruelty, gross sensuality and profound humanity co-exist side by side in his work. His effects are achieved by his unique style, its compression, fantastic imagery and above all the lurid landscapes. *Istoriya moyey golubyatni* (1926) is nostalgic in its tone and is devoted to Jewish life in Odessa. *Odesskiye rasskazy* (1931) are devoted to the criminal underworld of Odessa and combine his romanticism with a rich sense of humour.

Babel's plays are less remarkable but are still interesting. The two best, *Zakat* (1928) and *Mariya* (1933–5), deal with the fate of individuals and groups that have been pushed aside by the new age. [RDBT]

*Izbrannoye* (1966); *Collected Stories*, tr. W Morison and others (1957).

*I. B. Sta'i i materialy* (1928); Poggioli, *PS*.

**Babits, Mihály** (Szekszárd 1883–Budapest 1941). Hungarian novelist, essayist and poet. Born into the intelligentsia, he studied philosophy and became a schoolmaster; he retired in 1917 to write. He used varied styles, bold and unusual forms of language and poetry; the first of his six volumes of poetry, *Levelek Irisz koszorujából* (1909), showed his admiration for classical culture. His second volume of poetry, *Herceg ha megjön a tél is* (1911), indicates his weary spirit amid drab existence; his third, *Gólyakalifa*, appeared in 1916 (tr. anon., *King's Stork*, Budapest, 1948). *Isten kezében* (1916) and *A nyugtalanság völgye* (1920) reflect the shock of a pacifist at the Great War. Babits was representative of idealist philosophy and of the humanism of the conservative bourgeois; his polished style hides confusion in new circumstances and anxiety about the future of the Hungarian middle class, and its literature. His novel *Halál fiai* (1927) is a social study of the pre-war disintegration of the gentry and professional classes, while *Elza pilóta vagy a tökéletes társadalom* (1934) shows sardonic despair at society, and describes a Utopian state. By the thirties, Babits's lyricism was replaced by narrative prose. Defending the unrealistic 'new classicism' against the disturbances of the thirties, he tried to keep literature free of politics, but in later years realized the need for a more militant stand against the advent of fascism and war (*Jónás könyve*, 1940).

From 1929 he was editor of the literary magazine ⇨ *Nyugat*. Other notable works: *Az európai irodalom története* ('History of European Literature', 1935); *Karácsonyi Madonna* (1920); and his greatest novel, *Timár Virgil fia* (1922). He also translated Dante, Nietzsche, Bergson, and English and German poets. Several poems translated into English by W. Kirkconnell and others (in *A Little Treasury of Hungarian Verse*, Washington, 1947; *The Magyar Muse*, Winnipeg, 1933; *Modern Magyar Lyrics*, Budapest, 1926). [JFR]

*SEER*, XXII, 58 (1944).

**Bacchelli, Riccardo** (Bologna 1891– ). Italian novelist. He tried his hand at several genres: drama (*Amleto*, 1919, a remaking of *Hamlet*); philosophical satire (*Lo sa il tonno*, 1923); socio-psychological novel (*Una passione coniugale*, 1930; *Il fiore della mirabilis*, 1942; *L'incendio di Milano*, 1952, tr. K. Nott, *The Fire of Milan*, 1958); fiction of all kinds: religious (*Lo sguardo di Gesù*, 1948), humorous (*L'elmo di Tancredi e altre novelle giocose*, 1942), tragic (*Il* *brigante di Tacca del Lupo e altri racconti disperati*, 1942), uncanny (*La fine dell'Atlantide e altre favole lunatiche*, 1942: the last three reprinted in two volumes, *Tutte le novelle*, 1953); but he was perhaps at his best in the historical novel (*Il diavolo al Pontelungo*, 1927; *Il mulino del Po*, 1938–40, first 2 vols. tr. F. Frenaye, *The Mill on the Po*, 1952; vol. 3 tr. S. Hood, *Nothing New under the Sun*, 1955). In his wanderings through the wide narrative field he was only moderately experimental, and never allowed himself to forget the lesson of ⇨ Manzoni, from which he learned conservatism and formal dignity, and ⇨ Fogazzaro, who taught him how to cover his robust sensuality under a veil of Catholic unction. His ability to compromise between the old and the new, experiment and tradition, sex and religion, explains both the reservations of some critics and the favour granted him by the reading public.

*Il figlio di Stalin* (1953; tr. K. Nott, *The Son of Stalin*, 1956).

*Contemporanei*, ii; Falqui, *PNNI*; Robertis, *SN*; Biondolillo, *C.*

**Bachelard, Gaston.** ⇨ French Literary Criticism in the 19th and 20th Centuries.

**Bachmann, Ingeborg** (Klagenfurt 1926– ). Austrian poet. Influenced by Wittgenstein and Heidegger, on whom she wrote her Vienna doctoral thesis, her highly original poems, *Die gestundete Zeit* (1953) and *Anrufung des grossen Bären* (1956), aroused much interest at the time. They might be termed 'existential lyric poetry', being strongly confessional in character and apparently written to help her solve her own problems, above all of communication. Her radio-plays (*Der gute Gott von Manhattan*, 1958) and stories (*Das dreissigste Jahr*, 1961; tr. M. Bullock, *The Thirtieth Year*, 1964) have been somewhat overrated; she has translated ⇨ Ungaretti and worked with H. W. Henze, e.g. on the libretto for his opera *Prinz Friedrich von Homburg* (1960). [PB]

*Gedichte, Erzählungen, Hörspiele, Essays* (Munich, 1964); Bridgwater, *TCGV*; Hamburger and Middleton, *MGP*.

*I.B.: ein biographisch-bibliographischer Abriss* (Munich, 1962); *I.B.: Eine Einführung* (Munich, 1963); G. C. Schoolfield, in Keith-Smith, *ECGL*; Holthusen, *SW*; *GLL*, XVII, 3 (1964).

**Bächtold, A.** ⇨ Swiss-German Dialect Literature.

**Bachur, Elijah,** known also as **Levita, Tishbi** and **Germanus** (Neustadt 1468–Venice 1549). The earliest Yiddish writer. By profession a Hebrew teacher, he wrote the *Bovo Buch* (1540), and translated into Yiddish the Psalms (1545) and the Prayer Book (1562). [EE]

Waxman, *HJL*.

**Bacovia, George,** pseud. of George Vasiliu (Bacău 1881–Bucharest 1957). Rumanian poet. Unlike most Rumanian writers of his time, he took no active part in shaping his country's future, but led a humble and solitary life, noteworthy for material deprivation, ill-health and a series of nervous breakdowns. In 1898 he made his literary début in the Macedonskian review *Literatorul*. Five years of intense literary activity followed and, though he chiefly published in provincial reviews, his poetry attracted the attention of many contemporary writers. From 1903 to 1911 he studied law at Bucharest and Iaşi. Temperamentally unsuited for the Bar and unable to find a suitable post in other professions, he had to earn his living by supply teaching and as a clerk. His first collection of poems, *Plumb* (1916), won wide acclaim; written 1898–1903, they clearly show the influence of symbolism. His poetry evokes a sombre and deeply pessimistic world, in which the gaiety and promise of life is contrasted with nightmarish visions of society in the process of putrefaction and disintegration. Both the Kafkaesque elements of the exterior world and the nihilism, the monotony and loneliness of his interior reflections are expressed simply, without pretension or poetic artifice, but often with an awkwardness and naïveté that acquire a strength of their own in the macabre atmosphere he creates. Bacovia's poetry is distinguished by an acute feeling for music, the use of mood-colours, a limited background and the constant repetition of key words or phrases. A second volume of poetry, *Scîntei galbene* (1926), and a volume of prose-poems, *Bucăţi de noapte* (1926), also reflect the writer's inner world in which a losing battle is fought against insomnia and psychotic tendencies. But in the volumes of poetry *Cu voi* (1930) and *Comedii în fond* (1936) a more ironical attitude to life is found, together with several poems of social and political comment. Paradoxically, an underlying streak of optimism in the future of society can be traced throughout his work. This is given more explicit expression in *Stanţe burgheze* (1946) and in the posthumous cycle, *Stanţe şi versete*. His influence may still be felt today in the works of a number of young writers. [MI]

**Baena, Juan Alfonso de** (early 15th cent.). Minor Spanish poet. He compiled the *Cancionero* (1445) known by his name – a (dull) collection of court poetry, principally in Castilian with some Galician poems, including work by ⇨ Imperial, ⇨ Fernández de Jerena and ⇨ Villasandino. [JMC]

Ed. Menéndez y Pelayo, *PLC*, ii.

**Baggesen, Jens** (Korsør 1764–Hamburg 1826). Danish poet. His travels are recorded in his lively autobiographical *Labyrinten* (1792–3); much of his later life was spent in Paris. His versatility (he even wrote in German, and was popular in the aristocratic *salons* of Copenhagen) produced humorous poems in the style of ⇨ Wessel, naïve and sentimental verse, and some exquisite love lyrics. [ELB]

Å. Henriksen, *Den rejsende* (Copenhagen, 1961).

**Bagritsky, Eduard,** pseud. of Eduard Dzyubin (Odessa 1895–Moscow 1934). Russian poet. Son of a poor Jewish tradesman, he began writing at 13, though his pre-revolutionary verse – save for a paeon in praise of Mayakovsky – is uninteresting. He fought on the Persian front in the First World War and with Bolshevik partisans in the Civil War. In Odessa in the early twenties he was an enthusiastic propagandist for the Soviet regime and supported the ⇨ Constructivist movement. His *magnum opus* is *Duma pro Opanasa* (1926). Some 500 lines long, it shows the conscious influence of folk-balladry and ⇨ Shevchenko. It is the unrivalled epic poem of the Russian Civil War: its chief characters are Kogan, a Red Commissar, and Opanas, who joins the 'Green' peasant army of the anarchist Makhno. He later made an opera-libretto from it, which contains some very good lyric poetry.

In 1928 he moved to Moscow and published his important *Yugo-Zapad,* poems saturated with the warm atmosphere of the Black Sea, with a love of life, its pleasures and excitements; it introduced a welcome note of unashamed romanticism into the poetry of the twenties. His praise of vigour and heroism may have been in compensation for his own indifferent health; he died of asthma at 39. In Stalin's later years he ran into posthumous criticism on grounds of supposed decadence and political errors, but he remains among the best-loved poets in the Soviet Union today. [RM-G]

*Stikhotvoreniya i poemy* (1964); Gulland, *SRV*
Lugovskoy, *ARSP*; Markov, *MRP*.
E. P. Lyubareva, *E.B.* (Moscow, 1964).

**Bagryana, Elisaveta**, pseud. of E. Belcheva (Sofia 1893– ). Bulgarian poetess. In 1915 while reading literature at Sofia University, she contributed her first verse to *Săvremenna misăl*. She became the poetess of *Zlatorog*, the foremost Bulgarian inter-war periodical. Her *Vechnata i svyatata* (1927), *Zvezda na moryaka* (1932) and *Choveshko sărtse* (1936) contain some of the most mature modern Bulgarian poetry, expressing tenderness, vitality and a challenge to the anti-humanity of the modern world, symbolized for her in the sensitive seismograph's total insensitivity to human emotion. The intensity of her own feeling can be shared by the reader of her poem 'Elements'. Visits to Paris and Venice in 1928–9 inspired her 'From Other Shores', but her favourite theme is her homeland, especially the Black Sea and Nesebăr coast. More recently she has helped to edit the current literary monthly *Septemvri* and has published more verse, *Pet zvezdi* (1953). [VP]

*Izbrani proizvedeniya* (1957); Pinto, *BPV*.
Manning and Smal-Stocki, *HMBL*.

**Bahr, Hermann** (Linz 1863–Munich 1934). Austrian critic, dramatist and novelist. Influenced by French Symbolism he founded the Jungwien group. He anticipated the reaction against naturalism (*Zur Kritik der Moderne* 1890), championed the emergent neo-Romanticism (*Die Überwindung des Naturalismus*, 1891), and was a spokesman of ⇨ Expressionism (*Expressionismus*, 1916; tr. R. T. Gribble, *Expressionism*, 1925). His only outstanding works are *Die gute Schule* (1890), an Impressionistic or 'decadent' novel, and the play *Das Konzert* (1909; tr. B. Q. Morgan, *The Concert*, in *Chief Contemporary Dramatists*, ed. T. H. Dickinson,

Boston, Mass., 1921), a sophisticated Viennese farce. [PB]

*Essays*, ed. H. Kindermann (1964); *Kritiken*, ed. H. Kindermann (1964).
H. Kindermann, *H.B.* (Graz, 1955); *GLL*, XI, 3 (1958).

**Baïf, Jean-Antoine de** (Venice 1532–Paris 1589). French scholar and poet. Son of Henri II's ambassador to Venice, the humanist scholar Lazare de Baïf, he was taught by the humanist Dorat, along with Ronsard and Du Bellay, and was one of the original members of the ⇨ Pléiade; he had a large and varied literary output, but is not a great poet, though he can claim the distinction of helping, by his poems to 'Francine', to establish the alexandrine as a medium for love poetry instead of the decasyllabic line. He translated and adapted several classical plays, and his version of Plautus's *Miles gloriosus* was performed in 1567. He had a lively and inventive mind, and experimented with spelling reform and with '*vers mesurés*' (the attempt to use Greco-Latin metres in French verse); his rhythmic verse was written for musical accompaniment and cannot be judged alone. Another invention was what he called the '*vers baïfin*', a cumbersome 15-syllable line with the caesura after the seventh syllable. He seems never quite to have found his own style, nor achieved a satisfactory balance between erudition and emotion. [GJ]

*Œuvres en rime* (1573), ed. C. Marty-Laveaux (5 vols., 1881–90); *Le psautier de 1587*, ed. Yves le Hir (1963); Schmidt, *PSS*.

**Bąk, Wojciech** (Ostrów Wielkopolski 1907–Poznań 1961). Polish poet. He spent most of his life in Poznań, a western city with an old ecclesiastical tradition. He acquired fame as a religious poet with the publication of his *Brzemię niebieskie* (1934). Bąk survived the German occupation only to face persecution from the Communist regime, which drove him to a lunatic asylum. Here he continued to write poetry, which was later collected into a book *Zastygłe chwile* (1958), a record of mental suffering and also a protest against political insanity. [JP]

**Balassa, Bálint** (Zólyom 1554–Esztergom 1594). Hungarian magnate and Renaissance poet. His poetry reflects the pleasures of military life and his passionate love for 'Julia' – a symbol of perfect beauty and happiness. He created new verse-forms, of which one is universally known as the 'Balassi stanza'. Some well-known poems: 'In praise of the outposts' (1589), *Katonadal* (*Soldier's Song*) and *Boldogtalan vagyok* (*Farewell to my Love*), both tr. W. Kirkconnell in *The Magyar Muse*, Winnipeg, 1933. [JFR]

**Balbo, Cesare** (Turin 1789–Turin 1853). Italian politician and historian. A Piedmontese nobleman, his works have a strong Catholic bias (cf. *Storia d'Italia dal 476 al 774*, 1830; *Vita di Dante*, 1839, tr. F. J. Bunbury, *The Life and Times of Dante Alighieri*, 2 vols., 1852; *Meditazioni storiche*, 1843–5; *Sommario della storia d'Italia*, 1846, ed. E. Bianchi, 1937); but his insistence on the principle of Italian independence made him a leader of liberal-catholic thought before the first War of Independence against Austria. He advocated a federation of Italian states, its independence won by Piedmont, living in peaceful understanding with Austria, whose colonial interests must inevitably shift to the Balkans (*Delle speranze d'Italia*, 1844; ed. L. Taroni, 1944). In 1848 he became first constitutional president of the Council of Piedmont [RHC]

*Pagine scelte*, ed. N. Valeri (Milan, 1960).
*Minori*, iii.

**Balde, Jacobus** (Ensisheim, Alsace 1604–Neuburg 1668). German Latin poet. A Jesuit, the author of numerous poems, both sacred and secular, in excellent Latin. Eulogized in his own time as 'the German Horace', he was neglected till revived and translated by ⇨ Herder (*Terpsichore*, 1795). He is at his best as a lyric poet, but also wrote epics, satires, elegies, pastorals and a drama, *Jephtias*. Among his religious poems is an imitation of the famous *Cras amet qui nunquam amavit*, written in the metre of the original and inspired by the *Song of Songs*. [FB]

*Opera* (8 vols., Munich, 1729); *Ausgewählte Dichtungen* (1870).
G. Westermayer, *J.B.* (Munich, 1868); Mury-Sommervogel, *J.B.* (Strassburg, 1901); J. Bach, *J.B.* (Freiburg, 1904); A. Henrich, *Die lyrischen Dichtungen* (Strassburg, 1915); K. Viëtor, *Geschichte der deutschen Ode* (Munich, 1923).

**Baldini, Antonio** (Rome 1889–Rome 1962). Italian writer. One of the founders of *La Ronda*, a magazine upholding the traditional values of literature against an alleged decadence in standards of artistic taste and literary craftsmanship. Like most of the other *Rondisti*, he devoted himself to an ideal of stylistic refinement which he practised in several volumes of beautifully polished 'artistic prose'. His essays (*Michelaccio*, 1924; *Italia di Bonincontro*, 1940; *Beato tra le donne*, 1940; *Rugantino*, 1942; *Melafumo*, 1950, etc.) create an aesthetically self-contained world; life, as if literature were not part and parcel of it, is taken only as a literary pretext for delicate stylistic exercises, poetic meanderings of fantasy and tasteful capriccios. Baldini's prose is like a kaleidoscope; it is magical, colourful and entertaining, but one cannot see anything real through it. [GMC]

*Contemporanei*; Falqui, *PNNI*; Robertis, *SN*.

**Bálint, György** (1906–43). Hungarian journalist and critic. Author of a large number of masterly literary articles, reports, short stories and commentaries. He died in a Nazi labour camp. [JFR]

**Ball, Hugo** (Pirmasens 1886–Sant' Abbondio 1927). German poet, dramatist and critic. He worked with Max Reinhardt and was a producer at the Munich Kammerspiele (1913). He was a friend of Kandinsky and Marc. A pacifist intellectual, Ball went to Zürich in 1915 where he helped found ⇨ Dada. In 1917 he broke with the movement, seeing its poetry of revolt to be based on a diabolical egotism, and neither poetic nor creative ('the safety-valve of an abstract age has burst'). He was a fierce critic of the German intelligentsia (*Zur Kritik der deutschen Intelligenz*, 1919) with its cult of iconoclastic anti-art. He later became a Catholic, and wrote on *Die Folgen der Reformation* (1924) and on *Byzantinisches Christentum* (1923). His *Briefe 1911–1927* (1958) throw much light on Dada, abstract art, and the intellectual attitudes of his time. [PB]

*Gesammelte Gedichte* (1965); *Die Flucht aus der Zeit* (1927; new edn, Lucerne, 1946); Hamburger and Middleton, *MGP*.

**Bal'mont, Konstantin Dmitriyevich** (near Ivanovo-Voznesensk 1867–Paris 1943). Russian poet, living in exile after 1918. One of the early symbolists, his most striking verse collection is *Budem kak solntse* ('Let Us Be as the Sun', 1903), subtitled 'A Book of Symbols'. His philosophy of ecstatic liberty vaguely combines ideas of creative individualism derived from Nietzsche with socialist expectations learnt from Gor'ky. He wrote voluminously, but he lacked the temperament to rework original inspiration, and much is worthless.

Obolensky, *PBRV*.

**Balzac, Jean Louis Guez de** (Angoulême 1597–Angoulême 1654). French man of letters. He spent some years in travel, was at Leyden in 1615, and in Rome for eighteen months, aspiring it was said to high office in the state or to a bishopric. He got neither, but fame instead, through his letters, of which a small selection appeared in 1624 and which were added to through successive editions throughout the century. In an age when critical opinion was rare they supplied a means of civilized discussion comparable to the modern weekly. Elegant argument concerning the moral and social ideas of the time, this Balzac cultivates in treatises (*Le Prince*, 1631; *Le Barbon*, 1648; *Le Socrate Chrétien*, 1652) but most of all in his letters. Beside the chief classical writers he appears pompous and hollow, but he was their harbinger. He does not avoid platitudes, but often brings off the well-turned phrase and the vigorous sally. He gave offence to some, it appears, by comparing monks to the rats in the Ark. His letter to Corneille is a good example of his florid style: 'Votre *Cinna* guérit les malades; il rend la parole à un muet, ce serait trop peu dire, à un enrhumé.' [WGM]

*Les premières lettres*, ed. H. Bibas and K.-T. Butler (2 vols., 1933).

G. Guillaumie, *B. et la prose française* (Paris, 1927); Adam, *HLF*.

**Balzac, Honoré de** (Tours 1799–Paris 1850). French novelist. The creator of the *Comédie humaine*, a collection of interlocking novels and stories of which about ninety were completed in under twenty years. After a fairly long apprenticeship in Paris, and a calamitous attempt to earn his living as a printer (the first of many wild and financially disastrous schemes), he published *Les chouans* (1829), the first work he signed with his own name, and the first he allowed into the *Comédie humaine* later. In *Les chouans*, in the first *Scènes de la vie privée* (1830) and in the *Contes philosophiques* (1830–1), Balzac is inspired by prevalent literary fashions. Thereafter he gradually imposed his own personality on the French novel, although from 1836 the serial novel in the daily press became the major pace-setter, and Balzac found himself the rival by (financial) necessity of ⇨ Dumas and ⇨ Sue.

Most readers explore the *Comédie humaine* haphazardly, beginning with *Le curé de Tours* (1832), *Eugénie Grandet* (1833) or *Le père Goriot* (1834). A selective reading should certainly include *La peau de chagrin* (1831), *César Birotteau* (1837), *Illusions perdues* (three parts: 1837, 1839, 1843), *La rabouilleuse* (1841–2), and his last two novels, *La cousine Bette* (1846) and *Le cousin Pons* (1847). One is continually impelled to read more, because each book explores the same fictional world, uncovering aspects which shed new and unexpected light on the other novels one knows. Two features in particular draw attention to the unity of the *Comédie humaine*. One is the recurring characters: if a number of stories are set in Paris in the 1820s, the aesthetically bold idea of letting the characters from one book know characters from another seems reasonable and increases one's conviction of the reality of the world Balzac evokes. It does not mean, however, that individual novels lose their autonomy. The second aspect is more doctrinaire: in the 'Furne' collected edition of 1842–6, where the title *Comédie humaine* was first used, Balzac classified his stories in series (*Étude de mœurs*, *Études philosophiques*, etc.), and subdivided the *Étude de mœurs* into *Scènes de la vie privée*, *Scènes de la vie parisienne*, *Scènes de la vie de province*, etc. Both these features evolved naturally in the early 1830s, as Balzac's sense of the unity of the world he was creating grew.

Diversity is equally a characteristic of the *Comédie humaine*, mirrored by the variety of critical attitudes. To many, Balzac is essentially a realist, not only because his world convinces by its very size and complexity, but because it represents an acute observation of modern society. Marxists see in Balzac an intuitive analysis of capitalist society which corroborates their own account. Even the obscurer private dramas seem closely linked with the way of life of a whole community at a particular moment in the historical evolution of French society.

Others see the *Études philosophiques* as a key to understanding the *Comédie humaine*. Balzac had his own interpretation of Rousseau's criticisms of civilization, and showed thought as being always in conflict with instinctive vitality, and hence symbolizing a kind of death. In *La peau de chagrin* the choice between burning oneself out and vegetating is expressed allegorically, but it is implicit in many contrasts between one part of the *Comédie humaine* and another – between Paris and the provinces, between those who are loyal to the past and those who move with the times – and it is not an easy choice. (M. Bardèche, *Une lecture de Balzac*, 1964.)

It is not difficult to see in all this a dramatic working-out of personal conflicts rather than a considered political or philosophical comment. Balzac's fictional world was a compensation for all that the real world had failed to give him, but at the same time he had to be faithful to his own experience. If Balzac had been less a man of his time, the points where he disagreed with his age would have caused him less strain. Hence the moral ambiguity of so much of Balzac: the honest victims are seen as stupid because they vegetate, yet Balzac numbers himself among them; the men who dominate society are admired for their energy – they are creators, like Balzac – yet they are anti-social. The characters who move with the times are despicable, yet those who refuse to are not truly alive. Balzac is himself committed to an acquisitive society which he everywhere implicitly condemns. His subtlety is here: in the constant conflict between the external appearance and the vision which informs the work as a whole, between the need to accept and the need to reject the conventional labels of good and bad.

Balzac's shortcomings go hand in hand with his virtues. He is not the master of exquisite nuance – his style is too energetic and forthright for that, his psychology shrewd rather than subtle. One could not create such a monument as the *Comédie humaine* without exuberance, and exuberance can often go with tastelessness. The conventional values which attract Balzac intellectually without commanding his deepest allegiance are often rendered in conventional black-and-white patterns or a too explicit vocabulary, which pin-points the nature of the conflict but fails to transpose it completely into aesthetic terms. This intrusion of Balzac into his narration sometimes militates against the conviction engendered by the precision of the physical detail and the sense of perspective given by the artistic form. The popularity of Dumas and Sue did nothing to discourage this tendency to over-dramatize and over-simplify. At his best, Balzac's writing is marked by the opposite of these intrusive elements – by irony, by superbly chiselled dialogue.

Balzac's influence is incalculable, on novelists of many nations and of differing temperaments. He made the novel a vehicle for mature commentary on modern society, and showed how a novelist can impose his vision, his own universe, on generations of readers.

*La Comédie humaine*, ed. M. Bouteron and H. Lognon (40 vols., Conard edition 1912–40, and 11 vols., Pléiade, 1951–9); ed. P. Citron (7 vols., 1966–7); individual novels in Classiques Garnier; the Bibliophiles de l'Originale are bringing out an annotated photostat copy of Balzac's own edition of the *Comédie humaine* (1965ff.). *Correspondance*, ed. R. Pierrot (5 vols., 1960–69); *Lettres à l'etrangère* (4 vols., 1899–1950); *Morceaux choisis*, ed. J. Merlant (1950).

F. Marceau, *B. et son monde* (Paris, 1955); H. J. Hunt, *H. de B.* (1957) and *B.'s Comédie Humaine* (1959); *FS*, October 1958 (for biblio.); *ML*, December 1965 (for biblio.).

**Bamm, Peter,** pseud. of Kurt Emmrich (Hochneukirch 1897– ). German novelist. A ship's doctor, an army surgeon (1941–5) on the Russian front, since 1946 a freelance writer. His early writing consisted of humorously ironical weekly press articles, of which the best are collected in *Die kleine Weltlaterne* (1949). The 'essays on medicine' *Ex ovo* (1948) are in the same humorous vein. His first real success was *Die unsichtbare Flagge* (1952; tr. F. Herrmann, *The Invisible Flag*, 1962), a humane 'report' on his wartime experiences, with shrewd insights into the political naïveté and helplessness of the army; the 'invisible flag' is that of humanity. Bamm's later books, based on his travels, have been equally successful: *Frühe Stätten der Christenheit* (1955; tr. S. Godman, *Early Sites of Christianity*, 1958) and *Welten des Glaubens* (1958; tr. C. Holme, *The Kingdoms of Christ*, 1959). *Anarchie mit Liebe* (1962) is a collection of stories. [PB]

**Bances Candamo, Francisco de** (Sabugo 1662–Lezuza 1704). Spanish poet and dramatist. The last important figure in the tradition of ⇨ Góngora and ⇨ Calderón. His best play, *La piedra filosofal*, derives from *La vida es sueño*. A trained theologian, his curious interest in magic led him to write an *auto*, *El gran químico del mundo* (also after Calderón). He developed interesting dramatic theories in his defence of the theatre against Jesuit attacks: *Teatro de los teatros de los pasados y presentes siglos* (ed. Serrano y Sanz, *Revista de Archivos, Bibliotecas y Museos*, V and VI, 1902). His long poem in the style of Góngora, *El César africano*, has decorative merits, like many descriptive passages in his plays. His collected plays were published in two volumes in 1722. [JMC]

*Obras líricas*, ed. F. Gutiérrez (1949); plays in BAE 49 and 58.

F. Cuervo-Arango, *Don F.A. de B.C.* (Madrid, 1916).

**'Bandamanna Saga.'** ⇨ Icelandic Sagas.

**Bandello, Matteo** (Castelnuovo Scrivia 1485–Bassens, Agen 1561). Italian short-story writer. A wordly cleric, for a time Bishop of Agen (France), his life was spent in travel and diplomacy among the various courts of Italy. His vast *Novelliere* (214 stories in all; parts I–III, 1554; part IV, 1573) has no general narrative framework as in Boccaccio's *Decameron*. Instead, each story has a preface describing the circumstances in which it came to be written, or perhaps transcribed, for Bandello presents himself as an observer and recorder of actuality. The historical veracity of his 'settings' may be doubted, but the style, despite occasional rhetorical blemishes, is that of even, spoken narrative. The range is wide, with themes taken from history, literature and contemporary life, and Bandello was used by Shakespeare and other Elizabethans in search of plots. He lacks Boccaccio's dynamic feeling for the dramatic contours of a story, and his narrative tone is less varied, but he gives interesting sketches of Italian *cinquecento* life at all levels. [DGR]

*Tutte le opere*, ed. F. Flora (2 vols., 1934–5); *The Novels of M.B.*, tr. J. Payne (6 vols., 1890); *Certain Tragical Discourses of B.*, Belleforest's version tr. G. Fenton (1567, repr. 1898).

T. G. Griffith, *B.'s Fiction* (1955); Di Francia, *N; Minori*, ii; R. Pruvost, *M.B. and Elizabethan Fiction* (Paris, 1937).

**Bang, Herman** (Adserballe 1857–Ogden, Utah, U.S.A. 1912). Danish novelist and short-story writer. The son of a Danish clergyman, he became a journalist and literary critic, travelled in Scandinavia and wrote important essays on Naturalism. He died on a lecture tour. His first novel, *Haabløse Slægter* (1880), was banned as obscene. Of his many later novels only two have been translated into English, *Ludvigsbakke* (1896; tr. A. G. Chater, *Ida Brandt*, 1928) and *De uden Fædreland* (1906; tr. M. Busch and A. G. Chater, *Denied a Country*, 1927). Perhaps his best novels, such as *Ved Vejen* (1886) and *Tine* (1889), have not been translated, nor his fine short stories, with the exception of those in *Denmark's Best Stories* (tr. H. Astrup Larsen, N.Y., 1928). Bang is a realist and an exquisite psychologist, at his best when in his impressionistic style he describes the fate of small and insignificant people, the stepchildren of life; his own homosexuality made him feel an outcast himself and it is outcasts and outsiders he is best able to describe. [ELB]

H. Jacobsen, *H.B.* (4 vols., Copenhagen, 1954–66).

**Banville, Théodore de** (Moulins 1823–Paris 1891). French poet. Chief follower of Gautier's doctrine 'art for art's sake'. His masterpiece of virtuosity is *Odes funambulesques* (1857). He revised the ballade and the rondeau (*Trente-six ballades joyeuses*, 1873) and set out his elaborate principles of rhyme and rhythm in his *Petit traité de poésie française* (1872). A prolific writer of much occasional prose and several verse comedies, he contributed to *Le Parnasse contemporain* and was a friend and helper to many writers including the young Rimbaud who greatly admired his work. [WA]

*Poésies complètes* (3 vols., 1891–1907); *The Ballades*, tr. A. T. Strong (1913).
J. Charpentier, *T. de B.* (Paris, 1925).

**Barash, Asher** (Poland 1889–Israel 1952). Hebrew novelist and short-story writer. He went to Palestine as a young man and settled in Tel Aviv. He depicts the life of Jews in Galicia chiefly in his novels *Tmunot Mibet Mivshal-Haschechar* (1928) and *Ahava Zara* (1938). His later novels and short stories describe the new life in Israel in a simple, realistic style. He also edited an anthology of modern Hebrew poetry under the title *Mivchar Ha-shirah Ha-ivrit Hachadasha* (1938). [EE]

Klausner, *HMHL*; Waxman, *HJL*.

**Baratynsky, Y.** ⇨ Boratynsky, Y.

**Barbey d'Aurevilly, Jules-Amédée** (Saint-Sauveur-le-Vicomte 1808–Paris 1889). French writer. Of a royalist, Catholic family. Equally extreme in his *dandyisme* and his ultra-montane Catholicism (after 1841), his prolific work offers a dazzling if decadent display of flamboyant sensationalism and fervent spirituality, romantic affectation and affirmation of tradition (especially of the monarchy and the classics). Despite his imaginative flair and impassioned characters he is himself his own most fascinating creation, generous, proud, quarrelsome, idolized – and influential (on e.g. ⇨ Bloy, ⇨ Bernanos). His work includes essays (*Du dandyisme et de G. Brummel*, 1845), novels (*Une vieille maîtresse*, 1851; *L'ensorcelée*, 1854; *Le Chevalier des Touches*, 1864; *Un prêtre marié*, 1865), short stories (especially the famous *Les diaboliques*, 1874) and a vast series of literary studies, *XIXe siècle. Les œuvres et les hommes* (1860–95). [WA]

*Œuvres complètes* (17 vols., 1926–7); *Œuvres romanesques* (Pléiade, 1964); *The Anatomy of Dandyism*, tr. D. B. Wyndham Lewis (1928).
J. Canu, *B. d'A.* (Paris, 1945); R. Bésus, *B. d'A.* (Paris, 1958); J. Petit, *B. d'A. Critique* (Paris, 1963).

**Barbier, Auguste** (Paris 1805–Nice 1882). French poet and satirist Once famous for 'La Curée', satirizing the place-hunters who made capital out of the July revolution. His best collection is *Iambes* (1831), which contained further scathing condemnations of contemporary evils. In *Il pianto* (1833) there are poems lamenting the glorious past of Italy, in *Lazare* (1837) impressions of English industrialism. He influenced Hugo and was admired by the ⇨ Parnassians. He was elected to the Académie Française in 1869. [WA]

**Barbu, Ion,** pseud. of Dan Barbilian (Cîmpulung Muscel 1895–Bucharest 1961). Rumanian poet and mathematician. A student at the Faculty of Sciences at Bucharest, he took his degree in 1920, continued his studies at Göttingen, then became Professor at the Faculty of Sciences, Bucharest (1929). Author of numerous scientific treatises, one of the followers of the German school of mathematics (Gauss, Riemann, Klein) and of the Erlangen 'programme', Dan Barbilian is generally considered one of the founders of axiomatic algebra. A curious and rare example of a person pursuing a dual vocation, he made his début as poet in 1919, and from the very beginning received the notice of one of the most important critics of that period, Eugen Lovinescu, who likewise published numerous poems by him in his review *Sburătorul.* Three principal stages in his poetic evolution can be distinguished: between 1919 and 1920 his poetic ideal was ⇨ Parnassian, although the themes of his verses, expressing an exultant vitality that recalls the philosophy of ⇨ Nietzsche, are on the surface ill-suited to cold objectivity. There follows, between 1920 and 1924, a period of so-called 'Balkanism', in which he cultivated the Oriental picturesque in a lyricism that has a subtle, folkloristic musicality, of magic enchantment. From 1925 he adopted, following the example of Mallarmé, a type of poetic hermeticism, in which intellectual inspiration predominates. The volume *Joc Secund* (1930), in which the poet collects together his hermetic and part of his 'Balkanic' verses, is one of the most original books of poetry in Rumanian literary history. After 1930, he very rarely published verses, sometimes at intervals of years, concentrating on his studies of mathematics. His poetry – though insignificant in terms of quantity – has continued to exercise a great fascination on the Rumanian literary public and especially on the poets. A mathematician in his poetry too, he has created in his verses from the cycle *Joc Secund* a strange, lyrical algebra, in which the musical resources and the metaphorical allusions of the Rumanian language are used with an astonishing majesty. During the last few years of his life, he worked at a translation of Shakespeare's *Richard III*, of which the first three acts appeared in 1961. [MI]

**Barbusse, Henri** (Asnières 1873–Moscow 1935). French novelist. A journalist, his early attempts at poetry and fiction made little impression (*L'enfer*, 1908; tr. J. Rodker, *Inferno*, 1932). He became well known as a result of his experiences in the First World War in which he served with distinction as a volunteer but became disillusioned with war. *Le feu* (1916, Prix Goncourt; tr. F. Wray, *Under Fire*, Everyman, 1917) gives a strikingly realistic account of the lives of front-line troops, insisting that they are ordinary men who have been made to fight but have nothing to gain. *Clarté* (1918; tr. F. Wray, *Light*, 1919) and *Paroles d'un combattant* (1921) developed these ideas with less literary effect but more overt appeal to the international proletariat to unite against their capitalist masters. His literary stature tended to decline as his works became more militantly communist (*Les enchaînements*, 1925; *Lénine*, 1934; *Staline*, 1935, tr. V. Holland, 1935). [IHW]

J. Duclos, J. Freville, *H.B.* (Paris, 1946); P.-H. Simon, *L'esprit et l'histoire* (Paris, 1954); C. Wilson, *The Outsider* (1957); *Europe*, 119–20 (1955).

**Baretti, Giuseppe** (Turin 1719–London 1789). Italian writer and critic. One of the first Accademici Trasformati of Milan, in 1751 he went to London to enjoy greater intellectual freedom. There he directed the Italian Theatre, met Johnson, Reynolds and Garrick, and in 1760 published his *Dictionary of the English and Italian Languages.* He returned to Venice via France, Spain and Portugal, writing a series of controversial *Lettere familiari ai suoi tre fratelli* (1762–3), and in 1763 began publication of *La frusta letteraria*, a periodical written entirely by himself and censuring the superficial and frivolous in contemporary literature. The periodical was suppressed in 1765 and he returned to London in 1766, where he remained till his death, stirring the city with his *Account of the Manners and Customs of Italy* (1768) in reply to the surgeon Samuel Sharp's *Letters from Italy*, and with his fiery polemical work, *Discours sur Shakespeare et sur Monsieur de Voltaire* (1777), in defence of Shakespeare. [RHC]

*Opere*, ed. L. Piccioni (1911ff.); *Scritti*, ed. M. Menghini (1963); *Letterati memorialisti e viaggiatori del '700*, ed. E. Bonora (1951).

G. I. Lopriore, *G.B. nella sua 'Frusta'* (Pisa, 1940); M. Fubini, *Dal Muratori al B.* (Bari, 1954); N. Jonard, *G.B.* (Clermont-Ferrand, 1963); *Minori*, iii.

**'Barlaam et Josaphat.'** The legendary life of Josaphat, a Hindu prince, who is kept apart from the world by his father, but is converted nevertheless to Christianity by the saintly hermit, Barlaam. Josaphat becomes king, but retires from this world to seek fulfilment in the life of the spirit. He joins Barlaam in the desert, and dies a hermit.

Josaphat is none other than the Buddha. The story is derived from the legendary material about the Buddha, and a Greek adaptation of it dating from the 6th or 7th century A.D. was translated into Arabic. A later Greek version was translated into Latin in the 12th century. Several French versions of the story, including one by Gui de Cambrai, are found in the 13th century. English, German, Italian and Provençal versions follow in the next century.

The story, told with touching piety and a vehement belief in the purified and exalted life of the spirit, was known by buddhists, moslems, manichaeans, Christians and cathars. In its pure, mystical aspiration to the ideal life it has had wide appeal to all men of faith. In the Middle Ages its influence was widespread. [LTT]

Lavaud and Nelli, *T.*

E. C. Armstrong, *The French Metrical Versions of B. and J.* (Princeton, 1922); J. Sonet, *Le Roman de B. et J.* (Namur-Paris, 1949–52).

**Barlach, Ernst** (Wedel 1870–Güstrow 1938). German dramatist, sculptor and graphic artist. In 1906 he visited Russia and learnt there 'a Christian humility towards all things' – the decisive experience of his artistic life, which he spent after 1910 in solitude at Güstrow (Mecklenburg). His work was banned (and some of it destroyed) by the Nazis after 1933. His dramas are an extension of his work as a sculptor and designer (he made lithographic illustrations for some of his plays). The main plays are: *Der tote Tag* (1912), *Der arme Vetter* (1918), *Die echten Sedemunds* (1920), *Der Findling* (1922), and *Die Sündflut* (1924: Acts 3 and 4 tr. A. Halley and A. Page, *The Flood*, Northampton, Mass., 1960). All reflect a fervent mysticism, half Gothic and austere, half expressionistic and vitalistic, which broods on the opposition between God and world, to be overcome in a profounder cosmic emotion. [PB]

*Das dichterische Werk* (3 vols., 1956–9).

P. Fechter, *E.B.* (Gütersloh, 1957); W. Flemming, *E.B.: Wesen und Werk* (Berne, 1960); Hans Franck, *E.B. Leben und Werk* (Stuttgart, 1961); K. D. Carls, *E.B.* (Berlin, 1958); Natan, *GML*, iii.

**Baroja y Nessi, Pío** (San Sebastián 1872–Madrid 1956). Spanish novelist. The son of a Basque mining engineer, he received a medical training at Madrid University and took a doctoral degree in medicine at 21. He did not practise for long, but ran an aunt's bakery business in the capital before turning to a literary career. He began to write for periodicals in the nineties, and after a visit to Paris in 1899 he published his first book, *Vidas sombrías* (1900), which enjoyed some success in limited literary circles in Madrid. At that period he was aligned with a group of writers anxious to enliven the slow and apathetic rhythm of Spanish life, and many of the protagonists of his early novels are rebellious or reforming spirits violently opposed to traditional Spanish values (e.g. those of *La feria de los discretos*, 1905, and *Zalacaín el aventurero*, 1909). But his interest in countries other than Spain – reflected in his European travels – and in universal problems is apparent in the early novels too. A pessimism about human nature and the order of things is a feature of several of them, while others are set against an imaginary and vague rather than concrete Spanish or Basque background (*Paradox Rey*, 1906). But in spite of pessimistic tendencies, Baroja's characters do not submit easily to their fates. In style and in plot his novels express a willingness to face the inevitable uncertainties and adversities of human existence. He claimed that it was better to be ungrammatical and express life than to be extremely accurate and produce mere stylistic preciosities. His political and ideological scepticism increases in the later novels, however, and is nowhere more clearly expressed than in *Laura, o la soledad sin remedio*, published in 1939 on his return to Spain from France at the end of the Civil War. [ONVG]

*Obras completas* (1946–52); *Las inquietudes di Shanti Andía* (n.d.; tr. A. Kerrigan, *The Restlessness of Shanti Andía*, 1959).

Brenan, *LSP*; Eoff, *MSN*; *BHS*, XL (1963).

**Baronio, Cesare** (Sora 1538–Rome 1607). Cardinal and ecclesiastical historian. He succeeded St Philip Neri as superior of his Oratory. His *Annales ecclesiastici* (12 folios, 1588–1607) set out to prove the historical validity of the papal claims. In spite of a number of errors, his vast work marks a great advance in historical writing; it was continued by Rinaldi (1676–7), Laderchi (1728–37) and Theiner (1856). [FB]

*Annales*, ed. (with historical notes) J. D. Mansi and D. Georgius (38 vols., Lucca, 1738–59).

Kerr, *Life of C.B.* (1898); G. Calenzio, *C.B.* (Rome, 1907).

**Barrès, (Auguste-) Maurice** (Charmes-sur-Moselle 1862–Paris 1923). French novelist, essayist, Deputy. He filled over a hundred volumes, including his posthumous diaries, *Mes cahiers* (1929–57; extracts ed. G. Dupré, 1963), with his ambition to 'formulate', 'illustrate' and 'educate' the sensibility of his generation. To these ends he used a widely recognized (and imitated) mastery of the assertive and the ironical cadence; of the arresting axiom, silhouette, metaphor; of representative landscape with figures for the set-piece soliloquy or dialogue. Many were touched by some, if few by all, of his successive enthusiasms: solipsistic cult of the Self – *Sous l'œil des barbares* (1888), *Un homme libre* (1889); recovery of 'roots' in the hero- and ancestor-worshipping collective unconscious of 'the people' – *Le jardin de Bérénice* (1891), *Les déracinés* (1897), *La terre et les morts* (1899), *L'appel au soldat* (1900); promotion of traditions which preserve national 'energy' and 'continuity' behind frontiers broken by Bismarck and 'Kantianism', and threatened by the internationalism of 'Panama' financiers and Dreyfusard socialists – *Scènes et doctrines du nationalisme*, *Leurs figures* (1902), *Amori et dolori sacrum*, *Les amitiés françaises* (1903), *Les bastions de l'Est* (1905–21); celebration, in *La colline inspirée* (1913; ed. J. Barbier, 1962; extracts, Classiques Larousse, 1954), *La grande pitié des églises de France* (1914), *Une enquête aux pays du Levant* (1923), of a broadly assimilative Roman Catholic 'order' of civilization, able to incorporate the nation's polytheistic past, Christian present and scientific future, and to reconcile Barrès's still toughly defensive Lorrainer's frontier spirit, triumphant in his daily articles throughout the First World War, with a newly expansive 'inner Asia' of religious and erotic mysticism, freed in his post-war essays and last novel: *Le mystère en pleine lumière* (1926), *Un jardin sur l'Oronte* (1922). [PO]

P. Moreau, *M.B.* (Paris, 1946); I.-M. Frandon, *L'Orient de M.B.* (Geneva, 1952); J.-M. Domenach, *B. par lui-même* (Paris, 1954).

**Barrière, Théodore** (Paris 1823–Paris 1877). French playwright. Prolific author, alone or in collaboration, of more than a hundred farces and serious plays produced under the Second Empire. His vein is social satire and he creates a gallery of sharply observed types whose self-interest and stupidity are exposed with verve, e.g. *Les filles de marbre* (1853; tr./adapt. C. Selby, *The Marble Heart*, 1854), an unsentimental view of the world of courtesans; *Les faux bonshommes* (1856); *Les jocrisses de l'amour* (1865); and *Malheur aux vaincus* (1865). Two of his most successful plays were based on novels: *La vie de Bohème* (1849) and *Manon Lescaut* (1851). He lacks ⇨ Augier's moral seriousness and tends to violent incoherence in his serious plays. He also lacks a distinctive style and vision, but handles light comedy with some skill. [SBJ]

E. C. Byam, *T.B.: Dramatist of the Second Empire* (1938).

**Barros, João de** (Viseu ? *c.*1496–Pombal 1570). Portuguese chronicler and author of pedagogical and didactic works. The illegitimate son of a provincial fidalgo, he received a good classical education at the court of King Manuel I, where he attracted the attention of this monarch by writing a chivalresque romance, *Crónica do Imperador Clarimundo*, and was encouraged to undertake his grandiose history of Portuguese expansion. Apart from a voyage to Guinea in 1522, he never seems to have left Portugal; but from 1525 to 1567 he served first as Treasurer and then as Factor in the Casa da Índia at Lisbon, where the colonial administration was centralized. This enabled him to collect all the material which he needed for his projected history, planned on a global scale to include Asia, Africa and Brazil, together with more specialized works on the geography of the known world and on the seaborne trade of Asia. Of this ambitious project, only three *Décadas* dealing with Asia were published in his lifetime (1552–63); the draft of a fourth was edited by João Baptista Lavanha in 1615. His other works relating to Portuguese overseas expansion were either unfinished, lost or destroyed.

In 1532 he published one of his most important books, *Rópica Pnefma*, a discussion by several allegorical personages of moral, psychological and social problems. The work reveals strong Erasmian tendencies and was banned by the Portuguese Inquisition in 1581. In 1539–40, he published a pioneer *ABC*, *Gramática da língua portuguesa*, written for Indians and Africans learning Portuguese, accompanied by a *Diálogo em louvor da nossa linguagem*, and a complementary *Diálogo da viciosa vergonha*. His *Diálogo sobre preceptos morais em modo de jogo*, probably first published in 1540, had a second edition in 1563. Apart from other didactic and philosophical works which have been lost, he worked long hours at his official duties in the Casa da Índia, so it is hardly surprising that a paralytic stroke forced his retirement to Pombal in 1567. In his *Décadas*, João de Barros deliberately modelled himself on Livy, aiming to construct a truly monumental work which would endure for all time. His long, straggling sentences, and the moralizing speeches which he puts into the mouths of his principal characters make his *Décadas* heavy going in parts; and as an official historian he often (though not invariably) turned a blind eye to the seamy side of Portuguese activities in Asia. On the other hand, his work is of lasting value for the wealth of material it embodies concerning 16th-century Asia, including Arabic, Persian and Chinese sources which he had translated by competent individuals, one of whom was an educated Chinese slave bought for this specific purpose. [CRB]

A. Baião, *Documentos inéditos sobre João de Barros* (Coimbra, 1917); C. R. Boxer, *Three Historians of Portuguese Asia: Barros, Couto and Bocarro* (Macau, 1948); A. J. Saraiva, *História da cultura em Portugal*, ii and iii (Lisbon, 1955, 1961).

**Barthes, Roland.** ⇨ French Literary Criticism in the 19th and 20th Centuries.

**Basile, Giambattista,** pseud. Gian Alesio Abbattutis) (Naples 1575–Giugliano 1632). Italian short-story writer. His Italian writings are now forgotten and he is remembered only as author of the *Cunto de li cunti*, or *Pentamerone* (1634–6), a collection of fairy-tales written in a Neapolitan dialect which is orientated not towards the naïveté of popular art but towards the literary sophistication of *seicento* Baroque. The story of Princess Zoza's melancholy and her winning of a husband forms the framework of the 50 tales, and in this atmosphere of adventure, fantasy and magic, Baroque exuberance combines admirably with dialectal verve. Basile had Italian predecessors (e.g. ⇨ Straparola) in his cult of the fairy-tale, but his was the first major achievement in this minor genre in which he was followed by Perrault, ⇨ Gozzi and the brothers ⇨ Grimm. [DGR]

*Il Pentamerone*, Italian tr. B. Croce (1957); *Il Pentamerone or The Tale of Tales*, tr. Sir R. Burton (intr. E. R. Vincent) (1952).
Croce, *SSL*; C. Jannaco, *Il Seicento* (Milan, 1963).

**Basque Literature.** The tenaciousness of the Basques' sense of identity is shown most clearly in the preservation of their language in unfavourable circumstances, and in spite of 2,000 years of Romanization. Yet in other respects the Basques seem less attached to tradition. In general, they have always had short memories; when the Romantic movement aroused interest in the customs and traditions of this ancient European race very little could be brought to light. The epic poems which did enjoy a certain fame (the song of Lelo about the wars with Rome, and the song of Altabiscar which celebrated the victory of Roncesvalles) are little more than rather poor pastiches, even though the first dates from the 16th century.

The first evidence of Basque or *euskara* appears in Roman times in the names of people and more particularly of gods. They are found in Latin inscriptions, almost all of which were discovered in the old province of Aquitaine. After a fairly long absence of documentary evidence, traces of the language reappear, each time more numerous, from the 9th century onwards. The first two Basque sentences are two glosses, probably dating from the 10th century, mixed up with others in Romance in a manuscript from the monastery of San Millán de la Cogolla in the Rioja. It must be remembered that Basque was not a written language and that in the documents of the country Latin was replaced by Romance (Castilian, Aragonese or Gascon).

It is likely that the oral literature of the Middle Ages was already as rich and vital as it is today. The numerous fragments that survive demonstrate the popularity of the epic poems in irregular metre, inspired by the bloody battles and feuds that raged throughout the Basque country in the 14th and 15th centuries. Then, as now, improvisation based on traditional forms was usual, e.g. in the dirges that women composed and chanted over the body of a dead relative. The best example of this epic poetry has been transmitted orally in a poem that describes the assassination of the young Berteretch de Soule (*c.* 1440), when this region was still a feudal benefice of the king of England. Popular theatre has survived in Soule too – in the form of the so-called *pastorales* whose roots go back to the Middle Ages.

Written Basque is neither abundant nor varied. The first book, *Linguae Vasconum primitiae* by the priest Bernard Dechepare, was not printed until 1545. In its combination of religious feeling with profane love it resembles, although on a lesser scale, the Spanish *Libro de buen amor*. Dechepare's enthusiasm for the Basque language and his pride in being the first person to put it in print is very much in the spirit of the Renaissance.

The other important work of the 16th century had a quite different inspiration. Under the patronage of Jeanne d'Albret, the Queen of Navarre, Joanes de Leiçarraga, a priest who adopted the teachings of the Reformation, produced a dignified and skilful translation of the New Testament and of Calvinist works of doctrine published in La Rochelle in 1571.

Amongst Catholics the desire for religious instruction in their own language did not come about until after the Council of Trent. In Spain only catechisms of slight literary merit appeared, but a group of writers, all clerics, became established around Sare and St Jean de Luz in the region of Labourd. From 1617 onwards they published a number of books of instruction Two of these writers, Father Materre and Silvain Pouvreau, were Frenchmen who had learned the Basque language. The theologian Joanes de Etcheberri de Ciboure published three books of verse which achieve moments of lyricism in spite of their strong didactic element. The most important of this group was Pedro de Axular, born in 1556 in the Spanish province of Navarre. His *Guero* (1643), on the need for immediate repentance, is rightly regarded as the best example of Basque prose; discursive yet cohesive, it resembles the writing of Fray Luis de ⇨ Granada.

This religious literature soon found imitators in other regions. On the fringe was Arnaud d'Oihenart, historian known for his scholarly critical study *Notitia utriusque Vasconiae* (1638), and the author of a book of poems (1637) worth noting for their technical skill and the purity of the language. In addition he compiled a collection of proverbs like those of the two Huguenots, Sauguis, whose poems have been lost, and Jacques de Béla.

After the Treaty of Utrecht (1713) the centre of literary activity moved from the French to the Spanish part of the Basque country. Among the poets and the translators or adaptors of religious works one man can be singled out. He is Joanes de Etcheberri de Sara, a doctor who practised in Guipúzcoa; his ambitious project to introduce Basque into ordinary teaching failed, and his works remain unpublished to this day. Father Manuel de Larramendi (1690–1766), enthusiast for the Basque country and its language, brilliant orator and writer in Castilian and Basque, famous for his *Imposible vencido* (1729), a grammar of the Basque language, and his controversial *Diccionario trilingüe* (1736), was the most significant writer of the time. He was also the mentor and guiding force of a number of writers – Cardaberaz and Mendiburu and others, Jesuits like himself. His influence is still felt today.

In 1764 the Sociedad Bascongada de Amigos del País (Basque Society of Friends of the Country) was founded, which was to have so many members amongst the followers of the Enlightenment in Spain. Although the needs of the moment turned the *Caballeritos de Azcoitia*, as they were called, towards the sciences and technical matters, the arts were not neglected. The founder of this society, Xavier María de Munibe, Count of Peñaflorida, composed a bilingual comic opera *El borracho burlado* in 1764. However, this was not the first landmark in the Basque theatre; it was preceded by the delightful *Acto para la Nochebuena* by Pedro Ignacio de Barrutia, a native of the province of Alava, who died in 1759.

The work of the *Amigos del País* did not bear the fruit that might have been expected because of the wars against the French Convention (1793ff.) and Napoleon. Nevertheless its influence on the study and development of the Basque language was still being felt about 1800, the time of Wilhelm von ⇨ Humboldt's travels, and the time when the priest Juan Antonio Moguel wrote *Peru Abarca*, a novel in dialogue form which despite its moralizing intention is one of the most original and amusing books in Basque.

With the fabulists (Vicenta Moguel, the niece of Juan Antonio, Iturriaga, Archu, Goyhetche, etc.) an awareness of the needs of education invaded the field of poetry which until then had been the only non-didactic genre. For example the Basque Samaniego wrote his Castilian fables for the pupils at the Vergara seminary run by the *Amigos del País*. Jean-Martin Hiribarren wrote *Escaldunac* ('The Basques', 1853), a long descriptive poem about the country and the customs of its people. The work of Etchahun (1786–1862) is very different. The poems of this trenchant, vigorous improviser still live on in peoples' memories, and his own tragic story has been told by ⇨ Chamisso.

Romanticism was introduced into Basque literature by J.-A. Chaho (1810–58), a scholar and theosopher who wrote mostly in French. When he succeeded in restraining his flights of fancy his work shows that he recognized the value of many of the authentic elements of popular culture.

The religious writers were as numerous as ever; Juan Ignacio de Iztueta was the first secular prose writer to write on the dances (1824) and the history (1847) of Guipúzcoa. Prince Bonaparte (1813–91), who made the first study of Basque dialects, was also a patron of literature and published, amongst other things, many works of his Basque collaborators, including the translation of the Bible (London, 1859–65) by Captain Jean Duvoisin.

Poetry flourished and was further encouraged by special literary contests in the second half of the century. However the best lyric writers did not participate: Jean-Baptiste Elissamburu (1828–91), who had a fine command of verse and language, and Indalecio Bizcarrondo ('Vilinch', 1831–76), whose lack of education in no way impeded his mastery of expression. Of a lesser stature was José María Iparraguirre, although his *Gernikako Arbola* ('The Tree of Guernica', 1851) was immediately adopted as the Basque 'national anthem' and caused him to be exiled.

The end of the second Carlist war in Spain (1876) brought with it a curbing of autonomy. Side by side with new political currents a cultural movement emerged in the Basque cities. In San Sebastián, cradle of modern Basque theatre, Jose Manterola published his *Cancionero vasco* (1877–80), the first Basque anthology, and started the periodical *Euskal-erria* (1880–1918). From now on the number of books and periodicals increased. The study of history, language, literature and popular culture were firmly established with Arturo Campión, R. Ma. de Azkue, Julio de Urquijo and J. M. de Barandiaran. Through his political action Arana-Goiri gave Basque literature an entry into fields hitherto unknown. From many names the following deserve mention: Domingo Aguirre (1864–1920), author of the well-known novel *Garoa* (1912), a nostalgic picture of a Basque village; Evaristo de Bustinza ('Kirikino', 1866–1929), journalist and short-story writer; the essayist Jean Etchepare (1877–1935) and the poet Jules Moulier ('Oxobi', 1888–1958). Many people consider 'Xabier de Lizardi' (José Maria Aguirre, 1896–1933) to be the purest and most original lyric writer in Basque. Linked with his name must be that of his friend Nicolás de Ormaechea ('Orixe', 1888–1961), poet and prose writer, whose finest work of commitment is the poem *Euskaldunak* (1950, but written before 1936), a vast timeless picture of the Basque people.

The Spanish Civil War and the Second World War made a long break in literary output. Most publications appeared in America: the novels of Juan Ignacio Irazusta, the poetry and scholarly works of Joaquín de Zaitegui, etc. Today, literary activity is as great as at the best moments in the past, and more varied than ever before. In fact this little language apparently isolated and forgotten is as receptive as any to the winds of the world. [LM]

*Eskualdunen loretegia (1545–1800)*, ed. P. Lafitte (Bayonne, 1931) (anthology); *Milla euskal olerki eder*, ed. S. Onaindia (Larrea-Amorebieta, 1954) (anthology); *Textos arcaicos vascos*, L. Michelena (Madrid, 1964) (anthology). French tr. of Dechapare's verse in *Boletín de la Real Sociedad Vascongada de los Amigos del País* (San Sebastián, 1951–2, 1955); W. Webster, *Basque Legends Collected Chiefly in the Labourd* (1879); *Chants populaires du pays basque, paroles et musique originales*, ed. tr. J. D. J. Salaberry (Bayonne, 1870).

R. Gallop, *A Book of the Basques* (1930); J. Caro Baroja, *Los Vascos* (Madrid, 1958); L. Michelena, *Historia de la literatura vasca* (Madrid, 1960); L. Villasante, *Historia de la literatura vasca* (Bilbao, 1961).

**Bassani, Giorgio** (Bologna 1916– ). Italian novelist. He lived in Ferrara until 1943. After the war he worked in Rome as a film scriptwriter and publishers' reader. In 1955 he won a literary prize for *Gli ultimi anni di Clelia Trotti*, one in a series of short novels (later collected with the title *Storie ferraresi*, 1960) having as a common background the life of Ferrara Jews during the anti-semitic persecutions of the Fascist regime. Bassani paints some memorable figures: Geo Josz, the survivor of Buchenwald who, on his return home, finds himself a living unwelcome reminder of a past that even his own community tries to forget (*La lapide in via Mazzini*); Dr Fatigati slowly withdrawing into his homosexual obsession that will end in suicide, while at the same time the whole of society sinks into insanity (of which Fascism and anti-semitism are symptoms) culminating in the collective suicide of the Second World War (*Gli occhiali d'oro*, 1958; tr. I. Quigly, *The Gold-Rimmed Spectacles*, 1960); Pino Barilari, in whose life personal and political tragedy come at the same time (*Una notte del '43*). In his latest novels Bassani has continued to add to the picture of Jewish life in Ferrara during the thirties. *Il giardino dei Finzi-Contini* (1962; tr. I. Quigly, *The Garden of the Finzi-Continis*, 1963), the garden of a wealthy Jewish family where young Jews meet to play tennis after being forced to resign from the local club, becomes the symbol of lost humanity and innocence: within its idyllic grounds the narrator's love for the daughter of the family is allowed to grow, only to be brutally shattered by the dishuman reality outside its walls. *Dietro la porta* (1964) is a story of schoolchildren, in whose microcosm the novelist sees an embryonal representation of adult life, with its friendships, deceptions and inexplicable barriers between races, social classes and individuals. [GMC]

*Cinque storie ferraresi* (1956; tr. I. Quigly, *A Prospect of Ferrara*, 1956).
Ferretti, *LI*; Pullini, *RID*.

**Bataille, Henry** (Nîmes 1872–La Malmaison 1922). French writer of psychological melodramas. Once famous for *Maman Colibri* (1904), a 'strong' situation in which a middle-aged mother's passion for her son's friend is complicated by the veiled eroticism of her relations with the son himself. *La femme nue* (1908), *Les flambeaux* (1913), *Le phalène* (1913), all exploit notorious society scandals of the period involving the private lives of Debussy, the Curies, etc. [SBJ]

*Théâtre complet* (12 vols., 1922–9).
J.-B. Besançon, *Essai sur le théâtre d'H.B.* (Paris, 1928).

**Baudelaire, Charles-Pierre** (Paris 1821–Paris 1867). French poet. One of the greatest of all French poets and perhaps the most discerning art critic of the 19th century. He was the only son of an elderly father and a young mother. When not yet 6, he lost his father and in the following year, on his mother's remarriage, acquired a step-father, Col. (ultimately, Gen.) Aupick, whom he came to regard as both an interloper and an enemy. Baudelaire was sent to boarding school, in Lyons and Paris, and was unhappy there; his troubled childhood and rebellious adolescence had their logical outcome in his expulsion, at 18, from the famous Lycée Louis-le-Grand. Later that year (1839), he enrolled as a law student within the University of Paris, and having already contracted the venereal disease from which indirectly he was to die, soon drifted into a recklessly 'Bohemian' and dissolute way of life. Alarmed as much by his firm resolve to become a writer as by the 'unhealthy relationships' into which he had fallen, Aupick despatched him in 1841, as a remedial or disciplinary measure, on a long sea voyage round the Cape of Good Hope. Baudelaire's mood, however, remained one of unbending truculence, and after Mauritius he insisted on taking the next boat home. Yet the imaginative impact of the voyage was very great: it nourished his mind and art throughout the rest of his life, and one immediate sequel, on his return, was that he took as mistress a coloured girl, Jeanne Duval, and thus entered upon a long, stormy and poetically fruitful relationship that was at last painfully severed only in 1856. By now (1842), he had come into his father's inheritance, and acquired new opportunities for gratifying his expensive tastes in art (and love); inevitably, the family again took fright, and in 1844, to Baudelaire's deep mortification, transferred the effective control of his fortune to the notary Ancelle. From that time onwards, he became a 'remittance man', and plunged ever deeper into debts from which he never succeeded in extricating himself. He had by now written many of his poems in first draft, and had announced a collection under the provocative title *Les Lesbiennes*; in fact, however, his first publication was a review of the annual Paris art exhibition, *Le salon de 1845*, a prentice work that he almost immediately disavowed but which has interest as the first record of his lifelong admiration for Delacroix. Baudelaire's humiliation at the hands of his family, his straitened financial circumstances, his discouragement at the inadequacy (as he thought) of his literary achievement, his despair at the disorder of his emotional life – all these combined to drive him, in June 1845, to a suicide attempt which, although not without burlesque elements, was none the less a genuine cry for help. The cry was not altogether unanswered, Baudelaire regained some (temporary) favour with his family, and the next year or so was among the most notably productive periods in his life. In the *Salon de 1846*, in particular, he broke entirely fresh ground, virtually abandoning the conventional review of exhibits in favour of a brilliantly written aesthetic treatise. Another interesting publication was the novella, *La Fanfarlo*, with its ironic self-portrait of the poet 'Samuel Cramer'.

He was rescued from further disillusion and despair by the events of February 1848, which inspired him to surprising revolutionary, even Socialist, fervour. He joined in editing two short-lived Republican journals, associated with Champfleury, Courbet and other Realists, again announced his poems, but this time under a title, *Les Limbes*, which reflected his new-found social concerns, and even flirted briefly with utilitarianism in two essays proclaiming the social mission of art. But after the political disillusions of December 1851, he came increasingly under the influence of Edgar Allan Poe, in whom he saw a 'twin soul' and whose *Tales* he began assiduously to translate; he moved towards a strongly anti-didactic and 'purist' aesthetic, and on political and social questions took up an increasingly reactionary standpoint. A curious episode during this period was his Platonic (and, initially, anonymous) courtship of the wordly Mme Sabatier, for whom he wrote many of his most beautiful love poems; a second, more or less simultaneous relationship (both amorous and poetic) involved him with the actress Marie Daubrun.

In 1857, he at last brought out, under the title *Les fleurs du mal*, the book of poems which is his principal claim to glory; during the previous two years, he had worked untiringly at revising these poems and arranging them in the most logical and effective sequence. (The much-vaunted 'architecture' of the book amounts to no more than this.) In a style blending a notable freedom and range of imagery with a certain majestic, even 'classical', rhetoric, he lays bare, with a new directness, whole shrouded areas of human suffering, perversity and aspiration. Over a third of the poems are love poems – some among the most magical and idealistic in any language, others exploring pitilessly the degradations and corruptions of love. Further sections of this great if unequal collection evoke the terrible landscapes of inertia and despair, or hymn, more conventionally, the splendours and miseries of the poet's lot; there are poems of death, of protest and rebellion, of deep compassion for the unfortunate and dispossessed.

Certain of these poems published previously (1855, *Revue des Deux Mondes*) had by their audacity shocked the aesthetic puritans of the day; now, in the atmosphere of scandal surrounding Baudelaire's name, the authorities were moved to action. Legal proceedings were instituted, and in its eventual judgement the Court, as well as imposing substantial fines, ruled that 6 of the 101 poems were to be 'suppressed' as 'obscene or immoral'. This was a crushing blow, and provoked a long retreat into the blackest pessimism and misanthropy. But Baudelaire determined to make good the judicial excisions, and in 1861 published a new augmented edition of *Les fleurs du mal*; among the new poems written for this collection are several (*Le cygne*, *Le voyage*, *Danse macabre*) in which he reveals, through the scope and complexity of his social judgements, his true commanding stature as a 'moralist'. He had by now completed his translation of Poe; his prose writings attained a new richness and brilliance with his *Salon de 1859*, his essay (on the draughtsman Guys) *Le peintre de la vie moderne*, his passionate defence of Wagner against the contemporary musical 'establishment', his searching analysis of the effects of hashish and opium in *Les paradis artificiels*. He continued also with the writing (begun in the 1850s) of his *Petits poëmes en prose* (*Le spleen de Paris*), and of the intimate jottings to be gathered under the titles *Fusées* and *Mon cœur mis à nu*. (Neither of these projects was in fact realized until after his death.) In 1863, his poem *L'imprévu* marks a seeming return to the orthodox Catholic fold. In 1864, he was invited to Brussels to give a (disastrous) series of lectures; rooted by inertia and dogged increasingly by illness, he remained in Belgium until, in 1866, he was struck down with hemiplegic paralysis and transported to Paris, where he died in the following year.

Baudelaire is perhaps the first poet we recognize as being truly 'modern' and 'ours'. 'Modern', first of all, in his 'fraternal' feeling for sin and degradation, his ruthless self-awareness, his eye for the teeming pathos and mystery of city life; 'modern' in his refusal (implicit in the title *Les fleurs du mal*) to admit any restriction in the artist's choice of theme; 'modern' in his assertion of the spiritual intuitions (the 'correspondences') informing certain poetic symbols; 'modern', in his later poems, in his oblique interweaving of images and themes, and in his rejection of all overt moral recommendation. As for his supremacy as an art critic, this may be seen as the triumphant vindication of his own claim that it is the poet, infallibly, who makes the best critic of all. [FWL]

*Œuvres complètes*, rev. edn C. Pichois (Pléiade, 1966); *Correspondance générale*, ed. J. Crépet and C. Pichois (6 vols., 1947–53); *Lettres inédites aux siens*, ed. P. Auserve (1966); *Selected Verse*, ed. and tr. F. Scarfe (Penguin Poets, 1961); *The Painter of Modern Life and Other Essays* and *Art in Paris 1845–1862*, tr. and ed. J. Mayne (1964, 1965).

P. Mansell Jones, *B.* (1952); J. Prévost, *B.* (Paris, 1953); Enid Starkie, *B.* (1957); Alison Fairlie, *B.: Les Fleurs du Mal* (1960); F. W. Leakey, *B. and Nature* (1968) and 'B.: The Poet as Moralist', in Austin, *SMFL.*; L. J. Austin, *L'univers poétique de B.* (1956).

**Baudri of Bourgueil** (Meung-sur-Loir 1046–St Samson-sur-Risle 1130). Christian Latin historian and poet. Archbishop of Dol. He was the author of much Latin prose and verse, including a history of the conquest of Jerusalem by the crusaders (*Historiae Hierosolymitanae*), some lives of saints, and much light verse revealing a close study of Ovid and a love of the country. One of his lighter poems contains a detailed imaginative description of the bedroom of Adela, daughter of William the Conqueror. He defends his writing of love poetry on the ground that his own life is pure and that his characters express their own sentiments, not his. [FB]

Migne, *PL*, 160, 162, 166; P. Abrahams, *Œuvres poétiques de B. de B.* (Paris, 1926).

Raby, *CLP*, *SLP*.

**Bayle, Pierre** (Le Carla 1647–Rotterdam 1706). French Protestant scholar and critic. The son of a Huguenot pastor, he studied at Toulouse and Geneva, and later became professor of philosophy at the Protestant Academy of Sedan (1675); when this was dissolved in 1681, friends found him a similar appointment in Rotterdam, where he remained.

A critical rather than constructive thinker, in his first major work, *Pensées diverses sur la comète de 1680* (1682; ed. A. Prat, Paris, 1911), he attacks a contemporary superstition with both historical and philosophical arguments, and questions the necessity of a religious basis for morals. In 1684 he launched a monthly periodical *Nouvelles de la République des Lettres*, the first to offer the general reader a wide survey of European scholarship. He wrote polemics for the Huguenot cause, and in favour of general religious toleration (*Commentaire philosophique*, 1686), but here he incurred hostility from fellow-exiles, and was dismissed from his chair in 1693. He now devoted himself wholly to his very influential *Dictionnaire historique et critique* (1697, 2nd edn 1702; tr. P. Desmaizeaux *et al.*, 1734–8; *Selections*, tr. and ed. R. H. Popkin, 1965). This work, by its comparative analysis of evidence and its sceptical approach, supported by vast learning, revealed the unreliability of much that passed for historical knowledge, and emphasized the irreducible nature of many philosophical and theological dilemmas. It consequently became an arsenal for the critical thinkers of the Enlightenment, but it is questionable whether Bayle had any other philosophical intention than to support revealed religion by stressing the limitations of reason. Latterly Bayle turned away from historical studies to pursue philosophical and religious controversies in a series of amorphous volumes. His correspondence with learned contemporaries is extensive, and partly still unpublished. [WHB]

*Œuvres diverses* (Trévoux, 1737); *Choix de textes*, ed. M. Raymond (1948).

H. Robinson, *B. the Sceptic* (1931); É. Labrousse, *P.B.* (The Hague, 1963–4) (in French).

**Bazhan, Mykola** (Kamenets Podolskiy 1904– ). Ukrainian poet. Under futurist influence in his earliest poems, in his first collections (1926–7) he showed romantic *motifs* with high passions and powerful characters. Modernist-expressionist in style, with exquisite rich vocabulary, 'charged' epithets, rhythmic periods, he turns to historiosophic themes in his powerful epic poems: *Budivli* (1929), *Hofmanova nich*, *Trylohiya prystrasti*, *Sliptsi* (1930). Subjected to the Communist Party's severe criticism in the 1930s, which continued to some extent into the 1950s, he has treated, since 1934, socialist realism themes; an interesting example is his *Anhliys'ki vrazhennya* ('English Impressions', 1949; one poem, 'Big Ben', tr. in *SL*, 1, 1950) for which he was awarded a Stalin prize. One of the greatest masters of poetic language, his bold innovations are characterized by intellectualism and an inclination toward the abstract and contemplative. [VS]

*Tvory* (2 vols., Kiev, 1965); Andrusyshen and Kirkconnell, *UP*; Luts'ky, *LD*.
Luckyj, *LPSU*; *UCE*; *SL*, x (1964).

**Bazin, René** (Angers 1853–1932). French novelist. Studied and lectured in law (at Angers); elected to the French Academy (1903). As a boy he developed a deep love of the country and was fascinated by the landscape of Vendée as he travelled to the island of Noirmoutier for the holidays. Like Millet, whom he greatly admired, he became keenly interested in people who work on the land. His supreme achievement is his poetic novel *La terre qui meurt* (1899), a story set around Sallertaine (Vendée), dealing with the desertion of the soil by the younger generation lured away by the prospect of an easy life in developing cities. He believed in preserving the traditional patterns of life and showed in most of his novels that transgressors are doomed to failure. His sympathy for humble folk led him to study the lives of woodcutters, factory workers, priests, nursemaids and nuns. Influenced by his teacher Mgr Freppel, an Alsatian émigré, he turned his attention to the conflicts of loyalties in families living in Alsace after the German annexation of 1871. His novel *Les Oberlé* (1901) became particularly significant in 1919 and 1940 when Alsace changed hands twice again. His works appear as a vehement reaction against the naturalistic novels of Zola, but are no less important a contribution to the social history of their time. [HG]

*Les Noëllet* (1891); *De toute son âme* (1897); *Donatienne* (1902); *L'isolée* (1905); *Le blé qui lève* (1907); *Charles de Foucauld* (1920) (a biography).
J. S. Wood, *R.B., sa vie et son œuvre* (Paris, 1934); T. Catta, *Un romancier de vraie France, R.B.* (Paris, 1936); J. H. Leighton, *R.B. et l'Alsace* (Paris, 1953).

**'Beatrijs.'** Middle Dutch legend. The only surviving manuscript dates from 1374. The story itself is assumed to originate from the early 14th century or earlier (in view of the serious treatment of love, the courtly tone and the absence of didacticism). A nun eventually leaves her convent to marry the young man she has loved since childhood. Two children are born but after seven years he leaves her penniless and she takes to the streets for a living. Driven by remorse back to the convent, she finds that her absence was unnoticed because the Virgin Mary had done her Sacristan's duties for her. The unknown Flemish author took the legend, at second hand, from ⇨ Caesarius of Heisterbach's *Dialogus miraculorum*, and his moving and sensitive portrayal of Beatrijs' tragic dilemma inspires poets to this day (e.g. ⇨ Boutens, ⇨ Maeterlinck). [PK]

A. J. Barnouw, *The Miracle of Beatrice, A Flemish Legend of c. 1300* (1944); *Beatrice*, tr. E. Colledge in *Mediaeval Netherlands Religious Literature* (Leyden–London, 1965).

**Beaumarchais, Pierre-Augustin Caron de** (Paris 1732–Paris 1799). French dramatist and publicist. Brought up to his father's trade of clockmaker, his inventive skill early led to his appointment as court horologist. A rich marriage established his fortunes (and title) and he embarked on an adventurous career as financial speculator, confidential agent, and – ultimately – man of letters. His journey to Madrid in 1764, secretly for commercial negotiations with the Spanish government on behalf of a French financial syndicate, ostensibly to champion his sister, compromised by the prominent journalist José Clavijo, furnished material for Goethe's tragedy *Clavigo* (1774) and his own *Eugénie* (1767), an unsuccessful bourgeois drama in the Diderot manner. He undertook confidential missions for Louis XV and Louis XVI, and helped to supply arms to the American revolutionaries. He also sponsored the first complete edition of Voltaire's works (70 vols., Kehl, 1784–90). His complicated affairs involved him in numerous lawsuits, and the series of brilliantly conceived and often highly dramatic *Mémoires* (1773–5) against his adversaries made his literary reputation.

His first essays in comedy were *parades*, farcical sketches well spiced with obscenity – a genre then popular in noblemen's private theatres. One of these, *Jean-Bête à la foire*, furnished the basic situation for *Le Barbier de Séville* (1775; tr. J. Wood, Penguin

Classics, 1964). This play, without breaking with tradition, renewed French comedy by its revival of comedy of intrigue, by its gay vivacity and verbal wit, and by its re-creation of the traditional role of the scheming valet at a new level of ingenuity and complexity in Figaro, who shares many characteristics with his creator. His second masterpiece, *Le mariage de Figaro* (1778, staged after many difficulties 1784; tr. J. Wood, Penguin Classics, 1964), while no less brilliant, has stronger sentimental undertones and makes an older, less light-hearted Figaro the centre of a situation with clearly anti-aristocratic implications. In a third play, *La mère coupable* (1792), Figaro degenerates, however, into a prosy moralizer in an unconvincing sentimental melodrama. [WHB]

*Théâtre complet*, ed. R. d'Hermies (1952); *Théâtre* (Pléiade, 1949).

K. E. C. Cox, *The Real Figaro* (1962); R. Pomeau, *B., l'homme et l'œuvre* (Paris, 1956).

**Beauvoir, Simone de** (Paris 1908– ). French novelist and essayist. A brilliant student, she became a close friend of Sartre, and has played a leading part in the Existentialist movement. She taught in Marseilles, Rouen and Paris, and turned to literature during the Second World War. She is fiercely non-conformist in her outlook, and has reacted strongly against her bourgeois background. Her novels reflect many aspects of atheistic Existentialist thought and the characteristic social and political dilemmas of French left-wing intellectuals during the last thirty years. *L'invitée* (1943; tr. R. Senhouse and Y. Moyse, *She Came to Stay*, 1949) illustrates the Existentialist notion of a character becoming fully conscious of himself as a free, undetermined being through committing a wholly autonomous act. *Le sang des autres* (1944; tr. R. Senhouse and Y. Moyse, *The Blood of Others*, 1948) draws on events of the 1930s and of the French wartime Resistance movement to illustrate the supreme importance of freedom in life, a freedom which demands great courage, since God is deemed not to exist and since the reasons for living are, consequently, for men themselves to create. *Tous les hommes sont mortels* (1946; tr. L. Friedman, *All Men are Mortal*, N.Y., 1955) examines from the Existentialist angle the need to face the finality of death; what men had hoped to find in immortality they must now seek in life itself. *Les mandarins* (Prix Goncourt, 1954; tr. L. Friedman, 1957) is a vivid evocation of life in French intellectual circles in the 1940s; it is to some extent a *roman à clef*, and had been criticized as lacking the clear-cut philosophical drive of the earlier books; but, like all her writing, it reveals acute psychological insight, especially into the women characters. She has also published books of memoirs, notably *La force de l'âge* (1960; tr. P. Green, *The Prime of Life*, 1962), which not only reflect deeply felt personal experiences, but provide valuable evidence about the development of the Existentialist movement. Among her more important essays are: *Pour une morale de l'ambigüité* (1947) in which she stresses that moral values are not permanent or divinely imposed, but exist only insofar as men create them; and *Le deuxième sexe* (1949; tr. H. M. Paishley, *The Second Sex*, 1960) in which the author claims that, if women are subservient to men, this is due not to their natural inferiority, but to the deliberate subordination of women by men who dominate society; here again freedom is her ideal. Other important essays include *L'Amérique au jour le jour* (1954) and *Faut-il brûler Sade?* (1955). [CAB]

*Mémoires d'une jeune fille rangée* (1958; tr. J. Kirkup, *Memoirs of a Dutiful Daughter*, 1959); *La force des choses* (1963; tr. J. Kirkup, *The Force of Circumstance*, 1965).

H. E. Barnes, *The Literature of Possibility, a Study of Humanistic Existentialism* (1961); G. Hourdin, *S. de B. et la liberté* (Paris, 1962); J. Cruickshank, *The Novelist as Philosopher* (1962).

**Beccaria, Cesare** (Milan 1738–Milan 1794). Italian economist and criminologist. The leading representative of the Enlightenment in Italy. He derived from Montesquieu's *Lettres persanes* an early interest in philosophical and social problems. Encouraged by Alessandro and Pietro ⇨ Verri and other contributors to *Il caffè*, he wrote *Dei delitti e delle pene* (published anon. at Leghorn, 1764; tr. 1770 and 1880) – an instant immense success – a pioneering work in the movement of penal reform in France and parts of Italy. He became professor of political economy in Milan in 1768, in 1771 adviser to the Supremo Consiglio d'Economia Pubblica, and in 1791 member of the official penal reform commission. His *Ricerche intorno alla natura dello stile* (1770) is significant for challenging the authority of conventional forms in art, and for advocating a proper philosophical study of the true essence of artistic creation. [RHC]

*Opere*, ed. S. Romagnoli (2 vols., Florence, 1958); *Illuministi italiani*, iii, ed. F. Venturi (Milan, Naples, 1958).

A. De Marchi, *C.B. e il processo penale* (Turin, 1929); C. A. Vianello, *La vita e l'opera di C.B.* (Milan, 1938); *Minori*, iii.

**Becher, Johannes R.** (Munich 1891–Berlin 1958). German poet, novelist and critic. A pacifist, member of the Spartakusbund and then the Communist Party (1918–19), he escaped to Prague (1933) and went into exile in the U.S.S.R. (1935–45), where he edited the German section of *International Literature*; then in East Berlin he held 'cultural' posts (Minister of Culture, 1954). A sadly prolific poet since 1911 (*Der Ringende*, *Kleist-Hymne*) he was the leading political ⇨ Expressionist poet – his best collection is probably *Päan gegen die Zeit* (1918) – but his ultra-Expressionist technique soon became empty rhetoric. His early verse he later recanted in favour of the bombastic political hack-verse of his later years. His work illustrates the relation between poetry and politics in this century, but little is of intrinsic literary value. [PB]

*Sinn und Form, Zweites Sonderheft J.R.B.* (East Berlin, 1960) (with full bibliography).

**Becker, Knuth** (Hjørring 1891– ). Danish novelist. As a boy he was sent to a reformatory and later became a blacksmith and mechanic. He is the author of a long series (9 vols. by 1967) of autobiographical novels, begun in 1932 with *Det daglige Brød*, a novel cycle of high literary value. [ELB]

**Beckett, Samuel** (Foxrock, Dublin 1906– ). Irish novelist, dramatist, poet, resident in Paris. Equally at home in English and French, he has created a highly personal idiom and universe in novels and plays alike. His first published novel, *Murphy* (1938), written in English, reveals in conventional terms the essential features of his fiction which are ultimately diminished to a single consciousness concerned with itself, the ultimate solipsism. The early novels, *Murphy* and *Watt* (1953), utilize the sounds and humorous possibilities of the English language, but, with the changeover to French as the language of origin, there is a greater emphasis on analysis and the awkward, tramplike figures are gradually reduced to immobility. As a logical structure, language fails to bring order and clarity to an absurd world; yet, for the individual compelled to continue his quest for meaning in reality, it is the only weapon he has. The absurdity of the situation is described with irony and pathos. For Murphy, life is painful and difficult and he seeks to escape from physical existence, by negating his body, into a private world of the mind, sealed from the external fiasco; a realm of constantly changing forms enjoyed by the mental patients he looks after. Watt, a strange compulsive character, becomes a servant and attempts to describe his situation and relationship to other people, to name and describe objects and events which resist interpretation. The action of these novels takes place in real surroundings, but, with the French trilogy, one moves into the vaguer regions of the mind, the external world being gradually eliminated. In *Molloy* (1951; tr. P. Bowles and Samuel Beckett, 1955) the attempt to bring order to the confusion of life demonstrates the approximative and groping nature of language which develops through an association of images and ideas. For Molloy, physically immobile, past experiences are disjointed and language and thought is a buzzing in his head. Even Moran's disciplined life degenerates into chaos as he seeks Molloy. The bed-ridden hero of *Malone meurt* (1951; tr. Beckett, *Malone Dies*, 1956) spends his time awaiting death, telling stories and listing his possessions. With his body reduced to an almost foetal state, one follows the movement of a creative mind where language translates and becomes identified with the confused surging of thoughts and images which can only end in the silence of death. *L'innommable* (1953; tr. Beckett, *The Unnameable*, 1958) is the compulsive consciousness which can neither accept the fixed identity of a created character nor define itself. It is separated from the character it was or might have been by the fact that it constantly *becomes* something else. But, it is from the jumbled flux of language/consciousness that a possible past is created and the present apprehended. The disjointed phrases, without syntax, of *Comment c'est* (1961; tr. Beckett, *How It Is*, 1964) permutate the different parts of Bom and Pim's story as they crawl naked in the darkness and mud of existence. Beckett's prose work also includes the short stories of *More Pricks than Kicks* (1934), of *Nouvelles et textes pour rien* (1955) and *Têtes-mortes* (1967). He has written an excellent critical study: *Proust* (1931).

The central impulse of his theatre is the communication of disquiet, of that unease that comes from recognizing the fundamental 'absurdity' of the world. The technique he exploits to convey this experience owes much to the music hall and his peculiar power is to invest the patter, 'props' and 'business' of the cross-talk comedian with metaphysical intimations and to handle his clown/tramp figures (often reminiscent of Chaplin, always linked in a double-act: master and slave, victim and executioner) in such a way as to lead the audience towards sudden and unnerving confrontations with the haunting reality of death and decay. For the characters of his plays, living is simply entering into the habit of dying: there is the effort of living and the vanity of living. Characters are conscious of the slow and murderous passage of time and their unresting verbal activity is a kind of Pascalian 'diversion', at once a way of negating the decaying flesh through the operations of consciousness, a means of keeping the silence of death at bay and of redeeming their lives from insignificance through rhetoric and storytelling. Lucky's stream of nonsense in *En attendant Godot* (1952; tr. Beckett, *Waiting for Godot*, 1956), Krapp's mesmerized involvement with his own recorded voice in *Krapp's Last Tape* (1959) and the near-buried Winnie's social and sentimental chit-chat in *Happy Days* (1961) all testify to this. With the exception of the radio-play, *All That Fall* (1957), which has a realistically observed social setting, the characteristic Beckettian scene is a bare unlocalized space, like the vague terrain with a stunted tree of *En attendant Godot*, the bare room inhabited by Hamm and Clov in *Fin de partie* (1957; tr. Beckett, *Endgame*, 1958) or the unsituated grey urns in *Play* (1963). The characteristic Beckettian movement is towards the progressive extinction of human existence, as symbolized by the growing immobility of his characters, by their reduction (in *Happy Days* and *Play*) to mere trunks embedded in earth or tall urns, and distinguishable from other natural phenomena only by speech; inventive, rhythmic, precise speech that is often hilariously, yet painfully funny, giving to characters an individual voice and rescuing the drama from abstraction. For Beckett's theatre is not allegorical: it presents a certain vision of life and seems articulated about the maxim contained in his study of Proust: 'Art is the apotheosis of solitude.' His tramps are modern versions of Lear's 'unaccommodated man'; they suffer physically and are alone in a world full of obstacles, accidents and imperfections; invincibly trivial in the gathering darkness. He has also written *Acte sans paroles I* (1957; tr. Beckett, *Act without Words*, 1958) and the following radio-plays: *Embers* (1959), *Words and Music* (1962) and *Cascando* (1964). [RGV/SBJ]

R. N. Coe, *B.* (1964); J. Jacobsen and W. R. Mueller, *The Testament of S.B.* (1964); R. Federman, *Journey to Chaos: S.B.'s Early Fiction* (1965); P. Mélèse, *B.* (Paris, 1966); L. Janvier, *Pour S.B.* (Paris, 1966); J. Fletcher, *The Novels of S.B.* (1964); R. Cohn, *S.B.: The Comic Gamut* (1962); F. J. Hoffman, *S.B.: The Language of Self* (1962); Guicharnaud, *MFT*; Esslin, *TA*; Grossvogel, *FP*.

**Becque, Henry** (Paris 1837–Paris 1899). French dramatist. After an abortive start as the librettist of an opera (*Sardanapale*, 1867) based on Byron, he produced a comedy, *L'enfant prodigue* (1868), very much in the manner of ⇨ Sardou's 'well-made plays' though with characteristically bitter overtones. This was followed by *Michel Pauper* (1870) a striking study of a workman-inventor who marries the spoiled and selfish daughter of his rich backer. The attacks on unprincipled speculation and on the corrupting effects of luxury and easy money recall the drama of ⇨ Dumas *fils*, but they are conducted with impressive directness and sobriety. Becque's next play, *L'enlèvement* (1871), was in fact a crude copy of Dumas *fils* in its assault on the servitude of married women. Its failure provoked him into trying his hand at 'commercial' comedy with *La navette* (1878; tr. F. Tilden, *The Merry-Go-Round*, 1913) and *Les honnêtes femmes* (1880), two plays that add nothing to his range and technique. Though written 1872–3, his outstanding play, *Les corbeaux* (tr. F. Tilden, *The Vultures*, 1950) was produced only in 1882. It is a drama of human greed and unscrupulousness, conducted with great force and unflinching honesty, and focussing upon the struggle for a rich man's inheritance. There followed *La Parisienne* (1885; tr. J. Barzun, *Woman of Paris*, 1955), a mordant study of a typical *ménage-à-trois* of Parisian society, which strips bare characters unconscious of their own degradation. An unfinished play, *Les polichinelles* (1910, posth.), returned to the world of financial speculation and derisively reduced the characters to ciphers. Becque's dialogue is generally economical, tense and patterned, somewhere between natural speech and the literary language, though there is sometimes strain and clumsiness. The contained severity of the language creates a distinctive tone, like that of Flaubert alive with ironic distaste. Plot is simplified; asides and tirades greatly reduced, and the rhythm of the action consciously varied (e.g. Act I of *Les corbeaux*). He rejects Dumas *fils*' method of subordinating every facet of the plot to the 'effects' of a striking dénouement, but his almost Puritanical distrust of theatricality sometimes results in dryness and an excessive narrowing of range. [SBJ]

*Œuvres complètes* (4 vols., 1924).

A. Arnaoutovitch, *H.B.* (3 vols., Paris, 1927); E. Sée, *H.B. ou Servitude et grandeur dramatiques* (Paris, 1926); M. Descotes, *H.B. et son théâtre* (Paris, 1962); A. Antoine, *Mes souvenirs sur le théâtre libre* (Paris, 1922).

**Bécquer, Gustavo Adolfo** (Seville 1836–Madrid 1870). Spanish poet. His single collection of *Rimas* (probably mostly written 1859–61; publ. 1871) is the true point of departure for modern poetry in Spain. In contrast to the Romantic poetry of ⇨ Espronceda and his generation, the *Rimas* are written in half-tones. They are assonanced, simple in their metaphors and half-colloquial language, but subtle and sometimes rich in their music. In what may be seen as four interlocking sequences, Bécquer speaks first with wonder of his own functions as a poet, an instrument of nature, through whom inspiration flows; in the second he records with realistic vigour incidents from a love-affair – perhaps from several; in the third he turns inwards in bitterness and disenchantment making a somewhat Byronic display of his suffering, while the fourth is the distillation of a profound despair. The printed order of the poems is confused, being based on his notes made from memory after his original manuscript was destroyed. His *Cartas desde mi celda* (1864), letters written in the monastery at Veruela, are masterpieces of prose style. His verse is reminiscent sometimes of Musset and Spanish translations of Heine.

His life was unhappy. A painter by training, he came from Seville to Madrid to seek his fortune in journalism and the theatre, lived by miscellaneous writing, loved and parted from a woman (probably Elisa Guillén), and made an unfortunate marriage. In the end dream and reality became inseparable for him, and his *Leyendas* (1857–64), stories and descriptions in poetic prose, convey a haunted atmosphere of mystery and night-wandering. He learned most from Spanish folk-poetry, through which modern literary tradition gained vital contact again with its native soil, learning to abandon rhetoric and rhyme for half-rhyme and speech-rhythms. [JMC]

*Obras completas* (1950); *Rimas*, ed. J. P. Díaz (CC, 1963); *Tales and Poems of G.A.B.*, tr. H. F. W. Olmstead (1907); Cohen, *PBSV*; Blecua, *FLE*; Trend, *OBSV*.

J. P. Díaz, *G.A.B. Vida y poesía* (Montevideo, 1953); Rica Brown, *B.* (Barcelona, 1963); E. L. King, *G.A.B. From Painter to Poet* (Mexico, 1953).

**Beer, Johann** (St Georgen im Attergau 1655–Weissenfels 1700). German novelist. The son of a Protestant Austrian family which emigrated to southern Germany while he was still a boy, Beer early showed great musical talent and from 1677 was in the service of the Duke of Weissenfels as cantor, librarian and director of music. Published under a variety of pseudonyms (Jan Rebhu, Zendorius a Zendoriis, etc.), which for two centuries deceived the literary historians, the 21 novels now attributed to him are characterized by an exuberant love of narration for its own sake, a keen sense of humour which frequently expresses itself in fantastic, almost Rabelaisian satire, and a realism unparalleled in the 17th century. The novels are largely free of the moralizing tendencies of the age and are conceived primarily as entertainments. They draw freely on the chevalresque novel (*Ritter Hopfensack*), the contemporary 'political' novel (*Der politische Bratenwender*), the native tradition of moral satire (*Das Narrenspital*, ed. R. Alewyn, 1957) and the picaresque novel (*Jucundus Jucundissimus*) and show an obvious debt to the native German 'Volksbuch', as well as to ⇨ Moscherosch and ⇨ Grimmelshausen. In his longest and most important novels, *Teutsche Winternächte* (1682) and *Kurtzweilige Sommertäge* (1683; ed. W. Schmitt, 1958), Beer succeeds in creating what is in fact a new genre by his fusion of the picaresque and the courtly novel. [WAC]

*Gesammelte Werke*, ed. J. F. Fuchs (1960ff.).
R. Alewyn, *J.B.* (Leipzig, 1932); *MLR*, LVI, 2, 1961.

**Beer-Hofmann, Richard** (Vienna 1866–New York 1945). Austrian dramatist, poet and novelist of the neo-Romantic period. Of Jewish origin, he was closely associated with the Jungwien circle; first known for his slender *Novellen* (1893), his best works were the early wistful lyric 'Schlaflied für Mirjam' (1898; see *Verse*, 1941), and the play *Der Graf von Charolais* (1904), adapted from Massinger and Ford's *The Fatal Dowry*. His biblical trilogy *Die Historie von König David* (1933) remains incomplete; *Herbstmorgen in Österreich* (1944) are impressionistic autobiographical sketches. [PB]

*Gesammelte Werke* (1963).
S. Liptzin, *R. B.-H.* (New York, 1936); O. Oberholzer, *R. B.-H. Werk und Weltbild des Dichters* (Berne, 1947).

**Beets, Nicolaas** (Haarlem 1814–Utrecht 1903). Dutch author and poet. He enjoyed literature more than theology while training for the Ministry at Leyden. His first Byronic verse was acclaimed at the time but his fame rests on essays and short stories published in 1839 as *Camera obscura*, under the pseudonym Hildebrand. This was such a success that enlarged editions followed, the fourth (1854) being the final version. The humour may be unsubtle and even condescending, many effects (perhaps) imitated from Sterne, Lamb and Dickens, but the book's sentimental, humorous, sometimes satirical portrait of Dutch middle-class life made it a national legend. Equally fluent, entertaining (but never great) in e.g. literary essays, *Verscheidenheden meest op letterkundig gebied* (1859) the facile rhetoric of his later poetry was rejected by the aesthetic movement of the 1880s (⇨ Kloos). [PK]

*Dichtwerken* (5 vols., 1875–1900); *Hildebrands vorbereiding* (1956); Barnouw, *CA*.

**Behaim, Michael** (Sulzbach, Württemberg 1416–74). German poet. His great output is of scant literary value, but his place in literature is secured by his rhymed chronicles, above all that which tells of the Viennese uprising against Frederick III in 1462. He himself led a vagrant life and put his hand to many trades, and his chronicles are interesting documents on the social conditions of his age. [RT]

*Buch von den Wienern*, ed. T. von Karajan (Vienna, 1843); *Historische Lieder*, ed. T. von Karajan (Vienna, 1849).
H. Gille, *Die historischen und politischen Gedichte M.B.* (Berlin, 1910).

**Belinsky, Vissarion Grigor'yevich** (Sveaborg, Finland 1811–St Petersburg 1848). Russian literary critic. Belinsky was the son of a poor army doctor. As a student at Moscow University he joined the philosophical circle of Stankevich and became influenced by Schelling's philosophy. In 1832 he was excluded from the University for writing against serfdom and consequently engaged in journalism.

In 1834 he published his 'Literaturnyye mechtaniya' ('Literary Dreams') – a passionate article advocating pure art and complete freedom of the artist. Soon afterwards, under Bakunin's influence, he became interested in Hegel's philosophy. The misinterpretation of Hegel's principle 'all existing is rational' led him to an enthusiastic defence of the existing order in Russia.

His articles 'Ocherki Borodinskogo srazheniya', 'Mentsel, kritik Gete', 'Gore ot uma', were written in the spirit of Hegel's philosophy, but from 1840 onwards his views changed radically and he became a socialist and the central figure of the progressive Westernizers. In art he advocated social significance, and 'conformity with reality' became his main yardstick of artistic value. As he made no distinction between ethics and aesthetics a socially important work was for him also essentially significant artistically.

Belinsky saw Gogol' as a pioneer of the naturalistic school, was therefore bitterly disappointed in his 'Correspondence with Friends', and wrote him a passionate and bitter letter in which he called him a 'lost leader'.

Belinsky's temperament (his nickname was 'furious Vissarion') caused his frequent changes of opinion, but he always passionately believed in what he was preaching at the time. He not only reacted sensitively to all the contemporary literary events but gave in his articles a retrospect survey and analysis of Russian literature. His influence cannot be stressed too strongly. [MG]

*Polnoye sobraniye sochineniy* (13 vols., 1953–9).

N. Brodsky, *V.G.B.* (Moscow, 1946); H. E. Bowman, *V.B., a Study of the Origins of Social Criticism in Russia* (1954); A. Lavretsky, *Estetika B.* (Moscow, 1959); V. Nechayeva, *B. zhizn' i tvorchestvo* (Moscow, 1961); Hare, *PRST*; Poggioli, *PS*; Wellek, *HMC*; *Literaturnoye Nasledstvo*, 55–7 (1948–51); *Encounter*, 21, 26, 27 (1955); *SEER*, XXVII, 68 (1948).

**Belleau, Rémy** (Nogent-le-Rotrou 1528 ?–Paris 1577). French poet. A member of the ⇨ Pléiade. He studied in Paris at the Collège de Boncourt, and took part in the 1553 performance of ⇨ Jodelle's *Cléopâtre*. His particular characteristic, which appears in both his *Petites inventions* (1556) and his *Amours et nouveaux eschanges des pierres précieuses* (1576), is his delight in, and skill at describing little things – precious stones, tiny animals, fruits. But his interest in them is not limited to their charming or curious appearance. By his mythological references, by his evocation of the varied and mysterious properties of jewels, by the dynamic rhythm of his descriptions, he gives the impression that all these objects and creatures are part of a divinely ordered and harmonious universe. This seriousness of vision does not exclude touches of wit and preciosity, and conventional compliments to his friends and mistress.

He also published a translation in verse of the pseudo-Anacreon (1566) and a chaotic work called *La bergerie*, first published in 1565 – a mixture of prose and verse which includes, among its heterogeneous contents, some descriptions of the Château de Joinville-en-Bassigny where Belleau was living as tutor to the son of the Marquis d'Elbeuf. [GJ]

*Œuvres complètes* (3 vols., 1867, 1878); Schmidt, *PSS*.

**Bellman, Carl Michael** (Stockholm 1740–Stockholm 1795). Swedish poet and song-writer. The most original of Swedish 18th-century poets. Born into a family of good standing (one grandfather was professor of Latin at Uppsala, the other an influential clergyman in Stockholm), he received a careful private education. After a few years of clerical work, he went bankrupt and never afterwards regained full control of his finances. An incurable bohemian, he still found powerful patrons, among whom he was soon to count the King, Gustavus III. He was given the title of Secretary Royal and a sinecure; he was sometimes heard at court, but more often at the houses of the aristocracy and the wealthy bourgeoisie. For this fairly sophisticated audience he wrote – and performed – his poems and songs, for which he borrowed the popular tunes of the day, mainly from the French *vaudevilles* and *opéras comiques* but also from classical composers, such as Handel and Roman, Pergolesi and Haydn.

Bellman's adaptations reveal his instinctive musicality and to a limited degree bear his personal stamp, a sweet tunefulness and a lyrical tenderness particularly characteristic of the few melodies that can reasonably be ascribed to him. From a literary viewpoint his songs are remarkable for their imaginative combination of a rococo mythology with the often striking realism of his descriptions. They are remarkable too for the creation of characters such as Fredman, Mollberg, Movitz and Ulla Winblad, the immortal heroine of the chief cycle, *Fredmans epistlar* (1790); for the depiction of scenes of dancing and midnight revelling, and of delightful excursions to the surroundings of the capital. The 82 'epistles' together make up a world of the most astounding richness and variety: there are, besides serenades and moonlit townscapes, bantering conversations and heartsearching soliloquies; there are above all the delights of Venus and the forgetfulness of Bacchus. Bellman has often been accused of immorality, and he will continue to be a stumbling-block for puritans; he has also been seen as the apostle of unclouded enjoyment and the sheer delight of living. Yet Fredman's world is surrounded by shadows: it is only in the ecstatic moment that the knowledge of impending death fades In spite of a vast output of occasional verse his reputation rests almost exclusively on *Fredmans epistlar*, which were composed over a period of more than twenty years, and on a further collection, *Fredmans sånger* (1791), containing a miscellany of early drinking-songs and biblical parodies as well as later lyrics. He has been variously interpreted and evaluated by successive generations, as a 'Romantic' and as a 'realist'. The Jewish-Swedish poet and critic ⇨ Levertin saw in him not only a great poet but also a profound mind, a genius to be compared only with the greatest. [SAB]

*C.M.B.s Skrifter*, ed. Bellmanssällskapet (11 vols., 1921– ); *17 Songs*, tr. P. Britten Austin (Stockholm, 1965).

O. Sylwan, *B. och Fredmans epistlar* (Lund, 1943); A. Blanck, *C.M.B.* (Stockholm, 1943); N. Afzelius, *Myt och bild* (Stockholm, 1945);

*Bellmansstudier* (15 vols., Stockholm, 1924– ); *Kring B.*, ed. L. G. Eriksson (Stockholm, 1964); P. Britten Austin, *The Life and Songs of C.M.B.* (Malmö, 1967).

**Bely, Andrey,** pseud. of Boris Nikolayevich Bugayev (Moscow 1880–Moscow 1934). Russian novelist, poet and critic. Son of a Professor of mathematics he studied mathematics, zoology and philosophy at Moscow University; at the same time he interested himself in art and mysticism. Like ⇨ Blok, he was influenced by the philosophy and poetry of Vl. Solov'yov and he became a leading figure among the Russian ⇨ Symbolist poets. First known for a lyrical story in poetic prose, *Simfoniya* (*Vtoraya, dramaticheskaya*) (1902), he collaborated with ⇨ Bryusov in the publication of the journal *Vesy* (1904–9); his critical and philosophical articles, later collected in *Lug zelenyy* (1910), *Simvolizm* (1910) and *Arabeski* (1911) gave the new movement its theoretical basis. In 1914 he joined a Rudolf Steiner anthroposophical community in Switzerland. He returned to Russia in 1916 and at first welcomed the Bolshevik Revolution, but was soon disillusioned. He made a forlorn attempt to revive the Symbolist aesthetic in the journal *Zapiski mechtateley* (1919–22), read lectures on the theory of poetry to the Proletkul't, a school for writers from the proletariat, then emigrated again in 1921 only to return in 1923. In his last years he was left undisturbed; his works were published in small editions and largely ignored. But the influence of his style and ideas, directly on ⇨ Zamyatin and ⇨ Pil'nyak, and through them on other Soviet writers, ⇨ Fedin and ⇨ Leonov, was immense.

Bely, fascinated by both science and mysticism, saw Symbolism as a bridge between the rational and irrational. It was less an artistic movement than a religious *credo*, though he often subjected both these tendencies in himself to devastating irony. He was acutely aware of the forces of chaos threatening the order that man has imposed on experience; hence the frequent image of storms and tempests in his work. *Kotik Letayev* (1922) is a Joycean attempt to trace the growth of consciousness and the subjugation of chaos in the infant. But chaos is never wholly subdued. Even in Bely's intellectuals culture is only a veneer, concealing the savage. His novels invariably end tragically; the good and the rational are destroyed by the forces of chaos. In *Peterburg* (1913–16; tr. J. Cournos, 1960) European culture is overrun by Asiatic barbarism. After the First World War he became disillusioned in the West and came to regard the Bolsheviks as the last guardians of a beleaguered culture.

An important part of his large *œuvre* is his memoirs, his *Vospominaniya o Bloke* (1922), and the semi-autobiographical trilogy devoted to the pre-revolutionary epoch: *Na rubezhe dvukh stoletiy* (1930), *Nachalo veka* (1933), and *Mezhdu dvukh revolyutsiy* (1934).

As a prose-writer he is highly original. He shares certain features with ⇨ Gogol', the fondness for complex syntax, the delight in words for their own sake and an irrepressible sense of humour. But his prose is at the same time extremely sophisticated with its elaborate literary allusions (*Peterburg*) and its careful composition. The finest work in rhythmical prose is *Serebryanyy golub'* (1909). Surprisingly his poetry is simpler and less original than his prose. The best is in the collections *Zoloto v lazuri* (1904), *Pepel* (1909) and *Urna* (1909); much was later extensively and unwisely revised by the poet. The greater part is devoted to social and political themes, but Bely here only touches upon the problems that he explores and tries to solve in his novels.

His studies of rhythm and prosody in the classical Russian poets and above all his profound analysis of Gogol', *Masterstvo Gogolya* (1929), had a profound influence on the development of Formalism. [TJB/RDBT]

K. Mochul'sky, *A.B.* (Paris, 1955); O. A. Maslenikov, *The Frenzied Poets* (Berkeley, Cal., 1952); *LN*, 27–8 (1938); Poggioli, *PR*.

**Bembo, Pietro** (Venice 1470–Rome 1547). Italian writer. From 1513 to 1521 he was Papal Secretary to Leo X; in 1539, he was made Cardinal, and spent his last years actively involved in ecclesiastical matters. Though his works do not reach the first rank, he is an important figure in Italian literary history. A child of the Italian humanist movement, he was nevertheless convinced of the equality of the vernacular to Latin as a literary language, and the most important part of his literary activities consists of Italian works in which, by precept and example, he set out to raise the vernacular to the level of the classical tongues by correcting the disorganized linguistic and stylistic eclecticism of 15th-century Italian literature. His standards for Italian were identical with those he advocated for Latin – a rigorous imitation of the great writers of the past – in the case of Italian, Dante, and more especially Petrarch and Boccaccio.

His major Italian works are *Gli asolani* (1505; tr. R. B. Gottfried, Bloomington, Indiana, 1954), a dialogue on love, with neo-Platonic influences; *Prose della volgar lingua* (1525), a dialogue on the Italian language, his most important work; and *Rime* (1530). The influence of his example and advice on the subsequent development of Italian literature and of the Italian literary language can hardly be exaggerated. [CF]

*Prose e rime di Pietro Bembo*, ed. C. Dionisotti (1960).

G. Santangelo, *Il B. critico* (Florence, 1950).

**Ben-Ami,** pen-name of M. Rabinovitch (Ukraine 1858–Palestine 1932). Russian-Yiddish writer. As a supporter of Zionism among the Russian Jewish intelligentsia, he began writing in Russian, but later turned to Yiddish. In 1905 he emigrated to Switzerland and in 1925 to Palestine. [EE]

*Di Kinderishe yorn* (1904); *Ber der shooster* (n.d.); *A nacht in a klain shtetl* (n.d.).

Waxman, *HJL*.

**Benavente, Jacinto** (Madrid 1866–Madrid 1954). Spanish dramatist. Theatrically skilful, witty, but rarely profound, the best of his many plays are social satires, reflecting the world of the aristocracy (e.g. *Gente conocida*, 1896), the middle classes (e.g. *La losa de los sueños*, 1911) and the peasantry (e.g. *Señora ama*, 1908; CA). *Los intereses creados* (1909; CA), a satire on the business world, is interesting for its mixture of characters from the ⇨ *commedia dell'arte* with those of traditional Spanish theatre. He also attempted tragedies (e.g. *La noche del sábado*, 1903; CA), melodroma (e.g. *La malquerida*, 1913; CA – about incest) and, more successfully, children's fantasy plays (e.g. *La novia de nieve*, 1934). Nobel Prize, 1922. [JMC]

*Obras completas* (8 vols., 1947); *Comedias escogidas* (CA; 1958); *Plays*, tr. J. G. Underhill (N.Y., 1917–24).

W. Starkie, *J.B.* (1924); A. Lázaro, *Vida y obra de B.* (repr. Madrid, 1964).

**Ben Avigdor (Arieh Leib Shalkovits)** (Lithuania 1866–Karlsbad 1921). Hebrew writer. Instead of the Rabbinate for which he studied for many years, Ben Avigdor found his way to the idealistic Zionist movement B'nai Moshe founded by ⇨ Ahad Ha-am and became a dedicated fighter for the reform of the Hebrew language. The Hebrew publishing house Ahiasaf, which he founded and whose manager he became, was for 30 years the publisher of many important works of fiction, non-fiction and Hebrew translations of some of the most important historical, philosophical and biographical works in European languages. In 1890, he founded his own publishing house, Tushia, which published hundreds of works, including translations. His own literary activity was in the field of short stories of a realistic nature. His heroes are not the middle-class and rootless Jews of the Ghetto, but the labourer, the Jewish proletariat. *Leah Mocheret Dagim* (Warsaw, 1895) is a lively picture of a Friday morning in the Jewish market of Vilna, and *Ahava vechovah* (Warsaw, 1892) the story of Deborah the seamstress who sacrifices her youth and love for her sick mother. He wrote a historical novel, *Lifne Arba Meot Shanah* (Warsaw, 1893), describing the life of Jews in Spain before the expulsion in 1492, the expulsion itself and the problem of assimilation facing the Marannos. [EE]

Klausner, *HMHL*; Waxman, *HJL*.

**Benda, Julien** (Paris 1867–Fonteney-aux-Roses 1956). French novelist and thinker. From a Jewish bourgeois background, he had a passion for mathematics and a lifelong devotion to an ideal of Graeco-Roman order and abstraction. He remained unmarried. He wrote first in defence of Dreyfus, helped to edit Péguy's *Cahiers de la quinzaine* (1910–14), and made his name as an opponent of ⇨ Bergson: *Le bergsonisme* (1912), *Sur le succès du bergsonisme* (1914), and *Belphégor* (1919; tr. S. J. Lawson, 1929), which attacked the intellectual degeneracy of French social life. *La trahison des clercs* (1927; tr. R. Aldington, *The Great Betrayal*, 1934) is his most famous manifesto, proposing an ideal role of rational detachment for the intellectual who should be above mere emotional and practical concerns, and attacking contemporaries like Sorel, Maurras and Barrès. Benda's most significant novel, *L'ordination* (1913; tr. G. Cannan, *The Yoke of Pity*, 1913), tendentiously demonstrates his meaning by showing a *clerc* who betrays his interest in truth through concern for his sick child. A purist, he yet attacked the rival withdrawal from reality practised by symbolist poets and other devotees of pure literature: *La France byzantine* (1945). [AKT]

R. J. Niess, *J.B.* (Ann Arbor, 1956).

**Bengtsson, Frans G.** (Tossjö 1894–Ribbingsfors 1954). Swedish poet, essayist, novelist and historian. An erudite, witty and sometimes unorthodox scholar, he spent nearly twenty years at Lund improving his mind and exercising his numerous talents. A master of the informal essay in the English tradition, his subjects range from literary to military heroes, from bloody vendettas to peaceful country walks. He was very much opposed to the current preoccupation with psychology. A popular selection of his essays is found in *Tankar i gröngräset* (1953; tr. M. Roberts and E. Harley Schubert, *A Walk to an Ant Hill and Other Essays*, 1950). His genuine admiration for exceptional, strong and lonely personalities, his keen interest in warlike exploits and problems of strategy, combined with a contempt for utilitarian considerations made him singularly equipped to tackle the biography of *one* of his countrymen. *Karl XII:s levnad I–II* (1935–6; tr. N. Walford, *The Life of Charles XII*, 1960) is epic rather than analytic in approach. The style (in spite of none too rare lapses) shows the author's concern with a dignity appropriate to his essentially tragic subject. To a wider public he is best known for his rollicking novel of Viking times *Röde Orm I–II* (1941–5; tr. M. Meyer, *The Long Ships*, 1956). Its humour relies on deliberate anachronism and farcical episode but does not obscure the author's admiration for the heroic past. A volume of relaxed, idiosyncratic memoirs, *Den lustgård som jag minns*, appeared in 1953. [SAB]

*F.G.B. En minnesbok*, ed. G. Michanek (Uppsala, 1956).

**Benjamin, Walter** (Berlin 1892–Port Bou 1940). German essayist. Of outstanding philosophical critical ability, he had a poet's attitude to language which he regarded as the measure of all public values. He committed suicide while fleeing to Spain. His major essays include 'Über einige Motive bei Baudelaire' (1939), 'Zum Bilde Prousts' (1929), 'Karl Kraus' (1931), 'Franz Kafka' (1934), etc. The prose miniatures of the posthumous *Berliner Kindheit um Neunzehnhundert* (1950), a highly distinguished volume of memoirs, are a stylistic *tour de force*. An admirably representative selection of his work (*Illuminationen*, ed. S. Unseld) appeared in 1961. [PB]

*Schriften*, ed. T. W. Adorno (2 vols., 1955); *Briefe*, ed. G. Sholem and T. W. Adorno (2 vols., 1966).

T. W. Adorno, *Prismen* (Frankfurt a.M., 1955); *GLL*, XV, 4, 1962; *NM*, LXXVI, 1, 1964.

**Benjamin (Ben Jona) of Tudela** (fl. *c.* 1160–Spain 1173). The first great Jewish traveller. He visited Egypt, the Near East, Persia, Arabia and India and described his travels in *Masaot Rabbi Binyamin* (1st edn 1543), of which only fragments survive, but which has remained popular until modern times. [EE]

*The Itinerary of Rabbi Benjamin*, ed., tr., and comm. N. M. Adler (1907).

**Benn, Gottfried** (Mansfeld 1886–Berlin 1956). German poet. A practising Berlin doctor and army surgeon in both wars, his poetic work was banned by the Nazis in 1938, and by the Allies in 1945 (because of earlier pro-Nazi sympathies), but since then acclaimed – largely uncritically. His first poems, *Morgue* (1912) and *Söhne* (1913), were morbidly sensational, experimental, and brought him the reputation of an ⇨ Expressionist *enfant terrible,* sustained in 1917 by *Fleisch*. Much of this early poetry is bad, but from the mid-twenties onwards, in *Schutt* (1924), *Betäubung* (1925) and – most notably – *Spaltung* (1925), we find a new brilliant, ecstatic, highly associative Mediterranean poetry, described by Benn as 'intoxicatedly cerebral', or (in another of his definitions) as 'absolute poetry'. His later poetry is of another type, intellectual rather than vitalistic: *Statische Gedichte* (1948), *Fragmente* (1951), *Destillationen* (1953) and *Apèslude* (1955). Analytical, technically precise, written in the snappy, pseudo-scientific idiom of the mid 20th century, this classical modernism was highly influential in Germany. Essentially a cerebral (Apollonian) poet, his underlying theory of 'absolute poetry' or 'monologic art' is formulated in the brilliant *Probleme der Lyrik* (1951), discussed by T. S. Eliot in *The Three Voices of Poetry* (1953). An important but not a great poet, he sometimes substitutes poetic sleight of hand for genuine vision.

His *Gesammelte Werke* (4 vols., 1958–61) include critical and imaginative prose, e.g. the Expressionist *Gehirne* (1916), dramas, etc. [PB]

*Primal Vision. Selected Poetry and Prose*, ed. E. B. Ashton, tr. B. Deutsch *et al.* (1961); Bridgwater, *TCGV*; Hamburger and Middleton, *MGP*.

E. Buddeberg, *G.B.* (Stuttgart, 1961); E. Lohner, *G.B. Bibliographie 1912–1956* (Wiesbaden 1958); W. Lennig, *G.B.* (Reinbek, 1965); Hamburger, *RE*; Muschg, *ZDL*; I. Hilton, in Natan, *GML*, iii (1964).

**Benoît de Sainte-Maure** (fl. *c.* 1150). French poet from Touraine. He dedicated his successful *Roman de ⇨ Troie* to Eleanor of Aquitaine, and was commissioned by Henry II in 1174 to replace the *Roman de Rou* of ⇨ Wace with an *Estoire des ducs de Normandie*. Benoît's poem, in 43,210 octosyllabic rhymed couplets, carried the history of the Normans down to Henry I. He used the chronicles of Doon de Saint-Quentin (1000–20) and Guillaume de Jumièges, and, although he lacks Wace's verve, gives much valuable information about Norman customs. [LTT]

*Chronique des ducs de Normandie*, ed. F. Michel (3 vols., Paris, 1836–44); ed. C. Fahlin (2 vols., Uppsala, 1951–4).

**Ben Yehuda, Eliezer** (Perelman) (Vilna 1858–Jerusalem 1922). Hebrew scholar essayist and editor. His chief merit was the development of the Hebrew language as a spoken tongue. He founded his own periodical *Hazevi* in 1885 in Jerusalem, but was denounced to the Turkish authorities; the periodical was suspended and he himself imprisoned. After his release, he continued the struggle. His historical achievement in the field of linguistics is his dictionary of the Hebrew language, *Millon ha-lashon ha-ivrit* (Jerusalem/Berlin, 1908), now newly edited by the Hebrew Academy in Israel. [EE]

*Kol Kitve E.B.Y.* (2 vols., Jerusalem, 1929); *In Memoriam*, ed. J. Klausner (Jerusalem, 1924) (essays).

Spiegel, *HR*; Waxman, *HJL*.

**Ben-Zion, Simcha** (Simcha Alter Guttman) (Bessarabia 1870–Tel Aviv 1932). Hebrew story-writer. His heroes are the Jews of the Russian small town in the late 19th century, when the economic situation of the Jews in Bessarabia became almost desperate. Their numbers became depleted by the great wave of emigration to America and even their spiritual life became stagnant. The rise of the Zionist Movement is mirrored in some of his short stories, where the nationalist idea fills his younger heroes with a new ideal to replace the old ones. The *Kitve S.B-Z.* (2 vols., 1914; 2nd edn, Tel Aviv, 1951) comprise three cycles of stories. The first, *Be-Dor Yored*, depict the struggle for livelihood, the second, *Be-Dor Over*, the slow changes which engulf the Jews living in the Pale of Settlement, the transition from strict orthodoxy to Zionism. By contrast, the third group, *Mi-Toch Hafechah*, are pogrom stories of the outrages to feelings and sacred objects rather than painful recollections of physical assaults. [EE]

Klausner, *HMHL*; Waxman, *HJL*.

**Béranger, Pierre-Jean de** (Paris 1780–Paris 1857). French poet. He enjoyed an enormous reputation in the Europe of his time, as the poet of the people. After the fall of Napoleon he kept the flame of the Napoleonic tradition glowing in the memory of the people with such poems as *Les souvenirs du peuple*, in which an old peasant woman remembers seeing and speaking to the Emperor. His verses came to the notice of Lucien Bonaparte in 1804 which procured him a small pension. *Le Roi d'Yvetot* (1815 and 1821), satirizing the Restoration, earned him a spell in prison, where he began his *Chansons nouvelles* (1825). A fine (for his Bonapartism in *Chansons inédites*, 1828) was paid by public subscription, so popular had he become. After he published *Chansons nouvelles et dernières* in 1833 he lived in retirement. Not all his poems were political, many being gay and bawdy verses. There are many 19th-century English and American translations of the songs. [WA]

*Œuvres complètes* (1834); *Ma biographie* (1857; tr., *Memoirs*, 1858); *B. et son temps*, intr. notes etc., P. Brochon (1956).

**Berceo, Gonzalo de** (Upper Rioja, fl. first half of 13th cent.). Spanish poet. The first whose name has survived. Attached to the monastery of San Millán de la Cogolla, he may have been the abbot's notary. He wrote a number of devotional works in ⇨ *cuaderna vía* verse form: the lives of three local saints, Millán, Domingo de Silos, Oria; the martyrdom of a fourth, San Lorenzo; three works on the Virgin, including the well-known *Milagros de Nuestra Señora*; the *Sacrificio de la Misa* (concerning the symbolism of the Mass);

and a description of the Signs that will appear before the Last Judgement. The theory that he was also the author of the *Libro de* ⇨ *Alexandre*, advanced by some critics, is not generally accepted.

These works are mainly paraphrases of Latin prose originals. Berceo's adaptations are faithful to the substance of his models, and he repeatedly points out that he makes no statements without their authority; but he fills out the dry, impersonal skeletons of the originals with descriptions, dialogue, comments, etc., giving the stories the flavour and outlook of his own day. He calls himself *juglar* ('minstrel'), and his aim was to make these works available to a non-learned public. The *Vida de San Millán* is largely a propaganda work, seeking to justify the monastery's title to the annual tributes or 'Votos' it received from all over Castile. He was less naïve and more learned than he is often thought to be, or than he himself suggests, and he was capable of both humour and subtlety in narration. [GBG-M]

*Milagros de Nuestra Señora*, ed. A. G. Solalinde (CC); modern Spanish tr., Daniel Devoto (1957); *Vida de Santo Domingo de Silos* and *Vida de Santa Oria* (CA); *Cuatro poemas*, ed. C. C. Marden (1928).

G. Guerrieri Crocetti, *G. de B.* (Brescia, 1947); J. B. Trend, *B.* (1952); *RFE*, IX, 1922; *BHS*, XXXVIII, 1961; *NRFH*, XV, 1961.

**Berchet, Giovanni** (Milan 1783–Turin 1851). Italian poet. One of the group of Milanese writers mainly responsible for the introduction of Romantic ideas into Italy. At first an admirer and imitator of the neo-classical poets ⇨ Foscolo and ⇨ Monti, his wide knowledge of European literature (he translated works by Goldsmith, Gray, and Schiller) soon put him into contact with the most recent literary developments and theories. His *Lettera semiseria di Grisostomo* (1816), published pseudonymously, was the best-known and one of the most effective presentations of Romantic literary theory to Italian readers. Berchet also contributed to the Milanese periodical *Il conciliatore* (1818–19), an important vehicle of Romantic ideas. His best-known poems are *I profughi di Parga* (1821), and a group of *romanze* (simple narrative poems of a popular nature) including *Il romito del Cenisio* and *Le fantasie*. These were composed in London because as a supporter of the movement for Italian independence he was forced to leave Italy in 1821. Owing something to the influence of ⇨ Manzoni, they are animated by a genuine patriotic sentiment and nostalgia, but are uneven in composition. In 1829 he entered the household of Giuseppe Arconati, an exiled Italian nobleman living in Belgium. In 1837 he published a volume of translations of old Spanish ballads (*Vecchie romanze spagnuole*). He returned to Italy in 1848. [CF]

Kay, *PBIV*; Dionisotti, *OBIV*.

E. Petrini, *Lingua e poesia di G. Berchet* (Milan, 1951); *Belfagor*, 1959, 2.

**Berdichewski, Micah Joseph**, pseud. Micha Yoseph Bin Gorion (Podolia 1865–Berlin 1921). Hebrew novelist, essayist and philosopher. A prolific colourful and controversial figure from the town which was the cradle of Hassidism. For some years he represented extreme secularism in Jewish life. He chose as his motto the 'transvaluation of values', a concept borrowed from Nietzsche. Jews were more important to him than Judaism, and the renewal of the Jewish nation meant for him that Israel should be like any other people. He came into conflict with Achad Ha'am's spiritual Zionism. The characters of his short stories are both men of flesh and blood with a deep attachment to the soil, and disillusioned young men who had abandoned Jewish traditional life but have not managed completely to absorb European culture. He wrote revolutionary essays in a language borrowed from the Bible, the *Talmud* and even the *Zohar*. His essays in literary criticism took the form of subtle portraits of writers of his time (*Baerev*, Warsaw, 1910). Under the pseudonym of Bin Gorion he collected and adapted two volumes of oral legends from the close of the Bible down to his time (*Me-Ozar ha-Aggada*). They were also published in German. [EE]

*Kitve M.J.B-G.* (20 vols., Warsaw/Leipzig, 1921–5); Short stories: *Me-haavar Ha-karov* (1909); *Batim* (1920); *Garei Rehov* (1921).

Klausner, *HMHL*; Waxman, *HJL*.

**Berent, Wacław** (Warsaw 1873–Warsaw 1940). Polish novelist. He was educated in Zürich and Munich, obtaining a doctor's degree in marine biology. In 1933 he became a member of the Academy of Literature. He began his literary career at 22 with a remarkably mature novel, *Fachowiec*, in which he drew ironic conclusions from the Positivist idealization of work. His later books, each of them a new departure in subject matter, were progressively more stylized and less fictional. *Ozimina* (1911) describes one night in the winter of 1904 at a fashionable Warsaw house; the social occasion coincides with the outbreak of the war between Japan and Russia. The assembled guests talk, think, observe one another, reflect on the past and the future, groping for their personal and communal identity, until the shapes of myth are evoked at the end of the book. Berent's technique of associations within a restricted framework of time and place forestalled that of Joyce in *Ulysses* (1922). He even experimented with dream sequence.

*Żywe kamienie* (1918) disposes of conventional plot for the sake of a greater fluidity of scenes and characters, which are meant to re-create the anonymity of the Middle Ages. The language, too, echoes the whole undivided past: the poetry of vagabond monks, Christian and pagan beliefs, folk-tales and street cries. It is undoubtedly a difficult experiment, but civilized in its understanding of the European heritage.

Berent then turned to the 18th century, and in pursuing the origins of the Polish intelligentsia (e.g. *Diogenes w kontuszu*, 1937), relied on the literary possibilities of faithful documentation, as if he finally came to doubt the very tenets of fiction. [JP]

*Pisma* (8 vols., 1933–4).

**Bergelson, David** (Uman 1884–1952). Yiddish short-story writer and novelist. His career is divided by the Russian Revolution into two distinct periods. In the pre-revolutionary period, he took his subjects from the small Jewish towns; in the later phase he portrayed episodes of the hectic post-revolution years and became an ardent follower of the Soviet regime. He fell victim to the Stalinist purges. His novel *Noch Alemen* is considered one of the best in Yiddish literature. [EE]

*Ale lider fŭn D.B.* (6 vols., Berlin, 1922); *Penek* (Moscow, 1937); *Birobidjaner* (Moscow, 1935); *Di lider fŭn mayne lider* (Montreal, 1954).

J. Leftwich, *Yisröel. The First Jewish Omnibus* (rev. edn, 1963); Roback, *SYL*.

**Bergengruen, Werner** (Riga 1892–1962). German novelist and poet. A cavalry officer in the First World War and subsequently in the White Baltic campaign, then a student in Germany, he lived as a journalist in Berlin, later in Munich (1936). Converted to Catholicism, several of his works were banned by the Nazis and he emigrated to the Tirol, then Switzerland (1946). His first novels are historical, e.g. *Das grosse Alkahest* (1926; rev. edn, *Der Starost*, 1938). His most important work, the allegorical Renaissance-novel *Der Grosstyrann und das Gericht* (tr. N. Cameron, *A Matter of Conscience*, 1952), deals with the Machiavellian dualism of 'justice' based on expediency and justice as a matter of principle; modern parallels could also be found in the Luther-period novel: *Am Himmel wie auf Erden* (1940; banned). *Der letzte Rittmeister* (1952), a rambling series of tales (tr. E. Peters, *The Last Captain of Horse*, 1953), forms a trilogy with *Die Rittmeisterin* (1954) and *Der dritte Kranz* (1962).

Always looking for 'die metaphysische Pointe', he is an accomplished and polished story-teller, and his best novellas are: *Die drei Falken* (1937), *Der Tod von Reval* (1939), *Der spanische Rosenstock* (1940), and *Das Beichtsiegel* (1946). Poetry he sees as a song of praise, with all things as a symbol of higher reality; his main collections are *Dies irae* (1945) and *Die heile Welt* (1950). [PB]

H. Bänziger, *W.B. Weg und Werk* (Berne/Munich, 1961); G. Klemm, *W.B.* (Wuppertal-Barmen, 1954); E. Sobota, *Das Menschenbild bei B.* (Zürich, 1962) (with bibliography); *GLL*, II, 3, 1949.

**Berggol'ts, Ol'ga** (Petrograd 1910– ). Russian poetess. The daughter of a doctor, she studied at Leningrad University. After a brief, unhappy marriage to Boris ⇨ Kornilov, she married again and went to Kazakhstan as a journalist; subsequently she returned to Leningrad, worked in a factory, and published her first verses. In 1937 she was expelled from the Party, arrested, and incarcerated for two and a half years on trumped-up charges. She endured the siege of Leningrad; in 1942 her husband died of hunger. After Stalin's death in 1953 she helped to initiate the ⇨ 'Thaw' in literature, insisting on a return to intimate themes in poetry. Her verse is orderly, under-stated, with the feeling of unbearable emotion beneath its polished surface. Her wartime poetry – e.g. *Fevral'skiy dnevnik* (1942) – made her famous; but her rather sombre love-poetry, reminiscent sometimes of ⇨ Akhmatova, is equally good and her prose is also worthy of note. [RM-G]

*Stikhi. Proza* (1961); Gulland, *SRV*.
N. Bank, *O.B.* (Moscow–Leningrad, 1962).

**Bergman, Bo** (Stockholm 1869–Stockholm 1967). Swedish poet, novelist and story-writer. His early verse, e.g. *Marionetterna* (1903), showed a sceptical clarity and modulated disillusion similar to the mood of his friend ⇨ Söderberg (like him an outstanding portrayer of Stockholm). But the simplicity and precision of his poetry (more important than his prose, which is however by no means negligible) developed into an active, balanced humanism, including ripely varied love poetry. Among his principal books of verse are *Elden* (1917), *Livets ögon* (1922) and *Trots allt* (1931). His literary career (combined for many years with that of a civil servant and dramatic critic) has been exceptionally long; in his nineties he has published verse and prose of distinction, such as the novel *Vi vandrare* (1961), the poems *Makter* (1962) and the book of essays *Predikare* (1967).

S. Linder, *B.B.* (Stockholm, 1940); S. Arvidson, *B.B.* (Stockholm, 1945).

**Bergman, Hjalmar** (Örebro 1883–Berlin 1931). Swedish novelist, story-writer and dramatist. Amongst his narrowly realistic contemporaries, Bergman is an outsider, a man who follows a strange vision, and whose tragic sense of life is paradoxically offset by an incomparable sense of humour. As the fat, gawky son of an extroverted, authoritarian father, a bank manager in the small capital of a mining province, he appears to have found compensation not only in detached observation but above all in a heightened life of the imagination. Nearly all his works (apart from early experiments in a symbolist vein) contain elements of shrewd observation, but these invariably undergo a measure of change, or even distortion. *Hans nåds testamente* (1910) is bright and quixotic; *Komedier i Bergslagen* (1914–16) dark and grimly expressionistic; whereas *En döds memoarer* (1918), a major attack on the problem of the freedom of the will, mixes realistic and visionary scenes. He has himself spoken of 'caricature' as the first principle of his art. Because of his highly individual style, he had difficulty in establishing contact with his public, and when success finally came with *Markurells i Wadköping* (1919; tr. E. Classen, *God's Orchid*, N.Y., 1923), he distrusted his popularity. One of the funniest books in Swedish, it is at the same time deadly serious. Here as in the book that most critics consider his masterpiece, *Farmor och Vår Herre* (1921; tr. C. Napier, *Thy Rod and Thy Staff*, 1937), it is the small provincial town that forms the background with its quaint gentility, its gossip and scandals. The central characters are essentially lonely people: the ruthless Markurell with his almost insane love for his only son and child (who turns out not to be his) and 'Granny' in the latter book, who on her 78th birthday has to face the truth about herself and shed a lifelong illusion. In *Chefen fru Ingeborg* (1925; tr. E. Sprigge and C. Napier, *The Head of the Firm*, 1936) he ventures into Freudian territory with a description of the incestuous fascination of a middle-aged woman for her future son-in-law. The tragic resolution of the conflict makes clear the moral core of his art.

His plays *Marionettspel* (1917), short, fleeting pieces somewhat reminiscent of the mood and manner of ⇨ Maeterlinck, also explore the unconscious, here in the form of powers that mercilessly steal upon their helpless victims. More popular is *Swedenhielms* (1925; tr. H. Alexander and L. Jones in *Scandinavian Plays of the Twentieth Century*, N.Y., 1951), a gay and sparkling comedy about a Nobel Prize-winner and his family; while *Patrasket* (1928) is an entertaining, but also moving play about a Jewish business man, his family and relations. Bergman's last work was *Clownen Jac* (1930), a rambling, casual story marked by the difficulties surrounding its writing (he was by now a very sick man). Its hero, a celebrated clown, speaks in one place (like an *alter ego* of the author) about the price he has had to pay for his art: fear alone has been his driving-force, and the purpose of his art to make people laugh at fear. Bergman remained a moralist to the end. It was above all his uncompromising exploration of the ambivalence of all human emotions that made him a significant and profoundly independent writer. A selection of his letters, *Brev*, was published in 1964. [SAB]

*Samlede Skrifter*, ed. J. Edfelt (30 vols., 1949–58).
E. H. Linder, *Sju världars herre* (Stockholm, 1962); K. Jaensson, 'H.B.s diktning', in *Sanning och särprägel* (Stockholm, 1960); H. Levander, *H.B.* (Stockholm, 1957); S.R.E.K., *Verklighet och vision* (Stockholm, 1964); *Kring H.B.*, ed. S.R.E.K. (Stockholm, 1965).

**Bergroth, Kersti Solveig** (Viipuri 1886– ). Finnish dramatist, novelist and critic. Until 1920 she wrote in Swedish, but since then her works have been in Finnish. They include two rustic comedies in the Karelian dialect (*Anu ja Mikko*, 1932, and *Kuparsaare Antti*, 1956) which have enjoyed great popularity because of their lively dialogue and authentic Karelian atmosphere. The influence of Rudolf Steiner's anthroposophy can be seen in much of her work, and an emphasis on spiritual values as opposed to workaday materialism runs through her novels and essays and even the lighter journalistic pieces published over the signatures 'Asser' and 'Tet'. From 1927 to 1930 and again from 1934 to 1938 she edited avant-gardist literary periodicals. Her novels include *Kiirastuli* (1922), *Uusia sieluja* (1930), *Eläviä ja kuolleita* (1945), *Anja* (1949) and *Salaisuutemme* (1955). Under the pseudonym 'Mary Marck' she published a series of books for girls. She has also published poems, critical essays, and a travel book on Rome (1957), where she has lived since the 1950s. Her collection of essays has also been published in German, *Blick ins Leben* (1956). [IR]

**Bergson, Henri** (Paris 1859–Paris 1941). French philosopher. He studied at the École Normale and, after various secondary school posts, was appointed professor at the Collège de France in 1900. During the First World War he accomplished several cultural missions, notably in the United States, and from 1922 until 1925 was a member of the Commission Internationale de Coopération Intellectuelle. Elected to the French Academy in 1914, he was awarded the Nobel Prize for Literature in 1928.

Although directed locally against late 19th-century positivism and 'scientisme', Bergson's philosophy originates a new philosophical attitude, revolutionary in its impact on thought and literature, which may be summed up as a move from the abstract to the concrete. His criticism of Taine's associationism and 'psychological atomism' was that it studies mind from the outside and by analysis substitutes for what is given in experience, namely process, a combination of discrete parts – sensations, states, etc., all of which are abstractions. Philosophy, he declared, must return to 'the immediate data of consciousness' before conceptualization, and, to describe those without dislocating the organic wholeness of experience, a mode of 'inward' reflection is required which he called intuition.

In his epoch-making *Essai sur les données immédiates de la conscience* (1889; tr. F. L. Pogson, *Time and Free Will*, 1910) he shows how this is necessitated by the structure of consciousness itself. The essence of consciousness is *duration*: time, change, heterogeneity, pure quality, continuity. The intellect, for practical purposes, introduces measurement and substitutes for qualitative process an abstract, spatialized representation of discontinuous, homogeneous parts, quantitatively identical, transforming a 'se faisant' into a 'tout fait'. Intuition, on the contrary, is a way of 'thinking in duration'. A way, moreover, that opens up a perspective on human freedom, for the present of duration is the focal point of an accumulated past and an imminent future. Every act is a novel projection of the self, since, while grounded in the past, it emerges from it as a new act, 'like the fruit on the flower'.

In *Matière et mémoire* (1896; tr. N. M. Paul and W. Scott Palmer, *Matter and Memory*, 1911) Bergson develops, as against dualism, a mind-body theory which anticipates existentialism and phenomenology. He sees the self as 'in the world', acting in it through the 'body-subject'. Mind and body cooperate as one sense-giving activity. The body selects appropriate responses to a given situation from those stored up in the 'mémoire corporelle', while the mind similarly selects from its store of memory images. Each organizes its responses into fluid, dynamic schemas, and the two schemas (patterns of ideas and patterns of words, gestures, etc.) are then adjusted so as to project a sense or meaning, again through the body, in significant behaviour, speech or action – the whole formulation held together in a duration by a 'tension' of the will.

*L'évolution créatrice* (1907; tr. A. Mitchell, *Creative Evolution*, 1911) presents the creative process itself as the expression of an *élan vital*, projecting itself in forms which, once used, are discarded, to be taken up again, if need be, in new transformations. These discarded forms, says Bergson, remain as 'extinguished fragments which fall back as matter'. Matter, indeed, for Bergson, is not a radically different stuff from 'spirit', but simply spirit 'qui se dégrade'. Wherever there is repetition and dislocation there is materialization, as in dream or madness. Wherever there is concentration, duration, tension, there is 'spirit', with both a 'subjective', temporal side (the sense intended) and an 'objective', spatial side (the symbolic formulation). Spirit is novelty, and novelty is the use of old words or habitual gestures given new formulation by their integration into a new sense-giving act. Divorced from that act, and until they are taken up again in a new act and given another symbolic formulation, they fall back as disconnected, mechanized elements, like the dead words buried in the dictionary.

These considerations enable Bergson to propound his important distinction in *Les deux sources de la morale et de la religion* (1932; tr. R. Ashley Andra and C. Brereton, *The Two Sources of Morality and Religion*, 1935) between the 'closed' or formal and the 'open' or spiritual in religion and morals. Here again, he is not denying the importance of formal elements, since all senses find formal expression, but stigmatizing the 'intellectualist' error which dissociates the form (dogma, ritual) from the sense-giving act and hypostatizes what is, divorced from it, mere routine, habit or abstract concept, in short 'materialization'.

In *Le rire* (1900; tr. C. Brereton and F. Rothwell, *Laughter*, 1911), the work which bears most closely on aesthetics, Bergson, with examples taken mainly from Molière, defines the comic in terms of automatism and disconnexion. These arise whenever the self allows some *idée fixe* to control the will and express itself in repetitive, disjointed speech or action. Laughter is society's defence mechanism recalling the individual to the need to adjust himself to changing situations and to express his intentions in evolving patterns of behaviour and language. The Bergsonian aesthetic might be termed expressionist. The artist is gifted with a special intensity of perception which allows him to enter intuitively into the living reality of things and with the ability to embody his intuition in fresh imagery and colour, in a peculiarly evocative and dynamic symbolic formulation.

Bergson's philosophy, in the first decades of this century, was, alongside Pragmatism, the greatest liberating force from over-intellectualized modes of thought, while the revival of interest in it after 1940 points to the realization that it anticipates the existentialist and phenomenological view of the self as a sense-giving activity energizing in time. In this enlarged perspective the accusation of irrationalism made by Julien Benda and others misfires, since Bergson's aim, it is seen, was to show that rationality can only be understood when referred to its dynamic, concrete source in experience and action.

Bergson's influence on literature was profound, but diffuse rather than specific. The various attempts by writers to penetrate beneath the static images and facsimiles of the self and to render by new techniques the flux of consciousness intuitively perceived owe much to him. Virginia Woolf, Pirandello and Proust have all been mentioned in this connexion, although in the last case the similarities conceal a metaphysical difference, since permanence and identity, not time and heterogeneity, are the ultimates sought for. In France most decisive was the influence on Péguy and on the critics, Thibaudet and Du Bos. Symbolism, Futurism and Surrealism have other sources, but, in spite of major differences in aim and method, Valéry comes close to Bergson in his view of the self as an agent for the projection of meaning in dynamic symbolic forms. Generally, his literary influence runs parallel with his philosophical one, both working towards a new dynamic conception of thought and reality, freeing philosophers and writers from traditional modes of perception and explanation. [IWA]

*Œuvres* (Pléiade, 1959).

V. Jankélévitch, *B.* (Paris, 1931); *Études bergsoniennes* (Paris, 1942); R. Arbour, *H.B. et les lettres françaises* (Paris, 1955); I. W. Alexander, *B.: Philosopher of Reflection* (1957); H. Gouhier, *B. et le Christ des évangiles* (Paris, 1961).

**Berkowitz, Yitzhak Dov** (Slutzk 1885– ). Hebrew writer. Born in the Pale of Settlement in Russia, he went later to the United States and eventually to Palestine. Although best known for his fine Hebrew translations of the Yiddish stories of his father-in-law, ⇨ Sholem Aleichem, he wrote a realistic novel, short stories and a play on Jewish life in Eastern Europe and life in Israel. [EE]

*Kitve* (2 vols., Tel Aviv, 1936); *Menachem Mendel le-Eretz Israel* (Tel Aviv, 1936); *Rishonim Kivnei Adam* (Berlin, 1923).

Klausner, *HMHL*; Waxman, *HJL*.

**Bernanos, Georges** (Paris 1888–Paris 1948). French novelist and writer of polemical essays. His theme is the strife between good and evil, fought in the souls of a saintly elect. He shows how most people give themselves unconsciously to Satan from the earliest experience of disillusionment, after which the individual gradually loses his integrity, fabricating a false self, living a life of subterfuges and deceits and seeking to escape his true self by flights of all kinds, of which drugs and crimes are but the extreme form. In *Sous le soleil de Satan* (1926; tr. P. Morris, *Star of Satan*, 1940), Bernanos portrayed a priest fighting Satan tooth and nail, but whose mission is flawed through this excessive preoccupation with evil. In later novels he was to show a child-like simplicity as the life of grace which defeats through its very humility and candour the designs of Satan. Thus Chantal de Clergerie in *La joie* (1929; tr. L. Vanèse, *Joy*, 1948) and the parish priest of Ambricourt in the *Journal d'un curé de campagne* (1936; tr. P. Morris, *The Diary of a Country Priest*, 1954) are both able, through their self-sacrifice, to bring Christ's redemption to certain enslaved souls. Disturbing as is *L'imposture* (1927), a study of demoniacal possession, the *Journal* achieves greater aesthetic success, due in part to the implied parallel, in no way forced, between the seeming failure of the priest's tortured life and the Passion of Christ. The same Christocentric pattern is more audaciously woven in the unhappy experiences and suicide of an unlikeable girl of 14 in *Nouvelle histoire de Mouchette* (1937; tr. J. C. Whitehouse, *Mouchette*, 1966), a masterpiece of compassionate understanding. In the next nine years Bernanos published only polemical essays, the first of which, *La grande peur des bien-pensants*, in praise of Drumont, author of *La France juive* (1886), had already appeared in 1931. The best known of these digressive diatribes is *Les grands cimetières sous la lune* (1938; tr. P. Morris, *Diary of My Times*, 1938), a wholehearted indictment of Franco and the Spanish Church. He emigrated to South America in 1938, filled with disgust at the Munich agreement and in search of a livelihood. Two years before his death the publication of a defective edition of *Monsieur Ouine* (tr. G. Dunlop, *The Open Mind*, 1945) perplexed many critics. A study of evil in a Godforsaken village, this novel, not published in satisfactory form till 1955, presents a microcosm of the modern world. The incoherence of the narrative, with its juxtaposed fragments and unexplained occurrences, while it in some ways foreshadows the new novel of the post-war period, mirrors in fact the disruption of a parish which is spiritually dead, the incoherence of a world from which Christ has been banished. With *Dialogues des Carmélites* (tr. Gerard Hopkins, *The Carmelites*, 1961), a film script based on the martyrdom of a community of nuns during the Revolution which the writer completed just before he died, *Monsieur Ouine* represents the height of Bernanos's achievement. *Dialogues des Carmélites* is the most serene of his works, the simplest in expression and the most deeply Christocentric. [EB]

*Œuvres Romanesques suivies de Dialogues des Carmélites*, ed. A. Béguin (Pléiade, 1961); *Lettres aux Anglais* (1940; tr. H. L. Binsse and R. Bethell, in *Plea for Liberty*, (N.Y., 1944); *Un crime* (1935; tr. A. Green, *The Crime*, 1947); *Un mauvais rêve* (1950; tr. W. J. Strachan, *Night is Darkest*, 1953); *Les enfants humiliés* (1953; tr. anon., *Tradition of Freedom*, 1950).

*Bernanos par lui-même*, ed. Albert Béguin (Paris 1954); Hans Urs von Balthasar, *Le Chrétien B.*, tr. from German, M. de Gandillac (Paris, 1956); J. Scheidegger, *G.B. romancier* (Neuchâtel, 1956); M. Estève, *Le sens de l'amour dans les romans de B.* (Paris, 1959); W. Bush, *Souffrance et expiation dans la pensée de B.* (Paris, 1962); P. Hebblethwaite, S.J., *B.: an Introduction* (1965); M. Estève, *B.* (Paris, 1965); W. Bush, *L'angoisse du mystère, essai sur B. et M. Ouine* (Paris, 1966); *Études bernanosiennes* (1960ff.).

**Bernard, Jean-Jacques** (Enghien 1888– ). French playwright. Famous for a series of plays known as 'the theatre of silence': *Le feu qui reprend mal* (1921); *Martine* (1922); *Le printemps des autres* (1924); *L'invitation au voyage* (1924); *L'âme en peine* (1926) (all tr. J. L. Frith in *The Sulky Fire: Five Plays*, 1939). What distinguishes all these plays and some later ones, notably *Nationale 6* (1935), is a sober and discreet exploration of dreams, fears, passions which are hinted at and never made fully explicit. The inner life of a central character is evoked through broken phrases, tell-tale gestures and glances in an atmosphere that is usually heavy with ambiguity. Such is the situation in *Le feu qui reprend mal*, where the husband returning from captivity after the war suspects his wife's relationship with an American officer to whom she has been hospitable. The virtues of such a theatre are delicacy and sobriety; its defects, a tendency to portentousness and a failure to transcend an extraordinarily limited and banal world. Later attempts to extend his range (*Marie Stuart*, 1941; *Notre-Dame d'en-Haut*, 1950; *De Tarse, en Cilicie*, 1961) confirm the author's limitations. Interesting are his reflections in *Mon ami le théâtre* (1958). [SBJ]

*Théatre* (6 vols., 1925–46).
M. Daniels, *The French Drama of the Unspoken* (1953); Surer, *TFC*.

**Bernard of Clairvaux, St** (Fontaines 1090–Dijon 1153). Christian Latin writer. Cistercian monk (1113ff.) and first abbot of Clairvaux, one of the most famous religious houses in Europe. His influence, owing to his saintly life and overpowering personality, was enormous; his championship of Pope Innocent II was decisive. Strictly orthodox in his beliefs, he led the attack on ⇨ Abelard, Gilbert de la Poirée, and Arnold of Brescia. In 1146, at the Pope's suggestion, he preached the Second Crusade. Its failure disappointed him bitterly and probably hastened his death. St Bernard was a voluminous writer of theological treatises, letters, sermons, mystical works and poems. His *De diligendo Deo* (ed. and tr. E. G. Gardner, *The Book of St Bernard on the Love of God*, 1916) is one of the greatest of all medieval mystical books. As a preacher, he is at his best in his sermons on the *Song of Songs*. In all his writings he shows an extraordinarily intimate knowledge of the Bible. His honeyed poetical prose earned him the title of 'Doctor Mellifluus', but he could also be a biting satirist. [FB]

Migne, *PL*, 182–5; *Letters*, tr. and ed. B. Scott James (1952–3); *Select Treatises* (*De diligendo Deo* and *De gradibus humilitatis*), ed. W. Williams and B. R. V. Mills (1926).
V. Vacandard, *Vie de St B.* (2 vols., Paris, 1895); W. W. Williams, *St B. of C.* (1935); J. Leclercq, *St B.* (Paris, 1948).

**Bernard of Cluny (Bernard of Morlas, Morval, or Morlaix)** (fl. 1140). Christian Latin poet. Author of a famous Latin poem, *De contemptu mundi*, of about 3,000 lines, in an elaborate metre – dactylic hexameters rhyming in couplets, with internal rhymes in every line after the second and fourth dactyls: a a b, c c b. The greater part consists of a violent attack on contemporary abuses, relieved by beautiful descriptions of the heavenly Jerusalem. From J. M. Neale's paraphrase (in *The Rhythm of Bernard de Morlaix*, 1858) come the well-known hymns, 'Jerusalem the golden', 'Brief life is here our portion', and two others (⇨ Hymns, Latin). [FB]

Ed. H. C. Hoskier (1929); tr. H. Preble, *The Source of 'Jerusalem the Golden'* (Chicago, 1910).
Raby, *CLP*, *SLP*.

**Bernardes, Diogo** (Ponte da Barca 1530–? 1605). Portuguese poet. Little is known of his youth, except that he took minor orders in 1544 and spent some years in Lisbon. In 1576 he was a member of Pedro de Alcáçova Carneiro's embassy to Madrid, and in the following year is mentioned as occupying a court appointment (*moço de toalha*) to King Sebastian. In 1578 he accompanied the King on his disastrous expedition to Morocco, and was taken prisoner at Alqasr Kibir. Ransomed by 1582, he was made a member of the Order of Christ and granted a royal pension in that year and again in 1593.

Bernardes was one of the group of poets who recognized themselves disciples of ⇨ Sá de Miranda and, like Sá, he wrote in both the new Italianate forms and in the traditional metres. With ⇨ Camões he is the most euphonious sonneteer of his generation – so much so that his œuvre suffered grave depredations at the hands of certain admirers of Camões who considered that such good things should necessarily be attributed to the greater poet. Faria e Sousa even claimed that the three volumes of Bernardes's poetry were the collection of which Camões had been robbed, returning from Moçambique.

In 1594 he published his *Várias Rimas ao Bom Jesus*, containing his religious poetry, much of it dating from the time of his African captivity; and in 1596 two more volumes: *O Lima* and *Rimas Várias – Flores do Lima* (the latter including his early love poetry). According to tradition the charms of the river Lima caused Roman conquerors to forget their country, and its waters were compared with those of Lethe. The Lima is the central figure and the setting of his bucolic verse, and he peopled its banks with ancient spirits. [ARM]

*Obras Completas* (3 vols., CSC, 1945).

**Bernardes, Padre Manuel** (Lisbon 1644–Lisbon 1710). Portuguese theologian. Born of a middle-class family of civil servants, he took degrees at Coimbra in Philosophy and Canon Law and in 1674 became an Oratorian. A prolific writer, he devoted the rest of his days to penning sermons and spiritual tracts. Much of his work was published posthumously. Among his principal studies are *Pão Partido em Pequeninos* (1694), *Luz e Calor* (1696), *Exercícios Espirituais* (1707), and *Os Últimos Fins do Homem* (1728), but he is chiefly remembered for his *Nova Floresta* (5 vols., 1706–28), a vast collection of anecdotes and stories culled and adapted from a wide variety of sources. Intended for the spiritual and moral edification of the reader, the stories were arranged alphabetically according to their topic and had progressed as far as the letter *J*. They are especially characterized by the quality of the prose style and the vigour of the narration. Bernardes's apparently facile credulity, with regard to miracles and supernatural intervention at all times, has been the subject of no little subsequent debate. [RCW]

A. do Prado Coelho, *M.B.* (vol. I, Lisbon, 1942); F. de Almeida, *História da Igreja em Portugal*, iii (Coimbra, 1917).

**Bernardin de Saint-Pierre, Jacques-Henri** (Le Havre 1737–Éragny-sur-Oise 1814). French naturalist and novelist. With a lifelong love of the exotic awakened at 12 by a voyage to Martinique, he later abandoned thoughts of a missionary career to train as an engineer and then enter military service abroad. His two years in Mauritius provided material for his *Voyage à l'Île de France* (1773) and *Études de la Nature* (1784). A friend and disciple of Rousseau, with whom he shared a strong dislike of urban civilization, a taste for botany, and a belief in the goodness of natural man and the beneficence of nature, his literary success – which, with *Paul et Virginie* (1787; ed. V. P. Underwood, Manchester, 1942; tr. anon., 1923), was enormous – depended on the vogue for Rousseauistic ideas. This naïve and moral tale of youthful innocence in a tropical setting exercised a far-reaching influence on later Romantic literature by its lyrical and richly detailed descriptions of the exotic landscape of Mauritius. In later life he enjoyed considerable public eminence as a protégé of Napoleon, who much admired his books. [WHB]

M. Souriau, *B. de S.-P. d'après ses manuscrits* (Paris, 1905); Trahard, *MSF*.

**Bernart de Ventadorn** (fl. *c.*1145–1180). Provençal ⇨ troubadour. According to his Provençal biographer he was of humble birth, the son of the baker at the castle of Ventadorn. It is likely that he addressed his first songs to the wife of Ebles II of Ventadorn, likewise a troubadour. He sang at the courts of Eleanor of Aquitaine and count Raimon V of Toulouse, and is thought to have retired to the abbey of Dalon on the death of the count in 1194.

He wrote in the clear style of the *trobar leu* and his melodious language and vivid imagery lend lyric freshness to his best songs, e.g. 'Can vei la lauzeta mover' and 'Tant ai mo cor ple de joya', which still have an immediate appeal. Within an orthodox courtly cadre of homage and submission to the lady he exalts his sensual pleasure in all that surrounds him into an overwhelming feeling of *Jois*, and at other times he sinks into a mood of deep sorrow. Some poems written without this intense inspiration of feeling fall below the quality of his best work. He is unconcerned with general moral problems and attempts no genre other than the *canso* or love-song and the courtly debate or *tenso*. There survive 45 songs in many manuscripts and Bernart was much imitated by troubadours and Northern French *trouvères*. Some of his work was translated into verse in the *langue d'oïl*, and the direct influence of his imagery can be seen as late as the *Roman de la* ⇨ *Rose*. [LTT]

Ed. C. Appel (Halle a.S., 1915); ed. S. G. Nichols, jr, J. A. Galm, *et al.* (Chapel Hill, 1962); ed. M. Lazar (Paris, 1966).
*Filologia Romanza* ,VI, 1959.

**Berni, Francesco** (Lamporecchio 1497?–Florence 1535). Italian poet. Living mostly in Rome, he cultivated a style of earthy, burlesque parody, in reaction against the lofty, idealizing tenor of 16th-century Petrarchism. Occasionally there is a quick-witted, satirical incisiveness in his sonnets and *capitoli* which brings them to life, but often, despite the agility of his vigorous Tuscan, nothing more substantial emerges than the (not altogether unfashionable) jeer of irreverent protest. He also rewrote ⇨ Boiardo's *Orlando innamorato* (1541) in polished flowing Tuscan, taking considerable liberties. [DGR]

*Poesie e prose*, ed. E. Chiorboli (Geneva, 1934); *Rime*, ed. G. Macchia (1945); *The Orlando innamorato*, prose tr. W. S. Rose from Berni's version (1823); Lind, *LPIR*.
A. Sorrentino, *F.B. poeta della scapigliatura del Rinascimento* (Florence, 1933); *Minori*, ii.

**Bernolák, Anton** (Slanica 1762–Nové Zámky 1813). Slovak philologist. In his *Grammatica slavica* (1790) Bernolák was the first to codify a Slovak literary language, based on the dialects of western Slovakia. This language was employed by a number of writers in the early 19th century, notably the poet Ján Hollý, but it was superseded by the central Slovak language established in the 1840s by L'. ⇨ Štúr. [RA]

J. Pavelek, ed., *Gramatické dielo A.B.* (Bratislava, 1941); R. Auty, 'The Evolution of Literary Slovak', in *Transactions of the Philological Society* (1953).

**Bernstein, Henry** (Paris 1876–Paris 1953). French dramatist. He was popular in the *belle époque* for his hectic plays: *La rafale* (1905); *Le voleur* (1906; tr. J. A. Haughton, *The Thief*, 1915); *Samson* (1907); *L'assaut* (1912) and *Le secret* (1913). Contrived violence of situation, melodramatically inflated protagonists (like the financier in *Samson*, who engineers his own ruin so as to bring about the downfall of his wife's lover) take place against the décor of high society. Later plays, like *Judith* (1922), his rehandling of Biblical myth, *La galerie des glaces* (1925), a study of the self-doubts of a painter, and *La soif* (1950) mark no advance in power or technique. [SBJ]

L. Le Sidaner, *H. B.* (1931).

**Bershadsky, Isaiah**, pseud. of Isaiah Domachevitsky (Samoscha 1872–Warsaw 1910). Hebrew writer. Of the first of a generation of Hebrew writers who never went to Yeshivah, never had to rebel against his environment although he had received a traditional Jewish education. He loved the Hebrew language, but his attachment to Judaism was not the sentimental kind of his predecessors. He had an analytical mind, a rare descriptive ability, an eye for detail, psychological insight into human nature and deep sympathy for his characters which enabled him to write the first two realistic novels in Hebrew literature. From 1903 he was editor of the important periodical *Ha-Zeman* in Vilna. [EE]

*B'Eyn Matarah* (1890); *Neged ha-Zerem* (1901). Klausner, *HMHL*; Waxman, *HJL*.

**Bertran de Born** (*c.* 1140–Dalon Abbey, before 1215). French ⇨ troubadour. A feudal knight, of Hautefort in Périgord. There survive 8 love poems. The best known is the portrait of the 'dompna soisseubuda', the 'composite' lady endowed with an ideal quality taken from each noblewoman he admired. But his fame rests on his *sirventes* in praise of war. In 'Lo coms m'a mandat' (1181) he calls on the vassals and allies of Raimon V of Toulouse to come to his help against the king of Aragon and ends with the wish that the high barons may always remain angered with each other. In 1182, he drove his brother Constantin from the castle of Hautefort. Constantin enlisted the support of the viscount of Limoges and Richard Cœur de Lion, and, probably as a result of this quarrel, Bertran attended the court of Henry II in Normandy. He describes his dismay at this 'park of barons', devoid of luxury and munificence. Here he addressed some love-songs to Mathilda, daughter of Henry II and wife of Henry of Saxony, and also lent his voice in support of Henry the young king, who was jealous of the power of his brother Richard, Duke of Aquitaine. Bertran urged him in vigorous *sirventes* to fight for land and wealth in his own right. The young king took up arms but died on 11 June 1183. On 29 June, the army of Richard Cœur de Lion and Alphonso II of Aragon laid siege to Hautefort. Bertran surrendered on 7 July but was pardoned by Richard and remained loyal to him, notably during Richard's imprisonment in Austria. He also praised Conrad of Montferrat for his defence of Tyre against Saladin during the Third Crusade. In 1197 he entered the Cistercian abbey of Dalon.

Bertran scorned the arts of peace; merchants should be robbed, money wasted on frivolities such as gardens should be heaped high in the goblets to buy knights for the army. Life is to be felt only on the battlefield amidst 'trumpets, drums, pennants and ensigns', in the shock of combat when 'the fields will be strewn with pieces of helmets and shields, when there will be joy and tears, grief and delight . . .'. 'And if I live', he says, 'this will be my great happiness, and, if I die, my great deliverance.'

His original and highly evocative language earned him Dante's praise as the supreme troubadour in the art of singing of war (*De vulgari eloquentia*, II: 2). Dante also knew the long and extravagant Provençal biographies devoted to his life, especially to his friendship with the young king. In *Convivio*, IV, II, he praised his generosity, and in *Inferno*, xxviii, 118–42, described him carrying his severed head lantern-wise as one who had set the son at variance with his father. References to Bertran and the young king are found in collections of Italian short stories in the late 13th century, e.g. the second of the *Conti di antichi cavalieri* (*Giornale storico della letteratura italiana*, iii, 1884, 200–3), where Bertran, 'maestro del re giovene', teaches Saladin the art of courtly love. [LTT]

Ed. C. Appel (Halle, 1932); ed. A. Thomas (Toulouse, 1888); ed. A. Stimming (Halle, 1913); Hill and Bergin, *APT*.

S. Stroński, *La légende amoureuse de B. de B.* (Paris, 1914); Olin H. Moore, *The Young King, Henry Plantagenet (1155–1183) in History, Literature and Tradition* (Columbus, Ohio, 1925); *R*, LI, 1925.

**Bertrand, Louis Jacques Napoléon**, called 'Aloysius' (Ceva, Piedmont 1807–Paris 1841). French poet. Friend of ⇨ Sainte-Beuve, who published his prose poems as *Gaspard de la nuit* (1842; Paris, 1925). Described as *Fantaisies à la manière de Rembrandt et de Callot*, they reveal the current taste for the Gothic, the morbid, the dream. They influenced Baudelaire's *Le spleen de Paris* and the effusions of ⇨ Lautréamont. The title and some of the themes of *Gaspard de la nuit* were used by Ravel for his piano suite. [WA]

**Berzsenyi, Dániel** (Egyházashetye 1776–Nikla 1836). Hungarian poet. A nobleman living on his estate, he wrote odes, elegies and epistles mainly concerned with the moral regeneration of his class and of the nation, his aim being to awake heroic and patriotic spirit. Best-known poems: *A Magyarokhoz* (tr. W. Loew, *To the Hungarians*, in *Magyar Poetry*, 1908) and *Osztályrészem* (tr. ibid., *My Share in Life*, in *Magyar Songs*, 1887). [JFR]

**Bésus, Roger** (Bayeux 1915– ). French novelist. He trained as a civil engineer. Set against the rugged background of his native Normandy, his novels depict a central character brought into conflict with himself or his milieu, by falling victim to some obsessive and destructive urge: love and ambition in *Un homme pour rien* (1947), the will to dominate in *Le scandale* (1956), bewildered religious aspirations in *Louis Brancourt* (1955), devotion to a social outcast in *Les abandonnés* (1957). Though broken physically or socially, his tortured heroes finally acquire spiritual certainty and strength from their experience. In *Le refus* (1952) and *Cet homme qui vous aimait* (1953), where the subject and treatment are frankly Catholic, his affinity with ⇨ Bernanos is most apparent. [IHW]

*L'Âge Nouveau*, III, 1961.

**Betti, Ugo** (Camerino 1892–Rome 1953). Italian playwright. A magistrate by profession, he built several plays round the theme of the judicial inquiry (*Frana allo scalo nord*, 1932; *Il cacciatore di anitre*, 1934; *Ispezione*, 1942; *Irene innocente*, 1947; *La fuggitiva*, 1953), pointing to the collective responsibility of society for evil and sin, which only a Supreme Judge can adequately apportion. A lesser judge, however, would hardly welcome his handling of his theatrical inquests: often the evidence is vague and nebulous, with no precise reference to any real issues or problems; things always seem to happen in unlikely countries, where unmentioned 'high-placed persons' pull invisible strings; the motives behind the characters' actions remain obscure both to the characters themselves and to the audience. It is not therefore surprising that of Betti's 26 plays only a few were successful: *Corruzione al palazzo di giustizia* (1944), where the author is more explicit than usual in his strictures on judicial corruption; *Delitto all'isola delle capre* (1948; tr. H. Reed, *Crime on Goat Island*, 1960), the revenge of three lonely sex-starved women over the man who has satisfied and at the same time revealed their sexual obsession; *La regina e gli insorti* (1949), which, in spite of its oversimplified picture of the contrast between revolution and conservatism and its leaning towards melodrama, carries a simple message of redemption unclouded by pretentious metaphysical fumes. One should add to this list a charming comedy, *I nostri sogni* (1937), where Betti succeeded in finding a simple poetic style adequate to express a simple truth: that one should be contented with one's lot and not indulge in vain escapist dreams. Many of his less successful plays (e.g. *Marito e moglie*, 1943) seem to have been written with readers, not theatre audiences, in mind. [GMC]

*Tutte le opere* (1957); *Three Plays* (*The Burnt Flower Bed, The Queen and the Rebels, Summertime*), tr. H. Reed (1957).

F. Cologni, *U.B.* (Bologna, 1960); *Contemporanei*, ii; Robertis, *SN*; Biondolillo, *C.*

**Bèze, Théodore de** (Vézelay 1519–Geneva 1605). French theologian, political writer and dramatist. He was Calvin's right-hand man, his representative at the French court (where he had considerable personal influence on Charles IX) and his successor. He wrote prolifically, in Latin and French, on questions of theology and political theory (especially *Du droit des magistrats*, 1574, in which he examines the subject's right to revolt); he also produced one important literary work, a tragedy, *Abraham sacrifiant* (1550; Paris, 1945), in many ways a transitional work, with some elements of medieval drama – the Biblical subject, lack of *vraisemblance*, use of Satan as a character (dressed as a monk), and blend of comic and serious tone; but anticipating the classical theatre by its brevity, small number of characters, use of a chorus and simplicity of plot. Its chief features are its strong Protestant message (the importance of faith and its ultimate triumph) and the moving presentation of the relationship between Isaac and his parents. [GJ]

*Correspondance*, ed. H. Aubert (Geneva, 1960–3).

**Bezruč, Petr,** pseud. of Vladimír Vašek (Opava 1867–Olomouc 1958). Czech poet. The son of a Silesian grammar school teacher, he studied classical philology but became a postal official. After an early disappointment in love he never married and lived a very secluded life. In 1899 he began sending some striking poems anonymously to the magazine *Čas*. He posed as a rough and ugly miner speaking for the 70,000 Czechs of Silesia – outcasts who were being exploited by the mine owners, germanized and polonized by the authorities and neglected by the Prague politicians. First published in book form under the title *Slezské číslo* (1903), then as *Slezské písně* (1909, 1930), the collection was gradually expanded to about 80 poems. They are a dirge sung at the graves of his brothers, verses of scepticism, disillusion and nihilism. Among the social poems only 'Ostrava' suggests the advent of open revolt. [KB]

*Schlesische Lieder*, tr. R. Fuchs (Prague, 1937).
J. Janů, *P.B.* (Prague, 1947); F. Buriánek, *P.B.* (Prague, 1952).

**Bialik, Hayyim Nahman** (Ukraine 1873–Tel Aviv 1934). Hebrew poet. The greatest modern Hebrew poet both in content and in form. Primarily a lyricist, his poetry has great force, impulsiveness and passion. Having broken away from the traditional upbringing of the Talmudic high school he came under the influence of the Haskalah (Enlightenment). He moved to Odessa, where he met Ahad Ha-Am and other leading thinkers, and wrote his first poems, among them *El ha-Zippor* (1892), but was too shy to have them published; he made his début with an article in the Hebrew literary daily *Ha-Melitz*. But upon the encouragement received from his contemporaries, he published his poetry. His financial situation forced him in 1892 to leave Odessa for Zhitomir, where he married the daughter of a wealthy timber-merchant. During the four years he spent in the forests, he continued writing poetry, but eventually turned to teaching. While teaching, his reputation as the leading Hebrew poet was established by the publication of his first epic poem *Ha-Matmid* in *Ha-Shiloach*, ⇨ Ahad Ha'am's monthly. In 1900 he was able to return to Odessa, where, through the aid of his friend and patron, Ravnicki, he became a teacher at the recently established Hebrew school. This was the turning point in his life. His fame began to travel all over Europe, for his poems were translated into Russian and German. With Ravnicki, he established the publishing house 'Moriah', and later 'D'vir', which for twenty years issued many books in all fields of literary endeavour.

Bialik himself wrote stories and essays and tried his hand at translation (*Don Quixote* and Schiller's *Wilhelm Tell*) with great success. He remained in Russia during the First World War and even the first years of the Soviet regime, which did not molest him. But he soon left for Berlin and in 1923 settled in Palestine, where he reorganized the publishing house D'vir and for the rest of his life played the role of symbol and leader of the cultural revival in the new Jewish national home. But his poetic muse fell silent, and he wrote chiefly stories, fairy-tales and essays. In collaboration with Ravnicki, he collected and edited the legends of the Talmud and Midrash in *Sefer Ha'agada*. Bialik's poetry underwent a great change from the time he wrote *El ha-Zippor* to his last poem, *Yatmut*, which rates as his best, and which he wrote shortly before his death. The poems of his first ten years emanate an unbounded love for the ancient Judaism of the Bible and

Talmud. But this love soon became a tragic, nostalgic love for something that is doomed to extinction. Tormented by the dilemma of how a nation, dispersed as the Jews are, will live on, he wrote his classic poem, *Matei Midbar*, in which, as in his essays published at about that time, he became the rebuking and sternly reproving prophet. His admonishment of the people reaches a polished climax in the poem *Achen Gam ze Musar Elohim* (1905) and *B'ir Hacharega*, written after the Kisheneff pogrom, which he describes in a manner moving the reader to impotent rage as well as to tears. The revolt against Israel's oppressors suddenly turns into a revolt against Heaven, and the denunciation of cowardice and weakness becomes a summons to self and self-reliance. All his motifs, a longing for a full life on earth, the craving after love, the revolt against oppression and persecution, the vision of vengeance, the struggle between Judaism and other civilizations and the awesome vision of the End are concentrated in his most profound allegoric work, *Megillat Ha-Esh*. In lamenting the destruction of his people, Bialik also foreshadows a new beginning of a more complete life in that not all that is old will be cast away for the sake of the new, but only that part which has become obsolete and in place of it a new Jewish life would absorb all that is best in the new age. [EE]

*Kitve H.N.B.* (Tel Aviv, 1926); *Far Over the Sea* (Cincinnati, 1929); *Knight of Onions* and *Knight of Garlic* (N.Y., 1939); *Poems, From the Hebrew*, ed. L. V. Snowman (1929).

Waxman, *HJL*; Klausner, *HMHL*; Y. H. Ravnicki, *Dor ve-sofrov* (Tel-Aviv, 1927).

**Bidermann, Jakob** (Ehingen 1578–Rome 1639). German Jesuit writer. Professor of rhetoric in Munich, assistant of the General in Rome. Besides Latin verse and prose, he wrote plays, influential rather than great, especially *Cenodoxus* (1609). His themes, influenced by Loyola, are religious and philosophical: fortune, martyrdom, asceticism, and appearance and reality (cf. similar preoccupation in Calderón's *La vida es sueño*). He also wrote a Latin novel, *Utopia* (German tr. C. A. Hörl, *Bacchusia oder Fastnachtland*, 1677). [FB]

*Cenodoxus*, ed. E. Hederer (1958); *Philemon Martyr*, ed. M. Wehrli (1960); *Ludi theatrales sacri* (1666); *Epigrammatum libri tres* (1620); *Heroum ep stolae* (1633).

M. Sadil, *J.B., ein Dramatiker des 17. Jahrhunderts* (2 vols., Vienna, 1899–1900).

**'Biedermeier.'** The term is used of works of the years following German Romanticism, i.e. works written in the first half of the 19th century, especially in Southern Germany and Austria. The *Biedermeier* mood, which is particularly associated with the conservatism of Metternich's Austria, is one of moderation and of resigned acceptance of one's given lot. It is a *Biedermeier* moral that is presented in the *Besserungsstücke* of the popular Viennese stage, the plays of J. A. Gleich and Adolf Bäuerle; their successor in public favour, ⇨ Raimund, is often cited as an example of a *Biedermeier* writer, as also is ⇨ Stifter, while *Der Traum ein Leben*, a play in *Besserungsstück* form by ⇨ Grillparzer, contains the classic expression of *Biedermeier* philosophy. [WEY]

M. Greiner, *Zwischen B. und Bourgeoisie* (Göttingen, 1953); J. Hermand, *Die literarische Formenwelt des B.s* (Giessen, 1958); W. Höllerer, *Zwischen Klassik und Moderne* (Stuttgart, 1958).

**Bierbaum, Otto Julius** (Grünberg 1865–Dresden 1910). German poet and novelist. Co-founder of the art-journal *Pan* (1894) and with A. Heymel and ⇨ Schröder of the literary journal *Die Insel*, from which the Insel-Verlag was to develop. His most important publications include his edition of *Deutsche Chansons* (1900), his collection of lyric verse *Irrgarten der Liebe* (1901), and the grotesque novel *Prinz Kuckuck* (3 vols., 1906–7). He is remembered chiefly for showing the potentialities of cabaret-type (*Überbrettl*) songs and verses to express a variety of humour and sentiment – an important influence on ⇨ Brecht and the political poets of the 1920s. [PB]

P. Pollard, *Masks and Minstrels of New Germany* (1911); A. v. Klement, *O.J.B.: Bibliographie* (Vienna, 1957).

**Bijns, Anna** (Antwerp 1493–Antwerp 1575). Dutch poet. Her aggressive mockery of Luther and Reformation doctrines in her *Refereinen* makes most spirited use of ⇨ *rederijker* conventions at a time of decline. Two collections of 1528 and 1548 were followed by a third in 1567, in which militance gives way to devout resignation (publ. 1886). [PK]

L. Roose, *A.B. Een rederijker uit de hervormingstijd* (Gent, 1963).

**Bilderdijk, Willem** (Amsterdam 1756–Haarlem 1831). Dutch poet and dramatist. He spent an unhappy childhood as a cripple in his Protestant home. In 1795 he had to leave the country for refusing allegiance to the new government, and in London he contracted a liaison with Katherina Schweickhardt. A period of hardship in Brunswick was followed by his return to Holland as Louis Napoleon's tutor. A promised professorship did not materialize, but William I granted him an annuity which he supplemented by lecturing at Leyden.

A monumental and grotesque figure, his great talent and feeling made him appear the leader of a new golden age and think himself the chosen vessel of divine gifts, but his brilliant intellect is debased by lack of self-criticism and distorted by an egotistical and impulsive temperament. His originality and sometimes unbalanced passion are yet harnessed to neo-classical imagery and rococo flourish which mar the greater part of his work. His style is equally effusive whether he is expatiating on the evils of rationalism or the boiling of eggs. [PK]

*Napoleon. Ode* (1806); *Floris V* (1808); *De ondergang der eerste wareld* (1820), ed. J. Bosch, 1959 (unfinished epic); *Dichtwerken*, ed. I. da Costa (16 vols., 1856–9); *Geschiedenis des Vaderlands*, ed. H. W. Tydeman (13 vols., 1832–53); Barnouw, *CA*.

J. and A. Romein, *W.B.*, *Gefnuikt Genie* ('Erflaters van ouze beschaving', III, Amsterdam, 1956); M. J. G. de Jong and W. Zaal, *B.* (Kampen, 1960) (anthology with biographical commentary).

**Bildungsroman.** German 'educational novel' of which the prototype is ⇨ Goethe's *Wilhelm Meister*. ⇨ Novalis, Stifter, Keller, T. Mann. Some German scholars see already in Grimmelshausen's *Simplicissimus* an 'educational' interest in the development of the hero; on similar grounds they then include much of European fiction in this category (e.g. Dickens' *Great Expectations* etc.). Others make sub-classifications to distinguish between educational novels proper (*Erziehungsromane*), where some specific psychological theory is involved (⇨ Carossa, Hesse), general 'novels of development', wherever the hero's character evolves, and true *Bildungsromane* in the manner of Goethe, where an artistic temperament comes to terms with the demands of social life. [AKT]

*Dt. Vjschrift*, 35 (1961); R. Pascal, *The German Novel* (1956).

**Bill'-Belotserkovsky, Vladimir Naumovich** (Aleksandriya, Khersonskaya Gub. 1885– ). Russian playwright. A self-educated and widely travelled Jewish sailor, he was famous in the twenties for *Shtorm* (1925) and *Levo Rulya* (1925) – plays which raised the *agitka* to the level of the professional stage. His inspiration, however, did not outlast the immediate theme of the Revolution. His plays are crudely put together, almost all treat life at sea and are marked by passionate political pathos and rough humour. Since *Vokrug ringa* (1949) at the Moscow Theatre of Drama – the fruit of his experience in the U.S.A. (1911–17) – little more has been heard of him. [AP]

*Izbrannye Proizvedeniya* (2 vols., 1962).

I. Al'tman, 'V.N.B.-B.', in *Izbrannye Stat'i* (Moscow, 1957); K. Rudnitsky, *Portrety dramaturgov* (Moscow, 1961); Boguslavskiy, *KIRSD*.

**Billetdoux, François** (Paris 1927– ). French actor and playwright. Author of highly individual tragi-comedies of human impotence and despair in which the characters seek a temporary reprieve in drink or sex: *À la nuit la nuit* (1955); *13 pièces à louer* (1956); *Tchin-Tchin* (1959; tr. M. Rudkin, *Chin-Chin*, 1963); *Le comportement des époux Bredburry* (1960); *Va donc chez Törpe* (1961; tr. M. Rudkin, *Chez Torpe*, 1963). In all of these one encounters a rather Chekhovian search for the inexpressible in an idiom that makes rapid transitions from tenderness to violence and in a manner which relies on marked variations in tempo. This is obvious in *Tchin-Tchin*, where a man and woman whose marital partners are having an affaire enter into a drunken complicity that is, at once, shocking, comic and painfully moving. Billetdoux likes to proceed from an initial shock that disconcerts the spectator and throws him off his moral balance. Such is the situation in *À la nuit la nuit*, where the 'respectable' client of a Marseilles prostitute calls her mother, or in *Le comportement des époux Bredburry*, where a wife offers her husband for sale in the columns of a newspaper, or in *Va donc chez Törpe*, where all the guests at an inn have come there to commit suicide. These parables on the failure of love strike a curiously haunting note. Interesting too is his latest play, *Il faut passer par les nuages* (1964). [SBJ]

*Théâtre* (2 vols., 1961–4).

*Yale French Studies*, 29, 1962; Corvin, *TNF*.

**Billy, André** (Saint-Quentin 1882– ). French writer and critic. His religious upbringing provided material for his fiction; the early narrative *Bénoni* (repr. 1956) studies the 'mœurs d'église'. Author of many critical articles (cf. especially his regular contributions to *Le Figaro Littéraire*). He has written substantial studies of writers which have been described as 'lucid, readable, dependable, and without an index' (*Vie de Diderot*, 1932; *Vie de Balzac*, 2 vols., 1944; *Vie des Frères Goncourt*, 3 vols., 1956, tr. M. Shaw, *The Goncourt Brothers*, 1960; *Ce cher Stendhal*, 1958; *Mérimée*, 1959; *Huysmans et Cie*, 1962, etc.). Although a specialist in the 19th century, he has dealt with more recent times in such works as *Époque-1900* (1954), and *L'époque contemporaine* (*1905–1930*) (1956). A veteran laden with many honours (he is a member of the Académie Goncourt). [CAHR]

*Le lingue straniere*, x, 1, 1961; *Marginales*, XVII, 84/5, 1962.

**Bin Gorion, Micha Yoseph.** ⇨ Berdichewski, Micah Joseph.

**Bisticci, Vespasiano da** (Florence 1421–nr Florence 1498). Italian biographer. A Florentine bookseller, his *Vite di uomini illustri del tempo suo* (first publ. by Angelo Mai, 1839; ed. P. D'Ancona, E. Aeschlimann, 1951) presents an interesting gallery of 15th-century portraits. The 105 lives include Popes, rulers, statesmen, prelates and scholars (e.g. Nicholas V, Cosimo de' Medici, Bruni, etc.), and although literary naïveté limits his range and penetration, the good-nature and honesty of the humble bookseller make an agreeable impression as he recalls the great men whom he has been in contact with. [DGR]

*The Vespasiano Memoirs* (*Lives of Illustrious Men of the 15th Century*), tr. W. G. and E. Waters (1926, repr. 1963).

G. Caprin, 'V. d. B.', in *Il Quattrocento* (Sansoni, Florence, 1954); Varese, *PVQ*.

**Bizcarrondo, Indalego.** ⇨ Basque Literature.

**Björling, Gunnar** (Helsinki 1887–Helsinki 1960). Finnish-Swedish poet and essayist. A leading exponent of literary modernism in Finland, Björling is one of the most daring experimenters in Swedish. He can in a sense be regarded as a 'Dadaist' (⇨ Dada), but his poetry reflects a conscious philosophy, which he also expounded in a theoretical form and which accommodated impulses both from the Naturalism of the eighties and opposite trends deriving from Nietzsche and Bergson. His elliptical style, with its sublime disregard for the rules of grammar, aims at, and frequently attains to, a degree of concentration in which familiar objects and the emotions surrounding them are experienced as mystical essences. Freshness of perception is wedded to rare stylistic economy; the result can be breathtaking but also impenetrable. His lyrical single-mindedness won him the respect of his colleagues, and his contributions to *Quosego*, a literary magazine published during 1928 and 1929, became particularly influential with the younger generation, also in Sweden, but made little impression on a wider public. Björling's lyrical output, some 20 collections in all, include *Korset och löftet* (1925), *Kiri-ra!* (1930), *Solgrönt* (1933), *Det oomvända anletet* (1939) and *Luft är och ljus* (1946). It is easier to grasp the varied particularity and essential consistency of his poetic universe from selections such as *Träd står i sina rader* (1952: poems 1922–36) and *Du jord du dag* (1957). A selection of his aphoristic prose, *Så fjärran skäller*, was published in 1952. [SAB]

B. Holmqvist, 'G.B.', in *Modern finlandssvensk litteratur* (Stockholm, 1951); B. Carpelan, *Studier i G.B.s diktning 1922–33* (Helsingfors, 1960).

**Bjørnson, Bjørnstjerne** (Kvikne, Hedmark 1832–Paris 1910). Norwegian novelist, playwright and poet. He was the son of a country clergyman. In 1850 he went to Kristiania (now Oslo) to begin his University studies, but broke them off in 1854 to become a journalist and writer. He soon achieved success with his stories of peasant life: *Synnøve Solbakken* (1857; tr. J. Sutter, 1881); *Arne* (1858; tr. W. Low, 1890); and *En glad Gut* (1860; tr. Mrs W. Archer, *A Happy Boy*, 1896). These and his first plays, of which *Sigurd Slembe* (1862; tr. W. M. Payne, 1888) is the most important, all owed very much to the current National Romanticism. For a time he directed theatres in Bergen and Oslo. He spent many periods abroad in Italy, the United States, France and Germany, and edited various newspapers and periodicals. In 1865 he initiated the modern drama in Norway with his *De Nygifte* (tr. R. Farquharson Sharp,

*The Newly-Married Couple*, in *Three Comedies*, 1912) and followed it with a number of other plays on contemporary themes, of which the best known are *Redaktøren* (1874), *En Fallit* (1875), and *Kongen* (1877) (all three tr. R. Farquharson Sharp, *The Editor*, *The Bankrupt*, *The King*, in *Three Dramas*, 1914). In general, these plays suffer by comparison with the work of Bjørnson's great contemporary Ibsen; they have points of dramatic interest but their themes tend to be dated and they lack wider perspectives. However, *Over Ævne I* (1883; tr. E. Bjørkman, *Beyond our Power*, in *Plays*, 1913) and *Paul Lange og Tora Parsberg* (1898; tr. H. L. Brækstad, 1899) are superior in every respect and, especially *Over Ævne I*, represent considerable dramatic achievements.

Bjørnson's other prose work includes *Fiskerjenten* (1868; tr. W. Low, *The Fisher Lassie*, 1890); *Magnhild* (1877; tr. R. B. Anderson, 1883); *Kaptejn Mansana* (1879; tr. R. B. Anderson, 1882); *Det flager i Byen og paa Havnen* (1884; tr. C. Fairfax, *The Heritage of the Kurts*, 1892); *Paa Guds Veje* (1889; tr. E. Carmichael, *In God's Way*, 1890). Of these, *Fiskerjenten*, *Magnhild* and *Paa Guds Veje* will probably make the greatest appeal to the present-day reader. Elsewhere, and especially in the long *Det flager i Byen og paa Havnen*, Bjørnson's novels tend to be marred by didacticism, a turgid prose style, and excessive topicality.

In addition to his literary work, Bjørnson was throughout his life actively engaged in political and public affairs. He was celebrated as an orator, and Norwegian life of the second part of the 19th century is indelibly stamped with his personality. Like Henrik ⇨ Wergeland before him, he was often referred to as 'the uncrowned king of Norway'. However, it seems likely that, in the literary field, he will endure longest as a poet. He was the author of the words of the Norwegian national anthem, *Ja, vi elsker dette landet*, and many other poems which have become a permanent part of Norwegian poetic heritage. Many of them are to be found in his *Digte og Sange* (1870; tr. A. H. Palmer, *Poems and Songs*, 1915). [RGP]

*Samlede digterverker*, ed. F. Bull (9 vols., 1919–20); *The Novels of B.B.*, ed. E. Gosse (13 vols., 1895–1909).

C. Collin, *B. hans Barndom og Ungdom* (2 vols., Oslo, 1907, rev. 1923); J. Lescoffier, *B. La seconde jeunesse* (Paris, 1932); C. Gierløff, *B.B.* (Oslo, 1932); H. Larson, *B.B.* (1944) (in English); H. Noreng, *B.'s dramatiske diktning* (Oslo, 1954); P. Amdam, *Den unge B.* (Oslo, 1960); Downs, *MNL*.

**Bjørnvig, Thorkild** (Aarhus 1918– ). Danish poet and essayist. His first volume of poems, *Stjærnen bag gavlen* (1947), placed him among the most important and brilliant poets of his generation, and this view has been fully confirmed by his later poetry, *Anubis* (1955), *Figur og Ild* (1959), and *Vibrationer* (1966), which also includes some excellent translations of Rilke. [ELB]

**Blaga, Lucian** (Lancrăm 1895–Cluj 1961). Rumanian poet and philosopher. He was born in Transylvania the son of a priest. He finally became professor of philosophy in the University of Cluj in 1938. His philosophy is contained in three main works *Trilogia cunoașterii* ('The Trilogy of Knowledge', 1931–4), *Trilogia culturii* ('The Trilogy of Culture', 1936–7), and *Trilogia valorilor* ('The Trilogy of Values', 1946). As a prose-writer he will be remembered for the singularly fine oration *Elogiul satului românesc* ('Eulogy of the Rumanian Village') which he delivered when received into the Rumanian Academy in 1936, and for his volume of autobiography *Hronicul Si cîntecul vîrstelor* (1966). His first volume of poetry, *Poemele luminii*, appeared in 1919. There followed *Pașii profetului* (1921), *In marea trecere* (1924), *Lauda somnului* (1929), *Cumpăna apelor* (1933). He also wrote poetic dramas, including *Zamolxis* (1922), *Mesterul Manole* (1927) and *Avram Iancu* (1934). He became closely identified with the review *Gândirea*, edited from 1926 onwards by Nichifor Crainic. Blaga, ⇨ Arghezi and ⇨ Barbu are likely to remain as the three leading poets of the period 1919–45. [EDT]

**Blanchot, Maurice.** ⇨ French Literary Criticism in the 19th and 20th Centuries.

**Blanco White, Joseph** (Seville 1775–Liverpool 1841). Spanish and English poet and theologian. Of mixed Spanish and Irish extraction, he was brought up in a strict religious atmosphere and was ordained in 1800. But his university career at Seville and Osuna had fostered doubts and stimulated literary interests, and seeds of scepticism had been sown when at 15 he read the works of ⇨ Feijoo and ⇨ Fénelon. The first important religious crisis did not, in fact, occur until he was in Madrid in 1806. There he had a relationship with a woman who later bore him a child, and this and his extreme liberal views led him to leave Spain for England in 1810. His political ideas and literary talents soon found an outlet in journalism in both Spanish and English, and his *Letters from Spain* (1822), published under the pseudonym Leocadio Doblado, established his reputation as a writer in England. Later Coleridge thought his sonnet 'Mysterious Night' the finest in the English language. More dramatic, however, was the evolution of his religious ideas. He published his *Practical and Internal Evidence against Catholicism* and became an Anglican in the 1820s. And after periods in Oxford and Dublin, he moved to Liverpool in the 1830s and embraced Unitarianism. In spite of continual ill-health he was an important figure in both literary and religious circles; a friend of Lord Holland and Mrs Hemans, on the one hand, and admired by Pusey and Newman on the other. [ONVG]

*The Life of the Rev. J.B.W. Written by Himself*, ed. J. Hamilton Thom (3 vols., 1845).
Mario Méndez Bejarano, *Vida y obras de D. José María Blanco y Crespo* (Madrid, 1920).

**Blasco Ibáñez, Vicente** (Valencia 1867–Menton 1928). Spanish novelist. He studied law but early turned to journalism and writing serial novels in collaboration with a hack. His republican sympathies forced him to emigrate to France in 1890, and when he returned shortly afterwards he was constantly in conflict with authority over his political opinions. He wrote his best novels, however, in the period which followed, mostly against Valencian backgrounds. *Arroz y tartana* (1894) described lower-middle-class commercial life in the city, but Blasco was most successful when writing about country environments. *La barraca* (1898; ed. G. J. G. Cheyne, 1964; tr. F. H. Snow and B. M. Mekota, *The Cabin*, 1919) sets struggles between landlords and tenant-farmers, and rivalries and jealousies among the latter, against the background of the Huerta of Valencia. And *Cañas y barro* (1902) is a relatively unsentimental picture of life amongst fisherfolk and rice-growers in the same region. Blasco's political sentiments are often not far from the surface in these novels, but the facility with which he evoked powerful emotions and wrote dramatic narrative led him to seek easy popularity in subsequent novels – often the basis of film-scripts at a later date – notably in the bull-fighting story *Sangre y arena* (1908). After more political activity with the Republican Union in 1903 he left the country for South America in 1909. A further period in Spain followed during the First World War, after which the success of many of his novels (in Spanish and in translation) enabled him to retire to Menton. [ONVG]

*Obras completas* (3 vols., 1964–5).
Ecff, *MSN*.

**Blicher, Steen Steensen** (Vium 1782–Spentrup 1848). Danish poet and writer of short stories. A North Jutlander by birth, and the descendant of a long line of country parsons, he returned to his own home district after his student days at Copenhagen to become a country parson. Being unhappily married and constantly worried by financial troubles he spent much time away from his home, taking refuge in walking, shooting, talking to the gypsies on the Jutland moors and drinking.

As a student at Copenhagen he taught himself English in order to translate Ossian into Danish, and he came to admire Pope, Sterne and Goldsmith, whose *Vicar of Wakefield* he also translated (1837). Both as a poet and as a prose writer Blicher is closely linked with the scenery, the population and the language of his native region, and in an age of romanticism he stands out as a sober exponent of 18th-century rationalism and enlightenment. His poetry ranges from nostalgic sadness to vivaciousness, and the best of it is of high quality. *Trækfuglene* (1938) is his most famous collection, in which the birds of passage take on a symbolical meaning, with himself as a caged bird in the fine Prelude.

Blicher's main contribution to Danish literature are his *noveller*, some of which rank among the finest Danish 19th-century prose. The earliest and also the most famous of them is *Brudstykker af en Landsbydegns Dagbog* (1824), based on the story of Marie Grubbe which later inspired J. P. Jacobsen to write his novel of that name; other important stories are *Ak! hvor forandret*, *Præsten i Vejlby*, *Hosekræmmeren* and the sparkling dialect story *Æ Bindstouw*. Jutland is often the background of his tales, and a recurrent theme in them is the bitter realization that life does not keep its promises. [ELB]

*Twelve Stories*, tr. H. A. Larsen, intr. Sigrid Undset (Princeton, 1945); *From the Danish Peninsula* (*Poems and a Tale*), tr. H. A. Larsen *et al.*, ed. J. Smith (Copenhagen, 1957).

**Blixen, Karen, Baroness Blixen-Finecke,** also known as Isak Dinesen (Rungsted 1885–Rungsted 1962). Danish author. After studying art at Copenhagen, Paris and Rome she married her cousin, Baron Bror Blixen-Finecke in 1914. Together they went to Kenya to manage a coffee plantation. The marriage was dissolved in 1921. After their divorce she continued to run the plantation until a collapse in the coffee market forced her back to Denmark in 1931. Though she had written occasional contributions to Danish periodicals since 1905 (under the *nom de plume* of Osceola) her real début took place in 1934 with the publication under the name Isak Dinesen of *Seven Gothic Tales,* written in English. Set largely in 19th-century Europe, their atmosphere is exaggeratedly Gothic. Ornate prose and plots heavy with ritual and mystery combine to produce these exotic, self-parodying melodramas. Most of her subsequent books were published in English and Danish simultaneously, including *Out of Africa* (1937), a warm-hearted and deeply moving epitaph of a period which has now become remote history, and a novel, *The Angelic Avengers* (1947, under the name Pierre Andrézel). *Winter's Tales* (1942), *Last Tales* (1957), *Anecdotes of Destiny* (1958), *Shadows on the Grass* (1960) and *Ehrengard* (1963) are further collections of stories in which a sophisticated, aristocratic wit is put to work on a tradition of writing that has suffered from the lack of it. [ELB]

*Mindeudgave* (7 vols., 1964).

E. O. Johannesson, *The World of Isak Dinesen* (Washington, 1961); R. Langbaum, *The Gaiety of Vision: A Study of I.D.'s Art* (1964); C. Svendsen, ed., *I.D.: A Memorial* (N.Y., 1965).

**Bloem, Jakobus Cornelis** (Oudshoorn 1887–Kalenberg 1966). Dutch poet. In short poems reiterating the theme of nostalgia and frustration he expresses ⇨ Leopold's impasse in verse often as delicate as his, but progressively simpler. In this patient refinement of a single theme he left a modest work of great beauty which exemplifies his humble acceptance of the continuation of life despite man's inability to find his ideal in it. [PK]

*Verzamelde gedichten* (1947); *Lyrical Holland* (1954).

**Blok, Aleksandr Aleksandrovich** (St Petersburg 1880–St Petersburg 1921). Russian poet. Son of the Professor of Public Law in Warsaw, a neurotic and violent man. Mother and baby fled to her father, A. N. Beketov, the Dean of St Petersburg University, into an atmosphere of music and literature: his mother, aunts and grandmother translated Western authors and edited a family journal. Summers were spent in the country near Moscow, the landscape of Blok's poetry. Both parents remarried. In 1897 he made a trip to Germany and experienced his first love. At University he read Law to 1901, Philology to 1906. His first poetry, *Ante Lucem* (1898–1900) and *Stikhi o prekrasnoy dame* ('Verses about the Beautiful Lady', 1901–2, in book form in 1904), proclaims pure worship of the Mysterious Star, the Virgin (akin to V. ⇨ Solovyov's 'incorruptible eternal feminine'). These were the years of Blok's love for L. D. Mendeleyeva, the great chemist's daughter, whom he married in 1903. He lived in Symbolist and theatre circles, amidst fame, bohemianism and mutual infidelities. He travelled abroad (1909, 1910, 1913) and kept undying love for his wife. Later critics saw 'The Beautiful Lady' changing into 'The Stranger' and 'Russia'; Blok said: 'they understood nothing'.

Though not a politician, Blok turned to ⇨ Gor'ky, hailed the 1905 revolution, and grieved at its failure; he found 'the notion "citizen" liberating and healing' (to E. P. Ivanov, September 1908), read papers on *Russia and the Intelligentsia.* He wrote in lyrical prose 'On the Present State of Russian Symbolism' (1910), but told his mother: 'I am a social animal with a publicist's pathos and need for human contacts'. In 1916 he served behind the lines; in 1917 he was detailed to investigate the Tsar's Ministers, to sit on theatre committees, etc. He translated for Gor'ky's World Literature series, gave public recitations, wrote challenging articles: 'The Intelligentsia and the Revolution' (1918), 'The Downfall of Humanism' (1919). He suffered privations, exhaustion, choking, spasms, heart-disease. 'A poet by God's grace and a man of fearless sincerity' (Gor'ky), his last public speech was on Pushkin, 'killed not by a bullet but by the absence of air', and on the 'officials' who, ready to guide poetry into their own channels, infringe on its 'secret freedom' (*O naznachenii poeta*, 'On the Purpose of the Poet', 1921).

Personal and world events come to Blok as 'musical pressure'. His lyrics form cycles with explicit titles but intermingled in time and contradictory like himself. Amidst the fogs, gnomes and devils of *Rasput'ya* (1902–4), one poem shows deceived workers (*Fabrika*, 'The Factory', 1903), another (*Gorod*, 'The City', 1904–11) brings in black colours, new rhythms, cries of drink, vice and destitution, or a shot agitator (*Miting*, 'A Meeting', 1905). As if imprisoned, Blok sees 'Christ in chains and roses'. There is bitter romantic irony, self-mockery in the lyrical dramas *Balaganchik*, where the Bride is a cardboard doll, Pierrot's blood a fruit-juice, and *Neznakomka* ('The Stranger', 1906), the Star who, unrecognized by the drunken poet, walks away with a man, while in a lyric of that title a courtesan is a bearer of high mystery. Blizzards, black silks and carnal love are 'the power of the elements' in *Snezhnaya maska* ('Snow Mask', 1907); music and song bring another elemental moment in *Karmen* (1914). He awakes, 'to accept life'; sarcastic and virile, in powerful blank verse, with bold strokes he paints the sea and the shore, death and desire in *Vol'nyye mysli* ('Free Thoughts', 1907). Or he lives in the purple world of *Strashnyy Mir* ('Dreadful World', 1907–16). His own double, a skeleton, he whirls in a dance of death. The Muse, his tormentor, spells ruin, violation of sanctity and 'the cold and gloom of the days to come'. In *Yamby* (1907–14), storms abated he bends down to the poor and humiliated, 'before a storm sweeps our land', preparing for deeds in righteous anger. There is no cosiness, no rest, no escape into the dream-world of beauty (cf. *Solov'inyy sad*; 'Garden of Nightingales', 1915). A drama in Western setting *Roza i Krest* ('The Rose and the Cross', 1913) shows a 'joy that is suffering', the self-sacrifice of a Knight for his Lady's trivial affair with a page. *Vozmezdiye* ('Retribution' 1910ff., unfinished; prose Preface, 1919) was to be Blok's family 'Rougon-Macquart' story; but more than heredity, history moulds them. He vigorously sums up the epoch; but his own fate, the last off-spring, is unsolved.

He told Stanislavsky, 'Russia is the theme of my life', and she is seen personified in some early poems, in the article on 'The Child of Gogol' (1907), above all in *Stikhi o Rossii* (or *Rodina*; 'Verses about Russia', 1907–16). Here Blok's premonitions and his interplay of rhythms and imagery echo ancient Russian lore, folk-lore and several poets. He sees Russia as a New America of the steppes (1913; 'a new, not old America', he noted in 1919). Only the bourgeoisie is satirized. In 1918, aware in the quiet of the night of strange persistent sounds, Blok submitted, like a medium, to that 'elemental power' and wrote *Dvenadtsat'* ('The Twelve') in which rhythms vary from the beat of marches to romances, revolutionary songs, roundelays, ditties and slogans. A reaction to the threat of foreign intervention was *Skify* ('The Scythians', 1918). His last but one poem is to Pushkin and the Academy's Pushkin House (11 February 1921).

Blok foresaw his life 'so complex, difficult and festive' analysed 'with heaps of bad quotes'. Indeed, he lends himself to varying interpretations. The best commentary are his diary, notes, letters and articles. Be he romantic or symbolist related to some Western and many Russian poets, by his own melody, colours, rhythms and words always expressive of his themes, he is an individual tragic poet, yet also 'a child of light, a triumph of freedom'. To him, only 'confessional' works, in which an author had burnt himself to ashes, were great. [NG]

*Sobraniye sochineniy*, ed. V. Orlov, Surkov, Chukovsky (8 vols., 1960–3); ed. V. Orlov (2 vols., 1955); *Izbrannoye*, ed. V. Orlov (1954; Obolensky, *PBRV*).

S. Bonneau, *L'univers poétique d'A.B.* (Paris, 1946); C. H. Kisch, *A.B., Prophet of Revolution* (1960); F. D. Reeve, *A.B.: Between Image and Idea* (1962); K. Chukovsky, *Kniga o A.B.* (Petersburg, 1922); L. I. Timofeyev, *A.B.* (Moscow, 1957); V. N. Orlov, *A.B.* (Moscow, 1956); Andrey Bely, *Vospominaniya ob A.B.* intr. G. Donchin (Letchworth, 1964); N. Vengrov, *Put' A.B.* (Moscow, 1963); K. Mochul'sky, *A.B.* (Paris, 1948); R. Kemball, *A.B.: A Study in Rhythm and Metre* (Mouton, 1965).

**Bloy, Léon Marie** (Périgueux 1846–Bourg-la-Reine 1917). French novelist and thinker. He was early influenced by ⇨ Barbey d'Aurevilly, whom he glorifies in his autobiographical novel *Le désespéré* (1884), a book attacking the 'establishment' of his time (e.g. Brunetière, Bourget). His attack on conformism continued with other works like *La femme pauvre* (1897), *Les dernières colonnes de l'église* (1903) and *Le sang du pauvre* (1909), becoming increasingly coloured by his apocalyptic sense of the doom of bourgeois society, which he believed might be succeeded by the reign of the holy spirit. The story of his conversion by Catherine Emmerich, and of the other mystical experiences and spiritual upheavals in his long 'pilgrimage', is told in his most important *Journal*, beginning with *Mendiant ingrat* (1892–5) and ending with *À la porte des humbles* (1915–17). [AKT]

*L'œuvre complète* (1947 f.); *Journal*, ed. J. Bollery (1956–63); *Pilgrim of the Absolute*, tr. J. Coleman, H. L. Binsse (1947) (selections); *She Who Weeps: Our Lady of Salette*, tr. E. La Douceur (Freno, California, 1956); *Letters to his Fiancée*, tr. B. Wall (1937).

J. Bollery, *L.B.* (3 vols., Paris, 1947–54); A. Béguin, *L.B.* (Paris, 1948; tr. E. M. Riley, 1947); R. Heppenstall, *L.B.* (1953).

**Bluvstein, Rahel** (Poltava 1890–Jerusalem 1931). Hebrew poetess. She came to Palestine from the Ukraine as a pioneer in 1908. Her poetry has no trace of diaspora life but is pervaded by a love for the land of Israel and its people. [EE]

*Shirat Rahel* (Tel Aviv, 1954).

D. Kobler, *Four Rahels* (1947).

**Bobrowski, Johannes** (Tilsit 1917–Berlin 1965). German poet. A prisoner-of-war in Russia (1941–9), he lived in Berlin-Friedrichshagen as reader for the East German Union-Verlag. Awarded the 'Preis der ⇨ Gruppe 47' for 1962, he published *Sarmatische Zeit* (1961), *Schattenland Ströme* (1962), and *Wetterzeichen* (1966). A laconic, reticent poet, he wrote of the 'pastoral folk-world' of Eastern Europe and its long, hidden history; he used dramatic imagery and strongly counterpointed rhythms to bring out the metaphysical implications of this dark, haunting landscape peopled with mythological memories The stories *Boehlendorff* (1965) and *Mäusefest* (1965), and novels *Levins Mühle* (1964) and *Litauische Claviere* (1966) have the same background. [PB]

*Shadow Land. Selected Poems*, tr. R. and M. Mead (1966).

*J.B. Selbstzeugnisse und Beiträge über sein Werk* (E. Berlin, 1967); *FMLS*, II, 4, 1966; *GR*, XLI, I, 1966; *DU*, XVIII, 2, 1966.

**Bocage, Manuel Maria Barbosa du** (Setúbal 1765–Lisbon 1805). Portuguese poet. Portugal's most eminent 18th-century poet and leading pre-Romantic; also known by the Arcadian name of Elmano Sadino. A runagate character all his life, Bocage enlisted first in the infantry and later in the marine guard, his travels taking him to Rio, Goa and Macau. Returning to Lisbon in 1790 he joined the Nova Arcádia or Academia das Belas Artes and published the first volume of his *Rimas* in the following year, winning the acclaim of such prominent figures as Filinto Elísio and the Marquesa de Alorna. Owing to differences with José Agostinho de Macedo he was expelled from the *Nova Arcádia* in 1794 and because of his radical and anti-clerical views he was jailed three years later. After a 'cure' at the hands of the Inquisition he was released in 1799. The second volume of his *Rimas* was published in the same year and the third in 1804. The three remaining volumes appeared posthumously (1812, 1813, 1842). Though a writer of odes, epigrams and epistles, Bocage came to reject the narrow formalism of Filinto Elísio, and found the rhymes and rhythms of the sonnet best suited to his freer style and diction. Responding strongly to the varying influences of Young, Voltaire, Ossian and Rousseau, his frequently sombre verse is characterized by egotism, self-pity, masochism and pessimism. [RCW]

T. Braga, *B., sua Vida e Época Literária* (Oporto 1902); H. Cidade, *B.* (Oporto, 1936); Mar Talegre, *Três Poetas Europeus* (Lisbon, 1947).

**Bocángel y Unzueta, Gabriel** (Madrid 1608–Madrid 1658). Spanish poet, by profession a librarian. In recent years he has been recognized as one of the best of the followers of ⇨ Góngora, in his love-poetry and mythological poems full of pleasing colour and imagery. He has some good sonnets and a fine elegy, 'En la muerte de una Dama'. [JMC]

*Obras* (1946); *La lira de las musas. Selección*, ed. F. Salvá Miquel (1948); Cohen, *PBSV*.

**Boccaccio, Giovanni** (? 1313–Certaldo 1375). Italian story-writer and poet. About his early life we have only enigmatic references in his writings. He is now thought to have been born the illegitimate child of Boccaccio di Chelino at Florence or Certaldo (his self-composed epitaph reads 'patria Certaldum') and not, as used to be believed, in Paris. As a boy he was sent by his father to Naples to learn commerce and later law, and at Naples occurred the love-affair with the woman immortalized as Fiammetta in his writings and traditionally and romantically identified as Maria d'Aquino, natural daughter of King Robert himself. But the episode may be largely a creation of Boccaccio's imagination, a literary convention. At Naples he rejected his father's plans and turned to the life of writer and scholar; details are uncertain, but the influence of the Neapolitan court atmosphere on his early works is clear from the *Caccia di Diana* onwards. The lengthy prose romance *Filocolo* (begun *c.* 1336; ed. S. Battaglia, 1938) recounts the love of Florio and Biancofiore, with an accretion of many extraneous episodes, including a story-telling scene in Naples where among the tales related there appear two which are repeated in the Decameron. The *Filostrato* (*c.* 1335; in *Opere*, Vol. 2, ed. V. Branca, 1964; tr. R. K. Gordon, in *The Story of Troilus*, 1934) and the *Teseida* (1339–40; *Opere*, Vol. 2, ed. A. Limentani, 1964), both in *ottava rima*, tell respectively of Troilus and Cressida and Palamone and Arcita (both used by Chaucer).

When family circumstances summoned Boccaccio to Florence, probably in 1340, Naples remained a symbol of youth and pleasure. The earliest of the Florentine works, *Ameto* (1341–2; in *Opere*, Vol. 2, ed. A. E. Quaglio, 1964) and the *Amorosa visione* (1342; ed. V. Branca, 1945), represent ventures into medieval allegory with the influence of Dante particularly apparent in the *terza rima* of the *Amorosa visione*. Although the *Ameto* with its mixture of *terza rima* and prose narrative has a certain importance in the history of the Italian pastoral, neither of these works is successful or coherent in achieving its ostensible purpose of illustrating the refining and uplifting influence of love; Boccaccio's interests and abilities lie clearly outside such allegorical didacticism. Much more impressive are the *Elegia di Madonna Fiammetta* (ed. F. Ageno, 1954; tr. B. Young, intr. E. Hutton, 1926) and the *Ninfale fiesolano* (ed. V. Pernicone, 1937; tr. D. J. Donno, *The Nymph of Fiesole*, 1960), which also belong to the period immediately preceding the *Decameron*. The former, which relates the fluctuating anguish of Fiammetta abandoned by her lover Panfilo, has been described as the earliest psychological novel and also been regarded as reflecting Boccaccio's own relations with Fiammetta at Naples, albeit by turning the situation upside down. Whether this is so, or whether the genesis of the narrative is more literary, its dramatic firmness makes it the most effective of his minor works. The *ottava rima* of the *Ninfale fiesolano* too, is attractive, with its mythical theme, reminiscent of Ovid, set in the Tuscan countryside, and the two ill-starred lovers changed into Tuscan streams. At Florence Boccaccio held various minor offices and represented the commune on missions in North Italy, but his writing continued unabated, reaching its peak in the joyously serene *Il Decameron* (ed. G. Petronio, 1950; N. Sapegno, 1956; V. Branca, 1960; tr. R. Aldington, 1957), and then declining into the bitter misogynistic *Corbaccio* (*c.* 1365). In 1350 he met Petrarch and there began a friendship which lasted until Petrarch's death and had a profound cultural and psychological effect on the younger man. To his later years belong various Latin works, mostly of an erudite, compilatory nature (*Bucolicum carmen*, *De casibus virorum illustrium*, *De claris mulieribus*, *De genealogiis deorum gentilium*, *De montibus*, *silvis*, *fontibus*, etc.), and also the fruits of his admiration and study of Dante, the *Commento* (ed. D. Guerri, 1926) on the *Divine Comedy* and the *Trattatello in laude di Dante*.

The background to the *Decameron* is the Florentine plague of 1348, from which the narrators have escaped; its impact is memorably described in the introduction. The hundred stories vary considerably in achievement and substance, their aesthetic range encompassing comedy and tragedy, and their moral range both the meekness of Griselda and the effrontery of Ser Ciappelletto. Read sometimes as a social document illustrating Boccaccio's Italy, sometimes as a medieval, earthy counterpart of Dante's *Divine Comedy*, sometimes even as an early manifestation of the dawning spirit of the Renaissance, the *Decameron* is above all else a superb masterpiece of imaginative narrative. The best stories are interwoven with contemporary circumstance and detail. The characteristic conflict is between Fortune and a Human Nature more concerned with earthy self-preservation or self-indulgence than with abstract concepts of morality or religion; this produces a dynamic type of *novella* full of memorably dramatic scenes in which astuteness and tenacity usually triumph. [DGR]

*G.B. Opere*, ed. V. Branca *et al.* (12 vols., 1964ff.); *G.B.* (Ricciardi, 2 vols., 1952–65) (copious selection); *Ameto Corbaccio e lettere*, ed. N. Bruscoli, 1940; *Rime*, ed. V. Branca, 1958; *Genealogie deorum gentilium libri*, ed. V. Romano (1951); *Opere latine minori*, ed. A. F. Massera (1928); *De claris mulieribus*, tr. H. Parker, Lord Morley, *Forty-Six Lives* (1943), and G. A. Guarino, *Concerning Famous Women* (1964); Lind, *LPIR*.

V. Branca, *B. medievale* (Florence, 1956); Binni, *CI*; H. G. Wright, *B. in England from Chaucer to Tennyson* (1957); Auerbach, *M*; *Maggiori*.

**Boccalini, Traiano** (Loreto 1556–Venice 1613). Italian satirist. After spending most of his adult life in Papal service as administrator and judge, he went in 1612 to Venice, whose political freedom he much admired, and there published the first two *centurie* (1612, 1613) of his chief work, the *Ragguagli di Parnaso* (ed. L. Firpo, 1948; tr. Henry, Earl of Monmouth, 1656). The suspicion that he was poisoned in revenge for his denunciations of Spanish tyranny is now largely discounted.

The *Ragguagli* are satirical journalistic reports from the imaginary state of Parnassus, governed by Apollo and inhabited by famous men of all lands and ages. In this setting Boccalini attacks with lively irony the follies (chiefly political and literary) of his time. His anti-Spanish feelings appear more marked in the posthumously published *ragguagli* of the *Pietra del paragone* (1615). The work which he himself valued most was the *Osservazioni su Tacito* (publ. in *La bilancia politica*, etc., 1678), in which he derives moral and political maxims from Tacitus and discusses them, often in terms of contemporary events. This, however, lacks the vigour of his satire. [DGR]

C. Varese, *T.B.* (Padua, 1958); E. G. Gardner, *T.B. Satire and History in the Counter-Reformation* (1926); *Minori*, ii.

**Bodmer, Johann Jakob** (Greifensee 1698–Schönberg, Zürich 1783). Swiss critic. Bodmer was Professor of History at Zürich, but is remembered as an important theoretician and critic of literature. In the foreword to J. J. ⇨ Breitinger's *Critische Dichtkunst* (1739) and in his own *Abhandlung von dem Wunderbaren in der Poesie* (1740) he turns against the rationalistic approach to literature typical of ⇨ Gottsched and his followers, advocating in place of a slavish obedience to classical rules the liberty of the creative imagination and seeing in literature a repository of human emotions rather than the product of conscious, rational thought, thereby initiating one of the most acrimonious literary controversies of the 18th century. In his rejection of classical rules, the emphasis he places on the emotions and in his interest in the nature of poetic creation, he may thus be regarded as one of the precursors of *Sturm und Drang*, although he himself is far from the chaotic lawlessness and rampant irrationalism which characterized that movement. His translation of Milton (1732), together with his translations from Middle High German – his *Chriemhildens Rache und Klage* appeared in 1757 and an edition of the *Minnesang* in 1758 – opened the eyes of his generation to a new kind of poetry. His own creative works, a Biblical epic on Noah and a number of dramas, enjoyed little contemporary success and today are mere historical curiosities. [WAC]

*Auswahl*, ed. F. Ernst (1938); DLE; *Abhandlungen von dem Wunderbaren* (repr. Metzler, Stuttgart, 1967).

M. Wehrli, *J.J.B. und die Geschichte der Literatur* (Frauenfeld, 1936); H. Schöffler, *Das literarische Zürich 1700 bis 1750* (Leipzig, 1925); Cassirer, *PE*.

**Bødtcher, Ludvig** (Copenhagen 1793–Copenhagen 1874). Danish poet. An aesthete and an Epicurean, he lived in Italy for eleven years. The quality of his slender volume, *Digte* (1856), is very high, for he destroyed many of his poems, including those written to a young girl to whom he was engaged but who died before they were married. Some of his best poems have an Italian setting, e.g. 'Mødet med Bacchus' ('Meeting with Bacchus'), his most famous. [ELB]

*Samlede Digte* (1940).
Gosse, *SLNE*.

**Boethius, Anicius Manlius Severinus** (Rome *c.*480–Pavia 524). Roman philosopher. Of noble birth, he was in the service of Theodoric the Ostrogoth. Arrested in 523 on a false charge of treason, he was imprisoned at Pavia and then executed.

The intellectual link between classical times and the Middle Ages, Boethius's never-completed translation of Aristotle into Latin was the basis of much medieval philosophy. His textbooks on the *quad-*

*rivium* – music, arithmetic, geometry, astronomy – to which he was the first to give the generic name, remained in use for centuries. His most famous work, the *Consolatio philosophiae*, composed in prison, is in alternate sections of prose and verse. Its 39 poems are in 13 different metres and are all of great beauty. It deals with the problems of good and evil, man's free will and God's foreknowledge. Gibbon describes it as 'a golden volume, which claims incomparable merit from the barbarism of the times and the situation of the author', and its influence has been immense. It was translated into Anglo-Saxon by King Alfred, into English by Chaucer, Lydgate and (reputedly) Elizabeth I, into Old French by Jean de Meun, and before the end of the Middle Ages into German, Greek, Italian, Catalan and other languages. [FB]

Migne, *PL*, 63–4; *Theological Tractates and The Consolation of Philosophy*, ed. and tr. H. F. Stewart and E. K. Rand (Loeb, 1918); *Consolatio philosophiae*, ed. A. Fortescue and G. D. Smith (1925) (with bibliography).

H. F. Stewart, *B.* (1891); H. R. Patch, *The Tradition of B., a Study of his Importance in Medieval Culture* (N.Y., 1935); H. M. Barrett, *B., Some Aspects of His Times and Work* (1940); Duckett, *GMA*.

**Bogomil Literature.** ⇨ Old Bulgarian Literature.

**Böhme, Jakob** (Görlitz, Silesia 1575–Görlitz 1624). German philosopher. Largely self-taught and for many years a cobbler, he stands in the great German mystical and alchemical tradition deriving in part from the great mystics of the Middle Ages and their 16th-century successors, Franck, Weigel and the Anabaptists, and partly also from Paracelsus. Persecuted by the strictly orthodox Pastor Richter of Görlitz, his works circulated only in manuscript and were not published until after his death. His view of existence is at times almost Manichaean, at other times he comes near to pantheism. The main lines of his philosophy are laid down in his earliest work *Aurora oder Morgenröte im Aufgang* (1612; tr. J. Sparrow, 1914), which sees the world as being subject to two opposing principles, good and evil, light and darkness, both of which are aspects of God, his love and his anger. Nature is the manifestation of this conflict, God dwelling in nature as the soul dwells in the body. This view is developed somewhat in the *Beschreibung der drei Prinzipien göttlichen Wesens* (1618–19), where a triad of principles is postulated: good, evil and their manifestation, the 'materialistic' principle, while *Vom dreifachen Leben des Menschen* (1619–20; tr. J. Sparrow, *The Threefold Life of Man*, 1909) translates this theory into the spiritual life of mankind, the three principles appearing now as the three directions or aspects of the human will. The fundamental problem around which Böhme's philosophy revolves is how to reconcile the goodness and the omnipotence of God with the existence of evil, a problem which is solved in terms of the necessity of an antithesis in order to achieve full self-realization – hence the description of God in his primeval unity as a '*Nichts*' (nothing) or the '*Ungrund*' (bottomlessness), creation being the physical expression of the principle of negation, by which the 'Nothing' directs its will to 'Everything' ('*der Wille des Ungrundes zum Grund*').

Böhme writes in an often puzzlingly obscure, but vigorous style, and as the first important philosopher to write in German is often known as the 'philosophus teutonicus'. As a religious thinker, his influence spready widely in Germany, the Low Countries and England, while Schelling, Hegel and Baader are all indebted to his philosophy. In literature, his influence is particularly strong in the writings of ⇨ Angelus Silesius. [WAC]

*Werke*, ed. A. Faust (11 vols., Stuttgart, 1942ff.).

A. Faust, *J.B. als 'Philosophus Teutonicus'* (Stuttgart, 1941); W. E. Peuckert, *Das Leben J.B.s* (Jena, 1924); S. Hobhouse, *J.B., His Life and Teaching* (1950).

**Boiardo, Matteo Maria,** Count of Scandiano (Scandiano 1441–Reggio Emilia 1494). Italian poet. He served the Dukes of Ferrara as envoy and administrator. A humanist education enabled him to compose Latin allegorical eclogues and poems in praise of the house of Este, as well as make translations from Cornelius Nepos and others. In 1469 at Reggio he fell in love with Antonia Caprara, and this inspired his Italian *Canzoniere*. In 1480 he became governor of Modena, and by this time he was engaged on the *Orlando innamorato*. In 1487 he was appointed governor of Reggio, and there he died with the *Orlando innamorato* unfinished. His *Canzoniere* (called also the *Amorum tres libri*) sets him, with Politian and Lorenzo de' Medici, in the forefront of the *quattrocento* lyric. The collection is divided into three books and the mood proceeds by gradations from initial exultation through suspicion and jealousy to final religious renunciation of the things of the world. Despite a certain surface Petrarchism the uncomplicated spirit of the *Amorum tres libri* is quite different from that of ⇨ Petrarch's *Canzoniere*, and the dialect flavour of Boiardo's language contributes to the slightly quaint freshness of his lyrics. The *Orlando innamorato*, a chivalrous epic in *ottava rima*, tells of Roland in love. Fusing together the matter of the Carolingian legends and the spirit of the Breton cycle, Boiardo created the world of romance which ⇨ Ariosto inherited and developed further. The text has vigour and zest and some scenes, like the first one, describing Angelica's arrival, escorted by four giants at Charlemagne's banquet, are splendidly realized. But it has little structural order, and its episodes proliferate wildly in ever stranger directions; the characters consequently lack coherence. It remains a poem of occasionally magnificent fragments. Overshadowed by Ariosto's *Furioso*, and rewritten in more polished *cinquecento* style by ⇨ Berni and Domenichi, Boiardo's poem was forgotten until rediscovered and acclaimed in the 19th century. [DGR]

*Tutte le opere*, ed. A. Zottoli (1936–7); *Opere volgari*, ed. P. V. Mengaldo (1962); *The Orlando innamorato*, prose tr. W. S. Rose from Berni's version (1823); Lind, *LPIR*.

E. Carrara, *I due Orlandi* (Turin, 1935); E. Bigi, *La poesia del B.* (Florence, 1941); P. V. Mengaldo, *La lingua del B. lirico* (Florence, 1963); *Minori*, i.

**Boileau, Nicholas,** known as Despréaux (Paris 1636–Paris 1711). French poet and critic. He became a legend within his own lifetime, so much so that modern research has had to reconstruct his entire career. His beginnings as a satirist were those of a hired hack, working for a patron. Surviving versions of his early satires show them to have been more rough and more topical than what he consented to publish in the first collected edition of 1666. Gradually he escaped his libertin entourage and became attached, first to Molière, later (after 1670) to Racine and to the circle which met in the house of President Lamoignon. Mme de Sévigné has testified to the delight caused by his public readings, notably in 1672 of 4 cantos which when published in 1674 as *L'art poétique* gave him wide notoriety and became one of the famous books of Europe. These witty comments on his fellow poets, liberally seasoned with advice to young writers, were all too successful. Their satiric and topical intention, which made them a salon hit, was soon lost sight of and their author was revered as 'the lawgiver of Parnassus', his neat epigrams were treated as the classical code, as the theory according to which the works of Molière and Racine were written. Boileau in old age lent himself to this role, but scholars have since shown that he was the disciple of the French classical writers rather than their teacher. His reputation in the Age of Reason was enormous, and understandable, since as an opponent of all that was baroque he had exalted the role of reason in poetry: Pope's annotated copy of *L'art poétique* is still extant to show how seriously he was studied. Besides the *Art poétique* he published in 1674 a mock epic, *Le lutrin*, and a translation of Longinus on the Sublime. These, together with a dozen satires and as many *Épîtres*, all in verse, and some occasional pieces, established him as the most famous critic of the age, the French Dryden, or as Dryden himself put it 'a living Horace and a Juvenal'.

Boileau was more poetic and more versatile than his reputation. *Le lutrin* was the first successful parody of the grand style and formality associated with epic. To translate Longinus was even more revolutionary, for Longinus emphasizes just those elements in art which are contrary to cold reason: for Longinus poetry implies a power of imagination, an ability to express what transcends reason, in a word the Sublime. It was Boileau's translation which started the vogue of the Sublime in Europe. 'The Sublime', said Dr Johnson, 'is a gallicism which is now [1755] naturalized.' A recent scholar calls Boileau a Janus-like figure, who in the *Art poétique* feeds the Augustan tradition and by reviving Longinus prepares Romanticism.

Boileau's real merit perhaps was to be an arbiter of taste, insisting on high standards, on an agreed level of perfection, on the connexion between thought and style ('Ce que l'on conçoit bien s'énonce clairement', 'Un sonnet sans défaut vaut seul un long poème'). His taste was sure; the writers whom he respected count among the greatest of modern times and those whom he attacked are known only from his writings. By *raison* he meant not so much logic as good judgement ('Si je pense exprimer un auteur sans défaut, La raison dit Virgile et la rime dit Quinault'). Addison was proud to visit the old man in his retirement and commented: 'He heartily hates an ill poet.' [WGM]

A. F. Clark, *B. and the Classical Critics in England* (1925); Sister M. Haley, *Racine and the Art Poétique of B.* (1938); A. Adam, *Les premières satires de B.* (Paris, 1941); J. Brody, *B. and Longinus* (1958).

**Boisrobert, François Le Metel, Sieur de** (Caen 1589–Paris 1662). French man of letters. The son of Protestant parents, he trained for the law but preferred the Court and became attached to the Queen Mother, by whom he was commanded to translate ⇨ Guarini. Richelieu recognized his wit and resource and used him as literary agent to furnish plays and entertainments when required. Of his plays 18 are known, most of them tragi-comedies, several adapted from the Spanish. *La belle plaideuse* (1655) supplied Molière with material for the great scene in *L'avare* where the miser lends money incognito to his son. [WGM]

*Épîtres*, ed. M. Cauchie (2 vols., 1927).
É. Magne, *Le plaisant abbé de B.* (Paris, 1909); Tallemant, *Historiettes*, ed. Adam (Pléiade, 1960); Lancaster, *HFDL*.

**Boito, Arrigo** (Padua 1842–Milan 1918). Italian poet and composer, but known chiefly as librettist. Senator in 1912. He studied music at the Milan conservatoire, and in 1861 went to Paris, where he associated with Parnassians, realists and impressionists – hence on his return his close association with the Milanese ⇨ *Scapigliatura*. The initial failure of his long-projected opera *Mefistofele* (1868) made him abandon music in favour of poetry and libretti which he wrote for various composers, notably Verdi (*Otello*, 1887; *Falstaff*, 1893). His work reflects all the excesses of romanticism; his rejection of conventional forms (cf. *Il libro dei versi*, 1877) partly explains why *Mefistofele* ran at first for over six hours; and the content shows concern rather for the fantastic and macabre than for intimate poetic expression (cf. *Il Re Orso*, 1865). The corruption of Imperial Rome gave ample scope for these qualities in the tragedy *Nerone* (1901), the operatic version of which was performed posthumously under Toscanini in 1924. [RHC]

*Tutti gli scritti*, ed. P. Nardi (1942).
P. Nardi, *Vita di A.B.* (Milan, 1944); *Minori*, iv.

**Bojer, Johan** (Orkedalsøren, S. Trøndelag 1872–Oppdal, S. Trøndelag 1959). Norwegian novelist. Of humble origins, he had a variety of jobs before making his way as a prolific writer. Though much of his work attempts to explore psychological conflicts, it is firmly fixed in the Norwegian realist tradition and is little influenced by newer trends. His earliest novels were on political themes. In *Troens magt* (1903; tr. J. Muir, *The Power of a Lie*, 1908) and *Vort rige* (1908; tr. J. Muir, *Treacherous Ground*, 1912) he explores ideals and their motivation; in *Den store Hunger* (1916; tr. W. J. A. Worster and C. Archer, *The Great Hunger*, 1918), *Verdensansigt* (1917; tr. J. Muir, *The Face of the World*, 1919) and *Det nye tempel* (1927; tr. C. Archer and J. S. Scott, *The New Temple*, 1928) he poses a religious solution; and in *Folk ved sjøen* (1929; tr. A. Heni, L. Rourke and C. Archer, *Folk by the Sea*, 1931); *Den siste viking* (1921; tr. J. Muir, *The Last of the Vikings*, 1936), *Vor egen stamme* (1924; tr. A. G. Jayne, *The Emigrants*, 1926) he embodies a positive view of life in the depiction of the workaday toilings of the common people of Norway. It is in these novels that Bojer's qualities are best expressed: his narrative skill, his eye for significant detail and, above all, his capacity for making the reader warm to his everyday heroes. Elsewhere his work has tended to date and his psychology seems shallow. [RGP]

*Samlede romaner* (5 vols., 1942).
C. Gad, *J.B.* (Oslo, 1918); P. G. la Chesnais, *J.B.* (Paris, 1930); Beyer, *NL*.

**Böll, Heinrich** (Cologne 1917–    ). German novelist, short-story writer and radio playwright. The son of a sculptor, he began work in a bookshop, then served in the infantry throughout the war. After 1945 he took various jobs, becoming a free-lance writer in 1951. Böll's first two novels – *Der Zug war pünktlich* (1949; tr. Richard Graves, *The Train Was on Time*, 1956) and *Wo warst du Adam?* (1951; tr. M. Savill, *Adam, Where Art Thou?*, 1955) – are works of protest which show the despair of those involved in total and totally pointless war. His subsequent novels are concerned, more characteristically, with the aftermath of war. *Und sagte kein einziges Wort* (1953; tr. R. Graves, *Acquainted With the Night*, 1955) deals with the marital problems of a returned prisoner of war obsessed with death; here Böll points for the first time to the moral vacuum behind the post-war 'economic miracle' in Western Germany. *Haus ohne Hüter* (1954; tr. M. Savill, *The Unguarded House*, 1957) treats the same precarious prosperity and underlying cynicism and despair. The long story *Das Brot der frühen Jahre* (1955; tr. M. Savill, *The Bread of Our Early Years*, 1957) shows how love may overcome this cynical materialism. *Billard um halb zehn* (1959; tr. P. Bowles, *Billiards at Half Past Nine*, 1961) is concerned with a less topical issue, that of the private emotions and memories that act as a barrier between individuals and generations, and is stylistically the most elaborate, making greater use of interior monologue and flashback and (though highly praised) less easy to read. His latest novel, *Ansichten eines Clowns* (1963; tr. L. Vennewitz, *The Clown*, 1965), concerned with authentic existence and authentic 'Christianity' (influence of ⇨ Kierkegaard), is more simply written and marks a new departure.

Böll's most important collections of stories – *Wanderer, kommst du nach Spa . . .* (1950; tr. M. Savill, *Traveller, If You Come to Spa*, 1956), *So ward Abend und Morgen* (1956), *Unberechenbare Gäste* (1956), and *Doktor Murkes gesammeltes Schweigen* (1958; tr. in Waidson, *MGS*) contain sharply satirical protests against futile convention, futile prosperity, etc. Vivid, dramatic, increasingly humorous, they have not a little in common with Hemingway, Wolfgang ⇨ Borchert and Kafka, and are his most considerable achievement; indeed, Böll is one of the founders of the contemporary German American-style '*Kurzgeschichte*'. [PB]

*Erzählungen, Hörspiele, Aufsätze* (Cologne/Berlin, 1961); *Absent without Leave and Other Stories*, tr. L. Vennewitz (1967).

Ferdinand Melius, *Der Schriftsteller H.B. Ein biographisch-bibliographischer Abriss* (Cologne/Berlin, 1962); A. Nobbe, *H.B. Eine Bibliographie* (Cologne, 1961); H. E. Käufer, *Das Werk H.B.s 1949–1963* (Dortmund, 1963); W. J. Schwarz, *Der Erzähler H.B.* (1967); W. E. Yuill, in Keith-Smith, *ECGL*; *GLL*, XII, 1959; *GQ*, XXXIII, 2, 1960.

**Bonaventura, St** (John of Fidanza) (Bagnarea, nr Viterbo 1221–Lyons 1274). Italian Franciscan writer. Called by contemporaries the 'Seraphic Doctor' (cf. Dante's *Paradiso*, xii), canonized 1482. He studied and lectured at Paris, was elected Minister General of his order (1257) whose factious differences he worked to overcome; to this end he wrote his charming *Life of St Francis* (tr. E. G. Salter, 1904), in Latin prose, which the order adopted as the 'official' biography. His theological works are in the mystical, Platonizing tradition of St Augustine, ⇨ Bernard of Clairvaux, etc. The Latin poems attributed to him concentrate, like all early Franciscan verse, on the passion of Christ. 'In passione Domini' is well known in English as the hymn 'In the Lord's atoning grief'. [FB]

*Works*, ed. Franciscans of Quaracchi (10 vols., 1882–92).

É. Gilson, *La philosophie de St B* (1924; tr. 1938); R. Lazzarini, *San B., filosofo e mistico* (Milan, 1946); Raby, *CLP*.

**Bonnefoy, Yves** (Tours 1923– ). French poet and critic. Philosophical reflection on the value and mechanism of language produces a careful, involuted style in *Du mouvement et de l'immobilité de Douve* (1953), a series of short variations on the life and death of the loved woman, and *Hier régnant désert* (1958), *Pierre écrite* (1959) and *Anti-Platon* (1963), where he is preoccupied with the brilliant, impermeable existence of material things and obsessed with the darkness, fire and death that may be hidden beneath. He has also published *L'improbable* (1959) and *La seconde simplicité* (1961) essays resulting from his academic research into the history of art and poetry. His translations of Shakespeare (*Henry IV*, *Hamlet*, *Julius Caesar*, *The Winter's Tale*) are well known to the Parisian public. [CLC]

P. Jacottet, *Y.B.* (*N.R.F.* magazine, August 1958).

**Bontempelli, Massimo** (Como 1878–Rome 1960). Italian novelist and critic. After teaching for a few years, he devoted himself entirely to writing, and contributed to several well-known newspapers and magazines. In 1926 he started with ⇨ Malaparte a new review with the significant title *900: Cahiers d'Italie et d'Europe* (one of its foreign editors was Joyce) whose programme was to attack both the aesthetic formalism originating from the post-war *avant-garde* and the popular realism issuing from the 19th century. He defined as 'magical realism' his difficult position, precariously poised between opposite tendencies, and explained it as an effort to 'discover surreality in reality'. [GMC]

*Racconti e romanzi* (2 vols., 1961).
Falqui, *PNNI*; *Contemporanei*, i; Pullini, *RID*; Gargiulo, *LIN*; Robertis, *SN*; Biondolillo, *C*.

**Boraischa, Menahem,** formerly Goldberg (Poland 1888–New York 1949). Yiddish poet. He began to write devotional poetry, but Polish anti-semitism evoked his anger against his environment. His chief work is the two-volume poem *Der Geyer* (1943), a spiritual Odyssey. The leitmotif in his latter work is the Jew in a Gentile environment. [EE]

Roback, *SYL*.

**Boratynsky, Yevgeny** (Mara, near Tambov 1800–Naples 1844). Russian poet. His name is usually misspelt 'Baratynsky'. Born into an ancient noble family, he was educated at home, until joining an aristocratic Army cadet corps in Petersburg at the age of 12. At 16 he participated in a theft and was expelled, a catastrophe which left a permanent mark upon him. He re-enlisted as a private soldier at 18, but not until 1825 was he pardoned and made an officer. Shortly thereafter he resigned his commission, married an heiress, and lived uneventfully in Moscow until his death (on his first visit to Western Europe).

Drawn to poetry from his cadet years, he became an active member of Petersburg literary circles during Army service there and in Finland. From 1819 his poems appeared in the press, but were not published in book form until 1827. His early poems (including the lengthy *Eda*, 1825) betray his admiration for Pushkin, who praised him in turn; but in his last 15 years of life he asserted – sometimes aggressively – his own individualism, and it is for this later work that he is now remembered. Though it took at least half a century to achieve general acclaim, it places Boratynsky among the half-dozen or so really important Russian poets before the 20th century. Typically it is a thinker's poetry, calculatedly unmusical, sometimes epigrammatic and abrupt to the point of obscurity. A paradoxical, pessimistic investigation of the world's and the artist's problems replaces Boratynsky's early modish Romanticism. [RM-G]

D. Blagoy *et al.*, *Russkiye poety*, ii (Moscow, 1966); Obolensky, *PBRV*.
R. Poggioli, *Poets of Russia* (Cambridge, Mass., 1960).

**Borchardt, Rudolf** (Königsberg 1877–Trins, Tirol 1945). German poet, essayist and translator. A friend of ⇨ Schröder and ⇨ Hofmannsthal (see his correspondence, *Rede über H.*, etc.). His conservative, self-conscious sense of style (*Gespräch über Formen*, 1905) inspired many sensitive literary essays (e.g. 'Swinburne', 1909) and translations (e.g. Dante) into a blended medieval-modern German. His poetry tends to be over-formal and intellectual; his skill in fiction appears in e.g. 'Der unwürdige Liebhaber' (from the story collection *Das hoffnungslose Geschlecht*, 1929). [PB]

*Gesammelte Werke*, ed. M. L. Borchardt (8 vols., 1955–62).
W. Kraft, *R.B.* (Hamburg, 1961); Wiese, in *DDM*.

**Borchert, Wolfgang** (Hamburg 1921–Basel 1947). German short-story writer, dramatist and poet. Severely wounded on the Russian front, he was arrested and sentenced to death for 'defeatist' remarks about the Nazi regime, pardoned, sent back to the Eastern front, and finally discharged for health reasons. During and after the war he worked in a Hamburg theatre and cabaret. Friends sent him to Switzerland in 1947 in the hope of restoring his health, but he died the same year. In his vividly poetic prose sketches, remarkable for their style, rather than plot, he has left a monument of unique artistry to the desolation and disillusion of Germany in the immediate post-war years. His best-known work is the play *Draussen vor der Tür* (1947; tr. D. Porter, *The Man Outside*, in *The Prose Works of W.B.*, 1952, repr. 1966), included in *Das Gesamtwerk* (1949). [PB]

P. Rühmkorf, *W.B.* (Reinbek, 1961); *Interpretationen zu W.B.* (Munich, 1962); C. Urban, *W.B. Ein bibliographischer Versuch* (Hamburg, 1958); H. Popper, in *GML*, iii (1964); *GLL*, IV, 4 (1950); *GR*, XXVII (1952); *GQ*, XXXIII, 3 (1961).

**Bordewijk, Ferdinand** (Amsterdam 1884–Thettagne 1965). Dutch author. His short stories and novels written between the wars show his mastery of widely divergent styles, fantastic, grotesque, austere. His recurrent theme is the degradation of man by the impersonality of machines and institutions, by the artificiality of social groups or by sheer depravity. [PK]

*De wingerdrank* (1937); *Karakter, Roman van zoon en vader* (1938); *Drie toneelstukken* (1940); *Vyf fantastische vertellingen* (1947); *Blokken. Knorrende beesten. Bint* (1949); *Arenlezing uit De Korenharp* (1955); *Tien verhalen* (1956); *De aktentas* (1958); *Delta* (Spring 1958).
V. E. van Vriesland, *F.B.* (The Hague, 1949).

**Borel D'Hauterive, Pétrus** (Lyons 1809–Mostaganem 1859). French poet, novelist and translator. The most extreme of the young Romantic group of *bousingos* (with Gautier and Philothée ⇨ O'Neddy). He detested the bourgeoisie, called himself 'Le Lycanthrope', and believed only in the hatred of man for man. His poems are in *Rhapsodies* (1832), *Champavert, contes immoraux* (1833). He also translated *Robinson Crusoe* (1836) and wrote a novel, *Madame Putiphar* (1839). His intention was to scandalize and his works are full of exaggerated horrors. The last years of his life were spent in Algeria in the Colonial Service until he was dismissed for incompetence. [WA]

E. Starkie, *P.B. en Algérie* (1950), and *P.B.* (1954).

**Boreman, Yokutiel** (Russia 1825–Russia 1890). Hebrew novelist. Both his novels, *Ha-Shodedim ba-Zohoraim* (1887) and *Ha-Yetomim* (1896), deal with the pogroms in South Russia and their effect. His style is Biblical but his chief merit is in his skill in linking together a number of events which take unexpected turns and lead to curious situations. [EE]

Waxman, *HJL*.

**Borgen, Johan** (Oslo 1902– ). Norwegian novelist, short-story writer and playwright. A lawyer's son, he started as journalist and critic, and published his first collection of short stories, *Mot mørket*, in 1925; at this stage he was strongly influenced by Knut ⇨ Hamsun. In his subsequent work he has been much concerned with problems of identity and the operation of human personality in convention-ridden societies. His humoristic gifts also found expression in the popular collection of anecdotes, *Mumle Gåsegg* (1936). Since the war he has moved into the front rank of contemporary Norwegian novelists with his trilogy, *Lillelord* (1955), *De mørke kilder* (1956), and *Vi har ham nå* (1957), and with *Jeg* (1959). [RGP]

*Noveller i utvalg 1936–61* (1961).
Beyer, *NL*.

**Borgese, Giuseppe Antonio** (Polizzi Generosa 1882–Fiesole 1952). Italian literary critic and novelist. Holder of several University chairs in Italy and the United States, where he expatriated himself after the advent of the Fascist regime. His early studies (*Storia della critica romantica in Italia*, 1905; *G. D'Annunzio*, 1909) influenced the subsequent course of his critical and literary work. Because of his often emotional and psychological approach to art, he was the epigone of the Romantic critics in a philosophic-aesthetic age; in his novels (*Rubé*, 1921; *I vivi e i morti*, 1923), whose protagonists are sterile intellectuals who destroy themselves by too much thinking and too little acting, he showed himself as the last of the decadents. Perhaps his best writing is found in his volumes of short stories (*Novelle*, Milan, 1950). In his late years he devoted himself to generous but impracticable projects for a world government. [GMC]

L. Russo, *I Narratori* (Messina, 1951); Biondolillo, *C*; *Contemporanei*, i.

**Boris and Gleb** (d. 1015). Russian princes. Three accounts survive of the martyrdom of Boris and Gleb, the first Russian saints to be canonized. All of them may be ascribed to the 11th century, but it remains unclear which preceded or influenced the others. The account incorporated into the ⇨ *Russian Primary Chronicle* under the year 1015 is closely related to the more sophisticated, anonymous *Skazaniye* ('Tale') of the martyrdom. The third account, a competent hagiography known as the *Chteniye* ('Lection'), was written by the monk Nestor; it is markedly different in tone and content, and of lesser interest from the artistic point of view. The *Skazaniye* deservedly proved the most popular of the texts and was repeatedly copied in the Middle Ages. One of the ⇨ Russian spiritual verses was based on it.

The *Skazaniye* enriches the narrative as given in the Chronicle by the addition of lyrical passages (laments and prayers); it is particularly successful in its use of interior monologue (Boris is credited with simultaneous and different thoughts in his mind and in his heart). The work is well constructed; it contains some brilliant imagery.

Boris and Gleb (who were brothers) suffered death in the summer of 1015 at the hands of a close relative and fellow prince (Svyatopolk, according to the Russian records; Yaroslav, according to some recent investigators). Boris, in particular, died because he was willing to be killed rather than to kill. The theme of non-resistance to evil and of innocent suffering for the sake of others was thus introduced into Russian literature at an early date. [SH]

D. I. Abramovich, *Zhitiya svyatykh muchenikov Borisa i Gleba i sluzhby im* (Petrograd, 1916; Munich, 1967); S. A. Bugoslavsky, *Pam'yatki XI-XVIII vv. pro knyaziv Borisa ta Hliba* (Kiev, 1928).

**Bosboom-Toussaint, Anna Louisa Geertruida** (Alkmaar 1812–The Hague 1886). Dutch novelist. The English romantics inspired her *De Graaf van Devonshire* (1839); subsequent historical novels support the *Reveil* (cf. ⇨ Drost) in their idealization of evangelical protestantism; *Het Huis Lauernesse* (1840), the Leycester cycle (10 vols., 1846–55), *De Delftsche Wonderdokter* (1870) and many others. Her characterization and descriptive detail do not compensate for her prolix and archaic style, but when, in *Majoor Frans* (1874; tr. J. Akeroyd, *Major Frank*, 1885), she attempted a modern novel on the French model she matched her theme of female enfranchizement with a welcome emancipation of her own style. [PK]

*Volledige romantische werken* (25 vols., 1885–8).

**Boscán Almogáver, Juan** (Barcelona 1474?–Perpignan 1542). Spanish poet. His early work is in the 15th-century manner, but he was persuaded at a meeting with Andrea Navagero, the Venetian envoy (Granada, 1525), to experiment with the Italian metres. His achievements in this are uninspired and angular, but the example set was of the highest importance, especially to his friend ⇨ Garcilaso. He made an excellent translation of ⇨ Castiglione's *Cortegiano* (Barcelona, 1534; CA), a fundamental Renaissance manual, to which Garcilaso wrote a preface. The poems of the two were published together by Boscán's widow in 1543. [JMC]

*Obras poéticas*, ed. M. de Riquer (1957ff.); Trend, *OBSV*; Perry, *HASP*; Cohen, *PBSV*; Terry, *ASP*. Menéndez y Pelayo, *PLC*, xiii, xiv; M. de Riquer, *J.B. y su cancionero barcelonés* (Barcelona, 1945).

**Bosco, Henri** (Avignon 1888– ). French novelist. He has been writing since 1924 and first attracted wide attention with *Le Mas Théotime* (1945, Prix Théophraste Renaudot; tr. M. Savill, *The Farm Théotime*, 1946). All his work reflects his fascination with Provence, both its obvious charms, its natural beauty and its appealing inhabitants, who follow with simplicity and dignity a pattern of life unchanged over the centuries, and the less obvious mystery and violence, which lurks just beneath and sometimes rises to the surface. The latter theme is well illustrated in *Le Mas Théotime*, whilst *L'âne culotte* (1937) and its sequel *Le jardin d'Hyacinthe* (1946) develop from a simple tale of two country children into a powerful allegory based, with characteristic ambiguity, on peasant superstition and Christian myth. The chief substance of Bosco's novels, the poetic evocation of people, places and anecdotes, finds freer expression, away from the constraining needs of formal construction, in *Un oubli moins profond* (1961), a volume of childhood reminiscences. [IHW]

M. Primault, H. Lhong and J. Malrieu, *Terres de l'enfance* (Paris, 1961); Austin, *SMFL*.

**Bossuet, Jacques Bénigne** (Dijon 1627–Paris 1704). French orator. He was born of lawyer's stock, educated by the Jesuits of his native city and then at the Collège de Navarre, whose Principal, Nicolas Cornet, is chiefly known from the funeral oration which Bossuet pronounced upon him. He spent seven fruitful years in Metz as preacher and administrator, was for two years Bishop of Condom, for ten years tutor to the Dauphin and then from 1681 Bishop of Meaux for the rest of his life.

The so-called 'Eagle of Meaux', the greatest of French orators, was neither arrogant nor desirous of literary fame, but an unpretentious man, endowed in large measure with the qualities of a Burgundian, industry, thoroughness, attention to one thing at a time, grasp of essentials. He was a 'residing' bishop, a tireless Christian pastor. Almost all his works were occasional, that is in response to requests for sermons, for counsel, for decision in controversy. His devotion to his very unresponsive royal pupil seems to have been entire, involving him in immense research and labour of writing textbooks, two of which became famous: *Discours sur l'histoire universelle* (1681) and *Politique tirée de l'Écriture Sainte* (1709) but others should not be forgotten, e.g. *Traité de la connaissance de Dieu et de soi-même* (1722).

Much of Bossuet's life was spent in controversy. In Metz his discussions with Paul Ferry, the Reformed minister, set a new standard in courteous polemic. He played a leading role in the preparation of the Revocation (of the Edict of Nantes), voted for it, but is on record as having advised against persecution. His writings against the Protestants played a part in English religious controversy, notably his *Exposition de la doctrine catholique sur les matières de controverse* (1671), *Traité de la Communion sous les deux espèces* (1682), and most famous of all, *Histoire des variations des églises protestantes* (1688).

He was no less involved against adversaries within his own church. His leadership of the moderates in the affair of the royal claim to revenues of vacant benefices, known as La Régale, his role in the church assembly of 1680 (at which he preached a famous sermon on the unity of the Church) are thought to have prevented open breach with Rome. The debates with ➪ Fénelon and the Quietists caused even more stir. After much writing on both sides and dubious backstairs negotiations the Holy See condemned Fénelon, but in terms so moderate that both parties were dissatisfied and the chief result was the scandal of protracted polemic between leading Churchmen.

Since his death Bossuet has himself been a centre of controversy. Attacks have been made upon his character, even upon his celibacy, and still more upon his ideas. It was unfortunate that most of the positions which he chose to defend became rapidly discredited. He can indeed be seen as a man who was almost always wrong. He did everything to suppress Biblical criticism (chiefly in the person of Richard Simon). The whole basis of his claim that Protestants but not Catholics have varied in doctrine was destroyed by J. H. Newman in a famous essay. His wholesale condemnation of the theatre (*Maximes et réflexions sur la comédie*, 1694) does more credit to his heart than to his head. His providential explanation of history could not survive Voltaire. He once committed himself to the statement that 'hérétique est celui qui a une opinion'. Small wonder that for many he is still a monolithic symbol of reaction.

This is now seen to be an unfair estimate. There was at least nothing monolithic about the preacher. His eloquence depended in great part on his personal qualities: single-minded simplicity, dignity, a sense of the grandeur of religion and of the challenge of death, the great leveller. The balance and rhythm of his sentences in which he expresses great truths in plain and sometimes homely language are accessible to any with an ear for spoken French. Moreover those who praise Bossuet for his form and neglect his matter are now seen to be also unjust. He may have been constantly wrong but he has a place in the history of ideas. His sketch of world history was the only thing of its kind available to Gibbon and Rousseau. He is a fine Biblical exegete. His vision of the unity of the Church seems today more realistic than it did then. Some of his pages on the universal 'néant' of human endeavour have the modern ring of Sartre. [WGM]

Ed. Lachat (31 vols., 1862–6); *Correspondance*, ed. C. Urbain, E. Levesque (15 vols., 1909–25); *Oraisons Funèbres*, ed. Truchet (1961); *Œuvres*, ed. l'abbé B. Velat (Pléiade, 1961).

J. Lebarq, *Histoire critique de la prédication de B.* (Paris, 1891); G. Lanson, *B.* (Paris, 1891); A. Rébelliau, *B. historien du protestantisme* (Paris, 1909); A. G. Martimort, *B.* (Paris, 1953); R. Schmittlein, *B.* (Baden, 1954).

**Botev, Hristo** (Kalofer 1848–Mt Vola, Vratsa 1876). Bulgarian poet and publicist. Educated, like his father, in Odessa, he was fired by the same radical ideas of the Russian intelligentsia as his revolutionary colleague ➪ Karavelov. Sent back there for preaching socialism and anti-Turkish resistance in Kalofer in 1867 he joined instead the Bulgarian émigrés in Rumania. Here he developed his manifesto of Bulgarian social-revolutionary liberation in the biting satirical publicism of his journals, *Duma* ('Émigrés' Word', 1871), *Nezavisimost* ('Independence', 1873), *Budilnik* ('Alarum', 1873) and *Zname* ('Flag', 1874). He militantly opposed the policy of education and church autonomy advocated by some, notably Petko ➪ Slaveykov, to whose *Gayda* he had contributed his 'To my mother' (1867). On the handful of poems, of which this was the first, rests his literary fame and the compelling Botev legend, which has inspired every Bulgarian generation since.

In the simple, strong language of the folk-song, of which his mother was a reputed singer, he conveys the apotheosis of the *haydutin* (guerrilla), an age-old tradition culminating in his own death on the mountain no less than the agony of 'Haji Dimităr' and 'The Hanging of V. Levski', tragedies seemingly involving the whole of nature in his poems. They epitomize the excitement and despair of these émigrés wrestling to awaken their countrymen. They combine premonition and acceptance of a tragic destiny with a virile faith in the cause to which he finally gave his own life in an abortive expedition across the Danube to free his countrymen from the Turks. [VP]

*Săchineniya* (2 vols., 1950, 1960); Pinto, *BPV*.

A. Burmov, *H.B. Spomeni, vpechatleniya* (Sofia, 1945); M. Dimitrov, *H.B. Idei. Lichnost. Tvorchestvo* (Sofia, 1946); ed. A. Burmov and S. Bozhkov, *Sbornik 'H.B.'* (Sofia, 1949); Botev-Levski Institute's *Izvestiya* and *Sbornik* (3 vols., Sofia, 1954–9); Manning and Smal-Stocki, *HMBL*.

**Botto, Ján** (Vyšný Skalník 1829–Banská Bystrica 1881). Slovak poet. His masterpiece is *Smrť Jánošíkova* (1862), a romantic lyrical epic on the death of the Slovak Robin Hood figure Jánošík. Literary echoes of ⇨ Mickiewicz and ⇨ Mácha combine with techniques of Slovak and Serbian popular poetry to create a minor masterpiece of Slavonic romanticism. [RA]

*Súborné dielo* (1955).

R. Brtáň, *O Bottovej Smrti Jánošíkovej* (Bratislava, 1942).

**Bouhélier, Saint-Georges de** (Rueil 1876–Paris 1947). French poet and dramatist. A minor poet (*Chants de la vie ardente*, 1902; *Romance de l'homme*, 1912, etc.) and leader of the Naturiste group which reacted against the abstract and aethereal aspects of ⇨ Symbolism in favour of a more vital and concrete return to Nature. The characteristic themes of his poems – social idealism and a sense of human fraternity – recur in many of the plays on which his reputation chiefly rests. He tackled 'big' subjects again, e.g. the mystery of Christ in *Le roi sans couronne* (1906); the legend of Oedipus in *Oedipe, roi de Thèbes* (1919); the predicament of a modern Hamlet in *La célèbre histoire* (1928). But these, and his historical dramas – *Le sang de Danton* (1931), *Napoléon* (1933), *Jeanne d'Arc* (1934), *Le roi soleil* (1938) – are inadequately controlled, prone to verbal inflation and uncertain in tone. What survives is *Le carnaval des enfants* (1910), a moving poetic fable about human love, the power and suggestiveness of which is enhanced by an imaginative use of carnival masks. [SBJ]

D. Knowles, *La réaction idéaliste au théâtre depuis 1890* (Paris, 1934); G. Lanson, *L'œuvre dramatique de S.-G. de B.* (Paris, 1934).

**Bouilhet, Louis-Hyacinthe** (Cany 1822–Rouen 1869). French poet and dramatist. He is chiefly known as the schoolfellow and the lifelong friend of Flaubert. He achieved some success with his plays *Madame de Montarcy* (1856) and *La conjuration d'Amboise* (1866). He also wrote poems on historical and scientific subjects including *Melaenis* (1851) on Rome in the time of the Emperor Commodus and *Festons et Astragales*, dealing with the geological ages of the earth. [WA]

**Bourdaloue, Louis** (Bourges 1632–Paris 1704). French preacher. One of the great preachers in 17th-century Paris, especially after 1669 when ⇨ Bossuet had created a new vogue and was forced by other duties to withdraw from preaching himself. Contemporaries praise his 'divine' insistence on plain and prime truths. His style seems to have been quite unmodern, violent, high-pitched, yet attached to a careful script. His sermons are a guide to the behaviour of the middle and upper class of his day. [WGM]

E. Griselle, *Histoire critique de la prédication de B.* (Paris, 1929); Adam, *HLF*.

**Bourdet, Édouard** (Saint-Germain-en-Laye 1887–Paris 1945). French playwright. His plays offer two centres of interest: psychological analysis and social satire. The first, characterized by sobriety and discretion, operates chiefly on psychological cripples. Such is the case with Irène, the sexual invert who is the heroine of *La prisonnière* (1926); with Marguerite de Navarre consumed with a secret, incestuous passion in *Margot* (1935); with the depraved aristocrats of *La fleur des pois* (1932); or with the twisted invalid Agnès of *Hyménée* (1941). His satirical range is reflected in: *Vient de paraître* (1927), a vivacious caricature of the literary world; *Le sexe faible* (1929), an astringent attack on the power of money to corrupt marriage; *Fric-frac* (1937), a spirited farce which compares the world of tarts and crooks favourably with that of the scheming and hypocritical *petits bourgeois*; and *Les temps difficiles* (1934), a clinically severe portrait of rich industrialists. Too great a complicity with his pathological cases, too obtrusive a handling of the geometry of the well-made play and too marked a tendency to avoid the logic of his own satirical attacks inhibit Bourdet from becoming the important dramatist his work sometimes suggests he is. His tenure of office as Administrator of the Comédie-Française (1936–40) was marked by important reforms. [SBJ]

*Théâtre* (5 vols., 1948–61).
Surer, *TFC*; Lalou, *TF*.

**Bourges, Élémir** (Manosque 1852–Paris 1925). French novelist. Erudite author of ambitiously scaled novels in which he tried, through a fusion of myth, history, philosophy and symbol, to reverse Naturalism's tendency to diminish man. His conception of the form and dimension of the novel owes much to his admiration for the Greek tragic dramatists and the Elizabethans, and for symphonic music, notably Beethoven, Berlioz and Wagner. His lively novel of the Chouannerie, *Sous la hache* (written 1876, published serially 1883), was followed by impressive, though grandiose, frescoes full of heroic exaltation, e.g. *Le crépuscule des dieux* (1884); *Les oiseaux s'envolent et les fleurs tombent* (1893), a little unreal in its quest for a tragic sense in the career of a Russian grand duke; and *La nef* (1904–22), a huge, lyrical prose-poem (in two parts) on the Promethean theme. [SBJ]

*Œuvres complètes* (7 vols., 1929).
R. Schwab, *La vie d'E.B.* (Paris, 1948); A. Lebois, *Les tendances du symbolisme à travers l'œuvre d'E.B.* (Paris, 1952).

**Bourget, Paul Charles Joseph** (Amiens 1852–Paris 1935). French critic and novelist. His most important critical work is his *Essais de psychologie contemporaine* (1883; *Nouveaux essais*, 1885; rev. edn 1899) which analyses the moral sickness of France in scientific-sounding terms derived from Taine; Stendhal is seen as the precursor of the modern sensibility, which is traced through Baudelaire, Flaubert and others. Of his early novels, which are much concerned with erotic psychology, the best is *Le disciple* (1889; tr. anon., *The Disciple*, 1901). It shows the effect of positivist teaching on a student, who becomes the victim of his own experiment in love, in which his beloved takes her life and her brother avenges her; the teacher himself has religious inklings of his responsibility. Bourget was converted to Catholicism in 1901 and became increasingly conservative in outlook, sympathizing with 'Action française'. Of his later work, his short stories (e.g. *Drames de famille*, 1900; *Les détours du cœur*, 1908, etc.) are considered superior to his novels, which are too obviously ideological. ⇨ French Literary Criticism.

L. J. Austin, *P. B., Sa vie et son œuvre* (Paris, 1940); M. Mansuy, *P. B.* (Paris, 1961).

**Boursault, Edmé** (Mussy-sur-Seine, Burgundy 1638–Montluçon 1701). French man of letters. He was involved in polemic with Boileau and Molière. He wrote light verse and topical journalism (a sequel to the Gazette of Loret) and put on the stage *Le médecin volant*, *Le portrait du peintre* (attacking *L'école des femmes*), *Le mort vivant* (1662), *Les Nicandres ou les Menteurs qui ne mentent point* (1664) and *Les amours de Germanicus* (1673). [WGM]

Adam, *HLF*; Lancaster, *HFDL*.

**Bousoño, Carlos** (Boal, Asturias 1923– ). Spanish poet and critic. A Ph.D. of Madrid University, where he lectures, his first book of poems, written like the rest in fairly conventional forms, shows profound religious preoccupations, mildly blasphematory in the poet's juvenile desperation at failing to assert his faith in God; besides this 'theme' the book reveals the never-dying presence of Spain in Bousoño's poetry, and an airy amatory thread showing repressed anxieties of a somewhat obscure nature. In his second book, which does not mention God, he has a melancholy look at Death; love, still undefined and ambiguous, runs throughout; reality seems to evade the experience of the poet, who denies the value of the senses in his next two books. In the last, he escapes from his previous 'noche del sentido' into a mild joyful acceptance of the reality apprehended by his formerly despised senses. He is a very elegant poet, extremely vague in expression, of a rare consistency of style which the poet commands throughout. As a critic, Bousoño, departing from the stylistic methods of Dámaso ⇨ Alonso, shows outstanding perceptiveness and originality. His most ambitious work, *Teoría de la expresión poética*, is a valuable attempt to find a scientific basis for the study of poetry. For him 'Poetry is *communication*'; his definition of this term comes close to Eliot's conception of the 'objective correlative'. Though he falls into a contradictory 'relativism' and a tedious classification of poetic devices, he pinpoints the style of several contemporary Spanish poets; his contribution to the understanding of ⇨ Aleixandre's poetry is of major importance. [JMA]

Poetry: *Subida al amor* (1945); *Primavera de la muerte* (1946); *Hacia otra luz* (1952) (the first two books plus *En vez de sueño*); *Noche del sentido* (1957); *Poesías completas* (1960); *Invasión de la realidad* (1962). Criticism: *La poesía de Vicente Aleixandre* (1950); *Seis calas en la expresión literaria española* (1951) (with Dámaso Alonso); *Teoría de la expresión poética* (1952, 2nd edn, 1956).

**Boutens, Peter Cornelis** (Middelburgh 1870–The Hague 1943). Dutch poet and classical scholar. At first he is often obscure – his mystical conceptions are expressed in individualistic and impressionistic poetry in keeping with the aspirations of *De Nieuwe Gids* (cf. ⇨ Kloos, ⇨ Verwey). But in *Stemmen* (1907) and the following collections his mastery of rhythm and form transcends the very personal, cosmic symbolism of his remote aestheticism, in which 'every word is a symbol of profound significance'. His *Beatrijs* (1908) is written in blank verse of rare beauty, and his translations (from Homer, Aeschylus, Sophocles, Goethe, etc.) are unsurpassed. [PK]

*Verzamelde Werken* (6 vols, 1943–51); Grierson *F*; Barnouw, *CA*; Snell, *FFG*; Weevers, *PNEC*.

D. A. M. Binnendijk, *Een protest tegen de tijd* (Amsterdam, 1965).

**Boye, Karin** (Göteborg 1900–Alingsås 1941). Swedish poet, novelist and story-writer. One of the most popular and (in her best work) most impressive modern Swedish poets, she passed through phases of Christianity, socialism and psychoanalysis; but her writing (though showing various influences, including Eliot, whom she translated) is essentially the expression of an individual personality endowed with a clear will and tragic inner conflicts – she ended her own life, alone in a winter forest. Her books of poetry – *Moln* (1922), *Gömda land* (1924), *Härdarna* (1927), *För trädets skull* (1935), and (posthumously) *De sju dödssynderna* (1941) – express her constant striving for integrity and devotion, combined with profound awareness of the unconscious. Particularly famous are her poems on the pain, mystery and inevitability of growth and change, often using memorably direct symbolism from organic nature, such as the tree, and reinforced by apparently simple but subtly haunting rhythms. Her prose is less significant, except for the remarkable novel of a future totalitarian state, *Kallocain* (1940); in psychological depth and symbolic power it equals ⇨ Zamyatin's *We*.

M. Abenius, *Drabbad av renhet* (Stockholm, 1951); ed. M. Abenius and O. Lagercrantz, *K.B.: minnen och studier* (Stockholm, 1942).

**Božić, Mirko** (Sinj 1919– ). Croatian novelist and dramatist. He began to write while serving with the partisans. His most important works are the novels *Kurlani* (1952) and *Neisplakani* (1955) and the drama *Pravednik*. He describes in brutal and colourful naturalism two branches of a peasant family, the Kurlans, living in the rocky and infertile area of his home. His work sometimes invites comparison with that of ⇨ Leonov, but his humour, sympathy and toughness are his own. [EDG]

*SEER*, XL, 94 (1961); Kadić, *CCL*.

**Braak, Menno ter** (Eibergen 1902–The Hague 1940). Dutch critic. With du ⇨ Perron and Roelants he founded the polemical journal *Forum* (1932–5). He attacked cant and conformity, suspected all doctrinaire ideals (*Politicus zonder partij*, 1934), and attacked especially National Socialism (*Het national-socialisme als rancuneleer*, 1937); he committed suicide during the Nazi invasion. The candour of his style and his exposure of bogus values are more effective in his essays (*Het carnaval der burgers*, 1930; *Démasqué der schoonheid*, 1932) than in his novels: *Hampton Court* (1931), *Dr Dumay verliest* (1933). [PK]

*Verzameld Werk* (7 vols., 1949–51); Greshoff, *HL*; T.B. en du Perron, *Briefwisseling 1930–40* (1962– ).

H. Marsman, *M. ter B.* (Amsterdam, 1939); W. L. M. E. van Leeuwen, *Drie vrienden. H. Marsman, M. ter B., E. du Perron* (Utrecht, 1947); R. Henrard, *M.T.B. in het licht van Friedrich Nietzsche* (Hasselt, 1963).

**Brainin, Reuben** (Lodz 1862–New York

1939). Hebrew writer. He belonged to ⇨ Ben Avigdor's circle of 'new writing'; the first in modern Hebrew literature to write biographies of Hebrew writers. He also contributed short stories to the *Sifre Agorah* ('Penny Books') series started by Ben Avigdor, like his *Mi-Gibbore Yisrael*, whose hero Moses the bricklayer bears all the mishaps of life with equanimity but with undying hope. [EE]

*Mimisrach U-Mimaarav* (2 vols., Vienna, 1899); *Avraham Mapu* (Warsaw, 1900); *Peretz Smoleskin* (Warsaw, 1896); *Collected Essays* (2 vols., N.Y., 1923–37); *Chayye Herzl* (N.Y., 1919).
Waxman, *HJL*.

**Bräker, Ulrich** (Näbis, Toggenburg 1735–Wattwil 1798). Swiss writer. The uneducated son of a peasant farmer, he was pressed into the service of a Prussian recruiting officer, but deserted and returned home, where he earned his living as a weaver. He achieved fame with the publication of his autobiography *Lebensgeschichte und natürliche Abenteuer des armen Mannes im Toggenburg* (1789), a work of considerable interest for the light it casts on a remarkable human being and for the worm's-eye view it gives us of conditions in the mid 18th century. An autodidact of lively intelligence, he also published a critical work on Shakespeare (ed. W. Muschg, 1942). [WAC]

*Leben und Schriften*, ed. S. Voellony (3 vols., 1946).

**Brancati, Vitaliano** (Pachino 1907–Torino 1954). Italian novelist. After a short teaching spell in Catania he became a journalist in Rome, where he came into contact with the liberal intelligentsia. This experience broadened his outlook, changed his political convictions and developed his latent vocation to satirical moralism, admirably served by his keen observation and colourful style. In 1941 he published *Gli anni perduti*, a delightful caricature of middle-class provincial society, where the wasting of time in idle pursuits is raised to the dignity of art. In his subsequent novels he turned his penetrating eye on the strange phenomenon of *gallismo*, i.e. the amorous antics of the Southern males who, brought up in a matriarchal society ruled by men, where honour is synonymous with face-saving and morality with conformity, love is divorced from sex, and chastity is good only for women, display a form of aggressive eroticism which is thirty per cent frustrated virility, thirty per cent boasting and forty per cent wishful thinking (*Don Giovanni in Sicilia*, 1942). In extreme cases, *gallismo* is nothing but a symptom of impotence (*Il bell'Antonio*, 1949; tr. V. Kean, *Antonio, the Great Lover*, 1952). Brancati was so much concerned with the problem of sexual fulfilment thwarted by social conventions that he took it as the theme of his last novel, *Paolo il caldo* (posthumously published 1955); perceiving its obsessive monotony, he tried to vary it by introducing autobiographical material and social and political satire, thereby weakening the artistic unity of the novel. He wrote also short stories (*Il vecchio con gli stivali*, 1958), various essays and articles and a diary (*Diario romano*, 1961) which shows the limitations of his liberalism – a system of enlightened moral beliefs, without any clear awareness of their necessary political foundations. [GMC]

*Contemporanei*, ii; Pullini, *RID*.

**Brandão, Raul** (Foz do Douro 1867–Lisbon 1930). Portuguese novelist, journalist, dramatist and social historian. Brandão made his first impression on the literary world in the final decade of the 19th century, first as a writer of Naturalist short stories and later as a journalist for the periodical *Nefelibatas* and the *Correio da Manhã*. Even at this stage he concerned himself with the major themes of his life's work, the privations of the poor and their exploitation, be they peasants, seafarers or city workers, and his concept of life as a tragic farce. These themes informed his first major work, the *fin de siècle* novel *Memórias de um Palhaço* (1896), a work strongly influenced by Poe and Hoffmann which was re-cast thirty years later under the title *Morte do Palhaço*. During the early years of the 20th century he was particularly impressed by his reading of the Russian novelists, especially Dostoyevsky. It was this new dimension which gave vigour to his 3 great novels, *Os Pobres* (1906), *A Farsa* (1909) and *Húmus* (1917), to his *Teatro* (1923), and to his posthumous novel, *O Pobre de Pedir* (1931). These works, particularly the novels, are characterized by a poetic style and by philosophical meditations on the human condition, a debate into which he entered without any preconceived notions, frequently analysing the dichotomy of the personality, the distinction between the inner *ego* and the social *persona*. His conclusions are never finalized, constantly oscillating between mystical idealism and anarchist nihilism. Brandão's other works comprise 3 historico-social studies, *El-rei Junot* (1912), *A Conspiração de Gomes Freire* (1914) and *As Memórias* (1919–25–33), and 2 volumes of highly colourful journalistic reporting, *Pescadores* (1923) and *Ilhas Desconhecidas* (1927). During the last decade of his life he was closely associated with the Seara Nova movement. [RCW]

C. B. Chaves, *R.B.* (Lisbon, 1934); J. P. de Andrade, *R.B.* (Lisbon, 1963).

**Brandes, Edvard** (Copenhagen 1847–Copenhagen 1931). Danish critic and playwright, brother of Georg ⇨ Brandes. A distinguished Oriental scholar and a literary critic closely associated with the militant radicalism of his brother, he was influenced as a playwright by Ibsen. Best known among his plays is *Et Besøg* (1882; tr. W. Archer, *A Visit*, 1892). [ELB]

**Brandes, Georg** (Copenhagen 1842–Copenhagen 1927). Danish literary critic. The son of unorthodox Jewish parents, his extraordinary gifts as a literary scholar early made him the leader of the Danish radical intelligentsia. He was influenced during his formative years by Kierkegaard (on whom he wrote in 1877) and Goethe, in his literary understanding by both Taine and Sainte-Beuve (his dissertation was on Taine), and in his social views by John Stuart Mill (some of whose works he translated into Danish) and Hegel. The Scandinavian literary movement of the 1870s known as *Det moderne Gennembrud* owed much to his ideas, and he was closely associated with the leading men-of-letters of Denmark, Norway and Sweden, including Jacobsen, Drachmann, Pontoppidan, Ibsen, Kielland and Strindberg. But by his atheism (influenced by Feuerbach and Renan; see his *Sagnet om Jesus*, 1925; tr. E. Björkman, *Jesus, a Myth*, 1926) and political radicalism he made many enemies and was for years refused professorial appointment; he travelled widely and lived in Berlin in1877–83.

With his *Hovedstrømninger i det 19de Aarhundredes Litteratur* (1871ff.; tr. W. Archer, *Main Currents in 19th Century Literature*, 1901–5) he gained international fame, becoming known in England first for his *Disraeli* (1878; tr. Mrs W. Sturge, 1880) and *Eminent Authors of the 19th Century* (1886; tr. R. B. Anderson, N.Y., 1886; enlarged as *Creative Spirits of the 19th Century*, 1924), which includes essays on Andersen, John Stuart Mill, Renan, Tegnér, Flaubert, Paludan-Müller, Ibsen and Bjørnson.

Under the influence of Nietzsche, with whom he corresponded, Brandes became increasingly anti-democratic and developed a philosophy of 'artistocratic radicalism'; his essays appeared in England as *Friedrich Nietzsche* (1914; tr. A. G. Chater). Brandes's conception of the 'great man' is reflected also in his still valuable studies of *Shakespeare* (1895ff.; a best-seller in England, tr. W. Archer *et al.*, 1898), of *Voltaire* (1916-17; tr. O. Kruger and P. Butler, 1930), *Goethe* (1914-15; tr. A. W. Porterfield, 1936), *Michelangelo* (1921; tr. H. Norden, 1963) and *Julius Caesar* (1918). His other works on *Ibsen, Bjørnson* (tr. 1899), *Anatole France* (tr. 1908), *Ferdinand Lasalle* (tr. 1911), *On Reading* (tr. New York, 1906) were also widely read in England and America. He also published culturally intelligent accounts of his travels in Greece (*Hellas*, tr. N.Y., 1926), Russia (*Impressions*, tr. 1890) and Poland (tr. 1903). His neutralist attitude to the First World War lost him many friends (including Edmund Gosse and Georges Clemenceau); his views are expressed in *The World at War* (tr. C. D. Groth, 1917). [ELB]

G. Brandes, *Levned* (1906); *Correspondance de G.B.*, ed. P. Krüger (4 vols., Copenhagen, 1951–66).

E. Gosse, *Two Visits to Denmark* (1911); J. Moritzen, *G.B. in Life and Letters* (Newark, 1922); S. Møller Kristensen, 'G.B. Research: A Survey', in *Scandinavica*, III, 2, 1964.

**Branner, Hans Christian** (Ordrup 1903–Copenhagen 1966). Danish novelist and playwright. He first became known, after some years working for a Copenhagen publishing firm, for a radio drama and a novel *Legetøj* (1936), and is now recognized as the leading Danish novelist of his generation. His novels deal with loneliness, the dangers of fear, and of power; he shows a humanist's faith in man and, especially in his superb short stories, a subtle understanding of children. Among his collections of short stories the best are *Om lidt er vi borte* (1939) and *To minutters stilhed* (1944; tr. V. L. Vance, *Two Minutes of Silence*, Madison, 1966). His main novels are *Drømmen om en Kvinde* (1941), *Historien om Børge* (1942), *Rytteren* (1949; tr. A. I. Roughton, *The Riding Master*, 1951), and *Ingen kender*

*Natten* (1955; tr. A. I. Roughton, *No Man Knows the Night*, 1958).

Branner's success as a playwright began with a dramatization of *Rytteren* (1949), followed in 1951 by *Søskende* (tr. A. I. Roughton, *The Judge*, in *Contemporary Danish Plays*, 1955) and *Thermopylæ* (1957), a play set in the Occupation period. He has also written for the radio, including *Et Spil om Kærligheden og Døden* (1960). [ELB]

J. Vosmar, *H.C.B.* (Copenhagen, 1959); R. B. Vowles, Introduction to *Two Minutes of Silence* (1966).

**Brant, Sebastian** (Strassburg 1457–Strassburg 1521). German poet and satirist. He inaugurated the Alemannic tradition of moral satire which persisted throughout the 16th century. His *Narrenschiff* (1494; ed. F. Zarncke, 1854, repr. 1861; DNL 16, 1889; tr. E. H. Zeydel, *The Ship of Fools*, N.Y., 1944) is unquestionably the most important vernacular satire of the age. The original conception of the ship as a collecting place for the various fools who are to be transported to 'Narragonia' (Fool-land) is soon lost and in essence the work is a series of 112 short sermons in rather clumsy rhyming couplets in which Brant castigates almost every type of folly from bad behaviour at table to adultery and refusing to listen to the word of God, no distinction being made between real vices, moral and intellectual defects and simple foolishness. Not least owing to its woodcut illustrations – many of them were long ascribed to Dürer – the work enjoyed tremendous popularity throughout Europe and went through innumerable editions, translations and adaptations. It played a decisive role in the establishment of a European folly tradition, while in Germany it exerted a major influence on such writers as ⇨ Murner, Hans ⇨ Sachs, ⇨ Fischart, ⇨ Moscherosch and ⇨ Abraham à Sancta Clara.

Of Brant's other literary works, which included Lives of the Saints and a number of translations from the Latin, the only one of real importance was his edition of Freidank's *Bescheidenheit* in 1508. [WAC]

R. Newald, *Probleme und Gestalten des deutschen Humanismus* (Berlin, 1963).

U. Gaier, *Studien zu Sebastian Brants N.S.* (Tübingen, 1966); B. Könneker, *Wesen und Wandlung der Narrenidee im Zeitalter des Humanismus* (Wiesbaden, 1966).

**Brantôme, Pierre de Bourdeilles de** (Bourdeille 1540?–S. Crépin, Dordogne 1614). French memorialist. A courtier and soldier, he took to writing after being crippled in early middle age by a fall from a horse. His memoirs (*Recueil d'aucuns discours*, published posthumously in 1665) contain the lives of great captains and of princesses, and in the section known as the 'Dames galantes' he relates some scandalous episodes of the French court. These memoirs are worth reading, not just as 'gossip' but for their brisk, informal style and the picture they give of military and court life in the second half of the 16th century. [GJ]

*Recueil des dames*, ed. R. Gaucheron (1926; tr. anon. *Lives of Fair and Gallant Ladies*, 1934).

**Brasillach, Robert** (Perpignan 1909–Montrouge 1945). French novelist, political commentator and critic. Actively associated with the Fascist press during the 1930s (*Action française*, *Je suis partout*) and an enthusiastic collaborator, he was subsequently shot.

In his novels (*Le voleur d'étincelles*, 1932; *L'enfant de la nuit*, 1934; *Comme le temps passe*, 1937; tr. W. B. Wells, *Youth Goes Over*, 1938) he saw himself as the novelist of youth; his loose narratives are strewn with philosophic-cum-poetic discourses on the nature of happiness, memory, destiny, and, of course, the charm and mystery of youth. The influence of Proust and Gide is apparent almost to the point of pastiche. Some of his descriptions of Paris scenes have a genuine lyrical flavour and his characters include some brief but moving portraits. *Les sept couleurs* (1939) includes a glowing apologia of Fascism. His play, *La Reine de Césarée*, was performed in 1957; admirers have compared his *Poèmes de Fresnes* (1949) to *Iambes*; his critical writing, particularly *Corneille* (1938), is probably the most enduring aspect of his work. [IHW]

M. Jouhandeau, *Carnet de l'écrivain* (Paris, 1957); J. Isorni, *Le Procès de B.* (Paris, 1946); P. Vandromme, *R.B.* (Paris, 1956); Jean Madiran, *B.* (Paris, 1958).

**Brecht, Bertolt** (Augsburg 1898–Berlin 1956). German poet and playwright. The son of an industrialist, he studied medicine and served as an army medical orderly in 1918. He became *Dramaturg* at the Munich Kammerspiele (1921), then at the Deutsches Theater, Berlin (1924). His first poems, *Taschenpostille*, were published privately in

1926; in 1928, having divorced his first wife, he married the actress Helene Weigel. In the winter 1928–9 he was converted to Marxism. He escaped (1933) to Denmark, then (1940–41) via Sweden, Finland and the U.S.S.R. to California; he acquitted himself skilfully before the Committee for Un-American Activities in 1947, and then returned to Europe (Zürich). He settled in East Berlin in autumn 1949, when the Berliner Ensemble was founded, but in 1950 took Austrian nationality. In June 1953 the East German Workers' Revolt affected him deeply, but his Marxist faith remained intact; he received the Stalin Peace Prize in 1954.

Though essentially a poet, Brecht became famous as a playwright. His dramatic work of the early, quasi-Expressionistic period (pre-1928) consists of *Baal* (1922), *Trommeln in der Nacht* (1922), *Im Dickicht der Städte* (1924; tr. E. Bentley, *In the Swamp* in *Seven Plays*, N.Y., 1961), and *Mann ist Mann* (1927; tr. E. Bentley, *A Man's a Man* in *Seven Plays*, N.Y., 1961). Typical of their period, they are socially anarchical (non-Marxist), experimental in form, violent in imagery, and in a style reflecting diverse influences: Luther, Villon, Rimbaud, Kipling, folk proverbs, South German dialect, business jargon, etc.

Brecht embraced Marxism both out of political conviction and out of psychological need for discipline and commitment. From the late 1920s also dates his formulation of 'epic' theatre: a reaction against the traditional ('Aristotelian') theatre of illusion. By means of numerous 'distancing' devices (*Verfremdungseffekte*) the spectator is continually reminded that he is only watching a play; instead of becoming emotionally involved in the stage action, he should remain a dispassionate observer and judge. Brecht's aim then was to teach men to think, to shake or enrage them into revolutionary action against social injustice.

Although elements of epic theatre occur in all Brecht's plays, his poetic spontaneity inevitably carried him beyond the didactic limits of the (1930) 'Lehrstücke' with their doctrinal solutions, of *Die heilige Johanna der Schlachthöfe* (1929–30; tr. F. Jones, *St Joan of the Stockyards*, 1956), attacking capitalism with parodies of Schiller and Goethe, and of the anti-Nazi plays *Der aufhaltsame Aufstieg des Arturo Ui* (1941) and *Furcht und Elend des Dritten Reiches* (1935–8; tr. E. Bentley, *The Private Life of the Master Race*, 1944). He was even dismayed to hear how much he had won the Zürich première (1941) audience's sympathy for the unintentionally moving 'heroine' of his outstanding play *Mutter Courage* (written, 1939, published, 1949; tr. E. Bentley, *Mother Courage*, 1941) who should have 'illustrated' that wartime courage and causes are the phoney values of a corrupt class-system, but in fact embodies something of man's timeless (and classless) heroism. Again, the ideological issues raised by Galileo's dilemma (*Leben des Galilei*, 1938, published, 1955; tr. E. Bentley, *The Life of Galileo* in *Seven Plays*, N.Y., 1961) between private enterprise and totalitarian protection are not the point but only the setting of this truly tragic study of weakness and integrity. And it is a girl's love for a child and a prostitute's selfless goodness which inspire the dramatic and often lyrical vitality beneath the ironies of his other two outstanding plays: *Der kaukasische Kreidekreis* (1949; tr. E. Bentley, *The Caucasian Chalk Circle*, 1961) and *Der gute Mensch von Sezuan* (1938, published, 1953; tr. E. Bentley, *The Good Woman of Sezuan*, 1961). In *Herr Puntila und sein Knecht Matti* (1940–41; tr. G. Nellhaus and R. Grenier, *Mr Puntila and his Hired Man Matti*, 1954) the social message is eclipsed by numerous character-drawings. Brecht's dramatic and aesthetic theories (see *Schriften zum Theater*, 1957; partly tr. J. Willett, *Brecht on the Theatre*, 1963) were in fact modified considerably, especially in the 'Kleines Organon für das Theater' (1949).

A major poet, two of his sayings 'The truth is concrete' and 'The only truth is in the imagination', express a typical tension in his work, between the public and the private, the political and the lyrical, the rational and the emotional. He was influenced by Arthur Waley's translations from the Chinese and Japanese, by modern music – he worked with Kurt Weill on *Die Dreigroschenoper* (1929; tr. D. I. Vesey and E. Bentley, *The Threepenny Opera*, 1955), on *Aufstieg und Fall der Stadt Mahagonny* (1930; tr. G. Stern, *Rise and Fall of the City of Mahagonny*, 1956), and on *Die sieben Todsünden der Kleinbürger* (1933; tr. W. H. Auden and C. Kallmann, *The Seven Deadly Sins of the Petty Bourgeois*, performed 1959) and with Paul Dessau on the operatic version of his play *Die Verurteilung des Lukullus* (1941) – and particularly by the *Überbrettl* song. His own youthful guitar performances, gratingly tough yet emotionally powerful, are legendary. [PB]

*Plays I* (1961); *Plays II* (1963); *Selected Poems*, tr. H. R. Hays (1962); *Poems on the Theatre*, tr. J. Berger and A. Bostock (1961).

M. Esslin, *B., a Choice of Evils* (1959); J. Willett, *The Theatre of B.B.* (1959); M. Kesting, *B.B.* (Hamburg, 1959); R. Gray, *B.* (1961); P. Demetz, ed., *B.* (1961).

**Bredero, Gerbrand Adriaensz** (Amsterdam 1585–Amsterdam 1618). Dutch poet and playwright. The son of a shoemaker with a considerable talent as a painter, his world has the medieval severity of Jan Steen, though his intellect leans towards the Renaissance. 'Things may change' was his motto. The duality of his heart and mind (erotic temperament and unsophisticated loyalties *v.* Calvinistic allegiance and modern aspirations) contributes to the turbulent and ruthlessly honest love lyrics and devotional verse of the *Amoureus, boertigh en aendachtig liedboeck*. The versatile mastery of Renaissance form in many of these songs and sonnets is the more remarkable, coming from a man who confessed to a stubborn penchant for the past. His farces, the best of which are *Klucht van de Koe* (1612) and *Klucht van den Molenaar* (1613), are masterpieces of this medieval genre. He wrote two 5-act comedies. *Het Moortje* (1615), his free rendering of Terence's *Eunuchus*, does not quite succeed in disguising its hybrid relationship to Rome and Amsterdam. But in his *Spaanschen Brabander* (1618; tr. in preparation), a tragi-comedy similar in structure to a satirical review, he transposes with great humanity and wit the theme of the picaresque novel (⇨ *Lazarillo de Tormes*) to Amsterdam, where it pulsates anew with the jostling energy of a city suddenly flooded with the prosperity and corruption of new nationhood. Though a member of 'De Englantier' (cf. ⇨ Rederijkers) and Coster's Academy Bredero's true environment is the back streets of the capital. [PK]

*Werken*, ed. J. ten Brink *et al.* (3 vols., 1890); Barnouw, *CA*; Weevers, *PNEC*.

J. ten Brink, *G.A.B., Historisch-aesthetische studie* (3 vols., Amsterdam, 1888).

**Bregendahl, Marie** (Fly 1867–Copenhagen 1940). Danish novelist and short-story writer. At one time married to Jeppe ⇨ Aakjær. Famous for *En Dødsnat* (tr. M. Blanchard, *A Night of Death*, 1931). Her novels describe the people and scenery of Jutland with authentic realism, e.g. in *Billeder of Sødalsfolkenes Liv* (7 vols., 1914–23). [ELB]

P. Hesselaa, *M.B.* (Copenhagen, 1939).

**Breitinger, Johann Jakob** (Zürich 1701–Zürich 1776). Swiss critic. Taught ancient languages and edited with his friend ⇨ Bodmer *Discourse der Mahlern* (1721ff.), a moral weekly imitating Addison's *Spectator*. In *Critische Abhandlungen von der Natur, den Absichten und dem Gebrauch der Gleichnisse* (1740), and more notably in *Critische Dichtkunst* (1740), a tentative, empirical theory of literature, he rejects ⇨ Gottsched's admiration of French Classicism, praises Homer and Milton, advocates the observation of 'nature', and prefers imaginative and miraculous elements to rationalism in poetry. He helped shape ⇨ Klopstock's work. [LL]

*Critische Abhandlungen* (repr. Metzler, Stuttgart, 1967).

H. Schöffler, *Das literarische Zürich 1700 bis 1750* (Leipzig, 1925); J. W. Eaton, *Bodmer and B. and European Literary Theory* (1941).

**Bremer, Fredrika** (Åbo 1801–Årsta 1865). Swedish novelist and travel-writer. Once internationally famous for her novels *Grannarne* (1837; tr. M. Howitt, *The Neighbours*, 1842) and *Hemmet* (1839; tr. M. Howitt, *The Home*, 1843), she is now chiefly remembered as a pioneer for women's rights. Her novels, not dissimilar to those of Charlotte Brontë, are in part still very readable, although the author's romantic inclinations remain unreconciled to her achievement as a realistic writer. Of particular interest to English and American readers are *England om hösten 1851* (tr. L. A. H. Boulogne, *England in 1851*, 1853) and *Hemmen i den nya världen* (1853–4; tr. M. Howitt, *The Homes of the New World: Impressions of America*, N.Y., 1854). In London she visited the Exhibition, but her interest ranged much more widely; in particular she studied social work and charity institutions. She returned to Sweden a more confirmed liberal. Her own ideology she described as 'Christian socialism'. In an even more practical spirit she wrote *Hertha* (1856; tr. M. Howitt, 1856), a highly tendentious novel claiming equal rights for women. In spite of its artistic imperfection, it caused a storm of protest in its day. Her travelogues, *Livet i den gamla världen* (1860–2; tr. M. Howitt, *Two Years* *in Switzerland and Italy* and *Travels in the Holy Land*, 1861 and 1862), have kept their charm and freshness as an artless expression of the warm and lively personality of their author and as evidence of her considerable powers of observation and her intellectual capacity. *Fredrika Bremers brev* (letters) were published in 4 volumes (1915–20). [SAB]

S. Adlersparre and S. Leijonhufvud, *F.B.* (Stockholm, 1896); C. Cederblad, *F.B.* (Stockholm, 1945); G. Axberger, *Jaget och skuggorna* (Stockholm, 1951); S. A. Rooth, *Seeress of the Northland: Fredrika Bremer's American Journey 1849–51* (Philadelphia, 1955).

**Bremond, Henri** (Aix-en-Provence 1865–Arthez d'Asson 1933). French literary historian and critic. A Jesuit priest, he examined the religious content in literature. Although ultimately concerned with general trends, his method was to proceed from the study of individuals, with *Newman* (1905; tr. H. C. Corrance, *The Mystery of Newman*, 1907) and studies on, for instance, Pascal and George Eliot in *L'inquiétude religieuse* (1909); a novitiate spent in England had given him a profound knowledge of English life and letters. His unfinished *Histoire littéraire du sentiment religieux en France* (1916–36; tr. K. L. Montgomery, *A Literary History of Religious Thought in France*, 1928–36) is an extension of the same method, linking analyses of particular individuals with considerations of influence and historical parallels. More sympathetically inclined towards the mystical than towards the orthodox or rational, e.g. in *Apologie pour Fénelon* (1910), he defended Romanticism in *Pour le Romantisme* (1924), seeing a mystical impulse at the heart of Romantic inspiration, an idea developed in *Prière et poésie* (1926; tr. A. Thorold, *Prayer and Poetry*, 1927). Elected to the Académie Française in 1923. [IHW]

A. Autin, *H.B.* (1946); M. Martin du Gard, *Les Mémorables* (Paris, 1957); H. W. Decker, *Pure Poetry 1925–30* (1962).

**Brenner, Joseph Hayyim** (Novi Malini, Bulgaria, 1881–Jaffa 1921). Hebrew novelist. He came from the ghetto, studied in Yeshivah and privately in high school, enlisted and served in the Russian army but at the outbreak of the Japanese war in 1905 escaped to London where he lived in abject poverty editing the Hebrew periodical, *Hamoeorer* ('The Awakener'). Like most of his contemporaries he was attracted to Socialism and for a time became an adherent of the *Bund* (the Jewish Socialist movement). Soon, however, he found that he could not reconcile his deep-rooted Jewishness and love for the Hebrew language with the extreme tendencies of the movement and be became a Zionist. In 1908 he settled in Palestine where he became leader of the pioneer groups and a founder of the *Histadruth* (General Confederation of Labour). Having seen the beginning of the realization of Zionist dreams he was killed in the Arab riots of 1921. The stormy life he led is reflected in his writing which is chaotic, turbulent, yet full of compassion for his heroes. His novels are full of often irrelevant detail, rather a series of episodes than a coherent narrative; still they show a deep understanding of the varied situations of life. The novels portray life as he saw it in Russia and the London ghetto and later the struggles of early Jewish settlement in Palestine. His short stories (collected ed. 1898) are rooted in the poverty, misery and darkness of the ghetto. [EE]

*Kol kitve J.H.B.* (Tel Aviv, 1953ff.); *Ba-Choref; Me-Saviv le-nekudah; Me-ever le-Gevulin; Mikan Umikan; Ben Mayim le-Mayim; Shekol ve-Kisharon* (N.Y., 1920); *Min ha-Metzar* (short stories).

D. A. Friedman, *J.H.B.* (Berlin, 1923).

**Brennu-Njáls Saga.** ⇨ Icelandic Sagas.

**Brentano, Clemens** (Ehrenbreitstein 1778–Aschaffenburg 1842). German poet, novelist and dramatist. Brother of Bettina von ⇨ Arnim. While a student at Heidelberg, he founded with Arnim, Görres and others, the school of Romantic writers which devoted itself to the study of folklore and the cultural treasures of the German past. The Romantic doctrine of unfettered self-expression had a particularly destructive effect on him; the unsettled, irresponsible early life to which these seductive Romantic theories had lured him gave way later to a Catholicism of intense asceticism, and he spent six years in a monastery.

His name is inseparably linked with that of his brother-in-law Achim von ⇨ Arnim through the famous collection of German folk-poems, *Des Knaben Wunderhorn* (1805–8). His original literary productions are unequal. From his own idealized vision of the past, and in the tradition of the Romantic interest in cultural history, comes the drama *Die Gründung Prags* (1815), a highly coloured presentation of the legendary founding of the Bohemian capital by Libussa (cf. the drama of this name by ⇨ Grillparzer). His novel *Godwi* (1801) stands in the tradition of extravagant but unsuccessful Romantic essays in this genre. His most effective works, however, like those of many Romantic writers, are his shorter prose narratives – *Märchen* (fairy-tales) like *Gockel, Hinkel und Gackeleia* (1838) and short stories like *Die Geschichte vom braven Kasperl und dem schönen Annerl* (1817), which is one of the most perfect of all Romantic tales. [RT]

W. Hoffmann, *C.B.* (Bern, 1966); I. Seidel, *B.* (Stuttgart, 1944); Gundolf, *R*; Staiger, *ZE*; Tymms, *GRL*.

**Breton, André** (Tinchebray, France 1896–Paris 1966). French poet. One of the founders of the ⇨ Surrealist movement, he became its tireless spokesman, and his *Manifeste du surréalisme* (1924) outlines some basic tenets, proposing automatic writing as a means of furthering Freud's exploration of the unconscious. The two later manifestos (1930, 1942) define Surrealism more closely in the light of its evolution. Most of his theoretical essays have been collected in *Les pas perdus* (1924), *Point du jour* (1934) and *La clé des champs* (1953); his conception of art is expounded in *Le surréalisme et la peinture* (1928). His more personal writings show Surrealism in practice by careful survey of his own experiences. His best-known book is *Nadja* (1928; tr. N.Y., 1963), a poignant journal of his encounters with a strange woman in Paris, in which the supranormal and the everyday are intermingled. *Les vases communicants* (1932) and *L'amour fou* (1937) illuminate the close connexion between dream and reality, between subjective and objective events. Written in reaction to the war, *Arcane 17* (1945) reveals a nostalgia for the traditions of occultism and stresses the cult of Woman, the vehicle of man's regeneration. Breton never hesitated to defend his conception of love: unique, mad and divinatory. His *Poèmes* (1948), containing the disquieting juxtapositions and occasional felicities of the automatic method, have less an aesthetic than a documentary value. He is indeed more a poet in his prose writings, and most of all in his exemplary poetic attitude, one of uncompromising loyalty to Surrealism in its quest for revelation and liberty. [RTC]

*Poésie et autre* (1960).
C. Mauriac, *A.B.* (Paris, 1949); J. L. Bédouin, *A.B.* (Paris, 1950); M. Carrouges, *A.B. et les donneés fondamentales du surréalisme* (Paris, 1950).

**Bretón de los Herreros, Manuel** (Quel Logroño 1796–Madrid 1873). Spanish dramatist. Imitator of ⇨ Moratín. His well-turned, uncontroversial comedies survived the competition of romantic drama, which he occasionally parodied. Mainly about middle-class manners, his 150 plays are faintly satirical, repetitive, and in neat, unpretentious verse. Typical are *Marcela, o ¿a cuál de los tres?* (1831), about a young lady who scorns her three suitors; *Muérete ¡y verás!* (1837), in which a man pretends to be his own ghost; and *El pelo de la dehesa* (1840), in which a rich, good-hearted bumpkin from Aragón shows up the greed and frivolity of fashionable Madrid society. *Elena* (1834) may be a serious attempt at romantic drama but reads like a parody. [DR]

*Teatro* (CC, 1928).
G. Le Gentil, *Le poète M.B. de los H. et la société espagnole de 1830 à 1860* (Paris, 1909).

**Breton Literature.** The Breton language, closely related to Welsh and Cornish, was brought to Gaul by British emigrants in the 5th and 6th centuries. It is still spoken by about one million people in the Western half of the Breton peninsula. The history of Breton divides into three periods: Old Breton (to 12th century), Middle Breton (12th–17th centuries), Modern Breton. The only extant documents of Old Breton are proper names, a large number of glosses, and recently discovered fragments of medical and astronomical treatises. The documents of Early Middle Breton (12th–14th centuries) are even more meagre. The existence of a flourishing literature during these two periods is indirectly attested by the preservation until the 17th century of a complicated system of versification, which indicated an unbroken poetical tradition, and by the presence of Breton influences in European literature, especially French and English. Brittany played a great part in the diffusion of the Arthurian legend, the 'matière de Bretaigne', and Breton lais have been translated or imitated by Chaucer and by Marie de France (the Middle English poem *Sir Orpheo* is also said to be an adaptation from Breton). Most of this literature remained probably unwritten; any manuscripts have perished.

The collapse of the Breton monarchy under Norman attacks in the 10th century and its replacement by a 'Duchy' open to French and Anglo-Norman influences, brought about the decline of Breton as an administrative and literary language, and by the late Middle Ages it had become a rural vernacular with little original literature. Except for some light-hearted fragments interspersed in a Latin manuscript by a young scholar about 1350, the oldest literary work extant dates from 1450; it is a poem – of scant literary value – entitled *An dialog etre Arzur ha Guynglaff* ('The Dialogue of Arthur and Guynglaff') – the latter being identified with Merlin in Breton popular tradition. A long miracle play *Buez Santes Nonn hac he map Deuy* ('The Life of St Nonn and her Son Deuy') was completed towards the end of the 15th century; its main interest lies in its showing the preservation of the traditions of the mother country after nearly ten centuries of separation. The printing press was introduced in Brittany as early as 1484 and most 16th-century works are known in printed form. With few exceptions, the literature of this period is religious – miracle plays: *An Passion hac an Resurrection* ('Passion and Resurrection of our Lord'), *Buhez Santes Barba* ('The Life of St Barbara'), *Buhez Sant Gwenole* ('The Life of St Gwenole'); long poems: *Buhez Mabden* ('The Life of Man'), *Tremenuan an ytron Maria* ('The Agony of Our Lady'), *Pemzec leuenez Maria* ('The Fifteen Joys of Mary'), *Le Mirouer de la Mort* (French title; 'The Mirror of Death'); collection of hymns, devotional books in prose *Buez an itron Sanctes Cathell* ('The Life of St Catherine'). Of another miracle, *The Destruction of Jerusalem* (Breton title not preserved), and of a comedy, *Amouroustet eun den coz* ('The Old Man in Love'), only fragments have survived. Most of these works are anonymous. Their literary value is not great; most of them are translated or adapted from French or Latin, and their importance lies mainly in their prosody, which uses an intricate system of alliterations and internal rhymes, akin to the Welsh *cynghanedd*. These poems and plays were certainly the work of learned clerics, heirs to a poetical tradition going back to the period of Brittonic unity. This tradition became gradually extinct in the Early Modern Breton period, when most works were written by half-educated peasants and craftsmen; the old versification was abandoned, although traces of it lingered until the 19th century, and the comparatively unified literary language gave place to dialects.

The literature of the 17th and 18th centuries is copious, but of no great interest, lacking the metrical craftsmanship which redeems somewhat the monotony of Middle Breton poems. Exceptions to the general mediocrity are the anonymous tragedy *Genouefa a Vrabant* ('Genevieve of Brabant', *c.* 1650), well composed and skilfully written (with internal rhymes), and the comic poems by C. M. Le Lae (1745–91) *Ar C'hi* ('The Dog') and *Mikeal Morin*; although adapted from French, these two pieces are full of verve and humour, indeed superior to their models. There are very few texts in prose, mainly devotional works translated from French; one should also mention *Ar farvel goapaer* ('The Bantering Clown'), a comedy by Pascal Kerenveier (*c.* 1750), not very original but quite amusing.

The 19th century marks a renascence of Breton literature under two influences: the impact of Romanticism and the renewal of relations with Wales (a Breton delegation attended the Eisteddfod at Abergavenny in 1838). J. M. F. Le Gonidec (1775–1838), grammarian and lexicographer, undertook the creation of a literary language with a rational spelling, a unified grammar, and a vocabulary purged of needless French borrowings. His translation of the Bible (1827) is the first work in the standard language. His most gifted disciple, Théodore Hersart de la Villemarqué (1815–95) published in 1839 *Barzaz Breiz*, a volume of ballads and songs purported to have been collected among the Breton peasants. The book met with tremendous success and was partially translated into several languages (Tom Taylor, *Ballads and Songs of Brittany*, London, 1865; Carrington Bolton, *Breton Ballads Translated from the Barzaz Breiz*, Edinburgh, 1886). The style of these poems is remarkably concise and refined, and often reminiscent of early Welsh poetry; some of them deal with remote historical events and even with Celtic mythology. *Barzaz Breiz* was soon hotly attacked by critics who pointed out how different it was, both in style and content, from folk-songs found by other collectors, and accused La Villemarqué of forgery. It is now generally accepted that the ballads purporting to be of great antiquity (in spite of their quite modern language) are entirely made up, while the others, authentic in source, are 'touched up' to a greater or lesser extent. But *Barzaz Breiz* had great influence in two directions: by stimulating the study of folk literature and by contributing to the revival of national feelings, both in politics and in literature. The greatest name in folkloric research is F. Luzel (1821–95), who between 1868 and 1890 published four large volumes of ballads and songs and three of folk-tales.

In literature proper, one may mention the poets Auguste Brizeux (1803–58), better known for his French works, Prosper Proux (1811–75), hearty and often bawdy, and Joachim Guillôme (1797–1857), author of *Livr er Labourér* ('The Book of the Labourer'), the 'Breton Georgics'. The literature in prose remains largely dependent on folklore, but there are a few more original works, like the historical novel *Emgann Kergidu* ('The Battle of Kergidu'), by Lan Inisan (1826–91). The theatre – still mainly religious – is flourishing but remains almost entirely folkloric.

The literature of the early 20th century presents the same general features, but Welsh influence increases with the foundation in 1901 of the Gorsedd of Brittany, on the pattern and with the help of the Welsh Gorsedd. Among the numerous but very unequal authors of that period are Erwan Berthou 'Kaledvoulc'h' (1861–1933), author of the patriotic poems *Dre an delenn hag ar c'horn-boud* ('Through the Harp and the War-Horn'), Fransez Jaffrennou 'Taldir' (1879–1956), poet *An hirvoudou* ('The Sighs'), *An delenn dir* ('The Harp of Steel'), journalist and polemist, and Erwan ar Moal 'Dir na dor' (1874–1957), author of many stories and plays. But the only two really great authors of that period had no connexion with the Gorsedd. J. P. Kalloc'h (1888–1917), killed in the First World War, left a volume of verse, *Ar en deulin* ('On my Knees'), marked with a Christian and virile sadness which in some poems ('The Vision', 'Come, Holy Ghost') attains apocalyptic grandeur. Tangi Malemanche (1875–1953) is a playwright in prose and verse; *Gurvan, ar marc'heg estrañjour* ('Gurvan, the Strange Knight') is rightly regarded as his best work and probably the greatest masterpiece of Breton literature. He allies ruthless realism with a keen conscience of a spiritual reality behind the material appearances.

In the first two decades of the century F. Vallée (1860–1949) and Meven Mordiern (1878–1949) completed the task of philological unification and epuration begun by Le Gonidec, thus preparing the ground for a truly national literature. In 1925 the first literary review in Breton, *Gwalarn* ('North-West'), was established by a few young writers, the most promising of whom was Roparz Hemon (1900– ). Its aim was to break away from folklore and give Brittany a real literature, written by and for educated people determined to turn away from parochialism and French influence and to open windows on the outside world – this at the same time as the political movement was abandoning regionalism for nationalism. Nearly all important works published between 1925 and 1944 appeared either in *Gwalarn* or under its auspices, and Roparz Hemon contributed a large part of them. In his short stories *Kleier eured* and novels *Ar c'hoar henañ* and *Ar vugale fall* he describes with a mixture of pity and irony the life of the working people and petty bourgeoisie of Brest, his native town – a new development in a literature hitherto purely rural. But country life remains also a source of inspiration to many writers: the short stories of Jakez Riou (1899–1937) and the novels of Youenn Drezen (1899– ) – the former gentle and somewhat melancholy, the latter raw and truculent – have become classics. Themes undreamed of by the old writers have been treated: love in its most carnal as well as its purest aspect in *Sizhun ar Breur Arturo* by Y. Drezen; the ordeal of soldiers in the 1914–18 trenches in *Dremm an Ankou* ('The Face of Death', stories by Abeozen, 1896–1963), and even 'the shape of things to come' in *Enez ar Rod* ('The Island of the Wheel', by Xavier de Langlais, 1906– ). Poetry has also renewed itself, seeking inspiration in the legendary past of the Celts expressed in the Welsh and Irish epics, and rejuvenating Middle Breton prosody. Three poets are especially noteworthy. Roparz Hemon seeks in the old epics of Ireland an echo to an almost Byronic pessimism, expressed with a great wealth of rhythms and vocabulary in several long poems ('The pilgrim of the sea', 'The murder of Aife's only son', etc.). Maodez Glanndour (1909– ) is a religious poet like Kalloc'h, but in a much more serene way; his masterpiece is the long poem 'Imram'. G. B. Kerverziou (1908–51) in 'Epona' and 'Manos and Bena' found his inspiration in Celtic mythology and sought its metaphysical meaning. The theatre has also freed itself from folklore and broadened its outlook. Short dramas (clearly influenced by the Anglo-Irish school) have been written by Roparz Hemon, the woman writer F. R. Meavenn (1911– ) and others, but in a class by itself we must mention the pseudo-historical nine-act play *Nomenoe-oe!* by Jakez Riou, an extraordinary mixture of wild parody and deep poetry.

The Breton intellectual movement suffered a great setback during and after the Second World War, when many writers were killed, imprisoned or forced into exile. It has now recovered, in spite of ever-increasing material difficulties and of the governmental ban on the use of Breton in schools of all levels. Roparz Hemon, now living in Ireland, is still the dominant figure, but younger writers are gradually asserting themselves. Per Denez (1921– ) is a gifted poet and story-writer, unfortunately too sparing, Goulven Pennaod (1928– ) fought in the Vietnamese war and made his experience the subject of powerful stories and poems. Youenn Olier (1923– ), literary critic and novelist, Ronan Huon (1922– ), poet, Abanna (1928– ), poet and philosophical writer, etc., are also members of the new team. Jarl Priel (1885–1965), who in his later years turned to Breton literature, made a name for himself with a number of plays (*Tri devezhour evit an eost*), some maritime novels (*An teirgwern 'Pembroke'*), and a most interesting autobiography. Another stream of literature, nearer to popular tradition, is represented by Yeun ar Go (1897–1965), P. J. Helias (1914– ) and a few others. [JRFP]

T. Jones, 'Breton Literature', *Chambers' Encyclopædia*; H. Lewis, 'Breton Literature', *Encyclopædia Britannica*; J. Delalande, 'Littérature bretonne', *Encyclopédie de la Pléiade*, iii (Paris, 1958); F. Gourvil, *Langue et littérature bretonnes* (Paris, 1952); L. Herrieu, *La littérature bretonne* (Hennebont, 1942); J. Loth, *Chrestomathie bretonne* (Paris, 1890).

**Březina, Otokar,** pseud. of Václav Ignác Jebavý (Počátky 1868–Jaroměřice 1929). Czech poet. A schoolteacher, he wrote 5 books of poetry and one of philosophical essays. He never married and lived as a recluse in a small country town. It was his ambition to evolve a complete philosophical and artistic system, and the individual books, which connect with each other, interpret the gradation of spiritual life, from individual despair to salvation in the eternal brotherhood of all creation. He was inspired by Indian sacred writings, Christian mystics, occult works, Baudelaire, Schopenhauer, and modern scientific theories. In his *Tajemné dálky* (1895), *Svítání na západě* (1896), *Větry od pólů* (1897), *Stavitelé chrámu* (1899) and *Ruce* (1901) his abstract notions and visions are concretely expressed in rich poetic language, splendid metaphors and musical verse. He is the most typically symbolist and at the same time the most intellectual modern Czech poet. [KB]

P. Selver, *O.B. A Study in Czech Literature* (1921); O. Králík, *O.B.* (Prague, 1948).

**Brezovački, Tito** (Zagreb 1757–Zagreb 1805). Croatian dramatist and priest. He wrote in the Kajkavic dialect. His plays are mainly either religious or moral satires, the most outstanding being *Matija Grabancijaš djak* (1804) and *Diogeneš* (1804–5), both of which are still performed. [EDG]

Barac, *HYL.*

**Brieux, Eugène** (Paris 1858–Nice 1932). French dramatist. He was passionately concerned with social problems – and grossly overvalued by Shaw. A sentimental *Blanchette* (1892) details the perils of a country girl educated above her station, while *Les trois filles de M. Dupont* (1897; tr. St John Hankin, *The Three Daughters of M. Dupont*, in *Three Plays by B.*, 1911) exposes the dark underside of arranged marriages, sometimes in scenes of genuine edge and passion. He roused the public with *La robe rouge* (1900; tr. B. Miall, *The Red Robe*, 1916), an attack on the abuses of the judiciary, and scandalized them with two sensational plays on sexual problems: *Les Avariés* (1901; *Damaged Goods*, in *Three Plays*) which deals with the ravages of syphilis, and *Maternité* (1903; *Maternity*, in *Three Plays*), a plea for birth-control. [SBJ]

*Théâtre complet* (9 vols., 1921–30).

W. H. Scheifley, *B. and Contemporary French Society* (1917).

**Britting, Georg** (Regensburg 1891–1964). German poet and short-story writer. Well known in Germany for his collections of tales *Michael und das Fräulein* (1927), *Der bekränzte Weiher* (1937) and *Der Schneckenweg* (1941), their descriptive and often fairy-tale qualities remain somewhat provincial. He was an outstanding nature poet whose characteristic theme is the changing seasons and whose best work (*Der irdische Tag*, 1935; *Die Begegnung*, 1947; and *Unter hohen Bäumen*, 1951) shows fine, terse craftsmanship.

*Gesamtausgabe* (6 vols., 1957–61); Bridgwater, *TCGV*.

D. Bode, *G.B. Geschichte seines Werkes* (Stuttgart, 1962); D. Schug, *Die Naturlyrik G.B.s* (Erlangen–Nürnberg, 1963).

**Broch, Hermann** (Vienna 1886–New Haven, U.S.A. 1951). Austrian novelist and poet. In 1927 he gave up management of his father's textile concern to study mathematics, philosophy and psychology at Vienna University, then lived as a writer. After brief Nazi arrest (1938), intervention by foreign friends – including James Joyce – enabled him to emigrate to the U.S.A., where he received (amongst other grants) a Rockefeller Fellowship for philosophical and psychological research at Princeton and an Honorary Fellowship at Yale. Little known in England, and still underrated in Germany, Broch is a major writer, and one of the creators of the modern novel.

His important novels are *Die Schlafwandler* (3 vols., 1931–2; tr. W. and E. Muir, *The Sleepwalkers*, 1932), *Der Tod des Vergil* (1945; tr. J. Starr Untermeyer, *The Death of Vergil*, 1946), and *Die Schuldlosen* (1950). All three are what he himself called 'polyhistoric' ('polymath', 'epistemological') novels, and use a variety of technical devices to express his belief that art 'has social significance but at a metaphysical level' i.e. it makes men realize the metaphysical dimensions of experience (the self, God, death, etc.) without which society is doomed. Thus his characters have to come to terms with the irrational, most unforgettably in his masterpiece on Virgil, a visionary prose poem in which reality is mystically illumined in the 'timeless' moment before death. This work represents 'the only advance beyond Joyce in the matter of technical form' (*TLS*, 19 April 1963).

Apart from the novels *Die unbekannte Grösse* (1933; tr. W. and E. Muir, *The Unknown Quantity*, 1935) and *Der Versucher* (1953), Broch's other work includes a drama, *Die Entsühnung* (1934); short stories; critical essays; a volume of profoundly abstract poems; and the fragmentary *Massenpsychologie* (1959), part of an ambitious theoretical work on mass-hysteria. [PB]

*Gesammelte Werke* (10 vols., 1952–61).

*Dichter wider Willen, Einführung in das Werk von H.B.* (Zürich, 1958); E. Kahler, *Die Philosophie von H.B.* (Tübingen, 1962); T. Ziolkowski, *H.B.* (N.Y. and London, 1964); M. Durzak, *H.B.* (Reinbek, 1966); D. C. Cohn, *The Sleepwalkers* (Stanford, 1967); M. Durzak, *H.B.* (Stuttgart, 1967); *Philobiblon*, VI (1962) (bibliography).

**Brockes, Barthold Heinrich** (Hamburg 1680–Ritzebüttel 1747). German poet. The son of a wealthy patrician family, he travelled widely before settling down as a merchant in his home town. His monumental *Irdisches Vergnügen in Gott*, a poetic theodicy in 9 volumes (1721–48), was one of the most popular and influential literary expressions of the early Enlightenment. Schooled in the nature poetry of Thomson and Pope (whom he translated) and gifted with considerable powers of observation and description, Brockes is one of the first German poets of modern times for whom nature is more than a conventional backcloth, and his descriptive nature poetry heralds the awakening of a new feeling for nature and initiated a vogue which culminated in the poetry of Ew. v. ⇨ Kleist and ⇨ Haller. In his desire to demonstrate that this is the best of all possible worlds he frequently lapses into a flat-footed philistinism, which is redeemed only by its involuntary humour – even ravening wolves prove that God is good, since their pelts can keep us warm in the winter! [WAC]

*Werke*, ed. L. Fulda (DNL 39, 1884); *Auswahl*, ed. R. v. Delius (1920).

A. Brandl, *B.H.B.* (Innsbruck, 1878); H. W. Pfund, *Studien zu Wort und Stil bei B.H.B.* (Lancaster, 1935).

**Brod, Max** (Prague 1884–Tel-Aviv 1968). Austrian-German novelist, critic, philosopher. Friend and editor of ⇨ Kafka. A Zionist, he went to Israel in 1939, becoming literary director of the Habimah Theatre, Tel Aviv. His religious-philosophic fiction includes a Renaissance trilogy, *Ein Kampf um Wahrheit* (*Tycho Brahes Weg zu Gott*, 1916, tr. F. W. Crosse, *The Redemption of*

*Tycho Brahe*, 1928; *Reubeni, Fürst der Juden*, 1925, tr. H. Waller, *Reubeni, Prince of the Jews*, 1929; *Galilei in Gefangenschaft*, 1948), an anti-nihilist novel about Christ, *Der Meister* (1952; tr. H. Norden, *The Master*, 1951), and *Armer Cicero* (1955). He blends fiction and memoir in his novels about Kafka (*Zauberreich der Liebe*, 1928; tr. E. Sutton, *The Kingdom of Love*, 1930) and ⇨ Hofmannsthal (*Mira*, 1958). Other novels evoke Austrian high society (*Die Frau, nach der man sich sehnt*, 1927; tr. J. W. Hartmann, *Three Loves*, 1930) and the Prague of Brod's youth (*Beinahe ein Vorzugsschüler*, 1952; *Der Sommer, den man zurückwünscht*, 1952; *Rebellische Herzen*, 1952; *Jugend im Nebel*, 1959). *Streitbares Leben* (1960) is straight autobiography. His critical works include *Heinrich Heine* (1934; tr. J. Witriol, *Heinrich Heine, The Artist in Revolt*, 1956) and *Franz Kafka, eine Biographie* (1937; revised 1954, tr. G. H. Roberts, *The Biography of Franz Kafka*, 1947). He wrote a number of plays (e.g. *Abschied von der Jugend*, 1921; *Die Retterin*, 1917; *Der Fälscher*, 1920; *Lord Byron kommt aus der Mode*, 1929) and dramatized Kafka's *Das Schloss* (1953) and *Amerika* (1957). His theoretical works include *Heidentum, Christentum, Judentum* (1921), *Diesseits und Jenseits* (1946–7), *Das Diesseitswunder* (1949).

*Festschrift, Ein Kampf um Wahrheit* (1949) (bibliography).

**Bródy, Sándor** (Eger 1863–Budapest 1924). Hungarian writer. Although he called himself a 'naturalist', his way of expression is extremely varied, as are the subjects of his works. He used a flavoured, often old Hungarian language, but mixed it with Budapest colloquial. He often applied a mischievous, gossipy tone, which was much imitated by journalists. A journalist himself in his earlier years, in 1902 he started the periodical *White Book*, writing it himself. He produced mainly short stories, novels and plays. Major short stories: *Nyomor* ('Poverty', 1884); *Kaál Samu* (1897; tr. I. Farkas, *The Jest*, in *Hungarian Short Stories*, Budapest, 1962); novels: *A nap lovagja* (1902); *Rembrandt* (1925; tr. anon., N.Y., 1928); plays: *A dada* (1902); *A tanítónő* (1908). [JFR]

**Brorson, Hans Adolf** (Randerup 1694–Ribe 1764). Danish poet, and Bishop of Ribe. His religious poetry, influenced by Pietism, dwells mystically on the torments of Christ: *Troens rare Klenodie* (1739); *Svanesang* (posthumous 1765). [ELB]

*Samlede Skrifter* (3 vols., 1951–6).

L. J. Koch, *H.A.B.* (Copenhagen, 1932).

**Brunetière, Ferdinand.** ⇨ French Literary Criticism in the 19th and 20th Centuries.

**Bruni, Leonardo** (Arezzo *c.*1370–Florence 1444). Italian humanist and historian. Also known as Leonardo Aretino. Important in his education was the study of Greek, for in an age when the language was not widely known, he Latinized many works by Greek authors (e.g. Aristotle, Plato, Plutarch, Xenophon), drew on Polybius in his *Commentarii primi belli punici* (1421), on Xenophon's *Hellenica* in *Commentarii rerum graecarum* (1439) and on Procopius in *Commentarii de bello italico adversus Gothos gesto* (1441; tr. A. Goldyng, *The History of Leonard Aretine*, 1563). In 1405 he became a secretary to the Papal Curia, but after the Council of Constance he returned to Florence and held many public offices. From 1427 till his death he was Cancelliere of the republic.

Pride in Florence animates several of Bruni's writings, from the *Laudatio florentinae urbis* (*c.*1401) to the important second part of the *Dialogi ad Petrum Histrum* (1401–6) with its praise of Dante and Petrarch, and the *Historiae florentini populi* (begun *c.*1415; ed. E. Santini, 1914–16) which tells in 12 books the history of Florence from its foundation down to 1404, showing critical discrimination in selection of material. The *Rerum suo tempore in Italia gestarum commentarius* (1440; ed. C. di Pierro, 1926) is largely centred on his own observations in Rome and Florence.

He was notable also for his positive attitude to the vernacular, in which he wrote a Life of Dante (tr. P. H. Wicksteed, *The Early Lives of Dante*, 1904). Also extant are a number of speeches in both Latin and Italian and many letters (1405–44) which throw light on contemporary cultural life. [DGR]

*Humanistisch-philosophische Schriften*, ed. H. Baron (1928); Garin, *PLQ*; *Lettere*, ed. L. Mehus (1741).

H. Baron, *The Crisis of the Early Italian Renaissance* (Princeton, 1955), and *Humanistic and Political Literature in Florence and Venice* (Cambridge, Mass., 1955); B. L. Ullman, *Studies in the Italian Renaissance* (Rome, 1955); E. Garin, *Ialian Humanism* (tr. P. Munz, 1965); *Minori*, i.

**Bruno, Giordano** (Nola 1548–Rome 1600). Italian philosopher. He entered at 15 the monastery of S. Domenico at Naples, but in 1576 his intellectually rebellious temperament brought him into conflict with his superiors and he fled. Thus his rupture with the Church began, and much of the rest of his life was spent in wandering throughout Europe, publishing his Latin and Italian writings as he went. At Calvinist Geneva he again aroused opposition and passed on to Paris, where he published a comedy, *Il candelaio* (1582; tr. J. R. Hale in *The Genius of the Italian Theatre*, ed. E. Bentley, 1964), and London, where his most famous cosmological and ethical treatises in Italian appeared – *La cena de le ceneri*, *De la causa principio et uno*, *De l'infinito universo et mondi*, *Spaccio de la bestia trionfante* (all of 1584), and *De gl'heroici furori* (1585; tr. P. E. Memmo, 1964). In England, where he came into contact with Sidney and Greville, he made a considerable impact – and as usual, enemies. In 1585 he went back to Paris, made short stays in various German cities and finally, in 1591, he returned to Italy. Falling into the hands of the Inquisition at Venice in 1592, he was interrogated in Rome over a period of years, and when he refused to retract, he was burnt in 1600.

Conceiving in pantheistic terms an infinite universe informed by immanent, all-encompassing Mind, with which the human soul strives to achieve mystical union, Bruno regards uncritical acceptance of dogma and authority in any field as an invalid intellectual or cultural procedure. He is thus anti-Aristotelian in philosophy and anti-Petrarchan in literature. His importance and attractiveness lie not so much in any particular aspects of his teachings, such as his confused exposition of Copernican theory, as in his unswerving insistence on the freedom of the human mind and his belief that the quest for truth must be forward-looking not backward-looking. [DGR]

*Opera latine conscripta*, ed. F. Fiorentino *et al.* (1879–91); *Dialoghi italiani*, ed. G. Gentile (1958); *Candelaio*, ed. V. Spampanato (1923); *Cena de le ceneri*, ed. G. Aquilecchia (1955); *Opere di G.B. e di Tommaso Campanella*, ed. A. Guzzo and R. Amerio (1956).

G. Gentile, *G.B. e il pensiero del Rinascimento* (Florence, 1925); D. Singer, *G.B. His Life and Thought* (N.Y., 1950) (with an annotated translation of *The Infinite Universe of Worlds*); F. Yates, *G.B. and the Hermetic Tradition* (1964); *Minori*, ii.

**Bryusov, Valery Yakovlevich** (Moscow 1873–Moscow 1924). Russian poet, critic and novelist. With the publication of the three issues of his *Russkiye Simvolisty* (1894–5), containing imitations of and translations from the French ⇨ Symbolists by himself and other poets, Bryusov burst on to the literary scene. The critics of the day were outraged by these and by the exaggerations of his own verse in *Chefs d'œuvre* (1895) and *Me eum esse* (1897). His best work, written in a more restrained and personal style – a style which led ⇨ Bely to term him a 'poet of marble and bronze' – is found in the collections *Tertia Vigilia* (1900), *Urbi et Orbi* (1903) and *Stephanos* (1906), which greatly influenced the younger generation of Symbolists. A sco-founder in 1904 of the Moscow journal *Vesy* and its editor until it ceased publication in 1909, he played a major part in the popularization of Symbolism in Russia. His major prose works, the two novels *Ognennyy Angel* (1907–8) – on which Prokofiev based his opera *The Fiery Angel* – and *Altar' Pobedy* (1911–12) are set in 15th-century Germany and 4th-century Rome respectively.

From 1910 Bryusov was literary editor of the journal *Russkaya Mysl'* and worked mainly as a critic. After the Revolution he remained in Russia and in 1921 set up in Moscow the 'Higher Literary-Artistic Institute', becoming its first director. His later attempts to write 'scientific poetry' – *Dali* (1922), *Mea* (1924) – show distinct ⇨ Futurist influences; they are interesting, but on the whole unsuccessful.

He edited a number of Russian classical authors; he was especially attracted to Pushkin, whose work is dealt with in the posthumous volume of essays, *Moy Pushkin* (1929). He was also the author of a large number of translations, especially from the French – among them poems of Verlaine and Verhaeren (a poet with whom his own work has much in common) – and from the Armenian. [TJB]

*Stikhotvoreniya i poemy*, ed. Maksimov and Dikman (Leningrad, 1961)

D. E. Maksimov, *Poeziya V.B.* (1940); K. Mochul'sky, *V.B.* (Paris, 1962); G. Donchin, *The Influence of the French Symbolists on Russian Poetry* (The Hague, 1958); Poggioli, *PR.*

**Büchner, Georg** (Goddelau, Darmstadt 1813–Zürich 1837). German dramatist. A student of science and medicine, he threw himself into politics, publishing in 1834 a political pamphlet called *Der Hessische Landbote*, which attacked, under the class-warfare slogan 'Peace to the cottages, War on the palaces!', the tyranny in his native Hessen. He was in constant danger of imprisonment for his revolutionary activity, fled to Strasbourg and then to Zürich, where, within a few months of being appointed Privatdozent in Comparative Anatomy at the university, he died of typhus at 23. Most of these last few years were spent in the study of biology and medicine, which strengthened the materialistic beliefs which he had always held.

His literary reputation rests on 3 plays and a fragment of a short story. Of the former, the tragedy *Dantons Tod* (1835; opera by Gottfried von Einem, 1949) depicts the political and spiritual fall of a public figure whose fate is an ineluctable necessity, a product of what Büchner called 'the terrible fanaticism of history'. Against this heroic tragedy of the great man stands *Woyzeck* (1836), the pitiful tragedy of the small man, the helpless creature at the mercy of his masters, who, like his faithless mistress, see in him an object to be picked up as need or fancy moves, and cast aside when he is no longer wanted. *Woyzeck*, an unordered sequence of unfinished scenes, communicates a grotesque, pessimistic power; in Alban Berg's opera (1920) its intensity becomes almost unbearable. The third play is a comedy, *Leonce und Lena* (1836), whose Byronic hero suffers, like all Büchner's heroes, simply because he is part of life. Life is suffering; the only tenable philosophy is a pessimistic realism, a mute acceptance of the brutal facts of existence.

*Lenz* (1836) is a superb prose fragment in which Büchner described, with characteristic power and realism, the onset of the madness which befell the *Sturm und Drang* dramatist Reinhold Lenz, who personifies the type of the true poet. The words which he puts into the mouth of Lenz can stand as his own *credo*: 'From everything I demand Life, the possibility of Existence – then it is good. It is not our task to inquire whether it is ugly or beautiful.' [RT]

*Gesamtausgabe* (1958); *The Plays of G.B.*, tr. G. Dunlop (1952); *Lenz*, tr. M. Hamburger (1966).
A. H. J. Knight, *G.B.* (1951); C. Viëtor, *G.B. als Politiker* (Bern/Leipzig, 1939); H. Mayer, *G.B. und seine Zeit* (Wiesbaden, 1959); *G.B.*, ed. W. Martens (Darmstadt, 1965); Stern, *R.*

**Budé, Guillaume** (Paris 1467–Paris 1540). French humanist. After a somewhat riotous youth, at 24 he was seized with an insatiable thirst for learning and, thanks to his phenomenal memory, acquired an exceptional erudition. He translated Plutarch into Latin and in 1508 published his commentaries on the Pandects, which had a great influence on the study of Roman law. A treatise on ancient coins, *De asse et partibus* (1514), brought him to the attention of the king and he was asked by the court to produce a French translation (*Sommaire ou épitomé du livre de asse*, 1522). He enjoyed the favour of François I, whom he accompanied to the Field of the Cloth of Gold in 1520. At Budé's instance the king instituted the Royal Readers (in Hebrew, Greek, Latin and mathematics) who became in fact the founding members of the future Collège de France. He was the first Librarian of the Library at Fontainebleau, which was to be transferred to Paris as the Bibliothèque Nationale. He corresponded widely (with Erasmus and others), encouraged Rabelais in his studies and generally influenced the reviving interest in the Classics. Refusing to be buried with religious ceremonial, he has been suspected of Calvinist sympathies. Other works: *De l'institution du prince*, written in French (publ. 1547) and, especially, his *Commentarii linguae graecae* (1525). [FWAG]

J. Plattard, *G.B. et les origines de l'humanisme français* (Paris, 1923); J. Bohatec, *Budé und Calvin. Studien zur Gedankenwelt des französischen Frühhumanismus* (Graz, 1950).

**Buero Vallejo, Antonio** (Guadalajara 1916– ). Spanish dramatist. He was in prison for political reasons when awarded the Premio Lope de Vega in 1949 for his play *Historia de una escalera* (ed. H. Lester and J. A. Z. Bilbao, 1963), which was influenced in technique by contemporary American drama. His concern with dramatic form led him to the theatrical mastery of *En la ardiente escuridad* (1950), *Madrugada* (1953), *Irene o el tesoro* (1954) and *Hoy es fiesta* (1956; ed. J. E. Lyon and K. S. B. Croft, 1964; Fundación March prize). Of his new cycle of plays on historical themes, the first, *Un soñador para un pueblo* (1958) presents the popular rebellion against Carlos III's minister Esquilache in the 18th century, while *Las meninas* (1960) evokes the life and times of Velázquez; *El concierto de San Ovidio* (1962) is set in Paris in the years immediately before the French Revolution. Though never deliberately political, his drama is notable for its moral purpose and social content. [JLC]

*Teatro* (2 vols., B.A., 1959, 1962).

**Buffon, Georges-Louis Leclerc, Comte de** (Montbard 1707–Paris 1788). French scientist and stylist. The son of a cultivated Dijon lawyer, he early developed scientific interests, and became curator of the Jardin du Roi in 1739. His scientific researches, pursued on his Burgundian estates at Montbard, ranged over the whole field of living creatures and their environment, and were published from 1749 onwards in the 44 volumes of his *Histoire Naturelle* (tr. W. Kenrick *et al.*, 1775, etc.). Though often disputed by contemporaries, his views show many percipient insights, and are presented with an ordered and majestic lucidity which stylistically marks an epoch in scientific literature. In his *Discours sur le style* (1753) he insists that the foundations of good style are a firm intellectual grasp of one's material, orderly presentation, and a choice of vocabulary in keeping with the tone of the subject. This essay, epitomizing the classical literary ideal, has had an enduring influence on French education. [WHB]

*Œuvres philosophiques*, ed. J. Piveteau (1954).

L. Dimier, *B.* (Paris, 1919); Mornet, *SNF*; Sainte-Beuve, *CL.*

**Bulatović, Miodrag** (Omladina, Montenegro 1930– ). Serbian novelist. Brought up in a village in extreme poverty and disorder, he did not read a book until he was 16. His works include the collection of stories, *Djavoli dolaze* (1960), and the novels *Vuk i zvono* (1958) and *Crveni petao leti prema nebu* (1961; tr. E. D. Goy, *The Red Cockerel*, 1962). He symbolizes the war with its pitiless violence to the human personality before which man is helpless yet still responsible as an individual. In *Crveni petao leti prema nebu* the war has become everyday life in which the individual struggles to be a man, to affirm his own personality or else perish as a person. He is one of the most original writers in Yugoslavia today. His new novel, *Heroj na magarcu* (1965; tr. E. D. Goy, *A Hero on a Donkey*, 1966), deals with the theme of war and pornography. [EDG]

Kadić, *CSL.*

**Bulgakov, Mikhail Afanas'evich** (Kiev 1891–Moscow 1940). Russian dramatist and prose writer. He studied and briefly practised medicine (see *Zapiski Yunogo Vracha*). After indigent wanderings through Revolutionary Russia and the Caucasus, he settled in Moscow in 1921. Humorous, cultured and politically tolerant, his realism borders on the fantastic, like that of Gogol' or Dostoyevsky, though his fantasy is lighter. This tendency is striking in *Beg* (1927), a play 'in eight dreams' about the evacuation of the Whites and émigré life, and in the stories *Diavoliada*, *Rokovye Yaytsa*, *Sobacheye Serdtse*. *Master i Margarita* (published posthumously in 1966–7) is a key work, a brilliant novel on two planes: a Hoffmannesque fantasy about the devil and his henchman in modern Moscow, in which the crucifixion of Christ and penitence of Pilate are rendered with almost naturalistic realism. Despite the success of the Moscow Arts Theatre production of *Dni Turbinykh* (1926), described in his autobiographical *Teatral'nyy Roman* (1936–7, in *Novyy Mir*, 8, 1965), its sympathetic portrayal of White characters, apparent again in *Beg*, and the satirical treatment of NEP officials in *Zoykina Kvartira* (1926) led to growing RAPP criticism, which became violent after the play *Bagrovyy Ostrov* (1928). Later works treat the subject of the artist and the tyrant under the guise of historical characters: *Mol'yer* (staged 1936), *Don Kikhot* (staged 1940), *Pushkin* (staged 1943). He also wrote a brilliant biography, highly original in form, of his great literary hero Jean-Baptiste Molière (1932–3, publ. *Molodaya Gvardiya*, 1962). Fame, at home and abroad, came some quarter century after his death, and the publication of his literary heritage is not yet complete. [AP]

*Dramy i Komedii*, intr. V. Kaverin, notes K. Rudnitsky (1965); *Izbrannaya Proza*, intr. V. Ya. Lakshin (1966); 'Avtobiografiya', in *Sovetskiye Pisateli*, iii, (1966); 'Master i Margarita', in *Moskva* (ii, 1966; i, 1967).

K. Rudnitsky, in *Voprosy Teatra* (1966); V. Smirnova, in *Sovremennyy Portret. Stat'i* (1964); V. Kaverin, in *Sobraniye Sochineniy*, 6, 1966; S. Lyandres, in *Voprosy Literatury*, 9, 1966; P. Markov, in *Pravda Teatra. Stat'i* (1965); S. Yermolinsky, in *Teatr*, 9, 1966.

**Bull, Olaf** (Kristiania 1883–Oslo 1933). Norwegian poet. A son of the popular writer Jacob B. Bull, he started as a journalist. Later he devoted himself entirely to his writing and became one of the most important Norwegian poets of this century. He has points of resemblance with Collett

Vogt and ⇨ Wergeland, but his work was characterized from the start by great introspection coupled with a concrete awareness of life and nature. He published many collections of verse but his qualities are best expressed in *Metope* (1927). [RGP]

*Samlede dikte* (1934).

T. Greiff, *O.B.* (Oslo, 1952); E. Ofstad, *O.B.'s lyrikk* (Oslo, 1955); E. Wyller, *Tidsproblemet hos O.B.* (Oslo, 1959); Beyer, *NL.*

**Bunin, Ivan Alekseyevich** (Voronezh 1870–Paris 1953). Russian poet and writer. He was born into an ancient but impoverished noble family, studied at Moscow University, then worked for the rural administration in Central Russia; later he travelled in Europe and Asia. He was acquainted with Chekhov and joined Gor'ky's *Znanie* group of democratic writers, though an inborn scepticism and aristocratic aloofness prevented him from fully sharing their socio-political aspirations. Nor did he join any of the other pre-revolutionary literary movements. In 1909 he was elected an honorary member of the Academy of Sciences.

His first volume of poetry was published in 1891. The lucid, objective verse of his nature lyrics is in the tradition of 19th-century Russian poetry. In 1901 he received the Pushkin Prize for his nature poem *Listopad.* He translated Longfellow's *Hiawatha* and Byron's verse dramas (*Manfred, Cain*).

He is primarily famous for his prose. His main theme is the disintegration of the traditional pattern of Russian country life at the turn of the century recorded with an incisive, pitiless precision mingled with a tinge of regret, e.g. *Derevnya* (1910; tr. I. Hapgood, *The Village*, 1923), *Sukhodol* (1911) and *Grammatika lyubvi* (1915). In *Gospodin iz San-Frantsisko* (1915; in *The Gentleman from San Francisco and Other Stories*, tr. D. H. Lawrence *et al.*, 1934), his most famous work, powerful satire on Western bourgeois civilization is combined with the expression of a pessimistic philosophy that was to gain ascendancy in his later work.

In 1920 he left Russia and settled in France. In his evocations of the country of his youth the themes of love and death are prominent, e.g. *Mitina Lyubov'* (1925), *Solnechnyy udar* (1927), the semi-autobiographical novel *Zhizn' Arsen'yeva* (Part I translated as *The Well of Days*) for which he received the Nobel Prize (1933) and *Tyomneyy allei* (1943), his last cycle of stories. His later short stories are the product of extreme concentration, some of them being less than a page long.

A vast range of Russian idiom subjected to exacting aesthetic control, the recreation of atmosphere by the artistic use of detail, the rhythmic flow of his prose and a deliberate detachment are the main features of Bunin's writing. He continues the realist tradition of S. T. Aksakov, Turgenev, Tolstoy and Chekhov. [PH]

*Sobraniye sochineniy* (12 vols., Berlin, 1934–9): *Sobraniye sochineniy* (9 vols., 1965– ); *Tyomneyy allei* (N.Y., 1943).

V. Muromtseva-Bunin, *Zhizn' Bunina* (Paris, 1958); Mirsky, *HRL*; Poggioli, *PS*; Struve, *RLI.*

**Buonarroti, Michelangelo.** ⇨ Michelangelo Buonarroti.

**Bürger, Gottfried August** (Molmerswende, Harz 1747–Göttingen 1794). German poet. The wayward son of a Protestant pastor, he studied law and aesthetics at Halle and Göttingen, where he came into contact with the poets of the 'Göttinger Hain'. The wretchedness and poverty of his public life as a village magistrate and latterly as Professor of Aesthetics at Göttingen is matched by the unhappiness of his private life. His marriage to Dorette Leonhart, with whose sister Auguste – the 'Molly' of his love poetry – he was passionately in love, involved him in the scandal and heartbreak of a '*ménage à trois*', which ended only with Dorette's death in 1784. His marriage to Molly ended suddenly with her death a few months later, while a third marriage was dissolved after two years. His lasting claim to fame lies in his revitalization, under the influence of ⇨ Herder, of the ballad. His *Lenore* (1773), an adaptation of the *Sweet William's Ghost* of Percy's *Reliques*, earned him a European reputation: its subsumption of folk elements, its evocation of eerie, ghostly atmosphere and its rejection of the rationalism of the Enlightenment gave it an immediate and lasting appeal for the generation of the 'Storm and Stress' and subsequently for the Romantics, for whom it was a seminal work. Other ballads, *Die Weiber von Weinsberg* (1775), *Das Lied vom braven Mann* (1777) and *Der wilde Jäger* (1778), equally bear witness to his poetic powers. His love lyrics (*Elegie*, 1776; *Das Hohe Lied von der Einzigen*, 1778, etc.) are characterized by their intensely personal and direct quality. [WAC]

*Ausgewählte Werke*, ed. L. Kaim and S. Streller (1956).
W. Kayser, *Geschichte der deutschen Ballade* (Berlin, 1936).

**Busch, Wilhelm** (Wiedensahl 1832–Mechtshausen 1908). German artist and 'nonsense'-writer. He is famous for his caricatures and comic drawings as for his humorous writings. In the comic weekly *Fliegende Blätter* (1859ff.) he produced illustrated verse-stories (the earliest 'comic strip'?), of which the first, *Max und Moritz* (1865; tr. A. Esdaile, *Max and Maurice*, 1913), has been a household name in Germany ever since, along with: *Die fromme Helene* (1872), *Abenteuer eines Junggesellen* (1875), *Herr und Frau Knopp* (1876), *Julchen* (1877), *Balduin Bählamm, der verhinderte Dichter* (1881), etc. Busch's very real poetic ability is revealed in the collections *Kritik des Herzens* (1874) and *Zu guter Letzt* (1904). By comparison with, say, Edward Lear he is less whimsically fantastic, more down-to-earth in his satire. For other German 'nonsense' poets, ⇨ Morgenstern and Grass. [PB]

*Gesamtausgabe*, ed. O. Nöldeke (1943); ed. R. Hochhuth (2 vols., Gütersloh, 1959) (selection); *A Bushel of Merry Thoughts by W. B.* (1868) (one of several early English/American selections); *Jahrbuch der W.B.-Gesellschaft*, passim.

**Busta, Christine,** pseud. of C. Dimt (Vienna 1915– ). Austrian poet. She has won several prizes for her poetry, which has mainly religious themes and is written in traditional forms (selection in *Das andere Schaf*, 1959). Also verse for children (*Die Sternenmühle*, 1959), and short prose (*Bethlemitische Legende*, 1956). [PB]

Hamburger and Middleton, *MGP*.

**Butor, Michel** (Lille 1926– ). French novelist and critic. Trained as a philosopher, he taught in France and abroad (Egypt, Salonika, Geneva, Manchester) and began writing poetry. His first novel, *Passage de Milan* (1954), reveals the interrelation of people's lives in a block of flats. *L'emploi du temps* (1957; tr. J. Stewart, *Passing Time*, 1961) tells in diary form of the central character's attempt to preserve his identity and integrity in a large industrial town, and *La modification* (1957; tr. J. Stewart, *Second Thoughts*, 1958) traces the development of a man's awareness of his dishonest relationship with his wife and mistress. The function of writing is to explore the complexity of events within clearly defined areas of reality – the block of flats, a train journey, a town – and to discover the hidden meaning and bring order through rigorous artistic forms which parallel the social structures, thus enabling the individual to achieve a greater awareness of his environment. With *Degrés* (1960; tr. R. Howard, *Degrees*, 1962) the ordered narrative is replaced by a painstakingly detailed description of a lycée, and in *Mobile* (1963) Butor constructs a pattern of American society, a structural analysis, from quotations, descriptions and passages of poetry. His analyses of the development of the novel, *Répertoire I* (1960), *II* (1964), and his literary essays reveal a penetrating and imaginative critical mind. [RGV]

R.-M. Albérès, *B.* (Paris, 1964); *Écrivains d'aujourd'hui 1940–1960*, ed. B. Pingaud (Paris, 1960); J. Roudaut, *M.B. ou le livre futur* (Paris, 1964); G. Charbonnier, *Entretiens avec M.B.* (Paris, 1967).

**Buzzati, Dino** (Belluno 1906– ). Italian novelist. On the staff of the Milan newspaper *Corriere della Sera* since 1928, he began his literary career with two whimsical mountain stories (*Barnabò delle montagne*, 1933, and *Il segreto del bosco vecchio*, 1935) which may be read as children's tales, or moralities for grown-ups, or both. He then developed his flat and unvarnished style as a vehicle for weird and uncanny tales charged with mysterious Kafkaesque symbolism. In this way even a simple plot – e.g., *Il deserto dei Tartari* (1940; tr. S. C. Hood, *The Tartar Steppe*, 1952), the story of a frontier garrison waiting for an opportunity to prove its gallantry that never materializes – can imply profound truths that could not be made explicit because of the political situation. After several books of 'metaphysical fables' and short stories, some of them quite arresting and disturbing ('I sette messaggeri', 'Sette piani', 'Paura alla Scala', 'Il crollo della Baliverna', all collected in the volume *Sessanta racconti*, 1958), the initial freshness of inspiration seems to have worn out (*Il grande ritratto*, 1960; tr. H. Reed, *Larger than Life*, 1962). Buzzati's reply to critics who have long urged him to shrug off his Kafkian mannerism, *Un amore* (1963; tr. J. Green, *A Love Affair*, 1965), is another variation on the old theme of the dignified middle-aged man, irretrievably enslaved by a young shameless minx. [GMC]

Falqui, *PNNI*; *Contemporanei*, ii; Pullini, *RID*.

**Byliny.** The *byliny* are the heroic songs of Russia handed down from generation to generation of *skaziteli* or reciters and recorded by collectors mostly in the north of Russia, particularly in the vicinity of Lake Onega. The recording and collecting of *byliny* has been going on ever since the 17th century. The first printed collection was that of Kirsha Danilov (1804); the most scholarly and valuable collections, those of Gilferding and Rybnikov in the second half of the 19th century.

*Byliny* are poems of varying length, the average being some 300 lines long. They are and were usually sung to the accompaniment of a stringed instrument. They are bound by no hard and fast rules of composition; the singer does not learn his poem by heart: he has at his disposal a number of situations, characters and clichés. Consequently much depends on the *skazitel's* skill. The outline of the main themes, however, is more or less fixed by tradition and no great deviation of plot in most of the better-known *byliny* is discernible. The metrical system is tonic: each line has a fixed number of stresses (usually three), between which there is a varying number of unstressed syllables.

Many of the *byliny* have as their subject matter the exploits of the *bogatyri*, heroes such as Il'ya Muromets or Dobrynya Nikitich, who perform various feats of bravery or cunning usually in defence of their country against external enemies. The scene of this type of 'military' *bylina* is usually Kiev ruled by 'Vladimir the Fair Sun' (either Vladimir I or Vladimir II Monomakh) and the period – the 11th and 12th centuries, with, of course, considerable anachronistic additions (the enemies may be Tatars or Lithuanians or Poles for instance). Sometimes the heroes are endowed with superhuman qualities (e.g. Svyatogor and Volkh), a characteristic which points to their pre-historical origin. Many *byliny* have non-military subjects (Sadko, Vasily Buslayev, Dobrynya and Alyosha, for instance) and are non-heroic in theme, dealing with domestic rather than national topics. Those *byliny*, the heroes of which are Sadko and Vasily Buslayev, have as their setting Novgorod in the period of her independence from the end of the 12th century to the annexation of the republic by Moscow in 1478, and give an excellent picture of life in many sections of the community. [JLIF]

*Russian Folk Literature*, ed. D. P. Costello and I. P. Foote (1967).

M. N. Speransky, *Russkaya ustnaya slovesnost'* (Moscow, 1917); V. Ya. Propp, *Russkiy geroicheskiy epos* (Moscow, 1955).

# C

**Caballero, Fernán,** pseud. of Cecilia Böhl de Faber (Morgues, Switzerland 1796–Seville 1877). Spanish novelist. Her father translated A. W. ⇨ Schlegel and was a pioneer of the Romantic movement. She was of mixed German, Irish and Spanish descent, was three times married and moved in aristocratic circles. She collected peasant stories and the traditional *coplas* of Seville. Her traditionalist fervour overflows into her novels; they show no deep sense of character; they are Romantic in their sentimentality but strikingly realistic in their *costumbrista* descriptions of Andalusia. The best are *La gaviota* (1849; CA), about a young German doctor's unhappy marriage to an unsophisticated Andalusian girl who becomes a singer and is corrupted by city life, *La familia de Alvareda* (1856), *Elia* and *Clemencia* (1852). [JMC]

*Obras* (BAE, 136–40).

J. F. Montesinos, *F.C.: Ensayo de justificación* (Mexico, 1962); J. Herrero, *F.C.: Un nuevo planteamiento* (Madrid, 1963).

**Cabanillas, Ramón.** ⇨ Galician Literature.

**Cadalso, José** (Cadiz 1741–Gibraltar 1782). Spanish poet and essayist. After a period of travel and education in Europe he enlisted in the cavalry in 1762. There, although his original bent may have been politics or diplomacy, he remained until his death during the siege of Gibraltar. A period of exile from Madrid in 1768 and subsequently the death of an actress with whom he was in love (1771) seem to have led him to express his disillusionment about society and the nature of things in literary form. He wrote a play in the classical manner (*Don Sancho García*, 1771), some poems and a number of prose works, in which the vagaries of fortune, the destructive power of human passions and stoicism are some of the main topics. His best-known work, *Cartas marruecas* (finished early in 1774), analyses the nature of man and Spanish society in a series of letters between two Moors and a Spaniard; constructive criticism of Spanish society is offset by doubts about the progress of human society. His style is a mixture of wry humour and philosophical rhetoric. [ONVG]

*Noches lúgubres*, CC; *Cartas marruecas* (1966) and CC.

N. Glendinning, *Vida y obra de C.* (1963); ed. E. Allison Peers, *Liverpool Studies in Spanish Literature*, i (1940).

**Caesarius of Heisterbach** (*c.* 1180–*c.* 1240). German Cistercian. Known chiefly for his *Dialogus miraculorum*, a collection of exempla (stories intended to edify or instruct), read today either for amusement or for the light which they throw on medieval credulity. [FB]

Ed. J. Strange (Cologne, 2 vols., 1851); *The Dialogue on Miracles*, tr. H. von E. Scott and C. C. S. Bland, intr. G. G. Coulton (1929).

**Čaks, Aleksandrs.** ⇨ Latvian Literature.

**Calderón de la Barca, Pedro** (Madrid 1600–Madrid 1681). Spanish dramatist. His education at a Jesuit school and his study of law and theology at the universities of Alcalá and Salamanca are clearly reflected in his dramatic works. He wrote some 110 plays, of which many were performed in the public theatres between about 1623 and 1640. During the latter year he took part in the campaign against the Catalan rebels. He was ordained priest in 1651, and thereafter wrote only plays and masques, often on mythological subjects, for the court theatre of Philip IV, and the two *autos sacramentales* a year which were regularly commissioned by the city of Madrid.

Though they adhere to the framework of the *comedia* as established by ⇨ Lope de Vega, Calderón's plays are much more intellectual and stylized than those of his predecessor. His is a theatre of thought rather than experience, of concept rather than character. In the comedies of intrigue action tends to hang on some external device, such as the concealed door between two rooms in *La dama duende*. The late drama *El alcalde de Zalamea*, which derives closely from Lope's play of the same title, is exceptional both in its personal reminiscences of army life, and in its creation of an outstanding human character, the village mayor Pedro Crespo, who, when his daughter is abducted by an army captain, vindicates the right of the peasant to defend his honour.

In his most characteristic plays Calderón reflects the mood of a nation in decline. Violence and death, the horrific and the supernatural, are frequently portrayed, but always with the didactic purpose of persuading men to shun illusion and adhere to eternal values. *El príncipe constante* presents, in terms of Stoic philosophy and Thomist psychology, the steadfastness of a Christian prince martyred by the Moors. *El mayor monstruo los celos* deals with Herod and his wife Mariene, *La cisma de Inglaterra* with Henry VIII's marriage to Anne Boleyn; in each case it is the surrender of the main characters to worldly concerns – lust, jealousy, ambition, pride – which occasions their fall. In *La devoción de la Cruz* a husband's false conception of honour brings tragedy to his whole family, while Calderón's adaptation of the Faust legend in *El mágico prodigioso* uses disillusionment over physical beauty as a means whereby the pagan hero attains to a knowledge of the Christian God. The problems of real and illusory values are explored most fully in *La vida es sueño* (tr. J. B. Trend and F. Birch, *Life's a Dream*, 1925), where Prince Segismundo, confused between dream and waking, has to learn to distinguish the transient from the lasting elements in his experience.

Calderón has long been regarded as the chief exponent and upholder of the rigorous code of honour. Recent criticism has shown, however, that in plays like *El médico de su honra*, where for the sake of his reputation a husband murders an innocent wife on mere suspicion of her infidelity, Calderón makes plain the series of moral errors which has led to the dilemma, and suggests that under a system of true values concern for reputation would be replaced by compassion.

The elements of stylization are developed to the full in the late works. Both *autos* and mythological dramas make use of elaborate staging, music and formal movement. He shows his mastery of allegory in the *autos*, handling the most varied types of dramatic material in such a way as to give each of them relevance to some aspect of the Mass.

As we must not look primarily for verisimilitude in the action, so too in the dialogue natural speech frequently gives way, either to scholasticism – characters often tabulate and argue like contestants in a disputation – or to splendid rhetoric, rich in formal pattern, image and conceit. [MW]

*Obras completas*, ed. A. Valbuena Briones and A. Valbuena Prat (3 vols., Madrid, 1952–60); CA; CC; *Six Dramas of C.*, tr. E. Fitzgerald (1853, 1903).

A. Valbuena Prat, *C., su personalidad, su arte dramático, su estilo y sus obras* (Madrid, 1941); A. A. Parker, *The Allegorical Drama of C.* (1943); E. Frutos Cortés, *C. de la B.* (Barcelona, 1949); A. E. Sloman, *The Dramatic Craftsmanship of C.* (1958); ed. B. W. Wardropper, *Critical Essays on the Theatre of C.* (N.Y., 1965).

**'Calila e Dimna, o las fábulas de Bidpay.'** A 13th-century Spanish book of fables, translated from the Arabic *Kalila wa-Dimna*, which ultimately derived from a 4th-century Indian original. The Spanish version claims to have been commissioned by ⇨ Alfonso X, but this attribution is now considered doubtful. The book was intended as a *speculum principis* and consists of a series of moral fables, most of them told by two jackals called Calila and Dimna (Karataka and Damanaka in the Sanskrit original). The moral advice offered does not always coincide with orthodox Christian attitudes. The book's great popularity can be judged by the many versions in Arabic and other Oriental languages. The Spanish work follows the Arabic version more closely than John of Capua's 13th-century Latin translation and the other European versions which were usually based on Capua's translation. Some of the stories in the Spanish version were later used by Don ⇨ Juan Manuel in *El conde Lucanor*, and by other contributors to the extensive fable-book tradition which enjoyed great popularity in medieval Spain. [IM]

Ed. J. Alemany y Bolufer (1915); ed. A. G. Solalinde (1917); ed. Alberto Franco (Buenos Aires, 1948); ed. J. C. Keller and R. W. Linker (Madrid, 1967).

S. de Sacy, *Calila et Dimna, ou fables de Bidpa* (Paris, 1816); I. G. N. Keith-Falconer, *Kalīlah and Dimnah, or the Fables of Bidpai* (1885) P. de Gayangos, in BAE 51 (1860).

**Calvino, Italo** (Cuba 1923– ). Italian novelist. After neo-realist beginnings as a left-wing *engagé* writer (*Il sentiero dei nidi di ragno*, 1947, tr. A. Colquhoun, *The Path to the Nest of Spiders*, 1956; *Ultimo viene il corvo*, 1949, sel. tr. A. Colquhoun and P. Wright, *Adam One Afternoon and Other*

*Stories*, 1957: stories of the Resistance movement), he changed to lighthearted fables and stories full of a dry and sometimes bitter humour (*Racconti*, 1958, including all other stories published since 1945); then he wrote three entertaining *contes philosophiques*, half way between satire and fantasy (*Il Visconte dimezzato*, 1952; *Il Barone rampante*, 1957, and *Il Cavaliere inesistente*, 1959; collected in one volume with the title *I nostri antenati* in 1960, tr. A. Colquhoun, *The Cloven Viscount*, 1962, *Baron of the Trees*, 1959,and *The Non-Existent Knight*, 1962). One of his latest works is a meditative story (*La giornata di uno scrutatore*, 1963) about the uneasy relationship between religious, humanitarian and political beliefs. [GMC]

Pullini, *RID*; Mariani, *GNI*; Germana Pescio-Bottino, *C.* (1967).

**Camblak, Gregory.** ⇨ Serbian Medieval Literature.

**Camões, Luís de** (Lisbon *c.*1524–Lisbon 1580). Portuguese poet. His family came of the minor nobility of Galicia. Much has been surmised, little is known of his life. He went to Coimbra University, became a soldier, lost an eye fighting in Morocco, returned to Lisbon where his part in a street affray cost him a year in gaol. In 1553 he left for India and became acquainted with the whole field of Portuguese adventure as far as the China seas. Returning to Portugal, he had the misfortune to have the manuscript of his lyric poetry stolen on the way, but succeeded in publishing *Os Lusíadas*, dedicated to King Sebastian, from whom he received a poor and irregularly paid pension. In Lisbon he lived in extreme poverty and when he died was given a pauper's burial. His lyrical poetry was published posthumously (1595).

Admired in his own time (when the epic was regarded as the loftiest literary genre) principally as an epic poet, Camões now appears as the supreme peninsular lyric poet, more various than ⇨ Garcilaso, more copious than ⇨ León, more spontaneous than ⇨ Góngora. He is at once sensual and mystical, sensitive to physical beauty and by nature inclined to the spiritual refinements of Renaissance Platonism.

In Camões a rich emotional and intellectual nature is accompanied by a consummate gift of expression. He is a master of every verse-form from the traditional *redondilha* to the new Renaissance forms of sonnet, canzone, eclogue, ode, and elegy. His poetry marks the culmination of two distinct literary traditions.

Love is of course the principal theme of these lyrics. From the simple expression of instinct or feeling, Camões rises to considerations of his own destiny, to moral reflections, analyses of the inner life, and flights of mystical inspiration. It is the constant intellectual analysis of his own feelings which gives his poetry its idiosyncrasy: it is the depth of the poet's feeling which gives sanction to this intellectual analysis.

The poetic career of Petrarch provided the literary prototype. When normal satisfactions are made impossible by absence, death, or lack of reciprocal affection, physical love must be transformed into spiritual love. Eventually it becomes possible even to court the disdain of the beloved, to solicit her absence, so that love can work upon grief and *saudade* to the point of satisfaction at doing without the beloved. Love is the means of ascent to the absolute beauty propounded by Renaissance Platonism (*Babel e Sião*).

Camões's second theme is the unreason of the world (*Oitavas sobre o Desconcerto do Mundo*). The poet is conscious of the distinction between the moral worth of the individual and the place accorded him by society. His meditation upon the medieval theme of the distribution of rewards and punishments leads him to regret that wealth and power belong to those who seize them, not to those who deserve them. Nor is the profane crowd worthy of anything but scorn. Camões's use of the Renaissance themes of love and reason emphasizes the impossibility of attaining the beloved object, of finding a plan in the world's unreason. If man's constant search for happiness is indeed because he remembers the celestial world he once knew, the poet trusts that in that transcendent sphere a solution will be offered.

*Os Lusíadas* falls into the rare category of a successful Renaissance epic which is not burlesque. It is an epic of knowledge and its extension, rather than an epic of commerce, as Mickle called it. Camões reveals all a humanist's interest in classical cosmography and geography, in natural phenomena, in the manners of foreign peoples. He shows a close acquaintance with the works of the Portuguese historians, and is interested by travellers' tales. From personal experience he describes the lives and habits of sailors and all the incidents of a long sea voyage. The hero, it is clear, is no character from national history, but the Portuguese nation. Vasco da Gama and his associates, and those they meet on the way, move stiffly like figures in a pageant, making admirable and informative speeches. Some of these speeches, however (like that of the Velho do Restelo), are not admirable from the official point of view, and express the poet's condemnation of the lust for power and wealth which was one of the motive forces of this 'crusade'.

Camões's real interest (and this is reflected in the quality of his poetry) is more often evoked by the gods of Olympus who quarrel over the three Portuguese vessels making for India. Venus and Mars – for the Portuguese are amorous and warlike – favour them; Neptune is jealous, and Bacchus their avowed enemy. The gods recall the values of humanism, and reflect those ideals whose satisfaction Camões failed to find in this world. When the triumphantly returning Portuguese copulate symbolically with Tethys and her sea-nymphs, their amorous life transcends the miseries and limitations Camões had known in his own. The gods represent an aesthetic order superior to moral conventions and remind us that beauty is indeed the supreme value of the Renaissance.

Thus the human quandary so often expressed by Camões in his lyric poetry seems to find its solution in his epic.

He also wrote a classical comedy (*Enfatriões*), adapting Plautus, and two plays in the tradition of Gil ⇨ Vicente (*El-Rei Seleuco* and *Filodemo*). Five extant letters are written in a language which is colloquial, witty and richly imaged. [ARM]

*Obras Completas* (CSC); *Rimas*, ed. A. J. da Costa Pimpão (1953).

H. Cidade, *C. O Lírico, O Épico, O Dramático* (3 vols., Lisbon, 1936–50); J. Agostinho, *A Chave dos Lusíadas* (Porto, c.1920); A. dos Anjos, *Significado dos Lusíadas* (Lisbon, 1958); A. Ferrão, *C. e a Pátria* (Lisbon, 1930); C. Ferreira da Cunha, *C. e a Unidade da Língua* (Lisbon, 1957); H. H. Hart, *L. de C. and the Epic of the Lusiads* (1962); G. Le Gentil, *C. L'œuvre épique et lyrique* (Paris, 1954); C. Michaëlis de Vasconcelos, *Estudos Camonianos* (Lisbon, 1922); M. de Moarais Sarmento, *A Poesia Amorosa de C.* (Lisbon, 1959); J. Nogueira, *Dicionário e Gramática de Os Lusíadas* (Lisbon, 1960); O. Orico, *C. y Cervantes* (Madrid, 1948); J. A. Peixoto, *Ensaios Camonianos* (Lisbon, 1932); J. Régio, *Ensaios de de Interpretação Critica* (Lisbon. 1964); Reis Brasil, *O. Conceito do Amor em C.* (Lisbon, 1956), and *Os Lusíadas* (Lisbon, 1960); A. Ribeiro, *C. Camilo, Eça, e Alguns Mais* (Lisbon, c.1960); J. M. Rodrigues, *Os Lusíadas* (Lisbon, 1929); A. Sérgio, *C. de D. Sebastião* (Lisbon, 1890); F. W. P. Storck, *L. de C. Leben* (Paderborn, 1890).

**Campana, Dino** (Marradi 1885–Castel Pulci 1932). Italian poet. His genius, profoundly unstable, made him a wanderer living precariously off odd-jobs from Odessa to Buenos Aires. Like Rimbaud, whom he resembles and perhaps imitated, his published work amounts to a single volume of poems and poetic prose, *Canti orfici* (1914; supplemented by *Inediti*, 1941–2; *C.O. e altri scritti*, 1952), remarkable for a feverish 'visionary' imagery, a vision in which inner and outer experience appear fused and transfigured. His discovery of new possibilities of poetic expression (hailed as having symbolic and even mystical meaning) in his tormented and alienated sensitivity made him the precursor of much modern Italian poetry. [GD]

*Lettere* (1958).

G. Bonalumi, *Cultura e poesia in C.* (Florence, 1953); E. Falqui, *Per una cronistoria dei 'Canti Orfici'* (Florence, 1961); G. Gerola, *D.C.* (Florence, 1955); M. Petrucciani, *Poesia pura e poesia esistenziale* (Turin, 1957).

**Campanella, Tommaso** (Stilo di Calabria 1568–Paris 1639). Italian theologian, philosopher and poet. A Dominican, he was soon disciplined by his Order for his Telesian views, left Calabria (1589) for Naples and published his *Philosophia sensibus demonstrata* (1591), which brought another rebuke and a command to return to Calabria. Instead he went to Florence, Bologna and Padua, was arrested and tortured by the Inquisition (1594), imprisoned in Rome, perhaps with ⇨ Bruno, and forced to retract. Sent back to Calabria, Campanella planned a conspiracy to overthrow Spanish rule in southern Italy and establish a utopian, communistic state. He was arrested (1599), escaped execution by feigning madness and was imprisoned in Naples (1599–1626). In prison he wrote many of his most important works – much of his Italian verse, whose rugged power is unique in the *seicento*; the Italian version of the politically utopian *Città del sole* (1602; ed. A. Seroni, 1962; tr. T. W.

Halliday, *C.s City of the Sun*, in *Ideal Commonwealths*, ed. H. Morley, 1885); *De sensu rerum et magia* (1604); *Atheismus triumphatus* (1607), a radical apologia of Christianity; *Apologia pro Galilaeo* (1616; tr. G. McColley, *The Defense of Galileo*, Northampton, Mass., 1937); *Metaphysica* (1623); *Theologia* (1624). The speculative works reveal increasing acceptance of orthodox theology but distinguish insistently between the realms of theology and science. Released by the Spaniards (1626), he was immediately imprisoned in Rome by the Holy Office and regained complete liberty only in 1629 on the intervention of Urban VIII. His championing of ⇨ Galilei and continued Spanish suspicion of his politics made him flee (1634) to Paris where, an honoured figure in his last years, he published many of his works. [DGR]

L. Firpo, *Bibliografia degli scritti di T.C.* (Turin, 1940); *Opere* (vol. 1 only, containing *Poesie* and *Philosophia rationalis*), ed. L. Firpo (1954); *Opere di G. Bruno e T.C.*, ed. A. Guzzo and R. Amerio (1956); *Del senso delle cose e della magia*, ed. A. Bruers (1925); *Syntagma de libris propriis*, ed. V. Spampanato (1927); *Lettere*, ed. V. Spampanato (1927); *Theologicorum libri* (with Italian tr.), ed. R. Amerio (1949ff.); *The Sonnets of Michael Agnolo Buonarroti and T.C.*, tr. J. A. Symonds, etc. (1878); Kay, *PBIV*.

R. Amerio, *C.* (Brescia, 1947); E. G. Gardner, *T.C. and His Poetry* (1923; repr. 1930, in *Taylorian Lectures 1920–30*); R. Mondolfo, *Figure e idee della filosofia del Rinascimento* (Florence, 1963); *Minori*, ii.

**Camphuysen, Dirck Rafaelsz** (Gorcum 1586–Dokkum 1627). Dutch painter, Remonstrant minister and poet. His poetry gained a popularity second only to that of ⇨ Cats, although the theme of his songs is suffering as a means to grace. He was persecuted for his tolerant pacifism. [PK]

*Stichtelyke rymen* (published anon., 1624).

**Campoamor, Ramón de** (Navia, Asturias 1817–Madrid 1901). Spanish poet. He studied philosophy at Santiago and logic, mathematics and medicine at Madrid. At 18 he nearly became a Jesuit, but he finally made his career in politics. He edited a political periodical for some years before being appointed Governor of Castellón in 1847. He was already establishing his reputation as a poet by this time, having published a volume of *Poesías* in 1840 and *Ayes del alma* two years later. His early poetry was full of typically Romantic, sentimental and patriotic touches, and it was only in his *Dóloras* (1845) that he began to show signs of originality. These *dóloras* were short, concise poems, often in dialogue form, with an ironic or philosophical point reflecting his slightly pessimistic view of human nature. Later he wrote longer poems on broader philosophical and sentimental themes, of which the most important were *El drama universal* (1869) and *El tren expreso* (1874). But his main contribution to Spanish 19th-century poetry lay in his advocacy and practice of short poetic forms, sometimes deriving from the *coplas* of folk-poetry like his *Humoradas* (1886). These were a revolt against Romantic rhetoric and influenced several younger poets, notably Antonio ⇨ Machado. Together with his *Poética* (1883) they reflect most clearly their author's central preoccupation with poetry as a vehicle for ideas. Unfortunately most of his ideas no longer have much force, and some, like his belief in the intellectual supremacy of pale-skinned people over dark, have long since seemed absurd. [ONVG]

*Poesías*, CC; *Obras poéticas completas* (n.d.). Piñeyro, *RS*.

**Camus, Albert** (Mondovi, Algeria 1913–Villeblevin 1960). French novelist, dramatist, essayist, journalist and moralist. He caught with remarkable accuracy the mood of those coming to manhood at the end of the last war. Although born in extreme poverty, his inherent ability enabled him to attend the lycée, and later the university, in Algiers. Tuberculosis cut short a possible academic career but by this time (1937) he was supporting himself by a variety of jobs and had helped to write a 'collective' play *Révolte dans les Asturies* (1936). It was staged by the *avant-garde* Théâtre du Travail company which he founded with friends in 1935 (it became the Théâtre de l'Équipe in 1937) and in which he worked in turn as producer, adaptor, actor and theorist, the aim of the group being to provide good plays for working-class audiences and a small intellectual élite. His first collection of essays, *L'envers et l'endroit* (1937), gives a picture of his early life of poverty and contains a first indication of his later doctrine of 'the absurd' with its lyrical orchestration of such themes as happiness and suffering, natural beauty and the horror of death. These themes, taken further in the course of his travels in France,

Italy and Czechoslovakia, reappear in the 'pagan' essays of *Noces* (1938). Here we have clear evidence of his fundamentally mediterranean outlook and his opposition to what he considered to be the 'nordic gloom' of a Europe following 'history' rather than 'nature' and experiencing tortured self-consciousness rather than spontaneity.

Camus's concept of 'the absurd' includes experiences which defy rational explanation or seem to confound our sense of fair play and thwart our desire for a happy and coherent existence. Metaphysical alienation and the problem of suffering are recurrent themes in his work. He explored the features of contemporary nihilism in his first two plays published as *Le malentendu, suivi de Caligula* (1944; tr. S. Gilbert, *Caligula and Cross Purpose*, 1947). *Caligula* attempts to take nihilism to its devastating logical conclusion and curiously foreshadows (it was written in 1938) those latter-day 'mad emperors' Hitler and Mussolini. The absurd is also the theme of his brilliant first novel *L'étranger* (1942; tr. S. Gilbert, *The Outsider*, 1946) with its portrait of an 'outsider' who is condemned to death less for the killing of an Arab than for the fact that he never says more than he feels and refuses to conform in the way society expects. *Le mythe de Sisyphe* (1942; tr. J. O'Brien, *The Myth of Sisyphus*, 1955) is a philosophical essay about the same concept.

Camus had said at an early stage that the absurd must be regarded as a point of departure, not an end. His thinking – particularly during his experiences in the French Resistance – increasingly took the form of rebellion against nihilism in the name of humanity and in support of that moral coherence for which a sense of the absurd is really a form of nostalgia. This change is expressed in the four *Lettres à un ami allemand* (1945; in *Resistance, Rebellion and Death*, tr. J. O'Brien, 1960). Rebellion amounts to humane stoicism in his second novel, *La peste* (1947; tr. S. Gilbert, *The Plague*, 1948), with its account of the fight against an epidemic in Oran by characters whose important achievement is less their efficacity than their assertion of their human dignity. This is a richly symbolical novel with its references both to the German Occupation and to the more general human predicament. Somewhat similar material is used in the unsuccessful play *L'état de siège* (1948). The concept of rebellion as a moral and metaphysical idea is contrasted with the politico-historical concept of revolution in *L'homme révolté* (1951; tr. A. Bower, *The Rebel*, 1953).

Immediately after the last war Camus emerged from his activities with the clandestine press as one of the most influential journalists and leader-writers in France. Much of his journalism is collected in the three volumes of *Actuelles* published respectively in 1950, 1953 and 1958. Other essays compose *L'été* (1954).

His fourth play, *Les justes* (1950; in *Caligula and Three Other Plays*, tr. S. Gilbert, N.Y., 1958), has been more admired in Europe than in England. It has also been argued that his most successful work for the theatre is really to be found in his adaptations for the stage of ⇨ Larivey, ⇨ Calderón, ⇨ Lope de Vega, ⇨ Dostoyevsky, Faulkner and ⇨ Buzzati.

In his third novel, *La chute* (1956; tr. J. O'Brien, *The Fall*, 1957), he seemed to experience a temporary disillusionment and dissatisfaction with some of his previous ideas though he firmly rejected suggestions that it contains evidence of a turning to Christianity. In the following year (1957), in which he was also awarded the Nobel Prize, he published a collection of short stories *L'exil et le royaume* (tr. J. O'Brien, *Exile and the Kingdom*, 1958), which show his skill and virtuosity as a master of different prose styles as well as returning to some of his earlier ideas, presented in new formulations. Since his death two volumes of his notebooks have been published as *Carnets: Mai 1935–Février 1942* (1962; tr. P. Thody, *Notebooks, 1935–42*, 1963), and *Carnets: Janvier 1942–Mars 1951* (1964; tr. P. Thody, *Notebooks, 1942–1951*, 1966). [JC]

*Théâtre, récits et nouvelles*, ed. R. Quilliot (Pléiade, 1962); *Essais*, ed. R. Quilliot (Pléiade, 1965).

R. Quilliot, *La mer et les prisons* (Paris, 1956); G. Brée, *Camus* (New Brunswick, N.J., 1958); J. Cruickshank, *A.C. and the Literature of Revolt* (1959); P. Thody, *A.C.: 1913–1960* (1961); A. King, *C.* (1964).

**Cancioneiros.** The earliest Portuguese poetry has come down in three manuscript songbooks: the *Cancioneiro da Ajuda* (in the Ajuda Library, Lisbon); the *Cancioneiro da Vaticana*; and the *Cancioneiro Colocci-Brancuti* (in the Biblioteca Nacional, Lisbon), which once belonged to the 16th-century Italian humanist, Colocci. Their contents fall into three groups: *cantigas de* *amigo*, *cantigas de amor*, and *cantigas de escárnio*.

The enchanting poetry of the *cantigas de amigo* constitutes one of the supreme values of Portuguese literature. The earliest of these poems, attributed to Pai Soares de Taveiró, dates probably from 1189. If this marks the beginning of the cultivation of this kind of poetry by poets whose names have come down to us, that is only a stage in a tradition whose origins are much more ancient, and which has lasted into the present century. Leite de Vasconcelos heard similar parallelistic songs, called *retornadas*, sung in the district of Bragança.

The *cantigas de amigo* are parallelistic songs consisting of two series of distichs sung antiphonally, the last line of each distich forming the first line of the next in the same series. Between the two series there is change of assonance, without change of meaning. There is a refrain sung in chorus.

The *cantigas de amigo*, like the poems in the Chinese Book of Songs, are put in the mouths of women crying for their lovers. (One or two examples uttered by men are doubtless later derivatives.) In the *cantigas de amigo*, as in the early *Frauenlied*, dark colours predominate: the pain of parting, longing and waiting, anxiety about the lover's fidelity, grief for his loss, jealousy and frank desire. Besides the meeting at night and the parting at dawn (in the *alba*) there is the chance meeting at the well-head and elsewhere. The stag, in Portugal, is the symbol of the beloved man, taking the place of the falcon in other literatures. These scenes are recalled in monologue, or in conversation, usually with the girl's mother, who in certain sophisticated examples may even be her rival for the man's affections. Often there is description of natural scenery: peculiarly Portuguese are the beach-scenes where the girl watches the ship that bears her lover away (the *barcarolas*).

In addition there are *bailias*, the dance-songs of the community, *cantigas de romaria* or pilgrimage-songs, and *serranilhas* or *pastorelas* (always of French-Provençal origin) in which the girl meets by chance a gentleman, perhaps a knight on horseback, even the king's son.

In the *cantigas de amor* there appears in the place of the yielding, longing woman the sighing, serving man. This reflects the new knightly spirit of 12th-century Provence, which was propagated at Iberian courts by resident Provençal poets. Unhappily the *cantigas de amor* offer only a pale reflection of the psychological and linguistic richness of Provençal poetry. The expression is direct and almost imageless.

The last group, that of the *cantigas de escárnio* or *cantigas de mal-dizer*, fell also under the influence of the Provençal *sirventès*, but reflects an older tradition of satirical poetry, mostly concerned with the private life of the *jongleurs*, their alcoholic and venereal excesses.

The poems of the *Cancioneiros* are all attributed to authors, but biographical details are few. Among the *jograis* (*jongleurs*) may be named Airas Corpancho (no doubt a fat man), João Servando, Lourenço, Martim Codax, Martim de Ginzó, Meendinho. Among the *segrêis* (aristocrats who had turned professional poets) are Bernardo de Bonaval, Pêro da Ponte, João Baveca. The clergy are represented by Sancho Sanches, Airas Nunes, and perhaps Pêro Meogo.

Afonso Lopes de Baião was governor of the Sousa estates, 1253–77. Estêvão Coelho was father or brother of the Pêro Coelho who was brought to justice in 1360 for the murder of Inês de Castro. Estêvão da Guarda held various offices at the court of King Dinis. Fernão Velho lived at the court of Afonso III. Gonçalo Eanes de Vinhal distinguished himself at the siege of Seville by Alfonso X, and was rewarded with the lordship of Aguilar. João Soares Coelho took part in the conquest of the Algarve. Pai Gomes Charinho was created admiral by Alfonso X.

The largest single group of poems (138 in number) is attributed to King Dinis (d. 1325) who shows himself one of the supreme masters in his handling of popular themes, as well as one of the more interesting composers of *cantigas de amor*. The second largest group (of 56) is attributed to King Dinis's bastard, D. Afonso Sanches (d. 1329). Thereafter the indigenous poetry retreats to the folk from whom it had sprung. [ARM]

H. Lang, *Liederbuch des Königs Denis von Portugal* (1894); J. J. Nunes (ed.), *Cantigas de Amigo* (3 vols., 1926–8); *Canc. da Ajuda* (CSC); *Canc. da Bibl. Nac. antigo Colocci-Brancuti*, ed. E. P. and J. P. Machado (1947).

M. Rodrigues Lapa, *Das Origens da Poesia Lírica em Portugal na Idade Média* (Lisbon, 1929).

**Canetti, Elias** (Rutschuk, Bulgaria 1905– ). Austrian novelist, dramatist and essayist. After a polyglot upbringing he studied and stayed in Vienna; in 1938 he went to England. His concern with the psychology of fascism is reflected in the novel *Die Blendung* (1935; tr. C. V. Wedgwood, *Auto da Fé*, 1946), the speculative-analytical *Masse und Macht* (1960; tr. C. Stewart, *Crowds and Power*, 1962) and plays like *Die Komödie der Eitelkeit* (1934, published, 1950) and *Die Befristeten* (1956). [LL]

*E.C. Welt im Kopf*, intr. E. Fried (1962) (selections); *Dramen* (1964).

H. Daiber, 'E.C.', in *Wort in der Zeit*, 3 (1957); K. Löwenstein, 'E.C.', in *Bulletin L.-Baeck, Institut*, 11 (1960).

**Canth, Minna,** née Johnsson (Tampere 1844–Kuopio 1897). Finnish novelist and dramatist. Left a widow with seven children in 1879, she turned to writing plays and stories while earning a living by keeping a yarn-shop in Kuopio. She was a pioneer of realism in Finland, influenced by Ibsen, Björnson and Zola, whose works she read in the original. She became a sharp and fearless critic of social problems, fighting for woman's independence and against prejudices of every kind. In the early 1890s she became influenced by Tolstoy. *Papin perhe* (1891) and *Anna-Liisa* (1895) are her finest achievements, the former a play about family conflicts, the latter about an infanticide. In her short stories she deals with social abuses and the underdog. She is still one of the best Finnish playwrights with a natural ear for dialogue. [IR]

*Kootut teokset* (5 vols., 1917–44).

L. Hagman, *M.C.* (2 vols., Helsinki, 1906–11); H. Vilkemaa, *M.C.* (Helsinki, 1931); G. von Frenckell-Thesleff, *M.C.* (Helsinki, 1944).

**Čapek, Karel** (Malé Svatoňovice, Bohemia 1890–Prague 1938). Czech novelist, dramatist and essayist. The son of a country doctor, he studied philosophy in Prague, Berlin and Paris, worked as a journalist throughout his life and travelled extensively in Europe. His work gives new meaning to the precept of Protagoras, that man is the measure of all things: for he sees how man, noble and wretched, is menaced and mocked in our time. *Továrna na absolutno* (1922; tr. M. and R. Weatherall, *The Absolute at Large*, 1944) defends man against the Absolute by attempting to prove that there are no absolute values. But man's humanity is also menaced by himself; and in his plays *R.U.R.* ('Rossum's Universal Robots', 1920; tr. P. Selver, 1923), *Věc Makropulos* (1922; tr. P. Selver, *The Macropoulos Secret*, 1927), and *Adam the Creator* (1927; tr. D. Round, 1929), as well as in his novel *Krakatit* (1924; tr. L. Hyde, *An Atomic Phantasy*, 1948) he maintains that man's desire to become master of the universe by changing the natural order of things may mean the suicide of humanity. The trilogy *Hordubal* (1933), *Povětroň* (1934) and *Obyčejný život* (1934; tr. M. and R. Weatherall, *Hordubal – An Ordinary Life-Meteor*, 1949) fluctuates between determinist realism and romanticism; behind the optimistic theorizing there lies a profounder awareness of man's fate and a feeling of ultimate resignation.

His travel books and essays, e.g. *Letters from England* (1924, tr. P. Selver, 1925), uphold democracy not as a system of social organization but as a moral task demanding compassion and patience. Fascism and the German threat drew from him a protest in *Bílá nemoc* (1937; tr. P. Selver and R. Neale, *Power and Glory*, 1938) and the recognition that individual and national freedom must in the last resort be defended by force (*The Mother*, 1938, tr. P. Selver, 1939: a play inspired by Brecht's *Señora Carrar's Rifles*). His relativist humanism was characteristic of his age but did not fully come to grips with the problems posed by 20th-century mass societies.

*Spisy bratří*, (51 vols., 1929–47); Dílo bratří (1954– ).

I. Klíma, *K.Č.* (1962); W. E. Harkins, *K.Č.* (1962); O. Elton, *Essays and Addresses* (1939); *SEER*, xv, 1936–7.

**Čapek-Chod, Karel Matěj,** pseud. of K. M. Čapek (Domažlice 1860–Prague 1927). Czech novelist. Born of peasant stock in southern Bohemia. As a journalist in Prague he acquired a detailed knowledge of its society, from the underworld to scientific and artistic circles. He became the chief exponent of the Czech moral and analytical novel, constructed in accordance with a rigid determinist system. He is a consistent pessimist who does not believe that the world has a purpose. His best novels, *Turbina* (1916; tr. J. Chopin, *La Turbine*, Paris, 1916), *Antonín Vondrejc* (1917–18), and *Jindrové* (1921), portray the world as a hermetically closed prison whose inmates are helpless puppets performing a play on which they have no influence; he shows striking similarities with Camus and Sartre. He manages to convey the inescapable automatism of life and suggests that there is no other solution for man but to exist, simply because he is unthinkable as non-existent. [KB]

*Spisy* (18 vols., 1921–38); *La fille de Jaïre*, tr. J. Chopin (Paris, 1929).

F. Kovárna, *K.M.Č.-Ch.* (Prague, 1936); V. Šach, *K.M.Č.-Ch.* (Prague, 1949); R. Wellek, *K.Č.*, in *SEER*, XV, 43 (1936); A. Novák, in *SEER*, II, 4 (1923).

**Capetanakis, Demetrios** (Smyrna 1912–London 1944). Greek poet and critic. He studied political science and economics at Athens University and philosophy with Karl Jaspers at Heidelberg. There he came in contact with disciples of Stefan George, and the latter's ideas had for a time a considerable influence on his development. He returned to Greece in 1937 and began publishing philosophical and literary treatises. In 1939 he came to England with a British Council scholarship to continue his studies at Cambridge. His acquaintance with English literature and England, to which he was strongly attracted from the start, had remarkable effects on his artistic development: he started writing poetry in English, a language he scarcely knew before coming to England. His first English poem appeared in *Penguin New Writing* (1942), and other poems of his, as well as literary essays he wrote in English, were subsequently published in numbers of *New Writing and Daylight*. In spite of their limited vocabulary, his poems (sixteen published in all) are fluent and neat in structure and from their seeming simplicity emerge enigmatic messages and disturbing tones of tragedy. Of his essays his more notable are: *Dostoyevsky*, *Rimbaud*, *Charlotte Brontë*, *Notes on Some Contemporary Writers*. During his short stay in England he made many friends among well-known literary figures, especially with John Lehmann, Edith Sitwell and William Plomer. He died of leukaemia at Westminster Hospital. [SJP]

*D.K. A Greek Poet in England* (1947) (poems and articles).

**Capuana, Luigi** (Mineo, Catania 1839–Catania 1915). Italian realist novelist and critic. He broke off his university law studies to go to Florence in 1864 where he became drama editor of *La nazione*. His chief importance is in having introduced the theories of French naturalist writers into Italy, and in having encouraged ⇨ Verga in the development of his own form of realism – regionalism. In addition to many short stories (e.g. the collection *Le paesane*, 1894), many very successful children's fables (e.g. *C'era una volta*, 1882; *Scurpiddu*, 1898), many Sicilian-dialect plays (published collectively in *Teatro dialettale siciliano*, Palermo, 1911–12, vols. 1–3; Catania, 1920–1, vols. 4–5), he wrote several novels (e.g. *Giacinta*, 1879; ed. A. Cervieri, 1914); and his best work, *Il Marchese di Roccaverdina*, 1901; ed. G. R. Ceriello, 1957). His critical theories on naturalism envisaged the ultimate fusion of the novel into a purely scientific, impersonal, case-history. His obsession for superficial details made his characters too remote, and, as Verga remarked about Flaubert, realism tended to be mere reality. [RHC]

E. Scalia, *L.C. and His Times* (N.Y., 1952); C. Di Blasi, *L.C.: vita, amicizie, relazioni letterarie* (Catania, 1954); *Minori*, iv.

**Caragiale, Ion Luca** (Haimanale 1852–Berlin 1912). Rumanian writer of plays and short stories. His father's family was of Greek origin and connected with the theatre. He was initiated in his teens into a life of poverty and hard work, from which he seemed in his thirties to be emerging through the success of his plays. But his irritability and sarcasm alienated even friends, and after holding the post of Director-General of the National Theatre at Bucharest for only a few months (1888–9), he never again had a good job. In 1904 he inherited money and removed with his family to Berlin for the rest of his life.

His period of playwriting lasted a little over ten years. Beginning with *O noapte furtunoasă* (1879; tr. F. Knight, *A Stormy Night*, 1956), a comedy of Bucharest *petit bourgeois* life, it reached its zenith with his best play *O scrisoare pierdută* (1884; tr. ibid., *A Lost Letter*), a comedy of political intrigue in a provincial town, and ended with the grim drama of a peasant woman's revenge, *Năpastă*. *Năpastă* was not well received, and thereafter he wrote sketches and stories.

The sketches, two or three pages long, are scenes of contemporary life, sometimes set in the provinces, but more typically in the less fashionable quarters of the capital, the world of clerks and shopkeepers. Their liveliness is largely due to the admirable dialogue characteristic of the comic dramatist. His comedy is astringent, but detached; neither caressing nor arch, but without bitterness. He has, as Lamb said of Congreve, 'the strange power of interesting you all along in the pursuits of characters, for whom you absolutely care nothing'.

Among his finest work are *La hanul lui Mînjoală* (1898), a subtly ironical tale of the supernatural, and *Kir Ianulea* (1909), a longer tale which is adapted from Machiavelli's *Belfagor* and set in 18th-century Wallachia. [EDT]

*Opere*, ed. P. Zarifopol (1930ff.); *The Lost Letter and Other Plays*, tr. F. Knight (1956).

**Carco, Francis,** pseud. of François Carcopino (New Caledonia 1886–Paris 1958). French poet, novelist and bohemian. His adult life was spent in France and he lived mainly in Paris after 1910. He wrote studies of a number of painters, and a book on Verlaine (with whose poetry his own has several affinities), but he is best known as the novelist and poet of Montmartre. He writes, with a mixture of cynicism and sentimentality, of the criminals, pimps and prostitutes of the 'Butte' in such novels as *Jésus-la-Caille* (1914), *L'homme traqué* (1922), *Rien qu'une femme* (1924), *Rue Pigalle* (1927) and *Brumes* (1935). These picturesque, entertaining novels, enlivened by argot, do not always avoid emotional and verbal clichés (yet have a certain documentary value).

As a poet, Carco has been admired for the compassion and tenderness of his verse with its direct and unforced evocation of emotion and mood. His most successful collections are *La Bohême de mon cœur* (1912), *Mortefontaine* (1946) and *Poèmes en prose* (1948). In 1934 he wrote a fascinating account of his early life under the title *De Montmartre au Quartier latin*. [JC]

P. Chabaneix, *F.C.* (Paris, 1949); S. Weiner, *F.C.: The Career of a Literary Bohemian* (N.Y., 1952); A. Négis, *Mon ami C.* (Paris, 1953).

**Cardarelli, Vincenzo** (Corneto Tarquinia 1887–Rome 1959). Italian poet and prose writer. One of the founders of the influential literary magazine *La Ronda* (1919) and director of the review *La Fiera Letteraria* (1949). His cultivation of formal structure and style in poetry makes him appear a latter-day classic, follower of Leopardi. His other confessed master was Baudelaire and there is often authentic passion beneath the stylistic decorum and anguish behind his irony. At its best his language is deeply reflective, though his brilliance sometimes degenerates into mere sophistication in his verse. His poetic themes are mainly 'confessions of soul', objectified in a description of landscape or an analysis of a love situation; his love poems are, with those of ⇨ Pavese, among the finest of the century. He first became known for his *Prologhi* (1916) and his later works include *Viaggi nel tempo* (1920), *Favole e memorie* (1924), and many collections of poems (1936, 1942, 1946, 1949, 1958). [GD]

R. Risi, *V.C. prosatore e poeta* (Bern, 1951); B. Romani, *C.* (Padua, 1942); P. Bigongiari, *Poesia italiana del Novecento* (Milan, 1960).

**Carducci, Giosuè** (Val di Castello 1835–Bologna 1907). Italian critic, scholar and poet. The influences of his parents' patriotism, his classical education and his youthful enthusiasm for romantic writers produced a unique fusion of classical and romantic in his character. He became Professor of Italian Literature at Bologna University in 1860, senator in 1890, and received the Nobel Prize in 1906. As critic and literary historian, his work covered a vast field and marked important advances in the standards of scholarship. He is known chiefly for his poetry, characterized by his profoundly patriotic vision of the great historic past and future destiny of the regenerate Italy (cf. 'Nell'annuale della fondazione di Roma', 'Dinnanzi alle Termi de Caracalla', 'Alle fonti del Clitumno' in *Odi barbare*, 1877; and 'Cadore' in *Rime e ritmi*, 1898). Sometimes a mood of spiritual elation on beholding an old building in a beautiful natural setting produces fine poetry of almost religious fervour (e.g. 'Il canto d'amore' in *Giambi ed epodi*, 1867–9; 'Santa Maria degli Angeli' in *Rime nuove*, 1861–87; and 'La chiesa di Polenta' in *Rime e ritmi*) though his outspoken condemnation of Christianity in 'Alle fonti del Clitumno' is perhaps more typical of his religious views. Likewise he attacked the flaccid poetry of the late romantics, seeing himself as a poet-prophet-blacksmith, forging, in a period of national depression, a virile beautiful poetry capable of inspiring Italians to achieve their great destiny (*Inno a Satana*, 1869; 'Congedo' in *Rime nuove*; and 'Preludio' in *Odi barbare*). He experimented cleverly with classical metres in *Odi barbare* (1877–89), not as purely technical virtuosity but as the ideal medium for his grandiose theme. He admitted that his inspiration was too often self-conscious and literary; all the more welcome, therefore, are some poems in *Rime nuove* which express with elegance and restraint essentially lyrical themes of nostalgia for his carefree childhood in the gentle Tuscan Maremma ('Traversando la Maremma Toscana', 'Idillio Maremmano', 'San Martino', 'Visione davanti a San Guido'), of sorrow at the death of his son ('Funere mersit acerbo', 'Pianto antico'), or of an idyllic natural scene ('Il bove'). [RHC]

*Edizione Nazionale* (30 vols., 1935–40); *Antologia carducciana* (poesie e prose scelte), ed. G. Mazzoni and G. Picciola (9th edn., 1957); *C., A Selection*, tr. G. L. Bickersteth (1913); *The Barbarian Odes*, tr. W. Fletcher Smith (Menasha, Wisconsin, 1939).

A. Galletti, *C. il poeta, il critico* (Milan, 1948); N. Busetto, *G.C. l'uomo, il poeta il critico e il prosatore* (Padua, 1958); F. Flora, *La poesia e la prosa di G.C.* (Pisa, 1959); G. Natali, *G.C.* (Florence, 1961); Binni, *Cl*, ii; *Maggiori*, ii; Kay, *PBIV*; Dionisotti, *OBIV*.

**'Carmina Burana.'** A 13th-century collection of Latin poems, mostly anonymous, called after the abbey of Benediktbeuern, in Bavaria, to which the manuscript formerly belonged. Some items are serious (e.g. satires and crusade poems) but the majority are light. The versification shows a decided advance on the *Cambridge Songs*, the technique of some of the poems being practically perfect. Many items, as in the earlier collection, show liturgical influence, others the influence of vernacular poetry. Among the former are love-poems written in the metres of the great ⇨ sequences, *Veni sancte Spiritus*, and *Stabat mater*. Interest in the *Carmina burana* has grown in recent years owing to the use of a number of items in the collection as the text of a 'scenic cantata' by the Bavarian composer, Carl Orff. [FB]

Ed. J. A. Schmeller (Stuttgart, 1847, etc.); ed. A. Hilka and O. Schumann (2 vols., Heidelberg, 1930–41); *Auswahl*, ed. E. Buschor with German verse tr. (Wiesbaden, 1956) (50 poems); tr. in J. A. Symonds, *Wine, Women and Song* (1884, many repr.) (selections); Lindsay, *MLP*; Waddell, *MLL*.

Raby, *SLP*.

**Carner, Josep.** ⇨ Catalan Literature.

**Caro, Annibale** (Civitanova 1507–Rome 1566). Italian man of letters. A Renaissance courtier, he wrote a comedy *Gli straccioni* (publ. 1582) and some *Rime*, but is better remembered for his interesting and accomplished *Letters* to friends and particularly for his long standard translation of the *Aeneid* (Venice, 1581) into supple blank verse. [DGR]

*L'Eneide*, ed. A. Pompeati (1954); *Opere*, ed. V. Turri (1912); *Lettere familiari*, ed. A. Greco (3 vols., 1957–61); *Commedie del Cinquecento*, ed. A. Borlenghi (1959).

F. Sarri, *A.C.* (Milan, 1934); A Greco, *A.C. Cultura e poesia* (Rome, 1950); C. Oliveri, *L'Eneide del C.* (Turin, 1965); *Minori*, ii.

**Caro, Rodrigo** (Utrera 1573–Seville 1647). Spanish poet and antiquarian. Famous for his poem on the ruins of the ancient Roman settlement of Itálica, near Seville. Its fine rhetorical sweep derives from ⇨ Herrera and is unaffected by Gongorist mannerism. [JMC]

*Obras*, ed. M. Menéndez y Pelayo (2 vols., 1883–84); Cohen, *PBSV*; Blecua, *FLE*; Trend, *OBSV*.

*RFE*, XXIII, 1936.

**Carossa, Hans** (Tölz, Bavaria 1878–Rittsteig 1956). German novelist. A doctor who, in (conscious) contrast to the nihilism of many contemporaries, struggled to preserve a Goethean faith in life, to reconcile the vision of poetry with the facts of medicine. His major work is the autobiographical sequence: *Eine Kindheit* (1922; tr. A. N. Scott, *A Childhood*, 1933), *Rumänisches Tagebuch* (1924; tr. ibid., *A Roumanian Diary*, 1929) and *Verwandlungen einer Jugend* (1928; tr. ibid., *Boyhood and Youth*, 1931). The work has been rightly compared with Goethe's autobiography, both for its classic style and for its philosophy of organic growth and wholeness of a higher and essentially good order transcending pain. Of his 'autobiographical' novels, *Doktor Bürgers Ende* (1913) suggests what conflicts he himself transcended, while *Ungleiche Welten* (1951) tells of the 'sickness' caused by the Nazi regime. His poems (*Gesammelte Gedichte*, 1956), though interesting for the integrity of their perceptions, are in expression little more than competent. [PB]

*Sämtliche Werke* (2 vols., 1962).

A. Langen, *H.C. Weltbild und Stil* (Bielefeld, 1955); R. Hofrichter. *Three Poets and Reality* (New Haven, 1942); K. H. Silomon, *H.C. Eine Bibliographie* (Murnau, 1948); H. Schlegel, *Die Lyrik H.C.s* (Zürich, 1963); *GLL*, II (1938); III (1939); XI (1957).

**Carpelan, Bo** (Helsinki 1926– ). Swedo-Finnish poet. He aims at great clarity and simplicity in his verse, which shows the influence of Rabbe ⇨ Enckell and of the Swedish poetry of the forties. [IR]

**Carrillo y Sotomayor, Luis de** (Córdoba 1582/3–Puerto de Santa María 1610). Spanish poet and naval captain. His *Fábula de Acis y Galatea* and his theoretical *Libro de la erudición poética* (ed. M. Cardenal Iracheta, 1946) foreshadow ⇨ Góngora, though each worked independently from common Latin sources. Sometimes facile or awkwardly complex, there is true gravity in his sonnets on death and time, and brilliance in his reasonings on love and loss. His works were published posthumously in 1611. [JMC]

*Poesías completas*, ed. D. Alonso (1936); Cohen, *PBSV*; Blecua, *FLE*.
Alonso, *EEG*.

**Carvajal, Valentín Lamas.** ⇨ Galician Literature.

**Casanova di Seingalt, Giacomo Girolamo** (Venice 1725–Château Dux, Bohemia 1798). Italian adventurer, publicist and autobiographer. The talented son of a theatrical family, he was an avid student, and might have achieved distinction in any of several professions, but for his wild temperament. After unsuccessful beginnings in the Church and in music he went abroad in 1750, to France and Germany. On returning to Venice he was imprisoned for alleged impiety and magical practices, but eventually escaped and embarked on his notorious career as amorist and trickster in court circles all over Europe. He published several historical works in Italian, and a fantastic novel in French (*Icosaméron*, 1788), but his literary reputation, and personal notoriety, rests primarily on his autobiographical writings, the *Histoire de ma fuite des prisons de Venise* (1788; tr. A. Machen, 1925) and the posthumous *Mémoires* (tr. A. Machen, 1959–61), which narrate (and perhaps embroider) his adventures in a lively if sometimes imperfect French, and shed valuable light on the manners of the age. [WHB]

B. Dobrée, *C.* (1933); J. Rives Childs, *C.* (1961).

**Casona, Alejandro** (Tines 1900–Asturias 1965). Spanish dramatist. He lived in exile in Argentina. His plays are poetic and humorous in the tradition of Benavente; the best are *La sirena varada* (Lope de Vega Prize, 1934) and the charming *Prohibido suicidarse en primavera* (1937), both published in Buenos Aires (1940). [JMC]

*Obras completas* (Mexico, 1954ff.); *La sirena varada, Prohibido suicidarse en primavera, Nuestra Natacha*, etc. (BC).
A. Valbuena Prat, *Historia del teatro español* (Barcelona, 1956).

**Cassiodorus, Flavius Magnus Aurelius** (*c.* 485–*c.* 580). Monastic scholar. He served Theodoric the Ostrogoth, then became a monk and founded two monasteries at Vivarium, South Italy, where he encouraged the copying of manuscripts, both secular and sacred, pagan and Christian, thus acting as a link between classical and medieval culture. His letters, dating from his secular career, and written on behalf of Theodoric to the Emperors, to Alaric the Goth, and to many others, are valuable both historically and linguistically. In his *Institutiones divinarum et secularium litterarum* he lays down an educational programme for his monks, with instructions on the use of manuscripts, etc. His *History of the Goths* has been lost but is the foundation of a work by ⇨ Jordanes. [FB]

Migne, *PL*, 69–70; *Institutiones*, ed. R. A. B. Mynors (1937); *Records of Civilization*, tr. L. W. Jones (1946); *Variae*, ed. T. Mommsen (MGH, AA, XII, 1894); *The Letters of C.* (a condensed tr. of the *Variae*, etc.), tr. T. Hodgkin (1886).
E. K. Rand, *Makers of the Middle Ages* (N.Y., 1957); Duckett, *GMA*; Laistner, *TLWE*.

**Cassirer, Ernst** (Breslau 1874–New York 1945). German neo-Kantian philosopher. For many years Privatdozent in Berlin, then professor in Hamburg (1919–33). He left Hitler's Germany, going first to England, then Sweden (1935), and finally America (1941). His work is important also for the study of literature. In general he followed ⇨ Dilthey in relating the evolution of philosophy to the totality of spiritual culture, including religion and aesthetics; see in this connexion his *Erkenntnisproblem* ('Problem of Knowledge', 4 vols., 1906, 1908, 1923, 1941). *Freiheit und Form*, written during the First World War, expounds the idealistic tendencies of German culture and contains fine interpretations of Goethe and Schiller. His defence of 18th-century ideas against irrationalist, Romantic theories inspired many articles on Goethe, Kant and

Rousseau, and above all *Die Philosophie der Aufklärung* (1932; tr. F. C. A. Koelln, *The Philosophy of the Enlightenment*, Princeton, 1932). His major work, *Die Philosophie der symbolischen Formen* (1923–9; tr. R. Manheim, *The Philosophy of Symbolic Forms*, 1953–7), offers an inspiring account of the way mental images, from the most primitive totemism to the mathematical concepts of modern physics, produce that 'synthesis of world and mind' – a phrase which Cassirer borrowed from Goethe – which we know as reality. In each of the symbolic forms of language, art, religion and science 'man discovers and proves a new power – the power to build up a world of his own, an ideal world . . . [they] cannot be reduced to a common denominator . . . All these functions complete and complement one another' (*An Essay on Man*, 1944). [AKT]

*Idee und Gestalt* (Goethe, Schiller, Hölderlin, Kleist) (Berlin, 1921); *Language and Myth*, tr. S. K. Langer (N.Y., 1946); *The Logic of the Humanities*, tr. C. M. Howe (Yale, 1961); *The Individual and the Cosmos in Renaissance Philosophy*, tr. M. Domandi (1963).

*The Philosophy of E.C.*, ed. P. A. Schilpp (N.Y., 1958); C. A. Hamburg, *Symbol and Reality* (The Hague, 1956).

**Cassola, Carlo** (Rome 1917– ). Italian novelist. In 1942 he published two small volumes of stories, *La visita* and *Alla periferia*, and wrote a short essay, 'Il film dell'impossibile', in which he laid down the foundations of his aesthetic: the essence of beauty, in literature as in painting, is absence of motion, lack of life, timelessness; the artist, in his descriptions or pictures, creates a form of static beauty constantly alluding to movement, life, the flowing of time. In his novels, which he began to write ten years later, expanding ideas contained in his early stories (Fausto and Anna, Bube and his girl, Alfredo the Hunter, the communist alabaster workers of Volterra are all there), he remained true to his ideals, keeping strangely aloof from post-war literary currents. Both neo-realism and neo-formalism, however, influenced him in his search for absolute narrative objectivity and stylistic purity. He tells his stories (a typical example is 'Il taglio del bosco', 1954) simply and artlessly, and empties them deliberately of action and development (nothing ever *happens* in them) so that every smallest variation from absolute stillness, every single word in a threadbare linguistic structure, may be thrown into startling relief and acquire a new unsuspected meaning. Bearing in mind what has been said of the French *nouveau roman*, of which he is in many ways a forerunner, his stories are the nearest one can get to a non-story, and his style is a good example of the 'zero degree' of writing. Unable to avoid altogether the pitfalls of such perilous aesthetic theories, he has often become indiscriminate in his striving for complete objectivity, like a tape-recorder picking up all relevant and irrelevant sounds. His search for naked simplicity makes some of his recent novels, developed from early small-format stories, look more like blown-up photographs than good paintings. [GMC]

*Fausto e Anna* (1952; tr. Isobel Quigly, *Fausto and Anna*, 1960); *Il taglio del bosco* (1959) (containing most of his previous stories and novelettes); *La ragazza di Bube* (1960; tr. M. Waldman, *Bebo's Girl*, 1962); *Un cuore arido* (1961; tr. W. Weaver, *An Arid Heart*, 1964); *La visita* (1962) (containing his 1942 stories and 'Il film dell'impossibile'); *Il cacciatore* (1964).

Pullini, *RID*; Mariani, *GNI*; Ferretti, *LI*; Alberto, *SP*; R. Macchioni-Jodi, *C.* (1967).

**Castanheda, Fernão Lopes de** (Santarém 149 ?–Coimbra 1559). Portuguese chronicler. Illegitimate son of a Crown Judge (*Ouvidor*), who was appointed to this post at Goa in 1528, Castanheda was a Dominican novice for a short time before leaving the Order and accompanying his father to India. He claims to have served in many regions of the East, and he may have gone as far as the Moluccas before returning to Portugal at an uncertain date, traditionally 1538. He seems to have formed the plan of writing the history of the Portuguese in the East before going out to Goa; and on his return, he checked and collated the information he had acquired *in situ* by interviewing, throughout the length and breadth of Portugal, fidalgos and captains home from the Orient. Physically exhausted and financially impoverished by his strenuous researches, he accepted the post of Beadle and Archivist at the University of Coimbra, where he compiled 10 volumes of his *História do Descobrimento e Conquista da Índia pelos Portugueses*. The first *Livro* was published in 1551, thus beating the *Décadas* of João de ⇨ Barros by a short head, to the evident annoyance of the latter. Castanheda published another six *Livros* during his lifetime (1552–4), and an eighth was published posthumously by his sons in

1561. The remaining two *Livros* were suppressed by royal command, for reasons which are not clear, but fragments of the ninth were discovered and published in 1929. An edition of the first nine *Livros* was published by the Coimbra University Press in 1924–33. Partial translations in French, Spanish, Italian, and English had appeared between 1553 and 1582. His literary style is more primitive and pedestrian than that of Barros and ⇨ Couto, but where his work can be compared with the original documents it stands the test equally well. [CRB]

A. J. Saraiva, *História da Cultura em Portugal* (Lisbon, 1950ff.).

**Castelao, Alfonso R.** ⇨ Galician Literature.

**Castelo Branco, Camilo** (Lisbon 1825–São Miguel de Seide 1895). Portuguese novelist and short-story writer. An illegitimate child, orphaned at the age of ten, he was left to the care of various relatives, educated in small village schools in Trás-os-Montes, and soon turned to the tempestuous life that was to be characteristic of him. After a short-lived marriage in 1841, he (unsuccessfully) studied medicine at Coimbra and Oporto. As a bohemian journalist and serial writer in Oporto he became notorious for his amorous and literary intrigues. Mortified when one of his mistresses, Ana Plácidó, married a rich merchant (1850), he sought refuge in the priesthood. He left the seminary, however, without taking his vows (1852). His novels and stories were now in popular demand and in any case Ana was not permanently inaccessible. In 1859 he finally persuaded her to leave her husband and to flee to Lisbon with him. As a result he was arrested, imprisoned, but later acquitted. The episode provided the material for his most popular 'romance passional', *Amor de Perdição* (1862). The remainder of his life was more prosaic but overshadowed by tragedy. He finally married Ana, though the romance had by this time left their relationship. Their children provided no consolation for the blindness with which he was increasingly afflicted. The pressure of work was enormous; though *Amor de Perdição* had been a success, Camilo was never remotely prosperous. Though he received the title of Viscount in 1885, the burden was too much for him, and in 1895 he committed suicide.

The unstable vitality of his life is constantly reflected in his books, which are often partly autobiographical. Among his hundreds of novels and stories we can distinguish: novels of satire, usually a gentle reproof of the bourgeois nouveau-riche, such as *A Queda de um Anjo* (1866); the tales of provincial life, *Novelas dó Minho* (1875–6); *A Brasileira de Prazins* (1883); historical novels such as *O Judeu* (1867); novels of passion, *Onde está a Felicidade?* (1856), etc.

The only common factor in his work is an indulgent understanding of matters of the heart. His irony and scepticism saved him from the excesses of Romantic sentimentalism. Similarly his zestful vitality made him distrustful of the social moralizing of the 'realists'. His style is exuberant and richly vernacular; taken as a whole, his work remains remarkably fresh and impressive. [AJP]

*Obras*, ed. P. A. M. Pereira (1902) (new edn in preparation).

H. Lacape, *C.C.B.* (Paris, 1941); A. Ribeiro, *O Romance de C.* (Lisbon, 1961).

**Castelvetro, Lodovico** (Modena 1505–Chiavenna 1571). Italian literary critic and theorist. From 1529 he lived mainly at Modena, a centre of the reforming spirit in religion, but in 1560, after incurring the suspicion (later the condemnation) of the Holy Office, he began travelling through Europe, publishing in Vienna (1570) his translation of Aristotle's *Poetics* with a commentary (repr. 1967).

His other works include a commentary on Petrarch's *Rime* (1582), a commentary on 29 cantos of Dante's *Inferno* (ed. G. Franciosi, 1886) and the *Giunte al Ragionamento degli articoli e de' verbi di Messer Pietro Bembo* (1563; repr. in *Le prose di M. Pietro Bembo*, 1714), which is a commentary on Bembo's *Prose della volgar lingua*. It has also been suggested that he wrote the anonymous comedy *Gli ingannati* (1537), but this is not proven. [DGR]

*Opere varie critiche di L.C.*, ed. L. A. Muratori (1727).

G. Cavazzuti, *L.C.* (Modena, 1903); H. B. Charlton, *C.'s Theory of Poetry* (1913); Weinberg, *HLC*; B. Hathaway, *The Age of Criticism* (Ithaca, N.Y., 1962); *Minori*, ii.

**Castiglione, Baldassar** (Casatico, Mantua 1478–Toledo 1529). Italian writer and courtier. Member of an ancient aristocratic family, he received a thorough humanistic education, and acquired a refined appreciation of art. Essentially a courtier, his literary activities were spare-time occupations. In 1504, after an unhappy period in Mantuan employ, he entered the service of Guidobaldo da Montefeltro, Duke of Urbino. The ensuing years were the most satisfying of his life. He enjoyed the confidence of the Duke, who frequently entrusted important missions to him; and in his leisure moments he participated in the literary and intellectual activities of the court, then one of the most brilliant in Italy (cf. his dramatic eclogue, *Tirsi*, performed during the Carnival of 1506). After Guidobaldo's death in 1508, he remained in the service of the new Duke, Francesco Maria della Rovere, becoming in 1513 resident ambassador in Rome. In 1515 the expulsion of Francesco Maria from Urbino deprived him of a job, and in the years 1516–19 he lived quietly on his estates near Mantua.

Between the death of Guidobaldo and 1519, and probably mainly in the latter part of this period, Castiglione completed his major work, *Il libro del cortegiano* (1528; ed. V. Cian, 1946; tr. Sir T. Hoby, *The Book of the Courtier*, 1561, repr. 1959). This famous dialogue, which soon enjoyed a European circulation, is set in Urbino in 1507, and describes, in a series of imaginary discussions between the principle members of the court, the qualities of the ideal courtier. Written with considerable vivacity in a beautifully modulated classically inspired Italian, the book presents a deeply felt account of the ideals of Italian Renaissance court society at the moment of its greatest splendour, and ranks, with ⇨ Ariosto's *Orlando furioso*, as the supreme literary expression of that society's achievements. He also wrote a small number of excellent poems in Latin and Italian.

In 1519 he returned to Rome, now as Mantuan ambassador, and after further activities on behalf of his Mantuan masters, in 1524 entered Papal service. From that date until his death, he was Papal Nuncio in Spain. [CF]

J. Cartwright, *B.C., the Perfect Courtier* (1908); V. Cian, *Un illustre nunzio pontificio del Rinascimento* (Vatican City, 1951); R. Roeder, *The Man of the Renaissance* (N.Y., 1959).

**Castilho, António Feliciano de** (Lisbon 1800–Lisbon 1875). Portuguese poet. Almost totally blind from the age of 6, he was in his youth regarded as a prodigy by reason of his ability to rise above his affliction and attain academic and literary distinction. Having graduated at Coimbra in Canon Law, he devoted himself to translating many great works of literature into Portuguese and to penning neo-classical verse, largely in imitation of ⇨ Bocage and ⇨ Gessner, but with little of the former's pre-romantic *spleen*. His earliest collections were *Cartas de Eco a Narciso* (1821), *A Primavera* (1822) and *Amor e Melancolia* (1828). Two long and sombre poems, *A Noite do Castelo* (1836) and *Os Ciúmes do Bardo* (1838), were experiments in Romanticism, a movement which he came to repudiate, although his later championing of *D. Jaime*, a long narrative poem by the ultra-Romantic Tomás Ribeiro, in preference to the *Lusíadas* of Camões made his position curiously ambiguous. Many modern critics actually date Portuguese Romanticism from the publication of *A Noite do Castelo*, rather than from the more traditional 1825 (the date of Garrett's equally experimental epic *Camões*), and indeed several ultra-Romantics modelled their work on Castilho's two Romantic poems. Castilho's Romantic phase ended shortly after the publication of his *Quadros da História de Portugal* (1839), written under the influence of Herculano, and in 1842 he assumed the direction of the *Revista Universal Lisbonense*, in which he frequently censured Romanticism. After the publication of *Escavações Poéticas* (1844) – probably his most effective collection – he devoted himself for a number of years to agriculture in the Azores, to tracts on teaching methods, and to his translations, the choice of which revealed his *goût* for the sensual. By the fifties and early sixties his reputation had created for him a literary dictatorship whereby his preface to any young author's work had the value of both *nil obstat* and *imprimatur*. The grip of his ethereal neo-classicism was finally broken in three stages: by the *D. Jaime* question (1862), by the failure of his last collection *O Outono* (1863) and at the hands of Antero de Quental and Teófilo Braga in the *Questão Coimbrã* (1865). [RCW]

A. Salgado Júnior, 'A.F. de C.', in *Perspectiva da Literatura Portuguesa do Século XIX*, I (Lisbon, 1947); A. F. de Castilho, *Poesías* (Lisbon, 1943) (preface).

**Castillejo, Cristóbal de** (Ciudad Rodrigo 1492 ?–Vienna 1550). Spanish poet. An upholder of traditional models and an outspoken enemy of the Italianate innovations of ⇨ Boscán and ⇨ Garcilaso. He was page to the Archduke Ferdinand, then for ten years a Cistercian before leaving his monastery to act as secretary to his old master. His *Sermón de amores* (1542) and *Diálogo de mujeres* (1544) offer amusing reflections in the 16th-century manner on the lax life of the monastery, with (in the latter) satire against women; court life is satirized in his *Aula de cortesanos*. His love-poetry is charming and not obviously platonic (the lady's name changes rather frequently). His *Reprensión contra los poetas españoles que escriben en verso italiano* satirizes those who condemn the good old poets, ⇨ Mena, ⇨ Manrique, etc.; it is much below the quality of his best work, which breathes a new spirit into the old octosyllabic forms. His outstanding achievement is the *Canto de Polifemo*, based on Ovid – the only successful long poem of the period written outside the Italianate tradition. [JMC]

*Obras* (4 vols., CC, 1926–8); Cohen, *PBSV*; Trend, *OBSV*; Blecua, *FLE*; Terry, *ASP*.

C. L. Nicolay, *The Life and Works of C. de C.* (Philadelphia, 1910); J. M. de Cossío, *Fábulas mitológicas en España* (Madrid, 1952).

**Castillo Solórzano, Alonso de** (Tordesillas 1584–before 1648?). Spanish novelist and dramatist. He wrote short stories in the Italian style, and 3 picaresque novels, of which *La Garduña de Sevilla* (1634; CC) is still read; but despite the crimes committed by his pair of rogues, male and female, they fail to come to life, and there is no moral interest in their casual adventures. His best play, *El mayorazgo Figura*, gives a portrait of a pretentious idiot. [JMC]

P. N. Dunn, *C.S. and the Decline of the Spanish Novel* (1952); *RFE*, XV, 1928.

**Castro, Eugénio de** (Coimbra 1869–Coimbra 1944). Portuguese poet. He enjoyed the unique distinction of membership of the Spanish, Portuguese and Brazilian Academies and was for a number of years Director of the Faculty of Letters at Coimbra. He was the first poet to introduce ⇨ Symbolism into the Iberian literatures, the fruit of a visit to Paris in 1889. His was not merely the quasi-Platonic Symbolism of *correspondances* of Mallarmé, but rather the Symbolism-Decadentism of ⇨ Kahn, ⇨ Verhaeren and ⇨ Moréas. His four earliest Symbolist collections, *Oaristos* (1890), *Horas* (1891), *Silva* (1894) and *Interlúdio* (1894), were at first derisively received, but eventually became influential, pointing the way to Pessanha and Sá-Carneiro. The preface of *Oaristos* was a trenchant manifesto, deploring the poverty of Portuguese poetic language and calling for lush imagery and epithets which would appeal to all the senses, and for free use of such technical devices as alliteration and interior rhyme. All this Castro achieved in his own verse. The publication of *Belkiss* (1894) heralded a gradual return to a form of classicism in his verse, which was later coupled with an interest in folk-lore. Castro published in all some 30 collections, the most prominent apart from the foregoing being *Sagramor* (1895), *Salomé* (1896), *O Rei Galaor* (1897), *Constança* (1900), *Depois da Ceifa* (1901) and *Camafeus Romanos* (1921). [RCW]

R. Darío, *Los raros* (Madrid, 1918); M. de Unamuno, *Por tierras de Portugal y de España* (Madrid, 1911); F. Ramos, *E. de C. e a Poesia Nova* (Lisbon, 1943); *Biblos*, XXII, 1946.

**Castro, Guillén de** (Valencia 1569–Madrid 1631). Spanish dramatist. His early plays, written in Valencia, were romantic comedies in the manner of ⇨ Lope though still affected by the more primitive style of the Valencians. He then undertook three works on epic subjects – *El conde Alarcos* and the two parts of *Las mocedades del Cid* – but except in the *Mocedades* his verse and execution were unequal to the subject. Sober and free from baroque extravagance, he was at the same time dull and over-precise. The *Mocedades* profits from his use of language from the source *romances*. His play on the theme of *Don Quixote* leaves the Knight and the Squire on the margin, and focuses on the episode of Cardenio and Lucinda. He also dramatized Cervantes' interpolated tale, *El curioso impertinente*, and his *novela*, *La fuerza de la sangre*. He attempted classical subjects and also a realistic piece on an unhappy marriage, *Los mal casados de Valencia*, which seems to have been founded on experience, for he touches on the theme more than once. Corneille based his *Le Cid* on some scenes from the *Mocedades*. His collected plays were published in 2 parts (Valencia, 1618, 1625). [JMC]

BAE, 43; *Archivum Romanicum*, XIV (1930); *RH*, LXXXI (1933).

**Castro, Rosalía de** (Santiago de Compostela 1837–Padrón, Galicia 1885). Spanish poetess. At 19, she left her native Galicia for Madrid, where her first volume of poems in Castilian, *La flor*, was published in 1857. A year later, she married the Galician writer and archivist Manuel Murguía. Like ⇨ Bécquer, she contributed to *El museo universal*, the leading Madrid literary review of the time, and both poets show the influence of contemporary translations of Heine. Her mature verse is contained in 3 collections: *Cantares gallegos* (1863), *Follas novas* (1880) and *En las orillas del Sar* (1884). The first two of these are in Galician dialect: *Cantares gallegos*, a deeply felt re-creation of popular poetry and beliefs, immediately established her as the leading figure in the 19th-century Galician literary revival; *Follas novas* is more introspective and contains most of her finest personal lyrics, though her preoccupation with the collective problems of her region sets her apart from other contemporary poets. Both these attitudes are represented in *En las orillas del Sar*, her one important volume in Castilian. Though technically less assured than the *Rimas* of Bécquer, Rosalía's Castilian poems have a greater range, and their metrical variety anticipates the experiments of the Modernist movement. The natural speaking-tones of her best verse contrast strongly with earlier Romantic rhetoric, and the extreme honesty of her self-analysis makes her one of the most attractive and original of 19th-century women poets.

Rosalía de Castro was also a fluent writer of novels and stories in Castilian, though none of these reaches the level of her verse. Her most interesting work of fiction is *El caballero de las botas azules* (1867), a long satirical fantasy, in which the influence of E. T. A. ⇨ Hoffmann is combined with acute observation of contemporary society. [AT]

*Obras completas* (1958); *Cantares gallegos*, ed. R. Carballo Calero (Salamanca, 1963); *En las orillas del Sar*, ed. J. Alonso Montero (Salamanca, 1964); *Beside the River Sar*, selected poems, tr. S. G. Morley (California, 1937); *Poems*, tr. C. D. Ley (Madrid, 1964); Cohen, *PBSV*; Blecua, *FLE*.

R. Carballo Calero, *Aportaciones fundamentales a la literatura gallega contemporánea* (Madrid, 1955); J. L. Varela, *Poesía y restauración cultural de Galicia en el siglo* XIX (Madrid, 1958); J. A. Balbontín, *Three Spanish Poets* (1961); Cernuda, *EPC*; Cossío, *CAPE*.

**Catalan Literature.** (1) MEDIEVAL. No Catalan literature survives from the three centuries following the reconquest of Barcelona from the Arabs (801). Ot de Montcada wrote songs *c.*1048, but none survives. The long *Cançó de Santa Fe* was probably written in some monastery in the Catalan Pyrenees (*c.*1033–66), but philologists still dispute whether the language is Catalan or Languedocian, so close were they in that early period. A collection of Homilies at the close of the 12th century is the first text unquestionably Catalan. The Bible was translated into Catalan, but following the repression of the Albigensian heresy all copies were burned (1234).

A school of Catalan troubadours using Provençal for their poetry flourished from the middle of the 12th century through the 13th. The most eminent of them was Guillem de Cervera (fl. 1250–80). A number of the Catalan kings were among this group.

Two great figures appear in the transition from the 13th to the 14th centuries – Ramon Lull and Arnau de Vilanova. The first was a dynamic and complex personality – philosopher, theologian, novelist, poet, mystic and missionary (1233–1316). His enormous output of 243 works was in Latin and Catalan. The *Libre de Contemplació en Déu* (1272), an encyclopedic work of 365 chapters, and his utopia, *Blanquerna* (1285), were the first philosophical treatise and the first novel to be written in any Romance language. One part of the latter is the *Libre d'Amic e d'Amat*, an exquisite piece of mystical prose poetry. Arnau de Vilanova, doctor to kings and popes, wrote on medicine in Latin, and in Catalan on theology and religious reform.

The autobiographical Chronicles of James I, dealing with the conquests of Majorca and Valencia, and of Peter II, written by Bernat Desclot, both of the second half of the 13th century; of Ramon Muntaner, giving a vivid account of the Catalan expedition to Greece, of Peter III written by Bernat Descoll, both of the 14th century, are four masterpieces of narrative prose.

The advanced development of the Catalan Parliament has left us a rich collection of political oratory, a genre rare in medieval literatures.

Catalan texts of liturgical dramas probably date from the late 13th century, though Latin fragments appear in the 11th and references to them in the 10th. The *Misteri d'Elx*, which is still presented today, goes back to the 15th century. Documents and chronicles mention secular drama, but no text survives.

Francesc Eiximenis's encyclopedia, *Lo Cristià* (1379–86), is the last great work of the Middle Ages, and Bernat Metge's *Lo Somni* (1398) is the first to show the humanist influences emanating from Italy.

The novels of chivalry are remarkable for their realism and the absence of magic and of imaginary beings. *Curial e Güelfa* (*c.* 1460) was probably written by an unknown Catalan in Naples. The most outstanding, *Tirant lo Blanc* (*c.* 1455), was the work of a Valencian knight, Joan Martorell. It begins with the adventures of the Count of Warwick, followed by those of a young Breton knight, Tirant the White, who comes to London for a royal tournament. His later adventures echo those of Catalan knights in Greece and the Mediterranean.

The *Spill o Llibre de les Dones* (1456), a long poem of 10,000 5-syllable lines, by a Valencian doctor, Jaume Roig, is an amusing and misogynistic account of a rogue's wanderings through Valencia, Catalonia and France, and a true forerunner of the Castilian picaresque novel.

After Jordi de Sant Jordi, Ausiàs Marc (1397–1459) is the last of the great Catalan poets. His 128 poems, divided into *Cants d'Amor*, *Cants de Mort*, *Cants Morals* and *Cant Espiritual*, are meditations on these themes in the light of scholastic philosophy, and had a lasting influence on both Catalan and Castilian poets.

In the 16th century decadence set in, the result of complex economic, social, political and cultural factors, and lasted for 300 years.

(2) MODERN. Nevertheless there were signs of life towards the end of the 17th and of the 18th centuries, and the early 19th brought a lasting revival. Known as the *Renaixença*, it is closely linked with Liberalism and Romanticism.

Though a long neo-classical poem, *Lo Temple de la Gloria*, was probably written by Antoni Puig Blanc, a liberal exile in London (1815?) and another of these, M. Prat, published *Lo Nou Testament* (British and Foreign Bible Society, 1832; his translation of most of the Old Testament remains unpublished), the *Renaixença* is usually dated from the publication of a romantic poem, *Oda a la Pàtria*, by Bonaventura Aribau in 1833.

Religious plays in Catalan had never died out, but now drama in Catalan began to be used by the liberals for propaganda purposes as early as 1820–3.

The modern Catalan novel has evolved out of romantic novels based on episodes in Catalan history, written in Spanish by Catalans imitating Sir Walter Scott. Joan Cortada's 9 historical novels (1833–40) are the most representative of this group. In 1862 Antoni de Bofarull published the first historical novel in Catalan, *L'Orfaneta de Menargues*.

The medieval annual contest of the *Jocs Florals*, with prizes for the best poets, was revived in Barcelona in 1859, but owing to political troubles did not come to full fruition until the publication of the epic poems of Jacint Verdaguer (1845–1902), *L'Atlàntida* (1877), on the submersion of a mythical continent in the Atlantic, and *Canigó* (1886), episodes in the reconquest of Catalonia from the Moors in the Pyrenees. Both rank high for their descriptions of nature and the wealth of their poetic language. In the theatre Angel Guimerà (1847–1924) is the outstanding name. From historical tragedies in verse he turned to naturalistic drama. His *Terra Baixa* (1897), a rural drama, which was translated into most European languages, formed the basis of the opera *Tiefland*, by the German composer Eugen D'Albert.

From rural stories, like Vayreda's *La Punyalada* (1902), and *Solitud* (1906) by Victor Català (the pen name of a woman writer, Caterina Albert), the next development of the novel is the naturalistic works of Narcis Oller (1846–1930) depicting the Barcelona bourgeoisie (*La Febre d'or*, *Pilar Prim*, 1912). The exquisite tales of Joaquim Ruyra (1858–1939) are a reaction against Català's pessimism.

The years 1885–1910 are the most extraordinary and fertile period of the revival. The *modernista* movement brought European influences into Catalonia – the Pre-Raphaelites, the *Yellow Book*, Ibsen, Wagner, Nietzsche. The painter and writer Santiago Rusiñol (1861–1931) formulated its ideas. Adrià Gual fostered the theatre, influencing Catalan and, later, Spanish dramatists down to García Lorca. In music the movement produced Catalan operas and composers like Albéniz and Granados, and one great artist, Pau Casals. The young Picasso was active in Catalan *modernisme*, Gaudí reflects it in architecture and Joan

Maragall (1860–1911) was its best and most representative poet.

During a period when the novel was losing ground, Ignasi Iglesies (1871–1925) produced social dramas, and Catalan poetry remained at a high level. Most of the glory goes to the Majorcan poets, Joan Alcover (1854–1926) and Miquel Costa i Llobera (1854–1922), who were influenced by Carducci and the classical traditions of the Mediterranean.

After Maragall, poets such as J. Bofill i Mates (1878–1933) and above all Josep Carner (1884–1970), who came under Parnassian and symbolist influences, strove for perfection of form and purity of language. J. V. Foix (1894– ) expresses surrealism in verse, as Dali and Joan Miró express it in painting. Carles Riba (1893–1959), a Greek scholar and literary critic, wrote intellectual poetry of the highest quality, and Josep S. Pons (1886–1962), the greatest poet Roussillon has ever produced, is outstanding for the Virgilian freshness of his delicate verses.

Catalan literature, like the language and culture, has suffered persecution under the Franco regime. There was a total ban on Catalan books from 1939 to 1947, and their numbers are still severely limited. There is likewise total suppression of the Catalan press. Nevertheless Catalan literature continues to flourish, with increasing encouragement from the people. The current trend is towards the development of the novel, with Manuel de Pedrolo, influenced for a time by Kafka, eagerly experimenting with new forms, and a crop of young writers. Salvador Espriu (1913– ) writes poems of social significance in bitter and satirical terms. Josep Pla (1895– ) continues his prolific prose portraiture of contemporary Catalan society.

(3) BIBLIOGRAPHY. Joan Ruiz i Calonja, *Història de la Literatura Catalana* (Barcelona, 1954), covers the Middle Ages, the decadence and the modern period. For the first two periods the scholarly contributions of Jordi Rubió i Balaguer in the volumes of *Historia General de las Literaturas Hispànicas*, edited by G. Diaz Plaja (Barcelona, 1949 onwards) are the most complete and erudite.

An *Anthology of Catalan Lyric Poetry* (Oxford, 1953) covers all the periods, with an introduction and notes in English, and poems in Catalan.

Medieval literary texts in the collection, *Els Nostres Clàssics* (Barcelona), with some 100 volumes.

Professor E. Allison Peers published a biography of Ramon Lull (London, 1929) and an English translation of his *Blanquerna* (London, 1925). Ramon Lull's Catalan works have been published in Palma de Mallorca (22 vols., 1901–55). The series, *Biblioteca Perenne* (Barcelona, 1947ff.), includes the complete works of the most important modern writers (Verdaguer, Costa i Llobera, Rusiñol, Maragall, Guimerà, Torras i Bages, Narcis Oller, Emili Vilanova, Joaquim Ruyra, Joan Alcover . . .). Its companion series, *Biblioteca Excelsa*, includes the complete works of J. M. Lopez Picó, M. S. Oliver, J. M. de Sagarra, Guerau de Liost (J. Bofill i Mates), Llorenç Riber, E. d'Ors, Victor Català, and Josep Carner, plus an *Antologia de Contistes Catalans* (1850–1950) by Joan Triadu.

A recent work, *Poesia Catalana del Segle XX*, by Josep M. Castellet and Joaquim Molas (Barcelona, 1964) examines the poetry from a social point of view.

Carles Riba's *Obra Poètica* (Madrid, 1956), contains his poems in Catalan with Spanish translations. A selection of his poems in Catalan, with English translations by J. L. Gili, *Carles Riba: Poems*, has now been published (Oxford, 1964). The same firm has published a selection of poems by Josep Carner with English translations by Pearse Hutchinson. There is also a *Catalan Grammar* (1st edn 1943, 2nd edn 1952, 3rd edn 1967.) [BR]

**Cats, Jacob** (Brouwershaven 1577–The Hague 1660). Dutch poet. Some 50,000 copies of his works were sold in his lifetime. He studied arts and law at Leyden and Orleans. During a visit to Cambridge he met William Perkins, whose pietism greatly influenced him, as did the strict orthodoxy of Elizabeth van Valkenburg, whom he married in 1605. His drainage works in Holland and England made him a wealthy man with leisure to recast his earliest poems, *Sinne- en Minnebeelden* (1618; ed. J. Bosch, 1960) – 'edifying recollections', emblems in verse with engravings by Adriaan van der Venne, to give homely advice on love and marriage. The same sapient moralizing runs through the prolix dialogues between Joseph and Potiphar's wife in *Selfstryt* (1620).

He became pensionary (legal functionary) of Middleburgh and in 1623 of Dordrecht.

Here he wrote *Houwelick* (1625), an illustrated guide for the housewife from maidenhood to widowhood. *Trou-Ringh* (1637) also moralizes on Christian marriage and the home, dealing at great length, after an illusion to the spiritual marriage of Christ with the Church, with simple practical matters. The colourless respectability of his didactics is matched by the emotionless monotony of his alexandrines, but his powers of observation as a story-teller endure. One of the many illustrative anecdotes so typical of him and his medieval predecessors is the well-known *Spaans Heydinnetje* (ed. H. J. Vieu-Kuik, 1963), after Cervantes.

In 1630 his wife died. ('I saw 't was only dust that once had been my care, Ah, what delights us here is only vap'rous air.') In 1636 he was appointed Grand Pensionary of Holland and moved to The Hague. In 1652 he retired from diplomatic service to his country house. 'Father Cats' was revered till the mid 19th century by a middle-class public who admired his homely Calvinist doctrine. [PK]

Barnouw, *CA*.
Ed. P. Minderaa, *Aandacht voor Cats bij zijn 300-ste sterfdag* (Zwolle, 1962).

**Cavafy (Kavafis), Constantine Peter** (Alexandria 1863–1933). Greek poet. He came from a well-to-do mercantile family from Constantinople which had emigrated to Egypt in the early 19th century. English was his first language, and he spent part of his childhood in England. He returned to Alexandria when he was nine – his father had died in the meantime and the prosperity of his family had rapidly declined. Apart from brief visits to Constantinople, Paris, London and Athens he spent all his life in Alexandria, earning his living as a civil servant in the Egyptian Ministry of Public Works. His early poems, which he disclaimed emphatically, were very much under the influence of romanticism, and his highly original poetic genius did not reveal itself until he was middle-aged. The poems which he owned and had printed in *feuilles volantes*, which he constantly revised and improved, consist of 154 short pieces and a few longer ones, reminiscent at first sight of the epigrams or studied mimes of the Hellenistic poets, but totally different from the latter in their lack of formal grace and *insouciance*. The backcloth of Cavafy's poetry is an imaginary world of his own, set in the declining world of the Hellenistic East, Rome or Byzantium, which supplied him with a mythology and characters, dramatic situations and paradoxes, moments of doubt, deceit and transition through which he could comment on the present. His portrayal of emotion is nearly always calm and detached as if seen by an impartial observer; yet it would be wrong to assume that he is uncommitted. Conflicts between two equally potent beliefs, tensions produced in individuals by transitional moments in history, or transient moments of beauty are for him emotional states which are hardest to bear. His disillusionment and his ironic criticism of life, sharp though it often is, is never inhuman. All these facets of his work, and many more, are often subtly combined in one single poem (*Waiting for the Barbarians*, *The God Abandons Antony*, *Myres: Alexandria, A.D. 340*, *Kaisarion*) to produce a kind of poetry which is unique in European literature. His love poems are inspired by homosexual love and a nostalgia for unfulfilled desires and fugitive moments of pleasure and beauty. He achieves his unique artistic effects by using a language which is sometimes colloquial and sometimes deliberately stilted and prosaic. A world of an extraordinary dramatic vividness and complexity emerges from his poetry when read as a single whole. [SJP]

*Poiemata*, ed. G. P. Savidis (1963); *Poems*, tr. John Mavrogordato (1951); *The Complete Poems*, tr. R. Dalven (N.Y., 1961).
E. M. Forster, *Pharos and Pharillon* (1923); E. Keeley and P. Sherrard, *Six Poets of Modern Greece* (1960); P. Sherrard, *The Marble Threshing Floor* (1956); G. Seferis, *Dokimés* (Athens, 1962); T. Malanos, *O Poietés K.P.K.* (Athens, 1957); G. P. Savidis, *Oi Kavafikés Ekdóseis* (Athens, 1966).

**Cavalcanti, Guido** (Florence 1259?–Florence 1300). Italian poet. A friend of Dante, he was reputed to be a studious, bizarre and violent character, and even suspected of atheism. Active in Florentine politics, when the Guelphs split into the White and Black factions, he became an ardent supporter of the Whites. He was exiled to Sarzana with other ringleaders of both parties in 1300 when Dante was one of the Priors. Recalled from exile he died the same year.

He wrote about 50 *canzoni*, ballads and sonnets, almost all on the theme of love, and was the most effective of the ⇨ *Stil novo* poets. His mood alternates between ⇨

Guinizellian rapturous contemplation and a pessimistic recognition of the destruction and suffering which the tyrant Love imposes. Thus although he attempts a philosophical analysis of love, he is clearly also concerned with its impact as an emotional experience. Even in the difficult *canzone* 'Donna mi prega', where he is at his most uncompromisingly intellectual, he makes clear his view that love is an agency hostile to the life of reason. The various faculties of body and mind are personified by spirits and the tumult of love is portrayed in terms of the sufferings and protests of these spirits. It is an intensely dramatic portrayal, though one which seems to be dealing more with a phenomenon of human experience in general than the situation of any one human being in particular. [DGR]

*Rime*, ed. G. Favati (1957); Contini, *PD*; Salinari, *PLD*; Benedetto, *RDSN*; *Sonnets and Ballate*, tr. and intr. Ezra Pound (1912); Rossetti, *DC*; Lind, *LPIR*.

Figurelli, *DSN*; *Minori*, i.

**Cayrol, Jean** (Bordeaux 1911– ). French poet and novelist. His early poetry – *Le Hollandais volant* (1936) – was ⇨ Surrealist in inspiration, but his outlook and the general tone of his writing were transformed by his experiences during the last war. Arrested by the Gestapo in 1942, he was imprisoned in several places, but principally in the Mauthausen concentration camp. In *Miroir de la Rédemption* (1944) and *Poèmes de la nuit et du brouillard* (1945) these experiences are reflected in poems that show both a strong religious sense and a deep compassion for suffering humanity.

Cayrol's theory of the novel, chiefly set out in *Lazare parmi nous* (1950), shows his affinity with the later theorists of the *nouveau roman*. The concentration camp world mirrors the human condition which must be suffered as a means of eventual redemption. Dereliction, solitude, absence are the lot of man, prefigured by Lazarus and equally capable of resurrection. But in such a world and one's vision of it, objects take on unusual importance and can seem more accessible than human beings. The outcast of society – something like a secular Christ taking on himself the world's misery – is the protagonist of his trilogy *Je vivrai l'amour des autres* (1947–50) and a similar vision, sharpened by some incisive satirical writing, can be found in his other fiction: *La noire* (1949), *Le vent de la mémoire* (1952), *L'espace d'une nuit* (1954; tr. G. Hopkins, *All in a Night*, 1957), *Le déménagement* (1956), *La gaffe* (1957), *Les corps étrangers* (1959; tr. R. Howard, *Foreign Bodies*, N.Y., 1960) and *Le froid du soleil* (1963). [JC]

*Esprit*, XX, 3 (1952); *Lettres Nouvelles*, v, 54 (1957).

C. Lynes, 'J.C.', in *The Novelist as Philosopher*, ed. J. Cruickshank (1962).

**Cecchi, Emilio** (Florence 1884–Rome 1966). Italian essayist and critic. He was well known for his studies on English literature (*Rudyard Kipling*, 1911; *Storia della letteratura inglese secolo XIX*, 1915; *Scrittori inglesi e americani*, 1935 and 1947; *Emily Dickinson*, 1939; *I grandi romantici inglesi*, 1957) and Italian literature and art (*La poesia di G. Pascoli*, 1912; *Armando Spadini*, 1924; *Pittura italiana dell'Ottocento*, 1927; *Trecentisti senesi*, 1928, tr. L. Penlock, 1931; *La scultura fiorentina del Quattrocento*, 1956). Perhaps the most representative of those writers who, in the early 1920s, advocated from the pages of the literary magazine *La Ronda* a revival of stylistic formalism, exemplified by non-narrative rhapsodic compositions variously defined 'artistic proses', 'chapters' or 'elzeviers'. In this genre Cecchi soon distinguished himself by his arresting choice of words, richness of imagination, superb elegance of style, unfailing good taste and keen discernment (*Pesci rossi*, 1920; *L'osteria del cattivo tempo*, 1926; *Messico*, 1932; *Et in Arcadia ego*, 1936; *America amara*, 1940; *Corse al trotto e altre cose*, 1952, but including articles previously published in 1931, 1936 and 1941). This stylistic flamboyance which, though perfectly acceptable in his essays, was rather obtrusive in his early critical works, fortunately subsided in his more mature studies, e.g. *Di giorno in giorno* (1954) and *Libri nuovi e usati* (1958), a very illuminating survey of contemporary Italian literature from 1945 to 1958. [GMC]

Falqui, *PNNI*; Gargiulo, *LIN*; *I Contemporanei*, i.

**Čech, Svatopluk** (Ostředek 1846–Prague 1908). Czech poet, novelist and dramatist. At a time when decadence and scepticism were in the ascendant, he nearly succeeded in giving a new form to Czech nationalism by imbuing it with social and almost socialist ideas. His long allegorical poems, *Evropa* (1878) and *Slavie* (1884), advocate the solution of social and national problems not by force but by social and spiritual reform. His *Písně otroka* (1895) castigate the moral subservience of the Czechs to their Viennese masters and spur them to heroism. Among his satirical writings, the poem *Hanuman* (1884; tr. W. W. Strickland, 1894) on the civil war between two leaders of the apes, one a progressive, seeking to force a superficial human civilization on his subjects, and the other a nationalist coining the slogan 'Back to the ape!', acquires a strange topicality in our own time. [KB]

*Spisy* (30 vols., 1899–1910); *Lieder der Sklaven*, tr. E. Neumann (Karlsbad, 1933).
A. Novák, *Sv. Č.* (2 vols., Prague, 1921–3).

**Celan, Paul,** pseud. of P. Antschel (Czernowitz, Bukovina 1920–70). German poet. In 1942 his Jewish parents were murdered in a concentration camp, and Celan himself was sent to a forced labour camp. After 1948 he lived in Paris as a language-teacher and translator; he was married to the graphic artist Gisèle Celan-Lestrange. His first book of poems, *Der Sand aus den Urnen* (1948), was withdrawn after publication; his main work is contained in the collections *Mohn und Gedächtnis* (1952), *Von Schwelle zu Schwelle* (1955), *Sprachgitter* (1959), and *Die Niemandsrose* (1963). He also published translations of A. Blok, O. Mandel'shtam, Yesenin, Rimbaud, Valéry, and René Char, all since 1958. He wrote self-effacingly about his own poetry in an essay in *Die neue Rundschau* (1/1958) and in his booklet *Der Meridian* (1961).

Celan, who started writing poetry in order to 'outline reality' for himself, is a hermetic or neo-Surrealist poet, who has learned much from early ⇨ Expressionism (especially ⇨ Trakl), from ⇨ Goll, and from French ⇨ Surrealism. His metaphors are deliberately 'uprooted' and his meaning becomes more and more elusive; but his unique style and purity of diction make him the outstanding German poet to have emerged since 1945.

Bridgwater, *TCGV*; Hamburger and Middleton, *MGP*.
K. Krolow, in *Anstösse* (Hofgeismar, April 1959); S. S. Prawer, in Keith-Smith, *ECGL; GR*, XXXIX, 1, 1964.

**Celaya, Gabriel,** pseud. of Rafael Múgica (Hernani, Guipúzcoa 1911– ). Spanish poet. Of strong socialist views, great courage and considerable output; *Las cartas boca arriba* (1951) contains two of his finest poems, one addressed to the workman Andrés Basterra and the other to P.N. (Pablo Neruda). The first makes an impassioned plea for human solidarity, and the second gives a masterly analysis of the state of Spain. Both are long yet well disciplined, the latter being in an uncharacteristically regular verse form. His heroic story of the resistance to Franco, *Las resistencias del diamante* (1957), revives an old narrative form, but might have been better in sober prose. More interesting is *Cantata en Aleixandre* (1959), written for three voices, which is a hymn to poetry itself. *Exploración de la poesía* (1964) is an interesting analysis of his own poetic aesthetic. [JMC]

*Poesía 1934–1961* (1962).
Cano, *PESV*.

**'Celestina, La.'** Popular title of a Spanish prose work in dramatic form: *La Tragicomedia de Calisto y Melibea*. The tale is of a young gentleman who uses the services of the bawd Celestina to seduce a young woman of good family, and of the disaster that overtakes them all on account of their 'disorderly lusts'. Declaredly a moral work, this novel-in-dialogue is a subtle study of passion and easy-going villainy. Celestina herself is one of the greatest characters of all fiction, the perfect incarnation of a bawd, while the lovers, he in his pride and she in her single-minded sensuality, are more vivid and tragic even than Romeo and Juliet.

The text presents many problems. The first act is in an older type of language than the rest, and in the anonymous edition of 1500–1 (the 1st edition is of 1499) the author claims only to be continuing his work. In the edition of 1502 its 16 acts are increased by 5, which may be of other authorship. Most recent theories attribute the whole work except the first act to Fernando de Rojas, whose name is given in some introductory verses (a 22nd act was included in 3 reprints, but is now excluded as spurious). A second problem arises from the supposed Jewish content of the story. It is possible to read into this unhappy love-story references to the forcible conversion of the Jews, of which its author's parents were victims, and to the social gulf between *conversos* like himself and the old Christians.

According to this argument Melibea and her family were *conversos*, and perhaps still practised their old religion, while Calisto was of pure Christian descent. This would account for his failure to propose for her hand, and for the employment of the bawd, which is explained by opponents of this theory as implicit in the medieval convention of love. The basic inspiration of the work, however, is probably the orthodox medieval idea of the all-pervading results of sin, to which is added a certain humanistic fatalism.

*La Celestina* exercised great influence on the Spanish theatre and novel. It was translated by J. Mabbe in 1631. [JMC]

*Tragicomedia de Calixto y Melibea*, ed. Criado de Val and Trotter (1958), and many other editions; tr. J. Mabbe (repr. 1894); tr. P. Hartnoll (1959); tr. J. M. Cohen (Penguin Classics, 1964).
M. Menéndez y Pelayo, *La C.* (CA, n.d.), reprinted from *Orígenes de la novela*, vol. III (Madrid-Santander, 1943); Maria Rosa Lida de Malkiel, *Two Spanish Masterpieces* (Urbana, Ill., 1961) and *La originalidad artística de 'La C.'* (Buenos Aires, 1962); S. Gilman, *The Art of 'la C.* '(Madison, 1956); M. Bataillon, *La C. selon Fernando de Rojas* (Paris, 1961); A. Deyermond, *The Petrarchan Sources of la C.* (1961); A. Castro, *La C. como contienda* (1965).

**Céline, Louis-Ferdinand,** pseud. of Dr L-F Destouches (Paris 1894–Paris 1961). French writer. Of lower-middle-class origins. His hallucinatory style, and the cynicism and pessimism inherent in the hero's outlook, made his controversial first novel a best-seller: *Voyage au bout de la nuit* (1932; tr. John Marks, *Journey to the End of the Night*, 1934). The later novels, notably *Mort à crédit* (1936; tr. J. Marks, *Death on the Instalment Plan*, 1938), *D'un château à l'autre* (1957) and *Nord* (1960), are in the same vein. However, Céline was less jaundiced than appearances suggest: if his characters are always suffering, stupid and nasty, this is his way of persuading his contemporaries, by presenting an albeit exaggerated portrait, of the folly of their ways. If they were less stupid and nasty, he suggests, they would suffer less; but conversely, he observes, if they suffered less, they would be nicer. Similarly, the 'Jew' of his hysterical anti-Semitic pamphlets, which earned him exile and imprisonment, is a projection, taken from popular prejudice, of his own class's worst tendencies. His works are honest attempts to force man to dominate his weaknesses and to end the disgustingly alienated conditions of life of his contemporaries. Whence the nightmare style, suggesting a reality beyond the comprehension and control of the individual. [JNJP]

N. Debrie-Panel, *L-F.C.* (Lyons, 1961); Pol Vandromme, *L-F.C.* (Paris, 1962); 'L-F.C.', in *L'Herne*, 3 (Paris, 1963).

**Cellini, Benvenuto** (Florence 1500–Florence 1571). Italian goldsmith, sculptor and writer. Forced to flee Florence in 1523 after a violent brawl, one of many which punctuated his adventurous life, he was employed by Clement VII in Rome and was among the defending garrison in 1527; he claimed that it was he who shot the Connétable de Bourbon. Further spells of service followed, at Florence, Mantua, Rome and the Paris of Francis I, with intrigue and violence never far away. A charge of theft made by the bastard son of Paul III, for instance, landed him in the dungeon of Castel Sant'Angelo from which he was lucky to emerge alive after a long imprisonment. His last years were spent in Florence, where in 1558 he began dictating to an apprentice in his workshop an account of his life's adventures. The *Vita* was not published till 1728 (ed. M. Gorra, 1954; B. Maier, 1959; tr. G. Bull, *Autobiography of B.C.*, Penguin Classics, 1956). At a time when Italian prose was much concerned with acquiring literary dignity by diligent study of authorized models, Cellini's vigorous and irrepressible Tuscan has a refreshing directness. But what makes the *Vita* one of the most enjoyable books of the *cinquecento* is the roistering, feckless character of the author. Utterly impregnable in his monumental self-esteem, he shows himself honestly and tenaciously triumphing with incomparable zest over misfortune, malice and treachery. Both his private life as a pleasure-seeking, quick-tempered, but ingenuous male, and his professional life as an artist involved in the vicissitudes of *cinquecento* patronage provide him with a store of vivid anecdotes. The casting of the famous Perseus, the escape from Castel Sant'Angelo, the siege of Rome – these and other episodes provide unforgettable scenes, and despite immorality and killings, the final impression which this loquacious extrovert makes is amiable.

He also wrote treatises on the goldsmith's

art and on sculpture, and some undistinguished verse. [DGR]

*Le rime*, ed. A. Mabellini (1891); *I trattati dell'oreficeria e della scultura*, ed. L. De Mauri (1927); *Opere di B. Castiglione, G. Della Casa, B.C.*, ed. C. Cordié (1960).

T. Parodi, *Poesia e letteratura* (Bari, 1916); E. Carrara, *C.* (Turin, 1938); B. Maier, *Umanità e stile di B.C. scrittore* (Milan, 1952); *Minori*, ii.

**Celtis, Conrad** (Wipfeld, Schweinfurt 1459–Vienna 1508). Wandering Humanist scholar. He visited Italy, was crowned laureate by Frederick III (1487), lectured at various universities, established literary societies (e.g. at Mainz), and was appointed professor in Vienna by Maximilian I. He wrote much fine life-loving poetry in Latin (especially *Amores*), elegies, epigrams, odes and an unfinished epic on Theodoric. [FB]

*Epigramme*, ed. K. Hartfelder (1881); *Amores*, ed. F. Pindter (1934); *Odae*, ed. F. Pindter (1937); *Selections*, tr., comm. and ed. L. W. Forster (1948).

**Cendrars, Blaise,** pseud. of Frédéric Sauser (Chaux-le-Fonds 1887–Paris 1961). French-Swiss author. His constant wanderings round the globe made him think of himself as an international citizen, and many of his works are directly concerned with his travels. But these works – notably *L'homme foudroyé* (1945), *La main coupée* (1946), and *Bourlinguer* (1948) – are far from mere travelogues; they are attempts to isolate the ego he incessantly contemplated in his multifarious activities – businessman, film-director, jewel-peddler, journalist, etc. The heroes of his novels too – especially *Dan Yack* (2 vols., 1927 and 1929; tr. *Antarctic Fugue*, 1948), *Moravagine* (1926), *L'or* (1925; tr. H. L. Stuart, *Sutter's Gold*, 1926) – constantly attempt to stabilize their ego, either through acceptance and renunciation (*Dan Yack*), or feverish iconoclasm (*Moravagine*). Cendrars sees the personality as needing both to breathe in and to breathe out – systole and diastole, the two faces of activity – but finally his admiration is for those who, through adversity, acquire an inner resilience, as Suter in *L'or* and Galmot in *Rhum* (1930). His characters live and move on an epic scale and he has been praised for the resulting 'life-like' quality of his work (in fact due to skilful narrative art), which breaks with the French analytic tradition. [JNJP]

L. Parrot, *B.C.* (Paris, 1948); J. Buhler, *B.C.* (Paris, 1960).

**Cernuda, Luis** (Seville 1902–Mexico 1963). Spanish poet of the 'Generation of the Dictatorship'. Shy, introverted, resentful, Cernuda has much of the *poète maudit* about him: his work shows 'a vision of reality which is a defiant challenge to the fragile edifice of what we call good and evil' (O. Paz). His most characteristic poetry begins with *Un río, un amor* (1929), written whilst he was teaching in France and just after his mother's death. Here, the young pagan god who had appeared briefly in *Égloga, elegía, oda* (1927–8) takes on the first of his many incarnations to provide Cernuda's love-theme, and there begins the conflict between *realidad* (the real world in which the poet has to live and to which he makes a tentative approach) and *deseo* (the poet's idealized dream-world, constantly betrayed and rejected by the real world); this conflict was later (1935) to provide him with the collective title for his poetry. *Deseo* rises triumphantly in *Los placeres prohibidos* (1931) but the vacuum left by the passing of both love and betrayal pervades *Donde habite el olvido* (1932–3). In *Las nubes* (1937–8) he sees beyond the immediate conflict of the Civil War to the basically tragic nature of the Spaniard; and in *Como quien espera el alba* (1941–4), written in exile in England and Mexico, the poet at last finds some hope in abiding values (*A un poeta futuro*, *Vereda del cuco*). In his last years, his bitterness increased and his last book, *Desolación de la quimera*, includes attacks on fellow-poets, even Pedro ⇨ Salinas, who had encouraged his early work. His essay *Historial de un libro* (included in *Poesía y literatura*) throws much light on the composition of his poems. Many younger Spanish poets consider his work unsurpassed in this century. [GC]

*La realidad y el deseo* (3rd edn, Mexico, 1958); *Ocnos* (2nd edn, 1949); *Desolación de la quimera* (Mexico, 1962); *Estudios sobre poesía española contemporánea* (1957); *Poesía y literatura* (Barcelona, 1960).

*La Caña Gris*, 6–8, *Homenaje a L.C.* (Valencia, Autumn 1962); *Insula*, 207 (Madrid, February 1964); P. Silver, '*Et in Arcadia ego*': *a Study of the Poetry of L.C.* (1966); Cano, *PESV*; Vivanco, *PEC*.

**Cervantes Saavedra, Miguel de** (Alcalá de Henares 1547–Madrid 1616). Spanish novelist and dramatist. The son of an unsuccessful surgeon, he was brought up in various Spanish cities, and evidently studied for a time under an Erasmian humanist,

López de Hoyos. He was an omnivorous reader. He went to Italy in 1569, entered the household service of Giulio Acquaviva and then enlisted as a soldier. He fought heroically at the battle of Lepanto, where his left hand was maimed. After taking part in the military operations of Corfu, Navarino and Tunis, with his brother Rodrigo, he was captured at sea by the Turks and taken off to Algiers as a slave in 1575. He made four daring attempts to escape and was eventually ransomed in 1580. Back in Madrid, he wrote some plays and his first novel, *La Galatea* (1585). Economic necessity dogged him for the rest of his life, which was not brightened by an unhappy marriage to a girl eighteen years younger than himself or, later, by the squalid legal embroilments of his illegitimate daughter. He held several commissions in the public service, was a tax-collector and had the thankless task of commandeering provisions for the Armada. He applied for an administrative post in America without success, ran into trouble over his accounts, and suffered more than one imprisonment. He was living in Valladolid and was 58 in 1605 when *Don Quixote* Part I was published. The work brought him fame but little monetary benefit; however, he now began to publish in earnest. The *Novelas ejemplares* came out in 1613, the *Viaje del Parnaso*, a long allegorical, satirical, panegyric poem, in 1614; and in 1615 8 plays and 8 *entremeses* (one-act farces), together with *Don Quixote* Part II. His last novel, *Los trabajos de Persiles y Sigismunda*, was published posthumously in 1617. He wrote the moving farewell words of the dedication, and probably those of the prologue, four days before he died. His death was on 23 April 1616 (new style), Shakespeare's having occurred on the same date (old style).

Cervantes attempted every major literary form of his day, except the epic poem. But he was an uninspired poet as a rule and a disappointed dramatist, whose plays, though sometimes rich in possibilities, are technically defective. They were soon outmoded by those of ⇨ Lope de Vega. The short *entremeses*, mostly in prose, are superior. His works as a whole show on the one hand his taste for the variegated adventure and poetic idealism of romance, on the other his shrewd observation of life, together with a keen awareness of the literary consequences of both.

The unfinished *Galatea* was written in the fashionable medium of pastoral, for which he always retained an affection – it features in the *Quixote* – though he was quite capable on occasion of making fun of its remoteness from everyday life. He remodelled some of the situations and episodes of this novel in later writings.

The 12 *Novelas ejemplares* were, as he claimed, the first of their kind in Spain, and the best of them were an advance in the genre. They range from stories of adventure and amorous intrigue with conventionally idealized characters, like *La española inglesa*, to studies of low life full of social and moral observation, like *Rinconete y Cortadillo* and the *Coloquio de los perros*. *El celoso extremeño* contains an acute character study within its theatrical plot and has many points of resemblance to the tragic exemplary novel *El curioso impertinente*, included in *Don Quixote* I, perhaps the best *novela* Cervantes ever wrote.

*Persiles y Sigismunda* is a novel of the type of Heliodorus's *Ethiopic History*. It was intended to combine the best-selling qualities of the old romances with the artistic virtues and the intellectual and edifying appeal of good epic. The protagonists are too idealized, and many of the episodes seem too unreal, for the work to be congenial to the modern reader, but it enjoyed an international reputation in its day and did much to set the trend in Europe for the heroic romances of the 17th century. The *Persiles* is the product of much reading and of research into travel accounts and geographies of northern Europe generally accepted at the time. Though devoutly Catholic in tone, its pieces of religious symbolism are not held together in a satisfying pattern. Overloaded with incident and apparently finished in a hurry, the book is usually regarded as a noble failure.

*Don Quixote* is the successful exploitation of a brilliant idea. An amiable elderly gentleman addicted to reading romances of chivalry goes out of his mind and sets out as a doughty knight errant in search of adventure and to redress the wrongs in the world, as though it were really the world of his storybooks. This simple initial situation entailed the confrontation of literary fiction and real life within the overall fiction of Cervantes's novel. From the interaction of these different levels of creation emerges a multi-dimensional world which contains all the major elements of the modern novel.

The book's implications seem endless as the enigmatic relationships of the ideal and the real, the true and the illusory, madness and sanity, art and life, present themselves as themes in the context of human experience. The idealistic knight and his simple but astute squire Sancho Panza, compounded of contradictions, always themselves and continually changing, complete as individuals yet complementary to one another, stand at the centre of what is also a novel of external occurrences and encounters (often presented, directly or by inference, from different points of view). Events modify their characters, which in turn help to determine events, and this interplay gives the apparently rambling work an underlying coherence. Nevertheless, Part I, which generally speaking deals with the illusions of Don Quixote, is constructed with somewhat less firmness than Part II, which deals with his gradual disillusionment. Part II is a sadder and a profounder book, although it retains its humour to the end. Here Cervantes reaches that rare height where comedy and tragedy are indistinguishable.

Immensely and immediately successful in Spain, and internationally so soon after (Shelton's Part I was published in 1612 and Oudin's in France in 1614), *Don Quixote* did not, however, come fully into its own until the beginning of the 18th century – first of all in England. It was seen chiefly as a comic prose epic until the German Romantic writers discovered much of its wider and deeper (and sadder) significance. Since then, the book has been open to endless reinterpretation. Editions, translations, adaptations and imitations are innumerable. *Don Quixote*'s influence on the modern novel is inestimable. Fielding, Sterne, Smollett, Dickens, Flaubert, Twain, Dostoyevsky, Pérez Galdós, Unamuno and others are directly or indirectly indebted to it. Even the world of Kafka and problems that exercise Robbe-Grillet and Butor can be found in germ in *Don Quixote*. [ECR]

*Obras completas*, ed. R. Schevill and A. Bonilla (16 vols., Madrid, 1914–41); *Don Quijote*, ed. Riquer (London, 1962); tr. S. Putnam (1953), J. M. Cohen (Penguin Classics, 1950); *Exemplary Novels*, tr. MacColl (Glasgow, 1902).

J. Fitzmaurice-Kelly, *Life of C.* (1913); J. Ortega y Gasset, *Meditaciones del Quijote* (Madrid, 1957); A. Castro, *El pensamiento de C.* (Madrid, 1925); P. Hazard, *Don Quichotte de C.* (Paris, 1949); J. Casalduero, *Sentido y forma del Quijote* (Madrid, 1949); E. C. Riley, *C.'s Theory of the Novel* (1962).

**Césaire, Aimé** (Basse-Pointe, Martinique 1913– ). West Indian poet and dramatist. While studying in a Parisian lycée, Césaire met the Senegalese poet Senghor, and through him discovered enthusiastically his own racial roots in Africa. As a result, his pre-war book *Cahier d'un retour au pays natal* (1947) is a joyful collection of verse and prose poems where torrentuous adjectives evoke luxuriant scenes of tropical life, and close assonant rhythms figure the throbbing of the drums or the songs of the galley slaves. He reacts against the rational modes of thought imposed by Europe on Negroes, and turns to ⇨ Surrealism and uses typographical tricks in order to uncivilize objects and stress their primitive force and strangeness. But in his hands the French language occasionally shows its still young power in a flashing metaphor, and Europe still lives in him through multiple literary reminiscences. In his latest book, *Cadastre* (1961), Surrealism becomes almost hermetic. Meanwhile he has continued to write, in *Les armes miraculeuses* (1946) and *Ferrements* (1960), in lyrical protest against the abuse of colonialism and the inferiority complex of Negroes. During the struggle of Africa for freedom he has also written plays on the emotional politics of newly liberated states (*La tragédie du roi Christophe*, *Et les chiens se taisaient*) and an essay on Toussaint Louverture (1961). A communist at first, he became a 'progressist' in 1956. Since the war he has been a *député* representing Martinique in Paris. [CLC]

L. Kesteloot, *A.C.* (Paris, 1962).

**Cesareć, August** (Zagreb 1893–Zagreb 1941). Croatian novelist. A leading left-wing author, his works are full of social protest but also some psychological insight. His best-known work is the novel *Careva kraljevina* (1925). [EDG]

**Cesarić, Dobrisa** (Slovenska Pozega 1902– ). Croatian poet. At a time when experiment was the dominant trend, this popular (because accessible) poet adapted conventional verse to express his subtle and often poignant lyrical experiences. [EDG]

Ibrovac, *APY*; Lavrin, *AMYP*.
Kadić, *CCL*.

**Cesarotti, Melchiorre** (Padua 1730–Selvazzano, Padua 1808). Italian poet and critic. After teaching in Padua and Venice, he became professor of Hebrew and Greek at Padua University. A devoted follower of the French *Encyclopédie*, he later welcomed the French Revolution and Napoleon's arrival in Italy (see *Pronea*, 1807). His importance lies mainly in his widely-read and very influential translation of Macpherson's *Ossian* (1763); but equally important for their influence on Italian romanticism were his theoretical essays, especially the *Saggio sopra la lingua italiana* (1785; later *Saggio sulla filosofia delle lingue*, 1800). His views on the evolution of language paralleled ➪ Vico's theories of the evolution of society, and did much to soften the fixed purist attitude towards language. [RHC]

*Opere* (40 vols., 1800–13); *Opere scelte*, ed. G. Ortolani (2 vols., 1945–6); *Dal Muratori al C.*, iv, ed. E. Bigi (1960); *The Poems of Ossian . . . with a Translation of the Abbé C.'s Dissertation on the Controversy Respecting the Authenticity of Ossian*, J. M'Arthur (1806).

W. Binni, *M.C. e il preromanticismo italiano* (Florence, 1941); G. Marzot, *Il gran C. Saggio sul preromanticismo settecentesco* (Florence, 1949); *Minori*, iii.

**Cetina, Gutierre de** (Seville 1514/17–Mexico 1554/7). Spanish poet and soldier. He fought in Italy and Germany and met a violent death in Mexico. He followed ➪ Garcilaso in the new Italian metres, and is best known for his madrigal 'Ojos claros, serenos' and some effective sonnets. [JMC]

*Obras* (Seville, 1895); Trend, *OBSV*; Perry, *HASP*; Terry, *ASP*.

**Chagas, Frei António das,** monastic name of António da Fonseca Soares (Vidigueira 1631–Varatojo 1682). Portuguese poet and ascetic. A swashbuckling soldier who earned the nickname 'Capitão Bonina' ('Captain Daisy'), Soares fought in the Wars of the Restoration, then took refuge in Brazil for a period of years after killing a man in a duel. Returning to Portugal in 1656, he continued his military career until in 1663 he became a Franciscan. While soldiering he penned Baroque poetry in Spanish in imitation of ➪ Góngora, many of his compositions ultimately being included in the collections *Fénix Renascida* and *Postilhão de Apolo*. As a religious he became celebrated for his popular, flamboyant sermons, in which he made frequent use of 'props', and was regarded by the devout as possessing miraculous powers. Increasingly ascetic, he was influenced by the works of Kempis, Van Esch and the Spanish mystics, and took to writing spiritual tracts which taught fear of hellfire and self-identification with Christ's Passion. The 368 *Cartas Espirituais*, his masterpiece, constitute an outstanding example of Baroque prose, frequently enriched by military imagery, and are principally dedicated to the reader's conversion. [RCW]

M. de L. Belchior Pontes, *Bibliografia de António da Fonseca Soares* (Lisbon, 1950), and *Frei A. d. C., um Homem e um Estilo do Século XVII* (Lisbon, 1953).

**Chamfort, Sébastien-Roch Nicolas** (Clermont 1741–Paris 1794). French moralist and publicist. Of obscure origins, he became a familiar figure in Parisian literary circles, living largely by journalism and some dramatic work. His disillusionment with Parisian society made him an enthusiastic revolutionary, and he eventually became secretary of the Jacobin Club, but committed suicide during the Terror. His real achievement is a posthumous collection of maxims and anecdotes, intended to bear the title *Produits de la civilisation perfectionnée*, in which he attacks the corruption of his age. [WHB]

*Œuvres* (1960).

J. Teppe, *C.* (Paris, 1950).

**Chamisso, Adalbert von,** properly Louis Charles Adelaide de Chamisso de Boncourt (Château Boncourt, Champagne 1781–Berlin 1838). German poet and writer. A French nobleman, he emigrated with his parents to Germany and settled in Berlin in 1790. In 1815 he was appointed botanist to a three-year expedition round the world under the leadership of Otto von Kotzebue (*Entdeckungsreise in die Südsee und nach der Beringsstrasse*, 1821), and received on his return an official appointment in the botanical gardens in Berlin.

Chamisso's literary output was slight, but won for him already in his lifetime a firm place in German literature – a remarkable achievement for a man not writing in his native tongue. His reputation is based solely on the famous tale *Peter Schlemihls wundersame Geschichte* (1814; tr. W. Howitt, 1954) – the story of a man who, in return for earthly rewards, sells his shadow to the Devil – and on a modest group of lyric poems, some political, some purely lyrical like the set *Frauenliebe und -Leben*, which have become more widely known through

Schumann's song-cycle. The secret of his popularity lies in his poised blend of the conservative and the progressive, the intellectual and the emotional. [RT]

R. Riegel, *C.* (Paris, 1934); Mann, *ETD.*

**Champfleury,** pseud. of Jules Husson or Fleury (Laon 1821 – Sèvres 1889). French novelist. He applied the ideas of realism as formulated by the painter Courbet to literature and he wrote a manifesto of the Realist movement *Le réalisme* (1857). He was also an art historian and Director of the State porcelain factory at Sèvres. His novels include: *Chien-Caillou* (1847), *Les aventures de Mademoiselle Mariette* (1853), *Les souffrances de Professeur Delteil* (1856), and *Les bourgeois de Molinchart* (1855), a study of provincial life. Besides *L'histoire de la caricature* (1865–90), he also wrote studies of the Romantics, *Les excentriques* (1852) and *Les vignettes romantiques* (1883). [WA]

Ed. G. Desezyk (1958) (selections).

**Chamson, André** (Nîmes 1900–     ). French novelist. From stern Huguenot and Camisard stock, he spent his whole youth close to Mount Aigoual (Cévennes) and in his frequent climbs he discovered the meaning of personal courage and a justification for living. He qualified as an archivist, and was assistant keeper at Versailles (1933–9). During the Occupation he organized resistance in the Rouergue and in 1944 was colonel in the army of Liberation. In 1945 he became director of the art gallery of the Petit Palais in Paris and has been responsible for many memorable exhibitions. He was elected to the French Academy in 1956.

Much of his work has the Cévennes as background: *Roux le bandit* (1925), *Les hommes de la route* (1927), *Le crime des justes* (1928), *L'auberge de l'abîme* (1933), *Les quatre éléments* (1935), *Adeline Venician* (1956). He is not, however, solely a regional novelist and many of his novels reflect concern with contemporary events: *L'année des vaincus* (a critical view of Nazi Germany, 1934), *Rien qu'un témoignage* (the Spanish Civil War, 1937), *La galère* (events of 6 February 1934; 1939), *Le puits des miracles* (the Occupation, 1945). In his essay *L'homme contre l'histoire* (1927) and in the novel *Héritages* (1932), he protests against the determinist view of history. His favourite work, which best expresses his qualities as moralist, philosopher and poet, is the autobiographical novel of his youth *Le chiffre de nos jours* (1954). [HG]

Louise J. Hubbard, *The Individual and the Group in French Literature since 1914* (Washington, D.C., 1955).

**'Chansons de geste.'** Medieval French epic poems composed between the late 11th and the early 14th century, and chanted by *jongleurs* to a simple musical accompaniment. Extant scraps of the music resemble that used for the *Vies des Saints.* The poems, which vary in length from under 1,000 to more than 20,000 lines, are in monorhymed *laisses* or stanzas. The earlier poems in lines of 8 or 10 syllables use assonance, the later ones are in rhyme, usually with lines of 10 or 12 syllables.

More than 80 *chansons* are preserved and the events which they cover range from the 5th to the 10th centuries. Their true inspiration is the heroic age of Charlemagne, and his wars in Italy, Germany and Spain, and the reign of his son Louis the Pious. The subject matter and some of the characters have a general basis of historical truth, greatly amplified by legend and the inventions of the *jongleurs* who continuously refashioned the poems. Audiences in the 12th century considered many of the *chansons,* especially those dealing with Charlemagne, as true history.

There has been much discussion about the origins of these epics. Scholars in the 19th century believed that the gap between the historical event, the battle of Roncesvalles in 778, for example, and the *Chanson de* ⇨ *Roland* in the Oxford version was bridged by a tradition of oral or written works, possibly short songs composed immediately or soon after the event and since lost. In the early 20th century Joseph Bédier denied this theory, and saw the *chansons* as the original inventions of creative poets who had used snippets of historical information presented to them by monks in the monasteries on the pilgrim routes. Bédier's theory of a collaboration between cleric and *jongleur* is now suspect, and is disproved in the case of the oldest extant poem, the Oxford *Chanson de Roland.*

In the early 13th century, the *chansons de geste* were grouped in three cycles by Bertrand de Bar-sur-Aube, author of *Girard de Viane.* The *Geste du Roi,* to which belong the *Chanson de Roland* and about 20 other poems, was the most important, probably because its poems centre on the king and his vassals. These vassals, including the twelve peers of Charlemagne, play a more actively heroic role than their sovereign who is often left in the background, a wise and aged ruler symbolizing the might of an Empire which will ensure the defence and the furtherance of Christianity against the Saracens. Many of these epics are characterized by high ideals of feudal knighthood, of the search for prowess in the service of France, the Empire and Christendom.

The *Geste de Garin de Monglane*, sometimes called the cycle of Orange or of Guillaume d'Orange, contains 24 related songs about the exploits of Guillaume d'Orange and of his kinsmen, ancestors and heirs. This most popular hero was probably William, Count of Toulouse, who was entrusted by his cousin Charlemagne with the defence of Aquitaine. He fought the Moors near Narbonne in 793 and in 803 took part in the capture of Barcelona. He became a monk at Aniane in 804, and founded Gellone, now Saint Guilhem-le-Désert, near Montpellier, in 806. Witburgh, wife of the historical count of Toulouse, may have provided the name Guibourc for the wife of the epic Guillaume d'Orange. In this cycle of poems battles are fought nominally on behalf of a weak and ungrateful king Louis, but the true stake in the fighting is the survival and success of the family unit. Less idealistic than the *Geste du Roi*, the cycle concentrates on the struggle of individuals for themselves and their family.

This emphasis on the warrior as an individual is accentuated in the third cycle, the *Geste de Doön de Mayence*, or the cycle of rebel barons. In these epics a vassal revolts against the king and is defeated, as in *Gormont et Isembart*, *Girart de Roussillon*, or *Renaud de Montauban*. Alternatively he may wage lawless war against another vassal while the king remains an ineffectual bystander; a fine example of this type of epic is *Raoul de Cambrai*.

A group of epic poems known as the cycle of the First Crusade and including *La Chanson d'Antioche* and *Le Chevalier au Cygne*, was composed in the 12th century, amplified and refashioned in the following two centuries. These epics, although not based on the legendary history of France, used the form of monorhymed *laisses* made popular by the *chansons de geste*.

In spite of much repetition of epic phrases in the lesser *chansons de geste*, there lies beneath the apparently rough exterior of many poems such as the *Chanson de Roland* or the first half of the *Chanson de Guillaume*, poetic and dramatic inspiration of the highest order. The *chansons de geste* exercised wide influence on the literatures of Germany, Holland, Italy, Spain, England and the Scandinavian countries. [LTT]

J. Crosland, *The Old French Epic* (1951); J. Bédier, *Les légendes épiques, recherches sur la formation des c. de g.* (4 vols., Paris, 3rd edn, 1926–9); I. Siciliano, *Les origines des c. de g.* (Paris, 1951); M. de Riquer, *Les c. de g. françaises* (Paris, 2nd edn, 1957); J. Frappier, *Les c. de g. du cycle de Guillaume d'Orange* (2 vols., Paris, 1955–65); W. C. Calin, *The Old French Epic of Revolt: Raoul de Cambrai, Renaut de Montauban, Gormond et Isembard* (Geneva-Paris, 1962); Rychner, *CG*.

**'Chansons de toile'** (sewing-songs) or *d'histoire*. Short medieval French love-songs, of popular origin, in assonance. The earliest and best examples were composed about 1100, and may have complemented the early ⇨ *chansons de geste* which normally neglected the theme of love.

There survive 20 songs, 5 preserved by ⇨ Jean Renart in his *Guillaume de Dole*. The characters are usually noblewomen with delightful singing names, bele Erembor, bele Aiglentine, who desire the return of their loved ones, Raynaut, Doon, whose wooing is often abrupt and disdainful. Refrains frequently offer a lyrical contrast to the dramatic concision of the narrative.

After 1150 courtly terms and motifs became prevalent in these songs but did not destroy their simplicity. In the first quarter of the 13th century Audefroi le Bâtard, *trouvère* of Arras, unsuccessfully attempted to adapt the dying genre to courtly taste. His five surviving poems are rhymed and wordy. The *chanson de toile* is a possible source for the English popular ballad. [LTT]

K. Bartsch, *Altfranzösische Romanzen und Pastourellen*, i (Leipzig, 1870); G. Saba, *Les 'Chansons de toile' ou 'Chansons d'histoire'* (Modena, 1955); *R*, LXIX (1946–7); *Revue de littérature comparée*, XVI (1936); *Studi romanzi*, XXX (1943); *MLQ*, XXIV, 1963.

**Chapelain, Jean** (Paris 1595–Paris 1674). French critic. A dominant figure of the French classical scene, he did much to maintain the official connexions of literature with the state and to create the conditions of classical poetry and drama. He was less talented, but perhaps more representative, than ⇨ Boileau. His first works were translations, from the *Guzmán de Alfarache* of ⇨ Alemán (1619; 7 edns before 1650) and the *Adonis* of ⇨ Marino (1623). A founder member of the French Academy, he worked with Richelieu and was regarded as his spokesman. It fell to him to draw up the famous *Sentiments sur Le Cid*, in which possibly he had to be more severe than he personally felt. His letter to Godeau on the 'Twenty-four hours rule' for plays does not mention similar rules on place and action, showing that the famous Unities were not even formulated as late as 1630. His long-awaited *magnum opus* was a poem in 24 cantos on Joan of Arc, *La Pucelle* (1656), which sold well (6 editions are known before 1670), but killed his reputation as a poet. He served Colbert as he had served Richelieu and drew up the first lists which served the king in granting pensions to men of letters. [WGM]

*Opuscules critiques*, ed. A. C. Hunter (1936); G. Tallemant, *Historiettes*, ed. A. Adam (Pléiade, 1960).
G. Collas, *J.C.* (1911).

**Char, René** (Isle-sur-Sorgue 1907– ). French poet. His short passage through ⇨ Surrealism in his youth served mainly to provoke his personal style. Though *Le marteau sans maître* (1934) is full of startling images, the poet sounds a note of sobriety which is already his individual voice. Recognition did not come however till after the Second World War, in which he had played a courageous role as leader of a Resistance group in Provence. *Seuls demeurent* (1945) and *Feuillets d'Hypnos* (1946) relate some of these experiences, but the anecdote is transcended by the poet's vision of eternal values: the poetry is one of strength, yet full of tenderness. Since the war Char has lived in his native Vaucluse, close to his rural friends. His poems, now more and more exclusively in prose, have become taut and aphoristic, for he seeks patiently to release the energy potential in language, and to make of poetry an instrument of revelation, indeed a close ally of philosophy. He points to Herakleitos as a model – like him he combines imagery and compression of language in formulations of truth seized *sur le vif* and set down as illuminations of the unknown. His recent work includes a play, *Le soleil des eaux* (1949), the beautiful *Lettera amorosa* (1953) and *Recherche de la base et du sommet* (1955). [RTC]

G. Mounin, *Avez-vous lu Char?* (Paris, 1946); P. Berger, *R.C.* (Paris, 1951).

**Chardonne, Jacques** (Barbezieux 1884–1968). French novelist and essayist. A publisher and son of a rich Cognac-producing family, he explored in his first novel *L'épithalame* (1921; tr. anon., 1923) the dual theme which remained the *leitmotiv* of his work, love and marriage. *Le chant du bienheureux* (1927), *Les Varais* (1929) and *Claire* (1931) trace the subtle ebb and flow of feeling which underly a married couple's difficulty in trying to reconcile their initial relationship with the practical problems of marriage. The three novels of *Les destinées sentimentales* (1934–6; tr. W. J. Strachan, *The House of Barnery*, 1955) include political and social themes, but *Romanesques* (1937) brought a return to his earlier manner. *Les chimériques* (1948) and *Vivre à Madère* (1952) hardly maintained his previous reputation. *L'amour du prochain* (1932) and *L'amour, c'est beaucoup plus que l'amour* (1937) are essays in the *moraliste* tradition, whilst *Le bonheur de Barbezieux* (1938) is autobiographical. [IHW]

J. Guitton, *Études et rencontres* (Paris, 1959); R. Poulet, *La lanterne magique*, i (Paris, 1956); P. Vandromme, *C., c'est beaucoup plus que C.* (Paris, 1962).

**Charles d'Orléans** (Paris 1394–Amboise 1465). French poet. Nephew and godson of Charles VI and father of Louis XII. His mother, Valentine Visconti, duchess of Milan, died in 1408, his father, Louis d'Orléans, was murdered in 1407 by the hirelings of Jean sans Peur of Burgundy. After further misfortunes, including the death of his first wife in pregnancy, he was found lying among the dead at Agincourt and held prisoner in England at Windsor, Pontefract, Fotheringay, Bolingbroke and Wingfield in Suffolk. In 1441 he was ransomed, and, after a fruitless expedition to Italy, established his court at Blois, where he attracted many poets, including ⇨ Villon.

His extensive works include *La Retenue d'amours*, an allegorical and courtly initiation into the service of Love, many *ballades*, songs, *complaintes* and *rondeaux* and a moral poem *Le Livre contre tout péché*, written at the age of 10. His best poems are the *ballades*, written in England, which praise *Beauté*, probably his wife, and lament his exile; some of his *rondeaux* are finely worked. He occasionally composed in English, probably for Alice Chaucer, countess of Suffolk. His poetic style and courtly language and themes are an anachronism in the 15th century, but he is much more than a poet of graceful trifles. His musical sense of language, and elegance and sincerity of feeling, often melancholic ('Je suis celui au cœur vêtu de noir') put him in the company of François Villon as one of the outstanding French poets of his century. [LTT]

*Poésies*, ed. P. Champion (2 vols., 1927–56); *The English Poems of C. of O.*, ed. R. Steele (1941).
P. Champion, *Vie de C. d'O. (1394–1465)* (Paris, 1911); S. Cigada, *L'opera poetica di C. d'O.* (Milan, 1960); *MLN*, XLVII, 1932; *Revue des sciences humaines*, n.s. fasc. 90, 1958.

**Charron, Pierre** (Paris 1541–Paris 1603). French preacher and theologian. After studying philosophy and law, he turned to theology and became a priest and a well-known preacher. In 1588 he applied unsuccessfully for admission to the Carthusian order. In 1589 he met Montaigne: their friendship influenced Charron strongly and his *Trois livres de la sagesse* (1601; tr. 1670) are to some extent an attempt to systematize Montaigne's thought and develop its implications with regard to religion. The style is tiresomely heavy and pleonastic. The work was severely criticized in the 17th century for impiety, because of the terms in which he talks of atheism. He died of apoplexy before he could complete a new edition of the book. [GJ]

**Chartier, Alain** (Bayeux *c.*1390–*c.*1440). French poet and prose writer. He was secretary to Charles VI and was sent by Charles VII on missions to Germany, Venice and Scotland. His work was greatly influenced by Agincourt and the ensuing confusion in France. In the *Livre des quatres dames* (ed. G. Hirschel, 1929) written just after the battle, four ladies grieve for their lovers, killed, captive, missing and fugitive. His most famous poem, *La belle dame sans mercy* (1424; ed. A. Pagès, 1937), on the courtly theme of the lover dying of despair at his lady's cruelty, aroused such opposition that the poet had to make amends for his 'uncourtliness'. In his greatest prose work, the *Quadrilogue invectif* (1422; ed. E. Droz, 1923; ed. R. Bouvier, 1945), the knight, the people and the clergy blame each other for their country's plight, and France with eloquent and stirring words exhorts them to unity, courage and faith. His other works include the *Lay de plaisance* (1414; in *MLR*, XII, 1917), *Complainte contre la mort* (1424), *Bréviaire des nobles*, *Lay de paix*, an elegant *Débat du réveille-matin*, ballads, *rondeaux*, and love songs, and many Latin works including a satire on court life, *De vita curiali* (ed. F. Heuckenkamp, 1899), which also survives in a French version and was translated by Caxton into English. The authorship and chronology of some works attributed to him are still in dispute. His works survive in a large number of manuscripts. [LTT]

*La belle dame sans mercy et les poésies lyriques* ed. A. Piaget (Lille-Geneva, 2nd edn, 1949).
P. Champion, *Histoire poétique du XVe siècle*, i (Paris, 1923); J. E. Hoffman, *A.C. His Work and Reputation* (N.Y., 1942); *R*, XXX (1901); XXXI (1902); XXXIII (1904); XXXIV (1905) (for *Belle dame sans mercy*); LXXII (1951); LXXV (1954); *Mél. Roques*, vol. I (1951); *Review of English Studies*, n.s. IX (1958); *SP*, LV (1958); *MLR*, LVI (1961); LXI (1966).

**Chassignet, Jean-Baptiste** (Besançon 1571 or 1578–1635 ?). French poet. After a good humanist education and legal studies at Dôle, he became doctor of law and fiscal advocate at Gray. In 1594 he published *Le mépris de la vie et consolation contre la mort*, an edifying sonnet sequence which uses illness, violent death and war to prepare man for the end of existence. Obsessed by mutability, which he expresses by a vast range of similes drawn from the Bible, the classics and the contemporary neo-Stoics, he reaches at one go the heights of Baroque genius. Despite a certain monotony of expression, this youthful work has great facility of versification and well-chosen images. He also published verse paraphrases of the Minor Prophets (Besançon, 1600) and of 150 Psalms (Lyons, 1613). [FWAG]

*Le mépris de la vie*, selection ed. A. Müller (Geneva, 1953).
A. Müller, *Un poète religieux du xvie siècle: J.-B. C.* (Paris, 1951), and *La poésie religieuse catholique de Marot à Malherbe* (Paris, 1950); F. Ruchon, *BHR*, XV, 1953; J. Tortel, *Cahiers du Sud*, 1952.

**Chateaubriand, Vicomte François-René de** (Saint Malo 1768–Paris 1848). French writer, the tenth child of an old Breton family. His childhood was passed mainly at the family Château de Combourg with his adored sister Lucile. His army and literary career was broken off by the Revolution and he went to America in 1791, where the vast and utterly new landscapes were to have a decisive effect upon his understanding and writing. He returned to fight in the royalist *armées des émigrés*, was wounded at the siege of Thionville and escaped to England where he lived in great poverty from 1793 to 1800 supporting himself by translating. He also wrote *Les Natchez*, a long prose epic not published until 1826, and an *Essai historique, politique et moral sur les révolutions anciennes et modernes considérées dans leurs rapports avec la Révolution française* (London, 1797). He began the work of Christian apologetic later to be called *Le génie du Christianisme*. After returning to France in 1800 he made a sudden reputation with *Atala* (1801; tr. R. Heppenstall, 1963) in which the life story of Atala an Indian girl converted to Christianity is told to René, a French exile, by an old Indian, Chactas. It contains some of his most beautiful descriptive passages. In 1802 he won even greater acclaim with *Le génie du Christianisme*, which was published at the time when Roman Catholicism was returning into official favour. It included his most famous story, *René* (ed. A. Weil, Geneva, 1963; tr. R. Heppenstall, 1963), which was later published separately (1805). *René* reflects much of his own life; René, a romantic youth, tells the story of his love for his sister to an aged Indian and a missionary in the wilds of America. The atmosphere of irremediable melancholy is made overpowering by the sweeping beauty of the language; it inspired (or echoed?) the mood of *mal du siècle* in generations of Romantic readers. *Le génie du Christianisme* attracted the attention of Napoleon, who appointed Chateaubriand to a place in the embassy at Rome; he resigned in 1804 immediately on hearing the news of the execution of the duc d'Enghien. Thenceforth until the Empire fell he was in opposition. On his election to the Academy in 1811 his speech was so provocative that he was not allowed to read it. After Napoleon's abdication he became one of Louis XVIII's ministers at Ghent. In 1809 as a pendant to *Le génie du Christianisme* he published his *Les martyrs ou le triomphe de la religion chrétienne*, a prose epic in 24 books following the lives and love of two Greeks, Eudorus and Cymodocea, in the time of Diocletian to their martyrdom in Rome. In 1811 he began his autobiography, *Mémoires d'outre-tombe*, which was to occupy him until 1841 (not published till 1849–50; ed. M. Levaillant and G. Moulinier, 2 vols., Pléiade, 1960; selections tr. R. Baldick 1961). Perhaps his greatest work, it gave the greatest scope to his sublime egoism and the astonishing variety of his life. He draws striking pictures of his childhood in the great and gloomy Château of Combourg and the contrasting worlds of the France of the Revolution and the Empire. His pamphlet *De Buonaparte et des Bourbons* (1814), a piece of invective against Napoleon, was said by Louis XVIII to have been of more use to him than an army. However, the Restoration did not bring the great rewards that he had hoped for in the political field. He was disgraced in 1816 after writing his *La monarchie selon la Charte*. In 1821 he was made Minister at Berlin and the next year Ambassador in London. He played an important part at the Congress of Verona in 1823 in deciding to intervene in Spanish internal troubles and when he was appointed Foreign Minister he brought the Spanish war to a triumphant conclusion. After performing this service he was perfunctorily dismissed in 1824. He did not hold office again, and after the July revolution of 1830 he had to earn his living by his pen (greatly helped by Madame Récamier, who formed a company with authority to publish his memoirs after his death and guaranteed him a pension). The greatest French writer of his generation, his egoism, melancholy, romantic life of exile and passion, his fascination with the Gothic and the past, and his love of Shakespeare made him the father of French Romanticism; his return to Catholicism gave the greatest single impetus to the revival of the Catholic Church in his lifetime. [WA]

*Œuvres complètes* (12 vols., 1929–38).

J. Evans, *C. A Biography* (1939); A. Maurois, *C.* (Paris, 1938); P. Moreau, *C.* (Paris, 1956); J. M. Gautier, *Le style des mémoires* (Paris, 1959); F. Bassan, *C. et la Terre Sainte* (Paris, 1959); J. Mourot, *Études sur les premières œuvres* (Paris, 1962); A. Vial, *C. et le temps perdu* (Paris, 1963); *Revue de la littérature comparée*, 1949.

**Châteaubriant, Alphonse de** (Rennes 1882–Kitzbühel 1951). French novelist. Much of his sheltered youth in the medieval setting of his father's domain near Rennes passed into *Monsieur des Lourdines* (1911; tr. Lady T. Davidson, *The Keynote*, 1912; Prix Goncourt), a story of the conflict between an old nobleman of Vendée and his prodigal son who does not share his father's mystical attachment to the soil. He had studied the great painters passionately and planned a work on Poussin, but turned to literature in 1908. *La brière* (1923; tr. F. M. Robinson, *Passion and Peat*, 1927; Grand Prix du Roman; filmed 1924), one of the summits of the regional novel in France, paints a sombre picture of the isolated bogland region north of Saint-Nazaire where the redoubtable Aoustin fights for its freedom from the threats of industrialization. After visiting Germany in 1937, he wrote a eulogy of Nazism in *La gerbe des forces*, and during the Occupation edited the pro-German weekly *La gerbe*. He escaped to the Tyrol with the defeated German armies (in 1948 he was sentenced to death in France for collaboration). His *Cahiers* (1906–31), published in 1955, throw important light on his composition of *La brière*. [HG]

G. Roger, *Maîtres du roman de Terroir* (Paris, 1959); P. Vernois, *Le roman rustique de George Sand à Ramuz* (Paris, 1962).

**Chazal, Malcolm de** (Vacoas 1902– ). French prose writer. Living in semi-isolation on the island of Mauritius, he initiated himself into the occult relationships between nature and the senses, collecting his intuitions and baroque images in *Sens plastique*, which posits the sexual act as the mediator between birth and death. This strange book caused a literary sensation on its Paris publication in 1948. His later works, such as *La bible du mal* (Port Louis, 1952), expound an idiosyncratic mysticism not unlike Blake's. [RTC]

A. Breton, 'La Lampe dans l'Horloge', in *La clé des champs* (Paris, 1953).

**Chekhov, Anton Pavlovich** (Taganrog 1860–Badenweiler, Germany 1904). Russian dramatist and story-writer. Grandson of a former serf and son of an unsuccessful shopkeeper, he went to Moscow (1879) and studied medicine; to make ends meet he wrote sketches for comic papers. He qualified in 1884, but devoted himself soon to writing, contributing stories to *Novoye Vremya*. His stories became more than merely comical, increased in range of character and setting, and were more carefully written (before 1886 he said he never spent more than 24 hours on a story). He also wrote several short farces and the play *Ivanov* (1887).

Despite success, he was restless, disturbed by Tolstoy's ideas, and in poor health (T.B. symptoms appeared already in 1884). In 1890 he made a gruelling journey across Siberia to report on the convict settlement on Sakhalin, off the Pacific coast (*Ostrov Sakhalin*, 1893–4). In 1892 he bought a farm at Melikhovo, south of Moscow, and enjoyed country life, engaging also in charitable work (mainly educational and medical); in 1897 he collapsed. Consumption now forced him to live often in the Crimea or France.

His first famous play, *Chayka* (publ. 1896; tr. E. Fen, *The Seagull* in *Plays*, 1959), failed when first performed (1896), but became a triumphant success when staged by the Moscow Art Theatre (newly founded by Stanislavsky and Nemirovich-Danchenko) in 1898. It was followed by *Dyadya Vanya* (publ. 1897, tr. ibid., *Uncle Vanya*), *Tri Sestry* (1901; tr. ibid., *Three Sisters*), and *Vishnyovyy Sad* (1904; tr. ibid., *The Cherry Orchard*). Chekhov married Olga Knipper, an actress of the Moscow Art Theatre, in 1901; in later years he was a friend of Tolstoy and Gor'ky.

The pessimism which pervades and gradually dominates the humour of his work contrasts with his poised temperament and (occasionally) progressive opinions. He regarded *The Cherry Orchard* – the decline of country gentry, indulging in vain memories, regrets, hopes – as a farce (Mme Ranevskaya to be played 'by a comic old woman'). If his melancholy satire of characters sunk in passivity, dreaming of action, is very Russian (cf. stories *The Steppe*, *The Duel*), the frustrated longings of his provincial intelligentsia blighted by life's emptiness (cf. the plays) symbolize a universal modern malaise. Soviet criticism interprets this situation sociologically as ripe for revolution, but there is no evidence that Chekhov shared this view. Western criticism senses in his 'farce' a condition beyond social remedy, and profound disbelief. From the first a comic virtuoso, able to give new twists to conventional humorous situations, he was already a master of concentrated pathos and psychological insight by 1886 (cf. *Anyuta*), which he applied to children (*Sleepy*, 1888), adolescents (*Volodya*, 1887) and animals (*Kashtanka*, 1887), young people in crisis (*A*

*Nervous Breakdown*, 1888) and the elderly (*A Dreary Story*, 1889). Typical of his later stories are: *Ward No. 6* (1892), which Lenin found extremely harrowing; *Peasants* (1897), a sombre portrayal of primitive village life; and *The Lady with the Dog* (1899), a perfectly balanced story of a love-affair, where apparent triviality expresses profound understanding.

Influenced by French Naturalism, Chekhov gave the short story a psychological depth and a humorous focus on human moods, resignations and self-deceptions which has been influential (⇨ Bunin, ⇨ Kazakov) but unsurpassed. [AKT]

*Polnoye sobraniye sochineniy i pisem*, ed. S. D Balukhatyy *et al.* (Moscow, 1944–51); *The Oxford Chekhov* (1964– ) tr. R. Hingley; *Letters*, tr. C. Garnett (1920); *The Personal Papers*, intr. M. Josephson (N.Y., 1948).

R. Hingley, *C.* (1950); D. Magarshack, *C. the Dramatist* (1952) and *C. a Life* (1953); Mann, *ETD*; W. H. Bruford, *C. and his Russia* (1947) and *A.C.* (1957); T. Eckman (ed.), *A.C.* (Leiden, 1960); E. J. Simmons, *C.* (1963); F. L. Lucas, *The Drama of C., Synge, Yeats and Pirandello* (1963).

**Chelčický, Petr** (*c.*1390–*c.*1460). Czech peasant philosopher. A lonely figure, he opposed both the official Church, which he considered corrupt and beyond reform, and the Hussites who were fighting injustice by violence. A defender of primitive Christianity, he held in his treatises *Siet' viery*, *O trojiem lidu*, etc., that evil must be fought by spiritual means only. The true Christian must have nothing to do with public administration which is organized violence, or with commerce which thrives on the work of others, and only work as a peasant. Knowing no Latin, he wrote for the people in Czech, in a direct, colourful style which had considerable influence on the future development of Czech prose. Tolstoy acknowledged him as his precursor. [KB]

C. Vogl, *P.C. Ein Prophet an der Wende der Zeiten* (Zürich, 1926); V. Novotný, *P.Ch.* (Prague, 1925); F. O. Navrátil, *P.Ch.* (Prague, 1929); L. N. Tolstoy, *The Kingdom of God Is Within You*, tr. A. Delano (1894).

**Chênedollé, Charles-Julien de** (Vire 1769–Le Coisel 1833). French poet. A member of Mme de ⇨ Staël's circle at Coppet; he suffered an unhappy love for Chateaubriand's sister (Mme de Cand). Famous for *Le génie de l'homme* (1807), a didactic poem, and *Études poétiques* (1820), which show fresh feeling for nature and suggestions of Romantic manner. Exiled to Hamburg during the Revolution, he was a close friend of Rivarol and later wrote *L'esprit de Rivarol* (1810). He contributed to the romantic review *La Muse Française*. [WA]

**Chénier, André-Marie** (Istanbul 1762–Paris 1794). French poet. Of mixed Greek-French parentage, he went to France in early childhood and studied in Paris, where his Greek mother's cultivated salon, frequented by eminent scholars and writers, further stimulated his interest in classical antiquity and his growing awareness of a poetic vocation. After an unsuccessful attempt at a military career (1782–3) he spent four uncomfortably poor years in study and writing, developing feelings of ineffectualness and isolation which his experiences in London as secretary to the French ambassador (1787–90) merely reinforced, although his faith in poetry as a heroic calling never weakened. The Revolution drew him back to Paris. He plunged into political journalism as a liberal monarchist, and was arrested and guillotined during the last days of the Terror.

Almost nothing of his poetry appeared during his lifetime, and much was left unfinished; any chronological pattern is thus difficult to establish. In the *Bucoliques*, he draws upon his deep personal affinity with the Greek world to revivify the traditional use of classical themes in French poetry, most effectively perhaps in such dramatic vignettes as *L'aveugle* (a symbolic portrait of Homer in old age) and *La jeune Tarentine* (a lament for a young bride lost at sea). The *Élégies* and *Épîtres*, though still predominantly in an antique setting, reflect more directly the poet's own aspirations, unhappiness and sense of alienation. Finally, the *Iambes* and *Odes*, largely the product of the revolutionary years, reveal his gift for passionate, bitter rhetoric and – most movingly with *Comme un dernier rayon . . .*, written while he awaited execution – enshrine his heroic devotion to the liberal ideals which the Revolution was betraying and his heroic conception of the poet as the voice of the conscience of mankind.

Though not wholly exempt from the defects of the period, and sometimes uneven in quality, Chénier's work represents the peak of French poetic achievement in the 18th century. When first fully published in 1819 it had a considerable impact upon the

Romantic poets, and later also influenced the Parnassians. [WHB]

*Œuvres complètes*, ed. G. Walter (Pléiade, 1940); *Poems*, ed. F. Scarfe (1961).

G. Walter, *A.C., son milieu et son temps* (Paris, 1947); J. Fabre, *C., l'homme et l'œuvre* (Paris, 1955); F. Scarfe, *A.C.* (1964).

**Chénier, Marie-Joseph-Blaise** (Istanbul 1764–Paris 1811). French dramatist and poet. Brother of the above. He became known as a Jacobin orator during the Revolution, and achieved popularity with a series of propagandist historical plays (*Charles IX*, 1789), which foreshadow later Romantic drama. He also wrote revolutionary and patriotic verse; one of his odes, *Le chant du départ* (1794), rivalled *La Marseillaise* in popular fame. [WHB]

A. J. Bingham, *M.-J.C., Early Political Life and Ideas* (N.Y., 1939); A. Liéby, *Étude sur le théâtre de M.-J.C.* (Paris, 1901); Lénient, *La poésie patriotique en France*, ii (Paris, 1894).

**Chernyshevsky, Nikolay Gavrilovich** (Saratov 1828–Saratov 1889). Russian critic and novelist. Successor of Belinsky as leader of the Russian radical intelligentsia. His attitude to literature was rigorously utilitarian. He wrote extensively on economic and political as well as literary topics. His beliefs were embodied in the curious novel *Chto delat'* (1864; tr. B. R. Tucker, *What is to be done?*, 1883; revised edn, 1961) written in prison in 1863 (the following year he was exiled to Siberia, where he spent most of the rest of his life). This novel was in part an optimistic rejoinder to Turgenev's *Fathers and Sons*; Chernyshevsky's novel in its turn helped to provoke Dostoyevsky's *Notes from Underground*, an onslaught on the rationalism affirmed by Chernyshevsky.

*Polnoye sobraniye sochineniy*, ed. V. Ya. Kirpotin (15 vols., 1939–53); *Selected Criticism* (also of Belinsky and Dobrolyubov), ed. R. E. Matlaw (1962); *Selected Essays* (Moscow, 1953).

R. Lampert, *Sons against Fathers* (1965).

**Chiabrera, Gabriello** (Savona 1552–Savona 1638). Italian poet. After a stormy youth punctuated by duels and banishments, he held various diplomatic offices, won favour at Florence, Turin, Mantua and Rome, and died a successful literary figure, whose influence in Italy remained considerable in the 17th and 18th centuries.

Influenced by the ⇨ Pléiade (especially Ronsard), Chiabrera was little affected by the flamboyant Marinismo of his time. Proposing to reform Italian verse by imitating the Greeks, he cultivated many genres and introduced a variety of metrical forms. His tragedies (e.g. *Angelica in Ebuda*, *Erminia*, *Pentesilea*, *Ippodamia*) and epics (e.g. *La Gotiade*, *L'Amedeide*, *Firenze*) are nowadays forgotten, as are his many poems in various forms on religious or moral subjects. Some of his other dramatic compositions (especially the melodrama *Il rapimento di Cefalo*) preserve a certain interest, but he is remembered chiefly for his lyrical and narrative poems. Among many metrical adaptations of Greek forms he wrote *canzoni* in what endeavoured to be a Pindaric manner, but heroic sublimity was beyond him, and he achieved his best effects in the graceful musicality of light *canzonetta* rhythms. [DGR]

*Canzonette, rime varie, dialoghi*, ed. L. Negri (1952); Calcaterra, *LSA*.

F. Neri, *Il C. e la Pléiade francese* (Turin, 1920); E. N. Girardi, *Esperienza e poesia di G.C.* (Milan, 1950); *Minori*, ii.

**Chorell, Walentin** (Turku 1912– ). Swedo-Finnish dramatist and novelist. Author of uncompromisingly realistic plays and novels dealing with humanity at its most primitive level and with disturbed states of mind in which primitive instincts and inner conflicts are laid bare. His plays have received numerous performances outside Finland, notably in the Scandinavian countries and in Germany. [IR]

**Choromański, Michał** (Elizawetgrad 1904– ). Polish novelist. Brought up in Russia, which he left in 1924. He started his literary career by translating modern Polish poetry into Russian. Then came his short experimental novel *Biali bracia* (1931), followed by *Zazdrość i medycyna* (1932; tr. E. Arthurton, *Jealousy and Medicine*, 1946), which made his reputation in Poland and abroad. This is the study of an obsession, intensified by a circular time sequence. In some ways his experiments in the thirties show a similar preoccupation with objects and weather as do the novels of the now fashionable *nouveau réalisme*. For Polish readers his style, taut yet very precise, has the beauty and fascination of a re-acquired language. He has also published an excellent collection of 'ambivalent tales' (*Opowiadania dwuznaczne*, 1934). [JP]

Ordon, *TCPS*.

**Choynowski, Piotr** (Warsaw 1885–Otwock 1935). Polish short-story writer. A member of the Academy of Literature. *Kij w mrowisku* (1923) contains his best stories which in their treatment of uncertain, half-realized moods recall both Turgenev and Maupassant. In his novel *Kuźnia* (1919) the historical subject matter is more interesting than the presentation. The events described lead to the rising of 1863, and one of the characters is Joseph Conrad's father, Apollo Korzeniowski. [JP]

*Młodość, miłość, awantura* (1926; tr. K. Żuk-Skarszewska, *Youth, Love and Adventure*, 1940); Ordon, *TCPS*.

**Chrétien de Troyes** (12th cent.). French poet. Author of the best and earliest extant Arthurian courtly romances. Very little is known about his life. He was probably a native of Eastern Champagne and most of his active career was spent at Troyes at the court of Marie de Champagne, daughter of Eleanor of Aquitaine.

Chrétien probably wrote *Erec et Enide* (ed. M. Roques, 1952) in 1170, *Cligès* (ed. A. Micha, 1957) in 1176, *Yvain* (*le Chevalier au lion*, ed. M. Roques, 1960) and *Lancelot* (*le Chevalier de la Charrete*, ed. M. Roques, 1958) concurrently between 1177 and 1179 or 1181. He began the *Conte du graal* (or *Perceval*) for Philippe d'Alsace, count of Flanders, after 14 May 1181. He also wrote, possibly in his youth, two love songs, one of which, 'D'Amors, qui m'a tolu a moi', is inspired by the Provençal poem 'Quant vey la lauzeta mover' by ⇨ Bernart de Ventadorn. The story of *Guillaume d'Angleterre* (ed. M. Wilmotte, 1927), based on the legend of Saint Eustache, has also been ascribed to him.

In the opening lines of *Cligès*, he listed the works he had already written. Apart from *Erec and Enide*, these included the *Comandemenz Ovide*, the *Art d'amors*, a translation of Ovid's *Ars amatoria*, the *Mors de l'Espaule* (the story of Pelops), a work about king Mark and Iseut the Fair, and the *Muance de la Hupe, de l'Aronde et du Rossignol* which has survived as the poem *Philomena*, ascribed to a Crestiens li Gois in an *Ovide moralisé* of the 13th century. All these early works, apart from *Erec* and *Philomena*, have been lost.

To a clerical training and a grounding in the art of rhetoric Chrétien brought a knowledge of classical and Celtic mythology, of Cistercian thought, and of the code of courtly love found in the works of the ⇨ troubadours. His romances are outstanding in medieval European literature for the *sen* or inner meaning which he unobtrusively wove into them. His theme is usually the quest for self-knowledge of a knight who too easily has won an illusory happiness or high position to which as a person he is unfitted. In *Erec et Enide* both Erec and his wife have to undertake this quest of rehabilitation in order to find harmony within themselves, with each other and with society. Whereas Erec had neglected his knightly duties for love of his wife Enide, Yvain in *Le Chevalier au Lion* breaks his pledge to his wife Laudine, who is portrayed as a courtly *dame*. Yvain is humbled and becomes insane, but after many trials he is accepted back by society and Laudine. Supernatural occurrences from Celtic mythology are used skilfully in this romance. The story of *Cligès* follows the tradition of Oriental romances favoured in France in the late 12th century, but is linked with the Arthurian legend and forms part of the Breton cycle. In this romance Chrétien reproduces the framework of the ⇨ Tristan story in the triangle of the uncle, his wife Fenice, and her lover, the nephew, Cligès; but Chrétien's quest for harmony in life is opposed to the tragedy implicit in the Tristan story. Fenice uses a potion to preserve herself from her husband and to devote herself to Cligès. By her constancy, including the trial of simulated death, she eventually wins happiness in marriage to Cligès who succeeds his dead uncle as Emperor.

In *Lancelot*, or the *Chevalier de la Charrete*, he depicts the conflict in Lancelot's mind between the demands of his courtly love and quest for the abducted Guenevere, and his ingrained conception of knightly honour. His courtly devotion triumphs over all obstacles and he is rewarded by the Queen. He tells us that the story of Lancelot and its interpretation, or *sen*, was proposed to him by his patroness Marie de Champagne. This work was finished by another cleric Geoffroy de Leigni, with Chrétien's consent.

The *Conte du graal* or *Perceval* (ed. W. Roach, 1960), his last romance, was also his most important; it blends Celtic themes of fertility, the Waste Land and subsequent regeneration, with a Christian interpretation of the quest for *caritas* and God, which is gradually and enigmatically suggested in the symbolism of the ⇨ Grail. Perceval, an unthinking and egoistic character, fails in the tests he undergoes in the Grail castle. Made aware of his limitations and his earlier sins, he sets out on the quest to rediscover the Grail castle. A parallel quest undertaken by Gawain to find the Lance that Bleeds is intended to show the inadequacy of the courtly code in the Christian life. Chrétien died before finishing this work which inspired a major cycle of works on the Grail in 13th-century France. [LTT]

*Eric et Enide*, Fr. tr. R. Louis (1954); *Cligès*, Fr tr. A. Micha (1957); *Perceval*, Fr. tr. L. Foulet (1947), tr. R. W. Linker (Chapel Hill, 1952); *Arthurian Romances*, tr. W. W. Comfort (1913).
J. Frappier, *C. de T.* (Paris, 1957).

**Christiansen, Sigurd** (Drammen 1891–Drammen 1947). Norwegian novelist and playwright. The son of a tailor who failed in business, he spent almost the whole of his working life as a post-office official. He was very much concerned with ethical problems, working them out against the background of Norwegian small-town life; Dostoyevsky was a major influence on him. His most important works are the trilogies *Inngangen* (1925), *Sverdene* (1927), *Riket* (1929); and *Drømmen og livet* (1935), *Det ensomme hjerte* (1938), *Menneskenes lodd* (1945). By comparison, his most popular work, *To levende og en død* (1931; tr. E. Bjørkman, *Two Living and One Dead*, 1932), is lightweight, as is *Agner i stormen* (1933; tr. I. Anderson, *Chaff before the Wind*, 1934). His style is traditional and often turgid, and his pyschological and ethical explorations are frequently so meticulous as to become boring, but he made a massive contribution to 20th-century Norwegian literature. His plays are relatively unimportant. [RGP]

*Samlede verker* (9 vols., 1949–50).
E. Kielland, *S.C.* (Oslo, 1952); Beyer, *NL*.

**Christine de Pisan** (Venice *c.*1365–*c.*1431). French poet and prose writer. An Italian by birth, at the age of 5 she accompanied her father Thomas of Pisa, a learned Doctor in Astrology, to the court of Charles V. She received a good humanist education and married Étienne du Castel. She was widowed at 25, and resolved to support her three children by her writings. Her prolific prose works include *Le livre des trois vertus*, a treatise on the education of women; the *Livre des faicts et bonnes meurs du roi Charles* (ed. S. Solente, 1936–41) and *La cité des dames*, translated from Boccaccio. Helped by Jean Gerson, the famous philosopher, she took up the defence of her sex against the antifeminist attacks by Jean de Meung in the *Roman de la* ⇨ *Rose*, a *Querelle des femmes* which survived until Rabelais' *Tiers livre* (1545). Her poems include moral and didactic works, an epistle to Eustache Deschamps to which he replied with a *ballade*, a few intensely personal poems of grief, and many *ballades* commissioned on the theme of love. She also wrote a *Ditié en l'honneur de Jeanne d'Arc* and other patriotic works which Caxton translated. Further English translations of her writings were made in the 15th and 16th centuries. Her skill as a prose writer has been underestimated and several works are not yet published. [LTT]

*Œuvres poétiques*, ed. M. Roy (3 vols., 1886–96); *La vision Christine*, ed. Sister M. L. Towner (Washington, D.C., 1932); J. Moulin, *C. de P. Introduction, choix et adaptation* (1962); *Le livre de mutacion de fortune*, ed. S. Solente (3 vols., 1959–64); *The Book of Fayttes of Arms and of Chyvalrye tr. Caxton*, ed. A. T. P. Byls (1933); *Ballades, Rondeaux and Virelais*, ed. K. Varty (1965); *Livre de la Paix*, ed. C. C. Willard (The Hague, 1958).
M. Laigle, *Le livre des trois vertus* (Paris, 1912); E. Nyss, *C. de P.* (The Hague-Paris, 1927); M.-J. Pinet, *C. de P.* (*1364–1430*) (Lyons-Paris, 1927); *MLN*, XXIV (1909); *R*, XLVIII (1922); *Revue de littérature comparée*, V (1925); *Mél. Guiette* (1962).

**'Chudoto s Balgarina.'** ⇨ Old Bulgarian Literature.

**Chukovsky, Korney,** pseud. of N. I. Korneichuk (St Petersburg 1882–1970). Soviet writer. During the pre-war years he associated with *avant-garde* literary circles and collaborated on various papers and journals. In 1903 he went to London as correspondent of *Odesskiye novosti*, and became editor of the satirical journal *Signal* in 1905. He also collaborated on Gor'ky's *Parus*, *Pravda* and *Krasnaya nov'* as translator, critic and children's writer.

Chukovsky has written many reminiscences and portraits of Russian writers – Korolenko, Chekhov, Andreyev, Kuprin, Gor'ky, Blok, Mayakovsky, etc.; but his most important contribution to literary scholarship are his many works on Nekrasov, the most comprehensive being *Masterstvo Nekrasova* (1952). He has translated works by Dickens, Kipling, Wilde, Chesterton, Twain, Whitman (on whom he wrote a book in 1923) and O'Henry. His views on translation are given in *Vysokoye iskusstvo* (1941).

Particularly popular are his books for and about children e.g. *Krokodil* (tr. anon., *The Crocodile*, 1932), *Moydodyr* and *Doktor Aibolit*, a version of H. Lofting's *Dr Dolittle*. *Ot dvukh do pyati* (1933; tr. M. Morton, *From Two to Five*, Univ. of California, 1963) is a collection of anecdotes and stories by and about Soviet children, giving a revealing insight into their language and psychology over the decades.

He consistently fought, e.g. in *Zhivoy kak zhizn'* (1962), for the preservation of literary Russian and opposed the introduction of ugly sovieticisms. He held the Order of Lenin and an Oxford Honorary D.Litt. (1962).

*Litsa i maski* (1914); *Sobraniye sochineniy* (4 vols, 1964–6).

M. Petrovsky, *K.Ch.* (Moscow, 1962).

**Cicognani, Bruno** (Florence 1879– ). Italian novelist and playwright. He was born into a literary and musical family whose life he described in his absorbing autobiography *L'età favolosa* (1940). His early propensity for character sketches tinged with Tuscan *fin de siècle* realism after Fucini (*Sei storielle di nòvo conio*, 1917; *Il figurinaio e le figurine*, 1920) soon gave way to a more mature and searching analysis of his characters (*La Velia*, 1923; *Villa Beatrice*, 1931), not without certain touches of introspective morbidity (*La nuora*, 1954). His style has most of the virtues, but also some of the faults, of traditional Tuscan prose-writing: a certain old-fashioned nobility, fastidious choice of words, occasional idiomatic mannerism. He also wrote two moderately successful plays: *Bellinda e il mostro* (1927) and *Yò el Rey* (1949). [GMC]

Gargiulo, *LIN*; Pullini, *NIN*; Biondolillo, *C*; Pancrazi, *SO*; *Contemporanei*, i.

**Cid, Poema de Mio.'** A 12th-century Spanish epic poem, the only Spanish *chanson de geste* that has survived virtually intact (the later vernacular chronicles provide evidence of a considerable epic *genre*, including other lost versions of the same poem). The work relates the deeds of a Castilian *infanzón*, Rodrigo Díaz de Bivar, who became known as *Mio Cid* (Arabic *Sidī*, 'my lord') and as *El Campeador*. The poem is preserved in a single 14th-century manuscript which lacks the first folio. This lacuna probably contained the account of King Alfonso VI's anger with the Cid because of the latter's alleged embezzlement of tributes. The poem opens, therefore, with the Cid's departure into exile with his vassals and his resolve to regain his honour and the King's favour by exemplary deeds. These consist in attacking a number of strongholds outside Castile belonging to various Moslem and Christian rulers. The first *cantar* or song ends with the Cid imprisoning and subsequently releasing the Count of Barcelona. This first section has the greatest claim to historicity, although even here some events are suspect. The second *cantar* relates the capture of Valencia (the Cid's greatest military achievement), his reconciliation with Alfonso VI and the restoration of his honour. This *cantar* ends with the marriages of the Cid's daughters to the Princes of Carrión, arranged and imposed on the Cid by the King. The third *cantar* describes the breaking of the marriages, brought about by the Princes' dishonour in the Cid's household after their displays of cowardice. They strip and flog the Cid's daughters in a lonely oakwood and leave them for dead. This act dishonours both the Cid and the King, and the remainder of the *cantar* recounts the legal proceedings and duels that culminate in restitution of honour and the re-marriage of the daughters to princes from Navarre and Aragon. Most of the poem after the conquest of Valencia is probably fictitious although some of the details have been shown to be historical by Menéndez Pidal. Despite the fictitious elements, the poem has the stamp of authenticity throughout. It totally lacks the fantastic and legendary elements to be found in some European epics and in the later Spanish ballads concerning the Cid. The hero is delineated not only as a great military leader and loyal vassal, but also, in more rounded fashion, as a perfect husband, father, businessman and lawyer and as a devout Christian. The author skilfully provides him with a deuteragonist in the person of Minaya Álvar Fáñez, and the relationship with Alfonso VI is most subtly traced. The theme of honour and the legal aspects are strongly Germanic in character. The poem is written in typical epic form: assonanced *laisses* of varying length, each introducing a new development in the action. The lines usually have a clear caesura, but the hemistichs vary in length from 4 to 10 syllables, with those of 7 and 8 syllables predominating. There are no digressions and the descriptions are concise, realistic and almost cinematographic in their occasional brief concentration on a small detail of a scene, often producing a momentary sense of great pathos. [IM]

Ed. R. Menéndez Pidal (1944–6; CC; CA); modern Spanish version by A. Reyes (CA); English tr. L. B. Simpson (Berkeley, 1957), and W. S. Merwin (London, 1959).

R. Menéndez Pidal, *The Cid and his Spain* (London, 1934), *Poesía juglaresca* (Madrid, 1957), *La epopeya española a través de la literatura española* (Buenos Aires, 1945), and *En torno al poema del Cid* (Barcelona, 1963); D. Alonso, *Ensayos sobre poesía española* (Buenos Aires, 1947); *NRFH*, II (1948); E. V. De Chasca, *Estructura y forma en el P.M.C.* (Iowa, 1955), and *El arte juglaresco en al Cantar de Mio Cid* (Madrid, 1967).

**Cienfuegos, Nicasio Álvarez de** (Madrid 1764–Orthez 1809). Spanish poet. He opposed Napoleon, narrowly escaped execution by Murat, and was taken as a hostage to France. Influenced in his neo-classical manner by ⇨ Meléndez Valdés, he later developed Romantic characteristics (though Romantic sensibility was always trammelled by neo-classical poetic diction and the Romantics found him artificial). He walked the spring countryside in the melancholy spirit of Cowper, but is violent in his loves and resentments, and obsessed by the tomb. [JMC]

*Poesías* (BAE 67); Blecua, *FLE*.

**Ciminelli, Serafino de'**, known as Serafino Aquilano (Aquila 1466–Rome 1500). Italian poet. A court poet at Rome, Naples, Urbino, Mantua and Milan, he achieved phenomenal success, partly due to his gifts as a musician and an improviser and reciter of verse. In his *strambotti* and his sonnets he cultivated a flamboyant strain of Petrarchism full of *concetti* and rhetorical ingenuity (cf. ⇨ Tebaldeo). Although this lively, if extravagant and sometimes tasteless Petrarchism of the *quattrocento* was supplanted in the *cinquecento* by ⇨ Bembo's more rigorous 'literary' Petrarchism, Serafino's popularity, measured by the number of editions of his works, extended well into the 16th century, and he was translated and adapted by English poets of that century, from Wyatt onwards. [DGR]

*Le Rime*, ed. M. Menghini (1894; vol. I only); B. Bauer-Formiconi, *Die Strambotti des Serafino dall'Aquila* (Munich, 1967).

D'Ancona, in *Studi sulla letteratura italiana de' primi secoli* (Ancona, 1884); Croce, *PES*.

**Claudel, Paul** (Villeneuve-sur-Fère-en-Tardenois 1868–Paris 1955). French dramatist and poet. His distinguished career in the consular and diplomatic service which took him to many lands (in North and South America and the Far East as well as in Europe) and kept him away from Paris for long periods has been thought to account in part for the vigorous independence of his literary development and the exotic, grandiose settings of many of his works.

The key – or, for many, the stumbling-block – to the understanding of Claudel is his religion. Nearly all his work is in some sense an affirmation of his Roman Catholic faith and a form of proselytizing. This fact creates difficulties: those readers and critics who share his beliefs sometimes seem to fear that to find fault with his work is to attack the faith and tend to be too enthusiastically uncritical of his writings, while other Christians and many agnostics or atheists assume too readily an equally prejudiced and often uninformed aversion. By temperament, he was passionate, expansive and assertive. There is an obvious link between his nature and the kind of poetry and poetic drama he produced: his characteristic style is confident, buoyant (some would say bumptious), intensely lyrical and ejaculatory. The bold and energetic eclecticism of his richly exploratory imagery and the freedom he exercised in settings and plots make him seem nearer to Elizabethan or Spanish drama than to the traditions of the French theatre. He had little regard for rationalism and abhorred any views that smacked of determinism or what he envisaged as scientific materialism (his criteria and arguments are not all likely to please painstaking historians, scientists and linguistic philosophers). His religion brought him the experience of joy and, above all, of personal freedom and Grace that he needed. Its tenets also provided the means to give some order and coherence to the manifold and turbulent tendencies of his complex nature. The discovery and celebration of that coherence is the stuff of his drama.

His most important plays are *Tête d'or* (1890), *La ville* (1893), *La jeune fille Violaine* (1901), *L'échange* (1901), *Le repos du septième jour* (1901), *Partage de midi* (1906), *L'annonce faite à Marie* (1912 – a later version of *La jeune fille Violaine*), the trilogy *L'otage* (1911), *Le pain dur* (1918) and *Le père humilié* (1920) and *Le soulier de satin* (1928–9). Many of these works have more than one version. He sought, not always successfully, to give clearer symbolic significance and more disciplined form to the dramas he had first created out of his own problems without much thought for their presentation on the stage. The themes are metaphysical or religious, e.g. the nature of sacrifice and miracle, the mystery of the Communion of Saints, the workings of Providence, the relationship between evil and God's purpose. He is especially drawn to the theme of love between man and woman; he shows woman as the fount of great evil and great good, as capable of immense sacrifice and of fulfilling the role of Beatrice in bringing man to understand that their love can be completely realized only in the eternity of God's presence. It is within the framework of such themes that Claudel is able to communicate his strong sense of the hierarchy of all things and his conviction that our function is to serve God in the way God mysteriously chooses. The drama inherent in the dichotomies of the Christian religion is given epic dimensions. Though the plays are allegorical in varying degrees and the characters are often mouthpieces for different doctrines he wishes to expound, Claudel at his best can disarm much criticism and grip us by the very frankness of his dogmatism, by the variety of tones and forms he adopts (cf. his *Farces lyriques*, *Protée* (1914) and *L'ours et la lune* (1916): *Le soulier de satin* is his most daring attempt to transcend the limits of the theatre), by the appropriateness of the historical setting (cf. *L'annonce faite à Marie* and *Le soulier de satin*) and by the complexity of the characters' struggles along the different roads to God.

He eschewed traditional rhyme and metre and developed his own form of poetic prose; his free *verset* admirably conveys his ebullient genius as it swells and subsides. His best poetic work – such as *Cinq grandes odes suivies d'un Processional pour saluer le siècle nouveau* (1910), *La cantate à trois voix* (1913), *Corona benignitatis anni Dei* (1914), *Poèmes de guerre 1914–1916* (1922) and *Feuilles de saints* (1925) – rivals his plays in the expression of his baroque imagination. His essentially catholic appetite gives his poetry both its metaphysical intensity and its eager delight in the pulp of existence. After a period of French poetry containing much introversion, anguish and narrow aestheticism, he represents for many readers a kind of liberation and a return to a more traditional conception of the poet's function, namely, to sing with generous heart of our world's tumultuous beauty and wonder. Much influenced by Aquinas, he wrote pontifically on the poet's vocation (cf. his *Art poétique*, 1907) and, in the latter part of his life, devoted himself to Biblical commentary. [WNI]

*Théâtre*, ed. J. Madaule (2 vols., Pléiade 1956); *Œuvre poétique* (1 vol., Pléiade, 1957).

L. Barjon, *P.C.* (Paris, 1953); J. Bastien, *L'œuvre dramatique de P.C.* (Reims, 1957); E. Beaumont, *The Theme of Beatrice in the Plays of C.* (1954); H. Guillemin, *C. et son art d'écrire* (Paris, 1955); J. Madaule, *Le génie de P.C.* (Paris, 1933); J. Madaule, *Le drame de P.C.* (new edn, Paris, 1947).

**Claudius, Matthias** (Reinfeld, Lübeck 1740–Hamburg 1815). German journalist and poet. He was a son of the manse and although he abandoned the study of theology and his intention of entering the church, it was in an essentially pastoral capacity, as editor of the *Wandsbecker Bote*, that he achieved lasting fame. This local paper of a small village near Hamburg gained wide popularity under his editorship, not only amongst the common people for whose edification and instruction it was designed with its consciously naïve, popular tone, but also amongst the most important literary men of the day, and included amongst its contributors ⇨ Klopstock, ⇨ Herder and ⇨ Lessing. After the *Bote* ceased publication, Claudius continued to publish his articles and poems in *Asmus omnia sua secum portans oder sämtliche Werke des Wandsbecker Botens* (1775–1812, 8 parts).

The naïve, childlike, devoutly Christian quality of his contributions to the *Bote* is the hall-mark of almost all his mature poetry, which often has the same unobtrusive, popular educational aims. His range is somewhat limited: a number of songs of peasant life which today strike a somewhat false note, some hearty drinking songs ('Rheinweinlied'), jocular children's poems ('Der Winter ist ein rechter Mann') and a number of nature poems of which the fine 'Der Mond ist aufgegangen' is the most famous. The death of his brother Josias (1760) exerted a profound influence on the young Claudius, and many of his poems hover between a desire to welcome 'Freund Hain', as he calls death, and a love of life ('Der Tod und das Mädchen', 'Der Säemann säet den Samen'). [WAC]

*Werke*, ed. P. Suhrkamp (3 vols., 1941); ed. U. Roedl (Cotta-Klassiker, n.d.).

J. Rüttenauer, *Die Botschaft. Versuch über M.C.* (Munich, 1947); U. Roedl, *M.C.* (Berlin, 1934).

**Claussen, Sophus** (Helletoft/Langeland 1865–Gentofte 1931). Danish poet. With *Pilefløjter* (1899) he remains the foremost Danish Symbolist (influenced by French), also affecting the diabolic manner (*Djævlerier*, 1904) and pantheism, and achieving even a moral (and prophetic) tone as in 'Atomernes Oprør'. [ELB]

E. Frandsen, *S.C.* (2 vols., Copenhagen, 1950).

**Clement, Saint.** ⇨ Old Bulgarian Literature.

**Clopinel, Jean.** ⇨ *Rose, Roman de la.*

**Cocteau, Jean** (Maisons-Laffitte 1889–Milly-la-Forêt 1963). French man of letters. Active in literature, art, ballet, music and films, he associated, at one time or another, with some of the most gifted figures of modern European culture: poets like ⇨ Apollinaire and Max ⇨ Jacob; novelists like Radiguet and Blaise ⇨ Cendrars; painters such as Picasso, Chirico and Dufy; Diaghilev and the Ballets Russes; composers like Poulenc, Satie, Milhaud, Honegger and Stravinsky. His reputation chiefly rests on his work as poet, novelist, playwright and critic, but he has executed talented drawings and book-illustrations, decorated churches and public buildings, worked in glass, pottery and ceramics, composed music, performed as an actor, and written and directed highly original films. His poetic output – from *Le Cap de Bonne-Espérance* (1919), which characteristically exploits the topical aeroplane as the symbol of the poet's effort to transcend the visible world, to *Léone* (1945) with its angel-like figure accompanying the poet towards a transcendent realm – is marked by his playful fantasy and fascination with verbal craft. There is much merely modish virtuosity in, e.g., *Escales* (1920), poems about the passing loves of sailors; *Poésies* (1920) and *Vocabulaire* (1922); *Plain-Chant* (1923), with its return to classical metre and rhyme and its characteristic obsession with sleep and death; *L'Ange Heurtebise* (1925), self-conscious and rarefied; *Opéra* (1927) with its hint of personal grief lying below the surface; *Clair-Obscur* (1954) and *Cérémonial espagnol du phénix* (1961). *Discours du grand sommeil* (1920), a moving long poem about the suffering and friendship of the Great War, escapes these strictures.

Cocteau's talent as a novelist finds expression in: *Le Potomak* (1919), an apparently random collection of texts and drawings unified by the underlying sense of a spiritual quest involving the poet and his place in the world, together with its fantasticated sequence, *La fin du Potomak* (1939); *Le grand écart* (1923; tr. L. Galantière, *The Grand Ecart*, 1925), perhaps the most accomplished of his novels, a delicate and scrupulous analysis of a young man's 'sentimental education'; *Thomas l'Imposteur* (1923; tr. Dorothy Williams, *The Imposter*, 1957), a brilliantly self-conscious *tour de force* creating a detached and unreal world through which we follow the progress of the elegant poet-hero, oddly unmarked by the horrors of the Great War; *Les enfants terribles* (1929; tr. R. Lehmann, *Children of the Game*, 1955), a remarkable study of the destructive relationship of four young people caught up in a sinister, private world of their own making; and *Le fantôme de Marseille* (1933), a curious and equivocal *nouvelle* in which a young male delinquent disguised as a girl sets off a tragic sequence of events.

Cocteau came to the theatre via the ballet and his first ventures were sketches for two ballets written for Diaghilev's company: *Le dieu bleu* (1912) and *Parade* (1917), with décor by Picasso and music by Erik Satie. These were followed by a hilarious mime written for the celebrated clowns, the Fratellinis: *Le bœuf sur le toit* (1920) with décor by Dufy and music by Milhaud. His subsequent sketches for ballets include *Le train bleu* (1924), again for Diaghilev, *Le jeune homme et la mort* (1946) and *La dame à la licorne* (1953). His drama proper begins with *Roméo et Juliette* (1918, staged 1924), a poor adaptation of Shakespeare. There followed: *Les mariés de la Tour Eiffel* (1921), a gay and witty satire of bourgeois attitudes, inventively exploiting gramophones to comment on the action and speak the cliché-ridden dialogue; two adaptations of Sophocles – *Antigone* (1922; tr. C. Wildman, 1962), subsequently turned into an opera by Honegger (1927), and *Oedipe-Roi* (written 1922–5; tr. C. Wildman, *Oedipus-Rex*, 1962), a Latin version of which was later used by Stravinsky as the text for his 'opera-oratorio', *Oedipus-Rex* (1927), dressed and mounted by Cocteau in a striking production in 1952. His subsequent plays include: *Orphée* (1926; tr. C. Wildman, *Orpheus*, 1962), a fantastic version of the old myth, exploiting anachronism for comic and ironic effect; *La voix humaine* (1930; tr. C. Wildman, *The Human Voice*, 1951), a deft piece of boulevard theatre in which a woman pleads on the telephone with the lover who has abandoned her; *La machine infernale* (1934; tr. C. Wildman, *The Infernal Machine* 1962), a sophisiticated handling of the Oedipus story. *Les Chevaliers de la Table Ronde* (1937) and *Renaud et Armide* (1946), both attempt to resuscitate the world of poetic legend to accommodate Cocteau's distinctive concerns with the role of the poet and the tragic nature of true love. In *Les parents terribles* (1938; tr. C. Franck, *Intimate Relations*, 1962), the pure love of Michael for Madeleine disrupts the precarious order of a household caught in a web of equivocation and lies. *Les monstres sacrés* (1940; tr. E. O. Marsh, *The Holy Terrors*, 1962) is an amusing but conventional play about the eccentricities of the theatrical world, *La machine à écrire* (1941; tr. R. Duncan, *The Typewriter*, 1947), a thriller that serves as a pretext for a moralist's analysis of bourgeois vice and hypocrisy in a provincial setting. *L'aigle à deux têtes* (1946; tr. C. Wildman, *The Eagle with Two Heads*, 1962) is a pretentious melodrama in a Ruritanian setting, based on the mysterious death of Louis II of Bavaria, and *Bacchus* (1951), a fable about a carnival-king in Reformation Germany whose reign of love and freedom provokes hatred and his own sacrificial death. Cocteau has also written a series of 'monodramas' (i.e. sketches for a single voice) of which the best-known are *Le bel indifférent* (1940) and *Anna la bonne*. To his most celebrated films he has brought a brilliant, though sometimes over-ornate, visual imagination and a deeply poetic conception of fantasy, as in *Le sang d'un poète* (1932), *L'éternel retour* (1944), *La belle et la bête* (1945), *Orphée* (1949) and *Le testament d'Orphée* (1959). In spite of its formal inventiveness, surface brilliance and assured technique, much of his creative work lacks spontaneity and a larger human resonance and seems trapped in a world of private myth-making. His literary criticism, though sometimes subtle and suggestive, also exhibits a tendency to preciosity and self-conscious paradox, e.g. *Le rappel à l'ordre* (1926; tr. R. H. Myers, *The Call to Order*, 1926), *Essai de critique indirecte* (1932), *La difficulté d'être* (1947). Other volumes of a more journalistic and autobiographical character contain incidental critical reflections of some acuteness, e.g. *Opium* (1930; tr. E. Boyd, 1932), *Portraits-Souvenir* (1935; tr. M Crosland, *Paris-Album*, 1956), *La belle et la bête: Journal d'un film* (1946; tr. R. Duncan, *Diary of a Film*, 1950), *Maalesh* (1949), an account of a theatrical tour in the Near East, *Journal d'un inconnu* (1953; tr. A. Brown, *The Hand of a Stranger*, 1956), and *Le cordon ombilical* (1962). [SBJ]

*Œuvres complètes* (11 vols., 1946–51); *Théâtre complet* (2 vols., 1957).

A. Fraigneau, *C. par lui-même* (Paris, 1957); J. J. Kihm, *C.* (Paris, 1960); P. Dubourg, *La dramaturgie de C.* (Paris, 1954); N. Oxenhandler, *Scandal and Parade: the Theatre of J.C.* (1958); S. Mourgue, *C.* (Paris, 1965); Fergusson, *IT*; Guicharnaud, *MFT*; Grossvogel, *TCFD*.

**'Codex Suprashensis.'** ⇨ Old Bulgarian Literature.

**Coffin, Charles** (Buzancy, Ardennes 1676–Paris 1749). Rector of the University of Paris, author of 100 Latin hymns, many written for a revised edition of the Paris Breviary (1736). None has been incorporated into the Roman Breviary, but some ten are well known in English translations. [FB]

*Œuvres* (2 vols., Paris, 1755); *Hymnes du nouveau bréviaire de Paris*, ed. J. H. Newman (1838); *English Hymnal* (1906, rev. 1933).

S. W. Duffield and R. E. Thompson, *Latin Hymn-Writers and Their Hymns* (1889).

**Colette, Sidonie Gabrielle** (Saint-Sauveur-en-Puisaye 1873–Paris 1954). French novelist. She collaborated with her first husband Willy on the 5 novels of the Claudine series (1900–7). In her own *La vagabonde* (1911; tr. E. Mcleod, *The Vagabond*, 1954) and its sequel *L'entrave* (1913; tr. V. G. Garvin, *Recaptured*, 1931), she recounts the social progress and emotional vicissitudes of a heroine not unlike herself. *Chéri* (1920) and *La fin de Chéri* (1926; both tr. R. Senhouse, 1953), which established her as a major talent, describe a young man's tragic love for an older woman. *Duo* (1934) shows jealousy ineluctably destroying a marriage and with it the jealous husband; its sequel, *Le Toutounier* (1939), describes the widow's rehabilitation, as she returns to her sisters and thus to the reassuring world of childhood and adolescent femininity. The theme of childhood and motherhood are more delicately evoked in *La maison de Claudine* – no real connexion with the original Claudine (1922), *Sido* (1929; both tr. E. Mcleod, 1953) and *La naissance du jour* (1932; tr. R. Benet, *A Lesson in Love*, 1932); near autobiography, they illustrate Colette's instinctive love and almost carnal understanding of nature, especially animals.

Colette often studies a character at a critical stage of development. She traces subtle shifts of mood and feeling from the eve of a crisis, to the crisis itself and its aftermath. In many ways her work remains wedded to the turn of the century: the 'poetry' of the *demi-monde*, the cult of childhood and memory, a propensity for teenage characters, a diffuse moral sense based on personal integrity, etc. She has a distinctive feeling for the no-man's-land in personal experience, which lies between the senses and the emotions. [IHW]

*Œuvres complètes* (1948–50).
J. Cocteau, *C.* (Paris, 1955); M. Goudeket, *Près de C.* (Paris, 1956); E. Marks, *C.* (1960); M. Davies, *C.* (1961).

**Colin Muset** (fl. 1230–50). French ⇨ *jongleur* and poet. Active in Champagne and Lorraine. Occasionally affecting the courtly style, he prefers the joys of the countryside, food and wine and shelter in winter, to the vain search for happiness in courtly love. His lyrics are remarkable for their skilful composition, poetic fantasy and personal realism. He attracted the Irish poet J. M. Synge. [LTT]

*Les Chansons*, ed. J. Bédier (2nd edn, 1938).

**Colliander, Tito** (St Petersburg 1904– ). Swedo-Finnish novelist and short-story writer. He studied art in Helsinki, subsequently taught drawing at Porvoo, and travelled in France, Belgium and Algeria. Later acted as religious instructor (Greek Orthodox) in Swedish-speaking schools. His novels and stories are perceptive studies, written with deep intuitive sympathy, of passive, suffering characters, at the mercy of their passions. He sees the solution of their problems in religious mysticism. Though his novels tend to be weak in structure, they are undeniably powerful and moving. [TA]

**Colonna, Francesco** (Venice? 1433?–Venice? 1527). Italian writer and Dominican friar. Little is known about him. Author of a Renaissance literary curiosity, the linguistically hybrid *Hypnerotomachia Poliphili* ('The Strife of Love in a Dream'), published in the famous Aldine edition of 1499 but perhaps written considerably earlier. Ostensibly an account of the love of Polifilo for Polia, its real core is a series of descriptions of ancient art, especially architecture. Its prose is a bizarre amalgam of Latin and Italian. [DGR]

*Hypnerotomachia*, facs. of 1499 edn (London, 1904); ed. G. Pozzi, L. A. Ciapponi, 1964; Varese, *PVQ*.
M. T. Casella and G. Pozzi, *F.C. Biografia e opere* (Padua, 1959); Croce, *PES*.

**Colonna, Vittoria** (Marino 1490–Rome 1547). Italian poetess. Of a famous Roman family, she married in 1509 Ferrante d'Avalos, Marquis of Pescara, but his soldiering in the service of Charles V made her life a lonely one. His death of wounds after Pavia (1525) caused in her a profound religious crisis and she came into contact with several representatives of the movement for religious reform – Valdes, Ochino, Vermigli. Her piety made her a revered figure and she corresponded with many famous contemporaries. Cardinal Pole was at one time her spiritual adviser, and in a century of Platonic devotions ⇨ Michelangelo wrote poems to her. Her last years were darkened by the collapse of the power of the Colonna family.

Her Petrarchan *Rime* faithfully reflect her experience – idealization of her absent husband, celebration of his deeds, grief at his death, fidelity to his memory, hope to rejoin him, and finally religious devotion. Potentially a moving story, it becomes curiously frozen in the formalized tone of her verse. [DGR]

*Rime e lettere*, ed. G. E. Saltini (1860); *Carteggio*, ed. E. Ferrero and G. Müller (1892); *The 'In Memoriam' of Italy. A Century of Sonnets from V.C.* (1895); Bo, *LC*.
M. F. Jerrold, *V.C.* ... (1906); Croce, *PPP*; *Minori*, ii.

**Columbanus, Abbot of Bobbio, St** (Ireland 543–Bobbio 615). Monastic writer. Educated in Latin and Greek under Comgall at Bangor, he evangelized Frankish Gaul and founded monasteries at Luxeuil and Bobbio under a Rule of singular austerity. He was an exquisite prose writer, with a pure style free of *Hisperica famina*; his verse is light and charming, and seasoned with classical allusions. His works include *Instructiones, Regula monachorum, Regula coenobialis, Tractatus de paenitentia*, 6 letters and some 6 poems; there is a *Vita* by Jonas of Bobbio. [CEC]

Ed. and tr. G. S. M. Walker, *Scriptores Latini Hiberniae*, ii (Dublin, 1957); ed. W. Gundlach, MGH (letters and poems).

J. Laporte, *Revue Mabillon*, XLV (1955), XLVI (1956), LI (1961); Manitius, *GLLM*; Raby, *CLP*.

**Comenius,** Latinized name of Jan Amos Komenský (Uherský Brod 1592–Amsterdam 1670). Czech educationalist and writer. Educated in Herborn and Heidelberg, he became a priest of the Church of the Bohemian Brethren and taught until the decrees against non-Catholics in 1621. He worked abroad and was known all over Europe for his educational theories. *The Labyrinth of the World and the Paradise of the Heart* (1631; tr. Count F. Lützow, new edn, 1950) describes a pilgrimage through a city, i.e. contemporary society. With shrewdness and irony the pilgrim observes and comments on various estates and professions. Finding no justice he nearly despairs but finally returns to Christ, the only haven of security in the universe.

*Veškeré spisy*, 8 vols., (n.d.) Brno; *Opera didactica*, (Prague, 1957); *Korrespondence*, ed. Patera (1892), ed. J. Kvačala (1897, 1901); *The Great Didactic*, tr. M. W. Keatinge (N.Y., 1967); (selections) ed. J. Piaget (N.Y., 1967); ed. J. Sadler (1969).

J. Kvačala, *Die pädagogische Reform des C.* (1903-4); J. Sadler, *J.A.C.* (1966); Harvard Slavic Studies, I, 1953.

**Commedia dell'arte.** A type of theatre production developed in 16th-century Italy by troupes of travelling actors. Performances were largely improvised on the basis of stock comic situations and characters: a guardian or guardian figure (Pantaleone), a professional man, a braggart (often a soldier), servant tricksters (Arlecchino, Pulcinella), and young lovers (Columbina). Shakespeare, Ben Jonson, Molière, Lope de Vega, Goldoni, Gozzi, and others made use of these conventions; 19th-century English pantomime and Viennese popular theatre also derive from them.

W. Smith, *C.d'a.* (repr. N.Y., 1966); V. Pandolfi, *La c.d'a., Storia e testo* (5 vols., Florence, 1957–9).

**Commines or Commynes, Philippe de** (Renescure, Hazebrouck *c.*1445–Argenton 1511). French chronicler. In 1464 he entered the service of the comte de Charolais who later, as Charles the Bold, Duke of Burgundy, appointed him councillor and chamberlain. In 1472 he defected to Louis XI at a moment of crisis between France and Burgundy – tempted by rich rewards and a fellow-feeling for the political outlook and behaviour of the king. As the closest adviser of the French king he amassed vast wealth, and gained by marriage the lands of Argenton in Poitou. After the accession of Charles VIII he was imprisoned on a charge of high treason which was probably justified, and confined for nearly two years 'en la haulte chambre de la tour carree de la Conciergerie'. He lost a quarter of his wealth. In 1491 he returned to royal favour, went on the Italian expedition of 1494–5, and was sent as ambassador to Venice. On the death of Charles VIII he retired to private life, and engaged in a bitter and ultimately vain defence of his title to the lands and wealth he had acquired.

His *Memoirs* deal mostly with the reign of Louis XI and were written between 1464 and 1498 at the request of the Archbishop of Vienne; the last portion describes the Italian expedition of Charles VIII. Careful, perspicacious and reflective, he judges men and events dispassionately. His admiration for Louis XI does not blind him to the king's weaknesses and faults. The prime virtue for a statesman is mistrust: 'Et n'est pas honte d'estre suspicionneux . . . mais c'est grant honte d'estre trompé' (III: 5). And later: 'ceux qui gaignent out tousjours l'honneur' (V: 9). The frontal attack is to be avoided: expose the enemy's flank by diplomacy and bribery. He regards warfare as abhorrent for its destruction of order and prosperity, and despises the feudal chivalry. He admires the administration of England because violence is not perpetrated on the people there. He is opposed to taxation without the consent of the taxed, and insists that the king must make himself loved by his subjects.

His judgements and interest in the science and philosophy of politics often anticipate the Renaissance. But unlike Machiavelli, Commines protests his religious beliefs, and acknowledges the guiding hand of Providence on the thread of human affairs. His memoirs were reprinted several times in the 16th century and were translated into Latin, Italian, Danish, German, Flemish and English. They inspired Scott's *Quentin Durward*. [LTT]

*Mémoires*, ed. J. Calmette (3 vols, 1924–5); Pauphilet, *HCMA*.
G. Charlier, *C.* (Brussels, 1945).

**Compagni, Dino** (Florence *c.*1255–Florence 1324). Italian chronicler. A contemporary of Dante, he was involved in the political events in the city which form the background to the *Divine Comedy*. He sided with the *popolani*, opposed the Black Guelphs, and was a member of the government overthrown in 1301. His *Cronica* (composed 1310–12; 1st edn, Muratori, 1726) gives an impressively personal and dramatic account of his age. There is vigour in his portraits of the chief protagonists like Giano della Bella and Corso Donati, and patriotic and partisan passion in his denunciation of the men and policies which have ruined the city. His close knowledge of events, his strong moral judgements and the energy of his language make his account stand out against the general flatness of medieval chronicles. [DGR]

*Cronisti del Trecento*, ed. R. Palmarocchi (Milan, 1935); *The Chronicle of D.C.*, tr. E. C. M. Benecke and A. G. F. Howell (1906).
*Minori*, i.

**Condillac, Étienne Bonnot, Abbé de** (Grenoble 1714–Beaugency 1780). French thinker. Much influenced by the empiricist psychology of Locke and the Newtonian conception of scientific knowledge, in his *Essai sur l'origine des connaissances humaines* (1746) and *Traité des sensations* (1754) he attempted a rigorously systematic analysis of the phenomena of consciousness, on a purely sensory basis, excluding all metaphysical hypotheses, but neither materialist nor idealist in implication. Though not wholly in sympathy with them, he had considerable influence on Diderot and the *philosophes*, and strengthened the movement of reaction against Descartes and the other major 17th-century metaphysicians, whom he attacked in his *Traité des systèmes* (1749). [WHB]

*Œuvres philosophiques*, ed. G. Le Roy (3 vols. 1947–51).
G. Le Roy, *La psychologie de C.* (Paris, 1937); Cassirer, *PE*.

**Conon de Béthune** (*c.*1150–Constantinople *c.*1219). French ⇨ *trouvère*. Related to the houses of Hainault and Flanders, he took part in the Third Crusade (1189–91) and played a leading role as diplomat and orator on the Fourth Crusade. His 10 surviving authentic poems are abruptly varied; 2 crusading songs, a bitter debate between a knight and a *vieille coquette*, and courtly songs, submissive and at times aggressive towards his lady because of her treachery. Conon, soldier before courtier, a vigorous poet, was acquainted with ⇨ Bertran de Born and was among the first *trouvères* to imitate the Provençal lyric. He accepted courtly themes and style, but not the courtly conventions. [LTT]

A. Wallensköld, *Les Chansons de C. de B.* (Paris, 1921); Woledge, *PBFV*.

**Constant, Benjamin** or **Henri-Benjamin Constant de Rebecque** (Lausanne 1767–Paris 1830). French novelist. He studied at Oxford, Edinburgh and Erlangen, and was appointed chamberlain at Brunswick court. He had several liaisons with older women, including Madame de Charrière and Mme de ⇨ Staël. Her hold on him (1794–1811) was extraordinarily powerful, their relationship being marked by passionate jealousies and reconciliations. When his politics incurred Napoleon's disfavour, he shared Mme de Staël's exile in 1803. In 1813 he published from Hanover a pamphlet attacking Napoleon, *De l'esprit de conquête et de l'usurpation*. During the Hundred Days, however, he took office under Napoleon because of the latter's liberal promises. After the second restoration he went to London where in 1816 he published *Adolphe* (tr. C.Wildmann, 1959; L.W.Tancock, Penguin Classics, 1964), remarkable not only for its superb style but also for its psychological analysis of a passion which frequently recalls the author's affair with Mme de Staël. The hero seduces an older woman (Ellenore) out of vanity; she leaves her protector and her children to follow him until she realizes the inauthenticity of his feelings for her and she dies of grief. Adolphe realizes too late that the bondage of love may be better than a freedom without love. The novel exposes the helplessness of the will to escape egotism, and the death of spontaneity at the hands of analytic intelligence. Constant returned to France in 1818 where he became famous as the leader of the Liberal opposition in the Chamber and as a political journalist. His other publications in his lifetime include *De la religion considerée dans sa source, ses formes et ses développements* (1824–31) and *Mélanges de littérature et de politique*. His

*Journaux intimes* were not published fully until 1952. His *Cahier rouge* (1907; tr. N. Cameron, 1959) contains a fascinating account of his youth. *Cécile*, another fragmentary tale, autobiographical like *Adolphe*, was published 1951 (ed. A. Roulin).

*Œuvres*, ed. A. Roulin (Pléiade, 1957).
Ch. du Bos, *Grandeur et misère de B.C.* (Paris, 1946); H. Nicolson, *B.C.* (1949); H. Guillemin, *B.C. muscadin* (Paris, 1958); M. Levaillant, *Les amours de B.C.* (Paris, 1958); W. W. Holdheim, *B.C.* (1961).

**Constantine of Preslav.** ⇨ Old Bulgarian Literature.

**Constructivism.** A Soviet literary movement (1924–30) associated particularly with ⇨ Sel'vinsky, ⇨ Bagritsky, ⇨ Inber, and the still important critic K. L. Zelinsky (1896– ). It believed in employing verbal tools which were strictly appropriate to the literary task in hand; with Sel'vinsky this could lead to remarkable pastiche effects. But its doctrine was too hazy for it to aspire to the importance of its progenitor, ⇨ Futurism, or of the Constructivist movement in the visual arts. [RM-G]

**Coornhert, Dirck Volckertszoon** (Amsterdam 1522–Gouda 1590). Dutch humanist, Christian-stoical moralist, poet and engraver. He had a wide education, travelled abroad and made a study of the classics, translating e.g. Boccaccio's *Decameron* and 12 books of the *Odyssey*. His opposition to tyranny cost him a prison sentence and a period of exile in Cleve, where he taught etching to Goltzius. His undoctrinal ethic, *Zedekunst dat is Wellevenskunste*, appeared anonymously in 1586. In contrast to his ⇨ *rederijker* poetry, it is entirely modern in substance and style, and its sturdy and resonant prose makes it a landmark in the history of the Dutch language. [PK]

*Werken* (3 vols., 1633); *Zedekunst*, ed. B. Becker (1942).
H. Bonger, *D.V.C.* (Lochem, 1941).

**Copić, Branko** (Hašani 1915– ). Yugoslavian novelist. One of the most popular writers in Yugoslavia since 1945, he has published a large number of stories for both adults and children. His most important works, the novels *Prolom* (1952) and *Gluvi barut* (1957), are about the gradual winning over of the peasants in an area of Bosnia by the communist partisan leaders, and show the clashes of personality and point of view that made this a difficult task. His assessment is as critical of the communists as of the peasants. In 1958 he published the novel *Ne tuguj bronzana stražo*. [EDG]

*SEER*, XL, 94 (1961); Kadić, *CSL*.

**Coppée, François** (Paris 1842–Paris 1908). French poet and dramatist. Known as the *poète des humbles*. From imitation of ⇨ Leconte de Lisle in *Le réliquaire* (1865) and *Intimités* (1868), he developed his own 'plain' style in *Les humbles* (1872), *Le cahier rouge* (1874), *Promenades et intérieurs* (1875) and *Les récits et les élégies* (1878), to sing the joys and sorrows of the ordinary folk of Paris. He became well known for his short comedies *Le passant* (1869, with Sarah Bernhardt) and *Le luthier de Crémone* (1876) and romantic verse dramas *Severo Torelli* (1883), *Les Jacobites* (1885), and *Pour la couronne* (1895). After becoming a Roman Catholic in later life he wrote a novel of religious experience, *La bonne souffrante* (1898). He became a firm anti-Dreyfusard in the Dreyfus case and supported the anti-Semitic Ligue de la Patrie Française. He was elected to the Académie Française in 1884. [WA]

L. Le Meur, *La vie et l'œuvre de F.C.* (1932).

**Corazzini, Sergio** (Rome 1885–Rome 1907). Italian 'Crepuscolari' poet with ⇨ Gozzano, he displays a similar style blended of irony and melancholy, learnt partly in imitation of ⇨ Verlaine and ⇨ Laforgue. [GD]

F. Donini, *Vita e poesia di S. C.* (Turin, 1949).

**Corbière, Édouard Joachim,** known as **Tristan** (Coat-Congar, nr Morlaix 1845–Coat-Congar 1875). French poet. Son of a Breton sea-captain, he was born and lived in a Breton village. His work was little known until Verlaine included him in *Les poètes maudits* (1884). Completely deformed by arthritis at 16, he developed a sharply ironic and unsentimental attitude to life. He particularly admired the sailors and seafaring life of Brittany and his poems in *Gens de mer* (1873) are full of sailors' slang. His poem 'La Fin' is a reply to Hugo's *Combien de marins* and shows a strong reaction against the earlier Romantic's idealization of the sea. He scorned Romanticism as a disease but admired the stoicism of the seamen he knew. In writing about himself, e.g.

in 'Paria', he developed that irony and detachment which was to influence ⇨ Laforgue, the young T. S. Eliot and others: 'Je ne connais pas mon semblable;/Moi, je suis ce que je me fais./ – *Le Moi humain est haïssable . . ./* – Je ne m'aime ni ne me hais.' To match his attitude he also developed deliberate unevenness, even apparent clumsiness, of rhythm and mood. He travelled to Italy, the Near East (1871), settled briefly in Paris and died of tuberculosis. [WA]

A. Sonnenfeld, *L'œuvre poétique de T.C.* (Princeton, 1960); P. Newman-Gordon, *C., Laforgue, Apollinaire* (Paris, 1964).

**Corippus, Flavius Cresconius** (fl. 565). African poet. He wrote a Latin epic of much historical and geographical value, *Johannis* (or *De bellis Lybicis*), on the theme of the defeat of the Moors in North Africa by John, on behalf of the Emperor Justinian; its style is modelled on Virgil, Lucan and Claudian. He also wrote a panegyric, *In laudem Justini minoris*, on Justinian's successor, Justin II, interesting for its account of Byzantine court ceremony. [FB]

*Opera*, ed. J. Partsch (MGH, AA, III, 2, 1879). Duckett, *GMA*.

**Corneille, Pierre** (Rouen 1606–Paris 1684). French dramatist, often called 'le grand Corneille'. After a Jesuit education he worked as Crown Council in Rouen, and for many years kept playwriting as his leisure activity. For a new middle class he provided a new type of play, including both tragedies and comedies, and scored his first great success in late 1636 (or early 1637) with *Le Cid*. Originally called a tragi-comedy because of its happy ending, its subtitle was later changed to 'Tragédie' because of the gravity of the issues involved. Like other famous plays of the century (notably *L'école des femmes* and *Phèdre*) it sparked off a war of pens and wits which has been called 'La Querelle du *Cid*' and in which Richelieu seems to have had some hand, working through his newly captured Académie Française. Before *Le Cid* Corneille wrote chiefly comedies, that is plays of banter and irony, ending happily: *Mélite* (performed 1629 or 1630); *Clitandre* (1630); *La veuve* (1631); *La galerie du palais* (1633); *La Place Royale* (1633); *L'illusion comique* (1635). It was with this last (recently revived) comedy that the Spanish influence first appeared dominant in his work: *Le Cid* is in content little more than a dramatic working-over of a 3-day comedy by Guillén de ⇨ Castro (see on this influence Z. B. Segall, *Corneille and the Spanish Dramas*, N.Y., 1902). The succession of tragedies produced within five years of *Le Cid* made Corneille's reputation as a master of serious drama and indeed created the kind of play known as 'French classical tragedy'. *Horace* (1640) deals with Livy's story of the patriot who saved the state and murdered his pacifist sister. *Cinna* (1641) presents a conspiracy in which the tyrant captures his antagonists only to pardon them. *Polyeucte* (1643), which some think the finest of all, treats the social obligations of a martyr, caught between his aspiration towards a glorious death and his duty to his faithful wife. For more than forty years Corneille produced a series of such plays, often fantastic, usually in the heroic style and always full of incident (*La mort de Pompée*, 1642–3; *Rodogune*, 1644–5; *Théodore, vierge et martyre*, 1645–6; *Héraclius*, 1647; *Andromède*, 1650; *Nicomède*, 1651). The heroics indeed were less popular after the Fronde, and Corneille is said to have been disgusted by the attacks of Racine and the parodies of Molière. Discouraged by the failure of *Pertharite* (1651), he gave up writing for seven years. His attempt then to regain popularity with a further series (*Oedipe*, 1659; *La toison d'or*, 1661; *Sertorius*, 1662; *Sophonisbe*, 1663; *Othon*, 1664; *Agésilas*, 1666; *Attila*, 1667) was not successful.

Corneille will always be remembered for having created, almost single-handed, a new form of dramatic art: the serious play in alexandrine verse, deliberately artificial in its refusal to represent physical action and change of time and place, but thereby all the more able to concentrate on movements of the mind, on clash of will and temperament. Most of these plays start from a situation which calls for the utmost daring, and which clashes violently with the heroic temper or the demands of an ethical code. The conflict is stylized in the verse, almost like counterpoint. Thus, the patriot who recognizes nothing beyond the State which he is proud to serve, will declare:

Alba has named you; I know you now no more.

He is immediately answered by the voice of humanity:

Yet I know you: which cuts me to the core.

It does not matter much when and where or by whom such things are said. Corneille's classic lines have been awaited and savoured by French audiences for more than three hundred years. They are rhetorical, but rhetoric may give great dramatic pleasure. Nor is the rhetoric untrue, to history or to life. *Nicomède* (1651) is the transposition of the national crisis of France in 1650; it was acted with applause under the German occupation of 1942. [WGM]

*Œuvres complètes*, ed. A. Stegman (Paris, 1963); chief plays tr. L. Lockert (1957).

B. Dort, *P.C. dramaturge* (Paris, 1957); G. Couton, *C.* (Paris, 1958); R. Brasillach, *C.* (Paris, 1961); R. J. Nelson, *C.: His Heroes and Their Worlds* (Philadelphia, 1963); Ph. J. Yarrow, *C.* (1963).

**Corneille, Thomas** (Rouen 1625–Les Andelys 1709). French dramatist and polymath. He lived and wrote in the shadow of his brother Pierre. It seems that the elder did his best to advance the dramatic career of his much younger brother. He wrote no comedies in the late forties, when Thomas produced *Les engagements du hasard* (1649), *Le feint astrologue* (1650), *Don Bertran de Cigarral*, *L'amour à la mode* (1651) and *Le berger extravagant* (1652). Just before Molière's return to Paris, and during Pierre Corneille's absence from the theatre, Thomas achieved at the Marais theatre almost the greatest theatrical success of the century, with *Timocrate*, played it is said over eighty times. An adventure theme taken from La Calprenède and presented with both style and suspense, it certainly fitted the taste of Paris audiences. It has been called a romantic subject treated classically. Three later tragedies do not seem to have had any success. With ⇨ Quinault, Thomas Corneille is one of the chief purveyors of that new kind of dramatic entertainment often called French classical drama and which became the envy of Europe. [WGM]

Adam, *HLF*; Lancaster, *HFDL*.

**Coronado, Carolina** (Almendralejo 1823–nr Lisbon 1911). Spanish poet. She wrote tender love lyrics, sometimes recalling San ⇨ Juan de la Cruz (though she mourns a worldly love – an American diplomat), and sometimes anticipating ⇨ Bécquer in the poignancy of her lamentation. Her occasional poems have faded with the events they record. [JMC]

*Poesías* (Badajoz, 1953); Blecua, *FLE*.

R. Gómez de la Serna, *Mi tía C.C.* (Buenos Aires, 1942).

**Correia, Gaspar** (Portugal *c.* 1495–Malacca *c.* 1565 where he was murdered). Portuguese historian. The author of one work, the unclassifiable, amorphous and monumental *Lendas da Índia*. In 1512 he left Portugal for India on military service and spent the rest of his days there and in the Far East. He was for a time secretary to the great viceroy Afonso de Albuquerque, and was privy to many succeeding governors and viceroys. His work, embellished by his own very competent paintings and sketches, is not concerned with legends, despite its title, but is a sporadic diary or register of events and circumstances to which he was witness, its only fictional element being the character Lisuarte Pacheco. Though lacking the scholarship and linguistic expertise of such chroniclers of the Orient as Castanheda, ⇨ Barros and ⇨ Couto, Correia left to posterity a vigorous, colourful and highly detailed account of daily life in 16th-century Portuguese India, condemning its vices and excesses and calling for a return to traditional values. An outspoken radical – a possible cause of his murder in Malacca – he maintains at one point that a salutary lesson for those who abused their authority would be the public execution of a viceroy by royal decree. His work was suppressed and remained unpublished until the 19th century. [RCW]

A. F. G. Bell, *G.C.* (1924).

**Cortada, Joan.** ⇨ Catalan Literature.

**Coşbuc, Gheorghe** (Hordoul Năsăudului 1866–Bucharest 1918). Rumanian poet. The son of a priest, he lived as a boy the life of the Transylvanian countryside which is the inspiration of his poetry. His most famous poem, the fierce *Noi vrem pămînt* ('We Want Land!', 1894), is a most eloquent cry of rage from the mouths of the landless Rumanians in Transylvania. In 1889 he moved to Bucharest. In 1901, with A. Vlahuţă, he founded the review *Semănătorul*, which gave its name to a literary movement (Semănătorism) drawing on peasant life for its inspiration. [EDT]

**Ćosić, Dobrica** (Velika Drenova 1921– ). Serbian novelist. An ex-political commissar with Tito's partisans, his first novel, *Daleko ie sunce* (1951), concerns the problems of communist relations with the peasant ethos, and has more naturalness than is usual in such works. *Koreni* (1954), the first volume of an unfinished trilogy, traces Serbian history from the early 19th century; it failed because of too strained an experiment with style. *Deobe* (3 vols., 1961) analyses the psychological and social reasons motivating those who fought in the Četnik movement, seeing them as victims of circumstance and character rather than as criminals; an interesting study by a writer of the opposite camp. [EDG]

*SEER*, XL, 94 (1961); Kadić, *CSL*.

**Cosmas of Prague** (1045?–Prague 1125). Czech chronicler. Dean of Prague Chapter, he travelled widely as a student and later on diplomatic missions. His vividly written *Chronica Boëmorum* spans Bohemia's history from its mythological beginnings to the year of his death. An objective historian with sharp judgement and wit. [KB]

*Chronicle*, ed. B. Bretholz (MGH, 1923).
H. Jireček, *Kosmas a jeho kronika* (Prague, 1906).

**Cosmas, the Priest.** ⇨ Old Bulgarian Literature.

**Costa i Llobera, Miquel.** ⇨ Catalan Literature.

**Costa y Martínez, Joaquín** (Graus, Huesca 1844–Graus 1911). Spanish lawyer, politician and essayist. The eldest child in a family of eleven, he was the son of a humble Aragonese farmer. An uncle paid for his secondary education in Huesca and later helped him to embark on a brilliant university career in law when he became dissatisfied with his apprenticeship as an architect. He applied his keen powers of analysis and scrupulous attention to detail to both practical and theoretical matters. It is said that a carpenter was able to make a prototype of the first bicycle in Spain from the description he gave of one he had seen in the Paris Exhibition of 1867. And his success in law may have derived from the application of similar qualities. A setback led him to abandon a university post for legal practice in the seventies, but subsequently he made a series of notable contributions to Spanish legal history, and published articles on Spanish popular poetry (1881) as well as important studies of the agrarian problem of which he had first-hand knowledge from childhood (*Colectivismo agrario en España*, 1898). Later he was elected to the Cortes and, although he never took his seat, was a powerful advocate of reform and a constant critic of narrow traditionalism. His advice to Spaniards to lock up the tomb of the Cid with seven keys, and let in 'the winds of Europeanization' to bring health to the country, is much quoted. His probity and sincerity in all he undertook commanded universal respect. [ONVG]

J. B. Trend, *Origins of Modern Spain* (1934).

**Cotin, Charles** (Paris 1604–Paris 1682). French abbé and poet. He is chiefly known as the butt of Boileau in the *Satires* and of Molière in *Les femmes savantes*. He was an active member of *précieux* society and wrote pleasant and ingenious verse, probably for no other purpose than to entertain. His verse may be read in various editions of Boileau: *Despreau ou la Satire des satires*, *Œuvres galantes en prose et en vers* (1663). Molière's attack on him as Trissotin seems inexcusable. [WGM]

Mongrédien, *PP*.

**Couperus, Louis Marie Anne** (The Hague 1863–De Steeg 1923). Dutch novelist. His father and grandfather served in the Dutch East Indies, and most of his upbringing was in Batavia; he lived extensively in Italy. After some poor poetry, his first novel, *Eline Vere* (1889; tr. J. T. Grein, 1892), was an immediate success. The inertia of Eline's comfortless reaction to life becomes a destructive fatalism (echoing Tolstoy and Zola). The amoral realism and pessimistic individualism are typical of the fiction of the movement of 1880, though he was the only important writer entirely independent of it. After his marriage in 1891 he explored less naturalistic themes, in *Extaze* (1892; tr. A. Teixeira de Mattos and John Gray, *Ecstasy*, 1919) and – after a number of less important travel stories, fantasies on classical antiquity and symbolic fairy-tales – in *De Berg van Licht* (1906). Here decadent civilizations breed languid characters in keeping with Couperus's luxurious style. Where, as in *Psyche* (1898; tr. B. S. Berrington, 1908) and *Fidessa* (1899), he adds ingenuity to pure imagination he lapses into cerebral virtuosity. The novels set in the Dutch East Indies, e.g. *De Stille Kracht* (1900; tr. A. Teixeira de Mattos, *The Hidden Force*, 1922), develop a latent interest in 'De Andere', an occult force of destiny eluding the Westerner, yet dominating him. The

Inevitable overwhelms all but the strongest personalities in the other Hague novels, *De Boeken der kleine zielen* (4 vols., 1901–4; tr. A. Teixeira de Mattos, *The Small Souls*, 1914, *The Later Life*, 1915, *The Twilight of the Souls*, 1917) and *Van oude Menschen, de dingen die voorbijgaan* (1906; tr. A. Teixeira de Mattos, *Old People and the Things that Pass*, 1963).

The form of Couperus's art suggests a compound of Western dandy and oriental painter. Mannerisms and the passionless beauty of delicate composition provide an escape from the shadow of 'De Andere'. His amorality is easily mistaken for decadence and his detachment for superficiality. Cultivating leisureliness as an art, he delights in observing minutiae and in painting moods and atmosphere; see especially his short stories *Korte Arabesken* (1911). [PK]

*Verzamelde Werken* (12 vols., 1953–7); *Xerxes of de Hoogmoed* (1919; tr. F. H. Martens, *Arrogance, the Conquests of Xerxes*, 1930); *Babel* (1901; tr. A. A. Betham, n.d.); *De Komedianten* (1917; tr. J. M. Wilson, *The Comedians*, 1926); *De Bocken der kleine zielen* (4 vols., 1901–3; tr. A. Teixeira de Mattos, *The Books of the Small Souls*, 4 vols., 1914–18); *Majesteit* (1895; tr. A. Teixeira de Mattos, *Majesty*, 1921); *Eighteen Tales*, tr. J. Kooistra (1924); Snell, *FFG*; Greshoff, *HL*.

H. van Booven, *Leven en werken van L.C.* (Velsen, 1933); W. Blok, *Verhaal en lezer* (Groningen, 1960); Adam, *HLF*; M. Galle, *Couperus in de Kritick* (Amsterdam, 1963).

**Courier, Paul-Louis** (Paris 1772–Véretz, Indre-et-Loire 1825). French pamphleteer and scholar. He discovered the great Italian libraries while serving there as a soldier, came across a fragment of Longus, and after transcribing it poured ink over the manuscript (either by accident or design). He thus came to public notice with his *Lettre à M. Renouard sur une tache faite à un manuscrit de Florence* (1810), turning the affair into ridicule. On returning to France in 1812 he managed his estates in Touraine where he became an active worker for the rights of the peasants. His pamphlets, surpassed only by Pascal's *Lettres provinciales*, include *Pétition aux deux chambres* (1816); *Pétition pour des villageois qu'on empêche de danser* (1822); and *Le simple discours de P.L., Vigneron de la Chavonnière* (1821). He was murdered by a farm labourer whom he had dismissed. His *Œuvres complètes* (4 vols., 1829–30) contain his correspondence from Italy. [WA]

*Œuvres complètes*, ed. M. Allem (Pléiade, 1951).
P. Arbelet, *Trois solitaires* (*C., Stendhal, Mérimée*) (Paris, 1934); E. Fornairon, *Le mystère de la Chavonnière* (Paris, 1941).

**Courteline, Georges** (Tours 1858–Paris 1929). French playwright. A prolific humorous journalist who turned to the stage and made his reputation with a series of brilliant farces distinguished by their vivacious dialogue, acute sense of the contemporary social scene and assured, if sometimes brutal, handling of comic types. The scale of his farces is deliberately limited; he prefers rapid, short scenes to fully articulated acts. His basic comic insight relates to the way in which human beings are moulded and distorted by social and professional habits and rules. He brings this insight to bear, with gaiety and a sharp satirical sense, on military life: *Lidoire*, 1892; the law, as in *L'Article 330*, 1900, *Le gendarme est sans pitié*, 1899 and *Un client sérieux*, 1897; and on conjugal life in *Boubouroche*, 1893, *La paix chez soi*, 1903 (tr. V. and F. Vernon, *Peace at Home*, 1933), *La cruche* (1909). [SBJ]

*Théâtre complet* (1961).
J. Portail, *C., l'humoriste français* (Paris, 1928).

**Courtly Love.** ♢ Troubadours.

**Couto, Diogo do** (Lisbon *c.* 1543–Goa 1616). Portuguese chronicler. After a good education at the Jesuit College of S. Antão in Lisbon as a page in the service of the Infante D. Luís, he sailed for India in 1559, after the death of his patron. After ten years service as a soldier, mainly on the west coast of India, he returned to Lisbon with his friend Luís de ♢ Camões as a fellow-passenger from Moçambique onwards. Returning to Goa in 1571, he settled there for the remainder of his life. 'Braço às armas feito, e mente às musas dada', like the author of the *Lusíadas*, he seems to have contemplated continuing the *Décadas* of João de ♢ Barros before 1580; but it was only in 1595–1604 that he succeeded in organizing the archives at Goa in his dual capacity of chronicler and keeper, to which posts he had been appointed by the Crown against considerable opposition. Only the *Décadas* IV–VII (1602–16) were published in his lifetime, the others appearing at intervals between 1645 and 1778. A vitriolic work in which he denounced Portuguese abuses and errors in Asia, *Diálogo do Soldado Prático*, though drafted before 1578, was not published until 1790, but it circulated widely in manuscript. Couto, though a patriotic Portuguese and an ardent imperialist, prided himself on telling *verdades chãas* in his works, which are freely spiced with homely proverbs and personal reminiscences, as well as sometimes nearly choked by the brambles of classical erudition. Taken as a whole, they are essential for the history of the Portuguese in the East, and often throw valuable light on the history of the Asian peoples with whom they were in contact. [CRB]

A. Baião, *D. do C.: Décadas. Selecções* (2 vols., 1947).

A. F. G. Bell, *D. do C.* (1924); M. Rodrigues Lapa, *D. do C.: o Soldado Prático* (Lisbon, 1938); C. R. Boxer, *The Tragic History of the Sea, 1589–1622* (1959).

**Creangă, Ion** (Humuleşti 1837–Jassy 1889). Rumanian story-teller. Born in a peasant family in Moldavia, he studied for the priesthood at Jassy and was ordained deacon in 1859. His unconventional behaviour having caused conflict with his ecclesiastical superiors, he trained as a teacher. In 1872 he was both unfrocked and temporarily suspended from teaching. Nevertheless he was received into the literary circle 'Junimea' in 1875, being introduced by ⇨ Eminescu, who had first encouraged him to write. His work consists of *Poveşti* (tr. M. Nandriş, *Folk Tales from Roumania*, 1952), some 15 tales, and 4 chapters of his memories of childhood, *Amintiri din copilărie* (1881–8; tr. L. Byng, *Recollections*, N.Y., 1930). It is particularly dear to Rumanians for its strong flavour of the Moldavian countryside, its rich regional vocabulary, and its peculiar humour. [EDT]

*Opere*, ed. G. Calinescu (1953).

J. Boutière, *La vie et l'œuvre de I.C.* (Paris, 1930).

**Crébillon (fils), Claude-Prosper Jolyot de** (Paris 1707–Paris 1777). French novelist. Author of elegantly licentious tales and dialogues. *L'écumoire* (1734; tr. anon., 1735), a supposedly Japanese legend with a strongly erotic theme, suspected of also containing satirical allusions to distinguished contemporaries, earned him a spell of imprisonment. His most serious and rewarding novel, *Les égarements du cœur et de l'esprit* (1736; ed. R. Étiemble, 1961; tr. B. Bray, *The Wayward Head and Heart*, 1964), reflects his impressions of the fashionable world to which notoriety had gained him admittance and gives a striking picture of the cynical hedonism of the period. Its subtle psychological insights engage the reader's interest in, and even sympathy for, both the green and corruptible young Meilcour and his mature seductress, Mme de Lursay. The notorious *Le sopha* (1742; tr. B. Dobrée, 1951), also officially condemned, is a series of erotic episodes in a flimsily oriental setting, but not lacking in shrewd moral comment; *La nuit et le moment* (1755) is a sophisticated dialogue between expert practitioners in the 18th-century art of love. Despite his reputation, Crébillon succeeded his father as official literary censor in 1759.

His literary merit has often been obscured by moral prejudice, but his style has the elegant simplicity of the finest writing of the age, his psychological insight is considerable, and in his cool analysis of sophisticated licence he not merely looks forward to ⇨ Laclos but also stands in the classical tradition of the French moralists. [WHB]

*Œuvres complètes* (1777).

C. Cherpack, *An Essay on C. Fils* (Durham, N.C., 1962).

**Crébillon (père), Prosper Jolyot de** (Dijon 1674–Paris 1762). French dramatist. His three most successful tragedies, *Atrée et Thyeste* (1707), *Électre* (1708) and *Rhadamiste et Zénobie* (1711), established him as the major tragic dramatist in the barren period between Racine and Voltaire, but are now of interest only as evidence of a changing public taste. Within the formal conventions of classical tragedy they develop horrific and melodramatic effects, often with an implausible complexity of plot, and little depth or originality of characterization. Official literary censor after 1735, he returned to the theatre in unsuccessful rivalry with Voltaire, whose enemies supported him (*Catalina*, 1748; *Le Triumvirat*, 1754). [WHB]

*Théâtre complet*, ed. M. A. Vitu (1885).

M. Dutrait, *Étude sur la vie et le théâtre de C.* (Paris, 1895).

**Crepuscolari.** ⇨ Moretti, Gozzano, Corazzini.

**Crescas, Hasdai** (Barcelona 1340–Saragossa 1410). Hebrew philosopher. Chief Rabbi of Aragon, where he lived through the pogrom of 1391 of which he wrote a historical account. His *chef d'œuvre* is *Or Adonai*

(Ferrara, 1555), in which he denied the validity of Aristotle's system of physics by using the method of Talmudic argument. He exercised a great influence on ⇨ Pico della Mirandola and even upon ⇨ Galilei and Giordano ⇨ Bruno. [EE]

Husik, *HMJP*.

**Crétin, Guillaume** (Paris *c.* 1460–1525). French poet. A *rhétoriqueur*, he enjoyed a considerable reputation in his time, and in the next generation ⇨ Marot spoke approvingly of him as 'le bon Crétin aux vers équivoqués' and called him 'souverain poète'. Rabelais gives an unforgettable portrait of him as Raminagrobis in *Pantagruel*, Book Three, quoting a rondeau of his. His abundant work, including a *Déploration sur le trépas de feu Okergan* (i.e. the musician Ockegham); epistles; patriotic allegories on current events; and an unfinished epic, *La chronique française* (continued by René Macé), is a good example of the *rhétoriqueur* style: erudition, allegory and complicated verse forms. His works were published by his disciple F. Charbonnier in 1527, and by Coustelier in 1723. [FWAG]

*Œuvres poétiques*, ed. K. Chesney (1932).

P. Champion, *Histoire poétique du XVe siècle* (Paris, 1923); H. Guy, *Histoire poétique du XVIe siècle*, i (Paris, 1910).

**Creutz, Gustav Filip,** Count (Finland 1729–Stockholm 1785). Swedish poet. He belonged to the 'salon' of Fru Nordenflycht, and was a colleague of Count Gyllenborg, also a poet, in the court of chancery; they published their works together. His idyll *Atis och Camilla* (1762) was once much admired, as was his pastoral *Daphne*.

*Skrifter*, edn Svenska Litteratursällskapet (1913). *Och Camilla*, ed. G. Sahlberg (Stockholm, 1952).

**Crnjanski, Miloš** (Ilanča 1893– ). Serbian poet and novelist. One of the most original lyrical poets in modern Serbia, he has worked as a journalist and diplomat. His first poems, *Lirika itake* (1919), were followed by a lyrical prose diary, *Dnevnik Čarnojevića* (1921). He is also well known for his novel *Seobe* (1929), dealing with the Serbs in the Vojvodina at the end of the 17th century. His highly individual style expresses a powerful and often destructive temperament, using Serbian with great freedom and vitality. His work has had an immense influence on post-war writers. [EDG]

*SEER*, XXIII, 62 (1945); Lavrin, *AMYP*.

**Croce, Benedetto** (Pescasseroli 1866–Naples 1952). Italian critic and philosopher, remarkable for the range and coherence of his scholarship. As regards literature, his late Renaissance studies stand out amidst criticism extending from Dante to his own day (including foreign authors). He wrote histories of his native Naples, of Italy in the Baroque and modern periods, and of Europe 1815–1915, combining political-economic knowledge with cultural perspectives. Most important are his theoretical *Estetica* (1902; tr. D. Ainslie, new ed. 1967), *Logica* (1909), and studies of Vico and Hegel, who greatly influenced him. His dominant concern was with the relationship of knowledge to experience, to personal and social reality. His theory that in art meaningful form should be inseparable from experiential content provided his somewhat subjective yardstick of living greatness. Consistent with his views, which he made known journalistically in *La critica* (1903–1944), he took an active part in politics, e.g. against warmongers in 1915 and against the fascists in the 'twenties.

*Filosofia, poesia e storia* (selections ed. Croce, 1952); *An Anthology*, ed. C. Sprigge, 1966.

G. N. G. Orsini, BC, 1961.

**Crommelynck, Fernand** (Paris 1888–Paris 1969). Belgian playwright of Flemish ancestry and temperament, who became notorious for lyrical-grotesque farce, combining soft sentiment and brutal caricature. His masterpiece *Le cocu magnifique* (1921), beginning with a husband's effusions on his wife's beauty and ending with his offering her to others to avoid further uncertainty about her fidelity, is typical. Comic paradox is carried furthest in *Chaud et froid* (1934), and *Les amants puérils* (1921), *Tripes d'or* (1925), *Une femme qui a le coeur trop petit* (1934) enjoyed similar success.

*Théâtre complet* (1956– ).

A. Berger, *À la rencontre de F.C.* (Paris, 1947); Surer, *TFC*; Grossvogel, *TCFD*.

**Cronegk, Johann Friedrich von** (Ansbach 1731–Nürnberg 1758). German dramatist. Friend of ⇨ Gellert. He studied in Halle and Leipzig, travelled through Italy and France, and became Kammerjunker and Reichshofrat in Ansbach. His tragedies, *Codrus* (1758) and *Olint und Sophronia* (unfinished; publ. 1760), both in alexandrines, praise patriotism, stoic heroism and Christian martyrdom. His didactic allegory *Die verfolgte Komödie* (?1760) and his comedy *Der Misstrauische* (?1760) are also influenced by French Classicism, his poems *Einsamkeiten* (1757) by Young's and ⇨ Klopstock's melancholy. [LL]

*Schriften*, ed. J. P. Uz (2 vols., 1760); Killy, *DLTZ*.
Heitner, *GTE*; Schneider, *DDA*.

**Crónicas.** Medieval Portuguese chronicles before Fernão ⇨ Lopes. The most noteworthy early Portuguese chronicle is the *Segunda Crónica Geral de Espanha*, sometimes referred to as the *Crónica de 1344*, the year in which it was first compiled under the probable organization of D. Pedro, Count of Barcelos and natural son of King Dinis. The extant Portuguese text is, however, that of a second version, which was compiled towards the end of the 14th century and involved several modifications. The *Segunda Crónica Geral* was an adaptation and continuation of a Galician version of the *Primera crónica general* organized by Alfonso X of León and Castile. Among the sources of its additional material figured earlier Portuguese texts (now lost). These were the *Crónica do Mouro Rasis* (a translation from Arabic, still extant in a Castilian re-translation), legendary material concerning Afonso Henriques and contradictory versions of the dethronement of Sancho II. Both versions of the *Segunda Crónica Geral* exist in Spanish translations of the 15th and 16th centuries. The *Crónica* continues Iberian history as far as the Battle of the Salado (1340), although the Paris codex of the second version contains additional material, probably organized by the Constable D. Pedro, which prolongs the Portuguese account well into the reign (1438–81) of Afonso V.

The three *Livros de Linhagens* or *Nobiliários* include another prominent example of 14th-century historiography. Of these the first two, the fragmentary *Primeiro Livro* (*c.* 1270) and the *Livro Velho* (*c.* 1340), present little material other than genealogical tables (kept for legal reference) of noble families, although there are some exceptional passages. The third book, first edited *c.* 1340 (and almost certainly before the *Crónica de 1344* with which it has passages in common), is attributed to D. Pedro, Count of Barcelos, and exists in two distinct versions, both modified and amplified, which belong to the period 1360–75. They are principally distinguished by the inclusion in one of them of an account of the Battle of the Salado, a description which is celebrated for its high literary quality. The *Livro do Conde D. Pedro* differs from the other two *Nobiliários* in that it possesses an overall plan and moral and political aims. It uses genealogies and other historical material to stimulate a sense of solidarity and responsibility among the noble families of the whole Peninsula and to unite them against the infidel. This is particularly effected by relating the glorious deeds of ancestors.

Notable also are the *Crónicas Breves de Santa Cruz de Coimbra*, found in a 15th-century codex. Of the four *Crónicas*, the second is a ceremonial speech delivered in 1451, but the remainder date from the 14th century. The first is a series of random historical jottings and is of marginal interest, the attention of scholars focusing itself on the third and fourth documents. The third is a copy of certain of those chapters of the *Crónica de 1344* to be devoted to the first two Portuguese monarchs, while the fourth is a summary account of the first six reigns and bears a close resemblance to the treatment of those reigns which is found in the *Livro do Conde D. Pedro*. It is usually deduced that this fourth *Crónica* and then his *Nobiliário* were progressive preparations by D. Pedro for the compilation of the *Segunda Crónica Geral*. Other extant 14th-century chronicles include the *Relação da Vida da Rainha Santa Isabel*, the *Crónica do Mosteiro de S. Vicente* and the *Crónica da Conquista do Algarve*.

The first 15th-century chronicle to emerge was the *Crónica Geral do Reino de Portugal*, also known variously as the *Crónica de Cinco Reis*, the *Crónica dos Sete Primeiros Reis*, and the *Crónica de 1419*, the date of its earliest compilation. This was a paste-and-scissors work which went through several versions and amplifications, drawing on a wide range of material, including *inter alia* the *Crónica de 1344* and a Spanish translation thereof, the *Primera crónica general* and the *Crónica da Conquista do Algarve*. Its earliest compiler is thought by some scholars to have been Fernão Lopes. There belong also to the earlier part of the 15th century the *Crónica Breve do Arquivo Nacional* (1429) which is a concise summary of the first six reigns, and the *Crónica do Condestabre Nuno Álvares Pereira* (*c.* 1434) which is sometimes attributed to Fernão Lopes. [RCW]

R. Menéndez Pidal, *Crónicas generales de España* (1918); L. F. Lindley Cintra, *Crónica Geral de Espanha de 1344*, i and ii (1951, 1954); A. Herculano (ed.), *Portugaliae Monumenta Historica*, i, *Scriptores* (n.d.); A. de Magalhães Basto (ed.), *Crónica de Cinco Reis de Portugal*, i (1945); C. da Silva Tarouca (ed.), *Crónica dos Sete Primeiros Reis de Portugal*, i and ii (1952), iii (1953).

A. de Magalhães Basto, *A Tese de Damião de Góis em Favor de Fernão Lopes* (Porto, 1951), and review of same by L. F. Lindley Cintrina *Revista da Faculdade de Letras de Lisboa*, XVII (1951); H. Cidade, *Lições de Cultura e Literatura Portuguesas*, i (Coimbra, 1951); M. Rodrigues Lapa, *Lições de Literatura Portuguesa* (Coimbra, 1955).

**Cros, Charles** (Fabrezan, Aude 1842–Paris 1888). French poet and inventor (of colour photography and the gramophone). He was well known in the Paris of the seventies and eighties for his comic monologues, a form he is said to have invented, *Le hareng saur* and *Le bilboquet*, spoken by the actor Coquelin *aîné*. His well-wrought lyrics, prose poems and *rondes* were published in *Le coffret de santal* (1873), *Le fleuve* (1875) and the posthumous collection *Le collier de griffes* (1908). [WA]

J. Brenner and I. Lockerbie, *C.C.* (Paris, 1955).

**Cruz Cano y Olmedilla, Ramón de la** (Madrid 1731–Madrid 1794). Spanish dramatist. Of poor but possibly noble parentage, he showed an early ability as a poet and dramatist. He excelled in short intermezzi or *sainetes*, which were full of wit, slightly caricaturesque portraits of lower-class characters and lively dialogue. He began to make a name for himself with these in the sixties, and although he tried to write and translated a number of tragedies in the approved classical manner, only his comic writing was really successful. The easy popularity of his *sainetes* made him disliked by some Spanish intellectuals who favoured tragedy, and he may have been having his revenge when he produced mock-tragedies like *Manolo* (1769). In its way, however, his view of drama was as serious as that of his critics, and his satirical treatment of pretentiousness, hypocrisy and other vices in lower- and middle-class settings was more accessible to a wide public than the moral tragedies of his contemporaries. The nearness of his work to the people and its supposed embodiment of a Spanish national spirit appealed to 19th-century critics more particularly. In his lifetime he was patronized by the Spanish nobility, although he only earned a pittance as a minor government official. His earnings were not commensurate with his success in the theatre and his widow had to live on a pension from the Dukes of Osuna. [ONVG]

E. Cotarelo y Mori, *Don R. de la C. y sus obras* (Madrid, 1899); J. A. Cook, *Neo-Classic Drama in Spain* (1959); McClelland, *ORMS*.

**Csokonai-Vitéz, Mihály** (Debrecen 1773–Debrecen 1805). Hungarian poet. The greatest figure of the Hungarian Enlightenment period. Coming from poverty-stricken petty-bourgeois parents, at the famous College of Debrecen he neglected studies of theology in favour of poetry and natural science. His works show the influence of Italian Rococo and French Enlightenment but also of ribald college humour and Hungarian folk-poetry. Coming into conflict with pedantic college rules, he was expelled and henceforth led a wandering, drab existence; his drama *Tempefői* (1793) is the story of his struggle to obtain a livelihood as a poet. His love for 'Lilla' provided inspiration, first for rococo-style love-poems, later for elegies; his *Lilla* cycle (*A Reményhez*, 1798; tr. Z. de Vállyi, Stuart, *The Hope*, in *Magyar Poems*, 1911) and his volume of 'Odes' are the finest poetry of the Hungarian Enlightenment. His wish for social, political and cultural reform, and the spirit of Enlightenment, are expressed in his poems *Az estve* ('The Evening'), *Konstancinápoly*, *A lélek halhatatlansága* ('The Immortality of the Soul'), and *Az álom* ('The Dream'). His comic epic *Dorottya* (1799) describes problems of contemporary Hungary. Csokonai was a pioneer of the folk-style poetry taken up by many later Hungarian poets. [JFR]

Klaniczay, *HHL*.

**Cuaderna Vía** ('fourfold way'). The name given to the verse form normally used by poets of the Spanish *mester de clerecía*, or learned school, of the 13th and 14th centuries; the form was superseded at the beginning of the 15th century by the *arte mayor*. The term occurs in stanza 2 of the *Libro de* ⇨ *Alexandre* and refers to the structure of the stanza: 4 lines of 14 syllables (with a marked *caesura* dividing it into equal hemistichs, 7 and 7) with one fully consonantal rhyme through each stanza.

Agreement is general that it is not a native Spanish form. Two sources have been proposed: medieval Latin verse (similar forms occur in the *Carmina Burana* and elsewhere) and French moral poetry of the 12th century (e.g. the *poème moral*); in both cases, however, the normal line is of 13 syllables, not 14.

At one extreme, scholars generally are convinced of ◊ Berceo's metrical strictness and treat as suspect all irregular lines in the manuscripts of his works; at the other extreme, octosyllabic hemistichs occur in the *Libro de buen amor* with a frequency that seems to rule out both scribal error and mere slipshod inadvertence on the part of Juan ◊ Ruíz. [GBG-M]

J. D. Fitz-Gerald, *Versification of the 'Cuaderna Vía'* (N.Y., 1905); P. Henríquez Ureña, *La versificación irregular en la poesía castellana* (Madrid, 1920); R. Menéndez Pidal, *Poesía juglaresca y orígenes de las literaturas románicas* (Madrid, 1957); *Bulletin Hispanique*, XLIV, 1942; XLVIII, 1946.

**Cueva, Juan de la** (Seville 1550?–Seville 1610). Spanish poet and dramatist. Apart from a period in Mexico (1574–7) he spent most of his life in Seville. Most of his poems on bucolic, mythological and allegorical themes are unpublished, but a collection of historical ballads (*Coro Febeo*), a tedious epic poem (*Conquista de la Bética*) and an interesting verse treatise in which he champions the cause of historical progress in drama (*Ejemplar poético*) have all been printed. His fame rests mainly on his 14 plays, performed in Seville between 1579 and 1581. He is usually considered as one of the most important dramatists prior to Lope de Vega, especially as he was the first to introduce Spanish history and legend to the public stage; more interesting are his motives for this innovation. It seems that he adapted his sources so that they might parallel the political situation which arose in the Peninsula on the death of King Sebastian of Portugal at Alcazar-Kebir. His history-plays are object-lessons for Philip II, who had taken up an aggressive attitude towards the neighbouring kingdom in order to gain the throne for himself. *La muerte del rey don Sancho* shows how the Cid tried to dissuade Sancho from an unjustifiable attack on his sister and how he was punished through ignoring this advice. In *La libertad de España* Alfonso the Chaste decides to hand over his kingdom to Charlemagne, just as Cardinal Henry of Portugal (renowned for his chastity) contemplated handing over *his* country to Philip. Bernardo el Carpio saves Spain from Charlemagne just as later the Prior of Crato attempted, less successfully, to save Portugal from Philip. Some of Cueva's more novelesque plays are also best understood as political allegories. Leucino, in *El infamador*, has often been likened to Don Juan, but his attempts to seduce Eliodora with the assistance of a *Junta* of go-betweens and a braggart-soldier are best related to Philip's efforts to gain the throne of Portugal assisted by his *Junta de Portugal* and an army headed by the Duke of Alba, restored to favour after a period of disgrace to head the attack. Cueva's drama looks back to the politically engaged school-plays of the Jesuits, António Ferreira and Jerónimo Bermúdez, and forward to the *teatro de oposición* of ◊ Tirso de Molina. [AIW]

*Comedias y tragedias*, ed. F. A. de Icaza (1917); *El infamador, Los siete infantes de Lara, El ejemplar poético*, ed. F. A. de Icaza (1941).

A. I. Watson, *The Political Implications of the Drama of J. de la C.* (1965); *NRFH*, IX, 2, 1955; *BHS*, XXXII, 1, 1955.

**'Culteranismo'** (adj. *culto*, *culterano*). A literary style developed by ◊ Góngora and others, which dominated Spanish verse in the 17th century and also affected prose and the drama. It grew out of earlier Renaissance tendencies towards latinization of vocabulary and syntax, extravagant metaphor, somewhat stereotyped imagery and highly artistic construction of line and stanza. [CCS]

**Curel, François de** (Metz 1854–Paris 1928). French dramatist. Author of plays of ideas imbued with profound and, on occasion, ferocious pessimism, not always fully assimilated to living situations and characters. His career began with two plays produced at the Théâtre Libre in 1892: *L'envers d'une sainte*, a penetrating study of an embittered woman whose spiritual pretensions create a desert about her; *Les fossiles* (tr. B. H. Clark, *The Fossils*, in *Four Plays of the Free Theatre*, 1915), a harsh analysis of a noble family in decline which earned for him the reputation of a French Ibsen. There followed: *Le repas du lion* (1897), an ambitious confrontation of Capital and Labour which shows greater insight into the psychology of power than into social and economic conflicts; *La nouvelle idole* (1899), a dramatized debate involving symbolic figures who represent religion, science and humanism; *La fille sauvage* (1902), in which the machinery of an intellectual demonstration obtrudes even more obviously; *La danse devant le miroir* (1913), where the theme of deceiving egoism of love is orchestrated with some power and subtlety, and *L'âme en folie* (1919), a disenchanted treatment of human passion seen, in ironic counterpoint, in terms of the animal kingdom. [SBJ]

*Théâtre complet* (6 vols., 1919–24).

E. Braunstein, *F. de C. et le théâtre d'idées* (Paris, 1962); E. Pronier, *La vie et l'œuvre de F. de C.* (Paris, 1934).

**Curros Enríquez, Manuel.** ⇨ Galician Literature.

**Curtis, Jean-Louis** (Orthez 1917– ). French novelist. Formerly a teacher of English in a Paris *lycée*, he published his first novel, *Les jeunes hommes*, in 1946 but made his first real impact the following year with *Les forêts de la nuit* (Prix Goncourt; tr. N. Wydenbruck, *The Forests of the Night*, 1950); one of a spate of war novels written at the time, its originality lay in its ironical detachment from Resistance rhetoric and its sober but moving account of provincial life in occupied France. *Gibier de potence* (1949; tr. R. Chancellor, *Lucifer's Dream*, 1952) and *Chers corbeaux* (1951) are set in Paris, where with a mixture of compassion and irony Curtis records the efforts of young people in the turbulent post-war years to come to terms with the adult world and their own adulthood. An underlying theme of these novels, the hostility of society to youthful aspirations, is more explicitly developed in *Les justes causes* (1954; tr. H. Hare, *The Side of the Angels*, 1956), whilst *La parade* (1960) suggests the need of the individual to parry the ruthlessness of society by being equally ruthless. Unusually widely travelled for a French intellectual, Curtis sets *L'échelle de soie* (1956; tr. Schiff and E. Beddington Behrens, *The Silken Ladder*, 1957), a love story with tragic overtones, against an Italian background and in *Cygne sauvage* (1962) recounts a Franco-American love affair. [IHW]

R. Kanters, *Des écrivains et des hommes* (1952); *Cahiers des Saisons*, 13 (1958) and 29 (1962).

**Cyrano, Savinien de,** known as **Cyrano de Bergerac** (Paris 1619–Paris 1655). French playwright and writer of philosophical fiction. Of great versatility, he wrote numerous *Lettres* in a euphuistic style, political pamphlets, a tragedy, *La mort d'Agrippine*, a comedy, *Le pédant joué* (all 1654), and two fantastic voyages, *L'autre monde ou les états et empires de la lune* and *Les états et empires du soleil* (published posthumously, 1657 and 1662, after being purged of many religious and philosophical audacities) (tr. R. Aldington, *Voyages to the Moon and the Sun*, 1923). Only after 20th-century scholarship made the complete text of his novels available did his talent and originality receive full recognition – as the creator of a genre which combined aspects of the utopia, the imaginary voyage, the philosophical dialogue and embryonic science-fiction, and was highly suitable to the spreading and discussion of ideas.

He associated with writers well known for their heterodox opinions, was acquainted with all the philosophical trends of his period (Scholasticism, which he attacked, scepticism, Epicureanism as revived by Gassendi, Cartesianism, and the Italian philosophies of the Renaissance), and was aware of all the recent discoveries in astronomy and physics since Copernicus, Kepler and Galileo, and in medicine since Harvey. His novels show him as a keen and talented popularizer, and contain amazing forecasts of many later developments in science and technology such as the unity of matter, its atomic structure, phagocytes, aviation, the gramophone, and X-rays.

His rejection of the principle of authority in the realm of ideas, in favour of reason and the evidence of the senses, his positivism and his mechanistic outlook, together with his advocacy of technology as a means of improving man's lot, make him a precursor of the Enlightenment. At the same time, he viewed the universe as a gigantic animal, whose elements were themselves organized, endowed with spontaneity, and arranged according to a Scale of Being. This 'cironalité universelle', as he calls it, which makes nature one huge metaphor where all aspects are interrelated, sometimes contradicts his other attitude, but gives his vision and style great poetry. He could also write with a Voltairean satirical bite, and had command both of a colourful realism and of epic exaggeration. [AL]

*Les œuvres libertines de C. de B., parisien*, ed. F. Lachèvre (1921).
P. A. Brun, *S. de C. B., sa vie et ses œuvres* (Paris, 1893); J.-J. Bridenne, 'À la recherche du vrai Cyrano de Bergerac', in *L'Information Littéraire*, 5 (Paris, 1953).

**Czechowicz, Józef** (Lublin 1903–Lublin 1939). Polish poet. He was brought up in a provincial environment which his poetry reflects. This fidelity to a regional culture enabled him to be daring in his formal and even typographical experiments. After teaching in village schools he moved to Warsaw, worked on a children's weekly, then for the radio, and was considered, despite his reticence, a leading figure in the Vanguard movement (*Awangarda*).

With remarkable consistency Czechowicz perfected his metaphoric language and irregular metres, counterpointing his calm village themes with the urban restlessness of an uprooted intellectual. A whispering voice of premonition about some future catastrophy was occasionally heard in his volumes *dzień jak codzień* ('today as everyday', 1930) and *ballada z tamtej strony* ('the ballad from the other side', 1932), but it became a truly prophetic cry of despair in poems like 'żal' ('sorrow') from his last published book, *nuta człowiecza* ('the human clef', 1939).

Soon after the outbreak of the war, he returned to his native town and was killed by a German bomb. A subtle lyricist and an intuitive master of experiment, his regionalism is of the kind that can be found in Polish baroque idylls. [JP]

Peterkiewicz and Singer, *FCPP*.
*SEER*, XXXVII, 89 (1959).

# D

**Dąbrowska, Maria** (Russów, near Kalisz 1889–1965). Polish novelist. She is best known for her long family saga *Noce i dnie* (1932–4), consisting of 4 novels, in which the characters of women are particularly well drawn. The cycle shows the decay of a social structure, but it also asserts the resilient qualities in the Polish gentry. She has published a set of stories about landless peasants (*Ludzie stamtąd*, 1925) and translated Pepys into Polish. Her dramatic pieces are disappointing. Taken as a whole, her work continues the tradition of the Positivist novelists (e.g. ⇨ Prus). [JP]

Ordon, *TCPS*.
Kuncewicz, *MPM*.

**Dach, Simon** (Memel 1605–Königsberg 1659). German poet. The foremost representative of the school of middle-class poets in 17th-century Königsberg (Heinrich Albert, Robert Robertin, Christoph Kaldenbach, etc.). His occasional verse, commemorating births, marriages and deaths amongst the Königsberg bourgeoisie, is informed by a genuine warmth of feeling, a gentleness and a musicality which give them a distinctive personal note. He sings the praises of friendship (his most famous poem is *Der Mensch hat nichts so eigen*) and preaches moderation and a sound, unaggressively Protestant ethic, while his religious poetry in many ways anticipates the community hymns of ⇨ Gerhardt. He also wrote the libretti for two operas, *Cleomenes* (1635) and *Sorbiusa* (1644), for which his friend Heinrich Albert wrote the music. [WAC]

*Sämtliche Gedichte*, ed. W. Ziesemer (4 vols., 1936–8).
W. Ziesemer, *S.D.*, Altpreussische Forschungen 1 (1924).

**Dada.** The deliberately meaningless designation (Fr. 'hobby horse') of an anarchical literary and artistic movement, begun by the pacifist H. Ball, with Tzara, ⇨ Arp, and others at the Cabaret Voltaire in Zürich (1916). Its chaotic experiments with language, form, public performance, etc., were an affirmation of radical irrationality and futility as a protest against all bourgeois notions of meaning and order. Its most creative tendency was towards ⇨ Surrealism. [PB]

R. Motherwell, *The Dada Painters and Poets* (1948); W. Verkauf, *Dada – Monograph of a Movement* (1961) (with bibliography).

**Dagerman, Stig** (Älvkarleby 1923–Danderyd 1954). Swedish novelist, short-story writer and dramatist. He was characteristic of the forties in his preoccupation with fear and anxiety, death and destruction. As man and writer, he was obsessed with the idea of defeat and death, evident already in *Ormen* (1945), a novel remarkable for its stylistic brilliance, the intensity of its presentation, and the maturity with which the young writer handles the theme of unavoidable fear. Hemingway and Faulkner may be discernible influences on its style, while Camus and Kafka may have a share in its thought; but the book does not read like an imitation, and its message about the necessity of 'keeping one's eyes open in the dark' springs from the author's deepest convictions. In a more abstract fable, *De dömdas ö* (1946), Dagerman ventured to analyse the sickness of modern, social man. His theme is the destruction of seven shipwrecked people, representing as many failures of living, who together make up an overwhelming sum of suffering and human waste. His insight into pathological psychology is appalling, but the inflamed style and symbolic projections of the novel are curiously offset by the astringent stoicism of its final message. *Nattens lekar* (1947; tr. N. Walford, *The Games of Night*, 1960) is a collection of short stories which, apart from stating the *Angst*-ridden themes in a condensed form, also gives evidence of a dark humour; in some ways it is his most balanced work. One of the stories, *Den dödsdömde*, also exists in a dramatic version published in *Dramer om dömda* (1948; *The Condemned* in *Scandinavian Plays of the Twentieth Century*, Third Series, Princeton and N.Y., 1951). Here Dagerman gropes towards a form to convey the same intensity as his novels. The result is a kind of Expressionism, a static drama in which everything is geared to expressing the terror of death. The play has one dominant mood only. The same criticism applies to *Skuggan av Mart* (1948), which effectively introduces the 'anti-hero' on the stage. The two novels *Bränt barn* (1948; tr. A. Blair, *A Burnt Child*, 1950), exploring the Oedipus situation and written in short staccato sentences with an almost 'behaviourist' detachment, and *Bröllopsbesvär* ('Wedding Tribulations', 1949), a study of social degradation and defeat shot through with desperate tenderness, are generally less successful variations on the theme of his early work.

After 1949 he suffered from cramping inhibitions, with moments of release. His *Den yttersta dagen* (1952), a radio play set in his native Uppland, is filled with lyrical overtones of country life, but is basically a drama of guilt and reconciliation; *Tusen år hos Gud* ('A Thousand Years with God', 1954) is the introductory chapter to an unfinished novel. The posthumous volume *Vårt behov av tröst* (1955) contains poetry and short stories as well as a moving autobiographical sketch of the author's childhood on his grandfather's farm. A selection of his incisive topical verse, published over many years in a syndicalist paper in Stockholm, appeared in 1954 under the title of *Dagsedlar*. [SAB]

O. Lagercrantz, *S.D.* (Stockholm, 1958); K. Henmark, *En fågel av eld* (Stockholm, 1962); *Delta*, 11, 1957.

**Dahlstjerna, Gunno,** noble name of Gunno Eurelius (Öhr, Dalsland 1661–Pomerania 1709). Swedish poet. Land surveyor to Charles XI. He is remembered for his bombastic poem in praise of Charles XI, *Kunga-Skald* (Stettin, 1679); it manipulates Swedish, which he was anxious to improve, into alexandrines and *ottava rima*. He wrote a long popular ballad about Charles XII (*Götha kämpavisa om konungen och Herr Peder*, 1701) and translated ◊ Guarini's *Pastor fido*.

**Dalin, Olof von** (Vinberg, Holland 1708–Drottningholm 1763). Swedish poet. While tutor to the crown prince, the future Gustavus III, he was tried for political intrigue, acquitted, but banned from court (1756–61); his health was damaged and he destroyed some unpublished work. During his exile he completed his *Svea Rikes historia* ('History of the Swedish Kingdom', 4 vols., 1746–62). His best literary works are the satirical allegories, *The Story of the Horse* and *Aprilverk* (1738); they show the influence of Pope, just as his weekly, *Svenska Argus* (begun 1733), shows that of Addison, and his didactic epic, *Svenska Friheten* (1742), that of Thomson's 'Liberty'. For the new Royal Swedish Theatre he wrote a comedy (*Den afvundjuke*, 1738; tr. E. Swanson, *Envy*, 1876), a tragedy (*Brynhilda*, 1739) and a pastoral about King Adolphus Frederick's return from Finland. His collected writings, including much occasional verse, epigram, etc., were published in 1767.

*Sagan om hästen* (Stockholm, 1953).

**Dalmatian and Dubrovnik Literature.** The development of a literature in Serbo-Croat based on the literature of Renaissance Italy and centred in the cities along the Dalmatian coast presents a unique feature in Slavonic literature generally.

Split, Zadar, the island of Hvar and, especially, Dubrovnik (Ragusa) gradually became colonized by Slavonic-speaking people on the arrival of the Slavs in the Balkans from the 7th century onwards. By the 15th century the Slavs had dominated the old Roman population while adopting an aristocratic, urban civilization based largely on trade. The cities on the Adriatic coast came under Venetian rule and under the direct influence of Italian culture, sending their upper classes to Italian universities. Dubrovnik is unique in that it gained its independence in 1358 and became the trading centre for the whole of the Balkans. The earliest surviving document in Serbian is the trade treaty between Dubrovnik and ban Kulin of Bosnia (1189) while the medieval state of Serbia granted trade monopolies to Dubrovnik which continued to be the trading centre even after the arrival of the Turks, to whom it paid a yearly tribute as a return for being unmolested. Dubrovnik society was sharply divided between a small group of noble families and the commoners, many of whom achieved both wealth and education. Political power, however, was vested in a council of nobles.

The first literary works in Dubrovnik were in Latin. Classical education came through Italy during the 15th century. The first works in the vernacular relate only to the early 16th century.

The earliest works, however, stem from the town of Split, with the poetry of Marko

Marulić (1450–1524). Marulić was well known for his religious and moral writings in Latin, his *De institutione bene vivende* being published some twenty times and translated into Italian, French, German and Portuguese. Deeply influenced by Humanism, Marulić none the less rejected its secular spirit, remaining a staunch Christian. He seems to have been moved by patriotic feelings towards his own people and to have recognized their need for works written in their own tongue. In 1500 he translated *De imitate Christi* and in 1501 wrote an epic poem, *Judita*, telling the story of Judith and the slaying of Holofernes. Its message appears to be a call for Christian faith and unity in the struggle with the Turks who are clearly paralleled with Holofernes. Marulić adopted the trochaic decasyllabic line of the folk poetry, but with a rhyme occurring both at the caesura and the end. This form may have stemmed from Latin poetry. He wrote in the Čakavic dialect, but sometimes using Štovaic forms to facilitate the difficult rhyme pattern. Educated in Padua, Marulić showed the considerable influence of Italian poetry, although he appears also to have followed the classics. He also wrote another epic, of less literary value, *Suzana*, which again uses a Biblical story as a means of conveying a moral message. *Judita* was published in Venice in 1521 and again in 1522.

In the island of Hvar two writers appeared contemporaneously with Marulić, though both were younger men. Hanibal Lucić (1485–1558), influenced by ⇨ Ariosto and Pietro ⇨ Bembo, wrote the earliest secular verse drama to be written in Serbo-Croat, again in the Čakavic dialect. This was *Robinja*, dealing with a historical theme about the rescue of the daughter of a Croatian prince who had been sold into slavery after her father's death in battle against the Turks. In 1568 Petar Hektorović (1487–1572) published in Venice his *Ribanje i ribarsko prigovaranje*, a fishing eclogue which, although owing something to the Italian *ecloga pescatoria*, possesses a refreshingly realistic tone that lends it originality. It contains some of the first written examples of the folk songs, which makes it particularly important. Like all his contemporaries, Hektorović was Italian by education and also knew the classics, one of his earliest known works being a translation of Ovid's *Remedium amoris*. In the town of Zadar, Petar Zoranić (1508–70) published in Venice 1569 a pastoral novel, *Planina*, based on the novel *Arcadia* by the Italian Jacopo ⇨ Sannazaro. Unlike Hektorović, Zoranić was against realism, preferring the idealistic pastoral style.

The Venetian occupation of the Dalmatian towns led to little more being written there. The exception was Dubrovnik. Nikola Ranjina published in 1507 his collection of the poems of various poets, *Rańinin Zbornik* (repr. 1870), some fifty years before *Tottel's Miscellany* in England. The two poets mainly represented in this collection are Šiško Menčetić (1457–1526) and Djore Drzić (1461–1501), a nobleman and a commoner. Both were deeply influenced by Petrarch and the later Italian poets, adapting the form of the *strambotto* to the Štokavic dialect. Both show influences of Čakavic also, even though Dubrovnik was a Štokavic-speaking town. It is love poetry in the troubadour spirit (which came through Italian poetry) and its rise presents a problem to scholars. It would appear probable that it grew from the tradition of oral urban poetry and also of the lyrical folk songs, several poems in Ranjina's collection being obvious adaptations of folk songs. Most educated men in Dubrovnik knew Italian but few women knew it, and it may have been for the sake of women that poets took to writing in the vernacular. Certainly, Italian influence predominated, some of the poems being little more than free translations of Italian originals.

In the second half of the 16th century this poetry was refined in the works of Dinko Ranjina (1536–1607), who was influenced by the revival of classical influence in contemporary Italian poetry and began to abandon the rhyme at the caesura in his later poems, and also of Dinko Zlatarić (1558–1609), a rather more original poet than Ranjina, who wrote many poems, like the one on the death of his infant son, which possess direct and sincere feeling.

Throughout the period of the Reformation, Dubrovnik remained staunchly Catholic and this religious feeling led to much religious and moral poetry. The Benedictine monk Mavro Vetranić (1482–1571) wrote a moral epic, *Remetar*, as well as various religious and moral dramas. The rise of the carnival and masquerade and the pastoral drama in Italy led to similar works in Dubrovnik. Nikola Nalješković (1500–87) produced various comedies and eclogues; the masquerade, *Jedjupka*, is generally attributed to Ante Čubranović, of whom little is known. The most important achievement in drama, however, was that of Marin Držić (1520–67), who produced several comedies as well as masquerades and pastoral plays. These works were written to be performed by Držić's own company of players on feast days. Perhaps because of this, few of them have survived intact. The most famous of Držić's plays is *Dundo Maroje* (1550), one of the early Plautian comedies in Western literature, dealing with the well-worn theme of the miser.

The golden age of Dubrovnik literature came at the beginning of the 17th century, when Dubrovnik was dominated by the spirit of the Counter-reformation. In 1604 the Jesuits settled there bringing both a spirit of tendentiousness and a leaning to scholarship. The Jesuit Bartulo Kašić (1575–1660) published a grammar of the language *De institutiones illyricae* (1604) in Rome, urging the reformation of the orthography and demanding that the somewhat stylized poetic language be brought closer to that of the people.

Lyrical poetry continued with the works of such minor poets as Ivan Bunić (1594–1658) and Vladislav Minćetić (1600–66). The greatest writer of the period, however, was Gjivo Franje Gundulić (1588–1638), whose epic poem *Osman*, devoted to the downfall of the Sultan Osman and his wars with Poland, is one of the greatest works to be written in any Slavonic country at that time. It embodies a greater freedom of language than is to be found in the works of his predecessors and its tone is patriotic, recognizing the unity of the Slavs as one race. Two of its twenty cantos are missing and there is some doubt whether they were ever written. Gundulić also wrote a patriotic pastoral play, *Dubravka* (1628). Influenced by the *seicentismo*, he wrote several other dramas of which only some have survived. He also wrote religious poetry such as the collected translations of the psalms of David, *Pjesni pokorne kralja Davida* (Rome 1621; Venice 1630) and his own *Suze sina razmetnoga* (Venice 1622; 1623). Gundulić was a great admirer of Tasso, whose *La Gerusalemme liberata* he intended to translate but never did.

A follower of Gundulić was Junije Palmotić (1606–57), who wrote many dramas taken from classical and Italian originals, all of them morally tendentious in the spirit of the age.

With the opening of the Atlantic trade routes following the discovery of America, the Levantine trade declined and with it the prosperity of Dubrovnik. This decline was hastened by the disastrous earthquake in 1667 which destroyed most of the city, including its rich harbour. With the decline of its wealth and its ruling families, Dubrovnik's literature declined also, its last true representative being Ignjac Djordjić (1675–1737), a Jesuit who wrote a collection of poems on religious themes. During the 18th century Dubrovnik's literature was mainly one of translations, particularly the plays of Molière, and by the 19th century Dubrovnik had lost its independence to Napoleon and its writers were merely a part of the romantic nationalist revival that spread almost throughout the lands which today comprise Yugoslavia.

Always rather localized, the Renaissance literature of Dubrovnik and the Dalmatian cities exercised surprisingly little influence on the 19th-century writers, many of whom considered it merely an offshoot of Italian literature. Even today there is not the attention commensurate with its size and uniqueness. Its existence did, however, help the Croatian reformer ⇨ Gaj to choose Štokavic as the Croatian literary language and Gundulić's *Osman* certainly influenced ⇨ Mažuranić's *Smrt Smail-age Čengića*. [EDG]

*Stari pisci* (Yugoslav Academy, Zagreb, 1869ff.) (a series of definitive editions of Dalmatian literature).

V. Javarek, 'Three 16th-Century Dalmatian Poets', in *SEER*, 41 (1963–4); J. Torbarina, *Italian Influence on the Poets of Ragusa* (1931).

**Dam, Albert** (Virring 1880–     ). Danish novelist and short-story writer. Fame came to him very late in life. After his first two novels, published in 1906 and 1908, it was more than 25 years before his third novel was published in 1934. Then, after another long pause, came the important novels *Jomfruen og Soldaten* (1951) and *Dag saa lang* (1954), followed by three highly original collections of short stories, *Morfars By* (1958), *Syv Skilderier* (1962) and *Menneskelinien* (1965). These works – especially the fantastic and visionary short stories which have been compared with the *Spoon River Anthology*, with Isak ⇨ Dinesen's *Seven Gothic Tales* and with Johannes V. ⇨ Jensen's *Myter* – have made him a central figure in contemporary Danish literature. [ELB]

**Damião de Góis** (Alenquer 1501–Alenquer 1574). Portuguese humanist. Born of minor nobility, he served as *moço da câmara* at the court of Manuel I until 1523, and subsequently on various foreign missions for the king. He went to the Portuguese Factory in Flanders, and in 1529 to Lithuania, Poland, Denmark and Germany. He was painted by Dürer, lunched with Luther, visited ⇨ Melanchthon and became the friend of ⇨ Erasmus. In 1533 he was appointed Treasurer of the *Casa da Índia* but in 1534 abandoned this appointment and Portugal, preferring the jollity of northern Europe and the company of Erasmus in Fribourg. From 1534 to 1538 he lived in Padua, meeting ⇨ Bembo, and visiting Venice and Rome. In 1538 he settled in Louvain, married a Dutch lady from The Hague, and began to write. Here he produced his description of the siege of Diu (*De bello Cambaico*); the *Legatio magni Indorum Imperatoris* (*Presbyteri*) *Ioannis* (1532); the *Fides, Religio, Moresque Aethiopum sub imperio Preciosi Ioannis* (1540), inspired by his meeting the Ethiopian bishop Zaga Zabo at John III's court; the *Deploratio Lappianae Gentis* (1540); and the descriptions of Spain and of the city of Lisbon, which fall into well-defined Renaissance categories. All these works, of imperfect latinity, typify an attitude of Iberian humanism in attempting to mould cultivated public opinion.

Góis returned to Portugal as official historiographer and composed the chronicles of Prince John and Manuel I, the latter being his major work. In 1545 he was denounced to the Inquisitors in Evora by Simão Rodrigues, delegate in Portugal of the Society of Jesus, who had known him in Italy, and seems to have borne some private grudge. Rodrigues made two further denunciations to the Lisbon Inquisition in 1550, but no action was taken until 1571, when Góis was arrested and imprisoned.

From the evidence taken by the Holy Office we learn how one Portuguese humanist lived in the 16th century. We hear of the royal family visiting his house to inspect the objects of art it contained; and of the rich presents he made his friends, including a St Sebastian of coral and gold presented to King Sebastian. He often neglected mass, preferring to ride on Sunday mornings, and the songs he composed and sang after lunch with his Flemish friends were 'not the sort of songs that are sung here'. He did not strictly observe the fasts of the Church. His age enabled him to escape torture and the ultimate bonfire. In 1572, after 18 months' imprisonment, he was reconciled to Holy Mother Church, condemned to the usual penalties, but eventually allowed to return to Alenquer to die. It was rumoured that he had been murdered by his servants. [ARM]

*Crónica de D. Manuel*, ed. D. Lopes (1949–55); *Opúsculos históricos* (Porto, n.d.).

*Bibliographia Goesiana* in *Bol. da Soc. de Bibliophilos Barbosa Machado*, i, 1910; M. Bataillon, *O cosmopolitismo de D. de G.*

**Daniil the Prisoner** (fl. 12th or 13th cent.). Russian secular writer. Nothing is known of his background, life or origin. It is not known where he lived, when he wrote his one work, called in some copies a 'Supplication' (*Moleniye*) and in others an 'Address' (*Slovo*), or why, if at all, he was imprisoned. From a comparison of the redactions of his work and from internal and philological evidence it seems most likely that his Address (*Slovo*) was written in the mid 12th century to a prince of Southern Pereyaslavl' probably by a member of his bodyguard, and that the Supplication (*Moleniye*), addressed to a prince of Northern Pereyaslavl', was later adapted by an unknown redactor (a junior member of the prince's court?) to suit the conditions of the 1220s or the 1230s.

Both the Address and the Supplication are in the form of an appeal to a prince who is urged to rule by fear, to acquire a strong army and not to rely on his boyars. The aim of the work is to make the prince take pity on the writer, who is in some form of unspecified trouble and who offers him his intellectual services. The leit-motif of both redactions is the extollation of wisdom and understanding. The genre is that of the aphoristic epistle, a genre known to European and Byzantine literature, which may have flourished in Galich during the 12th and 13th centuries and influenced Daniil or his later redactor. Many of the aphorisms themselves can be traced back to Biblical or Byzantine sources; but some are clearly original. The style is pretentious and flowery with a tendency to punning, rhyming, alliteration and euphony; the aphorisms are often weakly linked together. [JLIF]

M. O. Skripil', 'Slovo Daniila Zatochnika', in *Trudy otdela drevnerusskoy literatury*, XI.

**Danilo.** ⇨ Serbian Medieval Literature.

**D'Annunzio, Gabriele** (Pescara 1863–Gardone Riviera 1938). Italian poet, dramatist and novelist. His first poems, *Primo vere* (1879) and *Canto novo* (1882), despite imitation of ⇨ Carducci, reveal a powerful poetic talent, with a fresh, sensual feeling of participation in natural phenomena. In 1882 appeared a collection of short stories, *Terra vergine*, followed in the next four years by two other collections; they were influenced by ⇨ Verga's *Vita dei campi*, but, like his early poems, and for the same reasons, possess considerable individuality.

Between 1881 and 1891 his life was centred on Rome. The extensive poetic production of this period did not fulfil the promise of his early works, revealing above all the unfortunate influence of sophisticated Roman life on the young provincial's impressionable and sensual nature. The best work of his Roman period is the novel *Il piacere* (1889; tr. G. Harding, *The Child of Pleasure*, 1898), which describes, with autobiographical elements, the disordered emotional life of a Roman nobleman. Of other novels reflecting his Roman experiences, the best (indeed, his best novel) is *Il trionfo della morte* (1894; tr. G. Harding, *The Triumph of Death*, 1898).

Between 1892 and 1894 he became acquainted with the works of Nietzsche, whose views on ethics and art exercised an unfortunate influence on much of his later work (cf. the novel *Le vergini delle rocce*, 1895, the long poem *Laus vitae*, 1903, and most of his dramatic production, initiated in 1898 with *La città morta*). More beneficial to his art was his relationship (1895–1904) with Eleonora Duse, of whom there is a portrait, at times cruelly realistic, in his celebrated novel *Il fuoco* (1900; tr. K. Vivaria, *The Flame of Life*, 1900). Inspired by her help and encouragement, he wrote his best works, the poems of *Alcione* (1904) and the play *La figlia di Iorio* (1904), in which there reappears, with an increased mastery of language and intensity of feeling, that delight in the natural world and that celebration of the forces of instinct which had characterized his earliest production. Also of this period is another excellent play, *Francesca da Rimini* (1901).

These works represent the summit of d'Annunzio's achievement as a writer. Though he continued to write prolifically, he added little to his artistic stature. Worthy of mention is the French play *Le martyre de Saint Sébastien* (1911), with incidental music by Debussy; also the autobiographical prose work *Notturno* (1921), written in 1916 when temporarily blinded as the result of an aeroplane crash on active service.

D'Annunzio's heroic war record, and his attempt to preserve for Italy the Dalmatian port of Fiume (1919–20), made him a national hero. He passed his remaining years in retirement at his villa, Il Vittoriale, on Lake Garda. [CF]

*Tutte le opere*, ed. E. Bianchetti (9 vols, 1942–50); Kay, *PBIV*.

G. Gatti, *Vita di G. d'A.* (Florence, 1956); A. Rhodes, *The Poet as Superman* (1959); M. Praz, *The Romantic Agony* (tr. 1960).

**Dante Alighieri** (Florence 1265–Ravenna 1321). Italian poet. No autograph of his survives; the chronology of many writings, including the *Divine Comedy*, is uncertain; any account of his life involves conjecture based on isolated references in his works.

Born of a Guelph family of the lower nobility, he married at an unknown date Gemma Donati who bore him at least three children; his domestic life is not mentioned in any of his works. The *Vita nuova*, a collection of lyrics linked by a prose commentary (usually dated 1292), tells of his youthful love for Beatrice, and although her identity, and indeed even her existence cannot be absolutely proven, it is generally accepted that she was Beatrice Portinari, the wife of Simone de' Bardi. Dante relates how at the age of 9 he first saw her, how nine years later she greeted him and he fell in love with her, how he concealed that love by a pretended devotion to two other ladies, and how on her death he found consolation in a 'donna gentile' (later described in the *Convivio* as a symbol of Philosophy). He concludes by promising to celebrate Beatrice more worthily in some future work. Though tenuous and problematic as autobiography, the book illustrates Dante's early literary education and his connexion with the ⇨ *Stil novo*.

There is more tangible evidence of his civic and political experience. In 1289 he fought at Campaldino against the Aretines, and from 1295 took an active part in the administration of the commune. In 1300 he was one of the Priors at a time when the more turbulent adherents of the Black and White Guelphs (including his friend Guido Cavalcanti) were exiled, and in 1301, when under tne wing of Charles de Valois the Black Guelphs gained control of the city, he was away on a mission to Boniface VIII. He never returned to Florence, for during his absence sentence of exile was pronounced, and his life of wandering began. After briefly participating in the efforts of the White Guelphs to reinstate themselves, he withdrew to become the lone advocate of a view which far transcended factional politics and came to encompass the whole of humanity seen in the universal light of God's purpose for the world. He lived for a time at Verona and, finally, Ravenna.

The unfinished treatises, the Italian *Convivio* and the Latin *De vulgari eloquentia*, are generally dated 1304–7. In the former, Dante sets out to analyse in a prose commentary 14 of his own canzoni (only 3 were in fact commented). The first attempt at sustained intellectual discourse in Italian prose, it also reveals the outlines of his own philosophical position. In the latter, he proclaims the literary pedigree of the Italian vernacular, and after rejecting in turn the various regional dialects of Italy, he arrives at the concept of a supreme vernacular 'illustrious and aulic' which surpasses them all, which is in all Italian cities but 'is not of any one of them'. Together, the treatises represent a stage of intense intellectual, linguistic and stylistic exploration, and it is tempting and not unreasonable to explain their unfinished state as due to the more compelling demands made on the now mature poet by the *Divina commedia*, perhaps begun in 1307, though the idea of the poem may go back even as far as the time of the *Vita nuova*.

The *Commedia* gives Dante's comprehensive view of man's temporal and eternal destiny. With Virgil as his guide, he descends the realistically portrayed circles of Hell to where Lucifer, like an evil worm, bores through the very centre of the world, and then in the Antipodes he climbs the mount of Purgatory. Here Virgil, the voice of temporal wisdom, disappears, his function exhausted, and through the luminous heavens it is Beatrice, the symbol of Theology, who guides him to the supreme bliss – the contemplation of God. It is a vast design, whose poetic texture varies from the realistically gross to the ecstatic visionary, and which ranges over the whole culture, theological and literary, of the Middle Ages. Supporting it is that interpretation of God's dual purpose for mankind, adumbrated in the *Convivio* and expanded in the *De monarchia*, which sees man destined for temporal happiness in this world under the sway of an undivided Empire, and eternal beatitude in the next, achieved through the guidance of an uncorrupted Church. His own age he sees as woefully astray on both counts, and it is from this discrepancy that the drama, both personal and universal, of the *Comedy* springs.

During Dante's exile, the Emperor Henry VII arrived in Italy (1310); this seemed to promise fulfilment of the poet's political hopes for a strong, universal empire. Before the expedition ended in the failure and death of the Emperor (1313), it called forth three of the most impressive of Dante's Latin *Epistolae* – to the rulers and people of Italy, to the citizens of Florence, and to the Emperor himself. One other work, the Latin treatise *De monarchia*, comes perhaps within the orbit of Henry's enterprise, but no firm dating is possible. It enunciates Dante's basic political theory with Church and Empire each divinely ordained and each independent of the other.

The two least interesting of his minor works, both in Latin, were composed in his last years – the *Quaestio de aqua et terra*, which is a dissertation on natural philosophy, and the two personal *Eclogues* written in correspondence with Giovanni del Virgilio. [DGR]

*Opere*, crit. ed. of the Società Dantesca (1921, repr. 1960); some useful commentaries on the *Divina Commedia* are those of Casini/Barbi, Scartazzini/Vandelli, and Sapegno; *Vita nuova*, ed. Barbi (1932); *Rime*, ed. Contini (1965); *Monarchia*, ed. Ricci (1965); *Convivio*, ed. Busnelli, Vandelli (1964); *De vulgari el.*, ed. Marigo (1957); *The Latin Works* ..., tr. Ferrers Howell, P. H. Wicksteed (1904); *Convivio*, tr. P. H. Wicksteed (1912); *The Divine Comedy*, tr. L. Binyon (1933–43); tr. D. L. Sayers, B. Reynolds (Penguin Classics, 1949–62); *Monarchy and Three Political Letters*, tr. Nicholl, Hardie (1954); *D.'s Lyric Poetry* (text, tr. and commentary), ed. K. Foster, P. Boyde (2 vols, 1967).

É. Gilson, *D. the Philosopher* (1948); U. Cosmo, *A Handbook to D. Studies* (1950); D'Entrèves, *D. as Political Thinker* (1952); M. Barbi, *Life of D.* (1955); E. Auerbach, *D. Poet of the Secular World* (1961); T. G. Bergin, *An Approach to D.* (1965); U. Limentani, ed., *The Mind of D.* (1965); Rossetti, *DC*; Binni, *CI*; *Maggiori*.

**Da Porto, Luigi** (Vicenza 1485–Vicenza 1529). Italian writer. He fought in Venetian service in the war of the League of Cambrai. His *Lettere storiche* (1509–13) reflect the course of the war. His fame rests on his one *novella*, the tale of *Giulietta e Romeo*, later used by ◊ Bandello and Shakespeare. [DGR]

*Novelle del Cinquecento*, ed. G. B. Salinari (Turin, 1955); *Lettere storiche*, ed. B. Bressan (1857); *Romeo and Juliet* (photographic reproductions of 1535 and 1539 Italian editions, with English translation), tr. M. Jonas (London, 1921); Di Francia, *N*; Roscoe, *IN*.

**Dara, G.** ◊ Albanian Literature.

**Dass, Petter** (N. Herøy, Nordland 1647–Alstahaug, Nordland 1707). Norwegian poet and hymnist. After studying theology in Copenhagen, he was a tutor and curate in Helgeland until 1689 when he got the living at Alstahaug. He was almost the only purely Norwegian writer of any importance between the end of the Middle Ages and the beginning of the 19th century. He was a man of strong personality, and after his death became an almost legendary figure in north Norway. As a writer he is chiefly remembered for his posthumously published verse cycle, *Nordlands Trompet* (1739; ed. D. A. Seip, 1958), a vigorous and affectionate account of the life, people and topography of his native Nordland, written in the baroque style. [RGP]

*Samlede Skrifter*, ed. A. Eriksen (3 vols., 1874–7).

H. Midbøe, *P.D.* (Oslo, 1947); Beyer, *NL*.

**D'Aubigné, Théodore Agrippa** (Pons, Saintonge 1552–Geneva 1630). French poet and historian. Sworn by his father to the support of the Protestant cause from his youth, he studied with zeal at Paris, Orleans, Geneva and Lyons, before joining the Huguenot forces at 16. From 1573 he served his friend Henri de Navarre as soldier, diplomatist and councillor, and it was on the field of battle that he began (*c.* 1577) composing *Les Tragiques*. After Henri's conversion in 1593, he retired into his Poitou domains to pursue his literary career; he undertook the *Histoire universelle*, which was burned immediately it appeared. He fled to Geneva (1620), where he spent the rest of his days, writing some of his less important works. His last years were marred by the scandalous behaviour of his son (whose daughter was to become Mme de Maintenon).

In his youthful love poetry, *Printemps* (publ. 1874; ed. A. Garnier and J. Plattard, 1932), written in praise of Diane Salviati, niece of Ronsard's Cassandre, the Petrarchan manner is strangely modified by his naturally violent and morbid imagination to produce a good example of the French Baroque. His greatest work, the *Tragiques* (publ. 1616; ed. B. Gagnebin and F. Desonay, 1948–52), was almost completely neglected till Sainte-Beuve drew attention to it in 1828. This fierce celebration of the justice of God, who will avenge his martyred saints, reads like the work of an Old Testament prophet, with its denunciations of the evils of society and of religious enemies. His vast vision of the universe, ranging from the lowliest peasant to the Lord of All, has a grandeur which outweighs the imperfections of composition and style. The *Histoire universelle* (1616–20), covering the period 1550–1602, is valued today for its many eyewitness accounts and some lively dramatic passages. He also wrote *Aventures du baron de Faeneste* (1617–30), a satirical attack on Papistry, in which the Gascon Faeneste represents attachment to outward show; the *Confession de Sancy* (1660), a parody of the reasons given by Huguenots who abjured their faith with Henri IV; and an autobiography, *Sa vie à ses enfants*. [FWAG]

*Œuvres complètes*, ed. A. de Rubles (1886–1909), with *Supplément*, J. Plattard (1925).

A. Garnier, *A. d'A. et le parti protestant* (Paris, 1928); J. Plattard, *Une figure de premier plan dans nos lettres de la Renaissance: A. d'A.* (Paris, 1931); I. Buffum, *A. d'A.'s 'Les Tragiques': A Study of the Baroque Style in Poetry* (New Haven, Conn., 1951).

**Däubler, Theodor** (Trieste 1876–St Blasien 1934). German poet. A wanderer through Europe, Asia Minor and Egypt, he is famous for his cosmological epic *Das Nordlicht* ('Florentine edition', 1910), and *Der sternhelle Weg* (1915), which contains the best of his lyric poetry. Though never entirely an ◊ Expressionist poet, he championed Expressionist art, and evolved a similar theory of colour-symbolism. His famous poem 'Millionen Nachtigallen schlagen' was a notable early experiment in sound-effects. A mystic, he sought to reveal the cosmic mystery through poetry; his poetry, rich in sensuous imagery, sometimes over-rhetorical, can be most beautiful in its Italian colouring. [PB]

*Dichtungen und Schriften*, ed. F. Kemp (1956); *Auswahl*, ed. H. Ulbricht (1951); Bridgwater, *TCGV*; Hamburger and Middleton, *MGP*; Wiese, *DDM*.

**Daudet, Alphonse** (Nîmes 1840–Paris 1897). French novelist. He was strongly influenced by his southern upbringing. He went to school at Lyons and in 1857 went to Paris to join his brother Ernest and try his hand at writing. His book of verse *Les amoureuses* was published the next year and in 1861 he started to contribute to *Le Figaro*. He became private secretary to the Duc de Morny, Napoleon III's half-brother and minister. Although he is chiefly remembered today for his sketches of Provençal life in *Lettres de mon moulin*, which were first published in *Le Figaro* (1866), and for his Tartarin books, he was also for a time one of the leaders of the naturalist school. He wrote several novels about the contemporary business, social and political scene such as *Fromont jeune et Risler aîné* (1874), which centres round a wallpaper factory in Paris; *Jack* (1876); *Le Nabab* (1877), the story of a peasant who makes a fortune in Africa and returns to enjoy his wealth in Paris only to be made the butt of spite and rumours which cause his death; *Les rois en exil* (1879); and *Numa Roumestan* (1881), interesting for its comparison of the southern and northern French characters. His burlesque novels, *Tartarin de Tarascon* (1872), *Tartarin sur les Alpes* (1885), *La défense de Tarascon* (1886), *Port-Tarascon* (1890), are about the hero of a small town on the Rhône who is constantly forced by his habit of telling elaborate stories of his great achievements to seek real adventures to bolster up his reputation. The first of the series is probably the most amusing. His style has always been admired. His other works include the play *L'Arlésienne*, for which Bizet wrote the incidental music (1872), and two volumes of short tales inspired by his service in the Garde Nationale during the Franco-Prussian war, *Les contes du lundi* (1873) and *Contes et récits* (1873). His son Léon (1868–1942) was also well known as a journalist and novelist and helped to found *L'Action Française*, the royalist and Catholic paper. [WA]

*Letters from my Mill*, tr. J. MacGregor (1966); *Tartarin of Tarascon* and *Tartarin in the Alps* (Everyman, 423).

G. Benoît-Guyod, *A.D.* (Paris, 1947); J. H. Bornecque, *Les années d'apprentissage d'A.D.* (Paris, 1952).

**Daumal, René** (Boulzicourt, Ardennes 1908–Paris 1944). French poet and prose writer. At 20 he founded the review *Le Grand Jeu*, dedicated to the high seriousness of poetry, as the art which is to reveal the secrets of life. He seems to have been in perpetual quest of the Absolute and to have thirsted after esoteric and arcane knowledge – he tells how he tried experimentally to know death in life – and became a disciple of Gurdijeff. Poor and tubercular, he subsisted on work as a translator. The books published in his lifetime, *Contre-ciels* (1936), a collection of poems, and two prose-works, *La grande beuverie*, a satire-fantasy (1939), and *Chaque fois que l'aube paraît*, essays (1940), reveal his originality less, perhaps, than the posthumous works. In the unfinished *Mont analogue* (1952; tr. R. Shattuck, postface Véra Daumal, *Mount Analogue*, 1959) he relates the curious adventure of a group of explorers seeking the mountain from whose top a new perspective on the universe is to be gained; thus Daumal symbolizes man's spiritual quest, which characteristically he sets firmly in the physical world. His wife collected his poems in *Poésie noire, poésie blanche* (1954); the title recalls his belief that 'poetry, like magic, is black or white, according as it serves the subhuman or the superhuman'. [FWAG]

A. Rousseaux, *Littérature du 20e siècle* (1955); *Schweizer Rundschau*, 55, 1955–6; *Marginales*, 68, 1959; *Critique*, 15, 1959.

**D'Aurevilly, B.** ⇨ Barbey d'Aurevilly.

**Dauthendey, Max** (Würzburg 1867–Malung, Java 1918). German poet and novelist (originally a painter). His world-wide travels are reflected in his impressionistic, often exotic poetry, little known during his lifetime, and still the subject of critical controversy. His main collections were: *Ultra Violett* (1893), *Reliquien* (1899), *Singsangbuch* (1909); the *Gesammelte Gedichte* appeared in 1931. Many of his poems contain orgies of light, colour and sound, an experimental synaesthesia, a pagan '*Weltfestlichkeitsgefühl*'. He also published humorous verse in the manner of ⇨ Busch: *Bänkelsang vom Balzer auf der Balz* (1905). His best-known novel is *Raubmenschen* (1911), and his play *Spielereien einer Kaiserin* (1910) enjoyed some success. [PB]

H. G. Wendt, *M.D., Poet-Philosopher* (N.Y., 1936).

**Davičo, Oskar** (Šabac 1909– ). Serbian poet and novelist. Imprisoned before the

Second World War for communist activity, he belonged to the modernist poets in Serbia; the influence of surrealism is still felt in his later poetry. Since the war he has published the novels *Pesma* (1952; tr. A. Brown, *The Poem*, London/Belgrade, 1959), *Beton i svici* (1956), *Radni naslov beskraja* (1958). His main theme is the problem of the communist personality amid the changes, crises and disappointments of creating a socialist state. His novels *Ćutuje*, *Tajne* and *Gladi* appeared in 1963. The novel *Bekstra* appeared in 1966. Davičo has published several editions of poetry of which the best known are *Pesme* (1938), *Zrenjanin* (1949), *Višnja za zidom* (1951) and *Kairos* (1959). [EDG]

Kadić, *CSL*; *SEER*, XL, 94 (1961).

**Da Vinci, Leonardo** (Vinci, Tuscany 1452–nr Amboise 1519). Italian artist and scientist. Apprenticed to Andrea del Verrocchio at Florence about 1467, he became the prototype of the Renaissance all-round man of genius. He was patronized by Lodovico il Moro, Cesare Borgia and Francis I. He once described himself as 'omo sanza lettere'; his writings, not prepared for publication, have been pieced together from manuscripts scattered through the libraries of Europe. They range over his vast artistic and scientific interests and cover such subjects as painting, the flight of birds, anatomy, and the movement of water. Free of *cinquecento* literariness, his prose has often an untutored forcefulness beyond the reach of the 'official' *letterati* of his time. [DGR]

*The Literary Works of L. da V.*, parallel Italian and English text, ed. J. P. Richter (1939); *Scritti scelti*, ed. A. M. Brizio (1953); *Scritti letterari*, ed. A. Marinoni (1952).
Kenneth Clark, *L. da V.* (1961); *Minori*, i.

**De Amicis, Edmondo** (Oneglia 1846–Bordighera 1908). Italian journalist and short-story writer. He worked for the Florentine journal *L'Italia militare*, contributing short stories and articles based on his own military experiences from 1865 to 1867. Their publication in one volume (*La vita militare*, 1868; tr. W. W. Cady, *Military Life in Italy*, N.Y., 1882) immediately brought him fame. A series of travel books followed (1872–9); and in 1883 appeared *Gli amici*, a long series of sketches on the theme of friendship. In 1886 he published his masterpiece, *Cuore* (tr. G. S. Godkin, *Heart*, 1895; S. Jewett, *The Heart of a Boy*, N.Y., 1960), short stories in the form of a school diary, and rapidly established as a children's favourite. At their best his works possess a warm-hearted idealism and a certain psychological perception that have given them lasting appeal, despite the strictures of Carducci, who despised the commonplace and sentimental in them. [RHC]

Ed. A. Baldini (2 vols., 1945–6).
M. Mosso, *I tempi del 'Cuore'* (Milan, 1925); G. Gerini, *E. de A. scrittore educatore* (Florence, 1952); P. Guarnieri, *E. de A.* (Rovigo, 1954); L. Gigli, *De A.* (Turin, 1962); *Minori*, iv.

**Debelyanov, Dimcho** (Koprivshtitsa 1887–Demirhisar, Greece 1916). Bulgarian symbolist poet. A fatherless, destitute childhood, followed by a threadbare existence eked out on minor posts in Sofia, did not dull his flair for poetry. He enjoyed the friendship of D. Podvărzachov, Liliev (his colleagues in translating from French literature and compiling a new *Antologiya* of Bulgarian poetry, 1910) and other symbolist writers. Their characteristic mystical quality recurs in his poetry, notably in the cycle 'The Legend of the Profligate Princess', as do also the rhythms of their melancholy, evocative music. His gift for 'singing from the heart' and his tragically fulfilled premonition of death on the battlefield in his poems ('Orphan's Song' and 'The Still Victory') have made him a legend and a link in the Bulgarian martyr-poet tradition of ⇨ Botev and ⇨ Vaptsarov. Like them, he died comparatively young in voluntary sacrifice. His poems, like theirs, are few but of enduring quality. [VP]

*Stihotvoreniya* (1957); Pinto, *BPV*.
M. Debelyanova, *D.B. Spomeni za moya brai* (Sofia, 1946); V. Rusaliev, *Zhivotăt, lyubovta i smărtta na D.B.* (Sofia, 1936); Manning and Smal-Stocki, *HMBL*.

**Dechepare, Bernard.** ⇨ Basque Literature.

**'De Heinrico.'** An anonymous poem written at the turn of the 10th century by a German cleric, in a mixture of Latin and German, the first half of each line being in Latin, the second half in German. The titular hero is Henry, second son of the Saxon emperor Henry I (d. 936), and the subject of the poem is his public reconciliation with his elder brother Otto, who had succeeded to his father's imperial throne as Otto I (the Great). The poem's eight strophes consist of either three or four lines each. [RT]

Braune, *AL*, 39.

**Dehmel, Richard** (Wendisch-Hermsdorf 1863–Blankenese/Hamburg 1920). German poet (after working for a fire-insurance company). A volunteer front-line soldier in 1914–18, he won the Iron Cross; influenced by Nietzsche he preached and practised rigorous self-discipline. He was a very considerable lyric poet, standing aside from poetic movements, though friendly with ⇨ Mombert and ⇨ Liliencron. Elemental and 'excessively masculine', his themes include social compassion and a desire to spiritualize sex. His best poetry has excellent rhythm; his weakness is rhetoric and didacticism. His best collection of poems is *Weib und Welt* (1896). [PB]

*Dichtungen, Briefe, Dokumente*, ed. P. J. Schindler (1963).

Bridgwater, *TCGV*; Rose, *MGLV*; *GR*, II, 1927; J. Bab, *R.D.* (Leipzig, 1926); *GR*, XI, 1936; *JEGP*, XXXV, 1, 1936.

**Deledda, Grazia** (Nuoro, Sardinia 1871–Rome 1936). Italian novelist. After her marriage in 1900, she moved to Rome; but her short stories and novels, written at first for magazines, continued to treat the wild landscape and the folk-lore of her native Sardinia. In earlier writings romantic descriptions dominated, but these gradually gave way to a more intense study of her taciturn characters struggling with a peculiar form of fatalism against their primitive background (e.g. *Tesoro*, 1897; *Elias Portolu*, 1903; *Marianna Sirca*, 1915). This lyrical treatment of man and nature is well expressed in her best works *Cenere* (1904; tr. H. H. Colvill, *Ashes*, 1908), *L'edera* (1908) and *La madre* (1920). After 1921 she abandoned the Sardinian background; but in essence her art remained the same (e.g. *Il segreto dell'uomo solitario*, 1921). She was awarded the Nobel Prize in 1926. Her autobiographical *Cosima* appeared posthumously in 1937 (ed. A. Baldini). [RHC]

*Romanzi e novelle*, ed. E. Cecchi (4 vols., 1941–55); *The Woman and the Priest*, tr. M. G. Steegmann, intr. D. H. Lawrence (1928).

E. De Michelis, *G.D. e il decadentismo* (Florence, 1938); L. Roncarati, *L'arte di G.D.* (Florence, 1948); *Contemporanei*, i.

**Delicado** or **Delgado, Francisco** (early 16th cent.). Spanish novelist living in Italy. His Italianate novel in the manner of *La* ⇨ *Celestina* entitled *El retrato de la Lozana andaluza* (1528; ed. Vilanova, 1952) was famous for indelicacy, its many prostitute characters, and lively dialect. [JMC]

M. Menéndez y Pelayo, *Orígenes de la novela*, iv (repr. Madrid/Santander, 1943).

**Delille, Jacques, Abbé** (Aigueperse 1738–Paris 1813). French poet, translator (Virgil, Milton, Pope) and Academician. Some original descriptive and didactic verse (*Les jardins*, 1782; *L'homme des champs*, 1802; *Les trois règnes de la nature*, 1808) exploited the current sentimental vogue for rural simplicity. In his easy flow there is an occasional note of recognizably Romantic feeling. [WHB]

*Œuvres complètes* (1824).
*Mercure de France*, July 1938.

**Della Casa, Giovanni** (Mugello? 1503–Rome 1556). Italian prose-writer and poet. After a youth of study and pleasure he entered the Church and became in 1544 Archbishop of Benevento. Later, as Papal Nunzio to Venice, his task in a time of religious ferment was to protect the cause of orthodoxy. In retirement near Treviso (1549–55) he composed his *Galateo, ovvero dei Costumi*, second only to ⇨ Castiglione's *Courtier* among the courtesy books of the Renaissance ('*galateo*' has passed into Italian as a noun meaning good manners). Entertaining in its acute and good-humoured portrayal of social behaviour, and vigorous Florentine prose, it illustrates the Renaissance preoccupation with the art of living. As a poet Della Casa cultivates a resonant and dramatic strain of Petrarchism, while his letters throw light on the contemporary scene. Shortly before his death he was recalled to Rome as Paul IV's Secretary of State. [DGR]

*Rime*, ed. A. Seroni (1944); *Opere di B. Castiglione, G. Della C. e B. Cellini*, ed. C. Cordié (1960); *Opere di B. Castiglione e. G. Della C.* ed. G. Prezzolini (1937); *Prose scelte*, ed. S. Ferrari (1957); *Galateo*, tr. R. S. Pine-Coffin (Penguin Classics, 1958).

L. Baldacci, *Il petrarchismo italiano nel Cinquecento* (Milan, 1957); *Minori*, ii.

**Della Valle, Federico** (Asti *c.*1560–Milan 1628). Italian tragedian. He worked at the court of Charles Emanuel I of Savoy in Turin, and was active also in Milan. He has been rediscovered only in the present century. He composed a youthful tragicomedy, *Adelonda di Frigia* (publ. 1629), but his best plays are tragedies on religious themes, *Judit* (1627) and *Ester* (1627), on

Biblical subjects, and *La reina di Scozia* (1628) on the fate of Mary Stuart, who is presented as a Catholic martyr. They show the dynamic influence of religion on conduct, not through abstract rhetoric but with real poetic feeling for the tragic in human situations. The direct forcefulness of his writing is little touched by the baroque grandiloquence of the *seicento*. [DGR]

*Tragedie*, ed. C. Filosa (1939); *Tutte le opere*, ed. P. Cazzani (1955); *Teatro del Seicento*, ed. L. Fassò (1956).

B. Croce, *Nuovi saggi sulla letteratura italiana del Seicento* (Bari, 1949); *Minori*, ii.

**'Demanda do Santo Graal.'** Romance of chivalry in Portuguese devoted to the quest for the Holy Grail. The novel, which is the allegorical and mystical expression of moral and religious teaching, is the account of the quest of the Arthurian knights Galahad, Bors and Percival for the Holy Grail in which Joseph of Arimathaea had caught the drops of blood of the crucified Christ. Peninsular interest in the *matière de Bretagne* had first revealed itself in the ⇨ *Cancioneiros*. In the last quarter of the 13th century Portuguese prose translations or adaptations were made of the Breton cycle, most probably from the now fragmentary French texts falsely attributed to Robert de Boron. There emerged the trilogy of *Josep ab Arimatia*, *Merlim* and the *Demanda do Santo Graal*, of which the second has now been lost, although there does exist a Spanish *Merlín*, which may well have derived from it. The *Demanda* and *Josep ab Arimatia* survived in 15th- and 16th-century manuscripts respectively. There exists a Spanish version of the *Demanda* in a 16th-century printed text, a version usually regarded as a translation of the Portuguese, although a few scholars adduce textual evidence to suggest that the Spanish and Portuguese texts derived separately from a lost common source which came between the French and Peninsular versions. The Portuguese text, however, is of particular interest as it constitutes the earliest example of Portuguese literary prose. [RCW]

Ed. A. Magne (3 vols., Rio de Janeiro, 1944; vol. I, 2nd edn, Rio de Janeiro, 1955).

M. Menéndez y Pelayo, *Orígenes de la novela*, i (Madrid, 1943); M. Rodrigues Lapa, *Lições de Literatura Portuguesa* (Coimbra, 1955); H. Thomas, *Spanish and Portuguese Romances of Chivalry* (1920); W. J. Entwistle, *The Arthurian Legend in the Literatures of the Spanish Peninsula* (1925).

**De Marchi, Emilio** (Milan 1851–Milan 1901). Italian novelist and short-story writer. A teacher by career, his writings are characterized by a strong moral and educative sense, for which some have compared him with ⇨ Manzoni, whose unqualified religious feeling and stylistic elegance, however, he lacked. The didactic element emerges openly in *L'età preziosa* (1887), which aims at developing spiritual qualities in youth – similar but inferior to ⇨ De Amicis's *Cuore*. He has also been compared with French naturalist writers for his vision of the sad reality of bourgeois life which he describes with serenity and good humour as effectively in the short stories, *Storie d'ogni colore* (1885), as in the better-known novels *Demetrio Pianelli* (1890; tr. M. Newett, 1905), *Arabella* (1892), *Giacomo l'idealista* (1897) and *Col fuoco non si scherza* (1901). The well-told detective novel *Il cappello del prete* (1888; tr. F. A. Y. Brown, *The Priest's Hat*, 1935) remains his most popular work. [RHC]

*Tutte le opere*, ed. G. Ferrata (2 vols., 1959–60).

V. Branca, *E. De M.* (Brescia, 1946); M. Monteverdi, *E. De M. romanziere* (Milan, 1963); *Guida*, 1959; *Minori*, iv.

**De Rada, J.** ⇨ Albanian Literature.

**De Roberto, Federico** (Naples 1866–Catania 1927). Italian critic and novelist. His literary career began with now-forgotten critical works; but after his close association in Florence and Milan with other writers, especially ⇨ Verga, he turned to narrative, his first collection of short stories (*Documenti umani*, 1889) containing mixed elements of Verga's regionalism and Bourget's psychological analysis. The latter tended to dominate in his novels (e.g. *Ermanno Raeli*, 1889; *L'illusione*, 1891, repr. 1959) in an excessively intellectual and coldly scientific way; though in his masterpiece, *I vicerè* (1894, repr. 1959; tr. A. Colquhoun, *The Viceroys*, 1962), this scientific objectivity is well suited to the historical and psychological study of three generations of an aristocratic Sicilian family in decline. [RHC]

G. Mariani, *F. De R. narratore* (Rome, 1950) V. Spinazzola, *F. De R. e il verismo* (Milan 1961); *Minori*, iv.

**Deroulède, Paul** (Paris 1846–Mont Boron Nice 1914). French poet and politician After serving in the Franco-Prussian war he founded the Ligue des Patriotes (1882 and was later imprisoned for subversive activities. His *Chants du soldat* (1872), *Nouveaux chants* (1875), *Chants patriotiques* (1882), *Chants du paysan* (1894), etc., are historically interesting as once popular expressions of revanchist jingoism. [WA]

**Déry, Tibor** (Budapest 1894– ). Hungarian novelist. Son of a wealthy manufacturer, he joined the family business and learned much about the life of workers, which he portrayed with analytical insight in his works. Although he joined the Communist Party early, revulsion at the crimes of the Communist Rákosi regime inspired his later works. As the uncompromising leader of the writers' fight for free artistic expression and against tyranny, he was imprisoned after the 1956 uprising (1957–60). Major novels: *Befejezetlen mondat* (1945), *Felelet* (1950–2), *Niki* (n.d.; tr. E. Hyams, *Niki, the Story of a Dog*, 1958) was translated into many languages. He has also written numerous short stories (*A Mess of Potato*, and *Odysseus*, 1956, tr. in *The Plough and the Pen*, ed. I. Duczynska and K. Polányi, 1963). [JFR]

Klaniczay, *HHL*.

**Derzhavin, Gavrila Romanovich** (nr Kazan 1743–Zvanka, Novgorod Region 1816). Russian poet. A poor nobleman, he attended Kazan school, became a private in the footguards (1762–72), and saw action as an officer during the Pugachov rebellion. He was transferred to the Civil Service (1777) and granted land and serfs. As Governor of Olonets (1784), then of Tambov, he earned a reputation for being honest, irrascible and outspoken. In 1791 he became Catherine II's secretary. He went on to be a senator (1793) and Minister of Justice (1802), retiring in 1803. He had married in 1778, was widowed in 1794, and remarried in 1795.

His extraordinary career is not unlike his 'ascent to Helicon prompted by nature, want and foes'. Having earlier scribbled verses for his fellow-soldiers, he first published in 1773 and became known by 1779. Though adhering to classicism, he was an innovator in his varied metre, irregular syntax, use of onomatopoeia; his vocabulary combined lofty Slavonic with rugged idioms. He sided with literary archaists yet hailed new talent: ⇨ Karamzin, ⇨ Zhukovsky, the schoolboy Pushkin. His range is wide, and whether his subject is national victory, friends, nature, civic exhortation or satirical invective, an ode on death or a panegyric, he is always personal; his love lyrics are subtly diverse and sensual. An epicurean with immense zest for life, he has a painter's eye for detail and colour. Poems to Catherine II are a portrayal, a personal tribute, and criticism of her Court (*Felitsa*, 1782, *Videniye Murzy*, 1783–90, *Razvaliny*, 1797). *Yevgeniyu Zhizn' Zvanskaya* (1807), idyllic, facetious and realistic, prefigures parts of Pushkin's *Yevgeny Onegin*. *Gimn Bogu* (1780–4; tr. Sir J. Bowring, *Ode to Deity*, 1861) is no less an apotheosis of Man than of his Creator. Keenly conscious of death, he claims survival as a poet who 'spoke of God with simplicity of heart, and told the truth, with a smile, to the Tsars' (*Lebed'*, *c.* 1805, *Pamyatnik*, 1796, free version from Horace). His last unfinished poem, *Reka Vremen*, shows, however, a pessimism and grandeur reminiscent of Ecclesiastes. His historically interesting memoirs (*Zapiski*, 1743–1812) are told in vivid, virile prose. [NG]

*Sochineniya*, edn Akademiya Nauk (9 vols., 1864–83); *Stikhotvoreniya* (1947).

V. F. Khodasevich, *G.D.*, edn Sovremennye Zapiski (Paris, 1931); D. D. Blagoy, *D.* (Moscow, 1944).

**De Sanctis, Francesco** (Morra Irpino, Avellino 1817–Naples 1883). Italian literary historian. A strong opponent of the restricted view of literature held by grammarians and purists such as his own teacher, Basilio Puoti. He himself taught at Turin, Zürich (in exile, 1856–9) and Naples (Professor of Comparative Literature, 1871–7). He was thrice appointed Minister of Education for the new Kingdom of Italy. Many published works were edited versions of his lecture-courses, and have a characteristically simple, yet elegant style. His work is incorporated largely in *Saggi critici* (1866), *Nuovi saggi critici* (1872) and the celebrated *Storia della letteratura italiana* (1870–1; tr. J. Redfern, *History of Italian Literature*, 1932) – written as a school textbook. Its second volume, over-hurriedly completed for the publisher, is supplemented by *Letteratura italiana del secolo XIX* (ed. Croce, 1897), a collection of lectures given at Naples (1872–4). As historian and critic his importance lies in his insistence upon the autonomy of art. He rejected preconceived ideas on form, and saw each work as a necessarily unique and inseparable fusion of content and form. His grasp of important general ideas and his intuition of literary qualities were remarkable, though in the *Storia* his concern to outline a pattern of national characteristics presents some inconsistencies. Incomplete and with some romantic prejudices, the *Storia* remains nevertheless the most vital and coherent history of Italian literature. [RHC]

*Opere complete*, ed. C. Muscetta (1951ff.); *Opere*, ed. N. Gallo (1961).

B. Croce, *Gli scritti di F. De S. e la loro varia fortuna* (Bari, 1917); G. Getto, *Storia delle storie letterarie* (Milan, 1942); L. Russo, *F. De S. e la cultura napoletana* (3rd edn, Florence, 1959); L. Biscardi, *De S.* (Palermo, 1960); W. Binni, *Carducci e altri saggi* (Turin, 1960); E. and A. Croce, *F. De S.* (Turin, 1964); *Minori*, iv.

**Desbordes-Valmore, Marceline** (Douai 1786–Paris 1859). French poetess. Her family was ruined by the Revolution; she briefly emigrated to Guadaloupe with her mother. She took up acting at the Opéra-Comique (1805) and the Odéon (1813), and married an actor, F. P. Lachantin, known as Valmore. Her verse, 'discovered' by Sainte-Beuve (who loved her daughter, Ondine), is charming but melancholy in its constant theme of love – inspired by a passionate and unhappy love affair (? with Henri de Latouche, 1785–1851, the first editor of André Chénier's work) and her feelings for her daughters. Her best volumes are *Élégies* (1819), *Élégies et poésies nouvelles* (1825), *Les pleurs* (1833), *Pauvres fleurs* (1839) and *Bouquets et prières* (1843). Her mood and style resembles that of Verlaine, who included her among his *Poètes maudits*. [WA]

M. G. Sesma, *Le secret de M.D.-V.* (1945); É. Jasénas, *M.D.-V. devant la critique* (Paris, 1962).

**Descartes, René** (La Haye 1596–Stockholm 1650). French philosopher and mathematician, also an important figure in literary history. Educated by the Jesuits, in the famous school of La Flèche, he took up science in the quest for reliable evidence. Never a bookish man, he decided to travel, and his life was spent in arduous meditation and in journeys, with the object 'd'apprendre à distinguer le vrai d'avec le faux, pour voir clair en mes actions et marcher avec assurance en cette vie' (*Discours*). He travelled to Switzerland, Italy (to see Galileo), Holland, England, Germany, Denmark, and finally to Sweden, by invitation of Queen Christiana, where the cold was too much for him and he died in the prime of life. His correspondents show how closely he kept in touch with the key figures of his day: Beekman, Kepler, Harvey, Bérulle, Richelieu, Huyghens. His mathematical and scientific works, which hardly concern us here, should be regarded as the occasion and inspiration of his treatises on method, such as the *Discours* itself of 1637, but also the Regulae: *Règles pour la direction de l'esprit*, of 1628, the *Méditations philosophiques* of 1641, the *Principes de la philosophie* of 1644 and the *Traité des passions de l'âme* of 1649.

It used to be held that Descartes supplied the basis and theory of French Classicism, and even Lanson was concerned to prove that Corneille and Descartes thought alike on the passions. Modern research puts these matters in a larger context, by considering him as an ardent student of Montaigne, to whose astringent and acute suggestions even the teachers of La Flèche had no convincing reply. At school, as Gilson says, Descartes was taught very much the same as he would have been taught in the 14th century. To Montaigne's pulverizing of scholasticism he could find no adequate traditional answer so was forced to seek along new lines. The process of the revolution which he thus accomplished in the history of ideas can be followed almost step by step, one may say in the *Discours de la méthode pour bien conduire sa raison et chercher la vérité dans les sciences* (ed. É. Gilson, 1925; G. Gadoffre, 1941, 1961; tr. E. S. Haldane and G. R. T. Ross, *Discourse on the Method . . .*, Chicago, 1952) which is now read not as a single argument but as a collection of fragments, inconsistent in places but representing Descartes' successive attacks on the whole problem of certainty. The first section seems to be part of what Descartes sent to J. L. G. ⇨ Balzac in 1628 as 'Histoire de mon esprit', the third and sixth deal with treatises published only in 1637; the fifth concerns questions aroused by Harvey's experiments on circulation of 1632. To read the famous *Discours* in this way is not to destroy its unity but to follow the tortuous path Descartes himself took to attain a new method.

It is a pity that the founder of modern philosophy has been thought of exclusively as a philosopher. His influence has perhaps been greatest on his contemporaries and on scientists, on men who doubted his con clusions but were inspired by his method. Voltaire said of him that he gave sight to the blind. We need to remember this when his errors are proclaimed. No doubt European thought was led on a false trail by many of Descartes' assertions, while his rigid separation of mind and matter helped to create an intellectual outlook alien to poetry. But his errors do not affect the boldness and range of the Cartesian attack, of his insistence on evidence, on clarity, on the necessity of doubt before any real certainty can be acquired. The last section of the *Discours* pictures scientists combining in a vast endeavour to demonstrate the unity of nature 'et ainsi nous rendre maîtres et possesseurs de la nature'. This is the man of whom Turgot said that he looked at nature 'like a man who, plunging a vast look down upon her, saw all of her at once'. [WGM]

*Œuvres*, ed. C. Adam and P. Tannery (12 vols., 1897–1913); *Œuvres et lettres*, ed. A. Bridoux (Pléiade, 1952).

É. Gilson, *Études sur le rôle de la pensée médiévale dans la formation du système cartésien* (Paris, 1930); A. Vartanian, *Diderot and D.* (Paris, 1953).

**Deschamps, Émile** (Bourges 1791–Versailles 1871) and his brother **Antony** (1800–69). French Romantic poets. Émile was one of the founders of *La Muse Française* (1823) and a friend of Hugo and Vigny. His writings which were mostly translations or imitations aroused interest in German, English and Spanish literature (*Études françaises et étrangères*, 1828; *Romeo and Juliet*, 1839; *Macbeth*, 1844). Antony translated Dante (1829) and lost his reason in 1834. [WA]

**Deschamps, Eustache,** called Morel (Champagne 1346–*c.* 1406). French poet. Disciple, and possibly nephew, of ⇨ Guillaume de Machaut. He has left many *ballades* and *rondeaux* on moral, patriotic or satirical themes, a prose treatise on versification, *Art de dictier et de faire ballades et chants royaux*, an anti-feminist satire *Miroir de mariage*, and two dramatic works including the famous *Farce de Maître Trubert et d'Antroignart* which uses the ⇨ *Pathelin* theme of the duper duped. He addressed a ballade to Chaucer whom he influenced. His vast output and devotion to the art of medieval rhetoric have obscured the importance and interest of his pungent views on contemporary society and of the analysis of his personal situation which he develops in his poetry. [LTT]

Ed. Marquis de Queux de Saint-Hilaire and G. Raynaud (11 vols., 1878–1904).

G. Raynaud, *E.D. Sa vie, ses œuvres, son temps* (Paris, 1904) (from vol. 11 of complete works); E. Hœpffner, *E.D.s Leben und Werke* (Strasbourg, 1904); *Modern Philology*, VIII, 1910; *RR*, II, 1911; *NM*, XXVII, 1926; *MLN*, XLII, 1927; *PMLA*, XLVIII, 1933; *RF*, LXII, 1950; *MLR*, LI, 1956, LIX, 1964; *Mél. Hœpffner*, 1949.

**Desfontaines, Pierre François Guyot, Abbé** (Rouen 1685–Paris 1745). French journalist and publicist. A notorious enemy of Voltaire (*La Voltairomanie*, 1738). As editor of *Observations sur les écrits modernes* (1735–43) and other periodicals, he did much to popularize English literature in France; he also translated *Gulliver* (1727), *Joseph Andrews* (1743), and several of Pope's works. A conservative critic, his *Dictionnaire néologique* (1726) defends the purity of the French language. [WHB]

T. Morris, *L'Abbé D. et son rôle dans la littérature de son temps* (Geneva, 1961).

**Desmarets, Jean,** Sieur de Saint-Sorlin (Paris 1595–Paris 1676). French man of letters. Little is known of his life beyond his literary polemics, where scholars have had to disentangle fact from legend, owing to another man of the same name having moved in the same circles. He was one of Richelieu's most active collaborators, indeed he affirms that the Cardinal persuaded him to write plays. One of these was an outstanding success at the Théâtre du Marais in 1637, with Montdory in the main part: *Les visionnaires* (ed. H. G. Hall, 1964). It is a likely source of a character in Molière's *Femmes savantes*; it was remembered in 1674 as being one of the three or four plays which, with *Le Cid*, were thought to inaugurate the revival of the French theatre. Desmarets wrote 2 epics, *Clovis* and *Esther* (1673), which has been called the most readable of the French Biblical epics of the century, and also a novel, *Ariane*, about Rome in the time of Nero, possibly read by Racine and even more probably by his audiences. Like *Les précieuses ridicules*, *Les visionnaires* seems to have given offence to individuals and the original version was toned down. It is a play which can still be read with pleasure. [WGM]

R. A. Sayce, *French Biblical Epic* (1955); Adam, *HLF*.

**Desmasures, Louis** (Tournai 1515–?1574). French dramatist. He was converted to Protestantism in Geneva while travelling back to France from a visit to Rome, and in 1562 had to leave France to avoid religious persecution. In 1566 he published his trilogy of plays about David – *David combattant*, *David triomphant*, *David fugitif*. Like ➪ Bèze's *Abraham* these plays are transitional between medieval mystery plays and 'classical' tragedy, for they contain some characteristics of both *genres*. They are rather repetitively didactic, but some of the *cantiques* and *cantiques à danser* of the chorus are very successful, and Desmasures also presents well the frustrated malice of Satan and the youthful naïveté of Saul's daughter wondering whether she is in love with David. The plays are of interest both as Protestant propaganda and as documents in the history of tragedy. He also translated many of the psalms, and Virgil's *Aeneid*. [GJ]

*Tragédies saintes*, ed. C. Comte (1907).

**Desnica, Vladan** (Zadar 1905–1967). Croatian short-story writer and novelist. He began to publish only after the Second World War: several volumes of stories, marked by their humour and perceptive insight into character, the novels *Zimsko letovanje* (1950), and *Proleća Ivana Galeba* (1957), and the play *Jakovljeve ljestvice* (1959). Above all a psychological writer, he perceives the paradoxical nature of mankind as being both humorous and tragic. He introduces the fantastic by mingling the musings of his characters with external reality. Of particular interest is *Proleća Ivana Galeba*, a good-humoured, gentle yet penetrating intellectual view of existence where tragedy is ever-present, both outside man and within. [EDG]

*SEER*, XL, 94 (1961).

**Desnos, Robert** (Paris 1900–Terezine 1945). French poet. An early ➪ Surrealist, he became in 1922 the leading exponent of automatism, when he astonished his friends with endless monologues, speaking his dreams aloud, while under a hypnotic trance. *Deuil pour deuil* (1924) is a typical product of the automatic method, where all conscious control by reason is abandoned. In *La liberté ou l'amour!* (1927) this combines with the Surrealist love of scandal to produce a novel of oniric eroticism. In 1930 Desnos broke with ➪ Breton and the group under rather childish circumstances. but continued to conciliate dream and reality in his writings. *Domaine public* (1953) is a posthumous collection of most of his poetry, from the Surrealism and dream-love of *À la mystérieuse* (1926) to the more formal verse of *Fortunes* (1942). He died of typhoid in a Czech medical camp. [RTC]

R. Buchole, *L'évolution poétique de R.D.* (Brussels, 1956); P. Berger, *R.D.* (Paris, 1960).

**Des Périers, Bonaventure** (Arnay-le-Duc *c.*1510–1544). French writer. Very little is known about his life, and the authenticity of his two major works has sometimes been disputed. Around 1535 he collaborated on the translation into French of the Bible undertaken by Olivetan, Calvin's relative. He also appears to have collaborated with Étienne Dolet on his *Commentarii linguae latinae*. He was in the service of ➪ Marguerite de Navarre for several years and was a friend of ➪ Marot. His main work, a series of four prose dialogues under the title *Cymbalum mundi* (ed. Nurse, Manchester, 1958), was published in 1537. It has on the whole always been considered an atheistic, in the sense of violently anti-Christian, satire, although from time to time critics have most strenuously attempted to find evidence to the contrary. He wrote a number of poems more or less in the style of Marot. He appears to have died by suicide in 1544, according to Henri ➪ Estienne. His collection of short stories, *Les nouvelles récréations et joyeux devis*, was published posthumously in 1558 (ed. La Monnoye, Amsterdam, 1735). [CAM]

*Œuvres françoises*, ed. L. La Court (1856).

L. Febvre, *Origène et Des P.* (Paris, 1942); D. Neidhart, *Das Cymbalum Mundi des B. des P.* (Paris and Geneva, 1959).

**Desportes, Philippe** (Chartres 1546–Bonport, Normandy 1606). French poet. The son of a wealthy tradesman. He entered the priesthood, then had a varied and nomadic career before becoming a secretary to the Duc d'Anjou, later Henri III. He became Henri III's recognized court poet succeeding Ronsard as 'Prince of poets', and received many benefices from the king including the abbacies of Tiron and Josaphat. After the assassination of Henri III, he offered his services to the Ligue, and later still to Henri IV. With his knowledge of Italian literature, he brought to French poetry an Italian complexity of rhetoric and a distinctive soft musicality – his famous '*doux-coulant*' style. His vocabulary is smaller than that of the ⇨ Pléiade, but there is no denying his technical skill and acute ear. Many of the rules of prosody attributed to his enemy ⇨ Malherbe can be found already applied in his writing. His verse is always polished, smooth, lucid. Too often it is also feeble: not because he is a court poet writing commissioned poetry, but because by this stage in the development of French poetry it was not enough to follow slavishly the Petrarchan convention with all its apparatus of sighs and tears and rocky hearts. His main work, apart from the *Amours*, is his translations of the Psalms (1592, 1595), which have more dignity than those of Marot. [GJ]

Ed. V. Graham (7 vols., Geneva, 1958–63); Schmidt, *PSS*.

J. Lavand, *P.D.* (Geneva 1936); M. T. Marchand-Roques, *La vie de P.D.* (Paris, 1949).

**Destouches, Philippe Néricault** (Tours 1680–Fortoiseau, Melun 1754). French dramatist. His early verse comedies (*L'ingrat*, 1712; *Le médisant*, 1715) prolong the Molière tradition of comedy of character, though with far less talent and profundity, and with a tendency to shift the emphasis from the comic to the morally edifying. In his best-known play, *Le glorieux* (1732), the *comédie larmoyante* of Nivelle de ⇨ La Chaussée is clearly foreshadowed. An interlude spent as a diplomatic agent in England (1717–23) is reflected in his adaptation of Addison's play *The Drummer* (*Le tambour nocturne*, 1733), but his later plays had little success. [WHB]

*Œuvres* (1822).

J. Hankiss, *P. N. D., l'homme et l'œuvre* (Debreczen, 1920).

**Deus, João de** (São Bartolomeu de Messines 1830–Lisbon 1896). Portuguese poet. He graduated in Law at Coimbra University, where his cheerful nature and bohemian habits made him very popular with his colleagues, but a rather slow student who took ten years to finish an ordinary five-year course. After a brief experience as editor of a provincial newspaper (1862–4), he settled in Lisbon. Here he published the first collection of his poems, *Flores do campo* (1869), which were very well received by the reviewers who were impressed by the clarity of his language and the candid beauty of his lyrics at a time when a lachrymose and rhetorical romanticism was the fashion. *Campo de flores* (1893) confirmed all the qualities of his first book. In 1876, he embarked on the preparation of a primer (*Cartilha maternal*) to teach small children how to read. After a strenuous campaign, he saw his method officially adopted in Portuguese schools. His pedagogical ideas are still followed today in the institutes that bear his name. [LSR]

Vitorino Nemésio, 'O Erotismo de J. de D.', in *Sob os Signos de Agora* (Coimbra, 1932).

**Deval, Jacques** (Paris 1894– ). French playwright. Author of highly successful light comedies ranging from the satirical to the sentimental. The early satirical comedies are acutely observed and have a distinct edge, whether they deal with the double life of a 'respectable' bourgeois in *Étienne* (1930); the disunity and disintegration of the family life of a successful barrister (*Mademoiselle*, 1932); or the sordid chronicle of three generations of a 'solid' family in *Prière pour les vivants* (1933). Though the touch is lighter in the hilarious *Tovaritch* (1934; tr./adapt. R. E. Sherwood, 1937), the predicament of Russian aristocrats in exile serving the family of a new-rich socialist deputy is exploited with a sharp satirical sense. [SBJ]

Surer, *TFC*; Sée, *TFC*.

**Deyssel, Lodewijk van,** pseud. of Karel Jan Lodewijk Alberdingk Thijm (Hilversum 1864–Haarlem 1952). Dutch author and critic. His considerable inherited critical talent was marred by a dilettante subjectivity in many of his essays which appeared in *De Nieuwe Gids* (⇨ Kloos) and *De Beweging* (which he and ⇨ Verwey founded). His novels, *Een Liefde* (1887) and *De kleine Republiek* (1888), echo French naturalism. Later he attempted impressionistic 'prose-poems' which ultimately (*Apocalyps*, 1893) degenerated into aesthetic verbiage. At the same time he wrote outstanding biographies on ⇨ Douwes Dekker (1891) and his own father (1892). [PK]

*Verzamelde opstellen* (11 vols., 1894–1911); Greshoff, *HL*.

F. Jansonius, *L.v.D.* (Lochem, 1952); H. M. G. Prick, *L.v.D. Dertien close-ups* (Amsterdam, 1964).

**Díaz del Castillo, Bernal** (Medina del Campo? 1492–Guatemala 1581). Spanish captain and chronicler. After two explorations of the Mexican coast, he joined Cortés in the march on Mexico and battles for the city. His realistic *Historia verdadera* (intended to refute that of ⇨ López de Gómara) shows Cortés in true proportion, dependent on his generals; there are sympathetic portraits of Montezuma and Aztec allies whose fate Díaz regrets. The colloquial style may be due to his having dictated the work when blind in old age; as *regidor* in Guatamala, he possessed great estates but still felt cheated of wealth. [JMC]

Ed. Cabañas (2 vols., Mexico, 1942, repr. 1960); tr. Maudslay (5 vols., 1908–16); tr. J. M. Cohen (Penguin Classics, 1963).

**Diderot, Denis** (Langres 1713–Paris 1784). French thinker, publicist and man of letters. The son of a prosperous cutler in Champagne, he was originally destined for the Church, but rebelled and persuaded his father to allow him to complete his education in Paris, where he graduated in 1732. There followed a ten-year period of some obscurity: for part of it Diderot was nominally a law student, but actually led a precariously bohemian, but studious, existence, eked out with tutoring and hack writing. In the early 1740s, however, he came into contact with three contemporaries of great future significance, for himself and for the age: d' ⇨ Alembert, ⇨ Condillac and J.-J. ⇨ Rousseau. His marriage in 1743 increased the economic pressure on his pen, and he published several translations of English learned works, and also a version of Shaftesbury's *Inquiry Concerning Virtue and Merit* (*Essai sur le mérite et la vertu*, 1745) with notes which constitute his first philosophical statements. In the original works that follow (*Pensées philosophiques*, 1746; *Lettre sur les aveugles*, 1749; *De l'interprétation de la nature*, 1753), from a preoccupation with religious and moral problems which issues in atheism and determinism his ideas develop towards concern primarily with questions of sense-perception (following Locke and Condillac), and hence with the whole field of mind–body relationships. His determinist materialism leads him also into surprisingly modern speculations concerning the origins and nature of life and the diversity of living forms. During this period he also published an erotic and satirical novel in the Oriental manner then fashionable, *Les bijoux indiscrets* (1748), but from 1746 onwards he became involved in editing the ⇨ *Encyclopédie*, which was his chief occupation for twenty years.

The late 1750s saw him also launching into new spheres of literary activity. His interest in the theatre was of long standing, and discontent with current theatrical achievement, coupled with a concern (derived from his philosophical position) to make the theatre a moral substitute for the pulpit, led him to propose a new kind of play, exemplified by his *Le fils naturel* (1757) and *Le père de famille* (1758), and discussed in the essays which accompanied them (partly in *Dramatic Essays of the Neo-Classic Age*, ed. H. H. Adams and B. Hathaway, N.Y., 1950). This was the *drame bourgeois*, a genre midway between the tragedy and comedy of classical convention in that it involved characters drawn from contemporary middle-class life in serious, potentially tragic, situations. His own plays had little success on the stage, and suffer from threadbare plots, naïve characterization and an implausible moral didacticism in the dialogue, but their settings are meticulously realistic, and his ideas bore fruit in the 19th-century tradition of theatrical realism. His second venture was into the realm of art. In 1759 he wrote for Grimm's privately circulated *Correspondance littéraire* a detailed account of the Paris *salon* exhibition for that year, the first of a series of articles continuing until 1781, which may be said to inaugurate art criticism as a form of serious journalism (*Salons*, ed. J. Seznec and J. Adhémar, 1957–63: in progress).

The year 1759 brought crisis in the affairs of the *Encyclopédie* and also a turning-point in Diderot's literary development: in subsequent years his creative energies, though mature and more vigorous, seem to have gone primarily into works written for himself and posterity, and remaining unpublished during his lifetime. His boldest philosophical and scientific speculations are brilliantly summarized in a trilogy of dialogues, *Entretien entre Diderot et d'Alembert*, *Le rêve de d'Alembert*, *Suite de l'entretien* (1769, first printed 1830), and some of their implications for sexual morality explored in a Tahitian setting in the *Supplément au voyage de Bougainville* (1772, publ. 1796). His continual interest in the theatre is reflected in an important analysis of the actor's art, *Le paradoxe sur le comédien* (1773, publ. 1830; tr. W. H. Pollock, 1958), and in a lively play which is partly a self-portrait, *Est-il bon? Est-il méchant?* (1782, publ. 1834). Prose fiction, however, was the field in which Diderot finally discovered new creative scope. *La religieuse* (1760, publ. 1796; tr. F. Birrell, 1959) is less an anticlerical satire than an attack on the contemporary social abuse of 'forced vocations' and a fictional examination of the moral and psychological aberrations induced by a physically unnatural environment; the study of a Lesbian prioress which forms its climax is one of the most powerful episodes in 18th-century French literature. *Le neveu de Rameau* (1761 or later; publ. 1823, but German tr. by Goethe, 1805; tr. L. W. Tancock, *Rameau's Nephew*, Penguin Classics, 1966) is a portrait in dialogue form of a feckless but gifted parasite and his milieu, a figure who both attracts and repels Diderot and who provides opportunity for discussing such major problems in his thought as the nature of morality and the relationship between the genius and society. Finally, *Jacques le fataliste* (1773, publ. 1796), a mock-picaresque novel in the vein of *Tristram Shandy*, raises the problem of morality and destiny, but also creates a vivid personality in Jacques, and in the longest of its many digressions, 'L'Histoire de Mme de la Pommeraye', fully reveals Diderot's genius as a narrative and descriptive artist.

His later years were outwardly uneventful, apart from his visit to St Petersburg (1773–4) at the invitation of Catherine II, to whom his library passed on his death. His correspondence (now being published in full by G. Roth, Paris, 1955ff.) is remarkable chiefly for the series of vivid, discursive and self-revelatory letters to his mistress Sophie Volland. [WHB]

*Œuvres complètes*, ed. J. Assézat and M. Tourneux (20 vols., 1875–7); *Œuvres*, ed. A. Billy (Pléiade, 1951); *D., Interpreter of Nature*, tr. J. Stewart and J. Kemp (1940) (selection).

L. G. Crocker, *The Embattled Philosopher* (1955); A. M. Wilson, *D., The Testing Years* (1957) (first volume of a full-scale biography).

**Diego, Gerardo** (Santander 1896– ). Spanish poet. Best known for his anthology of contemporaries' work, *Poesía española contemporánea* (1932; rev. edns. 1934ff.). His own *Fábula de X y Z* (Mexico, 1932) – a poem in the *creacionista* style of the Chilean poet V. Huidobro – typifies his light-hearted experimental manner. Though he took part in the neo-gongorist movement, his best poetry is more conservative, e.g. poems about *Soria* (1923), a town where he taught (like Antonio ⇨ Machado, whose influence is clear). Since the Civil War his themes have been principally religious (*Angeles de Compostela*, 1940; *Alondra de verdad*, 1943) or literary (*Glosa sobre Villamediana*, 1940). A recent collection, *La suerte o la muerte* (1963), is on the subject of bull-fighting and is not impressive. [JMC]

*Primera antología* (Buenos Aires, 1941; *CA*); *Antología (1918–40)* (Salamanca, 1958); Blecua, *FLE*; Trend, *OBSV*.

Alonso, *PEC*; Vivanco, *PEC*; Zardoya, *PEC*; Cano, *PESV*.

**Dietmar von Aist** (fl. *c.* 1170). German ⇨ Minnesinger, one of the earliest known. Member of a noble family of Bavaria. His few surviving poems, like those of the ⇨ Kürenberg, belong to a tradition of love-poetry older than that derived from the Romance-inspired ideal of courtly love which reached Germany in the last decades of the 12th century, for they depict the woman pining for the love of the man, not the worship of the woman by the man. [RT]

Kraus, *MF*.

C. v. Kraus, *Des Minnesangs Frühling. Untersuchungen* (Leipzig, 1939); Ehrismann, *GDL*.

**Digenis Akrites Basileios.** A legendary hero of Byzantium, around whose life and exploits an epic saga grew during the 10th century represented by numerous Greek folk ballads and a written epic existing in four Greek and one Russian version (Greek MSS of Grotta Ferrata – the earliest – Escorial, Trebizond and Athens-Andros). As his name indicates, he was 'of two races', his mother being the daughter of a Byzantine general and his father a Saracen emir who adopted the Christian faith; as a 'soldier of the border' (Akrites) he waged war on various marauders in the eastern borders of the Byzantine empire. The written epic is mostly biographical, relating his parentage, boyhood, his various adventures and death, and is strongly flavoured with borrowings from late Hellenistic romances, such as those of Heliodoros and Achilles Tatius. It contains descriptive passages of considerable beauty, and is of historical interest for the picture it gives of conditions in remote outposts of the empire. The ballads of the Akritic cycle deal with episodes from the life of the hero, and bear very little resemblance to the written epic. The figure of Digenis has captivated the imagination of modern Greek writers and poets who treat him as a symbol of modern and medieval Hellenism and its heroic spirit. [SJP]

J. Mavrogordato, *Digenes Akrites* (Oxford, 1956).

**Diktonius, Elmer** (Helsinki 1896–Helsinki 1961). Finnish-Swedish poet and prose writer. A frustrated composer, his poetry has a new, harsh and aggressive note. His literary ancestry is composite: Nietzsche, Strindberg and Whitman are the most prominent but in no way obscure his own strong personality. The early collections, such as *Hårda sånger* (1922) and *Taggiga lågor* (1924), already show most of his qualities: the abrupt, almost explosive rhythm, the crisp imagery, the unfearing frankness, and the general radicalism, both political and otherwise; and compensating for the occasional harshness there are a number of delightful poems about children. A new maturity and a fuller range are found in *Stenkol* (1927), in some ways his most original and dynamic book of verse. Here, too, the poet's pent-up revolutionary pathos – dating back to the days of the Finnish civil war of 1918 – emerges, as also in *Stark men mörk* (1930), which, however, marks the return of a taste for experiments. His prose is on the whole less successful, its eccentricity proving less of a help than a hindrance to the flow of the narrative; but *Janne Kubik* (1932), a fragmented story about a Red soldier in the civil war, is memorable. Later collections, such as *Jordisk ömhet* (1938), *Varsel* (1942) and *Annorlunda* (1948), show a much-mellowed Diktonius seeking a new equilibrium after forsaking the revolutionary attitude of his youth. The poet's generosity and his tenderness for people, animals, and things constantly shine through and are made all the more effective by the persisting ruggedness of his verse and occasional lapses of inspiration. [SAB]

O. Enckell, *Den unge D.* (Helsinki, 1946); B. Holmqvist, 'E.D.', in *Modern finlandssvensk litteratur* (Stockholm, 1951).

**Dilthey, Wilhelm** (Biebrich 1833–Seis am Schlern 1911). German philosopher. After 1882, professor in Berlin. His attempt to study psychic life in terms of a 'totality', both as regards individual experience and as regards the past cultural experience of society, was influential also for literary scholarship. Poets he believed able to conceive new images of life's mystery and wholeness, which analytical thought only subsequently understands. Myth, literature, religious beliefs and philosophical systems he wished to make the object of a 'science of the spirit' (*Geisteswissenschaft*, which he contrasted with the methods of the natural sciences. This would transcend contemporary tendencies towards historical relativism by showing a teleologically meaningful struggle of the human spirit in every epoch to grasp ever more fully the enigma of life and of its own activity. His most important writings concerned with literature are *Das Erlebnis und die Dichtung* (1905) and *Die Weltanschauung und Analyse des Menschen seit der Renaissance und Reformation* (1913). [AKT]

*Die grosse Phantasiedichtung und andere Studien zur vergleichenden Literaturgeschichte* (1954); *Von deutscher Dichtung und Musik* (1957); *Gesammelte Schriften* (14 vols., 1957–66).

W. Heynen, *D.s Psychologie des dichterischen Schaffens* (Halle, 1916); H. A. Hodges, *The Philosophy of W.D.* (1952).

**Dinesen, Isak.** ⇨ Blixen, Karen.

**Dinis, Júlio,** pseud. of Joaquim Guilherme Gomes Coelho (Oporto 1839–Oporto 1871). Portuguese novelist. After brilliant studies at the Academia Politécnica he became a lecturer in Medicine at the Escola Médica in Oporto, though frequently absent owing to a tubercular condition which brought about his premature death. Interested more in literature than in medicine, he is chiefly remembered for his 3 great novels, *As Pupilas do Senhor Reitor* (1867), *Uma Família Inglesa* (1868) and *A Morgadinha dos Canaviais* (1868), all first serialized as *folhetins* in the *Jornal do Porto*. Representing an intermediary stage between Romanticism and Realism, his work is influenced by Anglo-Saxon literature (particularly Dickens and Thackeray) and Balzac. Dinis had made a special study of psychology and his frequent interior monologues benefit from it. Whether depicting the lives of the country priest, the Oporto English or the rural 'squirearchy', his approach is fundamentally, though not utterly, one of optimism and idealization. Disaster, ugliness and the unpleasant in people and circumstances are frequently subdued and even suppressed, and have led to charges of superficiality in spite of his profound attention to detail in other respects. Nevertheless, his attacks on dictatorial clergy and on electoral corruption in *A Morgadinha* partly serve to redress the balance. His other, lesser, works comprise a collection of rather sensational Balzacian short stories entitled *Serões da Província* (1870), an unrevised and loosely knit novel, *Os Fidalgos da Casa Mourisca* (1871–2), *Poesias* (1873–4), *Inéditos e Esparsos* (1910) and the 6 *comédias* of his *Teatro* (1946–7). [RCW]

E. Moniz, *J.D. e a sua Obra* (2 vols., 1924; 6th edn, Oporto, n.d.); H. Woischnik, *J.D. als Romandichter und Liebespsychologe* (Cologne, 1940); J. Gaspar Simões, 'J.D.', in *Perspectiva da Literatura Portuguesa do Século XIX*, i (1947).

**Ditlevsen, Tove** (Copenhagen 1918– ). Danish woman writer. She has been known since 1939 for her poetry, brilliant short stories, and novels, especially *For barnets skyld* (1941) and *Barndommens gade* (1943). [ELB]

*Digte i udvalg* (1964).

**Djalski, Ksaver Šandor,** pseud. of Ljubo Bratić (Gredice 1854–Gredice 1935). Croatian novelist and short-story writer. One of the most important 19th-century realists, he wrote of the decay of the old Croatian nobility and gradually developed into a chronicler of Croatian society of the 1880s and 1890s. His tone is often reminiscent of Turgenev, whose lyrical and elegaic undertones and objective social portraiture he shares. His first works, *Illustrissimas Batorych* and the short stories *Pod starim krovovima* (1886), are among his best. Later social novels describe events in Croatian social and political life. An aristocrat and a pessimist by nature, he turned in later life to mysticism. His works are pervaded by a sense of melancholy often relieved by humour. [EDG]

*My Neighbour Dobromir Bosiljkovic*, in *SEER*, XVIII, 252 (1939).
Barac, *HYL*.

**Djordjić, Ignjac.** ⇨ Dalmatian and Dubrovnik Literature.

**Döblin, Alfred** (Stettin 1878–Emmendingen, Baden 1957). German novelist. In Berlin a practising doctor and psychiatrist, an early collaborator on H. ⇨ Walden's ⇨ Expressionist journal *Der Sturm*, and an active Socialist; after 1933 (when his books were banned) in exile in France and (1941) the U.S.A. He wrote fiction on an epic scale, at first in a style of Expressionist outpouring, later with more subdued realism. His recurrent theme is the conflict of power and weakness, of action and passion, of the world and the spirit, developed first in tne story of a pacifist revolutionary in China (*Die drei Sprünge des Wang-Lun*, 1915), then between General and Emperor in *Wallenstein* (1920), in futuristic accounts of machinery *v.* man (*Wadzeks Kampf*, 1918; *Giganten*, rev. edn 1931), in the rival mercenary and missionary interests of the Spanish colonizers in South America in the trilogy *Das Land ohne Tod* (1936 etc.), and in the clash of reaction and illusion in the revolutionary fiasco of 1918 (*Verratenes Volk*, etc., a trilogy, 1948–50). His style came most fruitfully to grips with reality (under the influence of Joyce's *Ulysses*) in his famous novel *Berlin-Alexanderplatz* (1929; tr. E. Jolas, *Alexanderplatz*, 1931); its psychological exposure – with interior monologue etc. – of the way simple-mindedness may be subjugated into crime seems now to have prophetic political implications, as does the subtler betrayal of self in *Pardon wird nicht gegeben* (1935; tr. T. and P. Blewitt, *Men without Mercy*, 1937). In his last psychological novel, *Hamlet oder die lange Nacht nimmt ein Ende* (1956), Jung's theory of archetypes seems to have inspired the interesting relation of old legends to a modern marital crisis. *Schicksalsreise* (1949) is autobiography; Döblin was converted to Christianity in 1940–1. *Der unsterbliche Mensch* (1946) and *Unsere Sorge, der Mensch* (1948) are religious writings. [PB]

*Ausgewählte Werke*, ed. W. Muschg (1960ff.).
R. Links, *A.D.* (Berlin, 1965); Wiese, *DDM*; Friedmann and Mann, *DLZJ*.

**Dobraczyński, Jan** (Warsaw 1910– ). Polish novelist. He fought in the campaign of 1939 and in the Warsaw rising of 1944, both experiences being recorded in his autobiography (*Gra w wybijanego*, 1962). Religious themes predominate in his many novels, which are widely read and translated. The best are *Wybrańcy gwiazd* (1948) and *Listy Nikodema* (1952; tr. H. C. Stevens, *The Letters of Nicodemus*, 1958). He has also analysed the 'impassioned' quality in the Catholic thought of ⇨ Bernanos, Bloy and ⇨ Papini (cf. *Gwałtownicy*, 1957). [JP]

**Dobrolyubov, Aleksandr Mikhaylovich** (St Petersburg 1876–?). Russian poet. Though he had composed poetry since he was a boy Dobrolyubov first appeared in print in his

19th year with a collection *Natura Naturans. Natura Naturata* (1895). In this, and in his second volume, *Sobraniye stikhotvoreniy, 1895–1898* (1900), he gave evidence of a colourful and vital personality, expressing itself in Decadent terms. Some of these (Satanism, for instance) were borrowed from the French Symbolists, in whom he was exceptionally well read. The year 1898 was a turning point in his extraordinary career. He underwent a conversion, rejected the intelligentsia and its culture and withdrew to the Solovki Monastery as a novice. But the Orthodox Church, while it provided some of the imagery for his later poetry, was not to prove a haven for him. Within half a year (though he was of middle-class background) he was on the roads as a peasant pilgrim. He consorted with sectarians and preached a kind of Christian-pantheist anarchism. Eventually he founded his own sect, one of whose principles was to reject military service. His idiosyncrasy led occasionally to brief (and unjustified) confinement in mental hospitals and – in view of the obtaining laws – somewhat more justified confinement in prison. Though at first he reappeared occasionally in his old environment, he eventually vanished among the people and it is not known where and in what circumstances he died.

After his conversion Dobrolyubov was reluctant to write ('on visible paper you will never express the Principal Truth and Mystery'). Nonetheless a final collection, *Iz knigi nevidimoy* ('From the Invisible Book', 1905), was published in which he recanted the views expressed in his earlier volumes and concentrated – to a degree unusual in Russian poetry – on religious themes. He made effective use of Biblical and ecclesiastical imagery and demonstrated a genuine feeling for popular rhythms. In this collection he moved effortlessly from prose poetry to largely unrhymed, alliterative verse. The intensity and sincerity of his feelings persuade one to accept his 'folly in Christ' as more than a mask. Though he is not a major poet, he is unjustly neglected. Dobrolyubov was a powerful influence on the young ⇨ Bryusov, who acted as one of his editors. [SH]

K. Mochul'sky, *Novyy Zhurnal*, XXXII, 1953.

**Dobrolyubov, Nikolay Aleksandrovich** (Nizhny Novgorod 1836–St Petersburg 1861). Russian critic and revolutionary thinker. He opposed art-for-art's sake attitudes with his socio-utilitarian critical articles in the journal *Sovremennik*; particularly important are his interpretations of Goncharov, Turgenev and Ostrovsky.

*Sobraniye sochineniy*, ed. B. I. Bursov *et al.* (9 vols., 1961ff.); *Selected Philosophical Essays*, tr. J. Fineberg (Moscow, 1948); *Selected Criticism*, ed. R. E. Matlaw (1962) (also of Belinsky and Chernyshevsky).

**Dobrovský, Josef** (Gyarmat 1753–Brno 1829). Czech philologist. The most important representative of the first phase of the Czech national revival, he rediscovered medieval and early modern Czech literature (*Geschichte der böhmischen Sprache und Litteratur*, 1792 and 1818), codified the modern Czech literary language (*Ausführliches Lehrgebäude der böhmischen Sprache*, 1809 and 1819) and laid the foundations of comparative Slavonic philology (*Institutiones linguae slavicae dialecti veteris*, 1822). [RA]

J. Horák, *J.D., 1753–1829* (Prague, 1929); *J.D., 1753–1953* (Prague, 1953) (critical articles, with Fr. summaries).

**Doderer, Heimito von** (Weidlingen, Vienna 1896–1966). Austrian novelist. Prisoner-of-war in Siberia (1916–20), then resident in Vienna. He first became well known for his novel *Ein Mord, den jeder begeht* (1938); his major novels are *Die Strudlhofstiege* (1951) and *Die Dämonen* (1956; tr. R. and C. Winston, *The Demons*, 2 vols., 1961). Influenced by ⇨ Proust and ⇨ Musil, his work is a systematic, sometimes humorous '*recherche du temps perdu*' – the rediscovery of the virtues of pre-1914 Austria through an analysis of the country's subsequent social history. A monumental novelist, his work has been overrated; it scarcely realizes the ambitious claims which he makes for the modern novel in his *Grundlagen und Funktion des Romans* (1959). [PB]

D. Weber, *H.v.D.* (Munich, 1963); *GLL*, XI, 3, 1958; *M*, XLVII, 1955; *MLR*, LXI, 1, 1966.

**Dolitzki, Menachem Mendel** (Bialystok 1856–Los Angeles 1931). Hebrew poet and Yiddish novelist. His poetry expresses the longing for Zion and he was the best-known exponent of the aspirations of the Choveve Zion movement. In his two Hebrew novels *Ben Lebaim* (serialized in *ha-Melitz*, 1884) and *Mi-bait u-mi-Chutz* (first serialized in 1890 and published separately 1891), h depicts all the horrors of the pogroms in Tsarist Russia. [EE]

*Der gebildete merder* (Chicago, 1897); *Shtarker fun Eisen* (N.Y., 1899).
Klausner, *HMHL.*

**Domanović, Radoje** (Kragujevac 1873–Belgrade 1908). Serbian short-story writer. A savage social satirist, his stories *Vodja* (1901) and *Danga* (1901) possess something of the atmosphere of terror and hopelessness of Kafka's *Trial.* [EDG]

Barac, *HYL.*

**Domentijan.** ⇨ Serbian Medieval Literature.

**Donelaitis, K.** ⇨ Lithuanian Literature

**Doni, Anton Francesco** (Florence 1513–Monselice 1574). Italian writer. Once a priest he became a bizarre literary adventurer. A prolific and undisciplined writer of racy Florentine prose, his most successful works were the *Mondi* (Book I 1552) and the *Marmi* (1552; ed. E. Chiorboli, 1928), collections of slangy dialogues on all sorts of subjects, full of anecdotes, satire, and strange speculations (even that the world is in motion!). His once famous *Moral filosofia* (1552) is a collection of rehashed fables, each illustrating a moral precept. [DGR]

*Aretino e D., Scritti scelti*, ed. G. G. Ferrero (1951); 8 tales tr. in Roscoe, *IN*; C. Ricottini Marsini-Libelli, *A.F.D. scrittore e stampatore* (Florence, 1960).
A. Momigliano, 'La maschera del D.', in *Studi di poesia* (Bari, 1938); Croce, *PES*; *Minori*, ii.

**Donnay, Maurice** (Paris 1859–Paris 1945). French playwright. First attracted attention with a witty, topical version of Aristophanes's *Lysistrata* (1892; tr. W. A. Drake, 1929) before passing on to a succession of brittle, elegant comedies of 'society' life in Paris, deftly constructed, resembling Noel Coward. In *Georgette Lemeunier* (1898) and *Amants* (1895; tr. B. H. Clark, *Lovers,* 1917) he moves with assurance through the ambiguous world of the *fin-de-siècle* kept-woman and indulges the brand of cynical sentimentality which secured him his public and which one finds in his later successes: *La douloureuse* (1897); *L'affranchie* (1898); *Éducation de prince* (1906); and *L'autre danger* (1902), perhaps one of the most popular. His plays on contemporary problems, like the marriage of Jew and Gentile in *Le retour de Jérusalem* (1903), had a reputation for daring in their day. [SBJ]

*Théâtre* (8 vols., 1908–27).
H. Duvernois, *M.D.* (Paris, 1929).

**Dons, Aage** (Frederikssund 1903– ). Danish novelist. Best known among his many contemporary novels are *Koncerten* (1935), *Soldaterbrønden* (1938; tr. T. Shiel, *The Soldiers' Well*, 1940), and *Her mødes alle veje* (1941). His best stories are collected in *Den gule Billedbog* (1943). [ELB]

**Dostoyevsky, Fyodor Mikhaylovich** (Moscow 1821–Petersburg 1881). Russian novelist. Second son of a doctor (who in 1839 was murdered by peasants on his farm), he graduated in St Petersburg as a military engineer (1843), but soon resigned his commission and devoted himself to writing. His first novel *Bednyye lyudi* (1846; *Poor Folk*), a sentimental tale of poor and oppressed city-dwellers, was acclaimed; but *Dvoynik* (1846; *The Double*) was coolly received. Dostoyevsky thought it important enough to have it reprinted as late as 1877; it discovers through analysis of paranoia in a humble clerk that psychological duality which underlies most later characterizations, his own personality perhaps, and his religious sense of life as a spiritual battlefield.

Arrested in 1849 as a member of a socialist group led by Petrashevsky, condemned to death, even taken to execution (countermanded at the last minute), he was sentenced instead to four years' hard labour, and then to serve as a private soldier. Imprisoned at Omsk until 1854, he then served in the army at Semipalatinsk until 1858, and was allowed to return to European Russia and resume his literary career in 1859. He married Marya Isayeva in 1857, but the marriage was not happy; it was probably in Siberia that he began to suffer from epilepsy (cf. Freud's essay 'D. and Parricide', 1928).

He published in 1859 two short humorous novels, *Dyadyushkin Son* (*Uncle's Dream*) and *Selo Stepanchikovo i yego obitateli* (*The Village of Stepanchikogo*, sometimes translated as *The Friend of the Family*); in 1860–2, an impressively restrained account of his prison experiences, *Zapiski iz myortvogo doma* (*Notes from the House of the Dead*); and in 1861 a diffuse and clumsy novel *Unizhennyye i oskorblennyye* (*The Insulted and the Injured*). Living now in St Petersburg, he collaborated with his elder brother Mikhail in publishing the journals *Vremya* (1861–3) and *Epokha* (1864–5). In 1862 he visited Western Europe, and related his experiences in *Zimniye zametki o letnikh vpechatleniyakh* (*Winter Notes on Summer Impressions*, 1863), including a lurid description of London. The short novel *Zapiski iz podpolya* (1864; *Notes from Underground*) is the prelude to his mature work; its solitary hero, an embittered clerk, is a nihilist who discovers the dark, destructive under-side of man's rational and social pretences.

In 1863 Dostoyevsky underwent a harrowing affair with Polina Suslova (cf. Paulina in *The Gambler*, Nastasya in *The Idiot*, Lizaveta in *The Possessed*), with whom he travelled in Western Europe; his consumptive wife and his beloved brother and collaborator Mikhail died in 1864. In heavy debt from compulsive gambling, and with dependent relatives, he composed his first great novel, *Prestupleniye i nakazaniye* (1866; *Crime and Punishment*). Before completing it, he dictated in one month another novel, *Igrok* (1866; *The Gambler*), to fulfil an undertaking to a publisher. His stenographer, Anna Snitkina, he married in 1867; 25 years younger, practical and devoted, she brought him regularity and children. Escaping creditors by living in Germany, Italy and Switzerland (1867–71), Dostoyevsky still gambled away the little money they had; but he wrote the major novels *Idiot* (1868–9; *The Idiot*) and *Besy* (1871–2; *The Devils*, or *The Possessed*), and a short novel *Vechnyy Muzh* (1870; *The Eternal Husband*). After returning to Russia in 1871, he became famous and modestly prosperous, and enjoyed a peaceful life with his family. He expounded patriotic, nationalistic opinions in articles published as *The Diary of a Writer*, at first (1873–4) in a conservative journal that he edited, subsequently (1876–7 and briefly in 1880–1) as an independent monthly publication. In 1875 appeared the involved and obscure novel *Podrostok* (*A Raw Youth*); finally in 1879–80 his greatest: *Brat'ya Karamazovy* (*The Brothers Karamazov*). His patriotic speech at the unveiling of the Pushkin memorial in Moscow in 1880 was a triumphant conclusion to his career.

Dostoyevsky was an avid reader of English and French novels and newspapers; his own masterpieces are stories of crime and mystery, brilliantly exploiting sensational devices – suspense, surprise, climax, juxtaposed humour and horror. Not simply for effect, however; for him danger and violence belong to the irrational mystery of life. Gambling offers Alexis in *The Gambler* what murder offers Raskolnikov in *Crime and Punishment:* a demonic chance to overcome the deeply felt absurdity of society's restrictions. He was inspired by missionary urgency to write about social iniquities; he understood them not sociologically, but psychologically. The meaning of suffering was religious, initiation into the secrets of self and salvation.

Liberals then regarded Dostoyevsky as a reactionary; though widely published in the U.S.S.R., official criticism since Gor'ky has been stern. And indeed he exposes the spiritual nihilism in revolutionary thought; shows the radical Raskolnikov what 'being above moral convention' means in the case of his decadent counterpart, Svidrigaylov; repeats the lesson for the profoundly modern intellectual, Ivan Karamazov, whose knowledge becomes murderous in the proletarian hands of Smerdyakov. And in *The Possessed* above all he analyses almost pathologically the evil mechanism of a revolutionary 'cell'. His most celebrated discussion of power and totalitarianism occurs in 'The Legend of the Grand Inquisitor' (*Karamazov*). In contrast to his dangerous supermen, he tried 'to depict a positively good man', notably in Prince Myshkin, the 'Idiot', the epileptic saint whose simplicity of heart is powerless to withstand the real destructiveness of the world's passions. But against Sonya (in *Crime and Punishment*) and Alyosha Karamazov, radiant in their Christian love and suffering, hell does not prevail. Dostoyevsky's construction and style are congested, even feverish, but if conventional realism seems clumsily, impatiently distorted, the emotional reality of his new vision is inescapable. [AKT]

*Sobraniye sochineniy*, ed. L. P. Grossman *et al.* (10 vols., 1956); tr. C. Garnett (12 vols., 1912–20); tr. D. Magarshack, *Crime and Punishment* (1951), *The Idiot* (1955), *The Devils* (1953), *The Brothers Karamazov* (1958) (all 4 in Penguin Classics); tr. J. Coulson, *Notes from the House of the Dead* (1956); tr. K. Fitzlyon, *Winter Notes on Summer Impressions* (1955).

K. Mochul'sky, *D.* (Princeton, 1967); E. H. Carr *D.* (1931, revised 1962); E. J. Simmons, *D* (1950); V. Seduro, *D. in Russian Literary Criticism* (1957); A. Yarmolinsky, *D.* (1957); J

Coulson, *D. A Self-portrait* (1962); R. Hingley, *The Undiscovered D.* (1962); *D.*, ed. René Wellek (*20th Century Views*, 16, 1962) (contains essays by Freud, D. H. Lawrence, Georg Lukács, *et al.*).

**Douwes Dekker, Eduard,** pseud. Multatuli (Amsterdam 1820–Nieder-Ingelheim 1887). Dutch author. Son of a ship's captain; an erratic genius, his revolutionary prose works appeared under the characteristic pseudonym of Multatuli ('I have suffered much'). His quixotic temperament, even as a boy, was ill-suited to sustained effort, and his first job, in an office, was no more successful than his school career. So he went to the East Indies in the Colonial Service. He made rapid progress, but was temporarily suspended because of his failure to account for funds. His enforced leisure enabled him to cast some of his dreams into writing. *Losse bladen uit het dagboek van een oud man* (1841, 1843–4) is a solipsistic extravaganza which confuses the will to greatness with greatness itself, though finding in self-sacrifice the mark of the hero. In 1846 he married Everdine van Wijnbergen, 'Tine' in his writings, was reinstated, and after a wild, spendthrift leave returned to the post of Assistant Resident of Lebak. With his hot-headed and overweening manner he soon crossed his superiors, who called for his resignation. Leaving his wife and small son behind, he returned home where, beleaguered by creditors and driven by righteous indignation, he wrote his masterpiece, *Max Havelaar* (1860; tr. R. Edwards, 1967), a self-justifying attack on the tyranny of Colonial commercial attitudes. Though the book caused a furore, it did not bring the writer the power he sought, despite the effective image of Max Havelaar (Douwes Dekker), the enlightened despot and champion of the exploited natives against the mentality of his smug, blind, lethargic and hypocritical countrymen.

The conflict between dream and reality then became an obsession. The passionate disillusionment of a neglected genius raved wildly against the anathemas of his perfectionism, or indulged in excesses of self-pity as in *Minnebrieven* (1861), an imaginary correspondence between Multatuli, Tine and Fancy (the Psyche-ideal inspired by an admiring niece). The remainder of his work, the most important of which is contained in random epigrams, comments, essays and anecdotes, published (to relieve his poverty) as his *Ideën* (1862–77), is highly individualistic and iconoclastic on the one hand and romantically quixotic on the other. In *Woutertje Pieterse* (collected from *Ideën* and ed. G. Stuiveling, 1950; tr. H. Evans, 1904), a romantic social satire inspired by Multatuli's own childhood, the young Wouter is 'a Faust, a Don Quixote in spirit'. Douwes Dekker's unorthodoxy made him the centre of heated controversy, not least for his attempt to put the triangular relationship of *Minnebrieven* into practice with Mini Hamminck-Schepel, whom he eventually married. At all events he broke the 'whispering quietude of Dutch literature' and was the precursor of the literary revival of 1880. [PK]

*Volledige Werken*, ed. G. Stuiveling (12 vols., 1950ff.); *Indonesia: Once More Free Labor*, tr. N. Steelink (1948); Barnouw, *CA*; *Delta* (Winter 1960/1).

J. and A. Romein, in *Erflaters van onze beschaving*, iv (1940); *100 Jaar Max Havelaar* (Rotterdam, 1962) (essays); A. L. Sötermann, *De structuur van 'Max Havelaar'* (Utrecht, 1966).

**Dovizi, Bernardo (Il Bibbiena)** (Bibbiena 1470–Rome 1520). Italian man of letters. A protégé of Leo X, a cardinal, and a patron of Raphael. Apart from historically valuable letters, he is remembered for the comedy *La Calandria* first performed at Urbino in 1513. Deriving from Plautus, and with the gullible old husband Calandro owing something to Boccaccio's Calandrino, the play acquires its impetus from the confusion caused when a twin brother and sister disguise themselves as members of the opposite sex. Despite repetitiveness of incident and lack of any deep penetration, the vigorous prose still keeps interest alive. [DGR]

*Commedie del Cinquecento*, ed. A. Borlenghi (1959); *Epistolario*, ed. G. L. Moncallero (2 vols., 1955–65); *The Follies of Calandro*, tr. O. Evans, in *The Genius of the Italian Theatre*, ed. E. Bentley (1964).

G. L. Moncallero, *Il Cardinale B.D. da B.* (Florence, 1953); M. T. Herrick, *Italian Comedy in the Renaissance* (Urbana, 1960).

**Drachmann, Holger** (Copenhagen 1846–Hornbæk 1908). Danish poet and novelist. Originally a painter and always a wanderer, of restless temperament and colourful individuality, he was by turns a socialist (from meeting dockworkers and escaped French *communardes* in London, 1871), a radical and realist disciple of G. ⇨ Brandes, a traditionalist praising marriage and home, a neo-romantic fairy-tale playwright, a bohemian poet inspired by a music-hall singer. His love lyrics and sea poems best express his volatile genius, though many works reflect the tensions of his many-sided experience, e.g. the novel *Forskrevet* (1890). English translations exist of *Smaa Fortællinger* (*The Cruise of the 'Wild Duck', and Other Stories*, tr. H.C.M., 1891); *Paul og Virginie under nordlig Bredde* (tr. F. E. Browne, *Paul and Virginia of a Northern Zone*, Chicago, 1895, and by F. E. Browne, as *Nana: A Story of Danish Love*, Chicago, 1901); the poem *Robert Burns* (tr. J. C. Bay, Holstebro, 1925) and the melodrama *Renæssance* (tr. L. M. Hollander, *Renaissance*, in *Poet-Lore*, No. 4, Boston, 1908). [ELB]

P. V. Rubow, *H.D.* (3 vols., Copenhagen, 1940–50).

**Dracontius, Blossius Aemilius** (fl. late 5th cent.). Christian Latin poet of Carthage, where he was a lawyer. Imprisoned during the Vandal invasion, he wrote a Biblical epico-didactic poem, *De laudibus Dei* (on the same theme as Milton's *Paradise Lost* and *Paradise Regained*). He bases his style on Virgil and Ovid and illustrates his theme not only from the Bible but from classical history and legend. He is supposed to have migrated later to northern Italy and to be the author also of some rhetorical hexameter verses on classical subjects and an *Orestis tragoedia*. [FB]

Migne, *PL*, 60; *Carmina*, ed. F. Vollmer (MGH, AA, XIV, 1905).

S. Gambier, *Le livre de la Genèse dans le poésie latine au cinquième siècle* (Paris, 1899); Duckett, *LW*.

**Drda, Jan** (Příbram 1915–Dobříš 1970). Czech novelist and dramatist. Steeped in the tradition of the Czech countryside and its people, he began as a simple storyteller (*Městečko na dlani*, 1940) but later, as a convinced Communist, played a leading role in establishing the prose of the new socialist reality. His short stories in *Němá barikáda* (1946) are a tribute to the heroism of the simple Czech people facing Nazism. His plays are marked by optimism, humour and popular flavour. An anxious regard for ideology had a detrimental effect on his talent. He opposed the 1968 invasion.

*Krásná Tortiza* (1952); *Hrátky s čertem* (1946); *Dalskabáty – hříšná ves* (1959).

F. Buriánek, *Současná česká literatura* (Prague, 1960).

**Drenova, A. S.** ⇨ Albanian Literature.

**Drezen, Youenn.** ⇨ Breton Literature.

**Drieu la Rochelle, Pierre** (Paris 1893–Paris 1945). French novelist, short-story writer and literary and political journalist and essayist. Fought in the First World War, and later remembered it both with horror and yet with nostalgia for its demands of manliness, loyalty and authority (see the war-poems of *Interrogation*, 1917, and *Fond de Cantine*, 1920; and the short stories, *La comédie de Charleroi*, 1934). He was deeply disturbed by the aftermath of political futility, moral disarray and desperate hedonism in which his own instability, *snobisme* and tormented sexuality all too closely involved him. A great admirer of ⇨ Barrès, deeply and permanently influenced by Nietzsche, he was obsessed by the idea of decadence. Thus, in *Mesure de la France* (1922), he patriotically condemns his fellow-countrymen for France's declining birth-rate, and for thus endangering her position in the modern world, which she could still retain if she were true to herself. However, his best works are undoubtedly the novels and short stories, often autobiographical, in which he depicts, with incisive vigour, if not without secret complicity, the general moral malaise of the French bourgeoisie (*Plainte contre inconnu*, 1924; *L'homme couvert de femmes*, 1925; *Le feu follet*, 1931; *Journal d'un homme trompé*, 1934; *Rêveuse bourgeoisie*, 1937, repr. 1960; *Gilles*, 1939, repr. 1962; *Récit secret, Journal, 1944–1945, Exorde,* (all three repr. in one vol., 1960). The flabby rottenness of politics under the declining Third Republic drove him in the mid 1930s into Doriot's national socialist Parti Populaire Français. Under the German occupation, he became editor of the *Nouvelle Revue Française* and in 1945, too proud to submit to the frequently unscrupulous settling of accounts that accompanied the end of the Second World War in France, he killed himself. His personal involvement in central political and moral problems of his age, his lack of cant, his penetrating intellect, the energy and accuracy of his writing and, indeed, his very human weaknesses make him the outstanding 'representative man' of the period between the wars and one of its important and prophetic writers. [DP]

*Mémoires de Dirk Raspe* (1966).

F. Grover, *D. la R.* (Paris, 1962).

**Drost, Aarnout** (Amsterdam 1810–Amsterdam 1834). Dutch author. The early promise of his journal *De Muzen* (1834) was confirmed by his historical novel, *Hermingard van de Eikenterpen* (1832). His remarkable talent and his evangelical romanticism were admired by ⇨ Potgieter and Bakhuizen, who completed and published his *Schetsen en verhalen* (1835). [PK]

**Droste-Hülshoff, Annette von** (Hülshoff 1797–Meersburg, Bodensee 1848). German poetess and novelist. Of aristocratic Westphalian descent, she lived a lonely, pious life on the family estate. Almost predictably, her eye was for the small-scale, the detached. She is the poet of the exquisite and the intimate, whether in verse or in prose. A collection of her poems was published in 1844, others appeared posthumously. Her most striking work is the prose idyll *Die Judenbuche* (1837–41; tr. L. Thomas, 1958), which blends natural description with moral vision and a powerful sense of supernatural forces. [RT]

*Sämtliche Werke*, ed. V. K. Shulte-Kemminghansen (1925ff.); *Poems*, ed. M. E. Atkinson (London, 1964).

C. Heselhaus, *A. v. D.-H.* (Halle, 1943); E. Staiger, *A. v. D.-H.* (Zürich, 1962); M. Mare, *A. v. D.-H.* (1965); Natan, *GML*.

**Druon, Maurice** (Paris 1918– ). French novelist. During the war he broadcast for the B.B.C. and was later a war correspondent. His first works, closely reflecting his war-time experiences, a volume of essays *Lettres d'un Européen* (1944) and a novel *La dernière brigade* (1946; tr. H. Hare, *The Last Detachment*, 1957), had little success. But *Les grandes familles* (Prix Goncourt, 1948; tr. E. Fitzgerald, *The Rise of Simon Lachaume*, 1952) established his reputation. The first of three novels forming the family cycle *La fin des hommes* (completed 1951; tr. H. Hare, *The Curtain Falls*, 1952–9), it deals with the decadence and corruption of the upper classes in the inter-war period, gradually dragging France to disaster. After two shorter novels, Druon undertook his most ambitious project to date: written with the help of a historian, two novelists and a scriptwriter, *Les rois maudits* (1955.f.; tr. H. Hare, *The Accursed Kings*, 1956.f) is a gaudy, multi-volume historical romance. He has also written a biography of *Alexander the Great* (1958; tr. H. Hare, 1960) and three plays, *Mégarée* (1942), *Un voyageur* (1953) and *La contessa* (1962). [IHW]

Criticus (M. Berger), *Le style au microscope*, ii (Paris, 1951); *Cahiers des Saisons*, 14 (1958–9); *Yale Review*, XLV, 4 (1956).

**Druyanov, Alter,** pseud. Abgad Haedrey (Vilna 1870–Palestine 1938). Hebrew essayist, historian, folklorist and editor. His greatest literary achievement is in the field of Jewish folklore and his introductory essay to his *Sefer Habedichot ve-Hachidud* (repr. Tel Aviv, 1964) is a fundamental work of Jewish humour. [EE]

Waxman, *HJL*.

**Druzhina-Osor'in, Callistratus.** ⇨ Russian Literature of the 17th Century.

**Držić, Djore** and **Marin.** ⇨ Dalmatian and Dubrovnik Literature.

**Duarte, Dom** (Lisbon 1391–Tomar 1438). King of Portugal (1433) and distinguished man of letters. He was the eldest son of John I and Philippa of Lancaster, the patron of Fernão ⇨ Lopes and the possessor of a library of more than eighty codices.

The accession of a bastard dynasty seems to have demanded self-justification, and called forth an almost exacerbated sense of responsibility. His own major work, the *Leal Conselheiro* was written for the gentlemen of his court, and takes the form of a meditation upon the virtues and vices, because for him the problems of government were essentially problems of conscience. Concern for the commonwealth is the inspiration of the work. The king's whole duty is towards his people, and his life must be to them exemplary. The *Leal Conselheiro* is a definition of moral standards for the monarch and his peers, because Duarte had a Confucian sense of the importance of example.

For a modern reader perhaps the greatest interest of the book lies in Duarte's reflexions based on his own observations and personal experience. He notes himself that these are often of more value than lessons extracted from books. Written into the *Leal Conselheiro* by this lover of reason and the moderating powers of the intelligence are a series of essays on the passions which make of Duarte a precursor of Montaigne and Descartes – on benevolence, love and friendship ('the desire to be loved does not arise in the case of friends, because they always think they are'); on pointless activity; on the value of outdoor exercise; a famous disquisition on the nature of *saudade*; on vain fancies; on mental attitudes ('it is better to doubt than to decide unreasonably'); on the history of his own neurasthenia. And the remedies he offers for the mental ills he describes are exercise, attentive reading and of course the practice of religion.

Duarte claimed that he paid more attention to the substance of his book than to its style, but for the feelings he is the first to describe in Portuguese he had largely to invent a new language, a language full of neologisms, its syntax naturally based on that of Latin, though he himself decried the excessive use of latinisms.

Duarte also wrote a treatise on riding: *Livro da ensinança de bem cavalgar toda sela.* [ARM]

*Leal Conselheiro*, ed. H. Cidade (Lisbon, n.d.).

**Du Bartas, Guillaume de Salluste, Seigneur** (Montfort 1544–Coudon 1590). French poet. Born of a prosperous family, he served Henri de Navarre at court and as ambassador to James VI of Scotland, who regarded his poetry highly and had published a translation of his *L'Uranie* in 1584. A convinced Huguenot, but free from fanaticism, he was read equally by Catholic and Protestant and achieved immense success, thanks to the edifying and didactic nature of his poems. His early work consists of vast moral epics, *Judith*, *L'Uranie*, *Le triomphe de la foi* and some lyrics, but the work that won him a reputation rivalling Ronsard's was *La semaine ou la Création du monde* (1578; ed. M. Braspart, with intr. in *D.B. poète chrétien*, 1947), an epic account, in alexandrine couplets, of the seven days of the creation. His classical learning and his strong Protestant faith inspires him with eloquence, as in the opening of the seventh canto so much admired by Goethe, but stylistic lapses (bathos, encyclopedic pedantry, an excessive adoption of Ronsard's ideas on neologisms and imitative harmony) caused him to fall from favour in the next century. Translations into foreign languages, by avoiding these stylistic features, assured him a European success. Sir Philip Sidney began a translation, but it was Joshua Sylvester's version, *Divine Weekes and Workes* (1608), which seems to have influenced Milton. The *Seconde semaine* (1584–1603; ed. M. Braspart, op. cit.), intended to take the story of man from the Garden of Eden, was never completed: the faults here are perhaps more obvious than in the first *Semaine.* [FWAG]

*Œuvres*, ed. U. T. Holmes, J. C. Lyons and R. W. Linker (3 vols., 1935–40); *La Semaine* in *ZRP*, 107 (1963); Mourgues, *MBPP*.
K. Reichenberger, *D.B. und sein Schöpfungsepos* (Munich, 1962).

**Du Bellay, Joachim** (Liré, Anjou 1522–Paris 1560). French poet. Son of a noble family, he studied law at Poitiers, where he began writing poetry and where, it is said, he met Ronsard. They recognized each other as kindred spirits and Du Bellay went to Paris to study with Ronsard and Baïf under the humanist Dorat at the Collège de Coqueret and to plan the reform of French poetry. In 1549 he published the *Défense et illustration de la langue française*, the manifesto of the ⇨ Pléiade, and a collection of verse, the *Olive*, the *Antérotique* and 13 odes. The *Olive*, a bookish but brilliant work of Petrarchan inspiration, was instrumental in acclimatizing the sonnet in France. Encouraged by Madame Marguerite, Henri II's sister, he dedicated a *Recueil de poésie* to her later in the same year; its 'official' poems are mostly dull works, but *À Madame Marguerite* gives a verse statement of some ideas of the *Défense*. Harassed by illness and deafness, Du Bellay accompanied his cousin, the Cardinal Jean du Bellay, to Rome on a mission which kept him in 'exile' for four years, leaving behind friends and doctrine. Out of the melancholy he felt before the ruins of the ancient city he created the *Antiquités de Rome* (1558), the first of his great sonnet sequences, while his increasing disillusion with the life of modern Rome and his homesickness for his beloved France (especially the Anjou) result in the even finer satirical-elegiac collection, *Regrets* (1558). The last two works show the abandonment of past theories (already in *À une Dame* he had renounced Petrarchism) and the adoption of a simpler, more direct style in recounting his personal emotions. In 1558 he also published his Latin *Poemata*, which, like the *Regrets*, are a kind of intimate journal and deal with the poet's love for Faustina, and the *Divers jeux rustiques*, containing peasant *chansons*, among them the *D'un vanneur de blé aux vents* imitated from the Latin poem of

Naugerius (or Navagero), and the satirical *Poète courtisan*. In 1557 he left Rome for France, but his last years were clouded by troubles, both domestic and official. Spenser translated some of du Bellay's sonnets as *Visions of Bellay*, 1569 (republished in *Complaints*), and the *Antiquités* as *Ruins of Rome*. [FWAG]

*Œuvres poétiques*, ed. H. Chamard (6 vols., 1907–31).

H. Chamard, *J. du B.* (Lille, 1900); V. L. Saulnier, *Du B.: l'homme et l'œuvre* (Paris, 1951); J. Vianey, *Les Regrets de J. du B.* (Paris, 1930); G. Dickinson, *Du B. in Rome* (Leyden, 1960).

**Dubillard, Roland** (Paris 1923– ). French playwright. His theatre tends to eschew plot and conventional dramatic effects in favour of a deliberate and stylized use of conversational banality, intended to suggest our human solitude and failure to communicate. His 'operetta for the spoken voice', *Si Camille me voyait* (1953) was followed by *Naïves hirondelles* (1961), a touching and poetic study of the break-up of friendship, and *La maison d'os* (1962), which explores the dying of a lonely, rich old man. He has also written a radio-play, *Le père*. [SBJ]

Corvin, *TNF*; Serreau, *HNT*.

**Du Bos, Charles.** ⇨ French Literary Criticism in the 19th and 20th Centuries.

**Dučić, Jovan** (Trebinje 1871–Gary, Indiana 1943). Serbian poet. Influenced at first by ⇨ Ilić, he spent several years in Paris (*c.* 1900) where he was deeply influenced by French poetry, especially ⇨ Symbolism. Throughout his career in the diplomatic service he wrote poetry with a perfection of form unknown in Serbian. He has, rightly, been criticized as a writer of limited scope and a representative of Art for Art's Sake, but in such poems as 'Jablanovi', 'Dubrovacki madrigal' and 'Dubrovacki poklisar' he achieves a deep lyrical sincerity and a subtle perceptive humour. In bringing the colour and chiselled form of French poetry to Serbian, a certain stiffness was perhaps unavoidable, but his best poems are among the finest in Serbo-Croat: *Jadranski soneti* (1898–1906), *Carski soneti* (in praise of Serbia) and the prose poems, *Pesme i prozi* (1902). He emigrated in 1941 to the U.S.A. [EDG]

*Sobrana djela* (7 vols., 1929); Ibrovac, *APY*; Lavrin, *AMYP*.

Barac, *HYL*; Kadić, *CSL*.

**Duclos, Charles Pinot** (Dinan 1704–Paris 1772). French moralist, historian and novelist. Of prosperous Breton middle-class origins, he entered Paris literary society as a young man, and won a reputation as a wit. His two early novels are now of little interest, but his major work is *Considérations sur les mœurs de ce siècle* (1750), a polished and shrewd, if somewhat abstract, moral analysis of French society from a humanely rationalist standpoint. He also published several historical works. He succeeded Voltaire as Royal Historiographer in 1750, and became permanent secretary of the Académie Française in 1755. [WHB]

*Œuvres complètes* (1855); *Considérations sur les mœurs*, ed. and intr. F. C. Green (Cambridge, 1939).

**Dudintsev, Vladimir Dmitriyevich** (Kupyansk, Ukraine 1918– ). Russian novelist, author of one of the principal works of the ⇨ Thaw, *Ne khlebom yedinym* (1956; tr. E. Bone, *Not By Bread Alone*, 1957), an account of the struggle of a talented engineer against bureaucracy, careerism and victimization. The hero is eventually vindicated, but the vices he attacks continue to flourish. In 1957 he was publicly reprimanded by Khrushchev for this work. [RDBT]

*Rasskazy* (1963).

Swayze, *PCL*; *Oktyabr'*, 12, 1956.

**Du Guillet, Pernette** (Lyons 1520?–Lyons 1545). French poetess. A friend of Scève (perhaps inspiring his *Délie*). Her poetic output is small but varied, ranging from rather austere imitations of ⇨ Scève to inconsequential '*coq à l'âne*' pieces. Many of the poems are melancholy in tone, and among the best are those expressing wistful longing. She often uses Platonic terminology and in this she is typical of the Lyons poets; she also uses Petrarchan images and antitheses, but she handles both these conventions with a delicate wit. [GJ]

*Rimes* (1545); Schmidt, *PSS*.

**Duhamel, Georges** (Paris 1884–1966). French novelist. The son of a doctor, he himself qualified as a doctor in 1909. His contacts with the 'unanimists' before the First World War developed his ideas on fraternity and social responsibility. He served as a front-line surgeon and his intense compassion for his fellow-men is reflected in two vivid war books (*Vie des martyrs*, 1917; tr. F. Simmonds, *The New Book of Martyrs*, 1918; *Civilisation*, 1918; tr. T. Conwil-Evans, 1919). His literary career began after 1918; he wrote many novels, essays, memoirs and books for and about children. An agnostic, he bases his view of life on humane values, and stresses the need for men to show understanding, tolerance and moderation in their dealings with others. He is much concerned with the problem of individual freedom in the modern world, and voices doubts about the value of the material progress achieved in the present century. His fame rests mainly on his two large novel cycles (the so-called *roman-fleuve*). In *Vie et Aventures de Salavin* (1930–2; tr. G. Billings, 1936), the title character reflects dramatically the dilemma of the ordinary man in the 20th century, who seeks salvation outside religion, who is weak, even ridiculous, but always appealing, because his intentions are worthy and because he remains aware of his potential, though unattainable, nobility of purpose and action. In the second cycle, the *Chronique des Pasquier* (1933–41; tr. B. de Holthoir, *The Pasquier Chronicles*, 1937–46) traces the development of a middle-class family between 1880 and 1920. Centred on Laurent Pasquier, who becomes a doctor, the novels reflect many of the social and philosophical issues of the period (e.g. the connexion between science and humanism). Duhamel's gifts of humour, sympathy for his characters and keen psychological observation are here very apparent. He was elected to the Académie Française in 1935. [CAB]

C. Santelli, *D., l'homme et l'œuvre* (Paris, 1947); W. Falls, *Le message humain de D.* (Paris, 1948); A. Terrisse, *D., éducateur* (Paris, 1951).

**Dumas, Alexandre** (père) (Villers-Cotterêts 1802–Puys, Dieppe 1870). French novelist and playwright. He was the grandson of the marquis Antoine-Alexandre Davy de la Pailleterie and a negress, Marie Dumas. His father took the name of Dumas, fought in the revolutionary armies, became a general and died in 1806. Dumas was brought up in poor circumstances and had little education. He found employment in the household of the future Louis-Philippe in 1822 and entrance into the *cénacle* of Charles ⇨ Nodier. He had started on a voracious process of self-education, reading Shakespeare, Scott and Schiller and soon began to write. The production of his *Henri III et sa cour* at the Théâtre Français in 1829 began twenty years of successful playwriting. It was followed by *Antony* (1831), and *La Tour de Nesle* (1832), a grisly melodrama about the debauches of Marguerite de Bourgogne and her sisters-in-law. His other plays include *Charles VII chez ses grands vassaux* (1831), *Don Juan de Marana* (1836), *Kean* (1836), *Mademoiselle de Belle-Isle* (1839), *Un Mariage sous Louis XV* (1841) and *Les Demoiselles de Saint-Cyr* (1843). In 1839 he began to devote his tremendous energies to writing historical novels, often using collaborators such as Auguste Maquet to suggest plots or historical backgrounds which would suit his talents. 'L'action et l'amour' were the staple of his novels, both treated with immense gusto and historical liberty. His most successful novel, *Le Comte de Monte-Cristo* (1844–5; tr. anon. *The Count of Monte Cristo*, Everyman, 1906), describes the return of Edmond Dantès, a Marseillais sailor, after years of wrongful imprisonment, as the fabulously rich and mysterious Count of Monte Cristo and his vengeance upon the villains who betrayed him in his youth. The exploits of the four famous musketeers, D'Artagnan, Athos, Porthos and Aramis are chronicled in three novels, *Les Trois Mousquetaires* (1844; tr. anon. *The Three Musketeers*, Everyman), *Vingt ans après* (1845) and *Le vicomte de Bragelonne* (1848–50). His other historical novels cover the period of the Wars of Religion in France (*La Reine Margot*, 1845, *La Dame de Monsoreau*, 1846); another long series, set before and during the Revolution, exploit the intrigues of Cagliostro and the Diamond Necklace affair (*Le collier de la reine*, 1850). Dumas wrote many of these novels for the newspapers as *romans-feuilleton* often in daily instalments. His unbelievable extravagance meant that he was constantly in debt and thus constantly forced to earn more by his pen. He also wrote numerous travel books, including a description of a journey to Russia, an enchanting description of his many pets, together with children's stories, *Histoire de mes bêtes* (1868), and a *Grand dictionnaire de cuisine* (1873). His *Mémoires* (tr. A. C. Bell, 1961) describe most amusingly his early life, his entry into Paris literary circles and the 1830 Revolution. [WA]

*Œuvres complètes* (286 vols., 1848–1900); *Théâtre complet* (15 vols., 1863–74).

J. Charpentier, *A.D.* (Paris, 1947); A. C. Bell, *A.D.* (1950); R. Gaillard, *A.D.* (1953); H. Clouard, *A.D.* (1955); A. Maurois, *Les Trois D.* (1957); L. Thoorens, *La vie passionnée d'A.D.* (1957).

**Dumas, Alexandre (fils)** (Paris 1824–Paris 1895). French dramatist. Natural son of Alexandre ⇨ Dumas. The circumstances of his own birth and upbringing made him an impassioned moralizer, obsessed with the problems of illegitimacy, adultery and prostitution. His early plays reflect these concerns without being hag-ridden by them. Such are: *La dame aux camélias* (1852; tr. E. Gosse, *Camille*, 1934) where the doomed passion of Marguerite Gautier a Second Empire courtesan, for Armand Duval, the son of a respectable family, achieves the status of a modern myth and contrives to touch us still, in spite of strained rhetoric and threadbare conventions; *Diane de Lys* (1853), a tedious and artificial melodrama of illicit love; *Le demi-monde* (1855; tr. B. H. Clark, *The Outer Edge of Society*, 1921), a sharp defence of society against the machinations of a gifted 'fallen woman'; *La question d'argent* (1857), where, in a manner foreshadowing Galsworthy's, that representative period figure, the shady financier, is repudiated by respectable society. There follow a series of more overtly didactic dramas in which the tone becomes increasingly portentous. Chief among these are: *Le fils naturel* (1858), a complicated intrigue about illegitimacy which titillated the contemporary audience by its obvious references to the author's own life; *L'ami des femmes* (1864), in which a curiously ambivalent de Ryons acts as director of conscience to erring Jane de Simerose and reconciles her with her neglectful husband; and *Les idées de Madame Aubray* (1867), an edifying study of charity in which a 'fallen woman' is redeemed and restored to society. Dumas's later plays bring a cloudy symbolism to bear on his familiar theses. This is the case with *La femme de Claude* (1873), in which Claude, representing morality and conscience, kills his wife Césarine, the Beast who symbolizes the adultress undermining French society. In much the same way, *L'étrangère* (1876), a melodramatic farrago involving a dissolute aristocrat, an intercepted love-letter and a duel, represents evil man in terms of a clinical symbolism about cancers in the body. Dumas's didactic passion easily slips out of control, but his stage-craft is often skilful and his plays have a good deal of movement and suspense, though the clinching dénouements are sometimes too crudely explicit. [SBJ]

*Théâtre complet* (10 vols., 1868–92).

F. A. Taylor, *The Theatre of A.D. fils* (1937); P. Lamy, *Le théâtre d'A.D. fils* (Paris, 1928); L. Lacour, *Trois théâtres: E. Augier, A.D. fils, V. Sardou* (Paris, 1880); M. d'Hartoy, *D. fils inconnu* (Paris, 1964).

**Duras, Marguerite** (Indochina 1914–    ). French novelist. At 18 she came from Indochina to Paris where she studied maths, law and political sciences at university. Time, the richness of its 'duration' containing both the natural maturation of events and boredom and decay, is at the heart of her fiction, and this duality is most apparent in love and passion. She explores extreme reactions of passivity and revolt. Conversation – used to great effect in the chance encounter of *Le square* (1955; tr. S. Pitt-Rivers and I. Morduch, 1959) – is a 'parallel' activity beside the fullness of developing relationships which are intuitively understood. In *La vie tranquille* (1944) Françou wilfully breaks the passivity of her family, but her marriage is the fruition of events to which she resigns herself. Similarly the old woman's stubborn struggle against nature, *Un barrage contre le Pacifique* (1950; tr. A. White, *A Sea of Troubles*, 1953), contrasts with her children's desire to leave their concession, a negation of present reality; *L'après-midi de M. Andesmas* shows the oppressive duration of the long wait for an expected visitor. The eventual acceptance of an existent love frees Anna from her quest for the ideal, *Le marin de Gibraltar* (1952). The difficulties of daily life together for married couples in *Les petits chevaux de Tarquinia* (1953; tr. P. DuBerg, *The Little Horses of Tarquinia*, 1960), the slow revelation of a latent passion in *Moderato cantabile* (1958), and the inevitable consummation of love in *10.30 du soir en été* (1960; tr. A. Borchardt, *10.30 on a Summer Night*, 1962) are explored in the fullness of their temporal evolution. Similar themes are developed in *Le ravissement de Lol V. Stein* (1964), *Le vice-consul* (1966) and *L'amante anglaise* (1967). [RGV]

Y. Berger, *M.D.* (Paris 1960); *Archives des Lettres Modernes*, 47 (1963); *Cahiers Renaud-Barrault*, 52, December 1965.

**D'Urfé, Honoré** (Marseilles 1567–Villefranche 1625). French author. He was involved in the Wars of Religion, fighting for the dying Ligue against the Crown forces. His masterpiece, *L'Astrée*, is set in the region he thus knew so well, the Forez, lying between Lyons and Clermont. Well read in Renaissance literature, he achieved a pastoral in imitation of ⇨ Sannazaro and ⇨ Montemayor which has surpassed both of them in popularity. *L'Astrée* has been called the first great French novel; its hero Céladon has become a symbol of the constant lover; its style and realism saved it from the mediocrity of most pastorals. La Fontaine and Rousseau confessed themselves its lifelong admirers. [WGM]

M. Magendie, *Du nouveau sur l'Astrée* (Paris, 1927).

**Dürrenmatt, Friedrich** (Konolfingen, Bern 1921– ). Swiss dramatist, novelist and critic. For a time a graphic artist, then theatre-critic for the Zürich weekly *Die Weltwoche*, he is now, with Max ⇨ Frisch, the most celebrated German-language dramatist of his generation. From his first extravagantly experimental tragi-comedy *Es steht geschrieben* (1947), he has continued to play with sensational stage effects, having a preference for parody and cabaret changes of mood. His unhistorical *Romulus der Grosse* (1949; rev. 1957) is again a 'comic' tragedy, while the grotesque 'comedy' *Die Ehe des Herrn Mississippi* (1952; rev. 1957) is violently incoherent, a kind of surrealistic skit on the breakdown of bourgeois values, underlined (or distorted?) by the deliberate formlessness of the play. The phantasmagoria *Ein Engel kommt nach Babylon* (1953; rev. 1957) was followed by the successful 'tragic comedy' *Der Besuch der alten Dame* (1956; tr. P. Bowles, *The Visit*, 1962), in which the grotesque revenge of a rich old woman exposes the money-worship and sham civic ideals of her native town in a garish satirical light. In *Die Physiker* (1962; tr. J. Kirkup, *The Physicists*, 1963), another bitterly grotesque tragi-comedy which ends with the world in the hands of a madman, the satire does not illumine at all profoundly the problem of moral responsibility in science to which it points. Dürrenmatt justifies his dramatic technique (in the essay *Theaterprobleme*, 1955), as being the only one valid for this apocalyptically absurd age. His clever use of theatrical situations and effects rarely disguises, however, their imaginative weakness. He has also written radio-plays, *Gesammelte Hörspiele* (1961; see especially *A Dangerous Game*, tr. R. and C. Winston, 1960), Kafkaesque short stories, *Die Stadt. Prosa I–IV* (1952), the paradoxically contrived detective novels *Der Richter und sein Henker* (1950; tr. C. Brooks, *The Judge and His Hangman*, 1954), *Der Verdacht* (1951), and *Das Versprechen* (1958; tr. R. and C. Winston, *The Pledge*, 1959). [PB]

*Komödien* (2 vols., 1957/64); *Four Plays*, 1957–62 (1964).

E. Brock-Sulzer, *F.D.* (Zürich, 1960); U. Jenny, *F.D.* (Velber, 1965); C. M. Jauslin, *F.D.* (Zürich, 1964); Hans Bänziger, *Frisch und D.* (Bern, 1960); Natan, *GML*, iii; *Modern Drama*, VIII (Lawrence, Kansas, 1965); *BA*. XXXIV, 1960; *GLL*, XV, 4, 1962; *TLS*, 11 January 1963.

**Durych, Jaroslav** (Hradec Králové 1886–Prague 1962). Czech novelist and poet. The son of a journalist, he lost his parents at an early age and was brought up by relations. As an army doctor he served at the front during the First World War and afterwards in the Czechoslovak Army from which he retired with the rank of colonel. As a writer he combines naturalism with mysticism in a Baroque manner, and his ardent if unorthodox Catholicism reveals itself in his sympathy with the proletarian. His monumental historical novel *Bloudění* (1929; tr. L. A. Hudson, *The Descent of the Idol*, 1935) is about the Thirty Years' War. Dealing with the rise and fall of Wallenstein, it is a startling and non-traditional portrayal of this tragic period in European history and it includes some profound psychological pictures of the Baroque era. [KB]

*Sebrané spisy* (12 vols., 1933–40).

J. Bartoš, *Kdo jest J.D.?* (Prague, 1930).

**Duun, Olav** (Jøa, N. Trøndelag 1876–Botne, Vestfold 1939). Norwegian novelist. The son of a farmer, he spent his youth fishing and farming in his native Namdalen. Later he qualified as a teacher and in 1908–27 he taught at a school at Botne on the Oslofjord. Essentially a *heimat* writer, his books are set in Namdalen and are written in a *Nynorsk* much modified by his own Trøndelag dialect. But there is nothing provincial about them; his theme is nothing less than man in his battle with the 'powers' (*menneske og maktene*). His chief work, the cycle of 6 novels *Juvikfolke* (1918–23; tr.

A. G. Chater, *The People of Juvik*, 1930–5), has been called 'a psychological history of Norway'. It is the saga of successive generations of one family from the Middle Ages up to the present day, showing their social and spiritual development from the primitive vitality of the first Juvikings to the self-sacrificing humanism of the most modern of them. The growth of conscience is also the theme of *Det gode samvite* (1916; tr. E. Bjørkman, *Good Conscience*, 1928). His last book, *Menneske og maktene* (1938; tr. R. G. Popperwell, *Floodtide of Fate*, 1960), a somewhat schematic study of the inhabitants of a small island which is overwhelmed by the sea, shows how specifically human qualities triumph over the dark workings of the 'powers'. Problems of good and evil are also debated with great intensity in the trilogy, *Medmenneske* (1929), *Ragnhild* (1931), *Siste leveåre* (1933). Duun is one of the most important Norwegian writers of this century; his work demonstrates the great literary possibilities of *Nynorsk*, but his use of this language form has hindered a wider appreciation of his work. [RGP]

*Minneutgave*, ed. R. Thesen (12 vols., 1949).

R. Thesen, *Menneske og maktene – O.D.'s dikting i vokster og fullending* (Oslo, 1945); A. G. Schjelderup, *Dikteren O.D.* (Oslo, 1945); D. Haakonsen, *O.D.* (Oslo, 1958).

**Du Vair, Guillaume** (Paris 1556–Tonneins, Lot-et-Garonne 1621). French philosopher and statesman. Clerk councillor to the Paris Parlement (1584) and deputy for Paris at the États Généraux of the Ligue (1593), he had great political influence. He circulated his most notable political speech, the *Exhortation à la paix*, in which he examined the claims of rivals to the French throne and opted for Henri de Navarre, provided he became a Catholic. Knowing of the Spanish marriage intrigues, he delivered the *Suasion de l'arrêt pour la manutention de la loi salique* (1593) to counteract their influence. In 1596 he was sent on a mission to Elizabeth I to negotiate a league against Spain and then to Provence as Governor to restore order there. First President of the Parlement of Aix in 1599, he became Bishop of Lisieux in 1617.

His literary importance is twofold: he was a master of a pure prose style, writing speeches notably free from contemporary faults (such as excessive classical references), and also a moralist of great philosophical importance in his day. In *De la sainte philosophie* (1580; ed. G. Michaut, 1945), *De la philosophie morale des Stoïques* (tr. Charles Cotton, 1664; Thomas James, *The Moral Philosophie of the Stoicks*, ed. R. Kirk, New Brunswick, N.J., 1951) and his translation, *Manuel d'Épictète* (*c.* 1585), he enrols Stoic philosophy into the service of Christianity. ⇨ Descartes, ⇨ Pascal and ⇨ Charron, among others, read him closely. During the siege of Paris he wrote a most polished Ciceronian dialogue, *Traité de la constance et de consolation ès calamités publiques* (ed. J. Flach and F. Funk-Brentano, 1915); in it three friends talk of constancy in adversity, providence and faith in the life to come. It was translated as *A Buckler against Adversitie* (1622). His *Traité de l'éloquence française* (ed. R. Radouant, 1908) attributes the poverty of French to the excessive erudition it was made to serve. Malherbe and others sought his advice. [FWAG]

*Actions et traités oratoires*, ed. R. Radouant (1911).

R. Radouant, *G. du V., l'homme et l'œuvre* (Paris, 1908); R. Naves, *L'aventure de Promothée* (Paris, 1943).

# E

**Early Hungarian Literature.** The nomadic Asian Magyar tribes which settled in what is now Hungary in the late 9th century spoke a language of the Finno-Ugrian group, but had no written literature until their conversion to Christianity in the early 11th century, from which time their culture began to develop.

From the 11th to the early 16th century, literature developed mainly in clerical Latin and consisted of chronicles (*Illustrated Chronicle*, 1358; *Prime Chronicle*, 1052), legends about saints and the *Gesta Romanorum*; these were the work of mostly foreign monks invited by Hungarian kings for the encouragement of Christianity and learning. The first literary writings in Old Hungarian were (in prose) a *Funeral Oration*, and (in verse) the *Laments of Mary*, both dating from the late 12th century. From the mid 15th to the early 17th century, Hungarian literature flourished, especially at the cultured court at Visegrád of King Matthias Corvinus (1458–90). Among the Humanist scholars, writers and Renaissance artists residing there were the famous poet Janus Pannonius (1434–72), who wrote in Latin (his works have recently been translated into Hungarian) and András Hess, a writer and printer who prepared the *Chronica Hungarorum*, a Hungarian history up to the 15th century.

From the time of the Reformation, and even earlier owing to the Hussite Movement, the use of Hungarian in literature became more and more prominent, in order to proclaim religious doctrines to a wider public. Preaching poets made their appearance beside writers who, like Hess, were often also pioneer painters. New forms of writing were created, such as the fables of Gáspár Heltai, Mihály Sztárai's dramas debating religious questions, the verse-chronicles of Sebestyén Tinódi-Lantos and the historical fiction of Albert Gergei (*Prince Árgirus*). ⇨ Bálint Balassa was, at the close of this period, the first poet to write in Hungarian. [JFR]

Klaniczay, *HHL*.

**Eberhard of Béthune** or **Bourges** (fl. *c.* 1210). French grammarian. His standard text book, the *Graecismus* (ed. J. Wrobel, Breslau, 1887), written in undistinguished verse, registers the contemporary trend against the pagan classics, though less extreme in tone than the work of ⇨ Alexander de Villa Dei; it largely replaced Priscian and Donatus. He is to be distinguished from Eberhard the German, author of the *Laborintus*. [CEC]

B. Hauréau, *Journal des Savants* (Paris, 1889); Manitius, *GLLM*.

**Ebner-Eschenbach, Marie von** (Zdislawitz 1830–Vienna 1916). Austrian *Novellen* writer. A noblewoman by birth and marriage (1848), she lived in Moravia and, from 1863, Vienna. After failures at drama (*Maria Stuart in Schottland*, 1860; *Marie Roland*, 1867; *Das Waldfräulein*, 1873; *Männertreue*, 1874; etc.) she wrote numerous regional *Novellen* about Austrian aristocrats and/or Czech peasants. Recalling Turgenev, her strength lies in concrete realism, acute psychology, terse dialogue and narrative skill; her limitations consist in her narrow range, occasional theatricality and didacticism. A humanist from a Catholic background, she opposes to social, psychological and metaphysical evil human conscience, discipline and charity. Her most noteworthy long stories are *Das Gemeindekind* (1887; tr. M. A. Robinson, *The Child of the Parish*, N.Y., 1893), *Lotti, die Uhrmacherin* (1889), *Unsühnbar* (1890), and *Glaubenslos?* (1893). Her best shorter stories appeared in *Erzählungen* (1875), *Neue Erzählungen* (1878), *Dorf- und Schlossgeschichten* (1884), and *Neue Dorf- und Schlossgeschichten* (1886). In *Aphorismen* (1880; tr. A. L. Wister, Philadelphia, 1883), *Parabeln, Märchen und Gedichte* (1892), *Altweibersommer* (1909), and *Aus einem zeitlosen Tagebuch* (1916) she communicates well-meaning commonplaces of wisdom, while *Meine Kinderjahre* (1906) and *Meine Erinnerungen an Grillparzer* (1916) are autobiographical. [LL]

*Gesammelte Werke*, ed. E. Gross (9 vols., 1961).

**Eça de Queirós, José Maria de** (Póvoa-de-Varzim 1845–Neuilly, Paris 1900). Portuguese novelist and critic. The illegitimate son of a magistrate, his early upbringing was left to his grandparents; at 5 he was sent to a boarding school in Oporto. At the University of Coimbra he read widely and the influence of the French and German Romantics is apparent in his remarkable lyric prose poems published individually and collected after his death as *Prosas Bárbaras* (1905). After briefly practising law in Lisbon, he committed himself wholeheartedly to the cause of reform proclaimed by the 'Generation of 1870' (cf. Antero de ⇨ Quental). He composed biting articles for *As Farpas* (cf. Ramalho ⇨ Ortigão) and gave one of the 'democratic lectures' (organized by Quental) on 'Realism as a New Expression of Art' (1871). Joining the Portuguese consular service (1872), he lived mostly abroad, where he wrote his great social novels: *O Crime do Padre Amaro* (1875), *O Primo Basílio* (1878) and *Os Maias* (not published until 1888). True to the convictions of his Lisbon lecture, Eça endeavoured to expose the vices and foibles of the dominant classes in Portugal, especially the bourgeoisie. He hoped to undermine the 'anti-progressive' sectors of society and to bring about a social revolution through national self-enlightenment. He commands a wealth of meaningful detail without impoverishing the basic narrative. His style is disarmingly straightforward, a model of literary objectivity. However, his reformist ambitions do tend to produce type characterization, with the result that few autonomous personalities emerge to transcend the rigidly defined milieu in which the action is set. Characters illustrate specific problems such as the pernicious influence of the Portuguese clergy or the defective basis of middle-class education. As social tracts the novels can be supremely effective. But perhaps human warmth is lacking.

Eça became more and more disillusioned. Nothing, he concluded, short of a national catastrophe could shake Portugal out of its torpor. In the final phase of his literary career he tended to take refuge in stylistic refinements and in an aimless dilettantism. Typical of this trend are *Correspondência de Fradique Mendes* (1900), *A Ilustre Casa de Ramires* (1900) and *A Cidade e as Serras* (1901). Living permanently in Paris, Eça looked at Portugal with the eyes of a blasé tourist. He married into an aristocratic family and at the time of his death he was living the comfortable life of the reformer reformed. [AJP]

A. J. Saraiva, *As Ideias de E. de Q.* (Lisbon, 1947); E. Guerra da Cal, *Lengua y Estilo de E. de Q.* (Coimbra, 1954); J. G. Simões, *E. de Q.* (Lisbon, 1964).

**'Ecbasis Captivi.'** A beast epic in rhymed Latin hexameters, written by an unknown German monk of Lorraine about 940. Through the allegorical events of the tale, which is based partly on Aesop and partly on the Biblical parable of the good shepherd, the poet preaches the renunciation of the world and the spiritual blessings of monastic life. [RT]

Ed. E. Voigt (1875); ed. K. Strecker (1935). Raby, *SLP*.

**Echegaray, José** (Madrid 1832–Madrid 1916). Spanish dramatist. He first became a professor of hydraulics, and published works on thermodynamics and higher geometry; later an interest in economics led him into politics as a liberal, and it was a period of exile in France in 1874 which made him turn to literature. He had always been interested in the drama and had in fact already written one or two plays, but *El libro talonario*, a moral work about jealousy and adultery, was the first to be performed (1874). The tension and morality of his plays is usually very simple: honesty struggles with family duties and wins in *O locura o santidad* (1877; tr. H. Lynch, *Folly or Saintliness*, 1895); prejudice with sincerity in *Los rígidos* (1889). Their appeal lies in cunning plot development with all kinds of *volte-faces*, dramatic irony, and rhetorical speeches. But frequently he adds a level of social comment on top of his basic moral theme, notably in *El gran galeoto* (1881; tr. E. Bontecou, *The Great Galeoto*, 1917), where the scandal-mongering of society itself causes the tragic scandal of the dénouement. This area of social comment in his work probably led him to take an interest in Ibsen, and *El hijo de Don Juan* (tr. J. Graham, *The Son of Don Juan*, 1895) was inspired by *Ghosts*. But his plays are in all respects much more simple than Ibsen's, although they enjoyed a great success in their time and won their author the Nobel Prize in 1905. [ONVG]

*Teatro escogido* (1959).

**'Eckenlied.'** German strophic heroic poem belonging to the Dietrich von Bern cycle and named after its hero Ecke. The original poem, the story of which is also found in the mid-13th-century *Thidrekssaga*, may itself have been composed about that time, but the extant sources are all later, and in some of them – as with the ➪ *Nibelungenlied* – the cruder elements of Germanic heroic legend have been played down in deference to the taste of courtly audiences. [RT]

Ed. J. Zupitza (1870).
H. Schneider, *Germanische Heldensage*, i (Berlin, 1928).

**Eckhart, Johannes,** known as **Meister Eckhart** (Hochheim, near Gotha *c.*1260–Cologne 1327). German mystic philosopher. The first of the great speculative mystics of Western Europe. He entered the Dominican order, held ecclesiastical posts in Saxony and Bohemia, and later taught in Paris, Strasbourg and Cologne. For Eckhart nothing has real existence but God: the existence of God's creatures is the existence of God Himself, and the relationship between Him and His creatures is the closest of all relationships. This line of thought approaches so nearly to pantheism that he was, not surprisingly, regarded as a heretic in many influential quarters, though he protested his orthodoxy. The purpose of human life, in his view, was the reunion of man with God through knowledge. His thought is often confused and contorted, his language, both in German and Latin, exuberant and highly metaphorical. [RT]

*Die deutschen und lateinischen Werke*, edn Dt. Forschungsgemeinschaft (Stuttgart, 1956ff.); German tr. H. Büttner (1965); J. M. Clark, *The Great German Mystics* (1949) (selections).
O. Karrer, *Meister E.* (Munich, 1926); J. M. Clark, *M.E. An Introduction* (with texts) (1957); F. C. Copleston, *A History of Philosophy*, iii (1953).

**Eddaic Poetry.** The anonymous poetry known as *eddaic* is chiefly preserved in a single Icelandic codex (Gl. kgl. sml. 2365 4to, in the Royal Library, Copenhagen). It was written *c.* A.D. 1270. Its contents are derived from earlier sources of smaller scope, but the written history of the poems cannot be traced back beyond *c.* A.D. 1200. A few additional poems and variant texts are found in other sources. The *Prose Edda* (➪ Snorri Sturluson) and the *Saga of the Völsungs* are particularly important in supplementing our knowledge of this poetic material.

The chief eddaic metres are developments of the Germanic long line, made up of 2 half-lines each with 2 beats or lifts and linked by alliteration. In Norse a strophic verse form was developed and with it a tendency to expect a regular number of syllables in the line. The youngest poems in *fornyrðislag* normally have 4 syllables to the half-line and 8 such lines to the stanza; older poems are much less regular. The other important metre is called *ljóðaháttr*, not paralleled in other Germanic languages. Here the unit is of 3 lines, 2 half-lines of *fornyrðislag* type linked by alliteration in the normal way, followed by a third line, usually with 3 lifts and with its own internal alliteration. This 3-line unit is usually found in pairs, making a stanza of 6 lines. The *ljóðaháttr* is not used for narrative, only for speech (which may, of course, describe action); *fornyrðislag* is used for both.

We do not know how this poetry was delivered. It is unlikely that it was sung, and there is no evidence to show that it had any instrumental accompaniment.

The major linguistic changes of the so-called Syncope Period must have taken place by the time the poems were composed. None of them can thus be older than *c.* A.D. 800, while the youngest were probably composed in the 12th century.

The first half of the collection contains mythological poems. Pride of place is given to the *Vǫluspá* (*Sibyl's Prophecy*), thought to have been composed by an Icelander about the end of the 10th century. It tells of the creation of the world, of the innocent age of the gods, spoilt by avarice and falsehood, of the death of Baldr, and of *Ragnarǫk*, the doom of the gods, when the world is finally destroyed after a great cataclysmic battle between the gods and the monstrous powers in which both perish. But after all has passed away, a new earth arises from ocean, and the innocent gods return. The superb imaginative order of the whole, the poet's mastery of language and his stern ethical interpretation are awe-inspiring.

Next comes the *Hávamál* (*Sayings of the High One* – Odin), a sequence of 5 or 6 poems. Some of it is certainly as old as the settlement of Iceland (A.D. 870–930) and shows clear signs of composition in Norway. Among its parts may be especially noted the first 77 stanzas which advise a man on how to behave in society and on what standards he should maintain. This hard-headed wisdom is expressed vividly and economically in the *ljóðaháttr* metre and often has a proverbial ring. Among later sections are a list of the magic effects a knowledge of runes can produce and a particularly interesting little poem in which Odin describes how he attained the arts of poetry and runes by a kind of self-immolation.

The other mythological poems are as follows. *Hymiskviða* and *Þrymskviða* tell myths of Thor as adventure stories. *Vafþrúðnismál* is a contest in mythological lore between Odin and a wise giant, where the lore and not the situation is important. In the *Alvíssmál* Thor questions a dwarf about the names of things among the different classes of beings (gods, men, elves, giants, dwarfs), where again it is the word-play, not the situation, which is important. *Hárbarðsljóð* is an altercation between Odin and Thor, in which each god boasts of his own accomplishments. *Lokasenna* describes how Loki insults all the gods and goddesses in turn and is finally quietened only by the return of Thor and the threat of his hammer. *Grímnismál* has a prose introduction and epilogue which provide a comparatively elaborate dramatic setting for the poem itself, a long monologue by Odin which seems to describe visions of the world of the gods, experienced by him as he undergoes torture by fire in the world of men. The poem called *Fǫr Skírnis* tells of Frey's love for Gerd, a giant maid, and of Skírnir's mission to woo her on Frey's behalf – promises and threats are of no avail but spellbinding curses produce her consent. Of the few poems of this kind not in the main codex of the *Edda*, the *Rígsþula* is the most interesting. It describes the origin of the social classes through the intervention of the god Heimdall, but the best things in it are the vivid descriptions of the typical appearance, dress, occupations and names of the thralls, the yeomen and the high-born. The poem shows marked connexions with a Celtic Irish background.

With the exception of the *Þrymskviða*, these poems are generally believed to be from heathen times. They are however poems, not hymns, and as pagan literature their significance is conceptual and iconographic rather than sacred and ritual.

The heroic poems of the *Edda* are: the *Lay of Vǫlund* (*Vǫlundarkviða*), which in the codex appears before the last of the mythological poems; 3 poems that have Scandinavian heroes and settings (the so-called Helgi lays); and 15 poems all connected with the legend of Sigurd the dragon-slayer and its extensions. Some of the younger poems in this group display great beauties of language and composition, and most of them show a novel interest in the psychological and sentimental life of the characters in the legend. But the outstanding poems are those that are commonly counted the oldest, probably composed not later than *c.* A.D. 900: the *Lay of Vǫlund*, the *Lay of Attila* (*Atlakviða*) and the *Lay of Hamdir* (*Hamðismál*). In these indomitable courage, heroic defiance and the absolute demands of vengeance are supreme. These oldest poems are 'epic-dramatic' in form, a mixture of narrative and dialogue; younger poems may be all dialogue or, after a short introduction, all monologue.

The *Lay of Vǫlund* has Wayland the Smith, well known in early Germany and England, as its central figure. It describes how he is left solitary after the departure of his valkyrie wife, and then tells of his capture by the gold-greedy king Nidud, of his maiming and confinement, and of his vengeance and escape. The astonishing thing is that the poet touches us more with compassion for all the sufferers in the story, Vǫlund and his enemies alike, than he does with horror at the cold cruelty of their actions.

The *Lay of Attila* (historical king of the Huns, died A.D. 453) tells how Gunnar (historical king of the Burgundians, died *c.*437) and Hǫgni, owners of the Niflung treasure, are invited home by Attila, their brother-in-law; how they die at his command but without revealing the secret of the hoard; and how terribly Gudrun, their sister and Attila's wife, avenged them. The poem is unrivalled in its abrupt energy and swift movement, its splendid language, often compressed and suggestive, and in its realization of the superb heroism of Gunnar and Hǫgni and the tight-lipped tragedy of the inexorable Gudrun.

The *Lay of Hamdir* tells how Gudrun incites her sons, Hamdir and Sǫrli, to avenge the death of their half-sister on Jǫrmunrekk (historical king of the East Goths, died A.D. 375), how they attack him and maim him and are killed themselves. It is a hard, spare, swift poem, beginning with a sense of fierce rage at the duty that compels the young men to seek vengeance and their own deaths, but ending with calm refuge in a classic statement of the heroic creed: 'We have fought well, we stand above the sword-weary slain of the Goths like eagles on a branch; we have won good fame, whether we die today or tomorrow; no man lives an evening after the Norns have passed their sentence.' And then, abruptly, 'There fell Sǫrli at the hall's gable, and Hamdir died behind the house.' [PGF]

*Norrøn fornkvæði*, ed. S. Bugge (Christiania, 1867); *Edda*, rev. ed. H. Kuhn (Heidelberg, 1962); *The Poetic Edda*, tr. H. A. Bellows (1923); tr. L. M. Hollander (Texas, 1962).
*Bibliography of the Eddas*, in *Islandica*, XIII (1920); XXXVII (1955).

**Edschmid, Kasimir,** pseud. of Eduard Schmid (Darmstadt, 1890–1966). German novelist and essayist. First famous as a spokesman for Expressionism (*Über den Expressionismus*, 1919; editor of *Tribüne der Kunst und Zeit*, 1918–22; *Die doppelköpfige Nymphe* (essays), 1920), he helped revive recent interest with *Frühe Manifeste. Epochen des Expressionismus* (1959) and *Lebendiger Expressionismus* (1961); his critical writings contain illuminating material but partisan judgements. His stories (*Die sechs Mündungen*, 1915, was one of the earliest works of expressionist prose) aim at a sustained ecstatic style (*Das rasende Leben*, 1916; *Timur*, 1917), and like the novel *Die achatenen Kugeln* (1920) are often sensationally erotic. *Lord Byron* . . . (1929; tr. E. Bennett, 1930; American title: *The Passionate Rebel*) portrays the poet's love for his half-sister. Extensive travels are recorded in many more urbane, cosmopolitan works, e.g. *Afrika* . . . (1930), *Glanz und Elend Südamerikas* (1931; tr. O. Williams, *South America* . . . 1932), of which the best are the many volumes about Italy (*Italien* . . ., 1935ff.). Among the best of his later fiction are the novel *Wenn es Rosen sind, werden sie blühen*, 1950 (about Georg ⇨ Büchner) and the exotic tales in *Der Bauchtanz* (1952); *Das gute Recht* (1946) is autobiographical. [PB]

*K.E.*, ed. G. Schab (1950).
L. Weltmann, *K.E.*: *der Weg, die Welt, das Werk* (Stuttgart, 1955).

**Eeden, Frederik van** (Haarlem 1860–Bussom 1932). Dutch poet, novelist and critic. With his medical and psychiatric training he was always keenly aware of his own duality between restless desire for a noble ethic and humiliating sensuality. Co-founder of *De Nieuwe Gids* (1885), in which appeared *De Kleine Johannes* (1885–1906; tr. and abr. L. W. Cole, *The Quest*, 1911), a symbolic account of a child's search for truth. His poetry, in *Ellen, een lied van de Smart* (1890), *Het Lied van Schijn en Wezen* (1895), and *Van de Passieloze Lelie* (1901), contains the individualism, eroticism and the quest for transcendental meaning, characteristic of the movement of 1880 (cf. ⇨ Kloos, ⇨ Verwey). In his psychological novel, *Van de koele meren des doods* (1900; tr. M. Robinson, *The Deeps of Deliverance*, 1902), and even in *De Broeders* (1894), the best of his plays, he fails to resolve the conflict between the spiritual and sensual urges in love (represented by Clara and Henriette in his *Dagboek*, 1932–46). The demon in him, which inspired his best work, seems only to have left him towards the end of his life when, after the collapse of his communist community at Walden and his divorce from Martha van Vloten, he embraced Roman Catholicism. [PK]

*Studies* (6 vols., 1890–1918); *De nachtbruid* (1909; tr. M. von Auw, *The Bride of Dreams*, 1913); Barnouw, *CA*; Snell, *FFG*.
H. W. van Tricht, *F.v.E. Denker en strijder* (Amsterdam, 1934); H. C. Rümke, *Over F.v.E.'s 'Van de koele meren des doods'* (Amsterdam, 1964).

**Effen, Justus van** (Utrecht 1684–Bois-le-Duc 1735). Dutch essayist and short-story writer. He revolted against the Gallomania of his times by writing moralizing and realistic prose in homespun Dutch for his own weekly *De Hollandsche Spectator* (1731–35), modelled on Addison and Steele. He travelled in England, met Newton, Pope, Swift. [PK]

Pritchard, *GE* (2 essays).

**Egeria** or **Aetheria** (fl. *c*.414–16). A nun of good birth from southern Gaul, or more probably northern Spain who made a pilgrimage to the Holy Places in the reign of Honorius and wrote an account to her co-religious. The (incomplete) record describes her visits to Sinai, the Holy Land, Edessa and Constantinople, and adds much traditional and topographical information. The second part gives a detailed and very important account of the Holy Week Liturgy at Jerusalem. The author is one of a number of aristocratic ladies who made the pilgrimage at this time, including the patrons of Jerome and Rufinus. Gamurrini's identification of her with Silvia, sister of the Prefect Fl. Rufinus, is no longer accepted; but there is much in favour of the view that she was a member of the Theodosian Imperial family. The narrative is written in a vivid, a colloquial style, and as the longest piece of vulgar Latin to survive from this period is of great interest to the philologist. [CEC]

*Itinerarium seu Peregrinatio ad loca sancta*, ed. E. Franceschini and R. Weber (Turnhout, 1958); and in *Corpus Christianorum*, 175 (Turnhout, 1961); ed. and Fr. tr. H. Petré, *Éthérie, journal de voyage*, in *Sources Chrétiennes*, 21 (Paris, 1948); English tr. M. L. McClure and C. L. Feltoe (1919).

W. van Oorde, *Lexicon Aetherianum* (Hildesheim, 1963); A. Lambert, *Revue Mabillon*, XXVII (1937), XXVIII (1938); M. v. Schanz, *Geschichte der römischen Literatur* (1890).

**Egge, Peter** (Trondhjem 1869–Oslo 1959). Norwegian novelist and playwright. He led a jack-of-all-trades existence in his early youth, but managed to publish his first novel in 1891. A prolific output followed, firmly anchored in the realist tradition and set in his native Trøndelag. His best book, *Hansine Solstad* (1925; tr. J. H. Jackson, *The History of an Honest Woman*, 1929), with its clear portraiture, skill in conveying atmosphere and setting, and sympathetic understanding of the ill-fated in life, is typical of his qualities. In the broadly descriptive *Inde i fjordene* (1920), class divisions in a rural community and the personal tensions they give rise to are depicted with understanding and insight. *Jægtvig og hans gud* (1923) is a psychological novel scrutinizing the nature of a poor shoemaker's call to found a new religion. His plays are comparatively unimportant. [RGP]

*Samlede verker* (6 vols., 1949).

B. S. Jystad, *P.E.* (Oslo, 1949); Beyer, *NL*.

**Egils Saga.** ⇨ Icelandic Sagas.

**Eglitis, Anšlavs.** ⇨ Latvian Literature.

**Ehrenburg.** ⇨ Erenburg.

**Ehrenstein, Albert** (Vienna 1886–New York 1950). Austrian ⇨ Expressionist poet. First published in ⇨ Kraus's *Fackel*, then a member of ⇨ Walden's *Sturm*-circle. His friend Oskar Kokoschka illustrated both his experimental narrative *Tubutsch* (1911, rev. 1914; tr. E. Posselt and E. Zistel, N.Y., 1946) and his collected poems *Mein Lied, Gedichte 1900–1931* (1931): the best are the early socio-political outbursts, others are humorous, erotic. He travelled widely in Africa and Asia, and finally left Germany in 1932; he translated much Chinese poetry and adapted the novel *Robbers and Soldiers* (tr. G. Dunlop, 1929). His other important prose includes *Selbstmord eines Katers* (1912) and *Briefe an Gott* (1922). [PB]

*Gedichte und Prosa* (1961).

Hamburger and Middleton, *MGP*.

**Eich, Günter** (Lebus, Oder 1907– ). German poet and radio-playwright (married to Ilse ⇨ Aichinger). After a first volume of poetry (*Gedichte*) in 1930, he made his name with the collections *Abgelegene Gehöfte* (1948), *Untergrundbahn* (1949) and *Botschaften des Regens* (1955). His latest collections are *Zu den Akten* (1964) and *Anlässe und Steingärten* (1966). His poetry aims to discover language, reality, self; it is increasingly 'the criticism of life'; his spare, wistful lyrical style has influenced younger poets. A leading radio-playwright, his plays (collected in *Fünfzehn Hörspiele*, 1966) are characterized by his use of Kafkaesque dream-situations to reveal modern man's subconscious mind; stylistically they show the same tactful artistry as his poetry. [PB]

Bridgwater, *TCGV*; Hamburger and Middleton, *MGP*; *ER*, XXI, Nov./Dec. 1961.

Walter Höllerer, postscript to *G.E.*, *Ausgewählte Gedichte* (Frankfurt a. M., 1960); Keith-Smith, *ECGL*; *TK*, 5, 1965.

**Eichendorff, Joseph Freiherr von** (Schloss Lubowitz 1788–Neisse 1857). German lyric poet and novelist. A Silesian nobleman by birth, he studied law at Halle, Heidelberg and Berlin, and entered the administrative service of the Prussian state (1816–44). Yet this government official, a respected figure in Berlin society, was the greatest of the German Romantic lyricists. Nature was for him a divine gift, and poetry was to be found wherever this divinity was honoured, wherever the work of God was unsullied by human hands. Man was meant to find his happiness in full absorption in the beauties – lighthearted and sombre, clearly grasped and vaguely sensed – of which nature is composed. Schumann, Mendelssohn and Richard Strauss are among the many composers who have been drawn to his poems.

He also wrote a long Romantic novel (*Ahnung und Gegenwart*, 1815), a Catholic-inspired history of German literature (*Geschichte der poetischen Literatur Deutsch-*

*lands*, 1857), and translated a number of Calderón's religious dramas. His principal prose work is the exquisite novelette *Aus dem Leben eines Taugenichts* (1826; tr. R. Taylor, *Memoirs of a Good-for-Nothing*, 1966). This idyll, with its utterly naïve, sometimes simple-minded, unswerving optimism, is among the most sincere, most perfectly wrought achievements of Romantic narrative fiction. [RT]

O. Seidlin, *Versuche über E.* (Göttingen, 1965); Natan, *GML*.

**Eilhart von Oberg** (fl. *c.* 1180). German epic poet. Author of the earliest known German version of the Tristan legend. Although a native of Saxony, he wrote not in his native Low German dialect but in the language and style of the Middle Franconian pre-courtly epic as represented by works such as ⇨ *Herzog Ernst*, *König* ⇨ *Rother* and the Strassburg *Alexander* of Pfaffe ⇨ Lamprecht. Of the early surviving Tristan epics, Eilhart's *Tristrant* is the closest to the lost Anglo-Norman poem of the mid 12th century from which the earliest known French, Anglo-Norman and German versions are independently descended. Eilhart's work belongs to the tradition of minstrel epic rather than sophisticated courtly epic; his style is episodic and his poetic technique limited. From later references and from the use made of it by later poets, his work can be seen to have enjoyed considerable popularity throughout the Middle Ages. [RT]

Ed. F. Lichtenstein (1877).

W. Golther, *Tristan und Isolde in den Dichtungen des Mittelalters und der neueren Zeit* (Leipzig, 1907); Ehrismann, *GDL*, ii.

**Einhard** or **Eginhard** (*c.* 770–Seligenstadt 840). Biographer of Charlemagne. He was educated at the famous Benedictine abbey of Fulda, whose abbot, Baugulf, sent him to the palace at Aachen where he became one of Charlemagne's intimates. For his artistic skill he was given charge of the public buildings and nicknamed Bezaleel (from Exodus xxxv, 30–4). His *Vita Karoli Magni*, modelled on the *De vitis Caesarum* of Suetonius, gives a striking portrait of the Emperor, his character, daily routine and government, and is outstanding among medieval biographies. The unreliable legend that Einhard married one of Charlemagne's daughters after a romantic love-affair appears from time to time in literature, as in De Vigny's poem 'La Neige'. [FB]

*Opera*, ed. A. Teulet (2 vols., Paris, 1840–3); *Vita Karoli Magni*, ed. H. W. Garrod and R. B. Mowat (1915); ed. with Fr. tr. L. Halphen (Paris, 1923; 1938); *Early Lives of Charlemagne*, tr. A. J. Grant (1907).

Duckett, *CP*.

**Ekelöf, Gunnar** (Stockholm 1907–Sigtuna 1968). Swedish poet and essayist. Perhaps the most original contemporary poet, he is an unrepentant individualist whose mature style is a curious mixture of esoteric, even cryptic allusions and simple, homely confessions. His mind is profound, but he impresses more through his persistence and subtleness than through the power and range of his experience. He has called his first collection, *Sent på jorden* (1932), a suicidal book. It reflects an outlook that is fundamentally divided; objects of perception appear in a trance-like field, strangely independent of the knowing subject. It has been regarded as inspired by French ⇨ Surrealism, though the poet denies any direct influence. In its formal aspect, the book brought a radical innovation to Swedish poetry. *Dedikation* (1934) is more cautious and by comparison his further output in the thirties appears deliberately extraverted, but also pale and occasionally even sentimental. *Färjesång* (1941) and *Non serviam* (1945) represent a new development. The style is again direct and forceful; intellectual analysis takes the place of idealized attitudes. Most important is the innovation (in Swedish) of large-scale musical (polyphonic) structures, most successfully in poems like 'Samothrake' and 'Absentia animi'. Further development of this technique is found in *Om hösten* (1951). An essay entitled 'The Way of an Outsider' is included in *Utflykter* (1947). Here Ekelöf speaks of a deep-seated sense of 'insufficiency' which prompts him ever to test the validity of his position; he further identifies the poet's prime task as that of 'becoming like himself'. (As a prose-writer he impresses by his rationality and the unadorned simplicity of his style.) In *Strountes* (1955) the rediscovery of meaning in discarded objects, thoughts and feelings is the formative principle. (The title means 'nonsense' and is itself a misspelling of a trivial word.)

A significant change in this as in two further collections, *Opus incertum* (1959) and *En natt i Otočac* (1961), is that they again favour the short poem. Indeed the fragment appears to hold a greater fascination for the later Ekelöf, to judge by *En Mölna-elegi* (1960). It is an elaborate composition, yet remains essentially a fragment. The elegy dwells on the plural modes of time, on the death which 'begins already in life', on the mystery of the 'Great Human' (a notion derived from Swedenborg). Though obscure, it occupies a key-position in his remarkably consistent work. *Dīwān över Fursten av Emgión* (1965) and *Sagan om Fatumeh* (1966) reveal his absorption in the Oriental world. Set in the hinterland of medieval Byzantium, they offer through their theme, the total dedication of love, an experience so intensely personal as to deserve the name of mysticism. He is also an eminent translator, particularly of French poetry, e.g. *Valfrändskaper* (1960). Since 1958 he has been a member of the Swedish Academy.

His last book of verse, *Vägvisare till underjorden* (1967), completes his 'Byzantine triptych'. It tells, in its central section, of a hypnagogic meeting between a novice nun and the devil in the Diocletian baths of Spalato (Split); this is a fiction in which the poet's entire consciousness is absorbed through mystical indentification. At his death Ekelöf commanded unique respect as the most original Swedish poet of the century. [SAB]

*Selected Poems of G.E.*, tr. M. Rukeyser and L. Sjöberg (N.Y., 1967).

R. Enckell, 'G. E.s lyrik', in *En bok om G.E.* (Stockholm, 1956); E. Lindegren, 'G.E., en modern mystiker', in *Kritiskt 40-tal* (Stockholm, 1948); G. Printz-Påhlson, *Solen i spegeln* (Stockholm, 1958); *Scandinavian Studies* (37, November 1965); *GR*, 40, 1965; *ASR*, L, iii, 2, 1965.

**Ekelund, Vilhelm** (Stehag 1880–Saltsjöbaden 1949). Swedish poet, essayist and aphoristic writer. The son of a village blacksmith, he studied at Lund, and became deeply learned. In the first seven years of the century, he published as many collections of poetry, including some pioneering free verse, e.g. *Melodier i skymning* (1902) and *Dithyramber i aftonglans* (1906). Among his models were Swedish regionalists such as Ola ⇨ Hansson, but also German Classicists such as ⇨ Hölderlin and ⇨ Platen. Hardly popular at the time, his poetry has won the admiration of later generations. The year 1908 marks a turning-point in his career: he exiled himself from Sweden; he also turned decisively to prose, finding poetry too soft and sentimental a medium for his temperament. His 25 prose works are even more exclusive in subject-matter and style, and in his later years they acquired the quality of intimate journals. Ever an individualist, he was rarely content to accept other men's ideas, yet in his isolation he depended on other men's writings. His career was a dialogue with great minds – Heraclitus, Plato and Pindar; Nietzsche and Stefan George; Goethe, Carlyle and Emerson; Swedenborg and Dostoyevsky. These, by turns, attracted him; others repelled him and provoked his contempt. The style of his essays and aphorisms is always highly personal, sometimes cryptic, witnessing his impatient and impassioned character. Important landmarks in this life of intellection are *Antikt ideal* (1909), which is strongly anti-Romantic with its Nietzschean cult of austerity; *Veri similia I–II* (1915–16), a mellower and more harmonious work in which the influence of Goethe can be felt; *Metron* (1918), which adopts the principle of moderation in aesthetics and ethics alike; *På hafsstranden* (1922), written in praise of sanity, courage and strength and attempting a synthesis of the Nordic and the Classical. Later books become either more polemical or more introspective. Ekelund was not only proud and aristocratic, but also sensitive and vulnerable. After returning from abroad in 1921, he lived an economically precarious and increasingly secluded life, enjoying the reputation of a sage, and supported by a small but ardent circle of admirers. [SAB]

A. Werin, *V.E. I–II* (Lund, 1960–1); K. A. Svensson, *V.E. Moralisten – kulturkritikern* (Hälsingborg, 1946); S. Lindqvist, *Dagbok och diktverk* (1966); *Svensk litteraturtidskrift*, 1, 1938.

**Ekkehart I** (*c.*900–973). A monk at the Abbey of St Gall in Switzerland. He was long considered the author of *Waltharius*, a Latin epic of nearly 1,500 hexameters (now ascribed to Geraldus, Bishop of Eichstätt in Bavaria from 882 to 912, formerly considered merely the writer of the prologue). *Waltharius* relates the adventures of Walter, Hagen and Hildegund, who had been held as hostages for the rulers of the Aquitanians, Franks and Burgundians by Attila, King of the Huns. The author is steeped in Latin poetry of classical and later centuries; he is particularly indebted to the *Thebaid* of Statius, to Virgil and to Germanic legends. [FB]

Ed. K. Strecker (1924, rev. 1947); ed. K. Langosch (Basel and Stuttgart, 1956).

*Studi Medievali*, XVIII, 1951; *Germanisch-romanische Monatsschrift*, IV, 1954; J. M. Clark, *The Abbey of St Gall* (1926); Raby, *SLP*.

**Ekkehart IV** (*c.*980–1060). A monk at the Abbey of St Gall in Switzerland. A pupil of ⇨ Notker. He wrote Latin religious verse (*Liber benedictionum*) for use in schools and a lively work called *Casus Sancti Galli*, a largely fictitious history of the abbey; its many entertaining stories display his keen humour and insight into character. [FB]

*Casus Sancti Galli*, ed. G. Meyer von Knonau (St Gall, 1877).

J. Egli, *Der liber benedictionum Ekkeharts IV* (1909); J. M. Clark, *The Abbey of St Gall* (1926).

**Elin Pelin,** pseud. of Dimităr Ivanov (Baylovo 1878–Sofia 1949). Bulgarian story-writer. Travel to France and Russia, residence in Sofia and his job as a librarian and curator of the Vazov Museum (1922–44) never weakened his attachment to Shopsko, the Sofia countryside of his upbringing, whence came the settings and characters of his stories. These *shopi* are sympathetically guyed in the yokel figures of *Pizho and Pendo*, humoresques in dialect conceived with A. Bozhinov, the caricaturist, for the satirical journal *Bălgaran* (1904–9). His early *Baladi v prosa* (1903) are also *genre* pieces; their burden is the *narodnik* social pathos typical of *Selska razgovorka* (1902–3), his brief 'monthly for peasants and teachers'. In 'A Career' these last face the problems arising from the urban pollution of his pastoral idyll in 'Samodiva'.

By the turn of the century he acquired the detachment and maturity to write 'The Windmill' and the rest of his *Razkazi* (I, 1904; II, 1911), still much read for their range of moods, evocative lyrical language and memorable village characters like Lazar Dăbak, Andreshko, *Nane* Stoichko – a whole gallery of dreamers, humiliated souls, canny priests, old foxes and gifted performers. In 'The Mowers' he puts in Blagolazh's simple words his celebrated defence of creative art and the imagination as the essence of humanity. 'That I have written stories from village life does not mean I am a *genre* writer (like T. ⇨ Vlaykov) – in all my works man has been my prime interest.' His humanist view was finally stated in 'How I Write', a talk to the Writers' Union on 3 May 1949.

Two longer stories unfold the tragedies of a patriarchal peasant family's decline (*Geratsite*, 1911) and of Enyo's land hunger that wrecks his brother and finally himself (*Zemya*, 1922). The uncompleted *Nechista sila* (1909), planned to be a novel, foreshadows in Father Gerasim's obsession the problems of balance between the flesh and the spirit, so subtly and divertingly treated in *Pod manastirskata loza* (1936), his last and own favourite story cycle.

The prose poems of a would-be painter and poet (*Cherni rozi*, 1928), and the piquant *feuilletons*, 'a topical book of topicalities' (*Az, ti, toy*, 1931), complete this author's works but for his 'only story on a socialist theme', 'Strina Doyna's Sparrows', in which the contemporary scene is typically viewed through a peasant-woman's eyes. He wrote also many tales and poems for children. [VP]

*Săbrani săchineniya* (10 vols., 1958–9); Pinto, *BPV*.

K. Genov, *E.P.: zhivot i tvorchestvro* (Sofia, 1956); P. Rusev, *Tvorchestvoto na E.P. do Balkanskata voyna* (Sofia, 1954); Manning and Smal-Stocki, *HMBL*; V. Pinto, in *SEER*, XLI, 96 (1962).

**Elísio, Filinto,** Arcadian pseud. of Padre Manuel do Nascimento (Lisbon 1734–Paris 1819). Portuguese poet. Filinto was the leading figure of the neo-classical Grupo da Ribeira das Naus, the rival of the Arcádia Lusitana of Cruz e ⇨ Silva, Correia ⇨ Garção and Reis Quita. He taught Latin to the future Marquesa de Alorna, the pre-Romantic poetess, who coined his Arcadian name. A pawn of Pombal, he was denounced to the Inquisition on the collapse of the latter's regime in 1777 and fled via Le Havre to Paris, where he remained in exile until his death. In Paris he won the friendship and admiration of the young Lamartine, who dedicated to him a poem in which he is described as 'le divin Manuel'. The last great formalist in the history of Portuguese verse, he adopted as his standards the works of Horace and the Portuguese poets of the 16th century, and in the course of his long life penned a vast collection of odes, epigrams, epistles and the like. Ever a champion of blank verse and of the purity of poetic diction, he presented his precepts in a long epistle, written at the age of 82 to his friend José de Brito, entitled *Da Arte*

*Poética Portuguesa*. In 1817–19 his *Obras Completas* were at last published in book form, though individual compositions had long been in circulation. His verse reveals his staunch opposition to oppression and clerical obscurantism, his exhilaration at the American and French Revolutions and, in the sombrely subjective nature of some of his lyrics, evidence of those pre-Romantic tendencies occasionally detectable in such earlier neo-classicists as Pina e Melo and Xavier de Matos. He was revered by ⇨ Bocage and exerted no little influence on the work of the Marquesa de Alorna and the young Garrett. [RCW]

T. Braga, *F.E. e os Dissidentes da Arcádia* (Oporto, 1901); H. Cidade, *Lições de Cultura e Literatura Portuguesas*, ii (Coimbra, 1948).

**Elissamburu, Jean-Baptiste.** ⇨ Basque Literature.

**Elsschot, Willem,** pseud. of Alfons de Ridder (Antwerp 1882–1960). Flemish author. His first novel, *Villa des roses* (1913), passed unnoticed, but in *Lijmen* (1924) his sober, ironic style made an immediate appeal. His subsequent short novels, e.g. *Kaas* (1933), *Tsjip* (1934), *Pensioen* (1937), *Het Been* (1938), *Het Tankschip* (1942), established his name as a sophisticated parodist unique in Flemish realism, while he has retained an undercurrent of sensitivity which keeps his writings from the detachment of sick humour. [PK]

*Verzameld werk* (1957); *Three Novels*, tr. A. Brotherton (1965).
B.-F. van Vlierden, *W.E.* (Bruges, 1958).

**Éluard, Paul,** pseud. of Eugène Grindel (Saint Denis 1895–Paris 1952). French poet. From 1919 to 1938 a leading member of the ⇨ Surrealist movement. Such important volumes as *Capitale de la douleur* (1926), *L'amour la poésie* (1929), *La vie immédiate* (1932) and *La rose publique* (1934) were written in close sympathy with Surrealism's desire to explore dreams, the unconscious and even various forms of mental alienation. (*L'immaculée conception*, which he wrote with ⇨ Breton in 1930, consists of exercises in simulating alienation.) He sought in the dream-like disorder of the subconscious a new freshness and originality of perception. His poems, with their mysterious images, elliptical syntax and sensuous language, show striking directness and purity of feeling, and are the outstanding work that Surrealism has left.

In the 1930s, affected by social and political events, he became a more committed writer and broke with the Surrealists. The generosity which had already made him a unique love poet was extended to all humanity. He finally joined the Communist Party in 1942 and became the most famous of the Resistance writers with *Poésie et vérité* (1942) and *Au rendez-vous allemand* (1944). He remained a sincere Communist until his death. His later poetry is calmer, less elliptical; despite frequent loss of intensity, works like *Poésie ininterrompue* (1946) combine the purity of his earlier work with a fine human concern. [IL]

*Choix de poèmes*, ed. A. Bosquet (1963); Hackett, *AMFP*.
L. Parrot and J. Marcenac, *P.É.* (Paris, 1953); L. Perche, *P.É.* (Paris, 1964); L. Decaunes, *P.É.* (Paris, 1965); Raymond, *DBS*.

**Elytis, Odysseus,** pseud. of Odysseus Alepoudelis (Crete 1912– ). Greek poet. His family originated from Lesbos. He studied law at Athens University and in 1940, when Mussolini's forces attacked Greece, fought as lieutenant in Albania. He now earns his living as a business man. He is one of the most eminent poets who appeared in the 1930s in the periodical *Nea Grammata* edited by G. Katsimbalis. His first two collections, *Prosanatolismoi* (1939; 'Orientations') and *Ilios O Protos* (1943; 'Sun the First'), contained poetry deeply tinged with surrealism. With a sensuous but delicately handled imagery they communicate brilliant visions of Greek nature and evoke the latent spirituality and mystery of the Aegean landscape. Heroism, death and love are treated with a daring interplay between visual imagery and the non-visual connotations of the words. His long poem *Iroiko Kai Penthimo Asma Ghia Ton Hameno Anthypolohagho tis Alvanias* ('A Heroic and Mournful Song on the Lieutenant Killed in Albania', 1945), beautiful in imagery and rhythm, achieves a rare lyrical intensity giving most poignant utterance to a whole range of emotions and ideas occasioned by the death of a young Greek soldier. After a long silence he published in 1960 two volumes of verse: *Exi Kai Mia Typseis Ghia Ton Ourano* ('Six and One Regrets for the Sky'), poems on various themes in which his earlier lyricism is somewhat subdued, the tone is contemplative and more deeply personal, and the manner still surrealist; and *Axion Esti*, his greatest so far, and most difficult work. As the title suggests (the first two words of a liturgical hymn to the Virgin meaning 'it is meet to bless Thee') it is modelled on the pattern of a Byzantine liturgy. Verse and prose (the 'lessons') alternate in a sequence of varied tones of emotion and complexities of imagery to evoke the 'genesis' and growth of a poet's consciousness projecting itself into the history, tradition, nature and life of Greece. In conception, language and technique it represents the poet's most mature phase. It is by any standards a major poem. [SJP]

*Poèmes* (1945; Greek text with Fr. tr. by R. Levesque); tr. E. Keeley and P. Sherrard, *Six Poets of Modern Greece* (with intro.) (London, 1960).

'Prolegomena to *Axion Esti*', L. N. Maronitis in *Epochés*, 29 (Athens, 1965).

**Embirikos, Andreas** (Braïla, Rumania 1901– ). Greek poet. Educated in Rumania, Russia, Athens and France, he lives in Athens and is by training and profession a psycho-analyst. He was the first to introduce genuine Surrealism into Greek poetry with a collection of verse entitled *Ypsikaminos* ('Blast Furnace', 1935), followed by *Endohora* ('Hinterland', 1945), a slender volume of poems written between 1934 and 1937, all in the true Surrealist manner. Embirikos is still active as a poet – some of his latest verse and prose has appeared in the Greek magazine *Pali* (nos 2, 3, and 5) and, in English translations, in *London Magazine* (October 1965, August 1966). He remains the pre-eminent representative of Greek Surrealism, acknowledging André Breton as his master, and using in his composition the technique of 'automatic writing' and *automatisme psychique*. His poetry abounds in glittering images and verbal picturesqueness; a fine sensibility directs his 'automatism' to produce brilliant effects in the best Surrealist tradition. [SJP]

*Amour Amour* (1966; Engl. tr. N. Stangos, A. Ross).

**Eminescu, Mihai** (Botoşani 1850–Bucharest 1889). Rumanian poet. His father, Gheorghe Eminovici, was a Rumanian from Bucovina, then in the Austro-Hungarian Empire. Mihai, though born in Moldavia, went to Cernăuţi, the capital of Bucovina, for his schooling. He gave his surname the characteristic Rumanian ending *-escu* in 1866. For a time he was prompter to a troupe of actors. Then in 1869 he went to study philosophy and law at Vienna University, and later to Berlin. He returned to Moldavia in 1874, as a librarian at Jassy. Had he been able to retain this post, his life would probably have been happier and more productive. He was a member of the literary circle *Junimea*, to whose journal *Convorbiri Literare* he had first contributed in 1870. In 1877 he became editor of the Bucharest newspaper *Timpul*. Six years of work which was too exacting for him ended in his mental collapse (1883); until his death periods of madness alternated with lucid intervals. The first collection of his poems appeared in 1885, edited by T. Maiorescu, the founder of *Junimea*. Though Eminescu received little recognition in his lifetime, he has come to be regarded as the greatest of Rumanian poets.

*Luceafărul* (1883), acclaimed as his masterpiece, is in 98 4-line stanzas, a sort of lyrical ballad, in which the Evening Star, for love of a mortal princess, wishes to renounce immortality, till he sees her in the arms of a page-boy. This poem shares the characteristics of his most masterly short lyrics; it weaves their motifs into a grand design. In a lyric such as 'Somnoroase Păsărele', commonplace ideas are expressed in language which for all its simplicity evokes an atmosphere of enchantment, largely because of the sensitive handling of the sounds of vowels and consonants. Such poetry evaporates in translation. [EDT]

*Opere*, ed. Perpessicius (1939ff.); *Poems*, tr. P. Grimm (Cluj, 1938).

T. Vianu, *Poesia lui E.* (1930).

**Encina, Juan del** (nr Salamanca 1469–León after 1529). Spanish poet and dramatist. In his youth he served the Duke of Alba, in whose palace his early bucolic pieces were presented to the accompaniment of his own music. He visited Rome (*c.* 1500), became a choirmaster, later took orders and went to Jerusalem to say his first mass; his poem *Trivagia* (1521) gives an account of his journey. Appointed prior of León, he enjoyed papal protection as an absentee cleric. His dramatic pieces are historically interesting as first steps towards a secular Spanish drama. Before visiting Italy he wrote mainly comic or religious pieces (*Auto de la pasión*), sometimes combining comic and religious elements (*Égloga de las grandes lluvias*). The comic rustic dialect (known as *sayagués*) spoken by his shepherds became conventional for stage rustics. His later eclogues show the influence of Italian pastoral drama; dialect is largely abandoned, love is treated more seriously, and classical deities are introduced. The *Égloga de Plácida y Victoriano* (1510) includes a character modelled on ⇨ Celestina. Though his plays were written for private performance they were included in successive editions of his *Cancionero* (7 edns between 1496 and 1516). This collection is prefaced by a treatise on the poetic art in Spain. [DR]

*Teatro completo*, ed. F. A. Barbieri; *Cancionero*, ed. Cotarzio (1928); *Cançionero, música de los siglos xv y xiv*, ed. Barbieri (1890); *Poemas*, ed. J. Givanee Mas (1940); Cohen, *PBSV*; Blecua, *FLE*; Trend, *OBSV*.
Crawford, *SDLV*, *SPD*.

**Enckell, Rabbe** (Tammela 1903– ). Finnish-Swedish poet, dramatist and essayist. He began his career with lyrical miniatures of a remarkable sensitivity and tenderness, e.g. *Flöjtblåsarlycka* (1925). Later collections became more meditative but continue to trace out in refined and sensuous detail the idyllic mood of the Finnish countryside. Gradually the mood darkens, but the style remains measured even in sorrow and resignation. His mature style has developed under a strong classical influence. Two verse dramas, *Orfeus och Eurydike* (1938) and *Iokasta* (1939), are important stepping-stones in this development. Its fullest expression is found in *Andedräkt av koppar* (1946), a collection of great intellectual stature. In particular the long poem 'O spång av mellanord' is remarkable for its probing intensity and resigned wisdom: a tragic sense of the transience of life has added a new dimension and a moral content to Enckell's verse. Later collections, e.g. *Sett och återbördat* (1950), *Skuggors lysen* (1953) and *Kalender i fragment* (1962), can be seen as a partial return to his early phase, but there is an element of detachment, even abstraction, which dampens the immediacy of the poet's perceptions. Further plays on classical themes show his love of Greek culture, but are not escapist: they are a lyrical poet's approach to contemporary problems and to human destiny. Chief among them are *Agamemnon* (1949), which broods on the theme of the defeat awaiting in victory, and *Hekuba* (1952), with its study of a great feminine character, who is also the eternal refugee. Reasoned and engaging statements of the poet's aesthetic convictions and general outlook are found in *Relation i det personliga* (1950), *Traktat* (1953), and more recently in *Essay om livets framfart* (1961). *Och sanning?* (1966) is a *journal intime*, its entries ranging from aphorisms to essays. [SAB]

B. Holmqvist, 'R.E.', in *Modern finlandssvensk litteratur* (Stockholm, 1951).

**'Encyclopédie.'** The *Encyclopédie ou Dictionnaire raisonné des sciences, des arts et des métiers* (17 vols. folio, Paris 1751–65, plus 11 vols. of plates, 1762–72) originated in 1745 in a relatively modest project by a group of Paris printers for a translation of Ephraim Chambers's *Cyclopaedia* (1728). ⇨ Diderot, by then an experienced translator, was appointed editor in 1747, with d' ⇨ Alembert as his colleague on the mathematical and scientific side. The enterprise was soon transformed into something much more amibitious: a wholly new encyclopedia, with numerous expert contributors, embracing the full extent of contemporary knowledge, including the technical, and based upon a clear system of classification, expounded by d'Alembert in his *Discours préliminaire*. In the hands of two such emancipated thinkers, the project inevitably became a vast demonstration of the powers and achievement of man as a rational being, and by implication a protest against religious and political forces which sought to fetter the mind in tradition.

The first 2 volumes appeared with full official approval in 1751 and 1752; clerical opposition then caused difficulties, but publication continued, though precariously. In 1757, however, when 7 volumes had appeared, conservative hostility reasserted itself in the atmosphere of heightened official fear of subversive ideas which followed Damiens' attempted assassination of Louis XV; d'Alembert resigned in 1758 and in 1759 the *Encyclopédie* was banned by royal decree. Diderot and his devoted assistant Jaucourt continued their editorial work clandestinely, however, and it became possible to publish the 10 outstanding volumes of text in 1765.

Diderot's team of at least 160 contributors included major figures such as ⇨ Buffon, ⇨ Holbach, ⇨ Montesquieu, ⇨ Rousseau and ⇨ Voltaire, but also many humble specialists and artisans for the articles on technical processes which formed an important and novel feature, and probably constituted the work's major attraction for the public. A substantial proportion of the articles, many of which are unsigned, was prepared however by Diderot himself (some 600 are positively attributable to him) and especially by Jaucourt.

The spirit of rationalist humanism which suffuses the whole work, and especially underlies its emphasis upon scientific and technical achievements, necessarily had unorthodox implications in religion and politics. Here circumspection was necessary, and there are unimpeachable articles by theologians, but scepticism, anticlericalism and pleas for liberty of conscience are everywhere insinuated. Politically the attitude is less radical, and less consistent, but there are attacks on despotism and privilege, and Montesquieu's principles of liberal monarchy perhaps command most assent. Nothing of this, however, was new in France by 1750, and the direct influence of the *Encyclopédie* on the public mind is difficult to assess. Many of the 4,000 subscribers to the first edition were probably already sympathetic to its attitude, and little is known concerning its accessibility to a wider public. It served however as a magnificent rallying-point for the whole movement of rational enlightenment, and its publication is itself evidence of the progress made by the middle years of the century. [WHB]

P. Grosclaude, *Un audacieux message: L'Encyclopédie* (Paris, 1951); J. Proust, *Diderot et l'Encyclopédie* (Paris, 1962).

**'Eneas, Roman d'.'** Medieval French romance written about 1160 by an unknown Norman, on the subject of Virgil's *Aeneid.* The influence of the *Roman de Thèbes*, the story of *Pyramus and Thisbe*, ⇨ Wace's *Brut*, and the bestiaries, is discernible in the work, which has 10,000 lines in octosyllabic rhyming couplets. There is much emphasis on the 'marvellous' and on the motif of love. The relationship between Aeneas and Lavinia is expanded into a love story in which the characters analyse their feelings in lengthy monologues which derive from Ovid and which served as a pattern to many later medieval French romances (⇨ Veldeke). [LTT]

Ed. J. Salverda de Grave (2 vols., Paris, 1925–31).

E. Faral, *Recherches sur les sources latines des contes et romans courtois du moyen âge* (Paris, 1913).

**Ennodius, Magnus Felix** (Arles 474–Pavia 521). Latin poet. Driven to Italy by Visigothic invasions, he became Bishop of Pavia. His voluminous Latin verse and prose include a panegyric of Theodoric, a guide to education, topographical poems, a number of hymns, a collection of epigrams (many indecent), and a life of St Epiphanius (tr. G. M. Cook, Washington, 1946), a predecessor at Pavia. His style is spoiled by colloquialisms, affectations and rhetorical exaggeration. [FB]

*Opera*, ed. G. Hartel, in *Corpus Scriptorum Ecclesiasticorum Latinorum*, vi (Vienna, 1882); ed. F. Vogel (MGH, AA, VII, 1885).
Duckett, *GMA*.

**Enríquez Gómez, Antonio** (Segovia ? 1602–Amsterdam 1660). Spanish poet, dramatist and novelist. Of Jewish descent, he was suspected of heresy and fled to France, became secretary to Louis XIII, and later declared Jewish faith in Amsterdam. His best work is a picturesque satirical novel in verse and prose, *El siglo pitagórico* (1644). His poetry, often satirical, is in the manner of ⇨ Quevedo; his dramas (school of ⇨ Lope) somewhat melodramatic and precious: *Academias morales de las Musas* (Bordeaux, 1642), *La Torre de Babilonia* (Rouen, 1647). ⇨ Galician Literature. [JMC]

BAE, 33 and 42; Cohen, *PBSV*.

**Enzensberger, Hans Magnus** (Kaufbeuren/Allgaü 1929– ). German poet and critic. Student of literature, languages and philosophy (doctorate 1955). He was programme editor with the South German Radio, visited the U.S.A. in 1957, and is now resident in Norway and a publisher's reader. Apart from 3 collections of verse, *die verteidigung der wölfe* (1957), *landessprache* (1960) and *blindenschrift* (1964), he has produced essays (*Einzelheiten*, 1962; *Politik und Verbrechen*, 1963) and translations of poems by William Carlos Williams (1962) and Pablo Neruda – an influence on his own work. He is the German Angry Young Man, a satirical poet, reminiscent of ⇨ Brecht, ⇨ Kästner, and other political poets and satirists of the 1920s. Learning also from Gottfried ⇨ Benn and e. e. cummings, his attacks on contemporary society and civilization, especially the Germany of the 'Economic Miracle', are brilliantly clever. Real personal commitment and real lyricism first entered his life with *blindenschrift*. [PB]

*Poems*, tr. M. Hamburger (1966); Bridgwater *TCGV*; Hamburger and Middleton, *MGP*. Holthusen, *KV*; Keith-Smith, *ECGL*.

**Eötvös, Baron József** (Buda 1813–Buda 1871). Hungarian writer. An aristocrat, he was a progressive Minister of Education both in the 1848–9 revolutionary government and after the 1867 compromise between Hungary and the Habsburgs. His works extend from his first sentimental novel *A karthausi* (1839) to *Magyarország 1514-ben* (1847), a widely based novelistic analysis of the peasants' revolt, and include *A falu jegyzője* (1845; tr. O. Wenckstern, *The Village Notary*, n.d.), a Dickensian description of provincial life, *A nővérek* (1857), a romantic novel, and also political pamphlets (on the emancipation of the Jews, 1840) and philosophical works. [JFR]

Reményi, *HWL*.

**Epic Theatre.** ⇨ Brecht, Bertolt.

**Erasmus, Desiderius** (? Gouda 1466–Basle 1536). Dutch humanist. The natural son of (?) a priest at Gouda, he later styled himself 'Rotterdammensis'. Educated by the Brethren of the Common Life at Deventer, he became an Augustinian canon at Steyn, near Gouda, and was ordained priest (1492). He studied in Paris (1495), visited Oxford (1499), Louvain (1502–4), Italy (1506–9); in England again he became friendly with Sir Thomas More, and taught at Cambridge (1511). After long periods in the Netherlands, he settled at Basle (1521), leaving its atmosphere of gathering religious dissension for Freiburg in Breisgau (1529–35).

His intellect and learning were famous throughout Europe, though his reputation eventually suffered because he did not take a decided stand on the great question of his time – the Reformation. His *Enchiridion militis christiani* stresses the importance of learning to the Christian life and is strongly antagonistic to the unreformed Church. His *Moriae encomium* (1511), or *Laus stultitiae* (tr. J. Wilson, *The Praise of Folly*, 1688; repr. Michigan, 1961), is a satire on the monastic life of his time and on the condition of the Church, which helped to prepare the way for the Reformation. His *Colloquia familiaria* (1518ff.), which again hold the monastic life up to contempt (with other lively dialogues on contemporary topics), and his Paraphrases of the New Testament (tr. 1548 and ordered to be placed in English parish churches beside the Bible) were famous for their spirit of rational humanism independent of authority. But the systematization of free learning into theological faction was odious to him; he was more a man of letters than a metaphysician. Though he attacked obscurantism and abuses of the clergy, he opposed Luther, believing in the unity of the Church: albeit ideally purified of superstitious accretions to the simple 'philosophia Christi'. To rediscover this truth – a luminous if unclear Renaissance ideal, which 'enlightened' Christian reason with the spirit of classical culture – he devoted himself to editing the works of the Fathers and to his epoch-making (if superseded) edition of the Greek New Testament, with a new translation into classical Latin. His style is not 'pure', i.e. smoothly imitative, but highly personal in its elegance; Latin was the language in which Erasmus naturally thought and spoke.

Amongst his most interesting work now is his correspondence (about 3,000 letters survive), which reflects his independence of spirit and humane common sense, despite ill-health and some fads. He lived as champion of a new learning and a new liberty; amidst the maxims of ancient literature (*Adagia*) he writes denunciations of rulers and princes. His thoughts echo in Shakespeare. [FB]

*Opera omnia*, ed. J. Leclerc (10 vols., Leyden, 1703–6); *Opus epistolarum*, ed. P. S. and H. M. Allen and H. W. Garrod (11 vols., 1906–47); tr. (from 1518) F. M. Nichols, *The Epistles of E.* (3 vols., 1901–17); *Opuscula*, ed. W. K. Ferguson (1933).

J. A. Froude, *E.* (1894); J. Huizinga, *E. of Rotterdam* (1924; tr. 1952, incl. a selection of letters); R. H. Murray, *E. and Luther* (1920); Preserved Smith, *E.* (1923), and *A Key to the Colloquies of E.* (Harvard, 1927); P. S. Allen, *The Age of E.* (1914), and *E., Lectures and Wayfaring Sketches* (1934); A. Renaudet, *Érasme et l'Italie* (Geneva, 1954).

**Erben, Karel Jaromír** (Miletín 1811–Prague 1870). Czech poet. The son of a farmer, he graduated in law and philosophy and became archivist of the city of Prague. He has a prominent place as a student and collector of Slavonic folk-tales and Czech folk-songs.

In his own collection of ballads, *Kytice* (1853), he artistically adapted themes of folk poetry, such as the demonic relationship between man and nature or the mysterious links between parent and child, and created sophisticated poems at once of universal and profoundly Czech appeal. [KB]

*Dilo*, ed. A. Grund (5 vols., 1938–40); *Pan-Slavonic Fairy Stories*, tr. (from E.'s collection) W. W. Strickland (1896–1907).
A. Grund, *K.J.E.* (Prague, 1935).

**Ercilla, Alonso de** (Madrid 1533–? Madrid 1594). Spanish poet. He served as page to Philip II, and fought in Chile against the savage Araucanians. His epic, *La Araucana* (Part I, 1569; II, 1578; III, 1589–90), based on his experiences in this war, is the best of the Spanish Renaissance; Cervantes and Voltaire praised the nobility of its speeches, and more recent critics the realism of its imagery and sympathetic portrayal of the Araucanians. Collectively they are the heroes of the poem; the greatness of the Spaniards lies in their having defeated so brave and persistent an enemy. The Spanish captains are well characterized, and the Chilean landscape magnificently presented. Though individual battle-scenes are good, the epic is badly constructed (III is full of digressions); the protagonists sound falsely rhetorical, echoes of Homer or ⇨ Garcilaso equally out of place, and much of the poetry pedestrian. [JMC]

*La Araucana*, ed. J. Toribio Medina (5 vols., Santiago de Chile, 1910–18); ed. Caillet-Bois (Buenos Aires, 1945); CA; Bk I, canto I, tr. W. Owen (Buenos Aires, 1945); *The Historie of Aravcana*, tr. George Carew (repr. Manchester, 1964).
Pierce, *HP*.

**Erdman, Nikolay Robertovich** (Moscow 1904– ). Russian dramatist. He was famous for a brilliant satire, *Mandat* (1924), staged by Meyerkhol'd and popular in provincial and amateur repertory; he was once regarded as the Soviet Gogol'. After *Samoubiytsa* (1928) and *Aktrisa*, he has written mainly scenarios for cartoon films. [AP]

E. Garin, *Vstrechi s Meyerkhol'dom* (Mogo, 1967).

**Erenburg, Il'ya Grigor'yevich** (Kiev 1891–Moscow 1967). Russian novelist, poet and journalist. Son of a middle-class Jewish family he emigrated in 1908 and lived in Paris until 1917. He returned to Russia before the Revolution but did not support the Bolsheviks and emigrated again in 1919. Until that time he had written mainly verse, influenced by the Symbolists and the Futurists; he continued to write in this medium sporadically, but from 1919 it is overshadowed by his prose. His first novel *Neobychaynyye pokhozhdeniya Khulio Khurenito* (1919; tr. A. Bostock and Y. Kapp, *Julio Jurenito*, 1958) is a cynical and fast-moving satire on all human (including Soviet) institutions. Most of his other novels of this period are superficial and sentimental like *Lyubov' Zhanetty Ney* (1924; tr. H. Matheson, *The Love of Jeanette Ney*, 1929); but *Rvach* (1925) is an unusually vivid and outspoken picture of the NEP period. The novel was bowdlerized by Erenburg for publication in the U.S.S.R.

In the 1930s he adapted himself to the new trends in Soviet literature. *Den' vtoroy* (1933; tr. A. Bakshy, *Out of Chaos*, 1934) was his contribution to the cult of the First Five-Year Plan. During the Spanish Civil War he worked as a war correspondent for *Izvestiya*. He finally settled in Russia soon after the German invasion. During the war he completed his novel *Padeniye Parizha* (1942; tr. G. Shelley, *The Fall of Paris*, 1945), for which he won a Stalin Prize, and devoted himself to journalism and anti-Nazi propaganda. He returned to novel-writing with *Burya* (1947; tr. E. Hartley and T. Shebunina, *The Storm*, 1949) which won another Stalin Prize, and *Devyatyy val* (1951; tr. T. Shebunina and J. Castle, *The Ninth Wave*, 1955), but these works are potboilers cashing in on the violently anti-Western campaign of those years.

Since the death of Stalin Erenburg has been in the vanguard of liberalization. His novel *Ottepel'* (1954; tr. M. Harari, *The Thaw*, 1955) may be superficial, but it was the first work to refer to the iniquities of Stalinism, and it gave its name to a new trend in Soviet literature, the ⇨ Thaw. No less important in this respect are his critical essays, collected in *Chekhov, Stendhal and Other Essays* (tr. A. Bostock and Y. Kapp, 1962) which are pleas for greater liberty for the Soviet artist. His memoirs *Lyudi gody, zhizn'* (1960–4; *Men, Years, Life Childhood and Youth, 1891–1917*; *First Years of Revolution, 1918–1921*; *Truce 1921–33*; *Eve of War, 1933–41*; *The War 1941–5*; *Post-War Years, 1945–54*, Pts I and II tr. A. Bostock and Y. Kapp, Pts III–VI tr. T. Shebunina and Y. Kapp, 1961–6) have played an important part in acquainting the younger generation of

Soviet Russia with the history and culture of Europe in this century. [RDBT]

*Sobraniye sochineniy* (9 vols., 1962–7).
T. K. Trifonova, *I.E.* (Moscow, 1952).

**Ermetismo.** A modern Italian school of poetry deriving from French symbolism a use of language as a medium not of description, nor even communication, but of exploration into private realms of association and evocation. ⇨ Montale, Quasimodo, Ungaretti.

F. Flora, *La poesia ermetica* (Bari, 1936).

**Ermold The Black** (fl. 825–850). A cleric of Aquitaine. He was banished by the Emperor Louis the Pious for inciting his son Pippin to revolt. He tried to regain the Emperor's favour with a Latin epic about his achievements: *De rebus gestis Ludovici Pii.* In elegiac couplets, it is full of phrases from Virgil, Ovid and other classical writers. It contains some vivid descriptive passages, e.g. a hunting scene, the siege and recapture of Barcelona after nearly a century of Moorish rule, and a fight between two champions. [FB]

Ed. Dümmler (MGH, PLAC, 1881–4); Migne, *PL*, 105; Fr. prose tr. in *Ermold le Noir*, ed. E. Faral (Classiques de l'histoire de France au moyen âge, 1932).
Raby, *SLP*.

**Ernst, Paul** (Elbingerode 1866–St Georgen, Steiermark 1933). German critic, dramatist, poet, etc. Abandoning the study of theology for literature, he was influenced by Naturalism and Marxism, then reacted decisively against both with *Der Weg zur Form* (1906) – in praise of neo-classicism and notably of the true Hero in drama – and *Der Zusammenbruch des Marxismus* (1918; rev. edn, *Die Grundlagen der neuen Gesellschaft*, 1930) – the hero again, now in Nietzschean guise as political leader – for which Ernst was fêted by the Nazi regime, when neo-classical drama became official national taste (cf. W. Scholz). As a dramatist he developed from Naturalistic plays (*Lumpenbagasch*, 1898) through neo-classical hero-tragedies (*Demetrios*, 1905; *Canossa*, 1908, etc.) to a 'form beyond tragedy', the 'drama of redemption' or 'meta-tragedy' (*Manfred und Beatrice*, 1912; *Preussengeist*, 1914, etc.). Ernst's novellas, e.g. *Komödianten und Spitzbubengeschichten* (1920) and *Geschichten von deutscher Art* (1928), were meant to (and perhaps did) regenerate the form by returning to simple narrative outline. But his *Kaiserbuch* (3 vols., 1923–8), an epic of past German glories, regenerated neither the form nor the nation. Ernst's poetry is at its solemn best in the aphorisms of *Gedichte und Sprüche*, their worldly-wise wisdom being expressed again by various 'great men' of history in the imaginary conversations of *Erdachte Gespräche* (1921). [PB]

*German Studies Presented to H. G. Fiedler* (1938); Fechter, *ED*; *MLR*, XLIV, 1 (1949).

**'Erotokritos.'** Greek narrative poem of 10,052 lines in 15-syllable, or *political*, metre arranged in rhymed couplets and composed during the 17th century in Venetian-occupied Crete by Vincenzos Kornaros, about whom little is known. It describes the love story of Aretousa, the daughter of a king of ancient Athens, and Erotokritos, the son of the king's counsellor, their difficulties and trials resulting from the king's opposition to their union, and the ultimate triumph of love when Erotokritos returns from exile in disguise, saves the king from his enemies and thereby wins his consent to marry his daughter. The poem draws on verse romances of adventure and chivalry written in Greek under Western influence, but for plot and disposition of material it is particularly indebted to the medieval French romance *Paris et Vienne* by Pierre de la Cypède. There are also echoes in it of Ariosto's *Orlando furioso*, while its imagery, the prolific use of similes and the dramatic manner of presentation of heroes and battle scenes is often reminiscent of the *Iliad*. The Cretan poet has adapted his work with great artistry to contemporary Greek susceptibilities and tastes – this is especially true of his delicate portrayal of the heroine – and, in general, with the copious use he makes of Cretan popular elements, he succeeds in investing it with a distinct Greek atmosphere and ethos. The language is the Cretan dialect of modern Greek, free from all archaisms and characterized by a remarkable raciness. Cretan literature which is responsible for some of the most promising post-Byzantine Greek works reaches with the *Erotokritos* its high-water mark. Both as regards poetic tone and feeling and technical perfection it is one of the masterpieces of Greek literature, and has enjoyed immense popularity throughout the Greek world. Its influence on the diction and style of subsequent Greek poets has been considerable. The poem was first printed in Venice in 1713 and there followed numerous popular editions. The only manuscript of it, illustrated with 120 miniatures, was bought at Corfu in 1725 and is now at the British Museum (Harleian Collection 5644). The English traveller and topographer, W. M. Leake, was the first to draw attention to the importance of the poem (*Researches in Greece*, 1814). [SJP]

*Erotokritos*, ed. S. Xanthoudides (1915).
J. Mavrogordato, *The Erotokritos* (1929).

**Ertel', Aleksandr Ivanovich** (Ksizova 1855–Moscow 1909). Russian novelist. He is remembered chiefly for his two panoramic novels, *Gardeniny, ikh dvornya, priverzhentsy i vragi* (1889, his masterpiece), and *Smena* (1891). In these he demonstrated a remarkable knowledge of, and sympathy with, the Russian countryside and its inhabitants. He was a master of popular idiom and his characters are subtly differentiated by means of their speech ('His popular language is not only exact, powerful and beautiful, it is also endlessly varied', noted Lev Tolstoy). Ertel's work was well received in his life-time. He had made his debut as a writer of short stories (1878), and he continued to publish stories until the end of the nineties. During the last decade of his life, however, he virtually retired from literature. [SH]

*Sobraniye sochineniy* (7 vols., 1909).
G. A. Kostin, *A.I.E. Zhizn' i tvorchestvo* (Voronezh, 1955).

**Esenin, Sergey.** ⇨ Yesenin, Sergey.

**Espinel, Vicente** (Ronda 1550–Madrid 1624). Spanish novelist, poet and musician. A friend of Cervantes and Lope de Vega. He is credited with the invention of the fifth string of the guitar and has a variety of *décima* (stanza of 10 octosyllables) named after him. His *Vida de Marcos de Obregón* (1618; CC, 1922) contains more true autobiography than do other picaresque novels, is more gently humorous, less bitterly disillusioned or urgently didactic. His *Diversas rimas* (1591) include youthful love poems, occasional verse and the first Spanish translation of Horace's *Ars poetica*. [DR]

*Diversas rimas*, ed. D. C. Clarke (N.Y., Hispanic Institute, 1956).
G. Haley, *V.E. and Marcos de Obregón. A Life and Its Literary Representation* (Providence, 1959).

**Espinosa, Pedro** (Antequera 1578–Sanlúcar 1650). Spanish poet. His anthology *Flores de poetas ilustres* (1605) assembled verse in the advanced style of ⇨ Góngora and the Antequera school, and is something of a landmark. His best original poem is the *Fábula del Genil*, in which mythology blends with nature imagery; two *Soledades* and some religious poems also have distinction. [JMC]

*Obras*, ed. F. Rodríguez Marín (1909); Trend, *OBSV*; Perry, *HASP*; Cohen, *PBSV*.
F. Rodríguez Marín, *P.E. Estudio biográfico, bibliográfico y crítico* (Madrid, 1907); *Homenaje a P.E.* (Seville, 1953); *LSS*, II (1946).

**Espronceda, José** (Almendralejo, Estremadura 1808–Madrid 1842). Spanish poet. He was educated mainly in Madrid as a pupil of the neo-classic poet Alberto Lista who encouraged his early poetic inclinations and wrote some stanzas for his epic fragment *El Pelayo*. But most of his subsequent work and life was romantic in character. His outspoken Liberalism led him to leave Spain shortly after the Restoration (1823), and he travelled through Portugal, England, Holland and France, in pursuit partly of freedom and partly of the daughter of another exile, Teresa Mancha. His affair with her continued after her marriage, but did not long survive when he carried her off from Paris to Spain. When she died Espronceda distilled the sadness of their relationship into the stanzas 'A Teresa' which formed a section of his long unfinished poem *El Diablo mundo*. In poetry, Byron was his greatest model, and he wrote of revolt and disenchantment in poems which are not unlike those of the English Romantic in spirit if not in letter. But like many of his contemporaries he also drew on historical and legendary Spanish themes, notably for his verse drama *El estudiante de Salamanca* (before 1840), based on popular ballads with roots in the Don Juan stories. In his finest work he reflects the uncertainty which characterized the political, social and philosophical views of the time. The protagonists of his works are often the outcasts of society: the hangman, the pirate, the prostitute and the rebel. He makes them the mouthpieces for his protests against the brutality, selfishness and injustice of man, and the uncertainty of existence. [ONVG]

*Obras poéticas completas*, ed. J. J. Domenichina (1936); *Obras poéticas* (1951).

P. H. Churchman, *Byron and E.* (1909); E. Allison Peers, *A History of the Romantic Movement in Spain*, i (1940); Piñeyro, *RS*; *BHS*, XL (1963).

**Estang, Luc** (Paris 1911– ). French poet, novelist and critic. Literary editor of *La Croix* (1940–55). Originally hailed as a promising poet – e.g. in *Les béatitudes* (1945) – he has since developed primarily into a religious novelist. The trilogy *Charges d'âmes* (1949–54) suggests religious anguish reminiscent of ⇨ Bernanos; Estang clearly prefers characters harried by remorse or doubt to those whose faith raises no problems. *L'interrogatoire* (1957) portrays a groping convert to Christianity in a Communist state. *L'horloger du cherche-midi* (1959), developing a theme already present in *Cherchant qui dévorer*, the second volume of the trilogy, shows a hero overwhelmed by remorse for the sins of his ancestors. Similarly weighed down by sin, this time his own, is the hero of *Le bonheur et le salut* (1961; tr. D. Folliot and E. Mosbacher, *The Better Song*, 1964). Estang's critical writing includes volumes on ⇨ Bernanos (1947), Jean de Boschère (1952) and ⇨ Saint-Exupéry (1956). [IHW]

**Estébanez Calderón, Serafín** (Málaga 1799–Madrid 1867). Spanish writer. His poetry and historical study (*De la conquista y pérdida de Portugal*) are forgotten, but he is remembered for his somewhat over-written *Escenas andaluzas* (1847; CA), a series of *costumbrista* essays on picturesque scenes, local customs, etc. He wrote under the pseudonym 'El solitario', and was also a well-known Arabic scholar. [JMC]

BAE, 78, 79.
J. F. Montesinos, *Costumbrismo y novela* (Valencia, 1960).

**Estienne, Henri II** (Paris *c.*1531–Lyons 1598). French humanist. He was the son of the first Robert Estienne, printer of classical texts and author of the *Thesaurus linguae latinae*. Henri was himself a printer, Hellenist and lexicographer. After a youth of travel and study, he joined his father in Geneva and published editions of Greek texts on which he had himself researched, including *Anacreon* (1554), the complete *Agamemnon* (1557), Diodorus Siculus, books xi-xx, which he had discovered (1559). Inheriting his father's press in 1559, he was compelled by the will to remain in Geneva as a Protestant. The *Traité de la conformité du langage français avec le grec* (?1565) is a defence of the French language to be set beside ⇨ Du Bellay's *Défense et illustration*. His *Apologie pour Hérodote* (1566; ed. P. Ristelhuber, 1879), a translation of the introduction to his Latin Herodotus, draws parallels between the strange stories accepted by antiquity and by the 16th century and satirizes the credulity of his contemporaries. This brought him into conflict with the Genevan church. His *Thesaurus graecae linguae* (5 vols., 1572) is a masterpiece of scholarship admirably matching his father's Latin work. In 1578 *Deux dialogues du nouveau langage français, italianisé et autrement déguisé*, a satire, in the form of a dialogue, directed against the Italianate French of the day, displeased Geneva and led him to retreat into France, where he was well received. In the next year he published the *Précellence du langage français* (ed. E. Huguet, 1896), a second and more important defence of French as a means of expressing ideas, was published in Paris. After a short spell in prison on his return to Geneva, he travelled abroad as much as possible. He is the author of the saying, 'Si jeunesse savait; si vieillesse pouvait'. [FWAG]

L. Clément, *H.E. et son œuvre française* (Paris, 1898–9).

**Etchahun.** ⇨ Basque Literature.

**Étienne de Bourbon** (*c.*1190–1261). French Dominican friar. He preached against the Albigenses and took part in inquisitions against them. His *Tractatus de diversis materiis praedicabilibus* is a collection of some hundreds of *exempla* or stories for the use of preachers, to help them to drive their teaching home. It was very popular throughout the Middle Ages. [FB]

Selection ed. A. Lecoy de la Marche (Paris, 1877).
J. T. Welter, *L'exemplum dans la littérature religieuse et didactique du moyen âge* (Paris, 1927).

**Ettinger, Salomon** (Warsaw 1799–Zhdanov 1855). Yiddish writer of poetry, fables and plays. The first to write in a modern style. His *Serkele* (1861) was the first modern play in Yiddish. He also wrote in Hebrew and Italian. [EE]

Waxman, *HJL*.

**Eugenius of Toledo** (*c.*600–658). Visigoth who became Bishop of Toledo. His numerous poems are on very varied subjects, with frequent metrical faults and tricks of ornamentation. One of the best known is a short poem in praise of the nightingale, whose song he asserts to be superior to that of the swan, the swallow and the parrot. [FB]

Migne, *PL*, 87; ed. F. Vollmer (MGH, AA, XIV); Lindsay, *MLP*.

**Evtushenko, Evgeny.** ⇨ Yevtushenko, Yevgeny.

**Ewald, Johannes** (Copenhagen 1743–Copenhagen 1781). Danish poet. The son of a Pietist clergyman, he began divinity at Copenhagen at 15, then in a turmoil of love and longing for fame ran away to fight in the Seven Years' War, first on the Prussian, later on the Austrian side. Broken in health, and in heart when his fiancée married another man, he graduated in 1762 only to lead an irregular and reckless life, addicted to alcohol; he died at 37.

Ewald is one of Denmark's greatest lyrical poets. In him 18th-century rationalism blends with new individualistic and emotional tendencies which make him a precursor of Danish Romanticism. His earliest poetry is didactic, in the style of Pope, and his first dramatic work classicistic, in the style of Corneille; but under the influence of Klopstock (who lived for a time in Denmark) he began to study Shakespeare, Ossian and the ballads collected by Percy. His tragedy *Rolf Krage* (1770), based on an ancient Danish legend, is the first example of Shakespearean influence in Danish literature, though in its style it still owes much to French classicism. *Balders Død* (1773; tr. G. Borrow, *The Death of Balder*, 1889) is the first Danish tragedy in blank verse. In 1780 his patriotic drama, *Fiskerne*, was performed in Copenhagen.

Ewald's true greatness lies, however, in his lyrical (and often very personal) poetry, some of which has been translated into English by W. Herbert, W. S. Walker, George Borrow, H. W. Longfellow, R. Buchanan, R. P. Keigwin, and others. Most famous among his many poems are 'The Bliss of Rungsted', 'Ode to the Soul', 'Little Gunver', 'King Christian' (now the Danish royal anthem) and the moving poem dictated on his death-bed, 'Udrust dig, Helt fra Golgatha'.

In 1775 he began to write his impressionistic memoirs which, in imitation of Sterne, he entitled *Levnet og Meninger* (posth. 1804); it is a series of 'confessions', in the manner of Rousseau, pathetic and humorous at the same time. [ELB]

*Ewalds samlede Skrifter* (6 vols., 1914–24).
E. Frandsen, *J.E.* (Copenhagen, 1939).

**Expressionism.** A literary and artistic movement, originating in Germany, in revolt against representational conventions and seeking new spontaneity and intensity of inner vision. Associated at first with the painting of the 'Brücke' (Dresden, 1905) and 'Der blaue Reiter' (Munich, 1911) groups, and with publications in the journals *Der Sturm* (ed. H. Walden, 1910ff.) and *Die Aktion* (ed. F. Pfemfert, 1911ff.), the term is now applied to all similar visionary styles, variously reflecting the shock of industrialization and war, in poetry (e.g. Trakl, Heym, Stadler), in drama (e.g. Hasenclever, Toller, Unruh, Kaiser), and prose (e.g. Döblin, Edschmid, Benn). [PB]

Anthologies: *Menschheitsdämmerung*, ed. K. Pinthus (1920; repr. 1959) (poetry); *Schrei und Bekenntnis*, ed. K. Otten (1960) (drama); *Ahnung und Aufbruch*, ed. K. Otten (1957) (prose); *Anthology of German Expressionist Drama*, ed. W. H. Sokel (Garden City, N.Y., 1963); *Der blaue Reiter*, ed. F. Marc, V. Kandinsky (1912; repr. 1966); Hamburger and Middleton, *MGP*.
Hamburger, *RE*; Sokel, *WE*; Garten, *MGD*.

**'Eyrbyggja Saga.'** ⇨ Icelandic Sagas.

**'Ezzos Gesang (Ezzolied).'** German strophic hymn written in Bamberg *c.* 1060 and sung on the crusade of 1064–5. Of Ezzo, the monk who names himself as the author of the text, nothing is known save that he wrote the hymn at the behest of Bishop Gunther of Bamberg (d. 1065). The hymn gives a miniature history of mankind from Creation to Salvation, and its historical importance in literature lies in the fact that it breaks a silence of a century and a half in the recorded tradition of German poetry. [RT]

Braune, *AL*, 43.

# F

**'Fabliaux.'** 'Contes à rire en vers', short medieval French verse tales, varying from 50 to about 1,000 lines, composed in satirical, burlesque, sometimes obscene style, usually on the subject of wantonness, adultery or other deceitfulness. Some stories tilt at religious subjects, St Peter winning at dice the souls in Hell given into the keeping of the ⇨ *jongleur* (*Saint Pierre et le Jongleur*). The mockery and satire, as in much medieval writing, is directed primarily against women and priests. The genre, of which about 150 examples have survived, emerged in the late 12th century and continued in the 13th and 14th centuries. The sources, authorship and audiences of this literary form are in dispute. Many of the stories are of folk origin, often with Oriental connexions, written by professional poets or *jongleurs*, and intended in some cases for the court and, in varying 'remaniements', for audiences of widely different social status. In English the basic genre of the *fabliau* can be discerned in some of the *Canterbury Tales*. [LTT]

*Recueil général et complet des fabliaux des XIIIe et XIVe siècles*, ed. A. de Montaiglon and G. Raynaud (6 vols., Paris, 1872–90); *Fabliaux*, sel. and ed. R. C. Johnston and D. D. R. Owen (1957); *Twelve Fabliaux from ms. fr. 19152 of the Bibliothèque Nationale*, ed. T. B. W. Reid (1958).

J. Bédier, *Les fabliaux, études de littérature populaire et d'histoire littéraire du moyen âge* (Paris, 5th edn, 1928); Per Nykrog, *Les fabliaux, étude d'histoire littéraire et de stylistique médiévale* (Copenhagen, 1957); J. Rychner, *Contribution à l'étude des fabliaux* (2 vols., Neuchâtel/Geneva, 1960); *RF*, LXXII (1960).

**Fabre, Émile** (Metz 1869–Paris 1955). French dramatist. Author of solidly constructed, sharply observed studies of social life. His satire ranges from the world of politics and business to that of life in the colonies. His dialogue is deft and rapid and conveys the sense of a finely controlled moral passion. Of considerable interest are: *L'argent* (1895); *La vie publique* (1901), a mordant study of local politics; *Les ventres dorés* (1905), a satire on the 'City'; *La maison d'argile* (1907), which probes personal psychology in divorce; and *Les vainqueurs* (1908). His *Notes sur la mise en scène* (1933) reflect the long experience of the theatre of a playwright who was also Administrator of the Comédie Française (1915–36). [SBJ]

*Théâtre* (5 vols., 1920–9).

A. Brisson, *Le théâtre et les mœurs* (Paris, 1907–12); C. H. Bissell, *Les conventions du théâtre bourgeois contemporain en France (1887–1914)* (Paris, 1930).

**Fadeyev, Aleksandr Aleksandrovich** (Kimry, Tver' 1901–Moscow 1956). Russian novelist. The son of poor parents, he joined the Communist Party in 1918. In the Civil War he fought in Siberia against Kolchak and the Japanese. This provided material for his first novel, *Razgrom* (1927; tr. R. Charques, *The Nineteen*, 1929), which brought him fame. Both the style and the characterization reveal the influence of L. Tolstoy, but in his philosophy of history he rejects Tolstoy's ideas. This work and the delineation of the hero were later taken as models for socialist realism. The unfinished *Posledniy iz Udege* (1929-36) is also devoted to the Civil War in Siberia and shows the supersession of capitalism by socialism there. His last novel, an account of youth resistance behind the German lines during the Second World War, *Molodaya Gvardiya* (1945), ran into official disapproval and was revised by Fadeyev several times.

His chief importance lies in the field of literary politics. In the 1920s he was a theoretician of the RAPP group, which held the culture of all non-socialist civilizations to be irrelevant and even harmful to the new proletarian culture. In 1932 when RAPP was disbanded he retracted these views and took up an important position in the secretariat of the Union of Soviet Writers. From 1946 he was its General Secretary. Khrushchev's denunciation of Stalinism at the XXth Party Congress (1956) and the rehabilitation of many writers for whose exile or execution he had been responsible are said to have led to his suicide. [RDBT]

*Sobraniye sochineniy* (5 vols., 1959–61).

V. Ozerov *A.F.* (Moscow, 1964).

**Faguet, Émile.** ⇨ French Literary Criticism in the 19th and 20th Centuries.

**Falcão, Cristóvão** (Portalegre ?1518–?1554). Portuguese poet. His name first appears as receiving a *moradia* (pension) at court in 1527. In 1542 he was in Rome on a diplomatic mission. A letter written from Rome by an agent of João III refers to Falcão and his imprisonment in Lisbon castle, which may have been on account of his affair with Maria Brandão. Clearly his crime was not serious since the king knew of it and had agreed to his going to Rome. In 1545 he was named factor and captain of the fortress of Arguim for three years, but evidently sold the office. In 1547 he was in Portalegre where a case on the grounds of assault was brought against him, and he was imprisoned but finally pardoned in 1551.

Tradition has it that he was 14 at the time of his love-affair with the 12-year-old daughter of the Flanders factor João Brandão, as a result of which he was imprisoned and she was probably sent to a convent. Only perhaps years later was this love-idyll transformed into the poems, the *Égloga* and the *Carta do preso*, now attributed to Falcão, and upon which his literary reputation rests.

The *Trovas de Crisfal* were first published in 1554, with the works of Bernardim ⇨ Ribeiro, by the Usques, a family of Portuguese Jews who set up a press in Ferrara, but there exists a broadsheet entitled *Trouas de Chrisfal*, probably of *c.* 1545, and probably later than the departure of the Usques from Portugal, because there are slight differences between this text and that of Ferrara. In the latter case the eclogue is attributed to its author Cristóvão Falcão, the contraction of whose names gives *Crisfal*.

None of Ribeiro's friends protested against the attribution, nor did the second edition of Ribeiro's works (in 1557) include what had been attributed to Falcão in the first. Falcão is to be regarded as an inspired imitator of Ribeiro whom he never personally knew. [ARM]

B. Ribeiro and C. Falcão, *Obras* (2 vols., Coimbra, 1923); *Crisfal*, ed. J. Régio (Lisbon, 1959).

**Falkberget, Johan** (Røros 1879–Røros 1967). Norwegian novelist. The son of a miner, he began work at the Røros copper mines at an early age. Later he was for a time a journalist. Most of his novels are set in his native region and are inspired by its history, traditions and life in the mines. His first novels had contemporary settings, but with *Eli Sjursdotter* (1913) he began the long series of historical novels which have made his name: *Lisbeth paa Jarnfjeld* (1915; tr. R. Gjelsness, *Lisbeth of Jarnfjeld*, 1930); *Sol* (1918); *Bjørneskytteren* (1919); *Den fjerde nattevakt* (1923); *Nattens brød – An-Magritt* (1940); *Plogjernet* (1946); *Johannes* (1952); *Kjærlighets veier* (1959). Finest of them is *Christianus Sextus* (6 vols., 1927–35), with its superb handling of historical material, its diversity, and profound understanding of human motives and aspirations, all conveyed in an individual lyric-epic style and pervaded by a deep humanism. [RGP]

*Verker* (12 vols., 1959).

E. Døhl, *J.F.* (Oslo, 1949); R. Thesen, *J.F.* (Oslo, 1959).

**Fallada, Hans,** pseud. of Rudolf Ditzen (Greifswald 1893–Berlin 1947). German novelist. His *Kleiner Mann – was nun* (1932; tr. E. Sutton, *Little Man What Now*, 1933), a moving documentary of a devoted young married couple struggling with unemployment and inflation, became world famous (twice filmed). Sharing with Brecht a profound (but less ideological and more sentimental) concern with the victims of our time, his *Wolf unter Wölfen* (1937; tr. P. Owens, *Wolf Among Wolves*, 1938) is a moving and tragic novel, a little-man's *War and Peace*, set in the squalid, inhuman post-1918 Germany. *Damals bei uns daheim* (1942) and *Heute bei uns zu Hause* (1943) are autobiographical; after Fallada's death a number of outstanding works appeared, including *Der Alpdruck* (1947), *Jeder stirbt für sich allein* (1949), and *Der Trinker* (1950; tr. C. and A. L. Lloyd, *The Drinker*, 1952). The following works also appeared in translation: *Who Once Eats out of the Tin Bowl* (tr. E. Sutton, 1934), *Once We Had a Child* (tr. Sutton, 1935), *Sparrow Farm* (tr. Sutton, 1937), *Old Heart Goes on a Journey* (tr. Sutton, 1936), *Iron Gustav* (tr. Philip Owens, 1940), and *That Rascal Fridolin* (tr. anon., 1959). Though little-known nowadays, Fallada is a great social realist novelist. [PB]

J. Manthey, *H.F.* (Reinbek, 1963); H. Neugebauer, I. M. Lange and H.-J. Geerdts, *Leonhard Frank – H.F.* (East Berlin, 1960); *GLL*, XXIX, 1, 1956.

**Faludy, György** (Budapest 1913– ). Hungarian poet and writer. Of bourgeois origins he studied in Budapest and Paris. Though primarily a lyrical poet, he first became well known through his free adaptation into Hungarian of Villon's ballads (1937). Between 1939 and 1946, he lived in emigration. Being a Humanist of Jewish descent, all publications of his works were destroyed by the Nazis, and later by the Communists, who also interned him in a prison-camp (1950–54). After the 1956 Hungarian uprising, he emigrated to Britain. Among his publications are: *Laudetur* (1938), a collection of medieval religious verse in translation: *Európai Költők Antológiája* (1938); *A Pompéji Strázsán* (1938); *Emlékkönyv a Rőt Bizáncról* ('A Keepsake Book of Red Byzantium', 1961); *Tragödie eines Volkes* (Vienna, 1958). [JFR]

*My Happy Days in Hell*, tr. K. Szász (1962) (autobiography).

**Fangen, Ronald** (Kragerø 1895–Fornebu, Oslo 1946). Norwegian novelist and playwright. His father was a mining engineer, his mother English. A precocious but lonely schoolboy, he soon took to writing. His early novels were weak but success came with the plays *Syndefald* (1920), *Fienden* (1922) – both influenced by German ⇨ Expressionism – and the more realistic *Den forjættede dag* (1926). However, his more permanent importance lies in his later novels, especially *Nogen unge mennesker* (1929) and its continuation *Erik* (1931); *Duel* (1932; tr. P. Wiking, 1934); *En kvinnes vei* (1933); *Mannen som elsket rettferdigheten* (1934). In these works he is particularly concerned with problems of human relationships, especially between young people, which he often explores with great psychological acuity. There is an advocacy of the Christian solution in his work (he joined the so-called Oxford Movement in 1934); thus his ideology stands in sharp contrast to that of his contemporaries ⇨ Hoel, ⇨ Krog and ⇨ Øverland. In *En lysets engel* (1945; tr. D. McKay, *Both are My Cousins*, 1949) he deals with a quisling, also in an ideological context. He was killed in an air disaster. [RGP]

*Samlede verker* (9 vols., 1948–9).
C. F. Engelstad, *R.F.* (Oslo, 1946); Beyer, *NL.*

**Fargue, Léon-Paul** (Paris 1876–Paris 1947). French poet. After a childhood clouded by illegitimacy, he abandoned his studies and neglected his father's ceramics workshops for the artistic haunts of Montmartre and Saint-Germain. He tried his hand at music and painting, but won fame as a conversationalist and a bohemian poet. He became a semi-legendary bachelor-orphan, a fashionable sight of Parisian night-life. He helped to direct the experimental review *Commerce* in the twenties, but wasted himself on mundane literary activity, publishing poetry occasionally and meticulously. He progressed from verse to prose poems and finally to lyrical essays. The best are in *Tancrède* (1895), *Nocturnes* (1905), *Poèmes* (1918), *Espaces* and *Sous la lampe* (1929), *Ludions* (1933), *Le piéton de Paris* (1939), *Haute solitude* (1941) and *Méandres* (1946). They are inspired by courteous cynicism and feverish, luxuriant tenderness for his fellowmen; and consist in nostalgic savourings of minutious confessions and of the overwhelming spleen and burning solitude of the modern industrial city. He is remembered mainly as a loving commemorator of the streets of Paris. His varied rhythms provide a firm but throbbing basis for bizarre images and audacious visions with an occasional whiff of surrealism. Valéry called him the 'prince of metaphors'. What he intended to be the 'ripe fruit of internal succulence' appears as a voluptuous flowering of multiple impressions and verbal acrobatics. [CLC]

*Poésies*, 1963.
E. de la Rochefoucauld, *L.-P.F.* (Paris, 1959).

**Fastnachtspiel.** German Shrovetide play. Short, usually in doggerel verse, produced by amateurs at Shrovetide, it derives ultimately from fertility cults and primitive festivals in celebration of the return of spring. With the urbanization of the *Fastnachtspiel*, the original peasant-hero naturally tends to become an object of scorn, and the primitive cult significance is translated into social satire, the fertility element surviving in the preoccupation with questions of marital harmony, while the beating out of winter lives on in the frequent slap-stick brawls and free fights. As a literary form it enjoyed its greatest development in Nürnberg at the hands of Volz, Rosenplüt, ⇨ Sachs and ⇨ Ayrer. In the Reformation period it was adapted for religious polemicism by the Swiss dramatist Niklaus Manuel. [WAC]

**Fayko, Aleksey** (Moscow 1893–     ). Soviet playwright. Educated as a historian, he became a club instructor (1921) and producer at the second studio of the Moscow Arts Theatre. *Ozero Lyul'* and *Uchitel'*

*Barbus* were staged by Meyerhold in the mid-twenties; *Kontsert*, one of his best works, was put on by the Teatr Revolyutsii in 1928 and so was his near-thriller *Chelovek s portfelem.* His theme is the intelligentsia's search for a 'third force' and a 'middle way' – a search doomed to frustration by the violence of the times. [AP]

*Dramy i komedii* (1958).
*Vstrechi s Meyerkhol'dom* (Moscow, 1967); Boguslavskiy, *KIRSD.*

**Fazekas, Mihály** (Debrecen 1766–Debrecen 1828). Hungarian poet and botanist. Editor of a scientific herbal, his poetry reflects the gardener, and stands for bourgeois commonsense. His main work is *Ludas Matyi*, a comic hexametric epic in popular tone; it is the finest poetic narrative among older Hungarian literature. [JFR]

**Fedin, Konstantin Aleksandrovich** (Saratov 1892–1970). Russian novelist. Of humble origin, he studied in Moscow and Germany, and was interned in Bavaria from 1914 to 1918. On his return he joined the Communist Party and served in the Red Army. He left the Party in 1921 and joined the ⇨ Serapion Brothers. His first book, *Pustyr'* (1923), turns its back almost entirely on contemporary events, but his novel *Goroda i gody* (1924; tr. M. Scammell, *Cities and Years*, 1962) deals with the problems and scruples of intellectuals in time of revolution; the spirit of the Serapion brothers is revealed in the formal device of a shuffled time-sequence. With this work Fedin revived the traditional novel in Soviet Russia. His second and finest novel, *Brat'ya* (1928), deals with the same problems and employs similar devices. In the centre of the story are three brothers; the oldest had made his name before the Revolution as a surgeon; the youngest is a Bolshevik. Torn between them is the middle brother, a composer, whose loyalties lie with his art rather than with any political creed. His later novels of the 1930s, *Pokhishcheniye Yevropy* (1935) and *Sanatoriy Arktur* (1939), continue to reflect his fascination with the contrast of 'old' Europe and 'young' Russia. During the war he produced memoirs of the early 1920s, *Gor'ky sredi nas* (1944), but the work ran into official hostility and the projected third volume was never written. Fedin was then engaged on a vast historical trilogy: *Pervyye radosti* (1945; tr. H. Kazanina, *Early Joys*, 1948), *Neobyknovennoye leto* (1948; tr. M. Wettlin, *No Ordinary Summer*, 1950) and *Kostyor* (Pt I, 1962), but these works are less interesting and suffer from historical falsification; his style too has lost its earlier poise and distinction. In 1959 he was appointed First Secretary of the Union of Soviet Writers.

*Sobraniye sochineniy* (9 vols., 1960–2).
B. Braynina, *K.F.* (Moscow 1962); Simmons *RFSI.*

**Feffer, Itzik** (Kiev 1900– ? 1948). Yiddish writer and poet. From a working-class Jewish family, he started his career as a compositor. The Bolshevik Revolution was one of his main subjects and he was highly regarded by the regime. He fought in the Red Army in both wars, and during the Second World War was a member of the Jewish Anti-fascist Committee and in this capacity toured England and the U.S.A. He was executed during the Stalinist purges after the war. [EE]

*Vegn zich* (1924); *A shteyn oif a shteyn* (1926); *Roitarmeyish* (1942); *Di Shotns fun Warshawer Geto* (1944).
Roback, *SYL.*

**Feijoo, Benito Jerónimo** (Casdemiro 1676–Oviedo 1764). Spanish essayist. He inherited from his father a certain facility as a poet but his main inclinations were towards theology, philosophy and science. He entered the Benedictine Order in 1690 and held various teaching posts and chairs of theology from 1721 until ill-health forced him to retire in 1739. He spent most of his life in Oviedo, in spite of numerous invitations to take up more important posts in Madrid. But although he went to the capital in 1725 to prepare the first volume of his *Teatro crítico universal* for publication, he seems to have preferred to make the mountain come to Mahomet, and much of his work, notably the *Cartas eruditas*, was the result of inquiries sent to him which might well not have been sent at all, had he been more accessible. His main intention was to eradicate superstitious beliefs and popular misconceptions, and where possible his methods were scientific. He often conducted the relevant experiments himself, although for the modern taste he was far too ready to accept the validity of his own investigations. At a period when the scientific approach was rare in Spain, his work was invaluable, and his wit and directness were a salutary antidote to the rococo rhetoric of his times. [ONVG]

*Essays or Discourses*, tr. J. Brett (1780); CC (selections).
G. Delpy, *L'Espagne et l'esprit européen. L'œuvre de F.* (Paris, 1936); McClelland, *ORMS*.

**Feirberg, Mordecai Zeev** (Novygrad-Volhynsk 1874–Novygrad-Volhynsk 1899). Hebrew writer. In his best-known long short story, *L'An* (tr. 1959), this short-lived writer, son of a fanatic Hassid, poignantly describes the conflict between the old and new generation of Jews, leaving the hero perplexed. [EE]

S. Rawidowitz, *M.Z.F.* (Berlin, 1923).

**Félibrige.** An association founded in 1854 by seven young poets who met at Avignon and Font-Ségugne and organized and inspired a renaissance of Provençal literature, language and customs in the 19th century. The word *félibres* was taken by them from an old song in which Jesus disputes in the temple with the seven Doctors of the Law 'Emé li set félibre de la lèi'. The new movement was immediately successful. A uniform orthography and grammar was accepted, and in 1855 Roumanille and Mistral founded the *Armana Provençau* ('Provençal Almanach') which became the leading periodical for new writing and for articles on Provençal life and customs. The *félibres* were: Frédéric ⇨ Mistral, Joseph Roumanille, Théodore ⇨ Aubanel, Paul Giera (1816–61), Jean Brunet (1823–94), Remy Marcellin (1832–1908) and Anselme Mathieu (1828–1925).

From 1861 to 1865 a Pan-latinist idea for a federation of Mediterranean cultures developed within the Félibrige, and took the extreme form among some of its adherents of separatist demands for Southern autonomy. In this Pan-latinist period much active support was given to the Catalan revival: Victor Balaguer, outlawed by Madrid, was welcomed at Beaucaire in 1867. Shortly afterwards Mistral composed his 'Coupo santo', a sort of *Marseillaise* for Provençals and Catalans which is still sung. An Italian period followed around 1874. In 1876 Mistral reconstituted the Félibrige into a Consistory of fifty *mantenedors* and *majorals* presided over by a Capoulié, and the fight to preserve the life and literature of Southern France was extended from Provence to all areas of the *langue d'oc*. The demand for the teaching of the *langue d'oc* in Southern French schools was recently agreed to by the French government.

Interest in the Félibrige and in creative writing in Provençal still animates cultivated circles in Southern France but is hampered by the dispute concerning the merits of Mistral's Rhodanien language and other dialects, especially the forms favoured by the *escola occitana* at Toulouse. [LTT]

E. Ripert, *Le Félibrige* (Paris, 1924) and *La renaissance provençale 1800–1860* (Paris/Aix-en-Provence, 1918); C. Camproux, *Histoire de la littérature occitane* (Paris, 1953); L. Alibert, *Grammatica occitana* (Toulouse, 1935); A. V. Roche, *Provençal Regionalism* (Evanston, Ill., 1954).

**Feliński, Alojzy** (Łuck 1771–Krzemieniec 1820). Polish playwright. He wrote a tragedy on the best models of the French classical theatre about Barbara Radziwiłł, whose marriage to King Sigismund Augustus in 1547 created a political crisis. First staged in Warsaw in 1817, *Barbara* was hailed as an exemplary national drama, but the romantic fashion set in soon after and its reputation suffered. The metre of the play, which is the 13-syllable line, has been particularly studied and praised. [JP]

**Felipe, León** (Tábala 1884– ). Spanish poet. He has written to be recited rather than read. His *vers-libre* is almost without artifice, except for some sparing use of assonance (he is often compared to Whitman). His concern for man's social condition has religious depth; but the divine is an ideal to be realized on earth, not contemplated in heaven. Poetry is the language of that ideal, the only glimpse beyond man's tragic isolation into a realm of justice and light. Its true language cannot yet be spoken – which is perhaps why his own style is often harsh, colloquial, at times blasphemous. He left Spain after the Civil War and settled in Mexico. [JMC]

*Obras completas* (Buenos Aires, 1964); *Versos y oraciones de caminante* (1917); *El hacha* (Mexico, 1939); *E ciervo* (Mexico, 1958); Blecua, *FLE*.
Cernuda, *EPC*; Vivanco, *PEC*.

**Fénelon, François de Salignac de la Mothe** (Fénelon 1651–Cambrai 1715). French churchman and man of letters. He was educated at home, then at the University of Cahors and the Jesuit college du Plessis in Paris. He took ecclesiastical orders as a member of Saint-Sulpice in 1675, rapidly became known as a successful preacher, was appointed to missions directed at the Protestants, first at the institution known as the Nouvelles Converties in Paris, then in Saintonge. A protégé of ⇨ Bossuet, he became tutor to the King's grandson, the Duc de Bourgogne, and in 1695 Archbishop of Cambrai.

The most dramatic episode of his sensational career sprang from his meeting Mme Guyon in 1688, a year after the Quietist doctrines of Molinos had been condemned by Rome. Lukewarm at first, he became by stages the adherent and confessor of a select circle who were attracted by her mystical views. He was, one may say, taken up by Mme de Maintenon, Mme de Beauvilliers and Mme de Chevreuse. But this honeymoon did not last long in such a nest of intrigue as the French court. Mme de Maintenon turned against the too popular abbé and worked with his rivals: Godet, Noailles, ⇨ Bourdaloue and above all Bossuet, who soon became persuaded that Mme Guyon was in error and her influence pernicious. A conference at Issy only widened the breach: each of the two men suspected the other. Bossuet thought Fénelon vain and deluded. Fénelon reproached Bossuet with violating the secret of the confessional. It was thus not clear whether his appointment to the see of Cambrai was promotion, or removal. Since he refused openly to approve or condemn Bossuet's *Instruction sur les états d'oraison* in 1696, his own *Explication des Maximes des saints sur la vie intérieure* (1697) was taken as defence of Mme Guyon, and defiance of his colleagues. Fénelon appealed to Rome in April 1697. The King sided with Bossuet, demanded that the Pope condemn Fénelon and refused to allow him to go to Rome to plead his own cause (both sides acted through agents). A private letter of 1696 divulged by Mme de Maintenon seems to have turned the scale and in March Fénelon was condemned by papal brief. In later years he seems to have had some return of royal favour, by reason of his continued opposition to Jansenism. But his real life was in his diocese, where he was revered and popular. As author of *Télémaque* (ed. A. Cohen) he was a European figure. This Homeric imitation was the most popular French work of the first half of the 18th century. When objection was raised at Oxford to Alan Ramsay (a Catholic) receiving an honorary degree the official reply was that a disciple of Fénelon deserved honour from the University.

His reputation is as disconcerting as his life. For the generation of Voltaire he was a churchman only in name, and in reality a *philosophe*, though on many issues he would have sided with Bossuet rather than with Voltaire. He saw the evils of absolutism and the necessity of institutions almost as clearly as Rousseau; he wanted tax reform, free trade, a peace policy instead of a war policy, and a rise in the standard of living of the poorest; he at least admitted the thought of civil toleration. Yet he also denounced individualism and rationalism. To the Duc de Chevreuse he wrote (and the best of him is in his letters): 'Be on your guard against your mind which has often deceived you...and against men of learning and logical argument.'

Fénelon's works are voluminous and mostly unread except by experts. [WGM]

H. Bremond, *Apologie pour F.* (Paris, 1910); É. Carcassonne, *F. l'homme et l'œuvre* (Paris. 1946); J. Goré, *L'itinéraire de F.* (Paris, 1957); R. Schmittlein, *L'aspect politique du différend Bossuet–Fénelon* (Paris, 1954).

**Ferlin, Nils** (Karlstad 1898–Penningby 1961). Swedish poet. After trying various trades from unskilled labour to journalism and acting (he found the job of commercial song-writer most congenial) he achieved recognition with his first book of verse *En döddansares visor* (1930). The personality which emerges here and in *Barfotabarn* (1933) and *Goggles* (1938) is that of a lonely man looking at society from the outside and appearing in various guises as bohemian, vagabond, misfit and clown, yet with a personal awareness akin to Villon's. Ferlin writes in the tradition of the popular song; but there is nothing naïve about his simple, melodious, sometimes careless verses. Satirical bitterness and scorn alternate with tenderness and sympathy for the underdog. The element of self-irony is conspicuous but would be more tonic were it not offset by an occasional note of self-pity. From the start the idea of death is prominent and not unfrequently leads the poet into Biblical territory. The later work contained in *Med många kulörta lyktor* (1944), *Kejsarens papegoja* (1951), and *Från mitt ekorrhjul* (1957) on the whole marks a decline. It shows the poet increasingly preoccupied with the fear of the meaninglessness of life and, as before, unable to embrace any simpl faith. Never a modernist, Ferlin – no doubt aided by inspired musical settings by various hands – achieved popularity with a wider public than any of his contemporaries, including ⇨ Boye, ⇨ Gullberg and ⇨ Martinson. [SAB]

A. Häggqvist, *F. Ungdomsåren* (Stockholm, 1942); *En bok om N.F.*, ed. S. Carlson and A. Liffner (Stockholm, 1954); Å. Runnquist, *Poeten N.F.* (Stockholm, 1958).

**Fernández, Lucas** (Salamanca 1474–Salamanca 1542). Spanish dramatist. His single volume, *Farsas y églogas al modo y estilo pastoril* (1514; ed. M. Cañete, 1867; facsimile ed. E. Cotarelo, 1929), contains 3 secular and 3 religious pieces. One of the former is simply a lyrical debate between a knight, a lady and a shepherd; another, on the subject of the *Miles gloriosus*, ends with music and a dance. His best play (in the manner of ⇨ Encina, but more pious) is the *Auto de la Pasión*, a drama voiced by the witnesses so graphically and movingly that there is no need for the Saviour himself to speak or be represented. The play ends with a fine *villancico* which joins the memory of the Nativity to the tragedy that has just been described. [JMC]

Crawford, *SDLV*; Wardropper, *HPL*.

**Fernández de Jerena, Garcí** (end of 14th cent.). Spanish poet. Allegedly he married a converted Mooress, retired with her to a hermitage, set out on a pilgrimage to Jerusalem, but stopped at Málaga, where he became a Moslem and made love to his sister-in-law. ⇨ Baena, who included his poems in his *Cancionero*, gives this disapproving account of Fernández's life. So little is really known of him that his name is sometimes taken as Ferrándes. His *Despedida del amor*, in which Love bids farewell to Spain, is one of several very pleasing lyrics that bear his signature. [JMC]

Cohen, *PBSV*.
L. Dolfuss, *Études sur le moyen-âge espagnol* (Paris, 1894).

**'Fernán González, Poema de.'** Mid-13th-century Spanish narrative poem. The work recounts, not altogether accurately, the deeds of Count Fernán González (895?–970), who fought to make the County of Castile politically independent of the Kingdom of León. The poem is preserved in a single 15th-century manuscript which has considerable lacunae (it breaks off at stanza 701). The anonymous author, long held to be a monk of the Castilian monastery of San Pedro de Arlanza, seems to have reshaped an epic version of the life (which has not survived) and fitted it into the ⇨ *cuaderna vía* form. The poem shows the partial influence of ⇨ Berceo, the *Libro de* ⇨ *Alexandre* and even the *De laude Hispaniae* of St Isidore. The long introductory section concerning the history of Spain up to Fernán González's birth holds little interest for the modern reader, but in the main narrative there are some good descriptions: the Battles of Lara, La Era Degollada and Hacinas, and the burial of the Count of Tolosa. The episode of the Horse and the Hawk, the treachery at Cirueña, Fernán González's imprisonment in Castroviejo and his release by the enamoured Princess Sancha are incidents that offer considerable interest. The author depicts the protagonist in epic terms: he is discreet, courageous, wise, generous, noble in his treatment of conquered enemies. The work appears to have been carefully planned and constructed, but is perhaps marred by a too overt nationalistic and propagandist tone. [IM]

Ed. C. C. Marden (Baltimore, 1904); ed. E. Serrano (1943); ed. R. Menéndez Pidal, in *Reliquias de la poesía épica española* (1951); ed. A. Zamora Vicente (CC); modern Spanish version, E. Alarcos Llorach (Valencia, 1955).
*Hispania*, XIII, 1930; *Bulletin Hispanique*, XXX, 1928; XXXIII, 1931; *HR*, XXII, 1954; XXIII, 1955; XXV, 1957.

**Ferreira, António** (Lisbon 1528–Lisbon 1569). Portuguese poet. He studied law at the University of Coimbra (where he came in contact with the distinguished humanist Diogo de Teive), and at 28 became a judge in the Relação at Lisbon, where he spent the rest of his life. He died of the plague. His poems were published in 1598 by his son under the title of *Poemas Lusitanos*.

Ferreira was perhaps the most distinguished of the Portuguese poets who welcomed the new poetic doctrine of ⇨ Sá de Miranda, certainly the most exemplary defender of poetry written in Portuguese (as opposed to Spanish or Latin) and the one most imbued with the ideals of classical scholarship. The life he preferred was one spent among books in a country retreat, far from the clamour of war and trade, which he hated. He was equally opposed to the ideal of the knight and of the mystic. He appears as a man of the Renaissance, a type not common in Iberia. In his poetry sweet reason triumphs; he can think in verse (and not very many of his countrymen do that). The tone is almost always elevated and serious, the expression vigorous and concise. He is concerned to form the mind of his reader as much as to appeal to his emotions. His models were Virgil, and especially Horace, and his poems were therefore cast in the classical forms of elegy, epistle, epigram and ode. It was natural that he should also write sonnets under the influence of Petrarch and the Italians, but with less success since his genius needed more room for its expansion. Perhaps his Epistles best reveal Ferreira's qualities.

His fame, however, rests especially upon *A Castro*, a tragedy in five acts upon the Greek model, in blank verse, with chorus and upon a national theme: the love of D. Pedro for Inês de Castro, and her murder, for reasons of state, at the behest of the prince's father, King Afonso IV. Ferreira's is the only successful attempt (among many made in both Spain and Portugal) to write classical tragedy.

He also wrote, with less success, two prose comedies in the tradition of Latin comedy – *Bristo* and *O Cioso*. [ARM]

*Obras completas* (2 vols., CSC, 1939).
J. de Castilho, *A.F. Estudos biographico-litterarios* (3 vols., Lisbon, 1865).

**Ferreira de Castro, José Maria** (Oliveira de Azeméis 1898– ). Portuguese novelist. He emigrated to Brazil in 1911, spending four years working on the rubber-plantations of Amazônia, and a further three years in Pará as a journalist and minor novelist. After another year touring Brazil he returned to Portugal in 1919, where he continued in journalism and published minor novels and a play. His first literary success was in 1928 with *Emigrantes*, his and Portugal's first great social novel. With a realism born of personal experience he used this loosely knit work to relate the many hardships of Portuguese emigrants to Brazil. His next novel, *A Selva* (1930), won him international acclaim, has been translated into seventeen languages and was a clear indictment of working conditions in the rubber-plantations of Brazil. The Social Realism apparent in his concern for the under-privileged continued in his next four novels, *Eternidade* (1933), *Terra Fria* (1934), *Tempestade* (1940) and *A Lã e a Neve* (1947), the last, probably the most powerful, a penetrating scrutiny of the lives of shepherds and textile-workers in the Covilhã area. In his later fiction, *A Curva da Estrada* (1950) and the *novella* entitled *A Missão* (1954), set respectively in Republican Spain and the France of 1940, he is concerned no longer with underdogs and their battle with superiors, but with man's battle with himself to choose a course of action in situations where political pressures make no decision easy. The author's journalistic talents, constant wide travels and avid interest for the arts have also borne fruit in three non-fictional works, *Pequenos Mundos e Velhas Civilizações* (1937–8), *A Volta ao Mundo* (1944) and *As Maravilhas Artísticas do Mundo* (1957–61). He has consistently refused to be considered as a candidate for the Nobel Prize. [RCW]

A. de Cabral, *F. de C.* (Lisbon, 1940); J. Brasil, *F. de C.* (Lisbon, 1961).

**Fet, Afanasy Afanas'yevich** (estate in Orlov district 1820–Moscow 1892). Russian poet. He used his German mother's name (Foeth); his parents married in 1822, but he took his father's name, Shenshin, only in 1873. He went to a German boarding-school in Estonia and to Moscow University (1838–44). He published his first collection of poems, *Liricheskiy Panteon*, in 1840; later he became a cavalry soldier. He loved but was too poor to marry 'Yelena'; they parted and she committed suicide. Fet never forgot this love. In 1850 appeared another collection, *Stikhotvoreniya* (ed. B. Ya. Bukhshtab, 1937; ed. P. P. Gromov, 1963). He was transferred to the Guards (1853) and commissioned. After travels abroad, he made a rich marriage (1856) and became a friend of Turgenev and Tolstoy. He retired to farm (1858), wrote conservative articles (1862) and his poems were re-edited and decried by the Radicals. In 1881 he moved to Moscow, translated Horace and other Latin poets, Goethe's *Faust*, and Schopenhauer, and published *Vecherniye ogni* (1883) and his memoirs in prose (3 vols.). He attempted suicide and died of heart-failure.

Beauty and art are supreme to Fet. His deceptively simple lyrics are brief; now precise, now elusive words fix the intensity of a moment. 'Anxiety and love spread in the air with nightingale's song.' Keenly imagined detail makes his landscape live: 'the golden eye-lashes of the stars', the hues of flowers, the specific cry of a bird, unmistakably Russian seasons or the time of the day, the variety of dawns. Impersonal verbs evoke summer lightning; nouns alone re-create a scene of love. He would wish 'to pour out his soul without words', for 'beauty does not need even songs'. Words are powerless, 'only kisses have power ... with the gentle caesura of lips, with the free rhythm of love'. There is nothing in the world but 'that childlike pensive gaze', 'the parting of the hair'. He can say 'I hear the whiff of former tenderness', use illogical metaphors, reiterate exclamations, each line enriching the theme and the melody. He seeks joy in the identity of the spirit and nature, yet life is often 'a fleeting dream'; he wonders 'what comes from free will and what is inevitable'.

Rejected by his 'anti-aesthetic' contemporaries, he inspired many decadents, ⇨ Blok and several composers. [NG]

*Polnoye sobraniye stikhotvoreniy*, ed. B. Ya. Bukhshtab (1937); Bowra, *BRV*.
R. F. Gustafson, *The Imagination of Spring: The Poetry of A.F.* (Yale University Press, 1966).

**Feuchtwanger, Lion** (Munich 1884–Los Angeles 1958). German novelist and dramatist. Prolific, and popular in many countries, he gave historical romances a new show of life with touches of modern psychology; he had a flair for situation, a readable style and liberal, humane sentiments. *Jew Süss* (1925; tr. W. and E. Muir, 1926), a world best seller, was filmed in England (1933), and other novels treat such 'plum' subjects as Elizabeth I and Mary, Josephus, Nero, the French Revolution and the Resistance (*Simone*, 1944). He collaborated with Brecht on the dramas *Eduard II* (after Marlowe), *Kalkutta* (1927) and *Die Gesichte der Simone Machard* (1942, in U.S.A.), having been associated with expressionist and socialist circles after 1918. Indeed, his personal fate as a pacifist, a left-wing Jewish intellectual, an editor in Moscow (*Das Wort*), interned in France and emigrating to America, is perhaps his most moving story; it is told in *Moskau* (1937; tr. I. Josephy, *Moscow 1937*, 1937), *Der Teufel in Frankreich* (tr. P. Blewitt, *The Devil in France*, 1941) and glimpsed in the trilogy *Der Wartesaal* (esp. *Erfolg*, tr. W. and A. Muir, *Success*, 1930, with its account of the Bavarian communist revolution in 1919). [PB/AKT]

*L.F.* (E. Berlin, 1959) (in 'Schriftsteller der Gegenwart'); Natan, *GML*, iii.

**Feuerbach, Ludwig Andreas** (Landshut 1804–Rechenberg, Nürnberg 1872). German philosopher. Son of the famous lawyer and criminologist Anselm Feuerbach, brother of the mathematician Karl Feuerbach and the archaeologist Anselm Feuerbach. Although a student of Protestant theology he had by the age of 21, under the impact of Hegelianism, turned against religion and committed himself to the radical mode of thought which was to make him the most fiery, most uncompromising prophet of philosophical materialism in Germany, the man who, with Marx and Engels, set the course of the proletarian revolution.

In his first major work, *Gedanken über Tod und Unsterblichkeit* (1830), he attacked belief in an afterlife and uttered his critical sentiment 'Man is a cobbler, and the earth is his last'. In *Das Wesen des Christentums* (1841; tr. G. Eliot, *The Essence of Christianity*, 1855) he declared that man had created God in his own image, and that religion both prevented the full understanding and enjoyment of physical and moral reality, and also hindered the emergence of a true philosophy of life.

The complement to these aggressive, mainly destructive works is *Grundsätze der Philosophie der Zukunft* (1843), which, having portrayed all deities as mere personifications of human fear, states his faith in human values, and in the supremacy of material reality. The essence of his philosophy, and of its importance for the 19th century, lies in a sentence from this work: 'The characteristic of the modern age is that man sees himself as divine and infinite, and that the individual feels these qualities within himself in his individuality.' [RT]

H. Arvon, *L.F. ou la transformation du sacré* (Paris, 1957).

**Feuillet, Octave** (Saint-Lô 1821–Paris 1890). French novelist. This very popular writer is known especially for his sentimental novel *Roman d'un jeune homme pauvre* (1858), whose hero refuses to marry the rich young heroine and destroys the proof which says that he is the rightful owner of her fortune. However, he inherits even greater wealth and so does marry her. His many novels include *Monsier de Camors* (1867), exposing the immoral outlook of society, and *Julia de Trécœur* (1872). He also wrote successful plays, *Le pour et le contre* (1853), *La belle au bois dormant* (1867) and *La partie des dames* (1884). Flaubert said his success had two reasons: '(1) the lower classes believe that the upper classes are like that; and (2) the upper classes see themselves there as they would like to be.' He was elected to the Académie Française in 1862. [WA]

**Feydeau, Ernest** (Paris 1821–Paris 1873). French novelist, stockbroker and archaeologist. He achieved notoriety in 1858 with his realist novel *Fanny*. His later novels, *Danile* (1859), *Sylvie* (1861) and *La Comtesse de Chalis* (1867), were less successful. [WA]

**Feydeau, Georges** (Paris 1862–Rueil 1921). French playwright. Son of Ernest ⇨ Feydeau. He was the author of highly successful and ingeniously constructed vaudevilles and farces, the effects of which depended on a wild logic applied to outrageously improbable initial situations and supported by rapid and witty dialogue. Cumulatively, the impact of these farces is undoubtedly mechanical, but there are numerous individual felicities of tone and invention, especially in: *La dame de chez Maxim* (1899), *L'Hôtel du Libre Échange* (1894; tr. P. Glenville, *Hôtel Paradiso*, 1956), *Un fil à la patte* (1899), *Occupe-toi d'Amélie* (1908; tr./adapt. Noel Coward, *Look after Lulu*, 1959), *Mais n'te promène donc pas toute nue* (1911). [SBJ]

*Théâtre complet* (9 vols., 1948–56).
Lalou, *TF*; Volz, *C*; *Cahiers Renaud-Barrault*, 32 (December 1960).

**Fichman, Yaakov** (Poland 1881–Israel 1918). Hebrew literary critic and poet. In 1901 he went to Odessa where he worked with ⇨ Bialik, who remained his lifelong friend. In 1918 settled in Palestine, where he became editor of the central literary periodical. Never attracted to the modernistic style of the twenties, he remained an adherent of the classical lyric tradition. He wrote Biblical poems, elegies, nature sonnets, collected and edited the literary heritage from the period of enlightenment to the present and wrote a fundamental study of the great masters of Hebrew letters. [EE]

Waxman, *HJL*; Klausner, *HMHL*.

**Fichte, Johann Gottlieb** (Rammenau 1762–Berlin 1814). German Romantic philosopher. He found his immediate point of departure in Kant. He bridged the Kantian distinction between noumena and phenomena by presenting the noumena as ideal projections of the realities in the human mind. Through this transcendental idealism Fichte replaced God by Absolute Mind – his term is *Ur-Ich*, Primeval Self. These ideas are contained above all in his *Grundlage der gesamten Wissenschaftslehre* (1794). In a somewhat different role he had a great effect on the Germany of his day with his patriotic addresses known as the *Reden an die deutsche Nation* (1808).

Artificial as his extreme idealist position was, it had a liberating effect on German writers at the turn of the 18th century. A modified, less extreme system derived from the *Wissenschaftslehre* was set out by ⇨ Schelling, whose influence on the German Romantics was even greater. [RT]

H. Engelbrecht, *J.G.F.* (N.Y., 1933); N. Hartmann, *Die Philosophie des deutschen Idealismus* (Berlin/Leipzig, 1923–9).

**Figueroa, Francisco de** (Alcalá de Henares 1536?–Alcalá de Henares 1617?). Spanish poet, soldier and friend of Cervantes. His poems, in the Italianate style of ⇨ Garcilaso, were published posthumously. His charming eclogue, 'Tirsi, pastor del más famoso río', is typical of the elegant pre-*culto* manner. His chief influences are Garcilaso and Petrarch, though many of his best poems are genuine re-creations. He wrote poetry in both Italian and Spanish, and is notable for his experiments in blank verse. [JMC]

*Poesías*, ed. A. González Palencia (1943); Cohen, *PBSV*; Trend, *OBSV*; Blecua, *FLE*; Terry, *ASP*.

**Filicaia, Vincenzo da** (Florence 1642–Florence 1707). Italian poet. Made senator by Cosimo III of Tuscany and later governor of Volterra and Pisa, he won fame in his lifetime with his odes and sonnets on civic, political, moral and religious themes (e.g. the 6 *canzoni* on the siege and liberation of Vienna in 1683), but his studied, figurative eloquence now finds little favour. He is remembered chiefly for his patriotic sonnets to Italy which linked him to the poets of the Risorgimento. [DGR]

*Poesie toscane*, etc. (1823, 1827); Calcaterra, *LSA*. G. Caponi, *V. da F. e le sue opere* (Prato, 1901).

**'Fioretti di San Francesco.'** An Italian collection of legends on the life and works of St ⇨ Francis and his followers, which was derived by an unknown author in the second half of the 14th century from a Latin text of the late 13th or early 14th century. The scene is for the most part Umbria or Marche in Central Italy, but little historical or biographical reliability attaches to the stories. Each of the 'little flowers' is a short account of an episode in the career of the saint or one of his followers, pointing the way to holiness via the Franciscan ideals of poverty and humility. The simple, direct narrative carries the reader along as the miracles and their consequences are related in a serene tone of untroubled conviction with frequent ingenuous touches of detail. There is no argument, but simply the recording and illustration of edifying events. The very real impact of the Saint's uncompromising example with his message of joy found in absolute sacrifice is better reflected in this work's artlessness than in any other of the copious Franciscan writings of the time. [DGR]

*Fioretti*, ed. M. Casella (1926); *The Little Flowers of St Francis*, tr. L. Sherley-Price (Penguin Classics, 1959).

**Firenzuola, Agnolo** (Florence 1493–Prato 1543). Italian writer. A worldly Vallombrosan monk in the Rome of Leo X and Clement VII, he there wrote the (incomplete) *Ragionamenti* (1525) and the (unrevised) *Asino d'oro* (1525). The *Ragionamenti* combine in a Decameron-like framework disquisitions on linguistic questions and Platonic love (cf. Bembo's *Asolani*) with short stories sometimes far from Platonic, while the *Asino d'oro* is a very free version of Apuleius in which the fable is adapted to Firenzuola's own experiences and the events of his time. In 1526 he was absolved from his vows and, racked by disease, spent the next eleven years in obscurity and silence. During a second period of activity at Prato (1538–41) he wrote the *Dialogo delle bellezze delle donne* (tr. C. Bell, 1892) and *La prima veste dei discorsi degli animali*, which is a partial version, via a Spanish intermediary (*Exemplario contra los engaños y peligros del mundo*) of the Indian *Panchatantra*. His chief works were all published posthumously (1548–50). [DGR]

*Opere scelte*, ed. G. Fatini (1957); *Opere*, ed. A. Seroni (1958); *Tales*, Eng. tr. (Paris, 1889); Roscoe, *IN*.
G. Fatini, *A.F.* (Turin, 1932); *Minori*, ii.

**Fischart, Johann,** also called Mentzer after his father who came from Mainz (Strassburg 1547–Forbach 1590). German poet and satirist. Fischart studied and travelled widely in Italy, France, Holland and England, took a doctorate in law in Basel in 1574 and subsequently held legal posts in Strassburg, Speyer and in Forbach near Saarbrücken. A writer with little talent for original work, he was a gifted translator and adaptor, his greatest achievement being his rendering of Rabelais's *Gargantua* under the title *Geschichtklitterung* (1575). Longer than the original, it replaces Rabelais's satire of scholasticism and the Church by the satire of contemporary manners and of the follies of mankind in general. Free rein is given to his distinctive love of grotesque exaggeration in situation and language and the style is characterized by a predilection for puns and paraphrase, veritable cascades of synonyms and a quickening of literary German with the language of the common people.

As the spokesman of the Protestant middle classes, Fischart revived the polemicism of the Reformation period in a series of bitterly aggressive attacks on Roman Catholicism in such works as the *Binenkorb des Heyligen Römischen Immenschwarms* of 1579 (an adaptation of the Dutch original of Philipp van Marnix) and the *Jesuiterhütlein* of 1580. A happier, more humane side of his literary activities is revealed by *Flöh Hatz, Weiber Tratz* (1573), a humorous treatment of the venerable theme of the hostility between fleas and women. Other non-polemical works include an adaptation of the 'Volksbuch' in *Eulenspiegel Reimensweiss* (1572), the mock encomion *Podagramisches Trostbüchlein* (1577) and the *Philosophisches Ehezuchtbüchlein* (1578) in which Fischart sets forth a strikingly enlightened view of marriage and womankind. [WAC]

*Affentheurlich Naupengeheurliche Geschichtklitterung*, ed. U. Nyssen (2 vols., Düsseldorf, 1963–4); DNL, 18 (1895).
A. Hauffen, *J.F.* (2 vols., Berlin, 1921–2); H. Sommerhalder, *J.F.s Werk* (Berlin, 1959).

**Fischer, Leck** (Copenhagen 1904–Gentofte 1956). Danish novelist and playwright. His novels, e.g. *Kontormennesker* (1933), are mainly concerned with everyday life. [ELB]

*Selskabsrejsen* (tr. J. F. S. Pearce, *The Mystery Tour*, in *Contemporary Danish Plays*, 1955).

**Fishta, G.** ⇨ Albanian Literature.

**'Flamenca.'** A celebrated Provençal verse romance of 8,000 lines, written about 1270(?) in the Rouergue by an unknown author, thought by some to have been called Bernardet. A perfect knight and educated man, Guilhem de Nevers, is overwhelmed by love for Flamenca who is held prisoner in a tower by her jealous husband, Archambaut de Bourbon. Guilhem takes the tonsure in order to declare his love during the most sacred moments of the Mass. Flamenca accepts Guilhem and later betrays her husband's trust when he repents of his jealousy. The story moves with a lighthearted gaiety touched with irony and has moments of despair. The love described is *amour passion* which impels Archambaut to monomaniacal jealousy and Guilhem to unworthy and hypocritical ruses. Incidental themes are the conflict between profane and divine love, the rivalry between knight and priest and the value of education for the nobility and for women. *Flamenca* is important as a medieval Art of Love and as a document of social customs. [LTT]

Lavaud and Nelli, *T*; *The Romance of Flamenca*, ed. and verse tr. M. J. Hubert and M. E. Porter (Princeton, 1962).

C. Grimm, *Étude sur le roman de F.* (Paris, 1930); G. Millardet, *Le roman de F.* (Paris, 1936); *ZRP*, LIII (1933); *SP*, LV (1958); *MAe*, XXXVI (1967).

**Flaubert, Gustave** (Rouen 1821–Croisset 1880). French novelist. Son of a surgeon. He failed his law examinations and was allowed to remain at home devoting himself utterly to literature. He became the perfect type of the literary man, giving up everything to the perfection of his art, even to the extent of breaking off his affair with Mme Louise Colet because it interfered with his writing. He lived with his mother after his father's death in 1846 at Croisset near Rouen, leaving this retreat only to travel – notably in Egypt and Turkey (1849–51) with his friend Maxime du Camp. He wrote slowly and painfully, labouring for over five years on *Madame Bovary* (1856–7 in *La Revue de Paris*; tr. G. Hopkins, 1948; tr. J. L. May, 1953). He and the editor were tried for offences against public morals, but were acquitted. Set in Normandy near Rouen, the novel tells the story of a woman whose dreams of romantic love, largely nourished by novels, find no fulfilment when she is married to a boorish country doctor. She has affairs first with a local landowner and then with a lawyer's clerk. She falls deeply into debt and commits suicide when her creditors threaten to tell her husband. The story gains its power from the carefully studied picture of the Norman town and country; the lovers with whom Emma Bovary tries to realize her dreams are as shoddy as the local leaders of society like M. Homais the apothecary. Flaubert, who in a famous remark identified himself with his heroine, was yet disgusted by his subject; his determination to find in *the style alone* the beauty which does not exist in banal reality produced a perverse masterpiece, rich in new techniques of impersonal, symbolic narrative.

In 1857 he went to Tunisia to collect material for his novel with a Carthaginian setting, *Salammbô* (1862; tr. E. Powys Mathers, 1950). He desired to write something utterly different from *Madame Bovary* and gave full rein to his passion for the exotic and the gorgeous. After the First Punic War Salammbô is priestess in the temple of the Goddess Tanit at a time when Carthage is besieged by mercenaries under the command of Mathô. Mathô steals the sacred veil of the Goddess, and Salammbô is forced to give herself to him to recover it. The novel ends with the defeat and death by torture of Mathô and the death of Salammbô from grief. Some critics have objected to the savagery of the novel and others to its excessive documentation. Flaubert followed this with *L'éducation sentimentale* (1869; tr. A. Goldsmith, *Sentimental Education*, 1941) of which he had written a first version between 1843 and 1845. Drawing again upon his schoolboy love for Mme Schlésinger, Flaubert tells the story of the life and education in love of Frédéric Moreau. Although the lives depicted are uneventful, Flaubert has preserved a period and a certain range of society with such skill that many prefer this to his other works. He then brought out his *La tentation de Saint Antoine* (1874; tr. L. Hearn, *The Temptation of St Anthony*, 1932) and *Trois contes: Un cœur simple, La légende de Saint Julien l'Hospitalier, Hérodias* (1877; tr. M. Savill, *Three Tales*, 1950). The temptation is a prose poem of great power and imagination and in the three stories Flaubert produced diverse examples of his ability; the story *Un cœur simple*, about a Norman domestic servant, is the best. His last work, *Bouvard et Pécuchet* (1881 posth.), a study in stupidity, was unfinished. The two copying clerks of the title buy a farm and embark on a series of experiments which are always doomed to disappointment. Flaubert had planned that they should end as they began, as copying clerks, writing out passages from the works they had consulted during their years of experiment thus unconsciously compiling a dictionary of errors and misconceptions. This part would have included their anthology, which was to have incorporated Flaubert's own *Dictionnaire des idées reçues* (tr. J. Barzun, *Dictionary of Accepted Ideas*, 1954), a collection of trite sayings he had kept throughout his life. It was to have been his greatest attack upon the bourgeois conventions and foolishness he loathed so violently. Flaubert died suddenly in 1880, his last years having been made uneasy by money worries because he had given up his fortune to help his niece's husband. During his life he had been a great letter writer and his correspondence (tr. F. Steegmuller, *Selected Letters*, 1954) is fascinating not only for the picture it gives of his own literary life but for his judgements and criticism on other writers. One of his most important correspondents was George Sand. A record of a walking tour in Brittany which he wrote with his friend Maxime du Camp, *Par les champs et par les grèves*, came out in 1885 posthumously. [WA]

*Œuvres*, ed. A. Thibaudet and R. Dumesnil (2 vols., Pléiade, 1946-8).

A. Thibaudet, *G.F.* (Paris, 1922); R. Dumesnil, *F.* (Paris, 1903), *G.F.* (Paris, 1947), *La vocation de G.F.* (Paris, 1961); A. K. Thorlby, *F.* (1959); F. Steegmuller, *F. and Madame Bovary* (1958); A. Fairlie, *F. Madame Bovary* (1962).

**Fléchier, Esprit** (Pernes 1632–Montpellier 1710). French professor turned preacher. He had great success with polite society as a contemporary of Bossuet. One of the Dauphin's tutors, he became Bishop, first of Lavaur and then of Nîmes. A gentle (some said affected) rather than an imposing orator, he had literary gifts (shown in his *Mémoires sur les grands jours d'Auvergne*) and a remarkable Christian character. [WGM]

A. Fabre, *F., orateur* (Paris, 1886); Adam, *HLF.*

**Fleming, Paul** (Hartenstein 1609–Hamburg 1640). German poet. The great emotional experience of Fleming's life was his disappointed love for Elsabe Niehus, whom he had met in Reval, while travelling on a trade mission to Russia and Persia. The lyrics inspired by this experience (*Ein treues Herze*, *Zur Zeit seiner Verstossung*) have a freshness, sincerity and immediacy of feeling which makes them unique in an age of gallant erotic verse. Although certain of his religious poems exhibit a tendency towards baroque conceits (*An meinen Erlöser*), the best of them show the same qualities as his love poetry. The most famous religious poem, 'In allen meinen Taten', still finds a place in most hymnals; the ode 'Lass dich nur nichts tauren', the embodiment of his entire trust in God, and the sonnet 'An sich', an expression of the poet's Christian stoicism, are in their simplicity, directness and manly quality amongst the finest the century produced. [WAC]

*Deutsche Gedichte*, ed. J. M. Lappenberg (BLVS 82/3, 1865); Killy, *DLTZ*.

H. Pyritz, *P.F.s deutsche Liebeslyrik* (Leipzig, 1932).

**Flodoard** or (**Frodoard**) **of Rheims** (Épernay *c.* 893/4–Rheims 966). Medieval historian and poet. Well trained in the school of Rheims (⇨ Gerbert of Aurillac), he was attached to the see all his life and personally involved in its chequered fortunes, though he never rose to be bishop. He wrote the *De Triumphis Christi sanctorumque Palestinae*, *De Triumphis Christi Antiochiae gestis*, *De Triumphis Christi apud Italiam* – among the most substantial verse works of the 10th century, and much esteemed by ⇨ Ratherius of Verona. His *Historiae ecclesiae Remensis*, which goes up to 952 (tr. F. Guizot, Paris, 1824), and *Annales*, for the period 919–66 (ed. P. Lauer, Collection de Textes, Paris, 1905), are very solid historical productions, though the latter work is unfinished and much inferior in style to his other writings. [CEC]

Migne, *PL*, 135 (1853).

Manitius, *GLLM*.

**Fogazzaro, Antonio** (Vicenza 1842–Vicenza 1911). Italian novelist and poet. He became senator in 1896. His novels have offended both those Catholics who feared his modernist views (expressed theoretically in *Ascensioni umane*, 1899) and those non-Catholics who found the religious content indigestible in any case. Polemics on the orthodoxy of his views began after the publication of the first two novels, *Malombra* (1881; tr. F. T. Dickson, *The Woman*, 1907) and *Daniele Cortis* (1885; tr. S. L. Simeon, 1890); and *Il Santo* (1905) and *Leila* (1910), the last two novels, were immediately placed on the Index. His best work, by many considered second only to Manzoni's *I promessi sposi*, was *Piccolo mondo antico* (1895; tr. W. J. Strachan, *The Little World of the Past*, 1962), the first of a loose cycle of four novels (*Piccolo mondo moderno*, 1901, *Il Santo*, 1905, *Leila*, 1910; tr. M. Prichard Agnetti, *The Man of the World*, 1907, *The Saint*, 1906, *Leila*, N.Y., 1911). It is a study of the dynamic conflict between the generous but naïve religious faith of Franco and the strictly logical reasoning of his wife Luisa that fails poignantly to help her accept the death of their child. The final reference to reconciliation and the future birth of a second child is an allusion to Piero, the protagonist of the next two novels. Fogazzaro is noted for the skill and humour with which he draws his numerous characters and also captures the natural beauty of the Italian lakes (see also the collection of poems, *Valsolda*, 1876). [RHC]

*Tutte le opere*, ed. P. Nardi (15 vols., 1931–45).
P. Nardi, *A.F.* (Milan, 1938); L. Portier, *A.F.* (Paris, 1937); A. Piromalli, *F.* (Palermo, 1959); C. Salinari, *Miti e coscienza del decadentismo italiano* (Milan, 1960); *Guida*, 1954; *Minori*, iv.

**Foix, J. V.** ⇨ Catalan Literature.

**Folengo, Teofilo** (Mantua 1491–Campese, Bassano 1544). Italian poet. A Benedictine who left and later rejoined his Order, he wrote poems in both Latin and Italian, but is chiefly remembered as the author of several macaronic works in which Latin and Italian are fused together to form curious linguistic hybrids. The best known is his *Baldus* (ed. U. E. Paoli, 1941), first published in *Maccheronee* (1517; ed. A. Luzio, 1927–8) under the pseudonym Merlin Cocai and developed in later editions. This burlesque epic in what still set out to be Latin hexameters achieves genuine comic vigour with its homely realism and dialect flavour. [DGR]

*Opere italiane*, ed. U. Renda (1911–14).
G. Billanovich, *Tra don T.F. e Merlin Cocaio* (Naples, 1948); E. Bonora, *Le Maccheronee di T.F.* (Venice, 1956); *Minori*, ii.

**Folquet de Marseille** (d. Toulouse 1231). French ⇨ troubadour. Of a Genoese merchant family settled in Marseille, he became prosperous and composed troubadour poetry as a pastime. He employed several ⇨ *jongleurs* and was well known at the courts of Aragon and Provence. His extant poems (1179–95) include 14 love songs, a *tenso* or debate, 2 crusading songs and religious poems. He praised and attacked love in an erudite style with borrowings from classical Latin much appreciated by his contemporaries. His metrical forms and melodies are excellently worked.

In 1195 he entered the Cistercian abbey of Toronet, became abbot in 1201 and bishop of Toulouse in 1205. Friend and protector of Saint Dominic, he harassed the Cathars and played a leading part in the defeat of the South and the heresy in the Albigensian Crusade. He encouraged the establishment of the University of Toulouse in 1229 (⇨ Hélinand) and was the only troubadour to gain a place in Dante's Paradise (ix: 64–108). [LTT]

*Le Troubadour F. de M.*, ed. and tr. S. Stroński (Cracow, 1910).

**Folz, Hans** (b. Worms, fl. late 15th cent.). German ⇨ Meistersinger and writer of Shrovetide plays. He founded the Meistersinger school at Nuremberg, which became in the 16th century the most famous of all centres of Meistersang. His Shrovetide plays, which have all the crudity and coarse humour characteristic of the *genre*, are, like his Meisterlieder, among the most important examples of their kind before Hans Sachs. [RT]

*Meisterlieder*, ed. A. L. Mayer (1908); *Shrovetide Plays*, ed. A. Keller (Stuttgart, 1858).
Ehrismann, *GDL*, ii.

**Fontane, Theodor** (Neuruppin 1819–Berlin 1898). German novelist. The son of a Gascon Huguenot father and a Cévennoise mother, Fontane was born and bred on the North Sea coast of Prussia. He was a pharmaceutical dispenser, a war correspondent in the Austrian Campaign of 1866 and in the Franco-Prussian War of 1870–1, and secretary to the Prussian Royal Academy of Arts. Author of 2 war books, 4 volumes of travels in Mark Brandenburg, a slim volume of ballads and another of impressions of London. Fontane wrote his first novel at the age of 56. He was able to bring to his fiction a lifetime's experiences from many spheres: commerce, service in the Army, the Civil Service, landed *Junkers* and ironical generals, small shopkeepers, the Jewish and Gentile *nouveaux riches*, Protestant parsons and Catholic *dévots*, conservative *Von und Zu's* and progressive schoolmasters, a few dogs and elegant

Englishmen and picturesque Austrians in the margin, marriages and divorces, bankruptcies and get-rich-quick schemes, duels and illnesses and the gentle sloping down of life towards death – he 'knew it all inside out', it was all merely waiting for him to set it down.

*Vor dem Sturm* (1878), his (and German literature's) masterpiece in the genre of the historical novel, shows Prussia in 1812–13, morally uncertain whether to attack Napoleon's defeated army. Inhuman chauvinism, the defence of the fatherland, the conservatism of the Prussian aristocracy, the ideals of the French Revolution – these are the concerns of his characters. But though the narrator's sympathies tend to be with the Prussian *Junkers*, it is the practical Christian of no social 'background', Konrektor Othegraven, whose resistance and death are fully vindicated – a pyrrhic victory not of German patriotism but of the ideals of the French Revolution.

'The woman's predicament' is the theme of *L'Adultera* (1882), *Cécile* (1886), *Irrungen* (1888), *Frau Jenny Treibel* (1893) and, most finely, of *Effi Briest* (1895; tr. D. Parmée, Penguin Classics, 1967). Fontane writes in a wholly undoctrinaire way: the exuberant charm and lively temperament of Effi, the superb characterizations of her parents and childhood companions in the Prussian countryside, and of her friends in the North Sea town to which she moves after her marriage – all these suggest a story innocent of wider, social implications. Yet her life, even the form of her violation of the social proprieties in an adulterous affair, is shown to be dominated by a social ambience – the severe code of Prussian aristocracy. Her outlook is wholly limited by the aspirations and taboos of her own class; she cannot conceive any independent aspiration of her own. She has a vague longing for that greater thing which neither her husband nor anyone else around her can appease, the longing for love. But this longing is neither strong nor intelligent, it remains childish or at best childlike. The consummation of the code (and the climax of the novel) is reached when her husband decides to fight a duel with the long-since-forsaken lover. His motive is neither jealousy nor a feeling of personal injury – it is his 'social conscience', the pressure of a social norm which is created and perpetuated by characters who neither fully believe in the norm nor in anything much else: having no other beliefs to live by, they are at once sustained and destroyed by its dictates.

*Unwiederbringlich* (1892; tr. D. Parmée, *Beyond Recall*, World's Classics, 1964), set in a north-German castle and at the court of Copenhagen, tells the story of Graf Holk's divorce from his melancholic and puritanical wife, of his return to her after his affair with a charming and worldly lady-in-waiting has come to an untimely end, and of his wife's suicide. In *Poggenpuhls* (1896), and especially in *Der Stechlin* (1898), the narrative structure recedes behind the evocation of milieu, action is replaced by character, mainly that of Graf Major Dubslav von Stechlin, rtd. Yet for all its indulgence in anecdotes, reminiscences and 'type-casting', this great *causerie* is not really shapeless. Its form is the form of decline – old Stechlin's decline – towards death. There are many signs, strewn throughout the story, of its approach: Dubslav's unsuccessful candidature for the *Reichstag*, his financial difficulties, his sceptical appraisal of the future of his class; and – in personal terms – a strange, almost sinister sense of personal dissolution as, shortly before his end, Dubslav rejects the advice of his doctor and turns to a local soothsayer who prescribes her own magical medicines. [JPS]

*Sämtliche Werke*, ed. W. Keitel (1962ff.).

C. Wandrey, *T.F.* (Munich, 1919); Mary-Enole Gilbert, *Das Gespräch in F.s Gesellschaftsromanen* (Leipzig, 1930); P. Demetz, *Formen des Realismus: T.F.* (Munich, 1964); T. Mann, in *Rede und Antwort* (1922); *Adel des Geistes* (1948); *Neue Schweizer Rundschau*, 16 (1948–9); *GLL*, N.S. 8 (1954–5); *GLL*, N.S. 15 (1961).

**Fontanella, Girolamo** (? Naples 1612?–Naples 1644?). Italian poet. Little is known about the life of this attractive follower of ⇨ Marino whose poems appeared in 3 volumes – *Ode* (1638), *Nove cieli* (1640) and *Elegie* (1645). His verse is emotionally slight, but pictorially lively. Colours, shapes and movements he conveys in a dynamic language rich in striking imagery, with a penchant for the slightly exotic: the carnation, the glow-worm, coral, a beautiful girl swimming. [DGR]

Croce, *LM*.

Ferrero, *MM*; Getto, *MM*.

**Fontanes, Louis, Marquis de** (Niort 1757–Paris 1821). French poet. Early poverty and bereavement led him to develop a poetic strain of introspective melancholy, congenial to readers of the 1780s, which foreshadows romanticism (*Le cri de mon cœur*, 1777; *Le jour des morts dans une campagne*, 1785), and still has harmonious appeal. He also sought inspiration in contemporary scientific achievement, and his verse *Essai sur l'astronomie* (1789) brought him acclaim. During the Directory he was exiled to England (where he befriended Chateaubriand), but subsequently had a successful political career under Napoleon and Louis XVIII. [WHB]

*Œuvres* (1839).

A. Wilson, *F.* (Paris, 1928).

**Fontenelle, Bernard Le Bovier, Sieur de** (Rouen 1657–Paris 1757). French thinker and man of letters. A nephew of Corneille, his earliest reputation was made as a salon poet and wit. His tragedy *Aspar* (1680) failed, and he then turned to prose, with *Nouveaux dialogues des morts* (1683; tr. J. Hughes, 1708), an essay in a fashionable classical genre in which he declares for the Moderns in the 'Battle of the Books' then beginning, and *Lettres diverses de M. le Chevalier d'Her**** (1683), a collection of imaginary love-letters in the tradition of Voiture. His intellectual preoccupations emerge in 1686 with two major works, *Entretiens sur la pluralité des mondes habités* (tr. J. Glanvill, 1929) and *L'histoire des oracles* (tr. S. Whatley, 1750). The former is a lucid exposition of astronomy according to Copernicus and Descartes, enlivened by speculations concerning life on other planets and elegantly presented in the form of after-dinner conversations with a Marquise. It represents the first major attempt to present scientific knowledge to the layman in an attractive literary form, and was highly successful. The latter, an adaptation of a Latin work by a Dutch scholar, A. Van Dale, attacks current belief in the demonic origin of the oracles of antiquity, and by attributing them to priestly trickery implies a similar explanation for the Christian supernatural. A third essay, *De l'origine des fables* (1724; but conceived before 1680), offers a rational analysis of the origin of myths, and hints that all religious belief has similar beginnings. In 1688, Fontenelle reasserted his belief in the superiority of modern over ancient literature in his *Digression sur les Anciens et les Modernes*.

He became permanent secretary of the Académie des Sciences in 1697, and his later writings are chiefly either scientific or connected with the Académie: his obituary eulogies of academicians are often model essays in biography. [WHB]

*Œuvres* (1818); *Entretiens* . . . and *Digression*, ed. R. Shackleton (1955).

L. Maigron, *F.* (Paris, 1906); J. R. Carré, *La philosophie de F.* (Paris, 1932).

**Fonvizin, Denis Ivanovich** (Moscow 1745–St Petersburg 1792). Russian dramatist. A senior civil servant from the educated gentry, he moved in 'enlightened' circles. A conversational wit (nicknamed 'the Vulture'), his Voltairean *Letter to my Servants* (1763) philosophized humorously on the purpose of the world. His two satirical comedies, *Brigadir* (1768) and *Nedorosl'* (1782; tr. *The Minor*, in *Masterpieces of the Russian Drama*, ed. G. R. Noyes, 1960), are outstanding for their time, and influenced by ⇨ Holberg, whose plays he had translated: they are tidily neo-classic, didactically reasoned, though with grotesque 'Russian' characterization. His liberal views appear in *The Minor*, where a brutal and primitive family of country gentry is portrayed almost as animals. The play's success emboldened Fonvizin to raise political and social questions publicly, which caused censorship of his articles. He travelled; see interesting *Letters from Abroad* (1777–8, 1784–5).

*Sobraniye sochineniy*, ed. G. P. Makogonenko (1959).

K. V. Pigarev, *Tvorchestvo F.* (Moscow, 1954); H. Rogger, *National Consciousness in Eighteenth Century Russia* (Cambridge, Mass., 1960).

**Forner, Juan Bautista Pablo** (Mérida 1756–Madrid 1797). Spanish critic. He won a prize with his *Sátira contra los abusos introducidos en la lengua castellana* (1782) and followed this with a defence of his country against an Englishman who asked 'Has Spain done anything for Europe?' (*Oración apologética por la España*, 1786). He was so violent in his polemics that he was prohibited from publishing without royal permission. His *Exequias de la lengua castellana* (1782) give an interesting account of Spanish literature. His occasional poems about the pleasures of retiring to the country are not remarkable. [JMC]

BAE, 63; *Exequias* (CC, 1925).

Menéndez y Pelayo, *HIE*.

**Forssell, Lars** (Stockholm 1928– ). Swedish poet, dramatist and essayist.

Versatile and enterprising, he has written poetry and plays of a traditional as well as an experimental kind, scripts for revues, comic films and radio, and lyrics for songs. He first verse, *Ryttaren* (1949), continues a Swedish tradition, but he was remarkable for his wide international orientation, especially towards English and American poetry. (He translated Pound into Swedish.) He caught the public eye with his second book of verse, *Narren* (1952). In spite of its intellectual quality, Forssell's poetry has a distinct tonality, and draws often on nursery-rhyme and rigmarole: it is rarely transparent, but enjoyable even when only partially understood. In its central section, the figure of a Clown serves as a focus for emotions that become directly accessible through mime and gestures. (The piece has been performed as a play.) Through his senseless fear of death and his concern for his lost dignity the Clown touches the reader deeply. It is through such *personae* that Forssell's early poetry functions, and in the sophisticated and slender collection, *C. F. Tietjens* (1954), the elusive title figure is alive with both fear and numbness. This agile, contemporary mind in search of its own identity is clearly close to its maker, yet different from an *alter ego*.

In *Telegram* (1957) Forssell comes still closer to speaking in his own voice; the style is accordingly simpler, at the same time more varied than ever. This intermittent and engaging simplicity returns and is fortified in *En kärleksdikt* (1960). Here at last the poet speaks without disguise in a tone both subdued and intense. The sensuousness of these poems is daring, yet humble in its frankness. His latest collection, *Röster* (1964), has once more a fuller range. In some poems pure virtuosity entails a loss of perspicacity, in others simplicity is victorious and Forssell now achieves a new precision and freedom. His works for the stage include *Kröningen* (1956), based on the Alkestis myth and presenting a hero acquainted with fear; *Mary Lou* (1962), a play about treason and divided loyalties, set in a broadcasting studio in Nazi Germany and having an American-born female counterpart of Lord Haw-Haw for its heroine; and *Söndagspromenaden* (1963), remarkable for its subtle interplay of make-believe and trite reality. Still a very young man, Forssell was responsible for the revaluation of Evert ⇨ Taube, the Swedish troubadour and song-writer; and he has published a book about Chaplin (1953). [SAB]

G. Printz-Påhlson, 'Bristens ironi', in *Solen i spegeln* (Stockholm, 1958); O. Lagercrantz, 'L.F.s masker', in *Svenska lyriker* (Stockholm, 1961); *Scandinavian Studies* (37, February 1965).

**Fort, Paul** (Reims en Champagne 1872–Paris 1960). French poet. The son of a miller, he dreamed through his youth in a world of fairies and romance before going to school in Paris, where Gide, Verlaine and Moréas introduced him to poetry. He founded and directed an *avant-garde* theatre, the Théâtre d'Art (now Théâtre de l'Œuvre), to which all the minor symbolists contributed, though he never belonged to their school (1890–3). He later edited, with Valéry, the review *Vers et Prose* (1905–14). He was a very abundant poet, regularly writing several pieces a day; the definitive edition of his *Ballades françaises* (1922–58) comprises 17 volumes. He also wrote *Mes mémoires* (1944) and *Les chroniques de France* (1922), a collection of historical plays. He saw himself as the last of the ⇨ *trouvères*; much of his work poses convincingly as folk-lore – songs and ballads in verse without formal pattern, with more assonance than rhyme, more liveliness than depth, more familiar realism than metaphor, more sentiment than emotion. The joys of Nature, the history of the provinces and colonies of France, simple love situations, are his typical themes; his vocabulary and ideas are prolix, loose, unkempt, but amiably facetious and lovingly human with a touch of unpretentious melancholy. [CLC]

*Anthologie des ballades françaises* (1941).

'Hommage à P.F.', *Flammes Vives* (1952); introduction to *Ballades françaises*, ed. A. Fontainas (1922).

**Fortunatus, Venantius** (nr Ceneda, Treviso *c.* 530–Poitiers ?609). Latin poet. Favoured at Sigbert's court (cf. *epithalamium*), then by the saintly Queen Radegund at Poitiers, where he became chaplain at her convent, later bishop. He wrote prose lives of a dozen Gallic saints, including St Radegund, and many poems, some light – e.g. thanking Radegund and her friend Agnes, the superior of the convent, for a present of eggs and plums, or apologizing for over-eating and over-drinking – others liturgical; e.g. the famous Easter processional 'Salve festa dies' and two hymns celebrating St

Radegund's reception of a relic of the true cross from the Emperor – 'Vexilla regis prodeunt' and 'Pange lingua gloriosi proelium certaminis'. [FB]

Migne, *PL*, 88; ed. F. Leo and B. Krusch (MGH, AA, iv, 1881); Lindsay, *MLP*.

D. Tardi, *F.* (Paris, 1927); S. Dill, *Roman Society in Gaul in the Merovingian Age* (1926); Duckett, *GMA*; Raby, *CLP*, *SLP*.

**Foscolo, Ugo** (Zante island 1778–Turnham Green, London 1827). Italian poet. A precocious period of political activity, represented in his early literary production by a play, *Tieste*, and several poems (e.g. *Bonaparte liberatore*), ended in October 1797, when the ceding of Venice to the Austrians forced Foscolo to leave the city. Patriotism continued to be the driving force of his life, and the years immediately following were largely spent with the Napoleonic armies, mainly in Italy. The hopes and despairs of his generation were expressed in his popular, if mediocre, epistolary novel *Ultime lettere di Jacopo Ortis* (first complete edition 1802). During this period he also wrote some odes and sonnets, several of which (e.g. the sonnet *Alla sera*) are outstanding.

His greatest work, the poem *Dei sepolcri*, was written probably in 1806, and published in 1807. Though owing much to the 18th-century European tradition of 'sepulchral' poetry, this poem transcends its models, and is the first great Italian 19th-century poetic achievement. Written in a difficult style, in unrhymed hendecasyllables, a metre much used by Italian pre-Romantic writers, the poem derives its greatness from the depth of meaning which Foscolo is able to impart to the symbol of the tomb, the melancholy significance of which in the case of the individual is more than outweighed by its value to those still alive, as a powerful testimony to the glories and sufferings of the past. This civic and patriotic theme, so characteristic of him, gives way at the end of the poem to the second great theme of his life and works, the value of art as the permanent shrine of human virtue and nobility.

In 1815, on the return of the Austrians to north Italy, Foscolo left his native country, and in 1817 settled in England. Before leaving Italy, he had written considerable parts of a long poetic work *Le Grazie*, celebrating the civilizing influence of beauty and the arts on human society. Though continually worked on in England, it remains incomplete; some of the fragments are of exceptional beauty.

Among his other writings are two further plays, a brilliant Italian translation of Sterne's *Sentimental Journey*, and some very interesting critical works. [CF]

*Edizione nazionale* (14 vols., 1933, in progress); Kay, *PBIV*.

E. R. Vincent, *The Commemoration of the Dead. A Study of the Romantic Element in the 'Sepolcri' of U.F.* (1936); E. R. Vincent, *U.F.* (1953); M. Fubini, *U.F.* (Florence, 1962).

**Fouqué, Friedrich Freiherr de la Motte** (Brandenburg 1777–Berlin 1843). German novelist and dramatist. A nobleman and the son of a Prussian general, he spent many years in military service, later retiring to his estate and finally to Halle, where he lectured on the history of literature. One of the most prolific of the German Romantic writers, most of his works – lyric poetry, large-scale prose romances, the dramatic trilogy *Der Held des Nordens* – have fallen into a not surprising oblivion. The work for which he is remembered is the fairy-tale *Undine* (1811), a poignant presentation of the popular story of the watersprite who marries a mortal – a theme which offered obvious possibilities to a Romantic mind steeped in the antithesis of the real and supernatural. The story was made the subject of an opera by E. T. A. ⇨ Hoffmann (1813), for which Fouqué himself compiled the libretto, and later by Lortzing (1845). [RT]

A. Schmidt, *F.* (Karlsruhe, 1958).

**France, Anatole**, pseudonym of Anatole-François Thibault (Paris 1844–Saint-Cyr-sur-Loire 1924). French man of letters. The only son of a Parisian bookseller of conservative opinions; initiated early into the world of antiquarian scholarship. His early journalism (1862–77) was of a conventional academic kind, ranging from a sensitive study of Alfred de Vigny (1868) to editions of the French classics, notably Racine and Molière, and a variety of articles on Terence, Apuleius, Rabelais Sully Prudhomme, Bourget and Zola. He also wrote a good many pieces of a historical and antiquarian character, especially on the French Revolution, which continued to haunt his imagination throughout his life. Some of these literary essays were subsequently published in *Le génie latin* (1913;

tr. W. S. Jackson, *The Latin Genius*, 1924). He published critical *feuilletons* regularly in the newspaper *Le Temps* (1887–93) and a selection of these were printed in *La vie littéraire* (4 vols., 1888–92; tr. A. W. Evans, D. B. Stewart and B. Miall, *On Life and Letters*, 1911–24). This body of critical opinion is marked by irony, elegance and erudition and reveals a deep affinity with the world of pagan antiquity and with the literary temper of 18th-century France. The essays, whether on Florian or Balzac, Euripides or Renan, Flaubert or George Sand, are highly subjective and allusive, deploying an easy and appreciative charm rather than any critical rigour or profound insight. These 'adventures of a soul among masterpieces' dissolves away in a wash of anecdote and reminiscence.

His creative work proper begins with a collection of poems in the Parnassian manner: *Poèmes dorés* (1873) and a poetic drama *Les noces corinthiennes* (1876), performed at the Odéon in 1902 and later (1922) made the subject of an opera with music by Büsser. The poetry is accomplished, graceful, derivative and unmistakably minor, though it affords an index to the intense sensuous feeling which so frequently lies below the surface of much of his later prose work. After an early conflict between science (especially Darwinian theory) and the 'poetry of Christianity', his fundamental philosophy emerges as an urbane scepticism later modified by the passion of ideological commitment. His fiction veers between nostalgia for the innocence and tenderness of childhood and involvement in the urgent appeal of the senses; between the romanced evocation of his own early years – *Le livre de mon ami* (1885; tr. J. L. May, *My Friend's Book*, 1913); *Pierre Nozière* (1899; tr. J. L. May, 1916); *Le petit Pierre* (1919; tr. J. L. May, *Little Pierre*, 1920) – and the oblique but potent rendering of sexual need, mildly pornographic at moments, which one encounters in the exotic tale *Thaïs* (1890; tr. R. B. Douglas, 1909), with its courtesan turned saint; or in *Le lys rouge* (1894; tr. W. Stephens, *The Red Lily*, 1908), a study of love and jealousy set in contemporary Florence. His prose works exploit a further vein: that of the philosophical and satirical tale. Some of these, like *Sur la pierre blanche* (1905; tr. C. E. Roche, *The White Stone*, 1910), are barely disguised intellectual dialogues about war, religion and democracy. Others, like *Le jardin d'Épicure* (1894; tr. A. Allinson, *The Garden of Epicurus*, 1908), have no fictional element and are simply erudite excursions over a wide field of knowledge. *La rôtisserie de la Reine Pédauque* (1893; tr. W. Jackson, *At the Sign of the Reine Pédauque*, 1912) and its companion volume, *Les opinions de M. Jérôme Coignard* (1893; tr. W. Jackson, *The Opinions of Jérôme Coignard*, 1913), self-consciously and laboriously revive 18th-century France to provide a framework for the scepticism, anti-clericalism and mild bawdiness of the author. Erudite pastiche cannot give life to these tales any more than it can vivify the pages of the *Contes de Jacques Tournebroche* (1908; tr. A. Allinson, *The Merrie Tales of Jacques Tournebroche*, 1910). The decisive shift in his career as a writer comes with his participation in the Dreyfus case on behalf of the convicted Jewish officer. It marks the first stage of his emergence as one of the 'representative men' of his epoch, bringing about his conversion to socialism (though the personality of Jaurès counted for much in this) and leading, in his declining years, to a precarious adhesion to the Communist Party. Subsequent work reflects this sharpened humane concern and its concomitant, a powerful distrust of clerical obscurantism. Such is the case with the pungent satirical portraits of French social and political life to be found in the four volumes of the *Histoire contemporaine*: *L'orme du mail* (1897; tr. M. P. Willcocks, *The Elm-Tree on the Mall*, 1910); *Le mannequin d'osier* (1897; tr. M. P. Willcocks, *The Wicker-Work Woman*, 1910); *L'anneau d'améthyste* (1899; tr. B. Drillien, *The Amethyst Ring*, 1919); *Monsieur Bergeret à Paris* (1901; tr. B. Drillien, *Monsieur Bergeret in Paris*, 1921). The same controlled passion vibrates in *L'île des pingouins* (1908; tr. A. W. Evans, *Penguin Island*, 1909), a robust though uneven satirical allegory of the evolution of mankind; *Les Dieux ont soif* (1912; tr. A. Allinson, *The Gods are Athirst*, 1913), a striking study of fanaticism during the French Revolution, which illuminates the presumption of ideology and the corruption of power; and *La révolte des anges* (1914; tr. W. Jackson, *The Revolt of the Angels*, 1914), an ambitious satire of Christianity. Socialism rescued him from becoming the playful sage of a *rentier* public but severe defects remain in his work: thin plots, bookishness, lack of formal and imaginative gifts, absence of human density. The style so much admired in his day is not a fully personal voice but a mutation of that of his models, especially Voltaire. A significant disjuncture occurs between the optimistic quality of his political speeches (e.g. *Vers les temps meilleurs*, 1906), and the negative and pessimistic tone of his later imaginative writing. He was awarded the Nobel Prize in 1921. [SBJ]

*Œuvres complètes* (25 vols., 1925–35); *La vie littéraire*, 5e série (1950); *Trente ans de vie sociale* (3 vols., 1949–67).

E. P. Dargan, *A.F. (1844–1896)* (Paris, 1937); A. Vandegans, *A.F.: les années de formation* (Paris, 1954); H. Chevalier, *A.F., the Ironic Temper* (1932); J. Suffel, *A.F.* (1946); J. Levaillant, *Essai sur l'évolution intellectuelle d'A.F.* (Paris, 1965); M.-C. Bancquart, *A.F. polémiste* (Paris, 1962).

**Francis, Saint,** originally Francesco Bernardone (Assisi *c.* 1182–Santa Maria della Porziuncola, Assisi 1226). Italian saint. The son of a rich merchant, he spent a youth of worldly pleasure. In his twenties, after a serious illness followed by mystical visionary experiences, came a change in his way of life. He restored a chapel in Assisi, and began to mingle with the poor and leprous. Cited by his father to appear before the Bishop of Assisi, he solemnly renounced all worldly possessions and embraced a life of evangelical poverty. He gathered adherents and in 1210 gained the approval of Innocent III. He travelled in Italy and the Near East in search of converts, and in 1223 the establishment of the Franciscan Order was approved by Honorius III. In 1224 he received the stigmata. He was canonized in 1228.

Apart from various Latin works (a critical edition was published by the Franciscans of Quaracchi in 1904), which contain his injunctions to his followers, he also wrote in Italian the celebrated *Cantico delle creature* (or *Cantico di Frate Sole*). Composed in rhythmical, irregularly rhymed lines and stanzas of uneven length, it is a fervent hymn of praise to be intoned like the liturgy; it has no parallel in contemporary writing. God is praised for all his works, for 'brother' sun, 'sister' moon and the stars, and finally, in a stanza traditionally held to have been written by Saint Francis just before he died, for 'sister' death which no man can escape. (⇨ Fioretti.) [DGR]

*Gli scritti di San F.d'A. e 'I Fioretti'*, ed. A. Vicinelli (1955); *Gli scritti di S.F.d'A.*, ed. V. Facchinetti (5th edn, 1957); *Opuscula S. Patris Francisci Assisiensis*, Quaracchi (repr. 1949); D. Attwater, *The Penguin Dictionary of Saints* (1965); L. F. Benedetto, *Il Cantico di frate Sole* (Florence, 1941).

P. Sabatier, *Life of St Francis of Assisi* (tr. 1894); Kay, *PBIV*; Lind, *LPIR*; Levasti, *MDT*; *Minori*, i.

**Franck, Sebastian** (Donauworth 1499–Holland 1542). German writer. Franck was successively Roman Catholic priest, Lutheran pastor and sectarian preacher. His *Paradoxa* (1534; ed. H. Ziegler, 1909) expresses his mystic view of the alienation of God and the world; he rejects all outward religious forms and dogmas as barriers between the believer and God – the believer needs only the inner light of the Holy Spirit and the Scriptures. A scholar, influenced by humanism, his *Chronica Zeytbuch und geschycht bibel* (1531) goes beyond a recital of historical facts and attempts to understand and interpret them symbolically; his linguistic interests bore fruit in the large collection of German proverbs he published in 1541. A man in many ways reminiscent of ⇨ Erasmus, his translation of the latter's *Encomion moriae* (1534) and his own *Kriegsbüchlein des Friedens* (1539), a work indebted to the *Querela pacis*, bears witness to the tolerance and humanity he possessed in such a high degree. [WAC]

*Sprichwörter*, ed. F. Latendorf (1876).

W. E. Peukert, *S.F.* (Munich, 1943).

**François de Sales, Saint** (Thorens, Savoy 1567–Lyons 1622). French religious moralist. After practising law for a short time, he was ordained priest (1593), worked as an evangelist among the Protestants of Savoy (1594–8) and became Bishop of Geneva in 1602. With Mme de Chantal he founded the Order of the Visitation for women (1610). He exercised great spiritual influence by his sermons (he preached in Paris in 1602 and 1619), his correspondence and his writings. In his sermons his main aim was to be understood by the humblest listener and to achieve this he used everyday comparisons. His range of correspondents was enormous: working gently, he taught a rational morality that was free from austerity and mysticism; spiritual perfection was easy and possible for all, including those that live in the world. This was the essential purpose of his most popular work, the *Introduction à la vie dévote* (1609; definitive edn, 1619; ed. C. Florisoone, 1928; tr. A. Ross, 1948): to reconcile the Christian life with the life of the world. Written in a graceful style and full of similes, it achieved great success, was translated into countless languages and was Jeremy Taylor's model for *The Rule and Exercises of Holy Living*. Saint François's other major work, *Traité de l'amour de Dieu* (1616), addressed to more advanced readers, is concerned with the human foundations of mysticism. He was canonized in 1665. [FWAG]

*Œuvres*, ed. H. B. Mackey and Fr Navatel (1892–1932); selected letters, tr. H. B. Mackey (1883ff).

H. Burton, *The Life of St F. de S.* (1926); E. Sanders, *St F. de S.* (1928); F. Vincent, *St F. de S. directeur d'âmes* (Paris, 1923); H. Brémond, *Histoire littéraire du sentiment religieux en France*, i (Paris, 1921).

**Frank, Leonhard** (Würzburg 1882–Munich 1961). German novelist and dramatist. A declared pacifist, whose books were 'banned and burned' in 1933; he emigrated to the U.S.A. His best-known novel, *Die Räuberbande* (1914; tr. C. Brooks, *The Robber Band*, 1928; filmed; with sequels 1927 and 1949), describes the adventures of a group of Würzburg boys ('brigands') in an idyllic setting but with revolutionary undertones. Of his other protest works, *Die Ursache* (1915; tr. ibid., *The Cause of the Crime*, 1928) attacks a coercive and repressive educational system, *Der Mensch ist gut* (1917) is a denunciation of war (widely read even before 1918), while *Der Bürger* (1924; tr. ibid., *A Middle-Class Man*, 1930) shows how society kills a man's native spirit; it is also interesting for its ⇨ Expressionistic film-technique, seen again in the novella *Die Entgleisten* (1929). The story *Carl und Anna* (1926; dramatized 1929; tr. ibid. 1929) enjoyed international success with its realistic yet sentimental account of the returned soldier who seduces the wife of a former comrade. *Links wo das Herz ist* (1952; tr. ibid., *Heart on the Left*, 1954) is a racy autobiographical novel. [PB]

M. Glanbrecht, *Studien zum Frühwerk L.F.s* (Bonn, 1965); C. Frank and H. Jobst, *L.F.* (Munich, 1962); *GQ*, XX (1947); *Neue Texte*, 2, 1962 (bibliography).

**Franko, Ivan** (Drogobych, Austria 1856–L'vov 1916). Ukrainian writer, scholar, critic, translator, journalist. His romantic novel *Petriyi i Dovbushchuky* (1875–6) was followed by a series of stories on the post-emancipation peasant's life, and another series centred on the Boryslav oil wells. Here, notably in *Boa Constrictor* (1878; tr. F. Solasko, *BC and Other Stories*, Moscow, 1957) and *Boryslav smiyet'sya* (1880–1), the rise of the capital and its conflict with labour is naturalistically portrayed in the manner of Zola, often dwelling upon the pathological. In another series (*Na dni*, 1880; *Do svitla*, 1890, etc.) he drew on his experience of imprisonment for socialist activities. Several sympathetic, fine psychological studies of children are found in his stories from school life (e.g. *Maly Myron*, tr. in *UQ*, iii, 1, 1946; 2 stories in Runge, 109). A number of realist stories feature the life of landowners and the rising intelligentsia (the novel *Perekhresni stezhky*, 1900, etc.).

Franko's early poetry was summed up in his celebrated collection *Z vershyn i nyzyn* (1887, enlarged 1893), mostly 'civic', revolutionary and naturalistic. *Ziv''yale lystya* (1896) and later collections introduce also a wide range of deeply lyrical poetry, richly varied in form. His chief narrative poem, *Pans'ki zharty* (1887), portrays peasant life realistically, while his philosophical *Smert' Kayina* (1889) is an original treatment of the theme of Byron's *Cain*. His crowning poem, *Moysey* (1905; tr. W. Semenyna, *Moses*, N.Y., 1938), on the problem of the nation and its leader, is a jewel of Ukrainian literature (cf. *UQ*, ii, 3, 1946; xii, 2, 1956; xiii, 2, 1957).

A prolific writer, he covered a vast range of subjects. Basically a realist, he employed in his social, psychological, satirical, historical (*Zakhar Berkut*, 1882; tr. T. Boresky, N.Y., 1944) novels and stories, and in his poetry, successively romantic, naturalist, impressionist, symbolist, and modernist devices. He also exercised an immense influence on the cultural, social and political life of his country. [VS]

*Tvory* (20 vols., N.Y., 1956–60; 20 vols., 1950–56; 30 vols., 1924–31); *Beiträge zur Geschichte . . .* (E. Berlin, 1963); *Poems and Stories*, tr. J. Weir (Toronto, 1956); *Selected Poems*, tr. P. Cundy (N.Y., 1948); Ewach, *USL*.

Manning, *UL*; Mijakovs'kyj and Shevelov, *TS*; *UCE*; *UQ*, XXII, 2 (1966); *UR*, XIII, 3 (1966); *Suchasnist'*, IV, 7 (1964).

**Frasheri, A., N., S.,** and **M.** ⇨ Albanian Literature.

**Frauenlob.** ⇨ Heinrich von Meissen.

**'Fredegar.'** The fictitious but convenient name for a vast historical compilation, the unoriginal elements of which are extracts or re-workings of the writings of Hippolytus, Jerome, Hydatius, ◊ Gregory of Tours, and ◊ Isidore of Seville. These are interspersed with additions, often of great intrinsic interest, by the compiler himself, for example the legend of the Trojan origin of the Franks. Book IV, known as the chronicle proper to distinguish it from the compilation, is an original history of Burgundy for the years 584–642, and together with the continuations to the year 768 found in some manuscripts forms an invaluable source for the history of Frankish Gaul. Indeed for much of this period it is the only contemporary source we possess. Fredegar's Latin is appallingly corrupt, and the chronicle is thus of great value to philologists also, as evidence of the development of Vulgar Latin. [MRM]

Ed. Krusch (MGH, Scriptorum Rerum Merovingicarum, ii); Migne, *PL*, 71; Book IV and continuations ed. and tr. Wallace-Hadrill (1960).

**Fredro, Aleksander** (Surochów, nr Jarosław 1793–Lvov 1876). Polish playwright. He came from a well-to-do noble family and at 16 joined the Polish army, taking part in the last campaigns of Napoleon. These experiences he later re-created in the book of memoirs, *Trzy po trzy* (1877), for which he devised a structure and style similar to that of *Tristram Shandy*. His first play was staged in Lvov in 1817. His best comedies, *Śluby panieńskie* (1832; tr. A. P. and M. M. Coleman, *Maiden's Vows*, 1940) and *Zemsta* (1834), expose the romantic 'magnetism of the heart' and the intrigue based on the family feud; their titles are half ironic. *Zemsta*, in particular, is original in the use of characters and the elements of parody. Its octosyllabic verse, too, has a subtle stylistic function, allowing swift dialogue and absurd verbal juxtapositions in rhymes. Few plays in verse have succeeded to such an extent with both kinds of surprise, the poetic and the comic.

Successful during his lifetime in the Lvov and Warsaw theatres, Fredro was suddenly silenced in 1835 by the callous attack of a minor but overpatriotic poet who thought his subjects, even love, to be too cosmopolitan. Although later Fredro wrote a few more comedies, he would not allow them to be either published or performed, and this had a bad effect on their quality. [JP]

*Pisma wszystkie*, ed. Pigoń (1955–8); *Damy i huzary* (1825; tr. F. and G. R. Noyes, *Ladies and Hussars*, 1925).
Krzyżanowski, *PRL*.

**Freiligrath, Hermann Ferdinand** (Detmold 1810–Cannstadt 1876). German poet. After working as an accountant in Amsterdam (1831–6) he gained fame with his romantically exotic *Gedichte* (1838). *Ein Glaubensbekenntnis* (1844), which necessitated his escape from Darmstadt to Brussels, Zürich and London, *Ça ira* (1846), and *Neue politische und soziale Gedichte* (1849–51), proclaiming left-wing liberal views, contain some of the best German revolutionary poetry. He also translated French, English and American romantic poets. After being acquitted of 'subversion' in Düsseldorf (1848) and editing the *Neue Rheinische Zeitung* in Cologne he resumed his 1846 London exile in 1851. From 1868 to 1874 he lived in Stuttgart and published *Neue Gedichte* (1870). While disapproving of Bismarck he welcomed the unification of Germany. [LL]

*Auswahl*, ed. R. Buchwald (1947); *Poems*, ed. M. F. Liddell (1947).
H. Eulenberg, *F.F.* (Berlin, 1948).

**French Literary Criticism in the 19th and 20th Centuries.** It is in the 19th century that French literary criticism really acquires the status of an important genre. Breaking away from the strait-jacket of Boileau's formal rules, and greatly exceeding the limits of Voltaire's rather conservative taste, the Romantics, led by Madame de Staël (1766–1817), Chateaubriand (1768–1848), Stendhal (1783–1842) and especially the youthful Victor Hugo of the 1820s and 1830s, spurn the carping enumeration of solecisms to exult vigorously in the fundamental diversity of beauty and the unpredictable freshness of poetic vision. Madame de Staël's *De l'Allemagne* (1813) concludes with a noble passage contrasting genuine creative enthusiasm with the 'arid' pleasures of the mere refined amateur. Stendhal, in his *Racine et Shakespeare* (part I, 1823 part II, 1825), demands an end to pseudo classical imitations and calls on his contemporaries to embark on bold new ventures. And Hugo, in the *Préface de Cromwell* (1827), revolutionizes aesthetics by showing the 'grotesque' as valuable in itself and also as a necessary complement to the 'sublime'. 'Genius *must* have inequalities,' he writes. 'There are no high mountains without steeply sloping gorges ... There are some "faults" which can take root only in masterpieces, some "defects" which are the exclusive privilege of certain very great writers ... The oak-tree, which has more than one analogy with Shakespeare, is peculiar in its stance, it has gnarled branches, its leaves are dark in colour, and its bark is rough and coarse, but it *is* the oak-tree.'

But the reaction against Romanticism is already seen by the early 1840s in the criticism of one of its first supporters. Charles Augustin Sainte-Beuve (1804–69), the greatest of all French critics and possibly the greatest European critic since Aristotle, had started by rehabilitating the lyric poets of the Pléiade in order to shed their lustre over Hugo and his school. But, in his massive *Port-Royal* (1840–59), his voluminous *Causeries du lundi* (1851–70) and the acid *Chateaubriand et son groupe littéraire sous l'Empire* (1860), he denigrates his former 'Romantic' idols and develops an entirely new conception of literary history. He now sees the critical faculty as essentially different from the creative genius of a poet or novelist. Criticism, he says, is never arrogant, stand-offish or self-opinionated, as 'inspired' writing usually is, but, spurred on by curiosity, it goes anywhere and everywhere, takes the most trivial details into account, and exudes sympathy and understanding for all. Nevertheless, it is quick to retrace its steps, change its opinions, and indulge in self-contradiction. Thus the Montaigne (1533–92) who flits like a bee from one literary flower to another and the chameleon-like Bayle (1647–1706) are the best models for the modern critic to follow.

Sainte-Beuve with his abhorrence of dogmatism and his skill in frequenting the most extravagant sects and factions of his day without being committed to any of them, is eager to show this kind of flexibility. He believes firmly, however, that the study of any work of literature must inevitably lead to the study of the man behind it. His constant aim is to produce literary 'portraits' which will capture 'the well-worn twitch in a man's face, his tell-tale smile, and even the tiny crannies in his skin'. He labours with tireless patience to suggest an infinitesimal nuance of personality and to define it unmistakably. His *Port-Royal*, in particular, commands respect, not only for the author's thorough mastery of his subject, his intimate knowledge of the smallest details of its topography, and his skilful use of digressions and contrasts, but, above all, for his brilliant composition of 'one large portrait with many individual portraits and medallions inserted in it'.

His other works have not stood the test of time to the same degree and his portraits of Chateaubriand as a hollow demigod, or of Balzac and Baudelaire as crude sensation-mongers, have been censured, notably by Marcel Proust in *Contre Sainte-Beuve*, as malicious, unperceptive, and, in so far as they fail to distinguish between the banal surface of a writer and his hidden creative self, fundamentally erroneous.

Sainte-Beuve, however, seminal as his work undoubtedly is, cannot be said to represent the whole range of trends and fashions in mid-19th-century French criticism. While he occupies the centre of the critical stage, Baudelaire, in the wings, pleads for 'a biased, strongly emotional, and politically coloured criticism which, in one sense, will be severely restricted but will, in another, offer us the longest perspectives possible'. This is true of Baudelaire's own paradoxical studies of Poe and Gautier, true also of Hugo's curiously imposing *William Shakespeare* (1864). Without adhering to any traditional dogma both poet-critics scrutinize the ultimate mysteries of symbolics and poetics and they thereby incur the hostility of those anachronistic neo-Catholics whose judgements are perhaps the most individualistic and provocative of the period. The inflammatory Louis Veuillot (1813–83) and histrionic Barbey d'Aurevilly (1808–89) add garish colours to the critical spectrum.

During the latter part of Sainte-Beuve's career one of his own disciples, Hippolyte Taine (1828–93), tries to use the eminently flexible method of *Port-Royal* and the *Lundis* for a more rigorously scientific approach to literature. Sainte-Beuve, he says, has shown us in *Port-Royal* the infinite detail of human nature but he has not shown the underlying *causes* of psychological phenomena. In the significant 1863 preface to his *Histoire de la littérature anglaise* Taine recognizes 'race', 'environment' and 'the combined and cumulative effect of both' as the three determining factors of literary development. Every effect, he claims, has a discernible cause, vice and virtue no less than vitriol and sugar, and literary fashions come and go in a clearly pre-determined manner. And, although Taine failed to counter Sainte-Beuve's objection that such a method eliminated all consideration of the indefinable quality of genius, his provocative generalizations have stimulated the most diverse critical inquiries, while his essays on Balzac, Stendhal and Saint-Simon remain intrinsically interesting and serve as models of his lapidary style.

After the *apogée* of Taine's influence, the concluding decades of the century present an extremely complex picture to the student of criticism and only a few outstanding trends can be noted here. Perhaps the opposition between Paul Bourget (1852–1935) and Ferdinand Brunetière (1849–1906) on the one hand and Anatole France (1844–1924) and Jules Lemaître (1853–1914) on the other is the most important of these.

In the *Essais de psychologie contemporaine*, a masterly series of studies that first appeared between 1881 and 1885, Paul Bourget emphatically regards Taine and Renan, along with Baudelaire, Flaubert and the curiously prophetic Stendhal, as the true mentors of a whole new generation. Yet he diagnoses spiritual maladies in the authors he admires. Flaubert, for him, is a 'nihilist', Renan a 'dilettante', Baudelaire a 'decadent' and Taine a dangerous devotee of Science who concedes even her most sweeping claims. He quotes with alarm Taine's dictum that Science 'is going to tackle the human soul' and comments that 'this phrase gives us M. Taine's whole work in a nutshell' and that it clearly implies a denial of the soul's 'spontaneity and freedom'. Eight years later, in his novel *Le disciple*, he developed this attack on Taine, irreparably damaged the philosopher's prestige, and incidentally provoked a lively polemic between Ferdinand Brunetière, the moralistic editor of *La Revue des Deux Mondes*, and the witty, freethinking literary columnist of *Le Temps*, Anatole France.

Brunetière's most controversial contribution to critical theory was his neo-Darwinian concept, expounded at the École Normale in the autumn of 1889, of the 'evolution' of literary genres. Thus he tried to show how tragedy as a genre is born, grows, reaches perfection, declines and finally dies. Or again how one particular genre is transformed into another, how, for example, the eloquent sermon of the 17th century was transformed into the lyrical poetry of the 19th. The theory may appear eccentric but Brunetière's solid critical studies of 17th- and early-19th-century authors and his 1898 *Manuel de l'histoire de la littérature française* bear few traces of its excesses and can still be read with profit. He is unsympathetic, however, to the 18th century, to the principle of 'individualism' and to the 'naturalists' of Zola's school.

There was, by the late 1880s, a general disillusionment with the extravagant claims on behalf of Science and the scientific method put forward by Taine and Renan in the heyday of the Second Empire and revived by Zola in his *Roman expérimental* (1880). Brunetière was one of many who proclaimed the 'bankruptcy' of Science and this change in the general intellectual climate naturally affected fashions in criticism. For this reason, although it contained many ingenious ideas, Émile Hennequin's (1859–88) little book on *La critique scientifique*, published shortly after the author's premature death, found only a handful of readers and has never been reprinted. Taine and his methods were losing ground and criticism of contemporary literature in the '*fin-de-siècle*' period tended to remain in the hands of the so-called 'impressionists', Anatole France and Jules Lemaître, both of whom ostensibly rejected any belief in objective literary criteria and asked nothing more from books than nonchalant epicurean delights. Yet France, in the early stages, was just as hostile to Zola as Brunetière had been, while Lemaître, although professing that contemporary literature gave him pleasure 'in the very marrow of his bones', poured so much ridicule on Verlaine and on all the 'symbolists' and 'decadents', that his criticism surpassed in severity Brunetière's execution of Baudelaire. Indeed, there is so little to choose between Brunetière's dismissal of 'the poor man's Beelzebub' and, for example, Lemaître's ironic 'translation' of Mallarmé's poem *Le Tombeau d'Edgar Poe* that we are bound to regard both these critics as equally unreliable guides to their period. In the whole of Brunetière's *Roman naturaliste* (1883), France's *Vie littéraire* (1888–92) and Lemaître's *Contemporains* (1885–1918) and *Impressions de théâtre* (1888–98) there is less understanding of contemporary literature than in a few characteristic pages of Huysmans' novel *À rebours* (1884). Even more significant are the *avant-garde* articles in the *Mercure de France* by Rémy de

Gourmont (1858–1915), who, in his defence both of Huysmans and of 'the excommunicate poets' whom the latter championed, rejects Brunetière decisively but clearly outdistances France and Lemaître also.

Academic criticism in the 1890s and in the early decades of the 20th century was represented in France not only by Brunetière but also by two other university professors, Émile Faguet (1847–1916) and, especially, Gustave Lanson (1857–1934). Although its partiality and limitations are becoming more apparent, Lanson's *Histoire de la littérature française* (1894) is still a valuable guide while some of his numerous articles and monographs, particularly those dealing with critical methodology, repay an even closer study. But Faguet was condemned as unperceptive by André Gide (1869–1950) and Lanson savagely parodied by his brilliant pupil Charles Péguy (1873–1914). Moreover, despite the soundness of their scholarship, some of Lanson's pupils, particularly Gustave Rudler (1872–1957) and Daniel Mornet (1878–1954), have incurred similar censure. Such a vocal representative of 'la nouvelle critique' as Roland Barthes, for example, has attacked Lanson and the 'lansoniens' for their pedantry, their excessive attention to biographical trivia, and their ideological archaism. While conceding the magnitude of their contribution to *non*-literary background knowledge, he points out that this, in itself, may well be a *dis*service to criticism. Not only does he accept the psychoanalysts' conclusion that biographical facts are frequently distorted or inverted in works of art. He affirms that, in any event, we should not be concerned with the spurious question of whether Proust's imaginary Baron Charlus 'was' or 'was not' Count Montesquiou but rather with the character's aesthetic value within the framework of a novel. To Barthes and other critics of the 1960s the Lansonian method seems a dangerous irrelevance.

Conversely, the two outstanding philosophical influences on French literary criticism in the 1900–35 period, those of Henri Bergson (1859–1941) and, a little later, Sigmund Freud (1856–1939), still have a contemporary impact. The combined effect of these two very different thinkers completely revolutionized the mental climate of writers and the reading public.

Bergson's first major work, his *Essai sur les données immédiates de la conscience* or 'essay on the immediate data of consciousness', appeared in 1889 and, along with the subsequent *Matière et mémoire* (1896) and *L'évolution créatrice* (1907), it influenced a whole generation of critics. Charles Péguy in his *Note sur M. Bergson et la philosophie bergsonienne* (1914), Jacques Rivière (1886–1925) in the admirable *Études* (1912, 1947) which characterize the sensibility of the pre-First World War generation as skilfully as Bourget had evoked the spirit of the 1880s, and Charles Du Bos (1883–1939) in his delicately intuitive *Approximations* (1921–32), are all steeped in the dynamic imagery of this epoch-making philosopher. But perhaps the most 'Bergsonian' critic of all is Albert Thibaudet (1874–1936) who, in significant works on Mallarmé (1912), Barrès (1921), Flaubert (1922), the philosophy of 'Bergsonism' itself (1924) and the 'physiology' of criticism (1930), develops the master's notion of an organic duration that cannot be expressed in spatial analogies, his belief that '*in*determination' is 'the true principle', and his doctrine of evolution based *not* on observation and reconstruction of what has already evolved but rather on immediate perception of the essential dynamism of the genetic process. Thibaudet's monographs and numerous articles have, of course, been superseded on many points of detail but his sense of the rhythm and continuity of literary development, his method of 'creation in criticism', and his study of literary 'generations' (all derived, in large measure, from Bergson) give his work an unmistakable quality and force.

Freud's *Three Essays on Sexuality* were published in the original as early as 1905 but it was not until 1923 that Reverchon's French translation appeared. The following year André Breton published his first Surrealist manifesto and, with renewed interest not only in Nerval, Baudelaire and Rimbaud but also in Dostoyevsky (whose correspondence was studied by Gide as early as 1908) and in such writers as de Sade (1740–1814) and Lautréamont (1846–70), oneirocriticism of the Freudian variety soon had a wealth of material to investigate.

The main stream of French criticism, however, soon diverged from Freud and, although obscure motivations and obsessional patterns of imagery attracted increasing attention, the most characteristic approach was phenomenological rather than psychoanalytical. In other words, literary structures were studied for their own sake and described both in depth and extension but they were not 'explained' by reference to real or supposed psychological 'causes'. The methods of Sainte-Beuve, Taine and Lanson, and indeed of their Freudian successors, were abandoned when 'the autonomous literary phenomenon', the work seen in and for itself rather than as an extension of the author's personality, was judged to be the only authentic critical datum. New methods were devised to approach literature and these have developed into the controversial '*nouvelle critique*' of the 1950s and 1960s.

So far as France was concerned, the originator of the phenomenological approach to literature was Gaston Bachelard (1884–1962), a pure scientist and a philosopher whose interests embraced not only physics, chemistry and the problem of time but also such unusual subjects as 'the psychoanalysis of fire' and 'the poetics of space'. In a series of major works showing the four mythical elements as the essential substance of the world 'created' by poets, he completely revolutionized the critic's approach to the study of imagery. His disciples, who include Georges Poulet, Jean-Pierre Richard, Jean Rousset, Jean Starobinski and Roland Barthes, are unanimous in their enthusiasm for the subtlety of his conception and the radical character of his conclusions. 'Before Bachelard,' wrote Georges Poulet in 1965, 'consciousness was the most ethereal thing in the world. But Bachelard made it impossible to describe consciousness as anything but concrete and difficult to perceive except through the layers of images covering it up. His revolution, therefore, was Copernican in scope. He has been the greatest explorer of the life of the mind since Sigmund Freud (although his was a very different path from Freud's).'

Many other ideologies have, of course, influenced contemporary French criticism. Existentialism has left its critical monuments in Jean-Paul Sartre's *Situations* (7 vols., 1947–65), in his study of Baudelaire (1947) and in his powerful *Saint Genet, comédien et martyr* (1952). The heterodox Marxism of the Hungarian 'critical realist' George Lukács has inspired the 'sociological' criticism of Lucien Goldmann. The linguistic theories of Ferdinand de Saussure, the poetics of the Russian formalists (who flourished from 1915 to 1930), the new social anthropology of Claude Lévi-Strauss, the theories of Bertolt Brecht and Alain Robbe-Grillet, the Joycean and explicitly anti-Crocean aesthetics of Umberto Eco, the agonized meditation of Kafka, even the narrator whom Proust portrays as incidentally constructing one work while he is impatiently waiting to compose another, are all among the many formative influences on Roland Barthes. And the pregnant fragments left by Mallarmé and Kafka, the unsatisfied yearnings of Rilke and the enigmas of Samuel Beckett are strong incentives to Maurice Blanchot's search for the great definitive book of all time.

Apart from an unmistakable hostility to the methods of the Lanson school there is, in fact, little common ground between the various '*nouveaux critiques*'. Admittedly, as phenomenologists, most of them tend to equate criticism with the description of imagic or stylistic patterns, with the study of 'structures' or 'themes' unrelated to hypothetical 'causes', and with approximation to a point of view intrinsic to the work itself. But their particular terrains and methods of investigation are widely different. Georges Poulet, for example, in his masterly studies of 'human time', is exploring regions remote from Blanchot's elusively Kafkaesque 'void' with its magnetic and destructive fascination. Jean-Pierre Richard shows us 'the interpenetration of interiority and exteriority' or, in other words, 'consciousness at grips with substance and not floundering in a vacuum'. Roland Barthes, on the other hand, emphatically rejects the view that 'subjects' can be squeezed like lemons. Since the apparently solid core of creativity is, for him, an emptiness or 'absence' which the writer evades in ever-widening symbolic patterns, he regards nothing as more sterile than the attempt to reduce a work to a mere explicit statement. On the contrary, the Barthesian critic endeavours to continue rather than arrest the original metaphorical process, to cultivate a new efflorescence of the writer's symbols, and to multiply cross-references between related images. Symbol is translated into symbol and 'literature' becomes the amalgam of the original work and its successive interpretations.

The dramatic and total renovation of Anglo-American criticism in the inter- and post-war years has been barely noticed by the '*nouveaux critiques*' but it would, for example, be interesting to compare William Empson's approach to 'ambiguity' wit

Barthes's definition of the symbol as a plurality of meanings, all of which, with the critic's collaboration, evolve dynamically in time. Or again we may compare Kenneth Burke's rejection of 'the heresy of paraphrase' and his wide utilization of semantics, Marxism, psychoanalysis and anthropology with the whole of Barthes's development from his early articles on 'the zero-point in writing' (1947) to his 'structuralist' study of Racine and, especially, his conclusions in *Critique et vérité* (1966). Only Jean Rousset, however, in his stimulating *Forme et signification* (1962) acknowledges a specific debt to Eliot, Empson, Richards and Warren.

Such periodicals as *Tel Quel* and *Critique*, to which Barthes, Blanchot and the other '*nouveaux critiques*' contribute, now enjoy the kind of authority that Sartre's *Temps modernes* enjoyed immediately after the war. But, in academic circles, suspicion has turned to open hostility. Barthes's *Sur Racine* (1963), in particular, has provoked a scathing reaction from the distinguished scholar Raymond Picard. In a brilliant pamphlet entitled *Nouvelle critique ou nouvelle imposture* (1965) Picard has attacked Barthes in a manner reminiscent of Faguet taking Baudelaire to task for his alleged solecisms. Barthes has replied no less pungently in *Critique et vérité* and Serge Doubrovsky has carried the debate further in the virulent but most illuminating pages of *Pourquoi la nouvelle critique* (vol. I, 1966). As Thibaudet once remarked, feuds like these are the very life-blood of a genre that can never reach a final dogmatic solution. They are exciting in themselves, they throw valuable light on fundamental aesthetic issues, and they bear eloquent testimony to the inexhaustible potency of the great literature which is their pretext and justification. [JGC]

Mme de Pange, *Mme de Staël et la découverte de l'Allemagne* (Paris, 1929); M. Proust, *Contre Sainte-Beuve* (Paris, 1954); H. Nicolson, *Sainte-Beuve* (1957); M. Regard, *Sainte-Beuve* (Paris, 1959); A. G. Lehmann, *Sainte-Beuve: A Portrait of the Critic, 1804–1842* (1962); P. Moreau, *La critique selon Sainte-Beuve* (Paris, 1964); J. Corbière-Gille, *Barbey d'Aurevilly, critique littéraire* (Paris, 1962); Sainte-Beuve, *Causeries du Lundi*, XIII, 249–84, *Nouveaux lundis*, VIII, 66–137; V. Giraud, *Essai sur Taine* (Paris, 1901, 6th edn, 1912); A. Chevrillon, *Taine. Formation de sa pensée* (Paris, 1932); S. Kahn, *Science and Aesthetic Judgment: A Study in Taine's Critical Method* (N.Y., 1953); J. Clark, *La pensée de Ferdinand Brunetière* (Paris, 1954); G. Saintsbury, *A History of Criticism* (vol. III, 7th edn, 1949); G. Rees, *Rémy de Gourmont. Essai de biographie intellectuelle* (Paris, 1940), 'The Position of Rémy de Gourmont' (*French Studies*, vol. IV, no. 4); P. M. Jones, *The Assault on French Literature* (1963); H. Peyre, *G. Lanson. Essais de méthode, de critique et d'histoire littéraire* (Paris, 1965); R. Arbour, *Henri Bergson et les lettres françaises* (Paris, 1955); Charles Du Bos, *Approximations* (new edn, Paris, 1965); A. Thibaudet, *Physiologie de la critique* (Paris, 1930); A. Glauser, *Albert Thibaudet et la critique créatrice* (Paris, 1952); J. Davies, *L'œuvre critique d'Albert Thibaudet* (Paris, 1955); M. Turnell, *Rivière* (1953); P. Thody, *Jean-Paul Sartre* (1960); I. Alexander, *The Phenomenological Philosophy in France*, G. Poulet, *Gaston Bachelard et la critique contemporaine* (both published in G. T. Clapton memorial volume, *Currents of Thought in French Literature*, 1965); G. Poulet, *Études sur le temps humain* (3 vols., Paris, 1950, 1952, 1964) *Les métamorphoses du cercle* (Paris, 1961), *L'espace proustien* (Paris, 1963); J.-P. Richard, *Littérature et sensation* (Paris, 1954), *Poésie et profondeur* (Paris, 1955), *L'univers imaginaire de Mallarmé* (Paris, 1961), *Paysage de Chateaubriand* (Paris, 1967); M. Blanchot, *L'espace littéraire* (Paris, 1955), *Le livre à venir* (Paris, 1959); P. Moreau, *La critique littéraire en France* (Paris, 1960); M. de Diéguez, *L'écrivain et son langage* (Paris 1960); J. Rousset, *Pour une lecture des formes* (introduction to *Forme et signification*, Paris, 1962); *Critics Abroad* (special no. *TLS*, 27 Sept. 1963); R. Molho, *La critique littéraire en France au XIXe siècle: ses conceptions* (Paris, 1963); R. Wellek, *Concepts of Criticism* (Yale, 1963); R. Barthes, *Le degré zéro de l'écriture* (Paris, 1953), *Sur Racine* (Paris, 1963), *Essais critiques* (Paris, 1964), *Critique et vérité* (Paris, 1966); R. Fayolle, *La critique* (Paris, 1964); R. Picard, *Nouvelle critique ou nouvelle imposture* (Paris, 1965); S. Doubrovsky, *Pourquoi la nouvelle critique: critique et objectivité* (Paris, 1966); Char, Poulet, Starobinski, *Maurice Blanchot* (special no. *Critique*, June 1966); Wellek, *HMC*.

**Fréron, Élie-Catherine** (Quimper 1718–Montrouge 1776). French journalist and critic. After serving his apprenticeship with ⇨ Desfontaines, he launched his first independent periodical in 1745. In 1754 he founded his most influential journal, *L'Année Littéraire*, and devoted the rest of his life to it. Conservative in his beliefs and literary tastes, but often a shrewd judge, he made enemies by his outspoken criticisms, especially among the *philosophes*, and became a major spokesman for established orthodoxy, enjoying court patronage. Voltaire's detestation of him is reflected in numerous attacks, notably in *L'Écossaise* (1760). [WHB]

F. Cornou, *E.F.* (Paris, 1922).

**Freuchen, Peter** (Nykøbing, Falster 1904–Alaska 1957). Danish novelist and Greenland explorer. An expert on Eskimo life, leader of Alaska expedition for M-G-M Studios' film *Eskimo* (1933), member of wartime Resistance, he fled to Sweden and the U.S.A. His colourful personality is reflected in novels (set mainly in Greenland): *Storfanger* and *Rømningsmand* (both tr. A. P. M. and E. Branden, *Eskimo*, 1932), *Nordkaper* (tr. E. Bjorkman, *The Sea Tyrant*, 1932), *Ivalu* (1930; tr. J. Jusztis and E. P. Ehrich, *Ivalu, the Eskimo Wife*, 1935), *White Man* (tr. anon., 1946), *The Law of Larion* (tr. anon., 1952), and autobiographical books *Arctic Adventure* (tr. anon., 1936), *It's All Adventure* (tr. anon., 1938) and *Vagrant Viking* (tr. J. Hambro, 1953). [ELB]

**Freud, Sigmund** (Vienna 1856–London 1939). Austrian psychoanalyst. Although his theory of the unconscious was based on his practical work as a doctor and as a teacher at the Vienna General Hospital, both its methodological implications and Freud's speculative cast of mind led him to make many suggestive observations on cultural matters. His most famous analyses of modern culture appear in *The Future of an Illusion* (1927) and *Civilization and its Discontents* (1930). His pronouncements on art and literature, many of them made *en passant* in his more technical works, reflect his broad personal culture: his family was Jewish, he was schooled in the classics, he read English and French fluently, and loved the work of Shakespeare and of Goethe. His most direct article on art is *Leonardo* (1910; tr. A. Tyson, Penguin Books, 1963), which relates themes and attitudes in da Vinci's work to childhood experiences; on literature, the essay *Dostoyevsky and Parricide* (1927) points to a neurosis, a destructive impulse turned inward, in Dostoyevsky's life (his epilepsy, his guiltless acceptance of punishment) and work (his preoccupation with the criminal and sinner). Elsewhere Freud suggests that art helps the neurotic by offering 'a path back from phantasy to reality' (*Introductory Lectures*, 1917). Unlike the uncontrolled manifestations of repression in neurosis and dreams, the language, e.g., of wit allows conscious expression to 'pleasure sources which have become inaccessible' (*Jokes and Their Relationship to the Unconscious*, 1905); a variant theory of acceptance and control is adumbrated in *Beyond the Pleasure Principle* (1920) with regard to tragedy. Such hints have given rise to much subsequent speculation on the function of art as a mode of instinctual liberation, as essentially a primary psychic progress, as related to the mentality of childhood. [AKT]

*Complete Psychoanalytical Works*, ed. J. Strachey (1955– ); *Collected Papers* (International Psychoanalytical Library, 1924–50).

L. Trilling, *F. and the Crisis of our Culture* (1955); *Art and Psychoanalysis*, ed. W. Phillips (N.Y., 1957); *F. and the 20th Century*, ed. B. Nelson (1958); H. Marcuse, *Eros and Civilization* (1962); *Psychoanalysis and Literature*, ed. H. M. Ruitenbeek (N.Y., 1964).

**Freytag, Gustav** (Kreuzburg 1816–Wiesbaden 1895). German novelist and dramatist. Born into a well-to-do middle-class Silesian background, he made political cause with the educated liberals of the mid 19th century, preserving at the same time a firm pro-Prussian mentality. He earned the respect of aristocracy and commoners alike, and at his death he was mourned as a national hero.

As a dramatist he pursued the realistic lines laid down by ⇨ Gutzkow, ⇨ Laube and others of the Young German movement. He laid out his theories in *Technik des Dramas* (1863), but his actual dramas preceded this: the most successful was the comedy *Die Journalisten* (1854), in which, as in his other dramas, he presented the virtues of a Protestant middle-class morality through efficient but passionless characters.

The same bourgeois values emerge from his novels, whose realism owes something to Dickens; the most memorable is *Soll und Haben* (1855). His *Bilder aus der deutschen Vergangenheit* (1859 ff.) are a series of historical sketches evoking the spirit of earlier ages. [RT]

*Gesammelte Werke*, ed. H. M. Elster (12 vols, 1926).

A. Horawitz, *G.F. als Dichter und Historiker* (Vienna, 1871); A. Kohut, *G.F. als Patriot und Politiker* (Berlin, 1916).

**Fridegård, Jan** (Hjulsta 1897–1968). Swedish novelist and story-writer. A portrayer (like ⇨ Lo-Johansson) of the Swedish *statare* (farm labourers) and one of the outstanding self-educated Swedish authors (like also Moberg, Eyvind ⇨ Johnson and

Martinson), his exceptionally harsh life as manual worker, soldier and unemployed man provided material for the series of four partly autobiographical novels, *Lars Hård* (1935–42), that produced at first a sensation by their apparently cynical brutality. Lars Hård is an unemployed ex-soldier, at odds with society, who gets into prison. The clash of anti-social individual and impersonal society that has shaped him is shown with ruthless yet ironic directness, deep and unsentimental comprehension, controlled intensity, and precisely chiselled style. Fridegård's later work is on the whole less remarkable, but his concern with society and history produced the notable novels *Trägudars land* (1940), *Gryningsfolket* (1944), and *Offerrök* (1949), where with originality and skill Viking times are depicted partly from the point of view of slaves.

E. Gamby, *J.F.: introduktion till ett författarskap* (Stockholm, 1956); *En bok om J.F.* (ed. E. Gamby) (Stockholm, 1957); K. Jaensson, 'Lars Hård', in *Sanning och särprägel* (Stockholm, 1960).

**Fried, Erich** (Vienna 1921– ). Austrian poet and translator. Living in London since 1938, he works for the B.B.C. Owing perhaps to his admiration for Hopkins, Joyce, e. e. cummings, perhaps to writing in a language not used in daily speech, his poetry (*Gedichte*, 1958; *Reich der Steine*, 1963, etc.) shows a self-conscious sense of the magic and mystery of words, especially of verbal affinities (indeed, puns), which he has explored in an effort to find real connexions between things, and reach a style to overcome his dominant feeling of *Auswegslosigkeit*. In recent collections, notably *und Vietnam und* (1966), verbal inventiveness is effectively allied with political commitment. [PB]

*Ein Soldat und ein Mädchen* (1961); *Kinder und Narren* (1965) (stories); Bridgwater, *TCGV*; Hamburger and Middleton, *MGP*.

**Friedrich von Hausen** (fl. 1170–1190). German ◊ Minnesinger. One of the earliest to introduce into German lyric poetry the motifs of Romance-inspired courtly love. Of noble birth, he belonged to a family which had its domain near Worms, and which prided itself on a tradition of loyal service to the house of Hohenstaufen. He accompanied Frederick Barbarossa on the crusade of 1189 and was killed in battle. He was intimately acquainted with the poetry of the ◊ troubadours and ◊ *trouvères*, and as well as introducing into German verse the tripartite strophic structure characteristic of Romance courtly lyric poetry, he wrote poems which are virtually German copies, both in subject-matter and in form, of known French and Provençal originals. His poetic talent is unmistakable, although in style and poetic technique he is both heavily dependent on his chosen models and somewhat limited in his means of expression. [RT]

Kraus, *MF*.
Ehrismann, *GDL*.

**Friedrich von Sonnenburg** (fl. late 12th cent.). German lyric poet. A native of the Tirol, remembered for his political poetry in favour, first of Ottokar II of Bohemia, then of his rival Rudolf of Habsburg, in the period of the interregnum. His verse owes much to ◊ Walther von der Vogelweide, particularly in the aggressiveness of its language. His religious *Sprüche* are entirely conventional. [RT]

Kraus, *DL*.

**Friis Møller, Kai** (Copenhagen 1888–Copenhagen 1960). Danish poet. An ardent Anglophile and Francophile he made some outstanding verse translations, especially of Kipling, Villon, Baudelaire, Verlaine, T. S. Eliot and Christopher Fry. He was also a fine original poet (*Digte*, 1910, and *Indskrifter*, 1920) and a literary critic feared for his sarcasm. [ELB]

**Frisch, Max** (Zürich 1911– ). Swiss dramatist and novelist. He spent his early years in journalism and in qualifying as an architect. Though he had offered Max Reinhardt a drama (*Stahl*) at 16, his best work has all been written since 1945; with ◊ Dürrenmatt he is now the leading post-war German-language dramatist. His first characteristic play, the farce *Die chinesische Mauer* (1946, revised 1955; tr. J. L. Rosenberg *The Chinese Wall*, N.Y., 1961) is a satire on dictators, brilliantly ironical in dialogue, experimental in form, and influenced by Brecht and Claudel. The socially challenging drama *Als der Krieg zu Ende war* (1949) was followed by *Graf Öderland* (1951, revised 1956 and 1961; tr. M. Bullock, in *Three Plays*, 1962), a scenic tragi-comedy or 'Moritat', which shows how the revolutionary desire for freedom achieves its ironical opposite. A dominant preoccupation with Frisch, the comedy *Don Juan oder die Liebe zur Geometrie* (1953), reveals the disparity between a man's reputation and his real identity; it is an outspoken attack on facile preconceived opinion. Even more outspoken is the one-act *Biedermann und die Brandstifter* (radio-play, 1953; drama, 1958; tr. M. Bullock, *The Fire Raisers*, 1962), a comedy and parable-play which attacks the complacent irresponsibility of the average citizen who appeases and encourages the fire-raisers, the amoral Everyman whose behaviour in an incendiary world is criminal. Frisch's greatest drama is *Andorra* (1961; tr. M. Bullock, 1962), a tragedy about anti-semitism and the destructiveness of complacency and prejudice; it is also the most Brechtian of his dramas.

After the immature novel *Jürg Reinhart* (1934) and the unremarkable *Die Schwierigen oder J'adore ce qui me brûle* (1943), he produced the surrealistic dream-story *Bin oder Die Reise nach Peking* (1946). His reputation as a novelist rests on *Stiller* (1954; tr. M. Bullock, *I'm not Stiller*, 1961), and *Homo Faber* (1957; tr. M. Bullock, 1959). *Stiller* examines the uncertain identity and relationships of a modern intellectual who denies his former self for the sake of (dull) personal integrity. His latest novel is *Mein Name sei Gantenbein* (1964; tr. M. Bullock, *A Wilderness of Mirrors*, 1965). [PB]

*Stücke* (2 vols., 1962).

E. Stäuble, *M.F.: Ein Schweizer Dichter der Gegenwart* (Amriswil, 1966); H. Karasek, *M.F.* (Velber, 1966); M. Wintsch-Spiess, *Zum Problem der Identität im Werk M.F.s* (Zürich, 1965) (with bibliography); Hans Bänziger, *Frisch und Dürrenmatt* (Berne, 1964); Natan, *GML*, iii.

**Frischlin, Nicodemus** (Balingen 1547–Hohenurach 1590). German dramatist. Professor of Poetry at Tübingen at 21, his ridicule of his pretentious academic colleagues and his attacks on the feudal nobility of his native Suabia (*Oratio de vita rustica*, 1578) involved him in quarrels, recriminations and persecutions which culminated in his death while trying to escape from prison. He wrote Biblical and historical dramas (*Rebecca*, 1576; *Helvetiogermani*, 1588), imitations of Aristophanes (*Priscianus vapulans* – a satire on the vulgar ambitions and crude Latin of his colleagues – 1578) and dramatized versions of Virgil (*Dido*, 1581). Most of his dramas suffer from a looseness of dramatic structure – sub-plots frequently crowd out the main action – but the comedies reveal a gift for accurate observation and great talent in the creation of living characters. Of his German dramas only the comedy *Frau Wendelgart* (1579), a treatment of the *Heimkehrermotif*, survives. His other writings include translations of Aristophanes into Latin and a Latin epic on the history of Israel. [WAC]

*Deutsche Dichtungen*, ed. D. F. Strauss (BLVS, 41, 1857).

D. van Abbé, *Drama in Renaissance Germany and Switzerland* (1961); G. Bebermeyer, *Tübinger Dichterhumanisten* (Tübingen, 1927).

**Frishman, David** (Lodz 1862–Berlin 1922). Hebrew writer. Born into a well-to-do enlightened family, his command of several European languages, especially German, afforded an opportunity of intimate knowledge of European literature which was to lead to a synthesis of Jewish and European tradition. He had an equally good grounding in traditional Hebrew sources and a deep love for the Hebrew language. He published his first short story at 18 in ⇨ Smolenskin's monthly, *Ha-Shachar*. His versatility made him sought after and he became a collaborator of Nahum ⇨Sokolov on the journal *He-Assif* and then assistant editor of *Ha-Yom*, the first Hebrew daily, started by Dr J. L. Kantor in 1884. When it ceased publication in 1888, he went to Breslau University whence he returned to Warsaw in the early nineties. Here he translated into Hebrew from German, French and English the works of Goethe, Heine, Anatole France, Byron, Shakespeare, Nietzsche, Tagore and several scientific works of history. During the First World War, he lived in Odessa and Moscow, and finally in Berlin, where he died. His chief contribution to Hebrew literature was as a short-story writer, although he was an eminent critic, poet and feuilletonist. As an observer of human nature, he introduced the feature of psychological emphasis and analysis of the mental state of his subject. Frishman's short stories fall into two main groups: the first, to which group belong *Yom ha-kippurim*, *Haskorat Neshamot* and *Tikkun Shel Shavuot*, describes the tragedies resulting from the apostasy of children leaving the narrow ghetto life. The second exemplified by *Mitzvah Tithadesh*, *Le-Erez Yisrael*, etc., contains sketches on the theme of struggles and unfulfilled passions of his neighbours. With love for his characters, a great deal of understanding and fine humour, Frishman sketches the conflict between the narrow confines of ghetto life and the wider life outside, intruding and luring away the inhabitants of the ghetto. His best stories are *Bamidbar* (Berlin, 1923), a series of Biblical stories using some episode or precept of the Pentateuch. [EE]

*Kolvitve D.F.*, ed. L. Frishman (20 vols., Warsaw, 1923–7).

Waxman, *HJL*.

**Fröding, Gustaf** (Alster 1860–Stockholm 1911). Swedish poet. What ⇨ Lagerlöf did in prose, Fröding did in verse – give his native province (Värmland) a place in the hearts of his countrymen and a voice of its own. Of a wealthy family, which soon fell on evil days through mental illness (in parents and several relatives), he himself was an invalid after 1880; during periods of comparative health he wrote against the heaviest odds. In 1898 he was finally certified (schizophrenia?). In 1880 he went to Uppsala but returned after a few years, bankrupt and without a degree. Condemned to live off his relatives, he felt his social disgrace and alienation acutely, seeking to hide them behind a humorous front or else seeking escape in alcohol. He enjoyed a degree of rehabilitation on joining the staff of the liberal *Karlstads-Tidningen* in 1887. Encouraged by ⇨ Heidenstam's example he prepared his first collection of verse, *Guitarr och dragharmonika* (1891). Its success was instantaneous: he treats of simple folk with reconciling humour and delicacy of feeling, and a lucid mastery of rhyme and rhythm, which was to make his gallery of Värmland figures a part of the family circle in every literate Swedish household. But already in the first book, there are intimations of deep, personal suffering; in *Nya Dikter* (1894) and still more in *Stänk och flikar* (1896), written on the verge of mental breakdown, his affliction provides him with his material or makes possible a rare degree of identification with other sufferers. The experiences which he had to report were often extraordinary and of a clearly hallucinatory nature; yet in his endeavour to transmute them into art one is made aware of his strong and noble) will to communicate on terms acceptable to the reader. Accordingly, clarity is maintained even on the threshold of Hades, e.g. 'Drömmar i Hades', and honesty and tenderness asserted in the face of ultimate degradation, e.g. 'Flickan i ögat'. On the other hand, his sense of inadequacy also inspired him to celebrate strong, virile personalities, and involved him in a long and tortured dialogue with himself on the nature of good and evil, leading him at times to identify with the defiant Lucifer or dream about the final reconciliation of Heaven and Hell through a revolt of all damned souls, among whom he counted himself. The focus of these speculations is 'the grail', a symbol of wholeness and an obscure concept which appears to be influenced more by Nietzsche's dreamt-of Superman than by Christian thought. In these collections Fröding's formative faculty is still unimpaired, and his reason grapples with visions rising out of the hinterland of the mind. In later collections, however, intellect and emotion no longer appear to work together; the result is arid abstraction and opaque imagery: the struggle goes on, but deprived of colour and sensuous urgency. A posthumous collection, written during a period of better health but still marked by the distance from the outside world, was published in 1913 under the title *Reconvalescentia*. In it we find the poet once more indulging in make-believe but also capable of a tired self-awareness, which is doubly moving when seen as the last flicker of his upright spirit. [SAB]

*Samlade Skrifter*, ed. R. Gison Berg (16 vols., 1917–22).

H. Olsson, *F., ett diktarproträtt* (Stockholm, 1950); J. Landquist, *G.F., en biografi* (Stockholm, 1956).

**Froissart, Jean** (Valenciennes 1337–*c.* 1404). French chronicler, poet, cleric and traveller. He came to England in 1361 and gained the patronage of the Queen, Philippa of Hainault, and access at the English court to many French and English lords whose protection he sought. He visited Scotland, started out on the Black Prince's expedition to Spain (1367), and went on the marriage procession of the Duke of Clarence to Milan. He met Chaucer at this time, saw Petrarch in Milan, and visited Bologna, Ferrara and Rome. After the death of his benefactress Queen Philippa (15 August 1369) he found fresh patrons in France; he became a close friend of Gui de Blois and Wenceslas of Brabant, by whose favour he held various appointments in the Church. The next twenty years were occupied with travel in Flanders and France, a visit to the brilliant court of Gaston-Phébus of Foix being especially memorable, and with writing up the sights and stories he had gathered. On 12 July 1395 he disembarked at Dover, did homage at the tomb of the Black Prince at Canterbury, and was welcomed again to the English court where Richard II accepted a volume of his complete poems. His chronicle continues to the year 1400.

The first book of the *Chroniques* was published in three versions. The earliest is based on the narrative of Jean le Bel, but the two later accounts incline more to the French cause and contain more of Froissart's own impressions. The second book was completed in 1387, the third in 1390; he was probably still revising the fourth when he died.

He compiled his *Chroniques* 'afin que les grans merveilles et li biau fait d'armes qui sont avenu par les grans guerres de France et d'Engleterre et des royaumes voisins . . . soient notablement registré', and to this end he 'ordered and put into prose the true information' he had received from the 'vaillans hommes, chevaliers et escuiers' who were taking part in these wars, and from the 'rois d'armes et leurs mareschaus' whose duty it was to recount the noble deeds of their lords. In these chronicles the Hundred Years War is seen vividly through the eyes of the feudal chivalry which fought the battles, besieged castles, repressed popular risings and massacred rebels. External pageantry, the colour of feudal warfare, are brilliantly displayed. No heed is given to the wide moral issues involved, e.g. in the suppression of the *Jacquerie*. The story is dramatic, alive, and, despite occasional inaccuracies, of great historical value. It was continued to 1444 by the Burgundian Monstrelet (d. 1453), and then to 1461 by Mathieu d'Escouchi. It was translated into English by J. Bouchier in 1523 and by Thomas Johnes in 1803–10 (5 vols. and numerous reprints). He also wrote a long verse romance, *Méliador* (ed. A. Longnon 1893–9), and various *lais*, *ballades* and other lyric pieces (ed. A. Scheler, Brussels, 1870–2). [LTT]

*Chroniques*, ed. S. Luce, G. Raynaud and A. and L. Mirot (13 vols., 1869–1957); Pauphilet, *HCMA*; *L'espinette amoureuse*, ed. A. Fourrier (1962).

F. S. Shears, *F. Chronicler and Poet* (1930).

**Fromentin, Eugène** (La Rochelle 1820–St Maurice 1876). French novelist, artist and art critic. He is remembered (apart from accounts of his travels, *Un été dans le Sahara*, 1857, and *Une année dans le Sahel*, 1859) for *Dominique* (1863), one of the great French novels of psychological analysis. This is a partly autobiographical study in which Dominique de Bray narrates the story of his early love for Madeleine d'Orsel and the sacrifice he makes in agreeing for her peace of mind never to see her again. Dominique gives up the promise of a literary career to go to the country where he manages his estates. Fromentin's charming *Maîtres d'autrefois* (1876), essays on Flemish and Dutch painters, contain some of the finest art criticisms ever written. [WA]

V. Giraud, *E.F.* (Paris, 1945); A. Lagrange, *L'art de F.* (Paris, 1952).

**Frug, Simon Samuel** (Herson, 1860–Odessa 1916). Yiddish poet. Born in a Jewish agricultural settlement in Southern Russia, he was free from the shackles of ghetto life and had little Jewish education. First distinguished himself as a Russian poet by his first published poem in 1880 in Odessa which brought him an invitation to St Petersburg where he became prominent in Russian literary circles. In 1888 he began to write in Yiddish, introducing modern standards to Yiddish poetry. [EE]

*Ale Werk Fun S.F.* (2 vols., 1904) (Yiddish). Roback, *SYL*; Waxman, *HJL*.

**Frugoni, Carlo Innocenzo** (Genoa 1692–Parma 1768). Italian Arcadian poet. Once considered supreme for his blank verse, though his *canzoni* lacked the elegance of other Arcadian poets. He enjoyed an enormously exaggerated reputation as court-poet at Parma, but this reputation was eclipsed as rapidly as the appointment itself; and he then lived in poverty until 1748, when Du Tillott commissioned him to write occasional poetry in Parma. The subjects were so trite, however (he himself saw the limitations of his poetry and was reluctant to publish collections), that he was even more vehemently attacked by later critics such as ⇨ Baretti and ⇨ Alfieri. Not even the defence of ⇨ Monti, who described him as 'uncorrupted father of corrupted children', could rescue his work from the scorn of posterity. [RHC]

*Opere poetiche* (15 vols., 1779–80); *Lirici del '700*, ed. B. Maier (1959).

A. Equini, *C.I.F. alle corti dei Farnesi e dei Borboni di Parma* (2 vols., Milan, 1919–20); C. Calcatterra, *Storia della poesia frugoniana* (Genoa, 1920).

**Fučík, Julius** (Prague 1903–Berlin 1943). Czech journalist and literary critic. Editor of several Communist papers, he travelled in the Soviet Union about which he wrote enthusiastically. Executed by the Gestapo for his part in the Communist underground movement, his prison notebook *Reportáž psaná na oprátce* (1945; tr. S. Jolly, *Report from the Gallows*, 1951) was smuggled out. [KB]

G. Fučíková, *J.F.* (Prague, 1955) (in English); G. Bareš, *J.F.* (Prague, 1950).

**Fucini, Renato** (Monterotondo, Massa Maritima 1843–Empoli 1921). Italian poet and prose writer. He studied agriculture, held a municipal post in Florence, later taught and became a school inspector. His intimate knowledge and evocation of the Tuscan countryside, people and dialect made his *Cinquanta sonetti in vernacolo pisano* (1872) most popular. His prose is perhaps better literature, especially *Napoli a occhio nudo* (1878) and the novellas *Nella campagna toscana* (1908) and *La maestrina* (1922). *Acqua passata* (1921) and *Fogli al vento* (1922) are autobiographical works.

A. Nicolai, *R.F.* (Pisa, 1921); Croce, *LNI.*

**Fulbert of Chartres** (*c.*975–1029). Italian writer of Latin verse and prose. Of humble birth, he studied at Reims under Gerbert (afterwards Pope Sylvester II). At Chartres he made the cathedral school famous for learning and subsequently became Bishop. He wrote in prose on theology and medicine, and much Latin verse, sacred and secular. He is best known for his Easter hymn, 'Chorus novae Jerusalem' ('Ye choirs of new Jerusalem'), for a monorhymed poem on the nightingale, and for his amusing versified tale, *In gestis patrum veterum*. [FB]

Migne, *PL*, 141; *An. Hym.*, 50.
*Church Quarterly Review*, CLI, 1926; Raby, *CLP*, *SLP*.

**Fulcher of Chartres** (Chartres 1058–Jerusalem ?1127). Medieval historian. A priest, he took part in the First Crusade and settled in the East as chaplain to Baldwin, Count of Edessa, later King of Jerusalem. He accompanied Baldwin on the Arabian expedition of 1100 and the campaign against the Turks in 1111. His work, *Gesta Francorum Jherusalem peregrinantium*, or *Historia hierosolymitana*, is an eye-witness account of all these events, unadorned and very reliable. ⇨ William of Tyre used it as a source for his *Historia*. Fulcher composed three versions, all beginning with the Council of Clermont in 1095, at which he was present, and ending in 1105, 1124 and 1127 respectively. Of these the last two are still extant. [MRM]

*RHC*, Hist. occ., iii; Migne, *PL*, 155; tr. Guizot, *CHF*, XXIV.

**Fulgentius Ruspensis, Fabius Claudius Gordianus** (Telepte in Byzacena 467–Ruspae 532). North African bishop and writer. The leading figure in the late-5th-century African literary 'renaissance', in the tradition of Augustine and Martianus Capella. Of aristocratic birth and good education, he abandoned a civil service career to enter the Catholic Church, where he suffered the persecution of the (Arian) Vandal king Thrasamund (496–523). On his election to the see of Ruspae (*c.*507/8) he was exiled to Sardinia with 60 other bishops from Byzacena, remaining there, apart from a brief respite, until the death of his persecutor allowed him to return to his see. His life was recorded in detail by the deacon Ferrandus immediately after his death.

Few of his sermons survive, though he won celebrity as a preacher; he wrote many works on doctrinal controversies, mostly from Sardinia, especially the *Contra Arianos*, *Ad Trasamundum regem libri III*, *De Trinitate ad Felicem notarium*, *De remissione peccatorum ad Euthymium*, *Ad Monimum libri III.* These follow Augustine closely, and are marked by simplicity, orthodoxy and unoriginality. His pretension to Greek culture only shows how little Greek survived in his day. Some scholars still maintain his identity with the contemporary African mythographer, Fabius Planciades Fulgentius. [CEC]

Ed. L. Mangeant, Migne, *PL* 65 (new edn, J. Fraipont, *Corpus Christianorum*, 91); *Vita*, Fr. tr. G. G. Lapeyre (Paris, 1932).
G. G. Lapeyre, *S.F. de R.* (Paris, 1929); *Studien zur Geschichte und Kultur des Altertums* v (Paderborn, 1911); G. Krüger, *Ferrandus und F., Harnack-Ehrung* (Leipzig, 1921); P. Godel, *Dictionnaire de théologie Catholique*, vi, 1 (Paris, 1947).

**Fussenegger, Gertrud** (Pilsen 1912–     ). Austrian novelist. Her native Bohemia inspired historical novels, e.g. *Geschlecht im Advent* (1937) and the outstanding *Die Brüder von Lasawa* (1948), the story of two brothers during the Thirty Years' War. Her most important works are *Das Haus der dunklen Krüge* (1951) and *Das verschüttete Antlitz* (1957), sociological novels giving a vivid picture of life in Bohemia from 1870 to 1945; the former has been compared with Thomas ⇨ Mann's *Buddenbrooks*, though lacking its aesthetic pessimism. Her psychological penetration is shown again in *Zeit des Raben, Zeit der Taube* (1960) and several volumes of *Novellen*, notably ... *wie gleichst du dem Wasser* (1951). She has also written poems: *Iris und Muschelmund* (1955). [PB]

Newnham, *GSS.*
*Wort in der Zeit*, VIII, 5, 1962.

**Füst, Milán** (Budapest 1888–1967). Hungarian poet. Also a novelist and critic, and a member of ⇨ *Nyugat*. The philosophy reflected in his works, written in a rather abstract style, is a search for fundamental human virtues and a longing for a purer world. His novels include: *Advent* (1923), *A feleségem története* (1942). *Látomás és indulat a művészetben* ('Vision and Impulse in the Arts') is an aesthetic essay [JFR]

**Futurism.** In Italy, a literary and artisti movement, largely associated with Marinetti, ⇨ Papini, ⇨ Soffici, ⇨ Govon Futurism in Russia had more lastin significance. It repudiated Marinetti an his enthusiasm for war. Its strongly word ed manifesto *Poshchyochina obshchestven nomu vkusu* ('A Slap in the Face fo Public Taste', 1912) was signed by Mayakovsky, ⇨ Khlebnikov, D. Burlyu (1882–     ) – a writer and painter wh emigrated to the U.S.A. – and A. Kruch onykh (1886–     ). They rejected the who Russian literary past (in particular the Symbolists), and demanded a new an experimental attitude towards languag The Futurists welcomed the Revolution; the 1920s, centring on Mayakovsky's *LEF* they were vigorous in literary polemics wit the ⇨ Proletarian and other groupings. A were dissolved in the early 1930s by th Soviet Government; but numerous trac of Futurism have lived on, e.g. in the wor of ⇨ Kirsanov, ⇨ Zabolotsky, ⇨ Vo nesensky. [RM-G]

V. Markov, *The Longer Poems of Velim Khlebnikov* (1962).

# G

**Gabirol or Ibn Gabirol, Solomon ben Judah** (Malaga *c.* 1020–Valencia *c.* 1057). Hebrew poet and Arabic philosopher. A protégé of ⇨ Samuel Ha-Nagid, began writing poetry at 16 and at 19 composed a Hebrew grammar in verse. He was a prolific and deeply religious liturgical poet, but his secular poetry was mainly concerned with his own cruel fate. His chief philosophical work, *Fons Vitae* (ed. C. Bäumler, 2 vols., 1945), written in Arabic, is extant only in Latin translation. Written in dialogue, it is a neo-Platonic work with elements from Aristotle and Philo. He influenced Duns Scotus, Spinoza and Schopenhauer. The Hebrew translation, *Mekor Chayim*, influenced the Kabbala. The work was not considered that of a Jewish author, and the true identity of 'Avicebron' was discovered by S. Munk. His *Royal Crown*, in Hebrew, explains his philosophy. [EE]

*Selected Religious Poems*, ed. I. Davidson, tr. I. Zangwill (1923).
Husik, *HMJP*.

**Gaboriau, Émile** (Saujon 1832–Paris 1873). French novelist. The originator of the detective novel or *roman policier* in France; his detective, Monsieur Lecoq, was a forerunner of Sherlock Holmes. Nearly all his best-known novels first appeared as *feuilletons* and they include *Le crime d'Orcival* (1867), *Le dossier no 113* (1867), *Les esclaves de Paris* (1868), *L'affaire Lerouge* (1866), *Monsieur Lecoq* (1869) and *La corde au cou* (1873). [WA]

**Gabriel y Galán, José María** (Frades de la Sierra 1870–Guijo de Granadella 1905). Spanish poet. Of humble birth and strong local associations, his feeling for the country is that of a minor Wordsworth. Work on the land, domestic love and a simple faith are the three virtues preached by this poet of rural Castile. His poetry is traditional and rather monotonous. But a single piece in any anthology contrasts favourably with the Romantic rhetoric of many of his contemporaries. His principal collections are *Castellanas* (1902), *Extremeñas* (1902), *Campesinas* (1904), and *Nuevas castellanas* (1905). [JMC]

*Obras completas* (1909); Trend, *OBSV*; Blecua, *FLE*.
A. Revilla Marcos, *G. y G. y su obra* (Madrid, 1923) (preface by M. de Unamuno).

**Gace Brulé** (fl. 1180–1200). French *trouvère*. A minor knight of Champagne, patronized by Marie de Champagne and the Duke of Brittany. Bowed and sighing beneath the yoke of courtly love, he achieved great fame in his own day and was widely imitated in the 13th century. His poetic inspiration came from the Provençal troubadours and especially from ⇨ Bernart de Ventadorn. Love, for Gace, determines the destinies of mortals and its judgements are irrevocable, and the poet dies an *amant martyr* in every song, or nearly so. The language of his surviving poems (69 authentic) is controlled, elegant and melodious. [LTT]

H. Petersen Dygve, *G.B., trouvère champenois* (Helsinki, 1951); *R*, LIX (1933).

**Gadda, Carlo Emilio** (Milan 1893– ). Italian novelist. He trained as an electrical engineer, and, after several years of practice in Italy and abroad, devoted himself entirely to writing. At first sight, he may appear as a writer of social satire (some of his etchings of middle-class and lower-class life have a Hogarthian sharpness and bite), but one soon discovers that he is not concerned with public morality but with literature: as a caricaturist deforms the human features, he distorts the stale humanistic-romantic literary clichés showing up their fundamental untruth (see his 'Meditazione breve circa il dire e il fare' in *I viaggi la morte*, 1958). His moral indignation is nothing more than a stylistic stimulus to the invention of a radically new literary technique: his fascination with language and rhetoric (he draws on the whole Italian lexical heritage: written, spoken, current, obsolete, technical, slang, dialectal and foreign words, and also roots, prefixes, suffixes which he skilfully welds together into new unique and irreplaceable words) has been called 'baroque' by some critics, but it is in fact more like a medieval writer's, for whom words are substances, things endowed with magical creative and regenerative powers, not mere substitutes for real objects or flimsy labels for flimsier ideas. This love for words, already apparent in his early works (*La Madonna dei filosofi*, 1931; *Il castello di Udine*, 1934; *L'Adalgisa*, 1944; now collected in *I sogni e la folgore*, 1955), where it could be mistaken for an eccentric taste for parody and pastiche, soon developed into the central motif of his art. Gadda willingly admits to lapsing occasionally into formal narcissim, nevertheless his style is not the usual kind of formalism, since it lays its emphasis, through a distortion of forms, on fact and substance; nor is it a variety of realism, since realism is never so word-wise and sophisticated, and takes into account, in spite of its name, only a part of the whole reality; it is something else, their looking-glass or polar image, held up to them to neutralize them both.

After several volumes of short stories (collected as *Accoppiamenti giudiziosi*, 1963), Gadda produced a novel which is by many considered his masterpiece, *Quer pasticciaccio brutto de via Merulana* (1957; tr. W. Weever, *That Awful Mess on Via Merulana*), written in standard Italian and three other dialects. Its deliberate obscurity is part of the author's private revenge upon that meretricious fabrication of the intellectual élite known as 'literature'; it is therefore only fair that a medieval screen of archaisms, puns and linguistic medleys should prevent the novel from harming the innocent layman. His latest novel, no less impenetrable, is *La cognizione del dolore* (1964). [GMC]

G. Devoto, *Studi di stilistica* (Florence, 1950).
*Contemporanei*, ii; Falqui, *PNNI*; Pullini, *NIN*; Gargiulo, *LIN*; Robertis, *SN*; Biondolillo, *C.*

**Gaiser, Gerd** (Oberriexingen, Württemberg 1908– ). German novelist. A fighter-pilot in the Second World War and then a painter; since 1949 a schoolteacher. His prizewinning first novel, *Eine Stimme hebt an* (1950), describes the efforts of a war-bewildered homecoming soldier to regain a positive outlook on life. His most accomplished *Die sterbende Jagd* (1953; tr. P. Findlay, *The Falling Leaf*, 1956) relates the physical and moral disintegration of a fighter squadron in Norway towards the end of the war; *Schlussball* (1958; tr. M. Waldman, *The Last Dance of the Season*, 1960) satirizes new-found affluence in contemporary Germany. His many short stories show the same shrewd discernment and economy of style: *Zwischenland* (1949), *Einmal und oft* (1956), *Gib acht in Domokosch* (1959), *Gazelle, grün* (1965). [PB]

Spender, *GGSS.*
C. Hohoff, *G.G., Werk und Gestalt* (Munich, 1962); H. Bieneck, *Werkstattgespräche mit Schriftstellern* (Munich, 1962); Keith-Smith, *ECGL.*

**Gaj, Ljudevit** (Krapina 1809–Zagreb 1872). Croatian writer and publicist. Founder of the Croatian Illyrian movement. Born in an area where the Kajkavic dialect was spoken, he was influenced by Pan-Slav thought in the Slavonic societies of Grac and Požun. He believed that the Southern Slavs formed a single group within the Slav nations and should be culturally united by a single literary language to enable their culture to develop. His linguistic theories were partly influenced by the work of ⇨ Karadžić and the Czechoslovak Pan-Slav thinkers. He wanted Croats to adopt the Štokavic dialect spoken by Serbs, Dalmatians and Slavonians together with the Latin alphabet with diacritic signs as used in Czech to make it phonetic. In Zagreb he started a periodical *Danica*, later *Danica Ilirska,* and gathered a large group of nationalist thinkers and publicists. The name Illyria was taken from the belief that the Balkan Slavs were descendants of the old Illyrians. In 1832–48 the Illyrians published a great deal of nationalist poetry, thus inaugurating modern Croatian literature, and engaged in many other cultural activities, arranging first performances of plays in Štokavic in Zagreb, forming cultural societies and reading rooms, etc. Gaj himself started a printing press.

Croatian nationalism conflicted with Hungarian nationalism, which refused to recognize Croatian autonomy. Thus in 1848 the Croats supported Vienna against the Hungarian revolution, only to receive much the same treatment afterwards as the Hungarian rebels. After 1849 Gaj lived in retirement, his popularity and influence gone. But his work was of lasting value: Croatian literature still uses Štokavic, and the Illyrian movement provided almost a the main mid-19th-century writers. (⇨ Vraz). [EDG]

J. Horvat, *L.G.* (Belgrade, 1960); Barac, *HYL.*

**Gałczyński, Konstanty Ildefons** (Warsaw 1905–Warsaw 1953). Polish poet. His early grotesque fantasies, like *Koniec świata* (1930), were followed by lyrical verse, mostly anarchistic and defiant, sometimes mixing religiously devout with erotic themes. The collected edition of 1937 (*Utwory poetyckie*) established his reputation, which widened considerably after the war (e.g. *Wiersze liryczne*, 1952), despite the occasional bathos of his versified propaganda. [JP]

Peterkiewicz and Singer, *FCPP.*

**Galdós, Pérez Benito.** ⇨ Pérez Galdós, Benito.

**Galician Literature.** Galician literature follows very closely the vicissitudes of Galician – a Romance language originally spoken in Galicia and Portugal (Galician-Portuguese). From the 12th to the 14th centuries this language was the vehicle of an outstanding lyric poetry. The political unification of Spain under Ferdinand and Isabella (1542) and the subsequent disbandment of Galician nobility marked the beginning of a long decadence of the language, relegated to dialectal status in Galicia while embarking on a large-scale development as official language in Portugal. In the 19th century, the influence of Romantic nationalist ideas brought forth a revival of Galician language and culture, which, under different forms, lasts to this day. This evolution applies only to the learned and official usage, as the vernacular never ceased to be spoken by the rural population (i.e. the great majority of Galicians). A number of Galician authors of all periods (Rodríguez del Padrón, Pardo Bazán, Valle-Inclán, Cela, etc.) have written exclusively or almost exclusively in Spanish, some of them with great distinction, and they belong properly to Spanish Literature.

Leaving aside the tangled problem of the origins of lyric poetry in the Iberian Peninsula, the fact seems to be that the great pilgrimages to Saint-Jacques of Compostella brought about a close relationship between Provençal and Galician poets. Galician popular songs were shaped by Provençal artistry and out of this process the remarkable Galician-Portuguese medieval minstrelsy was born. Airy musicality, a sometimes irreverent sense of humour, a stylized feeling of the landscape and a preference for pointed allusion rather than direct expression are the distinctive marks of its works. Medieval Galician poems are usually classified under the headings '*cantigas de amor*' (love-songs), '*cantigas de amigo*' (songs of the love-lorn girl) and '*cantigas de escarnio e maldizer*', violently satyrical. The *cantigas de amor* are the most original and beautiful, and certainly the most frequent. The metre of the compositions varies from the very short, four-syllable lines to the anapaestic hendecasyllable. The versification is mainly parallelistic. The 'corpus' of this poetry is basically contained in the collections called 'Cancioneiros'. The school reached its zenith in the 13th century (Airas Nunes, Martin Codax, Payo Gomez Charinho, Pero Meogo, Mendiño). In the 14th century the too ripe perfection of the poems by Xohan Zorro and King Dinis of Portugal ushers in the decadence.

Apart from the poets of the 'Cancioneiros', a place of his own must be given to King ⇨ Alfonso X of Castile and Leon for his *Libro de Cantigas de Santa María* ('Songs to the Virgin Mary').

From the middle of the 14th century onwards Galician poetry gives way increasingly to the rising Castilian literature, and after the 15th century there is practically no writing in Galician. In contrast, oral literature seems to have been very rich.

This popular tradition was at the root of the Galician revival in the 19th century. Such revival began when the Napoleonic invasion of the Peninsula (1808) left each region to organize by itself the patriotic resistance to the French. Versified propaganda in Galician urged the people to revolt against the invader. Some years later Romanticism began to influence Galician writers and to make them use the vernacular. Among these (called the 'Precursores' or 'Forerunners'), the poet Añón (1812–78), author of the collection *Poesías gallegas y castellanas* (1889), and the historian Benito Vicetto (1824–78), author of *Historia de Galicia* (Ferrol, 1865–74), are the most significant figures.

In 1863 a momentous book appears: the *Cantares gallegos* ('Galician Songs') by Rosalía de ⇨ Castro (1837–85), the most important single author in Galician literature. One must always bear in mind that neither Rosalía nor any other Galician writer of that period knew the medieval literary tradition of their country, as the Cancioneiros were edited and published only much later on. They had to substitute the popular songs for it, and thence the 'folkloric' character of much of their work.

Eduardo ⇨ Pondal (1835–1917) and Curros Enríquez (1851–1908) are with Rosalía the most highly regarded Galician writers. While Pondal's poetry is heroic, aristocratic, inspired by a largely legendary Celtic past, and cast in a vigorous, fiery language, Curros Enríquez, socially progressive and a free-thinker, saw himself as the political conscience of his people. His main works are: *Aires da miña terra* (Orense, 1880) and *O Divino Sainete* (Corunna, 1888).

In the wake of these three brilliant figures follow a number of poets, isolated from the development of European literature in those years. Such are, among others, Valentín Lamas Carvajal (1849–1906), author of *Espiñas, follas e frores* (Orense, 1876) and *A musa das aldeas* (Orense, 1927), Benito Losada (1824–91), author of *Soaces dun vello* (Corunna, 1886), and Manuel Leiras Pulpeiro (1854–1912). Their homespun tradition was continued more recently with marked originality by A. Noriega Varela (1869–1947), author of *Do Ermo* (Orense, 1920).

In 1906, the Galician Academy was founded in Corunna. To incorporate Galician culture with contemporary European thought was the task of the group centred in the twenties and early thirties round the magazine *Nos* ('Us') and the Seminario de Estudos Galegos. The most prominent members of that generation are: Ramón Otero Pedrayo (1888– ), author of *Arredor de sí* (Corunna, 1930) and *Ensaio sobre a cultura galega* (Lisbon, 1954); Vicente Risco (1874–1963), author of *O porco de pe* (Corunna, 1928); Alfonso R. Castelao (1886–1950), author of *Un ollo de vidro* (Ferrol, 1922), *Os vellos non deben namorarse* (Pontevedra, 1953), *As cruces de pedra na Bretaña* (Santiago, 1930), and *As cruces de pedra na Galiza* (Buenos Aires, 1949); and Ramón Cabanillas (1876–1959), author of *Vento mareiro* (Havana, 1915), and *Antifona da cantiga* (Vigo, 1951). They widened the horizons of Galician culture, too confined until then to lyrical expression.

The Spanish Civil War (1936–9) interrupted this development. The new regime suppressed all activities suspect of separatism. Some writers and artists died or went into exile. Nevertheless, in the post-war years 'Galaxia', a mostly non-profit-making publishing house, continued the promotion of regional language and literature, and Galician emigrants associations in Buenos Aires, Havana and New York, helped to foster Galician culture.

In 1965 a Chair of Galician Language and Literature was created at the University of Santiago de Compostela. Nowadays, a great diversification is noticeable in Galician writing, reflecting the preoccupation with contemporary problems increasingly felt by the new generations. [FP-BN]

*Escolma de Poesía Galega*, ed. X. M. Alvarez Blázquez and F. F. del Riego (4 vols., Vigo, 1952–9); *The Oxford Book of Portuguese Verse*, ed. A. F. Bell (1925); R. Cabanillas, *Antífona da Cantiga* (Vigo, 1951) (for oral poetry).

R. Carballo Calero, *Historia da Literatura Galega Contemporánea (1808–1936)* (Vigo, 1963); F. Fernández del Riego, *Manual de Historia de la Literatura Gallega* (Vigo, 1951); B. Varela Jácome, *Historia de la Literatura Gallega* (Corunna, 1951); J. L. Varela, *Poesía y restauración cultural de Galicia en el siglo XIX* (1958); A. F. Bell, *Portuguese Literature* (1922) (appendix, 'The Galician Revival').

**Galilei, Galileo** (Pisa 1564–Arcetri 1642). Italian scientist and writer. After studying at Pisa, he became (1589) lecturer in mathematics there. He had already made and described (*La Bilancetta*) a hydrostatic balance and he now began his lifelong work on dynamics (*De Motu*, *c.*1590; tr. I. Drabkin and S. Drake, *On Motion and on Mechanics*, Madison, 1960). He obtained the Chair of Mathematics at Padua (1592), and entered his most creative period, developing his research on motion, making instruments (e.g. his geometrical and military compass) and writing on many subjects. He still taught, at this time, the Ptolemaic cosmology, though in a letter to Kepler (1597) he claimed to be a Copernican by conviction. In 1609 he improved the Dutch-invented telescope and described his observations (unevenness of the moon's surface, satellites of Jupiter, etc.) in the sensational *Sidereus Nuncius* (1610; tr. S. Drake in *Discoveries and Opinions of Galileo* N.Y., 1957). Galileo called the moons of Jupiter the Medicean Stars, dedicated the treatise to Cosimo II and moved (1610) to Florence. His letter to Don Benedetto Castelli written in 1613 clearly endorsed the Copernican theory as did the impressiv

*Lettera a Madama Cristina di Lorena, Granduchessa di Toscana* (written 1615, publ. 1636; tr. S. Drake, in *Discoveries and Opinions of Galileo*, N.Y., 1957) which also discussed brilliantly the relationship between faith and science, proclaiming the independence of scientific research from theological dogma since they dealt with different kinds of truth. In 1616 the Church condemned the theory of Copernicus and Galileo was forbidden to propagate it. In bitter dispute with the Jesuit Grassi on the nature of comets he published *Il Saggiatore* (1623; tr. S. Drake, in *Discoveries and Opinions of Galileo*, N.Y., 1957), which biting irony and brilliant observations on scientific method make memorable, although Galileo was wrong in much of what he said concerning comets. Under Urban VIII he hoped for increased intellectual freedom and published his *Dialogo sui massimi sistemi del mondo* (1632; tr. S. Drake, *Dialogue Concerning the Two Chief World Systems*, Berkeley, Calif., 1953), which discussed the Ptolemaic and Copernican systems and clearly favoured the latter. Summoned to Rome, he renounced his views (1633). He spent the rest of his life confined to his villa at Arcetri, his last years darkened by ill-health and the death of his daughter, Sister Maria Celeste. His last and scientifically most important work, *Discorsi e dimostrazioni matematiche intorno a due nuove scienze attenenti alla meccanica* (Leyden, 1638; tr. H. Crewe and A. de Salvio, *Dialogues Concerning Two New Sciences*, repr. 1963), brought experimental method to bear on many problems and established the outlines of several areas of modern physics.

Pre-eminent as a scientist, Galileo was also a great writer. In addition to clarity and logic in exposition, his prose has also a varied literary texture. His dialogues are rich in dramatic debate and polemical irony, and their mood encompasses both pride in intellectual power and the humility and wonder of the great discoverer before the marvels of the universe.

In addition to his scientific works he left many *Letters* and some observations on Dante's *Inferno*, Ariosto's *Orlando furioso* and Tasso's *Gerusalemme liberata*. [DGR]

*Opere* (1929–39) (repr. of the Edizione Nazionale); *Opere*, ed. F. Flora (1953).

G. de Santillana, *The Crime of G.* (Chicago, 1955); A. Koestler, *The Sleepwalkers* (1959); R. Spongano, *La prosa di G., etc.* (Messina/Florence, 1949); A. Banfi, *G.G.* (Milan, 1961); *Minori*, ii.

**Gallego, Juan Nicasio** (Zamora 1777–Madrid 1853). Spanish poet. He suffered imprisonment as a liberal, and ended as secretary of the Academy and canon of Seville Cathedral. His ode 'Al dos de Mayo' (1808) is soberly rhetorical in the neoclassical style, but later poems on solemn occasions affect a more Romantic style, e.g. 'Elegía a la muerte de la Duquesa de Frías' (1830). He is at his best in his accomplished sonnets. [JMC]

*Obras poéticas* (1854); BAE, 68; Blecua, *FLE*; Trend, *OBSV*.

**Ganivet, Angel** (Granada 1865–Riga 1898). Spanish novelist and essayist. He studied law, philosophy and letters. After passing an examination for archivists he became a consul first in Amsterdam and then at Helsingfors and Riga. He committed suicide over a love imbroglio just when he was beginning to be known in Spain. His first provocative political novel, *La conquista del reino de Maya por el último conquistador español Pío Cid*, was published in 1897, and his best-known work, *Idearium español* (CA; tr. J. R. Carey, *Spain: An Interpretation*, intr. R. M. Nadal, 1946), came out the same year. Like other writers of his generation he tried to analyse the Spanish temperament and the political and moral situation of his country. He argued from geographical factors in the *Idearium* that Spain's conquest of an overseas empire was out of character, and maintained that his country was suffering from the psychological state of *aboulia*, or chronic apathy, from which she could recover if she returned to the spiritual values of her past rather than her material glories. He also contributed a number of essays on Scandinavian culture to Spanish periodicals, amongst them studies of Ibsen and Strindberg, who were beginning to be read in Spain at the time. [ONVG]

*Los trabajos del infatigable creador Pío Cid*, intr. E. Mallea (Buenos Aires, 1954).

M. Fernández Almagro, *Vida y obra de G.* (Madrid, 1952); *BHS*, XLII (1965); M. Olmedo Moreno, *El pensamiento de G.* (1965).

**Gaos, Vicente** (Valencia 1919– ). Spanish poet and critic. His earlier poetry on themes of love or religious questioning is finely written but often derivative (echoing

⇨ Garcilaso, Luis de ⇨ León, ⇨ Unamuno). His fourth and best collection, *Profecía del Recuerdo* (1956), achieves an individual style in its profound reflections on the reconciliation of opposites, of emotion and intellect, of beauty and death. More recent poems have lost this reflective equilibrium and tend to rage against conventional belief. His lecture *Poesía y técnica poética* (1955) discusses the collaboration of poet and critic, in the making of a poem. He taught literature for eight years in the U.S.A. and since then in various institutions in Spain, and has published two volumes of criticism: *La poética de Campoamor* (1955) and *Temas y problemas de literatura española* (1959). [JMC]

*Poesías completas* (1959).
Cano, *PESV*.

**Garborg, Arne** (Time, Rogaland 1851–Hvalstad, Bærum 1924). Norwegian novelist, poet, playwright and essayist. A farmer's son, he became a teacher, studied at Kristiania, then turned to writing. His early background and pietist upbringing, the suicide of his father, a feeling that he had betrayed his proper inheritance, and the fact that his youth coincided with a crucial stage in the development of Norwegian peasant society, all exercised a strong influence on his work. In *Bondestudentar* (1883), his best book, he documents, often ironically, the life and tribulations of a peasant-student in the capital, and his consequent rootlessness. Its implicit Naturalism was developed in *Mannfolk* (1886) and the monotone *Hjaa ho mor* (1890), and culminated in *Trætte Mænd* (1891), the journal of a decadent, where a turning point was reached. *Fred* (1892; tr. P. Carleton, *Peace*, 1930), in which the chief character is based on Garborg's father, marks in a sense a homecoming (it is set in his native region), and the beginnings of a faith of a Tolstoyan kind which he developed in his later books: *Den burtkomne Faderen* (1899; tr. M. J. Leland, *The Lost Father*, 1920); *Heimkomin Son* (1908); and the play *Læraren* (1896). The highly evocative verse cycle *Haugtussa* (1895), set to music by Grieg, and its less successful sequel *I Helheim* (1901) depict the ethos of the old peasant life of Jæren, and give perfect demonstrations of the literary possibilities of the *Nynorsk* in which most of his work is written. Perhaps first and foremost an intellectual, he was active in public debate and had many-sided interests, as may be seen from his *Kolbotnbrev* (1890), *Knudaheibrev* (1904), and *Dagbok* (6 vols., 1924–7). [RGP]

*Skriftir i samling* (8 vols., 1951).
R. Thesen, *A.G.* (3 vols., Oslo, 1933–6; abbr. 1-vol. edn, Oslo, 1947); J. A. Dale, *Studiar i A.G.'s språk og stil* (Oslo, 1950); Downs, *MNL*.

**Garção, Pedro António Correia** (Lisbon 1724–Lisbon 1773). Portuguese poet. He was educated by the Jesuits in Lisbon and studied Law at Coimbra University. His weak constitution prevented him from completing his studies and made him move to his home town. Later he married a wealthy widow who owned the small farm, or *quinta*, of the Fonte Santa, where he lived and which is often quoted in his poems. Through marriage he came also to an employment at the Casa da Índia, a sinecure which belonged to his wife. This comfortable material position enabled him to cultivate his poetic talents which were first made known to a small circle of friends at Coimbra. Following the neo-classical style of the age he moulded his odes and other lyrical verse on the pattern of Horace.

He soon won the respect of his colleagues, who invited him to form a literary association, Arcádia Lusitana, where, according to fashion, he adopted the pen-name of Córidon Erimanteu. His activity in this small academy was remarkable. Garção produced many papers on the art of poetry, which he conceived as an imitation of the Greek and Roman masters and a continuation of the classical tradition of the 16th century. Besides Horace he followed also the example of Virgil and attempted two comedies of bourgeois manners in the style of the Roman theatre. But this period of tranquillity and prosperity came to a sudden end; Garção lost his case in the courts over his wife's fortune, and in 1771 was arrested for unknown reasons by order of the Marquis of Pombal. In his poverty he adopted a stoic attitude of resignation and, in true Horacian verse, carped against the whims of fortune. Illness overcame him in prison, where he died before an order for his release had arrived. The complete works, *Obras Poéticas*, were published posthumously in 1778, and reprinted many times. [LSR]

*Obras Completas* (2 vols., 1957–8).

**García de la Huerta, Vicente Antonio** (Zafra 1734–Madrid 1787). Spanish dramatist. He was deeply implicated in the polemics of his period, and was exiled for ten years to Orán. Though saturated in the baroque tradition of the 17th century, he wrote a fine neo-classical play, *Raquel* (1778; Buenos Aires, 1930), the first of its kind to succeed on the Spanish stage. Simplicity and austerity, exalted ideas and nobility of thought were his aim. His theme was several times treated by 17th-century dramatists, the tragic love of 'the Jewess of Toledo' for Alfonso VIII, and her murder by his vassals. He followed Calderón in his use of conceits, but wrote in heroic hendecasyllabic verse. He wished to establish a form in which a national Spanish theatre could develop (entitled his own collection *Theatro Hespañol*, 1785–6), but nothing followed. His *Agamemnón Vengado* (Buenos Aires, 1930) is Sophocles's *Electra* watered down for some ladies who wanted to present a Greek tragedy. [JMC]

**García Gómez, Emilio** (Madrid 1905– ). Spanish translator (from Arabic). Professor of Arabic in the University of Madrid, famous for his translations in rhythmical prose of the Arabic poetry of medieval Spain, showing the relationship of Castilian forms and imagery to those of the Moorish emirates and still older Arabic traditions. He has also published a notable translation of *The Dove's Neck-Ring* by Ibn Hazm, *El collar de la paloma* (1952), with preface by J. Ortega y Gasset. [JMC]

*Poemas arábigoandaluces* and *Cinco Poetas Musulmanes* (CA, 1930 and 1945).

**García Gutiérrez, Antonio** (Chiclana/Cadiz 1819–Madrid 1884). Spanish dramatist. He studied medicine, then translated ⇨ Scribe and ⇨ Dumas *fils*, and achieved success with *El Trovador* (1836) and *Simón Bocanegra* (1843), later famous as Verdi's operas. He worked as a journalist in Cuba and Mexico and eventually became director of the Madrid Archaeological Museum. His best-known plays are *Venganza catalana* (1864; CC), a tragedy based on an incident from an old chronicle, and *Juan Lorenzo* (1865; CC), the drama of a man who was too good to take swift action when confronted with a popular uprising. With his liberal sympathies and subtle psychology (especially of feminine emotions) he sees his central figures not in romantic isolation, but in relation to the people.

He also wrote lyrical poems, light comedies, and the texts for *zarzuelas* (e.g. *El grumete*, 1853). [JMC]

N. B. Adams, *The Romantic Dramas of G.G.* (N.Y., 1922).

**García Lorca.** ⇨ Lorca, García.

**García Tassara, Gabriel** (Seville 1817–Ávila 1875). Spanish poet and diplomat. His romantic poetry is highly rhetorical, avoiding personal topics and dwelling largely on History, God and Nature. His most interesting poems are political: 'A Napoleón', 'A la guerra de oriente', 'Un himno al Mesías'. [JMC]

*Poesías* (1872); Blecua, *FLE*; Trend, *OBSV*.
J. M. Cossío, *Cincuenta años de poesía española (1850–1900)* (Madrid, 1960).

**Garcilaso de la Vega** (Toledo 1501–Nice 1536). Spanish poet, soldier and courtier. A very model of Renaissance Man. Of illustrious family, he was attached to the court of Charles V, and fought in Italy (1525), Austria (1529), Tunis (1535) and Provence, where he was mortally wounded when leading the attack on a tower. The great influences on his life and work were his unrequited love for Isabel Freire, a Portuguese lady-in-waiting to the Empress, and his discovery of the classics and of contemporary Italian literature. The Italianate verse-forms which were being used rather coldly by his friend ⇨ Boscán from 1526 were warmed into life by Garcilaso's genius, particularly during and after his sojourn in Naples (1532). There he found kindred spirits and was much loved. The body of his work is small – 3 eclogues, 5 *canciones*, 38 sonnets, 2 elegies, a blank-verse epistle – but is among the very finest in Spanish. It is outwardly tranquil and restrained, but deep currents of yearning and desperation run through it; the eclogues in particular are intensely moving in their evocation of Arcadian landscapes and the melancholy of love. His language is smooth and musical, deliberately unpretentious, wholly convincing, a new kind of Spanish selected and polished by a craftsman. Conventional religious feeling is absent from his work, being replaced by a vaguely spiritual Platonism of the kind then fashionable in Italy, with a few Stoical touches; the noises of war are scarcely heard. His work was published, with that of Boscán, by the latter's widow in 1543. It achieved instant popularity, and the poet remained for the rest of the Golden Age the one undisputed Spanish classic. [CCS]

*Obras*, ed. T. Navarro Tomás (1935); Trend, *OBSV*; Perry, *HASP*; Cohen, *PBSV*.
H. Keniston, *G. de la V.* (N.Y., 1922); M. Arce Blanco, *G. de la V.* (Madrid, 1930); R. Lapesa, *La trayectoria poética de G.* (Madrid, 1948); Alonso, *PE*.

**Gárdonyi, Géza** (Agárd 1863–Eger 1922). Hungarian novelist. Noted both as a humorist and as an idealist describing peasant life in characteristic simple style: *Az én falum*, 1898; *Göre Gábor kalandjai*, 1895–9 – a sequence of ten volumes about the problems of life seen through the eyes of a villager.

Historical novels: *Egri Csillagok* (1901), a widely read vivid picture of Hungarian life during the 16th-century Turkish invasion; *A láthatatlan ember* (1902), about Attila's Huns; *Isten rabjai* (1908), reflecting the 13th-century religious atmosphere. As a playwright he was at his best in *Bor* (1901). [JFR]

*SEER*, XXXIII, 80 (1954).

**Garnier, Robert** (La Ferté Bernard 1545–Le Mans 1590). French dramatist. He spent most of his life in the province of Maine, though he studied law in Toulouse (where he won prizes at the annual poetry competition of the *Jeux Floraux*) and later spent some time in Paris. After this, although he was in friendly contact with members of the ⇨ Pléiade, he lived in the provinces, where he held various legal posts culminating in his appointment as Lieutenant Criminel du Maine in 1574. Towards the end of his life he belonged to the ultra-Catholic Ligue for a brief period.

He published a volume of love poetry which is lost, some other poems (the best is probably his elegy on the death of Ronsard) and 8 plays: *Porcie* (1568), *Cornélie* (1572), *Hippolyte* (1573), *La Troade* (1578), *Marc-Antoine* (1579), *Antigone* (1580), *Bradamante* (1582), *Les Juifves* (1583). All are tragedies except *Bradamante* (drawn from an episode in Ariosto's *Orlando furioso*), which is an experiment in tragi-comedy, a *genre* which became very popular at the turn of the century. The tragedies are by later standards lacking in both dramatic action and psychological interest, and overloaded with sententious lines and elaborate figures of speech; but the rhetorical approach which causes this also produces fine effects. He handles language with great skill, whether building up to an almost unbearable climax of violent grief, marshalling arguments in a disputation, or expressing melancholy and despair in graceful, supple choric metres. His overriding preoccupation is with the sufferings of war, particularly civil war. [GJ]

*Œuvres complètes*, i, ed. L. Pinvert (1923); ii, ed. R. Lebègue (1949); iii (1952).
A. M. Witherspoon, *The Influence of R.G. on Elizabethan Drama* (1924).

**Garrett, Almeida** (Oporto 1799–Lisbon 1854). Portuguese dramatist, poet, novelist and statesman. The principal artistic innovator of the Portuguese Romantic movement. A product of the bourgeoisie, his early education was directed towards the classics; he went on to study Law at Coimbra (1816–20) where he became politically active on behalf of the Liberals. The Liberal Revolution of 1820 inspired him to write enthusiastic odes and a mediocre neo-classical tragedy, *Catão*, which contained heavy political allusions. Three years later, however, he was forced into exile by the absolutist reaction of 1823. As a refugee in England and France he first came into contact with the Romantic movement and the influence of this is apparent in his long poems *Camões* (1825) and *Dona Branca* (1826). Politically he was identified with the more radical wing of the émigré groups but, after various polemics, he accepted a *rapprochement* with the moderates and joined the Liberal army massing in the Azores in 1832 under Pedro IV. After participating in the siege of Oporto (1833) he was sent on diplomatic missions as representative of the new Liberal government. With the triumph of the radicals in 1837, he returned to Portugal and resumed his political activities, now as a parliamentary deputy. His main task, however, was the creation of a national Portuguese theatre. He founded an Academy of Dramatic Art and himself set about writing plays to constitute a national dramatic repertoire: *Um Auto de Gil Vicente* (1838), *O Alfageme de Santarém* (1841), and later the pseudo-classical historical tragedy *Frei Luís de Sousa* (1843). The dictatorship of Costa Cabral (1842–51) forced him out of public life, leaving him to concentrate on his literary interests. From this period date the *Romanceiro* (1843), a delightful collection of touched-up Portuguese ballads, *O Arco de Sant'Ana* (1845), a historical novel, and his best prose work *As Viagens na Minha Terra* (1846), a series of rambling autobiographical reflections interspersed with a semblance of plot. A great love affair with the Viscondessa da Luz at this time was also the inspiration for his best collection of personal lyric poetry, *Folhas Caídas* (1853). On the fall of Costa Cabral, he re-emerged politically in the 'Regeneration' movement. He was made a Viscount in 1851 and in 1852 became Minister of Foreign Affairs.

Throughout his life Garrett was passionately involved in the struggle to modernize ideas and society in Portugal and endeavoured to stimulate a progressive political consciousness in his readers. As a literary innovator he explored the drama and the novel (relatively untried in Portugal) and dug deep into the national psychology for his own inspiration. This conscious literary nationalism may seem contrived, but Garrett accurately reflects a significant transitional stage in Portugal's evolution. [AJP]

*Viagens na Minha Terra* (CSC); *Folhas Caídas, O Romanceiro, Camões e D. Branca* (CP); *Frei Luís de Sousa* (TL).

J. G. Simões, *A.G.* (Lisbon, 1964); A. J. Saraiva, *Para a História da Cultura em Portugal* (Lisbon, 1946).

**Garshin, Vsevolod Mikhaylovich** (Bachmut, Yekaterinoslav 1855–Petersburg 1888). Russian writer of stories. He became sensationally famous with *Chetyre Dnya* (1877), about a wounded soldier helpless on a battlefield (he fought in the war with Turkey in that year in order to share in the common people's suffering). Obsessed by the evil and suffering of the world and consumed by pity, he wrote a few fine stories, often allegorical, before melancholy drove him to suicide. Particularly remarkable is *Krasnyy tsvetok* (1883; tr. B. Isaacs, *The Scarlet Flower*, 1961), set in a lunatic asylum. His work is of narrow range but effectively intense.

*Sochineniya* (1951, repr. 1955, 1960, 1963); *The Signal* (stories), tr. R. Smith, 1912.

G. A. Byaly, *V.M.G.* (Moscow, 1955); Mirsky, *HRL*; Slonim, *MRL*.

**Gatti, Armand** (Monaco 1924– ). French dramatist and film-director. The most considerable figure of a group of contemporary French playwrights (Cousin, Prost, Vinaver) who react against the prevailing drama of aestheticism, absurdity or despair in favour of a theatre of social conscience and political involvement which owes much of its stage technique to ⇨ Brecht, Piscator and Meyerhold. Film-projection, turntables, moving belts, multiple settings, complicated lighting-plots create rapid oscillation of movement, breaking up temporal and spatial unity and suggesting the play of consciousness, the passage from reality to dream-states. Such are the techniques which mark Gatti's moving account of the failure of a workers' strike in *La vie imaginaire de l'éboueur Auguste Geai* (1962). The effect is to liberate a social theme from the limitation of social realism by creating a quasi-poetic dimension in which the brute facts are transmuted and move toward a more universal statement. This is true of other plays, notably *La deuxième existence du camp de Tatenberg* (1962), in which the horror of the concentration camps is conveyed through the medium of fantasy and draws on puppets, etc. The same idiosyncratic fantasy operates with great theatrical force in *Le crapaud-buffle* (1959), a play which has many allusions to contemporary politics, and in his treatment of the Sacco-Vanzetti case in *Chant public devant deux chaises électriques* (1964). His latest play is a communal spectacle – *Les treize soleils de la rue Saint-Blaise* (1968). [SBJ]

*Théâtre* (3 vols., 1960–2).

*ML*, XLV, 4 (1964); Corvin, *TNF*; Serreau, *HNT*.

**Gatto, Alfonso** (Salerno 1909– ). Italian poet, journalist (edited *Campo di Marte*, 1938) and prizewinner (Premio Savini, 1939; Gran Premio San Vincent, 1948). His southern temperament was expressed in the emotional impact and fluctuations of his first poems, *L'isola* (1932), sensual, melancholy, ecstatic, despairing, lacking in control yet rich in colourful landscape. *Morto ai paesi* (1937) developed greater complexities of language in the hermetic and even surrealist manner, but his sense of moral commitment brought him to a plainer style, especially during the war when he was the only 'clandestine' poet of Italian resistance. *Il capo sulla neve* (1946) shows a quality of participation in actual events similar to that of ⇨ Quasimodo's. [GD]

Robertis, *SN*; Macri, *ESPC*; Varese, *CLC*.

**Gautier, Théophile** (Tarbes 1811–Neuilly-sur-Seine 1872). French poet and writer. He began studying as an artist, a training which never left him in his poetry and in his art criticism. He became a friend of ⇨ Nerval and of ⇨ Borel and, like them, was a fervent Romantic. He hero-worshipped Hugo and was one of the leaders of the claque which ensured the success of *Hernani* (1830), when he scandalized the audience by appearing in a rose-coloured doublet. He gave up painting to write and for five years poured out a flood of extreme Romantic writings, including *Poésies* (1830), *Albertus ou l'âme et le péché* (1833) and *Les Jeunes-France, romans goguenards* (1833), largely autobiographical sketches of life among his set of Romantics, the *Bousingos*. These were followed by *Les grotesques* (1835), studies of old French authors, and in the same year his famous novel *Mademoiselle de Maupin* (ed. A. Boschot, 1955; tr. P. Selven, 1948). The preface to this long novel was a manifesto of his doctrine of *l'art pour l'art*, and the story with its pagan lack of morality expounded his own worship of beauty. In the year of its publication he got a job on the *Chronique de Paris* with the help of Balzac and thus began his long career as a journalist writing for *La Presse*, *Le Moniteur*, and *La Revue de Paris*. In 1836 he brought out a vampire story, *La morte amoureuse* and next year his *Fortunio*. For forty years he produced weekly criticism of literature, the arts and the theatre. He was one of the most popular literary figures of his time and a good idea of his personality and conversation can be gained from the ⇨ Goncourt *Journals*. His chief work, *Émaux et camées* (1852; ed. A. Bosch, 1954), largely consists of short lyrical poems in finely wrought stanzas, packed with colour, foreign inspirations and themes of which 'Symphonie en blanc majeur' is a good example. The famous poem 'L'art' expresses his belief in art as the sole and supreme value, and it became the creed of the Parnassian poets. These poems are finely interpreted by Berlioz's settings, *Nuits d'été*. His journalism was collected in *Les beaux-arts en Europe* (2 vols., 1855). He also brought out several travel books, among them *Caprices et zigzags* (1845), which included England, and *Voyage en Russie* (1867). Some of his finest prose is contained in the travel sketches and in his shorter tales like *Le pavillon sur l'eau*. Although he had played no part in politics he was badly affected by the 1870 war and died of a heart disease which dated from that time. His unfinished *Histoire du romantisme* was brought out in 1874. [WA]

*Contes fantastiques* (1962).

J. Tild, *T.G. et ses amis* (Paris, 1951); J. Richardson, *T.G. His Life and Times* (1958).

**Geel, Jacob** (Amsterdam 1789–Leyden 1862). Dutch critic and essayist. Librarian at Leyden. His classical style is unique in an age of romantic sentimentality. His critical tenets anticipate *De Gids* (cf. ⇨ Potgieter). He frequently uses the Platonic dialogue in *Onderzoek en Phantasie* (1838) to air his views on style and literary trends. He edited Theocritus, Polybius and others. [PK]

*Gesprek op den Drachenfels*, ed. J. C. Blandt Corstius (1963).

**Geibel, Emanuel** (Lübeck 1815–Lübeck 1884). German poet. 1838–40 tutor for Russian ambassador to Athens; Prussian royal pension from 1842, and 1868 when he settled in Lübeck; 1852–68 Bavarian royal pension, professorship and leadership (with ⇨ Heyse) of the 'Dichterkreis' in Munich. Conservative Christian and constitutional monarchist; he saw poets as priests. His successful lyrics – *Gedichte* (1840), *Zeitstimmen* (1841), *Zwölf Sonette für Schleswig-Holstein* (1845), *Juniuslieder* (1848), *Neue Gedichte* (1856), *Gedichte und Gedenkblätter* (1864), *Spätherbstblätter* (1877) – reflect contemporary taste: classical, idealistic, non-topical. His plays – notably *Brunhild* (1858; tr. G. T. Dippold, Boston, 1879), *Meister Andrea* (1858), *Sophonisbe* (1868) – imitate French and German classicism. He translated Greek, Latin, French, Spanish, and Portuguese poetry. [LL]

*Werke*, ed. W. Stammler (3 vols., 1920); *Dramen*, ed. F. Drexl (1915).

A. Kohut, *E.G.* (Berlin, 1915); H. Meinardus, *E.G. und die deutsche Dichtung seiner Zeit* (Münster, 1932).

**Geijer, Erik Gustaf** (Ransäter 1783–Stockholm 1847). Swedish poet, historian and political writer. Born into a family of progressive industrialists, his background made him alive to the emerging liberal ideas, but his theoretical studies, especially of German philosophy, made his career take a more conservative course until, in the 1820s, he was considered the mainstay of intellectual conservatism. Geijer visited England as a young man and recorded his impressions in detailed letters, later published in a book of memoirs *Minnen* (1834; tr. E. Sprigge and C. Napier, *Impressions of England 1809–10*,

1932). On his return he was appointed reader in history at Uppsala, later professor. He was among the founding members of the Götiska Förbundet (a patriotic and antiquarian society) in 1811, and (until ⇨ Tegnér joined the society) its chief spokesman. His lyrical output is slender but includes pieces that have become part of the national heritage, e.g. *Vikingen* and *Odalbonden* (1811), two complementary and no doubt idealized national type-figures, one standing for the spirit of adventure and one for the anonymous constructive force in society. In other poems he revived the simple style of the Scandinavian ballads, and together with another 'Goth' he edited the first scholarly edition of Swedish ballads, *Svenska Folkvisor* (1814–16). His theoretical treatises paved the way for the new German philosophy and thus the romantic school of literature in Sweden. Increasingly, however, his energies were claimed for the grand historical works *Svea Rikes Hävder* (1825) and *Svenska Folkets Historia* (1832–6; tr. J. H. Turner, *The History of the Swedes*, 1845), which was never completed. In mature years he returned to poetry with short, profoundly experienced poems of a musical and highly subjective character. Goethe was his literary model, while Schubert inspired him to settings of his own. In 1838 he surprised and shocked his old conservative friends by openly declaring his allegiance to the Liberal cause. This action, generally known as 'Geijer's apostasy', was of greater importance as a moral gesture than as an intellectual statement. In his lyrical poems he confesses to a sense of isolation but also gives expression to his unshaken belief in the future. His chief legacy to posterity is what he himself called 'the personality principle': a belief in his fellow-men as persons, no matter how humble or beclouded by adverse conditions. To his contemporaries Geijer was something of a free-thinker, yet his warm and trustful, undogmatic faith is unmistakable. [SAB]

*Samlade Skrifter*, ed. F. Landqvist (13 vols., 1923–31).

J. Landquist, *G. en levnadsteckning* (Stockholm, 1954); E. Norberg, *G.s väg från romantik till realism* (Stockholm, 1944); V. H. Spongberg, *The Philosophy of E.G.G.* (Rock Island, Ill., 1945).

**Gellert, Christian Furchtegott** (Hainichen, Saxony 1715–Leipzig 1769). German poet and novelist. Professor of Poetry and Rhetoric, and latterly of Moral Philosophy at Leipzig, Gellert is probably the best literary representative of the German Enlightenment before ⇨ Lessing. His verse is essentially mediocre, but simplicity and basic honesty, together with its strong moral, didactic aim, gave it popular appeal. The *Fabeln und Erzählungen* (1746–8; ed. F. Kemp, 1959), a collection of fables and moralizing tales, enjoyed a place in many middle-class homes second only to that of the Bible. The religious verses of the *Geistliche Lieder* (1757) were equally popular and the most famous, including 'Die Himmel rühmen des Ewigen Ehren' ('The heavens declare the Creator's glory') in the setting by Beethoven, still retain a place of honour in most hymn-books. His plays, in the style of the *comédie larmoyante*, were popular in their day, but are now forgotten; his novel, *Das Leben der schwedischen Gräfin von G****, is a strange but fascinating mixture of the decadent gallant novel, the social novel and the novel of character. [WAC]

DNL, 43; Killy, *DLTZ*; DLE.

F. Bruggemann, *G.s schwedische Gräfin* (Aachen, 1925); K. May, *Das Weltbild in G.s. Dichtung* (Frankfurt, 1928).

**Gelli, Giovan Battista** (Florence 1498–Florence 1563). Italian writer. He continued to practise his trade as shoemaker even after devoting himself to study and literature. An early member of the Accademia Fiorentina, he lectured there on Dante and Petrarch.

He wrote 2 comedies (*La sporta*, 1543; *L'errore*, 1556), a few poems, and a *Trattatello sull'origine di Firenze*, but his most significant works are 2 treatises in dialogue form. *I capricci di Giusto bottaio* (1548; tr. W. Barker, *The Fearful Fansies of the Florentine Couper*, 1568), which incurred the Church's displeasure, conveys in 10 dialogues between a Florentine cooper and his soul a commonsense exhortation to all men, even the humblest, to seek the truth. The better-known *Circe* (1549; tr. T. Brown, 1702, repr. ed. R. Adams, Ithaca, N.Y., 1963) contains 10 discussions on the human condition between Ulysses and eleven former human beings who have been turned into animals. Ten reject the prospect of returning to their human lives, but the elephant, who had been a philosopher, accepts Ulysses's view; the last dialogue celebrates the nobility of man's intellect. [DGR]

*Opere*, ed. I. Sanesi (1952); *Dialoghi*, ed. R. Tissoni (1967).

*Minori*, ii.

**Gelsted, Otto** (Middelfart 1888– ). Danish lyrical poet. Since his first collection (1920) he has called himself a 'revolutionary humanist' in search of clarity. He is a disciple of Hellas (and a fine translator of classical Greek poetry) as well as of Lenin and Freud. During the Occupation he escaped to Sweden and there wrote his only novel, *Flygtninge i Husaby* (1944), and also *Emigrantdigte* (1945). [ELB]

K. Vogel, *O.G.* (Copenhagen, 1965).

**Generation of 1898, The.** A group of modern Spanish writers, thus designated by ⇨ Azorín in his *Clásicos y modernos* (1913), and including ⇨ Ganivet, ⇨ Unamuno, ⇨ Benavente, ⇨ Baroja, ⇨ Machado.

**Generation of the Dictatorship.** ⇨ Cernuda, Guillén, Salinas.

**Genet, Jean** (Paris 1910– ). French novelist and dramatist. Perhaps no other contemporary French writer has assimilated his private obsessions so completely to his literary art as Genet. An abandoned, illegitimate child, he was brought up in institutions or by foster-parents until the age of ten. Thereafter his childhood was spent in reformatories and his youth and young manhood in a succession of European prisons. His highly poeticized, even precious, novels revive this scabrous and abject world of criminals, prostitutes and homosexuals, calling on a sumptuous and ceremonial language that strangely transmutes the dirt and excrement, violence and betrayal which recur in all he writes: *Notre Dame des Fleurs* (1944; tr. B. Frechtman, *Our Lady of the Flowers*, 1964), *Miracle de la rose* (1946; tr. B. Frechtman, *Miracle of the Rose*, 1965), *Pompes funèbres* (1947), *Querelle de Brest* (1947; tr. G. Streatham, *Querelle of Brest*, 1966). His autobiographical *Journal du voleur* (1948; tr. B. Frechtman, *Thief's Journal*, 1964) views the same territory in a more personal vein. The world of his plays is, at once, hierarchical and ritualistic. It rests to an explicit degree on the inversion of 'normal' values and the rite, which is central to all the plays, not only involves death and a sacrificial victim, but celebrates the triumph of 'evil', in so far as evil can be construed as the converse of the values upheld by bourgeois society. Through an equivocal world of masks and mirrors, characters move in search of identity, challenging the world of 'reality' with their potent obsessions and illusions, their primeval and spontaneous desires. Thus, in *Les bonnes* (1947; tr. B. Frechtman, *The Maids*, 1954) personal identity is elusive and approached, though never fully attained, by a series of impostures: the actor playing Solange is playing Solange the maid pretending to be Claire the maid, while the actor playing Claire is playing Claire the maid pretending to be the mistress of the house. Eventually, Claire is poisoned in the character of the mistress by Solange who already sees herself in the role of the murderess on trial. The magnetism of the convicted murderer Yeux-Verts in *Haute surveillance* (1947; tr. B. Frechtman, *Deathwatch*, 1954) comes from the fact that he presents his cell-mates with an identity to which they abortively aspire: Lefranc's murder of Maurice does not secure for him the authenticity, the aesthetic perfection enjoyed by Yeux-Verts. Perhaps the most ambitious metaphor of Genet's vision of the world is the brothel of illusions in *Le balcon* (1956; tr. B. Frechtman, *The Balcony*, 1958), where false bishop, judge and general play out their grandiose fantasies, emphasizing that their unreality is no greater than that of their counterparts in the real world outside the brothel where a revolution is in progress. The brothel is merely an image of the falsity and hollowness of all society. The same exploration of unreality characterizes the relations between Whites and Negroes in *Les Nègres* (1958; tr. B. Frechtman, *The Blacks*, 1960), a play within a play, in which the ritual murder of a white woman on-stage masks the real-life shooting of a Negro traitor off-stage. In *Les paravents* (1961; tr. B. Frechtman, *The Screens*, 1962) the racial issue is transposed in terms of the Algerian conflict, and the key to the paradox of the outcast Said's betrayal of his comrades lies in Genet's characteristic belief that men must repudiate the fate others impose on them. Genet's drama is too narrowly related to his private obsessions always to reach the level of universality he aspires to, but he often handles paradox with great force and illuminates the ambiguities of human choice. Interesting are his *Lettres à Roger Blin* (1966). [SBJ]

*Œuvres complètes* (vols. II–III, 1953).

J.-P. Sartre, *Saint G.: comédien et martyr* (Paris 1952); J. H. MacMahon, *The Imagination of J.G.* (1963); T. F. Driver, *J.G.* (1966); Guicharnaud, *MFT*; Esslin, *TA*; Grossvogel

*TCFD*; P. Thody, *J.G., A Critical Appraisal* (1968).

**George, Stefan** (Büdesheim, Bingen 1868–Minusio, Locarno 1933). German poet. A student of languages, he travelled widely, was associated with Mallarmé and Verlaine in Paris, and was deeply influenced by Spain. Selfconsciously dedicated to a life of the Spirit, despising the decadence of his age, he lived withdrawn amidst a circle of admiring disciples for (and with) whom he published the esoteric journal *Blätter für die Kunst* (1890–1919). Refusing honours offered to him by the Nazis, who (mistakenly) saw propaganda value in his visions of noble youths, exalted leaders and a new Reich, he went into voluntary exile (1933). George's first collections of note, *Hymnen* (1890), *Pilgerfahrten* (1891) and *Algabal* (1892), clearly show the influence of Mallarmé; besides Symbolist technique, however, there are characteristic aspirations towards exclusive 'superior' experiences (some of them extravagantly decadent!). His aesthetic philosophy of form in poetry is contained in the oracular manifesto *Über Dichtung* (1894). The collection *Die Bücher der Hirten- und Preisgedichte* (1895) is a rehearsal of spiritual attitudes in different historical costume (ancient Greek, medieval, oriental, etc.) as the poet searches for himself. With his so-called 'monochrome' period – *Das Jahr der Seele* (1897) and *Der Teppich des Lebens...* (1899) – George achieved a studied elegance, a perfection of form, a regularity of rhythm and purity of rhyme that remain the hallmarks of his best poetry. Particularly famous are the short autumnal inscapes of *Das Jahr der Seele* (reminiscent rather of Verlaine than of Mallarmé). Very different is the prophetic, quasi-mystical poetry of *Der siebente Ring* (1907), *Der Stern des Bundes* (1913), and *Das neue Reich* (1928), inspired by his curiously narcissistic worship of a 'divine' youth, Maximin, by ideas half-understood from Nietzsche, and by a typical German longing to realize in life the ideal vision of poetry. Such aspirations have been disastrously discredited; but where neither they nor the dubious figure of priest and prophet obtrude, a few poems reveal a rapturous quality of love. For the rest, in his somewhat monotonous obsession with form, George easily fell into a superficial and limited manner and lacked the depth and sympathy of greatness. [PB]

*Werke* (18 vols., 1927–34); *Poems*, tr. C. N. Valhope and E. Morwitz (1944); E. Morwitz and O. Marx, *The Works of S.G.* (North Carolina, 1949).

E. K. Bennett, *S.G.* (1954); U. K. Goldsmith, *S.G. A Study of his Early Work* (Colorado, 1959); G. P. Landmann, *S.G. und sein Kreis, Eine Bibliographie* (Hamburg, 1960); C. M. Bowra, *The Heritage of Symbolism* (1943); F. Schonauer, *S.G.* (Reinbek, 1960).

**'Georgslied.'** A fragmentary Old High German poem written by an anonymous cleric in the monastery of Reichenau *c.*900. Based on a lost Latin original, it is a hymn in honour of St George, written to be sung by the laity, and is the oldest surviving German poem devoted to the legendary achievements of a Christian saint and martyr. [RT]

Braune, *AL*, 35.
Ehrismann, *GDL*, i.

**Gerbert of Aurillac** (Pope Sylvester II). (Auvergne after 940–Rome 1003). Medieval scholar and man of affairs. After being educated in the monastery of Aurillac he studied music and mathematics at Ripoll in Spain (*c.*967–70), and taught as head of the school at Rheims (*c.*972–82), establishing a tradition of 'Christian Humanism', based on Cicero, continued by his pupil ⇨ Fulbert of Chartres. As a teacher he was famous for his mastery of every branch of learning; and he wrote important pioneering works on geometry and logic.

His political talents were exercised at the election of Hugh Capet (987) and in his own election to the see of Rheims; but he was forced to withdraw to the Imperial Court in 996. His admirer Otto III, fired by his ambitions for the restoration of Rome, made him Archbishop of Ravenna, and then Pope (999), but he died before much could be achieved. Later ages ascribed his extraordinary gifts and achievements to the devil. [CEC]

Ed. B. Pez, Migne, *PL*, 139 (1853); *Gerberti opera mathematica*, ed. N. Bubnov (Berlin, 1899); *Lettres de G.*, ed. J. Havet (Collection de Textes, Paris, 1889); *Letters of G.*, tr. H. P. Lattin (N.Y., 1961).

F. Weigle, *Deutsches Archiv für Erforschung des Mittelalters*, x (1953), xi (1954), xiv (1958), xvii (1961); F. Lot, *Bibliothèque de l'école des hautes études*, 147 (Paris, 1903); E. Amman, *Dictionnaire de théologie catholique* xiv, 2 (Paris, 1941); Manitius, *GLLM*.

**Gerhardt, Paul** (Gräfenhainichen, Saxony 1607–Lüssen a.d. Spree 1676). German poet.

A Lutheran pastor of the old school, he exhibited in his life a narrowness of outlook and a dogmatism in odd contrast with the soft and gentle quality of much of his religious poetry. In the Protestant tradition of preacher-hymn-writers he stands second only to Luther, and his work has a permanent place in the affections not only of German Protestants, but, in translation, of Christians throughout the English-speaking world. The best of his hymns – a collected edition, the *Geistliche Andachten*, was published in 1667 (tr. J. Kelly, *Spiritual Songs*, 1867) – such as 'Nun ruhen alle Wälder' ('The dutious day now closeth'), 'O Haupt voll Blut und Wunden' ('O sacred head, sore wounded') and 'Wach auf, mein Herz, und singe' are happily free from the excesses of baroque style and the crass dichotomy between God and the world which characterizes so much of the religious verse of the 17th century. In their simple directness and their naïve joy in the beauty of the created world ('Geh aus, mein Herz, und suche Freud') they are reminiscent of the folk-song. Significantly, however, it was not Lutheranism but Pietism that was most receptive to Gerhardt, since, while his hymns are community hymns, they are also characterized by an intensely personal element. [WAC]

*Dichtungen und Schriften*, ed. E. V. Cranach-Siehart (1949).

T. B. Hewitt, *P.G. as a Hymn-Writer and his Influence on British Hymnody* (1918); H. Petrich, *P.G.* (Gütersloh, 1914).

**Gersonides, Levi ben Gerson,** known as **Ralbag** (1288–Bagnols 1344). Provençal Hebrew philosopher and scientific writer. He invented a number of astronomical instruments and wrote commentaries to some books of the Bible. His *Milhamot Adonai* ('Wars of God') expounds the theme of revelation as against philosophy. [EE]

Husik, *HMJP*.

**Gerstenberg, Heinrich Wilhelm von** (Tondern 1737–Altona 1823). German writer, important mainly as a critic. His *Briefe über Merkwürdigkeiten der Literatur* (1766–70) herald the *Sturm und Drang* movement in their preoccupation with the sacred independence of genius, their adulation of Shakespeare, assertion of the rights of untrammelled emotion, and interest in folk-poetry and Ossian. His *Gedicht eines Skalden* (1766) imitates the bardic poetry of ⇨ Klopstock, while his drama *Ugolino* (1768) anticipates the new taste for heroic melodrama. [WAC]

DNL, 49 (selections).

K. Gerth, *Studien zu G.s Poetik* (Göttingen, 1960); A. M. Wagner, *G. und der Sturm und Drang* (Heidelberg, 1920–4); Garland, *SS*.

**Gervinus, Georg Gottfried** (Darmstadt 1805–Heidelberg 1871). German literary historian. He became professor in Göttingen in 1836 but was dismissed the following year, along with his colleagues (among them Jakob and Wilhelm Grimm) in the group known as the 'Göttingen Seven', for his liberal political views. He re-entered academic life in 1844 as professor in Heidelberg, and was a member of the Right-Centre party at the National Assembly of 1848 in Frankfurt.

In marked contrast to other eminent historians of his day such as Wackernagel and Goedeke, he held the view that literature is to be judged by the criteria not of aesthetics but of social and political policy: the justification of literature is the service of the community and the furtherance of national interests. A man of vast learning, in his *Geschichte der poetischen Nationalliteratur der Deutschen* (1835–42) he passes judgement on all authors from this politico-moral standpoint, criticizing some for their inattention to national interests in their choice of material, others for turning to private, small-scale literary genres like lyric poetry. Of all the figures he discusses, Lessing comes nearest to his ideal. His other two main works are *Shakespeare* (1849) and *Geschichte des 19. Jahrhunderts* (1855–66). [RT]

M. Rychner, *G.G.G.* (Berlin, 1922).

**Gessner, Salomon** (Zürich 1730–Zürich 1788). Swiss poet. Also painter (cf. *Briefe über die Landschaftsmalerei an Herrn Fuesslin*, 1772), publisher, civil servant. His European fame rested on his rhythmic prose *Idyllen* (1756; 1772). Inspired by Theocritus, they combine pastoral themes with Rococo sentiment; their peaceful idealization of nature aims to promote serenity through virtue. The prose epic *Der Tod Abels* (1758), the pastoral romance *Daphnis* (1754), and his *Gedichte* (1762) show ⇨ Klopstock's influence. [LL]

*Auswahl*, ed. H. Hesse (1922); *Works*, tr. anon. (1802); many 18th- and 19th-cent. translations; Killy, *DLTZ*.

P. Leemann-van Elck, *S.G.* (Zürich and Leipzig, 1930); Schneider, *DDA*.

**'Gesta Francorum.'** Medieval chronicle. The *Gesta Francorum et aliorum Hierosolymitanorum* is sometimes called the *Tudebodus abbreviatus* on the assumption that it is drawn from the chronicle of ⇨ Tudeboeuf, but this is doubtful. It is an account of the First Crusade, from 1095 to August 1099; the anonymous author was apparently a southern Italian. The *Gesta Francorum* was widely used as a source book by chroniclers, among them Baudri de Bourgueil, Guibert de Nogent, ⇨ Robert the Monk and ⇨ Giles de Paris. [MRM]

Ed. H. Hagenmeyer (Heidelberg, 1890); ed. B. A. Lees (Oxford, 1924); *RHC*, Hist. Occ. iii; tr. Bréhier (Paris, 1924); ed. and tr. R. Hill, *The Deeds of the Franks and the Other Pilgrims to Jerusalem* (London, 1962).

**'Gesta Romanorum'** ( ? *c.*1300). A collection of stories of unknown authorship, probably compiled by a cleric, and intended as a manual for preachers. It includes stories of Greek and oriental as well as Roman origin, and all have moral application. Popular and frequently re-written and expanded, it influenced later medieval writers and is the source of Chaucer's *Man of Law's Tale* and Shakespeare's *King Lear*. [FB]

Ed. H. Oesterley (Berlin, 1872); tr. C. Swan (1824, etc.), rev. W. Hooper (1876, repr. 1905.)

**'Gestes.'** ⇨ *Chansons de geste.*

**Gezelle, Guido** (Bruges 1830–Bruges 1899). Flemish poet. The son of a gardener, he was trained for the priesthood and taught at Roeselare seminary. Transferred for his powerful support of the Flemish movement to Bruges (1860) and the remote Courtrai (1871), he fell silent until his reinstatement in 1882. *Vlaemsche Dichtoefeningen* (1858), *Kerhofblommen* (1859) and *Gedichten, gezangen, gebeden* (1862) gave a foretaste of the lithe and supple measures of his greatest work, *Tydkrans* (1893) and *Rijmsnoer om en om het jaar* (1897). After nearly three centuries of total eclipse, he refashioned Flemish as a literary language. Abandoning the alexandrine, kept in vogue by ⇨ Bilderdijk, he blended elements of medieval Flemish and his own Western dialect, to express the wonder of his platonic and mystical lyricism. The apparent incompatability of pantheistic delights in a cleric has caused much controversy; paradoxically, it was his zest for life and visible beauty that had constantly to be submitted to the man-made disciplines of the Church. He is clearly a romantic with a simple, Franciscan love and trust of nature as the antithesis of adult sophistication and of his own waywardness. Despite the disapproval of his superiors he wrote as the prophet of Catholic nationalism in his journals *Rond den Heerd* (1865–71) and *Loquela* (1881). This humble but passionate genius not only gave the impetus to the revival of literary Flemish, he also handed to the many accomplished writers after him the clay of their craft. [PK]

*Werken*, ed. F. Baur (4 vols., 1949); tr. of 15 poems by C. and F. Stillman, *Lyra Belgica I* (N.Y., 1950); *Delta* (Spring 1961).

A. Walgrave, *Het leven van G.G.* (Amsterdam, 1924); A. van Duinkerken, *G.G.* (Brussels, 1958).

**Gfeller, S.** ⇨ Swiss-German Dialect Literature.

**Ghelderode, Michel de** (Ixelles, Belgium 1898–Brussels 1962). Flemish dramatist. His demonic vision of the sin and folly of men, whose lusts enslave them to evil, decay and death, has a ribald–grotesque quality reminiscent of Breughel or Bosch. In *Mademoiselle Jaire* (1934) a resurrected girl embraces the mouldering, root-tangled corpse of Lazarus. *Escurial* (1927; tr. L. Abel in *The Modern Theatre*, V, 1957) shows a king in decline surrounded by priest, jester, executioner, and howling dogs. A supernatural combat between the ghost of a bishop and his successor occurs in *Fastes d'enfer* (1929; tr. G. Hauger and G. Hopkins in *Seven Plays*, 1960).

*Théâtre complet* (5 vols., 1950–7); *Sortilèges et autres contes crépusculaires* (1962).

J. Francis, *M.G. dramaturge des pays de par deça* (Brussels, 1949); P. Vandromme, *G.* (Paris, 1963); A. Weiss, *Le monde théâtral de M. de G.* (Paris, 1966).

**Gheon, Henri,** pseud. of Henri Vangeon (Bray-sur-Seine 1875–Paris 1944). French dramatist and poet. He revived a medieval type of religious drama, acted by his company 'Les Compagnons de Notre-Dame' at the Vieux-Colombier theatre (1913), composing for it many facile plays like *La bergère au pays des loups* (1922; tr. F. J. Sheed, *St. Germaine of the Wolf Country*,

1932), *Le Noël sur la place* (1935; tr. E. Crozier, *Christmas in the Market Place. A nativity play*, 1944), *Le jeu des grandes heures de Reims* (1938), etc. Other books on the Curé d'Ars, St John Bosco, St Martin, St Vincent Ferrer, Ste. Thérèse de Lisieux, and also on Mozart, have been translated into English.

M. Deléglise, *Le théâtre d'H.G.* (Fribourg, 1947).

**Giacosa, Giuseppe** (Colleretto Parella, Aosta 1847–Colleretto Parella 1906). Italian dramatist. After the success of his one-act comedy in verse, *La partita a scacchi* (1873; tr. B. H. Clark, *The Wager*, N.Y., 1914), he abandoned his chosen legal profession and wrote many plays on widely different themes, characterized only by their easy appeal to popular taste – hence the sharp attacks of critics like Carducci. Writing firstly medieval period pieces (e.g. *Partita a scacchi*, *Trionfo d'amore*, 1875, tr. H. Cook, *The Triumph of Love*, 1887; *Fratello d'armi*, 1887), then 18th-century pieces (e.g. *Marito amante della moglie*, 1876), he later turned to prose dramas modelled on the French naturalist theatre (e.g. *Tristi amori*, 1887, tr. A. E. Trombly, *Unhappy Love*, Boston, 1916 – his best play; *Come le foglie*, 1900, tr. D. Robertson, *As the Leaves*, Chicago, 1908) and even on Ibsen's controversial *Doll's House* (*Diritti dell'anima*, 1894). He was the leading dramatist of this period. In collaboration with Luigi Illica, he also wrote the libretti of Puccini's *La Bohème* (1896), *Tosca* (1899), and *Madame Butterfly* (1903). [RHC]

*Teatro*, ed. P. Nardi (2 vols., 1948); *The Stronger*, tr. E. and A. Updegraph (N.Y., 1913) (three plays).
D. Donelli, *G.G.* (Milan, 1948); P. Nardi, *Vita e tempo di G.G.* (Milan, 1949); *Minori*, iv.

**Gide, André** (Paris 1869–Paris 1951). French novelist, critic, diarist, playwright and traveller. Gide's avowed intention of 'disturbing' his readers is primarily associated with his espousal of pagan values – particularly after his visits to North Africa between 1893 and 1896 – and his desire to liberate himself from the social, moral and sexual conventions of his strict Protestant and puritanical upbringing. He became a controversial figure, also for his views on colonialism, pacifism, communism, homosexuality, courtroom procedure, etc. Early affinities with the Symbolist movement (he had met Mallarmé and Valéry among others) are revealed in *Les cahiers d'André Walter* (1891), *Le traité du Narcisse* (1891) *Les poésies d'André Walter* (1892) and *Le voyage d'Urien* (1893). In 1896 he published *Paludes* (tr. G. Painter, *Marshlands*, 1953), a satire on literary conventionalism, but his first really striking work of moral 'subversion' is *Les nourritures terrestres* (1897; tr. D. Bussy, *Fruits of the Earth*, 1949) a series of lyrical exhortations to an imaginary young man, Nathanaël, who is urged to rid himself of the Christian sense of sin and to cultivate the life of the senses in sincerity and independence. Gide returned to the same themes and style of writing in *Les nouvelles nourritures* (1935).

In 1895 he married his cousin, Madeleine Rondeaux, and an acute conflict arose between her strict Christian values and his own desire for liberation together with strong homosexual leanings; *Et nunc manet in te* (published 1951; tr. J. O'Brien, *Madeleine*, 1953) is a moving essay in autobiography relating to this period. His writing drew much of its strength from the persistent battle within himself between the puritan and the pagan, the admirer both of the Bible and of Nietzsche, and many of his books represent in turn one or other of the two poles of his inner life. The 3-act play *Le Roi Candaule* (1901) swings right away from the message of *Les nourritures terrestres*, the novel *L'immoraliste* (1902; tr. D. Bussy, *The Immoralist*, 1930) returns to it, while *La porte étroite* (1909; tr. D. Bussy, *Strait is the Gate*, 1924) is a short novel in which he goes back to the themes of restraint and self-denial.

Gide himself divided his fiction into three categories. His satirical and partly farcical tales he called '*soties*', e.g. *Paludes* (1896), *Le Prométhée mal enchaîné* (1899) and *Les caves du Vatican* (1914; tr. D. Bussy, *The Vatican Cellars*, 1952). In this latter tale the hero, Lafcadio, lives 'dangerously' according to the Gidean formula and commits an apparently motiveless murder in conformity with Gide's doctrine of the psychologically liberating '*acte gratuit*'. Gide gives the term '*récits*' to ironically structured short novels told from the point of view of one single character e.g. *L'immoraliste*, *La porte étroite* *Isabelle* (1911), *La symphonie pastorale* (1919; tr. D. Bussy, *Two Symphonies*, 1931) *L'école des femmes* (1929), *Robert* (1930) *Geneviève* (1937) and *Thésée* (1946). Gide reserved the term '*roman*' for one work o fiction only: *Les faux-monrayeurs* (1926; tr. D. Bussy, *The Coiners*, 1950). The viewpoint is 'third person' and the structure of the novel is at once loose and extremely complex – imitating what Gide regards as the essential 'untidiness' of experience itself. The title refers to one of the groups making up the large cast of characters – some schoolboys who attempt to circulate counterfeit money. One of the major characters is a novelist, Édouard, who is writing a novel called *Les faux-monnayeurs* and whose literary diary is the counterpart of Gide's actual *Journal des faux-monnayeurs* (1926; tr. J. O'Brien, *Logbook of the Coiners*, 1952). In fact, *Les faux-monnayeurs* is constructed rather on the lines of a series of Chinese boxes. Despite Gide's attempt to espouse the disorder of life his preoccupation with various fictional techniques conveys an overall impression of extreme artificiality.

In 1908 he helped to found the influential French periodical *La Nouvelle Revue Française*. Six years later he published the first of his pieces of sharp social criticism with his impressions as a juror collected under the title *Souvenirs de la cour d'assises* (1914; tr. D. Bussy, *Recollections of the Assize Court*, 1941). Two later essays in the same spirit, published in the *NRF* 'Ne jugez pas' collection, are *L'affaire Redureau* and *La séquestrée de Poitiers*, both published in 1930. In the twenties and thirties Gide travelled widely and wrote increasingly on colonialism and communism. The former was roundly attacked in *Voyage au Congo* (1928) and *Le retour du Tchad* (1928; both included in *Travels in the Congo*, tr. D. Bussy, 1930) while his mixed attitude of admiration for and reservation about communism comes out in *Retour de l'U.R.S.S.* (1936) and *Retouches à mon Retour de l'U.R.S.S.* (1937).

From a relatively early date in his career he had written stimulating literary criticism, e.g. *Prétextes* (1903) and *Nouveaux prétextes* (1911). Later critical works are *Dostoïevsky* (1923; tr. D. Bussy, 1949), *Incidences* (1924) and *Essai sur Montaigne* (1929; tr. D. Bussy, *The Living Thoughts of Montaigne*, 1939).

Perhaps the most strikingly continuous feature of his work is its autobiographical and self-searching vein. In *Corydon* (1923; tr. H. Gibb, N.Y., 1950) he dealt with homosexuality very frankly, if in the form of a Socratic dialogue. Even more immediately personal is his autobiography *Si le grain ne meurt* (1926; tr. D. Bussy, *If it die...*, 1950) and his quite outstanding *Journal 1885–1939* (1939) to which were added in 1946 and 1950 respectively his diaries for the years 1939–42 and 1942–9 (tr. J. O'Brien, *The Journals of André Gide, 1889–1949*, 1953). These volumes contain some of the richest of Gide's meditations on life and on his own literary career which was crowned by the award of the Nobel Prize in 1947. He also carried on a voluminous correspondence with Jammes, Valéry, Claudel, Rilke and others. [JC]

*Œuvres complètes* (15 vols., 1932–9) (further vols. to be added).

J. Hytier, *A.G.* (Algiers, 1938); A. J. Guerard, *A.G.* (Cambridge, Mass., 1951); G. Brée, *A.G., l'insaisissable Protée* (Paris, 1953); P. Lafille, *A.G., romancier* (Paris, 1954); J. Delay, *La jeunesse d'A.G.* (2 vols., Paris, 1956–8); G. W. Ireland, *G.* (1963).

**Gijsen, Marnix,** pseud. of Joannes Alphonsius Albertius Goris (Antwerp 1899– ). Flemish author. After a book of expressionistic poems, *Het Huis* (1925), he turned to literary criticism. His first novel, *Het boek van Joachim van Babylon* (1948), was an immediate success, and his subsequent novels have taken the same sceptical but humane view of life, that conventional norms are generally a delusion. [PK]

*Klaaglied om Agnes* (1951); *De Vleespotten van Egypte* (1952); *De lange nacht* (1954); *Lucinda en de lotoseter* (1959); *Delta* (Summer 1958, Winter 1966/7).

M. Roelants, *M.G.* (Brussels, 1958).

**Gilbert, Nicolas-Joseph-Laurent** (Fontenoy-le-Château, Lorraine 1751–Paris 1780). French poet. Of humble provincial origins, but sure of his poetic talent, Gilbert was embittered by his failure to win recognition in the Parisian literary world, and came to attribute this to the hostility of the *philosophes*. His satirical verse (*Le dix-huitième siècle*, 1775) has a certain denunciatory eloquence, while he also writes in a melancholy, introspective mood (*Le poète malheureux*; *Les adieux à la vie*, 1780), which looks forward to the romantic poets. He became one of their martyr-heroes (A. de Vigny, *Stello*), but in fact his early death was the result of an accident and not of public neglect. [WHB]

*Œuvres complètes* (1823).

E. Laffay, *Le poète G.* (Paris, 1898); É. Faguet, *Histoire de la poésie française*, ix (Paris, 1936).

**Giles de Paris** (?–*c.* 1141). Medieval writer. Clerk of a church in Paris, then a Cluniac monk, he was made Cardinal-Bishop of Frascati in 1121. He travelled to the Holy Land in 1128 as legate of Honorius II, and in 1134 was in Aquitaine as legate of the anti-pope Anacletus. He wrote a life of Abbot Hugh of Cluny and of a history of the First Crusade, *Viae nostri temporis hierosolymitanae*. Written in hexameters, in six books, this begins with the siege of Nicaea and ends with the election of Godfrey of Bouillon as King of Jerusalem. Some of the material is drawn from the ⇨ *Gesta Francorum* and from ⇨ Robert the Monk. [MRM]

*Viae*, in *RHC*, Hist. Occ. v; Migne, *PL*, 155; *Vita S. Hugonis*, ed. L. de Heinemann, in MGH, xv, 2; Migne, *PL*, 159.

**Gil y Carrasco, Enrique** (Villafranca del Bierzo 1815–Berlin 1846). Spanish poet and novelist. His romantic poetry shows a delicate melancholy and a feeling for landscape, which also inspires many fine unrhetorical descriptions in his novels. The best is *El señor de Bembibre* (1844; tr. anon., *The Mystery of Bierzo Valley*, 1938), in the manner of Walter Scott: its setting is medieval, its main characters members of the Order of Templars. [JMC]

*Poesías líricas* (1873); *Obras en prosa* (1883); BAE, 74 (1954); Blecua, *FLE*; Trend, *OBSV*.

J. M. Goy, *E.G.* (Astorga, 1924).

**Gioberti, Vincenzo** (Turin 1801–Paris 1852). Italian philosopher and statesman. Ordained priest in 1825, Court Chaplain to Carlo Alberto, suspected unjustly of revolutionary activities, he was banished. In 1848 he became President of the Piedmontese Chamber of Deputies. In his purely philosophical works he opposed the eclecticism of Cousin and Rosmini in the field of ontology, and expounded an essentially Catholic concept that equated religion with civilization, so that he saw the Church as the vehicle of social progress (cf. *Introduzione allo studio della filosofia*, Brussels, 1840). Politically his importance lies in his leadership of the moderate federalist movement of liberal-catholics, claiming in his *Primato morale e civile degli Italiani* (Brussels, 1843) and the *Prolegomeni* (Brussels, 1845) that an independent regenerate Italy, a worthy centre of Christianity, was destined for moral leadership of the world. At first he supported federation under the Pope, but after the disillusionment of 1848–9, he shifted his allegiance to Piedmont, aggressively condemning reactionary elements in the Church, especially the Pope's temporal power and the Jesuit Order (cf. *Il Gesuita moderno*, Lausanne, 1846–7; *Del rinnovamento civile d'Italia*, 1851 – that led to his works being placed on the Index). [RHC]

*Opere*, ed. G. Massari (37 vols., 1861–6); *Edizione nazionale delle opere*, ed. E. Castelli (1938ff.) (incomplete).

G. Gentile, *I profeti del Risorgimento italiano* (Florence, 1923); G. Natali, *L'opera politica di V.G.* (Bologna, 1954); G. Gentile, *Rosmini e Gioberti* (Florence, 1958); *Minori*, iii.

**Giono, Jean** (Manosque 1895–1970). French novelist. He left school at 16 and worked in a bank until 1929, broken only by three years at the front in the First World War. His subsequent pacifism which led to his imprisonment for several months during the Second World War stems mainly from his lack of interest in social problems and his rejection of anything which limits the individual. The influence of his early reading (Virgil, Greek tragedy and above all Homer) and his own vivid imagination are reflected in the earliest works, *Accompagné de la flûte* (1924) and *Naissance de l'Odyssée* (1925). The success of *Colline* (1928) enabled him to leave his job and devote himself entirely to writing. His novels to the beginning of the Second World War are largely set against peasant backgrounds in Provence in which nature is described as a living force in which man can refind the harmony and depth which he has lost in town life. It is his descriptions of daily life that he expresses purpose and happiness and in the extremely simple characters such as Gagou (*Colline*) and Saturnin (*Un des Baumugnes*, 1929) one feels the mysterious participation in a hard way of life close to the rhythms of nature. He is optimistic in novels like *Regain* (1930) and *Un des Baumugnes*, where individual and communal growth and rejuvenation are dominant themes. But in *Que ma joie demeure* (1935; tr. K. A. Clarke, *Joy of Man's Desiring*, 1949) the characters do not fully accept the simple life and Bobi, the poetic central figure, cannot fulfil his ideal within the community, so that the vision of a richer society gives way to a greater stress on the individual's achievement of happi ıess through the working out of his own 'eelings and instincts. In the later novels, *Chroniques*, he continues to emphasize the ndividual's activity in life and especially n the face of crises – the epidemic in *Le ıussard sur le toit* (1951; tr. J. Griffin, *The Hussar on the Roof*, 1953) and the killer in *Un roi sans divertissement* (1946) – where, hrough his active participation, the hero ıchieves a greater intensity of experience. Giono broadened his field and no longer emained a simple apologist of the peasant ife, but it is the richness and fire of his anguage and poetry and his vivid imagina-ion which capture the reader's attention in ıis fiction. [RGV]

C. Chonez, *G. par lui-même* (Paris, 1961); J. Pugnet, *J.G.* (Paris, 1955); W. D. Redfern, *The Private World of J.G.* (1967).

**Gippius, Zinaida Nikolayevna** (Belev, Tula 1869–Paris 1945). Russian poetess. Wife of ⇨ Merezhkovsky, with whom she lived n exile. Her principal verse collections are *Sobranniye stikhov* (Moscow, 1904, 1910), *Stikhi* (Berlin, 1922), *Siyaniya* (Paris, 1938). Her search for formal, sometimes aphoristic perfection links her with the symbolist movement, while with her husband she hared mystical-religious interests. She writes on such themes as Providence, the vileness and misery of existence, the trans-endence of love and justice. *Zhivyye litsa* (Prague, 1925) is a book of memoirs about the poets she had known (Blok, Bryusov, and others), and *Zelyonoye kol'tso* (1916; tr. S. S. Koteliansky, *The Green Ring*, 1920), a play. She also wrote two novels and short tories in the psychological manner of Dostoyevsky.

**Giraldi Cinthio, Giambattista** (Ferrara 1504–Ferrara 1573). Italian tragedian, literary theorist and short-story writer. Professor of philosophy, then literature, at Ferrara and Pavia; author of the impor-ant Italian tragedy, *Orbecche* (1541). Much involved in contemporary discussions on the nature of tragedy, he interpreted Aristotle's precepts in terms of Senecan horror, and made *Orbecche* a veritable blood-bath. He composed 8 other tragedies, which illustrate his belief in the moral purpose of literature. His theoretical views re expounded in two treatises, *Intorno al comporre delle commedie e delle tragedie* (1554) and *Intorno al comporre dei romanzi* (1554). Similarly moralistic – and at times horrific – is his once popular collection of 113 *novelle*, *Hecatommithi* (1565). The framework and thematic grouping point clearly to the *Decameron*, but the artistic level is not high. The plot of Shakespeare's *Othello* derives from *Hecatommithi* iii:7; *Measure for Measure* from viii: 5. [DGR]

*Tragedie* (1583); *Scritti estetici*, ed. Daelli (Biblioteca Rara, 52–3, 1864); Roscoe, *IN*.
C. Guerrieri Crocetti, *G.B.G. ed il pensiero critico del sec. XVI* (Milan, 1932); P. R. Horne, *The Tragedies of G.C.G.* (1962); Weinberg, *HLC*.

**Giraudoux, Jean** (Bellac 1882–Paris 1944). French diplomat, novelist, playwright and critic. Born in the heart of rural France, he entered the diplomatic service in 1910 after a series of brilliant academic successes. Interrupted by the First World War, in which he was decorated for bravery, his diplomatic career was resumed in 1919 and continued without interruption until his retirement from official life in 1940. He occupied important diplomatic posts, notably as inspector of diplomatic and consular establishments (from 1934) and Director-General of Information (1939–40), the last a disastrous appointment. These interests are reflected in his memoirs: *Pleins pouvoirs* (1930), *Armistice à Bordeaux* (1945), *Sans pouvoirs* (1946).

His first major incursion into literature was with *Provinciales* (1909), a charming but mannered evocation of French country life seen through the eyes of a fanciful child. There followed a series of novels, precious in language, impressionistic in treatment, in which refinement often topples over into affectation. The novels are episodic and embody a highly personal vision of the world in which poetic myths are created for our amusement and distraction. The vision is essentially escapist, sometimes verging dangerously on a kind of poetic onanism. The world Giraudoux prefers is curiously matriarchal. His women are not hard-edged, isolated and competing atoms, like his men, but tied to the natural world and the world of other human beings by subtle and delicate filiations. It is they, above all, who uncover the poetic possibilities of ordinary existence in the imaged and mannered prose of: *L'école des indifférents* (1911); *Simon le pathétique* (first version 1918, definitive version 1926); *Elpénor* (1919); *Suzanne et le Pacifique* (1921), where the virgin Suzanne re-enacts the story of the Fall, electing to leave Paradise of her own free will; *Siegfried et le Limousin*

(1922), a characteristically fantasticated treatment of Germany, always a source of fascination for him; *Juliette au pays des hommes* (1924); *Bella* (1926), with its subtle and witty satire of current politics; *Eglantine* (1927); *Les aventures de Jérôme Bardini* (1930); *Combat avec l'ange* (1934); *Choix des élues* (1938), where, in an American setting, the loves of Jacques and Maléna are played out with poetic charm. A posthumous novel, *La menteuse*, appeared in 1958.

In Giraudoux's theatre there is small interest in psychological realism: character is metaphor or archetype, playing out universal themes in the form of debates of a highly stylized kind between opposed conceptions of human experience: human and divine in the brilliantly witty rehandling of myth in *Amphitryon '38* (1929; tr. S. N. Behrman, 1938); war and peace in the powerful confrontation of Hector and Ulysses in *La guerre de Troie n'aura pas lieu* (1935; tr. C. Fry, *Tiger at the Gates*, in *Plays I*, 1963); conventional and 'natural' morality in the amusing South Sea idyll of *Supplément au voyage de Cook* (1935); sacred and profane love in *Judith* (1931; tr. C. Fry in *Plays I*, 1963). His theatre is 'literary' in the sense that it confers supremacy on speech, but it depends in the highest degree on distinctively theatrical resources: lighting, movement, décor. Men respond to their destiny, their 'nature' in a generally predictable way but individuals may inflect the general course of events, though without altering the broad pattern. Such is the case with his treatment of the exigent heroine in *Électre* (1937; tr. W. Smith, *Electra*, in *The Modern Theatre I*, 1955) where the sense of inevitability is reinforced by the clairvoyance of the sinister Beggar. Giraudoux mistrusts divinities, which is to say any level of experience beyond the human. That is why Jupiter is outwitted by the delicious and resourceful symbol of human love, Alcmène, in *Amphitryon '38*, or why the knight and the sea-maiden in the romantic legend of *Ondine* (1939; tr. M. Valency, 1954) fail to sustain their love. The love of the human condition, conveyed with luminous tenderness and delicacy in his theatre, is central to his vision of life. Human love in all its imperfection transcends hollow patriotism in *La guerre de Troie*, survives the appeal of the ultimate poetry of immortal perfection held out by the Ghost to the unspoilt Isabelle of *Intermezzo* (1933; tr. M. Valency, *The Enchanted*, 1950), and challenges a vengeful Jehovah in *Judith*. The women who are the source and object of this love are natural, instinctive, candid; creatures of intuition endowed with a delicate and subtle sensibility. These very qualities often set them at variance with men, creatures of coarser fibre, peculiarly endowed for action. Generally, this conflict is reconciled in marriage (in many ways his plays represent the triumph of conjugal love), though the disharmony adumbrated in *Ondine* reaches painful proportions in the pessimistic *Sodome et Gomorrhe* (1943). Giraudoux sometimes succumbs to prettiness and sentimentality, but he handles myth and language with astonishing virtuosity, and below the surface dazzle one often glimpses a completely individual and arresting vision of the world, a vision that grows more sombre towards the end of his life, as the defeat of innocence in *Pour Lucrèce* (1953; tr. C. Fry, *Duel of Angels*, in *Plays I*, 1963) makes clear. The best of his criticism is contained in *Les cinq tentations de La Fontaine* (1938) and *Littérature* (1941). He has also written short stories (*Contes d'un matin*, 1952) and the scripts for two films: *Le film de la duchesse de Langeais* (1942) and *Le film de Béthanie* (1944). [SBJ]

*Théâtre complet* (16 vols., 1945–53); *Œuvre romanesque* (2 vols., 1955); *Œuvres littéraires diverses* (1958).

R. M. Albérès, *Esthétique et morale chez J.G.* (Paris, 1957); V. H. Debidour, *J.G.* (Paris, 1963); D. Inskip, *J.G.: The Making of a Dramatist* (1958); L. Le Sage, *J.G.: His Life and Works* (1959); C. Marker, *G. par lui-même* (Paris, 1952); Grossvogel, *TCFD*; Guicharnaud, *MFT*; Surer, *TFC*.

**'Gísla saga Súrssonar.'** ⇨ Icelandic Sagas.

**Giusti, Giuseppe** (Monsummano 1809–Florence 1850). Italian poet. The first volume of *Poesie* (Lugano, 1844 – later definitive edition, Florence, 1852, posth.) clearly shows the stages of his poetry from the youthful imitations either of classical poets or of popular satirical verse to his mature *Scherzi*, successful satires both profound and elegantly written – partly the result of his association with leading men of letters like ⇨ Manzoni and Capponi. Notable are the *Ghigliottina a vapore* (1833) advocating a useful instrument for an overworked tyrant Duke of Modena; *Lo stivale*

(1836), a rapid survey of Italian history; *Gingillino* (1845) – his best satire – against bureaucracy; and *Sant'Ambrogio* (1846), reflections on the presence of Austrian troops in Milan. There is an interesting *Epistolario* (1859, posth.) and a well-known collection of Tuscan proverbs. [RHC]

*Opere*, ed. Z. Arici (1955); *Epistolario*, ed. F. Martini (5 vols., 1932–56); *Poesie*, ed. N. Sabbatucci (1962); Kay, *PBIV*; Dionisotti, *OBIV*.

E. Bellorini, *G.G.* (Rome, 1923); P. De' Giovanni, *G.* (Milan, 1947); R. Schippisi, *G.* (Brescia, 1951); *Minori*, iv.

**Gjellerup, Karl** (Roholte 1857–Dresden 1919). Danish novelist. Under the influence of G. ⇨ Brandes he turned from theological studies to free-thinking radicalism (*Germanernes Lærling*, 1882), and later to Buddhism under the influence of Schopenhauer and Wagner. His only readable novels today are *Minna* (1889; tr. C. L. Nielsen, 1913), *Møllen* (1896), and *Pilgrimmen Kamanita* (1906; tr. J. E. Logie, *The Pilgrim Kamanita*, 1911); he shared the Nobel Prize in 1917 with ⇨ Pontoppidan. [ELB]

**Glazarová, Jarmila** (Malá Skála 1901– ). Czech novelist. The wife of a country doctor; after the last war she was the cultural attaché in Moscow and later a member of the Czechoslovak National Assembly. Her first novels, *Vlčí jáma* (1938) and *Advent* (1939), combine a portrayal of the hard life of peasants and workers in Silesia with an analysis of the social, personal and religious problems of modern woman. Social problems prevail in *Roky v kruhu* (1936). Her books, *Leningrad* (1950) and *Dnes a zítra* (1952), journalistic reports on the development of the new society both in the Soviet Union and Czechoslovakia, express strong faith in the future of the kind of social order being built in these countries. [KB]

*Dílo* (6 vols., 1953–60).

F. Buriánek, *Současná česká literatura* (Prague, 1960).

**Gleim, Johann Wilhelm Ludwig** (Ermsleben 1719–Halberstadt 1803). German poet. In the second Silesian War he served Wilhelm von Brandenburg-Schwedt, then became secretary to Leopold von Dessau; from 1747 he was secretary and canon at Halberstadt Cathedral. As leader of the 'Anacreontic' school he influenced ⇨ Uz, ⇨ Götz, ⇨ Klopstock and ⇨ Wieland. His *Lieder nach dem Anakreon* (1766) and *Oden nach dem Horaz* (1769) show his admiration for the two poets who, with Hagedorn, inspired him most. The songs of *Versuch in scherzhaften Liedern* (1740–1; repr. 1964) and *Lieder* (1745) glorify wine, love, and easy sociability in pastoral landscapes. His *Fabeln* (1756–7) teach Rococo virtues, while *Preussische Kriegslieder von einem Grenadier* (1758) strike a patriotic note. [LL]

*Sämtliche Werke* (4 vols., 1919–20).

E. Strobelt, *Die Halberstädter Anakreontik* (Leipzig, 1929); E. Ermatinger, *Barock und Rokoko in der deutschen Dichtung* (Leipzig, 1926); Schneider, *DDA*; Closs, *GGL*.

**Glišić, Milovan** (Gradac 1847–Dubrovnik 1908). Serbian short-story writer and dramatist. A socialist and realist, deeply influenced by Russian literature, especially Gogo'. All his stories and his play *Podvala* (1885) are directed against the social evils of the day. His most characteristic work is the story *Glava šećera* (1882), which satirizes the bureaucracy and its exploitation of the peasants. [EDG]

Popović, *JS*.

Barac, *HYL*.

**Glueckel von Hameln** (Hamburg 1645–Hamburg 1724). Jewish memoirist. Wife of a Hamburg Jewish merchant, she began writing her memoirs (*Die Memoiren Glückel von Hameln*, tr. B.-Z. Abrahams, *The Life of G. v. H.*, 1962) in Judeo-German after her husband's death in 1689. They shed a light on contemporary German life, the status of women in that period, the circle of court Jews and wealthy German merchants in the 17th century, the impact of the false Messiah Shabbetai Zevi, and the history of Yiddish. [EE]

**Gobineau, Joseph-Arthur de** (Ville d'Avray 1816–Turin 1882). French diplomat, novelist, historian. After employment in a gas company and the postal service, this son of impoverished gentry embarked on Parisian journalism with reviews of current fiction and poetry (the best of which were assembled in *Études critiques*, 1926) and articles of a historical and political character, frequently relating to the religion and culture of the East for which he had shown a precocious talent. Concurrently, he published largely forgotten historical novels in the manner of Walter Scott: *Les aventures de Jean de la Tour-Miracle* (1847;

tr. F. M. Atkinson, *The Lucky Prisoner*, 1926); *Nicolas Belavoir* (1847); *Ternove* (1848); and *L'Abbaye de Typhaines* (1867), perhaps the most accomplished. Chef de Cabinet to Tocqueville during the latter's brief tenure as Foreign Minister (1849), he subsequently entered the diplomatic service and was successively minister in Teheran, Athens, Rio de Janeiro and Stockholm. His distinctive intellectual and imaginative gifts emerged during these years of diplomacy. As historian and thinker, he published: *Essai sur l'inégalité des races humaines* (1853–5; tr. A. Collins, *The Inequality of Human Races*, 1915); *Trois ans en Asie* (1859); *Traité des écritures cunéiformes* (1864); *Les religions et les philosophies dans l'Asie Centrale* (1865); *Histoire des Perses* (1869), the last three of interest only to specialists. The essay on the races is marked by belief in the survival of the fittest; nostalgia for the feudal ideal and a tendency to link it with the early Germanic tribes; contempt for absolutist and centralized monarchy; and strong racial and historical pessimism. The essay is based on a kind of historical monism in which all social, political and cultural phenomena are reduced to the single factor of racial superiority with its implied correlation between miscegenation and cultural decay. The intellectual issues raised by these theories (later vulgarized as *Le Gobinisme* and brutally exploited by pan-Germanists and Nazis) inform the letters exchanged between Tocqueville and Gobineau and make of them one of the most fascinating debates of the 19th century (*Correspondance d'Alexis de Tocqueville et d'Arthur de Gobineau*, ed. M. Degros, 1959). Gobineau's extremely distinctive literary work is characterized by high intelligence, psychological finesse, elegant irony and a passionately idealistic conception of human love. The tone and manner often recall Stendhal, though he is not so assured. Memorable are his brilliant short stories, three of which were collected in *Souvenirs de voyage* (1872; tr. H. L. Stuart, *The Crimson Handkerchief and Other Stories*, 1927), while an exotic group were published under the title *Nouvelles asiatiques* (1876; ed. Pauvert, 1956; tr. J. L. May, *Tales of Asia*, 1947). He also wrote a striking novel, *Les Pléiades* (1874; ed. J. Mistler, 1946; tr. J. F. Scanlan, *Pleiads*, 1928), in which he fashions a golden myth of friendship, and *La Renaissance* (1877; ed. J. Mistler, 1947; tr. P. V. Cohn, 1913), a set of historical portraits and a vivid fresco of the Renaissance in dialogue form. His letters to his sister, *Comte de Gobineau et Mère Bénédicte de Gobineau: Correspondance 1872–1882*, ed. A. B. Duff (2 vols., 1958), are of great interest, as are *Lettres persanes*, ed. A. B. Duff (1957). [SBJ]

*Nouvelles*, ed. Pauvert (2 vols., 1956).

M. Lange, *Le Comte A. de G., étude biographique et critique* (Paris, 1924); M. Riffaterre, *Le style des Pléiades de G.* (Paris, 1957); J. Gaulmier, *Spectre de G.* (Paris, 1966); H. El Nouty, *Le Proche-Orient dans la littérature française* (Paris, 1958); J. Buenzod, *La formation de la pensée de G.* (1967).

**Goes, Albrecht** (Langenbeutingen, Württemberg 1908– ). German poet and novelist. Lutheran pastor and army chaplain in Russia. His poetry, *Gedichte 1930–1950* (1950), is in the religious tradition (cf. his *Mörike*, 1938) with a keen awareness of contemporary problems. Apart from essays (*Von Mensch zu Mensch*, 1949, etc.), Goes became widely known through two novellas about the Second World War: *Unruhige Nacht* (1949; tr. C. FitzGibbon, *Arrow to the Heart*, 1951), and *Das Brandopfer* (1954; tr. M. Hamburger, *The Burnt Offering*, 1956), the latter described by Martin Buber as 'a document of true humanity'. Each discovers, movingly and simply, a faith in the individual's ultimate capacity for goodness, greater than the senseless slaughter in Russia or (worse) the persecution of the Jews. He has also written numerous morality plays, e.g. *Das St Galler Spiel von der Kindheit Jesu*, 1959. [PB]

*Aber im Winde das Wort* (1963) (selection).

W. Janzen, *A.G.* (Diss, Manitoba, 1961).

**Goetel, Ferdynand** (Sucha 1890–London 1960). Polish novelist. During the First World War he spent a few years in Turkestan as a prisoner; later he escaped to India, and this had a profound influence on his writing. His exotic novel *Kar Chat* (1923; tr. M. Słomczanka and G. K. Murray, *The Messenger of the Snow*, 1931) anticipated the originality of *Z dnia na dzień* (1926; tr. W. Cooper, *From Day to Day*, 1931), in which Turkestan is relived in Cracow. 'The book is written in what I believe to be the totally new form of a diary by the leading character, in which he incorporates the text of a novel as he writes it' (Galsworthy's foreword). The sieving of experience through a disturbed memory and a disturbed awareness of the present is as fascinating as the narrative technique. Once an influential man of letters, Goetel had to escape from communist Poland and died destitute and half-blind in London. *Czasy wojny* (1955) describes his experiences in occupied Poland. [JP]

**Goethe, Johann Wolfgang von** (Frankfurt a. M. 1749–Weimar 1832). German poet. Goethe's range as a writer is truly tremendous: simple love lyrics and profound philosophical poems, straightforward nature poems and poems which express his scientific theories, novels and travelogues, verse idylls and satires, comedies, tragedies, short stories, scientific treatises, and critical and autobiographical works. The last of the great universal geniuses, in the course of a long life he engaged in a wealth of activities: poet, lawyer, politician and civil servant, botanist, zoologist, physicist, painter, theatre manager and literary critic. Yet there is nothing fragmentary about him, and his mature writings are the expression of the harmony he created by conscious effort out of the manifold experiences of a richly varied life. Herein lies his unique greatness as a man and as a poet, and perhaps more than in the case of any other European writer, his life and works form an indivisible whole, so that his work mirrors the course of his life and the development of his personality, or, as he himself puts it, all his works are fragments of a great confession.

It was under the influence of ◊ Herder, who opened his eyes to the greatness of Shakespeare and the beauties of folk-poetry while he was a student in Strassburg (1770), that he emerged as an important writer. The lyrics in which he commemorates his relationship with Friederike Brion, the daughter of a country parson in the neighbouring village of Sesenheim, sounded a note hitherto unheard in German literature in their directness, their naïve spontaneity and in their expression of powerful emotions in a language of great lyrical beauty ('Willkommen und Abschied', 'Mailied', 'Heidenröslein', etc.). His praise of Shakespeare in the *Rede zum Shakespeare-Tag* (1771) and the essay on architecture he contributed to Herder's *Von deutscher Art und Kunst* (1773) marked him as a theoretician of the ◊ *Sturm und Drang*, but it was through his creative writings that he exerted a decisive influence. His chaotically Shakespearean *Götz von Berlichingen* (1771–3) set the tone for the drama of the new movement in its medieval setting, in its adulation of the 'great individual' in the figure of Götz, the outlaw hero, and in its Rousseauistic rejection of an ignoble and degenerate society, while the epistolary novel *Die Leiden des jungen Werthers* (1774; tr. B. Q. Morgan, 1957) – the fruit of the disappointed love for Charlotte Buff which he had experienced while a lawyer at Wetzlar in 1772 – although basically a study in pathological sensibility, struck a powerful blow against the rationalism of the Enlightenment through its inherent glorification of the emotions and, incidentally, brought Goethe European fame.

During the period 1770–5 the restless sense of dissatisfaction and physical and emotional titanism which are fundamental to *Götz* and *Werther* resulted in the planning of a number of dramas which, with the exception of *Faust* and *Egmont*, were never written, but whose mood survives in the free rhythms of the magnificent poems 'Wanderers Sturmlied', 'Prometheus', and 'An Schwager Kronos'. With the move to Weimar in 1775, however, this mood is largely overcome. Here, as one of the principal ministers of the Duke, Goethe gained experience of practical life – mining, engineering, finance, etc. In the midst of practical tasks and under the benign influence of his spiritual mistress, Charlotte von Stein, the titanism of the early seventies gives place to the restrained humanism of such poems as 'Grenzen der Menschheit' and 'Das Göttliche' and to the emotional tranquillity of 'An den Mond' and 'Wanderers Nachtlied', although poems like 'Erlkönig' and 'Nur wer die Sehnsucht kennt' bear witness to his continuing awareness of the starkly tragic quality of human existence. This relatively unproductive early Weimar period, which saw many works begun, but few completed, was brought to a conclusion by the journey to Italy in 1786. Under the tremendous impression Italy made on him – the *Römische Elegien* (1788–90) and the *Italienische Reise* (1816–29; tr. W. H. Auden and E. Mayer, *Italian Journey*, 1963) recount his reactions in verse and prose – his creative urge quickened and long-neglected manuscripts and plans once more occupied him. It is now that the humanistic ideal towards which he had slowly been evolving gains its fullest expression in the statuesque classical drama *Iphigenie auf Tauris* (final version 1787) which typifies the mature Goethe in the restrained beauty of its verse, in its (not entirely satisfactory motivated) avoidance of tragedy and in its affirmation of '*reine Menschlichkeit*' (pure, sincere humanity, the harmonious expression of the highest in-dwelling qualities in man). *Iphigenie* expresses, in the cure of the fury-ridden Orestes at the hands of his sister, Goethe's own experience of the healing power of the pure humanity of Charlotte von Stein; *Torquato Tasso* (final version 1789) is equally autobiographical in its representation of the frustrations of the Italian poet in the tiny court of Ferrara, the comfort he draws from the company of a pure woman and above all in the suggestion of a harmonious synthesis of the poet and the man of practical affairs in the reconciliation of the irrascible Tasso with Antonio.

In the midst of these classical dramas the completion of *Egmont* (1787), with its wide historical canvas and its expression of Goethe's 'Storm and Stress' belief in the demonic forces which govern man's life, strikes a somewhat incongruous note and looks forward to the completion of the first part of his other 'Storm and Stress' fragment, *Faust*, after an intervening period of nearly twenty years, years which saw his friendship with ⇨ Schiller, the development of his scientific interests and the literary expression of his distrust of the French Revolution in the slight comedy *Der Bürgergeneral* (1793), the middle-class idyll *Hermann und Dorothea* (1797) and the enigmatic, classical tragedy *Die natürliche Tochter* (1803). The works of his post-classical period, the darkly symbolical novel *Die Wahlverwandtschaften* (1809; tr. H. M. Waidson, 1960), on the conflict of spontaneous emotional attraction and the social convention of marriage, and the cycle of poems, *West-östlicher Divan* (publ. 1819), the fruit of his discovery of the Orient in the poetry of the Persian poet Hafiz and simultaneously an expression of his relationship with Marianne Willemer, reveal a progressive deepening of his humane wisdom and a heightening of his poetic powers. The publication of *Wilhelm Meisters Wanderjahre* (1829) marked the completion of work on a theme which had occupied him since the 1770s (*Wilhelm Meisters theatralische Sendung*, 1777, remained unpublished) and had already gained expression in the semi-autobiographical novel of development *Wilhelm Meisters Lehrjahre* (1795–6; tr. T. Carlyle, 1812), the poetic expression of the typically Goethian concept of education for life by life itself: Meister is led by a benevolent fate through a rich variety of experiences to the point where he can become a useful member of the community. The *Wanderjahre* reflect in particular Goethe's interest in social problems, but in the extremely episodic form also seem to indicate a weakening of his powers.

It was not until shortly before his death that Goethe finished the work for which he is chiefly remembered, *Faust*. The drama had accompanied him from his student days and the original 'Storm and Stress' themes of titanic academic dissatisfaction, seduction and infanticide still constitute the heart of the profoundly moving Part One (publ. 1808), while Part Two is a vehicle for the scientific interests and the sibylline wisdom of the aged Goethe – already familiar from such poems as 'Urworte Orphisch' (1819) and often expressed in abstruse, esoteric symbolism. Fundamentally, however, the whole drama is a symbolical representation of the nature of Western European man in his unceasing activity and restless thirst for experience. It is these qualities which are the cause of Faust's pact with the devil and of his subsequent crimes and at the same time the reason for his ultimate salvation: activity will always result in error and crime, but activity is nonetheless the result of the divine spark in man and is therefore affirmed as positive in spite of its negative consequences.

Amongst his other writings the most important are *Zur Farbenlehre* (1810), a work on optics in which he sought to disprove the Newtonian theory of light, and *Dichtung und Wahrheit* (1811–31), the story of his life and times up to 1775.

The central idea in Goethe's thought is the concept of organic development. His botanical and zoological writings revolve around his theory of evolution from certain primary forms ('*Urphänomene*') and the principle of metamorphosis is held to be the basic law of all existence: the whole of nature is seen as being in a constant state of dynamic change and development. In his view of nature there is no dualism: God does not exist outside nature but is in-dwelling, and apparent conflicts serve only to produce heightened development (*'Polarität und Steigerung'*). The ethical task of man is to fit into this pattern of harmonious development: the Faustian principle of activity is in harmony with the dynamism of nature itself and, with external nature, man must learn to 'die and become'; above all, however, he must learn, like Wilhelm Meister, to recognize and respect the limits of his own physical and spiritual being. [WAC]

*Werke* ('Weimarer' or 'Sophienausgabe'), crit. edn (143 vols., 1887–1920); ed. E. Trunz (13 vols., 1952); *Dramatic Works*, tr. A. Swanwick (1846); *Faust*, tr. C. F. Coxwell (1932); *Poems and Ballads*, tr. W. E. Aytoun (1906).

E. Beutler, *Essays um G.* (Wiesbaden, 1946); W. H. Bruford, *Culture and Society in Classical Weimar* (1962); B. Fairley, *A Study of G.* (1947); H. A. Korff, *Geist der Goethezeit* (3 vols., Leipzig, 1923–41); G. Müller, *Kleine G.-biographie* (Bonn, 1947); H. Pyritz, *G.-Studien* (Cologne, 1962); R. Peacock, *G.'s Major Plays* (1959); W. Roxe *et al.*, *Essays on G.* (1949); E. Staiger, *G.* (3 vols., Zürich and Freiburg, 1952ff.); H. Trevelyan, *G. and the Greeks* (1942); E. Wilkinson and L. A. Willoughby, *G. – Thinker and Poet* (1962); Heller, *DM.*

**Gogol', Nikolay Vasil'yevich** (Sorochintsy, Poltava 1809–Moscow 1852). Russian novelist and dramatist. From a poor Ukrainian gentry family, he left school in 1828 and went to St Petersburg with hopes of a literary career. Some weak poetry met with scorn, and he became a government clerk. To forget his dreary life he wrote colourful stories of the Ukraine, *Vechera na khutore bliz Dikan'ki* (1831–2; tr. C. Garnett, *Evenings on a Farm near Dikanka*, 1926); these were well received, and he was encouraged by Pushkin. Interested in the picturesque aspects of history, he planned, but never wrote, vast historical works; he was briefly Professor of History at St Petersburg University (1834–5). *Mirgorod* (1835; tr. C. Garnett, 1928) contains four stories still with Ukrainian settings but greater imaginative range: *Old-World Landowners* is idyllic with an undercurrent of satire, *Taras Bulba* is romantically historical, and *Viy* is grimly fantastic; *The Tale of How Ivan Ivanovich Quarrelled with Ivan Nikiforovich* is uproariously (and painfully) satirical. *Arabeski* (1835) contains essays and stories, the latter (*Nevsky Prospekt*, *The Portrait* and *Notes of a Madman*) set in St Petersburg, shown in a dreamlike blend of the sordid and fantastic. The famous comic satire on provincial bureaucrats, *Revizor* (tr. D. J. Campbell, *The Inspector*, 1953), was staged in 1836.

From 1836 to 1848 Gogol' lived mostly abroad, often in Rome, whose magnificence fascinated him. In 1842 were published his satirical masterpiece, the first part of the novel *Mertvyye Dushi* (tr. D. Magarshack, *Dead Souls*, 1961), also his best-known short story *Shinel'* (tr. D. Magarshack, *The Overcoat*, 1956) and the comedy *Zhenit'ba* ('Marriage'). Deeply conscious of his responsibility as a leading Russian writer (especially after the death of Pushkin), his satires of bureaucracy and serfdom were interpreted by Belinsky as blows in the struggle for progress. But to Gogol' himself it was moral, rather than social or political evil that he was castigating, and he brooded over his own feelings of guilt and insufficiency. He laboured vainly at a second part to *Dead Souls*, which would show the transformation and regeneration of its negative characters, but burnt the manuscript (the positive characters in the surviving fragments are indeed lifeless). In 1847 he published *Vybrannyye mesta iz perepiski s druz'yami* ('Selected Passages from Correspondence with Friends'), a collection of moralizing essays defending the Tsarist regime and its institutions in a spirit of conservative religious orthodoxy; Belinsky's letter of denunciation became a declaration of faith for 19th-century Russian radicals. Gogol' made a pilgrimage to Palestine in 1848, but was unable to kindle in himself the warm faith he lacked. In his last years he became more and more a prey to despair and religious mania.

The roots of his satire lie in his own involved personality, riddled with anxieties and obsessions. His prosaic plots and mediocre scoundrels are seen in so grotesque a light, exaggerated with such uncanny caricature, that Chichikov's paper trade in dead serfs ('souls'), or the drab life of the poor clerk, Akakiy Akakiyevich, which hangs by the thread of a mere overcoat, or the farcical masquerading of Khlestakov as a government inspector, acquire a disturbing significance profounder than social satire, suggesting an artificiality in all human pretension, and often seeming to blur the distinction between people and things.

His style is a complex combination of colloquial and rhetorical elements. All that is elaborate and extreme in the Russian novel stems from him, just as the ideal of balance and simplicity stems from Pushkin. [AKT]

*Polnoye sobraniye sochineniy* (1937–52); *Works*, tr. C. Garnett (6 vols., 1922–8).

A. Bely, *Masterstvo Gogolya* (Moscow, 1934); V. Nabokov, *G.* (1944); J. Lavrin, *N.G.* (1951); D. Magarshack, *G.* (1957); G. A. Gukovsky, *Realizm G.* (Moscow, 1959).

**Goldfaden, Avraham** (Ukraine 1840–New York 1908). Yiddish playwright and poet. The father of the Yiddish theatre, he began writing light comedy in the early seventies, but was unable to produce his plays in Russia and therefore went to Jassy, Rumania, where in 1876 he founded the first professional Yiddish theatre. His success prompted others to form Yiddish troupes. He himself returned to Russia in 1880. Besides plays, he also wrote Hebrew poetry which he abandoned for Yiddish; he started a satirical weekly in Lemberg and another in Czernowitz. The Russian authorities eventually banned his theatre and, after a first successful visit to New York in 1887, he finally settled there in 1903. His plays and poems survive to the present day, and are even performed in Hebrew in Israel. [EE]

*Dos Yidele* (1866) (collected Yiddish Plays: *Di Yidene* (1896); *Di Rekruten* (1877); *Di Boobe mit'n ainikl* (1877); *Shmendrik* (1877/8); *Di shtume Kalle* (1877/8); *Kabtsanson und Hungerman* (1887); *Bar Kochbah* (1883); *Shulamith* (1889); *Doktor Almosado* (1898); *Ben Ami* (n.d.); *Di Kishef-Macherin* (n.d.).

B. Gorin, *Geschichte fun Iddishn Theater* (N.Y., 1929).

**Goldin, Ezra** (Russia 1867–Russia 1915). Hebrew writer. One of the first to express his attitude towards the rising nationalist movement. Most of his contemporaries were in favour of Jewish national aspirations and, although he endorsed them, Goldin expressed a fear that the secularization of Jewish life would lead to a substitution of material values for the old devotion to religion and learning which had upheld Judaism in the past. This is the general theme of his short stories and his novel, *Demon Yehudi* (1901). [EE]

Waxman, *HJL*; Klausner, *HMHL*.

**Goldoni, Carlo** (Venice 1707–Paris 1793). Italy's greatest comic playwright. Although he graduated at Padua University in 1731 his studies had been constantly interrupted by his passion for the theatre. His association with the company of S. Samuele at Venice led to his first success in 1734 – the popular drama *Belisario*. After a series of successful but now little-known tragicomedies, accompanied by more characteristic lively musical farces and *intermezzi*, *Momolo cortesan* in 1738 marked the real beginning of his reform of Italian comedy – the substitution of the author's own dialogue for the improvisation of the ⇨ *commedia dell'arte*. This change was only gradually accomplished and encountered stiff opposition to the end of his career. In all he wrote over 200 plays, many of the best (*La famiglia dell'antiquario*; *La bottega del caffè*, tr. H. B. Fuller, *The Coffee House*, 1925; *Il bugiardo*, tr. G. L. Fraser, *The Liar*, 1922; *La serva amorosa*) between 1748 and 1753, the year of his masterpiece, *La locandiera*; but bitter rivalry with Pietro Chiari and Carlo Gozzi's stubborn revival of the *commedia dell'arte* allowed him no complacency. In 1750, defying public feeling that he was 'finished', he arrogantly promised to write 16 new comedies in a year – and succeeded! In Paris, where he was invited in 1762 to revive the Comédie Italienne, he failed however to wean either public or actors from their attachment to the *commedia dell'arte*, and in 1765 began to teach Italian to the daughters of Louis XV, earning only a meagre pension. This, despite the success of *Le bourru bienfaisant* at the Comédie Française in 1771, left him destitute when, with the Revolution, it was withdrawn. He died a pauper. His memoirs (begun 1784, publ. 1787; tr. J. Black, 1926) are an important and pleasing document of 18th-century life. [RHC]

*Tutte le opere di C.G.*, ed. G. Ortolani (14 vols., 1935–56); *Opere*, ed. F. Zampieri (1954); *The Comedies of Goldoni* (*A Curious Mishap*, *The Beneficent Bear*, *The Fan*, *The Spendthrift Miser*), ed. H. Zimmern (1892); *The Good-Humoured Ladies*, tr. R. Aldington (1922); *The Servant of Two Masters*, tr. E. J. Dent (1952) *Three Comedies* (*La locandiera I rusteghi*, *Il ventaglio*), tr. C. Bax, E. and H. Farjeon, E M. Rawson (1961); *G. on Play-writing*, tr and compiled by F. C. L. van Steenderen (N.Y., 1919).

M. Apollonio, *L'opera di C.G.* (Milan, 1932) E. Rho, *La missione teatrale di C.G.* (Bari 1936); A. Gentile, *C.G. e gli attori* (Trieste 195 ); E. Caccia, *Carattere e caratteri nell commedia di G.* (Varese, 1958); G. Petronio. *G* (Palermo, 1958); *Guida* (1954); Binni. *CI* i *Maggiori*, i.

**Goldschmidt, Meïr Aron** (Vordingborg 1819–Frederiksberg 1887). Danish novelist. Of Jewish parents (and orthodox upbringing), he founded both the witty radical journal *Corsaren* (1840), famous for its attacks on Danish absolutism and its feud with Kierkegaard (1846), and later the more conservative journal *Nord og Syd* (1847). He travelled widely and considered settling in England (he himself translated his 3-volume novel *Hjemløs* (*Homeless*), 1861). His first significant novel was *En Jøde* (1845; tr. M. Howitt, *Jacob Bendixen, the Jew*, 1852); also in English are *Arvingen* (1863; tr. *The Heir*, 1865), *The Society of Virtue at Rome* (tr. anon., 1868), *Den flyvende Post* (1868–9; tr. C. Larsen, *The Flying Mail*, 1870), and some of his brilliant short stories, e.g. 'Avromche Nattergal' (tr. H. A. Larsen, *Denmark's Best Stories*, N.Y., 1928). His best novel, *Ravnen* (1867), has never been translated.

Goldschmidt's novels and stories are mostly concerned with Jewish life and traditions, and with the position of Jews in the Danish society. He is a master of style and ranks among the great novelists of Denmark. In 1877 he wrote his memoirs (*Livs erindringer og Resultater*), in which he expressed his philosophy of a belief in retributive justice. [ELB]

M. Brøndsted, *M.G.* (Copenhagen, 1965); E. L. Bredsdorff, *G.s 'Corsaren'* (Copenhagen, 1962).

**Goll, Iwan/Yvan** (St Dié, Vosges 1891–Paris 1950). German-French poet and experimental playwright. Beginning as an Expressionist, with poems in *Der Sturm* and *Der rote Hahn*, he founded the Rhein Verlag in Zürich (1914) – which published the first German translation of Joyce's *Ulysses* – where he met ⇨ Arp, ⇨ Werfel, ⇨ Jouve, ⇨ Romains and Joyce. With his wife, the poet Claire Goll, he moved to Paris (1919–39), where he was a friend of Picasso and Chagall, then to the U.S.A. (1939–47). In 1920, in the preface (written 1918) to his two 'Überdramen', *Die Unsterblichen*, Goll was the first (with ⇨ Apollinaire) to use the term *Überrealismus* (⇨ Surrealism). In 1924 the first (and only) number of his 'periodical' *Surréalisme* helped to establish the movement. Apart from his experimental dramas, and novels in French, he is a *major* lyric poet (collected *Dichtungen*, 1960), whose best-known work, the long cycle of poems *La Chanson de Jean sans terre* (1936; crit. edn, F. J. Carmody, Berkeley, Calif., 1962) was translated by William Carlos Williams and others as *Landless John* (San Francisco, 1944; new edn, intr. W. H. Auden, illustr. Chagall, Dali and Berman, N.Y., 1958). Other illustrators of his work include Picasso, Arp, Tanguy, Matisse. In *Traumkraut* (1951; outstanding with *Abendgesang*, 1954) Joyce's 'stream of consciousness' finds its poetic equivalent; the poems are based on visions induced by his last illness (leukemia). While Goll's imagery derives from free association (reminiscent of Dylan Thomas) it is most effectively controlled, though his artistry has for the most part only been fully realized by fellow artists. [PB]

Bridgwater, *TCGV*; Hamburger and Middleton, *MGP*.

F. J. Carmody, *The Poetry of Y.G.* (Paris, 1956); *Y.G. Quatre Études* (Paris, 1956); *Symposium* (Syracuse, N.Y., 1957); J. Müller, *Y.G. im deutschen Expressionismus* (East Berlin, 1962); D. Schaefer, *Die frühe Lyrik I.G.s* (Kiel, 1965) (dissertation); *GLL*, VIII, 3, 1955.

**Gombrowicz, Witold** (Małoszyce 1904–1969). Polish novelist. He began with the collection of short stories called *Pamiętnik z okresu dojrzewania* (1933). This moves in the violent borderlands of fantasy and dream, and its main themes are developed in the novel *Ferdydurke* (1937; tr. E. Mosbacher, 1961). Teasing and casual in tone, *Ferdydurke* probes deeply into the regressive appetites of man, into his adolescent and infantile obsessions. Evergreen schoolgirls, couples like the Youthfuls, the anal phraseology, are all part of the same hide-and-seek game, and the author advises the reader to 'start dancing with the book instead of asking for meanings'. After 1939 he lived in Argentina. There he wrote *Trans-Atlantyk* (1953), another experiment in style, and embarked on a long idiosyncratic diary. [JP]

*Pornografia* (1960; tr. A. Hamilton, 1966).
Ordon, *TCPS*.

**Gómez de Avellaneda, Gertrudis** (Puerto Príncipe, Cuba 1814–Madrid 1873). Spanish writer. She wrote conventionally romantic poetic dramas, poorly constructed but grandiosely tragic and eloquent, and once successful on stage (*Alfonso Munio*, 1844; *Saul*, 1849; *Baltasar*, 1858). The best of her love poems and a few deeply felt religious poems survive the bulk of her mediocre poetry (e.g. 'El miserere' or 'La ascensión'). She was twice widowed and this lent pessimistic depth to her natural piety. Her novel *Sab* (1841), about a slave in love with his master's daughter, is interesting for her childhood recollections of Cuba. [JMC]

*Obras* (4 vols., Havana, 1914); Blecua, *FLE*; Trend, *OBSV*.

**Gómez de la Serna, Ramón** (Madrid 1888–Buenos Aires 1963). *Avant-garde* Spanish writer. He developed a form of half-witty, half-poetic aphorism, 'humorous metaphors' in prose, which he called *Greguerías* (1910ff.; CA) and used to explore often surrealistic effects. His entertaining but facile talent enabled him to parody brilliantly international styles of the day in 6 *falsas novelas* (1926), to anticipate Pirandello in his *Teatro de soledad*, and draw biographical sketches of many writers and painters (*Lope de Vega*, *Goya*, etc.). His most famous novel is *El Rastro* (1918), vividly depicting the poor quarters of Madrid. His prolific writings include the autobiographical *Automoribundía*, 1948). [JMC]

*Obras completas* (Barabra, 1956ff.); CA, BC; *Mis mejores páginas literarias* (1957).

**Goncharov, Ivan Aleksandrovich** (Simbirsk, now Ulyanovsk 1812–St Petersburg 1891). Russian novelist. Son of a rich merchant family, he attended Moscow (1831–6), then Petersburg University (1837–52), and spent most of his life as a civil servant, eventually becoming a censor. Besides the publication of 3 novels, *Obyknovennaya istoriya* (1847; tr. C. Garnett, *A Common Story*, 1917), *Oblomov* (1859; tr. D. Magarshack, 1954), and *Obryv* (1869; tr. anon., *The Precipice*, 1915), the main event in his otherwise monotonous life was a voyage to Japan (1852–5) as secretary to a Russian mission, described in *Fregat Pallada* (1858). Both in himself and in his environment, he saw the clash between dreamy traditionalism (which could be well-meaning and imaginative) and vigorous practicality (which could be prosaically limited). This conflict is worked out in *A Common Story* with ingenious artificiality and in *The Precipice* with uneven diffuseness; but in *Oblomov* it is the foundation of one of the most profound Russian novels. The generous young nobleman Oblomov, incapable of action despite excellent intentions, loses the heroine to his practical friend Stolz, and eventually sinks into complete sloth, vegetating under the loving care of his simple landlady. Oblomov's inaction, conditioned by his upbringing, was declared by the radical critic Dobrolyubov to be typical of the Russian nobility; but the psychological implications are wider, and *Oblomov* is one of the principal Russian contributions to universal literature. [AKT]

*Sobraniye sochineniy* (8 vols., 1952–5).

J. Lavrin, *G.* (1954); G. A. Lensen, *The Russian Push towards Japan* (1959); A. G. Tseitlin, *I.A.G.* (Moscow, 1950); *SEER*, XXXVI, 87 (1958); Poggioli, *PS*.

**Goncourt, The Brothers, Edmond** (Nancy 1822–Champrosay 1896) and **Jules** (Paris 1830–Paris 1870). French writers. They formed one of the most famous literary partnerships. Sharing the same interests in literature and art, they wrote in collaboration, starting their careers with monographs on art and history, and produced, in 1854 and 1855, two social histories of French society during the Revolution and during the Directory. Their great work *L'art du dix-huitième siècle* (1859–75; tr. R. Ironside, 1948) contains most perceptive appreciations of Watteau, Boucher, Chardin and Fragonard. They were both passionate collectors and their interest in social history is reflected in their attitude to the novel. Their first novel, *En 1851*, had been a flop because of the *coup d'état* of that year, but gradually they built up an influential reputation as the originators of the *roman documentaire*. They set out to write novels as 'history which might have happened', taking the greatest pains to find out every detail necessary to set the scene. For example, for *Sœur Philomène* (1861) they studied hospital life from the inside, and for *Germinie Lacerteux* (1864; intr. M. Turnell, 1955) they made a study of one of their own servants who had served them faithfully for years while leading unknown to them a life of debauchery revealed only after her death from consumption. They are chiefly famous for the *Journal* (ed. R. Ricotte, 4 vols., 1956; selections tr. R. Baldick, 1962) which they began in 1851 and which was continued after the death of Jules in 1870 by Edmond; many conversations are reported verbatim and it is a fascinating source of information about French literary life from 1851 to 1895. Some of the most interesting entries are those describing the conversations at the Magny dinners with Sainte-Beuve presiding and with Gautier and a host of other famous figures including Turgenev. There are also passages describing life in Paris during the Franco-Prussian War and the Commune and, of course, Edmond's moving description of the mental disintegration and death of his brother. Edmond de Goncourt survived to become a well-known literary figure and his salon was a meeting place for writers. Proust parodied his style in the last book of *À la recherche du temps perdu.* Edmond did much to secure the recognition of Japanese art which was then becoming fashionable and he continued to write novels. These include *La fille Élisa* (1877), the story of a prostitute imprisoned for murder; *Les frères Zemganno* (1879), which deals with circus life; and *La Faustin* (1882), a study of an actress. On his death he left a sum of money to found the Académie Goncourt which awards the Prix Goncourt, the most famous French literary prize. [WA]

A. Billy, tr. M. Shaw, *The G. Brothers* (1960); R. Baldick, *The G.s* (1960).

**Góngora y Argote, Luis de** (Córdoba 1561–Córdoba 1627). Spanish poet. Of a cultured and distinguished family, he lived well as a student at Salamanca and as a prebendary of Córdoba cathedral in minor orders. In 1588 he was arraigned before the bishop for talking during mass, consorting with gossips, going to bullfights and writing profane verse; to the end of his days he was renowned as a wit, and he loved sociable discourse, music and public display. He was a good administrator and a tactful envoy, and he travelled widely on the chapter's business. A visit to the capital (1609) filled him with a disillusionment which is at the heart of his great poems. He composed the *Polifemo* and the first *Soledad* in a country retreat near Córdoba in 1612–13. The fame which these won him led him to renew his ambition for preferment, and he returned to Madrid in 1617 as a royal chaplain, in full orders; beset by money troubles and illness, he returned to Córdoba to die. In his person and in his poetry Góngora aroused strong feelings of devotion or detestation, and he revelled in conflict. His satirical verse made him many enemies, and the great poems of 1612–13 provoked one of the biggest literary wars of all time. Velázquez's portrait (1622) catches the sharp intelligence and the profundity of the man.

Something in his early verse foretold later greatness. He is a masterly maker of sonnets, handling the stock themes neatly and with a rich colour sense; his early *romances* show a fine sense of language, especially in its musical aspect, and a great zest for life; and his *letrillas* have both wit and humour. The poet gradually developed the style known as *gongorismo* or ⇨ *culteranismo*, in which he took to extremes the tendencies of earlier Renaissance verse, notably that of ⇨ Herrera. In this he subtly adapts to Spanish the richness of Classical Latin vocabulary and syntax, dislocating the normal word-order to achieve effects of balance and to enhance rhythms and rhymes. He revels in word-play and mythological allusion and devises elaborate metaphors which make us see new aspects of reality and new relationships. At 50 he ventured upon longer poems in keeping with the grandeur of this concept of poetry: *Oda a la toma de Larache* (1611), *Fábula de Polifemo y Galatea* (1612–13; ed. and intr. D. Alonso, 2 vols., 1961), and the *Soledades*, of which he almost completed two of the four planned (1612–17; ed. D. Alonso, with Spanish prose version, 3rd edn, 1956; tr. E. M. Wilson, 1965). The *Polifemo* uses, in highly artistic *ottava rima*, the tale of the Cyclops to portray man, love and evil in the setting of a primitive Sicily. In the more freely constructed stanzas and even more involved diction of the *Soledades* Góngora describes an ideal society, materially primitive but morally rich, viewed through the eyes of a wanderer from the outside world. It is a backward glance at the golden age of mankind, a hymn to the splendours of nature, a thesis about the harmony in which man once lived with nature, and a sermon about materialistic attitudes in the Spain of Philip III.

Góngora dominated Spanish verse throughout the 17th century, but his reputation declined in the 18th, and in the 19th he became a byword for obscurity and even poetic insanity. In our own time he has enjoyed an astonishing revival, thanks to the efforts of such scholars as Dámaso Alonso and to the discovery of his work by the fine young poets of the 1920s, who were deeply influenced by him. His place is now a very high one and he seems secure in it. [CCS]

*Obras poéticas*, ed. R. Foulché-Delbosc (3 vols., N.Y., 1921); *Obras completas*, ed. J. and I. Millé y Giménez (5th edn, 1961); Trend, *OBSV*; Perry, *HASP*; Cohen, *PBSV*.

M. Artigas, *Don L. de G. y A. Biografía y estudio*

*crítico* (Madrid, 1925); D. Alonso, *Estudios y ensayos gongorinos* (Madrid, 1955); D. Alonso, *La lengua poética de G.* (3rd edn, Madrid, 1961).

**Gonzaga, Tomás António** (Oporto 1744–Mozambique 1810). Portuguese pre-Romantic poet. He graduated in Law at Coimbra and, after a brief spell as a civil servant in Beja, became a magistrate in Vila Rica, the capital of the Brazilian state of Minas Gerais. Arrest for sedition led to imprisonment, eventual deportation to Angola and finally ten years' exile in Mozambique, where he chose to spend the rest of his days, once married into a wealthy family. While in Brazil he was the principal figure in the Escola de Minas, a group of Brazilian neo-classical poets. Jointly claimed by both Brazilian and Portuguese literatures, he is considered the leading lyricist of Brazil's colonial period. Writing under the Arcadian pseudonym of Dirceu, he dedicated many of his lyrics to a Brazilian girl known to us only as Marília. His major collection, *Marília de Dírceu*, was first published in 1792 in Lisbon, has known more editions than any other collection of lyrics in the language and is only surpassed in editions in any *genre* by the *Lusíadas* of Camões. Apart from minor poems he wrote also a juridical treatise (*Direito Natural*) and is thought to be the most probable author of the anonymous and inflammatory *Cartas Chilenas*. A complete critical edition of his works did not appear until 1942–4. Of his contemporaries, only Anastácio da Cunha matched the love-lorn melancholy of his lyricism, the quality of which lies in its melodious texture and profound subjectivism. [RCW]

*Obras Completas*, ed. M. Rodrigues Lapa (S. Paulo, 1942–4).

J. de Castro Osório, *Gonzaga e a Justiça* (Lisbon, 1950); A. Coutinho (ed.), *A Literatura no Brasil*, I i (Rio de Janeiro, 1955).

**González, Ángel** (Oviedo 1925– ). Spanish poet. One of the most recent 'realistic' generation, he writes with great restraint and a total absence of rhetoric. His short lines, deliberately anti-Romantic, show great human warmth, a resolute revolutionary spirit that is free from illusions, and an ultimate hope for '*paz y patria feliz,/ orden,/silencio*' – 'peace and a happy country, order, silence'. [JMC]

*Áspero mundo* (1955); *Sin esperanza con convencimiento* (Barcelona, 1961); *Grado elemental* (Paris, 1962).

**González, Diego Tadeo** (Ciudad Rodrig 1732–Madrid 1794). Spanish poet an Augustinian preacher. He was one of th first to reject the baroque tradition an return to the 16th-century manner of Lui de ◇ León; his translation of the 8th Psalr shows him at his best. His Eclogues an idylls were also once admired, while 'E murciélago alevoso', an invective agains the bold bat that disturbed his mistres while she was writing a poem, was fo long a popular burlesque. The first editio of his collected poems appeared in 179( [JMC]

BAE, 61; Blecua, *FLE*; Trend, *OBSV*.

**Gordon, Yehuda Leib,** writing unde pseudonym YLG (Vilna 1830–St Peter burg 1892). Hebrew novelist, poet an essayist. The most important poet of th Haskalah movement, he was the first t employ not only the Hebrew of Biblic style, but the most exact expressions c post-Biblical literature, thus the founder c a new style of Hebrew poetry. In 1879 wa imprisoned by Russian authorities as political conspirator and contracted a incurable disease in prison. When release became editor of *Ha-melitz*. His fir romantic poems had a Biblical setting o the love of King David and Michal (1857 later he dedicated another long, but n longer romantic, poem to King David. I 1860 he published a collection of fabl *Mishle Yehuda*, adapted from Talmudi legends and European fabulists. His poet work had a lasting influence on Hebre poetry. His works were first published i Russian and later in Israel. [EE]

A. B. Rhine, *L.G.* (Philadelphia, 1920).

**Gor'ky, Maksim,** pseud. of Aleksey Mi haylovich Peshkov (Nizhniy-Novgoro 1868–Moscow 1936). Russian novelist an dramatist. He lost his parents early and w sent out to work when only 8. He rea voraciously in his spare time and later bega to write himself. His first story, *Mak Chudra*, was published in 1892. He becan famous with the publication of two volum of short stories in 1898. Many of the stories are passionately romantic in the subject-matter and their ideals of supe human beauty and nobility, for examp *Starukha Izergil*' (1895); others, like *Na s* (1893), are grimly realistic descriptions the inhumanity of man to man. His be stories of this period, *Chelkash* (1895) ar

*Dvadtsat' shest' i odna* (1899; both in *Twenty-Six Men and a Girl*, tr. E. Jakovlev and D. B. Montefiore, 1902), combine these two conflicting tendencies with great power and tenderness. The early works culminate in his first novel *Foma Gordeyev* (1899; tr. H. Bernstein, 1928), a study of the decline of a Volga merchant-family.

Gor'ky was naturally a revolutionary and in 1901 he was arrested because of his openly seditious prose-poem *Burevestnik* (1901). The next year his election to the Academy of Sciences and Letters was annulled because of official disapproval. His plays, notably *Na dne* (1902; tr. M. Budberg, *The Lower Depths*, 1959), were greeted as political rather than literary events. His revolutionary activity came to a head during 1905 when he was arrested and imprisoned, but on the intervention of Western writers this sentence was commuted to exile. He went to America to collect funds for the Bolsheviks, but his mission boomeranged when it was revealed (by the Tsarist Embassy) that he was not married to his travelling companion. He was at once ostracized; in retaliation he wrote *Gorod Zholtogo D'yavola* (*The City of the Yellow Devil*, 1906), a vitriolic attack on the American way of life; and *Mat'* (1907; tr. I. Schneider, *Mother*, 1947), a novel about revolutionaries in a Russian industrial town. The tendentious nature of these works, however, adversely affected his literary reputation.

In 1907–13 Gor'ky lived mostly in Capri. Here he kept up his contacts with the Bolsheviks, but the works that he wrote at this time are less tendentious. The best of them, *Ispoved'* (1909; tr. R. Strunsky, *The Confession*, 1916), an attempt to found a new popular religion reconciling Marxism and Christianity, earned Lenin's disapproval and has been largely ignored by Soviet critics. Other works deal with the stagnation of Russian provincial towns, *Gorodok Okurov* (1910), and *Zhizn' Matveya Kozhemyakina* (tr. M. Wettlin, *The Life of M.K.*, 1960).

In 1913 he returned home, where he continued to support the Bolsheviks. But after the Revolution he became openly critical of their dictatorial methods. None the less he worked hard to keep cultural activity alive and to save writers from starvation by initiating a colossal project *Vsemirnaya literatura* (*World Literature*), a series of translations to embrace the classics of all ages and all races. At the same time he produced some of his finest works. He continued his autobiographical trilogy: *Detstvo*, *V lyudyakh* and *Moi universitety* (1913, 1918, 1923; tr. I. Schneider, *Autobiography*, 1953), and wrote his recollections of Tolstoy (1919; tr. S. S. Koteliansky and L. Woolf, 1948), perhaps his masterpiece.

Ostensibly because of ill-health, but partly on account of his disagreements with the leading Bolsheviks, Gor'ky went abroad again in 1921. He continued to keep in touch with young Soviet writers, however, and some of them visited him in Sorrento. His own work of this period harks back to his pre-Revolutionary themes, sometimes with new intensity as in *Delo Artamonovykh* (1925; tr. A. Brown, *The Artamonov Business*, 1935). The short stories *Karamora* (1924) and *Rasskaz o geroye* (1924) are among his most powerful and display his curious fascination with the ideas and methods of Dostoyevsky. But his last novel, the vast, unfinished *Zhizn' Klima Samgina* (1925–36; Pt I, tr. B. Guerney, *The Bystander*, 1930; Pts II, III, IV, tr. A. Bakshy, *The Magnet*, *Other Fires*, *The Specter*, 1931–38) is weak and formless.

Meanwhile his reputation inside Russia was declining. He was criticized for his contacts with Western intellectuals and his unwillingness to deal with contemporary Soviet subjects. In 1928 he returned to Russia for the summer; his impressions of the Soviet scene were recorded in a series of sketches *Po Soyuzu Sovetov* (1928–9), devoted to Soviet industrialization. After a few more visits he finally settled in Russia in 1931. His return was an occasion for national rejoicing, and he has since come to be regarded as the father of Soviet literature. In 1932 he became Chairman of the new Union of Soviet Writers and advocated socialist realism as the literary method of Soviet writers. His own novel *Mat'* was taken as the model. He had long been in poor health, but the circumstances of his death are still mysterious. It was later made the pretext for the arrest and execution of Yagoda, Chief of the NKVD.

Gor'ky's prose-style is undistinguished, his imagery frequently trite, and his longer works are shapeless. But his best work carries rare power and conviction. He had little imagination, but the breadth and variety of his experience easily made up for this deficiency. A convinced humanist, he was well aware of the baseness latent in human nature. Hence his lifelong feud with the work of Dostoyevsky, which none the less influenced him deeply. Yet for all his humanitarian ideals he instinctively admired physical strength even when misused; and it is these contradictory aspects of his nature which dictate much of his finest prose, *Dvadtsat' shest' i odna* and *Delo Artamonovykh.*

His plays suffer even more than his novels from his technical shortcomings. The pre-Revolutionary plays owe their success almost entirely to extra-literary circumstances. The later ones, *Somov i drugiye* (1931), *Yegor Bulychov i drugiye* (1931) and *Dostigayev i drugiye* (1932), form part of an uncompleted cycle of plays intended to cover Russian history from February 1917 to the 1930s. [RDBT]

*Sobraniye sochineniy* (30 vols., 1949–55) (most of Gor'ky's works are available in English translations).

A. S. Kaun, *M.G. and his Russia* (N.Y., 1931); B. V. Mikhaylovsky and Ye. B. Tager, *Tvorchestvo M.G.* (Moscow, 1958); *B. Byalik, M.G. dramaturg* (Moscow, 1962); S. Kastorsky, *G. khudozhnik* (Leningrad, 1963).

**Gorter, Herman** (Wormerveer 1864–Brussels 1927). Dutch poet. While still reading classics at Leyden he joined the circle of young poets of the 1880 movement. His first published poem and masterpiece, *Mei* (1889), shows the influence of Keats and ⇨ Verwey. The three cantos of this poem represent the carefree, adolescent discovery of beauty, the maturer desire to transcend mortality in 'pure' abstract verse and, finally, Mei's death after the poet's realization that he has sought the impossible. Striking associations and startlingly free style are developed further in the hypersensitive, experimental verse of *De School der Poezie* (1897, including an earlier collection of 1892). Here primordial urges inspire unrestrained imagery in some of the most intense poetry in Dutch. Gorter recognized that his orgies of feeling were carrying him to the verge of insanity, and, like others of the Movement, he turned to philosophy, to Spinoza and later Marx. A group of contemplative sonnets is followed by a translation of Spinoza's *Ethica* (1895). With H. ⇨ Roland Holst-van der Schalk he repudiated his 1880 individualism and bourgeois background; his long Marxist epic *Pan* (1916) is, however, psychologically so unconvincing that it highlights his isolation from the masses whose spokesman he claimed to be. [PK]

*Verzamelde Werken* (8 vols., 1948–52); *De groote dichters* (1935); *Twintig gedichten in handschrift*, ed. G. Stuiveling (1964); *H.G. Documentatio*, ed. E. Endt (1964); *Verzameld Lyrick tot 1905* (1966); Barnouw, *CA*; Snell, *FFG*; Weevers, *PNEC*.

H. Roland Holst, *H.G.* (Amsterdam, 1933).

**Gottfried von Neifen** (fl. mid 13th cent.). German ⇨ Minnesinger. Member of a noble Swabian family. His work set the tone for much of the Minnesang of the later 13th century. Building on the substitution of the village maiden for the noble lady of the court, he took the courtly lyric into an atmosphere of realism which recalls at times the world of folk-song, and in which directness of manner is sometimes synonymous with vulgarity. At the same time he is a keen observer of the social scene, and possessed of an effective poetic technique. [RT]

Poems and commentary in Kraus, *DL*.

**Gottfried von Strassburg** (fl. 1210). Medieval German poet. Author of a great epic, left incomplete, on the legend of Tristan and Isolde. The circumstances of his life are unknown, but it can be inferred that, though not of noble birth, he spent his life in the society of the well-born, and his work gives evidence both of remarkably wide learning and great poetic skill. It was through his *Tristan* that Wagner first met the legend which he treated in his opera *Tristan und Isolde*. [RT]

*Tristan*, ed. F. Ranke (1930; tr. A. T. Hatto, 1960).

G. Weber, *G. v. S. Tristan und die Krise des hochmittelalterlichen Weltbildes um 1200* (Stuttgart, 1953); D. de Rougemont, *Passion and Societ*y (1956).

**Gotthelf, Jeremias,** pseud. of Albert Bitziu (Murten 1797–Lützelflüh 1854). German Swiss novelist. After studying theology a Berne and Göttingen, he became a Protestant pastor in the Canton of Berne, livin from 1831 at the village of Lützelflüh. Hi first novel, *Der Bauernspiegel* (1837), give a critical picture of social conditions in th countryside where he lived. During his lifetime *Wie Uli der Knecht glücklich wir* (1841; tr. Julia Firth, *Ulric the Farm Servan* 1888), the humorous and realistic story c a farm-servant, was his best-known work its sequel, *Uli der Pächter*, appeared in 1848. Among his best novels are *Geld und Geist* (1843–4; tr. anon., *Wealth and Welfare*, 1866) and *Anne Bäbi Jowäger* (1843–4), both narratives of family life and farming; the former shows Emmental life in its idyllic aspects, while the latter begins as a satire and gradually acquires a more earnest manner. He frequently introduces didactic themes into his writing; his realism of characterization and of setting is immediately noticeable in his novels and in many of his shorter narrative works, as is his distinctive style. Of the shorter works, *Hans Joggeli, der Erbvetter* (1848) is a felicitous example. In a number of his tales set in the Bernese past Gotthelf introduces fantasy; the most widely known of these is *Die schwarze Spinne* (1842; tr. H. M. Waidson, *The Black Spider*, 1958), where a medieval plague-legend forms the inset-story to the account of a christening ceremony. [HMW]

H. Boeschenstein, *G.: Hans Joggeli, der Erbvetter* (1961); K. Fehr, *J.G.* (Zürich, 1954), *J.G.* (*Albert Bitzius*) (Stuttgart, 1967); W. Günther, *J.G. Wesen und Werk* (Berlin, Bielefeld, Munich, 1954); W. Muschg, *G. Die Geheimnisse des Erzählers* (Munich, 1931), *J.G. Eine Einführung in seine Werke* (Berne, 1954); H. M. Waidson, *J.G.* (1953).

**Gottschalk** (*c.*808–*c.*868). Given to the abbey of Fulda at an early age, Gottschalk was prevented from leaving his Order by ⇨ Hrabanus Maurus, then abbot of Fulda. After some years in the monastery of Orbais spent in studying the theology of St Augustine and St ⇨ Fulgentius of Ruspa, he became convinced of the doctrine of double predestination, that is, that the damned are predestined to Hell as the elect are to Heaven. For this heretical belief he was condemned in 848 by the council of Quierzy, under the direction of Hincmar, archbishop of Reims, to be flogged and then imprisoned. He thus found himself at the centre of a controversy which raged for many years and was never officially resolved. Among his opponents, besides Hincmar and Hrabanus Maurus, was John Scot Erigena, while his supporters included Ratramnus of Corbie, Prudentius, bishop of Troyes, Loup, abbot of Ferrières, and Rémi, archbishop of Lyon. Gottschalk at first burnt his confession of faith, under the effect of the flogging, but during his imprisonment wrote two new confessions, and resisted all Hincmar's attempts to make him recant, even when refused all rites on his deathbed. While in prison he also wrote a quantity of verse, not without merit. [MRM]

Migne, *PL*, 121 (confessions, letter to Ratramnus, extracts from Hincmar); MGH, PLAC, iii (poems); tr. F. Brittain, *Penguin Book of Latin Verse* (1962); ed. C. Lambot, *Spicilegium Sacrum Lovaniense*, 20 (1945) (theological and grammatical works).

**Gottsched, Johann Christoph** (Juditten, Königsberg 1700–Leipzig 1766). German critic. Before becoming a professor in Leipzig, he had exerted considerable influence on the intellectual and literary life of his age as editor of two periodicals, *Die vernünftigen Tadlerinnen* (1725–6) and *Der Biedermann* (1727–9). His *Versuch einer kritischen Dichtkunst* (1729) made him for a generation the principal theoretician and literary dictator of the Enlightenment (cf. ⇨ Bodmer, ⇨ Breitinger). Poetry, he held, was a matter of knowing and following the rules; the unities were to be observed and literature was to serve a moral, didactic aim. The wandering theatre with its emphasis on slapstick and crude theatrical effects and particularly 'Hanswurst', the commentator-clown, with his broad, often coarse humour, were rejected in favour of the works of French Classicism, which were declared to be the models native German dramatists should imitate. His wife's translations of Molière, his own *Der sterbende Cato* (1732) and the translated and adapted plays published in the 6 volumes of *Die deutsche Schaubühne* (1740–5) were intended as the nucleus of a German national drama. Though ridiculed by ⇨ Lessing, he did clear the ground for the creation of a serious national theatre. His *Grundlegung einer deutschen Sprachkunst* (1748) played a modest role in the establishment of a canon of correct German. [WAC]

*Gesammelte Schriften*, ed. E. Reichel (6 vols., 1901–6); DLE (*Aufklärung*); *Versuch*, photo repr. (1962).

E. Reichel, *G.* (2 vols., Berlin, 1908–12); E. Kriessbach, *Die Trauerspiele in G.s deutscher Schaubühne* (Halle, 1928); Cassirer, *PE*.

**Götz, Johann Nikolaus** (Worms 1721–Winterburg 1781). German poet. Studied at Halle (1739–42); French army chaplaincy (1748); church appointments at Forbach (1744ff.), Meisenheim (1754ff.), Winterburg (1761ff.). With ⇨ Gleim and ⇨ Uz the main exponent of German

Anacreontic poetry (combining the praise of 'wine, women, and song' with pastoral sentiment and Rococo middle-class morality). His works include *Versuch eines Wormsers in Gedichten* (1745), *Vermischte Gedichte* (ed. K. W. Ramler, 1785), the adaptions *Die Oden Anakreons in reimlosen Versen* (with Uz, 1746) and *Die Gedichte Anakreons und der Sappho* (1760). [LL]

Killy, *DLTZ*.

**Gourmont, Rémy de.** ⇨ French Literary Criticism in the 19th and 20th Centuries.

**Govoni, Corrado** (Tamara, Ferrara 1884–Rome 1965). Italian poet and novelist. Beginning in the style of the ⇨ 'Crepuscolari', he later belonged to the ⇨ Futurist group, and then to that of 'La Voce' in Florence. His more important collections are *Le fiale* (1903), *Fuochi d'artifizio* (1905), *Poesie elettriche* (1911), *L'inaugurazione della primavera* (1915), *Brindisi alla notte* (1924), *Il flauto magico* (1932), *Govonigiotto* (1943), *Aladino, lamento su mio figlio morto* (1946), *Preghiera al trifoglio* (1953). His technique of associative imagery tends to produce a 'catalogue' effect, though in the war years (particularly after his son was killed) he achieved some poetry of greater power. His novels, of which the most recent was *Uomini sul delta* (1960), are less important. [AKT]

*Poesie*, ed. G. Ravegnani (Milan, 1961).

**Gozzano, Guido** (Torino 1883–Aglie Canavese 1916). Italian poet. With ⇨ Corazzini the foremost of the 'Crepuscolari' (twilight) poets, whose style self-consciously reflects the decadent literary tastes of the *fin-de-siècle*. Deeply aware that the old order of society and culture was crumbling, he remained an ironic observer, evoking in tones of subdued melancholy a world of old houses and sleepy gardens, hospital wards and Sunday boredom, withered flowers, shabby paintings, dusty relics forgotten in attics, all the many little things (in a famous phrase) 'of bad taste'. Opposed to the rhetoric of D'Annunzio and affecting a discursive style near sometimes to prose, he is at his best in moments of playful poise between anguish and detachment. [GD]

*Le poesie* (1960).

**Gozzi, Carlo** (Venice 1720–Venice 1806). Italian writer. Brother of Gasparo ⇨ Gozzi, member of the purist Accademia dei Granelleschi. He is known chiefly for his opposition to the theatrical reforms of ⇨ Goldoni and for his attempted revival of the ⇨ *commedia dell'arte*. After his polemical attack against Goldoni and Chiari in *La Tartana degli influssi* (1757), Goldoni asserted that public approval of his innovations proved their desirability, to which Gozzi replied that the public was fickle enough to approve even of a children's fable on the stage. He proved the point with his famous *Fiabe*, the first – *L'amore delle tre melarance* (1761) – being so successful that 9 others followed (1761–5). With their mixture of regular comedy and improvisation they also appealed to the Romantics for elements of the grotesque and fantastic. His *Memorie inutili* (1797–8; tr. J. A. Symonds, *Useless Memories*, ed. P. Horne, 1962) reveal his artistic temperament and shed interesting light on 18th-century culture. [RHC]

*Opere* (14 vols., 1801–2); *Opere. Teatro e polemiche teatrali*, ed. G. Petronio (1962); *Letterati memorialisti e viaggiatori del '700*, ed. E. Bonora (1951); *Il mostro turchino*, tr. E. J. Dent, *The Blue Monster* (Cambridge, 1951); *C.G.'s Reflective Analysis of his Fable Entitled The Love of Three Oranges*, tr. J. A. Symonds (Boston, 1959).

G. B. Magrini, *I tempi, la vita e gli scritti di C.G.* (Benevento, 1883); M. Fubini, 'Arcadia e Illuminismo' in *Dal Muratori al Baretti* (Bari, 1954); *Minori*, iii.

**Gozzi, Gasparo** (Venice 1713–Padua 1786). Italian writer. Brother of Carlo ⇨ Gozzi. Though enduring great financial hardship and having to spend much time on hack translating during the period 1750–60, he was able to publish his *Lettere diverse* (1750–2) and the famous *Difesa di Dante* (1758). Between 1760 and 1762 he produced 3 journals, *La gazzetta veneta*, *Il mondo morale* and *L'osservatore veneto*, establishing a firm reputation for elegant style, sound judgement, good taste, and a concern for good traditions as well as a willingness (unlike his brother) to accept good innovations. His first satirical *Sermoni* on various themes appeared collectively in 1763, the last six posthumously in 1794. Appointed by the Magistero dei Riformatori in 1770 to prepare a plan of educational reform, his writings on the subject were notable for their adherence to the most advanced thought of his age. [RHC]

*Opere*, ed. A. Dalmistro (16 vols., 1818–20).

*Scritti scelti*, ed. N. Mangini (1960); *Letterati memorialisti e viaggiatori del '700*, ed. E. Bonora (1957); *La gazzetta veneta*, ed. A. Zardo (1956).

A. Zardo, *G.G. nella letteratura del suo tempo in Venezia* (Bologna, 1926); G. de Beauville, *G.G. Journaliste vénitien du 18e siècle* (Paris, 1937); M. Fubini in *Dal Muratori al Baretti* (Bari, 1954); *Minori*, iii.

**Grabbe, Christian Dietrich** (Detmold 1801–Detmold 1836). German dramatist. A jail supervisor's son, he studied law at Leipzig (1820–4). After attempts at acting and freelance writing in Berlin (1822–3), quarrels with Heine and Das ⇨ Junge Deutschland, and failure to secure ⇨ Tieck's help, he joined the Detmold civil service, which he eventually had to quit for irregularities. Unhappily married in 1833, he failed to find equilibrium in collaborating with ⇨ Immermann in Frankfurt from 1834. He died of TB and alcoholism. His work reflects both his neuroses and the contemporary loss of idealistic belief through rising pragmatism and materialism. Influenced by young Schiller, Byron and Shakespeare (whom he attacks in *Abhandlung über die Shakespearo-Manie*, 1827), his tragedies combine realism, loose epic structure, historical acuteness, bombast, violence, grotesque irony, determinism and nihilism. His heroes usually perish in conflicts between intellect and emotion, sensuality and spirituality, individuality and mass instincts, creating the impression of a destructive fate in a senseless universe. His *Dramatische Dichtungen* (1827) include the Gothic *Herzog Theodor von Gothland*, the literary and social comedy *Scherz, Satire, Ironie und tiefere Bedeutung* (1827; tr. B. Wright, *Comedy, Satire, Irony and Deeper Meaning*, 1955), and the Roman fragments *Marius und Sulla*. While *Don Juan und Faust* (1829) features legendary characters, *Kaiser Friedrich Barbarossa* (1829) and *Kaiser Heinrich VI* (1830) dramatize Hohenstauffen history. *Napoleon oder die hundert Tage* (1831) and *Die Hermannsschlacht* (posth. 1838) anticipate naturalistic, expressionistic and film techniques. [LL]

*Werke und Briefe*, ed. A. Bergmann (6 vols., 1960ff.).

E. A. H. C. Diekmann, *C.D.G.* (Detmold, 1936); A. Bergmann, *C.D.G.* (Detmold, 1954); A. Closs, *Medusa's Mirror* (1957); Koch, *IW*; Wiese, *DT*.

**Gracián y Morales, Baltasar** (Belmonte 1601–Tarazona 1658). Spanish moralist and novelist. Educated by the Jesuits, whom he joined (1619), frequenter of literary circles in Zaragoza and Madrid, he was censured for writing frivolous works. His first books are *El héroe* (1637), with Philip IV as the model hero, and *El político Fernando* (1640), an apology for Ferdinand the Catholic. *El discreto* (1646) describes the qualities required for such a man for whose guidance *El oráculo manual y arte de prudencia* (1647; tr. L. B. Walton, 1953) provides 300 maxims. This latter work influenced La Rochefoucauld, La Bruyère and Voltaire. The main themes treated are prudence, self-knowledge, the right use of reason, *desengaño*, and dissimulation. The style is a condensed, sententious prose, full of subtle conceits, and known as 'Conceptismo', which Gracián analyses with examples in the *Agudeza y arte de ingenio* (1648). His major work *El Criticón* (1651–3–7) was printed under the name García Morlanes (an anagram). This allegory is in three sections: youth, maturity, and old age. It describes the journey of Critilo (rational man) and Andrenio (natural man) through the world. They experience its deceptions and pitfalls until by the right use of reason and virtue they attain immortality. The basic pessimism is lightened by Christian ideas and an unexpected humour. Apart from his influence on French literature, Gracián was read in Germany – he had considerable effect on Schopenhauer, whose pessimism owes much to him. [JG]

*Obras completas*, ed. E. Correa Calderón (1944); *Oráculo manual*, ed. M. Romera-Navarro (1954); *El Criticón* (same editor, 1938); *El héroe*, *El discreto*, in CA.

A. Coster, *B.G., 1601–1658* (Paris, 1913; Sp. tr. 1947); E. Correa Calderón, *B.G. Su vida y su obra* (Madrid, 1961); A. F. G. Bell, *B.G.* (1921).

**Gracq, Julien** (Saint-Florent-le-Vieil 1910– ). French novelist and critic. History master in a Paris lycée, his first novel, *Au château d'Argol* (1939; tr. Louise Varèse, *The Castle of Argol*, 1951), did not win the wide recognition he was to achieve with *Un beau ténébreux* (1945; tr. W. Strachan, *A Dark Stranger*, 1951), *Le rivage des Syrtes* (1951), for which he was awarded – and declined – the Prix Goncourt, and *Un balcon en forêt* (1958; tr. R. Howard, *A Balcony in the Forest*, 1960). Deeply influenced by Surrealism – cf. also his *André Breton* (1948) and preface to *Les Chants de*

*Maldoror* (1947) – he draws freely on subconscious and oneiric experience. This technique combines with his use of ancient Celtic myth to give his novels a sense of mystery and quest, which the narrative never fully resolves and which, along with a fastidiously precise prose style, gives his writing its particular flavour. His critical works include *La littérature à l'estomac* (1950; tr. in *Transition*, 6, 1950) and *Préférences* (1961). His play *Le roi pêcheur* (1948) is a revival of the Grail legend; his translation of Kleist's *Penthesilea* (1954) is further evidence of his interest in mythological, chthonic subjects. [IHW]

G. Picon, *L'usage de la lecture*, ii (Paris, 1961); *N.R.F.*, 101 and 103 (Paris, 1961); Mourgue, *DDL*.

**Graf, Oskar Maria** (Berg a. Starnberger See 1894–1967). German novelist. A socialist, pacifist, humanitarian revolutionary. He took part in left-wing activities in Bavaria before 1933, emigrated to Czechoslovakia, and lived from 1938 in the U.S.A. His utopian novels (e.g. *Die Erben des Untergangs*, 1959) are weaker than his Bavarian peasant novels (*Bolwieser*, 1931, tr. M. Goldsmith, *The Station Master*, 1933; *Der harte Handel*, 1935; *Der Abgrund*, 1936, etc.) of which the best is the semi-autobiographical *Das Leben meiner Mutter* (1936–7, published 1947; *The Life of my Mother*, 1940). His short stories about peasant life include *Kalendergeschichten* (1958), *Das bayrische Dekameron* (1959), *Der grosse Bauernspiegel* (1962).

*Wir sind Gefangene* (1927; tr. M. Greek, *Prisoners All*, 1928) (autobiography).

E. Dabringhaus, *The Works of O.M.G.* (Michigan, 1957).

**'Grail, Cycle of the.'** A major cycle of works in medieval French deriving largely from the *Conte du Graal* (*Perceval*) by ⇨ Chrétien de Troyes. The symbols of the lance that wounds and lays waste and the cup, or horn, of plenty that restores happiness and abundance are found in early fertility rites. Chrétien combines the Celtic theme of the stricken Fisher King who must be healed and the Waste land that must be made fertile with the Christian theme of Perceval, a human soul sterile through ignorance, and redeemed by charity. As Perceval's character deepens, the Grail takes on a Christian meaning. Faced with the mystery of the Lance and Grail carried in procession, Perceval fails the test imposed on him because he lacks charity. The Grail, seen through his eyes, appears merely as a wide, deep dish for carrying food. When, after much suffering during his Quest for the Grail Castle, he turns to the Christian religion, he learns that the Grail contains a life-giving Eucharistic host. The combination of Lance and Grail in the procession in the Castle of the Fisher King could not fail to suggest to a 12th-century audience the Lance of Longinus and the Chalice of the Last Supper, relics preserved for centuries at Jerusalem. The inspiration of the Grail procession can be shown to be both Celtic and Christian: some scholars relate it to the rites used for the celebration of Mass in the Byzantine Church.

Chrétien died before completing his work. The stories of Perceval and of his courtly rival Gawain were taken up in four major and very long *Continuations* written in the first half of the 13th century. It is likely that the authors of these works were also using a source related to that followed by Chrétien.

Robert de Boron wrote his *Roman de l' Estoire dou Graal* shortly after 1200 and intended it to be an authoritative account of the origins of the Grail. Whereas Chrétien had hinted enigmatically at the Grail's symbolical Christian connexions, Robert de Boron defines it as the Chalice containing the Holy Blood gathered by Joseph of Arimathea. He describes how this Chalice was brought to Britain, a symbol of the New Testament and the evangelical power which would convert the country to Christianity.

The Cluniac influence of the abbey of Glastonbury, which can be discerned behind the work of Robert de Boron, is expressed directly in the *Perlesvaus*. This prose romance written in Franco-Picard, probably in England shortly before 1202 depicts the Grail Quest as a call to arms on behalf of the Church in order to convert the people to the New Law or Testamnent.

But the outstanding work concerning the Grail, and indeed all Arthurian material in medieval French, was the cyclical *Prose Lancelot*, sometimes called the Vulgate Version, compiled from older sources by various hands probably under a central direction between 1220 and 1230. The branches of this vast and fine work, which enjoyed great popularity, are the *Estoire del Saint Graal*, *Merlin*, *Lancelot*, *Queste del Saint Graal*, and *Mort Artu*. In the *Queste del Saint Graal*, the secrets of the Grail, the mysteries of God, are opened to Galahad, Lancelot's son, who has been destined by Grace for this revelation. In this work the most exalted Cistercian thought of the preceding century, especially the ideas of Saint Bernard of Clairvaux, find their finest expression in medieval French.

The Grail story also occurs in ⇨ Wolfram von Eschenbach's *Parzival*, in the Welsh *Peredur* and in the English *Sir Percyvalle of Galles* (15th century), *Joseph of Arimathie* (14th century) and the *History of the Holy Grail* by Henry Lovelich (15th century). [LTT]

*Le Roman de Perceval*, ed. W. Roach (Paris, 2nd edn 1960); *Robert de Boron, Le Roman de l'Estoire dou Graal*, ed. W. A. Nitze (Paris, 1927); *Le haut livre du Graal, Perlesvaus*, ed. W. A. Nitze *et al.* (2 vols., Chicago, 1932–7); *The Vulgate Version of the Arthurian Romances*, ed. H. Oskar Sommer (7 vols., Washington, 1909–13); *La Queste del Saint Graal*, ed. A. Pauphilet (Paris, 1949).

J. Marx, *La légende arthurienne et le Graal* (Paris, 1952); R. S. Loomis (ed.), *Arthurian Literature in the Middle Ages. A Collaborative History* (1959); U. T. Holmes, Jr, and Sister M. Amelia Klenke, *Chrétien de Troyes, and the Grail* (Chapel Hill, 1959); *RPh*, XVI, 1962. (⇨ Chrétien de Troyes).

**Granada, Luis de** (Granada 1504?–Lisbon 1588). Spanish writer. A Dominican whose devotional works were among the most popular of the Counter Reformation. The *Introducción del símbolo de la fé* (1583; CA) opens with a grand celebration of the beauties of the world, drawn from Pliny and laced with Biblical phrases. It is his finest work, written in a rhetorical style that owes much to Cicero and Quintilian; his feeling for nature resembles that of Luis de ⇨ León in his *Noche serena*. His earlier *Guía de pecadores* (1556; CC) is a moral treatise that stresses the need for personal piety. It was put on the Index (1559–76), but widely translated, being acceptable to Protestants as well as Catholics, its ascetic doctrine inspired by true human understanding; even Molière remarks in *Sganarelle*, '*La Guide des Pécheurs* est encore un bon livre.' [JMC]

BAE, 6, 8, 11; Bataillon, *EE*.

**Grass, Günter** (Danzig 1927– ). German poet and novelist. He first became known as a sculptor and draughtsman, and for grotesque short plays in the manner of ⇨ Beckett. His poems (with his own 'illustrations'), *Die Vorzüge der Windhühner* (1956), *Gleisdreieck* (1960) and *Ausgefragt* (1967), 'at once amusing, horrifying and strangely life-enhancing ... expose the false identities of modern man, the fragmentation of his world, his puzzlement, his littleness and his curious paradoxical courage in recognizing absurdity and facing it' (*TLS*, 23 September 1960). Reminiscent of Beckett's *Poems in English*, their elements of the 'Absurd' recur in the novel that has made Grass internationally famous: *Die Blechtrommel* (1959; tr. R. Manheim, *The Tin Drum*, 1961). The scenes which helped make it a *succès de scandale* are only incidental to its epic 'autobiographical' sweep, from German-Polish origins in Danzig through the Nazi period and the war to the night-clubs of the West. Its power lies in its 'style', the fantastic vision of its hero: a dwarf in an asylum, whose drum, the toy of his retarded childhood, beats through the illusions and forgetfulness of the adult world, to expose its follies and fears with a sensationally detached sophistication purporting to be naïve. Similar techniques and themes, with grotesque satire of Nazi violence, the war and its end, and post-war Germany, are employed in *Hundejahre* (1963; tr. R. Manheim, *Dog Years*, 1965). *Katz und Maus* (1961; tr. ibid., *Cat and Mouse*) is a novella. The controversial 'German tragedy' *Die Plebejer proben den Aufstand* (1966; tr. ibid., *The Plebeians Rehearse the Uprising*, 1967) fell short of the earlier playlets. [PB]

Hamburger and Middleton, *MGP*; Middleton, *GWT*.

Hamburger, *PE*; Keith-Smith, *ECGL*; *FMLS*, III, 2, 1967; *GR*, XL, 3, 1965; *M*, LVIII, 2, 1961.

**Grau, Jacinto** (Barcelona 1877– ). Spanish dramatist. Often self-consciously 'literary' in his traditional themes. *El conde Alarcos* (1917; BC) echoes the ⇨ *romance*, and *El hijo pródigo* (1918; BC) the Bible; *El señor de Pigmalión* (1930; BC) has affinities with Cervantes and ⇨ Pirandello. *Don Juan de Carillana* (1913) gives a stylized presentation of a rake in the autumn of his days, the theme also of his best play: *El burlador que no se burla* (1930; BC), with its egoistic hero, fatally attractive and insensitive to the pain of others. [JMC]

**Grazzini, Anton Francesco,** also called **Il Lasca** (Florence 1503–Florence 1584). Italian writer. An apothecary, he devoted himself to letters and was a founder member of the Accademia degli Umidi (later Accademia Fiorentina) in which he took the name Lasca. In his last years he was one of the group which developed into the Accademia della Crusca.

He edited collections of Florentine satirical verse and carnival songs and himself composed satirical poems (including the beginning of the mock-heroic, *La guerra dei mostri*), 7 comedies (*La gelosia* (1551), *La spiritata* (1561), *La strega*, *La sibilla*, *La pinzochera*, *L'arzigogolo*, *I parentadi*), and a collection of 22 mostly comic novelle (*Le cene*; one translated by D. H. Lawrence, *The Story of Dr Manente*, 1929), full of racy Florentine wit. [DGR]

*A.F.G.*, *Le cene*, ed. E. Emanuelli (1945); *A.F.G.*, *Teatro*, ed. G. Grazzini (1953); *A.F.G.*, *Scritti scelti in prosa e poesia*, ed. R. Fornaciari (rev. G. Grazzini, 1957); Croce, *PPP*.

Di Francia, *N*, i (Milan, 1924); *Minori*, ii; Roscoe, *IN*.

**Greban, Arnoul** and **Simon.** ⇨ Mystères.

**Green, Julien** (Paris 1900– ). French Catholic novelist. Of American parents who settled in France in 1895, he is completely bilingual, as is illustrated by *Memories of Happy Days* (1942), where he recalls, in simple but moving language, the lost happiness of his early life. Apart from six years (1939–45) spent in the U.S., and brief stays in Italy and the Scandinavian countries, he has remained in France. Most biographical details may be gained from the *Journal* (1928ff.; already 7 vols.; partly tr. J. Godofroi, *Personal Record 1928–39*, 1940; tr. A. Green, sel. K. Wolff, *Diary 1928–1957*, 1962) where he traces with deft and poignant touches his spiritual and literary development. Most striking is the author's ability to reach beyond exterior phenomena and create an awareness of some spiritual presence. The greatest influence in his life is Pascal, whose tragic portrait of 'man without God' determines to some extent the content and style of his novels. Murder, suicide, sadism and madness fill the novels with a 'gothic' atmosphere. *Adrienne Mesurat* (1927; tr. H. L. Stuart, *The Closed Garden*, 1928) and *Minuit* (1936; tr. V. Holland, *Midnight*, 1936), typical of his 'gothic' art, rely largely on darkness, and the sense of fear that it generates, to create a world of mystery which is not always free from exaggeration. His fictional world is, morally speaking, a neutral one, for it divests man of all ethical consciousness. The apathy of Philippe in *Épaves* (1932; tr. V. Holland, *The Strange River*, 1933) clearly demonstrates this. *Moïra* (1950; tr. D. Folliot, 1951), perhaps the best of his novels, is a departure from this world of darkness and amoral behaviour. It illustrates the struggle between the sensuality and spirituality of man.

Meditation on death, a heightened sense of evil, the felt presence of a spiritual realm, also animate his 3 plays: *Sud* (1953; tr. J. Green, *South*, 1955), *L'ennemi* (1954), and *L'ombre* (1956). [RB/SBJ]

*Œuvres complètes* (1960).

P. Brodin, *J.G.* (Paris, 1957); A. Fongaro, *L'existence dans les romans de J. G.* (Rome, 1954); C. Moeller, *Littérature du vingtième siècle et christianisme*, i (Tournai, 1962); J.-L. Prévost, *J.G. ou l'âme engagée* (Lyons, 1960); S. Stokes, *J.G. and the Thorn of Puritanism* (1955).

**Greenberg, Uri Zevi** (Galicia 1891– ). Hebrew writer. Spending his youth among the poorest and most oppressed Jews of Eastern Europe, he became embittered by the fate of his people and settled in Palestine in 1923. He borrows the style of the ancient Hebrew prophets and exhorts his people by pouring invective upon them for having brought the spirit of slavery to the land of redemption. His attacks upon the great powers, who he thinks have betrayed the Jewish people, are of equal fierceness but lack the mature technique of his contemporaries. [EE]

*Eima pedolah ve-yareach* (Tel Aviv, 1925); *Rechovot ha-nahar* (Jerusalem/Tel Aviv, 1951).

Waxman, *HJL*.

**Gregory of Tours** (Clermont-Ferrand *c.* 540–Tours 594). As Bishop of Tours (578) he came into close contact with the descendants of Clovis, the first Christian King of the Franks (*c.* 466–511). He and his four sons are prominent figures in Gregory's *Historia Francorum* (tr. O. M. Dalton, *History of the Franks*, 1927), represented like most of their followers as ruthless and cruel men, only nominally Christians. The book is vividly written, revealing a strong dramatic sense and great narrative skill. He also wrote a number of saints' lives. [FB]

Migne, *PL*, 71; *Historia Francorum*, ed. B. Krusch and W. Levison (MGH, *Scriptores Rerum*

*Merovingicarum*, 1951); Dill, *RSG*; Duckett, *GMA*; Laistner, *TLWE.*

**Gregory the Great, St** (Rome *c.*540–Rome 604). Elected Pope in 590, his writings include: 14 vols. of *Letters* (ed. P. Ewald and L. Hartman, MGH, *Epistolae i, ii*, 1891–9)), which reveal his vigour, commonsense, humanity – and occasional harshness; a *Regula pastoralis* (tr. J. Barmby, in *The Book of Pastoral Rule and Selected Epistles*, N.Y., 1895–8), written for the guidance of bishops, and accepted as authoritative for centuries; and *Dialogues* (tr. E. G. Gardner, 1911), relating many incredible miracles performed by saints, especially St Benedict, and telling many fascinating stories, which enjoyed great popularity throughout the Middle Ages. His part in establishing the so-called Gregorian Sacramentary, the Antiphonary, and the plain chant of the Roman singing school is disputed. The last of the Latin Fathers, his teaching mainly summarizes St Augustine. Though professing dislike of secular learning, he wrote an admirable Latin. [FB]

Migne, *PL* 75–9.
*Life and Miracles of St Benedict*, tr. A. Hoffmann (Collegeville, U.S.A., 1925); F. H. Dudden, *G. the Great* (2 vols., 1905); P. Battiffol, *St G. le Grand* (Paris, 1928); Duckett, *GMA*.

**Gresset, Jean-Baptiste-Louis** (Amiens 1709–Amiens 1777). French poet and dramatist. Educated by the Jesuits of Amiens and Paris, he won general acclaim while a novice of the Society with his poem *Ver-Vert* (1734; repr. Paris 1946), a polished piece of badinage describing the adventures of a parrot and gently mocking the nuns who owned it. This was ill received by the Church, and Gresset returned to secular life. He attempted tragedy, without success, but reached the height of his career with a comedy, *Le méchant* (1747), which stands out among contemporary plays for its epigrammatic, witty persiflage. He became a member of the Académie Française in 1748 and subsequently its Director, but later retired to Amiens and piety. [WHB]

*Œuvres complètes* (1811).
J. Wogue, *J.-B.-L. G.* (Paris, 1894).

**Grettis Saga.** ⇨ Icelandic Sagas.

**Grévin, Jacques** (Clermont-en-Beauvaisis 1538–Turin 1570). French dramatist, poet and doctor. His active Calvinism led to a quarrel with Ronsard, and finally to his exile in Turin. His best-known work is a vigorously rhetorical tragedy, *César* (1561), prefaced by a *Brief discours* in which he claims originality in the field of French tragedy. (⇨ Jodelle's *Cléopâtre* had been performed but not yet published.) His two comedies, *Les esbahis* and *La trésorière*, are sprightly and slightly licentious. He also published rather insipid love-poetry (*L'olimpe*), some religious poetry, and a work of satire (*La gélodacrye* – the title, a neologism, means tears and laughter). [GJ]

*Théâtre complet et poésies choisies*, ed. L. Pinvert (1922) (selections); Schmidt, *PSS*.

**Griboyedov, Aleksander Sergeyevich** (Moscow 1795–Teheran 1829). Russian dramatist. Author of *Gore ot uma* (1822–4; censored but widely known in MS; publ. 1833, though cut by censor; tr. as *Woe from Wit* in *Masterpieces of the Russian Drama*, ed. G. R. Noyes, 1960; annotated edn by D. P. Costello, 1951). Written in rhymed lines of varying length in iambic metre, it satirizes self-seeking and complacent Moscow society as one encountered by an idealist returned from travel. The characters, and many of the sparklingly pithy lines, have become proverbial; the play stands among the Russian classics alongside Pushkin and Gogol' (Griboyedov's few other works are not important). He was killed during disturbances in Persia, where he was a diplomat.

*Polnoye sobraniye sochineniy*, ed. N. K. Piksanov (3 vols., 1911–17); *Sochineniya* (1959).
H. Gifford, *The Hero of His Time* (1950).

**Grieg, Nordahl** (Bergen 1902–Berlin 1943). Norwegian poet, novelist and playwright. At 18 he went to sea and travelled widely. Later he studied at Oxford for a year, took a degree at Oslo, and was active as a writer and journalist. He made use of his experiences as a seaman in his first collection of poems *Rundt Kap det gode Haab* (1922), and in his highly successful novel *Skibet gaar videre* (1925; tr. A. G. Chater, *The Ship Sails On*, 1927). Later his experiences as a war correspondent in China and Spain, and two years in the Soviet Union, resulted in *Kinesiske dager* (1927), *Spansk sommer* (1937), and *Ung må verden ennu være* (1938). The man of action and the poet were inextricably combined in him, and in a sense his work is one long attempt to reconcile these two sides of his nature. The experimental play

*Barrabas* (1927) debates whether violence can serve the good, and in the play *Nederlaget* (1937; tr. E. Arkwright, *Defeat*, 1945) the theme is taken up again. The poems of *Norge i våre hjerter* (1929) celebrate the everyday heroes of Norway, facing danger in the line of work and duty; the collection of essays *De unge døde* (1932) commemorates the young dead of the First World War, Brooke, Sorley and Owen. For a time Marxism seemed to give the answer (the play *Vår aere og vår makt*, 1935) but in 1936–7 he published the periodical *Veien frem* to attack totalitarianism. The invasion of Norway in 1940 focused all his energies and beliefs; poetry and action became one. He served in Britain and Iceland, broadcasting, reporting and writing patriotic poems, *Friheten* (1943; tr. G. M. Gathorne-Hardy, *War Poems*, 1944). His nimbus as a war hero (he was killed on a bombing mission) still tends to colour assessment of his literary worth. [RGP]

*Samlede verker* (3 vols., 1952).

K. Egeland, *NG* (Oslo, 1953); F. J. Haslund, *N.G.* (Oslo, 1962); Beyer, *NL*.

**Grigorovich, Dmitry Vasil'yevich** (Simbirsk 1822–St Petersburg 1899). Russian novelist. After five years' uncompleted studies at the St Petersburg College of Engineering (where one of his fellow students was F. M. Dostoyevsky) Grigorovich became one of ⇨ Nekrasov's collaborators. In the mid-1840s he wrote the two stories which established his reputation: *Derevnya* ('The Village', 1846) and *Anton Goremyka* (1847). He followed these with a number of stories and novels, among which are *Rybaki* (1853; tr. A. S. Rappoport, *The Fishermen*, 1916) and *Pereselentsy* ('The Migrants', 1855–6). Most of his work was published before the sixties. Grigorovich then retired from the literary scene, to reappear only in the eighties.

Grigorovich (whose concern was to draw attention to the plight of the underprivileged) deserves to be remembered not for his somewhat melodramatic plots and oversimplified characterizations, but for his pioneer introduction of genuine Russian (albeit noble) peasants into his early stories ('The first attempt,' remarked Turgenev, 'to bring our literature closer to the people'). Turgenev himself was to follow the precedent set by Grigorovich's conscientious study of the peasant's language and milieu in his early *Zapiski okhotnika* ('A Hunter's Sketches'). Girgorovich was justly overshadowed by his great contemporaries, many of whom play a part in his memoirs. [SH]

*Polnoye sobraniye sochineniy* (12 vols., St Petersburg, 1896).

**Grigor'yev, Appolon Aleksandrovich** (Moscow 1822–St Petersburg 1864). Russian poet and critic. Grigor'yev, a fervent nationalist, was an early supporter of ⇨ Ostrovsky; in the last few years of his life he contributed critical articles to the journals edited by the brothers Dostoyevsky, *Vremya* and *Epokha*. He was largely unappreciated in his time. His irregular life prevented the full realization of his gifts; at the same time it often provided the inspiration for his poetry. Though much of his verse is rambling and uneven, there are passages which are striking in their immediacy, unusual in their theme and metre. His use of gypsy rhythms, in particular, delighted ⇨ Blok, his most influential admirer and (50 years after Grigor'yev's death) the first editor of his poetic works. For a full understanding of Blok it is important to read Grigor'yev.

In one of his critical articles Grigor'yev developed the concept of 'organic criticism': works of art were to be apprehended as expressions of a social and, more especially, a national entity, of the national soil or *pochva* (whence the term *pochvenniki*, 'men of the soil'). Grigor'yev's memoirs (1864; tr. R. Matlaw, *My Literary and Moral Wanderings*, N.Y., 1962) are of considerable interest. [SH]

*Izbrannyye proizvedeniya* (1959).

V. Knyazhnin, ed., *A.A.G. Materialy dlya biografii* (Petrograd, 1917).

**Grillparzer, Franz** (Vienna 1791–Vienna 1872). Austrian dramatist. He had a characteristically Viennese love-hate relationship to his native city. Grillparzer's work derives from diverse sources. *Die Ahnfrau* (1817) belongs to the school of '*Schicksalstragödien*' in the wake of Schiller's *Die Braut von Messina*; *Sappho* (1817; tr. A. Burkhard, 1953), treating the conflict between the poetess's vatic calling and her sensuous humanity, follows Goethe's *Torquato Tasso*. Following the play's great success Grillparzer was appointed court-playwright at the Burgtheater (1818–23), then keeper of the imperial archives until his retirement in 1856. The trilogy *Das goldene Vliess* (1821;

tr. A. Burkhard, *The Golden Fleece*, 1942) concentrates in the third part on the fate of Jason's wife, Medea, who is brought to Greece from her native island of Colchis; betrayed by her husband, she reasserts her 'barbaric' origins in a monstrous act of revenge. *König Ottokars Glück und Ende* (1825; tr. A. Burkhard, 1962) draws on the early history of Bohemia (as does *Libussa*, 1848, published 1872; tr. A. Burkhard, 1941); in the figure of the ruthless and ambitious Bohemian king (reminiscent of Richard III) the themes of personal and political hubris are powerfully linked, whereas the peace-loving Rudolf I, founder of the House of Habsburg, offers a not wholly adequate antagonist. In *Ein treuer Diener seines Herrn* (1828; tr. A. Burkhard, *A Faithful Servant of his Master*, 1941) Bancbanus, the Hungarian king's deputy, is involved in a series of intrigues, in the course of which he loses his young wife; this figure of the utterly loyal yet inadequate servant of the state embodies one of Grillparzer's favourite themes, the dilemma between spirituality and worldliness. *Des Meeres und der Liebe Wellen* (1831; tr. A. Burkhard, *Hero and Leander*, 1962) reinterprets the Greek tale of Hero and Leander, and again the dramatic interest lies in the fact that Hero is by nature unsuited to her priestly calling (as Medea was to the culture of Greece, and Bancbanus to political office). *Der Traum ein Leben* (1834, based on Calderón's *La vida es sueño*; tr. H. H. Stevens, *A Dream is Life*, 1946) represents a dramatically successful combination of realism and fairy-tale magic. As in *Ottokar*, the hero is driven by overweening ambition beyond the confines of the life allotted to him; but when disaster threatens, all his adventures are seen to have been but a dream. The comedy *Weh dem, der lügt* (1838; tr. H. H. Stevens, *Thou shalt not lie*, 1939), a resounding failure at the Burgtheater, is the last of Grillparzer's plays to be published in his lifetime; its serious moral theme – 'every lie, even the smallest, assaults the foundation of the entire human condition' – does not easily blend with the play's central figure, the scullion-boy Leon. His last three plays were published posthumously in 1872. In the weakest of them, *Die Jüdin von Toledo* (begun in 1824; tr. A. Burkhard, *The Jewess of Toledo*, 1953), the young and inexperienced Spanish king neglects the affairs of state, and his frigid English wife, for the young Jewess Rahel; the nobles solve his dilemma by murdering her, and the play closes as the king leaves with them on a holy crusade, leaving the regency in the queen's hands.

*Bruderzwist in Habsburg* (begun in 1827, all but completed in 1848; tr. A. Burkhard, *Family Strife in Hapsburg*, 1940) mirrors Grillparzer's disillusionment with the popular cause of the Revolution of 1848. The action centres on the Habsburg Emperor Rudolf II, his brother and successor to the throne, Matthias, and the religious and political turmoil preceding the Thirty Years' War; in addition, the lawlessness of the age is brought home to Rudolf through the doings of his natural son, Don Caesar. In his last play, *Libussa* (1841), the unwritten matriarchal order of a pastoral community is challenged by men clamouring for the rule of written laws. The new order, symbolized in the foundation of Prague, makes possible a more highly organized civilization; but Libussa, upholder of the old, becomes victim of the change. The tenor is elegiac and prophetic, but the play lacks the tension which makes of *Ein Bruderzwist* one of the few great political tragedies in German.

Grillparzer's dramas are written in a variety of classical metres (e.g. iambic pentameters), but sometimes the verse is strained and the imagery forced. Although disdainful of prose, his Novelle *Der arme Spielmann* (begun 1831, published 1848) is among the masterpieces of the century; significantly it is the only work he set in contemporary Vienna. The 'poor minstrel's' every action and encounter with reality is attended by pathetic or absurd failure. But the laconic presentation of this life through a 'psychologically curious' narrator ensures that the contrast between the hero's deprivations and the serenity and saintliness of his mind is achieved without a trace of sentimentality. [JPS]

*Sämtliche Werke*, ed. Sauer and Backmann (43 vols., 1909ff.).

J. Nadler, *F.G.* (1948); D. Yates, *F.G.* (first vol. only, 1946); W. Naumann, *G.: Das dichterische Werk* (Stuttgart, 1956); G. Baumann, *F.G.: sein Werk und das österreichische Wesen* (1954); E. Staiger, *Trivium*, iv (1946); Stern, *R.*

**Grimm, Friedrich Melchior,** Baron von (Regensburg 1723–Gotha 1807). German-born French journalist and critic. He lived in Paris 1749–90, becoming closely associated with the *philosophes*. In 1753 he launched his major journalistic enterprise, the *Correspondance littéraire* (ed. M. Tourneux, 1877–82), a bi-monthly critical review circulated privately in manuscript to a small number of princely subscribers, mostly German, and which he continued to edit until 1773. It included important contributions by Diderot, and evolved a new, more personal and discursive style of literary commentary. It throws invaluable light on the literature and society of the period. [WHB]

E. Scherer, *M.G.* (Paris, 1887); J. P. Smiley, *Diderot's Relations with G.* (Urbana, Ill., 1950); Wellek, *HMC*.

**Grimm, Jacob Ludwig** (Hanau 1785–Berlin 1863) and **Wilhelm Karl** (Hanau 1786–Berlin 1859). German philologists and literary scholars, the editors of the famous collection of folk-tales.

Jacob, elder of the two brothers, was one of the seven Göttingen professors dismissed from their posts in 1837 for their liberal political views, and was a delegate at the National Assembly in Frankfurt in 1848. He is legitimately regarded as the founder of the scientific study of the German language (*Geschichte der deutschen Sprache*, 1818), medieval German literature, and the culture of German antiquity – one of the greatest scholars that Germany has ever known, a man of extraordinary knowledge and phenomenal energy. His main independent works are the *Deutsche Grammatik* (4 vols., 1819–37), *Deutsche Rechtsaltertümer* (1828) and *Deutsche Mythologie* (1835).

Wilhelm, who shared his brother's fate as a professor at Göttingen, was appointed in 1841 to the University of Berlin, where he lived until his death. In addition to his many editions of medieval texts (*Freidank*, *Rolandslied*, Konrad von Würzburg's *Sylvester*, etc.), his contributions to the study of German culture include pioneering works on runes (*Über deutsche Runen*, 1826) and heroic legends (*Die deutsche Heldensage*, 1829).

The two greatest achievements of the Grimm brothers, however, spring from their cooperation: on the one hand, the great *Deutsches Wörterbuch*, started in 1854 and continued by Hildebrand, Weigand and a succession of later scholars; and on the other the famous *Kinder- und Hausmärchen* (3 vols., 1812–13), to this day the most famous collection of folk-tales in the world. Both reflect the Romantic revival of interest in the medieval past; the former represents the historical investigation of words, language and style, the latter revealed to the German people some of the treasures of their national folk-tradition, the narrative counterpart of the poems in *Des Knaben Wunderhorn*. They are the scholarly complement to the hazy, evocative medievalism of ⇨ Novalis, ⇨ Wackenroder, etc. [RT]

W. Schoof, *W.G.* (Bern, 1960), and *J.G.* (Bern, 1961).
Wellek, *HMC*.

**Grimmelshausen, Johann Jakob Christoffel von** (Gelnhausen 1625?–Renchen, Baden 1676). German novelist. His life mirrors accurately the uncertainties of the Thirty Years' War. Abducted by Croat irregulars as a boy, he served in both the Imperial and Swedish armies and rose to the status of regimental clerk. He was converted to Catholicism in 1646 and with the coming of peace was variously employed as a bailiff, a town clerk and a publican. Against this background of personal vicissitudes he wrote the greatest literary work of his age, *Der abenteuerliche Simplicissimus Teutsch* (1669; tr. A. T. S. Goodrick, *The Adventurous Simplicissimus*, 1912; tr. H. Weissenborn and L. Macdonald, 1963). Written under the influence of the Spanish picaresque novel and retaining many of the satirical elements proper to that genre, this realistic description of the life and adventures of Simplicissimus from his peasant boyhood to his retirement from the world as a man of middle age is full of incident; it is at one and the same time a novel of development, a representation of the pilgrimage of the Christian soul and a symbolical statement of the nature of existence itself. In the ascetic philosophy it advances and in its assertion of the inconstancy of human beings and of all created things, the work is one of the supreme expressions of the Christian pessimism of the age, but the story is told with a verve, a humour and a warmly sympathetic understanding of his fellow-men which bear striking testimony to Grimmelshausen's humanity and love of life.

The so-called *Simplicianische Schriften Die Landstörtzerin Courasche* (1670), *Der seltzame Springinsfeld* (1670) and *Das wunderbarliche Vogelnest* (1672), which take up themes and characters occurring in *Simplicissimus*, attempted unsuccessfully to repeat the success of his masterpiece. His *Dietwald und Amelinde* (1670) is an indifferent imitation of the courtly novel of the age and has little more than historical interest. [WAC]

*Simplicissimus*, ed. J. H. Scholte, NDL 302/9 (1939); *Simplicianische Romane*, NDL 246/8 (1923), 249/52 (1928), 288/91 (1931), 310/14 (1939); ed. A. Kelletat (1958).

R. Brie, *Die sozialen Ideen G.* (Berlin, 1938); E. Ermatinger, *Weltdeutung in G.s Simplicissimus* (Leipzig and Berlin, 1925); K. Fuchs, *Die Religiosität des J.J.C. v. G.* (Leipzig, 1935); W. Welzig, *Beispielhafte Figuren* (Graz/Köln, 1963).

**Grossi, Tommaso** (Bellano 1790–Milan 1853). Italian novelist and poet. He began with heavily romantic verse romances (*La fuggitiva*, 1815, in Milanese dialect; and *Ildegonda*, 1820). Of the same period is the satirical dialect poem against Classicism, *Matrimoni del sur cont Gabriell Verr* (1819) written in collaboration with the Milanese Carlo Porta. *Ildegonda*, with its stylized study of the Middle Ages and the languishing heroine, brought Grossi wide fame; but the popular epic *I Lombardi alla prima crociata* (1826), transformed by Verdi into opera and proclaimed by the Romantics as their answer to Tasso, was so severely attacked by some critics that Grossi abandoned verse for the novel. In 1831, undoubtedly influenced by his close friend ⇨ Manzoni, he began work on the historical novel *Marco Visconti* (1834; ed. A. Alberti, 1943; tr. A. F. Dugdale, 1876), whose vivid narrative, despite a similar sentimental romantic hotchpotch of fantasy and superficial erudition as in *Ildegonda* (tr. anon. 1859), made it one of the best historical novels of the century. [RHC]

*Opere* (1892); *Opere poetiche* (1877); Dionisotti, *OBIV*.

E. Flori, *Scorci e figure del romanticismo* (Rome, 1938); F. Fossati, *T.G.* (Lecco 1953); *Studi su T.G.* (Centenary Studies) (Milan, 1953); *Guida* (1959); *Minori*, iii.

**Grün, Anastasius,** pseud. of Anton Alexander Graf von Auersperg (Laibach 1806–Graz 1876). Austrian poet. Studied law in Vienna and Graz; travelled in Italy, France, England; country nobleman; member of 1848 Frankfurt and Austrian parliaments. His *Spaziergänge eines Wiener Poeten* (1821) and *Schutt* (1835) attack Metternich and advocate liberalism, democracy, 'Greater Germany'. The lyrics of *Blätter der Liebe* (1829), *Der letzte Ritter* (1830; tr. J. O. Sargent, *The Last Knight*, N.Y., 1871), *Gedichte* (1837), *Volkslieder aus Krain* (1850), the ballads of *Robin Hood* (1864), and the humorous epics *Die Nibelungen im Frack* (1843) and *Der Pfaff vom Kahlenberg* (1850) do not equal his political poems in importance. [LL]

*Sämtliche Werke*, ed. A. Schlossar (10 vols., Leipzig, 1907); ed. E. Castle (6 vols., Berlin, 1909).

R. Wächter, *A.G.s politische Dichtung* (1933); Koch, *IW*.

**Grundtvig, Nicolai F. S.** (Udby 1783–Copenhagen 1872). Danish poet, historian and educationalist. His influence has been immense: as a bishop whose controversial views still sway the strong Grundtvigian group; as an educationalist on whose ideas the Danish Folk High Schools are based; as a poet many of whose works have enjoyed unrivalled popularity; as a popularizer of the ideas of the Romantic school; as a highly unorthodox historian; and as an active liberal politician.

He was a most versatile writer, translating poetry and prose from Anglo-Saxon (e.g. *Beowulf*), from Latin (e.g. Saxo's *Gesta Danorum*), and from Old Icelandic (e.g. Snorri's *Heimskringla*) into Danish; writing large historical works about ancient Scandinavia (including a *Nordic Mythology*) as well as a *History of the World*, many personal poems, and a vast number of historical poems, popular songs, hymns, and versifications of Biblical stories. Best known outside Scandinavia for his educational ideas, it is his poetry – and especially his sacred poetry – which has made him a leading figure in Danish literature; most of it defies translation, partly because it is so closely linked with a liberal religious movement which has no parallel outside Denmark, partly because of his abundant use of Danish idioms. [ELB]

*Udvalgte Skrifter*, ed. G. Christensen and H. Koch (10 vols., 1940–50).

S. Johansen, *Bibliografi over N.F.S.G.s Skrifter* (5 vols., Copenhagen, 1948–54); N. Davies, *G. of Denmark* (1944); P. G. Lindhardt, *G.: An Introduction* (1951); H. Koch, *G.* (Ohio, 1952); Gosse, *SLNE*.

**Gruppe 47.** A loose association of German left-wing writers, established in 1947 by H. W. ⇨ Richter out of dissatisfaction with the Allied ban on the journal *Der Ruf* which he and ⇨ Andersch had edited. Richter has arranged meetings at least once every year since 1947; the proceedings, especially readings of unpublished work, have been broadcast and much discussed. The 'prize' has become one of the most coveted literary awards in Germany. [WPH]

*Almanach der Gruppe 47*, ed. H. W. Richter (Berlin, 1962); *Die Gruppe 47 und ihre Gäste*, H. Meyer-Brockmann (Munich, 1962).

**Gryphius, Andreas** (Glogau 1616–Glogau 1664). German poet and dramatist. Orphaned early in life, during his formative years he experienced the horrors of the Thirty Years' War. He travelled widely in France, England, Italy and Holland, spending six years as a student and lecturer in Leyden, where he came under the influence of the Dutch literary renaissance (⇨ Vondel, ⇨ Hooft, ⇨ Heinsius, etc.). His lyric poetry (*Sonn- und Feiertagssonette*, 1639; *Sonette*, 1643; *Kirchhofsgedanken*, 1657) is characterized by an intensely passionate awareness of the wretchedness of the human condition, the transience and vanity of the world, and a corresponding yearning for the peace and security of Heaven. These are stock themes in the 17th century, but Gryphius's verse transcends that of his contemporaries in its underlying personal note and in the power of his language.

His major tragedies (*Catharina von Georgien*, 1657; *Carolus Stuardus*, 1649–63 – intr. H. Powell, 1955; *Aemilius Paulus Papinianus*, 1659), which retain the classical unities and the chorus and make extensive use of allegory and the supernatural, may all be regarded as martyr tragedies and as such are a natural vehicle for Gryphius's pessimistic philosophy and rejection of earthly existence, the martyr welcoming death as a release from the distasteful prison of life; at the same time, however, they bear striking witness to his belief in the sublime ability of the human spirit to triumph over adversity. Viewed purely as dramas these plays are of little merit, being characterized primarily by their static quality, the passivity of the protagonists and by dialogue which consists either of inordinately long monologues or equally long passages of stichomythia. These same undramatic qualities are equally evident in his middle-class drama of conversion, *Cardenio und Celinde* (1647; intr. H. Powell, 1961). His comedies are more successful as plays and show him in a surprisingly different light in their, at times, heavy humour and their evident delight in the absurd (*Horribilicribrifax*, 1663; *Herr Peter Squentz*, 1663). *Die geliebte Dornrose* (1660), a comedy of peasant life written in Silesian dialect, is undoubtedly the most successful comedy of the century. [WAC]

*Werke*, ed. H. Palm, BLVS 183 (1878), 162 (1882), 171 (1884); DLE (*Barock*).

W. Flemming, *A.G. und die Bühne* (Halle, 1921); V. Mannheimer, *Die Lyrik des A.G.* (Berlin, 1904).

**Guarini, Giambattista** (Ferrara 1538–Venice 1612). Italian poet. Courtier at Ferrara, diplomat and secretary to several ruling families, he served also at Florence and Urbino. His lesser writings include a collection of *Rime*, a comedy (*L'idropica*), letters and various treatises on literary and political subjects, but his fame rests on his pastoral drama, or tragi-comedy as he defined it, *Il pastor fido* (1590; tr. Sir Richard Fanshawe, *The Faithful Shepherd*, 1647; repr. ed. W. F. Staton, W. E. Simeone, 1964). Written in emulation of ⇨ Tasso's *Aminta*, it gained great popularity throughout Western Europe. It dilutes the lyrical purity of Tasso's masterpiece in favour of complication of plot. The treatment is more discursive, the paraphernalia of shepherdom more prominent, there is moralizing and satire, and the action accords with Greek dramatic precepts. A thinly veiled voluptuousness and easy flowing verse made the play for long more acceptable in its varied texture than *Aminta*. [DGR]

*Opere*, ed. L. Fassò (1950); *Il pastor fido*, ed. G. Brognoligo (1914); *Teatro del Seicento*, ed. L. Fassò (1956).

E. Carrara, *La poesia pastorale* (Milan, 1908); M. Apollonio, *Storia de' teatro italiano* (Florence, 1938–51); *Minori*, ii.

**Guérin, Maurice de** (Château du Caya 1810–Château du Caya 1839). French writer. He was brought up by his devoted sister Eugénie after his mother's death in a lonely chateau near Albi. A friend of ⇨ Barbey d'Aurevilly in Paris, in 1832 he entered Lammenais's community at La Chesnaie. However, his nature was pagan rather than religious and when the community broke up he returned to Paris to support himself by teaching. He died of tuberculosis. In 1840 his prose poem *Le Centaure* for which he is best remembered was published in the *Revue des Deux Mondes* with a memoir by George Sand. In it the aged centaur Chiron relates the story of his youth to the young Melampus. Another prose poem, *Le Bacchante*, was also published posthumously as were his journal and other remains. His sister, Eugénie de Guérin (1805–48), was considered by Sainte-Beuve to be equally talented. She started writing her *Journal intime* for her brother in 1834 and continued it after his death. It was published in 1862. Matthew Arnold wrote appreciations of brother and sister in *Essays in Criticism* (1865). [WA]

*Œuvres* (2 vols., 1930).
Peyre, *LS.*

**Guerrazzi, Francesco Domenico** (Leghorn 1804–Cecina 1873). Italian poet, dramatist and novelist. He was deeply influenced by Byron, who arrived in Pisa in 1821 (cf. *Stanze alla memoria del Byron*, 1825). Engaged actively in the polemics between Classics and Romantics (cf. *Sul bello*, 1826), he wrote some early tragedies, but his most successful works were historical novels – *La battaglia di Benevento* (1827–8; tr. L. Monti, *Manfred*; *The Battle of Benevento*, 1875); *L'assedio di Firenze* (1836); *Beatrice Cenci* (1854; tr. C. A. Scott, 1858); *L'asino* (1857); *Il buco nel muro* (1862) – many of which were written during periods of imprisonment for political activities, for which he had been in trouble even before graduating at Pisa in 1824. Intensely patriotic, full of 'Byronic madness', macabre descriptions (cf. *Veronica Cybo*, 1837), long declamatory imprecations and digressions, these novels fail to appeal to modern taste but were highly influential in the Risorgimento. [RHC]

*Opere* (4 vols., 1849–50); *Scritti scelti*, ed. A. Cajumi (1955).
W. T. Elwert, *Geschichtsauffassung und Erzählungstechnik in den historischen Romanen F.D.G.* (Halle, 1935); *Minori*, iii.

**Guevara, Antonio de** (Treceño 1481?–Mondoñedo 1545). Spanish author of moral, political and theological works. After failing to get a position at court, he became a Franciscan. He was appointed Royal Preacher and Chronicler by Charles V, whom he accompanied to Tunis and Italy; he was an inquisitor and bishop of Guadix and Mondoñedo. His *Libro áureo de Marco Aurelio* (1528; ed. R. Foulché-Delbosc, 1929), a spurious autobiography, was expanded into the political treatise the *Relox de príncipes* (1529). This guide to princely and noble conduct was much translated. Its mannered style modelled on medieval ornate Latin prose had some influence in England as an indirect forerunner of Euphuism. His *Epístolas familiares* (1539, 1545; ed. J. M. de Cossío, 1950–2), a collection of open letters, sermons and essays, his *Década de Césares* (1539), based on Dion Cassius, Herodian and the *Historia Augusti*, his *Aviso de Privados* (1539), a guide for favourites, his *Menosprecio de corte y alabanza de aldea* (1539; ed. Martínez de Burgos, 1915), an elaborate exercise on the *Beatus ille* theme, and his *Arte de marear* (1539), on the origins and hardships of sea travel, all were once popular works and known in most of Europe. The *Oratorio de religosos* (1542; ed. P. Fr. J. B. Gomis, 1948), a guide to the religious life, and the *Monte Calvario* (1548, 1549), on Calvary and the Seven Last Words, were almost as popular in France and Italy. Never at a loss for an anecdote or example, he owed much of his success to the copious style in which he presented his moral maxims and his wonderful though often inaccurate learning. [JG]

*Prosa escogida*, ed. M. de Riquer (1943).
R. Costes, *A. de G.: sa vie, son œuvre* (Paris, 1925–6); J. Gibbs, *La vida de fray A. de G.* (Valladolid, 1961).

**Gui, Châtelain de Coucy** (d. 1203), probably Gui de Thourotte, governor of the castle of Coucy (1186–1203). French poet. A ⇨ *trouvère* whose love-songs and death and burial at sea during the passage from Andros to the Dardanelles on the Fourth Crusade won him a reputation as a tragic courtly lover. He became the hero (Renaut) of a late-13th-century romance which used the theme of the 'eaten heart'. [LTT]

Ed. A. Lerond (Paris, 1964); ed. F. Fath (Heidelberg, 1883); *Le Roman du Castelain de Couci et la Dame de Fayel*, ed. M. Delbouille (Paris, 1936); Woledge, *PBFV.*

**Guibert of Nogent** (Clermont-en-Beauvoisis 1053–1124). Abbot of Nogent-sur-Coucy; his history of the First Crusade (*Gesta Dei per Francos*) largely paraphrases the *Gesta Francorum* (by an anonymous Norman). His autobiography, *De vita sua sive monodiarum* (tr. C. C. S. Bland, 1926), is of value for its account of the commune of Laon, and of the manners and customs of the time, e.g. the method of instructing children by thrashing them. [FB]

Migne, *PL*, 156, 184.

**Guicciardini, Francesco** (Florence 1483–Arcetri, Florence 1540). Italian historian. Son of a patrician family, he became Florentine ambassador to Spain (1512–14) and held high papal offices. After the sack of Rome (1527) and the fall of the Medici in Florence, he retired to his villa and worked at his *Ricordi politici e civili* (ed. R. Spongano, 1951) and his *Considerazioni sui discorsi del Machiavelli.* He served the notorious Alessandro de' Medici (1534–7), and after his murder retired to write the *Storia d'Italia*, a vast account of Italy from 1492 to 1532 (tr. G. Fenton, 1579). Impressive in its detailed analysis of national corruption and calamity, his scepticism and aloofness make this a bleak masterpiece. Unlike ⇨ Machiavelli (whom he regards as an enthusiast) he sets no pattern or lesson; the largely sombre insights of his own political experience are expressed in the maxims of the *Ricordi*. Apart from the *Storia d'Italia* his works remained unpublished until the 19th century. [DGR]

*Opere*, ed. Panigada and Palmarocchi (9 vols., 1929–36); *Opere*, ed. V. De Caprariis (1953); *F.G., Selected Writings*, tr. M. Grayson (1965); *History of Italy and History of Florence*, tr. C. Grayson (1966) (selections).

V. Luciani, *F.G. and his European Reputation* (N.Y., 1936); F. Gilbert, *Machiavelli and G. etc.* (Princeton, 1965); R. Ridolfi, *Life* (tr. C. Grayson, 1967); Binni, *CI*; *Maggiori*.

**Guidi, Alessandro** (Pavia 1650–Frascati 1712). Italian poet. From the Farnese court at Parma he went to Rome and found a patron in Christina of Sweden. In 1691 he joined the newly founded Arcadian Academy. His early verse shows the influence of ⇨ Marino, but later he cultivated the Pindaric manner of ⇨ Chiabrera, aspiring ambitiously to become the Pindar of his century, and seeking a noble eloquence in canzoni of free stanzaic form. Author of a mythological drama, *Endimione*, he celebrated the great figures of his day and wrote loftily on historical and moral subjects, his best-known poem being a canzone, *Alla Fortuna*. He lacked creative, imaginative power, and his verse is now generally decried as frothy rhetoric. [DGR]

*Poesie di A.G.* (1787); Calcaterra, *LSA*.

T. L. Rizzo, *Dal Sei all'Ottocento* (Turin, 1931).

**Guilhem de Poitou** (1071–1127). The earliest known Provençal ⇨ troubadour. 7th count of Poitou and 9th duke of Aquitaine. A tempestuous ruler and a poet who 'desired always that which he could not have', he led a disastrous expedition to the Holy Land in 1101, and in 1120 at the head of 600 knights helped Alphonso of Aragon against the Almoravids. His reign was marked by his fruitless occupations of Toulouse and his unsuccessful strife with the Church and his feudal vassals. Orderic Vital describes him as bold, excellent and extremely joyous. His 13th-century Provençal biographer says he was 'one of the most courtly men in the world and one of the greatest deceivers of ladies, a good knight in the handling of arms, and generous in wooing'.

There survive 11 of his poems and these represent the earliest cultivated vernacular lyric in Europe. Five are in the form of burlesque or bawdy jests, with an underlying serious intention, the remainder, apart from a *congé*, are songs in which he seeks an uncertain love of the senses and the imagination. In 'Mout jauzens', he finds his supreme joy with a perfect *domna.* His poems are remarkable for their evocative language, self-doubt, humour and dislike of convention. His knowledge of music and versification probably derives from Church sources, especially from the paraliturgical *versus*. Much of his inspiration came from contemporary thought about love, from the cultivated background of the court of Poitou and from Ovidian and possibly Hispano-Arabic sources. [LTT]

*Les Chansons de Guillaume IX, duc d'Aquitaine*, ed. A. Jeanroy (2nd edn, Paris, 1927); Hill and Bergin, *APT*; *R*, LXVI (1940–1); *ZRP*, LXXVIII, 1962; *NM*, LXIX, 1968.

**Guilhem Montanhagol** (fl. 1233–*c.* 1258). Provençal ⇨ troubadour. His surviving work consists of 6 *cansos* or love songs, 7 *sirventes* of moral or political satire and a *partimen* or debate with ⇨ Sordello. He attended the court of Count Raimon VII of Toulouse, and knew James I of Aragon, Alphonso X of Castille, the counts of Foix and the lords of Moncade. He wrote in a clear direct style and was not interested in any intricate playing with rhyme or metre. He sang at a time when the Albigensian Crusade had uprooted the courtly society of the South and the Inquisition was extirpating the Cathar heresy. Described sometimes as a poet of chaste, spiritual love, an innovator among troubadours and a precursor of the *dolce* ⇨ *stil novo*, he is really a '*mantenedor*' of the courtly standards. He praises the values of *pretz* (social esteem), *valors* (inherent individual worth), *mesura* (moderation) and *onors* esteemed by earlier troubadours, and insists that these courtly qualities and hence the courtly code cannot be immoral or displeasing to God. [LTT]

Ed. J. Coulet (Toulouse, 1898); ed. P. Ricketts (Toronto, 1964); *FS*, XI, 1957.

**Guillaume de Lorris.** ⇨ *Rose, Roman de la.*

**Guillaume de Machaut** or **Machault** (*c.* 1300–Rheims 1377). French musician and poet. At 20 he became *clerc* to Jean of Luxembourg, King of Bohemia, whom he accompanied on campaigns in Poland, Italy, Germany and Russia. When the king fell blind Guillaume became canon of Rheims and devoted himself to music, poetry and hunting. In his sixties the love felt for him by a young noblewoman, Péronne of Armentières, inspired a correspondence which gives valuable information about his work.

He was acknowledged in his time as the chief of a school and was among the first poets to develop the *ballade* and *rondeau* in the fixed forms which were to make them increasingly popular in the 15th century. He refined the older *lai* and *virelai*, wrote 200 *ballades*, 42 to music, and invented the *double ballade*, a contrapuntal compromise between *ballade* and motet. His themes are usually courtly, but the *Voir Dit* (ed. P. Paris, 1875) is autobiographical. The musical settings of his lyrics have an astonishing melodic inspiration and his *Messe Notre-Dame* (or *Messe du Sacre*) is recognized as one of the outstanding musical compositions of the Middle Ages.

Among Machaut's longer narrative and didactic poems there survive the early *Dit dou Vergier*, an imitation of the *Roman de la* ⇨ *Rose*; two courtly debates, the *Jugement du roy de Behaingne* and the *Jugement du roy de Navarre*; the allegorical *Livre de la fontaine amoureuse*; *Confort d'Ami*, addressed to Charles of Navarre in captivity, and the historical poem *Prise d'Alexandrie ou Chronique du roi Pierre Ier de Lusignan* (ed. L. de Mas-Latrie, 1877). He especially influenced Eustache ⇨ Deschamps and Chaucer. [LTT]

Ed. E. Hœpffner (3 vols., incomplete, 1908–21); *Poésies lyriques*, ed. V. Chichmaref (2 vols., 1909); F. Ludwig, *G. de M. Musikalische Werke*, 3 vols. (Leipzig, 1926–30). A. Machabey, *G. de M.* (2 vols., Paris, 1955); *Revue musicale* (1930 and 1931); *Music and Letters*, XXXIX (1957); *ZRP*, XXX (1906); *R*, XLIII (1914); *Mod. Philology*, VII (1909–10); *PMLA*, XXX (1915); *MLN*, XXX (1915); *SP*, XXXVI (1939); J. Chailley, *Histoire musicale du Moyen Âge* (Paris, 1950).

**Guillén, Jorge** (Valladolid 1893– ). Spanish poet of the 'Generation of the Dictatorship'. His work, when complete, will consist of 3 volumes: *Cántico*, *Clamor* and *Homenaje*. *Cántico* (Buenos Aires, 1950) has occupied most of the poet's life, appearing in gradually augmented editions between 1928 and 1950. Here, he seeks '*una poesía pura*, ma non troppo'. He is 'the last free poet. After him, all are committed' (J. González Muela). His world is that which he can see around him from his individual 'crystal tower'. Dream, vision, immortality are outside his scheme of things, and pain and grief rarely intrude into the all-pervading exclamatory optimism. Guillén did not experience the crisis which turned his contemporaries Rafael ⇨ Alberti, ⇨ Lorca, ⇨ Aleixandre and ⇨ Cernuda away from *purismo* towards a more violent, sombre and subjective poetry in the period 1927–31. Only within the last ten years have the various published fragments of *Clamor* shown a concern with the more tragic side of life and with religious problems. He has also published, mainly during his post-Civil War residence in America, a number of critical works, notably *Language and Poetry* (Cambridge, Mass., 1961). [GC]

*Huerto de Melibea* (1954); *Luzbel desconcertado* (Milan, 1956); *Clamor: 1. Maremágnum* (Buenos Aires, 1957); *2. . . . Que van a dar en la mar* (Buenos Aires, 1960); *3. A la altura de las circunstancias* (Buenos Aires, 1963).

J. Casalduero, *Cántico de J.G.* (Madrid, 1953); P. Darmangeat, *J.G., ou le cantique émerveillé* (Paris, 1958); J. Gil de Biedma, *Cántico, el mundo y la poesía de J.G.* (Barcelona, 1960); J. González Muela, *La realidad y J.G.* (Madrid, 1962); R. Gullón and J. M. Blecua, *La poesía de J.G.* (Zaragoza, 1949); J. B. Trend, *J.G.* (1952).

**Guillôme, J.** ⇨ Breton Literature.

**Guimerá, Angel.** ⇨ Catalan Literature.

**Guinizelli, Guido** (Bologna *c.* 1235–Monselice *c.* 1276). Italian poet. A student of law and a judge, he was exiled by political opponents in 1274. Dante praises him (*Purgatorio*, XXVI) and his *Rime* have traditionally been regarded as the first expression of the *dolce* ⇨ *stil novo*. His most effective moment is that of ecstatic adoration of his lady. [DGR]

Benedetto, *RDSN*; Salinari, *PLD*; Contini, *PD*; Figurelli, *DSN*; Lind, *LPIR*; Rossetti, *DC*.

**Guiraut de Bornelh,** of Excideuil in Dordogne (fl.1170). Provençal ⇨ troubadour of humble birth. A cultured and skilful poet, he was called 'maestre dels trobadors' by his Provençal biographer. (Dante probably had this description of Guiraut in mind when he praised his favourite troubadour Arnaut Daniel in *Purgatorio*, xxvi). He was a 'Poet Laureate' among the troubadours. His courtly love-songs are orthodox and cerebral. He was skilled in the arts of rhetoric and excelled in the use of grandiloquent and sustained metaphor, and his language and rhymes are invariably elegant. He preferred to compose in the difficult style of the *trobar clus*, but in a literary debate or *tenso* with ⇨ Raimbaut d'Orange advocated the merits of the *trobar leu* or clear style. In his moralizing poems or *sirventes* he castigated social abuses with a directness and vigour which earned him Dante's praise as a poet of moral uprightness (*rectitudo*) (*De vulgari eloquentia*, II:2). His extant work includes 50 *cansos*, 15 moralizing poems, 3 *tensos*, 2 Crusading songs, 2 funeral laments (*planh*), a *pastorela*, a romance, a puzzle poem and a very successful *alba* or dawn song, 'Reis glorios, verais lums e clartatz'. [LTT]

*Sämtliche Lieder, G.B.*, ed. A. Kolsen (2 vols., Halle, 1910–35); Hill and Bergin, *APT*.

**Guiraut Riquier** (Narbonne *c.*1230/5–after 1292). Last of the major Provençal troubadours. Of modest parentage, he wrote his earliest poems at Narbonne, but he attended the courts of Castille 1270–9 and of Rodez 1280–5. A prolific and versatile writer, he left 89 poems in a wide variety of genres, and 15 rhymed epistles. His earlier love-songs addressed to the Duchess of Narbonne followed the traditional courtly pattern, but in his later years he turned away from profane love and composed several songs to the Virgin Mary and many didactic and moralizing poems. His most pleasing work is his sequence of 6 *pastorelas* in which he displays gaiety, wit and much dramatic skill. [LTT]

Ed. U. Mölk (Heidelberg, 1962); ed. S. H. Pfaff in Mahn, *Werke*, vol. IV (1853).
J. Anglade, *Le Troubadour G.R.* (Paris, 1905).

**Guitry, Sacha** (St Petersburg 1885–Paris 1957). French actor and playwright. His prodigious output of farce and light comedy utilized, with impudent candour and facility, increasingly thin material which the author justified by the opportunities it offered him of displaying his talents as a comedian. The earliest comedies are probably the best: *Le veilleur de nuit* (1911); *La prise de Berg-op-Zoom* (1912); *La jalousie* (1915). *Pasteur* (1919; tr. I. H. Brown, in *Chief Contemporary Dramatists, II*, 1921) and *Mozart* (1925) offer satisfying vehicles for character actors. [SBJ]

*Théâtre* (15 vols., 1959–64).
Surer, *TFC*; Lalou, *TF*.

**Guittone d'Arezzo** (Arezzo *c.*1235–? Florence 1294). Italian poet. He was the most considerable figure among the transitional Tuscan poets who followed the Sicilians and preceded the ⇨ *stil novo*. A Guelph, he lamented in a celebrated *canzone* the Ghibelline victory of Montaperti (1260). Soon afterwards came his religious conversion and he entered the order of the Knights of the Virgin Mary (or Frati Gaudenti). His important *Canzoniere* contains earlier poems on the conventional love themes of Sicily and Provence, and later ones on ascetic religious subjects. The manner of his *canzoni* and sonnets remains constant, however, in its cultivation of all the artifice and deliberate obscurity of expression inherent in the Provençal tradition of the *trobar clus*. It was against Guittone that the polemic of Dante and the Stilnovists was largely directed on the grounds of his harshness, obscurity and extravagant artificiality. But though often graceless, his verse does achieve more solid meaning and a firmer contact with life than the rather fragile poetic tradition of his Sicilian predecessors. [DGR]

*Le rime*, ed. F. Egidi (1940); *Le lettere*, ed. F Meriano (1922); Contini, *PD*; Salinari *PLD*.
A. Pellizzari, *La vita e le opere di G.d'A.* (Pisa 1906); A. Del Monte, *Studi sulla poesia er metica medievale* (Naples, 1953); C. Margueron *Recherches sur G.d'A.* (Paris, 1966); *Minori*,

**Gullberg, Hjalmar** (Malmö 1898–Böke bergsslätt 1961). Swedish poet. From working-class background, if only through adoption, he devoted himself to literary and classical studies at university and came to be regarded as an 'academic' poet. As such, he had no rival for popularity in the thirties, chiefly on account of his lucid language and elegant form. In fact there is a profound ambivalence in his poetry, which derives themes from the Christian tradition (Biblical and mystical) and from classical Greek culture. Success came fairly late with *Andliga övningar* (1932) and was consolidated with *Att övervinna världen* (1937). In between, the collections *Kärlek i tjugonde seklet* (1933) and *Ensamstående bildad herre* (1935) were characteristically different, one containing frank and sensuous love poetry, the other some tersely ironic comments on the cultural aspirations of modern man. In his main collections, however, he is much preoccupied with Christian themes. His tone is urbane and sophisticated, often casual, and he can be deliberately trivial in his choice of words or produce a self-conscious effect through his rhymes; yet he remains deeply committed to a mystical vision. *Fem kornbröd och två fiskar* (1942) brought little that was new, although, under the impact of the war in Europe, it included some patriotic poetry. There followed a lacuna in his productivity. When he returned, it was with poetry of a strikingly different kind, more akin to the work of the lyrical modernists. In *Dödsmask och lustgård* (1952) classical themes come to the fore, as the poet's earlier convictions are radically qualified or even reversed. A note of scepticism now prevails, but sustained by passion, not indifference. By the same token, the sacrifice of formal conventions is more than compensated by higher poetic density. His last two books of verse again mark a phase in his development. *Terziner i okonstens tid* (1958) and *Ögon, läppar* (1959) show him once more exercising his formal talents to the full. Yet there is a new freedom in the seemingly distracted perfection of the verse as well as in the unflinching honesty that informs it. Moreover, he was never more 'contemporary' than here. The last collection, written (or dictated) while he was in the grips of a severe muscular paralysis, can be regarded as his summing-up: it shows him unfailingly alert and responding to his situation with dignity and a simplicity that is rooted in gratitude and love.

As a distinguished translator of the classical Greek dramatists and of French, Spanish and Italian poets he has also made a great impact on Swedish readers. Some of his early verse is translated in *20th Century Scandinavian Poetry*, ed. M. S. Allwood (Mullsjö, 1950); some of the later in F. Fleisher, *Seven Swedish Poets* (Stockholm, 1963). [SAB]

C. Fehrman, *H.G.* (Stockholm, 1959); K. R. Gierow, *H.G.* (Stockholm, 1961); O. Holmberg, *H.G. En Vänbok* (Stockholm, 1966).

**Gumilyov, Nikolay** (Kronstadt 1886–Sevastopol 1921). Russian poet. The son of a naval surgeon, he was brought up in St Petersburg; at school he was taught by the distinguished poet Annensky. His first book appeared in 1905, while he was studying in Paris; it shows the influence of the Symbolist writer Bryusov. But in 1911 he and S. Goradetsky founded the Poets' Guild (cf. ⇨ Acmeism), a revolt against later symbolist vagueness and pretentiousness. In 1910 he married the poetess Anna ⇨ Akhmatova, but went off on two lengthy ethnographical trips to Africa; he enlisted in 1914 (decorated for bravery) and was divorced in 1918. His pre-war poetry is imbued with vigour, exoticism, a romantic love of heroism and adventure. The life and scenery of Africa powerfully influenced the next stage of his work. Shortly after the Bolshevik Revolution he returned to Russia, though a professed monarchist, and was active in literary projects, teaching and translating; in 1921 he was arrested and shot for alleged involvement in the anti-Soviet Tagantsev plot. Only in his last three years did he reach full poetic stature; his best book was *Ognenny Stolp* (1921). Moving away from his former style, reminiscent of both Kipling and the French Parnassians, his later poems have an uncanny intensity, with symbolic, sometimes apocalyptic, overtones: notable are *Muzhik* and *Zabludivshiysya tramvay*. Perhaps overrated by émigré taste for extra-literary reasons, Gumilyov's work has oddly enough had considerable influence in the U.S.S.R., although little has been republished there since the twenties; ⇨ Tikhonov, ⇨ Bagritsky and others developed his vein of romantic heroism. [RM-G]

*Sobraniye sochineniy* (4 vols., Regensburg, 1947; ed. G. P. Struve and B. A. Filippov); Obolensky, *PBRV*.
Strakhovsky, *CW*.

**Gundulić, Franje.** ⇨ Dalmatian and Dubrovnik Literature.

**Günther, Johann Christian** (Striegau 1695–Jena 1723). German poet. Unable to discipline his own passionate and sensual nature, he led a licentious life as a student and was rejected by the father he revered and the three women he loved at various stages of his career. His attempts to gain a foothold in life as Court Poet in Dresden and as a doctor of medicine were equally unsuccessful and he died in misery at 28. His collected verse was published posthumously (1724–35) and reveals a surprising range and variety of tones: satires and political poems, love poems, poems on friendship, student songs (including the German version of *Gaudeamus igitur*), drinking songs, religious poems and poems which, in the intensity of his search for God, border on the blasphemous; but almost everything that he wrote bears the stamp of his tragic life and personality. He anticipates the *Sturm und Drang* in writing about his own emotions and experiences; his 'Leonore' is not a figment of imagination in the baroque fashion, but a girl of flesh and blood, nor is the sorrow he expresses at losing her a conventional literary pose, but a genuinely experienced emotion. Equally, his religious poems mirror his struggle for faith or express his bitter regrets at a mis-spent life. The new content is matched by a new style: the metaphors, antitheses and conceits of the baroque have largely disappeared. He is not interested in language for ornamental effect, but as a means of self-expression and communication, and his own language, which is often reminiscent of that of the folk-song, has a directness and simplicity matched only by that of the younger Goethe, who recognized Günther as his precursor. [WAC]

*Werke*, ed. W. Krämer, BLVS, 275, 277, 279, 283, 286 (1930–7); ed. H. Dahlke (1958).

W. Krämer, *Das Leben des schlesischen Dichters J.C.* (Godesberg, 1950).

**Gutzkow, Karl Ferdinand** (Berlin 1811–Sachsenhausen 1878). German dramatist, novelist and journalist in Stuttgart, Frankfurt, Hamburg, Paris and Dresden (where he was *dramaturg* at the Hoftheater (1846–61)). Finally persecution mania led to aimless travelling. Most notable plays: the comedies *Zopf und Schwert* (1844), *Das Urbild des Tartuffe* (1844), *Der Königsleutnant* (1849), dramatizing part of Goethe's *Dichtung und Wahrheit*; the tragedies *Richard Savage* (1839), *Werner oder Herz und Welt* (1840), *Wullenweber* (1844), *Uriel Acosta* (1846; tr. H. Spicer, 1885) echoing ⇨ Lessing's *Nathan* and ⇨ Scribe. Most important novels: the Voltairean *Maha Guru, Geschichte eines Gottes* (1833); *Wally, die Zweiflerin* (1835; repr. 1965), which voiced religious doubts inspired by D. F. Strauss's *Das Leben Jesu* and led to his imprisonment for 'blasphemy' in Mannheim; *Die Ritter vom Geiste* (1850ff.), a rambling panorama of society and ideas influenced by ⇨ Immermann, ⇨ Sue, ⇨ Saint-Simon; *Der Zauberer von Rom* (1858ff.) advocating enlightened Catholicism. While a leading member of Das ⇨ Junge Deutschland and pioneer of social realism, his works suffer from bad craftsmanship and tendentiousness. He attacks romanticism, classicism, church, state, and vaguely demands rational humanity, justice, progress, freedom of thought and expression. His autobiographical writings include *Aus der Knabenzeit* (1852), *Rückblicke* (1875), *Die schöneren Stunden* (1875), *Lebensbilder* (1869ff.). [LL]

*Ausgewählte Werke*, ed. H. H. Houben (12 vols., 1908).

E. M. Butler, *The Saint-Simonian Religion in Germany* (1926); Dietze, *JD*.

**Guy (Guido) of Bazoches** (*c.* 1140–1203). Secular canon of Châlons, who took part in the Second Crusade and was present at the siege of Acre; remembered for his letters and some skilful Latin poems. [FB]

*An. Hym.* 50; selection from letters and poems, *Neues Archiv*, xvi (1891); Raby, *CLP*.

**Gyllensten, Lars** (Stockholm 1921– ). Swedish novelist and story-writer. A leading exponent of the new, intellectual approach to literature in Sweden with a characteristically international orientation. (He has had a scientific career, with numerous publications in the fields of embryology and histology; he teaches at the Karolinska Institutet, Stockholm.) His intellectualism and preoccupation with contemporary issues, political, ethical and religious, does not prevent him from realizing the individuality of his characters. He is a master of flexible prose with an outstanding ability to render current speech. His novels can be seen as experiments in character, studies in fundamental roles and attitudes, e.g. the short novel *Barnabok* ('Children's Book', 1952), which carries a gruesomely ironic title, being a study of a refusal to grow up which leads to isolation and mental decay. *Carnivora* (1953), subtitled 'conversational exercises', is a corrosive exposition of human meanness and egoism with a saving quantity of ironic detachment. In a number of more large-scale works, the novels *Senilia* (1956), *Senatorn* (1958) and *Sokrates' död* (1960), he has further explored man as a social being caught between his animal nature and the tyranny of ideologies on the one hand and the longing for an ideal and a personally meaningful existence on the other. His imaginative range is greater than ever in *Lotus i Hades* (1966), an evocation in poetic prose of fleeting memories of the dead of many ages. An enemy of ideologies and human rigidity, but a believer in vigilance and change, he has given a statement of personal convictions in *Nihilistiskt credo* (1964). He became a member of the Swedish Academy in 1966. His recent work has consolidated the regeneration of the philosophical novel in Sweden. In his masterly handling 'philosophy' becomes less of a discursive statement superimposed on the narrative than a fundamental attitude of persons or even of a fictional narrator, e.g. *Kains memoarer* (1963; tr. K. Bradfield, *The Testament of Kain*, 1967). [SAB]

K. E. Lagerlöf, 'Utbrytnings försök', in *Samtal med 60-talister* (Stockholm, 1965); *ASR*, LV, 2, 1967.

# H

**Haanpää, Pentti** (Pulkkila 1905–Pyhäntä 1955). Finnish novelist and short-story writer. When, in 1928, he published *Kenttä ja kasarmi*, a collection of short stories about life in the Finnish army, he was accused of communism, materialism and atheism. His work was virtually banned, though his social demands are now often taken for granted. When war came again and Haanpää underwent a patriotic 'conversion', he was fully rehabilitated. Writing with a powerful irony – sometimes misunderstood – he is one of the most sombre and pessimistic of Finnish authors, as his macabre themes indicate: an old woman devoured by worms, a group of drunks who drive one of their companions to the cemetery in a hearse to lay him in consecrated ground. In another story an old man, doubting the parson's word, resolves to test for himself the hypothesis of God's existence: he builds a great pyre and immolates himself on it, in the belief that in so doing he is going one better than Christ, since 'burning hurts more'. These events are described with almost cosmic detachment and deep humour; by subtle touches the situation is given philosophical significance. Light is shed on social implications, on human beliefs and the hypocrisy that goes with them. Haanpää's humour is hard and cruel. He sets human life against Nature, which remains indifferent to human purposes, and makes man and his preoccupations appear tragi-comically trivial and small. [AK]

*Kootut teokset* (10 vols., 1956–8); *Isännät ja isäntien varjot* (1935); *Korpisotaa* (1940; French tr. A. Sauvageot, *Guerre dans le désert bleu*, Paris, 1942); *Jauhot* (1949).

**Haavikko, Paavo** (Helsinki 1931– ). Finnish poet, dramatist and prose-writer. The most talented modernist of the 1950s, noted for the wide historical and geographical ambience of his imagery and precise handling of words and concepts. His imagination is as much at home in Ancient Rome as in the Germany of Luther or the Helsinki of today. The essential feature of his poetry, however, is an airy and delicate lyricism, in which the clarity and directness of the imagery (he has been called a 'Finnish Imagist') owes something to the influence of Chinese and Japanese poetry. The opposition between the world and the poet's own inner world is strongly brought out in *Talvipalatsi* (1959; tr. A. Hollo, *The Winter Palace*, in *Chelsea 17*, Gibraltar, 1961), an example of 'visionary metapoetry'. Of his plays, *Münchhausen* is concerned with the court of Catherine the Great and the division of Poland; *Nuket* takes its theme and its characters from Gogol's *Dead Souls*. He has also produced some experimental, rather bloodless prose, which aims at penetrating to the 'soul' of everyday things, but ignores the social background of characters and events. [RV]

*Runot 1951–1961* (1962); *Puut, kaikki heidän vihreytensä* (1966); Novels: *Yksityisiä asioita* (1960); *Toinen taivas ja maa* (1961); *Vuodet* (1962).

**Hacks, Peter** (Breslau 1928– ). German dramatist. Influenced by ⇨ Brecht, he joined the Berliner Ensemble in 1955. His best plays present Marxist interpretations of historical events, e.g. *Eröffnung des indischen Zeitalters* (1954, about Columbus) and *Die Schlacht bei Lobositz* (1956), based on U. ⇨ Bräker's chronicle, satirizing the Prussian army of the Seven Years' War. Other satires on the same period are *Der Müller von Sanssouci* (1958) and *Die Uhr geht nach* (1958), while *Die Sorgen um die Macht* (1958; revised 1962) deals with contemporary social problems in East Germany. [LL]

Kunisch, *HDG*.

**Hacohen, Shalom** (Poland 1772–Vienna 1845). Hebrew poet and dramatist. One of the many Jewish writers who, educated in the traditional way, joined the enlightenment movement. He first went to Germany but when less and less people there read Hebrew, he left for the Austro-Hungarian monarchy where he still found a large public. His best-known work is his verse play *Amal ve-Tirza* (1812). [EE]

Waxman, *HJL*.

**Hadewijch** (late 12th and early 13th cent.). Dutch mystic and poet. She was the leader of a lay group associated with a *béguinage*. Her authoritative tone suggests aristocratic birth, and she lived in Brabant. Her Augustinian pietism shows the influence of the French mystics Hugo and Richard of St Victor and above all of the Fleming William of St Thierry. Her spiritual *minnesanc* expresses in poetry of intense feeling and great beauty the neo-Platonic notion of the soul temporarily separated from its perfect image in eternity. The divinely created but finite emotion of human love is the experience by which the unknown ideal can be envisaged, and it is in terms of the most intimate and personal love that she sings of her yearning for the Beloved, and of her pain at her necessary separation from One of whom she is so unworthy. Her *Strophische gedichten* consists of 45 poems of various lengths, all probably written to music, many using Provençal courtly verse forms. The remainder of her work is intentionally didactic, whether in *Mengeldichten*, instruction in verse form, or her letters and *Visioenen* in prose. While these works are essential to an understanding of her esoteric mysticism and were even known where her poetry was not (e.g. in Bavaria, where she was given the name Adelwîp), it is her sublime lyricism that is unsurpassed in Dutch poetry, and a remarkable phenomenon in medieval Europe. [PK]

*Strofische gedichten*, ed. E. Rombants and N. de Paepe (1961); Barnouw, *CA*; Weevers, *PNEC*; *Mediaeval Netherlands Religious Literature*, tr. E. Colledge (1965).
*H. Een bloemlezing uit hare werken*, ed. J. van Mierlo (1950); P.J.-B., *H. d'Anvers* (Paris, 1954).

**Hadloub, Johannes** (fl. *c.* 1290–1320). Swiss lyric poet. His work belongs to the final phase of Minnesang (⇨ Minnesinger). He was of humble origin but affected in his poetry the ideals and attitudes of courtly love-poets. Of particular interest is his account of how members of the Zürich family of Manesse arranged for the collection and recording of Minnesang lyrics: this collection, known as the Manesse manuscript, forms the core of the largest single source of Middle High German lyric poetry. [RT]

*Die Schweizer Minnesänger*, ed. K. Bartsch (Frauenfeld, 1886).
Ehrismann, *GDL*.

**Hagedorn, Friedrich von** (Hamburg 1708–Hamburg 1754). German poet. He came to London as secretary of the Danish Ambassador (1729) and later worked for an English firm in Hamburg. His *Oden und Lieder* (collected edn 1742–52) are greatly indebted to Dryden, Gay and Horace, and their linguistic suppleness, grace and lightness of touch make him the foremost of the German Anacreontic poets. His didactic poems teach cheerful optimism, reasonableness rewarded by contentment, etc. His *Fabeln und Erzählungen* (1738–50), written largely under the influence of La Fontaine, enjoyed considerable popularity in their day. [WAC]

*Gedichte*, ed. A. Sauer (DLE 10, 1883).
K. Epting, *Der Stil in den Lyrischen und didaktischen Gedichten H.* (Stuttgart, 1929).

**Hagelstange, Rudolf** (Nordhausen 1912– ). German poet. His *Ballade vom verschütteten Leben* (1952; tr. H. Salinger, *Ballad of the Buried Life*, Chapel Hill, 1962) is the most successful long narrative poem by any German poet about his own time. The sonnet-cycle *Venezianisches Credo* (1946), privately circulated during the war, is an eloquent moral indictment of Nazism. All his work, informed by a love of freedom and a sense of the values of Western civilization, has a strong religious basis; but he is no less a master of the modern idiom. He has also written stories (*Wo bleibst Du, Trost?*, 1958, etc.), art books (*Art Treasures of Germany*, 1958, with E. Domke), and essays (*Es steht in unserer Macht*, 1953; *How do you like America?*, 1957, etc.). [PB]

*Lied der Jahre, Gesammelte Gedichte 1931–1961* (1961); Bridgwater, *TCGV*; Hamburger and Middleton, *MGP*.
*GR*, XXXIII, 2, 1958.

**Halas, František** (Brno 1901–Prague 1949). Czech poet. The son of a textile worker and self-educated by reading, he worked in a publishing house and finally in the Ministry of Information.

After a youthful period of proletarian poetry – 'The world, my love and revolution' was his own definition of his themes – he abandoned faith in a possible materialist solution and adopted extreme subjectivism. Death and nothingness became the primary reality, and life merely an illusion. At the time of Munich in 1938 his poems (*Torso naděje*, 1939) expressed the collective hope of the nation, but he was unable to keep in step

step with the crowd for long. In his last poems the apocalyptic vision of a last judgement which always overshadowed his verse, acquired a new urgency after the advent of the atom bomb. [KB]

*Sepie* (1927); *Kohout plaší smrt* (1930); *Tvář* (1931); *Staré ženy* (1935; tr. K. Offer, *Old Women*, 1948); *A co?* (1957).

B. Václavek, *Tvorbou k realitě* (Brno, 1935); *O Frant. Halasovi* (Bratislava, 1934).

**Halbe, Max** (Guettland, Danzig 1865–Gut Neuötting, Bavaria 1944). German dramatist. His *Jugend* (1893) enjoyed a Naturalistic vogue for its psychology of adolescent love. The break-up of an old social order in *Der Eisgang* (1892), *Der Strom* (1904), etc., resounds with now dated hopes for a new freedom. Less successfully than G. ⇨ Hauptmann, he attempted lyrical, romantic, humorous escapes from Naturalism (*Der Eroberer*, 1899; *Walpurgistag*, 1903; *Insel der Seligen*, 1906; etc.). His autobiographical *Jahrhundertwende* (1935) depicts intimately the literary world of Munich. [AKT]

**Haller, Albrecht von** (Bern 1708–Bern 1777). Swiss poet. A botanist and anatomist of European reputation, his scientific interests are reflected in his verse – his didactic poem, *Die Alpen* (1729), has footnotes with the Latin names of the plants mentioned. But this pedantry was accompanied by a linguistic power, a feeling for the majesty of the natural beauty of Switzerland and a pessimistic awareness of the questionable aspects of material and scientific progress which rendered it unique in an age of facile optimism and indifference to nature. In keeping with his age, however, he also wrote a number of weighty contemplative poems such as his theodicy, *Über den Ursprung des Übels* (1734). His early love poem *Doris* (1730) and the elegies he wrote on the death of his wife have a rare directness and sincerity. Towards the end of his life, he also wrote a number of political *romans à clef*, among them *Usong* (1771) and *Alfred, König der Angelsachsen* (1773). [WAC]

*Gedichte*, ed. H. Maync (Leipzig, 1923).

A. Ischer, *A.v.H. und das klassische Altertum* (Bern, 1928); A. Frey, *A.v.H.s Staatsromane* (Freiburg/B., 1928).

**Haller, P.** ⇨ Swiss-German Dialect Literature.

**Hallfreðar Saga.** ⇨ Icelandic Sagas.

**Hallgrímsson.** ⇨ Jónas Hallgrímsson.

**Hallgrímur Pétursson** (*c.* 1614–1674). Icelandic poet. After a childhood in poor circumstances, he received some schooling in Copenhagen, *c.* 1630–7. He then married and lived as an ordinary small farmer in Iceland until his ordination in 1644. In 1651 he moved to a better living, Saurbær in Hvalfjörður, which he held until his resignation in 1669; he was then suffering from leprosy. He was a capable and energetic farmer and priest. His most famous poems are the 50 hymns of commentary and meditation on the Passion, *Passíusálmar*, and the poem *Um dauðans óvissan tíma*, published together in 1666 and reprinted over 50 times since. They are outstanding for the tender sincerity of his piety, the colloquial vigour of his verse, and his ability to use familiar homely language in a heightened and austere way. [PGF]

Parts of the *Passion Hymns*, tr. in C. V. Pilcher, *Icelandic Meditations on the Passion* (N.Y., 1923) and *Icelandic Christian Classics* (Melbourne, 1950).

**Hamann, Johann Georg** (Königsberg 1730–Münster 1788). German writer. The decisive event in his life was the religious experience he underwent while a merchant in London in which he felt that he was given insight into the true meaning of the Bible. His religion conditioned everything he wrote, even to the aphoristic, semi-biblical style, rich and often obscure in meaning, which earned him the title of the 'Magus of the North' (the greater part of his life was spent in Königsberg), and he became one of the most important opponents of the rationalism of the Enlightenment. His most important works are the *Sokratische Denkwürdigkeiten* (1759), the *Kreuzzüge des Philologen* (1762) and the *Fünf Briefe, das Schuldrama betreffend* (1763) which may be regarded as seminal works for the ⇨ *Sturm und Drang* movement. Reason is rejected as a means of comprehending God or the nature of existence; the senses and the emotions are regarded as being coequal, if not superior, to reason in human nature, and human action, it is maintained, should proceed out of the totality of man's being; classical rules are dismissed as a fetter on the imagination of the poet, who is held to be possessed of a God-like independence in his creative work, and poetry is exalted as the mother-tongue of mankind. His influence was heightened by his personal relations with ⇨ Herder, whom he introduced to Shakespeare and Ossian. [WAC]

*Werke*, ed. J. Nadler (Vienna, 1949ff.); R. G. Smith, *J.G.H.* (1960) (with translated selection).
J. Nadler, *J.G.H.* (Salzburg, 1949).

**Hameiri, Avigdor**, pseud. of Emil Feuerstein (Hungary 1886–1970). Hebrew poet. Raised in a traditional Jewish atmosphere but deeply influenced by the Hungarian poet ⇨ Ady. In 1910 he founded the short-lived Hebrew periodical *Hayehudi*. Translated many Hungarian poets into Hebrew, among them *Tragedy of Man* by Madach which has become compulsory reading in Israeli schools. During the First World War he served in the Austro-Hungarian Army and fell prisoner to the Russians. His war-time novel *Hashigaon Hagadol* left a deep impression on modern Hebrew writers. After the war, he settled in Palestine and, upon the establishment of the State of Israel, became first editor of the Israeli equivalent of *Hansard*. [EE]

*Belivnat hasappit* (Jerusalem, 1962) (poems); *Hamaschiach halavan* (Tel Aviv, 1948) (novel); *Hamsked haran* (Tel Aviv, 1944) (short stories); *Mivchar sippurei A.H.* (Tel Aviv, 1954) (short stories).
Waxman, *HJL*.

**Hämmerli-Marti, S.** ⇨ Swiss-German Dialect Literature.

**Hamsun, Knut** (Lom, Oppland 1859–Grimstad 1952). Norwegian novelist, playwright and poet. Of peasant stock, he spent his youth in the province of Nordland in north Norway. He started work at an early age and led a jack-of-all-trades existence; in the 1880s he spent two periods in America. His first successful novel was *Sult* (1890; tr. G. Egerton, *Hunger*, 1899). His early work was a reaction against current Norwegian writers (including Ibsen), whom he criticized in lectures for their social preoccupations and their lack of understanding of 'the unconscious life of the mind'. His novel *Mysterier* (1892; tr. A. G. Chater, *Mysteries*, 1927) was intended as a demonstration of what the new literature should be. It is in many respects a remarkable work and in advance of its time, but it is not so readily accessible, nor has it been so popular, as his other novels of this period: *Pan* (1894; tr. J. W. McFarlane, 1956) and *Victoria* (1898; tr. A. G. Chater, 1929).

In his later work he forsook close scrutiny of the inner life of the individual and concerned himself more with the individual and society, and in particular with the perversion of the Self through contact with society. In novels like *Under høststjernen* (1906; tr. W. Worster, *Autumn*, in *Wanderers*, 1922), *En vandrer spiller med sordin* (1909; *With Muted Strings*, ibid.) and *Den sidste glæde* (1912; tr. P. Wiking, *Look Back on Happiness*, 1940) his hero is the wanderer – in fact, a lightly disguised Knut Hamsun. The wanderer also reappears later in his work, in the trilogy *Landstrykere* (1927; tr. E. Gay-Tifft, *Vagabonds*, 1930), *August* (1930; tr. E. Gay-Tifft, 1932) and *Men livet lever* (1933; tr. E. Gay-Tifft, *The Road Leads On*, 1937), but here the author's attitude to his hero August (one of his most memorable creations) is more ambivalent. In the novels *Børn av tiden* (1913) and *Segelfoss by* (1915), the consequences for the individual of the growth of modern town society are scrutinized; in *Markens grøde* (1917; tr. W. Worster, *The Growth of the Soil*, 1920), his best-known book, the wanderer comes to rest; at the same time, Hamsun seemed to be calling a war-weary world 'back to the soil'.

In spite of many predilections and prejudices (in his novels and in public pronouncements) he was not in essence a critic of society. His attitude to his characters is consistently marked by irony and ambivalence (his narrative technique is of particular interest), and the felicities of his style do not entirely disguise the void which surrounds human life as he sees it. The most considerable literary figure in Norway since Ibsen, his reputation now seems to have recovered from the setback it received because of his pro-Nazi attitude during the last war; on this his last, mainly autobiographical book, *På gjengrodde stier* (1949), provides an interesting but one-sided commentary. His plays and verse, though throwing interesting sidelights on his mind and art, are relatively unimportant. [RGP]

*Samlede verker* (15 vols., 1954–6).
H. A. Larsen, *K.H.* (1922); E. Skavlan, *K.H.* (Oslo, 1929); T. Hamsun, *K.H.* (Oslo, 1952); S. S. Nilson, *En ørn i uvær. K.H. og politikken* (Oslo, 1960); O. Øyslebø, *H. gjennom stilen* (Oslo, 1964); Gustafson, *SSN*; Downs, *MNL*; McFarlane, *TNL*.

**Hanka, Václav** (Hořiněves 1791–Prague 1861). Czech author. A gifted scholar and writer but a tortuous and eccentric character, he is best known for the leading part he played in the production of forged manuscripts of ostensibly medieval poetry in an attempt to enrich the Czech national literary heritage. Known as the manuscripts of Králové Dvůr and Zelená Hora, they were accepted until exposed as forgeries in the 1880s by J. Gebauer, T. G. ⇨ Masaryk and others. [RA]

*Rukopis královédvorský a zelenohorský,* ed. V. Vojtěch (1930); *The Queen's Court Manuscript, with Other Ancient Bohemian Poems, tr. from the Original Slavonic into English Verse,* tr. A. H. Wratislaw (1852).

J. Hanuš, *Česká literatura devatenáctého století* (2nd edn, Prague, 1911); S. E. Mann, 'Václav Hanka's Forgeries', in *SEER*, 36 (1957–8).

**Hansen, Martin A.** (Strøby 1909–Copenhagen 1955). Danish novelist. He dealt first with social problems (*Nu opgiver han*, 1935; *Kolonien*, 1937) then apparently escaping, during the Occupation, into fable with *Jonatans Rejse* (1941) and into a gay Reformation period-novel with *Lykkelige Kristoffer* (1945) – each with allusions to the present, however, which he approaches by way of myth in *Tornebusken* (1946) and *Agerhønen* (1948). The plight of a modern idealist is most skilfully handled in *Løgneren* (1950; tr. J. J. Egglishaw, *The Liar*, 1954). His collected works (10 vols., 1961) include essays on Scandinavian cultural history. [ELB]

T. Bjørnvig, *M.A.H.s digtning* (Copenhagen, 1949); and *Kains Alter* (1964); G. Printz-Påhlson, '*The Liar:* The Paradox of Fictional Communication in M.A.H.', in *Scandinavian Studies*, 36, 4 (1964).

**Hansson, Ola** (Grönby 1860–Buyukdere 1925). Swedish poet, prose-writer and essayist. A farmer's son, his exceptionally sensitive nature poetry captures the mood of his native province of Skåne. He is remembered chiefly for 2 slender volumes of verse, *Dikter* (1884) and *Notturno* (1886), and his early prose, which reveals his interest in the psychology of extraordinary or morbid states. His most important work in this genre, *Sensitiva amorosa* (1887), is a collection of sketches treating the intimate erotic reactions of feminine subjects and the irrational impulses that frustrate their love. The hostile reception of the work forced the author to leave his country to begin a restless itinerant life on the Continent. After 1890 he made a name for himself in Germany, and wrote a number of essays in German, notably on Strindberg and Nietzsche. His later production, which includes several autobiographical works, e.g. *Rustgården* (1910), and lyrical poetry, was read by decreasing numbers. Finally his isolation from Sweden became almost complete. Symptoms of paranoia help to explain this development. He married Laura Marholm, a German authoress, in 1889. After a period of Nietzscheanism, he became a follower of Julius Langbehn. Then he converted to Roman Catholicism, but never regained the sense of rootedness which gave his early work its distinctive quality. [SAB]

E. Ekelund, *O.H.s ungdomsdiktning* (Helsinki, 1930); H. Levander *Sensitiva amorosa* (Stockholm, 1944); I. Holm, *O.H.* (Lund, 1957); Borland, *NI.*

**Hardy, Alexandre** (Paris ?–Paris 1632). French dramatist. More is known about his plays than his life. He is said to have composed as many as 600, 30 of them published, 10 more known from the theatre records. Of his 12 tragedies most are taken from ancient historians popular in the Renaissance (*Coriolan*, *Lucrèce*, *Cornélie*). Most famous perhaps was *Marianne*, which inspired ⇨ Tristan's play of 1637 and possibly also ⇨ Hebbel. To the list of his comedies should now be added *Les ramoneurs* (ed. and attribution, A. Gill, TFM, 1957). [WGM]

Lancaster, *HFDL.*

**Harsányi, Zsolt** (Korompa 1887–Budapest 1943). Hungarian writer. His mainly biographical novels (*Liszt*, *Rubens*, *Munkácsy*, *Galilei*, etc.) were widely read bestsellers. His success was due to his well-chosen subject-matter and a style which appealed to the middle class; his real place in Hungarian literature is difficult to define. His work has been translated into many languages. *Eppur si muove* (tr. P. Tábori, 1963); *Immortal Franz* (tr. F. Stokes, N.Y., 1937); *Through a Woman's Eyes* (tr. unknown, N.Y., 1940); *The Star-Gazer* (tr. unknown, N.Y., 1939); *The Lover of Life* (tr. unknown, N.Y., 1942). [JFR]

Reményi, *HWL.*

**Harsdörffer, Georg Philipp** (Nürnberg 1607–Nürnberg 1658). German poet. Co-founder with ⇨ Klaj, of the Schäfer- und Blumenorden an der Pegnitz (1644), a middle-class literary society in Nürnberg which imitated the older, more aristocratic language societies, but laid special emphasis on the pastoral convention (Harsdörffer's pseudonym was Strefon). His manual of poetics, the *Poetischer Trichter* (3 parts, 1648–53), illustrates his rationalistic approach to poetry and represents a continuation and development of ⇨ Opitz – at times almost to the point of absurdity. Harsdörffer popularized the dactyl and saw the essence of poetry as lying in word music. His virtuosity in onomatopoeia, rhyme, etc., helped to make German a more supple medium for poetic expression. The *Frauenzimmergesprächspiele* (8 parts, 1641–9), collections of dialogues which aimed at raising the general cultural level and at inculcating more decorous and cultivated social behaviour, were popular in their day. [WAC]

W. Kayser, *Die Klangmalerei bei H.* (Leipzig, 1932); G. A. Narziss, *Studien zu den Frauenzimmergesprächspielen G.P.H.s* (Leipzig, 1928).

**Hartlaub, Geno(veva)** (Mannheim 1915– ). German novelist. Sister of Felix Hartlaub. She was a publisher's reader in Heidelberg from 1945, and in Hamburg from 1949; and has been a newspaper editor in Hamburg since 1956. Characteristic psychological themes, like self-realization, appear in *Noch im Traum* (1943) and, more questionably, in *Gefangene der Nacht* (1961), where Benjamin struggles to 'realize' what the Gestapo are doing to his family. *Der Mond hat Durst* (1963) borrows from C. G. Jung to interpret psychological disorders mythologically. [LL]

Kunisch, *HDG.*

**Hartmann von Aue** (fl. 1190–1210). Middle High German epic and lyric poet. One of the great masters of the classical courtly epic (with ⇨ Gottfried von Strassburg and ⇨ Wolfram von Eschenbach). He was *ministerialis* at a Swabian court and took part in the Emperor Henry VI's crusade of 1197. Of his poetic works we possess 4 extended narrative poems, 2 shorter allegorical love poems and 16 lyrics (13 love lyrics and 3 crusading lyrics). Of the narrative poems, two (*Erec* and *Iwein*) are secular epics based on works by ⇨ Chrétien de Troyes and belonging to the Arthurian cycle, while the other two (*Gregorius* and *Der arme Heinrich*) are religious works with an openly didactic purpose. He preaches above all the deal of restraint and moderation (*maze*) in human conduct. Literature is for him the instrument of a moral purpose: rhetorical devices and stylistic elegance are deliberately subordinated to the direct narration of an edifying sequence of events. [RT]

*Werke*, ed. F. Bech (3 vols., repr. 1934); *Der arme Heinrich, Gregorius*, ed. and intr. F. Neumann (1958).

P. Wapnewski, *H.v.A.* (Stuttgart, 1962); Ehrismann, *GDL*, ii.

**Hartzenbusch, Juan Eugenio** (Madrid 1806–Madrid 1880). Spanish dramatist and poet. Son of a German carpenter. His play *Los amantes de Teruel* (1837; CC, 1947; tr. H. Thomas, *The Lovers of Teruel*, 1938) is one of the most important of the Romantic era. Its atmosphere is melancholy, not passionate (as intended), and two revised versions forfeit spontaneity. His only other success among 69 plays, including fairy-tale pieces, was *La jura de Santa Gadea* (1845; CC, 1947), on an episode from the life of the ⇨ Cid. He translated Schiller's *Die Glocke*, and wrote some poetic fables. He was a good scholar, edited the 17th-century dramatists for the BAE, and was director of the Biblioteca Nacional from 1862. [JMC]

*Obras* (5 vols., 1887–92).

**Hašek, Jaroslav** (Prague 1883–Lipnice 1923). Czech novelist and short-story writer. The son of a teacher and a freelance journalist, he was a well-known figure in Prague bohemian circles before the First World War because of his practical jokes, anarchism and his own satirical Party of Moderate Progress Within the Limits of the Law. During the war he deserted from the Austrian Army and joined the free Czechoslovak forces in Russia fighting for his country's independence. In 1918 he joined the Russian Communist Party and served as a political commissar with the Red Army. Three years later he returned to Czechoslovakia to work on his main book, *The Good Soldier Schweik* (English version – with vulgar expressions and the cruder passages omitted – by P. Selver, 1930), as far as his health, undermined by alcoholism, permitted. The hero of this unwieldy and unfinished novel has been interpreted in many ways – as the 'little man' fighting officialdom by native wit and subterfuge, as the Czech patriot making fun of his Austrian rulers, or as a purely anarchistic, anti-social figure. There is no doubt some truth in all these interpretations; indeed, part of the success of Hašek's work is due to the ambivalent character of his hero. [RA/KB]

*The Tourist Guide*, tr. J. T. Havlů (Prague, 1962) (26 stories).

V. Menger, *Lidský profil J.H.* (Prague, 1946); F. Langer, *Byli a bylo* (Prague, 1963).

**Hasenclever, Walter** (Aachen 1890–suicide in Les Milles internment camp, France, 1940). German dramatist and poet. His play *Der Sohn* (1914, produced 1916) was a landmark in Expressionist drama with its typical theme of parricidal revolt, linked in later plays with politically naïve visions of all men liberated from ancient tyrannies (*Die Menschen*, 1918; *Der Retter*, 1919; *Jenseits*, 1920). Their symbolic action and declamatory style was later abandoned for more conventional comedy, e.g. *Ein besserer Herr* (1926), *Bourgeois bleibt Bourgeois* (musical comedy, with ⇨ Toller, 1928), *Christoph Columbus* ... (with ⇨ Tucholsky, 1932), *What Should a Husband Do?* (tr. Griffith, 1936), *Konflikt in Assyrien* (under pseudonym of Axel Kjellstrom: tr. G. Bullet, *Scandal in Assyria*, 1939). His film-scripts include that of *Anna Christie* (Greta Garbo, 1930). [PB]

*Gedichte, Dramen, Prosa*, ed. Kurt Pinthus (Reinbek, 1963).

A. Hoelzel, *W.H.'s Humanitarianism* (Boston, 1964) (dissertation); E. Zeltner, *Die expressionistischen Dramen W.H.s* (Vienna, 1961) (dissertation); Garten, *MGD*; Soergel, *DDZ*.

**Hauch, Carsten** (Frederikshald, Norway 1790–Rome 1872). Danish poet and novelist. While a student of zoology at Copenhagen he sent poems in admiration to ⇨ Oehlenschläger, who discouraged him from continuing. During a visit to Italy, where one of his legs was amputated, he began to write again, both poems and romantic plays. His most popular novels were *Vilhelm Zabern* (1834), *Guldmageren* (1836), and *En polsk Familie* (1839), and the historical novel *Robert Fulton* (1853; tr. 1868); his most interesting play *Søstrene paa Kinnekullen* (1849). He is greatest, however, as a lyrical poet, but only a few of his poems have been translated. [ELB]

K. Galster, *C.H.* (2 vols., Copenhagen, 1930–5).

**Hauff, Wilhelm** (Stuttgart 1802–Stuttgart 1827). German novelist and 'Märchen' writer. He studied theology in Tübingen, but became editor of Cotta's *Morgenblatt* and a freelance author in Stuttgart. He combined Romanticism with early Realism, and was influenced by Fielding, Goldsmith, ⇨ Jean Paul, the ⇨ Grimm brothers, and the *Arabian Nights*. His fame rests on his historical novel *Lichtenstein* (1826; tr. F. Woodley and W. Lander, 1846), a Swabian imitation of Walter Scott, and his fairy-tale cycles *Die Karawane*, *Der Scheich von Alessandria und seine Sklaven*, and *Das Wirtshaus im Spessart* (published in three *Märchenalmanache*, 1826–8). His episodic *Mitteilungen aus den Memoiren des Satans* (1825–6), *Phantasien im Bremer Ratskeller* (1827; tr. 1889), and his novel *Der Mann im Mond* (1825) contain humorous fantasy, satire and parody. The best of his 6 novellen are the realistic *Die Bettlerin vom Pont des Arts* (1826; tr. J. Nisbet, *A Constant Lover*, 1893) and the historical *Das Bild des Kaisers* (posth. 1828). [LL]

*Werke*, ed. G. Spiekerkötter (3 vols., 1961); ed. H. Engelhard (2 vols., 1961–2); *Eastern Fairy Tales*, 'revised and edited' R. Ingram (1949) (translation); *Fairy Tales*, tr. J. R. Edwards (1961).

H. Hofmann, *W.H.* (Frankfurt, 1902).

**Hauptmann, Gerhart** (Ober-Salzbrunn, Silesia 1862–Agnetendorf 1946). German dramatist, novelist and poet. Trained in agriculture, sculpture. At Jena university (history, philosophy, etc.) he became associated with ⇨ Holz in Berlin and achieved fame with his first play, *Vor Sonnenaufgang* (1889; tr. L. Bloomfield, *Before Dawn*, Boston, 1909), which caused an uproar at its première (Freie Bühne) and marked the birth of German naturalist drama. Besides portraying alcoholic degeneracy, it shocked with the hero's 'scientific' doctrine of determinism – which now seems tragically old-fashioned and 'unnecessary'. More original was *Die Weber* (1892; tr. T. H. Lustig, *The Weavers* in *Five Plays* by G.H., 1961), an 'epic' drama in five tableaux with no hero and little plot; but its cast of Silesian weavers come alive as a dramatic symbol of human misery in the industrial age and there is tragic pathos in the common helplessness of owner and worker, rebel and victim. *Florian Geyer* (1896) applies the same technique to the numberless masses of the Peasants' Revolt; successful (only since 1920s) for the 'poetry' of its stark realism and dialect. Even more conventional tragedies like

*Fuhrmann Henschel* (1898; tr. ibid.) and *Rose Bernd* (1903; tr. ibid.) make contact again with the timeless springs of tragedy through the same naturalistic medium, which takes in the Berlin underworld in *Die Ratten* (1910: the author's favourite, later filmed), and one of the few great comedies in German literature, *Der Biberpelz* (1893; tr. ibid.).

In the dream-play *Hanneles Himmelfahrt* (1893; tr. ibid.) and the 'fairy-drama' *Die versunkene Glocke* (1896; tr. C. H. Meltzer, *The Sunken Bell*, 1900), he discovered new (and once admired) poetry in Romantic flights from reality. Perhaps the finest blend of fantasy and realism is achieved in *Und Pippa tanzt* (1906). His fantasies seem always partly erotic in inspiration, typically about passionate young girls in ambiguously sensual-spiritual situations, having autobiographical implications perhaps (cf. *Das Buch der Leidenschaft* (1929–30)) and interpreted most strikingly in the novel *Der Ketzer von Soana* (1918; tr. B. Q. Morgan, *The Heretic of Soana*, 1960), where a priest is converted to a pagan-poetic gospel of nature. This later 'Naturalism' (half Nietzschean, half Hellenistic following a visit to Greece in 1907, cf. *Griechischer Frühling*, 1908) alternated in his later works with mystical themes (e.g. *Der grosse Traum*, an epic poem, 1942), which he examined with both sympathy and some psychological realism in the novel of a modern Christ, *Der Narr in Christo* (1910; tr. T. Selzer, *The Fool in Christ*, *Emanuel Quint*, 1912). Much of his prolific work has a cloudy grandeur of conception, but it is for the down-to-earth scenes of his earlier dramas that he is chiefly remembered. [PB/AKT]

*Das gesammelte Werk* (17 vols., 1942); *Sämtliche Werke* (Centenar Ausgabe), ed. H. E. Hass (10 vols., 1962ff.); ed. Stenzel (2 vols., 1956); *Dramatic Works*, ed. L. Lewisohn, tr. L. Lewisohn and others (9 vols., 1913–29).

H. F. Garten, *G.H.* (1954); Margaret Sinden, *G.H.: The Prose Plays* (Toronto, 1957); K. S. Guthke, *G.H. Weltbild im Werk* (Göttingen, 1961); T. Mann, *G.H.* (Gütersloh, 1953); C. F. W. Behl, *Wege zu G.H.* (Kitzingen, 1952); K. L. Tank, *G.H.* (Reinbek, 1959); *Hauptmann Centenary Lectures*, ed. K. G. Knight and F. Norman (1964); Natan, *GML*, I.

**Haushofer, Albrecht** (Munich 1903–Moabit 1945). German poet. He was shot for his part in the Hitler plot. His *Moabiter Sonette* (1946), written in prison, are remarkable as a poetic testimony to the German Resistance. He also wrote plays: *Scipio* (1934), *Sulla* (1938), *Augustus* (1939). [AKT]

**Havlíček Borovský, Karel** (Borová 1821–Prague 1856). Czech journalist, satirist and essayist. The son of a country merchant, he studied at a Jesuit seminary. Expelled from the seminary for writing a poem propagating Panslavism, he went as tutor to Russia where personal experience of social inequity and Tsarist despotism cured him of then current Panslavist ideas. In the revolutionary year 1848 he founded his own paper, *Národní noviny*, the first Czech daily, took an active part in political life and, elected deputy at the Reichsrat, fought for Czech national rights and constitutional reform even after many others had given up these causes as hopeless. In 1851 he was deported to Brixen in Tyrol. Released on account of illness in 1855, he died of tuberculosis.

His most original work is his unfinished satire *Křest sv. Vladimíra* (1876; tr. E. Altschul, *The Conversion of St Vladimir*, Cleveland, 1930), written in Brixen. It castigates the two institutions which he most hated – the absolutist regime and the established Church. His satires make him the greatest Czech satirist of modern times. Liberalism and rationalism are dominant in his essays in which he sharply reacts against romanticism. [KB]

*Politické spisy*, ed. Zd. Tobolka (5 vols., 1900–3); *Básnické dílo*, ed. J. Bělič (1951).

E. Chalupný, *H.* (Prague, 1929); B. Stanislav, *K.H.B.* (Prague, 1954); *SEER*, 3 (1924–5); 36 (1960–1).

**Háy, Gyula** (Julius) (Abony 1900– ). Hungarian dramatist writing chiefly in German. Lived in Germany (1919–33), then in Moscow till after the Second World War, when he returned to Hungary and was imprisoned (1956–60). His plays, based on Marxist ideology, include *Gott, Kaiser und Bauer* (1935), *Haben* (1938), *Das neue Paradies* (1938), *Gerichtstag* (1946), *Der Putenhirt* (1948), *Begegnung* (1953). Theatrical essays are contained in *Aus den Erfahrungen des Sowjet-Theaters* (1938; with M. Vallentin). [LL]

*Dramen* (2 vols., 1951–3).

**Hebbel, Christian Friedrich** (Wesselburen, Schleswig-Holstein 1813–Vienna 1863).

German dramatist. A mason's son, he suffered from poverty and lack of formal education. After working as a village clerk at 14, and unsuccessfully studying for the 'Abitur' at Hamburg in 1835, he attended university lectures at Heidelberg and Munich in 1836 with the assistance of Elise Lensing, who eventually bore him two illegitimate sons. After returning to Hamburg in 1839, he travelled on a Danish royal grant to Paris in 1843, Rome 1844, Naples in 1845; he visited Paris again in 1860, and London in 1862. In 1845 he settled in Vienna, where he married the actress Christine Enghaus in 1846, and gradually consolidated his fame. In 1849–50 he was literary editor of the *Österreichische Reichszeitung*. A self-taught artist and thinker, influenced by G. H. Schubert and Feuerbach, he independently developed 'Hegelian' ideas. His *Gedichte* (1842; 1848; coll. 1857), the epic *Mutter und Kind* (1859) and *Erzählungen und Novellen* (1855) are less important than his heavy historical or legendary plays which, neglecting social and political topicality, deal with metaphysical concepts and larger-than-life characters in a powerful if uneasy mixture of philosophy, psychology and semi-realistic stagecraft. In *Mein Wort über das Drama* (1843; tr. D. Barlow in *Selected Essays*, 1963), for which he received a doctorate, he defines his view of existence as a tragic conflict between individuals who, whether noble or base, incur guilt and destruction through their inherent striving for unrestrained self-expression, and a general order which they always disturb and often rejuvenate. By setting his plays at the turning-point of two epochs, personified by his protagonists, he achieves complex patterns of multi-layered dialectics. A frequent theme is the violation of women's dignity through men's inconsiderateness. In *Judith* (1840; tr. C. van Doren, Boston, 1914) he dramatizes the clash of heathendom and religion represented by an overbearing Assyrian general (portraying Napoleon) and a Hebraic widow, whose sense of divine mission is compromised by slighted love. In *Genoveva* (1843; cf. ⇨ Tieck's version) the heroine's beauty and virtue lead to martyrdom, while the villain-hero's dilemma between desire and conscience reflects Hebbel's own erotic confusions. In *Maria Magdalene* (1844; tr. B. Fairley, 1914), his only domestic tragedy, the middle-class heroine is destroyed in the conflict between sexual freedom and narrow-minded conventions. In *Herodes und Mariamne* (1850; tr. R. H. Allen, 1914, C. Dane, 1939) the archaic tyranny of the Jewish king drives the spiritually independent queen to suicide but cannot forestall the advent of Christ. In *Agnes Bernauer* (1852; tr. L. Pattee, Boston, 1909), expressing his post-1848 belief in state authority, the charm of the bourgeois heroine threatens the feudal hierarchy of Bavaria; only the acceptance of her execution can reconcile the ruler with his son and prevent civil war. In *Gyges und sein Ring* (1856; tr. L. H. Allen, *Gyges and his Ring*, 1914) the Lydian queen perishes through her conservatism and beauty, the king through his exhibitionist possessiveness and premature reforms. In the trilogy *Die Nibelungen* (1862; tr. H. Goldberger, *The Niebelungs*, 1921) psychological and metaphysical conflicts are fought out against the dual background of Teutonic myth and rising Christianity. Like Schiller, Hebbel did not live to complete his *Demetrius*. While the plays *Der Diamant* (1847), *Julia* (1848), *Ein Trauerspiel in Sizilien* (1851), *Der Rubin* (1851), and *Michel Angelo* (1851) are minor efforts, the *Tagebücher* (ed. F. Bamberg, 1885–7) contain a wealth of biographical and theoretical information. [AKT]

*Sämtliche Werke*, ed. R. M. Werner (24 vols., 1901–7); ed. H. Geiger (2 vols., 1961); ed. W. Vontin (2 vols., 1958).

E. Kuh, *Biographie F.H.s* (Vienna, 1877, 1907); O. Walzel, *H. und seine Dramen* (Leipzig and Berlin, 1913); P. Sickel, *F.H.s Welt- und Lebensanschauung* (Hamburg and Leipzig, 1921); G. B. Rees, *F.H. as a Dramatic Artist* (1930); E. Purdie, *F.H.* (1932); C. Augstein, *H. als Denker* (Berlin, 1947); J. Müller, *Das Weltbild F.H.s* (Halle, 1955); A. Meetz, *F.H.* (Stuttgart, 1962); Wiese, *DT*; Natan, *GML*.

**Hebel, Johann Peter** (Basel 1760–Schwetzingen 1826). German writer. He revived dialect verse in the *Alemannische Gedichte* (1803) and dialect narrative prose in the *Schatzkästlein des Rheinischen Hausfreundes* (1811; ed. C. P. Magill, 1955), the *Hausfreund* being a periodical he edited from 1808 to 1815. In his provincialism and his closeness to peasant life, his humour and realism, his Christianity and his concern to educate the common people who constituted the bulk of his readers he is a notable forerunner of his great compatriot Jeremias ⇨ Gotthelf. [WAC]

*Werke*, ed. W. Altwegg (3 vols.. Zürich, 1949). H. Bürgisser, *J.P.H. als Erzähler* (Horgen, 1929).

**Hečko, František** (1905–1960). Slovak novelist. He wrote two important novels of Slovak village life: *Červené víno* (1948) is perhaps the most successful Slovak specimen of this genre, but *Drevená dedina* (1951) suffers from the schematic application of the principles of 'socialist realism'. [RA]

*Dejiny slovenskej literatúry* (Bratislava, 1962).

**Hedberg, Olle** (Norrköping 1899– ). Swedish novelist. A prolific writer and a refined stylist in the 'French' tradition, he has enjoyed great popularity in Sweden since his early success with *Får jag be om räkningen* (1932). His chief preoccupation has been with the moral development of his characters, all recognizable types from a contemporary middle-class background. He has won a wide following among young readers through his frank descriptions of the hazards of youth, especially in the sphere of sex. *Bekänna färg* (1947) brought previously hinted-at religious problems to the fore. Basically a satirical moralist, he adds a note of distaste, even misanthropy in recent novels, e.g. *Dockan dansar, klockan slår* (1955) and *Djur i bur* (1959; tr. E. Harley Schubert, *Animals in Cages*, 1962). [SAB]

E. Andersson, *O.H.* (Stockholm, 1944); J. Kulling, *O.H.s romaner* (Stockholm, 1952).

**Hedenvind-Eriksson, Gustav** (Alanäs 1880–1967). Swedish novelist. Like ⇨ Koch he was a pioneer of the 'proletarian' writing that has been important in Swedish literature of the 20th century, but his colourful personality and experience made him an author of marked independence. For many years he led a roving life in Scandinavia and elsewhere, often as a workman in many different jobs; but he also pursued wide social and intellectual interests. His inside knowledge especially of the *rallare* (labourers employed particularly in railway construction) and of the hectic frontier-style activities in northern Scandinavia (neutral between the warring powers) during the First World War provided material for much of his writing. Earlier stories such as *Vid Eli vågor* (1914), *Tiden och en natt* (1918), and *En dröm i seklets natt* (1919), which sometimes combine vivid narrative with imaginative symbolism, were followed by a whole series of *rallare* novels, *De förskingrades arv* (1926), *Det bevingade hjulet* (1928) and *På friköpt jord* (1930). The author shows the rigorous development of northern Sweden and emphasizes both the individualism and the solidarity of the enterprising *rallare*, who sometimes went to work in Russia and other countries. With his keen interest in history and folk-lore he has subsequently written, e.g. *Fämt ländska sagor* (1941) and *Forms saga* (1949), besides striking autobiographical works, e.g. *Med rallarkärra mod dikten* (1944), several books of folk-tales and (in the 1950s) another series of epic novels on the dynamic modern history of northern Sweden and its timber.

O. Lindberger, *G.H.-E.* (Stockholm, 1945).

**Hegel, Georg Wilhelm Friedrich** (Stuttgart 1770–Berlin 1831). German philosopher. He published only four full-scale works: the *Phänomenologie des Geistes* (1807), the *Wissenschaft der Logik* (1812–16), the *Encyklopädie der Philosophischen Wissenschaften* (1817; revised 1827 and 1830) and the *Philosophie des Rechts* (1821); the rest of his major output consists of posthumous reconstructions of his lectures. In terms of cultural influence, Hegel is probably the most important of modern philosophers, not only in virtue of his relation to Marx, and of the support European theories of nationalism and 'social democracy' seemed to find in the *Philosophie des Rechts*, but also because of his impact upon nearly the whole range of the humanities. Thus the accelerated growth of intellectual history during the 19th and early 20th centuries continued to receive powerful stimulus from Hegel's phenomenology of culture long after his metaphysics had fallen into disrepute; Hegel's interpretation of Christian doctrine as a symbolic expression of 'philosophical truth' inaugurated modern philosophical theology; and many aestheticians, critics and poets have been irresistibly drawn to his dialectical categories. Central in this latter connexion are, firstly, Hegel's remarkable synthesis of organicist aesthetics and historicism in his *Vorlesungen über die Aesthetik* (1835–8); and, secondly, the fact that what is broadly true of Hegel's philosophy as a whole is also true of modern poetics: both attempt to give coherence to principles of disparity and conciliation, dissonance within harmony, transcendence and yet immanence, tension, paradox, irony. Significantly enough, recent scholarship shows that Hegel developed his characteristic modes of thought and utterance while he was absorbed in the aesthetic works of Diderot, Rousseau and Schiller. [MM]

W. Kaufmann, *Hegel: Reinterpretation, Texts and Commentary* (N.Y., 1965) (bibliography); A. C. Bradley, 'Hegel's Theory of Tragedy', in *Oxford Lectures on Poetry* (1909); A. Paolucci, 'Bradley and Hegel on Shakespeare', in *Comparative Literature*, XVI, 3 (Summer, 1964); G. Lukács, *Beiträge zur Geschichte der Aesthetik* (Berlin, 1954); B. Teyssèdre, *L'esthétique de Hegel* (Paris, 1958); G. Morpurgo-Tagliabue 'Attualità dell'estetica hegeliana', in *Il Pensiero*, 1–2 (1962); Wellek, *HMC*.

**Heiberg, Gunnar** (Kristiania 1857–Oslo 1929). Norwegian playwright. The most important of the post-Ibsen generation. His first and, in many ways, most successful play, *Tante Ulrikke* (1884), is in the tradition of the social play, and he often deals with topics of current interest, e.g. *Folkeraadet* (1897), treating them in a witty and provocative way, but always pointing a moral. *Kunstnere* (1893) and *Gerts have* (1894) are successful experiments, where light, allusive, erotically tinged conversation is more important than action. But his efforts to explore erotic relationships more deeply in *Balkonen* (1894; tr. Vickner and Hughes, *The Balcony*, 1922) and in *Kjærlighedens Tragedie* (1904; tr. E. Bjørkman, *The Tragedy of Love*, 1921) lack subtlety. He also published a number of collections of elegantly written essays and criticism. [RGP]

*Samlede dramatiske verker* (4 vols., 1917).
E. Skavlan, *G.H.* (Oslo, 1950); Beyer, *NL*.

**Heiberg, Johan Ludvig** (Copenhagen 1791–Bonderup 1860). Danish poet and playwright. The son of P. A. ⇨ Heiberg, a student of literature and aesthetics (with a dissertation on Calderón, who influenced his early dramas). After a visit to Paris he popularized French *vaudeville*-style comedy in Denmark. As Lector at Kiel (1822–5) he was influenced by Hegel, on whose ideas he based much of his literary criticism. Of his serious romantic plays, *Elverhøj* (1828) and *Syvsoverdag* (1840), the former has been a *pièce de résistance* of the Danish stage, but his most important work remains the apocalyptic verse-drama *En Sjæl efter Døden* (1841), an elegant and witty expression of his aristocratic philosophy. He wrote many poems of a philosophic nature as well as entertaining popular ballads. Married to Johanne Luise Heiberg, the leading actress of Denmark, he was director of the Royal Theatre, Copenhagen, and as critic a virtual dictator of literary taste in Denmark. [ELB]

M. Borup, *J.L.H.* (3 vols., Copenhagen, 1947–9).

**Heiberg, Peter Andreas** (Vordingborg 1758–Paris 1841). Danish poet and author. Influenced by the ideas of the French Revolution, his plays, novels, essays and poems attack absolutism and its misuses, satirizing specifically the monarchy and the German aristocracy in Denmark: for which he was exiled (1799). His play *Poverty and Wealth* was translated in 1799. [ELB]

H. Schwanenflügel, *P.A.H.* (Copenhagen, 1891).

**Heiðarvíga Saga.** ⇨ Icelandic Sagas.

**Heidenstam, Verner von** (Olshammar 1859–Övralid 1940). Swedish poet, novelist and essayist. Born into a noble family, he was attracted by the great, lonely personalities of history and in time came to be regarded not only as the spokesman of the literary 'nineties' but also as a somewhat remote figure of national status. In his youth he travelled extensively in South Europe and the Near East; settled for some years in Rome and Paris, where he studied painting, though with scant success. His *Vallfart och vandringsår* (1888), a collection of colourful verse, stood out from the often myopic and drab realism of the decade. His early poetry is strongly visual, its style by turns flamboyant and casual, most sincere in expressing longing for the distant homeland; this profound nostalgia forms the basis of his later patriotic works. Heidenstam followed up the success of his lyrical travels with a literary programme in the essay *Renässans* (1889), and soon found himself the leader of a new school of writers united by common aesthetic ideals, in particular a belief in the imagination as the prime poetic faculty. He consolidated his position with *Dikter* (1895), a collection of verse of remarkable emotional range. The ease with which the poet enters into one identity after another never ceases to astonish, but out of the bewildering richness of the book there emerges a patriotic strain, which for years to come was to prevail in Heidenstam's work and imbue it with an austere, even ascetic morality, stated in its most challenging form in the short cycle *Ett folk* (1899). The other important work of a similar cast is *Karolinerna* (1897–8; tr. C. W. Stork, *The Charles Men*, N.Y., 1920; London, 1933), book of stories dealing with Charles XII and his soldiers and written in a highly poetic, but sometimes strained and knotty style. It is a book full of inspired passages and often breathtaking scenes, yet lacking an epic current to carry the events. It exalts the heroic state of mind, rather than any individual hero. In a sequence of novels under the heading *Folkungaträdet* (1905–7; tr. *The Tree of the Folkungs*, 1925), he probes further into Swedish history, as far back as the clash between paganism and Christianity, to trace the forces that transform the lives of barbaric men. His last book of verse, *Nya dikter* (1915), marks his turning towards a classical ideal of life and literature. He now favours the short, lucid poem which is also a confession of his innermost thoughts and feelings without loss of dignity. He often achieves a simplicity reminiscent of Goethe's, and the humanist idealism which these poems embody places the mature Heidenstam in line with his compatriots ⇨ Tegnér and ⇨ Rydberg. In 1916 he was awarded the Nobel Prize. He wrote little after this time. His memoirs were published posthumously as *När kastanjerna blommade* (1941); similarly books of sketches, aphorisms and meditations. [SAB]

F. Böök, *V.v.H.* (2 vols., Stockholm, 1945–6); S. Björck, *V.v.H.* (Stockholm, 1947); A. Gustafson, 'Nationalism Reinterpreted', in *Six Scandinavian Novelists* (Princeton, 1940); Borland, *NI.*

**Heijermans, Herman** (Rotterdam 1864–Zandvoort 1924). Dutch playwright and author. As a socialist with a trenchant disdain for bourgeois hypocrisy, his drama, on such themes as anti-semitism and free love, became part of European theatre. *Op hoop van zegen* (1900; tr. L. Saunders and C. Heijermans-Houwinck, *The Good Hope*, 1928) takes up the cause of exploited fishermen, *Glück auf* (1911) of the miners. He wrote novels under the pseudonym Koos Habbema, sketches (pseud. Samuel Faulkand) and children's books. [PK]

*Ahasverus*, tr. C. Heijermans-Houwinck and J. J. Houwinck (1934); *The Rising Sun*, tr. C. St John (1926); *Saltimbanque*, tr. C. Heijermans-Houwinck and L. Saunders (1934).

. L. Flaxman, *H.H. and his Dramas* (The Hague, 1954); *H.H.* (Schrijvers Prentenboek II, Amsterdam, 1964).

**Hein, Piet** (Copenhagen 1905– ). Danish poet. Known for his 'grooks' (in Danish: *gruk*, a name invented by himself), which are short, aphoristic poems, many-faceted concentrated epigrams with ingenious expressions of both sense and common sense (e.g. 'I'd like to know/ what this whole show/ is all about/ before it's out'). Twenty volumes of *Gruk* (1940–63), written under his pen name Kumbel and illustrated by himself, have made him famous in Scandinavia. The first volume of *Grooks* (Cambridge, Mass., 1966) is likely to be followed by others. [ELB]

J. Hicks, 'P.H. – a Pixie Poet with a Slide Rule' in *Life International* (31 October 1966).

**Heine, Heinrich** (Düsseldorf 1797–Paris 1856). German poet and prose-writer. Born into a Jewish family in the Catholic Rhineland, the poor relation of a wealthy family, he felt an 'outsider' from the first. The tensions set up by this, coupled with his rejection by the girl he loved, partly account for the strange dualism of his terse early poetry, in which melodious sweetness is mingled with astringent satire. These early poems, on which his fame principally rests, are collected in the *Buch der Lieder* published in 1827, which has served composers as a seemingly inexhaustible reservoir of song-texts. (Serviceable translations from this and other collections: L. Untermeyer, *Poems of Heinrich Heine* (1938), Vernon Watkins, *The North Sea* (1955), E. Feise, *Poems of H.H.* (Pittsburgh, 1961).) A year before this 'Book of Songs', Heine published the first volume of his *Reisebilder* (tr. C. G. Leland, *Pictures of Travel*, in *The Works of H.H.*, 1892–1905), a new genre in which landscape description blends with irreverent comment on contemporary figures and institutions. After completing his studies at the universities of Bonn, Göttingen and Berlin, he was unable to find suitable employment in Germany. Attracted by the July Revolution, he moved to Paris in 1831 and settled there for the rest of his life, attempting to interpret German life and letters to the French in *Zur Geschichte der Religion und Philosophie in Deutschland* ('Remarks on the History of Religion and Philosophy in Germany', 1835) and French life and letters to the Germans in *Französische Zustände* ('Conditions in France', 1832) and *Lutetia* (1840–3 and 1854). The poetry he wrote in his early years in Paris tended more and more towards satire: it moves from the lyrics collected in *Neue Gedichte* (1844) to the two mock-epics which represent his highest flight as a satirist: *Deutschland. Ein Wintermärchen* (1844) and *Atta Troll* (1841–6).

In the last eight years of his life a painful paralytic illness confined Heine to what he himself called a 'mattress grave' in a Paris flat. This did not impair his wit and mental alertness, which shines more brightly than ever in the prose-works and recorded conversations of his final years. The most distinctive achievement, however, of this period are the poems and ballads collected in *Romanzero* (1852) and *Gedichte 1853 und 1854* (1854), in which pain and terror are presented and transfigured in often irreverent, often nightmarish, sometimes rambling but always fascinating verse.

Heine has left a number of autobiographical sketches, ranging from *Ideen, Das Buch le Grand* (1826) to *Geständnisse* ('Confessions', 1854). The bulk of his *Memoiren*, however, on which he worked in his last years, seems to have been destroyed by relatives with whom he fought a constant feud in his lifetime. He also wrote several essays on German folklore (*Elementargeister*, 1837; *Die Götter im Exil*, 1854); two ballet-scenarios on legendary themes; and two plays which – alone among all his many works – are of little interest.

In many of his poems, from the earliest to the last, he used the image of the 'double' or *Doppelgänger*: a fit symbol for this homeless poet who not only felt himself a Jew among Germans, a German among Frenchmen, a 'Hellene' among Jews, a rebel among the bourgeois and a conservative among revolutionaries, but who was also always divided against himself. It was from such self-division, however – romantic passion against mocking reason, and at the end a spirit that sought God against an intellect that refused to admit His existence – that he fashioned his best and truest poetry. [SSP]

*Sämtliche Werke*, ed. O. Walzel (Leipzig 1910/20); F. Ewen, *H. An Anthology* (N.Y., 1948); H. Bieber and M. Hadas, *H.H. A Biographical Anthology* (Pittsburgh, 1956).

E. M. Butler, *H.H. A Biography* (1956); W. Rose, *H.H., Two Studies of His Thought and Feeling* (1956); S. S. Prawer, *H.'s 'Buch der Lieder'* (1960) and *H. The Tragic Satirist* (1962); E. Galley, *H.H.* (Stuttgart, 1963).

**Heinesen, William** (Thorshavn 1900– ). Faroese poet and novelist. Has lived on the Faroe Islands since 1932 and writes in Danish; his best novels are *Blæsende gry* (1934), *Noatun* (1940; tr. J. Noble, *Niels Peter*, 1939), *Den sorte gryde* (1949), *De fortabte spillemænd* (1950), and *Det gode Haab* (1964). He has also published two volumes of essays and tales (1957 and 1960). [ELB]

*Digte i udvolg* (1955).

**Heinrich von Freiberg** (fl. *c.* 1280). German epic poet. Remembered, together with the somewhat older Ulrich von Türheim, as a continuator of the *Tristan* epic of ⇨ Gottfried von Strassburg, left unfinished at Gottfried's death. Building on the version of the Tristan legend used by ⇨ Eilhart von Oberg and Ulrich von Türheim – which belongs to a different tradition from that on which Gottfried drew – Heinrich tried to conclude the story in Gottfried's style and manner. The result, however, recalls Gottfried only in external and superficial respects: he does not attain to Gottfried's profound conception of love and of its fulfilment in death, and makes of Tristan a courtly Arthurian knightwho is activated by the conventional values of courtly love. And in the conclusion to his poem he holds up the tragic fate of Tristan and Isolde as a testimony to the transience of earthly happiness, exhorting his readers, in a manner utterly foreign to Gottfried, to turn to the True Love, which is the love of God. [RT]

Ed. A. Bernt (1906).

D. de Rougemont, *Passion and Society* (1956); Ehrismann, *GDL*.

**Heinrich von Meissen** (d. 1318). German lyric poet. His work belongs to the decadence of the classical ⇨ Minnesang. He is usually known under the soubriquet of Frauenlob, for his praise of ladies of noble birth (*vrouwen*). His poetry is characterized by overladen subtleties and complexities of thought, language and poetic form. Tradition ascribes to him the foundation in Mainz of the first school of ⇨ Meistersinger. [RT]

Ed. L. Ettmüller (1835 ff.); selection in modern German, tr. B. Nagel (1951).

**Heinrich von Melk** (fl. mid 12th cent.). Austrian monastic poet. He has been called 'the Juvenal of the age of chivalry'. His two narrative poems are fiercely moral in tone and interesting as bitter social commentary on the sins, physical and spiritual of the clerics. He fanatically preache asceticism and the imperative need of a corrupt mankind for abject repentance. [RT]

Ed. R. Heinzel and R. Kienast (Heidelberg, 1946).
R. Heinzel, *H.v.M.* (Berlin, 1867).

**Heinrich von Morungen** (fl. *c.* 1200). German ⇨ Minnesinger. A native of Thuringia. Of all courtly lyric poets before ⇨ Reinmar der Alte and ⇨ Walther von der Vogelweide, he is the artist with the strongest and most clearly defined personality. Within the conventions imposed by the ideal of courtly love he yet succeeds in communicating a sense of personal emotion which sets his poems apart from those of his contemporaries and makes them more readily approachable to modern readers. [RT]

Kraus, *MF.*
C. v. Kraus, *H.v.M.* (Göttingen, 1925).

**Heinrich von Neustadt** (fl. early 14th cent.). Austrian epic poet of the late courtly tradition. His principal work is *Apollonius von Tyrland*, the earliest known German version of the popular Greek adventure-story which was known in the Middle Ages in a variety of Latin translations. He was a physician and a man of wide learning; his work is full of matter culled from very varied sources of knowledge, but which is often planlessly and ostentatiously inserted into the course of the narrative. The values of the classical courtly epic, such as Love (*minne*) and Honour (*ere*), have lost their power, and only the external trappings remain. He also wrote a number of narrative religious poems. [RT]

Ed. S. Singer (Berlin, 1906).

**Heinrich von Wittenweiler** (fl. first half of 15th cent.). Swiss epic poet. Author of a famous poem known as the *Ring*. This compendious work is sustained by two of the most characteristic qualities of 15th-century German literature: a coarse delight in vulgar and often cruel comedy, and an insatiable urge for earnest moralizing. Through the colourful sequence of events that he describes, which take place both in court and peasant circles, the poet exposes in satirical and often grotesque manner the foibles of human conduct and offers his own didactic glosses upon them. Refinement, both of form and of content, is conspicuously absent, but for exuberance and *joie de vivre* the century can hardly show a comparable work. [RT]

Ed. L. Bechstein (Stuttgart, 1851).
Ehrismann, *GDL.*

**Heinse, Johann Jakob Wilhelm** (Langewiesen 1746–Aschaffenburg 1803). German novelist. His long pseudo-Greek poem in the style of ⇨ Wieland, *Laidion oder die Eleusischen Geheimnisse* (1774), in which the hetaera Lais gives an account of her life, shocked both Goethe and Wieland by its sensuality and lasciviousness, in spite of their admiration for its verse. His principal work, the novel *Ardinghello und die glücklichen Inseln* (1787), reflects his two years in Italy, as well as his interest in art and his passionately sensual nature. The work is a chaotic blend of genre pictures, travel journal, observations on life and art, Rousseau's philosophy and rank eroticism. The heaven-storming hero of the *Sturm und Drang* here appears as the *uomo universale* of the Italian renaissance: Ardinghello is successively painter, pirate and politician and knows neither limit nor law in the expression of his passionate personality. In its interest in art and artists the novel anticipates the *Künstlerroman* of the Romantics and is also one of the earliest Utopian novels of German literature – Ardinghello eventually founds a neo-Greek, Rousseauistic democracy on Paros and Naxos dedicated to the cultivation of sensual grace and beauty.

The partly autobiographical *Hildegard von Hohenthal* (1795–6), in which music takes the place of art in *Ardinghello*, appears to modify the uninhibited sensual freedom advocated in the latter work, but in reality reveals a mind as lustful as ever. [WAC]

*Werke*, ed. C. Schüddekopf (13 vols., 1902–25).
A. Jolivet, *W. H. Sa vie et son œuvre jusqu'en 1787* (Paris, 1922); E. Sulger-Gebing, *W.H.* (Munich, 1903).

**Heinsius, Daniel** (Ghent 1580–The Hague 1655). Dutch philologist and poet. Professor of poetry and Greek at Leyden, his importance lies rather in his considerable influence on ⇨ Opitz and ⇨ Gryphius than in his own Latin and Dutch poetry. His *Hymnus oft Lofsanck van Bacchus* (1614) and *Lofsanck van Jesus Christus* (1616) are curious expressions of the ambivalence in the Dutch renaissance between art and religion. [PK]

*Nederduytsche Poemata* (1616); *Bacchus en Christus*, ed. Ph. Rank, J. D. P. Warners and F. L. Zwaan (1965).
E. G. Kern, *The Influence of Heinsius and Vossius upon French Dramatic Theory* (Baltimore, 1949).

**Heissenbüttel, Helmut** (Wilhelmshaven 1921 – ). German poet. Author of *Kombinationen* (1954), *Topographien* (1956), and *Textbuch I, II, III, IV* and *V* (1960–65). His highly experimental (and controversial) combinations of words and phrases may appear no more than abstract exercises in technique. Animated by an 'insatiable desire for the inconceivable', he is, however, one of the most original poets of his generation, a master of 'discontinuous consciousness', sometimes reminiscent of ⇨ Dada. *Über Literatur* (1966) contains criticism of contemporary literature. [PB]

Bridgwater, *TCGV*; Hamburger and Middleton, *MGP*; Middleton, *GWT*.

**Hektorović, Petar.** ⇨ Dalmatian and Dubrovnik Literature.

**'Heliand'** ('Saviour'). A 9th-century alliterative epic poem in Old Saxon, relating the life and teaching of Christ. Together with the *Genesis* fragments, it provides all that has survived of Old Saxon poetry. The author is unnamed, but it is known that he undertook his task at the instance of Louis the Pious. The substance of the poem is drawn, not directly from the Vulgate but from the pseudo-Tatian Harmony of the Gospels, with additional matter taken from Gospel commentaries such as those of Bede and ⇨ Alcuin. The particular interest of the work lies in the way the religious narrative is assimilated to the form of the Germanic heroic epic, and Biblical scenes portrayed against a Germanic background. [RT]

*Heliand* and *Genesis*, ed. O. Behaghel (1958). Ehrismann, *GDL*, i.

**Hélinand de Froidmont** (nr Beauvais) (*c.* 1160 –after 1229). French *trouvère* at the court of Philip Augustus (1182–5), he became a Cistercian monk and was associated at the inauguration of the University of Toulouse in 1229 with ⇨ Folquet de Marseille, bishop of Toulouse, whose career curiously resembled his own. Author of lost poems and scientific writings, including a *Chronicon universale*, Hélinand is best known for his vivid *Vers de la mort*, 50 stanzas written (1194–7) on the theme of imminent and all-conquering death and showing some similarity to the later *danse macabre*. He gave his name to the metrical form of this poem, 12 octosyllables rhyming *aab aab bba bba*, which was much used by later poets writing on Death, especially in the 13th century. [LTT]

*Les vers de la mort*, ed. F. Wulff and E. Walberg (1905); modern Fr. tr. abbé J. Coppin (1930); *R*, 1, 1872; Woledge, *PBFV*, i (extract).

**Hellaakoski, Aaro** (Oulu 1893–Helsinki 1952). Finnish poet. He taught geography at Helsinki University and published a number of scientific works. The poems in his earliest collections (1916, 1918) were defiant, severely masculine and satirical in tone, full of scorn for stuffy middle-class attitudes. In *Me kaksi* (1920) there is an advance towards the creation of a genuine 'poetic self', with an evident conflict between head and heart. In the course of the twenties his poetry became more lyrical and more adventurous technically. *Jääpeili* (1928) contains some of his best lyrical work. There follows a long silence, after which progress towards real mastery can be traced through collections published in 1943 and 1946 to the mature achievements of *Hiljaisuus* (1949), *Sarjoja* (1952) and the posthumously published *Huomenna seestyvää* (1953). These collections reflect a profound religious crisis; without losing anything of his firm masculinity he has shaken off the dead weight of materialism and achieved a serene note of calmness and humility, acceptance and thankfulness. Other works include a novel and a collection of short stories, as well as aphorisms and essays. He was a sensitive interpreter both of literature and of the pictorial arts. [VKS]

*Runot* (1953).

**Hellström, Gustaf** (Kristianstad 1882–Stockholm 1953). Swedish novelist and journalist. After several years as a foreign correspondent in London, Paris and New York (he also wrote stories connected with his experiences and observations abroad), he emerged as a major author after returning to Sweden in 1923. He published over a long period a series of rather uneven autobiographical novels from *Dagdrömmar* (1921) to *I morgon är en skälm* (1952). He made a greater impact with three very fine social novels, showing distinct traces of English influence: *Snörmakare Lekholm får en idé* (1927; tr. F. H. Lyon, *Lacemaker Lekholm has an Idea*, 1930), *Carl Heribert Malmros* (1931) and *Storm över Tjurö* (1935). The first, clearly his most important work, traces with broad grasp and tragic comic insight the fortunes of a family in a provincial town during the best part of a century; the second weaves urgent moral and social questions into an intense presentation of a police chief and his problems; the third is a vivid picture of conflict in the microcosm of an isolated Swedish island.

H. Ahlenius, *G.H.* (Stockholm, 1934); B. Tomson, *G.H. och hans väg till Snörmakare Lekholm får en idé* (Stockholm, 1961).

**Heltai, Jenő** (Budapest 1871–Budapest 1957). Hungarian poet and playwright. Of his plays, generally built upon his chanson-like poetry, the best known is *A néma levente* (1930), a neo-romantic comedy in verse. He also produced numerous witty, light-hearted short stories and novels. [JFR]

**Helvétius, Claude-Adrien** (Paris 1715–Paris 1771). French philosopher. A wealthy tax-farmer, he cultivated the company of the major intellectual figures of the age, and shared their most radical ideas. In 1750 he resigned his appointment as Farmer-General to devote himself to philosophical studies, and published his major work, *De l'esprit*, in 1758 (ed. G. Besse, Paris, 1959 (abridged); tr. W. Mudford, 1807). Here he develops the sensationist psychology of Locke and extends it to the ethical and social fields, propounding a utilitarianism with materialist and atheist implications. The book occasioned a considerable scandal, which was a factor in the official decision to ban the *Encyclopédie* in 1759. [WHB]

*Œuvres complètes*, ed. P. L. Lefebvre de la Roche (1797).

A. Keim, *H., sa vie et son œuvre* (Paris, 1907); G. V. Plekhanov, *Essays in the History of Materialism* (1934).

**Hémon, Louis** (Brest 1880–Chapleau, Ont. 1913). French novelist. After a short stay in England, where he wrote short stories and articles for French magazines and three novels which he did not publish, he went to Canada in 1911. Life as a hired hand among French-Canadian settlers near Péribonka provided material for *Maria Chapdelaine* (1916; tr. W. H. Blake, N.Y., 1921), the novel which was to bring him only posthumous fame, for he died in a railway accident three years before it appeared. In his simple tale of a French-Canadian family living in an isolated settlement, faced by the harshness of nature, illness and death, the grimness of the picture is compensated by the courage of the pioneer settler. His novel, realistic and unidealized, influenced a whole generation of Canadian regional novelists (e.g. F. A. Savard's *Menaud, maître-draveur*, 1937). The success of *Maria Chapdelaine* allowed publication of *La Belle que voilà* (1923; tr. W. A. Bradley, *My Fair Lady*, 1923), *Colin-Maillard* (1924; tr. H. Richmond, *Blind Man's Bluff*, 1924), *Battling Malone, pugiliste* (1925), and *Monsieur Ripois et la Némésis* (1950; tr. W. A. Bradley, N.Y., 1924), which was a popular success as a film. [FWAG]

*The Journal of L.H.*, tr. W. A. Bradley (N.Y., 1924).

A. McAndrew, *L.H., sa vie et son œuvre* (Paris, 1936); D. Potvin, *Le roman d'un roman* (Paris, 1950).

**Hemon, Roparz.** ⇨ Breton Literature.

**Hennequin, Émile.** ⇨ French Literary Criticism in the 19th and 20th Centuries.

**Henningsen, Agnes** (Skovsbo 1868–Gentofte 1962). Danish novelist. Her novels, notably *Polens Døtre* (1901); *De spedalske* (1903); *Den elskede Eva* (1911); *Den store Kærlighed* (1917); *Kærlighedens Aarstider* (trilogy, 1927–30), caused a stir by their candid treatment of the erotic problems of women. Her charming and frank *Memoirs* (1941–55) are in eight volumes. [ELB]

**Herbert, Zbigniew** (Lvov 1924– ). Polish poet. A new voice to emerge after the political relaxation in 1956. His deliberate searching of conscience turns themes from history and myth (e.g. *Hermes, pies i gwiazda*, 1957) into personal statements; the dramatic monologue seems to be his natural form. Most representative is his volume *Studium przedmiotu* (1961). [JP]

**Herculano, Alexandre** (Lisbon 1810–Vale de Lobos 1866). Portuguese intellectual and historian. With ⇨ Garrett, the leading member of the first Romantic generation. Educated by the Oratorians, but precluded by his family's relative poverty from University. He read formidably and attained immense erudition. Being early involved with the Liberal cause in Portuguese politics, he was forced to emigrate in 1831 after participating in a plot against the reactionary monarchy of Dom Miguel. As a refugee in France, he made an assiduous study of

French literature. In 1833 he returned to Portugal as a common soldier in the victorious Chartist army of Dom Pedro and received the post of municipal librarian in Oporto. He did not sympathize with the more radical (Setembrista) wing of the Liberal party and, as pamphleteer, journalist and later parliamentary deputy, he devoted himself to a defence of moderate constitutional monarchy. In 1839 he was made director of the Royal Library at Ajuda, a post which left him ideally placed to undertake historical studies. His active political interests were temporarily curtailed by the reactionary dictatorship of Costa Cabral (1842–51), and during this period he devoted himself exclusively to his writing. Besides producing historical novels such as *O Bobo* (1843), he began to plan his two monumental works, *História de Portugal* and *História da Origem e Estabelecimento da Inquisação em Portugal.* When the first volume of the former appeared in 1846, Herculano immediately became the butt of clerical vilification. He was the first Portuguese historian to adopt an impartial scientific approach to his subject, and he poured scorn on the persistent superstitions, such as Christ's personal intervention at the battle of Ourique, which had so far bedevilled comprehensive histories of the country. Though himself a sincere Christian, he was henceforth violently attacked by the obscurantist Portuguese Church. After the fall of Costa Cabral in 1851, he re-entered politics, applying his lucid intelligence to the task of establishing a viable constitutional regime. He was actively involved in attempts to reform the Civil Code and was responsible for the introduction of civil marriage in Portugal. In 1867 he withdrew to his estate near Santarém, enjoying immense personal prestige until his death.

Conscious of the social responsibilities of the writer, his *História de Portugal*, a work of great scholarship, gives due prominence to social and economic factors in Portuguese history, and holds up for admiration the individual freedom of the Middle Ages. Human relationships, he implied, had degenerated since the Renaissance. Similarly in the *História ... da Inquisação* he set out to hearten his liberal supporters by revealing the sordid intrigues and multifarious motives which had given rise to the movement for 'religious purity' in Portugal. The lesson of the past was plain to see. [AJP]

J. Barradas de Cavalho, *As Ideias Políticas e Sociais de A.H.* (Lisbon, 1949); A. J. Saraiva, *H. e o Liberalismo em Portugal* (Lisbon, 1949).

**Herczeg, Ferenc** (Versecz 1863–Budapest 1954). Hungarian playwright and novelist. Of patrician German descent, he studied law, later contributed to *Pesti Napló*, and founded the weekly *Új Idők*. An extremely conservative writer, he described in a conversational tone the devil-may-care way of life of early-20th-century Hungarian gentry. Novels: *A Gyurkovits-lányok* (1893); *A Gyurkovits-fiúk* (1895). Most significant historical plays: *Pogányok* (1902); *Bizánc* (1904); *Árva László király* (1917); *A híd* (1925). Some of his plays were produced abroad; *Az ezüst róka* (1921) was the most successful. [JFR]

*SEER*, XXXI, 76 (1952).

**Herdal, Harald** (Copenhagen 1900– ). Danish poet and novelist. Born in a working-class milieu, he became a left-wing socialist, and the element of propaganda is noticeable in most of his social novels, but absent from his best lyrics, especially his fine love poetry, *Mennesket* (1937), *Nye Digte* (1944), and *Digte 1929–49* (1949). [ELB]

**Herder, Johann Gottfried** (Mohrungen, E. Prussia 1744–Weimar 1803). German writer. It was as the theoretician of the ⇨ *Sturm und Drang* rather than as a creative writer that Herder, who had come under the influence of ⇨ Hamann as a student in Königsberg, was to make his real contribution to German literature. Already in his earliest works he anticipates the main tenets of the movement: the *Fragmente über die neuere deutsche Literatur* (1766–7) maintain that poetry can only be understood in the context of the ethnic, geographical and cultural conditions under which it was produced, while the *Kritische Wälder* (1769) reiterate this relativist approach and see poetry as the expression of the indwelling *Kraft* (energy, power) of the poet. But it was his personal relations with Goethe in Strassburg in 1770 that enabled him to exercise decisive influence on the development of the *Sturm und Drang*. He brought home to the young poet the literary consequences of Rousseau's call for a return to nature and opened his eyes to the beauty of folk poetry (amongst which he included Ossian, Shakespeare, Homer and the Bible). The pre occupation with folk poetry was given full expression in *Von deutscher Art und Kunst* (1773), which may be regarded as the manifesto of the *Sturm und Drang* and to which Herder, as editor, contributed two essays: *Auszug aus einem Briefwechsel über Ossian und die Lieder alter Völker* and *Shakespear*. The *Briefwechsel* finally demolishes the literary rationalism of the Enlightenment by declaring folk poetry to be the only true poetry and seeing it not as the product of rational thought processes, but of ecstatic inspiration and intense emotion. In the essay on Shakespeare Herder develops the relativist theories of the *Fragmente*, rejecting the literature of Greece as a valid criterion by which to judge that of other peoples and other ages, and celebrating Shakespeare as the supreme irrational creative genius of the Germanic race and, like Lessing before him, pointing to Shakespeare as the natural model for contemporary German dramatists. The interest in native German folk poetry and the call to preserve it bore fruit in the 2-volume collection of folk-songs Herder published in 1778–9 (re-published in 1807 as *Stimmen der Völker in Liedern*), a collection which was to stimulate the Romantics (⇨ Arnim, ⇨ Brentano, Görres, the ⇨ Grimms) to do likewise.

At Goethe's suggestion Herder was called to Weimar as General Superintendent of the Lutheran church there in 1776. His later writings – especially *Ideen zur Philosophie der Geschichte der Menschheit* (1784–91), which in some respects anticipates Hegel – though concerned with philosophy and history rather than literature contributed to the cultural humanism of Weimar; cf. especially *Briefe zur Beförderung der Humanität* (1793–7). [WAC]

*Werke*, ed. F. Schultz (5 vols., 1939–43); ed. W. Dobbek (5 vols., 1958).

R. T. Clark, *H.'s Life and Work* (1955); A. Gillies, *H.* (1945); E. Kühnemann, *H.* (Munich, 1912); B. v. Wiese, *H.* (Leipzig, 1939); Natan, *GML*.

**Hérédia, José-Maria de** (La Fortuna, Santiago 1842–Château de Bourdonné, Hourdan 1905). French poet. Born in Cuba of a Spanish father and a French mother. He was educated in France, studied law, but soon devoted himself exclusively to poetry and was one of the first Parnassians. Many of the 118 sonnets of *Les trophées* (1893), upon which his fame rests, are perfect in technique. His imagination was fired by memories of the coral reefs and the rich forest of his childhood, by the works of art with which he came into contact or by the passive and detached contemplation of past civilizations. A famous line describes the battle of Actium as a reflection seen by Antony in Cleopatra's eyes. *Les trophées* consists of five groups: *La Grèce et la Sicile; Rome et les Barbares; Le Moyen Âge et la Renaissance; L'Orient et les Tropiques; La Nature et le Rève*. He also left a fragment of an epic *Les Conquérants de l'or*. From 1901 Hérédia was Keeper of the Bibliothèque de l'Arsenal, where Charles ⇨ Nodier had also held a post before him. He was elected to the Académie Française in 1894. [WA]

M. Ibrovac, *J.M. de H.* (Paris, 1923); U. V. Chatelain, *J.M. de H.* (Paris, 1930).

**Hermans, Willem Frederik** (Amsterdam 1921– ). Dutch author. His first novel, *Conserve* (1947), after earlier attempts at poetry, showed his potential as a bold experimentalist in prose, using film techniques to shift time sequences, locality and the positions of the reader and narrator. *De tranen der acacia's* (1949) and even more *Ik heb altijd gelijk* (1951) demonstrate his contention that 'writing is the creation of fallacy' by confronting deep emotion with absolute cynicism. But in *Het behouden huis* (1952) and *De donkere kamer van Damocles* (1958; tr. R. Edwards, *The Dark Room of Damocles*, 1962), a more orderly structure is reinforced with symbolism which hints at some moral values in man's self-alienation and chaos in war. In *Nooit meer slapen* (1966) the nihilism has gone, but man is still trying to find himself in a wasteland of few bearings, with memories only of a bogus past. *De god denkbaar denkbaar de god* (1956) stands apart as an intellectual 'anti-novel', deliberately intended to be as widely interpretable as possible. [PK]

*Delta* (Autumn, 1966).

**Hermlin, Stephan,** pseud. of Rudolf Leder (Chemnitz 1915– ). German poet. A communist, he lived in exile from 1936, returning to East Berlin in 1947. His early poetry was influenced by – and he was officially criticized for it – French ⇨ Surrealism, ⇨ Rilke and ⇨ Expressionism; and also by ⇨ Aragon, ⇨ Éluard and ⇨ Neruda (*Wir verstummen nicht*, 1945; *Zweiundzwanzig Balladen*, 1947). His later poems show the ideals of socialist realism (*Stalin*, 1949; *Der Flug der Taube*, 1952; *Dichtungen*,

1956). The style of his short stories developed similarly, from e.g. *Reise eines Malers nach Paris* (1947) to *Die Zeit der Gemeinsamkeit* (1949) and *Die Zeit der Einsamkeit* (1951). [LL]

Kunisch, *HDG*.

**Hernández, Miguel** (Orihuela, Alicante 1910 –Alicante 1942). Spanish peasant poet. He had little schooling, but by reading developed a precocious mastery of neo-gongorism (⇨ Góngora), winning fame with *Perito en lunas* (1933). He moved to Madrid, published a religious play (inspired by Calderón), *Quien te ha visto y quien te ve y sombra de lo que eras* (1934) and completed a social drama, *Los hijos de la piedra* (1935; unpubl.). There is a classic perfection, modelled on Garcilaso and L. de Vega, in the sonnets of *El raya que no cesa* (1936), many inspired by love for his future wife, the finest perhaps the elegy for his young friend and patron Ramón Sijé. An ominous image which recurs is of the bull that enters the ring knowing it must die. Influenced during the war by his friends ⇨ Aleixandre and ⇨ Neruda, and by his experiences as a Republican volunteer, his poems became direct, fervent and bellicose (*Viento del pueblo*, 1937); they were meant to be recited to the fighting troops – the kind of popular audience he had always desired. Apart from 4 satirical one-act plays, *Teatro en la guerra* (1937), he also wrote the more traditional verse-drama, *El labrador de más aire* (1937), before the tragic post-war years; he was kept in prison in Alicante, where he died of tuberculosis. His later, more tragic war poems in *El hombre acecha* (1939), above all his *Cancionero y romancero de ausencias* (1938–41) in the manner of the old songbooks, which dwell on his separation from his wife and son, are deeply moving in their simplicity. His final attitude was stoical, his last poems buoyant, without religious belief. Though known in Spain only through a tendentious selection, he has had great influence, not least by his example. [JMC]

*Obra escogida* (1952; Buenos Aires, 1958); *Poesía completa* (Buenos Aires, 1961); *Antología* (Buenos Aires, 1960); Blecua, *FLE*; Cohen, *PBSV*; Trend, *OBSV*.

J. Cano Ballesta, *La poesía de M.H.* (Madrid, 1963); C. Couffon, *Orihuela et M.H.* (Paris, 1964); Vivanco, *PEC*; Zardoya, *PEC*.

**Herrad von Landsperg** (d. 1195). Spiritual writer. She became Abbess of Hohenburg (Mont Saint-Odile) in Alsace in 1167, and devoted herself to reform. She wrote the celebrated *Hortus deliciarum* (1175; ed. J. Walter, Strasbourg, 1952), one of the most remarkable illustrated works of the high Middle Ages. With an allegorical interpretation of the history of salvation as its central theme, it embraces the whole of human knowledge then accessible. The authors drawn on include Ambrose, Augustine, Jerome, Leo the Great, Gregory the Great, Isidore of Seville, Bede, Smaragdus, Yves of Chartres, Peter Lombard and Peter Comestor. The unique manuscript was destroyed in the Strasbourg fire of 1870. [CEC]

*H. de L.* (Strasbourg, 1897); Manitius, *GLLM*.

**Herrera, Fernando de** ('El Divino') (Seville 1534–Seville 1597). Spanish poet, critic and literary theorist. He spent his whole life quietly in Seville, living on a small benefice, but wielding considerable influence upon the cultural life of the city through his membership of a circle of writers, artists and scholars under the patronage of the Conde de Gelves. To the Condesa (poetically named 'Luz') he addressed his love poetry – sonnets, elegies, *canciones* – over many years; this is as passionate as it is possible for Petrarchan-Platonic literary exercises to be, eloquent and powerful in its images, with mystical notes as he continued the cult after the death of the Countess. Of more enduring appeal are the splendidly rhetorical heroic odes, notably that for the victory at Lepanto (1571) and the sombre lament for the destruction of the Portuguese at Alcazarquivir (1578). These are remarkable for their use of Old Testament imagery and language (rarely attempted in Spanish) and for their vision of the Spaniards as a modern chosen people nobly doing God's work; the essence of Imperial Spain at the height of its power is perfectly expressed. Herrera published little of his verse during his lifetime (1582); the status of a posthumous edition (1619) is much debated still. He was a perfectionist, constantly retouching his work, and keenly aware of literary theory and tradition. His *Obras de Garcilaso de la Vega con anotaciones de F. de H.* (1580) is a massive exposition of ideas on literature and language. Its themes are that literature is a responsible *métier*, a craft to be learned, and that Spain deserved an elevated literary language befitting her imperial grandeur. A detailed policy for this elevation was laid down, and it had great influence on young poets of the time, among them ⇨ Góngora. Herrera's own language is rich and colourful, with a taste for Latinisms and stylistic peculiarities which were further developed by the next generation. Finally one should note his new orthography, based on very sound principles, and his two prose works: on the Lepanto war (1572) and the life of Sir Thomas More (1592). Much else has been lost. [CCS]

*Poesías*, ed. V. García de Diego (1914); *Rimas inéditas*, ed. J. M. Blecua (1948); *Poesías inéditas* (Sociedad de Bibliófilos Andaluces, 1870); Trend, *OBSV*; Perry, *HASP*; Cohen, *PBSV*.
A. Coster, *F. de H.* (Paris, 1908); O. Macrí, *F. de H.* (Madrid, 1959) (with anthology).

**Herrmann-Neisse, Max** (Neisse, Silesia 1886 –London 1941). German poet. Associated in Berlin with the ⇨ Expressionists, his own sensitive, sorrowful, personal poetry is more traditionally lyrical and simple in its expression of modern anguish and longings. (He also wrote comedies and novels.) [PB]

*Lied der Einsamkeit. Gedichte von 1914–41*, ed. F. Grieger (1961).
Bridgwater, *TCGV*; Hamburger and Middleton, *MGP*; R. Lorenz, *M.H.-N.* (Stuttgart, 1966).

**Hertz, Henrik** (Copenhagen 1798?–Copenhagen 1870). Danish poet and playwright. A disciple of J. L. Heiberg in light comedy (*Sparekassen*, 1836; *Amors Geniestreger*, 1830) and in his view of form as more important than content, emphasized in his versified *Genganger-Breve* (1830), which attacks many contemporaries (including Andersen). Of greater value are his romantic plays: *Svend Dyrings Hus* (1837), based on ballads and widely successful in Scandinavia, and *Kong Renés Datter* (1845; tr. T. Martin, *King René's Daughter*, 1850), popular in Victorian England. His novel *Stemninger og Tilstande* (1839) supposedly portrays ⇨ Kierkegaard. [ELB]

**Herwegh, Georg** (Stuttgart 1817–Baden-Baden 1875). German poet. After studying theology and law, he turned to writing political poems and essays. In 1843 he escaped from conscription to Switzerland and France. After the defeat of his 'deutsch-demokratische Legion' in the 1848 Baden uprising, he lived in Paris, Geneva and Zürich, till he could return to Baden-Baden in 1866. His philosophy was influenced by Feuerbach and Schopenhauer; his politics, despite his aristocratic tastes, by the radical liberalism and nationalism of Das ⇨ Junge Deutschland, and the socialism of Lassalle. His *Gedichte eines Lebendigen* (1841, 1843) and *Neue Gedichte* (posth. 1877), imitating ⇨ Béranger, express a vague if passionate longing for freedom and hatred of Prussian rule. Their violent rhetoric secured them a short-lived success. [LL]

*Werke*, ed. H. G. Werner (1967).
B. v. Wiese, *Politische Dichtung Deutschlands* (Berlin, 1931); Carr, *RE*; Koch, *IW*.

**Herzen, Aleksandr Ivanovich** (Moscow 1812 –Paris 1870). Russian philosopher and writer. He was the illegitimate son of a rich nobleman I. Yakovlev by a German governess. In 1829 he entered Moscow University where he became interested in political thought, particularly the socialism of Saint-Simon. In 1834 he was exiled to a series of provincial towns, which appalled him by their backwardness and corruption. He returned to Moscow, where he became, with ⇨ Belinsky, one of the leading 'Westernizers', believers in progress after the model of Western Europe, as a solution for Russia's problems. He published philosophical and scientific articles, stories and the novel *Kto vinovat?* ('Whose Fault?', 1847), an attack on outmoded systems of morality.

In 1847 he emigrated to Paris, where he was active during the 1848 revolution; but its failure was a severe shock to his Westernizing ideals, as can be seen from *S togo berega* (1851; tr. M. Budberg, *From the Other Shore*, 1956). He drew two conclusions from this experience; that the Western *bourgeoisie*, which he despised, was strong enough to crush a democratic revolution; and that there was more chance of socialism succeeding in Russia, where the power of the *bourgeoisie* and the Central Government was weaker than in Europe. Accordingly he now pinned his hopes on the Russian peasant-commune, in which he saw a pattern for socialism without any equivalent in Western Europe. He believed that the development of the commune could help Russia to avoid the capitalist phase which he had hitherto regarded as inevitable, and so enable Russia to take a 'short-cut' to socialism independently of Europe.

From 1852 to 1864 he lived in London, where his house became a meeting-place for *émigrés* of all nationalities. He set up a Russian printing-press whose publications, the annual *Polyarnaya zvezda* ('The Polestar', 1855–62) and the fortnightly *Kolokol* ('The Bell', 1857–67), served as a mouthpiece for his views and also as a forum for liberal comment on current affairs. They enjoyed a wide circulation inside Russia and did much to prepare public opinion for the emancipation of the serfs in 1861. But his influence inside Russia declined after his unpopular stand over the Polish insurrection of 1863. Although he tried to appeal to the new generation his natural distrust of violence made him now seem old-fashioned.

Herzen always stressed the need for individual freedom and responsibility, and his views were expressed with lucidity, wit and humanity. His unusual literary style sometimes violates grammatical usage but it is always clear and direct. His masterpiece is his book of memoirs, *Byloye i dumy* (mainly 1852–5; tr. C. Garnett, *My Past and Thoughts*, 1924–7). [RDBT]

*Sobraniye sochineniy* (30 vols., 1954–64).
M. Malia, *A.A. and the Birth of Russian Socialism* (1961); L. Piper, *Mirovozzreniye Gertsena* (Moscow, 1935); R. Labry, *A.I.H.* (Paris, 1928); Carr, *RE.*

**'Herzog Ernst.'** A German epic poem, preserved in various versions, the oldest of which dates from 1170–80 (ed. K. Bartsch, 1869). In the adventures of the hero are absorbed historical matter pertaining to the career of Liudolf, son of Otto the Great, and legendary motifs from various sources. This heroic poem was written for courtly audiences in the early period of courtly epic poetry; later German adaptations of this work are also extant, both in verse and in prose, as are verse and prose versions in Latin. [RT]

Ed. von der Hagen and Büsching (1908).
K. Bartsch, *H.E.* (Vienna, 1869).

**Hesse, Hermann** (Calw, Württemberg 1877–Montagnola, Lugano 1962). German novelist and poet. His father and maternal grandfather were missionaries in India; he himself ran away from theological school in Maulbronn. He worked as a bookseller before becoming a freelance writer (1904). After a visit to India (1911) he lived permanently in Switzerland (citizenship 1923), working for the Red Cross during the First World War. Hesse won many literary awards including the Nobel Prize (1946). His first well-known novel, *Peter Camenzind* (1904; tr. W. J. Strachan, 1961), describes how an artist-dreamer gropes towards a profounder understanding of the forces within himself and within nature, stifled by the deadly (educational) conventions shown in the more obviously autobiographical story *Unterm Rad* (1905; tr. W. J. Strachan, *The Prodigy*, 1957). Similar themes are treated in *Gertrud* (1910; tr. H. Rosner, 1955) and *Rosshalde* (1914), where spiritual and artistic integrity is jeopardized now by marital failures. *Demian* (1919; tr. W. J. Strachan, 1958), a considerable success with the post-war generation, and *Siddharta* (1922; tr. H. Rosner,1954), develop a Jungian mixture of depth psychology – Hesse underwent analysis – and Indian mysticism, probing the childhood memories and fantasy of adolescents, who have to accept these demonic fascinations as part of 'total reality'. The controversial *Der Steppenwolf* (1927; tr. W. Sorrell, 1965) discovers similar wild instincts in the split personality of an artist, leading him from bitter isolation to a dubious acceptance of life as a (humorous?) jumble of images in the 'magic theatre' of the imagination. *Narziss und Goldmund* (1930; tr. G. Dunlop, 1959) owed its success to its combination of nut-brown maidens and medieval monasteries, the poetry of the senses and profundities of the spirit, and its suggestion of some absolute in which they are all aspects of the same thing. Finally *Das Glasperlenspiel* (1943; tr. M. Savill, *Magister Ludi*, 1950), a Utopian *Bildungsroman* set in the future, envisages an elite of Rulers who achieve perfect self-fulfilment in a half-aesthetic, half-religious 'game' in which the dissonance of the world is resolved into order. Hesse is also known for his poetry (*Gedichte*, 1957), limited in range and essentially Romantic, for many short stories (see Waidson, *GSS*) of which the best is *Knulp* (1915), and for critical works, e.g. *Blick ins Chaos* (1920; tr. S. Hudson, *In Sight of Chaos*, Zürich, 1923). [PB/AKT]

J. Mileck, *H.H. and His Critics* (Chapel Hill, 1958); Hugo Ball, *H.H. Sein Leben und sein Werk* (Frankfurt/M., 1956); H. Waibler, *H.H., eine Bibliographie* (Bern, 1962); O. Bareiss, *H.H., eine Bibliographie* (2 vols., Basle, 1964); Th. Ziolkowski, *H.H.* (N.Y. and London, 1966), and *The Novels of H.H.* (Princeton, 1965); B. Zeller, *H.H.* (Reinbek, 1963); Nathan, *GML*, ii.

**Heym, Georg** (Hirschberg, Silesia 1887–Berlin 1912). German poet. Long underrated, he was, with ⇨ Trakl and ⇨ Stadler, the most important early Expressionist; influenced by Baudelaire and Rimbaud, he was obsessed with a sense of evil. *Der ewige Tag* (1911) and *Umbra vitae* (1912) are apocalyptic visions: of the monster metropolis in all its soulless misery and consuming solitude, and of the 'great war' which he prophesied. The same passionate outcry is heard in his short stories *Der Dieb* (1912; see Spender, *GGSS*). Although using traditional verse-forms to convey a modern vision, his poetry gains by the resultant tension. Dynamic imagery and syntax match the figures of evil that strut beneath the taut, impersonal rhythms of this major visionary poet. [PB]

*Gesamtausgabe*, ed. K. L. Schneider (1960); Bridgwater, *TCGV*; Hamburger and Middleton, *MGP*.

K. L. Schneider, *Der bildhafte Ausdruck in den Dichtungen G.H.s, Georg Trakls und Ernst Stadlers* (Heidelberg, 1954); K. Mautz, *Mythologie und Gesellschaft im Expressionismus. Die Dichtung G.H.s* (Bonn, 1961); E. Loewenson, *G.H.* (Hamburg, 1962); E. Krispyn, *G.H. and the Early Expressionist Era* (Pennsylvania, 1963) (dissertation); C. Eykmann, *Die Funktion des Hässlichen in der Lyrik G.H.s* (Bonn, 1965); H. Rölleke, *Die Stadt bei Stadler, H. und Trakl* (Berlin, 1966); *GR*, XXXVI, 1961; *JEGP*, LXIII, 1, 1964.

**Heym, Stefan,** pseud. of Hellmuth Fliegel (Chemnitz 1913– ). German novelist and journalist. After U.S. emigration and military service he went to East Berlin in 1953. He writes in English and German. The theme of individual struggle against tyranny recurs in the novels *Hostages* (1942; *Der Fall Glasenapp*, 1958 – about Czech resistance in Prague), *Crusaders* (1948; *Kreuzfahrer von heute*, 1950 – about the doubts of a U.S. psychological warfare officer), *Goldsborough* (1954; published in German with same title, 1954 – about a miners' strike in the U.S.A.) and in *Die Papiere des Andreas Lenz* (1963 – about the 1849 uprising in Baden-Pfalz). His short stories include *Die Kannibalen* (1956; *The Cannibals*, 1958). His political ideas are expressed theoretically in the essays of *Im Kopf sauber* (1954) and *Offen gesagt* (1957). [LL]

Kunisch, *HDG*.

**Heyse, Paul** (Berlin 1830–Munich 1914). German writer. A self-conscious stylist whose cultivation of beauty (and tendency to gloss over evil and suffering – he bitterly attacked the Naturalists) made him once popular but with time unreadable. Perhaps the most perfect technically of all his short stories is *L'Arrabbiata* (1855; tr. M. Wilson, 1867). He gave a celebrated (and characteristic) definition of the *Novelle* in his preface to the *Deutscher Novellenschatz* (24 vols., 1871ff.), the so-called '*Falkentheorie*' (from Boccaccio's 'model' *Tale of a Falcon*) that makes the story revolve about a 'strange happening'. He published translations (from Italian), unsuccessful plays (38 vols.) and novels, e.g. *Children of the World* (1872; tr. anon., 1882). He won the Nobel Prize in 1910. [PB]

Bennett, *HGN*.

**Hidalgo, José Luis** (Torres 1919–Madrid 1947). Spanish poet and painter. Famous for his final volume, *Los muertos* (1947), written as he was dying of tuberculosis; he wrestles passionately with this most immediate reality, questioning, almost hectoring God, who seems so absent, so incommunicative. His style has the starkness of ⇨ Unamuno. [JMC]

Cohen, *PBSV*.
Cano, *PESV*.

**Hierro, José** (Madrid 1922– ). Spanish poet. His *Cuanto sé de mí* (1957) might stand as epigraph to his *Poesías completas* (1962), since all his poetry is a kind of interim report, in a restrained undertone – 'so much as I know of myself'. He writes of his own life, of his four years' imprisonment as a boy after the Civil War, of his deeply felt private relationships, of his powerlessness in face of death, of his love of music, always deeply aware of himself as a man like many others – '*un hombre como hay muchos*'. A conscious craftsman, he yet says of his poetry that if it is read in a hundred years, it will be for its documentary significance alone. He proclaims his hatred of ivory-tower attitudes in his well-known 'Para un esteta'. There is a modern authenticity of feeling in his intimate tone and belief in personal values and a true economy of expression in his justly cadenced lines. [JMC]

*Libro de las alucinaciones* (1964); Cohen, *PBSV*.
Cano, *PESV*.

**Hildebert** (Lavardin 1056–Tours 1133). Christian Latin poet. Head of the cathedral school at Le Mans, Bishop of Le Mans, and finally Archbishop of Tours. A man of wide learning and a master of Latin versification. He paints the glory of pagan Rome and the splendour of its ruins in a fine elegy. In another, he praises the even more glorious Christian Rome of his own time. He wrote brilliantly also in accentual Latin verse, which in his hands at last reached perfection of rhythm and rhyme. There survive also letters, sermons, two lives, and treatises. [FB]

Migne, *PL*, 171; *An. Hym.*, 50.
B. Hauréau, in *Notices et extraits des mss de la Bibliothèque Nationale*, xxviii (part 2, 1878); A. Dieudonné, *H. de L.* (Paris, 1898); Raby, *CLP*, *SLP*.

**'Hildebrandslied.'** An anonymous fragmentary German poem probably written in the latter half of the 8th century. It is the sole surviving relic of Germanic heroic verse in the Old High German language, and as such of great historical importance. Of the poem 53 lines have survived. They tell how Hildebrand, who had fled from Odoaker in the entourage of Theodoric the Goth and has now returned to help his lord regain his lost Italian kingdom, is confronted in single combat by his son Hadubrand, whom he left behind when he fled and who is now among the bravest of Odoaker's warriors. The two men taunt each other and then begin to fight; the conclusion of the poem is missing but it is known from Nordic versions of the story that the father slays his son. Tradition and the Germanic concept of justice and duty take no heed of personal tragedy. And since justice exists by the will of God, the duel between father and son – a well-known motif in world literature – assumes religious significance: Hildebrand's personal tragedy cannot be avoided. It is in this interplay of ethical forces and individual fates that much of the historical and modern interest of the poem resides. [RT]

Braune, *AL*, 28.
Ehrismann, *GDL*, i.

**Hildesheimer, Wolfgang** (Hamburg 1916– ). German writer (formerly painter, studied in England) largely of satire with grotesque, even surrealistic distortion. Known for his short stories *Lieblose Legenden* (1952), *Ich trage eine Eule nach Athen* (1956), a novel, *Paradies der falschen Vögel* (1953), many radio-plays, especially *Begegnung im Balkanexpress* (1952, publ. 1955), and *Prinzessin Turandot* (1954, stage version publ. 1955 as *Der Drachenthron*), a radio-opera, *Das Ende einer Welt* (1954), in collaboration with Hans Werner Henze, and the play *Die Verspätung* (1962). [PB]

Spender, *GGSS*; Waidson, *MGS*.

**Hiller, Kurt** (Berlin 1885– ). German publisher, critic and essayist. Associated with the Berlin Expressionists, founder of the Activist movement (periodical: *Das Ziel* and other titles), later President of the Revolutionary Pacifists; his writings embody the ideal, typical of the period, of a left-wing revolution which should also be a spiritual regeneration of society, led by intellectuals (e.g. *Der Aufbruch zum Paradies*, 1922, repr. Hamburg, 1952; *Der Geist werde Herr*, 1922). [AKT]

*Köpfe und Tröpfe* (1950); *Rote Ritter* (1951).

**Hłasko, Marek** (Warsaw 1931–69). Polish short-story writer. He belongs to the literature of protest, which emerged after 1956. His bitter stories in the collection *Pierwszy krok w chmurach* (1956) were followed by *Ósmy dzień tygodnia* (1957; tr. N. Guterman, *The Eighth Day of the Week*, 1959), a novel about two young lovers in modern Warsaw, in which he achieves strong emotional contrasts against the bleak atmosphere of frustration and boredom. After *Cmentarze* (1958; tr. N. Guterman, *Next Stop – Paradise and the Graveyard*, 1961) he chose to live in exile. His tough but passionate style is reminiscent of early Hemingway. [JP]

**Hlaváček, Karel** (Prague 1874–Prague 1898). Czech poet. The son of a Prague worker, he combined literary talent with that of a designer but died of tuberculosis without fully realizing his potentialities. His collection of poems, *Pozdě k ránu* (1896), is the direct projection of a tortured and self-torturing mind; a cry against both nature and civilized life, its symbols express the unconscious condition of the soul. His *Mstivá kantiléna* (1898), using the setting of the 16th-century Dutch Gueux rebels, is an ironical call to a vain and already lost revolt.

The most original of the Czech exponents of aristocratic and decadent art, he is unique in reproducing the feverish dreams of a man who has nothing in common with the utilitarian world. His precise, musical verse had a great influence on modern Czech poetry. [KB]

*Dílo* (3 vols., 1930).

F. Soldan, *K.H., typ české dekadence* (Prague, 1930).

**Hochhuth, Rolf** (An der Werra, Nordhesse 1931– ). German dramatist. His play *Der Stellvertreter* (1963; tr. R. D. MacDonald, *The Representative*, 1963), dealing with the question of the responsibility of the Roman Catholic Church – in particular Pope Pius XII – and the German Catholic Zentrumspartei for the ascendancy of the Nazis, and the Church's complicity in atrocities against the Jews, aroused much controversy when it was produced by Erwin Piscator in Berlin and at subsequent productions elsewhere. The play's theatrical power stems from the author's use of heightened verse dialogue mixing colloquialisms with ecclesiastical and Nazi Party jargon. His other work, *Die Berliner Antigone* and *Inventur* (short stories) and a novel, *Victoriastr. 4*, set in his home town after the 1945 German collapse, remains unpublished in book form. [PB]

*Der Streit um H.s 'Stellvertreter'* (Basel/Stuttgart, 1963) (essays by Günther, Haas, Luft and others); *GR*, XXXIX, 3, 1964; XLII, 1, 1967.

**Hochwälder, Fritz** (Vienna 1911– ). Austrian playwright. (Emigrated to Switzerland in 1938.) He has used conventional dramatic forms and theatrical devices, often with historical settings, to explore ideological conflicts, most successfully between religion and politics in Spanish America in *Das heilige Experiment* (1941; adapted E. le Gallienne, *The Strong are Lonely*, 1956). Other aspects of persecution are dramatized in *Der Flüchtling* (1945; rev. 1955; filmed), which still bears the Expressionist traits of ⇨ Kaiser's original script, and *Der öffentliche Ankläger* (1948; tr. K. Black, *The Public Prosecutor*, 1958). Later works, e.g. *Die Herberge* (1956), attempt the form of modernized mystery and morality plays, including comic moralities. [PB]

F.H., 'Über mein Theater', in *GLL*, XII, 2 (1959); *M*, LVII, 1 (1965).

**Hoddis, Jakob van,** pseud. of Hans Davidsohn (Berlin 1884–1942: removed from Bendorf-Sayn mental hospital near Koblenz and murdered by Nazis). German poet. One of the most original and gifted cofounders of *Der neue Club* (in June 1910) in which the young experimental poets of Berlin held their 'Neopathetisches Kabarett' (cf. ⇨ Heym, ⇨ Hiller). Mentally sick from 1912, he remained in mental homes after 1914. His poem 'Weltende', published in the first issue of *Die Aktion* in 1911, was the first printed Expressionist poem; his collection *Weltende* (1918) was reprinted in 1958. His poems are conglomerations of images, almost *collages*; the rhythms are near-mechanical. This style marked the first breakthrough of modernism in German poetry. [PB]

Bridgwater, *TCGV*; Hamburger and Middleton, *MGP*; H. Schneider, *J.v.H.* (Basle, 1967).

**Hoel, Sigurd** (N. Odal, Hedmark 1890–Oslo 1960). Norwegian novelist and essayist. He began as a teacher and journalist, but soon became associated and identified with left-wing currents in Norwegian intellectual life. Early literary influences included ⇨ Hamsun and Kafka, but in *Syndere i sommersol* (1927; tr. E. Sprigge and C. Napier, *Sinners in Summertime*, 1930), the novel which established his reputation, he satirizes good-humouredly the pretensions of the younger generation, showing them to be just as convention-ridden as their elders, whom they despise. In *En dag i oktober* (1931; tr. S. and R. Bateson, *One Day in October*, 1933), an analysis of a number of middle-class marriages, his psychological insight comes into its own. There is greater warmth in *Veien til verdens ende* (1933), a psychological study of childhood; and in *Fjorten dager før frostnettene* (1934) his various qualities combine in his most impressive pre-war achievement. *Møte ved milepelen* (1947; tr. E. Ramsden, *Meeting at the Milestone*, 1951), a study of treachery, ranks very high, with its bold technique, penetrating insight and ethical seriousness; similar considerations apply to *Trollringen* (1958). Hoel has also published several collections of thoughtful and well-written essays. [RGP]

*Samlede romaner og fortellinger* (12 vols., 1950–8); *Essays i utvalg*, ed. N. Lie (1962).

A. Stai, *S.H.* (Oslo, 1955); K. Egeland, *Skyld og skjebne* (Oslo, 1960).

**Hoffman, Kai** (Copenhagen 1874–Lyngby 1949). Danish poet. Originally influenced by French Symbolism (e.g. *Liljer i Mørket*, 'Lillies in the Dark', 1899), he developed into a poet inspired by Danish scenery and everyday people, for instance in *Det grønne Land* (1931). [ELB]

**Hoffmann, Ernst Theodor Wilhelm** (or **Amadeus**) (Königsberg 1776–Berlin 1822). German novelist and composer. Having studied law he entered the Prussian civil service and held a number of legal posts in the eastern Prussian provinces. He had always wished, however, to live the life of an artist, and in 1808 he became Kapellmeister at the theatre in Bamberg. But the Bamberg theatre went bankrupt, a subsequent appointment as musical director with an operatic troupe lasted only a year, and the last nine years of his life were spent in the Prussian legal service as a judge at the Kammergericht in Berlin. Through the autobiographical character of Johannes Kreisler, above all in the unfinished novel *Kater Murr* (1819–21), he depicted his experiences at the hands of the Philistine society which, as Kapellmeister, he had served and despised. He proclaimed the greatness of Beethoven as a Romantic composer (*Über Beethovens Instrumentalmusik*, 1813) and offered an interpretation of Mozart's *Don Giovanni* (1812; tr. C. Lazare, 1960) which has influenced productions of this opera down to modern times. It was in reverence for Mozart that he changed his third name from Wilhelm to Amadeus. Little of his considerable music output is now remembered, but his opera *Undine* (1813), on the story by Fouqué, was well received and highly thought of in its day. Among his other operas is a setting of Goethe's morality *Scherz, List und Rache* (1799) and Brentano's *Lustige Musikanten* (1804).

As a man of letters Hoffmann is famed above all for his tales, in which he exploited the element of the grotesque and the bizarre in a manner unmatched by any other Romantic writer. Among these are short stories such as *Das Majorat* (1817; tr. C. Lazare, *The Legacy*, 1960) and *Das Fräulein von Scuderi* (1818; tr. M. Bullock, *Mademoiselle de Scudéry*, 1962; opera, *Cardillac*, by Hindemith, 1926, rev. 1953), and allegorical fairy-tales such as *Der goldene Topf* (1813; tr. C. Lazare, *The Golden Pot*, 1960). Perhaps the most gripping of his works in this vein is his one complete full-length novel, *Die Elixiere des Teufels* (1813–16; tr. R. Taylor, *The Devil's Elixirs*, 1963). This is also the side of Hoffmann presented in Offenbach's opera. [RT]

K. Ochaner, *E.T.A.H. als Dichter des Unbewussten* (Frauenfeld and Leipzig, 1936); H. Hewett-Thayer, *H. Author of the Tales* (Princeton, 1948); R. Taylor, *H.* (1963).

**Hoffmann** (known as) **Von Fallersleben, August Heinrich** (Fallersleben 1798–Corvey 1874). German poet. From 1823 he was a librarian, and from 1830 professor of German at Breslau. His *Unpolitische Lieder* (1840–41), advocating liberalism, democracy and patriotism, cost him his university position and forced him to lead a wandering life – partly in Zürich – from 1843 till his rehabilitation in 1848. From 1860 he was the ducal librarian at Corvey, Westphalia. Some of his political poems and the lyrics of notably *Lieder und Romanzen* (1821), *Die schlesische Nachtigall* (1825), *Alemannische Lieder* (1826), *Jägerlieder* (1828), *37 Lieder für das junge Deutschland* (1848), *Deutsches Volksgesangbuch* (1848), *Soldatenlieder* (1851–2), and *Gedichte und Lieder für Schleswig-Holstein* (1863) have a melodious folk-song quality. His autobiography, *Mein Leben*, appeared in 1868. He is famous for his song *Deutschland über alles* (1841). [LL]

*Auswahl*, ed. H. Benzmann (4 vols., 1924).
H. Gerstenberg, *Ein Lebensbild von H.v.F.* (Munich, 1916); Koch, *IW*.

**Hoffmeister, Adolf** (1902– ). Czech essayist, poet and dramatist (also a painter and outstanding cartoonist). By profession a lawyer, he took an active part in the left-wing artistic *avant-garde* movement between the wars. He left Czechoslovakia after the German occupation in 1939 and via internment camps in France, Morocco and Portugal finally reached the U.S.A. After the war he returned home and was appointed to a senior post at the Ministry of Information, and then became Czechoslovak Ambassador in Paris (1948–51).

His travel books, with his own illustrations, show a great gift of observation and a sense of humour. In *The Unwilling Tourist* (tr. Don Perris, 1942) he gives a witty and revealing report on the migration of nations in Hitler's Europe. His memoirs, serialized in *Literární noviny* (Prague, 1962–3), are a fascinating first-hand account of the European *avant-garde* movement between the wars. [KB]

*Kulturně-politický kalendář 1962* (Prague, 1961).

**Hofmannsthal, Hugo von** (Vienna 1874–Rodaun/Vienna 1929). Austrian poet, dramatist and essayist. A precocious genius, he captured in a few exquisite poems poignant impressions of the unity of life (and of a social tradition) menaced by disintegration. After the inevitable 'crisis' (described in the famous Chandos letter, *Ein Brief*

1902 – see *Selected Prose*, tr. M. Hottinger and T. and J. Stern, 1952) when language and reality seemed to lose any common coherence, his more self-conscious search for spiritual order, in personal experience and in the socio-cultural heritage of Europe, is expressed in (largely) dramatic and prose work. His essays are rich in insights into literature and art as symbols of civilization, and the poet he sees called to fulfil modern man's deepest need (e.g. 'Der Dichter und diese Zeit', 1907). His concern for, and faith in, European culture led him to found the Salzburg Festival in 1920 (with Max Reinhardt, *et al.*), and to formulate cloudily ineffectual notions of intellectual nationhood ('Das Schrifttum als geistiger Raum der Nation', 1927). In his early dramatic poems he had shown the aesthete as incapable of spontaneous experience or real relationships (*Gestern*, 1891; *Der Tor und der Tod*, 1893; see *Poems and Early Plays*, ed. M. Hamburger, 1961). In an effort to rediscover the true passions and interplay of tragedy he adapted Greek drama (e.g. *Elektra*, 1904) but achieved rather a sense of pathological abnormality. More successful was his revival of the medieval morality in *Jedermann* (1911) and *Das grosse Salzburger Welttheater* (1922; see *Selected Plays and Libretti*, ed. M. Hamburger, 1963), which do suggest a naïve participation in the old religious truths by means of a half convincing 'archaic' style. A revealing moment in the latter play shows the whole convention threatened by an outbreak of violence; this deepest of Hofmannsthal's fears after the First World War he wrestles with most profoundly in *Der Turm* (1925; rev. edn 1927; see ibid.), a tragedy which attempts to forge a language and a character strong enough to allow spiritual integrity to transcend defeat. The theme of integrity is presented in a humorous contemporary setting in *Der Unbestechliche* (1923) and more effectively in *Der Schwierige* (1921; see ibid.) where the disintegration of Viennese aristocratic society is subtly reflected in the hero's inability to express himself authentically in its language. The possibility of fuller and more 'significant' expression sustained his long cooperation with Richard Strauss (see their *Briefwechsel*, 1952), for whom he composed the opera libretti of *Der Rosenkavalier* (1911), *Ariadne auf Naxos* (1912), *Die Frau ohne Schatten* (1919), *Die ägyptische Helene* (1928) and *Arabella* (1933; tr. J. Gutman, N.Y., 1955). Neither of his later attempts at narrative prose, which he wrote at times with classic elegance, fully realized his lost ideal of the whole man, of life 'significantly' experienced and truth concretely expressed, and of love as the key to such spiritual reintegration: the allegorical fairy-tale (prose version of the opera), *Die Frau ohne Schatten* (1919) seems superficially arbitrary in its play with symbolic meanings, while the ⇨ *Bildungsroman Andreas* (1930; tr. M. Hottinger, 1936), though it achieved great sensual beauty of description in its opening adventures, remains an inscrutable fragment. [PB/AKT]

*Gesammelte Werke* (15 vols., 1946ff.); *Briefwechsel mit S. George* (1953); H. Weber, *H.v.H. Bibliographie des Schrifttums 1892–1963* (Berlin, 1966).

H. Hammelmann, *H.* (1957); *H. Studies in Commemoration*, ed. F. Norman (1963); Keith-Smith, *ECGL*; Staiger, *MDS*.

**Hofmann von Hofmannswaldau, Christian** (Breslau 1617–Breslau 1679). German poet. He came under the influence of Opitz while still at school and remained his disciple for the rest of his life, largely ignoring the innovations of Zesen and the Nürnbergers. His lengthy studies in Holland, followed by the usual 'grand tour', made him particularly receptive to foreign influences, especially the ideas of ⇨ Marino and Góngora. He translated ⇨ Guarini's *Pastor fido* (1652, publ. later), but is chiefly remembered for his Ovidian *Heldenbriefe* (1663), a series of pairs of letters in both prose and verse, allegedly written by the great lovers of history, and for his secular and religious lyrics, many of which were published only after his death. His undoubted artistry often covers hollowness or is a vehicle for rank sexuality. He uses words not as a means of communication but as decoration, consciously aiming at a witty elegance of expression, and many of his poems have an epigrammatic quality. He is a virtuoso of form, which is used for its own sake: 66 different strophic forms have been counted in his *œuvre*, and it was his style, with its superabundance of imagery, unexpected comparisons, conceits, overworked antithesis and paraphrase, which gave rise to the popular view of the Baroque as *Schwulst* (empty bombast). [WAC]

*Ausgewählte Gedichte*, ed. F. P. Greve (1907); Killy, *DLTZ*.

R. Ibel, *H.v.H.* (Berlin, 1928); E. Rotermund, *C.H.v.H.* (Stuttgart, 1963).

**Hojeda, Diego de** (Seville 1571?–Huánuco 1615). Spanish poet. Author of *La cristiada* (1611), an epic in 12 books on the Passion of Christ. He spent most of his life as a Dominican in Peru. *La cristiada* is his only known work and was probably written over many years. Outstanding passages in this richly embellished baroque narrative are the description of the splendours of heaven in Book II and that of the physical horrors of the Crucifixion in XI and XII. A digression on the Deadly Sins in Book I cites Henry VIII and Elizabeth I of England as embodying most of them. [DR]

BAE, 17; ed. Sister M. H. P. Corcoran (Washington, D.C., 1935); F. Pierce, *The Heroic Poem of the Spanish Golden Age* (Oxford, 1947) (selections).

**Holbach, Paul Heinrich Dietrich (or Thiry),** Baron d' (Heidelsheim 1723–Paris 1789). German-born French philosopher and publicist. Having inherited wealth and a French barony in youth, d'Holbach became the chief patron of the *philosophes*, for whom his home provided a headquarters. He contributed scientific articles to the ⇨ *Encyclopédie*, published anti-religious works of considerable vehemence (*Le Christianisme dévoilé*, 1761; tr. anon. 1795), and expounded an atheist materialism in his *Système de la Nature* (1770; tr. H. D. Robinson, 1955). He also published in translation numerous English anti-religious works. D'Holbach is scarcely an original thinker, but his independence and energy made him one of the most influential propagandists of the pre-revolutionary period. [WHB]

*Textes choisis*, ed. P. Charbonnel (Paris, 1957).

P. Naville, *Paul Thiry d'H. et la philosophie scientifique au XVIIIe siècle* (Paris, 1943); V. W. Topazio, *D.H.'s Moral Philosophy* (Geneva, 1956).

**Holberg, Ludvig,** Baron Holberg (Bergen 1684–Copenhagen 1754). Danish playwright, essayist and historian. Norwegian by birth, he studied at Copenhagen and soon settled permanently in Denmark, apart from long journeys, e.g. to England (1706–8) and to France and Italy (1714–16). Appointed professor of philosophy, then of metaphysics (which he despised), he finally became professor of history in 1730.

His mock-heroic poem *Peder Paars* (tr. B. Stromsoe, Lincoln, 1962), published under the *nom de plume* of Hans Mikkelsen in 1719–20, and nearly banned, won him literary fame, and he was invited to write for the first Danish theatre (opened by a French Company in 1722). Of his 32 comedies, 15 are comedies of character, 11 comedies of manner, and the rest mainly moral allegories. His most important plays are *Den politiske Kandestøber*, *Jeppe paa Bjerget*, *Jacob von Thyboe*, *Erasmus Montanus*, *Den Stundesløse*, *Den vægelsindede*, *Henrik og Pernille*, and *Maskarade*. The best English translations are by Hime (1912), Campbell and Schenck (New York, 1914), Alexander (Princeton, 1946 and 1950), and Spink (1957). The founder of Scandinavian drama, Holberg borrowed freely from the Classics and from Molière, which may explain why he is less known in England than in other European countries.

His satirical novel comparable with Swift's *Gulliver*, *Nicolai Klimii iter Subterraneum* (1741; tr. anon. 1742, *A Journey to the World Under-Ground by Nicolas Klimius*; tr. J. I. McNelis, *Journey of Niels Klim to the World Underground*, Lincoln, 1960), described – in Latin for safety – an enlightened Utopia; he also wrote many essays in the *Spectator* tradition, and historical works, of which several were translated into English. He was made a baron in 1746, having announced his intention of leaving his fortune to the famous college at Sorø. [ELB]

*Memoirs of L.H.* (tr. anon., 1827); *Selected Essays of L.H.*, tr. P. M. Mitchell (Lawrence, 1955).

G. Brandes, *L.H.* (Copenhagen, 1884); H. Brix, *H.s Komedier* (1942); O. J. Campbell, *The Comedies of H.* (Harvard, 1914); McFarlane, *TNL*; *TLS*, 29 January 1954.

**Hölderlin, Friedrich** (Lauffen, Württemberg 1770–Tübingen 1843). German poet. Hölderlin studied theology (with Hegel and ⇨ Schelling), but preferred to eke out an existence as a private tutor, rather than become the minister of a religion in which he found he could not believe. As a tutor in Frankfurt (1796–8) he underwent the most profound emotional experience of his life in his relationship with his employer's wife Suzette Gontard, the Diotima of his poetry. Dismissed by the jealous Gontard, he found employment in Switzerland and Bordeaux returning home in 1802 both mentally and physically ill. From 1806 until his death he was hopelessly, but harmlessly, insane.

With Goethe and Schiller, he shares the post-Winckelmann view of Greece as an ideal golden age in the development of mankind. The essentially intellectual concern of the Weimar classicists to revive the ideal harmony of ancient Greece is, in his case, quickened by intense religious fervour, and in his later poetry expresses itself in a mystical belief in the spiritual rebirth of mankind and the second coming of Christ, the latter being seen in his private neo-classical mythology as the brother of Dionysos and the intermediary between classical antiquity and occidental civilization.

Like Schiller, he was a Swabian, and his early hymnic poems to the ideal values of humanity, friendship, harmony and love ('Die Demut', 'Lied der Freundschaft') clearly show the influence of his great compatriot. It was not Schiller, however, but Klopstock who exercised a permanent influence on his poetry. With Klopstock he shares a quasi-religious belief in the dignity of the poet's calling and his own prophetic mission, and like Klopstock he writes in a consciously elevated, neo-classical style, cultivates the hexameter and is a master of the classical ode forms. The most difficult of all German poets, many of his later poems, in which he increasingly uses free rhythms, border on the incomprehensible in both language and thought.

For all his profoundly religious nature, he was incapable of belief in the traditional sense, and the poems of his middle period are years ahead of their age in their intense awareness of the pitiful fragility of human existence and their expression of a profound sense of isolation and loneliness – significantly it was not until the early decades of the present century that he was 'discovered' and it is only in the writings of poets such as ⇨ George, ⇨ Rilke and ⇨ Weinheber that he becomes important as a literary influence. He is alone in a cruelly inhospitable world ('Hälfte des Lebens'). He continues to believe in higher powers, but these latter are indifferent to man's fate ('Hyperions Schicksalslied'). Alternatively, man has destroyed the possibility of his own harmony by his titanism and alienated himself from nature ('Der Mensch'), and it is from his sense of alienation that his longing for Greece is to be understood ('Archipelagus'). His point of departure in his love poetry is his own experience in Frankfurt, but again his sense of alienation is evident in its joyless nature, in the view of love as a destructive force ('Der Abschied') or as something incapable of realization on earth ('Diotima'), destined to be fulfilled only in the hereafter ('Menons Klage um Diotima'). Nature is experienced pantheistically, the ancient Greek nature gods being resuscitated ('An den Äther', 'Da ich ein Knabe war...', 'Sonnenuntergang'), and although his descriptions and evocations of nature reveal poetic powers of the highest order, these are seldom introduced for their own sake, but almost invariably have symbolical overtones ('Der gefesselte Strom', 'Heimkunft').

While many of his more traditional lyrics are amongst the finest in the German language, it is in the so-called 'patriotic songs' of the late period ('Germanien', 'Patmos', 'Brot und Wein', 'Wie wenn am Feiertage') which deal with such themes as the mission of the poet, his yearning for classical Greece, the second coming of Christ and the rebirth of ancient Greece in the German fatherland, that his genius gains characteristic expression. It is here that his verse achieves unique heights in its ecstatic expression of his prophetic visions in powerful dynamic rhythms, strikingly original imagery and language which for all its near-incomprehensibility is strangely compelling in its emotive power and sense of tremendous urgency.

The epistolary novel *Hyperion* (1797–9) and the uncompleted drama *Empedokles* everywhere reveal the hand of the lyric poet and deal with themes common to the poems. Against the background of the unsuccessful revolt of the Greeks against the Turks (1770), *Hyperion* preaches the rebirth of religion and mankind and the return of the golden age through the agency of poetry and selfless love, while the self-immolation of the poet-philosopher Empedokles becomes a symbol for his own sense of alienation and desire to merge with the absolute. [WAC]

*Sämtliche Werke*, ed. F. Beissner (1944ff.); *Briefe*, ed. A. Beck (1954ff.); *Poems*, tr. and intr. M. Hamburger (1952).

R. Guardini, *H.* (Leipzig, 1938); L. S. Salzberger, *H.* (1952); Hamburger, *RE*.

**Höllerer, Walter** (Sulzbach-Rosenberg, Bavaria 1922– ). German poet and essayist. Since 1959 he has been professor of literature in West Berlin Technical University. He has made lecture tours in Europe and the U.S.A. and is editor of the magazines *Akzente* (since 1954, with H. Bender) and *Sprache im technischen Zeitalter* (since

1961). He has published essays on the arts, *Movens* (1960, with M. de la Motte and F. Mon), and literary criticism, *Zwischen Klassik und Moderne* (1958). His poems, notably in *Der andere Gast* (1952), show the influence of antiquity as well as imagistic and symbolistic tendencies, reducing lyrical emotion and logical thought to a minimum. He has also edited anthologies of recent poetry (*Transit*, 1956; *Junge amerikanische Lyrik*, 1961) and one-act plays (*Spiel in einem Akt*, 1961). [LL]

H. E. Holthusen, 'W.H.', in *Ja und Nein* (1954); P. Härtling, 'W.H.', in *in zeilen zu haus* (1957).

**Holstein, Ludvig** (Kallehave 1864–Copenhagen 1943). Danish poet. He is a Pantheistic worshipper of nature and a fastidious writer whose poetry is held in high esteem in Denmark. His first poems appeared in 1895, but his fame mainly rests on the volumes of poetry he published 1915–29, especially *Æbletid* (1920) and *Jehi* (1929). [ELB]

E. Frandsen, *L.H.* (Aarhus, 1931).

**Holthusen, Hans Egon** (Rendsburg 1913– ). German poet and critic. His post-war poems became famous for their apocalyptic sense of spiritual crisis (*Klage um den Bruder*, 1947; *Hier in der Zeit*, 1949; *Labyrinthische Jahre*, 1952); his influential essays, similarly inspired, critically examine what still authentically survives of traditional Western values especially in the work of contemporary German and English authors (*Der unbehauste Mensch*, 1951; *Ja und Nein*, 1954; *Das Schöne und das Wahre*, 1958; *Kritisches Verstehen*, 1961). *Das Schiff* (1956; tr. R. Kee and S. Hughes, *The Crossing*, 1959) is a selfconsciously philosophizing novel.

Bridgwater, *TCGV*; Hamburger and Middleton, *MGP*.
H. Salinger, in *Poetry*, LXXXII (Chicago, 1953); *GLL*, II, 2 (1949); IX (1950–1).

**Hölty, Ludwig Christoph Heinrich** (Mariensee, Hanover 1748–Hanover 1776). German poet. The most gifted of the student group – 'Hainbund' – at Göttingen. His poems (collected edn, 1782–3) express presentiments of his tragically early death of consumption. Melodious, with an elegiac note of unfulfilled longing, they are skilful in using the ode form, but somewhat limited in range: soft, delicate impressions of moonlit nights ('Die Mainacht'), poems to spring ('Frühlingslied'), and one or two expressions of worldly wisdom and practical morality (including the famous 'Übzimmer Treu und Redlichkeit'), together with occasional poems. Under the influence of Percy's *Reliques*, he wrote two ballads, 'Adelstan und Röschen' and 'Die Nonne' (1771–2, published in the *Musenalmanach* 1774–5) which deal with the theme of the abandoned girl and her revenge, which are notable for their love of the eerie and their introduction of ghosts.

*Werke*, ed. W. Michael (2 vols., 1914–18).
E. Albert, *Das Naturgefühl H.s* (Bonn, 1910).

**Holz, Arno** (Rastenburg, E. Prussia 1863–Berlin 1929). German poet and dramatist. His *Die Kunst: ihr Wesen und ihre Gesetze* (1891) formulated a famous theory of 'consistent' Naturalism ('art has the tendency to return to nature' – i.e. is 'reproductive' imitation limited only by its means). With Johannes Schlaf (1862–1941) he achieved a 'raw-life' sensation with the pointlessly stark Novellen *Papa Hamlet* (1889: under fashionably Scandinavian pseudonym) and the deliberately formless 'play' *Die Familie Selicke* (1890), which influenced G. ⇨ Hauptmann. Holz turned back to lyric poetry with his modernistic *Phantasus* (1898; various eds. 1926); he advocated (*Die Revolution der Lyrik*, 1899) 'inevitable' inner rhythms as opposed to meaningless conventional rhythms. His own recall Walt Whitman; structurally his poetry points forward to the futurism of ⇨ Stramm. [PB]

*Werke*, ed. W. Emrich and A. Holz (7 vols. 1961–4); ed. and sel. A. Döblin (Wiesbaden, 1951); Bridgwater, *TCGV*; Deutsch and Yarmolinsky, *Contemporary German Poetry* (N.Y., 1923).
H. Motekat, *Persönlichkeit und Werk* (Kitzingen, 1953); Emrich, *PV*.

**Honchar, Oles'** (Sukha, Poltava 1918– ). Ukrainian novelist and short-story writer. He came into prominence after the Second World War with his wartime, and later collective farm, themes, following socialist realism methods. There are also some romantic and highly poetical works. [VS]

*Tvory* (5 vols., 1966–7); *Standard-Bearers*, tr. N Jochel (1948); *Golden Prague* (1950); 'Perekop' *SL*, 11–12 (1958); 'Man and Arms', *SL*, 6– (1961); 'Tronka', *SL*, 6–7 (1964); short storie tr. in *SL*, 1 (1948); 2 (1949); 1 (1950); 5 (1951) 8 (1953); 3 (1954); 10 (1960).
*UCE; UR*, 1 (1960).

**Honorius 'of Autun'** (fl. near Regensburg *c.* 1120). Medieval scholar. His numerous works include the *De cognitione vitae*, in the Augustinian philosophical tradition, the encyclopedic *Imago mundi*, a collection of sermons under the title *Speculum ecclesiae*, the theological *Elucidarium*, and the *De luminaribus ecclesiasticis*, a history of Christian writers. [CEC]

Migne, *PL*, 172 (1854) (*De philosophia, De solis effectibus* and *Quaestiones* are not authentic); *Summa gloria, De offendiculo* and *De apostatis*, ed. I. Dieterich, MGH (1897).
Manitius, *GLLM*.

**Hooft, Pieter Corneliszoon** (Amsterdam 1581–The Hague 1647). Dutch poet. Exceptional in his detachment from religious and political parties and his cultivation of the new Renaissance art *an sich*. Whereas his countrymen discovered the new learning and art at second hand from France, he was privileged to see for himself the new masques, to visit Italian libraries and to take part in the debates on the Vulgate in Florence. He returned home at 22 with the truly humanist ambition to fashion Dutch into art as great and permanent as the stone of Greek sculpture. As sheriff of Muiden (1609) he could withdraw from party disputes in the capital, and in a spirit of stoical detachment, acquired from Montaigne and his friend H. L. ⇨ Spiegel ('better becalmed than blown too hard'), he played host to distinguished artists, musicians and diplomats. His cultured environment and the extravagance of his love poetry mark him as a natural aristocrat in a society of burghers. Yet the heart that is poured out in the courtly conventions of his Petrarchan sonnets also beats in sympathy with the simple men and women who are the heroes of his *Nederlandsche Historiën*. This chronicle of the Dutch Wars of Independence, started in 1628 after a close study and translation of Tacitus (1623–5), was his scholarly homage to his country to which he gave the last 21 years of his life; 27 books were completed, covering the years 1555–87; as a monument of Latin-inspired Dutch prose they survived as a model well into the 19th century.

Hooft's patriotism also inspired two tragedies, modelled on Seneca and providing a pacifist-stoical 'mirror for princes'. In *Geeraerdt van Velzen* (1613), based on a tradition of Floris V's murder at the Muiderslot, the treachery of the subject is shown to be a greater wrong than the tyranny of the ruler. In *Baeto oft Oorsprong der Hollanderen* (1617) the legend of the origin of the Dutch nation provides a model founder who, like so many of his countrymen (including his father), preferred exile to civil war. The same stoical counsel of moderation is given in his 13 edifying verses, and the simplicity of rural life is preferred to the sophistication of the Court in his pastoral play *Granida* (1605; tr. in preparation). In the rival suits of a prince and a shepherd for the hand of the princess Granida, the second, and more important motif, is that spiritual love is nobler than amorous delight. The contrary views of ⇨ Tasso's *Aminta* and ⇨ Guarini's *Il pastor fido* obviously impressed Hooft, whose songs and sonnets often seem to belie the theistic solemnity of the edifying verses and his deep understanding of marital love in e.g. the moving *Klaghte der Princesse van Oranjen over 't oorloogh voor 's Hartoghenbosch* (1629). The pagan, Platonic cult of beauty in Italy had sent him back to the functional austerity of Calvinist Holland with an erotic zest for life in which the whole perceptible world was experienced as a vision of perfection. Such was his genius as a poet, and so vivid was his imagination as an idealist, that his hyperbole is easily mistaken for reality. Yet the man who writes of small gains as triumphs, corrections as martyrdom, sorrow as agony and admiration as adoration, was happily married, first to Christina van Erp (1610) and, after her death in 1624, to Leonora Hellemans (1627).

His tragedies, *Achilles en Polyxena* (1589) and *Ariadne* (1602), and his renderings of Plautus's *Aulularia* as *Warenar* (1616) and of ⇨ Aretino's *L'ipocrito* as *Schijnheyligh* (1617) – as an attack on the Counter-Remonstrants – contribute less to his fame than his prose works (the *Historiën*, his essay on dramatic poetry, *Reden van de waerdicheit der Poesie*, and his letters) and above all his lyrical poetry which place him among the greatest renaissance writers. [PK]

*De Nederlandsche Historiën*, incl. G. Brandt's 'Levan van Hooft' (1703); *Volledige uitgave der gedichten*, ed. P. Leendertz and F. A. Stoett (2 vols., 1899); *Brieven*, ed. J. v. Vloten (1855); *Delta* (Winter 1959/60); Weevers, *PNEC*; Grierson, *F*; Barnouw, *CA*; *Hoofts Lyriek*, ed. C. A. Zaalberg (1963).
A. Romein-Vershoor, *P.C.H.* (Amsterdam, 1947); H. W. van Tricht *P.C.H.* (Arnhem, 1951).

**Hora, Josef** (Dobříň 1891–Prague 1945). Czech poet. A journalist by profession, he began with poems in praise of love for the earthly world, but the realization of social injustice marred his vision of a full and beautiful life. He joined a Communist daily and his volume *Pracující den* (1920) is a call to revolution. Unable to reconcile his individualism with collectivism, he left the Communist Party in 1929. The rhetorics of proletarian poetry changed into intimate lyrics and former optimism into melancholy. His *Struny ve větru* (1927) contain the motifs to which he was to remain faithful to the end; the motif of time, conceived as an isolated, independent entity, and those of death, silence, solitude, dreams and memory. In *Máchovské variace* (1936), published on the occasion of the hundredth anniversary of the death of ⇨ Mácha, he claimed the spiritual heritage of the great romantic. In *Zahrada Popelčina* (1940) he finally overcomes his tragic attitude to life. He gives up meditation and emotionalism and pours out verses pure in their sensualism and sheer melody. [KB]

*Dilo* (16 vols., 1950–61).
B. Václavek, *J.H.* (Prague, 1925); A. M. Píša, *J.H.* (Prague, 1947).

**Hortatzis, Georgios** (Crete, fl. end of the 16th century). The most considerable poet of the Greek literary renaissance in Venetian-occupied Crete. Little is known about his life. He wrote: the *Erophile*, a tragedy of love and horror inspired by the *Orbecche* of G. ⇨ Giraldi; the *Katzourbos*, a comedy of the ⇨ *commedia dell'arte* type; and (perhaps) the *Gyparis*, a *pastorale* based in the main on the *Calisto* of L. Groto. All three show him to be a consummate poet skilfully exploiting and adapting to Greek scenery and atmosphere dramatic fashions current in Italy. [SJP]

K. B. Sathas, *Kritikon Theatron* (1879); F. H. Marshall, J. N. Mavrogordato, *Three Cretan Plays* (1929); A. Embiricos, *La renaissance crétoise* (Paris, 1960); F. M. Pontani, *Teatro neoellenico* (Milan, 1962); *Katzourbos*, ed. L. N. Politis (Crete, 1964).

**Hostovský, Egon** (Hronov 1908– ). Czech novelist. He resigned his post in the Czechoslovak diplomatic service in 1948 when the Communists came to power, and now lives in the U.S.A. His novels combine thrilling plots with an analysis of the psychological and ethical problems of the contemporary intellectual. His heroes are displaced persons in both the literal and figurative sense. They live in a world of their own making in conflict with their surroundings. His first novels, such as *Případ profesora Körnera* (1937), are concerned with Jewish intellectuals, his later works, *Listy z vyhnanstvi* (1941; tr. A. Krtil, *Letters from Exile*, 1942), *Seven Times the Leading Man* (tr. F. Long, 1945), *Missing* (tr. E. Osers, 1952), *The Midnight Patient* (tr. P. H. Smith, 1955), *The Charity Ball* (tr. P. H. Smith, 1957). *The Plot* (tr. A. Backer and B. Wolfe, 1962) and *Three Nights* (tr. P. H. Smith, 1964) reveal, with compassionate irony, the fantastic mental world of refugees from Nazism and Communism. On one plane he states the case of a neurotic individual trying in vain to break out from his loneliness but on another, almost theological plane, he is preoccupied with man as a passive witness to a transcendental purpose he is unable to understand. [KB]

K. Sezima, *Mládí* (Prague, 1936).

**Houdar de La Motte, Antoine** (Paris 1672–Paris 1731). French critic, poet and dramatist. A friend of ⇨ Fontenelle and an extreme 'modern', La Motte advanced literary theories, based upon an unimaginative rationalism, which reduced poetry to an ornate (and ultimately indefensible) form of prose, and proposed the virtual abolition, in the name of common sense, of the conventions of classical French tragedy. His verse is aridly prosaic, and won little approval even from contemporaries. In the theatre, however, he neglected his own theories, and was more successful. His major tragedy, *Inès de Castro* (1723), the box-office success of the century, has historical interest as an early example of the tendency to introduce sentimentality and visual appeal into classical tragedy. [WHB]

P. Dupont, *Un poète-philosophe au commencement du XVIIIe siècle: H. de la M.* (Paris, 1898); Gilman, *IPF*; Lancaster, *FTLV*.

**Hrabal, Bohumil** (Brno 1914– ). Czech writer. A lawyer who worked successively as clerk, railwayman, travelling salesman, steel-worker, labourer and scene-shifter and devoted himself to writing only after 1962. In his short stories and novels, written in a rambling style and slangy language, he presents the anti-hero, an ordinary man grappling with reality. His novel *Ostře* *sledované vlaky* (1965) was turned into an internationally successful film (*Closely Observed Trains*, 1967). [KB]

**Hrabanus Maurus** (Mainz *c.* 780–Winkel am Rhein 856). Archbishop of Mainz (847). Studied under ⇨ Alcuin, who surnamed him Maurus and whose passion for learning and teaching ability he shared. He became famous as head of the Benedictine school at Fulda. He raised the intellectual level of the German clergy and encouraged monastic schools to educate men who had no intention of becoming clerics. In addition to verse epistles, didactic poems and hymns, his prolific prose includes *De institutione clericorum*, a treatise on the training of the clergy after Augustine, *De rerum naturis* (after ⇨ Isidore of Seville), Biblical exegesis, especially an influential commentary on St Matthew. [FB]

Migne, *PL*, 107–12; ed. E. Dümmler (Poems: MGH, PLAC II, 1884; Epistolae V, 1898).
Raby, *CLP*.

**Hrafnkels Saga.** ⇨ Icelandic Sagas.

**Hristov, Kiril** (Stara Zagora 1875–Sofia 1944). Bulgarian poet, dramatist and story-writer. Orphaned at 2, he was brought up by uncles and sent to the Trieste Naval Academy where he wrote his 'Morski soneti' (printed in *Misăl*, 1895), reminiscent of ⇨ Velichkov's seascapes. After publishing his *Trepeti* (1897), written in Naples, he left for Leipzig in 1898 and befriended Pencho ⇨ Slaveykov, whom, however, he soon deserted in the Vazov-Slaveykov polemic. After holding various posts in teaching, journalism and the National Library, he left Bulgaria 1923–38 to teach Bulgarian literature at Leipzig and Prague.

His wide range of writing includes plays like *Boyan magesnikăt* (1905) and *Răchenitsa* (1917), the novels *Tămni zori* (1920) and *Mechtateli* (1921), an epic *Cheda na Balkana* (1930), memoirs (1943), stories, literary articles and translations. His lyric verse marks him as the anacreontic poet without Bulgarian precedent, uninhibited (as he declares in 'Hymn') by 'the ordered life, reputation and ideals' or the social conscience which pervades Bulgarian literature. Inspired by 'love, delight in nature, anger at an affront... things straight from my personal life', he used to best effect the first two of these, nowhere more sensitively interwoven than in his poem 'First Love'. His *Slănchogledi* (1911), *Himni na zorata* (1911) and *Vălnolom* (1937) have enriched the Bulgarian tongue (extolled in his poem of that title) with a wealth of lyric poems and ballads on folk and historical themes. [VP]

*Izbrani stihotvoreniya* (1953); *Sbornik* (1943); Pinto, *BPV*.
S. Karakostov, *K.H. za sebe si* (Sofia, 1943); Manning and Smal-Stocki, *HMBL*.

**Hrotswith (Roswitha)** (fl. 950). A Benedictine nun at Gandersheim in Saxony; her 6 short plays in rhymed Latin prose, counterblasts to the licentiousness of the comedies of Terence, are founded on saints' legends and extol virginity. They are not without pathos and even comedy, though some are spoiled by 'lectures' on e.g. music, astronomy, arithmetic, borrowed from ⇨ Boethius. She also wrote 8 epic legends in leonine hexameters, an account of the founding of her convent, and an epic about Otto I. [FB]

Migne, *PL*, 137; ed. P. de Winterfeld (MGH, SRG, Berlin, 1902); ed. K. Strecker (Leipzig, 2nd edn, 1930); non-dramatic works tr. M. G. Wiegand (St Louis, 1936); plays tr. H. J. W. Tillyard (1923), C. St John (1923); *Abraham* and *Callimachus* tr. R. S. Lambert (1922–3); *Dulcitius* tr. Lindsay, *MLP*.
J. Aschbach, *Roswitha und Conrad Celtes* (Vienna, 1868); K. Young, *The Drama of the Medieval Church* (2 vols., 1933).

**Hucbald of St Amand** (*c.* 840–930). Learned monk and poet. Pupil of Heiric of Auxerre. He helped to reform the schools at Rheims (⇨ Flodoard, Gerbert). His principal work is the *Ecloga de Calvis* (ded. Hatto of Mainz), a philosophical defence of baldness in verse. The remarkable musical treatise, *Musica enchiriadis*, is probably not by him. [CEC]

Migne, *PL*, 132 (1853); *Verse*, ed. P. de Winterfeld in PLAC (1899).
Manitius, *GLLM*; Raby, *SLP*.

**Huch, Ricarda** (Braunschweig 1864–Schönberg 1947). German novelist, poet and critic. 'The first lady of Germany' (T. Mann). Her prolific work includes: romantic poetry (*Gesammelte Gedichte*, 1929), which seems now rather to strive for than achieve intense aesthetic experience; fiction, such as the famous study of decadence and passion in a Hanseatic family, *Erinnerungen von Ludolf Ursleu dem Jüngeren* (1893; tr. W. A. Drake, *Unconquered Love...*, 1931), which bathes its subject in a ⇨ Heyse-like lyrical style – so different from the philosophical intelligence informing ⇨ Mann's *Buddenbrooks* on this theme; historical prose 'epics' about Garibaldi (1906–7) and the Thirty Years' War (1912–14; new edn 1958); and scholarly works on the Holy Roman Empire (1934, 1937, 1939) and the Romantic Movement – *Die Romantik* (1951). [PB]

*Gesamtausgabe*, ed. W. Emrich (10 vols., 1966ff.).
H. Baumgarten, *R.H.* (Weimar, 1964); *GLL*, II (1948).

**Huchel, Peter** (Berlin-Lichterfelde 1903– ). German poet. Lived in France as translator, farm-labourer and freelance writer. He was a prisoner-of-war in Russia, then programme editor for East Berlin Radio, and editor-in-chief of the periodical *Sinn und Form* (1948–62). His early poetry is realistic *Heimatdichtung*, often pastoral or religiously inspired, its tone mainly elegiac or contemplative (*Gedichte*, 1948, 1950). But his latest collection, *Chausseen Chausseen* (1963), which includes the important topical cycle 'Das Gesetz', is altogether different: tersely modern, highly original and deeply lyrical. [PB]

Bridgwater, *TCGV*; Hamburger and Middleton, *MGP*.
E. Zack, *Der Dichter P.H.* (Berlin, 1953); *Akzente*, XII, 1965.

**Huet, Conrad Busken** (The Hague 1826–Paris 1886). Dutch critic, journalist and historian. A modernist (cf. *Brieven over den Bijbel*, 1858), he resigned from the Church rather than conform. He inclined towards French sophistication and the critical tenets of ⇨ Sainte-Beuve and ⇨ Taine, and his articles in *De Gids* (cf. ⇨ Potgieter) restored some perspective to Dutch literary criticism (cf. *Litterarische Fantasiën en Kritieken*, 26 vols., 1881–8). His later, historical work, best represented by *Het Land van Rembrandt* (1882), gains in brilliance what it loses in balance. [PK]

*The Land of Rubens*, tr. A. D. van Dam (1888); 'Thomas Carlyle' in Pritchard, *GE*.

**Hugh Primas** (fl. 1130). Latin poet. Of unknown origin, he taught for a time at Orleans and Paris and in later years lived on charity. He was a master of rhymed accentual Latin verse and of leonine hexameters. His verse extols wine, women and gambling, describes his hand-to-mouth existence and satirizes those who refused to help him and were niggardly. 'Primas' was a nickname conferred on him by his contemporaries, in recognition of his eminence as a poet. [FB]

Poems with German tr. in K. Langosch, *Hymnen und Vagantenlieder* (Basel, 1954).
Raby, *SLP*.

**Hugo, Victor Marie** (Besançon 1802–Paris 1885). French poet. The most prolific and versatile of the French Romantics, he was the second son of a colonel, later general in Napoleon's army, and as a child accompanied his father to Italy (1808) and Spain (1811–12). He was then educated in Paris, acquiring a lifelong admiration for Virgil and a taste for the metres and sonorities of Greek. At 15 he was congratulated by the Académie Française. Catholic and royalist, he aspired 'to be Chateaubriand or nothing'. His literary career began in 1819 with a triumph at the 'Jeux Floraux de Toulouse', followed by a first novel, *Bug-Jargal*, and the publication with his brothers Abel and Eugène of the *Conservateur Littéraire*. His first *Odes* (1822) were rewarded by Louis XVIII and enabled him to marry Adèle Foucher. He made his home a meeting-place for the rising generation of poets. He wrote for *La Muse Française* (1823–4) defending the new literature, but did not openly attack classicism until after the stir caused by his novel *Han d'Islande* in 1826. The theme of liberty is prominent in the *Odes et ballades*, and their preface of the same year. Simultaneously he gave free rein to fantasy and to great technical virtuosity, even more apparent in the final edition (1828), and in the *Orientales* (1829) with its famous preface advocating complete freedom of inspiration for poetry.

Similar principles had been invoked for romantic drama in the *Préface de Cromwell* (1827), proposing to replace the classical segregation of genres by contrasting tones on the model of Shakespeare, and to suppress the conventional three unities, the better to represent the complexity of life and man. The unity of action was retained, and reinforced by sub-plots. He emphasized that setting in place, time and customs formed part of the drama itself. Verse form was held to idealize natural expression. Despite obvious sources, the manifesto was fiery enough to confirm his leadership of the Romantic movement.

Success in the theatre was delayed. *Cromwell* was unsuitable, *Marion Delorme* (1829) withheld by the Censor (acted 1831); but in February 1830, after a hard battle, *Hernani* triumphed at the Comédie Française. Hugo continued writing for the stage with verse-dramas: *Le roi s'amuse* (1832) and *Ruy Blas* (1838), and in prose (*Lucrèce Borgia*, *Marie Tudor*, *Angelo*), until the failure of his dramatic epic, *Les Burgraves*, in 1843.

The first great novel, *Notre-Dame de Paris* (1831; tr. anon., Everyman, 1910), composed simultaneously with the early dramas, shares with them the concept of *fatality* dominating plot and characterization and achieves a sombre grandeur by its pessimism.

From 1830, Hugo's political, emotional and religious disquiet increased. He stressed the poet's social mission, but saw the July Monarchy crush the ideal of liberalism. After ⇨ Sainte-Beuve had broken his domestic happiness, he began (1833) the liaison with Juliette Drouet; it was to last until she died (1883). Finally, his religious belief, never orthodox, gave way to doubt. These themes are contrasted with social observation, family memories, joys of childhood, love and nature, in 4 volumes of lyrical poetry, *Les feuilles d'automne* (1831), *Les chants du crépuscule* (1835), *Les voix intérieures* (1837), *Les rayons et les ombres* (1840). In the first collection, the striking vision of resurrected mankind in the night of eternity ('La pente de la rêverie') and the poet's dionysiac affinities with nature ('Pan'), herald the subject-matter of *Les contemplations* (1856). Anguish of mind predominates in the second, intervenes in the third with 'Pensar', 'Dudar' and 'À Olympio' symbolizing the struggles of his superior genius. In the fourth volume, the prophet and visionary, seeking to guide humanity towards the future ('Fonction du poète'), probes the mysteries of death, destiny, nature and God. Exile was to accentuate these tendencies.

Hugo was elected to the Académie Française in 1841 and created Pair de France four years later. In the meantime, the death of his daughter Léopoldine and her husband at Villequier (1843) deeply affected him. He offset his grief by an active political life. He took little part in the 1848 revolution, at first supported the Prince President, but went into opposition and in July 1851 publicly denounced the intentions of *Napoléon le petit*. After trying unsuccessfully to organize resistance to the *coup d'état*, he went into exile, in Jersey until 1855, then in Guernsey until 1870.

His first care was to flay Napoléon III, while retaining his respect for the soldiers of the first Emperor. In this vein, the poems of *Les châtiments* (1853) are the most memorable; they pass from impassioned invective to parodies of popular songs, cast satire in epic form ('L'expiation') and prophesy the final victory of progress and freedom.

While composing *Les contemplations* (1853–5), Hugo explored spiritualism and various forms of occultism. The poems incorporate the familiar lyric themes, but retrace a spiritual autobiography centred on the loss of Léopoldine. He interrogated death ('À Villequier', 'Mors', 'Cadaver', 'Horror'). Haunted by a sense of light imprisoned in darkness and constantly drawn towards the infinite, he formulated an animist religion of love and expiation ('Explication', 'Saturne', 'Dolor') promising the end of evil ('Ce que dit la Bouche d'Ombre') and served by poets and thinkers of all time ('Les mages'). The theme was to be continued in 'Dieu' and 'La fin de Satan' (posthumous), but in the same cosmic framework, he expanded the epic of humanity in *La légende des siècles* (1859), recreated the spirit of the past and prophesied future greatness ('Le satyre', 'Pleine Mer–Plein Ciel'). In *William Shakespeare* (1864) he produced a key work redefining the means and mission of poetry. In 1865, the light-hearted *Chansons des rues et des bois* counterbalanced his oracular solemnity.

The later novels are dominated by an alert social conscience, concerned in *Les Misérables* (1862; tr. C. E. Wilbour, Everyman, 1906) with the victims of society and their rehabilitation by pity, illustrated by the ex-convict Valjean in his long struggle with the police officer Javert. He continued with *Les travailleurs de la mer* (1866; tr. anon., *Toilers of the Sea*, Everyman, 1911), *L'homme qui rit* (1869), *Quatre-vingt treize* (1874).

He was publicly acclaimed on his return from exile. After the Commune, he tried to reconcile the parties. Although nominated senator in 1876, he took little further part in public life. His fame heightened with further volumes of *La légende des siècles* (1877, 1883, 1885) and the popular *L'art d'être grand-père* (1877). *Les quatre vents de l'esprit* (1880) grouped satire, lyricism, epic and drama. In his last years, he lived his own apotheosis. He was mourned as a national hero and buried in the Panthéon.

Posthumous works include *Le théâtre en*

*liberté*; *Toute la lyre*; *Les années funestes*; *Dernière gerbe*; *Choses vues*; and recently, selections of drawings.

He was adept at recognizing and exploiting trends in contemporary thought; he owed much to the humanitarian mystics – Ballanche, Lamennais, Pierre Leroux, Jean Reynaud, among others – but with little selective discernment, he preferred elaboration to synthesis. His faith in his divine and prophetic mission, and in the religion he evolved, was complete. [BJ]

*Œuvres complètes* (45 vols., 1904–52); *Journal, 1830–1848* (1954); *Choix de poèmes*, ed. J. Gaudon (Manchester, 1957).

P. Berret, *V.H.* (Paris, 1927); M. Levaillant, *La crise mystique de V.H.* (Paris, 1954); G. Venzac, *Les premiers maîtres de V.H.*, and *Les origines religieuses de V.H.* (Paris, 1955); J. B. Barrère, *V.H.* (Paris, 1957); A. Py, *Les mythes grecs dans la poésie de V.H.* (Geneva, 1963).

**Hugo von Montfort** (1357–1423). German lyric poet. Much of his life was spent at the Viennese court, where he attained to a position of considerable influence and played a role of some importance in the Habsburgs' struggle against the Swiss (1385–8). In his poetry he is most at his ease in religious and didactic subjects, although in these, as in his love lyrics, his thoughts often move uncertainly from earthly joys to the virtues of moral earnestness. Of particular value is the fact that melodies to his poems have also been preserved. [RT]

Ed. K. Bartsch (1880); *Die Lieder H.v.M.*, ed. P. Runge (Leipzig, 1906) (for melodies).

**Hugo von Trimberg.** (*c.* 1230–*c.* 1313). German didactic poet. Although he is known to have written a number of other works as well, his only German work to have survived (certain Latin works of his are also extant) is the so-called *Renner* ('Runner' – a reference to the far-ranging content and discursive style of the work). His purpose in this unwieldy poem (of over 24,000 lines) is to provide a comprehensive system of ethics: building on the framework of the Seven Deadly Sins, he gives, in high-flown language and with a great display of learning, allegorical accounts of human weaknesses and emphatic exhortations to repentance. His concern is not with understanding human problems and temptations but with preaching, moralizing and instructing. [RT]

Ed. G. Ehrismann (1908–11).
Ehrismann, *GDL*, ii.

**Humboldt, Alexander von** (Potsdam 1769–Berlin 1859). German scientist and writer. Humboldt was probably the greatest geographer of his age and travelled extensively in Europe, South America (1799–1804) and central Asia (1829). He published in both French and German, aiming at a combination of the spirit of classical Weimar with natural science. His German writings (*Ansichten der Natur*, 1808; *Reise nach dem Ural, dem Altai und dem Kaspischen Meer*, 1837–42; and his masterpiece, *Kosmos*, 1845–62) are model travel books in their tempering of exact science with purity of style and a generous humanity. [WAC]

*Gesammelte Werke* (12 vols., 1889).
W. v. Hagen, *South America Called Them* (N.Y., 1945); C. Kellner, *A.v.H.* (1963).

**Humboldt, Wilhelm von** (Potsdam 1767–Schloss Tegel 1835). German politician and writer. In close contact with the great literary figures of the age, he contributed to Schiller's *Horen* and Goethe's *Propyläen.* He produced important works on aesthetics and literature (*Ästhetische Versuche*, 1799) and political theory (*Ideen zu einem Versuch, die Grenzen der Wirksamkeit des Staates zu bestimmen*, published sectionally, complete edn 1851), but his real achievement lay in the field of philology and linguistic philosophy, to which such works as the *Untersuchungen über die Urbewohner Spaniens vermittelst der baskischen Sprache* (1821) and *Über die Kawisprache auf der Insel Java* (1836–40) represent important contributions in their equation of language with spiritual energy and their view of language as reflecting the cultural development of humanity.

As a Prussian civil servant, Humboldt achieved permanent fame by his reformation of the Prussian education system after the defeat of Jena, a task which culminated in the foundation of the University of Berlin (1810). His liberalism was odious to the age of Metternich, however, and he was forced to resign in 1819. [WAC]

*Werke*, ed. A. Seitzmann, B. Gebhardt (16 vols., 1903ff.); ed. A. Flitner, K. Giel (1960ff.).

**Hurtado de Mendoza, Antonio** (Castro Urdiales 1586?–Saragossa 1644). Spanish poet and dramatist. A favourite of Philip IV, he wrote graceful *comedias* for the theatre at Aranjuez. His comedy of manners, *El marido hace mujer* is the source of Molière's *École des maris.* [JMC]

*Obras liricas y cómicas* (1728); BAE, 16, 42, 45. Blecua, *FLE*.

**Hurtado de Mendoza, Diego** (Granada 1503–Madrid 1575). Spanish poet, historian and humanist. He served Charles V in Italy where he collected important classical manuscripts (now in the Escorial library). Banished from court life by Philip II (1568), he devoted himself to poetry and study. He knew Latin, Greek, Hebrew and Arabic, and his outstanding work is a scathing history of the Morisco rebellion of 1568–70 (*La Guerra de Granada*, 1627) in the style of the Roman historians Sallust and Tacitus. His *Diálogo entre Caronte y el alma de Pedro Luis Farnaso* is an Erasmist satire. He excelled in malicious, indecorous verse in the old measures (rather than in the Italian metres of the ◊ Garcilaso school). The novel ◊ *Lazarillo de Tormes* has been attributed to him, though erroneously. [JMC]

Blecua, *FLE*; Trend, *OBSV*; Terry, *ASP*.
A. González Palencia and E. Mele, *Vida y obras de H. de M.* (3 vols., Madrid, 1941–3).

**Hus, Jan** (Husinec 1371?–Constance 1415). Czech theologian and religious reformer. A rector of Prague University who by his writings, preaching and martyrdom inspired the religious reform movement that came to bear his name, he has a place in literary history by virtue of his Czech and Latin sermons and of the letters which he wrote (in Czech) when he was imprisoned at Constance. [RA]

Czech writings ed. K. J. Erben (3 vols., 1865–8); *Letters with Introductions and Explanatory Notes*, tr. H. B. Workman and R. M. Pope (1904).
F. M. Bartoš, *Literární činnost M.J.H.* (Prague, 1948); R. R. Betts, 'J.H.', in *History* (1939); F. Lützow, *The Life and Times of Master J.H.* (1909).

**Hutten, Ulrich von** (Burg Steckelburg 1488–Ufenau, Lake Zürich 1523). German humanist. He came of a noble Franconian family, but as a young man led the life of a wandering scholar and soldier-poet in Germany and Italy, and in many ways personified the exuberant intellectual mood of his age. It is as a polemicist that he is chiefly remembered: he began with 5 pamphlets against the notorious Ulrich of Württemberg, but was soon involved in religious controversy, being largely responsible for the second volume of the *Epistolae obscurorum virorum* (1517). The 'first political German', he greeted the Reformation enthusiastically as an opportunity to rid Germany of the economic and political exploitation of the hated Italians and participated actively in the controversy with a series of Lucianic dialogues, written originally in Latin, but translated into German by Hutten himself and published as the *Gesprächbüchlein* in 1521, a work which in large measure inspired the outburst of satirical dialogues which accompanied the Reformation until 1525. In his fine poem 'Ich hab's gewagt mit sinnen' (1521), which seeks to vindicate his political attitude, he sounds a genuine lyrical note, which did not, however, awaken an echo in contemporary vernacular poetry. Disappointed by Luther's essentially unpolitical attitude, he joined the abortive revolt of the Imperial Knights in 1523, and died in exile, his dream of a strong centralized Germany shattered. [WAC]

*Die deutschen Dichtungen*, ed. D. Balke (DNL, 17, ii).
H. Holborn, *U.v.H. and the German Reformation* (New Haven, Conn., 1937).

**Huygens, Constantijn** (The Hague 1596–The Hague 1687). Dutch poet, musician, scientist and diplomat. The son of Christiaan, the scientist, he early acquired a fluent knowledge of seven languages and many of his own dialects. After reading law at Leyden he entered diplomatic service, travelling to Venice and several times to England, and becoming secretary to three successive Dutch princes.

He wrote for his own diversion, calling his poetry *Korenbloemen* (i.e. cornflowers in his field of labour). Though very personal, his work displays too much virtuosity to be consistently lyrical. He was, except for his scientific modernism, an orthodox, though not militant, Calvinist. Most of his work is either didactic or autobiographical. In *Batave Tempe dat is het Voorhout te 's Gravenhage* (1621), his glowing affection for his birthplace breaks through his ◊ Marinistic style. *Costelick Mal* (1622) mercilessly ridicules the display of Eve's sinfulness in the vanity of women's fashions. English puritanism appealed to him, and so did the poetry of Donne, whom he ranked 'prime poetarum', doing a number of remarkably faithful translations of his poems.

The *Uytlandighe Herder* (1622), like *Batave Tempe*, praises the countryside, but it also expresses his patriotism in terms of the exiled poet's longing for his homeland. His subsequent major works relate to his married life with Susanna van Baerle (his 'Sterre'), his further life in his country house, Hofwyck, and his latter years in The Hague; their greater mellowness and wisdom is at the expense of his earlier sparkle. Yet however intellectual the style and aristocratic the tone of most of his work, his affection for the lowest strata of society is manifest in his scurrilous *Tryntje Cornelisdr.* (1653; tr. in preparation), which is unlike his didactic, reflective and romantic work, except in the weakness of its structure. Because he took his art so casually, he is at his best in his witty and pointed epigrams, though his playful intellect is also capable of revealing as well as shielding his deepest emotions, as in *Sonetten op de Feestdagen.* [PK]

*Gedichten*, ed. J. A. Worp (9 vols., 1892–9); *Voet-maet, rijm en reden*, ed. F. L. Zwaan (1963); Barnouw, *CA.*

R. Colie, *Some Thankfulnesse to Constantine* (The Hague, 1956); A. G. H. Bachrach, *Sir Constantine Huygens and Britain* (Leyden, 1962– ); J. Smit, *Driemaal Huygens* (Assen, 1966).

**Huysmans, Georges Charles,** known as **Joris-Karl** (Paris 1848–Paris 1907). French novelist. Of Dutch descent, his name became a synonym for decadence. For thirty years he combined his writing with a minor job in the Sûreté. His first prose poems and sketches, *Le drageoir aux épices* (1874), and the novel *Marthe, histoire d'une fille* (1876; tr. R. Baldick, 1948), established him with Zola and the naturalists, and he contributed the story 'Sac au dos' to the *Soirées de Médan.* His more famous and characteristic work, however, is *À rebours* (1884; tr. R. Baldick, *Against Nature*, 1959), which depicts a hero, Des Esseintes, the frail descendant of an old family, determined to overcome his boredom by the refinement and unusualness of his tastes and sensations. This prototype of decadence, hypersensitive, aesthetically idealistic, morally ambiguous, religiously drawn to the occult, was admired in England by Oscar Wilde and his followers. In his later autobiographical novels he followed the career of a character called Durtal, who like himself arrived at Roman Catholicism by way of Satanism (*Là-bas*, 1891), was drawn to a Trappist monastery (*En route*, 1895), and Chartres (*La cathédrale*, 1898). This last has been much admired not so much as a novel but as a guide to Chartres cathedral. In the last novel, *L'oblat* (1903; tr. E. Perceval, *The Oblate*, 1924), Durtal becomes an oblate in a Benedictine monastery. Huysmans also wrote art criticism (*Trois primitifs*, 1905) and was one of the first to appreciate the Impressionists (*L'art moderne*, 1883). The fact that Des Esseintes in *À rebours* read Mallarmé, who was quite unknown at the time, did much for Mallarmé's reputation, and the latter wrote his poem *Prose pour Des Esseintes* as a token of gratitude. [WA]

*Œuvres complètes*, ed. L. Descaves (1928–40).

R. Baldick, *Life of J.-K.H.* (1955); H. R. T. Brandreth, *H.* (1963).

**Hviezdoslav,** pseud. of **Pavol Orszagh** (Vyšný Kubín 1849–Dolný Kubín 1921). Slovak poet and dramatist. The son of a Slovak farmer and a lawyer by profession, he was one of the main advocates of Czech-Slovak cooperation. His poetry is marked by patriotism and the strong principles of his Evangelical faith. He was a prolific writer and did much to raise Slovak literature from its provincialism. His novel in verse, *Hájnikova žena* (1884), shows him to be a strong protagonist of democracy and of social and economic justice. His cycle of sonnets, *Krvavé sonety* (1919), is a humanist's passionate protest against the madness of war. [KB]

*Sobrané spisy básnické* (15 vols., 1939–42).

A. Kostolný, *P.O.-H.* (Bratislava, 1949).

**Hymns, Latin.** The earliest Christians, being Jews, had no hymn-book but the Hebrew psalter. Their first converts in Europe, even at Rome, were Greek-speaking. When they began to supplement the psalms with original compositions in Greek, these followed their great exemplars by being written in prose, with parallelism as a prominent feature. A beautiful example of such compositions is the *Gloria in excelsis* of the Mass.

The first Latin hymns of the 4th century are still in prose and still exhibit the parallelism of the psalms. An outstanding example is the *Te Deum*, commonly ascribed to Niceta, a bishop in Yugoslavia (*c.* 370–441). Such prose compositions are today called canticles, the word 'hymn' being restricted to compositions in verse. The first to write verse hymns was St Hilary (*c.* 300–67), Bishop of Poitiers. Though he wrote in a popular metre – the trochaic tetrameter catalectic, used in both sacred and secular verse from Greek classical times to the present – his hymns were not popular. But St Ambrose (340–97), Bishop of Milan, had great influence on hymnody. His simple metre – the iambic dimeter, with 4 lines per stanza – remained the favourite for Latin hymn-writers; its modern equivalent, long metre (8.8.8.8.), is, next to the ballad metre, or common metre (8.6.8.6.), the most popular in English hymnody. Parallelism of thought is still evident in Ambrose's hymns, but later gradually disappears. Prudentius, who used a great variety of metres, wrote for private reading only, though excerpts became famous as hymns, e.g. *Corde natus ex parentis* ('Of the Father's heart begotten'), often used as a Christmas processional.

The practice of singing hymns was disseminated throughout Western Europe by the Rule of St Benedict (*c.*480–*c.*544), which required a hymn to be sung at each of the monastic Hours of Prayer. A number of well-known 'Ambrosians' probably date from the 6th century, e.g. the Compline hymn, *Te lucis ante terminum* ('Before the ending of the day'); also the Irish communion hymn *Sancti venite, Christi corpus sumite* (*c.*600). Fortunatus used the iambic dimeter for his *Vexilla regis prodeunt* ('The royal banners forward go') and the trochaic tetrameter catalectic for his *Pange lingua gloriosi praelium certaminis* ('Sing, my tongue the glorious battle') – two of the greatest hymns ever written. During the 6th century the classical metres are interpreted more and more freely in terms simply of accent (instead of quantity), and rhyme and assonance play a greater part.

The anonymous *Urbs beata Hierusalem* (the source of many later hymns on the theme of the heavenly Jerusalem, e.g. St Peter Damian's *Ad perennis vitae fontem*) probably dates from the 7th or 8th century, together with *Ave maris stella* – perhaps the favourite Marian hymn. The well-known Palm Sunday hymn, *Gloria, laus et honor*, is by Theodulph, Bishop of Orleans (*c.*750–821). The great *Veni creator Spiritus*, by an unknown writer, belongs to the 9th century. The Easter hymn *Chorus novae Jerusalem* ('Ye choirs of new Jerusalem') is by ⇨ Fulbert of Chartres. ⇨ Abelard wrote a whole book of hymns for Heloisa; over 100 survive, but the only one in common use is the immortal *O quanta qualia sunt illa sabbata* ('O what their joy and their glory must be').

The 13th century (when hymns were first used in St Peter's – such was Rome's conservatism) produced the magnificent Eucharistic hymns of St Thomas ⇨ Aquinas and Arnulf's *Salve caput cruentatum* ('O sacred head, sore wounded', best known in Bach's setting in the St Matthew Passion). The 14th century contributed the anonymous *Ave verum corpus*, which has been set to music by Byrd, Mozart and others, and the carols *Angelus ad Virginem* and *Quem pastores laudavere*. From the 15th century come *Jerusalem luminosa* ('Light's abode, celestial Salem'), attributed to ⇨ Thomas à Kempis, and Jean Tisserand's lilting Easter processional, *O filii et filiae*.

The Renaissance led to sweeping reforms in the liturgical books of the Roman rite. In the new breviary (1631) most of the medieval hymns based on accent were rewritten in correct classical metres and with a strictly classical vocabulary; but they lost much of their natural charm and simplicity. Only the hymns of Aquinas, *Ave maris stella* and a few others were left intact.

Despite papal injunctions, many of the secular clergy in France and (to a less extent) in Germany refused to conform to the revised breviary, and many new hymns were written between the mid 17th and the mid 19th century. All dioceses, however, had conformed to Roman use by 1875 – except Lyons, which still has special privileges. About a score of these new Latin hymns survive in English translations and are popular in Anglican churches, e.g. *Supreme quales arbiter* ('Disposer Supreme'), by Jean-Baptiste de Santeuil (1630–97), *Labente jam solis rota* ('As now the sun's declining rays') and *Jordanis oras praevia* ('On Jordan's bank'), both by Charles Coffin (1676–1749), and several by unknown authors, such as *Veni veni Emmanuel*, *Victis sibi cognomina* ('Conquering kings their titles take'), etc. Other Latin hymns of this period include the anonymous Easter hymn, *Finita jam sunt proelia* ('The strife is o'er'), Thomas Smith's *Te Deum Patrem colimus* (the Magdalen College May Day hymn), and *Adeste fideles*, probably written by J. F. Wade (1711–86). Pope Leo XIII (1810–1903) brought Latin hymnody back to its starting-point with a hymn written in Ambrosian quatrains for the new feast of the Holy Family (1892). [FB]

*An. Hym*; C. U. J. Chevalier, *Repertorium Hymnologicum* (6 vols., Louvain and Brussels,

1892–1920); *Ein Jahrtausend lateinischer Hymnendichtung*, ed. G. M. Dreves and C. Blume (2 vols., Leipzig, 1909); *Hymni Ecclesiae*, ed. J. H. Newman (1838); A. S. Walpole, *Early Latin Hymns* (1922); *Hymns Ancient and Modern, Historical Edition*, ed. W. H. Frere, with original texts of all translated hymns (1909); M. Britt, *The Hymns of the Breviary and Missal* (1936); J. Connely, *Hymns of the Roman Liturgy* (1957).

J. Stephán, *The 'Adeste Fideles,' a Study of its Origin and Development* (1947); *A Dictionary of Hymnology*, ed. J. Julian (1908); Raby, *CLP*.

**Hyry, Antti Kalevi** (Kuivaniemi 1931– ). Finnish modernist prose-writer. Author of neo-realistic short stories and novels, many of which have childhood or the static milieu of the countryside as their theme. His stories are told in a naïvely concrete, deliberately unsubtle style, from which ideas and attitudes are rigidly excluded. [R V]

Novels: *Kevättä ja syksyä* (1958); *Kotona* (1960); *Alakoulussa* (1964); short stories: *Maantieltä hän lähti* (1958); *Junamatkan kuvaus* (1962).

# I

**Ibn Ezra, Abraham Ben Meair** (Tudel 1092–Calahora 1167). Hebrew poet, grammarian, scientific and religious author. Left Spain before 1140 and wandered in Italy and Provence; visited London in 1158 where he wrote two short works. In his secular poems maintains a light, even jocular, vein; is philosophical in liturgical verse; his prose is erratic. One of the most gifted Jewish personalities who had not only a deep knowledge of but also great affection for the Hebrew language. His most important work is his commentary on almost the whole Bible in which he employed both philology and his neo-Platonic philosophy. [EE]

Husik, *HMJP*.

**Ibn Ezra, Moses** (Granada 1060–N. Spain 1139). Hebrew poet and literary critic. He was a high court official in Granada and as a patron of poetry encouraged the young ⇨ Judah Ha-levi. Although he wrote a large number of important and secular poems, his most important work is *Kitāb al-mumhādarah wal-mudhākarah*, in Arabic: a study and our chief source on the Spanish Hebrew poetic school. [EE]

Baer, *HJCS*; Husik, *HMJP*.

**Ibn Hasdai, Abraham** (d. Barcelona 1240). Hebrew writer and liturgical poet of the Spanish period. Besides poetry he also wrote philosophical works and adopted from the Arabic the fable of Barlaam and Josaphat under the title *Ben ha-Melech vehanazir* which, translated into Yiddish, was widely read. [EE]

J. Jacob, *Barlaam and Josaphat* (1896); Waxman, *HJL*.

**Ibsen, Henrik** (Skien, Telemark 1828–Kristiania 1906). Norwegian playwright and poet. The son of a well-to-do merchant, his father became bankrupt when he was 8, reducing the family to poverty; this is reflected in *Peer Gynt*. At 15 he was apprenticed to an apothecary in Grimstad where he remained for five years. There he started to study for university entrance with a view to reading medicine. This involved a study of Latin, and he became interested in the character of Catiline and resolved to write a drama on him. His knowledge of the theatre was practically nil and he had only written a few insignificant poems; the play, *Catalina*, was published in 1850 through the generosity of a friend but achieved no success. In the same year he went to live in Kristiania, where his next play *Kjæmpehøjen* (*The Warrior's Barrow*) was performed with some success. In 1851 he was appointed stage-manager at the newly established theatre in Bergen. His contract also required him to write a piece every year to mark the anniversary of the theatre, and while there he wrote *Norma* (1851); *Sankthansnatten* (1852); *Gildet paa Solhoug* (1856; *The Feast at Solhoug*); *Olaf Liljekrans* (1856); *Fru Inger til Østeraad* (1857; *Lady Inger of Østeraad*). Of these, only *Gildet paa Solhoug* and *Fru Inger til Østeraad* are of importance.

In 1857 he became director of the Norske Theater (The Norwegian Theatre) in Kristiania, founded to further the interests of a specifically Norwegian drama, but it was not a success and the years which immediately followed were the most miserable of his whole career. In addition, his plays *Hærmændene paa Helgeland* (1858; *The Vikings at Helgeland*) and *Kjærlighedens Komedie* (1862; *Love's Comedy*) had not been well received. Things brightened in 1863 when, having completed *Kongsemnerne* (1864; *The Pretenders*), he was awarded a scholarship which enabled him to travel to Rome. In Italy he wrote *Brand* (1866), which brought him a state pension, and *Peer Gynt* (1867). Thenceforward his reputation as a dramatist was firmly established, and, apart from short visits to Norway in 1874 and 1885, he continued to live abroad until 1891, either in Italy or in Germany.

With the appearance of *De unges Forbund* (1869; *The League of Youth*), his first prose play with a modern setting, the pattern was set, with the exception of *Kejser og Galilæer* (1873; *Emperor and Galilean*), for the rest of his work. A rough grouping is possible:

*Samfundets Støtter* (1877; *Pillars of Society*), *Et Dukkehjem* (1879; *A Doll's House*), *Gengangere* (1881; *Ghosts*), and *En Folkefiende* (1882; *An Enemy of the People*) are 'social' plays in the sense that society and its conventions are active agents in the affairs of the characters; in *Vildanden* (1884; *The Wild Duck*) and *Rosmersholm* (1886) the psychological nature of ideals and the idealist are especially scrutinized; in *Fruen fra Havet* (1888; *The Lady from the Sea*) and *Lille Eyolf* (1894; *Little Eyolf*) the theme of 'freedom with responsibility' is to the fore. *Hedda Gabler* (1890) may be regarded as a further comment on the nature of ideals, this time with a topical (decadent) twist; and in *Bygmester Solness* (1892; *The Master Builder*); *John Gabriel Borkman* (1896) and *Naar vi døde vaagner* (1899; *When we Dead Awaken*) we are 'down amongst the dead men'. But despite its apparent diversity, his work shows an extraordinary fundamental unity. Themes such as the idealist and the 'compact majority', the ineluctability of the past, the nature of vocation, are present almost everywhere.

Ibsen was not primarily a thinker or a philosopher, but a poet and craftsman, and it is the poet who illuminates, even in his apparently most social plays. He is the key-figure in modern drama, and the major influence on its later development. He perfected the conversation drama, and through his mastery of retrospective technique gave it a hitherto unequalled depth of perspective. Scarcely any other foreign author has been so thoroughly accepted in the English-speaking theatre. [RGP]

*Samlede verker*, ed. F. Bull, H. Koht, D. A. Seip (21 vols., 1928–57); *Samlede digterværker*, ed. D. A. Seip (7 vols., 1918); *The Collected Works of H.I.*, ed., with tr., W. Archer (12 vols., 1906–12); *The Oxford Ibsen*, ed. and part tr. J. W. McFarlane (8 vols., 1960– ); *Plays* (5 vols., tr. U. Ellis-Fermor and P. Watts, Penguin Classics, 1950ff.); *Early Plays*, tr. A. Ørbeck (1921); *Lyrics and Poems from I.*, tr. F. E. Garrett (1912); *Breve*, ed. H. Koht and J. Elias (2 vols., 1904); *The Correspondence of H.I.*, tr. M. Morison (1905); *H.I. Letters and Speeches*, ed. E. Sprinchorn (1964).

G. B. Shaw, *The Quintessence of Ibsenism* (1891, aug. edn 1913); H. J. Weigand, *The Modern I.* (1925); H. Koht, *H.I.* (2 vols., Oslo, 1928–9, rev. 1954; tr. R. L. McMahon and H. A. Larsen, 1931); M. C. Bradbrook, *I. the Norwegian* (1946, new edn 1966); B. W. Downs, *I. The Intellectual Background* (1946); B. W. Downs, *A Study of Six Plays by I.* (1950); J. Northam, *I.'s Dramatic Method* (1952); D. Haakonsen, *H.I.'s realisme* (Oslo, 1957); Downs, *MNL*; McFarlane, *TNL*.

**Icelandic Sagas.** Of the several kinds of prose narrative composed in medieval Iceland with the title 'saga', it is the group called Sagas of Icelanders, or less appropriately Family Sagas, which are the most original and valuable. They were written between *c.* 1200 and the early 14th century. With one probable exception, the names of their authors are unknown.

They usually describe a sequence of events in the period from the first settlement of Iceland, *c.* 870, down to the end of the first Christian generation *c.* 1030. The main story deals with one man or one family, the principal characters are historical persons and some of the facts must be true. The hero is above all a man of action and courage, but also often a poet, and verse by him and others may be given. In the end he dies tragically and vengeance for the dead hero is a common epilogue.

Conduct is judged in a fatalistic and heroic light. Death is not sought, but it must not be feared. A man's most precious possession is his honour or good name. No man is isolated, everyone is caught up in nets of kinship and friendship, and anyone may find himself called upon to fulfil duties that public opinion and established custom required – primarily duties of vengeance, whose aim is redress rather than punishment, restoring the damaged reputation of an individual and his family. Tragedy is fated, but the hero can die victorious none the less; by his conduct in life and his defiant courage at death he has challenged fate and ensured that his name will live.

Fate is conceived not only as external and inexplicable. Conduct springs from character, and character is also seen as destiny. The Icelandic hero is thus neither a puppet nor a *nonpareil*. He is a well-defined individual, flesh and blood, seen against an everyday background of familiar countryside and farming life. He is not necessarily wealthy o well connected, but he knows how to behave He is not faced by a villainous enemy but b a man who in another context might himsel be the hero; against the background o heroic standards and family duty there ma be right on both sides.

The author pretends to do no more tha record; he does not often describe people' thoughts or feelings but suggests them b describing action or physical reaction. The characters themselves are reticent in their speech. There is no background description for its own sake: if a place or an object is described it is in order to further the understanding or progress of the story. This lack of distraction means that the men and women of the story appear throughout in a clear and steady light. The narrative technique is thus limited, but powerful and concrete; the characters live not least through their natural, often laconic, dialogue. The emotions are elemental, however complex the story, and are seen against a simple and sharply defined social world.

From the first settlement of Iceland onward, tales about outstanding men were told and information about the past transmitted orally. Some tales may have remained substantially accurate in outline, especially if connected with some tangible reminder, such as a genealogy, a verse, an heirloom, or a place-name. Little scaldic verse of an occasional kind is self-explanatory and it must usually have been transmitted in a narrative framework. On the other hand, individual invention and adaptation were also introduced, and when the true origin of something was forgotten, stories were invented to explain it. Some of those who told the stories put their own verse into the mouths of the historical characters in their tales. Such oral tales were, however, only one source used by saga writers.

By the 13th century there was also a written vernacular literature. Saints' lives and homilies, antiquarian records about the past, histories of the reigns of the kings of Norway, existed in Iceland from about 1100 onwards. The matter preserved in them also depended on oral transmission, but its historical value is enhanced first because of the age of its recording and second because of the methods of the men who collected it. They sought reliable information about the past and applied critical standards in finding it. Apart from providing information, these men also influenced the desire of the saga authors to appear as judicious and neutral observers – a desire that plays an essential part in their self-effacing style and presentation.

The sources of each saga are very mixed. Sometimes the author follows an ancient local tale, true, garbled or false; sometimes he builds on the verse he knows, whether authentic or not; sometimes he draws material from earlier written records; sometimes he adapts a motive known from folktale or another saga, or an event that has occurred in his own contemporary world. But many episodes and links, the general organization of the narrative, and, above all, the realization of the characters through significant action and speech, are the work of his own imagination.

The range of the thirty or so extant sagas may be shown by a word of comment on a few of them.

Among the earliest are the *Heiðarvíga saga* ('Saga of the Battle on the Moor') and the *Hallfreðar saga* ('Saga of Hallfred'). The former traces the progress of a feud which culminates in a battle between men from two districts; by then the original cause of the feud is remote. It is sometimes confused in construction; the portrayal of the characters does not go deep; the presentation of the spoken word is fumbling. But the author's admiration for manliness, courage and generosity shines through the pettiness and violence. The hero of *The Saga of Hallfred* is an adventurous poet at the Norwegian court of King Olaf Tryggvason (995–1000). In Iceland he loved a girl whom he failed to marry, even though he could; trouble follows when he does not leave her or her husband alone. The theme recurs, with variations, in other sagas. Here there is no tragic outcome and the story has little unity; but we get a firm impression of Hallfred, likeable, tough, hot-tempered, sensitive and loyal, affected by the conversion to Christianity but reluctant to think ill of the heathen gods to whom his poetry owed so much.

From about 1225, in north-west Iceland, comes the graphic and moving *Gísla saga Súrssonar* ('Saga of Gisli'). A Norwegian prologue defines the central characters and explains their emigration to Iceland. Part one, skilfully constructed with parallelism of episodes, describes the events leading to Gisli's outlawry. Part two describes his life as an outlaw, his state of mind, bad dreams and fears of the life to come. The author conveys a sense of the outlaw's inner exhaustion when at last his end in battle comes.

The first saga on the scale of a full-length novel is the outstanding *Egils saga Skalla-Grímssonar* ('Saga of Egil'), probably by ⇨ Snorri Sturluson. A long prehistory concerning the relations and conflicts between his family and the kings of Norway sets the tone for Egil's own exploits. He is of enormous physical strength and stature, with a touch of the troll in his nature. Merciless and vengeful, as greedy for silver as he is for his rights, he is also attached by tight bonds to his kin, loyal and affectionate to his friend, delicately in love with his wife, and a master of poetry and rune-magic. Much of Egil's own great poetry is given in the saga.

Two other longer sagas written about the mid 13th century are the *Eyrbyggja saga* ('Saga of the Eyr-people') and the *Laxdœla saga* ('Saga of the Laxdalers'). From the middle west coast, with some characters in common, they yet differ greatly in outlook and atmosphere. The meandering narrative of the former runs from the Settlement down to the early 11th century, giving valuable descriptions of heathen ideas and customs, and some excellent stories of hauntings. The central figure, Snorri the Chieftain, is ruthless, cunning, and not of the noblest character. His opponent, Arnkell, is idealized as generous and fairminded; he dies in the feud, but the author apportions no blame. The *Saga of the Laxdalers* centres on the memorable tragic story of Gudrun, who makes her husband kill her former lover to satisfy her pride: a version of the heroic legend of Brynhild, Sigurd and Gunnar, played out among well-to-do families in a familiar Icelandic countryside. This tragedy is most powerfully presented, even though the main masculine characters are almost courtly abstractions, with a superiority and renown too effortlessly acquired.

The *Bandamanna saga* ('Saga of the Confederates') is the only saga (as distinct from some of the *þættir*, or short stories, about Icelanders) whose main theme is conceived throughout in terms of comedy. Avarice in a group of leading men is ridiculed, with overtones of social satire; some of the description has a burlesque quality. 'The first reasonable and modern comedy in the history of modern Europe' (W. P. Ker), it deserves to be better known.

The *Hrafnkels saga Freysgoða* ('Saga of Hrafnkel'), written late in the 13th century, is set in eastern Iceland, simply constructed with a few well-portrayed characters. Dialogue is smooth and incisive, with one remarkably natural speech by a woman. Long thought to be an orally preserved account of real events, comparative and critical study has shown that most of the action and some of the characters are imaginative creation.

The *Grettis saga* ('Saga of Grettir'), in the form we have it, was written about 1300 on the basis of an older written story. It is an extraordinary amalgam of local and family history, of everyday life in Iceland, of struggles against supernatural monsters, of motives drawn from folk-tale and romance. Grettir is a man of superb strength and daring, who by nature would turn his powers to good ends but is so dogged by misfortune that his best intentions cause death and bring revenge. Outlawed, he lives in hiding under a curse which has increased his moodiness and resentfulness and made him, the great hero, afraid of the dark. With great perception the author convinces us that the supernatural curse which is on him is essentially a projection of a fundamental element in Grettir's personality.

The longest and greatest of all the sagas is the *Brennu-Njáls saga* ('Saga of Njall'), written towards the end of the 13th century. The plot is complex, with great variety of incident and many shifts of place, and on the saga's vast canvas appears a host of living people. Yet, seen as a whole, it has a steady progressive order and an embracing unity. No other saga shows such perception and variety in the portrayal of character or such grandeur of design. The philosophy of this majestic historical novel accepts the heroic creed and the duty of vengeance, but also – above this, not in place of it – shows humanity at its highest foregoing atonement in Christian humility for the sake of peace, and death not as the instrument of blind fate but as a fulfilment of God's providence, inscrutable but full of promise and mercy. [PGF]

*Altnordische Saga-Bibliothek* (Halle, 1892–1929); *Islenzk fornrit* (Reykjavik, 1933– ); *Eirik the Red and other Icelandic Sagas*, tr. G. Jones (1961); other tr. listed in *Bibliography of the Sagas of Icelanders* in *Islandica*, I (1908), XXI (1935), XXXVIII (1957).

W. P. Ker, *Epic and Romance* (1896); G. Turville-Petre, *Origins of Icelandic Literature* (1953); P. Hallberg, *The Icelandic Saga*, tr. P. Schach (Nebraska, 1962).

**Iffland, August Wilhelm** (Hanover 1759–Berlin 1814). German dramatist. An actor of considerable talent, director of the National Theatre at Mannheim (1785–92) and subsequently of the National Theatre in Berlin. He popularized the '*coméd* *larmoyante*' in Germany, wrote some 65 plays, and in his day enjoyed a popularity which far exceeded that of either Goethe or Schiller. His plays appeal unashamedly to contemporary middle-class taste in their moralizing tendency, their sentimentality and their inevitable happy end, but the best of them (*Die Jäger*, 1785; *Die Hagestolzen*, 1793) show a first-class sense of the stage, introduce a number of interesting, effectively portrayed characters and in their middle-class setting convey a realistic picture of their age. [WAC]

*Ausgewählte Werke* (6 vols., 1859).
E. Kliewer, *A.W.I. Ein Wegbereiter in der Schauspielkunst* (Berlin, 1937).

**Iglesias de la Casa, José** (Salamanca 1748–Salamanca 1791). Spanish poet. His satirical *letrillas* are minor imitations of ⇨ Góngora and ⇨ Quevedo, though with some original wit, shrewd social observation and unconventional use of popular language. The first collected edition of his poems appeared in 1793. [JMC]

BAE, 61; Blecua, *FLE*.

**Iglesies, Ignasi.** ⇨ Catalan Literature.

**Ignjatović, Jakov** (Sent Andreja 1824–Novi Sad 1888). Serbian novelist. The first to write of town life. A realist, his novels are loosely constructed and the language rough and unpolished. He has been considered a follower of Balzac, but his novels are full of coincidence, black and white characters, etc. Yet there is some vitality in their realistic portrayal of the epoch, especially in the novels *Milan Navandžić* (1860) and *Vasa Respekt* (1875). [EDG]

J. Skerlić, *J.I.* (Belgrade, 1904); Barac, *HYL*.

**Igor's Campaign** (or **Armament**), **The Lay or Song) of.'** ⇨ *Slovo o Polku Igoreve.*

**larion, Metropolitan of Kiev** (mid 11th ent.). Russian churchman and homilist. ittle is known about his life. He was a riest at Berestovo, Grand Prince Yaro-av's summer residence outside Kiev, here he led an ascetic life. In 1051 he was ppointed metropolitan of Kiev by Yaro-av without, it appears, reference to Con-antinople. The only works which can be scribed to him are a short confession of ith and a long, florid address, or perhaps sermon, entitled *On Law and Grace*, written between 1037 and 1050. This consists of two parts: the first, theological and didactic in nature, contrasts the law given Moses by God and the Grace of Christ, or the Old and New Testaments; the second part contains a eulogy and prayer to Vladimir I, the baptizer of Rus' and the father of the grand prince. Scholars have placed a variety of interpretations on the work. Some say that it is anti-Byzantine in nature and that its purpose is to stress the independence of the Kievan Church from the jurisdiction of the Oecumenical patriarch; some consider that it was written to hasten the canonization of Grand Prince Vladimir; while others say that it celebrates the transfer of the metropolitan see to Kiev in 1037. Yet all agree that, though largely derivative, it is a work of high art combining the rhetorical devices of Byzantine homiletics with a sense of moderation and style. All the tricks of the orator's trade are to be found here – repetitions, exclamations, rhetorical questions, antitheses, metaphors, symbolism. The plan of the homily is strictly logical, and this gives it a sense of unity and a persuasive power not to be found in the works of other, purely imitative, homilists. *On Law and Grace* undoubtedly influenced generations of Russian panegyrists and homilists and enjoyed a remarkable popularity in the Middle Ages. [JLIF]

Lüdolf Müller, *Des Metropoliten Ilarion Lobrede auf Wladimir den Heiligen und Glaubensbekenntnis* (Wiesbaden, 1962).

**Ildefonsus** or **Hildefonsus of Toledo** (607–667). Hymn and liturgy writer. Bishop of Toledo in succession to ⇨ Eugenius III in 657; author of homilies (ined.), hymns and portions of the Mozarabic Liturgy; he also wrote a tract *De cognitione baptismi*, a collection of biographies *De virorum illustrium scriptis* (dependent on ⇨ Isidore), and the *De virginitate Beatae Mariae* (ed. V. B. Garcia, Madrid, 1937), his most celebrated work. He avoids rhetoric and cultivates clarity at the expense of style. [CEC]

Migne, *PL*, 96 (1850) (including spuria).
A. Braegelman, *The Life and Writings of St Ildefonsus of Toledo* (Washington, 1942); G. Bareille, *Dictionnaire de théologie catholique*, vii, 1 (Paris, 1922); Manitius, *GLLM*.

**Il'f, Ilya,** and **Petrov, Yevgeniy,** pseud. of Il'ya Arnol'dovich Faynzil'berg (Odessa 1897–Odessa 1937) and Yevgeniy Petrovich

Katayev (Odessa 1903–Sevastopol' 1942). Russian humorous writers. Working in close collaboration they produced 2 best-selling novels: *Dvenadtsat' stul'yev* (1928; tr. J. Richardson, *Twelve Chairs*, 1961) and its sequel *Zolotoy telyonok* (1931; tr. J. Richardson, *The Golden Calf*, 1962). Here they satirize the age-old Russian failings, inefficiency, red tape and racketeering that still flourish in spite of the Revolution; but the books are also remarkable imaginative achievements, combining acute observation, linguistic ingenuity and a touch of fantasy. *Odnoetazhnaya Amerika* (1937; tr. C. Malamuth, *Little Golden America*, 1937), based on their visit to the U.S.A., is rather more tendentious but still amusing. During Stalin's last years their satire was disapproved of, but it has since been restored to favour. [RDBT]

*Sobraniye sochineniy* (5 vols., 1961).
V. Galanov, *I.I. i Ye. P.* (Moscow, 1961).

**Ilić, Vojislav** (Belgrade 1860–Belgrade 1894). Serbian poet. The son of the minor romantic poet Jovan Ilić, he was forced by illness to spend much of his boyhood reading – Pushkin, Zhukovsky, as well as Russian translations of German poetry and the classics. His own poems are largely elegiac in tone. Those on village life often come close to prose description. His more imaginative poetry is set in classical times and imitates the characteristics of the classical hexameter. Not a great poet himself, his work heralded a complete breakaway from Serbian romanticism, exerting considerable influence on ⇨ Dučić, ⇨ Rakić, and ⇨ Šantić, thus leading to greater concentration on poetic form. His main volumes are : *Pesme* (1887), *Pitija* (1887), *Smrt Periklea* and *Argonauti na Lemnosn* (1889). His tragedy *Radoslav* (1882) treats a subject of Serbian history. [EDG]

*Djela* (2 vols., 1922); Ibrovac, *APY*.
Barac, *HYL*.

**Illyés, Gyula** (Rácegres 1902– ). Hungarian writer and poet. Son of an estate servant, he starved his way through university and started his career as a poet. His largely autobiographical *Puszták népe* (1936; tr. V. Biro, *People of the Pusztas*) is a sociographic work which has become a classic of its type. His background is reflected in many of his works, in which he gives critical analyses of contemporary social problems such as the future of the peasantry, the rift between village and town, the class war, etc. His vast and varied works include novels, short stories, essays (*Petőfi*; 1936), commentaries, film-scripts, and a large number of poems. Generally considered to be the greatest living Hungarian poet, he has attained highest stature in his heroic poetry: *Hunyadi keze* (1956); *Óda Bartókhoz* (1955); *Megy az eke* (1945) (all tr. in *The Plough and the Pen*, ed. I. Duczynska and K. Polányi, 1963). Illyés was also founder of the literary periodical *Magyar Csillag* (1941). [JFR]

Reményi, *HWL*; Klaniczay, *HHL*.

**Imber, Naftali Hertz** (Galicia 1856–New York 1902). Hebrew poet. Among the first settlers in Palestine, he left after some six years for the U.S. His poems, first published under the title *Barkai* (Jerusalem, 1886), sing of the return to Zion and of the new colonies in Palestine. Except for his poem *Hatikva* ('Hope') which was the anthem of the Zionist movement and is the national anthem of Israel, most of his writings are forgotten. [EE]

Waxman, *HJL*.

**Immermann, Karl Leberecht** (Magdeburg 1796–Düsseldorf 1840). German novelist and dramatist. He served in the Napoleonic wars, was a civil servant in Münster, Magdeburg, Düsseldorf; director of Düsseldorf theatre (1834–7). Rejecting liberalism and individualism, he believed in the Prussian state. His derivative plays include the comedies *Die Prinzen von Syrakus* (1821), *Das Auge der Liebe* (1824), *Die Schule der Frommen* (1829), the tragedies *Die Verschollene* (1822), *Cardenio und Celinde* (1826), *Andreas Hofer* (1835), *Merlin* (1832) – a Faustian hotch-potch of medieval myth, pantheism, gnosticism and neo-Platonism – and the trilogy *Alexis* (1832) dramatizing Russian history. His lyrical *Gedichte* (1822; 1830) were less successful than the anti-Romantic mock epic *Tulifäntchen* (1830). His best novels are a ⇨ *Bildungsroman* entitled *Die Epigonen* (1835), depicting the impact of industrialization, bourgeois interests, and materialism on a post-feudal, post-idealistic age, and *Münchhausen* (1838; partly tr. J. Oxenford and C. A. Feiling in *Tales from the German*, 1844), opposing to the attitudes personified by the mendacious baron a realistic idealized image of patriotic peasant mo ality. *Memorabilien* (1840ff.) contains autobiography and aesthetics, *Tristan und Isolde* (1841) unfinished romances. [LL]

*Werke*, ed. R. Boxberger (20 vols., 1883); *Auswahl*, ed. W. Deetjen (6 vols., 1923).
W. Fehse, *K.L.I.* (Magdeburg, 1940); M. Windfuhr, *I.s erzählerisches Werk* (Giessen, 1957).

**Imperial, Micer Francisco** (fl. early 15th cent.). Spanish poet. The son of a Genoese jeweller established in Seville. He was the first to bring Dante's influence to Spain. In verses that seem to mingle Spanish and Italian measures, he adapted parts of the *Purgatorio* to his own allegorical purposes, in the *Desir de los siete virtudes*. His work was anthologized by ⇨ Baena, and anticipated the sophisticated poems of Juan de ⇨ Mena. He was widely read, knowing also the latest books of chivalry and something of English, French and Arabic writing. ⇨ Santillana admired his work, which has reached us in what is probably a defective form. [JMC]

Menéndez y Pelayo, *PLC*, i; Trend, *OBSV*.

**Inber, Vera** (Odessa 1890– ). Russian poetess and writer. Brought up in a middle-class family, she spent four years in W. Europe before 1914 and published her first poems in Paris in 1912. In 1922 she moved to Moscow and became a journalist. She joined the ⇨ Constructivist movement. A brief poem on the death of Lenin, *Pyat' nochei i dney* (1924), is successful. Perhaps she has never produced a masterpiece, but her best work is in her longer poems: e.g. *Putevoy dnevnik* (1938), *Pulkovskiy meridian* (1943) and *Leningradskiy dnevnik* (1945); the two latter were written during the siege of Leningrad, which she lived through. Her prose is also of interest, particularly the short stories which evoke Odessa. [RM-G]

*Izbrannyye proizvedeniya* (2 vols., 1958); Lugovskoy, *RSP*; Newnham, *SSS*.

**Ineichen, J.** ⇨ Swiss-German Dialect Literature.

**Ingemann, B. S.** (Torkildstrup 1789–Sorø 1862). Danish poet and novelist. The son of a clergyman whose first sickly, romantic poems are now forgotten, unlike his historical novels glorifying the greatness of Denmark during the Middle Ages, and his so-called *Morgen- og Aften-Sange* which are still greatly admired for their childlike simplicity. The significance of the long narrative poem *Valdemar den Store og hans Mænd* (1824) and the novels *Valdemar Seir* (1826; tr. J. F. Chapman, *Waldemar, surnamed Seir, or the Victorious*, 1843), *Erik Menveds Barndom* (1828; tr. J. Kesson, *The Childhood of King Erik Menved*, 1846), *Kong Erik og de Fredløse* (1833; tr. J. F. Chapman, *King Eric and the Outlaws*, 1843), *Prins Otto af Danmark* (1835) – a cycle completed by the versified narrative *Dronning Margrethe* (1836) – may be likened to that of Sir Walter Scott's work. His hymn 'Through the Night of Doubt and Sorrow' has become very popular in England. [ELB]

C. Langballe, *B.S.I.* (Copenhagen, 1949).

**Ionesco, Eugène** (Slatina 1912– ). French playwright. Of Rumanian origin (which may partly account for his self-conscious attitude to the mechanisms of French), he is one of the acknowledged leaders of contemporary *avant-garde* drama in France. He creates a nightmare world energized by ferocious parody and resting on two basic tenets of *avant-garde* art: the fundamental isolation of man, and the breakdown of language. For Ionesco the failure of communication is related to man's alienation, as a result of the claims and forms of social organization, from what is most distinctively human in himself. Social order and authority are shown to be shams based on a typically bourgeois misconception of their 'logical necessity'. This view of society stems essentially from the experience of Nazism and finds its most explicit expression in a late play, *Le rhinocéros* (1960; tr. D. Prouse, in *Plays IV*, 1960) in which Ionesco dramatizes the conflict between mind and the Fascist glorification of nature by means of a fable about the progressive transformation of man into rhinoceros. The alienation of man is also seen in terms of the sterility of his moral and emotional life, a sterility Ionesco often conveys by using meaningless and mechanical platitudes, spasms of verbal delirium, or laboured parodies of logical argument. This can be seen at work in *La cantatrice chauve* (1950; tr. D. Watson, *The Bald Prima-Donna*, 1958) where routine and conformity reduce the marriage of a parodic English couple to an empty shell in a world in which identities are interchangeable because the sense of a fully individual existence has been lost. Ionesco's is in no sense a theatre of 'problem' plays, but a general argument seems to emerge through its images, metaphors; visual, rhythmic and choreographic effects. It is an argument in favour of expanding the conception of the real so as to embrace the absurd and the unreal; to transcend the rationally coherent and the psychologically probable, and to pierce through the social and political to the humanity we share and which he identifies with our 'anguish'. In this sense, Ionesco values subjectivity as the only counter to the fraud, violence, empty and automatic behaviour of the purely social realm. He values it in the shape of sexuality, a means of communication below the conscious or rational level, even when sexuality issues in curious forms, such as in the sordid eroticism of *Les chaises* (1952; tr. D. Watson, *The Chairs*, in *Plays I*, 1958), where the inanimate chairs crowd out the imaginary world of the two old people. This is preferable to the world in which sexuality is repressed, runs underground and emerges in violence, horror or despair. This characteristically is what happens in the social world of the bourgeoisie where love, Ionesco's convenient metaphor for the inner life, is distorted and frustrated in marriage, an institution devised to preserve society from the intolerable awareness of the power of sex. Hence, in *Amédée ou Comment s'en débarrasser* (1954; tr. D. Watson, *Amédée or How to Get Rid of it*, in *Plays II*, 1958), the enormous corpse growing in the room next door symbolizes the sterility and mutual misery of the relationship between Amédée and Madeleine for whom the routine of work and domesticity has killed love. The dementia of the Professor in the parable of power, *La leçon* (1951; tr. D. Watson, *The Lesson*, in *Plays I*, 1958), like the sadistic joy of Madeleine as she watches her husband tortured in *Victimes du devoir* (1953; tr. D. Watson, *Victims of Duty*, in *Plays II*, 1958), reinforces this insight. Significantly, Ionesco's women conspire to destroy love through marriage. In the absence of true and meaningful relationships, words take on an autonomous life of their own and victimize people. Thus, the pupil in *La leçon* is killed by a *verbal* onslaught, while the love-scene between Jacques and Roberte II in *Jacques ou la soumission* (1955; tr. D. Watson, *Jacques or Obedience*, in *Plays I*, 1958) is reduced to a constant reiteration of the word 'puss'. Balletic movement, feverishly accelerating verbal rhythms, and surrealistic fantasy distinguish this drama in which an ambiguous tension between 'comic' and 'tragic', between farce and fear is maintained by the play of contrasts, e.g. realism juxtaposed to fantasy in *Amédée*. His ideas on the theatre are available in *Notes et contre-notes* (1962) and *Journal en miettes* (1967). [SBJ]

*Théâtre* (4 vols., 1954–66).

Donnard, *I. dramaturge* (Paris, 1966); S. Benmussa, *I.* (Paris, 1966); R. N. Coe, *I.* (1961); P. Sénart, *I.* (1964); Esslin, *TA*; Guicharnaud, *MFT*; Grossvogel, *FPP*; Serreau, *HNT*.

**Iorga, Nicolae** (Botoşani 1871–Bucharest? 1940). Rumanian historian and politician. An enormously prolific writer, outstanding among the personalities of Rumania in the first forty years of this century. His gigantic output of historical writing is very uneven as literature; he tends to cumber his text with material that should be in footnotes. But when he set himself to write public lectures, he would shake himself free of detail and could be marvellously eloquent. As a literary critic his judgement was at times very faulty, as when he dismissed Arghezi's poetry as 'profoundly decadent verse'. Nevertheless under his editorship (1903–6) *Semănătorul* gave its name to the literary movement which drew its inspiration from Rumanian peasant life. [EDT]

**Irbe, Añdrejs.** ⇨ Latvian Literature.

**Iriarte, Tomás de** (Orotova, Tenerife 1750–Madrid 1791). Spanish poet. Once famous for his *Fábulas literarias* (1782; tr. R. Rockliffe, 1851), in which a variety of animals are made to discuss literary theories and to attack Iriarte's enemies. A great lover of music, he produced a long didactic poem, *La música* (1779), and a charming address to 'Haydn, músico alemán' on which his frail immortality now depends. [JMC]

**Irzykowski, Karol** (Błażkowa 1873–Żyrardów 1944). Polish novelist and critic. For a time chief stenographer at the Polish Diet and from 1933 a member of the Academy of Literature. Although he published several collections of critical essays, the most important being *Walka o treść* ('The Struggle for Content', 1929), it is his early and only novel *Paluba* (1903) which secures him a permanent place in literature, European as well as Polish.

It represents a pre-Freudian experiment in psychoanalytical fiction. The title itself is a cluster of meanings (one denoting a spiteful old woman), while the central character is called Strumieński (from *strumień*, stream). The story, in his own words, descends 'below the open deck of consciousness' and is concerned with 'bashful moments' in human behaviour. Strumieński concocts a private myth out of the memory of his dead wife, tries to live up to it during his second marriage, initiating others into his neurotic game, which in the end causes the death of his own child. The child's version of the myth is symbolized in the destructive enigma of the word *pałuba*. The plot and dialogue are reduced to bare essentials, whereas the character of Strumieński is further intersected by means of comments, cross-references and footnotes. A separate story and two explanatory essays complete this formidable structure. [JP]

*SEER*, XXX, 74 (1951).

**Isidore of Seville, St** (*c.* 570–636). Spanish churchman and scholar. He succeeded his brother as Bishop of Seville (*c.* 600), where he also founded a school and taught. He was a prolific writer celebrated particularly for his unreliable encyclopedia of the knowledge of his age. It is commonly called *Etymologiae*, because of his etymological explanations (often fantastic) of his various subjects. Popular throughout the Middle Ages, it kept alive knowledge of ancient culture and texts. His verses, composed for inscription over his bookcases, are interesting as showing what writers, both pagan and Christian, were represented in his library. His *De viris illustribus* continues the work of St Jerome. His world *Chronicon de sex aetatibus* (from creation to A.D. 615) is less important than the *Historia Gothorum, Wandalorum, Sueborum* which is a valuable historical source. The sum of medieval astronomy and meteorology is contained in his *De natura rerum.* He was active on Church councils and his *Regula monachorum* was widely used in the 7th and 8th centuries. [FB]

Migne, *PL*, 81–4; *Chronicon, Historia*, ed. T. Mommsen (MGH, AA, 1894); *Etymologiae*, ed. W. M. Lindsay (2 vols., 1911); *De natura rerum*, ed., with Fr. tr., J. Fontaine (Paris, 1960). E. Bréhaut, *An Encyclopaedist of the Dark Ages* (New York, 1912); P. Séjourné, *Le dernier Père de l'Église, Saint I.* (Paris, 1929); Laistner, *TLWE.*

**Isla, José Francisco de** (Villavidanes, León 1706–Bologna 1781). Spanish Jesuit writer. His semi-picaresque satire against pulpit orators, *Fray Gerundio* (1758–68; in CC), suffers from the inherent boredom of its subject. His own *Sermones morales* (1792–3) were highly regarded. Banished with his Order in 1767, while in Italy he translated ⇨ Lesage's *Gil Blas* into Spanish, believing (like Voltaire) it derived from Spanish sources. [JMC]

**Ivan IV** (1533–1584). Russian Tsar and a prolific epistle-writer. His letters – notably those addressed to ⇨ Kurbsky, to the Kirillo-Belozersky monastery and to Vasily Gryaznoy – are written in a style which can only be described as revolutionary. Carried away by the fire of his crude political theories, by the passion of his hatred or by his contempt for the object of his scorn, Ivan was the first Russian writer to combine the lofty traditional oratorical style with the earthy language of the stables, to attempt *jeux de mots*, to juxtapose the Biblical and the bawdy and to revitalize the moribund Russian language with the vocabulary of everyday speech. While his composition and sequence of thought are often chaotic, and although syntax often goes by the board in the heat of his impassioned diatribes, his rich picturesque language makes his epistles more readable than any other contemporary Russian polemical work. [JLIF]

*Poslaniya*, ed. D. S. Likhachov and Ya. S. Lur'ye (1951); *The Correspondence between Prince A. M. Kurbsky and Tsar Ivan IV of Russia 1564–1569*, ed. J. L. I. Fennell (1965).

**Ivanišević, Drago** (Trieste 1907–    ). A leading Croatian modernist poet. His wide European culture serves as a background to highly intellectual poetry reflecting man's predicament in a world of war and insecurity. [EDG]

*Dnevnik* (1957); *Karte na stolu* (1959).

**Ivanov, Vsevolod Vyacheslavovich** (Lebyash, Semipalatinsk 1895–Moscow 1963). Russian dramatist. Son of a teacher; he spent a wandering youth, working with a travelling circus, becoming a printer, wrestler, etc. After fighting as a partisan, he was brought to Petersburg by Gor'ky, becoming a member of the ⇨ Serapion Brothers (cf. style of *Tsvetniye Vetra*, 1922). His vivid descriptive powers, physically vital, free of introspection, exult in stories of war (*Partizany*, 1921) and colourful Asiatic landscape (*Vozvrashcheniye Buddy*, 1923), etc. His characters struggle with dark, individual passions amidst the storms of history. His first (preserved) play, a dramatization (1927) of his short story *Bronepoyezd No. 14–69* (1922; tr. G. Cowan and A. T. K. Grant, 1933) is based on a real incident recounted by the crew of an armoured train to whom he had been lecturing during the Civil War. The romantic treatment enabled Stanislavsky to realize his dream of 'showing the revolution through the soul of man'; it has been widely translated and staged abroad. Other plays about the Civil War are *Blokada* (1929), *Golubi Mira* (1937), and *Aleksandr Parkhomenko* (1941), based on his novel (1938) glorifying this partisan leader. His historical dramas include *Dvenadtsat' molodtsev iz tabakerki* (1936) about the murder of Paul I, *Lomonosov* (1953) and *Vdokhnoveniye* (1940) about the Time of Troubles in the 17th century. Much of his later work has still to be published. [AP]

*Sobraniye sochinenyy* (8 vols., 1958); *P'yesy* (1964); Faber, *RSS*; Reavey and Slonim, *SLA*; *I Live a Queer Life* (autobiography) (tr. anon., 1936).

*Molodaya Gvardiya*, 1, 1957; *Voprosy Literatury*, 1, 1962; N. Zaitsev, *Dramaturgiya V.I.* (Leningrad-Moscow, 1963) (for bibliography); *Literaturnaya Gazeta*, 2, 1964.

**Ivanov, Vyacheslav Ivanovich** (Moscow 1866–Rome 1949). Russian poet and philosopher. With the publication in 1901 of his first volume of poems, *Kormchiye zvyozdy*, he was at once recognized as a leading Symbolist poet. Together with ⇨ Bely, he became one of the chief theoreticians of the new movement, emphasizing in his critical works – *Po zvyozdam* (1909), *Borozdy i mezhi* (1916) – the mystical and religious aspects of the new poetry. A clash between this outlook and that of other poets, like Bryusov, who saw symbolism primarily as a poetic technique, led to a split in the movement, and in 1906 Ivanov became the leader of the short-lived 'mystical anarchist' group, originally formed by the poet Chulkov. After the Revolution he moved to Baku. From 1924 he lived in Italy, where he became a convert to Roman Catholicism.

Ivanov's early poetry – the best collections are *Eros* (1907) and *Cor Ardens* (1911) – tends to be rhetorical, pedantic and esoteric. He regards poetry primarily as a religious search and the poet as a hierophant. His later works, *Rimskiye sonety*, *Rimsky dnevnik 1944 goda*, are simpler, but he preserves in them his Platonic ideals, believing firmly in the existence of a higher reality, of which the objects of this world are but a reflection.

His philosophy, expressed in the works *Ellinskaya religiya Stradayushchego boga* ('The Hellenic Religion of the Suffering God', 1917) and *Dionis i pradionisiystvo* ('Dionysus and Proto-Dionysianism', 1923), is based on Nietzsche's dichotomy of Apollonian and Dionysiac; but whereas Nietzsche sees the religion of Dionysus as the anthithesis of Christianity, he believes it to be Christianity's forerunner. [TJB]

*Svet vecherniy. Poems by V.I.*, ed. D. Ivanov (Oxford, 1962).

*Oxford Slavonic Papers*, V (1954); Poggioli, *PR*.

**Iwaszkiewicz, Jarosław** (Kalnik 1894– ). Polish short-story writer and poet. Born in the Ukraine and educated in Kiev. His best work is of a sophisticated kind, whether in lyrical verse as represented by *Lato 1932*, or in the carefully written short stories, as in the collections *Młyn nad Utratą* (1936) and *Tatarak* (1960). His novels and plays, including one about Chopin's relations with George Sand (*Lato w Nohant*, 1936; tr. C. Wieniewska, *Summer at N.*, 1942) are of an inferior quality. [JP]

Kuncewicz, *MPM*.

# J

**Jacob, Max** (Quimper 1876–Drancy 1944). French *avant-garde* poet and occasional painter. A close friend of Picasso and ⇨ Apollinaire. His work is a paradoxical mixture of fantastic humour and mysticism. While writing poems which combine parody, pun, burlesque and verbal acrobatics of every kind, he lived a life of fervent piety. Jewish by birth, he was converted to Roman Catholicism in 1915, and in 1921 retired to live as a recluse at Saint-Benoît-sur-Loire. Arrested there in 1944 he died in Drancy concentration camp. In his years of retreat he wrote tirelessly, leaving fine mystic verse as well as curious Breton poems which have the naïve charm of folk poetry.

His most influential work was *Le cornet à dés* (1917), prose poems on apparently gratuitous subjects (a pointless anecdote, nightmarish vision, a sharp visual perception) in a brilliant style and masterly rhythms which inspired later innovators, particularly the Surrealists. The same qualities can be found in other volumes, notably *Le laboratoire central* (1921); *Les pénitents en maillot rose* (1925); *Derniers poèmes en vers et en prose* (1945). [IL]

Hackett, *AMFP*.
A. Billy, *M.J.* (Paris, 1947); Raymond, *DBS*.

**Jacobi, Johann Georg** (Düsseldorf 1740–Freiburg, Br. 1814). German journalist and poet. He founded the periodical *Iris* in Düsseldorf in 1774, aimed primarily at a female audience, but of sufficient standing to attract the collaboration of Goethe, ⇨ Gleim and ⇨ Heinse. When publication was suspended he collaborated in ⇨ Wieland's *Merkur*. After his appointment to a chair of aesthetics in Freiburg in 1784, he edited the *Taschenbücher*, a journal which from 1803 was renamed *Iris*.

As a lyric poet, he is usually classed with ⇨ Hagedorn and ⇨ Gleim as anacreontic. He possessed considerable talent in turning polished verses in the light, dallying mode of the gallic *poésie fugitive* and certain of his songs ('Willst du frei und lustig sein' and 'Sagt, wo sind die Veilchen hin?') were very popular in their day. [WAC]

*Werke* (3 vols., 1854) (selection).
J. O. Manthey-Zorn, *J.s 'Iris'* (Leipzig, 1905); G. Ransohoff, *Über J.G.J.s Jugendwerke* (Berlin, 1892).

**Jacobsen, Jens Peter** (Thisted 1847–Thisted 1885). Danish novelist and short-story writer. As a student at Copenhagen he was interested in both poetry and natural science, being profoundly influenced by Darwin, whose main works he translated into Danish and about whose ideas he wrote a series of essays. The poetry of his early years reflects his attempt to liberate himself from his own tendency to romantic dreams; most famous are the *Gurresange* (set to music by Schoenberg as *Gurre-Lieder*) and his first 'Arabesque'.

During the winter of 1871–2 he established close contact with G. and E. ⇨ Brandes and turned from romantic poetry to naturalistic prose; his first attempt, the short story *Mogens* (1872), is in idea, style and technique a classic of Scandinavian Naturalism. In Florence in the summer of 1873 Jacobsen received the first warning that he suffered from a serious tuberculosis which would leave him only a few years to live. Much of his later work is concerned with the problem of death.

Of his two novels, *Fru Marie Grubbe* (1876; tr. H. Astrup-Larsen, 1914) is a naturalistic novel after the model of Flaubert (though in its style possibly influenced by contemporary Danish translations of Turgenev), a *document humain* in which, against a background of 17th-century Denmark, the main character is seen as the victim of her own animal instincts. *Niels Lyhne* (1880; tr. H. Astrup-Larsen, 1919), is concerned with typical problems of the period and of Jacobsen himself: marriage *v.* free love, Christianity *v.* atheism (Jacobsen himself was a convinced atheist and this spiritually sensitive book has been called the 'Bible of atheism'), romantic dreaming *v.* a disillusioned acceptance of reality.

Jacobsen's short stories, *Mogens og andre Noveller* (1882; tr. A. Grabow, *Mogens and Other Stories*, 1921), are beautifully constructed masterpieces of artistic narration; his fastidious artistry is also revealed in the handful of poems published posthumously in 1886 (tr. P. Selver, *Poems*, 1920). He is a fine psychologist, reminiscent of Henry James, and his influence has been considerable – e.g. on the young Rilke. [ELB]

*Samlede Værker* (1924–9).

F. Nielsen, *J.P.J.* (Copenhagen, 1953); W. Rehm, *Gontscharow und J.* (Göttingen, 1963); Gustafsen, *SSN*.

**Jacobsen, Jørgen-Frantz** (Thorshavn 1900–Vejlefjord 1938). Faroese novelist and Copenhagen journalist. Apart from some volumes of essays (and his posthumously published *Journals*) he wrote perhaps the best novel by any Faroese writer, *Barbara* (1939; tr. E. Bannister, 1948). [ELB]

**Jacobus de Voragine** (Varazze, Genoa *c.* 1230–Genoa 1298). Dominican friar and Archbishop of Genoa, famous as a preacher throughout Italy. His two chief works are a history of Genoa (*Chronicon genuense* ed. G. Monleone, Rome 1941) and *Lombardica historia*, better known as the *Golden Legend* (*Legenda aurea*, ed. T. Graesse, Dresden and Leipzig, 1846; tr. G. Ryman and H. Ripperger, 1941), a collection of legends of the saints, grouped according to the liturgical calendar. Its (unhistorical) anecdotes and attractive style made it the most popular work of its kind in the Middle Ages. It was one of the first books to be printed anywhere (e.g. Caxton's English versions 1483, 1488; ed. F. S. Ellis, *The Golden Legend of William Caxton*, 3 vols., 1892; re-ed. F. S. Ellis, 7 vols., 1900). [FB]

M. de Waresquiel, *Le bienheureux J. de V.* (Paris, 1902).

**Jacopone da Todi** (Todi *c.* 1236–Collazzone, Umbria 1306). Italian poet. Composer of religious *Laude*. Tradition has it that after being shaken from a life of worldly pleasure by the death of his wife, *c.* 1268, he joined the Franciscan 'Spirituals', the most rigorous group of the Order, with whom he suffered persecution from Boniface VIII. His hymns of praise are intensely personal in their fervour. Whatever the immediate mood of the poem – aspiration to the love of God, denunciation of the values of the world, or specific condemnation of Boniface and the ills of the Church – the tone is taut and vibrant, the movement violent and dramatic. The world is ill, the senses are temptation, and they are loathed with a hatred which is feverish and intransigent. [DGR]

*Laudi, Trattato e Detti*, ed. F. Ageno (Florence, 1953); *Le Laudi*, ed. L. Fallacara (Florence, 1955); Contini, *PD*; Lind, *LPIR*; Kay, *PBIV*.

N. Sapegno, *Frate J.* (Turin, 1926); M. Apollonio, *J. da T.* (Milan, 1946); *Minori*, i.

**Jacques de Vitry** (*c.* 1160–1240). Celebrated preacher against the Albigenses, he took part in the Fifth Crusade and was present at the capture of Damietta. His popularity led to his election as Bishop of Acre, which he left later to become a cardinal. His sermons were interpolated with stories (*Exempla*) to entertain his hearers and emphasize his teaching. He collected many from oriental sources while in Palestine. He also compiled an account of the history, geography and natural history (real and fabulous) of the Holy Land and adjacent parts. [FB]

*Exempla*, ed. T. F. Crane (1890); ed. P. Lehmann (Munich, 1914); *Historia orientalis*, ed. J. Bongars in *Gesta Dei per Francos* (2 vols., Hanover, 1612); tr. A. Stewart, *History of Jerusalem* (1896).

I. Barroux, *J. de V.* (Paris, 1885).

**Jahnn, Hans Henny** (Hamburg, Stellingen 1894–Hamburg 1959). German novelist and dramatist. A pacifist, he lived in Norway from 1914 to 1918; an expert in organ-building and music, he founded in 1921 the Ugrino music publishing house in Hamburg. From 1933, when his writings were banned, to 1945, he ran a stud-farm (Bornholm). His controversial 'psychological' dramas, *Pastor Ephraim Magnus* (1919), *Die Krönung Richards III* (1921), *Der Arzt, sein Weib, sein Sohn* (1922), *Der gestohlene Gott* (1924), *Medea* (1926), *Armut, Reichtum, Mensch und Tier* (1933–48), and *Thomas Chatterton* (1955), show the violence of elemental, usually sexual, impulses. Though praised by W. Muschg as 'the greatest German prose-writer of our time', neither the experimental novel *Perrudja* (1929) nor the monumental trilogy *Fluss ohne Ufer* (begun 1933; publ. 1949–50; Vol. i, tr. C. Hutten, *The Ship*, N.Y., 1961) is widely known. Influenced by Freud and Joyce, his technique is difficult, imposing abstract, apparently arbitrary form and meaning (theoretically modelled on music and mathematics) on weird experiences, exotic, vicious, a half inner, half outer 'river' over which the individual has little control (or responsibility?). His *Die Nacht aus Blei* (1956) is Kafkaesque. [PB]

*Dramen* (2 vols., 1963–5); *Auswahl*, ed. W. Muschg (1959).

E. Lohner, in *Symposium*, VI (Syracuse, 1952); J. Mayer, *Verzeichnis der Schriften von und über H.H.J.* (Hamburg, 1967); H. Wolfheim, *H.H.J.* (Hamburg, 1966); R. Italiaander, *H.H.J. Zum 60. Geburtstag* (Hamburg, 1954), and *H.H.J.: Buch der Freunde* (Hamburg, 1960).

**Jakšić, Djura** (Srpska Crnja 1832–Belgrade 1878). Serbian poet, dramatist and short-story writer. His education was interrupted by the revolution of 1848 in which he took part. His ambition was to become a painter, but he was never able to complete his training nor, despite his many paintings, to make it his profession. Most of his life was spent as a provincial schoolteacher until, just before his death from tuberculosis, he was given a sinecure as corrector of the state press.

He began to write lyrical poetry in 1853 and later published three poetical dramas with themes taken from Serbian history – *Seoba Srbalja* (1863), *Jelisaveta* (1868), and *Stanoje Glavaš* (1878). His poems are, at their best, full of passion, colour and romantic temperament. One of his best is 'Na Liparu'. The deep blues, reds and golds of his pictures are reflected in his poetry. A literary autodidact, his work suffers from naïveté and his patriotic poetry is often marred by overstatement. His stories, despite their romantic setting, form a bridge between romanticism and realism in Serbian prose. His stormy and passionate nature makes him the most original of the Serbian romantics and his poetry is the most personal and spontaneous in Serbian 19th-century literature. [EDG]

Ibrovac, *APY*.
Barac, *HYL*.

**Jammes, Francis** (Tarbes 1868–Hasparren 1938). French poet. His family had exotic memories of their life in Martinique, but he always lived in Béarn and the Basque country. After a rebellious youth, he sought local recognition in the calm variety of village life, though it came to him less easily than the national reputation of a patriarch of poetry. The jaded Parisian men of letters of the late symbolist era came on pilgrimages to Jammes, whose fresh meditative poetry was a source of renewal. *De l'angélus de l'aube à l'angélus du soir* (1898) showed simple, sincere, sensitive feeling blended into a watered-down pantheistic romanticism. His themes were humble people and animals, the intricate life of the countryside, and simple passions in faintly gothic surroundings. A series of disappointed loves were sublimed into *Le deuil des primevères* (1901) and poetic novels such as *Clara d'Ellébeuse* (1899). Through sorrow he rediscovered his Christian faith, which inspires the hopeful *Clairières dans le ciel* (1906) and the slender *Géorgiques chrétiennes* (1912). After the war he collected 4-line verses similar in mood to *Haï Kaî* in the 4 volumes of *Quatrains* (1923–5), before finding his full maturity in *Ma France poétique* (1926), *De tout temps à jamais* (1935) and *Sources* (1936). In various essays about the Basque country and novels and prose poems forming village epics, he carries into prose the fine quality of his verse, based on primitive rhythms, virgin language, and the authenticating of rare images through bare words. [CLC]

R. Mallet, *F.J.* (Paris, 1961).

**Jansen, Cornelius** (1585–1638). French theologian. Bishop of Ypres for two years only, he died before the publication of his *Augustinus* (1640). This, and his lecture of 1627 called *Discours de la réformation de l'homme intérieur* and the *Livre de la fréquente communion* of Antoine Arnauld (1643), may be called the foundation texts of Jansenism. This movement, which in the 18th century became a political pressure group, was an attempt to recall modern man to the austerities of the Christian religion, as found in the writings of St Augustine. Jansen's inspiration, totally posthumous, was chiefly instrumental in such figures as Saint-Cyran, Richelieu's prisoner and spiritual director of the convent of Port-Royal, the Arnauld family, Pascal and a group of laymen known as the Solitaires. The movement has been brilliantly described in Sainte-Beuve's *Port-Royal*. [WGM]

A. Gazier, *Histoire générale du mouvement janséniste* (Paris, 1922); N. J. Abercrombie, *Origins of Jansenism* (1936); J. Orcibal, *Correspondance de Jansénius* (Paris, 1947).

**Jarchas.** ⇨ Mozarabic Lyric.

**Järnefelt, Arvid** (Pulkova (Russia) 1861–Helsinki 1932). Finnish novelist and short-story writer. Son of a general; brother of Eero Järnefelt the painter and Armas Järnefelt the composer. Their sister married the composer Jean Sibelius. Arvid graduated in law, but came under the influence of the movement inspired by Tolstoy and abandoned a legal career in favour of smallhold farming and writing. His 'conversion' is recounted in *Heräämiseni* (1894). Having begun as a realist and analyst of nationalist ideology (*Isänmaa*, 1893) he became a romantic and utopian prophet of the Tolstoyan doctrines, in the light of which he examined religious, social and economic problems (*Maaemon lapsia*, 1905; *Veneh-'ojalaiset*, 1909; *Hiljaisuudessa*, 1913). Having come to be regarded as a somewhat isolated phenomenon in Finnish literature, he made a surprisingly successful 'come-back' in the twenties with the excellent *Greeta ja hänen Herransa* (1925), a fine novel which treats a religious theme with great clarity and objectivity. This was followed by a 3-volume novel, *Vanhempieni romaani* (1928–30). [TA]

**Jarry, Alfred** (Laval 1873–Paris 1907). French writer and dramatist. Famous for his violent farce *Ubu Roi* (1896; tr. B. Wright, in *Four Modern French Comedies*, N.Y., 1960), which caused a scandal at its first production. The 'hero' Ubu is a caricature of bourgeois greed, cowardice and cruelty. He makes himself King of Poland in this free-wheeling burlesque of heroic theatre from Sophocles to Shakespeare. The unreality is heightened by Ubu's enormous paunch, grotesque head and pompous archaic language. He is, in fact, a monstrous puppet – the play was originally a schoolboy prank, inspired by puppet-plays, and the whole effect of the final work is due to its having retained the uninhibited ferocity of the world of Punch and Judy.

More Ubu works followed, both prose and plays (collected in *Tout Ubu*, ed. M. Saillet, 1962), which, together with the eccentricity and wild nonconformity of his own life, made Jarry a legend even before his early death. A posthumous work, *Gestes et opinions du Docteur Faustroll* (1911), with its exposé of the science of pataphysics, or science of imaginary solutions, completed his reputation as a dedicated exponent of absurdity in literature. Although in much of his work he never quite escaped from the artificiality, and even the mannered obscurity, of the Symbolist movement in which he has his roots, his work has had a fruitful effect on a long line of writers, from ⇨ Apollinaire and the Surrealists to the dramatists of the Theatre of the Absurd today. [IL]

*Œuvres complètes* (8 vols., 1948); *King Turd* (*Ubu enchaîné*), tr. B. Keith and G. Legman (1953).
J. H. Levesque, *A.J.* (Paris, 1951); L. Perche, *A.J.* (Paris, 1965); Esslin, *TA*; Shattuck, *BY*.

**Jaufré Rudel,** lord ('prince') of Blaye (fl. mid 12th cent.). Provençal ⇨ troubadour. His poems of earthly love are suffused by a mystical longing which is of Christian inspiration and may have led him to make his visit to the Holy Land in 1148. The most famous of the 6 poems that have survived is 'Lanquan li jorn son lonc en mai'. In this song he seeks happiness in an '*amor de lonh*', a distant love or love from afar, which may be love of God, love of the Virgin Mary, of the Holy Land or of the Countess of Tripoli. The legend of his love for this countess, which may have been invented by his 13th-century Provençal biographer, was referred to by Petrarch and inspired Browning, Swinburne, Rostand, Carducci, Heine and Heyse. [LTT]

*Les Chansons*, ed. A. Jeanroy (2nd edn, 1924); Hill and Bergin, *APT*.
*SP*, XLIX (1952); *MLN*, LVII (1942); LIX (1944); *R*, LXXI (1950).

**Jáuregui, Juan Martínez de** (Seville 1583–Madrid 1641). Spanish poet and literary critic. Although at first a professed opponent of *culteranismo* (in his preface to *Rimas*, 1618, and in *Discurso poético contra el hablar culto y oscuro*, 1624), Góngora's influence is clear in his fable *Orfeo* (1624) and his translation of Lucan's *Pharsalia* (publ. 1684). The latter is most striking in its accounts of naval battles; a wreck on the sea-shore is the theme of one of the best sonnets in *Rimas* (which are in the main gracefully classical in style). A particularly fine passage in *Orfeo* (suggestive of Shelley) describes the entrance to hell amidst a romantic landscape of crags, fens and thickets. [JMC]

*Orfeo* (1948); Blecua, *FLE*; Cohen, *PBSV*.
Jordán de Urríes, *Biografía y estudio crítico de J.* (Madrid, 1899); J. M. de Cossío, *Fábulas mitológicas en España* (Madrid, 1952).

**Jean Bodel** (*c.*1165–*c.*1210). French ⇨ *trouvère* of Arras at a time when the literary societies or ⇨ *puys* of that town offered encouragement and patronage to writers of every sort. He was about to set out for the Holy Land, probably on the Crusade of 1202, when he contracted leprosy. He marked his retirement from the world by a famous *congé* (ed. P. Ruelle, Paris, 1965) in which he took leave of a different friend in each of 41 stanzas. He has left several *pastourelles*, a successful epic, *La Chanson des Saisnes*, dealing with Charlemagne's war against the Saxons, and the excellent play, the *Jeu de saint Nicolas*. This ⇨ Miracle is used as a loose frame for Oriental scenes of Crusading fervour and Christian piety, and for tavern humour at Arras: in his lightly satirical approach and his handling of racy and realistic dialogue, he was far ahead of his time as a dramatist. For bibliography ⇨ Miracles. [LTT]

**Jean de Meun(g).** ⇨ *Rose, Roman de la.*

**Jean le Bel** (Liège *c.* 1290–Liège 1370). French chronicler. Canon of Saint-Lambert at Liège, author of one of the best medieval French chronicles, which deals with the years 1326–61 in France, England and Scotland. Jean had a powerful personality and loved elegant living. His chronicle was based on his own experience and on information given by eye-witnesses. ⇨ Froissart used it as a model for his early work. [LTT]

*Chronique*, ed. J. Viard and E. Déprez (2 vols., 1904–5); *Bibliothèque de l'école des chartes*, LXVI (1905); *Hist. litt. de la Fr.*, XXXVIII, 1941.

**Jean Paul,** pseud. of Johann Paul Friedrich Richter (Wunsiedel 1763–Bayreuth 1825). German novelist. The bitterness of his poverty-stricken youth is reflected in the savage satire of his early, unsuccessful works, *Grönländische Prozesse* (1783) and *Auszug aus den Papieren des Teufels* (1789); even when his novels and idylls had made him the most popular novelist of his age, he was never able to achieve any harmonious unity either in his writings or in his life. His prolific writings (60 volumes) are characterized by a highly developed sense of humour and an extreme formlessness – the plot is often slight and tends to be overlaid by a mass of digressions and interpolations. The mood of his works alternates between scepticism and emotionalism, between the 'Turkish bath of sentimentality and the cold shower of satire'; similarly his style varies between over-ornamentation worthy of the Baroque and passages of great lyrical beauty. His great novels (*Die unsichtbare Loge*, 1793, *Hesperus*, 1795; *Titan*, 1800-3; *Flegeljahre*, 1804–5) all deal with the same central problem: the achievement of a harmonious personality, the dangers of one-sidedness and the conflict of the ideal and the real. But it is not in the great world of the courts and upper-class society in which these novels move that he is at his best, but in the humorously and realistically portrayed little world of the petty bourgeoisie in the idylls (*Das Leben des vergnügten Schulmeisterlein Maria Wuz*, 1790; *Das Leben des Quintus Fixlein*, 1796; *Blumen-, Frucht- und Dornenstücke oder Ehestand, Tod und Hochzeit des Armenadvokaten F. St Siebenkäs*, 1796–7), for this is a world he knows and with which he can sympathize. He loves life even in its limitations and pettiness, but can still laugh at it uninhibitedly. His greatest achievement is in his psychological realism: with the exception of Lenette in *Siebenkäs*, his women do not reach the heights of his male characters, but his insight into masculine psychology, both normal and abnormal, is strikingly profound. The first of the bourgeois realist-humorists, his influence lives on in the 19th century in the writings of ⇨ Keller, ⇨ Raabe and ⇨ Mörike. [WAC]

*Werke*, ed. E. Förster (65 vols., 1826ff.); ed. W. Höllerer *et al.* (1960ff.); *Wit, Wisdom and Philosophy of J.P.F.R.*, ed. G. P. Hawley (1884).
M. Kommerell, *J.P.* (Frankfurt, 1933); J. Smeed, *J.P.'s Dreams* (1966); Wellek, *HMC.*

**Jean Renart** (fl. early 13th cent.). The most famous writer of medieval French romances after ⇨ Chrétien de Troyes. Works attributed to him are the *Escoufle* (*c.*1200–1202), *Guillaume de Dole* (between 1200 and 1226), and the *Lai de l'ombre* (1219–21), which he signed. The *Escoufle* (ed. H. Michelant, P. Meyer, 1894) deals with the love of Aelis, daughter of the Emperor of Rome, and Guillaume, son of Richard de Montivilliers. When Guillaume's father dies, the engagement of the two lovers is broken by the Emperor of Rome, and they flee. A vulture (*escoufle*) steals Aelis's purse and Guillaume, pursuing the bird, is separated from her. After many trials and wanderings the lovers meet again, are married and eventually become rulers of Rome.

*Guillaume de Dole* (ed. F. Lecoy, 1962) is concerned with the folklore motif of a wager on the chastity of a wife which is ignobly won by the would-be seducer who informs the husband of a birthmark on his wife's body. In this case the birthmark is in the shape of a rose, hence the original title *Li Romanz de la rose*, later suppressed to avoid confusion with the famous *Roman de la* ⇨ *Rose*. In *Guillaume de Dole* there are inserted in the story stanzas from songs in favour at the time, including the earliest known *chansons de danse* and *chansons de toile*, and poems of early ⇨ *trouvères* and ⇨ troubadours.

The *Lai de l'ombre* (ed. J. Orr, 1948) is a short (962 lines) but fine poem in which the most courteous knight sitting by a well is refused by the most courteous lady, has to take back his ring but gives it instead to her reflection in the well, thus winning her love.

Two other works in the *fabliau* genre are generally attributed to him: *Renart et Piaudoue* and the *Plaid de Renart de Dammartin*. *Galeran de Bretagne*, a romance close to the *Fresne* of ⇨ Marie de France, is not now thought to be his.

Tolerant, kindly and ironical, Jean Renart avoids courtly clichés and writes of courtly and everyday life with a familiar realism. [LTT]

Rita Lejeune-Dehousse, *L'œuvre de J.R.* (Paris-Liège, 1935).

**Jens, Walter** (Hamburg 1923– ). German novelist and critic. He teaches Classics at Tübingen. His best-known novel, *Nein – die Welt der Angeklagten* (1950), is a plea for political freedom and shows the eclipse of the 'last individual' in a totalitarian state. Its atmosphere of Orwellian fantasy links it with his subsequent novels: *Der Blinde* (1951; tr. M. Bullock, *The Blind Man*, 1954), *Vergessene Gesichter* (1953), and *Der Mann, der nicht alt werden wollte* (1954). In 1957 he published the prose parable *Das Testament des Odysseus*, which in its condemnation of war recalls the early pacifist novella *Das weisse Taschentuch* (1948), published under the pseudonym Walter Freiburger. Known also for radio-plays, classical translations and critical works: *statt einer literaturgeschichte* (1957), etc. [PB]

*W. J. Eine Einführung* (Munich, 1965).

**Jensen, Johannes Vilhelm** (Farsø 1873–Copenhagen 1950). Danish novelist, essayist and poet. His *Himmerlands Historier* (1898–1910) are *Heimat* literature of supreme quality, though few have been translated. His first important novel, *Kongens Fald* (1901; tr. P. Kirwan, *The Fall of the King*, 1933), was a protest against decadence and lack of vitality in his compatriots. Other, less important novels were inspired by his many travels to the Far East and America (the land of still vital drive). His main work is a novel cycle in 6 volumes, *Den lange Rejse* (1908–22; tr. A. G. Chater, *The Long Journey*, 1922), an attempt at a Darwinian counterpart to the Old Testament; the 'long journey' is that of mankind, from the baboon stage to the historical period. Elements from the Bible, ancient mythology, the Icelandic sagas and ancient historians, are compounded with details of geology, anthropology, archaeology and ethnography. Evolutionary ideas occur in many of his visionary *Myter* (1906–44; selection tr. C. A. Bodelsen, R. Bathgate, L. Cranfield, *The Waving Rye*, Copenhagen, 1958), a mixture of essays and tales which are probably his most original work, though his very varied poetry, collected in *Digte* (Copenhagen, 1952) is also highly rated. He owes much to the Icelandic sagas and to Heine, Whitman and Kipling. His theory of 'Gothic expansion' according to which the Scandinavian North was the starting-point of European and American civilization, is expounded in his many collections of pseudo-scientific and pseudo-philosophical essays, e.g. *Den gothiske Renæssance* (1901), *Introduktion til vor Tidsalder* (1915) and *Æstetik og Udvikling* (1923). In 1944 he was awarded the Nobel Prize for Literature. [ELB]

Johansen and Marcus, *J.V.J. En bibliografi I–II* (Copenhagen, 1933–51); L. Nedergaard, *J.V.J.* (Copenhagen, 1943); O. Friis, 'J.V.J.', in *Scandinavica* I, 2 (November 1962).

**Jesenský, Janko** (Turčiansky Sv. Martin 1874–Bratislava 1945). Slovak poet and novelist. Descended from the minor nobility and a laywer by profession, he deserted from the Austro-Hungarian Army during the First World War and joined the free Czechoslovak Army in Russia. Between the two wars he was Vice-President of the Slovak local administration. During the Second World War he lived in retirement and wrote illegal anti-fascist verses. His most successful work is the satirical novel, *Demokrati* (1st part 1934, 2nd 1937, tr. J. R. Edwards, *The Democrats*, Prague, 1961), dealing with the upper classes and political life in Slovakia in the inter-war years. [KB]

*Dejiny slovenskej literatúry* (Bratislava, 1960).

**Jilemnický, Peter** (Kyšperk-Letohrad 1901–Moscow 1949). Slovak novelist. Czech by birth, he came to Slovakia as a teacher in 1922 and began to write in Slovak. A member of the Communist Party, he went to the Soviet Union with a group of Slovak immigrants in 1926, studied at the State Institute of Journalism in Moscow, and returned to Slovakia to work as a journalist. Expelled from Slovakia in 1939, he taught in Bohemia until his arrest by the Gestapo in 1942. He spent the rest of the war in the Grieb and Dessau concentration camps and in 1947 he became cultural attaché at the Czechoslovak Embassy in Moscow. His best novels, *Pole neorané* (1932) and *Kus cukru* (1934), depict the class struggle of the industrial and peasant proletariat in Slovakia during the years of economic crisis. His *Kronika* (1947) is a chronicle of the heroic rising of the Slovak people against the Nazis. [KB]

J. Špitzer, *P.J.* (Bratislava, 1955).

**Jiménez, Juan Ramón** (Moguer, Andalucía, 1881–Puerto Rico 1958). Spanish poet and Nobel Prizewinner (1956). The successor of Rubén Darío in the development of modernism, his work echoes many French influences. His early impressionism (*Almas de violeta*, 1900) has a brilliance derived from the landscape of his native Andalusia. With *Diario de un poeta recién casado* (1917) his style undergoes a purge of decorative adjectives. In the 'pure poetry' of his middle period (generally in *vers-libre,* but as delicately cadenced as his former rhymed lines) he attempts to convey the feeling of an absolute moment without background, influenced partly by Tagore, whose work his wife was translating. The collections *Eternidades* (1918), *Piedra y cielo* (1919), *Poesía* (1923) and *Belleza* (1923) contain a number of magnificent poems in which experience seems to have been resolved into bare essences of light, water, absence. The reality of things, admitted again through the fuller imagery and metaphysical reflections of *La estación total* (Buenos Aires, 1946), lies ultimately in the Word of poetry. The poet's task of finding 'the exact name of things' is essentially religious, a revelation. God, with whom Jiménez is also preoccupied in some later poems, remains an abstraction, a kind of idealized unattainable fulfilment of desire and consciousness. More effective passages are inspired by nostalgia for his country and coloured by native imagery. His wife was of partly American descent and he lived in his later years in the U.S.A. and Puerto Rico. His portrait in poetic prose of himself as a boy with a donkey, *Platero y yo* (1917), is a children's classic. *Españoles de tres mundos* (Buenos Aires, 1942) contains sketches of his contemporaries. By his encouragement of younger poets and by founding a number of short-lived but important poetic reviews he made a unique personal contribution to the progress of Spanish poetry between the wars. [DLS]

*Autocrítica* (Barcelona, 1954); *300 poemas* (Barcelona, 1963); *50 Spanish Poems*, tr. J. B. Trend (1950).

G. Palau de Nemes, *Vida y obra de J.R.J.* (Madrid 1956); A. Sánchez Barbudo, *La segunda época de J.R.J.* (Madrid, 1962); S. R. Ulibarrí, *El mundo poético de J.R.J.* (Madrid, 1962).

**Jirásek, Alois** (Hronov 1851–Prague 1930). Czech historical novelist. A history master by profession, he took up the historical novel at a time when the genre was already in decline. Although his chief aim was to transpose the glorious Czech past into fiction in order to rouse the nation's political and nationalist consciousness, he managed to create more than mere didactic novels. Using a modern realistic method, he focused on the economic and social forces shaping the events in the various periods he was describing, and, instead of concerning himself with fictitious individuals, he made the popular masses his heroes. During the First World War he was among the leaders of the nation's resistance to Austria-Hungary. His novels, in particular those from the Hussite period, such as *Proti všem* (1894) and *Bratrstvo* (1899–1908), had a great political influence and are still widely read. [KB]

*Sebrané spisy* (47 vols., 1927–43); *Gaudeamus Igitur*, tr. E. Vilímová (Prague, 1961); *Stories and Legends of Old Prague*, retold by M. Cochrane Vojáček (1931).

Z. Nejedlý, *A.J.* (Prague, 1952) (in English).

**Jocs florals (Jeux floraux)**. A poetic competition in medieval Provençal instituted at Toulouse in 1323 by seven troubadours

(*La Sobregaya Companhia* or Consistory of *Gai Saber* or *Gaie Science*) who met under a laurel tree and invited the poets of the South to a concourse on 1 May 1324. The first prize, a golden violet, was awarded for a poem to the Virgin written by Arnaut de Castelnaudary who was also given a doctorate in *Gaie Science*. At later meetings further prizes were given; a silver marigold for a *danse* and a silver eglantine for a *sirventes* (moral poem) or ⇨ *pastourelle*. The competition, somewhat like those conducted earlier by the poetic ⇨ *puys*, was itself imitated in the 14th century, especially in Catalonia. In the 15th century the Consistory was endowed with property at Toulouse where it still organizes a *Jocs florals* at the beginning of May. It was attacked by Du Bellay in his *Défense et illustration de la langue française*. The founding of this poetic academy marks the end of the creative period of troubadour literature.

An important adjunct of the *Jocs florals* was the *Leys d'amors*, a compendium of rules of grammar and composition for the guidance of ambitious poets. This work was compiled by Guilhem Molinier, chancellor of the Consistory, and was promulgated in 1356 in a letter addressed to kings, princes, merchants and artists. Molinier imitated earlier Latin grammarians but distinguished between dialects and emphasized the importance of *le bon usage* as a criterion. The *Leys* are important for an understanding of the technical skill of earlier troubadours. ⇨ Félibrige and Troubadours. [LTT]

*Las leys d'amors*, ed. J. Anglade (4 vols., Toulouse, 1919); *Les joies du gai Savoir*, ed. A. Jeanroy (Toulouse, 1914); Jeanroy, *PLT*.

**Jodelle, Étienne** (Paris *c.* 1532–1573). French poet and playwright. He studied in Paris at the Collège de Boncourt and was soon associated with ⇨ Ronsard, ⇨ Du Bellay and ⇨ Belleau to the point that he is normally ranked as one of the poets of the Pléiade. His main fame rests on his introduction of classical tragedy and comedy in France through his plays *Cléopâtre* and *Eugène* (ed. E. Balmas, Milan, 1955) performed at the Collège de Boncourt in 1552 and celebrated by Ronsard in a famous poem. It has been customary since then to deny any literary value to his work. Recently, however, there has been a reappraisal. [CAM]

*Œuvres*, ed. C. Marty-Laveaux (2 vols., 1866); *Œuvres complètes*, I, ed. E. Balmas (1965).

E. Balmas, *Un poeta del Rinascimento francese: E.J.* (Florence, 1962).

**Johannes de Alta Silva,** or **Jean de Hauteseille** (fl. 1180–1200). French writer. Author of *Dolopathos sive de rege et septem sapientibus*, a Latin prose version of the Seven Sages, or Book of Sindbad, a collection of oriental stories popular all through the Middle Ages. [FB]

Ed. H. Oesterley (Strassburg, 1873); ed. A. Hilka (Heidelburg, 1913).

**Johannes Secundus (Johann Everts** or **Everaerts)** (The Hague 1511–Tournai 1536). Dutch Latin author. Secretary to the Archbishop of Toledo, later to the Bishop of Utrecht. His best prose work is a lively account of his travels in France and Spain. In verse, he wrote a touching tribute to his dead father and epitaphs on Erasmus, Katherine of Aragon, Sir Thomas More, and other celebrities of his time. In his *Basia* (tr. F. A. Wright, 1930), love-lyrics in the vein of Catullus, he rises to great heights; his influence on English love-poets of the Caroline and Restoration periods was great. [FB]

*Opera*, ed. P. Burman and P. Bosscha (2 vols., 1821).

**Johannes von Tepl** (also known as **Johannes von Saaz**) (Schüttwa, Bohemia *c.* 1355–*c.* 1414). Pre-Reformation German writer. Author of a well-known work *Der Ackermann aus Böhmen*, written *c.* 1400 in the form of a dialogue between a peasant whose wife has just died, and Death itself; the peasant, sad and embittered, curses Death, but Death calmly expounds how Man is destined to die and how God has ordained it thus; as he begins to understand, the peasant submits to the Divine will, and when God himself sets the seal of His approval upon the final relationship between the litigants, the peasant prays in submission for the salvation of his wife's soul.

The *Ackermann* stands at the beginning of the Humanistic tradition in Germany and is the most masterly piece of German prose to be written before the Reformation. It presents a confrontation between dogmatic Christianity and the new spirit of the Renaissance. The chief influence on the work is that of Petrarch's *De remediis utriusque fortunae*, which had already been translated into German. [RT]

Ed. and comm. A. Bernt and K. Burdach (3 vols., 1917–32); ed. L. Hammerich (Copenhagen, 1938); ed. M. O'C. Walshe (1951).

**John of Hanville** or **Hauteville** (fl. late 12th cent.). French Latin satirist. Author of a long allegorical satire in hexameters, *Architrenius*. A young man who regrets his wasted youth goes to Lady Nature to complain. On his way he visits the palace of Venus, the house of Gluttony, and then Paris. The Mountain of Ambition gives him an opportunity to satirize the princely courts of the city, and the Hill of Presumption leads him to attack the clergy and the doctors of the schools at Paris. When he at last finds Lady Nature she comforts him with a beautiful wife – Moderation, who is to bring rich gifts to him. [FB]

Text in T. Wright, *Anglo-Latin Satirical Poets* (1872).
Raby, *SLP*.

**John of the Cross.** ⇨ Juan de la Cruz.

**John Scotus Erigena** (*c.*810–*c.*877). Irish churchman and scholar. He was made head of the palace school at Paris by Charles the Bald, where he is believed to have studied Greek. His *De praedestinatione*, written in reply to Gottschalk on the doctrine of predestination, maintains that evil is in reality non-existent. His greatest work, *De divisione naturae*, written in dialogue form, attempts to reconcile the Christian idea of creation with the neo-Platonist theory of emanation. After his death it was suspected of pantheism and during the 13th century was condemned by provincial church councils. [FB]

Migne, *PL*, 122; ed. L. Traube (MGH, PLAC, iii, 1896).
E. K. Rand, *John the Scot* (N.Y., 1906); H. Bett, *J.S.* (1925).

**Johnson, Eyvind** (Boden 1900– ). Swedish novelist and story-writer. Largely self-educated (like ⇨ Moberg, ⇨Martinson, ⇨ Lo-Johansson, etc.), his intellectual culture and imagination are wide-ranging. After several striking works (several of them written in Berlin and Paris) in the 1920s and early 1930s, he created his masterpiece with a series of autobiographical novels (1934–7): *Nu var det 1914*, *Här har du ditt liv!*, *Se dig inte om!*, and *Slutspel i ungdomen*. Based on his hard early life in the far north of Sweden, they combine sophisticated flexibility of narrative and symbolic form with acute psychological insight, and are outstanding examples of the Swedish semi-autobiographical genre. His humanitarian and democratic convictions inspired both some plainly anti-Nazi stories and the allegorical *Krilon* trilogy (1941–3), huge and uneven but sometimes gripping. His long concern with experimental fictional form, and with periods and episodes of crucial significance, has flowered in several novels of arresting originality since the Second World War. Among them are his modern version of the Odyssey, *Strändernas svall* (1946; tr. M. Michael, *Return to Ithaca*, 1952); *Drömmar om rosor och eld* (1949) on the famous 17th-century French witchcraft trial at Loudun; *Molnen över Metapontion* (1957), interweaving ancient Greece and modern times; and *Hans nådes tid* (1960; tr. N. Walford, *The Days of His Grace*, 1965), an impressive presentation of totalitarianism and individuality, thought-control and brain-washing in the empire of Charlemagne – at the same time an effective political and historical novel, and a moving love story. His latest novel, *Livsdagen lång* (1964), is another study of the time motif, ranging freely from the 9th century to the present day, and also a subtle and imaginative love story. He also published a number of 'diaries', often in the form of thoughtful travel notes or even analytic essays, which offer glimpses of his literary workshop: *Dagbok från Schweiz* (1949), *Vinterresa i Norrbotten* (1954) and *Stunder, vågor* (1965). A substantial selection of his short stories was published in 1944 under the title *Sju liv*.

O. Holmberg, *Lovtal över svenska romaner* (1957); E. H. Linder, 'E.J.' in *Fem decennier av nittonhundratalet*, Pt 2 (1966); *Bonniers litterära magasin* (7, 1958, and 7, 1960).

**Johnson, Uwe** (Cammin/Pomerania 1934– ). German novelist. His *Mutmassungen über Jakob* (1959, Fontane Prize; tr. U. Molinaro, *Speculations about Jakob*, 1963), written in East Germany before his flight to the West, explores the uncertainties and confusions preceding the death of a worker unwillingly drawn into the Berlin conflict; it was acclaimed in the West for its implicit rejection of the facile conventions of socialist realism. The (improbable) appointment of a Hamburg journalist to tell the party-line story of an East German cycling champion in *Das dritte Buch über Achim* (1961; tr. U. Molinaro, *The Third Book about Achim*, 1966) poses a similar problem of representation and truth. His conception of his own task as a writer is discussed in the sketch, *Berliner Stadtbahn* (1960). His latest novel is *Zwei Ansichten* (1965). [PB/AKT]

K. Migner, *Das dritte Buch über Achim* (Munich, 1966); H. Popp, *Einführung in . . 'Mutmassungen'* . . . (1967); Reich-Ranicki, *DLWO*; *ER*, XXI (Nov./Dec. 1961); Middleton, *GWT*.

**John the Exarch.** ⇨ Old Bulgarian Literature.

**Joinville, Jean, Sire de** (1225–1317). French chronicler. Hereditary seneschal of Champagne, whose family had already established a tradition of service on the crusades. He took the cross in 1248, having mortgaged part of his lands in order to pay his expenses. With him he had nine knights and about seven hundred men. He tells us that as he left his home he dared not look round '*pour ce que li cuers ne me attendrisist dou biau chastel que je lessoie et de mes dous enfans!*' He was befriended by Louis IX, wounded five times at the calamitous battle of Mansourah and shared the captivity of the king, becoming his constant companion. In 1250–1 at Acre he wrote a *Credo*, a commentary in prose on the Nicene creed. He returned to France with Saint Louis in 1254; his joy was manifest, and he refused the king's later request to accompany him on the ill-fated crusade of 1270. He was already 80 when he began dictating his memoirs, the *Histoire de Saint Louis* (in Pauphilet, *HCMA*, tr. J. Evans, 1938), composed for the wife of Philippe le Bel, Jeanne de Navarre, who asked for a book '*des saintes paroles et des bons faits*' of Saint Louis; Jeanne died in 1305, and the work was dedicated in 1309 to her son, Louis le Hutin. Joinville deals primarily with the first crusade of Saint Louis, his relationship to the king and the king's character. He describes his own exploits with modest simplicity and his good sense frequently appears as a foil to the exalted and saintly outlook of Louis. His interest in his surroundings, in the Bedouin and Mamelukes, his eye for detail, and skilful narrative reveal a civilized humanity. [LTT]

J. and Villehardouin, *Chronicles of the Crusades*, tr. M. R. B. Shaw (Penguin Classics, 1963).

H. F. Delaborde, *J. de J. et les seigneurs de J.* (Paris, 1894).

**Jókai, Mór** (Komárom 1825–Budapest 1904). Hungarian novelist, the greatest Hungarian narrator and writer of romantic prose. Son of a rich burgher family in Komárom, he studied law in Budapest, where his first work appeared in 1845. He became a friend of ⇨ Petőfi, who introduced him to the literary world and with whom he cooperated in organizing a reform movement echoing the ideals of the French Revolution. Jókai contributed to ⇨ Kossuth's daily *Pesti Hírlap* and became editor of the periodical of the revolutionary 'Society of Ten' (1847). Later his radicalism changed to Liberalism, but he retained his belief in human rights; he was respected and popular for his idealism and growing fame abroad. In 1848, he married Róza Laborfalvi, a talented actress. The strongest side of his talent is his vivid imagination; his tales are fantastic, eventful and gripping. His psychology is somewhat oversimplified; his minor characters and episodes, however, show his talent for realism. He excels in descriptions of catastrophe (flood, storm, mining disasters, etc.) and of nature. His humour, anecdotal, epigrammatic style, glib dialogue and moving speeches are masterpieces which presented ideals and proved consolation to a public crushed by the defeat of the War of Independence (1848–9). Extremely creative, Jókai wrote over 100 novels. His themes are varied and set in various historical periods, many during the Turkish occupation; *Török világ Magyarországon* (tr. R. Nisbet Bain, *The Slaves of the Padishah*, 1902); *Erdély Aranykora* (tr. anon., *The Golden Age of Transylvania*, 1897); *A Janicsárok Végnapjai* (tr. R. Nisbet Bain, *The Lion of Janina, or the Last of the Janissaries*, n.d.), all appeared in the 1850s. Even more important are his novels dealing with the first half of the 19th century; the anecdotal *Egy Magyar Nábob* (1894; tr. R. Nisbet Bain, *A Hungarian Nabob*, 1898) and its continuation *Kárpáthy Zoltán*, show the political progress of the Reform Age (1825–48), whose cultural struggles are told in *Eppur si muove* (1872). *A Kőszivű Ember Fiai* (1869; tr. P. F. Bicknell, *The Baron's Sons*, 1900) is a grand prose-epic of the War of Independence. Jókai scrutinizes the problems of Hungarian capitalism in *Fekete Gyémántok* (1870; tr. A. Gerard, *Black Diamonds*, 1896), whose hero is a democratic-minded scientist working for the creation of a Utopian society; in *Az Aranyember* (1872; tr. H. Kennard, *Man with the Golden Touch*, Budapest, 1963), a disillusioned rich self-made man finds spiritual peace in an idyllic love on a desert island. *Rab Ráby* (1879; tr. anon., *The Strange Story of Ráby Rab*, 1909) outlines the various conflicts of the Hungarian Enlightenment. Sándor Rózsa, the legendary outlaw of the War of Independence, is the hero of the rustic, romantic and concise novel *Sárga Rózsa* (1892; tr. B. Danford, *The Yellow Rose*, 1909). Because of his ability to integrate instructive Hungarianism with an artistic universality, it has been possible to translate Jókai's works into most European languages. His paper *A Hon* ('Homeland') played a considerable part in public life from 1863. [JFR]

Reményi, *HWL*; Klaniczay, *HHL*.

**Jónas Hallgrímsson** (Hraun, Öxnadalur, N. Iceland 1807–1845). Iceland's chief romantic poet. Educated at Bessastaðir, he went to Copenhagen University (1832) and spent his life mainly in Denmark. He visited Iceland in 1837, and spent the summers 1839–42 in the countryside there, collecting materials for his studies as a naturalist. In Denmark he was one of the editors of the famous Icelandic periodical *Fjölnir*, short-lived but influential, in which many of his poems first appeared. He radically affected the course of Icelandic literature by his vision of the beauty of the Icelandic landscape and of the greatness of Iceland's past. His poems are marked by purity of language, by an outstandingly felicitous formal mastery, and by the clarity and precision of his descriptions of nature. He can be grave and fervent with a deep appreciation of true manliness and great nobility of feeling. He is perhaps nearer to the young Wordsworth than any other foreign poet. [PGF]

*Rit*, ed. Matthías Þórðarson (5 vols., Reykjavík, 1929–36).

**Jongleurs** (Provençal joglars). From Latin *joculatores*, public entertainers in the Middle Ages who might be mimes, jugglers, acrobats or performers with animals. In the 12th and 13th centuries the *jongleurs* attained fame in France, Spain and Italy by singing the lyrics of the ⇨ troubadours and ⇨ *trouvères*, ⇨ *chansons de geste* and lays. Their repertory of works was immense and to assist their memory manuscripts were copied out by fraternities of *jongleurs*. In the case of works written anonymously such as the epic, a *jongleur* might improvise or refashion an episode to suit his audience. A *jongleur* might be employed by a troubadour and could rise to the status of *trouvère* or troubadour and compose on his own account. [LTT]

E. Faral, *Les jongleurs en France au moyen âge* (Paris, 1910); Rychner, *CG*.

**Jordanes** (fl. 550). Germanic author of *De rebus Geticis* (or *Getica*) a history of the Goths (tr. C. C. Mierow, *The Gothic History of Jordanes*, 1915), admittedly taken (and probably often copied) from a lost work by ⇨ Cassiodorus, whose vision of Roman-Gothic unity perhaps inspired Jordanes, praise not only of Gothic greatness but also unexpectedly of Justinian (*De rebus Geticis*, Chap. LX). Most striking is the attribution of respectable classical ancestors (Scythians) to the Goths 'wiser than all other barbarians and almost like the Greeks'; one prince even fought at Troy. The best chapters (Sect. 3) describe Attila's invasion of Gaul. His *Romana* is a sketchy history of the world from the creation (based on Jerome, *et al.*), an intended Roman companion piece to the *Getica*, but uninformed except as to recent history. [FB]

Ed. T. Mommsen (MGH, AA, II, 1882). Duckett, *GMA*.

**Jørgensen, Johannes** (Svendborg 1866–Svendborg 1956). Danish poet and essayist. A leader of the neo-Romantic revival of the 1890s, his *Stemninger* (1892) show the influence of French symbolism. Though his collections of poems remain his greatest literary achievement, he became better known abroad as a religious prose writer after his conversion to Catholicism (1896) and especially after settling at Assisi. Among his best known works are *Pilgrimsbogen* (1903; tr. anon., *Pilgrim Walks in Franciscan Italy*, 1908) and *Lourdes* (1910; tr. I. Lund, 1914), his hagiographies, of which the most famous are of *St Francis of Assisi* (1907; tr. O'Conor Sloane, 1912), *St. Catherine of Siena* (1915; tr. I. Lund, 1938), and *St Bridget of Sweden* (1941–43; tr. I. Lund, 1954); and finally his memoirs, *Mit Livs Legende* (7 vols., 1916–28; tr. I. Lund, *An Autobiography*, 1928–9). The candid self-judgement of the early parts of these memoirs make them comparable to those of Augustine and Rousseau. [ELB]

*Udvalgte Digte, 1884–1944* (1946).

E. Frederiksen, *J.J.sungdom* (Copenhagen, 1946); W. Glyn Jones, *J.J.'s modne aar* (Copenhagen, 1963); and 'J.J. in the Centenary of his Birth', in *Scandinavica*, v, 2 (1966).

**Joseph of Volokolamsk** (*c.*1440–1515). Russian churchman, politician and polemicist. Of Lithuanian stock, Joseph took the tonsure at an early age. After experiencing life in a number of Russian monasteries, in 1477 he became abbot of the Borovsk monastery, which was closely linked with the grand-princely family. Two years later, after quarrelling with Ivan III, he founded his own monastery near Volok Lamsky. It became one of the richest religious foundations in Russia and certainly the most influential in the 16th century, for in it were trained numerous hierarchs and churchmen who propagated the views of their founder. Most of the rest of his life was spent in the monastery: from it he conducted empassioned campaigns against the heretical sect of the 'Judaisers', against Archbishop Serapion of Novgorod who was rash enough to excommunicate him, and against his ideological enemies, the so-called 'Non-possessors' or 'Trans-Volga Elders'. Nearly all his writings are connected with these three campaigns.

His major work, known from the 17th century onwards as *Prosvetitel'* ('The Enlightener'), contains an introduction and sixteen chapters. The entire voluminous work is devoted to refuting the teachings of the Judaisers. The first eleven chapters deal with the history of the sect up to 1491 and contain a denunciation of their teachings together with an exposition of the true teachings of the Church. Chapters XII to XVI, written later, take the history of the sect up to 1505 and deal largely with the question of how the heretics should be ferreted out, judged and punished. One of the most important questions discussed in the *Prosvetitel'* is the attitude of the Church to the State: in the earlier part (Chs VI and VII) Joseph advocates conditional obedience to the State and upholds the doctrine of the spritual supremacy of the Church. In the last chapter, however, written *c.* 1510–11, after the death of Ivan III and after the State had more or less satisfied Joseph's demands that the heretics be eradicated he put forward the theme of the absolute power of the autocrat: the tsar, as the representative of God on earth, has the right to punish both civil and ecclesiastical offenders and although 'by nature is like unto all men, by power is like unto Almighty God' – an idea patently borrowed from Agapetus.

His 'Monastic Rule' or 'Testament' is mainly concerned with the behaviour of monks in his monastery and contains stringent rules of discipline: in the short, or early, redaction of the work Joseph stresses the equality of the monks and the absence of personal possessions. In the long redaction, compiled probably just before his death, he refrains from mentioning the theme of equality of privilege or possession.

He also wrote a large number of epistles, many of which he incorporated into the above. His writing is largely of a compilatory nature. Massive and frequent quotations are used to bolster up his theological argumentation; frequently the quotations, which display an immense erudition, are linked together with considerable skill. His non-compilatory writing is concise, logical and stylistically uninteresting. He uses a turgid but clear language based largely on Old Church Slavonic. [JLIF]

*Poslaniya*, ed. A. A. Zimin and Ya. S. Lur'ye (1959).

Ya. S. Lur'ye, *Ideologicheskaya bor'ba v russkoy publitsistike kontsa XV – nachala XVI veka* (1960); N. A. Kazakova and Ya. S. Lur'ye, *Antifeodal'nyye yereticheskiye dvizheniya na Rusi XIV - nachala XVI veka* (1955).

**Jósika, Baron Miklós** (Torda 1794–Dresden 1865). Transylvanian-Hungarian writer. A Transylvanian aristocrat, he was the first to introduce historical novels into Hungarian literature, and is often called the Hungarian Walter Scott, having similar gifts for narrative prose. His first and greatest work is *Abafi* (1836), which covers the late 16th century period of Transylvanian history. [JFR]

Reményi, *HWL*.

**Jotuni, Maria** (Kuopio 1880–Helsinki 1943). Finnish fiction writer and dramatist. Beginning with short stories, she chose uneducated characters, in whom primitive reactions occur in their purest form. Love and death are her principal themes. A terse compressed style, relying mainly on dialogue and monologue, a keen eye for the humour of a situation, and a persistent undertone of tragedy, are already evident in her earliest collections (1905, 1907). In later volumes (1913, 1927) the naturalistic touches become rarer and a faint symbolism creeps in. *Tyttö ruusutarhassa* (1927) is one of the finest of all Finnish achievements in short-story writing. Similarly the longer tale *Arkielämää* (1909), describing a single summer day in the life of a small country community, with humorous and lyrical moments alternating like light and shade, is a subtle and delicate work of art.

As a dramatist, too, Jotuni was among the foremost of her generation. The early *Vanha koti* (1910) is a conventionally Ibsenesque family drama, but in later plays, particularly the comedies *Miehen kylkiluu* (1914), *Kultainen vasikka* (1918) and *Tohvelisankarin rouva* (1925), she displays a strong dramatic technique and a gift for satirical humour. *Olen syyllinen* (1929) is a study of guilt illustrated by the tragedy of Saul, while *Klaus, Louhikon herra* (1941) examines the impact of selfishness and violence on the sanctity and inviolability of the home.

The long novel *Huojuva talo* (published 1963) is an interesting study of human wickedness; though brilliant in some of its detail, its shape as a novel had not been fully worked out. Jotuni was an acute psychological observer: her realism is both firm and tender, and her ethical judgements are brought out by deft touches of humour and satire. One of the outstanding literary craftsmen of her generation. [VKS]

*Cœurs de femmes*, tr. J. L. Perret (Helsinki, 1929).

**Jouhandeau, Marcel** (Guéret, Creuse 1888– ). French novelist. He taught in Passy from 1912 until 1949. Between his first novel *La jeunesse de Théophile* (1921) and *L'école des filles* (1960), he wrote 70 works, a vast chronicle centred on the town of 'Chaminadour' (a name borrowed from a girl actress he had seen on a convent stage in Guéret in his youth). Here passions rage, crimes, vices and perversions abound but are given metaphysical significance by the author for whom God and Satan are absolute realities. For his ruthless dissection of human souls is a function of his belief that every human activity has its mystical counterpart; he detects the presence of the holy everywhere, especially in sin and abjection. His acute consciousness of human imperfection makes him remonstrate with God through his spokesman and double Monsieur Godeau (*Monsieur Godeau intime*, 1926; *Monsieur Godeau marié*, 1933, etc.). He has affinities with T. F. Powys (*The Only Penitent*) and sees the tragedy of the human condition in the rivalry between man and God and the possible failure of Creation. His is the heretic's approach to Christianity (cf. ⇨ Mauriac's near-orthodoxy), but his faith is no less solid and he is equally obsessed with the problem of salvation. [HG]

*Le jardin de Cordoue* (1938); *Chroniques maritales* (1938); *De l'abjection* (1939); *Essai sur moi-même* (1947).

C. Mauriac, *Introduction à une mystique de l'Enfer* (Paris, 1938); J.-L. Curtis, *Haute École* (Paris, 1950); J. Gaulmier, *L'univers de M.J.* (Paris, 1959).

**Jouve, Pierre Jean** (Arras 1887– ). French poet. He has lived mainly in Paris. The poetry of his mature years is religious in inspiration, and to its intense and mystical themes is allied a pattern of striking Freudian imagery (*Le paradis perdu*, 1929; *Les noces*, 1931; *Sueur de sang*, 1935; *Matière céleste*, 1937). War was seen by Jouve in apocalyptic, visionary terms; there are flashes of prophetic apprehension in *Kyrie* (1938), while in *La vierge de Paris* (1946), which remains his best-known collection, private meditation is counterpointed by the public disaster in an attempt to integrate guilt, suffering and vengeance. Later books explore the potentialities of poetry and the role of language: *Ode* (1950), *Langue* (1954), *Proses* (1960).

He is also an important novelist, e.g. *Paulina 1880* (1925), *La scène capitale* (1935), a considerable critic and essayist, a translator of Shakespeare, and the author of a measured autobiography, *En miroir* (1954). His powerful treatment of the themes of love and death and guilt, his strange, dense, haunting images, and the integrity of his artistic attitudes make him a remarkable figure in contemporary French poetry and the most notable successor to Baudelaire and Mallarmé. [MMC]

Starobinski, Alexandre, Eigeldinger, *P.J.J., poète et romancier* (Neuchâtel, 1946); M. Callander, *The Poetry of P.J.J.* (1965).

**Jovellanos, Gaspar Melchor de** (Gijón 1744–Vega 1811), Spanish poet, dramatist and politician. Studying law and theology at Alcalá University he met those members of his generation who were to lead the Enlightenment in Spain. Subsequently, a legal post in Seville (1768–78) introduced him to others, including Pablo de Olavide, who stimulated his interest in the drama as well as in education and economics. He wrote 2 plays, *El Pelayo* and *El delincuente honrado* (1773), the second clearly reflecting his interest in problems of guilt and innocence and the dramatic techniques of the French *comédie larmoyante*. His later work was mostly in the form of papers on economic, educational, artistic and literary subjects written for the guidance of the government or at the request of Academies. The most important of these was on agrarian reform (*Informe sobre la ley agraria*, 1794). He also wrote some effective satirical verse and was a prolific diarist and letter-writer. Perhaps his protection of artists and writers like Goya and ⇨ Meléndez Valdés, and the progressive system of education he introduced when he founded the Instituto Asturiano, were as valuable to Spain as anything he wrote. He fell from a ministerial post in 1798 suspected of Jansenist leanings, and was subsequently treated as a political subversive and exiled to Majorca. Lord and Lady Holland were active in trying to procure his release, and he returned to political power as a member of the Junta Central before his death. [ONVG]

*Diarios*, ed. M. Artola, BAE 85–86 (1956).
E. F. Helman in *Estudios hispánicos. Homenaje a Archer M. Huntington* (1952); John H. R. Polt, 'J. and his English Sources' in *Transactions of the American Philosophical Society*, New Series, Vol. 54, Pt 7 (Philadelphia, 1964).

**Jovine, Francesco** (Guardialfiera 1902–Roma 1950). Italian novelist. A teacher by profession, he began to write in his late twenties, but the best of his production is concentrated in the decade before his premature death. His stories (collected in *Racconti*, 1960) and novels (*Signora Ava*, 1942; *Le terre del Sacramento*, 1950, tr. A. Colquhoun, *The Estate in Abruzzi*, 1952) are mostly inspired by life in his native Abruzzi, with its old legends, customs and superstitions, on a background of poverty, social injustice and political unrest. A skilful blend of legend (the peasants, bypassed by civilization, out of time like mythical figures) and history (the struggle between Liberals and Bourbons in the 1850s, the occupation of feudal estates by the peasants in the 1920s) is the main characteristic of his 'poetic realism', and rates him as one of the best regionalist writers of the first half of this century. [GMC]

*Contemporanei*, ii; Pullini, *RID*.

**József, Attila** (Budapest 1905–Szárszó 1937). Hungarian poet. Of a Budapest working-class family whose father emigrated, he grew up in incredibly poverty-stricken circumstances. In his youth, however, he managed to study languages and to visit Vienna and Paris. He started writing at 17, when still at school, and became a free-lance poet. Becoming a Marxist, he joined the underground Communist Party but was expelled owing to doctrinal differences of opinion. As a member of the revolutionary group of poets of the early part of the 20th century, József was greatly influenced by the poetry of ⇨ Ady. Expressionism, impressionism, surrealism and the folk-style all affected his writings to some extent; in the re-discovery and refining of folk poetry, he followed a line similar to that taken in music by Bartók and Kodály, his contemporaries. After searching for an original style, he adopted a strict metre of closed syllables. An outstanding proletariat poet, his subjects vary enormously; though he often paints bleak rural scenes (*Holt Vidék*), his really characteristic subject is the drab, poor world of the working-class suburb, his homeland; *Külvárosi Éj* (1932; *A Város Peremén*, tr. J. C. W. Horne, *Upon the City's Outskirts*, Budapest, 1961). His poetry reflects a longing for love, humaneness, order, the triumph of intellect, and, increasingly, his inner struggles as an ill man (he became a schizophrenic, and eventually committed suicide by throwing himself in front of a train). Notable poems: '*Hazám*' ('My Homeland'); *A* '*Dunánál*' (tr. J. C. W. Horne, 'Beside the Danube', Budapest, 1948); '*Betlehemi Királyok*' (1929; tr. E. Kunz, 'The Kings of Bethlehem', Sydney, 1955); '*Én Nem Tudtam*' (tr. A. Nyerges, 'I did not know', Cleveland, 1947). Volumes of poetry: *Beggar of Beauty* (1922); *It's not me shouting, it's the earth rumbling* (1924); *Fatherless and Motherless* (1929); *Chop at the Roots* (1930). [JFR]

*Poems* (1966) (verse tr. by M. Beevor, M. Hamburger, T. Kabdebo, J. Székely, V. Watkins, ed. T. Kabdebo); *Poèmes choisis* (1961) (French verse tr. by P. Éluard, J. Cayrol, J. Cocteau and others, with preface by Guillevic).
Reményi, *HWL*; Klaniczay, *HHL*.

**Juan de la Cruz, San,** adopted name of Juan de Yepes y Alvárez (Fontiveros, Old Castile 1542–Úbeda 1591). Spanish poet and mystic. Also known as John of the Cross. Of humble origin, he became a Carmelite in 1563, joined Santa Teresa's movement to reform the Order and became spiritual director of her convent at Ávila in 1572. He was imprisoned by the unreformed Carmelites, escaped, and after some years spent in various monasteries was further persecuted and banished to a 'desert house' in Andalusia, where he died. His 3 great mystical poems in the Italian *lira* metre describe the emergence of the soul from the 'dark night' of purgation to attain union with God. They derive from the poetry of Garcilaso, perhaps by way of adaptations 'a lo divino', for the Carmelites were given to this kind of writing. They make use of Biblical images, e.g. from the Song of Songs, but attain a new music which soars like love-poems directed to a Divine Lover. A few poems in the *romance* metres and some religious glosses on popular refrains are less remarkable. He also wrote prose commentaries on his three mystical poems, of which only one is complete; they are sometimes pedantic, but helpful in elucidating his lofty symbolism. His *Obras espirituales* were published posthumously (1618); he was canonized 27 December 1726. [JMC]

*Obras*, ed. P. Silverio de Santa Teresa (5 vols., Burgos, 1929–31); *El cántico espiritual* (CC, Madrid); *Poesías completas* (1955); *Complete Works*, tr. E. A. Peers (3 vols., rev. edn 1953); *Poems*, tr. Roy Campbell (1960); Trend, *OBSV*; Perry, *HASP*; Cohen, *PBSV*; Terry, *ASP*.

P. Crisógono de Jesús Sacramentado, *S.J. de la C.* (1929; tr. K. Pond, 1958); D. Alonso, *La poesía de S.J. de la C.* (Madrid 1942) ; E. Orozco, *Poesía y mística* (Madrid, 1959).

**Juan Manuel, Infante don** (Escalona 1282–1349 ?). Spanish fabulist. A turbulent baron, and a nephew of Alfonso X of Castile. His *Libro de Patronio* or *Conde Lucanor* (1328–35; ed. A. González Palencia, 1942; ed. E. Moreno Baez, modernized version, 1953; tr. J. B. Trend, 1924) is a collection of 51 apologues or cautionary tales, which the steward or tutor Patronio uses to answer the questions of his pupil Lucanor. Each story points a moral. The framework is oriental, and came from the Jewish and Arabic wisdom literature. Many of the fables are Arabic also, though some are derived from Classical and even from more recent Spanish sources. Collections of such tales had appeared in Latin from the beginning of the 12th century, and Ramón Lull's works (⇨ Catalan Literature) abound in them. In form it recalls the *Arabian Nights*, but it contains no love stories. The tone is aloof and ironical, at times slightly humorous. His less well-known *Libro de los estados* (1330) reveals something more of its author's character and experience through his mouthpiece Julio, who comes to the court of a pagan king and converts his son (the finest incident in the book, modelled on the Buddhist legend of Barlaam and Josaphat). A very conscious artist, particularly that his works should be copied exactly, his laconic picturesqueness of expression is still striking. He also wrote an unfinished didactic novel, a book of advice for his son on such subjects as hawking and love, and a treatise on the Assumption. His poetry is lost. [JMC]

*Obras*, BAE, 51, ed. J. M. Castro y Calvo and M. de Riquer (Barcelona, 1955– ); *Libro de la caza*, ed. J. M. Castro y Calvo (Barcelona, 1945); *Crónica abreviada*, ed. R. L. and M. B. Grismer (Minneapolis, 1958).

J. M. Castro y Calvo, *El arte de gobernar en las obras de Don J.M.* (Barcelona, 1945).

**Judah ben Samuel Ha-levi** (Tudela *c.* 1080–Palestine, after 1143). Hebrew poet and Arabic philosopher. A physician who lived in Granada, Córdoba and Toledo, he took an active part in the literary life of his time. His early poetry was light and brilliant but became increasingly serious and of a national character. His poetry became ripest when he wrote his *Songs of Zion*. They followed his *Kuzari* (before 1140), an essay on national revival. In 1141 he set out on his longed-for journey to Palestine, but stopped on the way in Egypt. Among the Hebrew poets in medieval Spain, he is the most outstanding ; he was able to combine extraordinary power of language with sensitivity and sincerity. His religious and liturgical poems still survive in the prayer book of many Jewish communities. Of his life in Palestine nothing is known, but many legends surround his death there. [EE]

*Selected Poems*, tr. N. Salomon (Philadelphia, 1924); *Kitab-al-Khazari*, tr. H. Hirschfeld (2nd edn, London, 1931), and *Selections*, tr. I. Heinemann, *Kuzari : the Book of Proof and Argument* (1948).

R. Kayser, *The Life and Times of Yehudah Halevi* (1949); Baer, *HJCS*.

**Juhász, Gyula** (Szeged 1883–Szeged 1937). Hungarian poet. He started his career as a leading figure in the literary circle of Budapest University, and also member of ⇨ *Nyugat*, but gradually slipped into the background after becoming a teacher in various small provincial towns. His mood was made melancholy by loneliness and a hopeless love for 'Anna', an undeserving actress, which he expressed in tender lyrics of memories and yearnings. Juhász temporarily rose out of his lethargy first in 1908–11 while residing at Nagyvárad, then a centre of literary activity, and later owing to his sympathies for the 1919 Communist régime, when his poems (*A Sonnet to Work*) were inspired by humanist hopes and by ⇨ Ady's revolutionary ideals. Otherwise, Juhász's poetry, polished but inclining towards uniformity, includes impressionistic descriptions of the River Tisza region, and refined lyrics of solitude. Juhász wrote seven volumes of poetry, notably *Testamentom* and *Hárfa*, as well as some essays and stories. He committed suicide. [JFR]

Klaniczay, *HHL*; Reményi, *HWL*.

**Junge Deutschland, Das.** German literary and political movement of the 1830s. The document which became the policy statement of the group of writers who took this name to themselves – ⇨ Heine, Börne, ⇨ Gutzkow, Wienbarg, ⇨ Laube and Mundt – was Ludolf Wienbarg's *Aesthetische Feldzüge* of 1834. Their interest as a group was primarily political, not literary, and their political sympathies were radical left-wing. The idealistic, otherworldly pursuits of the Romantics they regarded as a betrayal of the true values of life, seeing the true subjects of human concern as the fate of mankind in the present, the moral and political challenge of the time, the fullness of life in the here and now. The inevitably restrictive and inhibiting effects of this attitude led to Heine's early defection from the group.

In 1835, under Prussian and Austrian pressure, the writings of the group were banned by the Bundestag. Heine and Börne had already sought political refuge in Paris, and the others dispersed to their individual interests. [RT]

H. Bieber, *Der Kampf um die Tradition* (Stuttgart, 1928); Dietze, *JD*; Brandes, *MCNL*.

**Jünger, Ernst** (Heidelberg 1895– ). German essayist and novelist. He ran away from school to enlist in the Foreign Legion (see *Afrikanische Spiele*, 1936; tr. S. Hood, *African Diversions*, 1954), volunteered in 1914, was commissioned, often wounded, and highly decorated for his leadership of storm-troops. His war experience – recorded in *In Stahlgewittern* (1920; tr. B. Creighton, *The Storm of Steel*, 1929, cf. many revised editions, esp. 24th edn 1942, *Ein Kriegstagebuch*), *Der Kampf als inneres Erlebnis* (1922), *Das Wäldchen 125* (1925; tr. B. Creighton, *Copse 125* 1930), and *Feuer und Blut* (1926) – influenced all his writing; its violence and pain he regarded not as aberrations but as revelations. His style (sometimes) mirrors the ecstatic clarity of perception which violent danger induced in him: a kind of aestheticism, an absolute focus on immediate things and sensations, transcending all personal feeling. This ideal of self-transcendence he developed into a totalitarian doctrine of society in *Die totale Mobilmachung* (1931), of the worker who achieves an ambiguous freedom through sheer achievement (*Der Arbeiter*, 1932). Though often quoted by Nazis, he remained critical of the regime, which had not realized the 'spirit' of his ideal. Later works, especially *Der Friede* (1943, circulated in typescript; tr. S. O. Hood, *The Peace*, 1948) and *Strahlungen* (1949) search for a more individual meaning in suffering and sacrifice. But his allegorical novels, e.g. *Auf den Marmorklippen* (1939; tr. S. O. Hood, *On the Marble Cliffs*, 1947), *Heliopolis* (1949), *Gläserne Bienen* (1957; tr. L. Bogan and E. Mayer, *The Glass Bees*, N.Y., 1961), which trace confusing conflicts between principles of anarchy and despotism, violence and contemplation, show little imaginative feeling for individual character. Most striking are passages of nature description, often minutely observed – he had studied zoology at Leipzig and Naples (1923–5) – which distinguish also many fine essays (e.g. *Blätter und Steine*, 1934) and travel books (e.g. *Eine Inselfuhrung*, 1948). [PB/AKT]

*Werke* (10 vols., 1960–65.).

J. P. Stern, *E.J.* (1953); G. Loose, *E.J. Gestalt und Werk* (Frankfurt/M., 1957); K. O. Paetal *E.J.* (Reinbek, 1962); *GLL*, II (1948–9) V (1951–2); *Philobiblon*, IV, 1960 (bibliography).

**Jünger, Friedrich Georg** (Hanover 1898– ). German poet, essayist and short story writer. Like his brother Ernst, h opposed Nazism. His famous poem 'Der Mohn' (1934) was an outspoken attack (secretly circulated) on the false heroism of Nazi Germany; in 1937 he emigrated to Überlingen, Switzerland. A classicist by inclination, he has continued and revived traditional forms, including the *Spruchdichtung* of the late Goethe. His essays, e.g. *Die Perfektion der Technik* (1946), *Griechische Mythen* (1947, revised 1957), *Orient und Okzident* (1948), *Rhythmus und Sprache im deutschen Gedicht* (1952), discuss the relation of literary forms and traditions to other cultural and ethical values. *Dalmatinische Nacht* (1950) are stories, *Grüne Zweige* (1951) and *Spiegel der Jahre* (1958) autobiography. Apart from numerous small collections (e.g. *Die Silberdistelklause*, 1947), his collected poems (*Gedichte*) appeared in 1950 and in a new edition in 1959. [PB]

Bridgwater, *TCGV*.
L. W. Forster, *German Poetry 1944–48* (1950); *Philobiblon*, VII, 3, 1964 (bibliography).

**Jungmann, Josef** (Hudlice 1773–Prague 1847). Czech author and philologist. He played an influential part in the re-creation of the Czech literary language in the early 19th century, not only by his philological work (especially his Czech-German dictionary, 1835–9) but also by his translations (Chateaubriand's *Atala*, 1805; Milton's *Paradise Lost*, 1811 etc.). [RA]

*Spisy* (3 vols., 1869–73); *Překlady*, ed. J. Dvořák and others (2 vols., 1953) (translations).
V. Zelený, *Život J.J.* (1883).

**Jung-Stilling, Johann Heinrich** (Grund bei Hilchenbach, Westphalia 1740–Karlsruhe 1817). German writer. Jung's addition of 'Stilling' to his name, a reference to 'die Stillen im Lande', a pietistic sect, indicates his deeply pietistic convictions. After a poverty-stricken youth, he underwent a profound religious experience at 22, in which he felt that he had surrendered himself completely to God. Feeling himself to be called to be a healer of men, he read medicine at Strassburg, where he met Goethe and Herder, subsequently practising successfully as an oculist, before devoting himself to the study and teaching of economics at Marburg. His great work was his autobiography (tr. R. O. Moon, *J.-S.: his Biography*, 1938), the first part of which, *Heinrich Stillings Jugend*, was published at the instigation of Goethe in 1777, but which was not completed until 1817, when the seventh part was published. In spite of its somewhat questionable belief in the author's status as the elect of God, the autobiography with its warm humanity and devout religious faith is a masterpiece of its kind and achieved immense popularity. He also wrote a number of novels directed against the unbelief of the age which today are largely forgotten. [WAC]

*Werke*, ed. S. C. von Kepff (12 vols., 1841–60).
H. R. G. Guenther, *J.S. Ein Beitrag zur Psychologie des Pietismus* (Munich, 1928).

**Junimea.** Rumanian literary circle. Titu Maiorescu (1840–1917), literary critic, professor and politician, was the leading spirit in its formation at Jassy in 1865. From *Junimea* there sprang in 1867 the periodical *Convorbiri Literare*, which maintained a high standard for eighty years until its disappearance with the coming to power of Communism. In the circle of 'Junimea', Eminescu and Creangă gave the first readings of many of their works. [EDT]

**Junqueiro, Abílio Manuel Guerra** (Freixo de Espada à Cinta 1850–Lisbon 1923). Portuguese poet. Of country gentry stock, educated at Coimbra University for the bureaucracy, appointed Portuguese ambassador to Switzerland in 1911, he began his literary career as a member of the *escola nova* in the wake of Antero de ⇨ Quental. The themes of the new poetry were to be those of social and political reform. Poetry was to concern itself with 'real' things, poets should adopt the outlook and methods of scientists, remembering that they live in an age of analysis, of criticism, and of observation. Thus he insists that the themes of art must be universal; justice is for him an artistic ideal; he does not differentiate between moral and aesthetic values – characteristics which show him as a ready follower of Hugo and an imitator of the Parnassians, though he was also influenced directly or indirectly by the satanism of Baudelaire.

Junqueiro satirized the romantic ideal of love in *A Morte de D. João* (1874); current clerical attitudes in *A Velhice do Padre Eterno* (1885); the House of Bragança in *Finis Patriae* (1890) which was inspired by the Ultimatum, and *A Pátria* (1896). His work culminated in *Os Simples* (1892) where his poetic powers are seen at their best: his grandiloquent tongue, his power of caricature, and his ability to give life to abstract ideas by literary characterization.

Hardly distinguished in mind and sensibility, his extraordinary verbal gift ensured him in his lifetime a popularity which it is now difficult convincingly to explain. His desk was that of a tribune of the people (though the number of *A Aguia* dedicated to him revealed his following among the élite). [ARM]

A. Cabral, *O talento e os desvarios de G.J.* (Lisbon, 1942); *Iberica*, v, 5 (1926); Lopes de Oliveira, *G.J.* (Lisbon, 1954).

**Juvonen, Helvi** (Iisalmi 1919–Helsinki 1959). Finnish poetess. Skilful in combining traditional forms with modern ideas and imagery. An isolated figure, who 'from her own soul gave a soul to natural phenomena, plants and animals' – as she said of Emily Dickinson, to whose poetry she was strongly attracted. Her religious 'self' is often represented in the poems by zoological images of shyness and withdrawal (bear, hedgehog, mole, tapir). She published 6 volumes, collected 1958. [RV]

*Sanantuoja* (1959); Ollilainen, *SF*.

# K

**Kabak, Abraham Aba** (Smorgon, Russia 1882–Jerusalem 1944). Russian Hebrew writer. One of the most prolific Hebrew writers, chiefly of novels. His first, *Levadah*, was published in 1905. It was followed by a number of sequels ending with *Nitzahon* 1923. Writing under the influence of Tolstoy, he showed the social and national problems of Jews living in an alien surrounding. This is particularly evident in his post-war novels written in Russia, whilst those written in Palestine leave the narrow confines of life in the ghetto and handle the wider conflicts of ordinary men and women. This is particularly true of his historical novel *Shlomoh Molkhoh* (1928–30). [EE]

*Bamishol Hazar* (2 vols., Tel Aviv, 1938). Waxman, *HJL*; Klausner, *HMHL*.

**Kačič-Miošič, Andrija** (Brist 1704–Zaostrog 1760). Croatian poet and publicist. A member of the Franciscan order, he taught philosophy and theology in Sibenik. Under the influence of the Englightenment he compiled a still valuable collection of prose and poetry concerning Serbian and Croatian history, *Razgovor ugodno naroda slovinskoga* (1756), in which he drew on the folk epic, whose style he copied, as well as on written sources. [EDG]

Barac, *HYL*.

**Kaden-Bandrowski, Juliusz** (Rzeszów 1885–Warsaw 1944). Polish novelist. An ardent follower of Marshal Pilsudski, he tried to assess the realities of modern Poland in his bulky novels (e.g. *Czarne skrzydla*, 1928–9). Despite its tendentious attack on peasant parliamentarians, the series *Mateusz Bigda* (1933) has great merits as a social document. His realism, however, is made overemphatic by his metaphoric style which seems to expose bulging muscles in each description. In his reminiscent mood he can be lyrical and humorous, as in his early short stories or in *Miasto mojej matki* (1925). [JP]

**Kaffka, Margit** (Nagykároly 1880– Budapest 1918). Hungarian writer. The first outstanding Hungarian woman author; a friend of ⇨ Ady. Born into the impoverished nobility, she became a provincial schoolmistress, then moved to Budapest to contribute to ⇨ *Nyugat*. After starting her literary career as a poetess, she took to writing short stories and novels. Her main interests were the moral and social problems of modern women. [JFR]

**Kafka, Franz** (Prague 1883–Sanatorium Kierling, nr Vienna 1924). Austrian novelist. He was the only son of a self-made Jewish businessman, whose dominant character obsessed him, influencing both his inability to marry, despite several engagements, and also his writings (see *Brief an den Vater*, 1919). Trained in law, he worked for a Prague Insurance Company until tuberculosis forced him to retire. He published too little during his lifetime to become known, he intended the incomplete manuscripts of his now most famous novels to be burnt after his death. His friend Max ⇨ Brod edited and published: *Der Prozess* (1925, written 1914–15; tr. W. and E. Muir, *The Trial*, 1955), *Das Schloss* (1926, written 1921–2; tr. ibid., *The Castle*, 1953), and *Amerika* (1927, written 1911–14; tr. ibid., 1938). Recognized above all since 1945 as one of the greatest European novelists, critics have differed considerably in their interpretation of his obscure meaning. This obscurity is of a unique kind, for it is expressed in a style that is a masterpiece of clarity. Not Kafka's art, but the world is incomprehensible; he has created a new kind of fiction to record the predicament of modern man, whose proudly lucid mind, heir to a spiritual tradition of great moral refinement, finds itself confronting an incomprehensible state of existence. Kafka's solitary central characters make the 'heroic' mistake of supposing that more resolution of purpose or ingenuity of mind would resolve the mystery. They are defeated at every turn by unexpected ramifications or new developments, which the author makes appear, however, not arbitrary, but in a sense 'necessary' – though without letting them fall within the hero's power to grasp or control. This nightmare necessity stems from some *basic* transformation in the character of existence: the hero finds himself inexplicably under arrest (*The Trial*), or transformed into an insect (*Die Verwandlung*, 1912; tr. W. and E. Muir, *Metamorphosis*, 1961), or trying to take up a job in a strange village where he believes, but no one can confirm, that he has been appointed to work (*The Castle*). The simplest human convictions – that one is innocent, that one deserves respect and affection, that one has a place in the world – have no basis in this altered reality. It is possible to interpret the transformation symbolically: as a way of showing the inappropriateness of man's (originally religious) assurance that the world is created and intended for individual human living (or in Marxist terms as a corruption of natural (?) human relations in society by capitalism). But the novels contain no such theoretical ideas and every attempt at allegorical interpretation runs into confusion. The hero experiences his monstrous dilemma like a seamless fabric of daily existence, in which his individual presence is an unwarrantable flaw: surely the reason for this flaw can be worked out, by tracing every conceivable thread to its end? But the threads have no end, the fabric no pattern. It is this negative vision which Kafka has seen with religious intensity, an intensity which makes any reading of his work as mere social satire, e.g. of bureaucracy, appear entirely superficial. For the depth of conviction with which he yet knows, within the endless relativity of existence, that its threads *absolutely* lead nowhere, transcends what reality allows to be known. This possibility of 'transcendence' is Kafka's only positive hope, the redeeming inspiration which persists in the absurd endeavours of his heroes, his own belief in any valid literary achievement – perhaps to save man in the very act of trying to unravel the meaning of his existence in terms which no longer make any sense, by showing him exactly what it is he is attempting. [PB/AKT]

*Beschreibung eines Kampfes* and *Beim Bau der chinesischer Mauer* (1931; tr. W. and E. Muir and T. and J. Stern, *Description of a Struggle and The Great Wall of China*, 1960); *Hochzeitsvorbereitungen auf dem Lande* (1953; tr. E. Kaiser and E. Wilkins, *Wedding Preparations in the Country*, 1954); *In der Strafkolonie* (1919; tr. W. and E. Muir, *In the Penal Settlement*, 1948–9); *Briefe an Milena* (1952; tr. T. and J. Stern, *Letters to Milena*, 1953).

H. Järv, *Die K. Literatur* (Malmo-Lund, 1961); M. Brod, *F.K. Eine Biographie* (Prague, 1954); G. Anders, *K.* (tr. 1960); W. Emrich, *F.K.* (Frankfurt/M., 1960); H. Politzer, *F.K.* (Ithaca, N.Y., 1962); K. Wagenbach, *K.* (Reinbek, 1964); W. H. Sokel, *F.K.* (Munich, 1964; London, 1966); Heller, *DM*.

**Kahn, Gustave** (Metz 1859–Paris 1936). French poet. Co-founder with ⇨ Moréas and Adam of *La Vogue et Le Symboliste*. His preface to *Palais nomades* (1887) justifies *vers libre*. More striking is his obstruse but rich imagery in *Chansons d'amant* (1891), *La pluie et le beau temps* (1895), *Limbes et lumières* (1895), *Livre d'images* (1897). He also wrote studies of Boucher, Fragonard, Rodin, and Baudelaire, and *Origines du symbolisme* (1939). [WA]

J. C. Ireson *L'œuvre poétique de G.K.* (Paris, 1962).

**Kailas, Uuno**, pseud. of Frans Uuno Salonen (Heinola 1901–Nice 1933). Finnish poet. The son of a farmer, at 18 he took part, like many of his schoolfellows, in the ill-fated Aunus expedition (to support the independence movement in Russian Karelia), a shattering experience which left its mark on him for life. Graduating from school in 1920, he went to university but soon discontinued his studies. He attempted a series of professions – journalist, advertising copywriter, temperance speaker, critic, translator – but could not settle down. Weakened by mental illness (schizophrenia) and a restless mode of life, he fell an easy victim to tuberculosis, from which a move to the warmer climate of Nice was unable to save him.

His first poetical attempts were unimpressive. Traces of the influence of German expressionism, which he himself introduced to Finland by publishing a set of translations (*Kaunis Saksa*, 1924), can be seen in the tormented early poetry, uneven and restless, in which he experimented uncertainly with forms and images. He was also attracted by and translated Baudelaire, and felt the same sensuous delight in the horrific products of a tragically obsessed imagination. With *Silmästä silmään* (1926) he was hailed as the foremost poet of the younger generation. Later, however, he disassociated himself from the boisterousness of ⇨ Tulenkantajat and his style became increasingly classical: terse, closely knit poetry, brooding ecstatically on 'Sleep and Death' (a collection published in 1931 had this title). The posthumous prose fantasies are of interest mainly as psychological case-material. [RV]

Ollilainen, *SF*; Tompuri, *VF*.
Allwood, *TCSP*.

**Kaiser, Georg** (Magdeburg 1878–Ascona 1945). German dramatist. Retiring from business life (including years spent in South America) because of ill-health, he became the leading Expressionist playwright. The author of 74 dramatic works, his dominant theme is the regeneration of man, brought about by shocks, accidents and desperate plights, which break the comfortable security of unthinking conventions, e.g. in the once famous *Von Morgens bis Mitternachts* (1916; tr. A. Dukes, *From Morn to Midnight*, 1920) where a bank clerk embezzles and absconds to 'live at last'. Perhaps the best plays are those in which spiritual transformation concerns not merely an individual but society: *Die Bürger von Calais* (1914), and the trilogy *Gas I* (1919; tr. H. Scheffauer, 1924), *Gas II* (1920) and *Die Koralle* (1920). In his Expressionist plays, he devised many techniques to bring out the *idea* (always more vital than the characters, who have no names, only functions, e.g. Billionaire, Citizen, Engineer, etc.); the language is stark, staccato, often declamatory (though the later works are more conventionally realistic). By comparison with both Naturalism and Neoclassicism, Kaiser's plays appeared both poetically alive and socially relevant, but his revolutionary naïveté and eloquent but sometimes unsympathetic or unlifelike figures are now of controversial merit. In 1933 his plays were banned; he emigrated to Switzerland in 1938. [PB]

*Stücke, Erzählungen, Aufsätze, Gedichte* (1966); *The Coral, Gas I* and *Gas II*, in *Twenty-Five Modern Plays*, ed. S. A. Tucker (1931).

W. Paulsen, *G.K. Die Perspektiven seines Werkes* (Tübingen, 1960); B. J. Kenworthy, *G.K.* (1957); Garten, *MGD*; Natan, *GML*, ii; Sokel, *WE*.

**Kaiserchronik.** ⇨ Konrad (Pfaffe Konrad).

**Kaleb, Vjekoslav** (Šibenik 1905– ). Croatian novelist and short-story writer. A schoolteacher before the war, he began to write at 35. His first collection of stories, *Na kamenju* (1940), depicted peasant life and its hardship. His novels, *Poniżene ulice* (1950), and *Beli kamen* (1955), dealing with the occupation, have earned him a considerable reputation in his own country. [EDG]

**Kaléko, Mascha** (Kladow 1912– ). German poet. She lives in New York, the wife of Chemjo Vinaver, the conductor and composer. Her poems: *Das lyrische Stenogrammheft* (1933), *Kleines Lesebuch für Grosse* (1934), and *Verse für Zeitgenossen* (1946) are lyrical *Zeitgedichte*; her 'melodious, mocking voice' (Thomas Mann) is reminiscent of Heine. [PB]

Bridgwater, *TCGV*.

**'Kalevala.'** The national epic of the Finns, a mythological poem of 50 cantos (22,795 lines) compiled by Elias ⇨ Lönnrot from folk poetry preserved by oral (sung) tradition and collected by him on his journeys among the eastern Finns. The poem opens with a description of the creation of the world and the supernatural birth of the principal hero, the eternal sage Väinämöinen; it ends when he departs from his people and is superseded by the son of Marjatta (i.e. by Christianity). The main body of the epic is concerned with the rivalry between Kalevala (the country of the Finns) and Pohjola ('the Northland'). The central theme is the wooing of the Maid of the North by the three Kalevala heroes: Väinämöinen the seer, Ilmarinen the wonder-working smith, and Lemminkäinen the warrior-adventurer. Ilmarinen wins the Maid by forgoing the Sampo, a magical object which will grind out eternal prosperity for Pohjola; a detailed description of the wedding marks the mid-point of the epic. Later the heroes of Kalevala steal the Sampo from Pohjola, but in the course of a sea-battle it is destroyed, and only fragments of it reach the shores of Kalevala to serve as a source of eternal good fortune. Towards the end of the poem comes a description of the wrath of Louhi, mother of the Maid, and her attempts at revenge, which are frustrated.

Into this framework are inserted episodes describing the amorous adventures of Lemminkäinen and the tragedy of the hero Kullervo (who dies on his own sword in expiation of his guilt as seducer of his sister), and other more lyrical episodes dealing with Väinämöinen's unsuccessful courtship of the maiden Aino and his playing on the five-stringed *kantele*, by which the whole of creation is enchanted.

The poem is in the traditional metre of old Finnish folk poetry, an octosyllabic trochaic line, with abundant use of alliteration and parallelism. Although the *Kalevala* is based throughout on traditional folk poems, and the number of linking lines actually composed by Lönnrot is negligible, the mass of material from which it was drawn had no unity of its own: the epic form was imposed upon it by Lönnrot with Homeric and other ancient models in mind, and throughout the work there is evidence of the activity of a conscious artist and the reflection of his personal ideas and conceptions.

The *Kalevala* has served as an important focus for Finnish nationalist feeling, and has provided inspiration and thematic material for many Finnish poets, artists and musicians. It has been translated into over 20 languages. The English poetical versions by J. M. Crawford (1888) and W. F. Kirby (1907) preserve the 8-syllabled trochaic line, but naturally fail to reproduce the subtleties of Finnish quantity and stress that are essential elements in the original metre: the resulting English metre is similar to that of Longfellow's *Hiawatha*, which was in fact partly inspired by an earlier German translation of the *Kalevala*. The prose version by F. P. Magoun, Jr (1963) may be found more readable. [VK]

K. Krohn, *Kalevalastudien I–I V* (Helsinki, 1924–8); E. N. Setälä, *Sammon arvoitus* (Helsinki, 1932); A. Turunen, *Lexique du Kalevala* (Helsinki, 1949); M. Haavio, *Väinämöinen, Eternal Sage*, tr. by Helen Goldthwaite-Väänänen (Porvoo, 1952); S. K. Langer, *Philosophy in a New Key* (N.Y., 1948); V. Kaukonen, *Elias Lönnrotin Kalevalan toinen painos* (Helsinki, 1956).

**Kallas, Aino** (Viipuri parish 1878–Helsinki 1956). Finnish writer. Daughter of the poet and folklorist Julius Krohn. In 1900 she married the Estonian scholar and diplomat Oskar Kallas. When she moved to Estonia, she threw herself with enthusiasm into the study of Estonian life and history. In her early stories, written in a realistic vein, she attacked the enslavers of the Estonian peasantry. Later, forbidden love became her central theme. In the collections published between 1904 and 1930 one can trace a steadily increasing mastery of the art of short-story writing. Her best works are perhaps the 'prose ballads', *Barbara von Tisenhusen* (1923; tr. A. Matson, 1925), *Reigin pappi* (1926; tr. A. Matson, *Eros the Slayer*, 1927) and *Sudenmorsian* (1928; tr. A. Matson, *The Wolf's Bride*, 1930) – interesting for the archaic, semi-Biblical language and for their powerful presentation of violent, instinctive love. Of a number of her stories she made stage adaptations, and some of these were later turned into operas by the Finnish composer Tauno Pylkkänen. Two other works of considerable merit are her biography of Lydia Koidula, *Tähdenlento* (1915), and the autobiographical novel *Katinka Rabe* (1920). *Löytöretkillä Lontoossa* (1944) recalls years in London (1922–34) when her husband was Estonian ambassador. The sufferings of the war years are reflected in 3 collections of poems, alive with an intense and glowing sadness. An exile in Stockholm 1944–53, she published 6 volumes of diaries and memoirs. All her books have appeared in Estonian. She has been translated into Dutch, Italian, Swedish, German and Hungarian. [VKS]

*Bathseba Saarenmaalta* (1932; tr. A. Matson, *Bath-Sheba of Saaremaa*, 1934); *Valkea laiva* tr. A. Matson, in *The White Ship* (a collection of Estonian stories in English translation, 1924).

**Kalloc'h, J. P.** ⇨ Breton Literature.

**Kalonymos ben Kalonymos** (Arles 1286–after 1322). Hebrew writer and scholar. Translator of many important scientific works from Arabic into Hebrew, and author of the satirical poem *Even Bochan* (Naples, 1489). He was a member of the famous Kalonymos family which produced over one hundred medieval Hebrew poets, writers and scholars. The liturgical poems (*Piyutim*) written in Mainz by *Kalonymos ben Moses of Lucca* (*c.*950) and his son *Meshullam* (*c.*976) survive in the synagogue service for the Day of Atonement. [EE]

Waxman, *HJL*; J. Chotzner, *Hebrew Humour* (1905).

**Kalvos, Andreas** (Zante 1792–Keddington by Louth 1869). Greek poet. He was educated in Italy, where he met and became closely associated with Ugo Foscolo, who exercised a considerable influence on his poetic development. When Foscolo went to Switzerland as a political refugee Kalvos followed him there (1816), and subsequently they came to England together. There for some unknown reason the two friends became estranged. Kalvos earned his living by translating religious works into Greek and by giving private lessons. He married an English wife, by whom he had a daughter, and when both died he returned to Italy for a while (1821); then to Switzerland, and afterwards to Corfu (1826), where he taught for a number of years as professor in the Ionian Academy. In 1852 he returned to England, he married an English wife again and lived until his death near Louth, Lincs., teaching in a girls' school run by his wife. His poetic output is small. Apart from a few Italian poems he wrote under the influence of Foscolo, he wrote only twenty odes in Greek, the first ten of which were published in Geneva as *I Lyra* (1824; intr. G. Seferis, 1942), and the rest in Paris (1826). In these the influence of the Italian classical school is manifest, but there is also a strong romantic streak in his verse. In style and language he is eccentric – he uses an archaic diction of his own making – and his poetry is ornamented with beautiful imagery and similes. Greece, and in particular the Greek War of Independence, supplies the subjects of his inspiration. [SJP]

K. Palamas, *Prota Kritika* (1912); H. Pernot, *La Grèce actuelle dans ses poètes* (Paris, 1921); *Nea Estia* (1946) (commemorative volume); M. Vitti, *A.K. e i suoi scritti in Italiano* (Naples, 1960).

**Kant, Immanuel** (Königsberg 1724–Königsberg 1804). German philosopher. His ideas were influential in forming the intellectual outlook of German *Klassik* (the Weimar period of Goethe, Schiller and Herder), and also of certain Romantic thinkers. The high place which art continued to enjoy in idealist thought owed much to Kant's definition in *The Critique of Judgement* (1790) of aesthetic pleasure as 'disinterested satisfaction'. Equally important was his conception of art as analogous to organic nature in that both exhibit a 'purposeless purposiveness'. The implication is that art unites opposites – and opposites are a characteristic feature of Kant's dualistic philosophy; it unites, for instance, the general with the particular, reason with imagination, the determinism of the phenomenal world with the freedom of human action. Although it is not clear how Kant intended the metaphysical implications of his thought to be taken, it is precisely these which most stimulated the literary and philosophical imagination of the period. Its generally enlightened, optimistic temper found confirmation in Kant's theories of the moral will, of the sublime, of the teleology of nature, etc., for its belief that there is an ultimate harmony between mind and universe. But whereas Kant had analysed the necessary limits and conditions governing man's spiritual relationship to the world in each of the three realms of epistomology, ethics and evaluative judgement (for which he wrote three separate *Critiques*) subsequent speculation transformed the relationship into mystiques of higher union, redemptive creativity, dialectical movement and tragic paradox. Thus, the metaphysics of ⇨ Fichte, ⇨ Schelling, ⇨ Hegel and ⇨ Schopenhauer variously derive from Kant. The profoundest influence of Kant's philosophy on an imaginative writer may be seen in Schiller, for whom it pointed the way from a naïve to a reflective understanding of ethical and aesthetic values. H. v. Kleist offers an interesting example of the kind of irrationalist response which could occur in a literary imagination. [AKT]

H. A. Korff, *Geist der Goethezeit*, iii (Leipzig, 1957); R. Wellek, *I.K. in England* (Princeton, 1931); E. Heller, *The Artist's Journey into the Interior* (1966); A. O. Lovejoy, *The Reason, the Understanding, and Time* (1961).

**'Kanteletar.'** A collection of Finnish folk-poetry published by Elias ⇨ Lönnrot in 1840–1 and consisting of 652 poems in the traditional Finnish trochaic folk-metre (cf. ⇨ *Kalevala*). Books 1 and 2 contain lyrical pieces, while Book 3 is devoted to ballads, legends and other narrative poems. The lyrics are predominantly mournful in tone with telling imagery drawn from nature or from everyday life; the singer laments his hard fate, his loneliness, his longing for an absent sweetheart or the death of a loved one. In the love songs, dancing songs and 'singer's words', however, the mood sometimes changes to intense joy. A special section is devoted to nursery and working songs, among which the grinding songs are of particular interest. The singer pours out his feelings as the handmill turns, and the work is lightened by the rhythm of the song. The boys' songs deal mostly with love and intended courtship, those of the men with disappointment in marriage or the premature approach of old age. The range of feeling is wide, with some humour and satire.

The narrative poems include not only ballads based on episodes in Finnish history, but also Finnish versions or variants of popular ballads well known in Central and Western Europe, e.g. *Valheritari* ('The False Knight') and *Lunastettava neito* ('The Maiden Held for Ransom'). Among the narratives with a Christian background, *Neitsyt Marian virsi* ('The Hymn of the Virgin Mary') and the Lazarus legend are noteworthy as artistic achievements of great beauty.

Selections have been published in Swedish, German and Hungarian. [VK]

German tr. H. Paul (Helsinki, 1882).

**Karadžić, Vuk Stefanovic** (Tršić 1787–Vienna 1864). Founder of the modern Serbian literary language. He took part in the Serbian rising against the Turks (1804–13), then took refuge in Vienna where he met the Slovene Panslav thinker, Jernej Kopitar, censor for the Slavonic publications in the Austrian Empire, who persuaded him to collect folk-songs and compile a dictionary and grammar. At that time literary Serbian was confined to the *Vojvodina* where writers used a mixture of church Slavonic and Russian. In 1814 Vuk published the first edition of his folk-songs (*Mala prostónarodna slaveno-srbska pjesmarica*) as well as a short grammar of Serbian (*Pismenica serbskova jezika po govoru prostova naroda*). In 1818 he published his great work, his dictionary (*Srpski Rjechnik*). For the rest of his life he continued to extend his collection of folk-songs, proverbs and folk-tales, revising his dictionary and campaigning to get his ideas accepted.

Vuk's reforms met considerable opposition, especially from the Serbian Orthodox Church in the Vojvodina, which considered him an agent of the Austrian government and the Catholic church and to be attempting to sever Serbian cultural ties with Russia. Particularly hateful to his opponents was his new orthography which adapted and simplified the Cyrillic alphabet so as to have one letter for each sound. His rule 'Speak as you write' gave Serbian a phonetic alphabet. These reforms were, however, accepted by the younger generation of writers, such as ⇨ Radičević, and in 1850 a group of Serbian and Croatian writers met and agreed to a standard spelling and grammar. In 1868 Vuk's orthography was officially recognized in Serbia.

Vuk turned writers' attention to the language and style of oral poetry as their main pattern, and this influence dominated until the late 1860s. He was also the first historian of the new Serbian state and his historical and ethnographical writings, e.g. *Miloš Obrenović* (1828), are a valuable source for our knowledge of the period. [EDG]

*Srpske narodne pjesme* (9 vols., 1891–1902); *Srpske narodne pripovijetke* (1897); *Srpske narodne polovice* (1900); *Gram i polem spisi* (3 vols., 1894–6); *Vukova prepiska* (7 vols., 1807–13).

Barac, *HYL.*

**Karamzin, Nikolay Mikhaylovich** (Simbirsk 1766–Petersburg 1826). Russian writer and historian. The son of a nobleman, he received a good secondary education in Moscow. An important influence on him was Novikov and his circle. Through them he became familiar with masonic ideas and with the trends in contemporary English and German literatures. In 1789 he visited Germany, Switzerland, France and England. On his return he founded *Moskovskiy Zhurnal* and became its main contributor (1791–2). He described his journey abroad in *Pis'ma russkogo puteshestvennika* (1789–90; tr. F. Jonas, *Letters of a Russian Traveller*, 1957), written under the varied influence of Sterne, Ossian, Thompson and Rousseau.

He was the main representative of the sentimental school in Russian literature. Its merits were: (1) the introduction of real human feeling, though exaggerated, into literary works; (2) the depiction of the 'small man' and everyday life. These elements laid the foundations of the so-called humanistic trend in Russian literature. His best-known work of fiction is his story *Bednaya Liza* (1792; tr. J. E. Elrington, *Poor Liza*, 1803), a sentimental account of the tragic end of a seduced and deserted girl. His poetry is sensitive and lyrical, but lacks originality.

In 1802 he started a historical and political journal *Vestnik Evropy* ('The Messenger of Europe'), but he soon gave up the editorship to become a court historiographer.

In 1811 he published a memoir *O drevney i novoy Rossii* (tr. R. Pipes, *On Ancient and*

*Modern Russia*, 1959). In it he expressed his views on the merits of a monarchistic and autocratic state.

The results of his research in Russian history were embodied in *Istoriya Gosudarstva Rossiyskogo* ('The History of the Russian State', 12 vols., 1816) – a colourful but one-sided account of Russian political history from the 9th to the 16th century. Notwithstanding its moralizing tendencies the work was a great success and became a classic.

He also made an important contribution to the reform of the Russian literary language. He attempted to clear it from too many Slavonic words, he adopted the construction of the spoken Russian and shortened the sentences. He also introduced new words into Russian. [MG]

*Bednaya Liza*, ed. W. Harrison (1964); *Russkaya Proza*, XVIII, v, vol. 2 (1950).

*SEER*, XIII (1954); XVIII (1959); *Zeitschrift für slav. Phil.*, 29/30 (1961/2).

**Karavelov, Lyuben** (Koprivshtitsa 1835–Ruse 1879). Bulgarian story-writer and publicist. Childhood travels with his cattle-dealer father and schooling in Plovdiv taught him much about his countrymen's life and their suppression by Greek and Turk. These impressions he used in the writings of a life spent almost wholly abroad in emigration. He went first to Moscow to read philology, but in fact ardently followed Russian radical and *narodnik* thought, studied ethnography and contributed to Russian periodicals the stories and studies of his homeland which form his *Pamyatniki narodnago byta bolgar* (Moscow, 1861) and *Stranitsy iz knigi stradaniy bolgarskago plemeni* (Moscow, 1868). His Gogolesque portraits of *dyado* Liben and *haji* Gencho in *Bălgare ot staro vreme* (1867) founded a whole line of elderly self-willed patriarchal heroes recurrent in Bulgarian literature.

No longer safe in Russia, he left in 1867 for Serbia, where he continued to preach radical ideas in his Serbian articles and stories, e.g. *Je li kriva sudbina?* (Novi Sad, 1869), modelled on Herzen's *Kto vinovat?* and Chernyshevsky's *Chto dyelat'?*. In 1869 he moved to Bucharest to join Levski and Botev in leading the Bulgarian revolutionary émigrés and publicizing their aims in his journals *Svoboda* ('Freedom', 1869–72) and *Nezavisimost* ('Independence', 1873–4). Broken by privation and Levski's betrayal in 1873, he turned to writing such 'pictures from Bulgarian life' as *Maminoto detentse* (Bucharest, 1875) and to educational journalism in his *Znanie* ('Knowledge', 1875–9). He lived just long enough to see his life's aim realized in Bulgarian independence. [VP]

*Săchineniya na L.K.*, i–vi (Sofia, 1942–3); Pinto, *BPV*.

B. Penev, *L.K. Zhivot–Lichnost–Tvoreniya* (Sofia, 1936); G. Konstantinov, *L.K.* (Sofia, 1936); M. Dimitrov, *L.K. Biografiya* (Sofia, 1959); Manning and Smal-Stocki, *HMBL*.

**Karinthy, Frigyes** (Budapest 1887–Budapest 1938). Hungarian writer. The best-known Hungarian humorist, and a member of ⇨ *Nyugat*. With a background of Budapest intelligentsia, he was a portraitist of urban life who strove to caricature and re-assess conventions of his time. His *Így Írtok Ti* ('The Way You Write', 1912) is a satirical panorama of the literary world, and a model of literary caricature. In *Tanár Úr Kérem* (1916), he draws a humorous and perceptive picture of the clash between adolescents and school. *Capillária* (1922) and *Utazás Faremidóba* (1916), further travel-stories of Swift's Gulliver, show Karinthy's quest for the grotesque and exotic. In his satires, he points out the absurdities of his age with brilliant use of paradox, irony and mock profundity. Though inclining towards scepticism, Karinthy was a sincere humanist. His most durable prose work is *Utazás a Koponyám Körül* ('Journey around my Skull', 1937), the accurate account of a brain-operation he underwent. Karinthy was also the translator of works by Swift, Heine, Mark Twain and Milne. [JFR]

Klaniczay, *HHL*; Reményi, *HWL*.

**Kārkliņš, Valdemārs.** ⇨ Latvian Literature.

**Karlfeldt, Erik Axel** (Folkärna 1864–Stockholm 1931). Swedish poet. Born on a farm in the province of Dalecarlia, he studied at Uppsala and later became a librarian in Stockholm. He was for a long time secretary of the Swedish Academy. In this capacity he was offered a Nobel Prize, which he declined, but the award was given to him posthumously in 1931. Karlfeldt is the voice of Dalecarlia in literature. His poetry is filled with the life of the province, its customs and traditions. He watches the march of the seasons and in particular loves to dwell on plants and flowers and to call them by their less-known names. Yet his aim is rarely to paint nature, rather to express a mood through natural symbols. The more conventional romantic strain of his first collection made room for a sense of rootedness and order in the two following collections, *Fridolins visor* (1898) and *Fridolins lustgård* (1901). Fridolin, the bachelor-poet, can perhaps be seen as a virile, communicative *persona* of Karlfeldt, who was shy and reticent. His technical mastery, in particular his strong sense of rhythm and word music, is fully developed in these two books, the latter of which contains his famous *Dalmålningar*, a selection of Biblical scenes in contemporary costume drawn in the manner of the simple folk-painters of his province. Here a past culture is re-created. The effect is at once humorous and nostalgic, but miraculously avoids both sentimentality and condescension. *Flora och Pomona* (1906) and *Flora och Bellona* (1918) reveal a more complex experience; they explore more daringly the darker sides of nature and the human soul. The poetic method is largely unchanged, but the mood it captures is often tinged with fear of moral dissolution, e.g. 'Häxorna' or with a new tenderness and melancholy, e.g. 'Träslottet' (on a visit to his mother's birthplace) and 'Sjukdom' (on his illness). His last collection, *Hösthorn* (1927), contains some of the most powerful poems in the language, e.g. the incomparable, richly orchestrated 'Vinterorgel', in which Nature through the sounds of the winds reveals her mysteries to the listening poet, and the solemn 'Höstpsalm', in which the poet stands on the threshold of a religious revelation. The collection as a whole is a summing-up of a remarkably consistent lyrical career. [SAB]

T. Fogelqvist, *E.A.K.* (Stockholm, 1941); K. Wennerberg, *Vårgiga och hösthorn* (Uppsala, 1944); C. W. Stork, *Arcadia Borealis* (Minneapolis, 1938) (introductory essay and a verse selection).

**'Karlmeinet.'** German epic poem, written *c.* 1300 in the area of the lower Rhine, possibly in Aachen. The title (*Carolus magnitus*, i.e. the young Charlemagne) applies properly only to the first part of the work; in fact the poem sets out to be a complete biography of the Emperor. It draws on material, both legendary and historical, that is treated in other medieval German poems (e.g. ⇨ Stricker's *Karl*); the section *Morant v. Galie* (ed. E. Kalisch, 1921) about Karl's wife who is accused of adultery exists also in a separate manuscript. Whether the whole work is the compilation of a single man is still open to question; the skill in characterization, however, together with the narrative vividness, are the undeniable marks of considerable literary accomplishment. [RT]

Ed. A. von Keller (Stuttgart, 1858).
M. A. Holmberg, *Karlmeinet-Studien* (Lund/Copenhagen, 1954); Ehrismann, *GDL*.

**Karpiński, Franciszek** (Hołosków 1741–Chorowszczyzna 1825). Polish poet. An impoverished nobleman from the south-east borders, he studied at the Jesuit academy at Lvov. He became famous for his pastoral love songs, but failed to secure a permanent literary patronage. His disillusionment is described in the poem *Powrót z Warszawy na wieś* (1784), which contains many informative details about his home and his mode of living.

Authenticity is the striking feature of his writing, and this alone lifts his subjects above the conventional sentimentality of the age. He could use sentimentality for a discreetly ironic purpose, as in his *Laura i Filon*, and needed to exercise his talent for adaptation and travesty. On the other hand, in poems like *Przypomnienie dawnej miłości* he would express emotion in an almost modern way, and it is therefore not surprising that the romantics thought so well of him. His devotional songs (*Pieśni nabożne*, 1792) are still sung; their lucid theology is by no means naïve and their language is free from obvious epithets. At 81 he completed his memoirs, *Pamiętniki*, disarmingly frank and youthful in style [JP]

Peterkiewicz and Singer, *FCPP*.

**Karyotakis, Costas** (Tripolis 1896–Preveza 1928). Greek poet. He earned his living as a civil servant and at the age of 32 he committed suicide. He published several collections of verse. He is above all a poet of disillusionment, bitter irony and despair with a fine and sophisticated sensibility in many ways *avant-garde* for his time. [SJP]

*Apanta*, ed. G. P. Savidis (2 vols., 1965).

**Kasack, Hermann** (Potsdam 1896–1966 German novelist, critic and poet. President of the German Academy. His fame rests largely on the widely discussed and translated novel *Die Stadt hinter dem Stro*

(1947; tr. P. de Mendelssohn, *The City Beyond the River*, 1953; opera in 1955, music by Hans Vogt), a political satire with a futuristic vision of life after death, reminiscent almost of Kafka in its hero's sense of alienation. He was influenced by ⇨ Loerke (whose diaries he edited, 1955) and regarded poetry as his main work, collected as *Das ewige Dasein* (1943); his novel *Das grosse Netz* (1952), stories *Der Webstuhl* (1949) and *Fälschungen* (1953), and essays *Mosaiksteine* (1956) have been less successful. [PB]

Keith-Smith, *ECGL*; *RLV*, XXX, 1964; *BA*, XXXI, 1 (1957).

**Kaschnitz, Marie Luise** (Karlsruhe 1901– ). German poet and short-story writer. From an old aristocratic family, she married the Viennese archaeologist Guido Freiherr von Kaschnitz-Weinberg. Her poems, *Gedichte* (1947), *Totentanz und Gedichte zur Zeit* (1948), *Zukunftsmusik* (1950), *Ewige Stadt* (1952), *Neue Gedichte* (1957), *Dein Schweigen – meine Stimme* (1962) and *Ein Wort weiter* (1965), are broadly religious in sensibility, humanistic in thought (with a cultivated historical consciousness), traditional (though very varied) in form, with effective free rhythms in *Zukunftsmusik*; her 'Roman Notebook' *Engelsbrücke* (1955) contains views on poetry. Apart from an interpretation of the *Griechische Mythen* (1943), she has written essays on the spiritual crisis of 19th-century man (*Menschen und Dinge*, 1945), radio-plays and short stories (*Das dicke Kind*, 1952). [PB]

*Überallnie* (1966) (selected poems); Bridgwater, *TCGV*; *Long Shadows*, tr. K. Bridgwater (Munich, 1966); *DR*, LXXXIV, 1958; *AGR*, XXXII, 4, 1965; *Schriften der Theodor-Storm-Gesellschaft*, XIV, 1965.

**Kašić, Bartulo.** ⇨ Dalmatian and Dubrovnik Literature.

**Kasprowicz, Jan** (Szymborze, nr. Inowrocław 1860–Harenda, Zakopane 1926). Polish poet. The first great writer of peasant origin in Poland, who absorbed folklore and gave it a new form of expression. Born in a village near Lake Gopło with which the oldest Polish legends are connected, he studied in Germany, but for political and financial reasons had to complete his education himself. Eventually he gained a professorship in comparative literature at Lvov.

His early poems, often clumsily worded, bordered on social *reportage*, and it took him more than ten years after the publication of *Poezje* (1889) to develop his individual form which he based on the metres and themes of medieval penitential hymns. The first four hymns appeared in the volume *Ginącemu światu* (1902), each an experiment in free verse and the musical pattern of associations. The images of his village childhood, however, recurred obsessively amidst ballad motives, fragments of myth and metaphysical queries, all seen through the beauty and terror of landscape. For once a genuine pathos of folklore was voiced. 'Ballada o słoneczniku' (1908) appeared in a volume of the same title, and is one of the best poems in the language.

The last phase in his life is well documented in the fascinating journal of his Russian wife, Maria Bunin, whom he married in 1911. *Księga ubogich* (1916) was, in fact, a memoir of reflections during everyday walks; *Mój świat* (1926) resembled peasant paintings on glass, naïvely realistic in detail and fantastic in colours. Here he identified the simple life around his home in the mountains with the retained vision of his childhood.

He was also a copious translator from Greek, German and especially from English (cf. his bold version of *Hamlet*, 1895, and his selection *Poeci angielscy*, 1907). But his importance lies in the structure of the longer poem. By using a technique of association he organized loose and fragmentary material into a pattern; he placed symbols in a clarifying context, sometimes at the risk of repetition. [JP]

*Dzieła*, ed. J. Kołaczkowski (1930); Peterkiewicz and Singer, *FCPP*; Pietrkiewicz, *PPV*; *SEER*, X, 28 (1931).

**Kassák, Lajos** (Érsekújvár 1887–1967). Hungarian poet. The chief representative of Hungarian abstract literature. In his youth he roamed Europe as a blacksmith and wrote of the desire of the working classes for a better future. In 1915, he launched the pacifist magazine *Tett* (Action), which was followed by *Ma* in 1916. Though left-wing in outlook, he proclaimed the independence of literature from politics. *Földem, virágom* (1935) is a collection of his poems, and *Craftsmen* (tr. W. Kirkconnell, in *A Little Treasury of Hungarian Verse*, Washington, 1947) is a typical example of his poetry. Significant prose works: two autobiographies, several novels and short stories. [JFR]

*Modern Language Journal* (February 1951).

**Kassner, Rudolf** (Gross-Pawlowitz, Moravia 1873–Sierre, Switzerland 1959). German cultural philosopher and critic. A friend of Rilke, Valéry, Yeats, and others, a great traveller (though a wheel-chair cripple) and connoisseur of many literatures, he stood for the old order of European culture, whose basic unity he tried to preserve and re-phrase in half-mystical, half-literary works. To the fragmented knowledge and values of the 20th century he opposed profoundly imaginative, indeed poetic visions of spiritual coherence of sense and soul and mind in man, and of nature and man and cosmos. Holding no 'philosophy', which he considered too abstract, he developed a *Physiognomik* (1932), i.e. an intuitive belief that true meaning is not conceptual but concrete; hence his interest in myth (*Die Mythen der Seele*, 1927, etc.). His best known work remains the early *Die Mystik, die Künstler und das Leben* (1900). It is perhaps in the 'concreteness' of his life's story that his private, precarious faith seems most impressive (*Buch der Erinnerung*, 1938). [PB]

*R. K. Gedenkbuch*, ed. A. C. Kensik and D. Bodmer (Zürich, 1953); Rychner, *A*; E. C. Mason, *Exzentrische Bahnen* (Göttingen, 1963).

**Kaštelan, Jure** (Zakucac 1919– ). Croatian poet. He began as a realist, taking his themes from the sufferings of the civil war and the German occupation. His later style has become more symbolic. His main works are the collections of poems *Pjetao na krovu* (1950) and *Malo kamena i puno snova* (1957), and his poetic drama *Pijesak i pena* (1958). [EDG]

**Kästner, Erich** (Dresden 1899– ). German satirist. His books were banned and burned (1933); he stayed in Germany 'to be an eye-witness and one day give evidence'. World-famous for his many subtly pedagogical children's books, especially *Emil und die Detektive* (1929; tr. E. Hall, *Emil and the Detectives*, 1960; filmed), the sentimental charm and verbal humour of his immensely popular novels, e.g. *Drei Männer im Schnee* (1935; tr. C. Brooks, *Three Men in the Snow*, 1935; filmed), *Die verschwundene Miniatur* (1936; tr. C. Brooks, *The Missing Miniature*, 1936), do not easily survive translation. His satire is best expressed in laconic poems, which skilfully shape conversational idiom to a fine point of wit and pathos (selection *Bei Durchsicht meiner Bücher*, 1946). His tragicomedy *Die Schule der Diktatoren* (1957) merely toys embarrassingly with its grim subject. [PB]

*Gesammelte Schriften*, ed. H. Kesten (7 vols., 1959); *Let's Face It. Poems by E.K.*, ed. P. Bridgwater (1963 (translations).

John Winkelman, *Social Criticism in the Early Work of E.K.* (1953), and *The Poetic Style of E.K.* (Lincoln, Nebraska, 1957); R. Bossmann *E.K. Werk und Sprache* (Brazil, 1955); L. Enderle, *E.K.* (Reinbek, 1966).

**Katayev, Valentin Petrovich** (Odessa 1897– ). Russian novelist and dramatist. Son of a schoolmaster, he volunteered for the Tsarist Army; during the Civil War he supported the Bolsheviks. He began writing in 1921. His best early work is *Rastratchiki* (1926; tr. L. Zarine, *The Embezzlers*, 1929), a lighthearted account of two naïve clerks who embezzle office funds and are in turn duped by more unscrupulous crooks. His novel about the first Five-Year Plan, *Vremya Vperyod* (1932; tr. C. Malamuth, *Forward, Oh Time*, 1933) is more orthodox, but remains fresh and humorous. His later work is less interesting with the exception of *Beleyet parus odinokiy* (1936; tr. C. Malamuth, *Lone White Sail*, 1937), a charming semi-autobiographical story of two boys in Odessa during the 1905 Revolution. It is part of a huge tetralogy (*Volny Chornogo Morya*, 1936–61). *Kvadratura kruga* (1928 tr. E. Lyons and C. Malamuth, *Squaring the Circle*, 1935) is his best comedy on the 'new morality' of the NEP period. Recent translations include *The Holy Well* (tr. M. Hayward 1967) and memoirs *The Grass of Oblivion* (tr. R. Dagleish 1969).

*Sobraniye sochineniy* (5 vols., 1956–7); Faber *RSS*; Guerney, *NRS*; Reavey and Slonim *SLA*; Yarmolinsky, *SSS*.

B. Braynina, *V.K.* (Moscow, 1960).

**Katona, József** (Kecskemét 1791–Kecskemét 1830). Hungarian playwright. Of middle-class background, he studied law then became an actor. With his five-act Shakespearean-style tragedy *Bánk Bán* (1814), he became the father of Hungarian drama. Written for a competition, it was not considered owing to its 'daring', and was published and performed only after

Katona's death; today it is unchallenged as a Hungarian classic. Its theme, though set in 13th-century Hungary, mirrors the problems of its author's time; hatred of foreign and tyrannical rule, and the poverty of the peasantry. Ban Bánk, regent of Hungary in the absence of King Andrew II, disarms a morally justified plot by the nobility on the life of the foreign Queen, Gertrudis. The outrage of his wife by the Queen's brother and the peasant Tiborc's staggering account of the misery of serfdom under the rule of the foreign court, however, lead Bánk to murder the Queen. This leads to his spiritual downfall, and almost Hamletian struggles with his own conscience. The exceptional psychological and theatrical qualities of *Bánk Bán* make it a masterpiece; it was the basis of F. Erkel's opera (1861). Katona's other works, such as *Žiska* and *Jeruzsálem pusztulása*, are of minor importance. [JFR]

Reményi, *HWL*; Klaniczay, *HHL*.

**Katyrev-Rostovsky, Prince Ivan.** ⇨ Russian Literature of the 17th Century.

**Katznelson, Jehuda Loeb** (pseud. Bukki ben Yogli) (Tchernigov 1847–St Petersburg 1917). Hebrew writer and scholar. One of the most forceful exponents of the idea that the physical and spiritual survival of Judaism is bound up with the land of Palestine. A physician by training, Katznelson wrote a penetrating study of the origin of hygiene among ancient Jews, *Yesodeh Tumah ve-Taharah* (1902). In his poetry and prose he wrote beautiful legends and fantastic tales. One of his best-known stories is the Song of the Nightingale, *Shviat ha-Zamir* (1903). He also wrote poetry and prose in Russian. [EE]

*Kevurot Neshamot* (1907); *Remach Avarim* (1908). Klausner, *HMHL*; Waxman, *HJL*.

**Kaverin, Veniamin,** pseud. of Veniamin Aleksandrovich Zil'ber (Pskov 1902– ). Russian novelist. The son of a musician, he joined the ⇨ Serapion Brothers in 1921; his first story appeared in the same year. From the first he was interested in complex plots and formal ingenuity and he took his subject-matter from a wide range. *Konets Khazy* (1926) is a story of the criminal underworld; *Skandalist ili vechera na Vasil'yevskom ostrove* (1928) and *Khudozhnik neizvesten* (1931; tr. P. Ross, *The Artist Unknown*, 1947) examine the attitudes of intellectuals to the Revolution and call for greater cultural liberty.

His subsequent works have been more conventional in their subject-matter and construction, but they are always well written and interesting. *Prolog* (1930) is devoted to the first Five-Year Plan. *Ispolneniye zhelaniy* (1936) and *Dva kapitana* (1940–5, awarded a Stalin Prize in 1946; Pt I, tr. E. L. Swan, *Two Captains*, 1942) reveal his ability to construct a good story. Since Stalin's death he has continued to campaign for greater intellectual and political liberty in *Otkrytaya kniga* (1949–56; part tr. B. Pearce, *An Open Book*, 1955), while his story *Sem' par nechistykh* (1962) indicates his continuing interest in criminal psychology. [RDBT]

*Sobraniye sochineniy* (6 vols., 1963–6.).

**Kazakov, Yuriy Pavlovich** (Moscow 1927– ). Russian short-story writer. His first stories appeared in 1953, and since then he has published comparatively little. A fine stylist, he builds his stories on atmosphere rather than on plot. He is interested chiefly in the inner world of human character; but this does not prevent him from achieving effects of great power, for instance the storm in *Man'ka* (1958). The brooding landscapes of northern Russia are often the setting for his solitary characters, sometimes adolescent as in *Goluboye i zelyonoye* (1956), or reprehensible as in *Otshchepenets*, later renamed *Trali-vali* (1959), or isolated as in *Arktur – gonchiy pyos* (1957), whose failings are unimportant beside their spiritual gifts. His individual style and approach have made him a controversial figure. He has been singled out by ⇨ Paustovsky for special praise, while in some sections of the press he has been attacked for decadence and pessimism. [RDBT]

*Goluboye i zelyonoye* (1963); *Y.K. Selected Short Stories* (in Russian), ed. G. Gibian (1963); *The Smell of Bread* (tr. M. Harari 1965).

**Kazantzakis, Nikos** (Herakleion, Crete 1885–Freiburg 1957). Greek novelist, poet, dramatist and traveller. He grew up amidst the bloody uprisings of the Cretans against Ottoman rule and for a time his family moved to the island of Naxos where he attended a French school run by Catholic friars. He later studied law at Athens. His first writings included numerous philosophical and literary essays, and translations of foreign works, mostly French and German. He wrote dramas, travel books, poems and several novels. A restless man, with an insatiable curiosity and avidity for experience, he travelled widely and incessantly in Europe, Asia and the Far East; his travel books, characterized by a romantic and intuitive grasp of people and landscapes, are notable. His intellectual explorations were equally wide: Bergson, Darwin, Nietzsche, Dante (whose *Divine Comedy* he translated very sensitively into Greek), Cervantes, Homer, Karl Marx, Lenin, Christianity, Buddhism.

His monumental epic, *I Odysseia* (1938; tr. K. Friar, *The Odyssey*, 1959), in 24 books and 33,333 lines (the number is of some occult significance), takes up the story of the Homeric Odyssey from the slaughter of the suitors and continues it with a new series of adventures upon which Odysseus embarks in search of a 'newer world'. He is presented alternately as a king, a warrior, an ascetic, a lover and a pilgrim, a hero not without a touch of the picaresque, who destroys old and withering civilizations, founds new ones, meeting in his wanderings lesser descendants of Buddha, Christ, Faust, Don Quixote, and questioning always the meaning of freedom as he searches for his soul and for God. It is a vast epic, having little depth, but much richness of symbol and imagery, and containing the full range of Kazantzakis's ideas and philosophical aspirations. His novels, written for the most part in his later years, are marked by a flamboyance in the treatment of heroes and situations and a great but uncontrolled energy. They have been widely translated and successful, especially *Vios Kai Politeia Tou Alexi Zorba* (1946; tr. C. Wildman, *Zorba the Greek*, 1952), *O Christos Xanastavronetai* (1954; tr. J. Griffin, *Christ Recrucified*, 1954), *O Kapetan Mihalis* (tr. J. Griffin, *Freedom and Death*, 1957), *O Ftohoulis tou Theou* (tr. P. A. Bien, *God's Pauper – St Francis of Assisi*, 1962), *O Teleftaios Peirasmos* (1959; tr. P. A. Bien, *Last Temptation of Christ*, 1960), and *Anafora Ston Greco* (tr. P. A. Bien, *Report to Greco*, 1965) a posthumous autobiographical novel. Kazantzakis spent the last decade of his life in Antibes, and died on the way back from a journey to China. [SJP]

*Greek Passion*, tr. J. Griffin (1959); *The Rock Garden*, tr. R. Howard (1963); *Japan, China*, tr. G. C. Pappageotes (1963); *Spain*, tr. A. Mims (1963); *Toda Raba*, tr. A. Mims (1964); *The Fratricides*, tr. A. G. Dallas (1965); *Travels in Greece*, tr. F. A. Reed (1966).

P. Prevelakis, *O Poietes Kai To Poiema Tis Odysseias* (Athens, 1958).

**Kazinczy, Ferenc** (Érsemlyén 1759–Széphalom 1831). Hungarian critic and neologist. After extensive education he became a county official, later district inspector of schools in Northern Hungary. In 1790 he established a short-lived periodical, *Orpheus*, advocating radical ideas. In 1795 he was imprisoned for seven years for his contacts with the secret Hungarian Jacobine society. After his release his vocation became that of remaking Hungarian culture. In 1811 he began the movement of linguistic, literary, and aesthetic reform, through epigrams attacking literary diehards who wished to keep Magyardom immune from Western influence.

He established many philological doctrines and enriched Hungarian diction with thousands of new words and idioms. His attempts to reform the language at will and create a suitable medium for his 'superior' style at the expense of practicality aroused much opposition. He obtained however the support of urban intelligentsia and his language reform was triumphant by 1819. It was the assertion of bourgeois progress at a time when political activity was barred and literature provided the sole means of its expression.

Kazinczy is the 'father of Hungarian criticism'. Although tending to overpraise in order to encourage budding writers, he enriched Hungarian critical intelligence and motivated new ideas on criticism. His own criticism dealt not so much with content, matter or originality but with style, tone and choice of words.

Not an outstanding creative artist, he was against originality but strove to copy bourgeois styles and literature from Western countries. To this end he translated works by Molière, Shakespeare, Goethe, Schiller, Lessing and Klopstock.

First to write sonnets in Hungarian, he also wrote elegies, odes and bucolics (published after his death in periodicals). Other works include *Poétai epistólák* (1819); *Tövisek és Virágok* (1811); *Pályám emlékezete* (1828); *Fogságom naplója* (1828); *Erdélyi levelek* (n.d.); *A mi nyelvünk* (n.d.; tr. W. Kirkconnel, *Our Tongue*, Winnipeg, 1933); *A sajka* (n.d.; tr. ibid., *The Boat*). [JFR]

Vorks and Letters, ed. Hungarian Academy (22 vols., 1890–1927).
*SEER*, XXIX, 72 (1950); XXXVIII, 91 (1960).

**Kedrin, Dmitry** (Bogodukhovo, Donbass 1907– ? 1945). Russian poet. From a mining village, he became a journalist and moved to Moscow (1931) where Gor'ky highly praised his poem *Kukla* (1932). He remained almost totally unknown during his life. His most remarkable long poem, *Zodchie* (1938), recounts a legend of Ivan the Terrible's cruel treatment of the architects of St Basil's Cathedral in Moscow; fascinated horror at gratuitous suffering forms an important element in his work. In the Second World War he was one of the few to express adequately the bewildered misery of the civilian population. Ironically, this timid and kindly poet was murdered by unknown assailants. His verse, angular and naïve, conveys pathos illumined with flashes of hope. [RM-G]

*Izbrannoye* (with introduction, 1957); Gulland, *SRV*; Lugovskoy, *RSP*.
P. A. Tartakovsky, *D.K.* (Moscow, 1963).

**Keller, Gottfried** (Zürich 1819–Kilchberg 1890). Swiss writer. The son of a carpenter, whose early death left the family in penury; on leaving school in 1834, he turned to desultory studies and painting. After two years in Munich (1840–2) he gave up painting for lack of talent. A first volume of poems (1846) brought him a scholarship from the Zürich town council, which enabled him to complete his education in Germany. He went to Heidelberg (1848), where he came under the influence of ⇨ Feuerbach, then to Berlin (1850–5); returning to Zürich, he became town clerk there (1861–71). The first version of his autobiographical novel, *Der grüne Heinrich*, begun in 1846, was completed in 1855 and met with a poor reception; it appeared in its final form (with a first-person narrator) in 1878–80 (repr. Munich, 1959; tr. A. M. Holt, *Green Henry*, 1960).

*Der grüne Heinrich*, the last directly Goethean ⇨ *Bildungsroman*, represents a fruitful compromise between the Goethean notion of 'becoming', of the human potentialities for positive development, and the trammels and responsibilities of social life. The novel describes the boyhood, adolescence and early manhood of Heinrich Lee, known from his manner of dressing (and also from a certain callowness) as 'Green Henry'. Through pride, affectation and fortuitous circumstances the boy comes to think of his minor talent for drawing and painting as a great gift; leaves his native Swiss town to study art in Munich, fails to make his way, and finally returns, *via* some unconvincing romantic detours, to a modest post in the civil administration of his home town. Honest and unsentimental, Keller's moral psychology exposes the effects of his hero's self-indulgence and insists on the finality of wrong-doing. Yet the 'educational' philosophy of the genre is seen when Heinrich readily assimilates a bad action into his experience 'because it belongs to my person, to my story, to my nature, otherwise it wouldn't have happened!'

Least successful in filling the social canvas of city life, Keller showed himself master rather of the miniature world of his *Die Leute von Seldwyla* (i, 1856; ii, 1874), 10 stories set in 'Seldwyla', an imaginary little Swiss town which, in its slothful and foolish ways, owes something to the 'Abdera' of Aristophanes and to ⇨ Wieland. Each story is built round a single mania, an *idée fixe*: a drastic cure for sulking; the quarrel between the families of a village Romeo and Juliet; a wastrel's ruin made good by a prudent wife and son; maniacal thrift; greed – which enables a Faustian cat to cheat a Mephistophelean magician; a snobbish regard for clothes; the love of titles and noble ancestry; the affectation of a housewife who has fallen in love with literature; religious bigotry. Sometimes the characters move jerkily, like marionettes; the charm of such stories lies in their life-like artifice. From wit, lighthearted irony, farce, burlesque and caricature, through oblique and direct social criticism, all the way to the tragic manner, harsh satire and the grotesque – his stylistic range is remarkably wide.

In *Sieben Legenden* (1872) he retells in the manner of fairy-tales episodes from the lives of the saints and of the Virgin Mary, offering natural and mundane motivations for miracles, and moral judgements for divine grace. *Züricher Novellen* (1878) continue some of the themes of *Die Leute von Seldwyla*. *Das Sinngedicht* (1881) is a series of stories held together by a young man's quest for a girl who will come up to his notion of ideal womanhood. In *Martin Salander* (1886) the social and political optimism of *Züricher Novellen* gives way to realistic accounts of the intrigues and infamies of contemporary *bürgerlich* society. To this theme, too, are devoted some of his remarkable satirical poems (e.g. 'Jesuitenzug 1843', 'Lied vom Schuft', and 'Die öffentlichen Verleumder'). [JPS]

*Sämtliche Werke*, ed. J. Fränkel and C. Helbing (1926–49); *Gesammelte Werke*, ed. H. Schumacher (1960).

E. Ermatinger, *G.K.s Leben, Briefe, Tagebücher* (Stuttgart, 1924–5); G. Lukács, *G.K.* (Berlin, 1946); H. Böschenstein, *G.K.: Grundzüge seines Lebens und Werkes* (Bern, 1947); Walter Benjamin, 'G.K.', *Schriften II* (1950); B. Rowley, *K: Kleider machen Leute* (1960); E. Ackerknecht, *G.K.: Geschichte seines Lebens* (Konstanz, 1961); L. Ziegler, *Dreiflügebild: G.K., H. Pestalozzi, A. Stifter* (Munich, 1961); Natan, *GML*; Pascal, *GN*; Silz, *RR*; Staiger. *MDS, ZE*.

**Kemény, Baron Zsigmond** (Alvinc 1814–Pusztakamarás 1875). Hungarian novelist. A Transylvanian nobleman, he studied medicine in Vienna and later became editor of the daily *Pesti Napló*. The basic tone of his novels is that of pessimism; he was an individualist who believed that life is lost if personality is abandoned.

Major novels: *Özvegy és leánya* (1857); *A rajongók* (1859); *Zord Idők* (1862); he wrote several historical essays. [JFR]

Reményi, *HWL*.

**Kerr, Alfred,** pseud of A. Klemptner (Breslau 1868–Hamburg 1948). German critic. A famous, eccentric and controversial critic during the golden age of the Berlin theatre (1890–1933; emigrated to England), he championed Naturalistic drama, especially ⇨ Hauptmann and Ibsen. Publishing in *Der Tag*, *Die neue Rundschau*, *Das Berliner Tageblatt*, his best criticism was collected in *Das neue Drama* (1904), then in *Die Welt im Drama* (5 vols., 1917; new edn G. F. Hering, 1964). Famous as much for his stylistic wit, verbal coinages, etc., as for his dramatic judgement (as a connoisseur of theatrical taste and technique), his reviews are often better than the plays which inspired them. Also known for travel impressions, e.g. *Die Welt im Licht* (repr. 1961, ed. F. Luft), and poems in an effective, 'functional' vernacular, capable of both satire and lyricism (selection: *Gedichte*, 1955). [PB]

**Kesten, Hermann** (Nuremberg 1900– ). German novelist. He escaped Nazism to Amsterdam (1933; ran anti-fascist press, Albert de Lange) and to New York (1940). His radical novels, *Josef sucht die Freiheit* (1927; tr. E. Sutton, *Josef Breaks Free*, 1930) and *Ein ausschweifender Mensch* (1929) successfully characterized a typical post-war mood of rebellion against conventional ties of family and fatherland. The anti-Hitler novel *Der Scharlatan* (1932) was followed by classically liberal studies of tyranny versus individualism in the Spain of *König Philipp II* (1938–53; tr. G. Dunlop, *I, the King*, 1939; part of a trilogy). Perhaps the best example of his critical realism is *Die Zwillinge von Nürnberg* (1947; tr. A. St James and B. B. Ashton, *The Twins of Nuremberg*, 1946), which reflects a nation's fate in the fortunes of one family between 1918 and 1945. His concern for freedom, tolerance and justice, mingled with sceptical irony, appears in his stories (*Die 30 Erzählungen*, 1962), plays (e.g. *Wunder in Amerika*, 1931, with ⇨ Toller), literary reminiscences (*Meine Freunde, die Poeten*, 1953) and criticism (*Die Unruhe des Geistes*, 1959). [PB]

Reich-Ranicki, *DLWO*.

**Keyserling, Hermann Alexander Graf** (Livonia 1880–Innsbruck 1946). German cultural philosopher. His attempt to refresh the rationalistic aridity of European thought and reorientate its confusions with the spiritual wisdom of other cultures, especially of the Orient (where he travelled widely), and to teach in his Schule der Weisheit in Darmstadt (1920) that further realization of personality which he called *Schöpferische Erkenntnis* (1922; tr. T. Duerr, *Creative Understanding*, 1929), enjoyed a vogue characteristic of the period. His best known work is *Reisetagebuch eines Philosophen* (1919–25; tr. J. H. Reece, *The Travel Diary of a Philosopher*). [AKT]

M. G. Parks, *Introduction to K.* (1934).

**Khlebnikov, Viktor** (Tundutovo, near Astrakhan 1885–Pskov prov. 1922). Russian poet. He substituted the Slavonic name Velimir (usually misspelt 'Velemir') for Viktor. As a child of well-to-do parents, he lived in Volhynia, Simbirsk and Kazan, where he attended university (and was in prison briefly for participation in student riots). At Petersburg University (1908) he met D. Burlyuk, with whom he hatched ⇨ Futurism. After 1910 he began his lifelong wanderings through Russia, virtually without money or belongings, apart from his fragments of prose and poetry scribbled on innumerable bits of paper. His early verse was startling: an experiment in rebuilding Russian poetry from its philological foundations upward. Other Futurists also sought to revivify language and find a new, more direct expression of feeling through 'metalogical' verbal coinages (*zaumny yazyk*), but only Khlebnikov's experiments are of lasting importance, and based on real knowledge of Slavonic linguistics and folk-lore. He quickly achieved notoriety through an incantatory poem (*Zaklyatie smekhom*, 1910) constructed from derivatives of the root *smekh* ('laughter'), but his work gained a reputation (which it has not yet shaken off) for formidable obscurity, and has never become adequately known to the reading public.

He actively supported the Revolution, though his vision of it was typically idiosyncratic, Slavophile–utopian; however, his observation of its consequences was sharp and realistic enough. His vagrant life continued through the Civil War; in Kharkov he was arrested by both sides, suffered appalling illnesses and privations, and yet continued insatiably to travel and to write. His last journey was with the Red Army to Persia (1921). Worn out by the effects of typhus and starvation, he died soon after his return from the South. His death was a tragedy, not only for its painful circumstances, but because of the fine quality of his later works, concerned less with neologisms and esoteric mythology, more with the living world: with the Revolution, e.g. *Nochnoy obysk* (1921); with friends, e.g. *Tri sestry* (1920); with Nature, e.g. *Poet* (1919). His shorter writings are mostly fragmentary and include perfect, lucid lyrics; all show great sensitivity to the feel of words and subtlety of rhythm. He was a master of technical effects (one poem has over 400 lines, each one a palindrome), and despite his individualism wove into his lines motifs out of the whole range of Russian verse, from ⇨ Derzhavin to the ⇨ *byliny*. His influence has yet to be fully felt. [RM-G]

*Sobraniye proizvedeniy* (5 vols., 1930–3); Gulland, *SRV*; Markov, *MRP*, *PG*.

V. Markov, *The Longer Poems of V. K.* (Berkeley, 1962); *RR* (October 1960).

**Khomyakov, Aleksey Stepanovich** (Moscow 1804–prov. Ryazan' 1860). Russian philosopher and poet. After studying in Moscow and fighting in the Turkish War (1828–9), his poems and religious essays soon made him a central spokesman for Slavophilism (with Kireyevsky). His *Neskol'ko slov*... ('A Few Words by an Orthodox Christian about Western Beliefs') (1831) rejected the 'rationalist' and materialist heresies of Protestantism and Catholicism in favour of Russia's orthodoxy, where the pure spirit of Christianity is preserved especially among the people. The same mystique of nation and creed inspires his rhetorical poetry. He also wrote tragedies *Yermak* (1832), *Lzhe-Dimitry* (1833).

*Sobraniye sochineniy* (1900–7); *Izbrannyye sochineniya*, ed. Arsen'yev (N.Y., 1955); *Stikhotvoreniya* (Prague, 1934).

N. V. Riasanovsky, *Russia and the West in the Teaching of the Slavophiles* (1952); P. K. Christoff, *An Introduction to Nineteenth-Century Russian Slavophilism. I: A. S. Xomjakov* (The Hague, 1961); H. Kohn, *Pan-Slavism* (1953); M. B. Petrovich, *The Emergence of Russian Panslavism* (1956).

**Khrabr the Monk.** ⇨ Old Bulgarian Literature.

**Khvyl'ovy,** pseud. of Mykola Fitil'ov (Trostyanets, Sumy 1893–Khar'kov 1933). Ukrainian writer. He began with impressionist urban and romantically rural poetry (*Molodist'*, *Dosvitni symfoniyi*, an industrial poem *V elektrychny vik*, 1921–2), but achieved fame with his short stories *Syni etyudy* (1923). After *Osin'* (1924), critics declared him the most brilliant of the younger writers, a true reformer boldly breaking with tradition, the only short-story writer of the Revolution worthy of wider and lasting interest. Basically impressionist, deeply sensitive to the music of words, in his staccato prose he often apostrophizes the reader, inducing him to participate in the creative process. A convinced idealist Communist, for him the revolution in the Ukraine was an organic link in the chain of bygone Cossack and peasant revolts. The ugly reality betraying his romantic ideals is satirized in *Revizor*, *Ivan Ivanovych* and in his *roman engagé*, *Val'dshnepy* (part 1, 1927; banned and no more publ.). This, and his pamphlets written in the great Literary Discussion of 1925–8 in which he advocated orientation towards Europe, not Moscow, brought a rebuff from Stalin, which started a Party campaign against him and his numerous followers, culminating in the 1933 mass arrests and deportations, when, unrepentant, he committed suicide. [VS]

*Stari poeziyi* (1931); *Tvory* (3 vols., 1927–30); *Val'dshnepy* (Salzburg, 1946); *Vybrani tvory* (1932); Luts'ky, *LD*; *Stories from the Ukraine*, tr. intr. G. S. N. Luckyj (N.Y., 1960).

Luckyj, *LPSU*; Manning, *UL*; *UQ*, I, 3 (1945); X. 4 (1954); XIV, 4, 1958; *UR*, II, 4, and III, 2/4 (1955–6); XII, 1 (1965); XIV, 4 (1958).

**Kianto, Ilmari,** original name Calamnius (Pulkkila 1874–1970). Finnish writer. He began with lyrical poetry in the 1890s, but soon turned towards realism under the influence of the Russian writers and of Zola and Strindberg. *Punainen viiva* (1909) and *Ryysyrannan Jooseppi* (1924) are Finnish classics, combining descriptions of backwoods poverty and social criticism with a penetrating analysis of the Finnish psyche. Tragedy and comedy intermingle in a happy amalgamation. Kianto also excelled in nature description. His large output includes novels, stories and amusingly outspoken memoirs. [IR]

**Kidde, Harald** (Vejle 1878–Copenhagen 1918). Danish novelist. His *Aage og Else* (1902–3) is a melancholy book about love and death, while *Helten* (1912) expresses his ascetic Christian piety. *Jærnet* (1918) was to have been part of a philosophically ambitious tetralogy, prepared while living in Värmland, Sweden. His wife, Astrid Ehrencron-Kidde (1874–1960), was also a novelist. [ELB]

J. M. Jensen, *H.K.* (Copenhagen, 1948).

**Kielland, Alexander** (Stavanger 1849–Bergen 1906). Norwegian novelist and playwright. The son of a wealthy merchant, he took a degree in law and went into business, but had strong literary interests; he was much influenced by ⇨ Kierkegaard and J. S. Mill. His short stories are skilful – *Novelletter* (1879; tr. R. L. Cassie in *Norse Tales and Sketches*, 1896; and W. Archer in *Tales of Two Countries*, 1891) and *To Novelletter fra Danmark* (1882; tr. R. L. Cassie, ibid.) – but his masterpiece is the novel *Garman og Worse* (1880; tr. W. Kettlewell, *Garman and Worse*, 1885), set in his native Stavanger (as most of his work is) and with characters largely modelled on his own family. It combines sensitive description of Nature and milieu, mellow characterization, with biting criticism of social injustice and hypocrisy. Its 'sequel' *Skipper Worse* (1882; tr. Henry John, Earl of Ducie, 1885) – the action in it precedes *Garman og Worse* – is less effective. Kielland was a literary radical *par excellence*. He scourged the official classes, attacked the clergy and educational system, championed the poor and oppressed, and scorned writers whose work did not contain a definite *tendens*. This, in his other work, *Else* (1881; tr. M. M. Dawson, 1894), *Arbeidsfolk* (1881); the trilogy *Gift* (1883); *Fortuna* (1884; tr. R. B. Flandreau, *Professor Lovdahl*, 1904), *Sankt Hans Fest* (1887), and *Sne* (1886; tr. Henry John, Earl of Ducie, *Snow*, 1887), often made for facile characterization, lack of perspective and organic unity. His last novel, *Jacob* (1891), seems to suggest disillusionment with his campaign for social reform. His plays are unimportant. [RGP]

*Samlede verker* (12 vols., 1949–50).

G. Gran, *A.L.K.* (Oslo, 1922); O. Storstein, *K. på ny* (Oslo, 1949); B. Kielland, *Min far A.L.K.* (Oslo, 1949); Downs, *MNL*.

**Kierkegaard, Søren** (Copenhagen 1813–Copenhagen 1855). Danish philosopher. As a child he was dominated by his father, a self-made man, who could never forget having once cursed God when he was a child. Young Søren was kept away from other children, in an atmosphere of religious gloom, in which performing actions in imagination was considered more important than performing them in reality. In his early undergraduate years at Copenhagen, where he studied aesthetics and philosophy, he went through a period of dissipation, which weighed heavily on his mind afterwards. After his father's death he took a degree in theology; he was a brilliant student, noted for his ironic wit and sarcasm. In 1840 he was engaged to Regine Olsen, but in spite of his love for her he broke off the engagement – after vainly attempting to make her do so in order that no one might think she had been jilted.

His fame rests mainly on works published 1843–6 under various *noms de plume*; they are a new genre of philosophical essay, having the religious urgency of Pascal's *Pensées* even where they assume the character of works of the imagination. *Enten-Eller* (1843; tr. D. and L. Swenson and W. Lowrie, *Either/Or*, 1944) analyses two of the so-called 'stages' of life, the aesthetic and the ethical; the author identifies himself with the imaginary characters of the book, e.g. Don Juan, the Seducer (in the 'novel' within the book, *Forførerens Dagbog*, *The Diary of a Seducer*), and the Judge, a respectable *paterfamilias*. The third (and to Kierkegaard the highest) 'stage', the religious stage, is analysed in *Stadier paa Livets Vej* (1845; tr. W. Lowrie, *Stages on Life's Way*, 1939). Between these two books lie other analyses of religious psychology, *Frygt og Bæven* (1843; tr. W. Lowrie, *Fear and Trembling*, 1941), *Gjentagelsen* (1843; tr. W. Lowrie, *Repetition*, 1941), *Philosophishe Smuler* (1844; tr. D. Swenson, *Philosophical Fragments*, 1936), and *Begrebet Angst* (1844; tr. W. Lowrie, *The Concept of Dread*, 1944). In 1843 he also published (under his own name) his first volume of *Opbyggelige Taler* (4 vols., tr. D. Swenson, *Edifying Discourses*, 1943–6). His *Afsluttende uvidenskabelig Efterskrift* (1846; tr. D. Swenson and W. Lowrie, *Concluding Unscientific Postscript*, 1941) acknowledges all the books previously published under pseudonyms.

In 1846 he provoked a bitter feud with *Corsaren* ('The Corsair'), a radical Danish satirical paper (ed. M. A. Goldschmidt), and the ridicule to which he was consequently subjected in the cartoons of that journal gave him the feeling of martyrdom. This is the subject of his next two books, *Sygdommen til Døden* (1849; tr. W. Lowrie, *The Sickness Unto Death*, 1941) and *Indøvelse i Christendom* (1850; tr. W. Lowrie, *Training in Christianity*, 1941). Other important works of this period are *Kjærlighedens Gerninger* (1847; tr. D. Swenson, *Works of Love*, 1946), *Christian Discourses, and the Lilies of the Field* (1849; tr. W. Lowrie, 1939), the autobiographical work *Synspunktet for min Forfatter-Virksomhed* written in 1848 but published posthumously in 1859 (tr. W. Lowrie, *The Point of View for my Work as an Author* 1939), and *For Self-Examination* (1851; tr. E. and H. Hong, 1940). These works all express Kierkegaard's highly personal philosophy which (consciously hostile to the dominant school of Hegel) conceives 'truth' in terms not of a generalized system but of a quality in individual experience. His word 'existential' emphasizes man's tragic situation in a world that is religiously not in harmony, but incommensurable, with the gifts and needs of his spirit. Thus the truth of Christianity must be realized existentially, not just intellectually; it is a call to heroic action, and ultimately to martyrdom.

A eulogy of the Primate of Denmark, delivered by his successor in a funeral sermon in 1854, sparked off Kierkegaard's last and most violent battle, when he attacked in articles, pamphlets and a journal, *Øjeblikket* ('The Moment'), edited and written by himself, what he called 'official Christianity' (*Kierkegaard's Attack upon 'Christendom'*, tr. W. Lowrie, 1944); he died in the middle of it, a lonely man with hardly a single follower. He has been 'discovered' only in the 20th century, and has influenced both modern Protestant theology and the Existentialist philosophy (e.g. of Heidegger). [ELB]

*Papirer* (20 vols., 1909–48); *Selections from the Writings of K.*, tr. L. M. Hollander (1923); *The Journals of S.K.: A Selection*, tr. A. Dru (1938); *The Diary of S.K.*, tr. G. M. Anderson (1960); *AK. Anthology* (tr. R. Bretall, 1946); *K.*, Sel. and introd. by W. H. Auden (1955); *Glimpses and Impressions of K.*, Sel. and tr. T. H. Croxall (1959); *S.K.: The Last Years: Journals 1853–55*, tr. R. Gregor-Smith (1965).

T. Haecker, *S.K.* (tr. A. Dru, 1937); W. Lowrie, *S.K.* (1938), *A Short Life of K.* (1943); T. H. Croxall, *K. Studies* (1948), *K. Commentary* (1956); Å. Henriksen, *Methods and Results of K. Studies in Scandinavia* (1951); J. Hohlenberg, *K.* (1954); J. Heywood Thomas, *Subjectivity and Paradox* (1957); H. Diem, *K.s Dialectic of Existence* (1959); F. Brandt, *S.K.* (tr. R. Spink, 1963); G. Price, *The Narrow Pass* (1963); J. Himmelstrup, *K.: International bibliografi* (Copenhagen, 1962); P. Rohde, *S.K.: An Introduction to his Life and Philosophy* (1963); H. Fenger, 'S.K.: A Literary Approach', in *Scandinavica*, III, 1 (1964).

**Kiila** ('The wedge, arrow-head'). A Finnish left-wing group of writers and artists, founded in 1936, aiming at spreading cultural-political ideas among the working classes. It has published six albums of prose and poetry, one anthology of poetry and two periodicals. Leading figures are Elvi Sinervo, Arvo Turtiainen, Jarno Pennanen and Anja Vammelvuo. [IR]

**Kilpi, Volter** (Kustavi 1874–Turku 1939). Finnish prose writer and librarian of the Turku University Library. Handicapped by early and increasing deafness, he read both deeply and widely. At the turn of the century he was the Finnish 'romantic' *par excellence*, an 'aesthete' and worshipper of beauty, whose ideas owed something to Pre-Raphaelite influences. His earliest literary works, the miniature novels *Bathseba* (1900), *Parsifal* (1902) and *Antinous* (1903), though containing little action, are ardent and ecstatic personal statements of the aesthetic experiences to be derived from love, music and the pictorial arts. He was also a theorist, his views reflecting the influence of Nietzsche, Schopenhauer, and Kierkegaard.

After a long silence he produced two admirable works of social criticism: *Kansallista itsetutkistelua* (1917) and *Tulevaisuuden edessä* (1918). He then wrestled with a great regional epic, the trilogy of novels: *Alastalon salissa* (1933), *Pitäjän pienempiä* (1934) and *Kirkolle* (1937). These present a finely drawn cross-section of life in an island parish during the closing phase of the history of the sailing-ship. He developed a stream-of-consciousness technique, and boldly exploited the possibilities of the Finnish language; his vocabulary is rich and wonderfully alive. Frequent flashes of humour and tenderness reflect sensitive human understanding, and this trilogy has come to be regarded as one of the outstanding Finnish literary achievements.

*Suljetuilla porteilla* (1938) is a book of religious reflexions. The unfinished *Gulliverin matka Fantomimian mantereelle* (1944) is an interesting criticism of modern life, and his skill in describing the sea and sailing is again evident. [VKS]

**Kinck, Hans Ernst** (Øksfjord, Finnmark 1865–Oslo 1926). Norwegian novelist, short-story writer, playwright and essayist. A doctor's son he spent his childhood in Setesdal and Hardanger, and there gained those insights into the psychology of the Norwegian rural communities which were to be decisive for his later work. His preoccupation with the clash of cultures, the problems of race, and the influence of tradition and environment showed itself in his very first novels. *Huldren* (1892) and *Ungt Folk* (1893; tr. B. T. Eyck, *A Young People*, 1929), and subsequently in *Sus* (1896) and *Hugormen* (1898) – published as *Herman Ek* (1923); *Fru Anny Porse* (1900); *Emigranter* (1904); *Præsten* (1907); *Sneskavlen brast* (3 vols., 1918–19), his most notable achievement. Artistically he is most successful in his many collections of short stories, especially the richly imaginative *Flaggermusvinger* (1896) and the more realistic *Fra hav til hei* (1897). Those of his plays which are set in Norway deal with similar themes as his novels, most effectively in the verse drama *Driftekaren* (1908) and its continuation *Paa Rindalslægret* (1925). He spent much time in Italy, studying Italian history, art and literature, and wrote a number of plays with Italian settings, but they are weak dramatically; he also wrote a historical-biographical study of the Renaissance, *Renæssanse-mennesker* (1916). He wrote prolifically about the problems of race and culture, both in short-story and essay form; the essay collections *Rormanden overbord* (1920) and *Kunst og kunstnere* (1928) are the most representative. [RGP]

E. Beyer, *H.E.K., I–II* (Oslo, 1956–65); D. Lea, *H.E.K.* (Oslo, 1941); R. Nettum, *En undersøkelse av H.E.K.s livsyn* (Oslo, 1949); Downs, *MNL*.

**Kingo, Thomas** (Slangerup 1634–Odense 1703). Danish poet. The son of a weaver of Scottish descent he became Bishop of Funen in reward partly for his literary ability, partly for his loyalty to absolutism. He is the greatest exponent of the baroque style in Denmark, better known for his divine than for his secular poetry. [ELB]

*Aandeligt Sjungekor* (1674/1681); *Vinterparten* (1689); *Salmebog* (1699).

C. Ludwigs, *T.K.* (Copenhagen, 1924).

**Kirill of Turov** (12th cent.). Russian churchman and homilist. Born in Turov, northwest of Kiev, he became a monk early in life and was later made bishop of Turov. He wrote some eight or nine homilies, two or three 'precepts' (*poucheniya*) and about twenty-two prayers. His sermons, the most important part of his work, are written to celebrate various church holidays. In them the form is all-important – the content plays a secondary role. They are largely derivative in style and inspiration, SS. John Chrysostom and Gregory the Theologian being the authors most heavily leaned upon by Kirill, but for sheer exuberance and wealth of imagery they are unexcelled in all medieval Russian homiletics. [JLIF].

I. P. Yeremin, 'Literaturnoye naslediye Kirilla Turovskogo', *Trudy otdela drevnerusskoy literatury*, xi, xii, xiii.

**Kirk, Hans** (Hadsund 1898–Copenhagen 1962). Danish novelist. The son of a country doctor, he took a degree in law, but left the Civil Service to share the existence of a group of Jutland fishermen. His first novel, *Fiskerne* (1928), is based on his experiences and this 'collective novel' is the finest example of Danish social realism. *Daglejerne* (1936) and *De nye Tider* (1939) were the first two volumes of a trilogy which was never completed because the manuscript was lost when, during the Occupation, he was interned as a Communist. Among his later works the most important is *Vredens Søn* (1950), a novel in which Jesus is interpreted as the first Communist, and a volume of memoirs, *Skyggespil* (1953). [ELB]

**Kirsanov, Semyon** (Odessa 1906– ). Russian poet. Son of a tailor. He moved to Moscow in 1925. His first book was *Pritsel*, published 1926. He was a keen supporter of the Soviet government, and close friend of ⇨ Mayakovsky, whom he accompanied on travels and public recitals (1927–8). He worked for many years as a journalist and as a war-correspondent. His poetry is uneven, but at its best it amazes by sheer verbal brilliance. His copious production of good work during four decades is (in the U.S.S.R.) unusual; perhaps his best single poem, the long *Tvoya Poema*, dates from the inauspicious year 1937. Basically a grief-stricken account of his wife's death from tuberculosis, its complicated assonances and rhythms, its kaleidoscopic dream-landscapes and breathless pathos are a linguistic *tour de force*. Another long poem, *Sem' dney nedeli* (1956), a sardonic allegory against bureaucratic heartlessness, notable for its humour, fantasy and pungency, was one of the most startling contributions to the ⇨ 'Thaw'. His volume *Etot mir* (1958) contains sympathetic impressions of travels in Western Europe, together with translations from foreign poets. Owing much to Mayakovsky (verbal bravura, fantasy) he remains uniquely original, highly intelligent, a master of neologism, of wit and of surprise. Little known abroad or translated. [RM-G]

*Lirika* (1962); *Odnazhdy zavtra* (1964); Gulland, *SRV*.

**Kirshon, Vladimir Mikhaylovich** (St Petersburg 1902– ? 1938). Russian dramatist. A leader of the Russian Association of Proletarian Writers and successful exponent of the principle that plays should be political in content with valid views on current events. His early plays, *Konstantin Terekhin* (1926), *Rel'sy gudyat* (1927) and *Khleb* (1930), caused a sensation; the second – *The Rails are Humming* – was staged in London (Little Theatre, 1928) and New York, and was widely translated. The third, 'Bread', is dramatically more convincing, but less well known outside Russia (where above all *Chudesnyy Splav* remains popular). He died as a result of 'false accusation' (*Teatral'naya Entsiklopediya*) and was rehabilitated in 1956. [AP]

*Dramaticheskiye proizvedeniya*, intr. N. Stal'sky (1957); *Izbrannoye* (1958); 'Avtobiografiya' in *Sovetskiye Pisateli*, iii (1966).
Gurvich, *Tri dramaturga* (Moscow, 1936); L. Tamashin, *V.K.* (Moscow, 1965); O. K. Borodina, *V.K.* (Kiev, 1964).

**Kisch, Egon Erwin** (Prague 1885–Prague 1948). German-Jewish novelist and journalist. After Communist activities in Vienna and Berlin, he worked as an editor in Prague. He took part in the Spanish Civil War (1937–8) and emigrated to New York in 1939 and later to Mexico (1940–46). He returned to Prague in 1947. He travelled all over the world as a journalist, using the realistic travelogue and newspaper report as a medium of social criticism. His works include: *Der rasende Reporter* (1925), *Zaren, Popen, Bolschewiken* (1927), *Asien gründlich verändert* (1932; tr. R. Reit, *Changing Asia*, 1935), *China geheim* (1933; tr. M. Davidson, *Secret China*, 1935); *Geschichten aus sieben Ghettos* (1934; tr. E. Bone, *Tales from Seven Ghettos*, 1948); *Landung in Australien* (1937; tr. J. Fischer, I. and K. Fitzgerald, *Australian Landfall*, 1937); *Entdeckungen in Mexico* (1947). [LL]

*Gesammelte Werke* (8 vols., 1960 ff.).
E. Utitz, *E.E.K.* (Prague, 1956).

**Kisfaludy, Károly** (Tét 1788–Pest 1830). Hungarian poet and playwright. The first really successful Hungarian playwright. Brother of Sándor ⇨ Kisfaludy, he broke away from his noble background to live a Bohemian life. His main plays are *A Tatárok Magyarországon* (1819); *Kérők* (1819); and *Csalódások* (1828). [JFR]

**Kisfaludy, Sándor** (Sümeg 1772–Sümeg 1844). Hungarian poet. A noble landowner, he spent some time in the Provence as a soldier, then as prisoner. His poetry reflects the historical pride of nobility. His most famous series of poems are the *Boldog Szerelem* (1807; tr. J. C. W. Horne, *Happy Love*, 1939), and *Kesergő Szerelem* (1801; tr. W. Kirkconnell, *Torments of Love*, in *The Magyar Muse*, Winnipeg, 1933). [JFR]

**Kiss, József** (Mezőcsát 1843–Budapest 1921). Hungarian poet. Son of a village publican, he was the first poet to interpret Hungarian-Jewish themes, keeping within a popular-nationalistic style. He later lived in Budapest, where he wrote a large amount of urban-style poetry. Typical poems: *The Kiss* (tr. W. Loew, in *Magyar Poetry*, N.Y., 1899); *Judith* (tr. W. Kirkconnell, in *The Magyar Muse*, Winnipeg, 1933). [JFR]

**Kivi, Alexis** (original name Stenvall) (Nurmijärvi 1834–Tuusula 1872). Finnish poet, dramatist and prose-writer. Son of a village tailor; despite poverty, he went to school in Helsinki, qualifying for the University in 1857. At that time Finnish, as a modern written language, was only just beginning to crystallize, with the eastern and western dialects competing for supremacy. The language of the Church and of the Finnish Bible, going back to the 16th century, was based on Western Finnish, but ⇨ Lönnrot's publication of the *Kalevala* had enriched the language by introducing Eastern Finnish elements. His style was based on the speech of Western Finland, but such was his genius and the vitalizing power of his imagination that the modern literary language of the Finns must be regarded as essentially his creation, and no subsequent writer has surpassed him in the handling of it.

It was the *Kalevala* that gave him the subject of his first important work, the tragedy *Kullervo*, with which he won first prize in a drama competition in 1860. For the semi-mythical atmosphere of the original folk poem he substituted a powerful rustic realism somewhat reminiscent of Ibsen's *Haermaendene på Helgeland*. The influence of Cygnaeus, in whose lectures the tragic element in the *Kalevala* had been analysed in the light of Shakespearean tragedy, was clearly evident. Simultaneously he was working on his superb rustic comedy, *Nummisuutarit*. Details of the plot were derived from ⇨ Holberg, but Holberg's satire is here replaced by an affectionate humour. Esko, the chief character, is a simple-minded, plain-spoken and stubborn country youth, who arrives at the home of his supposed bride only to find her celebrating her marriage to someone else. The play presents a wide range of country types, but essentially it is a comedy of primal innocence. With its palpable hits at certain aspects of the national character, it is still extremely popular. He also wrote 2 'Shakespearean' tragedies, *Karkurit* (1867) and *Canzio* (1868), and 2 interesting one-act plays: *Kihlaus* (1866), a rustic comedy, and *Lea* (1869), a powerfully poetical religious drama set in Palestine in New Testament times.

In poetry he developed his own half-romantic style, seen at its best in the idyllic narrative *Lintukoto*, in which an essentially mythical tale receives a realistic and 'folk' colouring. His masterpiece is the novel, *Seitsemän veljestä* (1870; tr. A. Matson, *Seven Brothers*, 1929). Set in a remote country area in the 1830s, the novel describes the adventures of a group of brothers who refuse to conform with the demands of society and flee into the forest to live as hunters. Here their boyish love of adventure leads them by degrees into a hopeless situation, their social conscience is awakened, and eventually they become respectable farmers with an honoured place in their rural society. The humour of the characterization and the enormous gusto of the narrative prevents the didactic side of the novel from becoming too obtrusive. Kivi's method of narration is highly original, and perhaps unique in modern European literature: the brothers are viewed, as it were, from a height like characters in a Homeric epic, while the comic solemnity of their deliberations and the vividly objective descriptions of their adventures also have an epic ring.

Kivi was the first Finn to adopt writing as his sole profession. Constant poverty and the harshness of his academic critics wore him out before his time. In his last years he suffered from a mental illness. But his life's work, the product of a single decade, has made him, a century later, the best-loved and most intensively studied of all Finnish authors. [LV]

*Kootut teokset* (4 vols., 1915–19).

V. Tarkiainen, *A.K., elämä ja teokset* (Helsinki, 1915); J. V. Lehtonen, *Runon kartanossa* (Helsinki, 1928); P. S. Elo, *A.K. persoonallisuus* (Helsinki, 1950); L. Viljanen, *A.K. runomaailma* (Helsinki, 1953); E. Ekelund, *A.K.* (in Swedish) (Helsinki, 1960).

**Kivimaa, Kaarlo Arvi** (Hartola 1904– ). Finnish poet, novelist, and essayist. Director of the Finnish National Theatre since 1949. After studies at Helsinki University and abroad (Paris, Berlin) he was an active literary and drama critic, member of the liberal-radical 'Torchbearer' group in the twenties, internationally known for his activities to promote theatrical research, cooperation and exchange of ideas. His literary output includes 12 collections of poetry, 3 plays, essays, short-stories and 5 novels, of which *Saari tuulten sylissä* has been translated into German (*Die Insel im Schoss der Winde*). [IR]

**Klabund,** pseud. of Alfred Henschke (Crossen/Oder 1890–Davos 1928). German writer. Consumption and years spent in sanatoria conditioned in him a sensually refined, virtuoso genius: as lyric poet (first published by ⇨ Kerr in *Pan*), ranging from *fin-de-siècle* impressionistic moods to intense Expressionist imagery and some satires and grotesques–*Morgenrot, K...* (1912), *Die Himmelsleiter* (1917), etc.; as an Oriental translator (*Dichtungen aus dem Osten*, 1954), whose feeling for *chinoiserie* is finely expressed in adaptations, e.g. *Der Kreidekreis* (1924; tr. J. Laver, *The Circle of Chalk*, 1929), a drama adapted again by Brecht, and the consciously exquisite story *Der letzte Kaiser* (1923) where beauty is menaced by violence: a characteristic fascination as appears in historical novels like *Pjotr* (1923; tr. H. G. Scheffauer, *Peter the Czar*, 1925), *Borgia* (1928, tr. L. Brink, N.Y., 1929), and *Rasputin* (1929). [PB/AKT]

*Gesammelte Werke* (7 vols., 1930–33); Bridgwater *TCGV*; Hamburger and Middleton, *MGP*.

H. Grothe, *K.* (Berlin, 1933); *GLL*, III (1939), IV (1950); *PQ*, XXXVII (1958).

**Klaj, Johann** (Meissen 1616–Kitzingen am Main 1656). German poet. With ⇨ Harsdörffer the founder of the Schäfer- und Blumenorden in Nürnberg (1644), his verse exhibits the same characteristics: exploitation of the pastoral convention, the extensive use of dactylic metre and onomatopoeia and the attempt to render visual impressions in terms of aural effects. His most important works are 'linguistic oratorios' such as the *Weihnachtsandacht* (1644), *Der leidende Christus* (1645) or *Der Engel und Drachen Streit* (1645), but like all the Nürnbergers, he also produced much occasional verse. His eye for detail distinguishes certain of his nature poems ('Spazierlust') but the attempts to create verbal music too often degenerates into a meaningless game. [WAC]

A. Franz, *J.K.* (Heidelberg, 1908).

**Kleist, (Bernd) Heinrich (Wilhelm) von** (Frankfurt a.d. Oder 1777–Wannsee, Berlin 1811). German dramatist. He came of an old Prussian military family (Ewald ⇨ Kleist was a distant relative), but detested military life and resigned his commission in 1799 to devote himself to mathematics and philosophy and the cultivation of his intellect. During the next ten years, in which he led a wandering existence (Paris, Switzerland, Königsberg, Dresden, where he edited *Phöbus*, and Berlin, where he edited the *Berliner Abendblätter*) Kleist produced some of the most remarkable dramas in German literature. He began with *Die Familie Schroffenstein* (1803), a theme somewhat reminiscent of *Romeo and Juliet*, after which he published nothing of importance until the happy period in Dresden which saw the completion of his two comedies *Amphitryon* (1807), a tragi-comic adaptation of Molière, and *Der zerbrochene Krug* (1808), a comedy of character and peasant intrigue set in a small Dutch village in which the splendidly conceived and realized village judge is called on to investigate a case in which he himself is the culprit – perhaps the finest comedy in the German language. In 1808 also he treated the tragic fate of the demonic, self-assertive Amazon queen in *Penthesilea*, and in 1810 created her innocent, self-yielding counterpart in the heroine of *Das Käthchen von Heilbronn*, a work rich in all the trappings of the Romantic chivalric drama. His patriotic hatred of the French and admiration for Prussia gained expression in two dramas *Die Hermannsschlacht* (1808, publ. 1821), a treatment of the defeat of Varus at the hands of Arminius in the battle of the Teutoburger Wald, in which Rome is intended to represent the France of Napoleon, and *Prinz Friedrich von Homburg* (1810, publ. 1821), in which Prussia, in the person of the Great Elector, is seen as uniting justice and mercy, but remarkable also for its psychological insight and the representation of a distinctly unheroic hero in Prince Friedrich.

Kleist was a completely unstable, almost schizophrenic personality, intensely ambitious, yet unsure of his gifts: his innate psychological *malaise* was heightened by the failure of his plays and the unsympathetic attitude of Goethe, to whom Kleist's passionate and unharmonious nature was repellant and who effectively spoilt *Der zerbrochene Krug*, when it was produced in Weimar, by insisting that the single act be divided into three, thereby disrupting its essential unity. Kleist's alternating fits of wild enthusiasm and periods of savage melancholia – he died by his own hand – are faithfully reflected in his works: episodes of great lyrical beauty alternate with scenes of the most frenzied brutality. It was, however, his misunderstanding of Kant's *Critique of Pure Reason* which was to give his works a characteristic theme. From Kant's analysis of the limits of cognition Kleist concluded that all human knowledge was based on illusion, or rather delusion, and that man could never know truth, but would always mistake the true for the false. In the tragedies God is either malicious or cruelly remote from the plight of his creatures; under the influence of passion man's feelings become confused and he inevitably misinterprets the truth of any given situation and from this misunderstanding tragedy arises. Even in the comedies the confusion of appearance and reality is never far from the surface and in every case comes near to overwhelming the protagonists in disaster. Only unreserved trust and love and the resignation of one's own will can mitigate man's tragic incapacity to see the truth.

The 8 short stories, of which the most important are *Michael Kohlhaas*, *Die Marquise von O.*, *Die Verlobung in St. Domingo* and *Das Erdbeben in Chile* (all tr. M. Greenburg, *The Marquis of O. and Other Stories*, 1963), all turn on the same metaphysical problem and are expressive of his savagely passionate incapacity to compromise, but are told in a style which replaces the tremendous emotional involvement of the dramas with a clinical detachment and objectivity. [WAC]

*Werke*, ed. H. Sembden (2 vols., 1952).

F. Braig, *H.v.K.* (Leipzig, 1925); F. Gundolf, *H.v.K.* (Berlin, 1924); W. Muschg, *K.* (Zürich, 1923); E. L. Stahl, *H.v.K.'s Dramas* (1948); C. Hohoff, *H.v.K.* (Hamburg, 1958); G. Blöcker, *Das absolute Ich* (Berlin, 1960).

**Kleist, Ewald Christian von** (Zeblin, Pomerania 1715–Frankfurt a.d.O. 1759). German poet. After anacreontic verse in the style of ⇨ Gleim, he sounded a more personal note in such lyrics as the famous 'An Wilhelminen' and the 'Grablied' of 1757. He is chiefly remembered for his long and incomplete descriptive poem *Der Frühling* (1749), which shows considerable indebtedness to ⇨ Brockes's translation of Thomson's *Seasons* and to ⇨ Haller's *Alpen*. Intended as a theodicy in the fashion of the early Enlightenment, it is conspicuous for its passionate love and glowing descriptions of nature, which are often tinged with a vague melancholy, and for its genre pictures of rural life. His high regard for the Prussia of Frederick the Great – he served as an officer and was fatally wounded at Kunersdorf – is reflected in his well-known *Ode an die preussische Armee* (1757). He also wrote an unsuccessful tragedy, *Seneca*, and a short epic, *Cissides und Paches*, but it was as the model for Major Tellheim in ⇨ Lessing's *Minna von Barnhelm* that he achieved literary immortality. [WAC]

*Werke*, ed. A. Sauer (3 vols., 1884).

H. Guggenbühl, *E.v.K.* (Zürich, 1948).

**Klinger, Friedrich Maximillan** (Frankfurt am Main 1752–Dorpat 1831). German dramatist. Imitative by nature, his *œuvre* is an omnium-gatherum of the principal dramatic tendencies of his generation. *Otto* (1775) is indebted to Goethe's *Götz* and *King Lear* and assembles almost all the stock elements of the ⇨ *Sturm und Drang*: medieval knights, sieges and battles, hostile brothers, a father who prefers his wicked son to his good one, a madman, murderers and the Inquisition (instead of the Fehmic Court of *Götz*). The chaotic structure – there is much action but little plot – is matched by the extravagant language: incomplete sentences, wild images and ejaculations intended to express emotions constantly at fever pitch. Again, *Das leidende Weib* (1775) is indebted to ⇨ Lenz in its technique and to ⇨ Lessing and Shakespeare in its content, while the plot of *Die Zwillinge* (1776) resembles that of ⇨ Leisewitz's *Julius von Tarent*. It was his *Wirrwarr* (1776), a *Romeo and Juliet* of the American War of Independence, which, renamed *Sturm und Drang*, gave the name to the movement of which Klinger is the typical representative. After his entry into the service of the Tsar in which he rose to high rank, he continued to write both dramas and novels, but these have no more than historical interest. [WAC]

*Werke* (2 vols., 1958).

O. Smoljan, *F.M.K.* (Weimar, 1962); Garland *SS*; Pascal, *GSD*.

**Klingsor, Tristan,** pseud. for Léon Leclère (La Chapelle-aux-Pots 1874– ). French poet and artist. A curious survival from th age of literary gentlemen who relied on th appeal of limited editions on thick pape One of the original symbolist group, h directed the review *La Vogue* (1895–1901). His verse is typical of the nineties: sensual love poems with mild erotic interest and an oriental background (*Schéhérazade*, 1903), lighthearted fantasies about fairy-tales, old-time carnivals, picturesque peasants, medieval legends, accompanied by semi-philosophical musings on Life (*Le valet de cœur*, 1908; *Humoresques*, 1921). More recently, he has graduated from pseudo-classical to pseudo-romantic verse with *Le tambour voilé* (1961). He paints, and has published some music and a few short plays, essays and monographies on minor aspects of the past. [CLC]

**Klitgaard, Mogens** (Valby, Copenhagen 1906–Aarhus 1945). Danish novelist. His first novel, *Der sidder en Mand i en Sporvogn* (1937), is about the white-collar proletariat of the 1930s; but his narrative talent and his fine sense of humour were given freer outlet in *Gud mildner luften for de klippede får* (1938), and the historical novels: *De røde Fjer* (1940) and *Ballade paa Nytorv* (1940). [ELB]

**Klonowic, Sebastian** (Sulmierzyce *c.* 1545–Lublin 1602). Polish poet. He was of burgher origin and used the name of Acernus for his Latin works. He wrote a guide in verse for the navigators of the Vistula (*Flis*, 1595), allegorical in its intention, but filled with particular and sometimes odd information about the raftsmen. The partial use of allegory and picturesque social detail characterize his other Polish poem, *Worek Judaszów* (1600). [JP]

**Kloos, Willem Johan Theodoor** (Amsterdam 1859–The Hague 1938). Dutch poet and critic. Co-founder and editor of the journal *De Nieuwe Gids* (cf. ⇨ Potgieter) (1885), and the inspired leader of the ('Tachtigers') 1880 poets who reacted against the stuffy 'vicarage' poetry of the 19th century with a new aesthetic idealism, influenced by the English Romantics (especially Shelley). Kloos's originally sound judgement and exquisite poetry gradually turned to unbalanced invective and self-adulation in his later prose and verse, when the other writers (cf. ⇨ Verwey) rejected his dictum that poetry should be the most personal expression of the most personal feeling. It was this tenet that governed his arrangement of ⇨ Perk's sonnets which is now also discredited. [PK]

*Verzen* (3 vols., 1894–1913); *Nieuwere literatuurgeschiedenis* (4 vols., 1897–1915); Barnouw, *CA*; Snell, *FFG*; Weevers, *PNEC*.

P. van Eeten, *Dichterlijk Labirint* (Amsterdam, 1963).

**Klopstock, Friedrich Gottlieb** (Quedlinburg 1724–Hamburg 1803). German poet. Almost from boyhood he felt himself called by God to become the 'Christian Homer' and the first three cantos of his great epic on the life of Christ, the *Messias*, appeared in the *Bremer Beiträge* while he was still a student (1748; tr. Miss Head, *The Messiah*, 1826). The twentieth and last canto did not appear until 1773, but the success of the first three was such as to make him a national figure almost overnight. In spite of its epic structure, the poem is essentially lyrical in its expression of the writer's at times almost ecstatic religious faith in language which in its rhythmic and musical quality, its dignity and emotive power was without parallel in German literature.

The *Messias* naturalized Greek hexameters in German literature; Klopstock's odes (collected edition 1771, but he continued to write them throughout his life) were to show him even more clearly as the 'apprentice of the Greeks' in his virtuosity in the use of the various classical ode forms. They treat principally of religion and nature, friendship and love and, latterly, politics. Like the *Messias*, they are written in a style remarkable for its dynamism – the active verb is the characteristic form – and infuse intensely personal emotions into neo-classical, consciously poetic, elevated diction – at times elevated to the point of obscurity.

His Biblical dramas (*Der Tod Adams*, 1757; *Salomo*, 1764) are forgotten today, while his 3 *Bardiete* (1769–87), dramatic poems on the life of Arminius (the name derives from a confusion of the Celtic 'bard' and Tacitus's 'barditus'), which bear witness to his patriotism and initiated the vogue of nationalistic, 'bardic' literature, possess only antiquarian interest. His plans for the establishment of an intellectual, cultural elite, announced in *Die deutsche Gelehrtenrepublik* (1774), remained a utopian dream.

As the culmination of the 'verbal art' of the baroque, his writings look to the past; in his liberation of the emotions and his concept of the *poeta-vates*, however, he anticipates Goethe and the *Sturm und*

*Drang*, but it is above all in the poetry of ⇨ Hölderlin, ⇨ Rilke and ⇨ Weinheber that his influence survives as a vital creative force. [WAC]

*Werke*, ed. K. A. Schleiden (1954).
E. A. Blackall, *The Emergence of German as a Literary Language* (1959); K. Viëtor, *Geschichte der deutschen Ode* (Munich, 1923); G. Kaiser, *K.* (Gütersloh, 1963).

**Klyuyev, Nikolay Alekseyevich** (Olonets prov. 1887–? 1937). Russian poet. Son of 'Old Believer' schismatics, in a remote Northern village, he early composed religious songs for his sect. His first collection of verse appeared in 1912, and was followed at brief intervals by several more. His work brought something new into Russian literature: true peasant poetry, saturated with the language, lore and religion of the Northern forests; it is never *faux-naïf*, but sophisticated and often esoteric. His attitude to the Revolution was uneasy; in a good deal of poetry he genuinely welcomed it, but in the spirit of the so-called 'Scythians' (who regarded it mystically as the fulfilment of Russia's religio-historical mission). Not surprisingly, he found himself less and less in sympathy with the Bolsheviks, who in turn considered him a *kulak* (wealthy peasant). In 1933 he was arrested and exiled; at Gor'ky's intercession he was released, but later re-arrested. He does not appear to have been 'rehabilitated' in the U.S.S.R. yet, and some of his later poetry may be lost. He was the senior member and inspirer of the important circle of 'peasant poets', in particular ⇨ Yesenin. The latter's suicide in 1925 inspired his most remarkable later poem, the long *Plach o Yesenine* ('Lament for Yesenin', 1927). [RM-G]

*Polnoye sobraniye sochineniy*, intr. B. Filippov (2 vols., N.Y., 1954); Markov, *MRP*; Obolensky, *PBRV*.

**'Knaben Wunderhorn, Des'.** ⇨ Arnim, Ludwig Achim von; Brentano, Clemens.

**Kniaźnin, Franciszek Dionizy** (Vitebsk 1750 –Końskowola 1807). Polish poet. He was educated to become a Jesuit, but after the dissolution of the order chose a literary career and spent his active years at the court of Prince Czartoryski at Puławy. He translated Horace and later Macpherson's Ossian (via French), wrote love poems, odes and mock-heroic verse, e.g. about a cat on a balloon expedition.

He himself supervised the complete edition of his poetic works (1787–8). The texts and the occasional footnotes show how passionately he was interested in both contemporary science and folklore. Melancholy by nature, he could not bear the loss of the country's independence in 1795 and the last years of his life were darkened by mental illness.

Much of his verse seems conventional at first reading, but a closer study reveals an inner conflict between heart and reason, an 18th-century mind straining to contain emotion. His *Erotyki* (1779) and his odes rely on the form to keep the balance. In *Babia Góra*, a verse-letter addressed to a friend going on a scientific expedition to the Carpathians, he anticipates romanticism in a manner very similar to that of Collins's *Ode on the Popular Superstitions of the Highlands.* [JP]

Peterkiewicz and Singer, *FCPP*; *SEER*, XXVIII, 71 (1950) (on Collins and Kniaźnin).

**Knudsen, Erik** (Slagelse 1922– ). Danish poet and playwright. His first volumes of poems, *Dobbelte Dage* (1945), *Til en ukendt Gud* (1947) and *Blomsten og Sværdet* (1949), gave him a leading place as an anti-lyrical poet, a disillusioned sceptic and a social satirist. Pop culture and the advertising industry are the chief targets of his satire, both in his essays, *Gallileis Kikkert* (1952), and in his witty plays, e.g. *Friedleben* (1954), his musicals, e.g. *Frihed det bedste Guld* (1961), and in his political farces, e.g. *Læn Dem ikke ud* (1966). [ELB]

*Digte 1945–58* (1958).

**Knudsen, Jakob** (Rødding 1858–Birkerød 1917). Danish novelist. An unorthodox Christian in the Grundtvigian movement, he was partly influenced by Carlyle; his novels reflect views opposed to the Welfare State: he believes in social inequality and attacks modern humanitarian attitudes. His main novels are *Den gamle Præst* (1899), *Lærer Urup* (1909), *Rodfæstet* (1911), and *Angst-Mod* (1912–14), two novels about Luther. [ELB]

C. Roos, *J.K.* (Copenhagen, 1954).

**Kobylyans'ka, Ol'ha** (Guru Humorulu Austria 1863–Chernovtsy 1942). Ukrainian novelist and short-story writer. Aged 16 she began writing in German, but changed to Ukrainian in 1886. Neo-romantic and modernist in style, her dominant theme is the 'aristocratism of the spirit', the cult of aestheticism, opposing the Philistine and the vulgar herd. It is often embodied in a girl's fight for emancipation, for example, in *Tsarivna* (1895). Contemporary social problems appear infrequently. *Zemlya* (1901) combines a realistic plot with mystical, romantic treatment of 'the power of the soil'. [VS]

*Tvory* (5 vols., 1962–3).
*UCE*; *UR*, x, 3 (1964).

**Koch, Martin** (Stockholm 1882–Avesta 1940). Swedish novelist. Although one of the pioneers of the Swedish *arbetardiktare* (working-class writers), he was born into the lower middle class and was given at least the beginning of an education. He had, however, first-hand experience as a painter's apprentice and as a temperance worker; later he became a journalist. His political convictions led him into full solidarity with the emerging labour movement, and his first important novel, *Arbetare* (1912), carries the subtitle 'a story about hatred'. Set in contemporary Stockholm, it reflects the sinister mood among workers following the general strike of 1909. The sense of moderation and the reformist spirit now typical of the Swedish labour movement are here shown to be the fruit of hard-won moral victory. In *Timmerdalen* (1913) the strike of saw-mill workers in a Norrland setting is based on a historical event: the novel is partly in the category *reportage*, but inspired by an almost religious sense of a just cause. Koch's most impressive work is the massive novel *Guds vackra värld* (1916). A study of gradual decay and centred on the criminal psyche, it gives uncanny insight into the Stockholm underworld, and its hero speaks the authentic dialect of vice. Against this sombre backcloth he sets pictures of a rural community in which old traditions and the Christian values are still alive; but how these should be transferred to society at large he seems unable to tell. After 1920 he wrote little. Various explanations have been given, the most plausible being the inability to control the subject-matter he most wanted to shape. Only at the very end of his life he returned to literature with a mellow, even humorous book of autobiographical stories, *Mauritz* (1939). [SAB]

T. Jonsson, *M.K.* (Stockholm, 1941); H. O. Granlid *M.K. och arbetarskildringen* (Göteborg, 1957).

**Kochanowski, Jan** (Sycyna 1530–Lublin 1584). Polish poet. The most important early Polish writer. Well educated in the universities of Cracow, Königsberg and Padua, he became a courtier after his return to Poland and was later appointed one of the king's secretaries. The death of Sigismund Augustus in 1572 loosened his ties with the court. The years of study abroad and the courtier's life influenced his Latin poetry and light sophisticated verses called *fraszki* (trifles). The latter were finally collected in a sumptuous volume (1584).

His best writing, however, came when he retired to his village Czarnolas and as a country squire found himself close to the Horatian ideal which he extolled in his *Pieśni*. The two sets of these songs together with the poetic versions of David's Psalter (*Psałterz Dawidów*, 1579) show a variety of form and a striking unity of lyrical tone. He also ventured into classical drama: *Odprawa posłów greckich*, a static play only 600 lines long, was performed in 1578, but failed to establish a theatrical tradition.

In 1580 he gave Polish literature its first masterpiece: a cycle of 19 laments (*Treny*), commemorating the death of his little daughter, Orszula. He had married late (at 40) and the loss of a favourite child in the final phase of his own life must have intensified the crisis, affecting all past achievements. In the 'Laments' a deeply personal voice asserts itself against literary conventions, the cold comforts of mythology and stoic philosophy, and shows up their uselessness. Yet the cycle ends in a medieval dream-vision, as if the poet needed two voices, humanist and medieval, to question his precepts of life. The vivid portrait of the child is the more moving for this absolute intellectual honesty of an old man.

He was creative in his use of the classical heritage as an author of Latin verse (e.g. *Lyricorum libellus*, 1580); he also understood the necessity for a stylistic norm and strove to establish it in the Polish language. In the end, he altered the native poetic diction, and his influence proved as vital as that of Spenser and Shakespeare on English verse. [JP]

*Dzieła polskie*, ed. J. Krzyżanowski (1955); *Poems by J.K.*, ed. G. R. Noyes (inferior renderings) (1928); Peterkiewicz and Singer, *FCPP*. *SEER*, XXXI, 75 (1952), XXXI, 77 (1953).

**Kochowski, Wespazjan** (Gaj nr Sandomierz 1633–Cracow 1700). Polish poet. A country squire, he took part in the military campaigns of his day. In 1683 he witnessed the delivery of Vienna by John III Sobieski. This great victory inspired him to write *Psalmodia polska* (1695), a cycle of 36 prose poems, in which he outlined a Messianic interpretation of Polish history. The immediate future, however, did not comply with his prognostications, for Turkey soon ceased to be a real danger to Poland. As a stylistic exercise his Psalmody has a particular relevance to the Messianic writing of the Polish romantics (⇨ Mickiewicz, ⇨ Słowacki, ⇨ Krasiński) who often clad their prophecies and admonitions in Biblical prose. He was also a prolific writer of verse and adapted some of John Owen's Latin epigrams. [JP]

**Kočić, Petar** (Stričići, nr Banja Luka 1877–1916 Belgrade). Bosnian writer. A fervent patriot and opponent of Austrian occupation. His stories are mainly satirical in character although they also contain realistic portrayals of human nature on the background of his native province. His stories were published together in 2 vols. (1928–31). Perhaps the most famous is the satire *Jazavac pred sudom.* Although his ability to create convincing characters and his satirical wit are beyond question, he remains a provincial writer, though unquestionably one of the best. [EDG]

**Kock, Charles Paul de** (Passy 1793–Paris 1871). French novelist. He was immensely successful writing bawdy sentimental novels about Paris life under the reign of Louis-Philippe. Among his large output there are *Georgette* (1820), *Gustave ou Le mauvais sujet* (1821), *Mon voisin Raymond* (1823), *L'amant et la lune* (1847). His novels were extremely popular abroad, especially in England (among Macaulay and Elizabeth Browning) and in Russia (the favourite though secret reading of Verkhovensky in Dostoyevsky's *The Devils*). [WA]

**Kolar, Slavko** (Palešnik 1891–1963). Croatian humorist, author of many stories dealing with the lives and ambitions of the little man. Perhaps his best-known works are the stories *Ili jesmo-ili nismo* (1933) and *Natrag u naftalin* (1946) as well as the play *Svoga tela gospodar* (1957). [EDG]

Kadić, *CCL.*

**Kölcsey, Ferenc** (Sződemeter, 1790–Pozsony 1838). Hungarian poet and essayist. Of noble origin, he became one of the leading spirits of the Enlightment Era as advocate of the new Western type bourgeoisie. Though now best known as author of the Hungarian national anthem *Himnusz* (1823; tr. W. Kirkconnel, *Hymn*, 1947), he wrote numerous poems, odes ('To Freedom', etc.) and essays on philosophy; *Parainesis* was his political-philosophic testimony. His short stories poignantly criticized contemporary society. He was the first to introduce folksongs into Hungarian literature. [JFR]

**Koliqi, E.** ⇨ Albanian Literature.

**Kollár, Ján** (Mošovce 1793–Vienna 1852). Slovak poet writing in Czech. In his time literary Slovak was not yet established. He studied in Jena, became an evangelical pastor in Pest and, in 1849, was appointed professor of Slavonic archeology at Vienna. He was the chief exponent of Panslavism, which he interpreted as cultural rather than political cooperation of all Slavs. His main work is *Slávy dcera* (1824, 1832, etc.), a cycle of sonnets which in subsequent editions grew to over 600 poems. It is a mixture of erotic, political and patriotic themes, of history and fiction, autobiographical anecdotes and moralizing maxims. He wanted to awaken a Slav consciousness by extolling the past glory of the Slavs, and pan-Slav cooperation for the sake of all mankind. Finally he assumed the role of supreme prophet and judge for all Slavs. His influence was great but only those of his sonnets which are closest both to the sentiment and the idiom of folk poetry are of lasting literary value. [KB]

A. Mráz, *J.K.* (Bratislava, 1952); *SEER*, 6 (1927–8); 31 (1952).

**Kolmar, Gertrud**, pseud. of G. Chodziesner (Berlin 1894–1943). German poet. She was murdered in a Nazi concentration camp, after a secluded life, apart from literary circles. Her best work begins with *Preussische Wappen* (1934), a cycle on the coats of arms of Prussian towns. A 1938 collection was destroyed when the concession to Jewish publishers ended. Her last and best cycle of poems, *Welten*, appeared in 1947; collected editions 195[illegible] and 1960, *Das lyrische Werk*. Her work has been compared to Emily Dickinson's, an[illegible] she is certainly one of the most, if not the most, outstanding woman poets in German. Her conventional early work was influenced by the *Volkslied*; she came to use the sonnet form with signal mastery, and in her last poems she employed a magnificent free verse line. She possessed a facility for precise observation reminiscent of ⇨ Droste-Hülshoff, but combined with it the power to evoke ultimate archetypes. All her poetry is highly distinguished, and she had the passionate integrity and range that come together only in a great poet. *Eine Mutter* (1965) is a story. [PB]

*Tag- und Tierträume* (1963) (selection); Bridgwater, *TCGV*; Hamburger and Middleton, *MGP*; *C*, x (1950).

**Konopnicka, Maria** (Suwałki 1846–Lvov 1910). Polish short-story writer and poet. Her copious verse is too often marred by naïve social or patriotic didacticism. There are, however, some notable exceptions, e.g. in the volume *Italia* (1901). She tried her hand at an epic subject and produced a mammoth poem about Polish peasant settlers in Brazil, having no direct knowledge of that country (*Pan Balcer w Brazylii*, 1910). Her short stories are on the whole free from her usual emotionalism and contain a few memorable portraits of working-class women (*Józefowa*, *Urbanowa*, *Banasiowa*). Ultimately her place in literature is ensured by her truly poetic book for children, *O krasnoludkach i o sierotce Marysi* (1895), about dwarfs and an orphan girl. [JP]

Peterkiewicz and Singer, *FCPP*; Scherer-Virski, *MPSS*.

**Konrad (Pfaffe Konrad).** German versifier of the mid 12th century, a cleric of Regensburg. He is known by two works: (1) the *Rolandslied* (ed. K. Bartsch, 1874), a glorification of Charlemagne and his knights based on the *Chanson de* ⇨ *Roland* and composed in the early 1130s; (2) the *Kaiserchronik* (ed. E. Schröder, 1892), the first extensive historical chronicle in the German language, written in halting and often highly imperfect metrical form, and consisting of a compendium of biographies of Roman and German emperors from Julius Caesar to Konrad III; the work breaks off in the middle of the poet's description of the preparations for the second Crusade (1147). [RT]

*Das Rolandslied*, ed. F. Maurer (Darmstadt, 1964); Ehrismann, *GDL*, II, 1.

**Konrad von Würzburg** ( ? –Basle 1287). Middle High German epic and lyric poet. One of the most influential writers in the later period of courtly literature, he was of middle-class origin and probably a native of Würzburg. The patrons he names in his works are from south-west Germany, and he eventually settled in Basle. His output testifies to a great versatility and energy. In the field of epic poetry he composed lengthy romances in the classical Middle High German tradition (*Partonopier*; *Trojanerkrieg*), shorter narrative poems, sometimes of allegorical intent, on historical and legendary subjects (*Heinrich von Kempten*; *Herzmaere*; *Der Welt Lohn*), and religious legends (*Alexius*; *Silvester*). In the realm of lyric poetry he wrote both love-songs and *Sprüche*. As his model he took ⇨ Gottfried von Strassburg, exploiting the earlier master's stylistic innovations and concentrating his attention, like almost all the poets of the late courtly tradition, on sophistications of form and subtleties of technique. But despite his efforts to equal the achievements of the classical Middle High German epic poets, his works lack the fire and inner conviction that make for powerful art. His talents are perhaps best employed in his shorter narrative poems of religious and allegorical content. [RT]

*Engelhard*, ed. P. Gereke (Halle, 1912); *Partonopier*, ed. K. Bartsch (Vienna, 1871); *Trojanerkrieg*, ed. A. von Keller (Stuttgart, 1858); *Kleinere Dichtungen*, ed. E. Schröder (Berlin, 1959); *Silvester*, ed. P. Gereke (Halle, 1925); *Alexius*, ed. P. Gereke (Halle, 1926).

K. Halbach, *Gottfried von Strassburg und K.v.W.* (Stuttgart, 1930); A. Moret, *Un artiste méconnu: C. de W.* (Lille, 1932); Ehrismann, *GDL*.

**Konstantin Filosof.** ⇨ Serbian Medieval Literature.

**Konstantinov, Aleko** (Svishtov 1863–Pazarjik 1897). Bulgarian satirist. Graduation in law at Odessa in 1885 prepared him for the Bulgarian bench (he became briefly Appeal Court prosecutor), but his integrity and idealism were fatal to such a career in the public life which he intrepidly criticized in his *feuilletons* and stories. An unsuccessful lawyer but gifted translator, he fed his craving for travel (he is still esteemed the patron of Bulgarian tourism) with visits to Paris in 1889 and Chicago in 1893. His travel notes, *Do Chicago i nazad* (1893), retain interest as a Bulgarian's blithe, yet revealing attempt – the first notable such – to size up the West and, by comparison, his own nascent society. The urge to unearth and show up that society's canker inspired his 'improbable tales of a contemporary Bulgarian' *Bay Ganyu* (1895), the best known and most controversial figure in Bulgarian literature. In anecdotes drawn from the personal experience of Konstantinov and his friends this brash, monstrous, yet touching pedlar of his native rose attar and rugs is pictured in Vienna, Prague, Dresden, St Petersburg and finally – a less acceptable partisan thug – on his home ground. Though Bay Ganyu failed to see that 'Europeans we are, yet still not quite', Konstantinov retained faith in this 'hero of our time', at least in his vitality and receptivity.

Assassination cut short the literary promise of *shtastlivetsa* ('the lucky'), as this fine personality styled himself and has since with a tragic irony come to be known. [VP]

*Săchineniya* (2 vols., 1957); Pinto, *BPV*.
G. Konstantinov, *A.K.: biografiya* (Sofia, 1946); M. Ralchev, *Istinskiyăt Bay Ganyu* (Sofia, 1944); Manning and Smal-Stocki, *HMBL*.

**Konstantinović, Radomir** (Subotica 1928– ). Serbian novelist. He writes in a difficult style about the individual faced with war and occupation and later with the threat of atomic destruction. His novels *Daj nam danas* (1958), *Mišolovka* (1956), *Čisti i prljavi* (1958) and *Izlazak* (1960; tr. E. D. Goy, *Exitus*, 1965) are works about mankind under strain. Basically an existentialist, he shows man's predicament as tragic. Even personal purity is in vain; for only by sharing the degradation of a historical period can man exist as a person. Yet, no matter how he acts, he cannot escape personal responsibility. His latest novel, *Ahasver* (1964), delves still deeper into the philosophical problem of individual existence and immortality. It is less concerned with society and views existence as a tragic inner dialectic of the person in search of his own reality. In 1966 he published a philosophical work, *Pentagram*, which goes far to explain the underlying sense of his novels. [EDG]

*SEER*, XL, 94 (1961).

**Korais, Adamantios** (Smyrna 1748–Paris 1833). Greek scholar and patriot. After studying medicine at Montpellier, he devoted himself to literature, living in Paris. He edited Theophrastus and part of Homer, produced a 'Library of Greek Literature' (17 vols., 1805–26) followed by *Parerga* (9 vols., 1809–27), and translated Herodotus into modern Greek. Most important was his attempt to assimilate literary or 'classical' Greek to the spoken idiom of the day; his *Atakta* (5 vols., 1828–35) contains the first dictionary of modern Greek. He was a prolific letter writer.

*Apanta*, ed. G. Valetas (Athens, 1964).
K. Amantos, *A.K.* (Athens 1933); K. Demaras, *K kai he epoche tou* (Athens, 1953).

**Kornilov, Boris** (Semyonovo, Nizhny-Novgorod province 1907–? 1939). Russian poet. The son of a teacher in a remote village, he studied in Leningrad. Briefly and unhappily married to Olga ⇨ Berggol'ts. His first book was *Molodost'* (1928). His unbridled life led to public censure; though enthusiastic for communism, he fell victim to Stalin's great purges. His ill-fated career has much in common with Pavel ⇨ Vasil'yev's; both had the daemon of the earlier generation of peasant poets (cf. ⇨ Yesenin) in them. Kornilov, however, lacks Vasil'yev's élan, and instead has a reflective philosophical note interwoven with fantasy in his verse. Most of his best poems are long – e.g. *Moya Afrika* – or of medium, discursive, length, e.g. *Mechta*, *Rusalka*. His involvement with Nature leads to fine semi-mystical passages. His poetry for children deserves attention. Since 1956 he has again been published in the U.S.S.R., but remains inadequately known both there and abroad. [RM-G]

*Stikhotvoreniya i poemy* (1960); Gulland, *SRV*; Lugovskoy, *RSP*.
G. Tsurikova, *B.K.* (Moscow-Leningrad, 1963).

**Korniychuk, Oleksander** (Khristinovka 1905– ). Ukrainian dramatist. He has a gift for uninhibited romantic pathos. An outstanding exponent of Socialist realism, he has been awarded several Stalin Prizes and numerous high Soviet decorations. His plays occupy a prominent place in the Soviet repertoire; those about the Revolution and the War, e.g. *Gybel' eskadry* (first publ. in 1934), *V Stepyakh Ukrayiny* (1941), *Front* (1942), are better than his rhetorical incursions into history (e.g. *Bogdan Khmel'nyts'ky*, 1939), which tend fatally towards the purple passage. He has also held various high Communist Party and government appointments. [AP/VS]

*Dramatychni tvory* (2 vols., 1955); Plays in tr.: *IL*, 12 (1935); *4 Soviet War Plays* (1944); *SL*, 8 (1961); *3 Soviet Plays* (Moscow, 1962).

Ya. S. Bilinkis, *Dramaturgiya A.K.* (Moscow, 1957); V. A. Gebel', *A.E.K.* (Moscow, 1957); *UCE*; *IL*, 4–5 (1939).

**Korolenko, Vladimir Galaktionovich** (Zhitomir 1853–Poltava 1921). Russian short-story writer. Of mixed Ukrainian and Polish origin he was educated in St Petersburg and Moscow. For his political activities he was exiled in 1879 and spent 1881–5 in Siberia. Here he gathered material for the story that brought him fame, *Son Makara* (1885; tr. M. Fell, *Makar's Dream*, 1916). On his return from exile he soon became known as a champion of the under-privileged (*V golodnyy god*, 1893). In the same year he visited America, and two years later joined the staff of *Russkoye bogatstvo*, a monthly journal of the Populist movement; he became its editor in 1904. His Populist sympathies led him to oppose the Communists and he did not support the Bolshevik Revolution of 1917.

His stories are memorable for their profound humanity and affectionate humour; but his finest work is his unfinished autobiography *Istoriya moyego sovremennika* (1909–22). Several of his stories are available in English translation. [RDBT]

*Sobraniye sochineniy* (10 vols., 1953–6).

G. A. Byaly, *V.G.K.* (Moscow-Leningrad, 1949).

**Koskenniemi, Veikko Antero** (original surname Forsnäs) (Oulu 1885–Turku 1962). Finnish poet, scholar and critic. Appointed Professor of Literature at Turku University 1921, he took German and French poetry as his special field, and became a leading authority on Goethe. As a critic he was far-sighted, conservative, and broad in his range. He enjoyed great prestige in Finland and had considerable influence on cultural policy. In 1948 he was chosen to be the representative of literature in the newly founded Finnish Academy.

His early poetry reflects the influence of the French Parnassians and the Swedish neo-romantics. Night, fate, death and homeland are the most frequent motifs. Of later influences by far the most important was that of the Greek and Latin classics; classical metres, forms and images abound in his poems. He also handled the sonnet form with considerable success. His lyrics were responsible for starting a trend towards classicism in Finnish poetry. [LV]

*Kootut teokset* (12 vols., 1956).

A. Mazon, *Un grand poète finnois* (Paris, 1920); L. Viljanen, *V.A.K.* (Helsinki, 1935).

**Kosor, Josip** (Trbounja 1879–Dubrovnik 1961). Croatian novelist and dramatist. An autodidact, he began writing stories of peasant life in Dalmatia and Slavonia. Later he wrote several dramas of wider significance, reflecting the influence of Tolstoy and Gorky. His most famous play, *Požar strasti* (1912; tr. F. S. Copeland, *Passion's Furnace*, 1917), portrays the elemental passions of the uneducated peasant in which love of the land is predominant. [EDG]

*Pomirenje* (1913; tr. J. M. Duddington, *Reconciliation*); *Nepobjediva Ladja* (1921; tr. P. Selver, *The Invincible Ship* (in *People of the Universe*, 1917)).

Barac, *HYL*.

**Kossuth, Lajos** (Monok 1802–Turin 1894). Hungarian statesman and political writer. Leading spirit of the 1848–9 Hungarian War of Independence and governor of Anti-Habsburg Hungary in 1849, after which he went into exile for the rest of his life. Coming from the landed gentry and starting his career as a lawyer, he soon became leader of the progressive opposition, seeking the advancement of his backward nation by revolution. As editor of the daily *Pesti Hírlap* (1841–4), he wrote articles and speeches that are still unchallenged gems of Hungarian prose; he was a perfect orator not only in Hungarian but also in English and other languages. Apart from numerous political writings, he wrote *Irataim az emigráczióból* (1880; tr. F. Jausz, *Memories of my Exile*, 1880). [JFR]

P. Szemere, *Politische Characterskizzen III: K.* (Hamburg, 1953); A. Somogyi, *L.K.* (Leipzig, 1894) (in German); G. Gracza, *Az 1848–9-iki magyar szabadságharcz története* (Budapest, 1894).

**Kostić, Laza** (Kovilje 1841–Vienna 1910). Serbian poet and dramatist. An extreme romantic, his poetry was criticized in his day for its excesses of imagery. Today he is considered to represent a greater freedom and imagination than most of his contemporaries. He translated Shakespeare, whose influence can be felt in his two historical dramas *Maksim Crnojević* (1866) and *Petar Segedinac* (1882). [EDG]

Ibrovac, *APY*.

Barac, *HYL*.

**Kosztolányi, Dezső** (Szabadka 1885–Budapest 1936). Hungarian poet and writer. Born into the provincial intelligentsia, he later lived in Budapest. He started his career as journalist and became a successful author of several novels, short stories and poems. He portrayed with psychological insight the moods of ordinary urban and country folk. His lyrical style was the most evocative of his time. [JFR]

*A véres költő* (1924; tr. Clifton P. Fadiman, *The Bloody Poet*, N.Y., 1927) (a novel about Nero); *Édes Anna* (1927; tr. A. Hegedűs, *Wonder Maid*, 1947) (novel); *A bús férj panaszai* (1924); *Esti Kornél* (1933) (short stories); *Szegény kisgyermek panaszai* (1910; two poems, tr. E. Kunz, 'The Map', 'The Trees of Üllői út', in *Hungarian Poetry*, Sydney, 1955).

**Kotlyarevs'ky, Ivan** (Poltava 1769–Poltava 1838). Ukrainian poet and playwright. In 1794 he began his chief work, *Eneyida*, a humorous adaptation of Virgil's *Aeneid*, which inaugurated modern Ukrainian literature. Its first 3 parts were published in 1798, appearing in full (6 parts) only in 1842. Aeneas, the Trojans, the gods are transformed into Ukrainian Cossacks and squires. Genuine idiomatic language, accurate ethnographic detail, warm folk humour and a sympathetic attitude to the people distinguish the book, endearing it to successive generations. He also introduced the modern metre (tonic-syllabic). Pictures from village life are shown in his equally important prose play with songs, *Natalka Poltavka* (1818), more serious and sentimental, with humanist and realist tendencies. It has always topped the Ukrainian repertoire. Influenced by his *Eneyida*, the anonymous *Eneyida navyvarat* (early 19th-century MS, publ. 1845) begins modern Byelor Russian literature. [VS]

*Povne zibrannya tvoriv* (2 vols., 1952–3); Ewach, *USL*; Meillet, *ALU*.
Andrusyshen and Kirkconnell, *UP*; Manning, *UL*; *Classical Weekly*, XXXVI, 8 (1942); *Die Welt der Slaven*, viii, 2 (1963).

**Kotsyubyns'ky, Mykhaylo** (Vinnitsa 1864–Chernigov 1913). Ukrainian prose-writer. First an ethnographic realist in ⇨ Nechuy's style (e.g. *Na viru*, 1891), he acquired an impressionist manner at the turn of the century influenced by Maupassant, Zola, Strindberg, Hamsun, Stefanyk as in *Na kameni* (1902), the psychological studies *Tsvit yabluni* (1902; tr. in *UR*, vii, 3–4, 1960), and the Chekhovian *Lyalechka* (1901). These modern techniques are often brought to bear upon 'social' themes arising from the 1905 revolution and subsequent reaction. The repercussions of these events in the village, the peasants' thirst for land, their rebellion and defeat, are similarly treated in his outstanding novel, *Fata morgana* (1903–10). One of the greatest Ukrainian prose-writers, he successfully applied new techniques to a democrat's view of life in a dark age; he was also a lone seeker after harmony in nature and life. [VS]

*Tvory* (6 vols., 1961–2); *Chrysalis and Other Stories* (Moscow, 1958); *UR*, XIII, 4 (1966).
Manning *UL*; *UCE*; *UR*, XI, 3 (1964).

**Kotzebue, August von** (Weimar 1761–Mannheim 1819). German dramatist. A prolific master of the dramatist's trade, his ability to create tension and surprise, his delightful 'gift' roles, witty, effective dialogue and uninhibited appeal to the sentimentality of the age assured him tremendous popularity. His earliest work, *Menschenhass und Reue* (1789), a sentimentalized *Sturm und Drang* theme of adultery and repentance, brought him international fame, and *Die deutschen Kleinstädter* (1803), a comedy of small-town life, is still occasionally produced. [WAC]

*Dramatische Werke* (10 vols., 1867ff.) (selection).

**Kovačić, Ante** (Marija Gorica 1834–Stenjevac 1889). The most original Croatian realist novelist. A member of the radical and extreme nationalist party of the *Pravaši*, his works are mainly satirical. Earlier novels reflect the influence of Turgenev but his last and best novel, *U registraturi* (1888), is influenced by Gogol', and is a mixture of fantasy and realism unequalled in Croatian literature. Its theme is the problem of the peasant boy, Ilija Kizmanović, who comes to live in the town, and his sufferings at the hands of his master. It is both a humorous and sympathetic portrayal of the village and a wild canvas of expressionist roguery and fantastic adventure. [EDG]

*Djela*, ed. M. Ratković (1950).
Barac, *HYL*.

**Kovačić, Goran Ivan** (Lukovdol 1913–Vrbuica 1943). Croatian poet. He began to write at school, published his lyrical poems in 1932. In 1942 he joined Tito's partisans. Most important works are his collection of poems in the Kajkavic dialect, *Ognji i rože* (1945), and his powerful long poem *Jama* (1944), telling of the inner experiences of a man blinded by the Ustaše, who escapes from a mass shooting by being buried in a pit beneath the bodies of his fellow-sufferers. [EDG]

Barac, *HYL*.

**Kozarac, Josip** (Vinkovci 1858–Koprivnica 1906). Croatian social novelist and short-story writer. He wrote chiefly of his native Slavonia, where he was employed as a forester. His novel *Mrtvi kapitali* (1890) deals with the lack of economic efficiency that leaves the land to go to ruin and fall into the hands of foreign exploiters. His main achievement is in his stories, especially in the lyrical prose poem *Slavonska šuma* (1905–11). [EDG]

Barac, *HYL*.

**Král', Janko** (Liptovský Sv. Mikuláš 1822–Zlaté Moravce 1876). Slovak poet. One of the first and most talented poets to write in the new Slovak literary language codified by ⇨ Štúr, Král' belonged to the radical wing of the Slovaks during the revolution of 1848–9. His ballads and lyrics express Panslavonic enthusiasm in powerful language, with many echoes of popular poetry. After the defeat of the revolution, he wrote little and his full poetic potentialities were never fully developed. [RA]

*Súborné dielo*, ed. M. Pišút (2nd edn 1959).
M. Pišút, *J.K.* (Bratislava, 1957); *SEER*, XXXIV, 83 (1955–6).

**Kramer, Theodor** (Nieder-Hollabrunn 1897–Vienna 1958). Austrian poet. He emigrated to England (1937–57), where much of his best poetry was written: *Verbannt aus Österreich* (1943), *Die untere Schenke* (1946), *Wien 1938 – Die grünen Kader* (1946), *Vom schwarzen Wein* (1956). *Einer bezeugt es* (ed. and intr. E. Chvojka, 1960) is a selection. [PB]

*Akzente*, IX, 2 (Munich, 1962); *GLL*, IX, 2 (1956).

**Kranjčević, Silvije Strahimir** (Senj 1865–Sarajevo 1908). Croatian poet. Sent to Rome to study for priesthood, he became disillusioned and returned to Zagreb where he qualified as a teacher; he spent his life in the profession, mainly in Sarajevo, where he edited the periodical *Nada*.

Croatian poetry had progressed little since the work of ⇨ Preradović, and Kranjčević's large body of poems came as something new and more profound. He combined his nationalism with a wider philosophy of life. His language and verse were rough-hewn and original, although he was probably influenced by ⇨ Njegoš. Having rejected religion, he saw man's fate as a Promethean struggle to express himself and solve the riddle of life. In 'Posljednji Adam' the last man's dying act is to trace a question mark in the snow. Christ is portrayed as a symbol of this tragic struggle to find certainty in a mortal existence. In 'Eli, eli, lama azavtani' Christ's last words are shown as a realization of the vanity of his faith. Yet if man is condemned to mortality, through work and human sympathy he may build a heaven on earth for as long as earth lasts. Always a radical, Kranjčević idealizes the worker as the source of all that is great in mankind in his poem 'Radniku'. One of the most individual poets of Croatia, he has had few direct followers. [EDG]

*Salvana djela* (2 vols., 1958); Ibrovac, *APY*; Lavrin, *AMYP*.
Barac, *HYL*.

**Krasicki, Ignacy** (Dubiecko 1735–Berlin 1801). Polish poet. He was a friend of the last king of Poland and had a brilliant career in the Church. An eclectic, he found the classical manner well suited to his temperament. As prince bishop he could, of course, risk ridiculing the religious orders in the anonymously published *Monachomachia* (1778) and follow it up with the mock-apology of *Antimonachomachia* (1780). After the first partition he became a subject of Frederick the Great of Prussia, but unlike Voltaire managed to make his stays at court quite amiable.

His fables (*Bajki i przypowieści*, 1779) and satires (*Satyry*, 1779) express the deeper moods of his moderately sceptical nature. The language of the fables is terse and lucid. Some of them, only four lines long, achieve a well-contrasted characterization through dialogue. His educational novel about Nicholas Try-All (*Mikołaja Doświadczyńskiego przypadki*, 1776) is derivative, especially in its Utopian part, but as an early example of fiction it has some importance in the Polish context. He also tried his hand at mock-heroic verse, but although he invented witty situations for his mice and cats in *Myszeidos* (1775), he gave the poem too weak a structure. A true classicist in his wide interests, he preferred literary miniatures. [JP]

*Dzieła wybrane* (ed. T. Mikulski, 1954); Peterkiewicz and Singer, *FCPP*.

P. Cazin, *Le Prince-évêque de Warmie* (Paris, 1940); *PR*, VI (Autumn, 1961).

**Krasiński, Zygmunt** (Paris 1812–Paris 1859). Polish dramatist and poet. He was dominated by the personality of his father, a wealthy aristocrat who became a loyal supporter of the Russian rule. Out of this prolonged conflict and a sense of guilt he created his type of visionary and Messianic literature which today seems more convincing in his dramas than in his lyrical verse. Once celebrated for his *Psalmy przyszłości* (1845) and *Przedświt* (1843), which proclaimed his faith in Poland's independence, he can still puzzle with his prophetic groping.

He envisaged a universal class conflict in his youthful play *Nieboska komedia* (1835; tr. H. E. Kennedy and Z. Umińska, *The Undivine Comedy*, 1924), wrote a haunting prose poem about the end of St Peter's Church (*Legenda*, 1840), and projected his fears about man's self-destructive urges in a strange piece in *terza rima*, beginning with the title line: 'Murder will spread by electric current'. Romantic in structure and mood, *Nieboska komedia* surprises with its almost modern sequences of crowd scenes and the Lenin-like portrait of the revolutionary leader.

Krasiński spent most of his life travelling, and behaved as if he were a clandestine writer, publishing his books abroad and under a veil of anonymity. His revealing correspondence includes letters to an English friend, the publicist Henry Reeve. [JP]

*Pisma*, ed. J. Czubek (1912); Peterkiewicz and Singer, *FCPP*.

M. M. Gardner, *The Anonymous Poet of Poland, Z.K.* (1919); *Z.K., Romantic Universalist*, ed. W. Lednicki (1964).

**Krasko, Ivan,** pseud. of Ján Botto (Lukovište 1876–Prague 1958). Slovak poet. A high state official and deputy of the National Assembly in the first Czechoslovak republic, he was greatly influenced in his poetry by the Czech decadents such as ⇨ Hlaváček. His books *Nox et solitudo* (1909) and *Verše* (1912) brought a new, reflective, impressionist and highly personal note into Slovak poetry. [KB]

*Dejiny slovenskej literatúry* (1960).

**Kraszewski, Józef Ignacy** (Warsaw 1812–Geneva 1887). Polish novelist. He wrote some 400 volumes. Many of these are historical novels, spanning a millennium, from which Poles still learn their history. His career began when the Polish novel was in its infancy (1830) and reflects changing fashions, from the whimsicality of Jean Paul and Gogol' to the realism of Balzac and Dickens. He was a careless writer and no book stands out as an achievement in language, not even the stylized vision of pagan Poland, *Stara baśń* (1876), which is still widely read. Besides historical themes, he tackled peasant life, as in *Jermoła* (1857; tr. M. Carey, 1891), which has a striking parallel in George Eliot's *Silas Marner* (1861); he introduced the gypsies in *Chata za wsią* (1854) and even wrote a *roman à thèse* about a blue-stocking.

He was banished from Russian Poland before the uprising of 1863 and settled in Dresden. There he published some of his topical novels under the pen-name of Bolesławita. His reputation abroad widened; several of his books were translated into English, including *Countess Cosel* and *Brühl* (tr. S. C. de Soissons, 1901 and 1902). Edmund Gosse wrote a perceptive foreword to *Żyd* (1866; tr. L. Kowalewska, *The Jew*, 1893). [JP]

Krzyżanowski, *PRL*.

**Kraus, Karl** (Jičin, Czechoslovakia 1874–Vienna 1936). Austrian poet and satirist. Founder and soon sole contributor of *Die Fackel* (1899–1936; repr. 1967ff.), a brilliantly idosyncratic periodical of social and literary criticism. Later he founded his Theatre of Poetry (in opposition to the Naturalistic theatre), at which he gave spellbound audiences readings of the dramatic and poetic classics, above all of Shakespeare. His essays include: *Sittlichkeit und Kriminalität* (1908), *Die chinesische Mauer* (1910), *Weltgericht* (1919), *Untergang der Welt durch schwarze Magie* (1922), *Literatur und Lüge* (1929) and *Die Sprache* (1937). Greatest by far of his dramas is the visionary-satirical 'tragedy of mankind', *Die letzten Tage der Menschheit* (1919), a vast assemblage of scenes which ironically 'document' the banality of an Apocalypse, the years 1914–19. His minor dramas were *Literatur* (1921, a parody of Werfel's *Spiegelmensch*), *Traumtheater* (1922), *Traumstück* (1922), *Wolkenkuckucksheim* (1923, a parody of Aristophanes's

*Birds*) and *Die Unüberwindlichen* (1928). He also wrote poetry (*Worte in Versen*, 9 vols., 1916–22), epigrams (*Epigramme*, 1927), aphorisms (*Sprüche und Widersprüche*, 1909; *Pro Domo et Mundo*, 1912; *Nachts*, 1919), translations of Shakespeare's sonnets (1933) and dramas (1934), and topical adaptations of Offenbach's libretti (*Zeitstrophen*, 1931). The range of his (untranslatably idiomatic) work is characteristic of his genius, at once profoundly, indeed religiously moral and aesthetically refined, tragically sensitive to every manifestation of the disastrous collapse he (fore)saw in Western values. His dominant concern was with language ('the crystallized tradition of the spirit of man') and its abuses, the unthinking rhetoric and clichés which, by making imagination dull and intelligence blunt, let conscience acquiesce in the inhumanities of modern times. [PB]

*Werke*, ed. H. Fischer (14 vols., Munich, 1955–66); *Poems*, tr. A. Bloch (Boston, 1930).

W. Kraft, *K.K. Beiträge zum Verständis seines Werkes* (Salzburg, 1956); O. Kerry, *K.K. Bibliographie* (Vienna, 1966); P. Schick, *K.K.* (Reinbek, 1965); C. Kohn, *K.K.* (Stuttgart, 1966); Heller, *DM*; *MLR*, LXI, 1, 1966.

**Kristensen, Tom** (London 1893– ). Danish poet and author of expressionist novels, *Livets Arabesk* (1921), *En Anden* (1923), *Hærværk* (1930; *Havoc*, tr. C. Malmberg, Madison, 1967), and poetry: *Mellem Scylla og Charybdis* (1943), *Den syngende Busk* (1949). He is a leading literary critic. [ELB]

*Udvalgte Digte* (1963); *1 min Tid* and *Aabenhjertige Fortielser* (1963-6) (memoirs).

**Kristoforidhi, K.** ⇨ Albanian Literature.

**Krklec, Gustav** (Udbiuja 1899– ). Croatian poet. He began writing during the First World War. Mainly a descriptive poet, whose descriptions serve to express an undercurrent of personal experience. His best works, written during the Second World War, are *Darovi Za bezimena* (1942) and *Tamnica vremena* (1944). Most of his poetry is conventional in form. [EDG]

*SEER*, XXIII, 62 (1945); Ibrovac, *APY*; Lavrin, *AMYP*.
Kadić, *CCL*.

**Krleža, Miroslav** (Zagreb 1893– ). Croatian dramatist, novelist, essayist and poet. Educated at the Ludoviceum military academy at Budapest, he served in the Austrian army 1914–18, then lived as a professional writer. The dominating figure of Croatian literature, his main talent is as a dramatist. A Marxist, influenced by his hatred of the manners and morals of the decadent Austrian empire and pre-war Yugoslavia, he writes as both a nationalist and a socialist.

His early plays, *Legende* (1933), on the themes of Christ, Michelangelo and Columbus, show the discoverer and the artist engaged in the noble if hopeless struggle of forging meaning out of existence. Art alone gives direction to man's life. His social dramas are of particular interest, especially the cycle of the Glembaj family, *U agoniji* (1931), *Gospoda Glembajevi* (1932) and *Leda* (1930), which trace the degeneration of a typical capitalist family in Croatia under Austro-Hungarian rule. He emphasizes that artistic perception and moral perception are akin and that the degeneration of the one involves the degeneration of the other. His novels are also important. *Hrvatski bog Mars* (1922) deals with the fate of Croatian peasants forced to perish unnecessarily in the Austrian army. *Povratak Filipa Latinovicza* (1932; tr. Z. G. Depolo, *The Return of Philip Latinovicz*, 1960) is about the struggles of an artist to regain his creativity in a world of provincial corruption. *Banket u Blitvi* (1938–9) is an allegorical account of dictatorship. As a poet he is an expressionist using words not descriptively but as images. His Kajkavic poems *Balade Petrice Kerempuha* (1936) mix satire and protest in a Breughelesque atmosphere. He was one of the first communists to protest against the narrow interpretation of art as socialist realism. He is steeped in the culture of Europe and is one of the best read of all Yugoslav writers. [EDG]

Lavrin, *AMYP*.
Barac, *HYL*; Kadić, *CCL*.

**Krog, Helge** (Kristiania 1889–Oslo 1962). Norwegian playwright and essayist. He began as a journalist and soon became known as a literary and dramatic critic, and as a contributor to the political and cultural debates of the day. His first play, *Det store Vi* (1917), is a merry attack on exploitation and the press. In subsequent plays, where the influence of Gunnar ⇨ Heiberg and ⇨ Ibsen can be detected, he depicts a number of women in their erotic and social relationships: Sonja in *Konkylien* (1929; tr. R. Campbell, *Happily ever After?*, 1934), who goes from man to man in order to be true to love; the Communist doctor Cecilie Darre in *Underveis* (1931; tr. H. Yourelle, *On the Way*, 1939), who refuses to marry though she has a child; and Vibeke in *Oppbrudd* (1936; tr. M. Linge, *Break-up*, 1939), who, like Nora in Ibsen's *A Doll's House*, breaks away from her busband to make a new life for herself. However, it is in his less pretentious, lighthearted pieces that Krog seems to be most himself: *På solsiden* (1927; tr. C. B. Burchardt, *On Life's Sunny Side*, 1939); *Blåpapiret* (1928; tr. R. Campbell, *The Copy*, 1934); *Treklang* (1933; tr. R. Campbell, *Triad*, 1934). He published many collections of brilliantly written, often controversial articles on a wide variety of topics. [RGP]

*Skuespill* (3 vols., 1948).
F. Havrevold, *H.K.* (Oslo, 1959); L. Longum, in *To kjærlighetsromantikere* (Oslo, 1959); Beyer, *NL*.

**Krolow, Karl** (Hanover 1915– ). German poet and critic. Beginning as a nature-poet in the manner of ⇨ Lehmann (besides some topical *Zeitgedichte*), he later helped establish surrealism, and is a master of the modernist metaphor (though criticized for merely following fashionable trends). The best of his 9 collections are *Die Zeichen der Welt* (1952) and *Wind und Zeit* (1954). He is a fine translator (from French, especially Apollinaire), and also writes criticism (*Aspekte zeitgenössischer deutscher Lyrik*, 1961). [PB]

*Gesammelte Gedichte* (1965); Bridgwater, *TCGV*; Hamburger and Middleton, *MGP*.
Holthusen, *JN*; G. Tonelli, *La nuova lirica tedesca: K.K.* (Palermo, 1961).

**Kronchmal, Nachman** (Brody, Ukraine 1785–Brody 1840). Hebrew philosopher. The first Jew in Eastern Europe to combine traditional Jewish learning with a thorough knowledge of contemporary European thought. He named his unfinished philosophical work *Moreh Nevuchei Hazeman* (1850) ('Guide for the Perplexed of our Time') after ⇨ Maimonides's work. His philosophy of Jewish history based on the concept of the 'national spirit' influenced thinkers and philosophers for generations. [EE]

*Kitve Renak*, ed. S. Rawidowicz (N.Y., 1924).
S. M. Stern, *The Jewish Historico-Critical School* (1901).

**Krúdy, Gyula** (Nyiregyháza 1878–Budapest 1933). Hungarian writer. Of gentry origin. He adopted an original poetic style in his novels. In blending past with present, deliberately losing the thread of his stories and creating a dreamy atmosphere, he was the forerunner of many present-day Western narrators. In all his writings, he portrays the decadent characters of a passing world. Major works: The *Szindbád* novels and short stories (1912); *A vörös postakocsi* (1913); *Boldogult úrfikoromban* (1930). [JFR]

*Poet Love* (Winter, 1948).
Reményi, *HWL*.

**Krusenstjerna, Agnes von** (Växjö 1894–Stockholm 1940). Swedish novelist. Of aristocratic origin and severe mental instability, she produced 3 cycles of novels that combined controversial sexual outspokenness with attack on the traditionalism of her class: the 3 volumes of the partly autobiographical *Tony* series (1922–6), the 7 volumes of the *von Pahlen* series (1930–5), and the 4 volumes (again partly autobiographical) of the unfinished *Fattigadel* series (1935–8). She was much influenced by her husband David Sprengel, a literary critic notorious for satirical malice. Despite the obvious morbidity of some of her work and its unevenness, it is an imposing achievement of erotic art in a broad psychological and biological sense. The final cycle is distinguished also by skilful construction and shrewd social depiction.

*Samlade skrifter*, 1–19, ed. F. Edfelt (1944–6).
O. Lagercrantz, *A.v.K.* (Stockholm, 1951).

**Krylov, Ivan Andreyevich** (Moscow 1769–St Petersburg 1844). Russian fable-writer. Son of a poor Army officer, the self-taught boy became in 1778 family bread-winner as a minor clerk in Tver', learning on his own French and German. Moving to St Petersburg (1782), he worked as a clerk, and wrote tragedies and comedies, then the satirical *Pochta Dukhov* (1789). He ran short-lived journals, got into trouble with the authorities (1794), suffered penury. After obscure years in the provinces, and having studied Italian, he returned to the capital. Translation of 3 fables by La Fontaine launched him; his 2 comedies were staged in 1806. He attempted lyrics and versions of Psalms, then took up fables. A booklet of 23 of them (1809), followed by others, brought success, a sinecure post in the Public Library of St Petersburg, honours and wealth. Allegedly lazy, he learnt English and, aged 60, Greek. His last fable is dated 1834; several were translated into many languages during his lifetime (Eng. tr. B. Pares, 1926).

Satirical journalism and comedies were his school. He overcame the solemnity of the 18th-century satire and the sentimental gentility of his rivals in the early 19th. His fables are brief and colloquial. He freed the verse, its metre, the disposition of rhyme and line, at times clinching it with one telling word. He used racy language and popular proverbs, the nation adopting his lapidary phrases. Linguistically, 'the *Fables* are a school of idiom' (Sir Bernard Pares).

Censorship quashed his early sharp political satire; he grew cautious. Yet all the evils of his day, his royal Eagles or the Fox in a Court of Law are unspared as are the gentry's snobbishness, gallomania and intellectual pretences. With a good-humoured archness he exposes universal foibles. Sympathetically though unsentimentally he shows the way of life and the world of the peasantry, 'the small fry', 'the roots'. He conveys the landscape, and his animals – be they from Aesop or La Fontaine – are familiar to the countryside and portrayed so that 'even his Ass is positively a Russian' (Gogol'). 'A foreigner studying his fables would gain a clearer notion of the Russian national character than by reading treatises on the subject' (Turgenev). [NG]

*Sochineniya*, ed. N. L. Stepanov (1955).
N. L. Stepanov, *I.A.K.*, *Zhizn' i tvorchestvo* (Moscow, 1949).

**Kuhlmann, Quirinus** (Breslau 1651–Moscow 1689). German poet. His extravagant personality combined a fanatical, proselytizing religious faith with extreme sensuality and eroticism. His early predisposition to religious mania was strengthened when he came into contact with disciples of Jakob Böhme while a student in Leyden (1673ff.): feeling himself called by God to preach the establishment of the 'Jesuelic Kingdom', he led a wandering life in Holland, England and Germany, everywhere persecuted as a dangerous heretic, and after an abortive attempt to convert the Sultan of Turkey, died at the stake in Moscow. He wrote epigrams (1666), a collection of sonnets (*Himmlische Liebesküsse*, 1671) remarkable for their combination of didacticism and visionary ecstasy, and the *Kühlpsalter* (1684–6). These 150 'psalms', the record of his mystical experiences, exhibit tremendous linguistic power, which at times anticipates the language of the Expressionists. His love of metaphor, and creation of unexpected and 'impossible' neologisms ('*pfeilen*', to 'arrow'; '*zentnern*', to 'hundredweight'; '*ewigst*', 'most everlasting') bear witness to the intensity of the emotions he sought to express. Although he exerted no permanent influence on either language or literature, it is in his expression of personal emotions in strikingly original form that his literary and historical significance lies. [WAC]

C. V. Bock, *Q.K. als Dichter* (Bern, 1957).

**Kuhn, J. G.** ⇨ Swiss-German Dialect Literature.

**Kukučín, Martin**, pseud. of Matej Bencúr (Jasenová 1860–Lipik, Yugoslavia 1928). Slovak novelist. As a physician he spent much of his life in Dalmatia and in Chile. His best novels, written in a realist style, are *Dom v stráni* (1903–4), describing social conflicts in the life of Dalmatian peasants, and *Mat' volá* (1926–7), set in the Croat colony in Punta Arenas. [KB]

*SEER*, XXII, 59 (1944).

**Kulish, Mykola** (Chaplynka, Kherson 1892–a Siberian prison camp 1942). Ukrainian playwright. Highly original and the most talented of his period, one of the greatest Ukrainian dramatists, he became famous with his first controversial tragedy, *97* (1924). In his Expressionist *Narodny Malakhiy* (1927–9) he created a modern Ukrainian Don Quixote (cf. *CSP*, i, 1956). His best play, *Patetychna sonata* (1929–31), a lyric drama of the 1917 Revolution, synthesizing music and words, has been compared to *Faust* and *Peer Gynt* (cf. *UQ*, v, 4, 1949). He was arrested and deported in 1934. [VS]

*Tvory* (N.Y., 1955); *P"yesy* (1960); Luts'ky, *LD.*
N. Kuzyakina, *Dramaturh M.K.* (Kiev, 1962); Luckyj, *LPSU*; *UCE*; *UQ*, xi, 3 (1955).

**Kulish, Panteleymon** (Voronezh, Sumy 1819–Borzna, Chernigov 1897). Ukrainian writer, translator, ethnographer and historian. Making his début with ethnographic short stories in 1841, in 1845 he started his celebrated historical novel-chronicle of the Cossack Ukraine in 1663, *Chorna Rada*, in the manner of Sir Walter Scott, completing it in 1857. His poems (after 1861) and plays are uneven in merit. He contributed immensely to Ukrainian also by translating the Bible, 11 plays of Shakespeare, etc. Though often in conflict with, and alienated from, his people, he stands in the Ukrainian tradition next to ⇨ Shevchenko. [VS]

*Tvory* (6 vols., 1908–10); Andrusyshen, and Kirkconnell, *UP*; Meillet, *ALU*.
Manning, *UL*; Mijakovs'kyj and Shevelov, *TS*; *UCE*.

**Kumičić, Evgenij** (Beršec 1850–Zagreb 1904). Croatian novelist. A member of the extreme nationalist party under Ante Starčević, his novels are tendentious. He became an ardent follower of Zola, and opposed to the gentler realism of ⇨ Šenoa, his novels failed to overcome romantic colouring and melodrama. They all attempt to expose the evils of Croatian society under Hungarian domination. His most famous novel is perhaps *Gospodja Sabina* (1884), showing the hypocrisy and immorality of Zagreb society, but his most successful work is his description of service in the Hungarian army, *Pod puškom* (1889). [EDG]

Barac, *HYL*.

**Kuncewicz, Maria** (Samara 1899– ). Polish novelist. Her best book is undoubtedly the character study of *Cudzoziemka* (1935; tr. B. W. A. Massey, *The Stranger*, 1944). Estrangement through the atmosphere of a provincial town gives a lyrical quality to her cycle of stories, *Dwa księżyce* (1933). She spent the war years in London and is now living in America. [JP]

Ordon, *TCPS*.

**Kundera, Milan** (Brno 1929– ). Czech writer and dramatist. The first Czech author to emphasize in his plays (*Majitelé klíčů*, 1962) and short stories (*Směšné lásky*; I 1963, II 1966, III 1968) the private and emotional spheres of the individual in contrast to the writers of the Stalinist period who saw man merely as a unit in the socialist collective. His novel *Žert* (1966) describes with wry humour the emotional and moral decline of a young man deformed by pseudo-socialist society. He is now (1971) debarred from publication and banned from public libraries.

**Kuprin, Aleksandr Ivanovich** (Narovchat, Penza 1870–Leningrad 1938). Russian short-story writer. He was trained at the Military Academy in Moscow and served as an officer 1890–4. After this he tried many occupations, among them acting and journalism, before devoting himself to literature. He was uninterested in politics; he could not accept the Bolshevik Revolution and emigrated. He finally settled in France, but returned to the Soviet Union in 1937, a sick and broken man.

His army experiences are reflected in many of his best works, notably *Poyedinok* (1905; tr. anon., *The Duel*, 1916), an attack on the artificial code of 'honour' and a revelation of the brutality and inefficiency of army life. Its appearance on top of the disasters of the Russo-Japanese War (1904–5) gave it a political relevance; but this is rare in his works. His best stories, *Granatovyy braslet* (1911; tr. L. Pasvolsky, *The Bracelet of Garnets*, 1917), and *Listrigony* (1911), extol the beauties of love and the simple life, and are free from moralizing or didacticism. His committed works like *Molokh* (1896), a denunciation of capitalism, and *Yama* (1910; tr. B. Guerney, *The Pit*, 1930), a study of prostitution, are tendentious and forced. He is an uneven writer; his best works are written in a clear and vigorous style, and he had a gift for telling a good story well. [RDBT]

*Sobraniye sochineniy* (9 vols., 1964); Faber, *RSS*.
A. Volkov, *Tvorchestvo A.I.K.* (Moscow, 1962).

**Kurbsky, Andrey Mikhaylovich** (? 1528–? 1588). Russian publicist and historian. One of the numerous minor and insignificant princes of Yaroslavl', he began his career in the army. During the 1550s and the early 1560s he occupied a series of relatively unimportant military commands. Although he was created *boyar* in 1556, which gave him the right nominally at least to participate in the government of the country, he seems to have taken no part in politics and to have spent most of his time soldiering. In 1564 he defected to the Lithuanian-Polish army, probably because he suspected that he was about to be liquidated by Ivan IV. He spent the rest of his restless life in Poland-Lithuania fighting against the Russians, squabbling with his neighbours and writing. He carried on a lengthy correspondence with Ivan IV, wrote a long history of Ivan – the first historical monograph in Russian – and a short account of the Council of Florence. His writings also include several letters to his friends and various attempts at translation from Latin to Russian.

His style is arid, repetitive and often clumsy; but both his correspondence and his history of Ivan are refreshingly free from long scriptural quotations, and he possessed a certain clarity of exposition and an ability to drive home his arguments which is usually lacking in the writings of his contemporaries. Muddle-headed and ill-informed though many of his political views were, his importance as a publicist lies in the fact that he was one of the very few articulate representatives of the *boyarstvo* capable of voicing the views of the opposition to autocracy. [JLIF]

*The Correspondence between Prince A.M.K. and Tsar Ivan IV of Russia 1564–1569*, ed. J. L. I. Fennell (1963); *K.'s History of Ivan IV*, ed. J.L.I. Fennell (1965).

**Kürenberg** (fl. mid 12th cent.). Name by which the earliest German ⇨ Minnesinger (strictly speaking, a native of Austria) is known. His poems, which are preserved in only one manuscript, represent the end of a tradition of love-poetry in which the relationship between man and woman is bluntly and realistically described, not idealistically envisioned as in the classical Minnesang of courtly love. The name Kürenberg occurs in one of the poems as the originator of the strophic form in which that and most of the other poems are written, but nothing is known of the poet. This strophic form is also that of the ⇨ *Nibelungenlied*, which in the 19th century led to speculation, now ignored, that he was also the poet of that epic. But whoever he was, his poems have a vividness of imagery and a forcefulness of manner that place them among the best of medieval German lyric poetry. [RT]

Kraus, *MF*.
M. Ittenbach, *Der frühe deutsche Minnesang* (Halle, 1939); Ehrismann, *GDL*.

**Kuzmin, Mikhail Alekseyevich** (Yaroslavl 1875–Leningrad 1936). Russian poet. His principal verse collections are *Aleksandriyskiye pesni* (1906), *Seti* (1908), *Osenniye ozyora* (1912), *Glinyanyve Golubki* (1914), *Paraboly* (1922). An aesthetic and somewhat mannered poet, his predilection was for the exquisite and the fragile, for decadent cultures of the past (Alexandria, rococo France), for intelligent artificiality. *Kuranty lyubvi* ('The Seasons of Love', 1907) is an 18th-century pastoral for which Kuzmin also composed the music. His ideal of 'beautiful clarity' renders his attempts at fiction rather lifeless. His comedy about St Alexis (*Komedii*, 1908) is characteristic of a rather light interest in religious themes, which became more serious in later years.

Obolensky, *PBRV*.

**Kvitka-Osnov''yanenko.** ⇨ Osnov''yanenko.

# L

**Labé, Louise** (Lyons 1524?–Parcieux-en-Dombes 1566). French poetess. One of the Lyons group of poets associated with ⇨ Scève and known as 'la Belle Cordière' because of her marriage to a rope-merchant, Ennemond Perrin. Her poetry, published in 1555, consists of 3 elegies and 23 sonnets: a remarkable collection of love-poems, some probably referring to an unhappy love-affair with the poet Olivier de Magny, a follower of Ronsard.

She uses the Petrarchan convention, with its frequent antitheses, to express a situation full of contradictions and complexities; her love flouts social conventions, but she will not disown it; it causes her pain, yet she glories in it. Her poems are both intellectual, in their play of images, allusions and argument, and sensual in their direct presentation of physical desire and delight. She also wrote a prose *Débat de Folie et d'Amour* (1555). [GJ]

Schmidt, *PSS*.

A. Jans, *L.L.* (Brussels, 1959); L. E. Harvey, *The Aesthetics of the Renaissance Love Sonnet* (1962).

**Labiche, Eugène** (Paris 1815–Paris 1888). French playwright. A brilliantly entertaining writer of gay farces, he produced alone, or in collaboration, some 160 plays which dominated the French 'light' theatre under the Second Empire. Like ⇨ Scribe, he exploited all the resources of the traditional French *vaudeville* – wildly improbable initial situations, knowing complicity with the audience, topicality, puns, rhymed couplets – but contained them within the framework of detailed, complicated and skilfully dovetailed plots. To this he added an exceptionally sure sense of dramatic rhythm, notably in his more fantasticated farces: *La fille bien gardée* (1850), *Le chapeau de paille d'Italie* (1851; tr. L. and T. Hoffman, *An Italian Straw Hat*, 1955), *La cagnotte* (1864). The action of *Le chapeau*, for example, is subjected to a wildly accelerating rhythm as Fadinard searches for the compromising straw hat in a variety of social settings, and this very rhythm reinforces the unreality of the central situation. Labiche's farces reflect keen observation of contemporary manners, notably of the middle and lower-middle classes of whose money-bound mediocrity he presents a gay but subversive picture in scores of farces, e.g. *Le voyage de Monsieur Perrichon* (1860; tr. M. Ivey, *The Journey of Mr Perrichon*, 1924), *La poudre aux yeux* (1861), *Célimare le bien-aimé* (1863), *La station Champbaudet* (1862), etc. In these, scheming lovers, pompous fathers, ineffably solemn and obtuse husbands go through the ritual motions of deceit, dowry-hunting, cuckoldry like so many animated puppets. Central to these farces are those blind, complacent automatons who are endlessly and vainly trying to control life which, in its energy, variety, accident and disorder, perpetually outwits them. [SBJ]

*Théâtre complet* (10 vols., 1878–9) (about a third of the plays); *Œuvres complètes*, ed. G. Sigaux (1967ff.).

P. Soupault, *E.L.* (Paris, 1945); Volz, *C.*

**La Boëtie, Étienne de** (Sarlat 1530–Germignan 1563). French translator and political writer. He translated Xenophon's *Oeconomicus*, but is best remembered for his *Discours de la servitude volontaire* or *Contr'un* (tr. H. Kurz, *Anti-Dictator*, N.Y., 1943), a youthful work of passionate protest against the tyranny of princes, reviving the doctrine of the sovereignty of the people. It was not published until 1576. As councillor of the Bordeaux Parlement he met Montaigne, who conceived a deep and lasting affection for him, and published his works in 1571, except for the *Contr'un* and the *Mémoire sur l'édit de janvier* (1562; ed. P. Bonnefon, 1922), a work which reveals his attachment to existing institutions. His sonnets are preserved by Montaigne in *Essais*, I, xxix. [FWAG]

*Œuvres*, ed. P. Bonnefon (1892) (lacks the *Mémoire sur l'édit*).

P. Bonnefon, *Montaigne et ses amis* (2 vols. Paris, 1898); G. Maze-Sencier, *Les vies close* (Paris, 1902).

**La Bruyère, Jean de** (Paris 1645–Versailles 1696). French satirist. Author of *Les caract* *ères* (1688; tr. H. van Laun, 1885, repr. 1963). A man of one book, but that book has put him among the immortals. Little is known of his short, unexciting life. He was probably educated by the Oratorians; he certainly qualified as a lawyer; from 1672 he held a financial post at Caen and in 1684 entered the household of Condé at Chantilly, first as tutor to the young Duke, then as librarian, finally as guest: '*en qualité d'homme de lettres, avec mille écus de pension*'. With the grandfather, le grand Condé, victor of Rocroi, he seems to have got on better than with his irascible son, Duke Henri Jules. A contemporary says that he was unpopular in so great a house, chiefly by his frantic efforts to avoid pedantry. The pungency evident in *Les caractères* and the scandal caused by his reception speech in the French Academy in 1693 suggest that he was not the most tactful of men, but any man of culture and learning would have found Chantilly a difficult home.

As to his book there have hardly been two opinions. An immediate and overwhelming success when published, it soon became a classic and it has been admired and copied by judges of the quality of Flaubert, Goncourt, Gide and Proust. The author disclaimed originality: 'one has only to think and speak correctly (*juste*)'. But he discovered an admirable means of laying bare the vanity of those who succeed in a competitive society, the envy of those who do not, the insolence of office and the tyrannies of money and fashion. So we meet Philémon, the man who wears the best clothes and jewels; these make him worth seeing; 'send me his clothes then, and keep the man'. We meet Ménippe, modelled on a marshall of France, an outstanding case of the unoriginal man: 'he neither speaks nor feels, he repeats'. We meet the omniscient gossip, Arrias, caught in defeat, bragging over the latest news of the ambassador's return... to the ambassador; and the famous Giton and Phédon, prototypes of a rich and a poor man, whose symmetrically listed gestures convey the ease of the wealthy and the uneasiness of the dependent. Or again, a short paragraph contains a sentence about a young and wealthy abbé who has inherited ten benefices, put side by side with the fact that over a hundred poverty-stricken families lack warmth and clothes and bread, and the reflection: 'Is future not clearly written here?'

Realism is not the word for this writing, brutal as are its social and moral revelations. All is transformed by the powerful imagination of a great style. All variations are employed, all rhetorical devices used. Dialogue, apostrophe, epigram, anticlimax, metaphor, all these and more serve their turn in a most brilliant parade. [WGM]

*Œuvres complètes*, ed. J. Benda (Pléiade, 1957).
P. Richard, *La B.* (1946); E. W. Gosse, *Three French Moralists* (1918).

**La Ceppède, Jean de** (Marseille *c.* 1548–Avignon 1623?). French poet. A Provençal man of law and a devout Catholic, he had unpleasant experience of the civil troubles from the Ligueurs. His *Théorèmes sur les mystères de la Rédemption* and the *Seconde partie des théorèmes spirituels sur la descente de Jésus-Christ aux enfers* (1613–21) have recently been rediscovered. The 515 sonnets attempt to pierce the obscure meaning of the figures and symbols God has encompassed us with, to suggest the mystical implications of the Passion and Resurrection of Christ and encourage meditation by a symbolism which is not far removed from Baudelaire's correspondances. He uses the Bible and the classics to explain the figures in a style marked by a wealth of metaphors from astrology, alchemy, the chase, etc. His preference for the picturesque, the theatrical, pathos, emphasis, movement makes him an excellent example of the Baroque. [FWAG]

F. Ruchon, *Essai sur la vie et l'œuvre de J. de La C* (Geneva, 1953) (with selection of poems); Mourgues, *MBPP*.

**La Chaussée, Nivelle de** (Paris 1692–Paris 1754). French dramatist. Created the *comédie larmoyante*, a mixed genre of verse-drama which proceeded by way of tears to a happy ending, and which was to lead to the *drame bourgeois* as conceived by ⇨ Diderot and executed by ⇨ Sedaine. He aimed at quickening consciences on moral and social problems by presenting them in a framework of moralizing sensibility. *Le préjugé à la mode* (1735) is typical. It portrays a man unfortunate enough to be in love with his wife in an age when uxoriousness is ridiculed. The audience, moved by Durval's plight and happy at his ultimate reconciliation with his wife, is expected to react critically towards such prejudices. Sentimentality is thereby combined with a reformist attitude ('il n'est pas possible qu'un préjugé si faux soit toujours invincible'). Other important plays include *La fausse antipathie* (1733), *Mélanide* (1741), *L'école des mères* (1744). The intrusion of a quasi-tragic tone into an essentially comic atmosphere is irritating, but the plays' insistence upon *sensibilité* and the great success many of them enjoyed point to the new wave of sentiment that invades French literature from La Chaussée's time onward. [HTM]

G. Lanson, *N. de La C. et la comédie larmoyante* (Paris, 1887); Trahard, *MSF*.

**Laclos, Pierre-Ambroise-François Choderlos de** (Amiens 1741–Taranto 1803). French novelist. A soldier by profession, he spent most of his life in garrison towns, ultimately reaching the rank of brigadier-general. Incensed at the obstacles to promotion placed in his way by social privilege, he resigned to become secretary to the dissident Duc d'Orléans (Philippe Égalité) during the early Revolution, and was arrested with him during the Terror, but escaped with his life. He resumed his military career under Napoleon, and died while serving in Italy.

His literary reputation rests upon one work, *Les liaisons dangereuses* (1782; tr. P. W. K. Stone, Penguin Classics, 1961). This is a novel in the epistolary form popularized by Richardson and Rousseau, but having affinities with 17th-century classicism in its close-knit structure and its concentration upon the searching psychological analysis of a small group of characters, to the virtual exclusion of background realism. The central figure, Mme de Merteuil, is a creation of great power. Conscious of her superior intelligence, and outraged from childhood by the unjustly inferior and restrictive status of women in the aristocratic world to which she belongs, she devotes her energies, beneath a cloak of respectability, to obtaining maximum sensual freedom for herself and to taking vengeance upon society by engineering the corruption of others. In these projects she has an accomplice, though of inferior mettle, in Valmont, much of the novel being concerned with the latter's seduction, in consultation with her, of a sensual young *ingénue* and a virtuous older woman, Mme de Tourvel, with whom he comes to fall in love. The novel ends with the downfall of the schemers, but the final note remains one of moral ambiguity. The depiction of a corrupt aristocratic society has a clearly satirical purpose, but beyond this the novel perhaps points to the ultimately nihilistic outcome of the application of 18th-century rationalist principles in the service of a daemonic egoism. [WHB]

*Œuvres complètes*, ed. M. Allem (Pléiade, 1951).
É. Dard, *Le Général C. de L.* (Paris, 1936); J. L. Seylaz, *Les liaisons dangereuses et la création romanesque chez L.* (Geneva/Paris, 1958); A. and Y. Delmas, *À la recherche des Liaisons dangereuses* (Paris, 1964).

**La Cour, Paul** (Rislev 1902–Roskilde 1956). Danish poet. After *Den galliske Sommer* (1927), he was influenced by contemporary French poetry, and with *Alt kræver jeg* (1938), *Levende Vande* (1946), *Mellem Bark og Ved* (1950) became recognized as a major poet. His novels are less important, but his reflections on poetry in *Fragmenter af en Dagbog* (1948) have been influential. [ELB]

*Udvalgte Digte* (1951).
P. Schmidt, *P.L.C.* (Copenhagen, 1963).

**La Fayette, Marie Madeleine de la Vergne,** Comtesse de (Paris 1634–Paris 1693). French novelist. Her father was tutor to the nephews of Richelieu. She wrote in an age when women could not avow authorship, and the degree of assistance she received from male friends has been much discussed. Brought up in the household of Anne of Austria, and later in the convent of Chaillot, founded by Henrietta Maria, whose life she wrote (published 1720), she married when 21 a widowed army officer eighteen years older. She bore him two sons but for some years they lived practically separated, he in Auvergne and she in Paris. Her acquaintance seems to have been a small circle of literary people: Ménage, her tutor and some said her lover, a man less pedantic than his reputation (cf. H. Ashton, *Lettres de Mme de L.F. et de Gilles Ménage*, 1924); Segrais, who served her as secretary and as literary adviser; ⇨ La Rochefoucauld and Mme de ⇨ Sévigné. Her tastes were artistic and cultured rather than scholarly; she did not read Latin easily. One source described how 'every afternoon' she would receive La Rochefoucauld and Segrais to read *Astrée* together. In the opinion of Boileau she was '*la femme de France qui avait le plus d'esprit et qui écrivait le mieux*'.

She seems to have written 3 works of fiction and some touched-up court memoirs *La Princesse de Montpensier* (1662) and *Zaïde* (1670) have now only historica interest, but *La Princesse de Clèves* (1678; tr. with introduction A. Ashton, 1925) is a classic. That it was thought a group product is clear from the English translation of 1679: 'The Princess of Cleves, the most famed Romance written in French by the greatest Wits of France....' It is in striking contrast to the novels most read by its author, the 3-volume tales of *La Calprenède* and *Mlle de Scudéry*; Mme de La Fayette's chief source was Brantôme, whose ebullience and realism she severely prunes. She concentrates on a single problem, a moment of adventure within a happy, and apparently successful marriage. It is a problem akin to that of Phèdre: what happens if marriage is shattered by a sudden and overwhelming new affection, such as the Princess in this book feels for the Duc de Nemours, despite her dutiful respect for her husband? Determined to act honourably, she avows to her husband her passion. This upright intent is turned to her ruin because unknown to husband and wife Nemours is by chance outside the window and overhears all. Since he does not keep the secret to himself, both parties feel betrayed by the other, the Prince dies unhappy and the Princess can only atone by refusing Nemours even when she is technically free. [WGM]

*Correspondence*, ed. A. Beaunier (1942).
H. Ashton, *Mme de La F. Sa vie et ses œuvres* (Cambridge, 1922); É. Magne, *Mme de La F.* (Paris, 1926).

**La Fontaine, Jean de** (Château Thierry 1621–Paris 1695). French scholar and poet. Deeply read in the classics, both ancient (he knew Platonic dialogues by heart) and modern. His first work was a translation from ⇨ Marino. At a time when poetry was thought of as either epic, or dramatic, or merely light verse, he discovered a way of imaginative expression without pomposity and of homely phrasing without bathos. Brought up in the countryside, where later as Maître des Eaux et Forêts he inherited his father's office, he spent his adult years mostly in Paris. He was for a short time attached to the Oratoire, and for much longer in touch with Port Royal. He seems to have obtained licence to practise as a lawyer, but is not on record as having done so. He found aristocratic patrons, including Fouquet, and was elected to the Academy. He translated a comedy of Terence, and practised the verse tale, or *Conte* with his collections of *Nouvelles en vers tirés de Boccace et de l'Arioste* (1665, 1666, 1671). The legend of regular meetings with Racine, Boileau and Molière may owe something to the four friends who figure in *Les amours de Psyché et de Cupidon* (1669). He also wrote some pieces of Christian verse, but the work of his life was *Fables choisies mises en vers par M. de La Fontaine*, published in three parts: 6 books in 1668, 5 more in 1678 and a twelfth (for the king's grandson, the Duc de Bourgogne) in 1694 (tr. E. Marsh, 1933). The poet seems to have died in the odour of sanctity after recanting his offences against public morals.

The tradition of the fable, from Aesop and Phaedrus onwards, supplied both subject and freedom of treatment. La Fontaine drew not only on these, and more recent collections (Nevelet and Haudent) but no doubt, thanks to his friendship with the traveller Bernier, on the Indian Pilpay (or Bidpai). Of these hackneyed and prosaic sources he made a wonderful and varied instrument, discovering a sort of halfway house between man and beast, where animals speak like men and men are described like animals. In this piety grave and gay intermingle, at the whim of the fancy. An apologue on Oak and Reed ends in a magnificent Virgilian echo. Jupiter's monkey (xii, 21) is a satiric agent. So are the Abderitans who scorn their wise man Democritus: 'who knows the universe but not himself' (viii, 26). In the greater fables, such as *Les animaux malades de la peste* (vii, 1), *L'homme et la couleuvre* (x, 1) or *Le paysan du Danube* (xi, 7) a moment of civilization is held in focus. The *Philosophe Scythe* (xii, 21), who went about in his garden 'everywhere correcting nature', may stand for all purists and puritans. Most features of French civilization are in fact suggested in these vignettes: tyranny, class hatred, litigation, roads, agriculture; and through all these the eternal poetic verities of death, love, vanity, happiness. The poet professed the approved classical aim 'to please and to instruct' (vi, 1) but the Ode to Pleasure ('Volupté') in his *Psyché* leaves no doubt as to the breadth of his delight in life and art. Never, as his contemporary Perrault observed, was any poet so justly called original. [WGM]

Ed. H. de Régnier (11 vols., 1883ff.); *Œuvres diverses*, ed. P. Clarac (1942); *Discours à Mme de la Sablière*, ed. H. Busson and F. Gohin (1938).

H. Taine, *La F.* (Paris, 1853); P. Wadsworth, *Young La F.* (Evanston, 1952); P. Clarac, *La F.* (Paris, 1947); M. Sutherland, *La F.* (1953); O. de Mourgues, *Ô Muse, fuyante proie, Essai sur la poésie de La F.* (Paris, 1962).

**Laforgue, Jules** (Montevideo 1860–Paris 1887). French poet, educated at Tarbes and Paris, reader to the Empress Augusta in Berlin (1881–6). He married an English governess Leah Lee and returned to Paris where he died of tuberculosis. He published only *Les complaintes* (1885) and *L'imitation de Notre Dame la Lune* (1886), but his influence has been widespread (e.g. on T. S. Eliot). Adopting the mocking cynical manner of ⇨ Corbière, he gave it a 'lunacy' and lightness that transform the basic melancholy of his inspiration. Using *vers libre*, the poem develops a free association of ideas, puns, images and startling juxtapositions. From Baudelaire he learned the new poetry of industrialized cities and an essentially urban wit and feeling. He depicts himself as the little man, half concealing himself behind what sometimes seems like a barrage of mockery. By bringing poetry back to the rhythms of everyday speech he is one of the most important innovators of modern poetry. His prose works *Moralités légendaires* (1887) contain 6 highly individual retellings of old stories. [WA]

*Œuvres complètes* (6 vols., 1925– ); *Derniers vers* (1890); *Selections*, ed. C. Pichois (1959); *Poems*, tr. P. Terry (Berkeley, 1958).

W. Ramsey, *J.L. and the Ironic Inheritance* (1953); M. J. Durry, *J.L.* (Paris, 1952); M. Collie, *L.* (1963).

**Lagerkvist, Pär** (Växjö 1891– ). Swedish poet, novelist and dramatist. His background is vividly portrayed in the autobiographical sketch *Gäst hos verkligheten* (1925; tr. E. Mesterton and D. W. Harding, *Guest of Reality*, 1936): early years in a small provincial town which retained vital links with the past and the simple life in the surrounding country, and then the painful process of liberation from the religious atmosphere of home. His main themes have been, on the one hand, the anxiety of a life deprived of meaning and hope, e.g. in the poetry of *Ångest* (1916) and in the Expressionist plays *Den svåra stunden* (1918) and *Himlens hemlighet* (1919); and, on the other hand, the tender resignation of the admirable prose fantasy *Det eviga leendet* (1920; *The Eternal Smile*, in *Guest of Reality*), the tentative acceptance of *Den lyckliges väg* (1921) and *Hjärtats sånger* (1926), two of his finest collections of verse, and, at the other extreme, the militant idealism expounded in *Det besegrade livet* (1927), a book of meditations and aphorisms. The chief works of the thirties are the play *Konungen* (1932), with its attempt to transcend dualism through a mythical scheme borrowed from Frazer; *Vid lägereld* (1932), which expresses the darkest pessimism in the most lucid poetic form; and *Bödeln* (1933; *The Hangman*, in *Guest of Reality*), a suggestive prose tale exploring the symbolic role of the hangman in the Middle Ages and in contemporary society. Lagerkvist's international fame rests largely on the two novels, *Dvärgen* (1944; tr. A. Dick, *The Dwarf*, 1953) and *Barabbas* (1950; tr. A. Blair, 1952), which won him the Nobel Prize in 1951. On a canvas filled with historical matter, the fundamental issue is the struggle between the human and the bestial, or between good and evil, rather than a concrete moral conflict. The earlier book is set in a Renaissance court, and the repugnant title figure is both a realistic study and a symbolic adumbration. As such he stands for the sterile, negative part of man and is consistently shown to be a reduced copy of his master, the Prince, whom he follows about like a shadow. Barabbas, on the other hand, is placed, as representative of all mankind, opposite the luminous figure of Christ. The sinister figure of the robber is Man deprived of the self-transcending capacity, but still human enough to feel his deprivation. Lagerkvist's later production is on the whole less memorable, although the poems in *Aftonland* (1953) include some of his finest, and the novel *Sibyllan* (1956; tr. N. Walford, *The Sibyl*, 1958), set in ancient Delphi, contains some of his most beautiful pages. It also introduces the figure of Ahasuerus, whose allegorical presence weighs rather heavily on the book. *Ahasverus' död* (1960; tr. N. Walford, *The Death of A.*, 1962) allows the Eternal Jew the right to die on abjuring 'religion', the curse of his life. In *Pilgrim på havet* (1962; tr. N. Walford, *Pilgrim at Sea*, 1964) the author's dialogue with himself is resumed, but it reaches what appears to be its final resolution in *Det heliga landet* (1964; tr. N. Walford, *The Holy Land*, 1966) on a note of peace and reconciliation, in which the Christian element is implied rather than expressly stated. [SAB]

*Modern Theatre; 7 Plays and an Essay*, tr. T. R. Buckman (University of Nebraska, 1966) (with introduction).

G. Fredén, *P.L. Från Gudstanken till Barabbas* (Stockholm, 1954); S. Linnér, *Livsförsoning och idyll* (Stockholm, 1954); and *P.L.s livstro* (Stockholm, 1961); *Synpunkter på P.L.*, ed. G. Tideström (Stockholm, 1966).

**Lagerlöf, Selma** (Mårbacka 1858–Mårbacka 1940). Swedish novelist and story-writer. Her childhood world, a small estate in Värmland, is the subject of a sequence of autobiographical works, which give an insight into the patriarchal way of life of a hundred years ago. They are *Mårbacka* (1922; tr. V. S. Howard, 1924), *Ett barns memoarer* (1930; tr. V. S. Howard, *Memoirs of My Childhood*, 1934) and *Dagbok* (1932; tr. V. S. Howard, *The Diary of Selma Lagerlöf*, 1936). Paralysed as a child (she retained a slight limp throughout her life), she experienced a dramatic and wonderful recovery. It is tempting to view her literary preoccupation with miraculous transformations in this connexion. In her work, fairy-tale, ghost-story and legend are not sharply separated from descriptions of the world of everyday affairs. A typical story ranges over all these spheres with the freedom of an age-old tradition. Recent research, however, has discarded the notion that she is a simple-minded provider of tales; it has demonstrated how she builds up complex patterns out of vivid episodes and symbolic material. In the 1880s she trained as a teacher in order to support herself after the family fortunes had suffered a serious decline. All the time she struggled with the abundant but recalcitrant material for her first book, *Gösta Berlings saga* (1891; tr. P. B. Flach, *The Story of Gösta Berling*, 1898). It portrays one fateful year in the life of a Värmland community. The ringleaders are the Ekeby 'cavaliers' who drive the lawful owner of the estate, the strong-minded major's wife, out on the road. Revelling, gambling and music-making take the place of work; the imagination and the life of the impulses are substituted for law and order. Beauty results, but chaos too. In the end, the return to order becomes the salvation of the hero and his high-spirited companions. The style of the book is a mixture of high-flown rhetoric and forceful directness. She was never quite to repeat the success of her first novel with its symbolic overtones and romantic colouring. In a more sober style and with more penetrating psychology she followed a group of Dalecarlian revivalists from their home parish to the Holy Land in the 2-volume novel *Jerusalem* (1901–2; tr. V. S. Howard, 1915–18). The first part makes an impressive study of the life of a rural community and the often subtle interplay of the individual and the collective. With its hero, Ingmar Ingmarsson, and his struggle for moral integrity Selma Lagerlöf has created her most memorable character, at once a rational being and a person subject to impulses he only partly understands. She also wrote several volumes of short stories, and a number of short but powerful novels, such as *Herr Arnes penningar* (1904; tr. A. G. Chater, *Herr Arne's Hoard*, 1923) and *Körkarlen* (1912; tr. W. F. Harvey, *Thy Soul Shall Bear Witness!*, 1921), both of them shot through with supernatural happenings. Her later novels, though still very readable, are generally considered less important. She was awarded the Nobel Prize in 1909. Shortly afterwards she bought back the manor at Mårbacka and restored it in a grandiose manner. It is now the shrine of a world-wide Lagerlöf cult. Her most famous book has probably been *Nils Holgerssons underbara resa* (1906–7; tr. V. S. Howard, *The Wonderful Adventures of Nils*, 1907), a work commissioned by the Primary School Board for the greater glory of the teaching of Swedish geography. In it, before the age of aviation, she envisaged a flight on gooseback which at one time captivated the youngsters of a whole world. [SAB]

*Skrifter* (12 vols., 1933).

Elin Wägner, *S.L.* (2 vols., Stockholm, 1943); F. S. de Vrieze, *Fact and Fiction in the Autobiographical Works of S.L.* (Assen, 1958); V. Edström, *Livets stigar* (Stockholm, 1960); G. Ahlström, *Den underbara resan* (Lund, 1958); V. B. Lagerroth, *Körkarlen och Bannlyst* (Stockholm, 1963).

**Laguna, Andrés** (Segovia 1499–Segovia 1560). Spanish doctor and satirist. Probably the author of the *Viaje de Turquía* (CA), an account in dialogue form of a captive's life in Turkey. The tone is Erasmist and anti-clerical, and the account of Turkish life appears to be first-hand, though there is no evidence that Laguna knew the country. His book remained unpublished till 1905. It is a minor masterpiece, tolerant, civilized and delicately ironic. [JMC]

Bataillon, *EE.*

**Lalić, Mihailo** (Trepča 1914– ). Serbian novelist. His main theme is the war in Montenegro and the problems of courage and suffering faced by the individual in a fratricidal struggle. His best novels are *Lelejska gora* (1957) and *Hajka* (1960), where he evolves a style of tough poetic symbolism beneath the realistic surface of his writing. [EDG]

*SEER*, XL, 94 (1961); Kadić, *CSL.*

**Lamartine, Alphonse Marie Louis Prat de** (Mâcon 1790–Paris 1869). French poet and statesman. Except for schooling, he spent his first twenty years in the country, mainly on his father's estate at Milly. His family's royalist sympathies prevented him, as a young man, from serving under Napoleon. Extremely active by nature, he experienced the melancholy caused by enforced idleness, drifted slowly away from religious belief, sought distraction in reading, poetry and lovemaking. He was sent to Italy in 1810 to avoid a socially impossible marriage and returned with memories of a brief liaison in Naples, later idealized in *Graziella* (1849). At first his ambitions were literary but met with no success. On the restoration of Louis XVIII, he joined the Royal Guard. His military career was interrupted by the Hundred Days, and he resigned three months after Waterloo. At 26, after a philosophical and religious crisis, he considered returning to the Christian faith. In October the same year, he met Mme Julie Charles at Aix-les-Bains. His passion for her acquired the significance of a spiritual rebirth. In December 1817 she died and was to relive as *Elvire* in the *Méditations poétiques* which, in 1820, brought fame to the poet.

That year he married Elizabeth Birch and entered the diplomatic service. The ten years spent in Italy are marked by a growing religious fervour expressed in *Nouvelles méditations* (1823), *La mort de Socrate* (1824), *Le dernier chant du Pélerinage d'Harold* (1825) and culminating in the mystical lyricism of the *Harmonies poétiques* (1830).

He was elected to the Académie Française in 1830. After the July revolution, he abandoned diplomacy for politics, but unsuccessful in the 1831 elections, he left for the Middle East. The death of his daughter Lydia during a visit to the Lebanon inspired a moving poem, *Gethsémani.* As Député for Bergues in 1833, he later opposed Guizot (1840). His opinions broadened from contact with the social mysticism of the period apparent in *À Némésis*, *Les révolutions* (1831), *Des destinées de la poésie* (1834) and a projected epic poem retracing the destiny of humanity. Only two episodes were completed: *Jocelyn* (1836) and *La chute d'un ange* (1838). For Lamartine, progress was social and spiritual, not industrial. He advocated, faithful to his upbringing, the return to the land. The social lyricism of his *Recueillements* (1839) is most evident in 'Utopie', password of contemporary aspirations.

In 1847 he published his political testimony in the *Histoire des Girondins.* He served as Minister of Foreign Affairs in the provisional government of 1848. He lost his popularity by siding with Ledru-Rollin in the suppression of the June uprising, was heavily defeated in the presidential election and retired from public life in December 1851.

During his declining years, he slaved to pay his debts: personal reminiscences in *Les confidences* and *Raphaël* (1849); novels, *Geneviève*, *Le tailleur de pierres de Saint-Point* (1851); numerous historical works, and from 1852 onwards, his interminable *Cours familier de littérature.* The inspiration of his *Méditations* returns for the last time in *La vigne et la maison* (1857).

His works reflect the phases in his life, and up to his *Recueillements*, the propensities of his generation. The affinity explains the popularity of the *Méditations.* The hesitation between reason, doubt and faith with undertones of Rousseau and Voltaire in 'Dieu', 'La providence à l'homme', and in the reply to Byron ('L'homme'), the religious sentiment in 'La foi', 'La prière', 'La semaine sainte', 'Le chrétien mourant', but tinged with pantheist unorthodoxy – 'L'hymne au soleil', 'Le temple' – the pessimism bred of despair ('L'ode au malheur'), all are in perfect harmony with the rising romantic mood, as is also the poetic ideal ('Enthousiasme', 'La gloire'). Equally concordant are the poems of despair, the memory of Elvire confided to Nature ('Le lac'), the mystery of human and divine love ('Immortalité' 'Invocation'), death seen as liberation

('Isolement'), and consolation too in nature ('Le souvenir', 'Le vallon', 'Le soir', 'L'automne'). This intimate poetry of the heart, with its sadness and exaltation prolonged in subtle verbal harmonies, renewed the concept of lyricism.

In subsequent volumes, meditation upon despair, faith and immortality reached a climax in 'Novissima verba' (*Harmonies poétiques*). Obvious similarities enabled the public to form a set image of the poet, confirmed by the lyricism of *Jocelyn*, but destroyed by *La chute d'un ange*. Yet Lamartine used in *La mort de Socrate* the idea of progress in religious ideals, and later placed it in an Italian setting for *Tristesse* and *La perte de l'Anio*. It is combined with the dogma of expiation and rehabilitation borrowed from Ballanche in the structure of the epic recounting through the nine incarnations of Cédar, the return to perfection after the initial fault. *Jocelyn* depicts the soul, purified by love, virtue and sacrifice, rising towards God. The lyricism recurs in *La chute d'un ange*, especially in 'Le chœur des Cèdres du Liban', but there are significant changes. Fantasy and violence dominate the scenes set in the corrupt civilization of Balbek. In contrast, the religious and social ideal is rationalist and deist, mixed with pantheism (*Fragment du Livre primitif*; ed. M.-F. Guyard, 1954). It foreshadows the social fraternalism of the *Recueillements* and opens the way to similar themes exploited later by Laprade. Although frequently imitated, his elegiac style was criticized by the Romantics for its classical affinities and excessive facility. Its originality lies in the suggestion of emotion through delicately sustained, natural imagery, widening out to a vision of the spiritual affinities between man, the universe and the divine. [BJ]

*Œuvres poétiques complètes*, ed. M.-F. Guyard (Pléiade, 1963).

M. Citoleux, *L.* (Paris, 1906); H. Guillemin, *Le Jocelyn de L.* (Paris, 1936), and *A. de L.* (Paris, 1940); M. Bouchard, *L. ou le sens de l'amour* (Paris, 1940).

**Lambert of Hersfeld** (*c.* 1025–1080). German Benedictine at Hersfeld. His *Annales* merely copy other 'annals' of the world from Genesis onwards, but of events between 1040 and 1070 he writes vividly from personal knowledge, e.g. the conflict between Pope Gregory VII and the Emperor Henry IV, Canossa, Hohenburg, etc., and in excellent Latin (modelled on Livy, Sallust). [FB]

Ed. O. Holder-Egger, MGH, SRG, xv (1894).

**Lampe, Friedo** (Bremen 1899–Berlin 1945). German short-story writer. Recognized only since publication of *Das Gesamtwerk* (ed. J. Pfeiffer, 1955), for his sensitive, iridescent prose with its vein of humorous fantasy that recalls ⇨ Walser and Katherine Mansfield (whom he admired). [PB]

Waidson, *MGS*; *GLL*, XIV (1960/1).

H. Piontek, *Buchstab-Zauberstab* (Esslingen, 1959) (chapter on Lampe).

**Lampedusa, Giuseppe Tomasi di** (Palermo 1896–Rome 1957). Italian novelist. A wealthy Sicilian prince, he lived an adventurous youth and a retired and studious middle age. In his last three years he wrote the novel that was to make him deservedly, but posthumously, famous, *Il gattopardo* (1958; tr. A. Colquhoun, *The Leopard*, 1960), a large fresco of Sicilian life in the 1860s, a bitter-sweet sceptical picture of an insular world where, in spite of major political and social upheavals, nothing changes that really matters, a world of violent contrasts where love and death, beauty and corruption, present and past, revolution and tradition, blend in one disturbing and intoxicating mixture. In 1958 the typescript of the novel was almost accidentally discovered by ⇨ Bassani, who immediately recommended it for publication. A second book, *Racconti* (1961; tr. A. Colquhoun, with one story omitted, *Two Stories and a Memory*, 1962), has since appeared; it contains 3 interesting and well-written stories and 8 revealing chapters of autobiographical memoirs. [GMC]

A. Vitello, *I Gattopardi di Donnafugata* (Palermo, 1963).

**Lamprecht (Pfaffe Lamprecht)** (fl. 1120). Early German poet and churchman. Author of a lengthy epic poem, *Alexander*, on the deeds of Alexander the Great, written *c.* 1120–30. Three distinct versions of the work are extant: that from Vorau, though incomplete, is the oldest, while those from Strassburg and Basle are later adaptations and continuations. Lamprecht's original is derived from an 11th-century French poem (only the opening of which has survived), itself based on Latin translations of the pseudo-Callisthenic romance which is the ultimate source of almost all the medieval literary works on the subject of Alexander. Although revelling in the great earthly achievements of his hero, Lamprecht emphasizes at the end that, like all men, Alexander too must die, and that worldly glory, even that of the greatest men, must perish. ⇨*Alexandre, Roman d'*. [RT]

*Das Alexanderlied*, ed. F. Maurer (Darmstadt, 1964); ed. K. Kinzel (Halle, 1884).
Ehrismann, *GDL*.

**Lange, Per** (Rungsted 1901– ). Danish poet. His refined verse is of a classical beauty; most important are the collections *Kaos og Stjærnen* (1926), *Forvandlinger* (1929) and *Orfeus* (1932). His best poems are selected in the volume *Relieffer* (1943). [ELB]

**Langgässer, Elisabeth** (Alzey, Rheinhessen 1899–Rheinzabern 1950). German poet and novelist. Part Jewish (though converted to Catholicism) she suffered Nazi persecution. A Christian nature-poet indebted to ⇨ Lehmann, her difficult, symbolic style, which blends mythical and mystical elements into a kind of private liturgy, has has been called 'magical realism'. Her best poems are in *Der Laubmann und die Rose. Ein Jahreskreis* (1947). Her major novels are *Das unauslöschliche Siegel* (1946) and *Märkische Argonautenfahrt* (1950), both dealing with conscience and the search for salvation, in an original, mythical-psychological style (seen at an early, almost surrealistic stage in *Proserpina*, 1932). *Der Torso* (1947) and *Das Labyrinth* (1949) are collections of stories. [PB]

*Gesammelte Werke*, ed. L. Rinser (5 vols., 1959–64); Bridgwater, *TCGV*.
E. Augsberger, *E.L.: Untersuchung ihrer dichterischen Leitmotive und Symbole* (Nuremberg, 1962); *ML*, XXXVI, 1 (1954).

**Lanson, Gustave.** ⇨ French Literary Criticism in the 19th and 20th Centuries.

**Larbaud, Valéry-Nicolas** (Vichy 1881–Vichy 1957). French man of letters. He inherited a considerable fortune, and devoted himself to reading, writing and travel, acquiring an extensive first-hand knowledge of the customs and culture of England, Italy, Spain and Portugal. In 1935, he was completely incapacitated for the rest of his life by a severe cerebral haemorrhage. His novels and stories, mostly inspired by his own experiences, sensitively delineate fine shades of feeling: *Fermina Marquez* (1911) studies the impact of two beautiful South American sisters on an exclusive boys' boarding-school: *A. O. Barnabooth* (1913; tr. *A. O. Barnabooth: His Diary*, 1924) is the journal of a blasé young South American millionaire who voyages throughout Europe in search of his authentic identity; *Enfantines* (1918) evokes impressions of childhood; *Amants, heureux amants* (1923) portrays men and women in love and, in part, makes use of the stream-of-consciousness technique employed in Joyce's *Ulysses*, which Larbaud helped to translate into French. He translated works by Sir Thomas Browne, Coleridge, Landor, Samuel Butler, Whitman and Arnold Bennett, and wrote a large number of critical articles on French and English literature (in *Ce vice impuni, la lecture*, 1925 and 1941). His other main works include notes on his European travels, *Jaune*, *bleu*, *blanc* (1927) and *Aux couleurs de Rome* (1938), and an interesting *Journal* (1953) which reveals that his cosmopolitan culture and restless wanderlust in no way diminished his abiding affection for France. [RG]

*Œuvres* (Pléiade, 1957).
G. J. Aubry, *V.L., sa vie et son œuvre: La jeunesse* (Monaco, 1949).

**Larivey, Pierre** (Troyes 1540?–Troyes 1611). French dramatist. Son of an Italian, he was the most important writer of comedy in 16th-century France. He published 6 comedies in 1579 including *Les esprits*, the most famous, and 3 more in 1611. They mark a real step forward in the rather uncertain development of comedy in France. They are prose adaptations of Italian plays, and their chief merit lies in their lively style, quick, inventive and admirably suited to the stage, a great improvement on the monotonous verse used by ⇨ Jodelle in the *Eugène*. [GJ]

**La Roche, Sophie von,** née Gutermann (Kaufbeuren 1731–Offenbach 1807). German novelist. A cousin and protégée of ⇨ Wieland, she achieved fame as the writer of sentimental, didactic novels which lay special emphasis on feminine psychology (*Geschichte des Fräuleins von Sternheim*, 1771). Her journalistic activities in her own periodical *Pomona* (1783) and her contributions to Jacobi's *Iris* (1775ff.) show her as a child of the Enlightenment who has, however, read her Rousseau, and aim at the moral, intellectual and phsycal education of her female readers. [WAC]

W. Milch, *S. de la R. Die Grossmutter Brentanos* (Frankfurt a. M., 1935).

**La Rochefoucauld, François,** Duc de (Paris 1613–Paris 1680). French classical moralist. Author of *Réflexions ou Sentences et maximes morales* (1665; tr. L. W. Tancock, 1959). Born into an old noble family, for two generations Protestant, the causes of his participation in the Fronde are obscure; he was no rebel at heart but vain and insistent on homage: much of his income went in costly litigation. Nor was he outstanding either in the field or in politics. And he was misled by (class ?) hatred of Mazarin and infatuation, first for Mme de Chevreuse and then for Mme de Longueville. His contemporaries are puzzled in their judgements of him; it says much for his qualities that he had and kept firm friends. His military career ended in a severe wound and in humiliation: at one point he was imprisoned by Richelieu. In retirement he composed the bitter reflexions which have made him famous. Their origin seems to have been a circle of friends, notably Mme de Sablé. His *Mémoires* (1664; tr. anon. 1684), ostensibly published, like the *Maximes*, to correct a pirated edition, are useful as a companion piece, offering here and there explanation or excuse for his role and his views.

As a retired *grand seigneur* La Rochefoucauld seems to have been a man of exquisite manners and considerable charm. Mme de la Fayette, who knew him best, may have sought his help in writing her novels; it is more likely that she influenced the *Maximes*. Scholars have not decided whether the Duke acted as secretary of the group in which the making of maxims was a social game, or (more likely) worked out his own epigrams and presented them for discussion.

His fame depends on the slim volume of 1665, the *Maximes*, of which six editions are known before 1700 and countless editions since. Nineteen longer pieces, known as the *Réflexions diverses*, seem to have been composed later. From the first, these outspoken judgements on contemporary behaviour aroused opposition; many maximes were withdrawn after the first edition. Modern scholars tend to account for their cynicism by the author's ill fortunes, and the double dealing and naked power-politics of the Fronde when passions were fanned not only by politics but by class antagonism and greed for power and wealth. But the *Maximes* are not all of this stamp. They unveil the protean energies of self-interest; they explore the real basis of courage; they affirm the majesty and the terror of death. They also suggest the limits of prudence, probe the gulf between words and deeds and show constant respect for chance and mood. They study such neglected qualities as indolence, of mind as of body, and weakness of character. The soul of their wit is brevity, a recognized mode of rhetoric which La Rochefoucauld raises to new heights. He is a master of exclusion, of suggestion by the barest comparison of terms, by a single, sober image; and his perception of self-interest and self-preservation lying deeper than all avowed principles anticipates modern psychiatry and earned him the admiration of readers like Nietzsche and Gide. [WGM]

Ed. J. Truchet (Garnier, 1967); selections, ed. E. Mora (1965) (bibliography).

É. Magne, *Le vrai visage de La R.* (Paris, 1923); P. Bénichou, *Morales du grand siècle* (Paris, 1948); M. Bishop, *Life and Adventures of La R.* (Cornell, 1951).

**Larra, Mariano José de** (Madrid 1809–Madrid 1837). Spanish essayist, novelist and playwright. His family were Liberals and lived 1814–18 in exile, mostly in France. On their return they had to live in relative retirement, and Larra was made aware of his country's social and political problems. Possibly studying at Valladolid then Madrid he took to social and literary criticism in 1828. He adopted the satirical methods of Cadalso, Jovellanos and Goya, using irony and caricature to attack the false values, indolence and hypocrisy of Spanish society. Marriage and financial difficulties in 1829 led him to write plays, and amongst them adaptations of ⇨ Scribe like *No más mostrador* (tr. J. S. S. Rothwell, *Trade is Odious*, 1853) reflected his interest in French literature, as did his adaptations of Jouy's articles. But he always tried to alter his French originals to suit his Spanish audience and criticized Spanish writers who failed to do likewise. In the Romantic tradition he involved himself in what he wrote, but never lost his ability to observe and analyse human behaviour in general and Spanish behaviour in particular. His amours and final suicide have helped to build up a legendary position for him as a Romantic. He also wrote a historical novel entitled *El Doncel.* [ONVG]

*Obras,* BAE 127–130 (1960); *Articulos,* CC.
E. MacGuire, *A Study of the Writings of D.M.J. de L.* (1919); Piñeyro, *RS.*

**Larramendi, Manuel de.** ⇨ Basque Literature.

**Larsen, Johannes Anker.** ⇨ Anker Larsen, Johannes.

**Larsen, Thøger** (Tørring 1875–Lemvig 1928). Danish poet. He mingles visionary cosmic elements with descriptions of Jutland scenery and people. [ELB]

*Udvalgte Digte* (1945).

**Lasker-Schüler, Else** (Elberfeld 1876–Jerusalem 1945). German Jewish poet. A colourful figure well known before the First World War when her neo-romantic, often exotic, vividly colourful poems full of intense personal fantasy and rich (if sometimes obscure) emotions were much admired – especially in the *avant-garde* literary circles in which she moved (she was married for a time to H. Walden, after being the companion of the vagabond poet Peter Hille (1854–1904), idealized in her *P.-H. Buch,* 1906) and which she fancifully reflected in the novel *Mein Herz* (1912) and essays (*Gesichte*). Her books were banned in 1933, and she lived in Jerusalem after 1937. Diffuse religious feelings and motifs inform some of her best poems in *Hebräische Balladen* (1913) and *Mein blaues Klavier* (1943). [PB]

*Gesammelte Werke,* ed. F. Kemp (3 vols., Munich, 1959–62); *Sämtliche Gedichte,* ed. F. Kemp (Munich, 1960); *Dichtungen und Dokumente,* selection ed. E. Ginsburg (Munich, 1951); Bridgwater, *TCGV*; Hamburger and Middleton, *MGP.*
K. J. Holtgen, *Untersuchungen zur Lyrik E.L.-S.s* (Bonn, 1958); G. Guder, *E.L.-S.* (Göttingen, 1966); *ML,* XLIII (1962); *C* (April 1950).

**La Taille, Jean de** (Bondaroy 1533?–Pithiviers 1608). French dramatist, pamphleteer and satirical poet. He may have been a Protestant, but fought in the royal army. He wrote 2 tragedies remarkable for a lively sense of theatre unusual in tragedy of the period, *Saül le furieux* (1572) and *La famine, ou les Gabéonites* (1573); in these plays he 'classicizes' his Biblical subjects by imitating parallel scenes and characters in ancient tragedy. In his treatise *L'art de la tragédie* (ed. F. West, 1939) he summarizes current theories of tragedy, making various recommendations as to construction, style and subject-matter. His other work includes a long poem, *Le prince nécessaire,* which is a verse adaptation of Machiavelli's *Prince.* [GJ]

*Œuvres,* ed. R. de Maulde (4 vols., 1878–82).

**Lateur, Frank** (pseud. Stijn Streuvels) (Heule 1871–1969). Flemish author. He was ⇨ Gezelle's nephew and the self-taught son of a baker. At the time of depression in the flax-growing areas, he wrote his first short stories *Lenteleven* (1899; tr. A. Taxeira de Mattos, *The Path of Life,* 1915). His fine, poetic observation of nature and human emotions were early recognized and his short stories regularly appeared in magazines. They were collected in *Zomerland, Zonnetij* (1900), *Doodendans* (1901) and *Dagen* (1903). His first novel, *Langs de Wegen* (1902), sets the inevitability of the natural cycle (the theme of *Zomerland*) against Man's mastery of his own destiny. This is further developed in *Minnehandel* (1904), six stories linked by their background of six seasons of the year, and in his masterpiece, *De Vlaschaard* (1907), a novel expressing the fatalism of his earlier work in the lyrical statement of an epic paradox that if the father is to survive in his son, the son must succeed the father. His work stagnated until *Prutske* (1922), the sensitive study of a child, and *Werkmensen* (1926), which contains *Leven en dood en den ast* (tr. in preparation), one of the finest short stories in the language. Inarticulate peasants provide poor material for dialogue, but asleep, as here, their thoughts and feelings have free rein. His style, like Gezelle's, shows the countryman's instinct for what is wholesome and good, and his genius set a corner of West Flanders in a cosmic perspective. [PK]

E. Janssen, *S.S.en zijn Vlaschaard* (Amsterdam, 1946); *Volledige Werken* (12 vols., 1957); *Delta* (Winter 1959/60).
F. de Pillecyn, *S.S.* in *Verzameld werk, IV* (1960); G. Knuvelder, *S.S.* (Brussels, 1964).

**Latini, Brunetto** (Florence *c.* 1220–Florence 1294/5?). Italian writer. A notary, he served the Guelph commune of Florence. After the Guelph disaster at Montaperti (1260), he spent six years in exile in France, and there did most of his writing. He returned to Florence after the Ghibelline defeat at Benevento (1266). The reverence and affection which Dante shows him (condemned as a Sodomite) in Inferno 15 have led many critics to accept that Dante was Brunetto's pupil, but this is not proven. His works include *Li livres dou Tresor* or simply *Tresor* (an encyclopedic survey of knowledge, written in French, ed. F. J. Carmody, 1948), and various Italian compositions – *Tesoretto* (an allegorical, didactic poem) and *Favolello* (a verse epistle on friendship) (both in *Poemetti allegorico-didattici del secolo XIII*, ed. L. Di Benedetto, 1941), and *La rettorica* (ed. F. Maggini, 1915), a version cum-commentary of the first 17 chapters of Cicero's *De inventione*. [DGR]

Contini, *PD*.

T. Sundby, *Della vita e delle opere di B.L.* (Florence, 1884); B. Ceva, *B.L. l'uomo e l'opera* (Milan/Naples, 1965); *Minori*, i.

**La Tour du Pin, Patrice de** (Paris 1911– ). French poet. Of an ancient noble family of Dauphiné who reappear at all stages of French history, he spent his childhood in Sologne developing a sense of mystic communion with nature, which forms the background to the symbols, myths and gothic settings in *La quête de joie* (1932). His rather colourless but evocative work was hailed by conservatives as a bastion of sound values challenging the surrealist monster. Since the war he has written mystical and theological verse, collected in *Une somme de poésie* (1946) and *Le second jeu* (1959), which are said to describe the attitude of the mature man in front of the world, and are intended to be followed by a crowning volume about man before God. [CLC]

E. Kushner, *P. de la T. du P.* (Seghers, 1961).

**Latvian Literature.** Latvian, Lithuanian and Old Prussian (extinct since the 17th century) form the Baltic branch of the Indo-European languages. Latvian is highly inflected; the verbs have a multitude of forms and derivatives; many nouns clearly show their archaic origin. The language is of a great age; and so is Latvian folk poetry, which reflects ancient Indo-European ethics, customs and beliefs. Krišjānis Barons published (1900–15) 35,789 folk-songs (later increased to 60,000) and a multitude of variants.

This oral tradition lives to the present day. But written literature, owing to the loss of political independence in the 13th century, did not evolve directly from folk poetry. Fostered by German clergymen, it started late; the first known book is the *Catechismus Catholicorum* (1585). Secular literature began in the 18th century with G. F. Stender. In the mid 19th century, Latvians themselves entered the literary scene with lyric and epic poetry. The first great novel, *Mērnieku laiki* by the brothers Kaudzītes, a masterly portrayal of Latvian peasant life, appeared in 1879.

The 1880s saw an efflorescence of literature, a wealth of diverse trends, an absorption and transmutation of foreign literary influences. But among the most outstanding authors are those who were firmly rooted in their Latvian antecedents: the poet-dramatist Rainis (1865–1929), who frequently used folklore themes and imagery, Blaumanis (1863–1908), with plays about peasant life, followed by Skalbe (1879–1945), whose fairy-tales reflect the ethics of folk poetry, and Virza (1883–1940), whose great prose poem *Straumēnī* extols the patriarchal farmstead. This tradition was continued by Veselis (1896–1962) in his legends, and by Zinaīda Lazda (1902–57), whose poetry comes close to the spirit of the folk-song. Folklore motifs appear also in the poetry of Gunars Saliņš, and folklore mystique in some of Velta Sniķere's work.

Interesting among the poets influenced by foreign trends is Aleksandrs Čaks (1902–50), an urban poet and admirer of Mayakovsky. He, in turn, has influenced Linards Tauns.

The only anthology of Latvian poetry in English translation, *A Century of Latvian Poetry*, by W. K. Matthews (1957), contains 71 poets of between 1856 and 1956. Matthews has unfortunately overlaid an entire century of poetry with the poetic diction of second-rate English Romantics of the 1890s.

Since the Soviet occupation, literature in Latvia has been inhibited by Party directives. But interesting new poets have emerged, e.g. Čaklais Belševica, Līvzemnieks, Vācietis, Ziedonis.

Of the poets in exile, Veronika Strēlerte (b. 1912), Sweden, has published five volumes of verse. Though capable of deep emotion, she has attained a poised serenity; her poems, with their clarity of thought and form, have a quiet, direct appeal. Muted, in simple words, she can express more than many a voluble poet. Velta Sniķere, London, has published a volume of poetry, *Nemitas minamais* (Kalnājs, Chicago, 1961). Hers is a private world, a poetry of diverse meanings and interpretations. She strips language and experience down to essentials; her concentrated poetic use of the Latvian language is admirably expressive. Her English poems do not show the same command of language. Linards Tauns (1922–63), U.S.A., author of two volumes of poetry, is an urban poet, sensitively, searchingly alive; his is a timeless town; both in living and inanimate things, the ancient past is as immediate to him as the present. Gunars Saliņš (b. 1924), U.S.A., writes with sensuous sophistication, with subtlety of mood and colour. Penetrating below the surface of things, he lends them a larger dimension, a radiant reality. Saliņš has published a volume of poetry, *Miglas krogs* (Grāmatu Draugs, U.S.A., 1957); from this volume, *Summer*; *Aquarelle* appeared in *The Texas Quarterly* (Spring, 1962; tr. Ruth Speirs).

Five of the novelists in exile deserve special attention. Knuts Lesiņš (b. 1909), U.S.A., writes with an endearingly calm wisdom and humanity. Unsentimental, with tolerant, kindly humour and quiet perceptiveness, he displays a sensitive understanding of human situations. He has published 3 novels and 5 volumes of short stories. A selection appeared in *The Wine of Eternity* (tr. Ruth Speirs, Minnesota University Press, 1957). Anšlavs Eglītis (b. 1906), U.S.A., with a sharp, intellectual humour and lively curiosity, covers a wide range of subjects. His psychology is sound; his plots capture the imagination. Eglītis has written poetry, plays and 11 volumes of short stories, the best volume being *Uguns pilsēta* (Zelta Ābele, Stockholm, 1946). Among the most outstanding of his 13 novels is *Homo Novus* (Grāmatu Draugs, U.S.A., 1960), a picaresque account of Latvian artists in pre-war Riga, bubbling over with wit and a prolific vocabulary. *The Best Seller*, a short story, appeared in *The Texas Quarterly* (Autumn, 1960; tr. R. Speirs). Although Valdemārs Kārkliņš (1906–64), U.S.A. wrote 10 novels his moment of achievement was his volume of short stories *Pie laika upes* (1951), with their almost tangible atmosphere of place and situation, and a sensitive insight into diverse facets of character and human behaviour. His short stories *The Tunnel* and *Encounter in the Dark* appeared in *The Hudson Review* (Autumn, 1959, Autumn, 1960; tr. R. Speirs), and *By the River of Time* in *The Texas Quarterly* (Spring, 1960; tr. R. Speirs). Guntis Zarinš (1920–65), London, published 4 novels and 2 volumes of short stories, between 1959 and 1964. He rapidly developed into a considerable writer, modern, sharp-edged, aware of the darker side of life. Andrejs Irbe (b. 1924), Sweden, sounds a new note in Latvian literature with his first volume of short stories *Mums nav svētvakaru* (Kalnājs, Chicago, 1962). His style, seemingly simple, is full of subtle nuances; his stories, seemingly fragmentary, have a completeness of their own. He shows the individual and at the same time the universally applicable and significant. A writer of high seriousness, Irbe is deeply concerned with man in the present day; but his is a large, universal view, and he penetrates both below and beyond the level of consciousness and experience. [RS]

*Latvian Literature*, tr. R. Speirs (1954).

**Laube, Heinrich** (Sprottau, Silesia 1806–Vienna 1884). German dramatist and novelist. A leader of Das ⇨ Junge Deutschland; expelled from Leipzig, where he edited *Zeitung für die elegante Welt* (1833); arrested for 'treason' in Berlin (1834–5), his writings were banned. Theatre critic in Leipzig (1840ff.); director of Vienna Burgtheater (1849–67), Leipzig Stadttheater (1869–71), Vienna Stadttheater (1872ff.) – see *Das Burgtheater* (1868), *Das norddeutsche Theater* (1872), *Das Wiener Stadttheater* (1875). Member of Frankfurt parliament (1848) – see *Das erste deutsche Parlament* (1849). His novels – voicing revolutionary ideas in a semi-realistic, sometimes historical manner – include the trilogy *Das neue Europa* (1833–7) and *Der deutsche Krieg* (1863–6). His *Reisenovellen* (1834–7) imitate Heine. His plays – including *Gottsched und Gellert* (1845), *Die Karlsschüler* (1846), *Struensee* (1847), *Prinz Friedrich* (1848), *Graf Essex* (1856) – combine political agitation with French stage-skill. His *Geschichte der deutschen Literatur* (1839–40) heralds social realism. [LL]

*Gesammelte Werke*, ed. H. H. Houben (50 vols., 1908–10).
Dietze, *JD*.

**Lauesen, Marcus** (Løjt Kirkeby 1907– ) Danish novelist of South Jutland. Famous mainly for *Og nu venter vi paa Skib* (1931; tr. A. G. Chater, *Waiting for a Ship*, 1933), *De meget skønne Dage* (1933; tr. I. Modin, *The Very Beautiful Days*, 1934), and *Mor* (1961). [ELB]

**Lautréamont,** so-called **Comte de,** pseud. of Isidore Ducasse (Montevideo 1846–Paris 1870). French writer of prose poems. Sent to be educated in France, he died after three years in Paris having spent his time writing strange poems. His 'title' seems to have been taken from the title of a novel by Eugène ⇨ Sue, *Lautréamont*, its hero being a super-Byron in his arrogance. His prose poems, *Les chants de Maldoror* (1868; tr. G. Wernham, N.Y., 1944), express his loathing of humanity through a Byronesque figure called Maldoror. His sadism, his voluntary self-abandonment to fantasies from the depths of his mind, his adoration of the sea as the cradle of thoughtless cruelty, led to his being acclaimed later by the surrealists as a forerunner. In a famous passage Maldoror watches shipwrecked sailors torn to pieces by sharks and then mates with the most dreadful shark of all. In the preface to his *Poésies* (1870), he made an ironical attack on the Maldoror type of literature. [WA]

*Œuvres complètes*, with prefaces by R. de Gourmont, A. Breton and others (1963).
M. Blanchot, *L. et Sade* (Paris, 1949); P. Soupault, *L.* (Paris, 1953); G. Bachelard, *L.* (Paris, 1963).

**Lavant, Christine,** pseud. of Christine Habernig (Gross-Edling, Lavanttal 1915– ). Austrian poet. Living in the country, she has a 'natural' lyric genius, capable of the passionate response and musical expression (if less profundity) shown in *Die unvollendete Liebe* (1948), *Die Bettlerschale* (1959), *Spindel im Mond* (1959), *Der Sonnenvogel* (1960), *Wirf ab den Lehm* (1961), and *Der Pfauenschrei* (1962). Her short stories *Das Kind* (1948), *Das Krüglein* (1949), *Baruscha* (1952), and *Die Rosenkugel* (1956) are largely autobiographical. [PB]

Schwebel, *CGP*.
*Symposium*, XIX, 1, 1965.

**La Varende, Vicomte Jean de** (Bonneville-Chamblac 1887–Paris 1959). French novelist and biographer. After studying at the École des Beaux-Arts and the Sorbonne he divided his energies between pursuits of the landed aristocracy and literature. Most of his writing asserts the grandeur of the Norman aristocratic tradition. A collection of short stories *Pays d'Ouche* (1936) first launched his type of hero – aristocratic, brave, proud of family and regional traditions, loyal to the Church and the throne. A further group of stories, *Les manants du roi* (1938), and the novels *Nez de cuir* (1937; tr. R. Wills Thomas, *Leather-Nose*, 1938) and *Le centaure de Dieu* (1938; tr. D. A. and R. Wills Thomas, *Centaur of God*, 1939) develop the theme. His later works include *Indulgence plénière* (1951), *La sorcière* (1954), *Le cavalier seul* (1957) and *La partisane* (1960). Among his biographies are studies of Anne of Austria (1938), William the Conqueror (1946), the Broglies (1950) and Saint-Simon (1955). Elected to the Académie Goncourt 1942, he resigned at the time of the liberation (1944). [IHW]

L. Barjon, *Monde d'écrivains* (Tournai, 1960); P. Brunetière, *L.V. le visionnaire* (Paris, 1959); P. Dolley, *L'œuvre de L.V. devant l'opinion* (1952); Collection Brimborions, 65, 67, 78, 82 (Liège, 1960ff.).

**Lavater, Johann Caspar** (Zürich 1741–Zürich 1801). Swiss writer and Protestant pastor. Influenced by Bodmer's doctrines at an early age. Of deep, almost mystical, religious disposition, he began with rhyming versions of the Psalms and a number of religious poems and patriotic *Schweizer Lieder* (1767ff.), written in the manner of ⇨Gleim's *Preussische Kriegslieder*, which achieved considerable popularity. His pietistic insight that religion and piety were not the product of rational thought but of irrational emotions (*Aussichten in die Ewigkeit*, 1768-78) had an immediate appeal for the *Sturm und Drang*. He is chiefly remembered for his *Physiógnomische Fragmente* (4 vols., 1775–8), where he develops the thesis that the human face is a 'magic mirror' of the soul. His Biblical drama *Abraham und Isaak* (1776) and his imitations of Klopstock in the *Messiaden* (1780–6) have only antiquarian interest. [WAC]

*Auswahl*, ed. E. Stähelin (1943); *Fragmente*, selection tr. G. E. Fosbrooke, *Character Qualities Outlined and Related* (1923).
C. Jannetzky, *J.C.L.* (Frauenfeld, 1928).

**Lavedan, Henri** (Orleans 1859–Paris 1940).

French dramatist. Author of successful comedies of manners and problem plays. The first include amusing studies of social decline and frivolity and are marked by an expansive and indulgent good humour, e.g. *Le Prince d'Aurec* (1894), in which the follies of an impoverished young aristocrat are redeemed by his mother, and *Les deux noblesses* (1897) in which the nobility go into trade. In a more moralizing vein were *Le Marquis de Priola* (1902), a highly theatrical study of a latter-day Don Juan, and *Le duel* (1905), a contrived drama in which two brothers, one a priest, the other – conveniently – an atheist, struggle for the soul of a duchess. He is an adroit technician, fully alert to all the ways of entertaining an audience, but without a distinctive vision or idiom. [SBJ]

R. Peter, *Le théâtre et la vie sous la IIIe République* (Paris, 1948); Filon, *DR*.

**Lavrenyov, Boris Andreyevich** (Moscow 1894–Moscow 1959). Russian dramatist, inspired by the fratricidal pathos of the Civil War. He is a romantic with an eye for character and tense situations; rarely profound or psychologically interesting, his plays move fast and grip the audience's attention and sympathy. They are often set against a naval background. [AP]

*Sobraniye sochineniy* (6 vols., 1965).

I. Eventov, *B.L. Kritiko-biograficheskiy ocherk* (Leningrad, 1951); I. Vishnevskaya, *B.L.* (Moscow, 1962).

**'Laxdœla Saga.'** ⇨ Icelandic Sagas.

**Laxness, Halldór** (Reykjavík 1902– ). Icelandic novelist. Of farming stock, he travelled widely in his youth, steeping himself in the movements of the time. He became a Roman Catholic; his novels *Undir Helgahnúk* (1924) and *Vefarinn mikli frá Kasmír* (1927) are from this period, and are noteworthy for their highly personal style. Later he turned Communist and aired his views in a volume of satirical essays *Albýðubókin* (1929). He made his name with *Þu vínviður hreini* (1931) and *Fuglinn í fjörunni* (1932; both translated as *Salka Valka*, F. H. Lyon, 1936; rev. 1963), and *Sjálfstætt fólk* (2 vols., 1934–5; tr. J. A. Thompson, *Independent People*, 1945). They were followed by *Ljós heimsins* (4 vols., 1937–40). All these books are conceived on the grand scale, taking as their subject rural life in Iceland – fishermen, a stubborn farmer, a poet of the people, who are raised to a monumental level in their everyday strivings in a hostile world. Social criticism is there, but it is the poetry, symbolism, and deep compassion with which these books are suffused which makes them memorable. Subsequently Laxness has written a number or novels with historical settings. the trilogy *Íslandsklukkan* (1943), *Hið ljósa man* (1944), *Eldur í Kaupinhafn* (1946), set in 18th-century Iceland; and *Gerpla* (1952; tr. K. John, *Happy Warriors*, 1958), a satirical novel in saga style, based on the *Fóstbrædra saga*. In *Atómstöðin* (1948; tr. M. Magnússon, *The Atom Station*, 1961), he returned to contemporary themes in a novel highly critical of post-war Iceland and American influence there; the same theme was taken up in the play *Silfurtunglið* (1954). *Paradísarheimt* (1960; tr. M. Magnússon, *Paradise Reclaimed*, 1962) is again satirical, at the expense of Mormons in Iceland. He effected a revolution in prose writing in Iceland, which hitherto had tended to be traditional in character. His own style is highly individual and polished, but his most endearing quality is the rich lyricism which pervades even his most critical passages. He is the most notable Icelandic writer of modern times. [RGP]

P. Hallberg, *Den store väveren* (Stockholm, 1954); I. Eskeland, *H.K.L.* (Oslo, 1955); S. Einarsson, *Islenzk bökmenntasaga* (Reykjavik, 1961); K. Karlsson, *H.K.L.* (Reykjavík, 1962); Einarsson, *HIL*.

**Lazarević, Laza** (Šabec 1851–Belgrade 1890). Serbian prose-writer. He studied medicine in Belgrade at a time when socialism and materialism, especially in their Russian form, were becoming popular with the Serbian intelligentsia. Sent to Berlin to complete his studies, he found its more individual West European life in conflict with the narrower duties and loyalties bred into him by his patriarchal background and by his dominating mother. His first story, *Švabica* (published posthumously *c.* 1878), deals with this conflict. From 1879, when he returned to Serbia, he published 8 stories dealing with various aspects of the same problem. These vary from an examination of the crushing of a man's character by patriarchal and ethical precepts in *Verter* (1880–1) to a lyrical expression of the positive value and stability offered to the individual by the family in *Na bunaru* (1880-

1) and *Prvi put s ocem na jutrenje* (1879). Some of these stories, such as *Skolska ikona* (1879), which appear to justify the old morality at the expense of the new, earned him the (false) reputation of being a conservative and a naïve optimist who idealized the patriarchal family. In some of his final stories, *Sve će to narod pozalatiti* (1880–1) and *Vetar* (1889), he attains considerable psychological depth. He was the most original 19th-century Serbian prose writer. [EDG]

Barac, *HYL*; Popović, *JS*; *SEER*, xxxv, 84 (1956).

**'Lazarillo de Tormes.'** Spanish satire, forerunner of the picaresque novel, which appeared anonymously at Alcalá, Burgos and Antwerp in 1554. Internal evidence shows it was written before 1539. Various authors have been suggested from Diego Hurtado de Mendoza to Sebastián de Horozco. Bataillon makes a case for Fray Juan de Ortega, a cultured Jeronymite. Lazarillo is a traditional character and much of the novel is folklore developed from the old story of the blind man's boy. Three sections attack the evil ways of churchmen and officials such as pardoners. The book begins with a long account of Lazarillo's initiation at the hands of an astute blind beggar, whilst the third *tratado* shows the stupidity of overscrupulousness in honour. Much of the anti-clerical satire is medieval in tone and not truly Erasmist, so claims that the author was an Erasmist must be treated with caution. The Inquisition objected to the pardoner episode duly omitted in the 1573 edition. The style is racy and colloquial, spiced with irony and excellent character studies. The book is a vivid picture of society's lower levels, but only reflects contemporary Spain in part. It was a universal success and translated into French (1561), English (1576; J. M. Cohen, 1962), Dutch (1579), German (1617), Italian (1622) and Latin (1623?). Two sequels (1555, anon.) and 1620 (Juan de Luna) are not in the same class. [JG]

Ed. J. Cejador (CC, 1914); fac. edn of 1544 edns (1959).

F. Maldonado de Guevara, *Interpretación del L. de T.* (Madrid, 1957); Bataillon, *EE*.

**Leal, António Duarte Gomes** (Lisbon 1848–Lisbon 1924). Portuguese poet. He led an agitated life in a stormy period of national politics in which an old monarchy was overthrown and the Republic proclaimed (1910). After he had left his secondary school, he worked for some time in a notary's office and soon became a popular figure in many of the literary and political groups then common in Lisbon. For a very short period he attended the Faculty of Arts, then turned to journalism and edited a satirical paper (1872). In 1875 he published his first book of poems, *Claridades do Sul*, which was immediately noticed for its marmoreal beauty and daring associations of imagery. His poetry is also haunted by the fascination of sin and by an anguished longing for absolute purity. Leal's violent campaigns as a pamphleteer against the Church and the Crown provoked a frustrated attempt on his life. But his ill-disciplined genius and his chaotic reading were a constant obstacle to the composition of an ambitious epic on cosmic evolution, *O Anticristo* (1884), of which he published different versions. Despite his anti-clericalism, Leal was evolving towards an acceptance of Christianity (*A História de Jesus*, 1883) and was finally converted to Roman Catholicism. [LSR]

Vitorino Nemésio, *Destino de G.L.* (Lisbon, 1953).

**Léautaud, Paul** (Paris 1872–Robinson 1956). French diarist and man of letters. Abandoned by his mother, he was brought up by his father, a prompter at the Comédie Française. His childhood, one of neglect and unhappiness, remained a bitter memory, reflected in his first story, *Le petit ami* (1903; tr. H. Hare, *The Child of Montmartre*, 1959). He edited (with Adolphe Van Bever) an anthology of Symbolist and post-Symbolist poetry, *Poètes d'aujourd'hui, 1880–1900* (1900). He worked for the *Mercure de France* (1908–40) and was for a time its dramatic critic (as 'Maurice Boissard'; see *Théâtre de Maurice Boissard, 1907–1925*, 1927). His criticism is outspoken and extremely personal, as are the literary judgements expressed in his *Journal littéraire* (19 vols., 1954–66), which began in the year 1893. Circumstances made a misanthropist of him, and he lavished his great resources of tenderness on animals. His love and care for a vast collection of dogs and cats is reflected in *Bestiaire* (1959), a posthumous collection of extracts from his works. He achieved a large public only towards the end of his life (and then rather as an eccentric than as a writer of note) through a series of interviews on the radio, *Entretiens avec Robert Mallet* (1951). [SMD]

M. Mormoy, *L.* (Paris, 1958); A. Rousseaux, *Littérature du XXe siècle* (1938); *Critique*, XVI, 163.

**Lebenson, Micha Joseph,** pen-name **Michal** (Wilno 1828–Wilno 1854). Hebrew writer. Son of Abraham Dov L. (Adam), a leader of the Haskalah movement in Lithuania and a poet and scholar of repute, he was trained in early youth both in Hebrew and European languages. At 13 he began translating the great German poets into Hebrew and in 1849 published *Harisoth Troja* from the German translation by Schiller of Virgil's *Aeneid*. When in 1849 he went to Berlin, he won the admiration of Y. L. Zunz, who advised him to abandon 'foreign godheads' for national themes. As a result he set out to compose Jewish historical poems, *Shirei Bath Zion* (1851). [EE]

*Kol Shirei Adam u-Michal* (6 vols., Wilno, 1895) (collected verse of father and son).
Klausner, *HMHL*.

**Leconte de Lisle, Charles-Marie-René** (Saint Paul, Reunion Island 1818–Louveciennes 1894). French poet. He travelled widely, came to France, studied law at Rennes, and settled permanently in Paris (1846), where he joined the staff of the Fourierist *La Phalange*. The abolition of slavery after the 1848 Revolution ruined his family and he was forced to support himself by journalism, tutoring and translating. His poetry expresses a fundamentally pessimistic view of life, but in a style opposed to Romantic subjectivity (cf. preface to *Poèmes antiques*, 1852). Although he accepted the atheism of the new positivist and scientific philosophies he could not subscribe to the belief in the inevitability of progress. Thus his poems, although cultivating a 'Parnassian' impassivity (especially through descriptions of nature), have a deep underlying feeling of hopelessness. His tropical childhood inspired an even more vivid vocabulary than that of Gautier, who was his first model; in his famous 'Midi', he describes ripe cornfields under the blazing sun, using all the violence of heat on an almost motionless landscape to evoke the feeling that 'nothing is living here, nothing is sad or joyful!'. *Poèmes antiques* (1852) are largely Greek in inspiration and reflect his friendship with the Hellenist L. ⇨ Menard. *Poèmes barbares* (1862) were inspired by Nordic mythology ('Le Cor d'Hialmar'), or Egyptian art and remains, or consist of evocations of tropical nature and wild animals. In the later 1860s his house became the meeting-place for the Parnassian group (⇨ Mendès, ⇨ Sully-Prudhomme, ⇨ Coppée, ⇨ Hérédia, ⇨ Villiers de l'Isle Adam, ⇨ Mallarmé). He accepted an imperial pension in 1864 and in 1872 he was given the sinecure post of librarian to the Senate. His later publications included *Les Érinnyes*, a tragedy based on Aeschylus's *Oresteia* (1873), and *Poèmes tragiques* (1884), and *Derniers poèmes* (posth. 1895). [WA]

*Poèmes choisis*, ed. E. Eggli (Manchester, 1943).
A. Fairlie, *L. de L.'s Poems on the Barbarian Races* (1947); P. Flottes, *L. de L., l'homme et l'œuvre* (Paris, 1954).

**Leeuw, Aart van der** (Delft 1876–Voorburg 1931). Dutch novelist and poet. In *Levensgestalten*, one of his *Liederen en Balladen* (1911), he resolved to banish the melancholy nature of his youth and to look for the joys of life. It was his discovery of Traherne that finally enabled him to reconcile dream and reality, and in his best novels, *Ik en mijn speelman* (1927) and *De kleine Rudolf* (1930), his heroes find the fulfilment of their creative longing in the wonder of mundane things. [PK]

*Verzamelde gedichten* (1950); *Miniatures*, in Greshoff, *HL*.
J. Noë, *A.v.d.L.* (Bruges–Utrecht, 1964).

**Le Fort, Gertrud von** (Minden 1876– ). German novelist and poet. From an old Huguenot family, she studied under E. Troeltsch, whose (Protestant) *Glaubenslehre* she edited (1925). Converted to Catholicism in Rome, her imagination was stirred both by the inner doctrine of redemptive suffering and self-effacing love and by the outer order of the historic Empire – themes which recur in psalm-like poems (*Hymnen an die Kirche*, 1924; *Hymnen an Deutschland*, 1932; etc.), novels (*Das Schweisstuch der Veronika*, 1928; tr. C. M. R. Bonacina, *The Veil of Veronica*, 1932; etc.), short stories (e.g. *Die Letzte am Schafott*, 1931; tr. O. Marx, *The Song of the Scaffold*, 1953; the basis for Poulenc's opera, *Dialogues des Carmélites*, 1956), collected as *Erzählende Schriften* (3 vols. 1956) and *Gesammelte Erzählungen* (1966) and essays *Die ewige Frau* (1934). *Aufzeichnungen und Erinnerungen* (1951) is autobiographical. [PB]

*Hymns to the Church*, tr. M. Chanler (1937).
A. Focke, *G.v.L.F., Gesamtschau und Grundlagen ihrer Dichtung* (Graz, 1960); I. O'Boyle, *G.v.L.F.* (Fordham, U.S.A., 1965); N. Heinen, *G.v.L.F.* (Luxemburg, 1955); Natan, *GML*, II (1963); *GLL*, XV, 4 (1962); *GLL*, VIII, 1 (1954).

**Le Gonidec, J. M. F.** ⇨ Breton Literature.

**Lehmann, Wilhelm** (Puerto Cabello, Venezuela 1882–1968). German poet, critic and novelist. Closely associated with ⇨ Loerke in initiating a new school of mythical nature-poetry, in which all things are mystical ciphers of the 'Green God', he combines mystical insight with precise observation to produce visually evocative poems. Though influencing e.g. ⇨ Langgässer, ⇨ Eich, ⇨ Krolow, his style is not modernist, but classical in the manner of Robert Graves and Robert Frost. Apart from poems – collected in *Meine Gedichtbücher* (1957), *Abschiedslust* (1962) and *Sichtbare Zeit* (1967) – he wrote literary essays, e.g. *Dichtung als Dasein* (1956) and *Kunst des Gedichts* (1961), and rhapsodically idyllic fiction, the novels: *Weingott* (1921); *Ruhm des Daseins* (1953); *Der Überläufer* (1962) and stories (*Verführerin, Trösterin und andere Erzählungen*, 1947, etc.). [PB]

*Sämtliche Werke* (3 vols., 1962); Bridgwater, *TCGV*; Hamburger and Middleton, *MGP*.
W. Siebert, *Gegenwart des Lyrischen Essays zum Werk W.L.s* (1967); D. Schug, *Die Naturlyrik G. Brittings und W.L.s* (Erlangen, 1963); H. Bruns, *W.L.* (Kiel, 1962); Keith-Smith, *ECGL*; *GLL*, XV, 4, 1962.

**Lehtonen, Joel** (Sääminki 1881–Huopalahti 1934). Finnish novelist and poet. He began as a journalist and translator, rapidly produced (1904–5) a substantial poem ('Perm') and 3 short lyrical novels, all strongly romantic and Nietzschean in inspiration, then travelled widely in Europe (principally in France and Italy) and published one or two novelistic travel books and some lyrical prose. His return to his native district of Savo, coupled with the outbreak of civil war in 1918, led to a marked change in his outlook: his awareness of nature was deepened, but at the same time his natural humour became tinged with satire and social criticism. The style and outlook of his best period are foreshadowed in the fine small-scale novel *Kerran kesällä* (1917). *Putkinotko* (1918–19), a long and humorously satirical apotheosis of laziness, is his finest work and one of the most brilliant of all Finnish novels. The satirical note is intensified in *Rakastunut rampa* (1922), *Sorron lapset* (1923) and *Punainen mies* (1925), which are written with great exuberance but little regard for form or structure.

Endeavouring to combat increasing depression he returned to sunny memories of childhood (*Onnen poika*, 1925; *Lintukoto*, 1929), or, despairing of human nature, took refuge in the study of animal psychology (*Rai Jakkerintytär*, 1927). The many-faceted *Sirkus ja pyhimys* (1927) can also be regarded as an attempt to preserve his humanity of outlook. But his last novel, the picaresque *Henkien taistelu* (1933), is a scathing satire. A collection of poems, *Hyvästijättö Lintukodolle*, appeared after his suicide in 1934; the mood is one of dejection and weariness. In Lehtonen a warm-hearted lyricist and a shrewd observer of human nature were constantly at war. He translated Boccaccio, A. France, Stendhal, Ibsen and Björnson. [VKS]

**Leino, Eino**, originally Eino Leopold Lönnbohm (Paltamo 1878–Tuusula 1926). Finnish poet and essayist. Beginning university in 1895, he soon became involved with the 'Young Finland' movement and devoted his time largely to writing, including journalism as a literary and dramatic critic and as a brilliant political columnist. He travelled widely after his first marriage broke up (1908), leading a bohemian existence to the detriment of his health. His genius was prolific and many-sided; outstanding as a poet, he was capable both of uninhibited lyrical spontaneity and formal discipline, informed by modern French and Scandinavian techniques. Early influenced by ⇨ Runeberg and Heine, his youthful romanticism gradually acquired darker nuances and greater introspective, even mystical depth. In his best collection, *Helkavirsiä* (I, 1903; II, 1916), he took material from the ⇨ *Kalevala* and ⇨ *Kanteletar*, stylizing the old legends and ballad form to express his deeply felt tragic affirmation of life. He sang ardently also of Finnish liberty, became embroiled in cultural-political controversy, and was bitterly attacked. He tried to resuscitate verse drama (some 20 plays in all; see especially *Naamioita*, 1905–11), produced nearly 30 volumes of poetry (*Talviyö*, 1905, and *Halla*, 1908, are among the best), a cycle of epic poetry, *Simo Hurtta* (1904–19), two allegories (*Mesikämmen* and *Ahven ja kultakalat*) and an animal story (*Musti*). His memoirs (*Elämäni kuvakirja*, 1925), many essays, on impressionistic history of Finnish literature (*Suomalaisen kirjallisuuden historia*, 1910), and fiction are full of brilliant passages. [IR]

*Kootut teokset* (16 vols., 1926–30); *Valitut teokset* (4 vols., 1934); *Kirjeet* (4 vols., 1960–2) *Pakinat* (2 vols., 1961); *Runot* (3 vols., 1961–4); Allwood, *TCSP*; Ollilainen, *SF*; Tompuri, *VF*.
Havu, *FL*.

**Leisewitz, Johann Anton** (Hanover 1752–Brunswick 1806). German dramatist. He wrote only one play, *Julius von Tarent* (1776; ed. A. Sauer, DNL 80, 1883), which treats the familiar theme of the *Sturm und Drang*, the hostile brothers. He avoids the worst crudities and callowness of his generation: the play shows careful dramatic construction and a considerable sense of the stage and as a favourite of the young Schiller exercised an influence on *Die Räuber*. [WAC]

*SD* (selections).
Garland, *SS*; Pascal, *GSD*.

**Leivick, Halpern** (Minsk 1888–New York 1962). Yiddish poet. Arrested and imprisoned for revolutionary activities in Russia 1906; sentenced to life imprisonment in 1912, he escaped while being transported to Siberia and settled in New York. This background, coupled with a deep resentment against a stern father and months spent in a TB sanatorium, are reflected in his poetry. His style is visionary, bordering on the mystical, but had the largest following among contemporary Yiddish poets. Published 20 prose dramas, 10 volumes of poetry, hundreds of essays and newspaper articles. [EE]

*Geklibene Verk* (5 vols., Vilno, 1925–8); *Liedel fun Gan Eden* (Chicago, 1937); *In Treblinka bin ich nit Gewen* (N.Y., 1945); *Mit der Sheris Hapleyta* (N.Y., 1947); *Di chassene fun Fernwald* (N.Y., 1949).
Roback, *SYL*.

**Lemaire de Belges, Jean** (Belges, now Bavay, Valenciennes 1473?–1515?). French poet. One of the last of the *rhétoriqueurs*, he spent most of his life at various princely courts. He visited Italy, and his poetry shows his admiration for Italian art and literature as well as for the poets of classical antiquity. His best works are probably *La concorde des deux langages* (1511; ed. J. Frappier, 1947), an allegorical plea for France and Italy to recognize their spiritual and cultural affinities, and the *Épîtres de l'amant vert* (1505; ed. J. Frappier, 1948) – the '*amant*' is a parrot belonging to his employer; in grief at her absence the bird commits suicide by throwing himself into the jaws of a dog. This is a light and witty piece of work, a graceful and amusing compliment to Marguerite d'Autriche. Lemaire is a technical virtuoso and often overdoes complicated rhyme schemes, punning rhymes, alliteration, echo-effects, etc. He also compiled a prose 'history' of the French nation, *Les Illustrations de Gaule* (1510–13). [GJ]

*Le temple d'honneur et de vertus*, ed. H. Hornik (1957).

**Lenau**, pseud. of Nikolaus Franz Niembsch von Strehlenau (Csatad 1802–Vienna 1850). German poet. Of mixed German and Hungarian parentage. A highly strung, unbalanced personality who ended his days in a mental asylum, he was obsessed with the elemental forces of nature, claiming to find living demons in the fields and streams, and seeing human life as an analogy to this view of nature. The expression '*Weltschmerz*' has come to be attached particularly to the mood of the lyric poetry by which he is most characteristically remembered (*Gedichte*, 1832, 1844; *Neuere Gedichte*, 1838). His slender output also includes fragmentary dramas on the subjects of *Faust* (1836–46; cf. the orchestral episodes by Liszt) and of Don Juan (cf. Richard Strauss's symphonic poem). [RT]

*Sämtliche Werke*, ed. E. Castle (6 vols., 1910–23); ed. H. Engelhard (1959); *Poems and Letters*, tr. and ed. W. H. Root (1964).
M. Schärffenberg, *N.L. Dichterwerk als Spiegel der Zeit* (Erlangen, 1935); J. Turóczki-Trotzler, *L.* (Berlin, 1961).

**Lenclos, Ninon de,** really Anne de (Paris 1620–Paris 1705). French feminist and wit. She owed her great reputation not only to her long life, her liaisons, and friendship with ⇨ Saint-Évremond, but to her gifts in handling light verse and skill in conversation. She wrote in prose *La coquette vengée* (1659), not unworthy of comparison with

Molière's *Précieuses ridicules* of the same year. [WGM]

*Letters*, ed. É. Magne (1925); Mongrédien, *PP* (prose).

**Lengyel, József** (Marcali 1896– ). Hungarian novelist. An active communist, his memoirs (eg. of the 1917–19 period in *Visegrádi utca*, 1957) are as important as his stories (*Elévült tartozás*, 1964). His arrest in 1937 and deportation to Siberia until 1955 did not destroy but deepened his inspiration, which both explores the reality of personal experience under mass (and brutal) treatment, and tries to understand what went wrong with the socialist ideal. *Igéző* (*The Spell*, tr. I Duczynska, 1964) is a characteristically moving story, while parts of *Reggeltől estig* (From morning to evening) have a power comparable with that of Solzhenitsyn. Part of a long novel was published in *Kortárs*, December 1968, entitled 'A Confrontation'.

*Szépirodalmi Könyvkiadó* (Budapest, 1966– ); *From Beginning to End* (memoirs, tr. I. Duczynska, 1968); *The Judge's Chair* (tr. I.D. 1968); *Acta Sanctorum* (stories in trans., 1971). *TLS*, 6 March 1969.

**Lengyel, Menyhért** (Balmazújváros 1880–1957). Hungarian playwright. He lived for many years in the U.S.A.; he wrote many successful plays, of which *Tajfun* (1909; tr. L. Irving, *Typhoon*, 1913) had world-wide success. Bartók's opera *The Miraculous Mandarin* was based on a play by him. [JFR]

**Lennep, Jacob van** (Amsterdam 1802–Oosterbeek 1868). Dutch novelist and scholar, son of the poet and scholar D. J. van Lennep. His poetry, influenced by ⇨ Bilderdijk and later by Scott, is far less important than his entertaining novel *Ferdinand Huyck* (2 vols., 1840; tr. A. Arnold, *The Count of Talavera*, 1880) and his informative edition of ⇨ Vondel. [PK]

*Romantische werken* (23 vols., 1856–72); *Poëtische werken* (13 vols., 1859–72); *De Pleegzoon* (1833; tr. E. W. Hoskin, *The Adopted Son*, N.Y., 1847); *De Roos van Dekama* (1836; tr. F. Woodley, *The Rose of Dekama*, 1846).

**Lenormand, Henri-René** (Paris 1882–Paris 1951). French dramatist. His pessimistic depiction of passions beyond man's control exploits Freud's theory of the unconscious. In *Le mangeur de rêves* (1922; tr. D. L. Orna in *Three Plays*, 1928) a mother's death before her daughter's eyes causes a trauma; *Le simoun* (1920) dwells on an incestuous father–daughter passion. The latter play, like *L'ombre du mal* (1924), compounds passion with the effects of tropical climate; others evoke weird effects (*Le temps est un songe*, 1919; *L'homme et ses fantômes*, 1924) or show decadent, helpless beings (*Les ratés*, 1930; *Le lâche*, 1925 – tr. op. cit.). *Le théâtre élizabéthain* (1933) and *Confessions d'un auteur dramatique* (2 vols., 1949) throw light on his aesthetic of the drama.

*Théâtre complet* (10 vols., 1925–49).
P. Blanchart, *Le théâtre de L.* (Paris, 1947); Robert E. Jones, *The Alienated Hero in Modern French Drama* (Athens, Georgia Univ., 1962).

**Lentini, Jacopo da** (early 13th cent.). Italian poet and notary at the court of Frederick II (sometimes referred to as 'Il Notaro'). His *canzoni* and sonnets constitute the most considerable extant collection of the Sicilian school. Their theme, characteristically Provençal, is chivalrous love. The poet is vassal, offering devotion to the lady and receiving disdain in return. He cultivates technical ingenuity, and is famous chiefly as the reputed inventor of the sonnet form. Dante quotes him in the *De vulgari eloquentia* and mentions him in the *Divine Comedy* (*Purg*. xxiv). [DGR]

C. Guerrieri Crocetti, *La Magna Curia* (1947); Salinari, *PLD*; Contini, *PD*; Panvini, *RSS*; Lind, *LPIR*; Rossetti, *DC*.

**Lenz, Jakob Michael Reinhold** (Sesswegen 1751–Moscow 1792). German dramatist. Influenced by Herder and Goethe while a private tutor in Strassburg, the ⇨ *Sturm und Drang* movement appealed to his chaotic, unstable nature – latterly he suffered from periodic insanity – and his *Anmerkungen übers Theater* (1774) is a typical statement of 'Storm and Stress' dramatic theory: French classicism and its rules are rejected; the main interest in drama should lie in the 'Kerls', the strong, ruthless characters; Shakespeare is celebrated as the great realist and the function of drama is declared to be the revelation of 'naked nature'. His fame as a dramatist rests principally on two plays, *Der Hofmeister* (1774), a partly autobiographical treatment of the Héloise and Abélard theme, and *Die Soldaten* (1776), the story of a middle-class girl who is seduced by an officer and eventually becomes a prostitute. *Der Hofmeister* is marred by a grotesque mixture of genres and a complete lack of unity of action, but both plays reveal Lenz's gifts as an accurate observer of reality and his strong social interests. His technique anticipates ⇨ Büchner and the Naturalists in its use of short abrupt scenes in realistic dialogue. Lenz also wrote several novels and a number of lyrics, certain of which ('Die Demut'; 'An den Geist') are amongst the most moving of their age. [WAC]

*Werke*, ed. F. Blei (5 vols., 1909–13); *SD*.
Garland, *SS*; Pascal, *GSD*.

**León, Luis de** (Belmonte, Cuenca 1527–Madrigal 1591). Spanish humanist, religious writer and poet. He joined the Augustinian order in 1544, obtained a chair in Theology at Salamanca in 1561 and secured others later. At a time of fierce academic rivalries he was denounced to the Inquisition (for criticizing the accuracy of the Vulgate text, for translating the *Song of Songs* into Spanish, etc.) and was imprisoned 1572–6. His profoundly Christian spirit inspired his Biblical commentaries in Latin and two remarkable prose works, *De los nombres de Cristo* (1583–5; ed. F. de Onís, 3 vols., 1914–21) and *La perfecta casada* (1583). He was much attracted to the pagan classics too, and his translations of Horace's *Odes* and Virgil's *Eclogues* and *Georgics* are unsurpassed. His modern fame rests upon a few of his 30 original poems, chiefly on those in the *lira* metre which he adopted from ⇨ Garcilaso. In these he expresses the eternal wonder of the poet at the mystery of the universe, and his yearning for a quiet life lived both for contemplation and for epicurean enjoyment. In several of these poems the setting is Horatian and the deeper thought Platonic, with a surprising absence of strictly Christian sentiment ('Qué descansada vida', 'A Francisco de Salinas', 'Noche serena', etc.); but the latter is strongly present in 'En la Ascensión'. He acknowledged that true mystical union was not for him; his approach was perhaps too speculative (on Pythagorean and Ptolemaic lines) and even scientific, even though his verse at times soars on an upward current of strong emotion. He was little known as a poet in his day; he referred modestly to his poems as *obrecillas* and never printed them. Quevedo's edition of 1631 made little impact, but from the late 18th century to our day his standing has been of the highest. [CCS]

*Obras completas castellanas* (1944); *Poesías*, ed. A. C. Vega (1955); *The Original Poems*, ed. E. Sarmiento (Manchester, 1953); Trend, *OBSV*; Perry, *HASP*; Cohen, *PBSV*.
A. F. G. Bell, *L. de L.* (1924); Alonso, *PE*.

**Léonard, Nicolas-Germain** (La Basse-Terre, Guadeloupe 1744–Nantes 1793). French poet. Educated in France, he held a minor diplomatic post in Liège, 1773–83, and then returned to Guadeloupe, serving there as a legal official. Poor health brought him back to France in 1791, and he died when about to re-embark. An unhappy early love affair, his illness, and nostalgia for both France and his native island give a sincere melancholy to his verse, and some subjective reality to the conventional yearnings of the pastoral idyll which, under the influence of the then popular ⇨ Gessner, became his natural poetic vehicle (*Idylles morales*, 1766; *Idylles et poèmes champêtres*, 1782). [WHB]

*Œuvres*, ed. V. Campenon (1798).
W. M. Kerby, *The Life . . . of N.-G.L.* (Paris, 1925); Barquissau, *PC*.

**Leonora Christina,** Countess Ulfeldt (Frederiksborg Castle 1621–Maribo 1698). Danish authoress. The daughter of King Christian IV (by his morganatic marriage), wife of Chancellor Count Corfitz Ulfeldt with whom, after his political disgrace, she fled to Sweden but was later imprisoned in the Castle of Bornholm; released, they both escaped abroad again. Count Ulfeldt was *in absentia* sentenced to death for high treason in Copenhagen in 1660. During a brief visit to England, where she came to reclaim money lent to Charles II during his exile, the King arranged for her to be arrested at Dover by the Danish authorities and taken to Denmark in 1663, where she was put into the Blue Tower of Copenhagen. Here she was kept prisoner for 22 years, without any sentence ever being passed. Reprieved in 1685, she spent her last years in a convent at Maribo.

Apart from some minor autobiographical sketches (including one in French, covering the period up to her imprisonment in the Blue Tower), she wrote in prison a detailed and moving account of her tribulations. Though her fate was well known before, *Jammers Minde* was only published in 1869 (tr., with the 'French autobiography', *Memoirs of Leonora Christina*, F. E. Bunnett, 1872) after the manuscript had been discovered among the possessions of remote descendants in Austria. In this most important prose work of Danish 17th-century literature, she reveals her impressive and proud character. [ELB]

Rousseau de la Valette, *The Life of Count Ulfeld and of the Countess Eleonora, his Wife* (tr. 1695).

**Leonov, Leonid Maksimovich** (Moscow 1899– ). Russian novelist and dramatist. He joined the Red Army in 1919 and was occupied mostly in journalistic work. His early stories, *Buryga* and *Tuatamur*, are imitative of ⇨ Leskov, ⇨ Remizov and ⇨ Zamyatin, but reveal unusual mastery of the language. He acquired fame with his first novel, *Barsuki* (1924; tr. H. Kazanina, *The Badgers*, 1947), a lively account of the enmity between village and city both before and after the Revolution. In *Vor* (1927; tr. H. Butler, *The Thief*, 1931) he traced the disillusionment, degradation and eventual redemption of a loyal Communist during the NEP period. Like his other work of this period it is heavily influenced by Dostoyevsky. In the 1930s, with *Sot'* (1930; tr. I. Montagu and S. Nolbandov, 1931) and *Skutarevsky* (1932; tr. A. Brown, 1936), his work becomes less independent. The themes are orthodox: industrialization, the re-education of the non-Communist intelligentsia and the unmasking of saboteurs; but the style and construction are complex and rewarding. In *Doroga na Okean* (1935; tr. N. Guterman, *Road to the Ocean*, 1944), however, he goes deeper and examines the problem of death for a devoted and active Bolshevik. His last novel, *Russkiy les* (1953), which was awarded a Lenin prize in 1956, is a cumbrous and over-written work. The fate of the Russian forest and the controversy over the best methods of felling become symbols for the history of the Russian people. The action takes place during the Second World War.

Leonov's plays are mostly psychological dramas and usually turn on events that have taken place several years previously but still dominate the present. All are carefully constructed and reveal the intricate characterization typical of his novels; structurally they show the influence of Gor'ky. *Nashestviye* (1942; *Invasion*, tr. in *Four Soviet War Plays*, 1944), which was awarded a Stalin Prize in 1943, is his best-known play; it has been turned into a film and an opera (composer Dekhteryov). *Obyknovennyy chelovek* (1940) and *Zolotaya kareta* (1946, revised 1955) are his finest plays and reveal his deepening preoccupation with moral problems. Since Stalin's death he has been mainly occupied in revising earlier works, notably *Vor* (1957–9), which has been re-interpreted as well as rewritten. [RDBT]

*Sobraniye sochineniy* (9 vols., 1960–2); *P'yesy* (1964); *Literatura i vremya. Izbrannaya publitsistika*, ed. V. V. Syakin (1964); tr. Yarmolinsky, *SSS*; Faber, *RSS*.

V. A. Kovalev, *Tvorchestvo L. L.* (Moscow, 1956); L. A. Fink, *Dramaturgiya L. L.* (Moscow, 1962); Muchnic, *GP*; Simmons, *RFSI*.

**Leont'yev, Konstantin Nikolayevich** (Kaluga 1831–Sergiyev posad 1891). Russian philosopher, writer and critic. He was the son of a landowner. He studied medicine at Moscow University, became a military surgeon in the Crimean War, spent ten years in the consular service in Turkey. After a religious conversion he went for a year to Mount Athos, then returned to Russia. He worked for a short time as a censor in Moscow, then settled in Optina Pustyn' and in 1891 became a monk.

Originally his philosophy was an immoral aesthetism. He remained true to the cult of beauty for the rest of his life but the element of immorality in his teaching was later replaced by Christian beliefs. Politically he was a conservative, and saw a danger to civilization in social levelling, democratization and the growing importance of the middle class in the West. He thought that if Russia stopped imitating the West it might lead the world to a great future. His social and political ideas are expressed in *Vostok, Rossiya i slavyanstvo* ('The East, Russia and Slavdom', 1885–6).

The main character of his literary works is the type of a Narcissistic superhero. The best known of his novels are *Egipetskiy golub'*, *Ditya dushi* and *Ispoved' muzha*.

In his works on literature Leontyev departed radically from the accepted doctrine that the 'golden age' of Russian literature began with Pushkin and continued until the end of the 19th century. Literature after Pushkin was for him in a state of decline, since the high aesthetic values had been replaced by polemical propaganda. It was in the field of pure literary criticism that he produced a masterpiece – *Analiz, stil' i veyaniye v romanakh grafa L. N. Tolstogo* (1890) – a masterly analysis of Tolstoy's literary methods. [MG]

*Sobraniye sochineniy* (12 vols., 1912–14); *Egipetskiy golub'*, *Ditya dushi* (N.Y., 1954).

N. Berdyaev, *L.*, tr. G. Reavey (1940); T. G. Masaryk, *The Spirit of Russia*, ii (1955); P. Milyukov, *Iz istorii russkoy intelligentsii* (1903); S. Frank, *Filosofiya i zhizn'* (St Petersburg, 1910); Hare, *PRST*.

**Leopardi, Giacomo** (Recanati 1798–Naples 1837). Italian poet. The eldest son of a provincial nobleman. His home life, dominated by his mother, a strong-willed woman of deep religious convictions but unresponsive character, provided an uncomfortable background to his early years, and was one of the causes of a sense of unhappiness which afflicted him in adolescence and never left him. His father, though unpractical and weak, was responsible for perceiving and encouraging his son's precocious intellectual talents, and, in the fine library of Casa Leopardi, Giacomo became by 1816 a classical scholar of exceptional ability. His intensive studies, however, had a serious and lasting effect on his health. Though he never abandoned his scholarly activities, poetry became his major medium of self-expression. At provincial Recanati, he was out of the main stream of Italian cultural life, and he never shared the literary theories of ◊ Manzoni and the Milanese Romantics. Yet his great poetry, the finest written in Italy in the 19th century, was not only highly original, but also contained more forward-looking elements than any written by supporters of Romantic theories.

Leopardi's poetic output is relatively small, and the central part is contained in one volume, the *Canti*. His first poems of significance, 'All'Italia' and 'Sopra il monumento di Dante' (both 1818), are patriotic in theme, and owe something to the encouragement and advice of his friend, the writer P. Giordani. These were followed (1819–21) by his first poems of real originality, a group of five lyrics known as *Idilli*, and including such famous poems as 'L'infinito' and 'La sera del dì di festa'. In these poems his bitter pessimism is already apparent, but also clear is the presence in his poetry of other elements, by virtue of which the negative aspects of this pessimism are transcended. After writing the *Idylls*, he turned (1821–2) to more philosophical subjects. With the exception of *Bruto minore*, an impressively stark and noble apologia for suicide, these poems are of uneven quality.

Between 1823 and 1828 he wrote no lyric poems. He did, however, compose, in 1824, the greater part of his major prose work, the *Operette morali* (tr. C. Edwardes, 1882), a series of 24 short dialogues and discourses describing various aspects of his attitude to life. In 1825 he made his first successful break with Recanati and his family home, and thereafter, though he returned to Recanati for two long spells, his life was passed, amidst illness and financial difficulties, away from home. In Bologna (1825–6) and Florence (1827 and 1830–3) he met many leading figures of Italian culture (including Manzoni), but made no lasting friendships; he remains essentially a solitary figure.

In 1828, his desire and ability to write lyric poetry returned (an event described in the poem 'Il risorgimento'), and in the next two years, largely during a period of residence at Recanati, he composed the 6 magnificent poems usually known as the second group of *Idylls*. Some of these ('A Silvia', 'Le ricordanze') are poems of nostalgia, recalling the lost hopes and illusions of youth; others ('Il sabato del villaggio', 'Canto notturno') express the poet's awareness of and compassion for the predicament of man, destined to unhappiness in a world ruled by an indifferent Nature. In 1830, at Florence, he met a young Neapolitan, Antonio Ranieri, who became his companion for the rest of his life. Also at Florence, he fell in love. The lady, Fanny Targioni Tozzetti, was more interested in Ranieri, and an odd, triangular affair ensued which terminated with the departure of Ranieri and Leopardi for Naples in 1833. It did, however, produce a group of 5 poems, outstanding among which are 'Il pensiero dominante', 'Amore e morte' and 'A se stesso'. In 'La ginestra' (1836), his most comprehensive poetic statement, we find, alongside the basic and characteristic theme of the insignificance of man in the face of an indifferent and omnipotent Nature, a sharp attack on contemporary optimism, and a moving statement of what the poet considered the proper basis for human solidarity.

Much valuable information concerning his life and thought is contained in the *Zibaldone*, a voluminous daybook which he kept from 1817 until 1832; and also in his correspondence. [CF]

*Tutte le opere*, ed. F. Flora (5 vols., 1940); *Canti*

tr. J. H. Whitfield (Naples, 1962) (parallel text); Kay, *PBIV*.

I. Origo, *L.: A Study in Solitude* (1953); J. H. Whitfield, *G.L.* (1954); G. Singh, *L. and the Theory of Poetry* (Lexington, Kentucky, 1964).

**Leopold, Jan Hendrik** ('sHertogenbosch 1865–Rotterdam 1925). Dutch poet. Deafness heightened his sense of spiritual isolation and vulnerability which makes his poetry the most sensitive and individualistic of *De Nieuwe Gids* (cf. ⇨ Kloos, ⇨ Verwey), to which he contributed in the nineties. Oriental mysticism offered his passive contemplation some hope for his 'unrequited longing', and he read and translated Persian poetry. He did not write a great deal but few poets have achieved the diaphanous texture and exquisite musicality of his verse. [PK]

*Verzameld Werk* (2 vols., 1951); Grierson, *F*; Barnouw, *CA*; *The Valley of Irdin. A Collection of Poems*, tr. P. J. de Kanter (1957); Weevers, *PNEC*.

J. M. Jalink, *Eine Studie über Leben und Werk des Dichters J.H.L.* (Bonn, 1949); N. A. Donkersloot, *Lotgevallen van een dichterschap* (Amsterdam, 1965); M. J. G. de Jong, *L.s 'Cheops'* (Leyden, 1966).

**Lermontov, Mikhail Yur'evich** (Moscow 1814–Pyatigorsk 1841). Russian poet. Brought up after his mother's death (1817) on his aristocratic grandmother's estate, away from his father, a retired officer of Scottish extraction. He enjoyed a good home education, three journeys to the Caucasus, then studied in the Moscow Noblemen's Pension and the University (1830–2), without sitting examinations. He began writing poetry and autobiographical dramas in prose. When first in love, he was derided; when seriously in love, the girl married another. He entered St Petersburg Guards' Cadet School, wrote bawdy verse and sought conflict and strife 'as if there were peace in storms': *Parus* (1832). As an officer in the Guards Hussars (1834), and in society life, his cynicism developed. In 1835 *Khadzhi Abrek* was published without his permission. He was arrested on Pushkin's death (1837) for a poem of invective – copied by hand in thousands – against Court circles; expelled from the Guards, sent to the Army in the Caucasus. Back in the capital, he became involved in a duel, and was banished again to the Caucasus (April 1840) just as his novel, *Geroi nashego vremeni* (tr. E. and C. Paul, *A Hero of Our Times*, 1958; P. Foote, Penguin Classics, 1966), appeared, and a book of verse (*October*). Twice cited for bravery, the Tsar refused the award. On leave in 1841, hoping to retire and to devote himself to literature (a second edition of the novel with his Foreword), he was ordered back to the forces. An officer, teased by him and goaded on by the poet's enemies, challenged him to a duel, in which Lermontov was killed outright.

A romantic in life as in literature, he was an embittered idealist. As if exiled from paradise, he fell into the reactionary world of Nicholas I and rebelled against the regime, the censorship, society, women (his love lyrics poignantly express fidelity and sadness – or scorn); defiantly he challenged Fate or God.

Pushkin, so different from him, is his lasting inspiration. He models on him his own *Kavkazskiy plennik* (1828), some lines surviving even in his *Demon* (1829–41, 5 versions; tr. A. C. Coolidge, *The Demon*, Leningrad, 1925). In Pushkin's vein is *Tambovskaya Kaznacheysha* (1836), much of it being a serious duologue with him, particularly on the nature and role of a poet. There are also echoes of Kozlov, Batyushkov, Ryleyev, while some early prose resembles Gogol', and (in the drama *Maskarad*, 1836) Griboyedov's free-iambic satire. Yet Lermontov's rhythms are individual: he is one of the first to write an octave (1831), he uses varied forms of ternary metre, a freer pattern of rhyme, sometimes masculine rhyme only, or blank verse of ⇨ *bylina* style. Fastidious, he constantly modified his recurrent themes and lines.

Affinity relates him to Western romantics. He shares their fascination with Napoleon. He is swayed by Byron, imitates him, longs for a similar destiny, then realizes his own identity: 'Like him an outcast but with a Russian soul' ('*Nyet, ya ne Bayron*' – 'No, I am not Byron', 1832). He follows Schiller's rhetoric of indignation, translates Heine, Goethe, André Chénier, etc. Typical romantic themes and images he makes his own. But his 'orientalism' is inspired by the Caucasus and by its folk-lore, which gives original stamp even to his Demon, otherwise a familiar Lucifer figure complete with angel and mortal love.

The device of a confession relieves his 'burden of self-knowledge'. Some 'I-lyrics' have dates as titles: *1831-go iyuniya 11 dnya*

('11 June 1831') sparkles with aphorisms ('in man alone the vicious and the sublime can meet'), or else he reveals his dreams and conflict with society: *Kak chasto*... ('How frequently, amid a crowd') (1840). Then he objectivizes himself in images: the sail, clouds, the crag, the oak-leaf. Yet he is reticent: *Ya ne khochy chtob svet uznal* ('I do not wish the world to know'), 1837. And he left neither diary nor correspondence. A confession, different from Constant's or Musset's, runs through his long poems to his psychological novel. A sense of predestination weighs upon his heroes, but fatalism leads to defiance and bold action.

Moral or philosophical issues preoccupy him. He has an intuition of 'the other world', but his attitude to it is contradictory: the Demon's 'proud enmity against Heaven' and his own sardonic thanks for all his suffering (*Blagodarnost'*, Gratefulness', 1840) alternate with prayerful contemplation: *Angel* (1831), *Kogda Volnuyetsya zhelteyushchaya niva* ('When sways the yellowing corn'), 1837, *Molitva* ('The Prayer'), 1837, 1839. Nature brings peace and harmony.

His musical and evocative nature-poetry gains force from precision of detail and colour (he could also paint and draw). It is masterful in *Mtsyri* (1840), where a rebellious novice roams day and night over the mountains.

The theme of revolt has wider political implications in the ballads, in *Posledniy syn vol'nosti* ('The last Son of Liberty'), 1830, *Novgorod* (1831), *Vadim* (1833–4) and the magnificent story of the times of John the Terrible *Pesnya pro tsarya Ivana Vasil'yevicha*...' ('The song of the Merchant Kalashnikov'), 1837. The present grieves him: *Duma* ('Meditation'), 1837; the very title of his novel 'of *our* times' is both a plea and an indictment. He juxtaposes his generation with the men of 1812 in *Borodino* (1837), where a veteran tells simply of heroism and of the horror of the war. He is the first realist poet of battle. Fighting under the clear Caucasian sky raises the question why man is always at strife: *Ya k vam pishu*... (1840). It is not military glory that stirs his patriotism. Sarcastic about his 'unwashed country' with its Tsars, he loves Moscow and, 'not knowing why', loves the northern landscape with its sad villages and peasants: *Rodina* ('My Country'), 1841.

He outlives his romanticism, 'freeing himself through verse' from his Demon who turns into a dandy: *Skazka dlya detey* ('A Tale for Children'), 1839. Bored with the 'deafening language' of the storms of nature and of the heart, he now likes 'nice weather in the morning and, in the evening, a quiet talk': *V al'bom S. N. Karamzinoy* ('For S. N. Karamzina's Album'), 1841. Even if a poet is like his derided and stoned (*Prorok* 'The Prophet', 1841), he would now accept the continuous process of life, with a song of love and the murmur of an oak-tree over his grave: *Vykhozhu odin ya na dorogu* ('Alone I come on to the road'), 1841.

We see his motifs again in Dostoyevsky and Blok; Tolstoy and Chekhov regard his prose as a model. Many of his lyrics were set to music, *The Demon* made into an opera by A. Rubinstein (1871), and *Borodino* and *The Cossack Lullaby* became popular songs. [NG]

*Sobraniye sochineniy* (4 vols., Moscow/Leningrad 1959); lyrics and *Borodino*, tr. in Bowra, *BRV*.
H. Troyat, *L'étrange destin de L.* (Paris, 1952); Y. Lavrin, *L.* (1959); J. Mersereau jr., *M.L.* (Southern Illinois Univ. Press, 1962); A. Ginsburg, *Tvorcheskiy put' L.* (Leningrad, 1940); B. Eichenbaum, *Stat'i o L.* (Leningrad, 1961).

**Lesage, Alain-René** (Sarzeau, nr Vannes 1668–Boulogne-sur-mer 1747). French novelist and dramatist. Trained for the law, he early abandoned it to become the first major French writer to live primarily upon the direct earnings of his pen. His output was consequently prolific: in addition to publishing numerous translations and adaptations, chiefly of Spanish plays and novels, from 1710 onwards, he also wrote over 60 plays – mostly farces, topical sketches and comic-opera librettos – for the Paris fairground theatres. His first truly original work dates from 1707: *Le Diable boiteux* (tr. anon., 1708; tr. J. Thomas, *Asmodeus*, 1924) uses a loose narrative framework of fantasy (borrowed from a Spanish novel) to present sketches of individuals and situations much in the manner of La Bruyère, which, despite the Spanish setting, gently satirize French foibles. In 1707 also he had some success with a one-act comedy, *Crispin rival de son maître* (ed. T. E. Lawrenson, 1961; tr. B. H. Clark, *Crispin, Rival of His Master*, N.Y., 1915) – a light-hearted comment, in a manner then popular, on the contemporary weakening of traditional class barriers. The note of social and moral criticism in *Turcaret* (1709; tr. R. Aldington, 1923) is much harsher: the play depicts the downfall of a wealthy tax-farmer, a ruthless and unscrupulous but vain and sexually gullible parvenu, at the hands of a group of schemers led by a quick-witted valet, Frontin, whose aim is to become a second Turcaret himself. It is however upon *Gil Blas* (1715–24–35; tr. Smollett, 1749) that his reputation has chiefly rested. This is a picaresque novel, Spanish in manner and setting, in which the multifarious adventures of an unheroic lad making his way in the world by his wits become the occasion for presenting vignettes, mostly satirical but sometimes sentimental, and always lively, of human behaviour at all levels of society. As in *Le Diable boiteux*, the emphasis is primarily upon moral analysis in the 17th-century manner, and the speed of the narrative precludes any real depth in characterization, but the book can still charm by its gently ironic humour and the cheerful vitality of its hero. [WHB]

*Œuvres complètes* (12 vols., 1828) (omits the fair-ground plays).

L. Claretie, *L. romancier* (Paris, 1890); E. Lintilhac, *L.* (Paris, 1893); H. C. Lancaster, *Sunset, a History of Parisian Drama, 1701–1715* (1945).

**Lesiņš, Knuts.** ⇨ Latvian Literature.

**Leskov, Nikolay Semyonovich** (Gorokhovo, Orel Province 1831–Petersburg 1895). Russian writer. Orphaned early, he entered the Civil Service at 16. His next post with an Anglo-Russian firm entailed travelling all over Russia, which gave him first-hand knowledge of the lives, customs and speech of many different strata of Russian society. He took up journalism in 1860, moved to Petersburg and published his first story, *Ovtsebyk*, at 32. His anti-nihilistic novels *Nekuda* (1864) and *Na nozhakh* (1872) resulted in his virtual isolation in the predominantly positivist literary circles of the time.

Leskov's stories are expanded anecdotes of crime, the exotic, bizarre or piquant, luridly embellished by his fertile imagination, his predilection for the incongruous, and his exuberant use of Russian vernacular. Many of them are narrated by characters of widely differing origin, often semi-educated, each using his particular colloquial idiom (incidentally providing amusing examples of 'folk etymology' that he overheard or invented himself). This narrative method, the *skaz*, was to be developed by ⇨ Remizov and ⇨ Zoshchenko.

The powerful concentration of his well-known *Ledi Makbet Mtsenskogo uyezda* (1865) is less typical of his originality than e.g. *Voitel'nitsa* (1865), the humorous story of a Petersburg procuress, *Ocharovannyy strannik* (1873), a masterpiece of storytelling, *Zapechatlennyi angel* (1873), or *Levsha* (1881). His best longer work is *Soboryane* (1872), one of several studies of the rural clergy. Drawn towards Tolstoy's religious teaching, he wrote a number of folk legends and Christmas tales revealing in their insight into peasant piety. His later works include pointed satires on the higher clergy and the bureaucracy.

His encyclopedic knowledge of little-known areas of Russian life and his linguistic virtuosity make him one of Russia's most original storytellers, while his erratic ideological evolution and his position as a humanitarian advocating no particular socio-political programme make him an exceptional and undeservedly neglected figure in 19th-century Russian literature. [PH]

*Sobraniye sochineniy* (11 vols., 1956–8); *The Musk-Ox and Other Tales*, tr. R. Norman (1944); *The Amazon and Other Stories* (1949) and *Selected Tales* (1962), tr. D. Magarshack.

L. Grossman, *N.S.L.* (Moscow, 1945); V. Setschkareff, *N.S.L.; Sein Leben und sein Werk* (Wiesbaden, 1959); *Oxford Slavonic Papers*, x (1962); Mirsky, *HRL*.

**Leskovar, Janko** (Valentinov 1861–Valentinov 1949). Croatian novelist. His works consist of 2 stories and 10 short novels. In 1905 he ceased to write altogether. His works deal with the psychological predicament of the educated man in provincial Croatia. He was deeply influenced by Turgenev. His best-known novel is *Sjene ljubavi* (1898). [EDG]

Barac, *HYL*.

**Leśmian, Boleslaw** (Warsaw 1879–Warsaw 1937). Polish poet of Jewish origin (his name was Lesman). He studied in Kiev, stayed for a time in Paris and wrote some of his early poems in Russian. Reluctant to commit himself to print, he published only 3 volumes of verse: *Sad rozstajny* (1912), *Łąka* (1920) and *Napój cienisty* (1936), but none of them contains inferior work. The first showed an integrating use of Symbolism. His volume *Łąka* stood out as a new landmark of style. By exposing the duplicity of myth and by exploiting freaks of nature such as lameness and disfigurement, he sought the true face of life, reflecting both sensuous ecstasy and ugly pain. In his poetry there walked many deaths 'holding one another by the hand', and God 'embraced the oak, crying'.

Leśmian seemed to be outside the current of literary fashions and reputations, a symbolist who would persist with his weird verbal coinages and macabre ballads set in the glossy wonderland of meadows and forests. He remained the poets' poet, an acquired taste, but not for the palate of vitalists or the pundits of social realism. The collected edition of his works had to wait until 1957. His originality is now undisputed. [JP]

Peterkiewicz and Singer, *FCPP*; *SEER*, XXXVII, 89 (1959).

**Lessing, Gotthold Ephraim** (Kamenz, Saxony 1729–Braunschweig 1781). German writer. To the horror of his pastor-father, he early deserted the study of theology and then of medicine to become one of the earliest free-lance writers in the history of German literature. It is in his re-orientation of German dramatic literature away from French models towards the naturalness of the English stage that his great achievement lies. This is the theme which appears in his earliest critical writings, *Beiträge zur Historie und Aufnahme des Theaters* (1749ff.), and occupies a central position in his two great critical periodicals, *Briefe, die neueste Literatur betreffend* (1759ff.), and the *Hamburgische Dramaturgie* (1767–8). His 54 contributions to the *Literaturbriefe* include criticisms of contemporary works, but are notable primarily for their utter rejection of ⇨ Gottsched and the artificiality of French classical drama. Naturalness and sincerity are declared to be valid literary criteria and in the famous 17th letter Shakespeare is held to be closer to the essence of classical Greek tragedy than Corneille, the conclusion being drawn that the English stage is a more natural model for German dramatists than the French one. Even native German popular drama is defended against the strictures of Gottsched, a Faust fragment being appended as evidence of the potentialities of native themes. The *Hamburgische Dramaturgie* is the fruit of his employment as resident critic at the national theatre in Hamburg: once again the rules of French classicism, particularly the unities of time and place, are rejected as unnatural and devitalizing, and Gottsched's importation of French models is declared to be a fetter on the development of native German drama; Aristotle's doctrine of catharsis is reinterpreted in the light of the self-identification of the audience with the protagonist and a call is made for rational motivation out of character and circumstance, Shakespeare again being celebrated as the great dramatic genius whom the German should imitate.

While his own dramatic works cannot be regarded as great literature, they nevertheless laid the foundations of modern German drama. The minor plays of his youth (from *Damon* to *Die Juden*) are still based on classical and French models. His first important play, *Miss Sara Sampson* (1755), in its combination of Richardson's sentimentality with the dramatic world of Lillo and Shadwell introduced the current English dramatic style and middle-class tragedy to the German stage. The middle-class milieu is preserved in the comedy *Minna von Barnhelm* (1767; tr. W. A. Steel and A. Dent, 1930), important for its treatment of immediately contemporary events – the situation of a wrongfully dismissed officer after the Seven Years' War and his relations with his fiancée. In spite of its contrived situations and stock comic devices, the play lives through its genuine characters and lively dialogue. The contrived quality, the sentimentality and a number of lines which simply do not 'come off' make *Emilia Galotti* (1772), a Virginia theme set in a petty Italian state, the least successful of his major plays, but again the drama has historical importance for its establishment of the middle-class tragedy as a distinct genre and its anticipation of the social criticism of the *Sturm und Drang*. His last play, *Nathan der Weise* (1779; tr. W. A. Steel and A. Dent, 1930), in which he already uses the blank verse of classical German tragedy, is the outcome of his defence of the free-thinker Reimarus against the attacks of the strictly orthodox Pastor Goeze of Hamburg. It is a dramatic counterpart to the rationalistic view of religion and the belief in the perfectibility of man which Lessing advances in *Die Erziehung der*

*Menschengeschlechts* (1780): the outward action of the play is neither convincing nor important, but in the person of the noble Jew, Nathan, in his tolerance and in his belief that true religion is not a question of dogma or faith but of ethical behaviour, the play expresses all the best tendencies of the age and achieves a timeless validity.

Of Lessing's minor works the only one of permanent importance is the *Laokoon* (1766; tr. W. A. Steel and A. Dent, 1930), which delimits the spheres of the plastic arts and literature, the former being seen as existing in space, the latter as existing in time, thereby destroying the facile interpretation of the Horatian '*ut pictura poesis*' and the spate of purely descriptive verse which the 18th century produced.

Although Lessing in many ways anticipated the 'Storm and Stress', its chaotic lawlessness was anathema to him and his true legacy is to be seen in the humanity of the Classical movement. It is in his personification of the best qualities of the German Enlightenment, in his intellectual honesty, his tolerance, his courageous search for truth and his respect and admiration for the in-dwelling powers of the human intellect, that his true significance lies. [WAC]

*Werke*, ed. J. Petersen (25 vols., 1925).
H. B. Garland, *L.* (1938); O. Mann, *L.* (Hamburg, 1949); B. v. Wiese, *L.* (Leipzig, 1931).

**Leucadio Doblado.** ⇨ Blanco White.

**Levertin, Oscar** (Gryt 1862–Stockholm 1906). Swedish poet, story-writer, essayist and critic. Of Jewish ancestry, he viewed Swedish history and culture with a measure of detachment but also with the enthusaism of an explorer from outside. Together with ⇨ Heidenstam he ushered in the more romantic style of the nineties, forgoing his earlier commitment to social realism. His early poetry in *Legender och visor* (1891) and *Nya dikter* (1894) is steeped in the culture of the European past. Old paintings and old poems are his favourite motifs, but they also serve as illustrations of the themes of love and death, which are mysteriously and inextricably interwoven in his mind. In his later verse he cultivated less exclusive interests. His last collection, *Kung Salomo och Morolf* (1905), shows him more openly personal than ever before. His poetic style is heavy, but darkly colourful and passionate. In his prose he is often most successful when writing in the style of a bygone age, as in his *Rococonoveller* (1899), set in the period most dear to him, that of King Gustavus III. He also approached that era in a more scholarly manner, while allowing his intuition ample scope. The result, e.g. his characterization of ⇨ Bellman in *Från Gustaf III:s dagar* (1896) and *Svenska gestalter* (1903), was highly successful, the classic formulation for Levertin's own generation. From 1897 to his premature death, he was associated with the *Svenska Dagbladet*, the organ of the literary nineties, and attained a position never held by a press reviewer before him, that of a leading national critic. [SAB]

F. Böök, *O.L.* (Stockholm, 1944); C. Fehrman, *L.s lyrik* (Lund, 1945); B. Julén, *Hjärtats landsflykt* (Stockholm, 1961).

**Levi, Carlo** (Torino 1902– ). Italian novelist. He trained as a doctor, but later devoted himself to politics, literature and painting. He became famous after the war with the publication of *Cristo si è fermato ad Eboli* (1945; tr. F. Frenaye, *Christ Stopped at Eboli*, 1948), which revealed to Italian readers a long neglected part of their own country, Lucania, where he was restricted in 1935–6 for his anti-fascist activities. The book, depicting with a painter's eye for shapes and colours, and a doctor's sensitivity to social and human problems, the Southern way of life in all its hopelessness, material poverty and spiritual richness, inaugurated the post-war trend to social realism and documentary novels, to which Levi himself later contributed a more sophisticated but artistically less convincing book, *Le parole sono pietre* (1955; tr. A. Davidson, *Words are Stones*, 1959), on Sicily. Other works are: *L'orologio* (1950; tr. J. Farrar, *The Watch*, 1952), a picture of political intrigue in Rome immediately after the war, and travel books, on Russia (*Il futuro ha un cuore antico*, 1956), Germany (*La doppia notte dei tigli*, 1959; tr. J. M. Bernstein, *The Twofold Night*, 1962) and Italy (*Un volto che ci somiglia*, 1960; *Tutto il miele è finito*, 1965). [GMC]

Falqui, *PNNI*; Pullini, *RID*.

**Levinski, Elchanan Leib,** pseud. **Rabbi Karov** (Vilna 1857–Odessa 1910). Hebrew publicist and novelist. One of the leaders of the Chovevei Zion Movement. Wrote a Utopian work, *Mass'a l'Eretz Israel be-*

*Shnat Tat* (Odessa, 1892), and travel sketches of Russia. [EE]

Waxman, *HJL.*

**Leys d'amors.** ⇨ Jocs florals.

**'Libro de buen amor.'** ⇨ Ruiz, Juan.

**Lichtenberg, Georg Christoph** (nr Darmstadt 1742–Göttingen 1799). German writer. Professor of physics in Göttingen, he wrote both strictly scientific works and numerous essays aimed at the spreading of popular enlightenment. He is remembered chiefly as a diarist and aphorist; his witty, sceptical and satirical turn of mind found natural expression in pithy sayings and aphorisms which tellingly characterize and often deflate the principal men and movements of his age. Goethe remarks that there is a problem lurking behind each one of his jests. He was a child of the Enlightenment, and although he had anticipated many of the theories of Lavater, he mocked the exaggeration of the latter's system; similarly he opposed the growth of sentimentality and the excessive Shakespeare-worship of the ⇨ *Sturm und Drang.*

He twice visited England, and his *Briefe aus England* (1776–8) reflect his interest in things English, including the theatre. He also wrote a perspicacious commentary on the engravings of Hogarth, *Ausführliche Erklärung der Hogarthschen Kupferstiche* (1794–9), in which, as in the work of Chodowiecki, whom he also admired, he saw a human reality nearer to the truth than the currently popular idealism of Winckelmann and his followers. [WAC]

*Werke*, ed. W. Grenzmann (1949); *Reflections of Lichtenberg*, sel. and tr. N. Alliston (1908).

W. Grenzmann, *L.* (Salzburg-Leipzig, 1939); H. Schöffler, *L.* (Linz, 1943); J. P. Stern, *L.* (Indiana Univ. Press, 1959).

**Lichtenstein, Alfred** (Berlin 1889–in action near Reims 1914). German poet. His 'Die Dämmerung' (modelled on ⇨ Hoddis's 'Weltende') was the second Expressionist poem to appear in print. Author also of a children's book (*Die Geschichte des Onkel Krause*, 1910), his collected *Gedichte und Geschichten* (1919; *Gesammelte Gedichte*, ed. K. Kanzog, 1962) reveal a subtle and sensitive talent which eschewed the more raucous tones of modernism. [PB]

*Gesammelte Prosa*, ed. K. Kanzog (Zürich, 1966); Bridgwater, *TCGV*; Hamburger and Middleton, *MGP.*

Hamburger, *RE.*

**Lidman, Sara** (Missenträsk 1923– ). Swedish novelist and dramatist. Born in a remote district of north Sweden, she studied at Uppsala; she spent long periods in Africa in the 1960s. She brought the regional novel back to life with outstanding success in *Tjärdalen* (1953), the charm of which is largely due to a skilful use of dialect and the economical yet evocative style of its writing. The intensity and maturity with which she depicted a moral conflict in the chief character are other notable features of this book. She confirmed her position with *Hjortronlandet* (1955), a novel more sparing in its use of dialect and closer to the collective novels of the 1930s, its theme being the poverty and cultural privations of a backward minority. Against this background the tragic destiny of a talented young girl is drawn up with poignant clarity. In *Regnspiran* (1958; tr. E. H. Schubert, *Rain Bird*, 1962) the concern is once more primarily with individuals, chiefly with the gifted, but egotistically callous Linda Ståhl. The book brings a beautiful realization of a provincial childhood, and touchingly introduces the theme of adolescent love, guilt, and betrayal. Its sequel, *Bära mistel* (1960), lacks the quality of effortlessness of the earlier books, and its psychology may appear somewhat schematic: it portrays Linda Ståhl later in life, tied to an unresponsive homosexual in hopeless love motivated by her need for atonement. After a journey to South Africa, which brought Lidman into personal contact with intransigent race laws, she has repeatedly manifested her solidarity with the oppressed African population. Her two latest novels, *Jag och min son* (1961) and *Med fem diamanter* (1964), are both set in Africa. As documents of indignation and protest, they have undoubtedly brought the underprivileged closer to Swedish readers in spite of a certain schematic simplification and, in the case of the first book, against the heavy odds of a thoroughly unsympathetic (white) hero. An account of her recent journey to North Vietnam, *Samtal i Hanoi*, in the form of a diary bearing the imprint of strong personal commitment and compassion, was published in 1966. [SAB]

L. Bäckström, *Under välfärdens yta* (Stockholm, 1959); *Bonniers litterära magasin*, 1957–63 and 1960–61.

**Lie, Jonas** (Øvre Eiker, Buskerud 1833–Fleskum, Ø. Bærum 1908). Norwegian novelist, playwright and poet. He spent most of his childhood in Tromsø in north Norway, where the immensity of the scenery and the customs and superstitions of the people made a lasting impression on him. He developed literary interests as a law student. Bankruptcy due to speculation in timber (1868) turned him to writing. His first book, *Den Fremsynte* (1870; tr. J. Muir, *The Visionary*, 1894), exploits the local colour of life in north Norway and through the person of the clairvoyant David Holst evokes its mystery. Subsequently, he wrote a long series of novels depicting the family life of the Norwegian middle classes. The best known of these are: *Lodsen og hans Hustru* (1874; tr. G. Tottenham, *The Pilot and his Wife*, 1877); *Familjen paa Gilje* (1883; tr. S. C. Eastman, *The Family at Gilje*, 1920); *Kommandørens Døtre* (1886; tr. H. L. Brækstad and G. Hughes, *The Commodore's Daughters*, 1892); *Et samliv* (1887).

Lie excels as a painter of milieu, which he often conveys in an impressionistic style. He became known in Norway as '*hjemmenes dikter*' (the poet of the home), a description which does rather less than justice to his talents and originality. In his naturalistic *Livsslaven* (1883; tr. J. Muir, *One of Life's Slaves*, 1895), the social criticism which elsewhere is implicit in his work receives full expression. However, his basic interest seems to have been in the inexplicable, in the vagaries of the human mind and human conduct, things for which the 'trolls' were responsible. This is very prominent in his collections of short-stories in fairytale style: *Trold I and II* (1891–2; tr. R. Nisbet Bain, *Weird Tales from Northern Seas*, 1893). His plays and verse are relatively unimportant. [RGP]

*Samlede dikterverker*, ed. P. Bergh (10 vols., 1920–1).

E. Lie, *J.L.* (Copenhagen, 1933); C. O. Bergström, *J.L.'s väg til Gilje* (Örebro, 1949); H. Midbøe, *Dikteren og det primitive* (4 vols., Oslo, 1964–6); Gustafson, *SSN*; Downs, *MNL*.

**Lilienblum, Moishe Leib** (Lithuania 1843–Odessa 1910). Hebrew poet, essayist and scholar. He was influenced by the Russian positivists and wrote a positivist-socialist treatise for Jewish youth, *Mishnah*. His autobiography, *Chatot Neurim* (1876), became his most famous book. [EE]

. Simon, *M.L.L.* (1912).

**Liliencron, Detlev von** (Kiel 1844–Alt-Rahlsted, Hamburg 1909). German poet. Aristocrat and officer on active service 1864, 1866, 1870; led a hand-to-mouth existence in America (1875–7); between local government posts and (1901) a State pension he associated with the Munich literary bohemia around ⇨ Bierbaum. His unconventional personality (and circumstances!), reflected in the humorous fantasy 'epic' *Poggfred* (1896–1906), discovered a new freshness of lyrical expression and form, anticipating the vivid compression of imagery typical of modern poetic styles. [PB]

*Gesammelte Werke*, ed. R. Dehmel (1910); *Ausgewählte Werke*, ed. H. Stern (1964).

H. Maync, *D.v.L.* (Berlin, 1920); Bridgwater, *TCGV*; *M*, XXXVII (1945).

**Liliev, Nikolay,** pseud. of N. Mihaylov (Stara Zagora 1885–Sofia 1960). Bulgarian symbolist poet. His studies in literature at Lausanne and commerce at Paris in 1905–12 prepared him for the variety of posts in teaching, government and research he held till his final appointment as director of the National Theatre in 1934.

From his first verse in 1905 he contributed to various periodicals, including *Zlatorog* (of which he became an editor), poems, articles on European literature and translations – plays of Shakespeare are among his distinguished renderings from many tongues. A leading symbolist poet, he sought in his *Ptitsi v noshta* (1919), *Lunni petna* (1922) and *Stihotvoreniya* (1932) an inner world of spiritual reality. His successful career did not diminish his sense of incompatibility with 'this century voracious for destruction', felt also by his less fortunate friend ⇨ Debelyanov. Over both hung a nostalgia for 'the paternal eaves' of their childhood and the characteristic symbolist pall, 'like the sadness of a verse from Verlaine'. Liliev survived his country's call and 'the machine-gun lulling its children by the Vardar in moonless embrace' to continue, in the tradition of ⇨ Yavorov, exploring the musical and evocative potentialities of Bulgarian verse. [VP]

*Izbrani stihotvoreniya* (1960); Pinto, *BPV*.

I. Meshekov, *N.L. – simbolist i romantik* (Sofia, 1936); Manning and Smal-Stocki, *HMBL*.

**Lind, Jakov** (Vienna 1927– ). German novelist of Jewish family. He escaped to

Holland in 1938, emigrated to Palestine, and now lives in London. His stories, *Eine Seele aus Holz* (1962; tr. R. Manheim, *A Soul of Wood*, 1964), and the novel *Landschaft in Beton* (1963; tr. R. Manheim, *Landscape in Concrete*) treat the horror and human degradation of persecution and death camp in an unheroic, macabre style. [LL]

Kunisch, *HDG*.

**Lindegren, Erik** (Luleå 1910–68). Swedish poet, critic and librettist. With ⇨ Vennberg, he was a leading name in the generation known as 'The Forties' in Swedish literature. Although he took part in the formulation of its pessimistic philosophy, it is chiefly through his poetic practice that he became influential. His second book of verse, the visionary *mannen utan väg* (1942; tr. R. Bates and L. Sjöberg, 'The Man without a Way' in *New Directions*, No. 20, N.Y., 1968), is one of the most radical poetic experiments ever undertaken in Swedish. It is based on a principle of free imagery and a full acceptance of the ambivalence of experience. Although reminiscent of surrealism, this poetry is more akin to an older brand of symbolism through its austere discipline of rhythm and structure. The collection consists of 40 'broken sonnets' and can be seen as an introverted preparation for action. The mood ranges from near-despair and impotence in the face of black events to irony and steely contempt, but eventually crystallizes into a measure of acceptance. By no means an instant success, *mannen utan väg* eventually became a canonical book for a whole generation. His third collection, *Sviter* (1947), met with readier response: some at least of its poems achieved a kind of popularity, e.g. 'Arioso', with its romantic diction and ecstatic sensibility, and 'Pastoralsvit', with its synthesis of intellect and emotion and its incomparable orchestration. In other parts there signed and elegiac mood persists, in yet others the note of bitterness and protest is heard again. A general characteristic, however, is the greater variation and freedom of the verse, which often achieves the quality of chamber-music. By comparison, his latest collection, *Vinteroffer* (1954), is cooler and more detached, its diction hieratically controlled, but simpler too. On the other hand, the subject-matter has not become more accessible. Prompted by an intense feeling of dissatisfaction, the poet appears to be now retracing, now anticipating some mystical experience. The imagery is accordingly consistent and speaks of distance, petrification, and icy cold space. In the incantatory 'En sång för Ofelia' he has written a masterpiece on the theme of the transience of beauty and the mystical longing for fulfilment. In recent years he has turned his attention to opera and retranslated the librettos for *Don Giovanni* and *Un ballo in maschera*; the latter restores the original Swedish atmosphere to the opera. He was responsible for the operatic version of ⇨ Martinson's *Aniara* (1959). His admirable translations of modern poetry (T. S. Eliot and St-J. Perse) should also be mentioned. In 1962 he became a member of the Swedish Academy. [SAB]

L. Bäckström, *E.L.* (Stockholm, 1962); K. G. Wall, 'mannen utan väg' in *Kritiskt 40-tal*, ed. K. Vennberg and W. Aspenström (Stockholm, 1948); B. Holmqvist, *Svensk 40-talslyrik* (Stockholm, 1951); G. Printz-Påhlson, *Solen i spegeln* (Stockholm, 1958).

**Linna, Väinö** (Urjala 1920– ). Finnish novelist. His first fiction was autobiographical, reflecting the passionate ambitions of a working-class youth and the influence, eagerly absorbed, of Dostoyevsky and Tolstoy. In a later phase he attempted a broader canvas, depicting his characters as members of a larger group. His first novel of this type was *Tuntematon sotilas* (1954; tr. anon., *The Unknown Soldier*, 1957), describing the everyday life of the Finnish soldier at the front, bringing out the psychological and social impulses and pressures affecting officers and men alike. Here a gift for vivid characterization is already evident. His particular field of interest has been the Finnish Civil War of 1918 and the complicated tangle of causes behind it. He shows in detail how the seeds of the war lay in a system of land tenure bristling with inequalities and in the unrealistic idealism of an intelligentsia devoid of any genuine understanding. He brings out the lack of political foresight with which the socialists behaved and which helped to make the tragedy inevitable. His political comment in, and in subsequent defence of, *Pohjantähden alla*, a trilogy (1959–62), have given rise to much controversy: he accused the historians of countenancing a 'white lie' by perpetuating the myth of a 'war of liberation' and of a White army actuated by purely idealistic motives. Linna's books have been translated into several languages. [AK]

**Linnankoski, Johannes,** pseud. of Vihtori Peltonen (Askola 1869–Helsinki 1913). Finnish prose-writer and dramatist. Largely self-educated, he began as a journalist in 1890 and by 1894 exerted considerable influence on Finnish nationalist thought. He was an ardent and persuasive public speaker, and published a manual for orators. He retired from public life in 1899 to devote himself entirely to writing. In his first play, *Ikuinen taistelu* (1903), the 'eternal conflict' between good and evil is eloquently and ardently presented. His best-known work is the thrice-filmed novel *Laulu tulipunaisesta kukasta* (1905; tr. W. Worster, *The Song of the Blood-Red Flower*, 1920), which tells the story of a young lumberjack, a kind of Finnish Don Juan; the romantic lyricism of the earlier chapters leads up to a dramatic and emotional declaration of ethical values. Two short Biblical plays and a few short stories also belong to his romantic period, but artistically his most durable achievement was the short realistic novel *Pakolaiset* (1908; tr. J. L. Perret, *Fugitifs*, Paris, 1929). [VKS]

**Lista y Aragón, Alberto** (Seville 1775–Seville 1848). Spanish poet and educationalist. He deeply influenced the Romantic generation (he was the founder of liberal San Mateo college, Madrid, co-founder of the free University, etc.). His poetry is traditional; his best-known 'La muerte de Jesús' distantly echoes ⇨ Herrera; 'La luna', his finest reflective poem, also recalls the 16th century. His conventional anacreontics only occasionally anticipate Romanticism; 'El himno del desgraciado', though on a Romantic theme, is completely Classical in treatment. [JMC]

*Obras poéticas*, BAE; Blecua, *FLE*.
*LSS*, I (1940); H. Juretschke, *Vida, obra y pensamiento de A.L.* (Madrid, 1951).

**Lithuanian Literature.** Lithuanian literature formed itself relatively late. The basic causes of this were unfavourable historical circumstances, late christianization, and the geographical situation of the country (between the Slavs and the Germans). From the formation of the Lithuanian state, in the second quarter of the 13th century, the Grand Dukes of Lithuania preoccupied themselves at first with the defence of the state, later with the expansion wars and gave little attention to cultural matters. Christianization and union with Poland at the end of the 14th century brought the Polish language, which very soon became the language of the upper classes and the clergy, while the Lithuanian language was reduced to the rank of a native dialect.

The first Lithuanian book, a lutheran Catechism by Martynas Mažvydas (? – 1563), was printed in 1547 in Lithuania Minor, a part of Lithuania since the conquest by the Teutonic Order under German rule. The purpose of the book was to spread the teachings of the Reformed Church in Lithuania Major and Samogitia. Shortly after, the Jesuits started to print books in Lithuanian, which were intended to stop the rapidly increasing influence of the Reformed Church. In the 16th and 17th centuries Lithuanian literature was dominated by religious and linguistic writings. The best noted writers of this time, Mikalojus Daukša (1527?–1613), Jonas Bretkūnas (1536–1602) and Konstantinas Sirvydas (1580–1631), laid the foundations for the written Lithuanian language.

During the 18th century Lithuanian literature, in Lithuania Major, sunk to the lowest mark. At the same time Lithuania Minor produced one of the most distinguished Lithuanian poets, Kristijonas Donelaitis (1714–80), whose idyllic poem *Metai*, written in classical hexameters, remains one of the highest achievements of Lithuanian poetry. Unfortunately this work of poetic genius remained unpublished until 1818 and therefore did not play any part in the further development of the Lithuanian literature of his time.

After the fall of the Polish-Lithuanian state in 1795, Lithuania became a part of the Russian Empire and had to confront a constant danger of Russianization. Several decades later, the first ideas of western romanticism reached Lithuania and gave birth to the movement of national resurrection. Of especially great importance in the further development of this movement were the Polish romanticists (⇨ Mickiewicz, ⇨ Słowacki, ⇨ Kraszewski, etc.), who worshipped the glorious past of Lithuania. The literature of national resurrection may be divided into two periods. In the first (passive) period (1818–83) the movement was characterized by idealization of the past and the will to regain national consciousness, both clearly reflected in the works of the best writers of this time (Simonas Daukantas, 1793–1864; Simonas Stanevičius, 1799–1848; Motiejus Valančius, 1801–75; Antanas Baranauskas, 1835–1902).

After the abortive insurrection of 1863, the Tsarist government prohibited the printing of books in Lithuanian. Lithuanian books were printed in East Prussia and smuggled into Lithuania illegally.

The second (active) period began with the publication of the newspaper *Aušra* and it lasted until the right to print books in Lithuanian was regained (1904). In this period the movement itself became a power to be reckoned with. The formation of written Lithuanian language was completed, the rules of versification established. The most important writers of this period (Jonas Basanvičius, 1851–1927; Vincas Kudirka, 1858–99; Vincas Pietaris, 1850–1902; Maironis, 1862–1932; Adomas Jakštas, 1860–1938) emphasized the effort of national, cultural and economical emancipation, which eventually would lead to the restoration of the Lithuanian state.

After the right to print books in Lithuanian had been restored, Lithuanian literature acquired more variety. Individual writers turned their attention to literary craftsmanship; the problems of literary form moved to the foreground. In this phase the literary scene was dominated by neo-romanticists (Vaižgantas, 1869–1933; Vincas Krėvė, 1882–1954), symbolists (Vydūnas, 1868–1953; Vincas Mykolaitis-Putinas, b. 1893; Balys Sruoga, 1896–1947; Faustas Kirša, 1891–1964), impressionists (Ignas Šeinius, 1889–1959; Jurgis Savickis 1890–1952) and realists (Jonas Biliūnas, 1879–1907; Antanas Vienuolis, 1882–1957).

In the early days of national independence (after 1918) Lithuanian literature was invaded by the followers of futurism, surealism, dadaism, etc., assembled around the literary magazine *Keturi Vėjai*, under the leadership of Kazys Binkis and Petras Tarulis. Very soon they were replaced by the so called 'generation of independence' (Jonas Aistis, Kazys Boruta, Bernardas Brazdžionis, Petras Cvirka, Juozas Grušas, Antanas Miškinis, Salomėja Neris, Henrikas Radauskas, Vytautas Sirijos Gira, Antanas Vaičiulaitis). The Second World War produced a new generation of writers, generally labelled 'existentialists'. During the great exodus of 1944 most of its representatives moved to Western Europe and later to the U.S.A., where they founded a literary magazine *Literatūros Lankai.* [AN-N]

**Littré, Émile** (Paris 1801–Paris 1881). French lexicographer. He studied medicine, edited medical journals and translated Hippocrates. A follower of Comte (cf. *Auguste Comte et la philosophie positive*, 1862), though not of Comte's later mystical ideas, he became the chief exponent of positivism, founding *La Revue de Philosophie positive* (1867). His most famous work is his *Dictionnaire de la langue française* (1863–73), the first scientific attempt to establish etymology and usage (largely from 17th- and 18th-century texts). [WA]

**Liutprand,** Bishop of Cremona (Pavia *c.* 920–972). Italian chronicler. As chancellor to King Berengar, he was sent as envoy to the Eastern Emperor, but was later disgraced and dismissed. His *Antapodosis* relates events in Germany, Italy and the East in 887–949 and satirizes Berengar, especially for meanness. He went over to Otto I, who made him Bishop of Cremona (962) and again sent him to Constantinople to ask for the hand of the Eastern Emperor's daughter for Otto II. His graphic account in *De legatione constantinopolitana*, especially of the Byzantine court (where he was ill received), is outstanding. [FB]

Ed. J. Becker (MGH, SRG, 1915); *Works*, tr. F. A. Wright (London, 1930).
R. W. Southern, *The Making of the Middle Ages* (London, 1953).

**Lizardi, Xabier de.** ⇨ Basque Literature.

**Ljubiša, Stepan Mitrov** (Budva 1824–Vienna 1878). Montenegrin writer. He based most of his stories on folk tales and on his knowledge of Italian literature. Romantic as these stories are, he is appreciated for his purity of style and language and for his local colour which makes him, for many critics, one of the first realists in Serbian literature. [EDG]

**Lobo, Eugenio Gerardo** (Toledo 1679–Barcelona 1750). Spanish poet. A late disciple of Góngora. Completely Gongorist in his romance, *Historia de Medoro y Zelima* this amateurish soldier was somewhat freer in his satires, and achieved a typically 18th-century style in one or two of his sonnets. At his death he was a general and governor of Barcelona. His poems were collected in *Selva de las Musas* (1717). [JMC]

BAE, 61; Blecua, *FLE.*

**Lobo, Francisco Rodrigues** (Leiria, *c.* 1580–near Lisbon, *c.* 1622). Portuguese author, probably of Jewish origin. He died tragically, drowning in the river Tagus not far from Lisbon. The poet spent almost all his life at Leiria, where he was well-acquainted with the House of Bragança. Having lived under the Spanish occupation, which lasted from 1580 to 1640, Lobo has expressed in his main work in prose *Corte na Aldeia e Noites de Inverno* (1619) the nostalgia for 'the golden age of the Portuguese', when they had their court in Lisbon with their own king. This book, written in dialogue form, is a brilliant work in the mannerist style and belongs to the tradition popularized in Europe by ♢ Castiglione's *Il cortegiano* (1582). Many witty stories are interspersed among long disquisitions on the qualities that make the perfect 'courtier' and the 'discreet' man, one of the ideals of the age. Lobo's reputation as a bucolic poet is high and entirely justified. Although he conveys already in his *Éclogas* (1605) the freshness of the rural scenery, it is in the pastoral trilogy, *A Primavera* (1601), *O Pastor Peregrino* (1608) and *O Desenganado* (1614), that he attains the absolute command of the verse and expresses, both with naturalness and sophistication, a deep sense of melancholy and weariness of the world. [LSR]

Ricardo Jorge, *F.R.L. – Estudo Biográfico e Crítico* (Coimbra, 1920); José Ares Montes, *Góngora y la Poesía Portuguesa del Siglo XVII* (Madrid, 1956); Maria de Lourdes Belchior, *Itinerário Poético de R. Lobo* (Lisbon, 1959).

**Loerke, Oskar** (Jungen, W. Prussia 1884–Berlin 1941). German poet. The son of a farmer, he lived mainly in Berlin (a reader for S. Fischer Verlag); member of the Prussian Academy. His *Naturlyrik*, imbued with a profound but obscure sense of cosmic mystery, was once admired and influential, especially on ♢ Lehmann. Sharing with Expressionism its mood of crisis, its abrupt, visionary imagery (and strictness of form), his tone is more quiet and meditative. Author also of essays on poetry – *Das alte Wagnis des Gedichts* (1961); collected *Gedichte und Prosa* (1958). [PB]

Bridgwater, *TCGV*; Hamburger and Middleton, *MGP.*

H. Kasack, *O.L.* (Frankfurt a.M., 1961); D. König, *O.L.s Gedichte* (Marburg, 1963) (dissertation).

**Logau, Friedrich von** (Borckuth 1604–Liegnitz 1655). German poet. He came of a noble Silesian family and after studying law spent many years administering the family estate which had suffered badly during the Thirty Years' War. From 1644 to 1653 he was in the service of the Duke of Brieg. During his life he published 3 collections of epigrams (1638, 1653, 1654), under the pseudonym of Salomon von Golaw, which combine the cynical wit of a satirically minded courtier with the simple proverbial wisdom of the common people and the profound moral seriousness of the devout Christian. He prefers the alexandrine rhyming couplet, but frequently uses the traditional *Knittelvers*; he can be direct to the point of bluntness, but generally his verse is characterized by a love of antithesis and a wealth of metaphors – the most famous being the one which inspired Keller's *Das Sinngedicht* (3. Tausend, X, 8). Besides castigating the perennial follies of mankind and expressing traditional wisdom, Logau is one of the chief opponents of the increasing gallicization of German cultural life. [WAC]

*Gedichte*, ed. G. Eitner (BLVS, 113, 1872); *Auswahl*, ed. H. Walter (1956).

P. Hempel, *Die Kunst F.L.* (Berlin, 1917).

**Lohenstein, Daniel Casper von** (Nimptsch 1635–Breslau 1683). German dramatist. Lohenstein practised law in Breslau and latterly held a post in the civil administration there. As a dramatist, his formal debt to his older compatriot, ♢Gryphius, is obvious: he writes in alexandrines, uses the chorus and frequently introduces allegorical figures, ghosts and dreams. In content, however, his dramas lack those high ethical ideals which are central to Gryphian tragedy. He was particularly interested in feminine psychology and the typical figure in his dramatic world is not the Christian martyr of Gryphius. but the political virago. His *Ibrahim* (1650) *Cleopatra* (1661), *Agrippina* (1665), *Epicharis* (1665) and *Sophonisbe* (1669) are creatures storm-tossed by the extreme violence of their passions and move in a world of political intrigue where the only constancy is to one's own advantage or to that of one's country. He has learnt from the wandering theatre and his plays are full of action and tension, though his characters tend to be larger than life, and he shows an almost perverted love of violence – torturings, rapes, suggested incest, suicides, etc. The action is matched by the extreme passion of the style – tremendous rhetorical outpourings of language more calculated to overwhelm than to enlighten. His heroic gallant novel, *Grossmütiger Feldherr Arminius* (1689–90), a treatment of Hermann's victory over the Romans, which is given contemporary political overtones, was perhaps the most popular novel of the age, but today has little more than antiquarian interest. [WAC]

*Trauerspiele*, ed. K. G. Just (3 vols., BLVS, 292/3/4, 1953ff.).

K. G. Just, *Die Trauerspiele D.C.v.L.* (Berlin, 1961); M. Wehrle, *Das barocke Geschichtsbild in L.s 'Arminius'* (Zürich, 1938).

**Lo-Johansson, Ivar** (Ösmo 1901– ). Swedish novelist and story-writer. A leading representative (with ⇨ Johnson, ⇨ Martinson, ⇨ Moberg and ⇨ Fridegård) of the largely self-educated authors in modern Swedish literature, after several years of rough life with various jobs in Sweden and abroad, writing also stories and reportage, he emerged as the principal portrayer (with Fridegård) of the grim existence of the Swedish *statare* (farm labourers) that he knew from his own early environment. He attempted to portray the depth and breadth of this harsh world – to write what he called 'collective' novels – in *Godnatt, jord* (1933) and *Traktorn* (1943), and in the stories of *Statarna* (1936–7) and *Jordproletärerna* (1941). A complement to this uneven but imposing corpus was *Kungsgatan* (1935), picturing the sordid proletarian vortex of Stockholm. His masterpiece however is *Bara en mor* (1939), where the *statare* theme is crystalized with mature judgement in the extremely moving life-story of a woman of that class. He has published a series of eight autobiographical novels, sometimes strikingly mellower than his earlier work, the first of which, *Analfabeten* (1951), is a monument to his father whose heroic struggle to achieve and maintain the status of an independent farmer has evidently been a moral example to the son. The fifth volume, *Författaren* (1957), is of particular interest for its vivid portraits and astute observation of the literary scene of the thirties. More recently he has returned to fiction, while giving free rein to his philosophic bent (earlier evidenced in various pamphlets). Prominent among these novels are *Lyckan* (1962), on the conditions of mature love, and *Elektra, kvinna år 2070* (1967), a satirical, yet warm-hearted fantasy of the future.

M. Edström, *I.L.-J.* (Stockholm, 1954); R. Oldberg, *I.L.-J.: en monografi* (Stockholm, 1957).

**Lomonosov, Mikhail Vasilyevich** (Kurostrov islet, White Sea *c.* 1711–St Petersburg 1765). Russian poet. A fisherman's son, he stands out like a great Renaissance figure. In 1730 he ran away to the Moscow ecclesiastical Slavo-Greco-Latin Academy, 1736–40 studied philosophy and sciences in Germany and married a German. From 1741 he lectured in St Petersburg Academy on physics and chemistry, organized the geography department, laboratories, glass factory, etc. The founder of Moscow University (1755), this man of encyclopedic mind and knowledge 'was himself our first University' (Pushkin).

The legislator of Russian literature, 'its Peter the Great' (Belinsky), he wrote *On Versification* (1739), *Rhetoric* (1748) and the first Russian *Grammar* (1754). A classicist, he elaborated the theory of the 'high', 'middle' and 'low' styles, differentiated between various Slavonic languages, emphasized the potentialities of Russian, advocated tonic instead of syllabic prosody and illustrated it with varieties of metre and the use of masculine rhyme. He composed didactic odes, heroic poems (*Peter I*, 1760), metric psalms, lyrics and epigrams, and a couple of weak tragedies. A great patriot, lover of studies and of peace, he is 'the poet-laureate of his country' rather than of the Tsars. Russia is his beloved, and more than by passion, he is 'carried away by the heroes' glory' (*To Anacreon*, 1757). A deist who sees the interrelation between philosophy, science, aesthetics and speech, he excels in lofty rhetoric and majestically concrete descriptions of natural phenomena (*Evening* and *Morning Meditation on the Divine Majesty*, 1748, 1751), while, by contrast, pungent popular Russian distinguishes his epigrams.

Although his verse was superseded in the 19th century, 'he stands before our poets as an Introduction before a book' (Gogol'). [NG]

*Polnoye sobraniye sochineniy* (10 vols., 1951–7); *Stikhotvoreniya*, ed. A. Morozov (Leningrad, 1954).

B. N. Menshutkin, *Russia's Chemist-Courtier-Physicist-Poet L.*, tr. J. Eyre, E. J. Webster (Princeton, 1952); A. Matrel, *M.L. et la langue littéraire russe* (Paris, 1933).

**Lönnrot, Elias** (Sammatti 1802–Sammatti 1884). Finnish folklorist and philologist. The son of a poor country tailor, he completed medical studies at Helsinki (1832). He became district medical officer at Kajaani in eastern Finland, which remained his base for 20 years. He made extensive collections of traditional folk poetry, and among the Lapps, the Estonians, and the Finnish tribes of Karelia and north-west Russia he collected much valuable linguistic material. From his collection of folk poetry he compiled a continuous 'folk epic' (⇨ *Kalevala*, 1835, enlarged 1849), which gave a tremendous impetus to the Finnish nationalist movement. He also published a collection of folk lyrics (⇨ *Kanteletar*, 1840–41), and collections of proverbs, riddles and incantations. As Professor of Finnish Language and Literature at Helsinki University (1853–62) he remained in the forefront of the nationalist movement and did much to bring about the adoption of Finnish as the second official language of the country (hitherto only Swedish had been recognized) and thus open up the possibility of a modern Finnish literature. The establishment of a standard literary Finnish was due largely to his efforts, and his Finnish-Swedish dictionary (1874–80) long remained a standard work on the language. The reform of the Finnish Hymn Book (1883) also owed much to him. A quiet, modest man, he was regarded in his old age as an honoured national patriarch, rising above all differences of opinion. [VK]

**Looy, Jacobus van** (Haarlem 1855–Haarlem 1930). Dutch author and painter. After a childhood in an orphanage he became a scholar at the Amsterdam Academy, won the Prix de Rome and travelled to Italy (1884–5), returning to Amsterdam via Spain and Tangiers. His short stories in *Proza* (1889) distinguished him as a vivid painter in words and a dreamer. In *Feesten* (1903) the enjoyment of other people's gaiety leaves no room for introspection. His third phase, his quest for his ideal is expressed in, the *Wonderlijke avonturen van Zebedeus* (1910), a satirical and often obscure fantasy. The autobiographical *Jaapje* (1917), *Jaap* (1923) and *Jacob* (1930), show his rare genius for recording the dreamy impressions of a child. [PK]

*Gekken* (1894); *Nieuw Proza* (1929); *Gedichten* (1932); *The Death of My Cat* in Greshoff, *HL.*

**Lope de Vega** (Madrid 1562–Madrid 1635). Spain's first great dramatist and an outstanding poet. As a young man he took part in the Spanish expedition to the Azores (1583) and sailed with the Armada (1588). His many love affairs, including several after he became a priest (1614), are reflected in his works and make his love-poetry, and the religious poems written in intermittent spasms of remorse, more personal than those of many contemporaries. Although he enjoyed immense literary prestige his life was tragic: he experienced the death of two wives, the blindness and madness of his last mistress, the death of two favourite sons and the abduction of a daughter by a courtier under royal protection (a situation he had treated in several dramas).

Lope de Vega's dramatic production was huge and influential. A contemporary admirer credits him with over 1,800 pieces, but of the 500 which survive (including *autos* and *entremeses*) a few are spurious. Through the success and volume of his plays he overwhelmed all competition and established the distinctive type of play which was to prevail in Spain for almost a century: the *comedia* in 3 acts written in a variety of metres, in which the eventful action on the stage may range widely in space and time, often combining two or more plots; a mixture of serious and comic elements (the latter provided by the 'gracioso' or comic servant) and of learned and popular styles; a poetic drama incorporating songs and sonnets, lyrical soliloquies and duets, and often making use of symbolism and of the metaphorical relations between different parts of the action. He defends this type of play against academic critics in his *Arte nuevo de hacer comedias* (1609), blaming his more 'vulgar' devices on the need to satisfy public taste. In this verse treatise he also declares that questions of honour make the most exciting subjects. The atrocities committed in honour's name in the plays of Lope de Vega and his followers have disturbed many critics, especially outside Spain. Scholars are not agreed on how far these Catholic dramatists, many of them priests, accepted the unchristian code which ruled their creatures. In Lope de Vega's own case, it seems probable that here, as in his private life, he was far from consistent.

His plays may be roughly classified as follows: (1) cloak and sword plays, or *comedias de capa y espada*, the largest single group, light comedies of intrigue usually set in the upper reaches of contemporary Madrid society, the love-story complicated by mistaken identity, disguises, simulations and dissimulations of love, chains of lovers, etc. (e.g. *La discreta enamorada*, *La noche toledana*, *El acero de Madrid*); (2) dramatizations of Bible stories and lives of saints (*La hermosa Ester*, *El divino africano* (St Augustine)); (3) pastoral plays (*El verdadero amante*, *Belardo furioso*, both early works); (4) mythological plays (*El laberinto de Creta*, *El amor enamorado*); (5) plays on Ancient history (*Las grandezas de Alejandro*, *Roma abrasada*); (6) plays based on novels of chivalry (*La mocedad de Roldán*, *Los celos de Rodamonte*), or (7) on Italian *novelle* (*El castigo sin venganza*, *El halcón de Federico*); (8) plays based on foreign history (*La imperial de Otón*, *El gran duque de Moscovia*); (9) plays based on Spanish history and legends (*Peribáñez*, *Fuenteovejuna*, *El caballero de Olmedo*, *El último godo*, *El bastardo Mudarra*).

Most of his best known serious plays belong to this last group. *Peribáñez* (1610?) and *Fuenteovejuna* (1613?), both set in the 15th century, show peasants driven to murder their tyrannical overlord in defence of their honour. Although the nobles are presented as wicked, the Kings of Castile appear as the just protectors of their subjects. *Peribáñez* is remarkable for its rustic lyricism, *Fuenteovejuna* for its inflammatory presentation of mob violence. *El caballero de Olmedo* (1620?–1625?), written around a snatch of an old folksong, but also looking back to *La ⇨ Celestina*, achieves a sinister air of mystery rare in Spanish drama. *El castigo sin venganza* (1631), based on a story by ⇨ Bandello, is a horrific tragedy of incest and revenge which shows the intensity and concentration of which this often diffuse and casual dramatist was capable.

As might be expected, Lope de Vega excels in the portrayal of lovers. He is also remarkable for his sympathetic and unpatronizing presentation of peasants. Otherwise, his chief virtues as a playwright are lyricism, inventiveness and neatness of plot. Though more inventive, more subtle in his emotional range which includes both passion and tenderness, and more influential, he is in general dramatic stature the Fletcher rather than the Shakespeare of Spanish drama.

Outside the drama, his earliest successful verses were *romances* in the new pastoral manner, which recounted the loves of Belardo and Filis – himself and Elena Osorio whom he loved in his twenties (he was later exiled from Castile for libelling her parents). In 1598 he produced a pastoral novel, *Arcadia*, inspired by ⇨ Sannazaro, and *La Dragontea*, an epic poem about Drake; in 1599, a narrative in *quintillas* of the life of Isidro, patron saint of Madrid. *La hermosura de Angélica* (1602) continues ⇨ Ariosto's *Orlando*, while *Jerusalén conquistada* (1609) feebly imitates ⇨ Tasso. Lope de Vega was once admired for the sonnets of *Rimas humanas* (1602) and of *Rimas sacras* (1614), which reflect his intensely sincere, if not lasting, repentance; but the best of his lyrical poetry is now thought to be found in the pious pastoral novel, *Los pastores de Belén* (1612), and in the autobiographical novel in dialogue, *La Dorotea* (1632). His traditional style, which he defended against the *culto* school (⇨ Góngora attacked the popular tone of Lope de Vega's poetry and plays), tends to wear thin except where it is inspired by experience of love or loss. He has true feeling for folk songs (which he often uses in his plays) and his own poems in this style may easily be taken for originals.

His other poems and novels are too numerous to list. His poetic *Laurel de Apolo* (1630) has bibliographical interest for its account of Spanish bards crowned on Helicon. Outstanding among the works of his last years are the mock epic about cats, *La gatomaquia* (1634), the eclogue, *Filis* (1635), which relates the abduction of his daughter, and *La Dorotea* (1632), modelled on *La Celestina* and inspired by his early love for Elena Osorio. Possibly begun in youth, the work looks back with wisdom and maturity on the false literary fantasies and factitious emotions that had once obscured reality. It is thought by some to be his greatest achievement, though others find it an unsatisfactory mixture of true autobiography and conventional fiction. [JMC/DR]

*Obras*, Real Academia Española (13 vols., 1916–30); *Obras escogidas* (1946); *Poesías líricas*

CC (2 vols., 1951–2); various plays in CC and CA; *La Dorotea*, ed. J. M. Blecua (1955); ed. E. S. Morby (Berkeley and Valencia, 1958); *El castigo sin venganza*, ed. C. A. Jones (Oxford, 1966); Alonso, *PE*; Blecua, *FLE*; Cohen, *PBSV*; Trend, *OBSV*.

H. A. Rennert y A. Castro, *Vida de L. de V.* (Madrid, 1919); R. Menéndez Pidal, *De Cervantes a L. de V.* (Madrid, 1935); S. G. Morley and C. Bruerton, *The Chronology of L. de V.s Comedias* (N.Y., 1940); K. Vossler, *L. de V. y su tiempo* (Sp. tr. from German, Madrid, 1940); M. Menéndez y Pelayo, *Estudios sobre el teatro de L. de V.*, ed. Sánchez Reyes (Santander, 1949); A. Zamora Vicente, *L. de V.* (Madrid, 1961).

**Lopes, Fernão** (*c.* 1380/90–*c.* 1460?). Portuguese chronicler. Probably of humble origins, and a notary by training; he worked for members of the Royal family, and was in charge of the National Archives (1418–54). Commissioned to record the history of the Portuguese monarchy, he produced the *Crónica de el-rei D. Pedro*, the *Crónica de el-rei D. Fernando* and the *Crónica de el-rei D. João* (2 parts), covering the years 1357–1411. He saw the feudal patterns of society beginning to disintegrate, and appreciated both the role of the bourgeoisie and artisan class in Lisbon and the relative insignificance of individual actions by princes and nobles. He attributed the successful defence of Portuguese sovereignty against Castilian machinations (1383–5) to the perseverance and patriotism of the common people; for the nobility, who had been willing to collaborate with Castile, Lopes had ill-disguised contempt. The use of direct speech, popular tales, down-to-earth allusions and local detail, allow him to capture the whole spirit of his age. Yet these imaginative elements do not detract from the value of his chronicles as historical documents. He eschewed the customary adulation of his patrons and portrayed events and characters with more impartiality than his contemporaries. [AJP]

*As Crónicas*, ed. A. J. Saraiva (Lisbon, n/d) (in modern Portuguese); *Quadros da Crónica de D. João 1* (TL); *Crónica de D. Pedro 1*, *Crónica de D. Fernando* (CP).

A. J. Saraiva, *F.L.* (Lisbon, 1953); A. E. Beau, *F.L.* in *Estudos*, i (Coimbra, 1959).

**Lopes de Mendonça, António Pedro** (Lisbon 1826–Lisbon 1865). Portuguese critic, journalist and novelist. His earliest major literary production was his sole novel, *Memórias de um Doido* (1846), which was only moderately successful. The Romantic egotism of its hero, Maurício, is moulded in the tradition of the novels of George Sand or of Vigny's *Chatterton*, but the narrative is reinforced by a 'Realism' involving the probing of the social depths in the manner of Balzac and Eugène Sue. Disappointed at the mixed reception of this work, Mendonça turned to political journalism and literary criticism and became one of the earliest masters in the genre of the *folhetim*. For a period he directed the periodical *Revolução de Setembro* (1846–57) and with a radicalism born of the study of Proudhon and Fourier he was frequently involved in polemics. His reputation was established by his *Estudos de Crítica e Literatura* (1849), re-cast as *Memórias da Literatura Contemporânea* (1855). Particularly celebrated was his 2-volume *Recordações da Itália* (1852–3), a widely read work which combined travelogue with literary journalism and a lightweight love-story, and which readily invited comparison with Garrett's *Viagens na minha Terra*. In 1858 he published two major monographs, *Damião de Góis e a Inquisição* and *José Agostinho de Macedo*, which assisted his appointment in 1860 to the chair of Modern Literature at the newly founded Curso Superior de Letras in Lisbon. Pressure of work, however, brought early insanity, a state in which he remained until his death. [RCW]

J. do Prado Coelho, *Lopes de Mendonça*, in *Perspectiva da Literatura Portuguesa do Século XIX*, i (Lisbon, 1947).

**López de Ayala, Pero** (Vitoria 1332–? 1407). Spanish chronicler and poet. Of noble Basque family (from Álava), he was educated for the Church, but became an active military and political figure under Peter the Cruel and the Trastamaras. He was twice a prisoner of war, after Nájera (1367) and Aljubarrota (1385). He retired to his estates in Álava from 1393, but was made Chancellor of the Realm in 1399. He wrote the official chronicles of the reigns of Peter the Cruel, Henry II and John I (and partly of Henry III), largely from first-hand knowledge, showing considerable objectivity and powers of selection. He remains the principal authority for the reign of Peter. His portrait of Peter, at the end of the chronicle, was the forerunner of the collections of historical portraits by Pérez de Gúzmán and Hernando del Pulgar. He also wrote a book on hunting birds. He translated several Latin works, including some of Livy, Boethius's *De consolatione*, Egidio Colonna's *De regimine principum* and Boccaccio's *De casibus virorum illustrium*.

His poetry is collected in a single miscellany known as the *Rimado de Palacio*, composed at various times between *c.* 1385 (some of it, probably, while imprisoned at Obidos) and his death. It is mostly in ◊ *cuaderna vía* form (of which it is the last example), but contains some interpolated songs in various lyric metres, and a 'dictado' in the new *arte mayor*. After making a general confession, formally arranged according to conventional categories (The Ten Commandments, The Seven Deadly Sins, The Seven Works of Mercy, etc.), and containing little personal revelation, he surveys the world from the standpoint of a devout but disillusioned elder statesman: he bemoans the state of the Church under the Great Schism, pillories different sections of society for their ruthless self-seeking and discusses how the country should be governed. The best-known section, 'Los Fechos del Palacio', is a satirical picture of a nobleman's frustrated attempts to gain audience with a harassed king in order to claim payment for his services. A further section serves as a framework for some songs of devotion, inspired by his imprisonment. The final section of the *Rimado* is a paraphrase of part of St Gregory the Great's commentaries on the Book of Job. It reflects Ayala's view of suffering as inflicted by God in order that men may prove their Christian loyalty. [GBG-M]

*Poesías*, ed. A. F. Kuersteiner (N.Y., 1920); ed. F. Janer, BAE, 57; *Crónicas de los Reyes de Castilla*, ed. C. Rosell, BAE, 66, 68; *El libro de la caza de las aves*, ed. J. Gutiérrez de la Vega, *Biblioteca, Venatoria*, iii (1879); in modern Spanish by J. Fradejas Lebrero (1959).

*Españoles ante la historia* (Buenos Aires, 1958); *Clavileño*, 29 (1954); *BHS*, XXXVIII (1961).

**López de Gómara, Francisco** (Gómara/Soria 1512–Seville 1572). Spanish historian. Secretary to Cortés and author of *Historia de las Indias* (1552). [JMC]

**López de Mendoza, Íñigo, Marqués de Santillana** (Carrión de los Condes 1398–Guadalajara 1458). Spanish poet and patron. A great nobleman, he took a leading part in the military and political affairs of his day; he corresponded with scholars, built up a fine library, imported books, acted as patron to poets and translators, and was perhaps the major figure in the Spanish 'pre-Renaissance'. Much of his verse is in the heavily Latinized manner, allegorical in form and stoic-didactic in sentiment; today he is read chiefly for his 10 *serranillas* (light lyrics on traditional knight-meets-shepherdess themes). His *Proemio* (ed. and intr. A. R. Pastor and E. Prestage, *Letter of the M. de S....* (in Sp.), Oxford, 1927) is an interesting conspectus of western European poetry as he knew it. His most ambitious allegorical poem, the *Comedieta de Ponça*, which mourns a naval defeat, is modelled on Dante, while *El infierno de los enamorados* borrows also from Petrarch. [CCS]

*Cancionero*, ed. R. Foulché-Delbose, NBAE, 19; *Canciones y decires*, CC; *Los Proverbios* (1928); *Obras*, ed. A. Cortina (Buenos Aires, 1946); *Prose and Verse*, ed. J. B. Trend (1940).

R. Lapesa, *La obra literaria del M. de S.* (Madrid, 1957).

**Lorca, Federico García** (Fuente Vaqueros 1898–Granada 1936). Spanish poet and dramatist. Also a talented musician. He studied in Granada and in 1919 went to the Residencia de Estudiantes in Madrid. In 1929, after the public success of the *Romancero gitano*, in the company of Fernando de los Ríos he left Spain for New York. On his return he co-directed La Barraca, a government-sponsored student theatrical company that toured the country, and in 1933 he visited Argentina. Just after the outbreak of the Civil War, in circumstances only now being clarified, he was shot by Nationalist partisans. His murder, combined with those aspects of his work which correspond to romantic foreign notions about Spain, inflated his poetic reputation abroad for some time. However, he is undoubtedly the most important Spanish dramatist of the century so far.

Besides the *Romancero gitano* (1928) and the *Llanto por Ignacio Sánchez Mejías* (1934) by which he is best known as a poet, he wrote, notably, *Canciones* (1927), *Poema del cante jondo* (1931), *Poeta en Nueva York* (1940), *Diván del Tamarit* (1940). Behind the persistently arresting and often surrealistic imagery of his poetry is a fresh and childlike eye for the external world (many of his early poems recall children's folk verse). Natural phenomena are continuall metamorphosed into human terms ('an arm of the night', 'the breasts of the moon'), producing a highly sensual world peopled by beings remarkably close to those of primitive mythologies, and coexisting on one plane with the poet or his characters. The gipsies of the *Romancero*, partly based on the real gipsies of Andalusia, are imaginary creatures of nature who live in a world of childlike innocence and popular religion, but also of passions, violence and death, persecuted above all by the deathly brutalism of modern civilization, personified by the Civil Guard (their traditional enemy in real life). An obsession with the death-in-life of civilization recurs through the tortured poems of *Poeta en Nueva York*, and with human mortality in the elegy for Sánchez Mejías, where death is the personal enemy faced in the bullring. Perhaps Lorca's greatest poetic achievement is the creation of an idiom at once traditional, modern and personal – indebted to folk poetry, to the old Arabic poets of Andalusia, to ⇨ Góngora, to modern poets, and yet unmistakably his own.

His early plays, lyrical and experimental, are animated by a spirit of revolt against the fashionable realism and middle-class ethos of the Madrid theatre of the time, and have resemblances with the works of ⇨ Cocteau, ⇨ Valle-Inclán and others. His puppet plays epitomize this revolt. *La zapatera prodigiosa* (1930) stands midway between his balletic farces and his later tragedies of frustrated womanhood. This is the theme of each of his 3 folk tragedies, *Bodas de sangre* (1933), *Yerma* (1934), *La casa de Bernarda Alba* (1936). *Doña Rosita la soltera* (1935) treats the same theme in a muted key in a period bourgeois setting. The first two plays are among the few successful poetic tragedies of this century, despite the difficulty of producing them convincingly. In all three tragedies the extreme emotional situations arising from the conflicts of passionate love, maternal feeling and the restraints of *honor* are secured by solid dramatic construction, the pertinence of imagery to theme and Lorca's practical knowledge of stage technique. In *Bernarda Alba* verbal poetry has been pared away to the point that this last of his plays stands on the verge of another sort of drama. His death came when he was at the height of his powers, full of new projects and never more conscious of his own capacity for development. [ECR]

*Obras completas* (1954); sel. and tr. by J. L. Gili (Penguin Books, 1960); *Three Tragedies*, tr. J. Graham-Luján and R. L. O'Connell (Penguin Books, 1961).

A. del Río, *Vida y obras de F.G.L.* (Zaragoza, 1952); F. Vázquez Ocaña, *G.L., Vida, cántico y muerte* (Mexico, 1962).

**Losada, Benito.** ⇨ Galician Literature.

**Loti,** pseud. of L. M. Julien Viaud, known as 'Pierre' (Rochefort 1850–Hendaye 1923). French novelist. A naval officer, nicknamed 'Loti' by native women in the South Seas, he evoked the atmosphere of faraway places in his prolific fiction. His sensualism, love of life and still more of love, gained its once popular charm from Loti's sense of the ephemeral and of death. The musicality of his simple prose has been highly praised. Among his most successful works are *Pêcheur d'Islande* (1886; tr. W. P. Baines, *Iceland Fisherman*, 1935), *Madame Chrysanthème* (1887; tr. L. Ensor, *Japan – Madame Chrysanthème*, 1915) and *Les désenchantées* (1906; tr. C. Bell, *Disenchanted*, 1906). He was elected to the Académie Française in 1891. [AKT]

K. G. Millward, *L'œuvre de P.L. et l'esprit fin de siècle* (Paris, 1955).

**Lubrano, Giacomo** (Naples 1619–1693). Italian poet. A Jesuit, famous both as a preacher and as an extravagantly flamboyant ⇨ Marinist. His *Scintille poetiche o poesie sacre e morali* (Naples, 1690) were published under the pseudonym Paolo Brinacio. His wide range includes many moral and religious themes, with typically spectacular displays of stylistic pyrotechnics. He is most effective in the descriptive bravura of brief vignettes, where esoteric subject, bizarre verbal juxtapositions and audaciously dramatic imagery produce an exciting vision of a brilliant, moving world impinging on the senses. [DGR]

Croce, *LM*.
Ferrero, *MM*; Getto, *MM*.

**Lucebert,** pseud. of Lubertus Jacobus Swaanswijk (Amsterdam 1924– ). Dutch poet and artist. He was the most accomplished of the individualistic 'poets of the fifties', and in his prophetic or humorous use of words he is a romantic revolutionary against society and its norms of behaviour and communication. Since

1963 he has preferred drawing to writing. [PK]

*1948–1963 gedichten* (1965); *Carcanet* (June 1963).

**Lucić, Hanibal.** ⇨ Dalmatian and Dubrovnik Literature.

**Ludwig, Otto** (Eisfeld 1813–Dresden 1865). German dramatist and novelist. Attached with an almost pathetic intensity to his native Thuringian village, he never set foot beyond the borders of Saxony. At 26 he began to study music with Mendelssohn in Leipzig but the pace of the city's physical and intellectual life upset him, and in spite of his fame after the production of his *Erbförster* in 1849, he remained withdrawn from society. His death came aiter years of sickness and disability.

To his studies in music Ludwig owed what he called the 'musical mood' – a world of colours and vague impressions. In this, as in other respects, he was influenced by ⇨ Hoffmann. His early works were Romantic in subject and in colour but those of his maturity show a realism akin to that of ⇨ Hebbel and of his friend ⇨ Freytag.

Of his plays, *Der Erbförster* remains the most effective. He also dramatized Hoffmann's story *Das Fräulein von Scudéri* (1848) and wrote a series of Shakespeare studies, published after his death. He is best remembered for his tragic novel *Zwischen Himmel und Erde* (1856; tr. W. Metcalfe, *Between Heaven and Earth*, 1911), a powerful story of character conflicts set in the small-town world to which he himself belonged. [RT]

*Werke* (1961ff.).
Brandes, *MCNL*

**'Ludwigslied'.** Anonymous Old High German poem. Devoted to the praise of the young King Louis III, ruler of the west Frankish kingdom in the line of Charles the Bald, and in particular to his victory over the Normans in the year 881, the poem, one of the most perfectly preserved pieces of Old High German literature, presents its hero as one fighting to defend the ideals of the Church, as a perfect Christian ruler. The narrative style is simple and direct, the manner assured. [RT]

Braune, *AL*.

**Lugovskoy, Vladimir** (Moscow 1901– Moscow 1957). Russian poet. The son of a teacher, he went to a military academy and in 1921 fought with the Red Army in Western Russia. He travelled widely in the U.S.S.R. and in Western Europe; in the forties he worked on the scenario of Eisenstein's film *Ivan the Terrible*. His poetry is bold and impressionistic, particularly when it deals with nature and the untamed landscape of Siberia and Central Asia. Military, revolutionary and heroic themes are common and he wrote some good love poetry. His early work owes something to the ⇨ Futurists though it is generally more straightforward and less technically daring than theirs. By the fifties he was a much-loved figure whose personality had considerable influence on the young generation of Soviet poets. [RM-G]

*Izbrannyye proizvedeniya* (2 vols., 1956); Gulland, *SRV*; Lugovskoy, *RSP*.
L. Levin, *V.L.* (Moscow, 1963).

**Lukács, Georg** or **György** (Budapest 1885– ). Hungarian critic and philosopher writing chiefly in German. Son of a titled banker, he early espoused communist ideas, took part in the 1919 revolution, then lived in Berlin till 1933, when he emigrated with J. R. ⇨ Becher to the U.S.S.R., where he became a theoretician of socialist realism. After accepting a chair in Budapest in 1945, he incurred party censure for the superior importance he gave to 'bourgeois' novelists like Balzac, Tolstoy and Thomas Mann. During the ⇨ Thaw he tried to shift emphasis from communist *v.* capitalist conflict to a broader front of rationalism, peace and progress united against irrationalism, war and reaction. He was briefly deported to Rumania after the 1956 uprising. His early *Theorie des Romans* (1920) attempted a phenomenology of the genre and diagnosed its 'crisis'. *Geschichte und Klassenbewusstsein* (1923) laid the foundations of Marxist criticism of literature as a reflection of social processes. Apart from writing on Lenin, Marx, Hegel, Nietzsche and Existentialism his best literary criticism is on 19th-century realism, e.g. *Essays über Realismus* (1948), *Der russische Realismus in der Weltliteratur* (1949), *Deutsche Realisten des 19. Jahrhunderts* (1952), *Balzac und der französische Realismus* (1951), *Der historische Roman* (1955; tr. H. and S. Mitchell, *The Historical Novel*, 1962). Other important works are *Thomas Mann* (1949; tr. S. Mitchell, *Essays on Thomas Mann*, 1964) and *Goethe und* *seine Zeit* (1947; tr. R. Anchor, *Goethe and his Time*, 1967). [LL]

*Gesamtausgabe* (Neuwied and Berlin, 1962 ff.); tr. J. and N. Mander, *The Meaning of Contemporary Realism* (1963) (selections); tr. E. Bone, *Studies in European Realism* (1950).

V. Zitta, *G.L.s Marxism* (1964); ed. F. Benseler, *Festschrift G.L.* (1965); Wellek, *HMC*.

**Lull, Ramon.** ⇨ Catalan Literature.

**Lunacharsky, Anatoliy Vasil'yevich** (Poltava 1875–Menton, on his way to take up appointment as ambassador to Spain 1933). Soviet literary critic, publicist and dramatist. Early revolutionary interests and reputation forced him to study abroad at Zürich under Avenarius whose doctrine of Empirio-Criticism influenced his philosophic plays, even after his close association with Lenin and the Bolsheviks (1904) led him to renounce it in his publicistic writings. He became the first People's Commissar for Enlightenment (1917–29) but his own plays were obscure and symbolistic. A collection of comedies entitled *Idei v maskakh* (1912), a philosophical drama about 'The Magi' (1919), subjects such as *Faust i Gorod* (1918) or *Osvobozhdennyi Don Kikhot* (1922), suggest the essentially bookish nature of his inspiration. Convinced, with ⇨ Blok, that melodrama is the natural drama of the people, he attempted it in the play *Yad* ('Poison', 1926). His critical writings are more memorable than his creative efforts. His pseudonyms include Voinov, Anyutin and Anton Levyy.

*Sobraniye sochineniy* (8 vols., 1963–7); *P'yesy*, ed., intr. A. Deych (1963); *O teatre i dramaturgii* (1958); *O kino* (1965); *Three Plays* (*Faust and the City*, *Vasilisa the Wise*, *The Magi*), tr. Magnus and Walter (1923); *On Literature and Art*, tr. anon. (Moscow, 1965).

N. A. Lunacharskaya-Rozenel', *Pamyat' sertsa, Vospominaniya* (Moscow, 1962); K. Chukhovsky, *Sovremenniki, Portrety i Etyudy* (Moscow, 1962); K. D. Muratova, *A.V.L.* (1964).

**Lundkvist, Artur** (Oderljunga 1906– ). Swedish poet, travel and story writer, novelist and critic. A leading contributor (with Harry ⇨ Martinson) to the anthology *Fem unga* (1929), which opened the door to modernism in Swedish literature, he introduced the group to writers such as Whitman, Sandburg, Masters, Lawrence as well as the Finnish writers ⇨ Södergran and ⇨ Diktonius. His early philosophy (generally labelled 'primitivism') was never given a coherent formulation, but included such contradictory elements as a cult of machines, primitive and proletarian life, Communism, Freudian psychology and a romantic view of sex. The assertiveness, not to say aggressiveness, of his early poetry, e.g. in *Naket liv* (1929) and *Svart stad* (1930), gave way to restless experimentation, its mood becoming more reflective and its manner revealing the influence of Surrealism, e.g. *Nattens broar* (1936). From the early thirties onwards he published several vivid books on his travels to Africa, China, Russia, Spain and South America. His untiring work in introducing foreign writers to Swedish readers has been of great importance. A prolific author, he has not only published over a dozen collections of verse, but more recently an impressive series of loose-limbed novels and collections of stories. His mature style bears the stamp of his intense, extravert nature. Even his best poetry is rhapsodic: its torrential imagery, although admirably fresh and precise, can become monotonous through the absence of an emotional focus. His ideas are often Utopian: he is a Marxist socialist, though relatively unconcerned with theory and dogma. *Vindingevals* (1956), a largely autobiographical novel, sketches the rural background from which as a young man he broke away to become a self-taught writer and critic. His later work includes *Agadir* (1961), a long poem on the great earthquake disaster there (of which the poet was himself a survivor) in expressive language; *Ögonblick och vågor* (1962), a collection of poetry which reads like a personal document of unusual directness; *Texter i snön* (1964), further meditations in verse; and *Självporträtt av en drömmare med öppna ögon* (1966), a vivid autobiography. [SAB]

K. Espmark, *Livsdyrkaren A.L.* (Stockholm, 1964); S. Carlson (ed.), *A.L. 3 mars 1956* (Stockholm, 1956).

**Lupus Servatus** (*c.*800–*c.*862). French churchman and writer. Abbot of Ferrières (Orleans), which he made a cultural centre. A pupil of ⇨ Hrabanus Maurus, he is famous for his *Letters* (ed. L. Levillian, 2 vols., 1927, 1935) in Ciceronian Latin of which about 130 survive. He engaged in controversy with ⇨ Gottschalk on the doctrines of St Augustine, but is a humanist rather than a theologian. [FB]

Migne, *PL*, 119.

C. H. Beeson, *L. of Ferrières* (Cambridge, Mass., 1930); Duckett, *CP*.

**Luther, Martin** (Eisleben 1483–Eisleben 1546). German theologian. He combined tremendous vitality and an intense conviction of the rightness of his cause with remarkable literary and poetic gifts. His private dissatisfaction with the penitential system of the Church, as expressed in the 95 theses of 1517, rapidly assumed major national and international proportions and by 1521 the breach with the Roman Church was irreparable and the Reformation a reality. His own doctrine of the priesthood of all believers, as well as the practical need to appeal from a hostile Pope to the Christian community at large, naturally prompted him to write in German, and the newly invented printing-press provided a ready vehicle for his 'literary magic' – the expression of the burning intensity of his religious convictions in rugged and essentially popular language. He was one of the earliest and probably the most effective of all publicists, and the great treatises of 1520 *Von der Freiheit eines Christenmenschen* ('On Christian Freedom') and *An den christlichen Adel deutscher Nation* ('To the Christian Nobility of the German Nation') are masterly, concise statements of the Protestant position and inaugurated an era of vernacular controversy which was entirely without parallel.

It was as the translator of the Bible (New Testament, 1522; Old Testament, 1534) that Luther was to exert an abiding influence, however. Consciously aiming at as wide an audience as possible and, while avoiding dialectal extremes, basing himself on his own native Saxon and the morphology of the language of the Saxon chancellery, Luther writes in a language which, constantly revised until 1545, went a long way towards establishing a norm for standard German. As a translator his aim, as he tells us in the letter on translation (*Sendbrief von Dolmetschen*, 1530), was above all to write clear, straightforward German such as would be understood and spoken by the common people: an undue regard for 'the letters of the Latin language' is rejected, since these are recognized as a poor guide for the writing of correct German. It is the combination of popular speech with a poetic dignity comparable to that of the Authorized Version which has caused Luther's translation to survive as a living work of literature, profoundly influencing the language and even the thought-patterns of successive generations of Germans, while other contemporary literal translations (14 between 1466 and 1518) enjoyed only ephemeral popularity.

Luther showed great skill as a translator and adaptor of fables and his *Table Talk* is invaluable for the understanding of a fascinating and outstandingly important human being, but of all his voluminous original writings, for the greater part on strictly theological topics, his hymns alone have survived as living literature. In all he wrote 41 – often consciously designed to inculcate Protestant theology in a more palatable form than tract or sermon – which in their rugged strength and their ability to express the emotions of the Christian community rapidly gained the status of folk-songs. Such hymns as 'Ein' feste Burg ist unser Gott', 'Aus tiefer Not schrei' ich zu Dir' and the children's carol 'Vom Himmel hoch da komm' ich her' – often sung in Luther's own settings – are not only the fountain-head of the German hymn-writing tradition, but are still, like his Bible, an essential part of the cultural inheritance of all Protestant Germans. [WAC]

*Werke* (Weimar, 1883) (in progress); *L.'s Primary Works*, tr. H. Wace and C. A. Buchheim (1896); *Hymns*, tr. L. W. Bacon (N.Y., 1883).

R. H. Bainton, *Here I Stand* (Nashville, 1950); L. Fébure, *Un Destin – M.L.* (Paris, 1928); J. Mackinnon, *L. and the Reformation* (4 vols., 1925–30); R. Pascal, *The Social Basis of the German Reformation* (1933); G. Ritter, *L. – Gestalt und Tat* (Gütersloh, 1962).

**Luxorius** (fl. 500–530). Roman poet. He lived in Africa under the Vandal kings and wrote grammatical works. He also left about a hundred epigrams in the style of Martial, in various metres. Nominally a Christian, he wrote many very indecent poems. [FB]

Epigrams in *Anthologia latina*, ed. F. Bucheler and A. Riese (2 vols., Leipzig, 1894–7).

M. Rosenblum, *L., a Poet among Vandals*, text and tr. (1961).

**Luyken, Jan** (Amsterdam 1649–Amsterdam 1712). Dutch poet, illustrator and mystic. His first poems, collected in *Duytse Lier* (1671), are love lyrics of great simplicity and charm. Later he repudiated his worldliness and, under the influence of Böhme, wrote many books of pietistic verse which he illustrated with his own etchings. In *Jesus en de Ziel* (1678), which traces his spiritual development, and in the remainder of his work, his spontaneity and personal conviction are never obscured by didactics or esoterism. [PK]

*Voncken der liefde Jesu* (1687); *Spiegel van het menselijk bedrijf* (1694); *Zedelijke en stichtelijke gezangen* (1704); Barnouw, *CA*.

J. Meeuwesse, *J.L. als dichter van de Duytsche lier* (Groningen, 1952).

**Luzán Cláramunt de Suelvas y Guerra, Ignacio** (Saragossa 1702–Madrid 1754). Spanish scholar and critic. His prose *La poética* (1737; Madrid 1937) follows ⇨ Muratori's *Della perfetta poesia* with its neo-classic rules. In poetry he began the attack on ⇨ Góngora and in his theatrical criticism accepted the unities, while praising Lope de Vega and Calderón. The controversy that followed affected all Spanish dramatists till the end of the century. In general, his point of view was liberal, admitting enjoyment to be more important than conformity. His own poetry aimed at dignity, but achieved only dullness. [JMC]

*Poesías*, BAE, 61; *Poética*, ed. J. Cano (Toronto, 1928).

J. G. Robertson, *Studies in the Genesis of Romantic Theory* (1923); Menéndez y Pelayo, *HIE*.

**Luzel, F.** ⇨ Breton Literature.

**Luzi, Mario** (Florence 1914– ). Italian poet, essayist and prizewinner (Gran Premio di St Vincent, 1949). A teacher whose learning is reflected in the cultural and philosophical perspective in which he sees the solitude, confusion and despair of modern man. There are echoes of T. S. Eliot in his metaphysical meditations on the meaning of experience, in which he reaches towards a new Christian realization. His best volumes are *Primizie del deserto* (1952) and *Onore del vero* (1957). [GD]

Golino, *CIP*.
Fortini, *M*.

**Luzzatto, Moses Chayim** (Padua 1707–Acre 1747). Hebrew poet, mystic and scholar. Son of a wealthy merchant, at the age of 17 wrote his first drama *Maasei Shimshon* (ed. A. M. Haberman, 1950). This was followed by a number of studies on Hebrew versification, *Leshon Limudim*, which contrasted the Italian neo-classic style with the earlier, Arabic style of Hebrew poetry. In 1727 he wrote an allegorical drama, *Migdal Oz*, which marks the beginnings of modern Hebrew drama. Subjected to persecution and excommunication, Luzzatto went to Amsterdam, where he continued his literary work and wrote *La-Yesharim Tehillah* (a morality play based on Guarini's *Pastor fido*), a gem of modern Hebrew poetry, and his most popular ethical work *Mesillat Yesharim* (1743; crit. edn with tr. M. M. Kaplan, 1936). [EE]

S. Ginsburg, *The Life and Works of M.C.L.* (1931) (with bibliography).

**Luzzatto, Shmuel David,** known as Shadal (Trieste 1800–Padua 1865). Hebrew writer, also wrote in Italian. Of a noble but poor family, in early youth planned to dedicate his life to regenerate his nation. From 1829 taught at the Padua Collegio Rabbinico which was eventually ruined owing to political events. The emotional, yet scientific attitude to Jewish religion and history of his prose pervades also his poetry, much of which is on national themes. He was a master of style. [EE]

*Kinnor Na'im* (2nd edn, 2 vols., 1913); *Collecte Essays* in *Mechkere Ba-Yahadut* (2 vols., 1913); *Autobiografia del S.D.L.* (1882).

S. Morais, *Italian Hebrew Literature* (1926).

# M

**Macedonski, Alexandru** (Craiova 1854–Bucharest 1920). Rumanian poet and prose-writer. The son of an army officer, he was a precocious poet, his first book appearing when he was 17. At 19 he edited his first review, *Oltul.* In 1880 he started another review, *Literatorul*, which was to appear on and off for the rest of his life. At a meeting of *Junimea* in 1882 he read his macabre poem *Noaptea de Noemvrie*, describing his own funeral. But the aggressiveness which brought him into conflict all his life was soon to alienate Maiorescu and his friends. An epigram against ⇨ Eminescu published when the latter had his mental breakdown brought such a storm upon Macedonski's head that in 1884 he escaped for a few months to Paris. In the following year his first poems in French were published; a collection, *Bronzes*, was published in 1897. His first volume of prose was *Cartea de aur* (1902).

His gifts did not match his ambition. He is at his best in highly wrought miniatures, such as his rondeaus (collected posthumously as *Poema rondelurilor*, 1927) and in his prose evocations of bygone Bucharest. But as editor of literary reviews and encourager of young poets (⇨ Arghezi made his debut in Macedonski's *Liga Ortodoxă*) and as the propagator of symbolist and symbolist-instrumentalist theories he is an important figure in Rumanian literature. [EDT]

*Opere*, ed. T. Vianu (3 vols., 1939–44).

**Mácha, Karel Hynek** (Prague 1810–Litoměřice 1836). Czech poet. His chief work, the lyrico-epic poem *Máj* (1836; *May*, tr. R. A. Ginsburg, 1932; H. H. McGoverne, Prague, 1949; S. Spender and K. Brusak, second canto only, in *Review – 43*, 2, 1943), personifies the Romantic revolt of the individual not only against society but also against the order of the Universe and the Absolute. In his poetry the impact of the Western romantics combines with the influence of Czech Baroque; but he differs from both – from the romantics in his metaphysics and from the Baroque in his titanic negation of God. All conscious life is nothing but a kind of metaphysical humiliation and spiritual suffering. Man, an eternal prisoner, mercilessly rotates in an eternal circle; if there is guilt it is beyond his comprehension and will. The force keeping the cruel circle rotating is love but this is denied to the individual who is condemned to be for ever alone. In many respects Mácha's attitude suggests that adopted later by the existentialists.

*Dílo* (3 vols., 1948–50).

F. X. Šalda, *M.* (Prague, 1936); H. Granjard, *M. et la renaissance nationale en Bohème* (Paris, 1957); *SEER*, xv, 44 (1937); *Review* 43, 2 (1943).

**Machado, Antonio** (Seville 1875–Collioure 1939). Spanish poet. He went to school in Madrid, became involved in its literary life in the 1890s and published some satirical comments on the social and literary scene in 1893. On a visit to Paris in 1899 he met Oscar Wilde and ⇨ Moréas; he returned to France in 1902, and most of his poetry at this period has a Verlainean musicality and melancholy, although he uses natural scenes to reflect his feelings in some of the poems in *Soledades* (1903) in a way that also recalls earlier Spanish poets like Rosalía de Castro and his contemporary ⇨ Villaespesa. A teacher of French by profession, he married his landlady's daughter when at a school in Soria (1909), and personal happiness and a new concern for Spain's political and social problems probably helped to liberate him from the *tristesse* of his early poems. He finds delight as well as sadness in Nature, in Spain and the human condition in the poems of *Campos de Castilla* (1912) and a style that is less narrowly subjective. Tensions between hope and despair are finely resolved in many of the poems, notably in 'Campos de Soria' and the long Biblical and mythological ballad 'La tierra de Alvargonzález'. The poet's growing concern for moral and social problems emerges still more strongly in a number of poems which appeared in the second edition of *Campos de Castilla* (1917). He criticizes Spanish apathy with mordant wit and advocates the sam energetic attitude to life as his friend ⇨ Unamuno. A new group of philosophical poems also appeared in the second edition of *Campos*. These were in part the consequence of his earlier enthusiasm for popular poetry, and in particular the Andalusian 'cantar' on which his father had been an authority; but in some respects they reflected continued interest in ⇨ Campoamor's *Humoradas* and Sem Tob's *Proverbs*. A few of them also embodied Bergson's theories about the richness of the world seen in the flux of time. Machado was reading Bergson at the time, and had also heard him lecture in Paris in 1911.

After his wife's tragic death in August 1912, he wrote a new series of deeply melancholic and personal poems. He moved from Soria to Baeza to escape his memories and immersed himself in philosophy as well as his teaching. More ironic and cryptic philosophical poems followed, and the same vein was later exploited in prose writings purporting to be the lessons given by two imaginary teachers, Abel Martín and Juan de Mairena; like Unamuno, he uses paradox and witticism to provoke thought in his readers. He wrote some fine poems to 'Guiomar', a lady with whom he fell in love when he was in Segovia (1917–31), and collaborated with his brother in writing a number of poetic dramas. He was a staunch Republican at the time of the Civil War and died in exile in France. [NG]

*Poesías completas* (CA); *Obras* (Buenos Aires, 1964).

J. B. Trend, *A.M.* (1953); H. T. Young, *The Victorious Expression* (1964) (with translations of Unamuno, Machado, Jiménez, Lorca); *Atlante*, II, 1954; *HR*, XXX (1962).

**Machado, Manuel** (Seville 1874–Madrid 1947). Spanish poet. Son of the folklorist Machado y Álvarez and elder brother of Antonio ⇨ Machado, with whom he went to Paris (1899, 1902), he saw himself (*Retrato*) as 'half Parisian and half gipsy'. His work reflects this view, being inspired in part by the French Parnassians (*Felipe IV*) and Verlaine (Cordura, *La buena canción*) and in part by Andalusian popular poetry (*Cante hondo*). Pejoratively referred to as 'Machado el malo' to distinguish him from Antonio, his attitude seems that of a dilettante writing for amusement. D. Alonso points out that he 'used a light touch to deal with serious subjects'; and his use of folk-poetry influenced many of his younger contemporaries. A librarian by career (Santiago, 1912, Madrid, 1914), he wrote much drama criticism and collaborated with his brother in writing plays, most successfully *La Lola se va a los puertos* (1930). [GC/NG]

*Poesía. Opera omnia lyrica* (1942).

M. Pérez Ferrero, *Vida de A.M. y Manuel* (Buenos Aires, 1952); R. Gullón, *Direcciones del modernismo* (Madrid, 1963); F. Vian, *Il 'modernismo' nella poesia ispanica* (Milan, 1935); Alonso, *PEC*.

**Machar, Josef Svatopluk** (Kolín 1864–Prague 1942). Czech poet. The son of poor parents, he became a bank clerk in Vienna. With ⇨ Masaryk he was the instigator and chief mouthpiece of the 'realistic' intellectual and moral movement, advocating action instead of sentimental nationalism. During the First World War he was imprisoned by the Austrian authorities and in 1919 was named Inspector General of the Czechoslovak Army. In his poetry he sets himself up as judge of his own nation, contemporary society and the whole of humanity throughout its history. In his *Tristium Vindobona* (1893) and *Golgatha* (1901) he takes a stand against the majority of his nation, against its illusions and its smugness. His novels in verse, *Zde by měly kvést růže* (1894) and *Magdalena* (1894), are mordant criticisms of bourgeois morality. The 9 volumes of his *Svědomim věků* (1906–26), an epic of humanity, dominated by his hostility to Christianity, express the opposite view to that of Hugo; blind humanity revolves in a spiral without sense or goal. [KB]

*Spisy* (52 vols., 1927–40); *The Jail*, tr. P. Selver (1922).

V. Martínek, *J.S.M.* (Prague, 1948).

**Machiavelli, Niccolò** (Florence 1469–Florence 1527). Italian political theorist and historian. He learned politics in the service of the Florentine republic (1498–1512). His experience is recorded in some minor works on contemporary political questions, and in the *Legazioni*, which not only give his impressions of Caterina Sforza, Cesare Borgia, etc., but also sketch the background against which the later works should be set. With the fall of the republic he was dismissed, soon suspected, imprisoned, and ordered to leave the city; he retired to a farm near San Casciano. Here he wrote his controversial *Principe* (in 1513; publ. 1532;

tr. G. Bull, Penguin Classics, 1961). This apparently cynical exposition of a creed of treachery and tyranny must be read in the context of his other political works, especially the *Discorsi*, and of the circumstances of the time. The Medici, restored to power in Florence and with Leo X elected Pope, seemed on the crest of a wave. Machiavelli, after the fumbling and failure of the republic, thought he saw for them the chance of creating a strong and stable state in an Italy ravaged by the foreigner; his dramatic treatise is inspired by this passionate hope. Its goal is noble; the rigorous means are imposed by necessity.

The *Discorsi* (completed *c.* 1519; tr. L. J. Walker, 1950), examining political institutions more broadly by reference to the evolution of the Roman republic, give his long-term views. His main concern is the same: security, which must be founded on law; and in this unconstrained context he proclaims the superiority of government by peoples over government by princes. In the *Arte della guerra* (1521) he expounds the virtues of a citizen army committed to the cause which it is defending. His last major work, the *Istorie fiorentine* (8 books completed by 1525), raises the study of history from mere chronicle to an evaluation of motives and causes. His comedy, *La Mandragola* (*c.* 1520), is strong in its satirical humour, cruelly improbable plot, and characterization of gullibility and astuteness and is much superior to his other comedy, *Clizia*. Women, marriage and the power of both in the world are satirized in the story *Belfagor*. [DGR]

*Opere*, ed. S. Bertelli, F. Gaeta (1960–65); *Opere*, ed. M. Bonfantini (1954); *Tutte le opere*, ed. F. Flora, C. Cordié (1949–50); *Il Principe* (with selections from *Discorsi, Istorie fiorentine*), ed. L. Russo (1943); *Florentine History*, tr. W. K. Marriott (1909); *Art of War*, tr. P. Whitehorne (1560). *The Prince*, tr. Edward Dacres (1640), and *The Florentine History*, tr. T. Bedingfield (1595), all in The Tudor Translations (1905); *M.'s Literary Works* (incl. *Mandragola, Clizia*, some letters, the *Dialogue on Language* and *Belfagor*), tr. J. R. Hale (1961).

J. H. Whitfield, *M.* (1947); F. Chabod, *M. and the Renaissance*, tr. D. Moore (1958); J. R. Hale, *M. and Renaissance Italy* (1961); R. Ridolfi, *The Life of Niccolo Machiavelli*, tr. C. Grayson (1963); Binni, *CI*; *Maggiori*.

**Madách, Imre** (Alsósztregova 1823–Budapest 1864). Hungarian playwright. After his studies, and his arrest for anti-Hapsburg views, he entered the Hungarian parliament. His minor works are overshadowed by *Az ember tragédiája* (1860; tr. J. C. W. Horne, *The Tragedy of Man*, Budapest, 1964), which was translated into over 20 languages; although not originally written for the stage, it earned him international recognition as the first Hungarian able to be classed with great Western playwrights.

In the fusion of drama and the deep symbolic philosophical issues involved, this play has been compared with Goethe's *Faust*. Madách was partly inspired in his pessimistic idealism by the collapse of the War of Independence (1848–9) and his bad marriage. He also felt the conflict between individuality and collectivism: the 15 scenes of the *Tragedy* alternate in character between individualistic and collective; tragedy is constant, in the former for the individual and caused by the mob, in the latter for the masses and caused by the rulers. The three chief characters, Adam, the enthusiastic optimist; Lucifer, the practical, sober materialist; and Eve, the cause of Adam's fall but also his means of escape, are also present throughout, though playing different roles. The various scenes deal with philosophical problems occurring all through the history of mankind, shown to Adam in a dream by Lucifer. [JFR]

*Works* (3 vols., 1892; 2 vols., 1942).

S. Hevesy, *Introduction to the Tragedy of Man* (N.Y., 1935); J. Gassner, *Master of the Drama* (N.Y., 1940).

**Maerlant, Jacob van** (nr Bruges *c.* 1225–Damme *c.* 1291). West Flemish poet. Known for historically influential didactic works (which brought knowledge of the ancients to the third estate) adapted from Latin originals, *Der Natueren Bloeme* (1269), *Rijmbijbel* (*c.* 1270), *Spieghel Historiael* (unfinished; ed. J. Franck, 1882), and for romances of chivalry from the French (*Alexander*, *Historie van Troyen*, ed. N. de Pauw, 1889–92). But his strophic poems have real originality (especially the 3 Martijn dialogues on theology and ethics), with some keen satire of clerical corruption. [PK]

*Strophische gedichten*, ed. J. Verdam and P. Leendertz Jr (1918); Barnouw, *CA*.

**Maeterlinck, Maurice** (Ghent 1862–Nice 1949). Belgian poet and dramatist (Nobel Prize, 1911). A leading figure in the Belgian and French Symbolist movements, he began as a poet (*Serres chaudes*, 1889 and *Douze chansons*, 1896) before establishing his reputation with a series of plays drawing on allegory, romance, legend and fairy-tale and seeking to create in misty and ill-defined settings an atmosphere suggestive of poetry and of a mystic, spiritual realm. *La Princesse Maleine* (1889; tr. G. Harry, 1892) expresses that brooding sense of mystery and fatality and that conception of characters as passive victims of nameless, circumambient forces which one encounters repeatedly in his plays. These themes recur in *L'intruse* (1890; tr. W. Wilson, *The Intruder*, 1892), where a family is held in a strange expectancy of death, and in *Les aveugles* (1890; tr. L. A. Tadema, *The Sightless*, 1895), where the sense of the unseen is oppressive. Elsewhere, as in *Pelléas et Mélisande* (1892; tr. L. A. Tadema, *Pelleas and Melisanda*, 1895), made memorable by Debussy's music, *La mort de Tintagiles*, (1894; tr. A. Sutro, *The Death of Tintagiles*, 1899), *Aglavaine et Sélysette* (1896; tr. A. Sutro, 1897) and *Ariane et Barbe-bleue* (1901; tr. B. Miall, 1901), the tone is less portentous but the excessive reliance on silence and enigma, on a language of self-conscious and often self-parodying simplicity; the recurrence of characters who are mere symbolic figments, sonambulists in a strange land, finally wearies or baffles the spectator, even though he is sometimes moved by the larger symbolic reverberations, the conflicts between light and darkness, physical and spiritual, human and divine. Even death – Golaud's vengeance on Mélisande, Sélysette throwing herself from the tower – sometimes seems less a tragic than an unreal gesture within a dream world. The optimistic allegory, *L'oiseau bleu* (1909; tr. A. T. de Mattos, *The Blue Bird*, 1909), seems to suggest a transcending of fatality and death and has a child-like charm of its own. *Monna Vanna* (1902; tr. A. Sutro, 1904), *Marie-Magdeleine* (1913; tr. A. T. de Mattos, 1910) and *Le Bourgmestre de Stilemonde* (1919; tr. A. T. de Mattos, *The Burgomaster of Stilemonde*, 1918) mark a shift away from allegory and fantasy toward social and psychological drama. Maeterlinck's essays brood characteristically on creation and death, e.g. *Le trésor des humbles* (1896), *La sagesse et la destinée* (1898), *La vie des abeilles* (1901; tr. A. Sutro, *The Life of the Bee*, 1901), *La mort* (1913), *Avant le grand silence* (1934; tr. B. Miall, *Before the Great Silence*, 1935), etc. He was much interested in spiritualism. [SBJ]

*Théâtre* (3 vols., 1901–2); *Théâtre inédit* (1959).

J. M. Andrieu, *M.M.* (Paris, 1962); A. Guardino, *Le théâtre de M.* (Paris, 1934); G. Compère, *Le théâtre de M.M.* (Paris, 1955).

**Maffei, Scipione** (Verona 1675–Verona 1755). Italian scholar. At first an Arcadian poet, his interest shifted gradually to scholarship. In 1710 he was co-founder with A. Zeno of the *Giornale dei Letterati d'Italia*, later continued with his *Osservazioni letterarie* (1737–40). In 1713 his successful tragedy *Merope* (tr. 1740; ed. G. R. Ceriello, Milan, 1954) brought European acclaim and marked a significant advance in the history of Italian tragedy. He rightly included it in his own selection of the best 12 tragedies – *Teatro italiano* (1723). His writings covered a vast field ranging from erudite historical study (e.g. his masterpeice *Verona illustrata*, 1732; and *Galliae antiquitates*, 1734) to controversial theological works (e.g. *Istoria teologica*, 1742; *Dell'impiego del denaro*, 1744) and others on economics, literature and the sciences (e.g. *Delle formazioni dei fulmini*, 1747). A polygraph representative of the best tradition of 18th-century Italian erudition. [RHC]

*Opere* (21 vols., 1790); *Opere drammatiche e poesie varie*, ed. A. Avena (1928); *Epistolario*, ed. C. Garibotti (2 vols., 1955).

G. Silvestri, *Un Europeo del '700. S.M.* (Treviso, 1954); G. Gasperoni, *S.M. e Verona settecentesca* (Verona, 1955); *Miscellanea maffeiana* (Verona, 1955); G. Toffanin, *L'Arcadia* (3rd edn, Bologna, 1958); G. Gasparini, *La tragedia classica dalle origini al M.* (Turin, 1963); *Minori*, iii.

**Magalotti, Lorenzo** (Rome 1637–Florence 1712). Italian writer, diplomat and scientist. Of noble Florentine family, he served the Medici, travelling all over Europe on diplomatic missions. He retired (1691) into a religious order, but after a short time resumed his secular career. His interests included science, philosophy, religion, languages and travel, and his writings are characterized by a mingling of scientific curiosity and aesthetic sensitivity. As secretary of the Florentine Accademia del Cimento he described in *Saggi di naturali esperienze* (1667; ed. E. Falqui, 1947) experiments carried out there in the tradition established by Galileo. His *Lettere scientifiche ed erudite* (publ. 1721) on various scientific topics, the *Lettere sugli odori* (publ. 1721) and the *Lettere sui buccheri* (1825; ed. M. Praz, 1945) on odours and perfumes are written in a prose which is sensitive and poetic, as well as meaningful. His religious and philosophical interests are reflected in *Lettere familiari contro l'ateismo* (ed. M. Praz, in *Lettere sui buccheri* etc., 1945). He also composed diplomatic reports and lively descriptions of foreign courts and countries, perhaps edited Carletti's *Ragionamenti* (a travel-book) and became well-known in many European capitals. His mediocre verse includes a frigid canzoniere (*La donna immaginaria*), some *Canzonette anacreontiche* and a dithyramb *La Madre selva*. [DGR]

*Le piú belle pagine di L.M.*, ed. L. Montano (1924); *Opere dei discepoli di G. Galilei* (vol. 1), ed. G. Abetti and P. Pagnini (1942); *Lettere odorose* (also contains *Canzonette*, *La Madreselva*), ed. E. Falqui (1943); *Scritti di corte e di mondo*, ed. E. Falqui (1945).

S. Fermi, *L.M. scienziato e letterato* (Piacenza, 1903); *Minori*, iii.

**Maimonides (Moses ben Maimon)**, known as **Rambam** (Córdoba 1135–Fostat (Old Cairo) 1204). Hebrew religious writer and Arabic philosopher. As a result of Almohade persecution of the Jews, his family left Spain in 1160 and lived in Fez; he then went for a short while to Palestine and eventually to Cairo where he was physician to the Sultan and Rabbi. He wrote important works on Jewish law: the 613 Commandments; a commentary in Arabic on the whole *Mishnah* (1168); and the greatest of all expositions of Jewish Law, *Mishne Torah* or *Yad Chazakah* (1180). His chief philosophical work, *Dalalat al-Ha'irin* (Heb. *Moreh Nevukin*; Heb. tr. Samuel ibn Tibbon and Judah al-Charizi; tr. M. Friedlaender, *The Guide of the Perplexed*, 3 vols., 1851–85; sel. tr. C. Rabin, 1952), was completed in 1190. In this work he presented the Jewish religion with the method of Aristotelian philosophy. Its influence was enormous upon Jewish and Christian philosophers (through several Latin translations, among others J. Buxtorf Jr, 1629). A bitter fight ensued after the appearance of the Hebrew translation between his partisans and opponents, resulting in a partial ban of the book. He also wrote *responsa* and medical works. [EE]

B. Bokser, *The Legacy of M.* (N.Y., 1950); *Essays on M.*, ed. S. W. Baron (N.Y., 1941); H. L. Roth, *The Guide to the Perplexed* (1948).

**Mairet, Jean** (Besançon 1604–Paris 1686). French dramatist. He appeared briefly in French literature at a decisive moment in the development of a classical style. It is strange that he should be remembered for his plays, which he stopped writing before he was 40. He seems to have been employed, along with the poet Théophile, by the Duc de Montmorency and then by the Comte de Belin. We get a glimpse of what patronage meant from ⇨ Tallemant, who says that Belin proposed a Roman subject to Mairet in order that the leading role be given to 'La Le Noir', his favourite actress. Mairet's early plays suggest a popular demand for dramatic pastorals, that is for witty imitations of the pastoral novel *L'Astrée*: *Chryséide et Arimand* (1625; ed. H. C. Lancaster, 1925), *Sylvie* (1626; ed. J. Marsan, 1905), *Sylvanire* (1636; ed. Otto, 1890). Apart from one comedy (*Les galanteries du Duc d'Ossone*, 1632) he exploited a new vein in tragedy: *Virginie* (1633), *Sophonisbe* (1634; ed. C. Dédéyan, 1945), *Le Marc-Antoine, ou La Cléopâtre* (1635), *Le grand et dernier Solyman* (1637). Finally he tried tragicomedy: *L'illustre corsaire*, *Roland furieux*, *Athenaïs* and *Sidonie* were all put on the stage between 1636 and 1641. These plays suggest that the audiences liked something approaching thrillers, story-plays making use of melodrama and romanesque improbability: 'a prince turned pirate rescues a princess, defeats a rival and finally regains a throne' (Lancaster). Even in *Solyman*, a tragedy, we have a girl in armour and an exchange of infants. Such plays make liberal use of dreams, oracles, long-lost relatives. At the same time he was among the first to see the tension and artistic pleasure to be derived from the 'regular' play in which interest is concentrated and focused on a moral issue, e.g. his queen Sophonisba, who dies for love of an enemy (a theme imitated by Corneille). The same play has excellent examples of the classical line ('*Il a puni ma faute en me la reprochant*'). In fact, with ⇨ Rotrou and Tristan, Mairet deserves some of the credit accorded to Corneille for inaugurating classical tragedy. [WGM]

**Majerová, Marie** (Úvaly 1882–Prague 1967). Czech novelist. Born in the Kladno mining area, she saw the hard life of the coalminers, worked as a journalist and joined the Communist Party when it was founded in 1921. Having spent several years in Paris amongst the anarchists from many lands, she por trayed this world in *Náměstí republiky* (1914). Her novel *Nejkrásnější svět* (1923) describes a country girl's path to Communism for which she eventually gives her life; *Siréna* (1935) is a large canvas of the economic and social changes in the Kladno region during four generations. Her best work is perhaps *Havířská balada* (tr. R. Finlayson-Samsour, *Ballad of a Miner*, Prague, 1960), a story of one human life, love and happiness struggling against the world. In her hands the socialist novel becomes a real work of art thanks to her passionate love for life, her understanding of the human heart, her talent to see poetry in ordinary things and her sense of humour. [KB]

J. Hájek, *Národní umělkyně M.M.* (Prague, 1952).

**Makriyannis, Yannis** (Avoriti 1797–Athens 1864). Greek memoirist. He came from a poor peasant family, and after an adventurous boyhood he fought with distinction in the Greek War of Independence and rose to the rank of General. He played a turbulent part in Greek politics during the reign of King Otho, whose absolutism he opposed fiercely. He taught himself to read and write late in life for the express purpose of writing his memoirs, one of the masterpieces of Greek prose in the demotic, distinguished for their vigorous style and their original and unconventional comments on personalities and events. They contain vivid scenes of powerful poetic beauty. [SJP]

*Apomnimonevmata*, ed. J. Vlachoyannis (1947); *The Memoirs of General Makriyannis*, tr. H. A. Lidderdale (1966).

**Maksim the Greek** (*c.*1470–1556). Greek Orthodox religious writer. Maksim (his lay name was Michael Trivolis) spent the last years of the 15th century in Humanist circles in Italy. Early in the 16th century he took the tonsure on Mt Athos where he soon achieved fame as a scholar. When in 1515 Grand Prince Vasily of Moscow asked for a translator from Mt Athos, Maksim was sent. He arrived in Moscow in 1518. Although at first knowing no Slavonic he translated a psalter with commentary as well as part of a commentary on the Acts of the Apostles. He then asked permission to return to Mt Athos. It was refused, and he spent the rest of his life in Muscovy. In 1525 he was arrested and accused of four main offences: interfering in Moscow's diplomatic relations with the Porte, attempting to undermine the autocephalous status of the Russian Church, defaming the Russian Church and saints for their attitude to ecclesiastical landownership, and spreading heretical teachings. But his real guilt was probably participation in the political opposition to the grand prince and his objection to Vasily III's uncanonical divorce in 1525. He spent six years as a prisoner in the Josephian monastery of Volokolamsk. In 1531 he was retried, together with ◊ Vasily Patrikeyev. Further charges of disseminating heretical doctrines, largely trumped up, were brought against him and he was once more sentenced to monastic confinement, this time in Tver' where conditions were milder and where he was able to write. In 1551 he was allowed to move to the Trinity monastery of St Sergy, where he died.

He wrote many religious treatises on many topics. His most important works are connected with: (a) the question of monastic landownership in which he ardently defended the cause of the disciples of ◊ Nil Sorsky; (b) the question of Church and State; (c) the need to free the Greeks from Turkish bondage and the need for the union of the Orthodox churches; and (d) the struggle with heresy, especially the remnants of the heresy of the Judaizers. [JLIF]

E. Denissoff, *Maxime le Grec et l'Occident* (Paris-Louvain, 1943); V. S. Ikonnikov, *Maksim Grek i yego vremya* (Kiev, 1915).

**Malaparte, Curzio,** pseud. Kurt Suckert (Prato 1898–Rome 1957). Italian political pamphleteer, journalist, satirical poet, playwright, film producer and novelist. He became a Fascist around 1922 but soon fell foul of the Party because of his impertinent heterodoxy. His French pamphlet *Technique du coup d'état* (1931) is said to have irritated Hitler, and earned him a short term of restricted residence. His war correspondences from the Russian front in 1941 (collected in 1943, *Il Volga nasce in Europa*; tr. D. Moore, *The Volga Rises in Europe*, 1957), angered the Nazi command, who had him confined to Finland; there he wrote his best book, *Kaputt* (1944), an apocalyptic vision of Europe crumbling under the senseless violence of war. His later experiences as Italian liaison officer with the Allies in Naples (1944) offered him the pretext for his most controversial novel, *La* *pelle* (1949; tr. D. Moore, *The Skin*, 1952), whose Goya-like surrealism was mistaken for documentary realism and caused great scandal. After three unsuccessful plays and a moderately successful film (*Cristo proibito*, 1951), he went back to journalism and took up again his pre-war role of literary *enfant terrible*, now rather unsuited to his age and experience. People grew less tolerant of his sniping, especially since it was difficult to understand from what position he was shooting: nationalism or cosmopolitanism, conservatism or progressivism, Right or Left? His international background and education made him see clearly the decadence of Europe, and turn to his land of adoption with all the passionate fervour of a man of foreign extraction. On the other hand his profound love for Italy made him grow intolerant of her parochial outlook, and open to broader cultural influences. In so far as both attitudes can be traced to a single motive, a sincere refusal of intellectual time-serving, they are not morally inconsistent. Malaparte failed to see, however, that they are also poles of a political choice that should be exercised outside and above the plane of personal morality. Thus his brilliant cynical moralism became a symptom of political disengagement and indifference, and what remains in his books of all the blood spilt in the wars, ultimately for political reasons, are only a few purple patches. [GMC]

*Contemporanei*, ii.

**Malczewski, Antoni** (Kniahinin 1793–Warsaw 1826). Polish poet. His brief life was rich in experience. He served in the army, travelled abroad and conquered the peak of Mont Blanc in 1818. After returning to Poland, he became involved with a mentally unbalanced woman, which deepened his recurring moods of melancholy. For her sake he dabbled in the then fashionable pursuit of Magnetism. His only published poem, *Maria* (1825), is unique in Polish romanticism for the intense lyrical precision of its narrative, unclouded by romantic effusion. It has the subtitle 'a Ukrainian tale' and is based on a true incident. Secretly married to a magnate's son, Maria brings on herself the revenge of her father-in-law and is murdered. The melodramatic themes of vengeance and crime are here transformed into a study of human emotions, the more memorable for the idiosyncratic use of language which abounds in metaphors of action and landscape images. *Maria* brought Malczewski no recognition, but the poem was hailed four years after his death by the critic Mochnacki, who used it to illustrate and justify the new movement in literature. Later comparisons with Byron, misleading and also unfair, were meant to flatter Malczewski. [JP]

Peterkiewicz and Singer, *FCPP*; Pietrkiewicz, *PPV*.

**Malemanche, Tangi.** ⇨ Breton Literature.

**Malherbe, François de** (Caen 1555–Paris 1628). French poet and critic. Plain-spoken, witty, industrious, he spent twenty years in Provence and achieved the ambition of so many, a summons to the Royal Court. An unattractive character but a strong personality (many stories are told of his probably deliberate confusion of rudeness and frankness), his judgements on his contemporaries are sharp and negative. ⇨ Tallemant says he had '*un grand mépris pour tous les hommes*'. But he is a great name in criticism because he insisted, both in precept and example, on careful writing, on the French and classical qualities of '*lucidité*, *volonté*, *calcul*' which were to be a dominant feature of the literature of the *grand siècle*. No wonder that Boileau hailed him as the first modern poet of France. Generations of schoolboys have been brought up on the cliché 'Enfin Malherbe vint' and have probably suspected that Boileau thought him a greater poet than Ronsard. Recent research has shown that his advent was not a great wonder and that he may have swelled, but could not have caused, the trend towards regular writing. [WGM]

R. Fromilhague, *M.* (Paris, 1954); R. Winegarten, *French Lyric Poetry in the Age of M.* (1954); Marcel Raymond, in *Baroque et Renaissance poétique* (Paris, 1955).

**Mallarmé, Stéphane** (Paris 1842–Valvins 1898). French poet. Like Baudelaire, by whom he was at first influenced, he turned away from reality towards an ideal world, possibly for similar psychological reasons in that he too lost one of his parents (his mother) in the early years of his childhood, as well as suffering a second blow in the death of his sister when he was 15. But, after a brief period of uncertainty in 1863 and 1864, Mallarmé, unlike Baudelaire, began to look for his ideal world in the realm of the intellect rather than of the emotions, and this may well be symbolized both by the cold, solitary princess who is the heroine of his dramatic poem *Hérodiade*, began late in 1864, and by the satyr of *L'après-midi d'un faune*, first written in the summer of 1865, who lets the nymphs he attempts to capture slip from his grasp.

After a struggle recounted in the group of 3 sonnets, 'Tout orgueil fume-t-il du soir', 'Surgi de la croupe et du bond' and 'Une dentelle s'abolit', he succeeded in defining the nature of his ideal world, and by 1868, when he wrote the first version of his important poem 'Ses purs ongles', he was convinced that beyond the real world there lies a void containing everything in essence and that the divine mission of the poet, proudly proclaimed in the sonnet 'Quand l'ombre menaça', is to express these essences lying beyond reality, to describe, not an individual flower, but the ideal, essential flower, '*l'absente de tous bouquets*', '*la notion pure*', as he was to call it almost twenty years later. To distil the essences of things in this way meant creating an intensely concentrated language and Mallarmé devoted the rest of his life, or as much of it as he could spare from his multiple occupations as an English teacher, translator, essayist and writer of occasional verse, to this exacting task which was ultimately intended to result in what he called his *Grand Œuvre*.

This project was never in fact carried out, but he also wrote a number of poems related to it, which he modestly referred to as '*études en vue de mieux*'. His 7 or 8 elegies, the best known being those addressed to Poe, Gautier, Wagner, Baudelaire and Verlaine, reflect his basic ideas in that their general theme is that death is not the end, since the essential quality of the dead person – his work in the case of a poet or composer – continues to live on. In the 6 or 7 sonnets inspired, between 1884 and 1887, by his mistress Méry Laurent, he is once more tempted, as he had been at the time of his marriage over twenty years before, by the real world of the senses, although in one of the later sonnets of the cycle, as the love affair waned, he turned back again to the ideal world of the intellect. In a third type of poem he reflects on his ultimate goal and what he has so far achieved. 'Le vierge, le vivace et le bel aujourd'hui', dealing with the poet's Hamlet-like inability to make a decisive move, is the most celebrated of the poems of this kind, while the most notoriously obscure example is the poem paradoxically entitled 'Prose', and addressed to Des Esseintes, the hero of ⇨ Huysmans's novel *À rebours*, in which Mallarmé acknowledges that up to that date, 1884, he has produced nothing, but excuses himself on the grounds that the task he has set himself is extremely difficult and promises that the fruits of his labours will now appear. They did not in fact do so, owing partly, no doubt, to the seductive charms of Méry Laurent and partly also, perhaps, to the increasing demands made on his time as a result of his growing reputation as one of France's outstanding poets. The same theme recurs a few years later in 'Salut', 'A nue accablante tu' and 'Au seul souci de voyager' in which he sadly recognizes that the sands are running out and that, at over 50, he has little or no chance of completing his task. But even if he had done so, even if he had written and published his *Grand Œuvre*, would it have survived? One can set down ideas in what one hopes is indestructible form, but fate can still intervene so that one's achievement is ignored and forgotten. This appears to be the theme of *Un coup de dés jamais n'abolira le hasard*, where this single sentence is interspersed with various qualifying parentheses and followed by a further qualification offering some consolation in the thought that ideas may still survive even if they have not been given tangible form.

*Un coup de dés* is Mallarmé's most ambitious experiment in that the irregular placing of the words on the page and the use of different kinds of type add to the general effect; but all his work, apart from the very early poems, has that extreme density and compression which makes its grammatical and syntactical structure so difficult to grasp. [CC]

*Poésies* (1956); *Œuvres complètes* (1951); *M.* (Penguin Poets, 1965) (poems with prose tr. ed. with intr. A. Hartley).

C. Chadwick, *M., sa pensée dans sa poésie* (Paris, 1962); A. R. Chisholm, *M.'s 'Grand Œuvre'* (1962); G. Michaud, *M., l'homme et l'œuvre* (Paris, 1953); P. O. Walzer, *Essai sur S.M.* (Paris, 1963).

**Mallet-Joris, Françoise** (Antwerp 1930– ). Belgian novelist. Educated in America and at the Sorbonne, she won a Sagan-type success with *Le rempart des Béguines* (1950; tr. H. Briffault, *Into the Labyrinth*, 1953), a tale of lesbianism and adultery, though serious critics recognized her mature understanding of character and her cool economical style, more than one comparing her with Laclos. In *La chambre rouge* (1953; tr. H. Briffault, *The Red Room*, 1956) the same heroine becomes involved in an unhappy love affair. In *Les mensonges* (Prix des Libraires 1956; tr. H. Briffault, *House of Lies*, 1958) the central situation – mother, father, illegitimate daughter – is again similar, but the style is quite different, deliberately *chosiste* where previously it had been precise and ironical. *L'empire céleste* (Prix Femina, 1959; tr. H. Briffault, *Cafe céleste*, 1959), an account – allegorical overtones – of life in a block of flats, and *Les personnages* (1960), France under Louis XIII, indicate a broadening of her canvas, without any blurring of her technique. [IHW]

*Lettre à moi-même* (1963; tr. P. O. Brian, *Letter to Myself*, 1964).

*Yale French Studies*, 27 (1961); Mourgue, *DDL*.

**Malmberg, Bertil** (Härnösand 1889–Stockholm 1958). Swedish poet and prose-writer. He has given an indirect description of his childhood and middle-class background in *Åke och hans värld* (1924; tr. M. Wenner-Gren, *Å. and his World*, N.Y., 1940) but also written a straight biography in *Ett stycke väg* (1950) and its sequel *Ett författarliv* (1952), an impressive piece of self-analysis. His first book of verse was the work of a precocious teenager, but with *Orfika* (1923) he began to achieve independence of his models, notably Schiller, Stefan George and Rilke (during 1917–26 he lived in Munich). In *Orfika* he embraces a dualistic view of the world, seeking to detach himself from crude experience and exalting the world of pure ideas. Characteristic of his early work is his rigorous concern with formal perfection. *Illusionernas träd* (1932), poised between pessimistic insight and feelings of gratitude and hope, is another milestone in his career. In *Dikter vid gränsen* (1935), by contrast, he solemnly prophesies coming disaster (in the spirit of Spengler). The verse has a hieractic movement, the effect of which may be hypnotic; but intellectually these poems are less convincing. After temporary association with the Oxford Movement, resulting in the confessions of *Sångerna om samvetet och ödet* (1938), he once more returned to melancholy self-examination. *Flöjter ur ödsligheten* (1941) expresses his sense of isolation, a mood which persists in *Under månens fallande båge* (1947). His last phase is marked by a new forceful directness, as if the inner censor has been made to withdraw; laconic brevity (tending towards fragmentation) replaces the wonted rhetorical architectonics, and a freer, more varied rhythm the impeccable regularity of his earlier verse. He himself claimed that a slight haemorrhage of the brain in 1947 altered the paths of his associations. Whatever the explanation, this late flowering brought the ageing poet close to the lyrical modernists of the day. Collections like *Men bortom marterpålarna* (1948), *Med cyklopöga* (1950), *Lek med belysningar* (1953) and *Klaviatur* (1955) will probably continue to be read by many who are immune to the 'older' Malmberg. [SAB]

A. Ahlberg, *B.M.* (Stockholm, 1939); A. Lundkvist, 'B.M.', in *Bonniers Litterära Magasin*, 1943; E. Bergman, *Diktens värld och politikens* (Lund, 1967).

**Malraux, André** (Paris 1901– ). French novelist, essayist, philosopher of art, archaeologist and publisher's editor. A revolutionary activist in China in the mid twenties, militant in the Spanish Civil War and in the Resistance, he has been prominent in the Gaullist movement since the war and Minister of State for Cultural Affairs since the inception of the Fifth Republic. A compellingly intense personality, a brilliant talker, a man of proven courage, Malraux - who for several generations of French readers was the very prototype of the 'committed writer' – is one of the spectacular figures of European literature in this century.

The legend surrounding his career as a 'man of action' (like one of his heroes, 'a man capable of acting – when necessary') for long caused him to be seen as a communistic chronicler of the times rather than as a truly imaginative novelist – and caused his adoption of the Gaullist cause in the early part of the Cold War period to be seen as a betrayal of the Left. In fact, however, there is a striking continuity underlying his career. He at no time subscribed philosophically to Marxism, he has always seen himself as an 'obsessive' novelist in the manner of Dostoyevsky rather than as a realist, and indeed observation in his writing is everywhere subservient to a profoundly Romantic meditation upon the metaphysical situation of modern man.

The originality of his earlier work resides in the fact that it was he who established in the French novel the idea of the 'absurd'. Already shocked, as a highly nervous and remote adolescent, by the stupidity as well as by the savagery of the First World War, he came to feel that liberal Europe had in effect committed suicide, that Reason had failed as much as Faith, that the progressive agnostic civilization emerging from 19th-century Europe following upon the 'death of God' had revealed its own hollowness and that modern European man was now 'dead' in his turn. Rejecting existing views of the personality as mere legends, he saw the individual as a 'monster of wish-fulfilment' locked up inside his own solitude and suffering. Driven by this view of the absurd and haunted by the sense that the only reality was death itself, he set out to live and to represent the metaphysical situation of the alienated European. Whence the hard, yet deeply vulnerable adventurer-hero asserting himself amid revolutionary strike action in Canton in *Les conquérants* (1928; tr. W. S. Whale, *The Conquerors*, 1929), or against the jungle in *La voie royale* (1930; tr. S. Gilbert, *The Royal Way*, 1935). Whence also, when this Nietszchean individualism is seen to fail, the attempt to re-create the climate of destiny of Greek tragedy in *La condition humaine* (1933; tr. A. Macdonald, *Man's Estate* – originally *Storm in Shanghai* – 1948). In this novel, for which Chiang Kai Shek's *coup* against the Communists in 1927 is merely the occasion, the darkly pessimistic view of life and of human relationships is to some extent balanced by a poetic assertion of the more positive values of dignity and fraternity.

In the middle and late thirties, Malraux became one of France's leading anti-Fascists, being active in a number of organizations and organizing a volunteer air-squadron to fight for the Republicans in Spain. His writings and his speeches of this period show a concern for the quality of individual living as well as pleading for brotherhood among men and, if he was often led to share a platform with the Communists, he generally contrived to distance his own position from theirs. His novel dealing with the early part of the war in Spain, *L'espoir* (1937; tr. S. Gilbert and A. Macdonald, *Days of Hope*, 1938), was written close to the events. Malraux himself regards it as his best.

Already before the Second World War – in which he had a spectacularly distinguished career – he had been haunted by the Spenglerian view that the rise and fall of civilizations reveals no continuity in human history, and he now turned to art for an image of the permanence of man. In the most important of his writings on art, *Les voix du silence* (1951; tr. S. Gilbert, *The Voices of Silence*, 1953), he argues the freedom of the artist from Marxian and Freudian determinisms, and attempts to show that art – the essential, eternal assertion of man's freedom over 'destiny' – transcends history. It is largely due to this shift in his preoccupations that Malraux moved to the Right after the war – insisting nevertheless, and though he had never been a Marxist, that he was opposing the threat from *Stalinism* to freedom and to culture rather than Communism as a force for social change.

Today, a mellower Malraux has been responsible, among other ministerial activities, for the cleaning and restoration of historic buildings in Paris. [CJ]

C. D. Blend, *A.M., Tragic Humanist* (Ohio, 1963); J. Delhomme, *Temps et destin* (Paris, 1955); W. M. Frohock, *A.M. and the Tragic Imagination* (Stanford, 1952); J. Hoffmann, *L'humanisme de M.* (Paris, 1963); G. Picon, *M. lui-même* (Paris, 1953); W. Richter, *The Rhetorical Hero* (1964).

**Mameli, Goffredo** (Genoa 1827–Rome 1849). Italian patriot and poet. After some undistinguished early love poetry, he played an important part in the events of 1847–9, especially with the publication of his celebrated patriotic poem *Fratelli d'Italia* (1847), later called the *Inno di Mameli*. It was set to music by M. Novaro, and since 1946 has been the Italian national anthem. [RHC]

Dionisotti, *OBIV*.
*G.M. La vita e gli scritti*, ed. A. Codignola (2 vols., Venice, 1927); E. Bertolti, *G.M. e la repubblica romana nel 1849* (Genoa, 1927).

**Mamin, Dmitry Narkisovich** pseudonym: Sibiryak; often known as Mamin-Sibiryak. (Perm' 1852–Petersburg 1912). Russian novelist and ethnographer. He was the son of a priest, studied veterinary surgery, then law, but left the University without completing the course. In 1877 he settled in the Urals. Most of his literary work depicts the life in the mines there: the profit-seekers, the tremendous squandering and short-lived riches, the stern military authorities. There is much action in his stories and many ethnographical details. Among the works of that period are *Boitsy* (1883), *Delo* (1883) and *Gornoye Gnezdo* (1884).

In 1891 he moved to Petersburg and at first continued to write about the Urals – *Zoloto* (1892); *Vesenniye grozy* (1893); *Khleb* (1895). The themes of his later works are drawn from the life of the capital – *Cherty iz zhizni Pepko* (1894); *Po novomu puti* (1895); *Padayushchiye zvezdy* (1899). He also wrote books for children. [MG]

*Polnoye sobraniye sochineniy* (12 vols., 1915–17); *Verochka's tales*, tr. R. Davidson (1922); *Tales for Alyounushka*, tr. Zheleznova (1957).
A. Gruzdev, *M.-S.* (Moscow, 1958).

**Mandel'shtam, Osip Emil'yevich** (Warsaw 1891–? Vladivostok 1938). Russian poet. Born of Jewish parents, he grew up in and near St Petersburg. He studied for a period at Heidelberg University (1910), and then at the University of St Petersburg. His friendship with the poet ⇨ Gumilyov, which dates from about 1910, led him to take an active part in 'The Poets' Guild', as a militant member of the ⇨ Acmeist school. His first volume of verse, *Kamen'*, appeared in 1913. His second volume of poetry, *Tristia* (1922), contains many of his masterpieces. It illustrates a gradual development of his style, away from the clear, solemn and slow-moving manner of his early verse towards a more elliptical and metaphorical language. This recondite style is still more evident in his third collection – the last to be published during his life-time – which appeared in 1928. His persecution by the Soviet authorities for his evident lack of ideological and literary conformism appears to have begun in earnest in the early 1930s. He was arrested in 1934 and was exiled first to Cherdyn', in the Ural region, and later (1935–7) to Voronezh in circumstances of which we still know little, but which, to judge from the veiled allusions and the tone of despair of his last poems, must have been harrowing. He was re-arrested in Moscow in 1938. The circumstances of his death are still uncertain: according to one version, he died in Eastern Siberia, on the way to a concentration camp.

Five themes figure prominently in his poetry: (1) The ambivalent face of St Petersburg, stately and classical, yet also dreamlike and insubstantial, of whose former glory and post-Revolutionary destitution he wrote in verses of haunting and poignant beauty; (2) the ideal of classical antiquity which, he hoped for a time, would restore balance and harmony to Russian post-Revolutionary culture; (3) the prophetic and liturgical function of poetry; (4) human love, which illustrates the polarity of joy and suffering, life and death; (5) the age of Revolution and the ensuing upheaval and tyranny, which provoked in him an awe-struck fascination, then a mixture of pity and terror, and finally a desperate urge to escape from the spiritual darkness of his confined environment to the promised land of ancient Greece and to the cultural values of Europe, both of which he recognized as his patrimony. [DO]

*Sobraniye sochineniy*, ed. G. P. Struve and B. A. Philippov, vols. 1 and 2 (Washington, 1964, 1966).
*The Prose of O.M.*, tr. with a critical essay, by C. Brown (Princeton, 1965); I. Bushman, *Poeticheskoye iskusstvo M.* (1964); W. Weidle, 'O poslednikh stikhakh Mandel'shtama', in *Vozdushnye Puti*, ed. R. N. Grinberg, II (N.Y., 1961); *RR*, 1 (1948).

**Mane, Mordecei Zevi** (nr Vilno 1860–nr Vilno 1887). Russian Jewish poet. One of the outstanding poets of Russian Jewry. He died at 27. Son of a poor schoolmaster, he won a place to the St Petersburg Academy of Arts and Crafts. He left behind a number of essays and poems which show great promise. Unlike other young poets, he did not write love poems, neither did he write, like his contemporaries, poems with a high moral purpose. In his writing, he gives evidence of a great love of nature, of a fear of impending death and of a great love of Zion. [EE]

*Kol Kitveh Maneh* (2 vols., 1946).
Waxman, *HJL*.

**Manger, Itzig** (Jassy 1900–1969). Yiddish poet. Son of a tailor whose literary talent was discovered when still at school in Czernowitz. From Jassy, he moved to Warsaw in 1929 and only left there at the outbreak of the Second World War. In 1941–51 he lived in London, and since then in New York. Writing both poetry and prose, he uses traditional motifs presented in a tuneful and artistic manner. [EE]

*Jubilee edition of his works* (Geneva–Paris, 1951); *Shtern Oifn Dach* (Bucharest, 1929); *Chumesh-lider* (2nd edn, 1936); *Noente Geshtaltn* (1938); *Volkens ibern dach* (London, 1947); *Hotsmach Spil* (London, 1947).
Roback, *SYL*.

**Mann, Heinrich** (Lübeck 1871–Los Angeles 1950). German novelist. Brother of Thomas

⇨ Mann, he once enjoyed more sensational fame, by exploring similar preoccupations with the predicament of the artist in bourgeois society but in far cruder terms of erotic fantasy and self-consciously amoral aestheticism (influenced by ⇨ D'Annunzio and admired e.g. by ⇨ Benn). The most extravagant of his works in this vein is the Renaissance 'orgy' *Die Göttinnen...* (1902–3; tr. E. Posselt and E. Glore, *Diana*, N.Y., 1929), while the most controlled and readable is *Die kleine Stadt* (1909; tr W. Ray, *The Little Town*, 1930) where for once artist and society meet in the humanly plausible and truly observed circumstances of an Italian town thrown into confusion by a visiting theatre company. That here the artistic cause is also socially progressive reflects the crystallization of Mann's anti-bourgeois attitude into socialism and a belief that literature should be politically committed (see essays like *Geist und Tat*, 1910, or *Zola*, 1915 – and Thomas Mann's analysis of this literary-political idealism as false in *Betrachtungen eines Unpolitischen*, 1918). His most memorable figure is Diedrich Hessling, who embodies the vanities and menace of the Wilhelmine authoritarian state in *Der Untertan* (1918; tr. anon., *Man of Straw*, 1947; part one of the trilogy, *Das Kaiserreich*, 1925), a role already rehearsed with the schoolmaster tyrant of Professor Unrat (1905; filmed as *Der blaue Engel*, 1928; tr. anon, *The Blue Angel*, 1932; *Small Town Tyrant*, 1944). While an active writer and speaker against Nazism (he was president of an association of émigré writers in Paris) he wrote in exile a monumental historical novel about Henry IV of France (*Die Jugend des Königs Henri Quatre*, 1935; tr. Eric Sutton, *King Wren: the Youth of Henri IV* (Eng.), *Young Henry of Navarre* (Amer.), 1937), inspired by his love of France and admiration for this ideally enlightened ruler, an exemplar of the natural and rational against all fanaticism. *Ein Zeitalter wird besichtigt* (1945) was a masterly autobiography. [PB]

*Gesammelte Werke* (1965ff.).

K. Schröter, *H.M.* (Reinbek, 1967); E. Zenker, *H.M.-Bibliographie* (Berlin, 1964); U. Weisstein, *H. M.* (Tübingen, 1962); Friedmann and Mann, *DLZJ*; Lukács, *HN*; Natan, *GML*; *GR*, XXX (1955); *Aufbau*, VI, 1950 (bibliography).

**Mann, Thomas** (Lübeck 1875–Kilchberg/Zürich 1955). German novelist. His father, Senator of the Hanseatic City of Lübeck, where their merchant family had been established for generations, inspired his conception of (and respect for) the 'Bürger'; from his part-Brazilian mother he derived his idea of the exotic artistic temperament. His father died in 1891, and after leaving school at Lübeck in 1893, Mann followed his mother and her other children to Munich, where he first worked in an insurance office, then became a part-time student at Munich university. Later in Italy (1896–7) with his elder brother Heinrich ⇨ Mann, he began *Buddenbrooks* (1901; tr. H. T. Lowe-Porter, 1924), the novel which confirmed the promise of his early successful stories, *Der Kleine Herr Friedemann* (1898; in *Stories of a Lifetime*, tr. ibid., 1961), and established him as a great writer. He married Katia Pringsheim (daughter of a Munich family of bankers and scholars) in 1905, and became father of six children. Humorous and tender aspects of his domestic experience are reflected in *Königliche Hoheit* (1909; tr. ibid., *Royal Highness*, 1916) and in such stories as *Herr und Hund* (1918) and *Unordnung und frühes Leid* (1926; both tr. in *Stories of a Lifetime*). A patriotic apologist during the First World War for the conservative, philosophical, musical traditions of German culture in his essays *Betrachtungen eines Unpolitischen* (1918), his hostility to Fascism, e.g. in the story *Mario und der Zauberer* (1930), brought Nazi denunciation, while he was abroad in 1933, and confiscation of his property; he settled in Switzerland at Küsnacht, formally broke with Hitler's Germany in an open letter to the University of Bonn, delivered warning political lectures (e.g. *Achtung, Europa!* 1938) and finally broadcasts to Germany, *Deutsche Hörer* (1945). In 1939 he took up a visiting professorship at Princeton University, retiring to California in 1941 and becoming a U.S. citizen in 1944. After frequent post-war visits to Europe he settled near Zürich in 1952. Among many literary honours he received the Nobel Prize (1929) and the Goethe Prize (1949).

Mann's distinctive style and literary method depend on his profound sense of intellectual irony: a play of thought and experience between opposites – opposing values, views of life, etc. His thought was influenced above all by ⇨ Schopenhauer, ⇨ Nietzsche and ⇨ Wagner. Thus his love for the latter's music affected the structure of *Buddenbrooks* – but is also ironically shown up as the very spirit of decadence. Schopenhauer's saintly denial of life, which alone leads to a vision of beauty and truth, is seen in ironically realistic terms as the decline of a Bürger family's business ability as it gains in spiritual refinement. And the hero actually misreads some Schopenhauer – and is carried away by Nietzschean thoughts of life affirmed (not denied) by a stronger, no longer decadent, type of man. Perhaps the most effective interplay artistically lies in the balance throughout between pessimistic metaphysical ideas and epically serene description.

The best-known stories, *Tonio Kröger* (1903) and *Der Tod in Venedig*, 'Death in Venice' (1911; both tr. ibid., *Stories of a Lifetime*), vary the way in which the same fundamental opposition between life and spirit may be expressed, in both the style and content of these accounts of the 'sick' artist. All conceivable variations are then developed in the ironical parody of a traditional German ⇨ *Bildungsroman: Der Zauberberg* (1924; tr. ibid., *The Magic Mountain*, 1927), which extends the same technique of diagnosis to the sick mind of contemporary civilization. The novel is set in a sanatorium where the once healthily ordinary hero experiences the typical fascinations, the moral and intellectual uncertainties, above all the confusing new knowledge of modern Europe – which seems to threaten death to its traditional culture. When he finally wins through to a healthier conception of man and returns to life, he finds himself ironically engulfed in the disaster of 1914.

During his émigré years Mann wrote of the Biblical exile in his trilogy *Joseph und seine Brüder* (1933–43; tr. ibid., *The Tales of Jacob*, 1934; *The Young Joseph*, 1935; *Joseph in Egypt*, 1938; *Joseph the Provider*, 1945). The exile is at last reconciled with his people, he mediates between his family's conventional way of life and the sophisticated intelligence of Egypt, between the inspiration of dreams and the scepticism of knowledge, i.e. between all the variant forms of Mann's opposing concepts of life and spirit, to achieve at last a truly enlightened humanity. But meanwhile his real homeland grew so unspeakably benighted in all aspects of its mind and life, that (for Mann) no literary convention could truly contain its aberration. *Doktor Faustus* (1947; tr. ibid., 1949) reflects this truth – the impossibility of expressing as 'literature' what happened in Nazi Germany – *obliquely*: through the story of a demonic musician's downfall, as seen through the naïve eyes of a fictitious author. Finally, in old age, Mann expressed in the humorous form of *Die Bekenntnisse des Hochstaplers Felix Krull* (1954; tr. ibid., *Confessions of Felix Krull Confidence Man*, 1958) the profound doubt underlying all his concern with art: whether the mind's search for beauty and truth, whether art, whether culture itself, might not ultimately be a mere pretence, a confidence trick.

Mann's many critical-philosophical and historical essays show the same level of originality and creative insight as his fiction (see, in English, *Essays of Three Decades*, 1947; tr. ibid.). [PB/AKT]

*Stockholmer Gesamtausgabe* (1938ff.); *Gesammelte Werke* (12 vols., 1956–60); *Briefe* (3 vols., 1961ff.).

K. W. Jonas, *Fifty Years of T.M. Studies, A Bibliography* (Minneapolis, 1955); R. H. Thomas, *T.M. The Mediation of Art* (1956); E. Heller, *The Ironic German* (1958); K. Schröter, *T.M.* (Reinbek, 1964).

**Manner, Eeva-Liisa** (Helsinki 1921– ). Finnish poet and prose-writer. She began as a writer of conventional poetry, regional in subject and expressing a deep nostalgia for Viipuri and the Karelian Isthmus (lost to the U.S.S.R. after the war). But her collection *Tämä matka* (1956, enlarged 1963) brought her to the forefront of the modernist movement: there was a new concentration of thought into imagery, an advance in precision of diction, and clear signs of the influence of T. S. Eliot. She uses free verse, and her poetry is extremely musical and auditive; the poems are often arranged so as to form a thematic or symphonic series. Her prose is nimbly surrealistic, and here too she experiments with musical effects. [RV]

Poetry: *Mustaa ja punaista* (1944); *Kuin tuuli pilvi* (1949); *Orfiset laulut* (1960); *Kirjoitettu kivi* (1966). Fiction: *Tyttö taivan laiturilla* (1951). Drama: *Eros ja Psykhe*; *Toukokuun lumi* (1965).

**Mannerkorpi, Juha** (Ohio, U.S.A. 1915– ). Finnish poet and novelist. The son of a clergyman, he graduated in philosophy and psychology. He has translated Camus, Sartre and Beckett. His early lyric poetry is conventionally contemplative, self-searching, often treating Biblical themes. His prose, however, with its distinct existentialist colouring, is experimenta both in style and in ideas; usually he has some complicated psychological problem or ethical conflict to examine. His laconic, uneventful short stories, often resembling internal monologues, have influenced modern Finnish prose. His plays have proved more successful on the radio than in the theatre. An increase of range, both in thought and in expression, is marked by the leisurely short novel *Vene lähdössä* (1961). [RV]

*Runot 1945–54* (1962). Stories: *Niin ja toisin* (1950); *Avain* (1955); *Sirkkeli* (1956). Novel: *Jyrsijät* (1958). Drama: *Pirunnyrkki* (1952); *Kirje* (1952); *Jälkikuva* (1966).

**Manninen, Otto** (Kangasniemi 1872–Helsinki 1950). Finnish poet. A lecturer on Finnish Language at Helsinki University and outstanding as a translator of ancient and modern European poetry, he produced the standard versions of the *Iliad* and the *Odyssey*, of works by Heine, Molière, Ibsen, Goethe and ⇨ Petöfi and of the complete poetical works of ⇨ Runeberg and ⇨ Topelius (who wrote in Swedish). His gifts as an original lyric poet are now beginning to receive the admiration they deserve: he was a supremely skilful artist, a master of brief and concise expression, of sensitivity combined with elegance, humour and verbal wit. His services to Finnish prosody were considerable, particularly in adapting such metres as the alexandrine and the classical hexameter. [VKS]

*Säkeitä*, I (1905), II (1910); *Virrantyven* (1925); *Matkamies* (1938); Ollilainen, *SF*.

**Manrique, Gómez** (Amusco 1412?–Toledo 1490?). Spanish poet and dramatist. He came of a noble family and took part in the civil struggles of his time. His *Representación del nascimiento de Nuestro Señor* is one of the few surviving liturgical plays of the century. His grave, melancholy poetry, not printed till 1885 (*Cancionero*, ed. Paz y Meliá), includes a satirical protest of a horse against a page, love-lyrics, and some pleasing religious pieces; his *Consejos* may have inspired the more famous *Coplas* of his nephew, Jorge ⇨ Manrique. [JMC]

*Regimiento de príncipes y otras obras*, CA; Blecua, *FLE*; Trend, *OBSV*; Menéndez y Pelayo, *PLC*.
Crawford, *SDLV*; Wardropper, *HPL*; *HR*, XXXIII (1965).

**Manrique, Jorge** (Paredes de Nava? 1440?–Garci-Muñoz 1479). Spanish poet. Of noble family, he was the nephew of Gómez ⇨ Manrique, great nephew of Santillana; he was killed in the Civil Wars. His love-songs, satires, and acrostic verses are merely typical of the time; his *Coplas por la muerte de su padre Don Rodrigo* (tr. H. Longfellow, 1833) is the most famous elegy in Spanish. Its reflections on the brevity of life and the vanity of all human deeds before eternity are expressed in colloquial language, rich in echoes from the Bible, Boethuis and the Church fathers. Like Gray's *Elegy*, it immortalized the commonplaces of its age. [JMC]

*Obra completa*, CA; *Cancionero*, CC; Blecua, *FLE*; Cohen, *PBSV*; Menéndez y Pelayo, *PLC*; Trend, *OBSV*.
A. Krause, *J.M. and the Cult of Death* . . . (California, 1937); E. P. Bergara, *J. M.* (Montevideo, 1945); P. Salinas, *J.M.* (Buenos Aires, 1947); Cernuda, *PL*.

**Manterola, Jose.** ⇨ Basque Literature.

**Manzoni, Alessandro** (Milan 1785–Milan 1873). Italian novelist. Apart from the years 1805–10, spent in France, he lived the whole of a long and retiring life in or near Milan. He began his literary career as a poet. His earliest poems followed the prevailing neo-classical trend, showing certain points of similarity with those of ⇨ Foscolo. In 1810, he returned to the active practice of the Catholic faith. This event brought about a change in his literary aims, which henceforth became identified with those of Italian Romanticism. His subsequent poetic works, including, among other compositions, *Inni sacri* (4 published in 1815; a fifth published in 1822), *Il cinque maggio* (1821) – an ode on the death of Napoleon – and the 2 verse dramas *Il Conte di Carmagnola* (1820) and *Adelchi* (1822), with their accompanying lyric choruses, represent a search for the most effective means of communication with the new and wider audience which he now wished to address, a search successfully concluded only with the abandonment of poetry and the composition of his historical novel, *I promessi sposi* (tr. A. Colquhoun, *The Betrothed*, 1951), upon which his reputation as the greatest Italian novelist rests.

The *Promessi sposi* was written between 1821 and 1827 (definitive edition 1840–2). Set in the province of Milan in the 17th century, during the Spanish occupation, the novel tells the story of two young peasants whose proposed marriage is prevented by the infatuation of the local lord for the bride. Fleeing from the persecution of this petty tyrant, the protagonists become involved in a series of adventures which take them further and further away from each other, at the same time bringing them into contact with men and events of more than local significance. Their oppressor is finally carried off by the outbreak of bubonic plague which decimated Milan and the surrounding area in 1629–30, and the two lovers are free to marry. The historical setting, with its patriotic undertones (the hardships of Italians under foreign rule), the choice of humble peasants as the central characters, the creation of a vivid and natural prose style, are all significant features of this work; but its real greatness lies in Manzoni's delineation of character. In the heroine, Lucia, in Padre Cristoforo, the Capuchin friar who helps the young couple in their hour of need, and in the saintly Cardinal of Milan, Federigo Borromeo, he has created three living examples of that pure and wholehearted Christianity which is his ideal. But his psychological penetration extends also to those who fall short of this standard, whether through weakness or through perversity, and the novel is rich in pictures of ordinary men and women, seen with a delightful irony and disenchantment which always stops short of cynicism, and which provides a perfect artistic balance for the evangelical fervour of his Christian ideal.

One of the masterpieces of Italian literature, the *Promessi sposi* was the last of his creative works. His interest in literary theory, however, did not decrease with age, and to his two early and fundamental explanations of Romantic doctrine (*Lettre à M. Chauvet*, 1820 – on the drama; *Lettera sul romanticismo*, written 1823, published 1846), he later added a work on the historical novel, and some interesting though fragmentary writings on linguistics. [CF]

*Tutte le opere*, ed. A. Chiari and F. Ghisalberti (1957 – in progress).

B. Reynolds, *The Linguistic Writings of A.M.* (1950); A. Momigliano, *A.M.* (Milan, 1952); A. Colquhoun, *M. and his Times* (1954).

**Mapu, Abraham** (Slobodka-Kovno 1808–Königsberg 1867). Hebrew novelist. At an early age he was known for his great erudition in Jewish studies. Later he studied Kabbalah (mysticism), and learned Latin and European languages. His first novel, *Ahavat Zion* (Vilna, 1853; tr. F. Jaffe, *Amnon, Prince and Peasant*, 1887), marked a turning point in Hebrew literature. Set in the time of the prophet Isaiah, it describes life and events of the time as if recounted by an eye witness. The book is fascinating despite the naïveté of the plot and the noticeable influences of the 18th-century French novelists. His second novel, *Ashmat Shomron* (Vilna, 1865), is set in the same period, has an even more complex plot and uses the same kind of imagery. [EE]

*In the Days of Isaiah*, tr. L. Shapiro (1902).

D. Patterson, *A.M.* (1964); *Kol kitvei A.M.* (Tel Aviv, 1950).

**Márai, Sándor** (Kassa 1900– ). Hungarian writer. A journalist of middle-class background, and the author of many short stories and novels, in which he analyses his characters with psychological insight. Though his writings conform to the middle class, he is often antagonistic towards its commonplace morality. He has lived in emigration since 1946. [JFR]

Major novels: *A búvár* (n.d.; tr. L. Wolfe, *The Diver*, 1936); *Szegények iskolája* (n.d.); *Egy polgár vallomásai* (1934); *A féltékenyek* (1937); *Válás Budán* (n.d.); *Vendégjáték Bolzanóban* (n.d.).

**Marbod** (Angers *c.* 1035–1123). Latin poet. Head of Angers cathedral school, later Bishop of Rennes. His *Liber lapidum* (tr. C. W. King, 1860), a poem in hexameters on the properties and supposed virtues of precious stones – some of them mythical – is among the best on this popular medieval subject. He also wrote hymns, love poems, saints' lives, and epistles in verse. Like his friend, ⇨ Baudri of Bourgueil, he had a great love for the beauty of nature and for country life. [FB]

Migne, *PL*, 171; *Poèmes*, ed., with Fr. tr., S. Ropartz (Rennes, 1873).

Raby, *CLP*, *SLP*.

**Marc, Ausiàs.** ⇨ Catalan Literature.

**Marcabru** (mid 12th cent.). The most original of the Provençal ⇨ troubadours. A Gascon of low birth, he greatly influenced the development of the Provençal courtly lyric. He attacked the amoral behaviour of the nobility, praised the concept of *Fin' Amors* ('pure, perfect love'), which though sensual aspires to moral improvement, and castigated *Fals' Amors*, a sensual and sterile love. He derived his ideas from the Augustinian theories of contemporary Christian philosophers, but applied them in inspired poetry to the doctrinally amorphous courtly society then developing in Southern France. His language, imagery and technical skill are those of a great poet. His vocabulary is strong and evocative, and he is the earliest exponent of the *trobar clus*, or 'obscure' style of composition, which has been much maligned because of its difficult symbolism. Over 40 of his works, dealing with love and social satire, and including a witty *pastorela* and a Crusading poem, the famous song of the *lavador* or 'cleansing-place', survive. [LTT]

*Poésies complètes du troubadour M.*, ed. J. M. L. Dejeanne (Toulouse, 1909); Hill and Bergin, *APT.*

*R*, XLVIII (1922); *ZRP*, XLIII (1923); *SP*, LI (1954); *Moyen Âge*, LXXIII (1967).

**Marceau, Félicien** (Cortenberg 1913– ). French novelist, essayist and dramatist. His fiction combines subtle observation, a vein of fancy and a vigorous and colourful idiom, e.g. *Chasseneuil* (1948); *Capri, petite île* (1951); *Chair et cuir* (1951); *Bergère légère* (1953; tr. D. Hughes and M. J. Mason, *The China Shepherdess*, 1957); *En de secrètes noces* (1953); *Les élans du cœur* (1955; tr. D. Hughes and M. J. Mason, *The Flutterings of the Heart*, 1957); *Les belles natures* (1957). He began in the theatre with a strained Elizabethan pastiche *Caterina* (1954) before striking his own idiosyncratic note in *L'œuf* (1956; tr. C. Frank, *The Egg*, 1958), a vivacious attack on the world's morality, exploiting the paradox of the 'little man' who only becomes acceptable when he has turned successful criminal. There follow: *La bonne soupe* (1959) another disenchanted, wry comedy involving a kept-woman on the decline; *L'étouffe-chrétien* (1961); *Les cailloux* (1962), and *La preuve par quatre* (1964), a gay and witty argument in favour of identifying the different facets of love with different women. Marceau exploits with great effect a central character whose monologue is 'illustrated' by inset scenes as he proceeds. He has also written stimulating critical essays, notably *Casanova ou l'Anti-Don Juan* (1949) and *Balzac et son monde* (1955). [SBJ]

*Théâtre* (2 vols., 1964–5); Boisdeffre, *HVLA*; Surer, *TFC.*

**Marcel, Gabriel** (Paris 1889–Paris 1964). French philosopher, dramatist and critic. Distinguished Christian existentialist thinker, deeply influenced by ⇨ Kierkegaard and much concerned with man as a creature striving to transcend himself in the direction of the divine (*Journal métaphysique*, 1927; *Être et Avoir*, 1935; *Homo Viator*, 1945, etc.). His drama is a direct reflection of these philosophic interests and, though it sometimes conjures up a metaphysical density rare in the theatre, it too often does so at the expense of life. This 'theatre of the soul in exile' suggests very well the tragic force of man's alienation in the world, but the climate is too intellectualized and the characters mere media for discourse. This is especially true of the early conflicts of conscience (e.g. *La chapelle ardente*, 1925; *Le chemin de Crète*, 1935; *Le Dard*, 1936), though *Un homme de Dieu* (1922) moves one by the anguish of a man of principle confronted by his wife's adultery. Later plays (*Rome n'est plus dans Rome*, 1951; *La dimension Florestan*, 1952; *Mon temps n'est pas le vôtre*, 1953) exploit topical themes but never quite lose their sense of intellectual contrivance, even when, as in *Rome n'est plus dans Rome*, the subject is the Cold War and the threat of Soviet occupation of France. Marcel is also a gifted critic of music and the theatre; reviews of the latter have been collected in *L'heure théâtrale* (1959). [SBJ]

J. Delhomme, *et al.*, *Existentialisme chrétien: G.M.* (Paris, 1947); S. Cain, *G.M.* (1963); J. Chenu, *Le théâtre de G.M. et sa signification métaphysique* (Paris, 1948); E. Sottiaux, *G.M. philosophe et dramaturge* (Paris, 1956).

**Marchena Ruiz, José** (Utrera 1768–Madrid 1821). Spanish poet. He abandoned a religious career to take part in the French Revolution, and became a protégé of Murat under Napoleon. He was such a good Latinist that he deceived German scholars with forged fragments of the *Satiricon.* He also translated Molière and Voltaire. He returned to Spain in 1820, and died unknown. His best poem, *A Cristo crucificado*, a product of his crisis of faith, is humanist in tone; he celebrates a Christ who came to liberate man. Generally his poetry is marred by his ethical and political preoccupations, but in this poem matter and manner agree. [JMC]

*Obras*, ed. M. Menéndez y Pelayo (Seville, 1896).

**Marguerite de Navarre** (Angoulême 1492–Odos, nr Tarbes 1549). Daughter of ➪ Charles d'Orléans, Count of Angoulême, and Louise de Savoie, and sister of Francis I. She was a most remarkable woman whose influence extended over political life, religion and letters. There is no doubt that the development of the Renaissance in France owes a great deal to her person and her influence. Michelet called her '*l'aimable mère de la Renaissance*'. In 1509 she married Charles, Duke of Alençon. After his death in 1525, she married, in 1527, Henri d'Albret, King of Navarre. Her daughter, Jeanne d'Albret (born 1528), was to be the mother of Henry IV. During the captivity of Francis I in Spain she played an important political role, culminating, after his release, in the conclusion of the Treaty of Cambrai. All her life she was interested in philosophy and literature. She encouraged poets and writers like ➪ Marot, ➪ Des Périers and Charles de Sainte-Marthe, whom she frequently protected from persecution by the religious authorities. She also encouraged to a certain extent the spreading of Luther's doctrines. Her own first publication was a religious poem, *Le miroir de l'Âme pécheresse* (1531), which was condemned by the Faculty of Theology of Paris (Sorbonne). Towards the end of her life she published another volume of poetry, *Les Marguerites* (1547; ed. F. Frank, 1873). She also wrote a number of plays in verse mainly on religious themes. Her collection of short stories imitated from ➪ Boccaccio's *Decameron*, the *Heptaméron* (ed. M. François, 1943), considered her greatest and most influential work, was published posthumously (1558–9). [CAM]

*Les dernières poésies de M. de N.*, ed. A. Lefranc (1896); *La Coche*, ed. F. Schneegans (1936); *Théâtre profane*, ed. V. L. Saulnier (1963); *La navire*, ed. R. Marichal (1956); *Petit œuvre devot et chrestien*, ed. H. Sckommodau (1956).

P. Jourda, *Tableau chronologique des publications de M. de N., Revue du XVIe*, 12 (1925); P. Jourda, *Répertoire chronologique et analytique de la correspondance de M. de N.* (Paris, 1930); P. Jourda, *Marguerite d'Angoulême, duchesse d'Alençon, Reine de Navarre* (2 vols., Paris, 1930); H. Sckommodau, *Die religiösen Dichtungen M. von N.* (Cologne, 1955).

**Mariana, Juan de** (Talavera 1535–Toledo 1624). Jesuit political theorist and historian. His *Historiae de rebus Hispaniae libri XXV* (Toledo, 1592), which he translated into Spanish in 1601, held the field for many years as the standard history of Spain and was known throughout Europe (English translation 1699). [CCS]

G. Cirot, *Mariana historien* (Bordeaux, 1905).

**Marie de France** (fl. late 12th cent.). The earliest known French poetess. She lived in England, knew Normandy, and was probably of noble birth. She was a woman of culture, knowing Latin and English as well as French, and an accomplished writer of great simplicity and charm. Her work can be dated from 1160–5 to about 1190. Several attempts have been made to identify her. It has been suggested, without definite proof, that Marie was an abbess of the abbey of Shaftesbury from 1181 to 1216, illegitimate daughter of Geoffrey Plantagenet (d. 1151), and hence the half-sister of Henry II of England.

It was to a king, and probably Henry II, that she dedicated her *lais*, poems of adventure and love, often with a Celtic background. In her Prologue she tells us that she had thought of translating some fine story from Latin into romance, but that since many had already engaged in this work, she had decided to retell the *lais* she had heard, presumably those sung by Breton minstrels. She was one of the first medieval French poets to write in this form and by far the most talented.

Among the most famous lays was *Le Fresne*, the story of the mother who abandons one of her twin daughters to save herself from an accusation of adultery; the child is left in an ash-tree near an abbey, is discovered and cared for, and is finally reunited with her parents. *Chèvrefeuille*, another lay, is a ➪ Tristan episode. But though attracted by Celtic themes, she is most interested in analysing the feelings of her characters. In *Lanval* she tells the story of the knight who is loved by Arthur's queen, accused by her before the king but rescued by his fairy mistress. This lay and *Eliduc*, the story of the husband in love with two wives, are her best works.

Her *Fables* she translated from English into French for a count William whom in the Prologue (31–2) she calls '*flurs de chevalerie, D'enseignement, de curteisie*'. Finally she wrote from a Latin model the *Espurgatoire Saint Patriz*, in which knight, Owein, is purged of his sin by trial. [LTT]

*Lais*, ed. A. Ewert (1958); ed. J. Lods (Paris, 1959); *Fables*, sel. ed. A. Ewert, R. C. Johnston (1942); *Espurgatoire*, ed. T. A. Jenkins (Philadelphia, 1894).

**Marinetti, Filippo Tommaso** (Alexandria 1876–Bellagio 1944). Italian poet and novelist. Founder of a short-lived artistic movement called ⇨ 'Futurism' which flourished in the first decade of the 20th century. Futurism, midway between Symbolism and Surrealism, advocated among other things: the destruction of all museums; the rejection of grammatical and syntactical rules in literature and, generally speaking, of all academic and traditional rules; the search for new media of artistic expression, including nonsense and onomatopoeic words in poetry, noise in music, etc.; and the tapping of new sources of inspiration, such as the new discoveries of science and technology (aircraft in particular) and the artist's unconscious mind freed from the usual restrictive patterns of logical association and time-space continuum. His movement, apparently progressive and revolutionary, was in fact profoundly reactionary, since it encouraged writers and artists to cut themselves off from history in order to cultivate morbid superhuman ambitions; and, by giving cultural iconoclasm a veneer of sophistication, it fostered the parochial complacency of a largely uneducated middle class. Thus the natural outcome of Futurism was isolationism in art and Fascism in politics. [GMC]

*Noi futuristi* (by M. and others) (Milan, 1933); *Catalogue of the Exhibition of Works by the Italian Futurist Painters* (containing the Initial Manifesto of Futurism), Sackville Gallery (London, 1912).

E. Settimelli, *M. l'uomo e l'artista* (Milan, 1921).

**Marinković, Ranko** (Vis 1913– ). Croatian dramatist and short-story writer. He writes mainly of Dalmatian provincial town life. His collection of stories, *Ruke* (1953), portrays the provincial psychology and the fate of the provincial individual faced with war and occupation. His drama, *Gloria* (1956), is one of the most popular in Yugoslavia. In 1966 he published his novel *Kiklop*, which has evoked considerable interest among Yugoslav critics. [EDG]

Kadić, *CCL*.

**Marino, Giambattista** (Naples 1569–Naples 1625). Italian poet. In 1598, while still at Naples, he was imprisoned in connexion with the death of a young woman whom he had got with child, and again when he forged documents in an attempt to save a friend from execution. He then fled to Rome and entered the service of Cardinal Pietro Aldobrandini. This took him to many cities in northern Italy, notably Venice, where he published in 1602 the first collection of lyrics later to become *La Lira*, and Turin, where his feud with a rival poet Murtola produced violent satirical verse on both sides and culminated in Murtola's attempt to assassinate him. Marino saw the hand of God in his deliverance from this danger and invited his friends to join him in giving thanks for the miracle. While still in Turin he was created *Cavaliere*, a title he always used thereafter. After a third imprisonment at Turin, he went to France in 1615 at the invitation of Maria de' Medici. There he was received with great honour, and it was in this period that his best-known works were published – poems describing paintings and sculptures in *La Galeria* (Venice, 1619), mythological and pastoral idylls in *La sampogna* (Paris, 1620), and an elaborate version of the story of Venus and Adonis in the *ottave* of *Adone* (Paris, 1623). This, his most celebrated poem, is weak and diffuse as narrative and is best read as a series of often splendid descriptive fragments. In 1623 he returned to Italy, to the lavish acclamation of Rome and his native Naples.

Marino revolted against the decorum and mediocrity of fading *cinquecento* Petrarchism. For repose and harmony he seeks to substitute excitement and wonder. There is an ardent sensuousness in his verse, and he delights in bizarre subjects and stylistic and technical *tours de force*. Alliterations, puns, *concetti*, onomatopeia, difficult rhymes and rhythms, and all the resources of a rich, lush vocabulary go to make up an ostentatious and aggressive technique which aims to take the reader's senses by storm. The term 'Marinismo' was coined to describe precisely this element of flamboyant virtuosity characteristic of much *seicento* verse. His weakness is that his poetic world is exclusively an outward one of colours, shapes and sounds, to be wondered at and enjoyed, but lacking the human dimension. Hence his failure as a narrative poet, and hence too the failure of his religious poem *La strage degl'innocenti* (cf. Crashaw's version of Book I, *Sospetto d'Herode*). Nevertheless, the vital surge of Baroque power is to be felt in almost all his writings, and as a descriptive poet he undoubtedly extended the range of Italian verse. [DGR]

*Poesie varie*, ed. B. Croce (1913); *Adone*, ed. G. Balsamo-Crivelli (1922); *Dicerie sacre e La strage degl'Innocenti*, ed. G. Pozzi (1960); *Lettere*, ed. M. Guglielminetti (1966).

M. Guglielminetti, *Tecnica e invenzione nell'opera di G.M.* (Messina/Florence 1964); J. V. Mirollo, *The Poet of the Marvelous. G.M.* (Columbia Univ. Press, 1963); H. Friedrich, *Epochen der italienischen Lyrik* (Frankfurt a.M., 1964); Croce, *SSL*; Ferrero, *MM*; Getto, *MM*; *Minori*, ii.

**Marivaux, Pierre Carlet de Chamblain de** (Paris 1688–Paris 1763). French playwright and novelist. The son of a provincial official of comfortable means, he was never more than a perfunctory law student in Paris, and from 1712 onwards he lived in the world of the literary salons. The loss of his inheritance in the collapse of Law's financial schemes in 1720–1 meant however that he had to take up writing in earnest, and the next twenty years were his most fruitful. His election to the Académie Française in 1742 seems to have marked the climax of his career, and in later life he produced relatively little.

After some false starts in parody, prose fiction and tragedy, he found his first true vein in comedy, in alliance with the then recently re-established Italian troupe in Paris, who offered him an acting tradition less artificial and more imaginative than that of the Comédie Française. The Italians staged two-thirds of his 30-odd plays. His most characteristic creations are comedies of love: in these, with great delicacy of feeling and psychological insight, and in language sometimes regarded as subtle to a fault (*le marivaudage*), he explores the stages by which men and women fall in or out of love, and creates comic effect by basing his plot upon the introduction of obstacles, often imaginary social barriers or false preconceptions, which make the characters unable to perceive or acknowledge their own true feelings until the dénouement. His two masterpeices in this manner are *Le jeu de l'amour et du hasard* (1730; tr. R. Aldington, *The Game of Love and Chance*, 1923) and *Les fausses confidences* (1737), but many lesser examples (*La surprise de l'amour*, 1722; *L'épreuve*, 1740) have great charm. In addition, he ranges over a variety of other styles of comedy, from the allegory (*Le triomphe de Plutus*, 1728) and the satirical fantasy (*L'île des esclaves*, 1725) to the sentimental moralizing play in the manner of Nivelle de La Chaussée (*La femme fidèle*, 1755).

His two major novels, *La vie de Marianne* (1731–41; ed. F. Deloffre, 1956; tr. anon., 1736–42; tr. Sir G. Campbell, 1889) and *Le paysan parvenu* (1734–5; ed. F. Deloffre, 1959; tr. anon., 1735), published in parts and both left unfinished, are fictional autobiographies which show a similar subtlety in psychological and moral analysis. Both depict the experiences of a young person of obscure origin in making a way in the world: Marianne by a combination of tearful innocence, coquettishness and self-conscious skill at winning sympathy, Jacob more dubiously by the exploitation of his personal attractiveness to older women and of his occasional altruistic impulses. The relative paucity of incident, as compared with the earlier picaresque novel (⇨ Lesage, *Gil Blas*), gives room for much fuller description, often vividly detailed and realistic, of various contemporary social milieux, and for much reflective moralizing. [WHB]

*Romans, Récits, etc.* and *Théâtre complet*, ed. M. Arland (2 vols., Pléiade, 1949).

G. Larroumet, *M., sa vie, ses œuvres* (Paris, 1882); F. Deloffre, *Une préciosité nouvelle: M. et le marivaudage* (Paris, 1955); K. N. McKee, *The Theater of M.* (1958); Trahard, *MSF.*

**Markisch, Peretz** (Polonoya 1895–? 1948). Yiddish poet and playwright. Originally wrote in Russian but in 1917 turned to Yiddish. From 1924 was one of the leading figures of the Kiev group of Soviet-Yiddish writers. With a large number of other Jewish writers was arrested during the Stalinist purges and at his trial denounced the methods by which 'confessions' had been obtained from them. His best works are those which give an epic account of Jewish heroism during the Nazi period, especially *Milchomeh* (1948) and *Der Oifshtand in Geto* (1947), a tribute to the Jewish heroes of the Warsaw Ghetto. [EE]

*Trot fun doires* (Moscow, 1966).
Roback, *SYL.*

**Marković, Svetozar** (Zaječar 1846–Trieste 1875). The first Serbian socialist. Sent as a student of engineering to Russia, h imbibed the positivist socialism of ⇨ Chernyshevsky and ⇨ Pisarev with which he returned to Serbia and began a movement for socialist decentralization and communes. He suffered political persecution for his faith and died of tuberculosis following a term in prison. His movement developed into the Serbian radical party.

As regards literature he preached the Russian critical realism as expounded by Chernyshevsky and his influence served to turn Serbian writers away from romantic poetry to the social novel and the short story. Particularly important was his drawing attention to Russian literature as a model for Serbian writers. In this way he served to create a new and more mature epoch in Serbian literature. [EDG]

**Marmontel, Jean-François** (Bort-les-Orgues, Corrèze 1723–Abloville, Eure 1799). French man of letters. A protégé of Voltaire, he failed in youth to impress as a dramatist, but succeeded later with his *Contes moraux*, slight but pleasantly written tales with a lesson, published in the *Mercure de France* (which he edited) from 1756 onwards (collected edn, 1761; selection tr. G. Saintsbury, 1895). He achieved notoriety with his longer philosophical tale *Bélisaire* (1766; numerous 18th-century trs), condemned by the Sorbonne for its advocacy of religious toleration. His most readable work today, however, is his *Mémoires d'un père* (1804; tr. B. Patmore, *Memoirs of Marmontel*, 1930), which give interesting impressions of distinguished contemporaries. He also contributed many literary articles to the ⇨ *Encyclopédie*. [WHB]

*Œuvres complètes*, ed. Saint-Surin (18 vols., 1818–19).

S. Lenel, *M.* (Paris, 1902).

**Marnau, Alfred (Fred)** (Bratislava 1918– ). Austrian poet and novelist. He has lived in England since 1939, where his poems first appeared in *Poetry in Wartime* (ed. M. J. Tambimuttu, 1942). The collections: *Seven Odes* (1944), *The Wounds of the Apostles* (1944), and *Death of the Cathedral* (1946) were bilingual (tr. E. O. Sigler); *Gesammelte Gedichte* (1946) and *Räuber-Requiem* (1961) appeared in Austria. *Der steinerne Gang* (1947; tr. author, *Free Among the Dead*, 1950) and *Das Verlangen nach der Hölle* (1952; tr. author, *The Guest*, 1957) are novels. An unfashionably rhetorical poet, frequently using a long, dynamic, Expressionistic line, his intense spiritual meditations are expressed in religious symbolism and dream imagery. [PB]

**Marner, Der** (fl. mid 13th cent.). Medieval German poet, chiefly of moral and didactic verse. He was of humble origins, a Swabian by birth, and according to a fellow-poet became blind in his old age and was murdered by an unknown assailant. His name ('The Mariner') may have been given to him by his contemporaries to characterize his nomadic life. He was a man of considerable learning, outspoken in his views and intolerant of opposition, and carried on a literary feud with certain of his contemporaries. Besides his many *Sprüche*, he has also left a handful of love lyrics, including 2 dawn-songs. [RT]

Ed. P. Strauch (Strassburg, 1876); Ehrismann, *GDL*.

**Marnix van St Aldegonde, Philips van** (Brussels 1540–Leyden 1598). Dutch poet and theologian. A nobleman in William's service, he had studied at Geneva under Calvin. Of his numerous polemical writings the most important is *Biëncorf der H. Roomscher Kercke* (1569), satirizing Roman Catholicism, translated into German in 1576 and 1579 and into English in 1598. His translation of the Psalms (1584), though a considerable improvement on Datheen's, did not replace his. In 1594 he was commissioned to translate the Bible. He may be the author of the national anthem, the *Wilhelmus* (tr. G. N. Clark in *Proceedings of the Anglo-Batavian Soc.*, 1940). [PK]

*Godsdienstige en kerkelijke geschriften*, ed. J. J. van Toorenbergen (3 vols., 1871–8).

**Marot, Clément** (Cahors 1496–Turin 1544). French poet. He followed his father, the poet Jean Marot, to Court in 1506 and became secretary to ⇨ Marguerite of Angoulême, sister of Francis I and later Queen of Navarre, towards 1519. Probably as early as 1515 he had written poetry in the style of the then fashionable school of the *rhétoriqueurs*, though he was soon to abandon their mannerisms, inspiration and versification, and to orientate French poetry towards the intelligent imitation of Greco-Latin models. In 1526 he was imprisoned for eating meat in Lent and was henceforth regarded as a Lutheran by his contemporaries. He was released after a few weeks; reimprisoned the following year for freeing a prisoner from the police, but again released shortly afterwards. In 1527 he became *valet de chambre* to Francis I. In autumn 1534, after the *affaire des Placards*, he fled and was condemned to death in his absence. He sought refuge first in Navarre, then at the Court of Renée de France, Duchess of Ferrara. In 1536 he had to flee from Ferrara to escape the Inquisition. After a stay at Venice he returned to France via Lyons where he was forced to abjure his errors (December 1536). He reoccupied his post at Court until 1542 when, no doubt because of the intensification of the persecution of Lutherans, he went for the second time into exile. He spent a year in Geneva with Calvin, then went on to Savoy and finally to Turin.

He is responsible for the majority of the reforms which the ⇨ Pléiade poets later claimed as their own. He introduced into French poetry the elegy, the epigram, the eclogue, the epithalam and probably wrote the first French sonnet. His translation of the Psalms is most important; in this work he created the metric forms ⇨ Ronsard was to make use of in his pindaric Odes. Many of his poems were never printed during his lifetime, although the number of editions of his various works published in the 16th century amounts to several hundred. His main publications include *L'adolescence clémentine* (1532), *La suite de l'adolescence clémentine* (*c.*1533), *Les œuvres* (1538). [CAM]

*Œuvres*, ed. G. Guiffrey and J. Plattard (5 vols., 1875–1931); ed. C. A. Mayer: *Les Épîtres* (London, 1958), *Œuvres satiriques* (London, 1962), *Œuvres lyriques* (London, 1964), *Œuvres diverses* (London, 1966).

C. A. Mayer, *Bibliographie des Œuvres de C.M.* (2 vols., Geneva, 1954); Ph. A. Becker, *C.M., sein Leben und seine Dichtung* (Munich, 1926); P. Villey, *Les grands écrivains du XVIe siècle, M. et Rabelais* (Paris, 1923); C. A. Mayer, *La religion de M.* (Geneva, 1960).

**Marshak, Samuil Yakovlevich** (Voronezh 1887–Moscow 1964). Russian poet and translator. He studied at the Regent Street Polytechnic and London University (1912–14). In the First World War he worked on the settlement of refugee children; thenceforth children dominated his work. Since 1923 innumerable books for children have flowed from his pen (English tr. in *Play*, tr. H. P. J. Marshall, 1943; *The Ice Cream Man*, etc., tr. D. Lawson and Z. C. Boyajian, 1943). As an editor in Leningrad he inspired the blossoming of children's literature which was a notable feature of the 1920s and early 1930s in the U.S.S.R.; he gathered a circle of brilliant young writers about him (⇨ Zabolotsky, Shvarts). His translations of English literature are classics in Russia; best known are his versions of Burns and a remarkable edition of Shakespeare's sonnets. His own poetry is simple, reflective and humanistic, and deals mostly with nature. [RM-G]

*Stikhi. Skazki. Perevody* (2 vols., 1955); *V nachale zhizni* (1961); *At Life's Beginning*, tr. K. H. Blair (1965); Lugovskoy, *RSP*; Markov, *PG*.

E. Vasil'yeva, *S.M. Teatr dlya detey* (Leningrad, 1924); B. Galanov, *S.Ya. M.* (Moscow, 1965).

**Marsilius of Padua** (Padua *c.*1275–1342). Italian writer and political philosopher. He was an eminent medical scholar and rector of Paris University (1313), where with the philosopher John of Jardun he composed the famous *Defensor pacis* (1324; ed. C. W. Prévite-Orton, Cambridge, 1928; R. Scholtz, Hanover, 1933; first Eng. tr. W. Marshall, 1535; tr. A. Gewirth, N.Y., 1956). It maintains that the State is in all respects a superior authority to the Church. At the same time, the State gets its authority from the people and the Emperor can be reproved or deposed by the people. The Church has no jurisdiction in its own right, either spiritual or temporal, but derives it from the State, which may withdraw it at will. The Church may not own property. Its hierarchy is of human origin. The Pope owes his prerogatives mainly to the Donation of Constantine, and his ecclesiastical authority is inferior to that of a General Council of the Church, consisting of clerics and laymen. Like Dante (though more radically secular), he supports the Emperor as a 'defender of peace', inspired by the struggle against the papacy by Louis IV, whom he accompanied to Italy, saw crowned 'by the people' (1328), 'depose' John XXII, 'appoint' Nicholas V by imperial decree, etc. Louis, in fact, disowned the *Defensor*, though bestowing favours on Marsilius, excommunicated like himself (1327). An unpublished manuscript at Oxford, *Defensor minor*, again combines often democratic ideas on Church questions with belief in Imperial omnipotence. [FB]

E. Emerton, *The Defensor Pacis of M. of P* (Harvard, 1920); A. Gewirth, *M. of P.. the Defender of Peace* (N.Y., 1951).

**Marsman, Hendrik** (Zeist 1899–drowned while fleeing to England 1940). Dutch poet, critic and novelist. A self-styled vitalist, he was the forceful spokesman for the younger poets who were more influenced by his critical work than by his poetry. His journal *Vrjie Bladen* succeeded *Het Getij* (1915–24) until it was replaced by ter ⇨ Braak's *Forum* in 1932. [PK]

*Verzameld Werk* (4 vols., 1947); Barnouw, *CA*; Greshoff, *HL*; *Delta* (Winter 1961–2).

W. L. M. E. van Leeuwen, *Drie vrienden. H.M., M. ter Braak, E. du Perron* (1963).

**Martín de la Plaza, Luis** (Antequera 1577–Antequera 1625). Spanish poet and priest. Espinosa drew freely on his lyrics for his *Flores de poetas ilustres* (1605). He continues the tradition of his fellow-townsman, Barahona de Soto, though he is more strongly influenced by ⇨ Herrera. His rich texture suggests the early ⇨ Góngora. But though a few of his poems are pleasing, they lack distinctive character, and could be mistaken for the work of many others. [JMC]

*Cancionero antequerano*, ed. D. Alonso and R. Ferreres (1950); Blecua, *FLE*; Cohen, *PBSV*; Trend, *OBSV*.

**Martin du Gard, Roger** (Neuilly-sur-Seine 1881–Bellême 1958), French novelist and dramatist. His father and forbears were all lawyers, but he studied history at the École des Chartes, where he qualified as an archivist. He served in the First World War and for a short period, immediately before and after, worked with Jacques Copeau at the Vieux-Colombier. He spent the rest of his life in strict seclusion, wholly dedicated to his writing.

His first novel, *Devenir!* (1908), depicts a would-be novelist who lacks the resolve to carry out his grandiose projects in literature and love. *Jean Barois* (1913; tr. Stuart Gilbert, 1950) traces the development of an intellectual torn, like many of his generation, between religious faith and scientific scepticism: it is notable for its presentation of the Dreyfus Case and its unusual dialogue form. His later works include two farces in the *fabliau* tradition, *Le testament du Père Leleu* (1913) and *La gonfle* (1928), *Un taciturne* (1931), a Naturalistic drama on the subject of homosexuality, *Vieille France* (1933; tr. John Russell, *The Postman*, 1954), mordantly sardonic sketches of French country life, the extremely frank *Notes sur André Gide* (1951; tr. John Russell, 1953) and a valuable account of his own literary development, *Souvenirs autobiographiques et littéraires* (1955).

Martin du Gard's reputation at present rests on *Les Thibault* (1922–40; complete tr. S. Haden-Guest and Stuart Gilbert, 1939–40), a family chronicle in the best traditions of 19th-century realism. The chief characters are Oscar Thibault, the autocratic bourgeois father, and his sons Jacques, the younger, who rebels against his Catholic background and becomes a revolutionary Socialist, and Antoine, the elder, a dedicated doctor who ends by questioning all the standards of modern civilization. The outstanding features of the work are the careful exploration of the relationships between the members of the Thibault family and those they love, the graphic account of the father's death in the sixth volume and the dramatic evocation of Europe on the eve of war in the seventh volume, for which he was awarded the Nobel Prize in 1937.

His reputation is likely to be revalued after the appearance of a number of works which, on his instructions, so far remain unpublished. These include his prolific correspondence, his journal and *Le journal du Colonel Maumort*, a vast novel on which he worked for the last eighteen years of his life. [RG]

*Œuvres complètes* (2 vols., 1955).

D. Boak, *R.M.G.* (1963); R. Gibson, *R.M.G.* (1961); R. Robidoux, *R.M.G. et la religion* (Paris, 1964).

**Martin of Braga** (Pannonia *c.* 510/20–Braga 579). Ecclesiastical writer. He came from Tours to Galicia at the request of Chararich king of the Suevi, and became bishop of Dumio in 556 and Archbishop of Braga before 972. He worked to give shape to the Catholic Church in Galicia, and moulded the baptismal liturgy in north-west Spain. He produced many short pastoral works written in simple, forceful language, such as the *De correctione rusticorum* and the *De trina mersione*; but his *De ira* and *Formula uitae honestae* (the latter having a wide currency in the Middle Ages as the *De quattuor uirtutibus cardinalibus* of 'Seneca' (reveal the breadth of his reading and remind us that he remained in contact with ⇨ Gregory of Tours. [CEC]

*Martini Episcopi Bracarensis Opera Omnia*, ed. C. W. Barlow (New Haven, 1950) (previously in Migne, *PL*, 72).

E. Amman, *Dictionnaire de théologie catholique* x, 1 (Paris, 1928); Manitius, *GLLM*.

**Martínez de la Rosa, Francisco** (Granada 1787–Madrid 1862). Spanish dramatist and statesman. He came to London to enlist help against Napoleon; he was twice exiled (1814–20; 1824–31) and twice prime minister (1820–3; 1831–4). His early plays and poems are influenced by ⇨ Moratín, his *Arte poética* (in *Obras literarias*, 1827), modelled on that of ⇨ Boileau. Impressed in France by the romantic writers, he attempted in French a historical drama, *Aben Humeya* (1830), then introduced the new style successfully in Madrid with *La conjuración de Venecia* (1834). His imitation of Scott in *Doña Isabel de Solís* (1837–46) is weak. [JMC]

*Obras dramáticas*, ed. J. Sarrailh, cc.

**Martínez de Toledo, Alfonso,** Archpriest of Talavera (1398–1470?). Spanish author of prose works, including the lives of San Isidoro and San Ildefonso. Best known for the *Corbacho*, or *Reprobación del amor mundano* (1438). Little is known of him, but he seems to have enjoyed favour in high places (he became chaplain to John II). The *Corbacho* (ed. Martin de Riquer, 1949; sel. tr. L. B. Simpson, *Little Sermons on Sin*, Berkeley, Calif., 1959), so called (though not by the author) after Boccaccio's misogynistic *Corbaccio*, is in 4 sections: it deals with the perils of worldly love; the vices and foibles of women; the four 'complexions' of men; and finally with astrology and free will, with a paraphrase of Boccaccio's allegory of Poverty and Fortune from the *De casibus virorum illustrium*. He illustrates his themes with examples from the traditional medieval stock, as well as from cases he claims to have observed in real life. He likes to portray his specimen characters, especially women, by putting dialogues and monologues into their mouths, a device recalling the dialogues of Andreas Capellanus's treatise on courtly love. He combines a mannered elegance and elaboration of style (with Latin-type constructions and hyperbaton) in his exposition, with a vivid, racy pastiche of popular speech in his dialogues and monologues. As with his predecessor Juan ⇨ Ruíz, his enthusiasm for his subject makes modern readers suspicious of the genuineness of his moralizing intention. [GBG-M]

*El Arcipreste de Talavera*, ed. M. Penna (Torino, 1955); *BSS*, v (1928); *BSS*, vi (1929); *Rev. del Bibl. Arch. y Mus.*, v (1928); *ZRP*, LXI (1941).

**Martínez Sierra, Gregorio** (Madrid 1881–Madrid 1948). Spanish dramatist and theatre director. A distant follower of ⇨ Benavente and translator of ⇨ Maeterlinck. Best known for *Canción de cuna* (1911, CA), a sentimental piece about a baby in a nunnery, and his unsuccessfully ambitious *Don Juan de España* (1921), which attempts a new version of the Don Juan theme. In the early years of the century he founded a number of important literary reviews, including *Helios* and *Renacimiento*. He also collaborated with Manuel de Falla in the ballet *El amor brujo* (1915). [JMC]

*The Plays of G.M.S.*, tr. H. Granville Barker and J. G. Underhill (2 vols., 1923).

**Martins, Joaquim Pedro de Oliveira** (Lisbon 1845–Lisbon 1894). Portuguese author and historian. He wrote voluminously on many fields of national and general history. Extraordinarily gifted as a writer, he usually lent great conviction to his theories and interpretations of social phenomena. He succeeds in combining a sweeping vision of great historical events with a moral judgement of the men involved in them. However, the massive amount of data with which he had to deal and the large field he intended to cover led him into many generalizations and even inaccuracies of fact. Entirely self-educated, he had to interrupt his regular studies at the age of 14. Martins also led a full life as a civil servant. He was successively a mine administrator in Spain (in the province of Córdoba), a director of the national railways and a minister of the treasury. His most impressive works are the *História da República Romana* (1885), *História de Portugal* (1879) and the *História da Civilização Ibérica* (1879). The last one, a critical interpretation of the history of Spain and Portugal, was widely known in both countries. [LSR]

Fidelino de Figueiredo, *História dum Vencido da Vida* (Lisbon, 1930); Óscar Lopes, *O.M. e as contradições da geração de 70* (Porto, 1946); António J. Saraiva, 'Três Ensaios sobre O.M.' in *Para a História da Cultura em Portugal* (Lisbon, n.d.).

**Martinson, Harry** (Jämshög 1904– ). Swedish poet, novelist, essayist and dramatist. *Nässlorna blomma* (1935; tr. N

Walford, *Flowering Nettles*, 1936) and its sequel *Vägen ut* (1936) describe his often bitter early years with poetic vividness and moral detachment. Orphaned at 6, he was passed round the parish in a pre-welfare, the-lowest-bidder-take-him spirit until, after many attempts at escape, he eventually signed on a small ship as a cabin boy. His subsequent life as a stoker and as an intercontinental vagabond is in part recorded in his travel books *Resor utan mål* (1932) and *Kap Farväl!* (1933; tr. N. Walford, *Cape Farewell*, 1936) in a highly individual, richly associative style. His breakthrough as a lyrical poet came with *Nomad* (1931; rev. edn 1943), which also exploits the travel motifs and childhood memories. In his early philosophy there is a strong belief in the goodness of nature, in human nobility, and in a collective purpose among the working classes. It has been summarily described as 'Primitivism', but from the start a note of scepticism and melancholy is discernible. In *Natur* (1934), a somewhat extravagant and jaggedly surrealistic collection, the mood can be almost despairing. During the thirties he published three further prose books which reveal his insight into and love for wild nature. *Passad* (1945) remains his greatest collection of verse, named after the equatorial winds that provided the poet with his central image, a symbol conveying his trust in the creative power of nature. Apart from many shorter poems, it contains a number of longer cycles that are equally remarkable, e.g. 'Passader', 'Hades och Euklides', and 'Li-Kan talar under trädet'. His prose works include the novel *Vägen till Klockrike* (1948; tr. M. Michael, *The Road*, 1955), a sympathetic study of the lives of tramps and social outcasts in an age of oncoming industrialism. The long narrative poem *Aniara* (1956; tr. H. McDiarmid and E. Harley Schubert, 1963), made up of 103 more or less firmly connected cantos, has far greater epic power. This haunting tale of a giant space-ship on an irreversible journey into the void has been read as an allegory of technological Man and his planet; yet the verbal invention, the symbolism (much of it grown from scientific concepts) and the individual destinies recorded make an immediate, often overwhelming effect. The lyrical collections *Cikada* (1953), *Gräsen i Thule* (1958) and *Vagnen* (1960) witness the poet's growing alienation in modern, technological society. More recently he has turned to the drama with *Tre knivar från Wei* (1964) He is a master of Swedish, a stylistic innovator comparable with Strindberg, an observer of nature akin to his great compatriot Linnaeus, and a poet uniquely combining learning with imagination, compassion with insight. Since 1949 he has been a member of the Swedish Academy, the first of the largely self-taught writers of working-class background to be elected. [SAB]

K. Jaensson, 'Återblick på H.M.', in *Sanning och särprägel* (Stockholm, 1960); T. Hall, *Vår tids stjärnsång* (Stockholm, 1958); I. Holm, *H.M.* (Stockholm, 1960); J. Wrede, *Sången om Aniara* (Stockholm, 1965).

**Martorell, Joan.** ⇨ See Catalan Literature.

**Martynov, Leonid** (Omsk 1905– ). Russian poet. Son of a railway employee, left school at 15 to become a journalist, and travelled widely in the U.S.S.R. Inspired first by ⇨ Mayakovsky, soon by ancient history and Old Russian culture. His first poems appeared in the late 1920s. After publishing his remarkable *Lukomor'ye* (1945) and *Ertsinsky Les* (1946), he was severely criticized and fell silent for ten years. Recently he has published a good deal of poetry in literary journals.

Many earlier poems are set in the deep forests and remote villages of Siberia. The most striking have the haunting strangeness of myths, sliding naturally from ancient times to Soviet Russia; a dominant theme is the search for the lost land of Lukomor'ye. Semi-allegorical, with its superficial simplicity and wry, reflective wit, its fine rhythms based on the cadences of speech, his style is entirely original. Since 1955 it has become more benign and less striking, like the Moscow countryside which is now its usual setting, without however losing its individuality. He has been underrated until recently in the U.S.S.R. and is scarcely known abroad. [RM-G]

*Stikhotvoreniya* (1961); Gulland, *SRV*; Lugovskoy, *RSP*.

**Marulić, Marko.** ⇨ Dalmatian and Dubrovnik Literature.

**Marxist Views on Art and Literature.** There is no systematic treatment of aesthetic problems in the works of Marx and Engels, but there are many passages that indicate their views on some fundamental issues. They concern (a) the place of art among the human activities; (b) art under capitalism; (c) the definition of 'realism'; (d) tragedy and comedy; (e) the assessment of individual writers.

(a) In the general conception of dialectical and historical materialism art is discussed as a specific part of the 'superstructure'. Its active role is indicated in its ability to contribute to important social-political changes. It is emphasized that the social determinations of art do not work mechanically, but only 'in the last analysis', and, because of the 'reciprocity' in this dialectical pattern of causation, art itself becomes a determining factor, not merely a determined one. The 'principle of uneven development' states that a higher social order does not necessarily produce a correspondingly high artistic achievement; (b) Capitalism – because of the fragmentation in the social body, the resulting isolationism, prosaic utilitarianism, the rule of money and gain, etc. – is described as being extremely unfavourable, or even hostile towards, artistic development; (c) 'Realism' is analysed not as one particular kind of style, but as the only adequate artistic attitude to reality; (d) Both tragedy and comedy are discussed as integral parts of a general conception of philosophy of history, and not simply as literary genres; (e) Writers who are discussed – e.g. Dante, Shakespeare, Shelley, Byron, Goethe, Schiller, Balzac, Sue, Chernyshevsky, Dobrolyubov, Herwegh, Heine – usually appear in broadest contexts, exemplifying general problems of aesthetic and social philosophy. (See Marx, *Economic and Philosophic Manuscripts of 1844*; *The German Ideology*; *Introduction to a Critique of Political Economy*; *The 18th Brumaire of Louis Bonaparte*; *Correspondence between Marx-Engels and Lassalle* and Engel's *Letters to Margaret Harkness and Minna Kautsky*; K. Marx, F. Engels, *Literature and Art*, 1947.)

Marx's followers have written a great deal on art and literature. Lenin raised the issue of the relationship between the Party and literature, and he insisted that art is a specific 'reflection' of reality. Trotsky centred his attention mainly on the issues of the relationship between art and revolution, and art and morality. By far the most systematic and complex elaboration of the Marxist conception of aesthetics can be found in ⇨ Lukács. Other outstanding Marxist works are: Plekhanov, *Art and Social Life*, W. E. Hartley and E. Fox (1953); Lenin, *On Socialist Ideology and Culture* (Moscow, 1955); Trotsky, *Literature and Revolution* (Michigan, 1960); *Their Morals and Ours* (N.Y., 1942); Lunacharsky, *On Literature and Art* (Moscow, 1965); F. Mehring, *The Lessing Legend* (Stuttgart, 1893); Gramsci, *Literature and National Life* (Turin, 1954); Caudwell, *Illusion and Reality* (1946, repr. 1950); W. Benjamin, *Origins of the German Drama* (revised Frankfurt a.M., 1963); E. Fischer, *The Necessity of Art* (Bostock, 1963). [ISM]

**Masaryk, Tomáš Garrigue** (Hodonín 1850–Lány 1937). Czech thinker and statesman. The son of a former serf, he rose to be successively Professor of Philosophy at Prague University, Deputy in the Austrian Reichsrat, leader of the campaign abroad for Czechoslovak independence during the First World War and first President of the Czechoslovak Republic. His philosophy of rationalist humanism influenced his conception of Czech history (*Česká otázka*, 1895) and his political programme. His *Rusko a Evropa* (1919; tr. E. and C. Paul, *The Spirit of Russia*, 1955) is a penetrating analysis of Russian thought and literature. In his war memoirs (*Světová revoluce*, 1925, abridged tr. Wickham Steed, *The Making of a State*, 1927) the record of historical events is intermingled with expositions of his political and philosophical ideas. The most attractive account of his life and ideas is contained in his conversations with Karel ⇨ Čapek (*President Masaryk Tells His Story*, 1934). [RA]

P. Selver, *M.* (1940).

**Masuccio.** ⇨ Salernitano, Masuccio.

**Matavulj, Simõ** (Sibenik 1852–Belgrade 1908). Serbian novelist. He lived as a teacher and professor. Widely read in French and Italian, he produced collections of stories based on life in various parts of Serbia, Dalmatia and Montenegro. His style is close to naturalism, being objective and impersonal, especially in his later years when he wrote of Belgrade. His most famous work is the humorous novel *Bakonja fra Brne* (1892), one of the best in Serbian. [EDG]

Popović, *JS.*
Barac, *HYL.*

**Matić, Dusan** (Ćuprija 1898– ). Serbian novelist and before 1941 a modernist poet. His novel *Kocka je bačena* (1957), about Serbian provincial life, purports to show how the growth of capitalism was already leading Serbia to the logical development of the communist revolution. [EDG]

*SEER*, XL, 94 (1961); Kadić, *CSL*.

**Matković, Marijan** (Karlovac 1915– ). Croatian dramatist. In the tradition of ⇨ Krleza. His *Vašar snova* (1959), *Heraclo* (1957) and *Ahilova baština* (1959) are among his most important works. The two latter unmask the cult of the hero, showing how men create heroes out of their own weakness. *Vašar snova* depicts the middle-class ethos. His dramas are predominantly intellectual with a well-developed sense of the theatre and a skilful use of the grotesque and the symbolic to express the problems which preoccupy modern man. [EDG]

**Matoš, Antun Gustav** (Tovarnik 1873–Zagreb 1914). Croatian poet, essayist and critic. Deserting from the Austrian army in 1898, he fled to Geneva and thence to Paris where he stayed till 1904. From Paris he brought the prevalent ideas of art with their insistance on aestheticism, publicizing both contemporary French and English literary ideas. His own poetry gave a new formal excellence to the Croatian language. His stories were popular for their mixture of psychological fantasy and realism. His essay on Baudelaire was the first of its kind in Croatia. As a critic, he was often eccentric, yet many of his judgements still stand; above all he broadened the cultural horizons of both Serbia and Croatian writers. [EDG]

*Sabrana djela*, i (1953), iii (1955); Lavrin, *AMYP*. Barac, *HYL*; Kadić, *CSL*.

**Matthew of Vendôme** (fl. 1160–1185). Medieval writer. A pupil of Bernard Silvester at Tours, then of ⇨ Hugh Primas at Orleans, where he himself taught grammar for some some time. Persecuted by a number of his colleagues he fled to Paris, where he spent ten years before eventually returning to Tours. He published a collection of model letters and a large number of poems, mostly on mythological themes; of these only the *Milo* survives, together with the *Liber Tobiae*, a metrical paraphrase of the Book of Tobit. But Matthew was more influential as a poetic theorist than a practising poet: his *Ars versificatoria* (*c.* 1175) is a fascinating and detailed treatise, enlivened by many examples and illustrations of his theories. [MRM]

Letters, ed. W. Wattenbach, in *Sitzungberichte der philosoph., philologischen und historischen Classe der Akademie der Wissenschaften zu München*, ii (1872); *Liber Tobiae*, Migne, *PL*, 205; *Milo*, ed. Haupt in *Exempla Poesis Latinae Medii Aevi* (1834); *Ars versificatoria*, ed. E. Faral in *Les arts poétiques* (Paris, 1924).

**Matute, Ana María** (Barcelona 1926– ). Spanish novelist. Her first novel, *Los Abel* (1948), shows some influence of Emily Brontë. She received the Premio Nacional de Literatura for *Los hijos muertos* (1958) and the Premio Nadal for *Primera memoria* (1960). Her other important novels are *Fiesta al Noroeste* (1953), *Pequeño teatro* (1954) and *El río* (1963). *Los niños tontos* (1957) is a short poetic novel of distinction. The most talented woman novelist of the post-Civil War generation, she achieves dramatic atmosphere and mystery, and a palpitating poetic quality especially in her descriptions of adolescence (*Los hijos muertos*, *Primera memoria*, *Los soldados lloran de noche*). Her protagonists are strange, solitary adolescents, who both love life and fear it. Her style is remarkable for delicacy and poetic power, though some novels lack a formal control. [JLC]

Alborg, *HANE*; Nora, *NEC*.

**Maupassant, Guy de** (nr Dieppe 1850–Passy 1893). French short-story writer and novelist. Brought up in Normandy, he was obliged to take a clerk's job in the Naval Ministry, but soon started a long literary apprenticeship to Flaubert and was introduced to Zola's circle. His first story to appear in print, 'Boule de suif', was one of the collection *Les soirées de Médan* published by Zola and his supporters in 1880. In the next eleven years he published some 300 stories and 6 novels; but mental disorders, syphilitic in origin, had progressively undermined his health, and he died after two years' insanity.

The subject matter of his stories is more varied than the average selection might suggest. Two clearly defined groups, including some of the most famous stories, are those which spring directly from his experience of the worlds of the minor civil servant and of the Norman peasant. Besides these, however, there are a vast number of less easily classifiable stories, often anecdotal and fragmentary in character – recitals of odd sexual encounters, of the ironies and brutalities of war, of the histories behind the outlaws and misfits of society. Up to a point he is concerned with the staple material of French realism; but the reality exposed includes the strange and unexplained as well as the more familiar elements of squalor, mediocrity and hypocrisy; and his excursions into the supernatural and hallucinatory – products of a growing presentiment of madness – are only the most strikingly personal features in a writer best known for his detached social observation.

Maupassant's loose affiliations with naturalism are implicitly renounced in the essay 'Le Roman' prefixed to his novel *Pierre et Jean* (1887). But his discipleship to Flaubert was backed up by affinities of outlook and temperament: he has the same pessimism, verging on moral and metaphysical nihilism; the same disgust at the philistinism of bourgeois life (modified by a certain pity for its more oppressed and impoverished practitioners); the same despairing assumptions about the quality and durability of human relations, especially those between the sexes. But life's inadequacies are not, as in Flaubert's case, measured against the sole and supreme value of art. He was dedicated to physical as well as literary activity; and the charm of the countryside and the Seine, the camaraderie of youth, the joys of rowing and fishing, are vividly present in his work. Only rarely, however (as in 'Mouche'), is an idyllic mood sustained, and then as a memory and not as a present reality. Usually the idyllic background serves only to set off violence or mediocrity or lost opportunity ('Le Trou', 'Deux Amis', 'Une partie de campagne'). Disillusion is in fact the central reality in Maupassant's work. An obsessively recurrent theme is that of recognition: a meeting with a long-lost child or relation on whom hopes or affections have been fixed only confirms the pathetic absurdity of human illusions ('Mon Oncle Jules', 'L'abandonné', 'Duchoux'); and reunions between friends of youth provoke a sharper satire of the almost routine decline into materialism and pomposity ('L'ami Patience', 'Le rosier de Madame Husson').

Maupassant rarely allows his characters completely unironic treatment; the isolated victim of life attracts his sympathy, but even here 'Garçon, un bock!', with its grotesquely pathetic hero, is more representative than the almost fully tragic 'Monsieur Parent'. Still more rarely are substantial positive values presented through character; these are at most fragmentarily suggested in figures outside regular society. The contrast in 'Boule de suif' between the prostitute's dignity and generosity and the callous, hypocritical bourgeois is responsible for the story's appeal; but a little farther along this road lies a consoling sentimentality into which Maupassant would not be tricked. Escape into comedy is frequent in the Norman stories ('La Ficelle', 'Le Diable', in a slightly different social setting 'La Maison Tellier'); for all the brutality and avarice of the Norman peasant his world has a robustness which makes it seem to us, as it did to Maupassant, a legitimate object for purely comic observation or farcical embroidery ('Toine').

It is difficult to generalize about the form of the stories. The ironic twist on which the very famous 'La Parure' ends is exceptional. A large proportion of stories are in fact deliberately removed from the immediately dramatic by being put into the mouth of a narrator. This serves Maupassant's personal vision in that the narrator can suggest a man who places himself outside normal acceptance of life and whose chief interest in it is to recall proofs of its incoherence or cruelty and examples of its transitory pleasures. Within this often leisurely framework, however, concision of expression is a constant. Maupassant's functional narrative style is removed from any concern for *écriture artiste*; and especially perhaps in the earlier stories there is a surface liveliness, a note of personal enjoyment in the irony, which differentiates him from Flaubert even in satiric mood.

The novels are of lesser interest, but some of them deserved to be read: *Une vie* (1883) and *Pierre et Jean* (1887) are fairly successful elaborations of subjects recurrent in the stories – the innocent victim of life and the discovery of a family secret and its psychological repercussions. *Bel-Ami* (1885), which relates the rise of an ambitious cad through journalism, has some good episodes; but the fact that he moves agains such a uniformly caddish world perhap makes for a certain loss of point in his progress, and enforces the appropriateness o the short story form to Maupassant' particular vision of the world. Very numer ous translations of Maupassant include a selection in Everyman Books (1934); and 3 vols. of selected stories and *Bel-Ami*, tr. H. Sloman (Penguin). [BLN]

*Contes et nouvelles* (2 vols.) and *Romans*, ed. A.-M. Schmidt (1959–60).

R. Dumesnil, *G. de M.* (Paris, 1947); A. Vial, *G. de M. et l'art du roman* (Paris, 1954); Henry James, *The House of Fiction* (1957); M. Turnell, *The Art of French Fiction* (1959); F. Steegmuller, *M.* (1950).

**Mauriac, François** (Bordeaux 1885–1970). French poet, novelist, playwright, biographer and critic. Sensitive and self-conscious, he was brought up in a middle-class Catholic milieu of which he was long the unwilling prisoner. Religious scruples and efforts to reconcile Catholicism and the flesh found expression in the poems of *Les mains jointes* (1909), and in the early novels, *L'enfant chargé de chaînes* (1913) and *La chair et le sang* (1920). With *Préséances* (1921), he added another theme, the denunciation of unthinking orthodoxy, whether of the bourgeois or the *bien-pensant*.

Success came with *Le baiser au lépreux* (1922), a study of crippling yearning for love, and with *Génitrix* (1923), where possessive love destroys. Here, as in *Le désert de l'amour* (1925), *Thérèse Desqueyroux* (1927) and *Le nœud de vipères* (1932), he vividly evokes a dark world in which human love seems impure and unsatisfactory, in which the family is torn by conflict and where sinful creatures struggle towards the light that only God's grace can grant. Criticism of his 'Jansenism' and Gide's jibe that in his work he achieved a compromise between God and Mammon caused him to re-examine his faith and its relation to art in a series of studies (*Jean Racine*, 1928; *Dieu et Mammon*, 1929; *Blaise Pascal et sa sœur Jacqueline*, 1931; *Souffrances et bonheur du Chrétien*, 1931; *Le romancier et ses personnages*, 1933). Acknowledging his responsibility to his readers, he sought to 'purify the source'. Recognizing in himself some exaggeration of man's helplessness in face of evil, he acknowledged that he had underestimated the power of love. There followed a happier novel of family union, *Le mystère Frontenac* (1933), *La fin de la nuit* (1935), in which Thérèse Desqueyroux is brought almost to salvation, and *Les anges noirs* (1936), where a simple priest successfully struggles against evil for the soul of a murderer. These and later novels are more serene; even where the *bien-pensant* is under attack (*La Pharisienne*, 1941), and the pure are menaced (*Galigaï*, 1952; *L'agneau*, 1954), there is more hope and charity, a less troubling evocation of sin.

Mauriac's scope is restricted; his theme is '*La misère de l'homme sans Dieu*'. The analysis and the conflicts are set in an unchanging milieu, but the drama, narrated in a sensuous and powerful style, has the intensity of classical tragedy. Though in the novel he made no technical innovations, he experimented in form by transposing his subjects into theatrical terms. *Asmodée* (1938) achieved considerable success; later plays, *Les mal aimés* (1945), *Passage du Malin* (1948), *Le feu sur la terre* (1951), *Le pain vivant* (1962) were less well received; Mauriac satisfied neither the boulevard nor the *avant-garde* public, though the plays are well constructed, the situations and the characters compelling.

He also turned to journalism (in *Le Figaro* and later in *L'Express*), often taking an unpopular line, as in his attack on Franco; he wrote for the Resistance, denounced the purge that followed the Liberation, supported General de Gaulle and was often involved in controversy.

His main achievement lies in the novel and has been publicly recognized (Grand Prix du Roman de l'Académie Française, 1925; Académie Française, 1933; Nobel Prize, 1952). [RJN]

*Collected Novels*, tr. G. Hopkins (1946ff.).

P.-H. Simon, *M. par lui-même* (Paris, 1953); M. Jarrett-Kerr, *Mauriac* (1954); C. Jenkins, *M.* (1965); K. Goesch, *F.M. Essai de bibliographie chronologique* (Paris, 1965).

**Maurice de Sully** (?–1196). Medieval sermon writer. A pupil of Peter Abelard, Maurice first held a chair in the university of Paris, then in 1160 succeeded Peter Lombard as bishop of Paris. His activities were many. Under his direction was begun the construction of the present cathedral of Notre-Dame; he was a zealous diocesan reformer; a politician of major importance under Louis VII and Philippe-Auguste; a partisan of Thomas à Becket in the church and state quarrel; and the greatest preacher of his day. His sermons, characterized by their simplicity, sound common sense and lively style, survive in both Latin and French versions. In the 13th-century collections of them enjoyed vast popularity and were used as preaching manuals in many parts of Europe. [MRM]

*Letters*, Migne, *PL*, 200; *Charters*, Migne, *PL*, 205; V. Mortet, *M. de S.* (Paris, 1890); C. A. Robson, *M. of S.* (1952).

**Maurois, André**, pseud. of Émile Herzog (Elbeuf 1885–Paris 1967). French writer, biographer and historian. Educated in Rouen – where he came under the lasting influence of his teacher ◊ Alain – and at the University of Caen. Subsequently he directed the family textile factory (cf. the autobiographical novel *Bernard Quesnay*, 1926; tr. B. W. Downs, 1927). He was an interpreter with British forces in the First World War. His gently ironic observation of the British inspired *Les silences du Colonel Bramble* (1918; tr. T. Wake and W. Jackson, *The Silence of Colonel Bramble*, 1940). The Anglo-Saxon world has continued to fascinate him (he lived in England and the U.S.A. during the Second World War). He is a prolific master of the '*vie romancée*', in which the line between critical biography and narrative art is hard to draw. Between *Ariel ou la vie de Shelley* (1923; tr. E. D'Arcy, 1935) and *Prométhée ou la vie de Balzac* (1965; tr. N. Denny, 1965) fall works on Disraeli (1927; tr. H. Miles, 1937); Byron (2 vols., 1930; tr. H. Miles, 1930), Voltaire (1932; tr. H. Miles, 1952), Proust (1949; tr. G. Hopkins, 1962), G. Sand (1952; tr. G. Hopkins, 1953), Hugo (1954; tr. G. Hopkins, 1956), Sir Alexander Fleming (1959; tr. G. Hopkins, 1963), and others. His novels include such analyses of the *haute bourgeoisie* as *Climats* (1928; tr. V. Schiff and E. Cook, *The Climates of Love*, 1957). The *Histoire d'Angleterre* (1937; tr. H. Miles, 1956) initiated his synoptic historical accounts. His interest in the English-speaking world is reciprocated: his works are widely available in English (cf. his *Histoire des États-Unis de Wilson à Kennedy*, 1963; tr. P. O'Brian, 1964). As well as critical and philosophical essays (*Magiciens et Logiciens*, 1935; *Un art de vivre*, 1939; tr. J. Whitall, 1960), he has written fantasies, and tales for children. Versatility is as striking a feature of his works as the fastidious yet direct style which informs them. He was elected to the Académie Française in 1938. [CAHR]

*Œuvres complètes* (1950).

M. Droit, *A.M.* (Paris, 1953); J. Suffel, *A.M.* (Paris, 1963); A. Maurois, *Portrait d'un ami qui s'appelait moi* (1959) (self-portrait).

**Maurras, Charles** (Martigues 1868–Tours 1952). French poet, critic, political philosopher and journalist. Chief doctrinaire of *Action Française*. Under his influence, this initially republican anti-dreyfusard group (1899) launched a newspaper (1908–44) to promote the restoration of a strong, hereditary French monarchy, alleging it to be the 'total' form of nationalism needed if the 'Real France' was to react effectively against a century of decay caused by the bureaucratic centralization of the Republic and the soft-headed democracy it owed to Protestant, Jewish, Masonic and 'immigrant' infiltrations. Maurras's 'empirical' rationale of monarchism was informed by a hierarchical concept of 'Order', derived from landscapes in his native Provence, Greek science and art, Roman, and English, politics, the laws of nature and of classical literature, kingship and corporative liberties in 15th- and 17th-century France, A. Comte's political positivism; cf. Maurras's *Anthinéa* (1901), *Enquête sur la monarchie* (1900–9); *Dictionnaire politique et critique* (1932–4). He was adept in persuasive simplification and continuity of exposition, and had a born partisan's capacity for imparting, and arousing, love and hate. Finely etched lyrics, prose reminiscences, and criticism (which, despite bias against Romantic individualism, shows sure taste) all reflect the sensuous, inward and scholarly qualities of his influential doctrine.

Between the wars, Rome condemned the political emphasis of his Catholicism, he was imprisoned for threatening Popular Front leaders with murder, the Pretender's press repudiated him, the Académie Française elected him, Hitler's ambitions made him campaign for rearmament *and* peace. When France fell, he ranged himself behind Pétain and (coining the ironically unrealistic slogan: 'France alone') against the Allies the Resistance *and* the Paris fascists; he was condemned to life imprisonment in 1945. Compassionately released in 1952, he died seven months later. His last task was to revise the *Œuvres capitales* (Paris, 1954) which would, he believed, vindicate him: '*On verra bien.*' [PO]

A. Thibaudet, 'Les idées de C.M.' in *Trente ans d vie française* (Paris, 1920); L. Rodiez, *M jusqu'à l'Action Française* (Paris, 1957); H Massis, *M. et notre temps* (Paris/Geneva, 1961)

**Mayakovsky, Vladimir Vladimirovich** (Bag dadi, now called 'Mayakovsky', Georgi 1893–Moscow 1930). Russian poet an playwright. One of the great revolutionary figures of 20th-century poetry. Son of a forester (minor gentry) who died in 1906; the family moved to Moscow to live on an inadequate pension. An active revolutionary in his teens, he was three times arrested and imprisoned; unable to finish school, he later studied art. Under the influence of David Burlyuk, he became one of the leaders of Russian ⇨ Futurism. In the years of the First World War he achieved notoriety in Moscow for his personal flamboyance, his proclivity for shocking the bourgeois, but above all for his incredible poetry, which from 1913 or so already bore the mature stamp of his unique style. He accepted unhesitatingly the October Revolution, devoted his creative energy to the young Soviet state, devised propaganda posters, slogans and rhymes, travelled the country reciting his verse, often in the company of like-minded poets. He founded (1923) and edited the journal *LEF* (*Left Arts Front*) and its successor *Noviy LEF* (*New LEF*); he engaged in often bitter literary polemics. He travelled to Western Europe and America, journeys reflected in several well-known poems. But this public activity did not preclude the complex and ultimately tragic personal life which occasioned his more intimate verse; the emotional triangle which arose when he met Lili Brik and her husband Osip in 1915 was not resolved until his death. Though disturbed and angered by the suicide of ⇨ Yesenin in 1925, he nevertheless shot himself at his flat in 1930 for reasons which have occasioned much speculation, but in which personal factors were probably dominant, rather than (e.g.) the harsh criticism of literary opponents on grounds of 'individualism'.

He dreamt of creating a new art that would correspond to a new order of society: and certainly his verse was revolutionary. Rejecting the traditions both of Symbolism and of the 19th-century classics, he juggled words and images into shocking new juxtapositions. He was a master of sound effects – unexpected assonances, rhymes and rhythms; his basic unit is the phrase or single stressed word (rather than the line or stanza), printed in 'stepped' lines (*s razbivkoy*) to stress the terse, declamatory effect. Aggressively eschewing sentimentality, 'fine writing', cliché images, facile melodiousness, his tone combines farce, tragedy and exaggerated reportage, with a vein of true fantasy – sometimes quasi-religious or blasphemous. His hard-boiled toughness hides great sensitivity.

The natural landmarks in his work are his longer poems and plays. They start in surprising fashion with *Vladimir Mayakovsky – A Tragedy*, written, directed and performed by its author in 1913. *Oblako v shtanakh* ('A Cloud in Trousers', 1914–15), *Fleyta-pozvonochnik* ('Backbone-Flute', 1915) and *Voyna i mir* ('War and the World', 1915–16, a pun on Tolstoy's novel) outraged the staider public but established his fame. The play *Misteriya-buff* (1918–21) and the poem *150,000,000* (1919–20) proclaimed his somewhat idiosyncratic revolutionary sympathies. *Vladimir Il'yich Lenin* (1924) and *Khorosho!* ('Okay!', 1927) treat public themes, while *Lyublyu* ('I Love', 1922) and *Pro eto* ('About This', 1923) spring from his emotional life. His two great satirical dramas, *Klop* ('The Bedbug', 1928–9) and *Banya* ('The Bath-house', 1929–30), based on contemporary life, at one time caused official misgivings by their sharpness. One of his greatest poems is *Vo ves' golos* ('At the Top of my Voice', 1930), which he did not live to complete; it is virtually a spiritual autobiography and testament. He also left unfinished a series of fragments which rank with the great love-poetry of our age. His most notable prose is *Kak delat' stikhi?* ('How to Make Poetry?', 1926; tr. G. Hyde, *How are Verses Made?* 1971), which analyses his motives and technique in composing a poem about Yesenin's suicide.

Though his poetry was remote from Socialist Realism (promulgated soon after his death), Stalin's remark that 'Mayakovsky was, and remains, the greatest Soviet poet' insured that posthumously he never fell from favour. Among poets his influence has been incalculably great: superficially, e.g. in the common adoption of his stepped lines and colloquialisms, and more profoundly on the young ⇨ Pasternak, ⇨ Aseyev, ⇨ Kirsanov, ⇨ Yevtushenko, R. Rozhdestvensky and ⇨ Voznesensky. [RM-G]

*Izbrannyye proizvedeniya* (2 vols., 1960) (6-vol. edn, 1927/30, 1934/8); H. Marshall, *M. and his Poetry* (1965) (intr. and translations); M. Hayward, G. Reavey (tr.), *The Bedbug and Selected Poetry*, ed. P. Blake (1962); Gulland, *SRV*; Lugovskoy, *RSP*; Markov, *MRP*, *PG*; Obolensky, *PBRV*.

Bowra, *CE*; L. Stahlberger, *The Symbolic System of M.* (The Hague, 1965).

**Mažuranić, Ivan** (Novi Vinodol 1814–

Zagreb 1890). Croatian poet. He received a classical education at the *gimnasium* in Fiume, was well read in German and Italian, and on coming into contact with the Illyrian movement in 1836, began contributing articles and poems to ⇨ Gaj's *Danica Ilirska*. In 1844 he supplied the two missing cantos for an edition of ⇨ Gundulić's *Osman* and in 1846 published his main work, the epic poem *Smrt Smail-age Čengića* (tr. J. M. Wiles, *The Death of Smail Aga*, 1918). He abandoned writing for politics, becoming president of the Croatian Assembly in 1872 and Ban of Croatia from 1873 to 1880.

*Smrt Smail-age Čengića* is, apart from the works of ⇨ Njegoš, the most distinguished poetic work in Serbo-Croat in the 19th century. It tells of a clash between Montenegrins and Herzegovinian Moslems which took place in 1840 when Smail aga Cengić was ambushed and killed while attempting to collect taxes. Mažuranić sees this theme as symbolic of the national struggle against tyranny but also makes Cengić a tragic figure, the victim of his own character and weakness that lead him inexorably to death and defeat. Using the traditions of Dalmatian literature and of folk poetry, he created a style having a freedom and versatility new in the Serbo-Croat language. [EDG]

Barac, *HYL*.

E. D. Goy, 'The Tragic Element in Smrt-Smailage Čengića', *SEER*, XLIV, 103 (1966).

**Mazzini, Giuseppe** (Genoa 1805–Pisa 1872). Italian patriot revolutionary and idealist. His intensely religious concept of the spiritual progress of humanity towards unity and brotherhood scarcely softened the violent methods he condoned in the pursuit of Italian unity and independence. From exile in Marseilles, disillusioned about the bungling of the uprising of 1831, he abandoned the secret society of Carbonari and formed his own association – Giovine Italia. For the first time came the demand for an independent united republic. In France and Switzerland he continued his revolutionary work on international lines (*Fede e avvenire*, 1835); but, although the idol of the oppressed, to governments he was the arch-conspirator. Banished from Switzerland in 1836, he went to London, where he lived for much of the remainder of his life, remote from political trends in Italy and failing to appreciate the ground gained by moderate opinion – largely due to repeated outrages committed by his own supporters. Although called to office in the short-lived Roman republic of 1848, his party was already discredited and the initiative had passed to the Kingdom of Piedmont. There was bitter antagonism between Mazzini and Cavour; yet national unity was achieved in 1860 not just through the diplomacy of Italy's 'maker' – Cavour – but also through the revolutionary methods of the 'apostle' – Mazzini – and Garibaldi. He had become a legend, but was forced to remain in exile.

In *I doveri dell'uomo* (1860; tr. T. Okey, *The Duties of Man*, 1894), with characteristic idealism, he attacked those socialist doctrines that stressed rights and ignored duties. In 1868 he moved to Switzerland to follow events in Italy more closely, watching sadly the class-war advocated by the first International (cf. *Agli operai italiani* and *Gemiti, fremiti e ricapitolazioni*, 1871). In 1872 he returned in disguise to die in Italy. At his funeral in Genoa there were 80,000 mourners. [RHC]

*Scritti editi e inediti* (106 vols., 1906–43); *Mazzini's Letters*, tr. A. De Rosen Jervis (1930).

G. O. Griffith, *Mazzini: Prophet of Modern Europe* (1932); U. Limentani, *L'attività letteraria di G. Mazzini* (Turin, 1950); R. V. Foa, *L'arte e la vita in G.M.* (Genoa, 1956); E. E. Y. Hales, *Mazzini and the Secret Societies* (1956); *Minori*, iv.

**Meckel, Christoph** (Berlin 1935– ). German poet and artist. He has an intense power of visual fantasy, more effective perhaps in his electrifying etchings (*Moel*, 1959; *Welttheater*, *Der Krieg*, *Die Stadt*, 1960) than in his prose (*Im Land der Umbranauten*, 1961; *Tullipan*, 1965) or poetry: *Tarnkappe* (1956), *Hotel für Schlafwandler* (1958), *Nebelhörner* (1959), *Wildnisse* (1962), and *Gedicht-Bilderbuch* (1964), where the imagery seems sometimes mere arbitrary ornament – reminiscent of Dada. [PB]

*Lyrik, Prosa, Graphik aus zehn Jahren* (Munich, 1965) (with bibliography); Hamburger and Middleton, *MGP*; Middleton, *GWT*.

*TLS*, 28 April 1961; Nonnenmann, *SG*.

**Mécs, László** (1895– ). Hungarian poet. A Catholic priest and teacher in Košice (Slovakia), he was for a time the literary rallying-point of the Hungarian minority in Czechoslovakia. Much of his poetry is an attempt to sustain Christian ideals; he is a singer of joy, faith and redemption. His poems, which have been translated into numerous languages, include *Rabszolgák* *énekelnek* (*Songs of Slaves*), *Alázat* (*Humility*) and *Az Ismeretlen Katona Sirján* (*On the Tomb of the Unknown Soldier*) all tr. W. Kirkconnell, 1964. After 1947 he disappeared into seclusion. [JFR]

Reményi, *HWL.*

**Medici, Lorenzo de'** (Lorenzo the Magnificent) (Florence 1449–Careggi 1492). Italian poet, statesman and patron of the arts. He wrote both stern spiritual *laudi* and hedonistic carnival songs, a verse exposition of Ficino's neo-Platonism (*l'Altercazione*) and the naturalistic *Caccia col falcone*, *Rime* of a Petrarchan flavour and a tale of rustic courtship in the *Nencia da Barberino*, elegant treatments of classical legends (*Ambra* and *Corinto*) and a *sacra rappresentazione*. This heterogeneity makes his literary personality enigmatic, but some of his verse is, with that of ⇨ Poliziano and ⇨ Boiardo, among the best of the century. [DGR]

*Opere*, ed. A. Simioni (2 vols., repr. 1939); *Scritti scelti*, ed. E. Bigi (1955); Lind, *LPIR.*
R. Palmarocchi, *L. de' Medici* (Turin, 1941); Binni, *CI*; W. Roscoe, *The Life of L. de' M.* (1795); C. M. Ady, *L. dei M. and Renaissance Italy* (1955); *Minori*, i.

**Medina Medinilla, Pedro de** (Seville? 1575–E. Indies, before 1621). Spanish poet. Known for his 'Égloga en la muerte de Doña Isabel de Urbina' – the first wife of Lope de Vega, who preserved and printed the poem, which is in the style of Garcilaso but original in its rare rustic realism. [JMC]

Blecua, *FLE.*

**Medrano, Francisco de** (Seville 1570–Seville 1607). Spanish poet. A Jesuit who left the order. He translated Horace and imitated him in his *odas*. Some sonnets have a religious moral, and one seems to speak of mystical experience. His delicate poetry, published posthumously, has only lately been appreciated. [JMC]

Cohen, *PBSV.*
D. Alonso and S. Reckert, *Vida y obra de Medrano* (2 vols., Madrid, 1948, 1958); *LSS*, II (1946).

**Mehring, Walter** (Berlin 1896– ). German poet and dramatist. His satirically aggressive, sometimes scandalous poems appeared in Walden's *Der Sturm*, or were sung at Reinhardt's Berlin cabaret 'Schall und Rauch'; 1920, co-founder of the left-wing 'Politisches Cabaret'. His satirical drama *Der Kaufmann von Berlin* (1929) was banned after production (by E. Piscator), *Die Höllische Komödie* (1932) before production. Years of exile after 1933 ended (1941) in the U.S.A., where he published poems, *No Road Back* (N.Y., 1944) and *Die verlorene Bibliothek* (1952; tr. R. and C. Winston, *The Lost Library*, 1951), his famous 'autobiography of (20th-century) culture'. *Berlin – Dada* (1959) describes his connexions with Dada, though his own poems, especially *Arche Noah SOS* (1951), the selection *Der Zeitpuls fliegt* (1958) and the *Neues Ketzerbrevier* (*Balladen und Songs*) (1962), remain 'functionally' realistic and satirically political. [PB]

*DR*, LXXXV (1959).

**Meilhac, Henri** (Paris 1831–Paris 1897). French playwright and librettist. Immensely popular author (in collaboration with Ludovic Halévy, 1834–1908) of gay, witty and cynical drawing-room comedies (*Frou-Frou*, 1869; *La petite Marquise*, 1874) and of highly diverting libretti for operettas by Offenbach which distil something of the essential spirit of Second Empire Paris: *La Belle Hélène* (1865), *La Grande-Duchesse de Gérolstein* (1867), *La vie parisienne* (1866), etc. The work of this talented duo is marked by extravagant complication of plot, irreverent parody and gay inventiveness of situation. [SBJ]

*Théâtre de M. et Halévy* (8 vols., 1900–2).
H. Parigot, *Le théâtre d'hier* (1893); Doumic, *SI.*

**Meistersinger.** German lyric poets of the 14th, 15th and 16th centuries, whose activity is the historical continuation of the *Spruchdichtung* (gnomic poetry) of the 13th century. The appellation 'master' originally connoted the achievement of high poetic excellence; soon, however, it acquired a social meaning and came to designate individual groups of such 'masterly' versifiers who founded private poetic lodges in various south German towns. The subject-matter of their poems is moralistic and predominantly religious. They erected strict rules of poetic form whose observance was pedantically insisted upon, rules derived initially from *Töne* (strophic patterns linked with the form of the melody to which the poem was sung) composed by the 12 so-called 'old masters' – the 13th-century lyric poets (⇨ Walther von der Vogelweide,

⇨ Reinmar von Zweter, the ⇨ Marner, etc.) who represented for the Meistersinger the zenith of formal excellence. A Meistersinger poem was prefaced by an acknowledgement of the old *Ton* to which it was written. In the late 15th century freedom was given to compose in original *Töne* but the air of forced pedantry and heavy-handed didacticism remained.

⇨ Heinrich von Meissen is generally considered the first Meistersinger, and is the legendary founder of the first 'school', in Mainz, at which formal instruction in the craft of Meistersang was given. Among the most famous schools that subsequently sprang up are those at Augsburg, Ulm, Strassburg and Nuremberg. The Bavarian poet Muskatblüt (fl. first half of 15th century) was one of the most capable Meistersinger whose work has come down to us, while to Hans Folz (fl. 1510), who, like Rosenblüt, was also a writer of Shrovetide plays, belongs the credit for breaking away from the slavish imitation of the 'old masters' and instituting the composition of new and original *Töne*. The best known of all Meistersinger, however, is Hans ⇨ Sachs (1494–1576), who made his native Nuremberg the most famous centre of Meistersang. Sachs wrote over 4,000 *Meisterlieder*. This era marks the apogee of this remarkable art-form, and although individual schools survived through the 17th and 18th centuries, and even into the early 19th, their one-time power of attraction could never be revived. [RT]

Texts: K. Bartsch, *Meisterlieder der Kolmarer Handschrift* (1862); E. de Groote, *Lieder Muskatblüts* (1852); A. L. Mayer, *Meisterlieder des Hans Folz* (1908). Music: G. Münzer, *Das Singebuch des Adam Puschmann* (1906); P. Runge, *Die Sangesweisen der Colmarer Handschrift und die Liederhandschrift Donaueschingen* (1896).

A. Taylor, *The Literary History of Meistergesang* (N.Y., 1937); A. Taylor and F. Ellis, *A Bibliography of Meistergesang* (Bloomington, 1936); B. Nagel, *Der deutsche Meistersang* (Heidelberg, 1952); B. Nagel, *Meistersang* (Stuttgart, 1962).

**Melanchthon, Philipp,** Graecized pseud. of Philipp Schwarzerd (Bretten, Baden 1497–Wittenberg 1560). German humanist. A disciple of Erasmus and nephew of ⇨ Reuchlin, he played a dominant role in the Reformation, and was Professor of Greek at Wittenberg. A man of sharper, neater mind than Luther, he gave the new faith its dogmatic basis in the *Loci communes* (1521) and the *Confessio augustana* (1530; tr. 1536). His educational theories and activities earned him the title of 'Praeceptor Germaniae' and his foundation of humanistic gymnasia on the twin basis of the classics and Christianity set a permanent stamp of the German educational system. [WAC]

*Werke*, ed. R. Stupperich (6 vols., 1951ff.); *Opera*, ed. C. G. Bretsclineider, *Corpus Reformatorum*, 1–28.

L. Stern *et al.*, *P.M. – Humanist, Reformator, Praeceptor Germaniae* (2 vols., Berlin, 1963); R. Stupperich, *Der unbekannte Melanchthon* (Stuttgart, 1961).

**Meléndez Valdés, Juan** (Ribera del Fresno, Badajoz 1754–Montpellier 1817). Spanish poet, lawyer and politician. He began to make a name for himself as a poet in the seventies while still a student at the University of Salamanca, where he was encouraged in legal studies as well as in his literary pursuits by José ⇨ Cadalso and, in letters, by ⇨ Jovellanos. The large number of French works on all subjects he read and collected at the same period also contributed considerably to his intellectual development. But the relatively advanced ideas on the law which he began to acquire as a student did not meet with the approval of his more conservative colleagues when he became a professor at Salamanca in the eighties, and he left the university for legal posts at Saragossa and Valladolid before taking up a ministerial position in Madrid in 1798. Unfortunately his friendship with Jovellanos caused him to be banished at the same time as the latter, and some of his political ideas led to a further period of exile from the court in the early 1800s.

In his private life and poetry there is a dualism between willing submission to order and external discipline on the one hand and a more vigorous independent spirit on the other. His secret marriage to a woman ten years his elder and moments of political restraint illustrate the one side, while his acute sense of graphic values and the observations of the world of the senses which distinguish some of his poetry from the more conventional neo-classics, reflects the other. His readiness to speak out against social injustice and to advocate concrete reforms also found an occasional outlet in his literature as well as in his life. [ONVG]

*Poesías selectas*, ed. P. Salinas, CC; Blecua, *FLE*; Trend, *OBSV*.

W. Colford, *J.M.V.* (N.Y., 1942); G. Demerson, *Don J.M.V. et son temps* (Paris, 1962).

**Mell, Max** (Marburg/Drau 1882– ). Austrian novelist, dramatist and poet. Praised (excessively) by ⇨ Hofmannsthal for his idyllic folk poems and fictional accounts of peasant faith and simplicities, and for the popular religious folk-plays: *Das Apostelspiel* (1923; tr. M. V. White, *The Apostle Play*, 1934), *Das Schutzengelspiel* (1923), and *Das Nachfolge-Christi-Spiel* (1927). *Barbara Naderers Viehstand* (1914) and *Mein Bruder und Ich* (1924) are two of his best stories; *Gedichte* (1953) is a selection of his nature poems. [PB]

*Prosa, Dramen, Verse* (4 vols., Munich, 1962).
I. Emich, *M.M. Der Dichter und sein Werk* (Vienna, 1957).

**Mel'nikov, Pavel Ivanovich** (pseud. Andrei Pechersky, often known as Mel'nikov Pechersky) (Nizhny Novgorod 1819–Nizhny Novgorod 1883). Russian novelist and ethnographer. He was the son of a small landowner, and spent his childhood in a district inhabited by the communities of the Old Believers (⇨ Russian Literature in the 17th Century). He graduated from the University of Kazan', taught history at Perm', then became a civil servant and an official historiographer of the sect of the Old Believers. All his literary works depict the life of the Old Believers, the theme often treated by ⇨ Leskov, occasionally by ⇨ Gor'ky. His early stories, *Krasil'nikovy* (1852), *Staryye gody* (1852), *Medvezhiy Ugol* (1857) and others, belong to the liberal trend in Russian literature. His main literary work is a novel developed from his earlier story *Za Volgoy – V lesakh* (1868–74) and its sequel *Na gorakh* (1875–81). He depicts in these novels colourfully and truthfully the life of the communities of the Old Believers. The text is full of folk-songs, proverbs and legends (e.g. the legend of the lost holy city of Kityezh). All this makes interesting reading. There is, however, no attempt made to explain the psychological reasons for the fanatic adherence of the Old Believers to their faith.

Among other works of Mel'nikov are: *Knyazhna Tarakanova* (1868); *Iz proshlogo* (1868); *Belyye golubi* (1869). [MG]

*Polnoye sobraniye sochineniy* (7 vols., 1909); *V lesakh* (1956); *Na gorakh* (1956).

**Melo, Francisco Manuel de** (Lisbon 1608–Lisbon 1666). Portuguese historian, moralist, essayist, playwright, poet and statesman. His family belonged to the highest ranks of Portuguese nobility, but (Portugal being united with Spain) he was educated in Madrid and began his military career in the Spanish navy. Much of his youth was spent in active service or at the Court of Madrid, then one of the most active cultural centres in Europe. He was sent by the Spanish favourite Olivares to Portugal on a mission of conciliation after popular uprisings against onerous taxation, to Flanders with a Portuguese regiment to fight the Dutch on Spain's behalf, and to Catalonia to participate in the suppression of the 1640 Catalan rebellion. He recorded these events in his *Epanáforas de vária História Portuguesa* (1660, in Portuguese, ed. E. Prestage, 1931) and the *Historia de los Movimientos y Separación de Cataluña* (1645, in Spanish). After restoration of an independent Portuguese monarchy in December 1640, his nationality made him suspect to Olivares; when he defected to the cause of the Braganza King Joao IV, his former services to Spain made him equally suspect in the eyes of the Lisbon Court. After attempting briefly to serve the new regime as soldier and diplomat, he was arrested, imprisoned and eventually banished to Brazil. Returning to Portugal in 1658, he was finally restored to royal favour and undertook important diplomatic commissions. He was also associated with the Academia dos Generosos, one of the 'academies' devoted at this period to the advancement of taste and erudition.

Melo exemplifies the 'discreto' ideal so assiduously cultivated in the Iberian peninsula since the Renaissance. He was the nobleman par excellence, cultured in peace, courageous in war, and fundamentally attached to the values of a cosmopolitan aristocracy. As a writer he was prolific, both in Spanish and Portuguese. His prose contains the subtle conceits and *double-entendres* of the *conceptismo* then in vogue, but these are not allowed to disturb the general clarity and fluency of his style. In moralizing vein he produced a *Carta de Guia de Casados* (1651; ed. E. Prestage, in *Ocidente*, 1953–4) giving an extremely reactionary view of the proper relationship between man and wife, and pseudo-picaresque novelettes such as *Relógios Falantes* and *Escritório Avarento* (both included in the *Apólogos Dialogais* published posthumously in 1721), in which he attacked the vices of government and contemporary politics. For the theatre he composed a satirical comedy *Auto do Fidalgo Aprendiz* (1676), similar in genre to the contemporary Spanish *comedias* and in theme to Molière's *Le bourgeois gentilhomme*. He even ventured into literary criticism and his *Hospital das Letras* (likewise in the *Apólogos Dialogais*) is the first critical history of Portuguese and Spanish literature. If we add to the above his voluminous correspondence (*Cartas Familiares*), his poetry, much of which is unduly Gongoresque (⇨ Góngora) or over-intellectualized, his polemical writings and his historical works, we appreciate the extraordinary diversity of his talents. He did not leave a masterpiece, but he is the supreme representative of the cultured bilingual aristocracy so active in Portugal in the first half of the 17th century. [AJP]

*Apólogos Dialogais* (CSC, 2 vols.); *Cartas Familiares* (CSC) (selection); *Relógios Falantes* (TL).

E. Prestage, *D. F. M. de Melo – Esboço Biográfico* (Coimbra, 1914).

**Mena, Juan de** (Córdoba 1411–Torrelaguna 1456). Spanish poet. He studied in Rome and held important posts at the Castilian court. He wrote numerous courtly lyrics, an allegorical tribute to his friend the Marqués de ⇨ Santillana (*La coronación*), and translated a medieval prose version of the *Iliad* into Spanish. His chief work is *El laberinto de fortuna* (ed. J. M. Blecua, 1943), also called *Las trescientas* (1444), a long poem in heavily rhythmical *arte mayor* metre. Its structure is Dantesque and medieval, but Mena has important imitations of Virgil and Lucan and makes much use of Ovidian mythology, which look forward to Renaissance poetic practice. The poem is basically a comparison of ancients with moderns; the latter come out poorly, and he has a contemporary message for them. Much of the verse is angular, but there are fine sections about battles, forebodings of tragedy and the macabre. His language is heavily Latinized and lofty in tone; he was much imitated for nearly a century and was widely read in the 16th and early 17th centuries, almost alone among medieval Spanish poets. [CCS]

Poems complete in NBAE, xix, ed. R. Foulché-Delbosc; Trend, *OBSV*; Perry, *HASP*.

M. R. Lida de Malkiel, *J. de M.* (Mexico City, 1950).

**Menard, Louis** (Paris 1822–Paris 1901). French poet. One of the earliest ⇨ Parnassians (cf. *Poèmes*, 1855); his Hellenism and pagan 'religion' strongly influenced ⇨ Leconte de Lisle. His principal work (verse and prose) is *Rêveries d'un païen mystique* (1876), and in many others pursues characteristic 19th-century ideas of universal religion. He took part in the 1848 insurrections (described in *Prologue d'une révolution*, 1849, for which he was imprisoned). [WA]

**Menčetić, Šiško.** ⇨ Dalmatian and Dubrovnik Literature.

**Mendele, Mocher Seforim** (Shalom Jacov Abramovitch) (Minsk 1835–Odessa 1917). Hebrew and Yiddish author. Alternatively known as the grandfather of Hebrew and of Yiddish literature. There were three phases in his literary career. After the publication of his novel *Ha'avot ve'ha-Banim* in 1868 in Hebrew, he wrote only in Yiddish until 1886 when, partly with translations into Hebrew of his own writings, partly by writing new works, he reverted to Hebrew. But his greatest achievement was the transformation of the Yiddish language, hitherto the colloquial idiom of masses of Jews, into a highly sophisticated literary language. His short stories and novels were a new feature in Jewish life in Eastern Europe, full of colour, satire and gentle criticism. No one before him wrote about the beauty of the countryside in which his heroes and his readers lived. Unlike his predecessors among the *Maskilim* (enlightened) who largely wrote under the influence of German thinkers, Mendele was deeply influenced by Russian literature, though he was familiar with German literature as well. By choosing the pseudonym Mocher Seforim (the bookseller), he sought to assume the traditional role of the travelling Jewish bookseller of his time, that of carrier or disseminator of knowledge, both religious and secular, who at the same time was the link between the Jewish communities dispersed as they were all over Russia and Poland. He travelled far and wide in Russia in his youth but in 1881 settled down as director of the Hebrew school in Odessa where, with the exception of a few short visits abroad, he spent the last 30 years of his life. During this time Odessa had become the centre of Jewish cultural and national activity and Jewish life and letters began to mirror the intensity of Jewish national aspirations largely as a reaction to increasing persecution and pressure. But Mendele, in daily touch with the leaders of the Zionist movement, never abandoned his belief in the permanence of the Jewish Diaspora. He therefore advocated the necessity of cultural, educational and social autonomy for the Jewish minority in the Diaspora. [EE]

In Hebrew: *Collected Works* (Berlin, 1922); *Michtav al davar ha-hinuch* (1856); *Mishpat Shalom* (1860); *Toldot he-Teva* (3 vols., 1862–72); *Sippurai Maasiot* (1881); *Ba-yamim ha-hem* (1899); *Massaot Binyamin Ha-shlishi* (1878). In Yiddish: *Collected Works* (17 vols., Cracow, 1911–12); *Fishke der Krummer* (1869; tr. G. Stillman, *Fishke the Lame*, 1960); *Die Takse* (1869); *Die Klatshe* (1873); *Der Prisiv* (1884); *Dos Vunsh-fingerl* (1899).

S. Gorelik, *Mendele* (Berlin, 1920); D. Patterson, *The Foundations of Modern Hebrew Literature* (London, 1961) (with translations); Klausner, *HMHL*; Waxman, *HJL*; Roback, *SYL*.

**Mendès, Catulle** (Bordeaux 1841–St Germain-en-Laye 1909). French poet, novelist and dramatist. Of Jewish origin. He was briefly married to Judith Gautier (daughter of Théophile), later to poetess Jane (née Matte). In 1859 he founded the *Revue Fantaisiste* to which the Parnassians first contributed, and told the history of their movement in *La légende du Parnasse contemporain* (1884). Acclaimed for his metrically skilful early verse, *Philoméla* (1864), and a Swedenborgian epic, *Hespérus* (1869), he succeeded also with stylized plays (e.g. *Médée*, 1898) and opera libretti (e.g. *Ariane*, 1906, with Massenet). He supported the Wagnerian cult (see his *Richard Wagner*, 1886, etc.) writing a novel about him and Ludwig II: *Le Roi Vierge* (1881). His prolific fiction has a characteristic element of erotic fantasy. [WA]

J. F. Herlihy, *C.M.* (Paris, 1936).

**Mendes Leal, José da Silva** (Lisbon 1818–Sintra 1886). Portuguese dramatist and pamphleteer. A successful diplomat and politician, he also won acclaim in the literary field, an acclaim which has not stood the test of time owing to the largely imitative and unoriginal nature of his work. He began by writing declamatory historical melodramas in the manner of Dumas *père*, his first production *Os Dois Renegados* (1839) achieving a resounding success which he never again equalled. There followed in rapid succession throughout the next decade *O Homem da Máscara Negra*, *O Pajem de Aljubarrota*, *D. Ausenda* and *D. Maria de Lencastre*, all of which vied with the plays of ⇨ Garrett and which surprisingly won the latter's approbation. Ever attentive to French modes he eventually switched to writing social drama in imitation of Dumas *fils* and Augier: *Os Homens de Mármore* (1854), *O Homem de Ouro* (1855), *Pobreza Envergonhada* (1858), *Pedro* (1861). There followed another tedious historical play, *Egas Moniz* (1861), and a period-comedy, *Os Primeiros Amores de Bocage* (1865). He experimented unsuccessfully with narrative fiction and was at his most effective as a pamphleteer and political journalist, his outstanding work in this *genre* being his *História da Guerra do Oriente* (1855), a vigorous piece of reporting on the Crimean War. He also published two verse collections, *Cânticos* (1858) and *Poesias* (1859), which enjoyed a certain vogue and which contain bombastic specimens of Ultra-Romantic heroic verse in the manner of Victor Hugo. [RCW]

**Mendes Pinto, Fernão** (? Montemor-o-Velho *c.* 1514–Almada 1583). Portuguese adventurer, author of the *Peregrinaçam* (1614; tr. H. Cogan, 1653), one of the few Portuguese books to circulate widely and repeatedly (in translations) beyond the national frontiers. The son of impoverished parents, after a picaresque boyhood and adolescence, Pinto sailed for the East in 1537. He led a roving and adventurous life in Asia for the next sixteen years, mainly in Indochina and the Far East. On the point of returning to Portugal with a sizeable fortune in 1554, he became a Jesuit novice in a fit of contrition for his misspent life, after seeing the arrival of the body of his former friend, St Francis Xavier, and attending its sumptuous interment at Goa. He then accompanied the Jesuit Provincial, Belchior Nunes Barreto, on an abortive diplomatic mission to Japan, where Pinto left the Society, apparently at his own request. He returned to Portugal in 1558, still with sufficient funds to marry and to buy a *quinta* at Almada, where he spent the remainder of his life writing his famous book.

Ever since its posthumous publication, the *Peregrinaçam* has lacked neither detractors nor defenders, and controversy over the author and his work still rages unabated in the learned world. Pinto's first editor, the Portuguese chronicler, Francisco de Andrade, and his first translator, the

Spanish chronicler, Herrera Maldonado, both confessedly tampered with the text, though probably not to any important extent. Proof-reading of the first edition, if carried out at all, obviously left a great deal to be desired; and we cannot tell how far Pinto's first two editors and the censors of his manuscript are responsible for some of the more palpable blunders and self-contradictions. Many of the facts and dates given in the work are demonstrably wrong and others are clearly taken from published works available to the author, such as Fr Gaspar da Cruz, O.P., *Tractado da China* (1570). But although critics continue to disagree violently about the factual content of the *Peregrinaçam*, there is general agreement nowadays that it is a literary masterpiece. It is also the only book of its kind, for, as Maurice Collis states, Pinto 'had no master and he has had no disciples; no book composed like the *Peregrination* was written before him, nor has any been written since'. [CRB]

G. Schurhammer, S.J., *Fernão Mendez Pinto und seine Peregrinaçam* (Leipzig, 1926); Georges Le Gentil, *Fernão Mendes Pinto, un précurseur de l'exotisme au XVI siècle* (Paris, 1947); Maurice Collis, *The Grand Peregrination* (1949); A. J. Saraiva in *História da Cultura em Portugal*, iii (Lisbon, 1962); Domingos Maurício, S.J., 'A Peregrinaçam de F. M. Pinto e algumas opinioes peregrinas', in *Brotéria* LXXIV (1962).

**Mendoza, Antonio Hurtado de.** ⇨ Hurtado de Mendoza.

**Mendoza, Íñigo de** (late 15th cent). Spanish poet. Franciscan at the court of Ferdinand and Isabel, who wrote a *Vita Christi* in *coplas* (1482); a poem on the subject of women, good and evil; and fragments intended as completion of the *Vita*. Of these the *Lamentación a la quinta angustia, cuando Nuestra Señora tenía a Nuestro Señor en los brazos* is outstanding, as is also his *Romance*, to be sung by the Seraphim. Satires accused him of leading a worldly life. (⇨ Montesino.) [JMC]

Blecua, *FLE*; Cohen, *PBSV*; Trend, *OBSV*. Wardropper, *HPL*.

**Mercantini, Luigi** (Ripatransone 1821–Palermo 1872). Italian patriot and poet. After playing an enthusiastic part in the events of 1847–9, he went into voluntary exile until 1852 to avoid Austrian persecution. As a poet, he was distinguished only by the sheer popularity of his patriotic poems, *Patriotti all'Alpi andiamo* (1848), *La spigolatrice di Sapri* (1857) and the famous *Inno di Garibaldi*, commissioned in 1859. [RHC]

*Canti di L.M.*, ed. G. Mestica (1885); Dionisotti, *OBIV*.

U. Biscottini, *Poeti del Risorgimento* (Leghorn, 1932).

**Mercier, Louis Sébastien** (Paris 1740–Paris 1814). French journalist and playwright. He was an early rebel against classical and aristocratic taste: he wrote *drames* based on humble everyday life, in the Diderot manner (*Le déserteur*, 1770; *La brouette du vinaigrier*, 1775), pre-romantic historical plays (*Childéric Ier*, 1774; *Molière*, 1776) and Shakespearian adaptations (*Les tombeaux de Vérone*, 1782; *Timon d'Athènes*, 1794) – all now of exclusively historical interest. Of more enduring appeal is his *Tableau de Paris* (1781; abridged tr. H. Simpson, 1933), a rambling collection of anecdotal material which takes the reader into every corner of the Parisian scene of his day. [WHB]

L. Béclard, *M.* (Paris, 1903); P. C. Monselet, *Oubliés et dédaignés* (Păris, 1885); H. T. Patterson, *Poetic Genesis: S.M. into Victor Hugo* (*Studies on Voltaire and the 18th Century*, xi, Geneva, 1960).

**Merezhkovsky, Dmitriy Sergeyevich** (St Petersburg 1865–Paris 1941). Russian novelist, poet and critic. In 1889 he married the poet Z. ⇨ Gippius. His collection of poems *Simvoly* (1892) and his article *O prichinakh upadka i o novykh techeniyakh sovremennoy literatury* ('On the Causes of the Decline of Modern Russian literature and of New Trends within It', 1893) pioneered the symbolist movement in Russia. He was widely read in classical and European literature and he led the trend towards cosmopolitanism that characterized Russian art at the beginning of the century. In 1903–4 he edited, with P. Pertsov, the review *Novyy Put'*, an important predecessor of *Vesy*.

He wrote little poetry after 1895, when he turned to prose. His historical trilogy *Khristos i Antikhrist* (1896–1905; tr. B. Guerney, 1928–31), on which his fame rests, attempts to reconcile the Greek cult of the body with the Christian cult of the spirit. This taste for antitheses characterizes his criticism too, notably his essays on Tolstoy and Dostoyevsky (1901), Gogol' (1909) and Lermontov (1909).

After 1917, he opposed the Bolsheviks

and he emigrated to Paris in 1919. Here his hatred of Bolshevism and contempt for the West's failure to suppress the Revolution eventually led him into a near Fascist position. He continued to write historical novels, among them *Napoleon* (1929), *Iisus neizvestnyy* (1932–3; tr. H. Matheson, *Jesus the Unknown*, 1937) and *Dante* (1939), but these works are invariably based on his old theme of Christ and Antichrist and their confrontation in the contemporary world; the somewhat pretentious style tends to undermine his noble intentions. [RDBT]

*Sobraniye sochineniy* (17 vols., 1911–13).
Struve, *RLI*; *SEER*, 36 (1957) and 42 (1963).

**Meri, Veijo** (Viipuri 1928– ). Finnish novelist and short-story writer. One of the outstanding younger writers, he is preoccupied with the problem of war. Though of the post-war generation, he is well acquainted with garrison life (his father was a non-commissioned officer). His choice of theme reflects the universal post-war mood of disgust with the senselessness of war and impatience with the idealism in which it tends to be cloaked. He believes that in war there is no such thing as heroism; chance pushes up against a man with a weapon in his hand, and makes him behave in such a way that a 'heroic deed' results. The fighting line is only a nominal frontier: destinies and the helplessness of the individual are the same on either side of it. This theme also appears in *Irralliset* (1959) and some of his other peacetime stories. The looseness of social ties, the decreasing importance of 'values' in human life, and the prevailing feeling of insecurity and distress are the problems most often treated in his books. The chain of causation, in peace as in war, can have the oddest beginnings and end in the oddest effects. Such a view of reality obviously lends itself readily to a grotesquely humorous treatment. His odd world is less brutally grotesque than that of Gogol', his great master, but equally fantastic in its oddity. He has been widely translated. [AK]

*Sujut* (1961; tr. into French in preparation); *Peiliin piirretty nainen* (1963); *Manillaköysi* (1957; French tr. Sylvain and Bolgár, *Une histoire de corde*, Paris, 1962); *Tukikohta* (1964) (a novel and a play); *Sotamies Jokisen vihkiloma* (1965 (play); *Everstin autonkuljettaja* (1966) (novel).

**Meriluoto, Aila** (Pieksämäki 1924– ). Finnish poetess. Her first volume of poems, *Lasimaalaus* (1946), showed a surprising maturity and had an unprecedented success with critics and public alike. Its appeal lay in a boldly virginal lyricism and a firm, uncompromising tone, combined with great clarity of expression. *Sairas tyttö tanssii* (1952) had the same intensity, but since then, under the impact of fresh influences (including Rilke) her poetry has become more restless and the problem of expression more troublesome. Of her translations, the most notable so far is that of Harry Martinson's *Aniara*. [RV]

*Pahat unet* (1958); *Portaat* (1961); *Asumattomiin* (1963); *Tuoddaris* (1965); Allwood, *TCSP*; Ollilainen, *SF*; Tompur *VF*.

**Mérimée, Prosper** (Paris 1803–Cannes 1870). French novelist. The son of an artist, he began his literary career with two hoaxes, the first *Le théâtre de Clara Gazul* (1825), the works of an imaginary Spanish woman dramatist, and the second, *La Guzla* (1827), fake translations of Illyrian national songs and poems. The latter were so good that they took in Pushkin, who had an amiable correspondence with Mérimée after he discovered the trick. He then published anonymously a novel in the popular historical style (of Scott), *Chronique du règne de Charles IX* (1829), set at the time of the Massacre of Saint Bartholomew. His first collection of tales, the short novel form of which he was a master, appeared under the title *Mosaïque* in 1833 and containes such stories as *Mateo Falcone* and *Le vase étrusque*. He brought a new flavour to the Romantic and historical themes he treated; savagery and extremes of passion are tempered by his objective manner of telling the tale and by his irony (cf. Pushkin, whose similar tales he helped to introduce to the west through his translations). Another collection, *Colomba* (tr. E. Marielle, Penguin Classics, 1965), came out in 1841, containing the Corsican-set tale of the title and *La Vénus d'Ille*. *Carmen* (tr. E. Marielle, 1965), his most famous work on which Bizet's opera was based, appeared in *Nouvelles* (1843). He also had a busy official life. He became Inspector General of Historical Monuments in 1834 and travelled throughout France classifying buildings and sites of interest and producing forceful reports on the need for preservation. He was a lifelong friend of the Empress Eugénie, became a senator during the

Second Empire and was the most prominent writer connected with the regime. His literary friendships ranged from Stendhal in his youth to Turgenev, who helped to maintain his interest in Russian history and literature. He lost much of his creative powers after the end of his long relationship with Mme Valentine Delessert in 1854. After years of ill-health he died heart-broken by the defeat at Sedan. Another friend of his was Mme de Beaulaincourt, the model for Proust's Mme de Villeparisis. Seven volumes of his important *Correspondance générale* up to 1855 have been published. [WA]

*Romans et contes*, ed. H. Martineau (Pléiade, 1951).

P. Trahard, *P.M.* (Paris, 3 vols., 1915-30); R. Baschet, *Du romantisme au second empire: M.* (Paris, 1959); A. Billy, *M.* (Paris, 1959); P. Léon, *M. et son temps* (Paris, 1962).

**Merrill, Stuart** (Hampstead, Long Island 1863–Versailles 1915). American-born French poet. He spent his childhood in Paris, returning to America to study law at Columbia University. Yielding to literary impulses while still in the States, he published first a collection of French verse, *Les gammes* (1887), then *Pastels in prose*, a volume of translations from recent French poets, including Banville, Baudelaire, Huysmans, Mallarmé, H. de Régnier and Villiers de l'Isle-Adam. In 1890 he settled in France and played an active role in the renewal of poetry, publishing at the same time numerous articles on French writers in leading American journals. His next poems, *Les fastes* (1891), are written, for the most part, in finished quatrains of short lines and have the qualities of an unemphatic preciosity; but some are incrusted with gem-like images in a style too *recherché* for our taste today. As he matured a deeper note entered his work. During his stay in the U.S.A., he had become interested in socialist ideas and aspirations and on returning to France he devoted a book of poems, *Les quatre saisons* (1900), to them. But although, like his compatriot ⇨ Vielé-Griffin, he avoided decadence, he left nothing strong enough to persist in face of the anxieties expressed in subsequent world poetry or the immense advance in irregular personal styles. [PMJ]

M. L. Henry, *La contribution d'un Américain au symbolisme français: S.M.* (Paris, 1927); Martino, *LF*; *Parnasse et symbolisme (1850–1900)* (Paris, 1935).

**Mesonero Romanos, Ramón de,** pseud. 'El Curioso Parlante' (Madrid 1808–Madrid 1882). Spanish essayist. His *Manual de Madrid* (1831) is full of interesting observation and curious research about the city. His articles on its social life are collected as *Panorama matritense* (1835–8) and *Escenas matritenses* (1842). He was one of the first and most influential of the 19th-century *costumbristas*, a good-humoured bourgeois who gently mocked the new-fangled and captured with nostalgic precision the ways of a society fast disappearing.

*Obras* (1881); *Escenas matritenses*, ed. F. C. Sainz de Robles (1945).

J. F. Montesinos, *Costumbrismo y novela* (Valencia, 1960).

**Messenius, Johannes** (Vadstena 1579–Uleåborg 1636). Swedish dramatist and poet. A professor of law at Upsala until imprisoned for plotting against Gustavus's government. His 6 historical plays (first edited Upsala 1886), part of a projected series of 50, contain some good ballad-style lyrics. He inspired several imitators, like Nikolaus Catonius, Andreas Prytz, Jacobus Rondeletius, whose dramas kept theatre alive in schools and university for a generation. Messenius also wrote a history of Sweden in Latin and two rhyme-chronicles in Swedish.

*Samlade Dramer*, ed. H. Schück (1886–8).

**Metastasio, Pietro** (Rome 1698–Vienna 1782). Italian poet and melodramatist. Son of a shopkeeper. Perhaps the most popular representative of Arcadianism, his two *canzonette – A Nice* and *La partenza* – are among the finest Arcadian poems; 40 editions of his works appeared during his lifetime. His first *poesie* (1717) included the tragedy *Giustino* (written at 14). The leading lady of the dramatic oratorio *Gli Orti Esperidi* (1721) – Marianna Benti Bulgarelli – fell in love with him, provided music lessons and encouraged him to write his first true melodrama, *Didone abbandonata* (1723; tr. J. G. Fucilla, *Dido Forsaken*, 1952) – a genre in which he excelled, elevating the drama so as to make it almost independent of the mediocre music that accompanied it (40 composers attempted fitting music for the *Didone*). With pretensions to the simplicity and dramatic tension of Greek tragedy, his mixture of heroism and inevitable galantry was nevertheless more akin to the French classical theatre – though lacking its psychological reality and intensity. He became Imperial Poet in 1730 and moved to Vienna, continuing to write melodramas but also an increasing amount of occasional poetry. With the decline of his inspiration he turned to a more scholarly study of classical authors, translating and commenting on Aristotle and Horace. His criticisms of the Aristotelian unities of Time and Place anticipated the views of Manzoni. [RHC]

*Tutte le opere*, ed. B. Brunelli (5 vols., 1943–54); *Teatro*, ed. R. Bacchelli (1962); sel. tr. J. Hoole (1767, 1800).

L. Russo, *M.* (Bari, 1945); C. Varese, *Saggio sul M.* (Florence, 1950); M. Apollonio, *M.* (Brescia, 1950); A. Trigiani, *Il teatro raciniano e i melodrammi di P.M.* (Turin, 1951); R. Giazotto, *Poesia melodrammatica e pensiero critico del '700* (Milan, 1952); W. Binni, *L'Arcadia e il M.* (Florence, 1963); Binni, *CI*, ii; *Minori*, iii.

**Meyer, Conrad Ferdinand** (Zürich 1825–Kilchberg, Zürich 1898). Swiss writer. From a wealthy patrician family, he long remained closely attached to his mother and sister, and did not marry until he was 50. At 27, and again at the end of his life, he suffered from acute melancholic depressions. He was brought up partly in French; only after the Prussian victory in 1871 did he decide to write in German.

His prose writings, mostly historical in subject, are no longer as highly esteemed as they were in the first decades of this century: psychology now makes us suspect his great 'renaissance' personages may be fantasy compensations for his own velleities, while recent history has shown up his cult of 'amoral' greatness. The novel *Jürg Jenatsch, eine Bündnergeschichte*, a considerable success on its publication in 1876, tells of the high adventures and gory death of a Swiss Lutheran parson of the early 17th century, whose heroic life is divided among patriotism, passion and Protestantism. In a scene before the altar of a Venetian church (Book ii, Chapter 3) are assembled all the elements of historical romance: a group of youthful warriors under a picture by 'maestro Titiano', seering amorous glances behind veils of black lace. Yet what his *tableaux* recall is not Titian but Hans Makart, whose luxuriant costume canvasses and stage décors were all the rage in the Second German Empire; the prose is not free from theatricalities, and an excess of verbs expressing violent emotion gives it the effect of breathlessness.

Of all the interpretations the life of St Thomas à Beckett has received, *Der Heilige* (1879) is surely the least commensurate with its subject, the conflict between King and Archbishop being explained by the former's seduction of the latter's daughter. *Der Schuss von der Kanzel* (1878, part of the collection *Kleine Novellen*, 1883), the story of a hunting parson, has touches of the same laconic humour which relieved some of the bathos of *Jürg Jenatsch. Die Hochzeit des Mönchs* (1884) and *Die Versuchung des Pescara* (1887), in medieval settings, explore again the 'great personality' worsted by a fate whose impact is echoed in the hero's conscience. *Zwanzig Balladen von einem Schweizer* (1864, revised in *Gedichte*, 1882) contain historical themes similar to those of his Novellen. Most of these stories are cast in the form of 'Rahmennovellen'; the 'frame-work' of a first-person narrator enables him not only 'to keep the subject [of the story] at a distance from myself and thus... to soften the harshness of the fable', it also makes it plausible for him to dispense with a moral judgement.

His lyrical poems belong to the *fin de siècle* and occasionally point the way beyond. Their short, firmly rhythmic lines are built from images in which natural and human objects blend effortlessly in the evocation of lyrical moods intimating the enticement of death. Dark surfaces and landscapes are briefly illuminated by sharp streaks of colour ('Auf dem Canal Grande', 'Erntegewitter'), a mood of sultry repose or melancholy issues in a moment of clarity and insight ('Schwüle', 'Eingelegte Ruder') – the very contrasts which in his prose make for melodrama are here perfectly contained and balanced. A sonnet-like impression of a nocturnal journey on the Lake of Zürich, 'Im Spätboot', envelops a moment of mystery, and again the poem ends on a note at once melancholy and enticing, 'Schmerz und Lust erleiden sanften Tod'.

Such poems as 'Die Felswand', 'Zwei Segel', 'Schwarzschattene Kastanie', 'Der römische Brunnen', 'Möwenflug', retrace objects in the outside world in such a way that their contours emerge as both precise and meaningful, as both reality and discrete symbols of reality. What these poems intimate is that near-identity of thing, word and experience which is characteristic of the imagist poetry of a later age (⇨ Rilke). [JPS]

*Sämtliche Werke*, ed. H. Zeller and A. Zäch (1958–63).

H. Maync, *C.F.M. und sein Werk* (Leipzig, 1925); A. Zäch, *C.F.M.* (Bern, 1945); R. Faesi, *C.F.M.* (Frauenfeld, 1948); H. Henel, *The Poetry of C.F.M.* (Madison, Wisconsin, 1954); L. Hohenstein, *C.F.M.* (Bonn, 1957); W. D. Williams, *The Stories of C.F.M.* (1962).

**Meyrink, Gustav,** pseud. of G. Meyer (Vienna 1868–Starnberg 1932). Austrian novelist. He lived for many years in Prague and converted from Protestantism to Buddhism. His grotesque fantasy-stories (three volumes of *Sonderbare Geschichten* appeared in 1909 as *Des deutschen Spiessers Wunderhorn*) are partly anti-bourgeois satire, partly romantic occultism. There are echoes of E. T. A. ⇨ Hoffmann, E. A. Poe, and similarities to ⇨ Kafka, especially in his best-known novel *Der Golem* (1915; tr. M. Pemberton, *The Golem*, 1928) incorporating his Prague experiences. His vision has apocalyptic overtones appropriate to world war in *Das grüne Gesicht* (1916) and *Walpurgisnacht* (1917). *An der Schwelle des Jenseits* (1923) is a confessional-philosophical work. [LL]

*Gesammelte Werke* (6 vols., 1917).
M.-E. Thierfelder, *Das Weltbild G.M.s* (Munich, 1953); E. Frank, *G.M.* (1957).

**Michaëlis, Karin** (Randers 1872–Copenhagen 1950). Danish novelist and short-story writer. Wife of Sophus Michaëlis, a Danish poet, she spent much time in the U.S.A. She early enjoyed international fame with stories like *Barnet* (1901; tr. J. N. Laurvik, *The Child: Andrea*, 1904) (translated into 15 languages); her greatest success came with the novel *Den farlige Alder* (1910; tr. B. Marshall, *The Dangerous Age*, 1912) about the erotic crisis of a woman in her forties. Also well known are *Elsie Lindtner* (tr. B. Marshall, 1912), *Glædens Skole* (tr. A. Skovgaard-Petersen, *The Governor*, 1912), *Mette Trap og hendes Unger* (tr. G.I. Colbron, *Venture's End*, 1927), *Den grønne Ø* (tr. R. Fyleman, *The Green Island*, 1935), *Little Troll* (written in English by the author and L. Sorsby, N.Y., 1946), and the once so popular 'Bibi'-books for teenagers (tr. R. Fyleman, 1934–5). Her own autobiography, *Vidunderlige Verden*, was written 1948–50. [ELB]

**Michaux, Henri** (Namur 1899– ). Belgian author. During a solitary childhood, he read mystics and symbolist poetry. His father forbade him to become a priest, and he travelled to South America and Asia as a sailor, bringing back travel notes showing enormous gifts of description (*Ecuador*, 1929, *Un barbare en Asie*, 1932). Encouraged by ⇨ Supervielle, he began publishing in Paris, where he settled in 1937 as director of a mystical review, *Hermès*. His first lyrical poetry (*Qui je fus*, 1927) shows the talents of a novelist and a moralist as well as of a poet; it is broadened in *La nuit remue* (1931), *Apparitions* (1946) and *Mouvements* (1954). He investigates the meanderings of the inner daydreaming mind (*Mes propriétés*, 1929, *Passages*, 1950), sometimes distorted by illness or drugs into hallucinations (*Épreuves, Exorcismes*, 1945); appeals against the crushing of the individual by society (*Un certain Plume*, 1930); parodies the absurd world in grotesque Gulliver-like fantasies (collected in *Ailleurs*, 1948). A seminal and entirely independent poet, he has achieved on his own the most ambitious aims of surrealism. His main theme, the conflict between inner and outer worlds, appears in penetrating quests into swarming mental facts, an estrangement of everyday objects and situations, and a naturalization of the fantastic. He has created a poetic character, *Plume*, the defencelesss featherweight man oppressed by tyrannical fellows and hardly master of his own personality – and reacted against him: first, cultivating lucidity and self-control almost as a mystic, and second, tailoring the outside world, sometimes violently, to wandering but not irresponsible requirements of his imagination. His prose is direct, clear, rhythmical, bubbling with maxims and verbal humour, poetic in its piercing metaphors. It includes drawings – he believes his painting more expressive than his poetry. [CLC]

*H.M. Selected Writings*, ed. R. Ellmann (London, 1952) (bilingual edition of *L'espace du dedans*, 1944, a 'definitive' collection of all the previous books).
P. de Coulon: *H.M. poète de notre société* (Neufchâtel, 1950).

**Michelangelo Buonarroti** (Caprese 1475–Rome 1564). Italian sculptor, architect, painter and poet. Apprenticed in Florence first to the Ghirlandaios and then to the sculptor Bertoldo, he attracted the attention of Lorenzo de' Medici and lived for a time in his palace, meeting there many writers and artists. Before the expulsion of Piero de' Medici in 1494 he left Florence, and in 1496 arrived in Rome. During this stay he sculpted the St Peter 'Pietà', and after returning to Florence in 1501 produced his 'David'. From now on, both in Florence and Rome he was engaged in some of his greatest long-term projects – from 1505 the tomb of Julius II, from 1508 the Sistine frescoes, from 1516 San Lorenzo and later the Medici chapel. In 1529 he was employed by the Florentine republicans as military engineer to fortify the city against the expelled Medici, but after their restoration he could still work for Clement VII and moved to Rome. In 1533 began his friendship with Tomaso de' Cavalieri and in 1538 that with Vittoria ◊ Colonna, to both of whom he wrote many poems platonic in tone. In 1541 he completed 'The Last Judgement', and his last years saw him engaged on the Paoline Chapel frescoes and his architectural work at St Peter's.

The writings of Michelangelo (*Rime*, 1st edn., 1623; ed. V. Piccoli, 1930; ed. G. Ceriello, 1954; ed. E. Girardi, 1967; tr. J. Tusiani, in *The Complete Poems*, 1961; and *Lettere*, 1st edn. G. Milanesi, 1875; ed. G Papini, 1910; tr. E. H. Ramsden, 1964) are a lesser expression of his genius. Many poems are incomplete fragments, but, in a century when the lyric is characterized by elegant form and conventional content, the best stand out by virtue of their dynamic, if jagged power. Despite their frequent lack of technical accomplishment, the resonance of an ultimate Dantesque or Shakespearian statement often lurks within them. Berni, contrasting him with the conventional Petrarchists of the time, observed: 'He says things and you say words.'

The *Lettere* (about 500 in number, covering the period 1496 – 1563) are for the most part personal notes to relatives, though a few are to notables like Vasari or Duke Cosimo. Unpretentious in tone, they deal simply and unaffectedly with the most humble, practical family questions. [DGR]

*Il Carteggio di M.*, ed. P. Barocchi, R. Ristori (1965f.); Lind, *LPIR*.

J. A. Symonds, *The Life of M.B.* (1892); F. Rizzi, *M. poeta* (Milan, 1924); G. G. Ferrero, *Il Petrarchismo del Bembo e le rime di M.* (Turin, 1935); H. Friedrich, *Epochen der italienischen Lyrik* (Frankfurt a.M., 1964); W. Binni, *M. scrittore* (Rome, 1965); R. J. Clements, *The Poetry of M.* (N.Y., 1965). *Minori*, i.

**Mickiewicz, Adam** (Zaosie/Nowogródek 1798–Constantinople 1855). Polish poet and 'national bard'. Chiefly known abroad as author of the epic poem *Pan Tadeusz* (1834; prose tr. G. R. Noyes, 1930). Born in the Lithuanian part of Poland, he was later to draw on his childhood memories to attain epic calm and distance. But already as a young man he made his University town, Vilna, the capital of the Polish romantic movement, borrowing themes from Lithuanian folklore for his early ballads and romances, which he collected in a first volume (*Poezje Tom pierwszy*, 1822).

These and other exercises in the new style, whether lyrical or narrative, were too self-conscious to be much disturbed by passion, but a sudden change came about in 1823 with the trial of Vilna students, in which he was implicated. Deported to Russia, he was in fact admitted to the best society, became friends with Pushkin, had love affairs, visited the Crimea. His book of sonnets, *Sonety* (Moscow, 1826), shows the quick stages in the process of relating new experience to his experiments with form. Adaptations from Petrarch appear alongside freshly recorded moods of love, followed by the confident display of artistry in the Crimean sonnets, where the sea and the mountains pulsate with energy and the condensed language glitters with oriental words.

Yet he could not forget his status as political deportee. He tried to outwit the censor with a cautionary medieval tale about patriotic revenge through treason (*Konrad Wallenrod*, 1828). In 1829 he was allowed to leave Russia and after a stay in Italy and Germany became an exile in Paris, aspiring to the role of national prophet. Some of the direct and bitter observations he had made in Russia were later added in the form of verse *reportage* to the third part of his play *Dziady* (1832; tr. C. Potocki of Montalk, *Forefathers*, 1944). In this play he traced back his mystical genesis to the trial and imprisonment in Vilna, and by extending the real events and people into the sphere of demons and angels, he sought to create an all-embracing romantic drama. From native folklore he took the cult of the dead, to which the title refers, and the character of Upiór, symbolizing an indefinable union of life and death. The whole work, seemingly formless, has a strange logic of its own.

Mickiewicz wanted *Dziady* to be his major achievement, and when he began *Pan Tadeusz*, he thought of it in terms of an idyllic tale; but it quickly took on epic dimensions. The village life of the Lithuanian gentry and Napoleon's campaign against Russia did not belong to a remote past, but to a time within memory. The result is that today *Pan Tadeusz* seems simultaneously archaic and modern, homely and exotic, and this perhaps explains its authority and its undeniable readability. Written in 13-syllable verse, the standard Polish metre, it sounds as convincing in descriptive passages as in dialogue. The romantic irony in the narrative is often turned against romanticism itself.

After *Pan Tadeusz*, Mickiewicz lived on for twenty years but wrote very little. His infatuation with mysticism of a cranky kind and the mental illness of his wife affected his imaginative powers. From 1840 to 1844 he lectured on Slavonic literatures at the Collège de France. He died during the Crimean War while on a mission in Turkey. [JP]

*Dziela* (1955); *Selected Poems*, ed. C. Mills (N.Y., 1956); *New Selected Poems*, ed. C. Mills (N.Y., 1957); D. Davie, *The Forests of Lithuania* (1959) (adaptations from *Pan Tadeusz*); *Pan Tadeusz*, tr. K. Mackenzie (1964); Peterkiewicz and Singer, *FCPP*.

M. Czapska, *La vie de M.* (Paris, 1931); W. Weintraub, *The Poetry of A.M.* (The Hague, 1954); *A.M. in World Literature*, ed. Lednicki (Berkeley, Calif., 1956).

**Mihaylovski, Stoyan** (Elena 1856–Sofia 1927). Bulgarian satirical poet. Like Velichkov, his contemporary and fellow-member of the '⇨Vazov circle', he was educated at the Constantinople lycée. He returned finally from his law studies in France in 1883 to a chequered career of senior posts in law, government and the university. Combatting evil by pen became his obsession. A restless, often vitriolic pessimist, he assumed in the first decades of Bulgarian independence the role of national tribune, relentlessly and often ingeniously castigating every evil he could detect – there were plenty – in contemporary government, society and press through a series of acidly scathing works such as *Poema na zloto* (1889), *Nashite pisachi i gazetari* (1893), *Filosoficheski i satiricheski soneti* (1895) and his most notable satire *Kniga za bălgarskiya narod* (1897), placed devastatingly in a Turkish setting. No term of vituperation, Bulgarian or borrowed, was spared in these attacks.

He introduced into Bulgarian verse a new range of intellectual and moral motifs, which are at their most readable in his original fables and forthright *pensées* ('Life and Literature' and 'Apothegms'). A full exposition of his thought is contained in his studies, on 'The Philosophy of Modern Bulgarian History' and 'The Decline and Collapse of States', which comprise *Metapolitika* (1940).

He edited the journals *Sofiyanets* (1879), *Narodny glas* (1880), *Nov zhivot* (1901–12) and, finally, *Napred* ('Forward', 1919), an attempt to rally and reorientate his country after a decade of war and defeat. [VP]

*Neizdadeni săchineniya* (i, 1940; ii, 1941); *Săbrani basni* (1939); *Izbrani proizvedeniya* (1960); Pinto, *BPV*.

I. Bogdanov, *S.M.* (*1856–1927*) (Sofia, 1947) and *S.M. kratka biografiya* (Sofia, 1947); Manning and Smal-Stocki, *HMBL*.

**Mikes, Kelemen** (Zágon 1690–Rodosto, Turkey 1761). Hungarian writer. A Transylvanian Hungarian with Jesuit education; as a page he accompanied into exile Ferenc Rákóczi II, leader of an unsuccessful nationalistic revolt, to France then Turkey. There he wrote his *Törökországi levelek* ('Letters from Turkey'), in the form of a series of letters to fictitious persons, recounting everyday incidents of the exiles at Rodosto. [JFR]

**Mikhalkov, Sergey** (Moscow 1913– ). Soviet dramatist, satirist, writer of children's verses and stories and scenarios for cartoon films. His satire exposes the imperfections of contemporary Soviet society (abuse of privilege in *Raki*, 1952; self-seeking at work in *Pamyatnik sebe*, 1959; sycophancy and careerism in academic circles in *Okhotnik*, 1956; the wrong kind of ambition for one's children in *Chuzhaya rol'*, 1954). He seems to have more feeling for children and animals than for grown-ups, about whom he writes with unsmiling distaste. [AP]

*Sobraniye sochineniy* (4 vols., 1963–4).

L. Kassil', *S.M.* (Moscow, 1954); B. Galanov, *S.M.* (Moscow, 1964); G. Yershov, V. Tel'pugov, *S.M.* (Moscow, 1956).

**Mikhaylovsky, Nikolay Konstantinovich** (Meshchovsk, Kaluga 1842–St Petersburg 1904). Russian philosopher and critic. Of noble birth, he was actuated by a profound social conscience. At the end of the 1870s he was connected with the terrorist group *Narodnaya Volya* and was exiled for four years from St Petersburg after the assassination of Alexander II in 1881. From 1892 until his death he was editor of the Populist journal *Russkoye bogatstvo*.

He was the last major philosopher of Populism. His thought was influenced by ⇨ Herzen and Lavrov and their passionate concern for the reunification of the different classes of Russian society; but at the heart of his system lies his belief that society was created for the individual and not *vice versa*. Accordingly in *Chto takoye progress?* he looked forward to a society which would emphasize the differences between individuals while minimizing those between the classes. Hence his idealization of the peasant community, for here ownership was equivalent with labour. This in his view developed personal qualities while benefiting society at the same time. He admitted that the factory which divorces ownership from work achieves greater efficiency, but believed that personal freedom was of greater value. Industrial society tended inevitably towards specialization and so to the loss of individual liberty, for human beings were reduced to mere cogs in a machine; and for him the image of the perfect society was a family, not a machine.

His views on progress, economics and the relationship of the peasantry and the proletariat differed sharply from those of the Darwinists and the Marxists. He accused Plekhanov and Lenin of ignoring psychological and moral factors, of sacrificing the individual to an impersonal society. The weakness of his position was his underestimation of the Russian *bourgeoisie*, whose rapid growth in the late 19th century had rendered many of his views anachronistic by the end of his life.

His literary criticism is usually directed by his social principles, but his essays *Desnitsa i shuytsa L'va Tolstogo* ('The Left Hand and the Right of L. Tolstoy', 1873), and *Zhestokiy talant* ('The Cruel Genius', 1883), on Dostoyevsky were ahead of their time. All his articles, even his most polemical works, are written with unusual wit and lucidity. [RDBT]

*Polnoye sobraniye sochineniy* (10 vols., 1909–13).
J. H. Billington, *M. and Russian Populism* (1958).

**Mikszáth, Kálmán** (Szklabonya 1847–Budapest 1910). Hungarian novelist. Born of a north-Hungarian country middle-class family, after studying law at Budapest he became a county clerk and later journalist or editor of several papers, including ⇨ Jókai's periodical *A Hon*. For many years a member of Parliament and friend of Prime Minister Tisza, he wrote numerous Parliamentary sketches. His early writings were greatly influenced by the romantic, anecdotal style of Jókai. Later, however, his work developed towards an individual brand of realism, that of the satirical sketch and the short story in which the anecdote is developed into vivid glimpses of reality, for example, *Az elfeledt fogoly*. In his works he maintained throughout an anecdotal construction, a romantic element and the description of idyllic love. A satirist of his own declining class, he views it with humour, a certain amount of forgiveness, but increasing pessimism. He first gained recognition with his volumes of short stories, *A Tót Atyafiak* (1881) and *Jó Palócok* (1881; tr. unknown, *The Good People of Palóc*, 1890). In his ballad-like short stories, he describes the experiences of his childhood and the lives of simple folk. *Beszterce Ostroma* is the tragic story of Count Pongrácz, a Don Quixote of the nobility who imagines himself to be the medieval lord of his castle; *Két Választás Magyarországon* is the satire of the political activities of the gentry. In his novel *Új Zrínyiász* (1898), also a satire of his times, he resurrects the 16th-century hero *Zrínyi* among contemporary circumstances as a bank manager. Even more unreserved is his criticism in *Különös Házasság* (1900; tr. G. Farkas, *Strange Marriage*, Budapest, 1964), the story of an unhappy 'arranged' marriage, which shows the unattainability of real love and happiness in a corrupt world. *A Noszti fiú esete Tóth Marival* (1908) is the tale of a greedy gentry family's unsuccessful intrigues to save their sinking fortunes by a beneficial marriage. His last great novel, *A fekete város*, is a tragic Romeo-and-Juliet story set in a 17th-century Hungarian town where the lovers are victims of the money-seeking feuds of declining gentry and unscrupulous middle class. [JFR]

*Szent Péter Esernyője* (1896; tr. B. W. Worswick, *St Peter's Umbrella*, Budapest, 1962).
Reményi, *HWL*; Klaniczay *et al.*, *HHL*.

**Miłosz, Czesław** (Szetejnie 1911– ). Polish poet, essayist and translator. He was born in Lithuania and is now living in America. His *Zniewolony umysł* (1953; tr.

J. Zielonko, *The Captive Mind*, 1962) analyses the impact of communism on four Polish writers named only as Alpha, Beta, Gamma, Delta; the portraits are sharply delineated. His pre-war poetry was preoccupied with catastrophic themes but formally tended towards a classicism now fully realized in discursive poems, such as *Traktat poetycki* (1957). His best lyrical verse is represented by *Światło dzienne* (1953). He has also published two novels. *Dolina Issy* (1955) evokes a childhood in the Lithuanian countryside. [JP]

**Milutinović Sarajlija, Sima** (Sarajevo 1791–Belgrade 1847). One of the first Serbian romantics, poet, historian and playwright. He was an eccentric figure in his day and a fervent patriot. He, like ⇨ Karadžić, collected folk-songs, but he lacked the same systematic and thorough approach to the task. His poetry was based upon both the folk-songs and his knowledge of German poetry. He experimented with the language to an extent that sometimes makes his works difficult to understand. For this reason he has probably been underestimated. His works include a long epic poem *Serbijanka* (1826), a tragedy *Miloš Obilić* (1837), and a history of Montenegro and also of the second rising under Miloš Obrenović (1815). He was the tutor of ⇨ Njegos, prince-bishop of Montenegro, and undoubtedly influenced his literary style. [EDG]

**Minnesinger.** Collective designation of the German lyric poets of the 12th and 13th centuries. Properly speaking, the term refers only to those whose poetry serves the ideal of courtly love (*Minne*), but in practice it is used of all the lyric poets of the period, whatever the subject-matter of their verse.

The German poetry of *amour courtois* derives both in form and content from Provençal and French models, although there are certain differences in tone. However, before this Romance influence made itself felt, there was already in existence a tradition of love-poetry quite different from that of *amour courtois*, a tradition characterized not by the man's utter self-commitment to the worship of ideal womanhood but by the yearning of the woman for the love of her chosen knight and by his indifference to her feelings. The poems of ⇨ Kürenberg, and certain of those ascribed to Dietmar von Aist, represent this tradition, which seems to have flourished above all in Austrian territory.

The Romance influence of courtly love first shows itself *c.* 1170, in the work of men such as Heinrich von Veldeke, ⇨ Friedrich von Hausen and ⇨ Rudolf von Fenis, who come from the Rhenish borderlands between France and Germany. The climax of this Romance-inspired poetry is reached with Reinmar von Hagenau (⇨ Reinmar der Alte), who flourished at the turn of the 12th century in Vienna.

The greatest German Minnesinger, ⇨ Walther von der Vogelweide, is more characteristically a poet of *Sprüche* (moral, political and religious poems) than of love-songs, though he has left a number of poems both in the tradition of *amour courtois* and in a direct, unaffected style that lies outside this tradition. As the conceits of courtly love began to lose their power, so this latter, direct style gained popularity, and the verse of Walther's younger contemporaries and successors, such as ⇨ Neidhart von Reuental, Gottfried von Neifen and ⇨ Tannhäuser, becomes more realistic and less refined, both in tone and in technique. ⇨ Ulrich von Lichtenstein (died *c.* 1275) is one of the few who strove to keep alive the dying ideals of courtly love.

As the name implies, Minnesang – love-songs and *Sprüche* alike – consists not only of verse but also of music. The individual Minnesinger normally wrote both, and as a servant of courtly society, he performed his songs in public. The earliest extant manuscripts of Minnesinger poems were only compiled about one hundred years after the songs themselves had been composed, and far fewer melodies have survived than texts. [RT]

*Des Minnesangs Frühling*, ed. C. von Kraus (1936) (the standard collection of poems from the early and central periods but excluding Walther von der Vogelweide); *Deutsche Liederdichter des 13. Jahrhunderts*, ed. C. von Kraus (1952–8) (post-Walther period only); K. Bartsch, *Deutsche Liederdichter des 12. bis 14. Jahrhunderts* (1914); I. Colvin, *I Saw the World* (1938).

E. Wechssler, *Das Kulturproblem des Minnesangs* (1909); Ehrismann, *GDL*; R. J. Taylor, *The Art of the Minnesinger* (1967).

**Miracles.** Medieval French plays in which 'a legend setting forth the life, or the martyrdom, or the miracles of a saint' were dramatized. Latin plays dealing with Saint

Nicholas, the conversions of Saint Paul and Saint Catherine are found from the end of the 11th century in Germany, England and then France, and were performed in the cathedral or monastic schools. These plays were associated with the liturgy, but readily included profane elements of satire and comedy. The earliest surviving example in French is the *Jeu de saint Nicolas* (ed. A. Henry, Brussels/Paris, 1962), written by ⇨ Jean Bodel and played in 1200, probably for the literary guild of Arras. The second is ⇨ Rutebeuf's *Miracle de Théophile* (1261; ed. G. Frank, Paris, 1925) an early version of the Faust theme, and the earliest French miracle play in which the Virgin appears.

From the 14th century survives a collection of forty *Miracles de Notre Dame* (ed. G. Paris and U. Robert, 8 vols., Paris, 1876–93), probably written for a guild or *puy* devoted to the Virgin. In these plays of usually less than 3,000 lines, a sinner is rescued by the dramatic and miraculous intervention of the Virgin. The subjects are taken from romances, ⇨ *chansons de geste*, folk-legends, chronicles and the lives of saints. The diversity of plot, the characterization and social comment give amusing insight into contemporary life. These plays use material from 13th-century collections of narrative poems about the miracles of the Virgin, especially the *Miracles narratifs de Notre-Dame* (ed. F. V. Koenig, Geneva, 1955–61ff.), composed in 1223 by Gautier de Coincy and based on the 12th-century *Miracula Virginis* of Hugues Farsit. [LTT]

P. R. Vincent, *The 'Jeu de saint Nicolas' ... A literary Analysis* (Baltimore, 1954); C. Foulon, *L'œuvre de Jean Bodel* (Paris, 1958); E. Roy, *Études sur le théâtre français du XIVe et du XVe siècle* ... (Paris, 1902); Frank, *MFD*.

**Mira de Amescua, Antonio** (Guadir 1574?–Guadir 1644). Spanish priest and dramatist. His most important play, *El esclavo del demonio* (1612), is about a man who makes a pact with the devil, but is rescued by his guardian angel who fights a duel for his soul. The style is violent and unbalanced; it wavers between the simplicity of Lope de Vega in his *Pastores de Belén* and the metaphoric brilliance of ⇨ Góngora. Of his other plays, *La mesonera del cielo*, is remarkable for its contrasts between sacred and profane love, and asceticism and action. The central character is a hermit who has abandoned his wife on their wedding day and, wearing the disguise of a young courtier, tracks down his sinful sister. Needless to say, the sister is brought to repentance. Though less prolific than many contemporaries, he also wrote *Autos sacramentales* (*Pedro Telonario*, CC), Biblical and historical plays (*El arpa de David*, *La rueda de la fortuna*) and comedies of intrigue (*La Fénix de Salamanca*). The poem 'Cancion real a una mudanza' is now known not to be his. ⇨ Sarabia, Juan de. [JMC]

*Teatro*, CC; BAE, 45.

**Miró, Gabriel** (Alicante 1879–Madrid 1930). Spanish novelist. Educated by the Jesuits at Orihuela and later studied law at Valencia University. Although he tried for a legal post in 1907 and 1908 to ease the financial burdens which a wife and three children brought him, his literary vocation was already apparent and he had published a series of short novels before that date. His first book appeared when he was only 20, but at that time he found it difficult to decide whether he most wanted to paint or write. Ultimately his painterly instincts seem to have found an adequate outlet in his novels, which are rich in descriptions of town scenes, landscapes and gardens. In most of his novels these are, in fact, an appropriate complement to a sensuous view of life and love, in which Nature and instinct are the most powerful forces of existence. His novels express the tensions between these and all that frustrates them: narrow religion and politics, fanaticism and cruelty. Nowhere does he embody this conflict more superbly than in *Nuestro Padre San Daniel* (1921; tr. C. Remfry-Kidd, *Our Father San Daniel*, 1930) and *El Obispo leproso* (1926). [ONVG]

*Obras completas* (1953).
R. Vidal, *G.M., Le style et les moyens d'expression* (Bordeaux, 1964); *BHS*, XLIV (1967).

**Mistral, Frédéric** (Maillane 1830–Maillane 1914). Provençal poet and leader of the Félibrige. He wrote in Provençal. The son of a wealthy farmer, he studied law at Aix-en-Provence but returned to Maillane in 1851 and rarely left Provence. He worked with ⇨ Roumanille to establish a uniform Provençal orthography and grammar. In 1859 he published *Mirèio*, a verse romance of tragic love, in epic form, which by its evocation of the life of Provence won immediate success and the praise of

Lamartine ('un pays est devenu un livre'). In a vulgarized form it was set to music by Gounod. *Calendau* followed in 1867 but was less popular than *Nerto* (1884), the medieval story of a maiden Nerto whose soul is sold to the devil by her dissolute father. Mistral's tragedy *La Rèino Jano* (1890) was his only failure. The celebrated *Lou Pouèmo dóu Rose*, the story of the Rhône since Roman times, appeared in 1897. His earlier collection of lyric verse *Lis Isclosd'Or* (1875) was complemented in 1912 by *Lis Oulivado*.

In his *Trésor du Félibrige* (1879–86) he compiled a vast and erudite dictionary of Provençal words and proverbs. He was for many years the mainstay of the *Armana Provençau* ⇨ (Félibrige), which also provided him with much material for his memoirs *Moun Espelido* (1906; Fr. tr. C. E. Maud, 1907). His immense correspondence is still largely unpublished. He used his Nobel Prize of 1905 for expanding and enriching the Museon Arlaten, the museum of Provençal life and customs which he established at Arles and which still flourishes as a testimony to his powerful genius (⇨ Aubanel). [LTT]

*Œuvres* (1887–1910) (with facing French trans.); *Prose d'almanach*, ed. P. Devoluy (1926); *Correspondance de F.M. et L. de Berluc-Pérussis, 1860–1902*, ed. B. Durand, intr. C. Rostaing (1955).

A. Thibaudet, *M., ou La république du soleil* (Paris, 1930); M. Decremps, *M. mage de l'Occident* (Paris, 1954); P. Lasserre, *F.M. poète, moraliste, citoyen* (Paris, 1918); E. Ripert, *La versification de F.M.* (Paris, Aix-en-Provence, 1917); D. Scheludko, *M.s Nerto* (Halle a.S., 1922); C. M. Girdlestone, *Dreamer and Striver; The Poetry of F.M.* (1937); P. Devoluy, *M. et la rédemption d'une langue* (Paris, 7th edn, 1941); R. Lyle, *M.* (1953); R. Aldington, *Introduction to M.* (1956); ⇨⇨ Félibrige.

**Młodożeniec, Stanisław** (Dobrocice 1895–Warsaw 1959). Polish poet. Born a peasant in a district rich in folklore, he studied in Cracow, becoming a prominent poet of the Futurist movement. His writing from that period has remained fresh and inventive partly because it is free from solemnity. One volume has the title *Kreski i futureski* ('Dashes and Futuresques', 1921) and contains his most popular poem 'Moskwa', in which ingenious sound effects and rhythms are produced from the arrangement of the words *tu, tam* ('here, there'). His later verse was more conventional. After the war he lived in London, but returned to Poland shortly before his death. [JP]

Peterkiewicz and Singer, *FCPP*.

**Mňačko, Ladislav** (Valašské Klobouky 1919– ). Slovak journalist and novelist. His novel *Smrť sa volá Engelchen* (1959; tr. G. Theiner, *Death is Called Engelchen*, Prague, 1961) is a partly autobiographical story of the punitive expedition of the S.S. units against the partisans in Slovakia during the Second World War. He was a staunch supporter of the official policy during the time when the Communist régime was persecuting even old guard Communists. During the subsequent period of liberalization he denounced these measures in *Oneskorené reportáže* (1964) in order, as he wrote, 'to document my own part of guilt in these events'. Later he depicted the stalinist era in Czechoslovakia in the novel *Ako chutí moc* 1968; tr. P. Stevenson, *The Taste of Power*, 1967), the life story of a high-ranking Communist functionary. In 1967 he went to Israel in protest against Czechoslovakia's attitude towards the Arab-Israeli conflict and left Czechoslovakia again after the 1968 invasion which he denounced in *Die siebente Nacht* (1968).

**Moberg, Vilhelm** (Algutsboda 1898– ) Swedish novelist and dramatist. Largely self-educated, he is of peasant origin from the province of Småland, the hard rural life and stony soil of which form the background of much of his work, often concerned with vigorous individualism and organic community, with tragic agrarian poverty and the problems of social, technical and psychological change and industrialization. These themes predominate in his earlier novels, in the partly autobiographical *Knut Toring* trilogy (1935–9; tr. E. Björkman, *The Earth Is Ours*, N.Y., 1940), and in the also partly autobiographical *Soldat med brutet gevär* (1944; condensed tr. G. Lannestock, *When I Was a Child* 1957).

He has also been an outspoken democratic publicist, as in the concentrated anti-Nazi historical novel *Rid i natt* (1941; tr. H. Alexander, *Ride This Night!*, N.Y., 1943), a pugnacious critic of bureaucracy and an exponent of frankness, sexual and otherwise. This last aspect caused a stir in the first of the series of four novels about Swedish immigrants to the United States in the 19th century that are his best-known books: *Utvandrarna* (1949; tr. G. Lannestock, *The Emigrants*, 1956); *Invandrarna* (1952; tr. G. Lannestock, *Unto a Good Land*, 1957); *Nybyggarna* (1956) and *Sista brevet till Sverige* (1959; both tr. in *Last Letter Home*, N.Y., 1961). These massively earthy volumes have had great success; they combine many of the features of a best-seller with some genuinely epic qualities. Moberg is also a versatile dramatist, known particularly for problem plays, such as the dramatization (in 1943) of his novel *Mans kvinna* (1933; tr. M. Heron, *Fulfilment*, 1953), and the dramatization of *Rid i natt* (1942). His original works for the stage at first reflected his early preference for corny, rustic farce, then his preoccupation with problems of married life. *Vår ofödde son* (1945), his dramatic masterpiece, has for its theme an illegitimate abortion and its shattering mental consequence for the frustrated, remorseful mother. Its deep, humanitarian pathos and its poetic quality in the presentation of one of the subsidiary characters, a young distracted girl, who believes herself to be the Virgin Mary, give the play a unique position in Moberg's production. A new pensive note is perceptible in his latest novel, *Din stund på jorden* (1963; dramatized 1967), in which an aged Swedish-American meditates upon his life and his destiny.

S. Mårtensson, *V.M.: en biografi* (1956) and *En bok om V.M.* (1953).

**Modena, Judah Aryeh (Leon)** (Venice 1571–Venice 1648). Hebrew poet and religious writer. A typical Renaissance figure, said to have had 26 different professions, was violently opposed to Kabbala. He travelled widely in Italy, taught in Ferrara and was Rabbi in Venice. A prolific writer, wrote an account of Jewish Rites for James I, *Historia degli riti hebraici* (1637; tr. E. Chilmead, *The History of the Rites... of the Jews*, 1650), and an autobiography, considered one of the earliest works of this kind, *Chaye Yehuda* (ed. A. Kahana, 1911). [EE]

S. A. Geiger, *L. de M.* (1856).

**Moguel, Juan Antonio.** ⇨ Basque Literature.

**Molière,** *nom de théâtre* of Jean-Baptiste Poquelin (Paris 1622–Paris 1673). French dramatist. Creator of French classical comedy. Educated by the Jesuits at the Collège de Clermont, he could have inherited his father's office as 'tapissier du Roi' (court furnisher), but at 21 he threw in his lot with other players who called themselves 'L'Illustre Théâtre'. This grand name did not save them from bankruptcy nor Molière (the name first occurs in an act of 1643) from prison for debt. Undeterred, he took to the provinces, where for thirteen years he practised his craft.

In 1658 he returned to Paris and attained notoriety almost at once by playing Corneille's *Nicomède* before the King, followed by what he called 'a little entertainment such as had won him some repute in the provinces', i.e. a farce (*Sganarelle ou le cocu imaginaire*, 1660, is an early example of this genre, *Les fourberies de Scapin*, 1671, a later sequence of Italian style *lazzi*). His troupe was adopted by Monsieur, and later (1665) by the King himself; he wrote romances and *comédie-ballets* for the court at Saint-Germain and Versailles (*George Dandin*, 1668), and for thirteen years kept his company going, writing as much as one-third of their material himself, until he died exhausted at the age of 51.

Little is known of his character. He is said to have been magnanimous but we do not know whether he was in the right against Racine, and his treatment of the abbé Cotin in *Les femmes savantes* suggests spite. That he had to face attacks from many quarters is certain. His private life was not happy. He married in 1662 Armande Béjart, a pretty and gifted but frivolous ingénue, who has probably contributed much to such delightful characters as Agnès and Célimène. Documents affirm her to have been the sister of Madelaine Béjart, who had been with Molière from the start of his career. Gossip asserted that she was the daughter, and thus possibly Molière's own daughter: hence his sharp rejoinder in the *Impromptu de Versailles* that his critics should keep off his private life.

The traditional picture of him is that of a man of reason, advocating in his plays the middle way. The facts suggest the opposite, a hot-tempered, choleric, generous man. He could not have chosen more incautious subjects: at least three of them had to be taken off because they were too risky. He had to rewrite *Les précieuses ridicules* (1659) and fight for the staging of *Tartuffe* (1664–9; tr. R. Wilbur, 1964), which brought him temporary affluence. His *Dom Juan* (1665) disappeared after a fortnight's run; there is no trace of an official ban, but it was never revived in Molière's lifetime.

Molière was clearly the big draw in his own theatre, as an actor, above all as a *farceur*. A disciple of Scaramouche, a pamphlet of 1672 shows him taking lessons from the master, before a mirror. He could apparently do what he liked with his face, and trained himself to make the slightest glance and gesture effective. He played in the manner of the ⇨ *commedia dell'arte*, training his actors to work out the full potential of an unscripted situation. Through all his work runs an innate instinct for drama, for driving a point to its explosive ending, the flash of comic revelation which his contemporary Hobbes spoke of as the 'sudden glory' which laughter alone confers. His dénouements were said to be weak until modern actors showed what good theatre they provided.

It is likely that he started acting behind a mask; his first successful Paris role was called Mascarille, or little mask. To the end he found comedy in pretence, pomposity, arrogance, in assumptions which events force his figures to abandon (the story of *Amphitryon*, 1668, taken from Plautus, offered an interesting variation on the theme of disguise). *Tartuffe*, in this as in so many respects, is Molière's most imaginative creation. He imagines a sensual man who adopts the mask of an ascetic. He does this with great acumen, skill and nearly complete success, but the play shows the sort of situation where a sensualist must reveal himself as such. So his diabolical efforts to impose himself on the head of the family and to inherit deeds and fortune are ruined by the biological impulse to tell the mistress of the house that he desires her, that he is not what he appears. Such glimpses of the way intelligence masks the will and the appetite are largely Molière's discoveries.

To take the better-known plays in order, *Les précieuses ridicules* (1659) was originally a polemic written for a patron against a coterie. In the present much-revised version provincial girls who think that all in Paris must be witty and wonderful are fooled by valets masquerading as their masters. They adore jargon ('*Voiturez-nous ici les commodités de la conversation*') and think the idea of physical marriage 'altogether shocking'. *L'école des femmes* (1662), a most original approach to pure comedy, concerns a man who worked out a plan to keep his wife faithful by giving her no education. The girl whom he thus deprives of knowledge is so artless without it that he falls for her himself. *Dom Juan*, founded on a popular Italian farce, is a running debate between the Sancho-like servant and the Quixotic lofty seigneur who despises all obligation, commercial no less than religious. In *Le misanthrope* (1666; ed. G. Rudler, 1947; tr. R. Wilbur, 1958), admired by George Meredith (in his *Essay on Comedy*), drawing-room discussion of frankness and plain speech turns against its protagonist, since plain speech, without good temper and equanimity, is much worse than politeness. Alceste is Molière's most enigmatic comic figure: he is on the side of right and honour, but passively and egotistically, mocking at things for not going his way: 'Justice is on my side and I lose my case'. *L'avare* (1668) takes its subject from Plautus, but the play runs on different lines. Its rhythmic prose suggests that its author had intended verse. Harpagon's mania shows the true comic dichotomy as Molière presents it elsewhere: the mind is perverse, deluded, cruel, while instinct and nature escape their control. The inhuman miser becomes human, and childish. There is laughter certainly, but incidental: the basic comic suggestion is incongruity, absurdity. *Le bourgeois gentilhomme* (1670) is perhaps the favourite for a modern audience. Jourdain is a social climber, without any of the unpleasantness we should expect. The war between fatuity in the master and sense in the servant is in the best farcical tradition. In *Les femmes savantes* (1672) Chrysale is a second Jourdain in his good nature, afraid of his blue-stocking wife. A poets' quarrel rephrases the comedy of the sonnet scene in the *Misanthrope*. With *Le malade imaginaire* (1673) the irony of events (that Molière died playing the part of a hypochondriac) tends to distract critical attention from the splendid comic treatment of jargon and expertise. The opposing forces of youth and sense in the persons of daughter and servant, and superstition and charlatanry in the doctors, are ranged ballet-like around the central figure, who is ill because the doctors say so, who fears death, but who is strong enough to walk when he forgets that he needs a stick. [WGM]

*Œuvres*, ed. E. Despois and P. Mesnard (13 vols. 1873–1900); ed. M. Rat (2 vols., Pléiade, 1956)
P. F. Saintonge and R. W. Christ, *Fifty Years o[f] M. Studies* (Baltimore, Md., 1952); R. Bray *M., homme de théâtre* (Paris, 1954); J. Gui

charnaud, *M. Une aventure théâtrale, Tartuffe – Don Juan – Le Misanthrope* (Paris, 1963).

**Møller, Kai Friis.** ⇨ Friis Møller, Kai.

**Møller, Poul** (Uldum, Vejle 1794–Copenhagen 1838). Danish poet and novelist. As professor of philosophy (Copenhagen, 1831) he taught ⇨ Kierkegaard, who admired him greatly. The author of many charming poems, he is known mainly for his novel *En dansk Students Eventyr* (written 1824 and published posthumously from an incomplete manuscript), remarkable for the realism and humour with which it deals with its romantic theme. [ELB]

V. Andersen, *P.M.* (Copenhagen, 1944).

**Molnár, Ferenc** (Budapest 1878–New York 1952). Hungarian playwright. Emigrated in 1940 and lived in Hollywood and New York. His plays, whose main features are satiric wit, brilliant technique and sentimentality mixed with humour, have been translated into many languages and achieved international success. *Liliom* (1909; tr. B. F. Glazer, 1921) is a dramatic mystery-play which was the basic script of the musical comedy and film *Carousel*; *Az Ördög* (tr. O. Herford, *The Devil*) tells of the conflict between a woman's social morality and subconscious desire. *Red Mill* illustrates the conflict between innocence and sensuality. Other well-known plays in translation: *Olympia*; *The Swan*; *Angel Making Music*; *Prologue to King Lear*; *Fashions for Men*; *Play in the Palace*.

He is also important as a novelist; his most popular novels are *A Pál Utcai Fiúk* (tr. L. Rittenberg, *The Paul Street Boys*, N.Y., 1927), in which he touchingly captures the beauty and torment of boyhood, and *Diary of a War Correspondent*. [JFR]

*The Plays of F.M.* (N.Y., n.d.) (in English with Foreword by D. Belasco).

**Molza, Francesco Maria** (Modena 1489–Modena 1544). Italian poet. Of notoriously dissolute life, he was an elegant composer of Latin verse. In Italian he left lyrics in Petrarchan vein, a few *novelle*, and some longer poems, the best known of which is a pastoral in *ottava rima*, *La ninfa tiberina*. [DGR]

*Poesie volgari e latine* (1747–54).
Bo, *LC*; Croce, *PES*.

**Mombert, Alfred** (Karlsruhe 1872–Winterthur 1942). German poet. After six years as a practising lawyer he devoted himself to writing and philosophico-scientific studies (mainly in Heidelberg). As a Jew he was sent to Gurs concentration camp (1940, France; Swiss friends finally secured his release). A friend of ⇨ Dehmel, Mombert's 'Cosmic-Impressionist' poetry develops a mythical cosmology in visionary hymns and 'Symphonic dramas' (*Aeon...* trilogy, 1907–10–11). *Der himmlische Zecher* (1909; repr. 1951) gives a representative selection of these grandiose inflations of personal fantasy, elaborated with much intellectual subtlety. [PB]

*Dichtungen*, ed. E. Herberg (1963).
H. Hennecke, *A.M.* (1952) (intr. and sel.); F. K. Benndorf, *M.* (Dresden, 1932) (with bibliography).

**Monnier, Henri** (Paris 1799–Paris 1877). French author, actor and caricaturist. He summed up the type of the prosperous bourgeois prominent under the July monarchy of Louis-Philippe in his character M. Joseph Prudhomme: first in *Scènes populaires* (1830), then in a play, *Grandeur et décadence de M. Joseph Prudhomme* (1852), finally in *Mémoires de M. Joseph Prudhomme* (1857). [WA]

**Montaigne, Michel Eyquem,** seigneur de (Château Montaigne, Périgord 1533– Château Montaigne, Périgord 1592). French essayist. Son of Pierre Eyquem, the first Lord of Montaigne, and of Antoinette de Louppes (*Lopes*), of converted Spanish Jewish stock. His devotion to his father was great. Raised to speak Latin as his mother tongue, he retained a markedly Latin turn of mind. He knew Greek, but preferred to use translations. After studying law he became eventually counsellor to the *Parlement* of Bordeaux. It was in this period that he met Étienne de ⇨ la Boëtie, whom he loved (partly in imitation of a Classical ideal of friendship) in death as in life. He married in 1565. After following the royal court in Paris and Rouen, he retired abruptly to his lands at Montaigne (1571), devoting himself to reading and reflecting in his library tower and to composing his *Essais* (1580; ed. J. Plattard, 1946; ed. A. Tilley and A. M. Boase, sel. with intro., 1962; tr. J. Florio, 1603; J. M. Cohen, 1958). As far as possible he kept out of the religious wars of his day, but sided with orthodoxy, authority and monarchy. In 1576 his interest in scepticism became markedly greater and he struck a medallion with his famous device, *Que sçay-je?* He suffered cruelly from gall-stones and, in 1580, journeyed through France, Germany and Italy, partly in search of curative waters, partly out of sheer curiosity. While in Rome he had his *Essais* approved by the ecclesiastical authorities with very slight modifications. Under royal pressure he became Mayor of Bordeaux in 1581, a post renewed for a further two years in 1583. He is sometimes criticized for not returning to the city during an outbreak of the plague. In 1586 he retired permanently to his estates, dying while preparing another edition of his *Essais*.

Both the word *essai* and its conception as a *genre* are essentially inventions of Montaigne. The title *Essais* was a modest one. He appears to have conceived an essay as an *assay*, a trial of an idea, of himself, of his judgement, of his experience. His books are divided not into essays but chapters: he probably thought of each chapter as containing a series of such *essais*. The order in which the chapters of the first two books are now read is not that in which they were written, but is that in which they were published (1580). The chapters written first tend to be short, less original and adventurous, and are decidedly stoic in tone, though later interpolations enrich them and deepen them. From the first he refuses to hide behind great names. He rarely quotes his sources: an idea has to stand on its own feet. He quotes poetry as an embellishment as much as an authority. He made numerous additions to his text, especially in 1588, when he added the Third Book as well. The posthumous edition of Marie de Gournay (1595) incorporates his last reflections.

His stoicism was a phase, but he continued to admire Seneca, treating him more independently. Even his early stoicism becomes a source of indolent comfort. He is often said to have become next a sceptic then an epicurean. This is partly true, but it over-simplifies a complex, personal philosophical development. The mature Montaigne is an eclectic, seeking stimuli to original thought in reading and conversation. Towards the end, Socrates (and with him, Plato) becomes his ideal, in so far as he had one. Plutarch, in Amyot's translation, influenced his thought and style. So too did Pyrrho, but his interest in the Ancients was progressively matched by interest in modern history and curiosity about the New World, which increased his awareness of the impermanence and arbitrariness of customs and institutions.

He presents the *Essais* as a book on a frivolous topic: himself. Refusing to believe that self-knowledge and self-study imply self-love, he examines his habits, thoughts, and emotions as they change from age to age, from moment to moment. He strives to isolate his *forme maîtresse*, the *form* which gives a permanence to his character despite change of *matter*. The quality he most admired was sound judgement: education should cultivate it – 'useful knowledge' is for professors, not gentlemen. Reading, discussion, conversation are a jousting match, not a war. He reads desultorily, and only books which are pleasing. If he studies, it is only pleasing books of moral reflection. He liked Pyrrhonist scepticism partly for its destruction of Lutheran dogmatism: if it destroyed any rational defence of his own catholicism he did not care (cf. his *Apologie de Raimond Sebond*, an author whose *Theologia naturalis* he translated for his father). Montaigne set no store by mere consistency. The frequent Latin quotations make his works difficult bedside reading, but his style has a richness, a concreteness, a directness, which seize one's attention and keep hold of it. [MAS]

*L'édition municipale* (1903–20); *Œuvres complètes*, ed. A. Thibaudet and M. Rat (Pléiade, 1962); *Essais*, ed. M. Rat (Garnier, 1962).

P. Villey, *Sources et évolution des Essais de M.* (2nd edn, Paris, 1933); H. Friedrich, *M.* (Bern, 1949) (in German; the best modern study); D. Frame, *M.* (1966).

**Montale, Eugenio** (Genoa 1896– ). Italian poet, translator and critic. Co-founder of the Turin review *Primo Tempo* (1922) and an early opponent of Fascism, he became director (1929–38) of the Gabinetto Vieusseux (a Florentine library and learned society), and since 1947 has been literary editor of the *Corriere della Sera*. His formative experience was the First World War and the sense of intellectual and cultural wasteland following it – not unlike that of Eliot, whom he translated and to whom he may owe certain stylistic developments, although his own imagery is often strikingly drawn from the barren, rocky Ligurian landscape; the fame he achieved with *Ossi di Seppia* (1925) shows how truly he had voiced the pessimism of this period. Uncompromising in his diagnosis of modern man's condition ('This only today we can tell you / what we are *not*, what we do *not* want'), harshly asserting factual realities, his bleak statement of man's 'stony suffering with no name' (like walking on a wall topped with 'sharp splinters of a bottle') gathers considerable poetic force – even if the symbolism of his sharply outlined figures is not always easy to interpret. (The 'closed' quality of his language, reminiscent in this of the tradition of Mallarmé, won for him the title of 'hermetic' poet – *ermetismo*, as the critic Francesco Flora called it.) In the interval until his next volumes of poems, *Le occasioni* (1939) and *Finisterre* (1943), he did not so much discover new sources of inspiration – let alone grounds for revising his pessimism – as deepen and 'interiorize' his original themes. His most recent volume is *La bufera* (1956). [GD]

*Poems*, tr. G. Kay (Edinburgh, 1964); Kay, *PBIV*.

R. Lunardi, *E.M. e la nuova poesia* (Padua, 1948).

**Montchrestien, Antoine de** (Falaise 1575?–Les Tourailles, Domfront 1621). French dramatist. Probably a Catholic by upbringing, though he was killed during a Protestant uprising in 1621, in which he was on the Protestant side. The sources of his tragedies include Greek legend and history (*Hector*, *Les Lacènes*), Roman history (*Sophonisbe*), the Old Testament (*Aman* and *David*) and contemporary history (*L'Écossaise*, about Mary Queen of Scots). They appeared from 1596 to 1604. Montchrestien was influenced by ⇨ Garnier, but is without Garnier's passionate concern with the evils of war, and his plays are pure exercises in style, often of great beauty, with noble development of commonplaces and Stoic themes (*L'Écossaise*) and elegant Petrarchan love poetry (*Aman*, *David*). They also contain an unpleasant macabre element, a refined playing on the reader's sensibility, as in the simultaneously decorative and horrible description of Mary Stuart's execution. He made considerable textual alterations to his plays after their original publication, but the theory that these were made at the instigation of ⇨ Malherbe appears to be incorrect. [GJ]

R. Lebègue, *La tragédie française de la Renaissance* (Brussels/Paris, 1943).

**Montemayor, Jorge de,** né Montemor (Montemor-o-Velho *c.* 1520–Piedmont 1561). Spanish poet and novelist. Portuguese by birth and musician by profession, he came to Spain in 1548 as *cantor* to the Infanta María, becoming *aposentador* to her sister Juana (1552–4). His roving ways led him to other parts of Spain, the Netherlands and to Italy where he died in an obscure affray possibly in Turin. In his *Cancionero* (1554, enlarged 1558, ed. A. González Palencia, 1932), he is a competent versifier in traditional and Italianate metres. His religious poems and Christmas play were placed on the Index of 1559. He also translated the first part of the Catalan poems of Ausiàs Marc. His fame rests on the pastoral novel *La Diana* (1559, ed. F. López Estrada, CC; E. Moreno Báez, 1955; tr. in Googe, *Eglogs, epytaphes and sonnets* (1565), repr. H. Thomas, 1920), the first in Spanish, widely read and translated, and praised by Cervantes for its prose though he thought the verses poor. Inspired by the Italian ⇨ Sannazaro's *Arcadia* (1481; tr. Spanish 1547), it owes something to the Novel of Chivalry in its more fantastic parts and to the shepherd scenes of the theatre. It is in part a *roman à clef*. This polished and leisurely work led to a fashion culminating in the *Astrée* (1607) of Honoré d'Urfé, and influenced Sidney, Spenser and Shakespeare. The continuation by Gil Polo supplies the second part Montemayor never wrote. [JG]

**Montesino, Ambrosio** (fl. early 16th cent.). Spanish religious poet and translator. A master of popular forms, which he turned with even greater charm than Íñigo de ⇨ Mendoza. Both were Franciscans and at the court of Ferdinand and Isabella. His description of the angel's coloured feathers, and the gold of his hair in his *coplas* in honour of John the Baptist displays him at his naïve best; like Íñigo, he is capable of falling into bathos. He translated the *Vita Christi* of Ludolf of Saxony and St Augustine's *Meditations*. [JMC]

*Cancionero* (1572) in BAE, 35; Terry, *ASP*.

**Montesquieu, Charles-Louis de Secondat,** Baron de La Brède et de (La Brède, Gironde 1689–Paris 1755). French social and political thinker and satirist. His family belonged to the lesser nobility of Guyenne, with a distinguished tradition of legal service in the Bordeaux *Parlement*. He accordingly trained for the law at Bordeaux and Paris (where he was in touch with some of the most emancipated minds), and inherited his uncle's office of president of that body in 1716. His real interests were intellectual and literary, however, and he laid the foundations of his fame by the publication (under a thin veil of anonymity) of *Les lettres persanes* in 1721 (ed. A. Adam, Paris, 1954; tr. Ozell, 1722; tr. J. R. Loy, 1961). This work is a series of letters, describing the reactions of two Persian visitors to France, and also providing a contrasting picture of oriental life, within a flimsy framework of fictional narrative. The attempt to make French readers see themselves through foreign eyes was not new, and the social satire is in a tradition well established by La Bruyère; but what chiefly distinguishes it – apart from the occasional irreverent allusion to religion and the eroticism of the harem episodes (which no doubt contributed substantially to its original success) – is the strongly marked political and social viewpoint upon which the criticisms are based. Montesquieu sees the France of his day as a country in grave danger of declining, from a condition in which liberty was preserved by the healthy divisions of social function and power within a traditional monarchical society, into a centralized royal tyranny: and the social vices and abuses he observes around him are interpreted as evidence for the imminence of this peril, rather than merely as examples of individual moral failings.

Montesquieu sold his Bordeaux presidency in 1726, was elected to the Académie Française in 1727, and in 1728 began a three-year European tour which took him principally to Italy and England, and greatly nourished his interest in political and social institutions. His next work, *Considérations sur les causes de la grandeur des Romains et de leur décadence* (1734; ed. H. Barckhausen, Paris, 1900; tr. anon., 1734), is a survey of Roman history, in lapidary French, which though factually uncritical seeks the underlying social forces which shaped, and explain, the pattern of events. His *magnum opus*, *De l'esprit des lois* (1748; ed. J. Brethe de La Gressaye, Paris, 1950–61; tr. T. Nugent, N.Y., 1949), is a vaster enterprise undertaken with the same preoccupations. Here, starting from a concept of law as expressing a relationship (like a scientific law), he analyses human institutions, and the positive laws which embody them, in terms of their dependence upon forms of government, upon the external relations of the state, upon national temperament, climatic and economic factors. The most influential part of the work, however, has been his analysis of the conditions which create political liberty, and his advocacy, based upon his reading of the English constitution, of a system of equilibrium based upon a separation of the legislative, executive and judicial powers of the state.

He also wrote some philosophical tales, and contributed the article 'Goût' to the ⇨ *Encyclopédie*. [WHB]

*Œuvres complètes*, ed. A. Masson (3 vols., 1950–5). R. Shackleton, *M., a Critical Biography* (1961); J. Dedieu, *M.* (Paris, 1913).

**Montherlant, Henry de** (Paris 1896– ). French novelist and dramatist. At first known mainly as a novelist, it is as a playwright that he has achieved most success, though he was 46 before he first had a play performed. His first novel, *Le songe* (1922; tr. T. Kilmartin, *The Dream*, 1962), written in praise of vigour, virility and a certain hardness, for fear of the corrosive effect of sentimentality, already reveals most of the themes his work was to express. Extolling instinct and honour, Montherlant there eschews all supposed weakness, typified especially by the acceptance or return of a woman's love. This view is further developed in *Les jeunes filles* (1936–9; tr. T. McGreevy, vol. 1, *Young Girls*, and J. Rodker, vol. 2, *Pity for Women*, 1937; J. Rodker, vol. 3, *The Demon of Good*, and J. Rodker, vol. 4, *The Lepers*, 1940), a tetralogy which examines at perhaps undue length the relationship of four women to a writer, for whom his art must have first place. Rejection awaits both the cultured woman who loves from the start and the attractive girl without culture or depth of character whose pleasure-giving capacity is extinguished the moment she loves. Only the casually encountered Arab girl, free from sentimental complications, causes no vexation, even though she is found to be physically leprous. The others, it is implied, are morally leprous, because they love, and cling. The basic theme of the best of his plays, as of his last novel, *Le chaos et la nuit* (1963), the tragic grandeur of a human destiny lived in austerity or isolation, unaffected by failure, is already apparent to some extent in *Les célibataires* (1934; tr. T. Kilmartin, *The Bachelors*, 1960), a Balzacian *roman de mœurs*, revealing through its irony a certain compassionate quality absent from *Le songe*, except where the war wounded are concerned, and from *Les jeunes filles*. In his impotent independence, his refusal to adapt himself, Léon de Coantré achieves a degree of grandeur, pointing the way, albeit quietly, to the high-principled heroics of Alvaro and Maraiana in *Le maître de Santiago* (1947; tr. J. Griffin, *The Master of Santiago*, with other plays, 1951). In these classically conceived historical plays, with their close texture, such as the above-mentioned, *La reine morte* (1942; tr. J. Griffin, ibid.), *Port-Royal* (1953) and *Le cardinal d'Espagne* (1960), the sense of honour, the refusal to compromise, personal pride, withdrawal from the world, and the anguish of a decision to be made by a man at war with himself, are the main elements of drama. Their most poignant expression is realized in *La reine morte*, where the grandeur of Ferrante, with his tragic dilemma, and the pride and sense of honour of the Infanta are counterbalanced by the lovingness of Inès as wife and mother. Always fraught with dramatic intensity, these plays do not perhaps involve deep resonances, the deepest being aroused by *La reine morte* and *Port-Royal*. This last play, with its theme of integrity and refusal to compromise, invites comparison with ⇨ Bernanos's *Dialogues des Carmélites*, the depth of vision of which it does not, however, attain.

Montherlant's finest work is probably *Le chaos et la nuit*, where the theme of an austere isolation is embodied in an exiled Spanish anarchist, the notion of a proud refusal to surrender being finely portrayed in the concluding identification of Celestino with the difficult death of a bull in the ring. Thus does his latest work reflect his life-long love of bullfighting, directly expressed in *Les bestiaires* (1926). With his changes of direction, his avowed aim of presenting the multifold aspects of man in all their contradictoriness, and refusing himself to be encased in any system, he has perhaps dispersed his energies in too diversified a course. [EB]

*Romans et œuvres de fiction* (Pléiades, 1959ff.) (collected novels and stories); tr. A. Brown, *Desert Love* (1957), P. Wiles, *The Matador* (1957), T. Kilmartin, *Chaos and Night* (1964); *Essais* (1963); tr. J. Wrightman, *Selected Essays* (1960); *Théâtre* (Pléiade, 1965).

J. de Laprade, *Le théâtre de M.* (Paris, 1950); P. Sipriot, *M. par lui-même* (Paris, 1953); G. Bordonove, *H. de M.* (Paris, 1954); N. Debrie-Pavel, *M.: l'art et l'amour* (Lyons, 1960); J. de Beer, *M. ou l'homme incombré de Dieu* (Paris, 1963); *La Table Ronde*, 148 (1960) and 155 (1960); J. Cruickshank, *M.* (1964); A. Marissel, *M.* (Paris, 1966).

**Monti, Vincenzo** (Alfonsine, Ravenna 1754–Milan 1828). Italian poet. He derived from his classical education a taste for the elegance of Virgil, but equally for the empty pomposity of the Arcadian poet ⇨ Frugoni. In 1781, following the success of some early Arcadian verse, he was invited to the Papal Court at Rome, where he spent most of the next fifteen years writing occasional poetry such as *Pellegrino apostolico* (1782) on Pius VI's journey to Vienna, the *Feroniade* (1784) on land reclamation in the Pontine marshes, and *Al signor di Montgolfier* (1784) on the first balloon ascent. An unhappy love-affair at this time provided inspiration for *Al Principe Don Sigismondo Chigi* and *Pensieri d'amore* (1783) – the latter, with its perhaps too faithful rendering of passages from Goethe's *Werther*, being unique among all his poetry for its emotional content.

He wrote classical tragedies – *Aristodemo* (tr. anon. 1854), acclaimed noisily in 1787; *Galeotto Manfredi* (1788), bearing obvious influences of Letourneur's translation of Shakespeare; and *Caio Gracco* (1800), typical, for all its eloquent rhetoric, of the essentially undramatic qualities of these works. Among his translations the *Iliad* (1786) is the acknowledged masterpiece. Though he knew no Greek and it was based on Latin and Italian translations, it was of exceptional beauty.

Justification for his being condemned for the fickleness of his political allegiance is found in the poems now deploring the French Revolution (*In morte di Ugo Bassville – La Bassvilliana*, 1793; tr. A. Lodge, *The Death of Bassville*, 1845), now welcoming Napoleon (*La Mascheroniana*, 1802; *Il bardo della selva nera*, 1806; *La spada di Federico II*, 1806), finally celebrating Napoleon's defeat and the return of Austria (*Il mistico omaggio*, 1815; *Il ritorno d'Astrea*, 1816). He was remarkably consistent, however, in the formal elegance of his poetry and in his insistence on the value of the imaginative and evocative use of mythology (cf. *La Musogonia*, 1793–7), as opposed to the emotional emphasis of the Romantics (cf. the polemical *Sermone sulla mitologia*, 1825). [RHC]

*Opere*, ed. M. Valgimigli and C. Muscetta (1953). F. Allevi, *V.M.* (Florence, 1954); C. Angelini, *La carriera poetica di V.M.* (Milan, 1960); Dionisotti, *OBIV*; Binni, *CI*; *Maggiori*, ii.

**Móra, Ferenc** (Kiskunfélegyháza 1879–Budapest 1934). Hungarian writer. Journalist and director of Szeged Museum, he was a virtuoso in the use of language, and has been called 'a musician of Hungarian prose'; an outstanding blender of romanticism and realism. Though an excellent novelist, his real genre is the short story.

Most important novels: *Ének a búzúmezőkről* (1927; tr. G. Halász, *Song of the Wheatfields*, 1930), a pacifist novel; *Hannibal föltámasztása* (1924), an ironical novel about the life of a provincial schoolmaster; *Az arany koporsó* (tr. E. Rácz, *The Golden Coffin*, Budapest, 1963), a historical novel about the early days of Christianity. [JFR]

Reményi, *HWL*; Klaniczay, *HHL*.

**Morando, Bernardo** (Sestri Ponente 1589–Piacenza 1656). Italian poet. A protégé of the Farnese family. He attempted various literary genres. He has the technical and psychological sophistication of the ⇨ Marinist school but without their usual imaginative vigour. He illustrates also a tendency, typical of his age, to dwell on abnormal aspects of reality which become repellent because of the 'outward' way in which they are scrutinized – a dwarf in love, a beautiful girl demented. He also wrote a prose romance, *Rosalinda* (1650). [DGR]

*Opere* (4 vols., 1662).
Croce, *LM*; Ferrero, *MM*; Getto, *MM*.

**Morante, Elsa** (Rome 1918– ). Italian novelist. Her first novel, *Menzogna e sortilegio* (1948), a long, romantic story of pride, prejudice and frustrated love, was followed nine years later by a minor masterpiece, *L'isola di Arturo* (tr. I. Quigly, *Arturo's Island*, 1959), the story of a boy's gradual awakening to love, when the joyful myths of childhood slowly give way to the disenchantment and suffering of maturity. *Lo scialle andaluso* (1964) contains 12 stories written between 1935 and 1951. In 1941 she married the novelist Alberto ⇨ Moravia. [GMC]

*Il mondo salvato dai ragazzini* (1968).
Pullini, *RID*; Bàrberi Squarotti, *NID*.

**Moratín, Leandro Fernández de** (Madrid 1760–Paris 1828). Spanish dramatist. At first a jewelry designer, he later held various official posts and ecclesiastical benefices. He was the son of a poet and dramatist, and won second prize in an Academy poetry competition at 18. His first surviving play, *El viejo y la niña*, was finished just eight years later, although the ecclesiastical censors prevented its performance until 1790. Subsequently he wrote 4 other original plays (of which the most famous is *El sí de las niñas*, 1805, about the marrying off of daughters against their will) and translated *Hamlet* (1798) and Molière's *L'école des maris* (1808), and *Le médecin malgré lui* (1814). He also wrote poetry, a prose satire on pedants (*La derrota de los pedantes*, 1789) and a historical work on the origins of the Spanish drama. Like his father's generation he respected the neo-classical theories of literature, and his comedies – notably *La comedia nueva* (1792) – exemplified orderliness of composition as well as of moral conduct. All his published works reflcct his belief in reason and the didactic function of literature. His accounts of his travels through Europe before 1796 and his letters show his wit and powers of observation. Both his literary and official careers were interrupted by the Peninsular War, and he lived in semi-retirement for several years during the reign of Ferdinand VII Fears for his future led him to flee to France in 1817. [ONVG]

*Teatro completo* (1944); CC, CA.
Brenan, *LSP*.

**Moratín, Nicolás Fernández de** (Madrid 1737–Madrid 1780). Spanish poet and dramatist. He is remembered for his part in the polemic against the traditional Spanish drama (*Desengaños al teatro español*, 1762–3) rather than for his plays in the French style that were never or seldom produced (e.g. *Lucrecia*, 1763; *Guzmán el Bueno*, 1777). His ode to the bullfighter Pedro Romero, and his even better known 'Fiesta de Toros in Madrid', though somewhat pretentious in language, have local colour (*El Poeta*, 1764). He tried many styles, from the Gongorist to the neo-classical and Horatian, and was particularly successful in his handling of the ballad (*romance*). His epic on the destruction of Cortés's ships (*Las naves de Cortés destruidas*, 1777) deservedly failed to get a prize from the Academy. [JMC]

*Poesías y Comedias* (1846) in BAE 2; *Poesías inéditas*, ed. Foulché-Delbosc (1892).
Blecua, *FLE*; Trend, *OBSV*.

**Moravia, Alberto,** pseud. of Alberto Pincherle (Rome 1907– ). Italian novelist. Owing to a serious and prolonged illness in adolescence, he had no formal education but plenty of time to read and write. His first novel, *Gli indifferenti* (1929; tr. A. Davidson, *The Time of Indifference*, 1953), a dry unemotional picture of petty middle-class corruption in Rome, caused a great sensation, especially since Fascism had succeeded in persuading the Italian literary establishment, already bent on idle formalistic pursuits, to avoid any reference to real problems and issues. The novel was therefore interpreted by many as a criticism of Italian society under Fascism. When, after a volume of short stories (*La bella vita*, 1935), he published his second novel, *Le ambizioni sbagliate* (1935; tr. A. Livingstone, *Wheel of Fortune*, 1938), the Fascist authorities obliged reviewers to ignore it. In order to express covertly what he could not say openly, Moravia then began to write short stories in a half surrealistic, half allegorical style (*I sogni del pigro*, 1940), thereby deceiving some critics into thinking that he had finally chosen the safer path of formalism. His third novel, *La mascherata* (1941; tr. A. Davidson, *The Fancy Dress Party*, 1947), was personally censored by Mussolini, who at first did not recognize himself in the grotesque South-Americanish dictator portrayed in the book; he later vetoed its reprint. Some of Moravia's best surrealistic tales appeared after the war in the volume *L'epidemia*: the title story, which tells of an unspecified country where people get so used to the nauseating symptom of a new epidemic – a carrion stench emanating from the head – as to enjoy it like an agreeable perfume, is a transparent allegory of Italy's political laxity during Fascism. A strong moralistic streak persists in all his novels published after the war, in which he presents a crude image of middle-class self-indulgence and hypocrisy and social alienation in a neo-capitalistic world. In 1952 the Roman Catholic Church put all his books on the Index.

Moravia's characters try to redeem their estrangement from one another and bridge indifference and boredom surrounding them by the only form of social intercourse open to them, sex; which in the circumstances becomes not an act of love but the confession of man's inability to love. In having sexual intercourse with a promiscuous woman a man communes in this confession with all the other men who had her before, and can thereby find some measure of comfort for his own spiritual impotence. This explains why the most sympathetic and warm-hearted of Moravia's characters are, after all, his prostitutes (*La Romana*, 1947; tr. L. Holland, *The Woman of Rome*, 1949), and why conjugal love and fidelity have no place in his novels (*L'amore coniugale e altri racçonti*, 1949; tr. A. Davidson, *Conjugal Love*, 1951; *Il disprezzo*, 1954; tr. A. Davidson, *A Ghost at Noon*, 1955).

In spite of its consistently high quality (a lean matter-of-factness where no word is inessential to stylistic perfection or in the logical development of the narration) his work has not benefited from continuous insistence on the same themes: Dino's 'boredom' in *La noia* (1960; tr. A. Davidson, *The Empty Canvas*, 1961) unrelieved by his frantic love-making to Cecilia, is basically the same as Michele's 'indifference' in *Gli indifferenti*, and stems from identical causes: 'the absurdity of a reality insufficient to persuade one of its real existence'. Moravia's attitude to literature in general, expressed in a book of unusually intelligent and penetrating essays (*L'uomo come fine, e altri saggi*, 1963; tr. B. Wall, *Man as an End*, 1965), deserves to be studied. [GMC]

*Bitter Honeymoon and Other Stories*, tr. B. Wall, *et al.* (1954); *Disobedience*, tr. A. Davidson (1950); *The Conformist*, tr. ibid. (1952); *Agostino*, tr. B. de Zoete (1952); *Racconti romani* (1954; tr. A. Davidson, *Roman Tales*, 1956); *La ciociara* (1957; tr. ibid., *Two Women*, 1957); *The Wayward Wife and Other Stories*, tr. ibid. (1961); *Nuovi racconti romani* (1959; tr. ibid., *More Roman Tales*, 1963); *L'automa* (1963; tr. ibid., *The Fetish*, 1964); *L'attenzione* (1965; tr. ibid., *The Lie*, 1966).

*M.*, ed. O. del Buono (Milan, 1962); G. Dego, *M.* (1966); A. Limentani, *A.M. tra esistenza e realtà* (Venice, 1962); Falqui, *PNNI*; Fernandez, *RI*; Flora, *SIC*; Pullini, *RID.*

**Moréas, Jean,** pseud. of Iannis Papadiamantopoulos (Athens 1856–Paris 1910). French poet born of Greek parents. He came to Paris in 1879. Much under the influence of Baudelaire and Verlaine, his first collection, *Les Syrtes* (1884), established him as a 'decadent'. In *Les Cantilènes* (1886), his preface claims the title of 'symboliste', as does his manifesto in *Le Figaro* (18 September 1886); the poems show a love of medieval and archaic terms. By the time he published *Le pèlerin passioné* (1891) he had become the leader of a new group, the

École Romane (Raynaud, R. de La Tailhède, ⇨ Maurras), inspired by antiquity. The poems typical of this phase were collected in *Poèmes et sylves 1886–1896* (1907). In his last works he became more and more classical in his style and themes, writing what are considered his best poems in *Les stances* (1899, bks i–ii; 1901, bks iii–vi; 1920, posth., bk vii). He wrote a play, *Iphigénie à Aulis*, after Euripides. [WA]

R. Niklaus, *J.M.* (Paris, 1936); C. Maurras, *Maîtres et témoins de ma vie d'esprit* (Paris, 1954); A. Embiricos, *Les étapes de J.M.* (Lausanne, 1955).

**Moreau, Hégésippe** (Paris 1810–Paris 1838). French minor Romantic poet. His collected poems, *Le Myosotis* (1838), contain poems of country life and the 'Ode à la faim'. He was employed as a proof-reader and ended his days in the workhouse. His prose *Contes à ma sœur* were published posthumously in 1851. [WA]

**Moreto y Cabaña, Agustín** (Madrid 1618–Toledo 1669). Spanish priest and court dramatist. He derived his plots from predecessors but gave them new elegance. His best play, *El desdén con el desdén* (ed. W. H. Jones, N.Y., 1935) (with episodes from ⇨ Lope), is a comedy, whose heroine believes herself incapable of falling in love; its lighthearted pretences and intrigues anticipate ⇨ Marivaux, and were imitated by Molière in *La Princesse d'Élide* and ⇨ Gozzi in *La principessa filosofa*. The 18th-century mood is present again, e.g. in *El lindo don Diego* (CA), a comedy about a fop, or in the setting (half Watteau, half *Figaro*) of *La confusión de un jardín*, which takes place at night in a tree-shaded garden. One volume of dramas was published in 1654 and two more in 1676. [JMC]

*Comedias escogidas* in BAE 39.

**Moretti, Marino** (Cesenatico 1885–1971). Italian novelist. He began as a poet in his early twenties, writing in a humble conversational style polemically opposed to current D'Annunzio-inspired bombast. The felicitous definition of 'crepuscular' first applied by G. A. Borgese to Moretti's *Poesie scritte col lapis* (1910) soon became the name of a poetic 'school' including Gozzano, Corazzini and others. Later Moretti turned to prose: he has produced some 17 novels and about as many volumes of short stories and personal memories. His narrative style is a direct descendant of his early 'crepuscular' manner: modest and unrhetorical; capable of delicate nuances. Moretti's themes are provincial frustration, the middling passions ruling the lives of common men; the weak resignation of the Christian underlings; the uneventful life of undistinguished people, which is nevertheless all they can hope for. However, within his narrow range of situations and emotions he succeeds in displaying considerable inventive gifts. His best-known novels are *Il sole del sabato* (1917), *La voce di Dio* (1920), *I due fanciulli* (1922, later rewritten with the new title *Il pudore*, 1950), *L'Andreana* (1935), *Il fiocco verde* (1948). A comprehensive selection of his short stories was published in 1959, under the title *Tutte le novelle*. [GC]

F. Casnati, *M.M.* (Milan, 1952); *Contemporanei*, i.

**Morgenstern, Christian** (Munich 1871–Merano 1914). German poet-philosopher. Translator of Ibsen and Strindberg. Influenced by Nietzsche, later by mysticism (Buddhist and Christian), finally by the anthropology of Rudolf Steiner; he was consumptive from his early teens. Neither his serious poems and epigrams inspired by his mysticism (*Einkehr*, 1910; *Wir fanden einen Pfad*, 1914) nor his love-poems (*Ich und du*, 1911) are as well known as his famous nonsense poems (*Galgenlieder*, 1905; *Palmström*, 1910). Palmström, von Korf, Palma Kunkel, the Nasobēm and the Gingganz are Lewis Carroll-like figures that lead their now immortal existence in realms where burlesque has profound metaphysical implications (Morgenstern was claimed as one of their own by the later writers in the 'absurd' tradition – the Dadaists). He strips language of its bourgeois conventions and pretensions by a grotesque literal interpretation of conventional phrases, and creates new objects by verbal analogies – yet not arbitrarily, but with a fine sense of the mysterious relationship (so soon to become problematic in modern philosophy) between words and things. [PB]

*Gesammelte Werke* (1965); *The Gallows Song*, tr M. Knight (1964).

M. Beheim-Schwarzbach, *C.M.* (Reinbek, 1964); F. Hiebel, *C.M., Wende und Aufbruch unseres Jahrunderts* (Berne, 1957); M. Bauer, *C.M Leben und Werk* (Munich, 1948); Natan *GML*, ii; *PEGS*, XXV (1957); *BA*, XII (1938); *GLL*, I, 2 (1948).

**Móricz, Zsigmond** (Csécse 1879–Budape

1942). Hungarian writer. The most important Hungarian writer of this century. Son of a peasant and a clergyman's daughter, he received a Calvinist education; enduring material hardships, he became a journalist. ⇨ Ady's works, and later friendship, provided a stimulus for his literary career, and he became editor of ⇨ *Nyugat*, gaining fame through his first published short story, *Hét Krajcár* (1909). Though at first influenced by ⇨ Jókai, ⇨ Mikszáth and the Naturalists, Móricz's individual form of expression became the highly realistic portrayal of the peasantry, gentry and small-town middle class. His characters are generally temperamental, often coarse, cruel or rebellious. His frequently returning theme is the conflict between heroes who strive for goodness and purity, and either their own shortcomings or the backward ideas of their environment. The problems depicted in his social studies are often those of married life, which is painted as the battlefield of the sexes. *A fáklya* (1917; tr. A. Lengyel, *The Torch*, N.Y., 1931) is the tragedy of an enthusiastic young priest, who, when confronted by the difficulties and old-fashioned conventions of his parish, tries to adapt himself but finally perishes. Similarly, the hero of *Úri Muri*, though himself a member of the gentry, tries to fight against the decadence of his class; the hopelessness of the struggle, however, leads to his suicide. In his novel *Légy jó mindhalálig* (tr. L. Körösi, *Be Faithful unto Death*, Budapest, 1962), which has been dramatized and filmed, he portrays himself in the pure and idealistic child hero who struggles 'unto death' against the evil world of adults. His other major novels, *Annácska*, *Rokonok* (1930–2), *Egy boldog ember* (1932–5), all contain strong criticism of society's shortcomings and crimes. The peasant world, whose atmosphere Móricz describes vividly from personal experience, provides the background for his short stories *Tragédia*, *Az ebéd*, *Szegény emberek* and *Egyszer jóllakni*. Other notable works: *The Romance of my Life* (1939), an autobiography; *Erdély* (1922–35), a historical trilogy about 17th-century Transylvania; *Rózsa Sándor* (1940–2), the story of a 19th-century outlaw; *A Százszínselyem keszkenő*, tr. L. Wolfe, *Shawl of Many Colours*, 1936; and *A Stipendium* (1936; tr. anon., *The Stipend*, Budapest, 1955) are short stories. [JFR]

Reményi, *HWL*; Klaniczay, *HHL*.

**Mörike, Eduard** (Ludwigsburg 1804–Stuttgart 1875). German poet. An outwardly uneventful life, spent as a student of theology at Tübingen, as curate in various Swabian villages with picturesque names, as pastor of Cleversulzbach (1834–43) and as valetudinarian in Bad Mergentheim and Stuttgart precipitated a slender volume of poems (*Gedichte*, 1838; augmented editions 1848, 1856 and 1867). These were at first regarded as of local interest only (Heine, for one, mocked them as typical products of Swabian provincialism); but gradually it dawned on German readers that what they here heard was the voice of a lyric poet who had few equals and no superiors. His poems are distinguished by a subtlety of rhythm which mirrors their subtlety of tone and mood; by a refusal to raise the voice or overemphasize which delays but in the end serves to enhance their emotional impact; by their presentation of half-tones of emotion, often symbolized – as in the famous 'On a Winter's Morning before Sunrise' – by the half-light of dawn or dusk; by the mythopoeic quality of such poems as 'At Midnight'; and by a refreshing sense of humour. Practically all sides of his genius are represented in Hugo Wolf's *Poems by Eduard Mörike, Set for Voice and Piano* (1889) which has been the greatest single factor in spreading Mörike's fame at home and abroad. The lyric poems constitute his greatest achievement; but he also published many translations from the Latin and Greek and a number of narrative prose-works, notably *Maler Nolten* (1832), a novel in the German tradition of the *Bildungsroman* or novel of education and personal development; and *Mozart auf der Reise nach Prag* (1856; tr. L. v. Loewenstein-Wertheim, *Mozart's Journey to Prague*, 1957), a short story based on an imaginary incident in the life of Mörike's favourite composer, which mingles – in a way wholly characteristic of his work as a whole – idyll and elegy, and which culminates in one of his finest poems: 'Consider, my Soul!'. [SSP]

*Sämtliche Werke*, ed. H. Mayne (Leipzig, 1909 and 1914); *Poems by E.M.*, tr. N. K. Cruickshank and G. F. Cunningham (1959).

M. Mare, *E.M. The Man and the Poet* (1957); S. S. Prawer, *Mörike und seine Leser* (Stuttgart, 1960); H. Meyer, *E.M.* (Stuttgart, 1961).

**Morpurgo, Rahel** (Trieste 1790–Trieste 1871). Hebrew poetess. The first Hebrew poetess, she wrote chiefly for special occasions. Her ode to the revolution of 1848 was translated into French and Italian. [EE]

*Collected Poems and Letters*, ed. V. Castiglione (1890).

**Morsztyn, Jan Andrzej** (? 1613–? 1693). Polish poet. He was the first of the neglected baroque writers to win recognition late in the 19th century, when both his picturesque life and his ornate verse seemed typical of the age. As courtier and statesman he served three kings of Poland to his great financial profit, but in 1683 he was charged with high treason, left the country and ended his life as a wealthy citizen of France.

His 2 collections of poems, *Kanikuła* (1647) and *Lutnia* (1661), include many translations and adaptations from ⇨ Marino, but he repaid his literary debts generously with experiments in language. His version of Corneille's *Le Cid*, which was performed in Warsaw (1662), is a model of intelligent and faithful translation. His personal manner is apparent in his courtly love songs (some addressed to Catherine Gordon, his Scottish wife), in penitential reflections as well as in obscene verses which he wrote with humorous gusto. [JP]

Peterkiewicz and Singer, *FCPP*.

**Morsztyn, Zbigniew** (?1620?–Königsberg 1689?). Polish poet. He was an active follower of Arianism, a sect exercising a considerable influence on Polish intellectual life in the 17th century, and he served the Radziwiłł family as a soldier, courtier and envoy. During the Swedish invasion he was wounded and taken prisoner; *Duma niewolnicza* reflects his state of mind at that time. After the edict of 1658, expelling the Arians from Poland, he chose exile in the principality of Prussia rather than abandon his beliefs. His *Pieśń w ucisku* is doubly convincing because it admits neither anger nor self-righteous piety. The Arian exodus deepened the religious poet in him.

The cycle *Emblemata* is his best lyrical achievement, and equally impressive as a record of mystical experience. It consists of 113 poems loosely based on the inscriptions from a book of emblems which has only recently been traced. Many of the Biblical mottoes are from Solomon's Song. The conceptual character of the emblems belongs to the baroque style, but in language he is far more ascetic than his contemporaries. This alone suggests an individuality strong enough to withstand the canons of required taste.

His occasional verses ring with the authentic tone of 'the homely muse' which is the title of his manuscript collection (*Muza domowa*). [JP]

**Moscherosch, Johann Michael** (Willstädt 1601–Worms 1669). German satirist. He suffered acute personal loss in the Thirty Years' War, before achieving a measure of security in various legal and administrative positions. A native of Alsace, he stands in the Alemannic tradition of moral satire established by ⇨ Brant and ⇨ Murner. His principal work, *Wunderliche und warhafftige Gesichte Philanders von Sittewald* (Part One, 1640; Part Two, 1643; ed. F. Bobertag, DNL 32), is based on the French translation of ⇨ Quevedo's *Sueños*. Women, sexual incontinence, hypocrisy, greed for money, the servility of courtiers, etc., are castigated, as well as a number of contemporary evils, in particular the gallicization of German cultural life (Part Two – *À la mode Kehrauss*). The narrative skill revealed in *Soldatenleben* (Part Two), a little picaresque novel which anticipates ⇨ Grimmelshausen's *Simplicissimus* in certain respects, never achieved full development, and his only other work is the *Insomnis cura parentum* (1643; ed. L. Pariser, 1893), the legacy of good advice left by a Christian father to his children.

A deeply moral and sincere writer, he is a spokesman of the Protestant middle classes and a prominent representative of the anti-courtly satirical tradition of the 17th century. [WAC]

*GLL*, VII (1953–4).

**Möser, Justus** (Osnabrück 1720–Osnabrück 1794). German historian. His essay on German history which he contributed to ⇨ Herder's *Von deutscher Art und Kunst* (1773) succinctly expresses the historical outlook of the *Sturm und Drang*. It was in fact the preface to his history of Osnabrück, *Osnabrücksche Geschichte* (1768ff.), a work which lays particular emphasis on the *Volk* and views history as an organic growth, and greatly influenced the Romantics. The *Patriotische Phantasien* (1774) may be regarded as one of the earliest monuments of German folklore in their accurate observation and recording of Westphalian life. [WAC]

*Sämtliche Werke*, ed. W. Kohlschmidt *et al.* (14 vols., 1954ff.).

F. Meinecke, *Über M.s. Geschichtsauffassung* (Berlin, 1932).

**Mounier, Emmanuel** (Grenoble 1905–Châtenay-Malabry 1950). French writer. *Agrégé* in philosophy, literary critic and essayist, intellectual leader in the Resistance, Catholic and Marxist sympathizer, controversialist, founder and editor of *Esprit*. Seeking to close the gap between communist and non-communist Frenchmen, he launched this periodical in 1932, and with it the Personalist movement, a non-party philosophy between Marxism and Existentialism. Influenced by ⇨ Bergson and ⇨ Péguy, he proposes a vitalistic dynamic individualism, and advocates an economic revolution and a new socialistic system, in which respect for the individuality of the person, and a prominently active Church, would give material implementation to the new ethical values, appropriate to our age, already recognized at theoretical level by academic theologians and philosophers, but, thinks Mounier, inadequately asserted by them, owing to fearfulness and illogical inertia, which cause them to cling to the forms of outmoded bourgeois-capitalist individualism. His claims to answer the needs of the apathetic and disorientated post-war youth receive some substantiation in the measured interest shown in him since his death.

He published some 170 articles, and collaborated in more, mostly in *Esprit*. His books include: *La pensée de Ch. Péguy* (with others), 1931, *Manifeste au service du Personnalisme* (1936; tr. the monks of Saint John's Abbey, *Personalist manifesto*, 1938) with several subsequent books on personalism, e.g. *Le personnalisme* (1950; tr. P. Mairet, *Personalism*, 1952); *L'affrontement chrétien* (1945), *Liberté sous conditions* (1946), *Traité du caractère* (1947; tr. C. Rowland, *The Character of Man*, 1956), *Introduction aux existentialismes* (1947; tr. E. Blow, *Existentialist Philosophies*, 1948), *La petite peur du XXe siècle: peur de quoi?* (1948; tr. C. Rowland, *Be not afraid*, 1951), *L'éveil de l'Afrique noire* (1948), *Carnets de route* (3 vols., 1950), *Communisme, anarchie et personnalisme* (posth. 1966). [JF]

C. Moix, *La pensée d'E.M.* (Paris, 1960); and *E.M., 1905–1950* (Paris, 1951) (repr. of special number of *Esprit*, December 1950); L. Guissard, *E.M.* (Paris, 1962); J. Conilh, *E.M., Sa vie, son œuvre, avec un exposé de sa philosophie* (Paris, 1966); J. Charpentreau and L. Rocher, *L'esthétique personnaliste d'E.M.* (Paris, 1966).

**Mozarabic Lyric.** The somewhat misleading name applied to the snatches in early Romance which occur as the final refrain (*kharja*) of some Arabic (and also Hebrew) strophic poems of a genre, the *muwaššah*, which originated in Muslim Spain in the 10th century and flourished in the 11th and 12th centuries A.D. They are called 'Mozarabic' because the dialect used is that of the Christian *mozárabes*, but since many Muslims (and Jews) also spoke this form of early Romance, there is no reason to associate the lyrics with any particular community. The themes – typically a maiden bewails to her mother or little sisters the absence of her beloved, often on the occasion of some festival – resemble those of the Galician *cantigas de amigo*, although the form is different. Arab theorists lay it down that in the *muwaššah* the *kharja* should be put into the mouth of a girl, may be in Romance, and if necessary may be borrowed from an existing poem. It is not unknown for Arabic poems of homosexual intent to terminate in one of these exclusively heterosexual refrains. Owing to the garbled state of the texts and the inherent ambiguities of the script, the correct reading must often remain subject to doubt. These lyrics, of scant intrinsic merit, have attracted great interest because they are the earliest monuments of Peninsular Romance and because of the light they might throw on the literary contacts between Arabic- and Romance-speaking peoples at a crucial period in the development of lyric poetry in Europe. To some they would appear to bring confirmation of the 'Arabic thesis' that the rise of the Provençal lyric, with its *muwaššah*-like strophic patterns, owes much to Arabic influence, but the authorities are by no means agreed that this is the true interpretation of the ambiguous facts, for it could be that the *muwaššah*, itself a phenomenon without parallel in Arabic literature, is an Arabic calque of a European model. [LPH]

*Les chansons mozarabes*, ed. S. M. Stern (1953).
*RFE*, XLIII (1960).

**Mrożek, Sławomir** (Borzęcin 1930– ). Polish satirist. He uses both nonsense and fantasy to dislodge the high seriousness of politics, and most of his stories in the collection *Słoń* (1957; tr. K. Syrop, *The Elephant*, 1962) deal with some obvious inefficiency or pretence. A cartoonist's hand can be detected in the outlines of his anecdotes. His short plays superficially resemble those of ⇨ Ionesco, but are in fact re-enacted anecdotes (e.g. 'The Police', 1958, 'The Turkey', 1960). *Tango*, his best-known play, was performed in London in 1966. Mrożek has the lightest touch among the Polish humorous writers who emerged after 1956. [JP]

*Six Plays*, tr. N. Bethell (1967); Kuncewicz, *MPM*.

**Mucha, Jiří** (Prague 1915– ). Czech author. His short stories *Problémy nadporučíka Knapa* (1946; tr. E. Osers, *The Problems of Lieutenant Knap*, 1945) and his novel *Spálená setba* (1948; tr. E. Osers, *Scorched Crop*, 1950) are based on his experience as a member of the Free Czechoslovak Army in the West during the Second World War. Wrongly accused of anti-state activities by the Communist régime in Czechoslovakia he was imprisoned and later confined to a forced labour camp. After being rehabilitated he gave a personal account of this period in *Studené slunce* (1968; tr. E. Osers, *Living and Partly Living*, 1967). His *Alphonse Mucha* (tr. S. Jolly, 1966) is a book of reminiscences about his father, the famous *art nouveau* painter. [KB]

**Mühsam, Erich** (Berlin 1878–Oranienburg 1934). German poet, dramatist and satirist. He edited anarchist periodicals like *Der arme Teufel* (Friedrichshagen, 1902), *Weckruf* (Zürich, 1905), *Kain* (Munich, 1911–19) and took a prominent part in Bavarian left-wing movements, for which he was imprisoned for six years in 1919. Further revolutionary activities led to his death in a Nazi concentration camp. His poems (*Die Wüste*, 1904; *Der Krater*, 1909; *Wüste, Krater, Wolken*, 1914; *Brennende Erde*, 1920; *Revolution*, 1925) and plays (*Die Hochstapler*, 1906; *Die Freivermählten*, 1914; *Judas*, 1921; *Staatsräson*, 1928) combine proletarian social criticism, anarchism and expressionist techniques. The manifestoes in *Alarm* (1925) and the treatise *Von Eisner bis Leviné* (1929) are theoretical writings on politics, while *Namen und Menschen* (published posthumously, 1949) is a more personal autobiography. [LL]

*Ausgewählte Werke*, ed. F. A. Hünich (1958 ff.). K. Hiller, 'E.M.', in *Köpfe und Tröpfe* (1950); N. Pawlowa, 'Die Dichtung E.M.s', in *Kunst und Literatur* (Berlin, 1959).

**Müller, Wilhelm** (Dessau 1794–Dessau 1827). German poet. One of the few to have come from a working-class family. In his lifetime he became known to a wide public for his political *Lieder der Griechen* (1821), but the abiding interest in his work derives from the collections of romantic, folk-song-like poetry (*Müllerlieder*, 1818; *Gedichte aus den Papieren eines reisenden Waldhornisten*, 1821; *Wanderlieder*, 1823), which captured to a degree unequalled by any other poet the simplicity and directness of the Volkslied. His poetry in this vein is the most perfect product of the enthusiasm evoked by ⇨ Brentano's and ⇨ Arnim's collection of folk-poetry, *Des Knaben Wunderhorn* (1805–8). The most famous of his poems are those which were set to music by Schubert in the song-cycles *Die Winterreise* (1827) and *Die schöne Müllerin* (1823). [RT]

Prawer, *PBGL*.

**Multatuli.** ⇨ Douwes Dekker, Eduard.

**Munibe, Xavier Maria de.** ⇨ Basque Literature.

**Munk, Kaj** (Maribo 1889–Hørbylunde 1944). Danish playwright and poet. Though he had written his first play as a schoolboy (*Pilatus*, printed 1938), he studied theology – being much influenced by Kierkegaard – took holy orders (1924) and became vicar at Vedersø, a little parish on the west coast of Jutland; here he married a local girl. Reading Shakespeare, Oehlenschläger and Ibsen he wrote *En Idealist* (1928; tr. R. P. Keigwin, *Herod the King* in *Five Plays by Kaj Munk*, 1953), which was staged in Copenhagen – and damned by the critics. Undeterred, he achieved success with *Cant* (1931; tr. R. P. Keigwin, ibid.), a verse drama about Henry VIII and Anne Boleyn, though *Ordet* (1932; tr. R. P. Keigwin, ibid.), about the reality of miracles, is a far better play. His new version of *Hamlet* (1935) was a complete failure; but a new production of *Herod* in 1938 established this play as one of his most successful. *Kærlighed* (1935; in part tr. R. P. Keigwin, *Love and Charity* in *The Norseman*, No. 1, 1949) reveals most clearly his strength and weakness as a playwright. For a time during the 1930s Munk admired Mussolini and Hitler, but in his play *Han sidder ved Smeltediglen* (1938; tr. R. P. Keigwin, *He Sits at the Melting-Pot* in *Five Plays*) he attacked the persecution of Jews; after the German occupation his resistance was so outspoken that his plays were banned. Apart from *Egelykke* (1940), a play about Grundtvig, he wrote a 'Resistance play' *Niels Ebbesen* (1942; tr. in *Scandinavian Plays of the 20th Century*, Princeton, N.J., 1945), a dramatic dialogue *Før Cannae* (1943; tr. R. P. Keigwin, *Before Cannae* in *Five Plays*), and a one-act play, *Ewalds Død* (1943; tr. R. P. Keigwin, *The Death of Ewald* in *The Norseman*, No. 6, 1949), which was produced under a different name. On 4 January 1944, Munk was taken from his vicarage by the Gestapo and murdered in a ditch on the main road to Silkeborg.

Munk's non-dramatic works include a number of travel books, essays, sermons, poems, and a volume of memoirs, *Foraaret saa sagte kommer*, published in 1942. [ELB]

*K.M. – Playwright, Priest and Patriot*, ed. R. P. Keigwin (1944) (sel. tr.).
R. P. Keigwin, *Introduction to Five Plays by K.M.* (1953); *Drama* (May 1949).

**Muratori, Ludovico Antonio** (Vignola, Modena 1672–Modena 1750). Italian historian. Of humble birth, he took holy orders and, as *dottore* at the Biblioteca Ambrosiana in Milan, soon distinguished himself for the collection of ancient inscriptions – *Anecdota latina* (1697–8). In 1700 he returned to Modena as archivist of Rinaldo I d'Este. His first great work of erudition was the *Antichità estensi* (1717–40), followed by *Rerum italicarum scriptores* (24 vols., 1723–38; new edn, 1900 ff. – the major collection of medieval manuscript sources), *Antiquitates italicae medii aevii* (6 vols., 1738–43 – studies of customs and institutions) and *Annali della storia d'Italia* (12 vols., 1744–9). Few medievalists have achieved his breadth of vision and his meticulous scholarship. His *Epistolario* (ed. M. Campori, 14 vols., 1910–22) – 6,000 letters addressed to many of the greatest contemporaries – contains remarkable evidence of his intellectual stature. [RHC]

*Opere varie* (36 vols, 1767–80); *Opere* (48 vols., 1790 ff.).
G. Bertoni, *L.A.M.* (Rome, 1926); M. Fubini, *Dal M. al Baretti* (Bari, 1954); F. De Carli, *L.A.M.* (Florence, 1955); G. Falco, 'L.A.M. e il preilluminismo', in *La cultura illuministica italiana* (Turin, 1957); *Minori*, iii.

**Murger, Henry** (Paris 1822–Paris 1861). French novelist of German extraction. Although of little education he frequented the haunts of lesser poets and painters of his time, living in appalling poverty. He became famous with *Scènes de la vie de bohème* (1847–9 in the *Corsaire*), which he dramatized with T. Barrière (1849); it is best known as Puccini's opera *La Bohème*. *Le pays latin* (1851), *Les buveurs d'eau* (1855) are less effective; he also wrote some minor poetry and the play *Le bonhomme jadis* (1852). [WA]

R. Baldick, *The First Bohemian* (1960).

**Murner, Thomas** (Oberehnheim 1475–Oberehnheim 1537). German satirist. He entered the Franciscan order at 15, and became famous as a teacher, preacher and fearless controversialist. As a native of Alsace, it was natural that his moral satires (*Doctor murners narrenbeschwerung*, 1512; *Der schelmen zunfft*, 1512; *Die Geuchmatt*, 1515) should show the marked influence of his great compatriot, ⇨ Brant – the *Narrenbeschwerung* even uses the woodcuts of *Das Narrenschiff* – but Murner excels him in his highly developed sense of humour, his waggishness and, as a preacher, in his closeness to the common people in thought and language. He castigated the obvious abuses of the Roman Church but hoped for a reformation without damage to the essential fabric of the faith. He became one of ⇨ Luther's fiercest opponents, once it became evident that Luther was destroying the whole penitential system of the Church. His *Von dem grossen Lutherischen Narren* (1522) builds on the folly tradition of his moral satires to burlesque Luther and the evangelical faith. His deep moral seriousness and devout faith, which often tend to be obscured by the waggishness and robust humour of the satires, are given true lyrical expression in his fine poem *Ain new Lied von dem undergang des christlichen glaubens* (1522). [WAC]

*T.M.s Deutsche Schriften*, ed. F. Schultz *et al.* (Strassburg, 1918ff.).
R. Newald, *Probleme und Gestalten des deutschen Humanismus* (Berlin, 1963).

**Musil, Robert (Edler von)** (Klagenfurt 1880–Geneva 1942). Austrian novelist. Abandoning military school (Mährisch-Weisskirchen), he qualified as an engineer (Brünn), later studied philosophy and psychology (D. Phil., Berlin, 1908). Distinguished also as an officer (1914–18; Ritterkreuz), he foresook brilliant opportunities to retire into writing. Ruined by the inflation, emigrating from Berlin, then Vienna, to escape Nazism, he died in poverty. He has been 're-discovered' only recently (e.g. in *Der Monat*, November 1950, and *Mod. Lang. Forum*, 37, 1952) and claimed as among the great novelists of the century, his reputation resting on the monumental work *Der Mann ohne Eigenschaften* (1930–43; rev. edn, 1952; tr. E. Wilkins and E. Kaiser, *The Man Without Qualities*, 1953–60). The novel explores one year, 1913–14, in the life of a brilliant Viennese intellectual who cannot commit himself to a career: an obviously 'subjective' theme which is treated, however, with intense intellectual objectivity. The complex synthetic style is what chiefly makes the novel remarkable (by conventional standards of character, plot, view of life, it appears 'fragmentary' and 'formless') – a 'spiritual expedition' to re-define experiences of which the conventional qualities and value no longer seem authentic. In this the 'hero's' dilemma is seen as symptomatic of a social condition; Musil is inspired by the same sense of cultural collapse as Rilke, Hofmannsthal, and the Expressionists (with whom he has been compared). His vision extends from an ironical Proust-like centre of reflection to relate both the inner and outer disorders of decadence, its perverse private passions and its futile public ideologies, its spiritual absurdities and its exposure to criminality and violence. His early work shows the same preoccupation (especially with erotic disturbance) in the novel *Die Verwirrungen des Jünglings Törless* (1906; tr. E. Wilkins and E. Kaiser, *Young Törless*, 1961), and the stories *Die Vereinigungen* (1911), *Drei Frauen* (1924), and in the drama *Die Schwärmer* (1921) and the farce *Vinzenz...* (1924). He published a selection of his essays, reviews, etc. in *Nachlass zu Lebzeiten* (1936). [PB]

*Torka and Other Stories*, tr. E. Wilkins and E. Kaiser (1965).
*Akzente*, 1 (1954); W. Berghahn, *R.M.* (Reinbek, 1963); H. Arntzen, *Satirscher Stil* (Bonn, 1960); K. Dinklage, *R.M.* (Hamburg, 1960); E. Kaiser and E. Wilkins, *R.M.* (Stuttgart, 1962); B. Pike, *R.M.* (1961); Jens, *DLG*; Natan, *GML*, III; *GQ*, 29 (1956); *Dt. Vierteljahrsschrift für Lit.*, 3, 1965.

**'Muspilli'** ('Fire of Purgatory'). A fragmentary alliterative Old High German poem of the early 9th century, telling of the Last Judgement and the fate of the soul after death. The motifs used in the poem are drawn from the Bible (above all from Revelations) and from early Christian sermons. The message of repentance is preached with an admonitory emphasis on the physical sufferings that await the unrepentent evil-doer, and in the extreme dualism of its outlook the poem is a typical product of the Christian mission in Germany. [RT]

Braune, *AL*, 30; Ehrismann, *GDL*, I.

**Musset, Alfred Louis Charles de** (Paris 1810–Paris 1857). French playwright, poet and novelist. He came of a literary family having strong affinities with the 18th century and the classical tradition. He was brought up in Paris and proved himself a brilliant pupil at the Lycée Henri IV. At 17 he was introduced to the romantic *cénacles* by Hugo's brother-in-law, Paul Foucher, and knew ⇨ Vigny, ⇨ Sainte-Beuve, Charles ⇨ Nodier and ⇨ Mérimée. After publishing a translation of de Quincey's *Opium Eater* (1828), he reproduced in his poems, *Contes d'Espagne et d'Italie* (1830), the themes and techniques of the moment, carried to new heights the frenzied violence of romantic passion ('Don Paëz', 'Portia') with fantasy exaggerated to the point of satire, while the opening lines of 'Mardoche' mocked Hugo. 'Les secrètes pensées de Raphaël' were an open declaration of independence; he stepped out of the battle, a decision confirmed by the *Dédicace* to *La coupe et les lèvres* (1832). Refusing the social dogma of Hugo, declining to distinguish between classic and romantic literatures, he admired the arts of Greece and of Renaissance Italy, adopting an almost classical harmony ('Vœux stériles').

His early poems coincide with a strong interest in drama. After the failure of his comedy *La nuit vénitienne* at the Odéon

(1830), he wrote plays entirely for his own satisfaction. Continuing in verse with a one-act tragedy, *La coupe et les lèvres*, and a charming frivolity, *À quoi rêvent les jeunes filles*, he published these with a parody of Hugo's oriental style – 'Namouna' – and an elegy – 'Le Saule' – in the first volume of *Un spectacle dans un fauteuil* (1832). The second volume, in prose, followed a year later with a drama, *Andrea del Sarto*; a tragi-comedy, *Les caprices de Marianne*, and *Fantasio*, a study of the bored, melancholic, romantic dreamer who, through love, changes his personality, discovers an exalted ideal and finally a secret equilibrium.

A contributor since 1830 to *Le Temps* and *La Revue de Paris*, he joined *La Revue des Deux Mondes* early in 1833 and met George ⇨ Sand. Their liaison began in July that year while Musset was finishing *Rolla*. They were parted by illness and incompatibility of temperament during the winter spent in Italy. Musset returned alone from Venice in March 1834. Attempted reconciliations broke down in bitterness, and the relationship ceased altogether a year later. The poet found refuge in dissipation.

During this period, *On ne badine pas avec l'amour* and the drama *Lorenzaccio* (1834) were influenced by George Sand, while *La confession d'un enfant du siècle* (1836) transposed the liaison into a novel.

From 1835 to late 1839, Musset wrote without slackening: plays, *Barberine*, *Le chandelier*, *Un caprice*, *Il ne faut jurer de rien*; 6 short stories; critical articles, including the anti-romantic *Lettres de Dupuis et Cotonet* (1836–7), echoed in the satirical poem, *Dupont et Durand*. The poetry, varied in tone, ranges from occasional verses to the elegy 'Lucie' and the meditation 'Espoir en Dieu'. The 4 famous *Nuits* express a slow change in mood from the silence of intense suffering (*La nuit de mai*, 1835) through the desolation of loneliness (*La nuit de décembre*, 1835) and the illusion of happiness in pleasure (*La nuit d'août*, 1836) to reconciliation with life and love (*La nuit d'octobre*, 1837). All except the second are dialogues with the Muse. In these poems Musset reached the height of his lyrical inspiration.

From 1840, he was stricken by ill-health and experienced increasing moral distress ('Tristesse'), aggravated by excesses. He was reconciled with Hugo and Nodier in 1843. The success of *Un caprice* in 1847 encouraged him to remodel certain plays for the Comédie Française. He was elected to the Académie Française in 1852. His rhythm slowed, but he continued to create: *Souvenir* (1841), *Une soirée perdue*, *Sur la paresse* (1842), *Sur trois marches de marbre rose* (1848), *Souvenir des Alpes* (1851), with other poems; *Mimi Pinson*, *L'histoire d'un merle blanc* and 3 other short stories; 7 comedies including *Il faut qu'une porte...* and *Carmosine* (1850).

Musset was more original in his theatre than in his poetry. The most gifted of his generation for the stage, he created in *Lorenzaccio* the greatest of the Romantic dramas, raised the conventional *proverbe* to drama with *On ne badine pas avec l'amour*, widened it to full comedy with *Il ne faut jurer de rien*. Allied to fantasy, elegance and a supreme lightness of touch, classical in tradition, his fine psychological insight – often subjective – never excludes lyricism. [BJ]

*Œuvres complètes*, ed. M. Allem (3 vols., Pléiade, 1954).

F. Gastinel, *Le Romantisme d'A. de M.* (Paris, 1932); M. Allem, *A. de M.* (Grenoble, 1948); J. Pommier, *Autour du drame de Venise* (Paris, 1958).

**Mustapää, P.**, pseudonym of Martti Haavio (Temmes 1899– ). Finnish poet. A member of the Finnish Academy, he is a distinguished scholar who has broken some new ground with his interpretation of ancient Finnish poetry. In his own poems he combines scholarly understanding with bold stylistic experiments, drawing deeply on folk poetry and classical literature, yet freely creative and individual in his expression. He reveals a warm feeling for nature, an attractive vein of mysticism, a shrewd and analytical mind and a subtle, ironical sense of humour. A delightful tragi-comic creation is Lindblad, the village tinsmith, who, though bashful in love, is not bashful at all when it comes to expounding the mysteries of life. In other poems, stories with an authentic historical and/or 'local' background are told in the style of an archaic ballad, fairground broadsheet, or Biblical 'legend'. There is seriousness beneath the fun. In his later collections he turns to more strictly classical metres, yet without relinquishing his earlier love of experiment. His inexhaustible metrical inventions, and in particular his studies in quantity and stress relationships, have contributed much to recent Finnish poetry. His

*Kootut runot* (1957) contains six collections of poems. He has also written eleven books of studies on folklore. [AK]

*Väinämöinen*, tr. Goldthwait-Väänänen (Helsinki, 1950); Allwood, *ICSP*; Ollilainen, *SF*; Tompuri, *VF*.

**Myrivilis, Stratis** (Mytilene 1892– ). Greek novelist and short-story writer. Educated in Lesbos and Athens where he studied law and literature at the university. In 1910 he joined the army and served until 1922 in the Balkan wars, the First World War and in the Greco-Turkish war. He began his career as a journalist and literary contributor to various periodicals. His first novel *I Zoi En Tafo* (1930), brought him into prominence as a writer of distinction. It is a realistic anti-war novel in the form of letters of a soldier to his sweetheart, a day by day account of the squalor and tedium, and of the effects of war on individuals. Images of violence, comic pathos and tragedy alternate with idyllic descriptions of nature. Pattern and rhythm, and a prose with carefully chosen vocabulary and cadence combine to make the book a poetic assertion of life and to endow it with a lasting artistic value. His second novel, *I Daskala Me Ta Chrysa Matia* (1933), is a love story set in his native island in an atmosphere of the aftermath of war, and reveals with sympathy and insight the perplexities and sufferings of ordinary folk. *I Panaghia I Gorgona* (1949; tr. Abbott Rick, *The Mermaid Madonna*, 1959), a novel also set in Lesbos, is a colourful study of island life with a poetic and humorous touch and a love for significant detail. Myrivilis has also written *nouvelles* and short stories showing in these too his accomplished craft as a writer. [SJP]

*Vassilis O Arvanitis, Ta Pagana, O Pan* (*nouvelles*); *Kokkines Istories, To Prasino Vivlio, To Galazio Vivlio* (short stories).

A. Karantonis, *Pezografoi Ghenias Tou '30* (Athens, 1962).

**Mystères.** Medieval French plays deriving from the liturgical dramas produced at Christmas and Easter, first in the churches, later in their precincts. These plays, depicting scenes such as the Nativity or Resurrection, were written originally in Latin and were usually staged with a 'simultaneous' juxtaposed *mise en scène*. In the 12th century the pseudo-Augustinian *Sermo contra Judaeos* was dramatized for performance at Christmas and became known as the *Ordo Prophetarum* or 'Procession of Prophets'. The earliest play in which the vernacular (Provençal) is found, with Latin, is the 12th-century *Sponsus* (ed. L. P. Thomas, Paris, 1951), the parable of the Wise and Foolish Virgins. The best example is the *Mystère d'* ⇨ *Adam*. *La Seinte Resurrecion* (crit. ed. J. M. Manly, M. K. Pope, J. G. Wright, 1943), less skilfully written, introduces the themes of Longinus the blind centurion, and Nicodemus.

In the 14th and 15th centuries the performance of mystery plays in the vernacular, and especially of those dealing with the Passion, was promoted throughout France by various confraternities. The most famous of these was the *Confrérie de la Passion*, licensed at Paris in 1402 by Charles VI. A narrative poem known as the *Passion des jongleurs* (about 1200, translated into English soon after) served as a source in France and England of many Passion plays, especially the important early 14th-century *Passion du Palatinus* (ed. G. Frank, Paris, 1922) and the *Passion d'Autun* (ed. G. Frank, Paris, 1934).

In the first half of the 15th century many *Mystères de la Passion* were composed and elaborately performed, the cost being borne by the *confréries*, the township, the Church or private patrons. Among the most famous were *La Passion de Semur* (9500 lines), of Burgundian origin, and *La Passion d'Arras*, attributed to Eustache Mercadé, long (25,000 lines), realistic but stiff. *Le Mystère de la Passion* by Arnoul Greban is the most popular and famous of all the French *Passions*, poetic, lyrical and tragic. It was reworked by Jean Michel, and performed at Angers (1486) '*moult triumphanment et sumptueusement*'. The plays by Mercadé, Greban and Michel were used, cut or expanded by other arrangers throughout France. An exuberantly prodigal performance at Bourges in 1536 of the very long *Actes des Apôtres* (61,000 lines), written possibly by Simon Greban helped by Arnoul his brother between 1452 and 1478, was said to have spread over many days. There were nearly 500 roles in this play.

The staging of Mysteries was ended in Paris in 1548 by decree of the *Parlement*. They were in discredit as irreverent, and as a profanation of the Bible, or as being unsuited to the new spirit of the 16th-century Renaissance. [LTT]

A. Pauphilet, *Jeux et Sapience du Moyen Âge* (Paris, 1941); *R*, XXII (1893); *Passion des Jongleurs* in *The Northern Passion . . .*, ed. F. A. Foster (2 vols., 1912–13); *La Passion provençale . . .*, ed. W. P. Shepard (Paris, 1928); *E. Marcadé, Le M. de la P.*, ed. J. M. Richard (Paris, 1893); *Le M. de la P. d'Arnoul Greban . . .*, ed. G. Paris and G. Raynaud (Paris, 1878) – modern adaptation in Pauphilet, above; Jean Michel, *Le M. de la P.*, ed. O. Jodogne (Gembloux, 1959).

G. Cohen, *Histoire de la mise en scène dans le théâtre religieux français du moyen âge* (Paris, 1926); E. Roy, *Le M. de la P. en France du XIVe au XVe siècle* (2 vols., Paris, 1905); K. Young, *The Drama of the Medieval Church* (2 vols., 1933); R. Lebègue, *Le M. des Actes des Apôtres . . .* (Paris, 1929); M. F. McKean, *The Interplay of Realistic and Flamboyant Art Elements in the French Mystères* (Washington, D.C., 1959); Frank, *MFD*.

# N

**Nachman of Bratzlav (Maharan)** (Miedzhybozh 1770–Uman 1811). Hebrew and Yiddish writer. As grandson of the Baal Shem Tov, the founder of Hassidism, he established his own Hassidic circle in Bratzlav. Unique narrator of fairy tales, about mankind, birds, animals, mountains, valleys, seas. First told his stories in Yiddish, and asked that they should be published after his death both in Yiddish and Hebrew. These were set down by his pupils and published under the titles, *Likkute Maharan* (2 vols., 1808–11) and *Sippure Maasiyot* (1815). [EE]

M. Buber, *The Tales of Rabbi Nachman*, tr. M. S. Friedman (N.Y., 1956).

**Nachmanides (Moses ben Nachman),** known as **Ramban** (Gerona 1194–Palestine *c.* 1270). Hebrew religious writer and poet. A Rabbi and physician in Gerona, he took part in the disputation of Barcelona of 1263. Besides composing a large number of legal works, he wrote some liturgical poems with strong cabbalistic overtones. In 1276 settled in Palestine where he completed his commentary on the Pentateuch. [EE]

S. Schechter, *Studies in Judaism*, i (1896).

**Nagibin, Yuriy Markovich** (Moscow 1920– ). Russian short-story writer. He served as a war-correspondent after being invalided out of the army. His first stories date from 1940. He became widely popular only with his collection *Trudnoye schast'ye* (1958). The war figures in many of his stories, even recent ones, *Boy za vysotu* (1957). Others are set in the capital, for example the semi-autobiographical *Chistyye prudy* (1961, 'Clean Ponds', i.e. a region of Moscow) and tend to deal with the problems of the younger generation. His latest collection *Pogonya* (1964) is set in the countryside and is devoted to hunting-stories. [RDBT]

*Y.N. Selected Short Stories*, ed. D. J. Richards (1963).

**Nagy, Lajos** (1883–1954). Hungarian socialist writer. As an illegitimate child, he went through many emotional and material hardships. His interest in social problems and dislike of injustice led him to join first the Socialist and later the underground Communist movement. He is at his best in short stories, sketches and commentaries. *A lázadó ember* (1944) and *A menekülö ember* (1954) are autobiographies. [JFR]

**Nalješković, Nikola.** ⇨ Dalmatian and Dubrovnik Literature.

**Naogeorg, Thomas,** Latin name of Thomas Kirchmair (Straubing 1511–Wiesloch 1563). German dramatist. A Lutheran preacher and the outstanding writer of Protestant Latin school drama before ⇨ Frischlin, his *Pammachius* (1538, German tr. 1539; ed. R. Froning, DNL, 22, 1894) uses all the devices of the humanist drama to deliver a swingeing attack on the Papacy. The Papacy, like its alleged founder Pammachius (the name means 'All-destroyer'), is held to be in league with the devil and all the 'abuses' of the Roman Church, its worldly power, its assertion of the supremacy of the Pope in matters of faith, its worship of images and sale of indulgences, are manifestations of its diabolical nature. Luther, on the other hand, is the true servant of Christ, and the play closes as he prepares to do battle with and overcome Pammachius and his agents. *Mercator* (1540; ed. J. Bolte, BLVS, 269/70, 1927), a treatment of the Everyman theme, contains similar attacks on the Roman Church. [WAC]

*ZfdA*, 54, 57.

**Nastasijevič, Momčilo** (Gornji, Milanovac 1894–Belgrade 1938). Serbian poet and dramatist. A lone figure who turned to the language of folklore to create a highly compressed vehicle for the expression of his mystical, national and religious philosophy. Difficult as a writer and so individualist in outlook as to limit his appeal to a minority, his influence on poetry since 1945 has increased owing to his bold experiments with language. [EDG]

'Gluhote' and 'Reci u Kamenu', E. D. Goy, *Annali*, IX (Naples, 1966).

**Nathansen, Henri** (Hjørring 1868–Lund, Sweden 1944). Danish playwright and novelist. Now mainly known for his play *Indenfor Murene* (1912), a *pièce de résistance* in the Danish theatre, concerned with the problems of Jews *v.* Gentiles. [ELB]

**Nazor, Vladimir** (Postire, Brač island 1876–Zagreb 1949). Croatian poet, novelist and essayist. His many works vary from lyrical poetry, mythological epic and poetic prose to stories and tales for children; he also translated Dante, Shakespeare and Baudelaire. His world is one of legend and myth with an underlying realism. Above all a poet of Pantheism, a worshipper of nature and the sun, his poems, influenced by his love of the classics, are often of considerable formal beauty and rare polish. *Lirika* (1910) made him famous but his epic *Ahasver* and novel *Pastir Loda* (1946) are now acclaimed as his major works. He joined Tito's partisans at 66 and published his diary of this period in 1945, returning to Zagreb as President of the Praesidium of the Croatian Sabor. [EDG]

*Djela*, ed. I. Vasic (29 vols., 1928ff.); Lavrin, *AMYP*; *SEER*, XXIII, 62 (1945), XXIV, 63 (1946).
Barac, *HYL*; Kadić, *CCL*.

**Nechuy**, pseud. of Ivan Levyts'ky (Stebliv, Kiev 1838–Kiev 1918). Ukrainian novelist. Influenced by Zola and the Goncourts, he produced broad canvases of Ukrainian life: *Mykola Dzherya* (1876), a post-emancipation peasant's search for a living in a factory, on the land, in fishing; *Kaydasheva sim"ya* (1878), about the poverty and ignorance of the peasantry; *Burlachka* (1876), about factory life; *Chorni khmary* (1871), about intelligentsia problems. A realist with strong naturalistic and ethnographic leanings, he ranks among the greatest Ukrainian novelists. [VS]

*Tvory* (10 vols., 1930; 10 vols., 1965– ).
Manning, *UL*; *UCE*.

**Negri, Ada** (Lodi 1870–Milano 1945). Italian poet. When still a young schoolmistress in a small primary school, she published a collection of poems (*Fatalità*, 1892) where social and humanitarian ideals, coupled with a certain defiance of comfortable middle-class morality, were voiced in a turgid and emotional style reminiscent of late Carducci and early D'Annunzio. This volume, which won her immediate literary fame, was followed between 1895 and 1943 by a further nine, whose sentimental idealism, aggressive feminism and ambiguous mysticism, displayed with greater formal refinement in spite of frequent lapses of taste, were often mistaken for major literary virtues. Her prose writings were better received by the readers, and some passages are still found in school anthologies. [GMC]

*Prose* (1954); *Poesie* (1956).
S. Grilli, *A.N. La vita e l'opera* (Milan, 1953); Croce, *LNI*; *Contemporanei*, i.

**Neidhart von Reuenthal** (*c.* 1180–*c.* 1250). German ⇨ Minnesinger. He was of noble birth and possessed a fief in northern Bavaria: in 1217–19 he was on Crusade in the Holy Land; *c.* 1230, for reasons not known, Otto II of Bavaria deprived him of his fief, whereupon he travelled to Austria and received a new fief from Friedrich der Streitbare, a ruler known for his patronage of men of letters. On this fief he apparently lived out the remaining years of his life.

Taking his lead from tendencies and sympathies in the work of his great older contemporary, ⇨ Walther von der Vogelweide, he evolved what has been called 'courtly village-poetry', in which, while still writing for the courtly society on which he was dependent, he described, with a wit sometimes benevolent but often aggressive, his encounters with the peasants, above all with peasant girls and their boorish suitors. Both in subject and in form his songs fall into two groups: summer songs, free in form, in which the joys of Nature's awakening are blended with the girls' delight in the dance; and winter songs, cast in the tripartite form of the courtly Minnesang, which are more serious and reflective in tone, but which also, like the summer songs, abound in satirical and often grotesque descriptions of life among the peasants. This is the particular aspect of his originality that attracted his contemporaries and gave the lead to so much of the lyric poetry of the middle and late 13th century. The song-melodies that are preserved show him to have been a very capable musician as well as a highly gifted poet with an original and incisive personality. [RT]

Ed. E. Wiessner (1923); W. Schmieder, *Die Lieder N.s v. R.* (Vienna, 1930) (contains facsimiles of texts and melodies).
A. T. Hatto and R. J. Tavlor. *The Songs of N.v.*

*R.* (1958) (contains melodies); A. Bielschowsky, *Geschichte der deutschen Dorfpoesie im 13. Jahrhundert I* (Berlin, 1890); W. Weidmann, *Studien zur Entwicklung von N.s Liedern* (Basle, 1947).

**Nekrasov, Nikolay Alekseyevich** (Nemirov, Podol'sk region 1821–St Petersburg 1877). Russian poet. Son of a debauched, tyrannical father – retired officer and landowner – and a gentle, educated, idolized mother (*Mat'*, 1868, 1876/7, and cf. the childhood impressions in *Rodina*, 1845, and of the estate Greshnevo on the Volga, with its over-burdened peasants, in *Na Volge*, 1860). He did not finish high school in Yaroslavl' (1832–6), returning home to hunt, ride, and write poetry. In 1838, in St Petersburg, he unofficially attended University courses, refusing the Army career prescribed by his father, and published a poem, *Mysl'* ('Thought'), in a journal. His allowance cut, he endured starvation, odd jobs, homelessness (cf. his prose piece *Peterburgskiye ugly*, 1844). His poems, *Mechty i zvuki* (1840), were a failure and he destroyed the book. In 1841–5 he tried journalism, adaptations of French vaudevilles (4 rejected, 10 staged); and he became a friend of ⇨ Belinsky. He wrote *Stateiki v stikhakh* (1843), and edited *Peterburgskiy Sbornik* (1846) with Herzen, Turgenev and Dostoyevsky. Subsequently he ran the quarterly *Sovremennik* ('The Contemporary') (launched 1836 by Pushkin), with I. Panayev, attracting new talent or, when short of copy, writing potboiler novels with Panayev's wife. In 1856 appeared a book of his poems (*Stikhotvoreniya*). This, 'The Bard of the People's Sorrows', sold well (6 editions in his lifetime); his journal was popular, and with business acumen he became rich. Lucky in cards and love-affairs, he bought estates, hunted, and moved in high society, while losing old literary friends and being torn by remorse (*Rytsar' na chas*, 1860). *Sovremennik* turned anti-aesthetic and radical with ⇨ Dobrolyubov and ⇨ Chernyshevsky. In March 1862 Nekrasov became its sole owner. It was banned for eight months in June; and closed down in 1866. Nekrasov then alienated the intelligentsia by writing some subservient verse. In 1868, he took over the journal *Otechestvennye zapiski* ('Notes of the Fatherland'), collaborating with ⇨ Saltykov.

Afflicted since 1853 with intestinal troubles, he tried cures abroad (1856, 1868, 1872–3), and went to the Crimea (1874), to one of his estates. Treatment failed: it was cancer. He returned to St Petersburg (October 1876) and in 1877 (4 April) married F. A. Viktorova – 'Zina' – a young uneducated girl who had lived with him since 1870; on 12 April a Viennese surgeon performed a colotomy. An anthology of his poems appeared and his *Posledniye pesni* ('Last Songs'). Hints of agonizing pain, poignant repentance for the discord between his life and his ideology aroused a wave of general sympathy. His funeral (30 December) became an enormous public manifestation.

Nekrasov is the master-poet of the peasant masses. 'I have dedicated my lyre to the People' (*Elegiya*, 1874). Intense emotion, intimate knowledge and rich idiom render this subject truly his own. 'Called to sing the sufferings of his incredibly patient nation' (*Neizvestnomu drugu*, 'To an unknown friend', 1867), he draws harrowing pictures of down-trodden serfs. If a peasant is cruel and crude and 'drinks until half-dying', he also 'works till dropping dead'. Identifying himself with these people, he can paint a greedy, harsh peasant who repents and sets out to collect for the churches (*Vlas*, 1854). So also 'the healing spaciousness' of the rye-fields brings him, an unbeliever, to the cross of the humble folk to implore forgiveness from 'the God of the oppressed and the mournful' (*Tishina*, 'Silence', 1857). But this 'Poet with the passion for suffering' (Dostoyevsky) is not overwrought with pity: 'A heart, which is weary of hatred, cannot learn how to love' (*Zamolkni muza*... 'Be silent, Muse...', 1855). He calls for vengeance. Some lines have revolutionary appeal. He greets the abolition of serfdom guardedly in *Svoboda* ('Freedom', 1861), since the masses are still destitute and illiterate. A former domestic serf's lot is hopeless: *Hey Ivan!* (1867). Yet his poems for children sparkle with humour: for instance, *General Toptygin* (1867), *Dedushka Mazay i zaitsy* ('Grandad Mazai and the Hares', 1870). Folk idiom resounds in many works which became songs, like *Korobeyniki* ('Pedlars', 1861) or *Zeleny shum* ('Green Rustle', 1862), etc. The folklore-inspired, racy masterpiece *Komu na Rusi zhit' khorosho* ('Who Can Live Happy in Russia?', 1864–76) combines sheer fun with drama and the apotheosis of suffering motherhood. In the magnificent *Moroz, Krasnyy nos*('Frost the Red-Nosed', 1863), fulfilment in work and love are only a memory to the widow as, in the snow-bound forest, she slowly freezes to death.

For his Muse is a peasant woman, now mournful, now wild, now teaching him to forgive his enemies – 'only the crown of thorn suited her sullen beauty' (*Muza*, 1851). The sight of a beaten peasant girl stirs up a cry: 'My sister... Muse!' Envious of 'a blessed poet' of peace, he must 'preach love through negation'.

Nekrasov's fame is firm. His exhortations to poets to be citizens, *Poet i grazhdanin* ('Poet and Citizen', 1856), are still relevant. His rhymed journalism, with its message of social justice, at times verbose, often satirical, has more than historical value, as also the moving stories of a returned Decembrist, *Dedushka* (1870), and the Decembrists' wives in Siberia, *Russkiye zhenshchiny* (1872–3). His 'freshness and power of feeling' (Chernyshevsky) has inspired generations. For ⇨ Mayakovsky he is 'one of ours'. The musical riches of his language, his imagery and style were rediscovered by the Symbolists; his peasant Russia is reborn in the Russia of ⇨ Blok. [NG]

*Polnoye sobraniye sochineniy i pisem*, ed. V. E. Yevgen'yev-Maksimov, A. M. Yegolin, K. I. Chukovsky (12 vols., 1948–53); *Stikhotvoreniya*, intr. A. M. Yegolin (1949); intr. V. P. Druzin, notes I. Z. Serman (1956); *Moroz*, ed. V. E. J. Holttum (1964); *Poems*, tr. J. M. Soskice (Worlds Classics, 1929); *Who Can be Free and Happy in Russia?*, tr. ibid. (1917); Bowra, *BRV*, *SBRV*; C. Corbet, *N. l'homme et le poète* (Paris, 1948); K. Chukovsky, *Masterstvo N.* (Moscow, 1952).

**Němcová, Božena** (Vienna 1820–Prague 1862). Czech woman novelist. Both parents being in domestic service, she spent five profoundly important years of early childhood with her grandmother, an upright, wise Czech country woman, in the village of Ratibořice. Marriage at 17 to a much older Czech customs official, who was greatly harassed by Austrian authorities for alleged political activity, brought frequent change of abode, social upheaval and financial hardship, but provided valuable opportunties for the study of country people and customs. Exhausted, sick and disappointed she died prematurely.

One of the leading personalities of late Czech romanticism, she is the first eminent Czech woman writer. She combines a romantic vision of country life and society with trained realistic observation. She practised her storytelling on folk and fairy tales, *Národní báchorky a pověsti* (1845–7), *Slovanské pohádky a pověsti* (1857–8). In *Babička* (1855; tr. E. Pargeter, *Granny*, Prague, 1962), a classic of the Czech novel, she gives in accomplished prose a poetically inspired portrait of unforgettable village characters and traditions. The central figure is her own grandmother. *Babička* was a world-wide success, translated into all Slavonic and many other languages. [RPH]

*Spisy* (*Ústav pro českov Literaturu*) (15 vols., 1950–61); J. Mukařovsky, *B.N.* (1950); M. Novotný, *Zivot B.N.* (6 vols., 1951–9).

Arne Novak, *Dějiny české literatury* (Prague, 1946); *Dějiny české literatury*, ii (Prague, 1960); Tille-Novotný, *B.N.* (Prague, 1939); Z. Nejedlý, *B.N.* (Prague, 1928).

**Németh, László** (Nagybánya 1901– ). Hungarian writer and dramatist. Son of a secondary-school teacher, he studied at Budapest, but gave up a medical career in favour of literature. He became one of the most important members of the ⇨ *Nyugat* group. A writer of wide erudition, style and imagery, the characteristics of his novels, *Gyász* (1935), *Kocsik Szeptemberben* (1937), *Szerdai Fogadónap* (1940), all containing autobiographical elements, are minutely accurate depictions of life and character. *Égető Eszter* (1956), a family saga, and *Iszony* (1947; tr. anon., *Revulsion*, 1965) are social studies showing the impenetrable inter-class barriers of his time, and depict especially the contemporary middle class and intelligentsia. *Medve Uccai Iskola*, and his other autobiographies, are candid, interesting treatments of factual observations. In his successful, mostly historical, plays (*Galilei*; *József II*; *A Két Bólyai*), the heroes stand unsuccessfully for the common good against an ignorant, insensitive public. Thought and dialogue are more important in Németh's plays than action. He has translated numerous works from Western and Slavonic languages into Hungarian, and is also noted for his essays, as well as studies in Hungarian cultural history. His many theoretical studies have been collected into six major volumes, notably *Készülődés* (1943) and *Kisebbségben* (1941). [JFR]

**Neruda, Jan** (Prague 1834–Prague 1891). Czech poet, short-story writer and essayist.

The son of a tobacconist and a charwoman, he knew the life of the poor of Prague from his own experience. After his university studies he worked as a teacher. In 1862 he joined the foremost Prague daily of his time, *Národní listy*, writing, until his death, literary and dramatic criticism and *feuilletons* on various subjects. His private life was very sad; he suffered much from bad health and after several emotional disillusionments never married. As a poet he began as a rebel but finally found refuge in a visionary conception of a nation which had been born king and then crucified like Christ, yet which will rise from the dead. His poems range from intimate lyrics of a reflective and analytical kind such as *Prosté motivy* (1883) to the visions of an ardent nationalist such as *Zpěvy páteční* (1896). In his prose Neruda, a radical cosmopolitan hating the upper classes and contemptuous of the petty bourgeois, paid much attention to social themes; the best example is *Trhani* (1868–71), stories of social outcasts employed on railway building. His *Povídky malostranské* (1878; tr. E. Pargeter, *Tales of the Little Quarter*, 1957) are realistic short stories about the inhabitants of Prague's oldest quarter, tinged with impressionism and bitter-sweet humour. His essays, precise in thought and perfect in style, successfully combine his impressions with clear-sighted comments of a true European. [KB]

*Spisy* (41 vols., 1906–15); (4 vols., 1921); (1950 ff.).

F. V. Krejčí, *J.N.* (Prague, 1902); M. Novotny, *Zivot J.N.* (Prague, 1951–6); *SEER*, XXVIII, 70 (1949).

**Nerval, Gérard de,** pseud. of Gérard Labrunie (Paris 1808–Paris 1855). French poet and author. The son of a doctor in the Napoleonic armies. His uncle had a library of occult books through which he was allowed to browse and which profoundly influenced him. He was a member of the *Jeune-France*, led by ⇨ Gautier and Pétrus ⇨ Borel. At 20 he published a remarkably able free translation of *Faust* which Goethe praised and which Berlioz drew upon for his *Damnation of Faust*. The attempts to make him learn a useful trade failed and he began a life of wandering which was to take him to Germany and the Near East (*Voyage en Orient*, 1851). In about 1831 he came under the spell of an idealized love for the actress, Jenny Colon, which was to last until 1838. It was an almost entirely cerebral passion, and was to have a deep effect upon his writings. He had a first mental breakdown in 1841 and until his suicide in 1855 he was rarely mentally balanced. It was towards the end of his life that his works were collected and published in book form. They include *Les illuminés ou les précurseurs de socialisme* (1853), studies of Cagliostro, Restif de la Bretonne etc., and *Petits châteaux de Bohème* (1853), which included the strange despairing sonnets 'Le Christ aux Oliviers'. The next year he brought out *Les filles du feu*, which includes his *Sylvie*, a dream-like story which hovers between reminiscences of his childhood and his love for Jenny Colon with two former loves obtruding themselves upon his memory. The sonnets of *Les chimères*, for which he is best remembered, were appended to this collection. Drawing on alchemy, the tarot, strange myths of the Egyptians, Greeks and other races, he mingled these themes with his own private obsessions and experiences; they include the sonnet 'El Desdichado', quoted by T. S. Eliot in *The Waste Land*. These sonnets often have moments of peerless beauty which haunt the mind, but Nerval himself said that this magic would disappear if attempts were made to explain them. He called them 'super-naturaliste' and they have been seen as the precursors not only of the Symbolists in their use of traditional imagery for private purposes but also of the Surrealists. The latter influence owes even more to *Aurélia* (1855), which describes his visions and the stages of his mental breakdown and is remarkable for its lucid depiction of hallucination. [WA]

*Œuvres*, ed. A. Beguin and J. Richer (2 vols., Pléiade, 1960); *Fortune's Fool*, selected poems tr. B. Hill (1959).

F. Carco, *G. de N* (Paris, 1953); R. M. Albérès, *G. de N.* (Paris, 1955); A. Lebois, *Vers une élucidation des Chimères de N.* (Paris, 1957).

**Nestroy, Johann** (Vienna 1801–Graz 1862). Austrian dramatist. After studying at Vienna University, he became a comic actor and writer of plays, of which over 70 have survived, for immediate performance. At first following ⇨ Raimund by using the traditional Viennese genre of the *Zauberspiel* (*Der böse Geist Lumpazivagabundus*, 1833), he soon abandoned this convention for comedies – such as *Das Mädl aus der Vorstadt* (1841) – with a realistic Viennese setting. Some of his plays have the lightness of pure farce (*Das Haus der Temperamente*, 1837; *Einen Jux will er sich machen*, 1842), but what distinguishes his writing is the aggressiveness of his satire. He usually borrowed his plots, and they are unimportant; the highlights of his plays are his satirical monologues and songs, composed with a linguistic dexterity at its best in *Der Talisman* (1840). His critical intelligence was always trained against empty conventionality, and this made him a natural parodist: *Judith und Holofernes* (1849), a parody of ⇨ Hebbel's *Judith*, is regarded as the classic German parody. Equally fine is *Die verhängnisvolle Faschingsnacht* (1839), directed against a drama by Karl von Holtei. Increasingly he incorporated his satirical shafts into plays with a positive didactic purpose, such as *Der Unbedeutende* (1846), upholding the solid virtues of the simple craftsman. [WEY]

*Gesammelte Werke*, ed. O. Rommel (1962) (re-issue).

Karl Kraus, *N. und die Nachwelt* (Vienna, 1912); Otto Rommel, *J.N.*, in *Sämtliche Werke*, XV (Vienna, 1930); F. H. Mautner, *J.N. und seine Kunst* (Vienna, 1937); *MLR*, 2, 1966.

**Netherlands Medieval Drama.** The oldest surviving plays in Dutch are the entirely secular *Abele Spelen*, perhaps the earliest in Europe (including *Lanceloet van Denerekmen*, tr. P. Geyl, 1924, E. Colledge, 1967; *Esmoreit*, tr. H. M. Ayres, 1924). Of the development of religious drama from the earliest liturgical mimes at church festivals to the mystery plays of the 15th century there is no trace, though a Latin Christmas play, *Officium Stellae*, is extant from the 11th century. The *Abele Spelen* were probably the outcome, as elsewhere in Europe, of a gradual secularization of religious themes, though they may have arisen out of a spontaneous addition of mime to the minstrels' popular ballads and lays. The four *Spelen* and six farces (*sotternieën* or *kluchten*) intended to follow them as a light (and bawdy) diversion probably date from the second half of the 14th century. Romantic themes similar to the exotic tales of chivalry and love in these plays were certainly dramatized in the following centuries, but only one has survived, Colijn van Rijssele's *Spiegel der Minnen*, which introduces burgher theatre early in the 16th century. The farce retained its popularity throughout the 16th century (in *esbatementen* and *tafelspelen*) and into the Renaissance (cf. ⇨ Bredero, ⇨ Hooft, ⇨ Huygens).

The only instance of a play cycle in the Netherlands is a seven-year series on the Joys of Mary, commissioned at Brussels and first performed 1448–55. Only *Die Eerste* and *Die Sevenste Bliscap van Maria* survive. The Biblical or hagiographical miracle play, however, is well represented, though only two plays are worth noting. *Het spel vanden heilighen sacramente vander Nyeuwervaert* is, exceptionally, the work of a northern poet (Breda, *c.* 1500), but the finest in this genre is undoubtedly *Markieken van Nieumeghen* (tr. H. M. Ayres, 1924, E. Colledge, 1965), written at about the same time at either Nijmegen or Antwerp. It is strikingly modern in its psychology and technique, for the renegade Emmeken's conversion is achieved by a most topical and realistic *dea ex machina*, the Virgin Mary enacted in a pageant-play 'Masscheroen', at which Emmeken is a spectator. The chapbook translation (ed. H. M. Ayres and A. J. Barnouw, 1932) of this play into English does little justice to the original. *Everyman*, on the other hand, is so similar in all respects to *Elckerlyc* that the priority of the Dutch has only recently been established. This morality, probably written by a priest, Pieter Doorlant, won a prize at the Antwerp *Landjuweel* (⇨ *Rederijkers*) *c.* 1485. [PK]

*Middelnederlandsche dramatische poëzie*, ed. P. Leendertz Jr (1897); *Nu Noch*, tr. E. Colledge in *Reynard the Fox and Other Mediaeval Netherlands Secular Literature* (Leyden–London, 1967) (*tafelspel*).

J. A. Worp, *Geschiedenis van het drama en van het tooneel in Nederland* (2 vols., Groningen, 1904, 1908).

**Netherlands Medieval Epic.** No early literature from the northern provinces has been preserved, and of the pre-courtly Germanic epic only fragments remain in Diets, the literary language of the South. There are, however, indifferent translations of some French ⇨ *chansons de geste* (e.g. *Het Roelantslied*, *Reinout van Montalbaen*) and one apparently original work *Karel ende Elegast* (12th or 13th century), a delightful tale of feudal reverence and dry humour, which probably originated in West Flanders and was translated in the German ⇨ *Karlmeinet*. Charlemagne is ordered by an angel to go out stealing, whereby he meets the incognito Elegast, whom he has unjustly banished. While Elegast is trying to make a thief of him he learns of a conspiracy on his life, which Elegast satisfactorily deals with in a duel. The courtly romances achieved more popularity than literary merit. An exception is the work of Hendrik van ⇨ Veldeke and Segher Diergodgaf's *'t Prieel van Troyen* and his adaptation from Benoît de Sainte-Maure, *Paerlement van Troyen.* There were oriental tales, such as Diederic van Assenedes' sentimental *Floris ende Blancefloer*, a translation from a Latin version of an Irish odyssey, *De reis van Sinte Brandaen*, and of course the Arthurian legend appeared in many versions down to van ⇨ Maerlant and the rise of the third estate.

The decline of courtly fashions in the face of more utilitarian requirements is well marked by *Van den Vos Reinaerde* (tr. A. J. Barnouw, 1967), an ageless masterpiece parodying the German epic and feudal society. Aernout, it is now generally agreed, here freely adapted *Le Plaid*, the best branch of the French *Roman de* ⇨ *Renart*. This was then rewritten and incorporated in Willem's substantially original epic (*c.* 1200) and skilfully revised in the extant version of *c.* 1250. Nothing is known about Aernout and Willem, except that they probably lived in East Flanders and that Willem did an earlier translation of a British romance *Madoc* which has not survived. In *Isengrimus* (12th century) another Fleming, Nivardus of Gent, gave the beasts from the earlier *Ecbasis Captivi* the names they have kept since, but this bitter attack on monastic life lacks the roguish sparkle and humanity of Willem's satire. It was unfortunately not Willem's but a diluted 14th-century version which was translated into English (ed. W. T. S. Stallybrass, 1924) and provided the Low German source of Goethe's *Reineke Fuchs.* [PK]

*Verwijs' Bloemlezing uit de Middelnederlandsche dichtkunst*, ed. C. C. de Bruin (3 vols., 1956–8); *Charles and Elegast* and extracts from *Wale wein*, tr. E. Colledge in *Reynard the Fox and Other Mediaeval Netherlands Secular Literature* Leyden–London, 1967).
Weevers, *PNEC.*

**Neumann, Stanislav Kostka** (Prague 1875–Prague 1947). Czech poet, novelist and essayist. Born of an old Prague family, he was always a rebel against his own class. As a student he was imprisoned by the Austrian authorities for his nationalist activities; in his next phase of individualist anarchism he edited a review propagating social utopianism; finally he embraced Communism. His first books are the work of an extreme and exclusive individualist, striking an anti-social and anti-Christian attitude and preaching a cult of paganism and sexual mysticism reminiscent of D. H. Lawrence. In his *Nové zpěvy* (1918) he finds truth and beauty in technological civilization, and in *Rudé zpěvy* (1923) he casts aside his personal griefs and pleasures and becomes the rhetorician of the revolution. His *Bezedný rok* (1945), written during the Nazi occupation, combines proletarian internationalism with Czech patriotism. [KB]

*Sebrané spisy* (22 vols., 1947–56).
J. Taufer, *S.K.N.* (Prague, 1956).

**Nexø, Martin Andersen** (Christianshavn 1869–Dresden 1954). Danish novelist. The story of his childhood in Copenhagen's slums, then as a shepherd boy, farm labourer and cobbler's apprentice, is movingly told in his *Memoirs* (1932–9; two first vols. tr. E. Watkins, *Under the Open Sky: My Early Years*, N.Y., 1938), which rank with those of Maxim Gor'ky. While living in Spain to recover from tuberculosis, his feelings of solidarity with the 'international' poor, which were to inspire all his revolutionary socialist writings, were further strengthened.

Apart from the remarkable travel book, *Soldage* (1903; tr. J. W. Hartmann, *Days in the Sun*, 1929), and some early fiction, Nexø's world fame as a 'proletarian writer' rests on the novel cycle *Pelle Erobreren* (4 vols., 1906–10; tr. J. Muir and B. Miall, *Pelle the Conqueror*, 1913–16), and the trilogy about 'Ditte', *Ditte Menneskebarn* (1917–21; tr. anon., *Ditte*: *Girl Alive!*, 1920; tr. A. G. Chater and R. Thirsk, *Ditte: Daughter of Man*, 1922; tr. A. and R. Kenney, *Ditte: Towards the Stars*, 1923): a working class *epos* about the Bornholm boy Pelle, a proletarian who becomes a trade unionist and a strike leader, and the girl Ditte, who is defeated and succumbs to the hardship of life. *Midt i en Jærntid* (1929; tr. T. Seltzer, *In God's Land*, 1933), a bitter attack on the mentality of well-to-do farmers, is inferior as a novel.

In 1922 Nexø visited the Soviet Union and (previously a Social Democrat) became an ardent Communist who faithfully toed the Party line. During the German occupation he was imprisoned but escaped via Sweden to Moscow. After the war he wrote a continuation of *Pelle*, a novel called *Morten hin Røde* (1945), about *Morten the Red*, his own *alter ego*, a not very successful mixture of memoirs and fiction. [ELB]

B. Houmann, *M.A.N. bibliografi* (Aarhus, 1961); W. A. Berendson, *M.A.N.* (1948): H. Slochover, *Three Ways of Modern Man* (N.Y., 1937); H. A. Koefoed, 'M.A.N. – Some Viewpoints', in *Scandinavica*, IV, I (1965).

**Nezval, Vitězslav** (Biskoupky 1900–Prague 1958). Czech poet, novelist and dramatist. The son of a teacher, he studied philosophy and then devoted himself entirely to literature. His literary beginnings were linked with the 'proletarian poetry' of the ⇨ Wolker group but he gradually developed his own idiom with elements of decadence, symbolism, dadaism and surrealism. Among his best longer poems are *Podivuhodný kouzelník* (1927), an apotheosis of the poet, 'a remarkable magician of imagination', who experiences the tastes, colours, sounds, forms and smells of the whole world and undergoes many metamorphoses; *Edison* (1928), a hymn to a civilization in which the old odic form is remoulded; and *Neznámá ze Seiny* (1929), which expresses both fascination and horror at night and death.

His novels, such as *Pan Marat* (1932), *Řetěz štěstí* (1936) and many others, are outstanding examples of the application of the surrealist theory of the automatic creative process. His drama in verse, *Dnes ještě zapadá slunce nad Atlantidou* (1956), is arresting for its new approach to the theme of Atlantis; the continent is destroyed by its own inhabitants who discover the secret of nuclear power and try to use it ruthlessly for world domination. [KB]

*Dilo* (24 vols., 1950ff.); *Zpěv míru*, tr. J. Lindsay and S. Jolly, *Song of Peace* (1951).
A. Jelínek, *V.N.* (Prague, 1961).

**'Nibelungenlied'** ('The Lay of the Nibelungs'). Medieval German heroic epic based on factual and mythological moments in Germanic history. The poem as we have it was written about 1200 but its constituent parts, like the story that it tells, go back to a far earlier date. Its authorship is unknown but its provenance appears to be Austrian.

The first part of the story centres on the legendary hero Siegfried – his love for Kriemhild, his wooing of Brunhild on behalf of the Burgundian king Günther, and his eventual assassination by Hagen; the second deals with the historical encounter between the Burgundians (Nibelungs) and the Huns, and the overthrow of the Burgundian kingdom – this latter event datable in history to the year A.D. 437. The poem is written in strophes of four long lines arranged in rhyming pairs, and though brutal and utterly un-courtly in subject-matter, reveals interesting attempts by the poet to soften the rougher outlines and bring the whole work closer to the taste of his 13th-century courtly audience.

Among the best-known modern works based on the Nibelungen saga are ⇨ Hebbel's dramatic trilogy *Die Nibelungen* (1862) and ⇨ Wagner's 4-part operatic cycle *Der Ring des Nibelungen* (1851–74). [RT]

*Das Nibelungenlied*, ed. H. de Boor (1956); tr. A. T. Hatto (1964).
F. Panzer, *Das Nibeungenlied* (1956).

**Nicolai, Christoph Friedrich** (Berlin 1733–Berlin 1811). German critic and novelist. Friend of M. Mendelssohn and ⇨ Lessing, whose *Literaturbriefe* he co-edited. In *Briefe über den itzigen Zustand der schönen Wissenschaften in Deutschland* (1755) and in his periodicals, *Bibliothek der schönen Wissenschaften und freien Künste* (1757–9) and *Allgemeine Deutsche Bibliothek* (1765–1804), he champions Enlightenment ideals, fighting ⇨ Gottsched, ⇨ Bodmer, ⇨ Breitinger, ⇨ *Sturm und Drang*, Romanticism, and following Boileau, Shaftesbury. A disciple of C. Wolff, he believes in happiness through reason and in the social utility of literature. His *Freuden des jungen Werthers* (1775) parodies Goethe, *Ein feiner kleiner Almanach* (1771 ff.) ⇨ Herder and ⇨ Bürger, *Vertraute Briefe von Adelheid B** an ihre Freundin Julie S*** (1794), Schleiermacher. The novels *Geschichte eines dicken Mannes* (1794) and *Leben und Meinungen Sempronius Gundiberts* (1798) attack Kant. *Das Leben und die Meinungen des Herrn Magisters Sebaldus Nothanker* (1773–6; repr. 1966; tr. T. Dutten, *The Life and Opinions of Sebaldus Nothanker*, 1798), a picaresque propaganda novel, advocates enlightened humanitarian Christianity against pietism and church orthodoxy. [LL]

K. Aner, *Der Aufklärer F.N.* (Giessen, 1912); M. Sommerfeld, *F.N. und der Sturm und Drang* (Halle, 1921); F. C. A. Philipps, *F.N.s. literarische Bestrebungen* (Hague, 1926); Schneider, *DDA*.

**Nielsen, Jørgen** (Paarup 1902–Copenhagen 1945). Danish novelist. His psychologically penetrating novels set in Jutland were only appreciated after his death. Most significant are *Offerbaal* (1929), *En Gaard midt i Verden* (1936), *Dybet* (1940) and *Et Hus splidagtigt med sig selv*. [ELB]

M. A. Hansen and K. Elfeldt, *J.N.* (Copenhagen, 1953).

**Nielsen, Morten** (Aalborg 1922–Copenhagen 1944). Danish poet. Killed in a wartime accident. His few collected poems, in *Efterladte Digte* (1954), established him as a leading poet of his generation. [ELB]

**Niemcewicz, Julian** (Skoki 1757–Paris 1841). Polish playwright, poet, novelist and translator. He showed more imagination in life than in writing, and is an ideal subject for biographers. His career coincided with the dramatic changes in Polish history: he was deputy at the last important Diet, took part in General Kościuszko's insurrection (1794), was imprisoned with him in Russia, accompanied him on his journey via England to the United States, stayed for a time in America, went back to Poland, witnessed the outbreak of the revolution in November 1830, acted as a political emissary in England, and lived ten more years in exile. His diaries and memoirs (*Pamiętniki czasów moich*, 1957) make fascinating reading.

Being curious and susceptible to literary novelties, he tried various forms (he translated, for instance, Monk Lewis's ballad *Alonzo the Brave and Fair Imogine* in 1802), but had no patience to perfect himself in one *genre*. Only his comedy *Powrót posła* (1790) showed his individuality, its popular success depending on the topical polemics in which he himself was involved. A topical interest, too, inspired his novel about the Polish Jews *Lejbe i Siora* (1821; tr. anon., *Levi and Sarah*, 1830). Here he used the epistolary form to lend authenticity to his information about the then exotic subject. He knew English well and translated Milton, Dryden, Pope, Gray, Johnson and even Wordsworth ('We are seven'). This is an important aspect of his literary career. [JP]

*Under their Vine and Fig Tree*, tr. and ed. M. J. E. Budka (Elizabeth, N.Y., 1965); Peterkiewicz and Singer, *FCPP*.

**Nietzsche, Friedrich** (Röcken, Saxony 1844–Weimar 1900). German philosopher and poet. Son of a Protestant pastor, his brilliance at Classics (Schulpforta, then Bonn and Leipzig) won him a Professorship at Basel (1869); close contact with ⇨ Wagner – at nearby Triebschen – was (with ⇨ Schopenhauer) a dominant intellectual influence. In 1879 ill health made him resign his chair; living restless, solitary and tormented in rented rooms in Sils Maria, Genoa, Turin, etc., he wrote the books which made him famous – alas, only after his total mental breakdown in 1889; he remained deranged until his death.

His work falls into three main periods. The first, that of 'Aesthetic Pessimism', develops a philosophy of culture based on *tragedy* as the greatest achievement of Greek civilization, which declined with Euripides, the moralist, and above all with Socrates and the search for philosophical truth (*Die Geburt der Tragődie*, 1872; tr. F. Golfing, *The Birth of Tragedy*, 1956). Other essays (*Unzeitgemässe Betrachtungen*, 1873–6) apply this revolutionary cultural lesson to the present, where only Schopenhauer and Wagner have understood it, while latter-day philosophers and scholars, optimistically pursuing the chimera of truth, amass meaningless knowledge that has no cultural coherence and by their insights undermine the spiritual values they seek to illumine

In his second period (1876–82) he appears 'to take sides against himself', pursuing knowledge with positivist bravura and condemning the romantic illusions of art. Behind every value he detects a 'human, all-too-human' weakness, or baseness, or self-deception (*Menschliches Allzumenschliches*, 1878–9). As this kind of modern knowledge spreads, European civilization will undergo a crisis of self-hatred, of nihilism. Only the few 'free spirits' strong enough to bear the prospect (and this is his desperate ideal) will experience as a spiritual dawn (*Morgenröte*, 1881) the coming of this 'gay science' (*Die fröhliche Wissenschaft*, 1882–7) whose basic pronouncement is that 'God is dead'.

From 1882 to 1888 Nietzsche developed his most characteristic ideas, the dangerously ambiguous doctrines that purport to point a way beyond that very collapse of all traditional values which they represent – the 'myths' of Eternal Recurrence (his symbol of a world of pure immanence, having no transcendent goal or meaning) and the new human creature who will survive the loss of transcendental illusions, the

Superman: *Also sprach Zarathustra* (1883–92; tr. R. J. Hollingdale, *Thus Spoke Zarathustra*, 1961), *Jenseits von Gut und Böse* (1886), *Zur Genealogie der Moral* (1887; tr. F. Golfing, *The Genealogy of Morals*, in *The Birth of Tragedy*, 1956), *Die Götzendämmerung* (1889; tr. W. Kaufmann, *Twilight of the Idols*, in *The Portable Nietzsche*, 1960), *Der Antichrist* (1888; tr. ibid.), *Nietzsche contra Wagner* and *Der Fall Wagner* (1888; tr. ibid.), *Ecce Homo* (1888) and the collection of fragments supposedly intended for the volume which was to sum up his philosophy: *Der Wille zur Macht*. This 'will to power' expressed his fundamental conception of existence, the endlessly self-perpetuating and self-aggrandizing energy, which, mankind is about to discover, is all that life consists of. Civilization with its moral restraints, its artistic and religious visions that life has higher meaning, has been the fantasy-creation of gregarious weaklings, who had thus to sublimate the frustration of their energies and gloss over facts too painful to bear. Once this is realized, a 'transvaluation of values' (on to a new basis of freely asserted will) will be needed, if man is to be able still to achieve anything noble, good, free (Nietzsche's *positive* vision remains shadowy). The profundity of Nietzsche's detailed anticipations and diagnoses of many aspects of modern literature and thought made his writing progressively influential in the 20th century (on historians, e.g. Spengler; philosophers, e.g. Heidegger; on many writers, among others Thomas Mann and Rilke; and politically through the facile abuse to which it lent itself as a justification of Fascism and anti-semitism). [PB/AKT]

*Musarion-Ausgabe* (23 vols. 1920–9); *Werke*, ed. K. Schlechta (1954).

*International N. Bibliography* (Chapel Hill, U.S.A., 1960); C. Andler, *N. Sa vie et sa pensée* (Paris, 1920–31); M. Heidegger, *N.* (Stuttgart, 1961); K. Jaspers, *N.* (Berlin, 1936); F. A. Lea, *The Tragic Philosopher* (1958); W. Kaufmann, *N.* (Princeton, U.S.A., 1950); R. J. Hollingdale, *N.* (1965); Heller, *DM*.

**Nievo, Ippolito** (Padua 1831–Padua 1861). Italian patriot poet and novelist. He wrote early poetry reminiscent of ⇨ Giusti and ⇨ Prati (*I versi*, 1854; *Le lucciole*, 1858), two tragedies (*Spartaco* and *I Capuani*) and short stories (noteworthy *Il varmo*, 1856); but he is known chiefly for his novels (*Angelo di bontà*, 1855; *Il conte pecoraio*, 1857; and especially *Le confessioni di un Italiano*, written in 1858, published 1867, posth.; tr. L. F. Edwards, *The Castle of Fratta*, 1957). *Le confessioni*, with their description of the emergence of a national spirit out of 18th-century decadence, has a moral purpose reminiscent of ⇨ Manzoni; and characterization and skilful humorous narrative make it one of the foremost novels of the century – despite its long digressions. For his part in the fighting of 1860 see the poems *Amori garibaldini* (1860). He died in a shipwreck. [RHC]

*Opere*, ed. S. Romagnoli (1952); *Teatro*, ed. E. Faccioli (1963).

A. Pesante, *Due manzoniani, I.N., E. De Marchi* (Trieste, 1930); N. Taroni, *I.N.* (Milan, 1932); G. Bozzetti, *La formazione del Nievo* (Padua, 1959); *Guida*, 1954; *Minori*, iv.

**Niger, Shmuel,** pseud. of Shmuel Charmi (Dukor, Minsk 1884– ). Yiddish literary critic and essayist. Champion of Yiddish language and literature which he considers as the chief instrument of Jewish spiritual survival. Started his literary life in Vienna, but had to leave after the Polish occupation at the end of the First World War. He settled in the United States, and wrote in Hebrew and Russian. His analytical studies of Yiddish writers are of great literary and historical value. [EE]

*Yiddishe Shreiber* (Warsaw, 1912); *Sholem Aleichem* (N.Y., 1928); *Mendele Moicher Sforim* (Chicago, 1936); *In Kampf far a Nayer Dersteeung* (N.Y., 1940); *H. Leivick* (Toronto, 1950); *Y. L. Perez* (Buenos Aires, 1952).

N. B. Minkoff, *S.N., vi a Kritiker* (N.Y., 1946).

**Nijhoff, Martinus** (The Hague 1894–The Hague 1953). Dutch poet and dramatist. Where his predecessors sought to make an eternally valid statement about the beauty in life as they saw it, Nijhoff anticipated the current emphasis on immanence by his creative transmutation of life in a crisis of materialistic doubt to provide some understanding for the immediate future. Hence his recurrent theme of the spiritual value of the physical world, childhood recollection and primordial innocence, expressed with the control, simplicity and power of his reverence for humanity as the epitome of the transient and eternal, the whole and the individual, the material and the transcendent. In both of his longer poems, *Awater* (1934) and *Het Uur U* (1942), a strange figure has a compelling attraction for those who are open-minded enough to understand his prophetic meaning. *Het heilig* *hout* (1950) contains three one-act plays, for Christmas, Easter and Whitsun. [PK]

*Verzameld Werk* (3 vols., 1954); *Delta* (Summer 1961).

F. Lulofs, *Verkenning door varianten* (The Hague, 1955); J. de Poortere, *M.N.* (Bruges, 1960); L. Wenseleers, *Het wonderbaarlijk lichaam* (The Hague, 1966).

**Nilin, Pavel Filippovich** (Irkutsk 1908– ). Russian novelist. His first stories date from 1936, but he became widely known only with *Zhestokost'*, a novel based on his experiences in the Security Services in Siberia. The hero succeeds in smashing a gang of anti-Soviet bandits, but at the cost of betraying the man who has made it possible. This conflict of conscience and political considerations ends with the hero's suicide. The tragic ending and the unusual theme made the book for some time the subject of controversy.

Many of his stories are set in Siberia. His heroes tend to be simple people, who are favourably contrasted with the intelligent, the successful and the ambitious. [RDBT]

*Znamenityy pavlyuk* (1960); *Zhestokost'*, ed. T. J. Binyon (1963); tr. J. Barnes, *Comrade Venka*, 1959.

N. F. Piyashev, *P.N.* (Moscow, 1962).

**Nil Sorsky** (1433–1508). Russian saint, mystic and writer. Little is known of his early life. Tonsured in the White Lake monastery of St Kirill, he was probably taught by the learned and influential Païsy Yaroslavov. He was present at the Council of 1490 in Moscow and was probably active in the Church's campaign against the heresy of the Judaisers. At some stage of his later life he travelled to Constantinople and Mount Athos where he studied hesychastic thought, patristic writings and Athonic monasticism. After this he founded his own '*skit*' – a small semi-eremitical community bound together not so much by strict discipline as by worship – on the Sor(k)a (hence 'Nil Sorsky'). He spent most of the rest of his life there, reading, 'interpreting the scriptures' and writing. At a Church Council in 1503 he allegedly attacked monastic landownership, probably at the instigation of Ivan III. It is not known when he was canonized.

Nil wrote two major works: the *Predaniye uchenikom*, a relatively early work (pre-1491) containing his instructions on how monks should live in a *skit*; and a 'Monastic Rule' in which he describes and analyses the various 'passions' which assail the body and recommends psycho-physical methods for overcoming them in the various phases of their occupation of the mind. As well as these he wrote several letters of spiritual comfort to his disciples and friends. He was the first Russian writer to describe the life of contemplation and to leave a detailed description of the method of attaining self-perfection. He advocated no harsh physical asceticism, rather moderation in fasting, in discipline and in church decoration: he was indeed the first Russian systematically to urge renunciation of worldly possessions. His writings are largely derivative and show little of that 'liberal critical spirit' which historians so often credit him with. Yet compilatory though his works are, they are imbued with considerable sincerity thanks to the flexibility of his style and the relative lightness of his touch. [JLIF]

F. von Lilienfeld, *N.S. und seine Schriften* (Berlin, 1963); Ya. S. Lur'ye, *Ideologicheskaya bor'ba v russkoy publitsistike kontsa XV-nachala XVI veka* (Moscow/Leningrad, 1960).

**Nilsson Piraten, Fritiof** (Vollsjö 1895– ). Swedish novelist and story-writer. A lawyer and renowned anecdotist (one of his yarns told how he acquired the extra name 'Piraten'), he became famous with the book *Bombi Bitt och jag* (1932; tr. P. Wiking, *Bombi Bitt*, 1933); often compared to *Huckleberry Finn*, it relates with rich humour the adventures of two boys in his native province of Skåne (the extreme south of Sweden). In later books, such as *Bokhandlaren som slutade bada* (1937), *Historier från Färs* (1940) and *Vänner emellan* (1955), the comical and grotesque are often penetrated by tragedy and by finely calculated shock, as in the writing of Hjalmar ⇨ Bergman. His most recent work is contained in the collections of stories *Flickan med bibelspråken* (1959) and *Millionären* (1965), which maintain the fastidious anecdotal quality of his early books.

M. v. Platen, 'Piratens två världar' in *Biktare och bedragare* (Stockholm, 1958).

**Nithard** (*c.*800–853 or 858). Medieval chronicler. Son of Charlemagne's daughter Bertha and of ⇨ Angilbert, Nithard was brought up at his grandfather's court. Unlike all other writers of his day he never took Orders, though he was commendatory abbot of Saint-Riquier, his father's abbey, and even exercised the functions of abbot for a time. At the request of Charles the Bald he wrote his *De dissensionibus filiorum Ludovici Pii*, a work remarkable for its grasp of both military and political matters. It outlines clearly the causes of the partition of the Carolingian Empire after Charlemagne's death, and in the third book is preserved the text of the famous Strassburg Oaths. Nithard's style is unpolished, but in historical insight he is without rival among his contemporaries. [MRM]

Ed. A. Holder-Egger (1882); ed. G. H. Pertz, MGH II; parallel French text, ed. P. Lauer (Paris, 1926).

**Nivard** (fl. 1150). German-born author of *Ysengrimus*. He migrated to Flanders and taught in the school of the famous monastery at Blandigny, Ghent. The *Ysengrimus* (ed. E. Voigt, 1884) is a long beast-epic in Latin verse on the old theme of the fox and the wolf. It is a collection of fables, interspersed with satires on monasticism. The wolf, who represents the monastics, is a blend of stupidity and avarice. He is tricked by the fox in one incident after another and comes to a violent end. He borrows freely from popular sources (⇨*Renart*). [FB]

L. Willems, *Étude sur l'Ysengrimus* (Ghent, 1895); Raby, *SLP*.

**Njegoš, Petar Petrović** (Njeguši 1813–Cetinje 1851). Montenegrin poet. Born Rade Tomov, he took his name from his native village (near Cetinje), was brought up by his uncle, the Prince-Bishop of Montenegro Petar I, whom he succeeded in 1830, taking the ecclesiastical name of Petar and ruling Montenegro till his death from T.B. Educated in a private school in Boka Kotorska and privately at the monastery of Cetinje, he had as his tutor Sima Milutinović, a Serbian romantic poet of some standing at that time, who cultivated in him an interest for poetry and philosophical thought. In 1833 and 1837 he made visits to Russia where he read Pushkin and ⇨ Zhukovsky. He also studied Hugo, Lamartine, Byron, Dante, and Milton, all of whom influenced his writings. In 1833 he published his first collection of poems, *Pustinjak cetinjski*. His main works are *Luča mikrokozma* (1845; tr. C. A. Manning, *The Rays of Microcosm*, Munich, 1953), the poetic drama *Gorski vjenac* (1847; tr. J. M. Wiles, *The Mountain Wreath*, n.d.) and the play *Lazni car Sćepan mali* (1851). His writing is philosophical in character. The long poem on the fall of man, *Luča mikrokozma*, places man's sin against God before creation, the world being seen as a place of punishment, lightened only by vague intuitions of man's divine nature. Some critics consider it to have been influenced by *Paradise Lost*. In *Gorski vijenac* his dialectical view of life, in which joy and suffering are both necessary facets of a tragic existence, is portrayed against a background of Montenegrin history and custom. His central theme is a philosophy of heroism. His style is highly individual, laconic but full of energy, drawing on the folk songs and proverbs of his people. [EDG]

*SEER*, XXX, 15 (1952).

**Nobre, António** (Oporto 1867–Foz do Douro 1903). Portuguese poet. His individuality forced him to interrupt his law studies at Coimbra University and seek a more congenial atmosphere at the Sorbonne in Paris, where he obtained his diploma in Political Science. Suffering from tuberculosis, he tried in vain to find a cure for his illness, staying for short intervals in Switzerland and Madeira, and even making a voyage to New York. Born in the affluent middle-class, Nobre retained a deep nostalgia for his childhood and adolescence, a happy period of his life which was spent between the fishing villages of northern Portugal and the family estate in the upper country. Both his stay in Paris, where he came to know the work of Verlaine and Laforgue, and his own illness exacerbated his egotism, the main inspiration of the poems he gathered in *Só* (Paris, 1892), mingling his vision of a patriarchal Portugal with the anguish of his solitude, which he disguised under an intentional narcissistic affectation. Two other books, *Despedidas* (1902) and *Primeiros Versos* (1921), were published posthumously. [LSR]

J. Gaspar Simões, *A.N., precursor da poesia moderna* (Lisbon, 1939); Guilherme de Castilho, *A.N.* (Lisbon, 1950).

**Nodier, Charles** (Besançon 1780–Paris 1844). French writer. He was persecuted in 1803 for a rhyming pamphlet against Napoleon, and later took various jobs, becoming editor of the tetraglot newspaper *Le Télégraphe Illyrien*. After 1814 he settled in Paris and in 1824 became librarian of the Bibliothèque de l'Arsenal. He was widely read in his lifetime especially for his novels which helped to spread the new Romantic themes, such as *Jean Sbogar* (1818), the story of an Illyrian Robin-Hood bandit (one of the heroes of Tatiana in Pushkin's *Eugene Onegin*), and *Trilby ou le Lutin d'Argail* (1822). His novel *Thérèse Aubert* (1819) influenced Sainte-Beuve's *Joseph Delorme*. He also wrote a melodrama, *Le vampire* (1820), and numerous works of lexicography, bibliography, entomology and criticism. He is chiefly remembered now as the founder of the first of the Romantic *cénacles* at his home at the Arsenal. The scenes of the gatherings where Hugo, de Vigny and other young romantics would come are excellently described in the *Mémoires* of Alexandre Dumas *père*. [WA]

M. Held, *C.N. et le romantisme* (Bern, 1949); R. Maixner, *C.N. et l'Illyric* (Paris, 1960); J. Richer, *C.N. 'dériseur sensé'* (Paris, 1962).

**Noot, Jonker Jan van der** (Brecht *c.* 1539–Antwerp *c.* 1595). The first truly Renaissance poet of the Netherlands. A frustrated opportunist, he spent a wretched life as a Calvinist exile in London and the Rhineland and as a Catholic in Antwerp. *Het Bosken* (London, 1570) is in the manner of the ◊ Pléiade and Petrarch. His prose *Het Theatre oft Toonneel* (London, 1568) was translated into French (1568), English (1569, with a contribution by Edmund Spenser) and German (1572). The first half of the original version of *Das Buch Extasis* (1576) was published in Dutch and French in 1579 as *Cort Begryp der XII Boecken Olympiados/Abregé des douze livres Olympiados* (ed. C. A. Zaalberg, 1956), followed in 1580 by *Lofsang van Braband/Hymne de Brabant* (ed. C. A. Zaalberg, 1958), which he vainly hoped would gain him an official appointment as Poet of the Province. His later poetry, much of it hack-work, was included in the *Poetische Werken* (1580–95). [PK]

Barnouw, *CA*; Weevers, *PNEC*.

**Nordström, Ludvig** (Härnösand 1882–Stockholm 1942). Swedish novelist, story-writer and publicist. Born in a small town on the coast of Northern Sweden, lovingly described as 'Öbacka' in innumerable stories, he was one of the first important authors to treat extensively the north of Sweden with its isolation and vast area, its economic resources and coastal towns, its hard climate and tough environment, and particularly its people. His mother was English, and he knew English literature (Sterne, Wells, Chesterton, etc.) and tradition (hence his concern with work, economics and practical religion, and perhaps his blend of commonsense and eccentricity). His large production is uneven; a good deal of it was designed to illustrate an odd social philosophy he called 'totalism'; but he was also a down-to-earth social reporter on actual conditions. His best work is to be found in some of his books of stories, such as *Fiskare* (1907), *Borgare* (1909) and *Herrar* (1910) – many of them collected in *Valda noveller* (6 vols., 1923) – showing (with effective use of dialect) the life of the north with broad perspective, pathos, and sometimes splendidly salty humour. The short, racy novel-chronicle *Planeten Markattan* (1937) combines a sweeping survey of economic expansion and social change with a sympathetic study of an actual man involved in it – his own father. Previously he had drawn engaging portraits of his parents and himself in *Tomas Lack* (1912) and *På hemväg till Öbacka* (1934).

G. Qvarnström, *Från Öbacka till Urbs* (Stockholm, 1954); T. Hallén, *L.N.* (Stockholm, 1952).

**Norwid, Cyprian** (Laskowo-Głuchy 1821–Ivry, Paris 1883). Polish poet. He lost his parents early and received little formal education. He grew up in the atmosphere of defeat after the rising of 1830, and in his adolescence acquired some fame as a poet in Warsaw. Allowed to travel abroad in 1842, he studied sculpture for a short time in Italy and then decided to become a voluntary exile. He was befriended in Paris by Chopin and some of the *émigré* writers, tried to improve his fortunes in America (1852), but returned disappointed and penniless to Europe. He lived for some months in the poorest district of London (cf. his poem *Larwa*), then moved to Paris. More and more estranged from his contemporaries, his writing ignored and even ridiculed, he continued to experiment with poetic diction, until after a life of poverty and solitude he died at a home for destitute Polish exiles. In 1888 his remains were transferred to a communal grave.

Among the few works printed during his lifetime, even the substantial volume *Poezje* (Leipzig, 1863) did not contain his best work. He failed to find a publisher for his experimental collection of poems, *Vademecum* (1866; ed. J. W. Gomulicki, 1962). He was unearthed from oblivion at the beginning of the present century, since when his poetry has been edited and studied by many modern critics who see in him not only the most important innovator of Polish poetic diction in the 19th century, but also a profoundly original mind.

Already in the dialogue *Promethidion* (1851), he moulded his syllabic verse on the rhythms of common speech. The subject is a discourse on the ultimate meaning of art, labour, beauty and love, held in a fashionable drawing-room, and it begins ironically with a typical conversation about Chopin. By 1866 he had developed the colloquialism of his metres into free verse proper, and later tried it out in a narrative sequence, *A Dorio ad Phrygium* (c. 1872). In this respect his experiments bring him nearer to the poetry of Browning, Laforgue and Pound, but his essentially religious interpretation of form offers a still more fascinating parallel with Hopkins. As a lonely innovator, he combined intellectual courage with instinctive foresight. He intended his manuscript collection *Vademecum* to be a guide to new poetry and he consciously displayed a variety of forms in it.

His thought, laced with irony, makes him an uncomfortable writer. He refused to be bullied by slogans and sham righteousness, whether political or social, orthodox or progressive; he stood for the dignity of the individual and for self-effacing honesty in artistic expression. This honesty forced him to examine the semantic nuances of words and to control the disintegration of everyday speech, of which he was aware, with precise metaphors. He spoke of Print-Pantheism and sensed the stupifying vulgarities of propaganda. His surviving letters show the growth of his intellect and, indirectly, comment on the first signs of the modern crisis as he perceived them already in the 19th century.

It is still difficult to assess the theatrical value of his poetic plays (such as *Zwolon*, 1851), and in particular his social comedies. They are rarely performed, and only stage productions could establish their tone and sophisticated manner. [JP]

*Wszystkie pisma*, ed. Z. Przesmycki (1937) (unfinished); Peterkiewicz and Singer, *FCPP*.
Scherer-Virski, *MPSS*; *Botteghe Oscure*, XXII (1958); *SEER*, XLIV, 102 (1966).

**Nossack, Hans Erich** (Hamburg 1901– ). German poet and novelist. A businessman before the war, his unpublished manuscripts (mostly dramas) were destroyed during air-raids on Hamburg (1943) – an experience reflected in *Nekyia* (1947), the 'report' by the sole survivor on a dead city and his own dead past, who questions the relevance of time and memory, and discovers in the physical chaos of 1945 a symbolic safeguard from spiritual corruption. *Interview mit dem Tode* (1948; 1950 as *Dorothea*) 'reports' again on the bombings which inspired also many of his *Gedichte* (1947). The novel *Spätestens im November* (1955) is a more conventional satire against a '*Grossindustrieller*' of the postwar boom. After a Kafkaesque parable, *Der Neugierige* (1955), his 'novel of a sleepless night', *Spirale* (1956), tells the surrealistic day-dreams of a man thinking back over his life, and in his despair passing judgement on himself. *Der jüngere Bruder* (1958), his best novel, shows another man's search for 'himself' in a characteristically satirical social setting. *Begegnung im Vorraum* (1963) are stories, *Die Rotte Kain* (1950), one of several dramas. [PB]

Spender, *GGSS*; Middleton, *GWT*.
Keith-Smith, *ECGL*; *GLL*, I, 1965; *DU*, 3, 1964; *Jahresring* (Stuttgart, 1962).

**Notker III, Labeo,** also known as Notker the German (d. 1022). Benedictine teacher and scholar. He was the youngest of the three celebrated monks of this name. He wrote both Latin and German works for use in the study of the Seven Liberal Arts in his monastery (St Gall), but his fame rests principally on his extensive translations into German (i.e. into the Alemannic dialect of his day) of authoritative Latin works on which the educational programme at the monastery school was based. He translated Boethius's *De consolatione philosophiae*, classical authors such as Aristotle, Virgil and Terence, and the influential schoolwork of Martianus Capella; in addition he translated, and wrote an accompanying commentary to, the Psalms and the Book of Job, but the latter has been lost. Of his original Latin writings, works on rhetoric and logic have survived, and there is also a *De musica* written in German. [RT]

*Die Schriften N.s und seiner Schule*, ed. P. Piper (1882–3).
Ehrismann, *GDL*.

**Notker Balbulus** (*c.*840–912). Benedictine monk and writer. He taught in the monastic school at St Gall in Switzerland and was famous for ⇨ sequences in unrhythmical prose, each consisting of a number of double strophes, together usually with a proem and a coda; each syllable of the text corresponds to one note of the melody. He may also be the author of *Gesta Karoli Magni* (ed. P. Jaffé, in *Monumenta Carolina*, Berlin, 1867; tr. A. J. Grant, in *Early Lives of Charlemagne*, 1907), a popular collection of good prose stories about Charlemagne (of little historical value). [FB]

*Notker der Dichter und seine geistige Welt*, ed. W. von den Steinen (Bern, 1948) (complete poems, partly tr., with intr.); Migne, *PL*, 131.

J. M. Clark, *The Abbey of St Gall* (1926); Raby, *CLP*.

**Novak, Vjenceslav** (Senj 1859–Zagreb 1905). Croatian novelist. He wrote about the Dalmatian provinces, producing evocative landscapes of the Adriatic littoral. Although a poet and dramatist, it is his novels that make him of importance especially *Pavao Šegota* (1888) and *Posljednji Stipančici* (1899). A realist, he exposed the squalor and suffering of his native province. True to his age and the influence of Zola, he ascribes the moral tragedy of human life to heredity and degeneracy. Despite certain naïveties of style, his works are written with human sympathy and often with considerable artistic perception. [EDG]

Barac, *HYL*.

**Novalis,** pseud. of Friedrich von Hardenberg (Wiederstedt, Mansfeld 1772–Weissenfels 1801). German Romantic poet and novelist. His short life was dominated by his love for Sophie von Kühn, who became his fiancée but died at 15. His will to live perished with her, and as by an act of will he died soon afterwards.

The small but priceless collection of pieces, most of them fragmentary, which make up his work, derives from the last five years of his life. A highly individualistic, mystic nature, he joined with the brothers ⇨ Schlegel, ⇨ Tieck and others in Jena to formulate the new Romantic theory of literature propounded in the journal *Das* ⇨ *Athenaeum* (1798–1800). His importance rests, however, less on his theoretical aphorisms than on the creative works in which he embodied the new principles. His two unfinished novels, *Die Lehrlinge zu Sais* and *Heinrich von Ofterdingen*, both published posthumously in 1802, carry the message that the true meaning of the world is to be sought in one's own self, and that a new Golden Age in the history of man will be heralded by the power of poetry and art. The latter work presents this picture in the allegorical tale known as *Klingsors Märchen*, which is the core of the novel.

In his *Hymnen an die Nacht* (1800), written in free verse (or rhythmic prose), he expressed the Romantic belief in the evocative power of a poetic language suffused with the qualities of music. The theme of these 6 odes is the desire for death (symbolized by night) which dominated Novalis's thoughts after the death of Sophie von Kühn; death is the gateway to true life, the moment of revelation: 'Life is the beginning of Death; Life is lived for the sake of Death.' He also wrote a number of hymns, two of which are in the German protestant hymnal.

His essay, *Die Christenheit oder Europa* (1799), argues (in an objective tone utterly different from that of the *Hymnen an die Nacht*) that the Catholic Church, which in the Middle Ages had unified all European civilization, must once again be made the rallying-point for a new, higher unity of spirit and activity in which the political and spiritual separatisms of contemporary Europe would be merged. [RT]

*Werke*, ed. P. Kluckhohn (1960f.).

W. Rehm, *Orpheus* (Düsseldorf, 1950); B. Heywood, *The Veil of Imagery* (The Hague, 1959); Dilthey, *ED*; Hamburger, *RE*; Strich, *DKR*.

**'Novellino, Il,'** also called the *Cento novelle antiche* (late 13th century). A collection of Italian *novelle* (ed. S. Lo Nigro, 1963; tr. E. Storer, 1925). The unknown author was almost certainly a Florentine. (Some critics see multiple authorship.) The 100 stories are briefly, often baldly, narrated with no regard for literary effect, and the material is drawn from a great variety of sources. Arthurian and Carolingian knights, Biblical characters, Roman emperors, Prester John, and the Old Man of the Mountains appear in kaleidoscopic sequence, and the only feature which gives a certain unity to the collection is a consistent exaltation of the typical medieval virtues of chivalry and courtesy. It is of interest as a forerunner of ⇨ Boccaccio's *Decameron*. [DGR]

Di Francia, *N*; Roscoe, *IN*.

**Novomeský, Laco** (1904– ). Slovak poet. Influenced by the poetic fashions of the inter-war period (proletarian poetry, symbolism, poetism), he reached artistic maturity just before the Second World War in poems which successfully fused personal experience and political conviction (*Svätý za dedinou*, 1939). Disgraced under the Communist regime and later rehabilitated, he returned to the 1930s in his autobiographical poem *Vila Teréza* (1963). [RA]

V. Reisel, *Poézia L.N.* (Bratislava, 1946).

**Núñez de Arce, Gaspar** (Valladolid 1834–Madrid 1903). Spanish poet, dramatist and Liberal politician. His poetry is declamatory and patriotically progressive; *Gritos del combate* (1875), containing poems exhorting Spaniards to rise above domestic strife, made him famous. His later philosophical and elegiac poems are more ponderous than profound, though the characteristic problem of science and faith is interestingly treated in *La última lamentación de Lord Byron* (1879). His plays have little dramatic life. [JMC]

*Obras dramáticas* (1879); Blecua, *FLE*; Trend, *OBSV*.

J. Romo Arregui, *Vida, poesía y estilo de G.N. de A.* (Madrid, 1946); J. M. de Cossío, *Cincuenta años de poesía española* (*1850–1900*) (Madrid, 1960).

**'Nyugat'** ('The West'). The dominating Hungarian literary periodical (1908–41). It appealed to the Budapest intelligentsia by its concern both with modern artistic trends (*l'art pour l'art*) and with political issues. E. Osvát (1877–1929) and A. Schöpflin (1872–1950) were its most distinguished critics. [JFR]

# O

**Obaldia, René de** (Hong Kong 1918– ). French poet, novelist and dramatist. Though first known for highly idiosyncratic novels (*Tamerlan des cœurs*, 1954; *Fugue à Waterloo*, 1956; *Le centenaire*, 1959), his current reputation rests on his plays which exploit a genuinely funny verbal inventiveness and a wide range of non-verbal scenic effects. He defends spontaneous human joy and feeling against the dehumanizing pressures of a world given over to space-travel, power politics and mass-communications, in such plays as the fantasticated murder mystery, *Genousie* (1960; tr. D. Watson, in *Jenousia and Seven Impromptus for Leisure*, 1965); *Le satyre de la Villette* (1963); and *Le cosmonaute agricole* (1965). [SBJ]

*Théâtre* (2 vols., 1966); *Sept impromptus à loisir* (1967); *Prose et théâtre*, ed. J.-L. Bory (1966).
P.-L. Mignon, *Le théâtre d'aujourd'hui de A jusqu'à Z* (Paris, 1966).

**Obey, André** (Douai 1892– ). French dramatist and actor-manager. Associated with the experimental theatrical group La Compagnie des Quinze (1930–6), which produced *Noé* (1931; tr. A. Wilmurt, *Noah*, 1934); *Le viol de Lucrèce* (1931; tr. W. Becker, *Venus and Adonis*, 1952); and *La bataille de la Marne* (1932). The last two strain unsuccessfully to reach a genuine poetic dimension but suffer from a self-conscious handling of myth and symbol. *Noé* has poetic freshness and skilfully exploits a sophisticated awareness of the relationship between the literal and the allegorical, though the candid strength of its folk elements sometimes slides into false naïvety. Obey's variations on the Don Juan myth – *Le trompeur de Séville* (1937) and *L'homme de cendre* (1950) – are more intellectualized but offer considerable psychological complexity. In *Lazare* (1952) he returns, with some power, to a Biblical myth. [SBJ]

*Théâtre*, I (1948).
Lalou, *TF*; Fergusson, *II*; Weinstein, *MDJ.*

**Obstfelder, Sigbjørn** (Stavanger 1866–Copenhagen 1900). Norwegian peot and short-story writer. He trained as an engineer, was in America, dreamt of becoming a composer, but never established himself; he was a typically *fin-de-siècle* figure and died of tuberculosis. He is the poet of the lonely, confused, but searching and erotically aware soul, who, to quote from one of his best-known poems, seems 'to have arrived on the wrong planet'. His work occupies a minor but distinctive position in Norwegian literature; *Digte* (1893; tr. P. Selver, *Poems*, 1920), the short story *Korset* (1896), and the unfinished *En præsts dagbog* (1900) are the most important. [RGP]

*Samlede skrifter*, ed. S. Tunold (3 vols., 1950).
J. F. Bjørnsen, *S.O.* (Oslo, 1959); A. Hannevik, *O. og mystikken* (Oslo, 1960); McFarlane, *TNL.*

**Oehlenschläger, Adam** (Copenhagen 1779–Copenhagen 1850). Danish poet and dramatist. Brought up at Frederiksberg Castle, at which his father was employed, he studied (without graduating) at Copenhagen, where the battle of 1801 inspired his first dramatic attempt. Public lectures in 1802 by the Norwegian scientist Henrik Steffens (and subsequently private discussion with him) on Goethe and the Romantic philosophy of ⇨ Fichte, ⇨ Schelling and the brothers ⇨ Schlegel made Oehlenschläger a convinced disciple of Romanticism. His poem *Guldhornene* (tr. G. Borrow, intro. E. Gosse, *The Golden Horns*, 1913) is generally recognized as introducing the new era in Danish literature (*Digte 1803*, publ. 1802, a volume which included romantic ballads and the lyric-dramatic poem *Sankt Hansaften-Spil*; tr. G. Borrow, *Midsummer Night's Play*, 1913). His *Poetiske Skrifter* (2 vols., 1805) added *Vaulundur's Saga*, a romantic legend of the mythological Wayland the Smith (tr. E. Kinnear, 1847), and the romantic fairy-tale play *Aladdin* (tr. T. Martin, 1857).

As the leading poet of Denmark Oehlenschläger went to Weimar where he met Goethe and also wrote his great patriotic tragedy *Hakon Jarl hin Rige* (tr. J. F. Chapman, 1857), and *Baldur hin Gode*, a Northern tragedy in Greek style (both published in *Nordiske Digte*, 1807). He went on to Pari where he wrote the tragedies *Palnatoke* (tr. J. F. Chapman, 1855) and *Axel og Valborg* (tr. J. F. Chapman, 1851), and then to Rome, where he wrote another tragedy, *Correggio* (tr. T. Martin, 1854). Returning to Denmark in 1809, he was appointed Professor of Aesthetics at Copenhagen soon after.

Oehlenschläger's later Northern tragedies, mostly inferior, have not been translated into English. Most outstanding among his later works are the two ballad cycles *Helge* (1814) and *Nordens Guder* (1819; tr. W. E. Frye, *The Gods of the North*, 1845). In 1829 he was laureated in Sweden as 'the poetic king of Scandinavia'. Many of his poems have been translated, by W. S. Walker, H. W. Longfellow, R. W. Buchanan, Lady Wilde, George Borrow, Robert Hillyer, C. W. Stork, R. P. Keigwin, and others, and it is for his lyrical poetry (rather than for his now largely forgotten dramas) that he remains one of Denmark's foremost writers. [ELB]

*Poetiske Skrifter*, ed. H. Topsøe-Jensen (5 vols., 1926–30).

V. Andersen, *A.O.* (3 vols., Copenhagen, 1899–1900).

**Olbracht, Ivan,** pseud. of Kamil Zeman (Semily 1882–Prague 1952). Czech writer. Son of Antal Stašek, the writer; he studied law before becoming a left-wing journalist and author. From 1945 he held high posts in the Prague Ministry of Information. Although diverted from writing by political and other interests, he produced at least two works, set in the years after the First World War, which place him among the leading Czech prose writers: *Podivné přátelství herce Jesenia* (1919) – a psychological novel of an artist's tortured evolution through work, friendship and love towards a higher moral stature; and his most mature novel, *Nikola Šuhaj loupežník* (1933; tr. R. Finlayson-Sansour, *Nikola Šuhaj – Robber*, Prague, 1954). This prize-winning book, translated into more than a dozen languages, is the story of a bandit in Sub-Carpathian Ruthenia, pre-war Czechoslovakia's easternmost land of forests, romance and Jewish mysticism. Like other characters in his books, Nikola Šuhaj is an outcast, in conflict with convention and civilization; yet he is something of a Robin Hood figure who symbolizes the people's rebellion against oppression, their love of freedom and yearning for justice.

Olbracht's other works include: *Žalář nejtemnější* (1918), a psychological novel of a blind man consumed with jealousy; *Anna proletářka* (1928), a tendentious political book; *Zamřížované zrcadlo* (1930), autobiographical impressions of the life of a political prisoner; and *Golet v údolí* (1937) (tr. *Valley of Exile*, Prague, 1965), stories from the life of Sub-Carpathian orthodox Jews. [RPH]

*Spisy* (15 vols., 1958).

B. Václavek, *Tvorbou k realitě* (Prague, 1937); A. M. Píša, *I.O.* (Prague, 1949).

**Old Bulgarian Literature.** After the disciples of St Cyril and St Methodius were expelled from Moravia, St Clement, St Nahum and St Angelarius travelled to Bulgaria in A.D. 885, taking with them the Slavonic translation of the Bible made by their masters, and the Slavonic liturgy used in Moravia and Pannonia. With the help and encouragement of Tsar Boris two schools subsequently to be very important in the creation and growth of Old Bulgarian Literature were founded: the Ochrida School became prominent owing to the activity of St Clement, and the Preslav school owing to its proximity to the Bulgarian court of Tsar Boris and his son Symeon who became its patrons.

St Clement of Ochrida was one of the prominent disciples of St Cyril and St Methodius and Tsar Boris sent him to Kutmitchevitza, a district in south-west Macedonia, where he developed missionary work on a large scale. Most impressive was his educational centre where in seven years he trained a large number of pupils some of whom were ordained priests. Tsar Symeon eventually promoted him Bishop of Drembitsa and Belitsa. St Clement devoted much time to the translation of the service books and just before his death, in A.D. 916, translated the triodium. In *Vita S. Clementis* we are told that he had to prepare sermons in clear and simple language for all festivals to be used by his priests to enlighten their parishioners. About 50 sermons are also ascribed to him, but only some dozen bear his name and are considered genuinely his. They have never been published together, but are dispersed in various Russian libraries and museums. They fall into two categories – didactic and panegyric. His *Vita* mentions that he also composed many hymns and prayers. Although St Clement's work did not have the distinguished literary form of the Preslav school, it was much closer to the people and thus had a greater educational value.

The Royal school of Preslav produced several illustrious scholars and theologians; one of its most gifted representatives was Constantine of Preslav, a pupil of St Methodius. While still a presbyter, he prepared the *Uchitelno Evangelie* ('The Gospel Commentary'), a work consisting of 51 sermons based on the Gospel readings appointed for each Sunday of the year, from Easter day to Palm Sunday. This work has come to us in several editions. In the synodic collection of the works of Constantine are ascribed: (1) the Alphabetical Prayer by Constantine the Philosopher; (2) the Prologue, followed by 51 sermons with the name of their authors at the headings, e.g. St John Chrysostom, St Cyril of Alexandria and Constantine the Presbyter (42nd sermon); (3) the structure of the Church and the liturgy; (4) the Chronicles. The Vienna edition is without the Alphabetical Prayer and the Prologue. The manuscript begins with the sermons. The complete work has never been published. In many manuscripts the Alphabetical Prayer, which is a religious poem of considerable merit, is ascribed to Constantine–Cyril, the brother of St Methodius. The Prologue is important because it tells how St Nahum urged Constantine of Preslav to undertake the work. Most sermons are translations from the Greek, but in some of them the introductions and conclusions are by Constantine himself. Both the structure of the Church and the liturgy and the Chronicles are pure translations from the Greek. Some scholars also ascribe to Constantine the service devoted to St Methodius.

As a bishop (A.D. 906) Constantine of Preslav translated from the Greek the 'Discourses against the Arians' by St Athanasius. The work was done under Symeon's instructions and copied by the monk Theodore Duks. It was a tremendous task to find and, in many cases, to create new words in an undeveloped language to express the complicated theological terminology of St Athanasius.

Another distinguished member of this school, John the Exarch, was a contemporary of Tsar Symeon. He admits that he was not a disciple of St Cyril and St Methodius but had heard of them. John translated 48 chapters out of 100 in the 3rd part of the famous book of St John of Damascus *De Fide Orthodoxa*. This translation became known in the Slavonic literature as *Nebesa* ('The Heavens'). It is preceded by a Prologue which is the only original part of the book. In it the author gives some information about himself and his approach as a translator. Like Constantine of Preslav the translation presented John with enormous difficulties and was little read.

John the Exarch's most important work was *Shestodnev* ('Hexameron'), written to prove the truth of the Biblical account of creation. The work begins with an introduction, at the end of which John humbly states that he compiled the material for his book from several writers such as St Basil the Great, St John Chrysostom and others. The book was very popular, among other things helping to introduce the Slavs to the field of natural science. At the beginning of the 6th oration there is a remarkable description of the Bulgarian capital, Preslav, and in several other places the king, his courtiers and the poor people in their straw huts are portrayed. Some of the many manuscripts in existence have miniatures. Several sermons on Festivals are also ascribed to John, but sufficient evidence has not yet been obtained to prove his authorship conclusively.

While on their mission to the West, St Cyril and St Methodius encountered what was known as the three-tongue heresy – i.e. that God should be worshipped only in Latin, Hebrew and Greek. Apparently the same 'heresy' existed in Bulgaria and the Monk Khrabr, also of the Preslav group, undertook to refute it. His name is not known outside the manuscript of his famous book, *O pismenekh* ('An Apology for Slavonic Letters'). It is possible that he used a pseudonym. Most scholars date the book between the end of the 9th and the beginning of the 10th centuries. The main task of the author was to defend the Slavonic writings and prove that they can coexist side by side with the Greek, Latin and Hebrew writings. While, Khrabr maintains, the Greek alphabet was created by many Hellenic heathens, the Slavonic one was created by one saintly man, i.e. Constantine–Cyril. Earlier the Slavs, according to the author, had used only very primitive signs for writing, but thanks to St Cyril they received a proper alphabet. Khrabr's work is both apologetical and polemical, thus introducing new literary forms to Old Bulgarian Literature.

When Bulgaria accepted Christianity from Byzantium it was natural that it should fall under its cultural influence and essential that many service and religious books should be translated. Since contacts with the West were insignificant, even the few Latin works that penetrated into Bulgaria came via the Eastern Roman Empire. It is important to remember that although Christianity was imposed by the Bulgarian king, the masses continued to be attached to their heathen rites and were thus ready ground for heretical tenets. This is why many of the Greek apocryphal works were translated and became widely known. Of the officially accepted literature, translations were made of: (1) Patristic literature, e.g. St Athanasius, St Cyril of Alexandria, St Basil the Great, St John Chrysostom and many others. (2) Legal codes, e.g. the Agrarian Law, the Law for Judging People, and the Ecloga. (3) *Vitae Sanctorum*, e.g. St Antony of Egypt and St Saba of Palestine. (4) Chronicles, e.g. John Malalas, Patriarch Nicephorus and George the Monk. The Old Bulgarian language was vastly enriched by this large number, and diversity, of translations. Tsar Symeon played an important role in this 'golden era' of Bulgarian literature by encouraging many to translate and write. Directly connected with Symeon is a translation of a collection of works by St John Chrysostom known as *Zlatostruy* ('Golden Stream'). Some of his contemporaries refer to him as 'an author of many works' and 'a man who loved books above all'. During the reign of Symeon, another large collection of commentaries on the gospels was compiled and, in 1073, copied for Prince Svyetoslav of Kiev.

Besides this official Church literature, which was often too scholarly to appeal to ordinary people, appeared many stories and legends that come close to the modern novel. Most of these are Greek translations and very few are of Bulgarian origin. It is difficult to establish exactly when this type of work appeared, although some of the translations must have been in circulation as early as the 10th century. The most popular tale was the story of Alexander the Great. It is full of phantasy about his birth, adventures and battles and his tragic death. Similar to this historical theme were stories connected with Troy. Among the stories of a didactic nature the most significant was 'Barlaam and Josaphat', based on the biography of Buddha. Although the legend was known in many languages it was translated from its Greek version. The other two popular tales of the same nature were *Stephanit and Ichnilat* and *Digenes Acritas.* The personality of Solomon, especially his wisdom and power over demons, was the source of many of these tales.

The first story with a Bulgarian theme was *Chudoto s Balgarina* ('The Miracle with the Bulgarian'). It was written in the 10th century and describes his adventures in Symeon's war against the Magyars. It has been suggested that it was written in a Greek monastery near the Bulgarian border and was translated into Old Bulgarian, but an Old Bulgarian origin is possible. The story concerns a private in Symeon's cavalry who tells of his exploits in the king's army and how, through a vision, he found three hoops under his dead horse's knee from which he made a cross endowed with a miraculous power.

Although in translation, all these stories are important because they were designed chiefly for the laiety and gradually permeated the masses to become part of their literary heritage.

After the acceptance of Christianity as a state religion the apocryphal stories began to be translated and circulated throughout Bulgaria. In the main they are based on Biblical stories, highly embellished by phantasy. Some of those associated with Old Testament themes were: 'Adam and Eve', 'The Book of Enoch', 'The Death of Abraham', 'The Vision of Isaiah', 'The Apocalypse of Baruch' and 'The Twelve Patriarchs'. New Testament themes were: 'The Childhood of Jesus' (Thomas Gospel), 'Mary Seeing the Torments of Hell', 'The Vision of Paul', 'A Dispute between Jesus and the Devil', the 'Revelation of John the Divine on Mount Tabor', the gospels of Nicodemus and Protevangelium, and several legends about Jesus. To this category also belong the apocryphal lives of Peter and John, Matthew the evangelist, the apostles Thomas, Philip and Andrew.

Many apocryphal works deal with eschatological themes and can be divided into three groups: (1) the Antichrist and the end of the world; (2) the terrible judgement; and (3) life after death. To this group belong the 'Sermon of Methodius of Patara', the 'Life of Macarius of Rome', the 'Sermon of Ipolitus' and many others.

A popular work with scientific data was

*Rasumnic* (known also as 'Questions and Answers' or 'Conversation between the Three Saints') ascribed falsely to St John Chrysostom, St Gregory the Divine and St Basil the Great. Among the questions it discusses are the composition and size of the sun, the moon and the stars, the distance between heaven and earth, and the creation of Adam and Eve. Another group is devoted to divination in which events are foretold from natural phenomena, e.g. thunder, and from the involuntary behaviour of the human body, e.g. the twitching of the eye. Works belonging to this group include: *Grămnic*, *Trepetnik*, *Kolednik* and *Lunnik*.

In many of the apocryphal works Bogomil (see below) doctrines and tendencies were interpolated during translations and the stories changed. Among the authors of these works the names of two heretical priests, Bogomil and Jeremiah, are met most frequently, although the latter appears a more prolific writer.

The apocryphal works give very interesting glimpses into the social, economic and religious aspects of the society of that period. For instance: 'Those who suppress the poor find themselves in hell', 'The money lenders are tortured in hell, because they accumulated unjustly riches from the poor'. 'The representatives of the Church have gone to hell, because they read the Holy Scripture without fulfilling their precepts.'

The priest (*pop*) Bogomil created an important religious and social movement during the first half of the 10th century which was deeply felt, not only among the south Slav and in Byzantium, but even in western Europe and which bore a rich literature. Their doctrinal book and most important source of information was the Secret Book (*Liber Sancti Johannis*), consisting of questions, supposedly put forward by John the Evangelist and answered by Jesus, about the activities of the Devil and his final Fall. Beside the New Testament books several of the apocryphal works already mentioned were considered part of the Bogomil literature. To these can be added the Bulgarian apocryphal chronicle, 'The Sea of Tiberius', and the Greek legend of the creation of the world. In addition, there are the writings attributed to the priest Jeremiah (according to some scholars Jeremiah and Bogomil are the same person): 'The Wood of the Cross', 'How Christ Became a Priest', 'The Holy Trinity', 'How Christ Ploughed with the Plough', 'How Christ Called Probus His Friend', 'The Questions of Jeremiah to the Mother of God', 'Falsehood about Fever and Other Illnesses'. Like the other apocryphal works it is improbable that these were original as they were known to the Greeks earlier.

From the antagonists of the Bogomil heresy the two most important sources are that of Cosmas, the Bulgarian priest, and the account to be found in the 'Dogmatic Panoply' of Euthymius Zigabenus.

Cosmas, the priest, was a 10th-century writer. His famous book 'Sermon against the Heretics' gives a significant description of the social conditions of Bulgaria at the time. The book begins with an introduction after which the author sets out to disprove the evil ways of the Bogomils, i.e. their beliefs, attitude to wealth, civil authority, sacraments, personal behaviour, etc., and sets against them the teaching of the Orthodox Church. He goes on to speak of monasticism, condemning some monks in their search for an easy life and praising the true representatives of monasticism. He also has some harsh words about the landowners and others of the privileged classes. He ends his sermon by summing up what he has said, speaks of evils that come as a result of the ungodly life and tries to find a solution to the problems. A satirical note is strong throughout.

During the 11th and 12th centuries Bulgaria was under the political domination of the Byzantine Empire. Although Basil II recognized the independence of the Bulgarian Church, whose seat became Ochrida, the archbishops and bishops were Greek and the policy in the main was the Hellenization of the Bulgarian Church. The Greek archbishops of Ochrida wrote several works on St Clement in Greek, e.g. Theophilact's *Vita S Clementis* which is also a substantial source of information on St Cyril, St Methodius and their disciples. The Old Bulgarian literary tradition continued especially in some monasteries. It is from this period (11th century) that some of the oldest glagolitic and Cyrilic manuscripts have come down to us. Of the glagolitic, the most important are: (1) the Four Gospels (*Codex Zographensis* and *Codex Marianus*); (2) the Evangelarium or liturgical gospel readings (*Codex Assemani*); (3) the Psalter (*Psalterium Sinaiticum*); (4) the Euchologium (*Euch. Sinaiticum*); (5) Homiletic literature (*Glagolita Clozianus*).

The two chief manuscripts in Cyrilic are: the Sava Gospel book (known as *Savvina kniga* or *Savva Book*) and *Codex Suprasliensis*, which is the largest extant Old Bulgarian manuscript. During this period the name of St John of Rila acquired great significance. George Scylitzes wrote his life which is extant only in Old Bulgarian translation. A long service was also written in his honour. The apocryphal works continued to be translated and some of them were permeated with Bogomil elements.

Three more works should be mentioned: (1) the popular life of St John of Rila (12th century, written in the Rila monastery), based on legends and containing many apocryphal elements; (2) the Salonica legend which narrates the life of St Cyril and how he converted the Bulgarians. Of no historical value, it is important as a literary document. In it the Bulgarians are described as a nation chosen by God; (3) the Bulgarian apocryphal chronicle divided into two parts, the first telling of the ascension of Isaiah (this resembles the 'Vision of Isaiah' with Bogomil elements) and the second consisting of a Chronicle in which Isaiah is told by God to lead the Bulgarians to their land. Historically it has no value and contains many Bogomil beliefs, but it is full of patriotic sentiments, e.g. that the Bulgarian kings were God-fearing, capable of giving riches to the country and collecting only small dues.

This outline of Old Bulgarian literature has shown how the work of St Cyril and St Methodius, originally in Moravia and Pannonia, was carried into and extended in Bulgaria. Through their disciples and other distinguished Bulgarian scholars and translators the Slavs became the proud heirs and preservers of Byzantine culture. This gave Bulgaria, and later other Slavs, the religious and political institutions of the Eastern Roman Empire and placed them on the level of the other Christianized nations of the world. [MK]

For the creation of two schools in Bulgaria: V. Jagić, *Entstehungsgeschichte der Kirchenslavischen Sprache* (Berlin, 1913); F. Dvornik, *Les légendes de Constantin et de Méthode, vues de Byzance* (Prague, 1933); E. Georgiev, *Raztsvetat na Bălgarskata literatura,* v IX–X vek (Sofia, 1962).

For St Clement of Ochrida: Migne, *PC*, compl. Gr. v. 126; N. L. Tunitsky, *Sv. Kliment, episkop Slovensky, Sergiev Posad* (1913); M. Kusseff, 'St Clement of Ochrida', in *SEER*, 1948.

For Constantine of Preslav: A. Gorsky i Nevostruev, 'Opisanie Slavyanskikh Rukopisey', *Moskovskoy sinodal'noy biblioteki*, II, 2 (Moscow, 1859); Yu. Trifonov, *Belezhki vărkhu uchitelnoto evangelie na episkopa Konstantina*, Sbornik V. N. Zlatarski (Sofia, 1925); A. Vaillant, *Discours contre les Ariens de saint Athanase, version slave et traduction en français* (Sofia, 1954).

For John the Exarch: K. Kalaydovich, *Ioann Eksarkh bolgarskiy* (Moscow, 1824); A. Leskien, 'Zum Šestodnev des Exarchen Johannes', *Archiv für slavische Philologie*, 26 (Munich, 1904); R. Aitzetmüller, *Das Hexaemeron des Exarchen Johannes* (Graz, 1958, 1960).

For Khrabr the Monk: A. Mazon, *Le moine Chrabr et Cyrille*, Sbornik V. N. Zlatarski (Sofia, 1925); V. N. Zlatarski, *Koy e bil Chernorizets Khrabăr? Istoria na bălgarskata dărzhava prez srednite vekove*, I, 2 (Sofia, 1927); K. M. Kuev, *Kăm văprosa za nachaloto na slavyanskata pismenost*, God. na Sof. univ. fil. fac. T.54 (Sofia, 1960); W. Wondrak z., *Kirchenslavische Chrestomanthie* (Göttingen, 1910) (text).

Translations: A. Popov, *Obsor khronografov ruskoy redaktsii*, vyp. 1 (Moscow, 1866); M. Wengart, *Byzantské kroniky v literature cirkevnéslavanské*, 1 (Bratislava, 1922); J. Dujčev, *Übersicht über die bulgarische Geschichtsschreibung. Antike und Mittelalter in Bulgarien* (Berlin, 1960).

Stories and Legends (works of fiction): A. N. Pypin, *Ocherk literaturnoy istorii starinnykh povestey i skazok russkikh* (St Petersburg, 1857); Iv. Snegarov, *Starobălgarskiyat razkaz 'Chudo na sv. Georgi s bălgarina' kato istoricheski izvor*, God. na Dukh. akademiya IV (XXX) (1954–5); Yord. Ivanov, *Starobălgarski raskazi* (Sofia, 1935).

Apocryphal works: V. Jagič, 'Opisi i izvodi iz nekoliko južnoslovinskih rukopisa', *Starine*, V (1873); VI (1874); IX (1877); X (1878); Yord. Ivanov, *Bogomilski knigi i legendi* (Sofia, 1925); Iv. Duychev, *Nay-stariyat slavyanski spisăk na zabranenite knigi*, God. na Bălg. bibl. inst. 'Elin Pelin', III (1952–3).

For the Bogomils: S. Runciman, *The Medieval Manichee* (1947); D. Obolensky, *The Bogomils* (1948) (both contain an extensive bibliography).

For Cosmas the Priest: M. G. Poprushenko, 'Kosma Presviter', *Bolgarskiy pisatel'* XV (Sofia, 1936); A. Vaillant, 'Le traité contre les Bogomiles du prêtre Cosmas', in *Revue d'étude slaves* (Paris, 1944); A. Vaillant et H. C. Puech, *Le traité contre les Bogomiles de Cosmas le Prêtre* (Paris, 1945).

For Old Bulgarian literature during the 11th and 12th centuries: Yord. Ivanov, *Zhitiya na sv. Ivana Rilski*, God. na Sof. universitet, 1st.-filolog. fac., kn.32 (1936); St Gečev, 'La Légende dite de Thessalonique', in *Studia historica-philologica Serdicensia*, 1 (1938); V. Sl. Kiselkov, sv. *Ivan Rilski – zhitiya* (Sofia, 1940).

**Old Church Slavonic** (also referred to as Church Slavonic and Old Bulgarian). A literary language, based – under the influence of Greek – on a Macedonian dialect of Bulgarian by the brothers Cyril (Constantine) and Methodius in the 9th century (⇨ Old Bulgarian Literature). The same brothers are also credited with the invention of at least one of the two alphabets (Glagolithic and Cyrillic) which were used to record the language. Of these, the Cyrillic was to gain greater currency; the Glagolithic has barely survived. The earliest surviving texts may be traced to the late 10th century. The first grammar appeared at the end of the 16th century (1586).

The Slavs are assumed to have shared a single language (the hypothetical Common Slav) in earlier centuries. By the time of Cyril and Methodius the various Slav languages had already taken shape, but there was sufficient common ground between them for Old Church Slavonic to act as a literary *lingua franca*. In particular, it provided the linguistic medium for the conversion to Christianity of the Slav nations (other than the Polish). Unlike the nations of Western Europe, the Southern and Eastern Slavs during the Middle Ages worshipped and heard the scriptures in a language of their own ('God created this language as perfectly as other tongues,' asserted Cyril, according to a Moravian legend of the 10th century).

The people of Great Moravia were the first to benefit from the new language, but the Bulgarians, Serbs and Russians were to be the principal legatees of Cyril and Methodius. Each of these nations was to modify the language lightly in accordance with its own vernacular. In Russia, Old Church Slavonic was to serve as, or was to provide the model for, the literary language until the end of the 17th century. Old Church Slavonic and Old Russian interpenetrated and enriched each other, and it is not always easy to assign a given text firmly to one language or the other (Ludolf, in his *Grammatica russica* of 1696, was oversimplifying the situation when he wrote, *loquendum est Russice et scribendum est Slavonice*). While an ⇨ Ilarion of Kiev adhered more closely to Old Church Slavonic, the compilers of the ⇨ Russian Primary Chronicle preferred Old Russian forms of expression. The reform of the alphabet under Peter the Great (1710) drew a visual as well as a linguistic distinction between the two. Under the Petrine dispensation the Russian vernacular was given new opportunities. ⇨ Lomonosov sought to give Church Slavonic a role in his scheme for three styles (1757): he proposed a high, a medium and a low style for literary Russian, of which the highest (for 'heroic verse, odes and prose discourses on matters of importance') was to be generously infused with, and dignified by, Church Slavonic elements. The theory was to be crudely interpreted by Shishkov (1803), who believed that the high style could and should consist almost entirely of Church Slavonic. Such schemes were soon to be abandoned altogether in 19th-century literary Russian, on the formation and integration of which ⇨ Pushkin was to exercise a powerful influence. Church Slavonic elements have become one of the standard ingredients of modern literary Russian. Church Slavonic vocabulary is most frequently drawn upon to express elevated feelings or abstract concepts.

Church Slavonic is still used in the public worship and private devotions of Orthodox Christians in Russia, Bulgaria and Yugoslavia. In Russia an attempt by the 'Living Church' in the early 1920s to replace Church Slavonic by the vernacular failed to gain popular support. In Yugoslavia, however, the Serbian Orthodox Church has recently authorized the alternative use of Serbo-Croat, side by side with Church Slavonic. [SH]

**Oles', Oleksander**, pseud. of Oleksander Kandyba (Verkhosuly, Sumy 1878–Prague 1944). Ukrainian poet. His first collection (1907) gained him immediate recognition and great popularity, and was followed by several others and poetic dramas. In his lyrics and nature poems he brought exceptional refinement, sincerity, melodiousness and new imagery into Ukrainian poetry. The 1905 revolution inspired him to powerful freedom poems, appealing for struggle against tyranny. Depressed and disillusioned by the subsequent reaction, he found renewed hopes in the February 1917 revolution and in the short spell of Ukrainian independence. after which, in 1919, he went abroad, and the elements of nationalism greatly strengthened in his poetry. The chief exponent of Ukrainian neo-romanticism, he is not only popularly recognized as an outstanding lyric and civic poet, but is also a poet's poet of great virtuosity. [VS]

*Poeziyi* (1964); Andrusyshen and Kirkconnell, *UP*; Ewach, *USL*.
Manning, *UL*.

**Olesha, Yuriy Karlovich** (Odessa 1889–Moscow 1960). Russian novelist and dramatist. During the Civil War he fought in the Red Army. His fame rests on the novel *Zavist'* (1928; tr. P. Ross, *Envy*, 1947), later dramatized as *Zagovor chuvstv*. In this work an efficient Soviet sausage-manufacturer is confronted by an anarchic and irresponsible individualist. The debate is conducted so ingeniously and ambiguously that the novel has been taken by some critics as favourable and by others as hostile to the Soviet system. Olesha's fear that man is being dehumanized by the cult of the collective appears also in his short stories, notably *Vishnyovaya kostochka* (1930). His play *Spisok blagodeyaniy* (1931; tr. A. R. MacAndrew, in *20th Century Russian Drama*, *A List of Assets*, 1963), expresses a cautious approval of the Soviet experiment, while deploring its crimes against the individual. *Tri tolstyaka* (1928) is a delightful fairy-story version of the Revolution. All his prose is admirably lucid and expressive; but this apparent simplicity often conceals profound anxieties and ambiguities.

After 1934 his work becomes less interesting; he confined himself mainly to journalism and collaborating on film-scenarios. In the late 1930s and again after the war he disappeared but returned to Moscow for the last years of his life. [RDBT]

*Povesti i rasskazy* (1965); Guerney, *NRS*; Reavey and Slonim, *SL*; Yarmolinsky, *SSS*.
L. Belinkov, *Y.O.* (Moscow, 1966).

**Oliver of Paderborn** (?–1227). Medieval chronicler. A native of Cologne, successively bishop of Paderborn and Cardinal-bishop of St Sabina. Oliver was present at the siege of Damietta and wrote from there two letters to Engelbert, archbishop of Cologne, which later formed the basis of his *Historia damiatana*, a reliable account of the Fifth Crusade. Bongars and other editors later attached one version of it, very misleadingly, to the work of ⇨ Jacques de Vitry. Oliver also wrote a *Historia regum terrae sanctae, 1096–1217*, chiefly valuable for the information it gives on Frederick I. [MRM]

Letters, ed. R. L. Röhricht in *Westdeutsche Zeitschrift für Geschichte und Kunst*, x (1891); *Opera*, ed. H. Hoogeweg (Stuttgart, 1894); tr. J. J. Gavigan (1948).

**Olsen, Ernst Bruun** (Nakskov 1923– ). Danish playwright. He began his career as an actor and a stage producer. From 1958 to 1961 he wrote radio plays in which he experimented with new poetic and satiric forms of expression, but he had his real breakthrough only with the Copenhagen production in 1962 of *Teenagerlove*, a sparkling satirical musical about pop idols and pop industry; the success of this play soon spread to the whole of Scandinavia. Politically and culturally he is a radical critic of the welfare society. His recent play *Bal i den Borgerlige* (1966) satirizes social-democratic respectability. [ELB]

**Olsson, Hagar** (Kustavi 1893– ). Swedo-Finnish novelist and critic. As a literary critic of Helsinki's leading Swedish evening paper during the twenties and thirties, she was the chief interpreter of the work of the younger generation of Swedo-Finnish writers. Her own creative works have progressed from the expressionism of the early novels, through stories and plays reflecting current trends and events, to the subjective lyricism and universal human themes of her later period. Her prose is to be found at its best in the 'legendary' novel *Träsnidaren och döden* (1940) and in the miniature fantasy *Kinesisk utflykt* (1949). [TA]

**O'Neddy, Philothée,** the anagrammatic pseud. of Théophile Dondey (Paris 1811–Paris 1875). One of the *bousingot* followers of Gautier and Borel. His verse was typical of the later and wilder Romantics (*Feu et flamme*, 1833). He also wrote short stories and a prose and verse romance of chivalry *L'histoire d'un anneau* (1842). In later life he became a dramatic critic. [WA]

**Onerva, L.,** pseud. of Hilja Onerva Lehtinen (Helsinki 1882– ). Finnish poetess, critic and translator from French. Her poetry reflects the inner conflicts of a highly civilized person trying to find a solution to her quest for truth. She is a meditative, intellectual poet, influenced by French culture and Nietzsche. Her works include a dozen collections of poetry (1904–52), a novel, *Mirdja* (1908), reflecting *fin-de-siècle* moods, and a two-volume biography of Eino ⇨ Leino (1932). Her poetry has been widely translated. [IR]

*Valitut runot* (1956); Tompuri, *VF*.

**Opatoshu, Josef,** adopted name of Opatofski (Poland 1887–New York 1954). Yiddish novelist. Studied in France and settled in the United States in 1907. One of the most prolific Yiddish writers of the century, influenced by I. L. ⇨ Peretz and ⇨ Sholem Ash. Introduced the historical novel into Yiddish literature. His novels are really a collection of short stories loosely connected. His short stories were published in the New York daily *Der Tog*. His most important works are: Der *Mishpet* (Warsaw, 1923); *Lehrer* (N.Y., 1920); *In Poilishe Velder* (N.Y., 1921) (also in Hebrew); and *Der letzter Oifshtand* (1948). [EE]

N. Maizl, *Y.O. Lebn an Shafn* (Warsaw, 1937).

**Opitz, Martin** (Bunzlau 1597–Danzig 1639). German poet. Verbal facility and literary flair made him the literary law-giver and model of his century. As a handbook of poetics, his *Buch von der deutschen Poeterey* (1624; ed. W. Braune, 1913) is unremarkable, being greatly indebted to Ronsard, ⇨ Scaliger, Horace and Aristotle. Its importance lies in its unequivocal statement of Opitz's belief in German as a language of equal poetic dignity with Italian or French, its handy formulation of literary rules (he treats literature as an intellectual exercise, despite lip-service to Genius) and above all in its insistence that natural stress should be the basis of German metre and not length of syllable. His activities as a theoretician were supplemented by the practical task of providing his fellow-countrymen with models worthy of imitation. Like all his generation, he did not distinguish sharply between translation and original composition and many of his *Teutsche Poemata* (1625; ed. G. Witkowsky, 1902) are unacknowledged translations of Heinsius, Petrarch and Ronsard. Equally, he gave models of high drama by his translations from Seneca and Sophocles, introduced the pastoral style into Germany in his version of Sydney's *Arcadia* and in his own *Schäferey von der Nymphen Hercynie*, and wrote the text of the first German opera, *Dafne* (in collaboration with Schütz). His translation of Barclay's *Argenis* provided a model for the political novel of the Baroque.

He is the embodiment of all the tendencies which gained expression in the work of the various language societies, and in his single-handed importation and naturalization of the achievements of the Italian, Dutch and French literary Renaissance he exercised a decisive influence on the whole of 17th-century German literature. [WAC]

*Trojanerinnen*, DLE, Barock, 5 (extracts).
F. Gundolf, *M.O.* (Munich, 1923); *Neue Heidelberger Jahrbücher* (1926).

**Orderic Vitalis** (Shrewsbury 1075–*c.* 1142). Latin chronicler and monk. He worked at St Évroul in Normandy, but kept his affection for England and revisited it on a number of occasions. His *Historia ecclesiastica* (ed. A. le Prévost, 5 vols., 1838–55; tr. T. Forester, *The Ecclesiastical History*, 4 vols., 1853–6) begins with Christ but is a mere compilation until he comes to events of his own time, in both England and Normandy. He is at his best when dealing with the careers of William I, William II, Henry I, and Robert of Normandy, and his character sketches of these are remarkably vivid. The book is badly arranged and written in affected Latin but gives much information about the social life and pastimes of his age. [FB]

Migne, *PL*, 188.

**Orfelin, Zaharija Stefanović** (Vukovar 1726–Novi Sad 1785). Serbian writer, engraver and publicist. One of the first Serbs in the Vojvodina to be influenced by rationalism. His main works are his biography of Peter the Great (1772) and his foundation of the first literary periodical, *Slavenosrpski magazin* (1768). He is also important for his poetry, some of which was written in the spoken language as opposed to the Russian-Slavonic of the period. In proclaiming the need to write in a language accessible to all, he was a forerunner of Obradović and ⇨ Karadžić. [EDG]

Barac, *HYL*.

**Ormaechea, Nicolás.** ⇨ Basque Literature.

**Orta, Garcia D'** (Castelo de Vide *c.* 1501–Goa 1568). Portuguese physician and botanist. Born in a 'New-Christian' family of Spanish-Jewish origin, recently settled in Portugal, Orta was educated at the Universities of Salamanca and Alcalá de Henares. After practising as a physician in his native town for a couple of years, he came to Lisbon in 1526, where he secured a university chair in 1530. Four years later he sailed for India in the fleet commanded by his friend and patron, Martim Afonso de Sousa, and settled at Goa where he soon developed a lucrative medical practice. He was personal physician to several viceroys and governors of Goa (one of whom granted him the lease of the island of Bombay) and also to several Indian princes, including the Sultan of Ahmadnagar. While preserving an appearance of strict Roman Catholic orthodoxy, Orta and most of his family secretly practised Jewish rites, a fact which only came to the cognizance of the Goa Inquisition after his death. His reputation rests on his *Colóquios dos simples e drogas e cousas mediçinais da Índia* (Goa, 1563), a remarkable work on four separate counts. It is a landmark in the history of materia medica and it is still quoted as an authority on some of the subjects of which it treats. It is the most interesting and original book published by the Portuguese in India during the 16th and 17th centuries, and the only one written by a layman. It probably contains more typographical errors than any other book ever issued from a printing press. It also contains the earliest published work of Luís de Camões in the form of a laudatory ode to the viceroy. The *Colóquios* are not confined to a discussion of Asian materia medica, but are enlivened by frequent digressions into such varied topics as Indian history and politics, the greatness of China, Luso-Spanish rivalry in the Moluccas, case-histories of some of Orta's patients, and anecdotes about elephants, cobras, and mongoose. They were admirably edited by the Count of Ficalho (2 vols., 1891–5). [CRB]

Augusto da Silva Carvalho, *G. d'O.* (Coimbra, 1934); C. R. Boxer, *Two Pioneers of Tropical Medicine: G. d'O. and Nicolás Monardes* (1963); *Revista da Junta de Investigações do Ultramar. G. d'O. Número Especial comemorativo do 4 centenário da publicação dos Colóquios* (Lisbon, 1963).

**Ortega y Gasset, José** (Madrid 1883–Madrid 1955). Spanish essayist and philosopher. He published his first article in a periodical just after graduating from Madrid University in 1902, and in spite of the fact that he spent some years studying philosophy at Marburg in Germany and was professor of metaphysics at Madrid for 25 years, he never ceased to seek non-academic outlets for his ideas. Altogether he produced a prodigious number of articles on a wide variety of topics and no single book of a narrowly philosophical nature. Many of his books are in fact collections of articles, and there is important philosophical material in his prologue to the Conde de Yebes' hunting memoirs (*Veinte años de caza mayor*). His most influential works have probably been his analyses of the Spanish and European scenes written in the twenties: *España invertebrada* (1921; tr. M. Adams, *Invertebrate Spain*, 1937), *La rebelión de las masas* (1929–30; tr. anon., *The Revolt of the Masses*, 1932) and *El tema de nuestro tiempo* (1923; tr. J. Cleugh, *The Modern Theme*, 1931). In all of these he purported to find patterns of development in history (whether Spanish or European) by which the present could be explained or its ills exposed. In one sense, this approach to historical situations was also an extension of his philosophical concern with the interrelationship of individuals and their circumstances, and the need for individuals to make their own lives in given circumstances. He first began to evolve these ideas in detail in his *Meditaciones del Quijote* (1914; tr. E. Rugg and D. Marin, *Meditation on Quixote*, intr. Julián Marías, 1964). Too often, however, his analysis of social and political trends and patterns is highly debatable. And his aim to make people think about their situation led him to dogmatize, oversimplify and strike rhetorical poses. His contribution to Spanish intellectual life was, nevertheless, considerable. He familiarized Spaniards with the ideas of Dilthey, Husserl and Spengler, and used his teaching, editing and writing to stimulate intellectual activity. His 'League for the Service of the Republic' was from a political point of view a counterpart in spirit to his university and literary work. [JMC]

J. Ferrater Mora, *O. y G.* (London, 1956).

**Ortigão, José Duarte Ramalho** (Oporto 1836–Lisbon 1915). Portuguese journalist and intellectual. Contact with ⇨ Eça de Queirós converted him to the cause of the reformist Generation of 1870 (⇨ Quental). With Queirós he produced *As Farpas* (1871ff.), a periodical satirical journal much influenced, at the outset, by the socialism of Proudhon; later positivism, under the influence of Teófilo Braga, became the dominant key. Ortigão's own revolutionary aspirations soon began to wane, and he became a 'vencido da vida' ('one defeated by life'). Indulging his youthful Romantic taste for the picturesque aspects of Portuguese life and customs, he began to apply his descriptive talents in the *Farpas* to the sort of effusions one might expect from the modern tourist office. He delighted in the exotic aspects of the ceremonies celebrating the Third Centenary of the death of Camões (1880). Slipping into a traditionalist frame of mind, he made his peace with the Portuguese monarchy and became a pillar of the established order. The last editions of *As Farpas* contained fierce attacks on the Portuguese republican party. [AJP]

*Obras Completas* (15 vols., edn Clássica, Lisbon, n.d.) (including *As Farpas*).
Cavalheiro, *A Evolução Espiritual de R.* (Lisbon, 1962).

**Orzeszkowa, Eliza** (Milkowszczyzna 1841–Grodno 1910). Polish novelist. Author of *Nad Niemnem* (1888). Her work is associated with the town of Grodno and its surrounding countryside. In this district, inhabited by Poles, White-Russians and Jews, she found the social and psychological contrasts for her noble but didactic fiction. In her novels about Polish Jews (*Eli Makower*, 1874, and *Meir Ezofowicz*, 1878; tr. I. Young, 1898) tolerance and assimilation are contrasted with extreme religious orthodoxy and exclusiveness. Herself an intelligent and humanitarian Polish patriot, she did not, however, believe in the future of Zionism.

In her early novel, *Marta* (1872), about a young widow in search of employment, as in her warning against the cosmopolitan aspect of socialism (*Widma*, 1881), she put her trust in theory rather than in what she observed. She could, however, be a most perceptive psychologist whenever she took an authentic story and reported it without giving too much local colour. In *Cham* (1889), her best book, she analyses the relationship between a neurotic woman from a provincial town and a middle-aged villager, probing into the nature of forgiveness and suicidal self-love. In *Dziurdziowie* (1888) she departed from sentimental notions about folklore and showed its brutal forces at work. [JP]

Scherer-Virski, *MPSS*.

**Osnov"yanenko,** pseud. of Hryhoriy Kvitka (Osnova, Khar'kov 1778–Khar'kov 1843). Ukrainian writer. His first Ukrainian novel, *Marusya* (1834; tr. F. Livesay, N.Y., 1940), which still preserves its appeal, is a romance in village setting, told in sentimental style with great sympathy and authentic ethnographic detail. *Serdeshna Oksana* (1841; tr. C. Moreau, *Oksana*, Paris, 1854), a story of betrayed love, has a greater element of realism. Such novels, together with his humorous stories (e.g. *Saldats'ky patret*, 1833), made him famous as the first modern Ukrainian prose writer. [VS]

*Tvory* (6 vols., 1956–7).
Manning, *UL*; *UCE*.

**Ossietzky, Carl von** (Hamburg 1887–Berlin 1938). German journalist. One of his country's most articulate pacifists, he contributed to, and ran, several newspapers and magazines, most notably *Die Weltbühne*, which he edited from 1926 to 1932. He spent several years in prison and Nazi concentration camps. He was awarded the Nobel Prize in 1936. [LL]

K. R. Grossman, *O.* (Munich, 1963); R. Koplin, *C.v.O.* (Berlin, 1964).

**Ostaijen, Paul van** (Antwerp 1896–Miavoye-Anthée 1928). Flemish experimentalist poet and essayist. From the grotesque, blatant and cynical expressionism of his 'metropolis lyricism' in *Music Hall* (1916), he passed through a phase of fraternal humanism (*Het Sienjaal*, 1918) to an orgy of nihilism and absurdity comparable with ⇨ Apollinaire (*Bezette Stad*, 1921). Hereafter he attempted complete 'organic expressionism' in what he termed objectivated lyricism in poetry, expressing only its own personality, not the poet's. [PK]

*Verzameld werk* (4 vols., 1952–3); *Delta* (Spring 1958).
P. Hadermann, *De kringen naar binnen* (Antwerp, 1965).

**Österling, Anders** (Hälsingborg 1884– ). Swedish poet and critic. After early aestheticism, he was deeply influenced by Wordsworth, and devoted his verse largely to comprehensive depiction of country life in the fertile Southern Swedish province of Skåne. His outstanding books – besides *Facklor i stormen* (1913) which with its darkly passionate love poems stands by itself – include *Idyllernas bok* (1917) and *Tonen från havet* (1933). He is an eminent translator of prose and poetry from English, French, German and Italian. His renderings of Wordsworth and Shelley deserve special mention. For many years he practised journalism as a literary critic, and from 1941 to 1964 was secretary of the Swedish Academy. A mellow volume of memoirs, *Minnets vägar*, was published in 196[illegible] revealing more of his literary interests an[illegible] connexions than of his intimate private emotions.

G. M. Silfverstolpe, 'A.Ö.'s Lyrik', in *Svensk litteraturtidskrift*, 1941.

**Ostrovsky, Alexander Nikolayevich** (Moscow 1823–Shchelykovo, Kostroma 1886). Russian dramatist. Son of a civil servant, he studied in the faculty of Law but had to leave the University after a disagreement with one of the professors. In 1843 he entered the civil service as a legal clerk. This brought him into close contact with the merchant class and the lower strata of the official world and gave him an intimate knowledge of the 'dark kingdom' which he later depicted in his plays. In 1885 he became the director of a dramatic school and was entrusted with choosing the repertoire of Moscow Imperial Theatres. His social and political opinions were close to those of the Slavofils but his sympathies are only indirectly reflected in his works.

He began his literary career as the writer of comedies drawn from the life of the merchant class. The dramatic tension of most of his plays arises from the relationship between wilful, domestic despots and their dependents. Among the best known of his early plays are: *Svoi Lyudi sochtemsya* (1850; tr. G. R. Noyes, *It's a Family Affair. We'll Settle it Ourselves*, 1917); *Bednaya nevesta* (1852; tr. J. L. Seymour and G. R. Noyes, *The Poor Bride*, 1933); *Bednost' ne porok* (1854; tr. G. R. Noyes, *Poverty is No Crime*, 1917).

He portrayed also the Russian officials. *Dokhodnoye mesto* (1856; tr. I. S. Colby and G. R. Noyes, *Easy Money*, 1926; D. Magarshack, 1944) gives a dark picture of bribery, despotism, servility and lack of education.

His masterpiece is his drama *Groza* (1859; ed. N. Henley, 1964; tr. F. Whyte and G. R. Noyes, *The Thunderstorm*, 1927; G. F. Holland and M. Morley, 1930). The action takes place in a provincial town on the Volga, and shows the domestic tragedy of a merchant and his young wife due to his despotic mother. The atmosphere is ignorance, intellectual stagnation and senseless coarseness set against the poetic background of dramatized landscape.

After the emancipation of the serfs (1861) Ostrovsky turned to historical plays (*Dmitry Samozvanets*, 1867), then concentrated his attention on the landowners class. The most outstanding among his later works are: *Na vsyakogo mudretsa dovol'no prostoty* (1868; tr. R. Ackland, *The Diary of a Scoundrel*, 1948), *Les* (1871; tr. C. V. Windlow and G. R. Noyes, *The Forest*, 1926), and *Volki i Ovtsy* (tr. I. S. Colby and G. R. Noyes, *Wolves and Sheep*, 1926; D. Magarshack, 1944).

Somewhat apart from his other works stands his fairy-tale *Snegurochka* (1873), a masterly build-up from various elements of Russian folklore, which became the libretto of Rimsky-Korsakov's opera (1881). His importance for the Russian theatre cannot be underestimated. He bridged the gap between Gogol' and Chekhov.

*Sobraniye sochineniy* (10 vols., 1959–60).

G. Vladykin, *A.N.O. v russkoy kritike* (Moscow, 1953); J. Patouillet, *O. et son théâtre de mœurs russes* (Institut Français, St Petersburg, 1912); L. M. Lotman, *A.N.O. i russkaya dramaturgiya yego vremeni* (Moscow/Leningrad, 1961).

**Oswald von Wolkenstein** (*c.* 1367–1445). Austrian ⇨ Minnesinger. His wanderings and variegated fortunes make his life read like a novel: he left his noble Tirolean home aged 10 and accompanied the Austrian army of Albrecht III on its Prussian campaign; after staying in Prussia for some years, he journeyed in northern and eastern Europe, in Mediterranean lands and North Africa, serving in a variety of humble capacities and learning many foreign languages. Even after he returned to his native soil he continued to look for adventure in the service of different lords.

His poetry reflects the vicissitudes of his life. His style is realistic and direct, and his poems – one group of which describes his travels and experiences and his reflections on life, while the other group consists of love-poems – abound with keenness of observation and liveliness. In later life religious concepts entered more and more into his poetry. Besides his verse, a considerable number of his melodies survive, and these include some very accomplished polyphonic compositions. [RT]

Ed. J. Schatz and O. Koller (Vienna, 1902) (includes text and music); ed. K. K. Klein (Tübingen, 1962) (text alone, with a few musical examples).

F. Mohr, *Das unhöfische Element in der mittelhochdeutschen Lyrik* (Tübingen, 1913); Ehrismann, *GDL*.

**Otčenášek, Jan** (Prague 1924– ). Czech novelist. One of the first to try to portray post-war development in Czechoslovakia.

His *Občan Brych* (1955) is a somewhat schematic portrait of a liberal bourgeois who, unable to adjust himself to a new reality, decides to escape abroad but returns to help with the building of Communism. Artistically more satisfactory is *Romeo, Julie a tma* (1958; tr. I. Unwin, *Romeo and Juliet and the Darkness*, Prague, 1960), a tenderly written story of the love of a Prague student for a Jewish girl whom he vainly tries to save from the Gestapo. [KB]

F. Buriánek, *Současná česká literatura* (Prague, 1960).

**Otero, Blas de** (Bilbao 1916– ). The outstanding Spanish poet of the post-war generation. He began under the influence of ⇨ Unamuno in his first book, *Cántico espiritual* (1942), which he refuses to reprint. In his early collections, *Ángel fieramente humano* (1950) and *Redoble de conciencia* (1951), deep tensions between social and religious beliefs and between love and sensuality are revealed in violent imagery and uneven accentuation; these powerful sonnets challenge comparison with ⇨ Quevedo. His later poetry makes a more deliberate effort to communicate with the working man, with whom he identifies himself. In *Pido la paz y la palabra* (1955) his tone becomes monotonously angry; some poems are fragmentary and ill-organized. *En castellano* (1959) contains only flashes of authentic poetry, yet his latest, *Que trata de España* (1964), is much more important. He has lived abroad but was no happier there than in Spain, where he now lives. His political poetry is subjective and anarchistic: 'peace and freedom' – to write and be heard. His censored anthology of early poems, *Ancia* (1958), has permanent value. [JMC]

*20 Poems* (Madison, 1964) (translation); Cohen, *PBSV*.
Cano, *PESV*.

**Otfrid** (*c.* 800–*c.* 870). Monk of Weissenburg. Author of a famous Old High German *Evangelienbuch* (ed. O. Erdmann, 1957), or Harmony of the Gospels. Among the four dedicatees of the work is King Louis the German (843–76), a grandson of Charlemagne, and according to Otfrid's declared purpose, his *Evangelienbuch* was intended to counteract the evil influences of the improper secular songs of the day. In short rhyming couplets, and with much wordy moralizing, he relates at great length the life and teaching of Christ, drawing both on the Vulgate and on the authoritative Bible commentaries of his age, such as those of ⇨ Alcuin and Bede. In form the *Evangelienbuch* represents a blend of the four-square rhythm of Germanic alliterative couplets with the end-rhyme technique taken from Christian Latin hymns. [RT]

Ehrismann, *GDL*.

**Otto of Freising** (*c.* 1115–Morimond 1158). Medieval chronicler. The son of the Margrave of Austria and a grandson of the Emperor Henry IV, after studying at Paris under Abelard and Hugh of St Victor he became a Cistercian at Morimond (Burgundy) and Bishop of Freising (*c.* 1138). In 1147 he took part in the disastrous Second Crusade, led by his half-brother, Conrad III, and Louis VII of France. Otto commanded part of the crusading army, but it was cut to pieces. He wrote the *Chronicon de duabus civitatibus* (ed. A. Hofmeister, MGH, SRG, 1912; tr. C. C. Mierow, N.Y., 1928), after St Augustine, but suggesting that both of the Two Cities were to be identified with the church; and the *Gesta Frederici* (ed. G. Waitz and B. de Simson, MGH, SRG, 1912; tr. C. C. Mierow, N.Y., 1953), a history of the earlier years of the reign of his nephew, Frederick I (Barbarossa). His Latin style is excellent and has been called a model of historical writing. [FB]

**Øverland, Arnulf** (Kristiansund 1889–1968). Norwegian poet. The son of a ship's engineer, he broke off his university studies to devote himself to literature. His first collections of verse, *Den ensomme fest* (1911) and *De hundrede violiner* (1912), full of youthful longing and loneliness, revealed a taut, expressive style. *Advent* (1915) has a more positive tone, and in *Brød og vin* (1924) he became the social critic and moralist. His socialist sympathies are also evident in *Berget det blå* (1927); *Hustavler* (1929); *Jeg besværger dig* (1934), and especially in the militant *Den røde front* (1937), but he is at the same time the sensitive, wide-ranging, passionate, though astringent poet. During the occupation of Norway his poems (published in *Vi overlever alt*, 1945) were distributed clandestinely and had great effect – he was arrested and sent to Sachsenhausen in 1942; they were followed by the collection *Tilbake til livet* (1946). His post-war poems

*Fiskeren og hans sjel* (1950); *Sverdet bak døren* (1956); *Den rykende tande* (1960); *På Nebo bjerg* (1962) are more symbolic in character. He also published some collections of short stories, two plays and a number of polemical writings. He was probably in his lifetime the leading Norwegian poet, and a notable figure in public life and debate.

*Samlede dikt* (3 vols., 1957); *Noveller i utvalg* (1939).

O. Gelsted, *A.Ø.* (Copenhagen, 1946); E. E. Johnsen, *Livets spiral* (1956); D. Haakonsen, *A.O. og den etiske realisme* (Oslo, 1966).

# P

**Paavolainen, Olavi** (Kivennapa 1903–Helsinki 1964). Finnish essayist. Starting as a ⇨ Tulenkantajat lyric poet (pen-name Olavi Lauri), he became well known as an essayist, an analyser of modernism (*Nykyaikaa etsimässä*, 1929, *Suursiivous*, 1932), and of Hitler's Germany (*Kolmannen valtakunnan vieraana*, 1936, *Lähtö ja loitsu*, 1937, *Risti ja hakaristi*, 1938). His war-time diaries (*Synkkä yksinpuhelu*, 'A Gloomy Monologue', 1946) reveal the same critical, questioning spirit characteristic of his earlier writings. [IR]

**Padilla, Juan de** (Seville 1468–Seville 1522?). Spanish poet and Carthusian. A follower of Juan de ⇨ Mena, he had read Dante and was much interested in allegory. His principal works are the *Retablo sobre la vida de Jesús Cristo* (1513) and *Las doce triunfos de los doce Apóstoles* (1521), which groups the apostles under the signs of the zodiac. He is at his best in his occasional secular *romances*. [JMC]

BAE, 35; Blecua, *FLE*; Cohen, *PBSV*.

**Pagnol, Marcel** (Aubagne 1895– ). French playwright. Pagnol exploits two veins: satirical comedy and sentimental comedy of manners. The former includes *Les marchands de gloire* (1925), in collaboration with Paul Nivoix, *Jazz* (1926) and *Topaze* (1928; tr. A Rossi, 1963). The first mounts an over-rhetorical but mordant attack on war profiteers and corrupt politicians; the second is a blast against the dehumanization of academic learning; the third brilliantly uses the fall of a scrupulous and ingenuous schoolmaster to expose the immorality of society. Pagnol's trilogy about Marseilles life (*Marius*, 1929, *Fanny*, 1931, *César*, 1937) has wildly funny moments, great vitality and pathos but suffers from its tendency to indulge vulgar and sentimental caricature. He has also written less successful plays (*Judas*, 1955, and *Fabien*, 1956) and been responsible for the dialogue of outstanding films, e.g. *La femme du boulanger* (1938), *La fille du puisatier* (1940). His autobiographical volumes (*La gloire de mon père*, 1957; *Le château de ma mère*, 1958; *Le temps des secrets*, 1960) have great charm. [SBJ]

*Théâtre complet* (1949).
Surer, *TFC*.

**Pakkala, Teuvo,** pseud. of Theodor Oskar Frosterus (Oulu 1862–Kuopio 1925). Finnish novelist and dramatist. A master of Finnish prose style, especially in his stories about children (e.g. *Lapsia*, 1895). In his full-length novels, in which he tried to give direct expression to his social conscience, his eye for detail and clear psychological insight are not balanced by an ability to fuse these details into an organized whole. His play *Tukkijoella* (1899) is still frequently performed. [TA]

**Palacio Valdés, Armando** (Asturias 1853–Madrid 1938). Spanish novelist. Educated in Oviedo, where he met ⇨ Alas, who later collaborated with him as a critic and became one of his closest friends. After finishing his studies in Madrid, he took to journalism and began publishing novels in the early 1880s. He shared his contemporaries' concern with religious and social problems and with theories of the novel. Though he admired the Naturalists he believed the novelist should select characters and events which were slightly out of the ordinary; he was also less pessimistic about human nature than the French Naturalists. His reputation for characterization, especially of women, was based on early novels like *Marta y María* (1883; tr. N. H. Dole, *The Marquis of Peñalta*, 1886), *La hermana San Sulpicio* (1889; tr. N. H. Dole, *Sister Saint Sulpice*, 1890) and *La fe* (1892; tr. Hapgood, *Faith*, 1892); but he was also interested in social groups and economic pressures as is evident from *José* (1885), in which he successfully captures the hard life of Asturian fishermen. He showed equal ability in recording the atmosphere of provinces he knew less well – Valencia in *La alegría del capitán Ribot* (1899; tr. M. C. Smith, *The Joy of Captain Ribot*, 1923) and Andalusia in *La hermana San Sulpicio*. Later his idealistic conception of life became more sentimentalized, and his autobiography

(*Novela de un novelista*) is difficult to stomach today. He outlived his reputation, which at the end of the 19th century was on a level with the great Russian writers. [ONVG]

*Obras, novelas y obras escritas* (1956).
A. F. G. Bell, *Contemporary Spanish Literature* (1933).

**Palacký, František** (Hodslavice 1798–Prague 1876). Czech historian. Born in Moravia and educated in Slovakia, he became influential in the Czech national revival movement, first as a writer and editor of the important *Journal of the Bohemian Museum*, and later as Chairman of the Slavonic Congress in Prague (1848) and an important political figure. His history of Bohemia, begun in German but continued in Czech, covers only the period to 1526 but has deeply influenced his compatriots by its conception of Czech history as 'contact and conflict' with the Germans and by its emphasis on the liberating role of the Hussite movement. [RA]

*Geschichte von Böhmen* (9 vols., 1836–67); *Idea státu rakouského* (1865).
J. Goll, *F.P.* in *Český časopis historický* (Prague, 1898); J. Fischer, *Myšlenka a dílo F.P.* (2 vols., Prague, 1926–7).

**Palamas, Kostis** (Patras 1859–Athens 1943). Greek poet. He lost both parents when he was 7 and was brought up by an uncle at Missolonghi, the town of origin of his family. At 18 he went to Athens and entered the Law School of the university but never graduated. He earned his living during his first years in Athens as a literary contributor to newspapers and periodicals. His critical articles were much admired, especially by the young poets of the day, for their fresh appraisal of Greek literary matters and for his wide knowledge of European literature and thought. This great capacity for reading and keeping abreast with current literary, philosophical and scientific ideas he sustained throughout his long life. In 1897 he was appointed secretary to the Faculties of Athens University, a post which he held until 1929. His enormous output in verse and prose, and the influence he exerted on Greek letters, entitles him to a central place in the literature of modern Greece. Not only was he one of the first and most militant supporters of the movement of the 1880s which eventually freed Greek literature from the cramping effects of a romantic purism and brought it back to its living forces, namely to the demotic and its literature, but he also led a group of young poets who sought to give new direction to Greek poetry by orientating it to Parnassian and Symbolist trends. Palamas's poetic collections, 18 in all, reveal his extraordinary mastery of the language, the wide range of his inspiration and his great rhythmic powers. The more outstanding are: *O Tafos* (1898; tr. D. A. Michalaros, *The Grave*, Chicago, 1930), a cycle of poems occasioned by the death of his five-year-old son. The poet's grief is communicated by an imagery evoking the dream-like quality of the child's world and alternating with tones of bewilderment at the spell cast by Death. *I Asalefti Zoi* (1904; tr. A. Phoutrides, *Life Immovable*, 1919), poems on a great variety of themes representing the whole range of his inspiration and technique. *O Dodecalogos Tou Gyftou* ('The Dodecalogue of the Gipsy', 1907, French tr. E. Clément, *Les douze paroles du tzigane*, 1931), a lyrical epic, perhaps his most ambitious composition 'integrating', as he wrote, 'all' his 'ideas'. The saga of Hellenism shortly before and after the fall of Byzantium is set forth in twelve cantos with a gipsy as principal actor whose moods, adventures and experiences provide the background to which the poet's eye is continually being carried back as situations and episodes open up and fade out until with deepening vision he discerns the dawn of a new era. The poem moves with lyrical onrush and striking imagery, Orphic ideas of retribution and rebirth being the underlying motif; in spite of its prolixity, it is a wonderful feat of virtuosity. *I Floghera Tou Vasilia* ('The King's Flute', 1910, French tr. E. Clément, *La flûte du roi*, 1934) another long poem in twelve cantos is inspired by an incident recorded by a Byzantine historian and deals with the exploits of Emperor Basil II, the Bulgar-slayer, the splendour and drama of the Byzantine empire. It was written at a time when the first stirrings of the struggle for the liberation of Greek Macedonia were heard, hence its predominant patriotic tone. Palamas's poetry is marked by an unusual mingling of influences – Classical Greece, modern Greece, Romanticism, Parnassianism, Symbolism, ancient and modern philosophies and religions are all echoed in it. He is on the whole a bookish poet, often obscure, at times rhetorical and self-conscious, but always impressive for his vigour and versatility. His numerous prose works include criticism, short stories, translations and letters. He also wrote a drama, *I Trisevgheni* (1902). [SJP]

*Complete Works*, ed. G. Katsimbalis (9 vols., 1965ff.); *Pages choisies*, French tr. A. Chendel (Éditions Nouveaux Cahiers, Switzerland, 1942).
Complete international biblio., G. Katsimbalis (1953).

**Palazzeschi, Aldo,** pseud. of Aldo Giurlani (Florence 1885– ). Italian poet and novelist. In his early poems *Riflessi* (1908) and *Poemi* (1909), he accepted from the poetic tradition of his time D'Annunzian rhythms ('La fontana malata' is a subtle parody of D'Annunzio's 'La pioggia nel pineto'), futuristic devices (the typographic layout of 'E lasciatemi divertire!'), crepuscular tones ('Il passo della Nazarene'). The apparent drabness and the commonplace themes of his prose-like verse are in fact a deliberate form of anti-rhetoric ('Pizzicheria', 'La passeggiata'). From prose-like verse to rhythmical prose there is but a small step: hence his admiration for Boccaccio, proclaimed in the preface to *Sorelle Materassi* (1934; A. Davidson, *Materassi Sisters*, 1953), perhaps his best novel, where with humour and finesse he paints the portrait of two elderly spinsters ruined by their rascally nephew. The contrast between the misguided ambitions of the young, and the materially wealthy but spiritually poor environment in which they have to grow up, appears again as the main theme of his later novels *I fratelli Cuccoli* (1948) and *Roma* (1953), where some of the early freshness of inspiration is however lost. [GMC]

*Poesie* (1930); *Tutte le novelle* (1937); *Opere giovanili* (1958); *I romanzi della maturità* (1961); *Il buffo integrale* (1966).
G. Getto, 'P. poeta', in *Poeti, critici e cose varie del Novecento* (Firenze, 1953); Bionđolillo, *C*; Gargiulo, *LIN*; Robertis, *SN*; Pullini, *NIN*; *Contemporanei*, i.

**Palitsyn, Avraamy.** ⇨ Russian Literature of the 17th Century.

**Palladius, Peder** (Ribe 1503–Copenhagen 1560). Danish theologian. His *Visitatsbog* (1543) is one of the finest literary documents of the victorious Lutheran Reformation. [ELB]

**Palmotić, Junije.** ⇨ Dalmatian and Dubrovnik Literature.

**Paludan, Jacob** (Copenhagen 1896– ). Danish novelist and essayist. In his early novels, of which the most important is *Fugle omkring Fyret* (1925; tr. G. I. Colbron, *Birds Around the Light*, 1928), he directs his irony against the optimistic materialism and 'Americanism' of the 1920s. His main novel, *Jørgen Stein* (1932–3; tr. C. Malmberg, Madison, 1966), is already a classic in Danish literature. He has since published mainly essays, aphorisms, satires and memoirs. [ELB]

O. Lundbo, *J.P.* (Copenhagen, 1943).

**Paludan-Müller, Frederik** (Kerteminde 1809–Copenhagen 1876). Danish poet and novelist. The son of a clergyman, he came under the spell of Byronism in his youth, and his early verse novel, *Danserinden* (1833), is an elegant pastiche of Byron which, with his mythological poem *Amor og Psyche*, was very popular. But after a serious illness (and his subsequent marriage to a very strong-willed lady) he came to scorn his early writings, and the former aesthete became a profoundly ethical writer who lived the life of a recluse. Many of his long narrative poems have Biblical or mythological motifs, e.g. *Venus* (1841), *Tithon* (1844), *Abels Død* (1845), *Kalanus* (1854) and *Adonis* (1874). In his important long verse novel, *Adam Homo* (1842–9), he depicts with scorching irony the emptiness of the life and career of a 'successful' citizen in his own time. *Ivar Lykkes Historie* (1866–73) was a less effective prose counterpart. [ELB]

V. Andersen, *P.-M.* (2 vols., Copenhagen, 1910); Brandes, *MCNL*.

**Pandurović, Sima** (Belgrade 1883–Belgrade 1960). Serbian poet. With Petković-Dis one of the first Serbian decadent poets, his poetic career was short and he ceased writing poetry after 1940. His poetry is essentially philosophical, full of bitter pessimism and despair. Before the First World War his poetry created considerable comment, being considered very *avant-garde*. [EDG]

Ibrovac, *APY*; Lavrin, *AMYP*.
Barac, *HYL*; Kadić, *CSL*.

**Panero, Leopoldo** (Astorga 1909–Astorga 1962). Spanish poet. After the Civil War he was one of the first to return to a formal style, conventional religious themes or evocations of landscape; at his best he is tender and reflective. His elegies for, and in the style of, Vallejo and ⇨ Lorca, reveal his limitations. His political 'Carta perdida a Pablo Neruda' (1953) also invites disadvantageous comparisons. [JMC]

*Poesía* (1963).
Alonso, *PEC*; Cano, *PESV*; Vivanco, *PEC*.

**Panfyorov, Fyodor Ivanovich** (Pavlovka, Simbirsk 1896–Moscow 1960). Russian novelist. The son of a peasant, he joined the Communist Party in 1926. His first stories appeared in 1918. Only his novel *Bruski* (1926–36; tr. S. Garry, *And then the Harvest*, 1939) is widely read today. This vast rambling epic of the benefits of collectivization was extravagantly praised when it first appeared, and soon afterwards no less violently attacked. It has now been restored to favour. At the end of his life he wrote an autobiographical story, *Rodnoye proshloye* (1956), which is of some interest. His style is clumsy and his constructional sense small. He was editor of the journal *Oktyabr'* from 1946 to 1954 and from 1957 until his death. [RDBT]

*Sobraniye sochineniy* (6 vols., 1958–9).
V. L. Grechishnikov, *Tvorchestvo P.* (Moscow/Leningrad, 1934).

**Panova, Vera** (Rostov-on-Don 1905– ). Soviet novelist, short-story writer and dramatist. She also wrote a film scenario based on her very successful short story *Seryozha* and other prose works. Her prewar plays imitate Gor'ky and, to a lesser extent, Chekhov, but her latest, *Devochki* (the story of two sisters evacuated to the Urals during the war), *Provody belykh nochey* (1961) and *Kak pozhivaesh' paren'?* (1962) are more individual. They are about the extreme vulnerability of youth in its first contacts and collisions with grown-up life. [AP]

*Izbrannye sochineniya* (2 vols., 1956).
L. A. Plotkin, *Tvorchestvo V.P.* (Moscow/Leningrad, 1962); Boguslavskiy, *KIRSD*.

**Panzini, Alfredo** (Senigallia 1863–Roma 1939). Italian novelist. For over 40 years he taught in secondary schools; the problem of how to reconcile his good old-fashioned professorial culture with the new demands of a rapidly evolving society, which his benign and slightly patronizing conservatism prevented him from fully understanding, is a constant characteristic of many of his works (*Il mondo è rotondo*, 1921; *Piccole storie del mondo grande*, 1901, 1919; *Viaggio di un povero letterato*, 1919; etc.). His most notable virtue is his sense of balance: he always sweetens his praise of the past and criticism of the present with a touch of humour; he always purifies his descriptions of women of some of their morbidity by diverting the reader's attention on some erudite quotation or classical tag (*Cos'è l'amore*, 1912; *Il diavolo nella mia libreria*, 1920; *Signorine*, 1921; *Il bacio di Lesbia*, 1937). His good taste is so consistent as to become slightly monotonous. Perhaps his best works are his travel reminiscences (*La Lanterna di Diogene*, 1909) where one finds pages of muted but sensitive and moving poetry. He also wrote a *Dizionario moderno* (1905, reprinted several times), an acute and humorous work of lexicography in the Johnsonian style. Most of his works are collected in *Sei romanzi tra due secoli* (1939) and *Romanzi d'ambo i sessi* (1941). [GMC]

*Io cerco moglie!* (1920; tr. F. T. Cooper, *Wanted – a Wife*, 1923).
Gargiulo, *LIN*; Biondolillo, *C*; *Contemporanei*.

**Paoli, Pier Francesco** (Pesaro ? –Rome? *c.* 1640). Italian poet. He spent much of his adult life at Rome in the service of the Savelli family. The chief early editions of his works are the *Rime* of 1609 and 1619 and the *Rime varie* of 1637. A ⇨ Marinist poet, though not one of the most extreme. His poems, many of them on women and love, have the character of elegant miniatures with, at times, a slightly ironical detachment, which makes him appear an agreeable, if not profound, salon poet. [DGR]

Croce, *LM*; Ferrero, *MM*; Getto, *MM*.

**Papadiamantis, Alexandros** (Skiathos 1851–Skiathos 1911). Greek short-story writer and novelist. His father was a priest and his mother came from a notable family of his native island. He went to school at Skiathos, Skopelos and the town of Chalkis in Euboea, and at the age of 20 he moved to Athens where he studied literature at the university. He led a secluded life in Athens making a precarious living by writing stories and serial novels for literary magazines and newspapers and by translating English and French works. Shortly before his death he returned to Skiathos. He is a writer with a rich fund of poetry and contemplation which he diffuses through his work giving it a glow of spirituality and symbolism. His short stories – some 200 of them – deal with the rough and picturesque life in small island communities or in poor Athenian suburbs, and the best of them are noted for their rapid narrative, their striking images of land – and seascape, their touches of humour, their vivid and brilliant scenes and characters who are treated with a human and optimistic sympathy and a delicacy of intuition. Papadiamantis was a devout Greek Orthodox and his ultimate message is one of compassion. Much of his work suffers from hasty composition. Among his longer stories, the novella *I Fonissa* ('The Murderess') should be singled out which, diffuse and formless though it is, reveals a powerful insight into the mind and soul of a peasant woman gradually going mad. The two historical novels of his youth are of little consequence. He writes in a language which is a mixture of archaic and ecclesiastical Greek interspersed with colloquialisms and dialectal idioms to add a touch of colour to a characteristic detail or to enliven the dialogue in his stories. [SJP]

*Complete Works*, ed. G. Valetas (6 vols., 1954–5).

**Papatsonis, Takis** (Athens 1895– ). Greek poet. He studied law and economics at the University of Athens, and travelled extensively in Europe, the Balkans and America. He was for many years a civil servant in the Ministry of Economic Affairs and is an expert in international trade and banking. His first poems appeared in the 1920s and were remarkable for their avant-garde tone and manner, presaging in many ways ideas and technical innovations which crystallized with the poetry of the 1930s. A strong religious feeling pervades his almost surrealist verse, whose deceptive simplicity often conceals acute introspection, and he uses natural imagery and colours with great subtlety to portray a particular situation or to enhance a contemplative mood. He has also written two travel books, *Askisi Ston Atho*, recording impressions from his visits to the monasteries of Mt Athos, and *Moldovlahika Tou Mythou*, a sensitive response to the atmosphere and landscape of Rumania as he saw it before the Second World War. His critical essays reveal wide knowledge of Greek and European literature and an original approach – notable among them are three studies on Dante. He has translated poems of Claudel, Aragon and Saint-John Perse. [SJP]

*Ekloge A, Ekloge B; O Tetraperatos Kosmos* (1967) (essays).

F. M. Pontani, *Osservatore Romano*, 29 February 1948; K. Paraschos, *Ellines Lyrikoi* (Athens, 1953).

**Papillon de Lasphrise, Marc de** (nr Amboise 1555–nr Amboise 1599). French poet and soldier. His love-poetry is addressed to various women, including a Benedictine novice ('Théophile'). His best poems ingeniously re-work the Petrarchan convention to express physical desire and its satisfaction. Other poems, in baby talk, are not successful. Weakened by wounds and illness, he passed the end of his life in pious retirement. [GJ]

Schmidt, *PSS*.

**Papini, Giovanni** (Florence 1881–Florence 1956). Italian essayist and pamphleteer. Author of more than 60 books of philosophical, literary and religious argument, founder or co-founder of several literary reviews, some influential (*Leonardo*, *Lacerba*), some less important. His life is a sequence of changes and contradictions: formerly a convinced cosmopolitan, he later became a staunch nationalist; he turned from agnosticism to Christianity (*Vita di Cristo*, 1921; tr. M. P. Agnetti, *The Story of Christ*, 1923), but did not spare the Church his criticism (*Lettere agli uomini di Papa Celestino VI*, 1946) and held most unorthodox views on demonology (*Il Diavolo*, 1954; tr. A. Foulke, *The Devil*, 1955); he joined the Futurist movement but later turned against it; he declared himself an enemy of academicism, rhetoric and erudition, but was thirsty for official recognition, a born rhetor, a voracious reader of too many books; his public image was that of an ebullient, aggressive, controversial writer (*Stroncature*, 1916), but his friends knew him as a simple, loving and patient man; one finds in his work sparks of genius amid fumes of stupidity, flashes of poetry and belches of vulgarity. However true and profound some of his self-confessions, diatribes and meditations (see *Un uomo – finito*, 1912; tr. P. Agnetti, *A Man – Finished*, 1924) may sound when taken in isolation, they appear false and shallow once seen in the context of their author's intellectual exhibitionism. In spite of their undeniable qualities (full-blooded vigour, a style with an unmistakable flavour, great imaginative powers), Papini's books owe their inner coherence less to formal control, artistic discipline or ideological consistency than to his uninhibited egotism and pseudo-Promethean arrogance, which unified all his contradictory attitudes into a sort of compatible system later to disguise its residual weaknesses through a religious conversion. It was not a reconciliation of opposite choices but a compromise which, coming from a respected author actively engaged in cultural debate, could not fail to confuse further the important issues (literary cosmopolitanism *v.* nationalism, cultural integration *v.* parochial isolation, art as a social phenomenon *v.* art for art's sake, free culture *v.* State ideology, and many more) at stake in Italy between the wars: a time when to compromise meant to play into the hands of Fascism and was tantamount to intellectual suicide. [GMC]

*Four and Twenty Minds*, tr. E. Wilkins (1923) (selected essays); *Gli operai della vigna* (1929; tr. A. Curtayne, *Labourers in the Vineyard*, 1930); *Dante vivo* (1933; tr. E. H. Broadus and A. Benedetti, 1944).

R. Ridolfi, *Vita di G.P.* (Milan, 1957); M. Gozzini, *Papini vivo* (Florence, 1959); F. Flora, *Dal Romanticismo al Futurismo* (Milan, 1925); Falqui, *PNNI*; Biondolillo, *C*; Gargiulo, *LIN*; *Contemporanei*, i.

**Paracelsus,** pseud. of Theophrastus Bombast von Hohenheim (Einsiedeln 1493–Salzburg 1541). German writer. He studied medicine at Ferrara, before teaching at the University of Basel. His rejection of the traditional authorities of the Middle Ages, Aristotle and Galen, combined with his irascible temperament, involved him in such conflicts with his orthodox colleagues that it became impossible for him to remain in Basel and in his later years he led the life of an itinerant doctor. His numerous writings, for the most part written in a powerfully vital German – he was one of the first university teachers to lecture in the vernacular – bear witness to his wide scientific, philosophical and religious interests. His medical theories are largely discounted today; though he replaced the authoritarian approach of the late Middle Ages by observation and free inquiry, he remains a neo-Platonist rather than a forerunner of the scientific method. Man, he held, was made up of three elements, salt, sulphur and mercury, and embodied three aspects, the physical, the spiritual and the divine. The microcosm, man, is the reflection of the marcocosm of the natural world which is made up of the same triad and in which God is in-dwelling. Like many another intensely religious spirit of the age, Paracelsus sought a way to God outside the doctrinaire teachings of either Lutherans, Zwinglians or Roman Catholics: love is for him the supreme virtue and purpose of mankind and he longed for a society free from the extremes of wealth and poverty, where all men were brothers.

He was scorned by his more educated contemporaries, but from the mid 16th century onwards he enjoyed ever-increasing popularity as one of the principal sources of 'pansophism'. His influence on Jakob ⇨ Böhme was considerable and survives in the writings of ⇨ Angelus Silesius and ⇨ Grimmelshausen, while much of Goethe's alchemical thought is unthinkable without him. [WAC]

*Werke*, ed. K. Sudhoff and W. Matthiessen (14 vols., 1922–33); ed. E. Goldhammer (1958ff.); ed. B. Aschmer (1926–32) (in modern German); *P. Selected Writings*, tr. N. Guterman (1951).

J. M. Stillman, *T.B. von H.* (Chicago, 1920); W. E. Peuckert, *P.* (Jena, 1924); H. M. Pachter, *Magic into Science* (1951); A. Koyre, *Mystiques, Spirituels, Alchémistes* (Paris, 1955).

**Pardo Bazán, Emilia,** Condesa de (La Coruña 1851–Madrid 1921). Spanish novelist and essayist. Poetry was her first love, and she studied foreign languages in order to be able to read French, German and English poets. Then she took up law to help her husband with legal studies. Subsequently an early enthusiasm for the work of ⇨ Feijoo blossomed into an interest in science and philosophy, and her first novel, *Pascual López* (1879), subtitled 'Autobiography of a medical student', made use of her newly acquired knowledge. Her scientific studies no doubt also led her to take an interest in the social analysis and novelistic techniques of Zola. She made daily visits to a tobacco factory in La Coruna in a search for naturalistic material, and her novel *La tribuna* (1882) and the collection of articles on Naturalism entitled *La cuestión palpitante* (1883) brought the Spanish polemics on Zola to a head. She was too ardent a Catholic to accept all Naturalistic theories without qualification, and travel in France brought the Russian novelists and Huysmans to her attention. Since these recognized the idealistic side of man she could enthuse about them, and in her own novel *La madre naturaleza* (1887) idealism triumphed although original sin had had its say in her earlier novel *Los pazos de Ulloa* (1886; tr. E. Harriet Hearn, *The Son of the Bondswoman*, 1908). Her preoccupation with social evils and their rectification is apparent in all her novels, and her interest in teaching found other outlets in essays, polemics and finally in a Chair of literature (1916). [ONVG]

*Obras completas* (1946ff.); *Novelas y cuentos completes* (2 vols., 1947).

C. Bravo-Villasante, *Vida y obra de E.P.B.* (Madrid, 1962); *BHS*, XXIX, 113 (1952).

**Parini, Giuseppe** (Bosisio, Brianza 1729–Milan 1799). Italian satirical poet. Son of a silk-merchant. Member of the Accademia dei Trasformati – like Baretti, Pietro Verri and Beccaria, respectful of good traditions but prepared also to accept new ideas. Ordained in 1754, he entered the household of the Duchessa Vittoria Serbelloni, for the next eight years observing closely the world of the aristocracy which he later satirized so effectively. (The famous *Dialogo sopra la nobiltà* was published in 1757, and the collection of satirical *Odi* in 1795.) Dismissed in 1762, he became immediately famous in 1763 for the publication of *Il mattino* (the first part of *Il giorno* – the remainder being published in 1765 and 1801; (tr. H. M. Bower, *The Day*, 1927) – in which he describes with pungent irony the daily round of a young nobleman. After his death a legend arose, due to the ardent praises especially of Foscolo in *Ortis* and *I sepolcri*, and later of Monti, Manzoni and Leopardi; Parini, who was a loyal Austrian subject, who condemned the French Revolution (cf. *Predaro i Filistei*, written the day of his death), whose satires ridiculed abuses of privilege rather than privilege itself, who stressed human dignity rather than equality, was transformed into an egalitarian precursor of the French Revolution and a fiery prophet of Italian independence. The artistry, sheer intellectual brilliance and the warm good-humoured humanity of his satires made him at all events the leading poet of the Italian Enlightenment. [RHC]

*Poesie e prose*, ed. L. Caretti (1951); *Opere*, ed. G. M. Zuradelli (2 vols., 1961).

E. Bruni, *Guida allo studio delle opere di G.P.* (Milan, 1955); W. Binni, 'Parini e l'Illuminismo', in *La cultura illuministica in Italia* (Turin, 1957); W. Binni, *Preromanticismo italiano* (Naples, 1959); L. Russo, *G.P.* (Pisa, 1959); N. Sapegno, *Poetica e prosa del P.* (Rome, 1960); G. Petronio, *P. e l'Illuminismo lombardo* (Milan, 1961); P. Giannantonio, *G.P.* (Naples, 1963); Binni, *CI*; *Maggiori*, ii.

**Parnassian.** A tendency in French poetry leading away from Romantic intimacies towards well-wrought imagery in the manner of Gautier and Baudelaire. The word derives from three collections of poems published by Lemerre as *Le Parnasse Contemporain* (1866, 1871, 1876), which included work by Leconte de Lisle, Hérédia, and even Verlaine and Mallarmé.

P. Martino, *Parnasse et symbolisme, 1850-1900* (Paris, 1925); M. Souriau, *Histoire du Parnasse* (Paris, 1929).

**Parny, Évariste-Désiré de Forges,** Vicomte de (Saint-Paul, Réunion 1753–Paris 1814). French poet. He was educated at Rennes, and served as an army officer, also making prolonged stays in his native island, where an unhappy love affair provided a source of elegiac inspiration. An Epicurean by temperament, and Voltairian in outlook, his verse is primarily erotic (*Poésies érotiques*, 1778; *Chansons madécasses*, 1787) or satirical (*La guerre des dieux*, 1799; *Goddam!*, 1804). His non-satirical poetry has the faded melodiousness of the period, but sometimes achieves an authentically pre-Romantic note of melancholy passion. [WHB]

*Œuvres* (4 vols., 1931).

Sainte-Beuve, *Portraits contemporains*, iii (Paris, 1855); Barquissau, *PC*.

**Pascal, Blaise** (Clermont 1623–Paris 1662). French man of science and man of letters. The first by profession and the second almost by accident, many regard him as the greatest of French prose artists, yet in the strict sense he wrote no books. He published results of his experiments, a number of broadsheets which became known as *Les lettres provinciales* (1656; ed. H. F. Stewart, 1926) and left unpublished, unfinished and in great disorder, a mass of notes for an Apology, now called *Les pensées* (written 1657–8; ed. L. Brunschvicg, 1897; ed. L. Lafuma, 1951; tr. J. Warrington, 1961; tr. A. Krailsheimer, Penguin Classics, 1966).

His father was a government official who moved to Paris in 1631, but was forced to move back to Clermont to avoid imprisonment for criticism of Richelieu's financial edicts. He trained his son to rigorous study (on what he called the principle of '*tenir l'enfant au-dessus de son ouvrage*') and to the company of men of science. He passed on his strong character to his children. Blaise himself had violent energy; he would attack problems fiercely and then lose interest (this was partly the result of a recurrent illness). He attacked opponents with vigour; Father Noel in the debates on the vacuum, Brother Saint Ange for preaching modernism in Rouen. One of his most brilliant (unpublished) essays is designed to show why conservatism in religion is as necessary as experiments are in physics. This *Fragment d'une Préface* anticipates by nearly a century D' ⇨ Alembert's division of the sciences in the ⇨ *Encyclopédie*.

He seems to have been a serious student, if not an adherent, of Jansenism from 1646. The crisis of his spiritual life came on the famous night of 23 November 1654: an account of which he carried on his person. Early in 1655 he was drawn into the dispute with the Jesuits which occupied him, though not exclusively, over several years. His scientific work went on, as did his preparation of a defence of the Christian position against agnostics. But from 1659 onwards his health gave him few intervals from pain and lassitude. Eventually he seems to have been killed by his doctors, who prescribed remedies which proved fatal.

His short life left its mark in mathematics, physics, religious controversy and literature. The two works on which his literary fame rests are different both in inspiration and intention. His aim in the *Lettres provinciales* was to distract public attention from the Sorbonne's censure of Jansenius. The title means, not letters from the provinces but to a Provincial, i.e. an official of the Society of Jesus. Pascal's technique is a model of destructive satire. Posing as the man in the street, he asks the plain meaning of terms such as '*pouvoir prochain*' and '*grace suffisante*' and puts his informants into most embarrassing positions. Not only this, but after the fourth letter he switches the whole debate from theology (on which as he admitted he was not too strong) to morals. The bulk of the book is in fact an attack on casuistry and on the Jesuit abuse of the practice of 'direction'. His *Pensées* have been rated as unique by some and as worthless by others. The blend of lucidity and eloquence is most impressive, and if his proofs of Christianity be thought feeble, we must remember that he wrote at a time when Biblical criticism was hardly invented, and that he himself denied the efficacy of rational proof. He preferred inducements to action rather than satisfactions of reason; his famous Wager was so intended, as inducement rather than as argument. The strong strain of scepticism, nourished on Augustine and Montaigne, led him to study such things as intuition ('*Le cœur a ses raisons que la raison ne connaît pas*') and habit (which he called '*la machine*' or '*l'automate*') and to work out the effects of will and motive in social action. This coupled with force, both of imaginative conception and of expression, led him to suggest an astonishing and modern dialectic. His fondness for paradox was such that one scholar speaks of the *Pensées* not as containing contradiction but as based on contradiction. [WGM]

*Œuvres complètes*, ed. J. Chevalier (Pléiade, 1954).

J. Steinmann, *P.* (rev. edn, Paris, 1962); R. E. Lacombe, *L'apologétique de P.* (Paris, 1958); J. Mesnard, *P. l'homme et l'œuvre* (Paris, 1951); Sainte-Beuve, *Port-Royal*, iii.

**Pascoais, Teixeira de,** pseud. of Joaquim Pereira Teixeira de Vasconcelos (Amarante 1877–S. João de Gatão 1952). Portuguese poet. He was the leader of the group of writers known as *saudosistas* which came together after the foundation of the Republic. Their work was published in the literary review, *A Águia*. *Saudosismo* now appears as a kind of synthesis of Pascoais's own poetic qualities. When he speaks of the genius of the race in his lectures on *O génio português* it is of his own genius that he is speaking; of his liking for English rather than French poetry; of his preference for what he calls 'sculptural' values to the musicality of the French symbolists; of his personal preference for such words and phrases as *luar*, *sombra*, *penumbra*, *silêncio*, *etéreo nume*, *névoa*, *fluido mágico*, *fantasma*, *vaga essência*. And when he writes approvingly of earlier Portuguese poets it is because he recognizes himself as their descendant. *Saudade* he attributes to the fusion in the Portuguese people of Roman and Semitic blood; it is compounded of paganism and Christianity. This synthesis brings about that pantheistic *saudosismo* which it is his constant effort to define in his poetry, being reflected in its 'broken gleams, and a stifled splendour and gloom'. By a verbal fusion of opposites, the poet implies the oneness of all things, a common end, that end being entry into a spiritual realm which is all-containing. In this general ascent *saudade*, which is the fusion of memory and desire, represents the binding force of love – the bond between the stone and the tree, the spirit and the body. All things being substantially the same, Pascoais can achieve in his poetry the most curious transpositions of words and ideas. God becomes the creature of man the creator. Evil is of divine origin, good of human. The poet dedicates a book to a tree and his sister. Those who visited him in his old age at Amarante, surrounded by half-naked children of whose paternity the visitor was never quite sure, found him a sage reconciled to Nature.

His poetry offers no material for the analysis of the human heart. The poet never, or rarely, speaks of himself. *Saudade* is for him an idea, the key to the future of human evolution. Love takes on cosmic proportions. He is a metaphysical poet whose great flights of imagination are best seen in his longer poems – *Maranos* (1911), *Regresso ao Paraíso* (1912).

Other works include *Para a luz* (still under the influence of ⇨ Junqueiro), *Sempre*, *Terra proibida*, *Vida etérea*, *As sombras*, and a series of prose works written in later life – *S. Paulo*, *S. Jerónimo*, *S. Agostinho*, and *Napoleão*. [ARM]

*Obras completas* (11 vols., Lisbon, n.d.); *A Era lusíada. Duas Conferências* (Porto, 1914); *Arte de ser Português* (1920); *Ultimos Versos* (Lisbon, 1953); *Cartas de P. e Unamuno* (1957).

G. Battelli, *T. de P.* (Lisbon, 1953); J. A. de Sant'Anna Dionísio, *O Poeta, essa ave Metafísica* (Lisbon, 1953); J. Sardoeira, *P.* (Lisbon, 1951).

**Pascoli, Giovanni** (San Mauro 1855–Bologna 1912). Italian poet and scholar (of classical philology and Italian literature). His perfectly formed and symbolically suggestive lyrics were once regarded as distinctively modern. The limitations of his intimate world (of children, flowers, birds), though less obvious than those of his later prophetic style (*Odi e inni*, 1906), seem now to mark his sensitivity – but perhaps not the fresher aspects of his language – as rather a product of the past century. His best poetry may be seen in *Canti di Castelvecchio* (1903); *Poesie* (10 vols., 1931–8). [GD]

B. Croce, *G.P.* (Bari, 1920); C. Curto, *La poesta di G.P.* (Turin, 1940); A. Galletti, *La poesiae l'arte di G.P.* (Bologna, 1924).

**Pasek, Jan Chryzostom** (*c.*1636–*c.*1701). Polish diarist. A nobleman from the district of Masovia, he lived through the turbulent reigns of John Casimir and John III, fighting the Swedish and Russian invaders, farming, selling corn in Danzig and attending Diets. Towards the end of his life he recorded his adventures in a book of memoirs (*Pamiętniki*, 1656–88; French tr. P. Cazin, 1922), a copy of which was discovered early in the 19th century and has since become one of the favourite Polish classics. He has consistent charm, whether he is making observations on the life in Denmark or on the behaviour of the Muscovite envoys, whether he is describing battles and the pleasures of looting or the election of the king and his own marital problems. When John III Sobieski takes a fancy to his pet otter and he has to part with it reluctantly, Pasek can express a complex mood with sentiment and wit.

The incomplete manuscript was at first badly edited, its Latin phrases pruned or translated, but now the stylistic variety of the memoirs is fully evident. Among the many diarists of the 17th century, Pasek stands out as a born writer who knows how to turn from novelistic scenes with dialogue to brisk anecdotes or digressions on matters of husbandry, from ornate baroque speeches to a simple peasant ditty. [JP]

*SEER*, XXXII, 79 (1954).

**Pasolini, Pier Paolo** (Bologna 1922– ). Italian poet, novelist and literary critic. He is also a scholar of popular and dialect poetry, was editor of an important *avant-garde* magazine, *Officina*, between 1955 and 1959, and has worked in the film industry as an actor, script-writer and producer. All his work is deeply motivated by his belief that the writer has a significant contribution to make towards the reform of social and political structures; as a reformer he must reject the dogmaticism of traditional literary style (which is nothing but the linguistic superstructure of the ruling classes) and must try to reproduce, with almost philological accuracy, the language of the common people. Hence his interest in popular poetry (he edited *Poesia dialettale del Novecento* with M. Dall'Arco, in 1952, and *Canzoniere italiano*, in 1955; see also his essays, *La poesia popolare italiana*, 1960), and his linguistic realism which may shock certain readers. Both his poems (the best known are *La meglio gioventù*, 1954; *Le ceneri di Gramsci*, 1957; *L'usignuolo della Chiesa Cattolica*, 1959) and novels (*Ragazzi di vita*, 1955; *Una vita violenta*, 1959; *Il sogno d'una cosa*, 1962) oscillate between autobiographical confession and the bitter sorrowful contemplation of life at its lowest level. [GMC]

Mariani, *GNI*; Pullini, *RID*; Ferretti, *LI.*

**Pasternak, Boris Leonidovich** (Moscow 1890–Peredelkino 1960). Russian poet and prose-writer. Born of Jewish parents (his father was a distinguished painter and his mother a concert pianist), he grew up and spent most of his life in or near Moscow. His early passion for music owed much to the personal influence of the composer Skryabin. A period of study of philosophy at Marburg (1912) was followed by his graduation at Moscow University. He published his first volume of verse in 1914 and two of his most outstanding collections of lyric poetry *Sestra moya zhizn'* and *Temy i variatsii* in 1922 and 1923. His most productive period as a poet lies between 1917 and 1923. Yet the following years remained rich in achievement. Two epic poems, in praise of the revolutionary movement, *Devyat'sot pyatyi god* and *Leytenant Shmidt*, both published in 1927, were followed by a new collection of lyric verse, *Vtoroye Rozhdeniye* (1932). In 1934, with the mounting pressure exerted by the Communist Party to ensure the ideological conformity of Russian writers and their acceptance of the principles of 'Socialist Realism', he stopped publishing new poetry for nine years. He translated works of foreign literature, notably Shakespeare, publishing remarkably successful versions of *Hamlet*, *Antony and Cleopatra*, *Romeo and Juliet*, *Othello*, *King Lear* and both parts of *Henry IV*. Once again in 1946, when the Party launched a new attack on deviationist writers, he fell silent, this time until Stalin's death in 1953. Since 1946 he had worked on his novel *Doktor Zhivago* which, banned in the Soviet Union, was published in Milan in 1957 (tr. M. Hayward and M. Harari, 1958). In 1958 he was awarded the Nobel Prize, but under severe political pressure and scurrilous attacks of the Soviet authorities, was forced to decline it.

His early poetry, which owed something to the combined though contrasting influences of ⇨ Blok and ⇨ Mayakovsky, is marked by a musical quality, an originality of imagery and diction, a sharpness of vision and an intense poetic passion. Its main themes are love, nature and poetic creation. His descriptions of the Russian countryside are especially unforgettable. After 1930 his poetry shows a gradual development away from modernism and experimentation towards a simpler, more direct and classical style. The supreme achievement of his new manner are the poems which form an appendix to *Doctor Zhivago*, and which reveal him as a great Christian poet, and his collection, *Kogda razgulyayetsya*, written in the last years of his life.

*Doktor Zhivago*, incomparably the greatest of his works of prose, is a novel conceived on a vast scale, shot through with religious imagery and philosophical reflection, and sketched against the background of the main events of Russian history during the first three decades of this century. Its descriptions of nature and treatment of human love reveal the author's mature poetic mastery. Though it is in no sense a political attack on the Soviet regime, it is profoundly at variance with its official ideology in its repudation of the philosophical inadequacy of Marxism and of the inhumanity of the Revolution, in its Christian interpretation of the problems of life and death, and in the prime emphasis it lays on the spiritual integrity of the individual and on the value of human compassion. [DO]

*Doktor Zhivago* (Russian Language edition) (Ann Arbor, Michigan, 1959); *Sochineniya*, ed. G. P. Struve and B. A. Philippov (3 vols., Ann Arbor, Michigan, 1961).

D. Davie, *The Poems of Doctor Zhivago* (1965); G. Struve, 'Sense and Nonsense about Dr Zhivago', in *Studies in Russian and Polish Literature*, ed. Z. Folejewski *et al.* (The Hague, 1962).

**Pastor Díaz, Nicomedes** (Lugo 1811–Madrid 1863). Spanish poet, politician, Rector of Madrid university. His few poems are remarkable for their romantic melancholy – inspired by an unhappy life – and their often morbid imagery. [JMC]

*Obras* (1866–7); Blecua, *FLE*; Trend, *OBSV*. Cossío, *CAPE*.

**Pastourelles.** Medieval French poems in which the poet or a knight attempts to seduce a shepherdess by conversation, gifts, promises. The shepherdess Marion (Marot), pledged to her rustic Robin, may be innocent, caustically witty, or forward. In a different type of *pastourelle* the poet meets a group of shepherds and shepherdesses and describes their country pastimes. The genre is of savant and aristocratic origin related to Virgil's *Bucolics* as interpreted by medieval commentators, and was doubtless intended as lighthearted relief to the courtly *canso* or love-song. A mark of the genre is the word *l'altrier* ('the other day') in the opening lines.

There survive 130 *pastourelles*, 50 anonymous, in northern French and 25 in medieval Provençal. The oldest is ⇨ Marcabru's (1130–48) *L'autrier jost' una sebissa*. Excellent examples were also written by ⇨ Jean Bodel and ⇨ Thibaut de Champagne. Some brutality and cynicism are introduced by late 13th-century Picard and Flemish poets of bourgeois origin, e.g. Perrin d'Angicourt, but the genre in this period is increasingly dramatized in poems by ⇨ Guiraut Riquier and Baude de la Quarrière, and in the *Jeu de Robin et Marion* in which ⇨ Adam de la Halle combines in one play many themes of earlier *pastourelles*. In the 14th and 15th centuries the genre is in decline, used for political purposes by ⇨ Froissart and Eustache ⇨ Deschamps and as a conventional setting for declarations of love by Oton de Granson and ⇨ Christine de Pisan. [LTT]

K. Bartsch, *Altfranzösische Romanzen und Pastourellen* (Leipzig, 1870).

E. Piguet, *L'évolution de la P. du XIIe siècle à nos jours* (Basle, 1927); M. Delbouille, *Les origines de la p.* (Brussels, 1926); W. P. Jones, *The P.* (Cambridge, Mass., 1931); *R*, XLIX (1923); *Speculum*, V (1930); *Harvard Studies*, XIII (1931).

**'Pathelin, La Farce de Maistre Pierre.'** The most famous medieval French farce, written before 1470 in which year the phrase *pateliner et faire du malade* is found in a legal document. The unknown author, who has been identified with Villon, Guillaume Alecis and others, probably lived in Paris and was acquainted with the legal profession. The incessant duper, the rascally lawyer Pathelin, is finally duped by his apparently simple client, the shepherd Aignelet. The final court scene between Joceaume, the merchant, and Pathelin and Aignelet who have robbed him of cloth and sheep respectively, is especially skilful. The characterization is sharp, the dialogue fast and witty, the plot coherent, and this farce, which recalls the early Molière, is still performed successfully. It was adapted by Brueys and Palaprat in *L'Avocat Pathelin* in 1706. [LTT]

*Maistre P.P.*, ed. R. T. Holbrook (Oxford, 1943); English adaptation by R. T. Holbrook (Boston, 1914).

*R*, LXXXII (1961); *ZRP*, LXXXI (1965); Frank, *MFD*.

**Paul the Deacon** (*c.* 720–Monte Cassino 799). Lombard historian. For many years an official under the Lombard rulers at Pavia and Benevento. After the conquest of the Lombards by Charlemagne in 773 he entered the Benedictine monastery of Monte Cassino. A prolific writer of Latin, his verse includes love poems addressed to Adelperga, a daughter of the last King of the Lombards, and a fine poem on Lake Como, showing keen appreciation of natural beauty. His prose includes an unfinished history of the Lombards. It contains many good stories, including the probable source of Poe's 'Descent into the Malestrom'. [FB]

Migne, *PL* (95); *Poems*, ed. E. Dümmler (MGH, PLAC, II, 1880), ed. K. Neff (Berlin, 1908); *Historia Langobardorum*, ed. L. Bethmann and G. Waitz (MGH, 1878; tr. W. D. Foulke, N.Y., 1907).

Laistner, *TLWE*; Raby, *CLP*, *SLP*.

**Paulhan, Jean** (Nîmes 1884–1968). French essayist and critic. He taught in Madagascar, then at the École Nationale des Langues Orientales Vivantes in Paris 1912–14, publishing a volume of Malagasy poetry, *Les Hain-Tenys Merinas* (1913). In 1919 he joined the *Nouvelle Revue Française* and was its editor from 1925 to 1940, in succession to Jacques ⇨ Rivière. In 1941 he founded, with Jacques Decour, the weekly *Les Lettres Françaises*. He was co-director, with ⇨ Arland, of the present *Nouvelle Revue Française* (revived by them in 1953). In 1945 he was awarded the Grand Prix de Littérature by the Académie Française for his work and was elected a member in 1963. He started his literary career with a series of short psychological tales which reveal an interest in subconscious states: *Le guerrier appliqué* (1915), *Le pont traversé* (1921), *La guérison sévère* (1925), etc. From his anthology onwards he had shown an interest in the nuances of language, in analysing what significance words have for modern man, and he abandoned fiction to devote himself to the critical study of such problems. In his best-known work, *Les fleurs de Tarbes* (1931), he studies the age of suspicion which literature has entered: *La terreur dans les lettres* is its sub-title. His works have since continued to be of a critical variety: *Clef de la Poésie* (1944), *F.F. ou le critique* (1945), *Braque le patron* (1946), etc. [SMD]

R. Judrin, *La vocation transparente de P.* (Paris, 1961); M.-J. Lefebve, *J.P., une philosophie et une pratique de l'expression et de la réflexion* (Paris, 1949); M. Toesca, *J.P., écrivain appliqué* (Paris, 1948).

**Paustovsky, Konstantin Georgiyevich** (Moscow 1892–1968). Soviet writer. He spent his childhood in Kiev. During the First World War and the Civil War he was a tramcar driver, medical orderly, factory hand, reporter and editor. In 1920 he met writers like Babel, whose influence he acknowledged, Il'f and Bagritsky in Odessa. Politically uncommitted for several years, he wrote dreamy stories of the sea and faraway exotic lands.

His youthful romanticism is echoed in his contributions to Five-Year Plan literature, e.g. *Kara-Bugaz* (1932) and *Sud'ba Sharlya Lonsevilya* (1933), in cyclic works like *Chornoye morye* (1936) and his historical sketches and plays. In the thirties he settled in Central Russia, which provided the setting for most of his mature work – short stories written in a simple, seemingly effortless idiom and containing nature descriptions unsurpassed in Soviet literature, e.g. *Meshchorskaya storona* (1939) and *Povest' o lesakh* (1948). A war correspondent in the Second World War, he wrote a novel and numerous lyrical stories with a wartime setting, e.g. *Snyeg* (1944). Many of his stories are pleas for tolerance, like *Telegramma* (1946) and *Starik v potyortoy shineli* (1956). His most remarkable work is the vast autobiographical *Povest' o zhizni* (1946–64; tr. M. Harari and J. Duncan, *Story of a Life*, 1964, *Slow Approach of Thunder*, 1965; *In That Dawn*, 1967ff.), reaching from the turn of the century to the early thirties; written in the tradition of Aksakov, Tolstoy and Gor'ky, it has earned him world-wide fame.

Paustovsky is a lyrical realist with a reverent love for the Russian countryside. His work is characterized by meticulous observation, an astonishing memory, evocative detail and a sensitive use of language. He states his views on literatry technique in *Zolotaya roza* (1955; tr. S. Rosenberg, *The Golden Rose*, 1961). Throughout, he has preserved his personal and artistic integrity, denouncing abuses in public life and low standards in literature. In 1956 he defended ⇨ Dudintsev's *Not by Bread Alone*, co-edited *Literaturnaya Moskva*, and edited *Tarusskiye stranitsy* in 1961, both of them sensations of the Khrushchev era. For over ten years he ran a seminar for young writers and has consistently given them his support and encouragement. His works, some of which have been filmed, are enormously popular with Soviet readers. As man and artist, he is the most revered figure in Soviet literature today (Order of Lenin, 1967). [PH]

*Sobraniye sochineniy* (6 vols., 1957–8); *Povest' o zhizni* (3 vols., 1966).
L. Levitsky, *K.P.* (Moscow, 1963).

**Pavese, Cesare** (S. Stefano Belbo 1908–Turin 1950). Italian poet and novelist, also well known as a translator of American literature. Although his fiction is one of the chief sources of post-war Italian realism, he cannot be called a realist in the strict sense of the word: he is not so much interested in the outside world as in how his protagonists (who in many cases can be identified with the writer himself) come to terms with their world. For Pavese, knowing and understanding is not seeing, but remembering; reality is a myth rediscovered, an image painstakingly clarified in a terse page of prose or in a few unsentimental lines of poetry (*Lavorare stanca* 1936, 1943; *Verrá la morte e avrá i tuoi occhi*, 1951). To remember a thing is really to see it for the first time. This is the key to his non-realistic use of recurrent images: the hills, the country roads, the empty town streets, the useless sea (many of which have later been translated into pictures by Italian film directors, such as Antonioni and Patroni-Griffi). But where truth resides so exclusively in the past, there can be little inspiration in the present time, or hope for the future. Pavese's destiny was fixed in the early 1930s when, as he tells us in his moving posthumous diary *Il mestiere di vivere* (1952; tr. A. E. Murch, *This Business of Living*, 1964), he first contemplated taking his own life. He committed suicide after twenty years of intellectual and sentimental loneliness, at the height of his literary reputation. The best of his consistently good literary production are perhaps his novels *Prima che il gallo canti* (1949), *Il compagno* 1947; tr. W. J. Strachan, *The Comrade*, 1962), *La luna e i falò* (1950; tr. L. Sinclair, *The Moon and the Bonfire*, 1952), which he himself described as 'the historical saga of his own time', whose themes are antifascism, prison, the Resistance movement, the post-war years, and whose characters are conceived as representatives of youth and middle age, of the workers and the intellectuals. [GMC]

*La spiaggia* (1941); *Paesi tuoi* (1941; tr. A. E. Murch, *The Harvesters*, 1962); *La bella estate*, etc. (1949); *Prima che il gallo canti*, etc. (1949); *Fuoco grande* (1959); *Among Women Only*, tr. D. D. Paige (1953); *The Devil in the Hills*, tr. D. D. Paige (1954); *The Political Prisoner*, etc., tr. W. J. Strachan (1955); *The House on the Hill*, tr. W. J. Strachan (1956); *The Beach* and *A Great Fire*, tr. W. J. Strachan (1963); *Poesie* (1961).

D. Lajolo, *Il 'Vizio assurdo'* (Milan, 1960); Fernandez, *RI*; Pullini, *RID*.

**Pázmány, Péter** (Nagyvárad 1570–Pozsony 1637). Hungarian archbishop (of Esztergom) and religious writer. He was a Protestant-born Jesuit convert; as head of the Hungarian Catholic Church, he also became a leading politician. He wrote several polemical religious books and pamphlets, his greatest work being *Isteni igazságra vezérlő kalauz* (1613). His translation of Thomas à Kempis is a masterpiece. [JFR]

**Pea, Enrico** (Seravezza 1881–Forte dei Marmi 1958). Italian novelist. Self-taught, he worked in his youth as a marble cutter, sailor, mechanic, pedlar. After a few years in Egypt, he came back to Tuscany, and took up writing and producing popular plays in a makeshift theatre he himself had helped build in Viareggio. His best writings are perhaps to be found in *Moscardino* (1922) and *Il servitore del Diavolo* (1931), where dreams, autobiographical memories, the wisdom distilled of various unusual experiences, and popular traditions, are blended into a sort of visionary lyrical prose not entirely proof against learned literary influences. His later collections of stories (*Il trenino dei sassi*, 1940) and novels (*Lisetta*, 1946; *Malaria di guerra*, 1946; *Peccati in piazza*, 1956) develop with greater stylistic maturity but possibly less poetic charm some of his early themes. [GMC]

Falqui, *PNNI*; Pullini, *NIN*; Gargiulo, *LIN*; Robertis, *SN*; Biondolillo, *C*; *Contemporanei*, i.

**Pedrayo, Ramón Otero.** ⇨ Galician Literature.

**Pedro de Axular.** ⇨ Basque Literature.

**Péguy, Charles** (Orléans 1873–battle of the Marne 1914). French poet and essayist. The orphaned son of a carpenter, he reached the École Normale Supérieure, where he became interested in social problems and started a publishing firm. He supported the Dreyfus cause, though his early poetic drama, *Jeanne d'Arc* (1897), shows patriotic and Catholic trends. He founded and edited the polemic review *Cahiers de la Quinzaine*, a spiritual guide to the period 1900–14; this and his death have made him a mystically ideal figure on the French scene. He veered away from the fashionable anti-clerical and international socialism (discussed in *Notre Jeunesse*, 1910) and reacted passionately (in *Clio*, 1909–12, *Note sur M. Bergson*, and *Note conjointe sur M. Descartes*, 1914) against modern intellectualism, preferring Faith and the French heritage, and the heroism represented by Corneille and Hugo (*Victor-Marie Comte Hugo*, 1910). These feelings, together with an almost heretic, pedestrian's view of religion, inspire *Le Porche du Mystère de la Deuxième Vertu* (1911) and *Le Mystère des Saints Innocents* (1912), long poems in Biblical stanzas; and a series of 'tapestries' or frescos, similar to the decorations of a church, in normal verse (*Sainte Geneviève*, 1912, *Ève*, 1913).

His passionate quest into the relationship between the everyday and the spiritual world of truth, honour and hope is reflected in his style: its ritual aspect stressed by scriptural borrowings, it succeeds, like Bach's music, in climbing through repetitions and laborious gropings from matter into a semi-hypnotic vision. [CLC]

*Œuvres en vers*, *Œuvres en prose*, ed. M. Péguy (Pléiade, 1958, 1963).

B. Guyon, *P.* (Paris, 1960); D. Halévy, *P. et les Cahiers de la Quinzaine* (N.Y., 1947); A. Dru, *P.* (1956); N. Wilson, *C.P.* (1965).

**Peire Cardenal** (*c.* 1180–1278). Provençal troubadour famed for his moralizing and satirical poems. A knight of modest means, he began a clerical education at Puy-en-Velay but 'feeling young, gay and handsome' left this and became secretary (*scribus*) of Count Raimon VI of Toulouse. He wrote a few love songs but refused to accept the artificiality of the courtly doctrine; he turned instead to moralizing poems. His main target was the extravagant and deceitful life of false monks and clerics. He affirmed his orthodox belief in the Church of Rome and was accordingly mild in his attitude towards the Albigensian Crusaders led by Simon de Montfort, and the establishment of the Inquisition in the South of France. He probably spent the last thirty years of his life at Montpellier. [LTT]

*Poésies complètes* . . ., ed. R. Lavaud (Toulouse, 1957); Hill and Bergin, *APT*.

**Pekkanen, Toivo** (Kotka 1902–Helsinki 1957). Finnish prose writer, and member of the Finnish Academy (1955–7). Some critics regard *Lapsuuteni* (tr. A. Blair, *My Childhood*, Wisconsin, 1966), an objective account of his childhood, as his most important work. It describes a Finnish working-class household, its members engaged in a long, stubborn battle for their daily bread. Others regard as his main achievement the great series of social novels known as the 'Kotka Epic', which depicts the slow and painful transformation of a Finnish community into an industrialized society, and the class conflicts arising out of this process. Frequently the action is observed through the eyes of a character who moves from a rural into an urban environment: beset by new problems of day-to-day life, he retains a stubborn courage which enables him to rise above them and view them from a higher spiritual standpoint than his workaday comrades; a courage which at the time suffuses the greyness of life with a kind of poetic radiance. This poetical quality in Pekkanen's writing has been greatly admired. A third approach to his work sees in it a powerful urge to analyse the secret and irrational forces of the human mind in symbolic terms. His message is, however, clear: we must step across all man-made frontiers, be they those of states or of groups with interests to defend. Men must stop living and writing as they have lived and written hitherto. The force that makes this change obligatory is Conscience, which in Pekkanen's world is always present, creating a 'divine discontent' in each individual at every turn. This is what gives such a deep glow of life even to the most ordinary characters in the 'grey world' of his books. His essential characteristic is an earnest artlessness, coupled with a respect for irrational forces and a firm faith in a happier future. [AK]

*Kootut teokset* (7 vols., 1957–8); *Tehtaan varjossa* (1932; Fr. tr. I. Spira, *À l'ombre de l'usine*, Paris, 1943); *Isänmaan ranta* (1937; French tr. S. and I. Anglade, *Aux rives de ma Finlande*, Paris, 1946); *Ihmisten kevät* (1935).

**Pellico, Silvio** (Saluzzo 1789–Turin 1845). Italian patriot and dramatist. He wrote classical tragedies with evident influences of ⇨ Alfieri and especially ⇨ Foscolo, the best known of which was *Francesca da Rimini* (1815; tr. A. O'D. Bartholeyno, 1915). During the polemics between Classics and Romantics (1816) he was at first undecided but eventually plumped for the latter, and contributed to the Romantic journal *Il Conciliatore*. His association with the *Carbonari* led to his arrest in 1820; but the death-sentence was commuted to imprisonment in the Austrian fortress of Spielberg, where he spent eight painful years. The famous *Le mie prigioni* (1832; tr. I. G. Capaldi, *My Prisons*, 1963), written after his release in 1830, are personal memoirs of the spiritual crisis and conversion which occurred during his imprisonment. Certain patriots despised its submissiveness, but it was an immediate success, acquiring an unintentional political interpretation – the condemnation of Austrian persecution. Its effect is said to have been as great as a major Austrian defeat on the battlefield. A later moral treatise, *I doveri degli uomini* (1834; tr. R. A. Vain, *On the Duties of Men*, 1869), placated those Catholic critics who viewed his conversion with suspicion, but antagonized patriots even more for its insistence on submission to authority. [RHC]

*Opere complete* (1857); *Scritti scelti*, ed. A. Romanò (1960); *Opere scelte*, ed. C. Curto (1964).

B. Allason, *La vita di S.P.* (Milan, 1933); A. Romanò, *S.P.* (Brescia, 1948); *Guida*, 1954; *Minori*, iii.

**Pennanen, Eila** (Tampere 1916– ). Finnish novelist, critic and essayist. A specialist on, and skilful translator of, English and American literature. *Ennen sotaa oli nuoruus* (1942) dealt with the social orientations of university students in wartime; this was followed by several well-constructed and psychologically extremely perceptive studies in female portraiture, written with matter-of-fact detachment in the modern manner. She has also experimented with a semi-romantic treatment of historical themes: one of her novels (*Valon lapset*, 1959) is about the early Quakers. Her best achievements have been in the field of the short story: in her descriptions of society and of urban life the women and children, dreamers and eccentrics are firmly portrayed by simple, unemphatic means; often the portrait is illuminated by a touch of satire. [RV]

*Kaadetut pihlajat* (1944); *Proomu lähtee yöllä* (1945); *Pilvet vyöryvät* (1947); *Leda ja joutsen* (1948); *Kattoparveke* (1950); *Pyhä Birgitta* (1954); *Mutta* (1963); *Mongolit* (1966). Stories: *Tornitalo* (1952); *Pasianssi* (1957); *Kaksin* (1961).

**Pereda, José Mariá de** (Polanco 1833–Santander 1906). Spanish novelist. Destined for the Artillery, he proved no good at mathematics when he went to Madrid to study in 1852. He took up literature seriously – supported by his rich family – beginning with newspaper articles and a number of plays, mostly composed and performed in Santander between 1858 and 1866. But he was first really noticed as a writer of short *costumbrista* pieces, describing the life of the Santander-Montaña region with a mixture of realism and sentimental affection. The first important collection of articles in this vein was his *Escenas montañesas* (1864). In contrast to the Santander which he loved, Pereda nearly always associated Madrid with political and moral corruption, gross materialism and social disorder. Early examples of this attitude are to be found in the short novels *La mujer de César* and *Los hombres de pró* (1872–6). The most notable later novel is *Don Gonzalo González de la Gonzalera*. In spite of his conservative politics and regional fervour, he was 'revolutionary' in his realistic use of popular speech. But he was at his best when describing the rugged spiritual qualities of the land and sea around Santander. He saw these as a complement to the social and religious character of the men who lived and worked there in his great sea novel *Sotileza* (1884) and in his fine novel of the mountain regions *Peñas arriba* (1895). [ONVG]

*Obras completas* (17 vols., 1913–24).

M. Mays, *A Sociological Interpretation of the Works of J.M. de P.* (Canton, Mo., 1926); J. F. Montesinos, *P. o la novela idilio* (Mexico, 1961).

**Peresvetov, Ivan** (fl. 16 cent.). Russian publicist. He spent the early part of his career as a soldier in the service of the king of Hungary, the *voevode* of Moldavia and the Holy Roman Emperor. During the 1530s he joined the service of the grand prince of Moscow. He evidently won favour at court by demonstrating (and manufacturing?) a new type of hussar shield fashioned in the Macedonian style and was given an estate on life tenure. In 1549 he wrote to Ivan IV complaining that his possessions were being pillaged by avaricious boyars and begging for protection; at the same time he handed over to the tsar two *tetradi* containing various allegorical narratives and projects for reforms. Nothing is known of his subsequent fate or death.

His writings are mostly of a political nature. They were designed to further the lot of the minor service gentry, to improve conditions in the army, to ameliorate the primitive judicial procedure, to abolish slavery and to ease the existing fiscal system by doing away with *namestnichestvo* and *kormleniye*. Most of his works are directed against the landowning aristocracy, who are branded as cowards, pacifists and traitors; their lust for wealth was, in his eyes, responsible for many of the evils of contemporary Russia. His criticisms and suggested reforms are contained in allegorical tales, the central characters of which are Constantine XI, Mahomet II and Peter IV of Moldavia. Constantinople falls because of the corrupt influence of the decadent boyars who ensnared the emperor; Mahomet is praised for his sound financial, military, juridical and social measures and for his uncompromising treatment of the grandees.

Owing to the proximity of his views to those of the tsar, some scholars have suggested that 'Peresvetov' was a pseudonym used by Ivan IV. However, there seems to be little doubt that Peresvetov did exist and did write the works attributed to him. [JLIF]

*Sochineniya*, ed. A. A. Zimin (1956).

A. A. Zimin, *I.S.P. i yego sovremenniki* (Moscow, 1958).

**Péret, Benjamin** (Nantes 1899–Paris 1959). French poet. The most faithful of the original members of the Surrealist movement. He never departed from automatic methods and made no concessions to 'art' or taste. In *Dormir, dormir dans les pierres*

(1929), each poem is a headlong succession of sparkling images formed by the irrational juxtaposition of commonplace verbal elements of which the most distinctive refer to food or objects in everyday use. His conviction that a poet must also be a revolutionary was expressed in the aggressive political satire of *Je ne mange pas de ce pain-là* (1936). [RSS]

Jean-Louis Bédouin, *B.P.* (Paris, 1961) (with selection).

**Peretz, Isaac Leib** (Zamosc 1851–Warsaw 1915). Hebrew poet. From a traditional Jewish background, in early youth he became an adherent of Haskalah and made his literary debut in *Ha-Shachar* in 1875 with some Hebrew poems attacking Hassidism. Unhappy in his personal life, he moved to Warsaw where he studied Law, but returned to practise as a lawyer in Zamosc, where he divorced his first wife, married for a second time and turned his attention to Yiddish, publishing his first story in 1888. From then on, he became a centre of Yiddish literature, not only for his own generation but influencing and guiding young writers. Influenced by major trends in European, chiefly Russian and German, literature, he founded a new school in his own field. His stories and plays combined a social outlook with national content, blending the best traditions of Jewish writing and philosophy of the past with modern trends. With ⇨ Mendele and ⇨ Sholem Aleichem he became one of the great classics of Yiddish literature. When barred from practising as a lawyer, he became an official of the Warsaw Jewish community and spent the last 25 years of his life in that great centre of Jewish life and letters. [EE]

*Ale Verk* (18 vols., Vilna, 1912); (12 vols., N.Y., 1920); *Stories and Pictures*, tr. H. Frank (Philadelphia, 1906).

M. Samuel, *Prince of the Ghetto* (1948).

**Pérez de Ayala, Ramón** (Oviedo 1880–Madrid 1962). Spanish novelist, essayist and poet. His Jesuit education, subsequent studies with L. ⇨ Alas at Oviedo University, and European travels profoundly influenced him. His first book (1904) initiated an unfinished cycle of poems with modernist tendencies, whose second part, *El sendero innumerable* (1916), is the better. In 1907 appeared the first of a clearly autobiographical, often vituperatively anti-clerical series of novels, best represented by *La pata de la raposa* (1912). They depict Sapin's apathy after the 1898 crisis.

With *Prometeo* (1916), his personal style crystallized in three symbolic 'poematic novels', harshly ironic and exquisitely written, using intercalated poems to original effect. He repeated this technique in the more realistic and humorous series *El ombligo del mundo* (1924). His final novels, notably the contrapuntal masterpiece on the problem of knowledge, *Belarmino y Apolonio* (1921), and *Tigre Juan* (1926) with its sequel *El curandero de su honra* (1928), experiment with musical forms and manipulate ideas through symbolic yet wittily authentic characters, the latter giving a new twist to the themes of honour and Don Juan. They established him as a stylist and innovator.

A war correspondent (1914–18) and dramatic critic (see *Las máscaras*, 1917, 1919), he became Republican Ambassador in London in 1932, but retired at the outbreak of Civil War to Argentina, where he wrote press articles (see *Obras completas*). Back in Spain (1955), he produced little, discouraged by a crippling censorship. [EJF]

*Obras completas* (1923ff.); *Obras completas*, i, ii, iii (1964ff.).

Norma Urrutia, *De 'Troteras' a 'Tigre Juan': Dos grandes temas de R.P. de A.* (Madrid, 1960); Nora, *NEC*.

**Pérez de Hita, Ginés** (Murcia 1544?–Murcia 1619?). Spanish writer. His *Guerras civiles de Granada* (2 parts, 1595 and 1601, tr. T. Rodd, 1803) is about the 15th-century Moslem state and the 1568 rebellion of the *moriscos*; it is in part a history but more a historical novel, interlarded with ancient and newly composed ballads. The book achieved great popularity in Spain, and in France, Germany and England, and helped to spread the notion of the romantic, chivalrous Moor. [CCS]

N. Acero y Abad, *G.P. de H. Estudio biográfico y bibliográfico* (Madrid, 1888).

**Pérez Galdós, Benito** (Las Palmas 1843–Madrid 1920). Spanish novelist. He wrote two vast cycles of novels and a number of plays. The *Episodios nacionales* (46 vols.) describe the important events of Spanish history from *Trafalgar* (1873; CA) to the Restoration. Some of the main characters are actual personages, others fictitious;

many details are the result of documentary research, but the basic conception is romantic, with glimpses of Galdós's own liberal and anti-clerical views. Like Balzac, he gives unity to this epic of Spanish national life by making some characters appear in consecutive books.

Though the *Episodios nacionales* remain his most popular work in Spain, the *Novelas españolas contemporáneas* are greater fiction. *Doña Perfecta* (1876) first tackles a contemporary problem with its account of a young liberal who comes to a stiflingly clerical town. *La desheredada* (1881) is the first of a series set in Madrid which he endows with a life as vivid as Balzac's Paris; it tells of a girl ruined by dreams above her station. *Tormento* (1884; tr. J. M. Cohen, *Torment*, 1952) is the study of another girl, caught in a relationship with a dissolute priest. *La de Bringas* (1884; CA; tr. G. Woolsey, *The Spendthrifts*, 1951) explores the ramifications of the Royal Palace with its penniless hangers-on among whom the pretentious spendthrift Rosalía Bringas pursues her long flirtation with grandeur and debt. Debt plays an important part also in *Miau* (1888; CA; tr. J. M. Cohen, *Miau*, 1963) about a pretentious family who lose their livelihood when the father, an elderly civil servant, loses his job through a change of government and eventually commits suicide. *Fortunata y Jacinta* (1886–7; CA), Galdós's masterpiece, is almost as long as *War and Peace*; it is concerned with four principal characters, a young man about town, his wife, his lower-class mistress and her husband – and of course with their society, above all with the city of Madrid and with the trades and business by which the characters live.

After *Miau*, Galdós became increasingly interested in abnormal psychology. In *Fortunata ...* Maxi, who marries the mistress, is crazy; the little grandson in *Miau* is epileptic and sees visions. Craziness, hallucination and religious mania play a part in most of the later novels. *Ángel Guerra* (1891; CA) is the story of an unbalanced man who, in an attempt to win the devout and inaccessible woman he loves, swings from agnosticism to Catholicism. The four novels which tell of the social ascent of the usurer *Torquemada* (1889–95) show him as obsessed by the notion of his dead son's divinity. *Nazarín* (1895) is the portrait of a priest who lives among the depraved and practises the lessons of the Sermon on the Mount in an original and quixotic fashion, while *Misericordia* (1897; CA) contrasts the unconscious piety of an old servant with the pretentious religiosity of her mistress, whom she supports. The poor-house atmosphere of this, his last important work, is magnificently sustained.

The *Novelas españolas contemporáneas* show Galdós to be the equal of the great 19th-century novelists of England and France. More realistic than Balzac, and less profoundly imaginative than Dickens, he nevertheless presents a *world* that is as authentic as theirs. His dramas and dramatic adaptations of novels are generally less successful, though *Realidad* (1892) is important in the history of realism in the Spanish theatre, and the anti-clerical *Electra* (1901) caused a political uproar. [JMC]

H. C. Berkowitz, *B.P.G. Spanish Liberal Crusader* (Madison, 1948); S. H. Eoff, *The Novels of P.G.* (St Louis, 1954); V. S. Pritchett, *Books in General* (1953); J. Casalduero, *Vida y obra de G.* (2nd edn, Madrid, 1951); A. del Río, *Estudios galdosianos* (Zaragoza, 1953); R. Gullón, *G.* (Madrid, 1960); H. Hinterhäuser, *Los episodios nacionales de P.G.* (Madrid, 1963); Eoff, *MSN*; *BHS*, XLII (1965).

**Perk, Jacques Fabrice Herman** (Dordrecht 1859–Amsterdam 1881). Dutch poet. The first of the young generation of 1880 (cf. ⇨ Kloos, Verwey). He died of T.B. but while convalescing in the Ardennes wrote *Mathilde*, a cycle of passionate sonnets on love and death. He was an admirer of Shelley, whose poem, *The Cloud*, inspired his *Iris* (1881). In 1882 Kloos arranged the first (incomplete) edition of *Mathilde* as a manifesto for the 1880 poets. [PK]

*Jacques Perks leven en werken* (4 vols., 1957–9) (complete works with biography); Barnouw, *CA*; Snell, *FFG*; Weevers, *PNEC*.

G. Stuiveling, *De wording van Perks 'Iris'* (Zwolle, 1963).

**Perrault, Charles** (Paris 1628–Paris 1703). French poet and fairy-tale writer. Member of a distinguished bourgeois family. He held administrative positions of importance under Colbert, who also encouraged him to reform the organization of the Académie Française. He became involved in polemics with Boileau and others, after maintaining the superiority of 'the moderns' in a poem *Le siècle de Louis le Grand* (1687) which resulted in the famous 'Querelle des anciens et des modernes'. Perrault's fame however, depends less on the works inspired by this dispute (*Apologie des femmes*, 1964, tr. R. Grant, *The Vindication of Wives*, 1954; *Parallèles des anciens et des modernes*, 1688–97; *Les hommes illustres qui ont paru en France depuis ce siècle*, 1696–70) than on a book which he evidently did not wish to be seen to take seriously and published under the name of his son Pierre: *Contes de ma mère Loye* (1697; tr. G. M. Gent, 11th edn 1719; tr. G. Brereton, *Fairy Tales*, Penguin Classics, 1957). With a few exceptions these stories are of popular origin, but are set down by Perrault in a style whose simplicity shows the highest art. [AKT]

A. Hallays, *Les Perrault* (Paris, 1926).

**Perron, Charles Edgar du** (Java 1899–Bergen 1940). Dutch author. Co-founder with ter ➪ Braak of *Het Forum* (1932–5), his outlook was cosmopolitan, impatient of national traditions, critical of provincial complacency (*Uren met Dirk Coster*, 1932). His best work is concerned with a re-appraisal of literary criticism, *Voor kleine parochie* (1932), and of human values, *De smalle mens* (1934). Besides poetry, novels and short stories, he wrote a fine biography of ➪ Douwes Dekker, *De Man van Lebak* (1937), and the autobiographical *Het land van herkomst* (1937). [PK]

*Verzameld werk* (4 vols., 1948–51); Ter Braak and du P., *Briefwisseling 1930–40* (1962– ); Greshoff, *HL*.

W. L. M. E. van Leeuwen, *Drie vrienden; H. Marsman, M. ter Braak, E. du P.* (Utrecht, 1947).

**Pers, Ciro di** (Pers, Friuli 1599–? San Daniele del Friuli 1663). Italian poet. He studied at Bologna where he met ➪ Achillini, one of the most celebrated Marinisti (➪ Marino) of the day. Disappointed in love, he became a Knight of Malta and later withdrew to a life of seclusion and study at San Daniele del Friuli, gaining a reputation for dignity and probity of character. In his *Poesie* (Florence, 1666; Venice, 1689) he combines two of the main trends of the Italian *seicento*. Many occasional sonnets are descriptive vignettes in characteristic Marinist vein, enlivened by audacious imagery, dramatic adjectives, and neatly rounded conclusion. Other poems on social and political themes are reminiscent of the manner of Fulvio Testi. In them he attacks the decadence and flabbiness of contemporary society, laments the calamities which have befallen Italy, and points to the frailty of human life. [DGR]

Croce, *LM*; Ferrero, *MM*; Getto, *MM*.

**Perse, Saint-John,** pseud. of Alexis Léger (Guadeloupe 1887– ). French poet. While studying in Pau and Bordeaux he wrote *Éloges* (1911; tr. A. Macleish, N.Y., 1944), inspired by his childhood on his parents' island in the West Indies; he later entered the French foreign service and worked in Peking, where *Anabase* (1922; tr. T. S. Eliot, 1930), an epic about the foundation of a town by nomads, reflected a visit to the grandiose ancient caravan trails. He held high positions at the Quai d'Orsay for 20 years, but left France in 1940 and was deprived of his nationality by the Vichy government. He has since lived mainly in the U.S., where he worked at the Library of Congress and lectured at Harvard. After a brief cry of despair (*Exil*, 1942) he published long impersonal poems where the events of Nature symbolize his sorrows (*Neiges*, 1944), the concept of regeneration through purification (*Pluies*, 1943) and the quests and energy of mankind (*Vents*, 1946). At the time of his marriage *Amers* (1957) treated outwardly of the love of the sea for the earth. In 1960 he wrote *Chronique* on the theme of old age, and was awarded the Nobel Prize. A poetic as well as a political exile, he has few attachments in modern poetry. His work – showing encyclopedic knowledge of natural history – is pantheistic and epic, but neither heroic nor episodic. He celebrates ageless ceremonials of Nature and expresses faith in the multiple resources of Man. He writes harmonious alliterating verse in the form of long prose stanzas, frequently using the rhetorical devices of litany and the enumerations dear to Renaissance artists. [CLC]

*Œuvre poétique* (1960).

R. Caillois, *Poétique de S.-J.P.* (Paris, 1954); A. J. Knodel, *S.-J.P.* (1965).

**Perzyński, Włodzimierz** (Opoczno 1877–Warsaw 1930). Polish dramatist. His smooth and deeply ironic comedies, though often revived, are underrated as works of literature. They resemble early Shaw in their daring unsentimental subjects, e.g. *Aszantka* (1907), about a *cocotte* from the proletariat, or *Szczęście Frania* (1909), which deals with illegitimacy. Even *Lekkomyślna siostra* (1907), where the charges against hypocrisy have dated, still asserts itself as theatre today. The secret of his dramatic authority lies in his dialogue, seemingly casual and lighthearted but, in fact, controlled by his acute sense of structure. His Polish is a model of colloquial grace and emphasis without rhetoric. His short stories and novels (e.g. *Raz w życiu*, 1925) seem to have lost their topical bite. [JP]

**Pessoa, Fernando** (Lisbon 1888–Lisbon 1935). Portuguese poet. His father died when he was 5 and two years later his mother married the Portuguese consul in Durban, where Pessoa was brought up. He matriculated at the University of Cape Town, where he won the Queen Victoria Prize for English Essay. In 1905 he returned alone to Lisbon where he matriculated at the University. In Portugal he continued to read and write in English, which was the language of his youthful erotic verse. In 1918 he published in Lisbon his *35 Sonnets* and in 1922 the three parts of his *English Poems*, all composed many years before. *The Times Literary Supplement* spoke of the 'ultra-Shakespearian Shakespearianisms' of this Portuguese writer.

The rest of Pessoa's life passed uneventfully in Lisbon. He earned a pittance from a number of commercial firms, composing free-verse or classical odes at the typewriter in the intervals of translating the firm's foreign correspondence. Many of the poems he wrote were published in literary reviews such as *Orfeu* and *Portugal Futurista*. He also wrote much prose on questions of aesthetics, and sketches for detective novels. The only book published in his lifetime was *Mensagem*, a collection of poems on patriotic themes, which won only a consolation prize in a national competition.

Pessoa wrote his poetry under his own name and under that of three heteronymous selves whose biographies he invented: Alberto Caeiro, Alvaro de Campos and Ricardo Reis. He claimed that he wrote the Caeiro poems as a result of inspiration; those of Campos when he felt a sudden impulse to write without knowing what; those of Reis after a period of abstract deliberation.

Caeiro is the poet for whom the world of the senses exists, in contradistinction to the metaphysical tendencies of Pessoa writing in his own name, whose poetry is one of concepts and mental states. Campos is the futurist poet who emphasizes the modern side of his creator. Aesthetic interest in the dynamism of machines provides the first theme of the poetry of Campos; the second is that of tedium vitae. Reis too is a man stricken with the grief of living, but he measures forces with destiny. A hellene by adoption, he attempts to perfect existence.

The heteronyms represent Pessoa's voyage of discovery of himself in the course of which he realized that extraordinary range of poetic values, and created that corpus of poems which have caused his countrymen to acclaim him as their greatest poet since Camões. [ARM]

*Obras completas*, ed. Atica (9 vols., 1945–65); *Antinous* (1918); *35 Sonnets* (1918); *English Poems* (1921); *Análise da Vida Mental Portuguesa. Ensaios Críticos* (Porto, 1950); *Cartas a J. G. Simões* (1957); *Cartas a A. Cortes-Rodrigues* (1959).

A. Casais Monteiro, *F.P. o Insincero Verídico* (Lisbon, 1954); J. de Entrambasaguas y Peña, *La Lírica de F.P.* (*Rev. de lit.*, 6, 1954); M. de Jong, *F.P. of het veelvoudig dichterschap* (The Hague, 1959); J. Nemésio, *Obra Poética de F.P.* (Lisbon, 1958); J. M. Parker, *Three Twentieth Century Poets* (1960); J. de Prado Coelho, *Diversidade e Unidade em F.P.* (Lisbon, 1949); A. Quadros, *F.P.* (Lisbon, 1960); J. de Sena, *O Poeta é um Fingidor* (Lisbon, 1961); J. G. Simões, *Vida e Obra de F.P.* (2 vols., Lisbon, 1951); M. de E. Tavares Monteiro, *Incidências Inglesas na Poesia de F.P.* (Lisbon, 1955).

**Pestalozzi, Johann Heinrich** (Zürich 1746–Brugg 1827). Swiss educationalist. He gave his theories fictional as well as non-fictional expression. In *Lienhard und Gertrud* (1781–7; tr. E. Channing, Boston, 1926), a realistic novel of peasant life, he shows how to educate a woman is to educate a family community, and in *Wie Gertrud ihre Kinder lehrt* (1801; tr. E. Holland, *How Gertrude Teaches her Children*, 1904), illustrates his own 'intuitive' educational method. [WAC]

*Werke*, ed. A. Buchmann *et al.* (Leipzig/Zürich, 1927ff.); *Auswahl*, ed. H. Barth *et al.* (1956).

J. A. Green, *The Life and Works of P.* (1913).

**Peter Damian (I), St** (Ravenna *c.*1006–Faenza 1072). Italian poet and satirist. An orphan, he took the name Damiani from a relative who adopted him. After a teaching career at Ravenna he joined the hermits of Fonte Avellana and became their abbot. His *Liber Gomorrhianus*, an outspoken attack on contemporary vices brought him to the notice of the reformer Hildebrand (later Pope Gregory VII); he became the trusted counsellor of three popes, cardinal bishop of Ostia, papal legate, etc. He surpassed Hildebrand in his denunciation of ecclesiastical corruption and clerical marriage, and was haunted by the thought of the Last Judgement. These features are evident in his writings, both prose and verse, e.g. in his poem *De die mortis*. Yet in this, as in his beautiful poem *Ad perennis vitae fontem* (ed and tr. S. A. Hurlbut, *The Song of S. P.D.*) Washington, 1928), a meditation on the glories of Paradise, he ranks among the great poets of his century. [FB]

Migne, *PL* (144–5); *An. Hym.* (48).
R. Biron, *S. Pierre Damien* (Paris, 1908); O. J. Blum, *St P.D.* (Washington, 1947).

**Peterkiewicz, Jerzy** (Fabianki 1916– ). Polish poet, now lives in London and writes in English. Born Pietrkiewicz. Of peasant origin, he transposed authentic people and places from his district into a highly metaphoric narrative poem, *Prowincja* (1936), serialized in a literary weekly. His later poems are constructed on parallel time sequences: in *Piąty poemat* (1950) the moment of death remains in the eye, telescoping life; in *Sielanka stołeczna* (1952; tr. Burns Singer and J.P., *Metropolitan Idyll*, *Botteghe Oscure*, XX, 1957) the memory of labour camps threatens the mock pastoral love set in Kensington Gardens. His play *Sami swoi* (*Us*, performed 1949) exposes the conventional image of Polish rural life. In 1953 he published *The Knotted Cord*, his first novel in English, followed by 6 others, e.g. *Isolation* (1959); *Inner Circle* (1966).

**Petersen, Nis** (Vamdrup 1897–Laven 1943). Danish poet, novelist and short-story writer. A vagabond with an addiction to drink, his poetry, published in one volume in 1949, is of a very high quality; better known outside Denmark are his 2 novels, *Sandalmagernes Gade* (1931; tr. E. Sprigge and C. Napier, *The Street of the Sandalmakers*, 1932), set in ancient Rome, and *Spildt Mælk* (1934; tr. C. Napier, *Spilt Milk*, 1935), set in contemporary Ireland. Many fine short stories appear in his collected works (8 vols., 1962). [ELB]

G. Albeck, *N.P.* (Copenhagen, 1949).

**Petković-Dis, Vladislav** (Čačak 1880–Drowned off Corfu 1917). Serbian poet. Like ⇨ Pandurović, he introduced the themes and style of decadence into Serbian poetry. Almost an autodidact, his poetry is more personal and less fundamentally pessimistic than that of Pandurović. Its popularity has revived since 1948. [EDG]

Ibrovac, *APY*; Lavrin, *AMYP*.
Barac, *HYL*; Kadić, *CSL*.

**Petőfi, Sándor** (Kiskőrös 1823–Battle of Segesvár 1849). Hungarian lyric poet; the most outstanding figure of Hungarian literature. Son of a country butcher, he received a haphazard schooling in various small provincial towns. Neglecting his studies, he was obsessed with acting and literature, and started writing poems at the age of 15. Living in extreme poverty, he wandered all over Hungary, joined the army, worked and acted at many places and became a friend of ⇨ Jókai. In his first published poems, 'A Borozó' and 'Szülőföldemen' (1842), he gave indication of great lyrical gifts; the first volume of his 'Poems' was published in 1844, after much adverse criticism. Moving to Budapest, Petőfi became associated with the young radical intellectuals of the Pilvax Café circle; he translated German, French and English works into Hungarian (his chief work being Shakespeare's *Coriolanus*), and in 1844 became assistant editor of the periodical *Pesti Divatlap*.

For his strong, self-assured personality, literature was an instinctive verbal manifestation of life; influenced by his Lowland peasant background, he had an extraordinary gift for genre-pictures and the folk-song. His first masterpiece of scenic poetry was *Az Alföld* (1844). *A Helység Kalapácsa* (1844) is a masterpiece of parody ridiculing the classical-epic school of poetry; *János Vitéz* (1845; tr. W. N. Loew, *János the Hero*, 1920), one of the finest poetic narratives of Hungarian literature, is the story of the fantastic, fairy-tale adventures of a peasant-soldier; it raised the folk-song type poem to a new, high standard.

Owing to bitterness caused by isolation, adverse criticism, disappointments in love and the ruin of his parents, Petőfi later sought more personal forms of self-expression than the folk-song, and his poetry developed towards the grand lyric. From 1846, his two main themes became those of love for his bride and of political idealism – nationalistic, liberal and revolutionary. His best-known love-poems are 'A Virágnak Megtiltani Nem Lehet', 'Reszket A Bokor',

'Rózsabokor A Domboldalon'; 'Hogy Hívjalak'; in 'Szeptember Végén' (1847) foreboding of ill looms over his happiness. Ultimately, political and social lyricism came to dominate all his poetic themes. Poems such as 'A Magyar Nemes', 'Pató Pál Úr' and 'Európa csendes, újra csendes' described the growing voice of popular discontent heralding the 1848 Revolution, whose 'Marseillaise' was his stirring *Nemzeti Dal* (1848). *Egy Gondolat Bánt Engemet* (1846) is proof of Petőfi's desire for action; indeed, after organizing the revolutionary 'Society of Ten' with Jókai (1847) during the War of Independence, he fought as a major in Transylvania against Russian Tsarist troops; he was not seen again after the Battle of Segesvár (July 1849).

Other notable works are: *A Tisza* (1847), *Az Apostol* (1848), *A Vén zászlótartó*, *Szécsi Mária*, *Négyökrös Szekér* (typical of his poetry). *A Hóhér Kötele* (1845) is a novel. His complete works were published in 1847. Of numerous translations of his works, *Sixty Poems by Alexander Petőfi*, tr. E. B. Pierce and E. Delmár (1948), is the most comprehensive and contains most works mentioned above. [JFR]

Reményi, *HWL*; Klaniczay, *HHL*.

**Petrarch (Petrarca), Francesco** (Arezzo 1304–Arquà 1374). Italian poet. His family had been exiled from Florence, and went to live in Provence when he was still a child. His studies began at Carpentras with Convenevole da Prato, and he read law with no enthusiasm at Montpellier and Bologna, returning in 1326 to the papal court at Avignon to take minor orders. Sonnet 211 of the *Canzoniere* tells how on 6 April 1327 he first saw Laura in the church of St Claire, and from this meeting stemmed the life-long experience which the *Canzoniere* relates. She is generally thought to have been Laure de Noves, the wife of Hugues de Sade, though other names have been suggested and some have doubted her very existence. At about this time there began also his connexion with the Colonna family, the first of a long succession of powerful patrons whose favours, together with his benefices, enabled Petrarch to devote himself throughout his whole life to study, travel and writing. Periods of travel alternated for a time with periods of studious seclusion in his house at Vaucluse. Together with the Italian poems ultimately collected in the *Canzoniere*, he began composing the first of his many Latin works, some of which were never completed, and others of which occupied him intermittently over a period of many years. His *Africa* (ed. N. Festa, 1926), a Latin epic on Scipio, on which he rested his greatest claims to fame, was begun *c.* 1338 at about the same time as the *De viris illustribus*.

In 1341 he was crowned with the laurel wreath at Rome after being examined by King Robert at Naples, and a year later began the intensely personal *Secretum*, perhaps the most interesting of the Latin works. Prompted by St Augustine, he analyses his own spiritual position in relation to the ultimate pattern of temporal and eternal values, and also examines the power of his own will to take what he knows to be the right path, thus laying bare the dilemma which runs through the *Canzoniere*. In 1343 Francesca was born, his second illegitimate child by an unknown woman; the same year he set out on another visit to Italy in the course of which he began the never completed *Rerum memorandarum libri* and discovered (probably at Verona) some letters of Cicero. After his return to Vaucluse in 1345, in a period which included a visit to his brother Gherardo, who had become a monk, he exalted the ideals of studious and religious solitude in the *De vita solitaria* and of monastic life in the *De otio religioso*, and composed also the eclogues later collected together to form the *Bucolicum carmen*. In 1347 he set out for Rome, inspired to high hopes by the deeds of Cola di Rienzo, but the worsening Roman situation diverted him to various north Italian cities, and in 1348 came news of the death of Laura and also of his patron Cardinal Colonna. In 1350 he was at Rome for the Jubilee, and although he returned to Provence and there perhaps began his Italian allegorical poem, the *Trionfi*, by 1353 he was back in Italy, which henceforth became his permanent home. The period 1353–61 he spent as the honoured guest of the Visconti at Milan, and then moved on to Venice, where the Senate put a house at his disposal, and in 1368 to Padua as the guest of Francesco da Carrara. Among the writings of these years were the two polemical outbursts against detractors, *Contra medicum quendam* and *De sui ipsius et multorum ignorantia*, and the medieval *De remediis utriusque fortunae*, and at this time too he began ordering the vast corpus of his *Epistolae*. These letters (especially the group entitled *Familiares* and the single letter to Posterity) rank second in interest only to the *Secretum* among his Latin writings. His last years were spent chiefly at Arquà in the Euganean Hills near Padua, where he lived with his daughter Francesca and her husband.

Despite the psychological interest of his Latin writings and also their paramount importance in any study of Renaissance Humanism, Petrarch's status as a great European writer depends mainly on the 366 Italian poems of his *Canzoniere*, which in his later years he affected to despise. Written in the Provençal-Sicilian tradition of love-poetry (there are a few political poems too), much of the *Canzoniere* is conventional: some of its sentimental attitudes, its restricted imagery and vocabulary, the conception of poetry as a rhetorical craft. Its greatness lies in Petrarch's supreme ability to modulate the rhythmical phrase to express his mood, and in the subtly and profoundly felt tension between eternal and religious aspirations and the appeal of present worldly attractions.

Of all Italian poets Petrarch has been the most influential. For centuries he was rated above Dante, and his influence was particularly strong in the *cinquecento*, not only in Italy, but throughout western Europe. Imitators, however, often failed to grasp the unity of the *Canzoniere*, seeing in it only a collection of sentimental themes or rhetorical devices to be copied or adapted at will. Thus, when the pendulum of taste swung away, the term 'Petrarchism' became a term of abuse to denounce artificiality of sentiment or expression. [DGR]

*Rime, Trionfi e Poesie Latine*, ed. F. Neri *et al* (1951); *Prose*, ed. G. Martellotti *et al.* (1955); *The Sonnets of P.*, tr. J. Auslander (1931); *The Triumphs of P.*, tr. E. H. Wilkins (Chicago, 1962); Lind, *LPIR*; Kay, *PBIV*.

U. Bosco, *P.* (Bari, 1965); J. H. Whitfield, *P. and the Renascence* (1943); E. H. Wilkins, *Life of P.* (Chicago, 1961); A. E. Quaglio, *F.P.* (Milan, 1967); Binni, *CI*; *Maggiori.*

**Petrescu, Cezar** (Cotnar 1892–Bucharest 1961). Rumanian novelist. In 1920 he left Bucharest for Cluj in Transylvania (which had just been united to Rumania), and there in 1921 he founded the review *Gîndirea*, most influential of the inter-war journals. He gave up the editorship in 1926 and devoted himself to writing cycles of novels on a Trollopian scale. *Intunecare* (1927) ranks with ⇨ Rebreanu's *Pădurea spînzuraților* as a classic description of the Rumanian campaign in the First World War. Of his later novels *Ochii strigoiului* (1942) is particularly impressive; it describes the tribulations of a young officer (a minor character in *Intunecare*) who lies unconscious for twenty years and then, escaping from hospital, finds himself lost in the Rumania of 1937. Petrescu has a vast vocabulary, a copious style in which repetition plays an artful part, and skill in handling large numbers of characters without losing the unity of the composition. [EDT]

**Petrov, Yevgeny.** ⇨ Il'f, Il'ya.

**Petrus Alfonsi** (1062–1110). A Spanish Jew converted to Christianity, whose collection of oriental tales, *Disciplina clericalis* (ed. A. Hilke and W. Söderhjelm, Heidelberg, 1911; tr. W. H. Hulme, Cleveland, 1919) was used as a source for the *Golden Legend* (⇨ Jacobus de Voragine) and the ⇨ *Gesta Romanorum* and widely translated. [FB]

**'Petruslied.'** Old High German hymn, written in Bavaria towards the end of the 9th century. The three verses make up a prayer to Saint Peter: each verse consists of two rhyming couplets sung by the priest, followed by the refrain 'Kyrie eleyson, Christe eleyson' sung by the congregation. In the sense that it is a religious song in the vernacular, composed for the instruction and participation of the masses, it has the historical claim of being the oldest German hymn. [RT]

Braune, *AL.*

**Pétursson.** ⇨ Hallgrímur Pétursson.

**Peyrefitte, Roger** (Castres 1907– ). French novelist. After a Jesuit education, he was a career diplomat 1931–40. He won wide critical acclaim for his first novel *Les amitiés particulières* (Prix Théophraste Renaudot 1944; tr. F. Giovanelli, *Special Friendships*, 1950), a sharply observed but moving account of affection and jealousy amongst the masters and boys in a Jesuit college. He did not achieve the same quality in ensuing works, including *Les amours singulières* (1949), an unsuccessful sequel to his first novel. *Les ambassades* (1951; tr. J. FitzMaurice, 1953) – adapted for the stage 1961 – brought an abrupt change of manner, with a satirical account of embassy life. *La fin des ambassades* (1953; tr. E. Hyams, *Diplomatic Conclusions*, 1954) pursued the same theme in more virulent vein. With *Les clefs de saint Pierre* (1955; tr. E. Hyams, *The Keys of St Peter*, 1957) he turned his satirical gaze to the Vatican. In *Jeunes proies* (1956), *L'exilé de Capri* (1959; tr. E. Hyams, *The Exile of Capri*, 1961) and *Notre amour* (1967) he returns with increasing frankness, to the homosexual theme, whilst *Chevaliers de Malte* (1957; tr. E. Hyams, *Knights of Malta*, 1960), and *La nature du Prince* (1963; tr. P. Fryer, *The Prince's Person*, 1966) keep up his attack on the Catholic establishment. [IHW]

D. Bourdet, *Pris sur le vif* (Paris, 1957); C. Garnier, *L'homme et son personnage* (Paris, 1955); *Kenyon Review*, XXIV, 3 (1962).

**Philip the Chancellor** (Paris *c.*1180–1236). Early French poet. Chancellor of the infant University of Paris, his severe rule brought him into frequent conflict with the students, the lecturers, the religious orders, and even the papacy. He was a prolific writer of verse, both French and Latin. Some of his Latin poems are satires on contemporary abuses, but he excels as a religious poet. Of over 100 surviving Latin hymns, the greatest are perhaps his lyrical carols (*cantiones*). A number of his poems are full of 'conceits' reminiscent of the metaphysical and 'précieux' poets of the 17th century. [FB]

*An. Hym.* 20, 21, 50.
Raby, *CLP*, *SLP*.

**Picard, Louis-Benoît** (Paris 1769–Paris 1828). French actor-manager and playwright. Author of some 100 vaudevilles and comedies which were especially popular during the Napoleonic period. He wrote a large number of meticulously observed comedies of manners, affording an amusing gallery of contemporary social types, e.g. *Médiocre et rampant ou le moyen de parvenir* (1797), *Duhautcours ou le contrat d'union* (1801), *Les provinciaux à Paris* (1802), *La vieille tante* (1811), and *Les deux Philibert* (1816). His keen eye for figures representative of social change inhibits Picard from exploring character or inventing situations and leads naturally to the heavy stylization and mechanical plotting which characterize some of his other plays, notably *La petite ville* (1801), which, after several metamorphoses, emerges as *The Merry Widow*, *Les marionnettes* (1806), and *Les ricochets* (1807; tr. B. H. Clark, *The Rebound*, 1915). In these, characters are deliberately manipulated like puppets, and music is often allied to the gay satire. [SBJ]

*Œuvres* (10 vols., 1821).
W. Staaks, *The Theater of L.B.P.* (Berkeley, Calif., 1952).

**Pichette, Henri** (Châteauroux 1924– ). French poet and playwright. He invented a theatrical style marked by verbal violence and a lyrical sense of outrage, features intended to suggest the horrors of modern European civilization. Virtuosity of image and metaphor creates a dramatic poem rather than a play and verbal luxuriance sometimes checks and inhibits the emergence of the larger theme: the protest of creative man (conceived as poet or lover) against the dehumanizing terror of war. This protest is central to *Les Épiphanies* (1947) and *Nucléa* (1952), one of the early failures of Jean Vilar's Théâtre National Populaire. The allegorical *Nucléa* has great theatrical impact, mounting an ambitious synthesis of dissonant modern music, human screams and vivid verbal effects which convey the sense of war by assaulting the sensibilities of the audience. Has published highly individual poems: *Apoèmes* (1947) and others. [SBJ]

Guicharnaud, *MFT*; Corvin, *TNF*.

**Pico della Mirandola, Giovanni** (Mirandola 1463–Florence 1494). Italian scholar and thinker. Studies at Bologna, Ferrara, Padua, Florence, Paris and Perugia, and a knowledge of Arabic and Hebrew, as well as Latin and Greek, brought within his grasp a wide range of philosophico-religious writings, which encompassed Averroism, neo-Platonism and the more esoteric mysteries of the Kabbalah, as well as Christian theology. Out of this vast area of knowledge he compiled his *Conclusiones* (1486) – 900 theses which he proposed to defend in debate at Rome, with the *Oratio de hominis dignitate* (publ. 1496) to introduce the discussion. When 13 of his propositions were judged heretical, he defended them in an Apologia, and though he declared his obedience to the Church, he was imprisoned at Vincennes in France. Quickly released through the intervention of Lorenzo de' ⇨ Medici and others, he returned to Florence and there composed (1489) the *Heptaplus*, a mystical inter pretation of the Genesis account of the Creation, and *De ente et uno* (1492), an attempt to reconcile Platonism and Aristotelianism. His last work was an attack on astrological superstition, *Disputationes adversus astrologos* (publ. 1496; ed. E. Garin, 1946–52), which he planned as part of a general apologia of Christianity. He was attracted in his last years by the reforming zeal of ⇨ Savonarola. His death may have been due to poisoning. [DGR]

*De hominis dignitate, Heptaplus, De Ente et Uno, scritti vari*, ed. E. Garin (1942); Garin, *PLQ*; *G.P.M. His Life by his Nephew* (*and Various Works*), tr. Sir Thomas More, ed. J. M. Rigg (1890); *A Platonic Discourse upon Love*, ed. E. G. Gardner (1914); E. Garin, *G.P. della M., Vita e dottrina* (Florence, 1937); *Minori*, i.

**Piferrer, Pablo** (Barcelona 1818–Barcelona 1848). Spanish poet, guitarist, music and art critic. He worked for a Catalan revival, and is remembered for 7 highly musical poems and for his contribution to *Recuerdos y bellezas de España* (1839–43), a picturesque account of the monuments of the Balearics and Catalonia. [JMC]

Blecua, *FLE*.
R. Carnicer, *Vida y obra de P.P.* (Madrid, 1963).

**Pil'nyak, Boris,** pseud. of Boris Andreyevich Vogau (Mozhaysk 1894– ? 1938). Russian novelist. Of mixed Volga German and Jewish descent, he had his first stories published in 1915. Some of them were later incorporated into the book that brought him fame, *Golyy god* (1922; tr. A. Brown, *The Naked Year*, 1928), an attempt to match the upheaval of the Civil War by disjointed narrative and a deliberate confusion of styles. He saw the Revolution as an elemental explosion, often symbolized in his works by a snow-storm, and as the triumph of peasant Russia over the artificial and alien civilization which he associated with Peter the Great and his capital (see *Sankt-Piter-Burkh*, 1921). These views were not popular with Soviet critics and two further stories, *Povest' o nepogashennoy lune* (1926) and *Krasnoye derevo* (1929; condensed tr., M. Hayward, *Mahogany* in *PR*, 1961, nos 3–4), brought him into disgrace. In an attempt to regain favour he rewrote *Krasnoye derevo* as a novel of the first Five-Year Plan, *Volga vpadayet v Kaspiyskoye more* (1930; tr. C. Malamuth, *The Volga Falls into the Caspian Sea*, 1932), but here too his sympathies lie with the old rather than the new world. With *O-Key* (1932), an attack on the American way of life, he again tried to regain favour, but unsuccessfully; he disappeared in the purges. His books have not yet been republished in the Soviet Union.

He was influenced by ⇨ Bely and ⇨ Remizov, but his ideas are largely his own. His best work belongs to the early and middle 1920s. He also travelled widely in Europe, Asia and America and left some interesting travel-notes on Japan and China: *Korni yaponskogo solntsa* (1927) and *Kitayskiy dnevnik* (1927). His early work exerted great influence on young Soviet writers, among them the Serapion brothers, in the 1920s. [RDBT]

*Sobraniye sochineniy* (8 vols., 1930).
*B.P. stat'i i materialy*, ed. V. Gofman, G. Gorbachov and N. Kovarsky (Leningrad, 1928); *SEER* 41 (1963).

**Pindemonte, Ippolito** (Verona 1753–Verona 1828). Italian poet. Known chiefly for his translation of the *Odyssey* (begun 1805, published 1822) and for ⇨ Foscolo's dedication to him in 1807 of the famous *I sepolcri*. He wrote Arcadian verse (*Le stanze*, 1779; *La Fata Morgana*, 1784), tragedies (*Ulisse*, 1777; *Arminio*, 1804), a satirical-autobiographical novel, *Abaritte* (1790), and some moralizing works (*Epistole*, 1800; *Sermoni*, 1819) – all less important for their intrinsic literary merit than as documents of Italian pre-romanticism. The influence of his long travels abroad and of his association with Alfieri and Foscolo can be seen in his melancholy sensitivity towards nature (*Poesie campestri*, 1788) and in his awareness of the social function of art (cf. his own reply to Foscolo's dedication – also entitled *I sepolcri*, 1808). [RHC]

*Le epistole, i sermoni, le prose e le poesie campestri* (2nd edn, 1893); *Poesie*, ed. A. Torri (1858); *L'Odissea*, ed. M. Valgimigli (1948); Dionisotti, *OBIV*.
B. Maier, *Lirici del '700* (Milan, Naples, 1959); O. Bassi, *Fra classicismo e romanticismo. I.P.* (Rome, 1934); W. Binni, *Preromanticismo italiano* (Naples, 1945); N. Bosco-Guillet, *Il P. attraverso il carteggio di Verona* (Turin, 1955); *Minori*, iii.

**Pinillos, Manuel** (Saragossa 1914– ). Spanish poet. Studied law at the University of Saragossa. An ex-civil-servant, he is a very prolific writer. At first influenced by the various post-Civil-War poetic 'fashions'

– the cult of memories, religious preoccupations, social awareness, etc. – in his sixth book, *La muerte o la vida* (1958), he showed the deep humanity and range of his poetic thought, together with a rare independence of style, which prompted one of his critics to compare his poetry to ⇨ Hölderlin's. From this book onwards, alternating free verse with more rigid – never too rigid – poetic forms, of at times Rilkean undertones, he has continued writing in a very personal way, deeply preoccupied with the metaphysical realities of the world he lives in, having achieved in his last books a serene and difficult intimacy, which, paradoxically, allows him to look at things in an almost detached manner. Perhaps his greatest merit lies in his refusal to follow current poetic trends in Spain, his weakness in a certain formal carelessness, due surely to his prolific production. [JMA]

*A la puerta del hombre* (1948); *Sentado sobre el suelo* (1951); *Demasiados ángeles* (1951); *Tierra de nadie* (1952); *De hombre a hombre* (1952); *La muerte o la vida* (1955); *El octavo día* (1958); *Débil tronco querido* (1959); *Debajo del cielo* (1960); *En corral ajeno* (1962); *Aún queda sol en los veranos* (1962); *Esperar no es un sueño* (1962); *Nada es del todo* (1963); *Atardece sin mí* (1964); *Lugar de origen* (1965).

**Pinski, David** (Mohilev 1872–Israel 1960). Yiddish playwright and novelist. Lived in Switzerland and Germany. Settled in America in 1899 but emigrated to Israel in 1950. His stories reflect the socialist ideas he embraced early on and to which he devoted most of his public activities. But in later years he turned to Jewish folklore and legends for his source material. He wrote several novels, the last being *Der Zurissener Mensch*, dealing with American Jewish life during the Second World War. His plays include: *Isaac Sheftel* (1899); *Di Muter* (1901); *Familie Ts'vi* (1905); *Der Oitzer*, tr. L. Lewisohn, *The Treasure* (1905). His volume of essays on Yiddish drama, *Dos Yiddishe Drama*, was published in 1909. [EE]

*In Yisroël*, ed. J. Leftwich (London, 1960).
Waxman, *HJL*.

**Pinto, Frei Heitor** (Covilhã? *c.*1528– ? *c.*1584, in exile). Portuguese theologian and humanist. Pinto became a monk of the Hieronymite order in 1543 and, gradually increasing in erudition, was transferred to Coimbra where in 1551 he assumed the chair of Scripture. By 1572 he had been made Provincial of his order. For opposing the Dual Monarchy and Spanish domination he was in 1583 exiled to Castile and that is the last we know of him. Though he was in 1570 rejected for the chair of Scripture in Salamanca, he was widely recognized as a considerable theologian and Biblical commentator and published commentaries in Latin on the prophecies of Isaiah, Ezekiel, Daniel, Nahum and Jeremiah. His great work, however, was the *Imagem da Vida Cristã* (part one, 1563; part two, 1572; ed. M. Alves Correia, 4 vols., 1958) which went through many editions before the turn of the century. Written in a style which on occasion verges on the Baroque, this work in eleven dialogues evinces penetrating theological insight, high literary aptitude and a welter of Humanistic erudition. Pinto, however, was no Erasmist. The fruit of extensive travels in Spain, France and Italy is readily apparent in the *Imagem*, which is further characterized by a clearly recognizable vein of Platonism. [RCW]

J. Carvalho, 'Frei Heitor Pinto e Frei Luis de Leon', in *Estudos sobre a Cultura Portuguesa do Século XVI*, ii (Coimbra, 1948); A. Soares and F. de Campos, *Prosadores Religiosos do Século XVI* (Coimbra, 1950); A. J. Saraiva, *História da Cultura em Portugal*, ii (Lisbon, 1955).

**Pinto Delgado, João** (? –Amsterdam after 1636). Portuguese Jewish poet. He wrote in Spanish a *Poema de la reina Esther* (ed. I. S. Révah, 1954) and *Historia de Rut*, both of some individuality, and a free version in *quintillas* of the Lamentations of Jeremiah, in which the Biblical imagery is heavy with personal feeling. [JMC]

Blecua, *FLE*.
*BHS*, XXXI (1954) and XXXII (1955).

**Piontek, Heinz** (Kreuzburg 1925– ). German poet and critic. His poetry (*Die Furt*, 1952; *Die Rauchfahne*, 1953; *Wassermarken*, 1957; *Mit einer Kranichfeder*, 1962) short stories (*Vor Augen*, 1955), criticism (*Buchstab, Zauberstab*, 1959), and a radio play (*Weisser Panther*, 1962) have established his reputation, at first as a nature poet in (inevitably) the manner of ⇨ Lehmann, then as an urban, more recently as a religious poet. He has shown almost too great versatility, easily catching the 'feel' of a style (he has made skilful translations of Keats) and hence many derivative echoes, but generally fulfils his ideal of 'open and transparent' clarity, reflected in the title of his latest collection, *Klartext* (1966). *Die mittleren Jahre* is a novel. [PB]

Bridgwater, *TCGV*; Hamburger and Middleton, *MGP*.
*GLL*, XIII, 1 (1959).

**Piovene, Guido** (Vicenza 1907– ). Italian novelist. In his first four novels (*Lettere di una novizia*, 1942, tr. E. Wilkins, *Confession of a Novice*, 1950; *La Gazzetta Nera*, 1943; *Pietà contro pietà*, 1946; *I falsi redentori*, 1949) he explored, with a rather abstract moralism clearly influenced by his philosophical training, the hidden depravity of 'normal' people, if this adjective can be applied to characters mostly from wealthy aristocratic background with a pious Catholic education. His characters seem to move aimlessly in a sheltered bourgeois world, unable to face the truth about themselves but pretending to express it in ambiguous self-confessions of real or imagined crimes. Piovene censures this world as if it were the only possible one, and therefore his criticism of it lacks vigour and bite. Even his strictures on contemporary society (*La coda di paglia*, 1961, a collection of articles published in Italian weeklies), though just and sensible, seem occasionally motivated by the same sterile pleasure that his characters feel in titillating their conscience. After an interval of fourteen years he wrote another novel, *Le Furie* (1963), a general review of his themes and stock characters, an attempt to exorcise the haunting phantoms of the past in autobiographical form. A writer in the ⇨ Fogazzaro tradition, he uses a slow-moving discursive style, with plenty of flashbacks, digressions, narrations within the narration. He also wrote 2 interesting travel books, *De America* (1953) and *Viaggio in Italia* (1957). [GMC]

*Contemporanei*, ii; Pullini, *RID*.

**Pirandello, Luigi** (Agrigento 1867–Rome 1936). Italian novelist and playwright. After his University studies in Germany, he settled in Rome as a professional man of letters. In 1894 he married beautiful Antonietta Portulano, the daughter of his father's business associate who had her brought up in claustral seclusion according to medieval Sicilian customs, never allowing his prospective son-in-law to talk to her before the marriage ceremony. When their parents' families, on whom they depended for support, were completely ruined by a flood, Antonietta, who had already had a nervous breakdown after the birth of her third son, was physically and mentally shattered by the news, and gradually lapsed into complete and dangerous insanity. Only when her presence in the family constituted a real threat to their daughter's safety did Pirandello agree to have his wife committed to an asylum, in 1918, when he had already written most of his narrative works in an effort to supplement his meagre teacher's income and support his family. Already by nature inclined to introspection and philosophizing, his personal tragedy provided him with most of his narrative and dramatic themes: the relativity of truth (*La Signora Frola e il Signor Ponza suo genero*, written in short-story form in 1915, later dramatized with the title *Così è se vi pare* and first produced in 1917; tr. A. Livingston, *Right you are* (*if you think so*), 1929); the tragicomic absurdity of human life (*La Patente*, 1911–19; *Caffè notturno – L'uomo dal fiore in bocca*, 1918–23; *Il giuoco delle parti*, 1918; tr. R. Rietty, *The Rules of the Game*, 1959); the uncertain boundaries between sanity and insanity (*Enrico IV*, 1922; tr. A. Livingston, 1929); the unbridgeable chasm of incomprehension between individuals (*Sei personaggi in cerca d'autore*, 1921; tr. A Livingston, *Six Characters in Search of an author*, 1929, tr. F. May, 1954). It is significant that out of 43 plays by Pirandello produced between 1910 and 1937, at least 28 are adaptations or straightforward dramatizations of earlier short stories written mostly between 1900 and 1918, that is, the most difficult period of the author's life. One can understand what he meant when he described (*La tragedia d'un personaggio*, 1911; *Colloqui coi personaggi*, 1915) how he was haunted, obsessed, persecuted by his dreams, who demanded to be fully realized as characters in a work of art: 'Born alive they wanted to live ...'. *Sei personaggi* is a transparent parable of the reasons why he had to give dramatic form to his fictional plots. His passionate insistence on his favourite themes had led some critics to look for a Pirandellian philosophy of life, and then judge his plays by its supposed shortcomings. But, in spite of his early claim that he was a writer of a philosophical nature, he was never a systematic philosopher, as he himself affirmed in 1935. He began his career as a southern realist, but his shrewd and psychologically penetrating study of the foibles, idiosyncracies, petty emotions and tragic passions of common men soon brought him to discover the impact of the 'unreal' on human life; the human personality split between two equally possible views of reality; the loss of personal identity, eroded by the passing of time, which makes fictional characters more real than live human beings; the relativity of human beliefs. Such a conception of life, based on contradiction, can hardly be expressed systematically: the philosophy of the all-pervading absurd must also be absurd. Pirandello's dialectic exercises must not be seen as an attempt to give formal dignity to his *Weltanschauung*, but rather as an attempt to translate into articulate words the inarticulate cries of the human mind tortured by pain and sorrow; to hint at the basic insecurity of the changeable human condition from which man tries to find refuge in abstract and therefore immutably fixed patterns of thought. Because he was an artist and not a philosopher, he soon realized that the many-sidedness of human reality could be described more effectively by moving from the single level of narrative prose, which needs only a reader to be realized, to the double level of dramatic action, which needs both actors and audience, and is naturally an apt medium to underline the ambiguity of the relationship between actors and characters, fact and fiction, form and substance. Then, in order to multiply the fragmentation of the levels of reality, he proceeded to destroy the dramatic conventions he had inherited and accepted in his early plays and to adopt new ones: the play within the play (*Sei personaggi*), the play outside the play (*Ciascuno a suo modo*), the scripted improvisation (*Questa sera si recita soggetto*). Thus he transferred the dissociation of reality from the plane of contents to that of form, achieving a nearly perfect unity between dramatic structure and ideas. He was undoubtedly one of the best interpreters of the crisis of middle-class values in the period between the two world wars, and his impact on the theatre was perhaps greater than his real artistic importance, although far from negligible, could justify. He was awarded the Nobel Prize for literature in 1934. [GMC]

*Novelle per un anno* (2 vols., 1956–7); *Tutti i romanzi* (1959); *Maschere nude* (2 vols., 1958); *Saggi, poesie e scritti vari* (1950) (with a complete bibliography); *The Late Mattia Pascal*, tr. A. Livingston (1923); *The Outcast*, tr. Leo. Ongley (1925); *The Old and the Young*, tr. C. K. Scott Moncrieff (1930); *Better Think Twice about It, and Twelve Other Stories*, A. and H. Mayne (1940); *Three Plays* (*Six Characters, Henry IV, Right You are!* (*If You Think So*)), tr. F. May and H. Reed (1929); *Each in his Own Way and Two Other Plays* (*The Pleasure of Honesty, Naked*), tr. A. Livingston (1924); *One-Act Plays*, tr. E. Abbott, A. Livingston, Blanche V. Mitchell (N.Y., 1928); *A Dream of Christmas, The Man with a Flower in his Mouth*, tr. F. May (1959); *Three Plays* (*The Rules of the Game, The Life I Gave You, Lazarus*), tr. F. May and R. Rietty (1959); *Short Stories*, tr. F. May (1965).

G. Giudice, *L.P.* (Turin, 1963); W. Starkie, *L.P.* (3rd edn 1965); Lander McClintock, *The Age of P.* (Indiana Univ., 1951); O. Büdel, *P.* (1966).

**Piron, Alexis** (Dijon 1689–Paris 1773). French dramatist and poet. He served his apprenticeship as a purveyor of farces and comic-operas to the Paris fairground theatres, and enjoyed a modest success with more ambitious tragedies (*Gustave Wasa*, 1733) and comedies (1728–34). His major work, however, is *La métromanie* (1738), one of the liveliest of 18th-century French comedies. Within the framework of an amusingly improbable plot, this satirizes the contemporary craze for versifying, and offers some vivid character-portrayals. He was also a witty writer of epigrams and light verse. [WHB]

*Œuvres complètes* (10 vols., 1928–31).

P. Chaponnière, *P., sa vie et ses œuvres* (Paris/Geneva, 1910).

**Pisarev, Dmitry Ivanovich** (Znamenskoye, prov. Orel 1840–Dubbeln, Riga 1868). Russian critic. He graduated at St Petersburg (1861), wrote philosophico-scientific and historical articles for *Russkoye Slovo*, and was arrested for a revolutionary article seized in a police-swoop on a secret press in 1862. While in prison he wrote famous pieces on the Realists, Auguste Comte, Pushkin and Belinsky. After his release (1866) he wrote further radical articles on the social order and the need for utilitarian reform. He was influenced by Chernyshevsky and Herzen, and had read Saint Simon, Owen and other European socialists.

His doctrines led him to underrate Pushkin as a 'mere' stylist.

*Sochineniya* (4 vols., 1955–6); *Selected Philosophical, Social and Political Essays*, tr. J. Fineberg (Moscow, 1958).

A. Coquart, *D.P. et l'idéologie du nihilisme russe* (Paris, 1946); René Wellek, *Continuity and Change in Russian Thought*, ed. E. J. Simmons (1955); H. Gifford, *The Hero of His Time* (1950); F. Venturi, *Roots of Revolution* (1960).

**Pisemsky, Aleksey** (prov. Kostroma 1820–Moscow 1881). Russian novelist and dramatist. Of poor noble family, he returned to his native province as a Civil Servant after graduating from Moscow; later in Petersburg he remained a gentleman muzhik, anti-radical, even reactionary. Several powerfully sardonic novels (with rough style, harsh characterization, but skilful construction), culminated in his masterpiece *Tysyacha dush* (1858; tr. I. Litvinov, *A Thousand Souls*, N.Y., 1959), a realistic picture of pre-reform Russia. His interest in plot made *Vzbalamuchennoye more* (1863) into a 'scandalous' thriller, with rich villains, courtesans, etc., and a satirical picture of young radicals. Outstanding among his plays is *Gor'kaya Sud'bina* (1859; tr. A. Kogan and G. R. Noyes, *A Bitter Fate*, in *Masterpieces of the Russian Drama*, ed. G. R. Noyes, 1960), a triangular tragedy of serf, wife and master. His sceptical independence caused him to be unduly criticized and underrated.

*Polnoye sobraniye sochineniy*, ed. B. B. Zelinsky (1910–11); *Sobraniye sochineniy*, ed. A. P. Mogilyansky (9 vols., 1953).

Mirsky, *HRL*; Slonim, *MRL*.

**Pistoia, Cino da** (Pistoia *c.*1270–Pistoia 1336). Italian poet. A famous jurist, he taught law in several universities. Like Dante, he set great hopes on the arrival in Italy of the Emperor Henry VII. He supported the imperial cause in his juridical writings and lamented the Emperor's death in a famous *canzone*. Though praised by Dante and Petrarch, his voluminous *Canzoniere* now seems curiously uneven. On the one hand there is mechanical imitation of the ⇨ *stil novo*, the already formalized modes becoming stiff and leaden; on the other hand, other lyrics are much freer and more personal. His laments for the absent beloved, his exile's longing for his native city, his portrayal of lonely suffering, often have a personal urgency which foreshadows the *Canzoniere* of Petrarch. [DGR]

*Le rime*, ed. G. Zaccagnini (Geneva, 1925); Benedetto, *RDSN*; Contini, *PD*; Lind, *LPIR*.

G. Zaccagnini, *C. da P. Studio biografico* (Pistoia, 1918); Rossetti, *DC*; *Minori*, i.

**Pixerécourt, Guilbert de** (Nancy 1773–Nancy 1844). French dramatist. Prolific author of comedies, vaudevilles, and above all melodramas, notably *Victor ou l'enfant de la forêt* (1798), *Coelina ou l'enfant du mystère* (1801; tr. J. Wallace, *Coelina or a Tale of Mystery*), *Valentine ou la séduction* (1821). He exploited popular taste for Gothic settings – castles, ruins, brigands, ghosts, vampires – but regularly rewarded virtue and punished vice. He influenced Hugo and Romantic drama.

*Théâtre choisi* (4 vols., 1841–3).

W. G. Hartog, *G. de P.* (Paris/Bruges, 1912); J. Marsan, *Le mélodrame de P.* (Paris, 1926); Descotes, *PT*.

**Platen, August, Graf von P. Hallermund (Hallermünde)** (Ansbach 1796 – Syracuse 1835). German poet and dramatist. His Aristophanic comedies satirize contemporary melodramas of fate (*Die verhängnisvolle Gabel*, 1826; *Der romantische Oedipus*, 1829). His poetry self-consciously aims at smooth perfection of form, using classical models (*Sonette aus Venedig*, 1825) or the Persian *ghazal*. His diaries (ed. Laubmann/Scheffler, 1896–9) and letters (ed. Scheffler/Bornstein, 1911–31) reveal inner torments and liberal political ideas.

*Werke*, ed. G. A. Wolff, V. Schweizer (2 vols; Leipzig, 1895).

R. Schlosser, *A. v. P.* (2 vols., 1910–13); H. Renck, *P.'s Politisches Denken und Dichten* (Breslau, 1910); K. Steigelmann, *P.'s Ästhetik;* Mann, *ETD*.

**Platonov, Andrey,** pseud. of Klimentov (Voronezh 1899–Moscow 1951). Soviet prose writer. After a volume (1922) of weak verse, he published short stories; two novels have not yet appeared in U.S.S.R. He lived by journalism. Of working-class origin, he took outwardly simple people as heroes, treating their inner lives with unmatched subtlety. A fine stylist, he was criticized in his lifetime, but influential on a new generation of Soviet writers.

*Izbrannoye* (Moscow, 1966); *The Fierce and Beautiful World* (tr. J. Barnes, 1971).

*Tvorchestvo A.P.*, ed. A. M. Abramov etc. (Voronezh, 1970).

**Pléiade, La.** The name given to seven 16th-century French poets grouped around Ronsard. (The name, an allusion to the constellation of the Pléiades, was originally given to seven Greek tragic poets writing in the reign of Ptolemy II.) Ronsard's 'brigade' consisted of Ronsard himself, ⇨ du Bellay, Pontus de Tyard, ⇨ Baïf, ⇨ Jodelle, ⇨ Belleau and Peletier, although the name of Dorat, their humanist teacher, was sometimes substituted for that of Peletier. The first spokesman of the school was du Bellay with his *Défense et illustration de la langue française* (1549), which aimed at restoring the dignity of the French language which humanists had neglected in favour of Greek and Latin. All languages were fundamentally equal and French was capable of dealing with the most serious themes, although it needed to be enriched by borrowings from Greek or Latin, the adoption of archaic, technical and dialect words, and a freer syntax. This new literary instrument was to be used to endow France with masterpieces imitated (but not translated) from Classical or Italian models: the native medieval tradition was rejected in favour of a learned, cultured art of high seriousness. The poet must not rely on natural facility, but must toil and study the rules of his art. Ronsard, in his *Abrégé de l'art poétique français* (1565) and elsewhere, laid down rules of versification (caesura, enjambement, masculine and feminine rhymes, hiatus), the best of which Malherbe was to adopt himself. Above all the Pléiade was responsible for the restoration of the alexandrine. The weakness of the Pléiade was its overly learned style and its excessive imitation of the classics, but it is noteworthy that both Ronsard and du Bellay gradually progressed towards a simpler, more personal style as they matured. [FWAG]

H. Chamard, *Histoire de la Pléiade* (4 vols., Paris, 1939–40).

**Plievier, Theodor** (Berlin 1892–Avegno/Lugano 1955). German writer of journalistic, Socialistic novels. Of working-class origins, he was a wanderer and a sailor. He lived in the U.S.S.R. 1933–45, and in 1947 he left Weimar (and an official post) for West Germany, then Switzerland. His tendentious early novels (*Des Kaisers Kulis*, 1929, about a sailors' revolt in 1919; *Der Kaiser ging, die Generäle blieben*, 1932; etc.) were once as sensationally successful as the violently 'documentary' account of the Russian campaign *Stalingrad* (1946; tr. H. L. Robinson, 1959) and sequels *Moskau* (1952; tr. S. Hood, 1953) and – with a change of heart about the Red Army – *Berlin* (1954; tr. L. Hagen and V. Milroy, 1956; reissued as *Rape of a City*, 1962). [PB]

H. Wilde, *T.P.* (Munich, 1965).

**Pogodin, Nikolay Fyodorovich,** pseud. of N. F. Stukalov (Don Province 1900–Moscow 1962). Soviet dramatist. Of peasant family, he spent a wandering childhood with his mother, who travelled from one Cossack village to another taking in sewing. Before turning to literature and journalism, he worked as a bookbinder and carpenter. He began to write for the stage during the thirties (the 'period of reconstruction') and this influenced the content of his plays, which were among the first to get away from the over-simplified revolutionary situation of 'us' (the good communists) versus 'them' (White Guards, saboteurs and kulaks) and to show the workman simply getting on with his job, adapting himself to and rising above the enormous difficulties of rebuilding his country's economy. His settings are the factory (*Poema o topore*, 1931; *Ten'*, 1931; *Moy drug*, 1933), the collective farm (*Posle bala* ,1934), a scientific expedition (*Sneg*, 1933), even a forced labour camp (*Aristokraty*, 1935; staged by 'Unity', London, 1937). He became a Soviet classic with his historical trilogy *Chelovek s ruzh'yom* (1937). *Kremlevskiye Kuranty* (1940; tr. A. Shrett, *Kremlin Chimes*, in *Three Soviet Plays*, Moscow, n.d.) and *Tret'yaya pateticheskaya* (1958), which represents the most successful attempt to date to put Lenin on the stage. His post-1954 work is distinguished by a tolerant attitude to the problems of youth and a vigorous 'humanism' (a Soviet word for interest in the individual). His plays have the rare virtue of depicting the good characters as genuinely more interesting and attractive than the bad. During his last years, he was editor of the periodical *Teatr*, which he made most forward-looking and unashamedly cultured. [AP]

*Sobraniye dramaticheskikh proizvedeniy* (5 vols., 1960–1); *Ocherki raznykh lyet* (1964).

N. Zaytsev, *N.P.* (Leningrad-Moscow, 1958); *Novyy Mir*, 12 (1960); E. D. Uvarva, *N.P.* (Moscow, 1959); N. Zaytsev, *Trilogiya N.P. o V. I. Lenine* (Leningrad, 1960); V. Baborykin, *Trilogiya* etc. (Moscow, 1962); Vl. Diyev, *Trilogiya* etc. (Moscow, 1965) Ya. Yargunovsky, *Teatr N.P.* (Saratov, 1964); F. M. Bykova, *Dram. trilogiya N.P. o Lenine* (Moscow, 1960).

**Polish Medieval Literature.** Poland was converted to Christianity in the second half of the 10th century, and this linked her early literature with the common Latin heritage of Europe. In comparison with the West, extant written records are fewer and later, especially in the vernacular. Prose is represented by sermons (e.g. *Kazania świętokrzyskie*, 14th century or earlier), psalms (e.g. *Psałterz floriański*, 14th century) and apocrypha (*Rozmyślanie przemyskie*, 15th century); poetry establishes itself as a continuous tradition during the 15th century.

There are isolated exceptions, like the song addressed to the Mother of God (*Bogurodzica*), undoubtedly the earliest Polish poem. It may have been composed towards the end of the 13th century, long before the foundation of Cracow University (1364), but its complex rhyme-scheme and abstract vocabulary suggest nothing primitive. *Bogurodzica* is a terse litany-like invocation, to which inferior stanzas were later added, emphasizing by contrast the sophisticated form of the older text.

A similar sophistication characterizes the representative Polish *planctus*, known as 'Lament of Our Lady under the Cross' (*Żale Matki Boskiej pod Krzyżem*, *c*.1450), which again displays a varied metrical pattern. Dramatic in the direct presentation of emotions, it could well be a fragment of an extinct mystery play for Good Friday. This lament is comparable in literary importance to *Quia amore langueo* in Middle English.

Other outstanding 15th-century poems are the dialogue between Master Polikarp and Death (*Rozmowa Mistrza Polikarpa ze Śmiercią*) and the Dying Man's lament (*Skarga umierającego*), the first evocative in its satirical detail, the second a moving penitential poem still echoing in folklore. A rhymed tract on table manners (written by a certain Słota) offers a contrast, both in vocabulary and in didactic tone, to the predominantly religious subjects in early Polish verse. These subjects, however, can be related to the main themes of medieval literature: to the songs of the Cross, the laments of the Virgin Mary, the carols, or the legends of saints (e.g. that of Saint Alexis in Polish).

Gaps, too, seem to indicate the trend within the national tradition. There is no medieval epic in Polish, no allegory of courtly love; religious verse seems to have led naturally to the supremacy of lyrical forms. Medieval themes were kept alive both by the Catholic Church which withstood the challenge of the Reformation, and by the continuity of folklore in a vigorously rural society. Rather as in Spain, the baroque style was to become a national style, because it took over and transformed the medieval heritage.

Even the 16th-century writers, though conscious of the new age, preferred to rely on the well-tested formulas of medieval literature. The best mystery play, 'The Story of Our Lord's Glorious Resurrection' (*Historia o chwalebnym Zmartwychwstaniu Pańskim*, *c*.1570, by Mikołaj z Wilkowiecka) survives as a seeming anachronism from the humanist era, but its vitality became evident when it was recently revived on the stage. ⇨ Rej, an ardent Protestant, remained a medieval moralist who felt at ease in versified debate, ⇨ Klonowic needed allegorical props in describing contemporary life, and even ⇨ Kochanowski, a humanist poet educated in Italy, used the medieval dream-vision in his most personal cycle of poems. This endurance of form helped to give literature a sense of national identity at a time when the Polish language was extending its influence in the united Polish-Lithuanian state.

Latin, too, had a paradoxically revitalizing effect. At first it was the only medium of expression. Chronicles were written in it, beginning with the work of Gallus the Anonymous in the 12th century, then hymns, tracts and elegies (e.g. Ianicius, 1516–43, a peasant's son). At the height of the Renaissance the great writers who altered poetic diction in the vernacular also produced remarkable poetry in Latin. Both Kochanowski and ⇨ Simonides found this bilingual practice an artistic stimulus and not a handicap. The growth of Polish as a literary medium in such close partnership with Latin seems to have given its users self-confidence rather than a sense of inferiority. It accounts partly for the many masterpieces created outside the strictly ethnic boundaries, and also for the universality of themes in 19th-century writing when Poland was no longer an independent state. [JP]

Peterkiewicz and Singer, *FCPP*.
*SEER*, XLI, 96 (1962); *Cambridge History of Poland*.

**Poliziano, Angelo** (Montepulciano 1454–Florence 1494). Italian poet. His real name was Ambrogini, but he became known as Poliziano from the Latin name of his birthplace (Mons Politianus). As a poor student in Florence his scholarly precocity made him a protégé of Lorenzo de' ⇨ Medici; for some time he was tutor in the Medici household, where he composed odes in Latin, epigrams in both Latin and Greek, the *Stanze per la Giostra* and his Italian lyrics. After 1480 he was professor of Greek and Latin in Florence, famous for his erudition.

With ⇨ Pontano the foremost Latinist of his time, he excelled also as a vernacular poet, rivalled only by Lorenzo de' Medici and ⇨ Boiardo. And although he wrote much less Italian verse than either of the other two, his quality may well be judged superior. His major work, the unfinished *Stanze per la Giostra* (ed. V. Pernicone, 1954), was begun to celebrate the victory in a tournament in 1475 of Lorenzo's brother Giuliano de' Medici, who was killed in the Pazzi conspiracy three years later. But the heroic theme is never broached, and the magnificent fragment which remains offers a fragile vision of love, beauty and youth seen under the shadow of death and conveyed with Botticellian poignancy. The *ottava rima* here acquires a suppleness and a descriptive delicacy learnt from the Latins. The same polish and lightness of touch distinguish his lyrics when he takes over popular forms and themes and gives them shimmering, palpitating life, as in the graceful, hedonistic *canzoni a ballo*. His *Orfeo*,a short court entertainment written for a Gonzaga celebration at Mantu in 1480, confirms the poetic gifts of Politian and gives him also some significance in the history of drama, since this version of the story of Orpheus is the first treatment of a non-religious subject in the traditional form of the *sacra rappresentazione*. [DGR]

*Le Stanze, l'Orfeo e le Rime*, ed. A. Momigliano (1945); *Rime*, ed. N. Sapegno (1967); Lind, *LPIR*; Kay, *PBIV*.

Arnaldi, *PLQ*; L. Malagoli, *Le Stanze e l'Orfeo e lo spirito del Quattrocento* (Rome, 1941); R. Lo Cascio, *Lettura del P.* (Palermo, 1954); F. de Sanctis, *Storia della letteratura italiana* (Bari, 1954); Binni, *CI*.

**Polo, Gaspar Gil** (Valencia *c.*1530–Barcelona 1585). Spanish writer. Lawyer and civil servant, he is remembered for his *Diana enamorada* (1564; ed. Ferreres, CC), an unfinished sequel to ⇨ Montemayor's *Diana*, in pleasing prose and embellished with charming and metrically adventurous poems; it was widely translated – into English by Bartholomew Young (1598, but the manuscript was known earlier, perhaps to Shakespeare for *Two Gentlemen of Verona*). [JMC]

Blecua, *FLE*; Trend, *OBSV*; Terry, *ASP*.

**Polo, Marco** (Venice 1254–Venice 1324?). Italian explorer of China and the Far East in the time of Kubla Khan. Returned from 25 years of travel, he was captured by the Genoese at the sea-battle of Curzola (1298), and while in prison the story of his journeys was taken down by Rustichello da Pisa. This version (probably in French) was the basis of his book which came to be best known as *Il Milione* (ed. L. F. Benedetto, 1928; tr. R. Latham, Penguin Classics). Despite its often exotic subject-matter, the main impression which it leaves is of direct, unadorned observation simply, even baldly recorded. [DGR]

*Minori*, i.

**Polo de Medina, Salvador Jacinto** (Murcia 1603–Alcantarilla 1676). Spanish poet, priest and moralist. His miscellany, *Academias del jardín* (1630), contains delicate poems of trees, flowers and moths. He is a light-weight Gongorist, who imitated ⇨ Quevedo's *Sueños*, and wrote comic fables and a treatise on prudence. [JMC]

*Obras escogidas*, ed. J. M. de Cossío (1931); Blecua, *FLE*; Cohen, *PBSV*; Trend, *OBSV*.

**Polotsky, Simeon.** ⇨ Russian Literature in the 17th Century.

**Pondal, Eduardo** (Ponte-Ceso, nr. Corunna 1835–nr. Corunna 1917). Leading poet in the Galician revival. He anticipated Rosalía de ⇨ Castro in the use of traditional measures, and wrote a melancholy poetry, pantheistic, and tragic in its pessimism. He identified himself with what he believed was the Celtic past of his native province, and endowed it with gods and bards. His style was restrained and his affinities rather with Camões' *Babel e Sião* than with anything in the Spanish tradition. ⇨⇨ Galician Literature. [JMC]

*Poesías*, ed. Academia Gallega (1935); Blecua, *FLE*; A. F. Bell, *Spanish Galicia* (1922) (translations); R. M. Anderson, *Gallegan Provinces of Spain* (N.Y., 1939) (translations).

J. L. Varela, *Estudios dedicados a Menéndez Pidal*, vi (Madrid, 1956); Cossío, *CAPE*.

**Ponge, Francis** (Montpellier 1899– ). French poet and essayist. After working for the *NRF*, he has been employed in a publishing firm and as a teacher at the Alliance Française. He was a militant communist from 1936 to 1946. A controversial poetic figure, he reacts against emotional and symbolic modes, and would limit poetry to a phenomenological discovery of insular objects. His aim is to express their differential qualities, thus synthesizing lyrical poetry and encyclopedias. He achieves this on a small scale through allegories, analogies, images and puns directed at their several facets and associations in dream and reality. He writes carefully chiselled prose poems, where thought and the creation of suitable rhetorical forms for each object appear to renew the value of words, the 'main secretion of Man'. His main works are *Le parti-pris des choses* (1942), *L'œillet, La guêpe, Le mimosa* (1946), *Proèmes* (1948) and *La rage de l'expression* (1952). Several minor works of interest have been collected in *Le grand recueil* (3 vols., 1961). [CLC]

J. P. Sartre, *L'homme et les choses* in *Situations I* (Paris, 1947); P. Sollers, *F.P.* (Paris, 1963).

**Pons, Josep S.** ⇨ Catalan Literature.

**Pontano, Giovanni** or **Gioviano** (Cerreto, Umbria 1429–Naples 1503). Italian Latinist. He spent his adult life in the service o the Aragonese rulers of Naples. When Ferdinand II was driven out, he transferred his allegiance to Charles VIII, and so when Ferdinand returned (1495) he lost his office.

Rivalled only by ⇨ Poliziano as a writer of Latin, he covered a wide variety of subjects. His prose includes works on astrology (*De rebus coelestibus*), philosophy (*De prudentia, De fortuna*, etc.), politics (*De principe liber*), an account of the war (1459–64) between Ferdinand I of Aragon and the Angevins (*De bello neapolitano*) and a series of at times lively dialogues (*Antonius, Asinus, Actius, Aegidius, Charon*). His verse too has a wide range – from *Urania* (hexameters on astrology) and *Lepidina* (a mythological account of the marriage of the god Sebeto to the nymph Parthenope), to personal lyrics and elegies. The *Parthenopei sive Amorum libri* combine with the traditional themes of the Latin love lyric an idyllic feeling for Nature, and the *Hendecasyllaborum seu Baiarum Libri* reflect the voluptuous atmosphere of Baia. His most attractive poems, however, are often those expressing the more intimate joys and sorrows of family life, as in *De amore coniugali* (including 12 famous lullabies), *Versus iambici* (on the death of his son Lucio), or the melancholy tomb-poetry and tender reminiscences of the *Tumuli*. [DGR]

*De Sermone*, ed. S. Lupi, A. Risicato (1954); *Carmina*, ed. J. Oeschger (1948); *I Dialoghi*, ed. C. Previtera (1943); Arnaldi, *PLQ*; Garin, *PLQ*.

A. Altamura, *G.P.* (Naples, 1938); Sparrow, *LVHR*; *Minori*, i.

**Pontoppidan, Henrik** (Fredericia 1857–Ordrup 1943). Danish novelist. The son of a Lutheran clergyman he broke off his engineering studies just before taking his degree in order to become a writer. After a vain attempt at practising a kind of Tolstoyan philosophy by living the life of a peasant in the country and marrying a peasant girl (the marriage was dissolved after some years), he soon established himself as one of the leading prose writers of Denmark. Among his many short novels and collections of short stories published between 1881 and 1907 the earliest have an undertone of strong social indignation, while others reflect his political radicalism (at times more akin to anarchism) and his pronounced anti-clericalism. His irony is directed against the worship of lyrical-romantic emotions, against the neo-Rousseauistic cult of Nature, and against the contemporary imitation of the Renaissance man. Only a small selection has been translated, e.g. *Mimoser* (1886; tr. G. Nielsen, *The Apothecary's Daughters*, 1890).

The first of his great novel cycles, *Det forjættede Land* (1891–5; tr. E. Lucas, *Emanuel, or Children of the Soil*, 1896; *The Promised Land*, 1896; *Dommens Dag* (1895) remains untranslated), deals with the heroic attempt and failure of a Tolstoyan clergyman to realize his ideals. Pontoppidan's main work, *Lykke-Per* (8 vols., 1898–1904), reflects his own experiences still more clearly in its account of the inhibiting effects of a Protestant background and upbringing. With *De Dødes Rige* (5 vols., 1912–16), these are perhaps the greatest novels in the Danish language, inspired by the author's profound pessimism about his compatriots, which reached its climax in his last, and most pessimistic novel, *Mands Himmerig* (1927). He wrote his *Memoirs* (4 vols.,

1933–40). In 1917 he shared the Nobel Prize with ⇨ Gjellerup. [ELB]

P. C. Andersen, *H.P.: En Biografi og Bibliografi* (1934).
C. M. Woel, *H.P.* (2 vols., Copenhagen, 1945); K. Ahnlund, *H.P.* (Stockholm, 1956); E. L. Bredsdorff, *H.P. og Georg Brandes*, i, ii (Copenhagen, 1964).

**Poot, Hubert Korneliszoon** (Abtswoude 1689–Delft 1733). Dutch poet, son of a farmer. He too readily aspired to the popularity of contemporaries whose talent was grossly inferior to his. Yet for the purity of some of his nature poetry he is justly called the last of the golden-age poets. [PK]

*Gedichten* (3 vols., 1722–35).

**Popa, Vasko** (Grebenac 1922– ). Serbian poet. Influenced by pre-war modernism, especially by ⇨ Nastasijevič, his remarkable poetry is deeply analytical, its text bristling with associations, its language distilled significance. His theme of human tragedy is mingled with a sense for the humorous and the grotesque. His best-known poems are *Belutak* and *Igre*. [EDG]

Lavrin, *AMYP*.
Kadić, *CSL*.

**Popović, Bogdan** (Belgrade 1863–Belgrade 1944). Serbian critic. He introduced the influence of French symbolism into Serbian literature drawing particular attention to the need to develop style and the formalistic side of Serbian literature, at that time much neglected. He founded and edited the literary periodical *Srpski Književni Glasnik*, perhaps the most important Serbian cultural periodical between the two world wars. Among his most important works is his anthology of modern Serbian poetry (1911) and his collection of critical studies *Članci i predavanja* (1932). He also wrote a host of articles on the theory of literature as well as studies of foreign writers. [EDG]

**Popović, Jovan Sterija** (Vršac 1806–Vršac 1856). Serbian poet and dramatist. Beginning with sentimental stories, he later wrote a satire on sentimentalism, *Roman bez romana* (1838). His best work was as a dramatic satirist, the most famous of his satirical plays being *Kir Janje* (1837). His dramas, still performed today, are greatly influenced by Molière. His poetry is extremely pessimistic and in archaic language, since he was an opponent of ⇨ Karadžić. [EDG]

Barac, *HYL*.

**Porcel, José Antonio** (Granada 1730?–?). Spanish poet. Though anxious to belong to the new school of Luzán, Porcel was the last of the Gongorists. He translated Boileau, but in the prologue to his *Adonis* praised 'the incomparable Cordoban'. The poem is in a diluted baroque style that derives indirectly from Góngora, by way of Porcel's fellow inhabitant of Granada, Pedro ⇨ Soto de Rojas. He was the last until Rubén Darío to admire the poet of the *Soledades*, of whom some passages in the *Adonis* are worthy. [JMC]

BAE, 61.
J. M. de Cossío, *Fábulas mitológicas en España* (Madrid, 1952).

**Postoli, F.** ⇨ Albanian Literature.

**Potgieter, Everardus Johannes** (Zwolle 1808–Amsterdam 1875). Dutch poet, essayist and critic. After an unhappy childhood in a middle-class home, an unsettled youth, he developed a romantic habit of identifying himself with an anonymous nobleman. A visit to Sweden and the influence of romantic poets (⇨ Tegnér) marked the end of his sentimental immaturity (cf. *Nalatenschap van de Landjonker*, 1835 – a title which he uses again in 1874 in his best cycle of poetry). Back in Amsterdam he met Bakhuizen van den Brink, with whom he founded *De Gids* (1837), a review of arts and science giving prominence to literature and theology. His repeated attacks on the flaccid complacency of his day and his plea for a return to the spirit of the Golden Age sharpened his critical perception from which his creative work benefited. *Jan Jannetje en hun jongste kind* (1841) is a good-humoured story satirizing the national spirit and *Het Rijksmuseum te Amsterdam* (1844) is a prose commentary in renaissance style on the national heroes of the 17th century. In poetry too he paid homage to past glories in *Liedekens van Bontekoe* (1840).

In 1848 he resigned from *De Gids* to study French and English literature, returning (1860–5) with Busken ⇨ Huet with whom he attended the tercentenary Dante festival in Italy. The result is *Florence* (1865), 'one continuous stream of praise to beauty which was re-echoed by the poets of the eighties'.

By applying his aesthetic standards to his own writing he raised his considerable talent from the nostalgic imitations of his early years to the melodious and subtle, if sometimes contrived, originality of his last short stories and poems. [PK]

*Werken* (18 vols., 1885–6); Barnouw, *CA*; Weevers, *PNEC*.

**Potocki, Wacław** (Wola Łużańska 1621–Łużna 1696). Polish poet. He is best known for his long epic poem *Transakcyja wojny chocimskiej* (*c.*1670, published 1850). Its subject is the Turkish attack on Poland in 1621, which was successfully repulsed at Hotin on the Dniester river, but the heroic theme apart, there runs throughout the poem a baroque obsession with exotic detail. The Turkish Emperor, Osman II, has all the trappings of the arch-enemy, like the Moor in the Spanish heroic tradition. Potocki led the life of a country squire and was a prolific writer of verse, narrative, religious, polemical and domestic. Much of it has only antiquarian interest, but when his wit glitters it can illuminate the paradox of his own violent times. [JP]

Peterkiewicz and Singer, *FCPP*.

**Poulet, Georges.** ◊ French Literary Criticism in the 19th and 20th Century.

**Povesti.** ◊ Russian Literature in the 17th Centuries.

**Prado, Adrían de** (early 17th cent.). Spanish poet and Jeronimite. His 'Canción real a San Jerónimo en Siria' is a baroque poem which describes an unknown picture of the saint. The language is bold and realistic, and the free verse has a pleasing roughness. The poem appears in the *Cancionero de 1628* (ed. J. M. Blecua, 1945), together with another poem by the same little-known author taken from manuscript. It appears also in Blecua, *FLE*. [JMC]

**Prados, Emilio** (Málaga 1899–Mexico 1962). Spanish poet who remained deeply Andalusian during voluntary exile in Mexico (1937–62). His earliest poetry contains echoes of folk-song varied by imagery drawn from the neo-Baroque. A characteristic theme is that of the *Jardín cerrado* (1946), the enclosed garden. He became a poet of solitude, echoing the mystics though lacking their faith; he felt himself isolated by the prison of the body from both love and reality. Later poems lament a lost country and distant childhood, always more real to him than Mexico. Forgotten but scrupulous to his last collection, *La piedra escrita* (1961). [JMC]

*Antologia 1923–1953* (Buenos Aires, 1954); Blecua, *FLE*; Trend, *OBSV*.
Zardoya, *PEC*.

**Prati, Giovanni** (Campomaggiore, Trento 1814–Rome 1884). Italian poet. A scandal following an early marriage (1834) dogged him all his life. His monarchist principles also led to trouble in Venice and Florence in 1848, after which he settled in Turin and became court-historian. He became senator in 1876. His early work was political and sentimental love-poetry showing the influence of Lamartine and Hugo (*Poesie*, 1835) and he gained wide popularity with the poem *Edmenegarda* (1841), whose essentially romantic view of contemporary bourgeois reality satisfied all but the critics. They attacked the vague musicality and sentimentality of his poetry, and were so hostile towards his 'epics' (e.g. *Rodolfo*, 1853; *Armando*, 1868) that he turned to a more precise, simple form of expression which, with his growing disillusionment, ironically produced what certain critics think his best poetry (*Psiche*, 1876; *Iside*, 1878). [RHC]

*Opere edite e inedite* (5 vols., 1862–9); *Poesie varie*, ed. O. Malagodi (2 vols., 1929–33); Dionisotti, *OBIV*.

G. Toffanin, *La seconda generazione romantica* (Naples, 1942); U. Bosco, *Aspetti del romanticismo italiano* (Rome, 1942); L. Fontana, *Saggio di una interpretazione di G.P.* (Genoa, 1947); S. Einaudi, *G.P. poeta d'amore* (Saluzzo, 1952); *Minori*, iv.

**Pratolini, Vasco** (Florence 1913– ). Italian novelist. Of working-class extraction, he did several manual jobs before taking up writing as a career. A left-wing Fascist, he soon got into trouble with the Party over the magazine *Campo di Marte* he had founded with the poet Alfonso Gatto in 1939. After its suppression, he joined the underground Resistance movement, taking an active part in the partisan struggle. He has since become one of the most influential left-wing novelists in Italy. His main concern is to make literature a relevant expression of the whole life of the whole people, and not simply a pastime for a small ruling minority. He has therefore studied in detail the two main structures of society: family

(*Il tappeto verde*, 1941; *Via de' Magazzini*, 1942; *Cronaca familiare*, 1947; *La costanza della ragione*, 1964), and the larger town community (*Il Quartiere*, 1945; tr. P. and P. Duncan, *A Tale of Santa Croce*, 1952; *Cronache di poveri amanti*, 1947; tr. anon., *A Tale of Poor Lovers*, 1949) and showed how the simplest acts of life take on a deeper meaning when situated in a wider context; and how, from a passive perception of their value, men can grow to a fully conscious acceptance of their social significance. The mere keeping alive against all odds on the one hand, and organized class struggle and political opposition on the other, are two different levels of the same protest of the working classes against the oppressiveness and injustice of society. This 'crescendo' from family to community life has been followed quite logically by a further widening of his perspective: a narrative history of Italian society from the 1890s to the present day (*Metello*, 1957; *Lo scialo*, 1960; *Bruno Santini*, tr. R. Rosenthal, 1965; *Allegoria e derisione*, 1966), which has aroused much interest and controversy. Many critics have seen in these novels a fracture between descriptive and reflective passages; in Pratolini's intentions, however, both the enchanted remembrance of things past and the lucid effort to understand the present are complementary aspects of the 'constancy of reason'; in other words, memory is seen as a part of dialectic process, not as a Proustian store. [GMC]

*Un eroe del nostro tempo* (1950; tr. E. Mosbacher, *A Hero of Today*, 1951).

*Contemporanei*, ii; Pullini, *RID*; Falqui, *PNNI*; Alberto, *SP*; F. Rosengarten, *V.P.: The Development of a Social Novelist* (1965).

**Preradović, Paula von** (Vienna 1887–Vienna 1951). Austrian poet. Granddaughter of Petar ⇨ Preradović, wife of Ernst Molden, editor of *Die Neue Freie Presse* and post-war *Die Presse* (arrested with him for involvement in the (1944) 'July conspiracy'). She wrote the new Austrian national anthem, and was much admired for her religious, essentially romantic, often poignantly nostalgic poetry (influenced by Rilke): *Südlicher Sommer* (1929), *Lob Gottes im Gebirge* (1936) and others. *Pave und Pero* (1940) is a *vie romancée* of her grandfather. [PB]

*Gesammelte Gedichte*, E. Molden (1951–2); *Meerferne Heimat*, ed. W. Röttinger (Graz 1961).

P. v. P., *Porträt einer Dichterin* (Innsbruck, 1955); R. Vospernik, *P.v.P.* (Vienna, 1961) (dissertation); *GLL*, VII, 4 (1954).

**Preradović, Petar** (Grabovnica 1818–Fahrfeld, Austria 1872). Croatian poet. Educated in German schools and finally in an Austrian military academy, he forgot his native language. In 1843, as a serving officer in the Austrian army, he came into contact with followers of ⇨ Gaj's Illyrian movement and began to relearn Serbo-Croat. Posted to Dalmatia, his first poem in the language, *Zora puca, Biće dana*, appeared in the periodical *Zora dalmatinskä*. This and other poems soon became very popular. Until 1850 his themes were mainly patriotic, but in his later works he turned to a form of Panslav mysticism, influenced partly by his interest in spiritualism. Always a reflective poet, his works become increasingly philosophical. In such poems as *Zvanje slavjanstva* he presents the Slavs as a nation embodying Christian love, whose task it is to implant it in the entire human race. One of the best educated of Croatian writers of the period, he had read German philosophy and translated Dante, Byron and Manzoni. [EDG]

Ibrovac, *APY*.
Barac, *HYL*.

**Preti, Girolamo** (Bologna 1582?–Barcelona 1626). Italian poet. He spent his life in the service of various Italian princes and prelates, his last employer being Cardinal Francesco Barberini, who took him to Spain. His sonnet, 'Penna immortal...', proclaims his poetic debt to ⇨ Marino, and his description of the mechanism of a clock is a famous example of the Marinist liking for difficult and unconventional subjects. But despite some stylistic flamboyance, he deplored the voluptuous tone in Marino and cultivated instead a more sentimental strain. His tenuous spirituality has made him appear to some as a precursor of the Arcadian reaction against Baroque excesses. [DGR]

Croce, *LM*; Ferrero, *MM*; Getto, *MM*.

**Prevelakis, Pandelis** (Rethymno, Crete 1909– ). Greek novelist, poet, playwright and art critic. He received his early education in Crete and later studied literature and history of art at the universities of Athens, Paris and Thessalonike. In 1939 he was elected Professor at the School of Fine

Arts, Athens. He started on his literary career with a lyrical epic, *Stratiotes* ('Soldiers', 1928), which showed great sensitivity and assurance in the handling of language. He wrote subsequently several cycles of lyrical poems which have appeared in two slender volumes, *Gymni Poiesi* (1939) and *I Pio Gymni Poiesi* (1941). But it is as a prose writer that he has attained his distinction. His first work, *To Chroniko Mias Politeias* (1938), a narrative full of picturesque details about life, characters and events in his native town, is written in a style of deliberate simplicity and remarkable freshness. The works that followed deal with the heroic saga of modern Crete: *Pandermi Kriti* (1945), a chronicle of the Cretan rising of 1866, and the *Kritikos* (1948–50), a trilogy, rank among the highest achievements of Greek historical fiction: the prose style is elaborate and sustains its rhythmical movement throughout; and the characters are types embodying the Cretan ideals of heroism and caste honour. His latest novels, *O Ilios Tou Thanatou* (tr. P. Sherrard, *The Sun of Death*, 1965) set in Crete during the First World War, *I Kefali Tis Medousas* (1963) and *O Artos Ton Angelon* (1966), are to a large extent autobiographical. Prevelakis's three plays, *To Iero Sfaghio* (1952), *O Lazaros* (1954), *Ta Heria Tou Zontanou Theou* (1955), deal with the problem of freedom and guilt as it emerges from the struggle of modern man to adjust himself in a world of obsolescent institutions and traditions. He has written numerous studies on literature and art; translations from Valéry and Calderón; and an excellent translation of Euripides's *Medea* into modern Greek. [SJP]

**Prévert, Jacques** (Neuilly-sur-Seine 1900– ). French poet. A member of the ⇨ Surrealist group in Paris for only a few years, he has retained its characteristic imagery, while some of his poems seem more purely dadaistic. His anarchic poems attack officialdom, be it church or state, with the humorous virulence exploited by ⇨ Péret; Prévert alternates these with poems of nostalgic or melancholy mood, songs of the Paris streets full of echoes of Villon and Apollinaire, many of which have become popular songs. He sketches poignant vignettes of underdogs in society, always ready to be moved by a poor girl's beauty or an old man's humiliation. Prévert's versatility adapts any tricks of speech to his purpose, juxtaposing puns, jerky repetitions and slang terms, in a racy style which sometimes risks becoming too facile. Above all his work is easy to understand, and *Paroles* (1946) has done much to introduce poetry to a wide audience of ordinary people. This best-seller has since been followed by *Spectacle* (1951), *La pluie et le beau temps* (1955), and *Histoires* (1963), all equally 'readable'. He has also written some playlets and several important film scenarios, including Carné's *Les enfants du paradis* (1945). [RTC]

*J.P.* (PMEP, 1966) (selection in French with verse tr. by L. Ferlinghetti).

P. Berger 'J.P.', in *Présences Contemporaines* (Paris, 1958); J. Queval, *J.P.* (Paris, 1955).

**Prévost d'Exiles, Antoine-François,** abbé (Hesdin, Artois 1697–Courteuil, nr Chantilly 1763). French novelist and journalist. In his adventurous life phases of sobriety alternated with wild escapades. After periods as a Jesuit novice, a soldier, a Benedictine priest, and a Protestant convert, he was forced to flee into exile in 1728 to escape imprisonment. Until 1734 he lived in England and Holland, incurring further troubles through large debts and, in England, a spell of imprisonment for forgery. However, he was allowed to return to France, re-entered the Benedictine order by papal consent, and became chaplain to the prince de Conti; but exile again became necessary in 1740 for allegedly writing certain satiric pamphlets. On his return (1742) he seems to have settled to a quieter existence, still complicated by too many mistresses and too little money, and to the end of his life he was a professional hack writer, at the mercy of the publishers, turning out translations and histories to pay his debts.

His *Mémoires et aventures d'un homme de qualité* (1728–31) cover 7 volumes. The first 6 constitute a picaresque adventure novel which is as undistinguished as volume 7, *Manon Lescaut*, is brilliant. Other novels include *Le philosophe anglais: Histoire de Cleveland* (4 vols.) which appeared in 1731 and *Le Doyen de Killerine* (1736). In addition, he was a journalist, editing 20 volumes of *Le pour et contre* (1733–40), a translator of English works such as Richardson's novels (*Paméla*, 1742; *Clarisse Harlowe*, 1751), and a historian and biographer.

In this mass of writings *Manon Lescaut* (ed. F. Deloffre and R. Picard, 1965; tr. L. W. Tancock, Penguin Classics, 1949) alone stands out. It is the tale of the chevalier Des Grieux's love for Manon Lescaut as told by the chevalier to the Homme de Qualité (the only link with the six preceding volumes). In the weak-willed but essentially refined character of Des Grieux, Prévost has transposed many of his own failings and aspirations. Manon appears through Des Grieux's eyes – charming, innocent, amoral. As she is made for the life of a demi-mondaine but has the ill-chance to win his undying love, so he, an aristocrat's son with a future full of promise, is cursed in meeting her. Character is destiny; the pair fatally ruin one another. The pure ineluctability of fate, reminiscent of Racine, is demonstrated against a background of corrupt Parisian society where money rules all. Des Grieux is the victim not only of his character but of his social situation too. Rejected by his family because of his pursuit of Manon, he has no money. Unable, as an aristocrat, to earn it by working, his only recourse is to gambling, which leads to debts, deceit and murder. Virtue is destroyed as passion comes to dictate his whole conduct. The novel is eminently classical in the sobriety of its style and concision of its recital, but by its stress on sensibility, by the wild force of the emotions portrayed, it already announces Rousseau and the Romantics. [HTM]

C.-E. Engel, *Le véritable Abbé P.* (Monaco, 1957); F. C. Green, *Minuet* (1935); P. Hazard *et al.*, *Études critiques sur Manon Lescaut* (Chicago, 1929); H. Roddier, *L'Abbé P.* (Paris, 1955); Auerbach, *M*; Trahard, *MSF.*

**Prishvin, Mikhail Mikhaylovich** (Khrushchov, Oryol 1873–Moscow 1954). Russian short-story writer. Son of a merchant family, and trained as an agronomist, he later became a naturalist and ethnographer. He was first published in 1907, but he acquired fame only after the Revolution; he is now one of the most popular of contemporary Russian writers. His work is quite independent of Bolshevik slogans. It is devoted almost entirely to nature, and man occupies often only a secondary position in it. His love of nature is based on precise and accurate observation, the fruit of a lifetime spent in wandering through Russia, and especially in the North. He has a rich and delightful sense of humour; some of his stories, while remaining strictly realistic, carry symbolic overtones (*Zhen'-shen'*, 1932; tr. G. Walton and P. Gibbons, *Jen Sheng: the Root of Life*, 1936). His masterpiece is his long autobiographical novel *Kashcheyeva Tsep'* (1923–30). Several of his short stories have been translated into English. [RDBT]

*Sobraniye sochineniy* (6 vols., 1956–7).
T. Khmel'nitskaya, *Tvorchestvo M.P.* (Leningrad, 1959); I. Motyashov, *M.P.* (Moscow, 1965).

**Prodromic Poems**. Byzantine satirical and begging poems, in the *political* (fifteen-syllable) verse, written in the twelfth century and addressed to Emperor John Comnenus and to his son. They are falsely attributed to the poet and scholar Theodoros Prodromos. They give a vivid picture of contemporary conditions and everyday life in Constantinople, and as they are the first continuous texts in the Byzantine vernacular they are of primary importance to the student of later Greek language and literature. [SJP]

D. C. Hesseling, H. Pernot, *Poèmes prodromiques en grec vulgaire* (Amsterdam, 1910).

**Proletarian Poetry.** An ill-defined literary movement in the early years of the U.S.S.R., when the *proletkul't* tried to create a true literature of the proletariat. Two major groupings arose: the *Kuznitsa* (smithy poets) and the ultra-left *Napostøvtsy* (on-guardists). Among the more talented poets were V. Kazin (1898–     ), N. Ushakov (1899–     ), I. Utkin (1903–45), M. Svetlov (1903–64), and the popular satirists A. Bezymensky (1898–     ) and Demyan Bedny (pseud. of Ye. Pridvorov, 1883–1945). [RM-G]

Lugovskoy, *RSP*; E. J. Brown, *The Proletarian Episode in Russian Literaure* (1953).

**Proust, Marcel** (Auteuil 1871–Paris 1922). French novelist. The younger son of an eminent Professor of Medicine and a wealthy Jewess to whom he remained inordinately devoted. Though he suffered from chronic asthma from the age of 9, he was able to attend the Lycée Condorcet, to complete a year's military service at Orléans (1889–90) and, in the 1890s, to become a conspicuous society figure. He entertained lavishly and assiduously frequented the most fashionable Paris *salons* of the day. After the death of his father (1903) and mother (1905), he became a recluse, only rarely emerging from his cork-lined bedroom at 102 Boulevard Haussmann, where he wrote a vast number of letters and devoted himself to the completion of *À la* *recherche du temps perdu* (tr. C. K. Scott Moncrieff and S. Hudson, *Remembrance of Things Past*, 1922–31). He completed a first version in 1912 and a year later, at his own expense, published the opening volume, *Du côté de chez Swann* (tr. C. K. Scott Moncrieff, *Swann's Way*). From then on, increasingly aware that he would not survive to express himself in another work, he drastically expanded his original manuscript. He lived to see the publication of *À l'ombre des jeunes filles en fleurs* (1919; tr. C. K. Scott Moncrieff, *Within a Budding Grove*), which was awarded the Prix Goncourt, *Le côté de Guermantes* (1920–1; tr. C. K. Scott Moncrieff, *The Guermantes Way*) and *Sodome et Gomorrhe* (1921–2; tr. C. K. Scott Moncrieff, *Cities of the Plain*). The remaining volumes, completed but not fully revised, are: *La prisonnière* (1923; tr. C. K. Scott Moncrieff, *The Captive*); *Albertine disparue*, now renamed *La fugitive* (1925; tr. C. K. Scott Moncrieff, *The Sweet Cheat Gone*), and *Le temps retrouvé* (1927; tr. S. Hudson, *Time Regained*).

His earlier published works did little to correct the impression, created by his youthful social life, that he was merely a cultured dilettante with a gift for mimicry. They include *Les plaisirs et les jours* (1896; tr. L. Varese, *Pleasures and Regrets*, 1950), a very elegant collection of stories and poems, with illustrations by Madeleine Lemaire, music by Reynaldo Hahn and a fulsome preface by Anatole France; his Ruskin translations, *La Bible d'Amiens* (1904) and *Sésame et lys* (1906); and *Pastiches et mélanges* (1914), a set of accomplished stylistic imitations, some of which had earlier appeared in *Le Figaro*.

Although critics were later able to link elements of these early works with *À la recherche du temps perdu*, it was only in the 1950s, with the discovery of a large cache of unpublished papers, that Proust was found to have begun serious preparatory work on his great novel as early as the mid-1890s: *Jean Santeuil* (1952; tr. G. Hopkins, 1955), written in the period *c.* 1895–1900, is virtually a first draft for the final work; in *Contre Sainte-Beuve* (1954; tr. S. Townsend Warner, *By Way of Sainte-Beuve*, 1958), he violently attacks the biographical approach to literary criticism, propounds the view that any worthwhile novel expresses the author's hidden self, and explores for memories of his own past very much like the hero of his great masterpiece.

*À la recherche du temps perdu*, a *summa* of Proust's views on a formidable range of major and minor topics, is a highly complex novel in which a number of dominant themes are intricately interwoven. Unity is ensured by the narrator-hero, who is clearly similar to though not wholly identical with Proust himself. With infinite care and patience, he sets out to resurrect his past life, from childhood to middle age, recalling the many people, places and events which most affected him. Of the more than 200 characters portrayed, the most memorable are the members of his own family circle, Swann, the wealthy dilettante, and Baron de Charlus, an arrogant homosexual with a genius for colourful invective. In the course of his odyssey, Marcel comes to realize that the whole of our past remains alive, hidden somewhere within us, and may be rediscovered, involuntarily, through sensory perceptions or the agency of works of art. Inspired by the creative artists he himself most admires, Elstir (the painter), Bergotte (the novelist) and, especially, Vinteuil (the musician), he resolves to recapture his past and hold it forever prisoner through Art, by writing the very novel the reader has just completed.

As well as the account of a literary vocation, *À la recherche du temps perdu* is a social comedy in which, after a protracted siege, the decadent aristocracy are finally overrun by the militant middle classes, and the vices and pretensions of each group are mercilessly exposed. Love, normal and abnormal, is no less cruelly analysed in a number of drawn-out liaisons, and in each case is depicted as a purely subjective emotion, fortuitously inspired and artificially sustained by such stimuli as absence or the threat of loss.

Proust is an accomplished and highly versatile stylist. His dialogues sensitively record the different idiosyncracies and speech-rhythms of his many characters, and his intricate and lavishly metaphorical sentences can be adapted to convey the most abstruse thoughts on the most lyrical of natural descriptions. His work, as a whole, is nevertheless uneven: it can rightly be criticized for *longueurs*, for its excessively bleak view of human personality and the inordinate space allowed for the theme of male and female homosexuality, but it amply repays re-reading as the unique testament of a sick but richly endowed personality. [RG]

G. Brée, *M.P. and Deliverance from Time* (1956); J. M. Cocking, *P.* (1956); A. Maurois, *The Quest for P.* (1950); G. Painter, *M.P.* (2 vols., 1959, 1965); G. Poulet, *L'espace proustien* (Paris, 1963); L. P. Quint, *M.P. sa vie, son œuvre* (Paris, 1946).

**Proux, Prosper.** ⇨ Breton Literature.

**Prus, Bolesław,** pseud. of Aleksander Głowacki (nr Hrubieszów 1845–Warsaw 1912). Polish novelist. He lost his parents early, and at 18 joined a group of insurgents, was wounded, taken to a Russian prison and after his family's endeavours released. This experience, followed by a spiritual crisis, had a profound influence on his character and indirectly on his writing. He went to Warsaw, but his plans to become a scientist were frustrated, for he had to give up his university studies, and instead drifted into journalism. Fortunately, his witty pen and talent for social observation secured him an influential public platform. In 1875 Prus began contributing *kroniki*, i.e. weekly articles, to *Kurier Warszawski*, a respectable daily, and for nearly forty years practised this form of social and humorous commentary.

In his short stories, published at the beginning of his journalistic career, the didactic tone often resembles that of his 'weekly chronicles'. Yet the provincial scenes in *Przygoda Stasia* (1879) and particularly in *Grzechy dziecińistwa* (1883) are drawn with a novelist's authority, while the gentle mockery of style reminds one of Chekhov. Indeed, Prus could not help revealing his sympathy for people despite his didactic intentions. As his imaginative writing grew alongside his weekly contributions, the social content gradually needed a wider interpretation.

His long story *Powracająca fala* (1880) is in this respect a transition to the novel proper. It describes a whole series of events and the relationship between the unscrupulous Adler, a German, and his reckless son is firmly attached to the realities of their factory and the surrounding Polish world. The moral at the end echoes the title: the wrong rebounds, it is a 'returning wave'. In 1886 Prus published his first novel, *Placówka*, and gave it a detailed village setting. The hero is a very unheroic peasant forced by circumstances to resist the pressure of an entire social group, in this case German settlers. Willy-nilly, he finds himself living on the outpost of a farm, isolated by fate and finally resigned to accept it. But new circumstances turn his seeming failure into victory.

Once Prus had touched on this positive meaning of failure, he tried to explore it in all his major novels, and the oblique way in which he would proceed from decaying society to noble individual and back suggests a personal preoccupation, uncertainty and regret. His greatest book and perhaps the best realistic novel in Polish fiction was engendered by a personal crisis which is also at the core of the hero's ultimate failure. Although the title *Lalka* ('The Doll', 1890) does not suggest the large canvas of a social novel, it is the Warsaw of 1878–9 which breathes life into every page; an accurate portrait of that city stands all the time behind the portraits of Prus's characters and this gives their features a double reality. The middle-aged hero, Wokulski, is being destroyed by an obsessive love for the frigid aristocratic doll, Izabela, whereas in society (he owns a prosperous store and is successful in financial speculations) he is a man of positive action. A personal conflict results, and it brings into play all the social factors around Wokulski: Warsaw big business with its Polish and Jewish representatives, the endangered aristocrats shifting to new positions, the shop assistants and the proletariat. The pundits of social realism canonized *Lalka* as a novel about feudal decay and capitalism, but this ignores both the highly personal vision of life and the moral analysis of failure.

After a less successful novel about emancipated women (*Emancypantki*, 1893), he conceived a brilliant idea for a historical novel about ancient Egypt, *Faraon* (1897; pedestrian tr. J. Curtin, *The Pharaoh and the Priest*, Boston, 1902). The brilliance lies in the analysis of a political mechanism and the struggles for power it generates and uses up. Here the conflict arises between the caste of priests and the youthful Rameses XIII, for whom Prus invented a reign. Again a noble but inexperienced hero has to fail in order to justify his own character as well as his function in both society and history. Prus's last and short novel, *Dzieci* (1909), is based on the events of 1905 and expresses his deep-rooted distrust of revolutionary psychosis.

His life and work was bound up with his immediate environment. Unlike his contemporary ⇨ Sienkiewicz, he travelled little, his movements being handicapped by agoraphobia. But even this restriction seems to have been beneficial to his talent, for it intensified his realism. [JP]

*Wybór pism* (1957); *Selected Polish Tales* (tr. E. C. Benecke, 1942); *SEER*, XXXIX, 92 (1960); *PR*, 4 (1963).

**Przybyszewski, Stanisław** (Łojewo 1868–Jaronty 1927). Polish novelist and playwright. He belongs to both Polish and German literature, but in both his reputation still appears vulnerable. During his years in Berlin he moved in the cosmopolitan circle of artists, knew ⇨ Strindberg, ⇨ Dehmel and Munch (about whose art he wrote in 1894). He married a Norwegian beauty and travelled widely. His German works, like *Totenmesse* (1893) or *Satanskinder* (1897), typified the *fin-de-siècle* decadence, and their tense style was meant to reveal 'the naked soul'.

In 1898 he arrived in Cracow and became the leader of the 'New Poland' movement, preaching the aesthetics of pure art. His tempestuous private life and bohemian habits contributed to his fame as much as his novels and plays, which he was now writing in Polish. But he still had successes abroad: e.g. his play *Śnieg* (1903; tr. O. F. Theis, *The Snow*, 1920) found an admiring public in Russia. Despite the exhibitionist manner of his dialogue, he was inventive: a character's own shadow is the revengeful visitor in his one-act play *Goście* (1901).

His 2 books of memoirs (*Moi współcześni*, 1926–30) preserve the personal myth, but somehow they voice a tormented sincerity through the make-believe. His style, both in Polish and in German, is stamped with the mannerisms of the period, but the imaginative mind behind it continues to fascinate. [JP]

M. Herman, *Un sataniste polonais: S.P.* (Warsaw, 1939).

**Psycharis, Yannis** (Chios 1854–Paris 1929). Greek scholar and novelist. Chiefly remembered for his *To Taxidi Mou* (1888), a polemical work written in an uncompromising demotic (popular) language and attacking the purist tradition in Greek literature and education. It sparked off a violent controversy over the language question which resulted in the gradual prevalence of the demotic in literature. [SJP]

**Pückler-Muskau, Fürst Hermann Ludwig Heinrich von** (Muskau 1785–Branitz 1871). German man of letters. One of the most colourful personalities of the 19th century. Born in Silesia, he served in the Russian army, travelled extensively in England, married the Countess of Pappenheim, a daughter of the Prussian chancellor Prince Hardenberg, and settled with her on his ancestral estate of Muskau, where he laid out magnificent gardens which brought him fame all over Europe. In 1826 he obtained a divorce, travelled in Egypt and the Middle East, and came again to England in search of a rich wife; when he failed to find one, he returned to Germany and remarried the Countess Pappenheim, living with her until his death on an estate near Cottbus, having sold Muskau to Prince Frederick of the Netherlands in 1846.

His *Briefe eines Verstorbenen* (1830; new edn, intr. Jost Hermand, Wisconsin, 1967), written in the language and style of aristocratic society and recalling, both in subject and in manner, Sterne's *Sentimental Journey*, was one of the most widely read books of the time. Its cosmopolitan confidence and sophisticated worldly wisdom, added to the almost legendary career of its author, brought him the reputation of a minor Byron. [RT]

E. M. Butler, *The Tempestuous Prince* (1929).

**Pugliese, Giacomino** (fl. early 13th cent.). Unidentified Italian poet of the so-called Sicilian school which flourished around the court of the Emperor Frederick II. Only a few poems of his are extant, but they are among the liveliest and freshest products of the Sicilians, who, by and large, stand in the conventional courtly love tradition of the troubadours. In him there is occasional dramatic liveliness, as in his celebrated *contrasto* between lover and lady – 'Donna di voi mi lamento'. [DGR]

Contini, *PD*; Salinari, *PLD*; Panvini, *RSS*; Rossetti, *DC*.

C. Guerrieri-Crocetti, *La Magna Curia* (Milan, 1947).

**Pujmanová, Marie** (Prague 1893–Prague 1958). Czech novelist and poet. Her main interest was the analysis of contemporary Czech society. Her trilogy, *Lidé na křižovatce* (1937), *Hra s ohněm* (1948) and *Život proti smrti* (1952), describes the fortunes of two families, one middle-class, the other a worker's family. It recaptures the atmosphere of the period from Hitler's rise to power to the end of the war, with emphasis on the anti-fascist struggle of the Communist workers and intellectuals. [KB]

M. Blahynka, *M.P.* (Prague, 1961).

**Pulci, Luigi** (Florence 1432–Padua 1484). Italian poet. Of limited formal education, but endowed with a bizarre intelligence, he was bound to Lorenzo de' ⇨ Medici by strong ties of affection. Among his lesser works are letters, satirical sonnets, the *Beca da Dicomano* (a poem in the manner of Lorenzo's *Nencia*), and a celebration in *ottava rima* of Lorenzo's triumph in a tournament in 1469.

He is best remembered for his *Morgante* (1483; ed. F. Ageno, 1955), a comic epic which he wrote at the instigation of Lorenzo's mother, Lucrezia Tornabuoni. The first version consisted of 23 cantos, in which Pulci took as model an anonymous, unfinished poem on Roland (*Orlando*). Later, using a different source (*Spagna in rima*), he added 5 more cantos, more elaborate in style, relating the drama of Roncevaux.

The *Morgante* illustrates how in the popular Italian *cantastorie* tradition the heroic material of the French romances has declined towards the broadly comic. There is still, in the ramblings of the poem, an official core of heroic action, but the Paladins have a raucous, plebeian tinge, Charlemagne is no more than a silly, petulant old man, and the language has become earthy and colloquial. The most characteristic expression of this gross spirit is the episode of Morgante and Margutte. Morgante is an amiable giant with a vast appetite and a congenital liking for violence, while Margutte is a demi-giant who blasphemously acknowledges a comic parody of the *credo* as his philosophy of life and claims to have a vast list of mortal sins to his credit. Later in the poem Pulci introduces another celebrated figure, the comic-serious devil Astarotte, who discourses with heterodox intelligence on science and theology and advocates religious tolerance.

Pulci's irreverent, bizarre handling of the chivalrous epic smacks of the Florentine street corner, and is very different from that of ⇨ Boiardo or, later, ⇨ Ariosto at the court of Ferrara. [DGR]

*Morgante e lettere*, ed. D. De Robertis (1962).

F. Foffano, *Il poema cavalleresco dal 15 al 18 secolo* (Milan, 1904); G. Getto, *Studio sul Morgante* (Florence, 1967); *Minori*, i.

**Pulpeiro, Manuel Leiras.** ⇨ Galician Literature.

**Pushkin, Aleksandr Sergeyevich** (Moscow 1799–St Petersburg 1837). Russian writer. Educated sensibly and liberally in his parents' home up to the age of twelve, then in the Lyceum of Tsarskoye Selo, an academy founded by Alexander I for gifted children from the nobility. He left school in 1817 with the reputation of a brilliant poet and having been given a purely nominal post in the Foreign Office spent three dissipated years in St Petersburg, keeping up with literary acquaintances made at school, writing light, often erotic, and always highly polished verse, and forming new friendships with many of those connected with the pre-Decembrist political societies. Although never a member of any of the secret revolutionary societies, his 'liberal' and 'revolutionary' poems were known to many of the conspirators. In 1820 he was exiled for his unprinted political poems which, mild though they may seem today, were construed by the authorities as inciting to revolution. After a trip to the Caucasus and the Crimea during which he fell under the spell of Byron, he was sent to Kishinev in Bessarabia, where during nearly three years of boredom and debauchery he wrote, *inter alia*, the two Byronic verse-tales, *Kavkazskiy plennik* (1822; *The Prisoner of the Caucasus*) and *Bakhchisarayskiy Fontan* (1824). In Odessa where he spent the last year of his southern exile he wrote most of *Tsygany* (1827; tr. J. Fennell, *The Gipsies*, in *The Penguin P.*, 1964), and started *Yevgeny Onegin* (1833; tr. V. Nabokov, 1964; B. Deutsch, Penguin Classics, 1965), both in sharp contrast to the exoticism and levity of his earlier work. In July 1824 he was transferred to his parents' estate at Mikhaylovskoye (north-west Russia). Here he spent two fruitful years under police surveillance: he produced a large amount of lyrical and folk poetry, wrote his great historical drama, *Boris Godunov* (1831; tr. P. L. Barbour, N.Y., 1953), continued *Yevgeny Onegin* and finished *Tsygany*. His liberal enthusiasm and spirit of protest seemed to flag, especially after the failure of the uprising of the Decembrists (14 December 1825), and in September 1826 he was freed from his 'disgrace' by the new tsar Nicholas I, who announced that he would henceforth be his censor. He was still, however, under the close surveillance of the secret police. For three years he wandered restlessly between Moscow and St Petersburg writing little. his only major work of this period was the epic poem *Poltava* (1829). In 1829 he managed to attach himself to the army which was fighting the Turks in Transcaucasia, but the change did little to alleviate his restlessness. Back in Russia, he engaged in journalism, and in the autumn of 1830 spent a remarkably productive three months at his parents' estate of Boldino where he finished the draft of the last chapter of *Yevgeny Onegin* and wrote *Domik v Kolomne* (1833; tr. E. F. B. Clark, *The Little House in Kolomna*, Slavonic Review, XV), the 'little tragedies' – short psychological studies in blank verse – several lyrical poems and the experimental *Povesti Belkina* (1831) in prose. In February 1831 he married Natalia Goncharova. For most of the rest of his life he was worried by debts, by rumours caused by his wife's behaviour and by the contemptuous attitude of tsar and society. He was unable to write much, except during his second stay in Boldino (October–November 1833) where he finished his prose history of the Pugachev rebellion, wrote two folk poems, *Skazka o mertvoy tsarevne* (1834; tr. O. Elton, *The Dead Princess*, in *Slavonic Review* II) and *Skazka o rybake i rybke* (1835; tr. O. Elton, *The Tale of the Fisherman and the Fish*, in *Verse from Pushkin and Others*, 1935), and produced the first draft of his epic poem *Mednyy vsadnik* (unpublished in his lifetime; tr. J. Fennell, *The Bronze Horseman*, in *The Penguin P.*, 1964). At the end of 1836, incensed by the scandalous rumours spread by his enemies, he challenged an officer in the Horse Guards, d'Anthes, to a duel. He was shot in the stomach and died on 29 January 1837. During the last few years of his life he wrote little: two prose works – *Kapitanskaya dochka* (1836; tr. Rosemary Edmonds, *The Captain's Daughter*, 1962) and *Pikovaya dama* (1834; tr. Rosemary Edmonds, *The Queen of Spades*) – one folk poem – *Skazka o zolotom petushke* (1835; tr. J. Fennell, *The Golden Cockerel*, in *The Penguin P.*, 1964) – and a few lyrical poems.

Pushkin's range and versatility as a writer were immense. He covered every genre of poetry known to Russian literature at the beginning of the 19th century, from the humorous epigram to the solemn heroic epic poem; he even introduced new genres into Russian literature, viz. the novel in verse, *Yevgeny Onegin*, and the psychological dramas in verse, *Motsart i Sal'eri* (1831; tr. J. Fennell, *Mozart and Salieri* in *The Penguin P.*, 1964), *Skupoy rytsar'* (1836; tr. A. F. D. Clark, *The Covetous Knight* in *The Works of Alexander Pushkin*, ed. A. Yarmolinsky, N.Y., 1936). In his prose works he experimented with style and mastered the technique of the short story and the short novel. His tragedy, *Boris Godunov*, was experimental both in form and in language and broke with the dry traditions of the 18th-century Russian theatre. His favourite, or at any rate his most frequently practised, genre was the long narrative poem, the *poema*, which he used as a vehicle for experimentation with language and subject-matter, for setting the reader intellectual problems to solve (see *Tsygany* and *Medny vsadnik*) and for attempting new techniques. The full extent of his poetic range is best seen in his short poems. Here he covers every conceivable poetic – and often unpoetic – subject from the bawdy joke to the majestic and sometimes pompous political pronouncement, from the cosy descriptions of life on the country estate to the grandiloquent portrayal of spectacular nature-scenes from erotic flirtation to resounding passion.

Pushkin's influence on his contemporaries and successors was immense. It was not just that he provided them with new genres, new subject-matter, introduced them to themes which had hitherto been considered totally unsuitable for verse or broke the old bonds of 'rules' which governed poetry, prose and drama. He created a new language which was free from excessive artificiality, archaism, stiffness and coyness, qualities which characterized the Russian literary language in the 18th and early 19th centuries, and he showed his fellow-writers how to make use of the immense possibilities of the Russian language, how to adapt technique to suit mood or subject-matter, and above all how to blend one manner of speech with another. Biblical and popular, archaic and modern – all types of language were usable and blendable, and were used and blended by him. Few poets or prose writers who followed him failed to acknowledge their debt to Pushkin. [JLIF]

*Sochineniya*, ed. B. V. Tomashevsky (1936); *Selected verse*, tr. J. Fennell (Penguin Poets, 1964) (selection with prose tr. and intro.).
E. J. Simmons, *P.* (1937); A. Slonimsky, *Masterstvo Pushkina* (Moscow, 1959); G. A. Gukovsky, *P. i problemy realisticheskogo stilya* (Moscow, 1957).

**Puy** or **Pui.** Medieval French fraternities of *jongleurs* and poets, which organized contests of lyric poetry. The most famous were at Puy-en-Velay, where a sparrow-hawk was usually awarded as a prize, in the late 12th century, and at Arras, which had bourgeois support, and produced in the 13th century many leading poets from ⇨ Jean Bodel to ⇨ Adam de la Halle. This Puy had a religious and profane character, being known as the *Puy Notre-Dame* and *Puy d'Amour*. A 'Prince', usually a rich bourgeois, to whom poems were dedicated, was elected annually and his duty was to pay for the feasting and the religious offices of the fraternity. [LTT]

# Q

**Quasimodo, Salvatore** (Modica 1901–1968). Italian poet, translator and critic. He was trained as an engineer, became professor of Italian literature at the Milan Conservatoire in 1935, and won the Nobel Prize for his lyrical poetry in 1959. His earlier collections contain many poems in the subtle manner of the ⇨ *ermetismo*: *Acque e terre* (1930), *Oboe sommerso* (1932), *Erato e Apollion* (1936), *Ed è subito sera* (1943). His symbolism owes less to foreign influences, however, than to his preoccupation with the classic forms of Mediterranean poetry (which inspired some masterly translations from the ancient poets); his evocations of the Sicilian landscape, people and past have the quality of myth or fable. Yet there is sometimes also a deliberate harshness, a refusal of illusion, a revolt which seems to lack human sympathy: until the experience of war, the years of *Giorno dopo giorno* (1943–6) – 'And how could we sing/with the alien foot upon our heart/with the dead abandoned in the squares/on the grass hard with ice ...'. Since then the voice which could sound so pitiless has developed a warmer tone, capable of rising to oracular authority, of ringing with moral indignation. His social conscience is concerned with concrete examples and scenes of human suffering. To bear witness to man's history in all the urgency of a particular time and place, and to teach the lesson of his courage, this has been Quasimodo's poetic task. His later collections (*La vita non è sogno*, 1949; *Il falso e vero verde*, 1956, containing his declaration *Discorso sulla poesia* in favour of 'poesia sociale'; *La terra impareggiabile*, 1958) are included in *Tutte le poesie* (Milan, 1960; tr. *Selected Writings*, N.Y., 1960). [GD]

*Q.* (PMEP, 1965) (selection tr. R. Bevan); Golino, *CIP*.

M. Stefanile, *Q.* (Padua, 1943); N. Tedesco, *S.Q.* (Palermo, 1959); Jones, *Italian Studies*, 1961.

**Queneau, Raymond** (Le Havre 1903– ). French poet and novelist. After being involved in ⇨ Surrealism, he attempted to reintroduce the spoken language into literary French, through the humorous anti-poems and droll rhymes of *Les Ziaux* (1943). A poetic autobiography (*Chêne et chien*, 1937) had already closed the gap between his personality and his projected image by describing his psychoanalysis, which explains a series of erotic stories written at that time (*Journal de Sally Mara*). A grammarian and a serious thinker on the gratuitous nature of inspiration, as well as a dignitary of the Order of Pataphysics (an Academy founded in memory of ⇨ Jarry), he has published a caricature of style containing 99 versions of the same story (*Exercices de style*, 1947; tr. B. Wright, *Exercises in Style*, 1958) and a do-it-yourself sonnet kit (*Cent mille milliards de poèmes*, 1961). *Le Chiendent* (1933) is an anti-novel based on a meditation around cartesianism, and *Les enfants du limon* (1937), a study of madness in literature. He has since written meticulously structured stories which play with the mechanics of illusion, where the cynical views of impervious characters and ubiquitous personalities and their adventures in slightly fantastic surroundings progress towards epic dimensions: *Saint Glinglin* (1948), *Le dimanche de la vie* (1952), *Zazie dans le métro* (1959; tr. B. Wright, *Zazie in the Metro*, 1960). Juliette Gréco's version of the poem 'Si tu t'imagines' helped to make him popularly known. He has collaborated in several films (he wrote the script for *Monsieur Ripois*). He is also the widely cultured editor of the Pléiade encyclopedia, and has written piercingly on the history and nature of mathematics (*Bords*, 1963). [CLC]

*Si tu t'imagines . . .* (1952) (collected poems); *Un rude hiver* (1939; tr. B. Askwith, *A Hard Winter*, 1948).

J. Bens, *Q.* (Paris, 1962); C. Simonnet, *Q. déchiffré* (Paris, 1962).

**Quental, Antero de** (Ponta Delgada, Azores 1842–Ponta Delgada 1892). Portuguese poet and left-wing intellectual. Born of aristocratic parents, he received a Catholic education, but as a student in Coimbra reacted against his background, becoming a prominent radical, later a Socialist. Rejecting the effete Romanticism of the literary schools then fashionable, he proclaimed the social function of literature and gave vent to his own revolutionary enthusiasm in his *Odes Modernas* (1865). He was also the moving spirit behind the progressive intellectuals known as the Generation of 1870 (or the Coimbra Generation), who attempted to remedy the intellectual stagnation in which Portugal was sunk. The group included Teófilo Braga, ⇨ Eça de Queirós, Oliveira ⇨ Martins and Ramalho ⇨ Ortigão; they organized a series of 'democratic lectures' at the 'Casino' in Lisbon, to enlighten Portugal about the radical trends in European thinking. Quental gave the first lecture significantly entitled 'The Causes of the Decadence of the Peninsular Peoples'. He was also associated at this time with the foundation of the Lisbon branch of the First International, and with a vague 'iberismo' involving proposals for federating Portugal with Spain. However, amidst this welter of political activity, Quental began to feel intensely disillusioned. The Portuguese working class did not correspond to his idealized concept of the proletariat. He was haunted by a consciousness of his own class origins, and found himself temperamentally in need of some transcendental justification for the phenomenon of life; after his rejection of the Christian God, he became enmeshed in the pseudo-rationalist verbiage of German metaphysics. Even here he could find no lasting escape from his persistent doubts, and his various collections of *Sonnets* document the suffering caused by his striving for a permanent reality. Philosophically, he shows no great originality in his dallying with nihilism, Buddhism, etc., but of his moral nobility there can be no doubt. After gradually withdrawing from public life, he committed suicide. [AJP]

*Sonetos* (CSC).
J. G. Simoes, *A. de Q.* (Lisbon, 1963); H. Cidade, *A. de Q.* (Lisbon, 1962).

**Quevedo y Villegas, Francisco Gómez de** (Madrid 1580–Villanueva de los Infantes 1645). Spanish poet, pamphleteer and satirist. The master of *conceptismo*. A brilliant student (of theology, law, classics and languages) at Alcalá University, he became one of a group of young blades at the court of Philip III. In his early thirties, perhaps as a result of a duel, he went to Italy and became secretary to the Duke of Osuna, on whose fall he was exiled to his estate. After ingratiating himself with the new king, Philip IV, and his favourite the Count-Duke of Olivares, he was recalled to Court and given a royal post, but fell again into disgrace for reasons probably connected with his satirical allusions in print to Olivares and his corrupt regime. After five years' imprisonment (1639–43) he ended his life in retirement.

His youthful satires – the only part of his wide literary production to retain a general appeal – are characterized by a fierce and elaborate wit, and are frequently parodies of established literary or epistolary forms. His picaresque novel, *La historia de la vida del Buscón* (publ. 1626, but begun some twenty years earlier), is a parody of the conventions and attitudes behind the Spanish picaresque tradition typified in Mateo Alemán's *Guzmán de Alfarache*. His *Sueños* or 'Visions' (also begun early, publ. 1627) are mainly a series of paradoxical, pun-crammed Hell-fire cartoons, a highly intellectualized *danse macabre* which reflects his doubts and preoccupations about the values and beliefs of his age. Beneath the chaotic review of types and professions there lies a disgust at the life he knew, expressed in scenes of agitated suffering which recall Bosch and may have influenced Goya's *Caprichos*. His other prose work includes political satire (*La hora de todos y fortuna con seso*, 1635–45), a development of the cartoon-technique apparent in earlier works; political and moral treatises in the Christian Stoic vein (the best known, perhaps, being *La vida de Marco Bruto*, 1644, a commentary on the Plutarch version); and pamphlets of a patriotic and religious nature (such as *España defendida*, 1609, and the anti-Teresan *Su espada por Santiago*, 1629).

Quevedo's large body of poetry is very varied in style and quality. His early love-sonnets, comparable with the 'colourist' verse of ⇨ Herrera and ⇨ Lope de Vega, are rich in erudition and conceits but doubtful in sentiment. His satirical verse often parodies popular song-forms such as the traditional ballads and the slang-songs set in the underworld of Seville. His targets are the usual ones: the social climber, the usurer, the old hag 'Renaissancing' herself. His best burlesques are often the most fantastic and scabrous ones, such as those entitled 'King Tarquin consults a duenna about his love affair, and she replies', or

'A husband who seeks an arrangement narrates his qualifications'. Among his serious sonnets are some extremely fine and moving ones, still in currency, on the passing of time and his country's decay. The celebrated *A S. M. el Rey don Felipe IV. Memorial*, an epistle in verse which is popularly supposed to have been discovered under the royal napkin, is a protest against the sad effects of delegating government to the royal favourite.

Quevedo, born with a club-foot and short-sighted, gives the impression in his work of sex turning sour in him, and in later life he was manoeuvred into an unhappy and short-lived marriage. Nevertheless, he was anything but unsocial; a 'pious rake', Court wit, matchless swordsman, he travelled widely and corresponded assiduously with the scholars of his age. Like Lope de Vega, he repented the levity of his youth in his later years and writings. 'I who have wasted the hours given to me in the cradle, as amends for my sins write Christian doctrine so that others may not imitate me, and I subscribe myself as a danger that all ought to avoid.' Posterity, however, chose to celebrate his more ebullient works. He personifies the brilliance and the tragedy of 17th-century Spain. [KG]

*Obras completas*, ed. L. Astrana Marín (3rd edn, 2 vols., 1943–5); ed. J. M. Blecua (1963ff.); *Epistolario completo*, ed. L. Astrana Marín (1946); *Works* (tr. anon., 3 vols., Edinburgh, 1798); tr. R. L. Estrange *et al.; Q. The Choice Humorous and Satirical Works*, ed. C. Duff (London, 1926); Trend, *OBSV*; Perry, *HASP*; Cohen, *PBSV*.

L. Astrana Marín, *Ideario de don F. de Q.* (Madrid, 1940); C. Campoamor, *Vida y obra de Q.* (Buenos Aires, 1945); A. Papell, *Q.: su tiempo, su vida, su obra* (Barcelona, 1947).

**Quinault, Philippe** (Paris 1635–Paris 1688). French dramatist. He supplied the public of Molière and Racine with exciting and well-planned plays, mostly sentimental in attraction and which have lost their hold on the stage. His most successful comedy was *La mère coquette* (1665). Among his tragedies were *La mort de Cyrus* (1656), *Amalasonte* (1657) and *Astrate, roi de Tyr* (1664). After 1670 he seems to have worked chiefly at operas, with Lulli. [WGM]

E. Gros, *P.Q.* (Paris/Aix-en-Provence, 1926).

**Quiñones de Benavente, Luis** (Toledo 1589?–Madrid 1651). Spanish writer and priest. A friend of ⇨ Lope de Vega; his popular one-act farces in verse, often intended to be sung, were played in the intervals of more serious dramas. Tirso de Molina praises him for substituting dancing for knockabout in these short pieces. He uses stock comic characters: braggart, doctor, notary, sacristan, etc. (e.g. *Los cuatro galanes, El doctor y el enfermo, Los sacristanes burlados*). [DR]

NBAE, XVII, XVIII.

**Quintana, Manuel José** (Madrid 1772–Madrid 1857). Spanish poet. He wrote patriotic odes, in majestic neo-classical style, during Napoleon's invasion. He was imprisoned (1814–20) as a liberal under Ferdinand VII, held office in the short-lived liberal regime that followed, and finally became tutor to Isabel II, who 'crowned' him laureate (1855); nobility of sentiment and rousing rhetoric remain his chief distinction. He based a (poor) tragedy, *El Duque de Viseo* (1801) on 'Monk' Lewis's *Castle Spectre*; his patriotic *Pelayo* (1805) is better. His prose lives, *Vidas de españoles célebres* (1807–33), and his letters to Lord Holland (1823–4) on Spanish affairs at the end of the liberal period are more interesting. [JMC]

*Obras completas*, BAE, 19, 67; *Poesías* (CC); Blecua, *FLE*; Trend, *OBSV*.

# R

**Raabe, Wilhelm** (Eschershausen 1831–Braunschweig 1910). German novelist. After attending Wolfenbüttel grammar school, he was a bookseller in Magdeburg from 1849, extra-curricular student at Berlin University from 1853, freelance writer from 1856. He toured Germany and Austria in 1859. After marrying in 1862, he lived in Stuttgart and from 1870 in Braunschweig. His basic pessimism is veiled by a sense of humour developing from facetiousness, through irony, into philosophic calm. He rejects 19th-century mechanization, materialism, and philistinism. His favourite characters – humble introverts and dreamers in cosy small-town surroundings – rise above external success or failure by leading rich inner lives. His numerous contemporary or historical novels and stories, influenced by ⇨ Jean Paul, Dickens, Thackeray, combine realism with social symbolism and moral comment. His successful first novel, *Die Chronik der Sperlingsgasse* (1857), is a lyrical, episodic idyll of old Berlin. In a loose trilogy, *Der Hungerpastor* (1864; tr. Arnold, *The Hunger-Pastor*, 1885) still allows an unworldly hero to win, and *Abu Telfan oder die Heimkehr vom Mondgebirge* (1868; tr. S. Delffs, *Abu Telfan; or, the Return from the Mountains of the Moon*, 1881) criticizes Germany in the detached manner of ⇨ Montesquieu's *Lettres persanes*, but *Der Schüdderump* (1870) grimly depicts the victory of utilitarian ambition. *Unruhige Gäste* (1886) praises a near-Christian heroine, while *Stopfkuchen* (1891) features Raabe's most memorable eccentric whose modest humanity defies the dehumanizing forces of Bismarck's age. The unfinished *Altershausen* hints again that childlike simplicity gets nearer the truth than worldly wisdom. His best Novelle is the socially critical adventure story *Die schwarze Galeere* in the collection *Ferne Stimmen* (1865). His most notable minor works are the novels *Die Kinder von Finkenrode* (1859), *Der Dräumling* (1872), *Horacker* (1876), *Alte Nester* (1879), *Das Odfeld* (1888), *Die Akten des Vogelsanges* (1895), and some Novellen in *Deutscher Mondschein* (1873) and *Krähenfelder Geschichten* (1879). [LL]

*Sämtliche Werke*, ed. K. Hoppe (24 vols., 1951ff.); *Werke*, ed. K. Hoppe (4 vols., 1961ff.).
H. Fehse, *W.R.* (Braunschweig, 1937); H. Pongs, *W.R.* (Heidelberg, 1958); B. Fairley, *W.R.* (1961).

**Rabelais, François** (1494 ?–1553 ?). French humanist. A Franciscan turned Benedictine, he abandoned the cloister to study medicine at Montpellier (1530). He took a doctorate there in 1537. By entering a Benedictine abbey about to be secularized, he became a lay priest (1536). His children were later legitimated. His patrons included Guillaume du Bellay, the seigneur de Langey, and Cardinal Jean his brother (whose private physician he was and with whom he visited Italy), Marguerite de Navarre and Cardinal de Châtillon.

*Pantagruel* (1532), a comparatively slight and partly popular work, already reveals Rabelais's genius as storyteller, satirist, propagandist and creator of comic situation and character (cf. Panurge). Chapter 8 is a serious eulogy of fertile matrimony and Christian humanist education. *Gargantua* (1534), now printed first, treats an earlier stage of his giants' history. It contains some of his best work. It mocks old-fashioned education beloved by Paris theologians; ridicules monks for uselessness, preferring Frère Jean's uncouth activeness to the vain repetitions of his fellows; preaches appeasement but not pacifism; contrasts superstition with Evangelism and, in the *Abbey of Thelema* ('will'), opposes the monastic ideal with a free society of noble Evangelicals, living under self-discipline in a community where riches and beauty are good and marriage the norm. The book ends pessimistically with reflections on the suffering of true Christians. Following an outburst of repression in late 1534, Rabelais abandoned his post of doctor at the Hôtel-Dieu at Lyons (1535). Despite royal support, his *Tiers Livre* (1546) was condemned and he fled. In this complex book, the giants are huge in wisdom, not body. Pantagruel the wise is contrasted with Panurge, the erudite, fluent, self-loving fool who cannot reconcile desires to marry with fears of cuckoldom. Rabelais's philosophy deepens into a syncretic Evangelical platonic stoicism with sceptical overtones. Pauline folly-of-the-Gospel is contrasted with worldly wisdom and worldly folly, but is reconciled with true wisdom. Chapter 48 is a bitter diatribe against canon law and monks for interfering in matrimonial affairs and permitting clandestine marriages. The *Quart Livre* of 1548, though incomplete, contains some of his funniest episodes, many indebted in conception to the French farce. The complete *Quart Livre* (1551) is his boldest work. The *Storm at Sea* mocks superstition while defending free-will; a war against the *Andouilles* ('Protestant Sausages') leads to a hilarious parody of chivalrous romances, but a visit to the *Papimanes* leads to a total rejection of Papal-centred religion as a comic perversion of Evangelical truth. The philosophy of the book develops further a profound Classical/Christian syncretism.

*L'Isle sonante* (1562) allegedly by Rabelais, and the so-called *Cinquiesme Livre* (1564) which incorporates it, are probably supposititious. Villey holds that anyone who thinks they are in part authentic must go and prove it. Rabelais also wrote some comic almanachs and edited learned works. Some of his works are lost.

His genius was recognized in his own day; his influence was immediate and great, but attempts to copy his characters, style, enormous vocabulary and colourful language have all failed. [MAS]

*Édition critique*, ed. Lefranc *et al.* (1913ff.); *Œuvres complètes*, ed. J. Boulenger (Pléiade, 1934); *Pantagruel, Tiers Livre* and *Quart Livre* in Droz, *Textes littéraires français*; tr. Sir T. Urquhart and P. A. Motteux (Everyman, 826, 827, 1954); J. M. Cohen (Penguin Classics, 1955).

J. Plattard, *L'œuvre de R.* (Paris, 1909); P. Villey, *Marot et R.* (Paris, 1923); M. Screech, *The Rabelaisian Marriage, Aspects of R.'s Religion, Ethics and Comic Philosophy* (1958); A. Krailsheimer, *R. and the Franciscans* (1963).

**Racine, Jean** (La Ferté-Milon 1639–Paris 1699). French tragic poet. He was the son of a customs official, his mother a Sconin, a strict religious family. His aunt, a nun at Port Royal, took special care of the boy who was orphaned early. He attended the Jansenist Collège de Beauvais and later the Collège d'Harcourt in Paris, but his essential education he received informally from the lay *solitaires* of Port Royal, in particular from Lancelot, Le Maître, Nicole and (his favourite) Hamon. Through a cousin of his father's he became acquainted with the world of fashion and of letters. An early ode was shown to Chapelain and a tragedy, *Amasie*, is spoken of in 1660 as having pleased certain actors. While his own friends Nicholas Vitart and the Abbé le Vasseur stimulated his inborn taste for writing, a stay with an uncle at Uzès (1661–2) soon dispelled an idea that he might enter the Church. The attraction of the Paris theatre in the season 1662–3 must have been great for so gifted a débutant and we may imagine Racine following closely the success of *L'école des femmes* and the so-called comic war; he already knew La Fontaine and soon met Boileau. It was in fact Molière who produced Racine's first tragedy, *La Thébaïde*, in June 1664, and who would have produced the second, *Alexandre le Grand*, in December 1665, had not the young dramatist removed it in course of rehearsal to the main tragic theatre at the Hôtel de Bourgogne. That he had now discovered his true talent was evident from the success of *Andromaque*, produced in the Louvre in November 1667, one of the great dates in the history of French theatre, like 1636 (⇨ Corneille, P.).

Meanwhile, Racine's new way of life had led to an open break with Port Royal; he defended Desmarets de Saint-Sorlin, author of *Les Visionnaires*, against Nicole's unfortunate expression that a writer of novels and plays was 'un empoisonneur public'. Racine's answer was brilliant, harsh and all too effective: in 1677 he was still seeking for a reconciliation with the pious men to whom he owed so much. But Racine's character is far from clear. His skill in polemic and certain facts about him suggest that he was a careerist. Yet the turning-points in his public life are all still unexplained. We do not know why he broke with Molière, nor why he wrote no more secular plays after 1677, when he married. His appointment as historiographer royal need surely not have caused such an absolute break. We do not even know whether, as is often said, he died in disfavour with the king. The accounts left by his sons seem tendentious: we need not assume that he was as pious as they make out – nor as wicked as the scandal associated with his mistresses has suggested.

Between 1667 and 1677 Racine produced 7 tragedies and 1 comedy, *Les plaideurs*

(1668). There was a postscript, in 1689–91, when he wrote 2 Biblical plays for the young ladies in Mme de Maintenon's school at Saint-Cyr; though neither was performed on any public stage until after his death, both now count among his great works. Racine claimed that he imitated only Euripides and Sophocles, but he owed more to his contemporaries, who for thirty years had attracted Paris audiences to a new type of serious drama and perfected its technique. ⇨ Corneille, ⇨ Tristan, ⇨ Rotrou, and others supplied him with a form and a framework within which he showed the destruction of human personality by its own agency, through ambition, passion, jealousy – forms, always, of what La Rochefoucauld called self-love. In verse sometimes magnificent and always musical his characters perceive and proclaim the bondage of man to instinct, the impossibility of satisfaction. They need only the barest minimum of incident to spark off their tragedy, for it lies in the human condition and not in events. The poet gives them a lucidity which intensifies their plight and our pity for their abandonment in a hostile world.

Racine's final, and many would say his finest, play expresses the tragedy of one who resists God, the creature in revolt against the creator, dying impenitent, as Port Royal had taught him that it was possible for men to do: *Pitiless God, Thou hast willed it all.* This is the cry of the abandoned, of those whom worldly power betrays into challenging even the deity.

In *Andromaque* (1667), the theme, probably inspired by Virgil, is that of the captive Andromache, and the vacillations of her captor Pyrrhus between her and the proud Hermione, on whom depends the sanity of Oreste. A most ingenious plot where a false step may bring four people to death. *Britannicus* (1669) is a rewriting of Tacitus's chapters on Nero as young emperor, poised between attraction for Junie and fear of his mother Agrippine. He listens to good and bad counsel and is pushed into crime by the mother's tyranny. A drama on the mysterious links between weakness and wickedness. *Bérénice* (1670) is a drama of three characters, where action is reduced almost to nothing. There remains a pure analysis of passion (hers for Titus who as Emperor cannot marry her, and that of Antiochus for her) in its extremes both of self-abasement and final self-transcendence and renunciation. *Bajazet* (1672) is a drama of the harem, in which a former slave, now queen, requires a prince to marry her, or to die. The prince's true (and younger) beloved urges him to dissemble to save both their lives – but in vain. In *Mithridate* (1673), Rome's most persistent enemy, King of Pontus, finds resistance within his own palace in the person of Monime, whom he commands to marry him and whose integrity is more resistant than any army. In *Iphigénie* (1674) modern psychological motivation is sought for an ancient myth, with a guilty scapegoat provided to save the innocent heroine. In *Phèdre* (1677) a queen avows love for her stepson, only to find that her husband still lives. Jealousy induces her to send him to death, conscience to admit her guilt before dying herself. In *Athalie* (1691), hardly a play for a girls' school, a pagan queen fights the God of the Jews, defies him, then admits his power over her. [WGM]

*Œuvres complètes*, ed. R. Picard (2 vols., Pléiade, 1960); *Phaedra, Andromache, Britannicus*, tr. G. Dillon (1961); *Iphigenia, Phaedra, Athaliah*, tr. J. Cairncross (Penguin Classics, 1964).

F. Mauriac, *La vie de J.R.* (Paris, 1928); G. Brereton, *J.R.* (1951); J. C. Lapp, *Aspects of Racinian Tragedy* (Toronto, 1955); J. Pommier, *Aspects de R.* (Paris, 1960); P. Butler, *Classicisme et baroque dans l'œuvre de R.* (Paris, 1959); E. Vinaver, *R. et la poésie tragique* (2nd edn, Paris, 1961); B. Weinberg, *The Art of J.R.* (Chicago/London, 1963).

**Radičević, Branko** (Slavonski Brod 1824–Vienna 1853). Serbian poet. The first major romantic poet in Serbia to abandon artificial patterns and write in a direct, personal tone and in the pure spoken language. His first poems were written in German while at the Serbian *gimnasium* at Sremski Karlovci, but in Vienna he met ⇨ Karadžić and was influenced by his linguistic reforms, which he vindicated in his volume of poetry *Pesme* (1847). Many of his lyrics are almost indistinguishable from the more erotic lyrical folk songs, but he also studied the German romantic poets and towards the end of his life began to introduce new and more sophisticated verse forms into Serbian poetry. His best-known poems, 'Djački rastanak' and the moving 'Kad mlidijah umreti', are typically romantic pieces expressing a unity between the poet's mood and nature. His works still retain their freshness and youthful sincerity and he is generally considered the founder of Serbian romantic poetry. [EDG]

Ibrovac, *APY.*
Barac, *HYL.*

**Radishchev, Aleksander** (Moscow 1749–St Petersburg 1802). Russian writer of prose and poetry. Studied in Germany, steeped in 18th-century French philosophy, he became a customs official and legal expert. Many poems, including 'Ode to Freedom', are revolutionary in spirit; but he is famous for one work in prose, published through an oversight of the police: *Puteshestviye iz Peterburga v Moskvu* (1790; tr. L. Wiener, ed. R. P. Thaler, *Journey from St Petersburg to Moscow*, 1958). It realistically describes the horrors of serfdom, autocratic tyranny, bureaucratic inefficiency, evidently to 'enlighten' Catherine, who is shown (allegorically) as blindfolded. But Radishchev was exiled to Siberia; rehabilitated by Alexander (1801), he cooperated in new projects for reform, but despaired and committed suicide. His clumsily written *Journey* became a symbol for the 19th-century intelligentsia, with its cry, 'my soul was afflicted with the sufferings of mankind'.

*Polnoye sobraniye sochineniy* (3 vols., 1938–52).
D. M. Lang, *The First Russian Radical* (1959).

**Radnóti, Miklós** (Budapest 1907–Györ 1944). Hungarian poet. The greatest writer of Hungarian anti-Fascist poetry. As a student he became the centre of a literary circle in Szeged. He first gained recognition as a translator (*Orpheus Nyomában*, 1943, including works from La Fontaine, Coctau, Shelley and others). The rebellious jauntiness of his early poems (*Pogány köszöntő*, 1930; *Lábadozó szél*, 1933) is gradually replaced by a presentiment of tragic death which overshadows even his happiest moods (*Tajtékos ég*, 1940); but he faces up to the danger (*Mint a Bika*) and in poems such as *Kortárs Útlevelére* (1934) and *Járkálj csak*, *Halálraitélt* (1936) he exhorts poets to speak out against injustice. His only relief from gloom was provided by his love for his wife and for nature. In his volumes of poems, *Újhold* (1935), *Meredek út* (1938), Radnóti developed a classical metre.

In 1944 he was taken to a concentration camp in Yugoslavia and later killed while being herded west by the retreating Germans. Up to his death, in the last two of his eclogues and other poems which were later found in his pockets, he recorded his experiences, protest against barbarity and his faith in a brighter future for mankind. [JFR]

Klaniczay, *HHL.*

**Raičković, Stevan** (Neresnica 1928– ). Serbian poet. He is one of the most interesting Serbian post-war poets (⇨ Popa). He writes nature poetry. He brings a modern sensibility to the relation of the human individuality to natural phenomena, to the colour and movement of trees, insects and grass, in which man finds expression for his profoundest emotional experiences. His verse is more conventional than that of many modern poets, but his language is marked by a rigid economy. [EDG]

*Pesma tišine* (1952); *Kasno leto* (1958); Lavrin, *AMYP.*
Kadić, *CSL.*

**Raimbaut, Count of Orange** (Provence). ⇨ Troubadour who flourished in the third quarter of the 12th century. An independent spirit, educated and witty, he refused to accept the traditionally submissive role of the courtly lover, and preferred *jois*, a positive attitude to the enjoyment of life, as the inspiration for his poetry. He began by composing in the obscure style, or *trobar clus*, and revealed great delicacy in his use of symbols. He was then persuaded by ⇨ Guiraut de Bornelh and others to simplify his style, and he developed the clearer but technically rich style of *trobar ric* in which he showed great skill with his choice of rhymes. In this he was a direct precursor of ⇨ Arnaut Daniel. [LTT]

*The Life and Works of the Troubadour R. d'O.*, ed. W. T. Pattison (Minnesota U.P., 1952).

**Raimon de Miraval** (Carcasses fl. *c.*1185–1213). Provençal ⇨ troubadour. A close friend of count Raimon VI of Toulouse, with whom he exchanged the pseudonym *Audiart*, he was acquainted with the great lords of the Carcasses, Pedro II of Aragon, Alphonso VIII of Castille and various Catalan nobles. After the loss of his castle to the armies of Simon de Montfort and the Southern defeat at Muret (1213), he went to Spain and entered the monastery at Lerida. In his courtly poetry he is not the submissive suitor seeking happiness in the love of an unapproachable lady. Instead of *jois* he seeks *pretz* or the social esteem of the courtly world in which he moves. Love has become an *art de plaire* in which flawless manners and brilliant and entertaining conversation (*solatz*) are essential. Both lover and lady must obey this code, and if the lady is at fault, the troubadour has the right to admonish, criticize, even leave her in order to preserve his own courtly reputation.

Miraval has left 37 *cansos* and 8 other poems in minor genres. His 13th-century biographers invented extensive amorous stories about him especially in connexion with the famous Loba de Pennautier who may be the *Mais d'amic* of his songs. He is highly praised by 13th-century authorities on courtly doctrine such as Raimon Vidal of Besalu and Matfré Ermengaud. In his *Documenti d'amore* (ed. Egidi, I, p. 270) Francesco da Barberino (1264–1348) states that he used a story by Miraval as the source of one of his tales in the *Fiori di novelle*, a collection which has unfortunately been lost. [LTT]

L. T. Topsfield, *Les poésies du troubadour R. de M.* (Paris, 1968); *MLR*, LI (1956).

**Raimund, Ferdinand** (Vienna 1790–Pottenstein 1836). Austrian dramatist. By profession an actor, he inherited a traditional Viennese form, the *Zauberspiel*, a dramatic fairy-tale with music and allegorical figures, centring around simple comic characters; he wrote his plays for production in the theatre where he performed. His marriage to an actress was short-lived, and his love for a bourgeois girl, Toni Wagner, was embittered by jealousy. This bitterness and his discontent both with the artistic limitations of the popular stage and with the fickleness of the theatre-going public find expression in his best plays – *Das Mädchen aus der Feenwelt* (1826), *Der Alpenkönig und der Menschenfeind* (1828) and *Der Verschwender* (1834), whose humour is tinged with melancholy but which conform to the spirit of Austrian ⇨ *Biedermeier* in teaching a moral of contented self-sufficiency. Raimund's literary aspirations misled him at times into attempting too high-flown a style, but he was the first to add genuine personal feeling to popular Viennese comedy. [WEY]

*Werke*, ed. F. Brukner and E. Castle (1924–34).
K. Fuhrmann, *R.s Kunst und Charakter* (Berlin, 1913); O. Rommel, *Die Alt-Wiener Volkskomödie* (Vienna, 1952).

**Rakić, Milan** (Belgrade 1876–Zagreb 1938). Serbian poet. One of the finest early 20th-century Serbian poets (with ⇨ Dučić he also reflects French influences). He lived in Paris (1898–1902), entered the diplomatic service, and was Yugoslav ambassador to Rome (1927–33). Not a prolific writer, his poems are limited to two small volumes. His poetry is more sensual than Dučić's and has a philosophical theme. Its underlying *motif* is a resigned and pessimistic sense of mortality and the relentless passage of time. Typical of his range of mood are the poems 'Minare', 'Oprostajna pesma' and 'Iskrena pesma'. [EDG]

*SEER*, XXIV, 263 (1946); Ibrovac, *APY*; Lavrin, *AMYP*.
Kadić, *CSL*; Barac, *HYL*; *SEER*, XVIII, 52 (1939–40).

**Ramler, Karl Wilhelm** (Kolberg 1725–Berlin 1798). German poet. He was a teacher at the Cadet School in Berlin, but it was as co-editor (with Sulzer) of the literary journal, *Kritische Nachrichten aus dem Reich der Gelehrsamkeit*, and a friend of E. von ⇨ Kleist, ⇨ Nicolai and ⇨ Lessing (with whom he skilfully refurbished the epigrams of Logau) that he exercised a modest influence on the intellectual life of his age. Though celebrated as the German Horace, his *Oden* (1767) and *Lyrische Gedichte* (1772), with their antique style allegory, classical allusions and private pseudo-mythology, have only historical interest. [WAC]

DNL, 45.
H. Freydanck, *Goethe und R.* (1928).

**Ramuz, Charles-Ferdinand** (Cully, Vaud 1878–Pully, Lausanne 1947). Swiss novelist. After eleven years in Paris he returned to Switzerland for good in 1914. His first novel *Aline* (1905), the story of a village girl who is seduced by a rich young man and who kills her child, displayed what was to be a characteristic simplicity of subject-matter and style. The chief works of his Paris period are *Aimé Pache, peintre vaudois* (1910) and *Vie de Samuel Belet* (1913; tr. M. Savill, *The Life of Samuel Belet*, 1951), both ⇨ *Bildungsromane* with an autobiographical content. On his return to Switzerland his writing became allegorical and acquired a Biblical tone, e.g. *La guérison des maladies* (1917), and was also inspired by the war, e.g. *Présence de la mort* (1922; tr. A. R. Macdougall and A. Comfort, *The Triumph of Death*, 1946). The period of his greatest novels followed, e.g. *La grand* *peur dans la montagne* (1926), *La beauté sur la terre* (1927; tr. anon., *Beauty on Earth*, 1938), *Adam et Ève* (1932), and *Derborence* (1935; tr. S. F. Scott, *When the Mountain Fell*, 1949). The last-named, perhaps his best, deals with an avalanche and the fate of a young villager who, weeks later, emerges from under the stones. His novels are set in his native region, in its mountains and woods, and portray the life of its peasants, closer to 'universal man' than city-dwellers. Ramuz incorporates aspects of the local dialect into his style. Although his studied simplicity may sometimes seem overdone, at his best, as in *Derborence*, he achieves works of considerable power. Besides his novels he has published a journal, volumes of reminiscences and essays, e.g. *Besoin de grandeur* (1937). He was a friend and collaborator of Stravinsky, e.g. *Histoire du soldat* (1918; tr. M. Flanders and K. Black, *The Soldier's Tale*, 1955). [SMD]

H. Cingria, *R., notre parrain* (Bienne, 1956); J. M. Dunoyer, *R., peintre vaudois* (Lausanne, 1959); G. Guisan, *R., ou le génie de la patience* (Lausanne, 1958).

**Ranjina, Dinko** and **Nikola.** ⇨ Dalmatian and Dubrovnik Literature.

**Ranković, Svetolik** (Moštanica 1863–Belgrade 1899). Serbian novelist. Deeply influenced by Russian literature, especially Dostoyevsky and Tolstoy, he introduced the psychological novel into Serbian. *Porušeni ideali* (1899) and *Seoska učiteljica* (1898) lacked life, but his first and best work, *Gorski car* (1897), an account of the fate of a Serbian bandit, is the first Serbian novel to examine the inner life of its characters and to portray the complex nature of crime. [EDG]

Barac, *HYL.*

**Rapin, Nicolas** (Fontenay-le-Comte 1535?–Poitiers 1609?). French lawyer and poet. Active in public life, he was a firm opponent of the Ligue and supporter of the king. Besides translations of Horace and Ovid, his work includes paraphrases of the 7 penitential psalms. In the title poem of his collection *Les plaisirs du gentilhomme champêtre* (1583) he recommends a retreat into rural life as an escape from the miseries and factions of the age. He also contributed to the verse sections of the *Satire Ménippée.* [GJ]

**Rapin, René** (Tours 1621–Paris 1687). French Jesuit and author of French and Latin works. He is chiefly remembered for his Latin poem on gardens, in 4 books, which has been translated into several languages. [FB]

*Renati Rapini Hortorum libri* iv, ed. I. T. McDonald, verse tr. J. Gardiner (Worcester, Mass., 1932).

C. Dejob, *De Renato Rapino* (Paris, 1881).

**Rashi,** abbreviation of Rabbi Shelomoh Itzhaki or Solomon Ben Isaac (Troyes 1040–Troyes 1105). Hebrew poet and religious writer. After studying in Worms and Mainz, he founded the Talmudic academy at Troyes. His commentaries on the Pentateuch and Talmud had immense influence on Jewish scholarship. French words (*Loazim*) scattered throughout his works have contributed to the study of early French. His liturgical poetry has simplicity and great depth. [EE]

S. Bernstein, *R. betor paytan* (1940); M. H. Liber, *R.* (English edn, 1906).

**Rasmussen, Halfdan** (Copenhagen 1915– ). Danish poet. Of working-class origin, he is a fine lyrical poet, and ever since his first volume of poems, *Soldat eller menneske* (1941), was published he has been a poet *engagé*; today he is Denmark's leading poet of social protest and social conscience in the nuclear age. At the same time he is also the country's leading writer of inspired nonsense poetry, of which several volumes have been published under the common title *Tosserier.* [ELB]

*Digte i Udvalg* (1953); *Tosserier i Udvalg* (1960).

**Rasmussen, Knud** (Jakobshavn, Greenland 1879–Gentofte 1933). Danish arctic explorer whose most important literary work is *Myter og Sagn fra Grønland*, i–iii (1921–5). [ELB]

**Ratherius** or **Ratharius of Liège (and Verona)** (*c.* 887–974). Medieval writer and man of affairs. Gifted and nobly born, he was trained at Lobbes in Hainault. He secured the bishopric of Verona in 931, but provoked deposition and imprisonment three years later. By political intrigues he secured restoration to Verona in 947 and again *c.* 962; and he also obtained the bishopric of Liège for a time. But he could never maintain any position for long, and spent his last years in exile. He lacked the worldliness necessary for political survival and the dignity to remain a martyr. Though in sympathy with the beginnings of the reform movement, he was essentially an isolated figure, exceptionally sensitive and self-aware for the period, and psychologically close to Augustine. His letters and autobiographical *Praeloquia* reveal his singular style – mannered and exaggerated, involuted and violent, and yet varied and powerful and able to convey a wide range of tone. [CEC]

Ed. P. and G. Ballerini (Verona, 1765); Migne, *PL*, 136 (1853); ed. F. Weigle, MGH (1949) (letters); A. Adam, *Arbeit und Besitz nach R. von V.* (Freiburg im Breisgau, 1927).

H. M. Klinkenberg, *Archiv für Kulturgeschichte*, 38 (1956); E. Amman, *Dictionnaire de théologie catholique*, xiii, 2 (Paris, 1937); Manitius *GLLM*.

**Raymond of Agiles** or **Aguilers** (fl. 1095–1100). Medieval chronicler and canon of Le Puy. He joined the First Crusade as chaplain to Count Raymond of Toulouse and at the siege of Antioch was involved in that curious incident, the Invention of the Holy Lance. ⇨ Tudeboeuf says that Raymond carried this relic before the Christian army at the battle of Ascalon the following year. Raymond was also present at the siege and taking of Jerusalem, and accompanied Count Raymond on a pilgrimage to the Jordan. His *Historia Francorum qui ceperunt Jerusalem* is full and detailed, largely an eye-witness account, and all the more reliable since he is careful to specify when his information has been obtained second hand. [MRM]

*RHC*, Hist. Occ., iii; Migne, *PL*, 155; tr. Guizot, *CHF*, xxi.

**Raynal, Paul** (Narbonne 1885– ). French dramatist. Self-consciously exploits the manner and structure of neo-classical tragedy in plays devoted to contemporary subjects. He restricts the action in space and time in a way that recalls the 'unities', and, by refusing to locate his characters in any precisely rooted milieu, hopes to avoid the resonances of naturalistic drama and so create a 'heroic' climate in which the protagonists can use heightened and intensified speech. The result is to produce strained rhetorical structures markedly deficient in their sense of life. This is true of *Le maître de son cœur* (1920, but written in 1909); *Le tombeau sous l'Arc de Triomphe* (1924; tr. C. Lewis, *The Unknown Warrior*, 1928), the most 'alive' of his plays in its confrontation between the psychology of the trenches and that of the civil population. Other works include *Au soleil de l'instinct* (1932); *La francerie* (1933), an encounter between three symbolic types played out against the sombre background of the battle of the Marne; *Napoléon unique* (1936), which concentrates on the conflict between love, in the shape of Josephine, and dynastic ambition; *A souffert sous Ponce-Pilate* (1939); and *Le matériel humain* (1947, but written in 1935), a grandiose fable about authority, involving a general, a corporal condemned to death, and a cloudy ethic of discipline and responsibility. [SBJ]

Surer, *TFC*; Sée, *TFC*.

**'Razón de Amor, La'** (early 13th cent.). The first known poem of any length written in Castilian. It is a love-poem in the Provençal manner by an anonymous author who claims to have been educated in France and Germany and to have lived in Lombardy. It tells of the meeting of two lovers in an orchard in the month of April, and is beautifully lyrical. The second part, burlesque in manner, describes a dispute bebetween water and wine. [JMC]

Blecua, *FLE*; Menéndez y Pelayo, *PLC*; Trend, *OBSV*.

L. Spitzer, *Sobre antigua poesía española* (Buenos Aires, 1962).

**Rebora, Clemente** (Milan 1885–1957). Italian poet. He was the foremost religious poet of modern Italy. He entered a monastry in 1929, after years of anguished meditation intensified by the shock of war experiences. [GD]

*Le poesie* (1947).

*Quaderno reboriano* (Milan, 1960) (various contributors); Bárberi Squarotti, *AR*.

**Rebreanu, Liviu** (Tîrlişiua 1885–Valea Mare 1944). Rumanian novelist. He was born the son of a teacher in the north of Transylvania, when that country was still part of the Austro-Hungarian empire. His secondary education was unusually varied; he attended Rumanian, German and Hungarian schools. He trained as an officer at Budapest, but in 1909 went to Bucharest to be a writer. His most famous novels are *Ion* (1920), a vast panorama of peasant life and Rumanian national feeling in Transylvania: *Pădurea spînzuraților* (1922; tr. A. V. Wise, *The Forest of the Hanged*, 1930), dedicated to 'my brother Emil executed by the Austro-Hungarians, on the Rumanian front, in 1917', a deeply felt tragedy of the First World War; and *Răscoala* (1933; tr. P. Crandjean and S. Hartauer, *The Uprising*, 1964), a sequel to *Ion*, vividly depicting the peasant revolt of 1907. In *Răscoala*, as in some of Cezar ⇨ Petrescu's novels, there is a crude violence which must have been more startling at the time of publication than now. [EDT]

**Rederijkers.** A popular and apposite corruption of French *rhétoriqueurs.* 'Cameren van Rhetorica' (Dutch 'chambers of rhetoric') spread rapidly from the French border in the 15th century and were organized like guilds with functions similar to those of the French dramatic societies (⇨ *puys*). There were chambers in the towns and villages of Brabant, Flanders and South Holland with their own names, slogans and symbols generally of religious significance. The members composed for special occasions, performed at all functions and organized recitals of their art, pageants and processions. Initially they were truly communal and democratic and produced only anonymous work under the name of the chamber. Yet they attracted the patronage of the nobility and had their own internal hierarchy: an influential citizen at the head with the title *coninc*, assisted by a *prins* or (later) *keizer*, and *dekens*, frequently church ministers who also had their assistants. Each chamber also had its own paid manager, the *factor*, and its jester (*nar* or *zot*). At the great annual festival, the lavishly organized *Landjuweel*, the chambers competed for prizes. *Elckerlijc*, the original of *Everyman*, won such a prize in Antwerp.

Though they considered drama to be the highest form of art, they practised all kinds of poetry and developed their own form of Refrain. This consisted of any number of stanzas of any length, each ending in a *stoc* (the basis of the theme?), and it always finished with an *envoi*, a stanza addressed to the Prince and introduced by this word or a derivation from it. The Refrain was used to great effect by Anna ⇨ Bijns in her trenchant attacks on Lutheranism. Towards the end of the 16th century the war and laws against organized meetings necessitated the closure of many of the chambers, and those that survived had lost much of their medieval character. Catholic belief was no longer the *raison d'être* of the chambers and their activities, and the original ideal of popular participation in intellectual and cultural expression was declining into mannerisms aped from the French court. Two chambers, however, justly retained their fame through the 17th century, Het Wit Lavendel and De Eglantier, the Amsterdam centres of the greatest of the Renaissance poets. The coteries which clung to the remnants of the chambers into the 19th century reflected the bankrupt standards and pedestrian tastes of the 18th century. [PK]

*Het Antwerpse Landjuweel van 1561*, ed. C. Kruyskamp (1962).

J. J. Mak, *De Rederijkers* (Amsterdam, 1944).

**Redi, Francesco** (Arezzo 1626–Pisa 1698). Italian writer and scientist. Physician to Ferdinand II and Cosimo III of Tuscany, and an experimental biologist, he composed several scientific pamphlets on his work. His verse includes numerous, love sonnets full of Petrarchan and *stilnovo* echoes, and more effective lighthearted poems in various short-lined metres which make witty use of rhyme and rhythm, diminutive suffixes and earthy, realistic vocabulary. His best-known poem is the dithyramb *Bacco in Toscana* (tr. Leigh Hunt, 1825) published in 1685 after 20 years of preparation. Here all his metrical virtuosity is displayed, as Bacchus, sampling the wines of Tuscany, and decrying such unworthy beverages as coffee, beer and English cider, is carried in sliding lurching rhythms to intoxicated bliss. [DGR]

*Lettere e consulti; Bacco in Toscana*, ed. V. Osimo (1927); *Naturali osservazioni ed esperienze*, ed. V. Osimo (1927); *Le piú belle pagine*, ed. P. Giacosa (1925); Calcaterra, *LSA*.

G. Imbert, *F.R. l'uomo* (Milan, 1925); *Minori*, iii.

**Regnard, Jean-François** (Paris 1655–Chateau de Grillon, Dourdan 1709). French playwright. Much travelled, a gambler, and fond of good living, he wrote successful plays for the Théatre-Italien and the Théatre Français. The best, *Le joueur* (1696) and *Le légataire universel* (1708), are polished examples of the comic art of the time, in which artificial situations lightly reveal social and psychological truths.

*Oeuvres complètes* (2 vols., Paris, 1854); *Le retour imprévu*, ed. S. D. Screech, 1930; *The Intriguing Chambermaid* (a comedy), Henry Fielding, 1734.

**Régnier, Henri de** (Honfleur 1864–Paris 1936). French poet and novelist. He began as a Parnassian (*Les lendemains*, 1885, *Apaisement*, 1886), then imitated symbolist techniques and *vers libre* (*Poèmes anciens et romanesques*, 1890), and achieved his most characteristic melancholy-nostalgic style in *Les jeux mystiques et divins* (1897), *Les médailles d'argile* (1900), *La cité des eaux* (1902) (about Versailles), *La sandale ailée* (1906), *Le miroir des heures* (1910). His aristocratic, if effete, good taste made him a favourite poet of the *belle époque* (Académie Française, 1911). The best of his fiction is in evocations of 17th- and 18th-century life of elegant pleasure (from *La double maîtresse*, 1900, to *Le voyage d'amour ou l'Initiation vénitienne*, 1930). [WA]

D. Parmée, *Classicisme et néo-classicisme dans l'œuvre d'H. de R.* (1939); E. Jaloux, *Souvenirs sur H. de R.* (Lausanne, 1941).

**Régnier, Mathurin** (Chartres 1573–Rouen 1613). French poet. He travelled to Rome, became a canon of Chartres (like his uncle ⇨ Desportes) and enjoyed a life of ease. He became famous for his (nineteen) satires, in the manner of Horace and Juvenal, and reflecting the ideas of Montaigne. Satire IX defends inspiration, imagination (even negligence) against Malherbe; satire XIII is a masterly study of a hypocrite, Macette, comparable with Roja's Celestina or Molière's Tartuffe. He also wrote *Elégies*, *Discours au roi*, a *Hyme sur la Nativité du Seigneur*, and occasional poems, publishing three editions (Paris, 1608, 1609, 1612).

*Oeuvres complètes*, ed. G. Raibaud (Paris, 1958); *Satires*, intr. and notes J.-A. Lacour (Paris, 1955).

J. Vianey, *M.R.* (Paris, 1969).

**Reinmar der Alte (Reinmar von Hagenau)** (born Alsace ? *c.*1170). German ⇨ Minnesinger. There is no documentary reference to him but from his own poetry, as well as from that of his younger contemporary ⇨ Walther von der Vogelweide, it can be concluded that he spent the greater part of his life as a poet at the court of Vienna, and that he died there in the first decade of the 13th century. His poetry represents the zenith of the German courtly love lyric in its strict 'classical' sense, and is characterized by a high degree of preciosity of feeling and contrived subtlety of form. [RT]

Kraus, *MF.*

K. Burdach, *R. der A. und Walther von der Vogelweide* (Halle, 1928); C. von Kraus, *Die Lieder R.s des A.* (Munich, 1919); Ehrismann, *GDL.*

**Reinmar von Zweter** (*c.*1200–*c.*1250). German moral and didactic poet. Chief representative of a long line of 13th-century *Spruchdichter*. In the course of an unsettled life he served a number of patrons, among them the rulers of the courts of Bohemia and Vienna. He was devoted to serious moral and religious virtues, and the overt purpose of his very considerable poetic output, which consists of religious, political, general moral, and formal love poetry, is to improve the mind and conduct of his audience. Probably the most characteristic of his poetic creations is the allegorical figure of Dame Honour (*Frau Ehre*), a personification of moral excellence, in whom the chivalric ideals of *Minne* amd *Ehre* (Courtly Love and Moral Virtue) are combined. [RT]

Ed. G. Roethe (1887).

Ehrismann, *GDL.*

**Reinoso, Félix José** (Seville 1772–Madrid 1841). Spanish poet and priest. His poem in two cantos, *La inocencia perdida* (1799), takes its subject from Milton. Its treatment, however, is of a conventional 18th-century type, relieved by occasional fine descriptions. [JMC]

BAE, 29; *Obras*, ed. A. Martin Villa (1872, 1879).

**Reizen, Abraham** (Kojdanov 1875–New York 1953). The first modern Yiddish poet of prominence with a highly individual style without great stresses but of a human quality which is almost unique. He wrote many short stories and sketches – a new departure in Yiddish literature in which the experiences of his childhood spent in abject poverty are vividly reflected. He founded and edited the weekly *Di Europeishe Literatur* from 1919 which was devoted to Yiddish translations from European languages. [EE

*Collected Works* (24 vols., N.Y., 1924).

N. B. Minkoff, *A.R., Der Dichter fun lid* (N.Y. 1936).

**Rej, Mikolaj** (Żórawno 1505–1569). Polish writer. He served as a courtier for time, then led the life of a prosperous country squire. He propagated the teachings of Luther, then turned to Calvinism. Thoug often described as the father of Polish literature, he comes, in fact, at the end of the ⇨ Polish medieval tradition. The year 1543, the date of his verse debate 'between the Squire, the Bailiff and the Parson', has conveniently been used to mark the beginning of a new epoch, but the static form of the dialogue and its moralizing belong to a much older literary convention. The same can be said of his other works, both in prose and in verse: they all have a didactic purpose in common. Certainly, Rej stood for the rights of the vernacular, as his dedications and prefaces repeatedly confirm. Moreover, his lack of formal education saved his busy pen from inhibitions in the choice of vocabulary and manner of expression.

He wrote as he must have spoken, and his representative collection *Zwierciadło* (1568) truly reflects the features of 16th-century Polish. It includes *Żywot człowieka poczciwego* which is his best-known work, proving him to be a shrewd observer of domestic and social scenes. His casual tone makes even the didactic nagging quite bearable. [JP]

Peterkiewicz and Singer, *FCPP*.

**Reljković, Matija Antun** (Svinjar 1732–Vinkovci 1798). Croatian poet and publicist. Taken prisoner while serving in the Austrian army during the Seven Years' War, he spent some time in Frankfurt where he was struck by the generally higher standard of living than in his native Slavonia. In 1762 he published his satirical poem *Satir ili divlji čovic* in which he slated the morals of his people and urged them to improve their material and moral conditions by an increase of diligence. In 1779 he published a second part to the poem. A conservative Catholic, he attacks the national customs as being immoral and relics of Turkish influence. His poetry is little more than versification and his real significance is as one of the first representatives of the Enlightenment in Croatia. [EDG]

Barac, *HYL*.

**Remarque, Erich Maria** (Osnabrück 1898–1970). German novelist. Wounded in the First World War, he became a teacher, businessman, journalist (for *Sport im Bild*). After the world success of his novel *Im Westen nichts Neues* (1929; tr. A. W. Wheen, *All Quiet on the Western Front*, 1929), 2½ million copies of which were sold in 25 languages in 18 months, he travelled, settled in Switzerland (1932–9; his books were banned in Germany), then in New York (U.S. citizenship, 1947), finally again in the Tessin. His best-seller re-lived a European trauma, recording its inhuman horrors in the very ordinary human words and reactions of an average soldier: a crude style by conventional criteria (e.g. of characterization) but perhaps the only one appropriate to the impersonal, unheroic violence of modern war – the doom both physical and spiritual of a whole generation. This latter theme runs again (less convincingly) through novels of post-war 'adjustment' (*Der Weg zurück*, 1931, tr. A. W. Wheen, *The Road Back*, 1931; *Drei Kameraden*, 1937, tr. A. W. Wheen, *Three Comrades*, 1937) and émigré life (*Flotsam*, 1940; tr. D. Lindley, repr. 1961; *Arc de Triomphe*, 1947; tr. W. Sorbell and D. Lindley, repr. 1961). Not even American (Hemingway-esque) techniques could give much literary significance to his popular *Zeit zu leben und Zeit zu sterben* (1954; tr. D. Lindley, *A Time to Live and a Time to Die*, 1954), *Der schwarze Obelisk* (tr. D. Lindley, *The Black Obelisk*, 1956), etc., though his play on the last days of Berlin, *Die letzte Station* (1956), was theatrically effective. *Die Nacht von Lissabon* (1962; tr. R. Mannheim, *The Night in Lisbon*, 1964) re-lives, less freshly, Europe's other nightmare of persecution and flight. [PB]

*Ludwig Renn/E.M.R.* (SG, 1965).

**Reményík, Sándor** (Kolozsvár 1890– Kolozsvár 1942). Transylvanian-Hungarian poet. Born into a middle-class Lutheran family, he contributed much to Transylvanian culture as a poet, critic and literary editor. He also worked for the important literary monthly *Erdélyi Helikon*. He is a regionalist, deeply concerned about the fate of Hungarians in Transylvania, under Rumanian rule since 1920; his tone is always humane, inspired by sincere religious beliefs. Notable poems: *Csillag a víz alatt* (*Star beneath the Water*); *Írjad, Poéta* (*Write, oh Poet*); *Erdély Magyarjaihoz* (*To the Magyars of Transylvania*), all tr. W. Kirkconnell, n.d. [JFR]

Reményi, *HWL*.

**Remizov, Aleksey Mikhaylovich** (Moscow 1877–Paris 1957). Russian writer. The son of a merchant, he was educated at Moscow University. He was exiled in 1897 for political activities and took no part in politics thereafter. After 1917, he found work translating and teaching under the Soviet regime. In 1921 he was allowed to go abroad for reasons of health, and in 1923 he settled in Paris. Unlike the other *émigrés* he did not attack the Bolsheviks; his *Slovo o pogibeli Russkoy zemli* ('Lament for the Ruin of the Land of Russia', 1921) recognizes the inevitability as well as the calamities of the Revolution.

Remizov is one of the most versatile and original of Russian writers. He himself named as his literary ancestors Gogol', Leskov and Dostoyevsky. From the latter comes the concern for humiliation and suffering, characteristic of his early stories, *Chasy* (1908; tr. J. Cournos, *The Clock*, 1924) and *Krestovyye syostry* (1910). From Gogol' and Leskov come his fascination with the nuances of colloquial speech and the possibilities of language, neologisms and original syntax. Hence too his interest in fantasy and in folk-legends and popular religion, both Christian and pagan. Dreams play an important part in all his work: *Epopeya* (1927) is a picture of the Revolution seen and interpreted through dreams. Remizov's most characteristic works take the form of free fantasies round memories and words, *Plyashushchiy demon* (1949) and *Podstrizhennymi glazami* (1951).

But he was also capable of simple straightforward narrative as in the stories about his wife *Olya* (1927; part tr. B. Scott, *On a Field Azure*, 1946) and *V rozovom bleske* (1952). His influence on ⇨ Zamyatin, ⇨ Prishvin and ⇨ Pil'nyak and through them on Soviet writers was considerable. [RDBT]

*Sobraniye sochineniy* (8 vols., 1910–12).
N. Kodryanskaya, *A.R.* (Paris, 1960).

**Renan, Ernest** (Tréguier 1823–Paris 1892), French moralist and orientalist. He abandoned his training for the priesthood under the influence of German ideas of Bible exegesis. He continued his studies while working as *répétiteur* in a school and won the Prix Volney for his *Essai historique et théorique sur les langues sémitiques* (1847). The revolutionary events of 1848 prompted his *L'avenir de la science* (not published till 1890) which declares faith in the liberation of mankind through science and through an intellectual *élite*. He obtained a post at the Bibliothèque Nationale and made his name by articles, collected as *Études d'histoire religieuse* (1857) and *Essais de morale et de critique* (1859), which preach also an aristocratic responsibility of the few towards the many who must be saved from slavery to material goals. He was sent on an archaeological expedition to Syria (accompanied by his beloved sister, who died there of a fever); his findings are included in his scholarly *Corpus Inscriptionum Semiticarum* (1881ff.). He was appointed to the chair of Hebrew at the Collège de France in 1862, but his description of Christ as 'an incomparable man' revived the opposition of the Catholic party and his course was prohibited; he was reinstated in 1871. His most widely known work, *La vie de Jésus* (1863), perfectly voiced the educated desire of his time to be reassured for its disbelief in the religious claims of Christianity by an enlightened enjoyment of the poetry and human achievements contained in the Bible story. Subsequent volumes, e.g. on the Apostles (1866) and St Paul (1869) and the Roman period, complete his *Histoire des origines du christianisme* (1863–83), to which he added an *Histoire du peuple d'Israël* (1887–93). Deeply shaken by the defeat of 1870, his historical works reflect his gradual acceptance of democracy, albeit with renewed strictures in *La réforme intellectuelle et morale* (1871). His *Souvenirs d'enfance et de jeunesse* (1833) show an eclectic enthusiasm for the primitive Celtic spirit, the Italy of Rome and Renaissance, and the Athens of antiquity ('Prière sur l'Acropole').

*Œuvres complètes*, ed. H. Psichari (10 vols., 1947–61).
H. W. Wardman, *E.R.A. Critical Biography* (1964); R. M. Chadbourne, *E.R. as an Essayist* (Cornell, Mass., 1957).

**Renard, Jules** (Châlons-sur-Mayenne 1864–Chitry-les-Mines 1910). French writer of drama and prose fiction. He began with an undistinguished collection of verse (*Les roses*, 1886) before turning to the descriptive prose sketches, fiction and plays on which his reputation as a minor classic rests. He has two veins: that of the moralist and that of an observer of natural phenomena. He views nature as if under a microscope but the extremely rigorous, almost scientific act of attention he brings to bear on discrete phenomena – leaves, feathers, shells – is sometimes given, through metaphor, a wholly idiosyncratic and poetic resonance. This is brilliantly in evidence in *Histoire* *naturelles* (1896; tr. T. W. Earp and G.W. Stonier, *Hunting with the Fox*, 1948), illustrated with masterly skill by Toulouse-Lautrec; *Bucoliques* (1898); *L'œil clair* (posth. 1913). His moral vision is haunted by the fear of being deceived or deceiving oneself and finds its stylistic equivalent in a prose both cryptic and laconic, pared down to fastidious notation and hostile to 'fine writing'. His novel of the miseries of an unhappy childhood, *Poil de carotte* (1894; tr. G. W. Stonier, *Carrots*, 1946) moves one by its ironic restraint, while he brings to the familiar conflict between artist and bourgeois society a sharp and unforgiving sense of the pettiness and self-deception of the world (*L'écornifleur*, 1892; tr. E. Hyams, *The Sponger*, 1957). His plays often transpose situations originally created in his fiction and display remarkable economy and bite in their punctilious observation of human failings. Most accomplished are: *Le plaisir de rompre* (1897); *Le pain de ménage* (1898); *Monsieur Vernet* (1903), the dramatization of *L'écornifleur*; and *La bigote* (1909), a powerful study of religious bigotry. His posthumous *Journal* is not simply a fascinating document on the contemporary literary scene, but reveals a kind of secular mystic in despair at the incommunicability of all experience. [SBJ]

*Œuvres complètes* (16 vols., 1925–7); *Lettres inédites, 1883–1910*, ed. L. Guichard (1957); *Dans la vigne de J.R.: inédits*, ed. L. Guichard (1966); *Théâtre complet*, ed. L. Pauwels (1957); *Journal*, ed. L. Guichard and G. Sigaux (1960).
L. Guichard, *J.R.* (Paris, 1961); P. Schneider, *J.R. par lui-même* (Paris, 1956).

**'Renart, Roman de.'** Cycle of medieval French versified stories, of which the earliest and best 15 branches were composed, mostly anonymously, between *c.*1174 and 1205. The sources are folklore, Greek and Roman fables, and similar works about animals in medieval Latin such as the *Ecbasis captivi* (930–40, or later) and the *Ysengrinus* (*c.*1150). The *Ysengrinus* appears to have influenced the oldest extant Renard story, Branch II, composed by Pierre de Saint-Cloud. In this work Renard is still the fox, the *goupil*, attempting to trap and deceive other animals. In Branch I, however, the *Jugement de Renart*, probably the finest of all the stories, Renard is a petty baronet, contemptuous of the laws of the realm of king Noble the Lion. This story was translated into Dutch by Willem, a Fleming, as *Reinaert de Vos*, and spread throughout Europe, being used by Chaucer and Goethe (*Reineke Fuchs*). Ysengrin, the wolf, accuses Renard of raping his wife, Hersent. Renard is summoned to the court and sentenced to be hanged, but is reprieved on condition that he takes the cross. Once at a safe distance, he mocks the court and hurls his pilgrim's staff at his enemies together with other unmentionable insults. His castle of Maupertuis is besieged, but Renard by a ruse inflicts on Fiere, Noble's Queen, the same undignified treatment he had accorded Hersent. Again he is tried and condemned, but his wife, Hermeline, arrives and buys his freedom from Noble.

The work satirizes not only the slander, hypocrisy, weakness and corruption of the courts, but also the literary genres practised in court circles. Much humour comes from the gentle parodies of the Arthurian romance, of the ⇨ *chanson de geste*, and of courtly behaviour in general, such as the dissimulation with which the Queen proposes a meeting-place to Renard.

Many further branches in the first half of the 13th century were amplifications of earlier material. After 1250 the cycle took a new turn; social and political satire becomes bitter and direct, and the fable loses its simplicity and charm in the *Couronnement de Renart* (before 1270) and *Renart le Novel* (*c.*1288). In the *Couronnement*, Renard, no longer happy at winning a chicken, ham, or eel, aspires to royal power. His true rival is no longer Ysengrin but Noble. The earlier malicious quips and pranks have given way to the calculated diplomatic perfidy of middle age. Renard teaches the monks his code of cunning behaviour. He ingratiates himself at court and is declared king. He returns from Palestine with a reputation for courage and holiness, is summoned to advise the Pope. *Renardie* is the key to all worldly success.

In *Renart le Novel*, by Jacquemart Gielée of Lille, the conflict between Renard and King Noble is secondary to the philosophical ideas, sermons and false erudition that weight it down. In one scene the whole Church, clerics and friars, cardinals, and the Pope at the helm, sail in Renard's ship which is covered with grey cloth woven of hypocrisy and idleness. Much satire is directed against the Knights Hospitallers and Templars, and the decline of feudal power before the onslaught of the skilled lawyer class is foretold. Renard, still the 'hero', is seen as a 'puante bête'.

*Renart le Contrefait* (in two versions, 1319–22 and 1328–41, together over 50,000 lines) is probably a collective work, but the authors are unknown, except for the famous '*épicier*' of Troyes, an unfrocked cleric. Overloaded with allegory and erudition, it is an uncut version of the material that Jean de Meung had trimmed for his continuation of the *Roman de la* ⇨ *Rose*. But Renard's bitter attacks on society have much historical interest. Renard is an old man, morose and heavy, with few flashes of his earlier gaiety. His former malice towards the nobles and the clergy has turned to a revolutionary denunciation of their privileges and taxes, and points unmistakably to the coming bourgeois revolution, the *Jacquerie*, and the true end of the feudal era.

A German adaptation of the early French branches was made by Heinrich der Glîchezâre (*Reinhart Fuchs*, *c.*1180). In the 13th century *Rainardo e Lesengrino* in hybrid French-Italian was written by an anonymous author who knew the earliest French branches. For *Renart le bestourné* ⇨ Rutebeuf. [LTT]

*Le Roman de R., Branches I–XIX*, ed. M. Roques (1948–63); *Le Couronnement de R., poème du treizième siècle*, ed. A. Foulet (Princeton, Paris, 1929); *R. le Novel*, ed. H. Roussel (1961); *Le Roman de R. le Contrefait*, ed. G. Raynaud and H. Lemaître (2 vols., 1914).

R. Bossuat, *Le Roman de R.* (Paris, 1957); J. Flinn, *Le Roman de R.* (Paris, 1964).

**Renn, Ludwig,** pseud. of Arnold Friedrich Vieth von Golssenau (Dresden 1889– ). German novelist. His First World War experiences made him into a pacifist and a writer; he joined the Communist Party in 1928, was imprisoned (1933–5) for 'literary high treason', escaped to Switzerland and became Chief-of-Staff, XI International Brigade, in the Spanish Civil War (*Der spanische Krieg*, 1955). After living in Mexico, he returned to East Germany in 1947. Renn's fame rests on his first novel, *Krieg* (1928; tr. W. and E. Muir, *War*, 1939; and sequel – *Nachkrieg*, 1930; tr. W. and E. Muir, *After War*, 1931), one of the great war books, rich in personal experience and truly sympathetic insight, yet tense and objective in style. His later novels, travel books, autobiographical sketchbooks and children's stories have received little attention in the West. [PB]

*L. R. zum 70 Geburtstag* (1960); *L.R.* (E. Berlin, 1956, in SG); *L.R./E.M. Remarque* (E. Berlin, 1965, in SG).

**Resende, Garcia de** (Évora *c.* 1470– Évora 1536). Portuguese chronicler. Compiler of the *Cancioneiro Geral* and chronicler of he reign of John II, he also wrote an interesting commonplace-book in verse entitled *Miscelânea*. He is recorded from 1491 onwards as private secretary (Moço da Escrevaninha) to John II, a king who liked poetry and thought it as important for a gentleman to know the *Coplas* of Jorge Manrique as the Paternoster. Resende also drew, and composed music. In 1514 he accompanied the Portuguese ambassador, Tristão da Cunha, to the court of Leo X as secretary of the embassy.

The *Crónica dos valerosos e insignes feitos del-Rei D. João II* (1545) is based on that of Rui de Pina, even to the choice of words, but interspersed with more personal memories and anecdotes of the time, where the reader may catch a glimpse of Portuguese life in the last two decades of the 15th century.

Such glimpses are more frequent in the *Miscelânea*, which first appeared in the 1554 edition of the *Crónica*, and which contains, as the sub-title states, 'a variety of descriptions of manners, events, and things which occurred in the author's lifetime'. It is a work of interest to the social historian.

The *Cancioneiro Geral* (1516) reflects Portuguese poetic taste during the reigns of John II and Manuel I. Among many poets now forgotten are found such famous names as Ribeiro, Sá de Miranda, Gil Vicente. It contains principally love-poetry (often under the influence of Petrarch) in the antithetical 15th-century manner, sometimes with a new note of Renaissance realism; secondly (probably the most readable group) poems by moralists like Álvaro de Brito Pestana, who were conscious of living in a period of rapid changes which many considered to be for the worse; thirdly, a kind of 'occasional poetry', generally satirical in intent if no longer in effect, descended from the earlier *cantigas de escárnio*. Resende himself is represented by a poem about Inês de Castro which is a good example of the 'hell of lovers' of medieval tradition.

In versification the *Cancioneiro Geral* proves the triumph of the *redondilha*, the heptasyllabic line with its *pé quebrado* of three or four syllables (though the *arte maior* was still favoured for grave topics). All poems in redondilha metre were called *trovas*, or occasionally *coplas*. These were subdivided into *esparsas* (poems of not less than eight or more than sixteen lines, and usually melancholy in tone); *vilancetes* (a seven-line gloss upon a two- or three-line fragment of (usually) traditional poetry, the last line of the gloss repeating verbally or with variants that of the *mote*); and *cantigas* (an eight- or ten-line gloss upon a *mote* of four or five lines, again with last-line repetition). [ARM]

*Cancioneiro Geral*, ed. A. J. Gonçalves Guimarãis (5 vols., 1910–17); *Miscelânea*, ed. A. J. Gonçalves Guimarãis (1917).

J. de Castro Osório, *Estudos sobre o Renascimento Português, O Testemunho de G. de R.* (1963).

**Restif** or **Rétif, Nicolas-Anne-Edmé,** known as **de la Bretonne** (Sacy, Yonne 1734–Paris 1806). French novelist and prose writer. Of peasant birth, he seems to have led a dissolute existence which took him into every dark corner of Parisian and provincial life. His vast output of rambling novels and memoirs, half fiction, half experience, often pornographic but shot through with sentimental moralizing (e.g. *Le paysan perverti*, 1775; *La paysanne pervertie*, 1785; *Monsieur Nicolas*, 1794, tr. R. C. Mathers, 6 vols., 1930–1) is now of little interest except for the light it sheds on the contemporary scene: here the most striking material, especially in its description of the Revolution, is *Les nuits de Paris* (1788–90; ed. H. Bachelin, 1960; tr. L. Asher and E. Fertig, *Nights of Paris*, N.Y., 1964). The most rewarding of his works from the literary standpoint however is *La vie de mon père* (1779; ed. M. Boisson, 1924), a vivid and in many ways noble picture of peasant life in 18th-century France. [WHB]

*L'Œuvre* (a selection), ed. H. Bachelin (9 vols., 1930–2).

C. R. Dawes, *R.* (1946); A. Tabarant, *Le vrai visage de R.* (Paris, 1936); Trahard, *MSF*.

**Retz, Jean François Paul de Gondi,** Cardinal Duc de (Montmirail 1613–Paris 1679). French man of letters. He led the life of an adventurer rather than a churchman ('*l'âme la moins ecclésiastique qui fût dans l'univers*'). His intrigues during the Fronde are reflected in his incomparable *Mémoires* (ed. E. Thomas, Pléiade, 1956; tr. anon., Everyman, 1917), written during his retirement (probably 1673–6). They were first published in 1715, saw fifteen editions within a century and are now regarded as a classic.

At the Jesuit college de Clermont, Retz was exceptional, for brilliance in languages, and for bad behaviour. He was given a canonry at Notre Dame when only 14, studied at the Sorbonne and attracted the attention of Richelieu as '*un esprit dangereux*'. In 1643 he was made *coadjuteur* of his uncle the Archbishop of Paris, with the title of Archbishop of Corinth *in partibus* (hence the satiric description of two of his pamphlets as First and Second Corinthians). Energetic in all things, his guiding principle throughout the Fronde was the defeat of Mazarin by any methods: plots with Spain, inflammable sermons, cabals, riots, pamphlets. These brought him a Cardinal's hat in 1652 but many vicissitudes. He was imprisoned, resigned his diocese, revoked his resignation, fell out with his clergy, and finally fled the country (see E. H. Kossmann's *La Fronde*, 1954). Louis XIV exiled him to his estates at Commercy on the Meuse, but used him more than once in papal negotiation. His very name has shared the inconstancy of his fortunes: it seems clear that he was always known as Rais.

His *Mémoires* are the only thing in his life that approach to reliable sincerity. Written at the request of a lady (Mme de Sévigné? or Mme de La Fayette?) that he at last tell the truth, men and affairs are judged here very much as they are in the *Maximes* of La Rochefoucauld, a contemporary whom he hated and who once nearly murdered him between the swing doors of the Parlement. In the absence of strong central power, parties will struggle for mastery and even for existence; the laws of this struggle are pitiless and depend on balance of forces. They may have little to do with beliefs or professions. Human conduct is thus shown as in a Molière comedy, from two sides, appearance and reality, words and deeds. Thoughts and beliefs are secondary to will and decision. Courage is a constant touchstone, and he repeatedly returns to what he calls '*une grande action*' – the ability, it seems, to ride events and to prevail against opposition. That he is a disciple of Machiavelli appears in his earlier, interesting and influential *La Conjuration de Fiesque*, a rewriting of a life of the Genoese conspirator by Mascardi. He substitutes for Mascardi's moral strictures praise of Fiesco's aristocratic intrepidity and independence of mind which made him prefer expediency to morality (cf. ⇨ Schiller). [WGM]

D. Ogg, *Cardinal de R.* (1912); L. Batiffol, *Cardinal de R.* (Paris, 1927); *FS* (1958); Adam, *HLF.*

**Reuchlin, Johannes** (Pforzheim 1455–Liebenzell, Württemberg 1522). German humanist. Although a lawyer by profession, he was one of the outstanding philologists of his day. He edited a Latin lexicon, *Vocabularius breviloquens* (1475), and translated Demosthenes and Xenophon, but it was as a hebraist that he achieved lasting fame, writing both text-books (*Rudimenta hebraica*, 1506) and mystical works on the Cabbala (*De arte caballistica*, 1517). It was his interest in Hebrew which involved him in the long quarrel with Pfefferkorn and the Dominicans, who were empowered by the Emperor to destroy all Jewish writings as blasphemous. The humanist in him, however, saw in these writings a reflection, even if an imperfect one, of God's purpose with man. His defence, *Epistolae clarorum virorum* (1514), a collection of letters from distinguished scholars assuring him of their support, suggested the greatest satire of the age, *Epistolae obscurorum virorum* (1515–17; probably written by Crotus Rubeanus and ⇨ Hutten) which purports to be a collection of letters written by Reuchlin's opponents, who are mercilessly pilloried for their stupidity and ignorance. His two Latin comedies, *Sergius* (1496) and *Henno* (1497), were models of humanist school drama. [WAC]

L. Geiger, *J.R., sein Leben und seine Werke* (Leipzig, 1871); H. Holstein, *J.R.s Komödien* (Halle, 1888).

**Reuter, Christian** (Kütten bei Zörbig 1665–? after 1712). German dramatist. His experiences as a student in Leipzig with his landlady, the hostess of the Red Lion, Frau Müller, and her son, Eustachius, inspired his two comedies *L'honnête femme oder die ehrliche Frau zu Plissine* (1695) and *Der ehrlichen Frau Schlampampe Krankheit und Tod* (1696) in which he satirizes the stupidity and vulgarity not only of Frau Müller, but of the bourgeoisie as a whole. Similarly the mock travel-book *Schelmuffskys Curiose und sehr gefährliche Reisebeschreibung* (1696; tr. W. Wayne, Chapel Hill, Ind., 1962) transcends the personal attack on Eustachius Müller in its grotesque satire of the ignorance of the *bourgeoisie* and their foolish aping of the grand tour of the nobility. The ebullient sense of humour, the realism and the sharp eye for the characteristic fault, whether of a person or class, which characterize these works are equally in evidence in Reuter's comedy of high life, *Graf Ehrenfried* (1700). [WAC]

*Werke*, ed. G. Witkowski (2 vols., 1916).
O. Denecke, *Schelmuffsky* (Göttingen, 1927); F. J. Schneider, *C.R.* (Halle, 1936).

**Reverdy, Pierre** (Narbonne 1889–Solesmes 1960). French poet. From 1910 he was a member of the ⇨ Apollinaire-Picasso *avant-garde* group. In 1917 he founded the review *Nord-Sud* which drew together the first Surrealists, but took little part in *avant-garde* activity, preferring an obscure, anonymous existence in harmony with the feeling of loneliness and strong spiritual doubt which runs through his work. In his early prose and verse poems, collected in *Plupart du temps* (1945), he projects this doubt into short, fragmentary poems of sharp visual detail, owing something to the example of Cubism in the rigorous organization of their brief, broken lines, and their feeling for plastic values, but going beyond Cubism in the impression of desolation they convey. Their stifled anguish reflects Reverdy's sense of a mystery in the universe which lies constantly beyond his understanding.

In 1926 he withdrew to live near the Abbey of Solesmes, hoping to find a solution in religious faith. In this he was unsuccessful, but he continued to live an ascetic existence until his death. He wrote several prose works there, the most important being *Le gant de crin* (1927) and *Le livre de mon bord* (1948), condensed reflections on literature, religion and life. The poetry written at Solesmes (collected in *Main d'œuvre*, 1949) reflects the same preoccupations as his earlier work, but with greater richness and complexity, both in the texture of the verse, shot through with natural images of stark sensuousness, and in the lyric note, which is fuller and more poignant. He is an exemplary and undervalued poet. [IL]

J. Rousselot, *P.R.* (1951) (selections and critical essay by M. Manoll); *MDF*, 344 (January 1962).

**Revius, Jacobus** (Deventer 1586–Leyden 1658). Dutch poet, ecclesiastical historian and biblical scholar who assisted in the *Staten Vertaling*. He is remembered as the Deventer parson who wrote the *Overysselsche Sangen en Dichten* (1630, ed. W. A. P. Smit, 2 vols., 1930–35). In both religious and profane songs and sonnets he is the prophet of axiomatic Calvinism. But the austerity of his teaching is imparted with a warmth of conviction which can inspire superb poetry. His emblematic treatment of Old and New Testament themes gives a baroque structure to his credo. [PK]

Barnouw, *CA*.

**Reymont, Władysław Stanisław** (Kobiele Wielkie, nr Radom 1867–Warsaw 1925). Polish novelist. His French-sounding name was originally a peasant nickname (from *rejment*, regiment), and the whole of his life seemed to bear this birthmark of paradox. The son of a village organist, he received little formal education, became in turn a tailor's apprentice (competent), a travelling actor (hopeless), a provincial railway clerk (melancholy), and later, by a grotesque intervention of fate, benefited financially from a railway accident. As with Gor'ky, life was his university, and through hard work and intelligent response to the changing reality about him, he released and channelled his wild talent, becoming in the end the author of a masterpiece, *Chłopi* (1902–9; tr. M. H. Dziewicki, *The Peasants*, 1925–6), which won him the Nobel Prize in 1924. There is an obsessive quality already in the village themes of his early short stories (*Śmierć*, *Suka*). But, strangely enough, Reymont's first ambitious novel depicted urban society. Lodz, the growing industrial city, forms the background of *Ziemia obiecana* (1899; tr. M. H. Dziewicki, *The Promised Land*, 1928). In this it resembles ⇨ Prus's novel about Warsaw, although Reymont relies rather on his talent for the grotesque, often creating situations and characters larger than life. *The Promised Land* taught him how to construct a mobile plot with a great number of people and a restricted place of action. This he was to bring to perfection in his village epic, but first he had to drain his memory of secondary experiences. In *Komediantka* (1896; tr. E. Obecny, *The Comedienne*, 1920) and its sequel he used his knowledge of seedy actors on the road.

His immediate reason for writing *The Peasants* was odd. During his stay in France he read Zola's *La terre* in Polish translation (he knew no French) and found its realism unconvincing. Later, he apparently checked on Zola's background and even thought of depicting 'the real French peasant' himself. Wisely he decided to write about the Polish village instead, and the first draft was finished in 1900. He was advised by a friend and critic to develop the epic possibilities of the novel and embarked on a new version in four volumes, corresponding to the four seasons. The last came out in 1909.

By enclosing the village community of Lipce within the cycle of the seasons he gave the novel both a natural unity and a continuous sense of time. In this epic conception each human act acquires the dimensions of myth, though the psychological motivation remains sound. The conflict between Boryna, a rich peasant, and his son Antek slowly reveals their instinctive and practical behaviour, until in the end both are exposed in their self-love. Antek asserts his will and uses his incestuous love for Jagna, Boryna's third wife, in order to identify himself with his father's authority. The subconscious drive for power finally comes to the surface of awareness when Antek, after his father's death, reaches the coveted goal and takes over the full inheritance in both a material and a spiritual sense. The villagers expel Jagna from their midst and Antek abandons her, conforming to the morals of the community. For him the process of identification has come full circle just as the year has turned around its seasons. Reymont's minor characters are sharply delineated against the magnified landscape. The language is stylized throughout and evokes a peasant idiom without narrowing it to one specific dialect.

By comparison, his historical trilogy (*Rok 1794*) is an honourable failure, and so is his curious novel about spiritualism and theosophy, *Wampir* (1911), in which the London setting causes a good deal of unconscious comedy. A melancholy atmosphere pervades his *Marzyciel* (1910), a clerk's view of the world from a small railway station. The world in *Bunt* (1924) is seen by animals: they rebel against man, but cannot live with their new freedom, and end by worshipping a gorilla. The fable is, however, less obviously political than Orwell's *Animal Farm*. [JP]

*Pisma*, ed. A. Bar (1948–51).
*SEER*, XVI, 47 (1938).

**Řezáč, Václav**, pseud. of Václav Voňavka (Prague 1901–Prague 1956). Czech novelist. His early novels show the psychology of the individual against the background of an unstable society with shattered moral values. After the Second World War he applied the method of socialist realism to portray the great economic and social changes in Czechoslovakia. *Nástup* (1951) and *Bitva* (1954) describe the difficulties in the frontier regions after the removal of the German population and the struggle of the Communists with those who wanted to renew the old capitalist order. He took the contemporary Party line and aimed at the ideological education of the masses. [KB]

*Dílo* (12 vols., 1953–61).
F. Götz, *V.R.* (Prague, 1957).

**Rhigas, Pheraios** (Velestino 1760–Belgrade 1798). Greek poet. He is chiefly remembered for his patriotic activity, his efforts to enlighten his fellow-countrymen then under the Turks by translating European works into Greek, and for his stirring patriotic songs – his *Thourios* was paraphrased by Byron as 'Sons of the Greeks, Arise.' His political activities in Vienna roused the suspicions of the Austrian authorities. He was handed over to the Turks and executed. [SJP]

A. Daskalakis, *Les œuvres de Rhigas Velestinlis* (Paris, 1937).

**Riba, Carles.** ⇨ Catalan Literature.

**Ribeiro, Aquilino** (Carregal da Tabosa 1885–Lisbon 1963). Portuguese writer. Author of more than seventy publications, including novels, *novelle*, collections of short stories, plays, essays, translations, editions, historical, critical and biographical studies and tales for children. His early life included imprisonment for revolutionary activities, escapes from jail, exiles in Paris (1907 and 1927), study at the Sorbonne, and membership of the *Seara Nova* movement; in later years he strongly supported the presidential campaigns of Opposition candidates Norton de Matos (1949) and Humberto Delgado (1958); he was decorated by the Brazilian government in 1952, elected to the Portuguese Academy in 1958, becoming its principal *sócio*, was first President of the Sociedade Portuguesa de Escritores, and was at one time a leading contender for the Nobel Prize. He died at the height of the fiftieth-anniversary celebrations of his first publication *Jardim das Tormentas*, a collection of short stories written while studying in Paris. Much of his work is characterized by his repudiation of the hypocrisy, exploitation and tyranny which he reveals at many levels of Portuguese society, by his desire for the removal of prejudices against physical love and by his admiration for the roguish wit and resourcefulness of the lower social strata. His early narrative fiction (his principal *genre*) was mainly confined to rustic life in his native province of the Beira Alta, but after settling in Lisbon on his return to Portugal in 1932 the life of the city became the predominant theme. Aquilino's prose is of especial interest for its lexical richness, for its colloquial and regional flavour and for the chromatic subtleties of its style. The breadth of vocabulary surpasses even that of Camilo Castelo Branco (whom Aquilino closely studied and admired) and has prompted the publication of a glossary. Aquilino's most important fictional works are the two collections of short stories, *Jardim das Tormentas* (1913) and *Estrada de Santiago* (1922), and the following novels: *A Via Sinuosa* (1918), *Terras do Demo* (1919), *Andam Faunos pelos Bosques* (1926), *Maria Benigna* (1933), *S. Banaboião* (1937), *Mónica* (1939), *Volfrâmio* (1944), *Lápides Partidas* (1945), *O Arcanjo Negro* (1947), *A Casa Grande de Romarigães* (1957) and *Quando os Lobos Uivam* (1958; tr. P. M. Pinheiro, *When the Wolves Howl*, 1963). This last work was banned for political reasons after the first printing, only normally being available in English translation. [RCW]

M. Mendes, *A.R.* (Lisbon, 1960); E. da Rocha Gomes, *Glossário sucinto para melhor compreensão de A.R.* (Oporto, 1950).

**Ribeiro, Bernardim** (Torrão 1482–Lisbon 1552). Portuguese poet and novelist. Virtually nothing is known of his biography save that he belonged in his youth to the courtly circles which produced the *Cancioneiro Geral* (1516). He was himself a contributor to this collection. He may possibly have been a converted Jew, since traces of Jewish influence have been seen in his style and imagery. He was the author of several *Éclogas* (*Obras completas*, CSC) and of the extraordinary, superficially pastoral, novel normally known as *O Livro da Menina e Moça* (ed. D. E. Grokenberger, 1947, and *Obras completas*, CSC). These works were published posthumously in 1554. The *Écloga de Crisfal* may be by him or by Cristovão ⇨ Falcão.

Ribeiro had an intimate understanding of all the subtleties of Petrarch's amorous dialectic, yet at the same time saw love not merely as a literary theme but as a vital force justifying and motivating individual existence. In *Menina e Moça* love engenders a sentimental fatalism in its victims, who can never find fulfilment; indeed, their absolute passion must end with the attainment of the beloved. Hence the strain of sensuous masochism which pervades the book and which can be identified with the origins of Portuguese *saudade*. The troubadour love ethic resuscitated by Ribeiro is necessarily amoral, a-Christian, and completely divorced from any notions of social or matrimonial obligation. The 'plot' is set in momentum by the psychology of the characters and subsequent events arise out of the nature of the passion gripping them. Images from nature are sensitively used to complement the delicate anguish of the protagonists, and the whole is related in a prose style of gentle rhythmic musicality identical in spirit to that of the *Éclogas*. Nowhere in contemporary European fiction can one find such acute penetration in the description of a man or woman in love. Every nuance from the first dim semi-realization to the full flood of rapturous captivation is faithfully recorded; and in addition he depicts the torments of amorous timidity and indecision with exquisite piquancy. As it has come down to us, *Menina e Moça* is fragmentary in form. The later chapters do not appear to be the work of Ribeiro himself, and there are flagrant inconsistencies between the contributions of different authors. [AJP]

A. Salgado jr, *A Menina e Moça e o Romance Sentimental do Renascimento*, in *Labor*, xii–xiv (Lisbon, 1940); A. J. Saraiva, 'Ensaio sobre a poesia de B.R.', in *Revista da Faculdade de Letras*, VII, 1/2 (Lisbon, 1941).

**Ribeiro, Tomás António** (Parada de Gonta 1831–Lisbon 1901). Portuguese poet, politician and diplomat. His earliest and most successful work was *Dom Jaime* (1862), of which the patriotic exordium has been particularly celebrated. In nine cantos rich in metrical experiments Ribeiro relates the resistance offered by a young *fidalgo* of the Beira Alta to the Philippine Monarchy. Often classed as a 'Realist' work because of its evident opposition to the contemporary idea of Iberian Union and because of its patches of prosaic language and imagery, *Dom Jaime* is moreover a vehicle for Hugoesque notions of social justice and human progress. Paradoxically, despite its being *engagé*, despite its obvious Romanticism, it was excessively lauded by the formalist neo-Classicist ⇨ Castilho, who was normally wont to repudiate both these trends in verse. Ribeiro's remaining works met with less success and comprise *A Delfina do Mal* (1868), another 'Realist' poem in ten cantos, the collection *Sons que Passam* (1868) which contained one celebrated poem, 'A Judia', *Vésperas* (1880) – oriental exotica – *Dissonâncias* (1890) and some minor prose works. [RCW]

P. Homem de Mello, *T.R.*, in *Perspectiva da Literatura Portuguesa do Século XIX*, I (Lisbon, 1947).

**Richard, Jean-Pierre.** ⇨ French Literary Criticism in the 19th and 20th Centuries.

**Richter, Hans Werner** (Bansin/Usedom 1908– ). German novelist. The son of a fisherman, he worked in a Berlin bookshop; he emigrated in 1933 to Paris but poverty forced him to return. Captured in the war (he was in a prisoner-of-war camp in the U.S.A.), he later founded the periodical *Der Ruf* (banned by the Allied Command), then ⇨ Gruppe 47, with which many left-wing writers have been associated, and became president of the German C.N.D. His fiction has mainly documentary interest: *Die Geschlagenen* (1949; tr. R. Kee, *The Odds Against Us*, 1950; 1961 as *Beyond Defeat*) exposes the inhumanity of the German high command in Italy, then the fanatical terror in an American prisoner-of-war camp ('not to whitewash us, but merely to make us understandable'). *Sie fielen aus Gottes Hand* (1951; tr. G. Sainsbury, *They Fell From God's Hand*, 1956) traces the experiences of twelve characters from different backgrounds between 1939 and 1950, when they meet in a displaced persons' camp. *Du sollst nicht töten* (1955), which shows how war destroys all moral values, is a formless work. *Spuren im Sand* (1953) is autobiographical. [PB]

**Rieti, Moses di** (called **Maestro Gaio**) (Rieti 1388–Rome *c.* 1460). Hebrew poet and historian, rabbi of Rome, physician to Pope Pius II. Was considered the Hebrew Dante, because in his *Mikdash Me'at* (ed. with biography as *Il Dante Ebreo* by J. Goldenthal, 1851) he imitated Dante's style. [EE]

C. Roth, *History of the Jews in Italy* (Philadelphia, 1946).

**Rifbjerg, Klaus** (Amager 1931– ). Danish poet, novelist and playwright. He is a gifted and versatile iconoclast whose poetry is often a challenge, e.g. *Under vejr med mig selv* (1956), *Konfrontation* (1960) and *Camouflage* (1961), whose novels are among the best of his generation (*Den kroniske uskyld*, 1958; *Operaelskeren*, 1966), and whose experiments with the theatre, as well as with television plays and films, have produced some interesting results. [ELB]

**Rigord** (Alais, Languedoc *c.*1150–*c.*1209). French chronicler. First a physician, then a monk, and finally Abbot of St Denis, his *Gesta Philippi Augusti* (ed. H. F. Delaborde, 1882–5) is a life of the King of France from his coronation in 1179 to 1206. Based largely on personal knowledge, the earlier part of the book is very flattering to the king, the latter part less so. The narrative is broken by a digression on the descent of the French nation from a legendary Francus. [FB]

**Rilke, Rainer Maria** (Prague 1875–Valmont, Montreux 1926). Austrian poet. One of the greatest lyrical poets of German literature, he dedicated his life to poetry as to a religious vocation. Though he travelled restlessly around Europe, meeting Tolstoy in Russia (1900), working as 'secretary' to Rodin in Paris (1905–6), enjoying aristocratic hospitality (especially at Castle Duino, near Trieste, as guest of Marie von Thurn und Taxis, 1910, 1912, 1914), meeting and corresponding with endless acquaintances (latterly with Valéry, whose work he translated in 1925 and imitated in *Poèmes français*, 1935), he was always solitary. Marriage could only be an impossible interlude (1901–2); his most appropriate 'home' (after 1922) was the medieval tower, little bigger than a hermit's cell, at Muzot (Valais). What Russia showed him was chiefly a new dimension of sensitivity, a spiritual 'openness', symbolized by landscape and people; what Rodin meant to him was a doctrine of impersonal work. Love he cherished as an inspiration, but shunned as an entanglement; his almost mystical insight into life was awakened by things rather than persons; even his voluminous correspondence was a medium for poetic meditation rather than personal contact.

His earliest poems (1899–4, collected as *Erste Gedichte*, 1913) already carry a sense of some greater reality glimpsed through their dreamy moods and impressions. His intuitions reach towards the 'depths' of experience: the realm of love and death, of sex and subconscious fears, of nature, of ecstasy, of pain. His evolving conception of this dark ground of existence is reflected in different phases of his work. *Das Stundenbuch* (1905; tr. A. L. Peck, *The Book of Hours*, 1961) intuits the psychological 'reality' behind the man-made myths and concepts of God; it charges medieval imagery with a new emotional content – and subtly inverts its meaning, so that religious symbols find their 'real' meaning in nature (or immanence). Or again, poverty is 'radiant' as an affirmation not of heaven but of the naturalness of life, the nakedness of death. And death is a mystico-erotic consummation, the fruit of the life process as sex is the seed. Typical and once popular expressions of this decadent confusion of spirituality and sensuality are *Geschichten vom lieben Gott* (1900; tr. N. P. Wydenbruck and D. H. Norton, *Stories of God*, 1932) and *Die Weise vom Leben und Tod des Cornetts Christoph Rilke* (1906; tr. Phillips and S. Schimanski, 1948).

The second phase is summed up in *Die Aufzeichnungen des Malte Laurids Brigge* (1910; tr. J. Linton, *The Notebook of M.L.B.*, 1930). It was a period of discipline, of learning to look at things, the ugly things, the daily existence of a modern city. The facile mysticism fades before a profounder sense of alienation and terror. The *Requiem* poems (1909; tr. J. B. Leishmann, 1949) look for salvation through art, which transmutes all personal feeling into the finished work. Characteristic poems in *Neue Gedichte* (1907; vol. 2, 1908; see *Poems 1906–1926*, tr. J. B. Leishmann, 1957) render experience with the concreteness of a pure 'thing', and are known as '*Dinggedichte*'. Their intense imagery is the fruit, however, not of detached impressionism but of an emotional communion with the non-personal ground of being, of a spiritual openness, indeed exposure to a reality not made in man's image. These 'descriptions' have the quality of myth or oracle, of a voice speaking in symbols from within a realm where it is not 'I' who feels or knows 'something' about 'it', but I and it become one in a single reality of feeling, the 'thing' itself of life – which also utters itself as word, as equally non-personal art, the thing as poem and the poem as thing. Rilke called this realm '*Weltinnenraum*' and the central truth of his mystical communings is: '*Gesang ist Dasein*' (song is being).

His sonnets to Orpheus (*Die Sonette an Orpheus*, 1923; tr. J. B. Leishmann, 1936) represent the ultimate lyrical perfection of this magic art which richly fuses words and things in a new creative relationship, a 'symbolism' having confusing religious implications. The very act of realizing the world's utter transcience, of accepting life and death as one, is *itself* holy, a hymn of praise, *itself* provides the deathless figure of transcendent meaning, the sheer beauty of the word that redeems. It is, as it were, the sheer act of man's kneeling that is the only 'measure' of holiness (see *Späte Gedichte*, 1934; tr. J. B. Leishmann, 1938). What this aesthetic mysticism means in personal terms, what it implies as regards the conventional values and beliefs of Western Culture, is expressed in the 10 great *Duineser Elegien*, (1923; tr. J. B. Leishmann, *Duino Elegies*, 1948). In surges of oracular inspiration over a period of ten years, each elegy brought some new insight into man's individual plight in a world whose traditional order is felt to be crumbling. What does it mean to love, to die, what does nature mean, and language? How shall man bear the immanent reality which he can no longer veil with his illusions? What justification, what hope can his pathetically exposed spirit have before the 'Angel', a figure conceived not as the highest form of individual being before God, but as a symbol of the overwhelming terror at the heart of a universe *without* God, where individuality counts for nothing and the distinction between living and dead is illusory? The poetic 'answer' offered by the *Elegies* lies in the depth with which the questions have been formulated, and in the doctrine of a redeeming power in the very act of poetic utterance (see 9th Elegy). [AKT]

*Sämtliche Werke*, ed. E. Zinn (1955ff.); trs.: *Auguste Rodin*, J. Lemont and H. Trausil (N.Y., 1919); *Elegies from the Castle of Duino*, V. and E. Sackville West (1931); *Poems*, J. Lemont (N.Y., 1943); *Duino Elegies*, R. Speirs, in *Poetry London* (1947); *Selected Letters*, R. F. C. Hull (1946); *The Life of the Virgin Mary*, S. Spender (1951); *Selected Works*, tr. G. C. Houston (1954) (prose).

W. Ritzer, *R.M.R. Bibliographie* (Vienna, 1951); H. E. Holthusen, *R.M.R.* (London, 1952); W. L. Graff, *R.M.R.* (Princeton Univ., 1956); H. F. Peters, *R.M.R.* (N.Y., 1960); R. Guardini, *R.M.R.* (Munich, 1953); E. C. Mason, *R.* (Edinburgh, 1963); C. M. Bowra, *The Heritage of Symbolism* (1943); Heller, *DM.*

**Rimbaud, Arthur** (Charleville 1854–Marseilles 1891). French poet. The son of an army officer who deserted his wife and family in 1860, he had an unhappy childhood, due to his embittered mother's harsh discipline, and this may well explain the fact that his life and work are characterized by a spirit of rebellion and a desire to escape which first came to the surface in 1870 when he was 15. Violently anti-clerical and anti-Christian, openly republican in his political sympathies, he refused to stay at school and ran away from his home in Charleville twice in the autumn of 1870 and a third time in the spring of 1871. All this is reflected in the astonishingly mature poems he wrote at that time, some of which viciously attack anyone in authority, from God, Napoleon III and Mme Rimbaud to customs officers on the nearby Belgian frontier and the local librarians, while others dream of a different world of total freedom. The most celebrated of these is 'Le bateau ivre', in which Rimbaud imagines himself as a boat drifting wildly down rivers, into seas and across oceans, completely out of control.

Immediately after writing this poem with its vivid and tumultuous imagery, he set off for Paris in September 1871, where he was welcomed by a poet ten years his senior, ⇨ Verlaine, whose unorthodox versification had appealed to him and to whom he had taken the precaution of writing to ask for help. Although he had written earlier (May 1871) his famous 'lettre du voyant' in which he had preached the '*dérèglement de tous les sens*' and claimed that the poet's duty is to sharpen his perception by submitting himself to every kind of experience and then to transmit what he perceives directly, without any conscious control, it was not until he joined Verlaine that he seriously began to put these ideas into practice. He wanted, as he said in 'Matinée d'ivresse', to get rid of the concept of good and evil, and he and Verlaine tried to live according to a new moral code, or rather amoral code, hoping to create a different world which was to be expressed through a different kind of poetry – '*les inventions d'inconnu réclament des formes nouvelles*'. Verlaine had already tried to loosen the bonds of traditional versification and Rimbaud quickly forged ahead of him in the direction of complete freedom of form. In May and June 1872, in poems such as 'Larme' and 'L'éternité' he began to break away from the strict rhyme schemes and the rigid patterns he had so far followed and soon went on to adopt the form of the prose poem in the group of about forty passages known as the *Illuminations*. Though the exact meaning of many of these attempts to convey a vision of another world is obscure, some of them such as 'Royauté', 'Matinée d'ivresse, 'Ornières', 'Veillées I', 'Mystique', 'Aube', 'Fleurs' and 'Barbare' have an undoubted poetic quality of a uniquely compelling kind that springs from the vividness of the imagery, the rhythm of the phrasing and the directness of the language.

Rimbaud's rebellion failed, however, and in the summer of 1873 he wrote *Une saison en enfer* which, again in an often obscure but nevertheless vivid and compelling prose, proclaimed the collapse both of his hope of creating a new, amoral society and of his attempt at writing a new, unconventional kind of poetry. He bitterly conceded that he had been living in a fool's paradise, that he had spent a season in hell rather than a season in heaven, that he and Verlaine, far from being '*l'époux divin*' and '*la vierge sage*' as they had tried to believe, had in fact been '*l'époux infernal*' and '*la vierge folle*', that his '*alchimie du verbe*' had been nothing more than a piece of senseless folly. But whereas Verlaine, from whom he finally parted in July 1873 after a violent quarrel, returned to a conventional pattern in both his life and his poetry, Rimbaud, in the face of his defeat, maintained a kind of passive resistance, preferring to withdraw rather than surrender. He abandoned writing altogether (though whether this was immediately after *Une saison en enfer*, when he was barely nineteen, or whether he continued to write for another year or two is not quite certain) and, in a sense, he also abandoned life, or at least society, and became a solitary wanderer, first through various countries in Europe, then out to the East Indies and finally down the Red Sea to Aden and Abyssinia where he engaged in exploring, gun-running and trading. Ill health forced him to return home in the spring of 1891 and six months later, while trying to make his way back to Abyssinia, he died in hospital in Marseilles at the age of 37, uninterested to the end in the extraordinary reputation he had acquired after Verlaine had written an essay on him in his *Poètes maudits* in 1884 and had published the *Illuminations* in 1886. His reputation has continued to grow ever since and he is probably responsible in no small measure for the increasing readiness of the 20th century to allow the artist to create his own mode of expression instead of conforming to an accepted pattern. [CC]

*Œuvres*, ed. S. Bernard (1960); *Selected Verse*, tr. O. Bernard (Penguin Poets, 1962) (prose tr. with intro.).

C. Chadwick, *Études sur R.* (Paris, 1960); W. M. Frohock, *R.'s Poetic Practice* (1963); C. A. Hackett, *R.* (1957); Enid Starkie, *A.R.* (1961).

**Ringelnatz, Joachim,** pseud. of Hans Bötticher (Wurzen 1883–Berlin 1934). German poet, painter and prose-writer. He ran away from school, spent four years at sea, and was subsequently a newspaper-boy, window-dresser, cigarette-vendor, librarian – and minesweeper captain (1914–18). Very successful in Hans von Wolzogen's Berlin cabaret *Schall und Rauch* with his *Turngedichte* and *Kuttel Daddeldu*, he became a travelling cabaret comedian, reciting his satirical grotesques (especially in Munich). Having some affinities with Dada – e.g. in prose *...liner Roma...* (1924) – his poems conceal a profounder moral sensibility beneath the nonsense. [PB]

*Und auf einmal steht es neben dir* (1960) (collected poems); *Mein Leben bis zum Kriege* (1931), *Als Mariner im Krieg* (1928) (autobiographical works); *Kasperle-Verse* (1954) (children's verse); Bridgwater, *TCGV*.

W. Kayser and H. P. des Coudres, *J.R.-Bibliographie* (Hamburg, 1960); H. Günther, *R.* (Reinbek, 1964).

**Rioja, Francisco de** (Seville 1583?–Madrid 1659). Spanish poet and librarian. He wrote love sonnets, stoical reflections, and a number of *silvas* addressed to various flowers in which he delicately exploits the *carpe diem* theme. He continued the manner of ⇨ Herrera and resisted the blandishments of Gongorism, although his use of colour is baroque enough. [JMC]

BAE, 32; *Poesías*, ed. Sociedad de Bibliófilos Españoles (1867); *Poesía*, in *Poesías sevillanas en la edad de oro* (1948); Trend, *OBSV*; Perry, *HASP*; Cohen, *PBSV*.

J. M. Cossío, *Poesía española, notas de asedio* (Madrid, 1936); *LSS*, II (1946).

**Riou, Jakez.** ⇨ Breton Literature.

**Risco, Vicente.** ⇨ Galician Literature.

**Rist, Johannes** (Ottensee, Hamburg 1607–Wedel 1667). German poet. The leading disciple of ⇨ Opitz in north-west Germany, he founded his own language society, the Elbschwanorden (1660) in opposition to the Deutschgesinnte Genossenschaft of ⇨ Zesen. He was for many years a Protestant pastor in Wedel, and it is for his religious verse (*Geistliche poetische Schriften*, 3 vols., 1657–9) that he is chiefly remembered. Many of his religious poems, such as the evening hymn 'Werde munter, mein Gemüte, und ihr Sinne geht herfür', are in the standard Lutheran tradition; others, such as the famous 'O Ewigkeit, du Donnerwort', use all the stylistic devices of the high baroque, anaphora, antithesis, paradox and hyperbole in order to overwhelm the reader by their sheer linguistic power.

His gallant secular verse (*Musa teutonica*, 1634; *Hirtenlieder und Gedichte*, 1656) is written in the stock Petrarchan and pastoral modes. Most of the numerous dramas he is known to have written have been lost. Amongst those that survive are a *Perseus* (1634) and the two 'peace plays' *Das Friedewünschende Teutschland* (1647; ed. H. Stümke, 1915), conspicuous for its treatment of a strictly contemporary theme – the state of Germany at the end of the Thirty Years' War – its use of allegory and its introduction of moral satire, and the more operatic *Das Friedejauchzende Teutschland* (1653). He also wrote an adaptation of Gautier's *Rodomontades*, *Capitan Spavento* (1635) and 6 *Monatsgespräche* (1663–8) in imitation of Harsdörffer's *Frauenzimmergesprächspiele*. [WAC]

*Irenomachia*, ed. W. Flemming, *DLE*, Barock 6. *Altpreussische Monatsschriften*, 47 (1910).

**Ritsos, Yannis** (Monembasia 1909– ). Greek poet. His first collection of verse, *Trakter* ('Tractors', 1934), brought him to the forefront of the new poetic movement in Greece of the 1930s. He has published numerous volumes of verse of which the best known are: *Epitaphios* (1936; parts have been set to music by M. Theodorakis); *To Tragoudi Tis Adelfis Mou* ('My Sister's Song', 1937); *Earini Symfonia* ('Summer Symphony', 1938); *Dokimasia* ('Trial', 1943); *Ydria* ('Pitcher' 1957); *To Dentro Tis Fylakis Kai I Gynaikes* ('The Prison Tree and the Women', 1963). Ritsos's poetry is intensely lyrical and is often coloured by his left-wing sympathies. His compositions are long. He blends successfully modern poetic techniques and conceptions with traditional diction and forms. He was arrested during the military *coup* of April 1967 and deported to an island prison. [SJP]

*Poiemata* (3 vols., 1961).

T. Sinopoulos, *Epochés*, 13 (1964); Ch. Lambrinos, *Epitheorisi Technis*, 17 (1964).

**Rivarol, Antoine Rivaroli,** known as Comte de (Bagnol, Linguadoca 1753–Berlin 1801). French polemical writer and journalist. The son of an innkeeper, he styled himself 'count' on making his way into French *salon* society. He achieved notoriety by writing satirical attacks against established figures like Delille (in *Lettres critiques sur le poème des jardins*, 1782) or Buffon and Mme de Genlis (in a parody of *Le songe d'Athalie*). He attacked all and sundry in *Le petit almanach de nos grands hommes* (1788), which he wrote in collaboration with another self-styled noble and published anonymously. As a journalis the wrote in defence of the monarchy and aristocracy, published a satirical *Petit dictionnaire des grands hommes de la Révolution* (1790), ironically dedicated to Mme de Staël, and *Une lettre à la noblesse française* (1792), published in Brussels where he emigrated with an adventuress, abandoning wife and children. His satire is witty linguistically, but shows no serious grasp of contemporary society or events. The success of his prize-winning essay for the Berlin Academy, *Discours sur l'universalité de la langue française* (1784), which defends the universal clarity of French, led him to plan a *Nouveau dictionnaire de la langue française*, but he only completed the plan and introduction. [AKT]

**Rivas, Duque de.** ⇨ Saavedra, Ángel de.

**Rivaudeau, André de** (Poitou 1538?–1580). French Protestant dramatist and poet. His Biblical tragedy in French, *Aman* (1566), was performed in Poitiers in 1561 while he was still a student there. It is the first 'humanist' religious tragedy, i.e. conforming to the 'classical' rules for tragedy (though ending happily), but rhetorical, lacking in action. He also published verse, some on Biblical subjects (e.g. in *Complaintes*), and a translation of Epictetus. [GJ]

**Rivière, Jacques.** ⇨ French Literary Criticism in the 19th and 20th Centuries.

**Robbe-Grillet, Alain** (Brest 1922– ). French novelist. Trained in Paris as an agricultural expert, he worked in the National Institute of Statistics, then in a research establishment on tropical fruits, which necessitated travel to Africa and the Antilles. With his first novels and essays he became an important exponent of the 'new novel', developing an individual idiom related to the general rejection of conventional character and plot. In *Les gommes* (1953) a detective investigating a murder finally kills the 'victim' and his attempt to impose meaning on reality is destroyed by forces beyond his control, recreating in modern form a parallel of classical tragedy. As in *Le voyeur* (1955; tr. R. Howard, 1959), where the world is seen through the eyes of a sadistic killer, reality cannot be moulded according to man's desires, for it exists outside him with an objective 'thereness'. In his provocative journalistic essays, collected in *Pour un nouveau roman* (1963; tr. B. Wright, *Snapshots and Towards a New Novel*, 1965), he emphasizes man's distance from physical reality, denying him the emotional comfort of describing the world in anthropomorphic terms, and in *Instantanés* (1962; tr. ibid., a collection of purely visual descriptive passages, all relationships are rendered spatially. In *La jalousie* (1957; tr. R. Howard, *Jealousy*, 1959) the objective descriptions of an impersonal eye are interwoven with a jealous husband's interpretation of an eternal triangle situation. *Dans le labyrinthe* (1959) is a fiction created from nothing in which the narrator's room, a picture on the wall and the story of a soldier delivering a dead man's possessions form a complex descriptive narrative. He extends his exploration of reality in *La maison de rendez-vous* (1965). His films *L'année dernière à Marienbad* (1961; tr. R. Howard, *Last Year at Marienbad*, 1962) and *L'immortelle* (1963) extend his visual explorations. [RGV]

B. Morrissette, *Les romans de R-G.* (Paris, 1963); B. Stoltzful, *A. R.-G. and the New French Novel* (S. Illinois Univ., 1964); J. Miesch, *R.-G.* (Classiques du XXe siècle, 1965); O. Bernal, *A.R.-G., le roman de l'absence* (Paris, 1964).

**Robert de Clari.** Knight of Picardy, who in his *Conquête de Constantinople* (ed. A. Pauphilet, *HCMA*; tr. E. Holmes McNeal, N.Y., 1936) gives a human and picturesque account of the Fourth Crusade which began in 1202. His style is conversational and, at times hesitant, but his record of the pleasures, griefs, complaints and fears of the lesser fighting man is interesting and valuable as a complement to the more authoritative chronicle by ⇨ Villehardouin. [LTT]

*R*, LVII (1931).

**Robert the Monk** (Reims 1055–Senuc 1122). Medieval chronicler. Elected abbot of St Rémi in 1095, he was deposed as a result of accusations (apparently false) made against him by Manasses, archbishop of Reims. He then became Prior of Senuc, but Manasses again having accused him of maladministration he was deposed by Calixtus II in 1121 and ended his days as a simple monk at Senuc. His *Historia hierosolymitana*, in eight books covering the years 1095–9, is based, as he states in his preface, on another work (in fact the ⇨ *Gesta Francorum*) with extra material added. Despite his apologies for its deficiencies his style is good, and the work became one of the most popular of its kind. [MRM]

*RHC*, Hist. Occ., iii; Migne, *PL*, 155; Guizot, *CHF*, xxiii; G. Marquardt, *Die Historia hierosolymitana des Robertus Monachus* (1892).

**Rode, Helge** (Copenhagen 1870–Frederiksberg 1937). Danish poet, playwright and essayist. A religious mystic and symbolist he played a dominant part in the neo-romantic poetic revival in Denmark during the 1890s, and his best poetry does not date – unlike his dramas, many of which are concerned with contemporary problems. He wrote polemical essays against the radical movement led by G. ⇨ Brandes. [ELB]

*Ariel* (1914); *Udvalgte Digte* (1945).

**Rodríguez, Claudio** (Zamora 1934– ). Spanish poet. His poetry, of reflective, Wordsworthian feeling, and founded on childhood memories and local sentiments, makes a deeply felt plea for human solidarity. His *Don de la ebriedad* (1953) won the Adonais prize; his shorter poems, *Conjuros* (1958), include several pieces of great originality. [JMC]

Cohen, *PBSV*.
Cano, *PESV*.

**Rodríguez del Padrón** or **de la Cámara, Juan** (Padrón *c.* 1405–? after 1440). Spanish poet and novelist. He was page to John II, and probably became a Franciscan. Baena included some of his poems in his *Cancionero*, which are generally melancholy confessions of disappointed love. Legend has said that he was in love with the Queen. He wrote *Triunfo de las donas*, a defence of women, and also a book about lineage, *Cadira del Honor*. His *Siervo libre de amor* (Buenos Aires, 1943) is a partly autobiographical novel in the manner of ⇨ Boccaccio's *Fiammetta*, in which is interpolated a tale of chivalry in the manner of *Amadís*, entitled *Estoria de los dos amadores Ardanlier e Liesa*. [JMC]

*Obras*, ed. A. Paz y Melia (1884); Blecua, *FLE*.
R. Schevill, *Ovid and the Renascence in Spain* (Berkeley, Cal., 1913).

**Rodulphus (Radulphus** or **Raoul) Glaber** (Burgundy before 1000–Cluny after 1046). Historian. He became a monk, but because of his quarrelsomeness was sent from one monastery to another (Dijon, Moutiers, Auxerre, Cluny). He wrote a history of his own times in an exceptionally lively and individual prose style. [CEC]

*Historiarum sui temporis libri V*, ed. M. Prou, (Collection de Textes, Paris, 1886); Migne, *PL*, 142; French tr. F. Guizot (Paris, 1824).
Manitius, *GLLM*.

**Roidis, Emmanuel** (Syros 1835–Athens 1904). Greek critic, short-story writer and novelist. Educated in Genoa and Syros and afterwards in Germany where he studied literature and philosophy. He travelled widely in Europe and the Balkans and in 1860 he settled in Athens earning his living as a writer and as a translator of foreign literary works, mainly French and English. His critical writings on poetry and on the language revealing his considerable literary *flair* exercised a great influence on contemporary Greek letters. He is chiefly remembered for his satirical novel *I Papissa Ioanna* (1886; tr. Lawrence Durrell, *Pope Joan*, 1954) which is based on the well-known medieval story about Pope John VIII being a woman. It is well written, and the story is well told, though Roidis's wit is somewhat contrived. The anti-clerical tone and bawdy humour of the book provoked the fury of the Greek Church who banned it. His short stories contain some good descriptions of Greek provincial life and sensitive character studies. [SJP]

*Apanta* (1911–14).

**Rojas, Fernando de** (*c.* 1465–1541). Spanish novelist of Jewish descent, *La* ⇨ *Celestina.*

**Rojas Villandrando, Agustín de** (Madrid 1572–Paredes de Nava? after 1618). Spanish dramatist. He wrote for a touring company, led an adventurous life and composed stock comedies. He is best known for *El viaje entretenido* (1603; NBAE, XXI) a novel in dialogue about travelling actors, which throws a great deal of light on stage conditions in his day. [JMC]

H. A. Rennert, *The Spanish Stage in the Time of Lope de Vega* (N.Y., 1909).

**Rojas Zorilla, Francisco de** (Toledo 1607–Madrid 1648). Spanish dramatist who wrote for the court theatre and was knighted by Philip IV. He is principally noted for his horrific tragedies of revenge. Though influenced by Calderón (with whom he collaborated), particularly in his rather tedious sacred plays, he seems more sympathetically human in his treatment of the problem of honour; his feminist play, *Cada cual lo que le toca*, was hissed in the theatre, while his tragedy of revenge, *Morir pensando matar* (before 1642; ed. R. R. MacCurdy, in CC, 1961), ends, as his *gracioso* remarks, without the conventional pile of corpses. The authorship of what was hitherto his best-known work, *García del Castañar*, has recently been questioned. This play (generally called *Del rey abajo ninguno*, CA, CC) is conventional in its theme that a king can do no wrong, but unorthodox in its development; its descriptions of the pleasures of country life are poetic in the best post-Gongorist style. Rojas also wrote some original cloak and sword comedies, and his plots were borrowed by T. Corneille, ⇨ Scarron, ⇨ Lesage, etc. The best known is *Entre bobos anda el juego* (? 1638, CA, CC), with its theme of an old man in love with a girl. [JMC]

*Teatro*, ed. F. Ruiz Morcuende (CC); *Comedias escogidas* (1861; 1908); BAE; *La vida en el ataúd*, ed. R. R. MacCurdy, in CC (1961).
Raymond R. MacCurdy, *F. de R.Z. and the Tragedy* (Albuquerque, 1958).

**'Roland, Chanson de.'** Oldest and most famous of the extant ⇨ *chansons de geste*. The Oxford version, the earliest and the best available, was composed in the late 11th century, probably before the First Crusade. Textual evidence and allusions in 9th-century monastic annals and Latin chronicles indicate that Roland's epic fight at Roncesvalles was known in legendary form in the 9th century, and was probably narrated in song by the 10th century. ⇨ Wace, in his *Roman de Rou*, using a statement by William of Malmesbury, describes how Taillefer sang a 'Song of Roland' as he rode before the Norman army into battle at Hastings. A Latin prose summary of a 'Song of Roland', somewhat similar to the Oxford version, and known as the *Nota emilianense*, was copied in Northern Spain into the margin of a manuscript about 1050.

The Oxford version, in 4,002 assonanced decasyllabic lines, was composed by an unknown poet of great skill and experience; the name Turoldus in the last line may refer to the author. The poet conceals his artistry, but the balance and harmony with which he invokes simultaneously the stress of epic battle, the strength and weaknesses of human character, and feudal devotion to the highest ideals, were never equalled in any later *chanson de geste*.

The story divides into four parts: (a) Ganelon's hatred of his stepson Roland, against whom he plots treachery with Marsile, the Saracen king; (b) the Saracen attack at Roncesvalles against the rearguard of Charlemagne's army, Roland's refusal to summon immediate help, the heroic deaths of the peers and of Roland, Charlemagne's revenge on Marsile; (c) Charlemagne's victory in Spain over Baligant, the lord of all Islam; (d) the return to France, Ganelon's trial and execution.

The poem has two major themes: that of Charlemagne's struggle against the Saracens, in which his knights fight for the Empire, for *dulce France*, for Christendom and their feudal honour, and the theme of the personal relationships between Charlemagne's vassals, the enmity dividing Ganelon and Roland, and to a lesser extent Roland's quarrel with Oliver at Roncesvalles and their reconciliation as Oliver dies. Both themes are skilfully related and yet developed separately.

The friendship between Roland and Oliver illustrates the epic ideal, classical and medieval, of *fortitudo* and *sapientia*. Roland is fearless, tenacious against disaster, but seeking his own glory. Oliver, prudent and moderate, throws into relief the heroic immoderation which impels Roland to risk and lose the rearguard.

The song uses historical facts. Charlemagne invaded Spain in 778 at the invitation of two Moslem emirs. He occupied Pamplona peacefully but was halted before Saragossa, and then began a withdrawal from Spain, probably because of renewed war on the Saxon frontier. On the way north he sacked Pamplona and took as hostage one of the emirs who had been his ally. Charlemagne's army was attacked, probably by a mixed force of Moslems and Basques in the mountain pass to the north of Roncesvalles, the rearguard was destroyed, and Roland, prefect of the Breton march, was slain, together with other nobles.

Versions of the song exist in medieval Latin, German, Basque, Scandinavian and Provençal. Roland figures in medieval English literature in *Roland and Vernagu* and *Sir Firumbras*, and in the poetry of ⇨ Boiardo and ⇨ Ariosto. [LTT]

*La Chanson de R.*, ed. F. Whitehead (1947); ed. J. Bédier (Paris, 1947); tr. Dorothy Sayers, *The Song of Roland* (Penguin Classics, 1957); tr. J. Crosland (1924).

E. Faral, *La Chanson de R.* (Paris, 1933); P. Le Gentil, *La Chanson de R.* (Paris, 1955); R. Menéndez Pidal, *La Chanson de R. et la tradition épique des Francs* (2nd edn, Paris, 1960).

**Roland Holst, Adriaan** (Amsterdam 1888– ). Dutch writer. Unlike ⇨ Leopold, whose sensitivity he shares (*Over den dichter Leopold*, 1926), he has a vision of an elemental, primordial elysium (*De Belijdenis van de Stilte*) which later (in *Voorbij de Wegen*) derives a specifically Celtic orientation from Yeats. In autoscopic visions he sees his double or his reflection as part of a corrupt and doomed world. The prose-poem *De Afspraak* (1925) and the poetry of *De Wilde Kim* (1925) set the tone of his later works, yearning for the era of man's innocence before the barbarisms of civilization. [PK]

*Verzamelde Werken* (4 vols., 1948–50); Barnouw, *CA*; *Delta* (Summer 1959).

**Roland Holst-van der Schalk, Henriette Goverdina Anna** (Noordwijk 1869–Amsterdam 1952). Dutch poet, dramatist and scholar. Her early sensitive and faultering sonnets and terzinas, which appeared in *De Nieuwe Gids* (cf. ⇨ Kloos), expressed the ideal which ennobles her whole work and life: 'Of all single things I love people most.' As a result of ⇨ Gorter's political influence she and her husband, the painter Richard Roland Holst, joined the Marxist socialists, and William Morris's vision of the New Birth released great political and literary activity in her. Social reforms and party quarrels engendered elation and sorrow in her collections of poetry until, with the advent of Stalin, she repudiated Communism. Her later, religious socialist verse is calmer in mood, but still unrestrained in form.

Among her collections are: *Sonetten en verzen in terzienen geschreven* (1895); *De Nieuwe Geboort* (1902); *Opwaartsche wegen* (1907); *De vrouw in her woud* (1912); *Tusschen tijd en eeuwigheid* (1934); *Thomas Moore* (1912) and other plays. Biographies include *Herman Gorter* (1933). She also wrote *Kapitaal en arbeid in de 19de eeuw* (1902) and other studies. [PK]

Barnouw, *CA*; Weevers, *PNEC*.

**'Rolandslied.'** ⇨ Konrad (Pfaffe Konrad).

**Rolland, Romain** (Clamecy 1866–Vézelay 1944). French novelist, playwright, musicologist, biographer and internationalist. He was much influenced as a young man by Tolstoy's philosophy of art and his faith in humanity, as well as by the intense idealism of Malwida von Meysenbug and her circle. His reputation as a musicologist was established by *Histoire de l'opéra en Europe avant Lully et Scarlatti* (1895) and he later published *Musiciens d'autrefois* (1908), *Musiciens d'aujourd'hui* (1908), *Voyage musical au pays du passé* (1920) and the 6-volume *Vie de Beethoven* (1928–45; partly tr. E. Newman, 1925 ff.). Through ⇨ Péguy he became associated with the *Cahiers de la quinzaine* from 1900 onwards and some of his plays, together with the 10 volumes of his 'roman-fleuve' *Jean-Christophe* (1903–12; tr. G. Cannan, 1910), were published as *cahiers*. He early became an enthusiast for the 'popular' theatre concept of Pottecher and others, explaining his ideas in *Le théâtre du peuple* (1903). Two trilogies written in this spirit were published as *Le théâtre de la révolution* (1909) and *Les tragédies de la foi* (1913).

In 1914 he attempted to defend his internationalist and pacifist ideals by appealing to the intellectuals of France and Germany to cooperate in the interests of peace. His essay *Au-dessus de la mêlée* (1915; tr. C. K. Ogden, *Above the Battlefield*, 1916) made him many enemies, but it also led to his being awarded the Nobel Prize in the same year. His novel *Jean-Christophe* was another factor, being widely admired. It brought together his interests and ideals in the story of a German musical genius who makes France his second home and becomes a vehicle for Rolland's views on music, social matters and understanding between nations. Other novels are *Colas Breugnon* (1919), *Clérambault* (1920), *Pierre et Luce* (1920) and *L'âme enchantée* which first appeared in 7 volumes between 1922 and 1933 (tr. V. Wyck Brooks, A. de Alberti *et al.*, *The Soul Enchanted*, 1927–35).

His biographies are of interest as much for the light they throw on his own mind as for their intrinsic subject-matter. They include *Vie de Beethoven* (1903), *Vie de Michel-Ange* (1908), *Vie de Tolstoï* (1911), *Mahatma Gandhi* (1924), *Vie de Ramakrishna* (1929), *Vie de Vivekananda* (2 vols., 1930) and *Péguy* (2 vols., 1944). These works, along with such collections of essays as *Quinze ans de combat*: *1919–34* (1934) and *Par la révolution, la paix* (1935), and autobiographical writings like *Le voyage intérieur* (1942), *Le périple* (1946), show the evolution of his thought towards a highly individual mixture of marxism and oriental mysticism. [JC]

P.-J. Jouve, *R.R. vivant* (Paris, 1920); C. Sénéchal, *R.R.* (Paris, 1933); A. R. Levy, *L'idéalisme de R.R.* (Paris, 1943); J.-B. Barrère, *R.R. par lui-même* (Paris, 1955) and *R.R. l'âme et l'art* (Paris, 1966).

**Rollenhagen, Georg** (Bernau 1542–Magdeburg 1609). German writer. A Lutheran preacher and pedagogue, his writings are didactic. His 3 dramas, *Abraham* (1569), *Tobias* (1576; ed. J. Bolte, *Neudruche* 285–7, 1930) and *Der reiche Mann und der arme Lazarus* (1590), quicken their biblical subjects with many traditional elements of moral satire and the inculcation of contemporary middle-class virtues. Equally, in his principal work, the mock epic *Froschmeuseler* (1595), the war between the frogs and the mice is a vehicle for religious, social and moral satire. Indebted in its central theme to the pseudo-homeric *Batrachyomachia*, *Froschmeuseler* is the most important German fable since *Reyncke de Vos*, with which it has many political elements in common. [WAC]

*Das Spiel vom reichen Mann*, ed. J. Bolte, Neudrucke 270–3 (1929).

**Rolli, Paolo** (Rome 1687–Todi 1765). Italian Arcadian poet. Renowned for the musicality and graceful simplicity of his verse (first poetry published in a collection of 1711). In 1715 he went to London where he remained for most of his life, teaching Italian to the daughters of George II, writing poetry and libretti for the Italian melodramas then popular in London. He also published in England several editions of the works of Italian classical authors, translated Milton's *Paradise Lost* and in 1728 wrote, in English, his polemical *Remarks upon M. Voltaire's Essay on the Epick Poetry of the European Nations*. He returned to Italy in 1747 and in 1753 published in Venice a collection of his best poetry – *De' poetici componimenti del signor P.R.* [RHC]

*Liriche*, ed. C. Calcaterra (1926); *Lirici del '700*, ed. B. Maier (1959).
T. Vallese, *P.R. in Inghilterra* (Naples, 1938).

**Romains, Jules**, pseud. of Louis Farigoule (Saint-Julien-Chapteuil 1885– ). French poet, dramatist and novelist. He was educated at the Lycée Condorcet and the École Normale Supérieure, Paris, where he passed his *agrégation* in philosophy (1909). After the First World War, he abandoned his career as a teacher to devote himself entirely to writing, having already made a name with collections of verse, two novels – *Mort de quelqu'un* (1911) and *Les copains* (1913) – and a play, *L'armée dans la ville*, performed at the Paris Odéon in 1911. During the twenties, his major successes were in the theatre, notably with the comedies *M. le Trouhadec saisi par la débauche* (1923), *Knock, ou le Triomphe de la médecine* (1923; tr. H. Granville Barker, 1935) and *Donogoo* (1930). In the thirties, he turned principally to the novel, beginning his major work, *Les hommes de bonne volonté* (27 vols., 1932–47; tr. W. B. Wells and G. Hopkins, *Men of Good Will*, 1933), which was mainly responsible for his election to the Académie Française in 1946. Since then, there has been a steady output of novels, short stories and essays, but none of these has matched the quality of his earlier work.

*Knock* is now an established classic of both stage and screen, and is typical of much of Romains's work in its theme of imposture and in its brilliant comic force. Moreover, it also has characteristic links with the philosophical theory of Unanimism which the author elaborated: the idea that social life is essentially dominated by groups bound together by a collective psychology. The same idea provided the principal inspiration for *Les hommes de bonne volonté*, with its study of the evolution of French and European society in the years 1908–33. It was these novels which led some critics to see Romains as the modern successor to Balzac, and he himself explained his aim in the series as being to '*saisir d'abord la vie et le mouvement de la société en elle-même, des groupes dont elle se compose, les courants psychiques qui la traversent et la modifient*'. [PHN]

M. Berry, *J.R., sa vie, son œuvre* (Paris, 1953); A. Cuisenier, *J.R. et les H. de B.V.* (Paris, 1954).

**'Romances.'** The Romantics used to think that Spanish *romances* or ballads were the poetry of the Spanish people. But although they eventually enjoyed a wide currency, in origin they were most probably short episodes from medieval epics and condensed versions of ⇨ *gestes*, sung or recited by individual troubadours. These short narrative and dialogue poems almost certainly gained in popularity at the expense of the longer *gestes*, and by the second half of the 14th century *romances* were being created in their own right about the events of the time. Apart from epic subjects like the Cid, and historical themes, sometimes (like the reconquest of Spain from the Moors) of recent date, traditional Spanish ballads were often based on Greek and Roman history, on the story of Roland and Oliver and the Arthurian legends. But there was also a type of ballad, originating in medieval lyric poetry, concerned with tales of infidelity and lovers' meetings ('*serranillas*'). And although the actual period at which *romances* of this sort came to be written is not known, some of them can be dated with certainty to the early years of the 15th century.

Ballads of all these kinds were well established by the middle of the 15th century. They were popular at the court of Alfonso V of Aragon in 1445, and Enrique IV, in 1462, commissioned a ballad about one of the Granada campaigns. The inven tion of printing necessarily helped their diffusion, and many of the ballads probably acquired a more fixed form as a result of being printed in chap-books at the end of the 15th century. The early chap-books usually, although not invariably, contained more than one ballad, or one ballad with one or more glosses on it, and the title page sometimes carried a crude woodcut illustration. Sometimes the name of the author of the ballad was given, although there are no grounds for considering many of the attributions authentic. It is clear, however, that some ballads were believed to be more than a hundred years old, since some are ascribed to Don Juan Manuel (1282–1345).

The next stage in the diffusion of the ballads was their collection in book form, the earliest volume of them, containing 155 items, being printed between 1547 and 1549. Many of these collections contained *romances* written by established poets, but it was the late 16th and early 17th century which saw a significant increase in the writing and re-writing of ballads by cultivated writers. Just as lutenist composers of the period wrote elaborate variations on popular themes, poets wrote new versions of the traditional stories. To the rudimentary narrative or dialogue form of the *romances*, in which brief descriptive passages were used to heighten the dramatic tension, these writers added conceits and verbal tricks, more extensive descriptions, moral points and so forth. Alternatively, poets would also write original narrative poems or imitate or parody traditional ballads. ⇨ Góngora, ⇨ Quevedo and ⇨ Lope de Vega all wrote these kinds of *romance* and some of their work was so truly popular in character that they were printed and widely circulated in chap-book form at the period. The stories of the traditional ballads were also widely used by playwrights at the time, and they provided plots for many dramatic works in the late 16th and 17th centuries. Dramatists could also use them to create a specific atmosphere at given moments in a play, and even a brief reference to a traditional ballad would, of course, have been sufficient to put the general public in mind of it, so well were they known.

The 18th century brought no real decline in knowledge of the ballads, although Spanish writers were trying to produce an international rather than national literature. They continued to be sung or recited in country areas, and flourished in chap-books. Cultivated writers like ⇨ Cadalso and Huerta in the middle of the century and ⇨ Meléndez Valdés at the end glossed and imitated them or used the octosyllabic form to express their own ideas and feelings much as Lope had done in the previous century. Furthermore collections of *romances* were included in volumes XVI and XVII of Ramón Fernández's *Parnaso español* (1796), the first to appear since the various editions of the *Romancero general* (1600–14). Outside Spain interest in Spanish ballads grew in Germany and England. In Spain itself Romanticism gave a new impetus to the use of ballads in the early 19th century. They seemed the most obvious source of national themes on which to draw for both drama and poetry and Agustín Durán published important collections of them between 1828 and 1835. ⇨ Zorrilla and the Duque de Rivas wrote numerous *romances* in the traditional manner but with highly coloured descriptions; ⇨ Espronceda based his verse drama *El estudiante de Salamanca* on the *romances* of *Lisardo el estudiante*. Later in the century the growing interest in folklore led scholars to record the various forms of ballads which had been passed down in the oral tradition, and the most impressive fruits of this work were the numerous publications on *romances* by Ramón Menéndez Pidal. A number of 20th-century Spanish poets have used the form, amongst them Antonio ⇨ Machado, ⇨ Pérez de Ayala, Juan Ramón ⇨ Jiménez and García ⇨ Lorca. Of these, the first two sought to preserve the atmosphere of the traditional ballad while Jiménez and Lorca injected their own poetic styles into the form as Góngora and Quevedo had done in the early 17th century. Jacinto ⇨ Grau and others based plays on ballad themes in the early decades of the century. No other country perhaps has preserved the ballad-singing tradition in quite the same way or to the same extent. But wireless and television are gradually eliminating *romances* even in country areas in Spain. In very isolated parts and in closely knit traditionalist communities like those of the Sephardic Jews outside Spain they may continue to survive a few generations. Amongst modern poets, however, the *romance* is largely a verse-form, nothing more. [ONVG]

*Spanish Ballads*, ed. C. C. Smith (1964).

W. J. Entwistle, *The Arthurian Legend in the*

*Literature of the Spanish Peninsula* (1925); W. J. Entwistle, *European Balladry* (1951); W. S. Merwin, *Some Spanish Ballads* (1961); E. M. Wilson, *Tragic Themes in Spanish Ballads* (1964).

**Romansh Literature.** When the senior librarian of the British Museum, who came from the Romansh-speaking part of Switzerland, was asked in 1775 to read a paper before the Royal Academy about his native language, he presented in his 'Account of the Romanish language' a translation into Romansh of the oldest French text, the *Serment de Strasburg* (A.D. 843). He showed that the old French – virtually still Latin – was almost identical with the Romansh translation. Romansh is in fact an ancient romance language between French and Italian, which used once to be spoken throughout the Alps from the Gotthard to Trieste and survives today in three areas divided from one another by German and Italian-speaking territories. These are Friaul with 800,000 inhabitants, who call their language 'Furlan' or 'Ladin', a further 20,000 Ladin-speaking people in the Dolomites, and 50,000 'Retoromans' in Grisons (Switzerland) who call their language Romansh or, in the Engadine, Ladin. Each of these three groups has developed its own literature, though that of the Ladin-speaking people of the Dolomites consists chiefly of an oral literature of fairy-tales, legends and folk-song. The literature of Friaul has an unbroken tradition which goes back to the 14th century; its richest periods occur in the second half of the 17th century and in the 18th and 19th, and it has enjoyed an astonishing revival during and after the Second World War. The Romansh literature of Grisons is even richer. Apart from some ancient rich resources of fairy-tales, legends and folk-songs, there is a political epic of 700 lines, the *Chanzun de la guerra da Müsch*, written by the statesman, Gian Travers of Zuoz, in 1527, and also a translation of the New Testament by the lawyer, Jachiam Bifrun in 1560. These works laid the foundations for a literary language in the Engadine which was soon used for hymns, Biblical dramas and other devotional writings, and also for legal works and chronicles. There also appear secular writings, particularly political songs and pamphlets, which reflect the sharply differing views arising in the 15th-century democractic foundation, the 'Freistaat der drei Bünde', which only joined the Swiss Federation in 1803 as the Canton of Graubunden. The religious and political freedom hymns by the Protestant preachers, Joannes and Martinus ex Martinis and the mystical psalms by the Benedictine of Mustèr (Disentis), are still impressive today. In the 19th century much fine lyrical poetry was written, above all by Gian Fadri Caderas, Gion Antoni Huonder and Alfons Tuor; even more powerful in its use of language is the lyrical-epic work of Giachen Caspar Muoth. The turn of the century is marked by the aesthetically self-conscious poetry of Peider Lansel and the earthy Novellen by the country doctor, Giachen Michael Nay, who both stand out against a large number of far from insignificant writers in this period. In the last 50 years there has been a great revival in all fields, through the poetry and stories of Gian Fontana, the charmingly humorous novellas of Schimun Vonmoos, Gian Girun and Guglielm Gadola, through the poetry also of Pater Alexander Lozza and Andri Peer (influenced by Eliot, ⇨ Éluard, ⇨ Prévert), the marvellously fresh cadences of Luisa Famos, the colourful novels and Novellas of Cla Biert and Toni Halter, and the Biblical dramas of Gian Belsch and the historical dramas of Jon Semadeni. [RRB]

*Studies in Modern Romansh Poetry in the Engadine*, tr. M. E. Maxfield (Cambridge, Mass., 1938); C. Decurtins, 'Geschichte der retoromanischer Literatur', in *Gröbers der romanischen Philologie*, ii (Strasburg, 1901); E. Piguet, 'La Suisse rétoromanche', in *Littératures de la Suisse* (Paris, 1938); R. R. Bezzola, 'Littérature Romanche', in *Encyclopédie de la Pléiade, Histoire des littératures*, ii (Paris, 1956).

**Ronsard, Pierre de** (Coutoure-en-Vendômois 1524–Saint-Côme-lès-Tours 1585). French poet. Born of a good Vendômois family and son of a man of letters, he entered court life as a page and in 1537–9 visited Scotland in the retinue of the two successive queens of James V. But his career was interrupted by early deafness and he withdrew to study for five years under Dorat at the Collège de Coqueret, with Baïf and du Bellay. With them and others he formed the revolutionary brigade known as the ⇨ Pléiade. In 1550 he published his *Odes*, giving France its first great lyrical poetry in the Pindaric vein, with the poet taking on the lofty role of celebrant of public events and critic of great contemporaries. Intended to be sung (we still have the original melodies of Janequin and others), these odes are marred by pedantry, and Ronsard soon turned to Horace, Catullus and others as less austere models. His *Odes*, like the *Amours* (1552), love poems addressed to Cassandre, were an immediate success and he soon became recognized as the 'Prince of Poets', enjoying the protection of Charles IX and Madame Marguerite, the king's sister; Mary Stuart admired him and was to send him a present while in prison. He received an annual stipend and the benefices of two priories. He followed with *Continuation des amours* (1555), *Nouvelle continuation* (1556), the heroic, epic and didactic *Hymnes* (1555–6), and during the civil wars, the *Institution pour l'adolesence du roi* (1562), a pedagogical and moral poem on the reciprocal duties of king and subject; the conciliatory *Discours des misères de ce temps* (1563), *Remontrance au peuple de France*, urging the nation to rally round the king; *Élégies, mascarades et bergeries*, lyrical poems for court entertainment, dedicated to Elizabeth I; and the not very successful epic, *La Franciade* (1572), abandoned after the fourth canto. On the death of Charles IX (1574), Ronsard retired gradually from public life, but at 50 wrote a new series of love poems, *Sonnets pour Hélène*, possibly to compete with the young Desportes: they were published in the 1578 edition of his works. They include some of his most perfect sonnets, among them the *Quand vous serez bien vieille*. The greatest French poet of his day, he was not esteemed in the next two centuries, regaining his rightful place only in the 19th century. [FWAG]

Ed. P. Laummonier (8 vols., 1914–19); ed. H. Vaganay (7 vols., 1923–4); ed. G. Cohen (2 vols., Pléiade, 1936).

P. Champion, *R. et son temps* (Paris, 1925); R. Lebègue, *R., l'homme et l'œuvre* (Paris, 1950); F. Desonay, *R. poète de l'amour* (3 vols., Brussels, 1952–9).

**Rørdam, Valdemar** (Dalby 1872–Copenhagen 1946). Danish lyrical poet. His poetry strongly reflects his patriotic feelings, e.g. 'Danmark i tusind Aar' ('Denmark during a Thousand Years', 1940). [ELB]

**Rosa, Salvatore** (Naples 1615–Rome 1673). Italian painter and satirical poet. He studied painting at Naples and worked in Rome (1635–40) and Florence (1640–9). From 1649 he lived mostly at Rome. Some features appearing in early biographies are now rejected as untrue. He was not involved in Masaniello's uprising (1647), nor was he a composer of music.

His *Lettere* reveal his cultural taste and severe and combative character, but his chief literary work is his collection of 7 *Satire in terza rima* (6 published *c.* 1694 and the last in 1876). The first, *La musica* (*c.* 1641), attacks contemporary music and the moral corruption surrounding it; *La poesia* (*c.* 1642), the most interesting, denounces the extravagances of *seicento* literature; *La pittura* is against genre painting; *La guerra* (1647) describes the miseries of war and refers to Masaniello's revolt; *L'invidia* (1652–3) is an attack on his personal detractors; *Babilonia* (begun 1657–8) lashes the vices of Papal Rome; *Tirreno* is a gloomy meditation on man's corruption and the futility of life. Although sporadically effective in the vigour of direct attacks, he lacks artistic finesse and discrimination, and too often descends to crude bludgeoning. [DGR]

*Poesie e lettere*, ed. G. A. Cesareo (2 vols., 1892); *Poesie e lettere inedite*, ed. U. Limentani (1950).

U. Limentani, *Bibliografia della vita e delle opere di S.R.* (Florence, 1955); U. Limentani, *La satira nel seicento* (Milan/Naples, 1961); Croce, *SSL*; *Minori*, iii.

**'Rose, Roman de la'.** Poem in octosyllabic couplets, of which the first part of some 4,000 lines was written between 1225 and 1237 by Guillaume de Lorris. The remaining 18,000 lines were composed in very different style by Jean de Meung some 40 years later.

When Guillaume de Lorris says that in his poem *'L'Art d'Amors est toute enclose'*, he means the doctrine of love of the Provençal troubadours; this he knew well together with earlier Arts of Love, including Ovid's *Ars amatoria* and the 12th-century *De arte honeste amandi* of Andreas Capellanus. He tells his dream in which he was admitted by *Oiseuse* to the Garden of Love where he found the courtly virtues such as *Déduit*, *Liesse*, *Largesse*, *Cortoisie*, *Doux Regard*, *Franchise* in possession, and the vices such as Hatred, Avarice, Hypocrisy and Envy excluded. He falls in love with the Rose, symbol of the lady and of the lady's love, but must listen first to the precepts of the god of Love. The progress of his love for the Rose is described in a delicately sustained allegory in which figures such as *Bel Accueil*, *Dangier*, *Pitié*, *Male Bouche*, represent the feelings of the lady and the influences acting on her, and *Nature* and *Raison* the desires and doubts felt by the lover. The allegorical figures are portrayed with a lightness and sensibility and simple elegance of style that make this poem a masterpiece of medieval literature.

Unfinished perhaps because of Guillaume de Lorris's death, the work was continued by Jean de Meung, Jean Clopinel (Meung-sur-Loire *c.* 1240–*c.* 1305), whose house in the rue Saint-Jacques in Paris was well known until its destruction in the 16th century. He was a man of the schools, acquainted with the Aristotelian and Averroist throught of the University of Paris of his day. He had little patience with courtly love, which he considered deceptive and illusory. He records various medieval attitudes to love, the misogynist, venal and rationalist, but to him it is chiefly the means to propagate the species. His rationalism judges whatever is contrary to Nature as wrong and perverted, and he digresses skilfully about the working of the universe, man's growth as a social animal, the role of free will, and the influence of the stars on man's destiny. The original story meant little to him. The tower in which Bel Accueil had been imprisoned is now taken by storm, and the lover is allowed to pick the Rose, but the action of the poem is only a thread to which long and important digressions are attached. The allegorical figures are no longer states of mind with a separate psychological existence. They express ideas about man and the Universe which are not inspired or original, but valuable as a balanced encyclopedic digest in the vernacular of the main scientific theories and philosophical controversies of the 12th and 13th centuries. The clear, robust French verse reflects an underlying optimism in Man's destiny.

Jean de Meung's misogynist views were later to stir ⇨ Christine de Pisan to indignation, and a quarrel broke out in the early 15th century between his adversaries and supporters. His misogynism belongs, in fact, to a clerical and literary tradition stemming back to the earliest Church fathers and beyond.

The *Roman de la Rose* enjoyed an immense success in manuscript form and in print. By 1538 forty editions had been printed, and Jean de Meung's poem was highly esteemed in the 16th century. The English *Romaunt of the Rose*, attributed to Chaucer, is a translation of the poem by Guillaume de Lorris and of part of Jean de Meung's continuation. [LTT]

*Le Roman de la Rose*, ed. E. Langlois (5 vols., 1914–24); ed. F. Lecoy (1956); tr. F. S. Ellis (3 vols., 1900); tr. H. W. Robbins (N.Y., 1962). G. Paré, *Les idées et les lettres au XIIIe siècle, Le Roman de la Rose* (Montreal, 1947); C. S. Lewis, *The Allegory of Love* (1950); L. Thuasne, *Le Roman de la Rose* (Paris, 1929); A. M. F. Gunn, *The Mirror of Love. A Reinterpretation of 'The Romance of the Rose'* (Lubbock, Texas, 1952); *Revue des Deux Mondes*, v (1926); *PMLA*, LXVIII (1953).

**Rosegger, Peter** (Alp bei Krieglach 1843–Krieglach 1918). Austrian moralist and humorous writer. His short stories and anecdotes in a simple, homely style and a tone of gentle yet insistent moralizing present cameos of the life of plain folk, above all of those in the rural districts of his native Styria. His most typical works are: *Die Schriften des Waldschulmeisters* (1875); *Der Gottsucher* (1883); *Das ewige Licht* (1897). [RT]

R. Latzke, *P.R.* (Weimar, 1943).

**Rosenfeld, Morris,** pseud. of Moshe Jacob Alter (Boksa 1862–New York 1923). Noted as the poet of the Jewish working class. Left Russia at the age of 20, lived for a while in London's East End working as a tailor, spent some years in Amsterdam as a diamond cutter and finally settled in New York in 1886. He sings primarily of the 'sweatshops' and the immense poverty of the Jewish proletariat with great force and conviction. He also wrote biographies of Yehudah Halevi and Heinrich Heine, and two operettas. [EE]

*The Works of Morris Rosenfeld* (6 vols., N.Y., 1908–10); *Songs from the Ghetto*, tr. Leo Wiener, in prose with Latin transcription of original (Boston, Mass., 1898).
Waxman, *HJL*.

**'Rosengarten.'** 13th-century Middle High German strophic epic. One of a number of narrative works derived from the situation presented in the second part of the ⇨ *Nibelungenlied* and belonging to the sequence of sagas attaching to the history of the Ostrogothic kingdom. The story concerns the duels fought at Kriemhild's behest by twelve Burgundian knights, custodians of the 'Rose Garden', against twelve warriors chosen from the ranks of Theodoric the Goth; Theodoric himself is matched against Kriemhild's husband Siegfried. The

Goths are victorious in all but one bout, which ends with the reconciliation of the two contestants. [RT]

Ed. G. Holz (1893). C. Brestowsky, *Der Rosengarten zu Worms* (1929).

**Rosenhane, Gustaf** (1619–1684). Swedish poet. He is remembered chiefly for his development of the sonnet form, which he learned from French models; *Venerid* (1680) is a cycle of 100 sonnets. He wrote a long rhyming poem about the Swedish language, which he was anxious to improve, and published a collection of 80 songs.

**Rostand, Edmond** (Marseilles 1868–Paris 1918). French playwright. After the probing severity of Ibsen and the harsh scrutiny of ⇨ Becque, Rostand's surface glitter, vivacity and apparent spontaneity seduced a public for whom Naturalism was identified with gloom. The warm, though vague, idealism animating his plays also provided relief from the political and social strains of the period. *Les Romanesques* (1894; tr. G. Fleming, *The Fantasticks*, 1912), handles with conscious though insipid charm a witty inversion of the plight of Romeo and Juliet and is followed by *La princesse lointaine* (1895; tr. H. D. Norman, *The Princess Far Away*, 1921), a fanciful revival of troubadour love, touched with moments of tenderness but essentially precious in style and feeling. From Romance legend, he moved to a Biblical subject, *La Samaritaine* (1897; tr. H. D. Norman, *The Woman of Samaria*, 1921) in which sacred and profane love are mingled with conspicuous vulgarity and sentimentality. Only with *Cyrano de Bergerac* (1897; tr. H. Wolfe, 1937) does he create a play in which preciosity of language, lyrical feeling and romantic *bravura* fuse to produce an exciting, compelling, though fundamentally factitious, theatrical experience. The contrived pathos and over-elaboration of *L'Aiglon* (1900; tr. B. Davenport, 1927), the play devoted to Napoleon's ill-fated son, are not wholly redeemed by scenes of brilliant theatricality, like that of the dead battalions on the plain of Wagram coming to life in the young prince's imagination. This was followed by *Chantecler* (1910; tr. H. D. Norman, *Chanticleer*, 1921), in many ways the most ambitious and original of his dramas. This allegory set in a farmyard, with the Cockerel as the Orphic voice and servant of truth challenged by the voices of vanity, mediocrity, hypocrisy and vulgarity in the shape of birds and beasts, has moments of power and suggestiveness, but is too often marred by verbal artifice and facility. An unfinished play, *La dernière nuit de Don Juan* (posth. 1921; tr. D. Bagley, *The Last Night of Don Juan*, 1963), also reaches out for symbolic significance. In his attempts to break out of the limits imposed by naturalistic drama, Rostand was greatly helped by brilliant interpreters, notably Coquelin and Sarah Bernhardt. [SBJ]

*Œuvres complètes illustrées* (7 vols., 1910–30).

J. W. Grieve, *L'œuvre dramatique d'E.R.* (Paris, 1931); A. Lautier and F. Keller, *E.R., son œuvre* (Paris, 1924).

**Rostworowski, Karol Hubert** (Rybna 1877–Cracow 1938). Polish playwright. He lived in Cracow, which had a well-established theatrical tradition, and his verse dramas continued the symbolist manner of ⇨ Wyspiański, but with diverse results. The play about Judas (*Judasz z Kariothu*, 1913) rises above the symbolism inherent in the subject, and so does his dramatic treatment of Caligula. In his later works he introduced peasant characters, and the first part of a trilogy, *Niespodzianka* (1929), is his best achievement. A peasant woman kills her own son without recognizing him after his return from America. The play is based on a true incident, but its theme has several parallels in European literature, from Zacharias Werner's *Der vierundzwanzigste Februar* to Rupert Brooke's *Lithuania* and Camus's *Malentendu*. [JP]

**Roth, Joseph** (Schwabendorf, Volhynia 1894–Paris 1939). Austrian novelist. His decisive experience and recurrent theme was the war and the collapse of Austro-Hungary in 1918, e.g. as seen by a disillusioned officer returning home in *Die Flucht ohne Ende* (1927; tr. anon., *Flight without End*, 1930). His most popular work, *Radetzkymarsch* (1932; tr. G. Dunlop, 1935), is a half ironical glorification of Imperial Austria, ending in the despair of the *Anschluss* (*Die Kapuzinergruft*, 1939). Perhaps his most accomplished novel is *Hiob* (1930; tr. D. Thompson, *Job*, 1933), the story of a modern wandering Jew. [PB]

*Gesammelte Werke*, ed. H. Kesten (3 vols., 1956); *Romane, Erzählungen, Aufsätze* (1964).

E. Wegner, *Die Gestaltung innerer Vorgänge in den Dichtungen J.R.s* (Bonn, 1963) (dissertation); Hohoff, *GU*.

**'Rother, König.'** A German epic poem written by an unknown author 1140–50, forming together with *Salman und Morolf*, *Oswald* and *Orendel* a group of minstrel epics from the pre-courtly period of Middle High German literature. The hero of the *Rother* romance is the Langobardic king Authari (reigned 584–90), and its subject-matter is his adventurous wooing of the Bavarian princess Theudelinde; the Rother legend spread northwards, and on Low German territory many of its basic motifs were transferred to the Osanctrix legend as preserved in the Thidrekssaga, so that both High German and Low German versions of the basic story can be called upon. In *König Rother* the ethical content is dominated by the heroic values of Germanic knighthood such as fealty and service; at the same time the humble milieu of the minstrels, from which the poem stems, stands in an interesting contrast to this heroic world. *König Rother* is the first extant heroic poem in German literature after the Old High German ⇨ *Hildebrandslied.* [RT]

Ed. H. Rückert (Leipzig, 1872); J. de Vries (1922). Ehrismann, *GDL*, II, 1.

**Rotrou, Jean de** (Dreux 1609–Dreux 1650). French dramatist. He spent his formative years in Paris but returned to his native town; he is known to have been a magistrate, and to have died, courageously, of the plague. With Corneille, whom he admired and publicly praised, he built up a repertory of modern plays, working for the traditional Hôtel de Bourgogne as Corneille did for the new theatre of the Marais. Both men were prolific; both took much material from the Spanish drama and both treated it in the same French way: Rotrou cut ⇨ Lope down to size as Corneille cut Guillén de ⇨ Castro. The result, which gave a quite new public pleasure, was the serious play known as '*tragicomédie*', involving danger but not always tragic disaster. Racine must have read (or seen) Rotrou's version of *Antigone* (1638). Corneille's *Nicomède* (1651) is built on the same plan as Rotrou's *Cosroès* (1648; ed. J. Scherer, 1950); his *Polyeucte* may well have inspired Rotrou's best play, about an actor converted when playing the part of a martyr, *Le Véritable Saint Genest* (ed. R. W. Ladborough, 1954). Such a situation is an excellent example of the baroque taste which Rotrou catered for. The point of a dramatic action in which the protagonist can '*d'une feinte en mourant faire une vérité*' is that stage martyrdom is itself theatrical illusion. Molière may have borrowed the name Célimène from a Rotrou play and Racine probably owes to his *Bélisaire* (1644) the tremendous scene in *Britannicus* where the hidden Emperor forces Junie to be cold to her lover. [WGM]

*Venceslas*, ed. T. F. Crane (1907).
J. Rousset, *Littérature de l'âge baroque en France* (Paris, 1953); Adam, *HLF*; Lancaster, *HFDL*.

**Roumanille, Joseph** (Saint-Rémy 1818–Avignon 1891). Provençal poet. His lifelong friendship with Mistral began in 1845 when Mistral attended the school in Avignon where he was teaching. A founder and organizer of the ⇨ Félibrige, his Provençal poetry, *Li Margarideto* ('Les Pâquerettes', 1847) and *Li Flour de Sauvi* ('Les Fleurs de Sauge', 1859) has a moralizing and didactic intention. He re-edited the celebrated Noëls of the 17th-century Saboly and wrote new works in this genre. In his polemical writings (1848–50) in defence of the Catholic church against the Socialists he showed a talent for dialogue and narrative which he later put to use in his best work, the many short stories in Provençal which profoundly influenced Alphonse Daudet and Paul Arène. [LTT]

C.-P. Julian and P. Fontan, *Anthologie du Félibrige provençal* (3 vols., Paris, 1921–4); *Actes . . . du Ier Congrès international de Langage et Littérature du Midi de la France* (Avignon, 1957); *Mél . . . I. Frank* (Université des Saarlandes, 1957).

**Rousseau, Jean-Baptiste** (Paris 1671–Brussels 1741). French poet. Of humble origins but good education, he was early accepted in the most distinguished literary circles, but his career was blighted by a quarrel which in 1712 caused him to be exiled (perhaps unjustly) as the author of libellous verse. His *Odes* and *Cantates*, much admired by contemporaries, are in the most arid classical manner, expressing commonplace feelings in abstract form by means of conventional myth and allegory, although they sometimes achieve a certain musicality as a result of considerable technical skill. His lighter *Épîtres* and *Épigrammes* have sometimes more vitality. [WHB]

*Œuvres*, ed. A. de Latour (1859).
H. A. Grubbs, *J.-B.R., his Life and Works* (Princeton, 1941); Gilman, *IPF*.

**Rousseau, Jean-Jacques** (Geneva 1712–Ermenonville nr Senlis 1778). French writer. One of the greatest of the 'universal geniuses' in 18th-century French literature, and the most tormented. Born a Protestant, he lost his mother at birth, and lived with his irresponsible father until the latter's expulsion from Geneva when his son was 10; thereafter he lived as an orphan. His unstable temperament, insatiable need for love, and deep sense of guilt explain his restless, wandering existence. An engraver's apprentice from 1727, he fled Geneva in 1728, and in Annecy encountered Mme de Warens, who for a time was to be his good angel and to whom he would return at intervals in the following years. She sent him to a hostel in Turin where he became a Catholic convert. Thereafter he was a footman, a seminarist, a music master, a tutor; his wanderings took him to many parts of Switzerland and France. In 1732 began a more settled phase, spent near Mme de Warens at Chambéry or the country house nearby at Les Charmettes, remembered by Rousseau in the *Confessions* (not very accurately) as an idyllic place; during these years he made up for many gaps in his education by voracious reading. However the calm was soon to be disturbed, and from 1740 he was rootless once more. In 1741 he set out for Paris and entered on a career in society, which included a sojourn abroad as secretary to the French ambassador in Venice (1743–4), but otherwise he lived in Paris, devoting time particularly to musical compositions. ⇨ Diderot invited him to collaborate in the *Encyclopédie*, almost exclusively on musical subjects. In 1746 he became attached to a servant-girl, Thérèse Levasseur, by whom he had, he claims, five illegitimate children whom he abandoned to the foundling home, an act (or even a crime, for the mortality rate in foundling homes was high even for that age) which caused him much remorse. The reputation which he enjoys today as a writer is entirely founded on works written from 1750 onwards, beginning with the *Discours sur les sciences et les arts* which won a competition organized by the Academy of Dijon and first acquired him some renown. Fame did not, however, bring happiness, but only greater isolation. The 1750s saw quarrels with *philosophes* like Voltaire and Diderot, who had formerly befriended him, and the pattern was to be repeated until his death. A relatively happy period with Mme d'Épinay and Mme d'Houdetot at L'Ermitage, near Montmorency (1756–7), came to a close in characteristic disunity, but led to another near the Maréchal de Luxembourg at Montmorency (1757–62), which was the most fruitful of his life. This ended in flight from arrest after publication of *Profession de foi du vicaire savoyard*, in which he attacked revealed religion and ardently supported a fideist form of deism. Thereafter he wandered desolately through England (1766–7 – an experience that saw the usual disastrous deterioration in human relations, this time with Hume in particular), Switzerland, France, the wretched peripatetic existence being interspersed by rare phases of contentment, particularly at Motiers, near Neuchâtel (1762–3). Much of the time he fled before his enemies; these miseries fed his persecution complex, and in seeing every man's hand against him, he rejected many who tried to help. However, some respite was granted in 1770, when he was found humble but quiet lodging in Paris, where he wrote his latest works.

The *Discours sur les sciences et les arts* (1750; tr. G. D. H. Cole, 1955) and the *Discours sur l'origine de l'inégalité* (1755; tr. G. D. H. Cole, 1955) both protest against existing society. In the first, he showed how the growth of civilization corrupted natural goodness; in the second he developed the same theme in relating the growth of society to the growth of inequality. These works identified him with the cult of the noble, happy savage, and revealed both a fervent moralist keen to stress individualist virtue in contrast to the fraudulent manners of society and a social critic who eloquently drew men's attention to the extent of human injustice and servitude. But he did not intend man to seek out his former primitive state; this was as irrevocably lost as the Garden of Eden, and a new social order must be attained. The *Lettre à d'Alembert sur les spectacles* (1758) emphasizes the moralistic aspect of his personality. The theatre is bad because it inculcates immorality; culture is alien to the good society. But subjective considerations play an important part in these apparently objective statements; in attacking the theatre, Rousseau is attacking Voltaire and the Encyclopedists, he is announcing his isolation like that of Alceste in ⇨ Molière's *Le misanthrope* whose cause he passionately defends.

Many characteristic themes are restated

in *La nouvelle Héloïse* (1761), Rousseau's great novel, which met with an immediate and enormous success. Virtue thrives when personal relations between individuals are simple and direct, when, furthermore, they take place against a background of nature, which alone can inspire and elevate the soul; a vision of the ideal society emerges. Equally important, however, and a major factor in its success, is the praise of passion, which is linked to virtue in a manner that anticipates the Romantics. How was one to inculcate virtue in the young? *Émile* (1762; tr. B. Foxley, 1930) tries to answer this question. The child must be protected from the harmful artifices of civilization and left free to enjoy to the full the moral influence of nature. As with many of Rousseau's works, *Émile* contains excellent ideas even for those who would not accept the world-view on which it is based, and it has become a landmark in the history of educational thought. The crowning work in the edifice of Rousseau's political philosophy is *Du contrat social* (1762; tr. G. D. H. Cole, *The Social Contract*, 1955), a work where eloquence gives way to dispassionate reasoning. The sovereign power in a state is not the prince, but the '*volonté générale*' of the people, who delegate him an authority that may at any time be revoked. Despite its unfortunate application under the Terror by men like Robespierre, despite the sometimes disturbing suggestions of totalitarianism, the work is best understood as the basic theory of democratic government. The later years of his life were given largely to more personal works, most notably *Les confessions* (written, 1765–70; tr. J. M. Cohen, Penguin Classics, 1953), a kind of '*autobiographie romancée*', misleading on fact but highly revealing of his psychology. In its insistence on the singularity of the individual ('*Si je ne vaux pas mieux, au moins je suis autre*') and on the inherently interesting nature of the complex individual soul, and in its lyrical evocation of nature, the work contains elements that will become characteristic of Romanticism. [HTM]

*Œuvres complètes* (3 vols., Pléiade, 1959– ).
J. H. Broome, *R.* (1963); R. Grimsley, *J.-J.R.* (1961); B. Groethuysen, *J.-J.R.* (Paris, 1949);. G. Lanson, 'L'unité de la pensée de J.-J. Rousseau', *Annales de la Société J.-J.R.*, viii (Paris, 1912); D. Mornet, *R.* (Paris, 1950); J. Starobinski, *J.-J.R.* (Paris, 1958); E. H. Wright, *The Meaning of R.* (1929).

**Roussel, Raymond** (Paris 1877–Palermo 1933). French novelist and dramatist. A rich eccentric whose exotic work was taken up by the French surrealists in the 1920s. In novels and plays alike, he displays a strong vein of fantasy (he was an admirer of Jules ⇨ Verne), a mixture of precise description and disquieting invention, and a great deal of verbal play which some have compared to Rabelais. *La doublure* (1896), a novel in verse, is wholly concerned with the varied encounters experienced by Gaspard, a failed actor, and his girl Roberte as they make their way, masked and supplied with confetti, through a carnival crowd in Nice. At one level, nothing really happens; at another, a whole world of mood and feeling is evoked. Similar elements distinguish his second verse-novel, *La vue* (1901), and the shifting and highly coloured fancies of *Impressions d'Afrique* (1910; tr. L. Foord and R. Heppenstall, *Impressions of Africa*, 1966), a prose narrative involving shipwreck of a motley crowd of travellers who produce a great gala performance, at once entertainment and symbolic investiture, for the local black Emperor. Another remarkable excursion into fantasy followed with *Locus solus* (1914), later adapted as a play by Pierre Frondaie (1922), following on Roussel's own theatrical version of *Impressions d'Afrique* (1911). Other original plays, greeted with hostility and incomprehension at their first performance, were: *L'étoile au front* (1924) and *La poussière de soleils* (1926). Their special quality was their power to create an imaginary universe, somewhere between the gay film fantasies of René Clair and the macabre explorations of *The Cabinet of Dr Caligari*, where Roussel's obsession with masks and impersonation could have free play. *Comment j'ai écrit certains de mes livres* (posth. 1935) contains some interesting autobiographical material. [SBJ]

*Œuvres complètes* (8 vols., 1963–4).
M. Foucault, *R.R.* (Paris, 1963); J. Ferry (ed.) 'R.R.', in *Bizarre*, 34–5 (1964); R. Heppenstall, *R.R.* (1966).

**Roussin, André** (Marseilles 1911– ). French actor and playwright. Versatile author of light comedy and farce. Inventive in his handling of situation, racy and droll in his dialogue, he has zest and assurance to match his mockery. He is good at the farce of wild inconsequence and arbitrary plot (*Am-Stram-Gram*, 1945) and better, though always in a broad and mechanical manner, in pushing improbable initial situations to the limit of their absurd logic, as in *La petite hutte* (1947; tr. N. Mitford, *The Little Hut*, 1951) and *Nina* (1949), where a deceived husband is so taken with his wife's lover that he does his best to advance his cause. He has written extravagant satirical farces of family life: *Les œufs de l'autruche* (1948); *Lorsque l'enfant paraît* (1951), and *La Sainte Famille* (1946). *Une grande fille toute simple* (1940) and *Bobosse* (1949; tr. A. Macrae, *Figure of Fun*, 1953) derive predictable fun from actors who cannot stop playing roles. [SBJ]

*Comédies* (6 vols., 1959–64); *La locomotive* (1967). Surer, *TFC*; Lalou, *TF*.

**Roy, Jules** (Rovigo, Algeria 1907– ). French novelist and critic. A regular officer who won the D.F.C. while in the R.A.F. during the war, he resigned in 1953 to become a full-time writer and journalist. His novels reflect his experience of warfare and flying with the R.A.F. in *La vallée heureuse* (Prix Théophraste Renaudot 1946; tr. E. O. Marsh, *The Happy Valley*, 1952) – the title refers to the Ruhr Valley – and *Le navigateur* (1954; tr. Mervyn Savill, 1955) and in Indochina – *La bataille dans la rizière* (1953). Like ⇨ Saint-Exupéry whom he has clearly chosen as his model – cf. his *Passion de S.-E.* (1951) – Roy goes beyond the straightforward recording of exciting experience, though this is an important element of his writing. He sees in the flier's need to base his action on a choice clearly made and courageously carried through in the face of danger, an image of man's need to base his life on a moral choice. His later works include *Les flammes de l'été* (1956), *Les belles croisades* (1959) and the plays *Les cyclones* (1954) and *Le fleuve rouge* (1957). His experience of war and knowledge of Algeria made his *La guerre d'Algérie* (1960; tr. R. Howard, *The War in Algeria*, 1961) an important contribution to the Algerian debate. [IHW]

*La femme infidèle* (1955); tr. J. R. Loy, *The Unfaithful Wife* (1956).
*YR*, XXVII, 2 (1954); *Twentieth Century*, CLXVIII, 1006 (1960); *TLS* (7 July 1961).

**Rozanov, Vasily Vasil'yevich** (Vetluga 1856–Sergiyev Posad 1919). Russian essayist and critic. After a pioneering study of Gogol' and Dostoyevsky (whose mistress, Polina Suslova he married), he became a controversial journalist on problems of marriage, sex and religion; critical (like Nietzsche) of Christianity's 'weakness', he extolled sex and the family. He is famous for collections of fragmentary essays, *Uyedinyonnoye* (1912; tr. S. S. Koteliansky, *Solitaria*, 1927) and *Opavshiye List'ya* (1913–15; tr. S. S. Koteliansky, *Fallen Leaves, Bundle One*, 1929). These are not confessions, but ingenious self-revelations of unusual literary and psychological originality, presenting the quintessence of the egotistical and unhygienic self. His writings on religion include *Russkaya Tserkov'* ('The Russian Church', 1909); *Tyomnyy Lik* ('The Dark Face', 1911); *Apokalipsis nashego vremeni* (1917–18; *The Apocalypse of our Times*, in *Solitaria*).

R. Poggioli, *R.* (1962); Mirsky, *HRL*; Slonim, *MRL*.

**Rozov, Victor Sergeyevich** (Yaroslavl' 1913– ). Soviet playwright. Studied in the theatrical school of Moscow's Theatre of the Revolution (1934–8) where he became an actor. Wounded 1941, he turned to acting in front-line theatres. He organized a children's and young people's theatre in Alma-Ata (Kazakhstan) before returning to Moscow as director of the theatre of The Central House of Culture for Railwaymen and student of the Gor'ky Literary Institute. He writes vividly of people as they are without losing either his sense of fun or a certain happy-go-lucky, curiously poetic optimism. He is best known outside the U.S.S.R. for his *Vechno Zhivyye*, filmed as *The Cranes are Flying* (1956), but he has to his credit a number of other pieces (mainly comedies) of equal charm. [AP]

*P'yesy* (1959).
A. Anastas'yev, *V.R.* (1966); *Teatr*, 6, 1963; *Novyy Mir*, 8, 1960; 3, 1964.

**Rückert, Friedrich** (Schweinfurt 1788–Neusess, Koburg 1866). German poet. He embarked on an academic career but left it to become editor of the Stuttgart *Morgenblatt*; this, too, he soon abandoned, and took to the study of Oriental languages, in which subject he was appointed professor at Erlangen in 1822. Later he became professor and Regierungsrat in Berlin. His long didactic poem, *Die Weisheit des Brahmanen* (1836–9), is a large collection of maxims and mottos, on all manner of subjects, derived from his readings in Hindu literature. He translated from Hindu and Persian (*Die Verwandlungen des Abu Seid*, 1826–37) and wrote German poems in Oriental verse-forms. Prolific but uncritical, his political verse (disguised as *Geharnischte Sonette* by 'Freimund Raimar', then openly in *Deutsche Gedichte*, 1814), love poetry *Liebesfrühling* (1823), and the ⇨ *Biedermeier Haus- und Jahrespoesie* enjoyed great bourgeois popularity. Mahler's song-cycle *Kindertotenlieder* (1902) consists of settings of five poems by Rückert. [RT]

H. Prang, *F.R.* (Schweinfurt, 1963).

**Rudolf von Ems** (fl. 1220–1250). Middle High German epic poet. The most influential poet of his generation and, with ⇨ Konrad von Würzburg, the acknowledged master, for the 13th century, of the verse-epic as inherited from the great poets of the classical era – ⇨ Hartmann von Aue, ⇨ Gottfried von Strassburg, and ⇨ Wolfram von Eschenbach.

His fecundity is matched by his learning, and the realism of his style is placed at the service of his didactic intent. There survive 5 narrative poems. In order of composition (1) *Der gute Gerhard* (ed. M. Haupt, 1840), which preaches the evils of *superbia*; (2) *Barlaam und Josaphat* (ed. F. Pfeiffer, 1843), the legend of how Barlaam converts the Indian prince Josaphat to Christianity; (3) *Alexander* (unfinished; ed. V. Junk, 1928–9) and (4) *Willehalm* (ed. V. Junk, 1905), both presentations, in their different ways, of the ideal of a chivalric hero; (5) *Weltchronik* (ed. G. Ehrismann, 1915), a history of the world from the viewpoint of the Christian Middle Ages, and one of the most frequently copied and adapted works in all Middle High German literature.

As he states them in the prologue to his *Alexander* and his *Willehalm*, Rudolf's aims are moral and instructive, and his acknowledged means of attaining his ends is by imitating the form and manner of the great masters of the past. These he names as Hendrik van ⇨ Veldeke, Hartmann, Wolfram and Gottfried; it is above all on Gottfried, however, that his own poetic style is based. [RT]

Ehrismann, *GDL*.

**Rudolf von Fenis** (fl. late 12th cent.). Swiss ⇨ Minnesinger. One of the early imitators of the Romance lyric of courtly love, and a poet particularly well acquainted with the songs of the ⇨ troubadours. His poems are wholly typical products of the age when German lyric poets were learning the concepts and techniques of the new Romance-inspired literature of chivalry. [RT]

Texts in Kraus, *MF*.

**Rueda, Lope de** (Seville *c.* 1505–Córdoba 1565). Spanish actor-dramatist. His full-length plays copied from Italian models are unimportant. He excels only in his *pasos* – prose interludes to be performed between acts of his own and others' loosely strung verse plays (a form developed by Cervantes). His stock characters, doctor booby, old thief, young thief, apprentice etc., speak in brisk dialogue with the rude wit of common life. [JMC]

*Obras*, ed. E. Cotarelo y Mori (1908); *Paso completos* (1944); CC; CA.

**Rueda, Salvador** (Málaga 1857–Málaga 1933). Spanish poet. Of considerable outpu and invention, he anticipated some innovations of the modernists, and exercised a early influence over J. R. ⇨ Jiménez. H spent most of his life in Málaga, and the bes of his uneven poems are brilliantly Andalusian in setting. He was one of the first Spanish writers to recognize the greatness o Rubén Darío, but himself died almos forgotten. [JMC]

*Poesías completas* (Barcelona, 1911).

**Ruíz, Juan,** Archpriest of Hita (fl. first hal of 14th cent.). Named as author of the *Libr de buen amor*, the most remarkable poeti work of the Spanish Middle Ages. Th *Libro* is dated, in its second version, 134 and reveals familiarity with the Tagus valle (Alcalá, Toledo, etc.) and the Sierra d Guadarrama. Outside the text nothing i known of the author, and all speculatio based on the text (e.g. on his supposed im prisonment) has proved fruitless. The wor is in ⇨ *cuaderna vía* form, with several inte polations in various lyric metres; it consist of a series of clearly fictitious love-affair told in the first person, that serve as framework for some 30 fables and othe anecdotes (introduced as *exempla* by th author or by one of his characters), 2 se piece allegories (a debate with the god c love and a Battle of Carnal Appetite Lent), songs to the Virgin and various othe digressions. The language is rich in rheto ical devices, vivid concrete imagery, pr verbs and *sententiae*, popular-style di logue; the narrative is marked by iron ambiguity and sudden changes of theme and attitude.

The *Libro* reflects a wide range of medieval culture, though often superficially. There are echoes of Ovid's *Ars amatoria*, the *Disticha Catonis*, Canonical writings, medieval Latin 'comedies', Goliard satire and parody, the French *pastourelle* (in burlesque form), Provençal courtly lyric terminology, the 13th-century French *arts d'aimer*, etc. The structure of the *Libro* recalls those of the Oriental frame-story and the Arabic/Hebrew *maqamat* and Arabic terms occur in the text; but no direct borrowing from Arabic or Hebrew literature has been established, while the fictional autobiography as a narrative device has precedents in medieval European literature. The *Libro* also reflects many facets of everyday life in New Castile, both rustic and urban.

The author's stated aim (in his prose prologue and at various points in the course of the work) is to warn the innocent, especially women, against the snares of worldly love. But his irony and ambiguity, coupled with the gusto with which he portrays love in action, have led many critics to dismiss his claims to have a serious moral purpose. But the Archpriest is incurably didactic, whatever the topic he touches on, and he is no hypocrite; though he is far from being a kill-joy. [GBG-M]

*Libro de buen amor*, ed. J. Ducamin (Toulouse, 1901); ed. J. Cejador (2 vols., CC); in modern Spanish verse by María Brey Mariño (Valencia, 1954); tr. E. K. Kane, *The Book of Good Love* (N.Y., 1933).

F. Lecoy, *Recherches sur le Libro de buen amor* (Paris, 1938); M. R. L. de Malkiel, *Two Spanish Masterpieces: the Book of Good Love and the Celestina* (Urbana, 1962); L. Spitzer, 'En torno al arte del Arcipreste de Hita', in *Lingüística e historia literaria* (Madrid, 1955); A. Castro, in *The Structure of Spanish History* (Princeton, 1954); *BHS*, XXXVIII (1957).

**Ruíz de Alarcón y Mendoza, Juan** (Mexico City 1581?–Madrid 1634), Spanish dramatist. With Lope, Tirso and Calderón, one of the four outstanding figures in Golden Age drama. His plays constitute a measured protest against some of the more artificial conventions prevailing in the comedies of pure diversion to which Lope had shown overmuch indulgence. In contrast to the latter's gigantic production Alarcón seems to have written only 20 plays before abandoning the theatre in 1626 for a governmental appointment. He is chiefly thought of as the author of Spain's best-known satirical comedy of character, *La verdad sospechosa* (*c.* 1619), imitated by Corneille in *Le menteur* (1643). It figures among 8 of his plays published in Madrid in 1628, the remaining 12 being published in Barcelona in 1634. Little is known about actual dates of composition or performance. The characteristic Alarconian *comedia* is a comedy of thesis in which character is expressed in terms of moral choice or action in a moral setting. But he did not write mere moralities: he wished the theatre to find its conscience and his work is a contribution in that direction. It reveals the influences of Terence. Seneca and Martial and illustrates a noble conception of virtue for its own sake. More recently his delight in portraying ethical superiority has been interpreted as a compensation-mechanism for his severe physical deformities. The character of D. Juan in *Las paredas oyen*, illustrating the triumph of moral over physical qualities, is thought to contain elements of self-portraiture in this respect. Other outstanding plays include *Los pechos privilegiados*, on the theme of loyalty to the monarch, *Ganar amigos*, on that of friendship raised to the plane of heroism, and *Mudarse por mejorarse*, which treats of constancy in love. *El tejedor de Segovia* is believed to have influenced Schiller's *Die Räuber* (1782). His plays were probably written more slowly and reflectively than was common among his contemporaries in Spain. Though they are occasionally marred by a too simple contrast between good and evil, this defect is usually offset by the polished technique and elevated tone. This last does not preclude warm attachment to the common things of life. Lyricism is, however, largely absent from his work. [DLS]

*Teatro* (3 vols., CC).

M. V. Melvin, *J. R. de A.* (Ann Arbor, Mich., 1942); A. Castro Leal, *J.R. de A.* (Mexico City, 1943).

**Rumanian Literature before 1850.** The first datable autograph in Rumanian is a private letter of 1521. There are undated manuscripts of Biblical translations, the texts of which have been ascribed by some to the previous century. Printing in Rumanian begins in the second half of the 16th century with translations of the scriptures and other religious texts. Creative writing (as distinct from tales and ballads handed down orally, which are undatable) starts in the early 17th century with vernacular chronicles. In the second half of the century we have the first experiments in versification. The first complete printed version of the Bible appeared in 1688. However the growth of Rumanian literature was checked during the period 1716–1821, when both Rumanian principalities were ruled by Greeks sent from Constantinople. As this period went on, modern Greek increasingly predominated as the language of polite society. After 1821, when there were again native Rumanian princes, the newly awakened national consciousness began in both principalities to find expression in literature. It had already done so among the Rumanians of Transylvania, then part of the Habsburg Empire, where in the 18th century priests of the Rumanian Uniate Church were inspired by their studies in the West to stress the Latin origin of the Rumanian language.

The language had now to be adapted to the expression of new concepts. A writer in 1825 says in a preface: 'In the state in which we now are, we cannot immediately produce great poets or famous authors whom we could receive into our schools as classics.... Those who build are building without materials, lacking even a dictionary from which we could find definite terms to express our ideas.' Eliade (Ioan Heliade Rădulescu) in Wallachia and Gheorghe Asachi in Moldavia were very active in starting the first journals and encouraging and printing translations and original writings. The prose of Constantin Negruzzi and the verse fables of Grigore Alexandrescu are the earliest creations of the new era which would still find general readers in Rumania. Vasile ⇨ Alecsandri made his début in the early 1840s. His publication of a collection of folk-poetry in 1852 was important for the development of other poets beside himself. A French translation of his *Doinas* in 1853 made his name known abroad and started an international reputation which culminated in 1878 when his poem *Cîntecul Gintei Latine* won a contest at Montpellier; the jury which awarded him the prize included Mistral. With the rise of Alecsandri Rumanian literature soon after 1850 had reached a stage where classics could emerge. [EDT]

**Runeberg, Johan Ludvig** (Pietarsaari 1804–Porvoo 1877). Finland's 'national poet'. The son of a sea captain, his family originally came from Sweden, and he wrote in Swedish. He graduated at the Turku Academy in 1827, spent two years as a private tutor in Central Finland, where the character of the region and its Finnish-speaking inhabitants made a deep impression on him, then studied further in Helsinki, where he taught classics at a Lyceum and at the University. Failing to obtain an Assistant Professorship (his interest in the Finnish nationalist movement and great intellectual influence over the students made the appointment politically inadvisable), he took a teaching post in Porvoo in 1837, and spent the rest of his life there.

His development as a poet was slow. In 1837 he published a severe criticism of the romantic Swedish literature which had influenced him in his youthful, sentimental period. The study of Serbian and Finnish folk poetry helped him in the discovery of his own natural style, which was ingenuous and sincere. His classical interests were reflected in his choice of descriptions such as 'idylls' and 'epigrams' for many of his best lyrics. In simple, unadorned, homely verse he wrote powerfully of the joys and sorrows of love and of the countryside of the Finnish interior. A well-known example of his early poetry is *Bonden Paavo*, a narrative poem extolling the patience and unselfishness of the pioneer farmer of the backwoods. Another narrative poem, *Elgskyttarne* (1832), was the first authentic description of the common people to be written in any northern European country. He used the epic hexameter, in imitation of Goethe and ⇨ Voss, in two other poems: *Hanna* (1836), which secured his reputation both in Finland and in Sweden, and *Julqvällen* (1841), the first to have patriotic heroism as its theme.

In the early years at Porvoo his poetry reveals a shift of interest towards religious speculation and romantic fantasy. At this time the extreme fundamentalist views of the Pietists were the subject of intense controversy. *Den gamle trädgårdsmästarens brev* (1837) and *Kyrkan* express a soulful pantheism and a mystical approach to Christianity. Meanwhile the romantic vein that now found expression in much of his work owed much to the influence of the Swedish poet ⇨ Almquist, e.g. in the narrative poem *Nadeschda* (1841), a Russian folk-tale retold in flexible unrhymed verse. But he achieved a new individuality, and intellectually his most important poem, with the epic *Kung Fjalar* (1844; tr. E. Magnusson, *King Fialar*, 1912), where he continues the attempt, begun in *Chrysanthos*, to reconcile the ideals of pagan antiquity with those of Christianity. The punishment of the hero's *hubris* is presented as a form of divine mercy. This is fine imaginative poetry, drawing its material from the Scandinavian sagas, ancient Greek tragedy, and the songs of Ossian. His last published work, *Kungarne på Salamis* (1863), is a tragedy in classical trimeters.

The quickening of Finnish national consciousness in the 1840s, due in great measure to the energy and influence of the philosopher J. V. Snellman, inspired *Fänrik Ståls sägner* (1848, 1860; tr. C. W. Stork, *Tales of Ensign Stål*, N.Y., 1938). The unsuccessful Swedo-Finnish war of defence against the Russians in 1808–9 provided Runeberg – via copious oral tradition, supplemented by one or two reference books – with abundant examples of courage in the performance of duty. The *Tales* consist of a series of poems about soldiers of all ranks. They are splendid ballads, leaping effortlessly from a mood of simple, often humorous realism to the heights of heroism and lofty sentiment. The relevance of Runeberg's glowing patriotism was felt again in 1939, and even the most modern schools of criticism still pay tribute to his superb plastic poetic technique and above all to the magical simplicity of his lyrics. [LV]

*Samlade arbeten* (8 vols., 1899–1902); *Samlade skrifter* (6 vols., 1933).

C. G. Estlander, *R. Skaldskap* (Helsinki, 1902); J. W. Söderhjelm, *J.L.R.* (2 vols., Helsinki, 1904, 1906); J. E. Strömborg, *Biografiska anteckningar om J.L.R.* (4 vols., Helsinki, 1927–31); R. Hedvall, *R. och hans diktning* (Helsinki, 1931); L. G. G. Tideström, *R. som estetiker* (Helsinki, 1941); Y. Hirn, *R.-gestalten* (Helsinki, 1942); L. S. Viljanen, *R. ja hänen runoutensa* (2 vols., Helsinki/Lund, 1944, 1948); G. Castrén, *J.L.R.* (Stockholm, 1950).

**Rung, Otto** (Copenhagen 1874–Copenhagen 1945). Danish novelist and short-story writer. Several of his novels are laid in the Far East, where he lived for a time, but he is at his best in his humorous descriptions of Copenhagen characters and milieux which he knew intimately. His best books are *Skyggernes Tog* (1909; tr. G. I. Colbron, *Shadows that Pass*, 1924), *Syndere og Skalke* (1918), and Copenhagen memoirs, *Fra min Klunketid* (1942). [ELB]

**'Ruodlieb'** (*c.* 1050). A Latin romantic epic written in leonine hexameters by a monk of Tegernsee in Bavaria. One of the earliest of German romances of adventure, it is of eastern origin. It relates the adventures of a poor knight whose services are rewarded by moral aphorisms intead of money, but who finds himself the possessor of treasure in the end. [FB]

Ed. F. Seiler (1882); ed. K. Langosch, *Waltharius, Ruodlieb*, etc. (1956).

W. Braun, *Studien zum Ruodlieb* (Berlin, 1962); Raby, *SLP*.

**Russian Historical Songs.** Russian historical songs have a certain amount in common with the ⇨ *byliny* but are less diffuse historically in that the subject matter is usually a more or less identifiable historical event and that less is left to the imagination of the performer.

The earliest events sung of are connected with the Tatar invasions of the 13th century, but the heyday of the historical song was the 16th and 17th centuries, particularly the epoch of Ivan IV (second half 16th century). Typical subjects are the massacre of the Tatars by the Tverites (the uprising of 1327); the capture of Kazan' by Ivan IV in 1552; Ivan's marriage to Mar'ya Temryukovna (The Song of Kostryuk); and the capture of Astrakhan' by Sten'ka Razin.

Historical songs, which were collected in much the same areas as the *byliny* (i.e. north Russia) as well as in the Cossack districts in the south and in the area of Moscow, were performed in a manner similar to the *byliny* by peasant reciters, who in most cases included them in their repertories alongside *byliny*. Metrically there is little difference although the historical song tends to have two rather than three stressed syllables per line. They are usually shorter than *byliny* (often less than 100 lines) and bereft of the latter's folkloric elements: there are fewer fossilized epithets, less stock situations and less repetition. As a result they are more factual, more realistic and as a rule less entertaining. [JLIF]

*Istoricheskiye pesni XIII–XVI vekov*, ed. B. N. Putilov and B. M. Dobrovol'sky (1960); *Russian Folk Literature*, ed. D. P. Costello and I. P. Foote (1967).

**Russian Literature of the 17th Century.** Both in Russian history and in Russian literature the 17th century was a period of transition from the medieval to the modern. Russian society was changing. The final enserfment of the peasants in 1649 strengthened the position of the *dvoryanstvo* (gentry), a new class which had developed in the 16th century with the creation of a centralized state, and they, together with the rising urban population, constituted a larger and more diverse potential reading public with new interests; a public hitherto more familiar with the oral tradition, which was now to exert a greater influence on written literature. Moreover, the foundations of the medieval Muscovite state had been undermined by the interminable and ultimately profitless wars of the 16th century, the extinction of the royal house in 1598, and the ensuing 'Smutnoye vremya' ('Time of Troubles') (1598–1613), with its civil strife and foreign invasions. The Church, no less than the state, was shaken by these events. Its subsequent attempts to re-assert its authority and to assume the leadership of the Christian Orthodox East made necessary the correction of errors in religious texts and minor reforms of ritual, and these were interpreted by many as an attack on the old Russian piety which had made Moscow the 'Third Rome'. The result was the great schism or *Raskol* of the mid 17th century, which weakened the Church and thus prepared the way for the gradual secularization of the state. Renewed and ever-increasing contacts with Western Europe, encouraged by the state, which had need of skilled craftsmen and mercenaries, opened the door to Western influences; and from 1654, when the Ukraine swore allegiance to Tsar Alexey Mikhaylovich (1645–76), Muscovy included within its frontiers a large area which for centuries had been under Polish domination, and therefore subject to cultural influences alien to the old Muscovite way of life. Many immigrants from the Ukraine and White Russia came to settle in Moscow in the second half of the century and, thanks to their higher level of education and culture, they were able to make an important contribution to the development of Russian literature.

In the early part of the century the 'Time of Troubles' produced a large number of polemical works; partisan accounts of contemporary events and impassioned appeals for support for this or that faction in the struggle for power. While primarily of historical value, the best of these stories are not without literary merit. Outstanding among them is the *Skazaniye* (1612, revised 1620; extracts tr. S. A. Zenkovsky, *Narrative*, 1963) of Avraamy Palitsyn (*c.* 1555–1627), a monk of the Trinity-St Sergius monastery, which examines the origins of the *Smuta* ('Troubles') and gives a graphic description of the siege of the monastery by Polish and Lithuanian troops; and also of interest is *Novaya povest' o preslavnom Rosiyskom tsarstve* ('A New Tale of the Most Glorious Russian Tsardom', 1610–11), a summons to the people of Moscow to emulate the citizens of Smolensk and oppose the Polish invaders. Most of these stories are written in a traditionally ornate rhetorical style; for example, *Plach o plenenii i o konechnom razorenii Moskovskogo gosudarstva* ('A Lament for the Capture and Final Devastation of the Muscovite State', 1612); but some, such as *Povest' o prestavlenii knyazya Mikhaila Vasil'yevicha Skopina-Shuyskogo* ('The Tale of the Death of Prince Mikhail Vasil'yevich Skopin-Shuysky', *c.* 1612), also reflect the influence of the epic oral tradition; while others point to an awakening interest in poetry and are interspersed with fragments of a pre-syllabic type of verse and metrical prose. Of these the most impressive is the *Povest' ot prezhnikh let* (1626; extracts tr. S. A. Zenkovsky, *The Tale of Former Years*, 1963), attributed to Prince Ivan Katyrev-Rostovsky (d. 1640), a calm, objective and comprehensive account of the *Smuta*, which clearly owes something to the Russian translation of Guido delle Colonne's narrative of the Trojan war. Another significant innovation is the deliberate break with the conventional black-and-white portraiture of the medieval period and the attempts at genuine character studies of Tsar Boris Godunov (1598–1605) and the pretender Dmitry to be found in such works as the *Khronograf* (1617) and the *Vremennik* ('Chronicle', 1610–28) of Ivan Timofeyev (d. *c.* 1629), an official of one of the Muscovite ministries.

The recognition in literature of the complexity of human character was a first step towards the acceptance of the life of the ordinary individual as a valid subject for a literary work; and it is in the 17th century that the first true biographies are written. Their debt to hagiography is, however, unmistakable. One of the earliest, *Povest' o Yulianii Lazarevskoy* (*c.* 1630; tr. S. A. Zenkovsy, *The Tale of Juliana Lazarevskaya*, 1963), a biography of his mother (d. 1604) written by the nobleman Callistratus

Druzhina-Osor'in, a layman and an official of the local judiciary in Murom, is at least in form and conception a hagiography; but the author's conception of a hagiography is a sign of changing values. Though the *Povest'* follows the hagiographical pattern, the author's aim was not didactic, since he was concerned to prove the sanctity of his mother rather than to hold up the story of her life as an example and an inspiration to others. Detailed, circumstantial descriptions of the private life of the subject are substituted for the generalizations and commonplaces of the traditional *vita*; and what emerges is therefore a biography, the portrait of an individual who lived at a particular time and in a particular place.

That the spirit of the times was changing hagiography into biography is also apparent from the literature of the Old Believers or *raskol'niki* (schismatics); and this is all the more remarkable since it was in defence of the old traditions of the Church that the *raskol'niki* opposed with such fanaticism the reforms introduced in 1653 by Patriarch Nikon. The obviously hagiographical designs of the anonymous author of *Zhitiye boyaryni Morozovoy* ('The Life of the Boyarina Morozova') did not prevent him from producing, against a background of realistically depicted scenes from contemporary Muscovite life, a sharply defined and convincing portrait of the boyar's wife, Theodosia Morozova (d. 1672), a schismatic who suffered persecution, torture and death for the sake of her beliefs.

But it was the leader of the Old Believers, the Archpriest Avvakum (1620/1–82), who was the boldest innovator and the most talented writer of the century. Arrested for his vehement rejection of the Nikonian reforms in 1653, he, together with his wife and young family, was exiled first to Tobolsk and later to Dauria, on the borders of Mongolia, which he reached by joining an expedition whose mission was to subjugate the hostile native population. Brought back to Moscow in 1664, he demonstrated that nine years of almost unbelievable hazards and hardships in the wilds of Siberia had not broken his spirit and he was soon banished to a settlement on the River Mezen in the far north. He returned to the capital in 1666, when a final attempt was made to reconcile him with the official Church and, when this failed, he was forcibly tonsured, excommunicated and exiled to Pustozersk. Here, incarcerated in an underground prison from 1670 until he was burnt as a heretic in 1682, he wrote the majority of his works, over 50 in number and including epistles, sermons, petitions and works of exegesis. Though undistinguished in their theology and thought, the language of these minor works alone would have established him as an outstanding writer of the 17th century, but they are overshadowed by his *Zhitiye* (1672–5; tr. J. Harrison and H. Mirrlees, *The Life of the Archpriest Avvakum*, 1924), the first genuine autobiography in Russian literature and one of the greatest works of the whole pre-Petrine period.

In itself the writing of an autobiography was a remarkable challenge to medieval religious and literary decorum, but, convinced that God had guided him in all that he did, Avvakum was not afraid to break with tradition in order to defend and propagate his conception of Orthodoxy; moreover, he was able to justify himself on the grounds that he was writing on the orders of his spiritual father and fellow-prisoner Epiphanius. The *Zhitiye* was a supreme act of faith: in its realism it was meant to speak for itself and to prompt the conclusion that the ordeals described could not have been survived without divine intervention; and that therefore the cause was right. The story is told in carefully selected and arranged episodes, enhanced at times by lyrical descriptions of nature which harmonize with the mood of the narrative, and brought to life by the skilful use of dialogue as a method of characterization, by Avvakum's humour, and by his command of invective. Essentially a work of propaganda directed towards the broad masses of the population, the *Zhitiye* was written in a language which they could readily understand, a vigorous and earthy colloquial Russian. The deceptive simplicity of the intimate, colourful style is a perfect foil to the dramatic nature of the story, and the effectiveness of the use of the contemporary language can be judged by the fact that permission to publish the *Zhitiye* was withheld until 1861, nearly two centuries after Avvakum's death.

The gradual secularization of literature was marked by the appearance of fiction, previously shunned as falsehood, in the *povesti* (tales) of the latter half of the century. It was accompanied by the emergence of a new hero, the average, historically unimportant man. Even when an authentic historical background was retained and the hero was given the name of a person who had actually lived, the writer was now no longer tied by the historical events of the period, since his hero had not played a prominent part in them. Consequently, fictitious episodes could be introduced, private lives examined, and human emotions analysed. Love takes its place as an important theme in literature, aided, no doubt, by the translation into Russian of Western picaresque novels.

The fictitious peregrinations and tribulations of a merchant's son, driven by love to sell his soul to the devil, are the subject of *Povest' o Savve Grudtsyne* (1670s; tr. S. A. Zenkovsky, *The Tale of Savva Grudtsyn*, 1963). Though regarded by some, because of the erotic theme and the realistic background descriptions, as the earliest Russian novel, the moral tone and the handling of the basic situation in the *Povest'* are purely medieval, with the hero a lay figure manipulated in his amorous adventures by the devil and eventually saved by a miracle. But the Church becomes an indirect target for attack in *Povest' o Karpe Sutulove*, which deals with another erotic motif familiar to many literatures, the successful defence of her virtue by a merchant's wife during the absence of her husband; for here two of the would-be seducers are a village priest and an archbishop. While *Provest' o Frole Skobeyeve* (tr. S. A. Zenkovsky, *The Tale of Frol Skobeyev*, 1963), the story of a successful seduction, in which the victim is a willing accomplice and the seducer prospers, is frankly amoral. This is a psychologically convincing novella which belongs in spirit and in language wholly to the modern period of literature. The originality of *Povest' o Gore i Zlochastii* (tr. S. A. Zenkovsky, *The Tale of Woe and Misfortune*, 1963), on the other hand, lies in its skilful combination of the traditions of didactic literature with those of epic and lyric folksongs. Though set in 17th-century Russia, and with a merchant's son as the anonymous hero, it is basically the Biblical tale of the Prodigal Son, beginning with the Fall of Man as the general proposition and progressing to the fall and ultimate salvation in a monastery of an individual sinner; but to tell the story the author has used the language, imagery, rhythms and some of the stock situations of the epic folk-song. The dualistic nature of the work is exemplified by the personification of Woe and Misfortune, a figure which owes its origins partly to a Christian conception of the devil and partly to a view of evil fate deriving from folklore.

The increasing influence of oral poetry on literature, an indication that the latter was becoming more democratic in its origins, is also apparent in the 'poetic' version of *Povest' ob Azovskom osadnom sidenii* ('The Tale of the Siege of Azov'). Originally a petition and report sent by the Cossack conquerors of Azov to the tsar after the siege of the city by the Turks in 1641, and written in the dry precise style of an official document, the 'poetic' version of the story, attributed to Feodor Ivanovich Poroshin, one of the defenders of Azov, takes its inspiration from earlier *voynskiye povesti* (military tales) and borrows from epic and lyric songs to lend colour and emotion to the descriptions of the siege.

The numerous satires and parodies of the 17th century, which gave expression to popular grievances and attitudes, are more characteristic examples of the part played in the birth of fiction by sections of Russian society which had hitherto made little contribution to written literature. The judicial system and the corruptness of judges were satirized in *Povest' o Shemyakinom sude* (tr. S. A. Zenkovsky, *The Tale of Shemyaka's Judgement*, 1963) and *Povest' o Yorshe Yorshoviche* (tr. S. A. Zenkovsky, *The Tale of Ruff, Son of Ruff*, 1963), a parody on litigation, written in the prescribed official jargon, in which the plaintiff and the defendant are fish. The Church was attacked in *Prazdnik kabatskikh yaryzhek* ('The Feast of Drunkards'), a parody on a church service, and *Kalyazinskaya chelobitnaya* ('The Petition of the Monks of Kalyazin Monastery'), a mock petition on behalf of 'persecuted' monks, forced by a 'harsh' archimandrite to fulfil their obligations and abandon their drunken habits. The use of the language and formulae of Church literature and official documents in these and other satirical tales only serves to emphasize the transitional nature of the period and the distance that literature had travelled since the outwardly pious days of the 16th century.

Though the poetry of the native oral tradition made its impact on Russian literature in the 17th century, the birth of modern Russian poetry is rather a product of Western influence, exerted through Poland, the Ukraine and White Russia. It was from here that syllabic poetry was imported, becoming firmly established in

Russian literature thanks chiefly to the activities of Simeon Polotsky (b. Samuil Emel'yanovich Petrovsky-Sitnianovich, Polotsk, 1629–80), a teacher, poet and dramatist. Educated at the most advanced Orthodox centre for the study of theology and the humanities, the Kievan Academy of Peter Mogila, which was modelled on the higher educational institutions of Western Europe, and later at a Jesuit College, he returned in 1656 to his native Polotsk, where he became a monk and a teacher, but moved to Moscow in 1664. Here he taught Latin to the officials of one of the Muscovite ministries and in 1667 became tutor to the royal family. He participated in the work of the Church Councils of 1666 and 1667, which deposed Patriarch Nikon but confirmed his reforms, and was generally active in the movement to spread education and enlightenment, advocating in particular the study of Latin and secular disciplines.

His literary output was enormous and varied, but he owes his place in Russian literature to his *virshi* (poetry), collected in *Vertograd mnogotsvetnyy* (1677–8), which contains the majority of his didactic poems, and *Rifmologion* (1680), which remained unfinished at his death and includes his plays and the panegyrical odes which he wrote in celebration of royal occasions or in honour of important members of the nobility. Also of some consequence for the development of Russian poetry was his verse translation of the Psalter, *Psaltyr' rifmotvornaya* (1680). His 2 plays, *Komidiya o bludnem syne* ('The Comedy of the Prodigal Son') and *Tragediya o Navkhodonosore tsare* ('The Tragedy of King Nebuchadnezzar') were also in syllabic verse, and both were modelled on the school dramas popular in Poland and the Ukraine. Consisting of a prologue, a number of scenes, and an epilogue, with an intermezzo between individual scenes, they closely followed the Biblical stories on which they were based and make few concessions to realism. The characters are anonymous and the development of the plot depends largely upon coincidence.

Simeon Polotsky used all the known measures of syllabic versification, but favoured lines of 11 or 13 syllables with a caesura and paired feminine rhymes. His poetry, which is typically baroque in style, spirit and its pursuit of the bizarre, covers a wide variety of genres and subjects, ranging from ancient mythology and history to zoology and mineralogy, but he remained above all a teacher rather than an inspired poet. The most important of his successors as practitioners of syllabic verse in the 17th century were Sil'vestr Medvedev (1641–91) and Karion Istomin (*c.* 1650–*c.* 1717), both of whom were monks employed at the printing house.

It is doubtful whether his plays were ever performed, but the Russian theatre did come into being on 17 October 1672, when, at the invitation of Tsar Alexey Mikhaylovich, the German pastor of the Lutheran church in Moscow, Johann Gregory, staged a performance of *Artakserksovo deystvo* (Artaxerxes (Ahasuerus)) in the royal village of Preobrazhenskoye. The play, which was in seven acts, was based on the story in the Book of Esther. In all probability it was originally written in German by Gregory himself and then translated into Russian, and the cast of 64 was recruited from among the inhabitants of the German quarter in Moscow. In June 1673 a start was made with the training of Russian actors, the majority of them immigrants from White Russia. The new company performed a number of plays on Biblical subjects, as well as an adaptation of part of Marlowe's *Tamburlaine* and a comedy on Bacchus and Venus, in Preobrazhenskoye and Moscow. But when Tsar Alexey Mikhailovich died in January 1676, theatrical performances were discontinued. [AS]

N. K. Gudzy, *Istoriya drevney russkoy literatury* (7th edn, Moscow, 1966); *Istoriya russkoy literatury*, ed. D. D. Blagoy, i (Moscow, 1958); D. Čiževskij, *History of Russian Literature from the Eleventh Century to the End of the Baroque* (The Hague, 1960); *Khrestomatiya po drevney russkoy literatury*, ed. N. K. Gudzy (Moscow, 1962); *Anthology of Old Russian Literature*, ed. A. Stender-Petersen (N.Y., 1954); *Medieval Russia's Epics, Chronicles and Tales*, ed. S. A. Zenkovsky (Cambridge, Mass., 1963); *Russkaya istoricheskaya biblioteka*, xiii (Moscow, 1909); *Skazaniye Avraamiya Palitsyna*, ed. L. V. Cherepnin (Moscow, 1955); *Novaya povest' o preslavnom Rosiyskom tsarstve*, ed. N. F. Droblenkova (Moscow/Leningrad, 1960); *Vremennik Ivana Timofeyeva*, ed. O. A. Derzhavina (Moscow/Leningrad, 1951); *Russkiye povesti XVII veka*, ed. I. P. Yeremin (Moscow, 1954); *Zhitiye protopopa Avvakuma, im samim napisannoye, i drugiye yego sochineniya*, ed. N. K. Gudzy (Moscow, 1960); A. N. Robinson, *Zhizneopisaniya Avvakuma i Epifaniya* (Moscow, 1963); P. Pascal, *Avvakum et les Débuts du Raskol* (Paris, 1938); Simeon Polotsky, *Izbrannyye soch.*, ed. I. P. Yeremin

(Moscow, 1953); *Artakserksovo deystvo*, ed. I. M. Kudryavtsev (Moscow, 1957); A. S. Orlov, *Perevodnyye povesti XII–XVII vekov* (Leningrad, 1934); V. P. Adrianova-Peretts, *Ocherki po istorii russkoy satiricheskoy literatury XVII v.* (Leningrad, 1937); D. S. Likhachev, *Chelovek v literature Drevney Rusi* (Moscow/Leningrad, 1958).

**'Russian Primary Chronicle'** (*Povest' Vremennykh Let* – 'The Tale of Bygone Years'). The *Chronicle* (of which the earliest surviving manuscripts are the *Lavrent'yevskiy spisok* of 1377 and the *Ipat'yevskiy spisok* of the mid 15th century) was compiled in the second decade of the 12th century at Kiev. Despite the prodigious efforts of scholars like Shakhmatov to determine the earlier history of the *Chronicle*, it remains uncertain how the text developed during the preceding century. Shakhmatov attempted to establish the existence of a sequence of redactions (dated 1039, 1073, 1111 and 1116) by the analysis of incongruities in the text of 1118. Though Shakhmatov's findings have been disputed, there can be no doubt that the *Chronicle* is a complex document and that the monk Nestor (to whom the authorship of the *Chronicle* was once attributed) must be regarded as one – albeit perhaps the principal – compiler among several. Much of the work on the chronicle was carried out in the Monastery of the Caves at Kiev.

The work is placed in perspective by a brief introductory history of mankind since the Flood, but its principal concern is the origin and present state of *Rus'*. This concern acts as a unifying agent throughout the work which, on another plane, is bound together by adherence to a chronology of Byzantine derivation. There are entries for most of the years between 852 and 1116, some more detailed than others. Many of the earlier entries (such as the impressive story of Oleg's death under the year 912) are clearly based on oral, folkloric sources. Others are of a documentary nature (several treaties, in particular that of 945, are quoted at length). From 1051 onwards, a number of eyewitness accounts are inserted, the most vivid of which is the narrative of Vasil'ko's blinding (1097). Monastic records, Byzantine chronicles, lives of saints and the compendium of Biblical and apologetic material known as the *Paleya* are also drawn upon.

As the *Chronicle*'s sources are varied, so is its style. Terse, factual entries are interspersed with passages of rhetoric; sober narrative prose is enlivened by the occasional introduction of dynamic rhythms derived from folklore. Some characters make their appearance in the chronicle simply as names, some as types. Others, such as the protagonists of the Vasil'ko story, are not only described with tact and psychological insight; they are also placed convincingly in their everyday context.

The *Chronicle* remains what it set out to be – one of our principal sources for the history of Kievan *Rus'*. The way in which the compilers select and comment on their material affords us an invaluable insight into the Russian mind of the early Middle Ages; the quality of the material allows it to be placed on a par with the finest of contemporary European chronicles. [SH]

Ed. V. P. Adrianova-Perets (2 vols., Moscow-Leningrad, 1950); tr. S. H. Cross and O. P. Sherbowitz-Wetzor, *The Russian Primary Chronicle. Laurentian Text* (Cambridge, Mass., 1953).

A. A. Shakhmatov, *Razyskaniya o drevneyshykh russkikh letopisnykh svodakh* (St Petersburg, 1908; The Hague, 1967).

**Russian Spiritual Verses ('dukhovnyye stikhi')**. The *dukhovnyye stikhi* are comparable to the ⇨ *byliny* in form and appeal. They have been current in Russia since at least the 17th century and were recited usually by professional or semi-professional minstrels (often blind men) outside churches or on fair-grounds. In the Ukraine and in White Russia, though not in Russia proper, a lyre would accompany the somewhat monotonous chants. Unlike the *byliny* (which survive principally in the north) the *dukhovnyye stikhi* have been preserved and collected – chiefly in the 19th century – throughout European Russia. They are still sung by amateurs, but – if recorded – they are rarely if ever published or discussed in Soviet works on folklore, no doubt owing to their religious content.

The religion (as well as the naïve and vivid imagery) of the verses deserves to be studied; it derives from, but is not altogether consonant with, that of the Orthodox Church. The themes of the verses are rarely taken from the canonical scriptures (Old Testament subjects are particularly rare, and the few New Testament subjects are treated idiosyncratically). Apocryphal and liturgical texts, the lives and icons of saints are among the principal sources drawn upon. References to (apparently) primeval

Good and Evil – *Pravda* and *Krivda* – have been ascribed to possible Bogomil influences; these are now usually discounted.

Most of the verses tend to centre on a single (often suffering) hero, such as Christ, his Mother, Yegory *khrabryy* (St George) and Alexey the Man of God. Of the latter subject more than fifty variants have been recorded. The verses, like the *byliny*, tend to have a tonic metre. There are two or three stresses to the line, with a variable number of unaccented syllables. However, there are also (much less interesting) verses composed in a syllabic metre of Polish origin. [SH]

P. Bezsonov, *Kaleki-perekhozhiye* (Moscow, 1861–4).

G. Fedotov, *Stikhi dukhovnyye* (Paris, 1935).

**Rutebeuf** (fl. 1250–80). French poet. A powerful and original poet who was born in Champagne and lived in Paris. Unlike earlier ⇨ *trouvères* he did not write musical accompaniments but concentrated on the verbal melody of his verse. His poetry is concerned with the reality of his daily existence, with moralizing, satire and religious devotion. Capable of extreme bitterness, he attacked the mendicant orders and those who care more for the body than the soul; he criticized Louis IX, and praised Guillaume de Saint-Amour in his fight against papal influence in the University of Paris.

A large number of his works survive: personal poems such as the *Mariage Rutebeuf*, the *Complainte*, the *Pauvreté Rutebeuf*, which describes with humour his way of life and love of gambling; poems inspired by events of his day, the Crusades of Louis IX, the loss of Constantinople; moralizing invective, the *Dit d'hypocrisie*, *Bataille des vices et des vertus* and the famous *Dit des Ribauts de Grève*; *Renart le bestourné*, an attack on the King and the religious orders in the form of ⇨ Renart allegory; lives of saints, *Vie de sainte Élisabeth*, *Vie de sainte Marie l'Égyptienne*; fabliaux; poems to the Virgin; a narrative ⇨Miracle and the dramatic *Miracle de Théophile*. [LTT]

*Œuvres complètes de R.*, ed. E. Faral and J. Bastin (2 vols., 1959–60).

E. Faral, *La vie quotidienne au temps de saint Louis* (Paris, 1942); *RPh*, IX (1956); XI (1957–8); XVI (1963).

**Ruusbroec, Jan van** (Ruusbroec 1293–Groenendaal 1381). Dutch mystic. Founder-prior of the Augustinian abbey at Groenendaal, where he wrote all but the first of his 11 prose treatises for other religious, the finest of which is *Die chierheit der gheestelker brulocht* (*c.*1350; tr. C. A. Wynschenk, *The Adornment of the Spiritual Marriage, etc.*, 1916). The compass of his thought and the excellence of his style earn him his place in European mysticism, and only ⇨ Hadewijch, whose system he developed, surpassed his lyrical ardour. His works were widely read in the Netherlands, influencing the *devotio moderna* and Thomas à Kempis, and were known throughout Germany, Spain, France and Italy. [PK]

*Werken* (4 vols., 1944); *Het Hantvingherlijn of van den blickenden steene*, tr. E. Colledge in *Mediaeval Netherlands Religious Literature* (Leyden–London, 1965).

**Rydberg, Viktor** (Jönköping 1828–Djursholm 1895). Swedish poet, novelist, scholar and thinker. The loss of his mother in 1834 and the subsequent dispersal of the family cast a shadow over his life, but placed her for ever in an idealized light in his memory. After giving up his studies at the university for economic reasons, he later became affiliated to the liberal *Göteborgs Handels-Tidning* and remained in the service of that paper for 20 years. Some of his early novels were published in it in serial form, e.g. *Den siste athenaren* (1859; tr. W. W. Thomas, *The Last Athenian*, Philadelphia, 1869), an analysis of the conflict between Christian fanaticism and Classical humanism in the days of Emperor Julian. The novel applies rather crude, black-and-white psychology to its theme (in the interest of hard-hitting Liberalism). An artistically more satisfying work is *Singoalla* (1857, rev. edn 1865; tr. J. Fredbärj, 1904), a romantic story which tells of the love of a medieval knight for a gipsy girl, probing the conflict between Christian and pagan elements in the mind of its hero. With *Bibelns lära om Kristus* ('The Teaching of the Bible concerning Christ', 1862) Rydberg achieved national fame. Adopting the criticism of Strauss and Renan, although with qualifications, he challenged the doctrine of Christ's divinity. The concept of an ideal man which he substituted may now appear lifeless and abstract, but his stand against the authoritarian Swedish Church profoundly influenced contemporary opinion. In the period following upon these polemical years, he suffered from prolonged states of depression; he devoted himself largely to his various researches, to the translation of Goethe's *Faust* (published in 1876), and to the problem of linguistic purism. From 1884, he was Professor of the History of Culture in the University of Stockholm. In that capacity he published his massive *Undersökningar i germanisk mythologi I–II* (1886–9; tr. R. B. Anderson, *Teutonic Mythology*, London, 1889 – vol. I only). It is, however, the two collections of verse, *Dikter* (1882 and 1891), that are his crowning achievement. His poetic diction is both lucid and musical; among his masters are ⇨ Tegnér and ⇨ Stagnelius, Goethe, ⇨ Lenau and Poe. His concern for harmonious form makes his verse somewhat abstract and diffuse, but does not impose restrictions on the thematic range. The first collection brings statements of his humanistic faith in liberated humanity, e.g. 'Kantat' and 'Drömliv', but generally he is as far removed from easy optimism as from retrospective patriotism. Rather his mind is a battle-ground for the opposing forces of the contemporary world. In the philosophical dialogue 'Prometheus och Ahasverus', the self-sacrificing idealist and the despairing materialist are brought face to face; in 'Grubblaren', the solitary humanist is all but overcome by his vision of a soulless, mechanical universe; 'Den nya Grottesången', finally, builds up a tremendous picture of suffering humanity enslaved by the very means of production: he could see no hope for an industrialized society and distrusted the Marxist formula in politics as much as the naturalist formula in aesthetics. The epilogue to his work was the historical novel *Vapensmeden* (1891). Set in his native town during the age of the Reformation, it once more depicts the clash between power-seeking bigotry and undogmatic, natural piety. At his death, he occupied a position on the Swedish cultural scene not dissimilar to that of his slightly older contemporary Matthew Arnold in England. [SAB]

*Skrifter*, ed. K. Warburg (14 vols., 1896–9).
K. Warburg, *V.R.* (Stockholm, 1900); V. Svanberg, *Novantiken i Den siste atenaren* (Uppsala, 1928); O. Holmberg, *V.R.s lyrik* (Stockholm, 1935).

**Ryl's'ky, Maksym** (Kiev 1895–Moscow 1964). Ukrainian poet, translator, scholar and critic. His first youthful collection, *Na bilykh ostrovakh* (1910), romantic and symbolist, was followed in 1918–29, his 'neo-classicist' period, by six others, from *Pid osinnimy zoryamy* to *Homin i vidhomin*, in which extremely fine closely observed life-with-nature poems and sensitive lyrics alternate with escapes into an exotic world of far-away places rich in characters from, and allusions to, ancient and modern European literature. In his *Pam''yatnyk* (1929), styled on Horace's 'Exegi monumentum' (*Od.* iii, 30), pessimistically judging his work, he yet hopes to be appreciated for 'having never been in the service of untruth'.

Imprisoned in 1931 and released in summer 1932, he wrote much in socialist realism style (e.g. the ode *Pisnya pro Stalina*), beginning with his next collection *Znak tereziv* (1932). *Zhaha* (1942), 'a poem-vision', written away from the German-occupied Ukraine, is a powerful expression of love for his country, remarkable for its organic fusion of various elements, from folk-lore to classicism and realism. *Mandrivka v molodist'* (1941–4), a long poem-memoir of his youth, was severely criticized for abandoning socialist realism in favour of 'naturalism and bourgeois objectivism', and in particular for its sympathetic presentation of some prominent men of Ukrainian culture; it was radically rewritten in 1957. Among his later work, *Vony mizh namy khodyat'* (from the cycle *Zymovi zapysy*, 1961), is notable for its courageous invective against the secret informers, 'the Judases' who, unrepentant, 'still walk in our midst, and mouth grand speeches at meetings', 'who have paved their way to careers and honours with anonymous letters'.

With his last, *V zatinku zhayvoronka* (1961) and *Zymovi zapysy* (1964), the number of his books of original poetry approached 30; he reached a crystalline clarity of expression, classic perfection, rich imagery, serenity, belief in the good and beautiful. The technical resources of his verse are manifold, and he is the supreme master of the language, deservedly regarded by many as the greatest Ukrainian poet of the mid-century. His translations from Shakespeare, Voltaire, Mickiewicz and many other poets from East and West (over 250,000 lines in all) are as masterful as his original work and have also greatly enriched Ukrainian. [VS]

*Tvory* (10 vols., 1960–2); Andrusyshen and Kirkconnell, *UP*; *SL*, 10 (1958); 10 (1960).
Luckyj, *LPSU*; *UCE*; *IL*, 7 (1943); 3 (1945); *UQ*, v, 3 (1949).

# S

**Sá de Miranda, Francisco de** (Coimbra 1481–Tapada 1558). Portuguese poet. He spent much of his youth at Court; his early poetry reflected the contemporary preoccupation with Petrarchan themes and was framed in the traditional peninsular verse-forms of *vilancete* and *cantiga*. In 1521 he went to Italy, where he became familiar with the new Renaissance forms of poetic expression and their new intimacy of poetic experience. Returning to Portugal in 1526, he enthusiastically propagated the Italian verse-forms in hendecasyllable measure. His eclogue *Alexo* and sonnets are the first known examples in Portuguese of the new style. He also produced a prose comedy *Os Estrangeiros* modelled on the Italian comedies of Ariosto and Bibbiena. Though enjoying the royal favour and considerable personal prestige, he suddenly threw up this existence and withdrew to his estates in Alto Minho to live the life of a gentleman farmer (1530). He still maintained an active correspondence with literary personalities of the epoch but his poetry came more and more to reflect his exasperation at what he regarded as the increasingly artificial sophistication of courtly and national values. He sought to register a protest at the disintegration of Portuguese society caused by the movement of overseas expansion. He looked back with nostalgia to the 'golden age' when men contented themselves with a life of rustic simplicity, buttressed against adversity by the patriarchal aspects of feudal relationships. The pastoral convention, as he conceived it, was rooted less in some classical paradise than in the Portuguese past. In his most interesting eclogue *Basto*, he presents a long debate between two shepherds who advocate, on one side, a position of anti-social individualism and, on the other, one of compromise sociability. Elsewhere, notably in his poetic *Cartas*, he directed his satire against the corruption of justice, the hypocrisy of the court favourites, the exhibitionism of the Church and the cupidity of the nation as a whole. As a social critic, he is second in his generation only to Gil ⇨ Vicente. [AJP]

*Obras Completas* (CSC); *Poesias Escolhidas* (TL).

A. J. Saraiva, *História da Cultura em Portugal*, ii (Lisbon, 1955).

**Saar, Ferdinand von** (Vienna 1833–Döbling 1906). Austrian poet and Novellen writer. He was an officer in 1849–59, then a freelance author; he committed suicide. His lyrical poems – notably *Gedichte* (1881), *Wiener Elegien* (1893), *Nachklänge* (1899) – and his mostly regional and psychologically realistic stories – including *Novellen aus Österreich* (1877; 1879), *Schicksale* (1889), *Herbstreigen* (1897), *Camera Obscura* (1901), *Tragik des Lebens* (1906) – show a refined, decadent sense of beauty and resignation. His tragedies, *Kaiser Heinrich IV* (1867) and *Thassilo* (1885), were failures. [LL]

*Das erzählerische Werk*, ed. J. F. Fuchs (3 vols., 1959).

M. Lukas, *F.v.S.* (Vienna, 1947); J. L. Hodge, *The Novellen of F.v.S.* (Pennsylvania, 1961).

**Saavedra, Ángel de, Duque de Rivas** (Córdoba 1791–Madrid 1865). Spanish poet and dramatist. He fought against Napoleon, was condemned as a liberal, had to live in exile in England, Malta and France, came back on the death of Ferdinand VII, suffered further brief exile, but returned finally as a conservative (prime minister, ambassador). He did much to establish Romanticism in Spain, after a literary conversion due in part to Canning's collaborator in the *Anti-Jacobin*, Hookham Frere. His narrative poem *El moro expósito* (1834), in the Scott tradition, tells the heroic story of Mudarra, the bastard brother of the legendary 'Siete infantes de Lara'. Its introduction, written by Antonio Alcalá-Galiano, is in effect the Spanish Romantic manifesto.

The *Hernani* (⇨ Hugo) of Spanish Romanticism was Saavedra's drama in prose and verse *Don Álvaro o la fuerza del sino* (1835), which provided the libretto for Verdi's *Forza del destino*. Fully romantic too were the *Romances históricos* (1841), historical ballads on medieval or Habsburg period subjects. 'Colour, light and shade, attract, seduce Saavedra (who) practised painting as well as literature' (Azorín). Today his verse seems mediocre compared with that of ⇨ Espronceda. [JMC]

*Obras completas* (1945); Blecua, *FLE*; Trend, *OBSV*.
'Azorín', *Rivas y Larra* (CA); E. A. Peers, *R. and Romanticism in Spain* (1923); *RH*, LVIII, (1923).

**Saba, Umberto** (Trieste 1883–Gorizia 1957). Italian poet. His homely style may be due partly to his upbringing in Trieste, which he regarded as a cultural backwater, partly to his preoccupation with the commonplace objects of daily existence, partly to his late-Romantic longing 'to live the life of everybody/to be like all, the men of everyday'. In the manner almost of a diarist rather than of a lyric poet, he notes and reflects on each detail of sentiment aroused by themes of love and youth and death. To his collected poems *Canzoniere* (1945) he added an autobiographical commentary: *Storia e cronistoria del Canzoniere* (1948). [GD]

Golino, *CIP*.
Bàrberi Squarotti, *Astrazione e Realta* (Milan, 1960).

**Sá-Carneiro, Mário de** (Lisbon 1890–Paris 1916). Portuguese poet. Of good family, he matriculated at Coimbra University, but shortly after went to Paris to study law (October 1912). He had in that year already published a play, *Amizade*, written in collaboration, and a book of short stories, *Princípio*. The rest of his short life (he committed suicide) was spent between Paris and Lisbon, where he enjoyed the friendship of Fernando Pessoa, at whose suggestion he began to write verses.

The theme of Sá-Carneiro's poetry is the disintegration of his own personality, and his poetry is the result of his awareness and contemplation of this process. 'Now thou art an O without a figure' might be a translation of a line from Sá-Carneiro. *Dispersão* is more than the title of his next collection of poems, published in 1914: it depicts a constant state of mind. In the first poem he contrasts the extraordinary adventure of the career of poet with the life of other, ordinary men, but the rest of the volume relates the failure of the author to realize his dream. In the poem which gives the collection its title he even looks forward to his death 'far off in the north, in a great capital'.

Sá-Carneiro then returned to writing prose, and published a most remarkable short novel, *A Confissão de Lúcio* (1914), and another collection of short stories, *Céu em Fogo* (1915).

The last collection of poems, *Indícios de Ouro*, touches upon the same themes but with marked technical advance. The French symbolists have had their influence, but by way of affinity, not imitation. There is an extraordinary richness of late-romantic imagery, used to exemplify the literary theory of *interseccionismo* (evolved by the poet and his friend Pessoa), which involves a wealth of interlocking images evoked by the poet's subjective imagination. In some of his last poems he strikes the domestic note of António Nobre. Sá-Carneiro may be a minor poet, but his work is of major interest from a technical viewpoint. His thematic poverty is compensated for by remarkable verbal audacities and the attainment of effects which can still be regarded as inedited in Portuguese. [ARM]

*Obras Completas*, ed. Atica (4 vols., 1945– ).
M. da G. Carpinteiro, *A Novela Poética de M. de S.-C.* (Lisbon, 1960); J. M. Parker, *Three Twentieth Century Poets* (1960); J. Régio, *Ensaios de Interpretação Crítica* (Lisbon, 1964); D. Woll, *Wirklichkeit und Idealität in der Lyrik M. de S.-C.s* (Bonn, 1960).

**Sacchetti, Franco** (Ragusa ? *c.* 1332–S. Miniato ? *c.*1400). Italian short-story writer and poet. He travelled extensively as a young man, but later settled in Florence and held many offices in the service of the commune. His *Sposizioni dei vangeli* (ed. A. Chiari, 1938) are a plain man's commentary on everyday issues arising from religious teaching, and his numerous poems in traditional 14th-century modes are respectable and pleasing minor verse, especially in one or two graceful ballads. He is best known for the *Trecentonovelle* (ed. E. Li Gotti, 1946; V. Pernicone, 1946) (in fact only 223 survive, some of them incomplete), which he compiled during his later years, and which show him as the best Italian short-story writer between ⇨ Boccaccio and ⇨ Bandello.

Though the Introduction mentions the *Decameron*, there is no kinship. Sacchetti does not use Boccaccio's elaborate framework and his range and ambitions are much more modest. He does not aim at tragedy or complication of plot or subtle delineation of character, but simply at bringing the comic or curious event briskly to life, drawing largely on the oral tradition and on direct observation for his material. Such dramatized anecdote has only limited potentialities, but it is sometimes effective, as in his accounts of quarrels developing into near-riots. The author's good sense and humour make him an attractive minor writer. [DGR]

*Opere*, ed. A. Borlenghi (1957); *Rime*, ed. A. Chiari (1936); Roscoe, *IN* (10 stories translated); E. Li Gotti, *F.S. Uomo discolo e grosso* (Florence, 1940).

Croce, *PPP*; Di Francia, *N*; *Minori*, *i*.

**Sachs, Hans** (Nürnberg 1494–Nürnberg 1576). German poet and dramatist. For the greater part of his life he exercised the trade of cobbler in Nürnberg and in his truly prolific writings – over 6,000 different works in almost every contemporary genre – appears as the spokesman of the Protestant middle class. He is conservative and limited in outlook, but his work is characterized by a sound commonsense, an instinctive moderation and above all by a naïve freshness and an uninhibited sense of humour which have not lost their appeal even today. He did not possess an inventive mind, but he was a tireless plunderer of other men's inventions – indeed, it is partly in his function as the popularizer and purveyor of classical, medieval and Renaissance themes that his cultural and historical significance lies: Terence and the Bible, the chivalresque novel and Boccaccio, the *Gesta Romanorum* and Pauli's collection of anecdotes *Schimpff und Ernst* all provided him with motifs. He wrote many *Meistergesänge* (⇨ Wagner commemorates him rather inaccurately in *The Mastersingers*), but it was in the *Schwank* and the *Fastnachtspiel* that he found the happiest medium for his gifts as an observer of everyday life, which he reproduces in delightfully realistic genre pictures. The best of the *Schwänke* (humorous anecdotes told in doggerel verse), *Das Schlauraffenland* (1530), *Sant Peter mit der gaiss* (1555), *Sant Peter mit den Lanczknechten im himel* (1556), are characterized by their genial good humour, their popular quality and their satirical, didactic purpose – he seldom fails to point the moral with unmistakable clarity. These same qualities are evident in the 81 *Fastnachtspiele* (dramatized anecdotes and incidents of everyday life produced originally at Shrovetide), which reject the extreme crudity of his predecessors, Folz and Rosenplüt, and are conspicuous for their liveliness and dramatic effectiveness: such *Fastnachtspiele* as *Der paur im egfeur* (1550), *Das heisse eysen* (1551) and *Der farendt schüler ins paradeis* (1557) can still hold a modern audience.

His more ambitious dramatic works (61 'tragedies', 64 'comedies') are by no means so successful; particularly the tragedies suffer from an almost grotesque incongruence between theme and execution. An early convert to Lutheranism, Sachs engaged in the Reformation controversy with a long allegorical poem greeting Luther as the nightingale of Wittenberg (1523), 4 satirical dialogues (1524) and also wrote the texts for a number of polemical illustrated broadsheets. [WAC]

*Werke*, ed. A. v. Keller and E. Goetze (26 vols., 1870–1908); tr. W. Leighton, *Merry Tales and Three Shrovetide Plays* (1910); tr. E. U. Ouless, *Seven Shrovetide Plays* (1930).

H. Cattanès, *Les 'Fastnachtspiele' de H.S.* (Smith College Studies in Mod. Langs., vol. 4, Strasbourg, 1923).

**Sachs, Nelly** (Berlin 1891–1970). German Jewish poet. She escaped from Nazi Germany, where other members of her family were murdered, with the help of Selma ⇨ Lagerlöf (whose German translator she is). After early stories, her major poetic work begins with *In den Wohnungen des Todes* (1946), and has been collected in *Fahrt ins Staublose* (1961), *Späte Gedichte* (1965), and *Zeichen im Sand. Die szenischen Dichtungen* (1962). Little-known outside Germany and Sweden (where she lived), she won the Nobel Prize in 1966. Her work is a noble monument to the sufferings of her people; with Paul ⇨ Celan she helped to restore the German language to humanity. [PB]

Middleton, *GWT*; *Selected Poems* (1968).

*N.S.*, ed. W. A. Berendsohn (Dortmund, 1963) (with bibliography); *N.S. zu Ehren* (Frankfurt a.M., 1961) (various authors).

**Sade, Donatien Alphonse François,** Comte, known as Marquis, de (Paris 1740–Charenton 1814). French novelist. Sade served as a cavalry officer in the Seven Years War, but by 1768 his debauched life led to his imprisonment. Another prosecution (for poisoning) sent him into exile in 1772, and he was again in prison 1777–90. During these years of confinement he wrote the novels which he published during the revolutionary period: *Justine ou les malheurs de la vertu* (1791), *Aline et Valcour* (1795; part of this, *Histoire de Sainville et de Léonore*, ed. G. Lély, Paris, 1962), *La philosophie dans le boudoir* (1795), *La Nouvelle Justine* (1797). These works are chiefly notable for their wealth of detail in the field of descriptive sexual pathology, where he often foreshadows Freud, but they also present an ethical outlook and a view of human nature which is an extreme form of hedonistic moral nihilism. His publications led to his renewed imprisonment in 1801, and in 1803 he was adjudged insane and committed to the asylum at Charenton. [WHB]

*Œuvres complètes*, ed. G. Lély (8 vols, 1966ff.); *De Sade Quartet*, tr. M. Crosland (1963) (4 extracts).

G. Gorer, *The Life and Ideas of the Marquis de S.* (1963); L. C. Crocker, *Nature and Culture: Ethical Thought in the French Enlightenment* (Baltimore, 1963).

**Sadoveanu, Mihail** (Paşcani 1880–Bucharest 1961). Rumanian novelist and short-story writer. One of the greatest Rumanian prose-writers, but not so great a novelist. He has a marvellous power of portraying the background of nature. His characters are less vivid than the scenery in which they live, the more sophisticated less convincing than the countrymen. The most praised of his peasant stories is *Băltagul* (1930), in which a widow tracks down the murderers of her husband. His gift of evoking the past is used to advantage in historical novels such as *Şoimii* (1904), *Fraţii Jderi* (vol. I, 1935; II, 1936; III, 1942) and *Nicoară Potcoavă* (1952). In *Mitrea Cocor* (1949; tr. P.M., 1953) he attempted socialist realism. [EDT]

**Sagan, Françoise** (Cajore 1935– ). French novelist. Educated in Paris. In simple, dispassionate prose her novels describe the attempts of amoral characters to escape solitude in brief liaisons, lasting love and happiness being impossible. For the sensualist Cécile (*Bonjour Tristesse*, 1954; tr. I. Ash, 1957), pleasure is ultimately tinged with pain. Dominique, in *Un certain sourire* (1956; tr. I. Ash, *A Certain Smile*, 1956), seeking momentary happiness in an *affaire*, finally resigns herself to loneliness, and the older Paule, *Aimez-vous Brahms?* (1959; tr. P. Wiles, 1960), accepts the fatality of an unhappy love rather than a new affair. The short duration of love is again the subject of *Dans un mois dans un an* (1957; tr. I. Ash, *Those without Shadows*, 1957). And in *Les merveilleux nuages* (1961; tr. A. Green, *Wonderful Clouds*, 1961) Josée cannot break up her marriage to Alan until he accepts its inevitability. The thinness of her material is even more apparent in her plays, sexual ballets in fashionable settings: *Château en Suède* (1960; tr. L. Hill, *Castle in Sweden*, 1962), *Les violons parfois* (1962), *La robe mauve de Valentine* (1963), *Bonheur, impair et passe* (1964). [RGV]

G. Mourge, *F.S.* (Paris, 1958).

**Saint-Amant, Antoine Girard,** Sieur de (Rouen 1594–Paris 1661). French poet. Famous in his own day as author of the Biblical epic *Moyse sauvé*, and as a disciple of ⇨ Marino. He seems to have been unfairly discredited by ⇨ Boileau and has recently been seen to be one of the liveliest and most gifted writers of verse between ⇨ Malherbe and ⇨ La Fontaine. [WGM]

Adam, *HLF.*

**Sainte-Beuve, Charles Augustin** (Boulogne 1804–Paris 1869). French critic and novelist. Early associated with the Romantics (see his article on Hugo's *Odes et ballades*), he produced the '*poésies et pensées*' of an imaginary poet supposedly died young – *Joseph Delorme* (1829). Other collections, together with the novel *Volupté* (1834), reflect his love affair with Hugo's wife, Adèle. His principle critical works are: *Critiques et portraits littéraires* (1836–9); *Port Royal* (1840–59) *Chateaubriand et son groupe littéraire sous l'Empire* (1861) *Les causeries du lundi* (1851–62), *Les nouveaux lundis* (1863–70). ⇨⇨ French Literary Criticism in the 19th and 20th Centuries. [WA]

*Œuvres*, ed. M. Leroy (4 vols., and Pléiade, 1949–55).

A. Billy, *S.-B. et son temps* (Paris, 1952); H. Nicolson, *S.-B.* (1957); M. Regard, *S.-B.* (Paris, 1960); A. G. Lehmann, *S.-B.* (1962).

**Saint-Évremond, Charles de Saint-Denis,** Sieur de (St Denis-le-Guast, Normandy 1613–London 1703). French critic. He spent more than half his days in exile in London, but was for a large circle an authority in matters of literary taste. He never mastered the English language but knew everybody of note and was buried in Westminster Abbey. An early satire, *Comédie des Académistes*, shows power of irony but not the charm of his *Conversation du Maréchal d'Hocquincourt* and of essays on classical and modern literature. The text of his works has been difficult to establish owing to his fashionable appeal, and absence from contact with his printers, one of whom is said to have challenged young authors with '*Faites-moi du Saint-Évremond*'. His life was written and his work published by his friend Des Maizeaux. [WGM]

Adam, *HLF*.

**Saint-Exupéry, Antoine de** (Lyons 1900–in action 1944). French novelist. He intended to enter the Navy, but turned to flying during his military service (1921–3). He was very active during the pioneering days of commercial aviation, and worked in Africa and South America. His early books, *Courrier Sud* (1928) and *Vol de nuit* (1931; tr. S. Gilbert, *Night Flight*, 1932), which reflect his experiences as a pilot, brought him immediate fame. He remained a man of action, however, travelled widely by air, and drew extensively on his experiences in his writing (*Terre des hommes*, 1939; tr. L. Galantière, *Wind, Sand and Stars*, 1939). He fought with the French Air Force (*Pilote de guerre*, 1942; tr. L. Galantière, *Flight to Arras*, 1942), then went to America after the fall of France. In 1943 he joined the French forces in North Africa. A major work, *Citadelle*, was published posthumously (1948; tr. S. Gilbert, *Wisdom of the Sands*, 1954). Flying and writing were inextricably linked in his life, and to both he brought a unique sense of dedication. Far from writing mere memoirs or adventure stories, he tried to depict the awesome wonder inspired in him by flying, which he believed brought him nearer to the heart of the mystery of existence. Through it he found self-fulfilment and a sense of human dignity; he realized the existence of a noble fraternity between disinterested and courageous men united in a common endeavour. Thus *Courrier Sud* evokes the thoughts and feelings of an airmail pilot stationed in West Africa who knows that his vocation as a flyer sets him apart from ordinary men. *Vol de nuit*, his masterpiece, blends a bare but dramatic action with profound moral reflections on the theme that happiness is to be found not in freedom or in human love, but in the acceptance of duty and in dedication to one's mission. In *Terre des hommes* he seeks wisdom through men's conquest of the skies which teaches them to know themselves better and unite in fraternal efforts that will lift them above individual emotions. The idealism of *Pilote de guerre* blends Christian and humanistic notions; it grew out of the need for new vision and dedication after the collapse of France. His vivid, incisive prose lends power to his ideas while a restrained lyricism inspires many meditations which reveal his profound faith in Man and in Life. His 'fairy-tale', *Le petit prince* (1945; tr. K. Woods, *The Little Prince*, 1944), derives its charm and popularity from its concealed seriousness. [CAB]

*Œuvres*, ed. R. Caillois (Pléiade, 1963).
Luc Estang, *S.-E. par lui-même* (Paris, 1956); C. François, *L'esthétique de S.-E.* (Paris, 1957); R. M. Albérès, *S.-E.* (Paris, 1961).

**Saint-Gelais, Mellin de** (Angoulême 1487–Paris 1558). French poet. Son of Octavien de Saint-Gelais, one of the *rhétoriqueurs*, he lived for some time in Italy, then became a priest, and royal almoner and librarian. He wrote graceful and witty light verse, in the style of ⇨ Marot, with the addition of Italian sophistication. He was one of the first poets to use the sonnet form (imitated from Italian) in French. He also adapted from ⇨ Trissino a tragedy, *Sophonisbe*, which was performed in 1559 but soon became merely a literary curiosity because it was written in a mixture of verse and prose, whereas all 'regular' French tragedies were in verse. The style is at times very fine, e.g. in passages of prose rhetoric such as Sophonisba's farewell to life. [GJ]

H. J. Molinier, *M. de S.-G.* (Rodez, 1910).

**Saint-Lambert, Jean-François,** Marquis de (Nancy 1716–Paris 1803). French poet. He owes his niche in literary history chiefly to having been, after Voltaire, the lover of Mme du Châtelet, and also of Mme d'Houdetot, who played a crucial role in the life of J.-J. ⇨ Rousseau. He was highly thought of as a poet, however, by some contemporaries. His long didactic poem *Les saisons* (1769) (which owes much to Thomson's *Seasons*), though artificial in manner and full of faded imagery, did something to turn French poetry back towards natural description. [WHB]

M. M. Cameron, *L'influence des 'Saisons' de Thomson sur la poésie descriptive en France (1759–1810)* (Paris, 1927); Sainte-Beuve, *CL*.

**Saint-Simon, Louis de Rouvroy,** Duc de (Paris 1675–Paris 1755). French memoir writer. He was the son of a father aged 68 and a mother aged 31, small of stature, vain, intractable, jealous of his privileges. Father transmitted to son a reverence for Louis XIII and brought him up in a private school to appreciate the twin loyalties of Church and State. He fought in the cavalry at Namur and Neerwinden, married at 20, left the army in pique at a missed promotion (1702) and lived at Court, where his wife was in 1710 a lady-in-waiting to the Duchesse de Berry. In 1715 he was made member of the Council of the Regency but after the death of the Duc d'Orléans in 1723 his influence and participation in public affairs declined. He retired to his estates at La Ferté near Chartres and spent his last twenty years writing.

The central subject of the *Memoirs* (tr. B. St John, 1963) is life at the French court in the later years of Louis XIV, the events, the people, the repercussions of war and politics. Saint-Simon was near the centre and exceptionally gifted: his memory, and industry in following clues of evidence, are prodigious. But he was also biased and passionate, constantly and easily carried away by anger and spite, as well as by admiration. A member of a dying class, he saw public events as illustrating his conviction that Louis XIV was letting down the nobility by paring its privileges and by choosing as servants of the state men of the middle class. He pounces on the tiniest scrap of infringement of privilege, he abhors the trend of things: 'this vile bourgeois reign'. He judges people by their attitude to etiquette and to precedence. On no great event can he be trusted to get the essentials in right proportion.

But the weakness of the historian is the glory of the artist. He is incomparable as a painter of scenes, of excited people, of public figures in private, of any kind of clash of temperament. His zest for the *ipsissima verba* and for their counterpart in gesture and tone is uncanny; he describes the unmentionable, the gross, the physical, the savage, the private. He is best on outbursts, lapses, passions, natural outcroppings of the brute beast in people taught to behave with decorum – the Sun King above all (apart from the author the chief figure of the book). Although Saint-Simon disliked him he does full justice to his royal qualities, dignity, presence of mind, tact, self-control, and is all the more impressive in describing those few cases where the royal temper was lost. Vocabulary and style correspond to the subject; he writes on the grand scale, with a rich profusion of words. Overwhelming in accumulation of detail he is no less a master of the single detail, the vignette, the characteristic feature or the single mordant expression. [WGM]

*Mémoires*, ed. G. Truc (7 vols., Pléiade, 1947–61); *Louis XIV at Versailles: a Selection from the Memoirs of S.-S.*, tr. and ed. D. Flower (1953).

H. Taine, *S.-S.* (Paris, 1856); A. Baschet, *S.-S.* (Paris, 1874); F. R. Bastide, *S.-S.* (Paris, 1957); Auerbach, *M.*

**Salacrou, Armand** (Rouen 1899– ). French dramatist. Vigorous and uneven playwright distinguished by his involvement in contemporary intellectual currents, notably Communism, and his responsiveness to the aesthetic experiments of his day, more especially Surrealism. He makes free use of fantasy and dream projections and generally aerates a basically naturalistic drama with forms and devices borrowed from a more consciously poetic theatre. This enables him to appeal to both intellectual and popular audiences. Of his earliest plays, *La boule de verre* (published 1924) remains unstaged while *Le casseur d'assiettes* (published 1924) had to wait until 1954 for a professional production. *Tour à terre* (1925), *Le pont de l'Europe* (1927) and *Patchouli* (1930) were all disastrous failures and Salacrou only reached the general public in 1931 with *Atlas-Hôtel*, a comic imbroglio involving a superbly funny would-be Napoleon of the tourist trade. The failures are significant in that their fantasy and poetic disorder were prematurely aimed at a public nurtured on naturalistic models. This early spontaneous poetic fancy later hardens into a more intellectualized conception as it is put to the service of a satiric vein of considerable force which attacks the hollowness and corruption of bourgeois society, undermining its persistent illusions. Such is the case with *Un homme comme les autres* (1936), a caustic comedy on the hypocrisy of married men, or *Histoire de rire* (1939; tr. L. Hill, *No Laughing Matter*, 1957) where the conventional sexual merry-go-round is given a bitter twist, or *Sens interdit* (1953) where time is reversed, life lived backwards and couples impatiently await their youth when they will not yet have been deceived. The attack on bourgeois society sometimes takes on a more fully political sense, as in *La terre est ronde* (1938), perhaps the most ambitious and impressive of his plays, where fascism clearly stands behind the study of Savonarola's fanaticism; or in *Boulevard Durand* (1961), a rather obvious piece of social realism, in which capitalist society is seen as accomplishing the martyrdom of a union leader. Salacrou's drama is distinguished by two other factors. First, at the level of technique, it is greatly preoccupied with the problem of time. This is reflected not only in the reversal of the time process in *Sens interdit*, but in *L'inconnue d'Arras* (1935), where Ulysse's whole life passes through his mind in flashback in the moment before he presses the trigger of the revolver he holds to his temple, and in the strikingly effective play about the Resistance, *Les nuits de la colère* (1946; tr./adapt. R. Morley, *Men of Darkness*, 1948), where the play's moral passion is illuminated by a flashback device. Secondly, this drama is animated by profound metaphysical unease, a deep-rooted sense of the contingent character of all life and a horror-stricken consciousness of the inevitability of death. Characters, therefore, are often notations of spiritual doubt and anguish, and a tragic temper makes itself disconcertingly felt through apparently banal situations. It is a drama which sometimes opens out upon a cosmic dimension. Such is the impression left by moments of *Une femme libre* (1934), where Jacques installs a model of the solar system in his house, or in *Une femme trop honnête* (1956) with its ironic references to divine indifference, or in *Dieu le savait* (1950), a debate on determinism. In his variety, vivacious handling of dialogue, assured theatrical sense and spiritual restlessness, Salacrou offers a drama of high interest. His memoirs (*Les idées de la nuit*, 1960) are full of insight. [SBJ]

*Théâtre* (8 vols., 1943–66); *La rue noire* (1967); *Entretiens avec P.-L. Mignon* (1966).

J. Van den Esch, *A.S., dramaturge de l'angoisse* (Paris, 1947); P.-L. Mignon, *S.* (Paris, 1960).

**Salazar y Torres, Agustín de** (Almazán, Soria 1642–Madrid 1675). Spanish dramatist. He won a prize in boyhood for reciting and expounding Góngora's *Soledades* in a Jesuit college in Mexico. His plays, written after his return to Spain in 1666, contain lyrics full of echoes from Góngora and Calderón. A most accomplished lyricist, he was content to write in the manner of other men. [JMC]

BAE, 42, 49; *Poetas novohispanos (1621–1721)*, ed. A. Méndez Plancarte (1944).

**Salernitano, Masuccio**, pseud. of Tommaso Guardati (Salerno 1415?–1475?). Italian short-story writer. His *Novellino* (1476; ed. A. Mauro, 1940; G. Petrocchi, 1957; tr. W. G. Waters, 1895) consists of 50 short stories. Unlike the *Decameron*, it has no general framework, and each story has its own dedication and introduction. The stories are, however, divided into groups, as Boccaccio's are, and in style too he tries to follow Boccaccio, despite an admixture of latinisms and southern dialectal forms. He is often fiercely satirical, interested more in attacking common moral targets (hypocrisy, corruption of priests, etc.) than in the aesthetic merits of his story. Such dramatic effects as he does occasionally achieve are broad and grotesque. [DGR]

Varese, *PVQ*; Roscoe, *IN*.

M. Fubini, *Studi sulla letteratura del Rinascimento* (Florence, 1947); G. Petrocchi, *M. S. e la narrativa napoletana del Quattrocento* (Florence, 1953).

**Salimbene, Fra,** originally Ognibene di Guido di Adamo (Parma 1221–*c.* 1290). Franciscan friar. He travelled widely and his *Chronicon* (ed. O. Holder-Egger in MGH, XXII; F. Bernini in *Scrittori d'Italia*, 1942; sel. tr. G. G. Coulton in *From St Francis to Dante*, 1960), covering the years 1167–1287, gives a vividly observed, amusing, tolerant picture of 13th-century life in France and Italy and of his own career. [FB]

N. Scivoletto, *Fra S. da Parma* (Bari, 1950).

**Salinas, Pedro** (Madrid 1891–Boston 1951). Spanish poet, playwright and critic. Of the 'Generation of the Dictatorship'. His attitude contrasts with that of his close friend ⇨ Guillén, the poet of the actual, the visible: '*Abrir los ojos. Y ver/sin falta ni sobra, a colmo/en la luz clara del día,/ perfecto el mundo, completo,*' as Salinas writes (*Seguro azar: Vocación*). In this visible world, the poet is superfluous: '*Tú, de sobra*'; so he closes his eyes to look beneath the surface: '*Cerrar los ojos. Y ver/ incompleto, tembloroso,/.../un mundo sin acabar,/ necesitado, llamándome.*' From his first book (*Presagios*, 1923), he stresses the contrast between the appearance of things and their true reality. His language is almost conversational, but his poetic conceits give a new vision of the most banal topics (*Fábula y signo*: *Los adioses*). Alone of his group, he is at ease in the machine-city, his 'chosen level', where he can translate into myth and legend not only the typist, but also her machine (*Fábula y signo: Underwood girls*), along with cars, trains, the cinema, radiators, light-bulbs and telephones. His love poetry (*La voz a tí debida, Rázon de amor*) extends the appearance/ truth conflict – the beloved's body in his arms, her truant mind and soul. After the Civil War, he lived in the United States, where nostalgia and illness brought to his last books a new tone of disillusionment. [GC]

*Poesías completas* (1956); *Volverse sombra y otrós poemas* (Milan, 1957); *Teatro completo* (Madrid, 1957); *Reality and the Poet in Spanish Poetry* (Baltimore, 1940); *Literatura española siglo XX* (Mexico, 1949); *La responsabilidad del escritor* (Barcelona, 1961).

H. Baader, *P.S.* ... (Cologne, 1956); P. Darmangeat, *P.S.* ... (Paris, 1955); C. Feal Deibe, *La poesía de P.S.* (Madrid, 1965); Alonso, *PEC*; Cano, *PESV*; Cernuda, *EPC*.

**Saliņš, Gunars.** ⇨ Latvian Literature.

**Salminen, Sally** (Vardö, Åland Islands 1906– ). Swedo-Finnish novelist. Achieved international success with *Katrina* (1936), a novel of life in the Åland Islands. This and a later novel, *Prins Efflam* (1953), have both been translated into English. [IR]

**Salons.** An invention of the Renaissance, and the most important vehicle of the social spirit which has inspired so much French literature. They should be distinguished both from the Academies of the 16th century (which Miss Yates has shown to be chiefly centres of learned discussion and largely masculine) and the scientific societies of the 17th century (which Professor Harcourt Brown describes as concerned with experiment and advance of the new knowledge). One of the first, and perhaps the most famous, was the Hôtel de Rambouillet, a house in the rue Saint Thomas du Louvre with tasteful décor inside and out, where a Court circle was welcomed by Catherine de Vivonne, Marquise de Rambouillet, and which from 1620 until the Fronde (and in a restricted form even later) provided entertainment of a quite new kind. Similar gatherings met in the rue du Tournon under Mme des Loges, in the rue des Augustins under Mme d'Auchy, in the Hôtel d'Albret and in the Hôtel de Nevers, under Mme du Plessis-Guenegaud. Some of these were suspect as centres of political opposition, but all were alike in that they provided social pastime by means of conversation, light literature, games, playlets, excursions and the like. They had their bourgeois counterparts for a more middle-class clientele, such as the Saturday parties of Mlle de ⇨ Scudéry. Several of them boasted a sort of literary majordomo or *poète attitré*, ⇨ Voiture in the Hôtel de Rambouillet, J. L. ⇨ Balzac in the *salon* of Mme des Loges. In a country only recently delivered from civil war such assemblies were a civilizing influence of the first importance. To meet people of both sexes, at leisure, talking not of war or hunting but of manners and tastes, this was novelty, and like all fashionable novelties, especially in France, the land of fashion, it produced affectation and pride and vanity, and in their train satire and slander. But these (even preciosity) were but by-products: the end-products, so to speak, were a cultured society which became the envy of Europe and a socially slanted literature which had an even greater claim to distinction. The French classical writers learned in the salons standards of conduct, of judgement, of reading and even of writing, which are embedded in their works. They learned to admire a social type called the *honnête homme* (to be distinguished from the church type known as *l'homme de bien*). Pascal called these people '*les gens universels*' and said that they were marked by modesty and taste. Their conversation can be inferred from the novels of Mlle de Scudéry and the epigrams of La Rochefoucauld, Mme de Sablé and the Abbé Esprit. Molière's finest play may be said to range around this basic issue of politeness, that quintessence of the salon spirit, which resists individualism (even that of high principle) in the interests of social cohesion.

In the 18th century the traditions of the salons continued, though with some changes. In the years 1715–33 the outstanding Paris salon was that of Mme de Lambert. Here, although the *précieux* concern with refinement of language and the subtleties of human psychology persisted, there was a new strain of intellectual seriousness: its habitués included the mathematician Mairan, Fontenelle (then Secretary of the Académie des Sciences), Montesquieu, the influential literary critics La Motte-Houdart and Mme Dacier, as well as such successful writers as Crébillon *père* and Marivaux. After Mme de Lambert's death the same group continued to assemble until 1749 as guests of Mme de Tencin. In the latter years of the *ancien régime* the most brilliant salons were those of Mme Du Deffand, which attracted major political figures (Turgot, the Duc de Choiseul) as well as men of letters and such distinguished foreign visitors as Gibbon, Hume, and Horace Walpole; of Mme Geoffrin – more bourgeois in tone, well disposed towards the new emancipated ways of thought, and frequented also by the major painters; and of Mlle de Lespinasse, originally a splinter-group from Mme Du Deffand's salon, which was primarily a social focus for some of the *philosophes* closely associated with the *Encyclopédie*. Such salons did not have the fertilizing influence of their 17th-century forerunners, but they provided an invaluable framework for cultivated living, and as a social link between the world of letters and high Court society they greatly smoothed the path of the writer in search of public recognition. WGM/WHB]

E. Magne, *Voiture et les années de gloire de l'Hôtel de Rambouillet* (Paris, 1912); M. Magendie, *La politesse mondaine* (Paris, 1925); Tallemant des Réaux, *Historiettes*, ed. A. Adam (Paris, 1960); M. Glotz and M. Maire, *Salons du 18e siècle* (Paris, 1945).

**Saltykov, Mikhail Yevgrafovich** (pseud. Shchedrin, often known as Saltykov-Shchedrin) (Spas-Ugol, Tver' prov. 1826–St Petersburg 1889). Russian novelist. Of old aristocratic descent, he held a post in the War Office till exiled to Vyatka for his satirical story *Zaputannoye delo* (1848). In 1856 he returned to Petersburg; in 1858–62 he held official posts in Kazan', then Tver'. He retired in 1868, to write. As a radical editor with Nekrasov of *Sovremennik* and *Otechestvennyye zapiski*, he became a leader of the radical intelligentsia. His voluminous work consists mainly of satirical sketches of many aspects of Tsarist Russia both previous and contemporary, especially officialdom, the nobility and the rising capitalists; censorship necessitated a roundabout style, and topical references now lack interest (e.g. *Istoriya odnogo goroda*, 1869–70). His concentrated *Skazki* (1884–5; tr. V. Volkhovsky, *Fables*, 1931) are less dated; but his masterpiece is the novel *Gospoda Golovlyovy* (1876; tr. N. Duddington, *The Golovlyov Family*, 1955), showing simply but relentlessly the decay of a family of provincial gentry. The terrifying figure of the hypocrite Iudushka is justly one of the most famous characters in Russian literature.

*Polnoye sobraniye sochineniy*, ed. V. Ya. Kirpotin (1933–41); *Sobraniye sochineniy* (1965ff.) K. Sanine, *S-Chtchédrine* (Paris, 1955); V. Ya. Kirpotin, *M.E.S-Shch.* (Moscow, 1955).

**Samain, Albert** (Lille 1858–Magny-les-Hameaux 1900). French poet. He survives as a discreet example of the *décadent* whose poems were widely read at the beginning of this century. A modest, sincere man of *petit-bourgeois* origin and unstable health, he cultivated a style that owed more to the Symbolist than to the Parnassian manner, without aiming at any originality of form or inspiration. The discovery François ⇨ Coppée made of *Au jardin de l'Infante* (1893) brought Samain's gifts of sensuous imagery and languorous rhythm into favour, and the collection, when augmented, was 'crowned' by the French Academy in 1898. In that year appeared a second collection, pseudo-classical in feeling, *Aux flancs du vase*. At the end of 1899, Samain helped to found a review which is still active, *Le Mercure de France*. The lure of his melancholy and the yearning expressed through sumptuous images and subdued rhythms persisted after his death at the age of 42, until the taste of a sterner time showed up the soft and *mièvre* qualities of much of his work. Nothing, however, could better suggest the amount of attention it once received than the fact that the well-known anthology, *Les poètes d'aujourd'hui*, in 1910 devoted over twice as much space to him as to Rimbaud. [PMJ]

L. Bocquet, *A.S.* (Paris, 1905); P. Martino, *Parnasse et symbolisme, 1850–1900* (1935).

**Samaniego, Félix María de** (La Guardia 1745–La Guardia 1801). Spanish fabulist. He admired then quarrelled with ⇨ Iriarte, to whom he is superior in breadth of interest and imaginative range. He translated or adapted in his *Fábulas morales* (1781–4) fables by Aesop, Phaedrus, La Fontaine and Gay. [JMC]

BAE, 61.

**Samuel Ha-Nagid, Samuel ben Yoseph ibn Nagdela** or **Nagrela** (Cordoba 993–Granada 1055). Hebrew poet of the 'Golden Age', successful business man, Arabic scholar. His poetry, noted for elegance rather than poetic depth, follows Arab models and is mainly didactic. He also wrote an introduction to the Talmud and grammatic works. [EE]

*Diwan*, ed. D. S. Sassoon (1934); *Kol shire Samuel Ha-N.*, ed. A. M. Haberman and M. Abramson (2 vols., 1947).
Waxman, *HJL*.

**Sánchez de Badajoz, Garci** (Écija? 1460?–Badajoz 1526?). Spanish poet. A member of the allegorical school. His delightful poems, admired by Herrera and ⇨ Lope de Vega, were printed in the *Cancionero general* of Hernando de Castillo (1511). His 'Lágrimas de mi consuelo' is most touching; he is said to have gone out of his mind for love and to have died mad. [JMC]

*Cancionero*, ed. R. Foulché-Delbosc, NBAE, 22; Blecua, *FLE*; Cohen, *PBSV*; Menéndez y Pelayo, *PLE*; Trend, *OBSV*; Terry, *ASP*.

**Sánchez Ferlosio, Rafael** (Rome 1927– ). Spanish novelist. His first and only novel, *El Jarama* (1956; tr. J. M. Cohen, *The One Day of the Week*, 1962), which won him the Nadal prize, is the best that has come out of contemporary Spain. It describes a single day in the lives of a group of young people, and moves slowly and skilfully from small scene to scene. The conversation, carefully imitated from life, is never flatly realistic; there are many touches of poetry in his descriptions. His *Industrias y andanzas de Alfanhuí* (1951) is a fantasy in an original form, the poetic-picaresque. [JMC]

**Sand, George,** pseud. of Amandine-Aurore-Lucie Dupin, Baronne Dudevant (Paris 1804–Nohant 1876). French novelist. She was brought up largely at Nohant, her family's country property which she later inherited and made famous. In 1822 she married the baron Dudevant, a retired army officer, and had two children. A certain wildness in her character could no longer be contained and she left her husband to go in 1831 to Paris, where she lived an independent existence famous for her trousers and effort to earn a living by writing. She at first collaborated with Jules Sandeau under the pseudonym Jules Sand and then in 1832 by herself she brought out her first successful novel, *Indiana*, under the name George Sand. *Indiana* was the first of several novels which are original for their assertion of woman's right to love and independence; it is the story of a woman who after many ups and downs finds perfect happiness in secluded love on the Île Réunion. This period of her life was taken up by the liaison with Alfred de ⇨ Musset which ended in 1834. Her novels of this time include *Valentine* (1832), *Lélia* (1833) and *Jacques* (1834). In *Mauprat* (1837) she told the story of a brute who is transformed by a woman's love. Musset never fully recovered from their relationship, while she moved on to fresh experiences. For nine years she was closely associated with Frédéric Chopin and she described their famous journey to Majorca in *Un hiver à Majorque* (1841). She had by now become fascinated by social and political questions and went through phases of Lamennais's Christian socialism and republicanism. These were reflected in the novels of what is considered her second period, such as *Le compagnon du tour de France* (1840) and *Le meunier d'Angibault* (1845). One of her most admired books was *Consuelo* (1842–3), a novel using the background of 18th-century musical life to introduce a host of strange situations, historical characters and strange ideas. Then she turned to the Berrichon countryside (around Nohant) to write the pastoral novels for which she is best remembered: *La mare au diable* (1846), *La petite Fadette* (1848) and *François le champi* (1847–8). These books have an exceptional freshness and charm and were the favourite reading of the young Marcel Proust. The ⇨ Goncourt journals have a good description by ⇨ Gautier of her well-regulated but strange existence at Nohant, where she entertained widely and had a theatre for which she wrote plays. She wrote an autobiography, *Histoire de ma vie* (4 vols., 1854–5). There are innumerable 19th-century translations of her work. [WA]

G. S. and A. de Musset, *Correspondance, journal intime*, etc., ed. L. Evrard (1956); *The Devil's Pool, Francis the Waif* (Everyman, 534).
M. L. Pailleron, *G.S.* (2 vols., Paris, 1938–43); A. Maurois, *Lélia. The Life of G.S.* (tr. 1952); E. Thomas, *G.S.* (Paris, 1959).

**Sandel, Cora,** pseud. of Sara Fabricius (Kristiania 1880– ). Norwegian novelist and short-story writer. She spent part of her childhood in Tromsø, lived for many years in France, and from 1921 mainly in Sweden. She had contributed articles to the Norwegian press, but made her debut as a novelist at 46 with *Alberte og Jacob* (1926; tr. E. Rokkan, *Alberta and Jacob*, 1962). This book and its sequels *Alberte og friheten* (1931; tr. E. Rokkan, *Alberta and Freedom*, 1965) and *Bare Alberte* (1939) embody the theme of all her work: the struggle of the artistically gifted girl, or woman, to realize herself in a hostile environment. Her psychological insight, her stylistic qualities, and eye for detail and milieu make this trilogy a central work in Norwegian literature of the inter-war years. She also published a number of collections of short stories but achieved her next major success with *Kranes konditori* (1945), a masterpiece of technical compression; it was also dramatized by Helge Krog and performed with great success. *Kjøp ikke Dondi* (1958; tr. E. Rokkan, *Leech*, 1960) is less sympathetic to the unfortunate woman, but all her old qualities are there unimpaired. [RGP]

*Samlede verker* (6 vols., 1950–1).
O. Solumsmoen, *C.S.* (Oslo, 1957).

**Sandemose, Aksel** (Nykøping, Denmark 1899–Copenhagen 1965). Norwegian novelist. He went to sea at an early age and had many jobs. His first books, of which *Klabautermanden* (1927, rev. 1932) and *Ross Dane* (1928) are the most important, were written and published in Denmark. In 1929 he settled in Norway (his mother was Norwegian), and henceforth wrote in Norwegian. *En sjømann går iland* (1931), like his earlier work, makes use of his experiences at sea and amongst the Scandinavian communities in Canada, but goes deeper and explores what was to become typical Sandemose territory: the genesis of love and hate, and the psychology of murder. In *En flyktning krysser sitt spor* (1933, rev. 1955; tr. E. Gay-Tifft, *A Fugitive Crosses his Tracks*, 1936), Espen Arnakke, who has committed a murder, continues these investigations by going back to his childhood. The whole book is an extraordinary patchwork of psychological and sociological observations, thought associations and symbols, compiled with great skill and insight; it was one of the most remarkable Norwegian books of the 1930s. *Vi pynter oss med horn* (1936; tr. E. Gay-Tifft, *Horns for Our Adornment*, 1939) combines crass realism with subtle technical innovation and spotlights primitive minds and beliefs on board the schooner *Fulton. Det svundne er en drøm* (1946), his most important post-war work, though basically a murder mystery, is a labyrinth of associations, operating on different levels of time, place, and consciousness, and full of wayward commentaries and reflections. *Tjærehandleren* (1945), *Alice Atkinson og hennes elskere* (1949), like *Varulven* (1958; tr. G. Lannestock, *The Werewolf*, 1966) and its sequel *Felicias bryllup* (1961), arc further variations on his central themes, love and murder. [RGP]

*Verker i utvalg* (8 vols., 1965–6).
C.-E. Nordberg, *S. den obesegrade* in 'Ord och Bild' (1960).

**'Sängerkrieg auf der Wartburg'** ('The Minstrels' Contest at the Wartburg'). Name given to a mid-13th-century German strophic narrative poem telling of a song-contest in the famous castle of Hermann of Thuringia between ⇨ Wolfram von Eschenbach, ⇨ Walther von der Vogelweide and other Minnesinger. Whether such a contest ever took place is doubtful; it is, however, at least certain that Hermann's Wartburg castle was a popular centre for the poets of the day, Wolfram and Walther among them. The central character is the legendary Heinrich von Ofterdingen, whose existence has never been proved but who was already regarded by the later 13th century as a historical personage. The whole subject is revived in Wagner's *Tannhäuser*, in which the figures of Ofterdingen and Tannhäuser are united in the character of the hero. Among the other Romantic revivals of the story and its characters are E. T. A. ⇨ Hoffmann's *Sängerkrieg auf der Wartburg* and ⇨ Novalis's novel *Heinrich von Ofterdingen.* [RT]

Ed. T. A. Rompelmann (1939).

**San José, Jerónimo de** (Mallén 1587?–Saragossa 1654). Spanish Carmelite poet and historian. He studied under Bartolomé Leonardo de ⇨ Argensola. He wrote a life of St John of the Cross, a history of his order, amusing letters and some well-phrased but sententious religious poems. [JMC]

*Cartas*, ed. J. M. Blecua in *Archivo de filología aragonesa*, I (1945); Blecua, *FLE*; Cohen, *PBSV*.

**Sannazaro, Jacopo** (Naples *c.*1456–Naples 1530). Italian poet. One of the group of writers and scholars who flourished at the Aragonese court at Naples. He was influenced by the great Latinist ⇨ Pontano, composed elegant Latin epigrams and elegies, several *Eclogae piscatoriae* (1526), and dedicated to Clement VII an ambitious attempt at a Christian epic, *De partu virginis* (1526; ed. A. Altamura, 1948). He wrote various pieces for court celebrations, Italian lyrics, and by 1489 had completed the greater part of the *Arcadia* (authorized publ. 1504). When in 1501 the Aragonese were overthrown, he followed Frederick into exile in France, returning to a life of retirement in Naples only after his patron's death in 1504.

Full of Petrarchan echoes, a gentle plaintiveness is a distinguishing feature of his *Rime* (1530). But it was his pastoral romance *Arcadia* which won him fame by establishing a literary form destined to achieve great European popularity. Its mingling of prose narrative and verse eclogues was derived from ⇨ Boccaccio's *Ameto*, while the borrowings from Virgil, Theocritus and other pastoralists are extensive. There are also some autobiographical elements: the chief figure, Sincero, is in some respects Sannazaro himself, and other characters depict friends at Naples, but there is no compelling expression of personal feeling, and the roots in literature are clearly stronger than the roots in life. By consolidating all the themes and motives dispersed in previous pastoral into a coherent idyllic world, he provided a new literary convention; its wistful ideal of tranquil, dignified seclusion supplied a spiritual need of the 16th and 17th centuries. [DGR]

*Opere volgari*, ed. A. Mauro (1961); *The Piscatory Eclogues*, ed. W. P. Mustard (Baltimore, 1914); *Arcadia and Piscatorial Eclogues*, tr. R. Nash (Detroit, 1966).

E. Percopo, *Vita di J.S.* (Naples, 1931); E. Carrara, *La poesia pastorale* (Milan, 1909); V. Borghini; *Il più nobile umanista del Rinascimento* (Turin, 1943); A. Altamura, *J.S.* (Naples, 1951); Arnaldi, *PLQ*; *Minori, i.*

**San Pedro, Diego de** (fl. late 15th cent.). Spanish author. Probably of Jewish descent. His two novels, *Arnalte y Lucenda* (1491) and *La cárcel de amor* (1492; ed. J. Rubió, 1941), contain motives of chivalry and of courtly love. Though their descent is from ⇨ Boccaccio's *Fiammetta*, they are subtler in their psychology than their models. The first, which ends with the suicide of a slighted lover, is imitated at the end of *La* ⇨ *Celestina*. Its style is rhetorical, and it has been described as the *Werther* of its day. It was translated into various languages including English. [JMC]

*Obras*, ed. S. Gili Gaya (1950).

**Santeuil, Claude de** (Paris 1628–Paris 1684). French hymnist. A priest attached to the seminary of Saint-Magloire, Paris, he wrote hymns for French diocesan liturgical books. His younger brother, **Jean-Baptiste de Santeuil** (Paris 1630–Dijon 1697), a canon regular at the Abbey of Saint-Victor, Paris, wrote 228 Latin hymns for various French dioceses. Some English translations are in common use, the best known is 'Disposer supreme'. [FB]

J.-B. de S., *Opera omnia* (3 vols., 1729); J. H. Newman, *Hymni Ecclesiae*, Part I (1838 and 1865) (selections); tr. in Isaac Williams, *Hymns of the Parisian Breviary* (1839).

L. A. Montalant-Bougleux, *J-B. de S., ou la poésie latine sous Louis XIV* (Paris, 1855); Sainte-Beuve, *CL*; S. W. Duffield and R. E. Thompson, *Latin Hymn-writers and their Hymns* (1889).

**Šantić, Aleksa** (Mostar 1868–Mostar 1924). Serbian poet. Educated in trade school in Ljubljana and Trieste, he belonged to a group of younger poets, including ⇨ Dučić, but unlike him did not come directly under French influence. His profoundly lyrical poetry draws more directly on native sources, and reflects the folk-songs and the oriental imagery prevailing in Bosnia and Herzegovina. Some of his poems, particularly the beautiful *Emina*, have been set to music. His patriotic poetry has remarkable vitality and originality. [EDG]

'Fields of Misery' in *SEER*, XXIX, 73 (1951) (tr. W. K. Matthews); Ibrovac, *APY*; Lavrin, *AMYP*.

Barac, *HYL*; Kadić, *CSL*.

**Santillana, Marquis de.** ⇨ López de Mendoza.

**Sanz, Eulogio Florentino** (Arévalo 1821–Madrid 1881). Spanish dramatist and poet. He achieved success with his sober romantic drama, *Don Francisco de Quevedo* (1848;

ed. R. S. Rose, Boston, 1917). A bohemian by disposition, he slept on park benches till he secured a post with a newspaper. His poems are ironic; one satirical sonnet, circulated in manuscript, was said to have prepared the ground for the revolution of 1854. He was an enthusiast for German poetry, and translated Heine admirably. He spent two years in the Berlin embassy, where he wrote his best-known poem, 'Epístola a Pedro', a verse letter to his editor, which describes a visit to the neglected tomb of the poet Enrique ⇨ Gil. His work has not been collected. [JMC]

Blecua, *FLE*.

**Sarabia, José de** (fl. early 17th cent.). Spanish poet. His 'Canción real a una mudanza' is generally attributed to the dramatist Antonio ⇨ Mira de Amescua. It is a delicately turned 'theme and variations' in a moderately baroque style, on the mutability and changing whims of woman. [JMC]

Blecua, *FLE*; Cohen, *PBSV*.

**Sarbiewski, Mathias Casimir** (Sarbiewo 1595–Warsaw 1640). Polish Jesuit poet. Versed in the classics (especially Horace, Pindar), and a voluminous writer of Latin verse both sacred and secular (e.g. fine patriotic odes and charming flower-poems), he was appointed by Pope Urban VIII to revise the Latin ⇨ hymns in the Roman Breviary, and converted a number from accentual into quantitative verse, depriving them of much of their charm and making some unrecognizable. [FB]

*Poemata omnia* (Staravies, 1812); sel. and tr. J. Kitchener (1821); *Wood-notes*, tr. R. C. Coxe (1848).

**Sardou, Victorien** (Paris 1831–Marly 1908). French playwright. One of the most popular and successful dramatists of the 19th century. Like ⇨ Scribe, whose technique he copied, he was a brilliant theatrical craftsman for whom the mechanics of dramatic action were everything. He had a strong sense of the internal economy of acts and scenes, a flair for complicated plots and a firm command of striking theatrical effects. In spite of these gifts, his plays conspicuously lack life and are marked by relentless vulgarity of feeling and insight. This tinsel and cardboard quality was precisely what Bernard Shaw epitomized in his derisive label 'Sardoodledom'. An abundant output included comedies of manners, like *Les pattes de mouche* (1860; tr. J. P. Simpson, *A Scrap of Paper*, 1889), *Nos intimes* (1861; tr. G. March, *Our Friends*, 1879), *La famille Benoîton* (1865), *Rabagas* (1872), which tilts at political life, and *Divorçons* (1880; tr./adapt. M. Mayo, *Cyprienne*, 1941). He also wrote melodramas: *Fédora* (1882; tr. H. Merivale, 1883), an involved play about revenge, which was set in Russia, and *Tosca* (1887), already so close to the operatic convention that Puccini found no difficulty in adapting it. His historical plays had considerable popular success: *Patrie!* (1869; tr. B. H. Clark, 1915), *Thermidor* (1891), and *Madame Sans-Gêne* (1893), in collaboration with Émile Moreau, a comedy about a laundress who marries a miller's son who becomes one of Napoleon's marshals. The great actress Sarah Bernhardt brought her talent and glamour to many of the roles. [SBJ]

*Théâtre complet* (15 vols., 1934–61).

G. Mouly, *Vie prodigieuse de V.S.* (Paris, 1931); R. Doumic, *Portraits d'écrivains* (Paris, 1892); L. Lacour, *Trois théâtres. E. Augier, A. Dumas fils, V.S.* (Paris, 1880); J. A. Hart, *S. and the Sardou Plays* (Philadelphia, 1913).

**Sarkia, Kaarlo** (Kiikka 1902–Turku 1945). Finnish poet. Original surname Sulin. As a university student at Turku he came under the influence of V. A. ⇨ Koskenniemi and became deeply interested in French lyric poetry, showing considerable skill as a translator of Baudelaire, Verlaine and Rimbaud; his version of Rimbaud's 'Bateau ivre' is a remarkable piece of virtuosity. His life-story is tragic: he suffered from tuberculosis, travelled vainly to Germany, Switzerland and Italy in search of health; the south inspired many motifs for his poems. Essentially a dreamer, he was passionately involved in the search for absolute beauty and perfection; he developed his metrical and rhythmical skill to a high degree of brilliance that sometimes took precedence over clarity of thought and shed a haze of romantic aestheticism over all he wrote. [RV]

*Runot* (1944); *Valikoima runoja* (1958); Ollilainen, *SF*; Tompuri, *VF*.

**Sarment, Jean** (Nantes 1897–      ). French playwright. Deft at conveying states of reverie and disenchantment, he creates a muted world in which the characteristic hero is an idealist at variance with the ugliness and mediocrity of real life. The remedy is often to embrace some form of escapism, like the textile merchant of *Peau d'Espagne* (1933) who pretends to be a well-connected English peer, or Hécube, the derisory schoolmaster of *Le discours des prix* (1934), who imagines a brilliant future for himself because an ex-pupil has become an influential politician. There are echoes of Pirandello (*Le pêcheur d'ombres*, 1921; tr. P. Ustinov *Fishing for Shadows*, 1940) and Shakespeare (*Le mariage d'Hamlet*, 1922) but the world conjured up is closest to Musset's. The melancholy charm survives best in *Je suis trop grand pour moi* (1924) and *Léopold le bien-aimé* (1927). [SBJ]

*RR*, 36 (1935); Surer, *TFC*; Lalou, *TF*.

**Sarpi, Paolo** (Venice 1552–Venice 1623). Italian theologian and historian. At 14 he joined the Servites, changing his name from Pietro to Paolo, and at 20 became court theologian at Mantua. There he met Camillo Olivo, who, as secretary to Cardinal Ercole Gonzaga, had acquired considerable knowledge of the inner workings of the Council of Trent. After a brief stay (1575) in Milan, the diocese of Cardinal Carlo Borromeo, he returned to Venice and soon rose in his Order. As Procurator-General of the Servites in 1585–8 at Rome he gained first-hand experience of the Curia. The next years at Venice he devoted to the study of, among other subjects, the physical sciences, coming into contact with ⇨ Galileo, who was then at Padua. Papal suspicion of Sarpi was manifested in the refusal to accept Venetian proposals to make him a bishop, and the gulf widened when he became theological adviser to Venice in her resistance to Papal authority. The dispute became more bitter with Paul V (1605), who excommunicated the Venetian Senate and proclaimed his interdict. This period (1605–7) was later described by Sarpi from the Venetian point of view in his *Istoria dell'Interdetto* (1624). The uneasy agreement of 1607 brought no reconciliation between himself and Rome, and an attempt on his life is alleged to have provoked the memorable pun – '*Agnosco stylum Romanae Curiae*'. After 1607 theological and political motives appear mingled (see his *Lettere ai Protestanti*, ed. M. Busnelli, 1931) in his contacts with Protestant states, whom he saw as natural allies of Venice against the Papacy and Spain.

His chief work was his intensely personal *Istoria del Concilio Tridentino* (London, 1619; ed. G. Gambarin, 1935; tr. N. Brent, *The historie of the Councel of Trent*, 1620), which depicts the Council of Trent as the culmination of a process of corruption which has led the Church away from primitive spiritual purity and produced the evils of papal authoritarianism and secular ambition. [DGR]

*Istoria dell'Interdetto, etc.*, ed. M. Busnelli and G. Gambarin (3 vols., 1940); *Scritti filosofici e teologici editi e inediti*, ed. R. Amerio (1931); *Scritti giurisdizionalistici* (post-interdict), ed. G. Gambarin (1958); *Istoria del Concilio tridentino*, intr. R. Pecchioli (2 vols., 1966).

G. Getto, *P.S.* (Florence, 1967); *Minori*, ii.

**Sarraute, Nathalie** (Russia, n.d.– ). French novelist. She studied literature and law and practised at the bar in Paris until 1939. Her first published work, *Tropismes* (1939, reprint 1957; tr. M. Jolas, *Tropisms and the Age of Suspicion*, 1964), a collection of short, detailed scenes of middle-class life and behaviour, reveals her preoccupation with psychological detail, and in the essays *L'ère du soupçon* (1956) she discusses other writers' analyses of behaviour and ways of developing them. For her the biological tropism, a reaction to a stimulus, describes the almost imperceptible movements concealed behind the social facade of gestures, actions and language, the authentic, constantly moving realm of instinctive reactions. The suspicion between a father and daughter and their reactions and attitudes to each other, *Portrait d'un inconnu* (1947, reprint 1956; tr. M. Jolas, *Portrait of a Man Unknown*, 1959), are described in fragmentary details by an anonymous narrator who reveals the same neurotic preoccupations with other people's behaviour as the nephew/narrator in *Martereau* (1954; tr. M. Jolas, 1964). In both novels the apparently unassailable pose of a bourgeois man of action contrasts with the authentic inner movements of the other characters who constantly react to words and actions, but even the objective identity of Martereau finally disintegrates, revealing an area of uncertainty behind the façade. With *Le planétarium* (1959; tr. M. Jolas, *The Planetarium*, 1961) the authentic level of human feelings contained in tropisms is frequently hidden behind social masks, as an aunt and nephew concern themselves with their bourgeois possessions and friends. *Les fruits d'or* (1963; Prix Formentor 1964;

tr. M. Jolas, *The Golden Fruits*, 1965), consisting of passages of dialogue and interior monologue, reveals, with humour, the changing attitudes to a novel which is itself never described and incidental to the reactions it arouses. [RGV]

G. Zeltner, 'N.S.', in *Mercure de France* (August 1962); J. Weightman, 'N.S.', in *Encounter* (June 1964); R. Micha, *N.S.* (Classiques du XXe siècle, 1966); Y. Belaval and M. Kranaki, *N.S.* (Paris, 1965).

**Sartre, Jean-Paul** (Paris 1905– ). French philosopher, novelist, playwright and critic. Chief exponent of atheistic existentialism in France. Brilliant academic studies at the École Normale Supérieure (1924–8) were followed by a two-year stint as research-student in Berlin and Freiburg, where Heidegger was Rektor (1932–4), and by teaching appointments. During the Fall of France (June 1940) captured and made prisoner of war. Released in April 1941, he returned to teaching in Paris and engaged in clandestine resistance to the occupying Germans, an experience which gave him the subject for his play *Morts sans sépulture* (1946; tr. K. Black, *Men without Shadows*, 1949) just as his experience of military defeat in 1940 inspired the third volume of his trilogy 'Les Chemins de la liberté', entitled *La mort dans l'âme* (1949; tr. G. Hopkins, *Iron in the Soul*, 1950). With the return of peace, he gave up teaching to devote himself entirely to writing. In 1945 he founded his own review, *Les Temps Modernes*, and subsequently he has played a vital role in the political and intellectual life of his time. His major philosophical work is contained in: *L'imagination* (1936; tr. F. Williams, *Imagination*, 1962); *Esquisse d'une théorie des émotions* (1939; tr. P. Mairet, *Sketch for a Theory of the Emotions*, 1962); *L'imaginaire* (1940); *L'être et le néant* (1943; tr. H. E. Barnes, *Being and Nothingness*, 1957); *L'existentialisme est un humanisme* (1946; tr. P. Mairet, *Existentialism and Humanism*, 1948); *Réflexions sur la question juive* (1946; tr. E. de Mauny, *Portrait of the Anti-Semite*, 1948); *Critique de la raison dialectique* (1960; Section I tr. H. E. Barnes, *The Problem of Method*, 1964). *L'Être et le néant* and *Critique* contain the essentials of Sartre's existentialist thought, the central insights of the first, seminal work having their radical subjectivity modified by the neo-Marxist sociological concepts of the second. *Critique* effects a synthesis of Sartre's political essays of the post-war period, from 'Matérialisme et révolution' (1946) (reprinted in *Situations III*, 1949) to 'Les Communistes et la paix' (1952–4) (reprinted in *Situations VI*, 1965), together with the articles on Algeria and colonialism reprinted in *Situations V*, 1964. The world of *L'être et le néant* is antithetically divided between a flickering and unstable consciousness abortively striving to attain self-coincidence and the dense solidity of external objects. In this setting, man is a derelict creature in a godless universe, an isolated and egocentric agent engaged in a constant duel to alienate the freedom of his neighbour. He moves within the endless babble of consciousness, powerless to shrug off the freedom innate in him and incapable of justifying the uses to which he puts it. All action fatally compromises his freedom and can only be pursued at the cost of his falling into the 'spirit of seriousness', into a condition, that is, in which he accepts certain values as given and transcendent realities and so betrays the central truth that man alone is the architect of his own values. The aim of *Critique* is to effect the transition from this realm of the tragic consciousness to the sphere of social co-operation. The earlier picture of human clashes viewed in terms of personal psychology is replaced by the picture of clashes resulting from economic scarcity. *Critique* shows how 'anti-man', the 'natural' denizen of a hostile world characterized by scarcity, can only survive by consenting to join a 'group' which is cemented together by 'fear, pledge and Terror'. The significance of the 'group' (which strongly resembles the apparatus of the Communist Party) lies not only in its willingness to use violence but in the connexion between its effectiveness as a group and the conspiratorial pledge embodying Terror which secures its cohesion and permanence. We move from the hero as libertarian individualist (*L'être et le néant*) to the hero as revolutionary terrorist (*Critique*). This gradual intellectual conversion illuminates the direction in which Sartre's imaginative writing moves. Hence the world of his short stories: *Le mur* (1939; tr. L. Alexander, in *Intimacy*, 1956) is a closed world in which the reflective consciousness is trapped in its own operations or morbidly alert to the threatening presence of others. This is the case with Hilbert who fires at random at his hated fellow-men before locking himself in a lavatory and finally surrendering to the judgement of society, as it is with Ibbieta captured by Falangists during the Spanish Civil War and sweating under the gaze of a 'scientific observer', or with poor deranged Pierre, in terror of hurtling statues in his sick-room. In *La nausée* (1938; tr. L. Alexander, *The Diary of Antoine Roquentin*, 1949; R. Baldick, *Nausea*, 1965), Sartre's first published novel, the dichotomy between the transparency of consciousness and the dense solidity of the external world, vividly illustrated by the hero's encounter with the chestnut tree, is transposed into social terms as a conflict between the insecure individual and the massive moral assurance of organized society, brilliantly satirized in Roquentin's visit to the Bouville art gallery. Sartre's trilogy of novels (1945–9) move away from this negative derision, harnessing political themes to fiction and showing with insight and astringency the obstacles which Mathieu, a typical bourgeois intellectual, finds standing in the way of total commitment. Caught, as he is, in a period of revolutionary change, his virtues, scruples, confusion achieve a representative status. Deeply attracted by notions of freedom and individualism, he is also drawn to the ideas of community and fraternity and fascinated by the efficacy which the Communist Party seems to offer. Hence, in *L'âge de raison* (1945; tr. E. Sutton, *The Age of Reason*, 1947) the world of politics filters in through the interstices of Mathieu's private predicament, that of finding the money to pay for an abortion, whilst in *Le sursis* (1945; tr. E. Sutton, *The Reprieve*, 1947) the hopes, fears and self-deceptions of Munich are interwoven in an ambitious technique of simultaneity, reflecting public and private concerns. With *La mort dans l'âme* (1949), the final volume of the trilogy, the nature of personal freedom is graphically related to the Fall of France within an epic framework that challenges comparison with Zola. Generally, the novels are brilliant at conveying the ambiguities of human choice, as they are at conjuring up the disquieting profusion of nature, the body's secret chemistry and the melancholy poetry of the urban scene.

Sartre's plays are in the highest degree dramas of intelligence, exciting and often subtle in the ideas they explore, animated by moral conflicts and sustained by a developed rhetorical sense. A persistent theme underlies all this drama: that of gearing personal freedom to social ends without falling into bad faith. The theme is least present in *Huis clos* (1945; tr. S. Gilbert, *In Camera*, 1946) and *Kean* (1954; tr. K. Black, 1954). The first, a brilliantly ironical treatment of bad faith, is set in the metaphorical hell of a Second Empire drawing-room and involves the moral evasion of a coward, a lesbian and an infanticide. The second, which stands in much the same relation to Sartre's output as Graham Greene's 'entertainments' do to his major novels, is an inventively handled study of insincerity in the life of a celebrated actor. The rest of Sartre's theatre responds more fully to the larger social dimension. Such is the case with his restatement of the Electra myth in *Les mouches* (1943; tr. S. Gilbert, *The Flies*, 1946) where the action is removed from the context of Greek piety and becomes a metaphysical confrontation and a fable about involvement in politics, acquiring an edge from its obvious relevance to the circumstances of the German occupation of France. *Morts sans sépulture* (1946) concentrates the predicament of existential choice within the moment of torture and relates private and public good, all within the framework of a brutal thriller. With *La putain respectueuse* (1946; tr. K. Black *The Respectable Prostitute*, 1949) the problems of bad faith and authentic choice are ironically located in a whore of the American South on whom the life of a hunted Negro depends, while *Les mains sales* (1948; tr. K. Black, *Crime passionnel*, 1949), reflecting Sartre's fascination with the tactics and apparatus of the Communist Party, shows how the meaning of personal integrity can be alienated by the historical situation in which one is placed, as Hugo, the young bourgeois convert to the Party, painfully discovers. With *Le Diable et le Bon Dieu* (1951; tr. K. Black, *Lucifer and the Lord*, 1953) we are offered Sartre's most ambitious attempt to illustrate in imaginative terms the conflict between means and ends, a conflict which bears on the nerve of his own relationship to the Communist Party and which he tries to 'distance' by setting it in the context of Reformation Germany, with a freebooting Goetz as hero. *Nekrassov* (1955; tr. S. and G. Leeson, 1956), a rather laboured farce, satirizes the theme of anti-communism in terms of the activities of an ingenious confidence trickster, but lacks the pace and technical sophistication required. In his latest play, *Les séquestrés d'Altona* (1959;

tr. S. and G. Leeson, *Loser Wins*, 1960), he returns to the obsessional universe of his earlier fiction, restating the potent theme of personal responsibility in terms of German war-guilt and atrocity and embodying it in a deranged Frantz who fabricates a private world of self-judgement in a secret upstairs room which strikingly recalls the setting of *John Gabriel Borkman*. Sartre has also written film scenarios of which the most successful are: *Les jeux sont faits* (1947; tr. L. Varèse, *The Chips Are Down*, 1948) and *L'engrenage* (1948; tr. M. Savill, *In the Mesh*, 1954). His brilliantly partial, often wilful but illuminating criticism of literature and art ranges from striking essays on Dos Passos, Faulkner, Mauriac, Giraudoux and Camus (in *Situations I*) to a highly provocative and suggestive essay on 'Qu'est-ce que la littérature', reprinted in *Situations III* (tr. B. Frechtman, *What is Literature?*, 1950), a dazzling though perverse study of *Baudelaire*; 1947, tr. M. Turnell, 1949), stimulating and idiosyncratic analyses of the painting of Tintoretto, Giacometti and André Masson (in *Situations IV*, 1964), and an ambitious and sometimes pretentious account of the art of Jean Genet: *Saint Genet; comédien et martyr* (1952; tr. B. Frechtman, *Saint Genet*, 1964). His autobiographical fragment, *Les mots* (1964; tr. I. Cléphane, *Words*, 1964), is a small masterpiece of ironic wit and wry disenchantment. Sartre declined the Nobel Prize for Literature in 1964. He has translated and adapted Euripides: *Les Troyennes* (1965). [SBJ]

*Théâtre complet illustré* (1962).

I. Murdoch, *S.: Romantic Rationalist* (1953); F. Jeanson, *S. par lui-même* (1954); P. Thody, *S.: a Literary and Political Study* (1960); R. Champigny, *Stages on S.'s Way* (Bloomington, Ind., 1959); F. Jameson, *S., the Origins of a Style* (Yale Univ., 1961).

**Sastre, Alfonso** (Madrid 1926– ). Spanish dramatist. Founder of the Grupo de Teatro Realista. He first made his mark with *Escuadra hacia la muerte* (1953), which was forbidden by the censorship for its anti-militarism. A committed writer and a dissentient, his plays are nonetheless rich in human and dramatic interest. Among the most remarkable are *La mordaza* (1954), *Muerte en el barrio* (1955), *El cuervo* (1957), *La sangre de Dios* (1955), *La cornada* (1960) and *En la red* (1961) about the underground independence movement in Algeria. Owing to their strong social and revolutionary content, they are seldom performed in Spain. [JLC]

*Teatro* (BA, 1960).

**'Satire Ménippée, La'** (1594). A political pamphlet written by a group of moderates who, though not all Protestants, opposed the Ligue and supported Henri IV. The contributors were Leroy, Jacques Gillot, Nicolas ⇨ Rapin, Jean Passerat, Pierre Pithou and Florent Chrestien. The full title of the work is *Satyre Ménippée de la vertu du Catholicon d'Espagne et de la tenue des Estats de Paris* ('Ménippée' is a reference to a Greek philosopher of the 3rd century B.C., who wrote satires which are lost). The pamphlet, a mixture of prose and verse, consists mostly of a parody of the assembly of the Estates General in 1593. The tone is one of vigorous mockery, except in the speech attributed to D'Aubray, representing the Third Estate, which is a serious and moving attack on the Ligue. The work gained immediate and wide popularity. [GJ]

**Sava, Saint.** ⇨ Serbian Medieval Literature.

**Savonarola, Girolamo** (Ferrara 1452–Florence 1498). Italian religious reformer. In 1475 he abandoned his home and became a Dominican. Preaching, first at Ferrara and later at Florence, with uncompromising moral rigour, his sincerity and force of character gave him a growing authority in the city; when Piero de' Medici fled in 1494, he became the chief figure in the republic, and from the monastery of S. Marco assumed a more pronounced political role, composing at this time his republican *Trattato circa il reggimento e governo di Firenze*. He proclaimed Christ ruler of Florence and denounced the evils of the Church, coming into conflict with the notorious Alexander VI, who excommunicated him. Finally the populace turned against him and he was arrested, tried, and burnt in front of the Palazzo Vecchio.

The interest of his writings is chiefly historical and psychological. In his *Laudi* he sometimes takes up the rhythm of the carnival song and he expresses in it his passionate religious yearnings. The sermons, many based on versions taken down by his hearers, develop from a fairly traditional form to a much more dramatic, personal style in which he moves directly from his text to discuss the issues of his time in fervent, often prophetic, language. [DGR]

*Opere*, ed. R. Ridolfi and others (1955ff.); *Poesie*, ed. V. Piccoli (1926); *Le lettere*, ed. R. Ridolfi (1933).

M. Ferrara, *S.* (Florence, 1952); R. Ridolfi, *The Life of G.S.*, tr. C. Grayson (1959); *Minori*, i.

**'Savvina Kniga.'** ⇨ Old Bulgarian Literature.

**Saxo Grammaticus** (*c.* 1150–*c.* 1206). Danish-born Latin chronicler. A cleric of whose life very little is known, he is the author of *Gesta Danorum* or *Historia danica* (ed. A. Holder, Strassburg, 1886; tr. O. Elton, *The First Nine Books of the Danish History of Saxo Grammaticus*, 1894). The earlier part, based on old Danish poems and Norwegian-⇨ Icelandic sagas, is mostly mythological. It includes legends of Balder, Toko the archer (the prototype of William Tell), Amleth (Shakespeare's Hamlet), and other mythical gods and heroes. The book becomes less legendary and more historical as it goes on. His Latin style is modelled on authors of the Silver Age, particularly Martiamus Capella. [FB]

**Sayanov, Vissarion** (1903– ). Russian poet. Born in Eastern Siberia, the son of a political exile. After attending Leningrad University (1922–5) he served in the Red Army; since 1927 he has been a professional writer and war-correspondent. A good deal of his poetry treats Communist and revolutionary themes with a spirit of enthusiastic participation. His best work, dating from the early thirties, is in his book *Zolotaya Olyokma* which describes the remote goldfields of Eastern Siberia; the poem from which the book takes its title is a tour-de-force, magically evoking an atmosphere and an age. His poems are not truly lyrical, tending to be descriptions or anecdotes; at its best his style has laconic vigour, simplicity and effective rhythm. He has also written prose works. [RM-G]

*Izbrannyye sochineniya* (2 vols., 1955); Gulland, *SRV*; Lugovskoy, *RSP*.

**Scaldic Poetry.** The composition of scaldic poetry was chiefly practised in early Norway and Iceland, although it was also known and appreciated to some extent in Sweden and Denmark as well as in the Norse colonies in the Faroes and the British Isles. Poems, long or short, attributed to more than 250 named poets, are extant, as well as a quantity of anonymous verse. This kind of poetry was in existence in the 9th century but we know nothing for certain of its origins. Its vogue lived on in Iceland but elsewhere it was over by the end of the 13th century.

Scaldic poems may be divided into two main sorts. There is first the long set poem, often a eulogy of a lord, alive or dead, with special stress on the virtues of warlike prowess and generosity, the former often illustrated by reference to specific events. (It is this which gives the poems their value as historical sources.) It was counted a more distinguished form when the stanzas were broken at intervals by a refrain (the poem was then called a *drápa*) than when they were not (when it was called a *flokkr*). Second, there is the occasional poem, usually a single stanza, sometimes two or three on one theme. The purpose of such verse is usually to make a statement of fact or feeling in connexion with particular circumstances. Narrative in them is momentary and incidental, and the poet does not usually wish to be didactic or to express general truths. It will be readily understood why scaldic verse comes to us embedded in a prose account of some kind.

The simpler eddaic metres are sometimes used, but in general metre, diction and imagery are complex. This is perhaps not least due to the fostering of scaldic poetry by aristocratic circles interested in sophisticated – even esoteric – learning of a mythological kind. The chief and typical scaldic form is called *dróttkvætt*, of which the example below will serve as illustration. Scaldic diction is difficult and distinctive, partly because the poets use many single words that are peculiar to poetry, and partly because they make the figure known as the *kenning* an essential part of their style. A *kenning* at its simplest consists of a 'base-word', which on its own will be remote or obscure in the context, and a 'definer'. Taken together the two will at once present an image and give a precise single sense. Common examples from the conventional stock are 'god of the sword' for warrior, 'fire of the sea' for gold. Such *kennings*, many of them with allusions to myths or legendary stories, can be richly extended and varied, and in the best examples there is a striking counterplay between the intellectual sense and the pictorial image.

Some idea of a typical *dróttkvætt* stanza and scaldic style will be given by the following stanza by Egill Skalla-Grímsson, probably composed about the middle of the 10th century. The regular alliterating letters and the syllables with half- and full-rhyme are italicized.

> Nú hefr *þ*rym-R*ǫgn*ir *þegn*a
> *þ*rótth*arð*r, en mik v*arð*ak
> *víti*, *v*árrar sv*eit*ar
> *v*íg*eld*s tíu f*elld*a,
> *þ*vít *sár*laxa *Sýr*ar,
> *send*r ór minni h*end*i,
> d*igr* fló *b*eint meðal *bjúg*ra
> *bifþ*orn Ketils r*if*ja.

Read literally this says: 'Now the endurance-hard god of the din of the battle-fire has felled ten men of our band, but I kept myself from blame, for the stout shuddering thorn of the goddess of wound-salmon, sent from my hand, flew straight between the curved ribs of Ketill.' Here the 'battle-fire' is the sword, whose din is battle, whose god is the fighter; 'wound-salmon' are swords, whose goddess is the valkyrie, and the valkyrie's 'shuddering thorn' is a spear. [PGF]

*Den norsk-islandske Skjaldedigtning*, ed. Finnur Jónsson (4 vols., Copenhagen, 1912–15); L. M. Hollander, *A Bibliography of Skaldic Studies* (Copenhagen, 1958); *The Skalds* (American-Scandinavian Foundation, 1945).

**Scaliger, Julius Caesar** (Castle La Rocca, Lake Garda 1484–Agen 1558). Humanist scholar. He claimed to belong to the famous Veronese family of La Scala and to have been a soldier and a Franciscan friar before settling as a physician at Agen (France). He was a violent controversialist with ⇨ Erasmus and others in Latin prose, a grammarian, a philosopher, and the author of a vast quantity of Latin verse. Through his commentaries on classical writers (*Poetices libri VII*, 1561) Aristotle's theory of the dramatic 'unities' was transmitted to French playwrights of the 17th century.

His son, **Joseph Justus Scaliger** (Agen 1540–Leyden 1609), was the greatest classical scholar of his time. He produced critical editions of Catullus, Tibullus, Propertius, and Manilius, and, by the publication of his *De emendatione temporum* (1583), revolutionized European attempts at chronology. He also wrote an autobiography (ed. G. W. Robinson, Cambridge, Mass., 1927). [FB]

M. de B de Laffore, *Jules César de Lescale* (Agen, 1960); J. Bernays, *J.S.* (Berlin, 1855); J. E. Sandys, *History of Classical Scholarship* (3 vols., 1903–8); V. Hall, *Life of J.C.S.* (Philadelphia, 1950); Weinberg, *HLC*.

**Scapigliatura, La.** A group of Italian writers and artists living in Milan between 1860 and 1880, described by Carducci as the third and last generation of romantics, reacting against bourgeois traditions in both art and social customs and, in general, seeking a greater degree of originality, subjectivity and immediacy in their work. The name derives from the novel of one of them – *La Scapigliatura e il 6 febbraio* (1862) by Cletto Arrighi (anagram of Carlo Righetti). Principal figures in the group were the acknowledged leader G. Rovani, A. ⇨ Boito, E. Praga, and C. Dossi. The only truly common characteristic was their disorderly way of life, rather than any coherent artistic programme. Their importance lies perhaps in the impulse given by them to later realist writers such as Verga. [RHC]

E. and C. Colombo, *Racconti della S.* (1942); G. Contini, *Racconti della S. piemontese* (1953); *Via del vivaio. Narratori della S.* (1960); *Poeti della S.*, ed. M. Petrucciani, N. Bonifazi (1962); *Lirici della S.*, ed. G. Finzi (1964).

P. Madini, *La s. milanese* (Milan, 1929); P. Nardi, *S. da G. Rovani a C. Dossi* (Bologna, 1924); W. Binni, *La poetica del decadentismo italiano* (Florence, 1949); E. Gennarini, *La s. milanese* (Naples, 1961).

**Scarron, Paul** (Paris 1610–Paris 1660). French poet and wit. Perhaps the most gifted of the pre-classical writers. His life was a torment, owing to a disease which deformed and later paralysed him. Yet he earned the esteem of great ladies, first Marie de Hautefort, then Françoise d'Aubigné, whom he married and who was to become Mme de Maintenon. He invented a style of writing known as the burlesque, which was a precursor of the critical attitude, in its challenge to conventional respect for literary forms. His parody of the *Aeneid*, *Virgile Travesti*, appeared in 7 books from 1648 to 1658. Even more versatile was his *Roman comique* (2 vols., 1651–7; ed. H. Bénac, 1951), a vigorous picaresque story of strolling players. He published short stories, two of which are important sources for Molière, and 8 comedies, the best known being *Jodelet, ou le maître valet* (1645), written for the contemporary comedian, and *Don Japhet d'Arménie* (1647). These are, in more than one sense, the nearest thing to Molière. A strong personality comes through them, which enabled him to maintain through years of pain the reputation of a wit. [WGM]

*TFM* (poetry).

P. Morillot, *S.* (Paris, 1888); E. H. Chardon, *P.S.* (Paris, 1903); E. Magne, *P.S.* (Paris, 1924).

**Scève, Maurice** (Lyons 1501?–Lyons 1564?). French poet. He may have studied in Italy as well as in Avignon, where he discovered what he believed to be the tomb of Petrarch's Laura. Already the acknowledged leader of the Lyons poets, in 1544 he published his masterpeice, *Delie, Object de plus haulte vertu*, a collection of 499 decasyllabic dizains, in groups separated by emblems (ed. I. D. McFarlane, 1966). The total number of stanzas and the number in each group probably have symbolic significance. There has been much discussion as to whether Delie is a real woman or whether the name is an anagram of 'L'Idée' – or both; the name also refers to the 'Delian' goddess Artemis-Selene-Hecate – the chaste huntress, the bright and fickle moon, the dark goddess of the underworld. The poem contains neologisms and syntactical boldness; some 'scientific' images introducing technical vocabulary; many Biblical and mythological allusions; a complex system of psychological categories; complicated thought, poetic density and ambiguity. But in this tight, argumentative language, and with the help of the Petrarchan and Platonic conventions, Scève explores some of the essential problems and conflicts of love – the paradoxical oneness and separateness of lovers; in the absence of the loved one, the pain that memory causes, which can only be eased by memory; the simultaneous presence of physical desire and of a feeling almost of awe and worship.

He also wrote an eclogue, *La Saulsaye* (1547), and a long didactic poem, *Microcosme* (1563), a history of mankind starting with Adam and Eve. [GJ]

*Œuvres poétiques complètes*, ed. B. Guégan (1927) *M.S., une étude ...*, ed. J.-P. Attal (1963) (with selections); Mourgues, *MBPP*.

V. L. Saulnier, *Le Prince de la renaissance, M.S.* (2 vols., Paris, 1948); P. Boutang, *Commentaires ...* (Paris, 1953); J.-P. Attal, *M.S.* (Paris, 1963).

**Schack, Hans Egede** (Sengeløse 1820–Schlangenbad 1859). Danish novelist. Primarily a politician and civil servant, his one novel, *Phantasterne* (1857), is a remarkable book about romantic day-dreams in conflict with sober acceptance of reality. His incomplete novel, *Sandhed med Modification*, was first published in 1954. [ELB]

**Schade, Jens August** (Skive 1903– ). Danish poet. Usually inspired by erotic experience, with cosmic insights, e.g. *Den Levende Violin* (1926). His verse satire, *Sjov i Danmark* (1928), is his most popular work. [ELB]

*Udvalgte Digte* (1962).

**Schaper, Edzard** (Ostrowo/Posen 1908– ). German novelist. He lived for many years in Estonia, fleeing to Finland (1940), and settled in Switzerland. His often historical novels are rooted in the Baltic and in his own Christian faith; his main themes are the suffering of the political prisoner, man's struggle for freedom against terror, and his need for a religiously based stoicism. His main novels are: *Der letzte Gast* (1927), *Die Insel Tütarsaar* (1934), *Die sterbende Kirche* (1935), *Der Henker* (1940), *Der letzte Advent* (1948), *Die Freiheit des Gefangenen* (1950), *Die Macht der Ohnmächtigen* (1951), *Der Gouverneur* (1954), *Die letzte Welt* (1956), *Attentat auf den Mächtigen* (1957) and *Das Tier* (1958; tr. N. Denny, *The Dancing Bear*, 1960). *Bürger in Zeit und Ewigkeit* (1956) is an autobiography. [PB]

*Gesammelte Erzählungen* (1965).

*ML*, XXXVIII (1957); W. Grenzmann, in *Dichtung und Glaube* (Frankfurt a.M., 1964).

**Scheffel, Joseph Viktor von** (Karlsruhe 1826–Karlsruhe 1886). German poet and novelist. He studied law, became a civil servant, then went to Rome to try painting; later he travelled in Germany, Italy and France. His cheerfulness hides a melancholy character, the pains of unhappy love, and an unsuccessful marriage (1864–5). *Der Trompeter von Säkkingen* (1854; tr. F. Brünnow, *The Trumpeter of Säkkingen*, 1877) is a folksy, medievalizing verse epic with lyrical interludes. His still famous 10th-century novel, *Ekkehard* (1855; tr. H. Easson, Everyman, 1906), resulting from research for an intended university career, combines *Entwicklungsroman* elements with vast historical knowledge, personal confession, and feeling for the South German countryside. His Novellen, *Hugideo* (1857; publ. 1883) and *Juniperus* (1866), suffer from antiquarianism, as does the lyrical cycle *Frau Aventiure* (1863).

The once immensely popular *Lieder* of *Gaudeamus* (1868; tr. C. G. Leland, 1872) glorify student conviviality and satirize scholarship. The *Bergpsalmen* (1870; tr. F. Brünnow, *Mountain Psalms*, 1882) strike a heavy note. [LL]

*Werke*, crit. ed. F. Panzer (1917ff.).

J. Proelss, *S.s Leben und Dichten* (Berlin, 1887); Koch, *IW*.

**Schehadé, Georges** (Alexandria 1910– ). French dramatist. His Lebanese origin is sometimes invoked to account for the fairy-tale atmosphere of his plays in which plot and psychological motivation have no importance. From his first play, *Monsieur Bob'le* (1951), he ushers in a theatre bathed in poetry in which reality and fantasy progressively merge; a world of childhood touched with dreams and innocence. A kind of exotic displacement of the real occurs in plays like: *La soirée des proverbes* (1954), in which a commonplace inn is given a poetic dimension; *Le voyage* (1961; tr. R. Baldick, 1963), where the characters respond to imaginary journeys; or *Les violettes* (1960), where the theme of the destruction of the world by scientific weapons undergoes a poetic metamorphosis. Each play is a puzzle in which puppet-like characters move through a forest of deceiving signs, like the young conscript in *Histoire de Vasco* (1956) who encounters soldiers clumsily disguised as girls or trees, towards a truth they never quite attain. He has also written *L'émigré de Brisbane* (1965).

Guicharnaud, *MFT*; Corvin, *TNF*; Serreau, *HNT*.

**Scheidt, Kaspar** (*c.* 1520–Worms 1565). German satirist. His only major work was the German version of Friedrich Dedekind's Latin satire *Grobianus. De morum simplicitate* (1549). St Grobianus ('grobe' = 'rude', 'vulgar'), the patron saint of rude and vulgar persons, had appeared first in ⇨ Brant's *Narrenschiff* (1494), and Dedekind's book takes up the idea, parodying the fashionable codes of etiquette of the late Middle Ages to produce a manual of bad behaviour. Scheidt's version, *Grobianus. Von groben sitten und unhöfflichen geberden* (1551; ed. G. Milchsack, 1882), is considerably longer than the original and gives enthusiastic and detailed instruction on how vulgar people eat, sneeze, cough, laugh, pick their teeth, etc., ostensibly in the hope that the reader will refrain from emulating them. The work went through many translations and adaptations and initiated the 16th-century vogue of 'vulgarity literature'. [WAC]

**Schelling, Friedrich Wilhelm Joseph von** (Leoberg 1775–Ragaz 1854). German Romantic philosopher. Building on the solipsist philosophy of ⇨ Fichte, which claimed to understand the meaning of life through the comprehension, and the uninhibited expansion, of the individual mind, and which saw nature as the expression of the human mind in absolute, he evolved a doctrine of identities or correspondences – the identity of the Real and the Ideal, of Being and Thought. This so-called *Naturphilosophie*, which has a certain kinship with pantheism, is propounded in *System des transzendentalen Idealismus* (1800), *Ideen zu einer Philosophie der Natur* (1801) and other works. His views were eagerly accepted by the early German Romantics – Novalis, the brothers Schlegel, Tieck – with whom he associated in Jena, as the expression in philosophical terms of their own aesthetic doctrines. His influence can also be traced in later Romantic writers such as E. T. A. Hoffmann. [RT]

*Werke*, ed. M. Schröter (1964).

Karl Jaspers, *S.* (Munich, 1955); E. Benz, *S.* (Zürich, 1955); N. Hartmann, *Die Philosophie des deutschen Idealismus* (Berlin/Leipzig, 1923, 1929); Wellek, *HMC*.

**Schendel, Arthur François Emile van** (Java 1874–Amsterdam 1946). Dutch novelist. His first important novels *Een Zwerver verliefd* (1904) and its sequel, *Een Zwerver verwaald* (1907), move in the evasive world of a dreamer's longing. He moved to Italy in 1921 and his Italian stories are less insubstantial (*Angiolino en de lente*, 1923; tr. W. C. Niewenhuis in Greshoff, *Harvest of the Lowlands*, 1945). With *Het Fregatschip Johanna Maria* (1930; tr. B. W. Downs, *The Johanna Maria*, 1935), the first of the Holland novels (in a 19th-century setting), characters and scene are sharply defined. Here, and in *De Waterman* (1933; tr. N. C. Clegg, 1963) and *Een Hollandsch drama* (1935; tr. M. S. Stephens, *The House in Haarlem*, 1940), the noblest aspirations of the tragic heroes fail to protect them from a Calvinistically conceived predestination. Atmosphere is evoked with true poetic mastery. Romantic elements appear again in *De wereld een dansfeest* (1938), *De Zeven tuinen* (1939), *Mijnheer Oberon en* *mevrouw* (1940); and *De Grauwe vogels* (1937; tr. M. S. Stephens, *Grey Birds*, 1939). [PK]

F. W. H. van Heerikhuizen, *Het Werk van A.v.S.* (Amsterdam, 1961).

**Scherfig, Hans** (Copenhagen 1905– ). Danish novelist. Originally a painter. His first novel, *Den døde Mand* (1937), like most of his others – among which the best are *Den forsvundne Fuldmægtig* (1938), *Det forsømte Foraar* (1940) and *Idealister* (1945; tr. N. Walford, *The 'Idealists'*, 1949) – is a witty and acid social satire disguised as a detective story. *Frydenholm*, a novel of the German occupation of Denmark, was published in 1962. [ELB]

**Schickele, René** (Oberehnheim, Alsace 1885–Sanary, Riviera 1940). German poet, novelist and dramatist. The son of a German father and a French mother, he championed ideas of a cultural *rapprochement*, indeed of a European community. He edited the pacifist periodical *Die weissen Blätter* (1913–20; 1915–18 in Switzerland). His best-known poems are in *Weiss und Rot* (1911) and *Die Leibwache* (1914), which won him a reputation as an Expressionist. Of his many novels and stories, the most substantial is the traditionally realistic trilogy set in Alsace, *Das Erbe am Rhein* (*Maria Capponi*, 1925; tr. H. Waller, 1928; *Blick auf die Vogesen*, 1927; tr. H. Waller, *Heart of Alsace*, 1929; and *Der Wolf in der Hürde*, 1931). His most successful drama was *Hans im Schnakenloch* (1916). His critical work included *Liebe und Ärgernis des D. H. Lawrence* (1935). [PB]

*Werke*, ed. H. Kesten (3 vols., 1960–61).
P. K. Ackermann, *R.S. a Bibliography* (Cambridge, Mass., 1956).

**Schiller, Friedrich** (Marbach a. Neckar 1759–Weimar 1805). German dramatist and poet. The fundamental theme of his dramatic, philosophical and aesthetic writings is his passionate concern with freedom. He began as a belated member of *Sturm und Drang*, with dramas of social and political revolt: *Die Räuber* (1781), with its unconditional Rousseauistic rejection of a corrupt and corrupting society; *Die Verschwörung des Fiesko zu Genua* (1783), a drama of republican revolt against political tyranny; *Kabale und Liebe* (1784), a sentimental middle-class tragedy which fearlessly pillories the corruption of the petty German courts and their flagrant disregard for elementary human values. With the publication of *Don Carlos* (1787), the drama of revolt gives place to historical tragedy in the grand manner, in iambic pentameters – instead of prose – and the call to political revolt is muted in the rhetorical plea which Marquis Posa addresses to Philip II of Spain to give his subjects liberty of conscience. The theme of personal and political freedom still bulks large in the classical works – in his last play, *Wilhelm Tell* (1804), it again becomes dominant – but the lesson of the French Revolution was not lost on the erstwhile revolutionary and the freedom with which the mature Schiller is primarily concerned is the ideal freedom of the human spirit to overcome physical constraint: both *Maria Stuart* (1800) and Joan of Arc in *Die Jungfrau von Orleans* (1801) assert their moral freedom and rise superior to the compulsion to which they are subjected. The *Wallenstein* trilogy (1798–9) – his greatest work in its almost complete lack of sentimentality and its avoidance both of the excesses of the early plays and of the rather forced philosophy of the later ones – and the neo-classical *Die Braut von Messina* (1803) explore the problem of human freedom from the point of view of fate: the inner, Shakespearean fate of character in *Wallenstein*; externalized, Sophoclean fate in the *Braut*.

Although Schiller is the foremost dramatist of German Classicism and shared Goethe's enthusiasm for the post-Winckelmann idealized conception of classical Greece, he is also akin to the baroque in his acute sense of the theatre, his predilection for antitheses, elaborate sets and operatic effects and his love of the 'mighty line'. The belief in the moral structure of the world which is fundamental to everything which Schiller wrote has more affinities with the Christianity of an earlier age than with the paganism of classical Weimar, and his suffering heroines who achieve their apotheosis by freely willing the inevitable and thereby rising superior to it are the secularized sisters of the Christian martyrs of ⇨ Gryphius. Essentially, however, Schiller is a child of the Enlightenment both in his love of liberty and in his belief in the perfectability of man and man's capacity for ethical self-determination. These views gained natural expression both in his writings on aesthetics, where beauty is defined as 'freedom in appearance', and in his philosophical attempts to transcend the

Kantian view of morality as the victory of the moral will over recalcitrant inclination. In the essay *Über Anmut und Würde* (1793) he argues that man is intended not merely to perform individual moral acts but to be a moral being, and postulates a '*schöne Seele*' or 'beautiful soul' in whom duty and inclination are in complete harmony – a concept given dramatic embodiment in Max and Thekla in *Wallenstein* and in Joan in the early acts of *Die Jungfrau*; where there is a Kantian conflict the result is not moral beauty, but moral greatness or 'sublimity' (the later Joan, Maria Stuart).

He was essentially a reflective writer whose emotions were aroused by ideas rather than by experiences and he produced little genuine lyric poetry. His reputation as a poet rests primarily on his powerful hymns to the ideal human values, brotherhood, hope, etc. (his 'An die Freude' provided the text for the last movement of Beethoven's Ninth Symphony), a number of philosophical poems ('Die Götter Griechenlands', 'Die Künstler', etc.) and numerous ballads ('Die Bürgschaft', 'Der Taucher', etc.), which everywhere reveal the hand of the dramatist.

The historical interests evident in his plays also bore fruit in his history of the revolt of the Netherlands (1788) and of the Thirty Years' War (1791–3), and from 1789 he held the chair of history at Jena, a post which helped him to develop a close and mutually beneficial relationship with Goethe in neighbouring Weimar (cf. *Briefwechsel*, ed. Goethe, 1824). His plays hold their own on the modern German stage not merely because of the filial piety with which they are regarded, but also by virtue of their sheer dramatic power. In its sententiousness and sentimentality much of his work is dated, but none the less it embodies some of the noblest aspirations of mankind. [WAC]

*Nationalausgabe* (43 vols., 1943– ); *Complete Works*, tr. S. T. Coleridge *et al.* (Philadelphia, 1870); F. Unger, *F.S. An Anthology for Our Time* (N.Y., 1959).

K. Berger, *S.* (Munich, 1912); H. B. Garland, *S.* (1949); W. Witte, *S.* (1949); E. L. Stahl, *S.'s Dramas. Theory and Practice* (1954); T. Mann, *Versuch über S.* (Frankfurt/Berlin, 1955); W. F. Mainland, *S. and the Changing Past* (1957); B. v. Wiese, *S.* (1959); G. Storz, *Der Dichter F.S.* (Stuttgart, 1963).

**Schlegel, August Wilhelm von** (Hanover 1767–Bonn 1845). German poet, critic and scholar. The family to which he and his brother Friedrich belonged was rich in literary talents (their father was Johann Adolf Schlegel; Johann Elias Schlegel was an uncle). In 1798 he became professor in Jena, where, with his brother, ➪ Novalis and ➪ Tieck, he laid the critical foundations of Romanticism. 1804–17 he travelled in the entourage of Mme de ➪ Staël, whose *De l'Allemagne* (1810) rests on his information and advice. Following the lead given by his brother, he took up the study of Oriental languages, becoming in 1818, in Bonn, the first professor of Indology in Germany.

He wrote dramas in the Classical style and a great deal of verse, but he was not an original creative mind. But his contributions to the German Romantic movement as a critic (e.g. *Vorlesungen über dramatische Kunst und Literatur*, 1809) and his translations of the *Bhagavadgita* (1823), the dramas of Calderón, and the poetry of Petrarch and Dante are of lasting importance. Above all, however, his memory lives in his monumental translation (with Tieck) of Shakespeare's dramas (1797–1810), a translation which still holds pride of place in German stage productions today.

His wife Caroline, one of the brilliant women in the Romantic circle, later married the philosopher Schelling. [RT]

A. Besenbeck, *Kunstanschauung und Kunstlehre A.W.S.s* (Berlin, 1930); Wellek, *HMC.*

**Schlegel, Johann Elias** (Meissen 1718–Soröe 1749). German dramatist. Educated at Schulpforta, he studied law and philosophy at Leipzig, and became secretary to the Saxon envoy in Copenhagen in 1743, and professor at the Soröe Academy in 1748. His theoretical *Die Komödie in Versen* (1740), *Vergleichung Shakespeares und Andreas Gryphs* (1741), *Abhandlung von der Nachahmung* (1742–5) and *Gedanken zur Aufnahme des dänischen Theaters* (1747) show his break with his teacher ➪ Gottsched, whom he also attacked with ➪ Gellert in the periodical *Bremer Beiträge*: he urges dramatists to please rather than instruct, demands national and middle-class subjects, and praises Shakespeare. Nevertheless his own tragedies, *Hekuba* (1736, rev. as *Trojanerinnen*, 1742–3), *Geschwister in Taurien* (1739, rev. as *Orest*, 1739–42), *Dido* (1739), *Hermann* (1740–1), and *Canut* (1746), remain largely under French classical influence. His comedies, *Der geschäftige Müssiggänger* (1741), *Der Triumph der guten Frauen* (1746), and *Die* *stumme Schönheit* (1747), combine French types and intrigues with well-observed characters and graceful dialogue. [LL]

*Ausgewählte Werke*, ed. W. Schubert (1963).

P. Wolf, *Die Dramen J.E.S.s* (Zürich, 1964); E. M. Wilkinson, *J.E.S., a German Pioneer in Aesthetics* (1945); Heitner, *GTE*; Wellek, *HMC*.

**Schlegel, Karl Wilhelm Friedrich von** (Hanover 1772–Dresden 1829). German poet and thinker. Younger brother of August Wilhelm ⇨ Schlegel and the most penetrating mind among the founders of the Romantic movement in Germany. In 1802 he went to Paris, then the centre of Oriental studies in Europe, to study Sanskrit, and introduced the language to Germany. This enthusiasm for the East, however, was short-lived; in 1808, the watershed of his career, he became converted to Catholicism, gave up his Oriental work and lived a private, if unsettled existence in Vienna, Frankfurt and elsewhere, studying world literature and cultural history.

His earliest work to attract attention was *Lucinde* (1799), a Romantic novel of free love which caused considerable scandal. His contribution to Romantic drama was *Alarcos* (1802), a Spanish *Ritterdrama* in which, following his definition of Romantic poetry (⇨ *Athenaeum*), he combined classical and Romantic elements.

It is, however, in his philosophical and aesthetic writings that his great importance lies. Idealist and impulsive by temperament, he built on the philosophy of ⇨ Fichte, declaring the primacy of the individual subjective mind in the search for knowledge, and the ultimate unity of art, philosophy and religion. He thus sought a justification of man in the cultural achievements of the past: at first he found this justification in classical antiquity (*Geschichte der Poesie der Griechen und Römer*, 1798), later in the East (*Über die Sprache und Weisheit der Indier*, 1808). The inadequacies of these cultural ideals led to his self-absorption in religion and to his conversion to Catholicism, in which he found the totality of meaning and experience that he desired. His later works, such as *Geschichte der alten und neuen Literatur* (1815) and *Philosophie der Geschichte* (1829), are to be viewed within this framework.

His wife Dorothea (1770–1839), herself a writer, was the daughter of the rationalist philosopher Moses Mendelssohn. [RT]

*Werke*, ed. E. Behler (Munich, 1958f.).

K. Horst, *Ich und Gnade* (Freiburg, 1951); L. Wirz, *F.S.s philosophische Entwicklung* (Bonn, 1939); Strich, *DKR*; Wellek, *HMC*.

**Schnabel, Johann Gottfried** (Sandersdorf, Bitterfeld 1692–Stolberg 1752). German novelist. A barber-surgeon in the army of Prince Eugen, of whom he wrote a biography (1736), and subsequently Court Physician to the Duke of Stolberg. His *Wunderliche Fata einiger See-Fahrer, absonderlich Alberti Julii* (4 parts, 1731–43) is the most important of the many German imitations of *Robinson Crusoe*. Better known as *Insel Felsenburg* – a title it owes to ⇨ Tieck – it combines an obvious utopian element, in its vision of an ideal society and its condemnation of contemporary social and political tendencies, with a distinctly sentimental outlook reminiscent of Richardson. The gallant novel, *Der im Irrgarten der Liebe herumtaumelnde Cavalier* (1738), takes up a theme of the *Insel Felsenburg* – the destructive nature of the sexual urge when not disciplined by marriage. [WAC]

*Die Insel Felsenburg*, ed H. Ullrich, DLD, 108–20 (1902); DLE (Aufklärung).

F. Brüggemann, *Utopie und Robinsonade* (Weimar, 1914).

**Schnack, Anton** (Rieneck, Franconia 1892– ). German poet. Brother of the novelist Friedrich Schnack (1888– ), and member of the German Academy. His experiences in the First World War inspired the vivid and deeply felt poetry of *Tier rang gewaltig mit Tier* (1920). Later volumes (e.g. *Der Annoncenleser*, 1948; *Jene Dame, welche*... also of stories and prose-miniatures (e.g. *Die bunte Hauspostille*, 1938; new edn 1946 as *Die Angel des Robinson*), are in a more lightly lyrical romantic vein. [PB]

Bridgwater, *TCGV*; Hamburger and Middleton, *MGP*.

**Schnitzler, Arthur** (Vienna 1862–Vienna 1931). Austrian dramatist and novelist (and practising Viennese doctor). His brilliant dramatic sketches, *Anatol* (1893), typified a decadent era in the figure of the sophisticated philanderer, helplessly entangled in successive love affairs, witty in his melancholy disillusion, fascinated by his erotic addiction. This recurrent Casanova theme (cf. *Casanovas Heimfahrt*, 1918; tr. E. and C. Paul, *Casanova's Homecoming*, 1954 *Casanova in Spa*, 1919) is seen less as a traditional adventure than as a neurotic compulsion (cf. his medical thesis on hypnotic treatments, his knowledge of Freud, and use of the 'subconscious' especially in novels, *Der Weg ins Freie*, 1908; tr. anon., *The Road to the Open*, 1923). The mood of decadence is effectively dramatized in *Der grüne Kakadu* (1899), where aristocrats on the eve of the French Revolution unknowingly court their doom in their perverse pleasures, and underlies other fashionable 'social problems' of class (*Das Vermächtnis*, 1897), of marriage and feminine freedom (*Zwischenspiel*, 1904), and of anti-Semitism (*Professor Bernhardi*, 1912; tr. H. Landstone, 1927). But the typical 'problem' is sex, the common denominator of all classes and people, as shown in *Reigen* (1900; tr. F. and J. Marcus, *Merry-go-round*, 1953; *La Ronde* in *The Modern Theatre*, II, N.Y., 1955; filmed) – a repetition of the same erotic 'moment' with a change now of the male, now of the female partner, until the first and the last in the social scale are coupled in this casual yet inescapable bond. Like a parody of the medieval dance of death, sex is now the ultimate reality which makes the conventional appearances of life seem unreal, a grotesque play-acting, the 'comedy of our souls' (as ⇨ Hofmannsthal wrote in his preface to *Anatol*), where even agonies are no more than dramatic episodes. Are not the dream fulfilments of the subconscious as real as the accidents of actual experience? (cf. *Paracelsus*, 1897). What divides playing at from being in love? How can love be proved, or honour, or anything? It can be a matter of life and death, as appears in two of his best works, the drama *Liebelei* (1895; tr. P. M. Shand, *Playing with Love*, 1914; *Light o' Love* in *Contemporary Drama*, ed. Watson, N.Y., 1932), and the story *Leutnant Gustl* (1901), where such episodes end in catastrophe – though they lack the substance of tragedy. [PB/AKT]

*Die dramatischen Werke* (3 vols., Frankfurt a.M., 1962); *Die erzählenden Schriften* (2 vols., Frankfurt a.M., 1961); *Briefwechsel mit Brandes* (1956).

H. W. Reichert and H. Salinger, *Studies in A.S.* (Chapel Hill, 1963); G. Baumann, *A.S.* (Frankfurt a.M., 1965); F. Derré, *L'œuvre d'A.S.* (Paris, 1966); S. Liptzin, *A.S.* (N.Y., 1932); Natan, *GML*, ii; *GLL*, II, 3, 1949; *Journal of the International A.S. Research Association* (Birmingham, N.Y., 1961ff.).

**Schnurre, Wolfdietrich** (Frankfurt a. M. 1920– ). German poet and short-story writer. A founder member of ⇨ Gruppe 47, he is known for his satirical social conscience (e.g. *Protest in Parterre*, 1957), his often charming humour (especially in animal stories, e.g. *Die Rohrdommel ruft jeden Tag*, 1951, and animal imagery in poems), his illustrations (e.g. to *Sternstaub und Sänfte*, 1953), for his moments of disturbing lyrical seriousness (poetry: *Kassiber*, 1956; *Abendländler*, 1957), above all for his radio plays, especially *Man sollte dagegen sein* (1953). *Eine Rechnung, die nicht aufgeht* (1958) is translated in *Modern German Stories* (1961, ed. H. M. Waidson). *Schreibtisch unter freiem Himmel* (1964) is a volume of bitterly polemical essays. [PB/AKT]

*Die Erzählungen* (1966); Bridgwater, *TCGV*; Hamburger and Middleton, *MGP*.
Nonnenmann, *SG*.

**Schönherr, Karl** (Axams, Innsbruck 1869–Vienna 1943). Austrian dramatist. A Tyrolean, he followed the example of ⇨ Anzengruber in writing dialect plays set among country folk. *Die Bildschnitzer* (1900) is a study of impoverished misery, while in the comedy *Erde* (1907) naked lust for land is frustrated by the physical resilience and sheer will to live of the central figure, Grutz. *Glaube und Heimat* (1910) is set in the Austrian Alps during the Counter-Reformation and illustrates a conflict between religious faith and the attraction of 'Erde', i.e. of the characters' attachment to their own land. He opposed the aestheticism of the Jung-Wien group: his plays deal with modern problems – those of the medical profession in *Der Kampf* (1920), that of the psychology of pretence in *Der Komödiant* (1924) – and in this respect his affinities are less with the Viennese tradition than with the Naturalists, though the figure of Grutz has an earthy vitality which is reminiscent of Anzengruber's peasant characters. [WEY]

*Gesammelte Werke*, ed. V. Chiavacci jr (1948).

**Schopenhauer, Arthur** (Danzig 1788–Frankfurt a. M. 1860). German philosopher. Although his main work, *Die Welt als Wille und Vorstellung* (1819; tr. R. B. Haldane and J. Kemp, *The World as Will and Idea*, 1883), appeared after most of the characteristic achievements of the Romantic movement, and did not come into its own until considerably later, it can in many ways be regarded as the most profoundly Romantic of philosophical treatises, a work which reflects more truly than those of ⇨ Schelling, ⇨ Fichte, etc. the spirit and the implications of the Romantic outlook.

Thus he held that the world was the mere shadow of a deeper, singular reality; that the mysterious meaning of this reality was revealed to man in art, above all in music; that traditional systems of ethics were irrelevant, and that the *nirvana* of Hinduism, the denial of human will and desire, represented the truest of attitudes towards the life of the present. His pessimism is the product of his postulate that the Will (the inscrutable power behind the World) is evil, conventional morality therefore meaningless, and life an Odyssey of suffering.

Of his contemporaries, ⇨ Grillparzer and ⇨ Hebbel in particular felt the force of his ideas; the strain of pessimism in writers as different as ⇨ Busch and T. ⇨ Mann also responded to the Schopenhauerian world-picture. But it is in Nietzsche, and even more in Wagner (Romanticism resolved into music; the cult of suffering and of salvation through love) that his influence is seen at its strongest. [RT]

*Sämtliche Werke*, ed. A. Hübscher (7 vols., 1947ff.); *The World as Will and Idea*, tr. R. B. Haldane, B. Kemp (repr. 1964); *Essays*, tr. T. B. Saunders (1942).

F. Nietzsche, *S. als Erzieher* (Leipzig, 1874); E. Seillière, *S.* (Paris, 1911); P. Gardiner, *S.* (1963); Stern, *R*; Wellek, *HMC*.

**Schoultz, Solveig von** (Porvoo 1907– ). Swedo-Finnish poet and novelist. Her poems are noted for the strength of their imagery and the liveliness of their rhythm; she uses both conventional and free metres. Her prose works show a subtle psychological understanding of children and of the emotionally abnormal. [IR]

**Schröder, Rudolf Alexander** (Bremen 1878–Bergen, Bavaria 1962). German poet and translator. Co-founder of periodical *Die Insel*, later Insel-Verlag. A revered traditionalist and pillar of the (Protestant) Church, his translations – from Homer to T. S. Eliot – tend to be formal but flat; his later religious poetry and hymns are inspired by genuine piety. *Die weltlichen Gedichte* (1940); *Die geistlichen Gedichte* (1949); *Hundert geistliche Gedichte* (1955). [PB/AKT]

*Gesammelte Werke* (6 vols., 1952–8); Bridgwater, *TCGV*.

K. Berger, *Die Dichtung R.A.S.s* (Marburg, 1954); Forster, *GP*; *GLL*, II, 1949.

**Schulz, Bruno** (Drohobycz 1893–Drohobycz 1942). Polish short-story writer. He was a schoolteacher in a provincial town which he transformed into a fantastic world of his own. His collection *Sklepy cynamonowe* (1934; tr. C. Wieniewska, *Cinnamon Shops*, 1963) is pervaded by a personal vision of Jewish life, with the prophet-like father at its centre; it constantly oscillates between delicate magic and obsessional realistic detail. There is some affinity between his world and that of ⇨ Kafka and Chagall. He was shot dead during the German occupation of Drohobycz, the town of cinnamon shops. [JP]

**Schwitters, Kurt** (Hanover 1887–Ambleside, England 1941). German poet and artist. An eccentric genius, whose style of abstract 'Collage' (assemblage of disconnected objects), a form of Dada, he called Merz. His poems appeared in the periodical *Der Sturm* (1919–24) and as *Anna Blume* (1922). [PB]

*Anna Blume und ich* (Zürich, 1965) (collected edn); Bridgwater, *TCGV*.

S. Themerson, *K.S. in England* (1958).

**Schwob, Marcel** (Chaville, Seine-et-Oise 1867–Paris 1905). French essayist and critic. He was born of an old-established family of Jewish intellectuals. Early associated with the *Mercure de France*, he was widely read in English and German, and had a scholarly interest in Villon and the criminal social origins of his language (*Étude sur l'argot français*, 1889; *Le jargon des coquillards en 1445*, 1890); *Spicilège*, 1896, contains essays also on R. L. Stevenson and Meredith. *Les vies imaginaires* (1896) reconstructs the lives and backgrounds of characters he met in his medieval reading. He was also the author of several symbolist tales, notably the collections *Le livre de Monelle* (1894) and *La croisade des enfants* (1896) which have their bases in oriental, medieval and classical legends. He translated *Hamlet* and Defoe's *Moll Flanders* (1893). His wife, Marguerite Moreno, has published her *Souvenirs* (1948). [WA]

P. Champion, *M.S. et son temps* (Paris, 1927).

**Scott, Gabriel** (Leith, Scotland 1874–Arendal 1958). Norwegian novelist. The son of a Norwegian seamen's pastor. His prolific but uneven work is particularly associated with the Sørlandet region of Norway. The historically based *Jernbyrden*

(1915; tr. K. Miethe and W. Katzin, *The Burden of Iron*, 1935) and its continuation *Enok Rubens levnedsløb* (1917) represent considerable achievements, and in the prose poem *Kilden* (1918; tr. S. and R. Bateson, *Markus the Fisherman*, 1931) his mystical-religious vision of the simple life lived close to nature receives masterly expression. The legend *Det gyldne evangelium* (1921; tr. W. Worster, *The Golden Gospel*, 1928) is also an expression of his religious faith. His children's book *Kari Kveldsmat* (1913; tr. A. Barstad, *Kari, a Story of Kari Supper from Lindeland*, 1931) contains some of his best work of its period. [RGP]

*Romaner i utvalg* (12 vols., 1946).
A. Beisland, *G.S.* (Oslo, 1949).

**Scribe, Eugène** (Paris 1791–Paris 1861). French dramatist. Father of the 'well-made play'. A prolific output of more than 300 plays, written alone or in collaboration (notably with Legouvé and Delavigne), included vaudevilles, light and serious comedies of manners, historical plays and libretti for light opera. After initial failures, he struck a successful vein with *Encore une nuit de la Garde Nationale* (1815), *Le solliciteur* (1817) and a gay fantasy, *L'ours et le Pacha* (1820). The years 1820–30 saw a succession of highly popular light comedies of manners (*comédies-vaudevilles*) in which Scribe added to the strain of topical satire, characteristic of traditional vaudeville, a complex structure of plot, surprise and effects, and a quick verbal wit. This is evident in his spirited satires of corrupt literary journalism: *La camaraderie* (1837) and *Le charlatanisme* (1825). His hostility to Romanticism, as to any large idealism, and his acute and 'knowing' suspicion of human self-interest, are reflected in a series of plays in which literary genius, revolutionary idealism or political principle are ruthlessly 'debunked'. Thus *Bernard et Raton* (1833; tr. anon., *The School for Politicians*, 1840) cynically deflates Romantic adulation of the revolutionary mob, just as the celebrated *Le verre d'eau* (1842; tr./adapt. W. E. Suter, *A Glass of Water*, n.d.) confidently ascribes the overthrow of the Duke of Marlborough, the pacification of Europe and the elevation of Bolingbroke to power to a trivial personal intrigue symbolized by the 'glass of water' which Queen Anne asks of her young admirer, Masham. At another level, Scribe's suspicion of the human heart and imagination is reflected in his comedies of love and marriage. The claims of passion, so dear to the Romantics, are exposed as disastrous aberrations in that cautionary tale *Malvina ou un mariage d'inclination* (1828) and in *Le mariage de raison* (1826), where a prudent marriage between a lady's maid and an old soldier with a wooden leg is preferred to a heady misalliance with an aristocrat. He confines adultery to the *drame* (e.g. *Dix ans de la vie d'une femme*, 1832, and *La passion secrète*, 1834) on the grounds that a calamity for the family cannot be a proper subject of comedy. Curious ambivalences, however, characterize some of the treatments of illicit passion – in *Oscar ou le mari qui trompe sa femme* (1842) he diverts the audience from the full sense of a really scabrous situation involving a newly married husband's attempted seduction of his fifteen-year-old pupil by permitting the wife, who intercepts the letter of assignation, to substitute herself for the pupil under the cover of darkness. Here, as in *Une chaîne* (1841; tr./adapt. S. Grundy, *In Honour Bound*, 1885), which deals with a man trying to discard his mistress, the mechanisms of evasion and deceit (intercepted letters, secret meetings, mischances) are more important than the experiences themselves. Scribe is significant as a gay master-mechanic who manipulates the plot with virtuosity and provides the boulevard theatre with its standard recipes. [SBJ]

*Œuvres complètes* (76 vols., 1874–85).
N. C. Arvin, *E.S. and the French Theatre, 1815–60* (1924); L. Allard, *La comédie de mœurs en France au 19e siècle, 1795–1830* (2 vols., Cambridge, Mass., 1923–33); Descotes, *PT*; Doumic, *SI*.

**Scudéry, Madeleine de** (Le Havre 1608–Marais 1701). French novelist. With greater gifts than her flashy brother Georges, she probably gave more pleasure to 17th-century readers, certainly in quantity, than greater artists. Her long (and for that reason, in that age, delightful) novels were the favourites of many circles and many generations. *Artamène ou le Grand Cyrus* (10 vols., 1649–53) and *Clélie, histoire romaine* (10 vols., 1654–60) are the best known of her many works in prose and verse. [WGM]

C. Aragonnès, *M. de S.* (Paris, 1934); D. MacDougall, *M. de S.* (1938).

**Sebastian, Mihai** (Brăila 1907–Bucharest 1945). Rumanian playwright and novelist. A traffic accident ended at 37 a very promising career as a playwright. Rumanian writers having made less of a mark in the theatre than in other branches of literature, his *Ultima oră* (1945) is probably the best comedy since Caragiale. Others are *Jocul de-a vacanţa* (1936) and *Steaua fără nume* (1943). Of his novels *Accidentul* (1940) shows his characteristic charm. The earlier comedies have sometimes a touch of Barri-esque sentiment. [EDT]

*Opere alese*, ed. V. Mîndra (1956).

**Sedaine, Michel-Jean** (Paris 1719–Paris 1797). French dramatist. Son of a mason, he found a patron and devoted himself to literature. After *Poésies fugitives* (1752), he turned to the theatre, writing the libretti of several comic operas (music by Philidor and Monsigny), including *Rose et Colas* (1764). In 1765 appeared his first *drame* and most important work, *Le philosophe sans le savoir* (ed. T. E. Oliver, 1913); thereafter his productions included a variety of plays (notably *La gageure imprévue*, a comedy, in 1768) and comic operas, among which *Richard cœur de lion* (1784) to music by Grétry was pre-eminent. He entered the Académie Française in 1786 but lost his membership when it was reconstituted in 1795. He died in poverty as a result of the Revolution.

*Le philosophe sans le savoir* is the best example in 18th-century France of a *drame bourgeois*, putting into practice the principles of Diderot. With its bourgeois characters in a carefully established setting and insistence more upon their family and professional *conditions* than their *caractères*, its social realism anticipates the 19th-century French novel. Its mixture of grave and gay seeks a *vraisemblance* closer to everyday life than that of classical tragedy. Its moralistic attitudes and praise for commerce accord well with the utilitarian and humanitarian temper of the times. A well-made play, interesting for its detailed observations and especially for what it reveals about contemporary dramatic theories, it lacks the acuteness of a Marivaux or a Beaumarchais. [HTM]

F. Gaiffe, *Le drame en France au XVIIIe siècle* (Paris, 1910); L. Günther, *L'œuvre dramatique de S.'* (Paris, 1908); I. O. Wade, 'The Title of Sedaine's *Le philosophe sans le savoir*', *PMLA*, XLIII (1928).

**Seedorff Pedersen, Hans Hartvig** (Aarhus 1892– ). Danish poet. His first volume, *Vinløv og Vedbend* (1916), like all the gay and vivacious lyrical poems of this charming and light-hearted Dionysian poet, are melodious and song-like, and are very popular. [ELB]

*Udvalgte Digte* (1942–52).

A. Hjort-Mouritzen, *H.H.S. Digter og Troubadur* (Copenhagen, 1950).

**Seferis, George,** pen-name of Seferiades (Smyrna 1900– ). Greek poet. He was educated in Athens and Paris where he studied law. In 1926 he entered the Greek diplomatic service, visiting London first as Vice-Consul and then Acting Consul-General (1931–4). The eve of the Second World War found him serving as Greek Consul in Albania, and after the fall of Greece he followed the Greek Government in exile and served in Crete, South Africa, Egypt, London and Italy. He returned to London as Counsellor of the Embassy (1951–3); he was then appointed Counsellor again at Ankara, then Ambassador in Lebanon, and finally Ambassador in London (1957–62). In 1962 he was awarded the William Foyle poetry prize, and in 1963 the Nobel Prize for literature, the first Greek to win these distinctions. Since his retirement he has lived in Athens and has devoted his time to literary work. The influence of the French symbolists, especially of Valéry, Rimbaud and Laforgue, in whose poetry he became deeply interested while a student in France, was decisive in his poetic development; while his acquaintance with the work of T. S. Eliot during his first visit to London helped to bring out more strongly his own originality and to give his poetry a new dimension. His *Strophe* ('Turning Point', 1931), a volume of lyrical poems of powerful symbolism, bare and sober in diction and precise in imagery, marked a departure from till then accepted ideals and conventions in Greek poetry. It was followed by *I Sterna* ('The Cistern', 1932), his most undecipherable poem, where the utmost economy of expression and a language totally devoid of aural effects allow full play to the evocative force of words. His later poems, *Mythistorema* (1935; tr. R. Warner, *Mythistorema*, 1960), *Imerologio Katastromatos A* (1940; tr. R. Warner, *Log Book I*, 1960), *Imerologio Katastromatos B* (1945; tr. R. Warner, *Log Book II*), *Kichli* (1947; tr. E. Keeley and P. Sherrard, *The Thrush*, 1960), *Imerologio Katastromatos C* (1955; tr. R. Warner, *Log Book III*) and several more, owe much in manner and method to Eliot's influence, although Seferis's vision and cast of mind are entirely different. He looks outward, at a landscape, an ancient site, or a particular situation, and evokes the reality of a past event, a myth, a state of mind, or a mood lurking underneath. He is allusive and hermetic as he searches for the unrhetorical yet telling phrase, and explores the solitary places of his restless and complex mind. His distinctive awareness of the modern world derives its sharpness and its meditative edge from a profound consciousness of his native tradition. A tone of nostalgia with an underlying despair – 'There is an absolute blackness behind the golden web of the Attic summer' – is characteristic of his poetry, and becomes more pronounced in his latest verse. He has also distinguished himself as a literary critic and a translator, e.g. of *The Waste Land*, *Murder in the Cathedral* and of poems by Ezra Pound, Sidney Keyes, Auden, Yeats, Gide, Éluard and others; the original texts of the *Song of Songs* and of the *Apocalypse* of St John acquire fresh glow in his skilful and sensitive renderings into contemporary Greek. [SJP]

*Poiemata* (1964); *Dokimés* (1962) (essays); *Antigraphés* (1965) (translations); *Tria Kryfá Poiemata* (1966); *The King of Asine and Other Poems*, tr. B. Spencer, N. Valaoritis, L. Durrell (1948); *Poems*, tr. R. Warner (1960); *Six Poets of Modern Greece*, tr. E. Keeley and P. Sherrard (1960); *On the Greek Style*, tr. Frangopoulos and R. Warner (1966); *Collected Poems*, W. E. Keeley and P. Sherrard (1967).

E. Keeley, 'T. S. Eliot and the Poetry of G. Seferis', in *Comparative Literature*, VIII, 3, 1956; *Gia Ton Seferi* (Athens, 1961) (commemorative volume).

**Segalen, Victor** (Brest 1878–Huelgoa, Finisterre 1919). French poet and novelist. A ship's doctor, he visited the dwelling of Gauguin (in Polynesia), who had died three months earlier. Out of this voyage came his first novel, *Les immémoriaux* (1907), published under the pseudonym of Max Anély, which describes Tahiti life from within, showing how the native views external nature and describing the loss of traditional mythology. Segalen's exoticism, here and in his later poems, seems rooted in an intense care for the diversity which the world is destroying. After a first visit to China in 1908, he organized an archaeological expedition in quest of monuments of the Han dynasty. The expedition was interrupted by the 1914 war, but had a profound effect on his poetry, the essence of which is found in prose poems in the Chinese manner, written in sober, exact language (*Stèles*, 1912, *Peintures*, 1916, *Équipée*, 1929; all edited with preface by P. J. Jouve, 1955). He died in mysterious circumstances at 41. Posthumous publications include *Orphée-roi* (1921), a mystical play, and *René Lys* (1922), a novel about China. He probably influenced ⇨ Claudel and Saint-John ⇨ Perse. [FWAG]

G. Bouillier, *S.* (Paris, 1961); *Cahiers du Sud* (1948, 1962).

**Seghers, Anna,** pseud. of Netty Radvanyi (Mainz 1900– ). German novelist. Wife of the Hungarian novelist Laszlo Radvanyi, she joined the Communist Party (1929), emigrated (1933) to France, Spain, Mexico (1941). Since 1947 a prominent figure in East Berlin (Stalin Prize). Her socialist realism, toughly tense, makes telling use of 'fact' and situation to gain powerful effects, e.g. in her prizewinning first novel (set in Brittany), *Der Aufstand der Fischer von St. Barbara* (1928; tr. M. Goldsmith, *The Revolt of the Fishermen*, 1929), and the famous escape story, *Das siebte Kreuz* (1941; tr. J. A. Galston, *The Seventh Cross*, 1943; filmed U.S.A.), which shows Resistance in prewar Nazi Germany. *Transit* (1947; tr. J. A. Galston, 1945) reflects the fate of refugees in Marseilles in 1940, *Die Toten bleiben jung* (1949; tr. anon., *The Dead Stay Young*, 1950) the catastrophic social evolution of Germany 1919–45, and *Die Entscheidung* (1959) the post-war division of the country. She is the author of many stories, e.g. *Der Ausflug der toten Mädchen* (1948), *Die Linie* (1950). [PB]

*Erzählungen* (2 vols., 1964).

F. Albrecht, *Die Erzählerin A.S.* (Berlin, 1965); I. Diersen, *S.-Studien* (Berlin, 1965); A. A. Volgina, *A.Z.* (Moscow, 1964); *GLL*, VIII, 2 (1955).

**Seidel, Ina** (Halle, Saale 1885– ). German novelist and poet. She is known for her nature poetry (*Gedichte 1905–1955*, 1957) and the Protestant, patriotic, feminine world of her often historical novels; the best known are: *Das Labyrinth* (1923; tr. O. Williams, 1932), about the 18th-century naturalist Georg Forster, *Das Wunschkind* (1930; tr. G. D. Gribble, *The Wish Child*, 1935), about a widowed mother and her only son during the Prussian Wars of

Liberation, and *Lennacker* (1938), about a vicarage during the centuries. Her most recent novel is *Michaela*... (1959). [PB]

K. A. Horst, *I.S. Wesen und Werk* (Stuttgart, 1956).

**Seifert, Jaroslav** (Prague 1901– ). Czech poet. In his early years, like other Czech poets of the time, he passed through the phases of 'proletarian poetry' and 'poetism', but by the thirties he had evolved his own poetic style whose stanzaic forms and uncomplicated imagery strike a more traditional note than the work of many of his contemporaries. His poems of Prague, especially those written during the years of German occupation (*Světlem oděná*, 1940), probably represent his most lasting achievement. [RA]

*Dílo* (6 vols., 1956–64).

**Seifried Helbling.** Name by which, erroneously, the author of a series of 15 satirical, didactic German poems of the late 13th century is known. The name occurs in one of the poems but not as a designation of authorship; the actual author, apparently an Austrian nobleman, is not known. The work, which often treats of events in contemporary Austrian history, belongs in the literary tradition of the ⇨ Stricker, while owing something also to the satirical presentation of peasant life in the poetry of ⇨ Neidhart von Reuental. [RT]

Ed. J. Seemüller (1866).

**Sel'vinsky, Il'ya** (Simferopol', Crimea 1899–Moscow 1968). Russian poet. Educated in a Catholic monastery school in Constantinople, then in Yevpatoríya. He fought with the Reds in the Civil War, entered Moscow University, earning money as a seaman, a factory-worker and an athletics instructor. In 1924–30 he was the leader of ⇨ Constructivism. His first book appeared in 1926; in the thirties he participated in an expedition to the Arctic, and fought in the war in Southern Russia.

Fascinated by the inflexions of speech, in early poems he uses experimental spelling, typography and punctuation to reproduce and build upon (for example) gipsy songs, Cossack balladry and – poetically best of all – children's language. Snatches of Ukrainian, Finnish, nonsensical and onomatopoeic syllables, indications of unorthodox stress and intonation are among his devices, used also in long poems and verse plays: *Ulyalaevshchina* (1927), *Pushtorg* (1929). Perhaps, because of official Soviet disparagement of 'formalism', his later work is orthodox and less interesting. [RM-G]

Gulland, *SRV*; *Izbrannyye proizvedeniya* (1960); Markov, *MRP*.

**Šem Tob Ibn Ardutiel Ben Isaac,** also called **Santob del Carrión** (fl. early 14th cent.). Spanish poet and rabbi. He dedicated his *Proverbios morales* to Pedro the Cruel. They are gnomic poems in the Eastern style, which draw their proverbial philosophy from Arabic and Hebrew, from Maimonides and Moses ben Ezra, but also from Spanish *refranes*. He claims that good saws are none the worse because a Jew quotes them – '*nin los enxemplos buenos porque judío los diga*'. He also wrote poetry in Hebrew, and a caballistic treatise. His general attitude is stoical and sometimes humorous. [JMC]

*Proverbios morales*, ed. I. González Llubera (Cambridge, 1947).

**Sénancour, Étienne Pivert de** (Paris 1770–Saint-Cloud 1846). French writer. Famous for his novel *Obermann*. He was brought up in Paris and intended for the church. However he went instead to Switzerland where his soul, already awakened by readings of Rousseau, Bernardin de Saint-Pierre and *Werther*, surrendered to the contemplation of Nature and his own melancholy. He made an unhappy marriage and returned to Paris, where he spent his patrimony and soon was forced to live by hack-writing. In 1804 he brought out *Obermann* (ed. A. Monglond, 1947, M. C. Jalard, 1965), a novel in letter form. In these letters over a long period the hero writes to a friend pouring out his frustrated feelings and his ennui from which he is unable to escape. The surroundings, the Alps and the Forest of Fontainebleau, take the place of a plot. Like *René* this work had a strong influence upon the Romantics affecting Balzac's *Le lys dans la vallée*, Sainte-Beuve's *Volupté*, and George Sand's *Lélia*. Matthew Arnold made him known to England through his poems *Obermann* and *Obermann Once More*. [WA]

*Rêveries*, ed. J. Merlant (1939).

A. Finot, *S. ou le myapothique* (Paris, 1947); B. Le Gall, *L'imaginaire chez S.* (1966); M. Raymond, *S.* (Paris, 1965); Peyre, *LS*.

**Šenoa, August** (Zagreb 1838–Zagreb 1881). Croatian novelist. Creator of the Croatian novel. He studied law in Prague and Vienna, where he became a journalist and theatre critic (1865). His novels, *Zlatarevo zlato* (1872), *Selijacka buna* (1877) and *Diogenes* (1878), adapt the historical tradition of Walter Scott to Croatia. They are full of the romantic paraphernalia of evil barons, mysterious strangers, sorcerers and phantoms. Yet they contain a serious patriotic message and, in later works, the romantic setting gives way to realism. Such stories as *Barun Ivica* deal with contemporary problems. His work is closely linked to the city of Zagreb and its history, which he studied to gain material for his novels, all based on authentic events. He was also important as a critic, editing the most influential literary periodical of the day, *Vienac*, and acting as director of the national theatre. He preached social realism, demanding that works should treat contemporary life and exert moral influence. His ideas governed a whole generation of Croatian writers. [EDG]

*Sabrana djela*, ed. A. Barac (20 vols., 1931–4); *Djela*, ed. A. Barac (4 vols., 1951).
Barac, *HYL.*

**Sęp-Szarzyński, Mikołaj** (*c.* 1550–Wolica 1580). Polish poet. Like many of his distinguished contemporaries he studied abroad, but otherwise little is known of his life. His poems were collected and published posthumously by his brother. This volume entitled *Rytmy abo wiersze polskie* (1601) contains the best sonnets in early Polish literature. Revolving round religious paradoxes, his imagination often leads him into syntactic clusters. This, however, seems to strengthen his appositions. A good illustration is the sonnet 'On the War we wage against Satan, the World and the Body'. The technique resembles that of the metaphysical poets. [JP]

Peterkiewicz and Singer, *FCPP.*
W. Weintraub, 'Some Remarks on the Style of M.S-S.', in *Vasmer Festschrift* (Berlin, 1956).

**Sequences.** An outstanding feature in the singing of Mass during the Middle Ages, sequences probably originated about the end of the 8th century.

The Gradual, a whole psalm sung between the Epistle and the Gospel in the early church, had been reduced to a couple of verses by the beginning of the Middle Ages. These were immediately followed by the singing of 'Alleluia', the final *-a* of which was sung to a long melody called the *jubilus.* The first sequences were unrhythmical prose texts sung to the *jubilus* – one syllable of the words to each note of the music.

During the 9th century it became the custom to divide the singing of the sequence between two groups of voices, the second group repeating the melody of the first. Prose sequences of this kind consequently consisted of a series of double strophes (or strophes and antistrophes) of varying lengths – sung, therefore, to different melodies – with the optional addition of a prelude or a coda, or both. ⇨ Notker Balbulus is outstanding as a writer of this type of sequence. Identity of structure between strophe and antistrophe was naturally often accompanied by parallelism of thought, thus reviving the outstanding characteristic of the psalms. A good example of this is the anonymous 10th-century sequence, *Cantemus cuncti melodum* ('The strain upraise of joy and praise'), called the Alleluyatic Sequence. In many sequences of this century we find that every line ends in *a*, thus echoing the final syllable of the Alleluia preceding them. In ⇨ Wipo's 11th-century Easter sequence *Victimae paschali*, the prose runs with a smooth rhythm, the first half is in varied assonances and the second half in full rhyme. The 12th-century Christmas sequence, *Laetabundus* ('Come rejoicing'), has developed still further, being in verse and displaying more rhyme, though the rhymes do not run all through, neither are they symmetrically placed. Each strophe and antistrophe ends in *a.* In the same century we reach at length the regular sequence wholly in verse, with symmetrically placed rhymes throughout.

Different sets of rhymes are used in each strophe and its antistrophe, except that they have a common final rhyme. Nearly all regular sequences have a trochaic basis. Their greatest exponent is ⇨ Adam of St Victor, a master of technique. St Thomas ⇨ Aquinas maintains the same high standard in his *Lauda Sion.*

Many of the finest regular sequences are regularized to such an extent that all their strophes (and consequently all their antistrophes) are of identical pattern so that the whole could be (and often is) sung to one repeated melody, like a hymn. Examples of this are the Golden Sequence *Veni sancte*

*Spiritus*, usually ascribed to Stephen Langton, and the anonymous Franciscan Sequence *Stabat mater*.

⇨ Thomas of Celano's *Dies irae*, sung as a sequence at requiems, was not intended for use as a sequence. Its stanzas are consequently not linked in pairs by their final rhymes. The same is true also of the anonymous Rosy sequence *Jesu dulcis memoria* which consists of nine monorhymed Ambrosian quatrains extracted from a longer poem. [FB]

*An. Hym.*, 53–5; *Lateinische Sequenzen des Mittelalters*, ed. J. Kehrein (Mainz, 1873); *Sequentiae ex Missalibus Germanicis, Anglicis, Gallicis, aliisque Medii Aevi*, ed. J. M. Neale (1852).

*A Dictionary of Hymnology*, ed. J. Julian (1908); Introduction to *The Winchester Troper*, ed. W. H. Frere (Henry Bradshaw Society, 1894); E. J. Wellesz, *Eastern Elements in Western Chant* (1947); *History of Byzantine Music and Hymnography* (1949); *Early Medieval Music up to 1300*, ed. A. Hughes, in *New Oxford History of Music*, ii (1954); J. M. Clark, *The Abbey of St Gall* (1926); Raby, *CLP*.

**Serafimovich, Aleksandr,** pseud. of Aleksandr Serafimovich Popov (Nizhne-Kumoyarskaya na Donu 1863–Moscow 1949). Russian novelist. The son of a Cossack officer, he studied at St Petersburg University. He became a Marxist and was imprisoned and exiled. His work first appeared in 1888, and his novel *Gorod v stepi* (1905–12) was widely read at the time. His fame rests, however, on his novel of the Civil War *Zheleznyy potok* (1924; tr. anon., *The Iron Flood*, 1935), dealing with the breakout of a Red Army from White encirclement. The depiction of the Communist hero won particular praise from Soviet critics; but when the prototype of the hero was arrested and shot in connexion with the Tukhachevsky affair, the book was temporarily suppressed. It soon returned to favour, and in 1943 he was awarded a Stalin Prize for his services to Soviet literature. [RDBT]

*Polnoye sobraniye sochineniy* (10 vols., 1940–3). V. I. Kurilenkov, *A.S.* (Moscow, 1950).

**Serao, Matilde** (Patras, Greece 1856–Naples 1927). Italian journalist and novelist. During her early years working in the Naples telegraph office, she also wrote short stories for local papers, and eventually joined the editorial staff of the *Corriere del Mattino*. In 1882 she moved to Rome, and after contributing to leading literary journals, co-founded with her husband the *Corriere di Roma*. The *Corriere di Napoli* and *Il Mattino* followed; and in 1904, separated from her husband, she founded and edited until her death *Il Giorno* (Naples). Her newspaper work was accompanied by a copious output of realist novels, some – especially her masterpiece *Il paese di Cuccagna* (1890; tr. anon., *The Land of Cockayne*, 1901) – distinguished for their vivid portrayal of Neapolitan life, but most bearing excessive traces of her characteristic feminine sentimentality (e.g. *La ballerina*, 1899; tr. anon., *The Ballet Dancer* and *On Guard*, 1901; *Suor Giovanna della Croce*, 1901; tr. anon., in the *Living Age*, *Sister Giovanna of the Cross*, July–September 1907). [RHC]

*Opere di M.S.*, ed. P. Pancrazi (2 vols., 1944–6). M. Sandri, *M.S. profilo* (Milan, 1922); L. Giusso, 'La grande borghese', in *Il viandante e le statue* (Milan, 1929); L. Russo, *I Narratori* (Milan, 1951); *Minori*, iv.

**Serapion Brothers, The.** Russian literary group founded 1921, dominated by ⇨ Zamyatin and ⇨ Shklovsky, who defended the vitality and independence of art against political commitment.

Reavey and Slonim, *SL*.

**Serbian Medieval Literature.** The literature of medieval Serbia is generally agreed to begin with St Sava (Raška 1174–Trnovo 1236), son of Stefan Nemanja (1114–1200), the founder of the Serbian state of Raska and the Nemnajić dynasty. Sava fled to Athos as a young man and became a monk. There he was joined by his father, Nemanja, after his abdication, and together they founded the Serbian monastery of Hilander. On his father's death, Sava returned to Raška and became Serbia's first archbishop.

The canonization of Nemanja as the monk Simeon led Sava to include an account of his life and death as a monk in the *tipikon* for the monastery of Studenica. This biography is written with far greater simplicity and personal feeling than is usual in hagiographical works of the period, avoiding as it does much of the tedious rhetoric and long quotations much valued in Byzantine works of the time. Sava's elder brother Stefan (d. 1227), who succeeded his father as ruler, also wrote a life of Nemanja as both saint and ruler, including much historical detail up to the time of his writing. Stefan wrote with more national tendentiousness than Sava, presenting Serbia as God's chosen nation.

In 1253, Domentijan, a monk at Hilandar, wrote lives of both Sava and Simeon. These were the fullest biographies of Serbian medieval literature. They are full of rhetoric and long prayers, but their content, especially regarding Sava, is of great interest, suggesting that much of it is drawn from legends and anecdotes that were prevalent about him. These two lives were revised by Teodosije sometime about the end of the 13th century. Teodosije inserts an element of nationalism and his style is far easier and more natural. The tradition of canonizing its kings led the Serbian state to favour hagiography and during the 14th century there probably arose a genre of official biography. Certainly this appears to be the case from the collection of short lives of rulers and archbishops attributed to Danilo II, archbishop of Raška (d. 1324), although, since they include rulers and hierarchs up to the end of the century, he could have been no more than the founder of the school. These biographies lack detail and are extremely tendentious in character.

After the defeat of the Serbs by the Turks at Kosovo 1389, the tradition of biography did not end. In the Serbian vassal state in the early 15th century the biography underwent considerable development in style. Konstantin Filosof, probably of Bulgarian origin, wrote a life of Stefan Lazarević in 1431 full of historical and geographical data. He was influenced by the reforms of language and style instituted by the Bulgarian literary school of Trnovo. Gregory Camblak, also a Bulgar, wrote the life of Stefan Decanški, probably in the year 1408. Finally in the 16th century the patriarch Paisije wrote a life of Uroś, the last of the Nemanjići.

Medieval Serbian literature is the source for much of our knowledge of Serbia at that time. Already the earliest works appear in Serbian recension of Church Slavonic, which suggests that there must have been a considerable amount of writing prior to Nemanja, few traces of which remain. [EDG]

**Serbo-Croat Folk Literature.** A rich literature which comprises folk-tales, proverbs, epic and lyrical songs. Some of these are of considerable age, particularly the lyrical songs. The age of the epic is difficult to determine, although the cycles of the Nemanjići and Kosovo probably relate to the 15th century. We owe much of our knowledge of folk literature to Vuk ⇨ Karadžić, whose collections of folk-tales (1853) and proverbs as well as his 6 volumes of the folk-songs (1841–66) are still definitive.

The folk-song consists of two distinct genres. The lyrical song, which is an unrhymed trochaic poem in lines of differing length, from the 4-syllabic to the 10-syllabic, is sung to a melody, traditionally by the women, hence its name, *Ženska narodna pesma* (female folk-song). These songs reflect a wide scheme of folk-life, tradition and custom, including relics of pagan beliefs and Christian traditions which have been influenced by earlier pagan custom. The epic song is usually in the 10-syllable trochaic line, unrhymed. It is usually recited in a monotone to the accompaniment of the one-stringed fiddle or *Gusli.* The folk-singers or *Guslari* were of great importance in the life of the people right up to the end of last century and the tradition was even perpetuated during the partisan war 1941–5. The epic poems are divided into various cycles of songs dealing with different episodes from a given theme or historical period. Two of the most popular and well-known cycles are those of Kosovo and of Marko Kraljević. The Kosovo cycle tells the legend of Kosovo, the betrayal of the Serbs by Vuk Branković, the assassination of Sultan Murath by Milos Obilić and the martyrdom of prince Lazar. Marko Kraljević was vassal ruler of Prizren under the Turks. Historically his claim to being a national hero would seem slender, but in the epic he is a type of Robin Hood embodying typical national virtues and also faults. He is not only a hero but also a humorous and extremely human character. Other cycles include those of the *Uskoci*, the pirates and brigands, the cycles concerning the struggles of the Montenegrins against the Turks and that of the Serbian rising (1804–13). [EDG]

H. Rootham, *Kosovo, Heroic Songs of Serbia* (1920); D. H. Lowe, *The Ballads of Marko Kraljević* (1922); S. Stanley, *Serbian Fairy Tales* (1917); J. Subotić, *Yugoslav Popular Ballads* (1932).

**Sercambi, Giovanni** (Lucca 1348–Lucca 1424). Italian short-story writer. One of the duller imitators of Boccaccio. About 20 of his stories are poor rehashes of tales from the *Decameron*. His 155 *Novelle* (ed. A. D'Ancona, 1871, 1886) are set in the framework of a group of people fleeing from the Lucchese plague of 1374 and telling stories to pass the time. He treats a great variety of themes – witty sayings, fables, religious legends, as well as earthy, realistic anecdotes. His style is worst when he aspires to ambitious 'literary' effects, best in racier, uninhibited pieces. He also recorded the history of his native city in *Croniche delle cose di Lucca*, 1164–1423 (ed. S. Bongi, 1892). [DGR]

Varese, *PVQ;* L. Russo, *Storia della letteratura italiana*, i (Florence, 1957); Di Francia, *N*.

**Sereni, Vittorio** (Luino 1913– ). Italian poet. His experience as prisoner of war is recorded in *Diario d'Algeria* (1946), his only publication since *Frontiere* (1941) and *Poesie* (1942). Learning from ⇨ *ermetismo* and the ⇨ *crepuscolari*, he developed a manner of idyllic reverie; despite a profounder tragic awareness in his *Diario*, his more typical gift is the distillation of a rare elegiac mood, a poetry of nostalgic impressions and sweet sadness, out of the experience of catastrophe. Convoys moving towards the frontier, city lights lost in the night.... 'Europe, Europe, who watch me / go down listless and absorbed / in a shadowy myth of mine / among the ranks of the brutes.' [GD]

Golino, *CIP*.
Antonielli, *AFM*; Fortini, *M*.

**Sévigné, Marie de Rabutin Chantal,** Marquise de (Paris 1626–Grigan 1696). The most famous of European letter writers, she lost both parents before she was 8, and was brought up by two uncles, one of whom, the Abbé Christophe de Coulanges, figures much in her correspondence. Married at 18 to a young Breton nobleman, by whom she had two children, she was left a widow at 25. To be a young widow was the most enviable passport to freedom in society and Mme de Sévigné had the temperament and the gifts to make the most of all social occasions. She was a favourite everywhere, and her letters show that she missed nothing and had a charming compliment for all. The King sought her company and even asked her to dance in the Royal Ballet. She was as intelligent as she was sociable, reading widely, able to discuss politics and even subjects usually forbidden to her sex. She seems to have been quite fearless and loyal to her friends. She championed Fouquet, and later the Jansenists, when to do so was to risk royal censure. Her memorial and literary monument is the long series of letters chiefly addressed to her daughter, giving a most animated picture of what went on in Paris, and of what was said and thought. They are outstanding as a social document and a work of style. Their fame does not rest on the more serious or philosophical of them, but on the achievement, unattempted elsewhere in the 17th century, of transmitting in language the essence of personal dealing, not ideas or feelings only, but the illusion of life usually found only in drama. These letters suggest drama on every page, the movement of conversation, the animation of social gatherings, the animosity beneath the politeness, the tension between individuals and conventions, between Paris and the provinces. Mme de Sévigné is a Parisian, and has an almost natural scorn for what is provincial. Writing from Les Roches, where the provincial assembly is being held, she is surprised to find that 'In this vast expanse of Bretons there are some men of intelligence'. She can berate her daughter in Provence that the Assembly of Languedoc dare to question its financial assessment, decided on in Paris. She is as it were conscious of being at the centre, able therefore to transmit the very atmosphere of centralization. Thus, she pays tribute to Louvois, saying that he is 'at the centre of so many things'. Proust, who modelled his Elstir on her, called her impressionistic technique 'the Dostoyevsky side of Mme de Sévigné: she shows us things in the order of our perceptions instead of explaining first the reason why they are there'. One of her frequent remarks is 'Everything is many-sided'. Her taste in literature, for instance, is not the result of argument or principle but of enthusiasm; Corneille transported her to a degree that made her impervious to Racine. [WGM]

*Lettres*, ed. E. Gerard-Gailly (3 vols., Pléiade, 1953–7).

H. Busson, *La religion des classiques, 1660–1685* (Paris, 1948); H. R. Allentuch, *Mme de S. A Portrait in Letters* (1964); Adam, *HLF*.

**Shapiro, Lamed** (Ukraine 1875–New York 1948). Yiddish novelist and essayist. A reformer of style, he caused a stir by his stories of the Tsarist pogroms and introduced a new theme into Yiddish literature with his sea stories. He translated into Yiddish the works of Victor Hugo, Sir Walter Scott, Dickens and Kipling. [EE]

Waxman, *HJL*; Roback, *SYL*.

**Shchedrin.** ⇨ Saltykov, Mikhail Yevgrafovitch.

**Shevchenko, Taras** (Moryntsi, Kiev 1814–St Petersburg 1861). Ukrainian poet. Born a serf; his parents died early through privation and hard work. He acquired an early passion for reading, copying poetry and drawing. This latter incurred his master's wrath when Shevchenko became a valet; but, deciding to have his serf trained as a portraitist, on their arrival in St Petersburg in 1832 he apprenticed him to a decorator. Sketching a statue on a 'white' night in 1835, Shevchenko was discovered by a fellow-countryman, the art student Soshenko, and introduced to the Ukrainian writer Hrebinka whose library was put at his disposal. Among his new friends were ⇨ Zhukovsky and the famous painter Bryullov, who together purchased his freedom in 1838. He subsequently enrolled at the Petersburg Art Academy and read and studied widely.

He had started writing *c.* 1832, but kept from his serfdom days only *Prychynna* (1837?). His first 8-poem collection, *Kobzar* (1840), immediately caught the imagination of the Ukrainian public, bringing him wide fame. More poems followed in 1841–4. There were Romantic ballads (*Prychynna*, *Topolya*, etc.), distinguished by genuinely Ukrainian settings and folklore elements. Romantic features also dominate his historical poems; the longest, *Haydamaky* (1841), deals with an 18th-century peasant rebellion; *Ivan Pidkova*, *Tarasova nich*, *Hamaliya*, are visions of Ukraine's heroic, but irretrievable past; the same nostalgia for the glorious Cossack era is prominent in *Dumy moyi* and *Do Osnov"yanenka*. He often returns to the tragic theme of a girl seduced, first expressed in the major poem of *Kobzar*, *Kateryna* (tr. M. Skrypnyk, Toronto, 1961). All this he wrote after leaving the Ukraine – hence the characteristic motif of home-sickness. When he returned (1843) he intensified his protest against social and national oppression in the poems of 1843–5, circulated in manuscript copies and unpublishable under Nicholas I. The most important are: *Son*, a panorama of the Empire, with slavery in the Ukraine, political prisoners in the Siberian gold mines, and the grotesquely pictured hierarchy in the capital, headed by the Tsar. Peter I is passionately denounced for his crimes against the Ukrainian people. *Velyky l'okh*, a 'mystery play', reveals Shevchenko's views on history: he deplores the Ukrainian Hetman Bohdan Khmel'nyts'ky's treaty with Moscow, condemns those Ukrainians who helped Peter I against Mazeppa, and accuses Catherine II of abolishing the vestiges of Ukrainian autonomy. His invective against Russian colonialism and military imperialism, cloaked by a hypocritical Christianity's 'civilizing mission', is most passionate in *Kavkaz*, devoted to the Caucasian peoples' resistance to Russian conquest (cf. *UQ*, XVI, 4, 1960). *Yeretyk* interprets the courageous stand and martyrdom of John Hus, the 15th-century Czech anti-Catholic leader, as part of the Slav struggle to break the German stranglehold. In *I mertvym, i zhyvym* he warns those who, rhapsodizing about the Ukraine's history, ignore the iniquities of serfdom, that the only way to avoid fratricidal bloodshed lies in justice and respect of Mother Ukraine.

In 1846, several Ukrainian intellectuals formed a secret Brotherhood of Cyril and Methodius to advocate a democratic union of all Slavs with independence and equality for each nation. Shevchenko, who had similar ideas (e.g. the dedication to Šafařík of *Yeretyk*, 1845), joined with enthusiasm. In 1847, the Brotherhood was denounced, and Shevchenko, about to take up an appointment at Kiev University, was sentenced for his manuscript poems to penal army service in Central Asia, with a rider in the Tsar's own hand: 'Under the strictest supervision and with a ban on writing and sketching.' This strictness varied, and in the first three years he wrote many exquisite lyrics, and afterwards several Russian novelettes. Of these, *Khudozhnik* is autobiographical; the theme of a talented serf appears also in other stories (e.g. *Varnak*; cf. Runge, 7); *Kapitansha* and *Naymychka* (also a poem, 1845) continued the seduction theme, while others portrayed the degeneration of the old landed gentry.

After the death of Nicholas and two years' perseverance by friends, Shevchenko was released (1857), though he was never free from police surveillance and chicanery. His first poem, *Neofity*, on early Christians, is an allegorical treatment of his own and others' modern martyrdom in the cause of freedom. In *Mariya* (1859), a poem of undeniable piety, the Mother of Jesus is humanized in an unorthodox way. In other poems his invective against tyrants often has the majestic style of Biblical prophecy. In the last year of his life, his poetry acquired a serene harmony with extreme economy of means and perfection of form.

He made the basic folk-song rhythms wonderfully musical, introduced new vocabulary, imagery, ideas, and instilled his own passionate, singularly articulate personality which was consonant with the people's innermost dormant longings. The fusion of the familiar with vast new horizons explains the grip of his poetry. While he is virtually the creator of the Ukrainian literary language, his abhorrence of injustice, his call to the people to break their chains and fight for freedom (the celebrated *Testament*, 1845), and his belief in mankind's better future make his appeal universal. [VS]

*Povne zibrannya tvoriv* (10 vols., 1939–64) (includes paintings); (6 vols., 1963–4); all poetry, tr. C. Andrusyshen, W. Kirkconnell, *Kobzar* (Toronto, 1964); *Selected Works* (incl. prose), ed. J. Weir, intr. Ye Kirilyuk (Moscow, 1964); *Song out of Darkness*, tr. V. Rich, ed. intr. V. Swoboda (1961); *Selections*, tr. J. Weir (Toronto, 1961); *The Poet of Ukraine. Selected Poems*, tr. intr. C. Manning (Jersey City, 1945); *The Kobzar of the Ukraine*, tr. A. Hunter (N.Y., 1961); *IL*, 2, 3 (1939).

*T. Sh. Bard of People's Freedom, a Collection of Essays* (N.Y., 1962); M. Rylsky, A. Deitch, *T. Sh. A Biogr. Sketch* (Kiev, 1964); D. Doroshenko, *T.Sh.*, pref. R. Seton-Watson (Prague, 1936); A. Jensen, *T.Sch.* (Vienna, 1916); Mijakovs'kyj and Shevelov, *TS*; *UCE*; *AUAU*, II, 2 (1952); *SR*, III, 7 (1924); XXXIV, 82 (1955); XL, 94 (1961); *UQ*, I, 2 (1945); V, 4 (1949); XII, 4 (1956); XX, 2 (1964); XI, 2, 4 (1964); XII, 1 (1965); *SL*, 3 (1964); *Slavic Review*, XXI, 4 (1962); *Suchasnist'*, IV, 3, 8, 12 (1964); *UR*, VIII–IX, 1–2 (1961–2).

**Shiroka, F.** ⇨ Albanian Literature.

**Shklovsky, Viktor Borisovich** (St Petersburg 1893– ). Russian writer and critic. He studied sculpture and architecture, and lived abroad 1922–3. A member of the ⇨ Serapion Brothers and closely associated with the Futurists ⇨ Khlebnikov and ⇨ Mayakovsky, he was one of the Formalist critics, believing that a work of art could be classified and evaluated in terms of its formal devices alone, and that its social, political and philosophical aspects were irrelevant; cf. *O teorii prozy* (1925); but his *Material i stil' v romane L. Tolstogo 'Voyna i mir'* (1928) tries to reconcile Formalism with Marxism. Also of interest are his 'novel in letters' *Zoo ill pis'ma ne o lyubvi* (1923) and critical essays *Khod konya* (1923).

After 1929 he turned to film-scenarios, but has re-emerged since the death of Stalin with such works as *Khudozhestvennaya proza* (1959), a new study of Tolstoy, *Lev Tolstoy* (1963), and the autobiographical *Zhili-Byli* (1964).

His autobiography *Sentimental Journey* has been translated into English (1970).

V. Erlich, *Russian Formalism* (1955).

**Shlevin, Benjamin** (Brest Litovsk 1913– ). Yiddish novelist. He lived in France before and volunteered for the French Army at the outbreak of the Second World War. In 1940, he became a prisoner of war, but survived and now lives in Paris where he has published a number of novels since the war. [EE]

*Di Yidn fun Belville* (1948); *Geven iz es nechtn* (1951); *Di vegen kraitsn zich* (1952).

**Shlonsky, Avraham** (Russia 1900– ). Hebrew poet. Went to Palestine in 1921 and, although he became one of its most virile poets whose lightness of form and magical rhythm grips the reader, he clearly shows the influence of Soviet Russian poets. In 1925, with Steinmann, he edited a literary periodical which marked the first revolt in Hebrew literature. He translated Pushkin, Shakespeare, Romain ⇨ Rolland and modern Russian poets and founded *Sifriat Poalim* ('Workers' Library'); since 1951 he has edited its literary quarterly *Orlogin.* [EE]

*Shirim* (1954); *Avnei Gvil* (1960).
Waxman, *HJL*; Klausner, *HMHL*.

**Shmelyov, Ivan Sergeyevich** (Moscow 1873–Paris 1950). Russian novelist. His most important works are *Chelovek iz restorana* (1910) and *Solntse myortvykh* (1925; tr. C. J. Hogarth, *The Sun of the Dead*, 1927). The former depicts, with moments of Dostoyevskyan power, the decadence of the wealthy, as seen by a simple waiter and pious father to whom son and daughter return after disastrous adventures in the world. The latter 'novel', told in the first person, without a proper plot, is remarkable for its scenes of the revolution in Soviet Russia and of the destruction of the White Army.

*Leto gospodne* (Paris, 1948); *Puti nebesnyye* (2 vols., Paris, 1937, 1948).

**Shneor, Zalman** (White Russia 1887–New York 1959). Yiddish writer. The son of the mystic S.Z. of Ladi, he had both traditional and worldly education. In his youth, he went to Odessa, at that time a centre of young Jewish writers and poets. Subsequently, he lived in Warsaw, Vilna, Switzerland, Berlin and, after the war, Paris. Like those who came from the narrow confines of the Pale of Settlement, he revolted against traditional Judaism. At the same time, he felt the sufferings of his people and the grave injustices done to it. His rebellious spirit pervades all his lyric works. He also wrote a number of nature poems, chiefly on the Alps and the Harz mountains. Into most of these, he injected a Jewish note. Gradually he turned to Zionism in which he, too, saw the solution of the Jewish problem. His best-known poem is the great ode *Vilna* depicting life in the ancient Jewish community known as Jerusalem in Lithuania. [EE]

*Noah Pandre* (1936); *Noah Pandre's Village* (1938). Klausner, *HMHL*; Waxman, *HJL*.

**Sholem Aleichem,** pseud. of Sholem Rabinovitch (nr Poltava 1859–New York 1916). Yiddish writer. With ⇨ Mendele and Peretz one of the most important Yiddish writers. He is distinguished by his very original style, a wry humour, with which he describes his characters. Indeed it is this humour which helped the Jew to meet and overcome the many vicissitudes of life, particularly in the oppressive atmosphere of Tsarist Russia. The inhabitants of the township of Woronka, where he spent his childhood and early youth, left an indelible impression upon him and the inhabitants of the fictitious town of *Kasrilivke* are all modelled on this. His childhood was marred by the death of his mother, his stepmother and the financial difficulties of his father. At 21 he became a Government Rabbi in Luben, and held this position for three years. During this time he wrote his first articles in Hebrew for *Ha-Melitz*. Having married his childhood sweetheart, he moved to Kiev where he devoted his entire life to writing and spent the fortune inherited from his father-in-law on financial transactions, publishing and sponsoring young writers. His financial adventures led to bankruptcy and his move to Odessa in 1890. The misfortune he experienced in the world of finance are typified by his hero Menahem Mendel. From 1883 he wrote almost exclusively in Yiddish and adopted his pen-name which is in fact the common form of greeting among Jews, meaning 'peace be unto you'. From 1888 he edited and published the first Yiddish literary annual, *Di Yiddishe Folksbibliothek*, the first periodical designed to raise the standard of Yiddish, and to pay its contributors. Always unlucky in commercial life, he became immensely popular as a story-teller and soon his name became a household word in thousands of Jewish homes. From 1905 on he travelled extensively in England, the United States, Germany, Italy and Switzerland, but at the outbreak of the First World War went to settle in the United States. His chief contribution to Yiddish letters and Jewish life is that he taught Jews to laugh at their own misfortunes. His humour is never far from the tragedies that lie underneath. Immensely prolific, his writings fill many volumes and range from novels to short stories, comedies, essays, sketches and an autobiography. He is translated into most European languages and is widely read and often performed on stage and screen. Internationally he is most certainly the best-known Yiddish author of his time. [EE]

*S.A.s Werk* (14 vols., N.Y., 1908–14); *Chayey-Adam* (Yiddish) (N.Y., 1920) (autobiography); *Stories and Satires*, tr. C. Leviant (1959); *Adventures of Mottel the Cantor's Son*, tr. H. and T. Kahana (1953); *Selected Stories*, tr. J. and F. Butwin (1958); *Old Country Tales*, tr. C. Leviant (N.Y., 1966).

I. Zinbert and S. Niger, *Zum Ondenk fun S.A.* (Petersburg, 1927); *Dos S.A. Buch* (N.Y., 1926); Roback, *SYL*; M. Samuel, *The World of S.A.* (N.Y., 1943).

**Sholokhov, Mikhail Aleksandrovich** (Kruzhilino na Donu 1905– ). Russian novelist. Of middle-class origin, he served with the Red Army during the Civil War. His first works were published in 1923. Later included in his collections of stories *Donskiye rasskazy* (1925; tr. H. C. Stevens, *Tales from the Don*, 1961) and *Lazorevaya step'* (1926), they reveal his gifts of direct and colourful language and his sense of the close bond between man and nature. But they were eclipsed by the appearance of his novel *Tikhiy Don* (1928–40; Pt I, *And Quiet Flows the Don*, 1934; Pt II, *The Don Flows*

*Home to the Sea*, 1940; both tr. S. Garry). This account of Don Cossack life between 1912 and 1922 in peace-time, war and revolution is remarkable for its objectivity. The atrocities of Reds and Whites are carefully balanced, and the Cossacks' later hopeless struggle against the central government is related no less impartially. The hero is torn tragically between his love for two women and his two loyalties, to the Cossacks and to the Bolsheviks; and yet for all his weakness and treachery he remains a tragic figure. The novel has been frequently revised and bowdlerized, but even so it still retains its power. Now regarded as one of the masterpieces of socialist realism, *Tikhiy Don* in fact defies most of its criteria. *Podnyataya Tselina* (1932–60; Pt I, tr. S. Garry, *Virgin Soil Upturned*, 1935; Pt II, tr. H. C. Stevens, *Harvest on the Don*, 1960) deals with the collectivization campaign in the Don region; this novel is more tendentious than *Tikhiy Don*, but it makes some show at objectivity; it is redeemed by its vigorous humour.

Sholokhov is happiest when dealing with people and events connected with the Don. His language is steeped in local dialect. When he goes outside these limitations as in the fragments from a projected epic *Oni srazhalis' za rodinu* (1943–4) and *Sud'ba cheloveka* (1956; tr. in Snow and Hansford-Johnson, *WT*, *A Man's Life*) his writing lacks the gusto of his other work.

He was awarded the Nobel Prize for Literature in 1964. [RDBT]

*Sobraniye sochineniy* (8 vols., 1956–9).

L. Yakimenko, *Tvorchestvo M.A.S.* (Moscow, 1964); Simmons, *RFSI*.

**Shteyn, Aleksandr Petrovich** (Samarkand 1906– ). Soviet playwright. In 1928–48 he lived in Leningrad, as a student, then journalist, short-story writer and dramatist. His first play, *Neft*, was written in 1929. In the thirties he worked for the cinema as well as for the stage, and during the war he served as a Naval Officer and took part in the defence of Leningrad. Leningrad (past and present), with her bleak history of revolution, war and hunger, with her bleak classical beauty and her heroic people sheltering like snow-bound swallows in her crumbling masonry, is his first theme. His second is the Baltic Fleet – blood-brother to the city of Peter and Lenin, product of the same harsh nursery, loyal and cantankerous, defending his lovely, immobile sister in time of war, seeking to mould her fate in time of civil strife, returning always to rest in her stately havens after hard labour on the cold, grey seas. [AP]

*P'yesy*, intr. N. Okhlopkov (1962); *Kinostsenarii* (1956); *O trude dramaturga*, ed. Ve. F. Pimonov (1957); *Dramy* (1966); *Povest' o tom . . .* (1965).

*Voprosy Literatury*, 3 (1962); Boguslavskiy, *KIRSD*.

**Shvarts, Yevgeny L'vovich** (Kazan 1896–Leningrad 1958). Soviet dramatist and children's writer. For sheer charm, his dramatized fairy-tales for grown-ups, whether written for the stage like *Golyy Korol'* (1934), *Ten'* (1940) and *Drakon* (1944; tr. M. Hayward and H. Shukman, *The Dragon*, in *Three Soviet Plays*, 1966) or for the puppet-theatre like *Skazka o poteryanom vremeni* (tr. L. Pargment, E. Titiev, *A Tale of Stolen Time*, N.Y., 1966) and *Volshebnik* (1948), or for the cinema like *Zolushka* ('Cinderella') and *Don Kikhot* are among the loveliest works of their kind produced in Europe since Hans ⇨ Andersen – from whom he often borrowed his subjects. He appears simple, but is often profound, eccentric, topical, wise and very funny. Gimlet-eyed for all that is mediocre, pretentious or evil, he believes in goodness. His Cinderella is an enchanting creature who deserves her good fortune, his Quixote one of the pure in heart who, we feel, will inevitably come to his appointed reward, his Launcelot no cardboard knight but a real hero, who 'meddles in other people's business' only because he has been privileged to turn the pages of the 'Book of Unrighted Wrongs', a chronicle of man's offences against man kept by the trees and the air and the earth itself in a far place beyond the Black Mountains. [AP]

*Kukol'nyy Gorod: P'yesy dlya teatra kukol*, intr. S. Dreyden (1959); *P'yesy*, intr. S. Tsimbal (1960); *Skazki, povesti, p'yesy* (1960); F. D. Reeve, *An Anthology of Russian Plays* (N.Y., 1961).

S. Tsimbal, *E.S.* (Leningrad, 1961); *My znali Y.S.* (Moscow–Leningrad, 1966).

**Sienkiewicz, Henryk** (Wola Okrzejska 1846–Vevey 1916). Polish novelist, known outside Poland only for *Quo vadis* (1896), a historical novel about Nero's Rome, vulgarized by a number of film versions, the earliest in 1912. In fact, he is a good stylist – though badly served by translators – and his total achievement and moral stature are considerable. He came from an impoverished noble family and made a social adjustment by joining the new intelligentsia which was spreading the gentry's culture into the towns. He studied at Warsaw, worked as journalist, published a first curious novel, set in Kiev (*Na marne*, 1872; tr. J. Curtin, *In Vain*, 1899), and developed his creative talent in short stories. In stories like *Szkice węglem* (1877) he combined humorous observation with social criticism, the latter often directed against the country squire who was opting out of his responsibilities after the emancipation of the peasants.

In 1876 he went to the U.S.A.; he was to do most of his later writing while travelling, and his Warsaw home became almost as temporary as the German or Italian hotels in which he would create his very Polish characters and scenes. The maturing influence on his mind is much in evidence in his *Listy z podróży do Ameryki* (1876–8; tr. C. Morley, *Portrait of America*, N.Y., 1959), which brilliantly recaptures the moods of an expanding country, especially in the Californian scenes.

A bitter short novel, *Bartek Zwycięzca* (1882), with its peasant hero enlisted in the Prussian army to fight the French, showed Sienkiewicz's skill in depicting battles, but even then none of his critics could predict the unparalleled success of his war trilogy (tr. J. Curtin, 1891–3). Its first part, *Ogniem i mieczem* ('With Fire and Sword'), began as a serial in May 1883, and with it grew the author's unprecedented and lasting popularity. Perhaps the choice of the 17th century for the historical setting had something to do with this instinctive response to the national ethos. In *Potop* ('The Deluge'), the second and the best part of the trilogy, he excels, like Dickens, in the portrayal of secondary characters. His style is more heightened in dialogue than in narrative; he had a perfect ear for the sounds of the past which he absorbed from memoirs (e.g. of ⇨ Pasek), documents and epic poetry. The 17th century literally speaks through the mouths of his characters, which accounts for their verisimilitude. Here pedestrian translators inevitably fail. The 'deluge' of the Swedish invasion allowed him to move freely about his novel, changing backgrounds and manipulating hundreds of events (the third part, *Pan Wolodyjowski*, 1888, is more restricted). He had, however, a weakness for the romantic intrigue where a beautiful heroine is kidnapped and rescued after a prolonged chase. The same formula reappears with slight variations in *Quo vadis* (1896; tr. C. J. Hogarth, 1941), *Krzyżacy* (1900; tr. A. Tyszkiewicz, *The Teutonic Knights*, 1943) and even in the charming book for children, *W pustyni i w puszczy* (tr. M. A. Drezmal, *In Desert and Wilderness*, 1945). Some critics therefore belittle his treatment of character. Yet he made a thorough analysis of a decadent man of leisure in *Bez dogmatu* (1891; tr. I. Young, *Without Dogma*, 1899), a novel written in diary form. Here once again his style triumphed over the introspective theme.

Having acquired fame at home and abroad, Sienkiewicz found himself in the role of spokesman for his country which was then ruled by three foreign powers (e.g. his open letter to Wilhelm II, 1906). But his patriotism was well informed, civilized and devoid of any self-righteousness. French writers who could not forgive him the success of *Quo vadis* attacked him with zenophobic hysteria. The award of the Nobel Prize for Literature in 1905 crowned his reputation in his own time, but it is now in decline outside Poland. New and better translations are needed to make a reassessment possible. Recently, Henry de ⇨ Montherlant has acknowledged the formative influence of *Quo vadis* [JP]

*Dzieła*, ed. J. Krzyżanowski (1948–55); *Tales from H.S.*, ed. M. M. Gardner (1931).

W. Lednicki, *H.S.* (The Hague, 1960); M. Kosko *Un 'best-seller' 1900, Quo vadis?* (Paris, 1960).

**Sieroszewski, Wacław** (Wólka Kozłowska 1860–Piaseczno 1945). Polish novelist. For his revolutionary activities he was deported to Siberia and lived among the Yakuts, whose customs he described in novels and in a Russian monograph (1896). He later travelled to China and Japan, and used his impressions of Asia for the exotic background of his many novels. The best of them are: *Na kresach lasów* (1894), *Ucieczka* (1904; tr. anon. as *A Flight from Siberia*, 1909) and *Beniowski* (1916). When the Polish Academy of Literature was established in 1933, he became its first president. [JP]

**Sigebert of Gembloux** (*c.*1030–Gembloux 1112). Benedictine chronicler. He lived at Gembloux in Belgium. An indefatigable and learned writer, he is chiefly known for his universal chronicle, *Chronographia*, covering the years 381–1111, which was very popular during the Middle Ages. He also wrote lives of saints and lives of the Abbots of Gembloux. He took the side of the Emperor during the struggle between Henry IV and Pope Gregory VII. [FB]

Migne, *PL*, 160; MGH, Scriptores, VI.
S. Hirsch, *De vita et scriptis S.G.* (Berlin, 1841).

**Sikelianos, Angelos** (Leucas 1884–Athens 1951). Greek poet. He received his early education in his native island, and afterwards studied law for a time at the University of Athens. He travelled widely in Europe, Egypt and America. He devoted himself entirely to literature and was for many years a dominant and colourful personality in the literary world of Greece. His first important work, *Alafroiskiotos* (1909), established him immediately as a poet of powerful lyricism and comparable only to ⇨ Palamas in linguistic resourcefulness. His vision embraces Greek tradition and myth in its entirety, and his inspiration is rich and profound, but often – especially in his earlier verse – uncontrolled. He was obsessed with Orphism and other ancient cults and philosophies and by using images and symbols from them and combining them with images and symbols from Christianity he sought to find a mystical unity embracing mankind and nature. A sharp awareness and enjoyment of the physical world (a prerequisite for the illumination of the mind) gives his poetry a robust sensuousness and optimism. His later poetry is more controlled and restrained and deeper in its mystical approach. Another obsession of his was the 'Delphic idea', which would bring mankind together and stimulate the birth of a new civilization. Together with his first, American-born wife he organized the highly successful Delphic festivals of 1927 and 1930, where ancient Greek plays and dances were performed in the ancient theatre of Delphi before a cosmopolitan audience. His poetic output was very prolific; he also wrote several verse-dramas distinguished more for their poetry than their dramatic skill. [SJP]

*Lyrikos Vios* (3 vols., 1946–7); *Antidoron* (1943); *Thymeli* (2 vols., 1950) (plays).
G. Katsimbalis, *Bibliografia A.S.* (1946); S. Baud-Bovy, *Poésie de la Grèce moderne* (Paris, 1946); P. Sherrard, *The Marble Threshing Floor* (1956); E. Keeley and P. Sherrard, *Six Poets of Modern Greece* (1960).

**Sillanpää, Frans Eemil** (Hämeenkyrö 1888–Helsinki 1964). Finnish novelist. The son of a tenant-farmer, he studied natural sciences at Helsinki, where he became a biological monist in outlook. He was also influenced by foreign literature, especially by ⇨ Hamsun and ⇨ Maeterlinck. He was awarded a Nobel Prize in 1939.

His first novel, *Elämä ja aurinko* (1916), describes a summer in the life of two young lovers; the central role is played by Nature, of which the human characters are merely one manifestation. The best novel of his early period is *Hurskas kurjuus* (1919; tr. A. Matson, *Meek Heritage*, 1938), which describes the impact of the Finnish civil war of 1918 on a passive character, a humble tenant-farmer; the treatment of recent history is open-minded and humane, with the emphasis on what is basic in human nature. There follows a period of Maeterlinckian mysticism and sympathetic naturalism, culminating in *Hiltu ja Ragnar* (1923), a short, closely knit novel. With *Nuorena nukkunut* (1931; tr. A. Matson, *The Maid Silja or Fallen Asleep While Young*, 1933), which has a young girl as its central character, Sillanpää achieved international fame, and the book was widely translated. The two chief characters of *Miehen tie* (1932), a novel of peasant life, are a man and a woman drawn together by an 'affinity of choice' which seems as irresistible as a force of nature; the treatment of the theme is reminiscent of D. H. Lawrence. This period ends with the novel-series *Ihmiset suviyössä* (1934), in which his style, with its melodious cadences, is at its finest. He has also written a large number of short stories, in which the prose style is predominantly meditative and lyrical. [AK]

*Kootut teokset* (12 vols., 1932–48); Tompuri, *VF*. T. Vaaskivi, *F.E.S.* (Helsinki, 1937); R. Koskimies, *F.E.S.* (Helsinki, 1948); Havu, *FL*.

**Silone, Ignazio,** pseud. of Secondo Tranquilli (Pescina 1900– ). Italian writer and politician. The novels he wrote in exile during the Fascist dictatorship (*Fontamara*, 1933; tr. G. D. and E. Mosbacher, 1934, reissued 1960; *Pane e vino*, 1937; tr. G. D. and E. Mosbacher, *Bread and Wine*, 1934, later rewritten as *Vino e pane*, 1955; tr. H. Fergusson II, 1964; *Il seme sotto la neve*, 1941; tr. F. Frenaye, *The Seed beneath the Snow*, 1943) won him immediate fame abroad, where he was acclaimed, in the rather distorted literary perspective of those years, as the most representative Italian writer of his generation. This view has never been confirmed by Italian critics and readers, despite their respect for him as an anti-fascist and a patriot.

For all his socializing beliefs and his devotion to the cause of the under-privileged Southern peasants, he is not a realist, nor is he the initiator of post-war Italian realism. *Fontamara*, with its blood-sucking landlords, over-corrupt officials and all too articulate peasants on whose shoulders Fate heaps mechanically misfortune after misfortune, is in fact no more realistic than any 18th-century political satire. This novel has, however, an artistic unity which is found lacking in some of his later novels (*Una manciata di more*, 1952; tr. D. Silone, *A Handful of Blackberries*, 1954; *Il segreto di Luca* ,1956; tr. D. Silone, *The Secret of Luca*, 1959; *La volpe e le camelie*, 1960; tr. E. Mosbacher, *The Fox and the Camellias*, 1960), where realistic descriptions and lyrical passages mingle with naïve symbolism and sententious tirades, and the author's strong and sincere humanitarian message is often carried by a weak narrative structure. [GMC]

*Scuola dei dittatori* (1938; tr. G. D. and E. Mosbacher, 1939; new ed. tr. W. Weaver, *The School for Dictators*, 1964).

C. Varese, *Cultura letteraria contemporanea* (Pisa, 1951); N. A. Scott, *Rehearsal of Discomposure* (1952).

**Silva, António Dinis da Cruz e** (Lisbon 1731–Rio de Janeiro 1799). Portuguese man of letters. He graduated in Law at the University of Coimbra and was appointed judge in Elvas (1764). He was held in high esteem by his superiors who sent him to Brazil with the mission of trying the leaders of a conspiracy against Portuguese colonial rule (1792). Silva, who began to write poetry as an undergraduate, became famous for his mock-heroic poem, *O Hissope*, composed at the time of his sojourn in Elvas. That city had been the scene of an ecclesiastical dispute over matters of etiquette between the bishop of the local see and his dean. Silva was quick in seizing his opportunity and around that episode he spun a lively satire against the declining values of a feudal order that had been shattered by King José's Prime Minister, the Marquis of Pombal. *Hissope* was begun *c.* 1768; but owing to the personal allusions made in it, it was never published in the author's lifetime, although it was circulated in manuscript. When it was printed for the first time, in Paris in 1802, it contained already many interpolations for which the author is not responsible. Silva also wrote many lyric poems in the neo-classical style.

With the exception of the *Hissope*, Silva's poetry is little read outside academic circles. [LSR]

*Poesias* (6 vols., 1807–17).

Teófilo Braga, *A Arcádia Lusitana* (Porto, 1899); Ruggiero Ruggieri, 'A.D. da C e S. e *l'Hissope*', in *Relazioni storiche fra Italia e il Portogallo* (Roma, 1940).

**Simenon, Georges** (Liège 1903– ). French novelist. A kind of autodidact or 'natural' amid the general sophistication of French writing, the phenomenally prolific Simenon turned out popular fiction for a number of years before launching his celebrated Maigret series in 1931. Some years later he abandoned his detective in order to attempt more ambitious novels, but he revived him at the end of the war – in a mellower version – as a second string. He is one of the very few who have come close to superseding the inherent limitations of the detective novel. The Maigret stories are often 'technically' imperfect, but this is merely a pointer to their great superiority over English products of the time (with their tendency to treat murder as a parlour-game, their emphasis on 'method', etc.). Maigret does not so much deduce as attune himself to the situation until he has grasped intuitively the motivation behind the crime – his authority springs essentially from his simplicity, his humanity and his sympathy. In his other novels too, Simenon catches very well the frustration, the loneliness, the inability to be himself of the ordinary, inarticulate person trapped in a situation. Among those which possess serious literary merits are *La vérité sur Bébé Donge* (1942; tr. G. Sainsbury, *The Trial of Bébé Donge*, 1952), *La neige était sale* (1948; tr. J. Petrie, *The Stain on the Snow*, 1953), and the semi-autobiographical *Pedigree* (1948; tr. R. Baldick, 1965). Many stories have appeared in Penguins. [CJ]

B. de Fallois, *S.* (Paris, 1961); T. Narcejac, *Le Cas 'S'*. (Paris, 1950; tr. *The Art of S.*, 1952).

**Šimić, Antun Branko** (Drinovci 1898–Zagreb 1925). Croatian poet. He was influenced by the symbolist-expressionist ideas brought to Croatia by ⇨ Matoš. His poetry is mainly subjective free verse and in this he was one of the earliest experimenters in the language. His output was not great. His main theme is the relation of his own existence to the world around him and his tone is often pessimistic. His poems *Preobraženja* were published in 1925. [EDG]

Lavrin, *AMYP*.
Kadić, *CCL*.

**Simon, Claude** (Tananarive 1913– ). French novelist. He began writing in 1946 but came into prominence with *Le vent* (1957; tr. R. Howard, *Wind*, 1959), *L'herbe* (1958; tr. R. Howard, *The Grass*, 1961), *La route des Flandres* (1960; tr. R. Howard, *The Flanders Road*, 1962), *Le Palace* (1962; tr. R. Howard, *The Palace*, 1964), *Histoire* (1967). These novels present a character in a state of emotional turmoil, obsessed with some incident in the past, or with the environment in which he finds himself. The effect of this obsession is to abolish order, perspective and, therefore, traditional 'story': the characters in their dazed state mix the present, past and possible future into an 'eternal present'. Simon employs the jumbled chronology and abrupt transitions of William Faulkner to render consciousness directly in all its confusion. His characters never escape from the mass of their experience, and never order it. This pessimism is expressed with a power and a sensuous richness which gives *La route des Flandres* an almost epic quality. [IL]

B. T. Fitch, L. Lesage, J. L. Seylaz in J. H. Matthews (ed.), *Un nouveau roman?* (Paris, 1964).

**Simonides, Simon** (Lvov 1558–Czernięcin 1629). Polish poet. Of burgher origin, he enjoyed the patronage of the enlightened statesman Zamoyski and in 1590 was made a noble. He consistently used the pen-name of Simonides, and there is no biographical authority for the Polonized version of his name (Szymon Szymonowicz) under which he appears in most reference books. His polished Latin verse won him admirers in his own country and abroad, but today he is remembered for his Polish idylls (*Sielanki*, 1614), a volume which not only established a native pastoral tradition, but also orientated it towards genuine folklore.

The best example is the idyll *Żeńcy* ('The Reapers'), based on a theme from Theocritus, but so rich in local detail and musical effects that it transcends the literary convention. Its deeper originality, rooted in pre-Christian mythology, comes from the set of songs which a peasant woman addresses to the sun, 'the eye of day', and the giver of all love and order. [JP]

Peterkiewicz and Singer, *FCPP*.
*SEER*, XXXIV, 82 (1955).

**Simonov, Konstantin Mikhaylovich** (Petersburg 1915– ). Soviet journalist, novelist, poet and playwright. He worked as a metal-cutter from the age of 15, was an evening student at the Literary Institute (1934–8), and war-correspondent 1939–45 (Mongolia). He wrote the Stalingrad novel *Dni i nochi* (tr. J. Fineberg, *Days and Nights*, 1945), some excellent war poetry, including the world-famous 'Wait for me' and 'Remember, Alyosha' (see *Friends and Foes, A Book of Poems*, tr. I. Zhukovitskaya, Moscow, 1951), and several war plays. One of these, *Russkiye Lyudi* (tr. *Four Soviet War Plays*, 1944), was staged by the Old Vic (1943) and in the U.S.A. After the war, Simonov visited (with writers' delegations) many countries inside and outside the Soviet bloc, wrote several retrospective novels (including the recently filmed *The Living and the Dead*), and a number of plays, many of them set outside the U.S.S.R. (*Russkiy Vopros* and *Tak i budet* have been translated and staged in England and America). War and the necessity for peace are the main themes of his works; his heroes are often professional journalists, more interesting for their reaction to topical problems than psychologically, as human beings perceived in depth. On the other hand, Simonov writes of his own country with profound feeling and integrity. In depicting the West, he betrays neither factual nor psychological ignorance; his timing and sense of situation are slick, his dialogue witty – and he is never dull. [AP]

*Sobraniye Sochineniy* (6 vols., 1966ff.); *Sochineniya* (3 vols., 1952–3); *Zhivye i myortvye* (2 vols., 1960); *P'yesy*, intr. K. Lomunov (1954).

L. Lazarev, *Dramaturgiya K.S.* (Moscow, 1952); I. L. Vishnevskaya, *K.S. Ocherk tvorchestva* (Moscow, 1966).

**Singer, Yisroel Joshua** (Lublin 1893–Los Angeles 1944). Yiddish novelist, a leader of 'moderns'. After the Russian Revolution of 1917, he went to live in Kiev and Moscow, but returned to Warsaw in 1928 where he spent the war years. Soon after, he emigrated to America. Some of his novels were dramatized. [EE]

*Perl un andere dertseilungen* (Warsaw, 1922); *Oi Nayer Erd* (Vilna, 1923); *Yoshe Kalb* (N.Y., 1932) (drama).
Roback, *SYL.*

**Sinyavsky, Andrey Donatovich,** pen-name: Abram Tertz (Moscow 1925– ). Russian novelist and critic. Sinyavsky graduated and took his *kandidat* degree at Moscow University during the last years of Stalin's reign, and their atmosphere permeates much of his fiction. He embarked on a career as a literary scholar and achieved a deserved reputation both by his teaching and his publications, e.g. a brilliant study (in collaboration with A. Menshutin) of the poetry of the first years of the Russian Revolution (*Poeziya pervykh let revolyutsii, 1917–20*, 1964), and a detailed and sensitive introduction to the poetry of his friend and mentor, Boris Pasternak (1965). Simultaneously, as novelist and short-story writer, he was establishing a reputation outside the U.S.S.R. under the pseudonym of Abram Tertz. His writings as Tertz were begun in 1956 and started to appear from 1959 in Western Europe and the U.S.A., both in translation and in the original. His novel *Sud idyot* (tr. *The Trial Begins*, 1960) and his collection of short stories *Fantasticheskiye Povesti* (1961; tr. *The Icicle and Other Stories*, 1963) are penetrating evocations of the terror that preceded Stalin's death (the arrest of Sinyavsky's father in 1951 made a lasting impact on him). His most notable achievement to date is the symbolic novel *Lyubimov* (1964; tr. *The Makepiece Experiment*, 1965).

Sinyavsky (together with his friend Yuli Daniel, whose pseudonym is Nikolay Arzhak) was arrested in September 1965 and accused of 'writing and sending abroad ... stories ... which contain slanderous statements against the Soviet system and are used by reactionary propaganda against the Soviet State'. The trial (at which the verdict was never in doubt) provoked an outcry from all parts of the world: non-Russian Communists and Soviet intellectuals were prominent among those who protested against the holding, the conduct and the outcome of the trial. Sinyavsky was sentenced to seven years' hard labour and thus followed the narrator of his *The Trial Begins* to the penal camps.

At his trial Sinyavsky spoke of 'the marvellous and the fantastic' as his favourite qualities: he delights in the power and the autonomy of the imagination, and his caustic wit (tempered by compassion), his free use of time and space, his 'phantasmagoric art with hypotheses instead of a Purpose' have nothing in common with routine Socialist Realism. His aim ('to be truthful with the aid of the absurd and the fantastic') links him with Gogol' and Dostoyevsky, and with the Russian experimental writers of the 1920s. [SH]

*Fantasticheskiy Mir Abrama Tertsa* (Washington, D.C., 1967) (collected works).
L. Labedz and M. Hayward, ed., *On Trial: The Case of Sinyavsky (Tertz) and Daniel (Arzhak)* (1967).

**Siwertz, Sigfrid** (Stockholm 1882– ). Swedish novelist, essayist, poet and dramatist. Like ⇨ Söderberg and Bo ⇨ Bergman an outstanding portrayer of Stockholm; after early ironical work resembling theirs he developed under the influence of Bergson a concern with energetic activity, as in the classic boys' novel *Mälarpirater* (1911); Mälaren is the great lake inland from Stockholm – sea, lakes and water in general have been frequent inspirations. Much of his large and fluent production, sometimes closely related to recent events, is merely competent. His acknowledged masterpiece is the novel *Selambs* (1920; tr. E. Classen, *Downstream*, 1922), a sombre, massive and superbly ferocious dissection of a rapacious capitalist family through the varying fates of five brothers and sisters, each unforgettably vivid. Although his later production includes a great many novels, his most memorable books have been volumes of linked short stories, such as *Sex fribiljetter* (1943), *Förtroenden* (1945) and *Trådar i en väv* (1957). He has also published books of memoirs which are notable for their candour and charm, e.g. *Att vara ung* (1948) and *Fåfäng gå...* (1957).

*Bonniers Litterära Magasin* (1932).
S. Stolpe, *S.S.* (Stockholm, 1933).

**Sjöberg, Birger** (Vänersborg 1885–Växjö 1929). Swedish poet and novelist. He never completed his schooling and for a time worked in his native town as a shop-assistant and then for several years as a journalist there and in Hälsingborg. During the first half of the twenties he was a popular entertainer with guitar and songs composed by himself. Published in 1922 as *Fridas bok*, these charming and amusingly ironic songs of life in a provincial town enjoyed enormous success. In 1924 he published a popular comic novel, *Kvartetten som sprängdes*. In 1926 appeared his third book, *Kriser och kransar*, an important collection of verse of remarkable modernity. The fundamental theme is the agonizing clash between convention and reality or dream and reality, and the craving for truth. The influence of Shakespeare (in a classical Swedish version) has been discerned in his verse, which with its bold innovations, especially in the use of contemporary vocabulary, has affected several subsequent poets. More of his poetry was published posthumously, e.g. *Minnen från jorden* (1940), *Syntaxupproret* (1955) and *Fridas tredje bok* (1956).

A. Peterson, *B.S. den okände* (Stockholm, 1944); G. Axberger, *Lilla Paris' undergång* (Stockholm, 1960); K. Jaensson, 'B.S.' in *Sanning och särprägel* (Stockholm, 1960); *Synpunkter på B.S.*, ed. L. H. Tunving (1966).

**Skerlić, Jovan** (Belgrade 1877–Belgrade 1914). Perhaps the most important Serbian critic and historian of literature and author of the standard history of literature, *Istorija nove srpske književnosti* (1914). His other works include a history of Serbian literature in the 18th century (1909), a monograph on Jakov ⇨ Ignjatović (1904) and Svetozar Marković (1910) as well as many critical articles and other shorter works.

He was both a socialist and a realist by persuasion. This tended often to bias his criticism, causing him to reject the new trends in Serbian poetry as being decadent. None the less he is the most important figure in the development of the study of Serbian literature and his works remain of importance to the present day. [EDG]

**Skram, Amalie** (Bergen 1847–Copenhagen 1905). Norwegian novelist. An unhappy childhood, followed by early marriage ending in divorce, are both reflected in the pessimism of her work and its concern with the (erotic) problems of women. Her frank expression of the female view on sex and marriage in *Constance Ring* (1885), *Lucie* (1888), *Fru Inés* (1891), and *Forraadt* (1892) shocked her contemporaries. But her most important work is *Hellemyrsfolket* (4 vols., 1887–98), a deeply pessimistic, deterministic depiction of successive generations of a family in decline. As a writer she lacked finesse, but her eye for milieu, her flowing narrative and passion still keep her best work alive. [RGP]

*Samlede verker* (6 vols., 1946).
A. Tiberg, *A.S.* (Oslo, 1910); B. Krane, *A.S. og kvinnens problem* (Oslo, 1951), and *A.S.s diktning* (Oslo, 1961); Downs, *MNL*.

**Sládkovič, Andrej,** pseud. of Ondrej Braxatoris (Krupina 1820–Radvaň 1872). Slovak poet. One of the leading poets of the school of ⇨ Štúr, he is best known for his lyrical epic *Marína* which shows the influence of Pushkin and ⇨ Kollár and is a remarkable achievement for a poet writing in a relatively untried literary language. [RA]

*Dielo*, ed. C. Kraus (2 vols., 1961).
V. Kochol, *Poézia Štúrovcov* (Bratislava, 1955).

**Slaveykov, Pencho** (Tryavna 1866–Como 1912). Bulgarian poet, critic and thinker. From his father, Petko ⇨ Slaveykov, he inherited his resilient individualism, interest in folklore and devotion to his country's cultural development. Crippled by illness in youth, he acquired, as no Bulgarian writer before, a wide critical knowledge of European literature. Pushkin, the Russian novelists, Nietzsche and Heine inspired his humanist idealism and rejection of 'Zola's "the beast in man" naturalism'. While reading aesthetics at Leipzig (1892–8) he tried to analyse genius in his *Epicheski pesni* (I, 1896; II, 1898) on Michelangelo, Beethoven, Shelley and Prometheus. This last, and the Balkan mountain to which he is chained, are recurring images symbolizing his own frustrations and physical sufferings (cf. the defiant martyr in 'Poet' and 'Bacho Kiro'). In 'The Carol-Singers', 'Boyko', 'Ralitsa', 'The Inseparables' and other ballad poems he endowed folk themes with new significance. See also his essays on folk love-songs *Narodnite lyubovni pesni* (1902) and *Nashite narodni pesni* ('Our Folksongs', 1904), also his *Shade of the Balkans* (London, 1904) and *Kniga na pesnite* ('The Book of Songs', 1917).

In 1898 he settled in Sofia, becoming assistant head of the State Library in 1902 and (after a season directing the National Theatre) its head in 1909. With the critic Dr K. Krăstev, he encouraged such rising talents as ⇨ Yavorov, ⇨ Todorov and ⇨ Hristov, himself developing in the monthly *Misăl* (1892–1908) the 'individualist' reaction against the conservative tradition of the ⇨'Vazov circle'. Their aim was to explore their heritage in a wide context of classical and modern European thought; the quest for absolute standards of literary excellence was to replace at last Bulgarian literature's age-long ecclesiastical and national commitments. To this Slaveykov contributed signally as author, critic and translator.

The impression that as a philosopher he could not write from the heart was dispelled by his lyrics *Săn za shtastie* (1907). In 1910 appeared *Na ostrova na blazhenite*, his anthology of imaginary poets, each characterized with numerous autobiographical and contemporary allusions. His most ambitious work, *Kărvava pesen* (1911–13), an epic poem on the tragic April 1876 rising against the Turks, remained unfinished at his death. [VP]

*Săchineniya* (8 vols., 1958–9); Pinto, *BPV*.
M. Nikolov, *P.S.: zhivot, lichnost i deynost* (Sofia, 1939); S. Slaveykova, *P.S.: biografichen ocherk* (Sofia, 1955); Manning and Smal-Stocki, *HMBL*.

**Slaveykov, Petko** (Trnovo 1827–Sofia 1895). Bulgarian poet. Deflected from monkhood by reading Father Paisy's *Istoriya slavenobolgarska* ('Slavo-Bulgarian History', 1872), he devoted his life to that appeal for Bulgarian national awakening. He taught in Tryavna 1849–52. Hounded by the Phanariot clergy and angered at their efforts 'to obliterate the Bulgarian book', he joined the Bulgarian colony in Constantinople in 1864 to press in his journals *Gayda* (1863–7) and *Makedoniya* (1866–72) for church autonomy, won finally by the Exarchate of 1870. For Protestant missionaries there he translated the New Testament into modern Bulgarian.

The education of his people in a Bulgarian nationhood proof to all Greek, Turkish and Catholic incursions motivated the varied assortment of writing he published from 1852 as journalist, entertainer, pedagogue, fabulist and ethnographer. His poetry, too, has usually some such *raison d'écrire*. Gergana's apologia for her Bulgarian home withstands the Turkish vizier's grandiloquent offers in his ballad *Izvorăt na belonogata* (1873). The resolve to cease writing ('I have no heart to sing', 1870) he soon withdrew in another elegy, 'My cruelty is curbed', identifying his own with his people's sorrows. He remains, despite some able predecessors like D. Chintulov and N. Gerov, the first modern Bulgarian poet of distinction.

The events of the April 1876 rising and ensuing Russo-Turkish War he witnessed in Stara Zagora, the firing of which tragically consumed his manuscripts and folklore materials – he was an assiduous collector of proverbs and songs. 'Grandpa Slaveykov', as this veteran came respectfully to be known as in independent Bulgaria, continued after the liberation of 1878 to campaign as journalist and Liberal politician for the Trnovo Constitution. He left an illuminating little *Avtobiografiya*, written in 1884. [VP]

*Săchineniya*, i–x (1963ff.); Pinto, *BPV*.
P. Dinekov, *P.R.S.: tvorcheski păt* (Sofia, 1956); S. Slaveykova, *P.R.S.: sluchki iz negoviya zhivot* (Sofia, 1957) and *Biografichen ocherk* (Sofia, 1958); Manning and Smal-Stocki, *HMBL*.

**Słonimski, Antoni** (Warsaw 1895– ). Polish playwright and poet. He will probably be best remembered for his prewar satirical comedies, e.g. *Murzyn warszawski* and *Rodzina* (1934), the latter notable for its witty juxtaposition of the Communist and the Nazi ideologies. His reflective lyrical verse gains in depth when moods of solitude are contrasted with the exotic scenery or the expatriate condition, as in the volumes *Droga na Wschód* (1924) and *Wybór poezji* (1944). He spent the war years in London and returned to Warsaw in 1946. [JP]

**'Slovo o Polku Igoreve'** ('The Lay of Igor's Army'). Anonymous Russian tale in rhythmic prose, generally considered to date from *c.* 1187. It is a remarkable work by any standards, and if genuine it must be considered the masterpiece of Old Russian literature. Telling the tale of an unsuccessful raid against the nomad Polovtsy headed by a minor prince, Igor' Svyatoslavich, of his capture and escape, it makes a powerful propagandist appeal against the disunity of the Russian principalities in the face of outside threats. Its style is highly allusive, digressive, embellished with poetic and rhetoric devices (notably metaphor), and sometimes obscure. It recalls certain techniques of oral heroic epos (cf. ⇨ Byliny) – consciously evoked by the author, it would appear, in the person of the bard Bayan – but the *Slovo*'s closely-textured and sophisticated manner point to a written, not improvised, origin. A curious and perhaps archaic feature is the *Slovo*'s paucity of Christian references.

Several later medieval works, notably the ⇨ *Zadonshchina*, appear to quote or paraphrase the *Slovo*. But it was subsequently forgotten until rediscovered in a single manuscript by Musin-Pushkin in the late 18th century. Destruction of this manuscript in the 1812 Moscow fire has complicated modern study of the *Slovo*. Persistent doubts about its authenticity have been revived in recent years by Mazon in France and Zimin in the U.S.S.R.; but theories that it might be an Ossianic forgery based on the *Zadonshchina* occasion even more difficulties than they would resolve. Our present text of the *Slovo* is certainly to some extent corrupt (many readings of individual words and phrases are still in doubt). [RM-G]

Obolensky, *PBRV*; *The Song of Igor's Campaign*, tr. V. Nabokov (London, 1960); *The Tale of the Armament of Igor*, ed. and tr. L. A. Magnus (London, 1915).

J. Besharov, *Imagery of the Igor' Tale* (Leiden, 1956); T. Čiževska, *Glossary of the Igor Tale* (1966).

**Słowacki, Juliusz** (Krzemieniec 1809–Paris 1849). Polish poet. The son of a University professor and educated in Vilna, he turned to writing with confidence, but the outbreak of the November rising which he witnessed in Warsaw altered his life abruptly and he had to shape his artistic personality in exile. He left Poland in 1831, travelled as a courier to England where he managed to see Kean in *Richard III*, and after a stay in Switzerland, settled in Paris amongst the émigrés. Here he published plays and volumes of poems at his own expense, receiving little attention, unlike ⇨ Mickiewicz, whom he regarded as his rival.

It was because of this unreciprocated feeling of rivalry that he explored the genesis of the tragic rising in his play *Kordian* (1834), scourged the national faults in bitter poems like *Grób Agamemnona*, and finally sought bardic self-gratification in the concept of the 'King-Spirit' being reincarnated throughout the history of his nation. He invented the ballad-like world of prehistoric Poland in order to interpret for himself the contradictions within the national character; his best tragedy, *Lilla Weneda* (1840), is based on the antithesis between the dreamy Weneds and the ruthless Lechits. When he was absorbing the tradition of Shakespeare and Calderón, he intuitively felt that the Spaniard was more akin to his own type of imagination, and beginning in 1840 with the theme of honour and revenge (*Mazepa*, tr. C. F. and C. D. Wells, 1929) he entered a new phase, progressively more mystical and baroque (e.g. *Sen srebrny Salomei*, 1844).

Though he never saw his plays acted, he established a tradition of poetic drama which was to influence the symbolists two generations later. His technique seemed so modern and 'synaesthetic' that a prominent critic wrote a study, 'Słowacki and the new art' (1902).

Slowacki certainly liberated the poetic diction of his age; his sentences, though heightened by metaphors and occasional pathos, have a brilliant and memorable fluency. He relied on models, as in *Beniowski* inspired by Byron's *Don Juan*, and had a tendency to leave works unfinished, but he could also construct a difficult poem. His *W Szwajcarii* (1839), for instance, is in one respect a landscape poem integrated with the changing emotions of love, and in another a medieval combat between human and divine love, framed by an idyll. These two conventions are imposed on loose autobiographical material. The same process is evident in the poems reflecting his experiences on a journey to the Middle East, which he undertook in 1836.

All through the years of his exile Słowacki corresponded with his mother, and his letters have become classics of Polish prose. [JP]

*Dzieła*, ed. J. Krzyzanowski (1952); Peterkiewicz and Singer, *FCPP*.

M. Kridl, *The Lyric Poems of J.S.* (The Hague, 1958); *SEER*, XXVIII, 70 (1949).

**Slutsky, Boris** (Slavyansk, Ukraine 1919– ). Russian poet. After studying in Moscow, he volunteered in 1941. His war experiences colour most of his complex and deeply probing early poetry. His work became known slowly; much of it was not published until some time after it was written, and his first book *Pamyat'* appeared in 1957. His importance in the Thaw period can hardly be exaggerated. His verse has the qualities most in demand during the last decade: personal, small-scale, unpretentious, based on detailed incidents which often have universal implications. He faces up honestly to moral complexities which cannot be easily unravelled. In form his verse is simple, toughly wrought, rather slow-moving; closer inspection reveals great sophistication in the handling of words and lyric form. [RM-G]

*Segodnya i vchera* (1961); Gulland, *SRV.*

**Smolenskin, Peretz** (Russia 1842–Merano 1885). Hebrew author. Leader of the National Progressive Movement. Attracted by the Haskala movement, he went to Vienna when 25 and, to his great dismay, discovered that enlightenment led to assimilation – that the enlightened Jews had little Judaism left. He found his own answer and, in his monthly periodical *Ha-shachar* ('The Dawn'), founded in 1869, proclaimed his beliefs that a great people cannot live on the past alone, it must have a faith in its own future. In a series of essays and books, he went on to prove his ideas of the Jewish future. At the same time, he was one of the new Hebrew novel's best protagonists. His great novel, a veiled autobiography, *Hatohe bedarke Hahayyim* (3 vols., 1868–85), was serialized in *Ha-shachar*, where he also published his two fundamental treatises: *Am Olam* ('The Eternal People', 1872) and *Et Lataat* ('Time to Plant', 1873). His last novel, *Kevurat Chamor* (1875–6), is considered his best. [EE]

*Sifre Peretz ben Moshe Smolenskin*, ed. L. Rosenthal (1887).
R. Brainin, *P.S.* (2 vols., 1896).

**Snikere, Velta.** ⇨ Latvian Literature.

**Snoilsky, Count Carl** (Stockholm 1841–Stockholm 1903). Swedish poet. After a pale and conventional beginning he developed into an independent artist during a journey to Spain and Italy in 1864. His early verse is collected in *Dikter* (1869) and is distinguished by its rhythmical vitality and its fresh, refined sensuousness. With *Sonetter* (1871) he further proved his formal mastery, but there is evidence, too, of a growing sense of isolation. In 1879 Snoilsky scandalized Swedish society by divorcing his wife and remarrying; he also left his post in the Foreign Office and went abroad once more. Shortly afterwards, he broke his by now prolonged silence with poetry of a new kind. His aspirations were to find a form which could speak directly to the hearts of simple men. Thus in the collection *Dikter* (1883) he addresses the working classes, symbolically renouncing his aristocratic privileges. However sincere this gesture may have been, it did not bridge the social gulf. He achieved wider acceptance with *Svenska bilder* (1886), in which the treatment of grand patriotic themes does not preclude a democratic note, as if the poet has found it easier to make contact with the people through meditating upon hardships suffered in the past and upon the glories of national leadership. The view of history implied may now appear naïve, but the portraits of Gustavus Wasa, Queen Kristina and other historical figures have been decidedly influential. Today Snoilsky is admired as a minor classic. [SAB]

*Samlade dikter* (5 vols., 1903–4); tr. C. W. Stork, in *Anthology of Swedish Lyrics from 1750 to 1925* (N.Y., 1930) (selection).
H. Olsson, 'Snoilskygestalten', in *Törnrosskalden och andra porträtt* (Stockholm, 1956).

**Snorri Sturluson** (W. Iceland 1179–Reykjaholt 1241). The outstanding literary personality of medieval Scandinavia and Iceland. He was brought up at Oddi, the home of an aristocratic and cultured family in the south of the country, 1181–1201. He lived then as a wealthy landowner, politician and lawyer, and was Lawspeaker of the Althing 1215–18, 1222–31. He visited Norway twice, 1218–20 (when he also went to Sweden) and 1237–9. In 1241 he was killed by his enemies.

Snorri was the author of the *Edda* (written before 1223; ed. F. Jónsson, Copenhagen, 1931), of *Óláfs saga helga* (tr. S. Laing, rev. J. Simpson, *The Olaf Sagas*, Everyman, 1964), of the *Heimskringla* (written *c.* 1223–35; ed. ibid., 4 vols., 1893–1901; B. Aðalbjarnarson, 3 vols., Reykjavík, 1941–51; tr. S. Laing, rev. P. Foote, Everyman, 1961; part tr. M. Magnusson and H. Pálsson, *King Harold's Saga*, Penguin Classics, 1966), and probably of *Egils Saga* (⇨ Icelandic Sagas). The *Edda* is a handbook of scaldic art and an invaluable storehouse of information. Part I, *Gylfaginning*, after a prologue in which the origin of the heathen gods is explained in euhemeristic fashion, retells myths in a colloquy framework. These are to aid the understanding of the old poetry since much conventional diction and imagery were drawn from mythological tales. Part II, *Skáldskaparmál*, is primarily a classification of various forms of poetic diction, especially kennings. Some explanatory passages tell myths or heroic tales which lie behind particular types of expression. Part III, *Háttatal*, is an 'enumeration of metres' in the shape of a poem of 102 stanzas in honour of King Hákon and Earl Skúli of Norway. Each stanza exemplifies a different form, although the differences between them do not always lie in basic metrical structure but in the systematic use of varying stylistic elements. The stanzas are accompanied by a prose commentary. As a poet, Snorri is correct, tasteful and extremely ingenious, but his fame rightly depends upon his prose stories, especially in the *Gylfaginning*. He writes with precision and delicacy, conveys dramatic effects with economy and force, and ranges with all propriety from the light-hearted to the grave. Throughout the reader is conscious of him as a graceful and ironic artist.

The *Heimskringla* is a history of the kings of Norway from the half-mythical origins of the dynasty down to the year 1177. It embodies his own great *Saga of Saint Olaf* in modified form. Snorri used all the older histories that were available, some of them comparatively extensive, and particularly of ⇨ Scaldic poetry both as a source of information and a means of verification. He has deep knowledge of human character, great abilities in describing action, giving lifelike dialogue, and composing set speeches, and extraordinary skill in organizing his materials to produce a rational and plausible historical narrative, with causes and effects clearly perceived. He imposes the larger pattern and unity of art without strain on his history. His lucid, unmannered prose had a formative influence on early Icelandic writing. [PGF]

*Bibliography of the Sagas of the Kings*, in *Islandica*, III (1910), XXVI (1937); S. Nordal, *S.S.* (Reykjavík, 1920); ⇨ Eddaic Poetry.

**Soares de Passos, António Augusto de** (Oporto 1826–Oporto 1860). Portuguese ultra-Romantic poet. Of middle-class origins, he graduated in law at Coimbra, and while still a student was already writing verse for the ultra-Romantic periodical *Novo Trovador*, of which he became the most prominent contributor. His collected *Poesias* first appeared in 1855. He died of a gradually worsening tubercular condition. Characterized by pessimism and radicalism, his verse owed no small debt to the philosophico-religious poetry of Herculano. Most celebrated are his two long poems *O Noivado do Sepulcro* and *O Firmamento*, the former being a macabre dirge which betrays the influence of Young's *Night Thoughts*, while *O Firmamento* unites the two themes of man's puniness in face of the cosmos and the dignity of his uphill strivings for progress, viewpoints reflecting his study of the works of Herculano and Laplace. [RCW]

J. do Prado Coelho, *A Poesia Ultra-Romântica*, ii (Lisbon, 1944); A. de Navarro, *S. de P.*, in *Perspectiva da Literatura Portuguesa do Século XIX*, i (Lisbon, 1947).

**Söderberg, Hjalmar** (Stockholm 1869–Copenhagen 1941). Swedish novelist, story-writer, dramatist and essayist; his upper-middle-class background is reproduced scrupulously in his writing to the exclusion of all other social strata. He was trained in the sceptical school of the eighties: his intellectual ancestry includes the younger ⇨ Strindberg, Georg ⇨ Brandes and Anatole ⇨ France. From the beginning a note of disillusionment is perceptible. In *Historietter* (1898) he developed the art of the short pointed story written in the lucid, economical style which was to become his hallmark. *Martin Bircks ungdom* (1901; tr. C. W. Stork, *Martin Birck's Youth*, N.Y., 1930) contains a poetic evocation of a childhood (closely modelled upon the author's). Its final chapters set forth (but do not render quite accessible) the pessimism and resignation of the maturing hero. *Doktor Glas* (1905; tr. P. B. Austin, *Doctor Glas*, 1963) explores the motives for a murder, but in the form of an intimate diary also portrays the changing moods and atmospheres of Stockholm. Behind its disillusioned view of humanity, there lies the author's conviction of the deterministic nature of the universe. Among Söderberg's finest work are the drama *Gertrud* (1906) and the novel *Den allvarsamma leken* (1912). Both are built round love stories, both are pessimistic and share a moral quality in the truthfulness of their characterization. In spite of the harsh clarity with which Söderberg sees his figures, it is obvious that he himself lacks robustness. His melancholy may be considered constitutional. After the First World War he wrote little in the way of fiction, but devoted a great deal of energy to a private campaign against Christianity. He made a notably determined stand against Nazism during the thirties (he had by then settled in Denmark). [SAB]

*Samlade verk*, ed. T. Söderberg and H. Friedländer (10 vols., 1943).

B. Bergman, *H.S.* (Stockholm, 1951); K. Jaensson, 'H.S.', in *Sanning och särprägel* (Stockholm, 1960); S. Rein, *H.S.s Gertrud* (Stockholm, 1962).

**Södergran, Edith** (St Petersburg 1892–Raivola 1923). Swedo-Finnish poetess. She developed tuberculosis in 1908; after the Russian Revolution she lived with her mother, in great poverty, at Raivola, Finland. The poems in the three collections she published between 1918 and 1920 glow with a defiant vitality and shape themselves into a powerful vision of the future: the world is seen, as it were, in a cosmic perspective. In her later poems a new note of resignation is sounded, intensely moving because of the unwavering calm with which she faces the inevitable end. [TA]

*Dikter* (1940).

G. Tideström, *E.S.* (Stockholm, 1949); O. Enckell, *Esteticism och nietzscheanism i E.S.s Lyrik* (1949), *Vaxdukshäftet* (1961).

**Soffici, Ardengo** (Rignano sull'Arno 1879–Forte dei Marmi 1964). Italian writer and painter. Between 1900 and 1907 he lived in Paris, where he came into contact with Picasso, ⇨ Apollinaire, Max ⇨ Jacob, Braque, etc. He was the first to make Rimbaud known to the Italian public in 1911. He took part in the ⇨ Futurist movement, in the First World War, and in Fascism with equal gusto and enthusiasm. After the war he was one of the driving forces behind the influential literary magazines *La Voce* and *Lacerba*. His best-known works are *Lemmonio Boreo* (1912), *Giornale di bordo* (1915), *Bif § 2f + 18. Simultaneità. Chimismi lirici* (1915), *Kobilek* (1918), *Principi di estetica futurista* (1922), *Ricordi di vita artistica e letteraria* (1930). Also worth mentioning is his *Itinerario inglese* (1947) which he wrote after a visit to England. [GMC]

U. Fasolo, *S.* (Florence, 1951); *Contemporanei*, i.

**Sofronov, Anatoly Vladimirovich** (Minsk 1911– ). Soviet writer of plays, songs and librettos. Brought up in Don Cossack country, he graduated from the literary faculty of the Rostov Pedagogical Institute. During the war, he was a front-line correspondent, was wounded and drafted to *Izvestiya*. His first play, *V odnom gorode*, was published in 1945, but his first real success was the light-hearted *Stryapukha* (1959), an immensely popular comedy with songs. Some score of his comedies and dramas – mostly interspersed with songs and music – are a permanent feature of the Soviet stage. His *Million for a Smile* was staged in London (1967). Like ⇨ Pogodin and ⇨ Panova, he is almost always on the side of youth. [AP]

*Izbrannyye proizvedeniya* (2 vols., 1955) (with autobiography); *O trude dramaturgov*, ed. Vl. F. Pimenov (Moscow, 1957); *Dramy i Komedii* (1964).

Boguslavskiy, *KIRSD*.

**Søiberg, Harry** (Ringkøbing 1880–Copenhagen 1954). Danish novelist. Turning from Socialist propagandizing, he became famous for *Heimat* literature, e.g. about religious stirrings in a community on the west coast, *De levendes Land* (1916–20). [ELB]

*Søkongen* (1926–30; vol. I, tr. E. Bjorkman, *The Sea King*, 1928).

**Sokolov, Nahum** (Vishgorod 1860–London 1936). Hebrew critic, biographer and Zionist leader. From a Hassidic home, he went early to Talmudic school where he soon excelled himself. Finding his way to the Haskalah, he devoted himself to secular studies and eventually mastered eight European languages. At 17, he published his first book, *Sinat Olam le-Am Olam.* He was on the staff of *Hatzefirah* which he later owned and edited for twenty years, becoming immensely popular. His leading articles gave guidance to Jews all over the world. His masterpiece, *Ishim* (3 vols., 1935), contains portraits of Hebrew writers and national leaders. Besides editing *Hatzefirah* he also edited *Heasif* and *Sefer Hashanah* (two literary annuals) and a bibliographical dictionary of Hebrew writers. But he is chiefly remembered as a Zionist leader and for his role with Chaim Weitzman in obtaining the Balfour Declaration of 1917. [EE]

Waxman, *HJL*; Klausner, *HMHL*.

**Soldati, Mario** (Turin 1906– ). Italian film-director and novelist. His early studies in a Jesuit school are reflected in his subtle casuistic moralism, his ironical but undetached criticism of Roman Catholic beliefs and education, his delicate treatment of erotic themes – as if sex were only a morbid alteration of the mind. His solid literary culture and elegant style make his well-constructed stories very enjoyable reading. His contributions to the cinema have a strong literary bias: eight of his films are adaptations of novels or short stories, including one by Moravia (*La provinciale*) and one by himself (*Fuga in Francia*). [GMC]

*America primo amore* (1935); *La verità sul caso Motta* (1941); *L'amico Gesuita* (1943); *Fuga in Italia* (1947); *A cena col commendatore* (1952; tr. anon., *The Commander Comes to Dine*, 1952); *Le lettere da Capri* (1954; tr. A. Colquhoun, *The Capri Letters*, 1954); *La Confessione* (1955, 1959; tr. R. Rosenthal, *The Confession*, 1958); *Il vero Silvestri* (1957; tr. A. Colquhoun, *The Real Silvestri*, 1960); *I Racconti* (1957); *La Messa dei villeggianti* (1959); *Storie di spettri* (1963); *Le due città* (1964).

Pullini, *RID*; Falqui, *PNNI*.

**Sologub, Fyodor,** pseud. of Fyodor Kuz'mich Teternikov (St Petersburg 1863–Leningrad 1927). Russian poet, novelist and dramatist. Of humble birth he was brought up by a rich family. He was a schoolmaster and inspector for twenty-five years, but resigned in 1907 in order to devote himself to literature. After the Bolshevik Revolution he continued to write, but he was seldom published. Since his death he has been largely ignored by Soviet critics.

Sologub began writing in 1886, but he achieved fame only in 1907 with the novel *Melkiy Bes* (1905–7; tr. R. Wilks, *The Little Demon*, 1962), a repulsive but fascinating vision of the pettiness and vulgarity of evil. His other major work, the trilogy of novels, *Tvorimaya legenda* (1908–12; tr. J. Cournos, *The Created Legend*, 1916), a symbolic tale in which Satanism, fantasy and contemporary politics are oddly interwoven, is less successful. To Sologub the world was essentially evil. Purity, goodness and beauty, usually symbolized in his work by childhood, nakedness and love, are shown to be ambiguous and even diabolic. His poetry, notably the collections *Plamennyy krug* (1908) and *Zhemchuzhnyye zvyozdy* (1913), contains the finest expression of his philosophy, the limpid simplicity of the vocabulary, syntax and structure contrasting weirdly with the perverse and evil content. [RDBT]

*Sobraniye sochineniy* (19 vols., 1913–14).

A. Chebotarevskaya (ed.), *O.F.S.* (St Petersburg, 1911); Poggioli, *PR*.

**Solomos, Dionysios** (Zante 1798–Corfu 1857). Greek poet. The first major poet of modern Greece whose work may be regarded as a real link of Greek with modern European literature, he was the son of a Zantiot nobleman of ancient Venetian descent and a Greek woman of humble origin. At 10 he was sent to Italy for his education, first to Cremona and afterwards to Pavia where he took a degree in law. In Italy he formed close friendships with the poets Manzoni and Monti, who had some influence on the early stages of his poetic development. He returned to Zante in 1818 and in 1822 he published his *Rime Improvvisate*, a collection of verse in Italian. At about this time he began giving himself more and more to the study of Greek, concentrating on folk-songs and on poetry written in the demotic. His first Greek lyrical poems, slight though they might be, strike a new note in Greek poetry by their simple diction and melodious versification. It was the Greek War of Independence, however, which caught his imagination and enlarged the scope of his poetry, his liberal spirit finding in it its highest inspiration and investing its heroic pattern with an allegorical significance. In 1823 he composed the *Ymnos Eis Tin Eleftherian* (in *Songs of Greece*, ed. M. C. Fauriel; tr. C. B. Sheridan, in *Songs of Greece*, 1825; partly tr. R. Kipling, *Greek National Anthem*, 1918), a poem of 158 quatrains with alternate rhymes, inspired by the War of Independence and marked by a swiftness and lyrical spontaneity. It established his reputation as a national poet and its first few stanzas were adopted in 1863 as the Greek national anthem. The *Poiema Lyriko Eis Ton Thanato Tou Lord Byron* ('Lyrical Poem on the Death of Lord Byron'), written shortly after the *Hymn*, repeats the manner and technique of the latter but lacks its sustained vigour. In 1828 he removed to Corfu where he spent his life brooding over major compositions, some begun at Zante and all found after his death in unfinished drafts with scribbled comments in Italian and Greek and numerous workings-over of individual lines. His creativeness was inhibited by his fastidiousness in composition and by German idealist philosophies with which his poetry became implicated in its mature phase. His chief posthumous works are: *O Lambros* (name of poem's hero), intended to be a dramatic epic in *ottava rima* (apart from a few lyrical songs) but soon abandoned. The hero is Byronic and the tone strongly romantic – a poem which cured Solomos of any romantic illusions; *O Kritikos* ('The Cretan', 1833), showing a definite change in power of expression, consists of several sections in 15-syllable metre, one of them being a masterly attempt to communicate by means of natural imagery and sounds the elusive splendour of a momentary vision; *Oi Eleftheroi Poliorkimenoi* (1827–49; partly tr. in R. Jenkins and P. Sherrard, *The Free Besieged*), with the siege of Missolonghi as theme, has overtones of a drama where Missolonghi symbolizes the ultimate triumph of man over the world of senses. It is Solomos's most ambitious work and exists in 3 drafts reflecting progressive stages in his search for aesthetic purity; *I Gynaika Tis Zakynthos* ('Woman of Zante'), a prose draft in apocalyptic style depicting a woman of obscene hideousness and intended perhaps for a poem on a 'Vision of Evil'; *O Porfyras* ('The Shark', 1849), occasioned by the death of a young Englishman killed by a shark off Corfu; between the interstices of fragmentary lines shimmers the image of a youth poised on the moment of his imminent destruction. Towards the end of his life Solomos returned to Italian compositions. He is a poet who strove for the perfect equipoise between form and content and aimed (especially in his latest poems) at communicating with words of complete simplicity experiences and truths that result when the poet's sensibility probes the uttermost limits of consciousness. [SJP]

*Apanta*, ed. L. Politis (1948–60).
R. J. H. Jenkins, *D.S.* (1940); P. Sherrard, *The Marble Threshing Floor* (1956).

**Soloukhin, Vladimir** (Alepin, nr Vladimir 1924– ). Russian writer. From a peasant family, he fought in the First World War, then attended the Gor'ky Literary Institute, in Moscow. His first poems (*Dozhd'v stepi* 1953) are orthodox in form, with a strong feeling for the natural world and for history. Only more recently has he developed a strongly original manner: he is unusual among present-day Soviet poets for his experiments in blank verse and broken, variegated rhythms. His feeling for Nature has deepened to include a note of intensely philosophical and moral inquiry. Perhaps a post-war heir to the 'peasant poet' tradition. He has also worked as a journalist and written short stories. [RM-G]

*Vladimirskiye prosyolki* (1958); *Imeyushchiy v rukakh tsvety* (1962); Obolensky, *PBRV*.

**Solovyov, Vladimir Sergeyevich** (Moscow 1853–Uskoye, Moscow 1900). Russian philosopher and poet. Studied at Moscow and Petersburg; travelled to England and Egypt (1875–6); lectured in philosophy at Moscow till forced to resign after defending the murderers of Alexander II. He turned from early radical, nihilistic thought to a complex humanitarian, Christian philosophy; drawing on knowledge of the Greek Fathers, Neo-Platonism, and personal mysticism, he attempted a universalist 'philosophy of life', to reconcile most diverse elements of experience: faith and knowledge, love and reason, the divine and human. He strove for the unification of the Orthodox Church with Rome, was a Panslavist (but enemy of the Slavophiles, cf. Khomyakov). Symbolist writers (⇨ Blok, ⇨ Bely) were influenced particularly by his doctrine of divine wisdom. His own poetry meditates on the mystic heart of love in striking images and mellifluous rhythms.

*Sobraniye Sochineniy*, ed. M. S. Solovyov (1901–7); *Stikhotvoreniya* (1921); trs.: N. Duddington, *The Justification of the Good* (1918); H. Rees, *Russia and the Universal Church* (1948); P. P. Zouboff, *Lectures on Godmanhood* (1944); N. Duddington, *A Solovyov Anthology*, ed. S. L. Frank (1950); Obolensky, *PBRV*.
V. V. Zenkovsky, *A History of Russian Philosophy* (1953).

**Solzhenitsyn, Aleksandr Isayevich** (Rostov-on-Don 1918– ). Soviet novelist. He graduated in physics at Rostov (1941), served in the artillery as an officer, was arrested on a false charge (1945), sentenced and put in prison and labour camps until 1956. In 1957 he was rehabilitated, no case against him being found. He taught mathematics and physics until 1962, when he made his name with *Odin den' Ivana Denisovicha*, the first story realistically portraying prison life under Stalin to appear in the Soviet Union (published only in *Novyy mir* by the liberal editor ⇨ Tvardovsky, 1962; tr. R. Parker, *One Day in the Life of Ivan Denisovich*, *Soviet Literature*, 1963, and into a somewhat Hemingwayesque idiom by M. Hayward and R. Hingley, 1963). *Novyy mir* carried in 1963 (January, July) stories satirizing everyday life, especially the bureaucratic 'Stalins' still powerful in the Soviet Union: *Sluchay na Stantsii Krechetova* (*An incident at Krechetovka Station*), *Matryonin dvor* (*Matryona's home*), *Dlya pol'zy dela* (tr. D. Floyd and M. Hayward, *For the Good of the Cause*, 1964), and *Zakhar-Kalita* (1966). For these and particularly his major novels

– *V kruge pyervom* (1968, tr. M. Guybon, *First Circle*) and *Rakovyy korpus* (1968, tr. N. Bethell and D. Burg, *Cancer Ward*) – which have been widely published outside but not in Russia, he won the Nobel Prize in 1970. *First Circle* describes the lives of scientists working in a research centre that is in fact a prison, *Cancer Ward* those of people condemned on health grounds to 'internment' or death. Sensational revelations of some facts of Soviet life at the time of Stalin's death and of Malenkov's deposition are here less important than psychological insight into the intensified experience of people under varying degrees of pressure and deprivation.

*Sochineniya*, Frankfurt, 1966; *Dva rasskaza*, tr. P. W. Blackstock, *We never make mistakes*, N.Y. 1963; *Les droits de l'écrivain* (interview, Paris 1969).

*S., A. Documentary Record*, ed. Labedz, 1970; G Lukács, *S.*, 1970.

**Somoza, José** (Piedrahita 1781–Piedrahita 1852). Spanish writer. Friend of ◊ Meléndez Valdés and ◊ Quintana. He wrote some fine sonnets in the pre-romantic style, of which 'La durmiente' appears in many anthologies, and some prose descriptions of the contemporary scene, *Memorias de Piedrahita* (1837) and *Recuerdos e impresiones* (1843). [JMC]

*Obras*, ed. Lomba y Pedraja (1904); BAE, 57; Blecua, *FLE*.

**Sønderby, Knud** (Esbjerg 1909–Thy 1966). Danish novelist, essayist and playwright. His best novels are *Midt i en Jazztid* (1931), *To Mennesker mødes* (1932), and *En Kvinde er overflødig* (1935), dramatized most successfully (1942; tr. I. A. Roughton, *A Woman too Many*, in *Contemporary Danish Plays*, 1955), followed by some one-act plays and a modern version of *Lysistrata*, *Kvindernes Oprør* (1955). As a literary essayist he is superb (*Samlede Essays*, 1961). [ELB]

**Sordello** (fl. mid 13th century). The most famous Italian troubadour. He wrote in medieval Provençal. A minor noble, he was born at Goito near Mantua and was active from about 1225 to 1270. Dante assigned him a prominent place as escort to Virgil in *Purgatorio* VI and VII, and knew his works as well as the story of his adventurous life. In 1226 he abducted Cunizza da Romano from her husband Count Ricciardo di san Bonifazio, possibly on the instructions of Cunizza's brothers, Ezzelino and Alberico da Romano. Sordello took refuge with these brothers but fled to France after a quarrel and visited Spain and Portugal. His main patron in France was Count Raimon Bérenger IV of Provence who held court at Aix. On the count's death in 1245 Sordello became the follower of his successor, Count Charles of Anjou. As a result of services rendered in the Italian campaign of 1266, during which he was taken prisoner and ransomed, Sordello was rewarded by Charles with fiefs in the Abruzzi where he probably died.

Of his forty surviving poems the most lively are his debates with other poets (*tensos* or *partimens*). In a famous *planh*, or lament for the nobleman Blacatz, he invites to the funeral feast the Emperor Frederick II, the kings of England, France and Aragon, and the counts of Champagne, Toulouse and Provence. Each ruler is urged to eat of the dead man's heart in order to gain some of his noble qualities and courage. He also wrote an important *Ensenhamen d'onor*, a didactic poem on the education and conduct proper to a courtier and a lover. [LTT]

*Le poesie*, ed. M. Boni (1954).

**Sorel, Charles,** Sieur de Souvigny (Paris 1602–1674). French writer. A talented satirist, he worked in the tradition of Rabelais and Cervantes and mocked the sentimental pastoral of his day (*Le berger extravagant*, 1627), tried his hand in the latest fictional genre in *Polyandre* (1648) and, most successfully, in his *Histoire comique de Francion* (1622; thirty editions before 1700; ed. E. Roy, TFM, 1928). The picaresque adventures of young Francion in Burgundy and in Paris, with robbers and tramps and women, are racily described and seem to have been enjoyed by Molière. [WGM]

E. Roy, *C.S.* (Paris, 1891).

**Sørensen, Villy** (Copenhagen 1929– ). Danish essayist and short-story writer. He began his career as a student of philosophy and a writer of fanciful tales, undoubtedly influenced by both Kierkegaard and Hans Christian Andersen. He has written three volumes of highly original tales, *Sære Historier* (1953; tr. M. Neiiendam, *Strange Stories*, 1956), *Ufarlige Historier* (1955) and *Formynderfortællinger* (1964), and two volumes of equally original philosophical essays, *Digtere og Dæmoner* (1959) and *Hverken-eller* (1961). [ELB]

**Sorge, Reinhard Johannes** (Flüelen, Switzerland 1892–Battle of the Somme 1916). German poet and dramatist. His first play, *Der Bettler* (1912), initiated Expressionism: by its theme – the Poet feels called to regenerate the people (rather than 'entertain'), struggles parricidally against the reactionary Father, etc.; and by its technique – the use of types (even numbered), chorus speaking, tableaux scenes, symbolic scenery, etc. After conversion to Catholicism he wrote mystical dramas, *Guntwar* (1914), *Metanoeite* (1915), and poems, *Nachgelassene Gedichte* (posth. 1925). [PB/AKT]

*Sämtliche Werke*, ed. H. G. Rötzer (3 vols., 1962–7) (vol. 3 has bibliography).
*MLR*, XXXII (1937); H. G. Rötzer, *R.J.S.s Theorie und Dichtung* (Erlangen, 1961 (dissertation)).

**Sosyura, Volodymyr** (Debal'tesvo, Donets Basin 1898–Kiev 1965). Ukrainian poet. He began writing in Ukrainian in 1918 when in the ranks of the national Army (mostly unpubl.; cf. *CSP*, iii, 1958, and Luts'ky, *LD*). He soon went over to the Red Army and acquired fame with *Chervona zyma* (1921) and *Osinni zori* (1924), deeply felt lyrical and heroic revolutionary verse. His historical poems, *Taras Tryasylo* (1926) and *Mazepa* (1929), reveal national romanticism. Severely criticized for *Sertse* (1931), he wrote little until 1937, since when he followed Party requirements, though not always successfully (the 1951 censure of his 'Love Ukraine' (1944) was internationally notorious). A neo-romantic of great sincerity and immediacy, he was the most popular Ukrainian poet of the inter-war period. [VS]

*Tvory* (3 vols., 1957–8); tr. M. Trommer, *Poems of Ukraine* (N.Y., 1939); Andrusyshen and Kirkconnell, *UP*; Luts'ky, *LD*; Luckyj, *LPSU*; *UCE*.

**Soto de Rojas, Pedro** (Granada 1584–Granada 1658). Spanish poet and canon of Granada cathedral. His masterpiece, *Paraíso cerrado para muchos, jardines abiertos para pocos* (1652), describes his garden in a *culto* style, which even at that time required notes for its elucidation. The garden itself was a work of art, the poem a work of art at second remove from nature, etc. It is the most original and extreme development of ⇨ Góngora's style in Spain. His early poems (*Desengaño de amor en rimas*, 1623) are simpler and less remarkable, though his third Eclogue contains luscious descriptions of fruit and flowers, and the poem which he wrote for a fiesta in 1609 has graphic passages on bulls and bull-fighting. [JMC]

*Obras* (1950); Blecua, *FLE*; Cohen, *PBSV*.
A. Gallego Morell, *P.S. de R.* (Granada, 1948); E. Orozco Díaz, *Introducción a un poema barroco granadino* (Granada, 1955).

**Sova, Antonín** (Pacov 1864–Pacov 1928). Czech poet. A journalist and finally director of the Prague Municipal Library, he began as an impressionist but later took a more objective attitude to reality. His *Ještě jednou se vrátíme* (1900) gives a utopian vision of humanity's future, a new kingdom built entirely by spiritual effort; his *Dobrodružství odvahy* (1906), influenced by events in Russia, welcomes the Revolution as a vengeance and punishment which the oppressors brought upon themselves. A born subjectivist, he is at his best when interpreting his own inner states and feelings through the medium of nature. [KB]

*Spisy* (20 vols., 1936–8).
J. Zika, *A.S.* (Prague, 1953).

**Soya, Carl Erik** (Copenhagen 1896– ). Danish playwright, short-story writer and novelist. The *enfant terrible* of contemporary Danish theatre, he shocks his audience by turning accepted ideas upside-down and by using daring (and sometimes crude) stage effects. His most interesting plays are *Parasitterne*, a grim social satire of 1929, *Den leende Jomfru* (1930), *Hvem er jeg?* (1932), which is perhaps his finest, and the 'neo-realistic' tetralogy: *Brudstykker af et Mønster*, *To Traade* (tr. *Two Threads* in *Contemporary Danish Plays*, 1955), *30 Aars Henstand*, and *Frit Valg*, written 1940–8, and all concerned with the problems of justice, the laws of life *v.* life's lawless accidents, and the idea of retribution. He is the author of many entertaining short stories, and of the novels *Min Farmors Hus* (1943; tr. A. C. Hansen, *Grandmother's House*, N.Y., 1966) and *Sytten* (1953–4; tr. C. Malmberg, *Seventeen*, N.Y., 1961). [ELB]

**Spanish Ballads.** ⇨ *Romances*.

**Spee, Friedrich von** (Kaiserwerth 1591–Trier 1635). German poet. A Jesuit who often ministered to condemned witches, his *Cautio criminalis* (anon., 1631) courageously attacks the mentality behind witch-hunts and the legal use of torture to extract confessions. His mystical poems, *Trutz-*

*nachtigall* (with a preface setting forth a non-⇨Opitzian poetics, 1649; ed. O. Holt, 1936), revolve around two themes: the love of Christ and the love of nature. The former expresses itself principally in the many poems which tell, in the fashion of the *Song of Songs*, of the yearning of the soul for her heavenly bridegroom, often in terms borrowed from the contemporary secular love lyric. Often also the conventional pastoral poetry of the age is adapted to express the love of the Good Shepherd searching for His shepherdess, the soul. Nature is seen as the creation and mirror of God, so that Spee's love of nature is a reflection of his love of God. Spee's charm lies in the way he treats these highly sophisticated themes in a completely unsophisticated way, and the best of his poems have a folksong quality which is reflected not only in the naïve, spontaneous joy in nature, but also in the simplicity of his basic four-line stanza form, in his iambic metre and simple rhyming schemes and in the use of dialect forms and turns of phrase taken directly from folk song. [WAC]

W. Kosch, *F.v.S.* (München-Gladbach, 1921); E. Rosenfeld, *Neue Studien zur Lyrik F.v.S.* (1963).

**Speroni, Sperone** (Padua 1500–Padua 1588). Italian man of letters. One of the most influential and erudite literary theorists of the *cinquecento*, his writings include undistinguished lyric poetry, critical discourses (e.g. on Virgil, Dante and Ariosto), numerous dialogues on a variety of cultural and social subjects – most significant is the *Dialogo delle lingue* (1542; ed. G. de Robertis, 1912) which influenced Du Bellay – and a tragedy, *Canace* (1546). The dialogue follows Bembo's *Prose della volgar lingua* and introduces Bembo himself as the authoritative speaker, while the tragedy with its incestuous theme sparked off a formidable literary controversy concerning the interpretation of Aristotle. [DGR]

*Opere* (1740).

F. Cammarosano, *La vita e le opere di S.S.* (Empoli, 1920); Weinberg, *HLC*; M. Herrick, *Italian Tragedy in the Renaissance* (Urbano, 1965).

**Spiegel, Henric Laurens** (Amsterdam 1549–Alkmaar 1612). Dutch poet and humanist. A moderate, nominal Roman Catholic, he withdrew from public life as a protest against the *Alteratie* of 1578, when the Calvinists gained control of Amsterdam. He was *factor* of 'De Eglantier' (cf. ⇨ *Rederijkers*) and from its political sanctuary he attacked all forms of tyranny in his *Nieuwe Jaerslieden* (1578–1601; ed. G. Degroote, 1957). The loss of five of his six children was further reason for his engrossment in study, influenced by ⇨ Coornhert's humanism (who wrote the preface for his Dutch grammar, *Twe-spraack van de Nederduitsche Letterkunst*, 1584). He is also almost certainly the author of three works on the art of rhetoric, but his most scholarly achievement is *Hertspiegel* (posth. 1614; ed. P. Vlaming, with other writings, 1723), a stoical monistic ethic in alexandrines, unfinished at 7 of the intended 9 cantos; there is much of Montaigne and Coornhert here, though it lacks the Christian essence of the *Wellevenskunst*. The unfinished *Lieden op 't Vader Ons* (ed. G. Degroote, 1956) complete the image of a scholar and patriot not only of great integrity and tolerance but also of a deep and humble faith. [PK]

*Twe-spraack, Ruygh-bewerp, Kort Begrip, Rederijck-kunst*, ed. J. H. Caron (1962).

J. F. Buisman, *De ethische denkbeelden van H.L.S.* (Wageningen, 1935).

**Spielhagen, Friedrich** (Mecklenburg 1829–Berlin 1911). German novelist. Grew up in Stralsund; studied in Berlin, Bonn and Greifswald; actor, schoolteacher in Leipzig from 1854, editor in Hanover from 1860, freelance writer in Berlin from 1862. Foremost German social-political novelist till the rise of Naturalism. In *Beiträge zur Theorie und Technik des Romans* (1883), *Neue Beiträge zur Theorie und Technik der Epik und Dramatik* (1898), and his autobiography, *Finder und Erfinder* (1890), he demands scientific objectivity – in the service of social didacticism. His own novels suffer from unconvincing characterization and black-and-white, rhetorical didacticism. His attitudes derive from Das ⇨ Junge Deutschland and Lassalle. He dislikes aristocrats, proletarian social-democrats, materialistic bourgeois; advocates middle-class liberalism and social justice. In *Problematische Naturen* (1861; tr. S. de Vere, *Problematic Characters*, N.Y., 1869), *Die von Hohenstein* (1864; tr. S. de Vere, *The Hohensteins*, N.Y., 1870), *Reih und Glied* (1866), and *Stumme des Himmels* (1894), he deals with personal problems and class distinctions. In *Durch Nacht zum Licht* (1862;

tr. S. de Vere, *Through Night to Light*, N.Y., 1870) and *Hammer und Amboss* (1869; tr. W. H. Browne, *Hammer and Anvil*, N.Y., 1870) he searches for a humane synthesis between economic-political rulers and subjects. In *Sturmflut* (1877; tr. S. E. A. H. Stephenson, *The Breaking of the Storm*, 1877) he equates the results of capitalistic speculation with a natural catastrophe. *Allzeit voran* (1871), *Was will das werden?* (1887), *Opfer* (1899) and *Ein neuer Pharao* (1899) attack Bismarck's Germany. *Faustulus* (1898) caricatures a Nietzschean superman. *Auf der Düne* (1857), *Die Dorfkokette* (1869; tr. J. L. Laird, *The Village Coquette*, 1875) and *Quisisana* (1885; tr. H. E. Goldschmitt, 1891) revive childhood memories. [LL]

*Sämtliche Werke* (29 vols., 1895–1904); *Sämtliche Romane* (1899ff.); *Meisterromane* (3 vols., 1929).

V. Klemperer, *Die Zeitromane F.S.s* (Munich/Weimar, 1913); M. Geller, *F.S.s Theorie und Praxis des Romans* (Bonn, 1917); F. Martini, *Deutsche Literatur im bürgerlichen Realismus* (Stuttgart, 1962); Koch, *IW*.

**Spinoza, Baruch** (Amsterdam 1632–The Hague 1677). Dutch philosopher. His orthodox Jewish family had emigrated from persecution in Portugal. He suffered excommunication and risked further persecution for his views; he refused gifts of money and even a teaching post in Heidelberg, preferring to live in humble circumstances, earning something as an optical lense grinder, free to pursue his ideal of truth. In this his life was consonant with his doctrine, for he understood finite things as negative limitations (only seeming important to man's limiting intelligence) of the one, infinite substance which Spinoza identified as God and which alone was real. His identification of God with reality, though argued in often highly abstract terms, which derive partly from Descartes, made a strong appeal to the literary imagination above all of Herder and Goethe a century later, confirming their own tendencies towards pantheism together with an almost irrationalistic belief in the 'inward energy' of nature and of history. Spinoza's *Ethics* (one of his *Opera posthuma*, 1677) was attractive to the ◊ *Sturm und Drang* generation also for its morality of self-assertion, the higher affirmation of our own being which is identical with the love of God; evil is considered to be merely the too limited love of our own finite individuality. The inherent ambiguity of Spinoza's attempt to regard God and nature, body and soul, as one may be judged from the fact that, while he continued to inspire in Romantic minds (like Coleridge and Shelley) a mystical awareness of the ideal unity of nature, he was admired by many in the 19th century as a scientific rationalist and materialist (e.g. by George Eliot, Renan, Flaubert). [AKT]

*Ethics, The Treatise on the Correction of the Understanding*, intr. G. Santayana (Everyman).

S. Hampshire, *S.* (1951).

**Spitteler, Carl** (Liesthal 1845–Lucerne 1924). Swiss poet and Nobel Prize winner (1919). Trained in theology, he became a tutor in Russia, then a schoolteacher in Bern, later a journalist (Basel *Grenzpost*). Influence on and by Nietzsche is controversial, but some similarity between Nietzsche's *Zarathustra* and Spitteler's major epics, *Prometheus und Epimetheus* (1881; tr. J. F. Muirhead, 1931) and *Olympischer Frühling* (1900 ff.; rev.1910) is clear; cf. his essays on Nietzsche in *Lachende Wahrheiten* (1898), and use of heroic mountain landscape, Biblical phrasing, modernized mythology (here refashioned from Homeric sources), cult of new spiritual strength and beauty, etc. – now seeming dated and artificial, a fantasy escape from bourgeois banalities. This aspect of his inspiration is reflected in the novel *Imago* (1906), an almost psychoanalytic study of erotic conflicts and sublimations in the artist. [PB/AKT]

*Sämtliche Werke*, ed. G. Bohnenblust *et al.* (12 vols., 1945–58); *Kritische Schriften* (1965); *Selected Poems*, tr. E. C. Mayne and J. F. Muirhead (1928).

E. M. Butler, *The Tyranny of Greece over Germany* (repr. 1958); F. Buri, *Prometheus und Christus* (Bern, 1945); W. Stauffacher, *C. Sp.s Lyrik* (Zürich, 1950).

**Sponde, Jean de** (Mauléon, Basses-Pyrénées 1557–Bordeaux 1595). French poet. Born and educated a Protestant, he was converted to Catholicism at the same time as his protector, Henri IV. In 1592 he was appointed lieutenant-general to the seneschalcy of La Rochelle. In his day he was known as humanist, jurist and translator (Homer, Hesiod, Aristotle's *Logic*) and his poems, mostly published in miscellanies, were neglected till rediscovered by Alan Boase in recent years (cf. *Poésies*, ed. A. M.

Boase and F. Ruchon, 1949; *Méditations sur les Psaumes*, ed. A. M. Boase, 1954). The metaphysical tendency typical of many late Renaissance French poets marks both his early love poems, which he repudiated (*Sonnets d'amour*), and his religious verse: *Sonnets et stances de la mort*, the long *Stances du sacré banquet et convive de Jésus-Christ* and the *Méditations sur les Psaumes avec un essai de quelques poèmes chrétiens.* Obsessed by the impermanence of life, he concentrates on one main theme: the conflict between the Christian's acceptance of death and the natural man's reaction to it. His impassioned verse is marked by the abrupt tone of colloquial speech, with elliptical questions and images following one another without transition. [FWAG]

Mourgues, *MBPP.*

**Sremac, Stevan** (Senta 1855–Soko Bauja 1906). Serbian novelist and short-story writer. His novels deal with provincial town life, principally in Srem and the town of Nis where he worked as a teacher; *Vukadin* (1903) portrays the squalor of existence among craftsmen and apprentices. Famous for his humorous novel *Pop Ćira i pop Spira* (1898), in which he was influenced by Gogo'l, his story *Ivkova Slava* (1895) became a classic of Serbian humour. His language contains many provincialisms, yet is very effective and one of the most mature styles of his period. [EDG]

Barac, *HYL.*

**Stadler, Ernst** (Colmar 1883–Ypres 1914). German poet. Rhodes scholar (1906–8) at Magdalen College, Oxford, he later held lectureships in German literature at the universities of Strasbourg and Brussels; he was appointed to Toronto in 1914, but joined up and was killed. With his friend ⇨ Schickele he had worked for a cultural *rapprochement* between France and Germany; he translated F. ⇨ Jammes, ⇨ Péguy, and others, this French influence being apparent in his own *Präludien* (1905). His volume *Der Aufbruch* (1914) is an outstanding collection of Expressionist poetry and was highly influential. The long irregular lines (reminiscent of Whitman) were a liberating example to other poets, together with his modern themes (some concern London's East End) and associative imagery. [PB]

*Dichtungen*, ed. K. L. Schneider (1955); Bridgwater, *TCGV*; Hamburger and Middleton, *MGP.* Schneider, *Der bildhafte Ausdruck in den Dichtungen Georg Heyms, Georg Trakls und E.S.s* (Heidelberg, 1954); H. Rölleke, *Die Stadt bei S....* (Berlin, 1966); K. Kraft, *E.S.* (Frankfurt a.M., 1932); Hamburger, *RE*; *DU*, XVII, 5 (1965).

**Staël, Anne-Louise-Germaine Necker,** Mme de (Paris 1766–Paris 1817). French novelist and writer. She was the daughter of the Swiss banker Jacques Necker, who was Minister to Louis XVI. From her earliest days she was accustomed to the conversation of the most brilliant minds of the day. Her mother had nearly married Edward Gibbon and she herself was proposed as a bride for Pitt the Younger. However, in 1785 she was married to the Swedish Ambassador to Paris, baron de Staël-Holstein, by whom she had three children before they separated in 1798. In 1792 she emigrated first to England and then to Switzerland to her property at Coppet. In 1794 there began her relationship with ⇨ Constant which was to last until 1811. She returned to Paris in 1797 and re-established her salon, bringing out her first important work *De la littérature considérée dans ses rapports avec les institutions sociales* (1800). This was revolutionary for its view that all literature reflects the social background which produced it. Here she ended with her belief in perfectibility, that scientific progress will also bring moral progress and she mortally offended Napoleon by comparing the France of her day with the Roman Empire in its decadence. Her salon became a centre for those liberals who were disaffected with Napoleon, Constant being one of the chief of these. Her originality was again shown in her two novels *Delphine* (1802) and *Corinne* (1807) in which modern woman makes her first appearance in literature. The character studies of both her heroines were largely founded upon her own strongly contradictory nature, longing as it was for a normal love and fulfilment on the one side and fame and success on the other. Napoleon exiled her in 1803, 1806 and finally in 1810, after the publication of her *De l'Allemagne* when nearly all the copies were destroyed. This work, which was brought out in England in 1813, compared France and Germany to the detriment of the former; it also made known in France the great German writers of the time. Contrasting the classical literature of the south, which derives from ancient paganism, with the romantic literature of the northern races, she stresses the importance of feeling over form. With Chateaubriand she was one of the chief forerunners of the Romantics in France. When she was in exile she divided her time between Coppet and travelling widely throughout Europe and her descriptions of what she saw, *Dix années d'exil* (1821), make fascinating reading. Her wit and strong intelligence ensured that she was always surrounded by people of intelligence: A. W. ⇨ Schlegel who acted as tutor to her children, Bonstetten, Sismondi and Madame Récamier. She also wrote plays for her private theatre at Coppet. In 1811 she married secretly a young Swiss officer, Albert Rocca, and with the Restoration returned to Paris and reopened her salon. [WA]

J. C. Herold, *Mistress to an Age* (1959).
Wellek, *HMC*.

**Staff, Leopold** (Lvov 1878–Skarżysko Kamienna 1957). Polish poet. His first book (*Sny o potędze*) appeared at the beginning of the century, when Symbolism was in fashion, the last in the year of his death (*Dziewięć muz*). Like Yeats, he could express fresh poetic ideas in his old age, for instance in *Wiklina* (1954), but his total output was so voluminous that it inevitably obscured his lyrical profile.

The range of his translations is impressive (e.g. Nietzsche, Goethe, Michelangelo, Petronius) and includes versions from the Latin of ⇨ Kochanowski. [JP]

**Staffeldt, Adolph Vilhelm Schack von** (Gartz 1769–Slesvig 1826). Danish poet. Profoundly influenced by ⇨ Bürger, ⇨ Klopstock and ⇨ Herder, his first lyrical ballads and philosophical-speculative poems (1803) were overshadowed by ⇨ Oehlenschläger but he is now recognized as a precursor of Danish Romanticism. [ELB]

*Samlede Digte* (1843–51).
H. Stangerup, *A.V.S.* (Copenhagen, 1940).

**Stagnelius, Erik Johan** (Gärdslösa 1793–Stockholm 1823). Swedish poet. A solitary, eccentric figure, who published little and made no great impact during his lifetime, but whose posthumous reputation has been all the greater. He was the son of a rural dean and, according to his father, well versed in the poets of antiquity long before going to the university. While at Uppsala, he deliberately oriented himself towards contemporary Romanticism; his reading included ⇨ Chateaubriand and ⇨ Schlegel as well as ⇨ Atterbom – but he made no personal contact with the leader of the Uppsala Romantics. About 1817, on taking up a junior post in the Civil Service, he appears to have undergone a severe spiritual crisis as a result of which he adopted a fervent, partly heterodox form of Christianity, derived from his study of Plato, Plotinus, Swedenborg and Schelling but also of obscure writers of other schools, Pythagoreans as well as Gnostics. From these elements he composed a highly personal poetic universe which bore the stamp of radical dualism. His poetic practice, however, appears to belie his philosophical doctrine. His style is highly coloured and richly sensuous, even when he fervently expounds the necessity of an ascetic life. He published a short Christian hexameter epic *Vladimir den store* (1817) on a Russian theme, *Liljor i Saron* (1821), a collection of devout poems plus a verse-drama (*Martyrerna*), and *Bacchanterna* (1822), another verse-drama in a classical form on the death and apotheosis of Orpheus through spiritual fortitude and purity of mind. Only the posthumous publication of his collected works, *Samlade skrifter* (1824–6), revealed the contradictions in the poet's mind to the full. Erotic and religious themes are curiously intertwined in his work: he invariably stated his religious quest in terms of his longing for a woman's love. Literary scholars have tried to identify 'Amanda', the lady of the poems, but it may be wiser to regard her as the symbol of an unfulfilled dream. In some ways an arch-romantic, Stagnelius's style is highly ornate and almost oriental in its splendour, but his argument is nearly always lucid, and his syntax as impeccable as that of ⇨ Tegnér. In his best poems he reaches a rare perfection of diction and rhythm, speaking with subdued intensity in a voice entirely his own, e.g. 'Uppoffringen', 'Endymion' and 'Suckarnes mystèr'. [SAB]

*Samlade skrifter*, ed. F. Böök (5 vols., 1911–19).
F. Böök, *S. Liv och dikt* (Stockholm, 1954); S. Cederblad, *Studier i S. i romantik* (Stockholm, 1923); S. Malmström, *Studier över stilen i S.s lyrik* (Stockholm, 1961); S. Bergsten, *Erotikern S.* (Uppsala, 1967).

**Stampa, Gaspara** (Padua *c.* 1523–Venice 1554). Italian poetess. She lived at Venice and there fell in love with Count Collaltino di Collalto; the fluctuating story of this love is recorded in her *Rime* (1554). Her poems rise above conventional Petrarchism by virtue of their intensity of feeling as she runs through the gamut of emotions from exultation to suspicion, reproach, and renewed self-abandonment. Some critics consider her to have been a courtesan. [DGR]

*Rime*, ed. A. Salza (1913); ed. G. R. Ceriello (1954).
G. A. Cesareo, *G.S.* (Naples, 1920); Croce, *PPP*; Lind, *LPIR*; Kay, *PBIV*; *Minori*, ii.

**Stanković, Borisav** (Vranje 1876–Belgrade 1927). Serbian short-story writer, novelist and dramatist. He studied law, spent a short period in Paris, then settled to a career as a civil servant. His stories are dominated by nostalgia for the old patriarchal life of Vranje with its oriental customs, which he has been misunderstood as criticizing. Sensual passion conflicts with patriarchal order, but he seems to revel in the resulting intensification of passion and brutal sensuality, which he finds beautiful. His two most important works, the drama *Koštana* (1907) and the novel *Nečista krv* (1911), both equate passion with life. In *Koštana* the hero, Mita, is oppressed by the passing of time and the end of youth with its love and passion. *Nečista krv* superficially deals with the decline of an aristocratic family, but its real emotional theme is the experience of the girl Sofka, forced to marry a child and to endure the desperate advances of her father-in-law. The very frustrations of the old order are idealized as a source of intense experience and imply a criticism of the more civilized life of the new Serbia. [EDG]

*Djela*, ed. D. Kostić (8 vols., 1928–30); *Sophka*, tr. Alec Brown (1932); *Stanoja*, tr. V. Dimitrijević in *SEER*, VI, 18 (1928).
Barac, *HYL*.

**Staring, Antonie Christiaan Wynand** (Gendringen 1767–De Wildenborch 1840). Dutch poet. Like ⇨ Potgieter, the only true poet of his generation, a romantic and a subtle humorist. Except for his earliest work his verse had none of the false sentiment of his contemporaries or the rhetorical emotionalism of ⇨ Bilderdijk. His narrative poetry shares what is best and shuns what is worst in ⇨ Cats, his epigrammatic wit rivals ⇨ Huygens's. Because writing was such an exacting discipline for him he published relatively little, but among his small number of nature lyrics are some of exceptional charm and beauty. [PK]

*Gedichten* (4 vols., 1836–7); *Schetsen* (1826); *Kleine Verhalen* (1837); Barnouw, *CA*.

**Starter, Jan Jansz** (London 1594?–Germany 1626). Dutch poet. His parents were English Brownists who fled to Amsterdam. Here he was a member of the 'Eglantier' (cf. ⇨ *Rederijkers*) until he moved to Leeuwarden where he founded a Chamber of Rhetoric, for which he wrote two tragi-comedies. In *De friesche Lusthof* (1621) he collected his popular community songs and his other slight but often pleasing poems. [PK]

**Stefan Nemanja.** ⇨ Serbian Medieval Literature.

**Stefanyk, Vasyl'** (Rusiv, Stanislav 1871–Rusiv 1936). Ukrainian short-story writer. His first collection, *Synya knyzhechka* (1899), was followed by several others in 1900–5. Concentrated economy of means, austere simplicity, laconic dialogue in a local West Ukrainian dialect which makes the author an impartial observer, characterize him as 'an absolute master of form' (I. Franko). Though his characters, mostly peasants, are never idealized, his stories are imbued with deep sympathy towards them in their tragedy – grinding poverty, family strife, ignorance, loneliness, expectation of death. Resuming writing in 1916, he finds notes of hope and active qualities in his former passive tragic characters.

In their poignancy, psychological insight, unbelievable concentration, his impressionist miniatures are peerless of their kind. [VS]

*Povne zibrannya tvoriv* (3 vols., 1949–54); 'Burglar', tr. G. Raffalovich, in *The New Age*, XVI, 6 (1914); 'Sons', tr. C. H. Andrusyshen, in *UQ*, III, 4 (1947).
Manning, *UL*; *UCE*.

**Steinberg, Judah** (Lipcani, Bessarabia 1861–Odessa 1908). Hebrew story-writer. Born in a small Bessarabian town of a Hassidic family, he spent the greater part of his life teaching Hebrew. He found his way to the movement of enlightenment and gradually acquired recognition as a writer. Living close to the people, full of sympathy for the dwellers of the ghetto, he excelled in a kind of short, sharp sketch of the simple people who bear their hard lot with dignity and even joy. The peculiar situation of Jews in a hostile environment and the psychological stresses imposed on them are mirrored in his stories like *Asher ben Asher*, *Teshuvah*, *Nizoz Kadosh* and *Brit Milah*. Of his novels, *Ba-Yomin ha-Hem* (tr. G. Yeshurun, *In those Days*, Philadelphia, 1915) was the only success. It is a simple story of Jewish soldiers press-ganged into military service during the reign of Nicolas I. [EE]

*Kol kitve J.S.* (Tel Aviv, 1959); *Zichronot*, tr. E. Solis Cohen jr, *The Breakfast of the Birds* (Philadelphia, 1917).

Klausner, *HMHL*; Waxman, *HJL*.

**Steiner, Franz Baermann** (Prague 1909–Oxford 1952). German poet and émigré Jewish scholar. Known for his work at the Institute of Social Anthropology in Oxford: *Taboo* (1956). His knowledge of foreign cultures and languages contributed to the wide range (re-creations of Greek myths, adaptations of folklore and literature, landscape impressions, etc.) of his studied, formally elegant poems and prose aphorisms; *Unruhe ohne Uhr* (ed. H. G. Adler, 1954) and *Eroberungen* (ed. H. G. Adler, 1964). [PB]

Bridgwater, *TCGV*; Hamburger and Middleton, *MGP*; *GLL*, VII (1954); XI (1958).

**Steinman, Eliezer** (Russia 1892–1970). Hebrew novelist and short-story writer. He presents the problems of the modern Jew torn between his heritage and the vicissitudes of modern civilization. Influenced by both Gor'ky, and other Russian writers, and by Freud, his novels, *Zugot* (Paris, 1930) and *Dudaim* (1930), are much concerned with the sexual problems of their heroes. [EE]

Waxman, *HJL*.

**Stendhal,** pseud. of Henri Beyle (Grenoble 1783–Paris 1842). French novelist. Son of a provincial lawyer with aristocratic pretensions, he sought through companionship with his grandfather (a doctor brought up on Voltaire) and through the study of mathematics an antidote to the bourgeois environment that he came to hate. In 1799 he left Grenoble for Paris with the (short-lived) intention of studying at the École Polytechnique. Through his cousin, Daru, future minister under Napoleon, he obtained a War Office post and was then sent to Italy, a country he came to love. He briefly served in the dragoons, returned to Paris (1802) where he frequented *salons* and theatres, and tried to set up in business in Marseilles, whither an *affaire* with an actress had taken him (1805). As a deputy to the Commissaire des Guerres, thanks again to Daru, he lived in Brunswick (1806–8); followed the campaigns to Vienna (1809), then to Russia (Moscow, 1812), now as auditor to the Conseil d'État. After the empire, he lived in Italy (1814–21), chiefly in Milan, but had to return to France, being politically suspect as a liberal. He led the life of a (poor) dandy, travelled in England (1821, 1826) and wrote. After the 1830 revolution he was appointed consul at Trieste, but refused *exequatur* by Metternich, and was sent to Civita-Vecchia (1831). Nostalgic for Parisian life, he returned frequently; he died there of apoplexy and was buried in the cemetery of Montmartre.

In his novels, analysis and passion, 18th-century rationalism and romantic fervour are curiously blended. Divorce from society is their starting point: whether aristocrat (*Armance*, 1827; tr. G. and S. Sale, 1960), peasant's son (*Le rouge et le noir*, 1830; tr. M. R. B. Shaw, *The Red and the Black*, 1953), or scion of a bourgeois family (*Lucien Leuwen*, 1834–5, publ. 1894; tr. L. Varèse, 1950), the hero is first defined by contrast to his environment. He refuses any form of authority that would impinge on his personal liberty, and, in defiance of both good sense and history, sets out to remake the universe in his own image. Alienation, however, does not lead the hero out of society, but deeper into it, for he is impelled by a curiosity to know, down to the smallest detail, the corrupt world that he wishes to escape. Concealing his opposition, he takes part in the intrigue of his day with the secret aim of proving to himself, by the very falseness of his conduct, the distance that separates him from his contemporaries. Hypocrisy becomes a means of preserving his youthful purity, but creates the risk that he will accept as genuine a counterfeit designed to mislead others. For only a few moments does he know happiness (the prison scenes in *Le rouge et le noir* and *La Chartreuse de Parme*, 1839); death comes early.

Stendhal was fascinated by what he called the emotional 'crystallization' of experience (*De l'amour*, 1822; tr. H.B.V., *On Love*, 1957), and by broader aspects of the psychology of perception. In *La Chartreuse de Parme* (1839; tr. L. Blair, *The Charterhouse of Parma*, 1960), a story of contemporary passion and political adventure on which he meditated for 7 years and wrote in 7 weeks, Stendhal skilfully oscillates between the viewpoint of two characters. Elsewhere he intrudes as an author, judging his hero's behaviour and responding to it. Perhaps his delayed success in the 20th century is due to his awareness that an observer, by his very existence, modifies what he perceives: 'I don't claim to portray things in themselves, but only their effect on me' (*La vie de Henry Brulard*, 1835–6, publ. 1890; tr. J. Stewart and B. C. J. G. Knight, 1958). In schematic diagrams in the margins of this autobiographical work he carefully plotted his position in relation to that of others. Stendhal's realism builds up a multi-dimensional structure out of a mass of precise observations.

J. Prévost asserts that, for Henri Beyle, the art of writing, the art of living and the art of thinking were one. The contradictions inherent in Stendhal's manner, which led to Valéry's view of him as a theatrical character, have been analysed by R. Blin as a subtle dialectic between self and other. Disguise evokes a more acute consciousness of self even as it provides the means of escape. Thus is created an interaction between opposing impulses, reflected in the abrupt rhythm of a prose that neglects all mere artifice of style, with the exception of irony. The exploitation of the reversal of meanings is seen by H. Levin as a formal technique of composition. [JA]

*Les œuvres*, ed. V. del Litto and E. Abravanel (18 vols., 1961–2); *Correspondance*, ed. H. Martineau and V. del Litto, vol. 1 (1962); *Féder* (from *Romans et nouvelles*), tr. H. R. L. Edwards (1960); *Lamiel*, tr. T. W. Earp (1952); *The Life of Haydn*, tr. R. Brewin (1818); *Life of Napoleon* (1956); *Life of Rossini*, tr. R. N. Coe (1957); *Memoirs of a Tourist* (abridged), tr. A. Seager (1962); *Memoirs of Egotism*. tr. H. and M. Josephson (1949); *Private Diaries of Stendhal* (*Journal*), tr. R. Sage (1954); *Racine and Shakespeare*, tr. G. Daniels (1962); *A Roman Journal* (*Promenades dans Rome*), tr. H. Chevalier (1957); *Rome, Naples and Florence*, tr. R. N. Coe (1959); *Selected Journalism* (from *Courrier anglais*), tr. G. Strickland (1959); *The Shorter Novels of Stendhal* (*Armance*, *Abbesse de Castro*, and selections from *Chroniques italiennes*), tr. C. K. S. Moncrieff (1946); *To the Happy Few* (selected letters), tr. N. Cameron (1952).

F. M. Albérès, *Le naturel chez S.* (Paris, 1956); G. Blin, *S. et les problèmes du roman* (Paris, 1954) and *S. et les problèmes de la personnalité*, vol. I (Paris, 1958); G. Durand, *Le décor mythique de 'La Chartreuse de Parme'* (Paris, 1961); F. C. Green, *S.* (1939); F. W. J. Hemmings, *S.* (1964); H. Martineau, *Le cœur de S.* (2 vols., Paris, 1952–3) and *L'œuvre de S.* (Paris, 1945); J. Prévost, *La création chez S.* (Marseille, 1942; Paris, 1951); Levin, *GH.*

**Sternheim, Carl** (Leipzig 1878–Brussels 1942). German dramatist. Once notorious for his series of plays satirizing the German middle class, *Aus dem bürgerlichen Heldenleben* (1922), the best being perhaps *Bürger Schippel* (1913); in them, stages in the Maske family's rise to power are shown in *Die Hose* (1911; tr. E. Jolas, *A Pair of Drawers*, in *Transition*, Paris, 1927), *Der Snob* (1913; tr. W. Katzin, *A Place in the World*, in *Eight European Plays*, N.Y., 1927) and *1913* (1913). Remarkable for their terse ('telegram') style, part parody, part pre-Expressionist earnest, the satire is ambiguous; it lacks the reassuring sense of the natural (cf. Molière, whom Sternheim admired), reveals his partial belief in the ruthless drives underlying the social self-advancement which he burlesques and is tinged with the nihilism of the period (cf. ⇨ Wedekind). His character 'types' have little interest apart from the 'problem' they illustrate, and with the changed conditions and outlook after 1918, his work declined. His last success, *Die Schule von Uznach* (1926), is in effect a conservative satire of post-war youth. His stories (e.g. the collection, *Chronik von des zwanzigsten Jahrhunderts Beginn*, 1918), even more radical in portraying primitive drives and in their experimental style, were admired by ⇨ Musil. [PB/AKT]

*Das Gesamtwerk*, ed. W. Emrich (8 vols., Berlin, 1963ff.).

Wendler, *C.S.* (Frankfurt a.M., 1966); H. Karasek, *C.S.* (Velber, 1965); Natan, *GML*, ii; Garten, *MGD*; *PQ*, XXXVI (1947).

**Stieler, Kaspar** (Erfurt 1632–Erfurt 1707). German poet. His *Geharnischte Venus* (1660, written under the pseudonym of Filidor der Dorfferer, ed. T. Raehse, Neudrucke 74/5, 1888) celebrates the pleasures of sensual love and the joys of the free, untrammelled existence of the soldier. He also wrote a comedy, *Wilmut* (1680), which has only antiquarian interest today, a manual of grammar and rhetoric, *Der teutsche Wolredner* (1688) and *Zeitungs-Lust und Nutz* (1697), an interesting expression of his views on the early newspaper. [WAC]

A. Koester, *Der Dichter der Geharnischten Venus* (Marburg, 1897).

**Stifter, Adalbert** (Oberplan, S. Bohemia 1805–Linz 1868). Austrian writer of Novellen and novels. The son of a poor weaver, he became a scholar at the Benedictine monastery of Kremsmünster, and as a student at the University of Vienna had to make his way by tutoring in the prosperous families of the aristocracy; for some time he hoped to become a professional painter. An unhappy love-affair, a difficult childless marriage, and the sudden death of a foster-child are the major emotional experiences of a life whose tenor is one of profound deprivation. After his disillusionment with the popular cause in 1848, he became a school-inspector in Linz, the capital of Upper Austria, where (except for occasional journeys) he lived to the end of his days. Various illnesses led to his retirement from his post in 1865; an intolerably painful cirrhosis of the liver led to his suicide on 28 January 1868.

Stifter's early stories (*Der Kondor*, 1840, the first version of *Die Mappe meines Urgrossvaters*, 1841) contain elements of fantasy that hark back to ⇨ Jean Paul; it is in *Der Hochwald* (1842) and *Abdias* (1843) that the main themes and narrative devices of his maturity are expressed for the first time; *Das alte Siegel* (1844), *Brigitta* (1844; tr. E. Fitzgerald, 1957), *Der Hagestolz* (1845), and *Der Waldgänger* (1847), as well as the five stories ('playthings for young hearts') collected in *Bunte Steine* (1853), represent the peak of his art as a writer of Novellen; whereas in some of the later stories (*Der fromme Spruch*, *Der Kuss von Sentze*, both 1866) the precarious balance of his finest works is upset and his style topples over into pedantry and tedium. Of his two completed novels, *Der Nachsommer* (1857) has become a classic in the language, whereas *Witiko* (1867) is one of those masterpieces more often praised than read.

In his stories the simple and unsophisticated means of the cautionary or almanach tale are used towards complex and far from naïve ends: thus he is in a sense too artless a writer to characterize by a manner of speech or through the consistent use of a narrative point of view. The settings are almost always rural and confined to a very small group (a married couple, a family, a village), the characters tend to be accounted for by 'humours' or centred on a single, invariably destructive passion. The relationships in which they live are determined by experience and natural age (teacher-pupil, father-son, old man-adopted youth), and by their God-given position (master-servant, knight-squire): it is in the world of Nature and of man-made things ('Geräthe') that Stifter achieves the equivalents of those nuances and configurations which the European realists trace out through the intrigues of society.

The narrative structures of his stories have some affinities with those of Henry James. Characters are endowed with a perfection of heart and mind which is impaired by the merest flaw, and through this flaw hostile fate enters their lives. The narrative devices are concentrated now on an infinitely gradual evocation of that perfection, now again on circumstantial description of the natural setting. His prose, always stately and elaborate, comes to acquire a liturgical, almost sacred character – detail is piled upon detail, as if to avert the calamity, the blow of untoward fate. At this point the structure divides. Some stories issue in a tragic conclusion, in which the blow of fate is fully motivated; in others the conclusion is absurd, intimating an unbridgeable chasm between the human and the divine; others again remain fixed in idyllic utopia.

*Der Nachsommer* combines these elements in the traditional form of the ⇨ *Bildungsroman*. Its main theme is the infinitely gradual, and thus designedly undramatic, sentimental education of a young man wholly susceptible to the examples of wisdom and beauty that surround him; no adversity modifies the influence of nature and of art to which he is subjected. Hidden behind an array of things and moods and characters all in perfect harmony, hidden deeply in the 'past' of the main narrative, lies a 'Novelle' of passion in which an episode from the life of the young man's aged mentor is retold; the Novelle is intended as the source of that wisdom from which the young man now benefits. Yet while the contrast between *what was* (the Novelle) and *what ought to be* (the main story) – between passionate discord and present idyll – is clear enough, the motivating connexion between the two is less convincing. Ultimately, it seems, Stifter is no more prepared to entrust his art to the logic of the human heart than to the actuality of the social and political world. The idyll, set out with an overwhelming strength of narrative purpose, with an immovable determination to avoid all calamity, is complete. Stifter's unique creative achievement lies in an act of propitiation – in the majestic *sostenuto* of the moments of tranquillity we know experience can yield. [JPS]

*Sämtliche Werke*, ed. A. Sauer *et al.* (Prague, etc., 1901 ff.); ed. M. Stefl (first versions of *Novellen*) (1950ff.); 'Bergkristall', from *Bunte Steine*, tr. J. R. Foster (1950).

A. R. Hein, *A.S.* (Wien, 1952); Urban Roedl, *A.S.* (Berlin, 1936; Bern, 1958); K. G. Fischer, *A.S.: Psychologische Beiträge* (Linz, 1961); E. Bertram, *A.S.* (1919); E. Lunding *A.S.* (Copenhagen, 1946); E. A. Blackall, *A.S.* (Cambridge, 1948); K. Hohoff, *A.S.* (Düsseldorf, 1949); W. Rehm, *A.S.* (Bern, 1951); Stern, *R.*

**Stigliani, Tommaso** (Matera, Basilicata 1573–Rome 1651). Italian poet. At first a friend of ⇨ Marino, he later became his bitter enemy and indulged in literary and personal polemics with him. His *Canzoniero* (1625) reveals Marinist tendencies restrained by a sense of literary discipline deriving from Petrarch and the classics, and to some extent he parodies the Marinist idiom. The *Del mondo nuovo* (1628) is a long poem on the exploits of Columbus, introducing love stories, magicians and demons, and owing a good deal to the Italian Romance tradition; *Dello occhiale* (1627) is a critical work which attacks, sometimes effectively, Marino's *Adone.* [DGR]

Croce, *LM*; M. Menghini, *T.S.* (Genoa, 1892); Ferrero, *MM*; Getto, *MM.*

**'Stil novo', or 'Il dolce stil novo'.** The 'sweet new style' introduced into Italian poetry by Guido ⇨ Guinizelli and his followers. The name is first used by Dante (*Purg.* xxiv. 57). In the past the 'dolce stil novo' has been described in terms of an intellectual and social revolution, which exalted nobility of mind and character ('*il cor gentile*') above nobility of birth, and in philosophical terms as an enriching and spiritualizing of the courtly love tradition of Provence and Sicily through the introduction into it of the ethical and religious teachings of medieval thought. The madonna of the Sicilian lyric thus became a woman-angel, God's emissary on earth through whom man catches a glimpse of the divine in the human scene. Modern scholarship tends to link the Stilnovists by theme and attitude to the preceding tradition which goes back to ⇨ Andreas Capellanus. Their homogeneity as a group is nowadays sought more in aesthetic attributes – language, imagery, and the heightened lyrical tension of their verse. (⇨ Guittone.) [DGR]

*Rimatori del Dolce Stil Novo*, ed. L. Di Benedetto (1939); Contini, *PD*; Salinari, *PLD.*

F. Figurelli, *Il Dolce Stil Novo* (Naples, 1933); C. Cordié, *Dolce Stil Novo* (Milan, 1942); Lind, *LPIR*; Rossetti, *DC*; Kay, *PBIV.*

**Stjernhjelm, Georg,** adopted name of Göran Lilja (Wika, Dalecarlia 1598–Stockholm 1672). Swedish poet and scholar. He travelled widely and wrote on philology, history, mathematics, science and philosophy. His greatest literary work is the allegorical poem in hexameters, *Hercules* (Uppsala, 1653), which debates the problem of duty and pleasure. He also wrote a mock serious epithalamium, *Bröllops – Besvärs Ihugkommelse*, and several works for performance at Queen Christina's court. Among his pupils were the poet brothers Johan and Samuel Columbus.

*Samlade Skrifter*, ed. J. Nordström (8 vols., 1924–51).

**Storm, Theodor** (Husum 1817–Hademarschen 1888). German novelist and lyric poet. He practised law in his native town, but the Danish occupation of Schleswig-Holstein (1853–64) forced him into exile in Potsdam and Heiligenstadt. After the Prussians defeated and ousted the Danes, he returned to Husum, elected to a high legal post which he held until 1880; he then retired to Hademarschen. He was a friend and correspondent of ⇨ Heyse, ⇨ Mörike, ⇨ Keller, ⇨ Fontane and ⇨ Turgenev. Beginning as a lyric poet, his poetry, apart from some political, patriotic and satirical pieces, centres around the preoccupations of love, solitude and death (for Storm, a lifelong agnostic, death was the ultimate 'agonizing enigma'). His lyric reached a climax with the cycle *Tiefe Schatten* (1865) written on the death of his first wife; but by now he was already beginning to concentrate on the Novelle, and eventually devoted himself entirely to this form. A recurrent concern in his stories is solitude, the isolation of man from man, mostly seen as the life-denying but almost inevitable concomitant of being human, and explored in various manifestations: incommunication (*Immensee*, 1849; in *St. Jürgen*, 1867), class tensions (*Drüben am Markt*, 1861), superstition or religious bigotry (*Renate*, 1878), the father-son relationship (*Hans und Heinz Kirch*, 1882), and social problems like alcoholism (*John Riew'*, 1885) or the situation of an ex-convict (*Ein Doppelgänger*, 1886). He wrote a number of historical Novellen (*Aquis submersus*, 1876; tr. G. Skelton, *Beneath the Flood*, 1962). His last and most achieved work is *Der Schimmelreiter* (1888; tr. G. Skelton, *The White Horseman*, 1962), the story of a dykemaster whose ambitions defy nature and alienate him from his fellows, and who is thereby destroyed. Most of the stories are set in his immediate homeland, but the impression they leave is not overridingly provincial. His narrative technique is characterized by a subjectivism far in advance of his time. [TR]

*Sämtliche Werke*, ed. P. Goldammer (1956).

R. Pitrou, *La vie et l'œuvre de T.S.* (Paris, 1920); F. Stuckert, *T.S.* (Bremen, 1955); F. Böttger, *T.S.* (Berlin, 1958); Natan, *GML*, i.

**Stramm, August** (Münster 1874–Russian front 1915). German poet and dramatist. Co-editor with ⇨ Walden of the Expressionist periodical *Der Sturm*, in which his work (refused publication elsewhere) first appeared: e.g. his drama, *Sancta Susanna* (also in *Gessammelte Dichtungen*, 2 vols., 1919), set to music by Hindemith. His characteristic, ejaculatory style is less successful in plays (other so-called 'Schreidramen' are *Die Haidebraut*, 1914, *Erwachen*, 1915, *Kräfte*, 1915, etc.) which shout about rather than realize the dreadful immediacy of experience, than in poems, with their startling syntax and vivid clusters of images. [PB]

*Das Werk* (1963); *Dein Lächeln weint* (1956); trs. in *Poet Lore*, XXV (Boston, 1914); Bridgwater, *TCGV*; Cohen, *PA*; Hamburger and Middleton, *MGP*.

E. Bozzetti, *Untersuchungen zur Lyrik und Drama A.S.s* (Cologne, 1961) (dissertation); Hamburger, *RE*; *Euph*, LVIII, 3, 1964; *Neuedt. Hefte*, 100 (1964).

**Straparola, Gianfrancesco** (Caravaggio *c.*1480–*c.*1557). Italian short-story writer. Little is known of him. He left an undistinguished *Canzoniere*, but is remembered only for his short stories, *Le piacevoli notti* (2 parts 1550–3; ed. G. Rua, 1927; tr. W. G. Waters, *The Nights of Straparola*, 1894). The setting of the collection is the island of Murano and the 75 stories, each followed by a verse riddle, are related by ladies and gentlemen in the suite of Ottaviano Sforza, Bishop of Lodi. Though his tone is pedestrian, his use of fairy-tale plots, which makes him a humble predecessor of ⇨ Basile, gives the collection a certain novelty. It was published many times in the 16th century. [DGR]

Di Francia, *N.*

**Strashimirov, Anton** (Varna 1872–Vienna 1937). Bulgarian story-writer, novelist and dramatist. An unsettled upbringing and unruly temperament impeded this gifted, energetic writer's career in teaching and politics. After reading literature and geography at Bern in 1895–7, he returned to teaching, writing and literary journalism. He edited *Nash zhivot* ('Our Life') with ⇨ Mihaylovski and ⇨ Hristov, *Demokraticheski pregled* ('Democratic Review') with ⇨ Vlaykov and, after the First World War, *Nashi dni* ('Our Days') and the progressive daily *Vedrina* ('Clarity').

By 1900 he had published his stories on village life, *Smyah i sălzi* (1897), *Zmey* (1900), and a novel on life after the 1886 *coup*, *Smutno vreme* (1899). There followed, from *Vampir* (1902) to *Vihăr* (1922) and *Horo* (1926), a succession of plays, stories and novels, at times verbose, tortured and uneven but often dramatic and convincing in their treatment of current events and emotional clashes in village life. Thus, the narodnik dilemma of the nineties is forcefully presented in *Krăstopăt* (1904).

Honoured by the Ministry of Education with an *Antologiya* (1922) of his works, he won awards from the Academy of Sciences for his *Esenni dni* (1902) and from the National Theatre for his plays *Svekărva* (1907) and *Otvăd* (1906); this last, like his novel *Robi* (2 vols., 1929–30), reflects his ardent espousal of the Macedonian cause. His interest in sociology, coupled with wide experience of his countrymen and the different regions of Bulgaria, inspired his *Kniga za bălgarite* ('Book about the Bulgarians, 1917) and *Nashiyăt narod* ('Our People', 1923). With his biographies of P. Karavelov, *Reformatorăt* (1934), and S. Stambolov, *Diktatorăt* (1935), he entered the field of his brother, the historian D. Strashimirov. His own life and aspirations are the subject of his *Tvorchestvo i zhivot* ('Creativity and Life', 1930). [VP]

*Săchineniya* (7 vols., 1962–3); *Sbornik A.S. – lichnost i delo* (1931); Pinto, *BPV.*

Manning and Smal-Stocki, *HMBL*.

**Straszewicz, Czeslaw** (Białystok 1904–Munich 1963). Polish novelist. His books are few but of great originality. He first made his reputation with the volume of short stories, *Gromy z jasnego nieba* (1936). *Turyści z bocianich gniazd* (1953) consists of two short novels, as inventive in their narrative technique as they are in their dialogue. The tourists of the title are Polish sailors choosing freedom in a South-American port. The vocabulary delights with its admixture of Spanish in the first tale, and with the bureaucratic convulsions of speech in the second, which describes post-war Poland. Straszewicz went to live in Uruguay, and died in Munich. [JP]

**Strēlerte, Veronika.** ⇨ Latvian Literature.

**Streuvels, Stijn.** ⇨ Lateur, Frank.

**Stricker (Der)** (fl. 1215–50). Middle High German poet. Of humble birth, he was probably a native of the Middle Rhine but was resident for many years, as his poems show, in Austria. He was an industrious producer of realistic narrative poems whose didactic intent is accompanied by the dry, factual presentation of scenes which afford interesting glimpses of the life of the time. The work for which he is chiefly remembered is his ambitious epic on the life of Charlemagne, *Karl der Grosse* (ed. K. Bartsch, 1857), which enjoyed great popularity in the 13th century. [RT]

F. von der Hagen, *Gesamtabenteuer* (1850) (shorter poems).
Ehrismann, *GDL.*

**Strindberg, August** (Stockholm 1849–Stockholm 1912). Swedish dramatist, novelist, story writer, poet and pamphleteer. An almost universally gifted but also incorrigibly subjective writer, he was driven by a need to clarify his complicated, often tortured life to write extensively about himself. The four volumes of *Tjänstekvinnans son* (1886–7, 1909; tr. E. Sprinchorn, *The Son of a Servant*, 1967) retrace his intellectual development but also give a most vivid description of his unhappy childhood and youth; the fears and jealousies of a hypersensitive child; parental severity and lack of understanding; the early loss of his mother; his frustrating Uppsala sojourns and fruitless search for social recognition; and finally his early triumphs and setbacks as a writer. *Le plaidoyer d'un fou* (written in French in 1887; published 1895; Swedish tr. J. Landquist and E. Staaff, *En dåres försvarstal*, 1920; tr. E. Schleussner, *The Confession of a Fool*, 1912) is a partly fictional and wholly vindictive account of his first marriage (1877–91) to Baroness Siri von Essen. *Inferno* (1897; tr. M. Sandbach, *Inferno*, 1962) and *Legender* (1898) cover an especially unsettled period of his life, after his second marriage (1893–7) to the Austrian journalist Frida Uhl had foundered and when, living alone in Paris occupied with divers experiments, chiefly alchemical ones, and occult studies, he turned again to religion. The final link in the chain, *Ensam* (1903), is a more meditative book written when his third marriage (1901–4) to the young Norwegian actress Harriet Bosse was drawing to a close.

Strindberg's first major work, the historical play *Mäster Olof*, was written in 1872 but published only in 1881 (tr. W. Johnson, in *The Vasa Trilogy*, Seattle, 1959). For a hero he had chosen the venerable 16th-century Protestant reformer, faced him with problems almost identical with his own and made him waver between idealism and scepticism. The episodic novel *Röda rummet* (1879; tr. E. Sprigge, *The Red Room*, 1967) made its author famous. Written with humour and dramatic verve, its stylistic brilliance has never been denied. With scathing satire of social hypocrisy and corruption Strindberg embarked upon his lifelong career as the scourge of the Establishment. Yet the book has another aspect earning it the title of ⇨ *Bildungsroman* with a hero who, at the price of happiness, is cured of idealistic illusions. Regarded as a leader by the Young Sweden group of writers, Strindberg only now took up the study of Zola but was so far from being a dogmatic naturalist that in *Lycko-Pers resa* (1882; tr. A. Paulson, *Lucky-Per's Journey*, N.Y., 1965) he combined social criticism with the allegorical form of a fairy-play. Following harsh professional criticism of a work of popular history, he responded violently with *Det nya riket* (1882), the most brilliant but also most personally damaging pamphlet ever to leave his pen. As a result he soon found the climate of his native country intolerable. Thus began a continental odyssey (1883–9), often harassed by financial hardship and marital stress.

In *Svenska öden och äventyr* (1882–91), *Utopier i verkligheten* (1885) and *Giftas, i–ii* (1884–6; tr. E. Schleussner, *Married*, 1913) he developed the (often long) short story into a vehicle of his personal convictions, philosophical, political or otherwise. On a much-debated issue of the time, the emancipation of women, he at first took up a moderate, even conservative position. On publication of the first part of *Giftas*, however, an action for blasphemy was brought against him. Although he was acquitted, the trial was too great a strain on his mind (evidence of a hysterical disposition dates back to his adolescence), and from now on ideas of persecution combined with uncontrollable jealousy became a source of worry both to himself and those near him.

The 'war of the sexes' provided the theme of the naturalist dramas *Fadren* (1887; tr. M. Meyer, *The Father*, 1964) and *Fröken Julie* (1888; tr. M. Meyer, *Miss Julie*, 1964), which soon made him internationally famous. In these grim plays he perfected his personal form of psychological analysis, the result of extensive reading in the field of psychology coupled with an uncommon gift for self-analysis. Formally not unrelated to Greek and Shakespearean tragedy, these plays show a remarkable concentration upon one theme, but intensity and economy of presentation here go with unrivalled feeling for the wordless action of one person upon another. In *Fordringsägare* (1888; tr. M. Meyer, *Creditors*, 1964) the centre of interest shifts to the 'battle of brains'; and in the one-act play *Den Starkare* (1889; tr. M. Meyer, *The Stronger*, 1964) the same motif is handled with a maximum of concentration: of its two roles, one is mute.

Strindberg's love for the Stockholm archipelago and his knowledge of its inhabitants have inspired the novels *Hemsöborna* (1887; tr. E. H. Schubert, *The People of Hemsö*, 1959), according to the author, 'an intermezzo scherzando between the battles', and the more sombre *I Havsbandet* (1890). The former is a Swedish classic and his most popular work, full of masterly descriptions of land and sea and remarkable also for the balance it achieves between humorous surface detail and tragic undercurrent. The latter is his most strictly naturalist prose work, a study of the destruction of a 'superman' (he had by now both read and corresponded with Nietzsche) in a lonely fight against hostile nature and fellow-men.

From the period of reorientation known as the Inferno crisis, he emerged as a self-styled disciple of Swedenborg and as an interpreter of providential signs. His turn to religion found its most powerful expression in *Till Damaskus, i–iii* (1898–1901; tr. G. Rawson, *The Road to Damascus*, 1959), of which the first (and vastly superior) part re-enacts his conversion in a universalized symbolic form and inaugurates an enlarged idea of a theatre in which conscious and subconscious elements may co-exist. This feature has led some, but not all, critics to classify the later Strindberg among the Expressionists. Further plays in a similar mode are *Advent* (1898); *Brott och brott* (1899; tr. E. Sprigge, *Crime and Crime*, 1963); *Påsk* (1900; tr. E. Sprigge, *Easter*, 1963); *Kronbruden* (1901); *Svanehvit* (1901; tr. E. Sprigge, *Swanhwite*, 1963). More successful with the public, though not dissimilar in spirit, were *Folkungasagan* (1899; tr. W. Johnson, *The Saga of the Folkungs*, Seattle, 1959), *Gustaf Vasa*; and *Eric XIV* (both 1899; tr. W. Johnson, in *The Vasa Trilogy*, Seattle, 1959), the beginning of a cycle of no less than 12 historical dramas; whereas *Dödsdansen, i–ii* (1900; tr. E. Sprigge, *The Dance of Death*, 1963) marks at least a partial return to the naturalistic manner in the savage analysis of a love-hate relationship on the eve of a silver wedding.

His early poetry is contained in *Dikter på vers och prosa* (1883) and *Sömngångarnätter* (1884), strikingly unconventional as well as charged with his bold temperament. His later verse is found in *Ordalek och småkonst* (1902–5). Formally independent, he mixes idyllic themes with passionate confessions, realistic hexameters with symbolist free verse. His major poetic achievement, however, is the uniquely original form of *Ett drömspel* (1901; tr. E. Sprigge, *A Dream Play*, 1963), the purpose of which is to convey the fleeting unreality of existence. In terms of sheer theatricality and emotional immediacy the play has no rival among his works; its melancholy mood has an almost oriental colouring, and its refrain 'Mankind's to be pitied!' strikes a note of universal compassion.

The venture of his later years was the Intimate Theatre which he set up together with the young director A. Falck. For its members he laid down the principles of acting in *Öppna brev till Intima teatern* (1908 f.; tr. W. Johnson, *Open Letters to the Intimate Theater*, 1966), and for its stage he conceived his 'Chamber Plays', the best known of which, *Spöksonaten* (1907; tr. E. Sprigge, *The Ghost Sonata*, 1963), is partly cast in the dream mode, partly given a realistic setting. The total effect, which proved disconcerting for contemporary audiences, was to dissolve the contours of the dramatis personae, even to blur the borderline between life and death. More easily accessible are *Oväder* (tr. M. Meyer, *Storm*, 1964), *Brända tomten* and *Pelikanen* (all 1907), of which the first comes closest to a realization of the intimate quality of chamber music, while the other two waver between resignation and the desire to unmask the hypocrisy of mankind. His farewell to the drama, *Stora landsvägen* (1909; tr. E. Sprigge, *The Great Highway*, 1963), reviews, behind not too heavy allegorical disguise, his own life in a spirit equally of rancour and humility.

Strindberg's last decade was far from peaceful. After the hostile reception of his satirical novel *Götiska rummen* (1904), he turned in fury against his former friends in *Svarta fanor* (1907), the most devastating *roman à clef* ever published in Sweden. The warfare was continued up to the end of his life and culminated in the 'Strindberg Feud' of 1910–12, a general showdown between radicals and the literary Establishment. The most complete insight into the mind of the ageing Strindberg is gained through *En blå bok*, *i–iv* (1907–12), a strange collection of aphorisms, meditations, pseudo-scientific ideas, polemics and memories. [SAB]

*Samlade skrifter*, ed. J. Landquist (55 vols., 1912–20); *August Strindbergs brev*, ed. T. Eklund (9 vols. to date, 1948 ff.); *Ur Ockulta dagboken*, ed. T. Eklund (1963; tr. M. Sandbach, *From an Occult Diary*, 1965).

M. Lamm, *S.s dramer, i–ii* (Stockholm, 1924–6); M. Lamm, *A.S.* (Stockholm, 1948); T. Eklund, *Tjänstekvinnans son* (Stockholm, 1948); G. Brandell, *S.s Infernokris* (Stockholm, 1950); G. Ollén, *S.s dramatik* (Stockholm, 1961); *Synpunkter på S.*, ed. G. Brandell (Stockholm, 1964); E. Sprigge, *The Strange Life of A.S.* (1949); B. M. E. Mortensen and B. W. Downs, *S.* (1949); *Essays on S.*, ed. R. Smedmark (Stockholm, 1966); G. Lindström, 'Strindberg Studies 1915–1962', in *Scandinavica*, II, 1 (1963).

**Strittmatter, Erwin** (Spremberg 1912– ). German novelist and dramatist. He worked as baker, waiter and labourer, and deserted during the Second World War. From 1947 he was a leading civil servant in East Germany. Later he became a newspaper editor and free-lance writer. His plays (e.g. *Katzgraben*, 1954; *Die Holländerbraut*, 1960), novels (*Ochsenkutscher*, 1950; *Tinko*, 1955; *Der Wundertäter*, 1957; *Ole Bienkopp*, 1963) and short stories (*Eine Mauer fällt*, 1952; *Paul und die Dame Daniel*, 1956) often incorporate autobiographical elements and treat the lives of rural characters in a spirit of socialist realism. [LL]

Kunisch, *HDG*.

**Stub, Ambrosius** (Gummerup 1705–Ribe 1758). Danish poet. A *studiosus perpetuus* and impoverished private tutor. His surviving poems were only published 13 years after his death. The best are gracious and easy-flowing (reminiscent of Herrick), and show great versatility as to metre and form – epigrams, drinking songs, religious poetry, love poems, and descriptive and didactic poetry. [ELB]

*Samlede Digte* (1961).

H. Brix, *A.S.* (Copenhagen, 1960).

**Stuckenberg, Viggo** (Vridsløselille 1863–Copenhagen 1905). Danish poet. Of the Symbolist school, his intimate, formally perfect poems are tender in their expression of sad resignation. His few novels are forgotten, but his best tales and legends are collected in *Vejbred* (1899; tr. U. Hook, *By the Wayside*, 1917). [ELB]

*Digte* (1886); *Flyvende Sommer* (1898); *Sne* (1901); *Samlede Værker* (1910–11).

J. Andersen, *V.S. og hans Samtid* (Copenhagen, 1944).

**Štúr, L'udovít** (1815–1856). Slovak philologist and poet. An ardent follower of Kollár, he played a leading part in evolving the Slovak literary language which he constructed from the dialects of central Slovakia. He published a grammar in 1846. By his untiring efforts to publicize the language he gained for it general acceptance among the Slovak writers against strong opposition from many Czechs and Slovaks who saw in the introduction of a special literary language for the Slovaks a danger to the common political struggle of the two nations. [KB]

H. Tourtzer, *L.Š. et l'idée de l'indépendance slovaque* (Cahors/Alençon, 1913); J. M. Hurban, *L'.Š.* (Bratislava, 1928–42); J. Linhart, *L'.Š.* (Prague, 1952); V. Kochol, *Poézia Štúrovcov* (Bratislava, 1955).

**'Sturm und Drang'** ('Storm and Stress'). A German literary movement. The name was invented by Christoph Kaufmann in connexion with Klinger's play *Wirrwarr* (1775).

The word is now associated with the early writings of Herder, Goethe and Schiller, together with the work of many minor authors, like Heinse, Lenz, Leisewitz, F. Müller, H. L. Wagner.

*Sturm und Drang. Dramatische Schriften*, ed. E. Loewenthal (Heidelberg, 1963).

Pascal, *GSD*; Garland, *SS*.

**Sudermann, Hermann** (Matziken, E. Prussia 1857–Berlin 1928). German dramatist and novelist. He exploited the vogue for Naturalistic social dramas, revivifying essentially old theatrical sentiments and situations (derived from e.g. ⇨ Dumas, ⇨ Sardou) with modern settings, and achieving early fame with his love tangle between rich and poor, *Die Ehre* (1889; tr. H. R. Bankhage, *Honor*, N.Y., 1915). The obvious 'star' role in *Heimat* (1893; tr. C. E. A. Winslow, *Magda*, in *Contemporary Drama*, N.Y., 1932; filmed) – the prima donna with a past revisits her conventional home – was played by Sarah Bernhardt, Duse, Mrs Patrick Campbell. Historical and Biblical plays (e.g. *Johannes*, 1898; tr. B. Marshall, *John the Baptist*, 1909) and Prussian country passions (e.g. *Johannisfeuer*, 1900; tr. C. Swickard, *Fires of St John*, Boston, 1904) were less successful than well-tried intrigues of scandal: e.g. *Es lebe das Leben* (1902; tr. E. Wharton, *The Joy of Living*, 1903). Damningly criticized by ⇨ Kerr, his fame soon waned; the one-act *Fritzchen* (in *Morituri*, 1896; tr. A. Alexander, 1912) is still respected. His novels derive some vitality from their Memelland folklore and regional realism: e.g. *Frau Sorge* (1887; tr. B. Overbeck, *Dame Care*, 1902). [PB/AKT]

K. Busse, *H.S.* (Stuttgart/Berlin, 1927); Garten, *MGD*; Natan, *GML*, ii.

**Sue, Eugène** (Paris 1804–Annecy 1857). French novelist. Famous in his day for his depictions of low life and crime in Paris. He came of a distinguished line of doctors and began his life as a ship's doctor, but retired (1829) to write novels of seafaring life. It was when he turned to Paris life with such works as *Les mystères de Paris* (1842–3; tr. anon., *The Mysteries of Paris*) that he achieved great success. He had a strong humanitarian feeling and introduced ideas of social reform into his sensational stories. Because of this he has been described as a coarser Dickens. With ⇨ Dumas *père* he helped to start the vogue for *feuilletons*. Other titles from his enormous output are *Le juif errant* (1844–5), *Les Sept péchés capitaux* (1847–9) and *Les mystères du peuple* (1849–56). [WA]

**Sukhovo-Kobylin, Aleksander** (Voskresensk, Moscow 1817–Beaulieu, Alpes Maritimes 1903). Russian dramatist. A rich nobleman and student of philosophy, his three plays, though little known abroad, are classics of the Russian theatre: *Svad'ba Krechinskogo* (1855; tr. R. Magidoff, *Krechinsky's Wedding*, 1961), *Delo* (1869) and *Smert' Tarel'kina* (1869). All three are excellently dramatic. The first is a comedy; the others are ferocious satires on officialdom, which he knew at first hand from his protracted trial when suspected of having murdered his mistress.

*Trilogiya* (1959); *Pis'ma* (1934).

K. L. Rudnitsky, *A.B.S.-K.* (Moscow, 1957); *SR*, XXIV (1946).

**Sullivan, Vernon.** ⇨ Vian, Boris.

**Sully-Prudhomme, René-François-Armand** (Paris 1839–Paris 1907). French ⇨ Parnassian poet who is chiefly remembered for the anthology piece *Le vase brisé*. He studied first science and then law but inherited enough to devote himself to literature. At first he wrote melancholy and sometimes sentimental poems but his interest in philosophy led him towards the more impersonal ideals of the Parnassians. The collections *Stances et poèmes* (1865), *Les épreuves* (1866) and *Les solitudes* (1869) belong to his first style but later in *La justice* (1878), *Le prisme* (1886) and *Le bonheur* (1888) he tried to turn philosophical systems into epic verse. One of his first publications was a translation of the first book of Lucretius, a task which foreshadowed his later interests. Towards the end of his life he devoted himself to prose. In 1901 he was awarded the Nobel Prize. [WA]

P. Flottes, *S.P.* (Paris, 1930).

**Sumarokov, Aleksandr Petrovich** (Villmanstrand, now Lappeenranta 1717–Moscow 1777). Russian dramatist and poet. In St Petersburg Sumarokov helped to found and was the first director (1756–61) of the first Russian public theatre, for which he also provided much of the repertoire. He composed 9 tragedies and 15 comedies, as well as several libretti for opera and ballet.

Sumarokov was a devoted protagonist of classical principles (he adapted and partially translated Boileau's *Art poétique*). Though he hardly deserved the title 'Racine of the North' which his first editor bestowed on him (his characters lack complexity and his plots deal somewhat too obviously with the conflict between love and duty) his verse tragedies are competently constructed in accordance with French classical standards, while the majority of his themes (*Dimitriy Samozvanets*, 1771; *Mstislav*, 1774) are taken from the Russian past. Sumarokov was an innovator in his use of such themes. Moreover, his were the first Russian tragedies in verse. The comedies of his maturity, such as *Rogonosets po voobrazheniyu* ('The Imaginary Cuckold', 1772), are written with delicacy and wit. However, the importance of Sumarokov's dramatic works in the formation of the Russian theatre has not ensured their survival on the stage, and it is more as a poet than as a playwright that he is read today.

His poetry is varied in metre, form and mood. He composed odes, elegies, eclogues, idylls, songs, fables and satires. His most successful poems are remarkable for the simplicity of their language, the lucidity of their thought and (despite his adherence to classical idiom) the sincerity of their feelings.

Sumarokov was an aristocrat by birth and inclination, but his turbulent nature, his pride and his forthrightness made it difficult for him to fit comfortably into high society. He fell into debt, was evicted from his house and died in poverty. Only the actors of Moscow acknowledged their indebtedness to him by purchasing a grave for him and by carrying him to it. [SH]

*A.P.S. Izbrannyye proizvedeniya*, ed. P. N. Berkov (1957).

**Supervielle, Jules** (Montevideo 1884–Paris 1960). French poet, novelist and playwright. The orphaned son of Basque bankers, he lived in Uruguay, Paris and Oloron in the Pyrenees. He published a dozen volumes of precise, easily accessible and traditionally built verse. He wrote in French, but was influenced more by South American than by French poetry – from it he inherited slightly conceited metaphors, and power derived from technical simplicity, with occasional playful fantasies and allegories. *Poèmes* (1919), *Gravitations* (1925), *Le forçat innocent* (1930), *Les amis inconnus* (1934), *La fable du monde* (1938), *Poèmes de la France malheureuse* (1941), *Oublieuse mémoire* (1949), *Naissances* (1951) and *Le corps tragique* (1959) repeat and deepen four main themes – lucid anxiety over the poet's heart condition, in the constant throbbing presence of Death; cosmic reflections, where a humanist and a spiritual idealist rediscovers and interprets the many links in the Universe and saves it from absurdity; a double longing for the exotic civilization in 'Creolopolis' and for the gentleness of France; and a 'pansympathy' with Nature. He has also written, in a poetic vein, delicate and humorous tales on fanciful, mythical or Biblical themes: *L'arche de Noé* (1938), *Premiers pas de l'univers* (1950), and novels and plays: *L'homme de la Pampa* (1923), *Bolivar* (1936), *Schéhérezade* (1949). [CLC]

*L'enfant de la haute mer*, tr. D. Japp and N. Nicholls, *Souls of the Soulless* (1933); *Le voleur d'enfants*, tr. A. Pryce-Jones, *The Colonel's Children* (1950).
Claude Roy, *J.S.* (Paris, 1953).

**Surrealism.** A literary and artistic movement originating in France, where it was defined by A. ⇨ Breton in his *Manifeste du surréalisme* (1924). It aimed to revive spontaneity of expression by exploring the Unconscious through dreams, automatic writing, *humour noir*, etc. ⇨ Apollinaire, Éluard, Aragon. [RTC]

*Les Manifestes du S.* (1962)
M. Raymond, *De Baudelaire au S.* (Paris, 1933); F. Alquié, *Philosophie du S.* (Paris, 1955); J.-L. Bédouin, *Vingt ans de S., 1939–1959* (Paris, 1961); M. Nadeau, *Histoire du S.* (2nd edn, Paris, 1964).

**Sutzkever, Abraham** (Lithuania 1913– ). Yiddish poet. Editor of the Yiddish quarterly *Di Goldene Keyt* in Tel Aviv. A leader of the 'Young Vilna' group before the war, he lived through Nazi occupation, escaped to Russia, and spent several years in Siberia. After the war he returned to Poland from where he emigrated to Israel. His poetic style is truly modern. [EE]

*Di Geheime Shtat* (Tel Aviv, 1948); *Di Festung* (N.Y., 1947); *Lider fun Ghetto* (N.Y., 1947); *Vilnoer Ghetto* (Buenos Aires, 1947); *Sibir* (1950; tr. J. Sonntag, *Siberia*, 1961).

**Svevo, Italo,** pseud. of Ettore Schmitz (Trieste 1861–Motta di Livenza 1928). Italian novelist. Born in a Jewish family of mixed German–Italian parentage (symbolized by his pen-name), in what was an important meeting point of three cultures in the Austro-Hungarian Empire. In spite of his commercial training he soon turned to literature, but his first novels, *Una vita* (1892; tr. A. Colquhoun, *A Life*, 1963) and *Senilità* (1898; tr. Beryl de Zoëte, *As a Man Grows Older*, 1932, reissued 1962), met with a disappointing reception. Paradoxically his decision to abandon literature and concentrate on his business led to sudden literary fame; since his business travels took him often as far as London, he decided to learn English: his teacher happened to be Joyce, who, after reading the two novels, encouraged him to go on writing. Svevo could follow his advice only after the First World War, and in 1923 published a third novel, *La coscienza di Zeno* (tr. Beryl de Zoëte, *Confessions of Zeno*, 1920, reissued 1962). Joyce passed it on to Benjamin Crémieux and Valéry ⇨ Larbaud who reviewed it enthusiastically in 1926, presenting Svevo to the European public as a major literary discovery. This was the beginning of the 'Svevo Affair': vexed by the fact that an Italian writer should have been first acclaimed abroad, some Italian critics tried to prove, in long articles about Svevo's alleged stylistic and even grammatical faults, that they had been right to ignore him; some others maintained that he had first been 'discovered' by Montale in an essay published a few months before Crémieux's article (Montale's essay is in I. Svevo–E. Montale, *Lettere*, Bari, 1966). It is doubtful, however, whether Montale's *Omaggio* would have aroused much interest without the French intervention. Svevo died two years later in a car crash.

Svevo's education, a synthesis of many different elements, and his cultural and political position (a businessman who loved literature, an Austro-Hungarian subject who loved Italy, a pacifist in the middle of a world war, a Jew) turned him quite naturally into an outsider with a marked taste for self-analysis and introspection, for which he has often been compared to Proust. The resemblance is external, however, for Svevo's themes are different (the loneliness of modern man; his inability to will and act, directly proportional to his skill in psychoanalysing himself; his wild dreams of love and glory and his actual frustrations), his field of observation more restricted (merchant middle-class in Trieste), and his style 'anti-literary' and undistinguished. This is not necessarily a weakness, since it suits admirably his characters' lack of distinction. [GMC]

*Tutte le opere* (1954); P. M. Firbank, *I.S.* (1966).

**Swiss-German Dialect Literature.** In German-speaking Switzerland standard ('high') German is only used in secondary schools, official circles, the press and Parliament. In private life (and at local political meetings) dialect is felt to be a bond of citizenship; it is used equally by all classes. There is, however, no 'Swiss' dialect as such; local dialects differ strikingly in intonation, grammatical form and vocabulary. There are considerable variations in accent and intonation between the Alpine dialects and those of N. Switzerland. Perhaps because of the great variety of dialect forms, efforts to abandon standard German have always been unsuccessful; to create an artificial 'Swiss language' seemed less valuable than to preserve the cultural linguistic connexions of German.

Swiss literature is characterized on the one hand by a wide variety of highly vernacular writing and on the other by conscious confrontation with literary German. There is virtually no Swiss writer who has written only in dialect, but there are also very few who have consistently avoided its use. Many, and in particular the greatest Swiss novelist, Jeremias ⇨ Gotthelf, have included dialect words, either consciously or unconsciously, in their German style and have thus enriched its vocabulary. (There had anyway been considerable uncertainty until the 18th century as to what is German and what dialect.)

An unashamedly mixed language is used by U. ⇨ Bräker (1735–98), whose Shakespeare essay and diary notes reveal naïve poetic gifts; his language is partly that of the age of sentimentality, but it lacks educated correctness. His younger contemporary from Central Switzerland, the Luzern clergyman, Josef Ineichen (1745–1818), makes much more consistent use of his local dialect in his morally solid and homely folksongs; he was already influenced here by romantic ideas. The Bern minister, Gottlieb Jakob Kuhn (1775–1849), makes similar use of dialect in folksongs which are still sung today. It was J. P. ⇨ Hebel, however, who first enriched Swiss dialect literature most significantly with his *Alemannische Gedichte*. Under the influence of romantic belief in regional writing lesser and major talents began to flourish in all areas of the country. Noteworthy is the Zürich writer, Johann Martin Usteri (1763–1827); influenced by J. H. ⇨ Voss and by Goethe's *Hermann und Dorothea* he produced idylls in 'Zürich-German' hexameters, *De Vikari* and *De Herr Heiri.*

The Canton of Bern still remains the most fruitful soil for dialect writing. The novels and stories of Rudolf von Tavel (1866–1934) portray with affection and accuracy the aristocratic tradition of the Bundesstadt (esp. in the Napoleonic period, *Ja gäll, so geit's*, 1901, *Der Houptme Lombach*, 1903, etc.). One of the more artistically gifted Professors of German, Otto von Greyerz, founded the Bern Heimatschutz Theater which still continues to produce exclusively dialect plays, and he is also the author of several good 'Heimatspiele'. Owing also to his efforts and those of the Zürich Professor, Albert Bachmann, there has been much scholarly research into dialects and dialect literature in the Swiss universities; this has led to a systematic dictionary, the *Schweizerisches Idiotikon*, and more recently a Swiss linguistic Atlas. The various radio stations also soon decided to encourage local dialect, and there have resulted several traditions of radio drama in dialect, each with its own style of presentation and its own more or less exaggerated folklore. Thus the Bern farmer has found his enthusiastic romantic exponent in Simon Gfeller (1868–1943). Simultaneously in neighbouring Solothurn, Josef Reinhart (1875–1957) was writing sensitive idylls, while in Aargau, Sophie Hämmerli-Marti (1868–1942) gave this style of writing a still more intimate flavour. Also from Aargau was Paul Haller (1882–1920) who used dialect to convey the earthy gloom of his naturalistic vision and created a deterministic portrait of environment in *Maria und Robert*; in the same vein is *Steibruch* (1939) by Albert J. Welti (1894–1965). In E. Switzerland dialect comedy and farce have flourished in the hands of Alfred Huggenberger, Kaspar Freuler, and H. Jenny, and to this generation belongs also the gifted poet from Schwyz, Meinrad Lienert (1865–1933).

In Basel the historian Jacob Burckhardt (1818–97) published a volume of dialect lyrics, *E Hämpfeli Liedli* (1857). Here also a tradition of satirical 'folk-cabaret' songs has survived into the age of industrial development; at carnival time, private clubs sing these satires on contemporary events. Swiss humorous periodicals, notably the *Nebelspalter*, have also encouraged topical poetry.

The *Deutschschweizerischer Sprachverein* and similar organizations help to keep alive dialect writing. Though much is mere sentimental, homespun 'Heimatpoesie', the work of Albert Bächtold from Klettgau shows how a narrowly regional peasant dialect may be used effectively for a series of novels wide in scope and profound in meaning. Albert Meyer has made a powerful translation of the *Odyssey* into Bernese. [KF]

O. v. Greyerz, *Dialekt-Literatur der deutschen Schweiz* (1924).

E. Ermatinger, *Dichtung und Geistesleben der deutschen Schweiz* (Munich, 1933); J. Nadler, *Literaturgeschichte der deutschen Schweiz* (1932); A. Zäch, *Die Dichtung der deutschen Schweiz* (1951); H. Trümpy, *Schweizer-deutsche Sprache und Literatur im 17. und 18. Jahrhundert* (*Schriften der Schweizer Gesellschaft für Volkskunde*, 36, 1955); *Sprachspiegel* (1945ff.) (the journal of the Swiss *Sprachverein*); *Schriftenreihe des Swiss Sprachvereins* (1964ff.).

**Symbolism.** A poetic movement originating in France and defined by J. Moréas in a *Figaro* article (18 September 1886). Despite often striking differences of style between Baudelaire (from whose poem 'Correspondances' the word derives), Verlaine, Rimbaud, Mallarmé and his circle, Laforgue, Kahn, Valéry and others, a common tendency may be observed to regard poetry as a means of transcending reality, and words as magic entities in themselves. The movement developed out of ⇨ Parnassianism and passed into ⇨ Surrealism; it had affinities with the decadent aestheticism of Huysmans and Villiers de l'Isle Adam. It was widely influential throughout Europe.

A. Symons, *The Symbolist Movement in Literature* (1899); C. M. Bowra, *The Heritage of Symbolism* (1943); A. G. Lehmann, *The Symbolist Aesthetic in France* (1950).

**Syrokomla, Władysław,** pseud. of Ludwik Kondratowicz (Smolhów 1823–Vilna 1862). Polish poet. Constant financial insecurity forced him to earn a living from books and he published much, his verse tales enjoying considerable popularity. The best of them is *Ułas* (1858), a war idyll from the Pripet Marshes. Like Crabbe he could occasionally voice poignant social criticism; his poem *Lalka* (1851) was meant to disturb the complacency of the gentry. He achieved subtle originality in the cycle *Melodie z domu obłąkanych*, written towards the end of his life, in which he touched on surrealistic images. [JP]

Peterkiewicz and Singer, *FCPP*.

**Szabó, Dezső** (Kolozsvár 1879–Budapest 1945). Hungarian novelist. Starting his career as a provincial schoolmaster, he later joined the ⇨ *Nyugat*. His novel *Az Elsodort Falu* (1919) showed traces of idolization of the Magyar race; he later became a right-wing extremist, but this period was followed by a courageous anti-German attitude in his writings. [JFR]

*SEER*, XXIV, 63 (1946); Reményi, *HWL*.

**Szabó, Lőrinc** (Miskolc 1900–Budapest 1957). Hungarian poet. Son of a provincial railwayman, in his youth he was a rebel against city life and culture as well as capitalism (*Kalibán*, 1923, and *A Sátán Műremekei*, 1926). Later works, such as *Te meg a világ* (1932) and *Különbéke* (1935), however, show his change of tone, which gradually swings to disenchantment and almost aimlessness, in spite of his becoming the oustanding figure among the ⇨ *Nyugat* poets of his time. Many of his poems deal with the world of children and of nature, others with his selfish but tender love; *A Huszonhatodik Év* (1956), consisting of 120 sonnets, is a poetic requiem for his deceased lover. *Tücsökzene* (1947–57) is an autobiography. Szabó first gained fame as a translator, and produced the best Hungarian versions of Shakespeare's sonnets, Goethe, Villon and Kleist; his volume *Örök Barátok* is a selection of translations from the poetry of many languages and ages. [JFR]

Reményi, *HWL*; Klaniczay, *HHL*.

**Szaniawski, Jerzy** (Zegrzynek 1887–1970). Polish dramatist. All his plays are written in a simple yet poetically elusive dialogue and most have a provincial setting. The best are *Ptak* (1923), *Żeglarz* (1925) with its Ibsen-like exposure of lie and truth, and *Adwokat i róże* (1929). The experience of the occupation is imprinted on his post-war play *Dwa teatry*. [JP]

**Széchenyi, Count István** (Vienna 1791–Döbling 1860). Hungarian political writer and pamphleteer. One of the greatest Hungarian statesmen of the 19th-century Reform Age. As a leading aristocrat, he urged revolutionary reforms and championed liberal ideas. Founder of the Hungarian Academy of Sciences and other institutions. His books and pamphlets furthered his political aims, major works being *Hitel* (1830), *Világ* (n.d.) and *Stádium* (n.d.). [JFR]

A. Zichy, *Biographical Sketch of Count Stephen S.* (n.d.).

**Szerb, Antal** (Budapest 1901–Balf 1945). Hungarian essayist, critic and fiction writer. Being of Jewish origin, he was barred from holding university posts; relying on his own energy, he wrote his remarkable *History of Hungarian Literature* (1934), followed by *History of World Literature* (1941), a *Study of English Literature* and several essays on literary subjects. Major novels: *Utas és holdvilág* (1937), a reflection of the literary orientation of his generation; *A Pendragon-legenda* (1934; tr. L. Halápy, *The Pendragon Legend*, Budapest, 1963), an ironic novel set in Wales; *Szerelem a Palackban* (tr. L. Wolfe, *Love in a Bottle*, 1936). Szerb died as a victim of Nazism. [JFR]

# T

**Tadijanović, Dragutin** (Rastušje 1905– ). Croatian poet. The simplicity of his large body of poetry in free verse often appears close to prose, but his subtle ability to create atmosphere and suggest tone belies the superficial facility of form. A poet of nostalgia, of the passing of time and man's loneliness in an existence where real communication is scarcely possible, his sincere and unpretentious manner is extremely individual. [EDG]

Ibrovac, *APY*; Lavrin, *AMYP*.
Kadić, *CCL*.

**Taine, Hippolyte Adolphe** (Vouziers 1828–Paris 1893). French critic, philosopher and historian. His anti-romantic, positivist doctrines – that 'vice and virtue are products, like vitriol and sugar', that literature is the product of deterministic forces ('la race, le milieu, le moment') – acquired through his style the quality of a *mystique* that helped inspire Zola's naturalism. His *Origines de la France contemporaine* (1875–93) sought the reasons for the 1871 defeat in the Revolution of 1789; his conservatism and nationalism influenced e.g. ⇨ Barrès. His determinist views appear strikingly in the preface to his *Histoire de la littérature anglaise* (1863; tr. H. van Laun, *History of English Literature*, 1871). ⇨⇨ French Literary Criticism in the 19th and 20th Centuries.

*Notes sur l'Angleterre* (1872; tr. E. Hyams, *Notes on England*, 1957); *Sa vie et sa correspondance* (4 vols., 1902–7; tr. R. L. Devonshire, 1902–8).
A. Chevrillon, *T. Formation de sa pensée* (Paris, 1932); S. J. Kahn, *Science and Aesthetic Judgement* (1953).

**Talev, Dimitǎr** (Prilep 1898–1966). Bulgarian novelist. Macedonian by birth and upbringing, he returned from study abroad in 1921 and became editor of the dailies *Makedoniya* and *Zora*. His novels and stories on historical themes from *Usilni godini* (3 vols., 1928–30) to *Samuil* (1958), *Hilendarskiya monah* (1962) and especially his penetrating and moving trilogy on the difficult times of his homeland's renascence, *Zhelezniyǎt svetilnik* (1952), *Ilinden* (1953) and *Prespanskite kambani* (1954), have made him the most considerable figure in Bulgarian literature since the Second World War. [VP]

Manning and Smal-Stocki, *HMBL*.

**Tallemant des Reaux, Gédéon** (La Rochelle 1619–Paris 1692). French writer. He published nothing but a few poems but left in manuscript a most unusual literary monument, a mass of short biographies and sketches now known as *Historiettes* (ed. A. Adam, Pléiade, 1963). He came of a wealthy Protestant family, enjoyed affluence, but was overtaken by bankruptcy, which it took many years and much litigation to clear; his married life was unhappy and his wife, reconciled to him, became a Catholic in 1685; he took the same step twenty years later, just before the Revocation. Long thought to be a gossip, fond of scandal and of indecency, he is now reckoned an important historical observer. His sources have been checked in many places and his veracity and reliability established. He is often indecent and has no scruples about detailing scandals in high places (the homosexual practices of Louis XIII for instance). But his many contacts in both middle-class and upper-class society coupled with an insatiable thirst for information allow him to present a more complete picture than even contemporary memoirs and letters. He misses nothing: he even notes that an undergraduate left the Sorbonne for the stage and took the name of Molière. [WGM]

E. Magne, *T. des R.* (Paris, 1922); E. Gosse (Taylorian Lecture, 1925).

**Talvio, Maila,** pseud. of Maria Mikkola, *née* Winter (Hartola 1871–Helsinki 1951). Finnish novelist and dramatist. After her marriage in 1893 her Helsinki home became an influential meeting-place for many of the leading literary figures and promising young writers of the day. V. A. ⇨ Koskenniemi, a convert to conservatism, joined her circle and became its most influential member. Her earlier books are regional in setting and high-minded in tone, drawing on the prosperous East Häme background of her own childhood and proclaiming their message in a spirit reminiscent of Ibsen or ⇨ Canth: the style, however, is undeviatingly romantic and even symbolic. Rather in the manner of ⇨ Lagerlöf, she examines the relations between the Finnish-speaking rural population and the Swedish-speaking squirearchs, priests and civil servants. The Tolstoyan view of life, as put forward in the novels of Arvid ⇨ Järnefelt, was not without influence on her. Later *romans à clef* are about poets she had known, satirical sketches of contemporary life, and light, nationalistically coloured historical novels about the Helsinki of earlier days. She was also a prolific essayist. Her main novels are: *Haapaniemen keinu* (1895); *Pimeänpirtin hävitys* (1901); *Juha Joutsia* (1903); *Niniven lapset* (1915); *Elämän kasvot* (1916); *Kurjet* (1919); *Kihlasormus* (1921); *Itämeren tytär* (3 vols., 1929–36; Fr. tr. H. Boisson, *La fille du Baltique*, Paris, 1945–6); *Linnoituksen iloiset rouvat* (1941), *Rukkaset ja kukkaset* (memoirs) (1947); and she wrote 10 plays, 6 collections of short satires, 5 volumes of speeches and memoirs. [RV]

T. Tuulio, *M.T.* (2 vols., Porvoo, 1963–4).

**Tamási, Áron** (Farkaslaka 1897–Budapest 1966). Hungarian novelist. His writings are all influenced by his Transylvanian peasant background, and his style contains elements of folk-tales and ballades. His best-known novels are the Ábel trilogy (1934), tales of the adventures of a wide-awake Székely peasant lad, *Szűzmáriás Királyfi* and *Jégtörő Mátyás*. He is the author of many successful plays and short stories: *Erdélyi Csillagok*; *Himnusz egy Szamárról* (tr. L. Wolfe, *In Praise of a Donkey*, 1936); *Rendes feltámadás* (tr. I. Duczynska, *Orderly Resurrection*, 1963). [JFR]

*SEER*, XXV, 64 (1946); Reményi, *HWL*.

**Tamayo y Baus, Manuel** (Madrid 1829–Madrid 1898). Spanish dramatist. Born into the theatre world, he married an actress, but ceased writing in 1870 to become director of the National Library and secretary of the Academy. His range was considerable; a romantic drama in the manner of Schiller on the subject of Joan of Arc; a national drama in verse, *La ricahembra* (1854); a more realistic historical drama in prose, on the subject of Juana 'the mad', *La locura de amor* (1855; CA), which is probably his best play; a classical tragedy in the style of ⇨ Alfieri, *Virginia* (1853), which he revised and improved at the end of his career; also various comedies and dramas of ideas. *Un drama nuevo* (1867; CA; tr. G. O. Fitzgerald and T. H. Guild, *A New Drama*, 1915), which is set in Shakespeare's England, uses the device of the play within a play and is technically his most advanced work. [JMC]

*Obras completas* (4 vols., 1898–1900).
R. Esquer Torres, *El teatro de T. y B.* (1965).

**Tannhäuser** (fl. mid 13th cent.). German lyric poet. His wandering life, taken together with certain motifs and references in his poetry, subsequently led to his identification in the popular imagination with the legendary knight who, having revelled in the sensual pleasures of the Venusberg, repents and seeks forgiveness of the Pope for his sins; a miracle proclaims that salvation which the Pope has said can never be his, but he has already returned in despair to the Venusberg and is never seen again.

The historical Tannhäuser was a Bavarian ⇨ Minnesinger whose poetry reflects the decaying tradition of the courtly ideals of classical Minnesang. The legend has been made the subject of many modern stories and poems, and forms the basis of ⇨ Wagner's opera. [RT]

J. Siebert, *Der Dichter T.* (Halle, 1934).

**Tansillo, Luigi** (Venosa 1510–Teano 1568). Italian poet. His active life, which included fighting the Turks, was spent in military and administrative service of the Spanish viceroys of Naples. His main works were *Il vendemmiatore*, an early poem in *ottava rima* whose occasional obscenity made it notorious, love sonnets which display an at times turgid melancholy, *capitoli* on social and domestic themes (*La balia*, *Il podere*), and the religious *Lagrime di San Pietro*. Though writing within the general context of *cinquecento* Petrarchism, he has some individuality, and there is a certain freshness about his portrayals of natural scenes; his exuberant and dramatic imagery anticipates the *seicento*. [DGR]

*Poesie liriche*, ed. F. Fiorentino (1882); *L'egloga e i Poemetti*, ed. F. Flamini (1893); *Il canzoniere*, ed. E. Percopo (1926).
*Minori*, ii.

**Tardieu, Jean** (St Germain-de-Joux 1903– ). French poet and dramatist. Brought up to be an artist (his parents a painter and a harpist), he wrote poems and plays from the age of 7. At 17 a nervous breakdown brought a revelation of poetic terror in the face of the world, and he interrupted his studies to settle into the artistic life of Paris. His early poems (in *Accents*, 1939; *Le témoin invisible*, 1943; *Jours pétrifiés*, 1947) are lyrical quests stressing psychological dualism, verging on the mystical, and written in sprung-rhythms tending towards prose. Though aiming at cosmic communion, he reacts against the tendency of French poetry to over-emphasize, and tries to objectivize experiences in poetic vision. After the war, influenced by ⇨ Prévert and ⇨ Queneau, he began to write humorous poems which returned ironically to the use of rhymes and classical rhythms; his best pieces question the value of language by a sudden estrangement of tool words and grammatical categories (*Monsieur Monsieur*, 1951; *Une voix sans personne*, 1954). The suspicion of imagery and ornament developed here he later exploited for dramatic radio sketches. There (in *Le guichet*, *L'A.B.C. de notre vie*, *Les amants du Métro*, *La serrure*), having to do without stage realism, he searches for archetypal human situations and strikes a delicate balance between satirical symbolism and poetic harmony achieved through burlesque, empty dialogue. [CLC]

*Choix de poèmes* (1961); *Théâtre de chambre* and *Poèmes à jouer* (1955 and 1958).

G.-E. Clancier, 'Une voix et des personnes', in *Mercure de France* (Paris, 1963).

**Tarsis, Juan de, Conde de Villamediana** (Lisbon 1582–Madrid 1622). Spanish poet. He led a dissolute life, gambled, fought, and was banished from court; returning under Philip IV, he was murdered, probably on suspicion of paying court to the Queen. His bitter satires had made him many enemies. He wrote love-poetry, funeral sonnets, masques and a *Fábula de Europa*, and was one of the earliest and aptest imitators of ⇨ Góngora's style. [JMC]

*Poesías* (1944); 'Fábula de Europa', in R. Alberti, *Églogas y fábulas castellanas* i (Buenos Aires, 1944); Trend, *OBSV*; Perry, *HASP*; Cohen, *PBSV*.

E. Cotarelo y Mori, *El C. de V.* (Madrid, 1886).

**Tasso, Bernardo** (Venice? 1493–Ostiglia 1569). Italian poet. The father of Torquato ⇨ Tasso. He was employed as diplomat, administrator and secretary by Ferrante Sanseverino and other minor rulers of Italy. Interested in cultivating in Italian the example of the Classics, he composed odes in the manner of Horace, made a version of Ovid's tale of Pyramus and Thisbe, and wrote also piscatory and pastoral eclogues.

He is chiefly thought of as one of those precursors of the *Gerusalemme liberata* who tried to reconcile the freedom and variety of ⇨ Ariostesque romance with the discipline, unity and high seriousness demanded by the classical epic. His *Amadigi* (1560; ed. Serassi, 1755), which enjoyed considerable popularity, was derived from a Spanish source and told the love of Amadigi and Oriana. Around this theme were woven others of an episodic nature which looked to the romance tradition. He followed the same procedure when developing one sub-plot of the *Amadigi* into a separate poem, the *Floridante* (ed. M. Catalano, 1931), which was completed and published by Torquato in 1587. [DGR]

*Rime*, ed. Serassi (1749).

E. Williamson, *B.T.* (Rome, 1951) (in English); *Minori*, ii.

**Tasso, Torquato** (Sorrento 1544–Rome 1595). Italian poet. The son of Bernardo ⇨ Tasso, with whom he went into exile when the Sanseverino family fell from favour. He studied at Padua, met there the influential Sperone ⇨ Speroni and published an epic *Rinaldo* (1562). To these years belong his love poems for Lucrezia Bendidio and Laura Peperara.

In 1565 began the connexion with the Este rulers of Ferrara which was to last for twenty years and brought him fame and favour, insanity and imprisonment. The products of the early, golden period were the joyous and uninhibited hedonistic pastoral drama *Aminta* (1573) and his epic *Gerusalemme liberata* (completed by 1575; ed. L. Caretti, 1957; tr. E. Fairfax, *Jerusalem Delivered*, 1600, intr. R. Weiss, 1962). But soon the doubts and shadows began to appear. Even before the publication of the *Gerusalemme* in 1581 had started a great polemic, Tasso began asking the advice of professional *letterati* and having misgivings about the standing of his poem in terms of current neo-Classical theory; the problem of reconciling its romance elements with the rigorous demands of Classical epic poetry gradually undermined his confidence. Together with literary doubts came religious doubts and fears. Obsessed with anxieties concerning his own orthodoxy, he insisted on being examined by the Inquisition. Later he added an allegory to the *Gerusalemme*, and by persistent revision transformed the *Liberata* into the frigid *Gerusalemme conquistata* (1593; ed. L. Bonfigli, 1934). From about 1577 signs of mental disorder began to appear. He complained constantly about his treatment at Ferrara, became subject to hallucinations and persecution mania, sometimes fleeing secretly from Ferrara in fear for his life. Eventually, by order of the Duke Alfonso he was confined at S. Anna in 1579 and remained there for the next seven years in a captivity at first rigorous but later relaxed. It was around this captivity that the legend grew up that he was punished for loving the Duke's sister Leonora. During the S. Anna period he composed many lyrics and also many of his prose dialogues on philosophical, aesthetic and social subjects, and at this time too pirated editions of his works kept appearing. On his release he left Ferrara and entered that last phase of his life which saw him moving restlessly between Mantua, Rome, Florence and Naples before finding peace in the monastery of S. Onofrio in Rome where he died. The chief literary products of these last years were his tragedy, *Re Torrismondo*, a drama of incest and betrayal in the wake of ⇨ Giraldi and Speroni, and a group of poems on religious themes, of which the *Sette giorni del mondo creato* is the best known.

The critical problem posed by the *Gerusalemme liberata* is whether and to what extent Tasso's natural lyrical tendencies, his quest for the idyllic, the sensuous, the mysterious, are inhibited by the theoretical demands of 'regular' epic on one side and the moral and religious pressures of the Counter-Reformation on the other. The reader may find a series of 'poetic' and 'non-poetic' moments. On one side the enchanted wood, the roles of Armida, Clorinda and Erminia and on the other the paraphernalia of epic – the troops, the battles, the speeches, God and his angels. Certainly the tensions of the *Gerusalemme* contrast sharply with the utter serenity of Ariosto's *Orlando furioso*. [DGR]

*Opere*, ed. B. Maier (1963–5); *Rime*, ed. A. Solerti (4 vols., 1898–1902).

E. Donadoni, *T.T.* (Florence, 1936); G. Getto, *Interpretazione del T.* (Naples, 1967); C. M. Bowra, *From Virgil to Milton* (1945); C. P. Brand, *T.T.* (1965); Lind, *LPIR*; *Maggiori*.

**Tassoni, Alessandro** (Modena 1565–Modena 1635). Italian writer. After studying at Bologna, Pisa and Ferrara, he became (1599) secretary to Cardinal Ascanio Colonna, whom he accompanied to Spain in 1602. From 1603 he was at Rome and began to be employed by the house of Savoy. In 1620–1 he served them in Piedmont, but either his difficult temperament or his anti-Spanish attitude, which they no longer shared, caused a break. He served Cardinal Ludovisi (1624–32) and spent his last years as an honoured literary figure at the Este court of his native Modena.

His chief work was *La secchia rapita* (1622, tr. J. Atkinson, 1825), a mock-heroic poem in *ottava rima*. It describes a war between Modena and Bologna which was fought over a bucket taken by the Modenese as a trophy from their rivals, and in which even the gods of Olympus become involved. The material of the poem is a mixture of history, legend and fantasy, and the manner part heroic, part realistic-ironical, with some satire of contemporary society and individuals. His other verse comprises undistinguished *Rime* and the weak first canto of a projected epic, *L'Oceano*, on the discovery of America.

Of his prose works, the *Considerazioni sopra le rime del Petrarca* (1609) attack Petrarchism rather than Petrarch himself, and the *Filippiche* (1615) are 2 vigorous anti-Spanish political tracts. The work to which he was most committed, the *Dieci libri di pensieri diversi* (1620), discusses science, ethics, politics, philosophy and literature. The best-known book is the 10th, in which Tassoni compares the ancient and modern worlds. On the whole his conclusions favour the moderns. [DGR]

*Opere*, ed. G. Rossi (1930); ed. G. Ziccardi (1952).

V. G. Rossi, *T.* (Milan, 1931); G. Reichenbach, *A.T.* (Turin, 1931); *Minori*, ii.

**Taube, Evert** (Göteborg 1890– ). Swedish poet and prose-writer. Famous for the vitality of his songs (written, composed, played and sung by himself), where as a modern troubadour he blends several traditions of poetry and song with gaiety, irony and the experiences of his early roving life (especially as a sailor), he has achieved in his best work a rare combination of artistry and popularity; the setting may be the coasts of Sweden, of the Mediterranean, or of South America, seen by a painter and heard by a musician. A representative selection of his songs, *Hjärtats nyckel heter sång*, was published in 1960. His versatile talent has also produced striking prose, for example *Vallfart* (1957), about Provence and troubadour poetry, and *Jag kommer av ett brusand' hav* (1952), largely about himself.

J. Karlzén, 'E.T.', in *Svensk litteraurtidskrift* (1949); L. Forssell, in *Poesi* (1950).

**Tauns, Linards.** ⇨ Latvian Literature.

**Tavel, R. von.** ⇨ Swiss-German Dialect Literature.

**Tchernichowski, Shaul** (Russia 1873–Tel Aviv 1943). Hebrew poet. His chief characteristic is that he brought a quality until then unknown to Hebrew poetry, a secular tendency emphasizing the will of Jews to be like all other nations, an emancipation from the ghetto, and sometimes even from Jewish tradition. There is a degree almost of paganism in his poetry. He does not find a conflict between his Judaism and the world at large. He was born in the Crimea, i.e. outside the Pale of Settlement, and although his parents were observant Jews, his early years were spent with his gentile contemporaries. He was 7 when he first became acquainted with the Hebrew language, and indeed it was his first teacher who implanted in him his deep love of it. His first composition was a long Hebrew Biblical poem; at 15 he went to Odessa to attend a commercial high school and after graduation prepared for university entrance examinations to be able to study medicine. Having failed these, he left Russia in 1899 and entered the University of Heidelberg. Already in Odessa he came into contact with the Chovevei Zion (Lovers of Zion) movement and the many writers and thinkers around it, among them the then young essayist Josef Klausner, who induced him never to write in any language but Hebrew. He stayed four years in Heidelberg and went on to Lausanne where he studied for another three years.

As a young man of fine physique and vivacity he led a gay life and was continuously entangled with women. All this is reflected in his poetry. In 1907 he returned to Russia and was employed as an itinerant doctor. When war broke out he was drafted as an army doctor. After the war he settled in Berlin and went to Palestine in 1930.

His poetry differs greatly from his predecessors' – indeed he is unique in Hebrew poetry for the sensuous beauty of his love-lyrics and nature poems. His songs are singing of a fleeting love that knows no disappointment and is ever ready for a new adventure. After the love-lyrics came the pantheistic songs to heathen gods. He was even nicknamed 'Hellene' and 'Heathen'; but he also sang of Biblical themes, choosing chiefly heroic themes, and he also wrote 'idylls' describing the life of the Jews in his native Crimea. Although he wrote prose, in this he never achieved the stature of his poetry. He was an unrivalled translator, especially in the accomplished, metrically true, translations of the *Epic of Gilgamesh*, the *Kalevala*, the *Iliad* and *Odyssey*. [EE]

*Shirim* (Tel Aviv, 1950).

L. Snowman, *T. and his Poetry* (1929); Waxman, *HJL*; Klausner, *HMHL*.

**Tebaldeo, Antonio** (Ferrara 1463–Rome 1537). Italian poet. Tutor in poetry to Isabella d'Este at both Ferrara and Mantua, and later secretary to Lucrezia Borgia after she became Duchess of Ferrara. The high midsummer of his life was among the artists and writers in the Rome of Leo X. The sack of the city in 1527 shattered this existence and cast a shadow over his remaining years. He cultivated a bizarre Petrarchism which depended for its effects on the elaboration of striking conceits in a musical context. He was a prolific poet, composing in Latin as well as the vernacular. His Italian verse includes eclogues, epistles, *capitoli*, and nearly 300 sonnets. A first edition of his Italian poems appeared without his consent in 1499, and there followed many editions in the first half of the 16th century. [DGR]

*Poesia del Quattrocento e del Cinquecento*, ed. Muscetta and Ponchiroli (1959).

Croce, *PES*; D'Ancona, 'Del secentismo nella poesia cortigiana del secolo xv', in *Studi sulla letteratura italiana dei primi secoli* (Ancona, 1884).

**Tegnér, Esaias** (By 1782–Växjö 1846). Swedish poet. Long honoured as the national poet of Sweden, Tegnér now occupies the position of an independent romantic and is as much admired for his brilliant letters as for his poetry. Of humble origin, the young Tegnér made a striking academic career and became professor of Greek at Lund in 1812. He remained there until his appointment to the see of Växjö in 1825. He had small inclination for theology, but showed great administrative ability; he also scandalized his diocesans through a succession of love-affairs. An illness in 1840 left him partially incapacitated. His mental instability appears to have been constitutional with pronounced manic-depressive trends. He belongs to the romantic generation of Swedish poets, but was temperamentally more akin to the preceding classicist era. He was profoundly influenced by Schiller and ⇨ Oehlenschläger. His most inspired lyrical poems have a rhetorical brilliance unknown to his models, and speak of his ecstatic belief in an ideal world, e.g. *Det eviga* (1810), *Skaldens morgonpsalm* (1812) and *Sången* (1819). He made his reputation, however, with a long patriotic poem, *Svea* (1811), which reads like a sermon to the nation and ends in a prophetic vision of national glory. Stylistically derivative, it reflects the current ideals of the recently founded 'Götiska förbundet' (Gothic Society), but the fire of the rhetoric is the poet's own. The greatest achievement of his maturity was *Frithiofs saga* (1825; tr. C. D. Locock, 1925), a romantic cycle on an Old Norse theme, in which he deliberately set out to humanize the Viking age. Posterity still finds much to admire in his verse narrative: its metrical variety, its stylistic terseness, its visual quality and, above all, the masterly handling of its theme of guilt and reconciliation. A strong element of Classical humanism is hidden behind what purports to be a Norse mythology; similarly the depiction of children and women is more akin to 18th-century sentimentalism. The poem has frequently been translated into English. Tegnér sometimes fell victim to black moods of increasing severity. Such a state, the very opposite of the elation which provided the basis for most of his lyrical poetry, is reproduced with Byronic bitterness in *Mjältsjukan* (Hypochondria, 1825); a more quiet resignation characterizes the two masterpieces of poetic diction, *Den döde* (1834) and *Avsked till min lyra* 1845). [SAB]

*Samlade skrifter*, ed. E. Wrangel and F. Böök (10 vols., 1918–25); *E.T.s brev*, ed. N. Palmberg (12 vols., 1953– ).

F. Böök, *E.T.: en levnadsteckning* (Stockholm, 1946); A. Werin, *E.T.: från Det eviga till Mjältsjukan* (Lund, 1934); G. Brandes, 'E.T.' (1876) in *Creative Spirits of the Nineteenth Century* (N.Y., 1923).

**Teirlinck, Herman Louis Cesar** (Sint-Jans Molenbeek 1879–Beersel-Lot 1967). Flemish author. The hero of *Mijnheer J. B. Serjanszoon, orator didacticus* (1908) shows much of the sparkling wit, cynicism and agnosticism of the author, who like ⇨ Gijsen and ⇨ Elsschot raised the Dutch novel out of its bourgeois environment. In his best novel, *Zelfportret of het galgemaal* (1955; tr. J. Brockway, *The Man in the Mirror*, 1963), his ironic detachment is expressed in the alter ego of the protagonist who can only judge his past life by attributing it to another being. [PK]

*Verzameld Werk* (8 vols., 1956–9).

**Tendryakov, Vladimir Fyodorovich** (Makorovskaya, Vologda 1923– ). Russian novelist. His first stories were published early in the fifties. They usually concern simple people who fail to rise to a sudden and unexpected challenge. Such stories as *Ukhaby* (1956; *Ruts*, tr. S. Hackel in Bearne, *Modern Russian Short Stories*, (1968), and *Troyka, Semyorka, Tuz* (1960) have indeed been attacked by Soviet critics for their unheroic pictures of contemporary Russia. His novel *Za begushchim dnyom* (1959), a semi-autobiographical work, also reveals his characteristic humanity and tolerance. His style is simple and expressive.

*Izbrannyye sochineniya* (2 vols., 1963); tr. *The Road*, in Yarmolinsky, *SSS*.

*Novyy Mir*, 7 (1962).

**Teodosije.** ⇨ Serbian Medieval Literature.

**Teresa de Jesús, Santa** (T. Sánchez de Cepeda y Ahumada) (Ávila? 1515–Alba de Tormes 1582). Spanish mystic. Of noble family, she had little formal education, her early reading being mostly novels of chivalry, replaced later by devotional works. She became a Carmelite, rising to Mother Superior. Her autobiography the *Vida* contains a graphic account in vivid down-to-earth prose of her early life, her nervous illnesses, her difficulties with no proper guide to help over her mystic experiences, her visions and locutions, and her spiritual growth. She completed her account of the Mystic Way in the *Castillo interior o tratado de las Moradas*, where she describes the seven stages of union with God in the form of 'mansions', using everyday similes to explain difficult theological terms. *El libro de las fundaciones* describes her reform of the Order and the foundation of 17 new convents of Barefoot Carmelites. She wrote a spiritual guide for the Ávila nuns in *El camino de la perfección* and a set of *Avisos espirituales* for her Order. In her *Poesías* she is a simple yet attractive poet. Over 400 letters survive in which she shows herself to be a person of shrewdness, overwhelming persistence, and possessed of a delightful sense of humour. Her manuscripts are in the Escorial Library and were published from 1581 on. She was canonized in 1622. [JG]

*Obras completas*, BAC, 1951–9; *Camino de perfección* and *Castillo interior*, CC; *Complete Works*, tr. A. Peers (1946) and *Letters* (1951); *Life*, tr. J. M. Cohen (1957).

Crisógono de Jesús Sacramentado, *Sta T. de J.* (Barcelona, 1936); M. Auclair, *S.T. of A.* (1953) (tr. from French); R. Hoornaert, *Sta T. d'A.* (Paris, 1951); R. Hoornaert, *St T. in her Writings* (1940) (tr. from French); G. Etchegoyen, *L'amour divin* (Bordeaux/Paris, 1923) (sources); A. Peers, *Studies of the Spanish Mystics* (1927).

**Tersánszky, J. Jenő** (Nagybánya 1888–1969). Hungarian writer. Earlier also a painter, he lived a half-literary, half-Bohemian life. His outspoken, informal style is close to naturalism. Novels: *Viszontlátásra, drága* (1917), the *Kakuk Marci* cycle (1923–35), whose characters are cheerful vagabonds, outcasts and rebels against all social convention. [JFR]

**Testi, Fulvio** (Ferrara 1593–Modena 1646). Italian poet. His erratic career was centred round the Este court at Modena. An early collection of anti-Spanish *Rime* (1617) which praised Carlo Emanuele I of Savoy caused his banishment, but he soon regained favour and office. In 1646 his intrigues with the French led to his imprisonment at Modena, where, probably of natural causes, he died.

After some early lyrics in the manner of ⇨ Marino, he found a limpid eloquence of his own in poems on moral and political themes – the vanity of wealth and power, the contrast between Italy's past glory and present decadence, etc. In an age of Baroque grandiloquence the moral seriousness of his various volumes of *rime*, although not poetically exciting, is distinctive. He also left some descriptively lively letters. [DGR]

*Opere scelte* (1817); *Lettere*, ed. M. L. Doglio (1967); Calcaterra, *LSA*.

A. Zamboni, *F.T.* (Turin, 1939); A. Belloni, *Il Seicento* (Milan, 1929); *Minori*, ii.

**Tetmajer, Kazimierz** (Ludźmierz 1865–Warsaw 1940). Polish poet and short-story writer. He was born in the mountain region of Podhale, which he later depicted in a set of excellent short stories, *Na skalnym Podhalu* (1903–10; sel. tr. H. E. Kennedy and Z. Uminska, *Tales of the Tatras*, 1941). On the whole, his prose seems to have withstood the test of time better than either his drama (e.g. *Zawisza Czarny*, 1901) or his lyrical verse which was very popular at the turn of the century. His themes alternated between modishly languid decadence and tough regionalism, but they suffered from facility of expression. He published much, but after the First World War a brain disease stopped his activities. He existed like a shadow of his fame until the occupation of Warsaw by the Germans. [JP]

Peterkiewicz and Singer, *FCPP*.

**Thaw, The.** The period of liberalization of the arts in Soviet Russia which followed the death of Stalin in 1953. Within this period there have been several 'freeze-ups', notably after the Hungarian Revolution of 1956, but the general trend has been towards relaxation of controls. These controls, however, have not yet been officially rescinded: they are simply applied less harshly and dogmatically.

The 'thaw' takes its title from ⇨ Erenburg's novel *Ottepel'* (1954; tr. M. Harari, *The Thaw*, 1955). But the first work of the new trend was Pomerantsev's article '*Ob iskrennosti v literature*' (*Novyy Mir*, 12, 1953), which declared that a work of art should be judged not by the canons of socialist realism but by the sincerity of the author. Pomerantsev was severely criticized, and the article had little effect on Soviet literary theory; but works critical of injustice, corruption and, by implication, of the state's infallibility began to appear. ⇨ Dudintsev's novel *Ne khlebom yedinym* (1956; tr. E. Bone, *Not by Bread Alone*, 1957) was the first and one of the most outspoken of them; and it prepared the way for such open denunciations of Stalinism as Solzhenitsin's description of life in a concentration-camp *Odin den' Ivana Denisovicha* (1962; tr. M. Hayward and R. Hingley, *One Day in the Life of I.D.*, 1963).

Other young writers who represent this critical attitude include ⇨ Yevtushenko, ⇨ Slutsky and V. Nekrasov. But older men, Erenburg and ⇨ Paustovsky, have also played a part. The publication of their memoirs and their public support of younger writers have done much to make the movement respectable.

A leading part in the 'thaw' has been played by the journal *Novyy Mir* ('New World'), edited by A. Tvardovsky, except from mid-1954 to mid-1958; and most of the major works of this trend, from Pomerantsev to Solzhenitsyn, have been published in its pages. [RDBT]

G. Gibian, *Interval of Freedom* (Univ. of Minnesota, 1960); Swayze, *PCL*; Hayward and Labedz, *LRSR*.

**'Thèbes, Roman de.'** Medieval French romance written about the middle of the 12th century by an unknown Norman. In about 10,000 lines of octosyllabic rhyming couplets it tells the story of Oedipus and the siege of Thebes. The basic source was the *Thebais* of Statius, adapted to the taste of the 12th century, with elements from the ⇨ *chanson de geste* and Crusade epics, but without the emphatic love interest which was later to become the major theme of the romance genre. [LTT]

Ed. L. Constans (1890).

E. Faral, *Recherches sur les sources latines des contes et romans courtois du moyen âge* (Paris, 1913); *PMLA*, XVI (1901); *Mél. Jeanroy* (Paris, 1928).

**Theodulph, Saint** (*c.*760–Angers *c.*821). Medieval Latin poet. Bishop of Orleans. Of Spanish origin, he was a prominent figure at the court of Charlemagne and called 'Pindar' in the emperor's literary circle. Louis the Fair, however, imprisoned him (818) for suspected conspiracy. He is said to have been released for composing the hymn 'Gloria laus et honor' used ever since in the Palm Sunday procession. His other poems, whether religious or courtly, do not reach the same level. He composed sermons, treatises, etc. [FB]

Migne, *PL*, 105; ed. E. Dümmler (MGH, PLAC, I, 1881); *An. Hym.*, 50.

C. Cuissard, *T. évêque d'Orléans* (Orleans, 1892); Raby, *CLP*, *SLP*.

**Theotokas, George** (Constantinople 1906–Athens 1966). Greek novelist, essayist and playwright. He studied in Paris and London, and was twice Director of the National Theatre of Athens (1945–6, 1950–2). He has written several novels, short stories, essays, a few poems and several plays. Many of his novels have been translated into several European languages. Notable among his novels are *Leonis* (1940), dealing with reminiscences of his childhood in Constantinople during the First World War, and *Argo* (1936; tr. M. Brook, A. Tsatsopoulos, *Argo*, 1951), giving a lively and realistic picture of Greek life, aspirations and events during the period 1920–30. He writes in an urbane and graceful style, with a good sense of humour and astute observation. He is one of the most distinguished Greek prose writers. [SJP]

**Thibaudet, Albert.** ⇨ French Literary Criticism in the 19th and 20th Centuries.

**Thibaut IV, Count of Champagne** (1201–Pamplona 1253). King of Navarre 1234–53, the most famous ⇨ *trouvère*. His policies were marked by vacillation and lack of perseverance. In 1226 he left the royal army besieging Avignon without leave of Louis VIII whose wife, Blanche of Castille, he is said to have loved. In 1239 he headed an unsuccessful Crusade, visited Jerusalem and returned home in 1240.

Complex, enigmatic and handsome, he found refuge in poetry and music. There survive 53 authentic poems. In his love songs he reanimates outworn courtly themes and phraseology with zestful imagery and occasional self-mockery. His debates (*jeux partis*), *pastourelles* and Crusading songs are written with verve, elegance and clarity. Language and music are carefully worked, and his use of allegory influenced the later French medieval lyric. His fame was immense: he was praised by Dante and by Étienne Pasquier in the 16th century. [LTT]

*Les chansons*, crit. ed. A. Wallensköld (Paris 1925); Woledge, *PBFV*.

R. Bray, *La préciosité et les précieux de T. de C. à Jean Giraudoux* (Paris, 1948).

**Thomas à Kempis (Thomas Hamerkem)** (Kempen, Cologne *c.*1380–Zwolle 1471). Augustinian monk. Educated by the Brothers of the Common Life at Deventer, he joined a newly founded congregation of canons regular at Mount St Agnes, near Zwolle. His writings include lives of Gerhard Groot, founder of the Brothers of the Common Life, and Radewyn, one of the earliest of the Brothers (both tr. J. P. Arthur, in *The Founders of the New Devotion*, 1905), treatises on the monastic life, devotional works and poems. Far above all these is the great *Imitatio Christi* (1418; tr. L. Sherley-Price, Penguin Classics, 1953), usually ascribed to him, written in prose of which much is rhythmical and even rhymed. This famous devotional manual, which is said to have been translated into more languages than any other book except the Bible, owes its wide appeal to the simplicity of its language, the transparent sincerity of its retiring author, and its quietistic, anti-worldly and anti-intellectual piety. [FB]

*Opera*, ed. M. J. Pohl (7 vols., Freiburg i. Br., 1902–22).
S. Kettlewell, *T. à K. and the Brothers of the Common Life* (2 vols., 1882); James Williams, *Thomas of Kempen* (1910).

**Thomas of Celano** (Celano, Abruzzi *c*.1200–? *c*.1255). Disciple and first biographer of St ⇨ Francis. Commissioned by Pope Gregory IX, he finished the *First Legend* in 1229, then wrote a *Second Legend* (1247), on the instructions of the Minister General of the Order, which supplements the first and gives more prominence to miracles. He also wrote a tract on the miracles of St Francis and a short Life of St Clare, foundress of the Franciscan sisters, or 'Poor Clares'. He is also generally considered the author of the great ⇨ sequence *Dies irae*. [FB]

*S. Francisci vita et miracula*, ed. E. d'Alençon (Rome, 1906); tr. A. G. Ferrers Howell, *The Lives of S. Francis by T. of C.* (1908).
Raby, *CLP*.

**Thoor, Jesse,** pseud of Peter Karl Höfler (Berlin 1905–Lienz 1952). Austrian poet. A self-taught man and writer (during exile a goldsmith and silversmith in London). An occasional poet with few literary connexions (formerly with political Expressionism), his collected *Die Sonnette und Lieder* (1956) are direct, rhetorical, Villonesque, with latterly some religious themes. [PB]

*Das Werk*, ed. M. Hamburger (Frankfurt a.M., 1965).
Hamburger and Middleton, *MGP*.

**Tieck, Ludwig** (Berlin 1773–Berlin 1853). German Romantic poet, novelist and dramatist. He joined the brothers ⇨ Schlegel, ⇨ Novalis, ⇨ Schelling and others in Jena, the centre of the early Romantic school. Not an original mind, but receptive, talented and practical-minded, he forms a bridge between the Enlightenment and Romanticism. Among his best romantic stories are the Märchen *Der blonde Eckbert* (1797) and *Der Runenberg* (1804), in which supernatural events are presented with a cool, almost terrifying objectivity. His novels *Franz Sternbalds Wanderungen* (1798) and *William Lovell* (1795–6) descend, like practically all 19th-century German novels, from Goethe's *Wilhelm Meister*. Later in his career he wrote social and historical short stories in a realistic tone far removed from that of his early Romantic Märchen.

His works for the stage include romantic tragedies such as the fate-drama *Karl von Berneck* (1795), *Genoveva* (1799) and *Kaiser Oktavianus* (1804), and – both more attractive and of greater interest in the history of the drama – the satirical comedies *Der gestiefelte Kater* (1797), *Die verkehrte Welt* (1798) and *Prinz Zerbino* (1799).

His publication of medieval lyrics (*Minnelieder aus dem schwäbischen Zeitalter*, 1803) and his share in the great Shakespeare translation undertaken by A. W. Schlegel (1797–1810) represent another side of his versatility and energy. He was the first editor of Novalis's works and also had a share in the works of his bosom companion Wackenroder. [RT]

*Werke*, ed. M. Thalmann (4 vols., 1963).
A. E. Lussky, *T.'s Romantic Irony* (1932); J. Trainer, *L.T.: from Gothic to Romantic* (The Hague, 1964); M. Thalmann, *L.T.* (Bern, 1955); Gundolf, *R*; Tymms, *GRL*.

**Tikhonov, Nikolay** (St Petersburg 1896– ). Russian writer. His parents were small tradesmen of serf descent, and he himself trained as a commercial clerk; volunteered in 1914, later fought with the Red Army. A member of the ⇨ Serapion Brothers (1921). His first volume shows startling maturity: *Orda* (1922) contains most of the few short poems which have made him famous. From 1922 he devoted himself to writing and to travel – at first in the Soviet Union, since 1935 also abroad. Much of his later work reflects his thirst for the picturesque and his extensive travels, particularly in Georgia: both verse – e.g. the collection *Ten' druga* (1936) – and prose – many romantic and adventurous stories and a novel *Voyna* (1931). He was on the Finnish front in 1939–40, and in Leningrad during its three-year siege. In 1944 he became President of the Writers' Union but was dismissed by Zhdanov in 1946 for toleration of ⇨ Zoshchenko and ⇨ Akhmatova. Nevertheless he has remained an important figure in official Soviet literary circles.

He is the supreme lyric poet of the Civil War; eschewing rhetoric, he conveys in a few powerful images the pathos and horror of gratuitous slaughter. Yet there is a note of hopefulness, of reticent, heroic stoicism, and a sense of the accomplishment of a higher purpose. His measured quatrains, precise imagery and perfect lyric form relate him to the Acmeists (especially ⇨ Gumilyov). In most later work, however, simplicity and neatness of wording remain while inspiration has gone. [RM-G]

*Sobraniye sochineniy* (6 vols., 1958–9); Gulland, *SRV*; Markov, *MRP*, *PG*; Obolensky, *PBRV*.
V. Moshin, *N.T.* (Moscow, 1960).

**Timofeyev, Ivan.** ⇨ Russian Literature of the 17th Century.

**Timoneda, Juan de** (Valencia ? –Valencia 1583). Spanish dramatist. He wrote two *autos sacramentales* which contain snatches from popular songs and popular turns of phrase. He also made some prose translations from Plautus. His *El patrañuelo* (1567; ed. F. Ruiz Morcuende, CC), retells stories from ⇨ Boccaccio, Massucio, Bandello, etc. As a publisher, he edited plays by Lope de ⇨ Rueda and others, a tragi-comedy called *Filomena* by an unknown author, some collections of anecdotes and one of *romances*. [JMC]

*Obras*, ed. E. Juliá Martínez (2 vols., 1947–8); Cohen, *PBSV*; Terry, *ASP*.
Crawford, *SDLV*.

**Tiraboschi, Girolamo** (Bergamo 1731–Modena 1794). Italian historian. A Jesuit priest, he taught at the Accademia di Brera in Milan, in 1766 publishing his first major work of erudition – *Vetera humiliatorum monumenta*. In 1770 he went to Modena to direct the Biblioteca Estense – the post previously held by ⇨ Muratori. Besides important historical works on Modena and the Este family's estate (*La biblioteca modenese*, 1781–6; *Memorie storiche modenesi*, 1793–4; *Dizionario topografico-storico degli stati estensi*, posth. 1824–5), he founded and edited the *Nuovo giornale dei letterati d'Italia* (1773–90) and published the two editions of his most famous work – *Storia della letteratura italiana* (1772–93) – for which he has been called the 'Muratori of Italian literature'. [RHC]

*Dal Muratori al Cesarotti*, vol. IV, ed. E. Bigi (Milan/Naples, 1960); V. Cian, *G.T.* (Modena, 1933); G. Getto, *Storia delle storie letterarie* (Milan, 1946).

**Tirso de Molina,** pseud. of Gabriel Téllez (Madrid ?1580–Almazán 1648). Spanish dramatist. Nothing is known of his origins or early life; a theory that he was the bastard son of the Duke of Osuna is now largely rejected. At an early age he became a monk in the Mercedarian Order, in the service of which he travelled widely in Spain and spent two years in the West Indies (1616–18). Meetings with ⇨ Lope de Vega, whose enthusiastic disciple he became, probably provided the stimulus for his dramatic career. He claimed to have written over 300 plays, of which some 80 are extant. Personal animosities may have prompted the Council of Castile's condemnation of his plays in 1625 for their bad influence. Thereafter he wrote little for the theatre, but collected and published 60 of his plays (5 vols., 1627–36), and rose to responsible positions in his Order.

His works vary from the trivial to the masterly. His comedies modify the general formula evolved by Lope in two ways. Firstly he intensifies the intrigue, regularly intertwining two or more plots, often based on the jealousies and stratagems of rival lovers. At its worst the action becomes too embroiled to follow, and there is a tedious reliance on conventional devices; but the best of these plays, such as *Don Gil de las calzas verdes* or *Marta la piadosa*, make excellent lively theatre. Secondly he shows more interest in character than his master, and particularly in slightly abnormal and strong female personalities. Many plots, like those of *La gallega Mari-Hernández* and *El amor médico*, centre on the disguises and other ruses employed by the heroine to win her chosen husband.

He is pre-eminent in his dramatizations of historical and Biblical material, and here too dominant women characters have a special attraction for him. The Jezabel of *La mujer que manda en casa*, the Ruth and Naomi of *La mejor espigadera*, and the widowed Queen of Castile who in *La prudencia en la mujer* defends her young son's throne against usurpers are among his most striking creations.

The text of *El burlador de Sevilla* is now known to be an imperfect version of an earlier play, which may or may not have been by Tirso; but as yet he must still be credited with this first dramatic presentation of the figure of Don Juan. The play was almost certainly intended as an attack on debauched and irresponsible young nobles, and as a lesson in moral theology: works must accord with faith, and reliance on a death-bed repentance will not suffice. Don Juan is here primarily the despicable deceiver; though he already transcends the author's conception far enough to become a universal figure.

There are also doubts about the authorship of *El condenado por desconfiado*, another fine theological drama published under his name, which seems something of a companion-piece to *El burlador*. Here a hermit is damned through reliance on his own good works, rather than on faith in the mercy of God.

He wrote two prose collections constructed on Boccaccian lines. *Los cigarrales de Toledo* (1624) contains a spirited defence of the Lopesque *comedia* and a lively tale from Italian sources, *Los tres maridos burlados*. *Deleytar aprovechando* (1635) is merely pious. His prose style is highly artificial, and contrasts with the natural, racy dialogue of many of his plays. [MW]

*Obras dramáticas completas*, ed. B. de los Río (3 vols., 1947–58); CA; CC.

R. Menéndez Pidal, *Estudios literarios* (Madrid, 1920, 1938); I. L. McClelland, *T. de M. Studies in Dramatic Realism* (1948); G. Mancini and others, *Studi tirsiani* (Milan, 1958); M. Penna, *Don Giovanni e il mistero di Tirso* (Turin, 1958); A. Nougué, *L'œuvre en prose de T. de M.* (Toulouse, 1962).

**Todi, Jacopone da.** ⇨ Jacopone da Todi.

**Todorov, Petko** (Elena 1879–Château d'Aix 1916). Bulgarian idyll-writer and dramatist. Tolstoy's morality and French socialism imbibed during his lycée studies in Toulouse inspired in 1898 his first *narodnik* tales of village life, *Ocherki i kartini,* and also his 'subversive' *Văzvanie kăm rusenskite grazhdani* ('Appeal to Ruse Citizens'), for which he was tried and acquitted. That year he resumed his education in Bern, then Berlin and Leipzig, where he wrote his thesis, *Slavyanite i bălgarskata literatura* ('The Slavs and Bulgarian Literature'). Stimulated by his friend and mentor, Pencho ⇨ Slaveykov, to study aesthetics and his native folklore, he turned to new symbolist paths and evolved his individual style in his plays *Zidari* (1902) and *Samodiva* (1904) and in his series of *Idilii* (a genre taken from J. Schlaf), published first in *Misăl*; he became an important member of the literary circle associated with this periodical. Like Slaveykov, he sought in folk themes new spiritual symbolical significance such as the snowdrop's meaning to the three ages of man in 'Kogato kokicheto tsăfne' ('When the snowdrop blooms'). His heroes are the outcasts of life, individualists unable to compromise with society in their quest for spiritual freedom, a birthright denied to himself in 'Orisnitsi' ('The Fates'). The language of these idylls is poetically embroidered with every resource of dialect and artistic skill to create a decorative, condensed style, new to Bulgarian prose.

He received a National Theatre award for *Părvite* (1907), his play on the old patriarchal generation's conflict with its successors. Of a frail constitution, he worked as librarian at the National Library, Sofia. [VP]

*Săbrani proizvedeniya* (3 vols., 1957–8); *Slavyanite i bălgarskata literatura* (1944); Pinto, *BPV*.

I. Kirilov, *P.T. biografichni nabroski* (Sofia, 1921); Manning and Smal-Stocki, *HMBL*.

**Tolentino de Almeida, Nicolau** (Lisbon 1740–Lisbon 1811). Portuguese satirical poet. Having studied Law at Coimbra he worked as a schoolteacher under the Pombal regime, first in Évora and later in Lisbon. After the fall of Pombal in 1777 he cultivated the new authorities, was rewarded with junior ministerial positions, and became a member of the Academy in 1780. Currying favour rid him of the poverty suffered in earlier years, although in his verse he continued to feign poverty until the last. Much of his earlier poetry appeared anonymously in an annual publication entitled *Miscelânea Curiosa e Proveitosa* (1779–83). In 1811 he finally published the two slim volumes of his *Obras Poéticas*. A third volume, *Obras Póstumas*, appeared in 1828 and an even completer edition of his works in 1861. A definitive edition is wanting. Although an appreciable slice of his work consists of conventional neo-classical odes, sonnets and so forth, his reputation rests on the satirical poems which have made him the foremost representative of the *genre* in Portuguese literature. His technique for the most part avoids the idealism of a Horace or the *saeva indignatio* of a Juvenal and is basically humorous and indulgent rather than bitterly mordant. Offering a kaleidoscope of contemporary Portuguese *mores*, he is frequently satirical at his own expense, appearing to adopt the opinions he wishes to ridicule. [RCW]

M. Rodrigues Lapa, *Vida e Obra de Nicolau Tolentino*, in *Seara Nova*, 797 (Lisbon, 1942); H. Cidade, *Lições de Cultura e Literatura Portuguesas*, ii (Coimbra, 1948).

**Toller, Ernst** (Samotschin, Posen 1893–New York 1939). German dramatist. A volunteer in 1914, wounded and invalided out in 1916, he was profoundly 'transformed' in outlook (politically to socialism) – a recurrent theme in his work. Imprisoned for his part in the Bavarian 'Räterepublik' (1919), he wrote Expressionist plays of martyrdom and revolt against the old order: *Die Wandlung* (1919; tr. E. Crankshaw and others, *Transfiguration*, in *E.T.*: *Seven Plays*, 1935) and *Masse-Mensch* (1920; tr. E. Crankshaw and others, *Masses and Man*). Their ecstatic style, symbolic characters, loosely connected tableaux, etc., give way to more realistic presentation in the Luddite play, *Die Maschinenstürmer* (1922; tr. E. Crankshaw and others, *The Machine Wreckers*) and a mood of profound despair at the post-war scene in *Hinkemann* (1923; tr. E. Crankshaw and others) and *Hoppla, wir leben* (1927; tr. E. Crankshaw and others, *Hoppla! Such is Life*). *Feuer aus den Kesseln* (1930; tr. E. Crankshaw and others, *Draw the Fires!*) is a plain historical dramatization of the Kiel naval mutiny; *Die blinde Göttin* (1932; tr. E. Crankshaw and others, *The Blind Goddess*; adapted also by D. Johnston as *Blind Man's Buff*, 1938) exposes the sacrifice of innocent people to the 'blindness' of the law. After emigrating in 1932, he lived in difficult circumstances, his work little known – despite translations, e.g. by S. Spender of *Pastor Hall* (1939) and lyrics by W. H. Auden in *No More Peace* (1937). *Eine Jugend in Deutschland* (1933; tr. E. Crankshaw, *I was a German*, N.Y., 1934) is autobiography; *Das Schwalbenbuch* (1923; tr. A. Dukes, *The Swallow-Book*, 1924) a collection of moving poems written in prison. He committed suicide. [PB]

*Prosa, Briefe, Dramen, Gedichte* (1961); *Letters from Prison* (including *The Swallow-Book*), tr. R. E. Roberts (1936).

W. A. Willibrand, *E.T. Product of Two Revolutions* (Oklahoma, 1941), and *E.T. and his Ideology* (Iowa, 1950); W. W. Malzacher, *E.T.* (Vienna, 1961) (dissertation); F. Droop, *E.T.* (Berlin, 1922); P. Signer, *E.T.* (Berlin, 1924); Garten, *MGD*; Sokel, *WE*; Natan, *GML*, iii.

**Tolstoy, Count Aleksey Konstantinovich** (St Petersburg, 1817–Krasny Rog, Chernigov district 1875). Russian poet. His parents had parted, but his childhood on his mother's Ukrainian estate was happy. After journeys abroad, he lived in St Petersburg, where he was playmate to the future Alexander II. A 'student' in the Moscow State archives (1834), then a diplomatist in Germany; at the Chancellery in St Petersburg (1840) he began writing poetry, and published a story, *Upyr'* (1841). At Court (1843) he chivalrously pleaded for other writers; in 1855 he joined the Army, but was prevented from fighting by illness. He became (1856) an aide-de-camp, then master of the hunt, to the Tsar; he retired in 1861 and married in 1863.

He sees art as a revelation of the eternal Idea: cf. *Tshchetno, khydozhnik, ty mnish'* (1856). Its call is divine: *Ioann Damaskin* (1852) leaves the Court for art; then a monk binds him to silence; the Virgin Mary frees him from his vow. Tolstoy defends 'pure art' yet is an eclectic in content and style. He writes the humorously biting *Istoriya Gosudarstva Rossiyskogo* ('History of the Russian State', 1868), or satirizes bureaucracy and the 'nihilists'. With the Zhemchuzhnikovs, he 'invents' an author, Koz'ma Prutkov, whose inconsequential pronouncements beget Russian nonsense verse.

His romantic works are *Don Juan* (1862), the Dantesque *Drakon* (1875), a translation (1868) of Goethe's *Die Braut von Korinth*, and vampire stories, one recalling a poem of his boyish passion for a lady's portrait (*Portret*, 1874). His ballads are somewhat operatic as is a historical novel, *Knyaz' Serebryany* (*c.*1843–63). His dramatic trilogy in verse (1866–70), *Smert' Ioanna Groznogo* (tr. G. R. Moyes, *Death of Ivan the Terrible*, N.Y., 1933), *Tsar' Fedor Ivannovich* (tr. J. Covan, *Tsar Fedor Ioannovich*, N.Y., 1922), *Tsar' Boris*, is a remarkable achievement. He sees events as governed by the rulers' personalities more than by historical forces and at times sacrifices facts for dramatic effect and vivid dialogue, but this is no mere 'costume theatre'. Its high moral message and the frank and penetrating psychological portrayal of the Tsars secured Tolstoy's renown as a historical dramatist. *Ivan* was staged, but the best play, *Fedor*, banned by the censorship, was first performed on 12 October 1898 in St Petersburg, and on 14th at the inauguration of the Moscow Arts Theatre.

Tolstoy's true genre is the melodious

nature and love lyric (many were set to music). A delicate touch conveys the atmosphere of landscape and seasons and portrays his only love. [NG]

*Sobraniye sochineniy*, intr. and notes I. Yampol'sky (4 vols., 1963–4); 'Koz'ma Prutkov', *Izbrannyye proizvedeniya*, intr. Desnitsky (1951); *Stikhotvoreniya* (1952); *P'yesy* (1959).
A. Lirondelle, *Le poète A.T.* (Paris, 1912).

**Tolstoy, Count Aleksey Nikolayevich** (Nikolayevsk, Samara 1882–Moscow 1945). Russian poet, novelist and dramatist. Of noble birth (he was a distant relative of Count L. ⇨ Tolstoy) he studied at the St Petersburg Technological Institute; his work was first published in 1905. He served in the White Army before emigrating in 1919. He returned in 1923 and became one of the most popular Soviet authors.

Tolstoy was a prolific and versatile writer. His early verse was admittedly influenced by the Symbolists, but his prose is assured from the start. One of the finest works of this early period is *Khromoy barin* (1912), with its characteristic blend of Homeric vitality and sentiment. In emigration he wrote the semi-autobiographical *Detstvo Nikity* (1919–22; tr. V. Dutt, *Nikita's Childhood*, 1945) and began an anti-Bolshevik novel, *Syostry*, an account of intellectual life in Russia on the eve of the Revolution. On his return to Russia this novel was heavily revised and eventually expanded into the historical trilogy *Khozhdeniye po mukam* (1919–41; tr. E. Bone, *The Road to Calvary*, 1945), for which he was awarded a Stalin prize in 1942. The completed work shows how the heroes become Communists, but as history it suffers from serious distortions.

Tolstoy reflected the confused and disillusioned period of the NEP in such stories as *Golubyye goroda* (1925; tr. in *Azure Cities*, ed. J. J. Robbins and J. Kunitz, 1929) and in *Vasiliy Suchkov* (1925; part tr. in *Bonfire*, ed. S. Konovalov, 1932). At the same time he was experimenting with science fiction, *Aelita* (1922) and *Giperboloid inzhenera Garina* (1926; tr. B. Guerney, *The Death-Box*, 1934). His tributes to Stalinism, *Khleb* (1937; tr. S. Garry, *Bread*, 1938), and the play *Ivan Groznyy* (1943) are crudely tendentious. But his unfinished novel *Pyotr Pervyy* (1929–45; tr. T. Shebunina, *Peter the Great*, 1956), originally planned in this spirit, transcends these limitations. In its subtly archaized style, its vigorous characterization, its wealth of incident and narrative momentum it overshadows all Tolstoy's earlier work and indeed most Soviet fiction. It was awarded a Stalin prize in 1941.

Tolstoy's genius was for story-telling; psychological analysis and philosophical speculation were not his strong points, though he occasionally indulged in them. With his exuberance, humour and narrative skill, he is sometimes vulgar, but always readable. [RDBT]

*Sobraniye sochineniy* (15 vols., 1946–53).
L. M. Polyak, *A.T.-Khudozhnik* (Moscow, 1964); M. Charny, *Put' A.T.* (Moscow, 1961).

**Tolstoy, Count Lev Nikolayevich** (Yasnaya Polyana 1828–Astapovo 1910). Russian novelist, dramatist and thinker. 'The aim of an artist is not to resolve a question irrefutably, but to compel one to love life in all its manifestations', wrote the author of *War and Peace* to an acquaintance. And some years earlier, the young Tolstoy had reminded himself in his notebook: 'The first condition of an author's popularity... is the love with which he treats all his characters.' Tolstoy's love of life and of the characters with which he peopled his many works, a love matched and tempered by his exceptional powers of observation and discrimination, makes him one of the undisputed giants of European literature.

He is remembered usually as a novelist, as the creator of *Voyna i mir* (1863–9; tr. R. Edmonds, *War and Peace*, 1957) and of *Anna Karenina* (1873–7; tr. R. Edmonds, 1954; both Penguin Classics). In fact he wrote only one other full-length (and rather less successful) novel, *Voskreseniye* ('Resurrection', 1899), and shorter works – stories and *nouvelles* – occupy much of the space in the 45 large tomes of his complete artistic works (a further 45 contain his diaries and correspondence). Moreover, his prose fiction has tended to overshadow his work as a dramatist: *Vlast' T'my* ('The Power of Darkness', 1886) is, in fact, an impressive tragedy; *Plody Prosveshcheniya* ('The Fruits of Enlightenment', 1890) is an effective satirical comedy.

The young Tolstoy was by no means confident that he should write. He was an aristocrat attached as a volunteer to the Russian army in the Caucasus when he published, anonymously, his first work, *Detstvo* (1852). This sensitive and already well-controlled evocation of his own childhood deserved and received acclaim. Two sequels to it appeared in the course of the next five years, *Otrochestvo* (1854) and *Yunost'* (1857; all tr. R. Edmonds, *Childhood, Boyhood, Youth*, Penguin Classics, 1964). Meanwhile, Tolstoy had joined the army and the Crimean War involved him in rather less glamorous warfare than that which he had experienced in the Caucasus. His three Sevastopol sketches (1855) (the third of which, *Sevastopol in August 1855*, was the first work to which he appended his full name) prepare one not only for the magnificent battle scenes of *War and Peace*, but also for his eventual advocacy of unconditional pacifism, an advocacy that was to influence profoundly 'a Transvaal Hindu' correspondent of his, M. K. Gandhi.

He worked intermittently on what was to prove his finest early work, *Kazaki* (1852–63; tr. R. Edmonds, *The Cossacks*, Penguin Classics, 1960), in which – as in his later and equally impressive *Khadzhi-Murat* (1896–1904) – he glorified the natural man of the Caucasus at the expense of the civilized and rootless European. He had eagerly devoured Rousseau's complete works in his youth, but the cult of the natural man was not to remain an academic one for him. At Yasnaya Polyana he owned several hundred peasants and he came to devote himself ever increasingly to their welfare, well aware of the peasants' limitations, but still more acutely aware of his own. He had already demonstrated his concern for the peasant problem in his *Utro pomeshchika* ('A Landowner's Morning', 1852–6); in 1859 he considered abandoning literature altogether and opened an experimental progressive school for peasant children at his home. A number of his works in subsequent years were composed for use in such schools: *Kavkazskiy plennik* ('A Prisoner in the Caucasus', 1872), for instance, was written for inclusion in his *Azbuka*, a primer that he hoped would be used throughout Russia. He was to devote the last thirty years of his life to the education not only of the local peasants but of the whole of Russia, indeed, of the whole world. Unlike the young Tolstoy he came to believe that the aim of the artist *was* to resolve questions irrefutably for the benefit of mankind.

However, nearly two decades of writing and of family life – he married in 1862 – separated him from this period as a preacher. *War and Peace* and *Anna Karenina* are the fruit of these years. The profligate bachelor was now a married man, a father, with a new insight into family life, and it is with family life that both the great novels, in their different ways, are concerned. One of the original reviewers of *War and Peace* considered it to be 'a complete picture of everything in which people find their happiness and greatness, their grief and humiliation': in the subtlety with which Tolstoy depicts and analyses the thoughts and emotions of his heroes, in his warm yet careful use of apparently insignificant detail to reveal their inner world he has few rivals. It is all the more impressive that *War and Peace*, with its fascinating depiction of so many different microcosms, should yet flow coherently as a whole towards what Tolstoy (who ends the novel proper with three dots) hesitates to call a conclusion.

When he was a young boy his elder brother told him of a little green stick which he had buried in the forest at Yasnaya Polyana; on it was engraved a secret formula which, once revealed, would inaugurate a golden age of universal love. The mature Tolstoy dedicated himself to the search for such a formula. In *Ispoved'* ('Confession', 1879) he described the religious crisis which led to his rejection of orthodox religion: in a number of subsequent works like *V chom moya vera?* ('What is my faith?', 1883–4) he outlined his new beliefs. He pruned the four Gospels of all supernatural elements, preached deism in the religious and anarchism in the political sphere and urged his readers to love all men and to do violence to no one. His beliefs were advocated in striking parables and short stories written in a new idiom, popular, vigorous and economical: *Skazka ob Ivane-durake* ('The Tale of Ivan the Fool', 1885), *Dva starika* ('Two Old Men', 1885), *Mnogo li cheloveku zemli nuzhno* ('Does a Man Need Much Earth?' 1886), *Khozyain i rabotnik* ('Master and Worker', 1894–5), *Otets Sergiy* ('Father Sergiy', 1890–8) and *Alyosha Gorshok* (1905). *Smert' Ivana Il'icha* (1884–6; tr. R. Edmonds, *The Death of Ivan Ilyich*, in *The Cossacks*, etc., 1960) deserves particular mention as an impressive *tour de force* in which the hero, not unlike Kafka's 'K' in *The Trial*, is unexpectedly subjected to seemingly unmerited anguish and death.

At this time Tolstoy dressed as a peasant and worked in the fields; for reasons that he stated in *Chto takoye iskusstvo?* ('What is

Art?', 1898) he considered his earlier work worthless; and he had no desire to gain financially from his current or his future work. In 1891 he renounced his copyright on work published after 1881; and in the following year he divided all his property between his wife, Sofya, and his nine surviving children. His wife accepted neither his teachings nor his new disciples and the rift between them was an open secret of which the couple's diaries were by no means the sole custodians.

His prestige in the last decade of his life was enormous, both in Russia and abroad; but he found no peace either in his home or, worse, in himself. At 82 he fled from home, 'leaving this worldly life in order to live out my last days in peace and solitude', as he wrote to his wife. His last shelter was the station master's house at Astapovo. Within a few days he was dead. He was buried, at his own request, near the place where his brother had hidden the mysterious little green stick. [SH]

*Polnoye sobraniye sochineniy*, ed. V. Chertkov (90 vols., 1928–58); *Works*, tr. L. and A. Maude (21 vols, 1928–37).

E. J. Simmons, *Leo T.* (1946); I. Berlin, *The Hedgehog and the Fox* (1953); R. F. Christian, *T.'s War and Peace: a Study* (1962); D. Leon, *T., his Life and Work* (1944); A. Maude, *The Life of T.* (1930); T. Redpath, *T.* (1960); J. Bailey, *T. and the Novel* (1966).

**Tommaseo, Niccolò** (Sibenik, Yugoslavia 1802–Florence 1874). Italian lexicographer, poet and novelist. After graduating in Law at Padua University in 1822, he began writing on varied literary and philosophical subjects. In 1827 he went to Florence to work on his *Dizionario dei sinonimi* (1830), which, with the *Dizionario della lingua italiana* (1858–79, edited in conjunction with B. Bellini, and completed by G. Meini), constitutes his most important work. An ardent patriot, he spent several years in exile (1833–9, 1849–54; cf. *Dell'Italia*, Paris, 1835; *Paris et le Monde*, Corfù, 1851). His staunch opposition to the Piedmontese monarchy is reflected in his *Cronichetta del 1865–66* (posth. 1940), and in his refusal to accept any official honours from the new Kingdom of Italy. His poetry (e.g. *Confessioni*, 1836; *Poesie*, 1872) and his novel, *Fede e bellezza* (1840), show a depth of psychological insight that was unfortunately spoiled by an excess of erudition. [RHC]

*Edizione Nazionale delle opere di N.T.* (1954ff.); *Opere*, anthology, ed. A. Borlenghi (1958); *Poesie e prose*, ed. P. P. Trompeo and P. Ciureanu (2 vols., 1959) (selection).

R. Ciampini, *Vita di N.T.* (Florence, 1945); A. Borlenghi, *L'arte di N.T.* (Milan, 1953); F. De Sanctis, *La scuola liberale e la scuola democratica*, ed. F. Catalano (Bari, 1954); *Minori*, iii.

**Tömörkény, István** (Cegléd 1866–Szeged 1917). Hungarian short-story writer. He was first a chemist, later director of Szeged Museum and journalist. He had the touch of a folklorist, but his regionalistic writings describe classically the life and customs of the peasants and artisans of the great Hungarian Plain. [JFR]

**Tompa, Mihály** (Rimaszombat 1817–Hanva 1888). Hungarian poet. A friend of ⇨ Petőfi. After the tragic end of the War of Independence (1849), he became a Protestant priest. During the period of strictest censure, he wrote allegorical poems about freedom, such as *A Madár fiaihoz* (tr. D. M. Stuart, *The Bird to his Sons*, 1911) and *A gólyához* (1852). [JFR]

**Topelius, Zachris** (Uusikaarlepyy 1818–Helsinki 1898). Finnish poet (writing in Swedish), novelist and scholar. Professor of Finnish History at Helsinki University (1863), Rector of the University (1875–8). Under the influence of Scott and Hugo, he founded the tradition of the Finnish historical novel. *Fältskärns berättelser* (5 vols., 1854–66) was his main work. He also wrote stories and plays for children: *Sagor* (4 vols., 1847–52) and *Läsning för barn* (8 vols., 1865–96). [IR]

*Samlade verk* (24 vols., 1899–1907).

Selma Lagerlöf, *Z.T.* (Stockholm, 1920); E. N. Tigerstedt, *Z.T.* (Helsinki, 1943); P. B. Nyberg, *Z.T.* (Helsinki, 1949).

**Topsøe, Vilhelm** (Skelskør 1840–Skodsborg 1881). Danish author. He was influenced by Dickens and Thackeray. Politically opposed to the radicalism of the 1870s, his most notable fiction (published anonymously) is *Jason med det gyldne Skind* (1875) and *Nutidsbilleder* (1878). [ELB]

V. Andersen, *V.T.* (Copenhagen, 1922).

**Torga, Miguel,** pseud. of Alfredo Rocha (S. Martinho de Anta 1907– ). Portuguese poet, dramatist, novelist and diarist. A medical practitioner in Coimbra, he is married to the eminent literary critic,

Andrée Crabbé Rocha. In his youth Torga was one of the group of poets associated with the periodical *Presença* (1927–40), but in 1930 he broke away with Branquinho da Fonseca, with whom he collaborated in the direction of the short-lived periodical *Sinal*. He later ran *Manifesto* and contributed to the periodical *Revista de Portugal* (1937–8), but finally emerged as an isolated figure, in his own words a 'rebel Orpheus'. A prolific and much re-edited author, he has published 13 verse collections, 4 plays, 10 works of narrative fiction, 2 volumes of travel impressions and from 1941 a *Diário*, of which successive volumes appear at two- or three-year intervals, and which contains poems, short essays and random jottings. Though strongly and often narrowly Iberian in spirit, his work is nevertheless of universal appeal and has often been discussed in the context of the Nobel Prize. His most representative verse collections are *O Outro Livro de Job* (1936), *Odes* (1946) and *Orfeu Rebelde* (1958). His poetry is a poetry of protest, not against God (for God he rejects, though using transcendental imagery), but against all existence, against life's struggle and its brevity, against the Fall of Adam and the futility of Calvary, against the unending toil of Sisyphus, that is, of Man himself. His major prose works are *Bichos* (1940), *Vindima* (1945) and *Portugal* (1950). Undoubtedly his most popular work, the first of these is a collection of short stories mainly about animals, but animals to which are assigned quasi-human emotions, and is concerned with the eternal cycle of birth, life and death, in which death is consistently accepted with stoic resignation, never with despair. The novel *Vindima* is a colourful account, rich in characters, of a disastrous grape-harvest on a Douro estate in which catastrophe succeeds catastrophe, and serves to illustrate that fatalism and pessimism in Torga which also inform his *Portugal*, a series of impressionistic regional essays. Prominent among his other prose works are the basically autobiographical romance *A Criação do Mundo* (1937–9) and the collections *Contos da Montanha* (1941) and *Novos Contos da Montanha* (1944) short stories depicting the harshness of life in his own somewhat backward native province of Trás-os-Montes. [RCW]

E. Lourenço, *O Desespero Humanista de Miguel Torga* (Coimbra, 1955); J. de Melo, *Miguel Torga* (Lisbon, 1960).

**Torre, Francisco de la** (mid 16th cent.). Spanish poet. Nothing is known about his life. The poems, which were in finished form. before 1594, were published by ⇨ Quevedo in 1631, as a counterblast to Gongorism. They are Italianate in style, the theme is platonic love, and the prevailing mood is melancholy. Torre shows love for the country and for night, and a pleasingly Arcadian sentiment in his 8 eclogues, the *Bucóliça del Tajo*. The best of his poems, however, are his sonnets, and his delicately modulated ode 'Claras lumbres del cielo'. [JMC]

*Poesías*, ed. A. Zamora Vicente, CC; Blecua, *FLE*; Cohen, *PBSV*; Trend, *OBSV*; Terry, *ASP*.

**Torres Naharro, Bartolomé de** (Torres ? Badajoz ?–Torres ? 1524?) Spanish dramatist and poet. At first a soldier, then a priest, he was shipwrecked, captured by the Moors, and later lived in Rome, where he met Juan del Encina and began by imitating his eclogues (*Dialogo del nacimiento*). His 7 *comedias* (*Propalladia*, 1517; ed. J. E. Gillet, 4 vols., Bryn Mawr, 1943–61) are defined in the preface as either based on observation or imagination (though also appearing to be true). In his first category the *Comedia soldadesca* presents a lively and uncomplicated picture of military life in Renaissance Italy. *Himenea*, by contrast, is the first 'Cloak and Sword' drama, and its treatment of the 'point of honour' anticipates Lope de Vega and Calderón; it has affinities with *La Celestina* in its contrasts between masters and servants. Another 'fantastic' comedy, *Serafina*, contains a delightful caricature of a pimping friar who calmly proposes a murder. Burlesque, macaronics and snatches of foreign tongues produce a cosmopolitan effect, characteristic of this Erasmist and expatriate friar. Each of his plays is preceded by a comic prologue using the *sayagués* dialect introduced by ⇨ Encina, and frequently obscene. His works were included on the Index in 1559, and reissued in expurgated form in 1573. He was an important forerunner of the Golden Age dramatists, but his lyric poetry looks back to the 15th-century *cancioneros*.

J. P. W. Crawford, *Spanish Drama before Lope de Vega* (Philadelphia, 1922).

**Torres Villarroel, Diego de** (Salamanca 1694–Salamanca 1770). Spanish adventurer. After a career which included begging, bull-fighting and compiling astrological calendars, he secured the chair of mathematics at Salamanca, where the subject had not been taught for a hundred and fifty years. His *Vida* (1743–58; in CC, CA; tr. W. C. Atkinson, *The Remarkable Life of Don Diego*, 1958) tells the story of his life in racy, aggressive language, and casts considerable light on Spain at this moment of her decadence. A complete egotist, he describes no other character, but takes a cynical objective view of his own. His prose style and that of his amusing burlesque poetry derive from ◊ Quevedo. He was a voluminous writer; but though there are interesting passages in *Sueños* (1743), sketches of Madrid life which take their title from Quevedo, he survives only in his self-portrait, one of the most engaging in the language. [JMC]

**Tóth, Árpád** (Arad 1886–Budapest 1928). Hungarian poet. One of the leading members of the ◊ *Nyugat* movement. Son of a struggling sculptor. His youth was beset with difficulties and he was forced to abandon his studies for a dull career in journalism. His melancholy though manly lyricism is tinged with the knowledge of early death and the yearning for a full, healthy life (after a long period of ill-health, he died of tuberculosis). His wide culture and refined sense of style linked him with Western literature, especially the late French symbolists. A pacifist, Tóth protested dynamically against the First World War and longed for a peaceful, humane world; in *Az Új Isten* (1919), he hailed the Communist government of that year. Though a lonely soul, he harboured affection especially for the simple, common man. Tóth's main themes are life and death, loneliness, peace and the beauty of nature; his lyric is refined and delicate. His major poems are: *Meddő Órán*; *Lélektől Lélekig*; *Elégia az Elesett Ifjú Emlékére*; *Tetemrehívás.* He was the foremost Hungarian translator in his day (notably of Baudelaire, Verlaine, Flaubert, Shelley and Milton). [JFR]

Klaniczay, *HHL*; Reményi, *HWL*.

**Toulet, Paul-Jean** (Pau 1867–Guéthary 1920). French poet and novelist. His childhood by the Pyrenees, a visit to his family in Mauritius (1886–8), followed by a year in Algiers, and later a trip to Indochina (1902–3), all left their mark on his work. He settled down to the life of a dandy and journalist in Paris, publishing novels on his own and in collaboration, and articles, stories, poems and maxims in various reviews. In 1912 ill-health and lack of money forced him to return to the south where he collected his previously scattered work.

His best novels are those of a satirist sharply observing human nature (*M. du Paur*, 1898), yet with a love for his own province (*La jeune fille verte*, 1920). His fantasy and irony reveal themselves more clearly in *Le mariage de Don Quichotte* (1902) and in his stories (*Comme une fantaisie*, 1918; *Béhanzigue*, 1920). He spent years polishing his most lasting works: the maxims of *Les trois impostures* (1922) where Toulet, disillusioned and sceptical, renews sometimes commonplace or unnecessarily brutal observations by his style: a striking image, a harmonious cadence, an elliptical turn; and his poems (*Les contrerimes*, 1921), in which he draws on personal experiences: of women, of nature in France and abroad, of opium which bathes many in an unreal haze. But he avoids any Romanticism with a precision of form that at times nears preciosity. In both maxims and poems he renews a classical tradition with an original sensibility and an elliptical brevity that does not exclude delicacy. [PC]

P.-O. Walzer, *P.-J.T., L'œuvre, l'écrivain* (Paris, 1949); H. Martineau, *La vie de P.-J.T.* (Paris, 1957–9) (in 5 booklets).

**Trakl, Georg** (Salzburg 1887–Cracow 1914). Austrian poet. Trained as a dispensing chemist, he served as a Medical Corps lieutenant and became deranged by his experiences after the battle of Grodek; he died from an overdose of drugs in a military hospital. Most of his poems appeared in Ludwig von Ficker's periodical *Der Brenner* from 1912 to 1914, and in two collections: *Gedichte* (1913) and *Sebastian im Traum* (1914). A surrealist-type early Expressionist, influenced by Baudelaire, Rimbaud, Hölderlin, and Dostoyevsky, he has written some of the most truly original poetry of the century. His vivid, visionary imagery is difficult to interpret, but conveys a sense of menacing immediacy in experience, a fascination with decay, and yet a struggle for spiritual order and glimpses of Christian faith. His radically disjointed syntax is expressive of a deep disquiet, and his very obscurity is radiant with a stark beauty – as if the Apocalypse had transfigured the familiar into the terrible. [PB]

*Gesammelte Werke*, ed. W. Schneditz (3 vols., 1949–53); *Decline. Twelve Poems*, tr. M. Hamburger (1952); *Twenty Poems*, tr. J. Wright and R. Bly (Madison, 1961); Bridgwater, *TCGV*; Hamburger and Middleton, *MGP*.

W. Ritzer, *T. Bibliographie* (Salzburg, 1956); *Erinnerung an G.T.* (Salzburg, 1959); W. Killy, *Über G.T.* (Göttingen, 1960); K. Schneider, *Der bildlafte Ausdruck in den Dichtungen Georg Heyms, G.T.s und Ernst Stadlers* (Heidelberg, 1954); O. Basil, *G.T.* (Reinbek, 1965); T. J. Casey, *Manshape that Shone* (1964); Hamburger, *RE*.

**Traven, Ben,** pseud. for a (? Bavarian émigré) novelist whose real identity and whereabouts are unknown. He certainly lived in Mexico for many years, working in every conceivable job from gold-prospector to midwife. His fiction tells his adventurous experiences, with a compelling flair for story and keen sympathy with all victims of oppression and inhumanity. The novels include: *Die Baumwollpflücker* (1926; tr. E. Brockett, *The Cotton Pickers*, 1956), *Das Totenschiff* (1926; tr. E. Sutton, *The Death Ship*, 1934), *Der Schatz der Sierra Madre* (1927; tr. B. Creighton, *The Treasure of the Sierra Madre*, 1956; internationally successful as a film), *Die Brücke im Dschungel* (1929; tr. anon., *The Bridge in the Jungle*, 1940), and *Der Karren* (1930; tr. B. Creighton, *The Carreta*, 1935; new German edition 1953 entitled *Die Carreta*). *Der Banditendoktor* (1954) are brilliant short stories. [PB]

*The Night Visitor and Other Stories*, intr. C. Miller (1967).

*GQ*, XXXVI (1963).

**Trenyov, Konstantin Andreyevich** (Kharkovskaya Guberniya 1876–Moscow 1945). Soviet dramatist. Of peasant extraction, he was educated in an Agricultural College and a Priest's Seminary. He wrote short stories about peasants' life and his first play, *Pugachovshchina* (1924), was 'a tragedy about the people' in an 18th-century peasant rising. Most successful was *Lyubov' Yarovaya*, the only Soviet play which the Moscow Art Theatre took to the World Exhibition in Paris in 1937; its careful treatment of the *individual's* reaction to the Revolution was thought to mark a new departure in the development of Soviet drama. [AP]

*P'yesy, Stat'i*, ed. E. Surkov (1952); *Zhivoy T. Sbornik vospominaniy* (Rostov, 1963).

E. Surkov, *K.A.T.* (Moscow, 1955); R. I. Faynberg, *K.A.T.* (Moscow/Leningrad, 1962); V. A. Diyev, *Tvorchestvo K.A.T.* (Moscow, 1960).

**Trillo y Figueroa, Francisco de** (Corunna 1618?–Granada? 1680?). Spanish poet. His themes are light and he is at his best in his *letrillas* and *romances*, which imitate ⇨ Quevedo. He makes clever use of *germanía*, or thieves' slang, and is sometimes pleasantly bawdy. His more serious poems, among which are some sonnets on Old Testament themes, are mere pretexts for tasteless hyperbole. Though a man of learning, he was at his best in the culto-popular vein. Apart from a mediocre epic poem, *Neapolisea* (1651), his principal collection is *Poesías varias* (1652). [JMC]

*Obras* (1951); Blecua, *FLE*; Cohen, *PBSV*.

A. Gallego Morell, *F. de T. y F.* (Granada, 1950).

**Trissino, Giangiorgio** (Vicenza 1478–Rome 1550). Italian scholar-poet and tragedian. From a patrician family, he received a humanistic education, becoming an ardent hellenizer. He suffered both domestic unhappiness and political exile (for his ideal of a restored Empire).

His views on literature were intellectually aristocratic. His approach was academic and theoretical, and he aimed at ennobling Italian literature by importing from Greek the 'missing' genres of tragedy and regular epic. Thus in 1524 he published the first Italian tragedy, *Sofonisba*, and in 1547–8 his *Italia liberata dai Goti*, which gave Italy its first 'serious' epic. In *Sofonisba*, based on Livy's story of the Carthaginian princess, he followed the conventions of Greek tragedy. He observed the unities of time and action, employed a chorus, did not divide the play into acts, and selected the *endecasillabo sciolto* (Italian blank verse) to reproduce the effects of the Greek. The play itself is inevitably stiff and academic, full of long declamations and stilted stichomythia. His *Italia liberata dai Goti* suffers from similar defects. He worked for twenty years at this epic on Belisarius's campaign against the Goths, and the result is more remarkable for its erudition than for its poetry. His scholarly and theoretical approach to the epic helped to create the literary environment responsible for some of the tensions observable in Tasso's *Gerusalemme liberata*. [DGR]

*Tutte le opere*, ed. S. Maffei (1729); *Scritti scelti*, ed. A. Scarpa (1950).

B. Morsolin, *G.G.T.* (Florence, 1894); M. Herrick, *Italian Tragedy in the Renaissance* (Urbana, 1965); Croce, *PES*, *PPP*; Weinberg, *HLC*; *Minori*, ii.

**Tristan,** pen-name of François l'Hermite (? 1601–1655). French playwright. One of the chief architects of French classical drama. Working alongside Mairet, ⇨ Rotrou and Corneille, he was possibly the most gifted of the four pioneers of that form of art which Racine was to perfect. Much of his career is obscure. We know from his entertaining autobiography *Le page disgracié* (1643) that he grew up in a great house, serving in turn the Duc de Verneuil, Scévole de Sainte-Marthe, the Marquis de Villars, the king (Louis XIII), his brother Gaston d'Orléans and the Duc de Guise, in whose house he died. Tristan's vices (notably gambling), like his virtues, are known only from his own writing. He would appear to have had a superb memory and the taste for reciting long passages of prose and verse. His surviving work consists of 4 tragedies, a pastoral, a comedy and a tragi-comedy, and 3 collections of light verse. His first tragedy, *La Mariane* (1637), produced (as all Corneille successes were to be) at the Marais theatre, was his masterpiece. It competed with *Le Cid* in contemporary esteem and was fortunate to find, in Mondory, a great actor for the figure of *Herod*, whose jealousy for his sensitive wife Mariamne is a splendid tragic theme, discovered for Tristan's generation by ⇨ Hardy. All his tragedies suggest this skill in selecting a notable paradox of human greatness for dramatic contemplation: *Penthée* (1637), *La mort de Sénèque* (1644), *La mort de Chrispe, ou les malheurs domestiques du grand Constantin* (1644), *La mort du grand Osman* (1647). He also wrote a play for Molière's first company, the Illustre Théâtre, and his comedy *Le Parasite* (1653) had the honour of being used for some passages in *L'étourdi*. In *La folie du sage* (1644) he dramatized an episode from his own life and incidentally introduced to the French stage the famous name of Palamède. [WGM]

TFM (plays).

N. M. Bernardin, *T.* (Paris, 1879); Adam, *HLF*; Lancaster, *FTLV*; *HFDL*.

**Tristan.** The poems on this theme in medieval French are generally thought to derive from a model, an *Ur-Tristan*, which may have been written between 1150 and 1160, and is now lost.

The most important surviving versions are those by Thomas and Beroul. Thomas, an Anglo-Norman, wrote between 1160 and 1170, and his poem has survived in fragments, of which the most important are a magnificent account of Iseult's attempt to save the dying Tristan, the espisode of the black-and-white sails, and the deaths of the lovers. Thomas, who was writing for a courtly audience, omitted several brutal incidents, including that of Iseult given by Mark to the lepers, and he analyses the motives, feelings and reactions of his characters. Thomas's poem was imitated in a German version by ⇨ Gottfried von Strassburg and in a Norwegian version.

Beroul, who was a *remanieur*, wrote between 1160 and 1170 and remained close to the original Celtic theme. The extant text from l. 2755 is probably the work of a later writer, about 1200. The whole fragment of 4,500 lines deals with the central part of the story in which Tristan and Iseult, having drunk the potion, fail to hide their love, are condemned to be burnt, escape to the forest of Morois, and then seek reconciliation with Mark. The poem consists largely of juxtaposed episodes described in ⇨ *jongleur* style with great simplicity and bare dramatic force. The characters act violently and on impulse, and Beroul sympathizes with Tristan and Iseult in their struggle against their tragic destiny. ⇨ Eilhart von Oberg appears to have used the same source as Beroul for the Middle High German *Tristan* which he wrote about 1180.

Two versions of an episode exist describing how Tristan, during his last exile, revealed himself to Iseult in the disguise of a madman: these are known as *La Folie Tristan* of Berne (derived from Beroul) and of Oxford (derived from Thomas).

⇨ Chrétien de Troyes wrote a poem on Mark and Tristan which is not extant. ⇨ Marie de France used an episode of Tristan's first exile in a *lai* called *Chievrefueil*. About 1230 a long prose *Tristan* was compiled, in which the Tristan legend was combined with that of Arthur. From this prose *Tristan* are derived Malory's *Morte Darthur*, the Italian *Tavola Ritonda* and the Russian *Tristan*. [LTT]

*The Romance of T. by Beroul*, ed. A. Ewert (1939); *Thomas, Le roman de T.*, ed. J. Bédier (2 vols., Paris, 1902–5); *Les fragments du T. de*

*Thomas*, ed. B. H. Wind (Leiden, 1950); *La Folie T. de Berne*, ed. E. Hoepffner (2nd edn, Strasbourg, 1949); *La F.T. d'Oxford*, ed. E. Hoepffner (2nd edn, Strasbourg, 1943); P. Champion, *Le Roman de T. et Iseut* (Paris, 1949) (adaptation of the prose *T.*).

G. Schoepperle, *T. and Isolt* (1913); *RPh*, VII (1953); *Moyen Âge*, LXIV (1958); LXVII (1961); *MLR*, LX (1965); E. Vinaver, *Études sur le T. en prose* (Paris, 1925).

**'Troie, Roman de.'** A medieval French romance of over 30,000 lines written by ⇨ Benoît de Sainte-Maure in octosyllabic rhyming couplets between 1154 and 1173. His sources were the *Historia de excidio Trojae* written by Dares Phrygius about A.D. 550 and the *Ephemeris belli Trojani* of Dictys Cretensis composed about A.D. 330. Dares claimed to have fought for the Trojans and Dictys for the Greeks. He also knew the *Roman de ⇨ Thèbes* and the *Roman d'⇨Eneas* and gave particular importance to the loves of Jason and Medea, Achilles and Polyxena and Troilus and Cressida (Briseida). This last episode, which he appears to have invented, was to become famous. It was transmitted by Guido delle Colonne in his late-13th-century Latin *Historia destructionis Trojae* to⇨Boccaccio, from whom it passed by means of Chaucer to Shakespeare.

Benoît starts with the quest of the Argonauts and describes in the style of the ⇨ *chanson de geste* the many battles fought before Troy, the wanderings of Odysseus, the fate of Orestes, the story of Andromache and the death of Pyrrhus. The poem is well written and provided a popular source of knowledge about the legends of Ancient Greece. French prose adaptations were made from the late 13th century and versions and translations exist in German, Italian, Spanish and Slavonic. Caxton's translation (about 1474) of a French prose version was the first book printed in English. [LTT]

Ed. L. Constans (5 vols., 1904–12); ed. K. Reichenberger (Tübingen, 1963; selections, 1964); *Le R. de T. en prose*, ed. L. Constans and E. Faral, i (Paris, 1913).

E. Faral, *Recherches sur les sources latines des contes et romans courtois du moyen âge* (Paris, 1913;) *R*, XLIII (1914).

**Troubadours.** Medieval poets from all stations in life, writing in Provençal, who created the first cultivated vernacular lyric poetry in Europe. Their best poetry, written 1100–1210, reflects the tastes and outlook of the Southern French courts. Troubadour influence spread in Europe to such an extent that Provençal came to be recognized in the early 13th century as the pre-eminent language for lyric composition and was used by many poets, French, Spanish, German, and especially Italian. All the great troubadours, except Raimbaut d'Orange, travelled widely and were esteemed and welcomed at the courts of Europe as creative poets and singers. In this they fared better than the ⇨ *jongleurs*, whose way of life and reception at court were often uncertain.

The first known troubadour was ⇨ Guilhem VII, count of Poitou, ninth duke of Aquitaine (1071–1127), and ancestor of Eleanor of Aquitaine (*c.* 1122–1204) and Marie de Champagne, the patroness of ⇨ Chrétien de Troyes. It has been suggested that Guilhem inherited a tradition of cultivated lyric poetry already established in the South of France. It is more likely that he was one of the earliest troubadours who were translating into verse a synthesis of 'new' ideas of love drawn from Ovid, from Platonic thought transmitted by Arab and Christian philosophers and idealized forms of love found in medieval Hispano-Arabic and Latin poetry. These 'new' ideas on profane love were developed by the courtly society of the 12th century into a type of feudal code, similar to that of knightly initiation in which the aspirant and submissive lover found his reward in devotion and service offered to the lady (*domna*) rather than in the fulfilment of his love. His reward came from the improvement of his *valor*, or inherent worth, and his *pretz* or reputation. This idealized form of physical and spiritual aspiration was known as *Fin 'Amors* (so-called 'courtly love') in distinction to *Fals 'Amors* or *Bass 'Amors* (⇨ Marcabru). Variations by troubadours on these ideas of love are found in each decade of the 12th century, one of the most extreme being the *amor de lonh* or 'love from afar' of ⇨ Jaufré Rudel.

Although the troubadour love-song or *canso* was addressed to the lady, it was concerned with the joy or despair of the poet. A courtly terminology developed in which words such as *Jois* ('joy') and *Jovens* ('youth') acquired a valuable range of deeper meanings.

Troubadour poetry lived on the patronage of the courtly society of Southern France, and when the Albigensian Crusade swept this away in the fighting which began in 1209 many troubadours migrated to Spain and Italy and others sought bourgeois patronage. ⇨ Guilhem Montanhagol fought a rearguard action in defence of courtly standards, but the troubadour *canso* became increasingly didactic and religious. In the poems of ⇨ Guiraut Riquier the courtly *domna* was replaced by the Virgin Mary, who provided the main poetic theme for the works submitted to the first ⇨ *Jocs florals* in 1324.

The *canso* or love-song of the troubadours was their highest lyric genre and demanded an elegant vocabulary and perfected technique, each new song requiring a fresh metrical scheme and melody. The 12th-century *canso* was composed in various styles, of which the most famous were the *trobar leu* or clear style, the *trobar clus*, an obscure and highly symbolical style which was out of favour by 1200, and the *trobar ric*, a carefully worked style in which emphasis was laid on the poetic value of individual words, intricate rhymes and versification. ⇨ Arnaut Daniel was the chief exponent of the *trobar ric* and was admired and imitated by Dante.

Other lyric genres demanding a less rigorous technique than the *canso* were the *sirventes*, which might be a moralizing poem (⇨ Guiraut de Bornelh, ⇨ Peire Cardenal) or a militant song dealing with current events and deeds of arms (⇨ Bertran de Born); the ⇨ *pastourelle*; the *joc partit* or *tenso*, a form of debate; the *planh* or funeral lament; the *alba*, ⇨ *aube* or dawn song; and the Crusading song. Some epic, romance and dramatic works of high quality survive in Provençal, including the splendid *Chanson de la Croisade Albigeoise*, the Arthurian romance *Jaufré*, ⇨ *Flamenca* and the 14th-century *Passion Provençale* (⇨ *Mystères*). ⇨⇨ Bernart de Ventadorn, Folquet de Marseille, Raimbaut of Orange, Raimon de Miraval, Sordello. [LTT]

Anthologies: J. Anglade (Paris, 1927), J. Audiau and R. Lavaud (Paris, 1928), A. Berry (Paris, 1930), Lavaud and Nelli, *T*; Hill and Bergin, *APT*; *La Chanson de la Croisade Albigeoise*, ed. E. Martin-Chabot (3 vols., Paris, 1931–61), with Fr. tr.

A. Pillet and H. Carstens, *Bibliographie der T.* (Halle-Saale, 1933); E. Levy (and C. Appel), *Provenzalisches Supplement-Wörterbuch* (Leipzig, 1894–1924); E. Levy, *Petit Dictionnaire Provençal-Francais*, 2nd edn (Heidelberg, 1923); H. Davenson, *Les T.* (Paris, 1961); E. Hoepffner, *Les T.* (Paris, 1955); H. J. Chaytor, *The T.* (1912); *The T. and England* (1923); *From Script to Print* (1945); J. Anglade, *Les T.* (Paris, 3rd edn, 1922); A. Jeanroy, *Histoire sommaire de la Poésie Occitane* (Paris, 1945); C. Camproux, *Hist. de la littérature occitane* (Paris, 1953); R. R. Bezzola, *Origines et formation de la littérature courtoise en Occident* (*500–1200*), 3 parts (Paris, 1958–62) and *R*, LXVI; R. Briffault, *Les T. et le sentiment romanesque* (Paris, 1945); R. Nelli, *L'érotique des T.* (Toulouse, 1963); M. Lazar, *Amour courtois et 'Fin'Amors'* (Paris, 1964); L. Pollmann; *Trobar Clus* (Münster, 1965); *Die Liebe in der hochmittelalterlichen Literatur Frankreichs* (Frankfurt, 1966); *Der provenzalische Minnesang*, ed. R. Baehr (Darmstadt, 1967) (essays); P. Belperron, *La Croisade contre les Albigeois* (Paris, 1945); and *La Joie d'Amour* (Paris, 1948); Andreas Capellanus, *The Art of Courtly Love* (N.Y., 1959); I. Frank, *Trouvères et Minnesänger*, i (Saarbrücken, 1952) (with good bibliography); Zoë Oldenbourg, *Massacre at Montségur: a History of the Albigensian Crusade* (N.Y., 1962); J. Chailley, *Histoire musicale du moyen âge* (Paris, 1950); Jeanroy, *PLT*; de Rougemont, *PS*.

**Trouvères.** Northern French counterpart of the Provençal troubadours by whose theories of love and technique of lyric composition they were profoundly influenced. Many 12th- and 13th-century *trouvères* were of noble birth, but in the 13th century a school of poetry of bourgeois inspiration arose in Picardy and was centred on the ⇨ Puy of Arras. ⇨⇨ Conon de Béthune, Gace Brulé, Gui de Coucy, Thibaut IV of Champagne, Adam de la Halle, Colin Muset, Jean Bodel, Hélinand, Rutebeuf, Troubadours and *Jongleurs*. [LTT]

**Troyat, Henri** (Moscow 1911– ). French novelist. His parents left Russia after the Revolution and settled in Paris in 1920. He received his secondary education at the Lycée Pasteur and took a degree in law. He entered the French civil service and worked for some years in the Préfecture of the Seine but resigned in 1941 to devote himself to his writing. He had been encouraged to take this step by early success. His first novel, *Faux jour* (1935), the story of a young man's disillusionment with his father, won the Prix Populiste and a fair degree of critical acclaim. His third, *L'araignée* (1938), the study of a young man's attempt to dominate his family, gained him the Prix Goncourt and a wide public. His literary career has continued to be successful. In 1959, at an unusually early age, he was elected to the Académie

Française. He has also written plays, e.g. *Les vivants* (1946) and *Sébastien* (1949), volumes of short stories, *La fosse commune* (1939), and biographies of Russian writers, e.g. *Dostoievsky* (1940; tr. N. Guterman, 1946) and *Pouchkine* (1946; tr. R. T. Weaver, 1951). The influence of Dostoyevsky was present in his studies of obsession such as *L'araignée*; the influence of Tolstoy is evident in the *romans-cycles* with which he has been chiefly occupied since 1947, especially in the first, *Tant que la terre durera* (1947–50; tr. D. Hapgood, *My Father's House*, 1952), which depicts the end of the pre-revolutionary Russia. His second epic, *Les semailles et les moissons* (1953–8), narrates the history of a family from southern France. Two others have followed: *La lumière des justes* (1959–63) and *Les Eygletière* (1965–6). His works, however, though eminently readable, do not approach the greatness of those of his masters. [SMD]

*Le mort saisit le vif* (1942); *Le signe du taureau* (1945); *Étrangers sur la terre* (1950; tr. A. Hinton, *Strangers in the Land*, 1958); *Grandeur natur* (1936; tr. J. Whitall, *One Minus Two*, 1938); *La neige en deuil* (tr. C. FitzGibbon, *The Mountain*, 1954).

**Tsvetayeva, Marina** (Moscow 1892–Yelabuga 1941). Russian poetess. Her father was a professor of art history, her mother working class; she was a prodigy who began writing at six and published *Vecherniy al'bom* in 1910; it caused a favourable stir. Despite her early admiration for writers like ⇨ Rostand, de Noailles, Bashkirtseva, her verse came straight from her heart, and her heart was remarkably complicated: capricious, violently passionate, half-aristocrat, half-rebel.

She travelled, studied at the Sorbonne, reacted strongly against the Revolution, counting it the work of Satan; her husband (S. Efron) fought throughout the Russian Civil War for the Whites. Much of her copious verse was overtly anti-Bolshevik. In 1922 she was allowed to go abroad. At first she was lionized among Russian émigrés, but her intense individualism made her no more at home in reactionary circles than in the Soviet Union; she never published the anti-Bolshevik collection which she had brought out with her. Fascism in Germany and Czechoslovakia, her poverty, her estrangement from the émigré literary world and family pressures made her return home in 1939. During the German invasion she was evacuated to the remote town of Yelabuga, and, having tragically lost members of her immediate family, she hanged herself.

Remarkable in her literary independence, she developed a compressed lyrical style, which at times is virtually a poetic shorthand. She loves the myth in miniature, abrupt yet incantatory rhythms, the expansive gesture that suddenly recalls an 18th-century ode, the hammer-blows of unrefined passion, a sudden rough colloquialism embedded in lofty or archaic diction. Since the ⇨ Thaw her work has been rediscovered in the U.S.S.R., and she has some influence on the younger poets. [RM-G]

*Izbrannyye proizvedeniya* (1965); Gulland, *SRV*; Obolensky, *PBRV*; Markov, *MRP*.

S. Karlinsky, *Marina Cvetaeva* (Moscow, 1966).

**Tucholsky, Kurt** (Berlin 1890–Hindäs, Sweden 1935). German satirist (and journalist for *Die Schaubühne*, later *Die Weltbühne*) often using pseudonyms – Theobald Tiger, Peter Panter, etc. His brilliant cabaret-style lyrics, full of Berlin wit and slang, attack and mock stuffiness, indifference, injustice, etc. His left-wing political satire is still remembered for its shrewd humour and moral intelligence. He committed suicide. [PB/AKT]

*Gesammelte Werke* (3 vols., 1960–1); sel., e.g. *Gruss nach vorn* (1947); *Zwischen Gestern und Morgen* (1952); *The World is a Comedy*, tr. and ed. H. Zohn (1957).

K. P. Schultz, *K.T.* (Hamburg, 1959); H. Prescher, *K.T.* (Berlin, 1959).

**Tudeboeuf** or **Tudebodus** (fl. *c.* 1100–1118). Medieval chronicler. A priest from Civray, in the diocese of Poitiers, he was of noble family. His *Historia de hierosolymitano itinere* (*c.* 1118) covers the events of the First Crusade from the arrival of the crusaders at Constantinople to the battle of Ascalon in 1099. The relationship between this chronicle and the ⇨ *Gesta Francorum* is still in some doubt. It seems most likely that Tudeboeuf's chronicle is based on the *Gesta*, with original interpolations drawn from his own experiences on crusade, but there are reputable scholars who still hold that the *Gesta* is based on Tudeboeuf. At all events ⇨ William of Tyre, who was careful about his sources, used Tudeboeuf's work. [MRM]

*RHC*, Hist. occ. iii; Migne, *PL*, 155.

**Tulenkantajat** ('The Torchbearers'). A group of Finnish writers in the twenties so named after a literary album, later periodical, published 1924–39. Originally influenced by contemporary Swedo-Finnish writers (Edith Södergran, Hagar Olsson) and by German expressionism, their aim was to lead Finnish literature towards international modes of expression, such as free verse, exotism, machine-romanticism. Leading figures in the group were Uuno ⇨ Kailas, Katri ⇨ Vala, Erkki Vala, Elina ⇨ Vaara, P. ⇨ Mustapää, Lauri ⇨ Viljanen, Ilmari Pimiä, Yrjö Jylhä, Olavi ⇨ Paavolainen and Mika Valtari. [IR]

**Turgenev, Ivan** (Oryol 1818–Bougival, nr Paris 1883). Russian novelist. From a gentry family, dominated in his boyhood by a tyrannical mother, he swore a 'Hannibal's oath' against serfdom and after studying at the universities of Moscow, St Petersburg and Berlin (1838–41), where he was influenced by German Idealism, he returned to Russia an ardent liberal and Westernist. He first became famous as the author of a series of brilliant, sensitive pictures of peasant life, *Zapiski okhotnika* ('A Sportsman's Sketches'), published in Nekrasov's *The Contemporary*, 1847–51 (sep. edn 1852). Though he had also written poetry (*Parasha*, 1843), plays – notably *Myesyats v derevne* (1890; tr. R. Newnham, *A Month in the Country*, 1962) which foreshadowed Chekhov – and short stories about Hamlet-like 'superfluous men' (e.g. *The Diary of a Superfluous Man*, 1850), his greatest work was to be done as a novelist. Exiled to his estate of Spasskoye in 1852 for an obituary on Gogol'. he wrote *Rudin* (1856), *Dvoryanskoye gnezdo* (1859; tr. J. Coulson, *A Nest of Gentlefolk*, 1959), *Nakanune* (1860; tr. C. Gardiner, *On the Eve*, 1950), *Otsy i deti* (1862; tr. A. Pyman, *Fathers and Children*, 1962), but was so disillusioned by the obtuse criticism which greeted this last work that he spent most of the rest of his life abroad, in Baden-Baden (1862–70) and Paris (1871–83), always close to the singer Pauline Viardot, to whom he formed a lifelong attachment. His last novels, *Dym* ('Smoke', 1867) and *Nov'* ('Virgin Soil', 1877), lacked the balance and topicality of his earlier work.

His novels are noted for the poetic 'atmosphere' of their country settings, the contrast between hero and heroine (influenced by the Onegin-Tatyana relationship in Pushkin's *Yevgeny Onegin*) and, above all, for the objective portrayal of heroes representative of stages in the development of the Russian intelligentsia during the period 1840–70. Although Turgenev was a 'man of the forties', believing that Russia should learn from the West, he could be critical of his own generation's Hamlet-like egoism (as in *Rudin*) and appreciative of those who believed that Russia should create her own national ideal (Slavophilism), as he demonstrated in Lavretsky, hero of *A Nest of Gentlefolk*. Though opposed to revolution, he could portray sympathetically the revolutionary aspirations of the younger, radical intelligentsia who became prominent after the Crimean War (1854–5), as he showed in Yelena, heroine of *On the Eve* (which refers to the eve of the emancipation of the serfs in 1861), and in the greatest of his heroes, the nihilist Bazarov, in *Fathers and Children*. He proved less successful as an advocate of European civilization (in *Smoke*), and his attempt in *Virgin Soil* to portray the young Populist revolutionaries of the late 1860s was as lukewarm as it was long-winded.

Remarkable for its balance and stylistic felicity, his finest work was based on contrasts between the types of Hamlet and Don Quixote, love and death, youth and age, coloured by nostalgia and increasingly by a pessimism which proclaimed the futility of human existence. But much of his work has the beauty of great, if miniaturist, art, to be seen especially in such stories as *Asya* (1858), *First Love* (1860; tr. I. Berlin, 1956), *Torrents of Spring* (1872; tr. D. Magarshack, 1959) and his exquisite *Poems in Prose* (1878–82). Awarded an honorary degree by Oxford University (1879), a friend of Flaubert, the Goncourts and Zola, the first Russian writer to enjoy an international reputation, the finest memorial to his art is probably that of his admirer, Henry James, who honoured him with the title of 'beautiful genuis'. [RF]

*Polnoye sobraniye sochineniy i pisem* (1960 ff., 28. vols.); *Works*, tr. C. Garnett (15 vols., 1894–9); *Literary Reminiscences*, tr. D. Magarshack (1958).

H. Granjard, *I.T. et les courants politiques et sociaux de son temps* (Paris, 1954); D. Magarshack, *T.* (1954); A. Yarmolinsky, *T.* (1959); R. Freeborn, *T.: The Novelist's Novelist* (1960).

**Tuwim, Julian** (Łódź 1894–Zakopane 1953). Polish poet. Born of Jewish parents in the industrial town of Łódź, he later lived in Warsaw, spent the war years in America, returning in 1946. Tuwim made his name with his first and probably best book of verse, *Czyhanie na Boga* (1919). Among his later volumes, *Siódma jesień* (1921) and *Treść gorejąca* (1936) are outstanding for their blend of brisk, essentially urban moods and languid lyricism. He had a gift for adaptation and topical travesty, which showed itself in his light verses, cabaret songs and skilful translations from Russian. His language at its best extracts poetic surprise from sudden turns of colloquial idiom and from the naïve charm of doggerel verse which he echoed in his otherwise meandering poem, *Kwiaty polskie* (1949). [JP]

Peterkiewicz and Singer, *FCPP*.

**Tvardovsky, Alexsandr** (Zagor'ye, nr Smolensk 1910– ). Russian poet and editor. Son of a blacksmith, he studied in Smolensk and undertook journalistic work; in 1936 he went to Moscow and continued to study. In the Second World War he was a correspondent at the front. His first poems were in *Put' k sotsializmu* ('Road to Socialism', 1931); but he became famous for his narrative poems, *Strana Muraviya* (1936), which recounts the peasant Morgunok's search for an agricultural Utopia ending in a *kolkhoz*, and *Vasiliy Tyorkin* (1941–5), the experiences of a simple countryman fighting in the war. Subsequently his best-known work has been another long poem *Za dal'yu dal' 1953–60*, 1961), a discursive commentary on Soviet Russia, notable for its treatment of Stalin's era. *Tyorkin na tom svete* (1963), a sequel to his earlier poem, castigates official shortsightedness. As editor of *Novyy mir* he has been an influential liberal in official circles. His poetry has modest value. Its texture is subtler than its superficial simplicity would suggest; the long poems make sensitive use of peasant speech, humour and fantasy. [RM-G]

*Sobraniye sochineniy* (4 vols., 1959); Gulland, *SRV*; Lugovskoy, *ARSP*; Obolensky, *PBRV*. A. M. Turkov, *A.T.* (Moscow, 1960).

**Twardowski, Samuel** (1600–?1661). Polish poet. Born in western Poland, educated at a Jesuit college, he led the life of a country squire. As a young man he accompanied his patron on a diplomatic mission to Constantinople. He vividly described their journey in 'The Most Important Embassy of the Illustrious Prince Zbaraski to Mustafa, the Most Mighty Sultan of the Turkish Empire, in the year 1621' (*Przeważna legacja*, etc. published 1633). Gilded with panegyrical adornments, it is a curious travel book in verse, which anticipates the baroque manner of his pastoral and heroic poetry.

His versified chronicles earned him the reputation of 'the Polish Virgil'. They were concerned with recent history; the first with the reign of Władysław IV, and the second, after the model of Lucan, recorded 'the civil war with the Cossacks, Tartars, Muscovy, then with the Swedes and Hungarians' (*Wojna domowa*, etc., published in full in 1681). Today he is more appreciated for his *Nadobna Pasqualina* (1655), a pastoral romance about a Lisbon lady's rivalry with Venus, which ends in the defeat of the goddess and the suicide of Cupid. The poem, supposedly based on an unknown Spanish source, was an inverted kind of propaganda for divine love. The denunciation of pastoral licence, however, allowed him to dazzle with his sensuous metaphors in a style which contrasts words of Slavonic and Latin origin. Similar features can be found in his pastoral opera *Daphnis* (1638). His work displays the specifically Polish characteristics of baroque. [FP]

Peterkiewicz and Singer, *FCPP*; Oxford Slavonic Papers, VI (1955).

**Tychyna, Pavlo** (Pisky, Chernigov 1891–Kiev 1967). Ukrainian poet. He began writing in 1910; his first collection, *Sonyashni klarnety* (1918), was unanimously acclaimed as the highest poetic achievement of the national revolution period. A symbolist and a pantheist, his Universe is pervaded by the sounds of cosmic music. In *Pluh* and *Zamist' sonetiv i oktav* (1920) the Revolution is a cosmic force, breaking everything, inspiring high hopes and despair. In the post-Revolutionary *Viter z Ukrayiny* (1924), his highest achievement, his faith in the people and his profound humanism blend in supreme harmony. After virtual silence for seven years, he published *Chernihiv* (1931) and *Partiya vede* (1934), since when he geared his poetry to Party requirements. A unique innovator in poetic expression, he was one of the most outstanding Ukrainian poets of this century. [VS]

*Tvory* (6 vols., 1961–2); Andrusyshen and Kirkconnell, *UP*; Ewach, *USL*; Luts'ky, *LD*. Luckyj, *LPSU*; *UCE*.

**Tynni, Aale** (Kolppana, Inkeri 1913– ). Finnish poetess. Her earliest poems, published on the eve of the Finnish Winter War (1939), displayed a serene and disciplined lyricism. In the forties her poetry quickly became more mature and broadened its range. Her verse style is spacious, musical and rhythmically brilliant. Her themes are the eternal themes of womankind, love and motherhood, but side by side with those we find another, that of the 'black riddle'. This is not merely the sinister counterpart of the beautiful in life: it also stands for the imperfection of human nature, the mysterious and fatal flaw in its structure. Her poems thus contain hidden dramatic possibilities. In recent years, too, her 'characters' have undergone a certain enrichment, and there has been an increasingly clear enunciation of her central message – that human life is lived on the brink of an abyss. An invaluable translator, her great work is an anthology of poetry, ranging from A.D. 1000 to the present day, selected from all European literatures, with the original and the translation side by side: *Tuhat laulujen vuotta* (1957). [AK]

*Kootut runot* (1955); Ollilainen, *SF.*

**Tyutchev, Fyodor** (Ovstug, Oryol 1803–Tsarskoye Selo 1873). Russian poet. After leaving Moscow University he worked at the Russian Embassy in Munich (1822–37), where he married into the Bavarian aristocracy and thoroughly absorbed German metaphysical Romanticism (he was a friend of Schelling and also of Heine, whom he translated, in addition to Goethe and Schiller). He spoke perfect French, reserving Russian for his poetry, which expresses an intense awareness of the cosmic reality behind life's outward appearance, an uncanny sympathy with the irrational, chaotic springs of existence, and an idealistic, tragic view of man's predicament. These Nature poems are mostly short, lyrical, pantheistic and mainly philosophical.

After slow progress in his diplomatic career and dismissal for absence without leave, he returned to Russia (1844) and was reinstated in government service. The later poetry mirrors his outward life, as the youthful verse expresses his secret inner world. The three French articles ('La Russie et l'Allemagne', 1844, 'La Russie et la Révolution', 1848, 'La Question Romaine', 1849) and the fiery messianic but inferior political poetry advocate the independence of native Russian culture from Western civilization and the unification of all Slavs; his tragic 'last love', full of 'bliss and hopelessness', produced lyrics of unequalled poignancy; finally, he continued to experience moments of mystical union with Nature, mellowed by deepening pessimism. He is one of the few men to write poetry of genius in his seventh decade. [RCL]

*Lirika*, ed. K. Pigarev (2 vols., 1965); *Versions from F.T.*, tr. C. Tomlinson (1960) (intr. by H. Gifford).

Stremooukhoff, *La poésie et l'idéologie de T.* (1937); Gregg, *F.T.: the Evolution of a Poet* (1965).

**Tzara, Tristan** (Moineste, Rumania 1896–Paris 1963). French poet. He founded the ⇨ Dada movement in Zürich in 1916. He used poetry as a weapon against Western culture which had betrayed itself by its easy acceptance of the First World War. He sought to destroy conventional language by recording words in the arbitrary order of spontaneous thought, ignoring syntax and logical sequence. His *Vingt-cinq poèmes* (1918) prove that out of this nihilism a new, fresh poetry could arise. He settled in Paris in 1920 and collaborated with the Surrealists from 1929 to 1934. In *L'homme approximatif* (1931), the perpetual flux of violent and elemental images suggests the primal disorder of Creation, while his later poems are more austere and controlled (e.g. *Midis gagnés*, 1939). After 1935, anguish at the solitude of the individual led him to turn to revolutionary action as a means of communication between men. [RSS]

R. Lacôte, *T.T.* (Paris, 1952) (with selections).

# U

**Uhland, Ludwig** (Tübingen 1787–Tübingen 1862). German poet. His lyric poetry, above all his ballads, catches with remarkable faithfulness the tone of popular poetry; his 'Guter Kamerad' and 'Der Wirtin Töchterlein' have become folk-songs alongside Heine's 'Lorelei'. He gave much of his energy to political activity, the climax of which was the famous 'Kaiserrede' delivered in the German National Assembly of 1848, of which he remained a member until its dissolution. [RT]

*Dichtungen, Briefe, Reden*, ed. W. Scheffler (1963).

**Ujević, Augustin** (Vrgovac 1891–Zagreb 1953). Croatian poet. He lived in Paris 1913–19 and in 1920 published his first volume of poetry, *Lelek sebra.* A freelance writer and journalist, he lived for art through which he sought an answer to the tragedy of modern man, without faith in life and disillusioned with all ideals. His deeply original talent explored new modes of poetic expression, portraying the individual confronted with naked existence, often coming close to a Buddhist view of life. His output of poetry, essays and translations was very extensive. [EDG]

*Odabrane pesme* (1956); Ibrovac, *APY*; Lavrin, *AMYP*.
Kadić, *CCL*.

**Ukrainian Literature.** The literature of Kievan Rus' of the 11th–13th centuries, ranging through various genres from the *Ostromir Gospel* (1056–7) to the unique heroic epic *Tale of the Armament of* ⇨ *Igor* (*c*.1187), inaugurates Ukrainian literature. Kiev, destroyed by the Mongol Horde in 1240, was incorporated in the 14th century into the Lithuanian-Polish state, and the literary tradition continued chiefly through the copying and supplementing of old writings; the *Galician-Volynian Chronicle* (1201–92) is noteworthy. In the 16th century several new translations of the Gospels into contemporary Ukrainian were produced under Protestant influence. The Orthodox-Catholic religious struggle of the 16th–17th centuries produced a rich polemical literature, the outstanding figures of which were Ivan Vyshens'ky (*c*.1550–1625) and, later, F. Prokopovych (1681–1736) and S. Yavors'ky (1658–1722). The late 16th century saw the beginning of poetry in syllabic verse form (e.g. I. Mazeppa's songs, early 18th century). Drama and comedy appeared in the early 17th century. In the historiographic genre, the so-called Cossack chronicles of the early 18th century are prominent.

The 1654 treaty of union between B. Khmel'nyts'ky's Cossack Hetman state and Moscow, which was the outcome of Ukrainian efforts to be free of the increasingly oppressive Polish overlordship, led during the following century to a gradual extinction of Ukrainian independence. Many intellectuals were transferred to Russia; the use of Ukrainian was discouraged, and in 1720 Peter I banned by decree all ecclesiastical printing in this language. (This ban still operates today.) Many writers adopted Russian, among them the famous peripatetic philosopher and poet H. Skovoroda (1722–94) and the anonymous author of *Istoriya rusov* (early 19th century), a patriotic fiction in chronicle form which influenced the works of ⇨ Shevchenko, P. ⇨ Kulish, Kostomarov, ⇨ Gogol', ⇨ Pushkin, Ryleyev. With I. ⇨ Kotlyarevs'ky's *Eneyida* (1798), Ukrainian literature is restored to its own language. Other writers followed suit, notably the fabulists P. Hulak-Artemovs'ky (1790–1865) and Ye. Hrebinka (1812–48) who also wrote prose in Russian, the prose-writer H. ⇨ Osnov''yanenko, and others. The Romantic cultural revival of the Western Ukraine, then under Austria, began with *Rusalka dnistrovaya* (1837); ed. M. Shashkevych, (1811–43, *et al*). The unsurpassed poetry of ⇨ Shevchenko came in 1840 as the pinnacle of the Romantic movement. whose social ideas found expression in the Brotherhood of Cyril and Methodius; its programme was written by M. Kostomarov (1817–85). Another of its members, P. Kulish, also deeply influenced the Ukrainian spiritual tradition. Both Romantic and realist, Marko ⇨

Vovchok started a new trend. In Bucovina, Y. Fed'kovych (1834–88) followed her example in prose, while his poetry was influenced by the German Romantics. The versatile S. Rudans'ky (1834–73), whose folk humour in *Spivomovky* (1857–8) is inimitable, the fabulist and elegist L. Hlibov (1827–93), and Ya. Shchoholiv (1824–98) were the chief Romantic realists in poetry.

The laws of 1876 and 1881, heavily restricting Ukrainian publishing in Russia and repealed only in 1905, hindered the development of realistic prose of this period: many works appeared either only abroad or after long delay. Prominence was attained by I. ⇨ Nechuy, P. Rudchenko (pseud. Myrny) (1849–1920), B.Hrinchenko (1863–1910), who was also a poet and the author of the celebrated dictionary, and especially I. ⇨ Franko. P. Hrabovs'ky (1864–1902) was another notable realist poet. Important in drama, uniting ethnographic Romanticism with realism, were M. Staryts'ky (1840–1904), M. Kropyvnyts'ky (1840–1910), I. Tobilevych (pseud. Karpenko-Kary) (1845–1907).

The period of modernism is highlighted in prose by ⇨ Kotsyubyns'ky, ⇨ Stefanyk, ⇨ Kobylyans'ka, ⇨ Vynnychenko; others of note were I. Semanyuk (pseud. M. Cheremshyna (1874–1927), L. Martovych (1871–1916), S. Panasenko (pseud. Vasyl'-chenko) (1878–1932), A. Teslenko (1882–1911), and B. Lepky (1872–1941) who wrote a tetralogy *Mazepa* (1926–9) and also poetry. ⇨ Ukrainka and ⇨ Oles' excelled in poetry; V. Samiylenko (1864–1925), P. Karmans'ky (1878–1956), M. Vorony (1871–1942), H. Chuprynka (1879–1921), and M. Chernyavs'ky (1867–1937) were also of note.

The 1917 fall of Tsarism and the Revolution freed the forces of Ukrainian national and cultural revival, and a vigorous literary life centred in many writers' organizations. P. ⇨ Tychyna was the greatest of the symbolists, while M. Semenko (1892–1939) was the prolific futurist leader. The neoclassicists, drawing inspiration from world literature, showed a most cultural attainment: ⇨ Ryl's'ky, M. Dray-Khmara (1889–1938), Mykola Zerov (1890–1941), P. Fylypovych (1891–1937), O. Burghardt (pseud. Yu. Klen) (1891–1947). The Vaplite organization (1925–8), led by ⇨ Khvyl'ovy, played a remarkable role. Other important prose writers were: the Impressionists, H. Kosynka (1899–1934), M. Ivchenko (1890–1939), A. Holovko (1897); the Romantics: Yu. Yanovs'ky (1902–54), A. Lyubchenko (1899–1945); the Expressionists: V. Pidmohyl'ny (1901–42) and I. Senchenko (1901); the humorist, O. ⇨ Vyshnya; the parodist, K. Bureviy (pseud. E. Strikha) (1888–1934). Other poets of note were ⇨ Bazhan, ⇨ Sosyura, M. Yohansen (1895–1937), O. Vlyz'ko (1908–34), Ye. Pluzhnyk (1898–1936), V. Svidzins'ky (1885–1941) and T. Os'machka (1895–1962). The outstanding dramatist was M. ⇨ Kulish.

This period ended in the 1933–8 deportations and extermination of over 100 writers; many others abandoned literature. Those that remained followed socialist realism methods, mostly eulogizing Stalin and the Soviet way of life. During the Second World War, Soviet Ukrainian writers joined in the war effort, and Ukrainian patriotism was not discouraged until 1946–51, when many writers were accused of nationalism or 'cosmopolitanism'. The post-1956 ⇨ Thaw started a gradual and half-hearted posthumous rehabilitation of some of the exterminated writers, and a few surviving deportees returned. The chief prose writers were: ⇨ Honchar, N. Rybak (1913), O. Dovzhenko (1894–1956), who was also a famous script-writer and film director, D. Drob"yazko (pseud. I. Wilde) (1907), M. Stel'makh (1912), V. Sobko (1912) and I. Gurevich (pseud. L. Pervomays'ky, 1908) who was also an eminent poet. Other notable poets include: A. Malyshko (1912), P. Voron'ko (1913) and I. Muratov (1912) who also writes prose. In drama, ⇨ Korniychuk was dominant. I. Kocherha's (1885–1952) philosophical plays stand apart.

After 1956, and particularly in 1961–2, new trends and young writers of great originality and promise appeared, including poets L. Kostenko (1930), M.Vinhranovs'ky (1936), I. Drach (1936), V. Korotych (1937), Ye. Hutsalo (1937), who also writes prose, and V. Symonenko (1935–63).

A number of writers were active outside the Soviet Ukraine. In the Western Ukraine, under Poland till 1939, there were the poets, Ye. Malanyuk (1897), S. Hordyns'ky (1906), Y. Lypa (1900–44), who also wrote prose, and O. Teliha (1907–42); and the prose writers, V. Karkhut (1905), Yu. Kosach (1909) and Ya. Galan (1902–49). Outside the Ukraine there were I. Bahryany (1907–63), I. Kyriak (1888–1955), V. Petrov (pseud. Domontovych) (1893–?), and the poets, Mykhaylo Zerov (pseud Orest) (1901–63). Ya. Slavutych (1918), V. Barka (1908), E. Andiyevs'ka (1931). [VS]

*Ukrayins'ki pys'mennyky. Bio-bibliogr. slovnyk* (5 vols., 1960–65); *Khudozhnya lit., vydana na Ukrayini za 40 r.* (1958); *Khrestomatiya davn'-oyi ukr. lit.* (1952); *Antologiya ukr. opovi-dannya* (4 vols., 1960); *Antologiya ukr. poeziyi* (4 vols., 1957); *Rozstrilyane vidrodzhennya, Antologiya 1917–1933*, ed. Yu. Lavrinenko (Paris, 1959); F. Livesay, *Songs of Ukraina* (London, 1916); R. N. Bain, *Cossack Fairy Tales* (London, 1916); H. Kowalsky, *Ukrainian Folk Songs* (Boston, Mass., 1925); Meillet, *ALU*; Andrusyshen and Kirkconnell, *UP*; Ewach, *USL*; Luts'ky, *LD*.

Luckyj, *LPSU*; *UQ*, x, 4 (1954); *UR*, II, 4, and III, 2/4 (1955–6); Manning, *UL*.

**Ukrainka, Lesya,** pseud. of Larysa Kosach (Novograd Volynskiy 1871–Surami, Georgia 1913). Ukrainian poetess. She began with lyric verse (*Na krylakh pisen'*, 1892, *Dumy i mriyi*, 1899, *Vidhuky*, 1902) where traditional patriotic *motifs*, evoking powerful revolutionary feelings, are enriched by themes and characters from world history and literature: the ancient Hebrews, Egypt, Rome; Sappho, Mary Stuart, etc. Her narrative poems, *Robert Bruce*, the Heinean *Davnya kazka* (1893), etc., led to her highest achievement, a series of dramatic poems in Biblical and historical settings, e.g. *U pushchi* (1909; cf. *CL*, viii, 2, 1956), *Cassandra* (1907), and *Kaminny hospodar* (1912), where the Don Juan theme is given an entirely new slant (cf. *MLQ*, xvi, 1, 1955). *Boyarynya* (1910), a psychological drama, has, exceptionally, a 17th-century Ukrainian and Russian setting, while *Lisova pisnya* (1911), her masterpiece, is based on the treasures of Ukrainian folklore. Among her chief themes are: the poet's duty in society, single-mindedness of spirit striving towards personal, social and national freedom, and universal psychological problems. She is one of the greatest representatives of Ukrainian modernism, and is of European stature. [VS]

*Tvory* (12 vols., 1927–30; 10 vols., 1963–5); *Spirit of Flame. A Collection*, tr. and intr. P. Cundy (N.Y., 1950); Andrusyshen and Kirkconnell, *UP*; Ewach, *USL*.

Manning, *UL*; *UCE*; *AUAU*, 1, 2 (1951); *UQ*, II, 3 (1946); III, 2 (1947); *UR*, III, 2 (1956); x, 3 (1963).

**Ulrich von Lichtenstein** (*c.*1200–1275). Austrian poet. Of noble birth, he was one of the last to subscribe to the ideals of chivalric society. In his *Frauendienst* (ed. R. Bechenstein, 1888), a verse romance interspersed with lyric poems, he paints a romantic and highly unrealistic picture of himself as the servant of Courtly Love, a nobleman devoted to all the affectations associated with this idealization of human passion. His aristocratic attitudes stand in strong contrast to the prevailing satirical and anti-*Minne* tendencies of his time. [RT]

R. Becker, *Wahrheit und Dichtung in U. von L. Frauendienst* (Halle, 1888).

**Ulrich von Winterstetten** (fl. mid 13th cent.). German Minnesinger. A member of a Swabian family of *ministeriales*. The majority of his lyric poems lie within the framework of conventional Minnesang, but he has also left a number of poems in which the values of courtly love are mocked at, and in which the influence of ⇨ Neidhart von Reuental and ⇨ Gottfried von Neifen is felt. He also composed five *Leiche* (longer lyric poems made up of a number of unequal sections) in the manner of ⇨ Tannhaüser. [RT]

Poems and commentary in Kraus, *DL*.

**Unamuno, Miguel de** (Bilbao 1864–Salamanca 1936). Spanish essayist, novelist and poet. Professor of Greek Language and Literature (1891), later Rector, of Salamanca University. Early interested in German philosophy, he translated Hegel's *Logic*; he also studied Spencer and the positivists and read Carlyle and romantic poets including ⇨ Leopardi, Wordsworth and Coleridge. His earlier works show Hegelian patterns of thesis and antithesis resolved into synthesis, e.g. the essays of *En torno al casticismo* (1895) and in the first novel *Paz en la guerra* (1897). At the turn of the century, after a religious crisis, signs of which were apparent in youthful positivist attempts to rationalize his faith, he discovered three other thinkers whose ideas he made his own: Bergson, ⇨ Kierkegaard (of whom he learnt through reading criticisms of Ibsen's *Brand*), and William James. In all of these the conflict between Faith and Reason (Intuition and Reason in the case of Bergson) was fundamental. He expresses this conflict himself in *Amor y pedagogía* (1902), where the scientific and logical view of life is seen as sterile; an anti-rationalist view is adopted in his eulogy of Don Quixote in *Vida de Don Quijote y Sancho* (1905; tr. H. P. Earle, *The Life of Don*

*Quixote*, 1927); his best-known work, *Del sentimiento trágico de la vida* (1913; tr. P. Smith, *The Tragic Sense of Life*, 1958), finally resolves the conflict in terms of doubt: uncertainty is seen as a source of strength and the only possible position from which to face existence. A related problem at this period is Free Will: does man exist independently of his Creator, and is he capable of original action? Unamuno worked out this problem in literary terms in the novel and the drama. The author is equated with the Creator, the characters with human beings, in novels like *Niebla* (1914; tr. W. Fite, *Mist*, 1928) and plays like *El hermano Juan* (1934). Unamuno's concern was nearly always with problems not of thought but of existence, affecting real issues in society as well as the individual (his political attitudes tended to be as provocative as much of his literary work and he was twice exiled). He chose styles and forms of expressions which provoked original thought in the reader, and, by extension, independent action. But there is also a side of his work in which tranquillity predominates, notably in his poems and in his descriptions of the Spanish countryside. [ONVG]

*Obras completas*, ed. M. García Blanco (16 vols., 1958); *Cancionero. Diario poético* (1953); *Teatro. Fedra. Soledad. . . .* (1954); *Essays and Soliloquies*, tr. J. E. C. Flitch (1925).

Arturo Barea, *U.* (1952); J. F. Mora, *U. A Philosophy of Tragedy* (1962).

**Undset, Sigrid** (Kalundborg, Denmark 1882–Oslo 1949). Norwegian novelist. The daughter of a well-known archaeologist, she worked in an office for a number of years, but published her first book in 1907. Much of her early experience went into the novel *Jenny* (1911; tr. W. Emme, 1921), a penetrating study of the life, loves and tragedy of an artistically gifted young woman, which was her first success. She achieved world fame with her historical trilogy *Kristin Lavransdatter* (1920–2; tr. C. Archer and J. S. Scott, 1930), a massive work, set in 14th-century Norway, and remarkable for its historical verisimilitude, firm characterization and tenacity of purpose. The series *Olav Audunssøn* (1925–7; tr. A. G. Chater, *The Master of Hestviken*, 1928–30) is less convincing. Subsequently she wrote a number of novels with contemporary settings, all marked by her conversion to Roman Catholicism in 1924: *Gymnadenia* (1929; tr. A. G. Chater, *The Wild Orchid*, 1931); *Den brændende busk* (1930; tr. A. G. Chater, *The Burning Bush*, 1932); *Ida Elisabeth* (1932; tr. A. G. Chater, 1933); *Den trofaste hustru* (1936; tr. A. G. Chater, *The Faithful Wife*, 1937). In these books she is occupied with moral and religious problems, particularly as they affect women. Taken individually, many of her novels seem overloaded with detail, monotonous, and lacking in ultimate significance, but in sum they form an impressive and meaningful achievement. She also published some volumes of essays, including *Etapper* (1929; tr. A. G. Chater, *Stages on the Road*, 1934), and lives of the Norwegian saints, *Norske helgener* (1937; tr. E. C. Ramsden. *Saga of Saints*, 1934). *Elleve aar* (1934; tr. A. G. Chater, *The Longest Years*, 1935) is largely autobiographical. [RGP]

*Middelalder-Romaner* (10 vols., 1949); *Romaner og fortellinger fra nutiden* (10 vols., 1949).

N. R. Anker, *Minn venn S.U.* (1946); A. H. Winsnes, *S.U., A Study in Christian Realism* (1953) (tr. from Norwegian); E. Steen, *Kristin Lavransdatter* (1959); Gustafson, *SSN*; N. Deschamps, *S.U. ou la morale de la passion* (Montreal, 1966).

**Ungaretti, Giuseppe** (Alexandria 1888–1970). Italian poet and translator. Professor of Italian Literature in São Paulo, Brazil (1936), and in Rome (1942). A friend of Apollinaire during student days at Paris, he was influenced by the work of Mallarmé and Valéry to concentrate on form and language, the primitive, evocative, indeed religious power within each word, which could be rediscovered only by purging poetry of rhetoric and sentimentality. As a volunteer, the war intensified his sense of a revolution, 'which necessarily had to start from the use of words', in man's self-awareness in the face of death; and in his war poems, *L'allegria* (1919), each with its given place and date, the word does seem to have 'stopped at every cadence of the rhythm, at every beating of the heart, isolating itself moment after moment in its truth'. Ungaretti's lead was followed by the post-war 'hermetic' movement and when his *Sentimento del tempo* appeared (1933) he could claim 'I have done everything for the new Italian poetry.' Though criticized for obscurity and aestheticism, at its best his language commands the dignity of a hard-won truth: 'When I find in this silence of mine / a word / carved, it is in my life / like an abyss'. For Ungaretti language is the real fabric of civilization, threatened now by 'a mad disintegration of words'.

In his later volumes, *La terra promessa* (1950) and *Un grido e paesaggi* (1952), critics have found him guilty of a kind of 'antirhetorical rhetoric' in the use of devices which seem to point to an impoverishment of sentimental and poetic themes. A. Mondadori edited Ungaretti's poems as *Vita d'un uomo* (Milan, 1947ff.; tr. A. Mandelbaum, *Life of a Man*, 1958). [GD]

*Vita d'un uomo* (*Poesie*, 6 vols.; *Traduzioni*, 3 vols.; *Prosadi viaggio e saggi*, 1 vol.) (Milan, 1947f.); Golino, *CIP*.

Antonielli, *AFN*; Bàrberi Squarotti, *AR*; Bigongiari, *PIN*; Pancrazi, *SO*; Gargiulo, *LIN*; Pasolini, *PI*.

**Unruh, Fritz von** (Koblenz 1885– ). German dramatist, officer and aristocrat. He resembles H. ⇨ Kleist in his concern with duty and noble insubordination in *Offiziere* (1912), *Louis Ferdinand Prinz von Preussen* (1913). His experience of the First World War made the ethics of honour and patriotism seem irrelevant (cf. the visionary poem *Vor der Entscheidung*, 1914; the war narrative written at Verdun, *Opfergang*, 1916, publ. 1918; tr. C. A. Macartney, *The Way of Sacrifice*, 1928). *Ein Geschlecht* (1917), a tragic drama in one act, is a statuesque masterpiece, achieving moments of Antique passion by its rhetoric and expressionist setting: the mother and her children on a hill-top cemetery. She stands against the inhuman soldiery and is martyred; but her youngest son preaches her message, rousing the soldiers to rebellion. *Platz* (1920) continues the struggle of Dietrich (the son) against authoritarian principle and base expediency (and under different names in *Rosengarten*, 1921; *Stürme*, 1922; *Heinrich von Andernach*, 1925; *Phaea*, 1930); but the pacifist idealism of these works, as of historical plays like *Bonaparte* (1927; tr. E. Bjorkman, 1929) or *Bismarck* (1955), lacks power. After 1932 in exile in France, then U.S.A., he unsuccessfully tried to re-establish himself in Germany after the war. Also translated: *The End Is Not Yet* (1947) and *The Saint* (N.Y., 1950). *Der Sohn des Generals* (1957) is autobiography. [PB/AKT]

*Die Dramen* (1960).

A. Kronacher, *F. v. U.* (N.Y., 1946); F. Rasche (ed.), *F. v. U. Rebell und Verkünder* (Hanover, 1965); Natan, *GML*, iii.

**Uppdal, Kristofer** (Beitstad, N. Trøndelag 1878–Olbu, S. Trøndelag 1961). Norwegian novelist and poet. He had various occupations and worked as an itinerant navvy ('*rallar*'). His most important work, the cycle of novels *Dansen gjenom skuggeheimen* (10 vols., 1911–24), depicting the emergence of an industrial proletariat in Norway, is epic in conception and vividly realized. He was more concerned with the psychology of social change than its political aspects. Of his verse, *Altarelden* (1920) is especially fine, and in the massive but obscure *Kulten* (3 vols., 1947) he enunciates, using a *rallar* as mouthpiece, a religious-philosophical system involving eternal recurrence. [RGP]

J. Pedersen, *K.U.* (Copenhagen, 1949); O. Solumsmoen, *K.U.* (Oslo, 1959).

**Urban, Milo** (Rabčica 1904– ). Slovak novelist. The author of a series of novels depicting modern Slovak society, the most successful being the first, *Živý bič* (1927), about life in a northern Slovak village during the First World War. During the period of the independent Slovak state (1939–45) he was a leading journalist in the service of the Fascist regime. His first novel after the Second World War surveys the events of 1938–9 from the point of view of Communism (*Zhasnuté svetlá*, 1958). [RA]

*Dejiny slovenskej literatúry* (Bratislava, 1960).

**Uspensky, Gleb Ivanovich** (Tula 1843–Novoznamenskoye 1902). Russian writer. Uspensky published his first story in 1862 and wrote prolifically during the following thirty years until the onset of mental and physical illness in 1892. He was the most influential of Russian Populist writers, though his concern with problems of the day is not so easily shared by readers of a later age. Much of his work is in the form of documentary sketches (*ocherki*), based on a close study of the life of the lower classes. The sketches are often lightly fictionalized in order to gain the reader's attention and to avoid clashes with the censor. Uspensky makes effective use of dialogue and monologue to enliven his narrative, the pedestrian character of which is due in part, at least, to the writer's reluctance to make anything but an immediate and straightforward report on situations that moved and appalled him.

Uspensky is remembered particularly for his defence of the peasant in such series of sketches as *Krest'yanin i krest'yanskiy trud* ('The Peasant and Peasant Labour', 1880) and *Vlast' zemli* ('The Power of the Earth', 1882). Unlike some of his fellow Populists, Uspensky was wary of idealizing the peasant's world, the decay of which he feared and recorded. [SH]

*Polnoye sobraniye sochineniy* (14 vols., 1940–54).
V. V. Bush, *Literaturnaya deyatel'nost' Gl. U. (Ocherki)* (?Moscow, 1927); J. Lothe, *G.I.U. et le Populisme russe* (Leiden, 1963).

**Usteri, J. M.** ⇨ Swiss-German Dialect Literature.

**Uz, Johann Peter** (Ansbach 1720–Ansbach 1796). German poet. A friend of ⇨ Gleim and ⇨ Götz from his student days in Leipzig, he collaborated with the latter in a translation of Anacreon (1746). In his original verse (*Lyrische Gedichte*, 1749) he sings the praises of friendship, love and wine in true anacreontic fashion, but is also capable of a deeper, more sincere note; his *An die Freude*, for instance, earned him the admiration of Schiller. The didactic poem, *Versuch über die Kunst, stets fröhlich zu sein* (1760), is touched by the spirit of the Enlightenment in its rationalistic regard for middle-class virtue and its declaration that permanent happiness is dependent on the possession of wisdom. [WAC]

*Sämtliche poetische Werke*, ed. A. Sauer (1964)

# V

**Vaara, Elina** (Tampere 1903– ). Finnish poet and translator. A member of ⇨ Tulenkantajat, she published a number of volumes of smoothly flowing poems, traditional in form and often legendary or exotic in theme. Her translations are of outstanding merit and represent her finest work: they include a selection of Swedish lyric poetry, selected poems by ⇨ Hölderlin, ⇨ Tasso's *Gerusalemme liberata*, the *Oresteia* of Aeschylus and Dante's *Divine Comedy*. [RV]

*Valitut runot* (1959) (selected poems); Ollilainen, *SF*.

**Vailland, Roger** (Paris 1907–1965). French novelist. A *Normalien* who had moved in surrealist circles and who had travelled widely as a journalist before the war, he came to the fore with *Drôle de jeu* (1945; tr. G. Hopkins, *Playing with Fire*, 1948). If this detached, ironical story of the Resistance did not immediately suggest that its author had himself been a militant and was to join the Communist Party in 1952, the hero, Marat, already indicates the central tension in Vailland: the conflict between an aristocratic individualism leaning towards hedonism and eroticism, and an aristocratic generosity open to the call of moral commitment and solidarity. The denial of Don Juanism in *Les mauvais coups* (1948) led to the more committed period of the early and mid fifties, although a novel such as *Beau masque* (1954) suffers from this self-imposed discipline, while even the striking *325,000 francs* (1955) betrays some self-consciousness. It is perhaps in the freer *La loi* (1957; tr. P. Wiles, *The Law*, 1958) and *La fête* (1960; tr. P. Wiles, *The Sovereigns*, 1960) that Vailland – who had now drawn away from the Communist Party – is most authentically himself. At his best, he was a lucid and a classically elegant writer, having a certain affinity with ⇨ Laclos (cf. Vailland's *Laclos par lui-même*, 1953). He has also written plays, the anti-religious *Héloïse et Abélard* (1947) and the anti-American *Le Colonel Foster plaidera coupable* (1952). [CJ]

**Vajanský, Svetozár Hurban** (Hlboké 1847–Turčiansky Sv. Martin 1916). Slovak poet and novelist. Founder of the modern Slovak novel. A staunch fighter for the rights of the Slovak people oppressed by the Magyars in the Austro-Hungarian Empire, he was several times imprisoned by the Hungarian authorities. In his best novels, *Letiace tiene* (1883) and *Suchá ratolest'* (1884), he depicts, in an idealizing fashion, contemporary Slovak life; in *Kotlín* (1901) he warns against progressive literary and philosophical ideas penetrating Slovak youth from Prague. He held the Slavonic East to be the only pure and vital force in Europe and opposed the influence of the morally corrupt and decadent West, believing in the messianic and liberating mission of Russia. [KB]

R. W. Seton-Watson, *Slovak Peasant Art* (1911). A. Mráz, *Na sté výročie narodenia S.H.-V.* (Bratislava, 1947).

**Vajda, János** (Pest 1827–Budapest 1899). Hungarian poet. He is the greatest Hungarian lyrical poet of the late 19th century. He was a friend of ⇨ Petöfi, ⇨ Jókai and other outstanding literary figures. Son of a forester, he spent his early youth in the country, became an actor and later a journalist. He was editor of, and contributed to, several literary papers. As a poet he gained little recognition before his death. This perhaps contributed to the pessimistic self-tormenting attitude reflected in poems such as *Az Üstökös* (*The Comet*) and *A Váli Erdőben* (*In the Forest of Vál*) (both tr. W. Kirkconnell, in *The Magyar Muse*, Winnipeg, 1933); others express his philosophical problems regarding existence and death ('Végtelenség', 'Vége van'). His suffering is also present in his love-poems, inspired by a lifelong unrequited love for 'Gina' (*Húsz év mulva*, 1876; *Harminc év mulva*, 1892). His love is a sensual, physical passion, at that time an entirely new concept in Hungarian poetry. He also wrote political poems, epics and novels. [JFR]

Reményi, *HWL*.

**Vala, Katri,** pseud. of Karin Alice Wadenström (Muonio 1901–Stockholm 1944). Finnish poet. The daughter of a forester, she trained as a primary school teacher. She rapidly became the leading female member of ⇨ Tulenkantajat group of poets. In their sensualism and ardent longing, her free-verse stanzas recall ⇨ Södergran; but the use of exotic imagery and of Tahitian and Ethiopian motifs reflect the current fashion for decorative verse. In the thirties her political views became more pronounced and she was regarded as one of the leading poets of the left wing; more important than her radical views, however, was her development of free verse techniques. [RV]

*Kootut runot* (1945) (collected poems); *Valikoima runoja* (1958) (selected poems); Allwood, *TCSP*; Ollilainen, *SF*; Tompuri, *VF*.

**Valaoritis, Aristotelis** (Lefkas 1824–Lefkas 1879). Greek poet. Educated in Italy, Switzerland and France, he represented his island in the Constituent Assembly of the Ionian Islands then under British protection and he joined nationalist agitations for their union with Greece. After their cession to Greece in 1864 he was repeatedly elected to the Greek Parliament. He left politics disillusioned and retired to his native island devoting himself entirely to literature. Apart from two main collections of verse, *Stihourghimata* (1847) and *Mnemosyna* (1857), containing pieces in moods of melancholy and self-indulgent pessimism, elegies and folk-style heroic ballads, he wrote three long and ambitious narrative poems: the *Athanasis Diakos*, inspired by the self-sacrifice of a hero of the Greek War of Independence; the *Kyra Frosyni*, dealing with the tragic story of a Greek woman with whom Ali Pasha of Yannina fell in love; and the *Foteinos*, his best but unfinished poem having as theme the heroic stand of a Greek against a Latin ruler of Frankish-occupied Lefkas. All three are characteristic of Valaoritis's style – romantic and Byronic in their treatment of heroes and resounding with patriotic ideas. He was much influenced by ⇨ Hugo, and he based his style and diction on that of the heroic Greek folk ballads, thereby succeeding in catching the ear of the public at a time when most poets of the newly established Greek kingdom wrote in a frigid archaic style. He exerted no small influence on the young poets of the 1880s, especially on ⇨ Palamas, who looked for a literature with national roots. [SJP]

*Vios Kai Ergha* (3 vols., 1907); *Poèmes patriotiques*, Fr. tr. J. Blancard (Paris, 1883).

**Valaoritis, Nanos** (Lausanne 1921– ). Greek poet. Great-grandson of the above. He received his secondary education in Athens and studied law at the university. Towards the end of the Second World War he left German-occupied Greece clandestinely and came to London, where he lived for several years. He settled subsequently in Paris for a time, and now lives in Athens. He has published two volumes of verse, *I Timoria Ton Magon* ('The Punishment of the Magi', London, 1947) and *Kentriki Stoa* ('Central Stoa', 1958), both of which contain pieces in a variety of metres and free-verse rhythms as well as prose poems. He has also written poetry in French and English, plays, translations, articles and reviews in various Greek and European literary magazines. In collaboration with Bernard Spencer and Lawrence Durrell he was responsible for a volume of translations of ⇨ Seferis's poetry into English, which was the first serious introduction of this poet to the English public. He is also responsible for the avant-garde magazine *Pali*, published in Athens since 1964. A post-surrealist poet and influenced to some extent by beat writing, Valaoritis is endowed with a distinctly Greek sensibility which is often expressed through visual imagery and allusions to myth and history. He is uncomfortably sensitive to messages of fear and evil latent in the correspondences of things and situations. His intimate tone and occasional flippancy often conceal a protest or the poet's deep concern for the human condition. [SJP]

**Valdés, Juan de** (Cuenca 1490?–Naples 1541). Spanish humanist, religious writer and critic. Educated at Alcalá, he knew Latin, Greek and Hebrew, and was an Erasmist with unorthodox religious views which led him to go to Rome (1531). He then went to Naples where he formed a group of religious reformers of like ideas. His *Diálogo de la doctrina cristiana* (1529) sets out his main theological ideas, these being summarized later in the *Ciento y diez consideraciones divinas* (1539). He also translated the Psalms. His *Diálogo de la lengua* (in manuscript, 1535; publ. 1737; ed. J. F. Montesinos, CC, 1928; F. F. Corso, 1940) is his major literary work with its discussion of the origins of modern Spanish, its treatment of vocabulary and style, orthography, etc. Valdés hated affected language and advocated writing as one spoke. He makes use of proverbs, favours the traditional ballad and works like ⇨ *Amadís de Gaula* and *La* ⇨ *Celestina*, but attacks the falsity of contemporary novels of chivalry. His views are eminently reasonable and reflect the good taste of a well-educated gentleman of the period. [JG]

D. Ricart, *J. de V. y el pensamiento religioso europeo en los siglos xvi y xvii* (Mexico, 1958).
Bataillon, *EE*.

**Valdivielso, José de** (Toledo 1560–Madrid 1638). Spanish poet and dramatist. Chaplain to the archbishop of Toledo. His *Romancero espiritual . . . del Santisímo Sacramento* contains *villancicos* (carols) in which sacred themes are treated in the metres, and with the child-like directness, of popular songs. Drums are beaten and trumpets sounded in Bethlehem for the Nativity, as for a village *fiesta*; the angels who attend the Virgin are white swans. His puns at times come near to burlesque; in one *romance* Christ on the cross is presented as the May King. The pious charm of this baroque folk poetry is far more sophisticated than it appears, and ⇨ Lorca borrowed some startling images from him. His *autos* contain lyrics of this same kind, some of them are renderings 'a lo divino' of secular themes. His longer poems in hendecasyllables are hybrids with occasional pleasing passages. [JMC]

*Romancero* (Madrid, 1880); *Autos*, BAE, 58; *Vida de San José*, BAE, 29; Blecua, *FLE*; Cohen, *PBSV*; Trend, *OBSV*.
B. W. Wardropper, *Introducción al teatro religioso de la edad de oro, 1500–1648* (Madrid, 1953).

**Valente, José Ángel** (Orense 1929– ). Spanish poet. He aims at 'the maximum of expression with the minimum of verbal construction'. The poems of *A modo de esperanza* (1955) are 'built upon actual facts', or incidents, a farewell or a meeting, the memory of someone long dead, the thought of a person whose identity escapes him, the search for reality. The poetry is stripped to its essentials: the confrontation with death and solitude, and there are strong political undertones throughout. *Poemas a Lázaro* (1960) moves towards symbolism, but is more open in its call for intellectual liberty; its range is wider, and its treatments more meditative and profound. His most characteristic poetry is urban, sparing of metaphor and elaboration, and very deeply felt. With Ángel ⇨ González and others of the Barcelona group he has been identified with a new socialist realism, but he has no programme. After spending some years in Oxford, he now lives in Geneva. [JMC]

Cohen, *PBSV*.
Cano, *PESV*.

**Valera, Cipriano de** (Seville 1532?–? after 1602). Spanish translator. He was a monk who turned Protestant and came to England, where he printed his translation of the New Testament, *El Nuevo Testamento* (1596), which is a revision of Casiodoro's Basle translation of 1569. It is the standard Protestant version and stylistically very pleasing. He was an abusive controversialist and translated Calvin. [JMC]

M. Menéndez y Pelayo, *Historia de los heterodoxos españoles*, 2nd edn, vol. v (Madrid, 1911–32).

**Valera, Juan** (Cabra, Cordova 1824–Madrid 1905). Spanish novelist. He took degrees in Jurisprudence at Granada and Madrid (1841–6). Poems written in his teens had won the approval of the great ⇨ Espronceda, and in 1844 his father financed the publication of a volume of poems, but Valera withdrew the whole edition when he learned that it was not selling. Friendship with the Duque de Rivas led to an unpaid post in the diplomatic service at Naples where Rivas was ambassador, and to posts in Rio de Janeiro and Petersburg (1847–57). Amorous entanglements (sometimes more platonic than he wished) filled his letters at the time and subsequently contributed useful raw material to his novels. His first abortive attempt at novel-writing was certainly autobiographical (*Cartas de un pretendiente*, 1849), and *Mariquita y Antonio* (1861) contains the text of one of his own letters and much other material germain to his affair with Magdalena Brohan in Petersburg. But he was in principle opposed to the use of real-life material in literature as is particularly evident from his articles attacking the Naturalist theories of Zola, *Apuntes sobre el nuevo arte de escribir novelas*.

He was less obviously affected than some of his contemporaries by the social problems of post-1868 Spain, and his novels rather reflect his concern to criticize complacency and hypocrisy of any kind. Pride and false idealism are the real objects of his irony in *Pepita Jiménez* (1874; tr. anon., ed. E. Gosse, 1891) and *Doña Luz* (1879: tr. M. J. Serrano, 1893), although some of his contemporaries read them as anti-clerical attacks on Catholic extremists. Similar themes recur in the later less ironical novels, *Juanita la Larga* (1895), etc.; though dealing here only indirectly with the Spanish scene, his concern for his country is abundantly evident in his articles, and in his descriptions of Andalusian landscape. Furthermore, his last major novel, *Morsamor* (1899), was clearly conceived as an antidote to the depression of Spain after the loss of Cuba in 1898. [ONVG]

*Obras completas*, intr. L. Aranjo (1942); ed. L. A. Costa (3 vols., 1947).

E. Fishtine, *D.J.V. the Critic* (1933); Havelock Ellis, *The Soul of Spain* (1937); J. F. Montesinos, *V. o la ficción libre* (Madrid, 1957); Brenan, *LSP*.

**Valéry, Paul** (Cette, now Sète 1871–Paris 1945). French poet, thinker, essayist and critic. His literary career began under the influence of the Symbolists (especially Mallarmé), his early poems being published in small reviews in the 1890s. But the appearance of his *Introduction à la méthode de Léonard de Vinci* (1895) and *La soirée avec Monsieur Teste* (1896) indicated that his interest had already shifted from the composition of poetry to the understanding of what poetry and art are and how any kind of artist achieves his effects. The famous *Cahiers* or notebooks (29 volumes, each of some 900 pages) were begun in 1894. The most pleasurable part of the day for him was the very early morning, when he feasted on silence, purity and potentiality, and when, throughout his life, he took delight in filling his notebooks with tenacious analyses of such subjects as language, philosophy, mathematics, physics, poetry, religion, politics, dreams, memory and the central problem of consciousness. It was not until 1912 that he seriously turned his attention again to the composition of poetry and began his longest and greatest poem, *La jeune parque*. Its completion and publication in 1917, followed by the poems of *Charmes* (1922), brought him immediate renown, which was consolidated by his publications in prose, in particular, by two dialogues in Socratic form, *Eupalinos ou l'Architecte* and *L'âme et la danse* (1921), and several volumes of notes and critical essays which reflect the manifold interests more fully disclosed by the posthumous publication of the *Cahiers*. The 1920s and 1930s saw him become the darling of the most exclusive Parisian salons and an eminent representative of the French cultural establishment both at home and internationally.

Ambivalence is one of his most vital traits. His writings reveal the tension in him between the aloof and often disabused analyst (his creation Monsieur Teste gives fullest expression to this side of him) and the vivacious Latin of powerful sensibility. Though the Teste in him scorned literature as a medium which, by its very nature, cannot have truth and clarity as its goals, he manifestly enjoyed writing and publishing. Many of the themes of his poems – such as the drama of poetic or intellectual creation and the relationship between waking and dreaming, being and knowing, necessity and contingency – clearly derive from his abstract speculations, yet the same poems display a superbly sensuous, often incandescent, lyricism (for one of the best instances of these characteristics, see *Ébauche d'un serpent*, in *Charmes*). The exceptional compactness and density of his poetry can convey both the depth of his involvement and the ironic detachment in which he excelled. As for his prose, his capacity for self-analysis and his passionate veneration of order, lucidity and control lent taut cogency to his native sensitivity in fine compositions on architecture, painting and dancing as well as in subtle studies of the problems of artistic composition. He wrote mordantly about the contemporary world (cf. *Regards sur le monde actuel*, 1931) and relished using his considerable talent for aphorism to expose what he saw as myths – literary and social as much as philosophical – in the name of the intellectual rigour and clarity which he found exemplified by the science and mathematics that so absorbed and excited him. If his talents and interests sometimes entailed what his severest critics regard as narcissistic cerebralism, esoteric aestheticism and perhaps lack of generosity, he is incontestably one of France's greatest and most original poets and an outstanding example for our age of a genius who saw no gulf between the so-called two cultures because he united them in himself so naturally and so triumphantly. [WNI]

*Œuvres*, ed. J. Hytier (2 vols., Pléiade, 1957, 1960) (for biography see introduction to vol. I; for bibliography see end of vol. II); *Cahiers* (1894–1945) (29 vols., 1957–61); tr. *The Collected Works of Paul Valéry*, ed. Jackson Mathews (N.Y., in progress).

J. Duchesne-Guillemin, *Études pour un P.V.* (Neuchâtel, 1964); J. Hytier, *La poétique de V.* (Paris, 1953); W. N. Ince, *The Poetic Theory of P.V.* (1961); J. R. Lawler, *Lecture de V.: une étude de 'Charmes'* (Paris, 1963); J. Robinson, *L'analyse de l'esprit dans les cahiers de V.* (Paris, 1963); F. Scarfe, *The Art of P.V.* (1954).

**Valla, Lorenzo** (Rome 1405–Rome 1457). Italian humanist. After studying at Rome he taught rhetoric at Pavia until his dispute with the jurists there obliged him to leave (1433). He entered (1435) the service of Alfonso of Aragon, who once intervened at Naples to protect him when his views on the origin of the Credo caused trouble with the priests (1444). After the election of Nicholas V, he established himself in Papal service at Rome.

His importance in the development of *quattrocento* thought derives ultimately from his central linguistic studies. The most substantial of his purely philological writings was the *Elegantiae latinae linguae* (publ. 1471), which sought to free Latin from medieval deformations and set up the Classical writers, especially Cicero and Quintilian, as models. In other works a spirit of free inquiry, allied to philological rigour, produced results of revolutionary significance for the study of history, religion, politics and philosophy. The *De falso credita et ementita Constantini donatione declamatio* exposed as a myth the alleged Donation of Constantine and thus undermined Papal claims to temporal power, while the *In novum testamentum ... Adnotationes* (publ. by ⇨ Erasmus, 1505) opened the way to textual criticism of the Bible. His most famous work was the treatise *De voluptate ac de vero bono* (1431), which resolves the dispute between Epicureanism and Stoicism in terms of a Christian acceptance of pleasure as a legitimate part of life. *De libero arbitrio* (*c.*1443; ed. M. Anfossi, 1934), however, sees faith, not reason, as man's best guide to an understanding of God's purpose. Viewed as a whole, his work illustrates the general *quattrocento* quest to reconcile with Christianity the newly felt *humanitas* of classical culture. [DGR]

*Il piacere*, ed. V. Grillo (1948) (Italian tr.); *Scritti filosofici e religiosi*, ed. G. Radetti (1953) (intr., Italian tr. and notes); *Opera omnia*, (Turin, 1962) (facsimile of Basle 1540 edn); *The Treatise of L.V. on the Donation of Constantine*, ed. C. B. Coleman (1922) (text and tr.); Garin, *PLQ*. C. Carbonara, *Umanesimo e Rinascimento: L.V. e Pico della Mirandola* (Turin, 1944); F. Gaeta, *L.V.* (Naples, 1955); E. Garin, *Italian Humanism* (to P. Munz, 1965); J. H. Whitfield, *Petrarch and the Renascence* (1943); *Minori*, i.

**Valle-Inclán, Ramón del** (Villanueva de Arosa 1869–Santiago de Compostela 1935). Spanish novelist, dramatist and poet. Born in Galicia, whose folklore pervades his work, he cultivated a fictitious personality. Sympathetic to Carlism, which became a recurring theme, his bohemianism and sharp wit made him a striking figure in Madrid literary circles. His earlier novels, notably the 4 *Sonatas* (1902–5), weave elegant and richly cadenced filigree patterns from the erotic adventures of a Galician Casanova. In a violent triptych about Galician feudalism, *Comedias bárbaras* (1907–8; 1922), his dramatic use of dialogue and manipulation of mass forces through shapes and gestures foreshadow his later style. Married to an actress (1907), and fascinated by the theatre, he wrote several original verse-plays – *Cuento de abril* (1910), *Voces de gesta* (1911) – some, such as *La marquesa Rosalinda* (1913), mocking modernist themes.

His best work came after 1918. Disgust with society and sympathy for the disinherited lead him to adopt, in plays he called '*esperpentos*', and in novels, a new 'aesthetic of systematic distortion' and a magnificently discordant style, anticipating today's theatre of the absurd. The first esperpentic play was *Luces de Bohemia* (1923), but the best and most actable is *Los cuernos de Don Friolera* (1925). His manifest antagonism towards Primo de Rivera's dictatorship (1923–30), and a second visit to Mexico (1922), inspired *Tirano Banderas* (1926), a gruesomely brilliant novel of a Latin American revolution; contempt for Alfonso XIII's reign lies behind the burlesque treatment of Isabel II's court in the two novels of *El ruedo ibérico* (1927–8). The Republic sent him to Rome as Director of the Spanish Academy of Art (1933), but he returned a year later to die in Galicia. [EJF]

*Obras completas* (1945).
F. Almagro, *Vida y literatura de V.-I.* (Madrid. 1943); G. Díaz-Plajas, *Las estéticas de V* (Madrid, 1965).

**Vallès, Jules** (Le Puy-en-Velay 1832–Paris 1885). French journalist and novelist. Of peasant stock and revolutionary views. He was imprisoned in 1853 and exiled (1871–80) for his part in the Commune. His London impressions were collected in *La rue à Londres* (1884); his racy political journalism in *Le cri du peuple* (1953). His reputation rests on several volumes of fiction, clearly transposed from life, where his savage indignation at injustice and inequality and his profound pity for the disinherited energize a rapid, mordant and vivid narrative. Such as the autobiographical 'Jacques Vingtras' trilogy *L'enfant* (1879), *Le bachelier* (1881), *L'insurgé* (1886); the stories about Parisian eccentrics and outcasts in *Les réfractaires* (1865); and the short novels *Un gentilhomme* (1869, serially) about a country squire who deserts his class, and *Les blouses* (serially, 1880). [SBJ]

*Œuvres* (8 vols., 1950–7).
G. Gille, *J. V.* (2 vols., Paris, 1941).

**Vančura, Vladislav** (Háje 1891–Prague 1942). Czech novelist. Though a doctor of medicine, he devoted himself fully to literature. He took part in many activities of left-wing writers before the war and was executed by the Germans during the occupation. A writer of firm Communist beliefs, he was nevertheless a convinced experimentalist as regards creative writing. The only thing his novels have in common is class hatred and linguistic inventiveness. The hero of *Pekař Jan Marhoul* (1924) is an ideal proletarian, living in a state of ideological intoxication, indifferent to material wealth, to misery and suffering, with a passion for work which enables man to build the world to his image. In his war novel *Pole orná a válečná* (1925) Vančura writes in an angry and cynical mood; *Markéta Lazarová* (1931) is a simple history of medieval robbers, a poem in prose in praise of brute force. His last novel, *Rodina Horváthova* (1938), suggests that he was about to take the path of socialist realism.

His main importance lies in his style; to tell the dramatic plot, he brings slang, archaisms, proverbial sayings, phrases of popular wisdom, and fancy metaphors into play with an amusing if somewhat tiring virtuosity. [RA/KB]

*Spisy* (16 vols., 1951–61).
K. Nový, *V.V.* (Prague, 1954); J. Mukařovský, *V.V.* (Prague, 1945).

**Van Lerberghe, Charles** (nr Ghent 1861–Brussels 1907). Belgian symbolist poet. He wrote melodious, dreamily sensuous poems (*Entrevisions*, 1898, *La chanson d'Ève*, 1904), and dramas: *Les flaireurs* (1890), *Pan* (1906). [WA]

L. Christophe, *Ch.v.L.* (1943).

**Vaptsarov, Nikola** (Bansko 1909–Sofia 1942). Bulgarian poet. Unable to read literature at the university (an ambition aroused by his mother), he was trained as an engineer in Varna (1926–32) and sailed the East Mediterranean, glimpsing 'the stars clustering over Famagusta'. His single book of poems, *Motorni pesni* ('Motor Songs', 1940), reflects his life as ship's engineer, factory hand, railway stoker and Communist agitator, inspiring a whole generation with its virile assertion of human dignity and 'new romanticism' of factories, foundries and 'engines singing in the blue sky'. There is tenderness too, in the evocation of springtime in his native Pirin and the farewell to his wife on the eve of his execution. For his part in the Resistance against German occupation this 'Bulgarian Mayakovsky' faced the firing-squad with the words of an earlier martyr poet, H. ⇨ Botev, defiantly on his lips. [VP]

*Săchineniya* (1959); *N.V. spomeni, pisma, dokumenti* (1953); Pinto, *BPV*.
Manning and Smal-Stocki, *HMBL*.

**Varchi, Benedetto** (Florence 1503–Florence 1565). Italian man of letters. His sonnets are in the tradition of post- ⇨ Bembo Petrarchism, and his *Ercolano* (published 1570; repr. 1880), a treatise on language emphasizes the Florentine pedigree of literary Italian. He made contributions to the study of Dante and Petrarch in the *cinquecento*, and in his theoretical writings on literature (see his *Lezzioni*, 1590) he interpreted Aristotle in Counter-Reformation terms by insisting on the supreme moral function of literature. His most substantial work, however, is the *Storia fiorentina* (publ. 1721; repr. 1963), which covers the period 1527–38. Commissioned by Cosimo I, it at times may be guilty of pro-Medici bias but on the whole is a useful contemporary record. [DGR]

G. Manacorda, *B.V. l'uomo, il poeta, il critico* (Pisa, 1903); Croce, *PES*.

**Varela, A. Noriega.** ⇨ Galician Literature.

**Varnhagen von Ense, Karl August** (Düsseldorf 1785–Berlin 1858). German diplomat and man of letters. Modelling his style on Goethe, he wrote numerous biographies and critical essays which were regarded by the 19th century as the perfection of literary style. He is remembered now for his social relationships with prominent men of his age, recorded in 14 volumes of diaries, and correspondence, e.g. with A. von ⇨ Humboldt. His highly gifted wife Rahel (1771–1833), née Levin, is remembered for her enthusiastic patronage of the arts and sciences in her Berlin salon, in which, as in that of her fellow-Jewess Henriette Hertz, many of the *avant-garde* writers and thinkers of the early 19th century gathered to display and discuss their work. Like those of her husband, her letters and occasional writings afford insights into the life of the cultured Berlin society of her day. [RT]

Hannah Arendt, *R.V.* (Munich, 1959); Georg Brandes, *Rahel, Bettina und Charlotte Stieglitz* (Leipzig, 1896).

**Vartio, Marja-Liisa** (Sääminki 1924– Savonlinna 1966). Finnish poet and novelist. She began by publishing poetry (*Häät*, 1952, *Seppele*, 1953), but became specially known as a skilful, ironic analyser of woman's psyche through her novels: *Se on sitten kevät* (1957), *Mies kuin mies, tyttö kuin tyttö* (1958), *Kaikki naiset näkevät unia* (1960), *Tunteet* (1962), *Hänen olivat linnut* (1967). [IR]

**Vas, István** (Budapest 1910– ). Hungarian poet. He worked as a clerk before the Second World War, then as a civil servant and editor. His early poetry attempted to uphold 'Biedermeier' values threatened by modern society; soon he turned to odes, influenced by ⇨ Babits and ⇨ Illyés, in praise of reason: *Öszi Rombolás* (1932), *Levél A Szabadságról* (1935), *Menekülő Múzsa* (1938), *Áldott Asszonyok* (1947). *Vallomás* (2nd edn, 1956) contains love poems. *Rapszódia Egy Öszi Kertben* (1960) includes poetry and travel notes. *Évek És Művek* (1958) is a collection of literary essays written from 1934 to 1956. *A Teremtett Világ* (1956) is a selection of poems from 1930 to 1956. [LL]

**Vasari, Giorgio** (Arezzo 1511–Florence 1574). Italian painter, architect and art historian. A pupil of Andrea del Sarto, he worked chiefly at Rome and Florence. His *Vite de' più eccellenti pittori, scultori ed architetti* (1st edn 1550; enlarged 1568; ed. C. L. Ragghianti, 1942–9; tr. G. Bull, 1965) is a series of single biographies, beginning with Cimabue and extending to Vasari's own day. A clear historical pattern nevertheless emerges. He sees the arts in decline since classical times, reawakening in Tuscany in the 13th century, progressing through the *trecento* and *quattrocento* to achieve supreme fulfilment in the golden age of Leonardo, Raphael, and above all Michelangelo. The term '*rinascita*' which Vasari used in this context of art history acquired vast resonance as it became extended to encompass a whole cultural phenomenon. And although the Middle Ages does not now seem the artistic void which Vasari saw, the pattern which he established nevertheless dominated European taste unchallenged for centuries, and still has considerable validity. The biographies are not always factually reliable, but interesting in their first-hand knowledge of techniques and individuals. [DGR]

J. Rouchette, *La renaissance que nous a leguée V.* (Paris, 1959); R. Carden, *The Life of G.V.* (1910); *Minori*, ii.

**Vasconcelos, Jorge Ferreira de** (*c.*1515–1585?). Portuguese playwright. Author of 3 comedies, *Eufrosina* (1555; ed.E. Asensio, 1951), *Ulissipo* (2nd edn 1618) and *Aulegrafia* (1619). His comedies were not written for theatrical production, but rather to be read like a novel, for they are excessively long and digressive. The running theme in these plays is love considered from a Platonic point of view. *Eufrosina* abounds in long debates over the validity of ideal love, and in *Aulegrafia* courtly love is ridiculed as an outdated conception in the positive bourgeois world of the Renaissance. The materialistic aspects of this new society, its hypocrisy and false morals are also amusingly criticized in *Ulissipo*, a play which gives an excellent picture of Portuguese middle-class life in Lisbon. Vasconcelos's comedies have established in Portugal the tradition of picaresque literature. [LSR]

A. da Costa Pimpão, 'As correntes dramáticas da literatura portuguesa do séc XVI' in *A Evolução e o Espírito do Teatro em Portugal*, i (Lisbon, 1947); Aubrey F. Bell, introduction to *Eufrósina* (Lisbon, 1918); Eugénio Asensio, preface to his edn of *Eufrosina* (Madrid, 1951).

**Vasily/Vassian Patrikeyev** (d. Volokolamsk monastery *c.*1532). Russian soldier, politician and publicist. He was a direct descendant of Gedimin of Lithuania. His great-grandfather, Patriky, entered the service of Vasily I in 1408, and for a century the Patrikeyevs played a leading role in the diplomatic, political and military life of Muscovy. After nearly a decade of distinguished service as a diplomat and soldier, he was disgraced in 1499 for an unspecified reason, forced to take the tonsure (his monastic name was Vassian) and banished to the White Lake monastery of St Kirill. His guilt, and his father's, was probably participation in the dynastic crisis of 1497–9, on the side of Ivan III's second wife Sofia Palaeologa, and her son Vasily, the future grand prince, who were themselves under a cloud at the time. In 1505 he was allowed to move to the hermitage of ♢ Nil Sorsky, where he became Nil's pupil and absorbed his teachings on the need for monastic poverty. About 1509 he was transferred to the Simonov monastery in Moscow; here he remained for twenty-two years, in close touch with the court of Vasily III. He carried out a long polemical campaign against ♢ Joseph of Volokolamsk, associated and collaborated with the learned Athonic monk ♢ Maksim the Greek, and took an active part in the literary conflicts of the day. He was tried in 1531 for objecting to the principle of monastic landownership, for tampering with sacred literature and for heresy, and was banished to the Volokolamsk monastery.

His writings are mainly polemical and directed against his ideological enemies, the so-called 'Possessors' or advocates of monastic landownership, and touch mainly on such topics as the corruption of contemporary monasticism and the correct way of dealing with heretics. His style is lively, vivid and pungent; his argumentation is sharp and shrewd; his writings are not bereft of humour and at times show a certain freedom of thought and even critical spirit. His influence as a writer and stylist, however, was disappointingly small owing to the ideological unacceptableness of his views. [JLIF]

N. A. Kazakova, *V.P. i ego sochineniya* (Moscow/Leningrad, 1960).

**Vasil'yev, Pavel** (Zaysan, Kazakhstan 1910–1937). Russian poet. Son of a mathematics teacher, he spent most of his childhood in Pavlodar and Omsk. This milieu is reflected in his poetry; he is the finest poet of the Siberian and Central Asian steppes. He was restless, precocious, hungry for new experience; at 15 he left school and went to Vladivostok, to become a merchant seaman, travelling to and from Japan. At 17 he first read his poems in public and published them in a Siberian journal. He left the sea and prospected for gold on the banks of the Lena; in 1928 he went to Moscow and studied at the Literary Institute. His best work dates from 1930–4; he then ran into sharp public criticism for his boisterously sensual dithyramb, *Stikhi v chest' Natali* ('Verses in honour of Natalya'), and for allegedly *kulak* sympathies (despite his enthusiasm for the early achievements of Communism in Siberia). He disappeared in the 1937 purges, probably because (as ♢ Erenburg conjectures in his memoirs) he 'drank and chattered' too much. He was neglected until 1956, though one of the most brilliant poets to have grown up in the Soviet Union. His verse is fast-moving, verbose, evocative of place and atmosphere; it is stamped with too great originality and too much love of life for him to be classed as no more than a belated representative of the Peasant Poet group. [RM-G]

*Izbrannyye stikhotvereniya i poemy*, intr. K. L. Zelinsky (1957); Gulland, *RSV*; Lugovskoy, *RSP*; Markov, *PG*; Obolensky, *PBRV*.

**Vauthier, Jean** (Bordeaux 1910– ). French playwright. Seizes on the conception of drama as a musical and rhythmic structure, emphasizing the tempo of action and dialogue, the importance of movement and gesture as keys to the inner life of characters, and the part played by sounds and inanimate objects in human situations. All his work is grounded in the conflict between persons or within a single person. His drama is fundamentally religious (it is usually contained within a closed room) and pointing, however obliquely, to a divine revelation that is almost always withheld, a divine voice almost never heard. The elements of parody and clowning are often very pronounced. Hence, in *Capitaine Bada* (1952) the squabbling, tyrannical Bada and his slave-wife, Alice, offer a parody of man in deluding quest of truth confronted by simple faith and love. By the final act, Bada's parodic acts of self-purification achieve for him a mental state in which he fancies he hears an unearthly music from behind the wall. In his pursuit of the ineffable, he climbs on to a cupboard, falls and dies before the source of the music is revealed as a radio playing in the courtyard.

The themes of sincerity and quest for truth recur in *Le personnage combattant* (1956), where the 'Character', a successful writer, returns to the shabby hotel room he had once lived in and tries to recreate in artistic form the pure idealism of his youth. His effort becomes a kind of parody of the sacred passion in which he is hampered and frustrated at every turn by sounds, physical objects and his own vulgarity and bad faith. *Le rêveur* (1960) develops a similar idea in terms of the conflict between a poetic dreamer and a commercialized scriptwriter, though there is far less tragic intensity. The most explicitly religious play is *Les prodiges* (1958), a disturbing encounter between corruption and grace in which Marc is led from the murder of the saintly old nurse Berthe at the hands of his mistress Gilly to a genuine revelation. He has also successfully adapted Machiavelli's *Mandragola* as *La nouvelle Mandragore* (1952), and written a scenario *Les abysses* (1963). [SBJ]

*Théâtre*, *I* (1953).

Michel Beaujour, 'An Introduction to the Theatre of J.V.', in *Yale French Studies*, 29 (1962); Guicharnaud, *MFT*; Corvin, *TNF*; Serreau, *HNT*.

**Vauvenargues, Luc de Clapiers,** Marquis de (Aix-en-Provence 1715–Paris 1747). French moralist. After a probably rather limited education, he served as an army officer, 1733–44, seeing active service in the War of the Austrian Succession. His health impaired, and disappointed at his lack of advancement, he resigned his commission to seek employment in the diplomatic service but increasing ill-health closed this avenue also, and he devoted the last few years before his early death to his literary interests, encouraged in these by such percipient friends as Mirabeau and Voltaire. His major work is a miscellany, *Introduction à la connaissance de l'esprit humain, suivie de Réflexions et de Maximes* (1746; tr. F. G. Stevens, *Reflections and Maxims*, 1940). This, though in many ways conventional in its approach and means of expression, shows an insight into human nature which often reflects his own unhappy experiences, and with its emphasis upon vigour and kindness as human ideals also reveals the essential nobility of his character. [WHB]

*Œuvres*, ed. D. L. Gilbert (2 vols., 1857).

M. Paléologue, *V.* (Paris, 1890); M. Wallas, *V.* (1928).

**Vazov, Ivan** (Sopot 1850–Sofia 1921). Bulgaria's 'national poet', novelist and story-writer. His literary flair, nourished on the French and Russian classics, survived paternal pressure for a business career. Sent to Rumania on apprenticeship in 1870, he contributed to the Bulgarian *Periodichesko spisanie* (then published in Braila) and met there the émigré revolutionaries whose characters and hardships appear in his *Nemili nedragi* (1883). Returning to Sopot, he joined the Revolutionary Committee; his *Pryaporets i gusla* (Bucharest, 1876) became the battle hymn of the April 1876 rising, the barbaric suppression of which he recorded in verse (*Tăgite na Bălgariya*, 1877) and prose (*Neotdavna*, 1881, and *Pod igoto*, 1886).

Provincial life in the newly independent Bulgaria, which he knew as judge in Berkovitsa (1879–80), is entertainingly presented in *Mitrofan i Dormidolski*, *Zagorka* (both 1881) and *Mihalaki Chorbaji* (1882). Devoting himself to public life in Plovdiv, the cultural capital till E. Rumelia's reunion with Bulgaria in 1885, he edited *Nauka* and the daily *Narodny glas* and with Velichkov compiled a first Bulgarian anthology of literature. During this period, he wrote of the countryside in his poems, *Gusla* (1881) and *Polya i gori* (1882), and sketches, *Edin kăt v Stara Planina* (1882), and of the old pre-liberation days in portraits of *Chichovtsi* (1884) and national heroes *Epopeya na zabravenite*, *I* (1881), *II* (1884). The Serbo-Bulgarian War inspired his verses *Slivnitsa* (1886). That year he fled from Stambolov's *coup* to Odessa, where he wrote the nostalgic verses *Zvukove* (1893) and most of his *Pod igoto* (tr. Edmund Gosse, *Under the Yoke*, 1894), a lively picture of local life and circumstances of the April Rising. It won recognition for Bulgarian literature abroad and became the Bulgarian 'national novel'.

Settling finally in Sofia in 1889, he engaged in politics (elected to parliament in 1894, he became Minister of Education 1897–9) and literary journalism (he edited his own *Dennitsa* and collaborated in S. Bobchev's *Bălgarska sbirka*). He wrote ceaselessly novels, i.e. *Nova zemya* (1896) and *Kazalarska tsaritsa* (1903), sketches from urban life, more travel notes and ballads and plays on old Bulgarian history. Indulging rarely in the more personal expression of his last poems *Lyulyaka mi zamirisa* (1911), he continued to the end 'to identify my whole existence with that of my people' in topical verse *Pod grăma na pobedite* (1914) and *Pesni za Makedoniya* (1916).

The mirroring of fifty crucial years of nascent nationhood has made this versatile prolific writer and dedicated patriot the true laureate of Bulgarian literature. [VP]

*Săbrani săchineniya*, I–XX (1955–7); Pinto, *BPV*.

I. Shishmanov, *I.V.: Spomeni i dokumenti* (Sofia, 1930); Petr Hristoforov, *I.V. La formation d'un écrivain bulgare, 1850–1921* (Paris, 1938); M. Arnaudov, *I.V.: zhivot i delo* (Sofia, 1937); Manning and Smal-Stocki, *HMBL*.

**Vega, Lope de.** ➪ Lope de Vega.

**Veldeke, Hendrik van** (*c*.1145–*c*.1200). Limburg poet and *ministerialis* of the Counts of Loon. His *Servatius* (*c*.1170), honouring the patron saint of Maastricht, is of particular note because it was written in the Limburg dialect and in rhyming couplets. His *Eneide* (ed. O. Behagel, 1882), a free rendering of the *Roman d'* ➪ *Enéas*, is a fine work extant only in the Thuringian dialect. ➪ Gottfried von Strassburg's homage to Hendrik as the originator of *rehte rime* has led to a tradition that, whatever his birthplace, he was a German poet. Nevertheless, there is little doubt that the Thuringian version was translated from a lost Limburg original. He certainly had less influence in the Netherlands than in Germany, where he was acknowledged as a pioneer in transmitting the new literary fashions of Romance courtly civilization (➪ Wolfram von Eschenbach). Rhymed verse was no novelty in Limburg, Brabant and Flanders (cf. the octosyllabic rhyming couplets in *Aiol* of about the same date) and in the Netherlands van ➪ Maerlant effectively discredited courtly poetry some eighty years later. Moreover ➪ Hadewijch's *minnesanc* provides independent support for the belief that there must have been a tradition in the Netherlands to account for the accomplished style of his songs. [PK/RT]

*Servatius*, ed. Th. Frings and G. Schieb (1956); *Des Minnesangs Fruhling*, ed. C. V. Krats (1961) (lyrics); *Eneide I*, ed. G. Schieb and Th. Frings (1964).

L. J. Rogier, *H.v.V.* (Maastricht, 1930); J. van Mierlo, *Onde in nieuwe bydragen tot het Veldeke-probleem* (Ghent, 1957); Weevers, *PNEC*.

**Vélez de Guevara, Luis** (Écija 1579–Madrid 1644). Spanish dramatist and novelist. Of his plays 80 survive (? out of 400). A disciple of ➪ Lope de Vega he specialized in historical dramas, the most famous of which, *Reinar después de morir* (CC, 1948), treats the love and death of the legendary-historical Inés de Castro. Intrigues, crimes, and scenes of high drama came easily to Vélez, an Andalusian steeped in the traditional poetry of the *romance* and the music of old songs His female characters are particularly powerful; Gila, the bandit-heroine of *La serrana de la Vera*, takes wild vengeance on her seducer whom she hurls down a cliff; and Doña Violante in *Lo que obliga el ser rey* is a villainess who 'administers poison in every word'. His novel *El diablo cojuelo* (1641; CC, 1918) derives from ➪ Quevedo's *Sueños* and as skilfully exploits nightmare detail. The devil lifts the roofs of a number of Madrid houses (for a student who has obligingly released him from a bottle) and we are shown what is going on beneath. The prose is extremely complicated, many of the conceits being based on proverbs turned upside down. ➪ Lesage took (and improved) the subject for *Le Diable boiteux*. [JMC]

BAE, 45.

F. E. Spencer and R. Schevill, *The Dramatic Works of L.V. de G.* (Berkeley, Calif., 1937).

**Velichkov, Konstantin** (Pazarjik 1855–Grenoble 1907). Bulgarian poet and *belles lettres* writer. After graduating in literature at the Sultan's *lycée*, Constantinople in 1874, he returned to teach in Bulgaria. *V tămnitsa* (1900) vividly records his memories of the 1876 rising, for complicity in which he himself suffered. In his subsequent literary and public career he was much associated with ➪ Vazov to whose *Nauka* he contributed a play and stories, and with whom he compiled the first Bulgarian anthology of literature in Plovdiv. A gifted painter, he spent 1887–9 penuriously studying art in Florence; his *Pisma ot Rim* (1895) were written during this exile from the Stambolov regime, the remaining years of which he lived in Constantinople, working on his *Tsarigradski soneti* (1899), *V tămnitsa* and translating the *Inferno*. Returning to Sofia in 1894, he became Minister of Education till 1897 and resumed his literary work, editing and writing for his periodical *Letopisi* ('Chronicles', 1899–1903). His retirement in southern France was devoted to his special interest: translating from French and Italian literature. [VP]

*Săchineniya*, i–ix (1911–15); Pinto, *BPV*.
S. Vasilev, *K.V.: lichnost i tvorchestvo* (Sofia, 1947); Manning and Smal-Stocki, *HMBL*.

**Venezis, Ilias,** pseud. of Mellos (Aivali, Asia Minor 1904– ). Greek novelist and short-story writer. He was taken prisoner in the Greco-Turkish War (1921–2) and spent some time in a forced labour camp. His first book, *Numero 31–328* (1931; French tr. *La grande pitié*, 1946), describing his experiences in captivity, is a realistic piece of writing of considerable vigour. It was followed by *Galini* (1939), a novel about a group of refugees from Asia Minor settling, and starting life anew, on a remote shore of Attica. It is a study of character and of situations and problems arising in a community of uprooted people; the tone is subdued and the style mellowed into an idyllic softness. The latter becomes more pronouncedly so in *Aeoliki Gi* (1943; tr. E. D. Scott-Kilvert, *Aeolia*, 1949), a novel, partly autobiographical, of childhood memories of life in an estate in Anatolia before the 1914 war. The heroes are mostly children and adolescents; the narrative is serene and dreamy, with a good deal of sentimentality and folklore elements in it. He is at his best, however, in his numerous short stories, especially in those with an Aegean background where he shows invention and skilful poetic handling of local colour and atmosphere. [SJP]

*O Manolis Lekas* (1928); *Aigaio* (1941); *Anemoi* (1944); *Ora Polemou* (1946) (all collections of short stories).
A. Sachinis, *I Synhroni Pezografia Mas* (Athens, 1951).

**Vennberg, Karl** (Blädinge 1910– ). Swedish poet and critic. As a spokesman for the generation of the Forties, Vennberg occupied a singularly influential position, complementary to that of ⇨ Lindegren. He has been important both as a theoretician and as a model for younger poets, even though his personal idiom soon was proved to be inimitable. Two collections of verse, *Halmfackla* (1944) and *Tideräkning* (1945), became classical statements of the sceptical outlook of the time. He had studied at Stockholm, being decisively influenced by the so-called Uppsala school of philosophy, in particular its emotive theory of value. The prevailing mood of his poetry is radical pessimism, a recurrent theme being the inadequacy of all beliefs and ideologies; but the tone which comes across to the reader can be positively exhilarating. It is as if he had been freed from private feelings to tackle the task of giving intellectual formulation and a voice to the universal woe. Pride in his dialectic powers is clearly discernible; but the controlled aridity and pungent irony are off-set by the intensely moral concern and the surprisingly exact perception of sensuous detail. He returned to poetry in a somewhat mellower mood with *Fiskefärd* (1949). Here the irony is more subdued and there is a novel note of personal resolution; there are even some tentative idylls. But later collections show that this relaxation of tension was only temporary. In *Gatukorsning* (1952) and *Synfält* (1954) the mood is again more guarded. They still accommodate the poet's personal feelings, but resignation is never far removed, nor ironic scepticism, though often with the additional nuance of self-irony. His stand during the fifties for 'Tredje ståndpunkten', the principle of non-committal in the political East–West tug-of-war, involved him in prolonged and taxing polemics. He has also been active as a reviewer in the Leftist press (with a reputation for over-kindness). His latest collection to date is *Tillskrift* (Postscript, 1960). It persists in a mood of self-examining resignation, but introduces a more concentrated style and emotionally more viable imagery. Here the war on beliefs and ideologies has practically ceased, and the absence of a personal belief has itself become a theme of deep poetical concern. [SAB]

E. Lindegren, 'K.V.' (in *Den unga Parnassen*, ed. N. G. Nässtrõm and M. Strömberg, Stockholm, 1947); G. Printz-Påhlson, 'V., orden och tingen', in *Solen i spegeln* (Stockholm, 1958); K. E. Lagerlöf, *Den unge K.V.* (Göteborg, 1967).

**Verdaguer, Jacint.** ⇨ Catalan Literature.

**Verde, Cesário** (Lisbon 1855–Lisbon 1886). Portuguese poet. One of the most important Portuguese poets of the 19th century, he was born into a wealthy middle-class family. His father owned a large farm in the suburbs of Lisbon and had also a hardware shop in the capital. Initially he had to turn his mind to practical affairs, and his intellectual pursuits were followed as a sideline. But when he began to write poetry, he brought into it his experience of a man of action who was well attuned to the spirit of the century. His poems reflect a heartfelt enthusiasm for machinery, and praise man's labour and industrial activity. The city becomes for him a subject of manifold suggestions, which he explores deftly by analysing the transition in Lisbon from a rural into an urban community. A true realist in all senses, he excels in the visual detail of his descriptions. In his lifetime Verde printed only a few poems in periodicals. His work, *O Livro de Cesário Verde* (1887), was edited posthumously by his friend Silva Pinto, who did not respect the chronological order in which the poems were composed. [LSR]

*Obra Completa de C.V.*, ed. Joel Serrão (1964).

**Verdugo y Castilla, Alfonso, Conde de Torrepalma** (Alcalá la Real 1706–Turin 1767). Spanish poet and diplomat. Ambassador in Vienna and Turin. *El Deucalión*, a mythological poem on the flood, has some of the strength and complexity of ⇨ Góngora. In his predilection for ruins, melancholy and death, however, he reflects the taste of his century, or even looks beyond to Romanticism. *El diluvio*, another poem on the subject of the flood, has passages of great power. [JMC]

BAE, 29, 61.

**Verga, Giovanni** (Catania 1840–Catania 1922). Italian dramatist and novelist. Senator in 1920. He abandoned his studies at Catania University and, after failures in journalism and some early patriotic novels (the unpublished *Amore e patria*; *I carbonari della montagna*, 1861–2; *Sulle lagune*, 1863), he went to Florence in 1865 and acquired immediate fame with the publication of *Storia di una capinera* (1871). His novels are generally considered as belonging to one of two distinct periods – the so-called *prima maniera* of early sentimental novels (*Una peccatrice*, 1866; *Eva*, 1875; *Tigre Reale*, 1873; *Eros*, 1875) and the so-called 'mature' works in which he turns from the false elegance of city life to the basic struggle for existence of under-privileged Sicilian peasants, as in the short stories *Nedda* (1874), *Vita dei campi* (1880), *Novelle rusticane* (1882; tr. D. H. Lawrence, *Little Novels of Sicily*, 1958). The theme was to receive fuller treatment in a complete cycle of novels – *I vinti* – of which, however, he wrote only the first two – *I Malavoglia* (1881; tr. E. Mosbacher, *The House by the Medlar Tree*, 1950), about the misfortunes of a family of hard-working fisherfolk; *Mastro Don Gesualdo* (1888; tr. D. H. Lawrence, 1928), about a builder who, like Mazzarò of *La roba* (*Novelle rusticane*), in his successful bid for material prosperity pathetically isolates himself from neighbours and family alike – and the first pages of *La duchessa di Leyra*, in which, with bitter irony, he continues his account of the ruined life of Don Gesualdo's daughter.

Verga's interest is essentially in an objective psychological study of the individual in relation to his community. Description is minimal, the narrative consisting often of a form of dramatic dialogue – in *I Malavoglia* of unique intensity and suggestiveness. His concept of realism, deriving little from Flaubert and Zola whom his friend Luigi Capuana had introduced to him, is explained in the short stories *Fantasticheria* and *L'Amante di Gramigna* (*Vita dei Campi*), and in the preface to *I Malavoglia*.

He was very successful also as a dramatist, the best-known works being *Cavalleria rusticana* (1883; tr. D. H. Lawrence, 1928; adapted for the libretto of Mascagni's opera in 1890) and *La lupa* (1896). [RHC]

*Opere*, ed. L. Russo (1955).

T. G. Bergin, *G.V.* (1931); L. Russo, *G.V.* (4th edn, Bari, 1947); A. Seroni, *La 'Nedda' nella storia dell'arte verghiana* (Lucca, 1950); A. Seroni, *V.* (Palermo, 1960); G. Viti, *V. verista* (Florence, 1961); G. Cattaneo, *G.V.* (Turin, 1963); Binni, *CI*; *Maggiori*, ii.

**Verhaeren, Émile** (nr Antwerp 1855–Rouen 1916). Belgian poet. He studied law, was called to the Bar, but devoted most of his life to literature. His early collection, *Les Flamandes* (1883), contains naturalistic descriptions of peasant life in Flanders. Under the influence of the French symbolists he wrote *Les soirs* (1888: tr. anon., 1918) and other volumes in which he showed great power in his *vers libres*, most sombrely in *Les débâcles* (1888) and *Flambeaux noirs* (1890). Finally, his characteristic later socialism, and belief in human energy and the brotherhood of man, appear in *Les campagnes hallucinées* (1893), *Les villages illusoires* (1895) and *Les villes tentaculaires* (1895). He is moved both by the epic progress of industry and the plight of the worker, the threatened countryside, beauty of hearth and home. His disregard for grammar and his repetitive violent phrasing recall Walt Whitman. He also published three volumes of gentler poetry, mostly love poems to his wife, *Les heures* *claires* (1896), *Les heures d'après-midi* (1905) and *Les heures du soir* (1911). A patriot of the people and culture of Flanders, he laments the destruction of war in *Les ailes rouges de la guerre* (1916). [WA]

P. Mansell Jones, *E.V.* (1957).

**Verlaine, Paul** (Metz 1844–Paris 1896). French poet. His first book of verse, *Poèmes saturniens* (1866), joined in the ⇨ Parnassian reaction against Romanticism and preached the virtues of classical order and clarity. In practice, however, a few poems, such as 'Soleils couchants' and 'Chanson d'automne', already revealed that, with his fundamentally weak and unstable character, he was better suited to a more hesitant and suggestive kind of poetry and that he was more at ease with the short line of 8 syllables or less than with the heavier 12-syllable alexandrine. The *vers impair*, with an odd number of syllables, whose use he was later to recommend in his Art poétique' as being '*plus vague et plus soluble*', also made its appearance, as well as unusual verse forms. *Fêtes galantes* (1869), transposing into words the make-believe atmosphere and moonlit settings of the paintings of Watteau and other 18th-century artists recently popularized by the ⇨ Goncourts, continued this trend towards a distinctly personal style, with half the poems written in octosyllabic lines, sometimes grouped in tercets, and others written in *vers impairs* of 7 syllables. In *La bonne chanson* (1870), however, love poems addressed to his future wife sound a note of optimism and confidence in firm and measured alexandrines, save for a few exceptions such as 'Avant que tu ne t'en ailles' and 'La lune blanche'. The note of uncertainty returns, however, along with the fleeting rhythms, in *Romances sans paroles* (1874) for, from the end of 1871, although he had been married for only about eighteen months, he was carried away by the fascination of ⇨ Rimbaud's forceful personality. Rimbaud encouraged him in his metrical innovations and *Romances sans paroles* makes extensive use of *vers impairs*, short lines and varied verse forms, as well as experimenting in matters of rhyme. But, as the melancholy tone of most of the poem suggests, the relationship between the '*époux infernal*' and the '*vierge folle*' (to use Rimbaud's terms) was never an easy one and it finally ended in a quarrel in Brussels in July 1873 during which Verlaine shot Rimbaud in the wrist. He was condemned to two years' imprisonment in the course of which, when his hoped-for reconciliation with his wife proved impossible, he returned to the Catholic faith in which he had been brought up, later trying, for several years after his release, to lead a new life. *Sagesse* (1881) resulted from this period of repentance, conversion and reform, during which Verlaine, perhaps in a subconscious reflection of this return to a conventional way of life, also tended to move away from the *vers impairs* and octosyllabic lines of the poems he was writing at the beginning of the period, such as 'Je ne sais pourquoi', 'Le ciel est par-dessus le toit' and 'Un grand sommeil noir', towards traditional rhythms, though still retaining a typical fluidity in, for example, the alexandrines of the group of ten sonnets, forming the centrepiece of *Sagesse*, in which he communes with God. *Jadis et naguère* (1884), as the title implies, is made up of poems written long before, some of the best of which had been excluded from *Sagesse* because they lacked the necessary moral content. Among these is the celebrated 'Art poétique', written in 1874 when he was at the height of his powers, with its peremptory opening and closing lines: '*De la musique avant toute chose / Et tout le reste est littérature*' Ironically enough, however, the musical quality which characterizes his best poetry largely disappeared after *Jadis et naguère* and most of the enormous quantity of verse and prose he turned out during the remainder of his life, in which he made great play with the parallel themes of the aspirations of the spirit and the temptations of the flesh, though he had, in fact, yielded entirely to the latter, is little more than mere 'literature'. [CC]

*Œuvres poétiques complètes* (1962); *Fêtes galantes, La bonne chanson, Romances sans paroles*, ed. V. P. Underwood (1963); *Selected Poems*, ed. R. C. D. Perman (1965).

A. Adam, *The Art of P.V.* (1963); P. Martino, *V.* (1951); J. Richer, *P.V.* (1953).

**Verne, Jules** (Nantes 1828–Amiens 1905). French adventure-story writer. His tales were generally first published in the *Musée des Familles* and included *Cinq semaines en ballon* (1863), an exciting account of a journey by balloon, *Voyage au centre de la terre* (1864), *Les aventures du Capitaine*

*Hatteras*, a tale of polar exploration (1866), *Vingt mille lieues sous les mers*, with its sinister Captain Nemo and his submarine, *Nautilus*, and his most famous story of all, *Le tour du monde en quatre-vingt jours*, with the Englishman Phileas Fogg and his valet Passepartout, who win a bet to go round the world in eighty days, a feat then considered almost impossible. His books have been translated into many languages, including English. [WA]

*The Omnibus J.V.* (Philadelphia, 1951) (translations).

M. A. de la Fuye, *M.J.V.* (Paris, 1953).

**Verney,** Father **Luís António** (Lisbon 1713–Lisbon 17?). Portuguese critic and educationalist. He studied theology at Évora and later theology and civil law at the University of Rome. In Italy he frequented prominent intellectual circles and studied the 'enlightened' authors of the age. He was particularly drawn to the philosophy of Locke and the English empiricists. Having thus assimilated the spirit of progressive European thinking, Verney returned to Portugal in 1742 as archdeacon of the cathedral of Évora. Invited by King João V to collaborate in the projected reform of the Portuguese educational system, he published 16 'letters' under the title of *O Verdadeiro Método de Estudar* (1746; CSC, 5 vols.). These were a bitter indictment of the rhetorical subtleties on which traditional Jesuit education was based. In their place Verney offered an educational programme directed towards the rational study of observed reality. An insistence on the empirical approach made him an ardent champion of the Natural Sciences, and in fields such as Medicine he demanded a practical basis for University courses in place of out-moded theory. He likewise combated the adulation of classical authors and advocated teaching modern European languages and literature. He was contemptuous of the baroque legacy of the 17th century, and indeed of all 'artificial' forms of expression, including poetry as a genre. But *O Verdadeiro Método de Estudar* constituted virtually the only intellectual event in 18th-century Portugal and many of its recommendations were implemented by the enlightened dictator Pombal in the 1772 reform of the University of Coimbra. [AJP]

**Verri, Alessandro** (Milan 1741–Rome 1816). Italian writer. Brother of Pietro ⇨ Verri and a leading contributor to *Il Caffè*. In 1766 he accompanied Cesare ⇨ Beccaria to Paris and London, and on his return to Italy he settled in Rome. There, away from the liberal influence of Milan, his outlook became more conservative and classical; though certain preromantic features still persisted in his works, for example in his translations of *Hamlet* (1768) and *Othello* (1777), in his first successful narrative – *Le avventure di Saffo* (1782; tr. anon., 1789) – with its evident influence of *Werther*, and in his best work – *Notti romane* (1792–1804; repr. Rome, 1945; tr. anon. 1825) – inspired by the discovery of the Scipios' tomb, but essentially in the popular sepulchral tradition of Young's *Night Thoughts*. His tragedies *Pantea* and *La congiura di Milano* (*Tentativi drammatici*, Livorno, 1779) are in Shakespearean style and are significant for their rejection of the classical unities. The correspondence with his brother is important. [RHC]

*Opere scelte* (2 vols., 1822).

V. Ucerra, *I romanzi di A.V. e l'influenza della letteratura francese e inglese* (Aversa, 1912).

⇨ Verri., Pietro.

**Verri, Pietro** (Milan 1728–Milan 1797). Italian writer and economist. Brother of Alessandro ⇨ Verri, responsible for many important economic reforms in Lombardy and also for gathering around him the leading liberal intellectuals – the contributors to *Il Caffè*, the most influential periodical (1764–6) of the Italian Enlightenment. Among his chief works are: *Meditazioni sulla felicità* (1763); *Memorie storiche sulla economia pubblica dello stato di Milano* (1768); *Riflessioni sulle leggi vincolanti principalmente nel commercio dei grani* (1769); *Meditazioni sull'economia politica* (1771); *Discorso sull'indole del piacere e del dolore* (1773); *Osservazioni sulla tortura* (1777, publ. 1804). See also the correspondence with his brother. [RHC]

*Opere varie*, ed. N. Valeri (2 vols., 1947ff.); *Dal carteggio di P. e A.V.*, ed. G. Seregni (1943); *Il Caffè*, ed. S. Romagnoli (1960).

S. Caramella, *I problemi del gusto o de l'arte nella mente di P.V.* (Naples, 1926); M. R. Manfra, *P.V. e i problemi economici del suo tempo* (Rome, 1932); C. A. Vianello, *La giovinezza di Parini, V. e Beccaria* (Milan, 1933); N. Valeri, *P.V.* (Milan, 1937); W. Binni, *Preromanticismo italiano* (Naples, 1948); C. Rosso, *L'Illuminismo francese e P.V.* (Turin, 1955); M. Fubini, 'P.V. e *Il Caffè*' and 'P.V. nel carteggio col fratello', in *La cultura illuministica in Italia* (Turin, 1957); D. Chiomenti Vassalli, *I fratelli V.* (Milan, 1960); *Minori*, iii.

**Verwey, Albert** (Amsterdam 1865–Nordwijk 1937). Dutch poet, critic and scholar. The early experience of death of both mother and father (cf. *In Memoriam Patris*, *Rouw om het Jaar*) influenced his first conception of poetry as a dream (*Persephone*) and then when his intimate friendship with ⇨ Kloos broke down, as a divine attribute of the soul (*Cor Cordium*). Later, realizing that feeling alone cannot engender great poetry (and was indeed the cause of Kloos's disintegration), he developed the monistic idea of the poet as the divinely inspired interpreter of God's universe.

At 17 he was a member of the individualist circle of '1880 poets' who launched *De Nieuwe Gids* in 1885, but his thought was nearer to Wordsworth than Shelley (cf. Kloos). After his marriage to Kitty van Vloten (1890) he withdrew to prepare himself for his vocation as a poet and leader; he admired and was influenced by ⇨ George. Apart from scholarly works on van der ⇨ Noot, ⇨ Vondel, ⇨ Spiegel and ⇨ Potgieter, and many essays, he wrote 3 dramatic poems, 20 books of verse (each more complex, esoteric and contemplative), and translated Dante (*Goddelijke Komedie*, 1923). With van Deyssel he founded *Het Tweemaandelijks Tijdschrift* (1894), continued as *De Twintigste Eeuw* (1902–5), while his own *De Beweging* (1905–19) was the centre of a reaction to the impressionism of *De Nieuwe Gids*. He was professor of Dutch literature at Leyden in 1925–35. At its best his poetry has the qualities which, in a lecture, he praised in Vondel: strength and gentleness harmoniously blended. [PK]

*Oorspronkelijk Dichtwerk* (2 vols., 1938); *Proza* (10 vols., 1921–3); German tr. S. George, *Zeitgen, Dichter I* (1904); *A.V. en Stefan George, De documenten van hun Vriendschap*, ed. M. Nijland-Verviey (1965); Greshoff, *HL*; Barnouw, *CA*; Snell, *FFG*; Weevers, *PNEC*.
M. Uyldert, *Uit het leven van A.W.* (1948–59); B. M. Baxter, *A.V.'s Translations from Shelley's Poetical Works* (Leyden, 1963); S. Vestdijk *A.V. en de Idee* (Amsterdam, 1965); T. Weevers, *Mythe en vorm in de gedichten van A.V.* (2 vols., 1965).

**Vesaas, Tarjei** (Vinje, Telemark 1897–1970). Norwegian novelist, short-story writer, playwright and poet. He attended a Folk High School, travelled, then ran his own farm in his native Vinje. His first books, especially the Klas Dyregodt series – *Fars reise* (1930), *Sigrid Stallbrokk* (1931), *Dei ukjende mennene* (1932), *Hjarta høyrer sine heimlandstoner* (1938) – contain much of that highly sensitive but quiet awareness of the psychological significance of the minutiae of experience, sense impressions and silence, which is characteristic of his work. *Sandeltreet* (1933) is pessimistic in tone, but *Det store spelet* (1934), one of his best books, and its continuation, *Kvinnor ropar heim* (1935), affirm the blessings of life lived close to the soil. A mood of impending catastrophe had pervaded the play *Ultimatum* (1934), and in the novels *Kimen* (1940; tr. K. G. Chapman, *The Seed*, 1966) and *Huset i mørkret* (1945), the latter an allegory of Norway during the occupation, destructive forces are let loose. Technically, too, with their tightly packed, symbolic style, they inaugurate a new period in his work, and lead on to the fine novel *Bleikeplassen* (1946 – dramatized 1953); *Tårnet* (1948); *Signalet* (1950); *Brannen* (1961); *Isslottet* (1963; tr. E. Rokkan, *The Ice Palace*, 1965). *Vårnatt* (1954) and the sensitive *Fuglane* (1957) are more concrete. His collection of short stories *Vindane* (1952), which won him a European literary prize, pinpoint his qualities as a lyricist and psychologist. He was one of the most highly regarded of Norwegian writers. He wrote in a *Nynorsk* which he refined to a most expressive literary instrument. [RGP]

*Noveller i samling* (1964).
R. Skrede, *T.V.* (Oslo, 1947).

**Veselinović, Janko** (Crnobavski Salaš 1862–Glogovac 1905). Serbian novelist. His stories of village life are often based on folk tales. Later works portray contemporary life in the countryside with more modern realism. His novel *Hajduk Stanko* (1896), an adventure story based on the Serbian rising 1804–13, was once extremely popular. [EDG]

Popović, *JS*.
Barac, *HYL*.

**Vestdijk, Simon** (Harlingen 1898– ). Dutch writer. He studied medicine, philosophy, psychology and music before collaborating on *Forum* (cf. ter ⇨ Braak). 'Writing faster than God can read', his prolific virtuosity, penetrating intellect and demonic exploration of the subconscious endow his 38 novels, 10 collections of short stories, 28 books of essays and 22 books of poetry with a cerebral brilliance. His social and cultural critique is always challenging (cf. his notorious essay *De toekomst der religie*, 1947). If his best work lacks greatness it is because of its clinical detachment, suggesting that he is exploring life without finding or giving a diagnosis (cf. *De kellner en de levenden*, 1949; *De doktor en het lichte meisje*, 1957). Even his autobiographical novels about the early life of Anton Wachter (4 vols. in 2, 1948–9) are overweighted with psychological analysis, and in this respect he is at his best in his short stories (e.g. *De dood betrapt*, *Het Veer*, 1935). [PK]

*Het vijfde zegel* (1937); V. M. ter Braak and van Dumkerken, *Nederlandsche Litterature van nu* (1937); *De nadagen van Pilatus* (1938); *Lier en Lancet* (1939); *Albert Verwey en de idee* (1940); *De Poolsche ruiter* (1946); *De Koperen tuin* (1950; tr. A. Brotherton, *The Garden Where the Brass Band Played*, 1965); *Door de bri van het heden* (1956) (anthology of poetry, short stories and essays); Greshoff, *HL*.

Menno ter Braak, *De duivelskunstenaar* (Amsterdam, 1945); A. Wadman, *Handdruk en handgemeen* (Utrecht, 1965).

**Vetranić, Mavro.** ◊ Dalmatian and Dubrovnik Literature.

**Vian, Boris** (Ville d'Avray 1920–Paris 1959). French novelist and playwright. He owed something to surrealism, Kafka and the vogue for science-fiction. Under the assumed name of Vernon Sullivan, he gained notoriety for several American-style 'tough' novels, notably *J'irai cracher sur vos tombes* (1947), but his serious fiction has much greater sophistication and range. After the tentative explorations of *Vercoquin et le plancton* (1946), *L'automne à Pékin* (1947) ushers in his familar universe, a kind of poetic fable charged with violence and fantasy in which the private experience of children challenges the values and assumptions of the adult world. Didiche and Olive, the unsentimentally observed children of *L'automne à Pékin*, distrust and despise their elders, as do Jöel and Citroën in *L'arrache-cœur* (1953), where he paints a horrifying delirium of maternal possessiveness, and the conflict between the secret, autonomous life of childhood and the tyranny of family and social life. This desire to penetrate, through all kinds of semantic looseness and confusion, to the heart of personal and emotional relations also distinguishes *L'herbe rouge* (1950), where Wolf's explorations are aided by a time-machine, and *L'écume des jours* (1947), a moving love-story. The satirical assault on social and political institutions is more explicit in the plays. Of these, the most successful is *Les bâtisseurs d'empire ou le Schmürz* (1959; tr. S. W. Taylor, *The Empire Builders*, 1962), a kind of music-hall epic of the decline of the social and military values of the bourgeoisie. Equally violent attacks on war are contained in *Équarrissage pour tous* (1950) and *Le goûter des généraux* (1963). Vian has also exalted love in his dramatization of the legends of the knights of the Round Table: *Le chevalier de neige* (1953). Some short stories have been collected in *Les lurettes fourrées* (1962). Other posthumously published work includes: *Le dernier des métiers* (1966); *Les fourmis* (1966); *En avant la zizique et par ici les gros sous* (1966); *Trouble dans les Andains* (1966). [SBJ]

*Théâtre* (1965).

D. Noakes, *B.V.* (1964); H. Baudin, *B.V. La poursuite de la vie totale* (Paris, 1966); J. Clouzet, *B.V.* (Paris, 1966); 'Les vies parallèles de B.V.', in *Bizarre*, 39–40 (1966); P. Kast, preface to *L'arrache-cœur* and *L'herbe rouge* (Paris, 1962); Corvin, *TNF*; Beigbeder, *TFL*; Serreau, *HNT*.

**Viau, Théophile (de)** (1590–1626). French poet. A free-thinker, imprisoned for his share in *Le parnasse satirique* of 1622, but author also of spirited nature poetry, and of a tragedy on *Pyrame et Thisbé* (1623). [WGM]

F. Lachèvre, *T. de V.* (Paris, 1909); A. Adam, *T. de V.* (Paris, 1925).

**Vicente, Gil** (Lisbon *c.*1470–Lisbon 1536). Portuguese dramatist and the greatest in Europe before Shakespeare. He has been identified with Gil Vicente the goldsmith who worked the first gold brought back by Vasco da Gama from India (1503) into a monstrance for the Hieronymites of Belém, was elected by the goldsmiths to represent them in the Casa dos Vinte e Quatro (1512) and named as master of the Lisbon Mint (1513). If this identification is incorrect – and one must remember the frequency of homonyms in Portugal at the time – little is known of Gil Vicente the dramatist beyond what can be gathered from his works. These made his reputation at court where from 1502 to 1536 no anniversary, no important occasion, was complete without the production of one of his plays.

His first work, the *Monólogo do Vaqueiro*

(1502), was written to amuse the Queen after childbirth. One must imagine him bursting into her room, with rustic presents of milk, eggs, and honey, reciting his piece. Behind this and other of his early plays lies the tradition of pastoral drama practised in Spain by ⇨ Encina. He was heir also to the tradition of the morality play, the farce, the parodied sermon and the *momos* performed at court. (These last were usually episodes from novels of chivalry or the Bible in simple dramatic form, yet with some wealth of stage effect.) But in much of his theatre Vicente turned to the life he saw around him for his subject-matter, abandoning medieval chivalry and the religious theatre. In the *Auto da Alma*, too, his masterpiece in the latter category, we see a human personality emerging from the world of medieval symbolism. Allegory gives way to observation.

An allegorical framework, however, allows him scope for the presentation of a variety of social types (*Autos das Barcas, Auto da Feira, Romagem de Agravados*). All Portuguese society offers itself to his biting wit, especially the clergy and the idle nobility (to which it was every man's aim to belong), and silly women and the men who made them silly. Vicente is not merely an anticlerical: he disapproved of indulgences, of empty-headed prayer, of a cult of the saints which was full of pagan reminiscences. He disapproved of the persecution of the Jews. He may have read Erasmus. He was a rationalist who preferred to try to discover natural causes for unparalleled events, instead of the hand of God (*Carta a D. João III*).

His theatre is essentially one of types, sometimes of allegorical figures becoming types (*Mofina Mendes*). Unforgettable are Frei Paço, the dandy priest, Frei Narciso, the pseudo-ascetic, angling for a bishopric; the procuresses, Branca Gil, and Brígida Vaz with her cushions; the Jews who appear as marriage-brokers (*Inês Pereira*) or enjoying a delightful family life (*Lusitânia*); the amorous fidalgo (*Quem tem farelos?*); the young women, Cassandra, Inês Pereira, Isabel; the children (*Rubena*); the negroes (*Clérigo da Beira, Frágua de Amor*), the gypsies (*Farsa das Ciganas*) and the goddesses who appear in disguise, talking like gypsies (*Lusitânia*). For Vicente also has a new feeling for the forces of nature. The tempests encountered by the Portuguese on their sea-voyages play a part in his drama, mountains and the seasons are personified, and the inhabitants of Olympus appear in human form (*Auto dos Quatro Tempos, Triunfo do Inverno*).

Psychological interest (never strong in the Iberian theatre) comes only as the result of the study of classical drama, but in certain of Vicente's plays (*Auto da Índia, O Velho da Horta, Inês Pereira*) we see him moving in this direction. These are also his most perfect dramatic constructions, because they have a real intrigue which gives unity to the action, though his adaptations from the romance of chivalry (*Dom Duardos, Amadís*) have easy continuity of narrative. All the characters who appear on his stage are wonderfully defined by their language, whether Portuguese or Spanish. He noted the archaisms of shepherds, Jews, and women, the conservative elements in the population, the professional phrases of doctors, the stereotyped speech of grandiloquent Castilians, and the sounds of the Portuguese spoken by negroes and gypsies. All this dramatic conversation is expressed in the most delicious verse of an unparalleled ease and fluency, so that the traditional heptasyllabic *redondilha* seems quite the most natural vehicle for social intercourse.

Many of the plays end with traditional elements of song and dance. Here too Vicente is revealed as a poet of exquisite lyricism, whether writing carols to the Virgin or an *ensalada* in which snatches of the Portuguese version of 'Stop tha' tickling, Jock' jostle with popular songs of the day and reminiscences of the *cantigas de amigo*.

The works of Gil Vicente were collected and published posthumously (1562) by his son and daughter who proved regrettable editors. In addition his works were at various times mauled by the Holy Office. Uncut remained only the *Monólogo do Vaqueiro, S. Martinho, As Ciganas, Quem tem farelos?*, some of the poems and his own epitaph. [ARM]

*Obras Completas* (CSC, 6 vols., 1942–4); *Obras Dramáticas Castellanas* (CC, 1962); *Lyrics of G.V. with Portuguese Text*, tr. A. F. G. Bell (1914); *Dom Duardos*, ed. D. Alonso (Madrid, 1942); *Barca do Inferno*, ed. C. D. Ley (Madrid, 1946); *Inês Pereira*, ed. I. S. Révah (*Bulletin Historique du Théâtre Portugais*, III, 2, and V, 2, 1952/4); *Deux autos méconnus de G.V.: Obra da Geração Humana – Auto de Deus Padre e Justiça e Misericórdia*, ed. I. S. Révah (1948).

A. Braamcamp Freire *G.V.* (Lisbon, 1947); J. de Carvalho, *Os Sermões de G.V. e a Arte de Pregar* (Lisbon, 1948); C. Michaëlis de Vasconcelos, *Notas Vicentinas* (Coimbra, 1912/19); A. E. Beau, *Estudos* (Lisbon, 1959); H. de Castro Guimarães, *A Sátira Vicentina* (Lisbon, 1958); V. Nemésio, *G.V. Floresta de Enganos* (Lisbon, 1941); J. de Oliveira, *G.V. e Auto da Alma* (Lisbon, 1952), and *A Visitação de G.V.* (Lisbon, 1953); O. de Pratt, *G.V.* (Lisbon, 1931); I. S. Révah, *Recherches sur les œuvres de G.V.* (Lisbon, 1951), and *Deux autos de G.V. restitués à leur auteur* (Lisbon, 1949); A. J. Saraiva, *G.V.* (Lisbon, 1943); L. Sletsjøe, *O Elemento Cénico em G.V.* (Lisbon, 1965); P. Teyssier, *La langue de G.V.* (Paris, 1959).

**Vicetto, Benito.** ⇨ Galician Literature.

**Vico, Giambattista** (Naples 1668–Naples 1744). Italian philosopher. Of humble birth. His chief work was his *Principii di una scienza nuova d'intorno alla natura delle nazioni*, the three successive editions of which (called *Scienza nuova prima*, 1725; *seconda*, 1729–30; *terza*, posth. 1744; tr. T. G. Bergin and M. H. Fisch, N.Y., 1961) elaborate his theory, starting with an acceptance of the cartesian *cogito* but then rejecting the excessively abstract mathematical reasoning that Descartes based on this. Faced with the choice between a perfect understanding of a philosophical system divorced from reality and an imperfect understanding of the reality of life, Vico chose the latter and developed his concept that, since men could only fully apprehend the reality of their own creations, the task of Philosophy should be the study of the universal principles underlying the history of nations. More important perhaps than his conclusions are certain stages of his argument, concerning for example the interpretation of ancient documents, the function of the imagination in the development of thought and the significance of myths in the early history of mankind. [RHC]

*Opere*, ed. F. Nicolini (6 vols., 1914–41); ed. F. Nicolini (Milan, Naples, 1953); *Autobiografia*, ed. M. Fubini (1960); tr. M. H. Fisch and T. G. Bergin, *The Autobiography of G.B.V.* (N.Y., 1944).

H. P. Adams, *The Life and Writings of G.V.* (London, 1935); M. Fubini, *Stile e umanità in G.B.V.* (Bari, 1946); G. Villa, *La filosofia del mito secondo G.B.V.* (Milan, 1949); T. Berry, *The Historical Theory of J.B.V.* (Washington, 1949); A. R. Caponigri, *Time and Idea. The Theory of History in J.B.V.* (Chicago, 1953); S. Banchetti, *Il significato morale dell'estetica vichiana* (Milan, 1957); *Minori*, iii.

**Vida, Marco Girolamo** (Cremona 1485–Alba 1566). Italian Latinist. Bishop of Alba, he attended the Council of Trent, and his *Constitutiones Synodales* is a statement of the ideals of the Counter-Reformation.

His chief work was the Latin epic *Christiad* (1535), on the story of the Redemption, but its elegant Virgilian style cannot save it from dullness. Also in hexameters is his *De arte poetica* (ed. T. Tristram, Oxford, 1722; tr. C. Pitt, 1725, repr. in A. S. Cook, *The Art of Poetry*, Boston, 1892), which enjoyed European fame for two centuries. He left too a poem on chess, *Scacchia ludus*, one on the silkworm (*Bombycum libri duo*) (both ed. T. Tristram, Oxford, 1722) and a prose treatise *De republicae dignitate* (ed. and Italian tr. A. Altamura in G. Toffanin, *L'umanesimo al Concilio di Trento*, 1955). [DGR]

M. Di Cesare, *V.'s Christiad and Vergilian Epic* (N.Y., 1964); Sparrow, *LVHR*.

**Vidric, Vladimir** (Zagreb 1875–Zagreb 1909). Croatian poet. One of the first Bohemian representatives of the *fin de siècle*, his poetry has a classical plasticity unique in Yugoslav poetry. His theme is the beauty of life and nature seen against their sadness and suffering. His work is limited in quantity and individual in character. [EDG]

Ibrovac, *APY*; Lavrin, *AMYP*.
Barac, *HYL*; Kadić, *CCL*.

**Vieira, António** (Lisbon 1608–Bahia 1697). Portuguese writer. A Jesuit and greatest of classical Portuguese prose-writers. Born in a working-class family with a strain of Negro blood, Vieira accompanied his parents to Bahia in 1614. He remained in Brazil for the next twenty-seven years, being educated at the Jesuit College in the colonial capital, where he entered the Society as a novice in 1623. Three years later, he wrote the Jesuit Annual Letter from Brazil, which is the earliest of his surviving writings and displays all the qualities which subsequently made him a celebrated writer. While continuing his theological and philosophical studies, he did some work in the *aldeias* or mission-villages of the Amerindians near Bahia, and he was already the most popular preacher in the colony by the time of his ordination in December 1634. He went to Portugal in 1641 with the emissaries who brought the news of Brazil's adhesion to

King John IV, whose interest, confidence and patronage he at once secured. Vieira on his side believed that the new king would realize the fulfilment of the Sebastianist prophecies which were so widely spread in Portugal. Even after King John's death in 1656, for many years he confidently expected that this monarch would arise from the dead and inaugurate the fifth Biblical universal monarchy under Portuguese leadership. Apart from acting as adviser on Brazilian affairs, Vieira was employed on various confidential diplomatic missions to France, the Dutch Republic, and Rome in 1646–50. Sent by his Superiors to the Maranhão mission-field in 1652, Vieira left the Court at Lisbon with considerable reluctance; but once arrived in the colony he displayed as much energy, zeal and ardour in the pursuit of souls as he had previously employed in the exercise of worldly wisdom. Owing to his outspoken criticism of the colonists for their enslavement of the Amerindians, he was arrested and deported with most of the other Jesuits from the Maranhão and Pará in 1661. The palace-revolution of June 1662 weakened Vieira's influence at court, and he was arrested by the Portuguese Inquisition, to which he had long been an object of dislike and suspicion, not only on account of his unorthodox Messianic and Sebastianist beliefs, but also because of his outspoken advocacy of toleration for the hated Marranos or 'New-Christians'. Sentenced in December 1667, shortly after another palace revolution had brought his friends to power, he was speedily released from confinement, but he never regained the influence he had once enjoyed at court. In 1669–75 he resided at Rome, where he was almost as popular a preacher as he had been at Lisbon, Queen Christina of Sweden and the Jesuit General, Oliva, being among his many admirers. Finally disillusioned with court politics after another sojourn at Lisbon, he returned to Bahia in 1681, where he remained until his death.

As Robert Southey observed in 1809, 'better Portuguese has never been written than that penned by this remarkable man'. He was the acknowledged master of Portuguese prose during his lifetime, and, unlike that of most great authors, his literary fame did not undergo even a temporary eclipse after his death. His letters, crisp, incisive and frequently spiced with pungent humour, are still as readable nowadays as they were 300 years ago. His sermons, though strongly tinged by *conceptismo*, are hardly affected at all by *cultismo*, and have always been regarded as oratorical masterpieces. Vieira in prose and ⇨ Camões in poetry are the two writers who are without peers in the Portuguese language. [CRB]

*Obras Escolhidas*, ed. A. Sérgio and H. Cidade (12 vols., 1951–4).

Raymond Cantel, *Les Sermons de V., étude du style* (Paris, 1959) and *Prophétisme et Messianisme dans l'œuvre d'A.V.* (Paris, 1960); C. R. Boxer, *A Great Luso-Brazilian, Figure. Padre A.V., S. J.* (*Diamante*, 5, London 1957).

**Viélé-Griffin, Francis** (Norfolk, Virginia, U.S.A. 1864–Paris 1937). Poet of French extraction. He settled in France as a young man, sharing his time between Paris and Touraine, for which province he felt an inspiring affection. His first verses appeared in the review *Lutèce*, and were gathered under the title *Cueille d'Avril* (1886). Other collections, such as *Les cygnes* (1887), *Joies* (1889) and *La chevauchée d' Yeldis et autres poèmes* (1893), helped to establish him as one of the most admired of the later Symbolists. With Bernaud Lazare and Paul Adam he founded a review called *Les Entretiens Politiques et Littéraires* (1890–2), in which appeared his theories for a new type of poetry based on emancipated versification. In practice he lived up to his principles and became one of the pioneers of the *vers libre*. Temperamentally he distinguished himself from most of his compeers by the optimism of his feelings, his fluent rhythms being spontaneously prompted by impulses of joy in existence and in the beauty of nature which are reflected in most of his titles. The cult of legendary heroism and sacrificial faith also provided motifs for his songs and themes for longer poems like *Phocas le Jardinier* (1898), the dramatic poem, *La légende ailée de Wieland le Forgeron* (1900), and those collected in *L'amour sacrée* (1903). This fresh lyricism and these imaginative fictions helped to revive the poetic atmosphere in France sixty years ago. But they lacked sufficient sense of realities to be secure against the onslaughts and horrors that have intervened. [PMJ]

*Poètes d'aujourd'hui* (1910) (selections).

J. de Cours, *V.-G.* (Paris, 1930); P. Martino, *Parnasse et Symbolisme (1850–1900)* (Paris, 1935).

**Vigna, Pier della** (Capua *c.*1180–? San Miniato or Pisa 1249). Italian poet. He belonged to the Sicilian school and was Chancellor under Frederick II. His story is told in the *Divine Comedy* (*Inferno* xiii). Only a handful of *canzoni* and one sonnet have come down to us. They are in typical Sicilian vein, technically accomplished compositions on the conventional theme of chivalrous love. [DGR]

Salinari, *PLD*; Contini, *PD*; Panvini, *RSS*
C. Guerrieri-Crocetti, *La Magna Curia* (Milan, 1947).

**Vigny, Alfred Victor de** (Loches 1797–Paris 1863). French Romantic philosopher poet. He came of a noble family with a long military tradition. Proud, generous, extremely sensitive, he acquired a protective reserve during an unhappy childhood, and further strengthened it during ten years' service as an army officer (1814–24, finally discharged 1827). As far as his military duties allowed, Vigny, a poet by inclination – his first volume of ten *Poèmes* was published in 1822 – frequented Parisian literary circles where he met Antoni and Émile Deschamps, ⇨ Nodier, H. de Latouche, and Hugo among other contributors to *La Muse Française* (1823–4). After his marriage to Lydia Bunbury in 1825, he settled in Paris and achieved success with a historical novel, *Cinq-Mars*, and the *Poèmes antiques et modernes* (1826). In 1829, he claimed to be the first of his generation to have given epic or dramatic form to a philosophical concept, and in this sense was acclaimed by Hugo and Deschamps as the inventor of *le poème*.

His contribution to romantic theatre is at first Shakespearian. An adaptation of *Romeo and Juliet* was not staged but the *More de Venise*, based on *Othello*, was performed in 1829 at the Comédie Française, as was his own drama, *La Maréchale d'Ancre*, two years later. A comedy, *Quitte pour la peur*, followed in 1833.

Although recognized as a master of the new poetry, he was outdistanced by Hugo. In 1830 he was conscious of two major setbacks. Instead of fame, his military career had brought boredom and servitude. In literature, he had not conquered the preeminence he felt his talents merited. Moreover, with the July revolution disappeared the last hopes of the class to which he belonged.

Between 1830 and 1837, he composed his prose 'epic of disillusion', undertaking the defence of the *parias*, outcasts and victims of society. These were: the poet-genius in *Stello* (1832), of which one episode, *Chatterton*, was rewritten for the theatre; the soldier in *Servitude et grandeur militaires* (1835) and the visionary in *Daphné* (1837, unfinished). The fate of the noble had been illustrated in *Cinq-Mars*. In spite of his ideal of peace in solitude, Vigny maintained from 1831 a stormy liaison with the actress Marie Dorval who, in the part of Kitty Bell, ensured the success of *Chatterton* (1835). He brought it to an end in 1838 during the spiritual and moral crisis following his mother's death. Putting aside all religious faith, he confided to poetry the anguish of further disillusion ('La mort du loup', 1838; 'Le Mont des Oliviers', 1839).

He returned progressively to public life, persisting in his efforts to help younger poets in need. He was elected to the Académie Française in 1845, becoming Directeur in 1849. Politics tempted him but he remained an observer, interested in theories of progress and order, hating war and acutely conscious of the reality of human suffering. His output during the last years was relatively small, being confined to some eleven poems, but his *Journal* shows that his powers of observation, warmth of human feeling and inspiration were not at fault.

Consistency of thought, purpose and style distinguished Vigny from his contemporaries. From 1820, the theme of human destiny in conflict with liberty ('La Prison') is evolved alongside a continuous meditation upon the ironic inhuman cruelty of divine 'Justice'. The latter weighs on the enforced solitude of genius ('Moïse', 1822); punishes filial affection in its servitor ('La fille de Jephté', 1820), mutual love ('Le déluge', 1824) and pity ('Èloa', 1824). A silent divinity imposed upon humanity a destiny of ignorance, evil, suffering and death. Religious and political systems are but further causes of servitude ('Paris', 1831). In the progress of ideas promise for the future lies with the disinterested genius, poet, artist, visionary or scientist. Society destroys what it fails to understand or fears, as is shown in *Stello* by the fates of Gilbert, Chatterton and Chénier. To survive, the poet must separate his ideal from political and social illusion, hide his secret in the solitude necessary for meditation. *Chatterton* went further. The 'page of philosophy' enacted before a public shocked by the hero's suicide was an indictment of materialist society.

The reasoned pessimism, necessary for survival, eventually leads to guarded optimism. The progression is traced in the *Poèmes philosophiques* published, for the most part, by Vigny in *La Revue des Deux Mondes* (1838–44) and collected after his death by Louis Ratisbonne under the title *Les destinées*. The poem of the same title (1849) warns mankind to expect almost the same rigour from Providence as from antique Fatality. The *majesty* of human suffering lies in the ability of the mind to conquer itself and Destiny through stoicism, distain and silence ('La mort du loup' – 'Le mont des oliviers' – 'Le silence'). Therein is to be found independence enabling the imagination to condense the vision of the ideal in the peerless diamond of poetry ('La maison du berger'). The ultimate triumph of ideas is foreseen in 'La bouteille à la mer' (1847) and confided to posterity in 'L'esprit pur' (1863).

The *Journal* reveals that Vigny's inspiration was intensely personal. The use of symbols renders the literary expression indirect and impersonal, even 'La colère de Samson' transposing the rupture with Marie Dorval. By creating a type of symbolical art giving life, form and beauty to abstractions, Vigny was an innovator.

His influence extends to two other fields. The avoidance of all effusion and the Attic cult of beauty foreshadow Leconte de Lisle. With *Chatterton*, symbol of persecuted genius, he fathered the myth of *le poète maudit*. [BJ]

*Œuvres complètes*, ed. F. Baldensperger (2 vols., Pléiade, 1948); *Les destinées*, ed. V. L. Saulnier (Geneva, 1947); *Mémoires inédits* (1958).

M. Citoleux, *A. de V.* (Paris, 1924); P. Flottes, *La pensée politique et sociale d'A. de V.* (Paris, 1927); G. Bonnefoy, *La pensée religieuse et morale d'A. de V.* (Paris, 1944); E. Lauvrière, *A. de V.* (2 vols., Paris, 1945); F. Germain, *L'imagination d'A. de V.* (Paris, 1963); B. de la Salle, *A. de V.* (Paris, 1963).

**Viita, Lauri Arvi** (Pirkkala 1916–Mäntsälä 1965). Finnish poet and novelist. He worked for a time as a carpenter (his father's trade). A poet of great original force, he often achieved an effect of powerful and moving solemnity by means of simple everyday imagery. He experimented with an aphoristic use of a simple, ballad-like 4-line stanza, as well as with long, impetuous accounts of cosmic visions, in which the symbolism is deeply stratified and variable in meaning. His first novel, *Moreeni* (1950), is a monumental work describing changing patterns of life and society in a provincial town during the Finnish civil war of 1918. *Entäs sitten, Leevi* (1965), his second to last novel, was published just before he was killed in a car accident. [RV]

*Valitut runot* (1958) (selected poems).

**Vilanova, Arnau de.** ⇨ Catalan Literature.

**Viljanen, Lauri Sakari** (Kaarina 1900– ). Finnish poet and critic. Professor of Finnish Literature at Helsinki (1954-67), principal literary critic (1926–50) of *Helsingin Sanomat*, for fifteen years a member of the editorial board of *Valvoja-Aika*, and for two years editor of *Parnasso*. His impressionistic, psychologically perceptive criticism made him one of the most influential reviewers of his generation: in the twenties he was closely associated with ⇨ Tulenkantajat. His essays and verse translations have done much to keep the Finns abreast of contemporary movements in European literature. As a poet he has pursued an independent line both in handling and remoulding traditional forms and in his innovations; a reflective, sometimes a rather dictatorial humanist. His finest poetry is in *Seitsemän elegiaa* (1957), dedicated to Jean Sibelius. [RV]

*Kootut runot* (1946) (collected poems); *Valikoima runoja* (1958) (selected poems); Tompuri, *VF.*

**Villaespesa, Francisco** (Laujar, Almería 1877–Madrid 1936). Spanish modernist poet who popularized the innovations of Rubén Darío. His former reputation has now declined. 'Rhythm, the great rebel, obeys me as a vassal,' he wrote; and his too easy rhythms proved his undoing. His themes range from history to nature, his style from romanticism to *fin-de-siècle* impressionism. In general his colours are strong and his tone gently melancholy. He also wrote plays in the modernist manner, of which *El alcázar de las perlas* (1911) was an outstanding success. His importance is seen today as having lain in his friendship with and influence on younger poets, especially ⇨ Jiménez, and in his having created and prepared the audience for their poetry. [JMC]

*Poesías completas* (1954); Blecua, *FLE*.

F. de Onís, *F. V. y el modernismo* (Madrid, 1937).

**Villalón, Cristóbal de** (beginning of 16th cent.–1558). Spanish humanist. Educated at Alcalá and Salamanca, he taught at Valladolid where he published a dialogue *La ingeniosa comparación entre lo antiguo y lo presente* (1539) and *El provechoso tratado de cambios y contrataciones de mercaderes y reprobación de usura* (1541). His essay in the style of Castiglione, *El Scolástico* (ed. M. M. y Pelayo, 1911), discusses the ideal university teacher and student. He attacks Nebrija on his method of teaching Latin in his *Gramática castellana* (1558). He is thought to be the Bachiller Villalón who wrote a classical play *Tragedia de Mirrha* (1536; ed. Foulché-Delbosc, 1908) based on Ovid. He has also been credited on slight evidence with being the 'Christophoro Gnosopho' named as author of *El crotalón* (ed. Fuensanta del Valle, 1871), a social satire in the style of Lucian with Erasmist elements intermingled with historical and fantastic sections written in vigorous prose of high quality. Though it was not printed until 1871 Cervantes may have seen it and been influenced in his *Coloquio de los perros*. The attribution to him of the *Viaje de Turquía* (possibly by Laguna) is certainly false. [JG]

Bataillon, *EE*.

**Villamediana, Conde de.** ⇨ Tarsis, Juan de.

**Villani, Giovanni** (Florence *c.*1276–Florence 1348). Italian chronicler. A Florentine merchant, he held many posts in the administration of the commune. The 12 books of his *Cronica* begin with the Tower of Babel, and, proceeding through a haphazard mixture of classical legend and Biblical tradition, go on to record the history of Florence down to 1348. Even the last 6 (from the arrival in Italy of Charles d'Anjou) make flat reading as he chronicles events year by year, generally without distinguishing the important from the unimportant. He sees human events as the unfolding of God's will, and claims the role of moral instructor as well as chronicler. Details of Florentine government and commerce are of specialist interest, but his chronicle has little of the drama of ⇨ Compagni's. After his death further books were added by his brother Matteo and his nephew Filippo, which took the story down to 1364. [DGR]

*Cronisti del Trecento*, ed. R. Palmarocchi (Milan, 1935); tr. R. E. Selfe, *Villani's Chronicle* (1906) (selections of the first 9 books).

**Villasandino, Alfonso Álvarez** (Villasandino, *c.*1345–1425?). Spanish poet at the court of Henry II and John I of Castile. He began by writing in Galician but changed to Castilian. His verse is uneven, and much of it seems to have been written to order. His topics are satirical, petitionary, amorous in the troubadour manner, religious and occasional. One of his best poems, which is in praise of Seville, 'Linda sin comparación/claridat y luz de España', earned him a hundred gold doubloons. His gross attack on a lady who had rejected one of his friends was no doubt also commissioned. His poems are given pride of place in Baena's *Cancionero*.

*Cancionero*, NBAE, XXII; Blecua, *FLE*; Cohen, *PBSV*; Trend, *OBSV*.

**Villegas, Esteban Manuel de** (Matute/Logroño 1585–Nájera 1669). Spanish poet. A lawyer by profession. His *Eróticas* (1618; CC, 1913), after Horace and Anacreon, contains charming, but slight idylls, which foreshadow the 18th century, when he was still admired; today he is remembered only for odd poems, e.g. 'Al céfiro', a Spanish version of sapphics. In trouble with the Inquisition, he omitted the controversial last book on free will in his version of ⇨ Boethius. [JMC]

BAE, 42, 61; Blecua, *FLE*; Cohen, *PBSV*; Trend, *OBSV*.

**Villehardouin, Geoffroy de** (1152–*c.*1212). French chronicler and marshal of Champagne. His *Conquête de Constantinople* (written after 1207; ed. E. Faral, 1938–9; Pauphilet, *HCMA*; tr. M. R. B. Shaw, *Chronicles of the Crusades*, Penguin Classics, 1963) is the earliest example of good French prose. He describes the Fourth Crusade in which he had taken a leading part; especially vivid are his exhortation to the Venetians in the basilica of Saint Mark, his delivery of the ultimatum to the Greeks before the onslaught on Constantinople, and the many sieges and battle scenes, which he sees as a strategist. He is not concerned with the European political intrigues which diverted the Crusade to Constantinople. A noble who lived by the feudal code of honour, he enjoyed a reputation for probity among the warring factions in the Crusade. His descriptions are bare, restrained in enthusiasm, and possessed of a certain beauty, as in the departure of the Crusading fleet from Corfu. His history finishes with the death in 1207 of the Marquis Boniface of

Montferrat, who had led the Crusade to Constantinople. Some time before 1220, his account was continued by Henri de Valenciennes. [LTT]

J. Longnon, *Recherches sur la vie de G. de V.* (Paris, 1939); *R*, LVII (1931); *Revue Historique*, CLXXVII (1936).

**Villemarqué, Théodore Hersart de la.** ⇨ Breton Literature.

**Villiers de l'Isle-Adam, P. H.,** Comte de (St Brieuc 1840–Paris 1889). French poet. His *Premières poésies* (1859) were romantic in type. He collaborated in the *Parnasse Contemporain*; published *Isis* (1862) and, at intervals during the next five years, the dramas *Elen* (1865), *Morgane* (1866), and the collection *Tribulat Bonhomet* (1887). A decade of silence ensued during which this descendant of a noble line suffered great poverty and affliction. In 1883 he reappeared with *Contes cruels*, recommended to the younger generation by Huysmans in *À rebours*. Thence until his death in 1889 he published a series of plays and tales. His complete works were edited in eleven volumes (1914–31).

He was a picturesque survival of an impoverished family steeped in traditions of grandeur and chivalry and fervently Catholic. At Paris, existing in severe straits, he devoted his energies to literary productions of a highly idealistic type, mingling horrific episodes with scenes of lofty beauty in prose of a rich poetical quality. Their author was sensitive to most of the fantastic thinking in his time, occult, spiritualistic, Wagnerian; he could even blend these modes with ideas drawn from modern science, as in the novel called *L'Ève future* (1886). But it is to the visionary drama, *Axël* (1890; tr. H. P. R. Fineberg, *Axel*, 1925), that one turns for the supreme achievement of imaginative gifts like his that triumph in excess. Axël, the young lord of Auërsperg, having tried to discourage interest in the treasure he knows to be concealed beneath his castle, descends one night to find in the family vault Sara, a novice escaped from a nunnery. Rosicrucian pursuits have led her to the clue. Sara attempts to kill Axël, but in the struggle each perceives the beauty of the other and they decide to die together by sharing a fatal potion. [PMJ]

*Sardonic Tales*, tr. H. Miles (1927). E. Wilson, *Axel's Castle* (1900); M. Daireaux, *V. de l'I.A.* (Paris, 1936); Bédier and Hazard, *LF.*

**Villon, François** (Paris 1431–after 1463). French poet. Proper name de Montcorbier, sometimes called des Loges. He was brought up by his benefactor Guillaume de Villon, chaplain of Saint-Benoît-le-Bétourné, whose name he adopted. After a disturbed student life he took the degree of Master of Arts in 1452. In 1455 he killed a priest in the cloister of Saint-Benoît, received letters of remission for this murder in 1456, but had to flee and wander through France (1456–60) after taking part in a theft at the College of Navarre. He visited Bourg-la-Reine, Angers (mentioned in his *Lais*), Bourges, Saint-Généron, and attended the court of ⇨ Charles d'Orléans at Blois. Imprisoned in 1461 at Meung-sur-Loire by the Bishop of Orleans, and freed by Louis XI when he passed through the town, he composed his *Testament* between December 1461 and March 1462. Arrested in November 1462 at the Châtelet on a charge of theft, he agreed to restore 120 gold crowns to the College of Navarre. In 1463, following an affray, he was condemned to be 'pendu et estranglé' but the sentence was quashed and Villon was banished from Paris for ten years.

His surviving work (about 3,000 lines) consists of the *Lais* or *Petit Testament*, the *Testament*, several *ballades*, the *Débat du cuer et du corps de Villon*, a few occasional poems and epistles and his epitaph, the *Ballade des pendus*. In the *Lais* 'legacies', he takes leave of Paris and bequeaths his worthless possessions lightheartedly to friends and enemies. In the *Testament*, a review of his misspent life and sufferings, he expresses his macabre interest in physical decay and death. His bequests in the *Testament*, lighthearted, moving and bitter, are a framework for his most famous *ballades* such as the *Ballade pour prier Nostre-Dame*, bequeathed to his mother, the *Ballade des dames du temps jadis* and the *Ballade de la belle Heaulmière*. Among *ballades* not included in the *Testament* are the *Ballade du Concours de Blois* ('Je meurs de seuf auprès de la fontaine') and his masterpiece the *Ballade des pendus*, 'Frères, humains qui après nous vivez', written under sentence of death.

In 1533 Marot published an edition of the 'meilleur poëte parisien qui se trouve', but Villon's fame lapsed from the 16th to the 19th century. His ideas and poetic forms, even his use of thieves' cant, are largely unoriginal, but his compassion for suffering humanity expressed under an ironical show of detachment, his direct, personal language and startling success with individual lines and refrains make him the outstanding French poet of the 15th century. Various poems by him have been translated by Rossetti, Synge, Swinburne and Henley. [LTT]

*Œuvres*, ed. A. Longnon (4th edn, 1958) (useful bibliography up to 1930); ed. L. Thuasne (3 vols., 1923) (with detailed commentary); ed. A. Mary (2nd edn, 1957); ed. R. Guiette (1964); trs. H. de Vere Stacpoole (London, 1913); H. B. McCaskie (London, 1946).

P. Champion, *F.V., sa vie et son temps* (2nd edn, Paris, 1933), and *Histoire poétique du XVe siècle* ii (Paris, 1923); I. Siciliano, *F.V. et les thèmes poétiques du moyen âge* (Paris, 1934); G. A. Bruneli, *F.V.* ... (Milan, 1961) (good bibliography); J. Fox, *The Poetry of V.* (London/Edinburgh, 1962).

**Vincent of Beauvais** (*c.*1190–*c.*1264). Medieval Latin writer and scholar. A Dominican who compiled an encyclopedia of medieval knowledge, *Speculum maius*, in 3 parts: (i) *Speculum naturale*, a summary of natural history, astronomy, geography, agriculture etc.; (ii) *Speculum doctrinale*, a practical manual of mechanical arts, building, military science and also of logic, grammar, philosophy and theology; (iii) *Speculum historiale*, an outline of the history of the world, mingled with much legend. Industrious but unoriginal, he quotes from nearly fifty authors, including Greek, Arabic and Hebrew writers, but probably only through the medium of Latin translations. [FB]

*Speculum maius*, ed. by Benedictines of Douai (4 vols., 1624).

L. Lieser, *V. von B. als Kompilator und Philosoph* (Leipzig, 1928); Taylor, *MM*.

**Vinje, Aasmund** (Vinje, Telemark 1818–Gran, Hadeland 1870). Norwegian poet and essayist. The son of a cottar, born in the humblest circumstances, he took a law degree at 38, but had first made his name as a journalist. In 1858 he founded the periodical *Dølen* to further the cause of *Nynorsk* which he had adopted as his own literary language. His best-known work, *Ferdaminni* (2 vols., 1861), is a discursive account, full of keen observation, humour and critical comment, of a journey to Trondheim for the coronation of Charles XV. His poems, *Diktsamling* (1864), are, on the whole, slight and sentimental. In 1863, on a visit to Britain, he published in Edinburgh his unflattering *A Norseman's View of Britain and the British*. [RGP]

*Skriftir i samling*, ed. O. Midttun (5 vols., 1916–21).

V. Vislie, *Å.V.* (Oslo, 1929); S. Skard, *A.O.V. og antikken* (Oslo, 1938); A. Bergsgaard, *A.V.* (Oslo, 1940); O. Midttun, *A.O.V.* (Oslo, 1960).

**Vinokurov, Yevgeny** (Bryansk 1925– ). Russian poet. From a soldier's family, he fought in the War, the theme of his earlier poetry. His poetry has much in common with ◊ Slutsky's, and shows most of the features typical of the best post-Stalin writers. It is unpretentious, precise, probing moral and psychological problems. He uses language carefully and lyrically, simply but not without subtlety; he eschews mental cliches, inexactitude, bombastic gestures. [RM-G]

*Stikhotvorenlya* (1964); Gulland, *SRV*; Obolensky, *PBRV*.

**Virgilius Maro Grammaticus** (fl. Southern Gaul *c.*600). Grammarian. He is responsible for the fifteen *Epitomae* and eight letters which afford a startling glimpse of what passed for learning in the Toulouse of the early 7th century – distortions of style akin to the *Hisperica famina*, and tall stories about scholarship; a charlatan perhaps, but a clever man, and a useful witness to contemporary trends in prose and verse writing. [CEC]

Ed. J. Huemer, *Virgilii Maronis grammatici opera* (Leipzig, 1886); *Epitomae*, ed. and tr. D. Tardi, *Les E. de V. de Toulouse* (Paris, 1928).

Manitius, *GLLM*; Raby *SLP*.

**Virta, Nikolay Yevgen'evich** (Tambovsk Guberniya 1906– ). Russian dramatist, journalist, novelist and librettist. The son of a village priest, he writes in strong and sombre colours of the Russian countryside. Two of his most successful plays, the '*Kulak*' tragedy *Zemlya* (1937) and *Dali dal'nye, ne oglyadnye* (1957), are based on the novels *Odinochestvo* and *Krutye Gory*. He writes best about subjects near to his heart – the fate of the country-dweller, *Golgofa* (1944), *Khleb nash nasushnyy* (1947) – rather than when attempting to depict a foreign scene as in *Zagovor*

*Obrechennykh* (1948), a play about Western warmongers, or *Prizrak brodit po Evrope* (1948). His plays have been frequently staged outside the U.S.S.R. [AP]

*P'yesy* (1958); *Letom nebo vysokoye*, in *Sov. Dramaturgiya*, 12 (1959); *Zhelannaya*, in *Sov. Dramaturgiya*, 2/24 (1961); *Sekrety firmy 'Klemens i Syn* (1964).

**Vischer, Friedrich Theodor** (Ludwigsburg 1807–Gmünden am Traunsee 1887). German writer on aesthetics. His influence in the late 19th century was second only to that of Hegel. Forthright and uncompromising by nature, he threw himself into political life and was a member of the moderate left-wing party in the National Assembly of 1848. Like his friend and fellow-Swabian David Friedrich Strauss, who was unlike him in so many other ways, he started as a Romantic and reached maturity as a firm realist. He left a number of philosophical and aesthetic works, and a satire on Goethe, *Faust, der Tragödie dritter Teil.* Of particular interest for an understanding of the intellectual currents of the age is his correspondence with Strauss (publ. 1952) and with ⇨ Mörike (publ. 1926). [RT]

O. Hesnard, *F.T.V.* (Paris, 1921).

**Vishnevsky, Vsevolod Vital'yevich** (Petersburg 1900–Moscow 1951). Russian dramatist. His well-known plays *Pervaya Konnaya* (1929), *Posledniy reshitel'nyy* (1931) and *Optimisticheskaya Tragediya* (1932) are among the most successful in turning the *agitka* into literature. The latter (filmed 1963) made a hit with its brilliant reconciliation of heroic outline and personal characterization. When his native Leningrad was under siege, he wrote the 'morale-raiser' *Raskinulos' morye shirokoye* (1942, with Kron and Azarev), and subsequently sought to immortalize his city's struggle for existence on stage and screen. It is a pity that he is also remembered for the sycophantic Stalinist play, *Nezabyvaemyy 1919* (1949). He is nevertheless regarded as a classic in the U.S.S.R. and has been widely played abroad. He has a gift for handling crowd scenes and romantic sweep of vision. [AP]

*Sobraniye Sochineniy* (5 vols., 1954; 6th vol., 1961); *Stat'i, dnevniki, pis'ma* (1961); *Izbrannoye* (1966).

O. K. Borodin, *V.V.* (Kiev, 1958); A. N. Anastas'yev, *V.V.* (Moscow, 1962); M. M. Sav-. chenko *V.V.* (Moscow 1957); V. Diyev, *V.V.* (Moscow, 1962); V. Sharapkov, *V.V.V.* (Kishnev, 1965); Vs. Azarov, *V.V.V.* (Leningrad, 1966).

**Vitrac, Roger** (Pinsac 1899–Paris 1952). French poet and playwright. Influenced by Dadaism and Surrealism, he published poems (e.g. *Connaissance de la mort*, 1927) but is best known for his work in the theatre, where he started off as an associate of ⇨ Artaud at the Théâtre Alfred Jarry. His idiom and technique owe much to the ferocious surrealist joke, on the one hand, and the style of the music-hall, on the other. He invests the comedian's patter with the full power to shock and mounts a sharp, satirical attack on the bourgeois world, often exploiting a racy cynicism. All this can be seen at work in *Les mystères de l'amour* (1927); in the subversive reversal of roles in *Victor ou les enfants au pouvoir* (1928); in the impudent use of bourgeois puppets in *Le coup de Trafalgar* (1934). *Le Camelot* (1936), *Le Loup-Garou* (1939), where the force of the anti-bourgeois attack is sharpened for being set in a nursing-home, and *Le sabre de mon père* (1951), all fruitfully exploit the same ribald and irreverent manner. *Les demoiselles du large* (1938) uncharacteristically attempts to explore a tragic dimension. [SBJ]

*Théâtre* (4 vols., 1948–64).

H. Béhar, *R.V. un réprouvé du Surréalisme* (Paris, 1966); Lalou, *TF*; Beigbeder, *TFL.*

**Vittorini, Elio** (Siracusa 1908–Milan 1966). Italian novelist and literary critic. The son of a railwayman, he had little formal education; after working on a building site in Northern Italy, was employed by a Florentine newspaper as a proof-reader. He learned English translating *Robinson Crusoe* in his spare time with the help of a typographer, and began to write for the literary magazine *Solaria.* The Fascist authorities soon took exception to his literary activities, stopped the publication in instalments of his first novel *Il Garofano rosso* (1933–5, 1948; tr. A. Bower, *The Red Carnation*, 1953) and interfered with the distribution of his second, *Conversazione in Sicilia* (1939). He kept out of the way for some time, earning a living as a translator, mainly of American literature (Saroyan, Faulkner, Erskine Caldwell, Hemingway), work which considerably influenced his own narrative style. After the war, he emerged as one of the leading left-wing intellectuals, opening on his new review *Il Politecnico* (1945–7) some of the most exciting cultural debates of our time (see *Diario in pubblico*, 1957). As a publisher's reader, he has selected, encouraged and published the work of many young writers.

Convinced that literature is a form of political engagement and that culture is relevant to the whole development of society, Vittorini has never shirked, like some other *engagé* writers, the tremendous problems such belief presents to a practising novelist, especially (in the light of the conspicuous failures of the so-called 'socialist realism') the relationship between new contents and traditional form. After three more novels (*Uomini e no*, 1945, a Resistance epic; *Il Sempione strizza l'occhio al Frejus*, 1947, a modern myth of the human condition; tr. E. Mosbacher, *Tune for an Elephant*, 1955; *Le donne di Messina*, 1949, a tale of community life), in which he experimented with objective non-descriptive techniques, he became so absorbed in his literary problems that he gave up writing novels altogether. Perhaps his preoccupation with narrative theory has done his progress more harm than good (his 1964 re-writing of his last novel seems to prove this point); however his positive influence on intellectual and artistic life in post-war Italy is due more to his achievements as a literary critic and organizer than to his own narrative work, and has undoubtedly earned him a place of great distinction in the history of Italian culture. [GMC]

*Conversation in Sicily*, tr. W. David (1949); *Erica, La Garibaldina*, tr. F. Keene and B. Wall, *Women on the Road* (1961).

S. Pacifici, *A Guide to Contemporary Italian Narrative* (N.Y., 1962); *Contemporanei*, ii; Pullini, *RID*; Fernandez, *RI*; Bàrberi Squarotti, *NID*.

**Vives, Juan Luis** (Valencia 1492–Bruges 1540). Spanish scholar. He studied at Paris and became a professor at Louvain (1519). His friend ⇨ Erasmus suggested he should write a commentary on St Augustine's *De civitate Dei* (publ. 1532 with dedication to Henry VIII). He spent some time in England, mostly at Corpus Christi College, Oxford, and enjoyed the favour of Henry VIII, Wolsey, and Catherine of Aragon. His support of her cause against Henry led to his banishment. His voluminous writings include devotional books, such as *Introductio ad sapientiam*, which ran to 50 editions; educational works such as *Exercitatio linguae latinae*, which had 99 editions, and *De instititione feminae*. Many of his ideas were far in advance of his age, perhaps most of all in the sphere of social reform. He was severely critical of scholastic philosophy and the hagiography of his time, appeared to lean towards communism, and had some idea of the theory of evolution. [FB]

*Opera omnia*, ed. G. Mayáns y Siscar (1782).

A. Bonilla y San Martín, *L.V. y la filosofía del renacimiento* (Madrid, 1903).

**Vladimir Monomakh** (1053–1125). Russian statesman, ruler and writer. The son of Grand Prince Vsevolod and a Greek princess, he was the outstanding statesman among the descendants of Yaroslav the Wise during the period before he acceded to the throne of Kiev in 1113. By his tact and intelligence he managed again and again to avert dissension and civil war. As grand prince he ruled firmly, minimized the danger of attack by the Polovtsy by carrying the war into their territory, and was respected and loved by his people.

His only known literary work is a 'Testament' to his sons (inserted in the Primary Chronicle, for some reason, under the year 1096, but probably written towards the end of his life). This is an amalgam of Biblical quotations, prayers, advice on how to run the State and live a goodly life, autobiographical notes and a record of his hunting exploits. Apart from the purely personal details of his life there is little in the work that can be called strictly original; many of the precepts themselves were *loci communi* in the Byzantine translated literature of the period. The form of the work was probably inspired by the popular genre of Instructions from Father to Son. But the language is fresh and exhilarating, containing a mixture of Old Church Slavonic and the vernacular, and the structure of the work is logical and well-conceived. The 'Testament' is the earliest known example of Russian 'literature' produced by a layman. [JLIF]

*Testament*, in *Povest' vremennykh let*, I, sub anno 1096, ed. Akad. Nauk (1950); tr. *The Russian Primary Chronicle*, ed. S. H. Cross and O. P. Sherbowitz-Welzer (Cambridge, Mass., 1953).

A. S. Orlov, *V.M.* (Moscow, 1946); G. P. Fedotov, *The Russian Religious Mind* (N.Y., 1960).

**Vlaykov, Todor** (Pirdop 1865–Sofia 1943). Bulgarian story-writer and publicist. After reading philology at Moscow and editing there Duvernois's Bulgarian dictionary, he returned to Bulgaria in 1888, imbued with Russian *narodnik* ideals. The similar movement among village teachers, promoted by him with H. Maksimov, to improve Bulgarian agrarian conditions is reflected in his early works, e.g. *Ratay* (1893) and *Kmetove* (1895) and his earlier village idyll *Dyadovata Slavchova unuka* (1885). In the *crise de conscience* precipitated by this last, N. Mihaylovsky's defence of Tolstoy the artist against Tolstoy the moralist justified to him 'a work of art as such, even if it preach no social ideal whatever'; this salvaged his literary vocation. However, only after a quarter century's dedication to public life as Deputy and a founder of the Radical Party during which he wrote only social, agrarian and political articles (vols. IV–VI of his *Săbrani săchineniya*) and edited *Demokraticheski pregled* ('Democratic Review', 1902–25), could he retire to fulfil the promise of *Lelya Gena* (1888) with further tragic female figures from the Bulgarian village in *Strina Venkovitsa i snaha i* (1925) and *Zhitie na edna mayka* (1926). His literary reputation could rest secure on his last work alone, the autobiographical trilogy *Prezhivyanoto* (1934–42), an evocation of his early years and incidentally an anthology of Bulgarian life between the 1860s and 1880s. The lifelong conflict between his literary and civic vocations and his attempts to reconcile them are analysed in his *Zavoi iz zhizneniya păt na edin pisatel i obshtestvenik* (1935). [VP]

*Săbrani săchineniya* (6 vols., 1925–31); *T.V. Sbornik: literaturno i obshtestveno delo* (1935); Pinto, *BPV*.

Manning and Smal-Stocki, *HMBL*; *SEER*, XXXII, 79 (1954); XXXVII, 88 (1958).

**Voiture, Vincent** (Amiens 1597–Paris 1648). French poet. The son of a wine merchant, he was the animating spirit of the ◊ *salon* entertainments of the Hôtel de Rambouillet. Voiture kept the company amused, invented practical jokes, organized competitions, or sonnets, or games or madrigals or rondeaux. In this last genre, the perfection of social verse, Voiture was a master, and his poems appear in modern anthologies. His tact, wit and gaiety counted greatly in an age of salons and was probably of greater influence than his written works. It was he, for example, who when Bossuet at the age of fifteen was invited to stage a short sermon at the Hôtel late one evening, remarked that he had never heard anyone preach 'ni si tôt, ni si tard'. His letters, frequently reprinted after a first collection in 1654, are a mirror of both the man and his milieu. [WGM]

E. Magne, *V. et l'Hôtel de Rambouillet* (2 vols., 1929–30).

**Vojnović, Ivo** (Dubrovnik 1857–Belgrade 1929). Croatian dramatist. Well acquainted with European literatures, especially with the symbolists, his dramas *Ekvinocija* and *Dubrovačka trilogija* (1902) are still among the greatest achievements of Yugoslav drama. The latter consists of three short plays beginning with the surrender of Dubrovnik to Napoleon and continuing up to the end of the 19th century. They deal with the passing of an aristocratic age and the human problem of change. [EDG]

*Sabrana dela* (4 vols., 1939); *Aeqvinoctium* (1895); *Smrt majke Jugovića* (1907); *Lazarevo vaskresenije* (1913); *Imperatrix* (1919); *Akord* (1916) (poems); tr. F. S. Copeland, *The Dying Republic*, *SEER*, I, 1 (1922).

Barac, *HYL*; *SEER*, XV (1927).

**Volodin, A.**, pseud of A. Lifshits (1919– ). Russian dramatist. His first play, *Fabrichnaya Devchonka* (1956), was the subject of heated polemics and his subsequent works, *Pyat' Vecherov* (1959; tr. A. Nicolaeff, *Five Evenings*, Minnesota, 1966), *V gostyakh i doma* (1960), *Moya starshaya sestra* (1961), *Idealistka* (1962) and *Naznacheniye* (1963), show remarkable independence and originality of thought. [AP]

*Teatr*, 4, 5, 6, 7 (1957); *Znamya*, 3 (1958).

**Voloshin, Maksimilyan Aleksandrovich** (Crimea 1877–Koktyebel' 1932). Russian poet. He lived for several years in Paris. His early poetry was much praised for its picturesque, impressionist quality, e.g. the sonnets 'to winter in the Crimea', often touched by a mood of personal nostalgia. He at first exalted the Revolution as a primordial force liberating Russia from foreign evils and war. His increasingly mystical outlook proved incompatible with the harsh reality of subsequent events, and he ceased writing. His most interesting last works are the 'stikhi sul terrore' in *Demony glukhonemyye* (Khar'kov, 1919).

**Voltaire**, pseud. of François-Marie Arouet (Paris 1694–Paris 1778). French writer. A universal genius of the 18th century; in his writings a dramatist, poet, philosopher, scientist, novelist, moralist, satirist, polemicist, letter-writer, historian; in his life a man who was imprisoned in the Bastille, spent years abroad in England and Prussia, was a courtier at Versailles, a wealthy landowner at Ferney and an ardent defender of such victims of religious intolerance as Calas. His long life and his voluminous writings, which often show a strong sense of *engagement* to the world around him, make of him a man who bestrides the Age of Enlightenment and in many ways is the epitome of it.

He was educated by the Jesuits, and soon began to appear in Paris society, particularly in free-thinking and neo-Epicurean circles. Satiric writings incurred nearly a year in the Bastille (1717–18), but he quickly regained a comfortable situation in Parisian society. This period came to an end when a quarrel with the influential Chevalier de Rohan led to exile in England (1726). The incident served to remind a man already given to radical views that a member of the Tiers État could not hope for fair treatment against the aristocracy. England showed him a society living in greater justice and freedom, and led on his return to France (1728 or 1729) to the *Lettres philosophiques* (1734). Their publication occasioned another scandal and forced him into retreat at Cirey, the isolated Champagne home of the Marquise du Châtelet, and for a decade he remained there, apart from brief visits to Paris, Prussia and the Low Countries. In 1744 he was recalled to Versailles and given official positions at Court; but the experience was sterile and disillusioning, and with Mme du Châtelet he withdrew first to the Duchesse du Maine's court at Sceaux and then to the court of ex-King Stanislas at Lunéville, where Mme du Châtelet's sudden death (1749) was yet another bitter blow. The following year he accepted Frederick II's invitation to his court in Berlin; the enthusiasm and affection shown at first on both sides gradually disappeared, and Voltaire departed in 1753, even more disenchanted with the world. Eventually he settled (1755) at Les Délices on the outskirts of Geneva, and later moved to Ferney (purchased in 1758), a few miles away inside France. There followed a more settled period which lasted almost to his death and in which, independent and powerful, he launched a series of vigorous attacks upon '*l'infâme*', his word for the various injustices, absurdities and cruelties imposed by the Roman Catholic Church. He remained at Ferney until 1778, when he went back to Paris for a visit that became an apotheosis. Rapturously acclaimed on all sides, he prolonged his stay and eventually, exhausted by the social life, died before he could return to Ferney.

The period before 1726 is notable mainly for poetic works, of which the play *Oedipe* (1718), the *Épître à Uranie* (1722) and the first version of his epic poem *La Ligue* (1723 – to be called *La Henriade* in a later version) are the most striking. The *Lettres philosophiques*, purporting to be an account of English society, reveal Voltaire's polemical and satiric gifts; the example of a land where things are better ordered than in France is consistently set before the reader. From the work emerges not only an attack upon French institutions, but the praise of political, social and religious liberty, the stress upon social utility as the touchstone of public institutions, and an advocacy of the experimental approach to science. Doubt is the beginning of wisdom and the basis of tolerance; man cannot attain to first truths, should therefore not seek to impose unverifiable beliefs upon others, but modestly resign himself to working usefully within those limits that the Creator seems to have assigned him – to observe and measure, and to improve the human lot where possible. These are tenets to which Voltaire held all his life.

The Cirey years are in part given over to scientific pursuits, from which emerge works like the *Éléments de la philosophie de Newton* (1738), testifying to his admiration for Newton's discoveries. But he continues to write poetry; *Le mondain* (1736) is an apology for luxury, while the *Discours en vers sur l'homme* (1738) is a philosophical survey of man in optimistic terms similar to those of Leibniz and Pope. Plays also appear frequently; among them *Mahomet* (1741), with *Zaïre* (1732) among his most accomplished tragedies. More importantly, the later 1740s see the appearance of his first published *conte*, *Zadig* (1747; tr. R. Aldington, 1959), written at Sceaux. As in most of his *contes*, ideas are foremost; the episodic plot structure, the slightly drawn characters, the lucidly astringent style are all subordinated to this end – a meditation upon the evils to which man is heir, particularly, in this case, those caused by human malice and stupidity. The conclusion is not without hope, and the work praises rational conduct designed to improve the human condition; but evil is an insoluble mystery. The same attitude emerges from his most famous *conte*, *Candide* (1759; tr. R. Aldington, 1959), though the atmosphere and conclusion bear somewhat darker overtones; the brilliant irony brings out the cruelty of a world in which human life and dignity are of little account. In Pangloss he is ridiculing the optimism of Pope, Leibniz and indeed himself in earlier years. Experience is a better teacher than the metaphysical Pangloss, and experience shows that pain and disillusionment are unavoidable. Nevertheless, despair is not the answer; '*il faut cultiver notre jardin*', however one interprets it, represents a counsel of courage and defiance. Such a spirit animates all his works of the Ferney years, a whole armoury of *philosophique* onslaughts on man-made injustice – such as *Traité sur la tolérance* (1763), *Dictionnaire philosophique* (1764; tr. P. Gay, 1962), *contes* like *L'Ingénu* (1767), *La Princesse de Babylone* (1768), and innumerable *Dialogues* and pamphlets that castigate fanaticism and intolerance. Voltaire, a firm believer in God, preaches a deist religion, free of 'superstitious' observances, self-interested priests and false traditions – the religion common, he feels, to all men beneath their different cults. All humanity shares a natural morality, and one must work towards giving it full play, thereby ending the wars and persecutions to which man's present ignorance, arrogance and selfishness still lead him. [HTM]

*Œuvres complètes*, ed. L. Moland (52 vols., 1877–85); *Romans et contes*, ed. R. Groos (Pléiade, 1950); *Œuvres historiques*, ed. R. Pomeau (Pléiade, 1957); *Mélanges*, ed. J. van den Heuvel (Pléiade, 1961); *Correspondence*, ed. T. Besterman (Geneva, Institut Voltaire, 1953–65).

G. Lanson, *V.* (Paris, 1906); R. Naves, *V.* (Paris, 1942); R. Pomeau, *La religion de V.* (Paris, 1956); N. Torrey, *The Spirit of V.* (1938); I. Wade, *V. and Mme du Châtelet* (1941).

**Vondel, Joost van den** (Cologne 1587–Amsterdam 1679). Dutch poet and dramatist. His Baptist parents fled from Antwerp, later settled in Amsterdam. He took over his father's hat-shop and in 1610, when he married Maeyken de Wolff, he moved into a hosiery business, which his wife looked after while he wrote. Renaissance poetic taste and technique he learnt from reading Du Bartas, most of whose works he translated (1607–17). The conflict between pagan culture and his Mennist faith he resolved, after a crisis in 1621, by interpreting his classical models as adumbrations of Christianity. He treated the stage as the *theatrum mundi*, developing biblical themes to illustrate archetypal virtues and vices; his iconographical conception of 'speaking pictures' influenced German Baroque drama (cf. ⇨ Gryphius). His first work of importance, *Het Pascha* (1612), a dramatized version of the Exodus, with an obvious parallel between the Israelites and the Calvinists' liberation from evil, also made him a national poet. Vondel was deeply involved in religious and political controversy. Polemical verse was a feature of the Chambers of Rhetoric (cf. ⇨ *Rederijkers*) and his sorties from the safety of the Brabantine Chamber to lampoon Oldenbarneveld's opponents, the theology of Predestination and the bigoted Church ministers in the capital nearly cost him his freedom. His dialogue so often echoes contemporary disputes that political allegories have (often mistakenly) been read into his plays. Two secular plays were, however, intended as political allegories: *Palamedes* (1625), a satire on Oldenbarneveld's judicial murder, and *Leeuwendalers* (1647), a pastoral fantasy anticipating the peace of Westphalia. The second book of Virgil's *Aeneid* provided another secular theme for the celebration of Amsterdam's greatness at the opening of its new theatre in 1637 – *Gijsbrecht van Aemstel*, his best-known play, which is still acted annually at the New Year. It contains the first indications of his gradual drift away from the austerity of Calvinism to the sacramental catholicity of the Church of Rome. It is dedicated to Hugo Grotius, whose *Sophompaneas* he had translated (1635), and who urged him to study the Greek dramatists. His drama became progressively more Roman Catholic in substance and more restrained in style, from *Gebroeders* (1640) and *Joseph in Dothan* (1640) to the masterpieces *Lucifer* (1654; tr. L. C. van Noppen, 1917), *Adam in Ballingschap* (1664; tr. W. Kirkconnell, in *The Celestial Cycle*, 1952) and *Jeptha* (1659), which he considered his best play, scrupulously adhering to the Aristotelian unities and even abandoning his usual alexandrine in favour of the pentameter. In his songs he is as musical and versatile as ⇨ Hooft and his numerous occasional poems provide a commentary on his times. His prolific translations from French, Latin and Greek reveal his humility and sense of high calling as a poet and his extensive theological poems are magnificent testimonials to his sincerity and integrity. The prefaces to his plays, and his *ars poetica*, the *Aenleidinge ter Nederduitsche Dichtkunste*, are written in an elegant and generally lucid prose. Though he accorded drama the highest place in poetic art, he embarked on an ambitious Constantine epic, and completed a shorter epic poem on John the Baptist. [PK]

*De werken van V.* (10 vols., 1927–37) (known as 'Wereldbibliotheek editie'); Barnouw, *CA*; Weevers, *PNEC*.

*Vondel-Kroniek* (1930–40); A. J. Barnouw, *V.* (Haarden, 1926); W. A. P. Smit, *Van Pascha tot Noah* (3 vols., Zwolle, 1956–62); K. L. Johannessen, *Zwischen Himmel und Erde* (Oslo, 1963); W. A. P. Smit and P. Brachin, *V.* (Paris, 1964).

**Voronsky, Aleksandr Konstantinovich** (Tambov 1884–Moscow 1935). Russian writer and critic. The son of a priest he joined the Communist Party in 1904. In the following years he was several times arrested and imprisoned. In 1921, on Gor'ky's advice, Lenin appointed him editor of the first Soviet literary journal, the monthly *Krasnaya Nov'*. Although he was a Marxist, he was sceptical of the claims made for proletarian art and insisted that the criterion for publication must be literary merit and not class or ideological considerations. His refusal to compromise led to his being removed from the editorship in 1927 and expelled from the Party. *Krasnaya Nov'* declined in significance from that date, and its place was taken by *Novyy Mir*. Voronsky reappeared briefly in the 1930s and was re-arrested for Trotskyism. He died in prison, and was posthumously rehabilitated in 1956.

He was also the founder in 1924 of *Pereval*, a literary group consisting mainly of Communists interested in aesthetic questions and not ideologically hide-bound. This group was liquidated during the purges of the 1930s.

His views on aesthetics were taken from Plekhanov and are expounded in his article *Iskusstvo, kak poznaniye zhizni i sovremennost'* (*KN*, 1923, No. 5: 'Art as Cognition of Life and the Present'). Apart from literary criticism he wrote some short stories and two fine volumes of memoirs, *Za zhivoy i myortvoy vodoy* (1927, 1929; tr. L. Zarine, *Waters of Life and Death*, 1936). [RDBT]

G. Glinka, *Na Perevale* (N.Y., 1954).

E. J. Brown, *The Proletarian Episode in Russian Literature* (1953).

**Vörösmarty, Mihály** (Nyék 1800–Budapest 1855). Hungarian poet. Leading personality of Hungarian Romanticism. With a background of impoverished nobility, he studied in Budapest, where he became a tutor, and later the editor of *Tudományos Gyüjtemény*, then the most prominent learned periodical. He was an artist of romantic, lyrical and epic poetry and drama, wrote stage criticism and also translated Shakespeare. Though he first made his mark with *A Bujdosók* (1823–28), a historical tragedy, it was due to his patriotic *Zalán Futása* (1825) that he was truly recognized. This is a classical-style, hexametric epic telling the inspiring story of the Hungarians' conquest of their country; it contains vivid battle-scenes and also a lyrical description of romantic love. Vörösmarty's portraiture, describing not actual features or landscapes but mood and atmosphere, is almost impressionistic. Later, abandoning the classical epic style, he turned to treating traditional popular themes and ballad-like poems of emotional appeal, such as 'Szép Ilonka' (1833), a romantic love-story with psychological characterization. Other notable romantic poems are 'Délsziget' (1826) and 'Tündérvölgy' (1827). *A Két Szomszédvár* (1831) is a narrative poem. In the 1830s, after the opening of the National Theatre in Budapest, Vörösmarty also became a playwright. In *Csongor és Tünde* (1831), a romantic but deeply philosophical drama with a fairy-tale theme, Csongor and Tünde seek and find happiness in their love; the prospects of finding it in glory, wealth and knowledge are represented by the various other characters. Csongor and Balga are portrayed as symbolizing idealism and realism, in the style of Don Quixote and Sancho Panza. Probably the finest of Vörösmarty's love lyrics is *Ábránd* (1840; tr. J. C. W. Horne, 'Fancy', Budapest, 1957). *A Merengőhöz* (1843; tr. N. de Vállyi, *To a Dreamer*, London, 1911) is a philosophizingly amorous ode, while *Gondolatok a Könyvtárban* (1844) discusses the reasons for and problems of the existence of mankind. Vörösmarty's most important patriotic poem, *Szózat* (1836; tr. W. Kirkconnel, *Appeal*, Winnipeg, 1933), demands unshakeable patriotism, and is regarded as being a second national anthem. His *Elöszó* (1851) is the story of the Reform Age (1825–48), the War of Independence and its suppression. In his swansong, and perhaps greatest lyrical poem, *A Vén Cigány* (1854; tr. W. Kirkconnel, *The Old Gypsy*, Winnipeg, 1933), Vörösmarty casts himself as the dying Gypsy musician, and expresses his fears of disaster for mankind, but ends on an optimistic note. [JFR]

Klaniczay, *HHL*; Reményi, *HWL*.

**Voss, Johann Heinrich** (Sommersdorf, Waren 1751–Heidelberg 1826). German poet. After a penurious youth he studied classics at Göttingen, where he became one of the leading members of the 'Göttinger Hain' group of poets (⇨ Hölty, etc.), but he is chiefly remembered as a translator. His rendering of the *Odyssey* into German hexameters (1781; *Iliad*, 1793) gained immediate popularity and in its poetic qualities has never been surpassed: as an example of the translator's art and in its cultural and literary influence it ranks second only to ⇨ Schlegel's translation of Shakespeare. In collaboration with his sons, he also translated many other classical authors including Virgil, Ovid and Horace as well as Shakespeare.

Although many of his lyrics (*Gedichte*, 1785–95) enjoyed wide popularity in their day, it is on his idylls (collected edition, 1801) that his reputation as a poet rests. In spite of a tendency to pedantic triviality, these genre pictures of village and country life constituted an important innovation in German literature in their description of contemporary reality in the hexameters of the Greek epic; the most successful of them, *Luise* (1795), served as a model for Goethe's *Hermann und Dorothea*. [WAC]

*Werke*, ed. A. Voss (5 vols., 1867).

**Vovchok, Marko,** pseud. of Markovych, née Vilins'ka, Mariya (nr Yelets, Oryol 1834–Nal'chik, Caucasus 1907). Ukrainian and Russian prose-writer. Her first collection of Ukrainian stories, *Narodni opovidannya* (1857), was an immediate success. An outstanding authority on folklore and folk language, she synthesized ethnographic romanticism with new realistic themes from rural life under serfdom. The stories, artistically powerful, harmonious, fresh and warm in manner, struck home by their implied social protest against the inhumanities of the whole system. Her Russian *Rasskazy iz narodnogo russkogo byta* (1859) are similar in tenor.

In 1860–7 she lived in Paris and frequently contributed to the *Magasin d'éducation et de récréation*, particularly children's stories, some of which were also published separately. *Maroussia* (1871), a romantic story in Ukrainian historical setting of a girl's patriotic heroism ending with her death in battle, originally in Ukrainian, was adapted by Hetzel in the *Magasin* (1878), serialized in *Le Temps* (1875), and had a phenomenal success in book form (Paris, 1878), being reprinted many times right into the 1960s and winning a prize from the Académie Française. While in Paris, she also wrote in Ukrainian (*Narodni opovidannya*, ii, 1862) and in Russian. Returning to Russia, she produced several problem and feminist novels and stories, mostly in Russian. She reached a new perfection in Ukrainian narrative prose as a vehicle for her humanist and realist pictures of the evils of serfdom; the position of woman was her particular concern. [VS]

*Tvory* (7 vols., 1964–6).

M. T. Latzarus, *La littérature enfantine en France* (Paris, 1923); O. Zasenko, *M.V. i zarubizhni lit.* (Kiev, 1959); Manning, *UL*; *UCE*; *UQ*, III, 2 (1947); XIV, 4 (1958).

**Voznesensky, Andrey** (Vladimir 1933– ). Russian poet. He trained as an architect; first poems published 1958, first volumes: *Mozaika* (1960), *Parabola* (1960). With his friend Yevtushenko the most celebrated post-Stalin poet. His remarkable cycle of 'lyrical digressions', *Treugolnaya grusha* (1962), was inspired by a visit to America; he has also travelled in Western Europe. Stylistically highly experimental and original, his puns, alliterations, verbal tricks, startling imagery and deliberate bathos may give a false impression of his poems as humorous exercises; in fact they are inspired by a sensitive concern for personal relationships and telling insight into the aspirations and problems of his generation in the U.S.S.R. and outside. [RM-G]

*Antimiry* (1963; tr. W. H. Auden *et al.*, with introduction, *Antiworlds*, 1967); Gulland, *SRV*; Obolensky, *PBRV*.

**Vratislav z Mitrovic, Václav** (1576–1635). Czech author. At 15 he took part in a mission to the Turkish Sultan in Constantinople, was imprisoned by the Turks, forced to serve on the galleys, and was released only after four years. His vivid account of his experience, *Příhody* (1599; tr. A. H. Wratislaw, *The Adventures of Baron Wenceslas Wratislaw of Mitrowicz*, 1862), is full of human interest and illustrative of the conditions of the Turks of the 16th century and of their relations with Christendom. [KB]

**Vraz, Stanko** (Cerovec 1810–Zagreb 1851). Croatian and Slovene poet. Although a Slovene, Vraz wrote most of his works in Croat, being influenced by Gaj's ideas of cultural unity. Despite some linguistic blemishes, his poetry is among the best produced within the Illyrian movement. As a critic Vraz was one of the first to draw attention to such writers as ⇨ Njegoš, as well as laying the foundation for Croatian critical theory. He edited the literary periodical *Kolo* and was responsible for encouraging the purely literary element of the Illyrian movement. [EDG]

Ibrovac, *APY*.
Barac, *HYL*.

**Vrchlický, Jaroslav,** pseud. of Emil Frída (Louny 1853–Domažlice 1912). Czech poet, dramatist and essayist. Studied philosophy and in 1893 was appointed Professor of Comparative Literature at Prague University.

A rich and powerful personality, he went through medieval, classical, renaissance and romantic phases and his work shows the impact of realism, symbolism and impressionism. Like Victor Hugo he attempted a summary of the spiritual development of humanity in a cycle of epic poems. It is here that his poetic achievement is most lasting. His highly personal lyrics have worn less well, though the best of them (*Strom života*, 1909, *Meč Damoklův*, 1912) have a general and timeless value. Modern readers can still admire his craftsmanship which, like his substitution of French and English for German literary models, was profoundly influential in the development of Czech poetry. He was, moreover, one of the first Czech writers to subordinate national and utilitarian criteria to aesthetic values. [RA/KB]

*Sebrané spisy* (65 vols., 1896–1913).
A. Jensen, *J.V. Étude littéraire* (Stockholm, 1894); M. Weingart, *J.V.* (Prague, 1921); A. Pražák, *Vrchlickému nablízku* (Prague, 1946).

**Vučo, Alexsandar** (Belgrade 1897– ). Serbian poet and novelist. Between the world wars he wrote surrealist poetry, then with D. Matić published the novel *Gluvo doba* (1940). The novels *Raspust* (1954; tr. A. Brown, *The Holidays*, 1959) and *Mrtve javke* (1957) deal with the drama of a typical intellectual who views retrospectively, while a prisoner in a concentration camp and later during the occupation, his youth and development, trying to determine his attitude towards what has taken place. [EDG]

*SEER*, XL, 94 (1961).

**Vynnychenko, Volodymyr** (nr Kherson 1880–Paris 1951). Ukrainian writer. Starting in 1902 with short stories, he soon became the most popular pre-revolutionary prose writer. His first collection, *Krasa i syla* (1906), was hailed by I. ⇨ Franko. Realistic, often naturalistic stories revealed deep, unexpected conflicts, and profound knowledge of facets of life hardly touched in Ukrainian literature: ex-peasant workers versus bosses; dockland underworld; barracks; prison (of which, as a prominent revolutionary, he had first-hand experience). In his interest in the pathological and sordid, the influence of Dostoyevsky and Maupassant is discernible. Psychological and moral problems predominate in his later work, where he preaches 'new morality' to the formula 'honesty with oneself' (from the title of the typical novel of this class: *Chestnost' s soboy*, 1st Russian edn 1911). If one's will, reason and heart are in harmony, any action, even killing, is moral. The hero of the last and best novel of this series, the constructionally fascinating *Zapysky kyrpatoho Mefistofelya* (1917), is treated satirically. Among his plays, largely psychological in the Ibsen and Chekhov sense, *Chorna pantera i bily medvid'* (1911) scored remarkable successes on the European stage of the twenties. Two 'Wellsian' novels stand out among his later work: the popular *Sonyashna mashyna* (1928) and his last *Nova zapovid'* (Neu Ulm, 1950). [VS]

*Tvory* (11 vols., Vienna, 1919).
*UCE.*

**Vyshnya, Ostap,** pseud. of Pavlo Hubenko (Grun', Sumy 1889–Kiev 1956). Ukrainian writer of humorous short stories. His popularity in the Ukraine is second only to ⇨ Shevchenko's. He began contributing to newspapers in 1921, then published dozens of collections, totalling by 1928 half a million copies. His work is distinguished by Ukrainian folk humour, popular speech, knowledge of the people, topicality and treatment of universal human foibles. In 1933 he was arrested and sentenced to death together with another writer, O. Dosvitny (1891–1934), on a trumped-up charge of planning assassinations, but this was commuted to ten years' exile in the north. Released in 1943, he wrote to current requirements of the Communist Party. But *Myslyvs'ki usmishky* (1954) is outstanding in his post-war work. [v s]

*Usmishky* (4 vols., 1928); *Tvory* (7 vols., 1963–4); 2 stories tr. in *25 Stories from the Soviet Republics* (Moscow, 1958).

# W

**Wace** (Jersey *c.*1100–*c.*1175). Anglo-Norman chronicler. Educated at Paris and at Caen (*clerc lisant* after 1135), then canon of Bayeux. He knew Henry I and Henry II personally. Five works, all in verse and in the vernacular, are extant: *La vie de Saint Nicolas* (ed. E. Ronsjö, Lund, 1942), a popular sequence of legendary stories current about the Saint; *La vie de Sainte Marguerite* (ed. E. A. Francis, Paris, 1932), a close translation of a Latin life of Saint Marguerite of Alexandria based on a Greek original; *La conception Nostre Dame* (ed. W. R. Ashford, Chicago, 1933), using three Latin sources, relates the life of the Virgin and may have been intended to promote a Feast of the Immaculate Conception in Normandy; and the famous long historical poems, the *Roman de Brut* and the *Roman de Rou.*

The *Brut* or *Geste des Bretons* (1155; ed. I. Arnold, 2 vols., Paris, 1938–40), dedicated to Queen Eleanor, is a free translation in 15,300 lines of Geoffrey of Monmouth's legendary *Historia regum Britanniae*, with some amplification and invention, and includes the stories of Lear and Arthur. Wace was especially successful in his courtly and attractive account of Arthur's adventures, which became a major source for the later Arthurian romances. He introduced the story of the Round Table, which is not in Geoffrey of Monmouth. The *Roman de Brut* was reworked by the Middle English poet, Layamon, shortly before 1205.

The *Roman de Rou* (Rollo the Viking) or *Geste des Normans* (1160–74; ed. H. Andresen, 2 vols., Heilbronn, 1877–9) is a history of the dukes of Normandy up to 1107, based on Latin chronicles and legends; it has considerable historical value. Wace stopped on learning that Henry II had entrusted the same task to a more fashionable rival, ➪ Benoît de Sainte-Maure. Wace's writing and literary influence have been underestimated. His language is clear and elegant, and his vocabulary rich and varied. [LTT]

*La partie arthurienne du 'R. de B.' de W.*, ed. I. Arnold and M. Pelan (Strasbourg, 1962); Woledge, *PBFV*; *Marche Romane*, IX (1960).

**Wackenroder, Wilhelm Heinrich** (Berlin 1773–Berlin 1798). German Romantic poet. Known only by two short but highly significant works in which his friend ➪ Tieck also had a part – the *Herzensergiessungen eines kunstliebenden Klosterbruders* (1797) and the *Phantasien über die Kunst* (1799). The suggestive importance to the German Romantic movement of the *Herzensergiessungen* can be seen in the title alone: extreme emotional subjectivity, art as religion, self-devotion to art as an act of religious commitment and worship. The works of Wackenroder and ➪ Novalis are in large measure the creative counterpart of the aesthetic doctrines preached in the ➪ *Athenaeum.* [RT]

J. Rouge, *W. et la genèse de l'esthétique romantique* (Paris, 1934).

**Wägner, Elin** (Lund 1882–Berg 1949). Swedish novelist and journalist. She was a leading feminist, in her early novels largely concerned with the work and position of women, e.g. *Pennskaftet* (1910). The First World War made her a pronounced pacifist; but her masterpiece, *Åsa-Hanna* (1918), a novel of extraordinary power, has little to do with contemporary events but much to do with fundamental moral problems. Set in the province of Småland she knew from childhood, it is one of the classic Swedish novels of country life. Afterwards, though her experience of international relief work after the war, lifelong involvement in the women's movement and informed attachment to Småland were often evident in her writing, her best novels deal both intensely and symbolically with practical religion and morality (she was influenced by Quakerism), marital conflict and self-fulfilment, as in *Den namnlösa* (1922) and *Silverforsen* (1924). Her half-mystical feminist convictions, presented in *Väckarklocka* (1941) failed to rouse the response she had hoped for. Her two-volume biography, *Selma Lagerlöf* (1942–3), however, is a sound and painstaking work, which, even if it does not always penetrate the complex personality of its subject, is both generous and illuminating.

H. Ahlenius, *E.W.* (Stockholm, 1936); H. Martinson, *E.W.* (Stockholm, 1949).

**Wagner, Richard** (Leipzig 1813–Venice 1883). German composer and poet. His music dramas represent the culmination of Romanticism. He drew upon the whole poetic heritage of German Romanticism, on the one hand by dramatizing legendary Romantic subjects – *Tannhäuser* (1845), *Lohengrin* (1850), the *Ring* (completed 1876), *Tristan und Isolde* (1865), *Parsifal* (1882) – on the other hand by bringing the arts together in a single art-form (*Gesamtkunstwerk*) dominated, and ultimately judged, by the art in which all Romantic values find their highest fulfilment – music. Wagner's own theoretical writings (*Das Kunstwerk der Zukunft*, 1850; *Oper und Drama*, 1851, etc.) do not admit the supremacy of one art over the others in the *Gesamtkunstwerk*; in addition he sought to convey in his libretti the philosophical meanings – derived in large measure from Schopenhauer – which he saw latent in his subjects, regarding his libretti as dramatic works *per se*. But in fact, with the exception of *Die Meistersinger von Nürnberg* (1862) – which has a certain interest in the context of 19th-century German comedy – and possibly also of the earlier *Fliegender Holländer* (1843), the texts have little independent value. [RT]

*Hauptschriften*, ed. E. Bücken (1956); *W. on Music and Drama*, ed. tr. A. Goldman, E. Spinchorn (N.Y., 1964).

O. Luening, *R.W. als Dichter und Denker* (Zürich, 1900); E. Newman, *W. as Man and Artist* (1925); Mann, *ETD*.

**Walafrid Strabo** (*c.* 808–849). Medieval Latin writer and scholar. Educated at the Benedictine monastery of Reichenau and later at Fulda under ⇨ Hrabanus Maurus. The Emperor Louis the Pious made him abbot of Reichenau (838). His prose writings include *De rebus ecclesiasticis*, a liturgical handbook, in which he defends the use of images and pictures as *litteratura illiterata* for teaching the simple. He was long considered the compiler of the *Glosa ordinaria*, the most popular Biblical exegesis for 500 years. His verse includes a Life of St Gall (the Irish founder of the monastery of that name) and *De visionibus Wettini*, an early work, in which Wettin, his tutor, visits hell, purgatory and paradise in a delirium, and sees the punishments of sinners and the rewards of saints. His best-known work is his charming poem *Hortulus* (tr. R. S. Lambert, 1923), in which he describes the flowers growing in his beloved garden at Reichenau and adds details of their medicinal uses. [FB]

Migne, *PL*, 113–14; ed. E. Dümmler (MGH, PLAC, II, 1884); *Life of S. Gall*, tr. M. Joynt (1927).

A. Jundt, *W.S.* (Cahors, 1907); Duckett, *CP*; Raby, *CLP*, *SLP*.

**Walden, Herwarth,** pseud. of Georg Lewin (Berlin 1878–?). German author and art critic, at one time married to E. ⇨ Lasker-Schüler. Founder of the Expressionist periodical *Der Sturm*, theorist of modernism in art, he arranged in Berlin exhibitions of futurist and cubist painting (1912–21). His writings include novels (*Das Buch der Menschenliebe*, 1916, etc.), expressionistic plays (*Sünde*, 1920, etc.) and poems (*Im Geschweig der Liebe*, 1925). He emigrated to the Soviet Union in 1930, where he disappeared *c.*1940. [AKT]

*Gesammelte Schriften* (Berlin, 1916).

M. Walden and L. Schneyer, *Der Sturm. Ein Erinnerungsbuch an H.W....* (Baden-Baden, 1954).

**Walschap, Gerard** (Zonderzeel 1893– ). Flemish novelist. In his work during the thirties a sceptical attitude to the establishment gradually hardens into an amoral revolt against Flemish Catholicism. *Trouwen* (1933), *Celibaat* (1944; tr. *Marriage and Ordeal*, 1963), *Een mensch van goeden wil* (1936), and *Het Kind* (1939) present man, in four widely different and brilliantly portrayed characters, at odds with his environment. In *Houtekiet* (1940) and its sequel *Nieuwe Deps* (1961) there is an echo of Knut ⇨ Hamsun in the vitalistic justification of life itself as the only law-giver. [PK]

*Denise* (1942); *Genezing door Aspirine* (1943, tr. *Cure through Aspirin*, 1960); *De française* (1957); *Delta* (Winter 1958/9).

B. F. van Vlierden, *G.W.* (Bruges, 1958).

**Walser, Martin** (Wasserburg, Bodensee 1927– ). German writer and radio producer. *Ein Flugzeug über dem Haus und andere Geschichten* (1955) and *Ehen in Philippsburg* (1957), his first novel, criticize the values of commercial life, the *Wirtschaftswunder*, and German middle-class pretensions to culture as a leisure activity; *Halbzeit* (1960) is his major novel of social criticism. His *Beschreibung einer Form, Franz Kafka* (1961) acknowledges his debt to Kafka. *Eiche and Angora* (1962; tr. anon., *The Rabbit Race*) is a play about the recrudescence of Nazism in contemporary Germany. *Überlebensgrosser Herr Krott* (1963) concerns itself with the inhumanity of big business in Brechtian, loosely epic scenes of social criticism, while his next play, *Der schwarze Schwan* (1964), returns to the theme of the 'Bewältigung der Vergangenheit'. His most recent novel, *Das Abstecher*, appeared in 1966. He has written several Hörspiele, one of which, *Der Umweg*, was presented in 1962 by B.B.C. radio as *The Detour*. It is a comedy of menace, criticizing the immorality of the affluent male business world in a farcically horrific triangular situation. Not a profound writer, but an important social critic in post-war Germany, he has won many national prizes. [MB]

**Walser, Robert** (Biel 1878–Herisau 1956). Swiss poet and novelist. He held minor clerical jobs until his breakdown in 1929, after which he lived in a mental hospital. Without ambition, horrified by pretentiousness, his works of poetry and poetic prose are microcosmic. Behind his 'charmed ironic clownishness' (C. Middleton) and childlike playfulness there lies a rejection of conventional perspective; against an unseen but felt background of spiritual nightmare, his vision of things has a startling simplicity and stylistic clarity which influenced Kafka. Apart from little known first editions (1904–25), selections, e.g. *Grosse kleine Welt* (1937), there are: *Dichtungen in Prosa* (5 vols., 1953–61), *Gedichte* (1909, repr. 1944), *Unbekannte Gedichte* (1958). [PB]

*Das Gesamtwerk*, ed. J. Greven (12 vols., Geneva, 1966ff.); *The Walk and Other Stories*, tr. intr. C. Middleton (1957).

R. Mächler, *Das Leben R.W.s* (Geneva, 1966); C. Seelig, *Wanderungen mit R.W.* (St Gallen, 1957); K. J. W. Greven, *Existenz ... im Werk R.W.s* (Cologne, 1960) (dissertation); O. Zinniker, *R.W. der Poet* (Zürich, 1947); Natan, *GML*, ii.

**Waltari, Mika** (Helsinki 1908– ). Finnish writer. Created Member of Finnish Academy in 1957. He has run the gamut of literary forms, from poems to detective stories, with a new book almost every year. A technical virtuoso in several fields, his more important work falls into two categories, the long historical novel and the short story. Most famous for the former, his purest artistic success is with the latter. The best known historical novel is *Sinuhe, egyptiläinen* (1945; tr. N. Walford, *Sinuhe the Egyptian*, 1949); it has had a long line of successors. These novels are set either in ancient times or the Middle Ages; each describes some great turning point in history, with the hero dimly sensing the shape of things to come, oppressed by a sense of futility and by pessimistic forebodings. Questions of religion, even of dogma, play an important part. In the shorter novels and the short stories there is a calmer contemplation of the unchanging problems of mankind, and often the mood is one of resignation. Here too men fail to understand one another, but not because of historical circumstances: it is inherent in the very nature of human beings. Their interests, their use of words, are such as to preclude any genuine contact or understanding. One way out of the impasse is through mystical experience, the other apparently through something very like common sense. Many of his plays and occasional writings seem to propose a naïvely realistic approach: a good-humoured acceptance of the world as it is, an ability to lose one's illusions without becoming embittered. [AK]

Tr. N. Walford, *Mikael Karvajalka* (1948; *Michael the Finn*, 1950, or *The Adventurer*, N.Y., 1950); *Mikael Hakim* (1949; *The Sultan's Renegade*, 1951, or *The Wanderer*, N.Y., 1951); *Vieras mies tuli taloon* (1937; *A Stranger Came to the Farm*, N.Y., 1952); *Johannes Angelos* (1952; *The Dark Angel*, 1953); *Kuun maisema* (1953; *Moonscape and Other Stories*, N.Y., 1954); *Valtakunnan salaisuus* (1959; *The Secret of the Kingdom*, N.Y., 1960); *Neljä päivänlaskua* (1949; tr. A. Beesley, *A Nail Merchant at Nightfall*, 1954); *Turms Kuolematon* (1955; tr. E. Ramsden, *The Etruscan*, 1957); *Feliks Onnellinen* (1958; tr. A. Blair, *The Tongue of Fire*, 1959); *Ihmiskunnan viholliset* (1964); *Ihmisen vapaus*, a short story (1952; tr. D. Barrett, 1952).

**Walter of Antioch,** called **The Chancellor** (fl. 1112–1126). Medieval chronicler. A French clerk, probably from Normandy, Walter was chancellor to Roger of Antioch from 1112 to 1119. His *Antiochena bella* is a history of the principality 1114–19, in two parts. The first described Roger's victories over the Saracen prince Ilghazi and Antioch's prosperity under Roger's government; the second concerns Roger's defeat and death at Ilghazi's hands. Walter himself was captured in that same battle, and his sufferings during his subsequent imprisonment affected his intellect, he says, apologizing for the stylistic inferiority of his work. Nevertheless it is invaluable not only as a source of factual information but even more for the excellent insight it gives us into the administration of a Frankish state in Outremer. [MRM]

Ed. H. Hagenmeyer (Innsbruck, 1896); *RHC*, Hist. Occ., v; Migne, *PL*, 155.

**Walter of Châtillon, or Lisle (Galterus de Insula)** (Lille *c.*1135–1184). Latin poet. He studied at Paris, became a canon at Reims, came to the court at Angers, and was sent on an embassy to England where he became very friendly with Becket and John of Salisbury. He taught at Châtillon, studied further at Bologna and Rome, went back to Reims and entered the service of the archbishop, for whom he wrote an epic, *Alexandreis*, on the exploits of Alexander the Great. In his last years he was a victim of leprosy. He was one of the most prolific and talented of secular medieval Latin poets. His satires, some written for the Feast of Fools, are mostly at the expense of the superior clergy. He is perhaps at his best in lyrical *pastourelles*, in which he rivals contemporary vernacular poets in one of their own chosen fields. [FB]

K. Strecker, *Die Lieder W. von C. in der Handschrift 351 von St Omer* (Berlin, 1925); *Moralisch-satirische Gedichte W. von C.* (Heidelberg, 1929); Raby, *SLP*.

**Walther von der Vogelweide** (*c.*1170–*c.* 1230). German poet. The greatest German lyric poet of the Middle Ages. His reputation stood high already in his own lifetime, yet there is only one documentary reference to him – in Bishop Wolfger von Passau's household accounts for the year 1203. From his writings and from references to him by contemporaries and successors it can be inferred that he was a member of the lesser nobility, that his early career as a professional poet was spent at the Viennese court, that for many years after being forced to leave Vienna, he wandered unhappily from one German court to another, and that finally, probably in the early 1220s, he was granted a fief by the Emperor Frederick II in return for the support which he had lent to the Hohenstaufen cause through his political lyrics. The fief in question was in all likelihood the *curia de Vogelweide* referred to in a 14th-century record as lying within the see of Würzburg. His last datable poem refers to events which took place in 1227.

He wrote love-poems, both within the framework of so-called 'courtly love' and outside it, but it is above all in his *Sprüche* – moral and political poems dealing with his personal relationship to his various patrons, with the struggle between Empire and Papacy, with the spiritual value of crusade and pilgrimage and with general moral issues of the time – that the force and originality of his personality are revealed. He was a fearless champion of the causes he espoused, and his outspoken views often brought him, not surprisingly, into disfavour with ecclesiastical and secular powers, but he never departed from his ethical principles. In his devotion to Christian virtues and his fierce concern for the moral well-being of the German people, he embodies many of the highest values expressed in the medieval concept of the Holy Roman Empire. [RT]

*Die Gedichte* (Lachmann edn), ed. H. Kuhn (Berlin, 1965).

W. Wilmanns, *Leben und Dichten W.v.d.V.s* (Bonn, 1916); K. H. Halbach, *W.v.d.V.* (Stuttgart, 1965).

**Wassermann, Jakob** (Fürth 1873–Altaussee 1934). German novelist and Jewish liberal intellectual. He rejected traditional religion (*Die Juden von Zirndorf*, 1897; tr. C. Brooks, *The Jews of Zirndorf*, 1933) to search for a new spirituality based on more modern, but now dated psychology. The heart's release from sloth ('*Trägheit*' was the catchword in *Caspar Hauser*, 1908) was found, in imitation of Dostoyevsky, in unconventional 'depths' – of erotic experience in *Die Geschichte der Jungen Renate Fuchs* (1900) or *Das Gänsemännchen* (1915; tr. A. W. Porterfield, *The Goose Man*, N.Y., 1922); of innocence corrupted (*Der Moloch*, 1902), raped (*Caspar Hauser*, tr. C. Newton, N.Y., 1928) or regained among outcasts (*Christian Wahnschaffe*, 1919; tr. L. Lewisohn, *The World's Illusion*, N.Y., 1930); and of criminal 'psychological' mysteries in the once famous detective novel, *Der Fall Maurizius* (1928; tr. anon., *The Maurizius Case*, 1930) and sequels, *Etzel Andergast* (1931; tr. C. Brooks, 1932) and *Joseph Kerkhovens dritte Existenz* (1934; tr. E. and C. Paul, *Kerkhoven's Third Existence*, 1961). This blend of lurid interests and social criticism (especially of injustice) has lost its once great popularity. Also in translation: *Gold* (N.Y., 1924) and *Faber* (1930 – from the cycle *Der Wendekreis*, 1920ff.). *Bula Matari* (1932) analyses explorer Stanley in terms of Conrad's *Heart of Darkness*; *Mein Weg als Deutscher und Jude* (1921; tr. S. N. Brainin, *My Life as German and Jew*, N.Y., 1933) is autobiography. [PB/AKT]

*Gesammelte Werke* (15 vols., 1932).
J. C. Blankenagel, *The Writings of J.W.* (Boston, 1942).

**Wedekind, Frank** (Hanover 1864–Munich 1918). German dramatist. The son of a fiercely democratic physician, he grew up in Switzerland, returned to Germany and became journalist, poet, actor and cabaret singer. Political poems published in *Simplicissimus* in 1899 caused him to be imprisoned for lèse-majesté. His first successful play, *Frühlings Erwachen* (1891; tr. F. J. Ziegler, *The Awakening of Spring*, Philadelphia, 1916), is a tragedy of 'natural' adolescence repressed, corrupted and destroyed by social convention. *Der Erdgeist* (1895; tr. S. A. Eliot, *Earth Spirit*, N.Y., 1914) and *Die Büchse der Pandora* (1904; tr. S. A. Eliot, *Pandora's Box*, N.Y., 1918) expose society in the sexually still more lurid light of Lulu, the demonically beautiful but soulless Woman – who finally falls victim to prostitution and a maniac murderer. *Der Marquis von Keith* (1901), *König Nicolo oder So ist das Leben* (1902; tr. F. J. Ziegler, *Such is Life*, Philadelphia, 1916), etc., variously exploit the satirical possibilities of his ambiguous erotic philosophy (cf. 'Über die Erotik', preface to the stories *Feuerwerk*, 1905), which seems too outraged at contemporary hypocrisy to take its own basic nihilism seriously. 'Laugh gentlemen, it's all very tragic', was the keynote of his notorious ballads at 'Die elf Scharfrichter' (Munich). In his style and his acting – with its suggestion of the puppet – he foreshadowed Expressionism and influenced Brecht. *Die vier Jahreszeiten* (1905) and *Lautenlieder* (1920) are poems and songs. [PB]

*Gesammelte Werke* (9 vols., 1912–21); *Prosa, Dramen, Verse* (1954); *Five Tragedies of Sex* (*Spring's Awakening, Earth Spirit, Pandora's Box, Death and Devil, Castle Wetterstein*), tr. B. Fawcett and S. Spender (1952).
A. Kutscher, *F.W.* (Munich, rev. edn, 1964); G. Seehaus, *F.W.* (1964); K. Völker, *F.W.* (Velber, 1965); Garten, *MGD*; Natan, *GML*, ii (1963); *GQ*, XXXIX, 2 (1966).

**Weerth, Georg** (Detmold 1822–Havana 1856). German poet and essayist. He was a friend of Marx and Engels and edited the radical left-wing *Neue Rheinische Zeitung* in Cologne. He emigrated to England and subsequently to Cuba. His only book published in his lifetime is *Leben und Taten des berühmten Ritters Schnapphahnski* (1849), a satire on the Prussian 'Junker'. His *Humoristische Skizzen aus dem deutschen Handelsleben* satirize Germany's liberal bourgeoisie. His poems, influenced by ⇨ Heine and ⇨ Freiligrath, express socialist views. [LL]

*Gesammelte Werke* (5 vols., 1956); *Ausgewählte Werke* (2 vols., 1963; 1 vol., 1966).

**Weil, Simone** (Paris 1909–Ashford, Kent 1943). French essayist. Daughter of a Jewish doctor, *agrégée* in philosophy, left-wing intellectual, factory-worker and farm-hand, Free French worker. During her life she published some essays and articles, and completed *L'enracinement*, 1949–50 (tr. A. Wills, *The Need for Roots*, N.Y., 1955), but other books which have appeared since 1947 are posthumous editings, following her indications of themes, of jottings from her *Cahiers* (1951–6, tr. A. Wills, *Notebooks*, 1956), or of lengthy letters and reflections sent to close friends (e.g. *Écrits de Londres et dernières lettres*, 1957; *Seventy Letters*, tr. Sir Richard Rees, 1965; *Sur la science*, 1966). Her analyses of her penetrating religious intuitions and hesitant attraction to Catholicism (*La connaissance surnaturelle*, 1950; *Lettre à un religieux*, 1951, tr. A. Wills, *Letter to a Priest*, 1953), her original re-shaping of theological notions (*L'attente de Dieu*, 1949, tr. E. Craufurd, *Waiting for God*, N.Y., 1959; *La pesanteur et la grâce*, 1947, tr. E. Craufurd, *Gravity and Grace*, N.Y., 1952), her interpretations of history, of Mediterranean religions, of Greek classics and Plato (*Intuitions pré-chrétiennes*, 1951, *La source grecque*, 1953, *Leçons de philosophie*, 1959), together with her detestations: bureaucracy, the dehumanization of labour, capitalism, fascism, communism and even syndicalism, Aristotle, Thomism, Rome and the Jews, align themselves – though not without some didacticism and distortion of fact or focus – with her views that the individual should constantly associate himself with whichever group is currently oppressed by organized force, trying to counterbalance the evil and injustice inseparable from any social authority (*La condition ouvrière*, 1951; *Oppression et liberté*, 1955, tr. A. Wills and J. Petrie, *Oppression and Liberty*, 1958; *Écrits historiques et politiques*, 1960). Suffering and self-abasement are to be sought as the means to moral oneness with God. Though sometimes considered difficult, mystical, paradoxical and visionary, she is nevertheless uniquely respected for her exceptional lucidity, intellectual integrity and profundity. The many nuggets of wisdom, ruthlessly refined of obscurity, pretension or excess verbiage, represent a conscious code of obligation of writer to reader much needed today, and continue to attract scholarly attention from a variety of sources. [JF]

M. M. Davy, *S.W.* (Paris, 1956); M. Thout, *Jalons sur la route de S.W.* (2 vols., Paris, 1959); G. Kempfner, *La philosophie mystique de S.W.* (Paris, 1960); E. Piccard, *S.W., Essai biographique et critique, suivi d'un catalogue raisonné des œuvres* (Paris, 1960); J. Cabaud, *L'expérience vécue de S.W. avec de nombreux inédits* (Paris, 1956) and *S.W., a Fellowship in Love* (1964); R. Rees, *S.W.* (1965).

**Weinert, Erich** (Magdeburg 1890–Berlin 1953). German poet and essayist. An engineer and painter before call-up in the First World War. From 1921 he was active as a writer and reciter of political cabaret poetry, and as a communist agitator in Berlin. He emigrated in 1933 to Switzerland, then to France. He lived mainly in Moscow, from 1935 to 1946, fighting in Spain (1937–9). He returned to East Berlin in 1946 to take up a high position in educational administration. His stories (*Der Tod für das Vaterland*, 1942; *Camaradas*, 1951) and poems (collected in *Der Gottesgnadenhecht*, 1923; *Politische Gedichte*, 1928; *Pflastersteine*, 1934; *Deutschland*, 1936; *Stalin spricht*, 1940; *Gegen den wahren Feind*, 1943; *Rufe in der Nacht*, 1947; *Gedichte*, 1950, and other volumes) show his political commitment in the form of satire or propaganda. [LL]

*Gesammelte Werke* (9 vols., 1955–60); *Zwischenspiel* (1950) (selections); *Gedichte, eine Auswah* (1956).

A. Kantorowicz, *E.W.*, in *Deutsche Schicksale* (1949); B. Kaiser, *E.W.* (1951).

**Weingarten, Romain** (1926– ). French playwright. Noted for avant-garde plays in which fantasy and exuberant verbal invention dissolve the everyday world in a kind of wild poetry, often comic, often savagely violent, and reminiscent of surrealist dreams. Such are: *Akara* (1948) with its bizarre game of cards followed by the death of mother and son; *Les nourrices* (1960) and *L'été* (1963). [SBJ]

Corvin, *TNF*; Serreau, *HNT*.

**Weinheber, Josef** (Vienna 1892–suicide? Kirchstetten, Lower Austria 1945). Austrian poet. After privations in youth (cf. autobiographical novel *Das Waisenhaus*, 1925) and unsuccessful early poetry, e.g. *Der einsame Mensch* (1920), he was politically and popularly acclaimed for the heroic odes (and incidentally Nazi sentiments) of *Adel und Untergang* (1934). His preoccupations were poetic and philosophical (see essays *Im Namen der Kunst*, 1936, and *Über die Dichtkunst*, 1947), but the Hölderlinesque, 'antique' measures and mood of *Späte Krone* (1936) and *Zwischen Göttern und Dämonen* (1938) seem now rather contrived. *Kammermusik* (1939) experiments with verbal and vowel effects; *Wien Wörtlich* (1935) contains more popular, partly dialect verse. [PB/AKT]

*Sämtliche Werke*, ed. Nadler and Weinheber (1953ff.); Bridgwater, *TCGV*.

H. Bergholz, *J.W. Bibliographie* (Bad Bocklet, 1953); J. Nadler, *J.W.* (Salzburg, 1953); F. Feldner, *J.W.* (Salzburg, 1965); *GLL*, VI, 2 (1953).

**Weise, Christian** (Zittau 1642–Zittau 1708). German writer. As a serious pedagogue – he was headmaster of the grammar school in Zittau for many years – Weise early abandoned the lighthearted witty note he struck in lyrics of *Der grünenden Jugend überflüssige Gedanken* (1668; ed. M. v. Waldberg, Neudrucke 242–5, 1914) for the heavy didacticism and satire of his widely read novels *Die drei Hauptverderber in Deutschland* (1671), *Die drei ärgsten Erznarren in der ganzen Welt* (1672) and *Die drei klügsten Leute in der ganzen Welt* (1675), which exploit the review technique and are reminiscent of ⇨ Moscherosch in their castigation of perennial and contemporary vices. The didacticism of the novels is equally evident in most of his rather wooden school-dramas, which include tragedies on Biblical and historical themes – the most famous is *Masaniello* (1683; ed. R. Petsch, Neudrucke 216–18, 1907) – and a number of derivative comedies, amongst them versions of the *Taming of the Shrew* and ⇨ Gryphius's *Squentz*. [WAC]

*Bäurischer Machiavell. Comödie von der bösen Catharina*, ed. L. Fulda, DNL, 39; *Der Niederländische Bauer*, ed. W. Flemming, DLE (Barock, 4).

W. Eggert, *C.W. und seine Bühne* (Berlin, 1935); R. Becker, *C.W.s Romane und ihre Nachwirkung* (Berlin, 1910).

**Weiss, Konrad** (Rauenbretzingen, Württemberg 1880–Munich 1940). German poet. Editor of the Catholic periodical *Hochland* (1905–20), then art-critic for the *Münchner Neueste Nachrichten*. A religious poet, treating themes from nature, history and art in a language showing baroque and liturgical influences, and the author also of plays (e.g. *Konradin von Hohenstaufen*, 1938), critical and scholarly prose, etc.: *Deutschlands Morgenspiegel* (2 vols., 1950); *Wanderer in den Zeiten* (ed. F. Kemp, 1958). [PB]

*Dichtungen und Schriften* (1961ff.); *Gedichte*, ed. F. Kemp (1948ff.); Bridgwater, *TCGV*.

C. F. Müller, *K.W.* (Freiburg, 1965); Hohoff, *GU*.

**Weiss, Peter (Ulrich)** (Nowawes, nr Berlin 1916– ). German novelist, dramatist, painter and film producer. He emigrated in 1934 to England, then to Czechoslovakia and Switzerland, eventually settling in Sweden in 1939. His 'micro-novel', *Der Schatten des Körpers des Kutschers* (1960) and the novel fragment *Das Gespräch der drei Gehenden* (1963) are experimental in their fragmentary view of reality and shapeless language. They show the influence of ⇨ Kafka, ⇨ Gide, ⇨ Moravia, ⇨ Beckett. *Abschied von den Eltern* (1961; tr. C. Levenson, *Leavetaking*, 1967) and *Fluchtpunkt* (1962; tr. C. Levenson, *Vanishing Point*, 1967) are autobiographical stories. His plays include *Die Verfolgung und Ermordung Jean Paul Marats dargestellt durch die Schauspieltruppe des Hospizes zu Charenton unter Anleitung des Herrn de Sade* (1964; tr. G. Skelton and A. Mitchell, *The Persecution and Assassination of Jean Paul Marat* . . . 1965; short title: *Marat/Sade*) which contains elements of the absurd and of ⇨ Brecht's 'epic' theatre, and *Die Ermittlung* (1965; tr. A. Gross, *The Investigation*, 1966), a reproduction of the Auschwitz trials in the form of an 'oratorio in 11 cantos'. [LL]

**Weisse, Christian Felix** (Arneberg 1726–Stötteritz, nr Leipzig 1804). German writer. Weisse is an essentially backward-looking literary figure: as editor of the periodical *Allgemeine deutsche Bibliothek* (1759–86) he ignored or even deprecated contemporary literary developments. His numerous comedies are mostly *comédies larmoyantes* in the manner of ⇨ Gellert, while his 10 tragedies are imitative and experiment with 17th-century modes (*Mustapha und Zeangir*, 1761; *Rosenmunde*, 1761) and with a combination of the French and English styles – *Richard III* (1759) is subjected to the classical unities and *Romeo and Juliet* (1768) is given a middle-class setting. His activities as a librettist and as editor of children's periodicals (*Der Kinderfreund*, 1775–82) were more in keeping with his temperament and talents and in these capacities he exercised a modest but not important influence on his age. [WAC]

J. Minor, *C.F.W.* (Innsbruck, 1881); Killy, *DLTZ*.

**Welhaven, Johan S.** (Bergen 1807–Kristiania 1873). Norwegian poet. A clergyman's son, he broke off his university studies to devote himself to literature, and became one of the leaders of the so-called 'Intelligence Party'. In 1846 he was appointed professor of philosophy. In his poems he treats themes from popular ballads, thus reflecting the current National Romanticism; elsewhere he is more personal, and in *Norges Dæmring* (1834), polemical. His work is well turned but rather narrow in scope, and suffers by comparison with his great contemporary, Henrik ⇨ Wergeland. Today he is probably best remembered for his feud with Wergeland, in which he advocated conservatism and the maintenance of the link with Denmark in literary and cultural matters. [RGP]

*Digte* (1839); *Nyere Digte* (1845); *Halvhundrede Digte* (1848); *Reisebilleder og Digte* (1851); *En Digtsamling* (1860); *Samlede skrifter* (3 vols., 1943).

A. Løchen, *J.S.W.* (Oslo, 1900); R. Andersen-Næss, *J.S.W.* (Oslo, 1959).

**Welti, A. J.** ⇨ Swiss-German Dialect Literature.

**Weöres, Sándor** (Pécs 1913– ). Hungarian poet. A master of almost every style. He translates from many languages and poets of different periods. His own philosophy is that of an escapist, to the point of extreme nihilism. [JFR]

**Werfel, Franz** (Prague 1890–Beverly Hills, U.S.A. 1945). Austrian poet, novelist and dramatist. Co-founder of the Expressionist series *Der jüngste Tag* (1913–21), he was the movement's most popular poet, partly because of the plain moral sentiments underlying his ecstatic style – the bonds uniting all men, the evil of war, etc. These recur in his modernist plays, e.g. *Die Troerinnen* (1914), an anti-war version of Euripides, and *Der Spiegelmensch* (1920), a *Faust*-like search for true self and unselfishness, and also in the more conventional historical drama, *Juarez und Maximilian* (1924; tr. G. W. Gabriel, N.Y., 1926), with its lesson of 'love thine enemy', and in religious plays (*Paulus ...*, 1926; tr. P. P. Levertoff, 1943; *Die ewige Strasse*, 1936; tr. L. Lewisohn, *The Eternal Road*, 1937; – see *Dramen*, ed. A. D. Klarmann, 2 vols., 1959). His fiction has been more successful and is psychologically revealing of a Jewish intellectual's ambivalent attitudes during a period of war and revolution, towards the old order (*Nicht der Mörder, der Ermordete ist schuldig*, 1920; *Barbara*, 1929), towards art (*Verdi*, 1924; tr. H. Jessiman, 1944), towards intellectuals (*Der veruntreute Himmel*, 1938, tr. M. Firth, *The Embezzled Heaven*; and *Stern der Ungeborenen*, 1946), towards the Catholic Church in the famous *Das Lied von Bernadette* (1941; tr. L. Lewisohn, *The Song of Bernadette*, 1958; filmed), written in gratitude for sanctuary found at Lourdes as he fled on foot to Spain in 1940. Also translated: *Die Geschwister von Neapel* (1931; tr. D. F. Tait, *The Pascarella Family*, 1932), about the trials of a banker's family in Fascist Naples, and *Die vierzig Tage des Musa Dagh* (1933; tr. G. Dunlop, *The Forty Days*, 1962), a historical study of mass persecution in Turkey. [PB/AKT]

*Gesammelte Werke*, ed. A. D. Klarmann (3 vols., 1948–54) (collected fiction); *Das Lyrischewerk*, ed. A. D. Klarmann (1967); *Poems*, tr. E. A. Snow (1945).

L. B. Foltin (ed.), *F.W. 1890–1945* (Pittsburgh, 1961); *GQ*, XXXIX, 1, 1966; Natan, *GML*, iii; *GQ*, XXXIX, 1, 1966.

**Wergeland, Henrik** (Kristiansand 1808–Kristiania 1845). Norwegian poet. A clergyman's son, he came to epitomize in his life and work the strivings and aspirations of the new Norway after 1814, with its Constitution, Storting, and its great measure of freedom in the new union with Sweden. Like ⇨ Bjørnson after him, he was not only a poet but was also untiringly active in public and political affairs, and earned for himself the title of the 'uncrowned king' of Norway. From his father he had inherited the ideals of the Age of Enlightenment, and gave practical expression to them in his work for the enlightenment of the common people, through his periodicals *For Almuen*, *For Menigmand* and *For Arbeidsklassen*. As a poet he expressed himself in the terminology of the Romantics, but even here, especially in his chief work, the monumental but uneven *Skabelsen, Mennesket og Messias* (1830), his optimistic cosmology is 18th century. In Norway, all evaluation of his poetic stature tends to be coloured by his importance as a national symbol. Much of his work was published unrevised and is frequently very uneven, extravagant and tasteless, but there is always an overriding vitality. At times he rose to great imaginative heights and produced dazzling felicities of language, and on such occasions justifies the esteem in which he is held as the greatest poet Norway has produced. Amongst his principal works are *Jan van Huysums Blomsterstykke* (1840); *Jøden* (1842); *Jødinden* (1844); *Den engelske Lods* (1844). His prolific output also included a number of plays, essays, and a history of the Norwegian constitution, *Norges Konstitutions Historie* (1841–3). [RGP]

*Samlede skrifter*, ed. H. Jæger, D. A. Seip, H. Koht (23 vols., 1918–40); *H.W.s skrifter*, ed. L. Amundsen and D. A. Seip (8 vols., 1957–62); *Poems*, tr. G. M. Gathorne-Hardy, I. Grøndahl, J. Bithell (1929).

H. Beyer, *H.W.* (Oslo, 1946); A. Kabell, *W.* I–II (Oslo, 1956–7); Y. Ustvedt, *Det levende univers* (Oslo, 1964); McFarlane, *TNL*.

**Werner der Gärtner** (fl. 1250–1280). German poet. Author of the Middle High German narrative poem *Meier Helmbrecht* (ed. F. Panzer, 1941; C. E. Gough, 1947), one of the most interesting and effective works in 13th-century German literature. The story is that of a farmer's son who, discontent with his humble social status, joins the retinue of a marauding knight; he enriches himself through the proceeds of robbery but is finally caught and horribly mutilated. Blind and crippled, he comes back to his father's house and is turned away; the peasants whom he has scorned and mocked set upon him and finally hang him.

The poem, which is characterized by a realistic and often coarse descriptive style, is meant to convey, through the example of Helmbrecht's terrible fate, a social and ethical message: that one should abide by the terms of one's given social position, and honour the precepts of one's parents; the wickedness and callousness of Helmbrecht's deeds, like his ultimate downfall, stem from his disobedience of these rules.

Of Werner der Gärtner ('William the Gardener'), who names himself in the last line of his poem, nothing is otherwise known. [RT]

**Wessel, Johan H.** (Vestby, Akershus 1742–Copenhagen 1785). Dano-Norwegian poet and playwright. A clergyman's son, he spent most of his short life in Denmark, where he led a penurious bohemian existence. He is chiefly remembered for his *Kierlighed uden Strømper* (1772), a mock five-act tragedy in classical style, intended as a satire on the current fashion in Danish drama. In it, missing stockings set the whole tragic apparatus in motion, but in uproarious parody. His talents as a versifier and satirist are also evident in his poems, epigrams, and short stories in verse. [RGP]

*Digte*, ed. F. Bull (2 vols., 1918).

S. Thomsen, *Kun en Digter. En Bog om J.H.W.* (Copenhagen, 1942).

**Weyssenhoff, Józef** (Kolano 1860–Warsaw 1932). Polish novelist. His aristocratic origin and connexions gave him a self-assured understanding whenever he chose to describe a cosmopolitan milieu or provincial snobbery. The best of his novels is his second, with the 18th-century type of title, *Żywot i myśli Zygmunta Podfilipskiego* ('The Life and Thoughts of Sigismund Podfilipski', 1898), in which the biographical form is ingeniously applied: since earnestness was all too often associated with homely subjects, he hit on an apt ironical device by introducing an earnest story-teller in whose homely style the life of that high-minded cad Podfilipski is recorded and glorified. This mock-biography was translated into German and French and much admired.

Weyssenhoff spoilt most of his other works either by pontificating on current problems (e.g. *Unia*, 1909, set in Lithuania), or by overplaying his aristocratic manner in style, both habits fatal to an ironist. However, his novels about Polish forests and hunting are full of charm and information, as *Soból i panna* (1911; tr. K. Żuk-Skarszewska, *The Sable and the Girl*, 1929). In his memoirs (*Mój pamiętnik literacki*, 1925) the sophisticated *raconteur* is strangely absent. [JP]

**Wickram, Georg** (Kolmar 1505–Kolmar *c.* 1562). German novelist. His earliest works, *Ritter Galmy* (1539) and *Reinhard und Gabriotto* (1551), are weak imitations of the chevalresque novel and the influence of the latter still persists in *Der Goldfaden* (1554) and *Der Jungen Knaben Spiegel* (1554), although both show traces of the middle-class element which was to be the characteristic feature of his most important novel *Von guten und bösen Nachbarn* (1556). This latter work breaks significantly new ground not only in its exclusively middle-class milieu and unquestioning affirmation of the ethic of the Protestant merchant class, but also in its use of letters, dreams and monologues to reveal the inner life of the characters and in the conscious attempt to write poetic prose. Wickram also wrote a number of Shrovetide plays and *Meistergesänge*, together with a highly successful collection of humorous anecdotes, *Rollwagenbüchlein* (1555). [WAC]

*Werke*, ed. J. Bolte and W. Scheel (8 vols., BLVS, 1901–6); *Der Jungen Knaben Spiegel* and *Von guten und bösen Nachbarn*, ed. F. Podleiszek, DLE (Volks- u. Schwankb. 7).

R. John, *Studien zu W.s Romane* (Munich, 1954).

**Widukind** (fl. 975). Saxon chronicler at the Benedictine abbey of Corvey in Saxony, celebrated as a centre of classical learning. In his *Res gestae Saxonicae* (ed. P. Hirsch and H. E. Lohmann, MGH, SRG, 1935), dedicated to the abbess Matilda, a daughter of Otto the Great, Widukind, like ⇨ Cassiodorus, seeks a respectable origin in antiquity for a race of newly converted barbarians. He finds it in survivors of the army of Alexander the Great. After describing their conversion to Christianity under Charlemagne he deals with the reign of Otto the Great. His Latin style, based on Sallust, is on the whole good. He lacks humour but tells some good stories and can describe vividly, e.g. the defeat of the Magyars at the Lechfeld. [FB]

**Wiechert, Ernst** (nr Sensburg, E. Prussia 1887–nr Zürich 1950). German novelist. His solitary imagination, obsessed by his native countryside, brooded on problems of spiritual regeneration (after early despairs, intensified by the First World War, and reflected in e.g. *Der Wald*, 1922, *Der Totenwolf*, 1924), which he sought in experience of nature, and 'natural' as opposed to urban life. This he conceives sometimes with mystic intensity, sometimes with pastoral sentimentality; fine examples are the story *Die Hirtennovelle* (1935), *Das einfache Leben* (1939; tr. M. Heyneman, *The Simple Life*, 1954) and *Die Jerominkinder* (1945–7; tr. R. Maxwell, *The Earth is Our Heritage*, 1951). His relationship to Christianity (at first antagonistic) e.g. in *Der Knecht Gottes Andreas Nyland* (1926) or his last *Missa sine Nomine* (1950; tr. M. Heyneman and M. B. Ledward, 1953), like his mystique of blood and heredity (e.g. *Die kleine Passion*, 1929), remains controversial; his 'religion' seems inspired by older pagan institutions (cf. *Die Magd des Jürgen Doscozil*, 1932, tr. E. Wilkins and E. Kaiser, *The Girl and the Ferryman*, N.Y., 1947). His opposition to Nazism was clear, and the months he spent in Buchenwald concentration camp are recorded in *Der Totenwald* (1945; tr. U. Stechow, *The Forest of the Dead*, 1947); other autobiographical volumes are *Wälder und Märchen* (1936) and *Jahre und Zeiten* (1949). Also translated: *The Baroness*, by P. L. T. Blewitt, 1936. [PB/AKT]

*Die Novellen und Erzählungen* (1962).
H. Ollesch, *E.W. Dichtung und Deutung* (Wuppertal, 1960); *Librarium*, 7 (Zürich, 1964) (with critical bibliography); *GLL*, III (1949–50); IV (1950–1); VII (1953–4); *M*, XLIII (1951).

**Wied, Gustav** (Holmegaard 1858–Roskilde 1914). Danish novelist and playwright. A pessimistic satirist who saw life as a meaningless dance of puppets controlled by the invisible hand of a lunatic, he ridiculed all classes of contemporary society in his short stories and novels, the best of which are *Livsens Ondskab* (1899), *Knagsted* (1902), and *Fædrene æde Druer* (1908). His satirical plays (which he called 'Satyr Plays') are full of a bitter and mocking humour; best known are the four one-act plays collected under the title *Adel, Gejstlighed, Borger og Bonde* (1897), the grotesque *Dansemus* (1905), and the two comedies *Autumn Fires* (tr. Glazer, Cincinnati, 1920) and *2 × 2 = 5* (tr. Boyd and Koppel, New York, 1923). He committed suicide. [ELB]

*Romaner, Skuespil, Noveller* (12 vols., 1966–7).
S. Houmøller, *G.W.* (Copenhagen, 1948); K. Ahnlund, *Den unge G.W.* (Copenhagen, 1964).

**Wieland, Christoph Martin** (Oberholzheim, Biberach 1733–Weimar 1813). German novelist and poet. Although groomed by Bodmer as the seraphic poet who would emulate ⇨ Klopstock, he was essentially pagan by nature and early abandoned the exaggerated and forced Christianity of such works as the *Empfindungen eines Christen* (1756) in favour of a more congenial philosophy. Many of his mature writings testify to his distrust of any kind of religious enthusiasm, which is invariably seen as the result of the frustration of the natural life of the senses; indeed, in his undoubted sensualism and barely concealed delight in *risqué* situations he seems merely to have gone from one extreme to the other. The sub-title of the *Abenteuer des Don Sylvio von Rosalva* (1763) – 'the victory of nature over enthusiasm' – proclaims the new outlook. It was not in Quixotic Spain, however, but in ancient Greece that Wieland, in anticipation of Goethe and Schiller, saw his ideal of a healthy and natural harmony of spirit and senses realized, and Greece provides the setting for the important novel of development *Geschichte des Agathon* (1766–7; part 3 1794), 'the first and only novel of the 18th century for the thinking man' (Lessing), which tells how a young man is cured of his foolish religious enthusiasm by a hetaira, a theme which recurs in the delightful verse idyll *Musarion* (1768) and in the late novels *Peregrinus Proteus* (1791) and *Aristipp* (1801). *Der goldene Spiegel* (1772), a political Arabian Nights entertainment, produced an invitation to go to Weimar as tutor to the young Duke, an invitation which gave Wieland financial security and inaugurated the fruitful connexion of Weimar with the world of literature. It was here that he edited *Der teutsche Merkur*, for years the most influential literary periodical in Germany, and it was here that he wrote the two works for which he is popularly remembered, *Die Geschichte der Abderiten* (1774), a witty satire on the narrow-mindedness and stupidity of the *bourgeoisie*, and *Oberon* (1780), a verse fairy-tale conspicuous for its light grace and musicality.

His prose translation of 22 Shakespearean plays helped to popularize Shakespeare in Germany and exercised great influence on the *Sturm und Drang* movement, while his two *Singspiele*, *Alkeste* (1773) and *Die Wahl des Herkules* (1773), anticipated the drama of German classicism. [WAC]

*Werke* (1909ff.).
F. Sengle, *W.* (Stuttgart, 1949); D. van Abbé, *C.M.W.* (1961); W. H. Bruford, *Culture and Society in Classical Weimar* (1962).

**Wiele, Joannes Stalpaert van der** (The Hague 1579–Delft 1630). Dutch priest and poet. His Counter-Reformation polemical writing (e.g. *Roomsche Reys*, 1624, and *Extractum Catholicum tegen verwarde hersenen*, 1631) show little of the fine artistry of his verse legend *Sint Agnes* or of his devotional songs in *Den Schat der Geestelijke Lofzangen* (1634), which are medieval rather than Renaissance in style and spirit. [P K]

Barnouw, *CA*.

**Wierzyński, Kazimierz** (Drohobycz 1894–1970). Polish poet. He was a member of the pre-war Academy of Literature and from 1940 lived in America. He began his career with spontaneous poems in praise of life and physical prowess, which culminated in his *Laur olimpijski*, awarded a literary prize at the Olympics of 1928. From the volume *Wolność tragiczna* (1936) he became preoccupied with national and heroic subjects, which were made more profound by the experience of exile. His best work is disciplined by careful metres and classical language. He also published *The Life and Death of Chopin* (1951), a biography. [J P]

*Selected Poems*, ed. C. Mills and L. Krzyżanowski (N.Y., 1959).

**Wildenvey, Herman** (Nedre Eiker, Buskerud 1886–Stavern 1959). Norwegian poet. He lived for three years in America and had various jobs. He returned to Norway in 1907 and achieved immediate success with his first collection of verse *Nyinger* (1907). Subsequently he published a large number of collections of poems, all marked by casual elegance, charm, wit and irony, but often (especially in the later collections) containing deeper layers of reflection and speculation. [R G P]

*Samlede dikt* (6 vols., 1945–52).
K. Haave, *H.W.* (Oslo, 1952).

**William of St Thierry** (Liège *c.*1085–*c.*1148). Benedictine and Abbot of St Thierry, near Reims, he resigned to become a simple Cistercian at Signy in the Ardennes. A close friend of St ⇨ Bernard of Clairvaux and an opponent of ⇨ Abelard, he left an unfinished life of the former and some polemics against the latter. He was also the author of a number of mystical works, such as *De vita solitaria* (ed. J. Metarm, tr. W. Shewring, *The Golden Epistle*, 1930), *De Deo contemplando* and *Speculum fidei*. [F B]

Migne, *PL*, 180.
J. M. Dechanet, *Guillaume de St-T.* (Paris, 1942).

**William of Tyre** (? Palestine *c.*1130–*c.*1190). French chronicler. Archbishop of Tyre under Baldwin IV, King of Jerusalem. His outstanding *Belli sacri historia* (tr. E. A. Babcock and A. C. Krey, N.Y., 1943), or *Historia hierosolymitana*, deals with the history of the Crusades from the preaching of Peter the Hermit in 1094 to the end of the year 1183. He has a remarkable power of bringing his characters to life and is an unusually exact historian among medieval writers. A French translation, *Chronique d'Outremer*, written about the year 1200, enjoyed very great popularity. [F B]

*Speculum*, XVI (1941); *RHC.* Hist. Occ. i and ii.
Migne, *PL*, 201.

**Winckelmann, Johann Joachim** (Stendal 1717–Trieste 1768). German art historian. His instinctive love of art survived the deprivations of his early years and, quickened by his affection for classical literature, bore fruit in two epoch-making works, *Gedanken über die Nachahmung der griechischen Werke in der Malerei und Bildhauerkunst* (1755) and *Geschichte der Kunst des Altertums* (1762; tr. G. H. Lodge, *The History of Ancient Art amongst the Greeks*, 1881). These are seminal works in their scientific approach to their subject, teaching the understanding of art out of the spiritual, material and sociological conditions under which it was produced. Greek art is seen as the supreme aesthetic achievement of mankind and its 'noble simplicity and quiet grandeur' are held to reflect the ideal combination of physical and spiritual beauty achieved by the Greek world – a view of Greece and of art which was to exercise immense influence on Weimar Classicism. [W A C]

*Werke*, ed. K. L. Fernow *et al.* (11 vols., 1808–25).
B. Valentin, *W.* (Berlin, 1931).

**Winkler, Eugen Gottlob** (Zürich 1912–Munich 1936). German poet and essayist. His work became known only after his suicide, when friends published *Dichter-*

*ische Arbeiten* (poems and stories, 1937) and *Gestalten und Probleme* (essays, 1937). Influenced by Valéry, he was a nihilist who struggled to find an absolute value in art and save himself by writing from existential despair. He both exemplifies and analyses spiritual tensions typical of much modern German literature. [PB]

Holthusen, *UM*; H. Piontek, *Buchstab-Zauberstab: Über Dichter und Dichtung* (Esslingen, 1959); *DR*, LXXXIII (1957).

**Winther, Christian** (Fensmark 1796–Paris 1876). Danish poet. Famous for his evocations of the scenery of Sealand and his fine love poems, e.g. the deliberately naïve 'Woodcuts' in his first *Digte* (1828). After a number of unhappy love affairs, he eventually married a divorced woman who had inspired some of his finest love lyrics: *Til Een* (1841–8). His main work is *Hjortens Flugt* (1855), a long narrative poem set in Sealand with a romantic plot inspired by Byron's *Mazeppa*. He lived in Paris after 1851 but was buried in Denmark. [ELB]

O. Friis, *Hjortens Flugt* (Copenhagen, 1961).

**Wipo** (d. *c.* 1050). Medieval Latin writer. Perhaps a Burgundian, he was chaplain to the Emperor Conrad II and his son and successor, Henry III. His life of Conrad shows him to have been a man of learning with a wide knowledge of classical Latin poets. His verse includes a collection of proverbs, a dialogue on government and education (*Tetralogus*) addressed to Henry III, a lament on Conrad II, and the Easter ⇨ Sequence 'Victimae paschali', which is one of the five sequences in the current Roman Missal. [FB]

Ed. H. Bresslau (MGH, SRG, 1915).
Raby, *CLP*.

**Wirnt von Grafenberg** (fl. 1204–10). Middle High German epic poet. A Frankish nobleman whose family domain lay in the district between Bayreuth and Nuremberg. He is remembered for his Arthurian verse romance *Wigalois* (ed. J. M. N. Kapteyn, 1926), the story of the son of Gawain and Florie, who is portrayed as an exemplary Christian knight. Stylistically the work owes much to ⇨ Hartmann von Aue and ⇨ Wolfram von Eschenbach. [RT]

**Witkiewicz, Stanisław Ignacy** (Cracow 1885–Jeziory 1939). Polish novelist. He had a restless and agile mind, was interested in philosophy, preached the aesthetics of 'pure form', painted, and indulged a weakness for shocking subjects. He was most original in his apocalyptic novels, *Pożegnanie jesieni* (1927) and *Nienasycenie* (1930), predicting a communist regime in Poland and a Chinese invasion of Europe. Sexual fantasies dominate the life of his oddly assorted characters, but the real oddity is his language, careless, verbose and woolly in syntax. His plays, too, suffer from this paradoxical impurity of form, although the conscious element of nonsense in them has much in common with the theatre of today (*Dramaty*, 1962). He committed suicide when the Soviet army crossed the Polish frontier in September 1939. [JP]

**Wittlin, Józef** (Dmytrów 1896– ). Polish novelist and poet. He now lives in New York. He is best known for his *Sól ziemi* (1935; tr. P. de Chary, *Salt of the Earth*, 1939), 'a novel about a patient infantryman', which is the first part of an unfinished trilogy. The psalmodic strain in his verse (e.g. *Hymny*, 1920) was intensified by the events of the last war and the experience of exile. He has also translated the *Odyssey* (1924). [JP]

**Woestijne, Karel van de** (Ghent 1878–Zwijnaerde 1929). Flemish poet. Member of the Laethem artist group (cf. *Laethemsche Brieve over de lente*, 1902), then collaborator on the *Van Nu en Straks* journal, he was a hypersensitive introvert who isolated himself from those who could not share the intensity of his feelings in his verse of luxurious diction and obscure meaning. In *De Modderen Man* (1920) his confessional lyricism reached an apex of bitterness and melancholy unparalleled in Dutch literature. In his 11 books of poems and 6 of prose he rarely finds relief from the torture of the sinner alienated from the beloved. [PK]

*Verzameld Werk* (8 vols., 1947–50); 21 poems tr. C. and F. Stillman in *Lyra Belgica I* (N.Y., 1950).

M. Rutten, *De lyriek van K.v.d.W.* (Liège/Paris, 1935), *De aesthetische oprattingen van K.v.d.W.* (Liège/Paris, 1943) and *Het proza van K.v.d.W.* (Liège/Paris, 1959).

**Wolff, Elisabeth,** *née* Dekker (Flushing 1738–The Hague 1804) and **Deken, Agatha** (Amsterdam 1741–The Hague 1804). Dutch novelists. In 1759 Elisabeth Dekker married Adriaan Wolff, a minister 30 years older than herself, and until his death in 1777 she read widely in literature and theology. She then set up house, first in De Rijp and later (1782) in Beverwijk, with Agatha Deken, an orphan who had been in domestic service. They eked out a living by their translations and novels.

Betje Wolff, an admirer of Rousseau and modernist thought, had already made her name with her spirited verse and prose before her association with the less gifted Aagje Deken. In 1782 their *Sara Burgerhart* appeared, an epistolary novel; Richardson's influence is unmistakable not only in the form, but in the moral purpose and the dedication to Dutch young ladies. Betje's own abortive elopement at 17 and Aagje's experiences as an orphan provide vivid material, but it is the wit and evocative realism of the character description which earns this book a place in European literature. Its success was repeated in *Willem Leevend* (1784–5), where virtue derived from a liberal Christianity is again extolled. Yet although greater psychological insight improves on the tendency to caricature in *Sara Burgenhart*, the book is too long (8 vols.) and too theological for modern tastes. The later novels, *Abraham Blankaart* (1787) and *Cornelia Wildschut* (1793), fail to maintain the originality and charm of their earlier work. [PK]

*Economische liedjes* (3 vols., 1780–1); ed. J. van Nieuwenhuis (1963) (anthology).

*Boeket voor Betje en Aagje* (Amsterdam/Antwerp, 1954) (8 essays and an anthology).

**Wolfram von Eschenbach** (fl. early 13th cent.). Medieval German poet. All that can be reasonably assumed about his life is that he belonged to a Bavarian family of the lower nobility, that he apparently served a succession of Franconian lords, and that at some time in the early 13th century he was at Hermann of Thuringia's famous castle of the Wartburg. He probably died shortly after 1220.

Although he has left a few lyric poems, it is in his epics *Parzival*, *Willehalm* (unfinished) and the fragment of the so-called *Titurel* that his characteristic greatness resides. *Parzival*, based principally on ⇨ Chrétien de Troyes' *Perceval*, is a ⇨ *Bildungsroman* of spiritual education and development, treating the two originally separate motifs of Parzival, 'the guileless fool', and the quest for the Holy Grail, in the framework of Arthurian legend. Wolfram preaches the gospel of otherworldly values and leads the mind from the empirical and the temporal to the ideal and the divine. Parzival's career, which culminates in the temple of the Grail, symbolizes chivalric life at its highest, in which the demands of God and of the world are brought together in a single ethico-religious principle. Wagner's music-drama *Parsifal* (1882) is based on this work.

The *Titurel* elaborates the story of Parzival and Sigune in the third book of *Parzival*, while *Willehalm* is a religious epic, based on a French ⇨ *chanson de geste*, which tells the story of the famous crusader William of Toulouse. [RT]

*Parzival und Titurel*, ed. K. Bartsch (1927–32); the latest edition of K. Lachmann's original edition of W.'s works is by E. Hartl (1930); *Parzival*, tr. E. H. Zeydel (1951).

G. Weber, *Der Gottesbegriff des Parzival* (Frankfurt, 1935); M. F. Richey, *Studies of W. v. E.* (1957).

**Wolker, Jiří** (Prostějov 1900–Prostějov 1924). Czech poet. He came to Prague to study law and took a leading part among the young poets who fostered 'proletarian art' after the First World War. He died young of tuberculosis. The main theme of his first book of poems, *Host do domu* (1921), is that of humble love between human beings, which could overcome all misery and injustice; love of 'the good Jesus Christ' mingles with admiration for 'great Russia and brave Lenin'. This semi-religious note disappears in *Těžká hodina* (1922) in which the poet takes leave of his boyhood to create a new world in accordance with his revolutionary beliefs. Wolker tried to find a new style, half realistic and half dream-like, devoid of rhetoric. Among his best poems are social ballads, skilfully adapting native folk-tradition to the proletarian ideology. [KB]

*Spisy* (4 vols., 1953–4).

V. Nezval, *W.* (Prague, 1925); Zd. Kalista, *Kamarád W.* (Prague, 1933).

**Wolkers, Jan Hendrik** (Oegstgeest 1925– ). Dutch author and sculptor. Within eighteen months he published *Serpentina's petticoat* (1961), short stories, *Kort Amerikaans*, a novel, and further short stories in *Gesponnen suiker*. He has remained a controversial bestseller ever since, but his later work, *Een roos van vlees* (1963; tr. J. Scott, *A Rose of Flesh*, 1967), *De hond met de blauwe tong* (1964), and *Terug naar Oegstgeest* (1965), shows a brilliant talent working over the same theme, ridiculing the conventions of the previous generation and positing only a ruthless amorality in its place. [PK]

*Delta* (Spring 1964).
*Misverstand omtrent J.W.* (*Fase* 5/6, 1964–5).

**Wołoszynowski, Julian** (Serby1898– ). Polish novelist. He first wrote verse, then skilfully adapted his poetic style to biographical and historical novels. His portrait of the romantic poet, *Słowacki* (1928), unlike the typical *vie romancée*, asserted poetry as a life force shaping events. His most original work is *Rok 1863* (1931) where the year itself, memorable in Polish history for the tragic January insurrection, is treated as a biographical subject. Real documents and note-books are integrated with the fictional story. Even the illustrations and decorative vignettes in this beautifully presented book date from 1863. After the war Wołoszynowski produced a volume of tales about Podole, the land of his childhood (*Opowiadania podolskie*, 1959). A true original, he is still deplorably underrated in official criticism. [JP]

**Wyspiański, Stanisław** (Cracow 1869–Cracow 1907). Polish dramatist and painter. He was born and spent most of his life in Cracow which nourished his imagination with its relics of the past. His poetic theatre in many ways continues the Polish romantic tradition, but formally is close to symbolism. Already in his first acted play, *Warszawianka* (1898), the dramatic effects depend on a virtually static situation which is charged with the collective mood of the participants. They in turn seem to be trapped by the atmosphere of the setting itself. With a painter's accuracy, Wyspiański always specified his décor to the last detail, and treated stage directions as comments on the text. This integration of diverse elements demanded a similar process in language, but he was too easily infatuated with words. Sonorous verbiage came also from his attempts to wed Greek mythology with recent Polish history, as in *Noc listopadowa* (1904).

A real wedding, however, gave him the material for his best play, perhaps the most original work in the Polish theatre. His friend, a poet, had married a peasant girl, and the couple, together with their guests from the village and from Cracow, were re-created in *Wesele*, which caused a sensation when performed in 1901. The representatives of both classes here speak the traditional verse of the puppet Nativity-play, and their small talk, flirtation or sophisticated games with words lead to the visitation of symbolic guests in the second act, who disturb their communal fears and hopes. The historic apparitions prove to have less power than the enigmatic Straw-man, a creature of folklore, who in the end makes the real guests behave like puppets in a dance of despair and stupor. The authentic atmosphere of *Wesele* is all-embracing: the content and form of the play were conceived together; local gossip, doggerel, history and peasant music became one.

Among his other plays only *Sędziowie* (1907) is outstanding. His few lyrical poems, especially those affected by his illness (he died of syphilis), have a tragic poignancy. [JP]

*Dziela zebrane*, ed. L. Płoszewski (1958); Peterkiewicz and Singer, *FCPP*; Pietrkiewicz, *PPV*.
C. Backvis, *Le dramaturge S.W.* (Paris, 1952); *SEER*, XXX (1933).

# X Y

**Xabier de Lizardi.** ◊ Basque Literature.

**Yavorov, Peyo,** pseud. of P. Kracholov (Chirpan 1878–Sofia 1914). Bulgarian poet and dramatist. During his service as telegrapher at various stations from 1893 to 1903, he read ardently socialism and poetry. His first poems 'Napred' ('Forward!'), 'Na edin pesimist' ('To a Pessimist') and 'Na nivata' ('In the Fields') won notice for their spirit of *narodnik* social protest. 'Kaliopa' caught the attention of Dr K. Krăstev and Pencho ◊ Slaveykov, who printed it in their *Misăl* (1903) and adopted him as 'Yavorov' into the *Misăl* literary circle. His *Stihotvoreniya* (1901) revealed a new range and power in Bulgarian poetry. Dominant in them, but for momentary vignettes like 'Prolet' ('Spring') and 'Ludimladi' ('Madcaps'), were the rhythms of pathos and tragedy: the devastation of the peasant's season-cycle at its zenith in 'Gradushka' ('Hailstorm'), the storm of swelling grief in 'Armentsi' ('Armenians') and 'Zatochenitsi' ('Exiles') and the elemental despair of 'Esenni motivi' ('Autumn Motifs').

His part in the Macedonian movement, for which he edited *Delo* ('The Cause', 1901–2) and *Svoboda ili smărt* ('Freedom or Death', 1902–3), was in the true ◊ Botev tradition. These experiences inspired his 'Hayduk Songs' and are recounted in *Haydushki kopneniya* ('A Hayduk's Yearnings', 1905–7) and the biography (1904) of his friend G. Delchev. Withdrawing in 1903 from this conflict, which he now found as uncongenial as socialism to his poetry, he became head librarian at the National Library and then (1908–13) artistic secretary to the National Theatre, where his at times ominously autobiographical tragedies, *V polite na Vitosha* (1911) and *Kogato grăm udari* (1912), were produced.

The psychological struggle, 'crucial to his poetic development' (Pencho Slaveykov) and already evident in 'Nosht' ('Night'), was resumed in *Bezsănitsi i prozreniya* ('Insomnia and Intuitions', 1907). To the symbolism here he was predisposed by his nature and earlier writing as well as influences during his visit to France of 1906–7. His last verses, *Podir senkite na oblatsite* ('In the Shadows of the Clouds') appeared in 1911.

A succession of emotional calamities finally fulfilled this poet's tragic destiny, culminating in an attempted and then, a year later, fatal suicide. [VP]

*Săbrani săchineniya* (5 vols., 1959–60); Pinto, *BPV*.

M. Arnaudov, *P.Y.*, *Lichnost, tvorchestvo, sădba* (Sofia, 1961); D. B. Mitov, *P.Y.*, *istoriko-literaturno izsledvane* (Sofia, 1957); G. Naydenova-Stoilova, *P.Y.*, *Letopis*, Acad. Sc. (Sofia, 1959) and *P.Y.*, *Pătyăt kăm dramata* (Sofia, 1962); Manning and Smal-Stocki, *HMBL*.

**Yawitz, Zeev Wolf** (Kolna, Poland 1847–London 1924). Hebrew writer. Although better known for his scholarly writing, which included a 9-volume history of the Jews (*Toldoth Israel*, 1894–1924) and Talmudic legends in the modern Hebrew idiom (*Mimei Kedem*, Warsaw, 1887), he was one of the first literary exponents of a Jewish renaissance in Palestine. The Zionist Movement meant for him not only a solution of the Jewish problem, but a form of religious expression. He lived in Palestine in 1888–9, where a new pioneering type of Jew was emerging, and it was their life which he most vividly described in his sketches, *Idylls* (Warsaw, 1893). [EE]

Klausner, *HMHL*; Waxman, *HJL*.

**Yepifaniy 'Premudry' 'The Wise'** (fl. *c.* 1400). Russian hagiographer. He was the outstanding representative in Russian literature of a late-medieval blossoming of Orthodox culture known as the 'Eastern Pre-Renaissance'. Almost nothing is known of his life, save that he was a monk of St Sergius's great Trinity monastery, and the biographer of St Sergius himself and of St Stephen, the apostle to the Permians. He was probably a native of Rostov (not Moscow); he knew St Sergius and St Stephen personally – probably also the notable icon-painters Andrei Rublyov and Feofan Grek. His two Lives break new ground in Russian literature: they are lengthy (some 100 pages), of complex construction, and partly composed in a novel style – rhetorical, rhythmical, semi-poetic – the so-called '*pletenye sloves*' ('braiding of words'). This is abstract, verbose, emotional, sometimes picturesque; its origins are usually traced to South Slav literary émigrés and a would-be return to Old Slavonic models, but it owes as much to the native Russian rhetorical tradition (⇨ Ilarion, Kirill) and Yepifaniy's unique talents. His work was long considered obscure and unreadable; its aesthetic importance is nowadays generally recognized. After his death his achievements were vulgarized by lesser writers, starting with the prolific Pakhomiy Serb (fl. *c.* 1450), whose hand can probably be seen in all extant versions of the Life of St Sergius. Certain other writings – notably a fine rhetorical panegyric on the life and death of the Grand Prince Dmitriy Donskoy – have been doubtfully attributed to him. [RM-G]

Chizhevsky, *HRL*; Zenkovsky, *Medieval Russia's Epics, Chronicles and Tales* (1964).

**Yesenin, Sergey** (Konstantinovo, nr Ryazan' 1895–Leningrad 1925). Russian poet. Brought up in the depths of the country by his peasant grandfather of an 'Old Believer' sect. He wrote verses from childhood on, and irrupted precociously into the pre-Revolutionary literary salons of Moscow and Petersburg; dressed in a peasant smock, chanting his subtly artless bucolic-religious verses, he was welcomed as an unlettered genius. Called up in 1916, he greeted the October Revolution enthusiastically, giving it a Utopian interpretation in several unmemorable poems, while his strong religious streak turned temporarily to blasphemy. He joined the Imaginist poets, being himself the protégé of the older peasant-poet ⇨ Klyuyev.

His earlier verse was mellifluous and beautiful but slight, with some monotony of style and subject. In the twenties his manner is harsher, more immediate, technically more varied, reflecting the worsening crises of his life. The lionized youth (described with acid wit by the unsentimental ⇨ Mayakovsky in *How to Make Poetry?*), posing half-consciously as the spontaneous voice of Holy Russia, became a tortured *déraciné* sophisticate. Previously he had lamented the passing of an idealized countryside, invaded by the modern age, with gentle melancholy; now he was torn by nostalgia for the home and youth he had irretrievably lost, and by the fatal attractions of the city with its taverns and prostitutes. The romantic appeal of Revolution – which inspired some excellent poetry in the verse-play *Pugachov* (1921) – clashed with regrets for the loss of the Russia he had grown up in and also with the harsh realities of Soviet life; his quandary is poignantly shown in two famous poems of 1924: *Rus' Sovetskaya* and *Rus' ukhodyashchaya*. He sought escape through frenzied travel, and a life so debauched it has become a legend. In 1919–21 he travelled all over the Soviet Union. In 1922 he married the American dancer Isidora Duncan; without a common language, they journeyed through Europe and America in a haze of riotous living. Disillusioned, he returned to the U.S.S.R. next year; in 1924 he was travelling again, to Persia, a relatively serene interlude. By now a hopeless alcoholic, continually in trouble for acts of 'hooliganism', shackled to undesirable friends, he sought refuge in another marriage; late in 1925 he hanged himself in a Leningrad hotel, after writing a farewell poem in his own blood. His suicide inspired Mayakovsky's *To Sergei Yesenin* and Klyuyev's *Lament for Yesenin*. His later poetry is poignant in its naked self-revelation: e.g. *My teper' ukhodim ponemnogu . . .* ('Little by little we are going away...', 1924); *Pis'mo k materi* ('Letter to my mother', 1924); *Chorny chelovek* (1925). Though disapproved of by Stalinist critics, he ranks in popularity with Pushkin and Mayakovsky among ordinary Russian readers. [RM-G]

*Sochineniya* (2 vols., 1956); Gulland, *SRV*; Lugovskoy, *ARSP*; Markov, *MRP*, *PG*; Obolensky, *PBRV*.
Slonim, *MRL*.

**Yevtushenko, Yevgeny** (Zima, nr Irkutsk 1933– ). Russian poet, from a mixed peasant-intellectual background. First poems: *Razvedchiki gryadushchego* ('Prospectors of the Future', 1952); his early masterpiece is the long *Stantsiya Zima* (1956; tr. P. Levi and R. M.-Gulland, *Zima Junction*, in *Selected Poems*, 1962), written in 1953, which presents the public and private problems tormenting him in the summer of 1953 (after Stalin's death), with fine lyrical and conversational passages. He reopened long forbidden themes. This, coupled with personal flamboyance, has led to frequent critical attacks in the U.S.S.R. (especially in 1957 and early in 1963); simultaneously he has achieved enormous popularity among Soviet youth. He writes copiously and unevenly; important volumes are *Stikhi raznikh let* (1959) and *Vzmakh ruki* (1962). Since 1960 he has travelled widely – to England, the U.S.A., etc. – and won international fame. The publication, originally in France, of *A Precocious Autobiography* (1963) caused much criticism in the U.S.S.R.; the book presents a vivid sequence of scenes from his life and an individualistic interpretation of Soviet history.

His apparently slapdash, but deliberately wrought poetry has moments of brilliance. He continually shifts from the most intimate to the most public themes, expressing personal involvement in humanity's problems, and striving to overcome the fragmentation of modern society. His Communist idealism does not preclude sombre moments. His style has less experimental sparkle than that of his colleague ⇨ Voznesensky; it owes much to the poets of the 1920s and 30s – notably to Mayakovsky, Kirsanov and Pasternak. [RM-G]

*Selected Poetry* (in Russian), intr. R. M.-Gulland (1963); *Selected Poems*, tr. P. Levi and R. M.-Gulland (PMEP, 1962); Gulland, *SRV*; Obolensky, *PBRV*; G. Reavey, *The Poetry of Y.Y.* (1966).

*Soviet Leaders*, ed. G. W. Simmonds (N.Y., 1967).

**Yovkov, Yordan** (Zheravna 1880–Plovdiv 1937). Bulgarian novelist and story-writer. Failing to complete his Sofia University law course, he returned to teach in the Dobruja of his upbringing (his village is now named Yovkovo) and to represent in literature the Bulgarian attachment to this fertile, heterogeneous, dominantly Bulgarian region adjoining Rumania, where he served on the Bulgarian Legation (1920–7). He subsequently worked for the Bulgarian Foreign Ministry.

His experiences as officer and war correspondent in the Balkan Wars and First World War inspired his first collection of stories, *Razkazi* (2 vols., 1917 and 1918). The nature of patriotism, bravery and sacrifice is his theme, but he conveys too the reality of war and the Bulgarian soldier's reaction to it in such portraits as Petranov, the *daskal* (village teacher) actor-enthusiast and self-styled Macbeth of *Treta smyana* ('Third Watch'), and Stoil, the peasant uprooted to the trenches in his finest story *Zemlyatsi* ('Countrymen').

The search for a Bulgarian *mystique* in the national awakening under the Turkish yoke inspired his *Staroplaninski legendi* (1927), set in the Balkan mountains of his birth. The same religious intensity of emotion marks the *dénouement* of *Zhetvaryăt* (1920), his novel of a feud in the Dobruja village of Lyulakovo. His other novel, *Chiflikăt kray granitsata* (1934), likewise set in the Dobruja, depicts the decay of a *chiflik* (great estate of Turkish times). Its heroine, Nona, and her mother belong to his fine gallery of female portraits, which include the title characters of his plays *Albena* (1930) and *Boryana* (1932), Sarandovitsa in *Vecheri v Antimovskiya han* ('Evenings at Antimovo Inn', 1928) and others in *Pesen na kolelata* ('The Wheels' Song', 1933), *Zhensko sărtse* ('A Woman's Heart', 1935) and *Ako mozheha da govoryat* ('If they could talk', 1936), 'they' in this last being the village animals, 'our brothers – like us they work and die'. These cycles of stories complete his picture of Bulgarian village life, portrayed with human sympathy and objective, epic sweep. His consistently fine prose remains an accepted model of modern Bulgarian style.

He wrote two satirical works: *Milionerăt* ('The Millionaire', 1930), a comedy reminiscent of Gogol's *Revizor*, and *Priklyucheniyata na Gorolomov* ('Gorolomov's Adventures', 1938), his unfinished sketches of a *narodnik* (populist) teacher. [VP]

*Săchineniya* (7 vols., 1956); *Sbornik Y.Y.* (1937); Pinto, *BPV*.

S. Kazandzhiev, *Y.Y.: 1880–1937* (Sofia, 1937); D. Minev, *Y.Y.: dokumenti* (Sofia, 1947); Yovkov memorial issues of *Zlatorog*, *Bălgarska misăl* and *Literaturen glas* for 1937; Manning and Smal-Stocki, *HMBL*.

# Z

**Zabłocki, Franciszek** (1754–Końskowola 1821). Polish dramatist. He wrote over 40 plays, adapted or modelled on the French theatre, and coloured them with local observations and allusions. The most characteristic was the comedy in verse, *Sarmatyzm* (1785) (the title could be rendered as 'Polishness'), which popularized the plot involving litigation, a feud between two noble families, a foray and reconciliation through marriage. This same plot is used in two major Polish classics, ⇨ Fredro's comedy 'The Revenge' and Mickiewicz's *Pan Tadeusz*. In his political verse he was master of invective. His rich idiomatic language served the lexicographer Linde with many examples. [JP]

Peterkiewicz and Singer, *FCPP*.

**Zabolotsky, Nikolay** (Kazan 1903–Moscow 1958). Russian poet. Son of an agronomist in backwoods of Vyatka; higher education in Leningrad. There he worked in children's publishing under ⇨ Marshak, with a remarkable group of young writers (incl. ⇨ Shvarts, D. Kharms (1905–42). Their circle 'OBERIU' provided his first literary milieu.

His first book, *Stolbtsy* (1929), was sensational. Satirizing the more vulgar and trivial sides of everyday Leningrad life in amusing and often shocking fashion, its poems brilliantly blend coarse realism and poetic fantasy, their style shifting from unexpected metaphor and simile characteristic of ⇨ Khlebnikov and other Futurists to rhythms, vocabulary and verbal conceits that half-parody the 18th century and Pushkin. The long poem *Torzhestvo zemledeliya* (1929–30, publ. 1933) is set in the countryside, but shows the same play of styles and pervasive fantasy. Succeeding volumes (1937, 1948, 1957) seem to show a new Zabolotsky – a smooth and measured poet, imbued with a kindly, sometimes melancholy humanism. This enigmatic change may have resulted from external pressures – he was strongly criticized for his earlier work, and after 1937 he spent a period in exile – but may also have corresponded with an inevitable development in his poetic mood. Certainly the later Zabolotsky is on examination seen to be linked to the earlier in some important respects: in his originality of imagery, echoes of classicism, and an intense anthropomorphizing interest in the natural world, plants and animals (cf. his magnificent epic fragments, *Lodeynikov*, 1932–47). His work is coloured throughout his life by a quasi-religious philosophical belief in the metamorphosis of all natural beings through death. He is coming to be recognized as one of the great names of Russian poetry – the greatest to have grown up in the Soviet Union.

*Stikhotvoreniya i poemy* (1965); *Stikhotvoreniya* (Washington, D.C., 1965); Gulland, *SRV*; Markov, *MRP*; Obolensky, *PBRV*; *Soviet Studies*, April 1971; A. Turkov, *N.Z.* (Moscow 1966).

**'Zadonshchina.'** Name generally applied to a medieval Russian tale of *c.*1385, extant in several versions, and written down by the monk Sofoniy of Ryazan'. It celebrates the defeat of Russia's Tatar overlords under Mamay by the armies of Dmitriy Donskoy, Grand Prince of Moscow, in 1380. It is chiefly remarkable for the use made by its author of passages quoted or imitated from the earlier tale (of a Russian defeat), ⇨ *Slovo o Polku Igoreve*. This deliberate literary device emphasizes the work's political implications: Dmitriy's victory on the Don avenges Igor's defeat on the Kayala. The tone is overtly Christian (unlike the *Slovo*). Its style – emotional and rhetorical – has been branded as clumsy, and the handling of material borrowed from the *Slovo* as unintelligent. Recent critics, however, have given the *Zadonshchina* high esteem in medieval Russian literature. [RM-G]

*Sofonija's Tale of the Russian-Tatar Battle on the Kulikovo Field*, ed. R. Jakobson and D. Worth (The Hague, 1963).
Chizhevsky, *HRL*; Zenkovsky, *Medieval Russia's Epics, Chronicles and Tales* (1964).

**Zakuto, Moses** (Amsterdam 1625–Mantua 1697). Hebrew dramatist, poet and mystic. In his youth a fellow-student of Spinoza, he was rabbi first in Venice, later in Mantua. The first Hebrew dramatist, whose plays, chiefly on Biblical themes, are modelled on contemporary Italian drama. His *Yesod Olam* (ed. A. Berliner, with biography, 1874), based on the Biblical legend of Abraham destroying his father's idols, was written in Amsterdam (1642). [EE]

*Toftèh Aruch* (Venice, 1715; ed. D. A. Friedman, with intr., 1923).
Waxman, *HJL*.

**Zamfirescu, Duiliu** (Plăineşti 1858–Agapia 1922). Rumanian poet and novelist. Though hailed in 1880 by ⇨ Macedonski in *Literatorul* as a future great poet, he did not achieve that rank. His poetry has a classic elegance; when this is combined with deep feeling, as in the opening stanzas of the lyric *Către Domnul*, the product is very fine. But it is as a novelist that Zamfirescu is better known. His series of 5 novels centring round the Comănesteanu family began in 1894 with *Viaţa la ţară* (tr. L. Byng, *Sasha*, 1926) and ended with *Anna* (1916). In spite of weaknesses of construction this cycle gave the Rumanian novel a prestige which it had hitherto lacked. [EDT]

**Zamyatin, Yevgeniy Ivanovich** (Lebedyan', Tambov 1884–Paris 1937). Russian novelist, dramatist and critic. He was a student and later a lecturer in naval engineering. In his youth he was for a time a member of the Bolshevik Party and was twice arrested and exiled. Although his first story was published in 1902, he became known only in 1913 with his stories of provincial stagnation *Uyezdnoye* and *Na kulichkakh* (1914), which was suppressed because of his criticisms of the army. In 1916 he came to England, an experience which is reflected in *Ostrovityane* (1918) and *Lovets chelovekov* (1921), biting satires on the hypocrisy and monotony of English life.

After the Revolution his independent and critical attitude to the new regime prevented him from receiving any important official post in the literary world. But he played a major part in the development of Soviet literature by forming the ⇨ Serapion Brothers in 1921. During these years he produced his finest work, including the novel *My* (1920, unpublished in Russia, first Russian edition, N.Y., 1952; *We*, tr. in B. Guerney, *Anthology of Russian Literature in the Soviet Period*, 1960), a prophecy of the future totalitarian state which influenced George Orwell's *1984*. In *Rasskaz o samom glavnom* (1924), perhaps his masterpiece, he rejects the idea that there is or can be any one solution to human problems. In 1929 he was disgraced because *My* had been published outside Russia, admittedly in a garbled version, four years earlier and without the author's permission; all creative work was now made impossible for him. After two years of victimization he wrote to Stalin and was allowed to leave the country. He settled in Paris, where he wrote a few short stories and began an unfinished novel, *Bich Bozhiy* (1938), in which he examines the tragic consequences of a new clash between a decaying West and a revitalized East. He died in poverty.

As a critic he was a believer in constant development and revolution. He pointed out that all established creeds had been regarded at first as heresies, before being overthrown in their turn by new 'heresies'. His views are summed up in his article *O literature, revolyutsii, entropii* (1924). The same views can be found in his fiction, in his disillusionment with the Revolution because it had ceased to be revolutionary, and in his plays *Ogni Svyatogo Dominika* (1920) and *Atilla* (1928), which were never performed.

Zamyatin, like his master ⇨ Bely, was concerned with the unity of form and content. In the story *Peshchera* (1932; *The Cave*, tr. in Yarmolinsky, *SSS*) the whole work evolves from a single image. *Lovets chelovekov* and *My* reflect the dehumanization of man in linguistic terms. At the same time he liked to introduce ideas from contemporary arts and sciences into his writing. Cubism and Einsteinian mathematics play an important part in the structure of *Rasskaz o samom glavnom* and *My*. [RDBT]

*Sobraniye sochineniy* (4 vols., 1929); *Rasskazy* (1963); *Litsa* (1955); *A Soviet Heretic: Essays* (tr. M. Ginzburg 1970).
D. J. Richards, *Z.* (1962).

**Zapolska, Gabriela,** pseud. of Gabriela Korwin-Piotrowska (Podhajce 1857–Lvov 1921). Polish dramatist. Daughter of a wealthy nobleman and a prima ballerina. She took to the stage, first in Poland, then tried her luck in Paris (Antoine's Théâtre Libre), but without much success. Her stay in Paris (1889–95), however, helped her own writing for the theatre.

During an illness in 1906 she wrote in a few days a sharp dramatic invective against provincial middle-class hypocrisy, *Moral-*

*ność pani Dulskiej*, which is now a classic in the Polish repertoire. The abominable heroine, her two teenage daughters and the ever-silent husband who utters one memorable sentence at the end of Act II are most original character studies. The dialogue keeps a brisk conversational tempo.

Among her other plays *Ich czworo* (1912), subtitled 'a tragedy of the stupid', fascinates with both its intentional and its occasionally unintentional vulgarity, but the prologue here illustrates the embarrassing lack of judgement which is apparent in her novels. Some of them were meant to shock, with titles like 'What one doesn't talk about', or 'What one doesn't even want to think about'. Their hysterical tone spoils the intended social protest. [JP]

**Zech, Paul** (Briesen, W. Prussia 1881–Buenos Aires 1946). German poet, novelist and dramatist. Leaving university to work as a miner, factory hand, etc., he was active as trade unionist, later as editor of Expressionist periodical *Das neue Pathos* (1913–14); briefly imprisoned in 1933, he emigrated to South America. His prolific writing reflects his surroundings (from the Ruhr to the Argentine) and social idealism. His robust yet sensitive machine-age poetry is seen at its best in early collections: e.g. *Das schwarze Revier* (1909 ff.), *Die eiserne Brücke* (1914). *Das trunkene Schiff* (1924) is an experimental 'scenic ballad', a combination of music, drama and film. [PB]

Bridgwater, *TCGV*.
F. Hülser, ed., *P.Z.* (Dortmund, 1961) (with bibliography).

**Żeromski, Stefan** (Strawczyn, nr Kielce 1864–Warsaw 1925). Polish novelist. He did not finish his secondary education, was for a time a private tutor, then a librarian, but finally established himself as a successful and very influential man of letters. In 1895 he published one volume of short stories in Warsaw (*Opowiadania*) and another in Cracow, under the pen-name of Zych. Both were concerned with social conditions, but in the collection which appeared in Austrian Poland he could attack Russian rule directly. This illustrates the evasive methods of literature under foreign censorship, but in Żeromski's case such a duality of purpose seems to run through all his writing.

He was a passionate hater of social evil and a nationalist in love with tradition; he wrote a pamphlet against snobbery but had a weakness for aristocratic heroes; he tackled epic themes in a diffuse lyrical language. This lyricism served him well in the early tales and in a short novel, *Wierna rzeka* (1912; tr. S. Garry, *The Faithful River*, 1943). In longer works, however, the structure suffered and the disparity between the ideal and the psychological motivation became apparent. This is true of his social novel, *Ludzie bezdomni* (1900), with its altruistic hero, a doctor; and of the Napoleonic rhapsody, *Popioły* (1904; tr. H. Stankiewicz-Zand, *Ashes*, 1928), where the brutal realities of war are at variance with the lyrical tone and philosophic digressions.

He caused a scandal with *Dzieje grzechu* (1908), and his Manichean fascination with evil recurs in later novels bearing titles like 'The Struggle with Satan'. His final message came in *Przedwiośnie* (1925), broken again by contradictory emotions. The novel begins with a horrific description of the bolshevik revolution and ends with a symbolic march of Warsaw workers, now living in a free state. His intimate diaries (recently published) throw some light on the genesis of his inner conflicts. [JP]

Dzieła, ed. S. Pigoń (1955–7).
Scherer-Virski, *MPSS*; *SEER*, XIV, 41 (1936); XXXVI, 87 (1958).

**Zesen, Philipp von** (Priorau, Dessau 1619–Hamburg 1689). German poet and novelist. Despite many years in Holland, he believed in the patriotic cultivation of German language and literature. He wrote a manual of poetics, the *Hochdeutscher Helikon* (1641), and founded his own language society, the Deutschgesinnte Genossenschaft, in Hamburg (1642). There were mystical overtones in his search for the 'Ursprache'; Zesen believed it was essentially onomatopoeic and that of all vernacular languages, German came closest to it. To re-create the primeval language in its purity he suggested Germanization of foreign loan words, e.g. 'Fenster' should be replaced by 'Tageleuchter' and, with involuntary humour, 'Nase' by 'Gesichtserker'. In the cause of 'purity' he also evolved his own private orthography and introduced onomatopoeic and verbal-musical effects into his verse – often to the exclusion of clear syntactical meaning.

His epistolary novel, *Die Adriatische Rosenmund* (1645; ed. M. H. Jellinek, Neudrucke 160–3, 1899), is remarkable for its interest in psychology, its combination of sentimental and pastoral elements and for its adult treatment of a contemporary theme – the separation of two lovers by their differing religions. *Assenat* (1670), a treatment of the Joseph story, and *Samson* (1679) typify their age in their combination of fiction, encyclopedic knowledge and Biblical didacticism. He also translated Scudéry's *Ibrahim* (1645) and de Garzan's *Sophonisbe* (1647). [WAC]

H. Körnchen, *Z.s Romane* (Berlin, 1912).

**Zeyer, Julius** (Prague 1841–Prague 1901). Czech poet, novelist and dramatist. Born of a wealthy family with a father of French-German ancestry and a Jewish mother, he was educated in German. But, captivated by the strange spirit of Prague and Czech history, he became a Czech writer by choice. Finding the political and cultural climate in Bohemia oppressive, he spent much of his life travelling abroad. Amongst his epic poetry the cycles *Vyšehrad* (1880) and *Karolinská epopeja* (1896) re-create old Czech and French legends respectively; his autobiographical novel in verse, *Troje paměti Víta Choráze* (1905), is evidence of his search for a new Catholic, gothic ideal. His best novels are *Jan Maria Plojhar* (1891), an analysis of the Czech character and fate, and *Dům u tonoucí hvězdy* (1895), whose atmosphere is reminiscent of his friend ⇨ Huysmans. His works are neo-romantic, mystical visions, narrated in surprisingly fresh and rhythmical language, such as only a writer unburdened by the Czech peasant tradition and trained in a foreign cultural environment could achieve. [KB]

*Sebrané spisy* (34 vols., 1901–7); *Inultus*, tr. Paul Selver in *Review-43*, 2 (1943).

M. Marten, *J.Z.* (Prague, 1910); J. Š. Kvapil, *Gotický Zeyer* (Prague, 1942).

**Zhukovsky, Vasily Andreyevich** (Mishenskoye, Tula 1783–Baden 1852). Russian poet. Natural son of Squire Bunin and a Turkish serf girl. Brought up on the estate, he studied in the Moscow Noblemen's Pension. In 1802, he published his translation of Gray's *Elegy*. From 1808 to 1810 he edited the journal, *The Messenger of Europe*. In 1812, when forbidden to marry his niece, he volunteered for and subsequently joined the Militia, witnessed Napoleonic battle, wrote *The Bard in the Camp of Russian Warriors* (Masha married another, and died in 1823). In 1815–16 he published the first edition of his poetry. From 1815 to 1839 he was at the Court, teaching Russian to the German wife of Nicholas and becoming tutor to the future Alexander II. Although Conservative and devout, he interceded for many writers and liberals. He retired in 1840, settled in Germany and married.

With him begins modern Russian poetry. His original work, small in extent, is perfect in its harmony of language, syntax and rhythm; he evokes the memory of his dead love and meditates on the nature of poetry – 'God in holy dreams of earth'. His elegiac nature poetry conveys 'the landscape of the soul' (Veselovsky). But he also wrote Russian fairy-tales in gently humorous verse.

Leader of pre-romanticism, he introduced the ballad-form (*Lyudmila*, 1808, from Bürger's *Lenora*; a cheerful *Svetlana* in national setting, 1812). As a translator and adapter, he familiarized Russian readers with contemporary Western poetry: ⇨ Schiller, ⇨ Hebel, ⇨ Wieland, ⇨ Uhland, La Motte ⇨ Fouqué, Goethe; Byron, Thomson, Dryden, Moore, Southey, etc. He enlarged the metric and rhythmical system of Russian prosody, achieved melodic simplicity of verse and enriched its psychological vocabulary. He translated, via German, the Persian *Rustam and Sohrab*, the Indian *Nal and Damayanti*, and in 1843–9, the *Odyssey* in hexameters, from a word by word translation and linguistic notes. His last work was *Ahasuerus, the Eternal Jew*. Many of his translations became classics of Russian literature. [NG]

*Sobraniye Sochineniy* (4 vols., 1959–60); *Stikhotvoreniya*, ed. V. Petushkov (1952).

A. N. Veselovsky, *V.A.Z. Poeziya chuvstva i serdechnogo voobrazheniya* (Leningrad, 1918); Ehrard, *V.A. Joukovski et le préromantisme russe*, ed. Bibliothèque de l'Institut Français de Léningrad, vol. XVII (Paris, 1938).

**Ziegler und Kliphausen, Heinrich Anselm von** (Radmeritz 1663–Leipzig 1696). German novelist. Although he imitated Hofmannswaldau's *Heldenbriefe* in his *Helden-Liebe der Schrifft des Alten Testaments* (1691), his fame rests entirely on his long novel *Die asiatische Banise oder das blutige doch muthige Pegu* (1689; ed. F. Bobertag, DNL 37, 1883). Based on actual events in the oriental kingdom of Pegu and ably exploiting the exoticism of the oriental setting (with verbatim quotation from a variety of sources, both historical and geographical), the book is a fantastic blend of travelogue, political treatise and gallant novel which, together with its sadistic elements, appealed to the taste of the age and enjoyed wide popularity. Although it is usually cited as being typically baroque, the novel also in some measure anticipates the sentimentality and the moral outlook of the 18th century. [WAC]

W. Pfeiffer-Belli, *Die asiatische Banise. Studien zur Geschichte des höfisch-historischen Romans* (Berlin, 1940).

**Zilahy, Lajos** (Nagyszalonta 1891– ). Hungarian novelist and playwright. Son of a civil servant, he studied law; as journalist, became editor of the daily *Magyarország* and of a literary periodical, *Híd* ('Bridge'). As a sarcastic critic of social injustice, of living Hungarian authors his works are the best known in the West; some of his plays have run on Broadway and been filmed. He has lived in New York since 1947. Major novels: *A Két Fogoly* (1931; tr. G. Collins and I. Zeitlin, *Two Prisoners*, 1931); *A Dühödt Angyal* (no Hungarian edition; tr. T. L. Harsner, *The Angry Angel*, 1953); *A Fegyverek Visszanéznek* (1936; tr. L. Wolfe, *The Guns look Back*, 1938); *Ararát* (n. d.; tr. J. Panker, *The Dukays*, 1949); *A Szökevény* (1930; tr. G. Halász, *The Deserter*, 1932). [JFR]

**Zimorowic, Bartłomiej** (Lvov 1597–*c.* 1680). Polish poet. Of burgher origin, he reached a prominent position in the city of Lvov. His Latin works are now completely over-shadowed by his *Sielanki nowe ruskie* (1663), a volume characteristic of both the Polish baroque and the pastoral *genre* which he endowed here with fresh regional features. Metaphysical queries, reprimands against bad versifiers, images of Judgement Day are fitted into a clearly localized landscape, or uttered by characters who otherwise behave like genuine rustics. The most moving baroque paradoxes, for instance, are to to be found in the idyll about the vine-dressers ('Winiarze'). The final two poems turn out to be war *reportage* bristling with topicality. The duality of mood permeating his idylls has a simultaneous effect, demanding lyrical tenderness and disgust, naïve enchantment and horror. This all-embracing style, however, extended the length of each poem. As he published his poetry under the name of his younger brother Szymon (who died at 21), the authorship of the volume *Roxolanki* (1654) is still disputed. [JP]

Peterkiewicz and Singer, *FCPP.*
*SEER*, XXXIV, 82 (1955).

**Zlatarić, Dinko.** ⇨ Dalmatian and Dubrovnik Literature.

**Zmaj, Jovan Jovanović** (Novi Sad 1833–Kamenica 1904). Serbian poet and doctor. He was very popular during his own lifetime. Much of his poetry is little more than versification and a great deal is occasional. His best poems are the lyrical *Djulići* (1864) and *Djulići uveoci* (1883), and his poems for children. He edited several humorous periodicals, from one of which he took the name *Zmaj* – dragon. He translated Lermontov, Goethe, Tennyson and Petöfi, and introduced greater variety of form into Serbian poetry, going beyond the style of the folk-songs which predominated at that time. [EDG]

Ibrovac, *APY*; Popovič, *JS.*
Barac, *HYL*; *SEER*, XIII, 37 (1934).

**Zmichowska, Narcyza** (Warsaw 1819–Warsaw 1876). Polish novelist. She worked as a governess, encouraged intellectual women, and was imprisoned for her patriotic activities. Her chief contribution to literature is a romantic novel *Poganka* (1846), in which fantasy mingles with acute psychological observation. The vampire-like heroine and the young man fascinated by her beauty and evil are symbolically linked by a portrait, which when destroyed destroys her as well. Cryptic and scented with eroticism, the book reminds one of the uneasy reality in *Wuthering Heights*. Her poetry is disappointing. [JP]

**Zola, Émile** (Paris 1840–Paris 1902). French novelist. He was brought up at Aix-en-Provence, the 'Plassans' of his novels. Once established in Paris, he led a very businesslike writer's life, interrupted only by his intervention in the Dreyfus affair. His novel series, *Les Rougon-Macquart* (1871–93), is the chief monument of the French Naturalist movement. The subtitle, *Histoire naturelle et sociale d'une famille sous le Second Empire*, suggests his two interconnected purposes: to embody in fiction 'scientific' notions – ultimately derived from ⇨ Taine – of the determination of human conduct by heredity and environment; and to use the realistic and symbolic possibilities of a hereditarily unbalanced family to portray critically certain aspects of a diseased society.

Zola makes absurdly pretentious claims for the novel in propagandist works like *Le roman expérimental* (1880), where he equates the novelist's 'inquiries' with those of the experimental scientist. Privately, however, he admits that his deterministic theories are only a hypothesis with which to give his work a coherent framework; and he never really believed the bogus science of Lucas's *Traité de l'hérédité naturelle*, on which the genealogical tree of his fictional family was based. Moreover, he soon realized the artistic dangers of his theories. His first important novel, *Thérèse Raquin* (1867; tr. L. W. Tancock, 1962), with its characters 'dominated by their nerves, deprived of free will' (*Preface*), inevitably turns into a medical horror story; and Zola subsequently decided to avoid an insistent hereditary fatalism. Nevertheless 'truth' remains his constant concern. This involved widening the novel's scope to include aspects of life which the bourgeois reader preferred to ignore; a refusal to abstract the psychological from the physiological in character; and realistic documentation at least as a starting-point for creation. The word *poème* also recurs in his notes; but his greatest achievements owe much to the tenacity of his scientific ambitions.

Of the early novels *La fortune des Rougon* (1871) and *La conquête de Plassans* (1874) offer views of provincial politics based on familiar anti-bourgeois and anti-clerical assumptions; and *Son Excellence Eugène Rougon* (1876), with its uniform devaluation of political motive, perhaps lends support to the charges of over-simplification made against his work. But detailed political realism was not to be his chief aim. The early novels, especially *La curée* (1872), already embody a more impressionistic vision of corruption. In *Le ventre de Paris* (1873), in which a returned exile of 1851 is betrayed by his own family, prosperous butchers in the Paris markets, Zola first reveals his distinctive power of evoking a vast oppressive ambience which dwarfs or destroys the individual. *Nana* (1880), in which the slum-girl turned *demi-mondaine* humiliates the class responsible for her former misery, is also perhaps best read as an impressionistic allegory. In *Pot-Bouille* (1882), a lurid, often comic picture of intrigues and adulteries behind the façade of a middle-class block of flats, it is again the stylized over-concentrated approach which produces the artistic effect – and which provoked renewed accusations of pornography and distortion.

Nevertheless, bourgeois susceptibilities apart, working-class society undoubtedly offered the ideal field for Zola's genius. Here there can be easier acceptance of the hypothesis of a society so conditioned that individual responsibility becomes meaningless, and 'exposure' has humanitarian as well as merely scandalous possibilities. *L'assommoir* (1877; tr. A. Symons, *Drunkard*, 1928, repr. 1958), Zola's first masterpiece, relates with pathos and humour the dissolution of a family in the Paris slums. The superb evocation is at once realistic and symbolic; Gervaise's decline is shown as inevitable, but the dangers of 'scientific' demonstration are avoided by her being given, innately, the very tendencies of the society which engulfs her. *Germinal* (1885; tr. L. W. Tancock, Penguin Classics, 1954) is an overpowering evocation of a mining community enslaved from birth to death by a remote and inexorable system. *La terre* (1887; tr. A. Lindsay, *Earth*, 1954) and *La débâcle* (1892) bring the same epic sweep to peasant and military life.

*Germinal* raises the problem of Zola's ideas. Though revolutionary action is not discredited, there may be some substance in the Marxist view that he presents his material statically and ultimately remains a defeatist observer. In a sense his progressive and scientific ideas work against one another, since he tends to see even his active characters as products rather than dynamic agents. Similarly *La joie de vivre* (1884) is partly an attack on the growing anti-scientific pessimism which so disappointed his positivist spirit; but Lazare is described so persistently in medical terms that we remain unsure whether we are reading a novel of positive ideas or another fatalistic impression of things as they are. *La bête humaine* (1890) is an unresolved confrontation of technical progress (exemplified by the railways) and the human animal's physiological fatalities; but the concluding novel of the series, *Le Docteur Pascal* (1893), offers a modified (if not very scientific) optimism. The progressive solution of Zola's doubts and obsessions, however, brought a lessening of creative power. There had been idealistic and idyllic elements in many earlier novels (e.g. *La faute de l'abbé Mouret*, 1875); but the last groups of novels, especially *Les quatre Évangiles* (1899–1903, uncompleted), with their more overt optimistic didacticism, are too obviously *romans à thèse*.

Zola's work has been criticized for complacent brutality, indifference to notions of free will, reduction of human psychology to a few all-powerful impulses; and the results of his scientific programme have seemed oddly close to the magnifying lyricism which he claimed to combat. But the critical tide has turned in his favour: the epic, visionary and mythical elements are coming to be valued for themselves and he is beginning to be acclaimed as a pioneer of the modern sociological imagination. [BLN]

*Œuvres*, ed. Le Blond (50 vols., 1927–9).

H. Barbusse, *Z.* (1932); G. Robert, *E.Z.* (Paris, 1952); A. Wilson, *E.Z.* (1952); F. W. J. Hemmings, *E.Z.* (2nd edn, 1966); J. H. Matthews, *Les deux Z.* (Geneva, 1957); M. Turnell, *The Art of French Fiction* (1959); Auerbach, *M*; Lukács, *SER*.

**Żółkiewski, Stanisław** (Turynka 1547–Cecora 1620). Polish soldier and diarist. As commander (*hetman*) of the Polish army in the campaign against Russia, he conquered Moscow and recorded his military experiences in a book of memoirs, *Początek i progres wojny moskiewskiej* (1612; tr. M. W. Stephen, *Beginning and Progress of the Muscovy War*, 1959), where a fascinating self-portrait is presented in the third person, after the manner of Julius Caesar. Its documentary value apart, the book is important in the development of Polish narrative prose. The English version has uncommon stylistic merits. [JP]

**Zoranić, Petar.** ⇨ Dalmatian and Dubrovnik Literature.

**Zorin, Dmitri Ivanovich** (? 1905– ). Russian dramatist, lawyer and journalist. His earlier plays *Sem'ya Komissara* (1936) and the comedy *Vozvrasheheniye Tarasa* (1948) aroused little comment, but he is now established as one of the first to have reacted against the 'cult of personality' and to have returned to the traditions of the twenties and early thirties, indeed, of all Russian historical drama since Pushkin's *Boris Godunov*, by attempting to show the part played by the masses in the historical process. *Vechnyy istochnik* (1957) and *Vesenyy Grom* (1961) both seek to re-establish the fact that the Russian people were largely responsible for the Russian Revolution. [AP]

*Vechnyy Istochnik* (1957); *Teatr*, 10 (1961).

**Zorrilla, José** (Valladolid 1817–Madrid 1893). Spanish romantic poet. His drama, *Don Juan Tenorio* (1844), is still most popular. He clothes the legend in romantic fancy-dress, makes Don Juan a popular hero and saves him from damnation by the love of a pure woman. Among the best of his historical plays are *El zapatero y el rey* (Part I, 1840, Part II, 1842), concerning Peter the Cruel, and *Traidor, inconfeso y mártir* (1849), a treatment of the King Sebastian of Portugal theme. His verses are sonorous, colourful and nostalgic ('a latter-day troubadour', Valera). His highly readable *Leyendas* range widely over Spain's past history; *Granada* (1852) is a fragment of a vast and learned reconstruction of Moorish Spain. Worldly success eluded him: fleeing from home, abandoning an elderly wife, he attached himself to the ill-fated Emperor, Maximilian of Mexico; shy and penniless, he was perpetually escaping from reality into a world of make-believe – the world too of his poetry.

*Obras completas* (1943); Blecua, *FLE*; Trend, *OBSV*; *Don Juan Tenorio*, ed. W. Mills (London, 1966).

N. Alonso Cortés, *Z., su vida y sus obras* (Valladolid, 1942).

**Zoshchenko, Mikhail Mikhaylovich** (Poltava 1895–Leningrad 1958). Russian humorous writer. He was wounded in the First World War and in 1918 volunteered for the Red Army. In 1921 he joined the ⇨ Serapion Brothers and soon achieved fame with his first book, *Rasskazy Nazara Il'icha Sinebryukhova* (1922). His stories, often extremely short, are written in the language of uneducated city-dwellers, a nonsensical mixture of slang and Soviet jargon. The humour is often coarse and the situations ludicrous; but behind this lies his awareness that the Revolution has not changed human nature. Snobbery, inefficiency and corruption are as rife as they were before 1917. His stories combine pity for the ordinary man, lost and bewildered in the new age, with contempt for his stupidity and pettiness.

He was from the first criticized for his 'malicious distortions' of popular speech;

in his work of the 1930s the language becomes more restrained and the note of melancholy deepens. In *Vozvrashchonnaya molodost'* (1933) and *Golubaya kniga* (1935) his declared intention of writing a real Soviet novel is belied by the style and outcome of the work. In the first the hero's youth is in fact not restored and the second is a parody of the Soviet approach to history.

During the war he began an autobiographical work *Pered voskhodom solntsa* (1943; part tr. J. Richardson, *Before Sunrise*, in *PR*, 1961, Nos. 3–4), in which he seeks the explanation of his hypochondria and melancholy in a series of harrowing reminiscences. The work was quickly suppressed – it was never completed – and with *Priklyucheniya obez'yany* (1946) led to his expulsion from the Union of Soviet Writers in 1946. His later work is of less interest.

Many of his works have been bowdlerized or revised in subsequent editions, often without his consent, so that the original texts are sometimes difficult to come by. Many of his stories have been translated into English. [RDBT]

*Sobraniye sochineniy* (8 vols., 1930); *Rasskazy* (N.Y., 1952); tr. in Guerney, *TRL*; Reavey and Slonim, *SL*; Yarmolinsky, *SSS*.

E. J. Simmons, *Through the Glass of Soviet Literature* (1953); *M.Z. Stat'i i materialy* (1928).

**Zrinyi, Miklós** (Csáktornya 1620–Csáktornya 1664). Hungarian poet. An aristocrat of Jesuit education, whose main work was *Szigeti veszedelem* (1645; tr. W. Kirkconnell, *The Peril of Sziget*, or *Zrinyias*, in *Hungarian Poetry*, Sydney, 1955), an epic inspired by the heroic defence of Szigetvár against the Turks. His finest prose work is *A török áfium ellen való orvosság* (1661). [JFR]

**Zschokke, Heinrich** (Magdeburg 1771–Aaran 1848). German writer. He led a varied life as actor, student and pastor, before settling in Switzerland, where he dabbled in politics. He was an extremely prolific writer and tried his hand successfully at a variety of literary modes from *Die schwarzen Brüder* (1791–5), a sensational novel about secret societies, and *Abällino* (1793, dramatized version 1795), a criminal story in the degenerate tradition deriving from *Sturm und Drang*, to moral, didactic stories reflective of his social and economic interests (*Das Goldmacherdorf*, 1817; *Die Branntweinpest*, 1837), and historical novels in the style of Scott (*Adderich im Moos*, 1826). He edited several journals and wrote a number of historical works, political pamphlets and memoires, together with a very popular, non-confessional devotional work, *Stunden der Andacht* (8 vols., 1809–16). [WAC]

*Schriften* (40 vols., 1825–8) (selection).

**Zuckmayer, Carl** (Nackenheim/Rhein 1896– ). German dramatist and poet. A volunteer and front-line soldier 1914–18. His first poems appeared in *Die Aktion* (1917); he joined ⇨ Brecht as Dramaturg at Reinhardt's Deutsches Theater (Berlin, 1924), but his attempts at modernistic drama failed. He found his true vein, a more homely, humorous 'naturalism', in the successful rustic comedy, *Der fröhliche Weinberg* (1925), with its characteristic mockery of a nationalist *Corpsstudent*. Vital rogues, circus stars, vagabond artists conflict colourfully with conformity (the flagging dramatic interest buttressed with dialect, historical scenery, etc.) in *Schinderhannes* (1927), *Katharina Knie* (1928), *Der Schelm von Bergen* (1934), *Bellmann* (1938; 1953 as *Ulla Winblad*), and most successfully in *Der Hauptmann von Köpenick* (1931; tr. D. Portman, *The Captain of Köpenick*, 1932), which satirized Prussian officialdom. He emigrated from Nazism to Austria, then the U.S.A. (1939); his best play, *Des Teufels General* (1946; filmed), explored the now grimmer conflict between military obedience and personal honesty in a Nazi general (modelled on Udet); after a less successful play about the French Resistance (*Der Gesang im Feuerofen*, 1950), *Das kalte Licht* (1955) treated the theme of integrity again in the case of a nuclear scientist turned traitor. His fiction (e.g. *Salware*, 1936; *Herr über Leben und Tod*, 1938) has remained little known, except for his Austrian idyll, *Der Seelenbräu* (1945), with its nature lyricism characteristic also of his poetry (*Gedichte 1916 bis 1948*). *Als wärs ein Stück von mir* (1966) is an (excellent) autobiography. [PB]

*Gesammelte Werke* (4 vols., 1960); *Carnival Confession*, tr. J. and N. Mander (1961); Bridgwater, *TCGV*.

*Fülle der Zeit* (Festschrift, 1956); I. Engelsing-Malek, '*Amor Fati' in Z.s Dramen* (Constance, 1960); W. Adling, *Die Entwicklung des Dramatikers, C.Z.* (Leipzig, 1956); Natan, *GML*, iii; Garten, *MGD*; *ML* xxxv, 2, 1954; *GQ*,

XXXIII, 1960; *MLN*, LXXVI, 1961; *M*, XLIV (1952), LII (1960).

**Zunzunegui, Juan Antonio de** (Portugalete/Vizcaya 1901– ). Spanish novelist. He began with tales and sketches rich in the local colour of his native Basque country (*Cuentos y patrañas de mi ría*, 1935). His true narrative powers emerge in his many long novels of which the most notable are *¡Ay estos hijos!* (1943), *El supremo bien* (1951), *La quiebra* (1947), *La vida como es* (1954), *El mundo sigue* (1960), and *Una mujer sobre la tierra* (1959, in Mexico, censored in Spain). He won the Premio Nacional de Literatura with *El premio* (1962) – a satire against literary prizes in Spain! He writes in the realistic tradition, influenced by ⇨ Pérez Galdós, particularly in the Madrid stories (*La vida como es*, *El mundo sigue*), which are perhaps his best. They are remarkable for their social satire and detailed observation of middle-class and working-class life. From personal experience he also depicted the business world of Bilbao, where he pessimistically sees money playing a Balzacian role. [JLC]

Alborg, *HANE*; Nora, *NEC*.

**Zurara, Gomes Eanes de** (*c.* 1420?–*c.* 1474?). Portuguese official court chronicler, succeeding Fernão ⇨ Lopes. By 1450 he had completed the *Crónica de D. João I*, begun by Lopes, though his contribution is now normally known as the *Crónica da Tomada de Ceuta*. Passionately devoted to the interests of the resurgent nobility, Zurara's work exalts their deeds and adventures. For Lopes's global view of Portuguese society, he substituted a restricted and partisan vision in which the collective role of the 'people' almost disappeared from history. He interpreted early imperial expansion in terms of individual exploits by his noble mentors. Thus his *Crónica da Tomada de Ceuta*, dealing with the campaign of 1415, takes little or no account of the powerful economic factors behind Portugal's first incursion into North Africa. He looked upon the enterprise purely as a vehicle of self-glorification for the 'Infantes', justified by a vague medieval spirit of Christian crusade. Similarly his *Crónica do descobrimento e conquista de Guiné* (publ. Paris, 1841; tr. E. Prestage, 1928) about Portuguese penetration into West Africa, is essentially a panegyric of the Infante, Henry the Navigator. He also wrote *Crónica do Conde D. Pedro de Meneses* and the *Crónica do Conde de D. Duarte de Meneses*. [AJP]

*Crónica da Tomada de Ceuta* and *Crónica dos Feitos de Guiné* in CP (selection); further selections in *Prosas Históricas* (TL).
A. J. Saraiva, *História da Cultura em Portugal*, i (Lisbon, 1950).

**Zweig, Arnold** (Glogau/Silesia 1887–1968). German Jewish novelist and essayist. A pacifist after 1914–18 experiences, and a Zionist, he emigrated to Palestine (1933), returned to East Germany in 1948, to become President of Academy of Arts (Lenin Peace Prize, 1958, etc.). First successful with *Novellen um Claudia* (1912; tr. E. Sutton, *Claudia*, 1930), depicting the sufferings of a hypersensitive young woman, his *Der Streit um den Sergeanten Grischa* (1927; tr. E. Sutton, *The Case of Sergeant Grischa*, repr. 1961), described by J. B. Priestley as 'the greatest novel on a war theme ... from any country', is inspired by a new sense of social realism and protest. A series of novels was planned, to expose bourgeois society, militarism, etc.: *Junge Frau von 1914* (1931; tr. E. Sutton, *Young Woman of 1914*, 1932), *Erziehung vor Verdun* (1935; tr. E. Sutton, *Education before Verdun*, 1936), etc. Interest attaches to *De Vriendt kehrt heim* (1933; tr. E. Sutton, *De Vriendt Goes Home*, 1936), for its reflection of Zionism, and to *Das Beil von Wandsbek* (1947; tr. E. Sutton, *The Axe of Wandsbek*, 1948) as a symbolic story about Nazism. His later work is little known outside East Germany. [PB]

*Ausgewählte Werke* (15 vols, 1955–63).
J. Rudolph, *Der Humanist A.Z.* (Berlin, 1955); Reich-Ranicki, *DLWO*.

**Zweig, Stefan** (Vienna 1881–Petrópolis, Brazil 1942). Austrian essayist and poet. His first lyrics (and translations of Verlaine, Verhaeren) are typical of *Jungwien* aesthetic impressionism (*Gesammelte Gedichte*, 1924). The First World War inspired *Jeremias* (produced in Zürich, 1917; tr. E. and C. Paul, 1929) – a series of dramatic *tableaux* denouncing war – and the ideals of supra-national European culture and of world citizenship, which he championed on his later wide travels. Best known for his biographical 'analyses', in terms of a psychology of demonic perils and creative triumphs, of great writers: Balzac, Dickens, Dostoyevsky, Nietzsche, and others (*Drei Meister*, 1920; tr. E. and C. Paul, *Three Masters*, 1930; *Romain Rolland*, 1920; tr. E. and C. Paul, 1921; *Der Kampf mit dem Dämon*, 1923) and Casanova, Stendhal, Tolstoy in *Drei Dichter ihres Lebens* (1928; tr. E. and C. Paul, *Adepts in Self-Portraiture*, 1929) – see the collected *Master Builders* (tr. E. and C. Paul, 1939). Emotional tensions provide the focus of his historical 'studies', e.g. *Maria Stuart* (1935; tr. E. and C. Paul, *The Queen of Scots*, 1950) with its neurotic Elizabeth I, while his stories (*Gesammelte Erzählungen*, 1936; tr. E. and C. Paul, *Kaleidoscope*, 1936) attempt a psychoanalytic typology of feeling. His sense of European cultural tradition and crisis is reflected in his *Sternstunden der Menschheit* (1927; tr. E. and C. Paul, *The Tide of Fortune*, 1940) and memoirs *Die Welt von Gestern* (1943; tr. E. and C. Paul, *The World of Yesterday*, 1943). He committed suicide with his wife. [PB/AKT]

*Complete Works* (Hallam Edn), tr. E. and C. Paul (1949ff.).

R. J. Klawiter, *S.Z. A Bibliography* (Chapel Hill, 1965) J. Romains, *S.Z.* . . . (N.Y., 1941); F. Zweig, *S.Z. The Biography of a Great European*, (1947); H. Arens (ed.), *A Tribute* . . . (1951); Natan, *GML*, II; *GLL*, V (1951–2).

# GUIDE TO ENTRIES BY LANGUAGE AND COUNTRY

European writers can be classified according to their nationality or according to the language in which they wrote; these two categories are often the same, but not always. These lists preserve most of the customary subdivisions, both of language and of nationality, which history has imposed on Europe. Lists based on only one of these principles would have included some authors in categories with which they are not usually associated.

At the end of these main lists (on p. 908), there is a shorter one containing entries which do not belong under a specific national heading, each with a page reference.

## ALBANIAN

See also article on **Albanian Literature,** p. 40

| | | |
|---|---|---|
| Dara, G. | 1765–1832 | writer of folk-songs |
| De Rada, J. | 1813–1903 | journalist, poet |
| Kristoforidhi, K. | 1827–95 | writer, bible translator, linguist |
| Shiroka, F. | 1859–1935 | poet |
| Fishta, G. | 1871–1940 | writer, editor |
| Drenova, A. S. | 1872–1947 | lyricist |
| Frashëri, M. | 1880–1949 | writer, translator, short-story writer |
| Koliqi, E. | 1903– | poet, short-story writer |
| Postoli, F. | 20th cent. | novelist |

## AUSTRIAN

| | | |
|---|---|---|
| Heinrich von Melk | fl. mid 12th cent. | monastic poet |
| Ulrich von Lichtenstein | *c.*1200–1275 | poet |
| Heinrich von Neustadt | fl. early 14th cent. | epic poet |
| Oswald von Wolkenstein | *c.*1367–1445 | Minnesinger |
| Raimund, F. | 1790–1836 | dramatist |
| Grillparzer, F. | 1791–1872 | dramatist |
| Nestroy, J. | 1801–62 | dramatist |
| Stifter, A. | 1805–68 | novelist and Novellen writer |
| Grün, A. | 1806–76 | poet |
| Ebner-Eschenbach, M. von | 1830–1916 | Novellen writer |
| Saar, F. von | 1833–1906 | poet, Novellen writer |
| Anzengruber, L. | 1839–89 | dramatist, novelist |
| Rosegger, P. | 1843–1918 | moralist, humorous writer |

| | | |
|---|---|---|
| Freud, S. | 1856–1939 | psycho-analyst |
| Schnitzler, A. | 1862–1931 | dramatist, novelist |
| Bahr, H. | 1863–1934 | critic, dramatist, novelist |
| Beer-Hofman, R. | 1866–1945 | dramatist, poet, novelist |
| Meyrink, G. | 1868–1932 | novelist |
| Schönherr, K. | 1869–1943 | dramatist |
| Hofmannsthal, H. von | 1874–1929 | poet, dramatist, essayist |
| Kraus, K. | 1874–1936 | poet, satirist |
| Rilke, R. M. | 1875–1926 | poet |
| Musil, R. | 1880–1942 | novelist |
| Zweig, S. | 1881–1942 | essayist, poet |
| Mell, M. | 1882– | novelist, dramatist, poet |
| Kafka, F. | 1883–1924 | novelist |
| Brod, M. | 1884–1968 | Austrian-German novelist |
| Broch, H. | 1886–1951 | novelist, poet |
| Ehrenstein, A. | 1886–1950 | expressionist poet |
| Preradović, P. von | 1887–1951 | poet |
| Trakl, G. | 1887–1914 | poet |
| Werfel, F. | 1890–1945 | poet, novelist, dramatist |
| Weinheber, J. | 1892–1945 | poet |
| Roth, J. | 1894–1939 | novelist |
| Doderer, H. von | 1896–1966 | novelist |
| Kramer, T. | 1897–1958 | poet |
| Canetti, E. | 1905– | novelist, dramatist, essayist |
| Thoor, J. | 1905–52 | poet |
| Hochwälder, F. | 1911– | dramatist |
| Fussenegger, G. | 1912– | novelist |
| Busta, C. | 1915– | poet |
| Lavant, C. | 1915– | poet |
| Marnau, A. | 1918– | poet, novelist |
| Aichinger, I. | 1921– | short-story writer |
| Fried, E. | 1921– | poet, translator |
| Bachman, I. | 1926– | poet |

## BASQUE

See also article on **Basque Literature,** p. 85

| | | |
|---|---|---|
| Pedro de Axular | 1556–? | religious writer |
| Dechepare, B. | fl. mid 16th cent. | religious writer |
| Manuel de Larramendi | 1690–1766 | orator, grammarian |
| Munibe, X. M. de | fl. second half of 18th cent. | composer of comic opera |
| Etchahun | 1786–1862 | poet |
| Moguel, J. A. | 18th–19th cent. | novelist |
| Manterola, J. | 19th–20th cent. | writer |
| Elissamburu, J.-B. | 1828–91 | poet |

| | | |
|---|---|---|
| Bizcarrondo, I. | 1831–76 | poet |
| Aguirre, D. | 1864–1920 | novelist |
| Ormaechea, N. | 1888–1961 | poet, prose writer |
| Lizardi, X. de | 1896–1933 | lyric writer |

## BELGIAN

See also FLEMISH

| | | |
|---|---|---|
| Verhaeren, É. | 1855–1916 | poet |
| Van Leberghe, C. | 1861–1907 | symbolist poet |
| Maeterlinck, M. | 1862–1949 | poet, dramatist |
| Crommelynck, F. | 1888–1969 | dramatist |
| Michaux, H. | 1899– | novelist, poet |
| Mallet-Joris, F. | 1930– | novelist |

## BRETON

See also article on **Breton Literature,** p. 140

| | | |
|---|---|---|
| Le Gonidec, J. M. F. | 1775–1838 | grammarian, lexicographer translator |
| Guillôme, J. | 1797–1857 | poet |
| Proux, P. | 1811–75 | poet |
| Villemarqué, T. H. de la | 1815–95 | poet |
| Luzel, F. | 1821–95 | writer of ballads, songs, folk tales |
| Malemanche, T. | 1875–1953 | dramatist |
| Priel, J. | 1885–1965 | dramatist, novelist |
| Kalloc'h, J. P. | 1888–1917 | poet |
| Drezen, Y. | 1899– | novelist |
| Riou, J. | 1899–1937 | short-story writer, dramatist |
| Hemon, R. | 1900– | dramatist, poet |
| Denez, P. | 1921– | story writer, poet |
| Huon, R. | 1922– | poet |

## BULGARIAN

See also articles on **Old Bulgarian Literature,** p. 577 and **Old Church Slavonic,** p. 582

| | | |
|---|---|---|
| Clement, Saint | 9th cent. | sermon writer, translator |
| Constantine of Preslav | 9th–10th cent. | religious writer, chronicler |
| John the Exarch | 9th–10th cent. | translator, compiler |
| Khrabr, the Monk | 9th–10th cent. | religious writer |
| *Alexander* | 10th cent. | epic tale |
| *Barlaam and Josaphat* | 10th cent. | didactic tale |
| Bogomil literature | 10th cent. | religious writings |

| | | |
|---|---|---|
| *Chudoto s Balgarina* | 10th cent. | chronicle-story |
| Cosmas, the Priest | 10th cent. | religious writer |
| Simeon, Tsar | 10th cent. | literary patron, author |
| *Codex Suprasliensis* | 11th cent. | Gospel translation |
| *Savvina Kniga* | 11th cent. | Gospel translation |
| Slaveykov, Petko | 1827–95 | poet |
| Karavelov, L. | 1835–79 | story writer, publicist |
| Botev, H. | 1848–76 | poet, publicist |
| Vazov, I. | 1850–1921 | poet, novelist, story writer |
| Velichkov, K. | 1855–1907 | poet, belles-lettres writer |
| Mihaylovski, S. | 1856–1927 | satirical poet |
| Konstantinov, A. | 1863–97 | satirist |
| Vlaykov, T. | 1865–1943 | story writer, publicist |
| Slaveykov, Pencho | 1866–1912 | poet, critic, thinker |
| Strashimirov, A. | 1872–1937 | story writer, novelist, dramatist |
| Hristov, K. | 1875–1944 | poet, dramatist, story writer |
| Elin Pelin | 1878–1949 | story writer |
| Yavorov, P. | 1878–1914 | poet, dramatist |
| Todorov, P. | 1879–1916 | idyll writer, dramatist |
| Yovkov, Y. | 1880–1937 | novelist, story writer |
| Liliev, N. | 1885–1960 | poet |
| Debelyanov, D. | 1887–1916 | symbolist poet |
| Bagryana, E. | 1893– | poet |
| Talev, D. | 1898–1966 | novelist |
| Vaptsarov, N. | 1909–42 | poet |

## CATALAN

See also article on **Catalan Literature,** p. 168

| | | |
|---|---|---|
| Lull, R. | 1233–1316 | philosopher, theologian, novelist, poet, mystic, missionary |
| Marc, A. | 1397–1459 | poet |
| Vilanova, A. de | fl. around 1300 | doctor, writing on medicine and theology |
| Martorell, J. | fl. mid 15th cent. | writer of novels of chivalry |
| Cortada, J. | fl. 1833–40 | writer of historical novels |
| Verdaguer, J. | 1845–1902 | epic poet |
| Guimerà, A. | 1847–1924 | dramatist |
| Alcover, J. | 1854–1926 | poet |
| Costa i Llobera, M. | 1854–1922 | poet |
| Iglesies, I. | 1871–1925 | writer of social dramas |
| Carner, J. | 1884–1970 | poet |
| Foix, J. V. | 1894– | poet |

## CROATIAN

See also article on **Serbo-Croat Folk Literature,** p. 715

| | | |
|---|---|---|
| Kačič-Miošič, A. | 1704–60 | poet, publicist |
| Reljković, M. A. | 1732–98 | poet, publicist |
| Brezovački, T. | 1757–1805 | dramatist, priest |
| Gaj, L. | 1809–72 | writer, publicist |
| Vraz, S. | 1810–51 | poet |
| Mažuranić, I. | 1814–90 | poet |
| Preradović, P. | 1818–72 | poet |
| Kovačić, A. | 1834–89 | novelist |
| Šenoa, A. | 1838–81 | novelist |
| Kumičić, E. | 1850–1904 | novelist |
| Djalski, K. S. | 1854–1935 | novelist, short-story writer |
| Vojnović, I. | 1857–1929 | dramatist |
| Kozarac, J. | 1858–1906 | novelist, short-story writer |
| Novak, V. | 1859–1905 | novelist |
| Leskovar, J. | 1861–1949 | novelist |
| Kranjčević, S. S. | 1865–1908 | poet |
| Matoš, A. G. | 1873–1914 | poet, essayist, critic |
| Vidrić, V. | 1875–1909 | poet |
| Nazor, V. | 1876–1949 | poet, novelist, essayist |
| Kosor, J. | 1879–1961 | novelist, dramatist |
| Kolar, S. | 1891–1970 | humorist |
| Ujević, A. | 1891–1953 | poet |
| Cesareć, A. | 1893–1941 | novelist |
| Krleža, M. | 1893– | dramatist, novelist, essayist, poet |
| Šimić, A. B. | 1898–1925 | poet |
| Krklec, G. | 1899– | poet |
| Cesarić, D. | 1902– | poet |
| Desnica, V. | 1905–1967 | short-story writer, novelist |
| Kaleb, V. | 1905– | novelist, short-story writer |
| Tadijanović, D. | 1905– | poet |
| Ivaniševič, D. | 1907– | poet |
| Kovačić, G. I. | 1913–43 | poet |
| Marinković, R. | 1913– | dramatist, short-story writer |
| Matković, M. | 1915– | dramatist |
| Božić, M. | 1919– | novelist, dramatist |
| Kaštelan, J. | 1919– | poet |

## CZECHOSLOVAKIAN

See also separate headings: CZECH and SLOVAK

### CZECH

| | | |
|---|---|---|
| Cosmas of Prague | 1045?–1125 | chronicler |
| Hus, J. | 1371?–1415 | theologian, religious performer |

| | | |
|---|---|---|
| Chelčický, P. | c. 1390–c. 1460 | peasant philosopher |
| Vratislav z Mitrovic, V. | 1576–1635 | autobiographical adventure writer |
| Comenius | 1592–1670 | educationalist writer |
| Dobrovský, J. | 1753–1829 | philologist |
| Jungmann, J. | 1773–1847 | translator, philologist |
| Hanka, V. | 1791–1861 | scholar, forger of medieval poetry |
| Kollár, J. | 1793–1852 | Slovak poet, writing in Czech |
| Palacký, F. | 1798–1876 | historian |
| Mácha, K. H. | 1810–36 | poet |
| Erben, K. J. | 1811–70 | poet |
| Němcová, B. | 1820–62 | novelist |
| Havliček Borovský, K. | 1821–56 | journalist, satirist, essayist |
| Neruda, J. | 1834–91 | poet, short-story writer, essayist |
| Zeyer, J. | 1841–1901 | poet, novelist, dramatist |
| Čech, S. | 1846–1908 | poet, novelist, dramatist |
| Masaryk, T. G. | 1850–1937 | thinker, statesman |
| Jirásek, A. | 1851–1930 | historical novelist |
| Vrchlický, J. | 1853–1912 | poet, dramatist, essayist |
| Čapek-Chod, K. M. | 1860–1927 | novelist |
| Machar, J. S. | 1864–1942 | poet |
| Sova, A. | 1864–1928 | poet |
| Bezruč, P. | 1867–1958 | poet |
| Březina, O. | 1868–1929 | poet |
| Hlaváček, K. | 1874–98 | poet |
| Neumann, S. K. | 1875–1947 | poet, novelist, essayist |
| Majerová, M. | 1882–1967 | novelist |
| Olbracht, I. | 1882–1952 | writer |
| Hašek, J. | 1883–1923 | novelist, short-story writer |
| Durych, J. | 1886–1962 | novelist, poet |
| Čapek, K. | 1890–1938 | novelist, dramatist, essayist |
| Hora, J. | 1891–1945 | poet |
| Vančura, V. | 1891–1942 | novelist |
| Pujmanová, M. | 1893–1958 | novelist, poet |
| Nezval, V. | 1900–1958 | poet, novelist, dramatist |
| Wolker, J. | 1900–1924 | poet |
| Glazarová, J. | 1901– | novelist |
| Seifert, J. | 1901– | poet |
| Halas, F. | 1901–49 | poet |
| Řezáč, V. | 1901–56 | novelist |
| Hoffmeister, A. | 1902– | essayist, poet, dramatist |
| Fučik, J. | 1903–43 | journalist, literary critic |
| Hostovský, E. | 1908– | novelist |
| Hrabal B. | 1914– | novelist and short-story writer |

| | | |
|---|---|---|
| Drda, J. | 1915–70 | novelist, dramatist |
| Mucha, J. | 1915– | novelist and short-story writer |
| Otčenášek, J. | 1924– | novelist |
| Kundera, M. | 1929– | novelist, dramatist and short-story writer |

## DALMATIAN AND DUBROVNIK

See also article on **Dalmatian and Dubrovnik Literature,** p. 210

| | | |
|---|---|---|
| Marulić, M. | 1450–1524 | religious and moral writer |
| Menčetić, Š. | 1457–1526 | poet |
| Držić, D. | 1461–1501 | poet |
| Vetranić, M. | 1482–1571 | moral and religious writer, dramatist |
| Lucić, H. | 1485–1558 | writer |
| Hektorović, P. | 1487–1572 | writer |
| Nalješković, N. | 1500–87 | writer of comedies and eclogues |
| Zoranić, P. | 1508–70 | novelist |
| Držić, M. | 1520–67 | writer of pastoral plays and comedies |
| Ranjina, D. | 1536–1607 | poet |
| Zlatarić, D. | 1558–1609 | poet |
| Kašić, B. | 1575–1660 | Jesuit grammarian |
| Gundulić, F. G. | 1588–1638 | writer, epic poet |
| Bunić, I. | 1594–1658 | poet |
| Minćetić, V. | 1600–1666 | poet |
| Palmotić, J. | 1606–57 | dramatist |
| Djordjić, I. | 1675–1737 | Jesuit poet |

## DANISH

| | | |
|---|---|---|
| Palladius, P. | 1503–60 | theologian |
| Arrebo, A. | 1587–1637 | poet |
| Leonora Christina | 1621–98 | autobiographical writer |
| Kingo, T. | 1634–1703 | poet |
| Holberg, L. | 1684–1754 | dramatist, essayist, historian |
| Brorson, H. A. | 1694–1764 | poet |
| Stub, A. | 1705–58 | poet |
| Wessel, J. H. | 1742–85 | Dano-Norwegian poet, dramatist |
| Ewald, J. | 1743–81 | poet |
| Heiberg, P. A. | 1758–1841 | poet, author |
| Baggesen, J. | 1764–1826 | poet |
| Staffeldt, A. V. S. von | 1769–1826 | poet |
| Oehlenschläger, A. | 1779–1850 | poet, dramatist |

| | | |
|---|---|---|
| Blicher, S. S. | 1782–1848 | poet, short-story writer |
| Grundtvig, N. F. S. | 1783–1872 | poet |
| Ingemann, B. S. | 1789–1862 | poet, novelist |
| Hauch, C. | 1790–1872 | poet, novelist |
| Heiberg, J. L. | 1791–1860 | poet, dramatist |
| Bødtcher, L. | 1793–1874 | poet |
| Møller, P. | 1794–1838 | poet, novelist |
| Winther, C. | 1796–1876 | poet |
| Hertz, H. | 1798 ?–1870 | poet, dramatist |
| Aarestrup, E. | 1800–1856 | poet |
| Andersen, H. C. | 1805–75 | writer of fairy-tales |
| Paludan-Müller, F. | 1809–76 | poet, novelist |
| Kierkegaard, S. | 1813–55 | philosopher |
| Goldschmidt, M. A. | 1819–87 | novelist |
| Schack, H. E. | 1820–59 | novelist |
| Topsøe, V. | 1840–81 | novelist |
| Brandes, G. | 1842–1927 | literary critic |
| Drachmann, H. | 1846–1908 | poet, novelist |
| Brandes, E. | 1847–1931 | critic, dramatist |
| Jacobsen, J. P. | 1847–85 | novelist, short-story writer |
| Bang, H. | 1857–1912 | novelist, short-story writer |
| Gjellerup, K. | 1857–1919 | novelist |
| Pontoppidan, H. | 1857–1943 | novelist |
| Knudsen, J. | 1858–1917 | novelist |
| Wied, G. | 1858–1914 | novelist, dramatist |
| Stuckenberg, V. | 1863–1905 | poet |
| Holstein, L. | 1864–1943 | poet |
| Claussen, S. | 1865–1931 | poet |
| Aakjær, J. | 1866–1930 | poet |
| Jørgensen, J. | 1866–1956 | poet, essayist |
| Bregendahl, M. | 1867–1940 | novelist, short-story writer |
| Henningsen, A. | 1868–1962 | novelist |
| Nathansen, H. | 1868–1944 | dramatist, novelist |
| Nexø, M. A. | 1869–1954 | novelist |
| Rode, H. | 1870–1937 | poet, dramatist, essayist |
| Michaëlis, K. | 1872–1950 | novelist, short-story writer |
| Rørdam, V. | 1872–1946 | lyrical poet |
| Jensen, J. V. | 1873–1950 | novelist, essayist, poet |
| Anker Larsen, J. | 1874–1957 | novelist |
| Hoffman, K. | 1874–1949 | poet |
| Rung, O. | 1874–1945 | novelist, short-story writer |
| Larsen, T. | 1875–1928 | poet |
| Kidde, H. | 1878–1918 | novelist |
| Rasmussen, K. | 1879–1933 | explorer, travel writer |
| Dam, A. | 1880– | novelist, short-story writer |
| Søiberg, H. | 1880–1954 | novelist |

| | | |
|---|---|---|
| Blixen, K. | 1885–1962 | story writer, novelist |
| Friis Møller, K. | 1888–1960 | poet |
| Gelsted, O. | 1888– | poet |
| Munk, K. | 1889–1944 | dramatist, poet |
| Becker, K. | 1891– | novelist |
| Seedorff Pedersen, H. H. | 1892– | poet |
| Kristensen, T. | 1893– | novelist, critic |
| Paludan, J. | 1896– | novelist, essayist |
| Soya, C. E. | 1896– | dramatist, fiction writer |
| Petersen, N. | 1897–1943 | poet, novelist, short-story writer |
| Kirk, H. | 1898–1962 | novelist |
| Heinesen, W. | 1900– | Faroese poet, novelist |
| Herdal, H. | 1900– | poet, novelist |
| Jacobsen, J.-F. | 1900–1938 | Faroese novelist, Copenhagen journalist |
| Abell, K. | 1901–61 | dramatist |
| Lange, P. | 1901– | poet |
| La Cour, P. | 1902–56 | poet |
| Nielsen, J. | 1902–45 | novelist |
| Branner, H. C. | 1903–66 | novelist, dramatist |
| Dons, A. | 1903– | novelist |
| Schade, J. A. | 1903– | poet |
| Fischer, L. | 1904–56 | novelist, dramatist |
| Freuchen, P. | 1904–57 | novelist, explorer |
| Hein, P. | 1905– | poet |
| Scherfig, H. | 1905– | novelist |
| Klitgaard, M. | 1906–45 | novelist |
| Lauesen, M. | 1907– | novelist |
| Hansen, M. A. | 1909–55 | novelist |
| Sønderby, K. | 1909–66 | novelist |
| Rasmussen, H. | 1915– | poet |
| Bjørnvig, T. | 1918– | poet, essayist |
| Ditlevsen, T. | 1918– | poet, novelist, story writer |
| Knudsen, E. | 1922– | poet, dramatist |
| Nielsen, M. | 1922–44 | poet |
| Olsen, E. B. | 1923– | dramatist |
| Sorensen, V. | 1929– | essayist, short-story writer |
| Rifbjerg, K. | 1931– | poet, novelist, dramatist |

## DUTCH

See also articles on **Netherlands Medieval Drama** and **Netherlands Medieval Epic** p. 565; **Rederijkers**, p. 643

| | | |
|---|---|---|
| Hadewijch | 12th–13th cent. | mystic, poet |
| Ruusbroec, J. van | 1293–1381 | mystic |

| | | |
|---|---|---|
| *Beatrijs* | 14th cent. | middle Dutch legend |
| Erasmus, D. | 1466–1536 | humanist scholar writing in Latin |
| Bijns, A. | 1493–1575 | poet |
| Coornhert, D. V. | 1522–90 | humanist, translator |
| Noot, Jonker J. van der | *c.* 1539–*c.* 1595 | poet |
| Marnix van St Aldegonde, P. van | 1540–98 | poet, theologian |
| Spiegel, H. L. | 1549–1612 | poet, humanist |
| Cats, J. | 1577–1660 | poet |
| Wiele, J. S. van der | 1579–1630 | priest, poet |
| Heinsius, D. | 1580–1655 | philologist, poet |
| Hooft, P. C. | 1581–1647 | poet |
| Bredero, G. A. | 1585–1618 | poet, dramatist |
| Camphuysen, D. R. | 1586–1627 | painter, poet |
| Revius, J. | 1586–1658 | poet, historian, scholar |
| Vondel, J. van den | 1587–1679 | poet, dramatist |
| Starter, J. J. | 1594–1626 | poet |
| Huygens, C. | 1596–1687 | poet, musician, scientist |
| Spinoza, B. | 1632–77 | philosopher |
| Luyken, J. | 1649–1712 | poet, illustrator, mystic |
| Effen, J. van | 1684–1735 | essayist, short-story writer |
| Poot, H. K. | 1689–1733 | poet |
| Wolff, E. | 1738–1804 | novelist |
| Deken, A. | 1741–1804 | novelist |
| Bilderdijk, W. | 1756–1831 | poet, dramatist |
| Staring, A. C. W. | 1767–1840 | poet |
| Geel, J. | 1789–1862 | critic, essayist |
| Lennep, J. van | 1802–68 | novelist, scholar |
| Potgieter, E. J. | 1808–75 | poet, essayist, critic |
| Drost, A. | 1810–34 | novelist |
| Bosboom-Toussaint, A. L. G. | 1812–86 | novelist |
| Beets, N. | 1814–1903 | essayist, story writer, poet |
| Douwes Dekker, E. | 1820–87 | author |
| Huet, C. B. | 1826–86 | critic, journalist, historian |
| Looy, J. van | 1855–1930 | story and autobiographical writer |
| Kloos, W. J. T. | 1859–1938 | poet, critic |
| Perk, J. F. H. | 1859–81 | poet |
| Eeden, F. van | 1860–1932 | poet, novelist, critic |
| Couperus, L. M. A. | 1863–1923 | novelist |
| Deyssel, L. | 1864–1952 | novelist, critic |
| Gorter, H. | 1864–1927 | poet |
| Heijermans, H. | 1864–1924 | dramatist, author |
| Leopold, J. H. | 1865–1925 | poet |
| Verwey, A. | 1865–1937 | poet, critic, scholar |

| | | |
|---|---|---|
| Roland Holst-van der Schalk, H. G. A. | 1869–1952 | poet, dramatist, scholar |
| Boutens, P. C. | 1870–1943 | poet, classical scholar |
| Schendel, A. F. E. van | 1874–1946 | novelist |
| Leeuw, A. van der | 1876–1931 | novelist, poet |
| Bordewijk, F. | 1884–1965 | novelist, story writer |
| Bloem, J. C. | 1887–1966 | poet |
| Roland Holst, A. | 1888– | poet |
| Nijhoff, M. | 1894–1953 | poet, dramatist |
| Vestdijk, S. | 1898– | novelist, essayist, poet |
| Marsman, H. | 1899–1940 | poet, critic, novelist |
| Perron, C. E. du | 1899–1940 | critic, biographer, novelist |
| Braak, M. t. | 1902–40 | critic |
| Achterberg, G. | 1905–62 | poet |
| Hermans, W. F. | 1921– | experimental novelist |
| Lucebert | 1924– | poet, artist |
| Wolkers, J. H. | 1925– | novelist, story writer |

## FINNISH

See also article on **Kiila**, p. 429

| | | |
|---|---|---|
| *Kanteletar* | (publ. 1840–1) | collection of folk poetry |
| *Kalevala* | (publ. 1849; 1887) | Finnish national epic |
| Lönnrot, E. | 1802–84 | folklorist, philologist |
| Runeberg, J. L. | 1804–77 | Finland's 'national poet' |
| Topelius, Z. | 1818–98 | poet, novelist, scholar (writing in Swedish) |
| Kivi, A. | 1834–72 | poet, dramatist, novelist |
| Canth, M. | 1844–97 | novelist, dramatist |
| Aho, J. | 1861–1921 | novelist |
| Järnefelt, A. | 1861–1932 | novelist, short-story writer |
| Pakkala, T. | 1862–1925 | novelist, dramatist |
| Linnankoski, J. | 1869–1913 | novelist, dramatist |
| Talvio, M. | 1871–1951 | novelist, dramatist |
| Manninen, O. | 1872–1950 | poet |
| Kianto, I. | 1874–1970 | novelist |
| Kilpi, V. | 1874–1939 | novelist |
| Kallas, A. | 1878–1956 | poet, novelist |
| Leino, E. | 1878–1926 | poet, essayist |
| Jotuni, M. | 1880–1943 | short-story writer, dramatist |
| Lehtonen, J. | 1881–1934 | novelist, poet |
| Onerva, L. | 1882– | poet, critic, translator |
| Koskenniemi, V. A. | 1885–1962 | poet |
| Bergroth, K. S. | 1886– | dramatist, novelist, critic |
| Björling, G. | 1887–1960 | Finnish-Swedish poet, essayist |

| | | |
|---|---|---|
| Sillanpää, F. E. | 1888–1964 | novelist |
| Södergran, E. | 1892–1923 | Swedo-Finnish poet |
| Hellaakoski, A. | 1893–1952 | poet |
| Olsson, H. | 1893– | Swedo-Finnish novelist, critic |
| Diktonius, E. | 1896–1961 | Finnish-Swedish poet, story writer |
| Mustapää, P. | 1899– | poet |
| Viljanen, L. S. | 1900– | poet, critic |
| Kailas, U. | 1901–33 | poet |
| Vala, K. | 1901–44 | poet |
| Pekkanen, T. | 1902–57 | novelist |
| Sarkia, K. | 1902–45 | poet |
| Enckell, R. | 1903– | Finnish-Swedish poet |
| Paavolainen, O. | 1903–64 | essayist |
| Vaara, E. | 1903– | poet, translator |
| Colliander, T. | 1904– | Swedo-Finnish novelist, short-story writer |
| Kivimaa, K. A. | 1904– | poet, novelist, essayist |
| Haanpää, P. | 1905–55 | novelist, short-story writer |
| Salminen, S. | 1906– | Swedo-Finnish novelist |
| Schoultz, S. von | 1907– | Swedo-Finnish poet, novelist |
| Waltari, M. | 1908– | writer |
| Chorell, W. | 1912– | Swedo-Finnish dramatist, novelist |
| Tynni, A. | 1913– | poet |
| Mannerkorpi, J. | 1915– | poet, novelist |
| Pennanen, E. | 1916– | novelist, critic, essayist |
| Viita, L. A. | 1916–65 | poet, novelist |
| Juvonen, H. | 1919–59 | poet |
| Linna, V. | 1920– | novelist |
| Manner, E.-L. | 1921– | poet, prose writer |
| Meriluoto, A. | 1924– | poet |
| Vartio, M.-L. | 1924–66 | poet, novelist |
| Anhava, T. | 1927– | poet, critic, essayist |
| Meri, V. | 1928– | novelist, short-story writer |
| Haavikko, P. | 1931– | poet, dramatist, prose writer |
| Hyry, A. K. | 1931– | novelist, story writer |

## FLEMISH

| | | |
|---|---|---|
| Maerlant, J. van | *c.* 1225–*c.* 1291 | poet |
| Gezelle, G. | 1830–99 | poet |
| Lateur, F. | 1871–1969 | novelist, story writer |
| Woestijne, K. van de | 1878–1929 | poet |
| Teirlinck, H. L. C. | 1879–1967 | novelist |
| Elsschot, W. | 1882–1960 | novelist |

| | | |
|---|---|---|
| Ostaijen, P. van | 1896–1928 | poet, essayist |
| Ghelderode, M. de | 1898–1962 | dramatist |
| Walschap, G. | 1893– | novelist |
| Gijsen, M. | 1899– | poet, critic, novelist |

## FRENCH

Authors who wrote in LATIN, PROVENÇAL or BRETON, and authors of SWISS or BELGIAN nationality are listed under each of these separate headings

See also articles on **Aube,** p. 69; **'Encyclopédie',** p. 253; **French Literary Criticism in the 19th and 20th Centuries,** p. 282; **Parnassian,** p. 596; **Pastourelles,** p. 599; **La Pléiade,** p. 617; **Puy** (or **Pui**), p. 632; **Salons,** p. 690; **Tristan,** p. 772; **Trouvères,** p. 774

| | | |
|---|---|---|
| *Roland, Chanson de* | late 11th cent. | epic poem |
| *Chansons de geste* | 11th–14th cent. | epic poems |
| Wace | *c.*1110–*c.*1175 | Anglo-Norman chronicler |
| Marie de France | fl. 12th cent. | poet |
| Benoît de Sainte-Maure | fl. *c.*1150 | poet |
| Conon de Béthune | *c.*1150–*c.*1219 | trouvère |
| *Adam, Mystère d'* | *c.*1150–70 | play in Anglo-Norman |
| Villehardouin, G. de | 1152–*c.*1212 | chronicler |
| Hélinand de Froidmont | *c.*1160–after 1229 | trouvère |
| Jean Bodel | *c.*1165–*c.*1210 | trouvère |
| Gace Brulé | fl. 1180–1200 | trouvère |
| *Thèbes, Roman de* | mid 12th cent. | romance |
| Chrétien de Troyes | 12th cent. | poet |
| *Eneas, Roman d'* | 12th cent. | romance |
| *Troie, Roman de* | 12th cent. | romance |
| *Chansons de toile* | 12th–13th cent. | love-songs |
| *Grail, Cycle of the* | 12th–13th cent. | cycle of allegorical poems |
| *Renart, Roman de* | 12th–13th cent. | cycle of stories |
| *Alexandre, Roman d'* | 12th–14th cent. | romance |
| *Fabliaux* | 12th–14th cent. | verse tales |
| *Mystères* | 12th–16th cent. | religious plays |
| Clopinel, J. | early 13th cent. | poet |
| Guillaume de Lorris | early 13th cent. | poet |
| Jean de Meun(g) | early 13th cent. | poet |
| Jean Renart | fl. early 13th cent. | writer of romances |
| Robert de Clari | 13th cent. | Knight of Picardy, chronicler |
| *Rose, Roman de la* | 13th cent. | allegorical poem |
| *Miracles* | 13th–14th cent. | religious plays |
| Thibaut IV, Count of Champagne | 1201–53 | King of Navarre, trouvère |
| Gui de Coucy | died 1203 | poet |
| Joinville, J. Sire de | 1225–1317 | chronicler |
| Colin Muset | fl. 1230–50 | poet |
| Adam de la Halle | *c.*1240–*c.* 1288 | poet |

| | | |
|---|---|---|
| Rutebeuf | fl. 1250–80 | poet |
| Jean le Bel | *c.* 1290–1370 | chronicler |
| Guillaume de Machaut | *c.* 1300–1377 | musician, poet |
| Froissart, J. | 1337–*c.* 1404 | chronicler, poet, cleric, traveller |
| Deschamps, E. | 1346–*c.* 1406 | poet |
| Christine de Pisan | *c.* 1365–*c.* 1431 | poet, prose writer |
| Chartier, A. | *c.* 1390–*c.* 1440 | poet, prose writer |
| Charles d'Orléans | 1394–1465 | poet |
| Greban, A. and S. | early 15th cent. | poets |
| Villon, F. | 1431–after 1463 | poet |
| Commines, P. de | *c.* 1445–1511 | chronicler |
| Budé, G. | 1467–1540 | humanist |
| Lemaire de Belges, J. | 1473?–1515? | poet |
| Saint-Gelais, M. de | 1487–1558 | poet |
| Marguerite de Navarre | 1492–1549 | poet, dramatist, story writer |
| Rabelais, F. | 1494?–1533? | humanist |
| Marot, C. | 1496–1544 | poet |
| *Pathelin, La Farce de Maistre Pierre* | 15th cent. | farce |
| Crétin, G. | *c.* 1460–1525 | poet |
| Scève, M. | 1501?–1564? | poet |
| Des Périers, B. | *c.* 1510–44 | translator, poet, satirist, story writer |
| Amyot, J. | 1513–93 | translator |
| Desmasures, L. | 1515–74 | dramatist |
| Bèze, T. de | 1519–1605 | theologian, political writer, dramatist |
| Du Guillet, P. | 1520?–45 | poet |
| Du Bellay, J. | 1522–60 | poet |
| Labé, L. | 1524?–66 | poet |
| Ronsard, P. de | 1524–85 | poet |
| Belleau, R. | 1528?–77 | poet |
| La Boëtie, É. de | 1530–63 | translator, political writer |
| Estienne, H. II | *c.* 1531–98 | humanist |
| Baïf, J.-A. de | 1532–89 | scholar, poet |
| Jodelle, É. | *c.* 1532–73 | poet, dramatist |
| La Taille, J. de | 1533?–1608 | dramatist, pamphleteer, satirical poet |
| Montaigne, M. E. | 1533–92 | essayist |
| Rapin, N. | 1535?–1609? | lawyer, poet |
| Grévin, J. | 1538–70 | dramatist, poet, doctor |
| Rivaudeau, A. de | 1538?–80 | dramatist, poet |
| Brantôme, P. de B. de | 1540?–1614 | memorialist |
| Larivey, P. | 1540?–1611 | dramatist |
| Charron, P. | 1541–1603 | preacher, theologian |
| Du Bartas, G. de S. | 1544–90 | poet |

| | | |
|---|---|---|
| Garnier, R. | 1545–90 | dramatist |
| Desportes, P. | 1546–1606 | poet |
| La Ceppède, J. de | *c.*1548–1623? | poet |
| D'Aubigné, T. A. | 1552–1630 | poet, historian |
| Malherbe, F. de | 1555–1628 | poet, critic |
| Papillon de Lasphrise, M. de | 1555–99 | poet, soldier |
| Du Vair, G. | 1556–1621 | philosopher, statesman |
| Sponde, J. de | 1557–95 | poet |
| D'Urfé, H. | 1567–1625 | pastoral novelist |
| François de Sales, Saint | 1567–1622 | religious moralist |
| Chassignet, J.-B. | 1571 or 1578–1635? | poet |
| Régnier, M. | 1573–1613 | satirical poet |
| Montchrestien, A. de | 1575?–1621 | dramatist |
| Jansen, C. | 1585–1638 | theologian |
| Boisrobert, F. Le M. | 1589–1662 | dramatist |
| Viau, T. | 1590–1626 | poet |
| Saint-Amant, A. G. | 1594–1661 | poet |
| *Satire Ménippée, La* | 1594 | political pamphlet |
| Chapelain, J. | 1595–1674 | critic |
| Desmarets, J. | 1595–1676 | dramatist, novelist, epic writer |
| Descartes, R. | 1596–1650 | philosopher, mathematician |
| Balzac, J. L. G. de | 1597–1654 | man of letters |
| Voiture, V. | 1597–1648 | poet |
| Hardy, A. | ?–1632 | dramatist |
| Tristan | 1601?–55 | dramatist |
| Sorel, C. | 1602–74 | novelist |
| Aubignac, F. H., Abbé d' | 1604–76 | critic |
| Cotin, C. | 1604–82 | abbé, poet |
| Mairet, J. | 1604–86 | dramatist |
| Corneille, P. | 1606–84 | dramatist |
| Scudéry, M. de | 1608–1701 | novelist |
| Rotrou, J. de | 1609–50 | dramatist |
| Scarron, P. | 1610–60 | poet, wit |
| La Rochefoucauld, F., Duc de | 1613–80 | classical moralist |
| Retz, J. F. P. de G. | 1613–79 | biographer, memoir writer |
| Saint-Évremond, C. de St-D. | 1613–1703 | critic |
| Cyrano, S. de (Bergerac) | 1619–55 | dramatist, writer of philosophical fiction |
| Tallemant des Reaux, G. | 1619–92 | biographer |
| Lenclos, N. de | 1620–1705 | feminist, wit |
| La Fontaine, J. de | 1621–95 | scholar, poet |
| Molière | 1622–73 | dramatist |
| Pascal, B. | 1623–62 | mathematician, religious writer |
| Corneille, T. | 1625–1709 | dramatist, polymath |
| Sévigné, M. de R. C. | 1626–96 | letter writer |

| | | |
|---|---|---|
| Bossuet, J. B. | 1627–1704 | orator |
| Perrault, C. | 1628–1703 | poet, fairy-tale writer |
| Santeuil, C. de | 1628–84 | hymnist |
| Bourdaloue, L. | 1632–1704 | preacher |
| Fléchier, E. | 1632–1710 | professor turned preacher |
| La Fayette, M. M. de la V. | 1634–93 | novelist |
| Quinault, P. | 1635–88 | dramatist |
| Boileau, N. | 1636–1711 | poet, critic |
| Boursault, E. | 1638–1701 | dramatist, poet, journalist |
| Racine, J. | 1639–99 | dramatist |
| La Bruyère, J. de | 1645–96 | satirist |
| Bayle, P. | 1647–1706 | scholar, critic |
| Fénelon, F. de S. de la M. | 1651–1715 | religious author, epic writer |
| Regnard, J.-F. | 1655–1709 | dramatist |
| Fontenelle, B. Le B. | 1657–1757 | scientific thinker, man of letters |
| Lesage, A.-R. | 1668–1747 | novelist, dramatist |
| Rousseau, J.-B. | 1671–1741 | poet |
| Houdar de La Motte, A. | 1672–1731 | critic, poet, dramatist |
| Crébillon (père), P. J. de | 1674–1762 | dramatist |
| Saint-Simon, L. de R. | 1675–1755 | memoir writer |
| Destouches, P. N. | 1680–1754 | dramatist |
| Desfontaines, P. F. G. | 1685–1745 | journalist, publicist |
| Marivaux, P. C. de C. de | 1688–1763 | dramatist, novelist |
| Montesquieu, C.-L. de S. | 1689–1755 | political thinker, satirist |
| Piron, A. | 1689–1773 | dramatist, poet |
| La Chaussée, N. de | 1692–1754 | dramatist |
| Voltaire | 1694–1778 | dramatist, poet, novelist, philosopher |
| Prévost d'Exiles, A.-F. | 1697–1763 | novelist, journalist |
| Duclos, C. P. | 1704–72 | moralist, historian, novelist |
| Buffon, G.-L. L., Comte de | 1707–88 | scientific author, stylist |
| Crébillon (fils), C.-P. J. de | 1707–77 | novelist |
| Gresset, J.-B.-L. | 1709–77 | poet, dramatist |
| Rousseau, J.-J. | 1712–78 | Swiss novelist, philosopher |
| Diderot, D. | 1713–84 | dramatist, publicist, novelist, philosopher |
| Condillac, É. B. | 1714–80 | philosopher |
| Helvétius, C.-A. | 1715–71 | philosopher |
| Vauvenargues, L. de C. | 1715–47 | moralist |
| Saint-Lambert, J.-F. | 1716–1803 | poet |
| Alembert, J. Le Rond d' | 1717–83 | scientist, man of letters |
| Fréron, É.-C. | 1718–76 | journalist, critic |
| Sedaine, M.-J. | 1719–97 | dramatist |
| Grimm, F. M. | 1723–1807 | journalist, critic |
| Holbach, P. H. D. | 1723–89 | philosopher, publicist |
| Marmontel, J.-F. | 1723–99 | story writer, memoir writer |

| | | |
|---|---|---|
| Beaumarchais, P.-A. C. de | 1732–99 | dramatist, publicist |
| Restif, N.-A.-E. | 1734–1806 | novelist, prose writer |
| Bernardin de Saint-Pierre, J.-H. | 1737–1814 | naturalist, novelist |
| Delille, J. | 1738–1813 | poet, translator, Academician |
| Mercier, L. S. | 1740–1814 | journalist, dramatist |
| Sade, D. A. F. | 1740–1814 | novelist |
| Chamfort, S.-R. N. | 1741–94 | moralist, publicist |
| Laclos, P.-A.-F. C. de | 1741–1803 | novelist |
| Léonard, N.-G. | 1744–93 | poet |
| Gilbert, N.-J.-L. | 1751–80 | poet |
| Parny, É.-D. de F. | 1753–1814 | poet |
| Rivarol, A. R. | 1753–1801 | satirist, polemical journalist |
| Fontanes, L., Marquis de | 1757–1821 | poet |
| Chénier, A.-M. | 1762–94 | poet |
| Chénier, M.-J.-B. | 1764–1811 | dramatist, poet |
| Staël, A.-L.-.G. N. Mme de | 1766–1817 | novelist, literary theorist |
| Constant, B. | 1767–1830 | novelist |
| Chateaubriand, Vicomte F.-R. de | 1768–1848 | novelist, religious and historical writer |
| Chênedollé, C.-J. de | 1769–1833 | poet |
| Picard, L.-B. | 1769–1828 | actor-manager, dramatist |
| Sénancour, É. P. de | 1770–1846 | novelist |
| Courier, P.-L. | 1772–1825 | pamphleteer, scholar |
| Pixerécourt, G. de | 1773–1844 | dramatist |
| Béranger, P.-J. de | 1780–1857 | poet |
| Nodier, C. | 1780–1844 | novelist, journalist |
| Stendhal | 1783–1842 | novelist |
| Desbordes-Valmore, M. | 1786–1859 | poet |
| Lamartine, A. M. L. P. de | 1790–1869 | poet, statesman |
| Scribe, E. | 1791–1861 | dramatist |
| Deschamps, É. | 1791–1871 | poet |
| Kock, C. P. de | 1793–1871 | novelist |
| Vigny, A. V. de | 1797–1863 | poet |
| Balzac, H. de | 1799–1850 | novelist |
| Monnier, H. | 1799–1877 | author, actor, caricaturist |
| Deschamps, A. | 1800–1869 | poet |
| Littré, É. | 1801–81 | lexicographer |
| Dumas, A. (père) | 1802–70 | novelist, dramatist |
| Hugo, V. M. | 1802–85 | poet, dramatist, novelist |
| Mérimée, P. | 1803–70 | novelist |
| Sainte-Beuve, C. A. | 1804–69 | poet, critic, novelist |
| Sand, G. | 1804–76 | novelist |
| Sue, E. | 1804–57 | novelist |
| Barbier, A. | 1805–82 | poet, satirist |
| Bertrand, L. J. N. | 1807–41 | poet |

| | | |
|---|---|---|
| Barbey d'Aurevilly, J.-A. | 1808–89 | novelist, essayist, critic |
| Nerval, G. de | 1808–55 | poet, novelist |
| Borel D'Hauterive, P. | 1809–59 | poet, novelist, translator |
| Guérin, M. de | 1810–39 | poet |
| Moreau, H. | 1810–38 | poet |
| Musset, A. L. C. de | 1810–57 | dramatist, poet, novelist |
| Gautier, T. | 1811–72 | poet, novelist |
| O'Neddy, P. | 1811–75 | poet, story writer |
| Labiche, E. | 1815–88 | dramatist |
| Gobineau, J.-A. de | 1816–82 | diplomat, novelist, historian |
| Leconte de Lisle, C.-M.-R. | 1818–94 | poet |
| Augier, É. | 1820–89 | dramatist |
| Fromentin, E. | 1820–76 | novelist, artist, art critic |
| Baudelaire, C.-P. | 1821–67 | poet, critic |
| Champfleury | 1821–89 | novelist |
| Feuillet, O. | 1821–90 | novelist |
| Feydeau, E. | 1821–73 | novelist, stockbroker, archaeologist |
| Flaubert, G. | 1821–80 | novelist |
| Bouilhet, L.-H. | 1822–69 | poet, dramatist |
| Goncourt, E. | 1822–96 | novelist, journal writer |
| Menard, L. | 1822–1901 | poet |
| Murger, H. | 1822–61 | novelist |
| Banville, T. de | 1823–91 | poet |
| Barrière, T. | 1823–77 | dramatist |
| Renan, E. | 1823–92 | moralist, orientalist |
| Dumas, A. (fils) | 1824–95 | dramatist |
| About, E. | 1828–85 | journalist, novelist |
| Taine, H. A. | 1828–93 | critic, philosopher, historian |
| Verne, J. | 1828–1905 | adventure-story writer |
| Aubanel, T. | 1829–86 | poet |
| Goncourt, J. | 1830–70 | novelist, journal writer |
| Meilhac, H. | 1831–97 | dramatist, librettist |
| Sardou, V. | 1831–1908 | dramatist |
| Gaboriau, É. | 1832–73 | novelist |
| Vallès, J. | 1832–85 | journalist, novelist |
| Becque, H. | 1837–99 | dramatist |
| Sully-Prudhomme, R.-F.-A. | 1839–1907 | poet |
| Daudet, A. | 1840–97 | novelist |
| Villiers de l'Isle-Adam, P. H. | 1840–89 | poet, dramatist |
| Zola, É. | 1840–1902 | novelist |
| Coppée, F. | 1842–1908 | poet, dramatist |
| Cros, C. | 1842–88 | poet, inventor |
| Hérédia, J.-M. de | 1842–1905 | poet |
| Mallarmé, S. | 1842–98 | poet |
| Mendès, C. | 1841–1909 | poet, novelist, dramatist |

| | | |
|---|---|---|
| France, A. | 1844–1924 | novelist, essayist, critic |
| Verlaine, P. | 1844–96 | poet |
| Corbière, É. J. | 1845–75 | poet |
| Bloy, L. M. | 1846–1917 | novelist, religious thinker |
| Deroulède, P. | 1846–1914 | poet, politician |
| Lautréamont, so-called Comte de | 1846–70 | writer of prose poems |
| Faguet, É. | 1847–1916 | critic |
| Huysmans, G. C. | 1848–1907 | novelist |
| Brunetière, F. | 1849–1906 | critic |
| Loti, P. | 1850–1923 | novelist |
| Maupassant, G. de | 1850–93 | short-story writer, novelist |
| Bourget, P. | 1852–1935 | critic |
| Bourges, É. | 1852–1925 | novelist |
| Bazin, R. | 1853–1932 | novelist |
| Curel, F. de | 1854–1928 | dramatist |
| Rimbaud, A. | 1854–91 | poet |
| Moréas, J. | 1856–1910 | poet |
| Lanson, G. | 1857–1934 | critic |
| Brieux, E. | 1858–1932 | dramatist |
| Courteline, G. | 1858–1929 | dramatist |
| Gourmont, R. de | 1858–1915 | critic |
| Samain, A. | 1858–1900 | poet |
| Bergson, H. | 1859–1941 | philosopher |
| Donnay, M. | 1859–1945 | dramatist |
| Hennequin, É. | 1859–88 | critic |
| Kahn, G. | 1859–1936 | poet |
| Lavedan, H. | 1859–1940 | dramatist |
| Laforgue, J. | 1860–87 | poet |
| Barrès, M. | 1862–1923 | novelist, essayist |
| Feydeau, G. | 1862–1921 | dramatist |
| Merrill, S. | 1863–1915 | poet |
| Régnier, H. de | 1864–1936 | poet, novelist |
| Renard, J. | 1864–1910 | dramatist, novelist |
| Viélé-Griffin, F. | 1864–1937 | poet |
| Bremond, H. | 1865–1933 | literary historian, critic |
| Rolland, R. | 1866–1944 | novelist, dramatist, musicologist, biographer |
| Benda, J. | 1867–1956 | novelist, thinker |
| Schwob, M. | 1867–1905 | essayist, critic |
| Toulet, P.-J. | 1867–1920 | poet, novelist |
| Alain (Émile Chartier) | 1868–1951 | essayist, philosopher |
| Claudel, P. | 1868–1955 | dramatist, poet |
| Jammes, F. | 1868–1938 | poet |
| Maurras, C. | 1868–1952 | poet, critic, political philosopher, journalist |

| | | |
|---|---|---|
| Rostand, E. | 1868–1918 | dramatist |
| Fabre, É. | 1869–1955 | dramatist |
| Gide, A. | 1869–1951 | novelist, critic, diarist, dramatist |
| Proust, M. | 1871–1922 | novelist |
| Valéry, P. | 1871–1945 | poet, essayist, critic |
| Bataille, H. | 1872–1922 | dramatist |
| Fort, P. | 1872–1960 | poet |
| Léautaud, P. | 1872–1956 | diarist, man of letters |
| Barbusse, H. | 1873–1935 | novelist |
| Colette, S. G. | 1873–1954 | novelist |
| Jarry, A. | 1873–1907 | dramatist |
| Péguy, C. | 1873–1914 | poet, essayist |
| Klingsor, T | 1874– | poet, artist |
| Thibaudet, A. | 1874–1936 | critic |
| Ghéon, H. | 1875–1944 | poet, dramatist |
| Bouhélier, St-G. de | 1876–1947 | poet, dramatist |
| Bernstein, H. | 1876–1953 | dramatist |
| Fargue, L.-P. | 1876–1947 | poet |
| Jacob, M. | 1876–1944 | poet |
| Roussel, R. | 1877–1933 | novelist, dramatist |
| Segalen, V. | 1878–1919 | poet, novelist |
| Apollinaire, G. | 1880–1918 | poet, essayist, art critic |
| Hémon, L. | 1880–1913 | novelist |
| Larbaud, V.-N. | 1881–1957 | man of letters |
| Martin du Gard, R. | 1881–1958 | novelist, dramatist |
| Billy, A. | 1882– | writer, critic |
| Châteaubriant, A. de | 1882–1951 | novelist |
| Giraudoux, J. | 1882–1944 | novelist, dramatist, critic |
| Lenormand, H.-R. | 1882–1951 | dramatist |
| Du Bos, C. | 1883–1939 | critic |
| Amiel, D. | 1884– | dramatist |
| Bachelard, G. | 1884–1962 | philosopher, critic |
| Chardonne, J. | 1884–1968 | novelist, essayist |
| Duhamel, G. | 1884–1966 | novelist |
| Paulhan, J. | 1884–1968 | essayist, critic |
| Supervielle, J. | 1884–1960 | poet, novelist, dramatist |
| Guitry, S. | 1885–1957 | actor, dramatist |
| Mauriac, F. | 1885–1970 | poet, novelist, dramatist, biographer, critic |
| Maurois, A. | 1885–1967 | novelist, biographer, historian |
| Raynal, P. | 1885– | dramatist |
| Romains, J. | 1885– | poet, dramatist, novelist |
| Alain-Fournier | 1886–1914 | novelist |
| Carco, F. | 1886–1958 | poet, novelist |
| Rivière, J. | 1886–1925 | critic |
| Bourdet, E. | 1887–1945 | dramatist |

| | | |
|---|---|---|
| Jouve, P. J. | 1887– | poet |
| La Varende, Vicomte J. de | 1887–1959 | novelist, biographer |
| Perse, St-J. | 1887– | poet |
| Bernanos, G. | 1888–1948 | novelist, essayist |
| Bernard, J.-J. | 1888– | dramatist |
| Bosco, H. | 1888– | novelist |
| Jouhandeau, M. | 1888– | novelist |
| Cocteau, J. | 1889–1963 | dramatist, novelist, poet, critic |
| Marcel, G. | 1889–1964 | philosopher, dramatist, critic |
| Reverdy, P. | 1889–1960 | poet |
| Obey, A. | 1892– | dramatist, actor-manager |
| Drieu la Rochelle, P. | 1893–1945 | novelist, short-story writer, journalist, essayist |
| Barthes, R. | 1894– | critic |
| Céline, L.-F. | 1894–1961 | writer |
| Deval, J. | 1894– | dramatist |
| Éluard, P. | 1895–1952 | poet |
| Giono, J. | 1895–1970 | novelist |
| Pagnol, M. | 1895– | dramatist |
| Artaud, A. | 1896–1948 | actor, producer, theorist |
| Breton, A. | 1896–1966 | poet |
| Montherlant, H. de | 1896– | novelist, dramatist |
| Tzara, T. | 1896–1963 | poet |
| Aragon, L. | 1897– | poet, novelist, journalist |
| Sarment, J. | 1897– | dramatist |
| Arland, M. | 1899– | novelist, critic |
| Audiberti, J. | 1899–1965 | poet, dramatist, novelist |
| Péret, B. | 1899–1959 | poet |
| Ponge, F. | 1899– | poet, essayist |
| Salacrou, A. | 1899– | dramatist |
| Vitrac, R. | 1899–1952 | poet, dramatist |
| Chamson, A. | 1900– | novelist |
| Desnos, R. | 1900–1945 | poet |
| Green, J. | 1900– | novelist |
| Prévert, J. | 1900– | poet |
| Saint-Exupéry, A. de | 1900–1944 | novelist |
| Sarraute, N. | 20th cent. | novelist |
| Achard, M. | 1901– | dramatist |
| Malraux, A. | 1901– | novelist, journalist, philosopher |
| Aymé, M. | 1902–67 | novelist, dramatist, short-story writer |
| Chazal, M. de | 1902– | prose writer |
| Queneau, R. | 1903– | poet, novelist |
| Simenon, G. | 1903– | novelist |
| Tardieu, J. | 1903– | poet, dramatist |
| Mounier, E. | 1905–50 | journalist, religious thinker |

| | | |
|---|---|---|
| Sartre, J.-P. | 1905– | novelist, dramatist, philosopher |
| Beckett, S. | 1906– | novelist, dramatist, poet |
| Blanchot, M. | 1907– | critic |
| Char, R. | 1907– | poet |
| Peyrefitte, R. | 1907– | novelist |
| Roy, J. | 1907– | novelist, critic |
| Vailland, R. | 1907–65 | novelist |
| Adamov, A. | 1908–70 | dramatist |
| Beauvoir, S. de | 1908– | novelist, essayist |
| Daumal, R. | 1908–44 | poet, prose writer |
| Brasillach, R. | 1909–45 | novelist, political commentator, critic |
| Weil, S. | 1909–43 | essayist |
| Anouilh, J. | 1910– | dramatist |
| Genet, J. | 1910– | novelist, dramatist |
| Gracq, J. | 1910– | novelist, critic |
| Schehadé, G. | 1910– | dramatist |
| Vauthier, J. | 1910– | dramatist |
| Cayrol, J. | 1911– | poet, novelist |
| Estang, L. | 1911– | poet, novelist, critic |
| La Tour du Pin, P. de | 1911– | poet |
| Roussin, A. | 1911– | actor, dramatist |
| Troyat, H. | 1911– | novelist |
| Ionescu, E. | 1912– | dramatist |
| Camus, A. | 1913–60 | novelist, dramatist, journalist |
| Césaire, A. | 1913– | poet, dramatist |
| Marceau, F. | 1913– | novelist, essayist, dramatist |
| Simon, C. | 1913– | novelist |
| Duras, M. | 1914– | novelist |
| Poulet, G. | 1914– | critic |
| Bésus, R. | 1915– | novelist |
| Curtis, J.-L. | 1917– | novelist |
| Druon, M. | 1918– | novelist |
| Obaldia, R. de | 1918– | poet, novelist, dramatist |
| Vian, B. | 1920–59 | novelist, dramatist |
| Richard, J. P. | 1922– | critic |
| Robbe-Grillet, A. | 1922– | novelist |
| Bonnefoy, Y. | 1923– | poet, critic |
| Dubillard, R. | 1923– | dramatist |
| Gatti, A. | 1924– | dramatist, film-director |
| Pichette, H. | 1924– | poet, dramatist |
| Butor, M. | 1926– | novelist, critic |
| Weingarten, R. | 1926– | dramatist |
| Billetdoux, F. | 1927– | actor, dramatist |
| Arrabal, F. | 1932– | novelist, dramatist |
| Sagan, F. | 1935– | novelist |

## GALICIAN

See also article on **Galician Literature,** p. 297

| | | |
|---|---|---|
| Añón | 1812–78 | poet |
| Losada, B. | 1824–91 | poet |
| Vicetto, B. | 1824–78 | historian |
| Pondal, E. | 1835–1917 | poet |
| Carvajal, V. L. | 1849–1906 | poet |
| Curros Enríquez, M. | 1851–1908 | poet |
| Pulpeiro, M. L. | 1854–1912 | poet |
| Varela, A. N. | 1869–1947 | poet |
| Risco, V. | 1874–1963 | writer |
| Cabanillas, R. | 1876–1959 | writer |
| Castelao, A. R. | 1886–1950 | writer |
| Pedrayo, R. O. | 1888– | writer |

## GERMAN

LATIN writers, and AUSTRIAN, SWISS GERMAN and HUNGARIAN authors writing in German are listed separately under each of these headings

See also articles on **Activism,** p. 32; **Biedermeier,** p. 113; **Bildungsroman,** p. 114; **Fastnachtspiel,** p. 263; **Gruppe 47,** p. 337; **(Das) Junge Deutschland,** p. 410; **Meistersinger,** p. 525; **Minnesinger,** p. 538; **'Sturm und Drang',** p. 748

| | | |
|---|---|---|
| *Hildebrandslied* | 8th cent. | fragmentary poem |
| Otfrid | *c.*800–*c.*870 | religious versifier |
| *Heliand* | 9th cent. | epic poem in Old Saxon |
| *Ludwigslied* | 9th cent. | Old High German poem |
| *Muspilli* | 9th cent. | Old High German poem |
| *Petruslied* | 9th cent. | Old High German hymn |
| *De Heinrico* | 10th cent. | epic poem |
| *Georgslied* | 10th cent. | Old High German poem |
| Notker III, L. | died 1022 | Benedictine teacher, scholar |
| *Annolied* | 11th–12th cent. | narrative poem |
| *Ezzos Gesang* (*Ezzolied*) | 11th cent. | strophic hymn |
| Lamprecht (Pfaffe Lamprecht) | fl.1120 | poet, churchman |
| Veldeke, H. van | *c.*1145–*c.*1200 | poet |
| Konrad (Pfaffe Konrad) | mid 12th cent. | versifier |
| Kürenberg | fl. mid 12th cent. | Minnesinger |
| Dietmar von Aist | fl. *c.*1170 | Minnesinger |
| Friedrich von Hausen | fl. 1170–90 | Minnesinger |
| Reinmar der Alte | *c.*1170–? | Minnesinger |
| Walther von der Vogelweide | *c.*1170–*c.*1230 | poet |
| Eilhart von Oberg | fl. *c.*1180 | epic poet |
| Neidhart von Reuenthal | *c.*1180–*c.*1250 | Minnesinger |

| | | |
|---|---|---|
| Hartmann von Aue | fl. 1190–1210 | epic and lyric poet |
| Friedrich von Sonnenburg | fl. late 12th cent. | lyric poet |
| *Herzog Ernst* | 12th cent. | epic poem |
| *Rother, König* | 12th cent. | epic poem |
| Konrad von Würzburg | died 1287 | epic and lyric poet |
| *Nibelungenlied* | *c.* 1200 | heroic epic |
| Heinrich von Morungen | fl. *c.* 1200 | Minnesinger |
| Reinmar von Zweter | *c.* 1200–*c.* 1250 | moral and didactic poet |
| Albrecht von Halberstadt | fl. early 13th cent. | epic poet |
| Wolfram von Eschenbach | fl. early 13th cent. | poet |
| Wirnt von Grafenberg | fl. 1204–10 | epic poet |
| Gottfried von Strassburg | fl. 1210 | poet |
| Stricker (Der) | fl. 1215–50 | poet |
| Rudolf von Ems | fl. 1220–50 | epic poet |
| Hugo von Trimberg | *c.* 1230–*c.* 1313 | didactic poet |
| Werner der Gärtner | fl. 1250–80 | poet |
| Gottfried von Neifen | fl. mid 13th cent. | Minnesinger |
| Marner, Der | fl. mid 13th cent. | poet |
| Tannhäuser | fl. mid 13th cent. | lyric poet |
| Ulrich von Winterstetten | fl. mid 13th cent. | Minnesinger |
| Eckhart, J. | *c.* 1260–1327 | mystic philosopher |
| Albrecht von Scharfenberg | fl. *c.* 1270 | poet |
| Heinrich von Freiberg | fl. *c.* 1280 | epic poet |
| Seifried Helbling | 13th cent. | poet (ascribed name) |
| *Eckenlied* | 13th cent. | heroic poem |
| *Rosengarten* | 13th cent. | Middle High German strophic epic |
| *Sängerkrieg auf der Wartburg* | mid 13th cent. | narrative poem |
| *Karlmeinet* | *c.* 1300 | epic poem |
| Heinrich von Meissen | died 1318 | lyric poet |
| Johannes von Tepl | *c.* 1355–*c.* 1414 | religious prose writer |
| Hugo von Montfort | 1357–1423 | lyric poet |
| Behaim, M. | 1416–74 | poet |
| Reuchlin, J. | 1455–1522 | humanist, translator, dramatist |
| Brant, S. | 1457–1521 | poet, satirist |
| Murner, T. | 1475–1537 | satirist |
| Luther, M. | 1483–1546 | theologian, translator, hymn writer |
| Hutten, U. von | 1488–1523 | humanist, translator, poet |
| Agricola, J. | *c.* 1494–1566 | theologian, compiler |
| Paracelsus | 1493–1541 | medical and religious writer |
| Sachs, H. | 1494–1576 | poet, dramatist |
| Melanchthon, P. | 1497-1560 | humanist |
| Franck, S. | 1499–1542 | religious writer, translator, compiler |
| Folz, H. | fl. late 15th cent. | Meistersinger |

| | | |
|---|---|---|
| Wickram, G. | 1505–*c.*1562 | novelist |
| Naogeorg, T. | 1511–63 | dramatist |
| Scheidt, K. | *c.*1520–65 | satirist |
| Ayrer, J. | *c.*1543–1605 | dramatist |
| Rollenhagen, G. | 1542–1609 | dramatist, mock-epic writer |
| Fischart, J. | 1547–90 | poet, satirist |
| Frischlin, N. | 1547–90 | dramatist |
| Albertinus, Ä. | *c.*1560–1620 | translator, adapter |
| Böhme, J. | 1575–1624 | philosopher |
| Bidermann, J. | 1578–1639 | Jesuit dramatist, poet |
| Spee, F. von | 1591–1635 | poet |
| Opitz, M. | 1597–1639 | poet |
| Moscherosch, J. M. | 1601–69 | satirist |
| Logau, F. von | 1604–55 | poet |
| Dach, S. | 1605–59 | poet |
| Gerhardt, P. | 1607–76 | poet |
| Harsdörffer, G. P. | 1607–58 | poet |
| Rist, J. | 1607–67 | poet |
| Fleming, P. | 1609–40 | poet |
| Gryphius, A. | 1616–64 | poet, dramatist |
| Klaj, J. | 1616–56 | poet |
| Hofmann von Hofmannswaldau, C. | 1617–79 | poet |
| Zesen, P. von | 1619–89 | poet, novelist |
| Angelus Silesius | 1624–77 | poet |
| Grimmelshausen, J. J. C. von | 1625?–76 | novelist |
| Stieler, K. | 1632–1707 | poet |
| Lohenstein, D. C. von | 1635–83 | dramatist |
| Weise, C. | 1642–1708 | novelist, poet, dramatist |
| Abraham à Sancta Clara | 1644–1709 | religious writer |
| Kuhlmann, Q. | 1651–89 | poet |
| Beer, J. | 1655–1700 | novelist |
| Ziegler und Kliphausen, H. A. von | 1663–96 | novelist |
| Reuter, C. | 1665–after 1712 | dramatist |
| Brockes, B. H. | 1680–1747 | poet |
| Schnabel, J. G. | 1692–1752 | novelist |
| Günther, J. C. | 1695–1723 | poet |
| Gottsched, J. C. | 1700–1766 | critic |
| Hagedorn, F. von | 1708–54 | poet |
| Gellert, C. F. | 1715–69 | poet, novelist |
| Kleist, E. C. von | 1715–59 | poet |
| Winckelmann, J. J. | 1717–68 | art historian |
| Schlegel, J. E. | 1718–49 | dramatist |
| Gleim, J. W. L. | 1719–1803 | poet |
| Möser, J. | 1720–94 | historian |

| | | |
|---|---|---|
| Uz, J. P. | 1720–96 | poet |
| Götz, J. N. | 1721–81 | poet |
| Kant, I. | 1724–1804 | philosopher |
| Klopstock, F. G. | 1724–1803 | poet |
| Ramler, K. W. | 1725–98 | poet |
| Weisse, C. F. | 1726–1804 | dramatist |
| Lessing, G. E. | 1729–81 | dramatist, critic, religious essayist |
| Hamann, J. G. | 1730–88 | religious thinker, literary theorist |
| Cronegk, J. F. von | 1731–58 | dramatist |
| La Roche, S. von | 1731–1807 | novelist |
| Nicolai, C. F. | 1733–1811 | critic, novelist |
| Wieland, C. M. | 1733–1813 | novelist, poet |
| Gerstenberg, H. W. von | 1737–1823 | critic, poet, dramatist |
| Claudius, M. | 1740–1815 | journalist, poet |
| Jacobi, J. G. | 1740–1814 | journalist, poet |
| Jung-Stilling, J. H. | 1740–1817 | autobiographical writer, novelist |
| Lichtenberg, G. C. | 1742–99 | diarist, aphorist |
| Herder, J. G. | 1744–1803 | philosopher, historical writer, critic |
| Heinse, J. J. W. | 1746–1803 | novelist |
| Bürger, G. A. | 1747–94 | poet |
| Hölty, L. C. H. | 1748–76 | poet |
| Goethe, J. W. von | 1749–1832 | poet, dramatist, novelist, thinker |
| Lenz, J. M. R. | 1751–92 | dramatist |
| Voss, J. H. | 1751–1826 | poet |
| Klinger, F. M. | 1752–1831 | dramatist |
| Leisewitz, J. A. | 1752–1806 | dramatist |
| Iffland, A. W. | 1759–1814 | dramatist |
| Schiller, F. | 1759–1805 | dramatist, poet, literary theorist |
| Hebel, J. P. | 1760–1826 | writer |
| Kotzebue, A. von | 1761–1819 | dramatist |
| Fichte, J. G. | 1762–1814 | philosopher |
| Jean Paul | 1763–1825 | novelist |
| Humboldt, W. von | 1767–1835 | philologist, literary and political theorist |
| Schlegel, A. W. von | 1767–1845 | poet, critic, scholar |
| Humboldt, A. von | 1769–1859 | scientist, travel writer |
| Hegel, G. W. F. | 1770–1831 | philosopher |
| Hölderlin, F. | 1770–1843 | poet |
| Zschokke, H. | 1771–1848 | novelist, historical and religious writer |
| Novalis | 1772–1801 | poet, novelist |
| Schlegel, K. W. F. von | 1772–1829 | poet, novelist, thinker |
| Tieck, L. | 1773–1853 | poet, novelist, dramatist |

| | | |
|---|---|---|
| Wackenroder, W. H. | 1773–98 | poet, novelist |
| Schelling, F. W. J. von | 1775–1854 | philosopher |
| Hoffmann, E. T. W. | 1776–1822 | novelist, composer |
| Fouqué, F. F. de la M. | 1777–1843 | novelist, dramatist |
| Kleist, H. von | 1777–1811 | dramatist, story writer |
| Brentano, C. | 1778–1842 | poet, novelist, dramatist |
| Arnim, L. J. von | 1781–1831 | poet, dramatist, novelist |
| Chamisso, A. von | 1781–1838 | poet, story writer |
| Arnim, B. von | 1785–1859 | letter-writer, essayist |
| Grimm, J. L. | 1785–1863 | philologist, literary scholar |
| Pückler-Muskau, Fürst H. L. H. von | 1785–1871 | memoir writer |
| Varnhagen von Ense, K. A. | 1785–1858 | diarist, biographer |
| Grimm, W. K. | 1786–1859 | philologist, literary scholar |
| Uhland, L. | 1787–1862 | poet |
| Eichendorff, J. F. von | 1788–1857 | lyric poet, novelist |
| Rückert, F. | 1788–1866 | poet |
| Schopenhauer, A. | 1788–1860 | philosopher |
| Müller, W. | 1794–1827 | poet |
| Immermann, K. L. | 1796–1840 | novelist, dramatist |
| Platen, A. Graf von P. Hallermund, | 1796–1835 | poet, dramatist |
| Droste-Hülshoff, A. von | 1797–1848 | poet, novelist |
| Heine, H. | 1797–1856 | poet, journalist, essayist |
| Hoffmann von Fallersleben, A. H. | 1798–1874 | poet |
| Grabbe, C. D. | 1801–36 | dramatist |
| Hauff, W. | 1802–27 | novelist, *Märchen* writer |
| Lenau, N. | 1802–50 | poet |
| Feuerbach, L. A. | 1804–72 | philosopher |
| Mörike, E. | 1804–75 | poet |
| Gervinus, G. G. | 1805–71 | literary historian |
| Laube, H. | 1806–84 | dramatist, novelist |
| Vischer, F. T. | 1807–87 | writer on aesthetics |
| Freiligrath, H. F. | 1810–76 | poet |
| Gutzkow, K. F. | 1811–78 | dramatist, novelist, journalist |
| Büchner, G. | 1813–37 | dramatist |
| Hebbel, C. F. | 1813–63 | dramatist |
| Ludwig, O. | 1813–65 | dramatist, novelist |
| Wagner, R. | 1813–83 | composer, poet |
| Geibel, E. | 1815–84 | poet |
| Freytag, G. | 1816–95 | novelist, dramatist |
| Herwegh, G. | 1817–75 | poet |
| Storm, T. | 1817–88 | novelist, poet |
| Fontane, T. | 1819–98 | novelist |
| Weerth, G. | 1822–56 | poet, essayist |

| | | |
|---|---|---|
| Scheffel, J. V. von | 1826–86 | poet, novelist |
| Spielhagen, F. | 1829–1911 | novelist |
| Heyse, P. | 1830–1914 | story writer, novelist |
| Raabe, W. | 1831–1910 | novelist |
| Busch, W. | 1832–1908 | artist, 'nonsense'-writer |
| Dilthey, W. | 1833–1911 | philosopher |
| Liliencron, D. von | 1844–1909 | poet |
| Nietzsche, F. | 1844–1900 | philosopher, poet |
| Sudermann, H. | 1857–1928 | dramatist, novelist |
| Hauptmann, G. | 1862–1946 | dramatist, novelist, poet |
| Dehmel, R. | 1863–1920 | poet |
| Holz, A. | 1863–1929 | poet, dramatist |
| Huch, R. | 1864–1947 | novelist, poet, critic |
| Wedekind, F. | 1864–1918 | dramatist |
| Bierbaum, O. J. | 1865–1910 | poet, novelist |
| Halbe, M. | 1865–1944 | dramatist |
| Ernst, P. | 1866–1933 | critic, dramatist, poet |
| Dauthendey, M. | 1867–1918 | poet, novelist |
| George, S. | 1868–1933 | poet |
| Kerr, A. | 1868–1948 | critic |
| Barlach, E. | 1870–1938 | dramatist |
| Mann, H. | 1871–1950 | novelist |
| Morgenstern, C. | 1871–1914 | poet-philosopher |
| Mombert, A. | 1872–1942 | poet |
| Kassner, R. | 1873–1959 | philosopher, critic |
| Wasserman, J. | 1873–1934 | novelist |
| Cassirer, E. | 1874–1945 | philosopher |
| Stramm, A. | 1874–1915 | poet, dramatist |
| Mann, T. | 1875–1955 | novelist |
| Lasker-Schüler, E. | 1876–1945 | poet |
| Le Fort, G. von | 1876– | novelist, poet |
| Däubler, T. | 1876–1934 | poet |
| Borchardt, R. | 1877–1945 | poet, essayist, translator |
| Hesse, H. | 1877–1962 | novelist, poet |
| Carossa, H. | 1878–1956 | novelist |
| Döblin, A. | 1878–1957 | novelist |
| Kaiser, G. | 1878–1945 | dramatist |
| Mühsam, E. | 1878–1934 | poet, dramatist, satirist |
| Schröder, R. A. | 1878–1962 | poet, translator |
| Sternheim, C. | 1878–1942 | dramatist |
| Walden, H. | 1878–? | author, art critic |
| Keyserling, H. A. Graf | 1880–1946 | philosopher |
| Weiss, K. | 1880–1940 | poet |
| Zech, P. | 1881–1946 | poet, novelist, dramatist |
| Frank, L. | 1882–1961 | novelist, dramatist |
| Lehmann, W. | 1882–1968 | poet, critic, novelist |

| | | |
|---|---|---|
| Ringelnatz, J. | 1883–1934 | poet, painter, prose writer |
| Stadler, E. | 1883–1914 | poet |
| Brod, M. | 1884–1968 | novelist |
| Feuchtwanger, L. | 1884–1958 | novelist, dramatist |
| Hoddis, J. von | 1884–1942 | poet |
| Loerke, O. | 1884–1941 | poet |
| Hiller, K. | 1885– | publisher, critic, essayist |
| Kisch, E. E. | 1885–1948 | novelist, journalist |
| Schickele, R. | 1885–1940 | poet, novelist, dramatist |
| Seidel, I. | 1885– | novelist, poet |
| Unruh, F. von | 1885– | dramatist |
| Ball, H. | 1886–1927 | poet, dramatist, critic |
| Benn, G. | 1886–1956 | poet |
| Herrmann-Neisse, M. | 1886–1941 | poet |
| Arp, H. | 1887–1966 | poet, sculptor |
| Heym, G. | 1887–1912 | poet |
| Ossietzky, C. von | 1887–1938 | journalist |
| Schwitters, K. | 1887–1941 | poet, artist |
| Wiechert, E. | 1887–1950 | novelist |
| Zweig, A. | 1887–1968 | novelist, essayist |
| Lichtenstein, A. | 1889–1914 | poet |
| Renn, L. | 1889– | novelist |
| Edschmid, K. | 1890–1966 | novelist, essayist |
| Hasenclever, W. | 1890–1940 | dramatist, poet |
| Klabund | 1890–1928 | poet, fiction writer |
| Tucholsky, K. | 1890–1935 | satirist, journalist |
| Weinert, E. | 1890–1953 | poet, essayist |
| Becher, J. R. | 1891–1958 | poet, novelist, critic |
| Britting, G. | 1891–1964 | poet, story writer |
| Goll, I. | 1891–1950 | poet, experimental dramatist |
| Sachs, N. | 1891–1970 | poet |
| Benjamin, W. | 1892–1940 | essayist |
| Bergengruen, W. | 1892–1962 | novelist, poet |
| Plievier, T. | 1892–1955 | novelist |
| Schnack, A. | 1892– | poet |
| Sorge, R. J. | 1892–1916 | poet, dramatist |
| Fallada, H. | 1893–1947 | novelist |
| Toller, E. | 1893–1939 | dramatist |
| Graf, O. M. | 1894–1967 | novelist |
| Jahnn, H. H. | 1894–1959 | novelist, dramatist |
| Kolmar, G. | 1894–1943 | poet |
| Jünger, E. | 1895– | essayist, novelist |
| Kasack, H. | 1896–1966 | novelist, critic, poet |
| Mehring, W. | 1896– | poet, dramatist |
| Zuckmayer, C. | 1896– | dramatist, poet |
| Bamm, P. | 1897– | novelist |

| | | |
|---|---|---|
| Brecht, B. | 1898–1956 | poet, dramatist |
| Jünger, F. G. | 1898– | poet, essayist, fiction writer |
| Remarque, E. M. | 1898–1970 | novelist |
| Kästner, E. | 1899– | satirist |
| Lampe, F. | 1899–1945 | short-story writer |
| Langgässer, E. | 1899–1950 | poet and novelist |
| Traven, B. | 20th cent. | novelist |
| Kesten, H. | 1900– | novelist |
| Seghers, A. | 1900– | novelist |
| Kaschnitz, M. L. | 1901– | poet, story writer |
| Nossack, H. E. | 1901– | poet, novelist |
| Haushofer, A. | 1903–45 | poet |
| Huchel, P. | 1903– | poet |
| Andres, S. | 1906– | novelist, dramatist |
| Eich, G. | 1907– | poet, radio playwright |
| Gaiser, G. | 1908– | novelist |
| Goes, A. | 1908– | poet, novelist |
| Richter, H. W. | 1908– | novelist |
| Schaper, E. | 1908– | novelist |
| Steiner, F. B. | 1909–52 | poet, scholar |
| Hagelstange, R. | 1912– | poet |
| Kaléko, M. | 1912– | poet |
| Strittmatter, E. | 1912– | novelist, dramatist |
| Winkler, E. G. | 1912–36 | poet, essayist |
| Heym, S. | 1913– | novelist, journalist |
| Holthusen, H. E. | 1913– | poet, critic |
| Andersch, A. | 1914– | novelist, short-story writer |
| Hartlaub, G. | 1915– | novelist |
| Hermlin, S. | 1915– | poet |
| Krolov, K. | 1915– | poet, critic |
| Hildesheimer, W. | 1916– | writer |
| Weiss, P. | 1916– | novelist, dramatist |
| Bobrowski, J. | 1917–65 | poet |
| Böll, H. | 1917– | novelist, story writer, radio playwright |
| Celan, P. | 1920–70 | poet |
| Schnurre, W. | 1920– | poet, story writer |
| Borchert, W. | 1921–47 | story writer, dramatist, poet |
| Heissenbüttel, H. | 1921– | poet |
| Höllerer, W. | 1922– | poet, essayist |
| Jens, W. | 1923– | novelist, critic |
| Piontek, H. | 1925– | poet, critic |
| Grass, G. | 1927– | poet, novelist |
| Lind, J. | 1927– | novelist |
| Walser, M. | 1927– | writer, radio producer |
| Hacks, P. | 1928– | dramatist |

| | | |
|---|---|---|
| Enzensberger, H. M. | 1929– | poet, critic |
| Hochhuth, R. | 1931– | dramatist |
| Johnson, U. | 1934– | novelist |
| Meckel, C. | 1935– | poet, artist |

## GREEK

See also article on **Prodromic Poems**, p. 626

| | | |
|---|---|---|
| Digenis Akrites Basileios | 10th cent. | legendary hero of Byzantium |
| Prodromic Poems | 12th cent. | Byzantine satirical and begging poems |
| Maksim the Greek | *c.* 1470–1556 | religious writer |
| Hortatzis, G. | fl. end of 16th cent. | poet |
| *Erotokritos* | 17th cent. | narrative poem |
| Korais, A. | 1748–1833 | scholar, patriot |
| Kalvos, A. | 1792–1869 | poet |
| Solomos, D. | 1798–1857 | poet |
| Valaoritis, A. | 1824–79 | poet |
| Roidis, E. | 1835–1904 | critic, short-story writer, novelist |
| Papadiamantis, A. | 1851–1911 | short-story writer, novelist |
| Psycharis, Y. | 1854–1929 | scholar and novelist |
| Palamas, K. | 1859–1943 | poet |
| Cavafy (Kavafis), C. P. | 1863–1933 | poet |
| Sikelianos, A. | 1884–1951 | poet |
| Kazantzakis, N. | 1885–1957 | novelist, poet, dramatist, traveller |
| Myrivilis, S. | 1892– | novelist, short-story writer |
| Papatsonis, T. | 1895– | poet |
| Seferis, G. | 1900– | poet |
| Embirikos, A. | 1901– | poet |
| Venezis, I. | 1904– | novelist, short-story writer |
| Theotokas, G. | 1906–66 | novelist, essayist, dramatist |
| Prevelakis, P. | 1909– | novelist, poet, dramatist, art critic |
| Ritsos, Y. | 1909– | poet |
| Capetanakis, D. | 1912–44 | poet, critic |
| Elytis, O. | 1912– | poet |
| Valaoritis, N. | 1921– | poet |

## HEBREW

| | | |
|---|---|---|
| Samuel Ha-Nagid | 993–1055 | poet |
| Alfasi, I. B. J. | 1013–1103 | poet, religious writer |
| Gabirol, S. B. J. | *c.* 1020–*c.* 1057 | poet, philosopher |
| Rashi | 1040–1105 | poet, religious writer |

| | | |
|---|---|---|
| Ibn Ezra, M. | 1060–1139 | poet, literary critic |
| Judah ben Samuel Ha-levi | *c.* 1080–after 1143 | poet, philosopher |
| Ibn Ezra, A. B. M. | 1092–1167 | poet, grammarian, scientific and religious writer |
| Maimonides | 1135–1204 | religious writer |
| Benjamin of Tudela | fl. *c.* 1160–73 | travel writer |
| Al-Harizi (Alcharisi), J. B. S. | *c.* 1165–1235 | poet |
| Nachmanides | 1194–*c.* 1270 | religious writer, poet |
| Ibn Hasdai, A. | died 1240 | writer, liturgical poet |
| Abulafia, T. | 1247–*c.* 1303 | poet |
| Kalonymos ben Kalonymos | 1286–1322 | writer, scholar |
| Gersonides, L. ben G. | 1288–1344 | philosopher, scientific writer |
| Aboab, I. | *c.* 1300 | ethical writer |
| Crescas, H. | 1340–1410 | philosopher |
| Albo, J. | *c.* 1380–1444 | philosopher |
| Rieti, Moses di | 1388–*c.* 1460 | poet, historian |
| Abravanel (Abarbanel), I. | 1437–1508 | philosophic writer |
| Abravanel (Abarbanel), J. | *c.* 1460–before 1535 | philosophic writer |
| Modena, J. A. | 1571–1648 | poet, religious writer |
| Zakuto, M. | 1625–97 | dramatist, poet, mystic |
| Luzzatto, M. C. | 1707–47 | poet, mystic, scholar |
| Nachman of Bratzlav | 1770–1811 | Hebrew and Yiddish writer |
| Hacohen, S. | 1772–1845 | poet, dramatist |
| Kronchmal, N. | 1785–1840 | philosopher |
| Morpurgo, R. | 1790–1871 | poet |
| Luzzatto, S. D. | 1800–1865 | writer (also wrote in Italian) |
| Mapu, A. | 1808–67 | novelist |
| Boreman, Y. | 1825–90 | novelist |
| Lebenson, M. J. | 1828–54 | poet, scholar |
| Gordon, Y. L. | 1830–92 | novelist, poet, essayist |
| Mendele Mocher Seforim | 1835–1917 | Hebrew and Yiddish novelist, story writer |
| Smolenskin, P. | 1842–85 | journalist, novelist |
| Lilienblum, M. L. | 1843–1910 | poet, essayist, scholar |
| Katznelson, J. L. | 1847–1917 | poet, story writer |
| Yawitz, Z. W. | 1847–1924 | historian, writer of documentary sketches |
| Peretz, I. L. | 1851–1915 | poet |
| Ahad Ha-am | 1856–1927 | philosopher, essayist |
| Dolitzki, M. M. | 1856–1931 | Hebrew and Yiddish poet, novelist |
| Imber, N. H. | 1856–1902 | poet |
| Levinski, E. L. | 1857–1910 | publicist, novelist |
| Ben Yehuda, E. | 1858–1922 | scholar, essayist, editor |
| Sokolov, N. | 1860–1936 | critic, biographer |
| Mane, M. Z. | 1860–87 | poet, essayist |

| | | |
|---|---|---|
| Steinberg, J. | 1861–1908 | story writer |
| Brainin, R. | 1862–1939 | biographer, story writer |
| Frishman, D. | 1862–1922 | short-story writer |
| Berdichewski, M. J. | 1865–1921 | novelist, essayist, philosopher |
| Ben Avigdor | 1866–1921 | novelist, story writer |
| Goldin, E. | 1867–1915 | novelist, story writer |
| Ben-Zion, S. | 1870–1932 | story writer |
| Druyanov, A. | 1870–1938 | essayist, historian, folklorist, editor |
| Bershadsky, I. | 1872–1910 | novelist |
| Bialik, H. N. | 1873–1934 | poet |
| Tchernichowski, S. | 1873–1943 | poet |
| Feirberg, M. Z. | 1874–99 | short-story writer |
| Brenner, J. H. | 1881–1921 | novelist |
| Fichman, Y. | 1881–1918 | literary critic, poet |
| Kabak, A. A. | 1882–1944 | novelist |
| Berkowitz, Y. D. | 1885–1967 | novelist, dramatist |
| Hameiri, A. | 1886–1970 | poet |
| Agnon, S. Y. | 1888–1970 | novelist, short-story writer |
| Barash, A. | 1889–1952 | novelist, short-story writer |
| Bluvstein, R. | 1890–1931 | poet |
| Greenberg, U. Z. | 1891– | essayist |
| Steinman, E. | 1892–1970 | novelist, short-story writer |
| Shlonsky, A. | 1900– | poet |

## HUNGARIAN

See also articles on **Early Hungarian Literature,** p. 242, for pre-16th-century authors; **'Nyugat' ('The West'),** p. 575

| | | |
|---|---|---|
| Balassa, B. | 1554–94 | poet |
| Pázmány, P. | 1570–1637 | religious writer |
| Zrinyi, M. | 1620–64 | poet |
| Mikes, K. | 1690–1761 | travel writer |
| Kazinczy, F. | 1759–1831 | critic, translator, language reformer |
| Fazekas, M. | 1766–1828 | poet, botanist |
| Kisfaludy, S. | 1772–1844 | poet |
| Csokonai-Vitéz, M. | 1773–1805 | poet |
| Berzsenyi, D. | 1776–1836 | poet |
| Kisfaludy, K. | 1788–1830 | poet, dramatist |
| Kölcsey, F. | 1790–1838 | poet, essayist |
| Katona, J. | 1791–1830 | dramatist |
| Széchenyi, Count I. | 1791–1860 | political writer, pamphleteer |
| Jósika, Baron M. | 1794–1865 | historical novelist |
| Vörösmarty, M. | 1800–1855 | poet |

| | | |
|---|---|---|
| Kossuth, L. | 1802–94 | journalist, political writer |
| Eötvös, Baron J. | 1813–71 | novelist |
| Kemény, Baron Z. | 1814–75 | novelist |
| Arany, J. | 1817–82 | lyrical, epic poet |
| Tompa, M. | 1817–88 | poet |
| Madách, I. | 1823–64 | dramatist |
| Petőfi, S. | 1823–49 | lyric poet |
| Jókai, M. | 1825–1904 | novelist |
| Vajda, J. | 1827–99 | poet |
| Kiss, J. | 1843–1921 | poet |
| Mikszáth, K. | 1847–1910 | novelist |
| Ambrus, Z. | 1861–1932 | novelist |
| Bródy, S. | 1863–1924 | short-story writer |
| Gárdonyi, G. | 1863–1922 | novelist |
| Herczeg, F. | 1863–1954 | dramatist, novelist |
| Tömörkény, I. | 1866–1917 | short-story writer |
| Heltai, J. | 1871–1957 | poet, dramatist |
| Ady, E. | 1877–1919 | poet |
| Krúdy, G. | 1878–1933 | novelist |
| Molnár, F. | 1878–1952 | dramatist |
| Móra, F. | 1879–1934 | novelist, story writer |
| Móricz, Z. | 1879–1942 | novelist, story writer |
| Szabó, D. | 1879–1945 | novelist |
| Kaffka, M. | 1880–1918 | poet, novelist, story writer |
| Lengyel, M. | 1880–1957 | dramatist |
| Babits, M. | 1883–1941 | novelist, essayist, poet |
| Juhász, G. | 1883–1937 | poet |
| Nagy, L. | 1883–1954 | short-story writer |
| Kosztolányi, D. | 1885–1936 | poet, novelist |
| Lukács, G. | 1885– | critic, philosopher, writing chiefly in German |
| Tóth, Á. | 1886–1928 | poet |
| Áprily, L. | 1887–1967 | poet |
| Harsányi, Z. | 1887–1943 | novelist (*vies romancées*) |
| Karinthy, F. | 1887–1938 | writer, humorist |
| Kassák, L. | 1887–1967 | poet |
| Füst, M. | 1888–1967 | poet |
| Tersánszky, J. J. | 1888–1969 | novelist |
| Reményik, S. | 1890–1942 | poet |
| Zilahy, L. | 1891– | novelist, dramatist |
| Déry, T. | 1894– | novelist |
| Mécs, L. | 1895– | poet |
| Lengyel, J. | 1896– | novelist |
| Tamási, Á. | 1897–1966 | novelist |
| Háy, G. | 1900– | dramatist, writing chiefly in German |

| | | |
|---|---|---|
| Márai, S. | 1900– | journalist, novelist |
| Szabó, L. | 1900–1957 | poet |
| Németh, L. | 1901– | writer, dramatist |
| Szerb, A. | 1901–45 | essayist, critic, fiction writer |
| Illyés, G. | 1902– | poet, novelist, essayist |
| József, A. | 1905–37 | poet |
| Bálint, G. | 1906–43 | journalist, critic |
| Radnóti, M. | 1907–44 | poet |
| Vas, I. | 1910– | poet |
| Faludy, G. | 1913– | poet, writer |
| Weöres, S. | 1913– | poet |

## ICELANDIC

See also articles on **Icelandic Sagas,** p. 386, and **Eddaic Poetry,** p. 244

| | | |
|---|---|---|
| Snorri Sturluson | 1179–1241 | poet |
| Hallgrímur Pétursson | *c.*1614–74 | poet |
| Jónas Hallgrímsson | 1807–45 | poet |
| Laxness, H. | 1902– | novelist |

## ITALIAN

Authors who wrote mainly in LATIN are listed under that heading

See also articles on **Crepuscolari,** p. 202; **Ermetismo,** p. 257; **La Scapigliatura,** p. 701; **'Stil novo'** (or **'Il dolce stil novo'**), p. 744

| | | |
|---|---|---|
| Francis, Saint | *c.*1182–1226 | religious poet |
| Vigna, P. della | *c.*1180–1249 | poet |
| Latini, B. | *c.*1220–1294/5? | poet, scholar |
| Guinizelli, G. | *c.*1235–*c.*1276 | poet |
| Guittone d'Arezzo | *c.*1235–94 | poet |
| Jacopone da Todi | *c.*1236–1306 | poet |
| Polo, M. | 1254–1324? | travel writer |
| Compagni, D. | *c.*1255–1324 | chronicler |
| Cavalcanti, G. | 1259?–1300 | poet |
| Dante Alighieri | 1265–1321 | poet |
| Pistoia, C. da | *c.*1270–1336 | poet |
| Aquino, R. d' | 13th cent. | poet |
| Lentini, J. da | early 13th cent. | poet |
| Pugliese, G. | fl. early 13th cent. | poet |
| *Fioretti di San Francesco* | 13th or 14th cent. | collection of legends about St Francis |
| *Novellino Il* | late 13th cent. | collection of *novelle* |
| Villani, G. | *c.*1276–1348 | chronicler |
| Petrarch, F. | 1304–74 | poet (also in Latin) |
| Boccaccio, G. | 1313–75 | short-story writer, poet |
| Sacchetti, F. | *c.*1332–*c.*1400 | short-story writer, poet |

| | | |
|---|---|---|
| Sercambi, G. | 1348–1424 | short-story writer |
| Sordello | fl. mid 13th cent. | troubadour (writing in Provençal) |
| Bruni, L. | 1370?–1444 | humanist, historian |
| Alberti, L. B. | 1404–72 | humanist, author of philosophical dialogues |
| Salernitano, M. | 1415?–1475? | short-story writer |
| Bisticci, V. da | 1421–98 | biographer |
| Pulci, L. | 1432–84 | poet |
| Colonna, F. | 1433?–1527 | prose writer (partly in Latin) |
| Boiardo, M. M. | 1441–94 | poet |
| Medici, L. de' | 1449–92 | poet |
| Da Vinci, L. | 1452–1519 | artist, scientist, prose writer |
| Savonarola, G. | 1452–98 | preacher, poet |
| Poliziano, A. | 1454–94 | poet (also in Latin) |
| Sannazaro, J. | *c.* 1456–1530 | poet (also in Latin) |
| Tebaldeo, A. | 1463–1537 | poet (also in Latin) |
| Ciminelli, S. de' | 1466–1500 | poet |
| Machiavelli, N. | 1469–1527 | political theorist, historian |
| Bembo, P. | 1470–1547 | writer of dialogues, poet |
| Dovizi, B. | 1470–1520 | dramatist, man of letters |
| Ariosto, L. | 1474–1533 | poet |
| Michelangelo Buonarroti | 1475–1564 | artist, poet |
| Castiglione, B. | 1478–1529 | dialogue writer |
| Trissino, G. | 1478–1550 | scholar-poet, tragedian |
| Straparola, G. | *c.* 1480–*c.* 1557 | short-story writer |
| Guicciardini, F. | 1483–1540 | historian |
| Bandello, M. | 1485–1561 | short-story writer |
| Da Porto, L. | 1485–1529 | letter and story writer |
| Molza, F. M. | 1489–1544 | poet |
| Colonna, V. | 1490–1547 | poet |
| Folengo, T. | 1491–1544 | poet |
| Aretino, P. | 1492–1556 | satirist, letter writer, dramatist |
| Firenzuola, A. | 1493–1543 | story and dialogue writer |
| Tasso, B. | 1493–1569 | poet |
| Alamanni, L. | 1495–1556 | poet |
| Berni, F. | 1497?–1535 | poet |
| Gelli, G. B. | 1498–1563 | dramatist, dialogue writer |
| *Commedia dell'arte* | 16th cent. | type of theatre production |
| Cellini, B. | 1500–1571 | artist, poet, theoretical and autobiographical writer |
| Speroni, S. | 1500–1588 | writer of dialogues, critic, poet |
| Della Casa, G. | 1503–56 | prose writer, poet |
| Grazzini, A. F. | 1503–84 | dramatist, verse and story writer |
| Varchi, B. | 1503–65 | historian, treatise writer |

| | | |
|---|---|---|
| Giraldi Cinthio, G. | 1504–73 | tragedian, literary theorist, short-story writer |
| Castelvetro, L. | 1505–71 | literary critic, theorist |
| Caro, A. | 1507–66 | poet, translator, man of letters |
| Tansillo, L. | 1510–68 | poet |
| Vasari, G. | 1511–74 | artist, art historian |
| Doni, A. F. | 1513–74 | dialogue, fable writer |
| Stampa, G. | *c.* 1523–54 | poet |
| Guarini, G. | 1538–1612 | poet |
| Tasso, T. | 1544–95 | poet |
| Bruno, G. | 1548–1600 | philosopher |
| Chiabrera, G. | 1552–1638 | poet |
| Sarpi, P. | 1552–1623 | theologian, historian |
| Boccalini, T. | 1556–1613 | satirist |
| Della Valle, F. | *c.* 1560–1628 | tragedian |
| Galilei, G. | 1564–1642 | scientist, prose writer |
| Tassoni, A. | 1565–1635 | epic and mock-heroic poet, treatise writer |
| Campanella, T. | 1568–1639 | theologian, philosopher, poet (also in Latin) |
| Marino, G. | 1569–1625 | poet |
| Stigliani, T. | 1573–1651 | poet |
| Achillini, C. | 1574–1640 | poet |
| Basile, G. | 1575–1632 | short-story writer |
| Preti, G. | 1582?–1626 | poet |
| Testi, F. | 1593–1646 | poet |
| Pers, C. di | 1599–1663 | poet |
| Paoli, P. F. | ?–*c* 1640 | poet |
| Morando, B. | 1589–1656 | poet |
| Fontanella, G. | 1612?–44? | poet |
| Rosa, S. | 1615–73 | painter, satirical poet |
| Lubrano, G. | 1619–93 | poet |
| Redi, F. | 1626–98 | scientific pamphlet writer, poet |
| Magalotti, L. | 1637–1712 | scientific prose writer |
| Filicaia, V. da | 1642–1707 | poet |
| Guidi, A. | 1650–1712 | poet |
| Vico, G. | 1668–1744 | philosopher |
| Muratori, L. A. | 1672–1750 | historian |
| Maffei, S. | 1675–1755 | scholar |
| Rolli, P. | 1687–1765 | poet |
| Frugoni, C. I. | 1692–1768 | Arcadian poet |
| Metastasio, P. | 1698–1782 | poet, melodramatist |
| Goldoni, C. | 1707–93 | comic dramatist |
| Algarotti, F. | 1712–64 | scientist, essayist |
| Gozzi, G. | 1713–86 | journalist, critic |
| Baretti, G. | 1719–89 | journalist, critic |

| | | |
|---|---|---|
| Gozzi, C. | 1720–1806 | dramatist, literary theorist |
| Casanova, G. G. | 1725–98 | adventurer, publicist, autobiographer |
| Verri, P. | 1728–97 | journalist, economist |
| Parini, G. | 1729–99 | satirical poet |
| Cesarotti, M. | 1730–1808 | poet, critic |
| Tiraboschi, G. | 1731–94 | historian |
| Beccaria, C. | 1738–94 | economist, criminologist |
| Verri, A. | 1741–1816 | journalist, translator, dramatist |
| Alfieri, V. | 1749–1803 | poet, dramatist |
| Pindemonte, I. | 1753–1828 | poet |
| Monti, V. | 1754–1828 | poet |
| Foscolo, U. | 1778–1827 | poet |
| Berchet, G. | 1783–1851 | poet |
| Manzoni, A. | 1785–1873 | novelist |
| Balbo, C. | 1789–1853 | politician, historian |
| Pellico, S. | 1789–1845 | patriot, dramatist |
| Grossi, T. | 1790–1853 | novelist, poet |
| Azeglio, M. d' | 1798–1866 | painter, novelist |
| Leopardi, G. | 1798–1837 | poet |
| Gioberti, V. | 1801–52 | philosopher, statesman |
| Tommaseo, N. | 1802–74 | lexicographer, poet, novelist |
| Guerrazzi, F. D. | 1804–73 | poet, dramatist, novelist |
| Mazzini, G. | 1805–72 | patriot, political writer |
| Giusti, G. | 1809–50 | poet |
| Aleardi, A. | 1812–78 | poet |
| Prati, G. | 1814–84 | poet |
| De Sanctis, F. | 1817–83 | literary historian |
| Mercantini, L. | 1821–72 | patriot, poet |
| Mameli, G. | 1827–49 | patriot, poet |
| Nievo, I. | 1831–61 | poet, novelist |
| Carducci, G. | 1835–1907 | critic, scholar, poet |
| Capuana, L. | 1839–1915 | novelist, critic |
| Verga, G. | 1840–1922 | dramatist, novelist |
| Boito, A. | 1842–1918 | poet, composer |
| Fogazzaro, A. | 1842–1911 | novelist, poet |
| Fucini, R. | 1843–1921 | poet, prose writer |
| De Amicis, E. | 1846–1908 | journalist, short-story writer |
| Giacosa, G. | 1847–1906 | dramatist |
| De Marchi, E. | 1851–1901 | novelist, short-story writer |
| Pascoli, G. | 1855–1912 | poet, scholar |
| Serao, M. | 1856–1927 | journalist, novelist |
| Svevo, I. | 1861–1928 | novelist |
| D'Annunzio, G. | 1863–1938 | poet, dramatist, novelist |
| Panzini, A. | 1863–1939 | novelist |
| Croce, B. | 1866–1952 | critic, philosopher |

| | | |
|---|---|---|
| De Roberto, F. | 1866–1927 | critic, novelist |
| Pirandello, L. | 1867–1936 | novelist, dramatist |
| Negri, A. | 1870–1945 | poet |
| Deledda, G. | 1871–1936 | novelist |
| Marinetti, F. T. | 1876–1944 | poet, novelist |
| Bontempelli, M. | 1878–1960 | novelist, critic |
| Cicognani, B. | 1879– | novelist, dramatist |
| Soffici, A. | 1879–1964 | writer, painter |
| Papini, G. | 1881–1956 | essayist, pamphleteer |
| Pea, E. | 1881–1958 | novelist |
| Borgese, G. A. | 1882–1952 | literary critic, novelist |
| Gozzano, G. | 1883–1916 | poet |
| Saba, U. | 1883–1957 | poet |
| Cecchi, E. | 1884–1966 | essayist, critic |
| Govoni, C. | 1884–1965 | poet, novelist |
| Campana, D. | 1885–1932 | poet |
| Moretti, M. | 1885–1971 | novelist |
| Palazzeschi, A. | 1885– | poet, novelist |
| Rebora, C. | 1885–1957 | poet |
| Corazzini, S. | 1885–1907 | poet |
| Cardarelli, V. | 1887–1959 | poet, prose writer |
| Ungaretti, G. | 1888–1970 | poet, translator |
| Baldini, A. | 1889–1962 | essayist, stylist |
| Bacchelli, R. | 1891– | novelist |
| Betti, U. | 1892–1953 | dramatist |
| Gadda, C. E. | 1893– | novelist |
| Alvaro, C. | 1895–1956 | novelist |
| Lampedusa, G. T. di | 1896–1957 | novelist |
| Montale, E. | 1896– | poet, translator, critic |
| Malaparte, C. | 1898–1957 | journalist, satirical poet, dramatist, novelist |
| Silone, I. | 1900– | novelist |
| Quasimodo, S. | 1901–68 | poet, translator, critic |
| Jovine, F. | 1902–50 | novelist |
| Levi, C. | 1902– | novelist |
| Buzzati, D. | 1906– | novelist |
| Soldati, M. | 1906– | film director, novelist |
| Brancati, V. | 1907–54 | novelist |
| Moravia, A. | 1907– | novelist |
| Piovene, G. | 1907– | novelist |
| Pavese, C. | 1908–50 | poet, novelist |
| Vittorini, E. | 1908–66 | novelist, literary critic |
| Gatto, A. | 1909– | poet, journalist |
| Pratolini, V. | 1913– | novelist |
| Sereni, V. | 1913– | poet |
| Luzi, M. | 1914– | poet, essayist |

| | | |
|---|---|---|
| Bassani, G. | 1916– | novelist |
| Cassola, C. | 1917– | novelist |
| Morante, E. | 1918– | novelist |
| Pasolini, P. P. | 1922– | poet, novelist, literary critic |
| Calvino, I. | 1923– | novelist |

## JEWISH

See separate headings: HEBREW and YIDDISH

## LATIN

See also article on **Hymns, Latin,** p. 382

| | | |
|---|---|---|
| Egeria | fl. *c.* 414–16 | pilgrimage writer (N. Spain) |
| Avitus | *c.* 450–*c.* 525 | epic poet (Provence) |
| Fulgentius Ruspensis, F.C.G. | 467–532 | bishop, writer (N. Africa) |
| Ennodius, M. F. | 474–521 | poet (N. Italy) |
| Boethius, A. M. S. | *c.* 480–524 | philosopher (Rome) |
| Cassiodorus, F. M. A. | *c.* 485–*c.* 580 | monastic scholar (S. Italy) |
| Dracontius, B. A. | fl. late 5th cent. | poet (Carthage) |
| Luxorius | fl. 500–530 | poet (Rome) |
| Martin of Braga | *c.* 510/20–79 | ecclesiastical writer (Galicia) |
| Fortunatus, V. | *c.* 530–609 | poet (N. Italy, France) |
| Arator | fl. 540 | poet, lawyer (Rome) |
| Gregory of Tours | *c.* 540–94 | religious and historical writer (C. France) |
| Gregory the Great, St | *c.* 540–604 | religious writer (Rome) |
| Columbanus, St | 543–615 | monastic writer (Ireland, France, Italy) |
| Jordanes | fl. 550 | Germanic historian of the Goths (Bulgaria) |
| Corippus, F. C. | fl. 565 | poet (Africa) |
| Isidore of Seville, St | *c.* 570–636 | churchman, scholar (Spain) |
| Eugenius of Toledo | *c.* 600–658 | poet (Visigoth) |
| Virgilius Maro Grammaticus | fl. *c.* 600 | grammarian (S. France) |
| Ildefonsus of Toledo | 607–67 | ecclesiastical writer (Spain) |
| Paul the Deacon | *c.* 720–99 | historian (N. Italy) |
| Alcuin | *c.* 735–804 | scholar (England, N. France) |
| Theodulph, Saint | *c.* 760–*c.* 821 | poet (France) |
| *Fredegar* | 8th cent. | historical compilation |
| *Sequences* | 8th cent. | religious literary genre |
| Einhard | *c.* 770–840 | biographer (Germany, France) |
| Hrabanus Maurus | *c.* 780–856 | religious writer (Germany) |
| Lupus Servatus | *c.* 800–*c.* 862 | letter writer (France) |

| | | |
|---|---|---|
| Nithard | *c.* 800–853 or 858 | historian (France) |
| Gottschalk | *c.* 808–68 | religious writer (Germany) |
| Walafrid, Strabo | *c.* 808–49 | religious writer (Germany) |
| John Scotus Erigena | *c.* 810–*c.* 877 | theologian (Ireland, France) |
| Angilbert | *c.* 814 | poet (France) |
| Ermold The Black | fl. 825–50 | epic poet (France) |
| Notker Balbulus | *c.* 840–912 | Benedictine writer (Switzerland) |
| Hucbald of St Amand | *c.* 840–930 | poet (France) |
| Ratherius of Liège | *c.* 887–974 | letter and autobiographical writer (France, Italy) |
| Flodoard of Rheims | *c.* 893/4–966 | historian, poet (France) |
| Ekkehart I | *c.* 900–973 | epic poet (Switzerland) |
| Liutprand | *c.* 920–72 | chronicler (Italy) |
| Gerbert of Aurillac | after 940–1003 | scholar (France) |
| Hrotswith | fl. 950 | dramatist, epic writer (Germany) |
| Fulbert of Chartres | *c.* 975–1029 | historian (France) |
| Widukind | fl. 975 | chronicler (Germany) |
| Ekkehart IV | *c.* 980–1060 | poet (Switzerland) |
| *Ecbasis Captivi* | 10th cent. | beast epic |
| Rodulphus Glaber | before 1000–after 1046 | historian (France) |
| Peter Damian, St | *c.* 1006–72 | poet, satirist (Italy) |
| Lambert of Hersfeld | *c.* 1025–80 | historian (Germany) |
| Sigebert of Gembloux | *c.* 1030–1112 | chronicler (Belgium) |
| Marbod | *c.* 1035–1123 | poet (France) |
| Baudri of Bourgueil | 1046–1130 | historian, poet (France) |
| *Ruodlieb* | *c.* 1050 | romantic epic |
| Wipo | died *c.* 1050 | poet, versifier (France) |
| Guibert of Nogent | 1053–1124 | historical and autobiographical writer (France) |
| Robert the Monk | 1055–1122 | chronicler (France) |
| Hildebert | 1056–1133 | poet (France) |
| Fulcher of Chartres | 1058–1127? | historian (France) |
| Petrus Alfonsi | 1062–1110 | writer of oriental tales (Spain) |
| Orderic Vitalis | 1075–*c.* 1142 | chronicler (N. France) |
| Abelard, P. | 1079–1142 | scholastic philosopher (France) |
| William of St Thierry | *c.* 1085–*c.* 1148 | religious writer (France) |
| Bernard of Clairvaux, St | 1090–1153 | poet, mystical and religious writer (France) |
| Raymond of Agiles | fl. 1095–1100 | chronicler (France) |
| *Gesta Francorum* | 11th–12th cent. | crusade chronicle |
| Giles de Paris | ?–*c.* 1141 | historical writer (France) |
| Tudeboeuf | fl. *c.* 1100–1118 | chronicler (France) |
| Maurice de Sully | ?–1196 | sermon writer (France) |
| Adam of St Victor | *c.* 1110–80 | writer (France) |

| | | |
|---|---|---|
| Walter of Antioch | fl. 1112–26 | chronicler (France) |
| Otto of Freising | *c.* 1115–58 | chronicler (S. Germany) |
| Honorius 'of Autun' | fl. *c.* 1120 | medieval scholar (Germany) |
| Albert of Aix | fl. *c.* 1121 | chronicler (France) |
| Alan of Lille | 1128?–1203 | humanist, poet (France) |
| Archpoet, The | *c.* 1130–*c.* 1165 | secular poet (Germany) |
| Hugh Primas | fl. 1130 | poet (France) |
| William of Tyre | *c.* 1130–*c.* 1190 | chronicler (France) |
| Walter of Châtillon | *c.* 1135–84 | poet (France) |
| Bernard of Cluny | fl. 1140 | poet (France) |
| Guy of Bazoches | *c.* 1140–1203 | poet, letter writer (France) |
| Nivard | fl. 1150 | epic poet (Belgium) |
| Rigord | *c.* 1150–*c.* 1209 | chronicler (France) |
| Saxo Grammaticus | *c.* 1150–*c.* 1206 | chronicler (Denmark?) |
| Alexander de Villa Dei | *c.* 1160–after 1203 | grammarian, encyclopedist (France) |
| Jacques de Vitry | *c.* 1160–1240 | preacher (France) |
| Matthew of Vendôme | fl. 1160–85 | poetic theorist (France) |
| Andreas Capellanus | fl. 1175–80 | theorist of courtly love (France) |
| Caesarius of Heisterbach | *c.* 1180–*c.* 1240 | didactic story writer (Germany) |
| Johannes de Alta Silva | fl. 1180–1200 | oriental story writer (France) |
| Philip the Chancellor | *c.* 1180–1236 | poet (France) |
| Étienne de Bourbon | *c.* 1190–1261 | didactic story writer (France) |
| Vincent of Beauvais | *c.* 1190–*c.* 1264 | encyclopedist (France) |
| Herrad von Landsperg | died 1195 | encyclopedic spiritual writer (France) |
| John of Hanville | fl. late 12th cent. | satirical poet (France) |
| Oliver of Paderborn | ?–1227 | chronicler (Germany) |
| Thomas of Celano | *c.* 1200–*c.* 1255 | biographer (Italy) |
| Albertus Magnus | 1206–80 | philosopher (Italy, France, Germany) |
| Eberhard of Béthune | fl. *c.* 1210 | grammarian (France) |
| Bonaventura, St | 1221–74 | theologian, poet (Italy) |
| Salimbene, Fra | 1221–*c.* 1290 | chronicler (Italy) |
| Aquinas, St T. | *c.* 1225–74 | philosopher, poet (Italy) |
| Jacobus de Voragine | *c.* 1230–98 | historian, hagiographer (Italy) |
| Arnulf of Louvain | fl. 1240–48 | religious poet (France) |
| Marsilius of Padua | *c.* 1275–1342 | political philosopher (Italy) |
| *Carmina Burana* | 13th cent. | collection of poems |
| *Gesta Romanorum* | *c.* 1300 | collection of didactic stories |
| Thomas à Kempis | *c.* 1380–1471 | religious writer (Holland) |
| Aeneas Silvius | 1405–64 | poet, letter and memoir writer (Italy) |
| Valla, L. | 1405–57 | humanist, thinker, philologist (Italy) |
| Pontano, G. | 1429–1503 | poet, philosopher (Italy) |

| | | |
|---|---|---|
| Poliziano, A. | 1454–94 | poet writing sometimes in Latin (Italy) |
| Sannazaro, J. | *c.* 1456–1530 | poet writing sometimes in Latin (Italy) |
| Celtis, C. | 1459–1508 | humanist scholar, poet (Germany) |
| Pico della Mirandola, G. | 1463–94 | scholar, thinker (Italy) |
| Erasmus, D. | 1466–1536 | humanist, scholar, thinker (Holland) |
| Scaliger, J. C. | 1484–1558 | humanist scholar, poet (France) |
| Vida, M. G. | 1485–1566 | occasional and epic poet (Italy) |
| Johannes Secundus | 1511–36 | poet, travel writer (Holland) |
| Baronio, C. | 1538–1607 | ecclesiastical historian (Italy) |
| Scaliger, J. J. | 1540–1609 | classical scholar (France, Switzerland, Holland) |
| Campanella, T. | 1568–1639 | theologian, philosopher, poet, writing sometimes in Latin (Italy) |
| Balde, J. | 1604–68 | poet (Germany) |
| Rapin, R. | 1621–87 | poet (France) |
| Spinoza, B. | 1632–77 | philosopher (Holland) |
| Coffin, C. | 1676–1749 | hymn writer (France) |

## LATVIAN

See also article on **Latvian Literature**, p. 461, for minor writers

| | | |
|---|---|---|
| Eglītis, A. | 1906– | novelist |
| Kārkliņš, V. | 1906–64 | novelist, short-story writer |
| Lesiņš, K. | 1909– | novelist |
| Strēlerte, V. | 1912– | poet |
| Tauns, L. | 1922–63 | poet |
| Irbe, A. | 1924– | short-story writer |
| Saliņš, G. | 1924– | poet |
| Sniķere, V. | 20th cent. | poet |

## LITHUANIAN

See also article on **Lithuanian Literature**, p. 481, for minor writers

| | | |
|---|---|---|
| Donelaitis, K. | 1714–80 | poet |

## NORWEGIAN

See also ICELANDIC

| | | |
|---|---|---|
| Dass, P. | 1647–1707 | poet |
| Wessel, J. H. | 1742–85 | Dano-Norwegian poet, dramatist |

| | | |
|---|---|---|
| Welhaven, J. S. | 1807–73 | poet |
| Wergeland, H. | 1808–45 | poet |
| Aasen, I. | 1813–96 | philologist, poet |
| Vinje, A. | 1818–70 | poet, essayist |
| Ibsen, H. | 1828–1906 | dramatist, poet |
| Bjørnson, B. | 1832–1910 | novelist, dramatist, poet |
| Lie, J. | 1833–1908 | novelist, dramatist, poet |
| Skram, A. | 1847–1905 | novelist |
| Kielland, A. | 1849–1906 | novelist, dramatist |
| Garborg, A. | 1851–1924 | novelist, poet, dramatist, essayist |
| Heiberg, G. | 1857–1929 | dramatist |
| Hamsun, K. | 1859–1952 | novelist, dramatist, poet |
| Kinck, H. E. | 1865–1926 | novelist, short-story writer, dramatist, essayist |
| Obstfelder, S. | 1866–1900 | poet, short-story writer |
| Egge, P. | 1869–1959 | novelist, dramatist |
| Bojer, J. | 1872–1959 | novelist |
| Scott, G. | 1874–1958 | novelist |
| Duun, O. | 1876–1939 | novelist |
| Uppdal, K. | 1878–1961 | novelist, poet |
| Falkberget, J. | 1879–1967 | novelist |
| Sandel, C. | 1880– | novelist, short-story writer |
| Undset, S. | 1882–1949 | novelist |
| Aukrust, O. | 1883–1929 | poet |
| Bull, O. | 1883–1933 | poet |
| Wildenvey, H. | 1886–1959 | poet |
| Krog, H. | 1889–1962 | dramatist, essayist |
| Øverland, A. | 1889–1968 | poet |
| Hoel, S. | 1890–1960 | novelist, essayist |
| Christiansen, S. | 1891–1947 | novelist, dramatist |
| Fangen, R. | 1895–1946 | novelist, dramatist |
| Vesaas, T. | 1897–1970 | novelist, short-story writer, dramatist, poet |
| Sandemose, A. | 1899–1965 | novelist |
| Borgen, J. | 1902– | novelist, short-story writer, dramatist |
| Grieg, N. | 1902–43 | poet, novelist, dramatist |

## POLISH

See also article on **Polish Medieval Literature,** p. 619

| | | |
|---|---|---|
| Rej, M. | 1505–69 | writer |
| Kochanowski, J. | 1530–84 | poet |
| Klonowic, S. | *c.*1545–1602 | poet |
| Żółkiewski, S. | 1547–1620 | soldier, diarist |

| | | |
|---|---|---|
| Sęp-Szarzyński, M. | *c.* 1550–80 | poet |
| Simonides, S. | 1558–1629 | poet |
| Sarbiewski, M. C. | 1595–1640 | Jesuit poet |
| Zimorowic, B. | 1597–*c.* 1680 | poet |
| Twardowski, S. | 1600–1661 | poet |
| Morsztyn, J. A. | 1613–93 | poet |
| Morsztyn, Z. | 1620?–1689? | poet |
| Potocki, W. | 1621–96 | poet |
| Kochowski, W. | 1633–1700 | poet |
| Pasek, J. C. | *c.* 1636–*c.* 1701 | diarist |
| Krasicki, I. | 1735–1801 | poet |
| Karpiński, F. | 1741–1825 | poet |
| Kniaźnin, F. D. | 1750–1807 | poet |
| Zabłocki, F. | 1754–1821 | dramatist |
| Niemcewicz, J. | 1757–1841 | dramatist, poet, novelist, translator |
| Feliński, A. | 1771–1820 | dramatist |
| Fredro, A. | 1793–1876 | dramatist |
| Malczewski, A. | 1793–1826 | poet |
| Mickiewicz, A. | 1798–1855 | poet, 'national bard' |
| Słowacki, J. | 1809–49 | poet |
| Krasiński, Z. | 1812–59 | dramatist, poet |
| Kraszewski, J. I. | 1812–87 | novelist |
| Żmichowska, N. | 1819–76 | novelist |
| Norwid, C. | 1821–83 | poet |
| Syrokomla, W. | 1823–62 | poet |
| Asnyk, A. | 1838–97 | poet |
| Orzeskowa, E. | 1841–1910 | novelist |
| Prus, B. | 1845–1912 | novelist |
| Konopnicka, M. | 1846–1910 | short-story writer, poet |
| Sienkiewicz, H. | 1846–1916 | novelist |
| Zapolska, G. | 1857–1921 | dramatist |
| Kasprowicz, J. | 1860–1926 | poet |
| Sieroszewski, W. | 1860–1945 | novelist |
| Weyssenhoff, J. | 1860–1932 | novelist |
| Żeromski, S. | 1864–1925 | novelist |
| Tetmajer, K. | 1865–1940 | poet, short-story writer |
| Reymont, W. S. | 1867–1925 | novelist |
| Przybyszewski, S. | 1868–1927 | novelist, dramatist |
| Wyspiański, S. | 1869–1907 | dramatist, painter |
| Berent, W. | 1873–1940 | novelist |
| Irzykowski, K. | 1873–1944 | novelist, critic |
| Perzyński, W. | 1877–1930 | dramatist |
| Rostworowski, K. H. | 1877–1938 | dramatist |
| Staff, L. | 1878–1957 | poet |
| Leśmian, B. | 1879–1937 | poet |

| | | |
|---|---|---|
| Choynowski, P. | 1885–1935 | short-story writer |
| Kaden-Bandrowski, J. | 1885–1944 | novelist |
| Witkiewicz, S. I. | 1885–1939 | novelist |
| Szaniawski, J. | 1887–1970 | dramatist |
| Dąbrowska, M. | 1889–1965 | novelist |
| Goetel, F. | 1890–1960 | novelist |
| Schulz, B. | 1893–1942 | short-story writer |
| Iwaszkiewicz, J. | 1894– | short-story writer, poet |
| Tuwim, J. | 1894–1953 | poet |
| Wierzyński, K. | 1894–1970 | poet |
| Młodożeniec, S. | 1895–1959 | poet |
| Słonimski, A. | 1895– | dramatist, poet |
| Wittlin, J. | 1896– | novelist, poet |
| Wołoszynowski, J. | 1898– | novelist |
| Kuncewicz, M. | 1899– | novelist |
| Czechowicz, J. | 1903–39 | poet |
| Choromański, M. | 1904– | novelist |
| Gombrowicz, W. | 1904–1969 | novelist |
| Straszewicz, C. | 1904–63 | novelist |
| Gałczyński, K. I. | 1905–53 | poet |
| Bąk, W. | 1907–61 | poet |
| Andrzejewski, J. | 1909– | novelist |
| Dobraczyński, J. | 1910– | novelist |
| Miłosz, C. | 1911– | poet, essayist, translator |
| Peterkiewicz, J. | 1916– | poet |
| Herbert, Z. | 1924– | poet |
| Mrożek, S. | 1930– | satirist |
| Hłasko, M. | 1931–1969 | short-story writer |

## PORTUGUESE

| | | |
|---|---|---|
| *Cancioneiros* | 12th–14th cent. | early song books |
| *Demanda do Santo Graal* | 13th cent. | chivalric romance |
| Lopes, F. | *c.* 1380/90–*c.* 1460? | chronicler |
| Duarte, Dom | 1391–1438 | King of Portugal, man of letters |
| *Crónicas* | 14th and 15th cent. | historical chronicles |
| Zurara, G. E. de | *c.* 1420?–*c.* 1474? | chronicler |
| Resende, G. de | *c.* 1470–1536 | chronicler |
| Vicente, G. | *c.* 1470–1536 | dramatist |
| Sá de Miranda, F. de | 1481–1558 | poet |
| Ribeiro, B. | 1482–1552 | poet, novelist |
| Castanheda, F. L. de | 149?–1559 | chronicler |
| Correia, G. | *c.* 1495–*c.* 1565 | historian |
| Barros, J. de | *c.* 1496–1570 | chronicler, author |
| Damião de Góis | 1501–74 | humanist |
| Orta, G. D' | *c.* 1501–68 | physician, botanist |

| | | |
|---|---|---|
| Mendes Pinto, F. | *c.*1514–83 | adventurer, author |
| Vasconcelos, J. F. de | *c.*1515–85? | dramatist |
| Falcão, C. | 1518–54 | poet |
| Camões, L. de | *c.*1524–80 | poet |
| Ferreira, A. | 1528–69 | poet |
| Pinto, H. | *c.*1528–*c.*1584 | theologian, humanist |
| Bernardes, D. | 1530–1605 | poet |
| Couto, D. do | *c.*1543–1616 | chronicler |
| Lobo, F. R. | *c.*1580–*c.*1622 | dialogue and pastoral writer |
| Pinto Delgado, J. | ?–after 1636 | poet |
| Melo, F. M. de | 1608–66 | historian, moralist, essayist, dramatist, poet |
| Vieira, A. | 1608–97 | letter and sermon writer |
| Chagas, A. das | 1631–82 | poet, ascetic |
| Bernardes, M. | 1644–1710 | theologian |
| *Arte de Furtar* | publ. 1652 | political and moral satire |
| Verney, Father L. A. | 1713–17?? | critic, educationalist |
| Garção, P. A. C. | 1724–73 | poet |
| Silva, A. D. da C. | 1731–99 | man of letters |
| Elisio, F. | 1734–1819 | poet |
| Tolentino de Almeida, N. | 1740–1811 | satirical poet |
| Gonzaga, T. A. | 1744–1810 | poet |
| Bocage, M. M. B. du | 1765–1805 | poet |
| Garrett, A. | 1799–1854 | dramatist, poet, novelist |
| Castilho, A. F. de | 1800–1875 | poet |
| Herculano, A. | 1810–66 | intellectual, historian |
| Mendes Leal, J. da S. | 1818–86 | dramatist, pamphleteer |
| Castelo Branco, C. | 1825–95 | novelist, short-story writer |
| Lopes de Mendonça, A. P. | 1826–65 | critic, journalist, novelist |
| Soares de Passos, A. A. de | 1826–60 | poet |
| Deus, J. de | 1830–96 | poet |
| Ribeiro, T. A. | 1831–1901 | poet, politician, diplomat |
| Ortigão, J. D. R. | 1836–1915 | journalist, intellectual |
| Azevedo, G. de | 1839–82 | poet |
| Dinis, J. | 1839–71 | novelist |
| Quental, A. de | 1842–92 | poet, left-wing intellectual |
| Eça de Queirós, J. M. de | 1845–1900 | novelist, critic |
| Martins, J. P. de O. | 1845–94 | author, historian |
| Leal, A. D. G. | 1848–1924 | poet |
| Junqueiro, A. M. G. | 1850–1923 | poet |
| Verde, C. | 1855–86 | poet |
| Brandão, R. | 1867–1930 | novelist, journalist, dramatist, social historian |
| Nobre, A. | 1867–1903 | poet |
| Castro, E. de | 1869–1944 | poet |
| Pascoais, T. de | 1877–1952 | poet |

| | | |
|---|---|---|
| Ribeiro, A. | 1885–1963 | novelist, story writer, essayist |
| Pessoa, F. | 1888–1935 | poet |
| Sá-Carneiro, M. de | 1890–1916 | poet |
| Ferreira de Castro, J. M. | 1898– | novelist |
| Torga, M. | 1907– | poet, dramatist, novelist, diarist |

## PROVENÇAL

See also articles on **Félibrige,** p. 265; **Jocs Florals (Jeux Floraux),** p. 401; **Troubadours,** p. 773

| | | |
|---|---|---|
| Guilhem de Poitou | 1071–1127 | troubadour |
| Bertran de Born | *c.*1140–before 1215 | troubadour |
| Bernart de Ventadorn | fl. *c.*1145–1180 | troubadour |
| Jaufré Rudel | fl. mid 12th cent. | troubadour |
| Marcabru | mid 12th cent. | troubadour |
| Guiraut de Bornelh | fl. 1170 | troubadour |
| Peire Cardenal | *c.*1180–1278 | troubadour |
| Raimon de Miraval | fl. *c.*1185–1213 | troubadour |
| Raimbaut, Count of Orange | fl. late 12 cent. | troubadour |
| Arnaut Daniel | fl. *c.*1200 | troubadour |
| Guiraut Riquier | *c.*1230/35–after 1292 | troubadour |
| Folquet de Marseille | died 1231 | troubadour |
| Guilhem Montanhagol | fl. 1233–*c.*1258 | troubadour |
| Sordello | fl. mid 13th cent. | troubadour (from Italy) |
| *Flamenca* | 13th cent. | verse romance |
| *Leys d'amors* | 14th cent. | treatise on poetry |
| Roumanille, J. | 1818–91 | poet |
| Mistral, F. | 1830–1914 | poet |

## RUMANIAN

See also articles on **Juminea,** p. 411 and **Rumanian Literature before 1850,** p. 673

| | | |
|---|---|---|
| Alecsandri, V. | 1821–90 | poet, dramatist |
| Creangă, I. | 1837–89 | story-teller |
| Eminescu, M. | 1850–89 | poet |
| Caragiale, I. L. | 1852–1912 | writer of plays and short stories |
| Macedonski, A. | 1854–1920 | poet, prose-writer |
| Zamfirescu, D. | 1858–1922 | poet, novelist |
| Coşbuc, G. | 1866–1918 | poet |
| Iorga, N. | 1871–1940 | historian, politician |
| Arghezi, T. | 1880–1967 | poet, prose-writer |
| Sadoveanu, M. | 1880–1961 | novelist, short-story writer |
| Bacovia, G. | 1881–1957 | poet |
| Rebreanu, L. | 1885–1944 | novelist |

| | | |
|---|---|---|
| Petrescu, C. | 1892–1961 | novelist |
| Barbu, I. | 1895–1961 | poet, mathematician |
| Blaga, L. | 1895–1961 | poet, philosopher |
| Sebastian, M. | 1907–45 | dramatist, novelist |

## RUSSIAN

UKRAINIAN authors are listed separately under that heading

See also articles on **Acmeism**, p. 31; **Constructivism**, p. 197; **Proletarian Poetry**, p. 626; **Russian Historical Songs**, p. 675; **Russian Literature of the 17th Century**, p. 675; **(The) Serapion Brothers**, p. 714; **'(The) Thaw'**, p. 760

| | | |
|---|---|---|
| Boris and Gleb (*Skazaniye* and *Chteniye*) | 11th cent. | accounts of their martyrdom |
| Vladimir Monomakh | 1053–1125 | statesman, ruler and writer |
| Ilarion, Metropolitan of Kiev | mid 11th cent. | churchman, homilist |
| *Russian Primary Chronicle* | *c.*1115 | history of Kievan Russia |
| *Slovo o Polku Igoreve* | *c.*1185 | heroic tale |
| Kirill of Turov | 12th cent. | churchman, homilist |
| Daniil the Prisoner | fl. 12th or 13th cent. | aphoristic epistle writer |
| *Istoricheskiye pesni* | 13th cent. onwards | historical songs |
| *Zadonshchina* | *c.*1385 | heroic historical tale |
| Yepifaniy | fl. *c.*1400 | hagiographer |
| Nil Sorsky | 1433–1508 | saint, mystic, writer |
| Joseph of Volokolamsk | *c.*1440–1515 | religious and political writer |
| Kurbsky, A. M. | 1528?–1588 | letter writer, historian |
| Vasily/Vassian Patrikyev | died *c.*1532 | polemical writer |
| Ivan IV | 1533–84 | epistle writer |
| Palitsyn, A. | *c.*1555–1627 | historical writer |
| *Russian Spiritual Verses* | 17th cent. onwards | traditional genre of oral poetry |
| Druzhina-Osor'in, C. | 17th cent. | biographical writer |
| Timofeyev, I. | died *c.*1629 | chronicle writer |
| Katyrev-Rostovsky, Ivan | died 1640 | historical writer |
| Avvakum, Archpriest | 1620/1–82 | epistle, sermon, exegesis writer |
| Polotsky, S. | 1629–80 | teacher, poet, dramatist |
| Lomonosov, M. V. | *c.*1711–65 | poet, literary theorist |
| Sumarokov, A. P. | 1717–77 | dramatist, poet |
| Derzhavin, G. R. | 1743–1816 | poet |
| Fonvizin, D. | 1745–92 | dramatist |
| Radishchev, A. | 1749–1802 | travel writer, poet |
| Karamzin, N. M. | 1766–1826 | novelist, historian, poet |
| Krylov, I. A. | 1769–1844 | fable writer |
| Zhukovsky, V. A. | 1783–1852 | poet |
| Aksakov, S. T. | 1791–1859 | author of fictionalized reminiscences |

| | | |
|---|---|---|
| Griboyedov, A. S. | 1795–1829 | dramatist |
| Pushkin, A. S. | 1799–1837 | poet, dramatist, story writer |
| Boratynsky, Y. | 1800–44 | poet |
| Tyutchev, F. | 1803–73 | poet |
| *Byliny* | first publ. 1804 | Russian heroic songs |
| Khomyakov, A. S. | 1804–60 | philosopher, poet |
| Gogol', N. V. | 1809–52 | novelist, dramatist |
| Belinsky, V. G. | 1811–48 | literary critic |
| Goncharov, I. A. | 1812–91 | novelist |
| Herzen, A. I. | 1812–70 | philosopher, writer |
| Lermontov, M. Y. | 1814–41 | poet, novelist |
| Sukhovo-Kobylin, A. | 1817–1903 | dramatist |
| Tolstoy, Count A. K. | 1817–75 | poet, dramatist |
| Turgenev, I. | 1818–83 | novelist |
| Mel'nikov, P. I. | 1819–83 | novelist, ethnographer |
| Fet, A. A. | 1820–92 | poet |
| Pisemsky, A. | 1820–81 | novelist, dramatist |
| Dostoyevsky, F. M. | 1821–81 | novelist |
| Nekrasov, N. A. | 1821–77 | poet |
| Grigorovich, D. V. | 1822–99 | novelist |
| Grigor'yev, A. A. | 1822–64 | poet, critic |
| Ostrovsky, A. N. | 1823–86 | dramatist |
| Saltykov, M. Y. | 1826–89 | novelist |
| Chernyshevsky, N. G. | 1828–89 | critic, novelist |
| Tolstoy, Count L. N. | 1828–1910 | novelist, dramatist, thinker |
| Leont'yev, K. N. | 1831–91 | philosopher, critic |
| Leskov, N. S. | 1831–95 | novelist, story writer |
| Vovchok, M. | 1834–1907 | Ukrainian-Russian story writer |
| Dobrolyubov, N. A. | 1836–61 | critic, revolutionary thinker |
| Pisarev, D. I. | 1840–68 | critic |
| Mikhaylovsky, N. K. | 1842–1904 | philosopher, critic |
| Uspensky, G. I. | 1843–1902 | writer of stories and documentary sketches |
| Mamin, D. N. | 1852–1912 | novelist, ethnographer |
| Korolenko, V. G. | 1853–1921 | short-story writer |
| Solovyov, V. S. | 1853–1900 | philosopher, poet |
| Ertel', A. I. | 1855–1909 | novelist |
| Garshin, V. M. | 1855–88 | writer of stories |
| Annensky, I. F. | 1856–1909 | poet, dramatist, critic |
| Rozanov, V. V. | 1856–1919 | essayist, critic |
| Chekhov, A. P. | 1860–1904 | dramatist, story writer |
| Serafimovich, A. | 1863–1949 | novelist |
| Sologub, F. | 1863–1927 | poet, novelist, dramatist |
| Merezhkovsky, D. S. | 1865–1941 | novelist, poet, critic |
| Ivanov, V. I. | 1866–1949 | poet, philosopher |
| Bal'mont, K. D. | 1867–1943 | poet |

| | | |
|---|---|---|
| Gor'ky, M. | 1868–1936 | novelist, dramatist |
| Gippius, Z. N. | 1869–1945 | poet |
| Bunin, I. A. | 1870–1953 | poet, documentary writer |
| Kuprin, A. I. | 1870–1938 | short-story writer |
| Andreyev, L. N. | 1871–1919 | novelist, dramatist |
| Bryusov, V. Y. | 1873–1924 | poet, critic, novelist |
| Prishvin, M. M. | 1873–1954 | stort-story writer |
| Shmelyov, I. S. | 1873–1950 | novelist |
| Kuzmin, M. A. | 1875–1936 | poet |
| Lunacharsky, A. V. | 1875–1933 | literary critic, publicist, dramatist |
| Dobrolyubov, A. M. | 1876–? | poet |
| Trenyov, K. A. | 1876–1945 | dramatist |
| Remizov, A. M. | 1877–1957 | story writer |
| Voloshin, M. A. | 1877–1932 | poet |
| Bely, A. | 1880–1934 | novelist, poet, critic |
| Blok, A. A. | 1880–1921 | poet |
| Chukovsky, K. | 1882–1970 | journalist, critic, children's author |
| Tolstoy, Count A. N. | 1882–1945 | poet, novelist, dramatist |
| Voronsky, A. K. | 1884–1935 | writer, critic |
| Zamyatin, Y. I. | 1884–1937 | novelist |
| Bill'-Belotserkovsky, V. N. | 1885– | dramatist |
| Khlebnikov, V. | 1885–1922 | poet |
| Aldanov, M. A. | 1886–1957 | novelist |
| Gumilyov, N. | 1886–1921 | poet |
| Klyuyev, N. A. | 1887–1937 | poet |
| Marshak, S. Y. | 1887-1964 | poet, translator |
| Akhmatova, A. | 1889–1967 | poet |
| Aseyev, N. | 1889–1963 | poet |
| Olesha, Y. K. | 1889–1960 | novelist, dramatist |
| Inber, V. | 1890– | poet, writer |
| Pasternak, B. L. | 1890–1960 | poet, prose writer |
| Bulgakov, M. A. | 1891–1940 | dramatist |
| Erenburg, I. G. | 1891–1967 | novelist, poet, journalist |
| Mandel'shtam, O. E. | 1891–1938 | poet |
| Fedin, K. A. | 1892–1970 | novelist |
| Paustovsky, K. G. | 1892–1968 | journalist, fiction writer, critic |
| Tsvetayeva, M. | 1892–1941 | poet |
| Fayko, A. | 1893– | dramatist |
| Mayakovsky, V. V. | 1893–1930 | poet, dramatist |
| Shklovsky, V. B. | 1893– | critic |
| Babel', I. E. | 1894–1941 | short-story writer, dramatist |
| Lavrenyov, B. A. | 1894–1959 | dramatist |
| Pil'nyak, B. | 1894–1938 | novelist |
| Bagritsky, E. | 1895–1934 | poet |

| | | |
|---|---|---|
| Ivanov, V. V. | 1895–1963 | dramatist |
| Yesenin, S. | 1895–1925 | poet |
| Zoshchenko, M. M. | 1895–1958 | humorous writer |
| Antokol'sky, P. | 1896– | poet |
| Panfyorov, F. I. | 1896–1960 | novelist |
| Shvarts, Y. L. | 1896–1958 | dramatist, children's writer |
| Tikhonov, N. | 1896– | poet, story writer |
| Il'f, I. | 1897–1937 | humorous writer |
| Katayev, V. P. | 1897– | novelist, dramatist |
| Leonov, L. M. | 1899– | novelist, dramatist |
| Platonov, A. | 1899–1951 | novelist, short-story writer, journalist |
| Sel'vinsky, I. | 1899–1968 | poet |
| Pogodin, N. F. | 1900–1962 | dramatist |
| Vishnevsky, V. V. | 1900–1951 | dramatist |
| Fadeyev, A. A. | 1901–56 | novelist |
| Lugovskoy, V. | 1901–57 | poet |
| Kaverin, V. | 1902– | novelist |
| Kirshon, V. M. | 1902–38 | dramatist |
| Petrov, Y. | 1903–42 | humorous writer |
| Sayanov, V. | 1903– | poet |
| Zabolotsky, N. | 1903–58 | poet |
| Afinogenov, A. | 1904–41 | dramatist |
| Erdman, N. R. | 1904– | dramatist |
| Martynov, L. | 1905– | poet |
| Panova, V. | 1905– | novelist, short-story writer, dramatist |
| Sholokhov, M. A. | 1905– | novelist |
| Zorin, D. I. | 1905– | dramatist, journalist |
| Kirsanov, S. | 1906– | poet |
| Shteyn, A. P. | 1906– | dramatist |
| Virta, N. Y. | 1906– | dramatist, journalist, novelist, librettist |
| Kedrin, D. | 1907–45 | poet |
| Kornilov, B. | 1907–39 | poet |
| Arbuzov, A. N. | 1908– | dramatist |
| Nilin, P. F. | 1908– | novelist |
| Berggol'ts, O. | 1910– | poet |
| Tvardovsky, A. | 1910– | poet, editor |
| Vasil'yev, P. | 1910–37 | poet |
| Sofronov, A. V. | 1911– | writer of plays, songs, librettos |
| Mikhalkov, S. | 1913– | dramatist, satirist, writer |
| Rozov, V. S. | 1913– | dramatist |
| Aliger, M. | 1915– | poet |
| Simonov, K. M. | 1915– | journalist, poet, novelist, dramatist |

| | | |
|---|---|---|
| Dudintsev, V. D. | 1918– | novelist |
| Solzhenitsyin, A. I. | 1918– | autobiograpical writer |
| Slutsky, B. | 1919– | poet |
| Volodin, A. | 1919– | dramatist |
| Nagibin, Y. M. | 1920– | short-story writer |
| Tendryakov, V. F. | 1923– | novelist |
| Soloukhin, V. | 1924– | writer |
| Sinyavsky, A. D. | 1925– | novelist, critic |
| Vinokurov, Y. | 1925– | poet |
| Kazakov, Y. P. | 1927– | short-story writer |
| Aksyonov, V. P. | 1932– | prose writer |
| Voznesensky, A. | 1933– | poet |
| Yevtushenko, Y. | 1933– | poet |
| Akhmadulina, B. | 1937– | poet |

## SERBIAN

See also articles on **Serbian Medieval Literature,** p. 714; **Serbo-Croat Folk Literature,** p. 715

| | | |
|---|---|---|
| Stefan Nemanja | 1114–1200 | biographer |
| Sava, Saint | 1174–1236 | monk, biographer |
| Domentijan | 13th cent. | monk, writer |
| Teodosije | late 13th cent. | biographer |
| Danilo | 14th cent. | Archbishop, writer |
| Camblak, G. | 14th–15th cent. | biographer |
| Konstantin Filosof | early 15th cent. | biographer |
| Orfelin, Z. S. | 1726–85 | writer, engraver, publicist |
| Karadžić, V. S. | 1787–1864 | founder of the modern Serbian literary language |
| Milutinović Sarajlija, S. | 1791–1847 | poet, historian, dramatist |
| Popović, J. S. | 1806–56 | poet, dramatist |
| Njegoš, P. P. | 1813–51 | Montenegrin poet |
| Ignjatović, J. | 1824–88 | novelist |
| Ljubiša, S. M. | 1824–78 | Montenegrin story writer |
| Radičević, B. | 1824–53 | poet |
| Jakšić, D. | 1832–78 | poet, dramatist, short-story writer |
| Zmaj, J. J. | 1833–1904 | poet, doctor |
| Kostić, L. | 1841–1910 | poet, dramatist |
| Marković, S. | 1846–75 | socialist writer |
| Glišić, M. | 1847–1908 | short-story writer, dramatist |
| Lazarević, L. | 1851–90 | prose writer |
| Matavulj, S. | 1852–1908 | novelist |
| Sremac, S. | 1855–1906 | novelist, short-story writer |
| Ilić, V. | 1860–94 | poet |

| | | |
|---|---|---|
| Veselinović, J. | 1862–1905 | novelist |
| Popović, B. | 1863–1944 | critic |
| Ranković, S. | 1863–99 | novelist |
| Šantić, A. | 1868–1924 | poet |
| Dučić, J. | 1871–1943 | poet |
| Domanović, R. | 1873–1908 | short-story writer |
| Rakić, M. | 1876–1938 | poet |
| Stanković, B. | 1876–1927 | short-story writer, novelist, dramatist |
| Kočić, P. | 1877–1916 | Bosnian story writer |
| Skerlić, J. | 1877–1914 | writer, critic, historian |
| Petković-Dis, V. | 1880–1917 | poet |
| Pandurović, S. | 1883–1960 | poet |
| Andrić, I. | 1892– | short-story writer, novelist |
| Crnjanski, M. | 1893– | poet, novelist |
| Nastasijevič, M. | 1894–1938 | poet, dramatist |
| Vučo, A. | 1897– | poet, novelist |
| Matić, D. | 1898– | novelist, poet |
| Davičo, O. | 1909– | poet, novelist |
| Lalić, M. | 1914– | novelist |
| Copić, B. | 1915– | Bosnian novelist |
| Ćosić, D. | 1921– | novelist |
| Popa, V. | 1922– | poet |
| Konstantinović, R. | 1928– | novelist |
| Raičković, S. | 1928– | poet |
| Bulatović, M. | 1930– | novelist |

## SLOVAK

| | | |
|---|---|---|
| Bernolák, A. | 1762–1813 | philologist |
| Kollár, J. | 1793–1852 | Slovak poet, writing in Czech |
| Štúr, L. | 1815–56 | philologist, poet |
| Sládkovič, A. | 1820–72 | poet |
| Král', J. | 1822–76 | poet |
| Botto, J. | 1829–81 | poet |
| Vajanský, S. H. | 1847–1916 | poet, novelist |
| Hviezdoslav | 1849–1921 | poet, dramatist |
| Kukučín, M. | 1860–1928 | novelist |
| Jesenský, J. | 1874–1945 | poet, novelist |
| Krasko, I. | 1876–1958 | poet |
| Jilemnický, P. | 1901–49 | novelist |
| Novomenský, L. | 1904– | poet |
| Urban, M. | 1904– | novelist |
| Hečko, F. | 1905–60 | novelist |
| Mňačko, L. | 1919– | journalist and novelist |

## SPANISH

Authors who wrote in LATIN, BASQUE, CATALAN or GALICIAN are listed separately under these headings. See also articles on **Aljamiado Literature**, p. 48, the literature of the Spanish Muslims; **'Culteranismo'**, p. 206; **(The) Generation of 1898**, p. 306; **Mozarabic, Lyric** p. 553; **'Romances'**, p. 662

| | | |
|---|---|---|
| *Cid, Poema de Mio* | 12th cent. | epic poem |
| *Auto de los Reyes Magos* | late 12th cent. | liturgical drama |
| *Alexandre, Libro de* | early 13th cent. | narrative poem |
| Alfonso X, El Sabio | 1221–84 | patron, writer |
| Berceo, G. de | early 13th cent. | poet |
| *Fernán González, Poema de* | mid 13th cent. | narrative poem |
| *Razón de Amor, La* | early 13th cent. | love poem |
| *Apolonio, Libro de* | mid 13th cent. | historical poem |
| *Calila e Dimna* | 13th cent. | book of fables |
| Juan Manuel, Infante don | 1282–1349? | fabulist |
| Šem Tob Ibn Ardutiel Ben Isaac | fl. early 14th cent. | poet |
| *Amadís de Gaula* | 14th cent. | chivalric romance |
| Ruíz, J. | fl. early 14th cent. | archpriest of Hita |
| López de Ayala, P. | 1332–1407 | chronicler, poet |
| Villasandino, A. Á. | *c.*1345–1425? | poet |
| López de Mendoza, Í. | 1398–1458 | poet, patron |
| Martínez de Toledo, A. | 1398–1470? | didactic writer, hagiographer |
| Fernández de Jerena, G. | end of 14th cent. | poet |
| Baena, J. A. de | early 15th cent. | poet |
| Imperial, Micer F. | fl. early 15th cent. | poet |
| Rodríguez del Padrón | *c.*1405 after 1440 | poet, novelist |
| Mena, J. de | 1411–56 | poet |
| Manrique, G. | 1412?–90? | poet, dramatist |
| Manrique, J. | 1440?–79 | poet |
| Sánchez de Badajoz, G. | 1460?–1526? | poet |
| Rojas, F. de | *c.*1465–1541 | novelist |
| Padilla, J. de | 1468–1522? | poet |
| Encina, J. del | 1469–1529 | poet, dramatist |
| Boscán Almogáver, J. | 1474?–1542 | poet |
| Fernández, L. | 1474–1542 | dramatist |
| Guevara, A. de | 1481?–1545 | moral, political and theological writer |
| Mendoza, Í. de | late 15th cent. | poet |
| San Pedro, D. de | fl. late 15th cent. | novelist |
| Valdés, J. de | 1490?–1541 | humanist, religious writer, critic |
| Castillejo, C. de | 1492?–1550 | poet |
| Díaz del Castillo, B. | 1492–1581 | captain, chronicler |
| Vives, J. L. | 1492–1540 | scholar |
| Laguna, A. | 1499–1560 | doctor, satirist |

| | | |
|---|---|---|
| *Celestina, La* | *c.* 1500 | novel in dialogue |
| Delicado (Delgado), F. | early 16th cent. | novelist |
| *Lazarillo de Tormes* | 16th cent. | early picaresque novel |
| Villalón, C. de | early 16th cent.–1558 | humanist |
| Montesino, A. | fl. early 16th cent. | religious poet, translator |
| Torres Naharro, B. de | ?–1524? | dramatist, poet |
| Timoneda, J. de | ?–1583 | dramatist |
| Garcilaso de la Vega | 1501–36 | poet, soldier, courtier |
| Hurtado de Mendoza, D. | 1503–75 | poet, historian, humanist |
| Granada, L. de | 1504?–88 | devotional writer |
| Rueda, L. de | *c.* 1505–65 | actor-dramatist |
| López de Gómara, F. | 1512–72 | historian |
| Cetina, G. de | 1514/17–1554/7 | poet, soldier |
| Teresa de Jesús, Santa | 1515–82 | mystic |
| Acuña, H. de | 1518?–1580? | poet, soldier |
| Montemayor, J. de | *c.* 1520–61 | poet, novelist |
| León, L. de | 1527–91 | humanist, religious writer, poet |
| Alcázar, B. del | 1530–1606 | poet |
| Polo, G. G. | *c.* 1530–85 | novelist |
| Valera, C. de | 1532?–after 1602 | translator |
| Ercilla, A. de | 1533?–94 | poet |
| Herrera, F. de | 1534–97 | poet, critic, literary theorist |
| Mariana, J. de | 1535–1624 | Jesuit, political theorist, historian |
| Figueroa, F. de | 1536?–1617? | poet, soldier |
| Aldana, F. de | 1537–78 | poet, soldier |
| Juan de la Cruz, San | 1542–91 | poet, mystic |
| Pérez de Hita, G. | 1544?–1619? | historical and ballad writer |
| Alemán, M. | 1547–1614? | novelist |
| Cervantes Saavedra, M. de | 1547–1616 | novelist, dramatist |
| Torre, F. de la | mid 16th cent. | poet |
| Cueva, J. de la | 1550?–1610 | poet, dramatist |
| Espinel, V. | 1550–1624 | novelist, poet, musician |
| Argensola, L. L. de | 1559–1613 | poet, historian |
| Valdivielso, J. de | 1560–1638 | poet, dramatist |
| Aguilar, G. de | 1561–1623 | dramatist |
| Argensola, B. L. de | 1561–1631 | poet, historian |
| Góngora y Argote, L. de | 1561–1627 | poet |
| Lope de Vega | 1562–1635 | dramatist, poet |
| Arguijo, J. de | 1567–1623 | poet, patron |
| Castro, G. de | 1569–1631 | dramatist |
| Medrano, F. de | 1570–1607 | poet |
| Hojeda, D. de | 1571?–1615 | poet |
| Rojas Villandrando, A. de | 1572–after 1618 | dramatist |
| Caro, R. | 1573–1647 | poet, antiquarian |

| | | |
|---|---|---|
| Mira de Amescua, A. | 1574?–1644 | priest, dramatist |
| Medina Medinilla, P. de | 1575–1621 | poet |
| Martín de la Plaza, L. | 1577–1625 | poet, priest |
| Espinosa, P. | 1578–1650 | poet |
| Vélez de Guevara, L. | 1579–1644 | dramatist, novelist |
| Quevedo y Villegas, F. G. de | 1580–1645 | poet, pamphleteer, satirist |
| Tirso de Molina | 1580–1648 | dramatist |
| Ruíz de Alarcón y Mendoza, J. | 1581?–1634 | dramatist |
| Carrillo y Sotomayor, L. de | 1582/3–1610 | poet, naval captain |
| Tarsis, J. de | 1582–1622 | poet |
| Jáuregui, J. M. de | 1583–1641 | poet, literary critic |
| Rioja, F. de | 1583?–1659 | poet, librarian |
| Castillo Solórzano, A. de | 1584–before 1648? | novelist, dramatist |
| Soto de Rojas, P. | 1584–1658 | poet, canon of Granada cathedral |
| Villegas, E. M. de | 1585–1669 | poet |
| Hurtado de Mendoza, A. | 1586?–1644 | poet, dramatist |
| San José, J. de | 1587?–1654 | Carmelite poet, historian |
| Quiñones de Benavente, L. | 1589?–1651 | writer, priest |
| Andrada, A. F. de | early 17th cent. | poet |
| Prado, A. de | early 17th cent. | poet |
| Sarabia, J. de | fl. early 17th cent. | poet |
| Calderón de la Barca, P. | 1600–1681 | dramatist |
| Gracián y Morales, B. | 1601–58 | moralist, novelist |
| Enríquez Gómez, A. | 1602–60 | poet, dramatist, novelist |
| Polo de Medina, S. J. | 1603–76 | poet, priest, moralist |
| Rojas Zorilla, F. de | 1607–48 | dramatist |
| Bocángel y Unzueta, G. | 1608–58 | poet |
| Moreto y Cabaña, A. | 1618–69 | priest, dramatist |
| Trillo y Figueroa, F. de | 1618?–1680? | poet |
| Salazar y Torres, A. de | 1642–75 | dramatist |
| Álvarez de Toledo, G. | 1662–1714 | poet, historian |
| Bances Candamo, F. de | 1662–1704 | poet, dramatist |
| Feijoo, B. J. | 1676–1764 | essayist |
| Lobo, E. G. | 1679–1750 | poet |
| Torres Villarroel, D. de | 1694–1770 | autobiographical adventure writer |
| Luzán Cláramunt de Suelvas y Guerra, I. | 1702–54 | scholar, critic |
| Isla, J. F. de | 1706–81 | Jesuit writer |
| Verdugo y Castilla, A. | 1706–67 | poet |
| Porcel, J. A. | 1730–? | poet |
| Cruz Cano y Olmedilla, R. de la | 1731–94 | dramatist |
| González, D. T. | 1732–94 | poet, preacher |
| García de la Huerta, V. A. | 1734–87 | dramatist |

| | | |
|---|---|---|
| Moratín, N. F. de | 1737–80 | poet, dramatist |
| Cadalso, J. | 1741–82 | poet, essayist |
| Jovellanos, G. M. de | 1744–1811 | poet, dramatist |
| Samaniego, F. M. de | 1745–1801 | fabulist |
| Iglesias de la Casa, J. | 1748–91 | poet |
| Iriarte, T. de | 1750–91 | poet |
| Meléndez Valdés, J. | 1754–1817 | poet |
| Forner, J. B. P. | 1756–97 | critic |
| Moratín, L. F. de | 1760–1828 | dramatist |
| Cienfuegos, N. Á. de | 1764–1809 | poet |
| Marchena Ruiz, J. | 1768–1821 | poet |
| Arriaza, J. B. | 1770–1837 | poet |
| Arjona y de Cubas, M. M. de | 1771–1820 | poet |
| Quintana, M. J. | 1772–1857 | poet |
| Reinoso, F. J. | 1772–1841 | poet, priest |
| Blanco White, J. | 1775–1841 | Spanish-English poet, theologian |
| Lista y Aragón, A. | 1775–1848 | poet, educationalist |
| Gallego, J. N. | 1777–1853 | poet |
| Somoza, J. | 1781–1852 | poet, memoir writer |
| Martínez de la Rosa, F. | 1787–1862 | dramatist |
| Saavedra, Á. de | 1791–1865 | poet, dramatist |
| Bretón de los Herreros, M. | 1796–1873 | dramatist |
| Caballero, F. | 1796–1877 | novelist |
| Estébanez Calderón, S. | 1799–1867 | poet, scholar, descriptive essayist |
| Arolas, J. | 1805–49 | poet, priest |
| Hartzenbusch, J. E. | 1806–80 | dramatist, poet |
| Espronceda, J. | 1808–42 | poet |
| Mesonero Romanos, R. de | 1808–82 | essayist |
| Larra, M. J. de | 1809–37 | essayist, novelist, dramatist |
| Pastor Díaz, N. | 1811–63 | poet |
| Gómez de Avellaneda, G. | 1814–73 | dramatist, poet |
| Gil y Carrasco, E. | 1815–46 | poet, novelist |
| Campoamor, R. de | 1817–1901 | poet |
| García Tassara, G. | 1817–75 | poet, diplomat |
| Zorrilla, J. | 1817–93 | poet |
| Piferrer, P. | 1818–48 | poet, guitarist, music and art critic |
| García Gutiérrez, A. | 1819–84 | dramatist |
| Sanz, E. F. | 1821–81 | dramatist, poet |
| Coronado, C. | 1823–1911 | poet |
| Valera, J. | 1824–1905 | novelist |
| Tamayo y Baus, M. | 1829–98 | dramatist |
| Echegaray, J. | 1832–1916 | dramatist |
| Alarcón, P. A. de | 1833–91 | novelist |
| Pereda, J. M. de | 1833–1906 | novelist |

| | | |
|---|---|---|
| Núñez de Arce, G. | 1834–1903 | poet, dramatist |
| Bécquer, G. A. | 1836–70 | poet |
| Castro, R. de | 1837–85 | poet |
| Pérez Galdós, B. | 1843–1920 | novelist |
| Costa y Martínez, J. | 1844–1911 | politician, essayist |
| Pardo Bazán, E. | 1851–1921 | novelist, essayist |
| Alas, L. | 1852–1901 | critic, novelist |
| Palacio Valdés, A. | 1853–1938 | novelist |
| Rueda, S. | 1857–1933 | poet |
| Unamuno, M. de | 1864–1936 | essayist, novelist, poet |
| Ganivet, A. | 1865–98 | novelist, essayist |
| Benavente, J. | 1866–1954 | dramatist |
| Blasco Ibáñez, V. | 1867–1928 | novelist |
| Valle-Inclán, R. del | 1869–1935 | novelist, dramatist, poet |
| Gabriel y Galán, J. M. | 1870–1905 | poet |
| Álvarez Quintero, S. | 1871–1938 | dramatist |
| Baroja y Nessi, P. | 1872–1956 | novelist |
| Álvarez Quintero, J. | 1873–1944 | dramatist |
| Machado, M. | 1874–1947 | poet |
| Machado, A. | 1875–1939 | poet |
| Grau, J. | 1877– | dramatist |
| Villaespesa, F. | 1877–1936 | poet |
| Miró, G. | 1879–1930 | novelist |
| Pérez de Ayala, R. | 1880–1962 | novelist, essayist, poet |
| Jiménez, J. R. | 1881–1958 | poet |
| Martínez Sierra, G. | 1881–1948 | dramatist, theatre director |
| Ortega y Gasset, J. | 1883–1955 | essayist, philosopher |
| Felipe, L. | 1884– | poet |
| Gómez de la Serna, R. | 1888–1963 | parodist, biographer, novelist |
| Salinas, P. | 1891–1951 | poet, dramatist, critic |
| Guillén, J. | 1893– | poet |
| Azorín | 1894–1967 | essayist, novelist, critic |
| Diego, G. | 1896– | poet |
| Alonso, D. | 1898– | critic, scholar |
| Aleixandre, V. | 1898– | poet |
| Lorca, F. G. | 1898–1936 | poet, dramatist |
| Prados, E. | 1899–1962 | poet |
| Casona, A. | 1900–1965 | dramatist |
| Zunzunegui, J. A. de | 1901– | novelist |
| Alberti, R. | 1902– | poet |
| Cernuda, L. | 1902–63 | poet |
| Altolaguirre, M. | 1905–59 | poet |
| García Gómez, E. | 1905– | translator |
| Panero, L. | 1909–62 | poet |
| Hernández, M. | 1910–42 | poet |
| Celaya, G. | 1911– | poet |

| | | |
|---|---|---|
| Pinillos, M. | 1914– | poet |
| Buero Vallejo, A. | 1916– | dramatist |
| Otero, B. de | 1916– | poet |
| Gaos, V. | 1919– | poet, critic |
| Hidalgo, J. L. | 1919–47 | poet, painter |
| Hierro, J. | 1922– | poet |
| Bousoño, C. | 1923– | poet, critic |
| González, Á. | 1925– | poet |
| Matute, A. M. | 1926– | novelist |
| Sastre, A. | 1926– | dramatist |
| Sánchez Ferlosio, R. | 1927– | novelist |
| Valente, J. Á. | 1929– | poet |
| Rodríguez, C. | 1934– | poet |

## SWEDISH

| | | |
|---|---|---|
| Messenius, J. | 1579–1636 | dramatist, poet |
| Stjernhjelm, G. | 1598–1672 | poet, scholar |
| Rosenhane, G. | 1619–84 | poet |
| Dahlstjerna, G. | 1661–1709 | poet |
| Dalin, O. von | 1708–63 | poet |
| Creutz, G. F. | 1729–85 | poet |
| Bellman, C. M. | 1740–95 | poet, song-writer |
| Tegnér, E. | 1782–1846 | poet |
| Geijer, E. G. | 1783–1847 | poet, historian, political writer |
| Atterbom, P. D. A. | 1790–1855 | poet |
| Almquist, C. J. L. | 1793–1866 | poet, novelist, dramatist, journalist, pamphleteer |
| Stagnelius, E. J. | 1793–1823 | poet |
| Bremer, F. | 1801–65 | novelist, travel writer |
| Topelius, Z. | 1818–98 | Finnish poet, novelist, scholar, writing in Swedish |
| Rydberg, V. | 1828–95 | poet, novelist, scholar, thinker |
| Snoilsky, Count C. | 1841–1903 | poet |
| Strindberg, A. | 1849–1912 | dramatist, novelist, story writer, poet, pamphleteer |
| Ahlgren, E. | 1850–88 | novelist, story writer |
| Lagerlöf, S. | 1858–1940 | novelist, story writer |
| Heidenstam, V. v. | 1859–1940 | poet, essayist |
| Fröding, G. | 1860–1911 | poet |
| Hansson, O. | 1860–1925 | poet, prose writer, essayist |
| Levertin, O. | 1862–1906 | poet, story writer, essayist, critic |
| Karlfeldt, E. A. | 1864–1931 | poet |
| Bergman, B. | 1869–1967 | poet, novelist, story writer |
| Söderberg, H. | 1869–1941 | novelist, story writer, dramatist, essayist |

| | | |
|---|---|---|
| Ekelund, V. | 1880–1949 | poet, essayist, aphoristic writer |
| Hedenvind-Eriksson, G. | 1880–1967 | novelist |
| Hellström, G. | 1882–1953 | novelist, journalist |
| Koch, M. | 1882–1940 | novelist |
| Nordström, L. | 1882–1942 | novelist, story writer, publicist |
| Siwertz, S. | 1882– | novelist, essayist, poet, dramatist |
| Wägner, E. | 1882–1949 | novelist, journalist |
| Bergman, H. | 1883–1931 | novelist, story writer, dramatist |
| Österling, A. | 1884– | poet, critic |
| Sjöberg, B. | 1885–1929 | poet, novelist |
| Björling, G. | 1887–1960 | Finnish-Swedish poet, essayist |
| Andersson, D. | 1888–1920 | poet, novelist, story writer |
| Malmberg, B. | 1889–1958 | poet, prose writer |
| Taube, E. | 1890– | poet, prose writer |
| Lagerkvist, P. | 1891– | poet |
| Södergran, E. | 1892–1923 | Swedo-Finnish poet |
| Olsson, H. | 1893– | Swedo-Finnish novelist, critic |
| Bengtsson, F. G. | 1894–1954 | poet, essayist, novelist, historian |
| Krusenstjerna, A. von | 1894–1940 | novelist |
| Nilsson Piraten, F. | 1895– | novelist, story writer |
| Diktonius, E. | 1896–1961 | Finnish-Swedish poet, prose writer |
| Fridegård, J. | 1897–1968 | novelist, story writer |
| Gullberg, H. | 1898–1961 | poet |
| Moberg, V. | 1898– | novelist, dramatist |
| Hedberg, O. | 1899– | novelist |
| Boye, K. | 1900–1941 | poet, novelist, story writer |
| Johnson, E. | 1900– | novelist, story writer |
| Lo-Johansson, I. | 1901– | novelist, story writer |
| Enckell, R. | 1903– | Finnish-Swedish poet |
| Colliander, T. | 1904– | Swedo-Finnish novelist, short-story writer |
| Martinson, H. | 1904– | poet, novelist, essayist, dramatist |
| Lundkvist, A. | 1906– | poet, travel and story writer |
| Salminen, S. | 1906– | Swedo-Finnish novelist |
| Ekelöf, G. | 1907–68 | poet, essayist |
| Schoultz, S. von | 1907– | Swedo-Finnish poet, novelist |
| Arnér, S. | 1909– | novelist, story writer, dramatist |
| Lindegren, E. | 1910–68 | poet, critic, librettist |
| Vennberg, K. | 1910– | poet, critic |
| Chorell, W. | 1912– | Swedo-Finnish dramatist, novelist |
| Ahlin, L. | 1915– | novelist, story writer |
| Gyllensten, L. | 1921– | novelist, story writer |

| | | |
|---|---|---|
| Dagerman, S. | 1923–54 | novelist, short-story writer, dramatist |
| Lidman, S. | 1923– | novelist, dramatist |
| Forssell, L. | 1928– | poet |

## SWISS (FRENCH)

See also article on **Romansh Literature,** p. 664

| | | |
|---|---|---|
| Rousseau, J.-J. | 1712–78 | novelist, philosopher |
| Amiel, H.-F. | 1821–81 | diarist |
| Ramuz, C.-F. | 1878–1947 | novelist |
| Cendrars, B. | 1887–1961 | novelist |

## SWISS (GERMAN)

See also article on **Swiss-German Dialect Literature**, p. 751

| | | |
|---|---|---|
| Rudolf von Fenis | fl. late 12th cent. | Minnesinger |
| Hadloub, J. | fl. *c.* 1290–1320 | lyric poet |
| Heinrich von Wittenweiler | fl. early 15th cent. | epic poet |
| Bodmer, J. J. | 1698–1783 | critic |
| Breitinger, J. J. | 1701–76 | critic |
| Haller, A. von | 1708–77 | poet |
| Gessner, S. | 1730–88 | poet |
| Bräker, U. | 1735–98 | novelist, story writer |
| Lavater, J. C. | 1741–1801 | writer, Protestant pastor |
| Ineichen, J. | 1745–1818 | dialect folksong writer |
| Pestalozzi, J. H. | 1746–1827 | educationalist |
| Usteri, J. M. | 1763–1827 | dialect poet |
| Kuhn, G. J. | 1775–1849 | dialect folksong writer |
| Gotthelf, J. | 1797–1854 | novelist |
| Keller, G. | 1819–90 | novelist, story writer |
| Meyer, C. F. | 1825–98 | poet, story writer |
| Spitteler, C. | 1845–1924 | poet |
| Tavel, R. von | 1866–1934 | dialect novelist |
| Gfeller, S. | 1868–1943 | dialect radio playwright |
| Hämmerli-Marti, S. | 1868–1942 | dialect novelist |
| Walser, R. | 1878–1956 | poet, novelist |
| Haller, P. | 1882–1920 | dialect novelist |
| Welti, A. J. | 1894–1965 | dialect novelist |
| Frisch, M. | 1911– | dramatist, novelist |
| Bächtold, A. | 1891– | dialect novelist |
| Dürrenmatt, F. | 1921– | dramatist, novelist, critic |

## UKRAINIAN

See also article on **Ukrainian Literature,** p. 779

| | | |
|---|---|---|
| Kotlyarevs'ky, I. | 1769–1838 | poet, dramatist |
| Osnov''yanenko | 1778–1843 | writer |

| | | |
|---|---|---|
| Shevchenko, T. | 1814–61 | poet |
| Kulish, P. | 1819–97 | novelist, story writer |
| Vovchok, M. | 1834–1907 | Ukrainian and Russian story writer |
| Nechuy | 1838–1918 | novelist |
| Franko, I. | 1856–1916 | writer, scholar, critic, translator, journalist |
| Kobylyans'ka, O. | 1863–1942 | novelist, short-story writer |
| Kotsyubyns'ky, M. | 1864–1913 | prose writer |
| Stefanyk, V. | 1871–1936 | short-story writer |
| Ukrainka, L. | 1871–1913 | poet |
| Oles', O. | 1878–1944 | poet |
| Vynnychenko, V. | 1880–1951 | novelist, story writer |
| Vyshnya, O. | 1889–1956 | short-story writer |
| Tychyna, P. | 1891–1967 | poet |
| Kulish, M. | 1892–1942 | dramatist |
| Khvyl'ovy | 1893–1933 | poet, story writer, novelist |
| Ryl's'ky, M. | 1895–1964 | poet, translator, scholar, critic |
| Sosyura, V. | 1898–1965 | poet |
| Bazhan, M. | 1904– | poet |
| Korniychuk, O. | 1905– | dramatist |
| Honchar, O. | 1918– | novelist, short-story writer |

## YIDDISH

| | | |
|---|---|---|
| Bachur, E. | 1468–1549 | writer |
| Glueckel von Hameln | 1645–1724 | memoir writer |
| Nachman of Bratzlav | 1770–1811 | Hebrew and Yiddish fairy-tale writer |
| Ettinger, S. | 1799–1855 | writer of poetry, fables, plays |
| Mendele Mocher Seforim | 1835–1917 | Hebrew and Yiddish novelist, story writer |
| Goldfaden, A. | 1840–1908 | dramatist, poet |
| Dolitzki, M. M. | 1856–1931 | Hebrew and Yiddish poet, novelist |
| Ben-ami | 1858–1932 | writer |
| Sholem Aleichem | 1859–1916 | writer |
| Frug, S. S. | 1860–1916 | poet |
| Rosenfeld, M. | 1862–1923 | poet, biographer |
| An-ski | 1863–1920 | author, dramatist |
| Pinski, D. | 1872–1960 | novelist, dramatist |
| Reizen, A. | 1875–1953 | poet |
| Shapiro, L. | 1875–1948 | novelist, essayist |
| Ash, S. | 1880–1957 | writer |
| Bergelson, D. | 1884–1952 | short-story writer, novelist |
| Niger, S. | 1884– | literary critic, essayist |

| | | |
|---|---|---|
| Opatoshu, J. | 1887–1954 | novelist |
| Shneor, Z. | 1887–1959 | poet |
| Boraischa, M. | 1888–1949 | poet |
| Leivick, H. | 1888–1962 | poet |
| Singer, Y. J. | 1893–1944 | novelist |
| Markisch, P. | 1895–1948 | poet, dramatist |
| Feffer, I. | 1900–1948 | writer, poet |
| Manger, I. | 1900–1969 | poet |
| Shlevin, B. | 1913– | novelist |
| Sutzkever, A. | 1913– | poet |

## YUGOSLAVIAN

See separate headings: CROATIAN, DALMATIAN and DUBROVNIK, SERBIAN

## GENERAL ARTICLES